A Concordance to the Plays of
WILLIAM CONGREVE

THE CORNELL CONCORDANCES

S. M. Parrish, *General Editor*

Supervisory Committee

M. H. Abrams
Donald D. Eddy
Ephim Fogel
Alain Seznec

POEMS OF MATTHEW ARNOLD, *edited by S. M. Parrish*
POEMS OF W. B. YEATS, *edited by S. M. Parrish*
POEMS OF EMILY DICKINSON, *edited by S. P. Rosenbaum*
WRITINGS OF WILLIAM BLAKE, *edited by David V. Erdman*
BYRON'S *DON JUAN, edited by Charles Hagelman, Jr., and R. J. Barnes*
THÉÂTRE ET POÉSIES DE JEAN RACINE, *edited by Bryant C. Freeman*
BEOWULF, edited by J. B. Bessinger, Jr.
PLAYS OF W. B. YEATS, *edited by Eric Domville*
POEMS OF JONATHAN SWIFT, *edited by Michael Shinagel*
PLAYS OF WILLIAM CONGREVE, *edited by David Mann*
POEMS OF SAMUEL JOHNSON, *edited by Helen Naugle*

A Concordance to the Plays of

WILLIAM CONGREVE

Edited by

DAVID MANN

Cornell University Press

ITHACA AND LONDON

First published 1973 by Cornell University Press.
Published in the United Kingdom by Cornell University Press Ltd.,
2-4 Brook Street, London W1Y 1AA.

International Standard Book Number 0-8014-0767-2
Library of Congress Catalog Card Number 72-13384

Printed in the United States of America by Vail-Ballou Press, Inc.

Library of Congress Cataloging in Publication Data
(For library cataloging purposes only)

Mann, David, date.
    A concordance to the plays of William Congreve.   (

    (The Cornell concordances)
    "Based on The complete plays of William Congreve, edited by Herbert Davis (Chicago and London: University of Chicago Press, 1967)"
    1. Congreve, William, 1670–1729—Concordances.
I. Congreve, William, 1670–1729.   Selected works.
1967.   II. Title.   III. Series.
PR3366.A3   822'.4   72-13384
ISBN 0-8014-0767-2

CONTENTS

PREFACE

This concordance, based on *The Complete Plays of William Congreve,* edited by Herbert Davis (Chicago and London: University of Chicago Press, 1967),[1] is not only the first concordance to Restoration drama, but also the first devoted entirely to dramatic prose. Since no manuscripts of Congreve's plays are extant, Davis used as his basic text the first quartos of the five plays, which probably come close to the language of the earliest stage performances. Although Davis' edition is unquestionably the best, superseding earlier collections of Congreve's plays by Hunt (1840), Ewald (1887, reissued 1956), Summers (1923), Dobrée (1925–1928), Krutch (1927), and Bateson (1930), it does have a few minor errors, mostly typographical. (Davis would no doubt have corrected these errors himself, had he not died shortly after the volume appeared in 1967.) Consequently, I have felt it advisable to compare his text with quartos held by the Lilly library (Indiana University), and by the Newberry, Huntington, Folger, Ohio State University, and University of Cincinnati libraries, and I have made a few corrections (see pp. xiii–xiv below). Nevertheless, citations of page and line, act and scene, throughout, are to the authoritative Davis text.

Preparation of the Concordance

Congreve's plays were punched on IBM cards using a Model 029 Keypunch to include full punctuation. Italics had to be ignored, and all ligatures (e.g., cœlestial) were divided into single letters. Lines too long to fit on one card were also divided, and three spaced periods were used to close the first card and to indicate a continuation of the line on the second card. Words hyphenated at the end of a line in Davis' edition were checked in the quartos, then reconstituted with or without the hyphen, as appropriate, and punched on the line on which they started, so as to avoid the partial words that would otherwise appear in the index.

---

[1] Used by permission of the University of Chicago Press. Davis did not try to reproduce the original quartos; therefore, his line and page arrangement is arbitrary. Since the lines of his text are numbered, I have followed them as printed, except for words divided at the end of lines: these I have joined for clarity. Unless otherwise mentioned, all act-scene-line references are to Davis' text.

To ensure accuracy, all punched cards were verified on a Model 059 Verifier, and a listing (print-out) of the cards was proofread. After final correction, data on the cards were transferred by an IBM 1401 Card Reader to magnetic tapes, and the concordance program was run. The indexing process was similar to that described in detail by James Painter in his "Programmer's Preface" to the Cornell *Concordance to the Poems of W. B. Yeats* (Ithaca, 1963). Using an IBM 120-character Model TN print chain, the concordance printing took place at the Miami University Computer Center in just under three hours. Copies of the complete tapes are available at the Miami University Computer Center and at the Lawrence University *London Stage* Information Bank.

The user must take careful note of several conventions of the automatic indexing. The hyphen, followed by the apostrophe, precedes the alphabet; and, following the hyphen or apostrophe, capital letters are normally indexed ahead of lower-case letters. The following sequences of index words will illustrate these principles: Hang, Hang-Dog, Hang'd, Hang't, Hanging, and Sea, Sea-Beast, Sea-Lover, Sea-calf, Sea-wit, Sea's, Seal. Words beginning with apostrophe, however (like " 'em," " 'gainst," and " 'tis"), have been moved to the place where they would fall were the apostrophe not present. Symbols such as "&" and "£," together with Arabic numbers, appear at the end of the concordance, following the alphabet. Abbreviations remain as they are in the first quartos (and hence in Davis); cross references are provided. All hyphenated compounds are fully indexed under their first element; the indexing of additional elements gives a cross reference to the first. Similarly, foreign phrases are treated as single units: "Someils du Matin" and "In vino veritas" are listed under the first word of the phrase, and the indexing of each subsequent word in the phrase provides a cross reference to the main entry. A separate listing of all non-English words and phrases, including Latin legal terms, may prove helpful to the user:

Beau-mond	Forma Pauperis
Belle-air (bel air)	Humanum est errare
Belles Assemblees	in statu quo
Billet doux	In vino veritas
boon mein (bonne mine)	Inprimis [Imprimis]
Certiorari	Je-ne-scay-quoysh
Consummatum est	l'etourdie
Corum Nobus [Coram Nobis]	Lapsus Linguae
Decimo Sexto	le Drole
douceurs	Mittimus
Drap-du-berry	Mon Coeur
Erra Pater	Nemo omnibus horis sapit °2
faux pas	Noli prosequi [Nolle Prosequi]

[2] The length of the asterisked phrase caused the computer to drop the final word from the concordance listing.

Non Compos
Non Compos mentis (Non compos mentis)
Pass par tout (Pass par toute)
Premunire
Probatum est (probatum est)
propria persona
qui vult decipi decipiatur °

sapiens dominabitur astris °
Signatum, Sigillatum, and Deliberatum
Someils du Matin
teste a teste (tete a tete)
Valet de Chambre (Valet de chambre)
via Lactea

Title Abbreviations

In the concordance print-out, each line is identified by the page number in the Davis text, an abbreviated title of the play, and act, scene, and line numbers. The title abbreviations are as follows (the date of the first quarto is in parenthesis):

DOUBL DLR	*The Double Dealer* (1694)
FOR LOVE	*Love for Love* (1695)
M. BRIDE	*The Mourning Bride* (1697)
OLD BATCH	*The Old Batchelour* (1693)
WAY WORLD	*The Way of the World* (1700)

Editorial Problems

The user of any concordance wants the important words and their locations. But the editor of a concordance to drama must decide whether or not to indicate what character spoke the words. He must face other decisions as well: Should stage directions be brought in? How much of the dramatist's vocabulary should be included in the index? What difficulties arise in indexing old spelling? These problems I resolved in the following ways.

First, in order to include the dramatic speaker, I assigned a numerical code to each character, and this was punched on the card with the line from the play. In the final printing, after the program had compiled the concordance, the speaker code was reconverted to the name. Under each index word, then, are lines from the plays which include that word; the speaker of the line is indicated at the left. The name appears as it is in the *dramatis personae*, except in the following instances, where it was necessary to use abbreviations.

Abbreviation	Full name
The Old Batchelour	
Barnaby	Servant to Fondlewife
Capt Bluff	Captain Bluffe
The Double Dealer	
Lady Ply	Lady Plyant
Lady Touch	Lady Touchwood
Lord Touch	Lord Touchwood

Abbreviation	Full name
	Love for Love
Mrs Fore	Mrs. Foresight
Singer-F	Singer (at Foresight's, Act III, scene 1)
Singer-V	Singer (at Valentine's, Act IV, scene 1)
Sr Sampson	Sir Sampson Legend
	The Mourning Bride
Manuel	Manuel, the King [3]
Osmyn-Alph	Osmyn [4]
	The Way of the World
Lady Wish	Lady Wishfort
Mrs Fain	Mrs. Fainall
Servant-M	Servant to Mirabell
Servant-W	Servant to Lady Wishfort
Sir Wilful	Sir Wilfull Witwoud

Congreve's prologues and epilogues are included in the concordance without speaker indication. Commendatory poems by other poets, such as Southerne's to *The Old Batchelour* and Dryden's to *The Double Dealer*, although printed in Davis' edition, were excluded from the concordance.

Since Davis provided line numbers for most stage directions, they could be punched in the normal way, but in order to distinguish them from spoken text, all stage directions are enclosed within parentheses and collected in Appendix A, "Stage Directions." They appear as well in the body of the concordance under the index word, such as "Exit." Those few directions not provided with line numbers fall at the beginning of scenes: in *The Way of the World* (II.i.), for example, "St. James's Park. *Enter* Mrs. Fainall *and* Mrs. Marwood." If the user finds the act and scene attached to a stage direction, but no line number, he need only look at the opening of the act or scene. Often "Exit" appears on a line by itself; in order that the user will know who left the stage, the name is supplied in the speaker indication:

Fainall: (Exit.) 398 WAY WORLD I.i.104

A simple count of Congreve's stage directions gives one a sense of his developing artistry. As a beginning playwright, Congreve relies heavily on stage directions, but the more he learns his craft, the fewer he needs. Thus his first play, *The Old Batchelour*, contains almost as many stage directions as the last two, *The Mourning Bride* and *The Way of the World*, combined. The following table shows the declining percentage of stage directions from play to play.

---

[3] Speech prefix "King" is usually given in the quarto text.
[4] Osmyn's assumed name, Alphonso, is added because of his disguised character through much of the play.

Play	Total lines	Stage directions	Per cent of stage direction per play
The Old Batchelour	2847	260	9.2
The Double Dealer	2992	223	7.5
Love for Love	3711	210	5.6
The Mourning Bride	2397	133	5.5
The Way of the World	3189	141	4.4

A count of a single stage direction, "Aside," shows the same decline: there are 42 asides in *The Old Batchelour*, 34 in *The Double Dealer*, 25 in *Love for Love*, 4 in *The Mourning Bride*, and 3 in *The Way of the World*.

Omitted words

To confine this concordance to one volume, eighty common words have been omitted and are listed here with only their frequencies. Although the casual user may have little interest in these words, they should be available, I feel, for the student of Congreve's language. I have therefore provided their locations in Congreve's texts in Appendix B, "Index of Common Words." Pronouns, auxiliary verbs, articles, conjunctions, and a few prepositions have been relegated to this appendix, whereas most adverbs and exclamations, and all hyphenated and contracted words, have been retained in the concordance proper. These eighty words are given below with their frequency of occurrence:

A	2772	HIM	732	OUR	161
AM	362	HIS	691	SHALL	400
AN	389	HOW	373	SHE	449
AND	3725	I	4109	SHOULD	187
ARE	606	IN	1521	SO	749
ART	105	INTO	126	THAT	1384
AT	446	IS	1064	THE	3303
BE	1227	IT	1163	THEE	243
BEEN	272	MAY	354	THEIR	143
BUT	1167	ME	1387	THEM	31
BY	461	MIGHT	81	THESE	88
CAN	292	MUST	301	THEY	293
COULD	109	MY	2064	THIS	746
FOR	1181	NAY	197	THOSE	70
FROM	275	NEITHER	42	THOU	453
HAD	309	NEVER	221	THY	272
HAS	457	NO	767	TO	3352
HAST	78	NOR	122	UP	151
HAVE	1331	NOT	1193	UPON	288
HE	887	OF	2327	US	154
HER	784	ON	283	WAS	414
HERE	220	OR	457	WE	290

WERE	242	WHOM	55	YET	228
WHAT	745	WHY	336	YOU	3172
WHEN	314	WILL	582	YOUR	1340
WHERE	151	WITH	969	YOURS	30
WHICH	231	WOULD	270		

This list is arbitrarily based on my reading of Congreve. A word such as "very" with 236 occurrences might have been omitted, but since Congreve often intends "very" to mean "truly," basing his sense of the word on the Latin root, I chose to retain it. Homographs raised particular difficulties. "Art," "might," and "will" in the list above appear in the concordance only where they occur as nouns. Moreover, "Ile" as a contraction, and "Ile" meaning "aisle" have been divided into two index entries. A partial listing for "May" was not necessary since Congreve never uses the word as a month or a proper name. Other oddities will not easily come to light. In *The Double Dealer* (II.i.245), for instance, Sir Paul's nickname for his daughter Cynthia is "Thy," which, as a pronoun, has been relegated to the Index. In the comedies, several characters abbreviate "he" to "a'," e.g., "here a' comes." Most of these abbreviations can be found in the concordance, but there are times when the apostrophe is missing and one must use Appendix B.

Corrections and Emendations

Without a long polemic on the question whether to emend or not to emend, let me here list the textual emendations I have made in the concordance. The first kind of emendation corrects an obvious error: "is she has not" to "if she has not" (WAY WORLD IV.i.428). A second type of emendation changes the first quarto to avoid confusion with a similarly spelled word ("fort" is replaced by "for't"—OLD BATCH III.i.247; "hast" is replaced by "haste"—OLD BATCH I.i.332). A variant of this second type changes proper names in order that their spelling be consistent—so that all spellings of a name are collected under one index entry. "Sir Paul Pliant" (DOUBL DLR I.i.54) was changed to "Sir Paul Plyant," the usual spelling. The exceptions, "Saph" and "Sapho" (DOUBL DLR) and "Spintext"/"Spintext" (OLD BATCH), have been retained as possible clues to the printing of the first quartos.[5] A third variety of emendation is made on the basis of the concordance. In the first quarto of *The Double Dealer* (I.i.383), for instance, Maskwell says, "Na, Madam" (later in the same speech—line 385—he uses "Nay"). On the basis of 196 uses of "nay" and this single "na," I emended the concordance line to "Nay, Madam," a correction made in the second quarto of 1706. A fourth kind of emendation occurs where exits had been overlooked in the first quartos and Davis did

[5] Fredson Bowers, "The Cancel Leaf in Congreve's *Double Dealer*, 1694," *PBSA*, 43 (1949), 78–82.

not include them; I added the following exits: DOUBL DLR II.i.469, III.i.261; FOR LOVE V.i.220. In addition, I have reversed two sets of lines because speeches are made by characters who have just left the stage (DOUBL DLR IV.i.510–511; WAY WORLD IV.i.434–435). The full list of emendations which follows incorporates corrections of errors noticed in reviews of Davis' edition: [6]

The Old Batchelour

p. 46:	I.i.332	for "hast" read "haste"
	I.i.335	for "by Business" read "my Business"
p. 67:	III.i.247	for "fort" read "for't"
p. 78:	IV.i.127	for "No—h" read "No-h"
p. 96:	V.i.9	for "Sylvia' " read "Sylvia's"
p. 97:	V.i.43	for "Tribulation-*Spin-text*" read "Tribulation *Spin-text*"
p. 110:	V.ii.108	for "Art military" read "Art-military"

The Double Dealer

p. 128:	I.i.54	for "*Pliant*" read "*Plyant*"
p. 137:	I.i.383	for "Na, Madam" read "Nay, Madam"
p. 142:	II.i.150–155	reverse line numbers in the margin to correct order
p. 150:	II.i.469	add "Maskwell: Exit."
p. 155:	III.i.188	for " 'if I" read "if I"
p. 157:	III.i.261	add "Maskwell: Exit."
p. 162:	III.i.449	for "Mr. *Careless*. . . ." read "Mr. *Careless*."
p. 172:	IV.i.186	for "you'r" read "you're"
p. 175:	IV.i.306–307	"Walking about" should be in brackets because it is a stage direction
p. 178:	IV.i.411	for "than" read "then"
p. 181:	IV.i.510–511	reverse lines, as Careless speaks before leaving the stage
p. 201:	V.i.519	for "*Lord Froth*" read "*Lady Froth*"; incorrect speech prefix

Love for Love

p. 213:	PRO.5	for "Th'unladen" read "Th' unladen"
p. 245:	II.i.372	for "Scoundrell" read "Scoundrel"
p. 259:	III.i.212	for "Body o'me" read "Body o' me"
p. 273:	III.i.732	for "Sailer" read "Sailor"
p. 290:	IV.i.554	for "keep is secret" read "keep it secret"
p. 300:	V.i.127	for "Body o'me" read "Body o' me"
p. 303:	V.i.220	add "Exit Jeremy."
p. 305:	V.i.317	for "*Robbin*" read "*Robin*"

The Mourning Bride

p. 352:	III.i.104	for "thinks't" read "think'st"
p. 362:	IV.i.43	for "th'approaching" read "th' approaching"
p. 368:	IV.i.304	for "thour't" read "thou'rt"
p. 374:	V.i.67	for "Slave. ." read "Slave."

[6] *TLS*, 8 June 1967, p. 510; Carl Klaus, *PQ*, 47 (1968), 364–365; G. Blakemore Evans, *JEGP*, 67 (1968), 148–149.

p. 374:	V.i.87	for "th'Encounter" read "th' Encounter"
	V.i.88	for "Directon" read "Direction"

The Way of the World

p. 398:	I.i.109	for "*at his Watch*" read "*on his Watch*"
p. 418:	II.i.333	for "*Millimant*" read "*Millamant*"
p. 432:	III.i.278	for "*Wishford*" read "*Wishfort*"
p. 435:	III.i.380	for "wasts" read "wastes"
p. 443:	III.i.697	for "*Faihall*" read "*Fainall*"
p. 456:	IV.i.428	for "is she has not" read "if she has not"
	IV.i.434– 435	reverse lines so Millamant speaks her line before leaving the stage
p. 459:	IV.i.551	for "*Wishfort,*" read "*Wishfort.*"
p. 464:	V.i.86	for "told you-long" read "told you long"
p. 477:	V.i.572	for "*Wishford*" read "*Wishfort*"

Variants

Variant lines, marked V before the line number, are so called because they represent alterations in the text after the first quarto, as shown in Davis' "Textual Notes," pp. 480–503. All substantive changes listed by Davis, as well as lines deleted, added, or emended, in a later revision, have been included as variants and marked with a V. A few of the deletions can be credited to Collier's attack on Congreve and his contemporaries; other deletions may have been caused by the staging of the play; and several lines, Congreve must have realized, were just in bad taste. Congreve's additions to his first-quarto text are mainly in *The Mourning Bride*, which he extensively revised. Some of these added lines had to be given letters (e.g., M. BRIDE V.i.86A, 86B, etc.).

Most of the emendations are those in Davis' "Textual Notes"; my own, listed earlier, are meant to clarify the text and give it unity. With the exceptions below, I have included variant lines which showed a substantive change, such as Foresight's declaration (FOR LOVE III.i.552) "I have consulted the Stars" (Q1), altered to "I have consulted the Science" (Q2). A slight change, even of one word, or the addition of one word, is recorded if there is a corresponding change in meaning. Usually, however, changes involving accidentals, punctuation, capitalization, and alternative spellings were not treated as variants. (One notable exception is Mincing's affected pronunciation of "Cremp" [WAY WORLD II.i.371—Q1], which is included.) I have not regarded as variants Congreve's transfer of words from one line to another unless there was at the same time a corresponding change in syntax and thus in meaning or emphasis. Nor have I included as variants those lines from poorly reprinted quartos (such as FOR LOVE, Q4, 1704), in which Congreve himself made no changes. The total number of lines marked V in the concordance comes to 788: this is composed of 109 deleted lines, 20 added lines, 649 variant lines (those slightly altered), and 10 emended lines. These 788 lines, added to the number of lines in the first editions, as printed in Davis (15,136), give a total of 15,924 lines of text included in the concordance.

Old-Style Spelling

One of the most difficult problems to attend to in preparing this concordance was the handling of Congreve's spelling. Old-style spelling needs extensive cross-referencing, and I found it necessary to arrange some "combination index entries" (discussed below). Moreover, I have provided a list of old-style spellings without cross references to a modern equivalent. This list, plus the cross references within the concordance, should aid the casual user as well as persons better acquainted with older spellings.

Words which, in current spelling practice, are joined, Congreve frequently separated; these remain divided: Every Body, Him Self, Any Bodies, Birth Day, To Morrow. The user can discover all the occurrences by checking one index entry (in the case of "To Day," see "Day"), taking care to note words divided by line endings ("To/Day").

Cross references were added in the concordance whenever I felt the user might encounter a problem: for instance, both "Curs" and "Currs" are cross-referenced so they will not be confused with "Curse." Congreve occasionally spelled the same word two or three different ways, and these may be separated by many pages in the concordance, like "Ægyptian" and "Egyptian." If the concordance user will look up the modern spelling, the cross references will direct him to variant spellings. Where two variant spellings are now both obsolete, such as "Affrick" and "Africk," or "Balkt" and "Bauk'd," a cross reference was provided to each old-style spelling. Cross references are not added whenever the pertinent index entries follow one another or fall close together alphabetically. Since most derivational forms are already grouped, no attempt was made to cross-reference natural index lists as: Dream, Dream't, Dreamer, Dreaming, Dreams, Dreamt; or Learn, Learn'd, Learned, Learnedly, Learning, Learnings, Learnt. Most words with prefixes ("Misapply'd," "Revisit," "Unswear") are not cross-referenced. Also where only old-style spellings exist without a modern equivalent, such as "Ake" (for "Ache"), no cross references are possible. To introduce them would have entailed extensive additions of new words and of index entries.

The following list of old-style spellings should assist the concordance user. Closely related derivative words and Congreve's variant forms are in parentheses; modern spelling, usage, or meaning is given in brackets.

OLD-STYLE SPELLING, WITH NO MODERN ENGLISH EQUIVALENT IN THE PLAYS

A-cross
A-drift
A-kin
A-new
A-pace
A-Propos
Adjoyning
Aera's [Eras]
Affrick (Africk)
Ake (Akes, Aking)
Asswage
Atchievments
Awakned
Ballance
Barr
Bartlemew [Bartholomew]
Befal (Befel)
Bely [Belie]
Benumn [Benumb]
Biggot
Bishoprick
Bisket
Broaker
Busie
Centinel [Sentinel]
Certifie
Chearful
Chelsey [Chelsea]
Chilness
Chimaera
Choak
Cholerick
Cholick [Colic]
Chymist (Chymistry)
Cloath (Cloats, Cloathing)
Coarse [Corpse]
Coblers
Cocquetts
Compleat
Coul [Cowl]
Courtsie
Critick (Criticks)

Cry'd
Defie
Denyal (Deny'd)
Desarts
Dishabilie
Dispence (Dispens'd)
Disswading
Doat (Doating, Doats)
Domestick
Drachm [OED: Dram]
Drein [Drain]
Dry'd
Dy'd
Eccho
Ecstasie (Ecstacies, Exstacy, Extacies)
Effigie
Epigrammatick
Expences
Extream (Extreams)
Fanatick
Fantoms
Fiz [physiognomy]
Flouds
Fortifie
Friers
Fulsamick [OED: Fulsome + ic]
Gaoler
Gashly [OED: Ghastly]
Gause
Gawdy
Gingling [Jingling]

Glew
Gole [Goal]
Gothick
Gratifie
Grutch [OED: Grudge]

Guzling
Hainous
Hapned
Haule
Hazle
Heroick
Hide-Park
Hieroglyphick (Hieroglyphicks)
Huffe
Iambicks
Ile [I'll, Aisle]
Impowr'd
Inchanted (Enchantress)
Incurr
Inhancing
Intire
Intreat
Jear
Joyntures
Jugler
Justifie
Lanthorn
Lawrel
Leach
Leacher
Lieve [Lief]
Listning
Loaden
Locketts
Loyns
Lunatick
Magick
Magnifie
Magpye
Male-contents [Malcontents]
Matchiavilian
Mathemacular [Mathematical?]
Mechanick
Melancholick
Mellon
Merchandize
Mimick
Mollifie
Mouldring

Musick (Musick-Master, Musick-Meetings)
Odly
Oeconomy
Outragious
Pallace (Pallaces)
Panegyrick (Panegyricks)
Pathetick
Peacefull
Pedantick
Perswading (Perswasion)
Petrifie
Physick (Physicks)
Picque
Pidgeons
Pistoll
Plaistred
Politick (Politicks)
Poyson'd (Poysoning's)
Preheminence
Publick
Purloyn'd
Quoif [Coif]
Rancling
Ransome
Ratifia
Ratifie (Ratify'd)
Rebell
Redned
Rekin [Wrekin]
Repell
Rhetorick
Rhime (Rhymes)
Riseings
Rustick
Sarazen
Satisfie
Satyre
Sawcy
Scapes ('scaping)
Secresie
Shewing (Shew'd)

Shrew'd	Strole (Stroling)	Toling	Tygers (Mountain-
Shrilness	Strugling	Topicks	Tyger)
Signifie	Sully'd	Touzle (Touz'd)	Uncomatible [*OED:*
Sooth [Soothe]	Surprize	Towr	Uncomeatable]
Sowre	(Surprizes)	Traiterous	Unsincere
Spys	Suspence	Trapt	[Insincere]
Stile [Style]	Swail'd	Tripple	Unstopt
Stilness	Syren	Try'd	Vagarie
Stoick	Tarr	Tumbril	Vernish
Stomacks	Teaze	Turbant [Turban]	Vertuous
Stop't	Threatned	Turky-Cock	Wilder'd
Streights [Straits]	Tift	Twitnam	[Bewildered]
Stroaking	Tipt	[Twickenham]	Yew [Ewe]

Some contractions Congreve punctuated several different ways; "Shan't," for example, is also written "S'an't," "Sant," "Shan'n't," "Shant," and "Sha'nt." Owing to capitalization (or the use of lower-case letters), apostrophes, and hyphens, other contractions were scattered in various parts of the concordance. To make the concordance easier to use, I decided to pull a number of these differently punctuated words together, listed below as "combination index entries," thus making them available in one place.

COMBINATION INDEX ENTRIES

Agad (24)	Agad, 5; agad, 14; A-Gad, 2; A-gad, 3.
Ashore (2)	ashore, 1; a-shore, 1.
Bible-Oath (3)	Bible-Oath, 2; Bible-oath, 1.
Faith (93)	faith, 39; Faith, 53; 'Faith, 1.
I'faith (12)	I'faith, 2; I-faith, 1; i 'faith, 2; i'Faith, 1; i'faith, 5; 'ifaith, 1.
I'gad (20)	I'gad, 16; I-gad, 1; I' Gad, 1; i'Gad, 1; Igad, 1.
I'th (7)	I'th', 3; i'th', 1; 'ith, 1; ith', 1; i'th, 1.
Ill-natur'd (5)	Ill-natur'd, 1; illnatur'd, 1; ill-natur'd, 3.
Mayn't (11)	mayn't, 8; may'nt, 2; maynt, 1.
S'bud (4)	S'bud, 1; 'sbud, 1; Sbud, 1; 'S'bud, 1.
S'death (12)	S'death, 4; 'sdeath, 1; 'Sdeath, 2; 'S'death, 3; 'S death, 2.
S'heart (21)	S'heart, 5; 'S'heart, 3; 'Shart, 1; 'Sheart, 12.
S'life (6)	S'life, 2; 'slife, 1; 'Slife, 2; 'S'life, 1.
T'other (35)	t'other, 30; 'tother, 1; T'other, 1; tother, 3.
Twould (8)	twould, 1; 'twould, 4; 'Twould, 2; 'twou'd, 1.
Womankind (3)	Womankind, 2; Woman-kind, 1.

Old-style spelling may serve as a key to pronunciation, thus giving us a greater understanding of Congreve's knowledge of dialects. Moreover, Congreve's spelling habits may tell us about dialect usage in the Restoration theatre. Certainly, Congreve was conscious of affected or dialectal pronunciation as a habit of speech. This is suggested in his famous letter to John Dennis of 10 July 1695, entitled "Concerning Humour in Comedy," in Dennis' *Letters on Several Occasions.*[7] Mincing's use of "Cremp," mentioned

[7] John C. Hodges, ed., *William Congreve: Letters and Documents* (New York: Harcourt, Brace and World, 1964), pp. 176–186.

earlier, also hints at dialect usage. Her frequent employment of "Mem" and "Laship" (and she is the only character to use them) shows us an individuality created by a stylized vocabulary. Another character who can be classified as a dialect speaker is Lady Wishfort's Shropshire nephew, Sir Wilfull Witwoud. Spellings of "Cozen," "Grutch," and "Rekin" suggest differences in pronunciation. Moreover, the spelling of contractions like "Do't" and "By'r" and of specialized constructions like "Becravated," "Beperriwig'd," and "Belike," suggests Sir Wilfull's Shropshire "lingo," as he would say.

Frequencies

A frequency list of Congreve's entire dramatic vocabulary appears in Appendix C, "Words in Order of Frequency," printed by computer and numerically arranged from the greatest number of usages to a single occurrence. It is not surprising in a concordance to prose drama that "I" should be the word most often used—4109 times. Other personal pronoun references, "My" (2064) and "Me" (1387), are among the ten most-used words. Another expected result is the high count or the distinctive usage of words connected with certain regions, occupations, or dominant interests. In *Love for Love*, for instance, Sailor Ben and Foresight the astrologer employ a great many specialized terms, the jargon of their professions: Ben's nautical expressions salt his every speech, and Foresight's astrological words dominate his language. Sir Sampson's special-interest vocabulary grows out of his ruling passion for getting an heir. In *The Old Batchelour*, Captain Bluffe's vocabulary shows his interest in things military, whereas Sir Joseph Wittoll, his Buckinghamshire patron, is always exclaiming, "Agad," or swearing "by the Lord Harry."

What might not have been predicted, however, is the large number of proper nouns Congreve employs. Most of these nouns are one-time usages, such as Lady Wishfort's inviting Mrs. Marwood to peruse her library: "*Quarles* and *Pryn*, and the *Short View of the Stage*, with *Bunyan's* Works to entertain you" (WAY WORLD III.i.65–67). Some are references to particular people and localities: Lady Wishfort's "I'll send for *Robin* from *Lockets*" (WAY WORLD III.i.104–105), or Ben's "I'll sail as far as *Ligorn*" (FOR LOVE V.i.352). Others are mentions of groups of people or specific places—*Nilus* (Nile River—FOR LOVE V.i.191), *Antegoa* (Antigua—FOR LOVE V.i.351)—and reminders of specific contemporary events—"the *Royal Oak* Lottery" (FOR LOVE I.i.88), "the Hermaphrodite, or the Naked Prince" (FOR LOVE III.i.161–162), and "his *Czarish* Majestie's Retinue" (WAY WORLD V.i.273).

With the concordance, too, one can accurately document for the first time the large number of words describing family relationships (genitive and plural usages are counted together in the following list): Aunt (60), Brethren (2), Brother (48), Child (40), Children (9), Cousin (39), Cozen (22), Daughter (47), Daughter-in-Law (1), Family (23), Father (119), Father-in-Law (2), God-father (1), Godmother (1), Godson (2), Grandson (2), Half Brother (4), Husband (111), Issue (4), Kinsman (1), Man-child (2), Mother (35), Mother-in-Law (2), Nephew (38), Niece (24), Off-spring (2), Papa (1), Parent (6), Relation (14), Sister (37), Son (56), Son-in-Law (2), Twin (1), Uncle (42), Widow (18), Wife (154). Add to these the servants, and there is quite a house full: Abigail (2), Andrew (1), Boy (36), Butler (4), Chambermaid (2), Chaplain (14), Coach-man (15), Cook (1), Creature (54), Footman (10), Maid (20), Messenger (7), Nurse (19), Servant (61), Steward (8), Valet de Chambre (2), and Waiting Women (1).

One other observation can be made by examining words used only once for a special occasion. Congreve's "proviso" scene, so-called, in Act IV of *The Way of the World* has often been singled out for critical praise because of the language in the marriage articles mutually agreed upon by Millamant and Mirabell. This scene contrasts sharply with two other scenes in the same act which treat marriage proposals: Sir Wilfull's fumbling efforts to woo Millamant fail miserably in the early part of the act, and Sir Rowland's (Waitwell's) amorous advances toward Lady Wishfort go awry at the end of the act. One reason the "proviso" scene (WAY WORLD IV.i.154–282) between Millamant and Mirabell is such an achievement is that Congreve creates a language explicitly for the occasion. In the following selection (WAY WORLD IV.i.245–277), the underlined words are used only once in the entire dramatic canon, or only once in *The Way of the World*, or several times but only in this scene:

Mirabell. Item, I Article, that you continue to like your own Face, as
 long as I shall. And while it passes Current with me, that you endeavour not to new Coin it. To which end, together with all Vizards for the day, I prohibit all Masks for the Night, made of oil'd skins and I know not what——Hog's-bones, Hare's-gall, Pig-water, and the marrow of a roasted Cat. In short, I forbid all Commerce with the Gentlewoman in *what-de-call-it*-Court. *Item,* I shut my doors against all Bauds with Baskets, and pennyworths of *Muslin, China, Fans, Atlases,* &c.—*Item* when you shall be Breeding—
Millamant. Ah! Name it not.
Mirabell. Which may be presum'd, with a blessing on our endeavours—
Millamant. Odious endeavours!
Mirabell. I denounce against all strait-Laceing, Squeezing for a Shape, till you mold my boy's head like a Sugar-loaf; and instead

of a <u>Man-child</u>, make me the Father to a <u>Crooked-billet</u>. Lastly to the <u>Dominion</u> of the *Tea-Table,* I submit.—But with *proviso,* that you exceed not in your <u>province</u>; but <u>restrain</u> your self to <u>Native</u> and Simple *Tea-Table* drinks, as <u>Tea, Chocolate</u> and *Cof-fee*. As likewise to <u>Genuine</u> and, Authoriz'd *Tea-Table* talk,— such as <u>mending</u> of <u>Fashions</u>, <u>spoiling</u> Reputations, <u>railing</u> at ab-<u>sent</u> Friends, and so forth—but that on no account <u>you</u> <u>encroach</u> upon the mens <u>prerogative</u>, and presume to drink <u>healths</u>, or <u>toste</u> fellows; for <u>prevention</u> of which; I <u>banish</u> all *Foreign Forces,* all <u>Auxiliaries</u> to the *Tea-Table,* as *Orange-Brandy,* all *Anniseed, Cinamon, Citron* and *Barbado's-Waters,* together with *Ratifia* and the most noble Spirit of *Clary,*—but for *Couslip-Wine, Poppy-Water* and all *Dormitives,* those I <u>allow</u>,—these *proviso's* admitted, in other things I may prove a tractable and complying Husband.

While Mirabell's alliteration and cataloging hold the speech together, it is the distinctive word choice that gives the entire scene its variety and vivacity.

Acknowledgments

Anyone who has ever worked with computers, data systems, and key-punch operations knows that the people who handle the machines are more important than the machines themselves. To Don McWhirter and Tom Blandin of Indiana University Data Systems; keypunch operators Car-ole Fischer, Vicki Elmore, and Jerome Williams; Jack Southard and Art Fiser of Miami University's Computer Center; and James A. Painter (who devised the first Cornell concordance program and has been improving it ever since), I extend my thanks for help, advice, and support. Above all, Sharon Bonner, formerly of Miami University's Computer Center, set the project going, and altered the existing poetry concordance program to a program that would index prose drama. In hammering out the final changes, Robert W. Rosen was indispensable: he wrote programs, punched cards, proofread, and suggested several refinements. His magnanimous ef-forts. have done much to bring this concordance to fruition.

I am also grateful for a financial grant-in-aid which came from the Indi-ana University Research Foundation in the summer of 1968; and, for a gen-erous letter in support of the project, I gratefully acknowledge a debt to the late William Riley Parker. Additional aid from the Miami University Research Committee kept the project on its feet.

Stephen M. Parrish, the general editor of the Cornell Concordance se-ries, has been demanding and encouraging. He has shared with me his wide experience in preparing computer concordances and has resolved several problems. I should also like to thank the other members of the concordance committee, especially Donald Eddy, for their help. The editorial assistance of Mary Jane Wilson at Cornell is greatly appreciated.

Suggestions and support from teachers and colleagues cannot be repaid, but I am grateful to Donald W. Baker, David S. Berkeley, the late Owen Dustin, Walter L. Fertig, Rufus Reiberg, Newton P. Stallknecht, Owen Thomas, and Samuel H. Woods, Jr.

Professor Spiro Peterson read and commented on the introduction after working with the text of the concordance. Mrs. Lydia Paul DuChateau, my mother Mrs. W. H. Lackey, and Cathy deserve personal thanks.

This concordance is dedicated to my friend and teacher Philip R. Wikelund; without him it might never have become a reality.

DAVID D. MANN

Miami University
Oxford, Ohio

A Concordance to the Plays of
WILLIAM CONGREVE

A Concordance to the Plays of
WILLIAM CONGREVE

```
A (2772)      see Alas-a-day, Jack-a-napes, Lack-a-day, Now-a-days, Teste a teste,
                  Tete a tete, Well-a-day
A-cross (2)
   Brisk:                  (Stands musing with his Arms a-cross.)        175  DOUEL DLR  IV.1  311
   Zara:        With haggar'd Eyes? why are your Arms a-cross    .   .  . 380  M. BRIDE   V.2   157
A-drift (1)
   Mrs Frail:   No, I'll leave you a-drift, and go which way you    .  . 286  FOR LCVE   IV.1  420
A-fore (1)
   Ben:         Sweet-Heart, a-fore I turn in; may-hap I may dream of  . 275  FOR LCVE   III.1 809
A-going (2)
   Heartwell:   Why whither in the Devils name am I a-going now?    .  .  62  OLD BATCH  III.1 V 63
   Setter:      'Tis but setting her Mill a-going, and I can drein her of  99  OLD EATCH  V.1   105
A-kin (1)
   Lady Touch:  a-kin to me, upon your account, and had a mind to create . 153  DOUEL DLR  III.1  88
A-new (1)
   Valentine:   shake off Age; get thee Medea's Kettle, and be boil'd a-new, 289  FCR LOVE  IV.1  522
A-pace (2)
   Scandal:     So, faith good Nature works a-pace; you were   .  .  .  . 278  FCR LCVE   IV.1   84
   Manuel:      But wearing now a-pace with ebbing Sand,    .   .  .  . 364  M. BRIDE   IV.1  107
A-Propos (1)
   Brisk:       Deuce take me very a-Propos and Surprizing, ha, ha, ha.  . 141  DOUBL DLR  II.1  125
A-Whoring (1)
   Bellmour:    (peeping). Damn'd Chance! If I had gone a-Whoring    .  .  92  OLD BATCH  IV.4  109
A' (9)
   Bellmour:    parted with his Bed in a Morning, than a' could have slept  37  OLD BATCH  I.1     3
   Heartwell:   such a place, about his Nose and Eyes; though a' has my  .  45  OLD BATCH  I.1   323
   Sir Joseph:  Oh here a' comes--Ah my Hector of Troy, welcome   .  .  .  51  OLD EATCH  II.1  139
   Sir Joseph:  Ay Bully, a Devilish smart Fellow, 'a will fight    .  .  .  51  OLD BATCH  II.1  150
   Silvia:      Will a' not come then?  .  .  .  .  .  .  .  .  .  .  .  60  OLD BATCH  III.1   1
   Lucy:        --a' receiv'd it, as if 'thad been a Letter from his   .  .  61  OLD EATCH  III.1  23
   Bellmour:    thou hast lost it. Ha, ha, how a' strugled, like an Old  .  63  OLD BATCH  III.1  91
   Sir Joseph:  by, I would as soon have let him a' had a hundred of my   .  68  OLD BATCH  III.1 277
   Sir Wilful:  don't think a' knows his own Name.  .  .  .  .  .  .  . 437  WAY WCRLD  III.1 474
A'dies (1)
   Waitwell:    What, my Rival! is the Rebell my Rival? a'dies.   .  .  . 458  WAY WCRLD  IV.1  518
A'has (2)
   Sir Wilful:  What dee do? 'Shart a'has lock'd the Door indeed I   .  . 447  WAY WCRLD  IV.1   92
   Sir Wilful:  What a Vixon trick is this?--Nay, now a'has seen me too-- 447  WAY WCRLD  IV.1   94
Abandon'd (7)
   Mellefont:   Hell and the Devil, is she abandon'd of all Grace--   .  . 156  DOUBL DLR  III.1 235
   Valentine:   abandon'd Wretch.  .  .  .  .  .  .  .  .  .  .  .  . 290  FOR LCVE   IV.1  543
   Zara:        Yes, Traytor, Zara; lost, abandon'd Zara,   .  .  .  .  . 346  M. ERIDE   II.2  248
   Zara:        And now abandon'd--say what then is Osmyn?    .  .  .  . 347  M. ERIDE   II.2  V308
   Osmyn-Alph:  Abandon'd o'er to love where Heav'n forsakes?   .  .  .  . 351  M. ERIDE   III.1  56
   Fainall:     to Millamant, and swear he has abandon'd the whole Sex  . 406  WAY WORLD  I.1   420
   Waitwell:    the last remaining glimpse of hope in my abandon'd  .  . 461  WAY WCRLD  IV.1  644
Abate (4)
   Heartwell:   you abate of your vigor; and that daring Blade which was  .  43  OLD BATCH  I.1   248
   Heli:        When Zara comes, abate of your Aversion.   .  .  .  .  . 352  M. BRIDE   III.1 106
   Sir Wilful:  how that the Peace holds, whereby that is, Taxes abate.  . 440  WAY WCRLD  III.1 575
   Fainall:     or abate one tittle cf my Terms, no, I will insist the more. 474  WAY WCRLD  V.1   477
Abated (1)
   Mincing:     Closet, till my old Lady's anger is abated. O, my old Lady  465  WAY WORLD  V.1   107
Abby (0)      see Westminster-Abby
Abhor (1)
   Marwood:     But not to loath, detest, abhor Mankind, my   .  .  .  . 416  WAY WORLD  II.1  237
```

About (continued)

Millamant:	(Repeating and Walking about.)		446	WAY WORLD	IV.1	51
	(This while Millamant walks about Repeating to her self.)		446	WAY WORLD	IV.1	80
Witwoud:	to whim it about--Why dost thou not speak? thou art both	.	453	WAY WORLD	IV.1	337

Abouts (1)

Valentine:	Widow: I know where abouts you are: Come, to the	.	223	FOR LOVE	I.1	272

Above (14)

Sharper:	You are above--I'me sure--a thought so low, to suffer	.	50	OLD BATCH	II.1	100
Setter:	--'Tis above us:--And, for Men of Quality, they are	.	102	OLD BATCH	V.1	231
Setter:	above it. So that Reputation is e'en as foolish	.	102	OLD BATCH	V.1	232
Sir Paul:	touch a Man for the World--at least not above once a	.	162	DOUBL DLR	III.1	433
Maskwell:	above it?	.	184	DOUBL DLR	IV.2	27
Sr Sampson:	above a stink.--Why there's it; and Musick, don't you	.	245	FOR LOVE	II.1	371
Ben:	and then you'll carry your Keels above Water, he, he, he.		262	FOR LOVE	III.1	335
Ben:	part d'ee see, I'm for carrying things above Board, I'm	.	263	FOR LOVE	III.1	388
Sr Sampson:	--is shot from above, in a Jelly of Love, and so forth;	.	307	FOR LOVE	V.1	381
Garcia:	'Tis scarce above a word; as he were born	.	335	M. BRIDE	I.1	372
Zara:	To love above him, for 'tis dangerous:	.	348	M. BRIDE	II.2	342
Zara:	This, to our mutual Bliss when joyn'd above.	.	381	M. BRIDE	V.2	202
Mirabell:	For Travel! Why the Man that I mean is above	.	400	WAY WORLD	I.1	199
Lady Wish:	dress above. I'll receive Sir Rowland here. Is he handsome?		429	WAY WORLD	III.1	172

Abroad (26)

Bellmour:	Vainlove, and abroad so early! good Morrow!	.	37	OLD BATCH	I.1	1
Bellmour:	abroad--went purely to run away from a Campagne;	.	47	OLD BATCH	I.1	369
Capt Bluff:	abroad? for every Cock will fight upon his own Dunghil.	.	51	OLD BATCH	II.1	153
Capt Bluff:	Oh excuse me Sir; have you serv'd abroad Sir?	.	52	OLD BATCH	II.1	185
Laetitia:	Sir, I seldom stir abroad.	.	90	OLD BATCH	IV.4	34
Capt Bluff:	I plant Laurels for my Head abroad, I may find the Branches	.	111	OLD BATCH	V.2	148
Snap:	if we don't make haste, the Chairmen will be abroad, and	.	224	FOR LOVE	I.1	298
Valentine:	He knows I don't go abroad.	.	225	FOR LOVE	I.1	360
Mrs Frail:	Unlucky Day, and wou'd not let me come abroad: But I	.	231	FOR LOVE	I.1	581
Valentine:	to come abroad, and be at Liberty to see her.	.	234	FOR LOVE	I.1	674
Foresight:	abroad? Is not my Wife come home? Nor my Sister, nor	.	235	FOR LOVE	II.1	2
Angelica:	by going abroad; nor secure you from being one, by	.	237	FOR LOVE	II.1	62
Angelica:	abroad; and if you won't lend me your Coach, I'll take a	.	237	FOR LOVE	II.1	67
Angelica:	you keep her at Home, if you're Jealous when she's abroad?		237	FOR LOVE	II.1	70
Angelica:	you keep her at Home, if you're Jealous of her when she's abroad?	.	237	FOR LOVE	II.1 V 70
Angelica:	Aunt gc abroad.	.	239	FOR LOVE	II.1	145
Jeremy:	time he has been abroad since his Confinement, and he	.	242	FOR LOVE	II.1	268
Valentine:	him: I came to Angelica; but since she was gone abroad, it	.	246	FOR LOVE	II.1	408
Foresight:	there is a contagious Frenzy abroad. How does Valentine?	.	306	FOR LOVE	V.1	333
Foresight:	I think she has not return'd, since she went abroad	.	306	FOR LOVE	V.1	336
Zara:	And force their Balls abroad, at this dead Hour.	.	355	M. BRIDE	III.1	210
Mrs Fain:	You were dress'd before I came abroad.	.	419	WAY WORLD	III.1	354
Lady Wish:	Foible's a lost Thing; has been abroad since	.	426	WAY WORLD	III.1	45
Foible:	are so early abroad, or Catering (says he) ferreting for	.	427	WAY WORLD	III.1	96
Lady Wish:	to chuse. When you have been abroad, Nephew, you'll	.	441	WAY WORLD	III.1	608
Lady Wish:	--At least before he has been abroad.	.	457	WAY WORLD	IV.1	482

Abruptly (1)

Lady Wish:	abruptly, when Sir Wilfull was to have made his addresses.		461	WAY WORLD	IV.1	617

Abscond (1)

	(They abscond.)	.	197	DOUBL DLR	V.1	377

Absence (7)

Bellmour:	Fondness and Impatience of his Absence, by choosing a	.	38	OLD BATCH	I.1	57
Bellmour:	of your absence, by my Spy, (for Faith, honest Isaac, I	.	94	OLD BATCH	IV.4	206
Maskwell:	my Lords absence all this while, and will to her Chamber	.	181	DOUBL DLR	IV.1	523
Maskwell:	my Lords absence all this while, she'll retire to her Chamber	.	181	DOUBL DLR	IV.1 V523
Valentine:	of Confinement, and absence from Angelica, force me to	.	225	FOR LOVE	I.1	341
Gonsalez:	The Multitude should gaze) in Absence of your Eyes.	.	332	M. BRIDE	I.1	245
Osmyn-Alph:	Dwell with thee, and revive thy Heart in Absence.	.	345	M. BRIDE	II.2	212

Absent (6)

Heartwell:	Livery--I am Melancholy when thou art absent;	.	73	OLD BATCH	III.2	78
Heartwell:	Livery--I am Melancholick when thou art absent;	.	73	OLD BATCH	III.2 V 78
Valentine:	What, you will allow an absent Lover--	.	231	FOR LOVE	I.1	554
Valentine:	Oh, why would Angelica be absent from my Eyes	.	289	FOR LOVE	IV.1	535
Manuel:	Not to be found? in an ill hour he's absent.	.	372	M. BRIDE	V.1	1
Mirabell:	Fashions, spoiling Reputations, railing at absent Friends, and	.	451	WAY WORLD	IV.1	268

Absolute (7)

Belinda:	that an absolute Lover would have concluded the poor	.	55	OLD BATCH	I.2	28
Lady Ply:	you? What did I Marry you for? Am I not to be absolute	.	144	DOUBL DLR	II.1	216
Angelica:	an absolute Sea-wit.	.	262	FOR LOVE	III.1	337
Angelica:	You're an absolute Courtier, Sir Sampson.	.	298	FOR LOVE	V.1	20
Angelica:	would neither have an absolute Wit, nor a Fool.	.	299	FOR LOVE	V.1	64
Tattle:	Who I, Sir? I'm an absolute Stranger to you and your	.	305	FOR LOVE	V.1	284
Lady Wish:	will ever endure such a Borachio! you're an absolute	.	455	WAY WORLD	IV.1	389

Absolutely (4)

Jeremy:	absolutely and substantially Mad, as any Freeholder in	.	295	FOR LOVE	IV.1	738
Sr Sampson:	Not absolutely married, Uncle; but very near it,	.	307	FOR LOVE	V.1	390
Lady Wish:	Face. This Wretch has fretted me that I am absolutely	.	428	WAY WORLD	III.1	142
Fainall:	Estate to my management, And absolutely make over my	.	473	WAY WORLD	V.1	435

Absolution (1)

Mellefont:	and with a little Pennance and my Absolution all this may		185	DOUBL DLR	IV.2	62

Abstracted (1)

	As any one abstracted Fop to shew.	.	479	WAY WORLD	EPI.	30

Abundantly (1)

Lady Froth:	O I Writ, Writ abundantly,--do you never	.	138	DOUBL DLR	II.1	13

Abus'd (11)

Capt Bluff:	you my Friend; Abus'd and Cuff'd and Kick'd.	.	70	OLD BATCH	III.1	349
Miss Prue:	I won't be call'd Names, nor I won't be abus'd	.	264	FOR LOVE	III.1	428
Angelica:	are very much abus'd in that Matter; He's no more Mad	.	299	FOR LOVE	V.1	87
Valentine:	You were abus'd, Sir, I never was Distracted.	.	310	FOR LOVE	V.1	504
Zara:	You know how I abus'd the credulous King;	.	347	M. BRIDE	II.2	293
Zara:	'Tis plain, I've been abus'd--Death and Destruction!	.	359	M. BRIDE	III.1	398

Abus'd   (continued)
Almeria: And living? yes, I will; I've been abus'd . . . . . 383 M. BRIDE   V.2   295
Marwood: Nature so abus'd by that Dissembler. . . . . 414 WAY WORLD II.1   164
Lady Wish: know you are abus'd. He who pretends to be Sir Rowland . 460 WAY WORLD IV.1   587
Mrs Fain: I am wrong'd and abus'd, and so are you. 'Tis . . . 466 WAY WORLD V.1   153
Mrs Fain: I tell you Madam you're abus'd--stick to . . . . . 466 WAY WORLD V.1   173
Abuse (4)
Vainlove: But is it not an Abuse to the Lover to be made a . . . 38 OLD BATCH I.1   60
Bellmour: As you say the Abuse is to the Lover, not the . . . 39 OLD BATCH I.1   63
Lucy: No Sirrah, I'le keep it on to abuse thee and leave thee . 65 OLD BATCH III.1 181
Vainlove: abuse Mercy, by committing new Offences. . . . . . 87 OLD BATCH IV.3   140
Abused (1)
Careless: abused by a pretended Coyness in their Wives, and . . . 180 DOUBL DLR IV.1   497
Academy (1)
Marwood: Here is an Academy in Town for that use. . . . . . 440 WAY WORLD III.1 586
Accent (2)
Tattle: Accent. . . . . 302 FOR LOVE   V.1   183
Leonora: It bore the Accent of a Humane Voice. . . . . . . 339 M. BRIDE   II.1   53
Accents (1)
Maskwell: same Words and Accents, when I speak what I do think; . 150 DOUBL DLR II.1   461
Accept (1)
Mirabell: But that you wou'd not accept of a Remedy from . . . 473 WAY WORLD V.1   450
Accepted (2)
Sharper: Sir Joseph--Your Note was accepted, and the . . . . 68 OLD BATCH III.1 284
Sir Joseph: They won't be accepted, so readily as the Bill, Sir. . . 68 OLD BATCH III.1 286
Access (1)
Osmyn-Alph: If Piety be thus debarr'd Access . . . . 350 M. BRIDE   III.1   28
Accessary (1)
Mirabell: not us be accessary to your putting the Ladies out of . . 409 WAY WORLD I.1   524
Accident (3)
Cynthia: Hand, it is an Accident of Fortune. . . . . 142 DOUBL DLR II.1   163
Lady Ply: O the unlucki'st Accident, I'm afraid I shan't . . . 178 DOUBL DLR IV.1   393
Mrs Frail: O, Sister, the most unlucky Accident! . . . . . . 309 FOR LOVE   V.1   440
Accidentally (1)
Angelica: you, till I accidentally touch'd upon your tender Part: But 296 FOR LOVE   IV.1   766
Accidents (1)
Mellefont: Causes and Accidents of Fortune in this Life! but to what . 187 DOUBL DLR IV.2   142
Accomplice (3)
Manuel: Confusion! then my Daughter's an Accomplice, . . . 367 M. BRIDE   IV.1   234
Manuel: Thou art Accomplice too much with Zara; here . . . . 373 M. BRIDE   V.1   51
Lady Wish: deceive me? hast thou been a wicked accomplice with that . 474 WAY WORLD V.1   481
Accomplish (4)
Mellefont: accomplish her designs; whether the hopes of her revenge, 129 DOUBL DLR I.1   96
Mellefont: accomplish her designs; whether the hopes of revenge, . 129 DOUBL DLR I.1 V 96
Maskwell: made this agreement, if I accomplish her designs (as I told 149 DOUBL DLR II.1   427
Lady Wish: more from you than all your life can accomplish--O don't . 466 WAY WORLD V.1   170
Accomplish'd (3)
Maskwell: Opportunity, accomplish'd my Design; I prest the yielding 136 DOUBL DLR I.1   369
Lady Ply: Person and Parts of so accomplish'd a Person, whose Merit . 169 DOUBL DLR IV.1   82
Jeremy: and so Accomplish'd a Gentleman. . . . . 302 FOR LOVE   V.1   205
Accomplishments (3)
Careless: is very well in her Accomplishments--but it is when my . 160 DOUBL DLR III.1 376
Fainall: For having only that one Hope, the accomplishment . . 413 WAY WORLD II.1   112
Lady Wish: accomplishment of your revenge--Not that I respect . . 458 WAY WORLD IV.1   508
Accomplisht (1)
Tattle: long receiv'd the passionate Addresses of the accomplisht 255 FOR LOVE   III.1   68
Accord (2)
              It seems like Eden, fruitful of its own accord. . . . 213 FOR LOVE   PRO.   17
Ben: civilly to me, of her own accord: Whatever you think of . 264 FOR LOVE   III.1   411
According (5)
Lucy: not appear to Day according to the Summons I brought . 66 OLD BATCH III.1 218
Mellefont: to their Tea, and Scandal; according to their Antient . 127 DOUBL DLR I.1   12
Mellefont: to their Tea, and Scandal; according to their Ancient . 127 DOUBL DLR I.1 V 12
Maskwell: Why thus--I'll go according to Appointment; . . . . 157 DOUBL DLR III.1 248
Buckram: Sir, it is drawn according to your Directions; there . . 308 FOR LOVE   V.1   429
Accordingly (1)
Setter: And my Relation; pray let her be respected accordingly. . 111 OLD BATCH V.2   140
Account (20)
Lady Touch: a-kin to me, upon your account, and had a mind to create . 153 DOUBL DLR III.1   88
Lady Ply: O las, no indeed, Sir Paul, 'tis upon your account. . . 172 DOUBL DLR IV.1   181
Lady Ply: day: I would look upon the Account again; and may be . 173 DOUBL DLR IV.1   216
Mellefont: turn to good account. . . . . 185 DOUBL DLR IV.2   63
Maskwell: up this Account, to all our satisfactions. . . . . . 194 DOUBL DLR V.1   244
Scandal: I'll give an account of you, and your Proceedings. . . 234 FOR LOVE   I.1   675
Mrs Frail: Account I have heard of his Education can be no Conjurer: 248 FOR LOVE   II.1   493
Tattle: self upon my Account; Gad, I was sorry for it with all my 258 FOR LOVE   III.1   177
Ben: Mess, I've had such a Hurricane upon your account . . 285 FOR LOVE   IV.1   360
Mrs Frail: My acccunt, pray what's the matter? . . . . 285 FOR LOVE   IV.1   362
Ben: fobb'd,--if I have got anger here upon your account, . . 286 FOR LOVE   IV.1   415
Foresight: Robin make ready to give an Account of his Plate and . 306 FOR LOVE   V.1   327
Osmyn-Alph: It sets a Debt of that Account before me, ... 347 M. BRIDE   II.2   289
Gonsalez: But she might wish on his Account to see him. . . . . 367 M. BRIDE   IV.1   231
Fainall: you of the slight Account you once could make of strictest 414 WAY WORLD II.1   180
Foible: Account, I'm sure you wou'd not suspect my Fidelity. . 427 WAY WORLD III.1   88
Mirabell: account. Well, have I Liberty to offer Conditions--that . 450 WAY WORLD IV.1   229
Mirabell: so forth--but that on no account you encroach upon the . 451 WAY WORLD IV.1   269
Lady Wish: Well Nephew, upon your account--ah, ... 472 WAY WORLD V.1   400
Mirabell: Madam, disquiet not your self on that account, to . . . 478 WAY WORLD V.1   613
Accounted (1)
Mirabell: ever been accounted Venial. At least think it is Punishment 472 WAY WORLD V.1   387
Accounts (1)
Fondlewife: by the way,--and I must have my Papers of Accounts . . 89 OLD BATCH IV.4   24
Lady Ply: I'll settle the Accounts to your Advantage. . . . . . 174 DOUBL DLR IV.1   265
Lady Ply: I'll settle Accounts to your Advantage. . . . . . . 174 DOUBL DLR IV.1 V265
Accumulated (1)
Manuel: Shall he accumulated under-bear. . . . . 368 M. BRIDE   IV.1   298

4

		PAGE	TITLE	ACT.SC	LINE
Accurs'd (1)					
Zara:	O this accurs'd, this base, this treach'rous King!	380	M. BRIDE	V.2	V168
Accursed (1)					
Manuel:	Now doom'd to die, that most accursed Osmyn.	368	M. BRIDE	IV.1	288
Accusation (4)					
Angelica:	'Tis an unreasonable Accusation, that you lay upon	314	FOR LOVE	V.1	627
Selim:	Your Accusation highly has incens'd	361	M. BRIDE	IV.1	4
Marwood:	that can confirm your groundless Accusation. I hate him.	414	WAY WORLD	II.1	154
Mrs Fain:	a false accusation, as false as Hell, as false as your Friend	466	WAY WORLD	V.1	154
Accusation's (1)					
Maskwell:	So that Accusation's Answer'd; on to the next.	135	DOUBL DLR	I.1	319
Accuse (4)					
Bellmour:	accuse my self.	93	OLD BATCH	IV.4	149
Angelica:	You can't accuse me of Inconstancy; I never told	254	FOR LOVE	III.1	27
Valentine:	But I can accuse you of Uncertainty, for not telling	254	FOR LOVE	III.1	29
Manuel:	(aside). How? better than my Hopes; does she accuse	348	M. BRIDE	II.2	359
Accusing (1)					
Lady Touch:	--I was accusing you of Neglect.	183	DOUBL DLR	IV.2	11
Acknowledge (4)					
Scandal:	forc'd you to acknowledge a Kindness for Valentine,	294	FOR LOVE	IV.1	689
Angelica:	acknowledge your Trick, and confess your Master's	295	FOR LOVE	IV.1	735
Valentine:	Sir, I'm come to acknowledge my Errors, and ask	310	FOR LOVE	V.1	500
Marwood:	Come, be as sincere, acknowledge that your Sentiments	410	WAY WORLD	II.1	31
Acknowledgment (10)					
Sharper:	So-h, O Sir I am easily pacify'd, the acknowledgment	49	OLD BATCH	II.1	62
Sir Joseph:	Acknowledgment! Sir I am all over acknowledgment,	49	OLD BATCH	II.1	64
Lady Ply:	should ever be wanting in a respectful acknowledgment	169	DOUBL DLR	IV.1	80
Scandal:	An Acknowledgment of Love from you, perhaps, may	277	FOR LOVE	IV.1	63
Angelica:	of Revenge--Acknowledgment of Love! I find you	277	FOR LOVE	IV.1	68
Zara:	Acknowledgment from Noble Minds. Such Thanks	336	M. BRIDE	I.1	416
Zara:	Deserve acknowledgment from Noble Minds.	336	M. BRIDE	I.1	V416
Almeria:	I'll drink my glad Acknowledgment--	382	M. BRIDE	V.2	260
Mirabell:	with all acknowledgments for your transcendent goodness.	472	WAY WORLD	V.1	407
Acorn (1)					
Lady Wish:	Acorn? Why didst thou not bring thy Thimble? Hast thou	425	WAY WORLD	III.1	30
Acquaint (7)					
Bellmour:	me Leave to acquaint you with it.--Do you carry on	98	OLD BATCH	V.1	66
Mrs Frail:	I'll acquaint you with a design that I have: To tell Truth,	248	FOR LOVE	II.1	486
Valentine:	Acquaint Jeremy with it, he may easily bring it	292	FOR LOVE	IV.1	616
Selim:	This Grant--and I'll acquaint you with the rest.	362	M. BRIDE	IV.1	60
Foible:	Madam, I beg your Ladyship to acquaint Mr. Mirabell	430	WAY WORLD	III.1	214
Mincing:	Mem, I come to acquaint your Laship that Dinner	441	WAY WORLD	III.1	614
Mincing:	Mem, I am come to acquaint your Laship that Dinner	441	WAY WORLD	III.1	V614
Acquaintance (17)					
Bellmour:	worth your acquaintance--a little of thy Chymistry Tom,	46	OLD BATCH	I.1	345
Sharper:	Well, Ile endeavour his acquaintance--you steer	47	OLD BATCH	I.1	385
Sharper:	since it has purchas'd me the friendship and acquaintance of	49	OLD BATCH	II.1	77
Vainlove:	here is a silent Witness of your acquaintance.--	88	OLD BATCH	IV.3	178
Vainlove:	here's a silent Witness of your acquaintance.--	88	OLD BATCH	IV.3	V178
Scandal:	most of your Acquaintance to the Life, and as like as at	232	FOR LOVE	I.1	618
Valentine:	few Acquaintance.	280	FOR LOVE	IV.1	179
Valentine:	an Old Acquaintance with a new Face.	292	FOR LOVE	IV.1	620
Mirabell:	I had rather be his Relation than his Acquaintance.	400	WAY WORLD	I.1	196
Mirabell:	You are very free with your Friends Acquaintance.	404	WAY WORLD	I.1	356
Waitwell:	Difficulty will be how to recover my Acquaintance and	424	WAY WORLD	II.1	557
Millamant:	has not the liberty of choosing one's Acquaintance, as one	432	WAY WORLD	III.1	297
Marwood:	of one Set of Acquaintance, tho' never so good, as we are of	432	WAY WORLD	III.1	300
Sir Wilful:	further acquaintance,--So for the present Cozen, I'll take	446	WAY WORLD	IV.1	77
Sir Wilful:	present, 'tis sufficient till further acquaintance, that's all--	447	WAY WORLD	IV.1	85
Millamant:	acquaintance; or to be intimate with Fools, because they	450	WAY WORLD	IV.1	218
Mirabell:	acquaintance be General; that you admit no sworn Confident,	451	WAY WORLD	IV.1	235
Acquainted (9)					
Sir Joseph:	been long acquainted; you have lost a good Jest for want	50	OLD BATCH	II.1	117
Setter:	acquainted with my parts) employs me as a Pimp: why	64	OLD BATCH	III.1	140
Sir Joseph:	are like to be better acquainted.	111	OLD BATCH	V.2	132
Mellefont:	acquainted with the Secret of my Aunt Touchwood's	129	DOUBL DLR	I.1	85
Lord Touch:	familiarly acquainted with it. This is a little Trick wrought	151	DOUBL DLR	III.1	14
Mrs Fore:	will hang us--He'll think we brought 'em acquainted.	250	FOR LOVE	II.1	569
Scandal:	Would he have Angelica acquainted with the Reason	276	FOR LOVE	IV.1	6
Fainall:	Marry her, marry her; be half as well acquainted	400	WAY WORLD	I.1	175
Sir Wilful:	somewhat wary at first, before I am acquainted;--But I	446	WAY WORLD	IV.1	75
Acquiesce (1)					
Sir Paul:	(aside to her). I acquiesce, my Lady; but don't snub so	159	DOUBL DLR	III.1	334
Acquir'd (1)					
Lady Wish:	has acquir'd Discretion to choose for himself.	432	WAY WORLD	III.1	265
Acquiring (1)					
Bellmour:	Mistresses of my own acquiring; must yet take Vainlove's	41	OLD BATCH	I.1	140
Acquit (7)					
Sharper:	trivial a Sum, will wholly acquit you and doubly engage	50	OLD BATCH	II.1	90
Sharper:	But how the Devil do you think to acquit your self	100	OLD BATCH	V.1	154
Valentine:	Well, but how did you acquit your self?	228	FOR LOVE	I.1	444
Tattle:	acquit our selves--And for my part--But your	257	FOR LOVE	III.1	135
Manuel:	Acquit thy self of those detested Names,	368	M. BRIDE	IV.1	286
Witwoud:	acquit him--That indeed I cou'd wish were otherwise.	403	WAY WORLD	I.1	312
Mrs Fain:	his Charge, of which his Enemies must acquit him.	412	WAY WORLD	II.1	76
Acquittance (1)					
Maskwell:	general acquittance--Rival is equal, and Love like Death	150	DOUBL DLR	II.1	449
Acres (1)					
Sharper:	Dirt, you have large Acres and can soon repay it--	50	OLD BATCH	II.1	109
Acrostick (1)					
Saygrace:	of an Acrostick, and be with you in the twinckling of an	194	DOUBL DLR	V.1	273
Act (18)	see Over-act				
Vainlove:	an Act of Oblivion.	110	OLD BATCH	V.2	103

5

Admirable (4)
    Mrs Fore: Countenance purely, you'd make an Admirable Player.   .   . 247   FOR LOVE   II.1 452
    Tattle: Admirable! That was as well as if you had been born   .   . 252   FOR LOVE   II.1 644
    Scandal: Humh!--An admirable Composition, faith, this   278   FOR LOVE   IV.1   92
    Scandal: have been told she had that admirable quality of forgetting 284 FOR LOVE   IV.1 334
Admiral (1)
    Mrs Frail: an Admiral and an eminent Justice of the Peace to be the . 231   FOR LOVE   I.1   578
Admiration (6)
    Fondlewife: O Lord! O strange! I am in admiration of your   .   .   .   93   OLD BATCH   IV.4 153
    Careless: Lady! that is the envy of her Sex, and the admiration of . 160   DOUBL DLR   III.1 381
    Careless: Lady! that is the envy of her own Sex, and the admiration of 160 DOUBL DLR   III.1 V381
    Gonsalez: Would feed his Faculty of Admiration.   332   M. BRIDE   I.1   242
    Gonsalez: Would feed its Faculty of Admiration.   332   M. BRIDE   I.1   V242
    Garcia: I've heard with Admiration, of your Friendship;   .   .   . 338   M. BRIDE   II.1   13
Admire (10)
    Sharper: the person in the World, whose Character I admire.   .   . 49   OLD BATCH   II.1   78
    Belinda: enjoyment of that Conversation you admire.   57   OLD BATCH   II.2   89
    Musician: Men will admire, adore and die, ... 60   OLD BATCH   II.2 197
    Bellmour: admire the Words.   60   OLD BATCH   II.2 205
    Sharper: which narrow Souls cannot dare to admire.--And   .   .   . 86   OLD BATCH   IV.3 127
    Belinda: --Don't you admire him?   87   OLD BATCH   IV.3 146
    Cynthia: If not, they like and admire themselves--And why is   .   . 167   DOUBL DLR   III.1 629
    Valentine: Which, to admire, we should not understand.   297   FOR LOVE   IV.1 816
    Witwoud: And for my part--But that it is almost a Fashion to admire 407   WAY WORLD   II.1 466
    Mirabell: such Society? It is impossible they should admire you,   . 421   WAY WORLD   II.1 437
Admirer (3)
    Lord Froth: admirer of my Lady Whifler, Mr. Sneer, and Sir Laurence   . 162   DOUBL DLR   III.1 461
    Lady Ply: respect--That he has own'd himself to be my Admirer   .   . 172   DOUBL DLR   IV.1 166
    Valentine: then ever, and appear more notoriously her Admirer in   .   217   FOR LOVE   I.1   51
Admires (1)
    Sr Sampson: a Man that admires a fine Woman, as much as I do.   .   .   . 298 FOR LOVE   V.1   19
Admiring (3)
    Mellefont: taken up, with admiring one another, and Brisk's   .   .   . 130 DOUBL DLR   I.1   134
    Angelica: In admiring me, you misplace the Novelty.   .   .   .   .   . 314 FOR LOVE   V.1   635
    Manuel: Who with such Lustre, strike admiring Eyes, ... 335   M. BRIDE   I.1   388
Admit (7)   see Readmit
    Vainlove: Madam, will admit of no farther reasoning.--But   .   .   . 88   OLD BATCH   IV.3 177
    Maskwell: Lord's Displeasure to a degree that will admit of no   .   . 154 DOUBL DLR   III.1 147
                 'Tis hard that they must every one admit;   .   .   .   .   . 204 DOUEL DLR   EPI.   31
                 Should Grants to Poets made, admit Resumption: .   .   .   393 WAY WORLD   PRO.   19
    Mirabell: acquaintance be General; that you admit no sworn Confident, 451 WAY WORLD   IV.1 235
    Marwood: Family, shou'd admit of Misconstruction, or make me   .   . 466   WAY WORLD   V.1   163
    Lady Wish: Testimony of your Obedience; but I cannot admit that   .   . 470 WAY WORLD   V.1   334
Admittance (6)
    Heli: Gave order to the Guards for my Admittance.   351   M. BRIDE   III.1 44
    Selim: That none but Mutes may have Admittance to him.   .   .   . 362   M. BRIDE   IV.1   58
    Zara: You order none may have Admittance to   .   .   .   .   .   . 365 M. BRIDE   IV.1 162
    Manuel: Her Warrant, have Admittance to the Moor.   .   .   .   .   . 365 M. BRIDE   IV.1 169
    Manuel: Have yet required admittance?   372   M. BRIDE   V.1   4
    Millamant: --He is without and waits your leave for admittance.   .   . 470 WAY WORLD   V.1   332
Admitted (4)
    Tattle: never be admitted beyond a Drawing-Room: I shall   .   .   . 230 FOR LOVE   I.1   517
    Zara: You give strict Charge, that none may be admitted   .   .   . 365 M. BRIDE   IV.1 V162
    Marwood: Visit is always a Disguise; and never admitted by a Woman   433 WAY WORLD   III.1 312
    Mirabell: allow,--these proviso's admitted, in other things I may   . 452   WAY WORLD   IV.1 276
Admitting (1)
    Musician: But admitting their Embraces, ...   60   OLD BATCH   II.2 199
Ado (2)
    Mellefont: much ado I prevented her doing me or her self a mischief: 130   DOUBL DLR   I.1   115
    Tattle: much ado to tell your Ladyship, how long I have been in   . 291   FOR LOVE   IV.1 576
Adopted (1)
                 So much she doats on her adopted Care.   .   .   .   .   .   . 393 WAY WORLD   PRO.   10
Ador'd (3)
    Bellmour: Yet is ador'd by that Biggot Sr. Joseph Wittoll, as the   . 46   OLD BATCH   I.1   356
    Bellmour: But tell me how you would be Ador'd--I am very   .   .   .   59   OLD BATCH   II.2 173
    Belinda: Then know, I would be Ador'd in Silence.   59   OLD BATCH   II.2 175
Adoration (1)
    Lady Touch: Where is that humble Love, the Languishing, that Adoration, 136   DOUBL DLR   I.1   350
Adore (6)
    Vainlove: will adore thee.   38   OLD BATCH   I.1   54
    Musician: Men will admire, adore and die, ...   60   OLD BATCH   II.2 197
    Mellefont: Let me adore thee, my better Genius! By Heav'n I   .   .   . 157   DOUBL DLR   III.1 257
    Brisk: No more I have I'gad, for I adore 'em all in your   .   .   . 176 DOUBL DLR   IV.1 336
    Manuel: Nor will I Victory in Camps adore: 337   M. BRIDE   I.1   453
    Manuel: Or lift his Eyes to like, where I adore?   348   M. BRIDE   II.2 357
Adoreable (1)
    Waitwell: --and till I have the possession of your adoreable Person, I 457 WAY WORLD   IV.1 491
Adored (2)
    Lady Froth: Oh my adored Mr. Brisk!   177   DOUEL DLR   IV.1 359
    Sir Paul: expectation of my Adored Charmer.   .   .   .   . 178 DOUBL DLR   IV.1 415
Adorer (1)
    Careless: Adorer dies.   170   DOUEL DLR   IV.1   88
Adorn'd (1)
    Gonsalez: Chariots of War, adorn'd with glittering Gems, ... 331 M. BRIDE   I.1   229
Adsbud (1)
    Setter: Adsbud who's in fault, Mistress Mine? who flung the   .   . 66   OLD BATCH   III.1 204
Adsheart (1)
    Sir Joseph: Teeth. Adsheart if he should come just now when I'm   .   . 68   OLD BATCH   III.1 278
Adslidikins (1)
    Sir Joseph: and get 50 Pieces more from him. Adslidikins, Bully, we'll   85   OLD BATCH   IV.3   63
Adultery (3)
    Fondlewife: of Adultery is? have you weigh'd it I say? For it is a very 77   OLD BATCH   IV.1   69
    Fondlewife: Devil's Pater-noster. Hold, let me see: The Innocent
                 Adultery.   92   OLD BATCH   IV.4 107
    Fondlewife: Adultery, and innocent! O Lord! Here's Doctrine!   .   .   . 92   OLD BATCH   IV.4 112

Advanc'd (2)

| Zara: | And as my Kinsman, honour'd and advanc'd you. . . . | 347 | M. BRIDE | II.2 | 296 |
| Mirabell: | Your bill of fare is something advanc'd in this latter | 450 | WAY WORLD | IV.1 | 228 |

Advance (3)

Mirabell:	whole Design, and put it in your Power to ruin or advance	417	WAY WORLD	II.1	281
Lady Wish:	shall die with Confusion, if I am forc'd to advance--Oh	429	WAY WORLD	III.1	159
Lady Wish:	no, I can never advance--I shall swoon if he shou'd	429	WAY WORLD	III.1	160

Advances (3)

Fainall:	she has made you Advances, which you have slighted?	397	WAY WORLD	I.1	83
Fainall:	wilfully neglect the gross advances made him by my Wife;	413	WAY WORLD	II.1	144
Lady Wish:	expect advances. No, I hope Sir Rowland is better bred,	429	WAY WORLD	III.1	161

Advantage (8)

Araminta:	find fools, have the same advantage, over a Face in a Mask;	86	OLD BATCH	IV.3	117
Setter:	Advantage.	102	OLD BATCH	V.1	235
Araminta:	We had better take the Advantage of a little of our	112	OLD BATCH	V.2	173
Lady Ply:	I'll settle the Accounts to your Advantage.	174	DOUBL DLR	IV.1	265
Lady Ply:	I'll settle Accounts to your Advantage.	174	DOUBL DLR	IV.1 V	265
Maskwell:	your own art that turned it to advantage.	187	DOUBL DLR	V.1	5
Valentine:	give Scandal such an Advantage; why, your running away	229	FOR LOVE	I.1	512
Lady Wish:	some Confusion.--It shows the Foot to advantage, and	445	WAY WORLD	V.1	30

Advantages (1)

| Lady Ply: | those Advantages: I know my own Imperfections--but . . | 159 | DOUBL DLR | III.1 | 349 |

Adventurer (1)

| Scandal: | he is a thoughtless Adventurer, ... | 234 | FOR LOVE | I.1 | 679 |

Adventures (2)

| Heartwell: | purpose, ever embarking in Adventures, yet never comes | 42 | OLD BATCH | I.1 | 199 |
| Marwood: | Adventures. . . . . | 440 | WAY WORLD | III.1 | 577 |

Adverse (1)

| Osmyn-Alph: | And Chaff, the Sport of adverse Winds; till late . . | 351 | M. BRIDE | III.1 | 60 |

Advice (8)

Lady Froth:	Advice.	142	DOUBL DLR	II.1	135
Angelica:	Therefore I ask your Advice, Sir Sampson: I have . .	299	FOR LOVE	V.1	60
Sr Sampson:	wou'd take my Advice in a Husband--	300	FOR LOVE	V.1	104
Angelica:	Hold, hold, Sir Sampson. I ask'd your Advice for a . .	300	FOR LOVE	V.1	105
Millamant:	act always by Advice, and so tedious to be told of ones	422	WAY WORLD	II.1	455
Witwoud:	Husband's advice; but he sneak'd off.	454	WAY WORLD	IV.1	382
Mirabell:	suspected--she did I say by the wholesome advice of .	476	WAY WORLD	V.1	544
Mrs Fain:	advice all is owing.	477	WAY WORLD	V.1	571

Advis'd (1)

| Manuel: | Be thou advis'd, and let me go while yet . . . . . | 369 | M. BRIDE | IV.1 | 328 |

Advise (8)

Lady Ply:	sake step in here and advise me quickly, before he sees.	178	DOUBL DLR	IV.1	403
Ben:	Heart. Look you, Friend, if I may advise you, when she's	310	FOR LOVE	V.1	490
Angelica:	I'll advise you, how you may avoid such another. Learn to	312	FOR LOVE	V.1	571
Zara:	What shall I say? Invent, contrive, advise	361	M. BRIDE	IV.1	23
Selim:	Might breed Suspicion of the Cause. Advise, ...	362	M. BRIDE	IV.1	46
Zara:	That too I will advise.	365	M. BRIDE	IV.1	149
Marwood:	Nay Madam, I advise nothing, I only lay before . . .	468	WAY WORLD	V.1	241
Mirabell:	any Obligation to me; or else perhaps I cou'd advise.--	473	WAY WORLD	V.1	452

Advises (2)

| Valentine: | Understanding. So Epictetus advises. . . . . . . | 216 | FOR LOVE | I.1 | 16 |
| Gonsalez: | My Lord, the Queen advises well. . . . . | 365 | M. BRIDE | III.1 | 156 |

Advocate (1)

| | Well, I'm his Advocate--by me he prays you, ... | 35 | OLD BATCH | PRO. | 17 |

Aegyptian (2)

| Valentine: | Piece of Aegyptian Antiquity, or an Irish Manuscript; you | 297 | FOR LOVE | IV.1 | 802 |
| Jeremy: | O Ignorance! (aside). A cunning Aegyptian, Sir, that . | 302 | FOR LOVE | V.1 | 193 |

Aera's (1)

| Osmyn-Alph: | I shall have liv'd beyond all Aera's then, ... | 343 | M. BRIDE | II.2 | 143 |

Aesop's (2)

| Sir Joseph: | in Aesop's Fables, Bully? A-Gad there are good Morals to | 101 | OLD BATCH | V.1 | 175 |
| Sir Joseph: | be pick'd out of Aesop's Fables, let me tell you that; and | 101 | OLD BATCH | V.1 | 176 |

Affair (17)

Barnaby:	And run the hazard to lose your affair so!	76	OLD BATCH	IV.1	38
Barnaby:	And run the hazard to lose your affair, Sir!	76	OLD BATCH	IV.1 V	38
Sir Paul:	my Posterity, he Thy? Can't you contrive that affair .	173	DOUBL DLR	IV.1	229
Scandal:	wicked, and Heav'n grant he may mean well in his Affair	267	FOR LOVE	III.1	522
Mrs Frail:	this Affair between you and me. Here you make love to .	272	FOR LOVE	III.1	687
Mirabell:	her with the Imputation of an Affair with a young . .	397	WAY WORLD	I.1	72
Mirabell:	Well, is the grand Affair over? You have been something	398	WAY WORLD	I.1	111
Mirabell:	The Persons concern'd in that Affair, have yet a . .	412	WAY WORLD	II.1	100
Lady Wish:	Confidence. I sent her to Negotiate an Affair, in which if	426	WAY WORLD	III.1	51
Marwood:	for him you had not been his Confessor in that Affair;	431	WAY WORLD	III.1	241
Marwood:	of Wit, but to blind her Affair with a Lover of Sense. If	433	WAY WORLD	III.1	313
Mrs Fain:	your Proxy in this Affair; but I have business of my own.	446	WAY WORLD	IV.1	68
Lady Wish:	will bind me to you inviolably. I have an Affair of moment	457	WAY WORLD	IV.1	467
Mrs Fain:	Ay, all's out, My affair with Mirabell, every . . .	464	WAY WORLD	V.1	81
Marwood:	Let us first dispatch the affair in hand Madam, . . .	465	WAY WORLD	V.1	136
Marwood:	no more with an affair, in which I am not Personally .	466	WAY WORLD	V.1	165
Lady Wish:	detection of this affair.	475	WAY WORLD	V.1	505

Affairs (12)

Setter:	She was pumping me about how your Worship's Affairs .	99	OLD BATCH	V.1	113
Setter:	Why, to be brief, for I have weighty Affairs depending:	105	OLD BATCH	V.1	341
Sir Paul:	The strangest posture of Affairs!	200	DOUBL DLR	V.1	503
Sir Paul:	Affairs may be in a very good posture; I saw her go into	200	DOUBL DLR	V.1	506
Foresight:	Crab was ascending, and all my Affairs go backward. .	235	FOR LOVE	I.1	13
Tattle:	with her own Affairs.	255	FOR LOVE	III.1	62
Angelica:	in your Affairs.	299	FOR LOVE	V.1	92
Sr Sampson:	Madam, all my Affairs are scarce worthy to be laid at .	299	FOR LOVE	V.1	94
Heli:	Our Posture of Affairs and scanty Time, ...	352	M. BRIDE	III.1	92
Waitwell:	Sir, your Affairs are in a prosperous way.	423	WAY WORLD	III.1	511
Lady Wish:	Affairs really I know not what to do--- (Calls)--Foible--I	431	WAY WORLD	III.1	256
Mirabell:	her affairs under your Countenance and tempt you to make	451	WAY WORLD	IV.1	237

Affect (5)

| Lucy: | not to affect his Masters faults; and consequently . . | 64 | OLD BATCH | III.1 | 147 |
| Cynthia: | He does not indeed affect either pertness, or . . . | 139 | DOUBL DLR | II.1 | 53 |

9

Affronts (1)
Marwood: liable to affronts. You will pardon me, Madam, If I meddle   466 WAY WORLD   V.1   164
Afore (1)
Ben: afore I ha' done with 'en. . . . . 265 FOR LOVE III.1   438
Afraid (40)
   Capt Bluff: Sir: I'me afraid you scarce know the History of the Late . 52 OLD BATCH   II.1   188
   Belinda: my Scl, I'm afraid you'l follow evil Courses. . . . . 55 OLD BATCH   II.2   52
   Bellmour: Or as you did to day, when half afraid you snatch'd   . 63 OLD BATCH III.1   95
   Sir Joseph: No, no, hang't I was not afraid neither--Tho' I . . . . 68 OLD BATCH III.1   271
   Silvia: afraid to believe you yet. . . . . 72 OLD BATCH III.2   54
   Fondlewife: lovely in the Eyes of Women--Sincerely I am afraid he . . 76 OLD BATCH   IV.1   28
   Sharper: I'me afraid I give too great a Proof of my own at this
                    time-- . . . . 79 OLD BATCH   IV.1   158
   Bellmour: may lie down;--quickly, for I'm afraid I shall have a Fit. 82 OLD BATCH   IV.2   87
   Laetitia: Does it hold you long? I'm afraid to carry you into . 83 OLD BATCH   IV.2   90
   Araminta: We are afraid not. . . . . 85 OLD BATCH   IV.3   83
   Sharper: afraid, you would not have given us leave to know you. . 86 OLD BATCH   IV.3   115
   Laetitia: come near it, I'm afraid 'tis the Devil; indeed it has
                    hoofs, ... 92 OLD BATCH   IV.4   133
   Fondlewife: I'm afraid, 'tis the Flesh, thou Harlot. Deare, with
                    the Pox. . . . . 92 OLD BATCH   IV.4   136
   Lord Froth: Wife? I'm afraid not. . . . . 141 DOUBL DLR   II.1   103
   Mellefont: Ha, ha, ha, I, a very Fury; but I was most afraid . . 149 DOUBL DLR   II.1   416
   Mellefont: Ha, ha, ha, ay, a very Fury; but I was most afraid . . 149 DOUBL DLR   II.1 V416
   Maskwell: I'm afraid my frailty leans that way--but I don't . 156 DOUBL DLR III.1   207
   Brisk: I'm afraid that simile wont do in wet Weather-- . . . . 164 DOUBL DLR III.1   517
   Lady Froth: I swear and vow I'm afraid so--And yet our . . . . . 165 DOUBL DLR III.1   547
   Lady Ply: O the unlucki'st Accident, I'm afraid I shan't . . . 178 DOUBL DLR   IV.1   393
   Sir Paul: amazed, and so overjoy'd, so afraid, and so sorry.—But 179 DOUBL DLR   IV.1   460
                 And are afraid to use their own Edge-Tools. . . . . 214 FOR LOVE   PRO.   38
   Scandal: Aye? Why then I'm afraid Jeremy has Wit: For . . . . 219 FOR LOVE   I.1   120
   Angelica: her Nature. Uncle, I'm afraid you are not Lord of the . 237 FOR LOVE   II.1   72
   Mrs Frail: and speak openly one to another; I'm afraid the World . 248 FOR LOVE   II.1   487
   Mrs Frail: O' my Soul, I'm afraid not--eh!--filthy . . . . . . 250 FOR LOVE   II.1   564
   Sr Sampson: glad to hear you say so; I was afraid you were in Love . 260 FOR LOVE III.1   258
   Scandal: Alas, Mr. Foresight, I'm afraid all is not right-- . . . 267 FOR LOVE III.1   513
   Scandal: Sir Sampson is hasty, very hasty;--I'm afraid he is not . 267 FOR LOVE III.1   520
   Mrs Fore: O, mighty restless, but I was afraid to tell him . . 270 FOR LOVE III.1   619
   Mrs Fore: --that I'm afraid you have a great many Confederates. . . 272 FOR LOVE III.1   703
   Scandal: I'm afraid the Physician is not willing you shou'd . . 277 FOR LOVE   IV.1   50
   Angelica: without I suck the Poyson from his Wounds, I'm afraid . 277 FOR LOVE   IV.1   75
   Valentine: Madam, you need not be very much afraid, for I . . . 294 FOR LOVE   IV.1   697
   Foresight: Mercy on us, I was afraid of this. . . . . 306 FOR LOVE   V.1   344
   Servant-M: afraid his Lungs would have fail'd before it came to our . 398 WAY WORLD   I.1   117
   Mirabell: tollerable Reputation--I am afraid Mr. Fainall will be . 412 WAY WORLD   II.1   101
   Foible: O las Sir, I'm so asham'd--I'm afraid my Lady . . . 423 WAY WORLD   II.1   513
   Mrs Fain: with Mirabell, and I'm afraid will discover it to my Lady. 430 WAY WORLD III.1   186
   Sir Wilful: I thank you for your courteous Offer. 'Sheart, I was afraid 441 WAY WORLD III.1   602
Africk (2)   see Affrick
   Almeria: Of Africk: There our Vessel struck the Shore, ... 329 M. BRIDE   I.1   126
   Gonsalvez: That being sav'd upon the Coast of Africk, ... 363 M. BRIDE   IV.1   84
After (78)
   Bellmour: glass after the Small-pox. . . . . 42 OLD BATCH   I.1   187
   Heartwell: think it time enough to be lew'd, after I have had the . 43 OLD BATCH   I.1   233
   Heartwell: so often drawn, is bound to the Peace for ever after. . . 43 OLD BATCH   I.1   249
   Heartwell: force a smile and pray, the Boy takes after his Mothers . 45 OLD BATCH   I.1   326
   Capt Bluff: Ay, ay, no matter--You see Mr. Sharper after all . . 53 OLD BATCH   II.1   210
   Setter: (Exit after her.) . . . . . . 67 OLD BATCH III.1   240
                            (After the Song, a Dance of Antick.) . 71 OLD BATCH III.2   25
   Laetitia: be mistaken after all this.--A handsom Fellow if he had . 81 OLD BATCH   IV.2   43
   Sharper: real Fanatick can look better pleas'd after a successful . 100 OLD BATCH   V.1   133
   Bellmour: --I got an Opportunity (after I had marry'd 'em) of . 100 OLD BATCH   V.1   149
   Capt Bluff: (Almost whispering, and treading softly after him.) . 101 OLD BATCH   V.1   190
   Mellefont: Custome, after Dinner.--But I made a pretence . . . 127 DOUBL DLR   I.1   13
   Mellefont: (after a pause). So then,--spight of my care and . . . 148 DOUBL DLR   II.1   374
   Maskwell: anon, after that I'll tell you the whole matter; be here in 149 DOUBL DLR   II.1   434
   Maskwell: must ever after be in awe of you. . . . . . . 157 DOUBL DLR III.1   256
   Sir Paul: nice, Gads-bud don't learn after your Mother-in-Law my . 174 DOUBL DLR   IV.1   248
   Sir Paul: (Reads) Hum--After Supper in the Wardrobe by the . . 178 DOUBL DLR   IV.1   408
   Sir Paul: Wife. Have I for this been pinion'd Night after Night for . 178 DOUBL DLR   IV.1   423
   Maskwell: You had best make haste, for after she has . . . . 181 DOUBL DLR   IV.1 V521
   Mellefont: Horn mad after your Fortune. . . . . 187 DOUBL DLR   IV.2   133
   Maskwell: No, no, I'll after him immediately, and tell him. . . 194 DOUBL DLR   V.1   259
                 runs out affrighted, my Lord after her, like a Parson.) . 202 DOUBL DLR   V.1   557
   Jeremy: be Canoniz'd for a Muse after my Decease. . . . . 218 FOR LOVE   I.1   75
   Valentine: to his Estate after his Death, to my younger Brother, he . 225 FOR LOVE   I.1   336
   Angelica: we were ever after to live under Ground, or at least making 237 FOR LOVE   II.1   83
   Mrs Fore: won't let him come near her, after Mr. Tattle. . . . 250 FOR LOVE   II.1   563
   Tattle: (Exit after her.) . . . . . 253 FOR LOVE   II.1   663
   Mrs Fore: Mr. Foresight is punctual, we sit up after him. . . . 269 FOR LOVE III.1   581
   Mrs Frail: Well, but if you shou'd forsake me after all, you'd . . 273 FOR LOVE III.1   728
   Sr Sampson: there never was a lucky Hour after the first opportunity. 283 FOR LOVE   IV.1   291
   Ben: look after a Husband; for my part I was none of her . 285 FOR LOVE   IV.1   375
   Ben: after all your fair speeches, and stroaking my Cheeks, . 286 FOR LOVE   IV.1   417
   Ben: it as you will, may-hap you may holla after me when I . 287 FOR LOVE   IV.1   442
   Mrs Fore: together; and after Consummation, Girl, there's no . . 288 FOR LOVE   IV.1   473
                 That after Death, ne're went to Hell, nor Heaven, . . 315 FOR LOVE   EPI.   16
   Zara: And after did solicite you, on his . . . . . . 366 M. BRIDE   IV.1   186
   Almeria: Gasping as it would speak: and after it, ... 371 M. BRIDE   IV.1   389
   Almeria: Gasping as it would speak: and after, see! . . . . 371 M. BRIDE   IV.1 V389
   Zara: Hast stung the Traveller; and, after, hear'st . . . 375 M. BRIDE   V.1   107
                 And after she has made 'em Fools, forsakes. . . . . 393 WAY WORLD   PRO.   8
                 So Save or Damn, after your own Discretion. . . . . 393 WAY WORLD   PRO.   40
   Fainall: after I left you; my fair Cousin has some Humours, that . 395 WAY WORLD   I.1   18
   Mirabell: aloud of the Vapours, and after fell into a profound . 396 WAY WORLD   I.1   31
   Fainall: the Monster in the Tempest; and much after the same manner. 401 WAY WORLD   I.1   220

10

After (continued)

		PAGE	TITLE	ACT.SC	LINE
Mirabell:	know you staid at Millamant's last Night, after I went.	407	WAY WORLD	I.1	450
Marwood:	I loath the name of Love after such usage;	415	WAY WORLD	II.1	219
Mrs Fain:	her Woman after him.	418	WAY WORLD	II.1	327
Mirabell:	us'd to have the Beau-mond Throng after you; and a Flock	418	WAY WORLD	II.1	329
Millamant:	enquir'd after you, as after a new Fashion.	419	WAY WORLD	II.1	348
Mirabell:	after an old Fashion, to ask a Husband for his Wife.	419	WAY WORLD	II.1	352
Mirabell:	mortifies, yet after Commendation can be flatter'd by it,	420	WAY WORLD	II.1	396
Millamant:	after all, not to have you—We shan't agree.	422	WAY WORLD	II.1	450
Millamant:	after all, there is something very moving in a love-sick	422	WAY WORLD	II.1	474
Foible:	the return of her Husband after Knighthood, with that	428	WAY WORLD	III.1	125
Foible:	of kissing your Ladyship's Hands after Dinner.	428	WAY WORLD	III.1	127
Foible:	of kissing your Ladyship's Hand after Dinner.	428	WAY WORLD	III.1	V127
Millamant:	Chambermaid after a day or two.	433	WAY WORLD	III.1	307
Marwood:	there, like a new masking Habit, after the Masquerade is	433	WAY WORLD	III.1	310
Lady Wish:	Will you drink any Thing after your Journey, Nephew,	441	WAY WORLD	III.1	599
Fainall:	'twere somewhat,--but to crawl after, with my Horns	442	WAY WORLD	III.1	636
Fainall:	disable him for that, he will drink like a Dane: after dinner,	443	WAY WORLD	III.1	672
Sir Wilful:	hope after a time, I shall break my mind--that is upon	446	WAY WORLD	IV.1	76
Mirabell:	What, after the last?	449	WAY WORLD	IV.1	166
Mirabell:	other till after grace?	449	WAY WORLD	IV.1	184
Millamant:	and dee hear, I won't be call'd names after I'm Married;	450	WAY WORLD	IV.1	194
Millamant:	for ever After. Let us never Visit together, nor go to a	450	WAY WORLD	IV.1	206
Millamant:	ever After. Let us never Visit together, nor go to a	450	WAY WORLD	IV.1	V206
Sir Wilful:	but he spits after a Bumper, and that's a Fault.	455	WAY WORLD	IV.1	414
Lady Wish:	but a Pattern for you, and a Model for you, after you were	465	WAY WORLD	V.1	145
Lady Wish:	be wrong'd after all, ha? I don't know what to think,--	466	WAY WORLD	V.1	181
Lady Wish:	think after all this, that my Daughter can be Naught?	467	WAY WORLD	V.1	203
Marwood:	after, talk it all over again in Commons, or before Drawers	467	WAY WORLD	V.1	226
Marwood:	after, talk it over again in Commons, or before Drawers	467	WAY WORLD	V.1	V226
Marwood:	'twere well. But it must after this be consign'd by the	468	WAY WORLD	V.1	230
Sir Wilful:	S'heart you'll have time enough to toy after	477	WAY WORLD	V.1	V599
Sir Wilful:	S'heart you'll have him time enough to toy after	477	WAY WORLD	V.1	599
	After our Epilogue this Crowd dismisses,	479	WAY WORLD	EPI.	1

After-Game (1)

Maskwell:	After-Game to play that shall turn the Tables, and here	181	DOUBL DLR	IV.1	529

Afternoon (7)

Bellmour:	our Afternoon Service to our Mistresses; I find I am	40	OLD BATCH	I.1	132
Bellmour:	our Afternoon Services to our Mistresses; I find I am	40	OLD BATCH	I.1	V132
Sir Joseph:	Fondlewife, as far as two hundred Pound, and this Afternoon	51	OLD BATCH	II.1	133
Setter:	This afternoon, Sir, about an Hour before my Master	99	OLD BATCH	V.1	100
Sr Sampson:	from it in the Afternoon; here's a Rogue, Dog, here's	243	FOR LOVE	II.1	297
Sir Wilful:	with you in London; we shou'd ccunt it towards Afternoon	437	WAY WORLD	III.1	448
Foible:	Mirabell disguis'd to Madam Millamant this Afternoon. I	461	WAY WORLD	IV.1	612

Afterwards (10)

Lady Ply:	you afterwards: For one does not know how ones mind may	147	DOUBL DLR	II.1	339
Tattle:	No, I'll come in first, and push you down afterwards.	253	FOR LOVE	II.1	654
Tattle:	afterwards, for it was talk'd of in Town--And a Lady of	258	FOR LOVE	III.1	174
Tattle:	and be sorry for't afterwards. I'd have you to know, Sir,	305	FOR LOVE	V.1	291
	Almeria meets the King and kneels: afterwards Gonsalez	332	M. BRIDE	I.1	268
Petulant:	Beg him for his Estate; that I may beg you afterwards;	409	WAY WORLD	II.1	517
Marwood:	a very fit Match. He may Travel afterwards. 'Tis a Thing	432	WAY WORLD	III.1	267
Millamant:	afterwards.	449	WAY WORLD	IV.1	165
Marwood:	we shall have leisure to think of Retirement afterwards.	465	WAY WORLD	V.1	137
Mirabell:	Let me be pitied first; and afterwards forgotten,	471	WAY WORLD	V.1	378

Agad (24)

Sir Joseph:	and frightn'd 'em away--but agad I durst not stay to give	47	OLD BATCH	II.1	9
Sir Joseph:	remembrance makes me quake; agad I shall never be	48	OLD BATCH	II.1	14
Sir Joseph:	Agad and so 'tis--why here has been more	48	OLD BATCH	II.1	19
Sir Joseph:	I rejoyce! agad not I Sir; I'me sorry for your loss,	48	OLD BATCH	II.1	35
Sir Joseph:	I rejoyce! agad not I Sir; I'me very sorry for your loss,	48	OLD BATCH	II.1	V 35
Sir Joseph:	because I never saw your face before, agad. Ha, ha, ha.	48	OLD BATCH	II.1	41
Sir Joseph:	agad.	48	OLD BATCH	II.1	46
Sir Joseph:	I do scorn a dirty thing. But agad 'Ime a little out of	50	OLD BATCH	II.1	105
Sir Joseph:	as it were to be--agad he's a brave Fellow--Pauh,	50	OLD BATCH	II.1	121
Sir Joseph:	my Bully, my Back; agad my heart has gone a pit	51	OLD BATCH	II.1	140
Sir Joseph:	Nay agad I hate fear ever since I had like to have	51	OLD BATCH	II.1	144
Sir Joseph:	Ay, this damn'd Modesty of yours--Agad if	53	OLD BATCH	II.1	214
Sir Joseph:	fire once out of the mouth of a Canon--agad he did; those	53	OLD BATCH	II.1	219
Sir Joseph:	mad? Or de'e think I'm mad? Agad for my part, I don't	68	OLD BATCH	III.1	265
Sir Joseph:	my Choller had been up too, agad there would have been	68	OLD BATCH	III.1	275
Sir Joseph:	Indifferent, agad in my opinion very indifferent	70	OLD BATCH	III.1	333
Sir Joseph:	No agad no more 'tis, for that's put up already;	70	OLD BATCH	III.1	346
Sir Joseph:	--A-Gad, t'other Glass of Madera, and I durst have attack'd	85	OLD BATCH	IV.3	68
Sir Joseph:	Free-loves! Sir Joseph, thou art a Mad-man. Agad, I'm in	86	OLD BATCH	IV.3	109
Sir Joseph:	Agad, it's a curious, fine, pretty Rogue; I'll speak	89	OLD BATCH	IV.4	32
Sir Joseph:	did a little while ago.--Look yonder.--A-gad, if	101	OLD BATCH	V.1	172
Sir Joseph:	in Aesop's Fables, Bully? A-Gad there are good Morals to	101	OLD BATCH	V.1	175
Sir Joseph:	let's hearken. A-gad, this must be I.--	102	OLD BATCH	V.1	204
Sir Joseph:	her little Bubbies? And--A-gad, I'm so over-joy'd--And	103	OLD BATCH	V.1	256

Again (131)

Heartwell:	that will fawn upon me again, and entertain any Puppy	42	OLD BATCH	I.1	190
Heartwell:	And it should be mine to let 'em go again.	43	OLD BATCH	I.1	226
Capt Bluff:	Ay! Then I honour him again--Sir may I crave your	52	OLD BATCH	II.1	171
Capt Bluff:	Gazette! Why there again now--Why, Sir, there are	52	OLD BATCH	II.1	192
Belinda:	Footman--Here, take 'em all again, my Mind's	57	OLD BATCH	II.2	98
Araminta:	it once again--You may like it better at second	60	OLD BATCH	II.2	208
Capt Bluff:	for the Mony, and if you would look me in the Face again	67	OLD BATCH	III.1	249
Sir Joseph:	Gentleman again?	67	OLD BATCH	III.1	257
Sharper:	I Gad and so I will: There's again for you.	69	OLD BATCH	III.1	320
Capt Bluff:	to thank you in: But in your Ear, you are to be seen again.	69	OLD BATCH	III.1	323
Silvia:	again, 'cause you'd have me be naught.	74	OLD BATCH	III.2	112
Silvia:	again, and had heard me.	74	OLD BATCH	III.2	146
Laetitia:	not surpriz'd me: Methinks, now I look on him again,	81	OLD BATCH	IV.2	44
Araminta:	May be he may not know us again.	84	OLD BATCH	IV.3	58

Again   (continued)

Speaker	Text	PAGE	TITLE	ACT.SC	LINE
Footman:	if your Ladiship would have the Coach come again for	88	OLD BATCH	IV.3	207
Bellmour:	'Tis an alarm to love.--Come in again, and	89	OLD BATCH	IV.4	6
Laetitia:	run in thy debt again. But this Opportunity is the Devil.	91	OLD BATCH	IV.4	92
Laetitia:	(aside). Misfortune! Now all's ruin'd again.	92	OLD BATCH	IV.4	108
Laetitia:	of your Embraces again, my Dear, if ever I saw his face	93	OLD BATCH	IV.4	151
Fondlewife:	Good again--A very civil Person this, and, I	94	OLD BATCH	IV.4	179
Lucy:	That may be, without troubling your self to go again	97	OLD BATCH	V.1	14
Sharper:	Here again, my Mercury!	105	OLD BATCH	V.1	333
Heartwell:	when I wed again, may she be--Ugly, as an old	112	OLD BATCH	V.2	159
Lady Touch:	Again, provoke me! Do you wind me like	137	DOUBL DLR	I.1	380
Lady Froth:	O prettily turn'd again; let me die, but you have	140	DOUBL DLR	II.1	85
Sir Paul:	again.	145	DOUBL DLR	II.1	269
Lady Touch:	--I dare swear he's sorry--and were it to do again, would	152	DOUBL DLR	III.1	77
Lady Touch:	Lord must not see him again.	154	DOUBL DLR	III.1	145
Lady Froth:	lines again (pulls out a Paper.) Let me see here, you know	164	DOUBL DLR	III.1	512
Lady Froth:	Mouth, to Laugh, and then put 'em in again--Foh.	165	DOUBL DLR	III.1	571
Lord Froth:	sending it to and again so often, this is the seventh time	166	DOUBL DLR	III.1	610
Careless:	Feet. (Aside.) I must say the same thing over again, and	170	DOUBL DLR	IV.1	101
Sir Paul:	again--The Law will allow it.	171	DOUBL DLR	IV.1	146
Lady Ply:	make up this Match again, because Mr. Careless said it	171	DOUBL DLR	IV.1	153
Lady Ply:	make up the Match again, because Mr. Careless said it	171	DOUBL DLR	IV.1	V153
Sir Paul:	so, I'm of that Opinion again; but I can neither find my	171	DOUBL DLR	IV.1	157
Lady Ply:	day: I would look upon the Account again; and may be	173	DOUBL DLR	IV.1	216
Lady Froth:	then joyn hands again; I could teach my Lord this Dance	177	DOUBL DLR	IV.1	367
Lady Ply:	this, your Right Hand shall be swathed down again to	180	DOUBL DLR	IV.1	V482
Sir Paul:	Nay but Madam, I shall offend again if you don't	180	DOUBL DLR	IV.1	V485
Lady Touch:	punish your fond, rash Contempt! Again smile!	198	DOUBL DLR	V.1	392
Jeremy:	upon you again. You're undone, Sir; you're ruin'd; you	218	FOR LOVE	I.1	85
Jeremy:	body be surpriz'd at the Matter--(Knocking)--Again! Sir,	221	FOR LOVE	I.1	182
Valentine:	again.--Pretty round heaving Breasts,--a Barbary	223	FOR LOVE	I.1	284
Trapland:	Sack; but you cannot expect it again, when I have drank it.	224	FOR LOVE	I.1	314
Trapland:	Sack; but you cannot expect it again, when I have drunk it.	224	FOR LOVE	I.1	V314
Scandal:	And how do you expect to have your Money again,	224	FOR LOVE	I.1	315
Tattle:	never see a Bed-Chamber again, never be lock't in a	230	FOR LOVE	I.1	518
Jeremy:	Sir, here's the Steward again from your Father.	234	FOR LOVE	I.1	661
Valentine:	wait cn you again presently.	234	FOR LOVE	I.1	663
Foresight:	send your Son to Sea again. I'll wed my Daughter to an	241	FOR LOVE	II.1	238
Sr Sampson:	Again! 'Ouns han't you four thousand Pound	246	FOR LOVE	II.1	396
Sr Sampson:	--If I had it again, I wou'd not give thee a Groat,	246	FOR LOVE	II.1	397
Miss Prue:	Well, we'll do it again.	252	FOR LOVE	II.1	637
Tattle:	That's right,--again my Charmer.	252	FOR LOVE	II.1	641
Tattle:	(Kisses again.)	252	FOR LOVE	II.1	642
Sr Sampson:	kiss me again and again, dear Ben.	260	FOR LOVE	III.1	274
Ben:	to ask you; well, you be'nt Marry'd again, Father, be you?	261	FOR LOVE	III.1	296
Ben:	Nay, what do's that signifie?--an you Marry again--	261	FOR LOVE	III.1	299
Sr Sampson:	Why then, I'll go to Sea again, so there's one for t'other, an	261	FOR LOVE	III.1	300
Ben:	and may hap may'nt get 'em out again when he wou'd.	261	FOR LOVE	III.1	313
Foresight:	gone again--And now I'm faint again; and pale again,	269	FOR LOVE	III.1	609
Ben:	Why that's true again; for may-hap one Bottom may	273	FOR LOVE	III.1	725
Sr Sampson:	Let me feel thy Hand again, Val: it does not	281	FOR LOVE	IV.1	206
Valentine:	What, is my bad Genius here again! Oh no, 'tis	282	FOR LOVE	IV.1	237
Mrs Frail:	Do with him, send him to Sea again in the next	284	FOR LOVE	IV.1	306
Mrs Frail:	So then you intend to go to Sea again?	285	FOR LOVE	IV.1	378
Tattle:	Hah! good again, faith.	292	FOR LOVE	IV.1	647
Singer-V:	And could again begin to Love and Live,	293	FOR LOVE	IV.1	653
Jeremy:	to lock wild again now.	295	FOR LOVE	IV.1	748
Jeremy:	What, is the Lady gone again, Sir? I hope you	296	FOR LOVE	IV.1	799
Tattle:	every Night--No, no, to marry, is to be a Child again,	303	FOR LOVE	V.1	245
Miss Prue:	What, must I go to Bed to Nurse again, and be a Child as	305	FOR LOVE	V.1	305
Scandal:	O I hope he will do well again--I have a Message	306	FOR LOVE	V.1	334
Ben:	neither--But I'll sail as far as Ligorn, and back again,	306	FOR LOVE	V.1	352
Ben:	Mess, here's the Wind chang'd again. Father, you and I	312	FOR LOVE	V.1	568
Heli:	When many Years were past, in Men again.	315	FOR LOVE	EPI.	18
Almeria:	That Osmyn lives, and I again shall see him.	338	M. BRIDE	II.1	11
Osmyn-Alph:	Where I may kneel and pay my Vows again	339	M. BRIDE	II.1	82
Almeria:	To meet again in Life, to know I have thee,	342	M. BRIDE	II.2	93
Almeria:	To see him thus again, is such profusion	342	M. BRIDE	II.2	106
Almeria:	O my strain'd Heart--let me again behold thee,	342	M. BRIDE	II.2	V112
Osmyn-Alph:	Could sleep till we again were met.	344	M. BRIDE	II.2	196
Osmyn-Alph:	Or we could sleep till we again were met.	344	M. BRIDE	II.2	V196
Almeria:	Sure we shall meet again.	345	M. BRIDE	II.2	209
Osmyn-Alph:	We shall; we part not but to meet again.	345	M. BRIDE	II.2	210
Osmyn-Alph:	I have not wherewithal to give again.	346	M. BRIDE	II.2	271
Zara:	If so, this Sable Curtain shall again	353	M. BRIDE	III.1	151
Zara:	And unseen. Is it my Love? ask again	353	M. BRIDE	III.1	153
Zara:	That Question, speak again in that soft Voice,	353	M. BRIDE	III.1	154
Zara:	And Lcok again, with Wishes in thy Eyes,	353	M. BRIDE	III.1	155
Almeria:	Thus, thus; we parted, thus to meet again.	355	M. BRIDE	III.1	245
Osmyn-Alph:	But till she's gone; then bless me thus again.	359	M. BRIDE	III.1	395
Manuel:	Will quickly waste, and give again the Day.	364	M. BRIDE	IV.1	108
Gonsalez:	I'th' Morning he must die again; e're Noon	366	M. BRIDE	IV.1	210
Almeria:	I shall again behold my dear Alphonso.	371	M. BRIDE	IV.1	394
Gonsalez:	Almeria widow'd, yet again may wed;	372	M. BRIDE	IV.1	446
Gonsalez:	They shout again! Whate'er he means to do	378	M. BRIDE	V.2	100
Almeria:	Ha! point again? 'tis there, and full I hope.	382	M. BRIDE	V.2	258
Almeria:	Giv'n me again from Death! O all ye Powers	383	M. BRIDE	V.2	291
Mirabell:	That's well. Do you go home again, d'ee hear,	398	WAY WORLD	I.1	127
Mirabell:	That's well. Do you go home again, d'ye hear,	398	WAY WORLD	I.1	V127
Fainall:	Life on't, you are your own Man again.	400	WAY WORLD	I.1	177
Witwoud:	to the Door again in a trice; where he wou'd send in for	405	WAY WORLD	I.1	374
Marwood:	flush again.	412	WAY WORLD	II.1	79
Fainall:	and would be a Widow, but that I have a Heart of	415	WAY WORLD	II.1	212
Millamant:	Yet again! Mincing, stand between me and his	419	WAY WORLD	II.1	341
Waitwell:	me, I am married, and can't be my own Man again.	424	WAY WORLD	II.1	561

Agree (8)
Bellmour: I have Directions in my Pocket, which agree with . . .   81   OLD BATCH   IV.2   31
Valentine: I agree to 'em, take Mr. Trapland with you, and let him . 224   FOR LOVE   I.1   319
Singer-V: But for relief of either Sex agree, ...   293   FOR LOVE   IV.1   663
Angelica: O you'll agree very well in a little time; Custom . . . 310   FOR LOVE   V.1   481
Marwood: agree with mine.   410   WAY WORLD   II.1   32
Millamant: after all, not to have you--We shan't agree.   422   WAY WORLD   II.1   450
Witwoud: out of Lovers--We agree in the main, like Treble . . .   435   WAY WORLD III.1   396
Fainall: and the Current of this Lewd Town can agree.   473   WAY WORLD   V.1   444
Agreeable (9)
Bellmour: much more agreeable, if you can counterfeit his Habit to
                 blind   39   OLD BATCH   I.1   88
Lady Ply: unaffected, so easie, so free, so particular, so agreeable-- 160   DOUBL DLR III.1   364
Brisk: all I'gad. I was fallen into the most agreeable amusement in 175   DOUBL DLR   IV.1   315
Mrs Fore: agreeable man; I don't quarrel at that, nor I don't think . 247   FOR LOVE   II.1   428
Angelica: there were such a thing as a young agreeable Man, with a . 299   FOR LOVE   V.1   62
Mirabell: agreeable. I'll tell thee, Fainall, she once us'd me with
                 that   399   WAY WORLD   I.1   163
Millamant: it--But 'tis agreeable to my Humour.   434   WAY WORLD III.1   373
Millamant: from the Agreeable fatigues of sollicitation.   449   WAY WORLD   IV.1   169
Millamant: morning thoughts, agreeable wakings, indolent slumbers, . 449   WAY WORLD   IV.1   188
Agreeably (1)
Laetitia: Nay, now.--(aside) I never saw any thing so agreeably . . 82   OLD BATCH   IV.2   79
Agreed (8)
Setter: the Knight of the Treachery; who has agreed, seemingly . 106   OLD BATCH   V.1   348
Vainlove: Agreed.   110   OLD BATCH   V.2   89
Heartwell: Agreed.   112   OLD BATCH   V.2   164
Cynthia: well when the Parties are so agreed--for when   168   DOUBL DLR   IV.1   14
Witwoud: disposal of me then. If I had not agreed to that, I might   440   WAY WORLD III.1   560
Mirabell: Then wee're agreed. Shall I kiss your hand upon the . . . 452   WAY WORLD   IV.1   280
Fainall: must be agreed unto, and that positively. Lastly, I will be 469   WAY WORLD   V.1   277
Sir Wilful: she and I are agreed upon the matter, before a Witness. . 470   WAY WORLD   V.1   322
Agreement (1)
Maskwell: made this agreement, if I accomplish her designs (as I told 149   DOUBL DLR   II.1   427
Agrees (1)
Manuel: Agrees expressly too with her Report.   366   M. BRIDE   IV.1   217
Aground (1)
Ben: wou'd you, and leave me aground?   286   FOR LOVE   IV.1   419
Ah (65)
Sir Joseph: the Devil--God bless us--almost if he be by. Ah--had he . 50   OLD BATCH   II.1   123
Sir Joseph: the Devil--bless us--almost if he be by. Ah--had he . .   50   OLD BATCH   II.1   V123
Sir Joseph: Oh here a' comes--Ah my Hector of Troy, welcome . . .   51   OLD BATCH   II.1   139
Sir Joseph: Ah, well said my Hero; was not that great Sir?   52   OLD BATCH   II.1   166
Setter: --That is, passively valiant and actively obedient. Ah! . 65   OLD BATCH III.1   152
Laetitia: Ah! Heav'n defend me! Who's this?   81   OLD BATCH   IV.2   15
Belinda: come this Way, till I put my self a little in Repair,--Ah!   83   OLD BATCH   IV.3   10
Belinda: come this Way, till I have put my self a little in
                 Repair,--Ah!   83   OLD BATCH   IV.3   V 10
Belinda: Ah so fine! So extreamly fine! So every thing in the . .   87   OLD BATCH   IV.3   148
Laetitia: Ah! There he is. Make haste, gather up your things. . .   89   OLD BATCH   IV.4   10
Fondlewife: Cholick. Ah!   93   OLD BATCH   IV.4   165
Laetitia: Ah cruel Dear, how can you be so barbarous? You'll . .   95   OLD BATCH   IV.4   230
Fondlewife: Ah, dissembling Vermin!   95   OLD BATCH   IV.4   233
Fondlewife: Ah! No, no, I cannot speak; my heart's so full--I . .   95   OLD BATCH   IV.4   248
Lucy: Ah, the Devil is not so cunning.--You know my . . .   98   OLD BATCH   V.1   74
Sir Joseph: Ah, honest Setter.--Sirrah, I'll give thee any . . .   104   OLD BATCH   V.1   281
Sir Joseph: Ah! O Lord, my heart akes--Ah! Setter, a   110   OLD BATCH   V.2   118
Lady Froth: and as much a Man of Quality! Ah! Nothing at all . .   139   DOUBL DLR   II.1   29
Lady Froth: I'm not asham'd to own it now; ah! it makes my heart .   140   DOUBL DLR   II.1   62
Lord Froth: Pleasant Creature! perfectly well, ah! that look, . .   140   DOUBL DLR   II.1   67
Lady Froth: Pray mind, my Lord; ah! he bows Charmingly; nay, my .   140   DOUBL DLR   II.1   76
Lady Froth: Ah! Gallantry to the last degree--Mr. Brisk, . . .   140   DOUBL DLR   II.1   81
Lord Froth: Ah, that's all.   141   DOUBL DLR   II.1   114
Sir Paul: unworthy Sinner--But if I had a Son, ah, that's my . .   161   DOUBL DLR III.1   415
Sir Paul: Alas, that's not it, Mr. Careless; ah! that's not it; .   161   DOUBL DLR III.1   426
Sir Paul: Ah! would to Heav'n you would, Mr. Careless; you . .   162   DOUBL DLR III.1   444
Lord Froth: upon the broad grin, all laugh and no Company; ah, then . 162   DOUBL DLR III.1   459
Careless: (in a Whining Tone). Ah Heavens, Madam, you . . .   169   DOUBL DLR   IV.1   85
Lady Ply: Ah! Very fine.   170   DOUBL DLR   IV.1   89
Careless: (Still Whining). Ah why are you so Fair, so   170   DOUBL DLR   IV.1   90
Lady Ply: and how--Ah, there's Sir Paul.   170   DOUBL DLR   IV.1   126
Sir Paul: every inch of him that resembles me; ah this Eye, this .   173   DOUBL DLR   IV.1   234
Sir Paul: --Ah! when I was of your Age Hussy, I would have . .   174   DOUBL DLR   IV.2   241
Brisk: practice.--Ah! My dear Lady Froth! She's a most . .   175   DOUBL DLR   IV.1   291
Brisk: my Approaches--Hem Hem! (Bows.) Ah Madam!   175   DOUBL DLR   IV.1   297
Brisk: what a happy Discovery. Ah my dear charming . . .   177   DOUBL DLR   IV.1   357
Lady Touch: Ah! (Shrieks.)   184   DOUBL DLR   IV.2   37
Jeremy: --Ah Pox confound that Will's Coffee-House, it has . .   218   FOR LOVE   I.1   87
Valentine: Bo-peep under her Petticoats, ah! Mr. Trapland? . . .   223   FOR LOVE   I.1   288
Mrs Frail: Ah Devil, sly Devil--He's as close, Sister, as . . .   250   FOR LOVE   II.1   542
Miss Prue: Ah, but I'll hold the Door with both Hands, and . . .   252   FOR LOVE   II.1   651
Foresight: Ah, good Mr. Scandal--   267   FOR LOVE   III.1   518
Jeremy: Ah, Sir, he's quite gone.   278   FOR LOVE   IV.1   119
Jeremy: Ah, you've hit it, Sir; that's the matter with him, Sir; . 279   FOR LOVE   IV.1   137
Sr Sampson: your Harmony of Chiromancy with Astrology. Ah! . . .   283   FOR LOVE   IV.1   285
Foresight: Ah, Sir Sampson, Heav'n help your Head--   283   FOR LOVE   IV.1   293
Sr Sampson: (aside). Odsbud I believe she likes me--Ah, ...   299   FOR LOVE   V.1   93
Sr Sampson: Possessions--Ah! Baggage--I warrant you for . . .   301   FOR LOVE   V.1   153
Jeremy: Ah Sir, if you are not very faithful and close in this
                 Business, ...   301   FOR LOVE   V.1   167
Mrs Frail: Ah Mr. Tattle and I, poor Mr. Tattle and I are-- . .   309   FOR LOVE   V.1   445
Almeria: I'll catch it--hark! a Voice cries Murder! ah! . . .   371   M. BRIDE   IV.1   V391
Lady Wish: Ah dear Marwood, what's Integrity to an Opportunity? .   426   WAY WORLD III.1   60
Millamant: Ah! to marry an Ignorant! that can hardly Read . . .   436   WAY WORLD III.1   426
Millamant: Ah Rustick! ruder than Gothick.   447   WAY WORLD   IV.1   109
Millamant: Ah l'etourdie! I hate the Town too.   448   WAY WORLD   IV.1   126

16

All   (continued)

All (continued)

		PAGE	TITLE	ACT.SC	LINE
Maskwell:	know then, that all my Contrivances were but Bubbles; till	149	DOUBL DLR	II.1	420
Maskwell:	you before) she has ingaged to put Cynthia with all her	149	DOUBL DLR	II.1	428
Maskwell:	--Treachery, what Treachery? Love cancels all the	150	DOUBL DLR	II.1	443
Maskwell:	Ties: But the Name of Rival cuts 'em all asunder, and is a	150	DOUBL DLR	II.1	448
Maskwell:	as your wise man, who is too hard for all the World, and	150	DOUBL DLR	II.1	455
Lord Froth:	more trifling--I charge you tell me--by all our	152	DOUBL DLR	III.1	62
Lady Touch:	Lord--Ha, ha, ha. Well but that's all--now you have	153	DOUBL DLR	III.1	90
Lady Touch:	harmless mirth--only misplac'd that's all--but if it	153	DOUBL DLR	III.1	95
Lady Touch:	you all; will you, my Lord?	153	DOUBL DLR	III.1	120
Maskwell:	confirm all, had there been occasion.	154	DOUBL DLR	III.1	130
Lady Touch:	Expedition indeed; for all we do, must be	154	DOUBL DLR	III.1	141
Maskwell:	enough. Pox I have lost all Appetite to her; yet she's a fine	155	DOUBL DLR	III.1	175
Maskwell:	deceive 'em all, and yet secure my self, 'twas a lucky	155	DOUBL DLR	III.1	190
Mellefont:	Soul, thou art villainously bent to discover all to me,	156	DOUBL DLR	III.1	205
Maskwell:	know whether I can in honour discover all.	156	DOUBL DLR	III.1	208
Maskwell:	know whether I can in honour discover 'em all	156	DOUBL DLR	III.1	V208
Mellefont:	All, all man, what you may in honour betray her	156	DOUBL DLR	III.1	209
Maskwell:	By this Light, I'm serious; all raillery apart--	156	DOUBL DLR	III.1	232
Mellefont:	Hell and the Devil, is she abandon'd of all Grace--	156	DOUBL DLR	III.1	235
Maskwell:	Conditions. For this Discovery will disarm her of all	157	DOUBL DLR	III.1	254
Lady Ply:	qualified in all those Circumstances, I'm sure I should	159	DOUBL DLR	III.1	340
Careless:	O your Ladyship is abounding in all Excellence,	160	DOUBL DLR	III.1	356
Sir Paul:	Well, well, my Lady reads all Letters first--Child,	161	DOUBL DLR	III.1	398
Sir Paul:	Summers-day--indeed she is, Mr. Careless, in all	161	DOUBL DLR	III.1	422
Lord Froth:	Heav'n, Sir Paul, you amaze me, of all things in	162	DOUBL DLR	III.1	457
Lord Froth:	the World--you are never pleased but when we are all	162	DOUBL DLR	III.1	458
Lord Froth:	upon the broad grin, all laugh and no Company; ah, then	162	DOUBL DLR	III.1	459
Cynthia:	think they are all in good nature with the World, and only	163	DOUBL DLR	III.1	482
Cynthia:	laugh at one another; and you must allow they have all	163	DOUBL DLR	III.1	483
Brisk:	Right, right, that saves all.	164	DOUBL DLR	III.1	522
Lady Froth:	Then I don't say the Sun shines all the day, but,	164	DOUBL DLR	III.1	523
Lady Froth:	that he peeps now and then, yet he does shine all the day	164	DOUBL DLR	III.1	524
Brisk:	With all my Heart and Soul, and proud of the vast	165	DOUBL DLR	III.1	556
Cynthia:	know, we have misapply'd the Name all this while, and	167	DOUBL DLR	III.1	631
Cynthia:	Perspective all this while; for nothing has been between us	168	DOUBL DLR	IV.1	25
Lady Ply:	of an intire resignation of all my best Wishes, for the	169	DOUBL DLR	IV.1	81
Lady Ply:	should die, of all Mankind there's none I'd sooner make	170	DOUBL DLR	IV.1	111
Careless:	through all my Pores, and will to Morrow wash me for	170	DOUBL DLR	IV.1	116
Lady Ply:	Oh, I yield my self all up to your uncontroulable	170	DOUBL DLR	IV.1	124
Sir Paul:	your Ladyship, that's all.	172	DOUBL DLR	IV.1	184
Lady Ply:	all--and highly honoured in that Title.	172	DOUBL DLR	IV.1	191
Sir Paul:	be this is all his doings--something that he has said;	172	DOUBL DLR	IV.1	201
Sir Paul:	be this is all his doing--something that he has said;	172	DOUBL DLR	IV.1	V201
Lady Ply:	By all means--Mr. Careless has satisfied me of	173	DOUBL DLR	IV.1	204
Lady Ply:	--but though I may read all Letters first by Prerogative,	173	DOUBL DLR	IV.1	211
Sir Paul:	her Example, that would spoil all indeed. Bless us, if you	174	DOUBL DLR	IV.1	250
Sir Paul:	Wedding Night, to die a Maid; as she did; all were ruin'd,	174	DOUBL DLR	IV.1	252
Sir Paul:	all my hopes lost--My Heart would break, and my	174	DOUBL DLR	IV.1	253
Cynthia:	I'm all Obedience, Sir, to your Commands.	174	DOUBL DLR	IV.1	257
Brisk:	you, and all that; and I did not think it had been in you.	174	DOUBL DLR	IV.1	268
Brisk:	So now they are all gone, and I have an opportunity to	175	DOUBL DLR	IV.1	290
Brisk:	Men like rich Fellows, are always ready for all Expences;	175	DOUBL DLR	IV.1	300
Brisk:	all I'gad. I was fallen into the most agreeable amusement in	175	DOUBL DLR	IV.1	315
Brisk:	the whole Province of Contemplation: That's all--	175	DOUBL DLR	IV.1	316
Brisk:	No more I have I'gad, for I adore 'em all in your	176	DOUBL DLR	IV.1	336
Lady Froth:	O be merry by all means--Prince Volscius	176	DOUBL DLR	IV.1	341
Brisk:	Seriously, ha ha ha. Gad, I have, for all I Laugh.	176	DOUBL DLR	IV.1	348
Lord Froth:	The Company are all ready--How now!	177	DOUBL DLR	IV.1	362
Lady Froth:	With all my heart.	177	DOUBL DLR	IV.1	383
Lady Ply:	and Premunire! I'm all over in a Universal Agitation, I	178	DOUBL DLR	IV.1	397
Lady Ply:	moment renounce all Communication with you.	179	DOUBL DLR	IV.1	443
Sir Paul:	Surprize! Why I don't know any thing at all, nor I don't	179	DOUBL DLR	IV.1	449
Sir Paul:	know whether there be any thing at all in the World, or	179	DOUBL DLR	IV.1	450
Sir Paul:	overjoy'd, stay I'll confess all.	179	DOUBL DLR	IV.1	466
Sir Paul:	matter of Fact is all his own doing.--I confess I had a	180	DOUBL DLR	IV.1	477
Sir Paul:	which lie all in your Ladishps Breast, and he being a well	180	DOUBL DLR	IV.1	479
Careless:	said all I could, but can't prevail--Then my Friendship	180	DOUBL DLR	IV.1	492
Careless:	--but all in vain, she would not hear a word upon that	180	DOUBL DLR	IV.1	500
Maskwell:	my Lords absence all this while, and will to her Chamber	181	DOUBL DLR	IV.1	523
Maskwell:	my Lords absence all this while, she'll retire to her Chamber	181	DOUBL DLR	IV.1	V523
Lord Touch:	she has told me all: Her good Nature conceal'd it as long	182	DOUBL DLR	IV.1	547
Maskwell:	intended this Evening to have try'd all Arguments to	182	DOUBL DLR	IV.1	577
Maskwell:	And so may all your Pleasures be, and secret as	184	DOUBL DLR	IV.2	33
Mellefont:	And may all Treachery be thus discovered.	184	DOUBL DLR	IV.2	35
Mellefont:	and with a little Pennance and my Absolution all this may	185	DOUBL DLR	IV.2	62
Lady Touch:	Eye o're all my future Conduct; and if I once relapse,	185	DOUBL DLR	IV.2	82
Lady Touch:	all, all! all's my own!	186	DOUBL DLR	IV.2	96
Lady Touch:	forgive all that's past--O Heaven, you will not ravish	186	DOUBL DLR	IV.2	103
Mellefont:	which (if possible) are greater--Though she has all the	186	DOUBL DLR	IV.2	123
Mellefont:	O I could curse my Stars, Fate, and Chance; all	187	DOUBL DLR	IV.2	141
Mellefont:	purpose! yet, 'sdeath, for a Man to have the fruit of all his	187	DOUBL DLR	IV.2	143
Mellefont:	sudden Whirlwind come, tear up Tree and all, and bear	187	DOUBL DLR	IV.2	146
Maskwell:	ruine all, consume my honest Character, and brand me	188	DOUBL DLR	V.1	30
Maskwell:	O, should it once be known I love fair Cynthia, all this	188	DOUBL DLR	V.1	38
Maskwell:	perish first, and from this hour avoid all sight and speech,	188	DOUBL DLR	V.1	41
Maskwell:	and, if I can, all thought of that pernicious Beauty. Ha!	188	DOUBL DLR	V.1	42
Lord Touch:	shalt have due reward of all thy worth. Give me thy hand	189	DOUBL DLR	V.1	56
Lord Touch:	--my Nephew is the alone remaining Branch of all	189	DOUBL DLR	V.1	57
Lord Touch:	Thou shalt enjoy it--if all I'm worth in	189	DOUBL DLR	V.1	74
Maskwell:	to treat openly of my Marriage with Cynthia, all must be	190	DOUBL DLR	V.1	90
Mellefont:	maze of thoughts, each leading into one another, and all	190	DOUBL DLR	V.1	104
Lady Touch:	indebted to him, if you knew all, damn'd Villain! oh, I am	191	DOUBL DLR	V.1	143

18

All (continued)

Speaker	Text	PAGE	TITLE	ACT.SC	LINE
Lady Touch:	indebted to him, if you knew all, Villain! oh, I am	191	DOUBL DLR	V.1	V143
Lady Touch:	What shall I do? how shall I think? I cannot think, --all	191	DOUBL DLR	V.1	154
Lady Touch:	Where she's serving you, as all your Sex	192	DOUBL DLR	V.1	164
Sir Paul:	That's a jest with all my heart, faith and troth,--	192	DOUBL DLR	V.1	171
Lady Touch:	me, and I'll renounce all Blood, all relation and concern	192	DOUBL DLR	V.1	181
Sir Paul:	all this for? Pooh, here's a joke, indeed--why, where's	192	DOUBL DLR	V.1	186
Sir Paul:	say truth, all our Family are Cholerick; I am the only	192	DOUBL DLR	V.1	196
Maskwell:	up this Account, to all our satisfactions.	194	DOUBL DLR	V.1	244
Mellefont:	are all in my Chamber; I want nothing but the Habit.	196	DOUBL DLR	V.1	344
Lady Touch:	and sooth me to a fond belief cf all your fictions;	197	DOUBL DLR	V.1	380
Lady Touch:	knew it would--by Heav'n, this is Cunning all, and	197	DOUBL DLR	V.1	387
Lady Touch:	knew it would--this is Cunning all, and	197	DOUBL DLR	V.1	V387
Lady Touch:	silent? Oh, I am wilder'd in all Passions! but thus my	198	DOUBL DLR	V.1	401
Lord Touch:	Pray forbear all Resentments for a while,	198	DOUBL DLR	V.1	421
Maskwell:	I grant you in appearance all is true; I seem'd	198	DOUBL DLR	V.1	423
Maskwell:	more than all the rest; though I would give a Limb for	199	DOUBL DLR	V.1	434
Maskwell:	that all this seeming Plot that I have laid, has been to	199	DOUBL DLR	V.1	437
Lord Touch:	for I know him to be all goodness,--yet my	200	DOUBL DLR	V.1	482
Lord Touch:	all the Company into this Gallery,--I'll expose the Strumpet,	200	DOUBL DLR	V.1	488
Lord Froth:	the prettiest amusement! but where's all the Company?	200	DOUBL DLR	V.1	495
Sir Paul:	but here's the strangest Revolution, all turn'd topsie	200	DOUBL DLR	V.1	497
Sir Paul:	All turn'd topsie turvey, as sure as a Gun.	200	DOUBL DLR	V.1	501
Brisk:	With all my Soul,--your Ladyship has made me	201	DOUBL DLR	V.1	538
Lady Ply:	they should be all deceitful alike.	202	DOUBL DLR	V.1	547
Lady Touch:	Curses seize you all.	202	DOUBL DLR	V.1	V561
Lord Touch:	you stare as you were all amazed,--I don't wonder at it,--	202	DOUBL DLR	V.1	564
Mellefont:	thou wonder of all Falsehood.	202	DOUBL DLR	V.1	571
Brisk:	This is all very surprizing, let me perish.	203	DOUBL DLR	V.1	578
	All have a Right and Title to some part,	204	DOUBL DLR	EPI.	15
	The dreadful men of Learning, all Confound,	204	DOUBL DLR	EPI.	17
Valentine:	therefore resolve to rail at all that have: And in that I but	217	FOR LOVE	I.1	35
Valentine:	follow the Examples of the wisest and wittiest Men in all	217	FOR LOVE	I.1	36
Valentine:	be reveng'd on 'em all; I'll pursue Angelica with more Love	217	FOR LOVE	I.1	50
Jeremy:	to be converted into Folio Books, of Warning to all	219	FOR LOVE	I.1	112
Valentine:	The Rogue has (with all the Wit he could muster	219	FOR LOVE	I.1	118
Jeremy:	Keep it? Not at all; it has been so very much stretch'd,	221	FOR LOVE	I.1	180
Valentine:	of Visitants in a morning, all soliciting of past promises;	221	FOR LOVE	I.1	190
Scandal:	any body that did not stink to all the Town.	226	FOR LOVE	I.1	402
Tattle:	to that by one that we all know--A Man too. Only to	227	FOR LOVE	I.1	424
Scandal:	Whom we all know.	227	FOR LOVE	I.1	426
Tattle:	Pooh, pooh, nothing at all, I only rally'd with you	228	FOR LOVE	I.1	445
Scandal:	Yes, Mrs. Frail is a very loose Woman, we all know	228	FOR LOVE	I.1	458
Valentine:	will prove all that he can tell her.	229	FOR LOVE	I.1	513
Mrs Frail:	will be all Otters: he has been bred at Sea, and she has	231	FOR LOVE	I.1	572
Scandal:	Ay, we'll all give you something.	231	FOR LOVE	I.1	587
Mrs Frail:	Well, what will you all give me?	232	FOR LOVE	I.1	588
Scandal:	Yes, all that have done him Favours, if you will	232	FOR LOVE	I.1	606
Valentine:	Pictures of all that have granted him favours, he has the	233	FOR LOVE	I.1	623
Valentine:	Pictures of all that have refus'd him: If Satyrs, Descriptions,	233	FOR LOVE	I.1	624
Scandal:	Ignorance, all in one Piece. Then I can shew you Lying,	233	FOR LOVE	I.1	630
Mrs Frail:	Pooh, this is all Invention. Have you ne're a	233	FOR LOVE	I.1	649
Foresight:	Hey day! What are all the Women of my Family	235	FOR LOVE	II.1	1
Foresight:	the Moon is in all her Fortitudes; Is my Neice Angelica at	235	FOR LOVE	II.1	6
Foresight:	Crab was ascending, and all my Affairs go backward.	235	FOR LOVE	II.1	13
Nurse:	and Amen with all my heart, for you have put on one	235	FOR LOVE	II.1	27
Foresight:	What, wou'd you be gadding too? Sure all Females	236	FOR LOVE	II.1	46
Foresight:	When Housewifes all the House forsake,	236	FOR LOVE	II.1	51
Angelica:	reap up all your false Prophesies, ridiculous Dreams, and	237	FOR LOVE	II.1	77
Angelica:	a Voyage to Greenland, to inhabit there all the dark	237	FOR LOVE	II.1	84
Foresight:	Gallant, Valentine, pay for all, I will.	238	FOR LOVE	II.1	117
Angelica:	Will you? I care not, but all shall out then--	238	FOR LOVE	II.1	118
Sr Sampson:	draw up Writings of Settlement and Joynture--All shall	240	FOR LOVE	II.1	194
Sr Sampson:	said of what's past, and all that is to come will happen.	240	FOR LOVE	II.1	198
Sr Sampson:	Candle, and that's all the Stars are good for.	240	FOR LOVE	II.1	201
Foresight:	How, how? Sir Sampson, that all? Give me leave to	240	FOR LOVE	II.1	202
Sr Sampson:	Reverence the Sun, Moon and Stars with all my heart.	242	FOR LOVE	II.1	247
Sr Sampson:	House, and make an Entertainment for all the Philomaths,	242	FOR LOVE	II.1	252
Sr Sampson:	Oh Sir, I understand you,--that's all, ha?	243	FOR LOVE	II.1	289
Valentine:	Yes, Sir, all that I presume to ask.--But what	243	FOR LOVE	II.1	290
Sr Sampson:	to me;--of all my Boys the most unlike me; a has a	243	FOR LOVE	II.1	306
Sr Sampson:	to me;--of all my Boys the most unlike me; he has a	243	FOR LOVE	II.1	V306
Sr Sampson:	With all my heart: Come, Uncase, Strip, and	244	FOR LOVE	II.1	337
Sr Sampson:	can't a private man be born without all these followers:	245	FOR LOVE	II.1	350
Valentine:	Fortune was provident enough to supply all the	246	FOR LOVE	II.1	394
Mrs Frail:	With all my heart, ours are but slight Flesh-wounds,	248	FOR LOVE	II.1	480
Mrs Frail:	and if we keep 'em from Air, not at all dangerous:	248	FOR LOVE	II.1	481
Mrs Fore:	Here 'tis with all my heart.	248	FOR LOVE	II.1	484
Miss Prue:	Oh good! how sweet it is--Mr. Tattle is all over sweet,	249	FOR LOVE	II.1	518
Mrs Fore:	They're all so, Sister, these Men--they	250	FOR LOVE	II.1	547
Mrs Frail:	Creature, that smells all of Pitch and Tarr--Devil	250	FOR LOVE	II.1	565
Tattle:	Yes, if you would be well-bred. All well-bred Persons	251	FOR LOVE	II.1	610
Tattle:	With all my heart,--Now then my little Angel.	252	FOR LOVE	II.1	638
Tattle:	and bred in Covent-Garden, all the days of your Life;--	252	FOR LOVE	II.1	645
Nurse:	O Lord, We're all undone--O you young Harlotry	253	FOR LOVE	III.1	10
Angelica:	Perswade your Friend, that it is all Affectation.	254	FOR LOVE	III.1	38
Tattle:	You say true, I beg your Pardon;--I'll bring all off--	255	FOR LOVE	III.1	65
Tattle:	No indeed, Madam, you don't know me at all, I	256	FOR LOVE	III.1	112
Scandal:	ask'd the Question. That's all.	256	FOR LOVE	III.1	128
Angelica:	fruitless he has found his Endeavours, and to confess all	257	FOR LOVE	III.1	143
Tattle:	Maids at the Chocolate-Houses, all the Porters of Pall-Mall	257	FOR LOVE	III.1	155
Tattle:	Maids at the Chocolate-Houses, all the Porters at Pall-Mall	257	FOR LOVE	III.1	V155
Tattle:	Garden; my own Landlady and Valet de Chambre; all who	257	FOR LOVE	III.1	158

19

All   (continued)

Character	Line	PAGE	TITLE	ACT.SC	LINE
Almeria:	I must be sacrific'd, and all the Vows	330	M. BRIDE	I.1	V172
Almeria:	Thro' all Impediments, of purging Fire,	330	M. BRIDE	I.1	182
Almeria:	I thank thee. 'Tis but this; anon, when all	331	M. BRIDE	I.1	196
Gonsalez:	Have all conspir'd, to blaze promiscuous Light,	331	M. BRIDE	I.1	222
Gonsalez:	As they were all of Eyes, and every Limb	332	M. BRIDE	I.1	241
Gonsalez:	As if they were all Eyes, and every Limb	332	M. BRIDE	I.1	V241
Manuel:	You, and yours, are all, in opposition	333	M. BRIDE	I.1	281
Manuel:	And yours are all like Daughters of Affliction.	333	M. BRIDE	I.1	V282
Manuel:	And all this high and ample Roof to ring	333	M. BRIDE	I.1	312
Manuel:	But should have smil'd that Hour, through all his Care,	333	M. BRIDE	I.1	316
Manuel:	Of that offensive black; on me be all	334	M. BRIDE	I.1	324
Manuel:	And Garcia's well-try'd Valour, all oblige me.	334	M. BRIDE	I.1	341
Garcia:	Dumbly declines all Offers: if he speak	335	M. BRIDE	I.1	371
Manuel:	All Eyes, so by Preheminence of Soul	336	M. BRIDE	I.1	422
Manuel:	To rule all Hearts.	336	M. BRIDE	I.1	423
Heli:	And when his Soul gives all her Passions Way,	338	M. BRIDE	II.1	31
Almeria:	It was a fancy'd Noise; for all is hush'd.	339	M. BRIDE	II.1	52
Almeria:	No, all is hush'd, and still as Death--'Tis dreadful!	339	M. BRIDE	II.1	58
Almeria:	Angels, and all the Host of heaven support me!	340	M. BRIDE	II.2	36
Almeria:	His Voice, I know him now, I know him all.	342	M. BRIDE	II.2	83
Almeria:	How is all this? All-powerful Heav'n, what are we!	342	M. BRIDE	II.2	111
Osmyn-Alph:	Perfection of all Truth!	343	M. BRIDE	II.2	128
Osmyn-Alph:	Perfection of all Faithfulness and Love!	343	M. BRIDE	II.2	V128
Almeria:	Indeed I wou'd--Nay, I wou'd tell thee all	343	M. BRIDE	II.2	129
Osmyn-Alph:	I shall have liv'd beyond all Aera's then,	343	M. BRIDE	II.2	143
Almeria:	And speak--That thou art here, beyond all Hope,	343	M. BRIDE	II.2	151
Almeria:	All Thought; that all at once, thou art before me,	343	M. BRIDE	II.2	152
Almeria:	As hurries all my Soul, and dozes my weak Sense.	343	M. BRIDE	II.2	155
Almeria:	It hurries all my Soul, and stuns my Sense.	343	M. BRIDE	II.2	V155
Osmyn-Alph:	There are no Wonders, or else all is Wonder.	344	M. BRIDE	II.2	180
Osmyn-Alph:	In all, and can continue to bestow,	344	M. BRIDE	II.2	189
Osmyn-Alph:	To part no more; my Friend will tell thee all;	345	M. BRIDE	II.2	205
Osmyn-Alph:	And he Heli. All, all he will unfold.	345	M. BRIDE	II.2	208
Osmyn-Alph:	Thus, do our Eyes, as do all common Mirrours	345	M. BRIDE	II.2	V221
Zara:	For all I've done, and all I have endur'd,	346	M. BRIDE	II.2	274
Zara:	Where all is lost, and I am made a Slave.	347	M. BRIDE	II.2	302
Zara:	Think on the Cause of all, then, view thy self:	347	M. BRIDE	II.2	305
Osmyn-Alph:	That tumbling on its Prop, crush'd all beneath,	347	M. BRIDE	II.2	321
Zara:	Than all the Malice of my other Fate.	348	M. BRIDE	II.2	339
Osmyn-Alph:	O my Antonio, I am all on Fire,	351	M. BRIDE	III.1	80
Osmyn-Alph:	Of Light, to the bright Source of all. There, in	353	M. BRIDE	III.1	132
Osmyn-Alph:	Of Light, to the bright Source of all. For there	353	M. BRIDE	III.1	V132
Osmyn-Alph:	Or all extended Rule of regal Pow'r.	353	M. BRIDE	III.1	138
Osmyn-Alph:	As still to meditate Revenge on all	354	M. BRIDE	III.1	171
Osmyn-Alph:	Will make all fatal. But behold, she comes	355	M. BRIDE	III.1	232
Osmyn-Alph:	My Life, my Health, my Liberty, my All.	355	M. BRIDE	III.1	236
Almeria:	So shou'd'st thou be at large from all Oppression.	357	M. BRIDE	III.1	302
Almeria:	Am I, am I of all thy Woes the worst?	357	M. BRIDE	III.1	303
Osmyn-Alph:	My All of Bliss, my everlasting Life,	357	M. BRIDE	III.1	304
Osmyn-Alph:	Soul of my Soul, and End of all my Wishes.	357	M. BRIDE	III.1	305
Osmyn-Alph:	What are all Racks, and Wheels, and Whips to this?	358	M. BRIDE	III.1	362
Osmyn-Alph:	Distress, Heav'n will repay; all Thanks are poor.	359	M. BRIDE	III.1	404
Osmyn-Alph:	Distress'd, Heav'n will repay; all Thanks are poor.	359	M. BRIDE	III.1	V404
Zara:	And all those Ills, which thou so long hast mourn'd;	361	M. BRIDE	III.1	456
Zara:	Reply at once to all. What is concluded?	361	M. BRIDE	IV.1	3
Selim:	The King, in full belief of all you told him,	361	M. BRIDE	IV.1	12
Selim:	The State of things will countenance all Suspicions.	362	M. BRIDE	IV.1	55
Manuel:	Give Order strait, that all the Pris'ners die,	364	M. BRIDE	IV.1	127
Manuel:	Let all else void the Room. Garcia, give Order	364	M. BRIDE	IV.1	131
Manuel:	Let all except Gonsalez leave the Room.	364	M. BRIDE	IV.1	V131
Manuel:	For doubling all our Guards; Command that our	364	M. BRIDE	IV.1	V132
Selim:	Madam, take heed; or you have ruin'd all.	366	M. BRIDE	IV.1	185
Almeria:	All Days, to me,	367	M. BRIDE	IV.1	257
Almeria:	Of all thy Race. Hear me, thou common Parent;	368	M. BRIDE	IV.1	278
Almeria:	And free of all bad Purposes. So Heav'ns	368	M. BRIDE	IV.1	290
Manuel:	Torn, mangl'd, flay'd, impal'd--all Pains and	368	M. BRIDE	IV.1	295
Almeria:	Then all is ended, and we both must die	368	M. BRIDE	IV.1	303
Almeria:	Yes, all my Father's wounding Wrath, tho' each	368	M. BRIDE	IV.1	307
Almeria:	And cleaves my Heart; I would have born it all,	369	M. BRIDE	IV.1	309
Almeria:	Nay, all the Pains that are prepar'd for thee:	369	M. BRIDE	IV.1	310
Manuel:	And all should follow to partake his Doom.	369	M. BRIDE	IV.1	334
Almeria:	Ye Winds and Waves, I call ye all to witness.	370	M. BRIDE	IV.1	360
Almeria:	And ghastly Head, glares by, all smear'd with Blood,	371	M. BRIDE	IV.1	388
Alonzo:	All that it can, your Lordship shall command.	372	M. BRIDE	IV.1	431
Manuel:	O, give me Patience, all ye Powers! no, rather,	373	M. BRIDE	V.1	35
Manuel:	And lash again the Hook--by Heav'n you're all	373	M. BRIDE	V.1	44
Perez:	By all that's holy, I'm amaz'd--	373	M. BRIDE	V.1	49
Manuel:	All Nature, Softness, Pity and Compassion,	374	M. BRIDE	V.1	63
Manuel:	What's thy whole Life, thy Soul, thy All, to my	374	M. BRIDE	V.1	71
Gonsalez:	And all as still, as at the Noon of Night!	376	M. BRIDE	V.2	5
Garcia:	The King? Confusion, all is on the Rout!	376	M. BRIDE	V.2	17
Garcia:	All's lost, all ruin'd by Surprize and Treachery.	376	M. BRIDE	V.2	18
Garcia:	Had enter'd long 'ere now, and born down all	377	M. BRIDE	V.2	34
Gonsalez:	Would all were false as that; for whom you call	377	M. BRIDE	V.2	40
Garcia:	But that we all should turn our Swords, against	378	M. BRIDE	V.2	66
Zara:	Thro' all the Gloomy Ways, and Iron Doors	379	M. BRIDE	V.2	133
Zara:	O now he's gone, and all is dark--	381	M. BRIDE	V.2	211
Leonora:	Zara all pale and dead! two frightful Men,	381	M. BRIDE	V.2	223
Almeria:	All things were well: and yet my Husband's murder'd!	382	M. BRIDE	V.2	242
Almeria:	I hope they murder all on whom they look.	382	M. BRIDE	V.2	246
Almeria:	O noble Thirst! yet greedy, to drink all--	382	M. BRIDE	V.2	V255
Almeria:	Drink all--O for another Draught of Death,	382	M. BRIDE	V.2	256
Almeria:	Giv'n me again from Death! O all ye Powers	383	M. BRIDE	V.2	291
	For Fortune favours all her Idiot-Race:	393	WAY WORLD	PRO.	6
	Each time they write, they venture all they've won:	393	WAY WORLD	PRO.	14

22

Alone   (continued)
Angelica:	methinks Sir Sampson, You shou'd leave him alone with	262	FOR LOVE	III.1	345
Miss Prue:	I can't abide to be left alone, mayn't my Cousin	262	FOR LOVE	III.1	352
Ben:	me alone as soon as I come home, with such a dirty dowdy	264	FOR LOVE	III.1	423
Ben:	And lie o' Nights alone.	274	FOR LOVE	III.1	767
Angelica:	Oh Heavens! You wont leave me alone with a	294	FOR LOVE	IV.1	693
Tattle:	No, nc, let me alone for a Counterfeit;--I'll be	303	FOR LOVE	V.1	219
Tattle:	a great Beauty and great Fortune reserved alone for me, by	304	FOR LOVE	V.1	270
	Our Authors Sin, but we alone repent.	323	M. BRIDE	PRO.	22
	Thus far, alone dues to the Wits relate;	323	M. BRIDE	PRO.	33
Almeria:	And Glutton-like alone devour.	328	M. BRIDE	I.1	86
Gonsalez:	While you alcne retire, and shun this Sight;	332	M. BRIDE	I.1	243
Garcia:	Alone to do, and did disdain to talk;	335	M. BRIDE	I.1	373
Manuel:	With speed--yet stay--my Hands alone can	336	M. BRIDE	I.1	411
Heli:	Leave me alone, to find and cure the Cause.	338	M. BRIDE	II.1	26
Almeria:	Invites me to the Bed, where I alone	340	M. BRIDE	II.2	16
Almeria:	How camest thou there? wert thou alone?	343	M. BRIDE	II.2	158
Almeria:	True; but how cam'st thou there? wert thou alone?	343	M. BRIDE	II.2 V158
	(A Prison. Enter Osmyn alone, with a Paper.)	349	M. BRIDE	III.1
Osmyn-Alph:	But 'tis torn off--why should that Word alone	350	M. BRIDE	III.1	22
Osmyn-Alph:	Off Slavery. O curse! that I alone	352	M. BRIDE	III.1	89
Selim:	The King, and were alcne enough to urge	361	M. BRIDE	IV.1	5
Gonsalez:	Her Mutes alone must strangle him or he'll	366	M. BRIDE	IV.1	211
Almeria:	Since thou'rt reveal'd, alone thou shalt not die.	368	M. BRIDE	IV.1	304
Almeria:	And yet alone would I have dy'd, Heav'n knows,	368	M. BRIDE	IV.1	305
Almeria:	But doubly thou, who could'st alone have Policy,	370	M. BRIDE	IV.1	380
Zara:	The Pace of thy Design; alone disguising	375	M. BRIDE	V.1	104
Selim:	Prescience is Heav'ns alone, not giv'n to Man.	375	M. BRIDE	V.1	116
	Gonsalez alone, disguis'd like a Mute, with a Dagger.)	376	M. BRIDE	V.2 V
Alonzo:	Attire; leaving alone to View, the bloody	379	M. BRIDE	V.2	117
Alonzo:	Alone the undistinguishable Trunk:	379	M. BRIDE	V.2 V117
Zara:	Yet Fate, alone can rob his mortal Part	381	M. BRIDE	V.2	195
Almeria:	For in the Tomb or Prison, I alone	381	M. BRIDE	V.2	216
Osmyn-Alph:	Forbear; my Arms alone shall hold her up:	383	M. BRIDE	V.2	278
Singer:	Then I alone the Conquest prize	435	WAY WORLD	III.1	387
Marwood:	And let me alone to keep her warm, if she should	443	WAY WORLD	III.1	665
Lady Wish:	be too long alone with Sir Rowland.	445	WAY WORLD	IV.1	40
	To think themselves alone the Fools design'd:	479	WAY WORLD	EPI.	24

Along   (14)
Belinda:	O Lord, No, I'll go along with her. Come, Mr.	88	OLD BATCH	IV.3	209
Sharper:	Nay, Prithee, leave Railing, and come along with	104	OLD BATCH	V.1	284
Sharper:	the narrow Joys of Wedlock. But prithee come along with	104	OLD BATCH	V.1	305
Brisk:	along with you.	129	DOUEL DLR	I.1	62
Mellefont:	Good Fortune ever go along with thee.	157	DOUEL DLR	III.1	262
Careless:	You bring that along with you, Sir Paul, that shall	159	DOUEL DLR	III.1	323
Sir Paul:	I can't tell you I'm so overjoy'd; come along with me	181	DOUEL DLR	IV.1	508
Maskwell:	and run the hazard along with you.	193	DOUEL DLR	V.1	207
Valentine:	Attendants that you begot along with me.	244	FOR LOVE	II.1	342
Mrs Fore:	Come, Miss, come along with me, and tell	265	FOR LOVE	III.1	444
Ben:	Oh here they be--And Fiddles along with 'em;	275	FOR LOVE	III.1	796
Foresight:	Aye, but pray take me along with you, Sir--	304	FOR LOVE	V.1	279
Ben:	along with her, she'll break her Cable, I can tell you that.	310	FOR LOVE	V.1	494
Manuel:	And laid along as he now lies supine,	374	M. BRIDE	V.1 V86B

Alonzo   (24)
	(Enter Alonzo.)	331	M. BRIDE	I.1	208
	(Exit Alonzo.)	331	M. BRIDE	I.1	212
	(Enter Alonzo.)	335	M. BRIDE	I.1	358
Manuel:	Now, what would Alonzo?	335	M. BRIDE	I.1 V358
Gonsalez:	One to my Wish. Alonzo, thou art welcome.	371	M. BRIDE	IV.1	417
	(Enter Alonzo.)	371	M. BRIDE	IV.1	418
Gonsalez:	I'm not i'th' Way at Present, gcod Alonzo.	371	M. BRIDE	IV.1	421
Gonsalez:	Do, my best Alonzo.	371	M. BRIDE	IV.1	424
Gonsalez:	Away, I've not been seen--haste good Alonzo.	372	M. BRIDE	IV.1	442
Gonsalez:	And say, I've not been seen--haste good Alonzo.	372	M. BRIDE	IV.1 V442
	(Exit Alonzo.)	372	M. BRIDE	IV.1	443
	(A Room of State. Enter King, Perez, and Alonzo.)	372	M. BRIDE	V.1
Manuel:	Ha! seize that Mute; Alonzo, follow him.	373	M. BRIDE	V.1	13
Manuel:	Ha! stop and seize that Mute; Alcnzo, follow him.	373	M. BRIDE	V.1 V 13
	(Exit Alonzo.)	373	M. BRIDE	V.1	14
	(Alonzo re-enters with a Paper.)	373	M. BRIDE	V.1	18
	(Alonzo follows him, and returns with a Paper.)	373	M. BRIDE	V.1 V 18
Gonsalez:	What Noise! some body coming? 'st, Alonzo?	376	M. BRIDE	V.2	10
	(Enter Garcia and Alonzo.)	376	M. BRIDE	V.2	15
Garcia:	Where? where? Alcnzo, where's my Father? where	376	M. BRIDE	V.2	16
Gonsalez:	What hast thou dcne, Alonzo?	379	M. BRIDE	V.2	109
Gonsalez:	Repent. Haste thee, Alonzo, hence, with speed,	379	M. BRIDE	V.2	125
Gonsalez:	Haste thee, Alonzo, haste thee hence with Speed,	379	M. BRIDE	V.2 V125
Osmyn-Alph:	Gonsalez and Alonzo, both of Wounds	383	M. BRIDE	V.2	305

Aloud   (11)
Araminta:	Bellmour last Night, and call'd him aloud in your sleep.	55	OLD BATCH	II.2	38
Laetitia:	aloud.)	91	OLD BATCH	IV.4	84
Sharper:	(Aloud.)	102	OLD BATCH	V.1	197
Heartwell:	The youthful Beast sets forth, and neighs aloud.	112	OLD BATCH	V.1	187
Lady Froth:	Three times aloud, as I love Letters--But	176	DOUBL DLR	IV.1	331
Lady Touch:	(aloud). Never, never! I'le grow to the	186	DOUBL DLR	IV.2	98
Scandal:	manner. For the Rogue will speak aloud in the posture of	226	FOR LOVE	I.1	370
Garcia:	Proclaim'd aloud by Perez, for Alphonso.	377	M. BRIDE	V.2	44
Garcia:	Pronounc'd aloud by Perez, for Alphonso.	377	M. BRIDE	V.2 V 44
Mirabell:	aloud of the Vapours, and after fell into a profound	396	WAY WORLD	I.1	31
Mirabell:	roar cut aloud as often as they pass by you; and when	409	WAY WORLD	I.1	526

Alphonso   (61)
Leonora:	Proposing by a Match between Alphonso	327	M. BRIDE	I.1	48
Almeria:	O Alphcnso, Alphonso! thou art too	327	M. BRIDE	I.1	52
Almeria:	Alphonso! O Alphcnso!	327	M. BRIDE	I.1 V 52
Almeria:	O Alphonso, Alphonso!	328	M. BRIDE	I.1	69
Almeria:	It was because thou didst not know Alphonso:	328	M. BRIDE	I.1	101

Already   (continued)

Zara:	Thou hast already rack'd me with thy stay;	. . . . .	361	M. BRIDE	IV.1	1
Selim:	But to serve you. I have already thought.	. . . . .	362	M. BRIDE	IV.1	40
Gonsalez:	Wedded already--what if he should yield?	. . . . .	371	M. BRIDE	IV.1	405
Gonsalez:	With which he seems to be already shaken.	. . . . .	371	M. BRIDE	IV.1	408
Gonsalez:	Sure Death already has been busie here.	. . . . .	376	M. BRIDE	V.2	3
Garcia:	The Earth already groans to bear this Deed;	. . . . .	378	M. BRIDE	V.2	75
Zara:	O friendly Draught, already in my Heart!	. . . . .	381	M. BRIDE	V.2	204
Witwoud:	This is a vile Dog, I see that already. No Offence!	. .	438	WAY WORLD	III.1	487
Fainall:	I am married already; so that's over,--my Wife has	. .	443	WAY WORLD	III.1	677
Fainall:	Wife to Grass--I have already a deed of Settlement of the		444	WAY WORLD	III.1	709
Waitwell:	hand I see that already. That's some body whose throat	.	460	WAY WORLD	IV.1	578
Lady Wish:	I'm a Person. Your Turtle is in Custody already; You shall		463	WAY WORLD	V.1	54
Foible:	Waitwell's gone to prison already.	. . . .	463	WAY WORLD	V.1	64
Marwood:	consent to, without difficulty; she has already but too		468	WAY WORLD	V.1	259
Fainall:	remainder of her Fortune, not made over already; And for		469	WAY WORLD	V.1	269
Sir Wilful:	Over-sea's once again; and with proviso that I Marry my		471	WAY WORLD	V.1	349
Lady Wish:	have wasted my spirits so to day already; that I am ready		478	WAY WORLD	V.1	609

Also (7)

Bellmour:	'em, but must also undertake the harder Task, of obliging		41	OLD BATCH	I.1	143
Fondlewife:	And will not that which tempted thee, also tempt others,	.	76	OLD BATCH	IV.1	56
Fondlewife:	yet thy Husband must also bear his part: For thy iniquity		77	OLD BATCH	IV.1	71
Valentine:	also deprive me of Reason, Thought, Passions, Inclinations,		244	FOR LOVE	II.1	340
Valentine:	also divest me of Reason, Thought, Passions, Inclinations	.	244	FOR LOVE	II.1	V340
Almeria:	Behold thou also, and attend my Vow.	. . . . . .	330	M. BRIDE	I.1	184
Zara:	Has also wrought this chilling Change of Temper.	. . .	379	M. BRIDE	V.2	146

Altar (2)

Manuel:	And raise Love's Altar on the Spoils of War.	. . .	337	M. BRIDE	I.1	451
Osmyn-Alph:	Or this vile Earth, an Altar for such Off'rings?	. . .	357	M. BRIDE	III.1	326

Altars (1)

Belinda:	Creature to have had Darts, and Flames, and Altars, and all		55	OLD BATCH	II.2	29

Alter'd (3)

Maskwell:	have been in a great measure kept by her, the case is					
	alter'd;	. . . .	155	DOUBL DLR	III.1	177
Foresight:	How! Am I alter'd any way? I don't perceive it.	. . .	268	FOR LOVE	III.1	571
Osmyn-Alph:	Am I so alter'd, or, art thou so chang'd,	. . . .	342	M. BRIDE	II.2	80

Although (1)

Fondlewife:	weighty Sin; and although it may lie heavy upon thee,	. .	77	OLD BATCH	IV.1	70

Altogether (3)

Sir Joseph:	that it was altogether out of fear, but partly to prevent		68	OLD BATCH	III.1	273
Witwoud:	in the World,--he wou'd not be altogether contemptible.	.	403	WAY WORLD	I.1	293
Witwoud:	altogether on his Parts.	. . . .	436	WAY WORLD	III.1	417

Always (51)

Bellmour:	Flesh and Blood cannot bear it always.	. . . .	41	OLD BATCH	I.1	145
Heartwell:	April-fools, is always upon some errand that's to no	. .	42	OLD BATCH	I.1	198
Sharper:	That's because he always sets out in foul Weather,	. .	42	OLD BATCH	I.1	201
Bellmour:	to himself in the World; he takes as much always of an	.	42	OLD BATCH	I.1	211
Belinda:	sake let it be with variety; don't come always, like the		59	OLD BATCH	II.2	169
Laetitia:	My affliction is always your Jest, barbarous Man! Oh	.	78	OLD BATCH	IV.1	103
Vainlove:	pleasure of a chase: My sport is always balkt or cut short		80	OLD BATCH	IV.1	176
Brisk:	trick; you're always spoiling Company by leaving it.	.	128	DOUBL DLR	I.1	22
Careless:	And thou art always spoiling Company by coming	. . .	128	DOUBL DLR	I.1	23
Lord Froth:	pleases the Croud! Now when I Laugh, I always Laugh	.	132	DOUBL DLR	I.1	204
Careless:	be always welcome to my privacy.	. . . . .	159	DOUBL DLR	III.1	324
Lord Froth:	so ready--she always comes in three bars too soon--and	.	163	DOUBL DLR	III.1	476
Brisk:	Spectacle; she's always chewing the Cud like an old Yew.		165	DOUBL DLR	III.1	568
Lady Froth:	Then she's always ready to Laugh when Sneer	. . .	165	DOUBL DLR	III.1	573
Brisk:	Daughter your self; you're always brooding over her like		174	DOUBL DLR	IV.1	272
Brisk:	Men like rich Fellows, are always ready for all Expences;		175	DOUBL DLR	IV.1	300
Lady Ply:	Night--and I thought to have always allow'd you	. . .	180	DOUBL DLR	IV.1	V483
Lord Touch:	I have always found you prudent and careful	. . .	181	DOUBL DLR	IV.1	535
Maskwell:	when Innocence and bold Truth are always ready for	. .	184	DOUBL DLR	IV.2	20
Careless:	always thought him.	. . . .	196	DOUBL DLR	V.1	346
Jeremy:	always a Fool, when I told you what your Expences would	.	217	FOR LOVE	I.1	42
Scandal:	where-ever it is, it's always contriving it's own Ruine.	.	219	FOR LOVE	I.1	121
Tattle:	for his Calumniation!--I thank Heav'n, it has always been		226	FOR LOVE	I.1	393
Foresight:	Well, Jill-flirt, you are very pert--and always	. . .	237	FOR LOVE	II.1	74
Sr Sampson:	your Wits,--You were always fond of the Wits,--	. . .	246	FOR LOVE	II.1	400
Miss Prue:	O Gemini! well, I always had a great mind to tell	. .	252	FOR LOVE	II.1	629
Miss Prue:	always tell a lie to a man; and I don't care, let my Father		264	FOR LOVE	III.1	397
Foresight:	He was always of an impetuous Nature--But	. . . .	268	FOR LOVE	III.1	551
Mrs Frail:	And will you love me always?	. . . .	273	FOR LOVE	III.1	738
Valentine:	his Nose always, will very often be led into a Stink.	. .	282	FOR LOVE	IV.1	254
Tattle:	and play with the same Rattle always: O fie, marrying is a		303	FOR LOVE	V.1	246
Miss Prue:	I don't know for what--And I'd rather be always a	. .	305	FOR LOVE	V.1	311
Miss Prue:	I don't know for what--And I'd rather be always	. . .	305	FOR LOVE	V.1	V311
Mrs Frail:	for my part I always despised Mr. Tattle of all things;	.	310	FOR LOVE	V.1	472
Angelica:	Passion: Here's my Hand, my Heart was always yours,	.	312	FOR LOVE	V.1	562
Angelica:	always lov'd your Son, and hated your unforgiving	. .	312	FOR LOVE	V.1	573
Angelica:	Coldness which I have always worn before you, should	.	313	FOR LOVE	V.1	606
Leonora:	And always did compassionate his Fortune;	. . . .	326	M. BRIDE	I.1	21
Almeria:	Never: For always Blessings crown that Posture.	. . .	369	M. BRIDE	IV.1	322
Mirabell:	She was always civil to me, till of late; I confess I	.	397	WAY WORLD	I.1	85
Mirabell:	always the more the Scandal: For a Woman who is not a	.	399	WAY WORLD	I.1	145
Fainall:	Nature, and does not always want Wit.	. . . .	401	WAY WORLD	I.1	222
Mirabell:	Not always; but as often as his Memory fails him,	. .	401	WAY WORLD	I.1	223
Witwoud:	Well, well, he does not always think before he	. .	403	WAY WORLD	I.1	307
Petulant:	Not I, by this Hand--I always take blushing	. . . .	409	WAY WORLD	I.1	536
Marwood:	I never lov'd him; he is, and always was	. . . .	412	WAY WORLD	II.1	72
Millamant:	act always by Advice, and so tedious to be told of ones	.	422	WAY WORLD	II.1	455
Lady Wish:	Mrs. Qualmsick the Curate's Wife, that's always breeding		425	WAY WORLD	III.1	22
Marwood:	Visit is always a Disguise; and never admitted by a Woman		433	WAY WORLD	III.1	312
Lady Wish:	Wit. And your great Wits always rally their best Friends	.	441	WAY WORLD	III.1	607
Millamant:	lastly, where ever I am, you shall always knock at the door		450	WAY WORLD	IV.1	224

Am (362)

Am'rous (2)
Singer: Or am'rous Youth, that gives the Joy;   435   WAY WCRLD III.1 383
Millamant: Like Phoebus sung the no less am'rous Boy.   448   WAY WCRLD IV.1   153
Amaz'd (9)
Bellmour: the deeper the Sin the sweeter. Frank I'm amaz'd at thy good 39   OLD BATCH I.1   92
Laetitia: (aside). I'me amaz'd; sure he has discover'd nothing--   . 77   OLD EATCH IV.1   79
Araminta: I'm amaz'd! This Insolence exceeds the t'other;--   .   .   . 87   OLD BATCH IV.3 156
Araminta: I'm amaz'd! This Insclence exceeds t'other;--   87   OLD EATCH IV.3 V156
Laetitia: Dear Husband, I'm amaz'd:--Sure it's a good   92   OLD BATCH IV.4 114
Mellefont: What at first amaz'd me; for I look'd to have seen   .   .   . 130   DOUBL DLR I.1   103
Lord Touch: (aside). I'm amaz'd, here must be something   152   DOUEL DLB III.1   44
Perez: By all that's holy, I'm amaz'd--   373   M. BRIDE   V.1   49
Millamant: think of it--I am a Sybil if I am not amaz'd to think   . 434   WAY WCRLD III.1 357
Amaze (1)
Lord Froth: Heav'n, Sir Paul, you amaze me, of all things in   .   .   . 162   DOUBL DLR III.1 457
Amazed (6)
Lady Froth: Etymology.--But I'm the more amazed, to find you   .   .   . 139   DOUBL DLR II.1   40
Mellefont: I am so amazed, I kncw not what to speak.   145   DOUBL DLR II.1 263
Mellefont: I am so amazed, I know not what to say.   145   DOUBL DLR II.1 V263
Cynthia: (aside). I'm amazed to find her of our side, for I'm   . 171   DOUBL DLR IV.1 161
Sir Paul: amazed, and so overjoy'd, so afraid, and so sorry.--But   . 179   DOUBL DLR IV.1 460
Lord Touch: you stare as you were all amazed,--I don't wonder at it,-- 202   DOUBL DLR V.1   564
Amazement (8)
Mellefont: Passion had ty'd her Tongue, and Amazement mine.--   .   . 130   DOUBL DLR I.1   108
Mellefont: Death and amazement,--Madam, upon my   147   DOUBL DLR II.1 353
Lord Touch: Hell and Amazement, she's in Tears.   185   DOUBL DLR IV.2   93
Lord Touch: Amazement shakes me--where will   198   DOUEI DLR V.1   406
Valentine: Between Pleasure and Amazement, I am lost--   312   FOR LOVE   V.1   565
Osmyn-Alph: Amazement and Illusion! Rivet me   341   M. EBIDE   II.2   46
Osmyn-Alph: Amazement and Illusion!   341   M. EBIDE   II.2 V 46
Selin: (Which breeds Amazement and Distraction) scme   361   M. EBIDE   IV.1   9
Amazing (2)
Osmyn-Alph: This exquisite, amazing Goodness, ... 343   M. EBIDE   II.2 145
Osmyn-Alph: This exquisite, this most amazing Goodness, ... 343   M. EBIDE   II.2 V145
Amazon (1)
Mrs Pain: There spoke the Spirit of an Amazon, a   411   WAY WORLD II.1   48
Amber (0)   see Fat-Amber-Necklace
Ambiguity (1)
Lady Touch: And such a smile as speaks in Ambiguity! Ten thousand   . 198   DOUEL DLR V.1   394
Ambition (2)
Garcia: Fatal Ambition! Hark! the Foe is enter'd: 378   M. EBIDE   V.2   88
Singer: When 'tis not with Ambition join'd;   435   WAY WCRLD III.1 378
Ambitious (1)
Gonsalez: For thee I've been ambitious, base, and bloody: .   .   . 378   M. EBIDE   V.2   83
Amen (3)
Saygrace: Ejaculation, in the pronouncing of an Amen, or before you 194   DOUEL DLR V.1   274
Nurse: and Amen with all my heart, for you have put on one   .   . 235   FOR LOVE   II.1   27
Nurse: Amen: Why, what's beccme of the Child?--Why Miss,   .   .   . 253   FOR LOVE III.1   2
Amends (3)
Bellmour: Promise to make her Amends quickly with ancther   .   .   . 100   OLD BATCH V.1   152
                   'Twere some Amends if they cculd reimburse: 323   M. BRIDE   PRO.   24
Painall: and any way, every way will make amends;--I'll   .   .   . 416   WAY WORLD I.1   243
Amid (1)
Almeria: Amid those Flames--but 'twas not so decreed.   329   M. EBIDE   I.1 V118
Amidst (4)
Almeria: Started amidst his Foes, and made Captivity his Refuge;   . 329   M. EBIDE   I.1   116
Almeria: Started amidst his Foes, and made Captivity   329   M. EBIDE   I.1 V116
Osmyn-Alph: And bear amidst the Foe, with conqu'ring Troops.   .   .   . 351   M. EBIDE III.1   82
Osmyn-Alph: Luxurious, revelling amidst thy Charms;   358   M. EBIDE III.1 359
Amiss (5)
Lady Froth: Dairymaid, and our Coach-man is not amiss; you know,   .   . 163   DOUEL DLR III.1 503
Mrs Fore: is well enough, and your Understanding is not a-miss.   . 272   FOR LCVE III.1 689
Gonsalez: 'Twere not amiss to question her a little, ... 367   M. BRIDE   IV.1 237
Lady Wish: --But a little Disdain is not amiss; a little Scorn is   . 429   WAY WCRLD III.1 164
Marwood: Thing amiss from your Friends, Sir. You are among your   . 438   WAY WORLD III.1 507
Amity (1)
Setter: What no Token of amity Lucy? you and I don't use   .   .   . 67   OLD EATCH III.1 234
Among (12)
Bellmour: greater resemblance of Theft; and among us lewd Mortals,   . 39   OLD EATCH I.1   91
Bellmour: Say ycu so?--Is that a Maxim among ye?   106   OLD EATCH V.1   368
Tattle: be distinguish'd among the Waiting-Women by the   .   .   . 230   FOR LOVE   I.1   520
Angelica: Beasts among the Twelve Signs, Uncle. But Cuckolds go   . 239   FOR LOVE   II.1 139
Foresight: But there's but one Virgin among the Twelve Signs,   .   . 239   FOR LOVE   II.1 141
Miss Prue: any more Lavender among my Smocks--ha, Cousin?   .   .   . 249   FOR LOVE   II.1 530
Sr Sampson: had a Son that was spoil'd among 'em; a good hopeful   .   . 299   FOR LCVE   V.1   81
Heli: Among the Troops who thought to share the Plunder,   .   . 351   M. BRIDE III.1   65
Zara: Are tainted; some among 'em have resolv'd   364   M. BRIDE   IV.1 143
Gonsalez: Among the followers of the Captive Queen, ... 372   M. BRIDE   IV.1 433
Mrs Fain: must find the means in our selves, and among our selves.   . 410   WAY WORLD II.1   2
Marwood: Thing amiss frcm your Friends, Sir. You are among your   . 438   WAY WORLD III.1 507
Amongst (6)
Sir Paul: peaceable Person amongst 'em.   192   DOUBL DLR V.1   197
Mrs Frail: Fie, Miss; amongst your Linnen, you must say   249   FOR LOVE   II.1 531
Valentine: Livelyhood amongst you. I have been sworn out of   .   .   . 280   FOR LOVE   IV.1 172
Mrs Frail: O see me no more,--for thou wert born amongst   286   FOR LOVE   IV.1 398
Zara: Stiff'ning in Thought; a Statue amongst Statues.   .   .   . 345   M. BRIDE   II.2 233
Painall: amongst other secrets of Matrimony and Policy, as they are 469   WAY WORLD V.1   275
Amoret (1)
Singer: As Amoret and Thyrsis, lay   71   OLD BATCH III.2   2
Amour (7)
Vainlove: another; for my Temper quits an Amour, just where   .   .   . 39   OLD BATCH I.1   77
Bellmour: all My Heart--It adds a Gusto to an Amour; gives it the   . 39   OLD BATCH I.1   90
Bellmour: Amour as he cares for, and quits it when it grows stale, or 42   OLD BATCH I.1   212
Tattle: Third Person--or have introduc'd an Amour of my   .   .   . 256   FOR LOVE III.1 118
Mirabell: forbad me. But for the discovery of that Amour, I am   . 397   WAY WORLD I.1   79
Mirabell: forbad me. But for the discovery of this Amour, I am   . 397   WAY WORLD I.1 V 79

Angelica   (continued)
Scandal: is of a piece with Mrs. Frail. He Courts Angelica, if
                we cou'd . . . . 291 FOR LOVE   IV.1 598
Tattle: (to Angelica). Madam, shall I wait upon you? . . 293 FOR LOVE   IV.1 675
Jenny: (aside to Angelica). Yes, Madam, Sir Sampson will wait . 296 FOR LOVE   IV.1 782
                              (Exeunt Angelica and Jenny.) . 296 FOR LOVE   IV.1 794
                (A Room in Foresight's House. Enter Angelica and Jenny.) . 297 FOR LOVE   V.1
Tattle: --the time draws nigh, Jeremy. Angelica will be veil'd . 302 FOR LOVE   V.1   197
Scandal: from him to your Niece Angelica. . . . . 306 FOR LOVE   V.1   335
Scandal: Angelica? . . . . 307 FOR LOVE   V.1   363
Mrs Fore: Sir Sampson and Angelica, impossible! . . . . . 307 FOR LOVE   V.1   365
                (Enter Sir Sampson, Angelica, with Buckram.) . 307 FOR LOVE   V.1   375
Sr Sampson: (Kisses Angelica.) . . . 307 FOR LOVE   V.1   392
                (Valentine goes to Angelica.) . . . 311 FOR LOVE   V.1   530
Angelica's (3)
Tattle: Upon my Soul Angelica's a fine Woman--And . . . . 228 FOR LOVE   I.1   456
Scandal: Angelica's Love for Valentine; you won't speak of it. . 254 FOR LOVE   III.1   46
Scandal: Angelica's Love to Valentine; you won't speak of it. . 254 FOR LOVE   III.1 V 46
Angels (2)
Almeria: Angels, and all the Host of heaven support me! . . . 340 M. BRIDE   II.2   36
Osmyn-Alph: And wafted thence, on Angels Wings, thro' Ways . . . 353 M. BRIDE   III.1 131
Anger (16)
Bellmour: peacefull one, I can ensure his Anger dormant; or should he 46 OLD BATCH I.1   352
Silvia: letter, in Anger or in Scorn? . . . . 61 OLD BATCH III.1   17
Sir Joseph: O Lord his Anger was not raised before--Nay, ... 70 OLD BATCH III.1 339
Silvia: were not Love, but Anger. . . . . 72 OLD BATCH III.2   69
Lucy: on't, both your Love and Anger satisfied!--All that can 75 OLD BATCH III.2 160
Vainlove: says; and often blush'd with Anger and Surprize:-- . . 99 OLD BATCH V.1   96
Araminta: no need to forgive what is not worth my Anger. . . . 106 OLD BATCH V.1   363
Lady Ply: anger.) Gad's my Life if I thought it were so, I would this 179 DOUBL DLR IV.1 442
Lady Touch: Anger melts. (weeps) Here, take this Ponyard, for my very 198 DOUBL DLR V.1   402
Ben: fobb'd,--if I have got anger here upon your account, . . 286 FOR LOVE   IV.1 415
Zara: Thy Anger cou'd not pierce thus, to my Heart. . . . 354 M. BRIDE   III.1 187
Zara: From my Despair, my Anger had its source; . . . . . 362 M. BRIDE   IV.1   29
Zara: And Anger in Distrust, both short-liv'd Pains. . . . 362 M. BRIDE   IV.1   33
Betty: They are gone Sir, in great Anger. . . . . 406 WAY WORLD I.1   415
Petulant: Enough, let 'em trundle. Anger helps Complexion, . . . 406 WAY WORLD I.1   416
Mincing: Closet, till my old Lady's anger is abated. O, my old Lady 465 WAY WORLD V.1   107
Angle (2)
Maskwell: Hypocrisie; oh 'tis such a pleasure, to angle for fair-faced 150 DOUBL DLR III.1 458
Foible: He! I hope to see him lodge in Ludgate first, and Angle . 428 WAY WORLD III.1 137
Angrily (3)
Sharper: How!   (Angrily.) . . . . . . 48 OLD BATCH II.1   42
Sharper: hundred Pound to lose?   (Angrily.) . . . . . 50 OLD BATCH II.1 127
Capt Bluff: (Angrily.) . . . . . 53 OLD BATCH II.1 226
Angry (33)
Sir Joseph: damn'd angry Fellow--I believe I had better remember . 48 OLD BATCH II.1   44
Araminta: Oh is it come out--Now you are angry, I am sure . . . 56 OLD BATCH II.2   58
Bellmour: Pauh, Women are only angry at such offences, to . . . 63 OLD BATCH III.1   98
Bellmour: whether thou wouldst have her angry or pleas'd. Couldst . 63 OLD BATCH III.1 103
Sir Joseph: angry, I'd tell him--Mum. . . . . 68 OLD BATCH III.1 279
Silvia: Frowns, and make calm an angry Face; will soften a . . 72 OLD BATCH III.2   66
Heartwell: 'Tis both; for I am angry with my self, when I am . . 72 OLD BATCH III.2   70
Cynthia: (aside). Impertinent Creature, I could almost be angry . 140 DOUBL DLR II.1   58
Sir Paul: Pray your Ladyship give me leave to be Angry-- . . . 144 DOUBL DLR II.1 199
Sir Paul: angry, that's my pleasure at this time. . . . . . 144 DOUBL DLR II.1 212
Sir Paul: never angry before in my Life, and I'll never be appeased 145 DOUBL DLR II.1 268
Lady Touch: Dear. Nay, by this kiss you shan't be angry. O Lord, I . 152 DOUBL DLR III.1   68
Lady Touch: But will you promise me not to be angry . . . . . 152 DOUBL DLR III.1   75
Lady Touch: --nay you must--not to be angry with Mellefont . . . 152 DOUBL DLR III.1   76
Cynthia: Pray don't be angry, Sir, when I swore, I had your . . 171 DOUBL DLR IV.1 142
Sir Paul: angry, Mr. Brisk. . . . . 174 DOUBL DLR IV.1 270
Lady Froth: angry than usual. . . . . 203 DOUBL DLR V.1   580
Angelica: Nay Uncle, don't be angry--If you are, I'll . . . . 237 FOR LOVE   II.1   76
Sr Sampson: What, thou art not angry for a Jest, my good Haly--I . 242 FOR LOVE   II.1 246
Tattle: Kiss me, you must be angry, but you must not refuse me. . 252 FOR LOVE   II.1 620
Tattle: If I ask you for more, you must be more angry,--but . . 252 FOR LOVE   II.1 621
Miss Prue: No, indeed; I'm angry at you.-- . . . . 252 FOR LOVE   II.1 633
Miss Prue: be angry;--and you shall push me down before you come . 252 FOR LOVE   II.1 652
Miss Prue: Will you? then I'll be more angry, and more . . . . 253 FOR LOVE   II.1 655
Ben: No, I hope the Gentlewoman is not angry; I mean all in . 262 FOR LOVE   III.1 341
Sr Sampson: help of a Parson, ha? Odd if he should I cou'd not be angry 265 FOR LOVE   III.1 461
Ben: than my heart.--He was woundy angry when I . . . . 286 FOR LOVE   IV.1 384
Ben: angry, be you? . . . . 286 FOR LOVE   IV.1 397
Almeria: (If such there be in angry Heav'ns Vengeance) . . . 330 M. BRIDE   I.1   189
Zara: I'm angry: you're deceiv'd. I came to set . . . . 360 M. BRIDE   III.1 417
Zara: Their red and angry Beams; as if his Sight . . . . 375 M. BRIDE   V.1   94
Witwoud: wou'd come off--Ha, ha, ha; Gad I can't be angry . . 406 WAY WORLD I.1   410
Millamant: O ay, and went away--Now I think on't I'm angry . . . 420 WAY WORLD II.1 378
Anguish (3)
Silvia: For I would know, though the anguish of my Soul; . . . 61 OLD BATCH III.1   15
Osmyn-Alph: A Torture--yet, such is the bleeding Anguish . . . . 356 M. BRIDE   III.1 251
Manuel: In waking Anguish? why this, on the Day . . . . . 367 M. BRIDE   IV.1 250
Anihilator (1)
Petulant: Witwoud--You are an anihilator of sense. . . . . . 453 WAY WORLD IV.1 345
Animal (1)
Belinda: troublesome Animal than a Parrot. . . . . 60 OLD BATCH II.2 214
Animate (2)
                May now be damn'd to animate an Ass; . . . . . . 315 FOR LOVE   EPI.   22
Garcia: The King in Person animate our Men, ... 377 M. BRIDE   V.2   36
Animosities (1)
Sir Joseph: Come we'll go take a Glass to drown Animosities. . . . 54 OLD BATCH II.1 246
Animosity (3)
Millamant: Is your Animosity compos'd, Gentlemen? . . . . . 435 WAY WORLD III.1 392
Witwoud: Raillery, Raillery, Madam, we have no Animosity . . . 435 WAY WORLD III.1 393
Witwoud: Animosity--The falling out of Wits is like the falling . 435 WAY WORLD III.1 395

Anniseed (1)
| Mirabell: | all Anniseed, Ciramon, Citron and Barbado's-Waters, together | 451 | WAY WORLD | IV.1 273 |

Anniversary (1)
| Careless: | with much Solemnity on his anniversary Wedding-night. . . | 158 | DOUBL DLR | III.1 279 |

Annuated (0)   see Super-annuated

Annul (1)
| Sir Paul: | Why then the revoking my Consent does annul, or . . . . | 171 | DOUBL DLR | IV.1 144 |

Anon (7)   see Anan
Fondlewife:	Nykin, ee, ee, ee,--Here will be the good Man anon, to .	79	OLD BATCH	IV.1 136
Maskwell:	anon, after that I'll tell you the whole matter; be here in	149	DOUBL DLR	II.1 434
Almeria:	I thank thee. 'Tis but this; anon, when all	331	M. BRIDE	I.1 196
Heli:	You may; anon, at Midnight, when the King	351	M. BRIDE	III.1 47
Manuel:	Militia are in Arms: We will anon	364	M. BRIDE	IV.1 V133
Gonsalez:	Yet stay, I would--but go; anon will serve--	371	M. BRIDE	IV.1 425
Zara:	And ever and anon, the Sight was dash'd	379	M. BRIDE	V.2 139

Another (107)
Vainlove:	another; for my Temper quits an Amour, just where . . .	39	OLD BATCH	I.1 77
Bellmour:	He's of another opinion, and says I do the drudgery .	43	OLD BATCH	I.1 222
Heartwell:	replies another--methink he has more of the Marquess of .	45	OLD BATCH	I.1 322
Bellmour:	but I see he has turn'd the Corner and goes another way. .	46	OLD BATCH	I.1 V340
Sharper:	another Course, are bound, ...	47	OLD BATCH	I.1 386
Sir Joseph:	I am quite another thing, when I am with him: I don't fear	50	OLD BATCH	II.1 122
Silvia:	Could we perswade him, that she Loves another--	61	OLD BATCH	III.1 39
Setter:	in another Court.	66	OLD BATCH	III.1 221
Heartwell:	one Guinea rhymes to another--And how they dance . . .	72	OLD BATCH	III.2 36
Laetitia:	would get another Wife--Another fond Fool, to break her .	78	OLD BATCH	IV.1 107
Vainlove:	than Sawcy, in another place.	87	OLD BATCH	IV.3 165
Araminta:	Another place! Some villainous Design to blast	87	OLD BATCH	IV.3 166
Bellmour:	trust thee with another Secret. Your Mistress must not .	98	OLD BATCH	V.1 54
Bellmour:	another Woman would the like Disappointment; but my . .	100	OLD BATCH	V.1 151
Bellmour:	Promise to make her Amends quickly with another . . .	100	OLD BATCH	V.1 152
Heartwell:	vexation, or any thing, but another Woman.--	108	OLD BATCH	V.2 40
Mellefont:	taken up, with admiring another, and Brisk's	130	DOUBL DLR	I.1 134
Mellefont:	Or, what say you, to another Bottle of	134	DOUBL DLR	I.1 286
Lady Touch:	another Caprice, to unwind my temper.	137	DOUBL DLR	I.1 392
Cynthia:	the World, for you are not only happy in one another, and	141	DOUBL DLR	II.1 97
Cynthia:	become more Conspicuous by setting off one another. .	142	DOUBL DLR	II.1 152
Maskwell:	will cheat no body but himself; such another Coxcomb, .	150	DOUBL DLR	II.1 454
Maskwell:	the forming of another Plot that I have in my head-- .	154	DOUBL DLR	III.1 160
Maskwell:	the forming another Plot that I have in my head-- . .	154	DOUBL DLR	III.1 V160
Cynthia:	laugh at one another; and you must allow they have all .	163	DOUBL DLR	III.1 483
Cynthia:	and hinder one another in the Race; I swear it never do's	168	DOUBL DLR	IV.1 13
Cynthia:	same Game, but forget one another; and 'tis because we .	168	DOUBL DLR	IV.1 17
Mellefont:	House this moment and Marry one another, without . .	168	DOUBL DLR	IV.1 28
Mellefont:	Devil, or another Woman.	187	DOUBL DLR	IV.2 153
Mellefont:	maze of thoughts, each leading into one another, and all .	190	DOUBL DLR	V.1 104
Valentine:	hate, for just such another Reason; because they abound in	217	FOR LOVE	I.1 38
Jeremy:	as much as they do one another.	217	FOR LOVE	I.1 48
Scandal:	Fortunes either expect another great Fortune, or a Fool. .	225	FOR LOVE	I.1 354
Valentine:	What, another Dun?	225	FOR LOVE	I.1 357
Valentine:	asunder; you are light and shadow, and shew one another; .	225	FOR LOVE	I.1 364
Scandal:	of secrets, another Vertue that he sets up for in the same	226	FOR LOVE	I.1 369
Tattle:	till another time--I'll double the number.	230	FOR LOVE	I.1 543
Scandal:	Impotence and Ugliness in another Piece; and yet one of .	233	FOR LOVE	I.1 632
Scandal:	another large Piece too, representing a School; where there	233	FOR LOVE	I.1 653
Angelica:	great unnatural Teat under your Left Arm, and he another; .	238	FOR LOVE	II.1 120
Nurse:	another Christian, (crying)	238	FOR LOVE	II.1 125
Foresight:	Come, I know Women tell one another--She is	239	FOR LOVE	II.1 150
Jeremy:	another truth, I believe you did, for I find I was born with	245	FOR LOVE	II.1 362
Valentine:	was easily turn'd another way; and at least look'd well on	246	FOR LOVE	II.1 409
Mrs Fore:	often done in Duels, take care of one another, and grow .	248	FOR LOVE	II.1 478
Mrs Frail:	and speak openly one to another; I'm afraid the World .	248	FOR LOVE	II.1 487
Mrs Frail:	have observ'd us more than we have observ'd one another. .	248	FOR LOVE	II.1 488
Scandal:	another upon yours--As she is chaste, who was never .	256	FOR LOVE	III.1 127
Ben:	A man that is marri'd, d'ee see, is no more like another .	262	FOR LOVE	III.1 315
Ben:	heard as far as another,--I'll heave off to please you. .	263	FOR LOVE	III.1 367
Ben:	were, to look one way, and to row another. Now, for my .	263	FOR LOVE	III.1 387
Scandal:	and I had Hopes of finding another opportunity of . . .	269	FOR LOVE	III.1 589
Mrs Fore:	And so you think we are free for one another?	272	FOR LOVE	III.1 684
Scandal:	And now I think we know one another pretty well. . . .	272	FOR LOVE	III.1 710
Scandal:	can Dream as much to the purpose as another, if I set about	275	FOR LOVE	III.1 814
Sr Sampson:	shalt have it as soon as thou hast set thy Hand to another	282	FOR LOVE	IV.1 234
Valentine:	another than Oyl and Vinegar; and yet those two beaten	282	FOR LOVE	IV.1 257
Ben:	man.--I had another Voyage to make, let him take . .	285	FOR LOVE	IV.1 376
Valentine:	and yet we'll Marry one another in spite of the Pope-- .	290	FOR LOVE	IV.1 559
Valentine:	Nay faith, now let us understand one another, ...	294	FOR LOVE	IV.1 706
Angelica:	Never let us know one another better; for the Pleasure of	296	FOR LOVE	IV.1 789
Jeremy:	understood one another before she went.	296	FOR LOVE	IV.1 800
Tattle:	one another now--Pshaw, that would be a foolish . . .	303	FOR LOVE	V.1 242
Tattle:	one another.	309	FOR LOVE	V.1 452
Angelica:	'Tis very unhappy, if you don't care for one another. . .	309	FOR LOVE	V.1 462
Ben:	Why there's another Match now, as tho'f a couple of .	310	FOR LOVE	V.1 487
Ben:	one another. I'm sorry for the Young Man with all my .	310	FOR LOVE	V.1 489
Angelica:	I'll advise you, how you may avoid such another. Learn to	312	FOR LOVE	V.1 571
Sr Sampson:	You're an illiterate Fool, and I'm another, and	313	FOR LOVE	V.1 583
Sr Sampson:	You're an illiterate Fool, and I'm another, ...	313	FOR LOVE	V.1 V583
	As one Thief scapes, that executes another.	323	M. BRIDE	PRO. 32
Almeria:	Another Lord; may then just Heav'n show'r down	330	M. BRIDE	I.1 187
Almeria:	Drink all--O for another Draught of Death, ...	382	M. BRIDE	V.2 256
Almeria:	--Oh, for another Draught of Death--What mean they? .	382	M. BRIDE	V.2 V256
Fainall:	No, I'll give you your Revenge another time, when . .	395	WAY WORLD	I.1 4
Mirabell:	grave Faces, whisper'd one another; then complain'd .	396	WAY WORLD	I.1 30
Servant-M:	behind one another, as 'twere in a Country Dance. Ours .	398	WAY WORLD	I.1 114
Mirabell:	I am of another Opinion. The greater the Coxcomb, .	399	WAY WORLD	I.1 144
Mirabell:	become her; and those Affectations which in another .	399	WAY WORLD	I.1 161
Witwoud:	from one Poet to another. And what's worse, 'tis as sure a	401	WAY WORLD	I.1 247

31

Answer'd (5)

Maskwell:	So that Accusation's Answer'd; on to the next.	. . . .	135	DOUBL DLR	I.1	319
Tattle:	answer'd, I was the famous Tattle, who had ruin'd so	.	257	FOR LOVE	III.1	164
Ben:	and Gad I answer'd 'n as surlily,--What tho'f he be	.	285	FOR LOVE	IV.1	369
Sr Sampson:	Are you answer'd now, Sir?	.	311	FOR LOVE	V.1	535
Mirabell:	to the Occasion; a worse had not answer'd to the Purpose.		417	WAY WORLD	II.1	276

Answered (3)

Brisk:	Was that he then, I'm answered, if Jehu was a Hackney	.	165	DOUBL DLR	III.1	549
Brisk:	Was he? I'm answered, if Jehu was a Hackney	. . . .	165	DOUBL DLR	III.1	V549
Maskwell:	I am answered.	.	182	DOUBL DLR	IV.1	569

Answers (4)

Lady Ply:	be making Answers, and taking that upon you, which	. .	159	DOUBL DLR	III.1	328
Manuel:	He answers well, the Character you gave him.	.	336	M. BRIDE	I.1	429
Mirabell:	How pertinently the Jade answers me! Ha? almost . . .		398	WAY WORLD	I.1	108
Mrs Fain:	him; But he answers her only with Singing and Drinking	.	452	WAY WORLD	IV.1	312

Antegoa (1)

Ben:	a Voyage to Antegoa--No, hold, I maynt say so . . .		306	FOR LOVE	V.1	351

Anthony (2)   see Antony, Tantony, Tony

Sir Wilful:	Yea but 'tis, by the Rekin. Brother Anthony! What Tony	.	438	WAY WORLD	III.1	516
Sir Wilful:	Lead on little Tony--I'll follow thee my Anthony,	. .	457	WAY WORLD	IV.1	476

Anticipated (1)

Fainall:	. . . to be an Anticipated Cuckold, ...		442	WAY WORLD	III.1	631

Anticipation (1)

Fainall:	. . . to be a Cuckold by Anticipation, ...		442	WAY WORLD	III.1	V631

Antick (1)

	(After the Song, a Dance of Antick.)		71	OLD BATCH	III.2	25

Antideluvian (1)

Sr Sampson:	your Antideluvian Families, Fellows, that the Flood could	.	298	FOR LOVE	V.1	40

Antidote (2)

Capt Bluff:	But? Look you here Boy, here's your antidote, here's	. .	51	OLD BATCH	II.1	146
Waitwell:	O, she is the Antidote to desire. Spouse, thou will't	.	459	WAY WORLD	IV.1	560

Antient (2)

Mellefont:	to their Tea, and Scandal; according to their Antient	.	127	DOUBL DLR	I.1	12
Almeria:	Whose antient Pillars rear their Marble Heads, . . .		339	M. BRIDE	II.1	60

Antipodes (4)

Sr Sampson:	seen the Antipodes, where the Sun rises at Midnight, and	.	241	FOR LOVE	II.1	208
Sir Wilful:	at your Antipodes. If I travel Aunt, I touch at your	.	456	WAY WORLD	IV.1	423
Sir Wilful:	Antipodes--your Antipodes are a good rascally sort of					
	topsy-turvy		456	WAY WORLD	IV.1	424

Antiquity (1)

Valentine:	Piece of Aegyptian Antiquity, or an Irish Manuscript; you	.	297	FOR LOVE	IV.1	802

Antlers (1)

Fainall:	budding Antlers like a young Satyre, or a Citizens Child.	.	442	WAY WORLD	III.1	633

Antonio (4)

Osmyn-Alph:	Where? ha! what do I see? Antonio here!		344	M. BRIDE	II.2	169
Osmyn-Alph:	Where? ha! what do I see? Antonio!		344	M. BRIDE	II.2	V169
Almeria:	More Miracles! Antonio too escap'd!		344	M. BRIDE	II.2	172
Osmyn-Alph:	O my Antonio, I am all on Fire, ...		351	M. BRIDE	III.1	80

Antony (1)

Sir Wilful:	Yea but 'tis, by the Rekin. Brother Antony! What Tony	.	438	WAY WORLD	III.1	V516

Anxious (2)

Heartwell:	(Our Sun declines,) and with what anxious Strife,	. .	112	OLD BATCH	V.2	192
Osmyn-Alph:	More Anxious Grief. This shou'd have better taught me;	.	353	M. BRIDE	III.1	127

Any (240)

Vainlove:	Ay, or any Body that she's about--		38	OLD BATCH	I.1	42
Vainlove:	word--Had you been there or any Body 'thad been the	. .	39	OLD BATCH	I.1	99
Bellmour:	Poor Rogue. Any hour of the day or night will serve her--		40	OLD BATCH	I.1	116
Bellmour:	self, nor suffers any Body else to rail at me. Then as I	.	41	OLD BATCH	I.1	169
Heartwell:	that will fawn upon me again, and entertain any Puppy	.	42	OLD BATCH	I.1	190
Bellmour:	Well come off George, if at any time you should be . .		44	OLD BATCH	I.1	286
Bellmour:	thy Talent will never recommend thee to any thing of	. .	45	OLD BATCH	I.1	300
Sharper:	Word is sufficient any where: 'Tis but borrowing so much		50	OLD BATCH	II.1	108
Capt Bluff:	Perhaps, Sir, there was a scarce any thing of moment	.	52	OLD BATCH	II.1	197
Capt Bluff:	Death, had any other Man interrupted me--	.	54	OLD BATCH	II.1	237
Bellmour:	Thoughts fly to any pitch, I shall make villainous Signs.		59	OLD BATCH	II.2	178
Setter:	Come I'le make you any reparation.		66	OLD BATCH	III.1	214
Sir Joseph:	any offence to you Sir.		68	OLD BATCH	III.1	294
Heartwell:	cannot distrust me of any skill in the treacherous Mystery--		72	OLD BATCH	III.2	58
Silvia:	give Mony to any naughty Woman to come to Bed to	. .	73	OLD BATCH	III.2	87
Silvia:	self--honest--Here, I won't keep any thing that's yours,	.	73	OLD BATCH	III.2	110
Laetitia:	does not think, that ever I had any such thing in my Head,		77	OLD BATCH	IV.1	81
Bellmour:	--But it is a Mistake which any Body might have made. .	.	81	OLD BATCH	IV.2	41
Bellmour:	Million of Pardons, and will make you any Satisfaction.	.	82	OLD BATCH	IV.2	58
Bellmour:	any Condition.		82	OLD BATCH	IV.2	78
Laetitia:	Nay, now.--(aside) I never saw any thing so agreeably	.	82	OLD BATCH	IV.2	79
Bellmour:	nor any thing, but thy Lips. I am faint with the Excess of		82	OLD BATCH	IV.2	85
Bellmour:	Bliss:--Oh, for Love-sake, lead me any whither, where I	.	82	OLD BATCH	IV.2	86
Belinda:	to the Fashion, or any thing in practice! I had not patience		84	OLD BATCH	IV.3	32
Araminta:	Bless me, Cousin! Why wou'd you affront any		84	OLD BATCH	IV.3	35
Setter:	Captain, I wou'd do any thing to serve you; but this .	.	104	OLD BATCH	V.1	274
Sir Joseph:	Ah, honest Setter.--Sirrah, I'll give thee any . . .		104	OLD BATCH	V.1	281
Belinda:	any body else. Jesus! how he looks already. Ha, ha, ha.		108	OLD BATCH	V.2	31
Belinda:	any body else. How he looks already. Ha, ha, ha.	. .	108	OLD BATCH	V.2	V 31
Heartwell:	vexation, or any thing, but another Woman.--		108	OLD BATCH	V.2	40
Heartwell:	How have I deserv'd this of you? Any of ye? Sir, have I	.	109	OLD BATCH	V.2	51
Heartwell:	Oh! Any thing, every thing, a Leg or two, or an . . .		109	OLD BATCH	V.2	75
Setter:	think, you and I have been Play-fellows off-and-on, any	.	111	OLD BATCH	V.2	142
Mellefont:	would have mirth continued this day at any rate; tho'	.	129	DOUBL DLR	I.1	68
Mellefont:	narrowly, and give me notice upon any Suspicion. As for	.	130	DOUBL DLR	I.1	137
Careless:	Aunts Aversion in her Revenge, cannot be any way so	. .	131	DOUBL DLR	I.1	159
Brisk:	me perish, do I never say any thing worthy to be Laugh'd	.	132	DOUBL DLR	I.1	195
Lord Froth:	Person, or when any body else of the same Quality does	. .	132	DOUBL DLR	I.1	202
Lord Froth:	when any of their foolish Wit prevails upon the side	. .	133	DOUBL DLR	I.1	229
Maskwell:	as I told you before. I can't deny that neither.--Any	. .	135	DOUBL DLR	I.1	314
Lady Touch:	I have: She is ready for any Impression I		137	DOUBL DLR	I.1	408
Lady Froth:	you're a Judge; was ever any thing so well-bred as my	. .	140	DOUBL DLR	II.1	82

Any   (continued)

Speaker	Text	PAGE	TITLE	ACT.SC	LINE
Brisk:	Never any thing; but your Ladyship, let me perish. . . .	140	DOUBL DLR	II.1	84
Lady Froth:	More Wit than any Body.	140	DOUBL DLR	II.1	92
Sir Paul:	And she shall make a Simile with any Woman in	145	DOUBL DLR	II.1	261
Sir Paul:	--gadsbud he does not care a Farthing for any thing . .	146	DOUBL DLR	II.1	277
Sir Paul:	dye of 'em, like any Child, that were cutting his Teeth--	146	DOUBL DLR	II.1	283
Sir Paul:	think that I'll grant you any thing; O Lord, no,--but .	148	DOUBL DLR	II.1	366
Maskwell:	any thing--Why, let me see, I have the same Face, the .	150	DOUBL DLR	II.1	460
Lady Touch:	my Thoughts in any thing that may be to my Cousin's .	151	DOUBL DLR	III.1	35
Lady Touch:	to receive an ill impression from any opinion of mine . .	151	DOUBL DLR	III.1	37
Lady Touch:	like to be suspected in the end, and 'tis a pain any longer	151	DOUBL DLR	III.1	39
Lady Touch:	and can believe any thing worse, if it were laid to his charge	151	DOUBL DLR	III.1	41
Lady Touch:	wish I had not told you any thing.--Indeed, my Lord, .	152	DOUBL DLR	III.1	69
Lady Touch:	towards me. Nay, I can't think he meant any thing .	153	DOUBL DLR	III.1	84
Lady Touch:	take any notice of it to him.	153	DOUBL DLR	III.1	92
Lady Touch:	heard any thing from him these two days.	153	DOUBL DLR	III.1	98
Lady Touch:	--nay, I won't tell you any more, till you are your .	153	DOUBL DLR	III.1	111
Maskwell:	time he attempted any thing of that kind, to discover it to	154	DOUBL DLR	III.1	154
Maskwell:	self any longer: and was just going to give vent to a Secret, ...	156	DOUBL DLR	III.1	201
Mellefont:	Like any two Guardians to an Orphan Heiress--	156	DOUBL DLR	III.1	216
Maskwell:	open: 'twill be hard, if then you can't bring her to any .	157	DOUBL DLR	III.1	253
Lady Ply:	Pray what have you about you to entertain any bodies .	159	DOUBL DLR	III.1	331
Lady Ply:	Pray what have you to entertain any bodies	159	DOUBL DLR	III.1	V331
Lady Ply:	rather attempt it than any thing in the World, (Curtesies)	159	DOUBL DLR	III.1	341
Lady Ply:	you, Mr. Careless I don't know any thing in the World I .	159	DOUBL DLR	III.1	353
Sir Paul:	and I think need not envy any of my Neighbours, blessed .	160	DOUBL DLR	III.1	385
Cynthia:	without any harmony; for sure, my Lord, to laugh out of .	163	DOUBL DLR	III.1	472
Cynthia:	Duty, any temptation of Wealth, your inconstancy, or .	168	DOUBL DLR	IV.1	36
Cynthia:	Hold--Never to Marry any Body else.	168	DOUBL DLR	IV.1	40
Cynthia:	it to be only chance, or destiny, or unlucky Stars, or any	169	DOUBL DLR	IV.1	60
Lady Ply:	declare in the face of the World, never any body gain'd so	169	DOUBL DLR	IV.1	72
Lady Ply:	The last of any Man in the World, by my purity;	169	DOUBL DLR	IV.1	78
Lady Ply:	that Mellefont had never any thing more than a profound .	171	DOUBL DLR	IV.1	165
Lady Ply:	any dishonourable Notions of things; so that if this be .	172	DOUBL DLR	IV.1	168
Lady Ply:	Conscience, or Honour, or any thing in the World.-- .	172	DOUBL DLR	IV.1	170
Sir Paul:	It becomes me, when there is any comparison made, . .	172	DOUBL DLR	IV.1	187
Lady Ply:	read Mr. Careless his Letter, that I can't forbear any longer	173	DOUBL DLR	IV.1	210
Sir Paul:	any of my Family that will bring Children into the World.	173	DOUBL DLR	IV.1	227
Lady Froth:	near any other Man. Oh here's my Lord, now you shall .	177	DOUBL DLR	IV.1	369
Lord Froth:	Any other time, my Dear, or we'll Dance it	177	DOUBL DLR	IV.1	381
Sir Paul:	Surprize! Why I don't know any thing at all, nor I don't .	179	DOUBL DLR	IV.1	449
Sir Paul:	know whether there be any thing at all in the World, or .	179	DOUBL DLR	IV.1	450
Sir Paul:	Commission--If I desired him to do any more than . .	180	DOUBL DLR	IV.1	471
Lord Touch:	in any thing that has concern'd me or my Family. . .	181	DOUBL DLR	IV.1	536
Lord Touch:	my Honour never to own any Discovery that you shall .	182	DOUBL DLR	IV.1	573
Lord Touch:	any body else.	189	DOUBL DLR	V.1	70
Lady Touch:	Marriage, and the promoting any other, without consulting	192	DOUBL DLR	V.1	180
Cynthia:	any thing that resists my will, tho' 'twere reason it self.	193	DOUBL DLR	V.1	205
Maskwell:	was, the finding it impossible to gain the Lady any other	193	DOUBL DLR	V.1	219
Cynthia:	Did Maskwell tell you any thing of the Chaplain's . .	196	DOUBL DLR	V.1	341
Maskwell:	every look you cheaply throw away on any other Object .	199	DOUBL DLR	V.1	435
Maskwell:	his Case is desperate, and I believe he'll yield to any .	199	DOUBL DLR	V.1	449
	(If there be any here) and that is Satire.	213	FOR LOVE	PRO.	32
Jeremy:	or any of these poor rich Rogues, teach you how to pay .	217	FOR LOVE	I.1	27
Jeremy:	away for any Misdemeanour; but does voluntarily dismiss .	218	FOR LOVE	I.1	69
Jeremy:	his Master from any future Authority over him-- . . .	218	FOR LOVE	I.1	70
Jeremy:	Ay, more indeed; for who cares for any Body that . .	219	FOR LOVE	I.1	129
Scandal:	Old Woman, any thing but Poet; a Modern Poet is worse,	220	FOR LOVE	I.1	146
Scandal:	more servile, timorous, and fawning, than any I have .	220	FOR LOVE	I.1	147
Valentine:	any forecast in her.	221	FOR LOVE	I.1	213
Scandal:	Angelica: And I think she has never given you any assurance	225	FOR LOVE	I.1	344
Valentine:	You know her temper; she never gave me any great . .	225	FOR LOVE	I.1	346
Scandal:	before they act, so they rarely give us any light to guess at	225	FOR LOVE	I.1	349
Scandal:	any body's else, that will never happen.	226	FOR LOVE	I.1	385
Valentine:	any thing that he says: For to converse with Scandal, is to	226	FOR LOVE	I.1	388
Tattle:	him, that the World shall think the better of any Person .	226	FOR LOVE	I.1	392
Scandal:	any body that did not stink to all the Town.	226	FOR LOVE	I.1	402
Tattle:	knows any thing of that nature of me: As I hope to be .	227	FOR LOVE	I.1	405
Tattle:	any body else.	227	FOR LOVE	I.1	412
Valentine:	sometimes. I did not think she had granted more to any .	229	FOR LOVE	I.1	487
Valentine:	Scandal, have pity on him; he'll yield to any	230	FOR LOVE	I.1	523
Tattle:	Any, any Terms.	230	FOR LOVE	I.1	525
Scandal:	of any Body that I know: you fancy that parting with .	234	FOR LOVE	I.1	677
Foresight:	I say you lie, Sir. It is impossible that any thing . .	235	FOR LOVE	II.1	11
Nurse:	Town,--Marry, pray Heav'n they ha' given her any . .	235	FOR LOVE	II.1	21
Nurse:	ever hear the like now--Sir, did ever I do any thing .	238	FOR LOVE	II.1	101
Nurse:	thing; feel, feel here, if I have any thing but like .	238	FOR LOVE	II.1	124
Nurse:	. . . or any Teats, but two that han't	238	FOR LOVE	II.1	V125
Angelica:	do with any thing but Astrologers, Uncle. That makes my	239	FOR LOVE	II.1	144
Jeremy:	before any Justice in Middlesex.	245	FOR LOVE	II.1	356
Mrs Fore:	is scandalous: What if any Body else shou'd have seen you	247	FOR LOVE	II.1	431
Mrs Fore:	alight as I did?--How can any Body be happy, while . .	247	FOR LOVE	II.1	432
Mrs Fore:	Why, was I ever in any of these places?	247	FOR LOVE	II.1	441
Mrs Fore:	Why, was I ever in any of those places?	247	FOR LOVE	II.1	V441
Miss Prue:	nay, there's Snuff in't;--here, will you have any-- .	249	FOR LOVE	II.1	517
Miss Prue:	any more Lavender among my Smocks--ha, Cousin? . . .	249	FOR LOVE	II.1	530
Mrs Fore:	Heart, to think that any body else shou'd be before-hand .	250	FOR LOVE	II.1	551
Tattle:	(coming up). Scandal, are you in private Discourse, any	254	FOR LOVE	III.1	42
Angelica:	never deny'd any thing in his Life.	255	FOR LOVE	III.1	78
Angelica:	never ask'd any thing, but what a Lady might modestly .	255	FOR LOVE	III.1	89
Tattle:	Brag! O Heav'ns! Why, did I name any body?	255	FOR LOVE	III.1	93
Tattle:	I hope to be sav'd; I never had it in my Power to say any	256	FOR LOVE	III.1	101

Any   (continued)

Speaker	Text	PAGE	TITLE	ACT.SC	LINE
Angelica:	cou'd have lik'd any thing in him, it shou'd have been his	260	FOR LOVE	III.1	246
Angelica:	any Man, and for any Man with a good Estate: Therefore	260	FOR LOVE	III.1	254
Sr Sampson:	want a little Polishing: You must not take any thing ill,	262	FOR LOVE	III.1	339
Miss Prue:	You need not sit so near one, if you have any thing	263	FOR LOVE	III.1	364
Ben:	not for keeping any thing under Hatches,--so that if you	263	FOR LOVE	III.1	389
Ben:	your self, Gad I don't think you are any more to compare	264	FOR LOVE	III.1	412
Miss Prue:	any more, he'll thrash your Jacket for you, he will, you	264	FOR LOVE	III.1	417
Scandal:	him, and all of us, more than any thing else?	266	FOR LOVE	III.1	484
Sr Sampson:	Body o' me, I don't know any universal Grievance,	266	FOR LOVE	III.1	485
Foresight:	How! Am I alter'd any way? I don't perceive it.	268	FOR LOVE	III.1	571
Foresight:	(looking in the Glass). I do not see any Revolution	269	FOR LOVE	III.1	600
Mrs Fore:	Devil; do you think any Woman Honest?	271	FOR LOVE	III.1	665
Jeremy:	light as his Pockets; and any body that has a mind to a	276	FOR LOVE	IV.1	35
Scandal:	Gone; why she was never here, nor any where else;	278	FOR LOVE	IV.1	96
Jeremy:	Good lack! What's the matter now? Are any more of	278	FOR LOVE	IV.1	98
Scandal:	any Remorse!	281	FOR LOVE	IV.1	213
Sr Sampson:	need any body hold it?--I'll put it up in my Pocket,	281	FOR LOVE	IV.1	231
Scandal:	thereby incapable of making any Conveyance in Law; so	283	FOR LOVE	IV.1	299
Mrs Frail:	Any fool, but a Husband.	287	FOR LOVE	IV.1	428
Mrs Fore:	her, and Jeremy says will take any body for her that he	288	FOR LOVE	IV.1	469
Angelica:	any body so.	291	FOR LOVE	IV.1	573
Tattle:	of Valentine's making any more Addresses to you, I have	291	FOR LOVE	IV.1	578
Foresight:	But he knows more than any body,--Oh	291	FOR LOVE	IV.1	603
Valentine:	Nay, now you do me Wrong; for if any Interest	295	FOR LOVE	IV.1	725
Jeremy:	absolutely and substantially Mad, as any Freeholder in	295	FOR LOVE	IV.1	738
Jeremy:	Bethlehem; Nay, he's as Mad as any Projector, Fanatick,	295	FOR LOVE	IV.1	739
Jeremy:	O Lord, Madam, did you ever know any Madman	295	FOR LOVE	IV.1	743
Jeremy:	Sir, your Father has sent to know if you are any	296	FOR LOVE	IV.1	770
Angelica:	Wou'd any thing, but a Madman complain of	296	FOR LOVE	IV.1	785
Sr Sampson:	a Lady any way--Come, come, let me tell you, you	298	FOR LOVE	V.1	24
Sr Sampson:	Has any young Rogue affronted you, and shall I cut his	298	FOR LOVE	V.1	42
Sr Sampson:	and 'twere pity you shou'd be thrown away upon any	298	FOR LOVE	V.1	52
Sr Sampson:	of any thing;--And if they commit Matrimony,	299	FOR LOVE	V.1	56
Angelica:	Fortune enough to make any Man easie that I can like; If	299	FOR LOVE	V.1	61
Jeremy:	comply with any thing to please him. Poor Lady, I'm	302	FOR LOVE	V.1	202
Tattle:	Marry any body before.	303	FOR LOVE	V.1	214
Miss Prue:	you; I have been looking up and down for you like any	303	FOR LOVE	V.1	223
Miss Prue:	thing, till I'm as tired as any thing in the World.	303	FOR LOVE	V.1	224
Tattle:	The Devil take me if ever I was so much concern'd at any	309	FOR LOVE	V.1	460
Tattle:	serious Kindness--I never lik'd any body less in my Life.	309	FOR LOVE	V.1	465
Tattle:	wish we could keep it secret, why I don't believe any of	310	FOR LOVE	V.1	476
Valentine:	that loses hope may part with any thing. I never valu'd	312	FOR LOVE	V.1	544
Jeremy:	any thing like it--Then how could it be otherwise?	313	FOR LOVE	V.1	594
Valentine:	Any thing, my Friend, every thing that looks like	313	FOR LOVE	V.1	602
Almeria:	By any Action, Word or Thought, to wed	330	M. BRIDE	I.1	186
Almeria:	Than any I have yet endur'd--and now	330	M. BRIDE	I.1	190
Zara:	If I on any Terms could condescend	335	M. BRIDE	I.1	393
Garcia:	I saw him not, nor any like him.	338	M. BRIDE	II.1	V 18
Osmyn-Alph:	Is knowing more than any Circumstance,	342	M. BRIDE	II.2	94
Almeria:	On any Terms, that thou dost wish me from thee.	356	M. BRIDE	III.1	257
Almeria:	Thus, better, than for any Cause to part.	356	M. BRIDE	III.1	263
Gonsalez:	At any time, in Albucacim's Court.	363	M. BRIDE	IV.1	103
Manuel:	Nor she her self, nor any of her Mutes	372	M. BRIDE	V.1	3
Mirabell:	I did as much as Man cou'd, with any reasonable	397	WAY WORLD	I.1	68
Mirabell:	She has Beauty enough to make any Man think so;	399	WAY WORLD	I.1	153
Mirabell:	of the Squire his Brother, any thing related?	400	WAY WORLD	I.1	211
Witwoud:	Lady? Gad, I say any thing in the World to get this Fellow	402	WAY WORLD	I.1	255
Witwoud:	wrong him neither--And if he had but any Judgment	403	WAY WORLD	I.1	292
Witwoud:	wrong him.--And if he had any Judgment	403	WAY WORLD	I.1	V292
Witwoud:	contradict any Body.	403	WAY WORLD	I.1	304
Mirabell:	Was there any mention made of my Uncle, or me? Tell	407	WAY WORLD	I.1	451
Witwoud:	'Tis what she will hardly allow any Body else;--	408	WAY WORLD	I.1	476
Petulant:	any thing before him.	408	WAY WORLD	I.1	498
Fainall:	you cannot resent any thing from me; especially what is	412	WAY WORLD	II.1	96
Fainall:	and any way, every way will make amends;--I'll	416	WAY WORLD	II.1	243
Fainall:	her of all she's worth, and we'll retire somewhere, any	416	WAY WORLD	II.1	245
Mrs Fain:	I believe my Lady will do any thing to get a Husband; and	418	WAY WORLD	II.1	308
Mrs Fain:	suppose she will submit to any thing to get rid of him.	418	WAY WORLD	II.1	310
Mirabell:	Yes, I think the good Lady wou'd marry any	418	WAY WORLD	II.1	311
Mincing:	with Poetry, it sits so pleasant the next Day as any Thing,	420	WAY WORLD	II.1	373
Waitwell:	Day! 'Tis enough to make any Man forget himself. The	424	WAY WORLD	II.1	556
Lady Wish:	my Features, to receive Sir Rowland with any Oeconomy of	428	WAY WORLD	III.1	141
Marwood:	Care, like any Chymist upon the Day of Projection.	431	WAY WORLD	III.1	248
Millamant:	Sure never any thing was so Unbred as that odious	432	WAY WORLD	III.1	284
Millamant:	hear it Madam--Not that there's any great matter in	434	WAY WORLD	III.1	372
Petulant:	No, no, it's no Enemy to any Body, but them that	436	WAY WORLD	III.1	420
Millamant:	at the Impudence of any Illiterate Man, to offer to make	436	WAY WORLD	III.1	423
Petulant:	Why shou'd a Man be any further from being	436	WAY WORLD	III.1	V428
Petulant:	married tho' he can't Read, any more than he is from being	436	WAY WORLD	III.1	429
Servant-W:	A Week, Sir; longer than any Body in the House,	437	WAY WORLD	III.1	457
Servant-W:	A Week, Sir; longer than any in the House,	437	WAY WORLD	III.1	V457
Marwood:	before they find one another out. You must not take any	438	WAY WORLD	III.1	506
Sir Wilful:	write my self; no offence to any Body, I hope; and Nephew	438	WAY WORLD	III.1	511
Lady Wish:	Will you drink any Thing after your Journey, Nephew,	441	WAY WORLD	III.1	599
Marwood:	will come to any Composition to save her reputation, take	442	WAY WORLD	III.1	661
Millamant:	Have you any business with me, Sir Wilful?	447	WAY WORLD	IV.1	113
Mirabell:	Have you any more Conditions to offer? Hitherto	450	WAY WORLD	IV.1	210
Witwoud:	staid any longer I shou'd have burst,--I must have been let	453	WAY WORLD	IV.1	327
Lady Wish:	You must not attribute my yielding to any sinister appetite,	458	WAY WORLD	IV.1	529
Lady Wish:	to any Lethargy of Continence--I hope	458	WAY WORLD	IV.1	531
Lady Wish:	you do not think me prone to any iteration of Nuptials.--	458	WAY WORLD	IV.1	532
Waitwell:	Spouse, hast thou any Cordial--I want Spirits.	459	WAY WORLD	IV.1	557
Mincing:	O yes Mem, I'll vouch any thing for your Ladyship's	465	WAY WORLD	V.1	121
Marwood:	of Court, where there is no precedent for a Jest in any	467	WAY WORLD	V.1	216
Lady Wish:	up all, my self and my all, my Neice and her all,--any	468	WAY WORLD	V.1	239

Any   (continued)
  Sir Wilful: fairer? If I have broke any thing, I'll pay for't, an it
                 cost a   470   WAY WORLD   V.1   318
  Lady Wish: How's this dear Neice? Have I any comfort?   .   470   WAY WORLD   V.1   323
  Mirabell: any Obligation to me; or else perhaps I cou'd advise.--   473   WAY WORLD   V.1   452
  Lady Wish: I'll consent to any thing to come, to be deliver'd from this   473   WAY WORLD   V.1   455
  Lady Wish: Ay, ay, any Body, any body.   474   WAY WORLD   V.1   469
  Mirabell: appear--you do not remember Gentlemen, any thing of   .   476   WAY WORLD   V.1   528
              Who pleases any one against his Will.   479   WAY WORLD   EPI.   8
              If any are so arrogantly Vain, ...   479   WAY WORLD   EPI.   25
              As any one abstracted Fop to shew.   479   WAY WORLD   EPI.   30
Apart (6)
              (Vainlove and Araminta talk a-part.)   108   OLD BATCH   V.2   21
  Maskwell: By this Light, I'm serious; all raillery apart--   .   156   DOUBL DLR   III.1   232
  Valentine: Hypocrisie apart,--The Comedy draws toward an   . . .   294   FOR LOVE   IV.1   707
  Marwood: must entertain themselves, apart from Men. We may   . .   410   WAY WORLD   II.1   22
              (Fainall and Mrs. Marwood talk a-part.)   441   WAY WORLD   III.1   610
  Lady Wish: (apart). Oh, he has Witch-craft in his Eyes and   472   WAY WORLD   V.1   408
Apartment (1)
    see Appartment
         (Araminta, Belinda, Betty waiting, in Araminta's Apartment)   54   OLD BATCH   II.2 V
Apartments (1)
  Fainall: another's Apartments, where they come together like the   .   396   WAY WORLD   I.1   52
Ape (2)
  Belinda: than your talking Impertinence; as an Ape is a much more   .   60   OLD BATCH   II.2   213
  Lord Froth: had brought the Ape into the World her self.   165   DOUBL DLR   III.1   566
Apishness (1)
  Bellmour: Well, I find my Apishness has paid the Ransome   60   OLD BATCH   II.2   218
Apocryphal (2)
  Fondlewife: is this Apocryphal Elder? I'll ferret him.   92   OLD BATCH   IV.4   118
  Fondlewife: Ha! This is Apocryphal; I may chuse whether I   . . .   95   OLD BATCH   IV.4   217
Apollo (2)
  Singer-F: A Nymph and a Swain to Apollo once pray'd, ...   258   FOR LOVE   III.1   200
  Singer-F: Apollo was mute, and had like t' have been pos'd, . . .   259   FOR LOVE   III.1   205
Apollo's (1)
  Sir Wilful: Let Apollo's Example invite us;   455   WAY WORLD   IV.1   418
Apologies (2)
  Mirabell: Have a care of such Apologies, Witwoud;--for   402   WAY WORLD   I.1   275
  Marwood: No Apologies, dear Madam. I have been very   431   WAY WORLD   III.1   252
Apology (4)
  Laetitia: there needs no farther Apology.   81   OLD BATCH   IV.2   47
  Maskwell: make some Apology to the Company for her own, and   . .   181   DOUBL DLR   IV.1   522
  Maskwell: made some Apology to the Company for her own, and   . .   181   DOUBL DLR   IV.1   V522
  Valentine: No Apology, good Mr. Scrivener, you shall be   224   FOR LOVE   I.1   324
Apostle (1)
  Angelica: only because the Butler had mislaid some of the Apostle   .   237   FOR LOVE   II.1 V 89
Apostle's (1)
  Angelica: only because the Butler had mislaid some of the Apostle's   237   FOR LOVE   II.1   89
Apothecary (1)
  Fainall: is your Apothecary. Next, my Wife shall settle on me the   .   469   WAY WORLD   V.1   268
Apparitions (1)
  Almeria: With Apparitions and affrighting Fantoms: 383   M. BRIDE   V.2   296
Appartment (1)
  Gonsalez: At my Appartment. Use thy utmost Diligence;   372   M. BRIDE   IV.1   441
Appear (20)
  Bellmour: faith upon second Thoughts, she does not appear to be so   .   41   OLD BATCH   I.1   171
  Lucy: not appear to Day according to the Summons I brought   .   66   OLD BATCH   III.1   218
  Bellmour: You appear concern'd, Madam.   82   OLD BATCH   IV.2   61
         (Heartwell and Lucy appear at Sylvia's Door.)   96   OLD BATCH   V.1 V 9
  Capt Bluff: shall appear by the fair Araminta, my Wife's permission.   .   110   OLD BATCH   V.2   109
          But in this Court, what difference does appear!   . . .   204   DOUBL DLR   EPI.   12
  Valentine: then ever, and appear more notoriously her Admirer in   . .   217   FOR LOVE   I.1   51
  Mrs Fore: Very well, that will appear who has most, ...   247   FOR LOVE   II.1   455
  Foresight: How does it appear, Mr. Scandal? I think I am very   . .   268   FOR LOVE   III.1   561
  Angelica: thing that wou'd make me appear to be too much concern'd   .   299   FOR LOVE   V.1   91
  Sr Sampson: Odzooks I'm a young Man, and I'll make it appear--   . .   301   FOR LOVE   V.1   140
  Foresight: How! I will make it appear that what you say is   . . .   304   FOR LOVE   V.1   274
          New Plays did then like Almanacks appear;   323   M. BRIDE   PRO.   3
  Lady Wish: O Dear, I can't appear till I'm dress'd. Dear   432   WAY WORLD   III.1   278
  Marwood: you wou'd but appear bare fac'd now, and own Mirabell;   .   433   WAY WORLD   III.1   314
  Marwood: unknown hand--for the less I appear to know of the truth   .   443   WAY WORLD   III.1   702
  Fainall: appear by the last Will and Testament of your deceas'd   .   469   WAY WORLD   V.1   281
  Mirabell: I must have leave for two Criminals to appear.   . . .   474   WAY WORLD   V.1   468
  Mirabell: and Penitent to appear, Madam.   475   WAY WORLD   V.1   507
  Mirabell: appear--you do not remember Gentlemen, any thing of   .   476   WAY WORLD   V.1   528
Appear'd (3)
  Sharper: (reads). Hum hum--And what then appear'd a fault,   . .   79   OLD BATCH   IV.1   156
  Scandal: Something has appear'd to your Son Valentine--   . . .   266   FOR LOVE   III.1   496
  Manuel: Thy senseless Vow appear'd to bear its Date, ...   333   M. BRIDE   I.1   299
Appearance (8)
  Fondlewife: while her good Husband is deluded by his Godly appearance   76   OLD BATCH   IV.1   30
  Bellmour: Madam? Those Eyes shone kindly on my first Appearance,   .   81   OLD BATCH   IV.2   21
  Laetitia: Appearance promised: The Piety of your Habit was   . . .   81   OLD BATCH   IV.2   25
  Maskwell: own Opinion; the appearance is very fair, but I have an   .   181   DOUBL DLR   IV.1   528
  Maskwell: I grant you in appearance all is true; I seem'd   . . .   198   DOUBL DLR   V.1   423
  Fainall: Faith this has an appearance.   443   WAY WORLD   III.1   667
  Lady Wish: appearance. He is as terrible to me as a Gorgon; if I
          see him, ...   470   WAY WORLD   V.1   336
  Lady Wish: brib'd a Villain to his Assassination; but his appearance   472   WAY WORLD   V.1   410
Appearances (1)
  Foresight: Appearances are prosperous--   268   FOR LOVE   III.1   553
Appearing (3)
  Mellefont: appearing to my Shipwrack'd hopes: The Witch has rais'd   .   148   DOUBL DLR   II.1   382
  Garcia: Of that appearing Love, which Zara bears   338   M. BRIDE   II.1   42
  Servant-M: was the last Couple to lead up; and no hopes appearing of   398   WAY WORLD   I.1   115
Appears (8)
  Jeremy: Spirit of Famine appears to me; sometimes like a decay'd   .   218   FOR LOVE   I.1   95

37

		PAGE	TITLE	ACT.SC	LINE

Approve (4)
Heartwell: Bellmour, I approve thy mirth, and thank thee. . . . . 111 OLD BATCH V.2 150
Approve, or Damn the Repartee and Rallery. . . . . . 204 DOUBL DLR EPI. 20
Alonzo: Lest you forbid; what then you may approve. . . . . 378 M. BRIDE V.2 98
Zara: And wait his coming to approve the Deed. . . . . . 380 M. BRIDE V.2 153

Appurtenances (1)
Belinda: and Appurtenances; O Gad! sure you would--But you . . . 55 OLD BATCH II.2 33

April-fools (1)
Heartwell: April-fools, is always upon some errand that's to no . . 42 OLD BATCH I.1 198

Apt (9)
Fondlewife: I profess a very apt Comparison, Varlet. Go in . . . . 76 OLD BATCH IV.1 45
Fondlewife: I profess a very apt Comparison, Varlet. Go . . . . 76 OLD BATCH IV.1 V 45
Vainlove: what she knows as well as I. (Aside). Men are apt to offend 87 OLD BATCH IV.3 137
Lady Touch: in my Temper, Passions in my Soul, apt to every provocation; 135 DOUBL DLR I.1 326
Valentine: Nay faith, I'm apt to believe him--Except . . . . . 227 FOR LOVE I.1 414
Tattle: Oh my Dear, apt Scholar. . . . . 253 FOR LOVE II.1 659
Scandal: I'm apt to believe there is something mysterious in his . 285 FOR LOVE IV.1 344
Angelica: apt to run more in Debt than you are able to pay. . . 313 FOR LOVE V.1 614
Mirabell: am not one of those Coxcombs who are apt to interpret a . 397 WAY WORLD I.1 86

Aquatical (1)
Foresight: and Aquatical Trigons. Know whether Life shall be long . 241 FOR LOVE II.1 214

Arabella (1)
Fainall: deed of Conveyance of the whole Estate real of Arabella . 476 WAY WORLD V.1 551

Arabian (1)
Foresight: Prophesie written by Messehalah the Arabian, and thus . 236 FOR LOVE II.1 49

Araminta (23)
Vainlove: But I saw my Araminta, yet am as impatient. . . . . 40 OLD BATCH I.1 135
Heartwell: What has he not drop't Anchor at Araminta? . . . . 42 OLD BATCH I.1 204
(Scene Changes to Lodgings Enter Araminta, Belinda.) . . 54 OLD BATCH II.2
(Araminta, Belinda, Betty waiting, in Araminta's Apartment) 54 OLD BATCH II.2 V
Belinda: that in his Breast. Araminta, come I'll talk seriously
to you . . . . 55 OLD BATCH II.2 30
Silvia: Respects, and peruse it! He's gone, and Araminta . . 61 OLD BATCH III.1 28
Bellmour: a kiss from Araminta. . . . . 63 OLD BATCH III.1 96
Bellmour: thou be content to marry Araminta? . . . . . . 63 OLD BATCH III.1 104
Vainlove: Nor I to marry Araminta till I merit her. . . . . . 63 OLD BATCH III.1 109
Lucy: with Araminta. . . . . 66 OLD BATCH III.1 223
Sharper: How! Araminta lost! . . . . 79 OLD BATCH IV.1 153
Sharper: Araminta. . . . . 79 OLD BATCH IV.1 162
Araminta and Belinda meeting.) . . . . 83 OLD BATCH IV.3
Belinda: Dear Araminta, I'm tir'd. . . . . 86 OLD BATCH IV.3 100
Setter: stood towards Madam Araminta. As, When you had seen . 99 OLD BATCH V.1 114
Sharper: Impossible! Araminta take a liking to a Fool! . . . 102 OLD BATCH V.1 196
(Enter Bellmour, Belinda, Araminta and Vainlove.) . . 106 OLD BATCH V.1 355
Vainlove: (to Araminta). Oh, 'twas Frenzy all: Cannot you forgive 106 OLD BATCH V.1 356
(Enter Bellmour, Belinda, Vainlove, Araminta.) . . . 108 OLD BATCH V.2 16
(Vainlove and Araminta talk a-part.) . . . 108 OLD BATCH V.2 21
Capt Bluff: shall appear by the fair Araminta, my Wife's permission. 110 OLD BATCH V.2 109
(Araminta and Belinda unmask.) . . 110 OLD BATCH V.2 117
Vainlove: (To Araminta.) . . . . 112 OLD BATCH V.2 V172

Araminta's (1)
(Araminta, Belinda, Betty waiting, in Araminta's Apartment) 54 OLD BATCH II.2 V

Aramintas (1)
Lucy: You know Aramintas dissembled Coyness has won, and . . . 61 OLD BATCH III.1 37

Arbitrary (2)
Sr Sampson: Authority, no Correction, no Arbitrary Power; nothing . 240 FOR LOVE II.1 177
Zara: And Native Right to Arbitrary Sway; . . . . 336 M. BRIDE I.1 397

Arbour (1)
Lady Touch: With Careless, in the close Arbour, he may . . . . 192 DOUBL DLR V.1 188

Arch'd (1)
Almeria: To bear aloft its arch'd and pond'rous Roof, ... 339 M. BRIDE II.1 61

Ardent (1)
Maskwell: Your Zeal I grant was Ardent, but misplac'd; . . . . 137 DOUBL DLR I.1 374

Ardors (1)
Lady Wish: Trances, and the Tremblings, the Ardors and the Ecstacies, 458 WAY WORLD IV.1 514

Ardour (2)
Maskwell: dissemble Ardour and Ecstasie, that's resolv'd: How . . 155 DOUBL DLR III.1 183
Osmyn-Alph: With the new-flushing Ardour of my Cheek; . . . . . 383 M. BRIDE V.2 282

Are (606)

Argo's (1)
Valentine: Argo's hundred Eyes be shut, ha? No body shall know, . . 290 FOR LOVE IV.1 552

Argues (1)
Witwoud: than a Woman constant; one argues a decay of Parts, as . 403 WAY WORLD I.1 320

Argument (10)
Bellmour: Husband: For 'tis an Argument of her great Zeal towards . 39 OLD BATCH I.1 64
Sharper: An argument of my little Passion, very good . . . . 42 OLD BATCH I.1 214
Bellmour: let me tell you, my standing Argument is depress'd in . . 59 OLD BATCH II.2 183
Bellmour: let me tell you, my most prevailing Argument is express'd in 59 OLD BATCH II.2 V183
Maskwell: an Argument that I Lov'd; for with that Art you veil'd . 136 DOUBL DLR I.1 362
Mellefont: to a man that she has overcome Temptations, is an argument 158 DOUBL DLR III.1 299
Sr Sampson: there's Latin for you to prove it, and an Argument . . 240 FOR LOVE II.1 205
Mirabell: her, but Millamant joining in the Argument, I rose and . 396 WAY WORLD I.1 37
Mirabell: You pursue the Argument with a distrust that seems . . 397 WAY WORLD I.1 95
Witwoud: No, no, his being positive is an Incentive to Argument, . 403 WAY WORLD I.1 323

Arguments (2)
Maskwell: Indignation; your Disposition, my Arguments, and happy . 136 DOUBL DLR I.1 368
Maskwell: intended this Evening to have try'd all Arguments to . . 182 DOUBL DLR IV.1 577

Aright (1)
Gonsalez: And try howe'er, if I've divin'd aright. . . . . . 367 M. BRIDE IV.1 238

Arise (4)
Lord Touch: Still gnawing that, whence first it did arise; . . . 203 DOUBL DLR V.1 595
Heli: If to arise in very deed from Death, ... 337 M. BRIDE II.1 5
Almeria: Sure, from thy Father's Tomb, thou didst arise! . . . 343 M. BRIDE II.2 156
Look out when Storms arise, and Billows roar, . . . 385 M. BRIDE EPI. 20

Arises (1)
Scandal: Why thence it arises--The thing is proverbially . . . 256 FOR LOVE III.1 123

Aristotle (1)
    Lady Froth: O yes, and Rapine, and Dacier upcn Aristotle 142   DOUBL DLR   II.1   138
Aristotle's (1)
                   Thus Aristotle's Soul, of old that was, ... 315   FOR LCVE   EPI.   21
Arithmetician (1)
    Valentine: thing; it's a Question that would puzzle an Arithmetician, 280   FOR LCVE   IV.1   175
Arm (6)
    Heartwell: Arm; nay, I would be divorced frcm my Virility, to be . . 109   OLD EATCH   V.2   76
    Careless: Arm--he cannot be ignorant that Maskwell means to . . . 196   DOUBL DLR   V.1   352
    Angelica: great unnatural Teat under your Left Arm, and he another; 238   FOR LCVE   II.1   120
    Sr Sampson: (Stretches his Arm as far as he can.) . . 281   FCR LCVE   IV.1   227
    Heli: To arm your Mind with Hope. Such Piety 352   M. BRIDE   III.1 117
    Alonzo: The Morsel down his throat. I catch'd his Arm, ... 373   M. ERIDE   V.1   24
Arm'd (2)
                   Arm'd with keen Satyr, and with pointed Wit, ...   35   OLD BATCH   PRO.   7
    Almeria: But I am arm'd, with Ice around my Heart, ... 331   M. ERIDE   I.1   217
Arming (2)
    Gonsalez: Still alive, were arming in Valentia: 363   M. ERIDE   IV.1   78
    Gonsalez: Were still alive, and arming in Valentia: 363   M. EBIDE   IV.1 V 78
Arms (35)
    Araminta: But that's not all; you caught me in your Arms   55   OLD BATCH   II.2   41
    Heartwell: more Ccnsuming Fire, a Womans Arms. Ha! well . . .   62   OLD BATCH   III.1 69
    Singer: Baffled and senseless, tir'd her Arms.   71   OLD BATCH   III.2 V 24
    Bellmour: your snowy Arms about his stubborn Neck; bathe his . . .   95   OLD BATCH   IV.4   237
                   I'th' Good Man's Arms, the Chopping Bastard thrives, . 125   DOUEL DLR   PRO.   29
    Mellefont: Grand Signior's, and that night he has his arms at liberty. 158   DOUEL DLR   III.1 283
    Mellefont: Grand Signior, and that night he has his arms at liberty. 158   DOUEL DLR   III.1 V283
    Brisk: (Stands musing with his Arms a-cross.) 175   DOUEL DLR   IV.1   311
    Sir Paul: Position of taking up Arms by my Authority, against my . 178   DOUEL DLR   V.1   413
    Lady Touch: anothers Arms; oh! that I were Fire indeed, that I might . 191   DOUEL DLR   V.1   151
    Jeremy: lying in the Arms of a needy Wit, before the Embraces of . 219   FOR LOVE   I.1   114
    Jeremy: great Beauty and Fortune into your Arms, whcm I have . . 302   FOR LCVE   V.1   178
    Jeremy: with his Arms would over-run the Ccuntry, yet no body . . 302   FCR LCVE   V.1   194
    Leonora: Had bless'd Anselmo's Arms with Victory, ... 327   M. BRIDE   I.1   39
    Manuel: So great in Arms, as thou art said to be, ... 336   M. BEIDE   I.1   431
    Almeria: Me in his leaden Arms, and press me close 340   M. EBIDE   II.2   21
    Almeria: O take me to thy Arms, and bear me hence, ... 342   M. FEIDE   II.2   84
    Osmyn-Alph: Why dost thou weep, and hold thee from my Arms, . . . 343   M. FRIDE   II.2   122
    Osmyn-Alph: My Arms which ake to fold thee fast, and grow . . . 343   M. FRIDE   II.2   123
    Zara: Why dost thou leave my Eyes, and fly my Arms, . . . 345   M. EBIDE   II.2   239
    Zara: And dc your Arms so lessen, what they conquer, . . . 348   M. EBIDE   II.2   362
    Heli: Are risen in Arms, and call for Chiefs to head . . . 351   M. EFIDE   III.1 70
    Osmyn-Alph: My Soul is up in Arms, ready to charge 351   M. BBIDE   III.1 81
    Osmyn-Alph: How run into thy Arms with-held by Fetters, ... 355   M. BRIDE   III.1 239
    Almeria: Upon me--speak, and take me in thy Arms-- 356   M. BRIDE   III.1 265
    Almeria: Thou canst not! thy poor Arms are bound and strive . . 356   M. BEIDE   III.1 266
    Osmyn-Alph: From these weak, strugling, unextended Arms; . . . 358   M. BRIDE   III.1 344
    Zara: About the time our Arms embark'd for Spain. 364   M. BRIDE   IV.1   121
    Manuel: Militia are in Arms: We will ancn 364   M. EBIDE   IV.1 V133
    Almeria: For bended Knees, returning folding Arms, ... 369   M. ERIDE   IV.1   325
    Gonsalez: Reserve, to re-inforce his Arms: at least 379   M. ERIDE   V.2   127
    Zara: With haggar'd Eyes? why are your Arms a-cross 380   M. EBIDE   V.2   157
    Zara: And fright him from my Arms--See, see, he slides . . . 381   M. EBIDE   V.2   208
    Osmyn-Alph: Forbear; my Arms alone shall hold her up: 383   M. BEIDE   V.2   278
    Fainall: Arms in full Security. But cou'd you think because the . 414   WAY WCBLD   II.1   147
Army (3)
    Sharper: Is that Bully of his in the Army? 46   OLD BATCH   I.1   365
    Valentine: an Army lead just such a life as I do; have just such Crowds 221   FOR LCVE   I.1   189
    Selim: Both in the State and Army. This confirms 361   M. BRIDE   IV.1   11
Arose (2)
    Zara: Thy Temples, till reviving Blood arose, ... 346   M. ERIDE   II.2   283
    Gonsalez: Of a Father's Fondness, these Ills arose; 378   M. EBIDE   V.2   82
Around (2)
    Almeria: But I am arm'd, with Ice around my Heart, ... 331   M. ERIDE   I.1   217
    Sir Wilful: Put the glass then around with the Sun Bcys; 455   WAY WCBLD   IV.1   417
Arous'd (1)
    Manuel: Say'st thou? by Heav'n thou hast arous'd a Thought, . . 367   M. BRIDE   IV.1   232
Arraign (1)
                   Who, to assert their Sense, your Taste arraign. 393   WAY WCBLD   PRO.   28
Arraignment (2)
    Vainlove: Offender must Plead to his Arraignment, tho' he have his . 87   OLD BATCH   IV.3   154
    Vainlove: Offender must Plead to his Arraignment, tho' he has his . 87   OLD BATCH   IV.3   V154
Arrant (2)
    Waitwell: That I'm an Arrant Knight-- 462   WAY WORLD   IV.1   647
    Foible: Or arrant Knave. 462   WAY WCBLD   IV.1   648
Arrantly (1)
    Lady Wish: Why I am arrantly flea'd--I look like an old peel'd Wall. . 429   WAY WORLD   III.1 148
Array'd (1)
    Manuel: There with his Turbant, and his Bobe array'd 374   M. BRIDE   V.1 V86A
Arrest (2)
    Snap: Gentlemen to Arrest in Pall-Mall and Covent-Garden; and . 224   FOR LCVE   I.1   297
    Foible: Effect, Mr. Fainall laid this Plct to arrest Waitwell,
                   when he 464   WAY WCBLD   V.1   71
Arriv'd (6)
    Sr Sampson: as my Son Benjamin is arriv'd, he is tc make over to him . 240   FOR LCVE   II.1   182
    Almeria: And thcu Anselmo, if yet thou art arriv'd 330   M. EBIDE   I.1   181
    Alonzo: The King is just arriv'd. 331   M. ERIDE   I.1 V210
    Alonzo: The beauteous Captive, Zara, is arriv'd, ... 335   M. EBIDE   I.1   359
    Alonzo: Your beauteous Captive, Zara, is arriv'd, ... 335   M. EBIDE   I.1 V359
    Zara: Some News, few Minutes past arriv'd, which seem'd . . 354   M. EBIDE   III.1 204
Arrival (1)
    Mirabell: Brother Sir Wilfull's arrival. 409   WAY WORLD   I.1   513
Arrive (1)
    Valentine: Evening, and learn the knack of Bhiming, you may arrive . 218   FOR LOVE   I.1   79
Arrived (1)
    Selim: Is since arrived, of more revolted Troops. 361   M. BBIDE   IV.1   7

Arrogance (2)

Speaker	Line	PAGE	TITLE	ACT.SC	LINE
Gonsalez:	Of his Arrogance yet; she looks concern'd.	337	M. BRIDE	I.1	444
Millamant:	Pedantick arrogance of a very Husband, has not so Pragmatical	449	WAY WORLD	IV.1	179

Arrogant (1)

Speaker	Line	PAGE	TITLE	ACT.SC	LINE
Gonsalez:	His arrogant Reply; she looks concern'd.	337	M. BRIDE	I.1	V444

Arrogantly (1)

Speaker	Line	PAGE	TITLE	ACT.SC	LINE
	If any are so arrogantly Vain,	479	WAY WORLD	EPI.	25

Arrow (1)

Speaker	Line	PAGE	TITLE	ACT.SC	LINE
Heartwell:	well--Yet I must on--'Tis a bearded Arrow, and	73	OLD BATCH	III.2	72

Art (105)   [usages as noun (17)]

Speaker	Line	PAGE	TITLE	ACT.SC	LINE
Silvia:	Art.	62	OLD BATCH	III.1	53
Lucy:	Hang Art, Madam, and trust to Nature for	62	OLD BATCH	III.1	54
Heartwell:	Lying, Child, is indeed the Art of Love; and Men are	72	OLD BATCH	III.1	56
Maskwell:	an Argument that I Love'd; for with that Art you veil'd	136	DOUBL DLR	I.1	362
Brisk:	Ladyship has not the Art of Surprizing the most Naturally	142	DOUBL DLR	II.1	131
Maskwell:	and dear dissimulation is the only Art, not to be known	150	DOUBL DLR	III.1	463
Maskwell:	your own art that turned it to advantage.	187	DOUBL DLR	V.1	5
	Each chusing that, in which he has most Art.	204	DOUBL DLR	EPI.	16
Scandal:	A Trifler--but a Lover of Art--And the	267	FOR LOVE	III.1	534
Foresight:	to try if I could discover it by my Art--hum, ha! I	304	FOR LOVE	V.1	259
Tattle:	In the way of Art: I have some taking Features, not	304	FOR LOVE	V.1	267
	Art may direct, but Nature is his aim;	324	M. BRIDE	PRO.	36
	And Nature miss'd, in vain he boasts his Art,	324	M. BRIDE	PRO.	37
Zara:	Who wish'd it so: a common Art in Courts.	366	M. BRIDE	IV.1	190
Foible:	I warrant you, Madam; a little Art one made your	429	WAY WORLD	III.1	151
Foible:	Picture like you; and now a little of the same Art, must	429	WAY WORLD	III.1	152
Millamant:	Tho' thou do'st thine, employ'st the Power and Art.	447	WAY WORLD	IV.1	105

Art-military (2)

Speaker	Line	PAGE	TITLE	ACT.SC	LINE
Capt Bluff:	a little Art-military, used--only undermined, or so, as	110	OLD BATCH	V.2	108
Sir Joseph:	Only a little Art-military Trick, Captain, only	110	OLD BATCH	V.2	112

Artful (2)

Speaker	Line	PAGE	TITLE	ACT.SC	LINE
Almeria:	And with his Artful Tongue, to gild and magnifie	331	M. BRIDE	I.1	215
Mirabell:	her Faults. Her Follies are so natural, or so artful, that they	399	WAY WORLD	I.1	160

Article (1)

Speaker	Line	PAGE	TITLE	ACT.SC	LINE
Mirabell:	Item, I Article, that you continue to like your own	451	WAY WORLD	IV.1	245

Articles (3)

Speaker	Line	PAGE	TITLE	ACT.SC	LINE
Sr Sampson:	thou'rt honest, and wilt perform Articles.	281	FOR LOVE	IV.1	215
Valentine:	Articles, I must this Morning have resign'd: And this I	294	FOR LOVE	IV.1	719
Millamant:	before you come in. These Articles subscrib'd, If I continue	450	WAY WORLD	IV.1	225

Artifice (6)

Speaker	Line	PAGE	TITLE	ACT.SC	LINE
Bellmour:	Since all Artifice is vain--and I think my self obliged	93	OLD BATCH	IV.4	157
Mellefont:	but a shallow artifice, unworthy of my Matchiavilian	148	DOUBL DLR	II.1	376
Maskwell:	afflicted, but rather laugh'd at the shallow Artifice, which	154	DOUBL DLR	III.1	135
Zara:	Thy shallow Artifice begets Suspicion,	375	M. BRIDE	V.1	102
Mirabell:	Curious? Or is this pretty Artifice Contriv'd, to Signifie	449	WAY WORLD	IV.1	157
Mirabell:	had a Face of guiltiness,--it was at most an Artifice which	472	WAY WORLD	V.1	385

Artimedorus (1)

Speaker	Line	PAGE	TITLE	ACT.SC	LINE
Mrs Frail:	. . . Artimedorus for Interpretation,	231	FOR LOVE	I.1	582

Arts (2)

Speaker	Line	PAGE	TITLE	ACT.SC	LINE
Zara:	What Arts I us'd to make you pass on him,	347	M. BRIDE	II.2	294
Fainall:	To let you know I see through all your little Arts--	413	WAY WORLD	II.1	136

As (870)

Speaker	Line	PAGE	TITLE	ACT.SC	LINE
	Grave solemn Things, as Graces are to Feasts;	35	OLD BATCH	PRO.	3
	And 'twas the prettiest Prologue, as he wrote it!	35	OLD BATCH	PRO.	21
Vainlove:	early Sallies are not usual to me; but Business as you see	37	OLD BATCH	I.1	6
Vainlove:	Element Ned--Well as high as a Flyer as you are, I	38	OLD BATCH	I.1	30
Vainlove:	So was true as Turtle--in imagination Ned, ha?	38	OLD BATCH	I.1	52
Bellmour:	Lover as like him as she can, and what is unlike she may	38	OLD BATCH	I.1	58
Bellmour:	As you say the Abuse is to the Lover, not the	39	OLD BATCH	I.1	63
Vainlove:	Faith I hate Love when 'tis forced upon a Man; as	39	OLD BATCH	I.1	94
Bellmour:	I wish I may succeed as the same.	39	OLD BATCH	I.1	101
Vainlove:	So that as he is often Jealous without a Cause, he's as often	40	OLD BATCH	I.1	109
Vainlove:	But I saw my Araminta, yet am as impatient.	40	OLD BATCH	I.1	135
Bellmour:	self, nor suffers any Body else to rail at me. Then as I	41	OLD BATCH	I.1	169
Bellmour:	Woman's a Woman, and that's all. As such I'm sure I shall	41	OLD BATCH	I.1	173
Sharper:	And here comes one who Swears as heartily he hates	41	OLD BATCH	I.1	176
Bellmour:	morning was none of her own? for I know thou art as	42	OLD BATCH	I.1	185
Bellmour:	unmannerly and as unwelcome to a Woman, as a Looking	42	OLD BATCH	I.1	186
Bellmour:	to himself in the World; he takes as much always of an	42	OLD BATCH	I.1	211
Bellmour:	Amour as he cares for, and quits it when it grows stale, or	42	OLD BATCH	I.1	212
Heartwell:	Good Mr. Young-fellow, you're mistaken; as	43	OLD BATCH	I.1	229
Heartwell:	able as your self and as nimble too, though I mayn't have	43	OLD BATCH	I.1	230
Bellmour:	may be as wicked as thou art at thy years.	43	OLD BATCH	I.1	252
Sharper:	Why if whoring be purging--as you call it--then I	44	OLD BATCH	I.1	291
Heartwell:	It will as soon blow North and by South--marry	44	OLD BATCH	I.1	294
Heartwell:	off as unconcern'd, come chuck the Infant under the chin,	45	OLD BATCH	I.1	325
Sharper:	Say you so? faith I am as poor as a Chymist and	46	OLD BATCH	I.1	347
Sharper:	would be as industrious. But what was he that follow'd	46	OLD BATCH	I.1	348
Bellmour:	Yet is ador'd by that Biggot Sr. Joseph Wittoll, as the	46	OLD BATCH	I.1	356
Bellmour:	though I believe he was heartily frightned, for as soon as	46	OLD BATCH	I.1	362
Bellmour:	Soldier, which now a'days as often cloaks Cowardice, as a	46	OLD BATCH	I.1	367
Bellmour:	take a drubbing with as little noise as a Pulpit Cushion.	47	OLD BATCH	I.1	381
Sir Joseph:	An it hadn't been for a civil Gentleman as came by	47	OLD BATCH	II.1	8
Sharper:	I've lost. (Looking about as in search.)	48	OLD BATCH	II.1	24
Sir Joseph:	Not I Sir, not I, as I've a Soul to be sav'd, I have	48	OLD BATCH	II.1	29
Sir Joseph:	found nothing but what has been to my loss, as I may say,	48	OLD BATCH	II.1	30
Sir Joseph:	and as you were saying Sir.	48	OLD BATCH	II.1	31
Sharper:	My loss, I esteem as a trifle repay'd with interest,	49	OLD BATCH	II.1	76
Sir Joseph:	call my Back; he sticks as close to me, and follows me	50	OLD BATCH	II.1	119
Sir Joseph:	as it were to me--agad he's a brave Fellow--Pauh,	50	OLD BATCH	II.1	121
Sir Joseph:	hundred Pound--I meant innocently as I hope to be sav'd	51	OLD BATCH	II.1	129
Sir Joseph:	Sir--a damn'd hot Fellow--only as I was saying, I let him	51	OLD BATCH	II.1	130
Sir Joseph:	Fondlewife, as far as two hundred Pound, and this Afternoon	51	OLD BATCH	II.1	133

As (continued)
Sir Joseph:	you shall see I am a Person, such a one as you would	. .	51	OLD BATCH	II.1	134
Sharper:	unless it be to serve my particular Friend, as Sir					
	Joseph here, ...	. .	51	OLD BATCH	II.1	159
Sir Joseph:	well--Ey the Lord Harry Mr. Sharper he's as brave a	. .	52	OLD BATCH	II.1	175
Sir Joseph:	Fellow as Cannibal, are not you Bully--Back?	. .	52	OLD BATCH	II.1	176
Capt Bluff:	Gazette--I'll tell you a strange thing now as to that--		52	OLD BATCH	II.1	194
Capt Bluff:	this time--as I hope for a Truncheon--this rascally	. .	53	OLD BATCH	II.1	202
Capt Bluff:	Gazette-writer never so much as once mention'd me--Not once		53	OLD BATCH	II.1	203
Capt Bluff:	by the Wars--Tock no more notice, than as if Nol. Bluffe		53	OLD BATCH	II.1	204
Capt Bluff:	O I am calm Sir, calm as a discharg'd Culverin--But	. .	54	OLD BATCH	II.1	241
Vainlove:	Rewards to indefatigable Devotion--For as Love is a	. .	58	OLD BATCH	II.2	140
Araminta:	Religion, as his Humour varies or his Interest.	58	OLD BATCH	II.2	149
Belinda:	What will you get by that? To make such Signs as . .	59	OLD BATCH	II.2	179
Belinda:	than your talking Impertinence; as an Ape is a much more	.	60	OLD BATCH	II.2	213
Lucy:	You may as soon hope, to recover your own Maiden-head,	.	61	OLD BATCH	III.1	7
Lucy:	as his Love. Therefore e'n set your Heart at rest, and	.	61	OLD BATCH	III.1	8
Lucy:	his Face--Receive it! why he receiv'd it, as I would one	.	61	OLD BATCH	III.1	20
Lucy:	of your Lovers that should come empty-handed; as a Court	.	61	OLD BATCH	III.1	21
Lucy:	--a' receiv'd it, as if 'thad been a Letter from his	.	61	OLD BATCH	III.1	23
Lucy:	on him, himself--Contrive a kind Letter as from her,	.	62	OLD BATCH	III.1	41
Silvia:	'Tis as hard to Counterfeit Love, as it is to conceal it:		62	OLD BATCH	III.1	51
Heartwell:	to shun as I would infection? To enter here, is to put on		62	OLD BATCH	III.1	66
Bellmour:	Or as you did to day, when half afraid you snatch'd	.	63	OLD BATCH	III.1	95
Setter:	As all lew'd projects do Sir, where the Devil prevents	.	64	OLD BATCH	III.1	117
Setter:	which Tribulation Spintext wears as I'm inform'd, upon	.	64	OLD BATCH	III.1	126
Setter:	one Eye, as a penal Mourning for the ogling Offences of	.	64	OLD BATCH	III.1	127
Setter:	uses me as his Attendant; the other (being the better	.	64	OLD BATCH	III.1	139
Setter:	acquainted with my parts) employs me as a Pimp: why	.	64	OLD BATCH	III.1	140
Setter:	means--I follow one as my Master, but the tother	. .	64	OLD BATCH	III.1	142
Setter:	means--I follow one as my Master, t'other	.	64	OLD BATCH	III.1	V142
Setter:	follows me as his Conductor.	.	64	OLD BATCH	III.1	143
Setter:	wary and soforth--And to all this valiant as Hercules	.	65	OLD BATCH	III.1	151
Setter:	. . . as a Clap is to the Pox.	.	66	OLD BATCH	III.1	V197
Setter:	though we were both in fault as to our Offices--	. .	66	OLD BATCH	III.1	213
Setter:	To answer you as briefly--He has a cause to be try'd	.	66	OLD BATCH	III.1	220
Sir Joseph:	by, I would as soon have let him a' had a hundred of my		68	OLD BATCH	III.1	277
Sir Joseph:	They won't be accepted, so readily as the Bill, Sir. . .		68	OLD BATCH	III.1	286
Sharper:	Ay thou inimitable Coward and to be felt--As		69	OLD BATCH	III.1	324
Sir Joseph:	his Business--He durst as soon have kiss'd you, as kick'd		70	OLD BATCH	III.1	359
Singer:	As Amoret and Thyrsis, lay		71	OLD BATCH	III.2	2
Singer:	O let me feed as well as taste, ...		71	OLD BATCH	III.2	7
Silvia:	You lock ready to fright one, and talk as if your Passion		72	OLD BATCH	III.2	68
Heartwell:	am grown very entertaining to my self, and (as I am	.	73	OLD BATCH	III.2	82
Silvia:	No, I'll die before I'll be your Whore--as well as I	.	74	OLD BATCH	III.2	124
Lucy:	Lord, Madam, I met your Lover in as much haste, as	.	74	OLD BATCH	III.2	147
Silvia:	to our Sex is as natural as swimming to a Negro; we	.	75	OLD BATCH	III.2	151
Lucy:	As you would wish--Since there is no reclaiming		75	OLD BATCH	III.2	155
Barnaby:	I did; and Comfort will send Tribulation hither as soon		76	OLD BATCH	IV.1	21
Barnaby:	as ever he comes home--I could have brought young . .		76	OLD BATCH	IV.1	22
Fondlewife:	and glow upon his Cheeks, and that I would as soon	. .	76	OLD BATCH	IV.1	32
Laetitia:	Heart--Well, be as cruel as you can to me, I'le pray for		78	OLD BATCH	IV.1	108
Laetitia:	that will love you as well as I have done: I shall be					
	contented		78	OLD BATCH	IV.1	110
Sharper:	great a Brute as to slight her.		80	OLD BATCH	IV.1	187
Laetitia:	prejudice of her Reputation--You look as if you had .		82	OLD BATCH	IV.2	64
Belinda:	as I was telling you--Pish, this is the untoward'st	.	83	OLD BATCH	IV.3	15
Belinda:	Lock--So, as I was telling you--How d'ye like		83	OLD BATCH	IV.3	16
Araminta:	No, no; you're very well as can be.		83	OLD BATCH	IV.3	18
Belinda:	Ay, O my Conscience; fat as Barn-door-Fowl: But . . .		84	OLD BATCH	IV.3	28
Belinda:	Creature, I warrant, was as full of Courtesies, as if I had		84	OLD BATCH	IV.3	40
Belinda:	Creature, I warrant, was as full of Curtsies, as if I had		84	OLD BATCH	IV.3	V 40
Sir Joseph:	has made me as light as a Grasshopper.--Hist, hist,	.	85	OLD BATCH	IV.3	65
Sharper:	There is in true Beauty, as in Courage, somewhat, . . .		86	OLD BATCH	IV.3	126
Sharper:	see, the Owls are fled, as at the break of Day. . . .		86	OLD BATCH	IV.3	128
Belinda:	rubb'd his Eyes, since break of Day neither, he looks as if		86	OLD BATCH	IV.3	130
Vainlove:	what she knows as well as I. (Aside). Men are apt to offend		87	OLD BATCH	IV.3	137
Sir Joseph:	As you say, Madam, 'tis pretty bad Weather, and . .		90	OLD BATCH	IV.4	39
	(As Fondlewife is going into the Chamber, she runs to Sir		90	OLD BATCH	IV.4	49
Fondlewife:	Man is in great torment, he lies as flat--Dear, you .		91	OLD BATCH	IV.4	95
Laetitia:	(Shrieks, as surpriz'd.)	. .	92	OLD BATCH	IV.4	124
Fondlewife:	as I should be, a sort of a civil Perquisite to a					
	Whore-master, ...		94	OLD BATCH	IV.4	184
Fondlewife:	Well, well, Sir, as long as I believe it, 'tis well	.	96	OLD BATCH	IV.4	267
Bellmour:	Well, It is as I say?		98	OLD BATCH	V.1	51
Bellmour:	Well, is it as I say?		98	OLD BATCH	V.1	V 51
Bellmour:	Nay, nay: Look you, Lucy; there are Whores of as . .		98	OLD BATCH	V.1	64
Bellmour:	That's as much as to say, The Pox take me.--Well . .		98	OLD BATCH	V.1	78
Setter:	I do suspect as much;--because why, Sir;--		99	OLD BATCH	V.1	112
Setter:	stood towards Madam Araminta. As, When you had seen	.	99	OLD BATCH	V.1	114
Sharper:	thy Mirth: Hear thee tell thy mighty Jest, with as much		100	OLD BATCH	V.1	138
Sharper:	Gravity as a Bishop hears Venereal Causes in the Spiritual		100	OLD BATCH	V.1	139
Sharper:	Court: Not so much as wrinkle my Face with one Smile; .		100	OLD BATCH	V.1	140
Bellmour:	discovering the Cheat to Sylvia. She took it at first, as		100	OLD BATCH	V.1	150
Sir Joseph:	Nay, Don't speak so loud.--I don't jest, as I . . .		101	OLD BATCH	V.1	171
Sir Joseph:	may dispose of your own Flesh as you think fitting, d'ye		101	OLD BATCH	V.1	184
Sir Joseph:	Prithee, What do you see in my face, that looks as . .		101	OLD BATCH	V.1	191
Setter:	What have such poor Rogues as I to do with Reputation?		102	OLD BATCH	V.1	230
Setter:	above it. So that Reputation is e'en as foolish . . .		102	OLD BATCH	V.1	232
Setter:	. . . as honesty.		102	OLD BATCH	V.1	232
Setter:	. . . a thing as Honesty.		102	OLD BATCH	V.1	V232
Sharper:	Why, thou art as musty as a New-married Man, ...		104	OLD BATCH	V.1	296
Setter:	As I suppose my Master Heartwell.		105	OLD BATCH	V.1	332
Sharper:	As how, dear dexterous Pimp?		105	OLD BATCH	V.1	340
Setter:	--Our Stratagem succeeding as you intended, ...		105	OLD BATCH	V.1	342
Setter:	--Our Stratagem succeeded as you intended, ...		105	OLD BATCH	V.1	V342

42

As   (continued)

Speaker	Text	PAGE	TITLE	ACT.SC	LINE
Lady Froth:	Just as the Sun does, more or less.	164	DOUBL DLR	III.1	532
Lord Froth:	O silly! yet his Aunt is as fond of him, as if she . . .	165	DOUBL DLR	III.1	565
Brisk:	great Beard that bristles through it, and makes her look as	166	DOUBL DLR	III.1	586
Cynthia:	Affliction, as to dissemble Mirth in Company of Fools--	167	DOUBL DLR	III.1	625
Cynthia:	I heard him loud as I came by the Closet-Door, and . . .	167	DOUBL DLR	IV.1	1
Mellefont:	Ay, Hell thank her, as gentle breezes moderate a . . .	167	DOUBL DLR	IV.1	7
Cynthia:	Touchwood, as you boasted, and force her to give her . .	169	DOUBL DLR	IV.1	48
Lady Ply:	me as a fine thing. Well, I must do you this justice, and	169	DOUBL DLR	IV.1	71
Lady Ply:	far upon me as your self, with Blushes I must own it, you	169	DOUBL DLR	IV.1	73
Lady Ply:	have shaken, as I may say, the very foundation of my . .	169	DOUBL DLR	IV.1	74
Lady Ply:	shall value my self as long as I live, I swear.	169	DOUBL DLR	IV.1	76
Sir Paul:	Indeed if this be made plain, as my Lady your . . .	172	DOUBL DLR	IV.1	171
Sir Paul:	the most beholden to Mr. Careless--As sure as can . . .	172	DOUBL DLR	IV.1	200
Sir Paul:	pound a Year upon the Rogue as soon as ever he looks me .	173	DOUBL DLR	IV.1	225
Sir Paul:	the young Rogue as like as you can.	173	DOUBL DLR	IV.1	231
Sir Paul:	Eye, as the House of Austria is by a thick Lip. . . .	173	DOUBL DLR	IV.1	240
Sir Paul:	--Gads-bud I could have done--not so much as you . . .	174	DOUBL DLR	IV.1	243
Sir Paul:	Wedding Night, to die a Maid; as she did; all were ruin'd,	174	DOUBL DLR	IV.1	252
Lady Ply:	and he looks charmingly, and he has charm'd me, as much as I	174	DOUBL DLR	IV.1	260
Brisk:	an Old Hen, as if she were not well hatch'd, I'gad, he? .	174	DOUBL DLR	IV.1	273
Lady Froth:	Just now as I came in, bless me, why don't you . . .	176	DOUBL DLR	IV.1	323
Lady Froth:	Three times aloud, as I love Letters--But	176	DOUBL DLR	IV.1	331
Sir Paul:	the Marriage Bed with reverence as to a sacred shrine, and	178	DOUBL DLR	IV.1	427
Sir Paul:	Chaste as Ice, but you are melted now, and false as Water.	179	DOUBL DLR	IV.1	431
Lady Ply:	De'e see here? Lock, read it? (Snatches the Letter as in	179	DOUBL DLR	IV.1	441
Sir Paul:	Why now as I hope to be saved, I had no hand in . . .	180	DOUBL DLR	IV.1	468
Lord Touch:	she has told me all: Her good Nature conceal'd it as long	182	DOUBL DLR	IV.1	547
Lord Touch:	as was possible; but he perseveres so in Villany, that she	182	DOUBL DLR	IV.1	548
Lord Touch:	know as well that you can't.	182	DOUBL DLR	IV.1	556
Maskwell:	And so may all your Pleasures be, and secret as . . .	184	DOUBL DLR	IV.2	33
Mellefont:	None, Hell has served you even as Heaven has	185	DOUBL DLR	IV.2	59
Lady Touch:	so damn'd a Sin as Incest! unnatural Incest!	186	DOUBL DLR	IV.2	100
	(As she is going she turns back and smiles at him.)	187	DOUBL DLR	IV.2	134
Lord Touch:	as is thy Vertue.	189	DOUBL DLR	V.1	49
Lord Touch:	Blank as well--I will have no reply--Let me	189	DOUBL DLR	V.1	64
Maskwell:	As to go naked is the best disguise.	190	DOUBL DLR	V.1	101
Lady Touch:	Where she's serving you, as all your Sex	192	DOUBL DLR	V.1	164
Lady Touch:	want you by this time, as much as you want her. . . .	192	DOUBL DLR	V.1	189
Maskwell:	is carried on as he would have it.	193	DOUBL DLR	V.1	234
Lord Touch:	her as much as reason--by Heav'n, I'll not be Wife-ridden;	196	DOUBL DLR	V.1	320
Maskwell:	I had laid a small design for to morrow (as Love . . .	196	DOUBL DLR	V.1	326
Maskwell:	your Lordship--but it may be as well done to night. . .	196	DOUBL DLR	V.1	328
Lady Touch:	And such a smile as speaks in Ambiguity! Ten thousand .	198	DOUBL DLR	V.1	394
Lady Touch:	thou hast deceiv'd me; but 'tis as I would wish,-- . .	199	DOUBL DLR	V.1	454
Lord Touch:	inform my Nephew, and do you quickly as you can, bring .	200	DOUBL DLR	V.1	487
Sir Paul:	turvy; as I hope for Providence.	200	DOUBL DLR	V.1	498
Sir Paul:	All turn'd topsie turvey, as sure as a Gun.	200	DOUBL DLR	V.1	501
Lord Touch:	you stare as you were all amazed,--I don't wonder at it,--	202	DOUBL DLR	V.1	564
	As Nature gave the World to Man's first Age, . . .	213	FOR LOVE	PRO.	13
	Or only shews its Teeth, as if it smil'd.	213	FOR LOVE	PRO.	34
	As Asses Thistles, Poets mumble Wit, ...	214	FOR LOVE	PRO.	35
	They hold their Pens, as Swords are held by Fools, . . .	214	FOR LOVE	PRO.	37
Jeremy:	as much as they do one another.	217	FOR LOVE	I.1	48
Jeremy:	terrify'd Countenance, that looks as if he had written for	219	FOR LOVE	I.1	105
Jeremy:	whole Tatter to her Tail, but as ragged as one of the . .	219	FOR LOVE	I.1	110
Jeremy:	Muses; or as if she were carrying her Linnen to the	219	FOR LOVE	I.1	111
	Paper-Mill, ...	219	FOR LOVE	I.1	111
Valentine:	You are as inveterate against our Poets, as if your . .	220	FOR LOVE	I.1	151
Scandal:	The World behaves it self, as it used to do on such . .	220	FOR LOVE	I.1	159
Scandal:	The World behaves it self, as it uses to do on such . .	220	FOR LOVE	I.1	V159
Jeremy:	Dozen Duns with as much Dexterity, as a hungry Judge . .	220	FOR LOVE	I.1	167
Valentine:	an Army lead just such a life as I do; have just such Crowds	221	FOR LOVE	I.1	189
Trapland:	have forborn as long--	222	FOR LOVE	I.1	247
Valentine:	Eyes to her Feet, as they steal in and out, and play at	223	FOR LOVE	I.1	287
Scandal:	Women of her airy temper, as they seldom think . . .	225	FOR LOVE	I.1	348
Valentine:	and as you set up for Defamation, he is a mender . . .	226	FOR LOVE	I.1	366
Scandal:	A mender of Reputations! aye, just as he is a keeper . .	226	FOR LOVE	I.1	368
Scandal:	favour, as a Doctor says, No, to a Bishoprick, only that it	226	FOR LOVE	I.1	377
Scandal:	Aye, such rotten Reputations as you have to deal . . .	226	FOR LOVE	I.1	396
Tattle:	knows any thing of that nature of me: As I hope to be .	227	FOR LOVE	I.1	405
Tattle:	Not a word as I hope to be sav'd; an errant Lapsus Linguae	228	FOR LOVE	I.1	442
Tattle:	Why then, as I hope to be sav'd, I believe a Woman . .	228	FOR LOVE	I.1	473
Valentine:	cannot avoid such a palpable Decoy as this was; the Ladies	229	FOR LOVE	I.1	502
Mrs Frail:	if he be but as great a Sea-Beast, as she is a Land-Monster,	231	FOR LOVE	I.1	570
Scandal:	Twelve Caesars, paultry Copies; and the Five Senses, as ill	232	FOR LOVE	I.1	602
Scandal:	represented as they are in himself: And he himself is the	232	FOR LOVE	I.1	603
Scandal:	most of your Acquaintance to the Life, and as like as at .	232	FOR LOVE	I.1	618
Valentine:	No indeed, he speaks truth now: For as Tattle has . .	233	FOR LOVE	I.1	622
Scandal:	I have many more of this kind, very well Painted, as you .	234	FOR LOVE	I.1	657
Foresight:	should be as I would have it; for I was born, Sir, when the	235	FOR LOVE	II.1	12
Angelica:	You know my Aunt is a little Retrograde (as you call it) in	237	FOR LOVE	II.1	71
Angelica:	last Invisible Eclipse, laying in Provision as 'twere for a	237	FOR LOVE	II.1	80
Sr Sampson:	White, Signatum, Sigillatum, and Deliberatum; that as soon	240	FOR LOVE	II.1	181
Sr Sampson:	as my Son Benjamin is arriv'd, he is to make over to him .	240	FOR LOVE	II.1	182
Valentine:	provide for me, I desire you wou'd leave me as you found .	244	FOR LOVE	II.1	335
Sr Sampson:	go naked out of the World as you came into't. . . .	244	FOR LOVE	II.1	338
Jeremy:	Nay, that's as clear as the Sun; I'll make Oath of it .	245	FOR LOVE	II.1	355
Jeremy:	Yes, I have a reasonable good Ear, Sir, as to Jiggs and .	245	FOR LOVE	II.1	373
Valentine:	'Tis as much as I expected--I did not come to see . .	246	FOR LOVE	II.1	407
Mrs Fore:	alight I did?--How can any Body be happy, while . . .	247	FOR LOVE	II.1	432
Mrs Fore:	No matter for that, it's as good a Face as yours. . .	247	FOR LOVE	II.1	460
Mrs Fore:	as you say, since we are both Wounded, let us do that is .	248	FOR LOVE	II.1	477
Mrs Fore:	as you say, since we are both Wounded, let us do what is .	248	FOR LOVE	II.1	V477
Mrs Frail:	Well, as an earnest of Friendship and Confidence; . .	248	FOR LOVE	II.1	485
Mrs Frail:	Ah Devil, sly Devil--He's as close, Sister, as . . .	250	FOR LOVE	II.1	542

44

45

As (continued)

		PAGE	TITLE	ACT.SC	LINE
Osmyn-Alph:	But as I may, I'll do. I have a Paper	352	M. BRIDE	III.1	108
Osmyn-Alph:	With Grief, as wou'd draw Tears from Inhumanity.	352	M. BRIDE	III.1	115
Osmyn-Alph:	I'll treasure as more worth than Diadems,	353	M. BRIDE	III.1	V137
Zara:	Away, as from Deformity and Horrour.	353	M. BRIDE	III.1	150
Zara:	As she, whose savage Breast has been the Cause	353	M. BRIDE	III.1	157
Zara:	Of these thy Wrongs; as she, whose barbarous Rage	353	M. BRIDE	III.1	158
Osmyn-Alph:	As still to meditate Revenge on all	354	M. BRIDE	III.1	171
Osmyn-Alph:	Or Being as you please, such I will think it.	354	M. BRIDE	III.1	184
Zara:	Swift as Occasion, I	354	M. BRIDE	III.1	201
Osmyn-Alph:	Can I repay, as you require, such Benefits.	355	M. BRIDE	III.1	214
Zara:	To give, than I've already lost. But as	355	M. BRIDE	III.1	216
Osmyn-Alph:	And tear her Virtues up, as Tempests root	355	M. BRIDE	III.1	229
Osmyn-Alph:	With such a Dagger, as then stuck my Heart.	356	M. BRIDE	III.1	277
Almeria:	As they have Strength to tear this Heart in sunder;	357	M. BRIDE	III.1	301
Osmyn-Alph:	As to be wretched with thee.	357	M. BRIDE	III.1	334
Almeria:	As on leavings of Calamity.	358	M. BRIDE	III.1	338
Osmyn-Alph:	O--thou dost talk, my Love, as one resolv'd,	358	M. BRIDE	III.1	341
Osmyn-Alph:	Conduct you forth, as not perceiving her.	359	M. BRIDE	III.1	394
Zara:	Trembling and weeping as he leads her forth!	359	M. BRIDE	III.1	396
Zara:	As you'll answer it, take heed	360	M. BRIDE	III.1	447
Zara:	As you'll answer it, look, this Slave	360	M. BRIDE	III.1	V447
Selim:	And as to your Revenge, not his own Int'rest,	361	M. BRIDE	IV.1	21
Gonsalez:	Which seem to intimate, as if Alphonso,	363	M. BRIDE	IV.1	77
Zara:	O certain Death for him, as sure Despair	363	M. BRIDE	IV.1	94
Zara:	Was cast upon my Coast, as is reported;	364	M. BRIDE	IV.1	117
Manuel:	Is Treason then so near us as our Guards!	364	M. BRIDE	IV.1	145
Zara:	(As there the Custom is) in private strangle	365	M. BRIDE	IV.1	154
Zara:	The Pris'ner, but such Messengers, as I	365	M. BRIDE	IV.1	163
Zara:	To see the Pris'ner, but such Mutes as I	365	M. BRIDE	IV.1	V163
Gonsalez:	As if she'd rather that she did not hate him.	366	M. BRIDE	IV.1	204
Gonsalez:	As she pretends--I doubt it now--Your Guards	366	M. BRIDE	IV.1	206
Gonsalez:	If Osmyn be, as Zara has related,	367	M. BRIDE	IV.1	229
Gonsalez:	For Osmyn's Death, as he's Alphonso's Friend.	367	M. BRIDE	IV.1	240
Manuel:	As they had wept in Bondage, and worn the Night	367	M. BRIDE	IV.1	249
Almeria:	Never, but as with Innocence, I might,	368	M. BRIDE	IV.1	289
Almeria:	Gasping as it would speak: and after it,	371	M. BRIDE	IV.1	389
Almeria:	Gasping as it would speak: and after, see!	371	M. BRIDE	IV.1	V389
Gonsalez:	Thee such Reward, as should exceed thy Wish.	372	M. BRIDE	IV.1	439
Manuel:	Is Osmyn so dispos'd, as I commanded?	372	M. BRIDE	V.1	6
Perez:	He lies supine on earth; as easily	372	M. BRIDE	V.1	8
Perez:	He lies supine on earth; with as much ease	372	M. BRIDE	V.1	V 8
Perez:	She might remove the fix'd foundation, as	372	M. BRIDE	V.1	9
Perez:	As loose the rivets of his bonds.	372	M. BRIDE	V.1	V 10
Manuel:	As to conceal th' Importance of his Errand.	373	M. BRIDE	V.1	17
Alonzo:	Soon as I seiz'd the Man,	373	M. BRIDE	V.1	21
Manuel:	Be dark'ned, so as to amuze the Sight.	374	M. BRIDE	V.1	85
Manuel:	And laid along as he now lies supine,	374	M. BRIDE	V.1	V86B
Zara:	Their red and angry Beams; as if his Sight	375	M. BRIDE	V.1	94
Selim:	He did: But then as if	375	M. BRIDE	V.1	98
Selim:	Yes: But then, as if he thought	375	M. BRIDE	V.1	V 98
Selim:	If I have fail'd in what, as being a Man,	375	M. BRIDE	V.1	117
Selim:	I needs must fail; impute not as a Crime,	375	M. BRIDE	V.1	118
Zara:	A Forfeit as thy Life: Somewhat of high	375	M. BRIDE	V.1	124
Zara:	Of those Ingredients mix'd, as will with speed	375	M. BRIDE	V.1	132
Zara:	Of such Ingredients mix'd, as will with speed	375	M. BRIDE	V.1	V132
Zara:	Such Liberty as I embrace my self,	376	M. BRIDE	V.1	137
Gonsalez:	And all as still, as at the Noon of Night!	376	M. BRIDE	V.2	2
Gonsalez:	Would all were false as that; for whom you call	377	M. BRIDE	V.2	40
Gonsalez:	Should make atonement by a Death as horrid;	378	M. BRIDE	V.2	71
Alonzo:	As but an hour ago, I'd not have done,	379	M. BRIDE	V.2	111
Zara:	As thou art now--And I shall quickly be.	380	M. BRIDE	V.2	186
Almeria:	And of a suddain I am calm, as if	382	M. BRIDE	V.2	241
	And now as unconcern'd this Mourning wear,	385	M. BRIDE	EPI.	3
	As if indeed a Widow, or an Heir.	385	M. BRIDE	EPI.	4
	As Sussex Men, that dwell upon the Shoar,	385	M. BRIDE	EPI.	19
Mirabell:	easie to know when a Visit began to be troublesome;	396	WAY WORLD	I.1	39
Mirabell:	I did as much as Man cou'd, with any reasonable	397	WAY WORLD	I.1	68
Servant-M:	behind one another, as 'twere in a Country Dance. Ours	398	WAY WORLD	I.1	114
Mirabell:	That I may see her before she returns to her Lady; and as	398	WAY WORLD	I.1	131
Fainall:	Are you Jealous as often as you see Witwoud	399	WAY WORLD	I.1	148
Mirabell:	They are now grown as familiar to me as my own Frailties;	399	WAY WORLD	I.1	172
Mirabell:	as well.	399	WAY WORLD	I.1	174
Fainall:	Marry her, marry her; be half as well acquainted	400	WAY WORLD	I.1	175
Fainall:	with her Charms, as you are with her Defects, and my	400	WAY WORLD	I.1	176
Fainall:	By no means, 'tis better as 'tis; 'tis better to Trade	400	WAY WORLD	I.1	207
Fainall:	Obstinacy--But when he's drunk, he's as loving as	401	WAY WORLD	I.1	219
Mirabell:	Not always; but as often as his Memory fails him,	401	WAY WORLD	I.1	223
Witwoud:	from the Fool my Brother, as heavy as a Panegyrick in a	401	WAY WORLD	I.1	245
Witwoud:	from one Poet to another. And what's worse, 'tis as sure a	401	WAY WORLD	I.1	247
Witwoud:	forerunner of the Author, as an Epistle Dedicatory.	401	WAY WORLD	I.1	248
Witwoud:	Hum, faith I don't know as to that,--I can't say	403	WAY WORLD	I.1	302
Witwoud:	as to that.--Yes, Faith, in a Controversie he'll	403	WAY WORLD	I.1	303
Witwoud:	than a Woman constant; one argues a decay of Parts, as	403	WAY WORLD	I.1	320
Witwoud:	Ay, ay, Friendship without Freedom is as dull as	404	WAY WORLD	I.1	357
Witwoud:	just when you had been talking to him--As	405	WAY WORLD	I.1	370
Witwoud:	soon as your Back was turn'd--Whip he was gone;	405	WAY WORLD	I.1	371
Petulant:	Well, well; I come--Sbud, a Man had as good	405	WAY WORLD	I.1	383
Petulant:	be a profess'd Midwife as a profest Whoremaster, at this	405	WAY WORLD	I.1	384
Mirabell:	Fame, wou'd shew as dim by thee as a dead Whiting's	407	WAY WORLD	I.1	454
Fainall:	Petulant you both will find Mirabell as warm a	407	WAY WORLD	I.1	463
Fainall:	Rival as a Lover.	407	WAY WORLD	I.1	464
Witwoud:	Now, Demme, I shou'd hate that, if she were as handsome	408	WAY WORLD	I.1	477
Witwoud:	as Cleopatra. Mirabell is not so sure of her as he thinks				
	for.	408	WAY WORLD	I.1	478
Witwoud:	Mirabell and he are at some distance, as my Lady Wishfort	408	WAY WORLD	I.1	483

As (continued)

		PAGE	TITLE	ACT.SC	LINE
Mirabell:	I thank you, I know as much as my Curiosity	409	WAY WORLD	I.1	507
Witwoud:	O rare Petulant; thou art as quick as a Fire in a . . .	409	WAY WORLD	I.1	519
Witwoud:	O rare Petulant; thou art as quick as a Fire in a . . .	409	WAY WORLD	I.1	V519
Mirabell:	roar cut aloud as often as they pass by you; and when . .	409	WAY WORLD	I.1	526
Mrs Fain:	of what we were, and as such fly from us.	410	WAY WORLD	II.1	8
Mrs Fain:	of what we were, and as from such fly from us.	410	WAY WORLD	II.1 V	8
Marwood:	of Life because they once must leave us; is as preposterous,	410	WAY WORLD	II.1	14
Marwood:	as to wish to have been born Old, because we one Day .	410	WAY WORLD	II.1	15
Marwood:	readmit him as its lawful Tyrant.	410	WAY WORLD	II.1	27
Marwood:	Come, be as sincere, acknowledge that your Sentiments .	410	WAY WORLD	II.1	31
Marwood:	as bad.	411	WAY WORLD	II.1	59
Mrs Fain:	Why, had not you as good do it?	411	WAY WORLD	II.1	60
Fainall:	You wou'd intimate then, as if there were a	413	WAY WORLD	II.1	126
Marwood:	in Honour, as indigent of Wealth.	415	WAY WORLD	II.1	197
Fainall:	bestow'd as the prodigality of your Love would have it, .	415	WAY WORLD	II.1	199
Mirabell:	Husband, as may be sufficient to make you relish your .	416	WAY WORLD	II.1	259
Millamant:	as fast through the Crowd--	418	WAY WORLD	II.1	334
Witwoud:	As a Favourite in disgrace; and with as few	418	WAY WORLD	II.1	335
Witwoud:	As a Favourite just disgrac'd; and with as few	418	WAY WORLD	II.1	V335
Millamant:	For I am as sick of 'em--	419	WAY WORLD	II.1	338
Witwoud:	As a Phisician of a good Air--I cannot help it . . .	419	WAY WORLD	II.1	339
Millamant:	enquir'd after you, as after a new Fashion.	419	WAY WORLD	II.1	348
Mincing:	with Poetry, it sits so pleasant the next Day as any Thing,	420	WAY WORLD	II.1	373
Millamant:	Lovers as fast as one pleases, and they live as long as one	420	WAY WORLD	II.1	404
Millamant:	pleases, and they die as soon as one pleases: And then if	420	WAY WORLD	II.1	405
Mirabell:	as a Mortification; for sure to please a Fool is some degree	421	WAY WORLD	II.1	439
Mirabell:	I say that a Man may as soon make a Friend by his . .	422	WAY WORLD	II.1	464
Mirabell:	Wit, or a Fortune by his Honesty, as win a Woman .	422	WAY WORLD	II.1	465
Millamant:	peevish--Heigho! Now I'll be melancholly, as	422	WAY WORLD	II.1	476
Millamant:	melancholly as a Watch-light. Well Mirabell, If ever you	422	WAY WORLD	II.1	477
Mirabell:	which they are not turn'd; and by one as well as another;	423	WAY WORLD	II.1	497
Waitwell:	to Business, Sir. I have instructed her as well as I				
	cou'd. If	423	WAY WORLD	II.1	509
Waitwell:	she can take your Directions as readily as my Instructions,	423	WAY WORLD	II.1	510
Foible:	Sir, I made as much haste as I could.	423	WAY WORLD	II.1	515
Foible:	But I told my Lady as you instructed me, Sir. That I .	423	WAY WORLD	II.1	519
Lady Wish:	An errant Ash colour, as I'm a Person. Look you how this .	425	WAY WORLD	III.1	6
Lady Wish:	then--(Exit Peg). I'm as pale and as faint, I look like .	425	WAY WORLD	III.1	21
Lady Wish:	thou go with the Bottle in thy Hand like a Tapster. As I'm	426	WAY WORLD	III.1	35
Marwood:	I saw her but now, as I came mask'd through	426	WAY WORLD	III.1	47
Lady Wish:	she has as good as put her Integrity into his Hands. . .	426	WAY WORLD	III.1	59
Lady Wish:	Prodigal's in Debt as much as the Million Lottery, or the .	428	WAY WORLD	III.1	133
Mrs Fain:	Mirabell's Uncle, and as such winning my Lady, to involve	430	WAY WORLD	III.1	191
Foible:	for, as they say of a Welch Maiden-head.	430	WAY WORLD	III.1	212
Foible:	of his success. I wou'd be seen as little as possible to				
	speak	430	WAY WORLD	III.1	215
Lady Wish:	As I'm a Person I am in a very Chaos to think I . . .	431	WAY WORLD	III.1	254
Millamant:	Sure never any thing was so Unbred as that odious . .	432	WAY WORLD	III.1	284
Millamant:	has not the liberty of choosing one's Acquaintance, as one	432	WAY WORLD	III.1	297
Marwood:	If we had the liberty, we shou'd be as weary	432	WAY WORLD	III.1	299
Marwood:	If we had that liberty, we shou'd be as weary . . .	432	WAY WORLD	III.1	V299
Marwood:	of one Set of Acquaintance, tho' never so good, as we are of	432	WAY WORLD	III.1	300
Marwood:	you might as easily put off Petulant and Witwoud as your	433	WAY WORLD	III.1	315
Millamant:	handsomer--And within a Year or two as young. . . .	434	WAY WORLD	III.1	359
Petulant:	It seems as if you had come a Journey, Sir;	438	WAY WORLD	III.1	489
Sir Wilful:	May be not, Sir; thereafter as 'tis meant, Sir. . . .	438	WAY WORLD	III.1	496
Witwoud:	Why Brother Wilfull of Salop, you may be as	439	WAY WORLD	III.1	531
Witwoud:	short as a Shrewsbury Cake, if you please. But I tell .	439	WAY WORLD	III.1	532
Marwood:	You intend to Travel, Sir, as I'm inform'd.	440	WAY WORLD	III.1	566
Sir Wilful:	French as they say, whereby to hold discourse in Foreign .	440	WAY WORLD	III.1	584
Fainall:	my Reputation,--As to my own, I married not for it; so .	443	WAY WORLD	III.1	684
Fainall:	that's out of the Question,--And as to my part in my .	443	WAY WORLD	III.1	685
Fainall:	honourable as you say; and if so, Wherefore should . .	443	WAY WORLD	III.1	692
Marwood:	to act Sir Rowland is with her. It shall come as from an .	443	WAY WORLD	III.1	701
Lady Wish:	and then as soon as he appears, start, ay, start and be				
	surpriz'd, ...	445	WAY WORLD	IV.1	27
Lady Wish:	Foible; bring her hither. I'll send him as I go--When .	445	WAY WORLD	IV.1	38
Millamant:	him hither,--just as you will Dear Foible.--I think I'll see	446	WAY WORLD	IV.1	61
Sir Wilful:	Cozen, I made bold to pass thro' as it were,--I think this .	447	WAY WORLD	IV.1	95
Sir Wilful:	Town, as Plays and the like that must be confess'd indeed.	448	WAY WORLD	IV.1	125
Sir Wilful:	However that's as time shall try,--But spare to speak and .	448	WAY WORLD	IV.1	137
Sir Wilful:	spare to speed, as they say.	448	WAY WORLD	IV.1	138
Sir Wilful:	When you're dispos'd, when you're dispos'd. Now's as .	448	WAY WORLD	IV.1	143
Sir Wilful:	When you're dispos'd. Now's as	448	WAY WORLD	IV.1	V143
Sir Wilful:	well as another time; and another time as well as now. .	448	WAY WORLD	IV.1	144
Sir Wilful:	there's no haste; it will keep cold as they say,--Cozen, .	448	WAY WORLD	IV.1	146
Mirabell:	--Like Daphne she as lovely and as Coy. Do you . .	449	WAY WORLD	IV.1	155
Millamant:	I expect you shou'd solicite me as much as if I	449	WAY WORLD	IV.1	162
Millamant:	Mistress. There is not so Impudent a thing in Nature, as the	449	WAY WORLD	IV.1	177
Millamant:	a morning as long as I please.	449	WAY WORLD	IV.1	191
Mirabell:	Then I'll get up in a morning as early as I please. . .	449	WAY WORLD	IV.1	192
Millamant:	Ay as Wife, Spouse, My dear, Joy, Jewel, Love, . . .	450	WAY WORLD	IV.1	197
Millamant:	never to be seen there together again; as if we were proud	450	WAY WORLD	IV.1	204
Millamant:	never be seen there together again; as if we were proud .	450	WAY WORLD	IV.1	V204
Millamant:	let us be as strange as if we had been married a great				
	while;	450	WAY WORLD	IV.1	208
Millamant:	and as well bred as if we were not marri'd at all. . .	450	WAY WORLD	IV.1	209
Millamant:	Trifles,--As liberty to pay and receive visits	450	WAY WORLD	IV.1	212
Mirabell:	Face, as long as I shall. And while it passes Current with .	451	WAY WORLD	IV.1	246
Mirabell:	drinks, as Tea, Chocolate and Coffee. As likewise to Genuine	451	WAY WORLD	IV.1	266
Mirabell:	and, Authoriz'd Tea-Table talk,--such as mending of .	451	WAY WORLD	IV.1	267
Mirabell:	Forces, and Auxiliaries to the Tea-Table, as Orange-Brandy,	451	WAY WORLD	IV.1	272
Millamant:	looks as if he thought so too--Well, you ridiculous . .	452	WAY WORLD	IV.1	294
Mrs Fain:	return to Sir Rowland, who as Foible tells me is in a fair	452	WAY WORLD	IV.1	302
Mrs Fain:	Petulant and he were upon quarrelling as I came by. . .	452	WAY WORLD	IV.1	314

49

Asturian (1)
  Lady Wish: before she came tc me, like Maritornes the Asturian in Don   426   WAY WCRLD III.1   37
Asunder (4)   see Sunder
  Bellmour: are never asunder--yet last night, I know not by what   .   . 46   OLD BATCH   I.1   358
  Maskwell: Ties: But the Name of Rival cuts 'em all asunder, and is a   150   DOUEL DLR II.1   448
  Valentine: asunder; you are light and shadow, and shew one another;   . 225   FOR LCVE   I.1   364
  Ben: An we were a League asunder, I'de undertake to hold   .   . 263   FCR LCVE III.1   369
At (446)
Atchievments (1)
  Setter: Sublimate, if you please, Sir: I think my Atchievments   . . 105   OLD BATCH   V.1   334
Atheism (2)
  Bellmour: Black Gown does Atheism--You must know he has been   . . . 47   OLD BATCH   I.1   368
  Bellmour: in an opinion of Atheism; when they may be so much   . . . 75   OLD BATCH IV.1   7
Atheist (1)
  Scandal: Parson, be Chaplain to an Atheist, or Stallion to an   . . 220   FOR LOVE   I.1   145
Athens (1)
  Scandal: of the Name, recall the Stage of Athens, and be allow'd   . 220   FOR LOVE   I.1   149
Atlas' (1)
  Valentine: and Atlas' Shoulders. Let Taliacotius trim the Calves of   . 289   FCR LCVE   IV.1   524
Atlases (1)
  Mirabell: of Muslin, China, Fans, Atlases, &c.--Item when you shall   . 451   WAY WORLD IV.1   254
Aton'd (1)
  Manuel: In Filial Duty, had aton'd and giv'n   333   M. BRIDE   I.1   291
Atone (1)
  Garcia: Ha! what? atone this Murther with a greater!   378   M. BBIDE   V.2   73
Atonement (1)
  Gonsalez: Should make atonement by a Death as horrid;   378   M. BEIDE   V.2   71
Attack'd (1)
  Sir Joseph: --A-Gad, t'other Glass of Madera, and I durst have attack'd 85   OLD BATCH IV.3   68
Attain (1)
  Lady Touch: you to attain your ends.   198   DOUEL DLR   V.1   419
Attempt (7)
  Maskwell: attempt.   148   DOUEL DLR II.1   388
  Lady Ply: rather attempt it than any thing in the World, (Curtesies)   159   DOUEL DLR III.1   341
  Zara: Attempt no Means to make himself away;   360   M. BRIDE III.1 V448
  Selim: Attempt to force his way for an Escape.   362   M. BBIDE   IV.1   54
  Manuel: And lcok that she attempt not on her Life.   370   M. BBIDE   IV.1   366
  Gonsalez: Th' Attempt: I'll steal, and do it unperceiv'd.   .   .   . 376   M. BBIDE   V.2   9
  Marwood: Confusion, or I'll perish in the attempt.   477   WAY WCRLD   V.1   566
Attempted (2)   see 'tempted
  Mellefont: I don't know what she might have attempted.   149   DOUEL DLR II.1   418
  Maskwell: time he attempted any thing of that kind, to discover it to 154   DOUEL DLR III.1   154
Attempts (1)
  Valentine: vain Attempts, and find at last, that nothing but my Ruine   312   FOR LCVE   V.1   547
Attend (17)
  Silvia: Jealousie attend her Love; and Disappointment meet his   . 61   OLD BATCH III.1   31
  Setter: I attend you, Sir.   96   OLD BATCH   V.1   8
  Setter: She has, Sir;--And I have it in Charge to attend   .   . 102   OLD BATCH   V.1   215
  Heartwell: What rugged Ways attend the Nocn of Life!   112   OLD BATCH   V.2   191
  Mellefont: I will; till then, success attend thee.   149   DOUBL DLR II.1   437
  Maskwell: Till then, Success will attend me; for when I meet   .   . 150   DOUBL DLR II.1   439
  Lord Touch: Days attend you both; mutual Iove, lasting Health, and   . 203   DOUEL DLR   V.1   588
  Lord Touch: Torture and shame attend their open Birth: 203   DOUEL DLR   V.1   593
  Foresight: and unconvertible Ignorance attend him.   283   FOR LCVE   IV.1   296
  Foresight: and unconvertible Ignorance attend him.   283   FOB LCVE   IV.1 V296
  Almeria: Behold thou also, and attend my Vow.   330   M. BBIDE   I.1   184
  Leonora: I will attend you.   331   M. BBIDE   I.1   207
  Garcia: Great Sir, at her Bequest, attend on Zara.   335   M. BBIDE   I.1   367
  Manuel: Did Zara, then, request he might attend her?   .   .   . 335   M. BBIDE   I.1   377
  Manuel: To one, where young Delights attend; and Joys   .   .   . 349   M. BBIDE   II.2   383
  Osmyn-Alph: My Friend, the Good thou dost deserve attend thee.   .   . 352   M. BBIDE III.1   123
  Zara: Attend me instantly, with each a Bowl   375   M. BBIDE   V.1   131
Attendance (2)
  Scandal: Attendance, and promis'd more than ever you intend to   . . 221   FOR LOVE   I.1   194
  Scandal: Attendance, and promis'd more than ever you intended to   . 221   FOR LOVE   I.1 V194
Attendant (2)
  Setter: uses me as his Attendant; the other (being the better   . . 64   OLD BATCH III.1   139
  Manuel: Let your Attendant be dismiss'd; I have   367   M. BBIDE   IV.1   245
Attendants (8)
  Valentine: Attendants that you begot along with me.   244   FOR LCVE   II.1   342
                         (Attendants to Almeria enter in
                         Mourning.)   332   M. BBIDE   I.1   264
                         (Enter the King, Perez, and Attendants.)   348   M. BBIDE   II.2   351
                         (Exeunt Garcia, Perez, and Attendants.)   364   M. BBIDE   IV.1   135
  Manuel: Away, off, let me go,--Call her Attendants.   .   .   . 369   M. BBIDE   IV.1   335
                         (Enter Leonora and Attendants.) 369   M. BBIDE   IV.1   336
  Almeria: (Exit with attendants.)   .   . 371   M. BBIDE   IV.1   395
                Guards and Attendants.)   382   M. BBIDE   V.2   274
Attended (7)
  Scandal: and the Uneasiness that has attended me ever since, brings 269   FOR LCVE III.1   591
  Manuel: (Symphcny of Warlike Musick. Enter the King, attended by   . 332   M. BRIDE   I.1   265
  Manuel: It is our Will she should be so attended.   335   M. BRIDE   I.1   362
  Perez: Perez and a Guard, and attended by Selim, and several   . 335   M. BBIDE   I.1   383
                But at some distance follow, thus attended.   .   .   . 336   M. BBIDE   I.1   407
  Waitwell: (Enter Zara attended by Selim.)   .   . 345   M. BBIDE   II.2   231
                my self--Married, Knighted and attended all in one   . . 424   WAY WORLD II.1   555
Attends (2)
  Garcia: Great Sir, at her Bequest, attends on Zara.   335   M. BBIDE   I.1 V367
  Garcia: If so, Unhappiness attends their Love   339   M. BBIDE   II.1   47
Attention (2)
  Mellefont: Patience purchase fclly, and Attention be paid with noise: 129   DOUBL DLR   I.1   69
  Scandal: when you had Charity enough to give me your Attention,   . 269   FOR LCVE III.1   588
Attir'd (1)
  Garcia: See, see, attir'd like Osmyn, where he lies.   .   .   . 377   M. BBIDE   V.2   61
Attire (3)
  Alonzo: I'll be so bold to borrow his Attire;   373   M. BBIDE   V.1   29

Author's (1)
```
               Why that's some Comfort, to an Author's fears,    . . . . 113  OLD BATCH  EPI.   15
```
Authority (6)
```
  Sir Paul:    Position of taking up Arms by my Authority, against my  . 178  DOUEL DLR  IV.1  413
  Lord Touch:  Authority--hereafter, you shall rule where I have Power.  . 189  DOUEL DLR  V.1    66
  Jeremy:      his Master from any future Authority over him--  . . . . 218  FCR LCVE   I.1    70
  Sr Sampson:  Authority, no Correction, no Arbitrary Power; nothing  . . 240  FCR LCVE   II.1  177
  Sr Sampson:  . . . with the lawful Authority of a Parent,  . . . . 244  FCR LCVE   II.1  331
  Sr Sampson:  Who gave you Authority tc speak, Sirrah? To  . . . . . 308  FOR LCVE   V.1   417
```
Authoriz'd (1)
```
  Mirabell:    and, Authoriz'd Tea-Table talk,--such as mending of  . . 451  WAY WORLD  IV.1  267
```
Authors (1)
```
               Our Authors Sin, but we alone repent.  . . . . . . . 323  M. ERIDE   PRO.   22
```
Auxiliaries (1)
```
  Mirabell:    Forces, all Auxiliaries to the Tea-Table, as Orange-Brandy, 451  WAY WCRLD  IV.1  272
```
Avail (1)
```
  Fainall:     somewhere else; For here it will not avail. This, my Lady  473  WAY WCRLD  V.1   441
```
Avarice (1)
```
  Heli:        Which Manuel to his own Use and Avarice,  . . . . . . 351  M. ERIDE   III.1   66
```
Avaunt (3)
```
  Lucy:        No no, avaunt--I'le not be slabber'd and kiss'd  . . . . 67  OLD BATCH  III.1  236
  Setter:      --Avaunt Temptation.--Setter, shew thy self a  . . . . 102  OLD EATCH  V.1   226
  Setter:      Criticks avaunt; for you are Fish of Prey,  . . . . . 125  DOUBL DLR  PRO.   12
```
Avenging (1)
```
  Gonsalez:    On me, on me, turn your avenging Sword.  . . . . . . 378  M. ERIDE   V.2    69
```
Averse (1)
```
  Mrs Fain:    Men are ever in Extreams; either doating or averse.  . . 410  WAY WCRLD  II.1    3
```
Aversion (13)
```
  Mellefont:   self favour'd in her aversion: But whether urged by her  . 129  DOUEL DLR  I.1    94
  Careless:    Aunts Aversion in her Revenge, cannot be any way so  . . 131  DOUEL DLR  I.1   159
  Mrs Fore:    now if we can improve that, and make her have an Aversion  248  FCR LCVE   II.1  501
  Scandal:     work a Cure; as the fear of your Aversion occasion'd his  . 277  FCR LCVE   IV.1   64
  Angelica:    Malice is not a more terrible Consequence of his Aversion,  299  FCR LCVE   V.1    77
  Heli:        When Zara comes, abate of your Aversion.  . . . . . . 352  M. ERIDE   III.1  106
  Mrs Fain:    Then it seems you dissemble an Aversion to  . . . . . 410  WAY WCRLD  II.1   18
  Marwood:     my Aversion further.  . . . . . . . . . . . . 411  WAY WORLD  II.1   51
  Mrs Fain:    By the Reason you give for your Aversion, one  . . . . 412  WAY WORLD  II.1  138
  Fainall:     dissembl'd your Aversion. Your mutual Jealousies of one  . 413  WAY WORLD  II.1  138
  Mrs Fain:    without Bounds, and wou'd you set Limits to that Aversion,  417  WAY WORLD  II.1  262
  Millamant:   Well, an illiterate Man's my Aversion. I wonder  . . . 436  WAY WCRLD  III.1  422
  Lady Wish:   Aversicn to the very sight of Men,--ay Friend, she  . . 466  WAY WCRLD  V.1   186
```
Avert (2)
```
  Araminta:    avert the cure: Let me have Oil to feed that Flame and  . 54  OLD BATCH  II.2    9
  Selim:       Avert it, Heav'n, that you should ever suffer  . . . . 375  M. ERIDE   V.1   113
```
Avoid (12)
```
               But by my Troth I cannot avoid thinking,  . . . . . . 125  DOUBL DLR  PRO.   23
  Mellefont:   prevent the success of her displeasure, than to avcid the  129  DOUEL DLR  I.1    92
  Lord Froth:  avoid giving them encouragement.  . . . . . . . . 133  DOUEL DLR  I.1   232
  Maskwell:    perish first, and from this hour avoid all sight and speech, 188  DOUEL DLR  V.1    41
  Scandal:     worthless great Men, and dull rich Rogues, avoid a witty  . 219  FCR LCVE   I.1   132
  Valentine:   cannot avoid such a palpable Decoy as this was; the Ladies  229  FCR LCVE   I.1   502
  Valentine:   are earnest,--I'll avoid 'em,--Ccme this way,  . . . . 246  FCR LCVE   II.1  411
  Angelica:    I'll advise you, how you may avoid such another. Learn to  312  FCR LCVE   V.1   571
  Almeria:     The good King flying to avoid the Flames,  . . . . . 329  M. ERIDE   I.1  V115
  Garcia:      The Friends perhaps are met; let us avcid 'em.  . . . . 339  M. ERIDE   II.1   49
  Fainall:     mov'd that tc avoid Scandal there might be one Man  . . . 396  WAY WORLD  I.1    56
  Mrs Fain:    one scandalous Story, to avoid giving an occasion to make  412  WAY WORLD  II.1  105
```
Avow (1)
```
  Manuel:      What dar'st thou to my Face avow thy Guilt?  . . . . . 369  M. BRIDE   IV.1  315
```
Awake (7)
```
  Heartwell:   Awake; Sigh much, Drink little, Eat less, court Solitude,  . 73  OLD BATCH  III.2   81
  Mellefont:   Where am I? sure, is it day? and am I awake,  . . . . . 147  DOUBL DLR  II.1  323
  Mellefont:   Where am I? is it day? and am I awake,  . . . . . . 147  DOUEL DLR  II.1 V323
  Lord Froth:  No, my dear; I'm but just awake.--  . . . . . . . 201  DCUBL DLR  V.1   525
  Miss Prue:   Life: For when I'm awake, it makes me wish and long, and  . 305  FCR LCVE   V.1   310
  Zara:        Forbidding rest; may stretch his Eyes awake  . . . . . 355  M. ERIDE   III.1  209
  Osmyn-Alph:  With the Breath of Love. Shine, awake, Almeria,  . . . . 383  M. ERIDE   V.2   285
```
Awakned (1)
```
  Setter:      Ha! what art, who thus maliciously hast awakned me,  . . 65  OLD BATCH  III.1  165
```
Away (66)
```
  Heartwell:   Pox I have pratled away my time--I hope you are  . . . . 46  OLD BATCH  I.1   331
  Bellmour:    ever he was loose, he ran away, without staying to see who  46  OLD BATCH  I.1   363
  Bellmour:    abroad--went purely to run away from a Campagne;  . . . 47  OLD EATCH  I.1   369
  Sir Joseph:  and frightn'd 'em away--but agad I durst not stay to give  47  OLD BATCH  II.1    9
  Lucy:        'twould disgust his nicety, and take away his Stomach.  . . 62  OLD BATCH  III.1   42
  Bellmour:    Ha, ha, ha, prithee come away, 'tis scandalous to  . . . 69  OLD BATCH  III.1  327
  Setter:      S'bud Sir, away quickly, there's Fondlewife just turn'd  . 75  OLD BATCH  IV.1    9
  Araminta:    No reply; but away.  . . . . . . . . . . . . 86  OLD BATCH  IV.3  106
               it away.)  . . . . . . . . . . . . . . . . 88  OLD EATCH  IV.3  180
  Sir Joseph:         (Stealing away upon his Tip-toes.)  .  .  101  OLD BATCH  V.1   186
  Heartwell:   Then good Councel will be thrown away upon  . . . . . 112  OLD BATCH  V.2   157
               Be ev'ry Monster of the Deep away;  . . . . . . . 125  DOUBL DLR  PRO.   14
  Sir Paul:    Thy, Thy, come away Thy, touch him not, come  . . . . . 145  DOUBL DLR  II.1  245
  Sir Paul:    I should, indeed, Thy--therefore come away; but  . . . . 146  DOUBL DLR  II.1  284
  Sir Paul:    providence has prevented all, therefore come away, when  . 146  DOUBL DLR  II.1  285
  Maskwell:    I know it; I met Sir Paul towing away Cynthia:  . . . . 148  DOUBL DLR  II.1  385
  Lady Touch:  toy away an hour in mirth.  . . . . . . . . . . 155  DOUBL DLR III.1  171
  Maskwell:    I know what she means by toying away an hour well  . . . 155  DOUBL DLR III.1  174
  Mellefont:   To run most wilfully and unreasonably away with  . . . . 168  DOUBL DLR  IV.1   38
  Lady Touch:  sake away my Lord, he'll either tempt you to extravagance,  186  DOUBL DLR  IV.2  128
  Mellefont:   away the very root and foundation of his hopes; What  . . 187  DOUBL DLR  IV.2  147
  Lord Touch:  our ancient Family; him I thus blow away, and constitute  . 189  DOUBL DLR  V.1    58
  Maskwell:    you, Borrow my Lords Chaplain, and so run away with  . . 193  DOUBL DLR  V.1   224
  Maskwell:    every look you cheaply throw away on any other Object  . . 199  DOUBL DLR  V.1   435
  Valentine:   Here, take away; I'll walk a turn, and digest what  . . . 216  FCR LCVE   I.1    3
  Jeremy:      (Aside and taking away the Books.)  . . . . . . . 216  FOR LOVE   I.1    6
```

Ay   (continued)

		PAGE	TITLE	ACT.SC	LINE
Sir Joseph:	Ay; Do, do, Captain, if you think fitting.--You	101	OLD BATCH	V.1	V183
Sir Joseph:	Ay, now it's out; 'tis I, my own individual Person.	102	OLD BATCH	V.1	206
Setter:	honest. Reputed honest! Hum: Is that all? Ay: For, to be	102	OLD BATCH	V.1	228
Sir Joseph:	Ay, ay, whatsoever, Captain, stick to that;	110	OLD BATCH	V.2	98
Vainlove:	Ay, ay, to this instant Moment.--I have past	110	OLD BATCH	V.2	102
Careless:	Hum, ay, what is't?	128	DOUBL DLR	I.1	40
Brisk:	Ay, my Lord, it's a sign I hit you in the Teeth, if you	132	DOUBL DLR	I.1	210
Lord Froth:	ay, there it is; who could resist! 'twas so my heart was made	140	DOUBL DLR	II.1	68
Mellefont:	Ay, my Lord, I shall have the same reason for my	141	DOUBL DLR	II.1	111
Lady Froth:	He, Ay, is not it?--and then I call my Lord	141	DOUBL DLR	II.1	126
Lady Ply:	Ay, for tho' I am not Cynthia's own Mother, I	146	DOUBL DLR	II.1	309
Mellefont:	Ha, ha, ha, a, a very Fury; but I was most afraid	149	DOUBL DLR	II.1	V416
Sir Paul:	Ay, so so, there.	160	DOUBL DLR	III.1	365
Sir Paul:	be Providence--ay, truly, Mr. Careless, my Lady is a great	160	DOUBL DLR	III.1	386
Lady Froth:	Ay, Charioteer does better.	164	DOUBL DLR	III.1	537
Lady Froth:	--Ay my Dear--were you? Oh filthy Mr. Sneer;	165	DOUBL DLR	III.1	561
Mellefont:	Ay, Hell thank her, as gentle breezes moderate a	167	DOUBL DLR	IV.1	3
Cynthia:	Ay, ay, what have we to do with 'em; you know we	168	DOUBL DLR	IV.1	31
Mellefont:	Ay, what am I to trust to then?	169	DOUBL DLR	IV.1	57
Cynthia:	Ay, but my Conscience never will.	171	DOUBL DLR	IV.1	147
Lady Ply:	Ay, but Sir Paul, I conceive if she has sworn,	171	DOUBL DLR	IV.1	150
Lady Ply:	Ungrateful Monster! He? Is it so? Ay, I see it, a Plot upon	179	DOUBL DLR	IV.1	444
Sir Paul:	Ay, but by your own Vertue and Continency that	180	DOUBL DLR	IV.1	476
Maskwell:	It must not be; nay, shou'd my Lady knew it--ay,	190	DOUBL DLR	V.1	92
Maskwell:	Tell him so! Ay, why you don't think I mean to	193	DOUBL DLR	V.1	227
Jeremy:	Ay, more indeed; for who cares for any Body that	219	FOR LOVE	I.1	129
Scandal:	Ay, we'll all give you something.	231	FOR LOVE	I.1	587
Mrs Frail:	Ay, but I hear she has a Closet of Beauties.	232	FOR LOVE	I.1	605
Mrs Frail:	Ay, let me see those, Mr. Tattle.	232	FOR LOVE	I.1	608
Foresight:	Odso, let me see; let me see the Paper--Ay,	240	FOR LOVE	II.1	186
Sr Sampson:	Haste, ay, ay; haste enough, my Son Ben will	240	FOR LOVE	II.1	192
Sr Sampson:	Ay boy--Come, thou shalt sit down by me.	281	FOR LOVE	IV.1	198
Tattle:	Ay; 'tis well enough for a Servant to be bred at an	302	FOR LOVE	V.1	186
Tattle:	Ay faith, so she will, Jeremy: You're a good Friend to	302	FOR LOVE	V.1	206
Tattle:	Ay, but your Father will tell you that Dreams come	303	FOR LOVE	V.1	240
Ben:	Who, Father? ay, he's come home with a Vengeance.	306	FOR LOVE	V.1	341
Gonsalez:	To set him free? Ay, now 'tis plain; O well	371	M. BRIDE	IV.1	413
Mirabell:	Ay; I have been engag'd in a Matter of some sort	399	WAY WORLD	I.1	136
Witwoud:	Ay, but no other?	401	WAY WORLD	I.1	241
Witwoud:	Ay, ay, my half Brother. My half Brother he is,	402	WAY WORLD	I.1	250
Mirabell:	Ay.	402	WAY WORLD	I.1	269
Mirabell:	Ay marry, what's that, Witwoud?	403	WAY WORLD	I.1	313
Witwoud:	Ay; but I like him for that now; for his want of	404	WAY WORLD	I.1	330
Witwoud:	Ay, ay, Friendship without Freedom is as dull as	404	WAY WORLD	I.1	357
Petulant:	Ay, Roxolana's.	406	WAY WORLD	I.1	401
Petulant:	Ay, ay, let that pass--There are other Throats	406	WAY WORLD	I.1	425
Petulant:	Ay teste a teste; But not in publick, because I make	408	WAY WORLD	I.1	500
Petulant:	Ay tete a tete; But not in publick, because I make	408	WAY WORLD	I.1	V500
Petulant:	Ay, ay, pox I'm malicious, Man. Now he's soft	408	WAY WORLD	I.1	503
Fainall:	Ay, I'll take a turn before Dinner.	409	WAY WORLD	I.1	509
Witwoud:	Ay, we'll all walk in the Park, the Ladies talk'd of	409	WAY WORLD	I.1	510
Mrs Fain:	Ay, ay, dear Marwood, if we will be happy, we	410	WAY WORLD	II.1	1
Mrs Fain:	Most transcendantly; ay, tho' I say it,	411	WAY WORLD	II.1	37
Marwood:	Ay!	413	WAY WORLD	II.1	111
Millamant:	Ay, that's true--O but then I had--	419	WAY WORLD	II.1	355
Millamant:	O ay, Letters--I had Letters--I am	419	WAY WORLD	II.1	359
Millamant:	Ay, poor Mincing tift and tift all the morning.	419	WAY WORLD	II.1	370
Millamant:	O ay, and went away--Now I think on't I'm angry	420	WAY WORLD	II.1	378
Mirabell:	Ay, ay, suffer your Cruelty to ruin the object of	420	WAY WORLD	II.1	389
Waitwell:	Ay there's the Grief; that's the sad change of Life;	424	WAY WORLD	II.1	562
Lady Wish:	Ay dear Foible; thank thee for that dear Foible.	428	WAY WORLD	III.1	139
Petulant:	Ay in the main--But when I have a Humour to	435	WAY WORLD	III.1	398
Witwoud:	Ay, when he has a Humour to contradict, then I	435	WAY WORLD	III.1	400
Witwoud:	Ay, upon Proof positive it must; but upon Proof	435	WAY WORLD	III.1	409
Witwoud:	Ay, ay, but that was for a while. Not long, not	440	WAY WORLD	III.1	556
Witwoud:	Ay, ay, but that was but for a while. Not long, not	440	WAY WORLD	III.1	V556
Witwoud:	and this Fellow was my Guardian; ay, ay, I was glad	440	WAY WORLD	III.1	558
Lady Wish:	and then as soon as he appears, start, ay, start and be surpriz'd,	445	WAY WORLD	IV.1	27
Millamant:	He? Ay, and filthy Verses--So I am.	446	WAY WORLD	IV.1	57
Millamant:	Ay, if you please Foible, send him away,--Or send	446	WAY WORLD	IV.1	60
Millamant:	him--Shall I? Ay, let the Wretch come.	446	WAY WORLD	IV.1	62
Millamant:	Ay, ay, ha, ha, ha.	448	WAY WORLD	IV.1	152
Millamant:	Ay as Wife, Spouse, My dear, Joy, Jewel, Love,	450	WAY WORLD	IV.1	197
Mrs Fain:	Ay, ay, take him, take him, what shou'd you	452	WAY WORLD	IV.1	286
Millamant:	Ay, go, go. In the mean time I suppose you have	452	WAY WORLD	IV.1	306
Lady Wish:	with him--Travel quoth a; Ay travel, travel, get thee gone,	456	WAY WORLD	IV.1	438
Witwoud:	Horrible! He has a breath like a Bagpipe--ay, ay,	457	WAY WORLD	IV.1	474
Lady Wish:	Ay dear Sir Rowland, that will be some	461	WAY WORLD	IV.1	636
Waitwell:	in spight of treachery; Ay and get an Heir that shall defeat	461	WAY WORLD	IV.1	643
Foible:	--a Bride, ay I shall be a Bridewell-Bride. Oh!	463	WAY WORLD	V.1	59
Mrs Fain:	Ay, all's out, My affair with Mirabell, every	464	WAY WORLD	V.1	81
Mrs Fain:	there, ay or your Friend's Friend, my false Husband.	466	WAY WORLD	V.1	155
Mrs Fain:	you? ay, like a Leach, to suck your best Blood--she'll	466	WAY WORLD	V.1	174
Lady Wish:	Aversion to the very sight of Men,--ay Friend, she	466	WAY WORLD	V.1	186
Lady Wish:	make it up, make it up; ay, ay, I'll Compound. I'll give	468	WAY WORLD	V.1	238
Lady Wish:	Ay, ay, I do not doubt it, dear Marwood: No,	468	WAY WORLD	V.1	248
Mirabell:	Ay Madam; but that is too late, my reward is intercepted.	473	WAY WORLD	V.1	457
Lady Wish:	Ay, ay, any Body, any body.	474	WAY WORLD	V.1	469
Lady Wish:	Ay, dear Sir.	475	WAY WORLD	V.1	V513
Witwoud:	Ay I do, my hand I remember--Petulant set his	475	WAY WORLD	V.1	525
Lady Wish:	Ay, ay, Sir, upon my honour.	476	WAY WORLD	V.1	534
Mirabell:	Ay, and over and over again; for I wou'd have you	477	WAY WORLD	V.1	596
Mirabell:	Ay, and over and over again; I wou'd have you	477	WAY WORLD	V.1	V596

```
Ay-h (1)
  Millamant:   Contemplation, must I bid you then Adieu? ay-h adieu.--my   449   WAY WORLD   IV.1  187
Aye (26)    see Ay
  Jeremy:      Aye, Sir, I am a Fool, I know it: And yet, Heav'n      .  .   217   FOR LOVE    I.1    40
  Scandal:     Aye? Why then I'm afraid Jeremy has Wit: For     .  .  .  .   219   FOR LOVE    I.1   120
  Scandal:     A mender of Reputations! aye, just as he is a keeper   .  .   226   FOR LOVE    I.1   368
  Scandal:     Aye, such rotten Reputations as you have to deal    .  .  .   226   FOR LOVE    I.1   396
  Foresight:   Aye indeed, Sir Sampson, a great deal of Money for   .  .    243   FOR LOVE    II.1  277
  Scandal:     Aye, your Husband, a Husband is an opportunity for     .  .   271   FOR LOVE    III.1 681
  Mrs Fore:    Aye; but you are such an universal Jugler,   .  .  .  .  .   272   FOR LOVE    III.1 702
  Mrs Frail:   Aye, but my Dear, we must keep it secret, till   .  .  .  .   273   FOR LOVE    III.1 718
  Sr Sampson:  See it, boy? Aye, aye, why thou do'st see it--   .  .  .     281   FOR LOVE    IV.1  219
  Sr Sampson:  Let thee hold it, say'st thou--Aye, with all   .  .  .  .    281   FOR LOVE    IV.1  229
  Tattle:      Aye, prithee, what's that?  .  .  .  .  .  .  .  .   .  .    292   FOR LOVE    IV.1  642
  Angelica:    (aside). Aye, but if I don't fit you, I'll be hang'd.   .    294   FOR LOVE    IV.1  699
  Angelica:    Aye; But that is not in your Power, Sir Sampson; for   .  .   300   FOR LOVE    V.1   121
  Jeremy:      Aye, Sir, she's just going to the Place of appointment.   .   301   FOR LOVE    V.1   166
  Tattle:      Aye, who's that?  .  .  .  .  .  .  .  .  .  .  .  .  .   .   301   FOR LOVE    V.1   170
  Tattle:      Aye? Who's he, tho? A Privy Counsellor?   .  .  .  .  .  .    302   FOR LOVE    V.1   192
  Jeremy:      Aye, Sir, hooded like a Hawk, to seize at first sight   .    302   FOR LOVE    V.1   199
  Foresight:   Aye, but pray take me along with you, Sir--   .  .  .  .     304   FOR LOVE    V.1   279
  Ben:         Aye, the same.   .  .  .  .  .  .  .  .  .  .  .  .  .  .     307   FOR LOVE    V.1   364
  Mrs Frail:   (to her). Aye, aye, it's well it's no worse--Nay,   .  .     310   FOR LOVE    V.1   471
  Tattle:      Aye, my Dear, so they will as you say.   .  .  .  .  .  .    310   FOR LOVE    V.1   480
  Lady Wish:   won't sit--I'll walk--aye I'll walk from the door upon his    445   WAY WORLD   IV.1   20
  Lady Wish:   be too sudden. I'll lie--aye, I'll lie down--I'll   .  .      445   WAY WORLD   IV.1   22
  Lady Wish:   Aye that's true; but in Case of Necessity; as of   .  .      468   WAY WORLD   V.1   263
B'w'y (2)    see Bu'y
  Sharper:     me, or I'll go and have the Lady to my self. B'w'y' George.   104   OLD BATCH   V.1   306
  Foible:      haste home and prevent her. Your Servant Sir. B'w'y   .      424   WAY WORLD   II.1  547
Babe (1)
               Into the sea, the New-born Babe is thrown,   .  .  .  .  .   125   DOUBL DLR   PRO.    3
Babies (1)
  Lady Wish:   Coats; Nay her very Babies were of the Feminine Gender,   .   467   WAY WORLD   V.1   190
Baby (1)
  Heartwell:   Baby for a Girl to dandle. O dotage, dotage! That ever   .    72   OLD BATCH   III.2   47
Babylon (1)
  Fondlewife:  of my house, thou Son of the Whore of Babylon; Off-spring  .   90   OLD BATCH   IV.4   65
Back (44)
  Bellmour:    image of Valour. He calls him his Back, and indeed they   .    46   OLD BATCH   I.1   357
  Sir Joseph:  at present; he have lay'd it all out upon my Back.   .  .  .   50   OLD BATCH   II.1  112
  Sir Joseph:  call my Back; he sticks as close to me, and follows me   .     50   OLD BATCH   II.1  119
  Sir Joseph:  through all dangers--he is indeed Back, Breast and Headpiece   50   OLD BATCH   II.1  120
  Sir Joseph:  my Bully, my Back; agad my heart has gone a pit   .  .  .      51   OLD BATCH   II.1  140
  Sir Joseph:  and Cloth to him. But Back, this Gentleman is one of the   .   52   OLD BATCH   II.1  168
  Sir Joseph:  Pray Mr. Sharper Embrace my Back--very   .  .  .  .  .  .      52   OLD BATCH   II.1  174
  Sir Joseph:  Fellow as Cannibal, are not you Bully--Back?   .  .  .  .      52   OLD BATCH   II.1  176
  Sharper:     Sir Joseph's Back.  .  .  .  .  .  .  .  .  .  .  .  .  .      54   OLD BATCH   II.1  249
  Belinda:     a high Roof, or a very low Seat--Stay, Come back here   .      57   OLD BATCH   II.2   96
  Setter:      Too forward to be turn'd back--Though he's a little   .  .     67   OLD BATCH   III.1 224
  Sir Joseph:  And good Nature, Back; I am good Natur'd and   .  .  .  .      67   OLD BATCH   III.1 243
  Sir Joseph:  Put up, put up, dear Back, 'tis your Sir Joseph begs, come    70   OLD BATCH   III.1 341
  Sir Joseph:  done behind his Back, than what's said--Come wee'l   .  .      70   OLD BATCH   III.1 361
  Heartwell:   will more easily be thrust forward than drawn back.   .  .     73   OLD BATCH   III.2   73
  Laetitia:    Your back was no sooner turn'd, but like a Lion, he   .  .     90   OLD BATCH   IV.4   52
  Fondlewife:  back.--Give me the Key of your Cabinet, Cocky--   .  .  .      91   OLD BATCH   IV.4   73
  Fondlewife:  go back of your word; you are not the Person I took you   .     94   OLD BATCH   IV.4  191
               kisses her hand, behind Fondlewife's back.)   .  .  .  .      95   OLD BATCH   IV.4  242
  Setter:      Voyage. Or have you brought your own Lading back?   .  .       96   OLD BATCH   V.1     3
  Bellmour:    No, I have brought nothing but Ballast back,--   .  .  .       96   OLD BATCH   V.1     4
  Sir Joseph:  That's you, Bully Back.   .  .  .  .  .  .  .  .  .  .  .     102   OLD BATCH   V.1   210
  Mellefont:   Heaven she laughs, grins, points to your Back, she forks  .   186   DOUBL DLR   IV.2  131
               (As she is going she turns back and smiles at him.)   .  .   187   DOUBL DLR   IV.2  134
  Maskwell:    back Stairs, and so we may slip down without being   .  .     194   DOUBL DLR   V.1   240
  Maskwell:    corner Chamber at this end of the Gallery, there is a back    194   DOUBL DLR   V.1   253
  Maskwell:    him in her stead, you may go privately by the back Stairs,    199   DOUBL DLR   V.1   446
  Lord Touch:  has this discover'd! I am confounded when I look back,   .    200   DOUBL DLR   V.1   470
  Tattle:      Have you not a back way?   .  .  .  .  .  .  .  .  .  .  .    229   FOR LOVE    I.1   510
  Tattle:      Is there not a back way?  .  .  .  .  .  .  .  .  .  .  .    229   FOR LOVE    I.1  V510
  Foresight:   of the first Magnitude. Take back your Paper of Inheritance;  241   FOR LOVE    II.1  237
  Nurse:       come in the back way.  .  .  .  .  .  .  .  .  .  .  .  .    253   FOR LOVE    III.1   12
  Scandal:     water, and lye upon your back, may be you may dream.   .  .   270   FOR LOVE    III.1 639
  Sr Sampson:  Mr. Buckram, bid him make haste back with the   .  .  .      281   FOR LOVE    IV.1  209
  Valentine:   shrivell'd; his Legs dwindl'd, and his back bow'd, Pray,     289   FOR LOVE    IV.1  520
  Ben:         neither--But I'll sail as far as Ligorn, and back again,     306   FOR LOVE    V.1   352
  Almeria:     Back to the Bottom of the boundless Deep,   .  .  .  .  .    342   M. BRIDE    II.2   85
  Almeria:     That thus relenting, they have giv'n thee back   .  .  .     342   M. BRIDE    II.2   89
  Manuel:      Entring he met my Eyes, and started back,   .  .  .  .  .    373   M. BRIDE    V.1    15
  Witwoud:     soon as your Back was turn'd--Whip he was gone;   .  .  .     405   WAY WORLD   I.1   371
  Mrs Fain:    I'll go with you up the back Stairs, lest I shou'd   .  .     430   WAY WORLD   III.1 221
  Lady Wish:   young. It will be time enough when he comes back, and   .     432   WAY WORLD   III.1 264
  Mirabell:    inscrib'd on the back may serve your occasions.   .  .  .    476   WAY WORLD   V.1   549
  Mirabell:    written on the back may serve your occasions.   .  .  .      476   WAY WORLD   V.1  V549
Back-stairs (1)
  Mrs Fain:    occasion, and slip down the back-stairs, where Foible   .    452   WAY WORLD   IV.1  304
Back's (1)
  Servant:     There, Sir, his back's toward you.   .  .  .  .  .  .  .     260   FOR LOVE    III.1 269
Backside (1)
  Jeremy:      So--Just the very backside of Truth,--But   .  .  .  .  .    296   FOR LOVE    IV.1  775
Backward (3)
  Bellmour:    little too backward, that's the truth on't.   .  .  .  .      93   OLD BATCH   IV.4  171
  Foresight:   Crab was ascending, and all my Affairs go backward.   .  .    235   FOR LOVE    II.1   13
  Osmyn-Alph:  We both have backward trod the paths of Fate,   .  .  .      342   M. BRIDE    II.2   92
Backwardness (1)
  Valentine:   to you. For you found her Vertue, upon the Backwardness   .   256   FOR LOVE    III.1 131
```

Banter (4)
Mrs Frail:	The World's end! What, do you mean to banter	247	FOR LOVE	II.1	448
Sr Sampson:	Hey day, Rascal, do you banter me? Sirrah, ...	279	FOR LOVE	IV.1	127
Sr Sampson:	d'ye banter me--Speak Sirrah, where is he, for I . .	279	FOR LOVE	IV.1	128
Tattle:	(aside) what do's the Old Prig mean? I'll banter him, and	304	FOR LOVE	V.1	263

Barbado's-Waters (1)
| Mirabell: | all Anniseed, Cinamon, Citron and Barbadc's-Waters, together | 451 | WAY WORLD | IV.1 | 273 |

Barbarian (1)
| Lady Wish: | this Barbarian, But she wou'd have him, tho' her Year was | 469 | WAY WORLD | V.1 | 303 |

Barbarities (2)
| Lady Ply: | lov'd you tenderly--'tis a barbarity of barbarities, and | 146 | DOUBL DLR | II.1 | 291 |
| Lady Ply: | loves you tenderly--'tis a barbarity of barbarities, and | 146 | DOUBL DLR | II.1 V | 291 |

Barbarity (5)
Lady Ply:	lov'd you tenderly--'tis a barbarity of barbarities, and	146	DOUBL DLR	II.1	291
Lady Ply:	loves you tenderly--'tis a barbarity of barbarities, and	146	DOUBL DLR	II.1 V	291
Valentine:	I would have an excuse for your Barbarity and . . .	244	FOR LOVE	II.1	321
Scandal:	manifest the cruel Triumphs of her Beauty; the barbarity	276	FOR LOVE	IV.1	25
Lady Wish:	Barbarity of a Muscovite Husband.	469	WAY WORLD	V.1	272

Barbarous (14)
Belinda:	O barbarous Aspersion!	55	OLD BATCH	II.2	45
Laetitia:	My affliction is always your Jest, barbarous Man! Oh . .	78	OLD BATCH	IV.1	103
Belinda:	Oh the most inhumane, barbarous Hackney-Coach! . .	83	OLD BATCH	IV.3	4
Laetitia:	Ah cruel Dear, how can you be so barbarous? You'll . .	95	OLD BATCH	IV.4	230
	A Barbarous Device, to try if Spouse, ...	125	DOUBL DLR	PRO.	5
Lord Froth:	Barbarous! I'd as lieve you call'd me Fool.	132	DOUBL DLR	I.1	186
Brisk:	O barbarous, to turn me into ridicule! Yet, ha ha ha. .	176	DOUBL DLR	IV.1	343
Tattle:	But how Barbarous that is, and how unfortunate for . .	226	FOR LOVE	I.1	391
Tattle:	O Barbarous! why did you not tell me--	229	FOR LOVE	I.1	494
Angelica:	O barbarous! I never heard so insolent a piece of . .	258	FOR LOVE	III.1	182
Valentine:	Oh, 'tis barbarous to misunderstand me longer. . .	295	FOR LOVE	IV.1	731
Zara:	He Looks not, minds not, hears not; barbarous Man! . .	346	M. BRIDE	II.2	244
Zara:	Of these thy Wrongs; as she, whose barbarous Rage . .	353	M. BRIDE	III.1	158
Millamant:	ha, ha; tho' I grant you 'tis a little barbarous, Ha, ha, ha.	434	WAY WORLD	III.1	344

Barbary (1)
| Valentine: | again.--Pretty round heaving Breasts,--a Barbary . . | 223 | FOR LOVE | I.1 | 284 |

Bard (1)
| Foresight: | translated by a Reverend Buckinghamshire Bard. . . . | 236 | FOR LOVE | II.1 | 50 |

Bare (8)
Heartwell:	profit than what the bare tillage and manuring of the Land	44	OLD BATCH	I.1	280
Lady Froth:	her Guns bare, and her Mouth open.--	165	DOUBL DLR	III.1	575
Maskwell:	mean now, is only a bare Suspicion of my own. If your .	183	DOUBL DLR	IV.1	583
Sr Sampson:	am not so old neither, to be a bare Courtier, only a Man of	298	FOR LOVE	V.1	22
Zara:	Thee bare, the naked Mark of Publick View.	360	M. BRIDE	III.1	442
Almeria:	Drag me, harrow the Earth with my bare Bosom. . . .	369	M. BRIDE	IV.1	337
Selim:	I bare my Breast to meet your just Revenge. . . .	375	M. BRIDE	V.1	122
Marwood:	you wou'd but appear bare fac'd now, and own Mirabell;	433	WAY WORLD	III.1	314

Bare-fac'd (1)
| Gonsalez: | Should have more Meaning than appears bare-fac'd. . . | 365 | M. BRIDE | IV.1 | 176 |

Bare-faced (1)
| Careless: | not the same bare-faced and in Masks,--and a Vizor . . | 158 | DOUBL DLR | III.1 | 308 |

Bare-foot (1)
| Waitwell: | I'll do't. In three weeks he shall be bare-foot; in a . | 458 | WAY WORLD | IV.1 | 521 |

Barely (1)
| Maskwell: | rather die, than seem once, barely seem, dishonest:-- . | 188 | DOUBL DLR | V.1 | 37 |

Bargain (5)
Maskwell:	see Love-bargain				
Maskwell:	earnest of that Bargain, to have full and free possession of	156	DOUBL DLR	III.1	229
Sr Sampson:	Here's a Rogue, Brother Foresight, makes a Bargain under	243	FOR LOVE	II.1	295
Ben:	leaky Vessel into the Bargain.	262	FOR LOVE	III.1	318
Jeremy:	bad Bargain, can't do better than to beg him for his .	276	FOR LOVE	IV.1	36
Mrs Fore:	towards it. I have almost made a Bargain with Jeremy, .	288	FOR LOVE	IV.1	465

Bargaining (1)
| Maskwell: | Listen, and be dumb, we have been bargaining . . . . | 156 | DOUBL DLR | III.1 | 214 |

Barking (1)
| Manuel: | And spend their Mouths in barking Tyranny. . . . . | 362 | M. BRIDE | IV.1 | 64 |

Barn-Elms (1)
| Mrs Frail: | or Barn-Elms with a man alone--something . . . . | 247 | FOR LOVE | II.1 | 439 |

Barn-door-Fowl (1)
| Belinda: | Ay, O my Conscience; fat as Barn-door-Fowl: But . . . | 84 | OLD BATCH | IV.3 | 28 |

Barnaby (2)
| | (Enter Fondlewife and Barnaby.) . . . | 75 | OLD BATCH | IV.1 | 13 |
| | (Exit Barnaby.) . . . . | 76 | OLD BATCH | IV.1 | 48 |

Baronet's (1)
| Tattle: | 'Tis very hard--Won't a Baronet's Lady pass? . . . . | 230 | FOR LOVE | I.1 | 530 |

Barr (2)
| | Than they who stand their Trials at the Barr; . . . | 204 | DOUBL DLR | EPI. | 9 |
| Marwood: | reputation worry'd at the Barr by a pack of Bawling . | 467 | WAY WORLD | V.1 | 210 |

Barrel (0) see Tar-barrel

Barren (1)
| Sharper: | And jealous as a barren Wife. . . . . | 112 | OLD BATCH | V.2 | 163 |

Bars (2)
| Lord Froth: | so ready--she always comes in three bars too soon--and . | 163 | DOUBL DLR | III.1 | 476 |
| Zara: | And Crash of rusty Bars, and creeking Hinges: . . . | 379 | M. BRIDE | V.2 | 138 |

Bartlemew (1)
| Witwoud: | In the Name of Bartlemew and his Fair, what have . . | 436 | WAY WORLD | III.1 | 437 |

Base (9)
Laetitia:	(aside). My Letter! Base Vainlove! Then 'tis too late . .	81	OLD BATCH	IV.2	34
Araminta:	Base Man! Was it not enough to affront me with . . .	87	OLD BATCH	IV.3	162
Maskwell:	Friendship to my Lord, and base Self-interest. Let me .	188	DOUBL DLR	V.1	40
Lord Touch:	Like Vipers in the Womb, base Treach'ry lies, . . .	203	DOUBL DLR	V.1	594
Zara:	The base Injustice thou hast done my Love.	361	M. BRIDE	III.1	454
Manuel:	Why art thou mute? base and degenerate Maid! . . .	367	M. BRIDE	IV.1	265
Gonsalez:	For thee I've been ambitious, base, and bloody: . . .	378	M. BRIDE	V.2	83
Zara:	O this accurs'd, this base, this treach'rous King! . .	380	M. BRIDE	V.2 V	168
Witwoud:	and Base. Ha, Petulant!	435	WAY WORLD	III.1	397

Basely (2)
  Almeria: And Vows I gave my Dear Alphonso, basely   . . . . . . 330 M. BRIDE   I.1 173
  Almeria: I gave my Dear Alphonso, basely broken.   . . . . . . 330 M. BRIDE   I.1 V173
Baseness (6)
  Araminta: young, and your early baseness has prevented its growing . 87 OLD BATCH   IV.3 172
  Maskwell: May so much Fraud and Power of Baseness find? . . . 150 DOUBL DLR   II.1 468
  Zara: This groveling Baseness--Thou say'st true, I know   . . 348 M. BRIDE   II.2 335
  Zara: Have I? Yet 'twere the lowest Baseness, now, ... 363 M. BRIDE   IV.1 96
  Marwood: Love inviolate? And have you the baseness to charge me . 414 WAY WORLD   II.1 174
  Marwood: do it my self I shall prevent your Baseness. . . . . 415 WAY WORLD   II.1 189
Bases (1)
  Lady Wish: the Bases roar Blasphemy. O, she wou'd have swooned at . 467 WAY WORLD   V.1 201
Bashful (1)
                But on my Conscience he's a bashful Poet; . . . . . . 35 OLD BATCH   PRO. 15
Bashfulness (1)
  Fainall: Sir Wilfull is an odd mixture of Bashfulness and   . . . 401 WAY WORLD   I.1 218
Baskets (1)
  Mirabell: my doors against all Bauds with Baskets, and penny-worths 451 WAY WORLD   IV.1 253
Bassa (1)
  Mellefont: Feet like a gull'd Bassa that has married a Relation of the 158 DOUBL DLR III.1 282
Bastard (1)
                I'th' Good Man's Arms, the Chopping Bastard thrives, . . 125 DOUBL DLR   PRO. 29
Baste (1)
  Lady Wish: Abigails and Andrews! I'll couple you, Yes, I'll baste you 463 WAY WORLD   V.1 52
Bastinado'd (1)
  Lady Wish: sleep, you Sot--Or as I'm a person, I'll have you
                bastinado'd . . . . 457 WAY WORLD   IV.1 462
Batchelor (1)
  Sharper: My old Batchelor married! That were a Jest. Ha, ... 105 OLD BATCH   V.1 319
Batchelors (1)
  Heartwell: Batchelors Fall: and upon the third, I shall be hang'd in   63 OLD BATCH III.1 82
Bathe (2)
  Bellmour: your snowy Arms about his stubborn Neck; bathe his   . . . 95 OLD BATCH   IV.4 237
  Garcia: And bathe it to the Hilt, in far less damnable   . . . . 378 M. BRIDE   V.2 79
Battle (1)
  Zara: That Gallant Moor, in Battle lost a Friend   . . . . . 337 M. BRIDE   I.1 437
Battle-dores (1)
  Witwoud: one another like two Battle-dores: For . . . . 435 WAY WORLD III.1 402
Bauds (1)
  Mirabell: my doors against all Bauds with Baskets, and penny-worths 451 WAY WORLD   IV.1 253
Bauk'd (1) see Balkt
  Heartwell: with you and bauk'd it? Did you ever offer me the Favour . 109 OLD BATCH   V.2 57
Baulk (1)
  Mellefont: you wont baulk the Frollick? . . . . 168 DOUBL DLR   IV.1 42
Bawd (7)
  Bellmour: when it disclosed the Cheat, which, that trusty Bawd of . 38 OLD BATCH   I.1 49
  Heartwell: Bawd.-- . . . . 112 OLD BATCH   V.2 160
  Lady Touch: I been Bawd to his designs? his Property only, a baiting
                place . . . . 191 DOUBL DLR   V.1 146
  Witwoud: Bawd troubl'd with Wind. Now you may know what the   . . 404 WAY WORLD   I.1 354
  Fainall: Why then Foible's a Bawd, an Errant, Rank, Matchmaking   . 442 WAY WORLD III.1 628
  Fainall: Bawd, And I it seems am a Husband, a Rank-Husband;   . . 442 WAY WORLD III.1 629
  Lady Wish: you? What, have you made a passive Bawd of me?--   . . . 463 WAY WORLD   V.1 49
Bawdy (2)
  Miss Prue: Why, It is not bawdy, is it Cousin? . . . . 249 FOR LOVE   II.1 533
  Lady Wish: where the Leud Trebles squeek nothing but Bawdy, and . . 467 WAY WORLD   V.1 200
Bawl (1)
  Mrs Fore: Fie, fie, Miss, how you bawl--besides, I   . . . . . . 249 FOR LOVE   II.1 507
Bawling (1)
  Marwood: reputation worry'd at the Barr by a pack of Bawling . . 467 WAY WORLD   V.1 210
Bay (1)
  Scandal: where the Religion is Folly? You may stand at Bay for a . 219 FOR LOVE   I.1 140
Bays (1)
                I swear, young Bays within, is so dejected, ... 113 OLD BATCH   EPI. 24
Be (1227)
Be'nt (1)
  Ben: to ask you; well, you be'nt Marry'd again, Father, be you? 261 FOR LOVE   III.1 296
Beads (2)
  Valentine: Get me a Coul and Beads, that I may play my part,--   . . 290 FOR LOVE   IV.1 560
  Lady Wish: Beads broken, and a Quilted Night-cap with one Ear. Go, . 462 WAY WORLD   V.1 17
Beams (2)
  Manuel: But that the Beams of Light, are to be stain'd   . . . . 367 M. BRIDE   IV.1 252
  Zara: Their red and angry Beams; as if his Sight   . . . . . 375 M. BRIDE   V.1 94
Bear (34)   see Under-bear
  Bellmour: Flesh and Blood cannot bear it always. . . . . 41 OLD BATCH   I.1 145
  Heartwell: I confess you that are Women's Asses bear greater   . . . 44 OLD BATCH   I.1 272
  Heartwell: and bear my Horns aloft, like one of the supporters of a   45 OLD BATCH   I.1 311
  Lucy: Calling should be expos'd and scandaliz'd--I cannot bear it. 66 OLD BATCH III.1 210
  Fondlewife: yet thy Husband must also bear his part: For thy iniquity   77 OLD BATCH   IV.1 71
  Lady Touch: How does he bear his Disappointment?   . . . . 154 DOUBL DLR III.1 133
  Mellefont: great Beard, like a Russian Bear upon a drift of Snow. You 158 DOUBL DLR III.1 292
  Mellefont: sudden Whirlwind come, tear up Tree and all, and bear . . 187 DOUBL DLR   IV.2 146
  Maskwell: full fruition of my Love, I'll bear the railings of a losing 190 DOUBL DLR   V.1 87
  Lady Touch: I cannot bear it, oh! what Woman can bear to be a Property? 191 DOUBL DLR   V.1 149
  Lady Touch: Too well thou know'st my jealous Soul cou'd never bear . . 198 DOUBL DLR   V.1 399
  Sr Sampson: Bear? that my Cubs might have liv'd upon sucking their . 246 FOR LOVE   II.1 390
  Ben: don't love You so well as to bear that, whatever I did, . 287 FOR LOVE   IV.1 435
  Manuel: Thy senseless Vow appear'd to bear its Date, ... 333 M. BRIDE   I.1 299
  Manuel: Bear hence these Prisoners. Garcia, which is he, ... 335 M. BRIDE   I.1 363
  Almeria: To bear aloft its arch'd and pond'rous Roof, ... 339 M. BRIDE   II.1 61
  Almeria: O take me to thy Arms, and bear me hence, ... 342 M. BRIDE   II.2 84
  Almeria: It is too much! too much to bear and live!   . . . . . 342 M. BRIDE   II.2 105
  Almeria: Of delight, I cannot bear it--I shall   . . . . 342 M. BRIDE   II.2 107
  Almeria: Of Joy, of Bliss--I cannot bear--I must   . . . . . . 342 M. BRIDE   II.2 V107
  Osmyn-Alph: Then, bear me in a Whirl-wind to my Fate;   . . . . . 343 M. BRIDE   II.2 140
  Osmyn-Alph: Is singled out to bleed, and bear the Scourge;   . . . . 350 M. BRIDE   III.1 30

Beauty   (continued)
```
   Tattle:      speak you:--And like me, for the Beauty which I say      .   . 252   FOR LOVE    II.1   618
   Scandal:     manifest the cruel Triumphs of her Beauty; the barbarity    . 276   FOR LOVE    IV.1    25
   Valentine:   gave Beauty, when it grafted Roses on a Briar. You are      . 292   FOR LOVE    IV.1   635
   Valentine:   of Love, and Menial Creature of your Beauty.   .    .   .   . 294   FOR LOVE    IV.1   704
   Sr Sampson:  Lady of your inccmparable Beauty and Merit.--If I    .   .  . 300   FOR LOVE     V.1    97
   Sr Sampson:  Beauty.   .    .    .    .    .    .    .    .    .    .    . 300   FOR LOVE     V.1   101
   Jeremy:      great Beauty and Fortune intc ycur Arms, whom I have    .  . 302   FOR LOVE     V.1   178
   Tattle:      a great Beauty and great Fortune reserved alone for me, by   304   FOR LOVE     V.1   270
   Manuel:      As by transcendent Beauty to attract    .    .    .    .   . 336   M. BRIDE     I.1   421
   Mirabell:    She has Beauty enough to make any Man think so;    .   .   . 399   WAY WORLD    I.1   153
   Witwoud:     t'other of Beauty.    .    .    .    .    .    .    .    .   . 403   WAY WORLD    I.1   321
   Mirabell:    Beauty dies upon the Instant: Fcr Beauty is the Lover's     . 420   WAY WORLD   II.1   393
   Millamant:   one was not handsome. Beauty the Lover's Gift--   .    .   . 420   WAY WORLD   II.1   402
   Millamant:   One no more owes one's Beauty tc a Lover, than   .    .   . 420   WAY WORLD   II.1   409
   Foible:      of her Beauty, that he burns with Impatience to lie at her   423   WAY WORLD   II.1   523
   Millamant:   than a decay'd Beauty, or a discarded Tost;    .    .    .   . 433   WAY WORLD  III.1   324
   Mirabell:    Beauty, and with her my Peace and Quiet; Nay all my      .  . 472   WAY WORLD    V.1   390
                To which no single Beauty must pretend:    .    .    .    . 479   WAY WORLD    EPI.    34
Beauty's  (2)
   Manuel:      In Triumph led; your Beauty's Slave.    .    .    .    .   . 335   M. BRIDE     I.1 V 392
   Manuel:      In pleasing Triumph led; your Beauty's Slave.   .    .    . 335   M. BRIDE     I.1 V392
Beaux  (1)
                Whole Belles Assemblees of Cocquetts and Beaux.   .    .   . 479   WAY WORLD    EPI.    36
Became  (1)
   Mirabell:    Hour less and less disturbance; 'till in a few Days it
                became  .    .    .    .    .    .    .    .    .    .    . 399   WAY WORLD    I.1   170
Because  (57)
                Because, you know, if it be damn'd to day,    .    .    .   . 35   OLD BATCH   PRO.    24
   Bellmour:    Business upon my hands, because it lay too heavy upon his:   41   OLD BATCH   I.1   141
   Sharper:     That's because he always sets out in foul Weather,   .   .  . 42   OLD BATCH   I.1   201
   Sir Joseph:  because I never saw your face before, agad. Ha, ha, ha.     . 48   OLD BATCH  II.1    41
   Fondlewife:  of the Wife of thy Boscm?--Because she is young and    .   . 76   OLD BATCH  IV.1    51
   Fondlewife:  thee marry Isaac?--Because she was beautiful and tempting,   76   OLD BATCH  IV.1    53
   Fondlewife:  and because I was obstinate and doating; so that my   .   . 76   OLD BATCH  IV.1    54
   Setter:      I do suspect as much;--because why, Sir:--   .    .    .   . 99   OLD BATCH   V.1   112
   Sir Joseph:  How now, Bully? What, melancholy because    .    .    .   . 103   OLD BATCH   V.1   260
   Mellefont:   of fcllowing you, because I had scmething to say to you in   127   DOUBL DLR   I.1    14
   Mellefont:   to fcllow you, because I had something to say to you in   . 127   DOUBL DLR   I.1 V 14
   Brisk:       I suppose that's because you Laugh at your own Jests,    . 132   DOUBL DLR   I.1   206
   Careless:    Well, but prithee don't let it be a great while, because    . 134   DOUEL DLR   I.1   265
   Maskwell:    Honesty, because you know I am a Rascal: But I would    .  . 136   DOUBL DLR   I.1   343
   Cynthia:     Because he has not sc much reascn to be fond of    .    .  . 141   DOUBL DLR  II.1   107
   Brisk:       Because my Lord's Title's Froth, I'gad, ha, ha, ha,    .   . 141   DOUBL DLR  II.1   124
   Mellefont:   because it's possible we may lcse; since we have Shuffled   . 142   DOUBL DLR  II.1   160
   Sir Paul:    No, 'tis because I won't be headstrong, because I    .   .  . 144   DOUBL DLR  II.1   230
   Brisk:       because you say the Sun shines every day.   .    .    .   . 164   DOUBL DLR III.1   518
   Cynthia:     My Mind gives me it wont--because we are    .    .    .   . 168   DOUBL DLR  IV.1    11
   Cynthia:     same Game, but forget one another; and 'tis because we   . 168   DOUBL DLR  IV.1    17
   Lady Ply:    make up this Match again, because Mr. Careless said it    . 171   DOUBL DLR  IV.1   153
   Lady Ply:    make up the Match again, because Mr. Careless said it   .  . 171   DOUBL DLR  IV.1 V153
   Sir Paul:    because he has a great veneration for your Ladiship.   .   . 172   DOUEL DLR  IV.1   180
   Lady Froth:  That's because I've no light, but what's by    .    .    .  . 201   DOUBL DLR   V.1   532
   Jeremy:      Diogenes, because he understands Confinement, and liv'd   . 217   FOR LOVE    I.1    30
   Valentine:   hate, for just such another Reason; because they abound in   217   FOR LOVE    I.1    38
   Tattle:      I will; because I have a tender for your Ladiship.   .   .  . 234   FOR LOVE    I.1   668
   Angelica:    only because the Butler had mislaid some of the Apostle's   . 237   FOR LOVE   II.1    89
   Angelica:    only because the Butler had mislaid some of the Apostle  . 237   FOR LOVE   II.1 V 89
   Scandal:     to Night, because he has scme Business to do in a Dream.   . 266   FCR LOVE  III.1   503
   Scandal:     Science, Because, says he, it teaches us to consider the   . 267   FOR LOVE  III.1   538
   Mrs Fore:    Night; because I'll retire to my own Chamber, and think   . 273   FOR LOVE  III.1   743
   Valentine:   Because thou wer't a Monster; cld Boy:--The    .    .    .  . 282   FOR LOVE   IV.1   262
   Angelica:    because I had a Mind to be rid of Mr. Tattle.   .    .    . 293   FOR LOVE   IV.1   686
   Angelica:    because I would have such an one in my Power; but I    .  . 299   FOR LOVE    V.1    75
   Almeria:     It was because thou didst not know Alphonso:    .    .    . 328   M. BRIDE    I.1   101
   Osmyn-Alph:  Because Captivity has robb'd me of a just Revenge.   .    . 336   M. BRIDE    I.1   434
   Almeria:     Tho' 'tis because thou lov'st me. Do not say   .    .    .  . 356   M. BRIDE  III.1   256
   Osmyn-Alph:  Because not knowing Danger. But look forward;    .    .   . 358   M. BRIDE  III.1   342
   Mirabell:    because he has not Wit enough to invent an Evasion.   .    . 404   WAY WORLD   I.1   338
   Witwoud:     You shall see he won't go to 'em because there's no    .   . 405   WAY WORLD   I.1   363
   Petulant:    Ay teste a teste; But not in publick, because I make    .  . 408   WAY WORLD   I.1   500
   Petulant:    Ay tete a tete; But not in publick, because I make   .   . 408   WAY WORLD   I.1 V500
   Marwood:     of Life because they once must leave us; as preposterous,   . 410   WAY WORLD  II.1    14
   Marwood:     as to wish to have been born Old, because we one Day   .  . 410   WAY WORLD  II.1    15
   Marwood:     Because I hate him.    .    .    .    .    .    .    .    . 411   WAY WORLD  II.1    69
   Fainall:     Arms in full Security. But cou'd you think because the   . 414   WAY WORLD  II.1   147
   Foible:      I told her Sir, because I did not know that you might   .  . 424   WAY WORLD  II.1   530
   Sir Wilful:  because when I make it I keep it.    .    .    .    .    .  . 440   WAY WORLD III.1   580
   Marwood:     have Foible provok'd if I cou'd help it,--because you know   443   WAY WORLD III.1   704
   Sir Wilful:  have been encouraged with a Bottle or two, because I'm   . 446   WAY WORLD  IV.1    74
   Millamant:   converse with Wits that I don't like, because they are your  450   WAY WORLD  IV.1   217
   Millamant:   acquaintance; or to be intimate with Fools, because they   . 450   WAY WORLD  IV.1   218
   Lady Wish:   Letter--I wou'd open it in your presence, because I    .  . 460   WAY WORLD  IV.1   570
   Sir Wilful:  frown desperately, because her face is none of her own;   . 471   WAY WORLD   V.1   362
Beckon  (1)
   Mrs Frail:   beckon Mr. Tattle to us.    .    .    .    .    .    .    . 259   FOR LOVE  III.1   221
Become  (13)
   Careless:    the Women have the more Musical Voices, and become    .  . 127   DOUBL DLR   I.1     9
   Careless:    the Women have more Musical Voices, and become    .    .  . 127   DOUBL DLR   I.1 V  9
   Sir Paul:    Brisk Jokes, your Lordships Laugh does so become you,    . 132   DOUBL DLR   I.1   188
   Cynthia:     become more Conspicuous by setting off one another.    .  . 142   DOUBL DLR  II.1   152
   Maskwell:    what was my Pleasure is become my Duty: And I have as   . 155   DOUBL DLR III.1   178
   Sir Paul:    O strange, what will become of me!--I'm so    .    .    .  . 179   DOUBL DLR  IV.1   459
   Nurse:       Amen: Why, what's become of the Child?--Why Miss,    .   . 253   FOR LOVE  III.1     2
   Zara:        Am I become so low, by my Captivity;    .    .    .    .  . 348   M. BRIDE   II.2   361
   Mirabell:    become her; and those Affectations which in another    .  . 399   WAY WORLD   I.1   161
```

62

Before   (continued)

Begging (3)
Lucy: Lord does his Mercers Bill, or a begging Dedication;   .   . 61   OLD BATCH III.1   22
             And some here know I have a begging Face.   .   .   .   .   . 316 FOR LOVE   EPI.   42
Waitwell: month out at knees with begging an Alms,--he shall   .   . 458 WAY WORLD IV.1 522
Begin (16)
Setter: Oh! I begin to smoak ye, thou art some forsaken Abigail,   . 65   OLD BATCH III.1 183
Vainlove: wrong her.--I begin to doubt.   99   OLD BATCH V.1   98
Belinda: Nay, I swear, I begin to pity him, my self.   .   .   .   . 109 OLD BATCH V.2   49
Careless: and begin to think them the better Company.   .   .   .   . 127 DOUBL DLR I.1   4
Careless: begin with her Honour, or her Vertue, her Religion, or   . 157 DOUEL DLR III.1 271
Cynthia: you had not chang'd sides so soon; now I begin to find it. . 172 DOUBL DLR IV.1 177
Brisk: Lord Froth wants a Partner, we can never begin without   . 174 DOUEL DLR IV.1 278
Mellefont: Should I begin to thank or praise thee, I should   .   .   . 194 DOUEL DLR V.1   245
Scandal: Well, begin then: But take notice, if you are so ill a   . 230 FOR LOVE   I.1   536
Miss Prue: Come, I long to have you begin;--must I make Love   .   . 251 FOR LOVE II.1   596
Singer-V: And could again begin to Love and Live, ... 293 FOR LOVE IV.1   653
Valentine: fancy I begin to come to my self.   .   .   .   . 294 FOR LOVE IV.1   698
Jeremy: Books backwards; may be you begin to read at the wrong   . 297 FOR LOVE IV.1   806
Fainall: It may be so. I do now begin to apprehend it.   .   .   . 413 WAY WORLD II.1   132
Fainall: It may be so. I do not now begin to apprehend it.   .   . 413 WAY WORLD II.1 V132
Sir Wilful: you are in good Health, and so forth--To begin with   . 439 WAY WORLD III.1 544
Beginner (1)
             Yet, may be, you'll encourage a beginner;   .   .   .   .   . 113 OLD BATCH EPI.   27
Beginning (1)
Sr Sampson: Beginning.   .   .   .   . 301 FOR LOVE   V.1   156
Begins (8)
Belinda: more, that begins with an, I burn--Or an, I beseech   . 59   OLD BATCH II.2   171
Careless: tho' she begins to tack about; but I made Love a great   . 157 DOUEL DLR III.1 266
Scandal: He begins to Chuckle;--ply him close, or he'l   .   .   . 224 FOR LOVE   I.1   292
Sr Sampson: Obligation--Lock you, as plain as can be, so it begins--   . 281 FOR LOVE IV.1   222
Jeremy: Yes, Madam; He has Intervals: But you see he begins   . 295 FOR LOVE IV.1   747
Zara: But now the Dawn begins, and the slow Hand   .   .   . 360 M. BRIDE III.1   440
Almeria: Oh I am lost--there, Fate begins to wound.   .   .   . 368 M. BRIDE IV.1   299
Witwoud: Now Petulant, all's over, all's well; Gad my head begins   . 453 WAY WORLD IV.1   336
Begon (5)
Heartwell: You've wrack'd my patience; begon, or By--   .   .   .   . 108 OLD BATCH V.2   41
Manuel: Away begon thou feeble Boy, fond Love, ... 374 M. BRIDE   V.1   62
Lady Wish: traytress, that I rais'd from nothing--begon, begon,   . 462 WAY WORLD V.1   3
Lady Wish: begon, go go,--that I took from Washing of old Gause   . 462 WAY WORLD V.1   4
Begone (3)
Fondlewife: Wife! My Dinah! Oh Schechemite! Begone, I say.   .   .   . 90   OLD BATCH IV.4   67
Belinda: let me begone.   .   .   .   . 109 OLD BATCH V.2   60
Foresight: Linnen, d'ee hear, begone when I bid you.   .   .   .   . 306 FOR LOVE   V.1   328
Begot (5)
Sr Sampson: And might not I have chosen whether I would have begot   . 244 FOR LOVE II.1   325
Valentine: Attendants that you begot along with me.   .   .   .   . 244 FOR LOVE II.1   342
Jeremy: begot me too;--Nay, and to tell your Worship   .   .   . 245 FOR LOVE II.1   361
Sr Sampson: married till Fifty; yet they begot Sons and Daughters till   . 298 FOR LOVE   V.1   38
Leonora: My Love of you begot my Grief for him, ... 327 M. BRIDE   I.1   37
Begotten (1)
Sr Sampson: upon the Issue Male of our Two Bodies begotten. Odsbud,   . 300 FOR LOVE   V.1   128
Begs (2)
Sir Joseph: Put up, put up, dear Back, 'tis your Sir Joseph begs, come   . 70   OLD BATCH III.1 341
Scandal: He begs Pardon like a Hangman at an Execution.   .   .   . 225 FOR LOVE   I.1   328
Begun (1)
Lucy: Ay, the Breach of Faith, which he has begun: Thou   .   . 65   OLD BATCH III.1 177
Behalf (1)
Zara: behalf--   .   .   .   . 366 M. BRIDE IV.1   187
Behave (4)
Fondlewife: talk to Cocky and teach her how a Wife ought to behave   . 79   OLD BATCH IV.1 137
Laetitia: Husband ought to behave himself--I shall be glad to   .   . 79   OLD BATCH IV.1 140
Fondlewife: think I don't know how to behave my self in the Employment   . 94   OLD BATCH IV.4 195
Maskwell: How am I to behave my self? You know I am your   .   .   . 136 DOUEL DLR I.1   339
Behaved (1)
Lady Ply: Have I behaved my self with all the decorum, and   .   .   . 145 DOUBL DLR II.1 252
Behaves (2)
Scandal: The World behaves it self, as it used to do on such   .   . 220 FOR LOVE   I.1   159
Scandal: The World behaves it self, as it uses to do on such   .   . 220 FOR LOVE   I.1 V159
Behaviour (7)
             So, standing only on his good Behaviour, ... 35   OLD BATCH PRO.   12
Lucy: Remember to Days behaviour--Let me see you with a   .   . 67   OLD BATCH III.1 232
Belinda: shall I be bound for your good Behaviour for the future?   . 86   OLD BATCH IV.3 135
             Then pray continue this your kind behaviour, ... 316 FOR LOVE   EPI.   43
Manuel: That join'd with his Behaviour, ... 335 M. BRIDE   I.1   379
             But pleads no Merit from his past Behaviour.   .   .   .   . 393 WAY WORLD PRO.   17
Mirabell: one whose Wit and outward fair Behaviour have gain'd a   . 417 WAY WORLD II.1   272
Beheld (6)
Almeria: For when my Lord beheld the Ship pursuing, ... 329 M. BRIDE   I.1   134
Leonora: Or I'm deceiv'd, or I beheld the Glimpse   .   .   .   . 344 M. BRIDE II.2   191
Zara: For saving thee, when I beheld thee first, ... 346 M. BRIDE II.2   275
Zara: When I beheld the Day-break of thy Eyes, ... 347 M. BRIDE II.2   286
Zara: And shall the Wretch, whom yester Sun, beheld   .   .   . 349 M. BRIDE II.2   364
Osmyn-Alph: The Book of Prescience, he beheld this Day;   .   .   .   . 353 M. BRIDE III.1   133
Behind (17)
Sir Joseph: done behind his Back, than what's said--Come wee'l   .   . 70   OLD BATCH III.1 361
             kisses her hand, behind Fondlewife's back.)   95   OLD BATCH IV.4 242
Singer: Prithee Cynthia look behind you, ... 143 DOUBL DLR II.1 186
Mellefont: Aunt: There must be more behind, this is but the first   . 148 DOUBL DLR II.1 377
Mellefont: --Oh that her Lord were but sweating behind this   .   . 183 DOUEL DLR IV.2   2
Mellefont: (Goes behind the Hanging.)   .   .   . 183 DOUEL DLR IV.2   6
Mellefont: (Goes behind the Hangings.)   .   .   . 183 DOUEL DLR IV.2 V 6
Maskwell: here before me; but 'tis fit I should be still behind hand,   . 183 DOUEL DLR IV.2   14
             (Enter Lord Touchwood, Maskwell softly behind him.)   . 185 DOUEL DLR IV.2   89
Cynthia: My Lord, let me entreat you to stand behind this Skreen,   . 197 DOUEL DLR V.1   374
Tattle: Closet, nor run behind a Screen, or under a Table; never   . 230 FOR LOVE   I.1   519
Miss Prue: my self from you behind the Curtains.   .   .   .   .   . 252 FOR LOVE II.1   649

66

Behind (continued)

Valentine:	behind Counters, as if Religion were to be sold in every	.	289	FOR LOVE	IV.1	502
	For when behind our Scenes their Suits are pleading,	.	315	FOR LOVE	EPI.	7
Servant-M:	behind one another, as 'twere in a Country Dance. Ours	.	398	WAY WORLD	I.1	114
Marwood:	Mr. Witwoud, your Brother is not behind	. . .	437	WAY WORLD	III.1	475
Lady Wish:	Chafeing-dish of starv'd Embers and Dining behind a	.	462	WAY WORLD	V.1	6

Behold (25)

Belinda:	to behold.--I undertook the modelling of one of their	. .	84	OLD BATCH	IV.3	33
Almeria:	Leave for a Moment to behold Eternal Bliss,	. . . .	330	M. BRIDE	I.1	179
Almeria:	Behold thou also, and attend my Vow.	. . . .	330	M. BRIDE	I.1	184
Almeria:	My Lord, my Eyes ungratefully behold	. . . .	332	M. BRIDE	I.1	246
Zara:	I might be pleas'd when I behold this Train	. . . .	336	M. BRIDE	I.1	398
Perez:	Yonder, my Lord, behold the Noble Moor.	. . . .	338	M. BRIDE	II.1	16
Leonora:	Behold the Sacred Vault, within whose Womb,	. . .	340	M. BRIDE	II.2	6
Osmyn-Alph:	Let me behold and touch her, and be sure	. . .	341	M. BRIDE	II.2	67
Almeria:	O my strain'd Heart--let me behold thee,	. . .	342	M. BRIDE	II.2	112
Almeria:	O my strain'd Heart--let me again behold thee,	. . .	342	M. BRIDE	II.2	V112
Osmyn-Alph:	Yet I behold her--Now no more.	. . . .	345	M. BRIDE	II.2	214
Osmyn-Alph:	Yet I behold her--yet--And now	. . . .	345	M. BRIDE	II.2	V214
Osmyn-Alph:	Upon my Thought; so, shall you still behold her.	. .	345	M. BRIDE	II.2	216
Osmyn-Alph:	So shall you still behold her--'twill not be.	. . .	345	M. BRIDE	II.2	V216
Zara:	Dare you dispute the King's Command? Behold	. . .	359	M. BRIDE	III.1	232
Manuel:	We will our self behold the Execution.	. . . .	364	M. BRIDE	IV.1	V128
Almeria:	O Earth, behold, I kneel upon thy Bosom,	. . .	368	M. BRIDE	IV.1	273
Almeria:	Behold a damp, cold Hand has drop'd a Dagger;	. . .	371	M. BRIDE	IV.1	390
Almeria:	I shall again behold my dear Alphonso.	. . .	371	M. BRIDE	IV.1	394
Leonora:	Alas, a little farther, and behold	. . . .	381	M. BRIDE	V.2	222
Almeria:	Behold me well; your bloody Hands have err'd,	. . .	382	M. BRIDE	V.2	247
Almeria:	Seest thou not there? behold who prostrate lyes,	. .	382	M. BRIDE	V.2	V264
Fainall:	opportunity to do it at full length. Behold the Original.		401	WAY WORLD	I.1	233
Mirabell:	never shall behold you more--	. . . .	471	WAY WORLD	V.1	375

Beholden (5)

Sir Paul:	I am mightily beholden to Providence--a poor	. . .	161	DOUBL DLR	III.1	V414
Lady Froth:	Oh, infinitely better; I'm extremely beholden	. . .	164	DOUBL DLR	III.1	V510
Sir Paul:	the most beholden to Mr. Careless--As sure as can	. .	172	DOUBL DLR	IV.1	200
Sir Paul:	this Conspiracy; still I am beholden to Providence, if it		179	DOUBL DLR	IV.1	433
Mrs Fore:	We're beholden to Mr. Benjamin for this	. . . .	275	FOR LOVE	III.1	V805

Beholding (5)

Sir Paul:	I am mightily beholding to Providence--a poor		161	DOUBL DLR	III.1	414
Lady Froth:	Oh, infinitely better; I'm extremely beholding	. . .	164	DOUBL DLR	III.1	510
Mrs Fore:	We're beholding to Mr. Benjamin for this	. . .	275	FOR LOVE	III.1	805
	(Beholding Osmyn as they unbind him.)		336	M. BRIDE	I.1	425
Osmyn-Alph:	That ever I should think, beholding thee,	. . . .	355	M. BRIDE	III.1	250

Being (61)

Heartwell:	occasions; till in a little time, being disabled or disarm'd,	. . . .	43	OLD BATCH	I.1	247
Bellmour:	being full of blustring noise and emptiness--	. . .	47	OLD BATCH	I.1	378
Sharper:	'Tis but trying, and being where I am at worst,	. . .	48	OLD BATCH	II.1	16
Araminta:	then we are in great danger of being dull--If my Musick-master	. . . .	58	OLD BATCH	II.2	152
Setter:	uses me as his Attendant; the other (being the better	. .	64	OLD BATCH	III.1	139
Setter:	Man of parts. That is without being politick, diligent, secret,	. . . .	65	OLD BATCH	III.1	150
Setter:	Setter what a treasure is here lost for want of being known.		65	OLD BATCH	III.1	153
Sir Joseph:	hundred Pound for being saved, and d'ee think, an there	.	67	OLD BATCH	III.1	255
Capt Bluff:	out your Trick, and does not care to be put upon; being a	.	69	OLD BATCH	III.1	297
Sir Joseph:	Ay Trick, Sir, and won't be put upon Sir, being a	. .	69	OLD BATCH	III.1	310
Sir Joseph:	I was in most danger of being ravish'd, if you go	. . .	90	OLD BATCH	IV.4	62
Lady Touch:	been a Father to you in your wants, and given you being?	.	135	DOUBL DLR	I.1	310
Maskwell:	convince you, from the necessity of my being firm to you.	.	136	DOUBL DLR	I.1	344
Lady Froth:	Nay, I beg your Pardon; but being Derived	. . . .	139	DOUBL DLR	II.1	38
Maskwell:	What d'e think of my being employ'd in the	. . . .	149	DOUBL DLR	II.1	397
Maskwell:	What d'ye think of my being employ'd in the	. . . .	149	DOUBL DLR	II.1	V397
Mellefont:	suppose when she apprehends being with Child, he never	. .	158	DOUBL DLR	III.1	286
Mellefont:	secures them from blushing, and being out of Countenance,	.	158	DOUBL DLR	III.1	312
Mellefont:	and next to being in the dark, or alone, they are most truly	158	DOUBL DLR	III.1	313
Lady Ply:	might be supposed to be capable of being qualified to make	.	159	DOUBL DLR	III.1	337
Lady Ply:	to conferr upon one that is wholly incapable of being	. .	159	DOUBL DLR	III.1	339
Brisk:	Incomparable, let me perish!--but then being an Heroick	.	163	DOUBL DLR	III.1	505
Sir Paul:	are a better Christian than to think of being a Nun; he?	.	174	DOUBL DLR	IV.1	255
Sir Paul:	which lie all in your Ladishops Breast, and being a well	.	180	DOUBL DLR	IV.1	479
Maskwell:	Leave it to my care; that shall be so far from being	. .	193	DOUBL DLR	V.1	210
Maskwell:	back Stairs, and so we may slip down without being	. .	194	DOUBL DLR	V.1	240
	And dare not bite, for fear of being bit.	. . .	214	FOR LOVE	PRO.	36
Jeremy:	Treats and your Balls; your being in Love with a Lady,	.	217	FOR LOVE	I.1	44
Angelica:	by going abroad; nor secure you from being one, by	. .	237	FOR LOVE	II.1	62
Mrs Fore:	they're in perpetual fear of being seen and censur'd?--	.	247	FOR LOVE	II.1	433
Mrs Fore:	fond of it, as of being first in the Fashion, or of seeing a new	. . . .	250	FOR LOVE	II.1	549
Tattle:	Church, once, an Enquiry being made, who I was, it was	.	257	FOR LOVE	III.1	163
Angelica:	love, I can't help it; no more than he can help his being a		278	FOR LOVE	IV.1	88
Angelica:	Man, or I my being a Woman; or no more than I can help	.	278	FOR LOVE	IV.1	89
Jeremy:	her being here.	. . . .	278	FOR LOVE	IV.1	101
Mrs Frail:	at being a Husband with that stubborn and disobedient	.	286	FOR LOVE	IV.1	408
Mrs Frail:	nothing but his being my Husband could have made me	.	310	FOR LOVE	V.1	473
Almeria:	We put to Sea; but being betray'd by some	. . . .	329	M. BRIDE	I.1	122
Osmyn-Alph:	Have cast me down to this low Being: or,	. . . .	354	M. BRIDE	III.1	176
Osmyn-Alph:	Or Being as you please, such I will think it.	. . .	354	M. BRIDE	III.1	184
Gonsalez:	That being sav'd upon the Coast of Africk,	. . . .	363	M. BRIDE	IV.1	84
Almeria:	And torn, rather than have reveal'd thy Being.	. . .	369	M. BRIDE	IV.1	313
Selim:	If I have fail'd in what, as being a Man,	. . . .	375	M. BRIDE	V.1	117
Zara:	My Errand, being chang'd from Life to Death,	. . . .	379	M. BRIDE	V.2	145
Zara:	And Purpose, being chang'd from Life to Death,	. . .	379	M. BRIDE	V.2	V145
Mirabell:	habitual to me, to remember 'em without being displeas'd.		399	WAY WORLD	I.1	171
Fainall:	with a little Loss, than to be quite eaten up, with being		400	WAY WORLD	I.1	208

Being   (continued)

		PAGE	TITLE	ACT.SC	LINE
Mirabell:	other will be rotten without ever being ripe at all.	401	WAY WORLD	I.1	217
Witwoud:	No, no, his being positive is an Incentive to Argument,	403	WAY WORLD	I.1	323
Witwoud:	being in Embrio; and if it shou'd come to Life; poor	408	WAY WORLD	I.1	488
Witwoud:	being there.	409	WAY WORLD	I.1	511
Mrs Fain:	another by being seen to walk with his Wife. This way Mr.	412	WAY WORLD	II.1	106
Millamant:	want a being.	421	WAY WORLD	II.1	412
Lady Wish:	O he's in less Danger of being spoil'd by his	431	WAY WORLD	III.1	262
Petulant:	Why shou'd a Man be ever the further from being	436	WAY WORLD	III.1	428
Petulant:	Why shou'd a Man be any further from being	436	WAY WORLD	III.1	V428
Petulant:	married tho' he can't Read, any more than he is from being	436	WAY WORLD	III.1	429
Petulant:	married tho' he can't read, than he is from being	436	WAY WORLD	III.1	V429
Fainall:	Cuckoldom be a discredit, being deriv'd from so	443	WAY WORLD	III.1	693
Mrs Fain:	Letter?--My Mother do's not suspect my being in the	464	WAY WORLD	V.1	75
Lady Wish:	ruine? Ungrateful Wretch! dost thou not owe thy being,	473	WAY WORLD	V.1	446

Bel air (1)

Lady Froth:	bel air or Brillant of Mr. Brisk; the Solemnity, yet	139	DOUBL DLR	II.1	V 49

Belief (7)

Araminta:	to a wrong Belief.--Unworthy, and ungrateful! Be	87	OLD BATCH	IV.3	173
Mellefont:	extravagant belief?	149	DOUBL DLR	II.1	411
Maskwell:	that letter, told me the Secrets of her heart. At length we	149	DOUBL DLR	II.1	426
Lady Touch:	and sooth me to a fond belief of all your fictions.	157	DOUBL DLR	V.1	380
Selim:	The King, in full belief of all you told him,	361	M. BRIDE	IV.1	12
Gonsalez:	Some ready of Belief, have rais'd this Rumour:	363	M. BRIDE	IV.1	83
Fainall:	Convert to endless Jealousie; or if they have belief, let it	444	WAY WORLD	III.1	718

Believ'd (11)

Bellmour:	She still is Vertuous, if she's so believ'd.	96	OLD BATCH	IV.4	274
Maskwell:	And why are Friends and Lovers Oaths believ'd;	150	DOUBL DLR	II.1	466
Lord Touch:	contrary too, before it had been believ'd--	151	DOUBL DLR	III.1	20
Maskwell:	(aside). That I believ'd; 'twas well I left the private.	184	DOUBL DLR	IV.2	30
Cynthia:	what you ne're could have believ'd from my suspicions.	197	DOUBL DLR	V.1	376
Mellefont:	Good Heavens! how I believ'd and Lov'd this	202	DOUBL DLR	V.1	573
Scandal:	not to be believ'd; and refuses the reputation of a Ladies	226	FOR LOVE	I.1	376
Angelica:	have believ'd it--Is this your Secresie?	258	FOR LOVE	III.1	184
Scandal:	not to be believ'd. Valentine is disturb'd, what can be the	268	FOR LOVE	III.1	547
Scandal:	This I have heard of before, but never believ'd. I	284	FOR LOVE	IV.1	333
Valentine:	should tell, yet she is not to be believ'd.	292	FOR LOVE	IV.1	646

Believe (109)

Bellmour:	More than they believe--Or understand.	37	OLD BATCH	I.1	16
Bellmour:	know and believe more than really we do. You read of but	37	OLD BATCH	I.1	20
Bellmour:	foppish and affected, but in my Conscience I believe the	41	OLD BATCH	I.1	167
Bellmour:	though I believe he was heartily frightned, for as soon as	46	OLD BATCH	I.1	362
Sir Joseph:	damn'd angry Fellow--I believe I had better remember	48	OLD BATCH	II.1	44
Sharper:	Hannibal I believe you mean Sir Joseph.	52	OLD BATCH	II.1	177
Araminta:	I can't tell, Cousin, I believe we are equally concern'd:	57	OLD BATCH	II.2	85
Araminta:	In my Conscience I believe you.	57	OLD BATCH	II.2	112
Capt Bluff:	By these Hilts I believe he frightned you into this	68	OLD BATCH	III.1	268
Capt Bluff:	Composition; I believe you gave it him out of fear, pure	68	OLD BATCH	III.1	269
Sir Joseph:	mischief done, that's flat. And yet I believe if you had been	68	OLD BATCH	III.1	276
Silvia:	I dare not speak till I believe you, and indeed I'm	72	OLD BATCH	III.2	53
Silvia:	afraid to believe you yet.	72	OLD BATCH	III.2	54
Heartwell:	believe it: Nay, thou shalt think so thy self--Only let me	74	OLD BATCH	III.2	122
Laetitia:	Nay, don't swear if you'd have me believe you; but	82	OLD BATCH	IV.2	69
Belinda:	Very courtly.--I believe, Mr. Vainlove has not	86	OLD BATCH	IV.3	129
Vainlove:	Did I dream? Or do I dream? Shall I believe my	88	OLD BATCH	IV.3	175
Fondlewife:	believe speaks truth.	94	OLD BATCH	IV.4	180
Fondlewife:	inclining to believe every word you say.	94	OLD BATCH	IV.4	186
Fondlewife:	will believe it or no.	95	OLD BATCH	IV.4	218
Bellmour:	That you may, Faith, and I hope you won't believe	95	OLD BATCH	IV.4	219
Fondlewife:	How! Would not you have me believe you, say	95	OLD BATCH	IV.4	222
Fondlewife:	Oh, that I could believe thee!	96	OLD BATCH	IV.4	256
Fondlewife:	Heh. How? No, stay, stay, I will believe thee, I	96	OLD BATCH	IV.4	259
Fondlewife:	Here, here, I do believe thee.--I won't	96	OLD BATCH	IV.4	262
Fondlewife:	believe my own Eyes.	96	OLD BATCH	IV.4	263
Fondlewife:	Well, well, Sir, as long as I believe it, 'tis well	96	OLD BATCH	IV.4	267
Fondlewife:	my Dear. Nay, I will believe thee, I do, Ifeck.	96	OLD BATCH	IV.4	270
Lucy:	Think: That I shou'd not believe my Eyes, and that	97	OLD BATCH	V.1	32
Lucy:	Nay, Mr. Bellmour: O Lard! I believe you are a Parson	97	OLD BATCH	V.1	37
Sharper:	No, Faith; I believe not.--Few Women, but	104	OLD BATCH	V.1	303
Lady Touch:	likes him so well, that she will believe it faster than I can	138	DOUBL DLR	I.1	413
Lady Froth:	Mellefont believe you Love him?	139	DOUBL DLR	II.1	42
Cynthia:	'Tis my Interest to believe he will, my Lord.	141	DOUBL DLR	II.1	101
Cynthia:	I believe he'll Love me better.	141	DOUBL DLR	II.1	104
Lady Froth:	Yes, I believe I have.--Mr. Brisk, come will	142	DOUBL DLR	II.1	143
Lord Touch:	I don't believe it true; he has better Principles	150	DOUBL DLR	III.1	4
Lord Touch:	Yes, I believe I know some that have been	151	DOUBL DLR	III.1	13
Lady Touch:	I am willing to believe as favourably of my Nephew as I	151	DOUBL DLR	III.1	24
Lady Touch:	How? Don't you believe that, say you, my	151	DOUBL DLR	III.1	27
Lord Touch:	You believe it then?	151	DOUBL DLR	III.1	33
Lady Touch:	to dissemble: I own it to you; in short I do believe it, nay,	151	DOUBL DLR	III.1	40
Lady Touch:	and can believe any thing worse, if it were laid to his charge	151	DOUBL DLR	III.1	41
Maskwell:	me to watch you. I believe he will hardly be able to	154	DOUBL DLR	III.1	138
Sir Paul:	You'll scarcely believe me, when I shall tell you why	161	DOUBL DLR	III.1	430
Sir Paul:	You'll scarcely believe me, when I shall tell you--	161	DOUBL DLR	III.1	V430
Sir Paul:	true--she's so very nice, that I don't believe she would	162	DOUBL DLR	III.1	432
Mellefont:	Hum, 'gad I believe there's something in't;--	168	DOUBL DLR	IV.1	19
Cynthia:	(aside). And for your Ladiship too, I believe, or else	172	DOUBL DLR	IV.1	176
Brisk:	Deuce take me I believe you intend to Marry your	174	DOUBL DLR	IV.1	271
Careless:	tho' by this Light I believe her Virtue is impregnable.	180	DOUBL DLR	IV.1	503
Mellefont:	May I believe this true?	185	DOUBL DLR	IV.2	79
Maskwell:	so to be; By Heaven I believe you can controul her power,	187	DOUBL DLR	V.1	3
Lady Touch:	yonders my Lord, I believe he's coming to find you, I'le	188	DOUBL DLR	V.1	7

Believe (continued)

Speaker	Text	PAGE	TITLE	ACT.SC	LINE
Maskwell:	his Case is desperate, and I believe he'll yield to any	199	DOUBL DLR	V.1	449
Scandal:	what they mean: But you have little reason to believe that	225	FOR LOVE	I.1	350
Valentine:	Nay faith, I'm apt to believe him--Except	227	FOR LOVE	I.1	414
Tattle:	Why then, as I hope to be sav'd, I believe a Woman	228	FOR LOVE	I.1	473
Scandal:	believe him.	232	FOR LOVE	I.1	607
Mrs Frail:	--I can't believe a word he says.	233	FOR LOVE	I.1	621
Foresight:	I believe you lie, Sir.	235	FOR LOVE	II.1	9
Sr Sampson:	That's more than I know, Sir, and I believe not.	244	FOR LOVE	II.1	316
Jeremy:	another truth, I believe you did, for I find I was born with	245	FOR LOVE	II.1	362
Mrs Frail:	O hang you; who'll believe you?--You'd be	250	FOR LOVE	II.1	554
Tattle:	Why you must say no, or you believe not, or you	251	FOR LOVE	II.1	607
Tattle:	Hum--Yes--But you must believe I speak	252	FOR LOVE	II.1	627
Miss Prue:	you should believe that; and I'll speak truth, tho' one should	264	FOR LOVE	III.1	396
Scandal:	Yes, Faith, I believe some Women are Vertuous too;	271	FOR LOVE	III.1	669
Scandal:	but 'tis as I believe some Men are Valiant, thro' fear--For	271	FOR LOVE	III.1	670
Mrs Fore:	Entertainment. I believe it's late.	275	FOR LOVE	III.1	806
Jeremy:	I hear a Coach stop; if it should be she, Sir, I believe he	276	FOR LOVE	IV.1	16
Sr Sampson:	Oons, I won't believe it; let me see him, Sir	279	FOR LOVE	IV.1	145
Sr Sampson:	shake--I believe thou can'st write, Val: Ha, boy? Thou	281	FOR LOVE	IV.1	207
Sr Sampson:	thine? I believe I can read it farther off yet--let me see.	281	FOR LOVE	IV.1	226
Sr Sampson:	Manners, that don't believe a Syllable in the Sky and	283	FOR LOVE	IV.1	287
Scandal:	I'm apt to believe there is something mysterious in his	285	FOR LOVE	IV.1	344
Ben:	All mad, I think--Flesh, I believe all the Calentures of	285	FOR LOVE	IV.1	356
Ben:	you too well, by sad experience;--I believe he that marries	287	FOR LOVE	IV.1	438
Ben:	you will go to Sea in a Hen-peck'd Frigat.--I believe that,	287	FOR LOVE	IV.1	439
Scandal:	I believe it is a Spring Tide.	289	FOR LOVE	IV.1	530
Angelica:	Mad as Valentine, I'll believe you love me, and the maddest	291	FOR LOVE	IV.1	587
Angelica:	by over acting Sobriety; I was half inclining to believe	296	FOR LOVE	IV.1	765
Sr Sampson:	(aside). Odsbud I believe she likes me--Ah,	299	FOR LOVE	V.1	93
Scandal:	'S'death it's a Jest. I can't believe it.	307	FOR LOVE	V.1	367
Ben:	believe it or no. What I say is true; d'ee see, they are	307	FOR LOVE	V.1	369
Ben:	Lawyer, I believe there's many a Cranny and Leak unstopt	309	FOR LOVE	V.1	431
Ben:	Pump to your Bosom, I believe we shou'd discover a foul	309	FOR LOVE	V.1	433
Ben:	believe the Devil wou'd not venture aboard o' your	309	FOR LOVE	V.1	435
Angelica:	But I believe Mr. Tattle meant the Favour to me, I	309	FOR LOVE	V.1	455
Tattle:	reason to hate her neither; but I believe I shall lead her a	309	FOR LOVE	V.1	467
Tattle:	wish we could keep it secret, why I don't believe any of	310	FOR LOVE	V.1	476
Tattle:	Easie! Pox on't, I don't believe I shall sleep to Night.	310	FOR LOVE	V.1	483
Sr Sampson:	believe what I say.	311	FOR LOVE	V.1	523
	And we, who know no better, must believe 'em.	315	FOR LOVE	EPI.	14
Leonora:	Believe me, Madam, I lament Anselmo,	326	M. BRIDE	I.1	20
Gonsalez:	But Tears of Joy. Believe me, Sir, to see you thus, has fill'd	332	M. BRIDE	I.1	V273
Osmyn-Alph:	You wrong me, beauteous Zara, to believe	354	M. BRIDE	III.1	169
Zara:	Can'st thou forgive me then! wilt thou believe	354	M. BRIDE	III.1	178
Almeria:	Confirm this Miracle! can I believe	383	M. BRIDE	V.2	292
Mirabell:	I confess this is something extraordinary--I believe	405	WAY WORLD	I.1	378
Marwood:	No; but I'd make him believe I did, and that's	411	WAY WORLD	II.1	58
Fainall:	--I believe you; I'm convinc'd I've done you wrong;	416	WAY WORLD	II.1	242
Mrs Fain:	I believe my Lady will do any thing to get a Husband; and	418	WAY WORLD	II.1	308
Millamant:	--No, now I think on't I'm pleas'd--For I believe	420	WAY WORLD	II.1	379
Mirabell:	That I believe.	423	WAY WORLD	II.1	518
Foible:	to him,--besides, I believe Madam Marwood watches	430	WAY WORLD	III.1	216
Fainall:	But let the Lover still believe. Or if he doubt, let it be only	444	WAY WORLD	III.1	715
Sir Wilful:	Infidels, and believe not in the Grape. Your Mahometan,	456	WAY WORLD	IV.1	443
Lady Wish:	friend, I can't believe it, No, no; as she says, let him prove	467	WAY WORLD	V.1	206

Belike (5)

Speaker	Text	PAGE	TITLE	ACT.SC	LINE
Sir Wilful:	in our Parts, down in Shropshire--Why then belike	437	WAY WORLD	III.1	449
Sir Wilful:	Why then belike thou dost not know thy Lady,	437	WAY WORLD	III.1	459
Sir Wilful:	Belike I may Madam. I may chance to sail upon	440	WAY WORLD	III.1	567
Sir Wilful:	Tony, belike, I may'nt call him Brother for fear of offence.	441	WAY WORLD	III.1	605
Sir Wilful:	Impatient? Why then belike it won't stay, 'till	441	WAY WORLD	III.1	616

Belinda (15)

Speaker	Text	PAGE	TITLE	ACT.SC	LINE
Bellmour:	damnably in Love; I'm so uneasie for not seeing Belinda	40	OLD BATCH	I.1	133
Bellmour:	damnably in Love; I'm so uneasie for not having seen Belinda	40	OLD BATCH	I.1	V133
Sharper:	What, is Belinda cruel, that you are so thoughtful?	41	OLD BATCH	I.1	150
	(Scene Changes to Lodgings Enter Araminta, Belinda.)	54	OLD BATCH	II.2	
	(Araminta, Belinda, Betty waiting, in Araminta's Apartment)	54	OLD BATCH	II.2	V
Araminta:	Belinda?	57	OLD BATCH	II.2	110
Bellmour:	make Signs. (Addresses Belinda in dumb shew.)	60	OLD BATCH	II.2	211
	Araminta and Belinda meeting.)	83	OLD BATCH	IV.3	
	(To Belinda.)	85	OLD BATCH	IV.3	85
	(Exeunt Belinda and Sharper.)	87	OLD BATCH	IV.3	151
	(Enter Belinda, Sharper.)	88	OLD BATCH	IV.3	194
	(Enter Bellmour, Belinda, Araminta and Vainlove.)	106	OLD BATCH	V.1	355
Bellmour:	(To Belinda.)	107	OLD BATCH	V.1	397
	(Enter Bellmour, Belinda, Vainlove, Araminta.)	108	OLD BATCH	V.2	16
	(Araminta and Belinda unmask.)	110	OLD BATCH	V.2	117

Belinda's (1)

Speaker	Text	PAGE	TITLE	ACT.SC	LINE
Bellmour:	Belinda's Pardon--	41	OLD BATCH	I.1	160

Bell (2)   see 'Passing-Bell

Speaker	Text	PAGE	TITLE	ACT.SC	LINE
Fondlewife:	of Bell and the Dragon.--Bless us! Ravish my	90	OLD BATCH	IV.4	66
Almeria:	Was it the doleful Bell, toling for Death?	370	M. BRIDE	IV.1	385

Belle-air (1)

Speaker	Text	PAGE	TITLE	ACT.SC	LINE
Lady Proth:	Belle-air or Brillant of Mr. Brisk; the Solemnity, yet	139	DOUBL DLR	II.1	49

Belles Assemblees (1)

Speaker	Text	PAGE	TITLE	ACT.SC	LINE
	Whole Belles Assemblees of Cocquetts and Beaux.	479	WAY WORLD	EPI.	36

Bellmour (37)

Speaker	Text	PAGE	TITLE	ACT.SC	LINE
	(The Street. Bellmour and Vainlove Meeting)	37	OLD BATCH	I.1	
Vainlove:	Bellmour, good Morrow--Why truth on't is, these	37	OLD BATCH	I.1	5
Sharper:	You Bellmour are bound in gratitude to stickle for	43	OLD BATCH	I.1	218
Sharper:	This must be Bellmour he means--ha! I have a	48	OLD BATCH	II.1	11

Bend   (continued)

| Almeria: | I bend to Heav'n with Thanks. . . . . | 332 | M. BRIDE | I.1 V251 |
| Almeria: | And bend my flowing Eyes, to stream upon   . . . . . | 368 | M. BRIDE | IV.1 274 |

Bended (2)

| Almeria: | For bended Knees, returning folding Arms, ... | 369 | M. BRIDE | IV.1 325 |
| Zara: | To hide, the rustling Leaves, and bended Grass   . . . | 375 | M. BRIDE | V.1 109 |

Bending (2)

| Almeria: | And long oppress'd with Woes and bending Cares, . . . | 340 | M. BRIDE | II.2 18 |
| Leonora: | And bending this way.   . . . . | 344 | M. BRIDE | II.2 193 |

Beneath (14)

Careless:	out a Wretched Life, and breath my Soul beneath your . .	170	DOUBL DLR	IV.1 100
Lady Touch:	Ground, be buried quick beneath it, e're I be consenting to	186	DOUBL DLR	IV.2 99
Lady Touch:	Ground, be buried quick beneath it, e're I'll be			
	consenting to	186	DOUBL DLR	IV.2 V 99
Maskwell:	weak, and shrinks beneath the weight, and cannot rise to	189	DOUBL DLR	V.1 79
Mrs Frail:	that lurk beneath that faithless smiling face.	286	FOR LOVE	IV.1 395
Gonsalez:	Which groan beneath the Weight of Moorish Wealth. . . .	331	M. BRIDE	I.1 228
Zara:	Beneath Mock-Praises, and dissembled State.	336	M. BRIDE	I.1 402
Leonora:	Beneath, are still wide stretch'd upon their Hinge, . .	340	M. BRIDE	II.2 12
Almeria:	To Seas beneath, where thou so long hast dwelt. . . .	342	M. BRIDE	II.2 86
Osmyn-Alph:	That tumbling on its Prop, crush'd all beneath, ...	347	M. BRIDE	II.2 310
Osmyn-Alph:	Would soar, and stoop at Victory beneath.	352	M. BRIDE	III.1 91
Manuel:	To cast beneath your Feet the Crown you've sav'd, . .	365	M. BRIDE	IV.1 159
Manuel:	How's this? my mortal Foe beneath my Roof!	373	M. BRIDE	V.1 33
Gonsalez:	And fall beneath the Hand of my own Son.	378	M. BRIDE	V.2 72

Benefactor (1)

| Bellmour: | Thou'rt a lucky Rogue; there's your Benefactor, ... | 68 | OLD BATCH | III.1 281 |

Benefactors (1)

| Maskwell: | Duty to Kings, Piety to Parents, Gratitude to Benefactors, | 150 | DOUBL DLR | II.1 446 |

Benefit (2)

| Sr Sampson: | damn'd Tyburn face, without the benefit o' the Clergy. . | 243 | FOR LOVE | II.1 307 |
| Valentine: | I shall receive no Benefit from the Opinion: For   . . | 254 | FOR LOVE | III.1 39 |

Benefits (3)

Sir Paul:	of using the common benefits of Nature?	178	DOUBL DLR	IV.1 V426
Osmyn-Alph:	Can I repay, as you require, such Benefits.	355	M. BRIDE	III.1 214
Lady Wish:	benefits that I have receiv'd from your goodness? To you I	465	WAY WORLD	V.1 126

Benign (1)

| Foresight: | here;--Methinks I look with a serene and benign   . . | 269 | FOR LOVE | III.1 601 |

Benjamin (10)

Mrs Frail:	Brother Benjamin is landed. And my Brother Foresight's	231	FOR LOVE	I.1 567
Sr Sampson:	as my Son Benjamin is arriv'd, he is to make over to him	240	FOR LOVE	II.1 182
Sr Sampson:	My Son, Sir; what Son, Sir? My Son Benjamin, ...	242	FOR LOVE	II.1 265
Angelica:	I swear, Mr. Benjamin is the verriest Wag in nature; .	262	FOR LOVE	III.1 336
Mrs Fore:	she cry?--Mr. Benjamin, what have you done to her? . .	265	FOR LOVE	III.1 440
Mrs Frail:	down into the Parlour, and I'll carry Mr. Benjamin into	265	FOR LOVE	III.1 448
Mrs Fore:	We're beholding to Mr. Benjamin for this	275	FOR LOVE	III.1 805
Mrs Fore:	We're beholden to Mr. Benjamin for this	275	FOR LOVE	III.1 V805
Mrs Frail:	Mr. Benjamin in Choler!	285	FOR LOVE	IV.1 358
Mrs Fore:	Here's Mr. Benjamin, he can tell us if his Father . .	306	FOR LOVE	V.1 339

Bent (5)

	Our Christian Cuckolds are more bent to pity;	125	DOUBL DLR	PRO. 27
Mellefont:	Let him alone, Brisk, he is obstinately bent not to . .	134	DOUBL DLR	I.1 280
Mellefont:	Soul, thou art villainously bent to discover all to me, .	156	DOUBL DLR	III.1 205
Valentine:	am not violently bent upon the Trade.--	220	FOR LOVE	I.1 153
Gonsalez:	They who are fled have that way bent their course. . .	363	M. BRIDE	IV.1 80

Benumm (1)

| Zara: | Benumm the living Faculties, and give   . . . . . . | 375 | M. BRIDE | V.1 133 |

Beperriwig'd (1)

| Sir Wilful: | thee, thou art so Becravated, and Beperriwig'd--   . . | 439 | WAY WORLD | III.1 518 |

Bepiss (1)

| Brisk: | holding your sides, and Laughing as if you would bepiss   . | 134 | DOUBL DLR | I.1 255 |

Berry (0)   see Drap-du-berry

Beseech (9)

Belinda:	more, that begins with an, I burn--Or an, I beseech . .	59	OLD BATCH	II.2 171
Lord Froth:	O, for the Universe, not a drop more I beseech . . .	134	DOUBL DLR	I.1 288
Careless:	O Lord, I beseech you, Madam, don't--	160	DOUBL DLR	III.1 366
Lady Ply:	O rise I beseech you, say no more till you rise . . .	170	DOUBL DLR	IV.1 107
Brisk:	O Lord I Madam! I beseech your Ladyship--	176	DOUBL DLR	IV.1 321
Sir Paul:	Hold, stay, I beseech your Ladiship--I'm so	179	DOUBL DLR	IV.1 465
Sir Paul:	this Letter--Nay hear me, I beseech your Ladiship: . .	180	DOUBL DLR	IV.1 469
Mellefont:	Nay, I beseech you rise.	186	DOUBL DLR	IV.2 97
Sr Sampson:	Sir, how, I beseech you, what were you pleas'd . . .	243	FOR LOVE	II.1 285

Beside (1)

| Millamant: | Complaisance for all the World beside. I swear, I never   . | 433 | WAY WORLD | III.1 337 |

Besides (27)

Heartwell:	No, besides my Business, I see a Fool coming this . .	46	OLD BATCH	I.1 335
Musician:	Nothing's new besides our Faces, ...	60	OLD BATCH	II.2 201
Bellmour:	of Lying and Swearing at the Years end. Besides, I have	60	OLD BATCH	II.2 222
Setter:	Pounds, and all her Rigging; besides what lies conceal'd .	102	OLD BATCH	V.1 224
Mellefont:	to be allarm'd. None besides you, and Maskwell, are . .	129	DOUBL DLR	I.1 84
Sir Paul:	It concerns me, and only me;--besides, I'm not to . .	144	DOUBL DLR	II.1 220
Lady Touch:	disadvantage; besides, I find, my Lord, you are prepared	151	DOUBL DLR	III.1 36
Brisk:	sounds great; besides your Ladyship's Coach-man having a	163	DOUBL DLR	III.1 507
Lady Ply:	him; and besides, I have been inform'd by Mr. Careless, .	171	DOUBL DLR	IV.1 164
Maskwell:	O my Lord! consider that is hard: besides, time . . .	182	DOUBL DLR	IV.1 565
Scandal:	besides, Angelica has a great Fortune of her own; and great	225	FOR LOVE	I.1 353
Mrs Fore:	Besides, it wou'd not only reflect upon you, Sister, but me.	247	FOR LOVE	II.1 434
Mrs Fore:	Fie, fie, Miss, how you bawl--besides, I	249	FOR LOVE	II.1 507
Tattle:	Lie--Besides, you are a Woman, you must never . . .	251	FOR LOVE	II.1 611
Valentine:	Sphere: when he Rises I must set--Besides, if I shou'd stay,	259	FOR LOVE	III.1 224
Angelica:	What signifie a Madman's Desires? Besides, 'twou'd . .	277	FOR LOVE	IV.1 79
Mrs Fore:	besides he hates both you and me.--But I have a . . .	288	FOR LOVE	IV.1 463
Servant-M:	dispatch, besides, the Parson growing hoarse, we were .	398	WAY WORLD	I.1 116
Fainall:	Faith, I am not Jealous. Besides, most who are engag'd .	399	WAY WORLD	I.1 141
Petulant:	stay'd longer--Besides they never mind him; they say .	408	WAY WORLD	I.1 497
Millamant:	I please my self--Besides sometimes to	421	WAY WORLD	II.1 441

Better   (continued)
Bellmour:	better quality.	.	45	OLD BATCH	I.1	301
Sir Joseph:	damn'd angry Fellow--I believe I had better remember	. .	48	OLD BATCH	II.1	44
Sharper:	better root in your shallow memory.	.	48	OLD BATCH	II.1	49
Sharper:	came half despairing to recover; but thanks to my better	.	49	OLD BATCH	II.1	83
Sir Joseph:	that's a better Jest than tother. 'Tis a sign you and I					
	ha'n't	.	50	OLD BATCH	II.1	116
Bellmour:	Talk to your self--You had better let me speak; for if my	.	59	OLD BATCH	II.2	177
Araminta:	it once again--You may like it better at second . . .	.	60	OLD BATCH	II.2	208
Setter:	uses me as his Attendant; the other (being the better	.	64	OLD BATCH	III.1	139
Sir Joseph:	Lord-Harry. I know better things than to be run through	.	67	OLD BATCH	III.1	253
Heartwell:	may get the better of my self.	.	74	OLD BATCH	III.2	130
Fondlewife:	I profess I do love thee better, than 500 Pound-- . . .	.	78	OLD BATCH	IV.1	129
Fondlewife:	impudence. Look at him a little better; he is more modest,	.	93	OLD BATCH	IV.4	154
Fondlewife:	the better for't.--I shall, Ifeck--What, dost	.	94	OLD BATCH	IV.4	194
Sharper:	real Fanatick can look better pleas'd after a successful	.	100	OLD BATCH	V.1	133
Bellmour:	Pshaw, No: I have a better Opinion of thy Wit. . . .	.	100	OLD BATCH	V.1	142
Vainlove:	sell you freedom better cheap.	.	109	OLD BATCH	V.2	80
Sharper:	Sir Joseph, you had better have pre-engag'd this . . .	.	111	OLD BATCH	V.2	120
Sir Joseph:	are like to be better acquainted.	.	111	OLD BATCH	V.2	132
Vainlove:	--That deserves a Fool with a better Title.-- . . .	.	111	OLD BATCH	V.2	137
Araminta:	We had better take the Advantage of a little of our .	.	112	OLD BATCH	V.2	173
Careless:	and begin to think them the better Company.	.	127	DOUBL DLR	I.1	4
Careless:	Nonsence better.	.	127	DOUBL DLR	I.1	10
Brisk:	better, you or I. Pox, Man, when I say you spoil Company	.	128	DOUBL DLR	I.1	28
Brisk:	better, you or I. Pshaw, Man, when I say you spoil Company	.	128	DOUBL DLR	I.1 V	28
Sir Paul:	Were you, Son? Gadsbud much better as it is-- . . .	.	131	DOUBL DLR	I.1	177
Cynthia:	I believe he'll Love me better.	.	141	DCUEL DLR	II.1	104
Lord Touch:	I don't believe it true; he has better Principles . .	.	150	DOUBL DLR	III.1	4
Lord Touch:	of an undesigning person, the better to bespeak his security	151	DOUBL DLR	III.1	9
Lady Touch:	Whatever it was, 'tis past: And that is better . . .	.	152	DOUBL DLR	III.1	54
Mellefont:	Let me adore thee, my better Genius! By Heav'n I . .	.	157	DOUBL DLR	III.1	257
Brisk:	Poem, had not you better call him a Charioteer? Charioteer	.	163	DOUBL DLR	III.1	506
Lady Froth:	Oh, infinitely better; I'm extremely beholding . . .	.	164	DOUBL DLR	III.1	510
Lady Froth:	Oh, infinitely better; I'm extremely beholden . . .	.	164	DOUBL DLR	III.1 V	510
Lady Froth:	Ay, Charioteer does better.	.	164	DOUBL DLR	III.1	537
Cynthia:	Why should I call 'em Fools? The World thinks better of	.	167	DOUBL DLR	III.1	626
Sir Paul:	are a better Christian than to think of being a Nun; he?	.	174	DOUBL DLR	IV.1	255
Sir Paul:	are a better Christian than to think of living a Nun; he?	.	174	DOUBL DLR	IV.1 V	255
Sir Paul:	here made? Why, this is better and more Miraculous than	.	180	DOUBL DLR	IV.1	505
Maskwell:	and what is yet better, I have served a worthy Lord to	.	188	DOUBL DLR	V.1	25
Lady Touch:	what I said to you, or you had better eat your own Horns,	.	192	DOUBL DLR	V.1	192
Maskwell:	we had better meet in the Chaplain's Chamber, here, the	.	194	DOUBL DLR	V.1	252
Maskwell:	Conditions,--if not, here take this; you may employ it					
	better, ...	.	199	DOUBL DLR	V.1	450
	The Lady Criticks, who are better Read, ...	.	204	DOUBL DLR	EPI.	21
Scandal:	by Heav'n to seize the better half.	.	219	FOR LOVE	I.1	135
Valentine:	Ruby-Lips! better sealing there, than a Bond for a Million,	.	223	FOR LOVE	I.1	279
Trapland:	No, no, there's no such thing, we'd better mind our .	.	223	FOR LOVE	I.1	281
Tattle:	him, that the World shall think the better of any Person	.	226	FOR LOVE	I.1	392
Mrs Frail:	That's somewhat the better reason, to my	.	234	FOR LOVE	I.1	669
Scandal:	Well, if Tattle entertains you, I have the better					
	opportunity	.	234	FOR LOVE	I.1	671
Foresight:	be better inform'd of this--(Aside)--Do you mean my .	.	241	FOR LOVE	II.1	230
Mrs Fore:	better Friends than before.	.	248	FOR LOVE	II.1	479
Miss Prue:	this way--Is not it pure?--It's better than	.	249	FOR LOVE	II.1	528
Miss Prue:	O Lord, I swear this is pure,--I like it better than .	.	252	FOR LOVE	II.1	624
Miss Prue:	better not speak at all, I think, and truly I won't tell					
	a lie	.	263	FOR LOVE	III.1	383
Sr Sampson:	Black-Guard or his shall get the better of the Day. .	.	267	FOR LOVE	III.1	511
Scandal:	looks better than he did.	.	270	FOR LOVE	III.1	627
Scandal:	No, no, you look much better.	.	270	FOR LOVE	III.1	644
Scandal:	Yes, Faith I do; I have a better Opinion both of you .	.	271	FOR LOVE	III.1	662
Jeremy:	bad Bargain, can't do better than to beg him for his .	.	276	FOR LOVE	IV.1	36
Scandal:	the mean time, if our Project succeed no better with his	.	278	FOR LOVE	IV.1	104
Scandal:	You'd better let him go, Sir; and send for him if there	.	280	FOR LOVE	IV.1	189
Sr Sampson:	indisposed: But I'm glad thou'rt better, honest Val. .	.	281	FOR LOVE	IV.1	203
Sr Sampson:	the Nose in one's Face: What, are my Eyes better than .	.	281	FOR LOVE	IV.1	225
Valentine:	The sooner the better--Jeremy, come hither-- . . .	.	290	FOR LOVE	IV.1	556
Scandal:	Madam, I am very glad that I overheard a better . .	.	294	FOR LOVE	IV.1	687
Jeremy:	better yet--Will you please to be Mad, Sir, or how? .	.	296	FOR LOVE	IV.1	771
Angelica:	Never let us know one another better; for the Pleasure of	.	296	FOR LOVE	IV.1	789
Sr Sampson:	your Feet; And I wish, Madam, they stood in a better .	.	300	FOR LOVE	V.1	95
Sr Sampson:	your Feet; And I wish, Madam, they were in a better .	.	300	FOR LOVE	V.1 V	95
Sr Sampson:	and Troth I like you the better--But, I warrant you, .	.	300	FOR LOVE	V.1	125
Jeremy:	my self better to you, Sir, than by the delivery of a .	.	302	FOR LOVE	V.1	177
Ben:	Mess, I fear his Fire's little better than Tinder; may hap	.	308	FOR LOVE	V.1	410
Mrs Fore:	(aside to Mrs. Frail). He's better than no Husband .	.	310	FOR LOVE	V.1	469
Angelica:	pardon me, if I think my own Inclinations have a better	.	311	FOR LOVE	V.1	533
	And we, who know no better, must believe 'em. . . .	.	315	FOR LOVE	EPI.	14
	But from the rest, we hope a better Fate.	.	323	M. BRIDE	PRO.	34
Gonsalez:	Has better done;	.	332	M. BRIDE	I.1	256
Gonsalez:	Has better done; in proving with his Sword	.	332	M. BRIDE	I.1 V	257
Zara:	Better I was unseen, than seen thus coldly.	.	346	M. BRIDE	II.2	257
Manuel:	(aside). How? better than my Hopes; does she accuse .	.	348	M. BRIDE	II.2	359
Manuel:	Better for him, to tempt the Rage of Heav'n, . . .	.	349	M. BRIDE	II.2	368
Heli:	Have Hopes, and hear the Voice of better Fate. . . .	.	351	M. BRIDE	III.1	63
Osmyn-Alph:	More Anxious Grief. This shou'd have better taught me;	.	353	M. BRIDE	III.1	127
Almeria:	No, no, 'tis better thus, that we together . . .	.	356	M. BRIDE	III.1	258
Almeria:	Thus, better, than for any Cause to part.	.	356	M. BRIDE	III.1	263
Zara:	You free: But shall return much better pleas'd, . .	.	360	M. BRIDE	III.1	418
Gonsalez:	Their Execution better were deferr'd, ...	.	363	M. BRIDE	IV.1	69
Gonsalez:	If I delay--'twill do--or better so.	.	371	M. BRIDE	IV.1	416
Garcia:	Better with this to rip up my own Bowels, ...	.	378	M. BRIDE	V.2	78
Selim:	You thought it better then-- but I'm rewarded. . . .	.	380	M. BRIDE	V.2	179
Mirabell:	better pleas'd if she had been less discreet. . . .	.	396	WAY WORLD	I.1	48

Better (continued)

Fainall:	Had you dissembl'd better, Things might have continu'd	.	397	WAY WORLD	I.1	66
Fainall:	By no means, 'tis better as 'tis; 'tis better to Trade	.	400	WAY WORLD	I.1	207
Mirabell:	You had better step and ask his Wife; if you wou'd . .	.	402	WAY WORLD	I.1	266
Petulant:	Aunt, that loves Catterwauling better than a Conventicle.		406	WAY WORLD	I.1	408
Petulant:	Aunt, who loves Catterwauling better than a Conventicle.	.	406	WAY WORLD	I.1	V408
Marwood:	'tis better to be left, than never to have been lov'd. To		410	WAY WORLD	II.1	12
Mirabell:	Addresses. A better Man ought not to have been sacrific'd		417	WAY WORLD	II.1	275
Foible:	The sooner the better, Madam.	.	428	WAY WORLD	III.1	121
Lady Wish:	expect advances. No, I hope Sir Rowland is better bred,	.	429	WAY WORLD	III.1	161
Foible:	I manag'd my self. I turn'd it all for the better. I told my		430	WAY WORLD	III.1	207
Marwood:	Months Mind, but he can't abide her--'Twere better . . .		431	WAY WORLD	III.1	240
Marwood:	'Twere better so indeed. Or what think you	.	433	WAY WORLD	III.1	308
Sir Wilful:	'Sheart, and better than to be bound to a Maker of . .	.	440	WAY WORLD	III.1	563
Lady Wish:	understand Raillery better.	.	441	WAY WORLD	III.1	609
Marwood:	can contrive to have her keep you better than you expected;		442	WAY WORLD	III.1	656
Marwood:	--the better I can play the Incendiary. Besides I would not		443	WAY WORLD	III.1	703
Fainall:	are you the better for this? Is this Mr. Mirabell's					
	Expedient?	.	475	WAY WORLD	V.1	493
Mrs Fain:	You had better give it Vent.	.	476	WAY WORLD	V.1	564

Betters (1)

| Sir Wilful: | Betters? . . . . | . | 439 | WAY WORLD | III.1 | 530 |

Betty (11)

	(Araminta, Belinda, Betty waiting, in Araminta's Apartment)		54	OLD BATCH	II.2	V
Belinda:	Prithee tell it all the World, it's false. Betty. (Calls)	.	56	OLD BATCH	II.2	61
	(Enter Betty.)	.	56	OLD BATCH	II.2	V 67
	(Exit Betty.)	.	56	OLD BATCH	II.2	V 71
	(Enter Betty, with Hoods and					
	Looking-glass.)	.	57	OLD BATCH	II.2	90
Araminta:	Betty, why don't you help my Cousin?	.	57	OLD BATCH	II.2	93
	(Exit Betty with the Things.)	.	57	OLD BATCH	II.2	V100
	Mirabell and Fainall Rising from Cards. Betty waiting.	.	395	WAY WORLD	I.1	
Mirabell:	Betty, what says your Clock?	.	398	WAY WORLD	I.1	105
Witwoud:	No Letters for me, Betty?	.	401	WAY WORLD	I.1	239
	(Exit Betty, and Coachman.)	.	404	WAY WORLD	I.1	352

Between (42) see Go-between

Lucy:	inform my self of what past between 'em to Day, and	.	. 62	OLD BATCH	III.1	45
Bellmour:	Lawyer, between two Fees.	.	. 63	OLD BATCH	III.1	92
Vainlove:	Or a young Wench, between pleasure and	.	. 63	OLD BATCH	III.1	V 93
Bellmour:	Come, I know the Intrigue between Heartwell and your	.	. 97	OLD BATCH	V.1	42
Lucy:	Alas-a-day! You and Mr. Vainlove, between you, have	.	. 98	OLD BATCH	V.1	47
Careless:	I'm mistaken if there be not a Familiarity between . .	.	. 131	DOUBL DLR	I.1	153
Careless:	between them are frequent. His Affection to you, . .	.	. 131	DOUBL DLR	I.1	163
Lady Froth:	then I had a way.--For between you and I, I had . .	.	. 138	DOUBL DLR	II.1	10
Mellefont:	Winnings to be Shared between us.--What's here, the .	.	. 143	DOUBL DLR	II.1	171
Maskwell:	to Morrow Morning, or drown between you in the . .	.	. 148	DOUBL DLR	II.1	387
Lady Froth:	Then you think that Episode between Susan, the . .	.	. 163	DOUBL DLR	III.1	502
Cynthia:	Between you and me.		168	DOUBL DLR	IV.1	9
Cynthia:	Perspective all this while; for nothing has been between us		168	DOUBL DLR	IV.1	25
Sir Paul:	between--	.	172	DOUBL DLR	IV.1	188
Lady Ply:	Consummation between us, and	.	179	DOUBL DLR	IV.1	V458
Mellefont:	I'll stand between you and this Sally-Port.	.	184	DOUBL DLR	IV.2	43
Careless:	with what imperfectly I over-heard between my Lord and	.	196	DOUBL DLR	V.1	337
Valentine:	I know no effectual Difference between continued . .	.	254	FOR LOVE	III.1	40
Mrs Fore:	this Affair between you and me. Here you make love to	.	272	FOR LOVE	III.1	687
Scandal:	'S'death do you make no difference between me and . .	.	284	FOR LOVE	IV.1	321
Angelica:	carried on, between you and me, it would oblige . .	.	300	FOR LOVE	V.1	109
Jeremy:	what a happy Exchange she has made, between a Madman	.	302	FOR LOVE	V.1	204
Valentine:	Between Pleasure and Amazement, I am lost-- . . .	.	312	FOR LOVE	V.1	565
Valentine:	between me and Heav'n; but Providence laid Purgatory	.	313	FOR LOVE	V.1	596
Leonora:	Entail'd between Valentia's and Granada's Kings; . .	.	327	M. BRIDE	I.1	44
Leonora:	Between Valentia's and Granada's Kings;	.	327	M. BRIDE	I.1	V 44
Leonora:	Proposing by a Match between Alphonso	.	327	M. BRIDE	I.1	48
Manuel:	Has thrust between us and our while of Love; . . .	.	363	M. BRIDE	IV.1	106
Zara:	Of strictest Friendship, was profess'd between . . .	.	364	M. BRIDE	IV.1	123
Almeria:	And step between me and the Curse of him, ...	.	368	M. BRIDE	IV.1	280
Fainall:	you monopolize the Wit that is between you, the Fortune	.	402	WAY WORLD	I.1	283
Witwoud:	no further--Between Friends, I shall never break my .	.	407	WAY WORLD	I.1	468
Witwoud:	Town,--and is between him and the best part of his Estate;		408	WAY WORLD	I.1	482
Fainall:	fellow-feeling between my Wife and Him.	.	413	WAY WORLD	II.1	127
Marwood:	between us.	.	415	WAY WORLD	II.1	192
Mrs Fain:	Match between Millamant and your Uncle.	.	418	WAY WORLD	II.1	304
Millamant:	Yet again! Mincing, stand between me and his . . .	.	419	WAY WORLD	II.1	341
Foible:	thought the former good Correspondence between your .	.	430	WAY WORLD	III.1	197
Marwood:	match between Millamant and Sir Wilfull, that may be an	.	443	WAY WORLD	III.1	669
Witwoud:	If there had been words enow between 'em to have . .	.	454	WAY WORLD	IV.1	361
Lady Wish:	become a botcher of second hand Marriages, between . .	.	463	WAY WORLD	V.1	51
Millamant:	that past between Mirabell and me, I have oblig'd him .	.	470	WAY WORLD	V.1	330

Betwixt (3) see 'twixt

Vainlove:	Or a young Wench, betwixt pleasure and		63	OLD BATCH	III.1	93
Osmyn-Alph:	Fooling the Follower, betwixt Shade and Shining. . . .	.	350	M. BRIDE	III.1	38
Marwood:	S'life, we shall have a Quarrel betwixt an Horse and an Ass,		438	WAY WORLD	III.1	505

Bewitch'd (1)

| Silvia: | has bewitch'd him from me--Oh how the name of . . . . | | 61 | OLD BATCH | III.1 | 29 |

Bewitching (1)

| Careless: | bewitching Fair? O let me grow to the ground here, and | . | 170 | DOUBL DLR | IV.1 | 91 |

Beyond (22)

Bellmour:	beyond Woman--	.	64	OLD BATCH	III.1	114
Vainlove:	I am not presuming beyond a Pardon.	.	106	OLD BATCH	V.1	360
Cynthia:	It's impossible; she'll cast beyond you still--I'll .	.	167	DOUBL DLR	IV.1	6
Sir Paul:	The Devil take me now if he did not go beyond my . .	.	180	DOUBL DLR	IV.1	470
Lord Touch:	beyond your Hopes.	.	183	DOUBL DLR	IV.1	591
Lord Touch:	her beyond the bounds of Patience.	.	195	DOUBL DLR	V.1	311
Tattle:	never be admitted beyond a Drawing-Room: I shall .	.	230	FOR LOVE	I.1	517
Tattle:	Gad so, the Heat of my Story carry'd me beyond my . .	.	258	FOR LOVE	III.1	185
Tattle:	beyond her Reputation--But I hope you don't know . .	.	258	FOR LOVE	III.1	187

Beyond   (continued)
  Scandal: Worldly Lucre carry you beyond your Judgment, nor . . . 268 FOR LOVE III.1 555
  Almeria: My Grief has hurry'd me beyond all Thought. . . . 328 M. BRIDE I.1   79
  Almeria: I might be his, beyond the Power of future Fate: . . 329 M. BRIDE I.1 139
  Osmyn-Alph: I shall have liv'd beyond all Aera's then, . . . 343 M. BRIDE II.2 143
  Almeria: And speak--That thou art here, beyond all Hope, . . 343 M. BRIDE II.2 151
  Gonsalez: Is far from hence, beyond your Father's Power. . . 370 M. BRIDE IV.1 377
  Gonsalez: And tho' I know he hates beyond the Grave . . . . 371 M. BRIDE IV.1 409
  Zara: I cannot feel it--quite beyond my reach. . . . 381 M. BRIDE V.2 210
  Fainall: Marriage, my Lady had been incens'd beyond all means of . 415 WAY WORLD II.1 203
  Marwood: this imposture. My Lady will be enraged beyond bounds, . 442 WAY WORLD III.1 663
  Lady Wish: furnishes with Blushes, and re-composing Airs beyond . 445 WAY WORLD IV.1   31
  Mirabell: when you are dwindl'd into a Wife, I may not be beyond . 450 WAY WORLD IV.1 230
  Lady Wish: This Insolence is beyond all Precedent, all . . . . 469 WAY WORLD V.1 298
Bias (1)
  Bellmour: perverts our Aim, casts off the Bias, and leaves us wide and 37 OLD BATCH I.1   11
Bib (1)
  Marwood: draw him like an Idiot, a Driveler, with a Bib and Bells. . 431 WAY WORLD III.1 237
Bible (1)
  Valentine: if you should ask him, whether the Bible saves more . . 280 FOR LOVE IV.1 176
Bible-Oath (3)
  Foible: Verses and Poems,--So as long as it was not a Bible-Oath, . 464 WAY WORLD V.1   99
  Foible: Poems,--So long as it was not a Bible-Oath, . . . 464 WAY WORLD V.1 V 99
  Foible: Yes indeed Madam; I'll take my Bible-oath of it. . . 474 WAY WORLD V.1 478
Bid (23)
  Belinda: Get my Hoods and Tippet, and bid the Footman call . .   56 OLD BATCH II.2   69
  Fondlewife: and bid my Cocky come out to me, I will give her some .   76 OLD BATCH IV.1   46
  Sir Paul: I bid you. . . . . 146 DOUBL DLR II.1 286
  Cynthia: and bid me meet him in the Chaplain's Room, pretending . 196 DOUBL DLR V.1 348
  Valentine: and bid her trouble me no more; a thoughtless two handed . 221 FOR LOVE I.1 210
  Scandal: of my Love. And d'ee hear, bid Margery put more Flocks . 222 FOR LOVE I.1 218
  Valentine: Scandal, don't spoil my Boy's Milk.--Bid . . . 222 FOR LOVE I.1 222
  Valentine: Sirrah, fill when I bid you.--And how do's . . . 222 FOR LOVE I.1 250
  Valentine: Bid him come in: Mr. Trapland, send away your . . 224 FOR LOVE I.1 304
  Tattle: And bid me ask Valentine. . . . . 229 FOR LOVE I.1 496
  Sr Sampson: Years--I warrant he's grown--Call him in, bid . . 259 FOR LOVE III.1 214
  Scandal: think I heard her bid the Coach-man drive hither. . . 276 FOR LOVE IV.1   13
  Sr Sampson: Mr. Buckram, bid him make haste back with the . . 281 FOR LOVE IV.1 209
  Foresight: Hussy--Do what I bid you, no Reply, away. And bid . . 306 FOR LOVE V.1 326
  Foresight: Linnen, d'ee hear, begone when I bid you. . . . . 306 FOR LOVE V.1 328
  Manuel: 'Tis false; 'twas more; I bid she should be free: . . 336 M. BRIDE I.1 V408
  Manuel: If not in Words, I bid it by my Eyes. . . . . 336 M. BRIDE I.1 V409
  Manuel: Her Eyes, did more than bid--free her and hers, . . 336 M. BRIDE I.1 410
  Mirabell: and adjourn the Consummation till farther Order; bid . 398 WAY WORLD I.1 128
  Millamant: thoughtfull and would amuse my self,--bid him . . 446 WAY WORLD IV.1   49
  Millamant: Contemplation, must I bid you then Adieu? ay-h adieu.--my 449 WAY WORLD IV.1 187
  Marwood: bid adieu to all other Thoughts. . . . . . . 468 WAY WORLD V.1 262
Biddy (2)
  Lady Froth: Biddy, that's all; just my own Name. . . . . 141 DOUBL DLR II.1 129
  Brisk: Biddy! I'gad very pretty--Deuce take me if your . . 142 DOUBL DLR II.1 130
Bide (1)
  Manuel: Hence, Slave, how dar'st thou bide, to watch and pry . 373 M. BRIDE V.1   39
Bids (1)
  Almeria: Curst be that Tongue, that bids me be of Comfort; . . 370 M. BRIDE IV.1 371
Big (3)
  Capt Bluff: (Looks big.) . . . . . .   70 OLD BATCH III.1 355
  Miss Prue: do what he will; I'm too big to be whipt, so I'll tell you 264 FOR LOVE III.1 398
  Marwood: found it: The secret is grown too big for the Pretence: . 433 WAY WORLD III.1 317
Big-Belly'd (1)
  Lady Wish: Impudence, more than a big-Belly'd Actress. . . . 463 WAY WORLD V.1   37
Bigger (1)
  Lady Wish: Traverse Rag, in a shop no bigger than a Bird-cage,-- . 462 WAY WORLD V.1   7
Biggot (1)
  Bellmour: Yet is ador'd by that Biggot Sr. Joseph Wittoll, as the . 46 OLD BATCH I.1 356
Bilbo's (1)
  Capt Bluff: must refund--or Bilbo's the Word, and Slaughter will . 68 OLD BATCH III.1 259
Bilboes (1)
  Ben: is marry'd, has as it were, d'ee see, his feet in the
    Eilboes, ... 261 FOR LOVE III.1 312
Bilingsgate (1)
  Bellmour: Oyster-woman, to propagate young Fry for Bilingsgate-- . 45 OLD BATCH I.1 299
Bilk (3)
  Lady Froth: There he's secure from danger of a bilk, . . . 164 DOUBL DLR III.1 540
  Brisk: exception to make--don't you think bilk (I know its . 164 DOUBL DLR III.1 544
  Brisk: good Rhime) but don't you think bilk and fare too like a . 165 DOUBL DLR III.1 545
Bilk'd (1)
  Jeremy: Sometimes like a bilk'd Bookseller, with a meagre . . 219 FOR LOVE I.1 104
Bill (7)
  Sharper: only dropt a Bill of a hundred Pound, which I confess, I . 49 OLD BATCH II.1   82
  Lucy: Lord does his Mercers Bill, or a begging Dedication; . 61 OLD BATCH II.1   22
  Sir Joseph: They won't be accepted, so readily as the Bill, Sir. . 68 OLD BATCH III.1 286
  Sr Sampson: day in a Bill of Four thousand Pound: A great deal of . 243 FOR LOVE II.1 275
  Sir Wilful: Gazetts then, and Dawks's Letter, and the weekly Bill, 'till 440 WAY WORLD III.1 552
  Mirabell: Your bill of fare is something advanc'd in this latter . 450 WAY WORLD IV.1 228
  Sir Wilful: Bill--Give me more drink and take my Purse. . . . 455 WAY WORLD IV.1 395
Billet (0)   see Crooked-billet
Billet doux (2)
  Mellefont: Ply her close, and by and by clap a Billet doux into her . 158 DOUBL DLR III.1 315
  Jeremy: Porter, worn out with pimping, and carrying Billet doux . 218 FOR LOVE I.1   96
Billing (1)
  Mirabell: --What, billing so sweetly! Is not Valentine's Day over . 423 WAY WORLD II.1 502
Billows (2)
  Zara: 'Till Surges roll, and foaming Billows rise, ... 380 M. BRIDE V.2 V166
    Look out when Storms arise, and Billows roar, . . . 385 M. BRIDE EPI.   20
Bills (1)
  Sr Sampson: Weekly Bills out of Countenance. . . . . 308 FOR LOVE V.1 399

Bind (2)
Mellefont:	He has Obligations of Gratitude, to bind him to	131	DOUBL DLR	I.1	149
Lady Wish:	will bind me to you inviolably. I have an Affair of moment	457	WAY WORLD	IV.1	467

Binds (1)
| Lord Touch: | Astonishment binds up my rage! Villany . . . . | 199 | DOUBL DLR | V.1 | 468 |

Bird-cage (1)
| Lady Wish: | Traverse Rag, in a shop no bigger than a Bird-cage,-- . . | 462 | WAY WORLD | V.1 | 7 |

Birth (6)
Bellmour:	birth, and the discovery must needs be very pleasant from	40	OLD BATCH	I.1	125
Heartwell:	punish'd with a Wife of Birth--be a Stag of the first Head	45	OLD BATCH	I.1	310
Lord Touch:	Torture and shame attend their open Birth:	203	DOUBL DLR	V.1	593
Zara:	And now just ripe for Birth, my Rage has ruin'd. . . .	354	M. BRIDE	III.1	196
Osmyn-Alph:	Give a new Birth to thy long-shaded Eyes, ...	383	M. BRIDE	V.2	286
Lady Wish:	whole Court upon a Birth day. I'll spoil his Credit with his	428	WAY WORLD	III.1	134

Bishop (1)
| Sharper: | Gravity as a Bishop hears Venereal Causes in the Spiritual | 100 | OLD BATCH | V.1 | 139 |

Bishoprick (1)
| Scandal: | favour, as a Doctor says, No, to a Bishoprick, only that it | 226 | FOR LOVE | I.1 | 377 |

Bisket (2)
| Ben: | Bisket. . . . . | 273 | FOR LOVE | III.1 | 737 |
| Ben: | Thus we live at Sea; eat Bisket, and drink Flip; put on a | 275 | FOR LOVE | III.1 | 800 |

Bit (3)
	And dare not bite, for fear of being bit.	214	FOR LOVE	PRO.	36
Gonsalez:	That bound, and foam, and champ the Golden Bit, . . .	331	M. BRIDE	I.1	232
Lady Wish:	ne'er a Brass-Thimble clinking in thy Pocket with a bit .	425	WAY WORLD	III.1	31

Bite (7)
Maskwell:	Fools! then that hungry Gudgeon Credulity, will bite at .	150	DOUBL DLR	II.1	459
	And dare not bite, for fear of being bit.	214	FOR LOVE	PRO.	36
Tattle:	--Pox on't, now could I bite off my Tongue.	258	FOR LOVE	III.1	189
Ben:	and the Green Girl together;--May hap the Bee may bite,	286	FOR LOVE	IV.1	386
Osmyn-Alph:	. . . where I will bite the Ground	358	M. BRIDE	III.1	V355
Witwoud:	Thou dost bite my dear Mustard-seed; kiss me for . .	454	WAY WORLD	IV.1	353
Sir Wilful:	let me bite your Cheek for that.	457	WAY WORLD	IV.1	473

Bitter (1)
| Almeria: | Drink bitter Draughts, with never-slacking Thirst. . . | 356 | M. BRIDE | III.1 | 262 |

Bitterest (1)
| Zara: | Than e'er thou could'st with bitterest Reproaches; . . | 354 | M. BRIDE | III.1 | 186 |

Blab (1)
| Tattle: | I am no blab, Sir. . . . . | 292 | FOR LOVE | IV.1 | 615 |

Black (16)
Bellmour:	Black Gown does Atheism--You must know he has been . .	47	OLD BATCH	I.1	368
Setter:	Cover Carnal Knavery--not forgetting the Black Patch, .	64	OLD BATCH	III.1	125
Lady Touch:	black!--O I have Excuses, Thousands for my Faults; Fire .	135	DOUBL DLR	I.1	325
Lady Touch:	a sedate, a thinking Villain, whose Black Blood runs .	135	DOUBL DLR	I.1	328
Scandal:	What don't I know?--I know the Buxom black . . .	223	FOR LOVE	I.1	268
Valentine:	A Lovely Girl, i'faith, black sparkling Eyes, soft pouting	223	FOR LOVE	I.1	278
Scandal:	Yes, mine are most in black and white.--And yet . .	233	FOR LOVE	I.1	626
Sr Sampson:	was to pay the Piper. Well, but here it is under Black and	240	FOR LOVE	II.1	180
Valentine:	Why does that Lawyer wear black?--Does he	280	FOR LOVE	IV.1	167
Valentine:	For she'll meet me Two Hours hence in black and white,	290	FOR LOVE	IV.1	561
Almeria:	Nor will I change these black and dismal Robes, . . .	329	M. BRIDE	I.1	145
Manuel:	Of that offensive black; on me be all	334	M. BRIDE	I.1	324
Foible:	into Black Friers for Brass Farthings, with an old Mitten.	428	WAY WORLD	III.1	138
Petulant:	If he says Black's Black--If I have a Humour to . . .	435	WAY WORLD	III.1	404
Waitwell:	must let me give you;--I'll go for a black box, which .	461	WAY WORLD	IV.1	633
Waitwell:	Black box at last, Madam.	475	WAY WORLD	V.1	511

Black-box (1)
| Lady Wish: | Comfort; bring the Black-box. . . . . | 461 | WAY WORLD | IV.1 | 637 |

Black-Guard (1)
| Sr Sampson: | Black-Guard or his shall get the better of the Day. . | 267 | FOR LOVE | III.1 | 511 |

Black's (1)
| Petulant: | If he says Black's Black--If I have a Humour to . . . | 435 | WAY WORLD | III.1 | 404 |

Blackwall (1)
| Sr Sampson: | French Fleet were at Anchor at Blackwall. . . . . . | 266 | FOR LOVE | III.1 | 488 |

Bladders (1)
| Sir Joseph: | in your sight, upon the full blown Bladders of repentance-- | 49 | OLD BATCH | II.1 | 59 |

Blade (1)
| Heartwell: | you abate of your vigor; and that daring Blade which was . | 43 | OLD BATCH | I.1 | 248 |

Blades (0)   see Gads-Daggers-Belts-Blades

Blame (14)
Setter:	Nay faith Lucy I'me sorry, I'le own my self to blame, . .	66	OLD BATCH	III.1	212
Lucy:	Reputation; And can you blame her if she stop it up with a	98	OLD BATCH	V.1	49
Lucy:	Reputation; And can you blame her if she make it up with a	98	OLD BATCH	V.1	V 49
Lady Touch:	My Lord, can you blame my Brother	150	DOUBL DLR	III.1	1
Lady Touch:	disorder--Yet, I confess, I can't blame you; for I think I	153	DOUBL DLR	III.1	113
Lady Touch:	been to blame--a ready Answer shews you were . . .	183	DOUBL DLR	IV.2	17
Mellefont:	You have been to blame--I like those Tears, ...	185	DOUBL DLR	IV.2	68
	Whether to thank, or blame their Audience, most: . .	204	DOUBL DLR	EPI.	3
Scandal:	Others excuse him, and blame you: only the Ladies are .	220	FOR LOVE	I.1	161
Gonsalez:	And her Deliverance; Is she to blame?	333	M. BRIDE	I.1	306
Manuel:	I tell thee she's to blame, not to have feasted . .	333	M. BRIDE	I.1	307
Osmyn-Alph:	I've been to blame, and question'd with Impiety . .	352	M. BRIDE	III.1	125
Fainall:	You were to blame to resent what she spoke only in . .	396	WAY WORLD	I.1	41
Fainall:	Pardon--No Tears--I was to blame, I cou'd not . . .	416	WAY WORLD	II.1	240

Blank (2)
| Vainlove: | No signing to a Blank, friend. . . . . | 110 | OLD BATCH | V.2 | 84 |
| Lord Touch: | Blank as well--I will have no reply--Let me . . . . | 189 | DOUBL DLR | V.1 | 64 |

Blankets (2)
| Mellefont: | him swaddled up in Blankets, and his hands and feet . | 158 | DOUBL DLR | III.1 | 290 |
| Sir Paul: | three Years past? Have I been swath'd in Blankets till I . | 178 | DOUBL DLR | IV.1 | 424 |

Blasphemous (1)
| Fondlewife: | Oh, how the blasphemous Wretch swears! Out . . . . | 90 | OLD BATCH | IV.4 | 64 |

Blasphemy (1)
| Lady Wish: | the Bases roar Blasphemy. O, she wou'd have swooned at . | 467 | WAY WORLD | V.1 | 201 |

Blast (3)
| Araminta: | Another place! Some villainous Design to blast . . . . | 87 | OLD BATCH | IV.3 | 166 |

Blast   (continued)
  Lady Touch: immediate Lightning blast thee, me and the whole World . 184 DOUBL DLR IV.2   45
  Zara: The bluest Blast of Pestilential Air, ... 359 M. BBIDE III.1 400
Blasted (3)
  Sharper: shrub of Mankind, and seeks Protection from a blasted . . 102 OLD EATCH V.1   208
  Osmyn-Alph: One, driv'n about the World like blasted Leaves . . . 351 M. BBIDE III.1   59
  Garcia: Blasted my Eyes, and speechless be my Tongue, . . . 377 M. BBIDE V.2   55
Blaze (3)
  Maskwell: within this Breast, which should it once blaze forth, would 188 DOUBL DLR V.1   29
  Gonsalez: Have all conspir'd, to blaze promiscuous Light, . . . 331 M. BBIDE I.1 222
  Witwoud: I confess I do blaze to Day, I am too bright. . . . 419 WAY WCRLD II.1 344
Blazing (1)
  Zara: The blazing Torrent on the Tyrant's Head; . . . . . 380 M. EBIDE V.2 V170
Bleak (1)
  Lady Wish: and Weaving of dead Hair, with a bleak blew Nose, over a . 462 WAY WORLD V.1   5
Bled (1)
  Almeria: How would thy Heart have bled to see his Suff'rings! . 327 M. BBIDE I.1   33
Bleed (6)
  Osmyn-Alph: Is singled out to bleed, and bear the Scourge; . . . 350 M. BBIDE III.1   30
  Zara: This Heart of Flint, 'till it shall bleed; and thou . 353 M. BBIDE III.1 167
  Osmyn-Alph: There, there, I bleed; there pull the cruel Cords, . 356 M. EBIDE III.1 291
  Almeria: I am the Sacrifice design'd to bleed; . . . . . . 382 M. BBIDE V.2 249
  Singer: That Heart which others bleed for, bleed for me. . . 435 WAY WORLD III.1 390
Bleeding (1)
  Osmyn-Alph: A Torture--yet, such is the bleeding Anguish . . . . 356 M. BBIDE III.1 251
Blemish (1)
  Araminta: and Malice of thy Sex, thou canst not lay a Blemish on . 87 OLD BATCH IV.3 168
Blend (1)
    And shining Features in one Portrait blend, ... 479 WAY WCRLD EPI.   33
Bless (40)
    He prays--O bless me! what shall I do now! . . . . . 35 OLD EATCH PRO.   19
  Sir Joseph: the Devil--God bless us--almost if he be by. Ah--had he . 50 OLD BATCH II.1 123
  Sir Joseph: the Devil--bless us--almost if he be by. Ah--had he . 50 OLD EATCH II.1 V123
  Araminta: Bless me! what have I said to move you thus? . . . . 54 OLD BATCH II.2   3
  Silvia: Bless me! you frighted me, I thought he had been come . 74 OLD EATCH III.2 145
  Laetitia: Bless me, what means my Dear! . . . . 77 OLD EATCH IV.1   73
  Laetitia: Bless me! What Fit? . . . . 82 OLD BATCH IV.2   88
  Araminta: Bless me, Cousin! Why wou'd you affront any . . . . 84 OLD EATCH IV.3   35
  Laetitia: Help me, my Dear,--O bless me! Why will you leave me . 90 OLD BATCH IV.4   47
  Fondlewife: Bless us! What's the matter? What's the matter? . . . 90 OLD BATCH IV.4   51
  Fondlewife: of Bell and the Dragon.--Bless us! Ravish my . . . 90 OLD BATCH IV.4   66
  Fondlewife: O bless me! O monstrous! A Prayer-Book? Ay, this is the . 92 OLD BATCH IV.4 106
  Araminta: Bless me! What have you done to him? . . . . . . 108 OLD BATCH V.2   45
  Careless: put it into her Sexes power to Ravish.--Well, bless . . 130 DOUBL DLR I.1 101
  Lady Froth: come together,--C bless me! What a sad thing . . . 139 DOUBL DLR II.1   22
  Lady Froth: a Woman of Letters, and not Write! Bless me! how can . 139 DOUBL DLR II.1   41
  Cynthia: Bless me, what makes my Father in such a Passion!-- . 144 DOUBL DLR II.1 204
  Cynthia: Bless me! Sir; Madam; what mean you? . . . . . 145 DOUBL DLR II.1 244
  Lady Ply: O name it no more--bless me, how can . . . . . . 147 DOUEL DLR II.1 344
  Lady Touch: His Defence! bless me, wou'd you have me . . . . . 151 DOUBL DLR III.1   31
  Sir Paul: her Example, that would spoil it all indeed. Bless us, if you 174 DOUBL DLR IV.1 250
  Lady Froth: Bless me, why did you call out upon me so . . . . . 176 DOUBL DLR IV.1 319
  Lady Froth: Just now as I came in, bless me, why don't you . . . 176 DOUBL DLR IV.1 323
  Lady Ply: You tell me most surprizing things; bless me . . . . 202 DOUEL DLR V.1 545
  Angelica: and the Goat. Bless me! there are a great many Horn'd . 239 FOR LCVE II.1 138
  Sr Sampson: My Son Ben! bless thee my dear Boy; body o' . . . 260 FOR LCVE III.1 270
  Mrs Fore: Bless me, what's the matter? Miss, what do's . . . 265 FOR LCVE III.1 439
  Foresight: Bless us! . . . . 266 FOR LCVE III.1 481
  Foresight: Indeed! bless me. . . . . 268 FOR LCVE III.1 574
  Sr Sampson: He recovers--bless thee, Val--How do'st . . . . . 281 FOR LCVE IV.1 194
  Foresight: Sampson, bless us! How are we? . . . . 283 FOR LCVE IV.1 278
  Angelica: Bless me, Sir Sampson, what's the matter? . . . . 300 FOR LCVE V.1 102
  Foresight: Bless us! How so? . . . . 309 FOR LCVE V.1 444
  Gonsalez: And bless this Day with most unequal Lustre. . . . . 331 M. EBIDE I.1 223
  Gonsalez: And bless this Day with most unequal'd Lustre. . . . 331 M. EBIDE I.1 V223
  Osmyn-Alph: Look up Almeria, bless me with thy Eyes, ... 341 M. BBIDE II.2   71
  Osmyn-Alph: But bless my Son, visit not him for me. . . . . . 350 M. EBIDE III.1   13
  Osmyn-Alph: But till she's gone; then bless me thus again. . . . 359 M. BBIDE III.1 395
  Mrs Fain: Bless me, how have I been deceiv'd! Why you . . . . 410 WAY WCRLD II.1   28
  Foible: disinherited. O you would bless your self, to hear what he 428 WAY WCRLD III.1 108
Bless'd (5)
  Cynthia: The Wise are Wretched, and Fools only Bless'd. . . . 167 DOUBL DLR II.1 634
  Leonora: Had bless'd Anselmo's Arms with Victory, ... 327 M. BBIDE I.1   39
  Heli: Most happily, in finding you thus bless'd. . . . . 344 M. EBIDE II.2 171
  Osmyn-Alph: And 'tis deny'd to me, to be so bless'd, ... 357 M. EBIDE III.1 333
  Osmyn-Alph: Frail Life, to be entirely bless'd. Even now, . . . 383 M. BBIDE V.2 301
Blessed (3)
  Lucy: That Woman sure enjoys a blessed Night, ... 75 OLD BATCH III.2 162
  Sir Paul: and I think need not envy any of my Neighbours, blessed . 160 DOUBL DLR III.1 385
  Sir Paul: blessed be Providence I may say; for indeed, Mr. Careless, 161 DOUEL DLR III.1 413
Blessing (12)
    Where, Poets beg'd a Blessing, from their Guests. . . . 35 OLD BATCH PRO.   4
  Bellmour: See the great Blessing of an easy Faith; Opinion . . . 96 OLD BATCH IV.4 271
  Vainlove: May I presume to hope so great a Blessing? . . . . 112 OLD BATCH V.2 171
  Sir Paul: Blessing, a fine, discreet, well-spoken woman as you shall 160 DOUBL DLR III.1 387
  Maskwell: Transports of a Blessing so unexpected, so unhop'd for, so 189 DOUBL DLR V.1   81
  Maskwell: consenting to my Lord; nay, transported with the Blessing 198 DOUBL DLR V.1 424
  Scandal: My Blessing to the Boy, with this Token . . . . . 222 FCR LCVE I.1 216
  Valentine: Your Blessing, Sir. . . . . 243 FCR LCVE I.1 273
  Valentine: What a Clock is't? My Father here! Your Blessing, Sir? . 280 FCR LCVE IV.1 193
  Sr Sampson: ask'd her Blessing, Sir; that Lady is to be my Wife. . 311 FOR LCVE V.1 519
  Valentine: But on my Knees I take the Blessing. . . . . . 312 FOR LCVE V.1 566
  Mirabell: Which may be presum'd, with a blessing on our . . . 451 WAY WCBLD IV.1 257
Blessings (5)
  Lady Touch: (kneeling). Eternal Blessings thank you-- . . . . . 186 DOUBL DLR IV.2   94
  Heli: For you, those Blessings it with-held from him. . . . 352 M. BBIDE III.1 119

Blessings   (continued)
Almeria:	Never: For always Blessings crown that Posture. . . .	. 369	M. BRIDE	IV.1	322
Almeria:	With Prayers and Blessings, and paternal Love. . . .	. 369	M. BRIDE	IV.1	326
Osmyn-Alph:	For Blessings ever wait on vertuous Deeds;	. 384	M. BRIDE	V.2	321

Blest (5)
Singer:	I die, if I'm not wholly blest.	. 71	OLD BATCH III.2		8
Maskwell:	Minute, and was blest. How I have Lov'd you since, . .	. 137	DOUEL DLR	I.1	370
Tattle:	No Man but the Painter and my self was ever blest .	. 232	FCR LCVE	I.1	610
Scandal:	Make Blest the Ripen'd Maid, and Finish'd Man. . .	. 275	FOB LCVE III.1		820
Osmyn-Alph:	That I indeed shou'd be so blest to see thee. . .	. 344	M. BRIDE	II.2 V165

Blew (3)
Sr Sampson:	your Ephemeris--The brightest Star in the blew Firmament	. 307	FOR LCVE	V.1	380
Lady Wish:	and Weaving of dead Hair, with a bleak blew Nose, over a	. 462	WAY WCRLD	V.1	5
Mincing:	found you and Mr. Fainall in the Blew garret; by the same	474	WAY WCRLD	V.1	487

Blind (12)
Vainlove:	Blind of?	. 38	OLD BATCH	I.1	61
Bellmour:	much more agreeable, if you can counterfeit his Habit to				
	blind	. 39	OLD BATCH	I.1	88
Sir Joseph:	I am blind.	. 53	OLD BATCH II.1		236
Araminta:	Woman's Obstinacy made me blind to what	. 88	OLD BATCH IV.3		191
Bellmour:	blind, I must not see him fall into the Snare, and . .	. 98	OLD BATCH	V.1	61
Lady Ply:	I know you don't Love Cynthia, only as a blind for your	. 148	DOUBL DLR	II.1	368
Scandal:	that all Women are not like Fortune, blind in bestowing	. 314	FCR LCVE	V.1	624
Osmyn-Alph:	Some swift and dire event, of her blind Rage, . .	. 355	M. BRIDE III.1		231
Zara:	Somewhat, to blind the King, and save his Life . . .	. 361	M. BRIDE	IV.1	24
Gonsalez:	O my Scn, from the blind Dotage	. 378	M. BRIDE	V.2	81
Marwood:	of Wit, but to blind her Affair with a Lover of Sense. If	. 433	WAY WCRLD III.1		313
Fainall:	Corrupt to Superstition, and blind Credulity. I am single;	. 444	WAY WCRLD III.1		719

Blinded (3)
Maskwell:	discover'd, and Mellefont can be no longer blinded.-- .	. 190	DOUBL DLR	V.1	91
Osmyn-Alph:	Lost in my self, and blinded by my Thoughts, ...	. 346	M. BRIDE	II.2	253
Gonsalez:	The King is blinded by his Love, and heeds . . .	. 365	M. BRIDE	IV.1	177

Bliss (9)
Bellmour:	you; tho' I by treachery had stcll'n the Bliss-- . .	. 38	OLD BATCH	I.1	51
Bellmour:	Bliss:--Oh, for Love-sake, lead me any whither, where I	. 82	OLD BATCH	IV.2	86
Scandal:	Sinners, and the faint dawning of a Bliss to wishing .	. 275	FOR LCVE III.1		817
Almeria:	Leave for a Moment to behold Eternal Bliss, ...	. 330	M. BRIDE	I.1	179
Almeria:	One Moment, cease to gaze on perfect Bliss, ...	. 330	M. BRIDE	I.1 V179
Almeria:	In liquid Light, and float on Seas of Bliss	. 340	M. BRIDE	II.2	28
Almeria:	Of Joy, of Bliss--I cannot bear--I must	. 342	M. BRIDE	II.2 V107
Osmyn-Alph:	My All of Bliss, my everlasting Life, ...	. 357	M. BRIDE III.1		304
Zara:	This, to our mutual Bliss when joyn'd above. . . .	. 381	M. BRIDE	V.2	202

Blisses (1)
Singer:	And exchanging harmless Blisses:	. 71	OLD BATCH III.2		5

Blister (1)
Almeria:	Lest the rank Juice should blister on my Mouth, . . .	. 382	M. BRIDE	V.2	268

Blisters (1)
Araminta:	Blisters will follow--	. 88	OLD BATCH	IV.3	182

Block (2)
Snap:	block up the Chocolate-Houses, and then our labour's lost.	224	FOR LCVE	I.1	299
Sr Sampson:	with him; twould be but like me, A Chip of the Old Block.	. 265	FOR LCVE III.1		462

Block-head (1)
Bellmour:	Pardon a thousand times.--What an eternal Block-head .	. 81	OLD BATCH	IV.2	39

Blockheads (2)
Brisk:	while your Blockheads, like poor needy Scoundrels, are	. 175	DOUBL DLR	IV.1	301
Fainall:	that all Europe should know we have Blockheads of all .	. 400	WAY WCRLD	I.1	202

Blood (39)   see Life-Blood
Bellmour:	Flesh and Blood cannot bear it always.	. 41	OLD BATCH	I.1	145
Sir Joseph:	with all my Heart, Blood and Guts Sir; and if you did but .	. 48	OLD BATCH	II.1	36
Belinda:	Blood, the--All over--C Gad you are quite	. 54	OLD BATCH	II.2	14
Silvia:	Rival fires my Blood--I could curse 'em both; eternal .	. 61	OLD BATCH III.1		30
Heartwell:	reflux of vigorous Blood: But milky Love, supplies the .	. 72	OLD BATCH III.2		49
Capt Bluff:	My Blood starts at that Fellow: I can't stay where he is;	. 86	OLD BATCH	IV.3	120
Mellefont:	pleaded Honour and nearness of Blocd to my Uncle; . .	. 130	DOUEL DLR	I.1	112
Careless:	wanton. Maskwell is Flesh and Blood at best, and				
	opportunities	. 131	DOUBL DLR	I.1	162
Lady Touch:	a sedate, a thinking Villain, whose Black Blood runs .	. 135	DOUBL DLR	I.1	328
Lady Ply:	have brought all the Blood into my face; I warrant, I am	. 147	DOUBL DLR	II.1	335
Lady Touch:	Fortune, but he must mix his Blood with mine, and Wed .	. 191	DOUBL DLR	V.1	127
Lady Touch:	me, and I'll renounce all Blood, all relation and concern	. 192	DOUBL DLR	V.1	181
Angelica:	to write poor innocent Servants Names in Blood, about a .	. 238	FOR LCVE	II.1	109
Ben:	as good Blood in my Veins, and a Heart as sound as a .	. 273	FOR LCVE III.1		736
Sr Sampson:	Words. Odd, I have warm Blood about me yet, I can serve	. 298	FOR LCVE	V.1	23
Sr Sampson:	Words. Odd, I have warm Blood about me yet, and can serve	. 298	FOR LCVE	V.1 V 23
Gonsalez:	And Captains of the Noblest Blood of Affrick, . . .	. 331	M. BRIDE	I.1	235
Manuel:	Such Detestation, bears my Blood to his:	. 333	M. BRIDE	I.1	309
Zara:	Thy Temples, till reviving Blood arose, ...	. 346	M. BRIDE	II.2	283
Osmyn-Alph:	Dead Father's Blood; Nay, which refus'd to hear . .	. 351	M. BRIDE III.1		76
Osmyn-Alph:	Think how the Blood will start, and Tears will gush . .	. 358	M. BRIDE III.1		347
Osmyn-Alph:	Then will I smear these Walls with Blood, dash my . .	. 358	M. BRIDE III.1		350
Osmyn-Alph:	Then will I smear these Walls with Blood, disfigure . .	. 358	M. BRIDE III.1 V350
Zara:	Quick; or, by Heav'n, this Dagger drinks thy Blood. .	. 362	M. BRIDE	IV.1	38
Manuel:	As they had wept in Blood, and worn the Night . .	. 367	M. BRIDE	IV.1	249
Almeria:	And ghastly Head, glares by, all smear'd with Blood, .	. 371	M. BRIDE	IV.1	388
Garcia:	What means this Blood? and why this Face of Horrour? .	. 377	M. BRIDE	V.2	29
Gonsalez:	In whose Hearts Blood this Ponyard yet is warm. . .	. 377	M. BRIDE	V.2	42
Garcia:	Dead, welt'ring, drown'd in Blood.	. 377	M. BRIDE	V.2	60
Garcia:	Our selves, and expiate with our own his Blood. . .	. 378	M. BRIDE	V.2	67
Gonsalez:	I who have spilt my Royal Master's Blood, ...	. 378	M. BRIDE	V.2	70
Garcia:	With more unnatural Blood. Murder my Father! . . .	. 378	M. BRIDE	V.2	77
Zara:	At once dissolve and flow; meet Blood with Blood. . .	. 380	M. BRIDE	V.2 V164
Leonora:	Will stab the Sight, and make your Eyes rain Blood. .	. 381	M. BRIDE	V.2	230
Leonora:	Rain Blood.--	. 382	M. BRIDE	V.2 V231
Almeria:	There, there I see him; there he lies, the Blood . .	. 382	M. BRIDE	V.2	234
Lady Wish:	With Mirabell! You call my Blood into my	. 426	WAY WORLD III.1		49
Mrs Fain:	you? ay, like a Leach, to suck your best Blood--she'll	. 466	WAY WCRLD	V.1	174

Blood-Hound (1)
  Sharper: Here, Frank; your Blood-Hound has made out the   . . .   99   OLD BATCH   V.1   107
Bloody (10)
  Alonzo: O bloody Proof, of obstinate Fidelity!   373   M. BRIDE   V.1   19
                                   (Enter Gonsalez, bloody.)   .   376   M. BRIDE   V.2   23
  Gonsalez: For thee I've been ambitious, base, and bloody: . . .   378   M. BRIDE   V.2   83
  Alonzo: Attire; leaving alone to View, the bloody   379   M. BRIDE   V.2   117
  Zara: Ha! prostrate! bloody! headless! O--start Eyes,   . .   380   M. BRIDE   V.2   162
  Zara: Ha! prostrate! bloody! headless! O--I'm lost,   . . .   380   M. BRIDE   V.2 V162
  Selim: I found the dead and bloody Body strip'd--   380   M. BRIDE   V.2   182
  Almeria: Behold me well; your bloody Hands have err'd,   . . .   382   M. BRIDE   V.2   247
  Osmyn-Alph: Themselves, their own most bloody Purposes.   . . .   383   M. BRIDE   V.2   308
  Osmyn-Alph: Has turn'd their own most bloody Purposes.   383   M. BRIDE   V.2 V308
Bloody-minded (2)
  Sir Joseph: inhumane Cannibals, the bloody-minded Villains would   .   47   OLD BATCH   II.1   3
  Fondlewife: Oh Traytor! I'm astonished. Oh bloody-minded   90   OLD BATCH   IV.4   59
Bloom (1)
  Mirabell: usher in the Fall; and withers in an affected Bloom.   .   418   WAY WORLD   II.1   320
Blooming (1)
  Manuel: Yet new, unborn and blooming in the Bud, ...   349   M. BRIDE   II.2   384
Blossom   see Out-blossom
  Fondlewife: Ay, I feel it here; I sprout, I bud, I blossom, I am   .   92   OLD BATCH   IV.4   126
  Sr Sampson: none of your forc'd Trees, that pretend to Blossom in the   298   FOR LOVE   V.1   35
Blot (1)
  Lady Ply: of Paper, for you to make a Blot upon--   145   DOUBL DLR   II.1   260
Blotted (1)
  Valentine: and blotted by every Goose's Quill. I know you; for I   .   292   FOR LOVE   IV.1   639
Blow (5)
  Bellmour: How George, do's the Wind blow there?   44   OLD BATCH   I.1   293
  Heartwell: It will as soon blow North and by South--marry   . . .   44   OLD BATCH   I.1   294
  Lord Touch: our ancient Family; him I thus blow away, and constitute   .   189   DOUBL DLR   V.1   58
  Alonzo: Was to Revenge a Blow the King had giv'n him.   . . .   377   M. BRIDE   V.2   50
  Garcia: This Deed--O dire Mistake! O fatal Blow!   377   M. BRIDE   V.2   57
Blown (2)   see Full-blown
  Sir Joseph: in your sight, upon the full blown Bladders of repentance--   49   OLD BATCH   II.1   59
  Belinda: You have occasion for't, your Wife has been blown   . .   108   OLD BATCH   V.2   36
Blows (3)
  Sharper: ill Wind that blows no body good: well, you may rejoyce   .   48   OLD BATCH   II.1   33
  Ben: it's an ill Wind blows no body good,--may-hap I have   .   287   FOR LOVE   IV.1   425
  Ben: it's an ill Wind blows no body good,--may-hap I have a   .   287   FOR LOVE   IV.1 V425
Blue (2)   see Blew
  Lady Froth: nothing, but a Blue Ribbon and a Star, to make him Shine,   .   139   DOUBL DLR   II.1   31
  Petulant: say 'tis Blue--Let that pass--All's one for that. If   .   435   WAY WORLD   III.1   405
Bluest (1)
  Zara: The bluest Blast of Pestilential Air, ...   359   M. BRIDE   III.1   400
Bluffe (14)
              (Sir Joseph Wittoll and Capt. Bluffe, cross the Stage.)   .   46   OLD BATCH   I.1   340
  Bellmour: a Title; he is call'd, Capt. Bluffe.   47   OLD BATCH   I.1   384
                                   (Enter Bluffe.)   .   51   OLD BATCH   II.1   138
  Capt Bluff: by the Wars--Took no more notice, than as if Nol. Bluffe   .   53   OLD BATCH   II.1   204
                                   (Enter Sir Joseph Wittoll, Bluffe.)   .   67   OLD BATCH   III.1   241
                                   (Enter Sir Joseph and Bluffe.)   . .   84   OLD BATCH   IV.3   57
  Belinda: Huffe, Bluffe, (What's your hideous Name?) be gone: .   85   OLD BATCH   IV.3   87
                                   (Exeunt Sir Joseph and Bluffe.)   .   86   OLD BATCH   IV.3   125
                                   (Enter Sir Joseph and Bluffe.)   . .   101   OLD BATCH   V.1   162
                                   (Bluffe frowns upon Sir Joseph.)   .   102   OLD BATCH   V.1   211
              (While Sir Joseph reads, Bluffe whispers Setter.)   .   103   OLD BATCH   V.1   273
  Setter: --Bluffe turns errant Traytor; bribes me to make a   . .   105   OLD BATCH   V.1   343
  Sharper: free Discharge to Sir Joseph Wittoll and Captain Bluffe; for   110   OLD BATCH   V.2   86
              (Re-enter Sharper, with Sir Joseph, Bluffe, Sylvia, Lucy,   .   110   OLD BATCH   V.2   95
Blush (8)
  Silvia: Nay don't stare at me so--You make me blush   72   OLD BATCH III.2   43
  Setter: but, tho' I blush to won it at this time, I must confess
                I am   105   OLD BATCH   V.1   336
  Lady Ply: ready to blush for your Ignorance.   159   DOUBL DLR III.1   333
  Sir Paul: neither,--but--Nay, don't Blush--   174   DOUBL DLR   IV.1   244
  Cynthia: I don't Blush Sir, for I vow I don't understand.--   .   174   DOUBL DLR   IV.1   245
  Lady Ply: O dear, you make me blush.   202   DOUBL DLR   V.1   550
  Valentine: asham'd of; and then we'll blush once for all.   . . .   290   FOR LOVE   IV.1   564
  Mirabell: you have made a handsome Woman blush, then you think   .   409   WAY WORLD   I.1   527
Blush'd (2)
  Singer: She frown'd and blush'd, then sigh'd and kiss'd,   . .   71   OLD BATCH III.2 V 19
  Vainlove: says; and often blush'd with Anger and Surprize:--   . .   99   OLD BATCH   V.1   96
Blushes (3)
  Laetitia: Thus strew'd with Blushes, like--   81   OLD BATCH   IV.2   14
  Lady Ply: far upon me as your self, with Blushes I must own it, you   .   169   DOUBL DLR   IV.1   73
  Lady Wish: furnishes with Blushes, and re-composing Airs beyond   .   445   WAY WORLD   IV.1   31
Blushing (3)
  Bellmour: she own'd it to my Face; and blushing like the Virgin Morn   .   38   OLD BATCH   I.1   48
  Mellefont: secures them from blushing, and being out of Countenance,   .   158   DOUBL DLR III.1   312
  Petulant: Not I, by this Hand--I always take blushing   409   WAY WORLD   I.1   536
Blustring (1)
  Bellmour: being full of blustring noise and emptiness--   47   OLD BATCH   I.1   378
Bo-peep (1)
  Valentine: Bo-peep under her Petticoats, ah! Mr. Trapland?   . . .   223   FOR LOVE   I.1   288
Board (2)
  Ben: part d'ee see, I'm for carrying things above Board, I'm   .   263   FOR LOVE III.1   388
  Almeria: Had born the Queen and me, on board a Ship   329   M. BRIDE   I.1   120
Board-Wages (1)
  Jeremy: Board-Wages. Does your Epictetus, or your Seneca here,   .   217   FOR LOVE   I.1   26
Boast (1)
  Osmyn-Alph: Esteem; to this she's fair, few more can boast   . . .   355   M. BRIDE III.1   225
Boasted (1)
  Cynthia: Touchwood, as you boasted, and force her to give her   .   169   DOUBL DLR   IV.1   48
Boasts (1)
              And Nature miss'd, in vain he boasts his Art,   . . .   324   M. BRIDE   PRO.   37

Boat (0)   see Cock-boat
Boat-swain (1)
  Ben: Wife; our Boat-swain made the Song, may-hap you may   . . 273 FOR LOVE   III.1 751
Bobb'd (0)   see Woman-bobb'd
Bobbins (1)
  Lady Wish: that, Changeling, dangling thy Hands like Bobbins before . 425 WAY WORLD III.1   14
Bobs (1)
  Sr Sampson: Gads bobs, does he not know me? Is he mischievous?   . . . 279 FOR LOVE   IV.1   155
Bode (2)
               Th' unladen Boughs, he sees, bode certain Dearth,   . . 213 FOR LOVE   PRO.   5
  Zara: Or does my Heart bode more? what can it more   . . . . . 380 M. BRIDE   V.2   147
Bodes (4)
  Valentine: Pox take 'em, their Conjunction bodes no good,   . . . 231 FOR LOVE   I.1   574
  Valentine: Pox take 'em, their Conjunction bodes me no good,   . . 231 FOR LOVE   I.1 V574
  Foresight: are mad to day--It is of evil portent, and bodes Mischief 236 FOR LOVE   II.1   47
  Foresight: Fruitful, the Head fruitful, that bodes Horns; the Fruit . 236 FOR LOVE   II.1   57
Bodies (10)
  Fondlewife: . . . I wish he has lain upon no bodies stomach but his own. 93 OLD BATCH IV.4 V165
  Lord Froth: Laugh at no bodies Jest but my own, or a Lady's; I assure 132 DOUBL DLR I.1 192
  Lady Ply: Pray what have you about you to entertain any bodies . 159 DOUBL DLR III.1 331
  Lady Ply: Pray what have you to entertain any bodies . . . . 159 DOUBL DLR III.1 V331
  Mrs Frail: Issue-Male of their two Bodies; 'tis the most superstitious 231 FOR LOVE   I.1   579
  Sr Sampson: upon the Issue Male of our Two Bodies begotten. Odsbud, . 300 FOR LOVE   V.1   128
               That, does from Bodies, we from Houses strole. . . . . 315 FOR LOVE   EPI.   20
  Almeria: Of Humane Bodies; for I'll mix with them, ... 339 M. BRIDE   II.1   75
  Leonora: These Bodies.   . . . . 341 M. BRIDE   II.2   62
  Marwood: very Master-Key to every Bodies strong Box. My Friend . 431 WAY WORLD III.1 228
Boding (4)
  Lady Touch: Heart, and gnaw it piece-meal, for not boding to me this . 184 DOUBL DLR IV.2   47
  Almeria: O my boding Heart--What is your Pleasure, ... 334 M. BRIDE   I.1   330
  Almeria: my boding Heart--What is your Pleasure, ... 334 M. BRIDE   I.1 V330
  Osmyn-Alph: The Cause and Comfort of my boding Heart. . . . . . 355 M. BRIDE   III.1 235
Bodkin (4)
  Mrs Fore: you lose this Gold Bodkin?--Oh Sister, Sister! . . . 248 FOR LOVE   II.1   466
  Mrs Frail: My Bodkin!   . . . . 248 FOR LOVE   II.1   467
  Mrs Frail: Bodkin?--Oh Sister, Sister!--Sister every way. . . . 248 FOR LOVE   II.1   470
  Mrs Fain: Bodkin, nor part with a Brass Counter in Composition for . 466 WAY WORLD V.1   176
Body (118)   see No-body
  Vainlove: Ay, or any Body that she's about--   . . . . . . 38 OLD BATCH I.1   42
  Vainlove: word--Had you been there or any Body 'thad been the . . 39 OLD BATCH I.1   99
  Vainlove: will, for you have made him fit for no Body else--Well-- . 40 OLD BATCH I.1   114
  Bellmour: self, nor suffers any Body else to rail at me. Then as I . 41 OLD BATCH I.1   169
  Heartwell: I am for having every body be what they pretend . . . 43 OLD BATCH I.1   253
  Sharper: state of his Body.   . . . . 44 OLD BATCH I.1   289
  Heartwell: Compound of the whole Body of Nobility. . . . . . 45 OLD BATCH I.1   328
  Sharper: ill Wind that blows no body good: well, you may rejoyce . 48 OLD BATCH II.1   33
  Capt Bluff: share in't. Tho' I might say that too, since I am no Body . 53 OLD BATCH II.1   200
  Capt Bluff: share in't. Tho' I might say that too, since I name no Body 53 OLD BATCH II.1 V200
  Araminta: you love him. I tell no Body else Cousin--I have not . . 56 OLD BATCH II.2   59
  Bellmour: --But it is a Mistake which any Body might have made. . . 81 OLD BATCH IV.2   41
  Araminta: body so? They might be Gentlewomen of a very good . . 84 OLD BATCH IV.3   36
  Belinda: his Mistress, is like a Body without a Soul. Mr. Vainlove, 86 OLD BATCH IV.3   134
  Bellmour: Here's no body, nor no noise;--'twas nothing . . . 89 OLD BATCH IV.4   1
  Laetitia: 'Tis no body but Mr. Fondlewife, Mr. Spin-text, lie . 91 OLD BATCH IV.4   85
  Belinda: any body else. Jesus! how he looks already. Ha, ha, ha. . 108 OLD BATCH V.2   31
  Belinda: any body else. How he looks already. Ha, ha, ha. . . 108 OLD BATCH V.2 V 31
  Brisk: by leaving it, I mean you leave No body for the Company . 128 DOUBL DLR I.1   29
  Brisk: from the body of our Society.--He, I think that's . . 128 DOUBL DLR I.1   37
  Careless: Body to Disinherit thy self: for as I take it this
               Settlement   . . . . 130 DOUBL DLR I.1   121
  Lord Froth: 'tis such a Vulgar Expression of the Passion! every body can 132 DOUBL DLR I.1   200
  Lord Froth: Person, or when any body else of the same Quality does . 132 DOUBL DLR I.1   202
  Lady Froth: More Wit than any Body.   . . . . 140 DOUBL DLR II.1   92
  Lady Ply: guilt of deceiving every body; Marrying the Daughter, . 147 DOUBL DLR II.1   315
  Lady Ply: And no body knows how Circumstances may   . . . . 147 DOUBL DLR II.1   325
  Lady Ply: Nature. I know Love is powerful, and no body can help . 148 DOUBL DLR II.1   356
  Lady Ply: necessity--O Lord, here's some body coming, I dare . . 148 DOUBL DLR II.1   362
  Maskwell: will cheat no body but himself; such another Coxcomb, . 150 DOUBL DLR II.1   454
  Maskwell: will be made a Fool of by no body, but himself: Ha, ha, ha. 150 DOUBL DLR II.1   456
  Lady Touch: Well but go now, here's some body coming. . . . . 153 DOUBL DLR III.1 122
  Maskwell: which no body but you ought to drink down. Your Aunt's . 156 DOUBL DLR III.1 202
  Lady Ply: face of the World that no body is more sensible of Favours 159 DOUBL DLR III.1 351
  Cynthia: Hold--Never to Marry any Body else. . . . . . 168 DOUBL DLR IV.1   40
  Lady Ply: declare in the face of the World, never any body gain'd so 169 DOUBL DLR IV.1   72
  Lord Touch: any body else.   . . . . 189 DOUBL DLR V.1   70
  Lord Touch: Then Mellefont has urg'd some body to . . . . . 195 DOUBL DLR V.1   309
  Lady Touch: Thou can'st deceive every body,--nay, ... 199 DOUBL DLR V.1   453
  Jeremy: Ay, more indeed; for who cares for any Body that . . 219 FOR LOVE   I.1   129
  Jeremy: body be surpriz'd at the Matter--(Knocking)--Again! Sir, 221 FOR LOVE   I.1   182
  Valentine: one day bring a Confinement on your Body, my Friend. . 221 FOR LOVE   I.1   200
  Scandal: any body that did not stink to all the Town. . . . 226 FOR LOVE   I.1   402
  Tattle: For there is nothing more known, than that no body . . 227 FOR LOVE   I.1   404
  Tattle: any body else.   . . . . 227 FOR LOVE   I.1   412
  Tattle: No matter for that--Yes, yes, every body knows . . 227 FOR LOVE   I.1   427
  Tattle: --No doubt on't, every body knows my Secrets-- . . 227 FOR LOVE   I.1   428
  Valentine: body.   . . . . 229 FOR LOVE   I.1   488
  Scandal: of any Body that I know: you fancy that parting with . 234 FOR LOVE   I.1   677
  Sr Sampson: be--hah! old Merlin! body o' me, I'm so glad I'm . . 240 FOR LOVE   II.1   184
  Sr Sampson: Body o' me, I have made a Cuckold of a King, and the . 241 FOR LOVE   II.1   222
  Foresight: King of Bantam, yet by the Body of the Sun-- . . . 241 FOR LOVE   II.1   232
  Sr Sampson: Body o' me, I have gone too far;--I must not . . . 242 FOR LOVE   II.1   241
  Sr Sampson: I think on't, Body o' me, I have a Shoulder of an Egyptian 242 FOR LOVE   II.1   249
  Sr Sampson: Body o' me, so do I.--Heark ye, Valentine, . . . 243 FOR LOVE   II.1   279
  Sr Sampson: Body o' me--   . . . . 244 FOR LOVE   II.1   320
  Sr Sampson: Body o' me, what a many headed Monster have . . . 244 FOR LOVE   II.1   343
  Sr Sampson: and unreasonable,--Body o' me, why was not I a . . . 246 FOR LOVE   II.1   389

Body (continued)

Mrs Fore:	is scandalous: What if any Body else shou'd have seen you	247	FOR LOVE	II.1 431
Mrs Fore:	alight as I did?--How can any Body be happy, while	247	FOR LOVE	II.1 432
Mrs Fore:	Heart, to think that any body else shou'd be before-hand	250	FOR LOVE	II.1 551
Tattle:	Brag! C Heav'ns! Why, did I name any body?	255	FOR LOVE	III.1 93
Sr Sampson:	Frail, you shall see my Son Ben--Body c' me, he's the	259	FOR LOVE	III.1 212
Sr Sampson:	Estate: Body o' me, he does not care a Doit for your	260	FOR LOVE	III.1 243
Sr Sampson:	My Son Ben! bless thee my dear Boy; body o'	260	FOR LOVE	III.1 270
Sr Sampson:	Dick, body o' me, Dick has been dead these two	261	FOR LOVE	III.1 292
Sr Sampson:	Body o' me, Madam, you say true:--Look	262	FOR LOVE	III.1 349
Sr Sampson:	Body c' me, I don't know any universal Grievance,	266	FOR LOVE	III.1 485
Sr Sampson:	Why, body o' me, out with't.	266	FOR LOVE	III.1 495
Sr Sampson:	or his Divination--Body o' me, this is a Trick to	267	FOR LOVE	III.1 505
Jeremy:	light as his Pockets; and any body that has a mind to a	276	FOR LOVE	IV.1 35
Sr Sampson:	Ready, body o' me, he must be ready; his	278	FOR LOVE	IV.1 116
Sr Sampson:	Body o' me, I know not what to say to him--	280	FOR LOVE	IV.1 166
Sr Sampson:	Body o' me, he talks sensibly in his madness--	280	FOR LOVE	IV.1 180
Sr Sampson:	pretty well now, Val: Body o' me, I was sorry to see thee	281	FOR LOVE	IV.1 202
Sr Sampson:	need any body hold it?--I'll put it up in my Pocket,	281	FOR LOVE	IV.1 231
Sr Sampson:	Val: And then no body need hold it (puts the Paper in his	281	FOR LOVE	IV.1 232
Sr Sampson:	in Expectation of a lucky Hour. When, body o' me,	283	FOR LOVE	IV.1 290
Ben:	it's an ill Wind blows no body good,--may-hap I have	287	FOR LOVE	IV.1 425
Ben:	it's an ill Wind blows no body good,--may-hap I have a	287	FOR LOVE	IV.1 V425
Mrs Fore:	her, and Jeremy says will take any body for her that he	288	FOR LOVE	IV.1 469
Valentine:	Argo's hundred Eyes be shut, ha? No body shall know,	290	FOR LOVE	IV.1 552
Angelica:	any body so.	291	FOR LOVE	IV.1 573
Mrs Fore:	body.	291	FOR LOVE	IV.1 602
Foresight:	But he knows more than any body,--Oh	291	FOR LOVE	IV.1 603
Valentine:	Mad, and will be Mad to every Body but this Lady.	296	FOR LOVE	IV.1 774
Sr Sampson:	--Body o' me, I have a Trick to turn the Settlement	300	FOR LOVE	V.1 127
Sr Sampson:	Odso, here's some body coming.	301	FOR LOVE	V.1 162
Jeremy:	with his Arms would over-run the Country, yet no body	302	FOR LOVE	V.1 194
Tattle:	Marry any body before.	303	FOR LOVE	V.1 214
Sr Sampson:	That he shall, or I'll burn his Globes--Body	308	FOR LOVE	V.1 395
Ben:	it will only serve to light up a Match for some body else.	308	FOR LOVE	V.1 411
Tattle:	serious Kindness--I never lik'd any body less in my Life.	309	FOR LOVE	V.1 465
Sr Sampson:	them and you, my self and every Body--Oons, Cully'd,	313	FOR LOVE	V.1 V585
Valentine:	Therefore I yield my Body as your Prisoner, and	313	FOR LOVE	V.1 615
Osmyn-Alph:	Shall I not hurt and bruise thy tender Body,	355	M. BRIDE	III.1 242
Osmyn-Alph:	Shall I not hurt or bruise thy tender Body,	355	M. BRIDE	III.1 V242
Manuel:	Remove the Body thence, 'ere Zara see it.	373	M. BRIDE	V.1 28
Gonsalez:	What Noise! some body coming? 'st, Alonzo?	376	M. BRIDE	V.2 10
Gonsalez:	No body? sure he'll wait without--I would	376	M. BRIDE	V.2 11
Alonzo:	My Lord, I've thought how to conceal the Body;	378	M. BRIDE	V.2 96
Alonzo:	Or who can wound the Dead?--I've from the Body,	379	M. BRIDE	V.2 114
	(They go to the Scene which opens and shews the Body.)			
Selim:	I found the dead and bloody Body strip'd--	380	M. BRIDE	V.2 161
Almeria:	(Coming nearer the Body, starts and lets fall the Cup.)	380	M. BRIDE	V.2 182
Osmyn-Alph:	Let 'em remove the Body from her Sight.	382	M. BRIDE	V.2 271
	Provided they've a Body to dissect.	383	M. BRIDE	V.2 311
Witwoud:	contradict any Body.	385	M. BRIDE	EPI. 18
Petulant:	Not I--I mean no Body--I know nothing	403	WAY WORLD	I.1 304
Witwoud:	'Tis what she will hardly allow any Body else;--	406	WAY WORLD	I.1 428
Millamant:	persecuted with Letters--I hate Letters--No Body knows	408	WAY WORLD	I.1 476
Petulant:	No, no, it's no Enemy to any Body, but them that	419	WAY WORLD	II.1 360
Servant-W:	A Week, Sir; longer than any Body in the House,	436	WAY WORLD	III.1 420
Sir Wilful:	write my self; no offence to any Body, I hope; and Nephew	437	WAY WORLD	III.1 457
Waitwell:	hand I see that already. That's some body whose throat	438	WAY WORLD	III.1 511
Lady Wish:	from no body that I know)--I have that honour for	460	WAY WORLD	IV.1 578
Lady Wish:	Ay, ay, any Body, any body.	460	WAY WORLD	IV.1 585
Fainall:	to hide thy Shame; Your Body shall be Naked as	474	WAY WORLD	V.1 469
		475	WAY WORLD	V.1 496

Body's (1)

Scandal:	any body's else, that will never happen.	226	FOR LOVE	I.1 385

Boil'd (2)

Maskwell:	that might have soon boil'd over; but--	182	DOUBL DLR	IV.1 558
Valentine:	shake off Age; get thee Medea's Kettle, and be boil'd a-new,	289	FOR LOVE	IV.1 522

Boils (1)

Bellmour:	kind Nature works, and boils over in him.	95	OLD BATCH	IV.4 240

Boistrous (1)

Heartwell:	or the Clown may grow boistrous, I have a Fly-flap.	108	OLD BATCH	V.2 35

Bold (10)

Sir Joseph:	may be so bold, what is that loss you mention?	49	OLD BATCH	II.1 80
Maskwell:	This discovery made me bold; I confess it; for by it, I	136	DOUBL DLR	I.1 364
Maskwell:	when Innocence and bold Truth are always ready for	184	DOUBL DLR	IV.2 20
	This time, the Poet owns the bold Essay,	214	FOR LOVE	PRO. 41
Tattle:	that--Nay more (I'm going to say a bold Word now) I	227	FOR LOVE	I.1 410
Zara:	And build bold Hopes, on my dejected Fate?	349	M. BRIDE	II.2 367
Alonzo:	I'll be so bold to borrow his Attire;	373	M. BRIDE	V.1 29
Lady Wish:	me dear Friend, I can make bold with you--There	426	WAY WORLD	III.1 64
Sir Wilful:	Cozen, I made bold to pass thro' as it were,--I think this	447	WAY WORLD	IV.1 95
Sir Wilful:	Not at present Cozen,--Yes, I made bold to	447	WAY WORLD	IV.1 114

Bolder (2)

Almeria:	Lead me, for I am bolder grown: Lead me	339	M. BRIDE	II.1 81
Almeria:	Lead me, for I am bolder grown: Lead on	339	M. BRIDE	II.1 V 81

Boldly (1)

Fondlewife:	for. Come, come, go on boldly--What, don't be asham'd	94	OLD BATCH	IV.4 192

Bolt (1)

Manuel:	And wrench the Bolt red-hissing, from the Hand	349	M. BRIDE	II.2 369

Bolts (2)

Osmyn-Alph:	With Bolts, with Chains, Imprisonment and Want;	350	M. BRIDE	III.1 12
Almeria:	O, I am struck; thy Words are Bolts of Ice,	358	M. BRIDE	III.1 367

Bombast (1)

	And now they're fill'd with Jests, and Flights, and Bombast!	315	FOR LOVE	EPI. 31

Bond (3)

Valentine:	Ruby-Lips! better sealing there, than a Bond for a Million,	223	FOR LOVE	I.1 279
Sr Sampson:	I'll lend you the Bond,--You shall consult your Lawyer,	301	FOR LOVE	V.1 138

Bond   (continued)
Valentine:	But where is the Bond, by which I am oblig'd to	. . . .	312	FOR LOVE	V.1 552

Bonds (8)
Maskwell:	Bonds of Friendship, and sets Men right upon their first	.	150	DOUBL DLR	II.1 444
Zara:	These Bonds, I look with loathing on my self;	. . .	336	M. BRIDE	I.1 400
Manuel:	Those Bonds! 'twas my Command you should be free:	. .	336	M. BRIDE	I.1 403
Almeria:	My Soul, enlarg'd from its vile Bonds will mount,	. . .	340	M. BRIDE	II.2 25
Osmyn-Alph:	In Bonds, the Frame of this exalted Mind?	. . . . .	347	M. BRIDE	II.2 323
Almeria:	O that thy Words had force to break those Bonds,	. . .	357	M. BRIDE	III.1 300
Perez:	Unlock the rivets of his bonds.	. .	372	M. BRIDE	V.1 10
Perez:	As loose the rivets of his bonds.	. .	372	M. BRIDE	V.1 V 10

Bone (3)
Heartwell:	The Bone when broken, than when made a Bride.	. . . .	108	OLD BATCH	V.2 15
Lady Wish:	shou'st be my Child, Bone of my Bone, and Flesh of	. .	465	WAY WORLD	V.1 140

Bones (2)   see Hog's-tones
Almeria:	Lead me o'er Bones and Skulls, and mouldring Earth	. .	339	M. BRIDE	II.1 74
Almeria:	I'll scrape 'till I collect his rotten Bones,	. . .	370	M. BRIDE	IV.1 349

Bonne mine (1)
Lady Ply:	So well drest, so bonne mine, so eloquent, so	. . . .	160	DOUBL DLR	III.1 V363

Booby (1)
Mrs Fore:	for the Booby, it may go a great way towards his	. . .	249	FOR LOVE	II.1 502

Booby-Brother (1)
Valentine:	World: You have heard of a Booby-Brother of mine, that	.	225	FOR LOVE	I.1 332

Book (10)   see Play-Book, Prayer-Book, Dooms-day-Book
	Patch upon one Eye, and a Book in his Hand.)	. . . . .	80	OLD BATCH	IV.2
Fondlewife:	(Sees the Book that Bellmour forgot.)	.	91	OLD BATCH	IV.4 99
Fondlewife:	(Taking up the Book.)	.	91	OLD BATCH	IV.4 105
Laetitia:	Book, and only tends to the Speculation of Sin.	. . .	92	OLD BATCH	IV.4 115
Scandal:	So says Pineda in his Third Book and Eighth Chapter--	.	267	FOR LOVE	III.1 532
Osmyn-Alph:	The Book of Prescience, he beheld this Day;	. . . .	353	M. BRIDE	III.1 133
Osmyn-Alph:	He in the Book of Prescience, he saw this Day;	. . .	353	M. BRIDE	III.1 V133
Petulant:	without Book--So all's one for that.	.	436	WAY WORLD	III.1 433
Foible:	Book and swore us upon it: But it was but a Book of	.	464	WAY WORLD	V.1 98

Book's (1)
Fondlewife:	a warm-hand, rather than fail. What Book's this?	. . .	91	OLD BATCH	IV.4 98

Books (7)   see Horn-Books
Bellmour:	when it may be the means of getting into a fair Lady's				
	Books?	. . . .	44	OLD BATCH	I.1 V267
	Several Books upon the Table.)	. . . .	216	FOR LOVE	I.1
Jeremy:	(Aside and taking away the Books.)	. . . . . .	216	FOR LOVE	I.1 6
Jeremy:	musty Books, in commendation of Starving and Poverty?	.	217	FOR LOVE	I.1 33
Jeremy:	to be converted into Folio Books, of Warning to all	.	219	FOR LOVE	I.1 112
Jeremy:	Books backwards; may be you begin to read at the wrong		297	FOR LOVE	IV.1 806
Lady Wish:	are Books over the Chimney--Quarles and Pryn, and the	.	426	WAY WORLD	III.1 65

Bookseller (1)
Jeremy:	Sometimes like a bilk'd Bookseller, with a meagre	. . .	219	FOR LOVE	I.1 104

Boon (1)
Lady Ply:	So well drest, so boon mein, so eloquent, so	. . . . .	160	DOUBL DLR	III.1 363

Boot (1)
Heartwell:	Cringing, and the drudgery of loving to boot.	. . . .	44	OLD BATCH	I.1 275

Boots (7)
Witwoud:	Smoke the Boots, the Boots; Petulant, the Boots;	. . .	438	WAY WORLD	III.1 494
Petulant:	Sir, I presume upon the Information of your Boots.	. . .	438	WAY WORLD	III.1 497
Sir Wilful:	satisfy'd with the Information of my Boots, Sir, if you will	438	WAY WORLD	III.1 499
Sir Wilful:	I pull off my Boots. Sweet-heart, can you help me to a	.	441	WAY WORLD	III.1 617
Lady Wish:	Boots here--Go down into the Hall--Dinner	.	441	WAY WORLD	III.1 621

Borachio (4)
Lady Wish:	will ever endure such a Borachio! you're an absolute	.	455	WAY WORLD	IV.1 389
	Borachio.	.	455	WAY WORLD	IV.1 390
Sir Wilful:	Borachio!	.	455	WAY WORLD	IV.1 391
Sir Wilful:	day Cozen--I am a Borachio. But if you have a mind to be	.	455	WAY WORLD	IV.1 410

Bore (6)
Mrs Fore:	What then, he bore it most Heroically?	.	287	FOR LOVE	IV.1 454
Leonora:	It bore the Accent of a Humane Voice.	.	339	M. BRIDE	II.1 53
Osmyn-Alph:	And bore contiguous Pallaces to Earth.	.	347	M. BRIDE	II.2 311
Osmyn-Alph:	The Care of Heav'n. Not so, my Father bore	.	352	M. BRIDE	III.1 126
Selim:	Who bore high Offices of Weight and Trust, ...	.	361	M. BRIDE	IV.1 10
Gonsalez:	While t'other bore, the Crown, to wreath thy Brow, . . .	378	M. BRIDE	V.2 V 86

Born (36)   see Hell-born, New-born
	We've a young Author and his first born Play; . . .	.	35	OLD BATCH	PRO. 11
Bellmour:	the Jest were over; even this may be born with, considering	44	OLD BATCH	I.1 270
Bellmour:	the Jest were over; even, that, may be born with,				
	considering	.	44	OLD BATCH	I.1 V270
Sharper:	Faith, Madam, the Talent was born with me:--I . . .	.	88	OLD BATCH	IV.3 198
	To know, if it be truly born of Wit.	.	125	DOUBL DLR	PRO. 11
Mellefont:	to him they have born the face of kindness; while her	.	129	DOUBL DLR	I.1 89
Lord Touch:	Sure I was born to be controuled by those I	.	195	DOUBL DLR	V.1 302
Lord Touch:	No sooner born, but the Vile Parent dies.	.	203	DOUBL DLR	V.1 596
	The Freedom Man was born to, you've restor'd,	. . .	213	FOR LOVE	PRO. 15
Foresight:	should be as I would have it; for I was born, Sir, when the	235	FOR LOVE	II.1 12
Foresight:	young and sanguine, has a wanton Hazle Eye, and was born	.	239	FOR LOVE	II.1 151
Foresight:	Well--Why, if I was born to be a Cuckold, ...	.	239	FOR LOVE	II.1 169
Sr Sampson:	can't a private man be born without all these followers:	.	245	FOR LOVE	II.1 350
Sr Sampson:	--Why nothing under an Emperour should be born . . .	.	245	FOR LOVE	II.1 351
Sr Sampson:	Fellow was not born with you?--I did not beget him,	. .	245	FOR LOVE	II.1 358
Jeremy:	another truth, I believe you did, for I find I was born with	245	FOR LOVE	II.1 362
Sr Sampson:	have been born without a Palate.--'S'heart, what shou'd	.	245	FOR LOVE	II.1 367
Jeremy:	and I came up Stairs into the World; for I was born	. .	245	FOR LOVE	II.1 381
Tattle:	Admirable! That was as well as if you had been born	. .	252	FOR LOVE	II.1 644
Mrs Frail:	O see me no more,--for thou wert born amongst	. . .	286	FOR LOVE	IV.1 398
Valentine:	Paper, when you first are Born; but you are to be scrawl'd	292	FOR LOVE	IV.1 638
Almeria:	Had born the Queen and me, on board a Ship	.	329	M. BRIDE	I.1 120
Almeria:	Which had been brave, tho' I had ne'er been born. . .	.	332	M. BRIDE	I.1 260
Garcia:	'Tis scarce above a word; as he were born	.	335	M. BRIDE	I.1 372
Manuel:	Born to excel, and to command!	.	336	M. BRIDE	I.1 420
Almeria:	For 'tis not to be born--What shall I say?	.	343	M. BRIDE	II.2 149

Born   (continued)
Osmyn-Alph:	Ere Reason can be born: Reason, the Power	. 350	M. BRIDE	III.1	35
Osmyn-Alph:	By him set down; when his pure Thoughts were born . .	. 353	M. BRIDE	III.1	129
Zara:	Not to be born--devise the means to shun it, ...	. 362	M. BRIDE	IV.1	37
Almeria:	And cleaves my Heart; I would have born it all, . .	. 369	M. BRIDE	IV.1	309
Garcia:	Had enter'd long 'ere now, and born down all	. 377	M. BRIDE	V.2	34
Marwood:	as to wish to have been born Old, because we one Day .	. 410	WAY WORLD	II.1	15
Foible:	Nay, if that had been the worst I cou'd have born: But he	. 427	WAY WORLD	III.1	89
Fainall:	a Cuckold in Embrio? Sure I was born with	. 442	WAY WORLD	III.1	632
Foible:	O that ever I was Born, O that I was ever Married, . .	. 463	WAY WORLD	V.1	58
Lady Wish:	I warrant you, or she wou'd never have born	. 467	WAY WORLD	V.1	196

Borrow (3)
Maskwell:	you, Borrow my Lords Chaplain, and so run away with .	. 193	DOUBL DLR	V.1	224
Valentine:	thou can'st not borrow Money of me; Then what . .	. 292	FOR LOVE	IV.1	627
Alonzo:	I'll be so bold to borrow his Attire;	. 373	M. BRIDE	V.2	29

Borrowing (1)
| Sharper: | Word is sufficient any where: 'Tis but borrowing so much . | . 50 | OLD BATCH | II.1 | 108 |

Bosom (18)
Araminta:	when you named him, and press'd me to your Bosom .	. 55	OLD BATCH	II.2	42
Fondlewife:	of the Wife of thy Bosom?--Because she is young and .	. 76	OLD BATCH	IV.1	51
Bellmour:	not afford one warm Dish for the Wife of his Bosom. .	. 106	OLD BATCH	V.1	379
Sir Paul:	whomsever he receives into his bosom, will find the way .	. 178	DOUBL DLR	IV.1	421
Ben:	Pump to your Bosom, I believe we shou'd discover a foul .	. 309	FOR LOVE	V.1	433
Almeria:	Within its cold, but hospitable Bosom.	. 326	M. BRIDE	I.1	12
Almeria:	Leonora, in thy Bosom, from the Light, ...	. 341	M. BRIDE	II.2	44
Osmyn-Alph:	And stain thy Bosom with the Rust of these	. 355	M. BRIDE	III.1	243
Almeria:	Tread on me, spurn me, am I the bosom Snake . . .	. 357	M. BRIDE	III.1	298
Almeria:	Tread on me: What, am I the bosom Snake	. 357	M. BRIDE	III.1 V298
Osmyn-Alph:	Then Garcia shall lie panting on thy Bosom, . . .	. 358	M. BRIDE	III.1	358
Almeria:	O Earth, behold, I kneel upon thy Bosom, ...	. 368	M. BRIDE	IV.1	273
Almeria:	Drag me, harrow the Earth with my bare Bosom. . . .	. 369	M. BRIDE	IV.1	337
Manuel:	Frighted, and fumbling one hand in his Bosom, . . .	. 373	M. BRIDE	V.1	16
Alonzo:	He snatch'd from out his Bosom this--and strove . .	. 373	M. BRIDE	V.1	22
Zara:	I'll creep into his Bosom, lay me there;	. 381	M. BRIDE	V.2	206
Osmyn-Alph:	Of cordial Sighs; and re-inspire thy Bosom . . .	. 383	M. BRIDE	V.2	284
Marwood:	Bosom?	. 414	WAY WORLD	II.1	178

Bosome (1)
| Lady Wish: | Viper, thou Serpent, that I have foster'd, thou bosome . | . 462 | WAY WORLD | V.1 | 2 |

Bossu (1)
| Brisk: | presume your Ladyship has Read Bossu? . . . . . | . 142 | DOUBL DLR | II.1 | 137 |

Botcher (1)
| Lady Wish: | become a botcher of second hand Marriages, between . . | . 463 | WAY WORLD | V.1 | 51 |

Both (71)
Bellmour:	So Fortune be prais'd! To find you both within, . . .	. 57	OLD BATCH	II.2	114
Bellmour:	When Wit and Reason, both, have fail'd to move; . .	. 60	OLD BATCH	II.2	224
Silvia:	Rival fires my Blood--I could curse 'em both; eternal .	. 61	OLD BATCH	III.1	30
Lucy:	Yes, I know both Master and Man to be--	. 65	OLD BATCH	III.1	173
Setter:	though we were both in fault as to our Offices-- . .	. 66	OLD BATCH	III.1	213
Sir Joseph:	am both Sir; what then? I hope I may be offended, without	. 68	OLD BATCH	III.1	293
Heartwell:	'Tis both; for I am angry with my self, when I am . .	. 72	OLD BATCH	III.2	70
Lucy:	on't, both your Love and Anger satisfied!--All that can	. 75	OLD BATCH	III.2	160
Lucy:	Whom Love and Vengeance both at once delight. . .	. 75	OLD BATCH	III.2 V163
Laetitia:	they are both new to me.--You are not what your first .	. 81	OLD BATCH	IV.2	24
Belinda:	and laugh at the Vulgar.--Both the great Vulgar and the	. 87	OLD BATCH	IV.3	144
Fondlewife:	Nay, I find you are both in a Story; that, I must . .	. 93	OLD BATCH	IV.4	161
Capt Bluff:	Husband--But here, both these are from Persons of great .	. 103	OLD BATCH	V.1	269
Lady Froth:	Lord and I had been both of your Temper, we had never .	. 139	DOUBL DLR	II.1	21
Sir Paul:	O, sweet Sir, you load your humble Servants, both . .	. 159	DOUBL DLR	III.1	325
Cynthia:	both so willing; we each of us strive to reach the Gole, .	. 168	DOUBL DLR	IV.1	12
Cynthia:	both willing; we each of us strive to reach the Gole, . .	. 168	DOUBL DLR	IV.1 V 12
Cynthia:	meeting: We Hunt in Couples where we both pursue the .	. 168	DOUBL DLR	IV.1	16
Lady Ply:	both Letters.--(Puts the wrong Letter hastily up, and				
	gives him	. 174	DOUBL DLR	IV.1	263
Sir Paul:	be Damn'd for a Judas Maccabeus, and Iscariot both. O .	. 178	DOUBL DLR	IV.1	418
Lord Touch:	remember how we are both indebted to him.	. 191	DOUBL DLR	V.1	140
Lady Touch:	Both indebted to him! yes, we are both	. 191	DOUBL DLR	V.1	142
Lord Touch:	Days attend you both; mutual Love, lasting Health, and .	. 203	DOUBL DLR	V.1	588
	For every one's both Judge and Jury here;	. 204	DOUBL DLR	EPI.	13
	And when but two were made, both went astray; . .	. 213	FOR LOVE	PRO.	19
Valentine:	he is perfectly thy reverse both in humour and				
	understanding;	. 226	FOR LOVE	I.1	365
Mrs Frail:	Foresight has cast both their Nativities, and prognosticates	231	FOR LOVE	I.1	577
Scandal:	there are some set out in their true Colours, both Men and	233	FOR LOVE	I.1	627
Mrs Fore:	as you say, since we are both Wounded, let us do that is .	. 248	FOR LOVE	II.1	477
Mrs Fore:	as you say, since we are both Wounded, let us do what is .	. 248	FOR LOVE	II.1 V477
Miss Prue:	Ah, but I'll hold the Door with both Hands, and . . .	. 252	FOR LOVE	II.1	651
Scandal:	and I hope I shall find both Sol and Venus in the sixth .	. 271	FOR LOVE	III.1	651
Scandal:	Yes, Faith I do; I have a better Opinion both of you .	. 271	FOR LOVE	III.1	662
Mrs Fore:	besides he hates both you and me.--But I have a . . .	. 288	FOR LOVE	IV.1	463
Tattle:	Oh, Madam, look upon us both. There you see the ruins .	. 291	FOR LOVE	IV.1	580
Valentine:	without a Reverse or Inscription; for Indifference has both	297	FOR LOVE	IV.1	811
Sr Sampson:	faith and troth you speak very discreetly; For I hate both a	299	FOR LOVE	V.1	68
Angelica:	Man, submits both to the Severity and insolent Conduct of	299	FOR LOVE	V.1	73
Sr Sampson:	Joy Uncle Foresight, double Joy, both as Uncle and				
	Astrologer;	. 307	FOR LOVE	V.1	378
Angelica:	try'd you too, and know you both. You have not more .	. 312	FOR LOVE	V.1	575
Almeria:	Both, both--Father and Son are now no more. . . .	. 327	M. BRIDE	I.1 V 53
Osmyn-Alph:	We both have backward trod the paths of Fate, . . .	. 342	M. BRIDE	II.2	92
Osmyn-Alph:	And twice escap'd, both from the Wreck of Seas, . .	. 344	M. BRIDE	II.2	173
Osmyn-Alph:	And twice escap'd, both from the Rage of Seas . . .	. 344	M. BRIDE	II.2 V173
Almeria:	One Cup, the common Stream of both our Eyes, . . .	. 356	M. BRIDE	III.1	261
Zara:	Perdition catch 'em both, and Ruine part 'em. . . .	. 359	M. BRIDE	III.1	402
Selim:	Both in the State and Army. This confirms	. 361	M. BRIDE	IV.1	11
Zara:	And Anger in Distrust, both short-liv'd Pains. . . .	. 362	M. BRIDE	IV.1	33
Almeria:	Then all is ended, and we both must die	. 368	M. BRIDE	IV.1	303
Manuel:	Lest I forget us both, and spurn thee from me. . . .	. 369	M. BRIDE	IV.1	317

Bowls (continued)
  Zara: Let 'em set down the Bowls, and warn Alphonso . . . . 380 M. BRIDE   V.2 149
                (A Mute kneels and gives one of the
                Bowls.) . . . . 381 M. BRIDE   V.2 199

Bows (6)
  Sir Joseph: your favour.   (Bows.) . . . . . 49 OLD BATCH II.1   61
  Lady Froth: Pray mind, my Lord; ah! he bows Charmingly; nay, my   . 140 DOUBL DLR II.1   76
             (He bows profoundly low, then kisses the Glass.)   . . 140 DOUBL DLR II.1   79
             (He kisses her, and bows very low.) . . 172 DOUBL DLR IV.1 196
  Sir Paul: (Bows and gives the Letter.) . . 173 DOUBL DLR IV.1 219
  Brisk: my Approaches--Hem Hem! (Bows.) Ah Madam! . . . 175 DOUBL DLR IV.1 297

Box (7)   see Black-box, Side-Box, Snuff-Box, Snuff-box, Tobacco-Box
  Buckram: this Box, if he be ready to sign and seal. . . . 278 FOR LOVE   IV.1 115
  Angelica: seen Fifty in a side Box by Candle-light, out-blossom Five 298 FOR LOVE   V.1   31
  Marwood: very Master-Key to every Bodies strong Box. My Friend . . 431 WAY WORLD III.1 228
  Waitwell: must let me give you;--I'll go for a black box, which . . 461 WAY WORLD IV.1 633
            (Enter Waitwell with a Box of Writings.) 475 WAY WORLD V.1 508
  Waitwell: Black box at last, Madam. . . . . . 475 WAY WORLD V.1 511
  Mirabell: what that Parchment contain'd--(undoing the Box.) . . 476 WAY WORLD V.1 529

Boxes (1)
  Lord Froth: Boxes.--I swear,--he, he, he, I have often . . . . . 133 DOUBL DLR I.1 230

Boy (26)
  Heartwell: force a smile and cry, ay, the Boy takes after his Mothers 45 OLD BATCH I.1 326
  Capt Bluff: But? Look you here Boy, here's your antidote, here's . . 51 OLD BATCH II.1 146
           Enter Heartwell and Boy.) . . . . 107 OLD BATCH V.2
                (Exit Boy.) . . . . 107 OLD BATCH V.2   8
          (Enter Boy with a Letter, ... 160 DOUBL DLR III.1 392
          (Enter Boy and whispers Sir Paul.) . . 163 DOUBL DLR III.1 488
  Sir Paul: success. Boy, tell my Lady, when she has done, I would . 163 DOUBL DLR III.1 498
  Sir Paul: end--He? A brave Chopping Boy.--I'll settle a Thousand . 173 DOUBL DLR IV.1 224
  Scandal: My Blessing to the Boy, with this Token . . . . . 222 FOR LOVE   I.1 216
  Sr Sampson: Nor no more to be done, Old Boy; that's plain-- . . . 240 FOR LOVE   II.1 172
  Sr Sampson: Boy? . . . . 243 FOR LOVE   II.1 281
  Sr Sampson: My Son Ben! bless thee my dear Boy; body o' . . . 260 FOR LOVE   III.1 270
  Sr Sampson: Odsbud, and I'm glad to see thee, kiss me Boy, . . . 260 FOR LOVE   III.1 273
  Sr Sampson: I warrant thee Boy, Come, come, we'll be gone; . . . 263 FOR LOVE   III.1 357
  Sr Sampson: Ben's a brisk Boy: He has got her into a Corner, Father's 265 FOR LOVE   III.1 457
  Sr Sampson: know me, Boy? Not know thy own Father, Val! I am . . 279 FOR LOVE   IV.1 157
  Sr Sampson: thou do, Boy? . . . . 281 FOR LOVE   IV.1 195
  Sr Sampson: Ay boy--Come, thou shalt sit down by me. . . . . 281 FOR LOVE   IV.1 198
  Sr Sampson: shake--I believe thou can'st write, Val: Ha, boy? Thou . 281 FOR LOVE   IV.1 207
  Sr Sampson: See it, boy? Aye, aye, why thou do'st see it-- . . . 281 FOR LOVE   IV.1 219
  Sr Sampson: Pocket.) There Val: it's safe enough, Boy--But thou . . 282 FOR LOVE   IV.1 233
  Valentine: Because thou wer't a Monster; old Boy:--The . . . 282 FOR LOVE   IV.1 262
  Manuel: Away begon thou feeble Boy, fond Love, ... 374 M. BRIDE   V.1   62
  Singer: 'Tis not to wound a wanton Boy . . . . . . 435 WAY WORLD III.1 382
  Millamant: I prithee spare me gentle Boy, ... 447 WAY WORLD IV.1   98
  Millamant: Like Phoebus sung the no less am'rous Boy. . . . 448 WAY WORLD IV.1 153

Boy's (2)
  Valentine: Scandal, don't spoil my Boy's Milk.--Bid . . . 222 FOR LOVE   I.1 222
  Mirabell: a Shape, till you mold my boy's head like a Sugar-loaf; and 451 WAY WORLD IV.1 261

Boys (8)
  Brisk: Boys, Boys, Lads, where are you? What, do you give . . 128 DOUBL DLR I.1   20
  Sr Sampson: to me;--of all my Boys the most unlike me; a has a . . 243 FOR LOVE   II.1 306
  Sr Sampson: to me;--of all my Boys the most unlike me; he has a . . 243 FOR LOVE   II.1 V306
  Scandal: Girls, and growing Boys. . . . . 275 FOR LOVE   III.1 818
          Of Roaring Gamesters, and your Damme Boys. . . . 315 FOR LOVE   EPI.   29
  Sir Wilful: We'll drink and we'll never ha' done Boys . . . 455 WAY WORLD IV.1 416
  Sir Wilful: Put the glass then around with the Sun Boys; . . . 455 WAY WORLD IV.1 417

Brag (3)
  Scandal: go brag somewhere else. . . . . 255 FOR LOVE   III.1   92
  Tattle: Brag! O Heav'ns! Why, did I name any body? . . . 255 FOR LOVE   III.1   93
  Fainall: have something to brag of the next time he makes Court 406 WAY WORLD I.1 419

Bragging (2)
  Mellefont: Nay, then you have her; for a woman's bragging . . . 158 DOUBL DLR III.1 298
  Scandal: Foppery, Vanity, Cowardise, Bragging, Lechery, . . 233 FOR LOVE   I.1 631

Brags (1)
  Tattle: Pooh, I know Madam Drab has made her Brags in . . . 227 FOR LOVE   I.1 419

Brain (4)
  Mellefont: Hell is not more busie than her Brain, nor contains more . 129 DOUBL DLR I.1   77
  Cynthia: turn your Brain. . . . . 138 DOUBL DLR II.1   7
  Maskwell: it my Brain or Providence? No Matter which--I will . . 155 DOUBL DLR III.1 189
  Ben: has turn'd her senses, her Brain is quite overset.
          Well-a-day, ... 286 FOR LOVE   IV.1 404

Brains (1)
  Scandal: with his Brains in his Belly, and his Heart where his Head 233 FOR LOVE   I.1 645

Branch (2)
  Lord Touch: --my Nephew is the alone remaining Branch of all . . 189 DOUBL DLR V.1   57
  Sr Sampson: Fourscore. I am of your Patriarchs, I, a Branch of one of . 298 FOR LOVE   V.1   39

Branches (2)
  Capt Bluff: I plant Laurels for my Head abroad, I may find the Branches 111 OLD BATCH V.2 148
  Marwood: why not the Branches? . . . . 443 WAY WORLD III.1 696

Brand (1)
  Maskwell: ruine all, consume my honest Character, and brand me . . 188 DOUBL DLR V.1   30

Brands (1)
  Almeria: But brands my Innocence with horrid Crimes, . . . 368 M. BRIDE   IV.1 282

Brandy (5)   see Cherry-Brandy, Orange-Brandy
  Belinda: You stink of Brandy and Tobacco, most Soldier-like. Foh. . 85 OLD BATCH IV.3   88
  Scandal: Then I have a Lady burning of Brandy in a Cellar . . 233 FOR LOVE   I.1 639
  Scandal: Then I have a Lady burning of Brandy in a Cellar . . . 233 FOR LOVE   I.1 V639
  Peg: Brandy? . . . . 425 WAY WORLD III.1   10
  Fainall: Winter Evenings Conference over Brandy and Pepper, . . 469 WAY WORLD V.1 274

Brandy-sellers (1)
  Lady Wish: Brandy-sellers Bulk, or against a dead Wall by a
          Ballad-monger. . . . . 462 WAY WORLD V.1   13

Bridewell-Bride (1)
Foible:	--a Bride, ay I shall be a Bridewell-Bride. Oh!	. . . .	463	WAY WORLD	V.1	59

Bridge (0)   see Knights-bridge
Bridle (1)
| Mellefont: | Witch in her own Bridle. | . . . . | 167 | DOUEL DLR | IV.1 | 5 |

Brief (3)
Lucy:	To be brief then; what is the reason your Master did	. .	66	OLD BATCH	III.1	217
Setter:	Why, to be brief, for I have weighty Affairs depending:	.	105	OLD BATCH	V.1	341
Sr Sampson:	thy own Father, and this is honest Brief Buckram the Lawyer.	279	FOR LOVE	IV.1	158

Briefly (1)
| Setter: | To answer you as briefly--He has a cause to be try'd | . . | 66 | OLD BATCH | III.1 | 220 |

Bright (6)
Almeria:	To that bright Heav'n, where my Alphonso reigns,	. . .	330	M. ERIDE	I.1	183
Gonsalez:	The Sun, bright Conquest, and your brighter Eyes,	. . .	331	M. EEIDE	I.1	221
Osmyn-Alph:	Of Light, to the bright Source of all. There, in	. . .	353	M. EEIDE	III.1	132
Osmyn-Alph:	Of Light, to the bright Source of all. For there	. . .	353	M. EEIDE	III.1	V132
Witwoud:	I confess I do blaze to Day, I am too bright.	. . . .	419	WAY WORLD	II.1	344
Sir Wilful:	And that makes him so bright,	. . . .	455	WAY WORLD	IV.1	420

Brighter (1)
| Gonsalez: | The Sun, bright Conquest, and your brighter Eyes, | . . . | 331 | M. EBIDE | I.1 | 221 |

Brightest (1)
| Sr Sampson: | your Ephemeris--The brightest Star in the blew Firmament | . | 307 | FOR LOVE | V.1 | 380 |

Brightness (3)
Manuel:	In opposition to my Brightness, you	. . . .	333	M. BRIDE	I.1	V281
Manuel:	To my Brightness, like Daughters of Affliction.	. . .	333	M. BRIDE	I.1	282
Osmyn-Alph:	What Brightness, breaks upon me, thus thro' Shades,	. .	353	M. EBIDE	III.1	140

Brillant (2)
| Lady Froth: | Belle-air or Brillant of Mr. Brisk; the Solemnity, yet | . | 139 | DOUEL DLR | II.1 | 49 |
| Lady Froth: | bel air or Brillant cf Mr. Brisk; the Solemnity, yet | . | 139 | DOUEL DLR | II.1 | V 49 |

Bring (50)
Araminta:	hearing. You'l bring my Cousin.	. . . .	60	OLD BATCH	II.2	209
Capt Bluff:	go--and bring it me hither. I'le stay here for you.	. .	67	OLD BATCH	III.1	251
Bellmour:	would bring her to administer Remedies for my Distemper.	.	95	OLD BATCH	IV.4	213
Sir Joseph:	I warrant, I'll bring you into the Ladies good Graces.	.	103	OLD BATCH	V.1	263
Sharper:	Hist,--Bellmour: If you'll bring the Ladies, make	. .	107	OLD BATCH	V.1	390
Heartwell:	you? Did I bring a Physician to your Father when he lay	.	109	OLD BATCH	V.2	54
Brisk:	Enough, enough; Careless, bring your Apprehension	. .	129	DOUEL DLR	I.1	61
Maskwell:	open: 'twill be hard, if then you can't bring her to any	.	157	DOUEL DLR	III.1	253
Careless:	You bring that along with you, Sir Paul, that shall	.	159	DOUEL DLR	III.1	323
Sir Paul:	could bring it about, Mr. Careless.	. . . . . .	162	DOUEL DLR	III.1	449
Sir Paul:	He? And wilt thou bring a Grandscn at 9 Months	. .	173	DOUEL DLR	IV.1	223
Sir Paul:	any of my Family that will bring Children into the World.	.	173	DOUEL DLR	IV.1	227
Lord Touch:	inform my Nephew, and do you quickly as you can, bring	.	200	DOUEL DLR	V.1	487
Jeremy:	What our Endeavours can, and bring this day,	. . . .	213	FOR LOVE	PRO.	24
Jeremy:	bring you to; your Coaches and your Liveries; your	. .	217	FOR LCVE	I.1	43
Valentine:	himself, or were resolv'd to turn Author, and bring the	.	219	FOR LGVE	I.1	106
Valentine:	one day bring a Confinement on your Body, my Friend.	.	221	FOR LCVE	I.1	200
Tattle:	Well, I can't help it,--you must bring him up;	. . . .	225	FOR LCVE	I.1	359
Valentine:	bring me into Disgrace with a certain Woman of Quality--	.	227	FOR LCVE	I.1	425
Angelica:	What did I say? I hope you won't bring me to	. . . .	229	FOR LCVE	I.1	497
Tattle:	Look to it, Nurse; I can bring Witness that you have a	.	238	FOR LCVE	II.1	119
Sr Sampson:	You say true, I beg your Pardon;--I'll bring all off--	.	255	FCR LCVE	III.1	65
Sr Sampson:	But I'll bring him a Parson to tell him, that the Devil's a	267	FOR LGVE	III.1	508
Scandal:	Liar--Or if that won't do, I'll bring a Lawyer that	.	267	FOR LGVE	III.1	509
Foresight:	of a rightful Inheritance, will bring Judgments upon us.	.	268	FOR LCVE	III.1	545
Foresight:	Do I? And d'ye hear--bring me, let me see--	. . . .	270	FOR LCVE	III.1	645
Mrs Frail:	the turning of the Tide, bring me the Urinal;--And I	.	270	FOR LCVE	III.1	647
Mrs Fore:	upon me, if we could bring it about.	. . . . . .	287	FOR LCVE	IV.1	461
Valentine:	if in one of his mad fits he will bring you to him in her	.	288	FOR LCVE	IV.1	471
Sr Sampson:	Acquaint Jeremy with it, he may easily bring it	. . .	292	FCR LCVE	IV.1	616
Sr Sampson:	Fall; and Bud when they should bring forth Fruit. I am of	.	298	FOR LCVE	V.1	36
Almeria:	bring your Fore-castle Jests upcn your Father? But I shall	308	FOR LCVE	V.1	423
Leonora:	They must to me bring Curses, Grief of Heart,	. . .	327	M. EBIDE	I.1	62
Manuel:	And grant, that Time may bring her some Belief.	. . .	329	M. EEIDE	I.1	151
Manuel:	That cnly Zara's Mutes, or such who bring	. . . .	365	M. EBIDE	IV.1	168
Manuel:	Watch her returning Sense, and bring me Word:	. . .	370	M. BRIDE	IV.1	365
Fainall:	When thou hast endued him, bring me his Bcbe;	. . .	374	M. EBIDE	V.1	83
Betty:	Petulant and Witwoud.--Bring me some	. . . . .	398	WAY WCBLD	I.1	102
Betty:	Did not the Messenger bring you one but now, Sir?	. .	401	WAY WORLD	I.1	240
Coachman:	Did not a Messenger bring you one but now, Sir?	. . .	401	WAY WORLD	I.1	V240
Lady Wish:	You must bring two Dishes of Chocolate and a	. . .	404	WAY WORLD	I.1	350
Lady Wish:	Acorn? Why didst thou not bring thy Thimble? Hast thou	.	425	WAY WCBLD	III.1	30
Mirabell:	Foible; bring her hither. I'll send him as I go--When	.	445	WAY WCRLD	IV.1	38
Lady Wish:	bring you home in a pretended fright, when you think you	.	451	WAY WCRLD	IV.1	240
Waitwell:	Comfort; bring the Black-box.	. . . .	461	WAY WCRLD	IV.1	637
Lady Wish:	And may I presume to bring a Contract to be	. . . .	461	WAY WCRLD	IV.1	638
Foible:	Bring you will; but come alive, pray.	. . . . .	461	WAY WCRLD	IV.1	640
Mincing:	Peace and Quietness by my good will: I had rather bring	.	464	WAY WCRLD	V.1	87
Marwood:	sober, and to bring him to them. My Lady is resolv'd to	.	465	WAY WORLD	V.1	114
	Quoif like a Man Midwife to bring your Daughter's	. .	467	WAY WOBLD	V.1	213

Bringing (2)
Careless:	effectually chown, as in bringing forth a Child to				
	Disinherit	. . . .	131	DOUEL DLR	I.1	160
Fainall:	Wife's--Why she had parted with hers before; so bringing	.	443	WAY WCRLD	III.1	686

Brings (5)
Bellmour:	had a little Experience, that brings to my mind--	. .	60	OLD BATCH	II.2	223
Maskwell:	you, brings me certain Ruin. Allow it, I would betray you,	.	136	DOUBL DLR	I.1	341
Scandal:	and the Uneasiness that has attended me ever since, brings		269	FCR LCVE	III.1	591
Ben:	I warrant that brings 'em, an' they be within bearing.	.	274	FOR LOVE	III.1	794
Almeria:	And Joy he brings to every other Heart,	. . . . .	330	M. EBIDE	I.1	169

Brink (2)
| Maskwell: | Mellefont upon the brink of Ruin, and left him nought | . | 137 | DOUEL DLR | I.1 | 378 |
| Maskwell: | Mellefont upon the brink of Ruin, and left him none | . | 137 | DOUEL DLR | I.1 | V378 |

Briny (1)
| Zara: | Pale and expiring, drench'd in briny Waves | . . . . . | 346 | M. EBIDE | II.2 | 277 |

Brisk (43)

		PAGE	TITLE	ACT.SC	LINE
	(Enter Brisk.)	128	DOUBL DLR	I.1	19
Mellefont:	O' my word, Brisk, that was a home thrust; you	128	DOUBL DLR	I.1	31
Mellefont:	No, no, hang him, he has no tast.--but dear Brisk	128	DOUBL DLR	I.1	43
Mellefont:	No, no, hang him, he has no taste.--but dear Brisk	128	DOUBL DLR	I.1 V	43
Mellefont:	Truth. Prithee do thou wear none to day; but allow Brisk	129	DOUBL DLR	I.1	71
	and Brisk.)	131	DOUBL DLR	I.1	171
Sir Paul:	but Mr. Brisk--where is he? I swear and vow, he's a	132	DOUBL DLR	I.1	181
Sir Paul:	Brisk Jokes, your Lordships Laugh does so become you,	132	DOUBL DLR	I.1	188
Sir Paul:	With all my heart.--Mr. Brisk you'll come to	133	DOUBL DLR	I.1	218
Lord Froth:	Brisk to have Wit; my Wife says, he has a great deal. I	134	DOUBL DLR	I.1	274
Mellefont:	Let him alone, Brisk, he is obstinately bent not to	134	DOUBL DLR	I.1	280
Lady Froth:	Belle-air or Brillant of Mr. Brisk; the Solemnity, yet	139	DOUBL DLR	II.1	49
Lady Froth:	bel air or Brillant of Mr. Brisk; the Solemnity, yet	139	DOUBL DLR	II.1 V	49
	(Enter Lord Froth, Mellefont, Brisk.)	139	DOUBL DLR	II.1	57
Lady Froth:	Ah! Gallantry to the last degree--Mr. Brisk,	140	DOUBL DLR	II.1	81
Lady Froth:	Brisk has a World of Wit?	140	DOUBL DLR	II.1	87
Lady Froth:	Communicating all to Mr. Brisk.	142	DOUBL DLR	II.1	140
Lord Froth:	No, no, I'll allow Mr. Brisk; have you nothing	142	DOUBL DLR	II.1	141
Lady Froth:	Yes, I believe I have.--Mr. Brisk, come will	142	DOUBL DLR	II.1	143
	(Exit Lady Froth and Brisk.)	142	DOUBL DLR	II.1	146
	(Enter Lady Froth and Brisk.)	163	DOUBL DLR	III.1	501
Cynthia:	Fie Mr. Brisk, 'tis Eringo's for her Cough.	165	DOUBL DLR	III.1	569
Cynthia:	Fie Mr. Brisk, Eringo's for her Cough.	165	DOUBL DLR	III.1 V	569
Lady Froth:	Oh you made a Song upon her, Mr. Brisk.	166	DOUBL DLR	III.1	588
Lady Froth:	--Come, my dear Cynthia, Mr. Brisk, we'll go see	167	DOUBL DLR	III.1	615
	(Enter Brisk.)	174	DOUBL DLR	IV.1	266
Sir Paul:	angry, Mr. Brisk.	174	DOUBL DLR	IV.1	270
Sir Paul:	Good strange! Mr. Brisk is such a Merry Facetious	174	DOUBL DLR	IV.1	274
Lady Froth:	O Heavens Mr. Brisk! What's the matter?	175	DOUBL DLR	IV.1	312
Lady Froth:	thought Mr. Brisk could have been in Love, ha ha ha. O	176	DOUBL DLR	IV.1	333
Lady Froth:	Brisk, ha ha ha.	176	DOUBL DLR	IV.1	353
Lady Froth:	Oh my adored Mr. Brisk!	177	DOUBL DLR	IV.1	359
Lady Froth:	purely, but I vow Mr. Brisk, I can't tell how to come so	177	DOUBL DLR	IV.1	368
Lady Froth:	Mr. Brisk?	177	DOUBL DLR	IV.1	375
Sir Paul:	the Garden with Mr. Brisk.	200	DOUBL DLR	V.1	507
	(Enter Lady Froth, Brisk.)	201	DOUBL DLR	V.1	516
Lady Froth:	My dear, Mr. Brisk and I have been Star-gazing,	201	DOUBL DLR	V.1	519
Lady Froth:	Well, I swear, Mr. Brisk, you understood	201	DOUBL DLR	V.1	528
Lord Froth:	Mr. Brisk, my Coach shall set you down.	202	DOUBL DLR	V.1	554
Sr Sampson:	Ben's a brisk Boy: He has got her into a Corner, Father's	265	FOR LOVE	III.1	457
Foible:	By Storm, Madam. Sir Rowland's a brisk Man.	429	WAY WORLD	III.1	175
Lady Wish:	Is he! O then he'll Importune, if he's a brisk	429	WAY WORLD	III.1	176
Lady Wish:	O I'm glad he's a brisk Man. Let my	429	WAY WORLD	III.1	180

Brisk's (1)

Mellefont:	taken up, with admiring one another, and Brisk's	130	DOUBL DLR	I.1	134

Bristles (1)

Brisk:	great Beard that bristles through it, and makes her look as	166	DOUBL DLR	III.1	586

British (1)

Sir Wilful:	But let British Lads sing,	456	WAY WORLD	IV.1	455

Broad (1)

Lord Froth:	upon the broad grin, all laugh and no Company; ah, then	162	DOUBL DLR	III.1	459

Broader (1)

Sir Wilful:	round the Edges, no broader than a Subpoena. I might expect	439	WAY WORLD	III.1	542

Broaker (1)

Lady Wish:	you were Catering for Mirabell; I have been broaker for	463	WAY WORLD	V.1	48

Broke (11)

Belinda:	I have broke the ice for you, Mr. Vainlove, and so I	87	OLD BATCH	IV.3	142
Mellefont:	suspicions just,--but see the Company is broke up,	131	DOUBL DLR	I.1	168
Brisk:	Let me see, let me see, my Lord, I broke my Glass that	135	DOUBL DLR	I.1	291
Sir Paul:	poor Father,--and that would certainly have broke my	146	DOUBL DLR	II.1	280
Maskwell:	for your Passion broke in such imperfect terms, that yet	198	DOUBL DLR	V.1	414
Jeremy:	Sir, I have a most broke my Heart about him--I can't	279	FOR LOVE	IV.1	131
Jeremy:	Sir, I have almost broke my Heart about him--I can't	279	FOR LOVE	IV.1 V	131
Manuel:	Unus'd to wait, I broke through her Delay,	337	M. BRIDE	I.1	456
Mirabell:	good old Lady broke thro' her painful Taciturnity, with an	396	WAY WORLD	I.1	35
Millamant:	a Flame--I have broke my Fan--Mincing, lend me yours;	432	WAY WORLD	III.1	288
Sir Wilful:	fairer? If I have broke any thing, I'll pay for't, an it	470	WAY WORLD	V.1	318
	cost a				

Broken (7)

Heartwell:	The Bone when broken, than when made a Bride.	108	OLD BATCH	V.2	15
Mrs Fore:	I cannot say that he has once broken my Rest, since we	270	FOR LOVE	III.1	623
Foresight:	Truly Mr. Scandal, I was so taken up with broken	284	FOR LOVE	IV.1	340
Almeria:	I gave my Dear Alphonso, basely broken.	330	M. BRIDE	I.1	173
Manuel:	Which I'd have broken.	334	M. BRIDE	I.1	356
Osmyn-Alph:	When broken Echoes of a distant Voice,	343	M. BRIDE	II.2	160
Lady Wish:	Beads broken, and a Quilted Night-cap with one Ear. Go,	462	WAY WORLD	V.1	17

Brooding (1)

Brisk:	Daughter your self; you're always brooding over her like	174	DOUBL DLR	IV.1	272

Broods (1)

	O'er which she broods to hatch the Changling-Kind.	393	WAY WORLD	PRO.	8

Brook (1)

Manuel:	So ill can brook Captivity;	336	M. BRIDE	I.1	432

Broom-sticks (3)

Lady Wish:	with Broom-sticks. Call up the Wenches.	457	WAY WORLD	IV.1	463
Lady Wish:	with Broom-sticks. Call up the Wenches with broom-sticks.	457	WAY WORLD	IV.1 V	463

Brothel (1)

Heartwell:	hot Brothel. Ask no Questions.	105	OLD BATCH	V.1	324

Brother (48)
see Booby-Brother

Lady Touch:	My Lord, can you blame my Brother	150	DOUBL DLR	III.1	1
Lady Touch:	my Niece? how know you that my Brother will consent,	191	DOUBL DLR	V.1	128
Lady Touch:	that you're a Fool, Brother?	192	DOUBL DLR	V.1	166
Jeremy:	Younger Brother shou'd come from Sea, he'd never look	218	FOR LOVE	I.1	84
Valentine:	was sent to Sea three Years ago? This Brother, my Father	225	FOR LOVE	I.1	333
Valentine:	to his Estate after his Death, to my younger Brother, he	225	FOR LOVE	I.1	336
Mrs Frail:	Brother Benjamin is landed. And my Brother Foresight's	231	FOR LOVE	I.1	567

```
                                                          PAGE   TITLE      ACT.SC LINE

Bubling (1)
  Almeria:    Yet bubling from his Wounds--O more than savage!    . . . 382  M. BRIDE     V.2  235
Buckets (1)
  Bellmour:   Tyrant there and I, are two Buckets that can never come  . 57  OLD BATCH    II.2 118
Buckinghamshire (1)
  Foresight:  translated by a Reverend Buckinghamshire Bard.   . . . . 236  FOR LOVE     II.1  50
Buckram (9)
  Sr Sampson: D'ye see, Mr. Buckram, here's the Paper sign'd  . . .  . 278  FOR LOVE     IV.1 112
  Sr Sampson: thy own Father, and this is honest Brief Buckram the Lawyer. 279  FOR LOVE     IV.1 158
  Sr Sampson: Mr. Buckram, bid him make haste back with the    . . .  281  FOR LOVE     IV.1 209
                          (Re-enter Jeremy with Buckram.)    . .  282  FOR LOVE     IV.1 236
                          (Exit Buckram.)    . . . . .  282  FOR LOVE     IV.1 245
              (Enter Sir Sampson, Angelica, with Buckram.)  . . 307  FOR LOVE     V.1  375
  Sr Sampson: be even with you, I won't give you a Groat. Mr. Buckram is 308 FOR LOVE     V.1  424
  Sr Sampson: Very good, Sir--Mr. Buckram, are you  . . . . . .  311  FOR LOVE     V.1  513
  Sr Sampson: Come, come, Mr. Buckram, the Pen and Ink.  . . . . . 311  FOR LOVE     V.1  528
Bucks (1)                      see Gads-bud
  Sir Joseph: The same Sir, of Wittoll-hall in Comitatu Bucks.  . . .  49  OLD BATCH    II.1  71
Bud (12)
  Fondlewife: Ay, I feel it here; I sprout, I bud, I blossom, I am  . .  92  OLD BATCH    IV.4 126
  Sir Paul:   Gads bud! I am provoked into a Fermentation, as   . . . 143  DOUBL DLR    II.1 195
  Sir Paul:   Hum, gads bud she says true,--well, my Lady,  . . . . 145  DOUBL DLR    II.1 238
  Sir Paul:   gads bud she's a Wife for a Cherubin! Do you think her   145  DOUBL DLR    II.1 265
  Sir Paul:   you, while you take aim at my Wife? Gads bud I was  . . 145  DOUBL DLR    II.1 267
  Sir Paul:   Gad's bud, she's a fine person--   . . . . . . . . 159  DOUBL DLR    III.1 347
  Sir Paul:   should hear--Gad's bud, you may talk of my Lady  . . . 160  DOUBL DLR    III.1 373
  Sir Paul:   Gad so, gad's bud--Tim, carry it to my Lady, you  . . 161  DOUBL DLR    III.1 395
  Sir Paul:   Gads bud, I am transported! give me leave to kiss  . . 172  DOUBL DLR    IV.1 192
  Sir Paul:   whether I fly on Ground, or walk in Air--Gads bud, she   172  DOUBL DLR    IV.1 198
  Sr Sampson: Fall; and Bud when they should bring forth Fruit. I am of  298  FOR LOVE     V.1  36
  Manuel:     Yet new, unborn and blooming in the Bud,   . . . . . 349  M. BRIDE     II.2 384
Budding (1)
  Fainall:    budding Antlers like a young Satyre, or a Citizens Child. 442  WAY WORLD    III.1 633
Buffet (1)
  Sharper:    loves to buffet with the Winds, meet the Tide and sail in  42  OLD BATCH    I.1  202
Buffoonry (1)
  Belinda:    now; could you but see with my Eyes, the buffoonry of  . 55  OLD BATCH    II.2  31
Build (4)
  Careless:   build upon. . . . . . . . . . . . . . . . . 130  DOUBL DLR    I.1  132
  Maskwell:   Honour was not of my seeking, nor would I build my   . . 189  DOUBL DLR    V.1   72
  Zara:       And build bold Hopes, on my dejected Fate?   . . . . 349  M. BRIDE     II.2 367
              To build on that might prove a vain Presumption,  . . 393  WAY WORLD    PRO.  18
Building (1)
  Vainlove:   In Castles ith' Air of thy own building: That's thy  . . 38  OLD BATCH    I.1   29
Bulging (1)
  Almeria:    And bulging 'gainst a Rock, was dash'd in pieces.  . . . 329  M. BRIDE     I.1  127
Bulk (1)
  Lady Wish:  Brandy-sellers Bulk, or against a dead Wall by a
                Ballad-monger. . . . . . . . . . . . . . 462  WAY WORLD    V.1   13
Bull (2)
  Angelica:   Spirits and the Celestial Signs, the Bull, and the Ram,  . 239  FOR LOVE     II.1 137
  Sir Wilful: and a Bull, and a Whore and a Bottle, and so conclude  . 439  WAY WORLD    III.1 547
Bully (12)
  Sharper:    Is that Bully of his in the Army?  . . . . . . .  46  OLD BATCH    I.1  365
  Sir Joseph: my Bully, my Back; agad my heart has gone a pit  . . .  51  OLD BATCH    II.1 140
  Sir Joseph: Ay Bully, a Devilish smart Fellow, 'a will fight  . . .  51  OLD BATCH    II.1 150
  Sir Joseph: Fellow as Cannibal, are not you Bully--Back?  . . . .  52  OLD BATCH    II.1 176
  Sir Joseph: you--Why what a Devil's the Matter, Bully, are you  . .  68  OLD BATCH    III.1 264
  Sir Joseph: What, Bully?  . . . . . . . . . . . . . . .  70  OLD BATCH    III.1 344
  Sir Joseph: and get 50 Pieces more from him. Adslidikins, Bully, we'll 85  OLD BATCH    IV.3  63
  Sir Joseph: Bully, dost thou see those Tearers? (Sings.) Look you what  85  OLD BATCH    IV.3  66
  Sir Joseph: in Aesop's Fables, Bully? A-Gad there are good Morals to  . 101  OLD BATCH    V.1  175
  Sir Joseph: How's this! Good Bully, hold your breath, and   . . . 102  OLD BATCH    V.1  203
  Sir Joseph: That's you, Bully Back.  . . . . . . . . . . . 102  OLD BATCH    V.1  210
  Sir Joseph: How now, Bully? What, melancholy because  . . . . . 103  OLD BATCH    V.1  260
Bum (1)
  Valentine:  shape, and a Jut with her Bum, would stir an Anchoret:  . 223  FOR LOVE     I.1  285
Bum-baily (2)
  Witwoud:    Bum-baily, that I grant you,--'Tis Pity faith; the  . . 403  WAY WORLD    I.1  299
  Witwoud:    Bum-baily, that I grant you,--'Tis Pity; the  . . . . 403  WAY WORLD    I.1 V299
Bumper (3)
  Sir Wilful: For a Bumper has not its Fellow.  . . . . . . . . 455  WAY WORLD    IV.1 402
  Sir Wilful: but he spits after a Bumper, and that's a Fault.  . . . 455  WAY WORLD    IV.1 414
  Sir Wilful: Fellows--If I had a Bumper I'd stand upon my  . . . . 456  WAY WORLD    IV.1 425
Bundle (1)
  Careless:   There's Saygrace tripping by with a bundle under his  . 196  DOUBL DLR    V.1  351
Bunyan's (1)
  Lady Wish:  Short View of the Stage, with Bunyan's Works to entertain . 426  WAY WORLD    III.1  66
Burden (2)
  Almeria:    May lay the Burden down, and sink in Slumbers  . . . . 340  M. BRIDE     II.2  19
  Witwoud:    a Mule, a Beast of Burden, he has brought me a Letter  . 401  WAY WORLD    I.1  244
Burdens (1)
  Heartwell:  burdens, are forced to undergo Dressing, Dancing, Singing,  44  OLD BATCH    I.1  273
Buried (3)
  Lady Touch: Ground, be buried quick beneath it, e're I be consenting to 186  DOUBL DLR    IV.2  99
  Lady Touch: Ground, be buried quick beneath it, e're I'll be
                consenting to  . . . . . . . . . . . . . 186  DOUBL DLR    IV.2 V 99
  Marwood:    reflect that Guilt upon me, which should lie buried in your 414  WAY WORLD    II.1 177
Burn (5)
  Belinda:    more, that begins with an, I burn--Or an, I beseech  . . 59  OLD BATCH    II.2 171
  Lady Touch: and Recesses of my Soul.--Oh Mellefont! I burn;  . . . 137  DOUBL DLR    I.1  398
  Lady Touch: burn the vile Traytor.  . . . . . . . . . . . 191  DOUBL DLR    V.1  152
  Sr Sampson: That he shall, or I'll burn his Globes--Body  . . . . 308  FOR LOVE     V.1  395
  Lady Wish:  Uneasie I wou'd burn it--speak if it do's--but  . . . 460  WAY WORLD    IV.1 572
Burning (5)
  Heartwell:  But proves a burning Caustick when apply'd.  . . . . 108  OLD BATCH    V.2   13

                                    91
```

Burning (continued)

Brisk:	spite, by the Gods! and burning envy.--I'le be	128	DOUEL DLR	I.1	26
Scandal:	Then I have a Lady burning of Brandy in a Cellar	233	FOR LOVE	I.1	639
Scandal:	Then I have a Lady burning Brandy in a Cellar	233	FOR LOVE	I.1	V639
Zara:	--Rain, rain ye Stars, spout from your burning Orbs	380	M. BRIDE	V.2	V168

Burnishes (1)

Marwood:	before, but it burnishes on her Hips. Indeed, Millamant, you	433	WAY WORLD	III.1	319

Burns (4)

Maskwell:	Yet I am wretched--O there is a secret burns	188	DOUEL DLR	V.1	28
Osmyn-Alph:	Burns dim, and glimmers with expiring Light.	357	M. BRIDE	III.1	324
Foible:	of her Beauty, that he burns with Impatience to lie at her	423	WAY WORLD	II.1	523
Foible:	Impatience in which Sir Rowland burns for the dear hour	428	WAY WORLD	III.1	126

Burrough (1)

Mellefont:	Hold, Madam, you have no more holes to your Burrough,	184	DOUEL DLR	IV.2	42

Burst (7)

Brisk:	I shall burst else.--And yonder your Uncle my Lord	128	DOUBL DLR	I.1	53
Lord Touch:	Yes, I will contain, tho' I cou'd burst.	199	DOUEL DLR	V.1	430
Heli:	I know his Noble Heart would burst with Shame	338	M. BRIDE	II.1	33
Osmyn-Alph:	O I could tear and burst the Strings of Life,	352	M. BRIDE	III.1	87
Almeria:	Thy Heart will burst, thy Eyes look red and start;	356	M. BRIDE	III.1	273
Zara:	Split Heart, burst ev'ry Vein, at this dire Object:	380	M. BRIDE	V.2	V163
Witwoud:	staid any longer I shou'd have burst,--I must have been let	453	WAY WORLD	IV.1	327

Bury (1)

Osmyn-Alph:	And bury me alive;	358	M. BRIDE	III.1	355

Busie (3)

Mellefont:	Hell is not more busie than her Brain, nor contains more	129	DOUBL DLR	I.1	77
Lady Ply:	I'm busie, Sir Paul, I wonder at your	163	DOUEL DLR	III.1	491
Gonsalez:	Sure Death already has been busie here.	376	M. BRIDE	V.2	3

Busied (4)

Bellmour:	and keeps him busied in the search.	42	OLD BATCH	I.1	207
Maskwell:	So, why so, while you are busied in making your	193	DOUBL DLR	V.1	222
Almeria:	Are busied in the General Joy, that thou	331	M. BRIDE	I.1	197
Almeria:	Are wrap'd and busied in the general Joy,	331	M. BRIDE	I.1	V197

Business (47)

Vainlove:	early Sallies are not usual to me; but Business as you see	37	OLD BATCH	I.1	6
Vainlove:	Sir--(Shewing Letters.) And Business must be follow'd,	37	OLD BATCH	I.1	7
Bellmour:	Pox o' Business--And so must Time, my	37	OLD BATCH	I.1	9
Bellmour:	Business!--And so must Time, my	37	OLD BATCH	I.1	V 9
Bellmour:	Friend, be close pursued, or lost. Business is the rub of Life,	37	OLD BATCH	I.1	10
Bellmour:	nothing. Come come, leave Business to Idlers, and Wisdom	37	OLD BATCH	I.1	22
Bellmour:	Business is not my Element--I rowl in a higher Orb	38	OLD BATCH	I.1	27
Vainlove:	I do Wine--And this Business is none of my seeking; I	39	OLD BATCH	I.1	95
Bellmour:	Business upon my hands, because it lay too heavy upon his:	41	OLD BATCH	I.1	141
Bellmour:	No faith, not for that--But there's a Business of	41	OLD BATCH	I.1	151
Sharper:	Prithee what mighty Business of Consequence canst	41	OLD BATCH	I.1	154
Heartwell:	No, besides my Business, I see a Fool coming this	46	OLD BATCH	I.1	335
Lucy:	in the name of opportunity mind your own Business.	61	OLD BATCH	III.1	9
Sir Joseph:	his Business--He durst as soon have kiss'd you, as kick'd	70	OLD BATCH	III.1	359
Laetitia:	No you shan't neglect your business for me--No	78	OLD BATCH	IV.1	131
Lucy:	An Executioner qualified to do your Business. He has	97	OLD BATCH	V.1	18
Bellmour:	Well, Your Business with me, Lucy?	97	OLD BATCH	V.1	39
Setter:	the Business is undone.	103	OLD BATCH	V.1	241
Sir Joseph:	No, no, Never fear, Man, the Lady's business shall	103	OLD BATCH	V.1	242
Mellefont:	My Business here, was humbly to petition:	113	OLD BATCH	EPI.	18
Mellefont:	excuse me, I have a little business.	128	DOUBL DLR	I.1	44
Maskwell:	Cynthia; that did my business; that convinced your Aunt,	149	DOUBL DLR	II.1	422
Lady Touch:	your Temper. I'll make an excuse of sudden Business to	153	DOUEL DLR	III.1	117
Maskwell:	about our business, it shall be Tithes in your way.	194	DOUEL DLR	V.1	279
Maskwell:	the business in hand--have you provided a Habit for	195	DOUEL DLR	V.1	283
Lord Touch:	My thoughts were on serious business, not	197	DOUEL DLR	V.1	365
Valentine:	I cannot talk about Business with a Thirsty Palate.--	222	FOR LOVE	I.1	238
Trapland:	Hold, Sweet-heart.--This is not to our Business:	222	FOR LOVE	I.1	245
Trapland:	business.--You're a Wag.	223	FOR LOVE	I.1	282
Valentine:	No faith, we'll mind the Widow's business, fill	223	FOR LOVE	I.1	283
Trapland:	business must be done, are you ready to--	224	FOR LOVE	I.1	301
Trapland:	I hope you forgive me, my business requires--	225	FOR LOVE	I.1	326
Tattle:	it their Business to tell Stories, and say this and that of	227	FOR LOVE	I.1	431
Foresight:	for Business, Mercury governs this hour.	236	FOR LOVE	II.1	42
Mrs Frail:	Yes marry will I--A great piece of business to	246	FOR LOVE	II.1	418
Scandal:	So faith, your Business is done here; now you may	255	FOR LOVE	III.1	91
Scandal:	to Night, because he has some Business to do in a Dream.	266	FOR LOVE	III.1	503
Sr Sampson:	directed by a Dreamer, an Omen-hunter, and defer Business	283	FOR LOVE	IV.1	289
Jeremy:	Ah Sir, if you are not very faithful and close in this Business,	301	FOR LOVE	V.1	167
Manuel:	An unforeseen, unwelcome Hour of Business,	363	M. BRIDE	IV.1	105
Betty:	Yes; what's your Business?	400	WAY WORLD	I.1	182
Mirabell:	Petulant, about that Business.	406	WAY WORLD	I.1	424
Waitwell:	to Business, Sir. I have instructed her as well as I cou'd. If	423	WAY WORLD	II.1	509
Mrs Fain:	your Proxy in this Affair; but I have business of my own.	446	WAY WORLD	IV.1	68
Millamant:	Have you any business with me, Sir Wilfull?	447	WAY WORLD	IV.1	113
Millamant:	business.--	448	WAY WORLD	IV.1	141
Foible:	at this Juncture! this was the business that brought Mr.	461	WAY WORLD	IV.1	611

Buss (1)

Fondlewife:	buss poor Nykin--And I wont leave thee--I'le lose all first.	78	OLD BATCH	IV.1	118

Bustle (2)

Angelica:	Neighbourhood--What a Bustle did you keep against the	237	FOR LOVE	II.1	79
Painall:	Proof, and something of a Constitution to bustle thro' the	415	WAY WORLD	II.1	213

But (1167)

Butcher'd (1)

Sir Joseph:	have Butcher'd me last night: No doubt, they would	47	OLD BATCH	II.1	4

Butler (4)

Angelica:	only because the Butler had mislaid some of the Apostle's	237	FOR LOVE	II.1	89
Angelica:	only because the Butler had mislaid some of the Apostle	237	FOR LOVE	II.1	V 89
Miss Prue:	Robin the Butler, he says he loves me, and he's a Handsome	305	FOR LOVE	V.1	317

Call   (continued)

Speaker	Text	PAGE	TITLE	ACT.SC	LINE
Ben:	No matter what I can do? don't call Names,--I	287	FOR LOVE	IV.1	434
Ben:	I don't know what you may call Madness--But	307	FOR LOVE	V.1	372
Scandal:	Call 'em, Jeremy.	313	FOR LOVE	V.1	604
Almeria:	To thee, to thee I call, to thee Alphonso.	340	M. BRIDE	II.2	32
Osmyn-Alph:	I did, and thou didst call me.	343	M. BRIDE	II.2	157
Osmyn-Alph:	I did, and thou, my love, didst call me; thou.	343	M. BRIDE	II.2	V157
Osmyn-Alph:	And thought, I heard thy Spirit call Alphonso.	344	M. BRIDE	II.2	163
Osmyn-Alph:	O call not to my Mind what you have done,	347	M. BRIDE	II.2	288
Heli:	Are risen in Arms, and call for Chiefs to head	351	M. BRIDE	III.1	70
Osmyn-Alph:	I hear 'em call to lead 'em on to Liberty,	351	M. BRIDE	III.1	83
Zara:	So kindly of my Fault, to call it Madness;	354	M. BRIDE	III.1	179
Zara:	And call it Passion; then, be still more kind,	354	M. BRIDE	III.1	181
Zara:	And call that Passion Love.	354	M. BRIDE	III.1	182
Osmyn-Alph:	Is this to call thee mine? O hold my Heart;	357	M. BRIDE	III.1	329
Osmyn-Alph:	To call thee mine? yes, thus, ev'n thus, to call	357	M. BRIDE	III.1	330
Zara:	You more. One that did call himself Alphonso,	364	M. BRIDE	IV.1	116
Zara:	You mcre. One who did call himself Alphonso,	364	M. BRIDE	IV.1	V116
Manuel:	Away, off, let me go,--Call her Attendants.	369	M. BRIDE	IV.1	335
Almeria:	Ye Winds and Waves, I call ye all to witness.	370	M. BRIDE	IV.1	360
Gonsalez:	Would all were false as that; for whom you call	377	M. BRIDE	V.2	40
Fainall:	Mother. If you marry Millamant you must call Cousins	400	WAY WORLD	I.1	194
Mirabell:	will construe an Affront into a Jest; and call downright	401	WAY WORLD	I.1	230
Witwoud:	and something more by the Week, to call on him	405	WAY WORLD	I.1	360
Witwoud:	found out this way, I have known him call for	405	WAY WORLD	I.1	366
Fainall:	Call for himself? What dost thou mean?	405	WAY WORLD	I.1	368
Witwoud:	himself, that I mean, call for himself, wait for himself, nay	405	WAY WORLD	I.1	375
Mirabell:	or I shall call your Interpreter.	406	WAY WORLD	I.1	433
Petulant:	well bred, he's what you call a--What-dee-call-'em.	408	WAY WORLD	I.1	505
Lady Wish:	With Mirabell! You call my Blood into my	426	WAY WORLD	III.1	49
Witwoud:	slabber and kiss cne another when they meet, like a Call of	439	WAY WORLD	III.1	535
Sir Wilful:	Tony, belike, I may'nt call him Brother for fear of offence.	441	WAY WORLD	III.1	605
Lady Wish:	Ods my life, I'll send him to her. Call her down,	445	WAY WORLD	IV.1	37
Sir Wilful:	All's one for that,--yes, yes, if your Concerns call you,	448	WAY WORLD	IV.1	145
Lady Wish:	with Broom-sticks. Call up the Wenches.	457	WAY WORLD	IV.1	463
Lady Wish:	with Broom-sticks. Call up the Wenches with broom-sticks.	457	WAY WORLD	IV.1	V463
Lady Wish:	Call in the Dancers;--Sir Rowland, we'll	459	WAY WORLD	IV.1	566
Mrs Fain:	prepare to vouch when I call her.	465	WAY WORLD	V.1	119
Lady Wish:	Out Caterpillar, Call not me Aunt, I know thee	470	WAY WORLD	V.1	312
Sir Wilful:	--'Sheart, I'll call him in,--an I set on't	471	WAY WORLD	V.1	351
Foible:	Entertainment are yet within Call.	478	WAY WORLD	V.1	606

Call'd (16)

Speaker	Text	PAGE	TITLE	ACT.SC	LINE
Bellmour:	a Title; he is call'd, Capt. Bluffe.	47	OLD BATCH	I.1	384
Araminta:	Bellmour last Night, and call'd him alcud in your sleep.	55	OLD BATCH	II.2	38
Boy:	think they call'd him.	107	OLD BATCH	V.2	3
Lord Froth:	Barbarous! I'd as lieve you call'd me Fool.	132	DOUBL DLR	I.1	186
Brisk:	know the Sun is call'd Heav'ns Charioteer.	164	DOUBL DLR	III.1	509
Valentine:	you call'd me. But here I am, and if you don't mean to	244	FOR LOVE	II.1	334
Mrs Fore:	place call'd the World's-End? I'll swear you can keep your	247	FOR LOVE	II.1	451
Tattle:	True; I was call'd Turk-Tattle all over the Parish--	258	FOR LOVE	III.1	168
Miss Prue:	I won't be call'd Names, nor I won't be abus'd	264	FOR LOVE	III.1	428
Ben:	know her, Sir. Before she was Marry'd, she was call'd	273	FOR LOVE	III.1	752
Sr Sampson:	Weather; and destroy that Usurper of a Bed call'd a	308	FOR LOVE	V.1	406
	Whom, as I think they call'd--Py--Pythagories,	315	FOR LOVE	EPI.	12
Osmyn-Alph:	How I'm not call'd Alphonso, now, but Osmyn;	345	M. BRIDE	II.2	207
	Sure scribbling Fools, call'd Poets, fare the worst.	393	M. BRIDE	PRO.	2
Millamant:	and dee hear, I won't be call'd names after I'm Married;	450	WAY WORLD	IV.1	194
Millamant:	positively I won't be call'd Names.	450	WAY WORLD	IV.1	195

Called (1)

Speaker	Text	PAGE	TITLE	ACT.SC	LINE
Fondlewife:	called a Cuckold, Heh. Is it not so? Come, I'm	94	OLD BATCH	IV.4	185

Calling (1)

Speaker	Text	PAGE	TITLE	ACT.SC	LINE
Lucy:	Calling should be expos'd and scandaliz'd--I cannot bear it.	66	OLD BATCH	III.1	210

Callous (1)

Speaker	Text	PAGE	TITLE	ACT.SC	LINE
Valentine:	come forth with lab'ring Callous Hands, a Chine of Steel,	289	FOR LOVE	IV.1	523

Calls (9)   see Cat-calls

Speaker	Text	PAGE	TITLE	ACT.SC	LINE
Bellmour:	image cf Valour. He calls him his Back, and indeed they	46	OLD BATCH	I.1	357
Belinda:	Prithee tell it all the World, it's false. Betty. (Calls)	56	OLD BATCH	II.2	61
Araminta:	your Sex--Who's there? (Calls.)	58	OLD BATCH	II.2	155
Mrs Fore:	(Calls.)	270	FOR LOVE	III.1	V629
Osmyn-Alph:	Who calls that wretched thing, that was Alphcnso?	340	M. BRIDE	II.2	35
Almeria:	Now calls me Murderer, and Parricide.	368	M. BRIDE	IV.1	284
Almeria:	My Father's Voice; hollow it sounds, and calls	371	M. BRIDE	IV.1	V392
Almeria:	The Tomb it calls--I'll follow it, for there	371	M. BRIDE	IV.1	393
Lady Wish:	Affairs really I know not what to do-- (Calls)--Foible--I	431	WAY WORLD	III.1	256

Calm (11)

Speaker	Text	PAGE	TITLE	ACT.SC	LINE
Capt Bluff:	O I am calm Sir, calm as a discharg'd Culverin--But	54	OLD BATCH	II.1	241
Silvia:	Frowns, and make calm an angry Face; will soften a	72	OLD BATCH	III.2	66
Heartwell:	Damn your pity. But let me be calm a little.--	109	OLD BATCH	V.2	50
Lady Touch:	--Calm Villain! How unconcern'd he stands, Confessing	135	DOUBL DLR	I.1	323
Lady Touch:	Nay, but will you be calm--indeed it's	152	DOUBL DLR	III.1	72
Lady Touch:	Now, now, now I am calm, and can hear	198	DOUBL DLR	V.1	410
Almeria:	(aside). Damn'd, damn'd Dissembler! Yet I will be calm,	326	M. BRIDE	I.1	8
Zara:	Yet I'll be calm--Dark and unknown Betrayer!	359	M. BRIDE	III.1	406
Almeria:	And of a suddain I am calm, as if	382	M. BRIDE	V.2	241

Cals (0)   see D'ee-cals

Calumniation (1)

Speaker	Text	PAGE	TITLE	ACT.SC	LINE
Tattle:	for his Calumniation!--I thank Heav'n, it has always been	226	FOR LOVE	I.1	393

Calves (1)

Speaker	Text	PAGE	TITLE	ACT.SC	LINE
Valentine:	and Atlas' Shoulders. Let Taliacotius trim the Calves of	289	FOR LOVE	IV.1	524

Cam'st (2)

Speaker	Text	PAGE	TITLE	ACT.SC	LINE
Almeria:	True; but how cam'st thou there? wert thou alone?	343	M. BRIDE	II.2	V158
Osmyn-Alph:	What Noise! Who's there? My Friend, how cam'st	350	M. BRIDE	III.1	39

Cambridge (2)

Speaker	Text	PAGE	TITLE	ACT.SC	LINE
Jeremy:	upon a Gentleman at Cambridge: Pray what was that	216	FOR LOVE	I.1	18

PAGE TITLE ACT.SC LINE

		PAGE	TITLE	ACT.SC	LINE
Cambridge	(continued)				
Jeremy:	my Head--I have been at Cambridge.	302	FOR LOVE	V.1	185
Came (36)					
Sir Joseph:	An it hadn't been for a civil Gentleman as came by	47	OLD BATCH	II.1	8
Sharper:	came half despairing to recover; but thanks to my better	49	OLD BATCH	II.1	83
Belinda:	the Equipage of a Wife and two Daughters, came to Mrs.	84	OLD BATCH	IV.3	24
Laetitia:	came open mouth'd upon me, and would have ravished a	90	OLD BATCH	IV.4	53
Fondlewife:	Well Sir, And what came you hither for?	94	OLD BATCH	IV.4	177
Mellefont:	then came the Storm I fear'd at first: For starting from my	130	DOUBL DLR	I.1	113
Cynthia:	I heard him loud as I came by the Closet-Door, and	167	DOUBL DLR	IV.1	1
Lady Froth:	Just now as I came in, bless me, why don't you	176	DOUBL DLR	IV.1	323
Sr Sampson:	you or no? Ouns who are you? Whence came you?	244	FOR LOVE	II.1	326
Sr Sampson:	What brought you into the World? How came you here,	244	FOR LOVE	II.1	327
Valentine:	I know no more why I came, than you do why	244	FOR LOVE	II.1	333
Sr Sampson:	go naked out of the World as you came into't.	244	FOR LOVE	II.1	338
Jeremy:	and I came up Stairs into the World; for I was born	245	FOR LOVE	II.1	381
Valentine:	him: I came to Angelica; but since she was gone abroad, it	246	FOR LOVE	II.1	408
Tattle:	came down in her Coach and Six Horses, and expos'd her	258	FOR LOVE	III.1	176
Ben:	Thought if it came about, Sir,	274	FOR LOVE	III.1	782
Ben:	If some of our Crew that came to see me, are not gone;	274	FOR LOVE	III.1	790
Ben:	Why, Father came and found me squabling with yon	285	FOR LOVE	IV.1	363
Almeria:	He came to me, and beg'd me by my Love,	329	M. BRIDE	I.1	136
Heli:	And as your self made free, hither I came	344	M. BRIDE	II.2	177
Osmyn-Alph:	What would you from a Wretch, that came to	346	M. BRIDE	II.2	258
Osmyn-Alph:	What would you from a Wretch, who came too	346	M. BRIDE	II.2	V258
Zara:	I'm angry: you're deceiv'd. I came to set	360	M. BRIDE	III.1	417
Zara:	I came prepar'd to die, and see thee die--	380	M. BRIDE	V.2	V165
Zara:	Nay, came prepar'd my self to give thee Death--	380	M. BRIDE	V.2	V166
Fainall:	came in, and was well receiv'd by her, while you	395	WAY WORLD	I.1	20
Mirabell:	all in her own Name, my old Lady Wishfort came in.--	395	WAY WORLD	I.1	24
Servant-M:	afraid his Lungs would have fail'd before it came to our	398	WAY WORLD	I.1	117
Mrs Fain:	You were dress'd before I came abroad.	419	WAY WORLD	II.1	354
Mirabell:	knew I came to impart a Secret to you, that concern'd my	421	WAY WORLD	II.1	430
Mirabell:	But how you came to know it--	422	WAY WORLD	II.1	484
Lady Wish:	before she came to me, like Maritornes the Asturian in Don	426	WAY WORLD	III.1	37
Marwood:	I saw her but now, as I came mask'd through	426	WAY WORLD	III.1	47
Mrs Fain:	Petulant and he were upon quarrelling as I came by.	452	WAY WORLD	IV.1	314
Witwoud:	yes the fray is compos'd; my Lady came in like a	453	WAY WORLD	IV.1	329
Mrs Fain:	He's horridly drunk--how came you all in	454	WAY WORLD	IV.1	379
Camest (3)					
Almeria:	How camest thou there? wert thou alone?	343	M. BRIDE	II.2	158
Almeria:	But still, how camest thee hither? how thus?--Ha!	344	M. BRIDE	II.2	166
Almeria:	But still, how camest thou hither? how thus?--Ha!	344	M. BRIDE	II.2	V166
Camlet (1)					
Witwoud:	out and piec'd in the sides like an unsiz'd Camlet,--Yes,	453	WAY WORLD	IV.1	328
Camp (1)					
Zara:	Or Love, that late at Night still lights his Camp,	354	M. BRIDE	III.1	207
Campagn (1)					
Capt Bluff:	Campagn, had a small Post there; but no matter for that--	52	OLD BATCH	II.1	196
Campagne (1)					
Bellmour:	abroad--went purely to run away from a Campagne;	47	OLD BATCH	II.1	369
Camphire (1)					
Waitwell:	Dear Madam, no. You are all Camphire and	459	WAY WORLD	IV.1	545
Camps (1)					
Manuel:	Nor will I Victory in Camps adore:	337	M. BRIDE	I.1	453
Can (292)					
Can'st (11)					
Bellmour:	Nay let's see the Name (Silvia!) how can'st thou be	38	OLD BATCH	I.1	38
Lady Touch:	Thou can'st deceive every body,--nay,	199	DOUBL DLR	V.1	453
Sr Sampson:	shake--I believe thou can'st write, Val: Ha, boy? Thou	281	FOR LOVE	IV.1	207
Sr Sampson:	can'st write thy Name, Val?--Jeremy, step and overtake	281	FOR LOVE	IV.1	208
Valentine:	thou can'st not lie with my Wife? I am very poor, and	292	FOR LOVE	IV.1	626
Valentine:	thou can'st not borrow Money of me; Then what	292	FOR LOVE	IV.1	627
Tattle:	pretty Fellow, and can'st carry a Message to a Lady, in a	302	FOR LOVE	V.1	181
Osmyn-Alph:	Hast thou thy Eyes, yet can'st not see Alphonso?	342	M. BRIDE	II.2	79
Zara:	Can'st thou forgive me then! wilt thou believe	354	M. BRIDE	III.1	178
Sir Wilful:	Well prithee try what thou can'st do; if thou	437	WAY WORLD	III.1	464
Sir Wilful:	can'st not guess, enquire her out, do'st hear Fellow? And	437	WAY WORLD	III.1	465
Can't (113)					
Vainlove:	once raised up in a Woman, the Devil can't lay it, till she	40	OLD BATCH	I.1	103
Bellmour:	But she can't have too much Mony--There's	41	OLD BATCH	I.1	165
Sharper:	Pshaw you can't want a hundred Pound. Your	50	OLD BATCH	II.1	107
Capt Bluff:	of my Pallat, you can't relish a Dish of Fighting without	51	OLD BATCH	II.1	163
Capt Bluff:	see it; Sir I say you can't see; what de'e say to that now?	53	OLD BATCH	II.1	235
Belinda:	Ha, ha, ha, (you must pardon me I can't help Laughing)	55	OLD BATCH	II.2	27
Belinda:	play the Game, and consequently can't see the Miscarriages	55	OLD BATCH	II.2	34
Belinda:	Pish, I can't help dreaming of the Devil sometimes,	55	OLD BATCH	II.2	39
Araminta:	I can't tell, Cousin, I believe we are equally concern'd:	57	OLD BATCH	II.2	85
Bellmour:	Yet all can't melt that cruel frozen Heart.	59	OLD BATCH	II.2	166
Heartwell:	Houses and Coblers Stalls--Death, I can't think	63	OLD BATCH	III.1	84
Sir Joseph:	I can't help it.	67	OLD BATCH	III.1	244
Sir Joseph:	confess he did in a manner snap me up--Yet I can't say	68	OLD BATCH	III.1	272
Belinda:	ha, ha, I can't for my Soul help thinking that I look just	83	OLD BATCH	IV.3	12
Capt Bluff:	My Blood rises at that Fellow: I can't stay where he is;	86	OLD BATCH	IV.3	120
Laetitia:	(aside). I'm so distracted, I can't think of a Lye.--	92	OLD BATCH	IV.4	119
Bellmour:	a word on't.--But I can't help telling the truth, for my	95	OLD BATCH	IV.4	220
Capt Bluff:	extremity! You can't, in honour, refuse to carry him a	101	OLD BATCH	V.1	188
Sharper:	Death, it can't be--An Oaf, an Ideot, a Wittal.	102	OLD BATCH	V.1	205
Lord Froth:	He, he, he, I swear that's so very pretty, I can't	132	DOUBL DLR	I.1	212
Brisk:	O Lord, why can't you find it out?--Why there	133	DOUBL DLR	I.1	248
Careless:	you suppose I can't tell you?	134	DOUBL DLR	I.1	261
Brisk:	can't tell how to make him Apprehend,--take it	134	DOUBL DLR	I.1	277
Maskwell:	as I told you before. I can't deny that neither.--Any	135	DOUBL DLR	I.1	314
Lady Ply:	now, who are you? What am I? 'Slidikins can't I govern	144	DOUBL DLR	II.1	215
Lady Ply:	what did I say? Jealous! no, no, I can't be jealous, for I	148	DOUBL DLR	II.1	370
Maskwell:	of Doors; and to--ha, ha, ha, I can't tell you for Laughing,	149	DOUBL DLR	II.1	401

Can't (continued)

Speaker	Text	PAGE	TITLE	ACT.SC	LINE
Lady Touch:	That I can't tell: nay, I don't say there was--	151	DOUBL DLR	III.1	23
Lady Touch:	What if you can't.	152	DOUBL DLR	III.1	60
Lady Touch:	towards me. Nay, I can't think he meant any thing	153	DOUBL DLR	III.1	84
Lady Touch:	disorder--Yet, I confess, I can't blame you; for I think	153	DOUBL DLR	III.1	113
Maskwell:	Pox on't that a Man can't drink without quenching his	155	DOUBL DLR	III.1	185
Maskwell:	open: 'twill be hard, if then you can't bring her to any	157	DOUBL DLR	III.1	253
Careless:	'Pox I can't get an Answer from her, that does not	157	DOUBL DLR	III.1	270
Careless:	I can't get an Answer from her, that does not	157	DOUBL DLR	III.1	V270
Lady Froth:	can't hit of her Name; the old fat Fool that Paints so	166	DOUBL DLR	III.1	581
Brisk:	I can't hit of her Name neither--Paints de'e say?	166	DOUBL DLR	III.1	584
Cynthia:	And he that can't live upon Love, deserves to die in	168	DOUBL DLR	IV.1	34
Careless:	can't help it.	170	DOUBL DLR	IV.1	102
Careless:	O Heaven! I can't out-live this Night without	170	DOUBL DLR	IV.1	113
Lady Ply:	read Mr. Careless his Letter, that I can't forbear any longer	173	DOUBL DLR	IV.1	210
Sir Paul:	my Posterity, he Thy? Can't you contrive that affair	173	DOUBL DLR	IV.1	229
Brisk:	The Deuce take me, I can't help laughing my self neither,	176	DOUBL DLR	IV.1	344
Brisk:	The Deuce take me, I can't help laughing my self,	176	DOUBL DLR	IV.1	V344
Lady Froth:	purely, but I vow Mr. Brisk, I can't tell how to come so	177	DOUBL DLR	IV.1	368
Careless:	said all I could, but can't prevail--Then my Friendship	180	DOUBL DLR	IV.1	492
Sir Paul:	I can't tell you I'm so overjoy'd; come along with me	181	DOUBL DLR	IV.1	508
Sir Paul:	to my Lady, I can't contain my self; come my dear Friend.	181	DOUBL DLR	IV.1	509
Maskwell:	I am sorry, my Lord, I can't make you an answer;	182	DOUBL DLR	IV.1	V552
Lord Touch:	know as well that you can't.	182	DOUBL DLR	IV.1	556
Sir Paul:	Gad'sbud, I can't find her high nor low; where can	192	DOUBL DLR	V.1	162
Brisk:	perish,--I can't answer that.	201	DOUBL DLR	V.1	535
Scandal:	have fair Play for your Life. If you can't be fairly run down	220	FOR LOVE	I.1	142
Valentine:	Well, I can't help it,--you must bring him up;	225	FOR LOVE	I.1	359
Tattle:	I am strangely surpriz'd! Yes, yes, I can't deny't, if	229	FOR LOVE	I.1	481
Mrs Frail:	--I can't believe a word he says.	233	FOR LOVE	I.1	621
Servant:	I can't tell indeed, Sir.	235	FOR LOVE	II.1	14
Foresight:	No, I know you can't, Sir: But I can tell, Sir, and	235	FOR LOVE	II.1	15
Foresight:	No, I know you can't, Sir: But I can tell and	235	FOR LOVE	II.1	V 15
Sr Sampson:	can't a private man be born without all these followers:	245	FOR LOVE	II.1	350
Mrs Frail:	--Lord, where's the comfort of this Life, if we can't have	246	FOR LOVE	II.1	424
Mrs Fore:	But can't you converse at home?--I own	247	FOR LOVE	II.1	426
Tattle:	can't tell--	251	FOR LOVE	II.1	608
Miss Prue:	O fie, now I can't abide you.	252	FOR LOVE	II.1	643
Angelica:	You can't accuse me of Inconstancy; I never told	254	FOR LOVE	III.1	27
Angelica:	I can't. Resolution must come to me, or I shall	259	FOR LOVE	III.1	229
Miss Prue:	I can't abide to be left alone, mayn't my Cousin	262	FOR LOVE	III.1	352
Scandal:	Can't you guess at what ought to afflict you and	266	FOR LOVE	III.1	483
Ben:	to do with me--Nay, I can't say that neither; he has	272	FOR LOVE	III.1	714
Jeremy:	that was so near turning Poet yesterday morning, can't be	276	FOR LOVE	IV.1	4
Jeremy:	bad Bargain, can't do better than to beg him for his	276	FOR LOVE	IV.1	36
Angelica:	Mr. Scandal, you can't think me guilty of so much	277	FOR LOVE	IV.1	42
Angelica:	in my Power nor Inclination; and if he can't be cur'd	277	FOR LOVE	IV.1	74
Angelica:	and involuntary; if he loves, he can't help it; and if I don't	278	FOR LOVE	IV.1	87
Angelica:	love, I can't help it; no more than he can help his being a	278	FOR LOVE	IV.1	88
Scandal:	for I can't resolve you; but I'll inform your Master. In	278	FOR LOVE	IV.1	103
Jeremy:	Sir, I have a most broke my Heart about him--I can't	279	FOR LOVE	IV.1	131
Jeremy:	Sir, I have almost broke my Heart about him--I can't	279	FOR LOVE	IV.1	V131
Valentine:	For my part, I am Truth, and can't tell; I have very	280	FOR LOVE	IV.1	178
Valentine:	I can't tell whether I know it or no.	281	FOR LOVE	IV.1	218
Mrs Frail:	throw himself away, he can't do it more effectually than	287	FOR LOVE	IV.1	460
Valentine:	Sot, can't you apprehend?	295	FOR LOVE	IV.1	745
Tattle:	you can't solve this; stay here a Quarter of an Hour, and	305	FOR LOVE	V.1	297
Miss Prue:	Man; and if I can't have one, I wou'd go to sleep all my	305	FOR LOVE	V.1	309
Ben:	Why Father and--the Young Woman. I can't hit	307	FOR LOVE	V.1	361
Scandal:	'S'death it's a Jest. I can't believe it.	307	FOR LOVE	V.1	367
Ben:	can't deny it: But, Father, if I might be your Pilot in this	308	FOR LOVE	V.1	413
Mrs Frail:	I can't speak it out.	309	FOR LOVE	V.1	446
Ben:	enough to hold her, and if she can't drag her Anchor	310	FOR LOVE	V.1	493
Valentine:	can't love enough.	313	FOR LOVE	V.1	612
	I can't reflect without an aking Heart,	315	FOR LOVE	EPI.	36
	But we can't fear, since you're so good to save us,	315	FOR LOVE	EPI.	38
Witwoud:	Hum, faith I don't know as to that,--I can't say	403	WAY WORLD	I.1	302
Witwoud:	wou'd come off--Ha, ha, ha; Gad I can't be angry	406	WAY WORLD	I.1	410
Witwoud:	Faith, my Dear, I can't tell; she's a Woman and a	408	WAY WORLD	I.1	492
Millamant:	Faults--I can't bear it. Well, I won't have you Mirabell	422	WAY WORLD	II.1	456
Millamant:	Unless by the help of the Devil you can't imagine;	423	WAY WORLD	II.1	485
Millamant:	Without the help of the Devil you can't imagine;	423	WAY WORLD	II.1	V485
Foible:	I'll be gone; I'm sure my Lady is at her Toilet, and can't	424	WAY WORLD	II.1	543
Waitwell:	me, I am married, and can't be my own Man again.	424	WAY WORLD	II.1	561
Waitwell:	me, I'm married, and can't be my own Man again.	424	WAY WORLD	II.1	V561
Foible:	Mirabell can't abide her.--(Enter Footman.) John--	430	WAY WORLD	III.1	218
Marwood:	Months Mind, but he can't abide her--'Twere better	431	WAY WORLD	III.1	240
Lady Wish:	O Dear, I can't appear till I'm dress'd. Dear	432	WAY WORLD	III.1	278
Petulant:	married tho' he can't Read, any more than he is from being	436	WAY WORLD	III.1	429
Petulant:	married tho' he can't read, than he is from being	436	WAY WORLD	III.1	V429
Servant-W:	Really Sir, I can't tell; here come so many here, 'tis	437	WAY WORLD	III.1	470
Sir Wilful:	I can't tell that; 'tis like I may, and 'tis like I may	440	WAY WORLD	III.1	578
Sir Wilful:	some can't relish the Town, and others can't away with	448	WAY WORLD	IV.1	129
Millamant:	all ye douceurs, ye Someils du Matin, adieu--I can't do't, 'tis	449	WAY WORLD	IV.1	189
Lady Wish:	friend, I can't believe it, No, no; as she says, let him prove	467	WAY WORLD	V.1	206
Sir Wilful:	frown, she can't kill you;--besides--Hearkee she dare not	471	WAY WORLD	V.1	361

Canary (2)

Speaker	Text	PAGE	TITLE	ACT.SC	LINE
Sr Sampson:	but a new Tax, and the loss of the Canary Fleet.	266	FOR LOVE	III.1	486
Sr Sampson:	but a new Tax, or the loss of the Canary Fleet.	266	FOR LOVE	III.1	V486

Cancels (1)

Speaker	Text	PAGE	TITLE	ACT.SC	LINE
Maskwell:	--Treachery, what Treachery? Love cancels all the	150	DOUBL DLR	II.1	443

			PAGE	TITLE	ACT.SC	LINE
Candidly (1)						
Lady Wish:	favourably, Judge Candidly and conclude you have found	.	459	WAY WORLD	IV.1	552
Candle (4)						
Angelica:	Siege? What a World of Fire and Candle, Matches and	. .	237	FOR LOVE	II.1	81
Nurse:	and tuck you up, and set the Candle, and your Tobacco-Box,		238	FOR LOVE	II.1	103
Sr Sampson:	Candle, and that's all the Stars are good for.		240	FOR LOVE	II.1	201
Witwoud:	Like Moths about a Candle--I had like to have . . .		418	WAY WORLD	II.1	331
Candle-light (1)						
Angelica:	seen Fifty in a side Box by Candle-light, out-blossom Five		298	FOR LOVE	V.1	31
Candle's (1)						
Waitwell:	his head, and then go out in a stink like a Candle's end	.	458	WAY WORLD	IV.1	524
Candour (1)						
	But as with Freedom, judge with Candour too.		324	M. BRIDE	PRO.	40
Cann (1)						
Ben:	to her, than a Cann of Small-beer to a Bowl of Punch. . .		264	FOR LOVE	III.1	413
Cannibal (1)						
Sir Joseph:	Fellow as Cannibal, are not you Bully--Back?		52	OLD BATCH	II.1	176
Cannibals (1)						
Sir Joseph:	inhumane Cannibals, the bloody-minded Villains would . .		47	OLD BATCH	II.1	3
Cannot (75)						
	I cannot stay to hear your Resolution.		35	OLD BATCH	PRO.	27
Bellmour:	Flesh and Blood cannot bear it always.		41	OLD BATCH	I.1	145
Heartwell:	--Now could I curse my self, yet cannot repent. O . .		63	OLD BATCH	III.1	76
Lucy:	Calling should be expos'd and scandaliz'd--I cannot bear it.		66	OLD BATCH	III.1	210
Singer:	I cannot, dare not, must not hear:		71	OLD BATCH	III.2 V	11
Silvia:	--I cannot look.		72	OLD BATCH	III.2	44
Heartwell:	cannot distrust me of any skill in the treacherous Mystery--		72	OLD BATCH	III.2	58
Heartwell:	Now by my Soul, I cannot lie, though it were to serve a .		72	OLD BATCH	III.2	59
Laetitia:	poor Heart, while it holds; which cannot be long, with .		77	OLD BATCH	IV.1	92
Sharper:	cannot digest it.		80	OLD BATCH	IV.1	173
Sharper:	which narrow Souls cannot dare to admire.--And . . .		86	OLD BATCH	IV.3	127
Fondlewife:	Ah! No, no, I cannot speak; my heart's so full--I . .		95	OLD BATCH	IV.4	248
Bellmour:	cannot err.		96	OLD BATCH	IV.4	272
Vainlove:	(to Araminta). Oh, 'twas Frenzy all: Cannot you forgive	.	106	OLD BATCH	V.1	356
Heartwell:	--And I cannot in gratitude (for I see which way thou .		111	OLD BATCH	V.2	151
	But by my Troth I cannot avoid thinking, ...		125	DOUBL DLR	PRO.	23
Careless:	Faith I cannot help it, you know I never lik'd him; . .		131	DOUBL DLR	I.1	147
Careless:	Aunts Aversion in her Revenge, cannot be any way so . .		131	DOUBL DLR	I.1	159
Brisk:	Lactilla may be,--'gad I cannot tell.		141	DOUBL DLR	II.1	128
Sir Paul:	find Passion coming upon me by inspiration, and I cannot .		144	DOUBL DLR	II.1	207
Sir Paul:	find Passion coming upon me by inflation, and I cannot .		144	DOUBL DLR	II.1 V207	
Sir Paul:	provoked to fury, I cannot incorporate with Patience and .		144	DOUBL DLR	II.1	223
Lady Ply:	Why, gads my life, Cousin Mellefont, you cannot . . .		146	DOUBL DLR	II.1	297
Lady Touch:	to be unknown which cannot be prevented; therefore let .		152	DOUBL DLR	III.1	55
Sir Paul:	affliction, and my only affliction; indeed I cannot refrain		161	DOUBL DLR	III.1	416
Cynthia:	But that cannot be properly said of them, for I . . .		163	DOUBL DLR	III.1	481
Lady Ply:	O that's so passionate and fine, I cannot hear it . . .		170	DOUBL DLR	IV.1	97
Careless:	so transported I cannot speak--This Note will inform .		171	DOUBL DLR	IV.1	129
Mellefont:	Imagination cannot form a fairer and more plausible . .		187	DOUBL DLR	IV.2	150
Maskwell:	weak, and shrinks beneath the weight, and cannot rise to .		189	DOUBL DLR	V.1	79
Maskwell:	head that cannot fail: Where's Cynthia?		190	DOUBL DLR	V.1	116
Lord Touch:	I cannot do too much, for so much merit.		191	DOUBL DLR	V.1	123
Lady Touch:	impossible, it cannot be,--he Love Cynthia! what have .		191	DOUBL DLR	V.1	145
Lady Touch:	I cannot bear it, oh! what Woman can bear to be a Property?		191	DOUBL DLR	V.1	149
Lady Touch:	What shall I do? how shall I think? I cannot think, --all .		191	DOUBL DLR	V.1	154
Careless:	Arm--he cannot be ignorant that Maskwell means to . .		196	DOUBL DLR	V.1	352
Mellefont:	'Tis loss of time--I cannot think him false.		197	DOUBL DLR	V.1	354
	So till the Thief has stoll'n, he cannot know		204	DOUBL DLR	EPI.	6
	But tho' he cannot Write, let him be freed		204	DOUBL DLR	EPI.	35
	At least from their Contempt, who cannot Read. . . .		204	DOUBL DLR	EPI.	36
Valentine:	I cannot talk about Business with a Thirsty Palate.-- .		222	FOR LOVE	I.1	238
Trapland:	Sack; but you cannot expect it again, when I have drank it.		224	FOR LOVE	I.1	314
Trapland:	Sack; but you cannot expect it again, when I have drunk it.		224	FOR LOVE	I.1 V314	
Valentine:	cannot avoid such a palpable Decoy as this was; the Ladies		229	FOR LOVE	I.1	502
Scandal:	Painter, that I cannot know the Person by your Picture of .		230	FOR LOVE	I.1	537
Valentine:	We are the Twin-Stars, and cannot shine in one . . .		259	FOR LOVE	III.1	223
Scandal:	with you--But my Mind gives me, these things cannot . .		267	FOR LOVE	III.1	523
Mrs Fore:	I cannot say that he has once broken my Rest, since we .		270	FOR LOVE	III.1	623
Angelica:	am to hope for--I cannot speak--But you may tell me, .		277	FOR LOVE	IV.1	59
Valentine:	Thou liest, for I am Truth. 'Tis hard I cannot get a . .		280	FOR LOVE	IV.1	171
Foresight:	How! I cannot Read that knowledge in your Face, . . .		291	FOR LOVE	IV.1	610
Almeria:	It may my Fears, but cannot add to that.		339	M. BRIDE	II.1	72
Heli:	Yet cannot find him--Hark! sure 'tis the Voice . . .		340	M. BRIDE	II.2	2
Almeria:	Of delight, I cannot bear it--I shall		342	M. BRIDE	II.2	107
Almeria:	Of Joy, of Bliss--I cannot bear--I must		342	M. BRIDE	II.2 V107	
Almeria:	Be mad--I cannot be transported thus.		342	M. BRIDE	II.2	108
Almeria:	Why? why? to know it, cannot wound me more, ...		356	M. BRIDE	III.1	278
Almeria:	--I cannot speak.		359	M. BRIDE	III.1	392
Zara:	O Curse! I cannot hold--		360	M. BRIDE	III.1	430
Zara:	But cannot bear to find thee thus, my Osmyn-- . . .		380	M. BRIDE	V.2 V167	
Zara:	I cannot feel it--quite beyond my reach.		381	M. BRIDE	V.2	210
Witwoud:	not, I cannot say; but there were Items of such a Treaty .		408	WAY WORLD	I.1	487
Fainall:	you cannot resent any thing from me; especially what is .		412	WAY WORLD	II.1	96
Witwoud:	As a Phisician of a good Air--I cannot help it . . .		419	WAY WORLD	II.1	339
Mirabell:	Point of the Compass to which they cannot turn, and by .		423	WAY WORLD	II.1	496
Peg:	Lord, Madam, your Ladyship is so impatient--I cannot .		425	WAY WORLD	III.1	17
Marwood:	O Madam, you cannot suspect Mrs. Foible's		426	WAY WORLD	III.1	55
Foible:	cannot chuse but be grateful. I find your Ladyship has his .		430	WAY WORLD	III.1	204
Millamant:	--But that cannot be--Well, that Thought makes . . .		434	WAY WORLD	III.1	361
Servant-W:	Why truly Sir, I cannot safely swear to her Face in a .		437	WAY WORLD	III.1	461
Fainall:	too by this time--Jealous of her I cannot be, for I am					
	certain, ...		443	WAY WORLD	III.1	680
Sir Wilful:	Christian--I cannot find by the Map that your Mufti is .		456	WAY WORLD	IV.1	446
Lady Wish:	Testimony of your Obedience; but I cannot admit that .		470	WAY WORLD	V.1	334
Lady Wish:	Traytor,--I fear I cannot fortifie my self to support his		470	WAY WORLD	V.1	335
Lady Wish:	to sink under the fatigue; and I cannot but have some fears		478	WAY WORLD	V.1	610

97

Canon (1)
  Sir Joseph: fire once out of the mouth of a Canon--agad he did; those   53 OLD BATCH II.1 219
Canonical (1)
  Betty: Turn'd of the last Canonical Hour, Sir. . . . . . . 398 WAY WORLD I.1 106
Canoniz'd (1)
  Jeremy: be Canoniz'd for a Muse after my Decease. . . . . . . 218 FOR LOVE I.1 75
Canst (15)
  Sharper: Prithee what mighty Business of Consequence canst . . . 41 OLD BATCH I.1 154
  Fondlewife: canst reach, th' hast experimented Isaac--But Mum. . . 77 OLD BATCH IV.1 63
  Sharper: In her choice I gad--But thou canst not be so . . . . 80 OLD BATCH IV.1 186
  Araminta: and Malice of thy Sex, thou canst not lay a Blemish on . 87 OLD BATCH IV.3 168
  Bellmour: How canst thou be so cruel, Isaac? Thou hast the . . . 95 OLD BATCH IV.4 234
  Mrs Frail: Why canst thou love, Porpoise? . . . . 287 FOR LOVE IV.1 433
  Almeria: Thou canst not tell--thou hast indeed no Cause. . . . . 326 M. BRIDE I.1 19
  Zara: Thou canst not mean so poorly, as thou talk'st. . . . . 348 M. BRIDE II.2 331
  Zara: O no, thou canst not, for thou seest me now, ... 353 M. BRIDE III.1 156
  Zara: Thou canst not owe me more, nor have I more . . . . 355 M. BRIDE III.1 215
  Almeria: Thou canst not! thy poor Arms are bound and strive . . 356 M. BRIDE III.1 266
  Manuel: O Impious Parricide! now canst thou speak? . . . . 368 M. BRIDE IV.1 272
  Manuel: Hear me; then, if thou canst, reply, know Traitress, . 368 M. BRIDE IV.1 300
  Witwoud: Revenge--and hear me, if thou canst learn to write . . 454 WAY WORLD IV.1 372
  Mrs Fain: Say'st thou so Foible? Canst thou prove this? . . . . 464 WAY WORLD V.1 91
Cant (3)
  Careless: some such Cant. Then she has told me the whole History of 157 DOUBL DLR III.1 272
  Careless: I'm almost at the end of my Cant, if she does not yield . 170 DOUBL DLR IV.1 95
  Millamant: Sweet heart and the rest of that Nauseous Cant, in which . 450 WAY WORLD IV.1 198
Cantharides (2)
  Marwood: Cantharides, or sat upon Cow-Itch. . . . . 467 WAY WORLD V.1 222
  Marwood: Cantharides, or sate upon Cow-Itch. . . . . 467 WAY WORLD V.1 V222
Canting (1)
  Lucy: a Mumper in Love, lies Canting at the Gate; but never dare 66 OLD BATCH III.1 193
Cap (1)   see Night-Cap, Night-cap
  Marwood: They may prove a Cap of Maintenance to . . . . . 442 WAY WORLD III.1 649
Capable (4)
  Maskwell: could have contriv'd to make me capable of serving you, . 157 DOUBL DLR III.1 245
  Lady Ply: might be supposed to be capable of being qualified to make 159 DOUBL DLR III.1 337
  Sr Sampson: but a Groat in his Pocket, may have a Stomach capable . . 245 FOR LOVE II.1 353
  Mirabell: they are not capable: Or if they were, it shou'd be to you 421 WAY WORLD II.1 438
Capitulating (1)
  Capt Bluff: --I'm capitulating with Mr. Setter for you. . . . . . 104 OLD BATCH V.1 280
Caprice (1)
  Lady Touch: another Caprice, to unwind my temper. . . . . . . 137 DOUBL DLR I.1 392
Caprices (1)
  Lady Wish: Here I am ruin'd to Compound for your Caprices . . . . 466 WAY WORLD V.1 150
Capricious (1)
  Sharper: so Capricious a Lover. . . . . 42 OLD BATCH I.1 209
Capricorn (2)
  Sr Sampson: Brother Capricorn. . . . . 241 FOR LOVE II.1 234
  Foresight: Capricorn in your Teeth, thou Modern Mandevil; . . . . 241 FOR LOVE II.1 235
Capt (2)
      (Sir Joseph Wittoll and Capt. Bluffe, cross the Stage.) . 46 OLD BATCH I.1 340
  Bellmour: a Title; he is call'd, Capt. Bluffe. . . . . . . 47 OLD BATCH I.1 384
Captain (20)
  Sir Joseph: Zooks, would the Captain would come; the very . . . . 48 OLD BATCH II.1 13
  Sharper: Captain, Sir Joseph's penitent. . . . . 54 OLD BATCH II.1 240
  Sharper: I wait on you Sir; nay pray Captain--You are . . . . 54 OLD BATCH II.1 248
  Sharper: Hey day! Captain, what's the matter? You can tell. . . . 69 OLD BATCH III.1 295
  Sir Joseph: O Lord, O Lord, Captain, come justifie your . . . . 69 OLD BATCH III.1 306
  Sir Joseph: Captain, will you see this? Won't you pink his . . . 69 OLD BATCH III.1 311
  Sir Joseph: dear Captain, don't be in Passion now, he's gone-- . . . 70 OLD BATCH III.1 340
  Sir Joseph: To that Face I grant you Captain--No, no, ... 70 OLD BATCH III.1 356
  Belinda: O monstrous filthy Fellow! Good slovenly Captain . . 85 OLD BATCH IV.3 86
  Sir Joseph: Ay; Do, do, Captain, if you think fit.--You . . . . 101 OLD BATCH V.1 183
  Sir Joseph: Ay; Do, do, Captain, if you think fitting.--You . . . . 101 OLD BATCH V.1 V183
  Sir Joseph: Captain: Take it--All the World know me to be a Knight, . 101 OLD BATCH V.1 193
  Setter: Sir Joseph and the Captain too! undone, undone! I'm . . 103 OLD BATCH V.1 239
  Setter: Captain, I wou'd do any thing to serve you; but this . . 104 OLD BATCH V.1 274
  Setter: to be cheated, that the Captain may be so in reality. . . 106 OLD BATCH V.1 349
  Sharper: free Discharge to Sir Joseph Wittoll and Captain Bluffe; for 110 OLD BATCH V.2 86
  Sir Joseph: Ay, ay, whatsoever, Captain, stick to that; . . . . 110 OLD BATCH V.2 98
  Sir Joseph: No, no, Captain, you need not own, Heh, heh, ... 110 OLD BATCH V.2 105
  Sir Joseph: Only a little Art-military Trick, Captain, only . . . . 110 OLD BATCH V.2 112
  Heli: The Captain influenc'd by Almeria's Power, ... 351 M. BRIDE III.1 43
Captains (1)
  Gonsalez: And Captains of the Noblest Blood of Affrick, ... 331 M. BRIDE I.1 235
Captiv'd (1)
  Osmyn-Alph: To a vile Prison, and a captiv'd Wretch; . . . . . 351 M. BRIDE III.1 53
Captivate (1)
  Osmyn-Alph: Might hope to captivate the Hearts of Kings. . . . . . 355 M. BRIDE III.1 227
Captive (12)
  Lord Froth: a Captive first, and ever since 't has been in Love with . 140 DOUBL DLR II.1 69
  Lady Ply: help it, if you are made a Captive? I swear it's pity it . 148 DOUBL DLR II.1 359
  Almeria: I was a welcome Captive in Valentia, ... 329 M. BRIDE I.1 110
  Alonzo: The beauteous Captive, Zara, is arriv'd, ... 335 M. BRIDE I.1 359
  Alonzo: Your beauteous Captive, Zara, is arriv'd, ... 335 M. BRIDE I.1 V359
  Zara: The fall'n, the lost, the Captive Zara. . . . . . 347 M. BRIDE II.2 307
  Zara: The fall'n, the lost, and now the Captive Zara. . . . . 347 M. BRIDE II.2 V307
  Gonsalez: Your beauteous Captive, Zara, can inform, ... 363 M. BRIDE IV.1 101
  Zara: I am your Captive, and you've us'd me Nobly; . . . . . 364 M. BRIDE IV.1 136
  Gonsalez: But how prevent the Captive Queen, who means . . . . . 371 M. BRIDE IV.1 412
  Gonsalez: Among the followers of the Captive Queen, ... 372 M. BRIDE IV.1 433
  Garcia: The Traytor Perez, and the Captive Moor, ... 377 M. BRIDE V.2 38
Captivity (8)
  Almeria: Started amidst his Foes, and made Captivity his Refuge; . 329 M. BRIDE I.1 116
  Almeria: Started amidst his Foes, and made Captivity . . . . . 329 M. BRIDE I.1 V116
  Manuel: Must have some other Cause than his Captivity. . . . . 335 M. BRIDE I.1 376

Captivity   (continued)

			PAGE	TITLE	ACT.SC	LINE
Zara:	To like Captivity, or think those Honours,	. . . .	335	M. BRIDE	I.1	394
Manuel:	So ill can brook Captivity;	.	336	M. BRIDE	I.1	432
Manuel:	So hardly can endure Captivity;	.	336	M. BRIDE	I.1	V432
Osmyn-Alph:	Because Captivity has robb'd me of a just Revenge.	. .	336	M. BRIDE	I.1	434
Zara:	Am I become so low, by my Captivity;	.	348	M. BRIDE	II.2	361

Car'd (1)

Jeremy:	and keeping Company with Wits, that car'd for nothing	.	217	FOR LOVE	I.1	46

Card-matches (1)

Witwoud:	of Lovers, Madam, than of making so many Card-matches.	.	420	WAY WORLD	II.1	408

Cardan (1)

Sr Sampson:	your Quadrates?--What did your Cardan and your	. . .	283	FOR LOVE	IV.1	283

Cardinal (1)

Sr Sampson:	and so forth, large enough for the inside of a Cardinal,					
	this	.	245	FOR LOVE	II.1	387

Cards (4)

Cynthia:	Then I find its like Cards, if either of us have a good	.	142	DOUBL DLR	II.1	162
Scandal:	Cards, sometimes, but that's nothing.	.	271	FOR LOVE	III.1	667
	Mirabell and Fainall Rising from Cards. Betty waiting.	.	395	WAY WORLD	I.1	
Fainall:	. . . She might throw up her Cards;	.	442	WAY WORLD	III.1	V653

Care (54)

Bellmour:	I'le take care, he shall not be at home. Good! Spintext! Oh	39	OLD BATCH	I.1	84
Capt Bluff:	out your Trick, and does not care to be put upon; being a	69	OLD BATCH	III.1	297
Sharper:	confess, I have taken care to improve it; to qualify me for	88	OLD BATCH	IV.3	199
Setter:	under Hatches.--Ha! All this committed to my Care! . . .	102	OLD BATCH	V.1	225
Lady Touch:	Insolent Devil! But have a care,--provoke me not; . . .	135	DOUBL DLR	I.1	321
Sir Paul:	--gadsbud he does not care a Farthing for any thing . .	146	DOUBL DLR	II.1	277
Mellefont:	(after a pause). So then,--spight of my care and . .	148	DOUBL DLR	II.1	374
Maskwell:	passage from her Chamber, which I'll take care to leave .	157	DOUBL DLR	III.1	252
Mellefont:	don't care for her.	157	DOUBL DLR	III.1	269
Sir Paul:	but have a care of making rash Vows; Come hither to me, .	173	DOUBL DLR	IV.1	207
Mellefont:	O Madam, have a care of dying unprepared, I	184	DOUBL DLR	IV.2	54
Maskwell:	Leave it to my care; that shall be so far from being .	193	DOUBL DLR	V.1	210
Jeremy:	that did not care a Farthing for you in your Prosperity; .	217	FOR LOVE	I.1	45
Tattle:	To be free with you, I have--I don't care if I own . .	227	FOR LOVE	I.1	409
Mrs Frail:	take care of my own. Well; but I'll come and see you one .	232	FOR LOVE	I.1	597
Angelica:	Will you? I care not, but all shall out then-- . . .	238	FOR LOVE	II.1	118
Foresight:	Hum--truly I don't care to discourage a young	243	FOR LOVE	II.1	308
Mrs Frail:	take great care when one makes a thrust in Fencing, not to	248	FOR LOVE	II.1	474
Mrs Fore:	often done in Duels, take care of one another, and grow .	248	FOR LOVE	II.1	478
Mrs Frail:	I don't care; I won't be seen in't.	250	FOR LOVE	II.1	576
Tattle:	Pooh, Pox, you must not say yes already; I shan't care .	251	FOR LOVE	II.1	604
Sr Sampson:	Estate: Body o' me, he does not care a Doit for your .	260	FOR LOVE	III.1	243
Miss Prue:	I don't know what to say to you, nor I don't care . .	263	FOR LOVE	III.1	378
Ben:	tho'f they love a man well enough, yet they don't care to	263	FOR LOVE	III.1	392
Miss Prue:	always tell a lie to a man; and I don't care, let my Father	264	FOR LOVE	III.1	397
Scandal:	Pleasure, so you have taken care of Honour, and 'tis the .	271	FOR LOVE	III.1	682
Scandal:	least I can do to take care of Conscience.	271	FOR LOVE	III.1	683
Ben:	We're merry Folk, we Sailors, we han't much to care for. .	275	FOR LOVE	III.1	799
Valentine:	drive distinct Trades, and Care and Pleasure separately .	289	FOR LOVE	IV.1	506
Jeremy:	I'll take care, and--	290	FOR LOVE	IV.1	566
Jeremy:	care every thing shall be ready.	293	FOR LOVE	IV.1	672
Sr Sampson:	the next Morning.--Odso, have a care, Madam.	299	FOR LOVE	V.1	59
Angelica:	Have a care, and don't over-act your Part--If . . .	301	FOR LOVE	V.1	157
Ben:	Well, well, take you care of your own Helm, or you . .	308	FOR LOVE	V.1	420
Angelica:	'Tis very unhappy, if you don't care for one another. .	309	FOR LOVE	V.1	462
Angelica:	Have a care of large Promises; You know you are . . .	313	FOR LOVE	V.1	613
Angelica:	Have a care of Promises; You know you are	313	FOR LOVE	V.1	V613
Manuel:	But should have smil'd that Hour, through all his Care, .	333	M. BRIDE	I.1	316
Manuel:	Garcia, be it your Care to make that search. . . .	337	M. BRIDE	I.1	448
Manuel:	Garcia, that Search shall be your Care:	337	M. BRIDE	I.1	V448
Heli:	The Care of Providence, sure left it there, . . .	352	M. BRIDE	III.1	116
Osmyn-Alph:	The Care of Heav'n. Not so, my Father bore	352	M. BRIDE	III.1	126
Zara:	To be the Care of weeping Majesty?	360	M. BRIDE	III.1	426
Garcia:	But I'll omit no Care, nor Haste; and try	379	M. BRIDE	V.2	106
	So much she doats on her adopted Care.	393	WAY WORLD	PRO.	10
Mirabell:	Have a care of such Apologies, Witwoud;--for . . .	402	WAY WORLD	I.1	275
Marwood:	I care not--Let me go--Break my	416	WAY WORLD	II.1	225
Mirabell:	Care is taken for that--She is won and worn . . .	417	WAY WORLD	II.1	288
Marwood:	Care, like any Chymist upon the Day of Projection. . .	431	WAY WORLD	III.1	248
Marwood:	--But let the Mine be sprung first, and then I care not if	444	WAY WORLD	III.1	706
Fainall:	I care not if I leave 'em a common Motto, to their common	444	WAY WORLD	III.1	722
Waitwell:	Law? I care not for Law. I can but die, and 'tis in .	461	WAY WORLD	IV.1	623
Lady Wish:	--I may say it; for I chiefly made it my own Care to .	466	WAY WORLD	V.1	183
Fainall:	perfected, which I will take care shall be done with all .	469	WAY WORLD	V.1	293

Careful (2)

Lord Touch:	I have always found you prudent and careful . . .	181	DOUBL DLR	IV.1	535
Fainall:	which you like a careful Aunt had provided for her. .	469	WAY WORLD	V.1	285

Careless (53)

	(Enter Careless, Crossing the Stage, with his Hat, Gloves,	127	DOUBL DLR	I.1	
Brisk:	ground? Mortgage for a Bottle, ha? Careless, this is your	128	DOUBL DLR	I.1	21
Brisk:	said it out of thy Company.--Careless, ha? . . .	128	DOUBL DLR	I.1	39
Brisk:	Enough, enough; Careless, bring your Apprehension . .	129	DOUBL DLR	I.1	61
Brisk:	--My Lord, Careless, is a very honest Fellow, but . .	133	DOUBL DLR	I.1	250
Brisk:	now, you come up to me--nay, prithee Careless be . .	133	DOUBL DLR	I.1	253
Lord Froth:	O foy, Mr. Careless, all the World allow Mr. . . .	134	DOUBL DLR	I.1	273
Lord Froth:	O foy, Mr. Careless, all the World allows Mr. . . .	134	DOUBL DLR	I.1	V273
	(Enter to him Careless.) . . .	157	DOUBL DLR	III.1	263
Sir Paul:	Shan't we disturb your Meditation, Mr. Careless: . .	159	DOUBL DLR	III.1	321
Lady Ply:	breeding to think Mr. Careless did not apply himself to me.	159	DOUBL DLR	III.1	330
Lady Ply:	Mr. Careless, If a person that is wholly illiterate . .	159	DOUBL DLR	III.1	336
Lady Ply:	rather. (Curtesies). But I know Mr. Careless is so great a	159	DOUBL DLR	III.1	343
Lady Ply:	you, Mr. Careless I don't know any thing in the World I .	159	DOUBL DLR	III.1	353
Sir Paul:	be Providence--ay, truly, Mr. Careless, my Lady is a great	160	DOUBL DLR	III.1	386
Sir Paul:	Careless, if it were not for one thing--	160	DOUBL DLR	III.1	391

Carry'd (continued)
Peg: and carry'd the Key with her. 425   WAY WORLD III.1   19
Lady Wish: would not have carry'd it thus. Well, that was my Choice, . 469   WAY WORLD V.1   305
Carrying (5)
Laetitia: (aside). How! Heav'n forbid! that will be carrying the . 78   OLD BATCH IV.1   119
Jeremy: Porter, worn out with pimping, and carrying Billet doux . 218   FOR LOVE I.1   96
Jeremy: his Proportion, with carrying a Poet upon Tick, to visit . 218   FOR LOVE I.1   99
Jeremy: Muses; or as if she were carrying her Linnen to the
              Paper-Mill, ... 219   FOR LOVE I.1   111
Ben: part d'ee see, I'm for carrying things above Board, I'm . 263   FOR LOVE III.1   388
Cart (1)
            How we shou'd end in our Original, a Cart. 315   FOR LOVE EPI.   37
Case (13)   see Comb-Case
Lady Touch: such a Case as this, demonstration is necessary. . . . 151   DOUBL DLR III.1   18
Maskwell: have been in a great measure kept by her, the case is
              alter'd; 155   DOUBL DLR III.1   177
Maskwell: his Case is desperate, and I believe he'll yield to any . 199   DOUBL DLR V.1   449
Ben: tell'n so to's face: If that's the Case, why silence gives 263   FOR LOVE III.1   393
Ben: Case, you should not marry her. It's just the same thing, . 308   FOR LOVE V.1   414
            With Nature's Oafs 'tis quite a diff'rent Case, . . . 393   WAY WORLD PRO.   5
Mirabell: were a Case of more steady Contemplation; a very tranquility 423   WAY WORLD II.1   492
Sir Wilful: Enough, enough, Cozen, Yes, yes, all a case-- . . . 448   WAY WORLD IV.1   142
Sir Wilful: Orthodox--Whereby it is a plain Case, that Orthodox is a . 456   WAY WORLD IV.1   447
Foible: Law in that case before I wou'd meddle or make. . . . 463   WAY WORLD V.1   45
Marwood: have your Case open'd by an old fumbling Leacher in a . . 467   WAY WORLD V.1   212
Lady Wish: Aye that's true; but in Case of Necessity; as of . . 468   WAY WORLD V.1   263
Fainall: Consent is not requisite in this Case; nor Mr.
              Mirabell, your 473   WAY WORLD V.1   438
Cases (1)
Petulant: rest which is to follow in both Cases, a Man may do it . 436   WAY WORLD III.1   432
Cash (1)
            And wanting ready Cash to pay for Hearts, ... 315   FOR LOVE EPI.   9
Cassandra (1)
Scandal: I prophesie it, and I wou'd not have the Fate of Cassandra, 268   FOR LOVE III.1   546
Cast (9)   see O'er-cast
Cynthia: It's impossible; she'll cast beyond you still--I'll . . 167   DOUBL DLR IV.1   6
Lady Froth: cast off, and meet me at the lower end of the Room, and . 177   DOUBL DLR IV.1   366
Mrs Frail: Foresight has cast both their Nativities, and prognosticates 231   FOR LOVE I.1   577
Sr Sampson: Heart: Hang him, Mungrel; cast him off; you shall see the . 260   FOR LOVE III.1   260
Osmyn-Alph: Have cast me down to this low Being: or, ... 354   M. BRIDE III.1   176
Zara: Was cast upon my Coast, as is reported; 364   M. BRIDE IV.1   117
Manuel: To cast beneath your Feet the Crown you've sav'd, . . . 365   M. BRIDE IV.1   159
Gonsalez: Then cast my Skin, and leave it there to answer it. . . 376   M. BRIDE V.2   13
Lady Wish: you should lean aside to Iniquity who have been Cast in . 465   WAY WORLD V.1   143
Cast-serving-man (1)
Lady Wish: to a Cast-serving-man; to make me a receptacle, an . . 463   WAY WORLD V.1   35
Castanets (1)
Witwoud: Ears like a pair of Castanets. 454   WAY WORLD IV.1   363
Castle (0) see Fore-castle
Castles (1)
Vainlove: In Castles ith' Air of thy own building: That's thy . . 38   OLD BATCH I.1   29
Casts (1)
Bellmour: perverts our Aim, casts off the Bias, and leaves us wide and 37   OLD BATCH I.1   11
Casuist (1)
Capt Bluff: Anatomist, Lawyer or Casuist in Europe; it shall decide a . 53   OLD BATCH II.1   230
Cat (2)   see Civet-Cat, Tabby-Cat
Ben: if you shou'd give such Language at Sea, you'd have a Cat . 264   FOR LOVE III.1   408
Mirabell: marrow of a roasted Cat. In short, I forbid all Commerce . 451   WAY WORLD IV.1   251
Cat-calls (1)
Scandal: Coats, Steinkirk Cravats, and terrible Faces; with Cat-calls 234   FOR LOVE I.1   655
Catalogue (1)
Mirabell: rote. The Catalogue was so large, that I was not without . 399   WAY WORLD I.1   166
Catastrophe (1)
Sharper: I'm in haste now, but I'll come in at the Catastrophe. . 107   OLD BATCH V.1 V393
Catch (8)
Maskwell: but you to catch at for Prevention. 137   DOUBL DLR I.1   379
Osmyn-Alph: I'll catch it 'ere it goes, and grasp her Shade. . . . 341   M. BRIDE II.2   53
Zara: Perdition catch 'em both, and Ruine part 'em. 359   M. BRIDE III.1   402
Manuel: Should I hear more; I too should catch thy Madness. . . 370   M. BRIDE IV.1   362
Almeria: I'll catch it--hark! a Voice cries Murder! 'tis . . . 371   M. BRIDE IV.1   391
Almeria: I'll catch it--hark! a Voice cries Murder! ah! . . . 371   M. BRIDE IV.1 V391
Witwoud: before it can catch her last Words. 421   WAY WORLD II.1   422
            They from each Fair One catch some different Grace, . . 479   WAY WORLD EPI.   32
Catch'd (1)
Alonzo: The Morsel down his throat. I catch'd his Arm, ... 373   M. BRIDE V.1   24
Catechis'd (1)
Lady Wish: to have been Catechis'd by him; and have heard his long . 467   WAY WORLD V.1   197
Catechisme (1)
Miss Prue: What, is it like the Catechisme?--Come then 251   FOR LOVE II.1   600
Catering (2)
Foible: are so early abroad, or Catering (says he) ferreting for . 427   WAY WORLD III.1   96
Lady Wish: you were Catering for Mirabell; I have been broaker for . 463   WAY WORLD V.1   48
Caterpillar (1)
Lady Wish: Out Caterpillar, Call not me Aunt, I know thee . . . 470   WAY WORLD V.1   312
Catterwauling (2)
Petulant: Aunt, that loves Catterwauling better than a Conventicle. 406   WAY WORLD I.1   408
Petulant: Aunt, who loves Catterwauling better than a Conventicle. 406   WAY WORLD I.1 V408
Caudle-Cup (1)
Angelica: little Nutmeg-Grater, which she had forgot in the Caudle-Cup 238   FOR LOVE II.1   110
Caught (8)
Heartwell: caught in one my self. 45   OLD BATCH I.1   297
Araminta: But that's not all; you caught me in your Arms . . . 55   OLD BATCH II.2   41
Heartwell: Office--Not one Inch; no, Foregod I'me caught-- . . . 62   OLD BATCH III.1   74
Heartwell: Office--Not one Inch; no, Foregad I'me caught-- . . . 62   OLD BATCH III.1 V 74
Mellefont: foresight, I am caught, caught in my security,--yet this was 148   DOUBL DLR II.1   375
Heli: So to be caught in an unguarded Hour, ... 338   M. BRIDE II.1   30

Caught   (continued)
  Mrs Fain: So, if my poor Mother is caught in a Contract,   . . .   417   WAY WORLD II.1 296
Caus'd (4)
  Silvia: Lust. Oh that I could revenge the Torment he has caus'd-- . 61 OLD BATCH III.1 32
  Silvia: Oh that I could revenge the Torment he has caus'd-- . 61 OLD BATCH III.1 V 32
  Angelica: How! I thought your love of me had caus'd this . . . . 294 FOR LOVE IV.1 722
  Zara: Has caus'd this Melancholy and Despair. . . . . . 337 M. BRIDE I.1 440
Causation (1)
  Scandal: Causation of Causes, in the Causes of things.   . . . . 267 FOR LOVE III.1 539
Cause (51)
  Vainlove: So that as he is often Jealous without a Cause, he's as
                   often . . . . 40 OLD BATCH I.1 109
  Bellmour: for the Cause. . . . . 42 OLD BATCH I.1 196
  Sharper: Cause, I'me not for it. . . . . 51 OLD BATCH II.1 161
  Capt Bluff: sufficient Cause; Fighting, to me's Religion and the Laws. 52 OLD BATCH II.1 165
  Capt Bluff: Controversie or split a Cause-- . . . . 53 OLD BATCH II.1 231
  Setter: To answer you as briefly--He has a cause to be try'd . . 66 OLD BATCH III.1 220
  Silvia: again, 'cause you'd have me be naught. . . . . . 74 OLD BATCH III.2 112
  Heartwell: You are the principal Cause of all my present Ills. . . 109 OLD BATCH V.2 66
  Brisk: your self--I look grave, and ask the cause of this . . 134 DOUBL DLR I.1 256
  Lady Touch: But those which cause my disquiet, I am . . . . . 152 DOUBL DLR III.1 50
  Lady Touch: and fresh cause of fury from unthought of . . . . . 191 DOUBL DLR V.1 156
  Maskwell: I am to learn the cause. . . . . 198 DOUBL DLR V.1 415
  Scandal: Cause of that? And Sir Sampson is hurry'd on by an unusual 268 FOR LOVE III.1 548
                 But there's the Devil, tho' their Cause is lost, . . . 323 M. BRIDE PRO. 25
                 He wou'd not lose thro' Prejudice his Cause; . . . . 324 M. BRIDE PRO. 41
  Leonora: Your Griefs, there is no Cause-- . . . . 326 M. BRIDE I.1 16
  Leonora: Or moderate your Griefs; there is no Cause-- . . . . 326 M. BRIDE I.1 V 16
  Almeria: Peace--No Cause! yes, there is Eternal Cause. . . . 326 M. BRIDE I.1 17
  Almeria: No Cause! Peace, peace; there is Eternal Cause. . . . 326 M. BRIDE I.1 V 17
  Almeria: Thou canst not tell--thou hast indeed no Cause. . . . 326 M. BRIDE I.1 19
  Almeria: Peace--No Cause! yes, there is Eternal Cause. . . . 326 M. BRIDE I.1 17
  Almeria: Thou hadst no Cause, but general Compassion. . . . 327 M. BRIDE I.1 34
  Leonora: Cause, ... 327 M. BRIDE I.1 36
  Manuel: Must have some other Cause than his Captivity. . . . 335 M. BRIDE I.1 376
  Garcia: Let's haste to follow him, and know the Cause. . . . 338 M. BRIDE II.1 24
  Heli: Leave me alone, to find and cure the Cause. . . . . 338 M. BRIDE II.1 26
  Zara: Think on the Cause of all, then, view thy self: . . . 347 M. BRIDE II.2 305
  Heli: Zara the Cause of your restraint, may be . . . . 352 M. BRIDE III.1 95
  Heli: When they shall know you live, assist your Cause. . . 352 M. BRIDE III.1 103
  Zara: As she, whose savage Breast has been the Cause . . . 353 M. BRIDE III.1 157
  Osmyn-Alph: The Cause and Comfort of my boding Heart. . . . . 355 M. BRIDE III.1 235
  Almeria: Thus, better, than for any Cause to part. . . . . 356 M. BRIDE III.1 263
  Osmyn-Alph: Hell, Hell! have I not Cause to rage and rave? . . . 358 M. BRIDE III.1 361
  Selim: Might breed Suspicion of the Cause. Advise, ... 362 M. BRIDE IV.1 46
  Selim: Have Cause to fear his Guards may be corrupted, . . . 362 M. BRIDE IV.1 51
  Gonsalez: She fear'd her stronger Charms, might cause the Moor's 366 M. BRIDE IV.1 224
  Manuel: Whence is thy Grief? give me to know the Cause, . . . 367 M. BRIDE IV.1 262
  Gonsalez: No matter--give me first to know the Cause . . . . 377 M. BRIDE V.2 30
  Alonzo: And has declar'd the Cause of his Revolt, ... 377 M. BRIDE V.2 49
  Garcia: But what imports the Manner, or the Cause? . . . . 377 M. BRIDE V.2 64
  Garcia: We have no time to search into the Cause . . . . 378 M. BRIDE V.2 91
  Zara: It may be, that the Cause, and Purpose of . . . . 379 M. BRIDE V.2 144
  Zara: It may be, that the Cause of this my Errand . . . . 379 M. BRIDE V.2 V144
                 And therefore to the Fair commends his Cause. . . . 385 M. BRIDE EPI. 28
  Fainall: in his Love. What cause had you to make Discoveries . . 414 WAY WORLD II.1 158
  Mrs Fain: You have been the cause that I have lov'd . . . . . 417 WAY WORLD II.1 261
  Lady Wish: a Person who wou'd suffer racks in honour's cause, dear 459 WAY WORLD IV.1 553
  Waitwell: a good cause--my Lady shall be satisfied of my Truth . 461 WAY WORLD IV.1 624
Causes (6)
  Sharper: Gravity as a Bishop bears Venereal Causes in the Spiritual 100 OLD BATCH IV.1 139
  Mellefont: Causes and Accidents of Fortune in this Life! but to what . 187 DOUBL DLR IV.2 142
  Jeremy: do's Causes at Dinner time. . . . . 220 FOR LOVE I.1 168
  Scandal: Causation of Causes, in the Causes of things. . . . 267 FOR LOVE III.1 539
  Osmyn-Alph: Whom Chance, or Fate working by secret Causes, . . . 354 M. BRIDE III.1 172
Caustick (1)
  Heartwell: But proves a burning Caustick when apply'd. . . . . 108 OLD BATCH V.2 13
Caution (4)
  Maskwell: prevent your Plot, yet I would have you use Caution and . 154 DOUBL DLR III.1 139
  Maskwell: hiss, they must be stung into experience, and future
                   caution, ... 194 DOUBL DLR V.1 265
  Scandal: Caution-- . . . . 267 FOR LOVE III.1 517
  Gonsalez: But why that needless Caution of the Princess? . . . 366 M. BRIDE IV.1 221
Cautions (1)
  Mirabell: having it seems receiv'd some Cautions respecting your . 476 WAY WORLD V.1 541
Cautious (1)
  Mrs Fain: Thank Mr. Mirabell, a Cautious Friend, to whose . . . 477 WAY WORLD V.1 570
Cave (1)
  Heartwell: Cave of that Enchantress and which consequently I ought . 62 OLD BATCH III.1 65
Caves (1)
  Almeria: And Monumental Caves of Death, look Cold, ... 339 M. BRIDE II.1 65
Cease (5)
  Leonora: For Heaven's sake, dear Madam, cease . . . . . . 326 M. BRIDE I.1 V 15
  Leonora: O cease, for Heaven's Sake, assuage a little, ... 330 M. BRIDE I.1 165
  Almeria: One Moment, cease to gaze on perfect Bliss, ... 330 M. BRIDE I.1 V179
  Almeria: Will cease his Tyranny; and Garcia too . . . . . . 340 M. BRIDE II.2 23
  Mrs Fain: Jealousies are insupportable: And when they cease to Love, 410 WAY WORLD II.1 5
Celebrate (1)
  Manuel: Which was design'd to celebrate thy Nuptials? . . . 367 M. BRIDE IV.1 251
Celebrated (1)
  Scandal: these is a celebrated Beauty, and t'other a profest Beau. I 233 FOR LOVE I.1 633
Celestial (2)
                 see Coelestial
  Foresight: ridiculing that Celestial Science. . . . . 237 FOR LOVE II.1 75
  Angelica: Spirits and the Celestial Signs, the Bull, and the Ram, . 239 FOR LOVE II.1 137
Cell (4)
  Osmyn-Alph: In a dark Corner of my Cell, I found . . . . . . 350 M. BRIDE III.1 6

Cell   (continued)
  Osmyn-Alph: Is this dark Cell, a Temple for that God? . . . . . 357 M. BRIDE III.1 325
  Manuel: And let the Cell where she'll expect to see him, . . 374 M. BRIDE V.1 84
  Almeria: O let me seek him in this horrid Cell; . . . . . . 381 M. BRIDE V.2 215
Cellar (4)
  Scandal: Then I have a Lady burning of Brandy in a Cellar . . 233 FOR LOVE I.1 639
  Scandal: Then I have a Lady burning Brandy in a Cellar . . . 233 FOR LOVE I.1 V639
  Jeremy: in a Cellar. . . . . 245 FOR LOVE II.1 382
  Sir Wilful: the Sun's a good Pimple, an honest Soaker, he has a Cellar 456 WAY WORLD IV.1 422
Censorious (3)
  Fainall: Fie, fie Friend, if you grow Censorious I must leave . 397 WAY WORLD I.1 99
  Mirabell: Censorious. . . . . 412 WAY WORLD II.1 102
  Millamant: I'll take my Death, Marwood, you are more Censorious, . 433 WAY WORLD III.1 323
Censur'd (1)
  Mrs Fore: they're in perpetual fear of being seen and censur'd?-- . 247 FOR LOVE II.1 433
Censure (6)
  Sharper: not what, forced me. I only beg a favourable Censure of this 79 OLD BATCH IV.1 160
  Laetitia: Impudent. Won't you censure me for this, now;--but 'tis . 82 OLD BATCH IV.2 80
  Vainlove: Censure of the first finder. . . . . 88 OLD BATCH IV.3 189
  Lady Touch: You censure hardly, my Lord; my Sister's . . . . . 151 DOUBL DLR III.1 11
  Angelica: Censure of the World: And she that marries a very Witty . 299 FOR LOVE V.1 72
               Impartial Censure, he requests from all, ... 324 M. BRIDE PRO. 43
Center (1)
  Singer-V: Love hates to center in a Point assign'd, ... 293 FOR LOVE IV.1 660
Centinel (1)
  Gonsalez: Nor Centinel, nor Guard! the Doors unbarr'd! . . . 376 M. BRIDE V.2 1
Centre (3)
  Lord Touch: Plyant has a large Eye, and wou'd centre every thing in . 151 DOUBL DLR III.1 6
  Heli: Let Heav'n with Thunder to the Centre strike me, . . 337 M. BRIDE II.1 4
  Perez: She might remove the Centre of this Earth, ... 372 M. BRIDE V.1 V 9
Cerberus (1)
  Valentine: If I can give that Cerberus a Sop, I shall be at rest
               for one . . . . 222 FOR LOVE I.1 225
Ceremony (5)
  Mellefont: That I have seen, with the Ceremony thereunto . . . 158 DOUBL DLR III.1 280
  Mrs Fore: Mr. Tattle might have us'd less Ceremony. . . . . . 293 FOR LOVE IV.1 681
  Marwood: undergoing the Ceremony. . . . . 411 WAY WORLD II.1 56
  Petulant: the Parish-Priest for reading the Ceremony. And for the . 436 WAY WORLD III.1 431
  Lady Wish: --and dispence with a little Ceremony. . . . . . . 457 WAY WORLD IV.1 489
Certain (16)
  Bellmour: A very certain remedy, probatum est--Ha, ha, ha, . . 63 OLD BATCH III.1 88
  Heartwell: yet a more certain Sign than all this; I give thee my Mony. 73 OLD BATCH III.2 85
  Maskwell: you, brings me certain Ruin. Allow it, I would betray you, 136 DOUBL DLR I.1 341
  Mellefont: has confess'd to me that but at some certain times, that is
               I . . . . 158 DOUBL DLR III.1 285
               Th' unladen Boughs, he sees, bode certain Dearth, . . 213 FOR LOVE PRO. 5
  Tattle: bring me into Disgrace with a certain Woman of Quality-- 227 FOR LOVE I.1 425
  Scandal: Are you certain? You do not look so. . . . . . . 268 FOR LOVE III.1 568
               So t'other can foretel by certain Rules . . . . . 323 M. BRIDE PRO. 11
  Heli: Anselmo's Memory, and will, for certain . . . . . 352 M. BRIDE III.1 V102
  Selim: 'Tis certain Heli too is fled, and with him . . . . 361 M. BRIDE IV.1 8
  Zara: O certain Death for him, as sure Despair . . . . . 363 M. BRIDE IV.1 94
  Zara: Most certain; though my Knowledge is not yet . . . 364 M. BRIDE IV.1 146
  Alonzo: My Lord, for certain truth, Perez is fled; . . . . 377 M. BRIDE V.2 48
  Zara: I have a certain Remedy for that. . . . . 381 M. BRIDE V.2 V189
  Fainall: too by this time--Jealous of her I cannot be, for I am
               certain; . . . . 443 WAY WORLD III.1 680
  Mirabell: your hands as Witnesses to a certain Parchment. . . 475 WAY WORLD V.1 524
Certainly (7)
  Vainlove: for you to Course. We were certainly cut out for one . 39 OLD BATCH I.1 76
  Heartwell: Certainly, irrecoverably married. . . . . 105 OLD BATCH V.1 315
  Sir Paul: poor Father,--and that would certainly have broke my . 146 DOUBL DLR II.1 280
  Mellefont: Excellent Maskwell, thou wer't certainly meant for . . 193 DOUBL DLR V.1 235
  Angelica: Effects of his own Merit. For certainly Mr. Tattle was . 255 FOR LOVE III.1 77
  Jeremy: you'll certainly be the Death of a Person that has a most 301 FOR LOVE V.1 168
  Marwood: Certainly. To be free; I have no Taste of . . . . 410 WAY WORLD II.1 20
Certainty (2)
  Lady Ply: is no certainty in the things of this life. . . . . 147 DOUBL DLR II.1 329
  Mellefont: my hopes, my certainty! . . . . 157 DOUBL DLR III.1 259
Certificate (3)
  Jeremy: Certificate of Three Lines--only to certifie those whom . 217 FOR LOVE I.1 65
  Mirabell: Have you the Certificate? . . . . 398 WAY WORLD I.1 122
  Mrs Fain: by producing a Certificate of her Gallants former . . 417 WAY WORLD II.1 298
Certifie (1)
  Jeremy: Certificate of Three Lines--only to certifie those whom . 217 FOR LOVE I.1 65
Certiorari (1)
  Sir Paul: Certiorari. . . . . 144 DOUBL DLR II.1 201
Chaf'd (1)
  Zara: And with it dry'd thy wat'ry Cheeks; then chaf'd . . 346 M. BRIDE II.2 V282
Chafe (2)
  Fondlewife: Let her clap a warm thing to his Stomach, or chafe it with 91 OLD BATCH IV.4 97
  Fondlewife: Let her clap some warm thing to his Stomach, or chafe it
               with . . . . 91 OLD BATCH IV.4 V 97
Chafeing-dish (1)
  Lady Wish: Chafeing-dish of starv'd Embers and Dining behind a . 462 WAY WORLD V.1 6
Chaff (1)
  Osmyn-Alph: And Chaff, the Sport of adverse Winds; till late . . 351 M. BRIDE III.1 60
Chafing (1)
  Zara: And with it dry'd thy wat'ry Cheeks; chafing . . . 346 M. BRIDE II.2 282
Chagrin (1)
  Belinda: Vainlove--Lard I have seen an Ass look so Chagrin, . . 55 OLD BATCH II.2 26
Chain (1)
  Singer-V: Then never let us chain what should be free, . . . 293 FOR LOVE IV.1 662
Chain'd (1)
  Ben: chain'd to an Oar all his life; and may-hap forc'd to tug a 262 FOR LOVE III.1 317

Chase (continued)
   Mirabell: that here the Chase must end, and my pursuit be Crown'd, . 449 WAY WORLD IV.1 158
Chaste (4)
   Sir Paul: Chaste as Ice, but you are melted now, and false as Water. 179 DOUBL DLR IV.1 431
   Scandal: another yours--As she is chaste, who was never   . 256 FOR LOVE III.1 127
   Singer-F: E're a Nymph that was Chaste, or a Swain that was True.   258 FOR LOVE III.1 203
   Singer-F: And the Nymph may be Chaste that has never been Try'd.   259 FOR LOVE III.1 208
Chastity (2)
   Sr Sampson: more Illustrious than the Moon; for she has her Chastity   242 FOR LOVE II.1 258
   Waitwell: Frankincense, all Chastity and Odour. . . . . . 459 WAY WORLD IV.1 546
Chatter (1)
   Almeria: I chatter, shake, and faint with thrilling Fears.   .   . 358 M. BRIDE III.1 369
Cheap (2)
   Sharper: are; that you have so cheap an opportunity of expressing . 49 OLD BATCH II.1 88
   Vainlove: sell you freedom better cheap. . . . . 109 OLD BATCH V.2 80
Cheaply (1)
   Maskwell: every look you cheaply throw away on any other Object . 199 DOUBL DLR V.1 435
Chearful (1)
              There's Humour, which for chearful Friends we got,   . . 213 FOR LOVE PRO. 29
Cheat (14)
   Bellmour: when it disclosed the Cheat, which, that trusty Bawd of   38 OLD BATCH I.1 49
   Sharper: Ha, ha; 'Twill be a pleasant Cheat.--I'll plague   99 OLD BATCH V.1 86
   Bellmour: discovering the Cheat to Sylvia. She took it at first, as   100 OLD BATCH V.1 150
   Maskwell: will cheat no body but himself; such another Coxcomb, . 150 DOUBL DLR II.1 454
   Maskwell: (aside) to cheat you, as well as the rest.   .   . 154 DOUBL DLR III.1 161
   Maskwell: cheat my Lord.   190 DOUBL DLR V.1 119
   Maskwell: may not discover you in the Coach, but think the Cheat   193 DOUBL DLR V.1 233
   Maskwell: me to cheat 'em; and if they will not hear the Serpent's   194 DOUBL DLR V.1 264
   Maskwell: gratifie your taste, and cheat the World, to prove a
               faithful   199 DOUBL DLR V.1 438
   Scandal: Yes, several, very honest;--they'll cheat a little at . 271 FOR LOVE III.1 666
   Sr Sampson: Contrivance, what to cheat me? to cheat your . . . 311 FOR LOVE V.1 509
   Mirabell: Cheat. The Ugly and the Old, whom the Looking-glass   420 WAY WORLD II.1 395
   Lady Wish: is a cheat and a Rascal.--   460 WAY WORLD IV.1 588
Cheated (2)
   Setter: to be cheated, that the Captain may be so in reality.   . 106 OLD BATCH V.1 349
   Capt Bluff: Oh, the Devil, cheated at last! . . . . . . 110 OLD BATCH V.2 110
Checquer'd (1)
   Foresight: bad, some good, our lives are checquer'd, Mirth and   . 236 FOR LOVE II.1 35
Cheek (2)
   Osmyn-Alph: With the new-flushing Ardour of my Cheek; . . . . 383 M. BRIDE V.2 282
   Sir Wilful: let me bite your Cheek for that. . . . . . 457 WAY WORLD IV.1 473
Cheek'd (0)   see Cherry-cheek'd
Cheeks (7)
   Fondlewife: and glow upon his Cheeks, and that I would as soon   . . 76 OLD BATCH IV.1 32
   Lady Ply: my Honour; your guilty Cheeks confess it; Oh where   . . 179 DOUBL DLR IV.1 445
   Foresight: Cheeks have been gather'd many Years;--ha! I do not   . 269 FOR LOVE III.1 603
   Ben: after all your fair speeches, and stroaking my Cheeks,   . 286 FOR LOVE IV.1 417
   Zara: And with it dry'd thy wat'ry Cheeks; chafing . . . 346 M. BRIDE II.2 282
   Zara: And with it dry'd thy wat'ry Cheeks; then chaf'd   . 346 M. BRIDE II.2 V282
   Fainall: Cheeks, and sparkling from your Eyes.   . . . . 413 WAY WORLD II.1 141
Cheer (2)
   Maskwell: No sinking, nor no danger,--come, cheer up; . . . 148 DOUBL DLR II.1 391
   Sr Sampson: Sunday:--Come, Cheer up, look about thee: Look   . 265 FOR LOVE III.1 465
Cheerfulness (1)
   Osmyn-Alph: Look round; Joy is not here, nor Cheerfulness.   .   . 346 M. BRIDE II.2 261
Cheese (0)   see Cream-cheese
Cheese-curd (1)
   Ben: You Cheese-curd you,--Marry thee! Oons I'll Marry a   . 264 FOR LOVE III.1 425
Chelsey (1)
   Mrs Frail: had gone to Knights-bridge, or to Chelsey, or to
               Spring-Garden, ... 247 FOR LOVE II.1 438
Cherry (1)
   Peg: The red Ratifia does your Ladyship mean, or the Cherry . 425 WAY WORLD III.1 9
Cherry-Brandy (1)
   Lady Wish: A Pox take you both--Fetch me the Cherry-Brandy . 425 WAY WORLD III.1 20
Cherry-cheek'd (1)
   Araminta: I warrant, plump, Cherry-cheek'd Country-Girls.   . . . 84 OLD BATCH IV.3 27
Cherubin (1)
   Sir Paul: gads bud she's a Wife for a Cherubin! Do you think her   145 DOUBL DLR II.1 265
Chew (2)
   Sharper: Thou hast a sickly peevish Appetite; only chew Love and   80 OLD BATCH IV.1 172
   Valentine: Eyes; shut up your Mouth, and chew the Cud of   . . 216 FOR LOVE I.1 15
Chew'd (1)
   Lady Froth: I have seen her take 'em half chew'd out of her . . 165 DOUBL DLR III.1 570
Chewing (1)
   Brisk: Spectacle; she's always chewing the Cud like an old Yew.   165 DOUBL DLR III.1 568
Chide (1)
   Sharper: chide him about Sylvia. . . . . 104 OLD BATCH V.1 294
Chief (3)
   Jeremy: O Sir, for that Sir, 'tis my chief Talent; I'm as secret   . 302 FOR LOVE V.1 190
   Mirabell: What, is the Chief of that noble Family in Town,   .   . 400 WAY WORLD I.1 187
Chiefly (2)
   Heartwell: My Talent is chiefly that of speaking truth, which I   . 45 OLD BATCH I.1 302
   Lady Wish: --I may say it; for I chiefly made it my own Care to   . 466 WAY WORLD V.1 183
Chiefs (1)
   Heli: Are risen in Arms, and call for Chiefs to head   . . . 351 M. BRIDE III.1 70
Child (39)   see Male-Child, Man-child
   Heartwell: Child--A meer Infant and would suck. Can you   . . . 72 OLD BATCH III.2 51
   Heartwell: Lying, Child, is indeed the Art of Love; and Men are   . 72 OLD BATCH III.2 56
   Heartwell: lov'd; but that fashion is chang'd, Child.   . . . 73 OLD BATCH III.2 104
   Araminta: You were about to tell me something, Child,--   . . . 83 OLD BATCH IV.3 21
               So, does our Author, this his Child commit   . . . 125 DOUBL DLR PRO. 9
   Careless: effectually shown, as in bringing forth a Child to
               Disinherit . . . . 131 DOUBL DLR I.1 160
   Sir Paul: dye of 'em, like any Child, that were cutting his Teeth--   146 DOUBL DLR II.1 283

Chocolate-Houses (3)
Snap:	block up the Chocolate-Houses, and then our labour's lost.	224	FOR LOVE	I.1	299
Tattle:	Maids at the Chocolate-Houses, all the Porters of Pall-Mall	257	FOR LOVE	III.1	155
Tattle:	Maids at the Chocolate-Houses, all the Porters at Pall-Mall	257	FOR LOVE	III.1	V155

Choice (5)
Sharper:	In her choice I gad--But thou canst not be so	80	OLD BATCH	IV.1	186
Lady Ply:	my second choice.	170	DOUEL DLR	IV.1	112
Angelica:	if I were obliged to make a Choice, I declare I'd rather	260	FOR LOVE	III.1	255
Sir Wilful:	'tis like you may--Here are choice of Pastimes here in	448	WAY WORLD	IV.1	124
Lady Wish:	would not have carry'd it thus. Well, that was my Choice,	469	WAY WORLD	V.1	305

Choler (1)
Mrs Frail:	Mr. Benjamin in Choler!	285	FOR LOVE	IV.1	358

Cholerick (2)
Sir Joseph:	mischief--For he was a devilish cholerick Fellow: And if	68	OLD BATCH	III.1	274
Sir Paul:	say truth, all our Family are Cholerick; I am the only	192	DOUEL DLR	V.1	196

Cholick (6)
Laetitia:	Spin-text, has a sad Fit of the Cholick, and is forced to lie	91	OLD BATCH	IV.4	78
Laetitia:	you of the Cholick.	91	OLD BATCH	IV.4	87
Fondlewife:	confess. But, what--not to be cured of the Cholick? Don't	93	OLD BATCH	IV.4	162
Fondlewife:	Cholick. Ah!	93	OLD BATCH	IV.4	165
Bellmour:	Fit of the Cholick, to excuse my lying down upon your	94	OLD BATCH	IV.4	211
Laetitia:	Mr. Spin-text was ill of the Cholick, upon our bed. And	95	OLD BATCH	IV.4	245

Choller (1)
Sir Joseph:	my Choller had been up too, agad there would have been	68	OLD BATCH	III.1	275

Choose (2)   see Chuse
Lady Wish:	has acquir'd Discretion to choose for himself.	432	WAY WORLD	III.1	265
Millamant:	wear what I please; and choose Conversation with regard	450	WAY WORLD	IV.1	215

Choosing (3)   see Chusing
Bellmour:	Fondness and Impatience of his Absence, by choosing a	38	OLD BATCH	I.1	57
Garcia:	Choosing this lonely Mansion of the Dead,	337	M. BRIDE	II.1	2
Millamant:	has not the liberty of choosing one's Acquaintance, as one	432	WAY WORLD	III.1	297

Chopping (2)
	I'th' Good Man's Arms, the Chopping Bastard thrives,	125	DOUBL DLR	PRO.	29
Sir Paul:	end--He? A brave Chopping Boy.--I'll settle a Thousand	173	DOUEL DLR	IV.1	224

Chose (1)
Osmyn-Alph:	And only for his Sorrows chose this Solitude?	346	M. BRIDE	II.2	260

Chosen (1)
Sr Sampson:	And might not I have chosen whether I would have begot	244	FOR LOVE	II.1	325

Christian (9)
Belinda:	make her look like a Christian,--and she was sensible	84	OLD BATCH	IV.3	42
	Our Christian Cuckolds are more bent to pity;	125	DOUBL DLR	PRO.	27
Sir Paul:	are a better Christian than to think of being a Nun; he?	174	DOUEL DLR	IV.1	255
Sir Paul:	are a better Christian than to think of living a Nun; he?	174	DOUBL DLR	IV.1	V255
Nurse:	another Christian, (crying)	238	FOR LOVE	II.1	125
Lady Wish:	the Turks--for thou are not fit to live in a Christian	456	WAY WORLD	IV.1	440
Sir Wilful:	Christian--I cannot find by the Map that your Mufti is	456	WAY WORLD	IV.1	446
Sir Wilful:	To drink is a Christian Diversion,	456	WAY WORLD	IV.1	450
Sir Wilful:	Aunt, why you must an you are a Christian.	471	WAY WORLD	V.1	382

Christnings (1)
Witwoud:	like ten Christnings--I am tipsy with laughing--If I had	453	WAY WORLD	IV.1	326

Chronicled (1)
Heartwell:	Chronicled in Ditty, and sung in woful Ballad, to the	63	OLD BATCH	III.1	80

Chuck (2)
Heartwell:	off as unconcern'd, come chuck the Infant under the chin,	45	OLD BATCH	I.1	325
Sr Sampson:	Come, Chuck, satisfie him, answer him;--	311	FOR LOVE	V.1	527

Chuckle (1)
Scandal:	He begins to Chuckle;--ply him close, or he'l	224	FOR LOVE	I.1	292

Church (2)
Bellmour:	to Church in the Morning?--May be it may get	112	OLD BATCH	V.2	177
Tattle:	Church, once, an Enquiry being made, who I was, it was	257	FOR LOVE	III.1	163

Churches (1)
Valentine:	Oh, Prayers will be said in empty Churches, at	289	FOR LOVE	IV.1	500

Chuse (5)
Fondlewife:	Ha! This is Apocryphal; I may chuse whether I	95	OLD BATCH	IV.4	217
Sr Sampson:	Odsbud, Hussy, you know how to chuse, and so do I;	301	FOR LOVE	V.1	143
Foible:	cannot chuse but be grateful. I find your Ladyship has his	430	WAY WORLD	III.1	204
Lady Wish:	to chuse. When you have been abroad, Nephew, you'll	441	WAY WORLD	III.1	608
Fainall:	consider'd; I will only reserve to my self the Power to chuse	468	WAY WORLD	V.1	266

Chusing (1)
	Each chusing that, in which he has most Art.	204	DOUBL DLR	EPI.	16

Chymist (3)
Sharper:	Say you so? faith I am as poor as a Chymist and	46	OLD BATCH	I.1	347
Jeremy:	Chymist, Lover, or Poet in Europe.	295	FOR LOVE	IV.1	740
Marwood:	Care, like any Chymist upon the Day of Projection.	431	WAY WORLD	III.1	248

Chymistry (1)
Bellmour:	worth your acquaintance--a little of thy Chymistry Tom,	46	OLD BATCH	I.1	345

Cicero (1)
Bellmour:	Superscription (Takes up the Letter.) than in all Cicero--	38	OLD BATCH	I.1	34

Cinamon (1)
Mirabell:	all Anniseed, Cinamon, Citron and Barbado's-Waters, together	451	WAY WORLD	IV.1	273

Cinnamon-water (1)
Coachman:	Glass of Cinnamon-water.	404	WAY WORLD	I.1	351

Circle (6)
Lord Touch:	her own Circle; 'tis not the first time she has mistaken	151	DOUBL DLR	III.1	7
Maskwell:	I that had wanton'd in the wide Circle of your	199	DOUBL DLR	V.1	431
Maskwell:	I that had wanton'd in the rich Circle of your	199	DOUEL DLR	V.1	V431
Sr Sampson:	not keep the Devil out of his Wives Circle.	241	FOR LOVE	II.1	228
Sr Sampson:	not keep the Devil out of his Wife's Circle.	241	FOR LOVE	II.1	V228
Singer-V:	But runs with Joy the Circle of the Mind.	293	FOR LOVE	IV.1	661

Circling (2)
Lord Touch:	Circling Joys, tread round each happy Year of your long	203	DOUBL DLR	V.1	589
Almeria:	The circling Hours, that gather all the Woes,	330	M. BRIDE	I.1	153

Circling   (continued)
    Manuel: Where, ev'ry Hour shall roll in circling Joys;   . . . . 349 M. BRIDE   II.2   387
Circulation (1)
                    Stroling from Place to Place, by Circulation.   . . . . 315 FOR LOVE   EPI.   33
Circumstance (4)
    Lady Ply: dare swear every Circumstance of me trembles.--O your . . 178 DOUBL DLR   IV.1   398
    Osmyn-Alph: Is knowing more than any Circumstance, ... 342 M. BRIDE   II.2   94
    Manuel: Is manifest from every Circumstance.   . . . . . 366 M. BRIDE   IV.1   214
    Marwood: True, 'tis an unhappy Circumstance of Life, ... 410 WAY WORLD   II.1   9
Circumstances (3)
    Lady Ply: And no body knows how Circumstances may   . . . . . 147 DOUBL DLR   II.1   325
    Lady Ply: qualified in all those Circumstances, I'm sure I should . 159 DOUBL DLR   III.1 340
    Mirabell: my knowledge his Circumstances are such, he must of   . 478 WAY WORLD   V.1   614
Cite (1)
    Angelica: I cite Valentine here, to declare to the Court, how   . . 257 FOR LOVE   III.1 142
Citizen (1)
    Ben: fair a Face, as a Citizen or a Courtier; but for all
                    that, I've   . . . . 273 FOR LOVE   III.1 735
Citizens (1)
    Fainall: budding Antlers like a young Satyre, or a Citizens Child. . 442 WAY WORLD   III.1 633
Citron (1)
    Mirabell: all Anniseed, Cinamon, Citron and Barbado's-Waters, together 451 WAY WORLD   IV.1   273
Cits (1)
                    The Cuckoldom, of Ancient Right, to Cits belongs.   . . . 204 DOUBL DLR   EPI.   28
City (4)
                    I know not one Moor-Husband in the City.   . . . . . 125 DOUBL DLR   PRO.   28
    Jeremy: Trade, if he had set up in the City--For my part, I never . 218 FOR LOVE   I.1   91
    Foresight: In the City?   . . . . 288 FOR LOVE   IV.1   499
    Valentine: Shop. Oh things will go methodically in the City, the   . 289 FOR LOVE   IV.1   503
Civet-Cat (1)
    Ben: stink; he shall smell more like a Weasel than a Civet-Cat, 265 FOR LOVE   III.1 437
Civil (12)
                    He's very civil, and entreats your Favour.   35   OLD BATCH   PRO.   13
    Sir Joseph: An it hadn't been for a civil Gentleman as came by   . . . 47   OLD BATCH   II.1   8
    Fondlewife: Good again--A very civil Person this, and, I   94   OLD BATCH   IV.4   179
    Fondlewife: as I should be, a sort of a civil Perquisite to a
                    Whore-master, ... 94   OLD BATCH   IV.4   184
    Belinda: that will do a civil thing to his Wife, or say a civil
                    thing to   . . . . 108 OLD BATCH   V.2   30
    Mrs Frail: no Creature perfectly Civil, but a Husband. For in a little 231 FOR LOVE   I.1   563
    Mrs Frail: Civil!   . . . . 234 FOR LOVE   I.1   667
    Valentine: A couple of very civil Proverbs, truly: 'Tis hard to   . 256 FOR LOVE   III.1 129
    Ben: words however. I spoke you fair d'ee see, and civil.--As . 264 FOR LOVE   III.1 403
    Mirabell: She was always civil to me, till of late; I confess I   . 397 WAY WORLD   I.1   85
    Sir Wilful: 'Sheart the Gentleman's a civil Gentleman, Aunt,   . . . 471 WAY WORLD   V.1   345
Civility (4)
    Lord Touch: Respect for Love, and made Sir Paul jealous of the Civility 151 DOUBL DLR   III.1 8
    Mrs Frail: good Breeding, for it begets his Civility to other People. 231 FOR LOVE   I.1   565
    Tattle: Foresight mean by this Civility? Is it to make a Fool of me? 251 FOR LOVE   II.1   592
    Garcia: And with a haughty Mien, and stern Civility   . . . . 335 M. BRIDE   I.1   370
Civiller (1)
    Valentine: which are but a civiller sort of Duns, that lay claim to   . 221 FOR LOVE   I.1   191
Civilly (1)
    Ben: civilly to me, of her own accord: Whatever you think of   . 264 FOR LOVE   III.1 411
Claim (2)
    Valentine: which are but a civiller sort of Duns, that lay claim to   . 221 FOR LOVE   I.1   191
    Lady Wish: Neice exerts a lawfull claim, having Match'd her self by   . 472 WAY WORLD   V.1   417
Clamours (2)
    Osmyn-Alph: To Victory; their Shouts and Clamours rend   . . . . 351 M. BRIDE   III.1 84
    Gonsalez: Perdition choak your Clamours--whence this   . . . . 376 M. BRIDE   V.2   24
Clap (5)
    Setter: . . . as a Clap is to the Pox.   66   OLD BATCH   III.1 V197
    Fondlewife: Let her clap a warm thing to his Stomach, or chafe it with 91   OLD BATCH   IV.4   97
    Fondlewife: Let her clap some warm thing to his Stomach, or chafe it
                    with   91   OLD BATCH   IV.4 V 97
    Mellefont: Ply her close, and by and by clap a Billet doux into her . 158 DOUBL DLR   III.1 315
    Witwoud: --Then trip to his Lodging, clap on a Hood and Scarf,   . 405 WAY WORLD   I.1   372
Claret (1)
    Sir Wilful: hard Word, Aunt, and (hiccup) Greek for Claret.   . . . . 456 WAY WORLD   IV.1   448
Clary (1)
    Mirabell: with Ratifia and the most noble Spirit of Clary,--but   . 451 WAY WORLD   IV.1   274
Clash (3)
    Belinda: Nor are ever like--Yet we often meet and clash.   . . . 58   OLD BATCH   II.2   120
    Petulant: clash; snugs the Word, I shrug and am silent.   . . . 407 WAY WORLD   I.1   447
    Fainall: another, have made you clash till you have both struck   . 413 WAY WORLD   II.1   139
Claws (1)
    Gonsalez: And cling, as if with Claws they did enforce   . . . . 332 M. BRIDE   I.1   239
Clay (1)
    Alonzo: But what are Kings reduc'd to common Clay?   . . . . 379 M. BRIDE   V.2   113
Clayie (1)
    Almeria: To his cold clayie Breast: my Father then, ... 340 M. BRIDE   II.2   22
Clean (2)
    Saygrace: with a clean starch'd Band and Cuffs.   . . . . . . 195 DOUBL DLR   V.1   286
    Ben: clean Shirt once a Quarter--Come home and lie with   . . 275 FOR LOVE   III.1 801
Cleanly (1)
    Bellmour: the sweeter Breath, for the more cleanly conveyance. But   . 44   OLD BATCH   I.1   258
Clear (7)
    Laetitia: if I can clear my own innocence to my own Deare.   . . . 93   OLD BATCH   IV.4   169
                    Let's have a fair Tryal, and a clear Sea.   . . . . 125 DOUBL DLR   PRO.   15
    Lady Touch: temperately bad, what excuse can clear?   . . . . . 136 DOUBL DLR   I.1   329
    Cynthia: Why if you give me very clear demonstration that it   . . 169 DOUBL DLR   IV.1   58
    Jeremy: Nay, that's as clear as the Sun; I'll make Oath of it   . 245 FOR LOVE   II.1   355
                    For a clear Stage won't do, without your Favour.   . . 316 FOR LOVE   EPI.   44
    Fainall: So, so, why this point's clear,--Well how do we   . . . 443 WAY WORLD   III.1 697
Clear'd (1)
    Garcia: To have his Jealousie confirm'd or clear'd   . . . . 338 M. BRIDE   II.1   41

Cleaves (1)
Almeria: And cleaves my Heart; I would have born it all, ... 369 M. BRIDE IV.1 309
Cleft (1)
Osmyn-Alph: At length, imprison'd in some Cleft of Rock, ... 351 M. BRIDE III.1 61
Cleopatra (1)
Witwoud: as Cleopatra. Mirabell is not so sure of her as he thinks
             for. . . . . 408 WAY WORLD I.1 478
Clergy (2)
Sr Sampson: damn'd Tyburn face, without the benefit o' the Clergy. . 243 FOR LOVE II.1 307
Foible: put upon his Clergy--Yes indeed, I enquir'd of the . . 463 WAY WORLD V.1 44
Clerk (1)
Petulant: S'life, Witwoud, were you ever an Attorney's Clerk? . . 440 WAY WORLD III.1 554
Clifted (1)
Gonsalez: Their Hold, thro' clifted Stones; stretching, and staring, 332 M. BRIDE I.1 240
Cling (2)
Sr Sampson: young Spendthrift forc'd to cling to an Old Woman for . 260 FOR LOVE III.1 263
Gonsalez: And cling, as if with Claws they did enforce . . . . . 332 M. BRIDE I.1 239
Clink (1)
Zara: And Howls of Slaves condemn'd; from Clink of Chains, . 379 M. BRIDE V.2 137
Clinking (1)
Lady Wish: ne'er a Brass-Thimble clinking in thy Pocket with a bit 425 WAY WORLD III.1 31
Cloak (4)
Setter: precise Band, with a swinging long Spiritual Cloak, to . 64 OLD BATCH III.1 124
Bellmour: and even dar'd Discovery--This Cloak my Sanctity, . . . 80 OLD BATCH IV.2 5
Bellmour: (Throwing off his Cloak, Patch, &c.) . . 81 OLD BATCH IV.2 13
Bellmour: Enter Laetitia and Bellmour, his Cloak, Hat, &c. lying . 89 OLD BATCH IV.4
Cloaks (1)
Bellmour: Soldier, which now a'days as often cloaks Cowardice, as a 46 OLD BATCH I.1 367
Cloath (1)
Almeria: And cloath their Nakedness with my own Flesh; . . . . 370 M. BRIDE IV.1 350
Cloathing (3)
Setter: sully'd iniquities and Cloathing. . . . . 66 OLD BATCH III.1 191
Laetitia: Rather, sure it is a Wolf in the cloathing of a Sheep. . 93 OLD BATCH IV.4 142
Fondlewife: Thou art a Devil in his proper Cloathing, ... 93 OLD BATCH IV.4 143
Cloaths (5)
Sharper: Are you so extravagant in Cloaths Sir Joseph? . . . . 50 OLD BATCH II.1 113
Setter: Shifting Cloaths for the purpose at a Friend's House of . 106 OLD BATCH V.1 351
Valentine: My Cloaths are soon put off;--But you must . . . . 244 FOR LOVE II.1 339
Mirabell: Has the Taylor brought Waitwell's Cloaths home, . . . 398 WAY WORLD I.1 124
Millamant: does one's Cloaths. . . . . 432 WAY WORLD III.1 298
Clock (11)
Mellefont: This very next ensuing hour of Eight a Clock, is . . . 169 DOUBL DLR IV.1 52
Lady Touch: 'Tis Eight a Clock: Methinks I should have . . . . 183 DOUBL DLR IV.2 8
Lord Froth: what a Clock is't? past Eight, on my Conscience; my . . 200 DOUBL DLR V.1 493
Foresight: he's at leisure--'tis now Three a Clock, a very good hour 236 FOR LOVE II.1 41
Foresight: At Ten a Clock, punctually at Ten. . . . . . . 265 FOR LOVE III.1 472
Sr Sampson: Figures of St. Dunstan's Clock, and Consummatum est shall 266 FOR LOVE III.1 477
Mrs Fore: Clock. Mr. Scandal, your Servant-- . . . . . . 268 FOR LOVE III.1 577
Valentine: What a Clock is't? My Father here! Your Blessing, Sir? . 280 FOR LOVE IV.1 193
Mirabell: Betty, what says your Clock? . . . . 398 WAY WORLD I.1 105
Mirabell: One a Clock! (looking on his Watch) O y'are come-- . . 398 WAY WORLD I.1 109
Mirabell: Feathers, and meet me at One a Clock by Rosamond's Pond. 398 WAY WORLD I.1 130
Clocks (1)
Valentine: Clocks will strike Twelve at Noon, and the Horn'd Herd . 289 FOR LOVE IV.1 504
Clog (1)
Osmyn-Alph: Would hold thee here, and clog thy Expedition. . . . . 352 M. BRIDE III.1 110
Cloister'd (1)
Sharper: have their Year of Probation, before they are cloister'd in 104 OLD BATCH V.1 304
Clos'd (2) see Long-clos'd
Maskwell: Lips be ever clos'd. (Kisses her.) And thus--Oh who . . 184 DOUBL DLR IV.2 25
Osmyn-Alph: But now, and I was clos'd within the Tomb . . . . 349 M. BRIDE III.1 1
Close (18)
Bellmour: Friend, be close pursued, or lost. Business is the rub of
             Life, ... 37 OLD BATCH I.1 10
Bellmour: Oh here he comes, stand close let 'em pass. . . . . 46 OLD BATCH I.1 V339
Sir Joseph: call my Back; he sticks as close to me, and follows me . 50 OLD BATCH II.1 119
Bellmour: by those healing Lips.--Oh! press the soft Charm close . 82 OLD BATCH IV.2 73
Sharper: purpose. Setter, stand close; seem not to observe 'em; and, 101 OLD BATCH V.1 164
Mellefont: close her Eyes, till she had seen my ruin. . . . . . 130 DOUBL DLR I.1 118
Mellefont: close her Eyes, till they had seen my ruin. . . . . . 130 DOUBL DLR I.1 V118
Mellefont: Ply her close, and by and by clap a Billet doux into her 158 DOUBL DLR III.1 315
Lady Froth: --Shall you and I do our close Dance to show . . . . 177 DOUBL DLR IV.1 374
Lady Touch: With Careless, in the close Arbour, he may . . . . 192 DOUBL DLR V.1 188
Scandal: He begins to Chuckle;--ply him close, or he'l . . . . 224 FOR LOVE I.1 292
Mrs Frail: Ah Devil, sly Devil--He's as close, Sister, as . . . . 250 FOR LOVE III.1 542
Jeremy: Ah Sir, if you are not very faithful and close in this
             Business, ... 301 FOR LOVE V.1 167
Tattle: close, ha? . . . . 302 FOR LOVE V.1 189
Tattle: Close Dog! A good Whoremaster, I warrant him . . . . 302 FOR LOVE V.1 196
Foresight: O, Mr. Tattle, your Servant, you are a close Man; . . . 304 FOR LOVE V.1 256
Almeria: Me in his leaden Arms, and press me close . . . . 340 M. BRIDE II.2 21
Zara: Cover us close--or I shall chill his Breast, ... 381 M. BRIDE V.2 207
Closely (1)
Almeria: Who knew our Flight, we closely were pursu'd, ... 329 M. BRIDE I.1 123
Closer (2)
Valentine: closer--that none may over-hear us;--Jeremy, I can tell you 290 FOR LOVE IV.1 557
Marwood: without you cou'd have kept his Counsel closer. I shall . 431 WAY WORLD III.1 242
Closet (8)
Fondlewife: Fifty? I have the Summ ready in Gold, in my Closet. . . 89 OLD BATCH IV.4 30
Fondlewife: (Goes into his Closet.) . . 89 OLD BATCH IV.4 31
Lady Touch: Kindness--but will you go into your Closet, and recover . 153 DOUBL DLR III.1 116
Maskwell: you can in his Closet, and I doubt not but you will mould 155 DOUBL DLR III.1 166
Maskwell: My Lady is just gone down from my Lords Closet, . . . 181 DOUBL DLR IV.1 515
Maskwell: My Lady is just gone into my Lords Closet, ... 181 DOUBL DLR IV.1 V515
Tattle: Closet, nor run behind a Screen, or under a Table; never 230 FOR LOVE I.1 519
Mrs Frail: Ay, but I hear he has a Closet of Beauties. . . . . 232 FOR LOVE I.1 605

Cockatrice (2)
  Heartwell: My Wife! By this Light 'tis she, the very Cockatrice   . . 111 OLD BATCH   V.2   125
  Foresight: reveng'd on you, Cockatrice; I'll hamper you--You   . . . 238 FOR LCVE   II.1 114
Cocky (17)
  Fondlewife: and bid my Cocky come out to me, I will give her some . .   76 OLD BATCH IV.1   46
  Fondlewife: Nay Cocky Cocky, nay dear Cocky, don't cry, I was   . . .   78 OLD BATCH IV.1 100
  Fondlewife: Nay Cocky. . . . .   78 OLD BATCH IV.1 105
  Fondlewife: Oak--I profess I can hold no longer--Nay dear Cocky--   .   78 OLD BATCH IV.1 115
  Fondlewife: What not love Cocky! . . . .   78 OLD BATCH IV.1 126
  Fondlewife: I wont be dealous--Poor Cocky, Kiss Nykin, Kiss   . . .   79 OLD BATCH IV.1 135
  Fondlewife: talk to Cocky and teach her how a Wife ought to behave   .   79 OLD BATCH IV.1 137
  Fondlewife: By Cocky. . . . .   79 OLD BATCH IV.1 147
  Fondlewife: By Cocky, by, by. . . . .   79 OLD BATCH IV.1 150
  Fondlewife: (without). Cocky, Cocky, Where are you Cocky?   . . .   89 OLD BATCH IV.4   8
  Fondlewife: Cocky, Cocky, open the door . . . .   89 OLD BATCH IV.4   11
  Fondlewife: back.--Give me the Key of your Cabinet, Cocky--   . . .   91 OLD BATCH IV.4   73
Cocquetts (1)
                Whole Belles Assemblees of Cocquetts and Beaux. . . . . 479 WAY WORLD EPI.   36
Coelestial (1) see Celestial
  Foresight: Coelestial Spheres, know the Signs and the Planets, and
                their . . . . 241 FOR LCVE   II.1 211
Coeur (0)   see Mon Coeur
Coffee (2)
  Mirabell: drinks, as Tea, Chocolate and Coffee. As likewise to Genuine 451 WAY WORLD IV.1 266
  Sir Wilful: And be damn'd over Tea-Cups and Coffee. . . . . . 456 WAY WCRLD IV.1 454
Coffee-House (1)
  Jeremy: --Ah Fox confound that Will's Coffee-House, it has   . . 218 FOR LCVE   I.1   87
Coffee-Houses (1)
  Valentine: Occupy the Family. Coffee-Houses will be full of Smoak   . 289 FOR LCVE   IV.1 507
Coffee-houses (1)
  Capt Bluff: went every day to Coffee-houses to read the Gazette my   .   53 OLD BATCH II.1 208
Cogitations (1)
  Lucy: Of thy most vile Cogitations--Thou poor, Conceited   . .   65 OLD EATCH III.1 167
Coheiresses (1)
  Petulant: Relations--Two Coheiresses his Cousins, and an old   . . 406 WAY WCRLD   I.1 407
Coin (1)
  Mirabell: me, that you endeavour not to new Coin it. To which end,   . 451 WAY WORLD IV.1 247
Colberteen (1)
  Lady Wish: Yellow Colberteen again; do; an cld gnaw'd Mask, two   . . 462 WAY WORLD   V.1   15
Cold (21)
  Sharper: warming her when she should be cold? . . . . . .   44 OLD BATCH   I.1 265
  Bellmour: kick this Puppy without a Man were cold, and had nc   . .   70 OLD BATCH III.1 328
  Bellmour: kick this Puppy unless a Man were cold, and had no   . .   70 OLD BATCH III.1 V328
  Laetitia: to lie at peace in my cold Grave--Since it will . . .   78 OLD BATCH IV.1 111
  Bellmour: Well, I promise.--A promise is so cold.-- . . . . .   82 OLD BATCH IV.2   71
  Araminta: (aside). So cold! . . . .   87 OLD BATCH IV.3 141
  Belinda: Company, and at last serv'd up ccld to the Wife. . . . 106 OLD EATCH   V.1 377
  Lord Touch: find ycu so cold in his Defence. . . . . 151 DOUBL DLR III.1   30
  Careless: overspreads my face, a cold deadly dew already vents   . 170 DOUBL DLR IV.1 115
  Lady Touch: Cold indifference; Love has no Language to be heard.   . 184 DOUEL DLR IV.2   23
  Sr Sampson: in Winter? Not at all--It's a Plot to undermine Cold   . 308 FOR LOVE   V.1 405
  Almeria: Within its cold, but hospitable Bcsom. . . . . . 326 M. BRIDE   I.1   12
  Almeria: And Monumental Caves of Death, look Cold, ... 339 M. BRIDE   II.1   65
  Almeria: To his ccld clayie Breast: my Father then, ... 340 M. BRIDE   II.2   22
  Zara: Traytour, Monster, cold and perfidious Slave; . . . . 348 M. BRIDE   II.2 340
  Zara: Cold, cold; my Veins are Icicles and Frost. . . . . 381 M. BRIDE   V.2 205
  Almeria: Yet I will take a cold and parting Leave, ... 382 M. BRIDE   V.2 266
  Osmyn-Alph: The Words of Joy and Peace: warm thy cold Beauties,   . 383 M. BRIDE   V.2 281
  Sir Wilful: an you be so cold and so courtly! . . . . 439 WAY WORLD III.1 525
  Sir Wilful: there's no haste; it will keep ccld as they say,--Cozen,   . 448 WAY WORLD IV.1 146
Coldly (1)
  Zara: Better I was unseen, than seen thus coldly. . . . . 346 M. BRIDE   II.2 257
Coldness (3)
  Maskwell: interpret a Coldness the right way; therefore I must   . . 155 DOUBL DLR III.1 182
  Angelica: Coldness which I have always worn before you, should   . 313 FCR LCVE   V.1 606
  Fainall: else now, and play too negligently; the Coldness of a   . 395 WAY WORLD   I.1   6
Collect (2)
  Almeria: I'll scrape 'till I collect his rotten Bones, ... 370 M. BRIDE   IV.2 349
  Mirabell: And this is the Sum of what you cou'd collect last   . . 408 WAY WORLD   I.1 494
Collected (1)
  Almeria: The dire collected Dews, on my poor Head; . . . . . 330 M. BRIDE   I.1 160
Collection (1)
  Tattle: I have a pretty good Collection at your Service, some   . . 232 FOR LOVE   I.1 599
Colour (7)
  Vainlove: Ha! It has a Colour.--But how do you know . . . .   99 OLD BATCH   V.1 110
  Selim: However, for a Cclour, tell him, you . . . . . . 362 M. BRIDE   IV.1   50
  Gonsalez: Which wears indeed this Colour of a Truth; . . . . 363 M. BRIDE   IV.1   79
  Almeria: And stain the Colour of my last Adieu. . . . . . 382 M. BRIDE   V.2 269
  Mrs Pain: You change Colour. . . . . 411 WAY WORLD II.1   68
  Lady Wish: An errant Ash colour, as I'm a Person. Look you how this . 425 WAY WCRLD III.1   6
  Marwood: You have a Cclour, what's the matter? . . . . . . 432 WAY WCRLD III.1 286
Coloured (0)   see Party-coloured
Colours (1)
  Scandal: there are some set out in their true Colours, both Men and 233 FOR LCVE   I.1 627
Comb (1)   see Cox-Ccmb
  Mincing: The Gentlemen stay but to Comb, Madam; and . . . . 434 WAY WORLD III.1 368
Comb-Case (1)
  Belinda: Almanack, and a Comb-Case; the Mother, a great Fruz-Towr,   .   84 OLD EATCH IV.3   52
Combin'd (1)
  Manuel: Rank Traytors; thou art with the rest combin'd; . . . 373 M. BRIDE   V.1   45
Combust (1)
  Foresight: will be combust; and then I may do well. . . . . . 270 FOR LOVE III.1 649
Come (371)
                But now, no more like Suppliants, we come; . . . . .   35 OLD BATCH PRO.   5
  Bellmour: nothing. Come come, leave Business to Idlers, and Wisdom .   37 OLD BATCH   I.1   22
  Bellmour: Would thou hadst come a little sooner, Vainlove   . . . .   42 OLD BATCH   I.1 194

Come (continued)

Come (continued)

Speaker	Text	PAGE	TITLE	ACT.SC	LINE
Sir Paul:	Thy, Thy, come away Thy, touch him not, come	145	DOUBL DLR	II.1	245
Sir Paul:	Innocent! why heark'ee, come hither Thy,	146	DOUBL DLR	II.1	275
Sir Paul:	would kill me; they would never come kindly, I should	146	DOUBL DLR	II.1	282
Sir Paul:	I should, indeed, Thy--therefore come away; but	146	DOUBL DLR	II.1	284
Sir Paul:	providence has prevented all, therefore come away, when	146	DOUBL DLR	II.1	285
Lady Ply:	Nay, nay, rise up, come you shall see my good	148	DOUBL DLR	II.1	355
Maskwell:	Come, trouble not your head, I'll joyn you together e're	148	DOUBL DLR	II.1	386
Maskwell:	No sinking, nor no danger,--come, cheer up;	148	DOUBL DLR	II.1	391
Mellefont:	of her violence at last,--if you had not come as you did;	149	DOUBL DLR	II.1	417
Maskwell:	don't know, but she may come this way; I am to meet her	149	DOUBL DLR	II.1	433
Lord Touch:	--Pho, 'tis nonsense. Come, come; I know my Lady	150	DOUBL DLR	III.1	5
Lord Touch:	mutual Peace to come; upon your Duty--	152	DOUBL DLR	III.1	63
Lady Touch:	the Company, and come to you. Pray, good dear my Lord,	153	DOUBL DLR	III.1	118
Lady Touch:	let me beg you do now: I'll come immediately, and tell	153	DOUBL DLR	III.1	119
Maskwell:	help--tho' I stood ready for a Cue to come in and	154	DOUBL DLR	III.1	129
Maskwell:	come to?	155	DOUBL DLR	III.1	197
Maskwell:	I'm glad you're come, for I could not contain my	156	DOUBL DLR	III.1	200
Maskwell:	Ha, ha, how gravely he looks--Come, come, I	157	DOUBL DLR	III.1	243
Maskwell:	you shall have notice at the critical minute to come and	157	DOUBL DLR	III.1	249
Mellefont:	themselves in a Vizor Mask. Here they come, I'll leave you.	158	DOUBL DLR	III.1	314
Sir Paul:	How does my Girl? come hither to thy Father, poor	162	DOUBL DLR	III.1	455
Footman:	Your Ladiships Chair is come.	166	DOUBL DLR	III.1	605
Lady Froth:	--Come, my dear Cynthia, Mr. Brisk, we'll go see	167	DOUBL DLR	III.1	615
Lady Froth:	Wont you? What not to see Saph? Pray, My Lord, come	167	DOUBL DLR	III.1	621
Careless:	'Slife yonder's Sir Paul, but if he were not come, I'm	171	DOUBL DLR	IV.1	128
Sir Paul:	but have a care of making rash Vows; Come hither to me,	173	DOUBL DLR	IV.1	207
Sir Paul:	understand, and you shall understand, come don't be so	174	DOUBL DLR	IV.1	247
Sir Paul:	Merry, I'll come and look at you by and by--Where's	175	DOUBL DLR	IV.1	281
Brisk:	(sings). I'm sick with Love, ha ha ha, prithee come (walking	175	DOUBL DLR	IV.1	306
Lady Froth:	purely, but I vow Mr. Brisk, I can't tell how to come so	177	DOUBL DLR	IV.1	368
Brisk:	Come my Lord, I'll wait on you--(To her) My charming	177	DOUBL DLR	IV.1	384
Lady Ply:	come to Bed.	180	DOUBL DLR	IV.1	V488
Sir Paul:	I can't tell you I'm so overjoy'd; come along with me	181	DOUBL DLR	IV.1	508
Sir Paul:	to my Lady, I can't contain my self; come my dear Friend.	181	DOUBL DLR	IV.1	509
Lady Touch:	Come, come, good my Lord, my Heart	187	DOUBL DLR	IV.2	138
Mellefont:	sudden Whirlwind come, tear up Tree and all, and bear	187	DOUBL DLR	IV.2	146
Lord Touch:	Ccme, I beg your pardon that I over-heard	189	DOUBL DLR	V.1	52
Maskwell:	way into it, so that you need not come thro' this Door	194	DOUBL DLR	V.1	254
Lord Touch:	Here's Company--come this way and tell	196	DOUBL DLR	V.1	329
Maskwell:	Come, why do you dally with me thus?	197	DOUBL DLR	V.1	385
	(Cynthia, and Lord Touchwood, ccme forward.)	199	DOUBL DLR	V.1	466
Sir Paul:	O, here they ccme.	201	DOUBL DLR	V.1	515
Lord Froth:	Come my dear, shall we take leave of my Lord	202	DOUBL DLR	V.1	551
Jeremy:	Younger Brother shou'd come from Sea, he'd never look	218	FOR LCVE	I.1	84
Valentine:	Trapland come in.	222	FOR LCVE	I.1	223
Valentine:	Come sit you down, you know his way.	222	FOR LCVE	I.1	235
Valentine:	your handsome Daughter--Come a good Husband to	222	FOR LCVE	I.1	251
Valentine:	serve his Friend in Distress, tho' I say it to his face. Come,	223	FOR LCVE	I.1	262
Valentine:	Say you so, I'faith: Come, we'll remember the	223	FOR LOVE	I.1	271
Valentine:	Widow: I know where abouts you are: Come, to the	223	FOB LOVE	I.1	272
Valentine:	Bid him come in: Mr. Trapland, send away your	224	FOR LCVE	I.1	304
Jeremy:	No Sir, but Mr. Tattle is come to wait upon you.	225	FOR LCVE	I.1	358
Tattle:	--Come, let's talk of something else.	228	FOR LCVE	I.1	443
Tattle:	not what--Come, let's talk of something else.	228	FOR LCVE	I.1	448
Scandal:	Come then, sacrifice half a Dozen Women of good	230	FCR LCVE	I.1	526
Scandal:	Reputation to me presently--Come, where are you	230	FOR LOVE	I.1	527
Tattle:	O unfortunate! she's come already; will you have Patience	230	FOR LOVE	I.1	542
Mrs Frail:	Daughter is come out of the Country--I assure you,	231	FCR LCVE	I.1	568
Mrs Frail:	Unlucky Day, and wou'd not let me come abroad: But I	231	FOR LOVE	I.1	581
Mrs Frail:	you give me now? Come, I must have something.	231	FOR LOVE	I.1	584
Mrs Frail:	take care of my own. Well; but I'll come and see you one	232	FCR LOVE	I.1	597
Scandal:	No, no; come to me if you wou'd see Pictures.	232	FOR LCVE	I.1	615
Mrs Frail:	Come, let's hear 'em.	233	FOR LCVE	I.1	635
Mrs Frail:	Well, I'll ccme, if it be only to disprove you.	234	FOR LCVE	I.1	659
Mrs Frail:	Well, I'll come, if it be but to disprove you.	234	FOR LCVE	I.1	V659
Valentine:	I'll come to him--will you give me leave, I'll	234	FCR LCVE	I.1	662
Mrs Frail:	No, I'll be gone. Come, who Squires me to the	234	FOR LCVE	I.1	664
Valentine:	to come abroad, and be at Liberty to see her.	234	FCR LCVE	I.1	674
Foresight:	abroad? Is not my Wife come home? Nor my Sister, nor	235	FOR LOVE	II.1	2
Nurse:	Wee'st heart, I know not, they're none of 'em come	235	FOR LOVE	II.1	19
Angelica:	come home--You'll have a Letter for Alimony to	239	FOR LCVE	II.1	134
Angelica:	let no Mankind come near the House, but Converse with	239	FOR LOVE	II.1	136
Foresight:	How? how? is that the reason? Ccme, you know	239	FOR LOVE	II.1	146
Foresight:	--Come, you shall have my Coach and Horses--	239	FOR LOVE	II.1	148
Foresight:	Come, I know Women tell one another--She is	239	FOR LOVE	II.1	150
Foresight:	But come, be a good Girl, don't perplex your poor Uncle,	239	FOR LOVE	II.1	157
Angelica:	out my Aunt, and tell her, she must not come home.	239	FOR LOVE	II.1	162
Sr Sampson:	said of what's past, and all that is to come will happen.	240	FOR LOVE	II.1	198
Sr Sampson:	Did you come a Voluntier into the World? Or did I	244	FOR LCVE	II.1	330
Sr Sampson:	With all my heart: Come, Uncase, Strip, and	244	FOR LOVE	II.1	337
Sr Sampson:	your Friend and Servant--Come Brother Foresight.	246	FOR LOVE	II.1	404
Jeremy:	I told you what your Visit wou'd come to.	246	FOR LOVE	II.1	406
Valentine:	'Tis as much as I expected--I did not come to see	246	FOR LOVE	II.1	407
Valentine:	are earnest,--I'll avoid 'em,--Come this way,	246	FOR LCVE	II.1	411
Mrs Fore:	liking of you. Here they come together; and let us contrive	249	FOR LOVE	II.1	503
Mrs Fore:	liking you. Here they come together; and let us contrive	249	FOR LOVE	II.1	V503
Mrs Fore:	won't let him come near her, after Mr. Tattle.	250	FOR LOVE	II.1	563
Mrs Frail:	Come, Faith let us be gone--If my Brother	250	FOR LOVE	II.1	570
Miss Prue:	Come, must not we go too?	251	FOB LOVE	II.1	585
Miss Prue:	Come, I long to have you begin;--must I make Love	251	FOB LOVE	II.1	596
Miss Prue:	What, is it like the Catechisme?--Come then	251	FOB LOVE	II.1	600
Miss Prue:	be angry;--and you shall push me down before you come	252	FOR LOVE	II.1	652
Tattle:	No, I'll come in first, and push you down afterwards.	253	FOR LOVE	II.1	654
Nurse:	Miss, I hear her--Come to your Father, Child:	253	FOR LOVE	III.1	5

Speaker	Text	Page	Title	Act.Sc	Line
Nurse:	come in the back way.	253	FOR LOVE	III.1	12
Tattle:	and come off as you can.	254	FOR LOVE	III.1	24
Scandal:	No don't; for then you'l tell us no more--Come, I'll	258	FOR LOVE	III.1	190
Sr Sampson:	Is Ben come? Odso, my Son Ben come? Odd,	259	FOR LOVE	III.1	210
Valentine:	Estate, and I'll defer it as long as I can--Well, you'll come	259	FOR LOVE	III.1	227
Angelica:	I can't. Resolution must come to me, or I shall	259	FOR LOVE	III.1	229
Scandal:	Come, Valentine, I'll go with you; I've something in	259	FOR LOVE	III.1	231
Ben:	But I'll tell you one thing, and you come to Sea in a	262	FOR LOVE	III.1	330
Sr Sampson:	you Ben; this is your Mistress,--Come Miss, you must	262	FOR LOVE	III.1	350
Sr Sampson:	No, no. Come, let's away.	263	FOR LOVE	III.1	354
Sr Sampson:	I warrant thee Boy, Come, come, we'll be gone;	263	FOR LOVE	III.1	357
Ben:	Come Mistress, will you please to sit down, for an you	263	FOR LOVE	III.1	360
Ben:	Come, I'll haule a Chair; there, an you please to sit, I'll	263	FOR LOVE	III.1	362
Ben:	me alone as soon as I come home, with such a dirty dowdy	264	FOR LOVE	III.1	423
Mrs Fore:	Come, Miss, come along with me, and tell	265	FOR LOVE	III.1	444
Mrs Frail:	out.--Come, Sir, will you venture your self with me?	265	FOR LOVE	III.1	450
Sr Sampson:	Sunday:--Come, Cheer up, look about thee: Look	265	FOR LOVE	III.1	465
Scandal:	what it may come to--But it has had a Consequence	266	FOR LOVE	III.1	493
Scandal:	Come, come, Mr. Foresight, let not the Prospect of	268	FOR LOVE	III.1	554
Scandal:	Passion. But come a little farther this way, and I'll tell you	269	FOR LOVE	III.1	596
Scandal:	Come, I know what you wou'd say,--you think	272	FOR LOVE	III.1	694
Ben:	Come, I'll sing you a Song of a Sailor.	273	FOR LOVE	III.1	740
Ben:	come, my Lads, let's have a round, and I'll make one.	275	FOR LOVE	III.1	797
Ben:	clean Shirt once a Quarter--Come home and lie with	275	FOR LOVE	III.1	801
Angelica:	my want of Inclination to stay longer here--Come, Jenny,	278	FOR LOVE	IV.1	90
Valentine:	strange! But I am Truth, and come to give the World	280	FOR LOVE	IV.1	164
Sr Sampson:	Ay boy--Come, thou shalt sit down by me.	281	FOR LOVE	IV.1	198
Sr Sampson:	No, no, come, come, sit you down, honest	281	FOR LOVE	IV.1	200
Sr Sampson:	No, no, come, come, sit thee down, honest	281	FOR LOVE	IV.1	V200
Valentine:	the Lawyer with an itching Palm; and he's come to be	282	FOR LOVE	IV.1	238
Mrs Fore:	impertinent and impudent,--and would have come to	284	FOR LOVE	IV.1	328
Mrs Frail:	Lover, and give him his discharge, and come to you.	285	FOR LOVE	IV.1	352
Ben:	the Sea are come ashore, for my part.	285	FOR LOVE	IV.1	357
Mrs Frail:	whistled to by Winds; and thou art come forth with Finns	286	FOR LOVE	IV.1	400
Ben:	Young Woman--and may-hap may come to an	287	FOR LOVE	IV.1	440
Ben:	won't come too.	287	FOR LOVE	IV.1	443
Mrs Frail:	O Sister, had you come a minute sooner, you would	287	FOR LOVE	IV.1	449
Mrs Fore:	come, stand aside a little, and tell me how you like the	288	FOR LOVE	IV.1	476
Valentine:	come;--Dost thou know what will happen to morrow?	288	FOR LOVE	IV.1	490
Valentine:	come there.	288	FOR LOVE	IV.1	498
Valentine:	come forth with lab'ring Callous Hands, a Chine of Steel,	289	FOR LOVE	IV.1	523
Valentine:	The sooner the better--Jeremy, come hither--	290	FOR LOVE	IV.1	556
Foresight:	Neice, he knows things past and to come, and all the	291	FOR LOVE	IV.1	604
Valentine:	fancy I begin to come to my self.	294	FOR LOVE	IV.1	698
Angelica:	not have the Impudence to persevere--Come, Jeremy,	295	FOR LOVE	IV.1	734
Angelica:	a Masquerade is done, when we come to shew Faces;	296	FOR LOVE	IV.1	790
Angelica:	Well, have you been there?--Come hither.	296	FOR LOVE	IV.1	781
Angelica:	Leave me, and d'ye hear, if Valentine shou'd come,	297	FOR LOVE	V.1	9
Sr Sampson:	a Lady any way--Come, come, let me tell you, you	298	FOR LOVE	V.1	24
Sr Sampson:	--Come, don't despise Fifty; odd Fifty, in a hale	298	FOR LOVE	V.1	26
Sr Sampson:	With all my Heart;--Come in with me, and	301	FOR LOVE	V.1	137
Angelica:	you come to it.	301	FOR LOVE	V.1	151
Sr Sampson:	Say you so, Hussy?--Come lets go then;	301	FOR LOVE	V.1	160
Sr Sampson:	Odd, I long to be pulling down too, come away--	301	FOR LOVE	V.1	161
Sr Sampson:	Odd, I long to be pulling too, come away--	301	FOR LOVE	V.1	V161
Tattle:	Ay, but your Father will tell you that Dreams come	303	FOR LOVE	V.1	240
Tattle:	I'll come and explain it to you.	305	FOR LOVE	V.1	298
Foresight:	Rogue! Oh, Nurse, come hither.	305	FOR LOVE	V.1	322
Mrs Fore:	be come Home.	306	FOR LOVE	V.1	340
Ben:	Who, Father? ay, he's come home with a Vengeance.	306	FOR LOVE	V.1	341
Ben:	they'd ne're make a Match together--Here they come.	307	FOR LOVE	V.1	374
Sr Sampson:	way to come to it, but by the North-East Passage.	308	FOR LOVE	V.1	428
Valentine:	Sir, I'm come to acknowledge my Errors, and ask	310	FOR LOVE	V.1	500
Sr Sampson:	ready?--Come, Sir, will you sign and seal?	311	FOR LOVE	V.1	514
Sr Sampson:	Come, Chuck, satisfie him, answer him;--	311	FOR LOVE	V.1	527
Sr Sampson:	Come, come, Mr. Buckram, the Pen and Ink.	311	FOR LOVE	V.1	528
Sr Sampson:	now, Sir? Will you sign, Sir? Come, will you sign and	311	FOR LOVE	V.1	538
Almeria:	Come, heavy-laden with the oppressing Weight	330	M. BRIDE	I.1	155
Osmyn-Alph:	To thee with twining? Come, come to my Heart.	343	M. BRIDE	II.2	124
Almeria:	And thou hast heard my Prayer; for thou art come	343	M. BRIDE	II.2	132
Osmyn-Alph:	Should come and see the straining of my Eyes	345	M. BRIDE	II.2	203
Zara:	I come to mourn with thee; to share my Griefs,	346	M. BRIDE	II.2	268
Heli:	Presuming on a Bridegroom's Right--) she'll come.	351	M. BRIDE	III.1	50
Osmyn-Alph:	She'll come; 'tis what I wish, yet what I fear.	351	M. BRIDE	III.1	51
Osmyn-Alph:	She'll come, but whither, and to whom? O Heav'n!	351	M. BRIDE	III.1	52
Osmyn-Alph:	Time may have still one fated Hour to come,	354	M. BRIDE	III.1	198
Osmyn-Alph:	You do not come to mock my Miseries?	360	M. BRIDE	III.1	420
Osmyn-Alph:	Come, 'tis much.	360	M. BRIDE	III.1	431
Osmyn-Alph:	Come, 'tis too much.	360	M. BRIDE	III.1	V431
Manuel:	To talk with you. Come near, why dost thou shake?	367	M. BRIDE	IV.1	247
Gonsalez:	Things come to this Extremety? his Daughter	371	M. BRIDE	IV.1	404
Almeria:	Shew me, for I am come in search of Death;	381	M. BRIDE	V.2	220
Almeria:	And come prepar'd to yield my Throat--they shake	382	M. BRIDE	V.2	250
Fainall:	another's Apartments, where they come together like the	396	WAY WORLD	I.1	52
Mirabell:	One a Clock! (looking on his Watch) O y'are come--	398	WAY WORLD	I.1	109
Witwoud:	Come, come, you are malicious now, and wou'd	403	WAY WORLD	I.1	287
Witwoud:	Come come, don't detract from the Merits of my	403	WAY WORLD	I.1	294
Petulant:	Well, well; I come--Shud, a Man had as good	405	WAY WORLD	I.1	383
Petulant:	Places. Pox on 'em I won't come.--Dee hear, tell 'em	405	WAY WORLD	I.1	386
Petulant:	I won't come.--Let 'em snivel and cry their Hearts	405	WAY WORLD	I.1	387
Witwoud:	wou'd come off--Ha, ha, ha; Gad I can't be angry	406	WAY WORLD	I.1	410
Mirabell:	How! hearkee Petulant, come hither--Explain,	406	WAY WORLD	I.1	432
Petulant:	Uncle, have you not, lately come to Town, and lodges by	407	WAY WORLD	I.1	435

116

Come   (continued)
Mirabell:	Come, thou art an honest Fellow, Petulant, and shalt	. .	407	WAY WORLD	I.1	443
Mirabell:	O Raillery, Raillery. Come, I know thou art in	. . .	407	WAY WORLD	I.1	448
Mirabell:	thee, then Mercury is by the Sun: Come, I'm sure thou	. .	407	WAY WORLD	I.1	456
Witwoud:	something of an Uncle to Mirabell, who is lately come to	.	408	WAY WORLD	I.1	481
Witwoud:	being in Embrio; and if it shou'd come to Life; poor	. .	408	WAY WORLD	I.1	488
Marwood:	Come, be as sincere, acknowledge that your Sentiments	. .	410	WAY WORLD	II.1	31
Marwood:	I have done hating 'em; and am now come to	. . . .	411	WAY WORLD	II.1	45
Fainall:	Come, you both love him; and both have equally	. . .	413	WAY WORLD	II.1	137
Fainall:	Come, I'm sorry.	. . . .	416	WAY WORLD	II.1	224
Fainall:	Nay, this is Extravagance--Come I ask your	. . . . .	416	WAY WORLD	II.1	239
Fainall:	--'Sdeath they come, hide your Face, your Tears--	. .	416	WAY WORLD	II.1	247
Mrs Fain:	Female Frailty! We must all come to it, if we	. . . .	418	WAY WORLD	II.1	314
Millamant:	Come, don't look grave then. Well, what do you	. . .	422	WAY WORLD	II.1	462
Mirabell:	the force of Instinct--O here come my pair of Turtles	. .	423	WAY WORLD	II.1	501
Foible:	dress till I come--(Looking out.) O Dear, I'm sure	. .	424	WAY WORLD	II.1	544
Mirabell:	Come Sir, will you endeavour to forget your self	. .	424	WAY WORLD	II.1	552
Peg:	come at the Paint, Madam; Mrs. Foible has lock'd it up,	.	425	WAY WORLD	III.1	18
Lady Wish:	--Wench, come, come, Wench, what art thou doing,	. . .	425	WAY WORLD	III.1	23
Lady Wish:	of Nutmeg? I warrant thee. Come, fill, fill.--So--again	.	425	WAY WORLD	III.1	32
Lady Wish:	O Marwood, let her come in. Come in good	. . . .	426	WAY WORLD	III.1	40
Foible:	come down pretty deep now, she's super-annuated (says	.	427	WAY WORLD	III.1	100
Lady Wish:	come? Or will a not fail when he does come? Will he be	.	429	WAY WORLD	III.1	156
Lady Wish:	come? Or will he not fail when he does come? Will he be		429	WAY WORLD	III.1 V	156
Mrs Fain:	come too late. That Devil Marwood saw you in the Park	.	430	WAY WORLD	III.1	185
Foible:	is so impatient, I fear she'll come for me, if I stay.	.	430	WAY WORLD	III.1	220
Lady Wish:	Come, come Foible--I had forgot my Nephew will be	. .	432	WAY WORLD	III.1	274
Foible:	Mr. Witwoud and Mr. Petulant, are come to Dine with	. .	432	WAY WORLD	III.1	276
Millamant:	Mincing, tell the Men they may come up. My Aunt is not		433	WAY WORLD	III.1	325
Servant-W:	Really Sir, I can't tell; here come so many here, 'tis	.	437	WAY WORLD	III.1	470
Petulant:	It seems as if you had come a Journey, Sir;	. . . .	438	WAY WORLD	III.1	489
Witwoud:	to consent to that, Man, to come to London. He had the	.	440	WAY WORLD	III.1	559
Mincing:	Mem, I come to acquaint your Laship that Dinner	. . .	441	WAY WORLD	III.1	614
Mincing:	Mem, I am come to acquaint your Laship that Dinner	. .	441	WAY WORLD	III.1 V	614
Marwood:	will come to any Composition to save her reputation, take		442	WAY WORLD	III.1	661
Marwood:	to act Sir Rowland is with her. It shall come as from an		443	WAY WORLD	III.1	701
Marwood:	she knows some passages--Nay I expect all will come out	.	444	WAY WORLD	III.1	705
Fainall:	If the worst come to the worst,--I'll turn my	. . .	444	WAY WORLD	III.1	708
Lady Wish:	they are together, then come to me Foible, that I may not		445	WAY WORLD	IV.1	39
Millamant:	come another time.	. . . .	446	WAY WORLD	IV.1	50
Millamant:	him--Shall I? Ay, let the Wretch come.	. . . . .	446	WAY WORLD	IV.1	62
Mrs Fain:	O Sir Wilful! you are come at the Critical Instant. There's	446	WAY WORLD	IV.1	70
Sir Wilful:	see, to come and know if that how you were dispos'd to	.	447	WAY WORLD	IV.1	115
Millamant:	may be your Relations. Come to Dinner when I please,	.	450	WAY WORLD	IV.1	219
Millamant:	before you come in. These Articles subscrib'd, If I continue	450	WAY WORLD	IV.1	225
Millamant:	Come, Cozen.	. . . .	456	WAY WORLD	IV.1	434
Witwoud:	Come Knight--Pox on him. I don't know what to	. . .	457	WAY WORLD	IV.1	470
Witwoud:	come will you March my Salopian?	. . . . . .	457	WAY WORLD	IV.1	475
Lady Wish:	Bring what you will; but come alive, pray	. . . . .	461	WAY WORLD	IV.1	640
Lady Wish:	come alive. O this is a happy discovery.	. . . . .	461	WAY WORLD	IV.1	641
Waitwell:	Dead or Alive I'll come--and married we will be	. . .	461	WAY WORLD	IV.1	642
Waitwell:	Nephew. Come my Buxom Widdow.	. . . . . .	461	WAY WORLD	IV.1	645
Foible:	come to no damage--Or else the Wealth of the Indies	. .	463	WAY WORLD	V.1	31
Mincing:	six thousand Pound. O, come Mrs. Foible, I hear my old	.	465	WAY WORLD	V.1	116
Fainall:	I come to make demands,--I'll hear no	. . . . .	469	WAY WORLD	V.1	288
Lady Wish:	come two more of my Egyptian Plagues too.	. . . .	470	WAY WORLD	V.1	309
Sir Wilful:	no more words. For what's to come to pleasure you I'm	.	470	WAY WORLD	V.1	320
Millamant:	on Mirabell to come in Person, and be a Witness that I give	470	WAY WORLD	V.1	328
Sir Wilful:	let him come in; why we are sworn Brothers and fellow	.	471	WAY WORLD	V.1	346
Sir Wilful:	once, he shall come in; and see who'll hinder him.	. .	471	WAY WORLD	V.1	352
Mirabell:	me not, by turning from me in disdain,--I come not to	. .	471	WAY WORLD	V.1	372
Sir Wilful:	you nothing, Aunt--Come, come, Forgive and Forget	. .	471	WAY WORLD	V.1	381
Lady Wish:	I'll consent to any thing to come, to be deliver'd from this	473	WAY WORLD	V.1	455
Fainall:	If it must all come out, why let 'em know it, 'tis but	.	474	WAY WORLD	V.1	475
	They scarcely come inclining to be Pleas'd:	. . . .	479	WAY WORLD	EPI.	6

Comedies (1)
| Mellefont: | But does your Lordship never see Comedies? | . . . . | 133 | DOUBL DLR | I.1 | 222 |

Comedy (1)
| Valentine: | Hypocrisie apart,--The Comedy draws toward an | . . . | 294 | FOR LOVE | IV.1 | 707 |

Comers (1)
| Setter: | opened for all Comers. In Fine thou art the high Road to | . | 66 | OLD BATCH | III.1 | 196 |

Comes (56)
Sharper:	I'm sorry to see this, Ned: Once a Man comes to his	. .	41	OLD BATCH	I.1	147
Sharper:	And here comes one who Swears as heartily he hates	. .	41	OLD BATCH	I.1	176
Heartwell:	that comes; like a Tumbler with the same tricks over and	.	42	OLD BATCH	I.1	191
Heartwell:	purpose, ever embarking in Adventures, yet never comes	.	42	OLD BATCH	I.1	199
Bellmour:	Oh here he comes, stand close let 'em pass.	. . .	46	OLD BATCH	I.1 V	339
Sir Joseph:	Oh here a' comes--Ah my Hector of Troy, welcome	. .	51	OLD BATCH	II.1	139
Araminta:	which comes pretty near my own Opinion of Love and	. .	58	OLD BATCH	II.2	154
Barnaby:	as ever he comes home--I could have brought young	. .	76	OLD BATCH	IV.1	22
Bellmour:	Hypocrites.--Oh! she comes.	. . . . . .	80	OLD BATCH	IV.2	8
Belinda:	Oh Gad, here comes the Fool that din'd at my Lady	. .	84	OLD BATCH	IV.3	55
Setter:	Talk of the Devil--See where he comes.	. . . . .	100	OLD BATCH	V.1	131
Cynthia:	formality; for which I like him: Here he comes.	. . .	139	DOUBL DLR	II.1	54
Maskwell:	Thirst. Ha! yonder comes Mellefont thoughtful. Let me	.	155	DOUBL DLR	III.1	186
Maskwell:	Here he comes, now for me--	. . . . .	155	DOUBL DLR	III.1	194
Sir Paul:	Tears when it comes in my mind.	. . . . . .	161	DOUBL DLR	III.1	417
Lord Froth:	so ready--she always comes in three bars too soon--and	.	163	DOUBL DLR	III.1	476
Brisk:	the Day. Here she comes, I'll seem not to see her, and try		175	DOUBL DLR	IV.1	303
Lady Ply:	O yonder he comes reading of it, for Heavens	. . . .	178	DOUBL DLR	IV.1	402
Maskwell:	you had best steal into her Chamber before she comes, and		181	DOUBL DLR	IV.1	516
Maskwell:	comes the Man that I must Manage.	. . . . . .	181	DOUBL DLR	IV.1	530
Mellefont:	she comes--Little does she think what a Mine is just ready		183	DOUBL DLR	IV.2	4
Maskwell:	comes opportunely--now will I, in my old way,	. . .	190	DOUBL DLR	V.1	97
Maskwell:	Chamber. When Cynthia comes, let there be no Light, and	.	195	DOUBL DLR	V.1	293
Cynthia:	Here he comes.	. . . .	196	DOUBL DLR	V.1	339

Comes (continued)

Character	Text	PAGE	TITLE	ACT.SC	LINE
Jeremy:	Sir, your Father's Steward says he comes to make	224	FOR LOVE	I.1	302
Valentine:	Shew her up, when she comes.	229	FOR LOVE	I.1	506
Jeremy:	comes to pay his Duty to you.	242	FOR LOVE	II.1	269
Angelica:	But whence comes the Reputation of Mr. Tattle's	256	FOR LOVE	III.1	121
Ben:	But an he comes near me, may-hap I may giv'n a Salt Eel	264	FOR LOVE	III.1	421
Scandal:	Well, I'll try her--'tis she, here she comes.	276	FOR LOVE	IV.1	18
Scandal:	comes Tyrannically to insult a ruin'd Lover, and make	276	FOR LOVE	IV.1	24
Valentine:	Prophecy comes, Truth must give place.	283	FOR LOVE	IV.1	275
Mrs Frail:	O' my Conscience, here he comes.	285	FOR LOVE	IV.1	353
Valentine:	Where is she? Oh I see her--she comes, like Riches,	290	FOR LOVE	IV.1	541
Angelica:	Mr. Scandal, I only stay till my Maid comes, and	293	FOR LOVE	IV.1	685
Almeria:	For with him Garcia comes--Garcia, to whom	330	M. BRIDE	I.1	171
Alonzo:	The Lord Gonsalez comes to tell your Highness	331	M. BRIDE	I.1	209
Manuel:	Whence comes it, valiant Osmyn, that a Man	336	M. BRIDE	I.1	430
Heli:	When Zara comes, abate of your Aversion.	352	M. BRIDE	III.1	106
Osmyn-Alph:	Will make all fatal. But behold, she comes	355	M. BRIDE	III.1	232
Gonsalez:	That were too hard a Thought--but see she comes.	367	M. BRIDE	IV.1	236
Manuel:	'Tis well--that when she comes to set him free,	374	M. BRIDE	V.1	77
Manuel:	But see she comes; I'll shun th' Encounter; do	374	M. BRIDE	V.1	87
Manuel:	But see she comes; I'll shun th' Encounter; thou	374	M. BRIDE	V.1	V 87
Fainall:	He comes to Town in order to Equip himself for	400	WAY WORLD	I.1	197
Witwoud:	No, no, he comes to his Aunts, my Lady Wishfort;	409	WAY WORLD	I.1	514
Marwood:	Ha, ha, ha; he comes opportunely for you.	412	WAY WORLD	II.1	85
Fainall:	Nothing remains when that Day comes, but to sit down	413	WAY WORLD	II.1	115
Mirabell:	Here she comes i'faith full sail, with her Fan spread	418	WAY WORLD	II.1	323
Lady Wish:	Thou must repair me Foible, before Sir Rowland comes; or	429	WAY WORLD	III.1	149
Marwood:	now I'll have none of him. Here comes the good Lady,	431	WAY WORLD	III.1	246
Lady Wish:	young. It will be time enough when he comes back, and	432	WAY WORLD	III.1	264
Sir Wilful:	time; and rail when that day comes.	441	WAY WORLD	III.1	612
Lady Wish:	Rowland comes by?	444	WAY WORLD	IV.1	9
Mirabell:	Contract? and here comes one to be a witness to the	452	WAY WORLD	IV.1	281
Marwood:	have Overseen. Here comes Mr. Fainall. If he will be satisfi'd	468	WAY WORLD	V.1	243

Comfort (29)

Character	Text	PAGE	TITLE	ACT.SC	LINE
	But for your Comfort, it falls out to day,	35	OLD BATCH	PRO.	10
Heartwell:	Tune of the Superanuated Maidens Comfort, or the	63	OLD BATCH	III.1	81
Fondlewife:	say you with his Wife? With Comfort her self.	76	OLD BATCH	IV.1	20
Barnaby:	I did; and Comfort will send Tribulation hither as soon	76	OLD BATCH	IV.1	21
Fondlewife:	hath already defiled the Tabernacle of our Sister Comfort;	76	OLD BATCH	IV.1	29
Laetitia:	(aside). How my heart akes! All my comfort lies in	94	OLD BATCH	IV.4	202
	Why that's some Comfort, to an Author's fears;	113	OLD BATCH	EPI.	15
	The Poet's sure he shall some comfort find:	125	DOUBL DLR	PRO.	32
Mellefont:	There's comfort in a hand stretch'd out, to one	148	DOUBL DLR	II.1	389
Lord Touch:	And be each others comfort;--let me	203	DOUBL DLR	V.1	586
Mrs Frail:	--Lord, where's the comfort of this Life, if we can't have	246	FOR LOVE	II.1	424
Foresight:	a Watch-light, and lay the Crums of Comfort by me.--	270	FOR LOVE	III.1	641
Foresight:	great Comfort to me. Hem, hem! good Night.	271	FOR LOVE	III.1	654
Almeria:	But 'tis the Wretches Comfort still to have	328	M. BRIDE	I.1	82
Almeria:	Comfort me, help me, hold me, hide me, hide me,	341	M. BRIDE	II.2	43
Osmyn-Alph:	The Cause and Comfort of my boding Heart.	355	M. BRIDE	III.1	235
Osmyn-Alph:	Thee mine, were Comfort, Joy, extremest Exstacy.	357	M. BRIDE	III.1	331
Gonsalez:	Have Comfort.	370	M. BRIDE	IV.1	370
Almeria:	Curst be that Tongue, that bids me be of Comfort;	370	M. BRIDE	IV.1	370
Osmyn-Alph:	O my Heart's Comfort; 'tis not given to this	383	M. BRIDE	V.2	300
Marwood:	No, it is not yet too late--I have that Comfort.	416	WAY WORLD	II.1	235
Waitwell:	that Satisfaction.--That wou'd be some Comfort to	458	WAY WORLD	IV.1	503
Lady Wish:	Comfort; bring the Black-box.	461	WAY WORLD	IV.1	637
Mrs Fain:	that's my Comfort.	464	WAY WORLD	V.1	83
Foible:	Indeed Madam, and so 'tis a Comfort if you knew all,	464	WAY WORLD	V.1	84
Lady Wish:	shall be mad, Dear Friend is there no Comfort for me?	470	WAY WORLD	V.1	307
Lady Wish:	How's this dear Neice? Have I any comfort?	470	WAY WORLD	V.1	323
Mirabell:	hopes of future Comfort.	472	WAY WORLD	V.1	391
Lady Wish:	Ah Mr. Mirabell, this is small comfort, the	475	WAY WORLD	V.1	504

Comfortably (1)

Character	Text	PAGE	TITLE	ACT.SC	LINE
Sir Paul:	see--if it becomes me to say so; and we live very comfortably	160	DOUBL DLR	III.1	388

Comical (2)

Character	Text	PAGE	TITLE	ACT.SC	LINE
Belinda:	Oh; a most Comical Sight: A Country-Squire, with	84	OLD BATCH	IV.3	23
Maskwell:	No, but it's a Comical design upon mine.	156	DOUBL DLR	III.1	212

Coming (47)

Character	Text	PAGE	TITLE	ACT.SC	LINE
Heartwell:	incumbrances is like coming to an Estate overcharg'd with	44	OLD BATCH	I.1	278
Heartwell:	No, besides my Business, I see a Fool coming this	46	OLD BATCH	I.1	335
Setter:	the Corner, and's coming this way.	75	OLD BATCH	IV.1	10
Servant:	My Mistress is coming, Sir.	80	OLD BATCH	IV.2	V 2
Bellmour:	Freedom of his Bed: He not coming home all Night, a	82	OLD BATCH	IV.2	51
Araminta:	No matter,--I see Vainlove coming this way,--	85	OLD BATCH	IV.3	77
Fondlewife:	I'll shut this door, to secure him from coming	91	OLD BATCH	IV.4	72
Bellmour:	But, you were a little unlucky in coming so soon, and	94	OLD BATCH	IV.4	188
Laetitia:	Indeed, my Dear, I was but just coming down stairs,	95	OLD BATCH	IV.4	243
Setter:	mine. Here's Company coming, if you'll walk this way,	106	OLD BATCH	V.1	352
Careless:	And thou art always spoiling Company by coming	128	DOUBL DLR	I.1	23
Lord Froth:	here is Company coming.	135	DOUBL DLR	I.1	V296
Sir Paul:	find Passion coming upon me by inspiration, and I cannot	144	DOUBL DLR	II.1	207
Sir Paul:	find Passion coming upon me by inflation, and I cannot	144	DOUBL DLR	II.1	V207
Lady Ply:	necessity--O Lord, here's some body coming, I dare	148	DOUBL DLR	II.1	362
Lady Ply:	despair neither,--O, they're coming, I must fly.	148	DOUBL DLR	II.1	372
Lady Touch:	Well but go now, here's some body coming.	153	DOUBL DLR	III.1	122
Careless:	coming, and I shall never succeed while thou art in sight--	157	DOUBL DLR	III.1	265
Cynthia:	are so near that we don't think of coming together.	168	DOUBL DLR	IV.1	18
Lady Touch:	yonders my Lord, I believe he's coming to find you, I'le	188	DOUBL DLR	V.1	7
Mrs Frail:	Hey day! I shall get a fine Reputation by coming	230	FOR LOVE	I.1	546
Mrs Frail:	I shall get a fine Reputation by coming	230	FOR LOVE	I.1	V546
Foresight:	pretty good that too; but then I stumbl'd coming	236	FOR LOVE	II.1	33
Angelica:	May, I'll declare how you prophecy'd Popery was coming,	237	FOR LOVE	II.1	88
Servant:	Sir Sampson is coming down to wait upon you--	239	FOR LOVE	II.1	160

118

Coming   (continued)
    Miss Prue: O Lord, she's coming--and she'll tell my . . . . . 253 FOR LOVE   III.1   15
    Tattle: shou'd have wish'd for her coming. . . . . 253 FOR LOVE   III.1   18
    Tattle: (coming up). Scandal, are you in private Discourse, any . 254 FOR LOVE   III.1   42
    Mrs Frail: Foresight, and Sir Sampson coming. Sister, do you take Miss 265 FOR LOVE III.1 447
    Sr Sampson: Rogue's sharp set, coming from Sea, if he should not stay 265 FOR LOVE III.1 459
    Mrs Fore: Hold, here's my Sister coming toward us. . . . . . . 273 FOR LOVE   III.1 747
    Mrs Frail: (to Jeremy). O Lord, her coming will spoil all. . . . 291 FOR LOVE   IV.1   590
    Valentine: I must be plain. (Coming up to them.) I am Truth, and hate 292 FOR LOVE IV.1 619
    Tattle: Pox cn't, there's no coming off, now she has said . . 293 FOR LOVE   IV.1   679
    Sr Sampson: Odso, here's some body coming. . . . . 301 FOR LOVE   V.1   162
    Jeremy: Well, Sir, I'll go and tell her my Master's coming; . 303 FOR LOVE   V.1   215
                 Take your Revenge upon the coming Scenes: . . . . . 323 M. BRIDE   PRO.   30
    Garcia: And I cou'd pity 'em. I hear some coming, ... 339 M. BRIDE   II.1   48
    Osmyn-Alph: (Coming forward.) . . . 341 M. BRIDE   II.2   48
    Manuel: Your coming has prevented me Almeria; . . . . 367 M. BRIDE   IV.1   243
    Gonsalez: What Noise! some body coming? 'st, Alonzo? . . . . 376 M. BRIDE   V.2   10
    Zara: And wait his coming to approve the Deed. . . . . . 380 M. BRIDE   V.2   153
    Almeria: (Coming nearer the Body, starts and lets fall the Cup.) 382 M. BRIDE   V.2   271
    Mirabell: he waits for himself now, he is so long a coming; O I ask 405 WAY WORLD I.1 379
    Lady Wish: Is Sir Rowland coming say't thou, Foible? . . . . . 444 WAY WORLD   IV.1   1
    Foible: Sir Wilfull is coming, Madam. Shall I send Mr. Mirabell 446 WAY WORLD IV.1   58
    Mrs Fain: is coming; and in my Conscience if she should see you, . 452 WAY WORLD IV.1 300
Comitatu (1)
    Sir Joseph: The same Sir, of Wittoll-hall in Comitatu Bucks. . . . 49 OLD BATCH   II.1   71
Command (17)
    Brisk: shall Command me from the Zenith to the Nadir.-- . . . 128 DOUBL DLR I.1   50
    Sir Paul: Lady Plyant shall Command Sir Paul; but when I am . . 144 DOUBL DLR II.1 222
    Lord Touch: command this time; for 'tis the last, in which I will assume 189 DOUBL DLR V.1 65
    Lord Touch: should Command: my very Slaves will shortly give me . 195 DOUBL DLR   V.1 303
    Manuel: You stand excused that I command it. . . . . 334 M. BRIDE   I.1 326
    Manuel: It shall be your Excuse that I command it. . . . . 334 M. BRIDE   I.1 V326
    Garcia: At least, to talk where he must not command. . . . 335 M. BRIDE   I.1 374
    Manuel: Those Bonds! 'twas my Command you should be free: . 336 M. BRIDE   I.1 403
    Manuel: Born to excel, and to command! . . . . 336 M. BRIDE   I.1 420
    Zara: Dare you dispute the King's Command? Behold . . . 359 M. BRIDE   III.1 377
    Manuel: For doubling all our Guards; Command that our . . 364 M. BRIDE   IV.1 V132
    Manuel: Rise, I command thee rise--and if thou would'st . 368 M. BRIDE   IV.1 285
    Alonzo: All that it can, your Lordship shall command. . . . 372 M. BRIDE   IV.1 431
    Perez: It was your Majesty's Command, I should . . . . . 374 M. BRIDE   V.1   57
    Manuel: One moment's Ease? Hear my Command; and look . . . 374 M. BRIDE   V.1   72
    Zara: Think fit, I'll leave thee my Command to die. . . 375 M. BRIDE   V.1 127
    Millamant: think he wou'd obey me; I wou'd command him to shew . 433 WAY WORLD III.1 339
Commanded (2)
    Ben: d'ee see that was none of my seeking, I was commanded . 263 FOR LOVE III.1 373
    Manuel: Is Osmyn so dispos'd, as I commanded? . . . . . . 372 M. BRIDE   V.1   6
Commanding (1)
    Osmyn-Alph: Of God-like Mould, intrepid and commanding, ... 355 M. BRIDE   III.1 223
Commands (8)
    Cynthia: I'm all Obedience, Sir, to your Commands. . . . . . 174 DOUBL DLR   IV.1 257
    Maskwell: Commands. . . . . 181 DOUBL DLR   IV.1 534
    Saygrace: You have no more Commands? . . . . 195 DOUBL DLR   V.1   296
    Sr Sampson: I have not been honour'd with the Commands of . . 298 FOR LOVE   V.1   13
    Sr Sampson: not wash away. Well, Madam, what are your Commands? . 298 FOR LOVE   V.1   41
    Jeremy: Appetite to be fed with your Commands a great while; . 301 FOR LOVE V.1   172
    Foible: not doubt of Success. If you have no more Commands Sir, . 424 WAY WORLD II.1 542
    Millamant: Plot, as you were misinform'd; I have laid my commands . 470 WAY WORLD V.1   327
Commenc'd (1)
    Zara: Commenc'd? not knowing who you were, nor why . . . . 347 M. BRIDE II.2 299
Commence (1)
    Lady Wish: At a time when you shou'd commence an . . . . . . 455 WAY WORLD   IV.1 392
Commend (2)
    Millamant: If they did not commend us, we were not handsome! . . 420 WAY WORLD II.1 400
    Millamant: Now you must know they could not commend one, if . . 420 WAY WORLD II.1 401
Commendation (5)
    Belinda: Commendation of that filthy, awkward, two-leg'd Creature, 54 OLD BATCH II.2   5
    Jeremy: musty Books, in commendation of Starving and Poverty? . 217 FOR LOVE I.1   33
    Mirabell: with her, and was guilty of a Song in her Commendation: . 397 WAY WORLD I.1   70
    Fainall: Commendation wou'd go near to make me either Vain . . 402 WAY WORLD I.1 262
    Mirabell: mortifies, yet after Commendation can be flatter'd by it, . 420 WAY WORLD II.1 396
Commendatory (1)
    Witwoud: Funeral Sermon, or a Copy of Commendatory Verses . . 401 WAY WORLD I.1 246
Commended (1)
    Sharper: I know, she commended him all the while we were . . . 102 OLD BATCH V.1 200
Commends (1)
                 And therefore to the Fair commends his Cause. . . . 385 M. BRIDE   EPI.   28
Commerce (1)
    Mirabell: marrow of a roasted Cat. In short, I forbid all Commerce . 451 WAY WORLD IV.1 251
Commiseration (1)
                 Damn him the more; have no Commiseration . . . . . 393 WAY WORLD   PRO.   24
Commission (3)
                 But hold--I am exceeding my Commission; . . . . . . 113 OLD BATCH   EPI.   17
    Sir Paul: Gallery. If Sir Paul should surprize us, I have a Commission 178 DOUBL DLR IV.1 409
    Sir Paul: Commission--If I desired him to do any more than . . 180 DOUBL DLR   IV.1 471
Commission'd (1)
    Scandal: into their Titles and Estates; and seems Commission'd . 219 FOR LOVE I.1   134
Commit (10)
    Bellmour: commit my self to lasting Durance. . . . . 112 OLD BATCH   V.2   167
                 So, does our Author, this his Child commit . . . . 125 DOUBL DLR   PRO.   9
    Maskwell: thy Beauty gild my Crimes; and whatsoever I commit of . 150 DOUBL DLR II.1 441
    Lady Touch: or commit some himself. . . . . 186 DOUBL DLR   IV.2 129
    Scandal: into Obscurity and Futurity; and if you commit an Error, . 267 FOR LOVE III.1 515
    Sr Sampson: of any thing;--And if they commit Matrimony, ... 299 FOR LOVE   V.1   56
    Sr Sampson: 'tis as they commit Murder; out of a Frolick: And are . 299 FOR LOVE V.1   57
    Manuel: To seem is to commit, at this Conjuncture. . . . . 334 M. BRIDE   I.1 321
    Zara: This Slave commit no Violence upon . . . . 360 M. BRIDE   III.1 448

120

Constant   (continued)
  Almeria: Than Trees, or Flint? O Force of constant Woe!   326   M. EBIDE   I.1   7
  Witwoud: than a Woman constant; one argues a decay of Parts, as   . 403   WAY WCRLD   I.1   320
Constellation (1)
  Sr Sampson: Thy Wife is a Constellation of Vertues; she's the   . . . 242   FOR LCVE   II.1   256
Constitute (1)
  Lord Touch: our ancient Family; him I thus blow away, and constitute   . 189   DOUEL DLR   V.1   58
Constitution (3)
  Maskwell: You are merry, Sir, but I shall probe your Ccnstitution.   . 156   DOUEL DLR III.1   223
  Sr Sampscn: Constitution, is no such contemptible Age.   298   FCR LCVE   V.1   27
  Fainall: Proof, and something of a Constitution to bustle thro' the 415   WAY WCRLD   II.1   213
Constrain'd (1)
  Mirabell: with a constrain'd Smile told her, I thought nothing was so 396   WAY WCRLD   I.1   38
Constrained (1)
  Lord Froth: constrained my Inclinations to Laugh.--He, he, he, to   . . 133   DOUEL DLR   I.1   231
Constru'd (1)
  Zara: And what was Charity, he constru'd Love.   349   M. EBIDE   II.2   380
Construe (1)
  Mirabell: will construe an Affront into a Jest; and call downright   . 401   WAY WCRLD   I.1   230
Consult (6)
  Maskwell: Let us go and consult her, my life for yours, I   190   DOUBL DLR   V.1   118
  Sir Paul: I must consult my Wife,--he talks of disinheriting his   . 192   DOUEL DLR   V.1   174
  Angelica: Let me consult my Lawyer concerning this Obligation;   . . 301   FCR LCVE   V.1   134
  Sr Sampson: I'll lend you the Bond,--You shall consult your Lawyer,   . 301   FCR LCVE   V.1   138
  Sr Sampson: and I'll consult a Parson; Odzooks I'm a Young Man: . . 301   FCR LCVE   V.1   139
  Mrs Fain: waits to consult you.   452   WAY WCRLD   IV.1   305
Consultation (1)
  Maskwell: Consultation may be over.   149   DOUBL DLR   II.1   436
Consulted (4)
  Foresight: have consulted me for the time. Well, but we'll make   .   . 240   FOR LCVE   II.1   190
  Scandal: Men; but they were such as you--Men who consulted   . .   . 267   FCR LCVE   III.1   529
  Foresight: as to this marriage I have consulted the Stars; and all   . 268   FOR LCVE   III.1   552
  Foresight: as to this marriage I have consulted the Science; and all . 268   FOR LCVE   III.1 V552
Consulting (1)
  Lady Touch: Marriage, and the promoting any cther, without consulting   192   DOUEL DLR   V.1   180
Consume (2)
  Maskwell: ruine all, consume my honest Character, and brand me   .   . 188   DOUBL DLR   V.1   30
  Zara: Scorch and consume the curst perfidious King.   380   M. EBIDE   V.2 V171
Consuming (1)   see Self-consuming
  Heartwell: more Consuming Fire, a Womans Arms. Ha! well   62   OLD BATCH III.1   69
Consummated (1)
  Foible: your Lady-ship: for if he had Consummated with your   .   . 463   WAY WCRLD   V.1   42
Consummation (3)
  Lady Ply: Consummation between us, and   179   DOUEL DLR   IV.1 V458
  Mrs Fore: together; and after Consummation, Girl, there's no   . .   . 288   FCR LCVE   IV.1   473
  Mirabell: and adjourn the Consummation till farther Order; bid   .   . 398   WAY WCRLD   I.1   128
Consummatum est (1)
  Sr Sampson: Figures of St. Dunstan's Clock, and Consummatum est shall . 266   FOR LCVE   III.1   477
Contagious (1)
  Foresight: there is a contagious Frenzy abroad. Hcw does Valentine?   . 306   FCR LCVE   V.1   333
Contain (8)
  Heartwell: Damn'd, damn'd Strumpet! Cou'd she not contain her   . .   . 107   OLD BATCH   V.2   5
  Maskwell: Look ycu, Madam, we are alone,--pray contain   136   DOUBL DLR   I.1   359
  Maskwell: I'm glad you're come, for I could not contain my   . .   . 156   DOUEL DLR III.1   200
  Careless: said--Oh! (Aside.) I shall never contain Laughter.   . .   . 170   DOUEL DLR   IV.1   123
  Sir Paul: to my Lady, I can't contain my self; come my dear Friend. . 181   DOUEL DLR   IV.1   509
  Mellefont: temper can contain? They talk of sending Maskwell to   .   . 187   DOUEL DLR   IV.2   148
  Lord Touch: Yes, I will contain, tho' I cou'd burst.   199   DOUEL DLR   V.1   430
  Zara: (Aside.) Confusion! yet I will ccntain my self.   359   M. EBIDE   III.1   411
Contain'd (1)
  Mirabell: what that Parchment contain'd--(undoing the Box.)   . .   . 476   WAY WCRLD   V.1   529
Contains (2)
  Mellefont: Hell is not more busie than her Brain, nor contains more   . 129   DOUBL DLR   I.1   77
  Waitwell: Contains the Writings of my whole Estate, and deliver   . . 461   WAY WCRLD   IV.1   634
Contemner (1)
  Foresight: Contemner of Sciences, and a defamer of Vertue.   241   FOR LOVE   II.1   240
Contemplation (6)
  Mellefont: How now, Jack? What, so full of Contemplation   155   DOUBL DLR III.1   198
  Brisk: the whole Province of Contemplation: That's all--   . .   . 175   DOUEL DLR   IV.1   316
  Tattle: Oh Madam, those are Sacred to Love and Contemplaticn.   . . 232   FOR LOVE   I.1   609
  Mirabell: were a Case of more steady Contemplation; a very tranquility 423   WAY WORLD   II.1   492
  Mrs Fain: your Mistress up to the Ears in Love and Contemplation,   . 446   WAY WCRLD   IV.1   71
  Millamant: Contemplation, must I bid you then Adieu? ay-h adieu.--my   449   WAY WCRLD   IV.1   187
Contemplative (2)
  Bellmour: thought a Contemplative Lover could no more have   37   OLD BATCH   I.1   2
  Lucy: Contemplative Pimp.   65   OLD BATCH III.1   164
Contempt (3)
  Lady Touch: punish your fond, rash Contempt! Again smile!   198   DOUEL DLR   V.1   392
                At least from their Contempt, whc cannot Read.   204   DOUEL DLR   EPI.   36
  Foresight: What, is he gone, and in contempt of Science! Ill Stars   . 283   FCR LCVE   IV.1   295
Contemptible (6)
  Cynthia: contemptible in exposing their Infirmities.   165   DOUBL DLR III.1   579
  Cynthia: contemptible by exposing their Infirmities.   165   DOUBL DLR III.1 V579
  Sr Sampson: Constitution, is no such contemptible Age.   298   FOR LCVE   V.1   27
  Angelica: Fifty a contemptible Age! Not at all, a very fashionable   . 298   FOR LOVE   V.1   28
  Fainall: Kind too Contemptible to give Scandal.   399   WAY WORLD   I.1   143
  Witwoud: in the World,--he wou'd not be altogether contemptible.   . 403   WAY WCRLD   I.1   293
Contending (1)
  Zara: To have contending Queens, at dead of Night   360   M. EBIDE   III.1   427
Content (10)   see Self-content
  Capt Bluff: I am content to retire--Live a private Person--   53   OLD BATCH   II.1   211
  Bellmour: thou be content to marry Araminta?   63   OLD BATCH III.1   104
  Vainlove: Could you be content to go to Heaven?   63   OLD BATCH III.1   105
  Cynthia: O Lord, not I, Madam; I'm content to be a   139   DOUEL DLR   II.1   18
  Scandal: and be content only to be made a Fool with other reasonable 278   FOR LOVE   IV.1   107
                And a less Number New, would well content ye.   323   M. EBIDE   PRO.   2

Content   (ccntinued)
```
Almeria:     Or, ever taste content, or peace of Heart,    . . . .  . 329  M. BRIDE    I.1   147
Fainall:     content you shall enjoy your own proper Estate during  . . 468  WAY WCRLD   V.1   252
Sir Wilful:  Pound. And so let that content for what's past, and make  . 470  WAY WCRLD   V.1   319
Millamant:   I am content tc be a Sacrifice tc your repose   . . .  . 470  WAY WCRLD   V.1   325
```
Contented (5)
```
Bellmour:    contented with the slavery of honourable Love in one  . . 40   OLD BATCH   I.1   138
Laetitia:    that will love you as well as I have done: I shall be
               contented  . . . . . . . . . . . . . . . . . . . .  . 78   OLD BATCH   IV.1  110
Lady Ply:    hold you Contented. . . . . . . . . . . . . . . .  . . 144  DOUEL DLR   II.1  203
Sir Paul:    Hold your self Contented, my Lady Plyant,--I  . . . . . 144  DOUEL DLR   II.1  206
Mirabell:    will ycu be contented with the first ncw, and stay for the 449  WAY WOBLD   IV.1  183
```
Contents (1)   see Male-Contents
```
Bellmour:    Upon the Perusal I found the Contents so charming, that  . 82   OLD BATCH   IV.2  53
```
Contiguous (1)
```
Osmyn-Alph:  And bcre contiguous Pallaces to Earth. . . . . . . .  . 347  M. BRIDE    II.2  311
```
Continence (2)
```
Fainall:     This Ccntinence is all dissembled; this is in order to  . 406  WAY WCRLD   I.1   418
Lady Wish:   to any Lethargy of Continence--I hope  . . . . . .  . . 458  WAY WCBLD   IV.1  531
```
Continency (1)
```
Sir Paul:    Ay, but by your own Vertue and Continency that  . . . . 180  DOUEL DLR   IV.1  476
```
Continu'd (1)
```
Fainall:     Had ycu dissembl'd better, Things might have continu'd  . 397  WAY WCRLD   I.1   66
```
Continual (1)
```
Sir Paul:    me and my Wife, with continual Favours.  . . . . . .  . 159  DOUEL DLB   III.1 326
```
Continually (1)
```
Vainlove:    Ay, am I not? To be continually starting of Hares  . . . 39   OLD BATCH   I.1   75
```
Continue (10)
```
Araminta:    But if you continue your Humour, it won't be very  . . . 57   OLD BATCH   II.2  86
Jeremy:      Now Heav'n of Mercy continue the Tax ufon  . . . . .  . 217  FOR ICVE    I.1   61
Tattle:      Very true, Sir, and desire to continue so. I have no  . . 305  FOR LCVE    V.1   287
             Then pray continue this ycur kind behaviour,  . . . .  . 316  FOR LCVE    EPI.  43
Osmyn-Alph:  In all, and can continue to bestow, . . . . . . . .  . 344  M. BRIDE    II.2  189
Marwood:     have him ever to continue upon the Rack of Fear and  . . 411  WAY WCRLD   II.1  63
Fainall:     that ly permitting her to be engag'd, I might continue  . 414  WAY WCRLD   II.1  145
Mirabell:    and yet continue to be in Love, is to be made wise from the 423  WAY WCRLD   II.1  499
Millamant:   before you ccme in. These Articles subscrib'd, If I continue 450  WAY WCRLD   IV.1  225
Mirabell:    Item, I Article, that you continue to like your own  . . 451  WAY WCRLD   IV.1  245
```
Continued (2)
```
Mellefont:   would have mirth continued this day at any rate; tho'  . . 129  DOUEL DLR   I.1   68
Valentine:   I know no effectual Difference between continued  . . . 254  FCB ICVE    III.1 40
```
Continues (2)
```
             (Scene Continues. Enter Lady Wishfort and Foible.)  . . . 444  WAY WCBLD   IV.1
             (Scene Continues. Lady Wishfort and Foible.)  . . . . . 462  WAY WCRLD   V.1
```
Contract (8)
```
Sr Sampson:  Contract. . . . . . . . . . . . . . . . . . . . .  . . 300  FCR LCVE    V.1   116
Mrs Fain:    So, if my pocr Mother is caught in a Contract,  . . . . 417  WAY WCRLD   II.1  296
Mirabell:    Contract? and here comes one to be a witness to the  . . 452  WAY WCRLD   IV.1  281
Waitwell:    And may I presume to bring a Contract to be  . . . . . 461  WAY WCBLD   IV.1  638
Millamant:   my hand to this flower of Knight-hood; and for the Contract 470  WAY WCRLD   V.1   329
Millamant:   and insist upon the contract still. Then 'tis the last
               time he  . . . . . . . . . . . . . . . . . . .  . . 470  WAY WCRLD   V.1   339
Sir Wilful:  melt, I can tell you that. My contract went no further  . 472  WAY WCRLD   V.1   396
Lady Wish:   resign the Contract with my Neice Immediately.  . . . . 472  WAY WCRLD   V.1   404
```
Contract's (1)
```
Lady Touch:  The Contract's void by this unheard of Impiety.  . . . . 150  DOUBL DLR   III.1 3
```
Contracted (3)
```
Manuel:      Garcia, what's he, who with contracted Brow,  . . . . . 336  M. BRIDE    I.1   424
Lady Wish:   contracted to Night. . . . . . . . . . . . . . .  . . 428  WAY WCRLD   III.1 120
Foible:      she'll be contracted to Sir Rowland to Night, she says;-- 430  WAY WCBLD   III.1 210
```
Contracting (1)
```
Fainall:     Contracting her self against your Consent or Knowledge;  . 469  WAY WCRLD   V.1   283
```
Contradict (10)
```
Tattle:      Manners than to contradict what a Lady has declar'd.  . . 229  FOR LOVE    I.1   479
Foresight:   contradict you, and tell you, ycu are ignorant. . . . . 240  FCR LCVE    II.1  203
Tattle:      speak what you think: Your words must ccntradict your  . . 251  FCB LCVE    II.1  612
Tattle:      thoughts; but your Actions may contradict your words. . . 251  FCR LCVE    II.1  613
Mirabell:    and Ccmplaisance enough not to ccntradict him who shall  . 399  WAY WOBLD   I.1   154
Witwoud:     contradict any Body. . . . . . . . . . . . . . . .  . 403  WAY WCBLD   I.1   304
Petulant:    contradict. . . . . . . . . . . . . . . . . . . .  . 435  WAY WCBLD   III.1 399
Witwoud:     Ay, when he has a Humour to contradict, then I  . . . . 435  WAY WCRLD   III.1 400
Witwoud:     contradict too. What, I know my Cue. Then we contradict  . 435  WAY WCBLD   III.1 401
```
Contradicted (2)
```
Lady Ply:    Conduct, should be contradicted in a matter of this  . . 144  DOUBL DLR   II.1  218
Millamant:   Nay, he has said nothing neither; but he has contradicted  432  WAY WOBLD   III.1 292
```
Contradiction (3)
```
Heartwell:   when 'tis out of Obstinacy and Contradiction--But  . . . 74   OLD BATCH   III.2 127
Fondlewife:  Good lack! I profess the Spirit cf contradiction  . . . 75   OLD BATCH   IV.1  16
Witwoud:     Contradictions beget one another like Jews. . . . .  . . 435  WAY WCRLD   III.1 403
```
Contraries (2)
```
Valentine:   Dutch Almanacks are to be understood by contraries. But  . 297  FOR LCVE    IV.1  809
Tattle:      by Contraries, Child--O fie; what, we must not love  . . 303  FOR LCVE    V.1   241
```
Contrary (8)
```
Bellmour:    of a Husband, as of a Creature contrary to that soft,  . . 106  OLD BATCH   V.1   381
Lady Touch:  Mellefcnt, will convince her of the contrary.  . . . . . 138  DOUBL DLR   I.1   416
Lord Touch:  contrary too, before it had been believ'd--  . . . .  . 151  DOUBL DLR   III.1 20
Scandal:     Lady; it is contrary to his Character--How one may  . . . 229  FOR LCVE    I.1   490
Ben:         speak cne thing, and to think just the contrary way; is as
               it  . . . . . . . . . . . . . . . . . . . . .  . . 263  FOR LOVE    III.1 386
Ben:         Lapland-Witch as soon, and live upon selling of contrary  . 264  FOR LOVE    III.1 426
Ben:         Lapland-Witch as soon, and live upon selling contrary  . . 264  FOR LCVE    III.1 V426
Mirabell:    end I so us'd my self to think of 'em, that at length,
               contrary  . . . . . . . . . . . . . . . . . . .  . 399  WAY WORLD   I.1   168
```
Contribute (2)
```
Lady Wish:   Contribute much both to the saving of your Life; and the  . 458  WAY WORLD   IV.1  507
Mirabell:    force comply. For my part I will Contribute all that in  . 478  WAY WOBLD   V.1   615
```

Corner-House   (continued)
 Bellmour: Corner-House, and I'll tell you by the way what may   .   . 107   OLD BATCH   V.1   402
Corner-house (2)
 Sharper: Corner-house.   104   OLD BATCH   V.1   286
 Heartwell: not near that House,--that Corner-house,--that   .   .   . 105   OLD BATCH   V.1   323
Coroner's (1)
 Fainall: Coroner's Inquest, to sit upon the murder'd Reputations of 396   WAY WORLD   I.1   53
Correct (1)
   For so Reform'd a Town, who dares Correct?   393   WAY WORLD   PRO.   32
Correction (1)
 Sr Sampson: Authority, no Correction, no Arbitrary Power; nothing   .   . 240   FOR LOVE   II.1   177
Correspondence (3)
 Selim: Concerning Osmyn's and his Correspondence   361   M. BRIDE   IV.1 V 13
 Foible: thought the former good Correspondence between your   .   . 430   WAY WORLD III.1   197
 Lady Wish: Correspondence to his Passion?   445   WAY WORLD   IV.1   13
Corresponding (1)
 Selim: Concerning Osmyn's corresponding with   361   M. BRIDE   IV.1   13
Corrupt (4)
 Setter: O Lord, Sir, What d'ye mean? Corrupt my honesty.   .   . 103   OLD BATCH   V.1   247
 Lady Wish: corrupt Integrity it self. If she has given him an
   Opportunity, ... 426   WAY WORLD III.1   58
 Fainall: Corrupt to Superstition, and blind Credulity. I am single; 444   WAY WORLD III.1   719
 Marwood: Wishfort go to Mrs. Fainall and Foible). These Corrupt   . 474   WAY WORLD   V.1   473
Corrupted (2)
 Selim: Have Cause to fear his Guards may be corrupted,   .   .   . 362   M. BRIDE   IV.1   51
 Gonsalez: Corrupted; how? by whom? who told her so?   366   M. BRIDE   IV.1   207
Corum Nobus (1)
 Lady Ply: your face; for now Sir Paul's gone, you are Corum Nobus.   . 146   DOUBL DLR   II.1   299
Cost (6)
   But that late knowledge, does much hazard cost,   .   .   . 204   DOUBL DLR   EPI.   4
   There's no recov'ring Damages or Cost.   323   M. BRIDE   PRO.   26
 Waitwell: and Innocence, tho' it cost me my life.   461   WAY WORLD   IV.1   625
 Sir Wilful: fairer? If I have broke any thing, I'll pay for't, an it
   cost a   470   WAY WORLD   V.1   318
 Sir Wilful: By'r Lady a very reasonable request; and will cost   .   . 471   WAY WORLD   V.1   380
 Mirabell: For each deceiver to his cost may find, ... 478   WAY WORLD   V.1   622
Costive (1)
 Valentine: O the Devil, what damn'd Costive Poet has given   .   .   . 255   FOR LOVE   III.1   73
Cotten (1)
 Sr Sampson: see 'em hug and cotten together, like Down upon a   .   . 260   FOR LOVE   III.1   265
Cou'd (75)
 Bellmour: I cou'd think of nothing all Day but putting 'em in practice 82   OLD BATCH   IV.2   54
 Araminta: You who cou'd reproach me with one Counterfeit,   .   .   . 106   OLD BATCH   V.1   361
 Belinda: (to Bellmour). O my Conscience, I cou'd find in my   .   . 106   OLD BATCH   V.1   364
 Bellmour: That were a miserable Wretch indeed, who cou'd   .   .   . 106   OLD BATCH   V.1   378
 Heartwell: Damn'd, damn'd Strumpet! Cou'd she not contain her   .   . 107   OLD BATCH   V.2   5
 Heartwell: And Adam, sure, cou'd with more Ease abide   108   OLD BATCH   V.2   14
 Lady Froth: see little Saph. I knew you cou'd not stay.   .   .   . 167   DOUBL DLR III.1   622
 Lady Froth: Heaven's I thought you cou'd have no Mistress but the   . 176   DOUBL DLR   IV.1   334
 Lady Touch: Too well thou know'st my jealous Soul cou'd never bear   . 198   DOUBL DLR   V.1   399
 Lord Touch: Yes, I will contain, tho' I cou'd burst.   199   DOUBL DLR   V.1   430
 Maskwell: World of Love, cou'd be confin'd within the puny Province 199   DOUBL DLR   V.1   432
 Valentine: Pox on her, cou'd she find no other time to fling   .   . . 221   FOR LOVE   I.1   207
 Sr Sampson: the twinckling of a Star; and seen a Conjurer, that cou'd 241   FOR LOVE   II.1   227
 Mrs Fore: (aside). O Devil on't, that I cou'd not discover   .   . 248   FOR LOVE   II.1   471
 Mrs Frail: Now if I cou'd wheedle him, Sister, ha? You understand   . 248   FOR LOVE   II.1   495
 Mrs Fore: A cunning Cur; how soon he cou'd find out a   250   FOR LOVE   II.1   544
 Tattle: There's no occasion for a Lie; I cou'd never tell a Lie   . 253   FOR LOVE   III.1   21
 Angelica: wou'd if you cou'd, no doubt on't.   255   FOR LOVE   III.1   95
 Sr Sampson: Cou'd neither Love, nor Duty, nor Natural Affection   .   . 259   FOR LOVE   III.1   238
 Angelica: cou'd have lik'd any thing in him, it shou'd have been his 260   FOR LOVE   III.1   246
 Mrs Fore: They have quarrel'd just as we cou'd wish.   264   FOR LOVE   III.1   433
 Sr Sampson: help of a Parson, ha? Odd if he should I cou'd not be angry 265   FOR LOVE   III.1   461
 Sr Sampson: we are Fools as we use to be--Oons, that you cou'd   .   . 283   FOR LOVE   IV.1   280
 Scandal: she cou'd grant 'em.--Madam, I'm your humble Servant,   . 284   FOR LOVE   IV.1   337
 Ben: and if so be that he cou'd get a Woman to his mind, he'd . 286   FOR LOVE   IV.1   381
 Scandal: is of a piece with Mrs. Frail. He Courts Angelica, if
   we cou'd   291   FOR LOVE   IV.1   598
 Sr Sampson: How, Madam! Wou'd I cou'd prove it.   299   FOR LOVE   V.1   89
 Angelica: cou'd not make me worthy of so generous and faithful a   . 312   FOR LOVE   V.1   561
 Valentine: If my happiness cou'd receive Addition, this Kind   .   . 312   FOR LOVE   V.1   579
 Garcia: And I cou'd pity 'em. I hear some coming, ... 339   M. BRIDE   II.1   48
 Almeria: If I cou'd speak; how I have mourn'd and pray'd,   .   . 343   M. BRIDE   II.2   130
 Almeria: Without thee cou'd not cure.   343   M. BRIDE   II.2   134
 Zara: Cou'd one that lov'd, thus torture what she lov'd?   .   . 353   M. BRIDE   III.1   161
 Zara: Cou'd one who lov'd, thus torture whom she lov'd?   .   . 353   M. BRIDE   III.1 V161
 Zara: And Detestation, that cou'd use thee thus.   353   M. BRIDE   III.1   163
 Zara: Thy Anger cou'd not pierce thus, to my Heart.   .   .   . 354   M. BRIDE   III.1   187
 Osmyn-Alph: That I cou'd almost turn my Eyes away, ... 356   M. BRIDE   III.1   253
 Osmyn-Alph: Grief cou'd not double thus, his Darts against me.   .   . 356   M. BRIDE   III.1 V283
 Almeria: Curst my own Tongue, that cou'd not move his Pity.   .   . 370   M. BRIDE   IV.1   372
 Almeria: Curst these weak Hands, that cou'd not hold him here;   . 370   M. BRIDE   IV.1   373
 Mirabell: I did as much as Man cou'd, with any reasonable   .   .   . 397   WAY WORLD   I.1   68
 Witwoud: that's the Truth on't, if he were my Brother, I cou'd not 403   WAY WORLD   I.1   311
 Witwoud: acquit him--That indeed I cou'd wish were otherwise.   . 403   WAY WORLD   I.1   312
 Mirabell: And this is the Sum of what you cou'd collect last   .   . 408   WAY WORLD   I.1   494
 Marwood: Faith by Marrying; if I cou'd but find one   411   WAY WORLD   II.1   53
 Fainall: Arms in full Security. But cou'd you think because the   . 414   WAY WORLD   II.1   147
 Fainall: Pardon--No Tears--I was to blame, I cou'd not   .   .   . 416   WAY WORLD   II.1   240
 Mirabell: what a Butler cou'd pinch out of a Napkin.   418   WAY WORLD   II.1   313
 Millamant: Ha, ha, ha. What wou'd you give, that you cou'd help   . 422   WAY WORLD   II.1   458
 Mirabell: cou'd not help it.   422   WAY WORLD   II.1   461
 Waitwell: to Business, Sir. I have instructed her as well as I
   cou'd. If   423   WAY WORLD   II.1   509
 Foible: what shall I say?--Alas, Madam, cou'd I help it, if I   . 427   WAY WORLD III.1   85
 Foible: Nay, if that had been the worst I cou'd have born: But he 427   WAY WORLD III.1   89

Cou'd (continued)

		PAGE	TITLE	ACT.SC	LINE
Marwood:	without you cou'd have kept his Counsel closer. I shall	431	WAY WORLD	III.1	242
Millamant:	Things! without one cou'd give 'em to one's	433	WAY WORLD	III.1	306
Millamant:	O silly! Ha, ha, ha. I cou'd laugh immoderately.	433	WAY WORLD	III.1	335
Millamant:	--If you cou'd but stay for me, I shou'd overtake you	434	WAY WORLD	III.1	360
Sir Wilful:	--You cou'd write News before you were out of your	439	WAY WORLD	III.1	548
Sir Wilful:	of Furnival's Inn--Ycu cou'd intreat to be remember'd	439	WAY WORLD	III.1	550
Sir Wilful:	then to your Friends round the Rekin. We cou'd have	439	WAY WORLD	III.1	551
Painall:	Encrease of fortune,--I cou'd have worn 'em tipt with	442	WAY WORLD	III.1	646
Marwood:	have Foible provok'd if I cou'd help it,--because you know	443	WAY WORLD	III.1	704
Witwoud:	Left 'em? I cou'd stay no longer--I have laugh'd	453	WAY WORLD	IV.1	325
Witwoud:	That's the Jest, there was no dispute, they cou'd	453	WAY WORLD	IV.1	332
Waitwell:	me, If I cou'd but live so long as to be reveng'd on that	458	WAY WORLD	IV.1	504
Foible:	Pray do but bear me Madam, he cou'd not marry	463	WAY WORLD	V.1	38
Foible:	first, to secure your Lady-ship. He cou'd not have bedded	463	WAY WORLD	V.1	41
Foible:	cou'd have told you long enough since, but I love to keep	464	WAY WORLD	V.1	86
Mrs Fain:	I cou'd wish. Now Mincing?	464	WAY WORLD	V.1	102
Lady Wish:	My Nephew was non Compos; and cou'd not	469	WAY WORLD	V.1	286
Mirabell:	Consider Madam, in reality; You cou'd not receive	472	WAY WORLD	V.1	383
Lady Wish:	Tongue;--When I did not see him I cou'd have	472	WAY WORLD	V.1	409
Mirabell:	any Obligation to me; or else perhaps I cou'd advise.--	473	WAY WORLD	V.1	452
Mirabell:	You have dispos'd of her, who only cou'd have	473	WAY WORLD	V.1	458
Mirabell:	partial Opinion and fondness of you, she cou'd never have	476	WAY WORLD	V.1	543
Couch (5)					
Lord Froth:	Lady's is the most inviting Couch; and a slumber there, is	200	DOUBL DLR	V.1	494
	a Couch disorderly dress'd, Scandal by him.)	279	FOR LOVE	IV.1	149
Lady Wish:	receive him in my little dressing Room, there's a Couch--	445	WAY WORLD	IV.1	23
Lady Wish:	Yes, yes, I'll give the first Impression on a Couch--I wont	445	WAY WORLD	IV.1	24
Lady Wish:	nothing is more alluring than a Levee from a Couch in	445	WAY WORLD	IV.1	29
Cough (2)					
Cynthia:	Fie Mr. Brisk, 'tis Eringo's for her Cough.	165	DOUBL DLR	III.1	569
Cynthia:	Fie Mr. Brisk, Eringo's for her Cough.	165	DOUBL DLR	III.1	V569
Coul (1)					
Valentine:	Get me a Coul and Beads, that I may play my part,--	290	FOR LOVE	IV.1	560
Could (109)					
Could'st (6)					
Mellefont:	outwitted Woman.--But tell me, how could'st thou thus	149	DOUBL DLR	II.1	408
Zara:	Than e'er thou could'st with bitterest Reproaches;	354	M. BRIDE	III.1	186
Osmyn-Alph:	O could'st thou be less killing, soft or kind,	356	M. BRIDE	III.1	282
Zara:	I know thou could'st; but I'm not often pleas'd,	360	M. BRIDE	III.1	423
Almeria:	But doubly thou, who could'st alone have Policy,	370	M. BRIDE	IV.1	380
Gonsalez:	Could'st thou procure with speed,	372	M. BRIDE	IV.1	436
Couldst (2)					
Bellmour:	whether thou wouldst have her angry or pleas'd. Couldst	63	OLD BATCH	III.1	103
Almeria:	That thus couldst melt to see a Stranger's Wrongs.	327	M. BRIDE	I.1	31
Councel (1)					
Heartwell:	Then good Councel will be thrown away upon	112	OLD BATCH	V.2	157
Council (3)					
Capt Bluff:	I'll call a Council of War within to consider of my	70	OLD BATCH	III.1	363
Valentine:	. . . the Council, and Generals of	221	FOR LOVE	I.1	188
Heli:	Where not far off some Male-Contents hold Council	352	M. BRIDE	III.1	V100
Counsel (4)					
Heli:	Where not far off some Male-Contents hold Counsel	352	M. BRIDE	III.1	100
Zara:	But for thy fatal and pernicious Counsel.	380	M. BRIDE	V.2	178
Marwood:	without you cou'd have kept his Counsel closer. I shall	431	WAY WORLD	III.1	242
Sir Wilful:	let her keep her own Counsel in the mean time, and cry	456	WAY WORLD	IV.1	429
Counsellor (1)					
Tattle:	Aye? Who's he, tho? A Privy Counsellor?	302	FOR LOVE	V.1	192
Counsellour (1)					
Osmyn-Alph:	My Friend and Counsellour; as thou think'st fit,	352	M. BRIDE	III.1	104
Count (1)					
Sir Wilful:	with you in London; we shou'd count it towards Afternoon	437	WAY WORLD	III.1	448
Counted (1)					
Lady Wish:	The Miniature has been counted like--But	427	WAY WORLD	III.1	79
Countenance (14)					
Bellmour:	Countenance. But, to tell you something you don't know.	100	OLD BATCH	V.1	148
Bellmour:	Frank, Will you keep us in Countenance.	112	OLD BATCH	V.2	170
Mellefont:	secures them from blushing, and being out of Countenance,	158	DOUBL DLR	III.1	312
Careless:	Countenance.	160	DOUBL DLR	III.1	371
Lady Ply:	O fy, Sir Paul, you'l put me out of Countenance	172	DOUBL DLR	IV.1	189
Jeremy:	terrify'd Countenance, that looks as if he had written for	219	FOR LOVE	I.1	105
Mrs Fore:	Countenance purely, you'd make an Admirable Player.	247	FOR LOVE	II.1	452
Mrs Fore:	Countenance:--But look you here now,--where did	248	FOR LOVE	II.1	465
Sr Sampson:	Weekly Bills out of Countenance.	308	FOR LOVE	V.1	399
Selim:	The State of things will countenance all Suspicions.	362	M. BRIDE	IV.1	55
Mirabell:	Countenance, with your senseless Ribaldry; which you	409	WAY WORLD	I.1	525
Mirabell:	put another out of Countenance.	409	WAY WORLD	I.1	535
Millamant:	Countenance, 'tis impossible I shou'd hold mine. Well,	422	WAY WORLD	II.1	473
Mirabell:	her affairs under your Countenance and tempt you to make	451	WAY WORLD	IV.1	237
Counter (1)					
Mrs Fain:	Bodkin, nor part with a Brass Counter in Composition for	466	WAY WORLD	V.1	176
Counter-work (1)					
Mellefont:	fire; but I shall counter-work her Spells, and ride the	167	DOUBL DLR	IV.1	4
Counterfeit (10)					
Bellmour:	much more agreeable, if you can counterfeit his Habit to blind	39	OLD BATCH	I.1	88
Silvia:	'Tis as hard to Counterfeit Love, as it is to conceal it:	62	OLD BATCH	III.1	51
Sharper:	Fault: This Letter, that so sticks in thy Maw, is Counterfeit;	99	OLD BATCH	V.1	108
Araminta:	You who cou'd reproach me with one Counterfeit,	106	OLD BATCH	V.1	361
Maskwell:	surprize your Aunt and me together: Counterfeit a rage	157	DOUBL DLR	III.1	250
Cynthia:	'Tis not so hard to counterfeit Joy in the depth of	167	DOUBL DLR	III.1	624
Angelica:	Madness counterfeit.	295	FOR LOVE	IV.1	736
Jeremy:	Counterfeit, Madam! I'll maintain him to be as	295	FOR LOVE	IV.1	737
Tattle:	No, no, let me alone for a Counterfeit;--I'll be	303	FOR LOVE	V.1	219
Scandal:	No really, Sir; I'm his Witness, it was all Counterfeit.	311	FOR LOVE	V.1	506

Counterfeited (5)
Scandal:	upon the Superscription: And yet perhaps he has				
	Counterfeited	226	FOR LOVE	I.1	374
Scandal:	in the Superscription: And yet perhaps he has Counterfeited	226	FOR LOVE	I.1	V374
Valentine:	Gods have been in counterfeited Shapes for the same Reason;	294	FOR LOVE	IV.1	701
Angelica:	Transport in your Soul; which, it seems, you only				
	counterfeited,	294	FOR LOVE	IV.1	723
Valentine:	counterfeited Madness; I don't know but the Frolick may	311	FOR LOVE	V.1	525

Countermin'd (1)
Sir Joseph:	countermin'd, or so--Mr. Vainlove, I suppose you know . .	110	OLD BATCH	V.2	113

Counters (1)
Valentine:	behind Counters, as if Religion were to be sold in every .	289	FOR LOVE	IV.1	502

Counterwork (1)
Manuel:	By Heav'n I'll meet, and counterwork this Treachery. . .	374	M. BRIDE	V.1	66

Countess (1)
Capt Bluff:	Quality. Here, here's from a Countess too. Hum--No . . .	103	OLD BATCH	V.1	267

Countless (1)
Osmyn-Alph:	This countless Summ of Tenderness and Love, ...	343	M. BRIDE	II.2	138

Countries (1)
Sir Wilful:	Countries.	440	WAY WORLD	III.1	585

Country (17)
Vainlove:	It must be a very superstitious Country, where such . .	39	OLD BATCH	I.1	66
Sharper:	my Country, or my Religion, or in some very Justifiable .	51	OLD BATCH	II.1	160
Sir Paul:	Fortune, a good Estate in the Country, some houses in .	161	DOUBL DLR	III.1	408
Lady Froth:	I may suppose the Dairy in Town, as well as in the Country.	163	DOUBL DLR	III.1	504
Scandal:	vain! Who would die a Martyr to Sense in a Country . .	219	FOR LOVE	I.1	139
Mrs Frail:	Daughter is come out of the Country--I assure you, . .	231	FOR LOVE	I.1	568
Mrs Frail:	never been out of the Country.	231	FOR LOVE	I.1	573
Jeremy:	Country Dances; and the like; I don't much matter your .	245	FOR LOVE	II.1	374
Miss Prue:	our old fashion'd Country way of speaking ones mind;-- .	252	FOR LOVE	II.1	625
Tattle:	or the Naked Prince. And it is notorious, that in a Country	257	FOR LOVE	III.1	162
Jeremy:	with his Arms would over-run the Country, yet no body .	302	FOR LOVE	V.1	194
Servant-M:	behind one another, as 'twere in a Country Dance. Curs .	398	WAY WORLD	I.1	114
	(Enter Sir Wilfull Witwoud in a Country Riding Habit, and .	436	WAY WORLD	III.1	443
Witwoud:	think you're in the Country, where great lubberly Brothers	439	WAY WORLD	III.1	534
Millamant:	I Nauseate walking; 'tis a Country diversion, I . . .	448	WAY WORLD	IV.1	121
Millamant:	loath the Country and every thing that relates to it. . .	448	WAY WORLD	IV.1	122
Sir Wilful:	the Country,--'tis like you may be one of those, . . .	448	WAY WORLD	IV.1	130

Country-Dance (1)
	(They pretend to practice part of a Country-Dance.) . .	177	DOUBL DLR	IV.1	371

Country-Girls (1)
Araminta:	I warrant, plump, Cherry-cheek'd Country-Girls.	84	OLD BATCH	IV.3	27

Country-Squire (1)
Belinda:	Oh; a most Comical Sight: A Country-Squire, with . .	84	OLD BATCH	IV.3	23

Country's (1)
Zara:	Driv'n by the Tide upon my Country's Coast, ...	346	M. BRIDE	II.2	276

Couple (11)
Belinda:	see a couple, I'll give you their History.	87	OLD BATCH	IV.3	150
Lord Froth:	Don't you think us a happy Couple?	140	DOUBL DLR	II.1	95
Cynthia:	I vow, my Lord, I think you the happiest Couple in . .	141	DOUBL DLR	II.1	96
Sir Paul:	with Lambs, and every Creature couple with its Foe, as .	144	DOUBL DLR	II.1	225
Valentine:	A couple of very civil Proverbs, truly: 'Tis hard to .	256	FOR LOVE	III.1	129
Valentine:	There's a couple of Topicks for you, no more like one .	282	FOR LOVE	IV.1	256
Scandal:	contrive to couple 'em together--Heark'ee--.	291	FOR LOVE	IV.1	599
Sr Sampson:	Aunt? Not at all, for a young Couple to make a Match .	308	FOR LOVE	V.1	404
Ben:	Why there's another Match now, as tho'f a couple of .	310	FOR LOVE	V.1	487
Servant-M:	was the last Couple to lead up; and no hopes appearing of	398	WAY WORLD	I.1	115
Lady Wish:	Abigails and Andrews! I'll couple you, Yes, I'll taste you	463	WAY WORLD	V.1	52

Couples (1)
Cynthia:	meeting: We Hunt in Couples where we both pursue the . .	168	DOUBL DLR	IV.1	16

Couplets (3)
Sir Paul:	making Couplets.	201	DOUBL DLR	V.1	513
Lord Froth:	Couplets.	201	DOUBL DLR	V.1	514
Valentine:	--I'll have you learn to make Couplets, to tag the . .	218	FOR LOVE	I.1	77

Coupling (1)
Servant-M:	Sir, there's such Coupling at Pancras, that they stand .	398	WAY WORLD	I.1	113

Courage (7)
Heartwell:	courage, which you shew for the first year or two upon all	43	OLD BATCH	I.1	246
Sharper:	There is in true Beauty, as in Courage, somewhat, . . .	86	OLD BATCH	IV.3	126
Cynthia:	have once resolved; and a true Female courage to oppose .	193	DOUBL DLR	V.1	204
Lady Touch:	not Courage; no, I know thee well: but thou shalt miss .	197	DOUBL DLR	V.1	388
Angelica:	Courage at this time. To tell you the Truth, I'm weary of .	298	FOR LOVE	V.1	46
Zara:	Than your high Courage suffers you to see;	364	M. BRIDE	IV.1	110
Mirabell:	What, Courage?	403	WAY WORLD	I.1	301

Course (11)
Vainlove:	for you to Course. We were certainly cut out for one . .	39	OLD BATCH	I.1	76
Sharper:	may say Marriage is entring into a Course of Physick. . .	44	OLD BATCH	I.1	292
Sharper:	another Course, are bound, ...	47	OLD BATCH	I.1	386
Jeremy:	that I reckon it will break of course by to morrow, and no	221	FOR LOVE	I.1	181
Trapland:	And I desire to know what Course you have taken . . .	222	FOR LOVE	I.1	240
Gonsalez:	They who are fled have that way bent their course. . .	363	M. BRIDE	IV.1	80
Zara:	And kindle Ruine in its Course. Think'st thou	375	M. BRIDE	V.1	96
Zara:	And kindle Ruine in its Course. Dost think	375	M. BRIDE	V.1	V 96
Fainall:	must be his of Course.	402	WAY WORLD	I.1	284
Mirabell:	You are not in a Course of Fools?	421	WAY WORLD	II.1	447
Lady Wish:	desperate Course.	478	WAY WORLD	V.1	612

Coursers (1)
Heartwell:	All Coursers the first Heat with Vigour run;	112	OLD BATCH	V.2	194

Courses (1)
Belinda:	my Sol, I'm afraid you'l follow evil Courses. . . .	55	OLD BATCH	II.2	52

Court (21)   see Tennis-Court, What-de-call-it-Court
Bellmour:	importunity at Court; first creates its own Interest, and	58	OLD BATCH	II.2	133
Lucy:	of your Lovers that should come empty-handed; as a Court .	61	OLD BATCH	III.1	21
Setter:	in another Court.	66	OLD BATCH	III.1	221
Heartwell:	Awake; Sigh much, Drink little, Eat less, court Solitude, .	73	OLD BATCH	III.2	81
Sharper:	Court: Not so much as wrinkle my Face with one Smile; . .	100	OLD BATCH	V.1	140

Creatures (5)
```
  Araminta:    Ay, Ccusin, and 'tis a sign the Creatures mimick    .   .   .  60   OLD BATCH  II.2   215
  Belinda:     my Dear,--I have seen such unhewn Creatures since,--Ha,      83   OLD BATCH  IV.3    11
  Belinda:     Out-landish Creatures! Such Tramontanae, and Foreigners   .  84   OLD BATCH  IV.3    31
  Mellefont:   We are your Lordships Creatures.  .   .   .   .   .   .   . 203   DOUEL DLR   V.1   585
  Tattle:      O, the Two most unfortunate poor Creatures in the   .   .  309   FOR LCVE    V.1   442
```
Credibly (1)
```
  Mirabell:    be credibly inform'd.   .   .   .   .   .   .   .   .   .  402   WAY WCRLD   I.1   267
```
Credit (7)
```
  Sir Joseph:  Limbo--But Sir I have a Letter cf Credit to Alderman    .   51   OLD BATCH  II.1   132
  Gonsalez:    I am a little slow of Credit, Sir,   .   .   .   .   .   . 366   M. EBIDE   IV.1   200
  Mirabell:    the Credit of the Nation, and prohibit the Exportation of  400   WAY WCRLD   I.1   205
  Mirabell:    fix'd a Father's Name with Credit, but on a Husband? I  . 417   WAY WORLD  II.1   269
  Mrs Fain:    I ought to stand in some degree of Credit with   .   .   . 417   WAY WCRLD  II.1   278
  Lady Wish:   whole Court upon a Birth day. I'll spoil his Credit with his 428  WAY WCRLD III.1   134
  Marwood:     to give credit against your Friend, to the Aspersions of  . 474  WAY WCRLD   V.1   484
```
Creditors (3)
```
  Jeremy:      Mouths of your Creditors? Will Plato be Bail for you? Or   217  FOR LCVE    I.1    29
  Scandal:     and gratifying your Creditors.   .   .   .   .   .   .   . 221  FOR LCVE    I.1   197
  Valentine:   of my Creditors for their Money, and my own impatience  . 225  FOR LOVE    I.1   340
```
Credulity (3)
```
  Vainlove:    Pox o' my sawcy Credulity.--If I have lost   .   .   .   . 100  OLD BATCH   V.1   125
  Maskwell:    Fools! then that hungry Gudgeon Credulity, will bite at  . 150  DOUEL DLR  III.1   459
  Fainall:     Corrupt to Superstition, and blind Credulity. I am single; 444  WAY WOBLD III.1   719
```
Credulous (3)
```
  Lady Touch:  She is so Credulous that way naturally, and   .   .   .   . 138  DOUEL DLR   I.1   412
  Zara:        You kncw how I abus'd the credulous King;  .   .   .   .   . 347  M. EBIDE   II.2   293
  Fainall:     of his pretended Passion? To undeceive the credulous   .  414  WAY WCRLD  II.1   159
```
Creeking (1)
```
  Zara:        And Crash of rusty Bars, and creeking Hinges:   .   .   . 379  M. BBIDE    V.2   138
```
Creep (1)
```
  Zara:        I'll creep into his Bosom, lay me there;   .   .   .   .  381  M. BBIDE    V.2   206
```
Creeps (1)
```
  Mellefont:   belonging--for on that night he creeps in at the Bed's   . 158  DOUEL DLR  III.1   281
```
Cremp (1)
```
  Mincing:     'Till I had the Cremp in my Fingers I'll vow Mem.   .   . 419  WAY WORLD  II.1   371
```
Crept (2)
```
  Leonora:     Have stoll'n frcm Bed, and to his Priscn crept:   .   .   . 326  M. EBIDE    I.1    25
  Zara:        Confess, and point the Path which thou hast crept.   .   . 375  M. BBIDE    V.1   110
```
Crest (2)
```
  Fainall:     Crest.  .   .   .   .   .   .   .   .   .   .   .   .   .  444  WAY WORLD III.1   723
  Sir Wilful:  Wilfull will do't, that's my Crest--my Motto I have forgot. 455  WAY WCRLD  IV.1   405
```
Crew (1)
```
  Ben:         If scme of our Crew that came to see me, are not gone;   . 274  FOR LOVE  III.1   790
```
Crew's (0)   see Ships-Crew's
Cries (9)   see Cry's, Crys
```
  Lucy:                             (Cries)   .   .   .   .   .   .   .   66  OLD BATCH III.1  V211
               Joseph, almost pushes him down, and Cries out.)   .   .   . 90  OLD BATCH  IV.4    50
  Laetitia:                         (Cries.)   .   .   .   .   .   .   .   95  OLD BATCH  IV.4   232
  Sir Paul:                         (Cries.)   .   .   .   .   .   .   .  161  DOUEL DLR  III.1   418
  Lady Ply:                         (Cries.)   .   .   .   .   .   .   .  170  DOUEL DLR   IV.1   121
  Ben:         Let her cry: The more she cries, the less she'll--she   . 265  FCR LCVE  III.1   441
  Scandal:     Service of your Sex. He that first cries out stop Thief, is 272 FCB LCVE  III.1   698
  Almeria:     I'll catch it--hark! a Voice cries Murder! 'tis   .   .   . 371  M. BBIDE   IV.1   391
  Almeria:     I'll catch it--hark! a Voice cries Murder! ah!   .   .   . 371  M. EBIDE   IV.1  V391
```
Crime (3)
```
  Lady Ply:    strike him with the remorse of his intended Crime.   .   . 145  DOUEL DLR  II.1   273
  Lady Ply:    not stay. Well, you must consider of your Crime; and   .  148  DOUEL DLR  II.1   363
  Selim:       I needs must fail; impute not as a Crime,  .   .   .   .  375  M. BBIDE    V.1   118
```
Crimes (4)
```
  Lady Touch:  more moved with the reflection of his Crimes, than of his  136  DOUBL DLR   I.1  V330
  Maskwell:    thy Beauty gild my Crimes; and whatsoever I commit of   .  150  DOUBL DLR  II.1   441
  Almeria:     But brands my Innocence with horrid Crimes,   .   .   .   . 368  M. EBIDE   IV.1   282
  Osmyn-Alph:  Whose Virtue has renounc'd thy Father's Crimes,   .   .   . 383  M. BBIDE    V.2   316
```
Criminals (1)
```
  Mirabell:    I must have leave for two Criminals to appear.   .   .   . 474  WAY WCRLD   V.1   468
```
Crimine (1)
```
  Lady Ply:    when 'tis Dark. O Crimine! I hope, Sir Paul has not seen  . 174  DOUEL DLR   IV.1   262
```
Crimson (1)
```
  Zara:        And curl their Crimson Heads, to kiss the Clouds!   .   . 380  M. EBIDE    V.2  V167
```
Cringing (1)
```
  Heartwell:   Cringing, and the drudgery of loving to boot.   .   .   .   44  OLD BATCH   I.1   275
```
Crips (2)
```
  Mincing:     and is so pure and sc crips.   .   .   .   .   .   .   .  420  WAY WORLD  II.1   374
  Witwoud:     Indeed, so crips?   .   .   .   .   .   .   .   .   .   . 420  WAY WCRLD  II.1   375
```
Critical (2)
```
  Maskwell:    you shall have notice at the critical minute to come and  . 157  DOUBL DLR  III.1   249
  Mrs Fain:    O Sir Wilfull; you are come at the Critical Instant. There's 446  WAY WORLD  IV.1    70
```
Critically (1)
```
  Careless:    And here's this Cox-Comb most Critically come to   .   .  128  DOUBL DLR   I.1    17
```
Criticism (1)
```
  Brisk:       tho' to prevent Criticism--only mark it with a small   .  165  DOUEL DLR  III.1  V551
```
Criticisms (1)
```
  Brisk:       tho' to prevent Criticisms--only mark it with a small   . 165  DOUEL DLR  III.1   551
```
Critick (4)
```
  Lady Ply:    Critick and so fine a Gentleman, that it is impossible for  159  DOUBL DLR  III.1   344
  Scandal:     Praise for Praise, and a Critick picking his Pocket. I have 233  FOR LOVE    I.1   652
               And know each Critick by his sowre Grimaces.   .   .   .  385  M. BRIDE    EPI.    6
  Mincing:     You're such a Critick, Mr. Witwoud.   .   .   .   .   .   . 420  WAY WORLD  II.1   376
```
Criticks (7)
```
               But then you cruel Criticks would so maul him!   .   .   . 113  OLD BATCH   EPI.   26
               Criticks avaunt; for you are Fish of Prey,   .   .   .   . 125  DOUBL DLB   PRO.   12
               The Lady Criticks, who are better Read,   .   .   .   .  204  DOUBL DLR   EPI.   21
  Scandal:     are huge Proportion'd Criticks, with long Wigs, Lac'd   . 233  FOR LOVE    I.1   654
               Criticks to Plays for the same end resort,   .   .   .   . 385  M. EBIDE    EPI.   15
               So Criticks throng to see a New Flay split,   .   .   .   . 385  M. EBIDE    EPI.   25
```

Criticks   (continued)

Dally (2)
| Lady Touch: | Death, do you dally with my Passion? | 135 | DOUBL DLR | I.1 | 320 |
| Maskwell: | Come, why do you dally with me thus? | 197 | DOUEL DLR | V.1 | 385 |

Dam (3)
Lord Touch:	Wife! Dam her,--she'll think to meet him in that	200	DOUEL DLR	V.1	483
Fainall:	hate my Wife yet more, Dam her, I'll part with her, rob	416	WAY WCRLD	II.1	244
Fainall:	Dam him, that had been mine--had you not made	442	WAY WCRLD	III.1	643

Damage (3)
Foible:	come tc no damage--Or else the Wealth of the Indies	463	WAY WCRLD	V.1	31
Lady Wish:	No damage? What to Betray me, tc Marry me	463	WAY WCRLD	V.1	34
Lady Wish:	Hospital for a decay'd Pimp? No damage? O thou frontless	463	WAY WCRLD	V.1	36

Damages (1)
| | There's no recov'ring Damages or Cost. | 323 | M. EBIDE | PRO. | 26 |

Dame (1)
| Mirabell: | Waitwell shake his Ears, and Dame Partlet rustle up her | 398 | WAY WCBLD | I.1 | 129 |

Damme (1)
| | Of Roaring Gamesters, and your Damme Bcys. | 315 | FOR LCVE | EPI. | 29 |

Damn (11)
	To save our Plays, or else we'll damn your Pit.	35	OLD BATCH	PRO.	9
Heartwell:	Damn her let her go, and a good riddance--Yet so	74	OLD EATCH	III.2	114
Capt Bluff:	Damn your Morals.	101	OLD BATCH	V.1	178
Capt Bluff:	Damn your Morals: I must revenge th' Affront done	101	OLD BATCH	V.1	180
Heartwell:	Damn ycur pity. But let me be calm a little.--	109	OLD BATCH	V.2	50
	You gain your End, and damn 'em when you've done.	113	OLD BATCH	EPI.	30
	You gain your Ends, and damn 'em when you've done.	113	OLD BATCH	EPI. V	30
	Let Nature work, and do not Damn too soon,	125	DOUBL DLR	PRO.	16
	Approve, or Damn the Repartee and Rallery.	204	DOUEL DLR	EPI.	20
	Damn him the more; have no Commiseration	393	WAY WCBLD	PBO.	24
	So Save or Damn, after your own Discretion.	393	WAY WCRLD	PRO.	40

Damn'd (34)
	Because, you know, if it be damn'd to day,	35	OLD EATCH	PRO.	24
Vainlove:	Zeal passes for true Devotion. I doubt it will be damn'd	39	OLD BATCH	I.1	67
Sir Joseph:	Um--Ay this, this is the very damn'd place; the	47	OLD BATCH	II.1	2
Sharper:	damn'd unlucky place--	48	OLD BATCH	II.1	18
Sir Joseph:	damn'd angry Fellow--I believe I had better remember	48	OLD BATCH	II.1	44
Sir Joseph:	Sir--a damn'd hot Fellow--only as I was saying, I let him	51	OLD BATCH	II.1	130
Sir Joseph:	Ay, this damn'd Modesty of yours--Agad if	53	OLD BATCH	II.1	214
Lucy:	Neither; but what was ten times worse, with damn'd,	61	OLD BATCH	III.1	18
Heartwell:	thou Delicious, Damn'd, Dear, destructive Wcman!	63	OLD BATCH	III.1	77
Sharper:	Never leave this damn'd illnatur'd whimsey Frank?	79	OLD EATCH	IV.1	171
Bellmour:	(peeping). Damn'd Chance! If I had gone a-Whoring	92	OLD EATCH	IV.4	109
Sir Joseph:	no Quality at all, 'tis such a Damn'd ugly Hand.	103	OLD BATCH	V.1	272
Heartwell:	Damn'd, damn'd Strumpet! Cou'd she not contain her	107	OLD EATCH	V.2	5
Maskwell:	She has a damn'd penetrating head, and knows how to	155	DOUBL DLR	III.1	181
Brisk:	engaging Creature, if she were not so fond of that damn'd	175	DOUBL DLR	IV.1	292
Sir Paul:	be Damn'd for a Judas Maccabeus, and Iscariot both. O	178	DOUEL DLR	IV.1	418
Lady Touch:	Be Damn'd.	184	DOUEL DLR	IV.2	50
Lady Touch:	so damn'd a Sin as Incest! unnatural Incest!	186	DOUEL DLR	IV.2	100
Mellefont:	Confusion, my Uncle! O the damn'd Sorceress.	186	DOUEL DLR	IV.2	111
Lady Touch:	indebted to him, if you knew all, damn'd Villain! oh, I am	191	DOUBL DLR	V.1	143
Jeremy:	you, or be damn'd with your Works: But to live even	218	FOR LOVE	I.1	73
Sr Sampson:	damn'd Tyburn face, without the benefit o' the Clergy.	243	FOR LOVE	II.1	307
Valentine:	O the Devil, what damn'd Costive Poet has given	255	FOR LCVE	III.1	73
Tattle:	damn'd sort of a Life.	309	FOR LOVE	V.1	468
	May now be damn'd to animate an Ass;	315	FOR LOVE	EPI.	22
	For that damn'd Poet's spar'd whc draws a Brother,	323	M. EBIDE	PRO.	31
Osmyn-Alph:	What dc the Damn'd endure, but to despair,	358	M. EBIDE	III.1	365
Zara:	(aside). Damn'd, damn'd Dissembler! Yet I will be calm,	359	M. EBIDE	III.1	406
Manuel:	With damn'd Conspirators, to take my Life.	368	M. EBIDE	IV.1	271
	Of a damn'd Poet, and departed Muse!	385	M. BBIDE	EPI.	12
Sir Wilful:	And be damn'd over Tea-Cups and Coffee.	456	WAY WORLD	IV.1	454
	But that they have been Damn'd for want of wit.	479	WAY WORLD	EPI.	13

Damnable (1)
| Garcia: | And bathe it to the Hilt, in far less damnable | 378 | M. EBIDE | V.2 | 79 |

Damnably (2)
| Bellmour: | damnably in Love; I'm so uneasie for not seeing Belinda | 40 | OLD EATCH | I.1 | 133 |
| Bellmour: | damnably in Love; I'm so uneasie for not having seen Belinda | 40 | OLD EATCH | I.1 V133 |

Damnation (7)
Mellefont:	(aside). Hell and Damnation! this is my Aunt; such	145	DOUEL DLR	II.1	270
Lord Touch:	No, no, no--Damnation!	153	DOUBL DLR	III.1	93
Mellefont:	Damnation!	186	DOUEL DLR	IV.2	105
Lady Touch:	Damnation proof, a Devil already, and Fire is his Element.	191	DOUEL DLR	V.1 V153
Lord Touch:	of unheard of Treachery. My Wife! Damnation! my	200	DOUBL DLR	V.1	472
Manuel:	Damnation!	369	M. EBIDE	IV.1	340
Fainall:	Very likely Sir, What's here? Damnation! (Reads) A	476	WAY WCRLD	V.1	550

Damns (1)
| Valentine: | Souls in Westminster-Abby, or damns more in Westminster-Hall? | 280 | FOR LOVE | IV.1 | 177 |

Damp (2)
| Zara: | Strike, damp, deaden her Charms, and kill his Eyes; | 359 | M. BRIDE | III.1 | 401 |
| Almeria: | Behold a damp, dead Hand has drop'd a Dagger; | 371 | M. BRIDE | IV.1 | 390 |

Damp'd (2)
| Osmyn-Alph: | This Den for Slaves, this Dungeon damp'd with Woes; | 357 | M. BRIDE | III.1 | 327 |
| Garcia: | The Horrour of that Thought, has damp'd my Rage. | 378 | M. EBIDE | V.2 | 74 |

Dampness (1)
| Careless: | your favour--I feel my Spirits faint, a general dampness | 170 | DOUBL DLR | IV.1 | 114 |

Damps (1)
| Almeria: | And all the Damps of Grief, that did retard their Flight; | 330 | M. BBIDE | I.1 | 158 |

Dams (1)
| | For that damn'd Poet's spar'd who dams a Brother, | 323 | M. BBIDE | PRO. | 31 |

Damsel (1)
| Setter: | Good Words, Damsel, or I shall--But how dost | 65 | OLD EATCH | III.1 | 171 |

Danc'd (2)
| Heartwell: | Why 'twas I Sung and Danc'd; I gave Musick to | 72 | OLD BATCH | III.2 | 32 |
| Sr Sampson: | warrant you, if he danc'd till Doomsday, he thought I | 240 | FOR LOVE | II.1 | 179 |

Dance (19)   see Country-Dance

Speaker	Quote	PAGE	TITLE	ACT.SC	LINE
	(After the Song, a Dance of Antick.)	71	OLD BATCH	III.2	25
Silvia:	If you could Sing and Dance so, I should love to look	72	OLD BATCH	III.2	30
Heartwell:	one Guinea rhymes to another--And how they dance	72	OLD BATCH	III.2	36
	(A Dance.)	112	OLD BATCH	V.2	181
Brisk:	Froth won't Dance at your Wedding to Morrow; nor	129	DOUBL DLR	I.1	56
Sir Paul:	Go, go Child, go, get you gone and Dance and be	175	DOUBL DLR	IV.1	280
Lady Froth:	then joyn hands again; I could teach my Lord this Dance	177	DOUBL DLR	IV.1	367
Lady Froth:	--Shall you and I do our close Dance to show	177	DOUBL DLR	IV.1	374
Lord Froth:	Any other time, my Dear, or we'll Dance it	177	DOUBL DLR	IV.1	381
Ben:	you shall see, that we Sailors can Dance sometimes, as well	274	FOR LOVE	III.1	791
	(Dance.)	275	FOR LOVE	III.1	798
Sr Sampson:	and yet you shall live to dance at my Wedding; faith and	307	FOR LOVE	V.1	384
Sr Sampson:	Dance in via Lactea.	307	FOR LOVE	V.1	387
Scandal:	tho' it be Morning, we may have a Dance.	313	FOR LOVE	V.1	601
	(Dance.)	313	FOR LOVE	V.1	618
Servant-M:	behind one another, as 'twere in a Country Dance. Ours	398	WAY WORLD	I.1	114
	(Dance.)	459	WAY WORLD	IV.1	568
Sir Wilful:	Dance in the mean time, that we who are not Lovers, may	477	WAY WORLD	V.1	601
	(A Dance.)	478	WAY WORLD	V.1	607

Dancers (3)

Speaker	Quote	PAGE	TITLE	ACT.SC	LINE
Lady Wish:	And are the Dancers and the Musick ready,	445	WAY WORLD	IV.1	11
Foible:	Madam, the Dancers are ready, and there's one with a	459	WAY WORLD	IV.1	549
Lady Wish:	Call in the Dancers;--Sir Rowland, we'll	459	WAY WORLD	IV.1	566

Dances (2)

Speaker	Quote	PAGE	TITLE	ACT.SC	LINE
Heartwell:	here Silvia, here are Songs and Dances, Poetry and Musick	72	OLD BATCH	III.2	34
Jeremy:	Country Dances; and the like; I don't much matter your	245	FOR LOVE	II.1	374

Dancing (4)

Speaker	Quote	PAGE	TITLE	ACT.SC	LINE
Heartwell:	burdens, are forced to undergo Dressing, Dancing, Singing,	44	OLD BATCH	I.1	273
Cynthia:	As dancing without a Fiddle.	163	DOUBL DLR	III.1	479
Lady Wish:	lectures, against Singing and Dancing, and such Debaucheries;	467	WAY WORLD	V.1	198
Witwoud:	in a maze yet, like a Dog in a Dancing School.	477	WAY WORLD	V.1	591

Dandle (1)

Speaker	Quote	PAGE	TITLE	ACT.SC	LINE
Heartwell:	Baby for a Girl to dandle. O dotage, dotage! That ever	72	OLD BATCH	III.2	47

Dane (1)

Speaker	Quote	PAGE	TITLE	ACT.SC	LINE
Fainall:	disable him for that, he will drink like a Dane: after dinner,	443	WAY WORLD	III.1	672

Danger (16)

Speaker	Quote	PAGE	TITLE	ACT.SC	LINE
Vainlove:	a Venture which he's in danger of losing. Read, read.	39	OLD BATCH	I.1	81
Araminta:	then we are in great danger of being dull--If my Musick-master	58	OLD BATCH	II.2	152
Heartwell:	on't--I'le run into the danger to lose the	63	OLD BATCH	III.1	85
Sir Joseph:	were no danger, I'le be so ungrateful to take it from the	67	OLD BATCH	III.1	256
Sir Joseph:	I was in most danger of being ravish'd, if you go	90	OLD BATCH	IV.4	62
	I will not say, we'd all in danger been,	125	DOUBL DLR	PRO.	21
Maskwell:	No sinking, nor no danger,--come, cheer up;	148	DOUBL DLR	II.1	391
Lady Froth:	There he's secure from danger of a bilk,	164	DOUBL DLR	III.1	540
Foresight:	danger of Hanging.	243	FOR LOVE	II.1	310
Scandal:	why shou'd a Man court Danger, or a Woman shun	271	FOR LOVE	III.1	671
Ben:	at these years, there's more danger of your head's aking	286	FOR LOVE	IV.1	383
Osmyn-Alph:	Because not knowing Danger. But look forward;	358	M. BRIDE	III.1	342
Zara:	Shall I prevent, or stop th' approaching Danger?	362	M. BRIDE	IV.1	43
Zara:	You're too secure: The Danger is more imminent	364	M. BRIDE	IV.1	109
Lady Wish:	O he's in less Danger of being spoil'd by his	431	WAY WORLD	III.1	262
Lady Wish:	danger.	474	WAY WORLD	V.1	466

Dangerous (5)

Speaker	Quote	PAGE	TITLE	ACT.SC	LINE
Maskwell:	Gamester--but shou'd he find me out before! 'tis dangerous	190	DOUBL DLR	V.1	88
Mrs Frail:	and if we keep 'em from Air, not at all dangerous:	248	FOR LOVE	II.1	481
Scandal:	it more dangerous to be seen in Conversation with me, than	272	FOR LOVE	III.1	695
Zara:	To love above him, for 'tis dangerous:	348	M. BRIDE	II.2	342
Mirabell:	Why do we daily commit disagreeable and dangerous	417	WAY WORLD	II.1	265

Dangers (2)

Speaker	Quote	PAGE	TITLE	ACT.SC	LINE
Sir Joseph:	through all dangers--he is indeed Back, Breast and Headpiece	50	OLD BATCH	II.1	120
Zara:	The Dangers which I 'tempted to conceal you.	347	M. BRIDE	II.2	292

Dangling (2)

Speaker	Quote	PAGE	TITLE	ACT.SC	LINE
Lady Wish:	that, Changeling, dangling thy Hands like Bobbins before	425	WAY WORLD	III.1	14
Lady Wish:	a little dangling off, Jogging in a thoughtful way--Yes--	445	WAY WORLD	IV.1	26

Daphne (1)

Speaker	Quote	PAGE	TITLE	ACT.SC	LINE
Mirabell:	--Like Daphne she as lovely and as Coy. Do you	449	WAY WORLD	IV.1	155

Dar'd (2)

Speaker	Quote	PAGE	TITLE	ACT.SC	LINE
Bellmour:	and even dar'd Discovery--This Cloak my Sanctity,	80	OLD BATCH	IV.2	5
	Not one has dar'd to lash this Crying Age.	214	FOR LOVE	PRO.	40

Dar'st (5)

Speaker	Quote	PAGE	TITLE	ACT.SC	LINE
Zara:	Dost fear so much, thou dar'st not wish. The King!	348	M. BRIDE	II.2	347
Manuel:	What dar'st thou to my Face avow thy Guilt?	369	M. BRIDE	IV.1	315
Manuel:	Hence, Slave, how dar'st thou bide, to watch and pry	373	M. BRIDE	V.1	39
Manuel:	Dar'st thou reply? Take that--thy Service? thine?	374	M. BRIDE	V.1	69
Zara:	I'll give thee Freedom, if thou dar'st be free:	376	M. BRIDE	V.1	136

Dare (28)

Speaker	Quote	PAGE	TITLE	ACT.SC	LINE
Capt Bluff:	Good Mr. Sharper speak to him; I dare not look	54	OLD BATCH	II.1	238
Bellmour:	Faith, Madam, I dare not speak to her, but I'll	60	OLD BATCH	II.2	210
Lucy:	a Mumper in Love, lies Canting at the Gate; but never dare	66	OLD BATCH	III.1	193
Singer:	I cannot, dare not, must not hear:	71	OLD BATCH	III.2	V 11
Silvia:	I dare not speak till I believe you, and indeed I'm	72	OLD BATCH	III.2	53
Belinda:	Of a very ancient one, I dare swear, by their Dress.	84	OLD BATCH	IV.3	38
Sharper:	which narrow Souls cannot dare to admire.--And	86	OLD BATCH	IV.3	127
Lady Froth:	call it? I dare Swear you won't guesse--The Sillibub,	141	DOUBL DLR	II.1	122
Cynthia:	Pray, Sir, stay, hear him, I dare affirm he's innocent.	146	DOUBL DLR	II.1	274
Lady Ply:	necessity--O Lord, here's some body coming, I dare	148	DOUBL DLR	II.1	362
Lady Touch:	--I dare swear he's sorry--and were it to do again, would	152	DOUBL DLR	III.1	77
Lady Ply:	dare swear every Circumstance of me trembles.--O your	178	DOUBL DLR	IV.1	398
Mellefont:	No, no; ha, ha, I dare swear thou wilt not.	193	DOUBL DLR	V.1	229
Cynthia:	I dare answer for him.	200	DOUBL DLR	V.1	480
	And dare not bite, for fear of being bit.	214	FOR LOVE	PRO.	36
Scandal:	Yes, but I dare trust you; We were talking of	254	FOR LOVE	III.1	45

Dare   (continued)
Angelica:	I dare swear you wrong him, it is his own--And	255	FOR LOVE	III.1	75
Valentine:	Not once, I dare answer for him.	256	FOR LOVE	III.1	108
Osmyn-Alph:	But who shall dare to tax Eternal Justice!	350	M. BRIDE	III.1	32
Zara:	Dare you dispute the King's Command? Behold	359	M. BRIDE	III.1	377
Zara:	Regard me well; and dare not to reply	375	M. BRIDE	V.1	128
Mrs Fain:	Mirabell, and I dare promise you will oblige us both.	412	WAY WORLD	II.1	107
Marwood:	worse than when you had her--I dare swear she had given	442	WAY WORLD	III.1	651
Millamant:	never sure in Love. O, I hate a Lover, that can dare to think,	449	WAY WORLD	IV.1	175
Mrs Fain:	my own Innocence, and dare stand by a tryall.	466	WAY WORLD	V.1	178
Mrs Fain:	my own Innocence, and dare stand a tryall.	466	WAY WORLD	V.1	V178
Marwood:	That condition I dare answer, my Lady will	468	WAY WORLD	V.1	258
Sir Wilful:	frown, she can't kill you;--besides--Hearkee she dare not	471	WAY WORLD	V.1	361

Dares (6)
Capt Bluff:	--He sucks not vital Air who dares affirm it to this	70	OLD BATCH	III.1	353
Bellmour:	O my Conscience she dares not consent, for fear	112	OLD BATCH	V.2	175
	Tho Satire scarce dares grin, 'tis grown so mild;	213	FOR LOVE	PRO.	33
Zara:	A Slave, not daring to be free! nor dares	348	M. BRIDE	II.2	341
Manuel:	What's he that dares be Rival to the King?	348	M. BRIDE	II.2	356
	For so Reform'd a Town, who dares Correct?	393	WAY WORLD	PRO.	32

Daring (3)
Heartwell:	you abate of your vigor; and that daring Blade which was	43	OLD BATCH	I.1	248
Zara:	A Slave, not daring to be free! nor dares	348	M. BRIDE	II.2	341
Manuel:	'Tis daring for a God. Hence, to the Wheel	349	M. BRIDE	II.2	371

Dark (15)
Mellefont:	Malice, like a Dark Lanthorn, onely shone upon me,	129	DOUBL DLR	I.1	90
Mellefont:	Malice, like a Dark Lanthorn, only shone upon me,	129	DOUBL DLR	I.1	V 90
Mellefont:	and next to being in the dark, or alone, they are most truly	158	DOUBL DLR	III.1	313
Lady Ply:	when 'tis Dark. O Crimine! I hope, Sir Paul has not seen	174	DOUBL DLR	IV.1	262
Mellefont:	dark--	186	DOUBL DLR	IV.2	V126
Lord Touch:	upon Villany! Heavens, what a long track of dark deceit	199	DOUBL DLR	V.1	469
Angelica:	a Voyage to Greenland, to inhabit there all the dark	237	FOR LOVE	II.1	84
Valentine:	not a word. Hymen shall put his Torch into a dark Lanthorn,	290	FOR LOVE	IV.1	549
Osmyn-Alph:	In a dark Corner of my Cell, I found	350	M. BRIDE	III.1	6
Osmyn-Alph:	And promises a Day to this dark Dwelling!	353	M. BRIDE	III.1	141
Almeria:	Give thy Soul Way, and tell me thy dark Thought.	356	M. BRIDE	III.1	274
Osmyn-Alph:	Is this dark Cell, a Temple for that God?	357	M. BRIDE	III.1	325
Zara:	Yet I'll be calm--Dark and unknown Betrayer!	360	M. BRIDE	III.1	439
Gonsalez:	Ha! sure he sleeps--all's dark within, save what	376	M. BRIDE	V.2	6
Zara:	O now he's gone, and all is dark--	381	M. BRIDE	V.2	211

Dark'ned (1)
| Manuel: | Be dark'ned, so as to amuze the Sight. | 374 | M. BRIDE | V.1 | 85 |

Darling (4)
Almeria:	Some unsuspected hoard of darling Grief,	328	M. BRIDE	I.1	84
Lady Wish:	Darling. Paint, Paint, Paint, dost thou understand	425	WAY WORLD	III.1	13
Millamant:	shall I leave thee? My faithful Solitude, my darling	449	WAY WORLD	IV.1	186
Fainall:	Wishfort, must be subscrib'd, or your Darling Daughter's	473	WAY WORLD	V.1	442

Darted (2)
| Zara: | And thrill'd thee through with darted Fires; but thou | 348 | M. BRIDE | II.2 | 346 |
| Zara: | His Eyes like Meteors roll'd, then darted down | 374 | M. BRIDE | V.1 | 93 |

Darts (3)
Belinda:	Creature to have had Darts, and Flames, and Altars, and all	55	OLD BATCH	II.2	29
Osmyn-Alph:	Grief wou'd not double thus, his Darts against me.	356	M. BRIDE	III.1	283
Osmyn-Alph:	Grief cou'd not double thus, his Darts against me.	356	M. BRIDE	III.1	V283

Dash (6)   see Slap-dash
Ben:	Anchor at Cuckolds-point; so there's a dash for you, take	287	FOR LOVE	IV.1	441
Almeria:	Kill me, kill me then, dash me with thy Chains;	357	M. BRIDE	III.1	297
Osmyn-Alph:	Then will I smear these Walls with Blood, dash my	358	M. BRIDE	III.1	350
Osmyn-Alph:	And dash my Face, and rive my clotted Hair,	358	M. BRIDE	III.1	V351
Manuel:	Sudden I'll start, and dash her with her Guilt.	374	M. BRIDE	V.1	V86F
Zara:	Dash your encountering Streams, with mutual Violence,	380	M. BRIDE	V.2	V165

Dash'd (4)
Almeria:	And bulging 'gainst a Rock, was dash'd in pieces.	329	M. BRIDE	I.1	127
Osmyn-Alph:	But dash'd with Rain from Eyes, and swail'd with Sighs,	357	M. BRIDE	III.1	323
Zara:	And ever and anon, the Sight was dash'd	379	M. BRIDE	V.2	139
Osmyn-Alph:	Yet am I dash'd to think that thou must weep;	383	M. BRIDE	V.2	303

Date (6)
Sharper:	present Date hereof.--How say you?	110	OLD BATCH	V.2	88
	For in One Year, I think they're out of Date.	323	M. BRIDE	PRO.	6
Manuel:	Thy senseless Vow appear'd to bear its Date,	333	M. BRIDE	I.1	299
Waitwell:	Enough, his date is short.	461	WAY WORLD	IV.1	621
Fainall:	Your date of deliberation Madam, is expir'd. Here is	472	WAY WORLD	V.1	414
Mirabell:	Elder Date than what you have obtain'd from your Lady.	476	WAY WORLD	V.1	555

Daughter (34)
Sir Paul:	Do you think my Daughter, this pretty Creature;	145	DOUBL DLR	II.1	264
Lady Ply:	you think to reverse Nature so, to make the Daughter the	146	DOUBL DLR	II.1	306
Mellefont:	The Daughter procure the Mother!	146	DOUBL DLR	II.1	308
Mellefont:	The Daughter to procure the Mother!	146	DOUBL DLR	II.1	V308
Lady Ply:	guilt of deceiving every body; Marrying the Daughter,	147	DOUBL DLR	II.1	315
Lady Ply:	no sin,--but then, to Marry my Daughter, for the	147	DOUBL DLR	II.1	350
Lady Touch:	Plyant, if he refuse his Daughter upon this Provocation?	150	DOUBL DLR	III.1	2
Sir Paul:	Daughter, and a fine dutiful Child she is, though I say it,	161	DOUBL DLR	IV.1	412
Lady Ply:	made plain--I don't see how my Daughter can in	172	DOUBL DLR	IV.1	169
Brisk:	Daughter your self; you're always brooding over her like	174	DOUBL DLR	IV.1	272
Valentine:	your handsome Daughter--Come a good Husband to	222	FOR LOVE	I.1	251
Mrs Frail:	Daughter is come out of the Country--I assure you,	231	FOR LOVE	I.1	568
Foresight:	my Daughter?	235	FOR LOVE	II.1	3
Sr Sampson:	his Right of Inheritance. Where's my Daughter that is to	240	FOR LOVE	II.1	183
Foresight:	send your Son to Sea alone. I'll wed my Daughter to an	241	FOR LOVE	II.1	238
Tattle:	I was reveng'd upon him, for he had a handsom Daughter	258	FOR LOVE	III.1	172
Foresight:	but methinks your Love to my Daughter was a Secret I	304	FOR LOVE	V.1	257
Foresight:	marry my Daughter without my Consent?	304	FOR LOVE	V.1	283
Tattle:	Daughter, Sir.	305	FOR LOVE	V.1	285
Tattle:	more love for your Daughter, than I have likeness of you;	305	FOR LOVE	V.1	288
Manuel:	My Daughter should have revell'd at his Death.	333	M. BRIDE	I.1	310

Day (continued)

Jeremy:	much to seek in playing the Madman to day.	276	FOR LOVE	IV.1	5
Sr Sampson:	Hey day, Rascal, do you banter me? Sirrah,	279	FOR LOVE	IV.1	127
Valentine:	Westminster-Hall the first Day of every Term--Let me see	280	FOR LOVE	IV.1	173
Valentine:	had inform'd you of to Day, but you were gone, before	294	FOR LOVE	IV.1	720
Foresight:	Hey day! What time of the Moon is this?	305	FOR LOVE	V.1	286
Angelica:	The Miracle to Day is, that we find	314	FOR LOVE	V.1	636
	These Walls but t'other Day were fill'd with Noise	315	FOR LOVE	EPI.	28
Almeria:	Ev'n on the Day when Manuel, my Father,	329	M. BRIDE	I.1	111
Almeria:	That Day, that fatal Day, our Hands were joyn'd:	329	M. BRIDE	I.1	133
Almeria:	And in one Day, was wedded, and a Widow.	329	M. BRIDE	I.1	141
Gonsalez:	Be every Day of your long Life like this.	331	M. BRIDE	I.1	220
Gonsalez:	And bless this Day with most unequal Lustre.	331	M. BRIDE	I.1	223
Gonsalez:	And bless this Day with most unequal'd Lustre.	331	M. BRIDE	I.1	V223
Manuel:	Upon this solemn Day, in these sad Weeds?	333	M. BRIDE	I.1	280
Manuel:	That Life, which Heav'n preserv'd. A Day bestow'd	333	M. BRIDE	I.1	290
Manuel:	To see that Sable worn upon the Day	333	M. BRIDE	I.1	295
Manuel:	To day--Retire, divest your self with speed	334	M. BRIDE	I.1	323
Manuel:	This Day we triumph; but to morrow's Sun	334	M. BRIDE	I.1	342
Manuel:	Fix'd her by Force, and snatch'd the doubtful Day.	337	M. BRIDE	I.1	457
Manuel:	Her shining from the Day, to gild this Scene	348	M. BRIDE	II.2	353
Zara:	And me; presume to day to plead audacious Love,	349	M. BRIDE	II.2	366
Zara:	Presume to day to plead audacious Love,	349	M. BRIDE	II.2	V366
Manuel:	And Love, shall wing the tedious-wasting Day.	349	M. BRIDE	II.2	388
Osmyn-Alph:	The Book of Prescience, he beheld this Day;	353	M. BRIDE	III.1	133
Osmyn-Alph:	He in the Book of Prescience, he saw this Day;	353	M. BRIDE	III.1	V133
Osmyn-Alph:	And promises a Day to this dark Dwelling!	353	M. BRIDE	III.1	141
Manuel:	Will quickly waste, and give again the Day.	364	M. BRIDE	IV.1	108
Manuel:	In waking Anguish? why this, on the Day	367	M. BRIDE	IV.1	250
Manuel:	Nor shall the guilty Horrours of this Day	367	M. BRIDE	IV.1	255
Almeria:	Henceforth are equal; this the Day of Death,	367	M. BRIDE	IV.1	258
Osmyn-Alph:	Then double on the Day reflected Light.	383	M. BRIDE	V.2	287
Mirabell:	Not at all: I happen to be grave to day; and you are	395	WAY WORLD	I.1	15
Mirabell:	hopes, one Day or other to hate her heartily: To which	399	WAY WORLD	I.1	167
Fainall:	He is expected to Day. Do you know him?	400	WAY WORLD	I.1	189
Witwoud:	--I have no Luck to Day.	402	WAY WORLD	I.1	280
Witwoud:	once a Day at publick Places.	405	WAY WORLD	I.1	361
Marwood:	as to wish to have been born Old, because we one Day	410	WAY WORLD	II.1	15
Fainall:	You don't look well to Day, Child.	412	WAY WORLD	II.1	89
Fainall:	Nothing remains when that Day comes, but to sit down	413	WAY WORLD	II.1	115
Millamant:	O I have deny'd my self Airs to Day. I have walk'd	418	WAY WORLD	II.1	333
Witwoud:	I confess I do blaze to Day, I am too bright.	419	WAY WORLD	II.1	344
Mincing:	with Poetry, it sits so pleasant the next Day as any Thing,	420	WAY WORLD	II.1	373
Mirabell:	--What, billing so sweetly! Is not Valentine's Day over	423	WAY WORLD	II.1	502
Waitwell:	Day! 'Tis enough to make any Man forget himself. The	424	WAY WORLD	II.1	556
Marwood:	at this time of day.	426	WAY WORLD	III.1	44
Lady Wish:	whole Court upon a Birth day. I'll spoil his Credit with his	428	WAY WORLD	III.1	134
Marwood:	Care, like any Chymist upon the Day of Projection.	431	WAY WORLD	III.1	248
Millamant:	Chambermaid after a day or two.	433	WAY WORLD	III.1	307
Sir Wilful:	time; and rail when that day comes.	441	WAY WORLD	III.1	612
Mrs Fain:	You are very fond of Sir John Suckling to day,	446	WAY WORLD	IV.1	55
Mirabell:	together with all Vizards for the day, I prohibit all Masks	451	WAY WORLD	IV.1	248
Sir Wilful:	day Cozen--I am a Borachio. But if you have a mind to be	455	WAY WORLD	IV.1	410
Lady Wish:	Vehemence.--But a day or two for decency of	458	WAY WORLD	IV.1	496
Mrs Fain:	thing discover'd. This is the last day of our living together,	464	WAY WORLD	V.1	82
Witwoud:	Hey day! what are you all got together like Players	475	WAY WORLD	V.1	521
Lady Wish:	have wasted my spirits so to day already; that I am ready	478	WAY WORLD	V.1	609

Day-break (1)

Zara:	When I beheld the Day-break of thy Eyes,	347	M. BRIDE	II.2	286

Day's (1)

Gonsalez:	And of a piece with this Day's dire Misdeeds.	379	M. BRIDE	V.2	123

Days (19)   see Dog-days, Now-a-days

	How this vile World is chang'd! In former days,	35	OLD BATCH	PRO.	1
Capt Bluff:	Hannibal was a very pretty Fellow in those Days, it must	52	OLD BATCH	II.1	180
Heartwell:	the Jest of the Town: Nay in two Days, I expect to be	63	OLD BATCH	III.1	79
Lucy:	Remember to Days behaviour--Let me see you with a	67	OLD BATCH	III.1	232
Heartwell:	Ay, ay, in old days People married where they	73	OLD BATCH	III.2	103
Lady Touch:	heard any thing from him these two days.	153	DOUBL DLR	III.1	98
Lord Touch:	These two days! Is it so fresh? Unnatural	153	DOUBL DLR	III.1	99
Lady Froth:	spent two days together in going about Covent-Garden to	165	DOUBL DLR	III.1	563
Lord Touch:	Days attend you both; mutual Love, lasting Health, and	203	DOUBL DLR	V.1	588
Jeremy:	Three days, the Life of a Play, I no more expect it, than to	218	FOR LOVE	I.1	74
Tattle:	be receiv'd but upon Publick Days; and my Visits will	230	FOR LOVE	I.1	516
Tattle:	and bred in Covent-Garden, all the days of your Life;--	252	FOR LOVE	II.1	645
Osmyn-Alph:	Days,	343	M. BRIDE	II.2	136
Almeria:	All Days, to me,	367	M. BRIDE	IV.1	257
Mirabell:	Hour less and less disturbance; 'till in a few Days it became	399	WAY WORLD	I.1	170
Marwood:	wou'd now and then find Days of Grace, and be worn for	433	WAY WORLD	III.1	302
Sir Wilful:	of late Days.	440	WAY WORLD	III.1	553
Sir Wilful:	these days, Cozen, in the mean while, I must answer in	447	WAY WORLD	IV.1	111
Marwood:	hear nothing else for some days.	468	WAY WORLD	V.1	236

De (0)   see Valet de Chambre, Valet de chambre, What-de-call-it-Court

De'e (10)

Capt Bluff:	see it; Sir I say you can't see; what de'e say to that now?	53	OLD BATCH	II.1	235
Araminta:	So, how de'e like the Song, Gentlemen?	60	OLD BATCH	II.2	203
Sir Joseph:	mad? Or de'e think I'm mad? Agad for my part, I don't	68	OLD BATCH	III.1	265
Brisk:	I can't hit of her Name neither--Let me see; Paints de'e say?	166	DOUBL DLR	III.1	584
Lady Ply:	De'e see here? Look, read it? (Snatches the Letter as in	179	DOUBL DLR	IV.1	441
Tattle:	De'e you think you can Love me?	251	FOR LOVE	IV.1	602
Ben:	then put off with the next fair wind. How de'e like us?	275	FOR LOVE	III.1	803
Mrs Frail:	How de'e now, Sir? Can I serve you?	290	FOR LOVE	IV.1	545
Tattle:	But in short, de'e see, I will hold you a Hundred Pound	291	FOR LOVE	IV.1	608
Tattle:	Why de'e think I'll tell you, Sir! Read it in my Face?	292	FOR LOVE	IV.1	612

Dead (31)
```
Laetitia:      you; and when I am dead with grief, may you have one   .  .   78   OLD BATCH   IV.1   109
Lady Touch:    Thunder strike thee Dead for this Deceit,  .  .  .  .  .  . 184   DOUEL DLR   IV.2    44
Sr Sampson:    Support, like Ivy round a dead Oak: Faith I do; I love to . 260   FOR LOVE    III.1  264
Sr Sampson:    Dick, body o' me, Dick has been dead these two   .  .  .  . 261   FOR LOVE    III.1  292
Ben:           Mess, and that's true: marry I had forgot. Dick's dead   . 261   FCB LOVE    III.1  294
Ben:           Mess, that's true: marry I had forgot. Dick's dead   .  . 261   FOR LCVE    III.1 V294
Sr Sampson:    Gone! What, he is not dead?  .  .  .  .  .  .  .  .  .  . 278   FOR LOVE    IV.1   120
Jeremy:        No, Sir, not dead.  .  .  .  .  .  .  .  .  .  .  .  .  . 278   FOR LCVE    IV.1   121
Valentine:     and we'll be Marry'd in the dead of Night.--Eut say   .  . 290   FOR LCVE    IV.1   548
Garcia:        Choosing this lonely Mansion of the Dead,  .  .  .  .  . 337   M. ERIDE    II.1     2
Osmyn-Alph:    And growing to his dead Father's Shrowd, roots up   .  .  . 341   M. EBRIDE   II.2    39
Osmyn-Alph:    Nor Dead, nor Shade, but breathing and alive!   .  .  .  . 341   M. EBRIDE   II.2    55
Osmyn-Alph:    Dead Father's Elood; Nay, which refus'd to hear   .  .  . 351   M. EBRIDE   III.1   76
Zara:          And force their Balls abroad, at this dead Hour.   .  .  . 355   M. EBRIDE   III.1  210
Zara:          To have contending Queens, at dead of Night   .  .  .  . 360   M. EBRIDE   III.1  427
Zara:          When he is dead, I must despair for ever.  .  .  .  .  . 362   M. EBRIDE   IV.1    30
Almeria:       Behold a damp, dead Hand has drop'd a Dagger;   .  .  .  . 371   M. EBRIDE   IV.1   390
Gonsalez:      The Moor, is dead. That Osmyn was Alphonso;   .  .  .  . 377   M. EBRIDE   V.2     41
Garcia:        Dead, welt'ring, drown'd in Blood.   .  .  .  .  .  .  . 377   M. EBRIDE   V.2     60
Alonzo:        Or who can wcund the Dead?--I've from the Body,   .  .  . 379   M. EBRIDE   V.2    114
Selim:         I found the dead and bloody Body strip'd--   .  .  .  .  . 380   M. EBRIDE   V.2    182
Zara:          'Tis not that he is dead: for 'twas decreed   .  .  .  .  . 380   M. EBRIDE   V.2    187
Leonora:       Zara all pale and dead! two frightful Men,   .  .  .  .  . 381   M. EBRIDE   V.2    223
Almeria:       Is it at last then so? is he then dead?   .  .  .  .  .  . 382   M. BRIDE    V.2    232
Almeria:       What dead at last, quite, quite, for ever dead?   .  .  . 382   M. EBRIDE   V.2    233
Almeria:       That Sense, which in one Instant shews him dead   .  .  . 383   M. EBRIDE   V.2    294
Mirabell:      Fame, wou'd shew us dim by thee as a dead Whiting's  .  . 407   WAY WCRLD   I.1    454
Waitwell:      Dead cr Alive I'll come--and married we will be   .  .  . 461   WAY WCRLD   IV.1   642
Lady Wish:     and Weaving of dead Hair, with a bleak blew Nose, over a  . 462   WAY WCRLD   V.1      5
Lady Wish:     Brandy-sellers Bulk, or against a dead Wall by a
               Eallad-monger.  .  .  .  .  .  .  .  .  .  .  .  .  .  . 462   WAY WCRLD   V.1     13
```
Deaden (1)
```
Zara:          Strike, damp, deaden her Charms, and kill his Eyes;   .  . 359   M. EBRIDE   III.1  401
```
Deadliest (1)
```
Manuel:        Succeeding that, in which our deadliest Foe,   .  .  .  . 333   M. BRIDE    I.1    296
```
Deadly (1)
```
Careless:      overspreads my face, a ccld deadly dew already vents   .  . 170   DOUBL DLR   IV.1   115
```
Deaf (6)
```
Singer:        For Thyrsis deaf to Loves allarms,   .  .  .  .  .  .  . 71    OLD BATCH   III.2 V 23
Miss Prue:     to say, I can hear you farther cff, I an't deaf.   .  .  . 263   FOR LOVE    III.1  365
Osmyn-Alph:    But Heav'n was deaf, Heav'n heard him not; but thus,   .  . 350   M. EBRIDE   III.1   24
Osmyn-Alph:    The Spirit which was deaf to my own Wrongs,   .  .  .  . 351   M. EBRIDE   III.1   74
Osmyn-Alph:    Deaf to revenge, and the loud Crys of my   .  .  .  .  . 351   M. EBRIDE   III.1   75
Zara:          Thou like the Adder, venomous and deaf,   .  .  .  .  . 375   M. EBIDE    V.1    106
```
Deal (16)
```
Sharper:       No, I'll deal fairly with you.--'Tis a full and   .  .  . 110   OLD EATCH   V.2     85
Lord Froth:    Brisk to have Wit; my Wife says, he has a great deal. I  . 134   DOUBL DLR   I.1    274
Lady Froth:    a great deal of Wit: Mr. Mellefont, don't you think Mr.  . 140   DOUEL DLR   II.1    86
Lady Froth:    An infinite deal!   .  .  .  .  .  .  .  .  .  .  .  .  . 140   DOUEL DLR   II.1    90
Mellefont:     Pretious Aunt, I shall never thrive without I deal with the 187   DOUEL DLR   IV.2   152
Lady Froth:    me, O Parnassus, you have an infinite deal of Wit.   .  . 202   DOUEL DLR   V.1    542
Scandal:       Aye, such rotten Reputations as you have to deal   .  .  . 226   FOR LOVE    I.1    396
Sr Sampson:    day in a Bill of Four thousand Pound: A great deal of  .  . 243   FOR LCVE    II.1   275
Foresight:     Aye indeed, Sir Sampson, a great deal of Money for   .  . 243   FCB LOVE    II.1   277
Mrs Frail:     I'll swear you have a great deal of Impudence, and   .  . 247   FCR LOVE    II.1   453
Mrs Frail:     I'll swear you have a great deal of Confidence, and   .  . 247   FOR LCVE    II.1  V453
Angelica:      deal of Temptation.   .  .  .  .  .  .  .  .  .  .  .  . 257   FOR LCVE    III.1  138
Scandal:       it is with a great deal of Consideration, and Discretion,
               and  .  .  .  .  .  .  .  .  .  .  .  .  .  .  .  .  . 267   FOR LCVE    III.1  516
Witwoud:       --Faith and Troth a pretty deal of an odd sort of a small 403   WAY WORLD   I.1    290
Lady Wish:     great deal in the first Impression. Shall I sit?--No I  . 445   WAY WORLD   IV.1    19
Witwoud:       Thou art a retailer of Phrases; and dost deal in   .  .  . 453   WAY WORLD   IV.1   346
```
Dealers (1)   see Plain-Dealers
```
Fondlewife:    we still suspect the smoothest Dealers of the deepest  .  . 77    OLD BATCH   IV.1    61
```
Dealing (2)   see Double-Dealing, Plain-dealing
```
Lord Touch:    Proof, that I may justifie my Dealing with him to the  .  . 182   DOUBL DLR   IV.1   563
Mirabell:      with plain Dealing and Sincerity.   .  .  .  .  .  .  . 422   WAY WORLD   II.1   466
```
Dealous (2)
```
Laetitia:      you been dealous of me still.   .  .  .  .  .  .  .  .  . 78    OLD BATCH   IV.1   133
Fondlewife:    I wont be dealous--Poor Cocky, Kiss Nykin, Kiss   .  .  . 79    OLD BATCH   IV.1   135
```
Dealt (2)
```
Almeria:       And Woe shou'd be in equal Portions dealt.   .  .  .  . 356   M. BRIDE    III.1  288
Lady Wish:     dealt in when I took you into my house, plac'd you next  . 462   WAY WORLD   V.1     20
```
Dear (167)
```
Bellmour:      Let me see--How now! Dear perfidious Vainlove.   .  .  . 38    OLD BATCH   I.1     35
Bellmour:      Let me see, Laetitia! Oh 'tis a delicious Morsel. Dear  . 39    OLD EATCH   I.1     73
Belinda:       Ay! nay Dear--prithee good, dear sweet Cousin no   .  . 54    OLD BATCH   II.2     1
Silvia:        How, dear Lucy.   .  .  .  .  .  .  .  .  .  .  .  .  . 61    OLD BATCH   III.1    36
Heartwell:     thou Delicious, Damn'd, Dear, destructive Woman!   .  .  . 63    OLD EATCH   III.1   77
Sir Joseph:    dear Captain, don't be in Passion now, he's gone--   .  . 70    OLD BATCH   III.1  340
Sir Joseph:    Put up, put up, dear Back, 'tis your Sir Joseph begs, come 70    OLD EATCH   III.1  341
Heartwell:     Yet I must--Speak dear Angel, Devil, Saint, Witch; do  .  . 72    OLD BATCH   III.2   41
Heartwell:     No, no, dear ignorance, thou beauteous Changel'ng   .  . 72    OLD BATCH   III.2   62
Laetitia:      Bless me, what means my Dear!  .  .  .  .  .  .  .  .  . 77    OLD EATCH   IV.1    73
Laetitia:      Unkind Dear! Was it for this, you sent to call me? is  .  . 77    OLD BATCH   IV.1    87
Fondlewife:    Nay Cocky Cocky, nay dear Cocky, don't cry, I was   .  . 78    OLD BATCH   IV.1   100
Fondlewife:    Oak--I profess I can hold no longer--Nay dear Cocky--   . 78    OLD BATCH   IV.1   115
Fondlewife:    That's my good Dear--Come Kiss Nykin once   .  .  .  . 79    OLD BATCH   IV.1   143
Belinda:       Lard, my Dear! I am glad I have met you;--I   .  .  .  . 83    OLD BATCH   IV.3     1
Belinda:       my Dear,--I have seen such unhewn Creatures since,--Ha, . 83    OLD BATCH   IV.3    11
Belinda:       like one of 'em:--Good Dear, pin this, and I'll tell you. 83    OLD BATCH   IV.3    13
Belinda:       --Very well.--So, thank you my Dear.--But   .  .  .  . 83    OLD BATCH   IV.3    14
Belinda:       And sc--But where did I leave off, my Dear? I was   .  . 83    OLD BATCH   IV.3    19
Belinda:       Dear Araminta, I'm tir'd.   .  .  .  .  .  .  .  .  . 86    OLD BATCH   IV.3   100
Fondlewife:    Nay, prithee, Dear, Ifeck I'm in haste.  .  .  .  .  . 89    OLD EATCH   IV.4    19
```

Dear   (continued)

		PAGE	TITLE	ACT.SC	LINE
Fondlewife:	Kiss, Dear,--I met the Master of the Ship	89	OLD BATCH	IV.4	23
Laetitia:	Help me, my Dear,--O bless me! Why will you leave me	90	OLD BATCH	IV.4	47
Laetitia:	my Dear?	91	OLD BATCH	IV.4	71
Laetitia:	(aside). What can I do now! Oh! my Dear, I have	91	OLD BATCH	IV.4	76
Laetitia:	him. Dear Fortune, help me but this once, and I'll never	91	OLD BATCH	IV.4	91
Fondlewife:	Man is in great torment, he lies as flat--Dear, you	91	OLD BATCH	IV.4	95
Laetitia:	Mr. Spintext's Prayer-Book, Dear.--(aside) Pray	91	OLD BATCH	IV.4	100
Laetitia:	Dear Husband, I'm amaz'd:--Sure it's a good	92	OLD BATCH	IV.4	114
Laetitia:	In the Name of the--Ch! Good, my Dear, don't	92	OLD BATCH	IV.4	132
Laetitia:	Indeed, and indeed, now my dear Nykin--I never	93	OLD BATCH	IV.4	139
Laetitia:	of your Embraces again, my Dear, if ever I saw his face	93	OLD BATCH	IV.4	151
Laetitia:	No, indeed Dear.	93	OLD BATCH	IV.4	160
Laetitia:	Ah cruel Dear, how can you be so barbarous? You'll	95	OLD BATCH	IV.4	230
Laetitia:	Indeed, my Dear, I was but just coming down stairs,	95	OLD BATCH	IV.4	243
Laetitia:	Indeed, my Dear, I was but just come down stairs,	95	OLD BATCH	IV.4	V243
Laetitia:	Oh! Oh! Where is my Dear.	96	OLD BATCH	IV.4	261
Fondlewife:	my Dear. Nay, I will believe thee, I do, Ifeck.	96	OLD BATCH	IV.4	270
Sharper:	As how, dear dexterous Pimp?	105	OLD BATCH	V.1	340
Brisk:	Oh, my dear Mellefont, let me perish, if thou art not the	128	DOUBL DLR	I.1	33
Mellefont:	No, no, hang him, he has no tast.--but dear Brisk	128	DOUBL DLR	I.1	43
Mellefont:	No, no, hang him, he has no taste.--but dear Brisk	128	DOUBL DLR	I.1	V 43
Brisk:	But prithee dear Rogue, make haste, prithee make haste,	128	DOUBL DLR	I.1	52
Mellefont:	Sir Paul, my wise Father-in-Law that is to be, my Dear	130	DOUBL DLR	I.1	138
Lady Touch:	How, how? Thou Dear, thou precious	137	DOUBL DLR	I.1	404
Lady Froth:	O my Dear Cynthia, you must not rally your	138	DOUBL DLR	II.1	8
Lady Froth:	My Lord, I have been telling my dear Cynthia,	140	DOUBL DLR	II.1	60
Lady Froth:	leap, I vow I sigh when I think cn't: my dear Lord! ha,	140	DOUBL DLR	II.1	63
Lady Froth:	O that Tongue, that dear deceitful Tongue! that	140	DOUBL DLR	II.1	71
Brisk:	O dear, Madam--	140	DOUBL DLR	II.1	V 89
Lord Froth:	O your humble Servant for that, dear Madam;	141	DOUBL DLR	II.1	109
Lord Froth:	about you to shew him, my Dear?	142	DOUBL DLR	II.1	142
Mellefont:	dear Jack, how hast thou Contrived?	149	DCUEL DLR	II.1	431
Maskwell:	and dear dissimulation is the only Art, not to be known	150	DOUBL DLR	II.1	463
Lord Touch:	By my Life, my Dear, I will.	152	DOUBL DLR III.1		59
Lady Touch:	Dear. Nay, by this kiss you shan't be angry. O Lord, I	152	DOUBL DLR III.1		68
Lady Touch:	the Company, and come to you. Pray, good dear my Lord,	153	DOUBL DLR III.1		118
Mellefont:	How, how, for Heaven's sake, dear Maskwell?	157	DOUBL DLR III.1		247
Lord Froth:	Hee, hee, hee, my Dear, have you done--	165	DOUBL DLR III.1		558
Lady Froth:	--Ay my Dear--were you? Oh filthy Mr. Sneer;	165	DOUBL DLR III.1		561
Lady Froth:	O the dear Creature! Let's go see it.	166	DOUBL DLR III.1		608
Lord Froth:	I swear, my Dear, you'll spoil that Child, with	166	DOUBL DLR III.1		609
Lady Froth:	seen her these two hours.--The poor dear Creature	166	DOUBL DLR III.1		613
Lady Froth:	--Come, my dear Cynthia, Mr. Brisk, we'll go see	167	DOUBL DLR III.1		615
Lady Ply:	Embraces--Say thou dear dying Man, when, where,	170	DOUBL DLR	IV.1	125
Lady Ply:	Nay, not to interrupt you my Dear--only	173	DOUBL DLR	IV.1	214
Lady Ply:	(Having read the Letter). O dear Mr. Careless, I	174	DOUBL DLR	IV.1	258
Brisk:	practice.--Ah! My dear Lady Froth! She's a most	175	DOUBL DLR	IV.1	291
Brisk:	what a happy Discovery. Ah my dear charming	177	DOUBL DLR	IV.1	357
Lord Froth:	--No, my Dear, do it with him.	177	DOUBL DLR	IV.1	376
Lord Froth:	Any other time, my Dear, or we'll Dance it	177	DOUBL DLR	IV.1	381
Sir Paul:	to my Lady, I can't contain my self; come my dear Friend.	181	DOUBL DLR	IV.1	509
Mellefont:	No; my Dear, will you get ready--the things	196	DOUBL DLR	V.1	343
Lady Froth:	My dear, Mr. Brisk and I have been Star-gazing,	201	DOUBL DLR	V.1	519
Lady Froth:	Oh, no, I love it viclently,--my dear you're	201	DOUBL DLR	V.1	523
Lord Froth:	No, my dear; I'm but just awake.--	201	DOUBL DLR	V.1	525
Lord Froth:	I've some of my own, thank you, my dear.	201	DOUBL DLR	V.1	527
Lady Ply:	O dear, you make me blush.	202	DOUBL DLR	V.1	550
Lord Froth:	Come my dear, shall we take leave of my Lord	202	DOUBL DLR	V.1	551
Foresight:	of the Head is Horns--Dear Neice, stay at home--	236	FOR LOVE	II.1	58
Tattle:	Yes, my Dear--I think I can guess--But	251	FOR LOVE	II.1	583
Tattle:	Oh my Dear, apt Scholar.	253	FOR LOVE	II.1	659
Miss Prue:	O Dear, what shall I say? Tell me, Mr. Tattle, tell	253	FOR LOVE	III.1	19
Sr Sampson:	My Son Ben! bless thee my dear Boy; body o'	260	FCR LOVE	III.1	270
Sr Sampson:	kiss me again and again, dear Ben.	260	FCB LOVE	III.1	274
Foresight:	My Dear, pray lend me your Glass, your little	269	FOR LOVE	III.1	582
Mrs Frail:	Aye, but my Dear, we must keep it secret, till	273	FOR LOVE	III.1	718
Scandal:	Dear, too considerable to be forgot so soon.	284	FOR LOVE	IV.1	317
Mrs Frail:	But, my Dear, that's impossible; the Parson and	310	FCR LOVE	V.1	478
Tattle:	Aye, my Dear, so they will as you say.	310	FOR LOVE	V.1	480
Leonora:	For Heaven's sake, dear Madam, moderate	326	M. BBIDE	I.1	15
Leonora:	For Heaven's sake, dear Madam, cease	326	M. BBIDE	I.1	V 15
Almeria:	Thy dear Resemblance is for ever fixt;	328	M. BBIDE	I.1	75
Almeria:	And Vows I gave my Dear Alphonso, basely	330	M. BBIDE	I.1	173
Almeria:	I gave my Dear Alphonso, basely broken.	330	M. BBIDE	I.1	V173
Gonsalez:	Dear Madam, speak, or you'll incense the King.	367	M. BBIDE	IV.1	266
Almeria:	Not Osmyn, but Alphonso is my Dear,	370	M. BBIDE	IV.1	358
Almeria:	I shall again behold my dear Alphonso.	371	M. BBIDE	IV.1	394
Witwoud:	My Dear, I ask ten thousand Pardens;--Gad I	402	WAY WORLD	I.1	270
Witwoud:	Friend.--No, my Dear, excuse me there.	403	WAY WORLD	I.1	315
Witwoud:	Empresses, my Dear--By your What-dee-call-'ems	406	WAY WORLD	I.1	399
Witwoud:	charm me, dear Petulant.	406	WAY WORLD	I.1	414
Witwoud:	Faith, my Dear, I can't tell; she's a Woman and a	408	WAY WORLD	I.1	492
Mrs Fain:	Ay, ay, dear Marwood, if we will be happy, we	410	WAY WORLD	II.1	1
Fainall:	My Dear.	412	WAY WORLD	II.1	87
Fainall:	O my Dear I am satisfy'd of your Tenderness; I know	412	WAY WORLD	II.1	95
Millamant:	Dear Mr. Witwoud, truce with your Similitudes:	419	WAY WORLD	II.1	337
Mrs Fain:	But dear Millamant, why were you so long?	419	WAY WORLD	II.1	345
Foible:	O dear Sir, your humble Servant.	424	WAY WORLD	II.1	536
Foible:	dress till I ccme--(Looking out.) O Dear, I'm sure	424	WAY WORLD	II.1	544
Lady Wish:	wrought upon Foible to detect me, I'm ruin'd. Oh my dear	426	WAY WORLD III.1		53
Lady Wish:	Ah dear Marwood, what's Integrity to an Opportunity?	426	WAY WORLD III.1		60
Lady Wish:	in. (Exit Peg.) Dear Friend retire into my Closet, that I	426	WAY WORLD III.1		62
Lady Wish:	me dear Friend, I can make bold with you--There	426	WAY WORLD III.1		64
Foible:	Impatience in which Sir Rowland burns for the dear hour	428	WAY WORLD III.1		126
Lady Wish:	Ay dear Foible; thank thee for that dear Foible.	428	WAY WORLD III.1		139

154

Defend   (continued)
Nurse: Marry Heav'n defend--I at Midnight Practices . . . . . 238 FOR LOVE   II.1   98
Witwoud: defend most of his Faults, except one or two; one he has, 403 WAY WORLD I.1   310
Foible: defend my self? O Madam, if you knew but what he promis'd 463 WAY WORLD V.1   29
Defer (6)
Lord Touch: know he's no way to be rewarded but in her. I'll defer my 191 DOUBL DLR V.1   138
Maskwell: you please, defer the finishing of your Wit, and let us talk 194 DOUBL DLR V.1   278
Valentine: Estate, and I'll defer it as long as I can--Well,
              you'll come . . . . 259 FOR LOVE   III.1 227
Sr Sampson: defer Signing the Conveyance. I warrant the Devil will . 267 FOR LOVE   III.1 506
Sr Sampson: directed by a Dreamer, an Omen-hunter, and defer Business 283 FOR LOVE   IV.1   289
Perez: Your Majesty one Moment to defer . . . . 359 M. BRIDE   III.1 380
Deferr'd (2)
Gonsalez: Their Execution better were deferr'd, ... 363 M. BRIDE   IV.1   69
Manuel: Wherefore I have deferr'd the Mariage Rites, ... 367 M. BRIDE   IV.1   254
Defiance (2)
Marwood: Face, that goodly Face, which in defiance of her . . . 433 WAY WORLD III.1 321
Sir Wilful: in defiance of you Sir, and of your Instrument. S'heart an 473 WAY WORLD V.1   424
Deficient (1)
Foible: Confidence in your Ladyship that was deficient; but I . 430 WAY WORLD III.1 196
Defie (5)
Bellmour: --Gad, I defie thee.-- . . . . 100 OLD BATCH V.1   143
Mellefont: I go this moment: Now Fortune I defie thee. . . . . . 181 DOUBL DLR V.1   525
Foresight: I defie you, Hussie; but I'll remember this, I'll be . . 238 FOR LOVE   II.1   113
Mrs Fain: me. I defie 'em all. Let 'em prove their aspersions: I know 466 WAY WORLD V.1   177
Mrs Fain: I despise you and defie your Malice--You . . . . . . 475 WAY WORLD V.1   498
Defil'd (1)
Maskwell: there was Revenge in view; that Womans Idol had defil'd . 137 DOUBL DLR I.1   375
Defiled (1)
Fondlewife: hath already defiled the Tabernacle of our Sister Comfort; 76 OLD BATCH IV.1   29
Deform'd (1)
Scandal: neither Deform'd, nor a Fool. . . . . 272 FOR LOVE   III.1 691
Deformity (2)
Almeria: Will fly my pale Deformity with loathing. . . . . . . 340 M. BRIDE   II.2   24
Zara: Away, as from Deformity and Horrour. . . . . 353 M. BRIDE   III.1 150
Degenerate (1)
Manuel: Why art thou mute? base and degenerate Maid! . . . . . 367 M. BRIDE   IV.1   265
Degree (8)
Heartwell: that noble passion, Lust, should ebb to this degree--No . 72 OLD BATCH III.2   48
Laetitia: that I should love to this degree! yet-- . . . . . . 78 OLD BATCH IV.1   104
Lady Froth: Ah! Gallantry to the last degree--Mr. Brisk, ... 140 DOUBL DLR II.1   81
Maskwell: Lord's Displeasure to a degree that will admit of no . . 154 DOUBL DLR III.1 147
Valentine: doat on at that immoderate Degree, that your Fondness shall 313 FOR LOVE   V.1 V609
Marwood: I think she do's not hate him to that degree . . . . 413 WAY WORLD II.1   128
Mrs Fain: I ought to stand in some degree of Credit with . . . . 417 WAY WORLD II.1   278
Mirabell: as a Mortification; for sure to please a Fool is some degree 421 WAY WORLD II.1   439
Degrees (1)
Millamant: to endure you a little longer, I may by degrees dwindle into 450 WAY WORLD IV.1   226
Deity (1)
Vainlove: Deity, he must be serv'd by Prayer. . . . . 58 OLD BATCH II.2   141
Dejected (2)
              I swear, young Bays within, is so dejected, ... 113 OLD BATCH EPI.   24
Zara: And build bold Hopes, on my dejected Fate? . . . . 349 M. BRIDE   II.2   367
Delay (5)
Lord Touch: delay. . . . . 152 DOUBL DLR III.1   80
Maskwell: to delay--let me think--shou'd my Lord proceed . . . . 190 DOUBL DLR V.1   89
Manuel: Unus'd to wait, I broke through her Delay, ... 337 M. BRIDE   I.1   456
Gonsalez: If I delay--'twill do--or better so. . . . . 371 M. BRIDE   IV.1   416
Waitwell: For decency of Funeral, Madam. The delay will . . . . 458 WAY WORLD IV.1   498
Delay'd (1)
Osmyn-Alph: Delay'd: nor has our Hymenial Torch . . . . 357 M. BRIDE   III.1 321
Delia (1)
Musician: Poor, old, repenting Delia said, ... 59 OLD BATCH II.2   191
Deliberate (1)
Marwood: 'Tis false, you urg'd it with deliberate Malice-- . . . 414 WAY WORLD II.1   182
Deliberation (3)
Belinda: No; upon deliberation, I have too much Charity . . . . 57 OLD BATCH II.2   104
              For Dulness on mature Deliberation. . . . . 393 WAY WORLD PRO.   25
Fainall: Your date of deliberation Madam, is expir'd. Here is . . 472 WAY WORLD V.1   414
Deliberatum (1)
Sr Sampson: White, Signatum, Sigillatum, and Deliberatum; that as soon 240 FOR LOVE   II.1   181
Delicate (1)
Mirabell: You have a Taste extreamly delicate, and are for . . . 395 WAY WORLD I.1   11
Delicious (4)
Bellmour: Let me see, Laetitia! Oh 'tis a delicious Morsel. Dear . 39 OLD BATCH I.1   73
Heartwell: thou Delicious, Damn'd, Dear, destructive Woman! . . . 63 OLD BATCH III.1   77
Sharper: To her Man--A delicious Mellon pure and consenting . . 79 OLD BATCH IV.1   165
Bellmour: made a delicious Voyage, Setter; and might have rode at . 96 OLD BATCH V.1   5
Delight (9)
Lucy: Whom Love and Vengeance do at once delight. . . . . . 75 OLD BATCH III.2 163
Lucy: Whom love and Vengeance both at once delight. . . . . 75 OLD BATCH III.2 V163
Valentine: me Signal Service in my necessity. But you delight in . . 223 FOR LOVE   I.1   259
Gonsalez: My Eyes with more Delight, than they can hold. . . . . 332 M. BRIDE   I.1   274
Heli: In least Proportion to the vast Delight . . . . . . 338 M. BRIDE   II.1   9
Almeria: Of delight, I cannot bear it--I shall . . . . 342 M. BRIDE   II.2   107
Osmyn-Alph: O may'st thou never dream of less Delight; . . . . . 383 M. BRIDE   V.2   289
Mirabell: incumbrance of their Lives. How can you find delight in . 421 WAY WORLD II.1   436
Singer: If there's Delight in Love, 'tis when I see . . . . . 435 WAY WORLD III.1 389
Delights (2)
Manuel: To one, where young Delights attend; and Joys . . . . 349 M. BRIDE   II.2   383
Waitwell: been solacing in lawful Delights; but still with an Eye . 423 WAY WORLD II.1   508
Deliv'rance (1)
Leonora: Sent in my Sighs and Pray'rs for his Deliv'rance; . . . 327 M. BRIDE   I.1   28
Deliver (5)
Messenger: Wilfull, which I am charg'd to deliver into his own Hands. 400 WAY WORLD I.1   184
Foible: Letter, who must deliver it into your own hands. . . . 459 WAY WORLD IV.1   550

Deliver (continued)
  Waitwell: Contains the Writings of my whole Estate, and deliver . . 461   WAY WORLD IV.1 634
  Mirabell: I have sent my Servant for it, and will deliver it to you, . 472   WAY WORLD   V.1 406
  Mirabell: deliver this same as her Act and Deed to me in trust, and . 476   WAY WORLD   V.1 546
Deliver'd (7)
  Bellmour: strein to be deliver'd of a Secret, when he has miscarried .   40   OLD BATCH   I.1 127
  Sharper: deliver'd of it.   79   OLD BATCH   IV.1 168
  Bellmour: Letter was deliver'd to me by a Servant, in the Morning: .   82   OLD BATCH   IV.2   52
  Heartwell: thou hast deliver'd me. 111   OLD BATCH   V.2 153
  Marwood: deliver'd with so significant Gesture, shou'd be so   . . 434   WAY WORLD III.1 346
  Marwood: I will contrive a Letter which shall be deliver'd   . . . 443   WAY WORLD III.1 699
  Lady Wish: I'll consent to any thing to come, to be deliver'd from this 473 WAY WORLD   V.1 455
Deliverance (3)
  Sharper: in a manner--Pay'd down for your deliverance; 'twas so   .   50   OLD BATCH   II.1 102
  Almeria: In Mourning, and strict Life, for my Deliverance . . . 333   M. BRIDE   I.1 285
  Gonsalez: And her Deliverance; Is she to blame? 333   M. BRIDE   I.1 306
Delivery (1)
  Jeremy: my self better to you, Sir, than by the delivery of a   . 302   FOR LOVE   V.1 177
Deluded (7)
  Fondlewife: while her good Husband is deluded by his Godly appearance   76   OLD BATCH   IV.1   30
  Angelica: deluded with vain Hopes. Good Nature and Humanity . . 277   FOR LOVE   IV.1   72
  Angelica: am I deluded by this Interval of Sense, to reason with a . 295   FOR LOVE   IV.1 729
  Gonsalez: O Wretch! O curs'd, and rash, deluded Fool! 378   M. BRIDE   V.2   68
  Foible: been deluded by him, then how shou'd I a poor Ignorant,   . 463   WAY WORLD   V.1   28
Deludes (1)
  Gonsalez: And deludes your Sense. Alphonso, if living, ... 370   M. BRIDE   IV.1 376
Demands (2)
  Mirabell: your demands are pretty reasonable. 450   WAY WORLD   IV.1 211
  Fainall: I come to make demands,--I'll hear no 469   WAY WORLD   V.1 288
Demm (1)
  Mrs Fore: Oh, Demm you Toad--I wish you don't 249   FOR LOVE   II.1 538
Demme (1)
  Witwoud: Now, Demme, I shou'd hate that, if she were as handsome . 408   WAY WORLD   I.1 477
Demonstration (7)
  Lady Ply: Demonstration, answer me directly--but I have not   . . 146   DOUBL DLR   II.1 303
  Lady Touch: such a Case as this, demonstration is necessary. . . 151   DOUBL DLR   III.1   18
  Lord Touch: There should have been demonstration of the 151   DOUBL DLR   III.1   19
  Cynthia: Money, He should give me a very evident demonstration . . 168   DOUBL DLR   IV.1   46
  Cynthia: Why if you give me very clear demonstration that it . . 169   DOUBL DLR   IV.1   58
  Scandal: A very desperate demonstration of your love to   . . . 225   FOR LOVE   I.1 343
  Scandal: So, why this is fair, here's Demonstration with a   . . 257   FOR LOVE   III.1 147
Demonstrative (1)
  Lord Touch: make me. Can you give me a demonstrative Proof? . . . 182   DOUBL DLR   IV.1 574
Den (1)
  Osmyn-Alph: This Den for Slaves, this Dungeon damp'd with Woes; . . 357   M. BRIDE   III.1 327
Denials (1)   see Denyal
  Angelica: his Sollicitations and my Denials. 257   FOR LOVE   III.1 144
Denies (2)
  Vainlove: That Tongue, which denies what the Hands have   . . .   88   OLD BATCH   IV.3 183
  Angelica: Ha, ha, ha, you see he denies it. 295   FOR LOVE   IV.1 742
Denounce (1)
  Mirabell: I denounce against all strait-Laceing, Squeezing for   . 451   WAY WORLD   IV.1 260
Denunciations (1)
  Bellmour: Well; 'Midst of these dreadful Denunciations, and   . . 112   OLD BATCH   V.2 165
Deny (19)
  Belinda: I deny it all.   55   OLD BATCH   II.2   48
  Fondlewife: I warrant you, than to deny it. Come, Were you two never .   93   OLD BATCH   IV.4 155
  Lady Touch: you deny it? 135   DOUBL DLR   I.1 307
  Maskwell: as I told you before. I can't deny that neither.--Any   . 135   DOUBL DLR   I.1 314
  Maskwell: No, that I deny; for I never told in all my Life: . . 135   DOUBL DLR   I.1 318
  Maskwell: of Love, have told me. Why should you deny it? Nay, . . 137   DOUBL DLR   I.1 385
  Lady Ply: be so peremptory as to deny it; when I tax you with it to . 146   DOUBL DLR   II.1 298
  Lady Ply: refuse it; I swear I'll deny it,--therefore don't ask me, . 147   DOUBL DLR   II.1 333
  Lady Ply: nay you shan't ask me, I swear I'll deny it. O Gemini, you . 147   DOUBL DLR   II.1 334
  Lady Ply: Hear you, no, no; I'll deny you first, and hear . . . 147   DOUBL DLR   II.1 338
  Scandal: a Whisper; and deny a Woman's name, while he gives you   . 226   FOR LOVE   I.1 371
  Sr Sampson: under Hand and Seal--Can you deny it? 243   FOR LOVE   II.1 301
  Valentine: Sir, I don't deny it.-- 243   FOR LOVE   II.1 302
  Mrs Fore: You deny it positively to my Face. 247   FOR LOVE   II.1 458
  Mrs Frail: deny it positively to Your Face then. 247   FOR LOVE   II.1 462
  Tattle: Handsome, you must deny it, and say I flatter you-- . . 252   FOR LOVE   II.1 616
  Mrs Frail: in short, I will deny thee nothing. 293   FOR LOVE   IV.1 674
  Ben: can't deny it: But, Father, if I might be your Pilot in this 308 FOR LOVE   V.1 413
  Mirabell: You had the Tyranny to deny me last Night; tho' you   . . 421   WAY WORLD   II.1 429
Deny'd (8)
  Sir Paul: deny'd my self the enjoyment of lawful Domestick   . . . 179   DOUBL DLR   IV.1 428
               Thus poor Poets the Favour are deny'd, ... 204   DOUBL DLR   EPI.   29
               Poor Poets thus the Favour are deny'd, ... 204   DOUBL DLR   EPI. V 29
  Angelica: never deny'd any thing in his Life. 255   FOR LOVE   III.1   78
  Scandal: which you deny'd to all his Sufferings and my
               Sollicitations 294   FOR LOVE   IV.1 690
  Osmyn-Alph: And 'tis deny'd to me, to be so bless'd, ... 357   M. BRIDE   III.1 333
  Osmyn-Alph: To grasp and reach what is deny'd my Hands; 358   M. BRIDE   III.1 346
  Millamant: O I have deny'd my self Airs to Day. I have walk'd   . . 418   WAY WORLD   II.1 333
Deny't (1)
  Tattle: I am strangely surpriz'd! Yes, yes, I can't deny't, if . 229   FOR LOVE   I.1 481
Denyal (1)   see Denials
  Belinda: My Denyal is premeditated like your Malice--Lard, . . .   55   OLD BATCH   II.2   50
Denying (2)
  Scandal: all night, and denying favours with more impudence, than . 284   FOR LOVE   IV.1 336
  Scandal: all night, and denying that she had done 284   FOR LOVE   IV.1 V336
Departed (3)
  Zara: Alphonso, privately departed, just 364   M. BRIDE   IV.1 120
  Zara: Alphonso, secretly departed, just 364   M. BRIDE   IV.1 V120
               Of a damn'd Poet, and departed Muse! 385   M. BRIDE   EPI.   12

Device (2)

		PAGE	TITLE	ACT.SC	LINE
	A Barbarous Device, to try if Spouse, ...	125	DOUBL DLR	PRO.	5
Mirabell:	much prejudice; it was an Innocent device; tho' I confess it	472	WAY WORLD	V.1	384

Devil (72)

		PAGE	TITLE	ACT.SC	LINE
Vainlove:	once raised up in a Woman, the Devil can't lay it, till she	40	OLD BATCH	I.1	103
Bellmour:	like her; for the Devil take me if I don't love all the .	41	OLD BATCH	I.1	174
Heartwell:	you save the Devil the trouble of leading you into it: Nor	43	OLD BATCH	I.1	241
Bellmour:	Who the Devil would have thee? unless 'twere an .	45	OLD BATCH	I.1	298
Heartwell:	Ay there you've nick't it--there's the Devil upon	45	OLD BATCH	I.1	317
Heartwell:	Devil--Oh the Pride and Joy of Heart 'twould be to me, .	45	OLD BATCH	I.1	318
Heartwell:	relations--when the Devil and she knows, 'tis a little .	45	OLD BATCH	I.1	327
Sir Joseph:	the Devil--God bless us--almost if he be by. Ah--had he .	50	OLD BATCH	II.1	123
Sir Joseph:	the Devil--bless us--almost if he be by. Ah--had he . .	50	OLD BATCH	II.1	V123
Belinda:	Fancy--This Love is the Devil, and sure to be in Love .	54	OLD BATCH	II.2	12
Belinda:	Pish, I can't help dreaming of the Devil sometimes; . .	55	OLD BATCH	II.2	39
Belinda:	Devil take Bellmour--Why do you tell me of him?	56	OLD BATCH	II.2	57
Belinda:	to trust you to your self. The Devil watches all opportunities;	57	OLD BATCH	II.2	105
Belinda:	Devil, wrapt in Flames--I'll not hear a Sentence . .	59	OLD BATCH	II.2	170
Bellmour:	But how the Devil dost thou expect to get her if . .	63	OLD BATCH	III.1	110
Setter:	As all lew'd projects do Sir, where the Devil prevents .	64	OLD BATCH	III.1	117
Setter:	Devil could know you by instinct?	66	OLD BATCH	III.1	206
Heartwell:	Yet I must--Speak dear Angel, Devil, Saint, Witch; do .	72	OLD BATCH	III.2	41
Laetitia:	run in thy debt again. But this Opportunity is the Devil.	91	OLD BATCH	IV.4	92
Laetitia:	come near it, I'm afraid 'tis the Devil; indeed it has hoofs, ...	92	OLD BATCH	IV.4	133
Fondlewife:	Indeed, and I have Horns, Deare. The Devil, no. . . .	92	OLD BATCH	IV.4	135
Fondlewife:	Thou art a Devil in his proper Cloathing, ...	93	OLD BATCH	IV.4	143
Lucy:	Ah, the Devil is not so cunning.--You know my . .	98	OLD BATCH	V.1	74
Setter:	Talk of the Devil--See where he comes.	100	OLD BATCH	V.1	131
Sharper:	But how the Devil do you think to acquit your self .	100	OLD BATCH	V.1	154
Heartwell:	(aside). Hell, and the Devil! Does he know it? But, .	104	OLD BATCH	V.1	298
Bellmour:	Hold, hold. What the Devil, thou wilt not draw . .	108	OLD BATCH	V.2	42
Capt Bluff:	Oh, the Devil, cheated at last!	110	OLD BATCH	V.2	110
	But how?--Just as the Devil does a Sinner. . . .	113	OLD BATCH	EPI.	28
Careless:	Exquisite Woman! But what the Devil, does she . .	130	DOUBL DLR	I.1	119
Careless:	Smile, no, what the Devil should you smile at, when .	134	DOUBL DLR	I.1	260
Lady Touch:	Insolent Devil! But have a care,--provoke me not; .	135	DOUBL DLR	I.1	321
Lady Touch:	Well, mollifying Devil!--And have I	137	DOUBL DLR	I.1	372
Mellefont:	(aside). Incest! O my precious Aunt, and the Devil .	146	DOUBL DLR	I.1	312
Mellefont:	Hell and the Devil, is she abandon'd of all Grace-- .	156	DOUBL DLR	III.1	235
Mellefont:	the last Minute of her Reign, unless the Devil assist her in	169	DOUBL DLR	IV.1	53
Cynthia:	Well, if the Devil should assist her, and your Plot .	169	DOUBL DLR	IV.1	55
Cynthia:	was the Devil, I'll allow for irresistable odds. But if I find	169	DOUBL DLR	IV.1	59
Cynthia:	thing but the very Devil, I'm inexorable: Only still I'll	169	DOUBL DLR	IV.1	61
Sir Paul:	The Devil take me now if he did not go beyond my . .	180	DOUBL DLR	IV.1	470
Mellefont:	Devil, or another Woman.	187	DOUBL DLR	IV.2	153
Maskwell:	word,--how the Devil she wrought my Lord into . .	190	DOUBL DLR	V.1	110
Mellefont:	The Devil he has! what's to be done?	190	DOUBL DLR	V.1	113
Lady Touch:	Damnation proof, a Devil already, and Fire is his Element.	191	DOUBL DLR	V.1	V153
Scandal:	what the Devil has not your Poverty made you Enemies .	219	FOR LOVE	I.1	127
Valentine:	And how the Devil do you mean to keep your . . .	221	FOR LOVE	I.1	178
Mrs Frail:	to see Fellows in a Morning. Scandal, you Devil, are you	230	FOR LOVE	I.1	547
Mrs Frail:	O Devil! Well, but that Story is not true. . . .	233	FOR LOVE	I.1	641
Angelica:	and that you Suckle a Young Devil in the Shape of a .	238	FOR LOVE	II.1	121
Sr Sampson:	not keep the Devil out of his Wives Circle. . . .	241	FOR LOVE	II.1	228
Sr Sampson:	not keep the Devil out of his Wife's Circle. . . .	241	FOR LOVE	II.1	V228
Mrs Fore:	(aside). O Devil on't, that I cou'd not discover .	248	FOR LOVE	II.1	471
Mrs Frail:	Ah Devil, sly Devil--He's as close, Sister, as . . .	250	FOR LOVE	II.1	542
Mrs Frail:	Creature, that smells all of Pitch and Tarr--Devil . .	250	FOR LOVE	II.1	565
Mrs Fore:	together is as bad--And he's such a sly Devil, he'll never	250	FOR LOVE	II.1	574
Scandal:	Why, is the Devil in you? Did not I tell it you for a .	255	FOR LOVE	III.1	59
Valentine:	O the Devil, what damn'd Costive Poet has given . .	255	FOR LOVE	III.1	73
Sr Sampson:	defer Signing the Conveyance. I warrant the Devil will .	267	FOR LOVE	III.1	506
Sr Sampson:	shall out-lie the Devil. And so I'll try whether my .	267	FOR LOVE	III.1	510
Mrs Fore:	Devil; do you think any Woman Honest?	271	FOR LOVE	III.1	665
Valentine:	and you shall see me act St. Dunstan, and lead the Devil	282	FOR LOVE	IV.1	241
Sr Sampson:	What the Devil had I to do, ever to beget Sons? . . .	282	FOR LOVE	IV.1	260
Ben:	believe the Devil wou'd not venture aboard o' your . .	309	FOR LOVE	V.1	435
Tattle:	The Devil take me if ever I was so much concern'd at any	309	FOR LOVE	V.1	460
	But there's the Devil, tho' their Cause is lost, . .	323	M. BRIDE	PRO.	25
Millamant:	Unless by the help of the Devil you can't imagine; . .	423	WAY WORLD	II.1	485
Millamant:	Without the help of the Devil you can't imagine; . .	423	WAY WORLD	II.1	V485
Foible:	(aside). So, the Devil has been before hand with me, .	427	WAY WORLD	III.1	84
Mrs Fain:	come too late. That Devil Marwood saw you in the Park .	430	WAY WORLD	III.1	185
Witwoud:	I hope so--The Devil take him that remembers	437	WAY WORLD	III.1	477
Foible:	mischeivous Devil told Mr. Fainall of your Ladyship then?	464	WAY WORLD	V.1	80

Devil's (9)

		PAGE	TITLE	ACT.SC	LINE
Sir Joseph:	you--Why what a Devil's the Matter, Bully, are you . .	68	OLD BATCH	III.1	264
Sir Joseph:	Why, the Devil's in the People, I think.	91	OLD BATCH	IV.4	68
Fondlewife:	Devil's Pater-noster. Hold, let me see: The Innocent Adultery.	92	OLD BATCH	IV.4	107
Fondlewife:	ripe-horn-mad. But who, in the Devil's name, are you? Mercy on	92	OLD BATCH	IV.4	127
Heartwell:	What the Devil's all this to me.	110	OLD BATCH	V.2	93
Careless:	Wit, In what? Where the Devil's the Wit, in not . .	133	DOUBL DLR	I.1	246
Sr Sampson:	But I'll bring him a Parson to tell him, that the Devil's a	267	FOR LOVE	III.1	508
Mirabell:	reported to be in Labour. The Devil's in't, if an old woman	397	WAY WORLD	I.1	76
Marwood:	Woman! The Devil's an Ass: If I were a Painter, I wou'd	431	WAY WORLD	III.1	236

Devilish (5)

		PAGE	TITLE	ACT.SC	LINE
Sir Joseph:	Ay Bully, a Devilish smart Fellow, 'a will fight . . .	51	OLD BATCH	II.1	150
Sir Joseph:	mischief--For he was a devilish cholerick Fellow: And if .	68	OLD BATCH	III.1	274
Jeremy:	You'll grow Devilish fat upon this Paper-Diet. . . .	216	FOR LOVE	I.1	5
Sr Sampson:	devilish Handsom.--Madam, you deserve a good Husband, .	298	FOR LOVE	V.1	51
Sr Sampson:	Odd, you're devilish Handsom; Faith and Troth, you're .	301	FOR LOVE	V.1	141

Did   (continued)

Speaker	Text	PAGE	TITLE	ACT.SC	LINE
Cynthia:	Love, and so much Wit as your Ladyship has, did not	138	DOUEL DLR	II.1	6
Lady Froth:	then your Bow! Good my Lord, bow as you did when I	140	DOUEL DLR	II.1	73
Lady Froth:	Did my Lord tell you? Yes I vow, and the Subject	141	DOUEL DLR	II.1	120
Lady Ply:	you? what did I Marry you for? Am I not to be absolute	144	DOUEL DLR	II.1	216
Lady Ply:	I did not think it a sin,--but still my honour, if it were	147	DOUEL DLR	II.1	349
Lady Ply:	what did I say? Jealous! no, no, I can't be jealous, for I	148	DOUEL DLR	II.1	370
Mellefont:	of her violence at last,--if you had not come as you did;	149	DOUEL DLR	II.1	417
Maskwell:	Cynthia; that did my business; that convinced your Aunt,	149	DOUEL DLR	II.1	422
Maskwell:	This was a Master-piece, and did not need my	154	DOUEL DLR	III.1	128
Mellefont:	Did not she tell you at what a distance she keeps him. He	158	DOUEL DLR	III.1	284
Lady Ply:	breeding to think Mr. Careless did not apply himself to me.	159	DOUEL DLR	III.1	330
Brisk:	He? e'gad, so I did--My Lord can sing it.	166	DOUEL DLR	III.1	589
Lady Ply:	--Why did you kneel so long? I swear I was so	170	DOUEL DLR	IV.1	108
Lady Ply:	transported, I did not see it.--Well, to shew you how	170	DOUEL DLR	IV.1	109
Sir Paul:	did you swear, did that sweet Creature swear! ha? How	171	DOUEL DLR	IV.1	139
Sir Paul:	Did your Ladiship call?	173	DOUEL DLR	IV.1	213
Sir Paul:	Wedding Night, to die a Maid; as she did; all were ruin'd,	174	DOUEL DLR	IV.1	252
Brisk:	you, and all that; and I did not think it had been in you.	174	DOUEL DLR	IV.1	268
Lady Froth:	Bless me, why did you call out upon me so	176	DOUEL DLR	IV.1	319
Brisk:	Not I, let me perish--But did I! Strange! I confess	176	DOUEL DLR	IV.1	325
Brisk:	Dream that did in a manner represent a very pleasing	176	DOUEL DLR	IV.1	327
Brisk:	Object to my imagination, but--But did I indeed?--To	176	DOUEL DLR	IV.1	328
Brisk:	see how Love and Murder will out. But did I really name	176	DOUEL DLR	IV.1	329
Lady Froth:	did you talk of Love? O Parnassus! Who would have	176	DOUEL DLR	IV.1	332
Lady Ply:	Has he been Treacherous, or did you give his insolence a	179	DOUEL DLR	IV.1	439
Sir Paul:	did you give me this Letter on purpose he? Did you?	179	DOUEL DLR	IV.1	461
Lady Ply:	Did I? Do you doubt me, Turk, Sarazen? I	179	DOUEL DLR	IV.1	462
Sir Paul:	The Devil take me now if he did not go beyond my	180	DOUEL DLR	IV.1	470
Lady Ply:	Did you so, Presumption!	180	DOUEL DLR	IV.1	481
Sir Paul:	Madam, Sister, my Lady Sister, did you see my	191	DOUEL DLR	V.1	159
Maskwell:	(aside). This I fear'd. Did not your Lordship tell	195	DOUEL DLR	V.1	312
Cynthia:	Did Maskwell tell you any thing of the Chaplain's	196	DOUEL DLR	V.1	341
Lord Touch:	Still gnawing that, whence first it did arise;	203	DOUEL DLR	V.1	595
Jeremy:	Was Epictetus a real Cook, or did he only write	216	FCR LCVE	I.1	10
Jeremy:	that did not care a Farthing for you in your Prosperity;	217	FCR LCVE	I.1	45
Valentine:	I was much oblig'd to you for your Supply: It did	223	FOR LCVE	I.1	258
Trapland:	Mr. Scandal, you are Uncivil; I did not value your	224	FOR LCVE	I.1	313
Scandal:	any body that did not stink to all the Town.	226	FCR LCVE	I.1	402
Tattle:	her, and did I know not what--But, upon my Reputation,	227	FCR LCVE	I.1	421
Tattle:	she did me wrong--Well, well, that was	227	FCR LCVE	I.1	422
Scandal:	and ha, ha, ha, well, go on, and what did you say to her	227	FCR LCVE	I.1	439
Valentine:	Well, but how did you acquit your self?	228	FOR LCVE	I.1	444
Valentine:	sometimes. I did not think she had granted more to any	229	FCR LCVE	I.1	487
Tattle:	O Barbarous! why did you not tell me--	229	FCR LCVE	I.1	494
Valentine:	What did I say? I hope you won't bring me to	229	FCR LCVE	I.1	497
Nurse:	and swear now, ha, ha, ha, Marry and did you ever see the	235	FOR LCVE	II.1	23
Angelica:	Neighbourhood--What a Bustle did you keep against the	237	FOR LCVE	II.1	79
Angelica:	Tinderboxes did you purchase! One would have thought	237	FOR LCVE	II.1	82
Nurse:	Doings with my Masters Worship--Why, did you	238	FOR LCVE	II.1	100
Nurse:	ever hear the like now--Sir, did ever I do any thing	238	FOR LCVE	II.1	101
Sr Sampson:	Did you ever hear the like! Did you ever hear the like!	244	FOR LCVE	II.1	319
Sr Sampson:	what I please? Are not you my Slave? Did not I beget you?	244	FOR LCVE	II.1	324
Sr Sampson:	Did you come a Volunteer into the World? Or did I	244	FOR LCVE	II.1	330
Sr Sampson:	Fellow was not born with you?--I did not beget him,	245	FOR LCVE	II.1	358
Sr Sampson:	did I?--	245	FCR LCVE	II.1	359
Jeremy:	another truth, I believe you did, for I find I was born with	245	FOR LCVE	II.1	362
Valentine:	'Tis as much as I expected--I did not come to see	246	FOR LCVE	II.1	407
Mrs Fore:	alight as I did?--How can any Body be happy, while	247	FOR LCVE	II.1	432
Mrs Fore:	Countenance:--But look you here now,--where did	248	FOR LCVE	II.1	465
Mrs Frail:	Well, if you go to that, where did you find this	248	FOR LCVE	II.1	469
Mrs Frail:	take you, you confounded Toad--why did you see	250	FOR LCVE	II.1	566
Mrs Fore:	Nay, why did we let him--my Husband	250	FOR LCVE	II.1	568
Valentine:	me whether you did or no.	254	FOR LCVE	III.1	30
Valentine:	me whether you did or not.	254	FOR LCVE	III.1 V	30
Scandal:	Nor good Nature enough to answer him that did	254	FOR LCVE	III.1	33
Scandal:	Why, is the Devil in you? Did not I tell it you for a	255	FOR LCVE	III.1	59
Tattle:	Brag! C Heav'ns! why, did I name any body?	255	FOR LCVE	III.1	93
Foresight:	I protest I honour you, Mr. Scandal--I did not think	267	FCR LCVE	III.1	540
Scandal:	And did not use to be so.	270	FOR LCVE	III.1	621
Scandal:	looks better than he did.	270	FOR LCVE	III.1	627
Mrs Fore:	Did you ever hear such a Toad--heark'ee	271	FOR LCVE	III.1	664
Mrs Fore:	Pish, you'd tell me so, tho' you did not think	272	FCR LCVE	III.1	707
Valentine:	It may be so--I did not know you--the World	280	FCR LCVE	IV.1	159
Sr Sampson:	Why did I ever marry?	282	FOR LCVE	IV.1	261
Foresight:	What says he? What, did he prophesie? Ha, Sir	283	FOR LCVE	IV.1	277
Sr Sampson:	your Quadrates?--What did your Cardan and your	283	FOR LCVE	IV.1	283
Scandal:	he did not foresee, and more particularly relating to his	284	FOR LCVE	IV.1	312
Scandal:	And did not?	284	FOR LCVE	IV.1	330
Mrs Fore:	Did not! with that face can you ask the	284	FOR LOVE	IV.1	331
Scandal:	How did you rest last night?	284	FOR LOVE	IV.1	339
Ben:	put'n into a passion; but what did I know that, what's that	285	FOR LOVE	IV.1	367
Ben:	Graceless, why did he beget me so? I did not get my self.	286	FOR LOVE	IV.1	391
Ben:	don't love You so well as to bear that, whatever I did,	287	FOR LOVE	IV.1	435
Valentine:	Fortune; and Honesty will go as it did, Frost-nip't in a	288	FOR LOVE	IV.1	493
Jeremy:	O Lord, Madam, did you ever know any Madman	295	FOR LCVE	IV.1	743
Angelica:	I did not think you had Apprehension enough to be	296	FOR LOVE	IV.1	762
Angelica:	Where is Sir Sampson? Did you not tell me, he	297	FOR LOVE	V.1	1
Tattle:	O fie, Miss, why did you do so? and who told you so,	303	FOR LCVE	V.1	233
Miss Prue:	Who? Why you did; did not you?	303	FOR LOVE	V.1	235
Tattle:	Night, and did not so much as dream of the matter.	303	FOR LOVE	V.1	238
Miss Prue:	Well, but don't you love me as well as you did	304	FOR LOVE	V.1	248
Tattle:	--And I'm going to be Married just now, yet did not	305	FOR LOVE	V.1	293
Foresight:	Did he so--It'll dispatch him for't presently;	305	FOR LOVE	V.1	321
Tattle:	I did, as I hope to be sav'd, Madam, my Intentions	309	FOR LOVE	V.1	457
	And this our Audience, which did once resort	315	FOR LOVE	EPI.	25

163

Did   (continued)

		PAGE	TITLE	ACT.SC	LINE
	And thus our Audience, which did once resort	315	FOR LOVE	EPI. V	25
	New Plays did then like Almanacks appear;	323	M. BRIDE	PRO.	3
	The Dearth of Wit they did so long presage,	323	M. BRIDE	PRO.	15
Leonora:	And always did compassionate his Fortune,	326	M. BRIDE	I.1	21
Leonora:	He did endear himself to your Affection,	327	M. BRIDE	I.1	45
Almeria:	Why did he not use me like an Enemy?	327	M. BRIDE	I.1	67
Almeria:	But I did promise I would tell thee--What?	328	M. BRIDE	I.1	98
Leonora:	I never did presume to ask the Story.	328	M. BRIDE	I.1	108
Almeria:	The Queen too, did assist his Suit--I granted,	329	M. BRIDE	I.1	140
Almeria:	And all the Damps of Grief, that did retard their Flight;	330	M. BRIDE	I.1	158
Gonsalez:	And cling, as if with Claws they did enforce	332	M. BRIDE	I.1	239
Garcia:	Alone to do, and did disdain to talk;	335	M. BRIDE	I.1	373
Manuel:	Did Zara, then, request he might attend her?	335	M. BRIDE	I.1	377
Garcia:	My Lord, she did.	335	M. BRIDE	I.1	378
Manuel:	Her Eyes, did more than bid--free her and hers,	336	M. BRIDE	I.1	410
Osmyn-Alph:	I did, and thou didst call me.	343	M. BRIDE	II.2	157
Osmyn-Alph:	I did, and thou, my Love, didst call me; thou.	343	M. BRIDE	II.2	V157
Zara:	O Heav'n! how did my Heart rejoice and ake,	347	M. BRIDE	II.2	285
Zara:	What did I not? Was't not for you, this War	347	M. BRIDE	II.2	298
Osmyn-Alph:	So did it tear the Ears of Mercy, from	350	M. BRIDE	III.1	26
Zara:	I did not know the Princess Favourite.	359	M. BRIDE	III.1	415
Zara:	You more. One that did call himself Alphonso,	364	M. BRIDE	IV.1	116
Zara:	You more. One who did call himself Alphonso,	364	M. BRIDE	IV.1	V116
Zara:	I've heard, her Charity did once extend	365	M. BRIDE	IV.1	181
Zara:	And after did solicite you, on his	366	M. BRIDE	IV.1	186
Gonsalez:	As if she'd rather that she did not hate him.	366	M. BRIDE	IV.1	204
Almeria:	Did ever Father curse his kneeling Child!	369	M. BRIDE	IV.1	321
Almeria:	O that I did, Osmyn, he is my Husband.	370	M. BRIDE	IV.1	356
Selim:	He did: But then as if	375	M. BRIDE	V.1	98
Zara:	Than did that Scene of complicated Horrors.	379	M. BRIDE	V.2	143
Almeria:	Had they or Hearts, or Eyes, that did this Deed?	382	M. BRIDE	V.2	236
Mirabell:	I did as much as Man cou'd, with any reasonable	397	WAY WORLD	I.1	68
Betty:	Did not the Messenger bring you one but now, Sir?	401	WAY WORLD	I.1	240
Betty:	Did not a Messenger bring you one but now, Sir?	401	WAY WORLD	I.1	V240
Marwood:	No; but I'd make him believe I did, and that's	411	WAY WORLD	II.1	58
Fainall:	And wherefore did I marry, but to make lawful Prize of a	415	WAY WORLD	II.1	206
Mrs Fain:	of which you have been the occasion? Why did you	417	WAY WORLD	II.1	263
Witwoud:	you met her Husband and did not ask him for her.	419	WAY WORLD	II.1	350
Millamant:	Mirabell, Did not you take Exceptions last Night?	420	WAY WORLD	II.1	377
Millamant:	Mirabell, Did you take Exceptions last Night?	420	WAY WORLD	II.1	V377
Millamant:	If they did not commend us, we were not handsome!	420	WAY WORLD	II.1	400
Mirabell:	I would give something that you did not know, I	422	WAY WORLD	II.1	460
Waitwell:	That she did indeed, Sir. It was my Fault that she	423	WAY WORLD	II.1	516
Waitwell:	did not make more.	423	WAY WORLD	II.1	517
Foible:	I told her Sir, because I did not know that you might	424	WAY WORLD	II.1	530
Lady Wish:	Me? What did the filthy Fellow say?	427	WAY WORLD	III.1	92
Millamant:	swear I did not mind you.	434	WAY WORLD	III.1	349
Fainall:	but I'le be hang'd if she did not put Fam in her Pocket.	442	WAY WORLD	III.1	V654
Foible:	Yes Madam; but my Lady did not see that part; We	464	WAY WORLD	V.1	78
Sir Wilful:	I hope I committed no Offence Aunt--and if I did I	470	WAY WORLD	V.1	316
Lady Wish:	Tongue;--When I did not see him I cou'd have	472	WAY WORLD	V.1	409
Mirabell:	suspected--she did I say by the wholesome advice of	476	WAY WORLD	V.1	544

Did'st (2)

Almeria:	Did'st thou not say, that Racks and Wheels were	357	M. BRIDE	III.1	311
Lady Wish:	Did'st thou not hear me, Mopus?	425	WAY WORLD	III.1	8

Didst (10)

Fondlewife:	vigorous, and I am Old and impotent--Then why didst	76	OLD BATCH	IV.1	52
Almeria:	--If thou didst!--	328	M. BRIDE	I.1	90
Almeria:	And when I said thou didst know nothing,	328	M. BRIDE	I.1	100
Almeria:	And when I told thee thou didst nothing know,	328	M. BRIDE	I.1	V100
Almeria:	It was because thou didst not know Alphonso:	328	M. BRIDE	I.1	101
Manuel:	It looks as thou didst mourn for him: Just as	333	M. BRIDE	I.1	298
Almeria:	Sure, from thy Father's Tomb, thou didst arise!	343	M. BRIDE	II.2	156
Osmyn-Alph:	I did, and thou didst call me.	343	M. BRIDE	II.2	157
Osmyn-Alph:	I did, and thou, my Love, didst call me; thou.	343	M. BRIDE	II.2	V157
Lady Wish:	Acorn? Why didst thou not bring thy Thimble? Hast thou	425	WAY WORLD	III.1	30

Die (44)   see Dye

Musician:	Men will admire, adore and die,	60	OLD BATCH	II.2	197
Capt Bluff:	Death and Hell to be affronted thus! I'll die before	70	OLD BATCH	III.1	336
Singer:	I die, if I'm not wholly blest.	71	OLD BATCH	III.2	8
Silvia:	No, I'll die before I'll be your Whore--as well as I	74	OLD BATCH	III.2	124
Laetitia:	won't you speak to me, cruel Nykin? Indeed, I'll die, if	95	OLD BATCH	IV.4	246
Brisk:	thing, Laughing all the while as if you were ready to die	134	DOUBL DLR	I.1	268
Lady Froth:	O prettily turn'd again; let me die, but you have	140	DOUBL DLR	II.1	85
Sir Paul:	die of 'em, like a Child, that was cutting his Teeth--	146	DOUBL DLR	II.1	V283
Cynthia:	And he that can't live upon Love, deserves to die in	168	DOUBL DLR	IV.1	34
Mellefont:	And you won't die one, for your own, so still	169	DOUBL DLR	IV.1	63
Lady Ply:	should die, of all Mankind there's none I'd sooner make	170	DOUBL DLR	IV.1	111
Sir Paul:	Wedding Night, to die a Maid; as she did; all were ruin'd,	174	DOUBL DLR	IV.1	252
Sir Paul:	Gads-bud, would that were Matter of Fact too. Die and	178	DOUBL DLR	IV.1	417
Lady Touch:	I'le hold my breath and die, but I'le be free.	184	DOUBL DLR	IV.2	53
Maskwell:	rather die, than seem once, barely seem, dishonest:--	188	DOUBL DLR	V.1	37
Jeremy:	Sir, it's impossible--I may die with you, starve with	218	FOR LOVE	I.1	72
Scandal:	vain! Who would die a Martyr to Sense in a Country	219	FOR LOVE	I.1	139
Sr Sampson:	live; and leave you a good Jointure when I die.	300	FOR LOVE	V.1	120
Almeria:	No, it shall never be; for I will die first,	330	M. BRIDE	I.1	175
Almeria:	Die ten thousand Deaths--Look down, look down	330	M. BRIDE	I.1	176
Zara:	Thou shalt die.	360	M. BRIDE	III.1	434
Osmyn-Alph:	Then you may know for whom I'd die.	360	M. BRIDE	III.1	437
Zara:	More than his Crown, t'impart 'ere Osmyn die.	361	M. BRIDE	IV.1	19
Gonsalez:	Till Osmyn die. Mean time we may learn more	363	M. BRIDE	IV.1	70
Manuel:	Give Order strait, that all the Pris'ners die,	364	M. BRIDE	IV.1	127
Gonsalez:	I'th' Evening Osmyn was to die; at Mid-night	366	M. BRIDE	IV.1	208
Gonsalez:	I'th' Morning he must die again; e're Noon	366	M. BRIDE	IV.1	210
Manuel:	Now doom'd to die, that most accursed Osmyn.	368	M. BRIDE	IV.1	288

Die (continued)
    Almeria: Then all is ended, and we both must die   368   M. BRIDE   IV.1   303
    Almeria: Since thou'rt reveal'd, alone thou shalt not die.   . . . 368   M. BRIDE   IV.1   304
    Zara: Think fit, I'll leave thee my Command to die.   . . . 375   M. BRIDE   V.1   127
    Zara: I can but die with thee to keep my Word.   376   M. BRIDE   V.1   139
    Garcia: Or to repell their Force, or bravely die.   379   M. BRIDE   V.2   107
    Zara: I came prepar'd to die, and see thee die--   380   M. BRIDE   V.2 V165
    Zara: We both should die. Nor is't that I survive;   380   M. BRIDE   V.2   188
    Marwood: that Love shou'd ever die before us; and that the Man so . 410   WAY WORLD   II.1   10
    Millamant: pleases, and they die as soon as one pleases: And then if 420   WAY WORLD   II.1   405
    Lady Wish: shall die with Confusion, if I am forc'd to advance--Oh . 429   WAY WORLD III.1   159
    Waitwell: before I die--I wou'd gladly go out of the World with . 458   WAY WORLD   IV.1   502
    Lady Wish: I shall faint, I shall die, I shall die, oh!   460   WAY WORLD   IV.1   594
    Lady Wish: I shall faint, I shall die, oh! 460   WAY WORLD   IV.1 V594
    Waitwell: Law? I care not for Law. I can but die, and 'tis in   . 461   WAY WORLD   IV.1   623
Dies (8)
    Careless: Adorer dies.   170   DOUBL DLR   IV.1   88
    Lord Touch: No sooner born, but the Vile Parent dies.   203   DOUBL DLR   V.1   596
    Manuel: Is pass'd; if you revoke it not, he dies.   364   M. BRIDE   IV.1   113
    Manuel: For on my Soul he dies, tho' thou, and I, ... 369   M. BRIDE   IV.1   333
    Selim: (Dies.)   380   M. BRIDE   V.2   185
    Zara: (Dies.)   381   M. BRIDE   V.2   212
    Mirabell: Beauty dies upon the Instant: For Beauty is the Lover's . 420   WAY WORLD   II.1   393
    Witwoud: Rotation of Tongue, that an Eccho must wait till she dies, 421   WAY WORLD   II.1   421
Diet (0)   see Paper-Diet
Diff'rent (1)
                  With Nature's Oafs 'tis quite a diff'rent Case, ... 393   WAY WORLD   PRO.   5
Difference (4)
    Lady Froth: difference.   139   DOUBL DLR   II.1   56
                  But in this Court, what difference does appear!   . . . 204   DOUBL DLR   EPI.   12
    Valentine: I know no effectual Difference between continued   . . 254   FOR LOVE   IV.1   40
    Scandal: 'S'death do you make no difference between me and   . . 284   FOR LOVE   IV.1   321
Different (3)
    Maskwell: and Fidelity to Friends, are different and particular   . 150   DOUBL DLR   II.1   447
                  (Mellefont, Maskwell, from different Doors.)   . . 161   DOUBL DLR   IV.1 V512
                  They from each Fair One catch some different Grace,   . 479   WAY WORLD   EPI.   32
Difficult (1)
    Setter: is so difficult--   104   OLD BATCH   V.1   275
Difficulties (2)
    Tattle: you,--I know you love to untie Difficulties--Or if   . . 305   FOR LOVE   V.1   296
    Mrs Fain: her in those Difficulties, from which Mirabell only must . 430   WAY WORLD III.1   192
Difficulty (2)
    Waitwell: Difficulty will be how to recover my Acquaintance and   . 424   WAY WORLD   II.1   557
    Marwood: consent to, without difficulty; she has already but too . 468   WAY WORLD   V.1   259
Difficulty's (1)
    Careless: (aside). So, so, so, this difficulty's over.   181   DOUBL DLR   IV.1 V510
Diffide (1)
    Bellmour: --What Diffide in me, Lucy?   97   OLD BATCH   V.1   46
Diffus'd (1)
    Almeria: Which are diffus'd thro' the revolving Year, ... 330   M. BRIDE   I.1   154
Dig (2)
    Almeria: Let me go, let me fall, sink deep--I'll dig, ... 370   M. BRIDE   IV.1   347
    Almeria: I'll dig a Grave, and tear up Death; I will;   370   M. BRIDE   IV.1   348
Digest (2)
    Sharper: cannot digest it.   80   OLD BATCH   IV.1   173
    Valentine: Here, take away; I'll walk a turn, and digest what   . . 216   FOR LOVE   I.1   3
Digestion (1)
    Sr Sampson: dissected, he has his Vessels of Digestion and Concoction, 245   FOR LOVE   II.1   386
Dignity (2)
    Bellmour: Dignity with the rest of his Brethren. So I must beg   . . 41   OLD BATCH   I.1   159
    Setter: somewhat fall'n from the Dignity of my Function; and   . 105   OLD BATCH   V.1   337
Diligence (2)
    Gonsalez: At my Appartment. Use thy utmost Diligence;   372   M. BRIDE   IV.1   441
    Mirabell: Your Diligence will merit more--In the mean   424   WAY WORLD   II.1   533
Diligent (1)
    Setter: Man of parts. That is without being politick, diligent,
                  secret, ...   65   OLD BATCH III.1   150
Dim (2)
    Osmyn-Alph: Burns dim, and glimmers with expiring Light.   357   M. BRIDE   III.1   324
    Mirabell: Fame, wou'd shew as dim by thee as a dead Whiting's   . 407   WAY WORLD   I.1   454
Dim'd (1)
    Almeria: But want a Guide: for Tears have dim'd my Sight.   . . . 381   M. BRIDE   V.2   221
Diminish (1)
    Mirabell: diminish in their value, and that both the giver loses the 449   WAY WORLD   IV.1   172
Din (1)
    Zara: Is seen, or heard. A dreadful Din was wont   379   M. BRIDE   V.2   135
Din'd (2)
    Belinda: Oh Gad, here comes the Fool that din'd at my Lady   . .   84   OLD BATCH   IV.3   55
    Sir Wilful: my Aunt han't din'd yet--Ha, Friend?   437   WAY WORLD III.1   450
Dinah (1)
    Fondlewife: Wife! My Dinah! Oh Schechemite! Begone, I say.   . . .   90   OLD BATCH   IV.4   67
Dine (3)
    Vainlove: Well good Morrow, let's dine together, I'l meet at   . .   40   OLD BATCH   I.1   129
    Foible: Mr. Witwoud and Mr. Petulant, are come to Dine with   . 432   WAY WORLD III.1   276
    Millamant: dine in my dressing room when I'm out of humour   . . . 450   WAY WORLD   IV.1   220
Dined (1)
    Sir Joseph: (aside). The great Fortune, that dined at my Lady   . .   86   OLD BATCH   IV.3   108
Dining (1)
    Lady Wish: Chafeing-dish of starv'd Embers and Dining behind a   . . 462   WAY WORLD   V.1   6
Dining-Room (1)
    Jenny: He's at the great Glass in the Dining-Room, Madam,   . . 297   FOR LOVE   V.1   3
Dinner (13)
    Mellefont: Custome, after Dinner.--But I made a pretence   . . . 127   DOUBL DLR   I.1   13
    Jeremy: do's Causes at Dinner time.   220   FOR LOVE   I.1   168
    Nurse: Dinner--good lack-a-day, ha, ha, ha, O strange; I'll vow . 235   FOR LOVE   II.1   22
    Fainall: Ay, I'll take a turn before Dinner.   409   WAY WORLD   I.1   509

Dinner (continued)

Foible:	of kissing your Ladyship's Hands after Dinner. . . .	. 428	WAY WORLD	III.1 127
Foible:	of kissing your Ladyship's Hand after Dinner. . . .	. 428	WAY WORLD	III.1 V127
Lady Wish:	here before Dinner--I must make haste.	. 432	WAY WORLD	III.1 275
Mincing:	Mem, I come to acquaint your Laship that Dinner . .	. 441	WAY WORLD	III.1 614
Mincing:	Mem, I am come to acquaint your Laship that Dinner	. 441	WAY WORLD	III.1 V614
Lady Wish:	Boots here--Go down into the Hall--Dinner . . .	. 441	WAY WORLD	III.1 621
Fainall:	disable him for that, he will drink like a Dane: after dinner, ...	. 443	WAY WORLD	III.1 672
Millamant:	may be your Relations. Come to Dinner when I please,	. 450	WAY WORLD	IV.1 219
Foible:	Dinner. She sent the Letter to my Lady, and that missing	. 464	WAY WORLD	V.1 70

Dinner's (1)

| Lady Wish: | before you eat? Dinner's almost ready. . . . . . | . 441 | WAY WORLD | III.1 600 |

Diogenes (1)

| Jeremy: | Diogenes, because he understands Confinement, and liv'd | . 217 | FOR LOVE | I.1 30 |

Dire (9)

Almeria:	And Heat of War, and dire Revenge, he fir'd.	. 329	M. BRIDE	I.1 114
Almeria:	The dire collected Dews, on my poor Head;	. 330	M. BRIDE	I.1 160
Zara:	No, no, it must be Hatred, dire Revenge, ...	. 353	M. BRIDE	III.1 162
Osmyn-Alph:	Some swift and dire event, of her blind Rage, . . .	. 355	M. BRIDE	III.1 231
Manuel:	That Wit of Man, and dire Revenge can think, ...	. 368	M. BRIDE	IV.1 297
Manuel:	Yet somewhat she must mean of dire Import, ...	. 370	M. BRIDE	IV.1 363
Garcia:	This Deed--O dire Mistake! O fatal Blow!	. 377	M. BRIDE	V.2 57
Gonsalez:	And of a piece with this Day's dire Misdeeds. . . .	. 379	M. BRIDE	V.2 123
Zara:	Split Heart, burst ev'ry Vein, at this dire Object:	. 380	M. BRIDE	V.2 V163

Direct (7)

Mellefont:	For Heaven's sake, Madam, to whom do you direct . . .	. 145	DOUBL DLR	II.1 250
	And suffers Judges to direct the Jury.	. 204	DOUBL DLR	EPI. 11
Foresight:	Houses. Can Judge of Motions Direct and Retrograde, of	. 241	FOR LOVE	II.1 212
Sr Sampson:	Helm, Sirrah, don't direct me.	. 308	FOR LOVE	V.1 419
	Art may direct, but Nature is his aim;	. 324	M. BRIDE	PRO. 36
Sir Wilful:	nor the Weather-Cock your Companion. I direct my . .	. 440	WAY WORLD	III.1 571
Lady Wish:	the direct Mold of Vertue? I have not only been a Mold	. 465	WAY WORLD	V.1 144

Directed (7)

Bellmour:	find it directed to Mr. Vainlove. Gad, Madam, I ask you a	. 82	OLD BATCH	IV.2 57
Mellefont:	where it was directed. Still it gave me less perplexity to	. 129	DOUBL DLR	I.1 91
Boy:	'Tis directed to your Worship.	. 161	DOUBL DLR	III.1 397
Maskwell:	self, and some ill Chance might have directed malicious	. 189	DOUBL DLR	V.1 44
Sr Sampson:	directed by a Dreamer, an Omen-hunter, and defer Business	283	FOR LOVE	IV.1 289
Foresight:	I will be directed by you.	. 293	FOR LOVE	IV.1 670
Marwood:	unhappily directed to miscarry.	. 434	WAY WORLD	III.1 347

Direction (5)

Bellmour:	was to come by your direction.--But I laid a trap . .	. 94	OLD BATCH	IV.4 208
Manuel:	Thou follow, and give heed to my Direction.	. 374	M. BRIDE	V.1 88
Manuel:	Follow me, and give heed to my Direction.	. 374	M. BRIDE	V.1 V 88
Mirabell:	That was by Foible's Direction, and my Instruction,	. 418	WAY WORLD	II.1 305
Lady Wish:	my direction to Sir Wilfull.	. 472	WAY WORLD	V.1 418

Directions (3)

Bellmour:	I have Directions in my Pocket, which agree with . .	. 81	OLD BATCH	IV.2 31
Buckram:	Sir, it is drawn according to your Directions; there . .	. 308	FOR LOVE	V.1 429
Waitwell:	she can take your Directions as readily as my Instructions,	423	WAY WORLD	II.1 510

Directly (1)

| Lady Ply: | Demonstration, answer me directly--but I have not . . | . 146 | DOUBL DLR | II.1 303 |

Directs (1)

| | There, as instinct directs, to Swim, or Drown. . . . | . 125 | DOUBL DLR | PRO. 4 |

Dirt (5)

Bellmour:	may extract Gold from that Dirt.	. 46	OLD BATCH	I.1 346
Sharper:	Dirt, you have large Acres and can soon repay it-- . .	. 50	OLD BATCH	II.1 109
Sharper:	Mony is but Dirt Sir Joseph--Mere Dirt.	. 50	OLD BATCH	II.1 110
Sir Joseph:	But I profess, 'tis a Dirt I have wash'd my Hands of . .	. 50	OLD BATCH	II.1 111

Dirt-pies (1)

| Ben: | for her to learn her Sampler, and make Dirt-pies, than to | 285 | FOR LOVE | IV.1 374 |

Dirty (3)

Sir Joseph:	I do scorn a dirty thing. But agad 'Ime a little out of	. 50	OLD BATCH	II.1 105
Ben:	me alone as soon as I come home, with such a dirty dowdy	. 264	FOR LOVE	III.1 423
Valentine:	Master's Shop in the morning, may ten to one, dirty his	. 289	FOR LOVE	IV.1 509

Disable (1)

| Fainall: | disable him for that, he will drink like a Dane: after dinner, ... | . 443 | WAY WORLD | III.1 672 |

Disabled (1)

| Heartwell: | occasions; till in a little time, being disabled or disarm'd, ... | . 43 | OLD BATCH | I.1 247 |

Disadvantage (1)

| Lady Touch: | disadvantage; besides, I find, my Lord, you are prepared | . 151 | DOUBL DLR | III.1 36 |

Disagree (1)

| Gonsalez: | Sometimes concur, and sometime disagree; . . . . . | . 366 | M. BRIDE | IV.1 196 |

Disagreeable (2)

| Cynthia: | time, is as disagreeable as to sing out of time or out of | 163 | DOUBL DLR | III.1 473 |
| Mirabell: | Why do we daily commit disagreeable and dangerous . . | . 417 | WAY WORLD | II.1 265 |

Disappoint (4)

Vainlove:	I should disappoint her if I did not--By her	. 80	OLD BATCH	IV.2 188
Sharper:	Now, were I ill-natur'd, wou'd I utterly disappoint . .	. 100	OLD BATCH	V.1 137
Maskwell:	Mean? Not to disappoint the Lady I assure you-- . . .	. 157	DOUBL DLR	III.1 242
Mellefont:	think it is not in the power of Fate to disappoint my hopes--	. 157	DOUBL DLR	III.1 258

Disappointed (7)

Brisk:	be disappointed?	. 134	DOUBL DLR	I.1 270
Careless:	Then I shall be disappointed indeed.	. 134	DOUBL DLR	I.1 279
Scandal:	explaining my self to you--but was disappointed all this day;	. 269	FOR LOVE	III.1 590
Scandal:	that all his measures are disappointed.	. 283	FOR LOVE	IV.1 300
Valentine:	I have been disappointed of my only Hope; and he . .	. 312	FOR LOVE	V.1 543
	And how they're disappointed if they're pleas'd! . .	. 385	M. BRIDE	EPI. 14
	And how they're disappointed when they're pleas'd! . .	. 385	M. BRIDE	EPI. V 14

Disappointing (1)

| Mirabell: | Play, and disappointing the Frolick which you had to pick | 451 | WAY WORLD | IV.1 242 |

Disappointment (4)
```
   Silvia:      Jealousie attend her Love; and Disappointment meet his   .  61  OLD BATCH III.1   31
   Bellmour:    another Woman would the like Disappointment; but my      . 100  OLD BATCH  V.1  151
   Lady Touch:  How does he bear his Disappointment?   . . . . . . .       154  DOUBL DLR III.1  133
   Manuel:      And give her Eyes yet greater Disappointment.   . . . .    374  M. BRIDE   V.1   82
Disarm (1)
   Maskwell:    Conditions. For this Discovery will disarm her of all   .  157  DOUBL DLR III.1  254
Disarm'd (3)
   Heartwell:   occasions; till in a little time, being disabled or
                   disarm'd,   . . . . . . . . . . . . . . . . . . .        43  OLD BATCH  I.1  247
   Mellefont:   having disarm'd her; in a gust of Passion she left me, and 130  DOUEL DLR  I.1  116
   Lady Touch:  disarm'd my Soul.   . . . . . . . . . . . . .               198  DOUEL DLR  V.1  404
Disbanded (1)
   Foible:      some disbanded Officer I warrant--Half Pay is but   . .    427  WAY WORLD III.1   97
Discarded (1)
   Millamant:   than a decay'd Beauty, or a discarded Tost;   . . . . .    433  WAY WORLD III.1  324
Discernable (1)
   Foible:      Madam. There are some Cracks discernable in the white   .  429  WAY WORLD III.1  145
Discerning (3)
                In which, we do not doubt but they're discerning,   . .    204  DOUEL DLR EPI.   25
   Painall:     somewhat too discerning in the Failings of your Mistress.  399  WAY WORLD  I.1  157
   Mirabell:    And for a discerning Man, somewhat too passionate   . .    399  WAY WORLD  I.1  158
Discharg'd (2)
   Capt Bluff:  O I am calm Sir, calm as a discharg'd Culverin--But   .     54  OLD BATCH II.1  241
   Almeria:     Discharg'd this Debt, incumbent on my Love.   . . . .      330  M. BRIDE   I.1  193
Discharge (3)
   Sharper:     free Discharge to Sir Joseph Wittoll and Captain Bluffe; for 110 OLD BATCH  V.2   86
   Mrs Frail:   Lover, and give him his discharge, and come to you.   .    285  FOR LOVE  IV.1  352
   Zara:        Against your State: and fully to discharge   . . . .       364  M. BRIDE  IV.1  140
Discipline (1)
   Fondlewife:  Ay, here's Discipline!   . . . . . . . . . . .              92  OLD BATCH IV.4  113
Disclaim (2)
   Brisk:       threatens to disclaim you for a Son-in-Law, and my Lord    128  DOUBL DLR  I.1   55
   Scandal:     Do, I'll dye a Martyr, rather than disclaim my   . . .     269  FOR LOVE III.1  595
Disclos'd (2)
   Singer-F:    But sagely at length he this Secret disclos'd:   . . .     259  FOR LOVE III.1  206
   Gonsalez:    He there disclos'd himself to Albucacim,   . . . . .       363  M. BRIDE  IV.1   85
Disclose (1)
   Marwood:     Disclose it to your Wife; own what has past   . . . .      415  WAY WORLD II.1  191
Disclosed (1)
   Bellmour:    when it disclosed the Cheat, which, that trusty Bawd of  .  38  OLD BATCH  I.1   49
Discompose (2)
   Foible:      discompose you when you were to receive Sir Rowland.   .   461  WAY WORLD IV.1  620
   Marwood:     record; not even in Dooms-day-Book: to discompose the   .  467  WAY WORLD  V.1  217
Discomposed (1)
   Maskwell:    I am concern'd to see your Lordship discomposed--   . .    195  DOUEL DLR  V.1  305
Discourage (2)
   Foresight:   Hum--truly I don't care to discourage a young   . . .     243  FOR LOVE  II.1  308
   Scandal:     discourage you--But it is palpable that you are not
                   satisfy'd.   . . . . . . . . . . . . . . .              268  FOR LOVE III.1  560
Discourse (8)
   Bellmour:    discourse of their diseases and infirmities? What fine Lady 42 OLD BATCH  I.1  182
   Araminta:    Discourse--Pray oblige us with the last new Song.   . .     59  OLD BATCH II.2  187
   Araminta:    to find me in discourse with you.--Be discreet.--   . .     86  OLD BATCH IV.3  105
   Careless:    Madam,--if your Ladyship please, we'll discourse of this in 163 DOUBL DLR III.1  494
   Tattle:      (coming up). Scandal, are you in private Discourse, any   . 254 FOR LOVE III.1   42
   Ben:         Discourse with you, an 'twere not a main high Wind   . .   263  FOR LOVE III.1  370
   Sir Wilful:  Discourse to the Lady, Sir: 'Tis like my Aunt may have     440  WAY WORLD III.1  572
   Sir Wilful:  French as they say, whereby to hold discourse in Foreign   440  WAY WORLD III.1  584
Discourses (3)
   Maskwell:    for those free discourses which I have had with my self.   189 DOUBL DLR  V.1   51
   Scandal:     Discourses, and sometimes rather think him inspir'd than   285 FOR LOVE  IV.1  345
   Marwood:     those insipid dry Discourses, with which our Sex of force  410 WAY WORLD  II.1   21
Discov'ry (1)
   Maskwell:    upon the Rack; and made discov'ry of her last Plot: I hope 199 DOUBL DLR  V.1  462
Discover (23)
   Musician:    Never let him all discover,   . . . . . . . . . .           59  OLD BATCH II.2  194
   Lucy:        may discover something in my Masque--Worthy Sir, a   . .     65  OLD BATCH III.1  155
   Heartwell:   a naked Truth, which I'm ashamed to discover.   . . .       72  OLD BATCH III.2   64
   Laetitia:    Sure, when he does not see his face, he won't discover   .   91  OLD BATCH IV.4   90
   Heartwell:   hold:--If he shou'd not, I were a Fool to discover it.--    104  OLD BATCH  V.1  299
   Maskwell:    so little time must of necessity discover. Yet he is
                   apprehensive                                            154  DOUBL DLR III.1  136
   Maskwell:    time he attempted any thing of that kind, to discover it to 154 DOUBL DLR III.1  154
   Mellefont:   Soul, thou art villainously bent to discover all to me,    156  DOUBL DLR III.1  205
   Maskwell:    know whether I can in honour discover all.   . . . .       156  DOUBL DLR III.1  208
   Maskwell:    know whether I can in honour discover 'em all   . . .      156  DOUBL DLR III.1 V208
   Maskwell:    thought a vent; which might discover that I lov'd, nor     188  DOUBL DLR  V.1   35
   Maskwell:    discover the whole and real truth of the matter to him,    190  DOUBL DLR  V.1   98
   Maskwell:    may not discover you in the Coach, but think the Cheat     193  DOUBL DLR  V.1  233
   Mrs Fore:    (aside). O Devil on't, that I cou'd not discover   . .      248  FOR LOVE  II.1  471
   Valentine:   Company but Angelica, that I may discover my design to     291  FOR LOVE  IV.1  595
   Foresight:   to try if I could discover it by my Art--hum, ha! I   .    304  FOR LOVE   V.1  259
   Ben:         Pump to your Bosom, I believe we shou'd discover a foul    309  FOR LOVE   V.1  433
   Marwood:     O if he shou'd ever discover it, he wou'd   . . . .        411  WAY WORLD II.1   61
   Mrs Fain:    you will discover the Imposture betimes; and release her   417  WAY WORLD II.1  297
   Mirabell:    and discover Beauties in it: For that reflects our Praises, 420 WAY WORLD II.1  397
   Mrs Fain:    with Mirabell, and I'm afraid will discover it to my Lady. 430 WAY WORLD III.1  186
   Foible:      Discover what, Madam?   . . . . . . . . .                   430  WAY WORLD III.1  187
   Marwood:     Discover to my Lady your Wife's conduct;   . . . . .       442  WAY WORLD III.1  659
Discover'd (21)
   Setter:      his Youth; and some say, with that Eye, he first discover'd 64 OLD BATCH III.1  128
   Laetitia:    (aside). I'me amaz'd; sure he has discover'd nothing--   .   77  OLD BATCH IV.1   79
   Laetitia:    (aside). I am discover'd:--And either Vainlove is   . .      82  OLD BATCH IV.2   59
   Bellmour:    discover'd.   . . . . . . . . . . . . . . .                  92  OLD BATCH IV.4  111
   Sir Paul:    discover'd--But let me see to make an end on't.--   . .     178  DOUBL DLR IV.1  407
```

Discover'd   (continued)

171

Do   (continued)

Speaker	Line	PAGE	TITLE	ACT.SC	LINE
Bellmour:	Kind Looks and Actions(from Success)do prove,	60	OLD BATCH	II.2	225
Silvia:	but I'le do my weak endeavour, though I fear I have not	62	OLD BATCH	III.1	52
Heartwell:	Well, Why do you not move? Feet do your	62	OLD BATCH	III.1	73
Bellmour:	heartily? I'de do a little more good in my generation first,	63	OLD BATCH	III.1	107
Setter:	As all lew'd projects do Sir, where the Devil prevents	64	OLD BATCH	III.1	117
Setter:	Gentlemen I do most properly appertain--The one	64	OLD BATCH	III.1	138
Setter:	I do swear to the utmost of my power.	66	OLD BATCH	III.1	216
Sharper:	This is a double Generosity--Do me a Kindness	68	OLD BATCH	III.1	289
Sharper:	What do you mutter about a time, Rascal--You	69	OLD BATCH	III.1	315
Singer:	Dearest Thyrsis, do not move me,	71	OLD BATCH	III.2 V	12
Singer:	Do not--do not--if you Love me	71	OLD BATCH	III.2 V	13
Heartwell:	ha? Speak Syren--Cons why do I look on her!	72	OLD BATCH	III.2	40
Heartwell:	Yet I must--Speak dear Angel, Devil, Saint, Witch; do	72	OLD BATCH	III.2	41
Heartwell:	--I tell thee I do love thee, and tell it for a Truth,	72	OLD BATCH	III.2	63
Silvia:	one. But do you intend to Marry me?	73	OLD BATCH	III.2	94
Lucy:	first. I know that will do--walk in and I'le shew	75	OLD BATCH	III.2	158
Lucy:	Whom Love and Vengeance do at once delight.	75	OLD BATCH	III.2	163
Laetitia:	Tyrannize--Go on cruel Man, do, Triumph over my	77	OLD BATCH	IV.1	91
Fondlewife:	Kiss kiss, ifeck I do.	78	OLD BATCH	IV.1	123
Fondlewife:	I profess I do love thee better, than 500 Pound--	78	OLD BATCH	IV.1	129
Belinda:	O frightful! Cousin, What shall we do? These things	85	OLD BATCH	IV.3	75
Vainlove:	Did I dream? Or do I dream? Shall I believe my	88	OLD BATCH	IV.3	175
Laetitia:	(aside). Ruin'd, past redemption! What shall I do?	90	OLD BATCH	IV.4	45
Laetitia:	(aside). What can I do now! Oh! my Dear, I have	91	OLD BATCH	IV.4	76
Laetitia:	think that I have nothing to do but excuse him; 'tis enough,	93	OLD BATCH	IV.4	168
Fondlewife:	Here, here, I do believe thee.--I won't	96	OLD BATCH	IV.4	262
Fondlewife:	my Dear. Nay, I will believe thee, I do, Ifeck.	96	OLD BATCH	IV.4	270
Lucy:	An Executioner qualified to do your Business. He has	97	OLD BATCH	V.1	18
Lucy:	I warrant you--Do you go and prepare your Bride.	97	OLD BATCH	V.1	21
Bellmour:	me Leave to acquaint you with it.--Do you carry on	98	OLD BATCH	V.1	66
Bellmour:	--If you do, I'll spoil all.--I have some private	98	OLD BATCH	V.1	68
Bellmour:	Reasons for what I do, which I'll tell you within.--In	98	OLD BATCH	V.1	69
Lucy:	you; but if you do deceive me, the Curse of all kind,	98	OLD BATCH	V.1	76
Vainlove:	Ha! It has a Colour.--But how do you know	99	OLD BATCH	V.1	110
Setter:	I do suspect as much;--because why, Sir:--	99	OLD BATCH	V.1	112
Sharper:	But how the Devil do you think to acquit your self	100	OLD BATCH	V.1	154
Sir Joseph:	Ay; Do, do, Captain, if you think fit.--You	101	OLD BATCH	V.1	183
Sir Joseph:	Ay; Do, do, Captain, if you think fitting.--You	101	OLD BATCH	V.1 V183	
Sir Joseph:	Prithee, What do you see in my face, that looks as	101	OLD BATCH	V.1	191
Sharper:	Well, I'll go and inform your Master; and do you	102	OLD BATCH	V.1	218
Setter:	What have such poor Rogues as I to do with Reputation?	102	OLD BATCH	V.1	230
Setter:	Captain, I wou'd do any thing to serve you; but this	104	OLD BATCH	V.1	274
Setter:	do deserve the Epithet.--Mercury was a Pimp too;	105	OLD BATCH	V.1	335
Setter:	do condescend to be scandalously employ'd in the	105	OLD BATCH	V.1	338
Belinda:	that will do a civil thing to his Wife, or say a civil thing to	108	OLD BATCH	V.2	30
	How say you, Sparks? How do you stand affected?	113	OLD BATCH	EPI.	23
	Let Nature work, and do not Damn too soon,	125	DOUEL DLR	PRO.	16
Brisk:	Boys, Boys, Lads, where are you? What, do you give	128	DOUEL DLR	I.1	20
Mellefont:	do, they'll fall asleep else.	128	DOUEL DLR	I.1	48
Mellefont:	this Juncture it will do me Service.--I'll tell you, I	129	DOUEL DLR	I.1	67
Mellefont:	Truth. Prithee do thou wear none to day; but allow Brisk	129	DOUEL DLR	I.1	71
Mellefont:	Addresses, she has endeavour'd to do me all ill Offices with	129	DOUEL DLR	I.1	87
Mellefont:	It is so. Well, the Service that you are to do me,	130	DOUEL DLR	I.1	124
Mellefont:	It is so. Well, the Service you are to do me,	130	DOUEL DLR	I.1 V124	
Careless:	them, you do not suspect: For all her Passion for you.	131	DOUEL DLR	I.1	154
Careless:	them, you do not suspect: Notwithstanding her Passion for you.	131	DOUEL DLR	I.1 V154	
Mellefont:	to do me Service; and he endeavours to be well in her	131	DOUEL DLR	I.1	156
Lord Froth:	O foy, Sir Paul, what do you mean? Merry! O	132	DOUEL DLR	I.1	185
Brisk:	me perish, do I never say any thing worthy to be Laugh'd	132	DOUEL DLR	I.1	195
Maskwell:	I do not.	135	DOUEL DLR	I.1	308
Lady Touch:	Death, do you dally with my Passion?	135	DOUEL DLR	I.1	320
Maskwell:	Rogue still, to do you Service; and you are flinging	136	DOUEL DLR	I.1	337
Lady Touch:	Again, provoke me! Do you wind me like	137	DOUEL DLR	I.1	380
Maskwell:	same Fire? Do you not Love him still? How have I this	137	DOUEL DLR	I.1	387
Lady Touch:	O' Maskwell, in Vain I do disguise me from	137	DOUEL DLR	I.1	396
Lady Froth:	O I Writ, Writ abundantly,--do you never	138	DOUEL DLR	II.1	13
Lady Froth:	the very Phosphorus of our Hemisphere. Do you understand	139	DOUEL DLR	II.1	32
Lady Froth:	ha, ha, do you remember, my Lord?	140	DOUEL DLR	II.1	64
Lord Froth:	D'e think he'll Love you as well as I do my	141	DOUEL DLR	II.1	102
Lord Froth:	Heavens! that can never be; but why do you	141	DOUEL DLR	II.1	105
Brisk:	but when I do--keen Iambicks I'gad. But my Lord	141	DOUEL DLR	II.1	117
Lady Froth:	is my Lord's Love to me. And what do you think I	141	DOUEL DLR	II.1	121
Mellefont:	For Heaven's sake, Madam, to whom do you direct	145	DOUEL DLR	II.1	250
Sir Paul:	Do you think my Daughter, this pretty Creature;	145	DOUEL DLR	II.1	264
Sir Paul:	gads bud she's a Wife for a Cherubin! Do you think her	145	DOUEL DLR	II.1	265
Maskwell:	same Words and Accents, when I speak what I do think;	150	DOUEL DLR	II.1	461
Maskwell:	and when I speak what I do not think--the very same--	150	DOUEL DLR	II.1	462
Lady Touch:	to dissemble: I own it to you; in short I do believe it, nay,	151	DOUEL DLR	III.1	40
Lady Touch:	--I dare swear he's sorry--and were it to do again, would	152	DOUEL DLR	III.1	77
Lord Touch:	Confusion and Hell, what do I hear!	153	DOUEL DLR	III.1	86
Lady Touch:	let me beg you do now: I'll come immediately, and tell	153	DOUEL DLR	III.1	119
Lady Touch:	Expedition indeed; for all we do, must be	154	DOUEL DLR	III.1	141
Lady Touch:	I'll do it--I'll tell him you hindred	155	DOUEL DLR	III.1	162
Maskwell:	mischief, what mischief I shall do, is to be paid with	156	DOUEL DLR	III.1	219
Maskwell:	mischief, what mischief I do, is to be paid with	156	DOUEL DLR	III.1 V219	
Sir Paul:	do so no more; d'ye hear, Tim?	161	DOUEL DLR	III.1	399
Sir Paul:	no, no, you shoot wide of the mark a mile; indeed you do,	161	DOUEL DLR	III.1	427
Sir Paul:	year to an Old Man, who would do good in his Generation?	162	DOUEL DLR	III.1	435
Lord Froth:	then, what do they laugh at? For you know laughing	163	DOUEL DLR	III.1	477
Brisk:	I'm afraid that simile wont do in wet Weather--	164	DOUEL DLR	III.1	517
Lady Froth:	No, for the Sun it wont, but it will do for the	164	DOUEL DLR	III.1	519
Cynthia:	Ay, ay, what have we to do with 'em; you know we	168	DOUEL DLR	IV.1	31

Speaker	Text	PAGE	TITLE	ACT.SC	LINE
Lady Ply:	me as a fine thing. Well, I must do you this justice, and	169	DOUBL DLR	IV.1	71
Sir Paul:	Thou art my tender Lambkin, and shalt do what	171	DOUBL DLR	IV.1	132
Sir Paul:	There it is, Madam; Do you want a Pen and Ink?	173	DOUBL DLR	IV.1	218
Sir Paul:	Girl? Do gads-bud, think on thy old Father; Heh? Make .	173	DOUBL DLR	IV.1	230
Sir Paul:	Pshaw, Pshaw, you fib you Baggage, you do	174	DOUBL DLR	IV.1	246
Lady Froth:	see me do it with him.	177	DOUBL DLR	IV.1	370
Lady Froth:	--Shall you and I do our close Dance to show	177	DOUBL DLR	IV.1	374
Lord Froth:	--No, my Dear, do it with him.	177	DOUBL DLR	IV.1	376
Lady Froth:	--I'll do it with him, my Lord, when you are	177	DOUBL DLR	IV.1	377
Lady Ply:	now, Sir Paul, what do you think of your Friend Careless? .	179	DOUBL DLR	IV.1	438
Lady Ply:	now I find was of your own inditing--I do Heathen, . . .	179	DOUBL DLR	IV.1	456
Lady Ply:	I do, see my Face no more;	179	DOUBL DLR	IV.1	457
Lady Ply:	Did I? Do you doubt me, Turk, Sarazen? I	179	DOUBL DLR	IV.1	462
Sir Paul:	Commission--If I desired him to do any more than . . .	180	DOUBL DLR	IV.1	471
Careless:	effects that will have, but I'll be sure to tell you when				
	I do, ...	180	DOUBL DLR	IV.1	502
Careless:	What do you mean?	181	DOUBL DLR	IV.1	507
Maskwell:	may work upon him: then, for me to do it! I have . . .	182	DOUBL DLR	IV.1	566
Maskwell:	My Duty to your Lordship, makes me do a severe	183	DOUBL DLR	IV.1	588
Maskwell:	I confess you do Reproach me when I see you	183	DOUBL DLR	IV.2	13
Lady Touch:	O. What shall I do? say? whither shall I	185	DOUBL DLR	IV.2	57
Lady Touch:	your Pride--Do but conceal my failings, and forgive-- .	185	DOUBL DLR	IV.2	86
Mellefont:	me; I never had more need of him--But what can he do? .	187	DOUBL DLR	IV.2	149
Maskwell:	Why do I love! yet Heaven and my waking	188	DOUBL DLR	V.1	33
Maskwell:	Little do you think that your Aunt has kept her	190	DOUBL DLR	V.1	109
Lord Touch:	I cannot do too much, for so much merit.	191	DOUBL DLR	V.1	123
Lady Touch:	What shall I do? how shall I think? I cannot think, --all	191	DOUBL DLR	V.1	154
Maskwell:	do so?	193	DOUBL DLR	V.1	228
Maskwell:	Nay, good Mr. Saygrace do not prolong the time, . . .	194	DOUBL DLR	V.1	276
Saygrace:	middle of a Sermon to do you pleasure.	195	DOUBL DLR	V.1	281
Saygrace:	middle of a Sermon to do you a pleasure.	195	DOUBL DLR	V.1	V281
Maskwell:	You could not do me a greater,--except--	195	DOUBL DLR	V.1	282
Maskwell:	do not speak, that she may not distinguish you from .	195	DOUBL DLR	V.1	294
Maskwell:	Come, why do you dally with me thus?	197	DOUBL DLR	V.1	385
Lady Touch:	Ha! do you mock my Rage? then this shall	198	DOUBL DLR	V.1	391
Lord Touch:	Ha! O poison to my Ears! what do I hear!	198	DOUBL DLR	V.1	427
Maskwell:	be otherwhere employ'd--do you procure her Night-Gown, .	199	DOUBL DLR	V.1	444
Lord Touch:	I do him fresh wrong to question his forgiveness; . .	200	DOUBL DLR	V.1	481
Lord Touch:	inform my Nephew, and do you quickly as you can, bring .	200	DOUBL DLR	V.1	487
Lord Froth:	How do you mean? My Wife!	200	DOUBL DLR	V.1	502
Lord Froth:	How? where, when, what to do?	201	DOUBL DLR	V.1	508
Mellefont:	your hand;--do you hold down your head? Yes, I am . .	202	DOUBL DLR	V.1	569
Lord Touch:	let me hasten to do Justice, in rewarding Virtue and wrong'd	203	DOUBL DLR	V.1	582
	In which, we do not doubt but they're discerning, . .	204	DOUBL DLR	EPI.	25
Jeremy:	in a Tub, go to Prison for you? 'Slife, Sir, what do you .	217	FOR LOVE	I.1	31
Jeremy:	as much as they do one another.	217	FOR LOVE	I.1	40
Valentine:	Yes, I do; I'll write a Play.	217	FOR LOVE	I.1	63
Jeremy:	I do at a Horse-Race. The Air upon Banstead-Downs is .	218	FOR LOVE	I.1	93
Valentine:	But tell me what you would have me do?--What do . . .	220	FOR LOVE	I.1	157
Valentine:	But tell me what you would have me do?--What does . .	220	FOR LOVE	I.1	V157
Scandal:	The World behaves it self, as it used to do on such .	220	FOR LOVE	I.1	159
Scandal:	The World behaves it self, as it uses to do on such .	220	FOR LOVE	I.1	V159
Valentine:	And how the Devil do you mean to keep your	221	FOR LOVE	I.1	178
Valentine:	an Army lead just such a life as I do; have just such Crowds	221	FOR LOVE	I.1	189
Valentine:	Scandal, learn to spare your Friends, and do not . . .	221	FOR LOVE	I.1	198
Valentine:	Drink first. Scandal, why do you not Drink?	223	FOR LOVE	I.1	255
Snap:	must do our Office, tell us.--We have half a dozen . .	224	FOR LOVE	I.1	296
Scandal:	And how do you expect to have your Money again, . . .	224	FOR LOVE	I.1	315
Scandal:	Not know 'em? Why, thou never hadst to do with . . .	226	FOR LOVE	I.1	401
Tattle:	never could meddle with a Woman that had to do with .	227	FOR LOVE	I.1	411
Scandal:	To tell what? Why, what do you know of Mrs. . . .	228	FOR LOVE	I.1	463
Tattle:	Nay, what do you mean, Gentlemen?	229	FOR LOVE	I.1	492
Tattle:	Mum--O Madam, you do me too much Honour.	231	FOR LOVE	I.1	551
Mrs Frail:	Pooh, No I thank you, I have enough to do to	232	FOR LOVE	I.1	596
Nurse:	--O Lord, what's here to do?--I in unlawful	238	FOR LOVE	II.1	99
Nurse:	ever bear the like now--Sir, did ever I do any thing .	238	FOR LOVE	II.1	101
Angelica:	Do Uncle, lock 'em up quickly before my Aunt	239	FOR LOVE	II.1	133
Angelica:	do with any thing but Astrologers, Uncle. That makes my	239	FOR LOVE	II.1	144
Foresight:	something; tell me, and I'll forgive you; do, good Neice .	239	FOR LOVE	II.1	147
Foresight:	Do you laugh?--Well Gentlewoman, I'll--	239	FOR LOVE	II.1	156
Foresight:	be better inform'd of this--(Aside)--Do you mean my .	241	FOR LOVE	II.1	230
Foresight:	But what do you know of my Wife, Sir Sampson? . . .	242	FOR LOVE	II.1	255
Foresight:	a young Man, I wonder what he can do with it! . . .	243	FOR LOVE	II.1	278
Sr Sampson:	Body o' me, so do I.--Heark ye, Valentine, ...	243	FOR LOVE	II.1	279
Sr Sampson:	Excuse! Impudence! why Sirrah, mayn't I do	244	FOR LOVE	II.1	323
Valentine:	I know no more why I came, than you do why	244	FOR LOVE	II.1	333
Sr Sampson:	'Oons, what had I to do to get Children,--	245	FOR LOVE	II.1	349
Sr Sampson:	he do with a distinguishing taste?--I warrant now he'd .	245	FOR LOVE	II.1	368
Mrs Frail:	What have you to do to watch me?--'S'life I'll . . .	246	FOR LOVE	II.1	415
Mrs Frail:	do what I please.	246	FOR LOVE	II.1	416
Mrs Fore:	What do you mean Sister?	247	FOR LOVE	II.1	442
Mrs Frail:	Was I? what do you mean?	247	FOR LOVE	II.1	443
Mrs Frail:	The World's end! What, do you mean to banter	247	FOR LOVE	II.1	448
Mrs Frail:	Not by a Dozen Years wearing.--But I do	247	FOR LOVE	II.1	461
Mrs Fore:	as you say, since we are both Wounded, let us do that is .	248	FOR LOVE	II.1	477
Mrs Fore:	as you say, since we are both Wounded, let us do what is .	248	FOR LOVE	II.1	V477
Mrs Fore:	I do; and will help you to the utmost of my	248	FOR LOVE	II.1	497
Miss Prue:	What makes 'em go away, Mr. Tattle? What do	251	FOR LOVE	II.1	581
Miss Prue:	they mean, do you know?	251	FOR LOVE	II.1	582
Miss Prue:	No! what then? what shall you and I do together? . .	251	FOR LOVE	II.1	587
Tattle:	do as she would be done by--Gad I'll understand it so. .	251	FOR LOVE	II.1	594
Miss Prue:	Well, we'll do it again.	252	FOR LOVE	II.1	637
Nurse:	to do?--O the Father! A Man with her!--Why, ...	253	FOR LOVE	III.1	8
Miss Prue:	Father, what shall I do now?	253	FOR LOVE	III.1	16
Scandal:	Only for the affectation of it, as the Women do for . .	254	FOR LOVE	III.1	36

Do   (continued)

		PAGE	TITLE	ACT.SC	LINE
Tattle:	For Heaven's sake, if you do guess, say nothing; Gad,	258	FOR LOVE	III.1	194
Sr Sampson:	Support, like Ivy round a dead Oak: Faith I do; I love to	260	FOR LOVE	III.1	264
Ben:	Father, and how do all at home? How do's Brother Dick,	261	FOR LOVE	III.1	290
Ben:	Why an you do, You may run the risk to be overset,	262	FOR LOVE	III.1	334
Miss Prue:	do what he will; I'm too big to be whipt, so I'll tell you	264	FOR LOVE	III.1	398
Ben:	end;--And may-hap I like you as little as you do me:--	264	FOR LOVE	III.1	405
Ben:	Whipping no more than you do. But I tell you one thing,	264	FOR LOVE	III.1	407
Ben:	What, do you mean that fair-Weather Spark that was	264	FOR LOVE	III.1	419
Mrs Frail:	Lord, what shall we do, there's my Brother	265	FOR LOVE	III.1	446
Mrs Frail:	Foresight, and Sir Sampson coming. Sister, do you take Miss	265	FOR LOVE	III.1	447
Scandal:	to Night, because he has some Business to do in a Dream.	266	FOR LOVE	III.1	503
Sr Sampson:	Hoity toity, What have I to do with his Dreams	267	FOR LOVE	III.1	504
Sr Sampson:	Liar--Or if that won't do, I'll bring a Lawyer that	267	FOR LOVE	III.1	509
Scandal:	Nay, nay, 'tis manifest; I do not flatter you--But	267	FOR LOVE	III.1	519
Scandal:	methinks he does not look as he used to do.	268	FOR LOVE	III.1	550
Scandal:	you do not know your self.	268	FOR LOVE	III.1	564
Scandal:	Do you sleep well o'nights?	268	FOR LOVE	III.1	566
Scandal:	Are you certain? You do not look so.	268	FOR LOVE	III.1	568
Scandal:	Do, I'll dye a Martyr, rather than disclaim my	269	FOR LOVE	III.1	595
Foresight:	(looking in the Glass). I do not see any Revolution	269	FOR LOVE	III.1	600
Foresight:	Cheeks have been gather'd many Years;--ha! I do not	269	FOR LOVE	III.1	603
Mrs Fore:	How do you do, Mr. Foresight?	269	FOR LOVE	III.1	613
Scandal:	Do so, Mr. Foresight, and say your Pray'rs;--He	270	FOR LOVE	III.1	626
Foresight:	Do you think so, Mr. Scandal?	270	FOR LOVE	III.1	630
Foresight:	Do I? And d'ye hear--bring me, let me see--	270	FOR LOVE	III.1	645
Foresight:	will be combust; and then I may do well.	270	FOR LOVE	III.1	649
Mrs Fore:	Well; and what use do you hope to make of	271	FOR LOVE	III.1	659
Scandal:	Yes, Faith I do; I have a better Opinion both of you	271	FOR LOVE	III.1	662
Mrs Fore:	Devil; do you think any Woman Honest?	271	FOR LOVE	III.1	665
Scandal:	least I can do to take care of Conscience.	271	FOR LOVE	III.1	683
Ben:	to do with me--Nay, I can't say that neither; he has	272	FOR LOVE	III.1	714
Ben:	something to do with me. But what do's that signifie? If	272	FOR LOVE	III.1	715
Jeremy:	bad Bargain, can't do better than to beg him for his	276	FOR LOVE	IV.1	36
Sr Sampson:	Hey day, Rascal, do you banter me? Sirrah,	279	FOR LOVE	IV.1	127
Sr Sampson:	How now, what's here to do?--	279	FOR LOVE	IV.1	150
Valentine:	is full--There are People that we do know, and	280	FOR LOVE	IV.1	160
Valentine:	People that we do not know; and yet the Sun shines	280	FOR LOVE	IV.1	161
Buckram:	Sir, I can do you no Service while he's in this	280	FOR LOVE	IV.1	183
Buckram:	Condition: Here's your Paper, Sir--He may do me a	280	FOR LOVE	IV.1	184
Sr Sampson:	thou do, Boy?	281	FOR LOVE	IV.1	195
Sr Sampson:	Val: How do'st thou do? let me feel thy Pulse--Oh,	281	FOR LOVE	IV.1	201
Sr Sampson:	what to do, or say, nor which way to go.	282	FOR LOVE	IV.1	250
Sr Sampson:	What the Devil had I to do, ever to beget Sons?	282	FOR LOVE	IV.1	260
Mrs Fore:	Oh Sister, what will you do with him?	283	FOR LOVE	IV.1	305
Mrs Frail:	Do with him, send him to Sea again in the next	284	FOR LOVE	IV.1	306
Mrs Fore:	What do you mean? I don't understand you.	284	FOR LOVE	IV.1	315
Scandal:	'S'death do you make no difference between me and	284	FOR LOVE	IV.1	321
Foresight:	opinion in this matter, and do reverence a man whom the	285	FOR LOVE	IV.1	349
Mrs Frail:	Sister, do you stay with them; I'll find out my	285	FOR LOVE	IV.1	351
Ben:	how shall I do to set her to rights.	286	FOR LOVE	IV.1	405
Ben:	No matter what I can do? don't call Names,--I	287	FOR LOVE	IV.1	434
Mrs Frail:	throw himself away, he can't do it more effectually than	287	FOR LOVE	IV.1	460
Foresight:	Mr. Tattle--Pray, what do you know?	291	FOR LOVE	IV.1	611
Valentine:	Scandal) What, do you look strange upon me?--Then	292	FOR LOVE	IV.1	618
Tattle:	Do you know me, Valentine?	292	FOR LOVE	IV.1	622
Valentine:	My Friend, what to do? I am no Married Man, and	292	FOR LOVE	IV.1	625
Angelica:	Do you know me, Valentine?	292	FOR LOVE	IV.1	631
Singer-V:	Since women love to change, and so do we.	293	FOR LOVE	IV.1	664
Scandal:	outragious, and do mischief.	293	FOR LOVE	IV.1	669
Mrs Frail:	Thou shalt do what thou wilt,	293	FOR LOVE	IV.1	673
Tattle:	that--Madam, will you do me the Honour?	293	FOR LOVE	IV.1	680
Valentine:	Nay, now you do me Wrong; for if any Interest	295	FOR LOVE	IV.1	725
Angelica:	pretending to a sound Understanding; as Drunken men do	296	FOR LOVE	IV.1	764
Sr Sampson:	a Man that admires a fine Woman, as much as I do.	298	FOR LOVE	V.1	19
Sr Sampson:	Women think a Man old too soon, faith and troth you do	298	FOR LOVE	V.1	25
Angelica:	Will you? well, do you find the Estate, and leave the	300	FOR LOVE	V.1	130
Sr Sampson:	Odsbud, Hussy, you know how to chuse, and so do I;	301	FOR LOVE	V.1	143
Tattle:	her, poor Creature--I swear I do it hardly so much in	302	FOR LOVE	V.1	207
Tattle:	O fie, Miss, why did you do so? and who told you so,	303	FOR LOVE	V.1	233
Foresight:	Mercy on us, what do these Lunacies portend?	305	FOR LOVE	V.1	302
Foresight:	Hussy--Do what I bid you, no Reply, away. And bid	306	FOR LOVE	V.1	326
Scandal:	O I hope he will do well again--I have a Message	306	FOR LOVE	V.1	334
Ben:	before you shall guess at the matter, and do nothing else;	306	FOR LOVE	V.1	353
Sr Sampson:	Why you impudent Tarpaulin! Sirrah, do you	308	FOR LOVE	V.1	422
Scandal:	Favours, either on those who do not merit, or who do not	314	FOR LOVE	V.1	625
Scandal:	For a clear Stage won't do, without your Favour.	316	FOR LOVE	EPI.	44
Almeria:	Why do I live to say you are no more?	327	M. BRIDE	I.1	55
Almeria:	I thank thee--indeed I do--	328	M. BRIDE	I.1	94
Almeria:	Indeed, I do, for pitying thy sad Mistress;	328	M. BRIDE	I.1 V	95
Almeria:	If ever I do yield, or give consent,	330	M. BRIDE	I.1	185
Garcia:	Alone to do, and did disdain to talk;	335	M. BRIDE	I.1	373
Leonora:	What do I see? O Heav'n! either my Eyes	340	M. BRIDE	II.2	9
Osmyn-Alph:	Where? ha! what do I see? Antonio here!	344	M. BRIDE	II.2	169
Osmyn-Alph:	Where? ha! what do I see? Antonio!	344	M. BRIDE	II.2 V	169
Osmyn-Alph:	Thus, do our Eyes, like common Mirrours	345	M. BRIDE	II.2	221
Osmyn-Alph:	Thus, do our Eyes, as do all common Mirrours	345	M. BRIDE	II.2 V	221
Zara:	What Joy do I require? if thou dost mourn,	346	M. BRIDE	II.2	267
Zara:	O, why do I relate what I have done?	347	M. BRIDE	II.2	297
Zara:	And do your Arms so lessen, what they conquer,	348	M. BRIDE	II.2	362
Osmyn-Alph:	So do. I will with Patience wait my Fortune.	352	M. BRIDE	III.1	105
Osmyn-Alph:	But as I may, I'll do. I have a Paper	352	M. BRIDE	III.1	108
Zara:	So thou dost think; then, do but tell me so;	353	M. BRIDE	III.1	164
Almeria:	Tho' 'tis because thou lov'st me. Do not say	356	M. BRIDE	III.1	256
Osmyn-Alph:	What do the Damn'd endure, but to despair,	358	M. BRIDE	III.1	365
Osmyn-Alph:	You do not come to mock my Miseries?	360	M. BRIDE	III.1	420

175

Do   (continued)

Speaker	Line	PAGE	TITLE	ACT.SC	LINE
Zara:	I do.	360	M. BRIDE	III.1	421
Manuel:	Hell, Hell! do I hear this, and yet endure!	369	M. BRIDE	IV.1	314
Gonsalez:	If I delay--'twill do--or better so.	371	M. BRIDE	IV.1	416
Gonsalez:	Do, my best Alonzo.	371	M. BRIDE	IV.1	427
Gonsalez:	I think thou would'st not stop to do me Service.	371	M. BRIDE	IV.1	427
Gonsalez:	I've seen thy Sword do noble Execution.	372	M. BRIDE	IV.1	430
Manuel:	But see she comes; I'll shun th' Encounter; do	374	M. BRIDE	V.1	87
Gonsalez:	Th' Attempt: I'll steal, and do it unperceiv'd.	376	M. BRIDE	V.2	9
Garcia:	Nothing remains to do, or to require,	377	M. BRIDE	V.2	65
Gonsalez:	They shout again! Whate'er he means to do	378	M. BRIDE	V.2	100
Zara:	Then, wherefore do I pause?--give me the Bowl.	381	M. BRIDE	V.2	198
Almeria:	--I do not weep! The Springs of Tears are dry'd;	382	M. BRIDE	V.2	240
	But what unequal Hazards do they run!	393	WAY WORLD	PRO.	13
Fainall:	Women do not easily forgive Omissions of that Nature.	397	WAY WORLD	I.1	84
Mirabell:	That's well. Do you go home again, d'ee hear,	398	WAY WORLD	I.1	127
Mirabell:	That's well. Do you go home again, d'ye hear,	398	WAY WORLD	I.1	V127
Fainall:	You do her wrong; for to give her her Due, she has	399	WAY WORLD	I.1	151
Fainall:	He is expected to Day. Do you know him?	400	WAY WORLD	I.1	189
Fainall:	opportunity to do it at full length. Behold the Original.	401	WAY WORLD	I.1	233
Mirabell:	I do from my Soul.	401	WAY WORLD	I.1	237
Witwoud:	Wit: Nay, I'll do him Justice. I'm his Friend, I won't	403	WAY WORLD	I.1	291
Witwoud:	this is nothing to what he us'd to do;--Before he	405	WAY WORLD	I.1	365
Petulant:	If I do, will you grant me common Sense then, for	407	WAY WORLD	I.1	458
Mirabell:	Faith I'll do what I can for thee; and I'll pray that	407	WAY WORLD	I.1	460
Fainall:	Why do you think so?	408	WAY WORLD	I.1	479
Mirabell:	Do you.	408	WAY WORLD	I.1	502
Mirabell:	You do?	408	WAY WORLD	I.1	V502
Witwoud:	do with the Fool?	409	WAY WORLD	I.1	516
Marwood:	despise 'em; the next thing I have to do, is eternally to	411	WAY WORLD	II.1	46
Marwood:	of ill usage; I think I shou'd do my self the violence of	411	WAY WORLD	II.1	55
Mrs Fain:	Why, had not you as good do it?	411	WAY WORLD	II.1	60
Mrs Fain:	So do I; but I can hear him nam'd. But what	411	WAY WORLD	II.1	70
Mrs Fain:	Do I? I think I am a little sick o' the suddain.	412	WAY WORLD	II.1	80
Fainall:	It may be so. I do now begin to apprehend it.	413	WAY WORLD	II.1	132
Fainall:	It may be so. I do not now begin to apprehend it.	413	WAY WORLD	II.1	V132
Marwood:	You do me wrong.	413	WAY WORLD	II.1	142
Fainall:	I do not--'Twas for my ease to oversee and	413	WAY WORLD	II.1	143
Fainall:	And wherefore do you hate him? He is Insensible,	414	WAY WORLD	II.1	155
Marwood:	Shame and Ingratitude! Do you reproach me?	414	WAY WORLD	II.1	171
Marwood:	be meritorious, that I have been vicious. And do you	414	WAY WORLD	II.1	176
Marwood:	do it my self I shall prevent your Baseness.	415	WAY WORLD	II.1	189
Fainall:	Why, what will you do?	415	WAY WORLD	II.1	190
Marwood:	Hands, do--I'd leave 'em to get loose.	416	WAY WORLD	II.1	226
Mirabell:	Why do we daily commit disagreeable and dangerous	417	WAY WORLD	II.1	265
Mrs Fain:	I believe my Lady will do any thing to get a Husband; and	418	WAY WORLD	II.1	308
Witwoud:	Do Mrs. Mincing, like a Skreen before a great Fire.	419	WAY WORLD	II.1	343
Witwoud:	I confess I do blaze to Day, I am too bright.	419	WAY WORLD	II.1	344
Witwoud:	Is that the way? Pray Madam, do you pin up your	419	WAY WORLD	II.1	363
Millamant:	Come, don't look grave then. Well, what do you	422	WAY WORLD	II.1	462
Lady Wish:	Fetch me the Red--The Red, do you hear, Sweet-heart?	425	WAY WORLD	III.1	5
Foible:	Nay, 'tis your Ladyship has done, and are to do; I	427	WAY WORLD	III.1	74
Lady Wish:	do with him in the Park? Answer me, has he got nothing	427	WAY WORLD	III.1	82
Lady Wish:	Affairs really I know not what to do--(Calls)--Foible--I	431	WAY WORLD	III.1	256
Millamant:	O Madam, why so do I--And yet the Creature	434	WAY WORLD	III.1	355
Petulant:	rest which is to follow in both Cases, a Man may do it	436	WAY WORLD	III.1	432
Sir Wilful:	Well prithee try what thou can'st do; if thou	437	WAY WORLD	III.1	464
Sir Wilful:	Do you speak by way of Offence, Sir?	438	WAY WORLD	III.1	503
Marwood:	Well, how do you stand affected towards	443	WAY WORLD	III.1	674
Fainall:	So, so, why this point's clear,--Well how do we	443	WAY WORLD	III.1	697
Lady Wish:	And--well--and how do I look, Foible?	445	WAY WORLD	IV.1	15
Sir Wilful:	What dee do? 'Shart a'has lock'd the Door indeed I	447	WAY WORLD	IV.1	92
Millamant:	I swear it will not do its part,	447	WAY WORLD	IV.1	104
Sir Wilful:	Indeed! Hah! Look ye, look ye, you do? Nay,	448	WAY WORLD	IV.1	123
Mirabell:	--Like Daphne she as lovely and as Coy. Do you	449	WAY WORLD	IV.1	155
Mirabell:	But do not you know, that when favours are conferr'd	449	WAY WORLD	IV.1	170
Millamant:	Fainall, what shall I do? shall I have him? I think	452	WAY WORLD	IV.1	284
Mrs Fain:	do?	452	WAY WORLD	IV.1	287
Witwoud:	Do, rap thy self up like a Wood-louse and dream	454	WAY WORLD	IV.1	371
Lady Wish:	and his Family. Beastly Creature, I know not what to do	456	WAY WORLD	IV.1	437
Lady Wish:	I do with this beastly Tumbril?--Go lie down and	457	WAY WORLD	IV.1	461
Lady Wish:	This will never do. It will never make a Match.	457	WAY WORLD	IV.1	481
Waitwell:	am tantaliz'd on a rack; And do but hang Madam, on the	457	WAY WORLD	IV.1	492
Waitwell:	am tantaliz'd on the rack; And do but hang Madam, on the	457	WAY WORLD	IV.1	V492
Lady Wish:	you do not think me prone to any iteration of Nuptials.--	458	WAY WORLD	IV.1	532
Lady Wish:	If you do, I protest I must recede--or	459	WAY WORLD	IV.1	534
Waitwell:	I do not, I do not--	459	WAY WORLD	IV.1	540
Lady Wish:	Indeed you do.	459	WAY WORLD	IV.1	541
Waitwell:	I do not, fair shrine of Vertue.	459	WAY WORLD	IV.1	542
Waitwell:	Sure? am I here? do I live? do I love this Pearl of	461	WAY WORLD	IV.1	606
Lady Wish:	go, go, starve again, do, do.	462	WAY WORLD	V.1	8
Lady Wish:	--do, drive a Trade, do, with your three penny-worth	462	WAY WORLD	V.1	11
Lady Wish:	Yellow Colberteen again; do; an old gnaw'd Mask, two	462	WAY WORLD	V.1	15
Foible:	No, no, dear Madam. Do but hear me, have but a	462	WAY WORLD	V.1	24
Foible:	Pray do but hear me Madam, he cou'd not marry	463	WAY WORLD	V.1	38
Marwood:	Friend, what do you mean?	466	WAY WORLD	V.1	157
Mrs Fain:	I know what I mean Madam, and so do you; and	466	WAY WORLD	V.1	158
Lady Wish:	Ay, ay, I do not doubt it, dear Marwood: No,	468	WAY WORLD	V.1	248
Lady Wish:	no, I do not doubt it.	468	WAY WORLD	V.1	249
Sir Wilful:	Look up Man, I'll stand by you, 'sbud an she do	471	WAY WORLD	V.1	360
Witwoud:	Ay I do, my hand I remember--Petulant set his	475	WAY WORLD	V.1	525
Mirabell:	appear--you do not remember Gentlemen, any thing of	476	WAY WORLD	V.1	528
Lady Wish:	to do that--	477	WAY WORLD	V.1	576
Mirabell:	do for Musick?	477	WAY WORLD	V.1	604
	So Poets oft, do in one Piece expose	479	WAY WORLD	EPI.	35

Do's (23)
Bellmour:	How George, do's the Wind blow there?	44	OLD BATCH	I.1	293
Bellmour:	What do's he mean?	46	OLD BATCH	I.1	338
Sir Joseph:	(aside). What a dickens do's he mean by a trivial	50	OLD BATCH	II.1	92
Cynthia:	and hinder one another in the Race; I swear it never do's	168	DOUBL DLR	IV.1	13
Jeremy:	do's Causes at Dinner time.	220	FOR LOVE	I.1	168
Valentine:	Sirrah, fill when I bid you.--And how do's	222	FOR LOVE	I.1	250
Scandal:	I am surpriz'd; what, do's your Father relent?	225	FOR LOVE	I.1	330
Ben:	Father, and how do all at home? How do's Brother Dick,	261	FOR LOVE	III.1	290
Ben:	Nay, what do's that signifie?--an you Marry again--	261	FOR LOVE	III.1	299
Ben:	for's Supper, for all that. What do's Father mean to leave	264	FOR LOVE	III.1	422
Mrs Fore:	Bless me, what's the matter? Miss, what do's	265	FOR LOVE	III.1	439
Ben:	something to do with me. But what do's that signifie? If	272	FOR LOVE	III.1	715
Scandal:	Well, Is your Master ready; do's he look madly, and	275	FOR LOVE	IV.1	1
Tattle:	(aside) what do's the Old Prig mean? I'll banter him, and	304	FOR LOVE	V.1	263
Mirabell:	He is the only Man that do's, Madam.	412	WAY WORLD	II.1	91
Marwood:	I think she do's not hate him to that degree	413	WAY WORLD	II.1	128
Mirabell:	Do's that please you?	420	WAY WORLD	II.1	381
Lady Wish:	Uneasie I wou'd burn it--speak if it do's--but	460	WAY WORLD	IV.1	572
Mrs Fain:	Letter?--My Mother do's not suspect my being in the	464	WAY WORLD	V.1	75
Mrs Fain:	Do's your Lady and Mirabell know that?	465	WAY WORLD	V.1	112
Sir Wilful:	An he do's not move me, wou'd I might never	472	WAY WORLD	V.1	392
Sir Wilful:	An he do's not move me, wou'd I may never	472	WAY WORLD	V.1 V392
Millamant:	Why do's not the man take me? wou'd you have	477	WAY WORLD	V.1	594

Do'st (17)
Sr Sampson:	if there is too much, refund the Superfluity; Do'st hear	243	FOR LOVE	II.1	280
Sr Sampson:	if there be too much, refund the Superfluity; Do'st hear	243	FOR LOVE	II.1 V280
Sr Sampson:	I'll speak gently--Val, Val, do'st thou not	279	FOR LOVE	IV.1	156
Sr Sampson:	He recovers--bless thee, Val--How do'st	281	FOR LOVE	IV.1	194
Sr Sampson:	Val: How do'st thou do? let me feel thy Pulse--Oh,	281	FOR LOVE	IV.1	201
Sr Sampson:	Do'st thou know this Paper, Val: I know	281	FOR LOVE	IV.1	214
Sr Sampson:	See it, boy? Aye, aye, why thou do'st see it--	281	FOR LOVE	IV.1	219
Manuel:	By Heav'n thou lov'st me, and I'm pleas'd thou do'st:	333	M. BRIDE	I.1	275
Zara:	That having seen it, thou do'st turn thy Eyes	353	M. BRIDE	III.1	149
Almeria:	Why do'st thou heave, and stifle in thy Griefs?	356	M. BRIDE	III.1	272
Manuel:	What Husband? who? whom do'st thou mean?	370	M. BRIDE	IV.1	354
Manuel:	Wilder than Winds or Waves thy self do'st rave.	370	M. BRIDE	IV.1	361
Sir Wilful:	Sir; your Lady is my Aunt, Sir--Why, what do'st	437	WAY WORLD	III.1	453
Sir Wilful:	can'st not guess, enquire her out, do'st hear Fellow? And	437	WAY WORLD	III.1	465
Sir Wilful:	i'faith! What do'st thou not know me? Ey'r Lady nor I	439	WAY WORLD	III.1	517
Sir Wilful:	'Sheart why do'st not speak? Art thou o'er-joy'd?	439	WAY WORLD	III.1	519
Millamant:	Tho' thou do'st thine, employ'st the Power and Art.	447	WAY WORLD	IV.1	105

Do't (17)
Mellefont:	I'll do't.	169	DOUBL DLR	IV.1	50
Cynthia:	And I'll do't.	169	DOUBL DLR	IV.1	51
Lady Ply:	Drink the less you Sot, and do't before you	180	DOUBL DLR	IV.1 V487
Lord Touch:	ha, I'll do't, where's Mellefont, my poor injured Nephew,--	200	DOUBL DLR	V.1	478
Jeremy:	(to Scandal). I'll do't, Sir.	293	FOR LOVE	IV.1	667
Manuel:	Why dost thou start? Resolve to do't, or else--	374	M. BRIDE	V.1	75
Marwood:	By all my Wrongs I'll do't--I'll publish to	415	WAY WORLD	II.1	194
Sir Wilful:	then; if I say't, I'll do't: But I	440	WAY WORLD	III.1	581
Sir Wilful:	that--for if so be that I set on't, I'll do't. But only for he	447	WAY WORLD	IV.1	84
Millamant:	all ye douceurs, ye Someils du Matin, adieu--I can't do't, 'tis	449	WAY WORLD	IV.1	189
Sir Wilful:	Word, and I'll do't--Wilfull will do't, that's the Word--	455	WAY WORLD	IV.1	404
Sir Wilful:	Wilfull will do't, that's my Crest--my Motto I have forgot.	455	WAY WORLD	IV.1	405
Sir Wilful:	will do't. If not, dust it away, and let's have tother round--	455	WAY WORLD	IV.1	412
Sir Wilful:	Cozen, with the hard Name,--Aunt, Wilfull will do't, If	456	WAY WORLD	IV.1	427
Waitwell:	I'll do't. In three weeks he shall be bare-foot; in a	458	WAY WORLD	IV.1	521
Sir Wilful:	on't, I must do't. And if these two Gentlemen wou'd	477	WAY WORLD	V.1	586

Doat (5)
Fondlewife:	does not thy Wife love thee, nay doat upon thee?--	77	OLD BATCH	IV.1	58
Maskwell:	of a Girl. No--yet tho' I doat on each last Favour	199	DOUBL DLR	V.1	433
Valentine:	doat on at that immoderate rate, that your Fondness shall	313	FOR LOVE	V.1	609
Valentine:	doat on at that immoderate Degree, that your Fondness shall	313	FOR LOVE	V.1 V609
Marwood:	and seem to doat like Lovers; but 'tis not in our	410	WAY WORLD	II.1	24

Doating (2)
Fondlewife:	and because I was obstinate and doating; so that my	76	OLD BATCH	IV.1	54
Mrs Fain:	Men are ever in Extreams; either doating or averse.	410	WAY WORLD	II.1	3

Doats (2)
Lucy:	No, you're out; could we perswade him, that she doats	62	OLD BATCH	III.1	40
	So much she doats on her adopted Care.	393	WAY WORLD	PRO.	10

Doctor (1)
Scandal:	favour, as a Doctor says, No, to a Bishoprick, only that it	226	FOR LOVE	I.1	377

Doctrin (1)
Vainlove:	Preach this Doctrin to Husbands, and the married Women	38	OLD BATCH	I.1	53

Doctrine (1)
Fondlewife:	Adultery, and innocent! O Lord! Here's Doctrine!	92	OLD BATCH	IV.4	112

Does (104)
Bellmour:	faith upon second Thoughts, she does not appear to be so	41	OLD BATCH	I.1	171
Sharper:	pains to sow: he does the drudgery in the Mine, and you	43	OLD BATCH	I.1	220
Bellmour:	Black Gown does Atheism--You must know he has been	47	OLD BATCH	I.1	368
Lucy:	Lord does his Mercers Bill, or a begging Dedication;	61	OLD BATCH	III.1	22
Capt Bluff:	out your Trick, and does not care to be put upon; being a	69	OLD BATCH	III.1	297
Bellmour:	Well and how Setter hae, does my Hypocrisy fit me hae?	75	OLD BATCH	IV.1	3
Bellmour:	Does it sit easy on me?	75	OLD BATCH	IV.1	4
Fondlewife:	does not thy Wife love thee, nay doat upon thee?--	77	OLD BATCH	IV.1	58
Laetitia:	does not think, that ever I had any such thing in my Head,	77	OLD BATCH	IV.1	81
Fondlewife:	--Nay look you now if she does not weep--'tis the fondest	78	OLD BATCH	IV.1	98
Vainlove:	All Naturally fly what does pursue:	80	OLD BATCH	IV.1	190
Laetitia:	Does it hold you long? I'm afraid to carry you into	83	OLD BATCH	IV.2	90
Laetitia:	Sure, when he does not see his face, he won't discover	91	OLD BATCH	IV.4	90
Laetitia:	Let the wicked Man answer for himself; does he	93	OLD BATCH	IV.4	167
Heartwell:	(aside). Hell, and the Devil! Does he know it? But,	104	OLD BATCH	V.1	298

177

Dog   (continued)

Manuel:	Swear thou hast never seen that foreign Dog,	368	M. BRIDE	IV.1	287
Witwoud:	This is a vile Dog, I see that already. No Offence!	438	WAY WORLD	III.1	487
Witwoud:	in a maze yet, like a Dog in a Dancing School.	477	WAY WORLD	V.1	591

Dog-days (1)
Waitwell:	--by this hand I'd rather be a Chair-man in the Dog-days	459	WAY WORLD	IV.1	563

Dog-star (1)
Zara:	Would, like the raging Dog-star, scorch the Earth,	375	M. BRIDE	V.1	95

Dogs (2)
Sr Sampson:	able Fellow: Your Sampsons were strong Dogs from the	301	FOR LOVE	V.1	155
Petulant:	Dogs, and read Romances--I'll go to bed to my	454	WAY WORLD	IV.1	376

Doily (1)
Marwood:	one Suit, tho' never so fine. A Fool and a Doily Stuff	433	WAY WORLD	III.1	301

Doing (11)
Laetitia:	Oh, but what am I doing!	82	OLD BATCH	IV.2	83
Bellmour:	Doing! No Tongue can express it,--not thy own;	82	OLD BATCH	IV.2	84
Mellefont:	much ado I prevented her doing me or her self a mischief:	130	DOUBL DLR	I.1	115
Sir Paul:	be this is all his doing--something that he has said;	172	DOUBL DLR	IV.1	V201
Sir Paul:	matter of Fact is all his own doing.--I confess I had a	180	DOUBL DLR	IV.1	477
Maskwell:	but what is my distraction doing? I am wildly talking to my	188	DOUBL DLR	V.1	43
Valentine:	doing good.--Scandal, Drink to me, my Friend Trapland's	223	FOR LOVE	I.1	260
	Is doing painful Penance in some Beau,	315	FOR LOVE	EPI.	24
Lady Wish:	--Wench, come, come, Wench, what art thou doing,	425	WAY WORLD	III.1	23
Lady Wish:	doing?	427	WAY WORLD	III.1	71
Mrs Fain:	doing.	464	WAY WORLD	V.1	67

Doings (3)
Sir Paul:	be this is all his doings--something that he has said;	172	DOUBL DLR	IV.1	201
Nurse:	Doings with my Masters Worship--Why, did you	238	FOR LOVE	III.1	100
Nurse:	Miss I say, God's my Life, here's fine doings towards--	253	FOR LOVE	III.1	9

Doit (1)
Sr Sampson:	Estate: Body o' me, he does not care a Doit for your	260	FOR LOVE	III.1	243

Doleful (2)
Bellmour:	Chimes of Verse were past, when once the doleful	108	OLD BATCH	V.2	18
Almeria:	Was it the doleful Bell, tolling for Death?	370	M. BRIDE	IV.1	385

Dolefull (1)
Sir Wilful:	dolefull Sigh more from my fellow Traveller and 'tis	472	WAY WORLD	V.1	398

Domestick (3)
Sir Paul:	deny'd my self the enjoyment of lawful Domestick	179	DOUBL DLR	IV.1	428
Scandal:	Domestick Thief; and he that wou'd secure his Pleasure,	271	FOR LOVE	III.1	676
Witwoud:	Domestick. But I talk like an old Maid at a Marriage, I	402	WAY WORLD	I.1	258

Dominabitur (0)
see Sapiens dominabitur astris

Dominion (1)
Mirabell:	Lastly to the Dominion of the Tea-Table, I submit.--	451	WAY WORLD	IV.1	263

Don (1)
Lady Wish:	before she came to me, like Maritornes the Asturian in Don	426	WAY WORLD	III.1	37

Don't (265)

	(I don't know whether I shall speak to please you)	35	OLD BATCH	PRO.	18
Vainlove:	has don't.	40	OLD BATCH	I.1	104
Bellmour:	like her; for the Devil take me if I don't love all the	41	OLD BATCH	I.1	174
Bellmour:	Faith I don't know, he's of a temper the most easie	42	OLD BATCH	I.1	210
Heartwell:	so much Mercury in my Limbs; 'tis true indeed, I don't	43	OLD BATCH	I.1	231
Heartwell:	is it out of discretion, that you don't swallow that very	43	OLD BATCH	I.1	242
Heartwell:	don't expect should ever recommend me to People of	45	OLD BATCH	I.1	303
Sir Joseph:	O Lord forget him! No no Sir, I don't forget you--	48	OLD BATCH	II.1	40
Sharper:	Sir your humble Servant--I don't question but you	49	OLD BATCH	II.1	87
Sir Joseph:	I am quite another thing, when I am with him: I don't fear	50	OLD BATCH	II.1	122
Sir Joseph:	I don't know, but I'le present you--	51	OLD BATCH	II.1	154
Belinda:	Man--you don't know what you said, your Fever has	54	OLD BATCH	II.2	6
Belinda:	Man--you don't know what you've said, your Fever has	54	OLD BATCH	II.2 V	6
Araminta:	I wonder Cousin you should imagine, I don't	55	OLD BATCH	II.2	20
Araminta:	Bellmour meet. You don't know that you dreamt of	55	OLD BATCH	II.2	37
Araminta:	Prithee don't be so Peevish.	56	OLD BATCH	II.2	64
Belinda:	Prithee don't be so Impertinent.	56	OLD BATCH	II.2	65
Araminta:	Betty, why don't you help my Cousin?	57	OLD BATCH	II.2	93
Belinda:	sake let it be with variety; don't come always, like the	59	OLD BATCH	II.2	169
Bellmour:	O very well perform'd--But I don't much	60	OLD BATCH	II.2	204
Setter:	What no Token of amity Lucy? you and I don't use	67	OLD BATCH	III.1	234
Sir Joseph:	mad? Or de'e think I'm mad? Agad for my part, I don't	68	OLD BATCH	III.1	265
Sir Joseph:	dear Captain, don't be in Passion now, he's gone--	70	OLD BATCH	III.1	340
Silvia:	Nay don't stare at me so--You make me blush	72	OLD BATCH	III.2	43
Silvia:	them--O Gemini, I hope you don't mean so--For I	73	OLD BATCH	III.2	88
Heartwell:	thee--There thou hast don't, all my Resolve melted in	74	OLD BATCH	III.2	135
Heartwell:	thee--There thou hast don't, all my Resolves melted in	74	OLD BATCH	III.2 V135	
Fondlewife:	Nay Cocky Cocky, nay dear Cocky, don't cry, I was	78	OLD BATCH	IV.1	100
Laetitia:	Go naughty Nykin, you don't love me.	78	OLD BATCH	IV.1	122
Laetitia:	indeed you sant. Nykin--if you don't go, I'le think	78	OLD BATCH	IV.1	132
Sharper:	However I hope you don't mean to forsake it, that	80	OLD BATCH	IV.1	181
Laetitia:	Nay, don't swear if you'd have me believe you; but	82	OLD BATCH	IV.2	69
Belinda:	--Don't you admire him?	87	OLD BATCH	IV.3	146
Fondlewife:	Alack poor Man.--No, no,--you don't know the	91	OLD BATCH	IV.4	81
Fondlewife:	Ay, ay, lie still, lie still; don't let me disturb you.	91	OLD BATCH	IV.4	88
Laetitia:	In the Name of the--Oh! Good, my Dear, don't	92	OLD BATCH	IV.4	132
Fondlewife:	Fleece here!--You don't love Mutton?--you Magdalen	93	OLD BATCH	IV.4	145
Fondlewife:	confess. But, what--not to be cured of the Cholick? Don't	93	OLD BATCH	IV.4	162
Fondlewife:	for. Come, come, go on boldly--What, don't be asham'd	94	OLD BATCH	IV.4	192
Fondlewife:	think I don't know how to behave my self in the Employment	94	OLD BATCH	IV.4	195
Laetitia:	you don't.	95	OLD BATCH	IV.4	247
Lucy:	for your Brother's Chaplain. Don't you see that stalking	97	OLD BATCH	V.1	15
Bellmour:	Nay, don't be in Passion, Lucy;--I'll provide a	98	OLD BATCH	V.1	57
Bellmour:	the Mistake of me: I'll marry 'em.--Nay, don't pause;	98	OLD BATCH	V.1	67
Bellmour:	Countenance. But, to tell you something you don't know.	100	OLD BATCH	V.1	148
Sir Joseph:	Hush, hush: Don't you see him?	101	OLD BATCH	V.1	169
Sir Joseph:	Nay, Don't speak so loud.--I don't jest, as I	101	OLD BATCH	V.1	171
Sir Joseph:	and his primitive Braying. Don't you remember the Story	101	OLD BATCH	V.1	174
Sir Joseph:	Prithee, don't speak so loud.	101	OLD BATCH	V.1	179
Capt Bluff:	Not at all. Don't I know him?	104	OLD BATCH	V.1	276

Don't   (continued)

		PAGE	TITLE	ACT.SC	LINE
Careless:	Lady, I don't see what you can expect from the Fruit.	131	DOUBL DLR	I.1	166
Lord Froth:	O foy, don't misapprehend me, I don't say so, for	132	DOUBL DLR	I.1	197
Brisk:	'tis, in the not Laughing—don't you Apprehend me?	133	DOUBL DLR	I.1	249
Brisk:	Pshaw, pshaw, prithee don't interrupt me.—But I	134	DOUBL DLR	I.1	262
Careless:	Well, but prithee don't let it be a great while, because	134	DOUBL DLR	I.1	265
Maskwell:	I would not be a Traytor to my self: I don't pretend to	136	DOUBL DLR	I.1	342
Lady Touch:	perswade her. But I don't see what you can propose from	138	DOUBL DLR	I.1	414
Maskwell:	I know it.—I don't depend upon it.—	138	DOUBL DLR	I.1	417
Lady Froth:	those Two hard Words? If you don't, I'll explain	139	DOUBL DLR	II.1	33
Lady Froth:	a great deal of Wit: Mr. Mellefont, don't you think Mr.	140	DOUBL DLR	II.1	86
Lord Froth:	Don't you think us a happy Couple?	140	DOUBL DLR	II.1	95
Lady Ply:	please—therefore don't provoke me.	145	DOUBL DLR	II.1	237
Lady Ply:	Fiddle, faddle, don't tell me of this and that, and	146	DOUBL DLR	II.1	301
Lady Ply:	refuse it; I swear I'll deny it,—therefore don't ask me,	147	DOUBL DLR	II.1	333
Lady Ply:	Heart? May be you don't think it a sin,—they say	147	DOUBL DLR	II.1	346
Lady Ply:	some of you Gentlemen don't think it a sin,—may be	147	DOUBL DLR	II.1	347
Lady Ply:	it is no sin to them that don't think it so;—indeed, If	147	DOUBL DLR	II.1	348
Lady Ply:	don't be melancholly, don't despair,—but never	148	DOUBL DLR	II.1	365
Lady Ply:	don't be melancholick, don't despair,—but never	148	DOUBL DLR	II.1	V365
Lady Ply:	I know you don't Love Cynthia, only as a blind for your	148	DOUBL DLR	II.1	368
Lady Ply:	must not Love you,—therefore don't hope,—but don't	148	DOUBL DLR	II.1	371
Maskwell:	why you don't know, that while I plead for you, your	148	DOUBL DLR	II.1	392
Mellefont:	I don't know what she might have attempted.	149	DOUBL DLR	II.1	418
Maskwell:	don't know, but she may come this way; I am to meet her	149	DOUBL DLR	II.1	433
Lord Touch:	I don't believe it true; he has better Principles	150	DOUBL DLR	III.1	4
Lady Touch:	That I can't tell: nay, I don't say there was—	151	DOUBL DLR	III.1	23
Lord Touch:	(half aside). I don't know that.	151	DOUBL DLR	III.1	26
Lady Touch:	How? Don't you believe that, say you, my	151	DOUBL DLR	III.1	27
Lord Touch:	No, I don't say so—I confess I am troubled to	151	DOUBL DLR	III.1	29
Lady Touch:	I don't know; I am very unwilling to speak	151	DOUBL DLR	III.1	34
Lady Touch:	—Don't ask me my Reasons, my Lord, for they are	151	DOUBL DLR	III.1	42
Lady Touch:	don't press me.	152	DOUBL DLR	III.1	52
Lord Touch:	Don't oblige me to press you.	152	DOUBL DLR	III.1	53
Lady Touch:	make me lay my heart before you, but don't be thus	152	DOUBL DLR	III.1	65
Lady Touch:	it; well remember your promise, my Lord, and don't	153	DOUBL DLR	III.1	91
Lady Touch:	Lord, I don't know: I wish my Lips had	153	DOUBL DLR	III.1	109
Lady Touch:	self. Pray, my Lord, don't let the Company see you in this	153	DOUBL DLR	III.1	112
Maskwell:	Woman, and I lov'd her once. But I don't know, since I	155	DOUBL DLR	III.1	176
Maskwell:	Woman, I lov'd her once. But I don't know, since I	155	DOUBL DLR	III.1	V176
Maskwell:	I'm afraid my frailty leans that way—but I don't	156	DOUBL DLR	III.1	207
Mellefont:	don't care for her.	157	DOUBL DLR	III.1	269
Careless:	Nay, I don't despair—but still she has a grudging	158	DOUBL DLR	III.1	304
Sir Paul:	(aside to her). I acquiesce, my Lady; but don't snub so	159	DOUBL DLR	III.1	334
Lady Ply:	you, Mr. Careless I don't know any thing in the World I	159	DOUBL DLR	III.1	353
Careless:	O Lord, I beseech you, Madam, don't—	160	DOUBL DLR	III.1	366
Lady Ply:	so fine limbs, so fine linen, and I don't doubt but you have	160	DOUBL DLR	III.1	368
Sir Paul:	true—she's so very nice, that I don't believe she would	162	DOUBL DLR	III.1	432
Lady Froth:	Then I don't say the Sun shines all the day, but,	164	DOUBL DLR	III.1	523
Lady Froth:	too, you know, tho' we don't see him.	164	DOUBL DLR	III.1	525
Brisk:	exception to make—don't you think bilk (I know its	164	DOUBL DLR	III.1	544
Brisk:	good Rhime) but don't you think bilk and fare too like a	165	DOUBL DLR	III.1	545
Brisk:	rather an Epigrammatick Sonnet; I don't know what to	166	DOUBL DLR	III.1	592
Lady Froth:	—I swear, my Lord, you don't Love poor little Sapho	167	DOUBL DLR	III.1	614
Cynthia:	are so near that we don't think of coming together.	168	DOUBL DLR	IV.1	18
Mellefont:	that we only have in view, I don't see but we have it in	168	DOUBL DLR	IV.1	21
Mellefont:	I don't know why we should not steal out of the	168	DOUBL DLR	IV.1	27
Cynthia:	Pray don't be angry, Sir, when I swore, I had your	171	DOUBL DLR	IV.1	142
Lady Ply:	made plain—I don't see how my Daughter can in	172	DOUBL DLR	IV.1	169
Sir Paul:	I humbly thank your Ladiship—I don't know	172	DOUBL DLR	IV.1	197
Sir Paul:	neither,—but—Nay, don't Blush—	174	DOUBL DLR	IV.1	244
Cynthia:	I don't Blush Sir, for I vow I don't understand.—	174	DOUBL DLR	IV.1	245
Sir Paul:	understand, and you shall understand, come don't be so	174	DOUBL DLR	IV.1	247
Sir Paul:	nice, Gads-bud don't learn after your Mother-in-Law my	174	DOUBL DLR	IV.1	248
Lady Froth:	Just now as I came in, bless me, why don't you	176	DOUBL DLR	IV.1	323
Brisk:	Ladiship—Let me perish, I don't know whether to	176	DOUBL DLR	IV.1	337
Lady Froth:	No the Deuce take me if I don't Laugh at my	176	DOUBL DLR	IV.1	351
Lord Froth:	don't like this familiarity.	177	DOUBL DLR	IV.1	373
Sir Paul:	Surprize! Why I don't know any thing at all, nor I don't	179	DOUBL DLR	IV.1	449
Sir Paul:	Nay but Madam, I shall offend again if you don't	180	DOUBL DLR	IV.1	V485
Careless:	Subject: Then I writ a Letter to her; I don't know what	180	DOUBL DLR	IV.1	501
Maskwell:	No matter, Sir, don't trouble your head, all's in	190	DOUBL DLR	V.1	106
Lady Touch:	ought to be served; making you a Beast. Don't you know	192	DOUBL DLR	V.1	165
Lady Touch:	Why then you don't know half your	192	DOUBL DLR	V.1	169
Sir Paul:	of things; I don't know what to make on't,—gad'sbud	192	DOUBL DLR	V.1	173
Sir Paul:	Nephew; and I don't know what,—look you, Sister,	192	DOUBL DLR	V.1	175
Cynthia:	I don't know whether I have Love enough,—	193	DOUBL DLR	V.1	202
Mellefont:	I don't understand you.	193	DOUBL DLR	V.1	216
Maskwell:	Tell him so! Ay, why you don't think I mean to	193	DOUBL DLR	V.1	227
Lord Touch:	we don't presently prevent the Execution of their plots;—	200	DOUBL DLR	V.1	477
Sir Paul:	The Company, gad'sbud, I don't know, my Lord,	200	DOUBL DLR	V.1	496
Lady Froth:	I don't know how long.	201	DOUBL DLR	V.1	520
Lord Touch:	you stare as you were all amazed,—I don't wonder at it,—	202	DOUBL DLR	V.1	564
Jeremy:	Paper; you don't mean to write!	217	FOR LOVE	I.1	62
Jeremy:	sit at the Door, that I don't get double the Stomach that	218	FOR LOVE	I.1	92
Scandal:	Jeremy speaks like an Oracle. Don't you see how	219	FOR LOVE	I.1	131
Jeremy:	if you don't like my Negotiation, will you be pleas'd to	221	FOR LOVE	I.1	183
Valentine:	Scandal, don't spoil my Boy's Milk.—Bid	222	FOR LOVE	I.1	222
Scandal:	The Morning's a very good Morning, if you don't	222	FOR LOVE	I.1	233
Scandal:	What don't I know?—I know the Buxom black	223	FOR LOVE	I.1	268
Snap:	if we don't make haste, the Chairmen will be abroad, and	224	FOR LOVE	I.1	298
Valentine:	He knows I don't go abroad.	225	FOR LOVE	I.1	360
Tattle:	To be free with you, I have—I don't care if I own	227	FOR LOVE	I.1	409
Tattle:	Who I? Upon Honour I don't know whether she be	228	FOR LOVE	I.1	465
Tattle:	O inhumane! You don't expect their Names.	230	FOR LOVE	I.1	532
Tattle:	O inhuman! You don't expect their Names.	230	FOR LOVE	I.1	V532

Don't (continued)

Speaker	Text	PAGE	TITLE	ACT.SC	LINE
Scandal:	Well, on that Condition--Take heed you don't	230	FOR LOVE	I.1	544
Angelica:	find who's in Conjunction with your Wife. Why don't	237	FOR LOVE	II.1	69
Angelica:	Nay Uncle, don't be angry--If you are, I'll	237	FOR LOVE	II.1	76
Foresight:	But ccme, be a good Girl, don't perplex your poor Uncle,	239	FOR LOVE	II.1	157
Foresight:	they dcn't know it themselves.	241	FOR LOVE	II.1	225
Foresight:	Fellow? I don't like his Physiognomy.	242	FOR LOVE	II.1	264
Valentine:	Sir, I don't deny it.--	243	FOR LOVE	II.1	302
Foresight:	Hum--truly I dcn't care to discourage a young	243	FOR LOVE	II.1	308
Valentine:	you call'd me. But here I am, and if you don't mean to	244	FOR LOVE	II.1	334
Sr Sampson:	above a stink.--Why there's it; and Musick, don't you	245	FOR LOVE	II.1	371
Jeremy:	Country Dances; and the like; I don't much matter your	245	FOR LOVE	II.1	374
Mrs Fore:	agreeable man; I don't quarrel at that, nor I don't think	247	FOR LOVE	II.1	428
Mrs Frail:	upon you?--I don't doubt but you have thought	247	FOR LOVE	II.1	436
Mrs Fore:	Poor innocent! you don't know that there's a	247	FOR LOVE	II.1	450
Tattle:	strangely--pretty Miss, don't let 'em perswade you	249	FOR LOVE	II.1	536
Mrs Fore:	Oh, Demm you Toad--I wish you don't	249	FOR LOVE	II.1	538
Tattle:	have such a thought--sure you don't know me?	250	FOR LOVE	II.1	541
Mrs Frail:	a Confessor--He thinks we don't observe him.	250	FOR LOVE	II.1	543
Mrs Frail:	--she looks so wholscme;--we're stir, I don't	250	FOR LOVE	II.1	557
Mrs Frail:	I don't care; I won't be seen in't.	250	FOR LOVE	II.1	576
Tattle:	No, nc, they don't mean that.	251	FOR LOVE	II.1	586
Angelica:	I swear I don't think 'tis possible.	255	FOR LOVE	III.1	80
Angelica:	I don't understand you now. I thought you had	255	FOR LOVE	III.1	88
Scandal:	wou'd have told me; I find, Madam, you don't know	256	FOR LOVE	III.1	110
Tattle:	No indeed, Madam, you don't know me at all, I	256	FOR LOVE	III.1	112
Tattle:	beyond her Reputation--But I hope you don't know	258	FOR LOVE	III.1	187
Scandal:	No dcn't; for then you'l tell us no more--Come, I'll	258	FOR LOVE	III.1	190
Valentine:	I don't know but my Father in good Nature may press me	259	FOR LOVE	III.1	225
Ben:	that be all--Pray don't let me be your hindrance; e'en	261	FOR LOVE	III.1	301
Ben:	don't much stand towards Matrimonie. I love to roam	261	FOR LOVE	III.1	309
Miss Prue:	I don't know what to say to you, nor I don't care	263	FOR LOVE	III.1	378
Ben:	tho'f they love a man well enough, yet they don't care to	263	FOR LOVE	III.1	392
Miss Prue:	always tell a lie to a man; and I don't care, let my Father	264	FOR LOVE	III.1	397
Miss Prue:	plainly, I don't like you, nor love you at all, nor never will,	264	FOR LOVE	III.1	399
Miss Prue:	that's more: So, there's your answer for you; and don't	264	FOR LOVE	III.1	400
Ben:	for your Love or your liking, I don't value it of a Rope's	264	FOR LOVE	III.1	404
Ben:	your self, Gad I don't think you are any more to compare	264	FOR LOVE	III.1	412
Sr Sampson:	Body o' me, I don't know any universal Grievance,	266	FOR LOVE	III.1	485
Scandal:	No, nct yet; nor Whirlwind. But we don't know	266	FOR LOVE	III.1	492
Foresight:	How! Am I alter'd any way? I don't perceive it.	268	FOR LOVE	III.1	571
Mrs Fore:	this Project? You don't think, that you are ever like to	271	FOR LOVE	III.1	660
Ben:	don't think I'm false-hearted, like a Land-man. A Sailor	273	FOR LOVE	III.1	732
Angelica:	Mr. Scandal, I suppose you don't think it a Novelty,	276	FOR LOVE	IV.1	20
Angelica:	I don't like Raillery from a serious Face--pray	276	FOR LOVE	IV.1	27
Angelica:	don't play Trick for Trick, may I never taste the Pleasure	277	FOR LOVE	IV.1	67
Angelica:	make me uneasie--If I don't see him, perhaps my	277	FOR LOVE	IV.1	80
Angelica:	and involuntary; if he loves, he can't help it; and if I don't	278	FOR LOVE	IV.1	87
Scandal:	nor I don't know her if I see her; nor ycu neither.	278	FOR LOVE	IV.1	97
Scandal:	For Heav'ns sake softly, Sir, and gently; don't	279	FOR LOVE	IV.1	152
Sr Sampson:	Hold, hold, don't you go yet.	280	FOR LOVE	IV.1	188
Sr Sampson:	Manners, that don't believe a Syllable in the Sky and	283	FOR LOVE	IV.1	287
Mrs Fore:	What do you mean? I don't understand ycu.	284	FOR LOVE	IV.1	315
Ben:	No matter what I can do? don't call Names,--I	287	FOR LOVE	IV.1	434
Ben:	don't love You so well as to bear that, whatever I did,	287	FOR LOVE	IV.1	435
Ben:	them marry you, as don't know you:--Gad I know	287	FOR LOVE	IV.1	437
Angelica:	I never lov'd him till he was Mad; but don't tell	291	FOR LOVE	IV.1	572
Tattle:	Tell, Madam! alas you don't know me--I have	291	FOR LOVE	IV.1	575
Angelica:	(aside). Aye, but if I don't fit you, I'll be hang'd.	294	FOR LOVE	IV.1	699
Angelica:	the Fool you take me for; and you are Mad and don't	296	FOR LOVE	IV.1	792
Sr Sampson:	--Come, don't despise Fifty; odd Fifty, in a hale	298	FOR LOVE	V.1	26
Angelica:	Have a care, and don't over-act your Part--If	301	FOR LOVE	V.1	157
Miss Prue:	Well, but don't you love me as well as you did	304	FOR LOVE	V.1	248
Tattle:	you're a Woman, and don't know your own mind.	304	FOR LOVE	V.1	253
Miss Prue:	I don't know for what--And I'd rather be always a	305	FOR LOVE	V.1	311
Miss Prue:	I don't know for what--And I'd rather be always	305	FOR LOVE	V.1	V311
Ben:	I don't know what you may call Madness--But	307	FOR LOVE	V.1	372
Sr Sampson:	Helm, Sirrah, don't direct me.	308	FOR LOVE	V.1	419
Angelica:	'Tis very unhappy, if you don't care for one another.	309	FOR LOVE	V.1	462
Tattle:	wish we could keep it secret, why I don't believe any of	310	FOR LOVE	V.1	476
Tattle:	Easie! Pox on't, I don't believe I shall sleep to Night.	310	FOR LOVE	V.1	483
Sr Sampson:	don't mean to sleep.	310	FOR LOVE	V.1	486
Sr Sampson:	That's as much as to say, I lie, Sir, and you don't	311	FOR LOVE	V.1	522
Sr Sampson:	counterfeited Madness; I don't know but the Frolick may	311	FOR LOVE	V.1	525
Valentine:	I vow, I don't much like this Transmigration,	315	FOR LOVE	EPI.	32
	Grant Heaven, we don't return to our first Station.	315	FOR LOVE	EPI.	34
Witwoud:	him, dcn't let's talk of him;--Fainall, how does your	402	WAY WORLD	I.1	254
Witwoud:	don't know what I say: But she's the best Woman in the	402	WAY WORLD	I.1	259
Witwoud:	don't know what I say: she's the best Woman in the	402	WAY WORLD	I.1	V259
Fainall:	'Tis well you don't know what you say, or else your	402	WAY WORLD	I.1	261
Mirabell:	I don't find that Petulant confesses the Superiority	402	WAY WORLD	I.1	285
Witwoud:	Come ccme, don't detract from the Merits of my	403	WAY WORLD	I.1	294
Fainall:	You don't take your Friend to be overnicely bred.	403	WAY WORLD	I.1	296
Witwoud:	Hum, faith I don't know as to that,--I can't say	403	WAY WORLD	I.1	302
Mrs Fain:	My Husband. Don't you see him? He turn'd	412	WAY WORLD	II.1	82
Fainall:	You don't look well to Day, Child.	412	WAY WORLD	II.1	89
Millamant:	Come, don't look grave then. Well, what do you	422	WAY WORLD	II.1	462
Millamant:	Sententious Mirabell! Prithee don't look with that	422	WAY WORLD	II.1	467
Millamant:	Face. Ha, ha, ha--Well I won't laugh, don't be	422	WAY WORLD	II.1	475
Foible:	I don't question your Generosity, Sir: And you need	424	WAY WORLD	II.1	541
Lady Wish:	Don't answer me. I won't know: I'll be surpriz'd. I'll be	429	WAY WORLD	III.1	173
Marwood:	you don't mitigate those violent Airs.	433	WAY WORLD	III.1	334
Marwood:	'Tis your Brother, I fancy. Don't you know	436	WAY WORLD	III.1	439
Sir Wilful:	don't think a' knows his own Name.	437	WAY WORLD	III.1	474

Don't (continued)

Speaker	Text	PAGE	TITLE	ACT.SC	LINE
Marwood:	Friends here, tho' it may be you don't know it--If I	438	WAY WORLD	III.1	508
Marwood:	Don't you know this Gentleman, Sir?	438	WAY WORLD	III.1	513
Sir Wilful:	. . . I don't stand shill I, shall I,	440	WAY WORLD	III.1	580
Millamant:	Ah don't be Impertinent--My dear Liberty,	449	WAY WORLD	IV.1	185
Millamant:	never bear that,--Good Mirabell don't let us be familiar	450	WAY WORLD	IV.1	200
Millamant:	converse with Wits that I don't like, because they are your	450	WAY WORLD	IV.1	217
Millamant:	now, and don't say a word.	452	WAY WORLD	IV.1	297
Millamant:	now, don't say a word.	452	WAY WORLD	IV.1	V297
Witwoud:	Come Knight--Pox on him. I don't know what to	457	WAY WORLD	IV.1	470
Lady Wish:	No, don't kill him at once Sir Rowland, starve	458	WAY WORLD	IV.1	519
Waitwell:	Here's a Villain! Madam, don't you perceive it,	460	WAY WORLD	IV.1	597
Waitwell:	don't you see it?	460	WAY WORLD	IV.1	598
Foible:	No, good Sir Rowland, don't incurr the Law.	461	WAY WORLD	IV.1	622
Lady Wish:	No, dear Sir Rowland, don't fight, if you	461	WAY WORLD	IV.1	626
Mrs Fain:	I don't understand your Ladyship.	466	WAY WORLD	V.1	147
Lady Wish:	more from you than all your life can accomplish--O don't	466	WAY WORLD	V.1	170
Lady Wish:	be wrong'd after all, ha? I don't know what to think,--	466	WAY WORLD	V.1	181
Sir Wilful:	take Shipping--Aunt, if you don't forgive quickly; I shall	472	WAY WORLD	V.1	395

Done (110)

Speaker	Text	PAGE	TITLE	ACT.SC	LINE
Sharper:	His name, and I have done.	47	OLD BATCH	I.1	382
Sir Joseph:	mischief done I perceive.	48	OLD BATCH	II.1	20
Sharper:	If he had Sir, what then? he could have done no	50	OLD BATCH	II.1	125
Capt Bluff:	done but an humble Servant of yours, that shall be nameless,	52	OLD BATCH	II.1	198
Capt Bluff:	Scipic and others have done it.	53	OLD BATCH	II.1	212
Sir Joseph:	mischief done, that's flat. And yet I believe if you had been	68	OLD BATCH	III.1	276
Sir Joseph:	you had put on your fighting Face before, you had done	70	OLD BATCH	III.1	358
Sir Joseph:	done behind his Back, than what's said--Come wee'l	70	OLD BATCH	III.1	361
Heartwell:	I'm impatient till it be done; I will not give my	74	OLD BATCH	III.2	138
Barnaby:	I have done Sir, then farewell 500 Pound.	76	OLD BATCH	IV.1	18
Barnaby:	done there till you come.	76	OLD BATCH	IV.1	35
Fondlewife:	And nothing can be done here till I go--So that	76	OLD BATCH	IV.1	36
Laetitia:	that will love you as well as I have done: I shall be contented	78	OLD BATCH	IV.1	110
Vainlove:	done.	88	OLD BATCH	IV.3	184
Heartwell:	I'm impatient till it be done.	97	OLD BATCH	V.1	13
Capt Bluff:	Damn your Morals: I must revenge th' Affront done	101	OLD BATCH	V.1	180
Sir Joseph:	be done. What--Come, Mr. Setter, I have over-heard all,	103	OLD BATCH	V.1	243
Araminta:	Bless me! What have you done to him?	108	OLD BATCH	V.2	45
Sharper:	all Injuries whatsoever, done unto you by them; until the	110	OLD BATCH	V.2	87
Sharper:	'Tis done, those Gentlemen are witnesses to the	110	OLD BATCH	V.2	100
	Now the Deed's done, the Giddy-thing has leasure	113	OLD BATCH	EPI.	8
	You gain your End, and damn 'em when you've done.	113	OLD BATCH	EPI.	30
	You gain your Ends, and damn 'em when you've done.	113	OLD BATCH	EPI.	V 30
Maskwell:	Cynthia? Which c're to Morrow shall be done,--had	137	DOUEL DLR	I.1	389
Mellefont:	the Storm, and her Ministers have done their Work; you	148	DOUEL DLR	II.1	383
Lord Touch:	Before I've done, I will be satisfied.	153	DOUEL DLR	III.1	107
Sir Paul:	success. Boy, tell my Lady, when she has done, I would	163	DOUEL DLR	III.1	498
Lady Froth:	And when at night his labour's done,	164	DOUEL DLR	III.1	535
Lord Froth:	Hee, hee, hee, my Dear, have you done--	165	DOUEL DLR	III.1	558
Sir Paul:	Left Eye! A 1000 [Pound] for this Left Eye. This has done	173	DOUEL DLR	IV.1	235
Sir Paul:	--Gads-bud I could have done--not so much as you	174	DOUEL DLR	IV.1	243
Sir Paul:	Person, he, he, he. No, No, I have done with her. I have	174	DOUEL DLR	IV.1	275
Sir Paul:	done with her now.	174	DOUEL DLR	IV.1	276
Mellefont:	done, left you to your self.--You're in a kind of Erasmus	185	DOUEL DLR	IV.2	60
Maskwell:	What have I done?	188	DOUEL DLR	V.1	16
Maskwell:	that I have done, would look like Rivals Malice, false	188	DOUEL DLR	V.1	39
Mellefont:	The Devil he has! what's to be done?	190	DOUEL DLR	V.1	113
Lord Touch:	were it possible it shou'd be done this night.	196	DOUEL DLR	V.1	321
Lord Touch:	Instruct me how this may be done, you shall	196	DOUEL DLR	V.1	324
Maskwell:	your Lordship--but it may be as well done to night.	196	DOUEL DLR	V.1	328
Trapland:	business must be done, are you ready to--	224	FOR LOVE	I.1	301
Scandal:	No doubt on't. Well, but has she done you wrong, or	228	FOR LOVE	I.1	476
Scandal:	Yes, all that have done him Favours, if you will	232	FOR LOVE	I.1	606
Sr Sampson:	Nor no more to be done, Old Boy; that's plain--	240	FOR LOVE	II.1	172
Sr Sampson:	to be done, but for him to offend, and me to pardon. I	240	FOR LOVE	II.1	178
Foresight:	things were done, and the Conveyance made--	240	FOR LOVE	II.1	188
Sr Sampson:	be done to Night--No matter for the time; prithee,	240	FOR LOVE	II.1	195
Mrs Fore:	often done in Duels, take care of one another, and grow	248	FOR LOVE	II.1	478
Tattle:	do as she would be done by--Gad I'll understand it so.	251	FOR LOVE	II.1	594
Tattle:	to no purpose--But since we have done nothing, we must	253	FOR LOVE	III.1	22
Scandal:	So faith, your Business is done here; now you may	255	FOR LOVE	III.1	91
Ben:	done; may-hap you may be shame-fac'd, some Maidens	263	FOR LOVE	III.1	391
Ben:	afore I ha' done with 'en.	265	FOR LOVE	III.1	438
Mrs Fore:	she cry?--Mr. Benjamin, what have you done to her?	265	FOR LOVE	III.1	440
Angelica:	more than he has done by himself: and now the Surprize	277	FOR LOVE	IV.1	82
Scandal:	all night, and denying that she had done	284	FOR LOVE	IV.1	V336
Foresight:	Pray what will be done at Court?	288	FOR LOVE	IV.1	496
Mrs Frail:	No, no, we'll keep it secret, it shall be done	290	FOR LOVE	IV.1	554
Valentine:	one anothers Faces, till we have done something to be	290	FOR LOVE	IV.1	563
Valentine:	is done, and I will be Mad no longer.	295	FOR LOVE	IV.1	750
Angelica:	a Masquerade is done, when we come to shew Faces;	296	FOR LOVE	IV.1	790
Angelica:	a Masquerade is done, when we come to shew our Faces;	296	FOR LOVE	IV.1	V790
Angelica:	I can tell you how that may be done--But it is a	299	FOR LOVE	V.1	90
Tattle:	No, Sir; 'tis to be done Privately--I never make	304	FOR LOVE	V.1	280
Angelica:	I have done dissembling now, Valentine; and if that	313	FOR LOVE	V.1	605
Scandal:	Well, Madam, You have done Exemplary Justice,	313	FOR LOVE	V.1	619
Gonsalez:	Has better done;	332	M. BRIDE	I.1	256
Gonsalez:	Has better done; in proving with his Sword	332	M. BRIDE	I.1	V257
Gonsalez:	What she has done, was in excess of Goodness:	334	M. BRIDE	I.1	318
Almeria:	No, no, thy Griefs have done this to thee.	342	M. BRIDE	II.2	116
Almeria:	No, no, thy Griefs, I know, have done this to thee.	342	M. BRIDE	II.2	V116
Zara:	Is it well done? Is this then the Return	345	M. BRIDE	II.2	235
Zara:	For all I've done, and all I have endur'd,	346	M. BRIDE	II.2	274
Osmyn-Alph:	O call not to my Mind what you have done,	347	M. BRIDE	II.2	288

Done   (continued)

Speaker	Line	PAGE	TITLE	ACT.SC	LINE
Zara:	O, why do I relate what I have done?	347	M. BRIDE	II.2	297
Zara:	Have I done this? tell me, am I so curs'd?	354	M. BRIDE	III.1	197
Zara:	That done, I leave thy Justice to return	355	M. BRIDE	III.1	219
Zara:	The base Injustice thou hast done my Love.	361	M. BRIDE	III.1	454
Zara:	But say, what's to be done? or when, or how	362	M. BRIDE	IV.1	42
Selim:	That Execution may be done in private.	362	M. BRIDE	IV.1	47
Manuel:	What's to be done?	365	M. BRIDE	IV.1	148
Alonzo:	Conclude it done. Where shall I wait your Lordship?	372	M. BRIDE	IV.1	440
Alonzo:	Which done, he drew a Ponyard from his side,	373	M. BRIDE	V.1	26
Gonsalez:	'Twere done--I'll crawl and sting him to the Heart;	376	M. BRIDE	V.2	12
Garcia:	O whence, or how, or wherefore was this done?	377	M. BRIDE	V.2	63
Garcia:	What's to be done? the King's Death known, will strike	378	M. BRIDE	V.2	93
Alonzo:	Require me not to tell the Means, till done,	378	M. BRIDE	V.2	97
Gonsalez:	What hast thou done, Alonzo?	379	M. BRIDE	V.2	109
Alonzo:	As but an hour ago, I'd not have done,	379	M. BRIDE	V.2	111
Zara:	The King; tell him, what he requir'd, I've done:	380	M. BRIDE	V.2	152
Leonora:	Feeling Remorse too late, for what they've done.	381	M. BRIDE	V.2	225
	The Tragedy thus done, I am, you know,	385	M. BRIDE	EPI.	1
Fainall:	Have we done?	395	WAY WORLD	I.1	2
Fainall:	What have you done with Petulant?	402	WAY WORLD	I.1	278
Marwood:	I have done hating 'em; and am now come to	411	WAY WORLD	II.1	45
Fainall:	The Injuries you have done him are a proof: Your interposing	414	WAY WORLD	II.1	157
Marwood:	the World the Injuries you have done me, both in my	415	WAY WORLD	II.1	195
Fainall:	--I believe you; I'm convinc'd I've done you wrong;	416	WAY WORLD	II.1	242
Millamant:	have done thinking of that; think of me.	423	WAY WORLD	II.1	488
Lady Wish:	But what hast thou done?	427	WAY WORLD	III.1	73
Foible:	Nay, 'tis your Ladyship has done, and are to do; I	427	WAY WORLD	III.1	74
Marwood:	No. What has he done?	432	WAY WORLD	III.1	290
Millamant:	Nay, he has done nothing; he has only talk'd--	432	WAY WORLD	III.1	291
Marwood:	over, and we have done with the Disguise. For a Fool's	433	WAY WORLD	III.1	311
Mrs Fain:	--what they have done by this time I know not. But	452	WAY WORLD	IV.1	313
Mrs Fain:	--what they may have done by this time I know not. But	452	WAY WORLD	IV.1	V313
Sir Wilful:	We'll drink and we'll never ha' done Boys	455	WAY WORLD	IV.1	416
Marwood:	done. I am sorry my Zeal to serve your Ladyship and	466	WAY WORLD	V.1	162
Fainall:	perfected, which I will take care shall be done with all	469	WAY WORLD	V.1	293

Dont (2)

Speaker	Line	PAGE	TITLE	ACT.SC	LINE
Silvia:	dont I know my Father lov'd my Mother, and was married	73	OLD BATCH	III.2	101
Laetitia:	No you dont.	78	OLD BATCH	IV.1	124

Doom (4)

Speaker	Line	PAGE	TITLE	ACT.SC	LINE
Manuel:	His Doom	364	M. BRIDE	IV.1	112
Manuel:	And all should follow to partake his Doom.	369	M. BRIDE	IV.1	334
Almeria:	For he is gone to doom Alphonso's Death.	370	M. BRIDE	IV.1	374
	But pray consider, ere you doom its fall,	479	WAY WORLD	EPI.	3

Doom'd (1)

Speaker	Line	PAGE	TITLE	ACT.SC	LINE
Manuel:	Now doom'd to die, that most accursed Osmyn.	368	M. BRIDE	IV.1	288

Dooms-day-Book (1)

Speaker	Line	PAGE	TITLE	ACT.SC	LINE
Marwood:	record; not even in Dooms-day-Book: to discompose the	467	WAY WORLD	V.1	217

Doomsday (1)

Speaker	Line	PAGE	TITLE	ACT.SC	LINE
Sr Sampson:	warrant you, if he danc'd till Doomsday, he thought I	240	FOR LOVE	II.1	179

Door (37)   see Barn-door-Fowl, Chamber-door, Closet-Door

Speaker	Line	PAGE	TITLE	ACT.SC	LINE
Footman:	Only to the next door, Madam; I'll call him.	58	OLD BATCH	II.2	158
Belinda:	Jut-Windows, and her Mouth the great Door, most hospitably	84	OLD BATCH	IV.3	47
Fondlewife:	Cocky, Cocky, open the door	89	OLD BATCH	IV.4	11
Laetitia:	(Opens the Door.)	89	OLD BATCH	IV.4	21
Fondlewife:	I'll shut this door, to secure him from coming	91	OLD BATCH	IV.4	72
Bellmour:	like an uncivil Person, you knock'd at the Door, before	95	OLD BATCH	IV.4	215
Laetitia:	when you knock'd at the door; and the Maid told me,	95	OLD BATCH	IV.4	244
	(Heartwell and Lucy appear at Sylvia's Door.)	96	OLD BATCH	V.1	V 9
Bellmour:	Ha! Is not that Heartwell at Sylvia's Door; be gone	97	OLD BATCH	V.1	10
Setter:	They're at the Door: I'll call 'em in.	112	OLD BATCH	V.2	180
Maskwell:	lie conceal'd there; otherwise she may Lock the Door	181	DOUBL DLR	IV.1	517
Lady Touch:	Hold, let me Lock the Door first.	184	DOUBL DLR	IV.2	28
Lady Touch:	(Goes to the door.)	184	DOUBL DLR	IV.2	29
Maskwell:	way into it, so that you need not come thro' this Door	194	DOUBL DLR	V.1	254
Maskwell:	(Goes to the Chamber Door and knocks.)	194	DOUBL DLR	V.1	271
Jeremy:	sit at the Door, that I don't get double the Stomach that	218	FOR LOVE	I.1	92
Miss Prue:	Ah, but I'll hold the Door with Hands, and	252	FOR LOVE	II.1	651
Nurse:	Open the Door--Open the Door Miss--I hear you	253	FOR LOVE	III.1	6
Nurse:	(knocks) Ods my Life, won't you open the Door? I'll	253	FOR LOVE	III.1	11
	(Tattle and Miss Prue at the Door.)	253	FOR LOVE	III.1	V 14
Tattle:	(Thrusts her in, and shuts the Door.)	254	FOR LOVE	III.1	25
Scandal:	(Goes to the Door.)	258	FOR LOVE	III.1	193
Jeremy:	Mr. Scandal is with him, Sir; I'll knock at the Door.	279	FOR LOVE	IV.1	147
Jeremy:	(Goes to the Door.)	296	FOR LOVE	IV.1	779
	(Garcia leads Almeria to the Door, and returns.)	334	M. BRIDE	I.1	352
Leonora:	Are false, or still the Marble Door remains	340	M. BRIDE	II.2	10
Gonsalez:	There lies my way, that Door is too unlock'd.	376	M. BRIDE	V.2	4
Witwoud:	to the Door again in a trice; where he wou'd send in for	405	WAY WORLD	I.1	374
Lady Wish:	won't sit--I'll walk--aye I'll walk from the door upon his	445	WAY WORLD	IV.1	20
Mrs Fain:	lock the Door.	447	WAY WORLD	IV.1	89
Sir Wilful:	What dee do? 'Shart a'has lock'd the Door indeed I	447	WAY WORLD	IV.1	92
Sir Wilful:	think--Nay Cozen Fainall, open the Door--Pshaw,	447	WAY WORLD	IV.1	93
Millamant:	lastly, where ever I am, you shall always knock at the door	450	WAY WORLD	IV.1	224
Lady Wish:	her foot within the door of a Play-house. O my dear	467	WAY WORLD	V.1	205
Lady Wish:	her foot within the door of a Play-house. O dear	467	WAY WORLD	V.1	V205
Sir Wilful:	(Goes to the Door and hems.)	471	WAY WORLD	V.1	V353

Door-keepers (1)

Speaker	Line	PAGE	TITLE	ACT.SC	LINE
Tattle:	and Covent-Garden, the Door-keepers at the Play-House,	257	FOR LOVE	III.1	156

Door's (2)

Speaker	Line	PAGE	TITLE	ACT.SC	LINE
Sir Wilful:	Door's inchanted--.	447	WAY WORLD	IV.1	96
Sir Wilful:	your Servant--I think this door's lock'd.	448	WAY WORLD	IV.1	147

Doors (10)

Speaker	Line	PAGE	TITLE	ACT.SC	LINE
Fondlewife:	near my Doors. I say, he is a wanton young Levite and	76	OLD BATCH	IV.1	26
Laetitia:	Oh! Won't you follow, and see him out of Doors,	91	OLD BATCH	IV.4	70
Maskwell:	of Doors; and to--ha, ha, ha, I can't tell you for Laughing,	149	DOUBL DLR	II.1	401

Dress   (continued)

PAGE   TITLE   ACT.SC LINE

Dress'd (6)
              (Sir Wilfull Witwoud in a riding Dress, ...   436   WAY WORLD III.1 V443

		PAGE	TITLE	ACT.SC	LINE
	a Couch disorderly dress'd, Scandal by him.)	279	FOR LOVE	IV.1	149
Jeremy:	to be so dress'd; and she is so in Love with him, she'll	302	FOR LOVE	V.1	201
	(Enter Valentine dress'd, Scandal, and Jeremy.)	310	FOR LOVE	V.1	496
Mrs Fain:	You were dress'd before I came abroad.	419	WAY WORLD	III.1	354
Lady Wish:	O Dear, I can't appear till I'm dress'd. Dear . . .	432	WAY WORLD	III.1	278
Servant-W:	Morning, before she is dress'd. 'Tis like I may give a	437	WAY WORLD	III.1	462

Dressing (7)

		PAGE	TITLE	ACT.SC	LINE
Heartwell:	burdens, are forced to undergo Dressing, Dancing, Singing,	44	OLD BATCH	I.1	273
Millamant:	dressing; their Folly is less provoking than your Mallice,	433	WAY WORLD	III.1	326
Millamant:	dressing here; their Folly is less provoking than your Mallice,	433	WAY WORLD	III.1	V326
Servant-W:	Sir, my Lady's dressing. Here's Company; if you	437	WAY WORLD	III.1	445
Sir Wilful:	Dressing! What it's but Morning here I warrant . . .	437	WAY WORLD	III.1	447
Lady Wish:	receive him in my little dressing Room, there's a Couch--	445	WAY WORLD	IV.1	23
Millamant:	dine in my dressing room when I'm out of humour . . .	450	WAY WORLD	IV.1	220

Dressing-Room (3)

		PAGE	TITLE	ACT.SC	LINE
Maskwell:	an hour, yonder in my Lady's Dressing-Room: go by the .	194	DOUBL DLR	V.1	239
Maskwell:	the Chaplain's habit, wait for Cynthia in your Dressing-Room:	199	DOUBL DLR	V.1	442
Lord Touch:	Dressing-Room,--was't not so? And Maskwell will	200	DOUBL DLR	V.1	484

Drest (2)

		PAGE	TITLE	ACT.SC	LINE
Lady Ply:	So well drest, so boon mein, so eloquent, so	160	DOUBL DLR	III.1	363
Lady Ply:	So well drest, so bonne mine, so eloquent, so	160	DOUBL DLR	III.1	V363

Drew (2)

		PAGE	TITLE	ACT.SC	LINE
Sharper:	chance which drew me hither; ay here, just here, this spot	48	OLD BATCH	II.1	22
Alonzo:	Which done, he drew a Ponyard from his side, . . .	373	M. BRIDE	V.1	26

Drift (2)   see A-drift

		PAGE	TITLE	ACT.SC	LINE
Mellefont:	great Beard, like a Russian Bear upon a drift of Snow. You	158	DOUBL DLR	III.1	292
Fainall:	turn'd a drift, like a Leaky hulk to Sink or Swim, as she	473	WAY WORLD	V.1	443

Drink (29)

		PAGE	TITLE	ACT.SC	LINE
Sir Joseph:	by the Lord Harry he says true; Fighting, is Meat, Drink .	52	OLD BATCH	II.1	167
Heartwell:	Awake; Sigh much, Drink little, Eat less, court Solitude, .	73	OLD BATCH	III.2	81
Lord Touch:	Ladys, and Drink a Dish of Tea, to settle our Heads. .	132	DOUBL DLR	I.1	217
Lord Touch:	Ladies, and Drink a Dish of Tea, to settle our Heads. .	132	DOUBL DLR	I.1	V217
Maskwell:	Pox on't that a Man can't drink without quenching his .	155	DOUBL DLR	III.1	185
Maskwell:	which no body but you ought to drink down. Your Aunt's .	156	DOUBL DLR	III.1	202
Lady Ply:	Drink the less you Sot, and do't before you	180	DOUBL DLR	IV.1	V487
Valentine:	Drink first. Scandal, why do you not Drink?	223	FOR LOVE	I.1	255
	(They Drink.)	223	FOR LOVE	I.1	256
Valentine:	doing good.--Scandal, Drink to me, my Friend Trapland's .	223	FOR LOVE	I.1	260
	(They Drink.)	223	FOR LOVE	I.1	277
Ben:	Thus we live at Sea; eat Bisket, and drink Flip; put on a .	275	FOR LOVE	III.1	800
Valentine:	Is the Lawyer gone? 'tis well, then we may drink . .	280	FOR LOVE	IV.1	191
Almeria:	Drink bitter Draughts, with never-slacking Thirst. . .	356	M. BRIDE	III.1	262
Selim:	Drink not the Poyson--for Alphonso is--	380	M. BRIDE	V.2	184
Almeria:	O noble Thirst! yet greedy, to drink all--	382	M. BRIDE	V.2	V255
Almeria:	Drink all--O for another Draught of Death, ...	382	M. BRIDE	V.2	256
Almeria:	I'll drink my glad Acknowledgment--	382	M. BRIDE	V.2	260
Almeria:	From his pale Lips; I'll kiss him e'er I drink, . . .	382	M. BRIDE	V.2	267
Lady Wish:	brought! Dost thou take me for a Fairy, to drink out of an	425	WAY WORLD	III.1	29
Lady Wish:	Will you drink any Thing after your Journey, Nephew, .	441	WAY WORLD	III.1	599
Fainall:	disable him for that, he will drink like a Dane: after dinner, ...	443	WAY WORLD	III.1	672
Mirabell:	mens prerogative, and presume to drink healths, or toste .	451	WAY WORLD	IV.1	270
Sir Wilful:	Bill--Give me more drink and take my Purse.	455	WAY WORLD	IV.1	395
Sir Wilful:	We'll drink and we'll never ha' done Boys	455	WAY WORLD	IV.1	416
Sir Wilful:	Head and drink a Health to 'em--A Match or no Match, .	456	WAY WORLD	IV.1	426
Sir Wilful:	To drink is a Christian Diversion, ...	456	WAY WORLD	IV.1	450
Sir Wilful:	drink, to give her to him again,--I wou'd I might never .	472	WAY WORLD	V.1	394

Drinking (4)

		PAGE	TITLE	ACT.SC	LINE
Foible:	Sir Wilfull is set in to Drinking, Madam, in the Parlour. .	445	WAY WORLD	IV.1	36
Mrs Fain:	him; But he answers her only with Singing and Drinking .	452	WAY WORLD	IV.1	312
	(Enter Witwoud from drinking.)	453	WAY WORLD	IV.1	322
Lady Wish:	'tis with drinking your Health--O' my Word you are . .	455	WAY WORLD	IV.1	407

Drinks (6)

		PAGE	TITLE	ACT.SC	LINE
Trapland:	--my Service to you Mr. Scandal--(Drinks)--I	222	FOR LOVE	I.1	246
Valentine:	(Drinks.)	222	FOR LOVE	I.1	253
Trapland:	(Drinks.)	224	FOR LOVE	I.1	291
Zara:	Quick; or, by Heav'n, this Dagger drinks thy Blood. .	362	M. BRIDE	IV.1	38
Zara:	(Drinks.)	381	M. BRIDE	V.2	203
Mirabell:	drinks, as Tea, Chocolate and Coffee. As likewise to Genuine	451	WAY WORLD	IV.1	266

Driv'n (2)

		PAGE	TITLE	ACT.SC	LINE
Zara:	Driv'n by the Tide upon my Country's Coast, ...	346	M. BRIDE	II.2	276
Osmyn-Alph:	One, driv'n about the World like blasted Leaves . . .	351	M. BRIDE	III.1	59

Drive (6)

		PAGE	TITLE	ACT.SC	LINE
Bellmour:	I could be well enough pleas'd to drive on a Love-bargain,	60	OLD BATCH	II.2	220
Scandal:	think I heard her bid the Coach-man drive hither. . .	276	FOR LOVE	IV.1	13
Valentine:	drive distinct Trades, and Care and Pleasure separately .	289	FOR LOVE	IV.1	506
Witwoud:	and Mask, slap into a Hackney-Coach, and drive hither .	405	WAY WORLD	I.1	373
Lady Wish:	--do, drive a Trade, do, with your three penny-worth .	462	WAY WORLD	V.1	11
Lady Wish:	go, drive a trade,--these were your Commodities . . .	462	WAY WORLD	V.1	18

Driveler (1)

		PAGE	TITLE	ACT.SC	LINE
Marwood:	draw him like an Idiot, a Driveler, with a Bib and Bells. .	431	WAY WORLD	III.1	237

Driving (1)

		PAGE	TITLE	ACT.SC	LINE
Lady Froth:	And there his whipping and his driving ends;	164	DOUBL DLR	III.1	539

Drole (0)   see Le Drcle

Drop (5)

		PAGE	TITLE	ACT.SC	LINE
Lord Froth:	O, for the Universe, not a drop more I beseech . . .	134	DOUBL DLR	I.1	288
Mellefont:	Industry grown full and ripe, ready to drop into his mouth,	187	DOUBL DLR	IV.2	144
Mellefont:	Industry grow full and ripe, ready to drop into his mouth,	187	DOUBL DLR	IV.2	V144
Mrs Fain:	drop off when she's full. Madam you sha'not pawn a . . .	466	WAY WORLD	V.1	175
Mrs Fain:	drop off when she's full. Madam you shan't pawn a . .	466	WAY WORLD	V.1	V175

188

Dy'd (7)
```
Sir Joseph:    dy'd cf a fright. But--  . . . . . . . . . . .  51   OLD EATCH  II.1  145
Almeria:       To Heav'n and thee; and sooner wou'd have dy'd--  . . . 343   M. ERIDE   II.2  127
Almeria:       And yet alone would I have dy'd, Heav'n knows,  . . . 368   M. ERIDE   IV.1  305
Zara:          He dy'd unknowing in my Heart.  . . . . . . . .  381   M. ERIDE   V.2   190
Zara:          But Oh, he dy'd unknowing in my Heart.  . . . . .  381   M. ERIDE   V.2  V190
Fainall:       I thought you had dy'd for her.  . . . . . . .  408   WAY WCRLD  I.1   473
Lady Wish:     O Sir Rowland, the hours that he has dy'd  . . . .  458   WAY WCRLD  IV.1  511
```
Dye (2)   see Die
```
Sir Paul:      dye of 'em, like any Child, that were cutting his Teeth--  146  DOUEL DLR  II.1  283
Scandal:       Do, I'll dye a Martyr, rather than disclaim my  . . . 269   FOR LCVE   III.1  595
```
Dying (5)
```
Lady Ply:      Embraces--Say thou dear dying Man, when, where,  . . . . 170  DOUEL DLR  IV.1  125
Sir Paul:      Dying Ned. Careless. . . . . . . . . . . . .  178   DOUEL DLR  IV.1  416
Mellefont:     O Madam, have a care of dying unprepared, I  . . . 184   DOUEL DLR  IV.2  54
Gonsalez:      With dying Words, to offer at your Praise.  . . . 332   M. ERIDE   I.1   254
Almeria:       Or dying Groans frcm my Alphonso's Breast?  . . . 371   M. ERIDE   IV.1  386
```
Dyingness (1)
```
Lady Wish:     sort of a dyingness--You see that Picture has a sort of  . 429  WAY WCRLD  III.1  168
```
E'en (7)
```
Sharper:       Faith e'en give her over for good-and-all; you can  . . . 41   OLD BATCH  I.1   161
Setter:        above it. So that Reputation is e'en as foolish  . . . 102   OLD BATCH  V.1   232
               Women and Wits are used e'en much at one;  . . . . . . 113   OLD BATCH  EPI.  29
Mellefont:     and Cutt, let's e'en turn up Trump now.  . . . . . 142   DOUBL DLR  II.1  161
Ben:           that be all--Pray don't let me be your hindrance; e'en  . 261   FCB LCVE   III.1  301
Ben:           And just e'en as he meant, Sir, . . . . . . . 274   FCR LCVE   III.1  785
Jeremy:        just as he was poor for want of Money; his Head is e'en as  276  FCR LCVE   IV.1  34
```
E'er (6)
```
Almeria:       E'er next we meet--  . . . . . . . . . . . .  345   M. BRIDE   II.2  V209
Zara:          Than e'er thou could'st with bitterest Reproaches;  . . . 354   M. ERIDE   III.1  186
Manuel:        Hence, e'er I curse--fly my just Rage with speed;  . . . 369   M. BRIDE   IV.1  316
Almeria:       From his pale Lips; I'll kiss him e'er I drink,  . . . 382   M. BRIDE   V.2   267
Fainall:       nodding Husband would not wake, that e'er the watchful  . 414   WAY WCRLD  II.1  148
Fainall:       been false, I had e'er this repaid it--'Tis true--Bad you  . 415   WAY WCRLD  II.1  201
```
E'gad (1)
```
Brisk:         He? e'gad, so I did--My Lord can sing it.  . . . . . 166   DOUEL DLR  III.1  589
```
E'n (1)
```
Lucy:          as his Love. Therefore e'n set your Heart at rest, and  . 61   OLD EATCH  III.1  8
```
E're (11)
```
Maskwell:      Cynthia? Which e're to Morrow shall be done,--had  . . . 137   DOUEL DLR  I.1   389
Singer:        Cynthia frowns when e're I Woo her,  . . . . . . 143   DOUEL DLR  II.1  179
Maskwell:      Come, trouble not your head, I'll joyn you together e're  . 148   DOUBL DLR  II.1  386
Lady Touch:    the love of you, was the first wandring fire that e're
                 misled  . . . . . . . . . . . . . . . . . 185   DOUEL DLR  IV.2  76
Lady Touch:    Ground, be buried quick beneath it, e're I be consenting to  186  DOUEL DLR  IV.2  99
Lady Touch:    Ground, be buried quick beneath it, e're I'll be
                 consenting to  . . . . . . . . . . . . . . 186   DOUEL DLR  IV.2  V 99
Maskwell:      lov'd Embraces, could e're be fond of an inferiour Slavery.  . 198  DOUEL DLR  V.1   426
Foresight:     Egyptian Mummy, e're she shall Incorporate with a  . . 241   FOR LCVE   II.1  239
Singer-F:      E're a Nymph that was Chaste, or a Swain that was True.  . 258   FOR LCVE   III.1  203
Miss Prue:     What, and must not I have e're a Husband then?  . . . 305   FCR LCVE   V.1   304
Gonsalez:      I'th' Morning he must die again; e're Noon  . . . . 366   M. BRIDE   IV.1  210
```
Each (31)
```
Bellmour:      in the Mine; well, we have each our share of sport, and each  43  OLD BATCH  I.1   223
Sharper:       May each succeed in what he wishes most.  . . . . . 47   OLD BATCH  I.1   388
               Were each to suffer for his Mothers Sin:  . . . . 125   DOUEL DLR  PRO.  22
Maskwell:      When each, who searches strictly his own mind,  . . . 150   DOUEL DLR  II.1  467
Lord Froth:    And each Morning wears a new one;  . . . . . . 166   DOUEL DLR  III.1  600
Cynthia:       both so willing; we each of us strive to reach the Gole,  . 168   DOUEL DLR  IV.1  12
Cynthia:       both willing; we each of us strive to reach the Gole,  . 168   DOUEL DLR  IV.1  V 12
Mellefont:     maze of thoughts, each leading into one another, and all  . 190   DOUEL DLR  V.1   104
Lady Touch:    meanings lurk in each corner of that various face. O! that  198  DOUEL DLR  V.1   395
Maskwell:      of a Girl. No--yet tho' I doat on each last Favour  . . 199   DOUEL DLR  V.1   433
Lord Touch:    And be each others comfort;--let me  . . . . . . 203   DOUEL DLR  V.1   586
Lord Touch:    Circling Joys, tread round each happy Year of your long  . 203   DOUEL DLR  V.1   589
               Each chusing that, in which he has most Art.  . . . 204   DOUEL DLR  EPI.  16
               To cultivate each Year a hungry Soil;  . . . . . 213   FOR LCVE   PRO.  2
               We hope there's something that may please each Taste,  . 213   FOR LCVE   PRO.  26
Valentine:     fill each Man his Glass. . . . . . . . . . . 223   FOR LCVE   I.1   263
Almeria:       Feed on each others Heart, devour our Woes  . . . . 356   M. BBIDE   III.1  259
Almeria:       Thy second self should feel each other Wound,  . . . 356   M. EBIDE   III.1  287
Almeria:       But sink each other, lower yet, down, down,  . . . 358   M. BBIDE   III.1  371
Almeria:       But sink each other, deeper yet, down, dcwn  . . . 358   M. BBIDE   III.1  V371
Almeria:       To Morrow, and the next, and each that follows,  . . 367   M. EBIDE   IV.1  259
Almeria:       Yes, all my Father's wounding Wrath, tho' each  . . 368   M. EBIDE   IV.1  307
Zara:          Attend me instantly, with each a Bowl  . . . . . 375   M. EBIDE   V.1   131
Zara:          Of Sense: His Soul still sees, and knows each Purpose,  . 381   M. BBIDE   V.2   196
               And know each Critick by his sowre Grimaces.  . . . 385   M. BBIDE   EPI.  6
               Each time they write, they venture all they've won;  . 393   WAY WCRLD  PRO.  14
Marwood:       affect Endearments to each other, profess eternal
                 Friendships,  . . . . . . . . . . . . . . 410   WAY WCRLD  II.1  23
Mirabell:      For each deceiver to his cost may find,  . . . . . 478   WAY WORLD  V.1   622
               Yet each pretends to know the Copy'd Face.  . . . . 479   WAY WORLD  EPI.  20
               They from each Fair One catch scme different Grace,  . 479   WAY WORLD  EPI.  32
```
Eager (3)
```
Heartwell:     'tis true you are so eager in pursuit of the temptation,
                 that  . . . . . . . . . . . . . . . . . 43   OLD BATCH  I.1   240
Lucy:          doubt will be eager enough to day, to swallow the  . . . 61   OLD BATCH  III.1  12
Singer:        He trembling, cry'd, with eager haste,  . . . . . 71   OLD BATCH  III.2  6
```
Ear (5)
```
Capt Bluff:    to thank you in: But in your Ear, you are to be seen again.  69  OLD EATCH  III.1  323
Jeremy:        Yes, I have a reasonable good Ear, Sir, as to Jiggs and  . 245   FOR LCVE   II.1  373
Zara:          Worthy your private Ear, and this your Minister.  . . 364   M. BBIDE   IV.1  130
Sir Wilful:    your Ear, prithee who are these Gallants?  . . . . 437   WAY WORLD  III.1  469
Lady Wish:     Beads broken, and a Quilted Night-cap with one Ear. Go,  . 462   WAY WORLD  V.1   17
```

Earlier (1)
Zara: My self will fly; and earlier than the Morn, ... 354   M. EBIDE   III.1   202
Earliest (1)
Singer-V: To you I should my earliest Off'ring give;   293   FCB LCVE   IV.1   654
Early (6)
Bellmour: Vainlove, and abroad so early! good Morrow; I . . .   37   OLD BATCH   I.1   1
Vainlove: early Sallies are not usual to me; but Business as you see 37   OLD BATCH   I.1   6
Araminta: young, and your early baseness has prevented its growing . 87 OLD BATCH   IV.3   172
Scandal: I must work her into the Project. You keep early Hours, . 269 FOR LCVE   III.1   579
Foible: are sc early abroad, or Catering (says he) ferreting for . 427 WAY WCBLD III.1   96
Mirabell: Then I'll get up in a morning as early as I please.   . . 449 WAY WCBLD IV.1   192
Earnest (7)
Lucy: in gocd earnest, you kiss so devoutly.   97   OLD BATCH   V.1   38
Bellmour: fitter Husband for her.--Ccme, Here's Earnest of my good . 98 OLD BATCH   V.1   58
Capt Bluff: time, here's Earnest. (Gives him Money). Come, Knight; . 104 OLD BATCH   V.1   279
Maskwell: earnest of that Bargain, to have full and free possession of 156 DOUEL DLR III.1   229
Valentine: are earnest,--I'll avoid 'em,--Ccme this way,   . . .   246 FOR LCVE   II.1   411
Mrs Frail: Well, as an earnest cf Friendship and Confidence; . .   248 FOR LCVE   II.1   485
Jeremy: is almost mad in good earnest, with the Joyful News of   . 278 FOR LCVE   IV.1   100
Ears (13)
Sir Joseph: Love, up to the Ears. But I'll be discreet, and husht.   . 86 OLD BATCH   IV.3   110
Vainlove: Eyes, cr Ears? The Vision is here still.--Your Passion,   . 88 OLD BATCH   IV.3   176
Maskwell: Ears this way. . . . . 189 DOUEL DLB   V.1   45
Lord Touch: Ha! O poison to my Ears! what dc I hear! . . . . .   198 DOUBL DLR   V.1   427
Valentine: about without gcing together by the Ears--heigh ho! . . 280 FOR LCVE   IV.1   192
Almeria: To fill my Ears, with Garcia's valiant Deeds;   . . .   331 M. BRIDE   I.1   214
Almeria: Nor will my Ears be charm'd with sounding Words,   . .   332 M. BBIDE   I.1   248
Osmyn-Alph: So did it tear the Ears of Mercy, from . . . . . .   350 M. EBIDE   III.1   26
Osmyn-Alph: My Ears, and reach the Heav'ns; where is the King? . . 352 M. BRIDE   III.1   85
Mirabell: Waitwell shake his Ears, and Dame Partlet rustle up her . 398 WAY WCBLD I.1   129
Mirabell: you tender your Ears be secret. . . . .   398 WAY WCBLD   I.1   132
Mrs Fain: your Mistress up to the Ears in Love and Contemplation,   . 446 WAY WCBLD IV.1   71
Witwoud: Ears like a pair of Castanets. . . . .   454 WAY WCBLD   IV.1   363
Earth (24)
Capt Bluff: be nothing, Nothing in the Earth.   52   OLD BATCH   II.1   182
                Unless transplanted to more kindly Earth. . . . . . 213 FCB LCVE   PRO.   6
Almeria: And bend thy Glorious Eyes to Earth and me;   . . . . 330 M. EBIDE   I.1   180
Manuel: When my first Foe was laid in Earth, such Enmity, . . 333 M. EBIDE   I.1   308
Almeria: Lead me o'er Bones and Skulls, and mouldring Earth . . 339 M. BBIDE   II.1   74
Almeria: Yet green in Earth, rather than be the Bride . . . . 339 M. EBIDE   II.1   77
Osmyn-Alph: To Earth, and nail me, where I stand, ye Powers;   . . 341 M. EBIDE   II.2   47
Almeria: To Earth, to Light and Life, to Love and me,   . . .   342 M. EBIDE   II.2   90
Zara: See, where he stands, folded and fix'd tc Earth,   . . 345 M. EBIDE   II.2   232
Zara: Ev'n then. Kneeling on Earth, I loos'd my Hair, . . . 346 M. EBIDE   II.2   281
Osmyn-Alph: And bore contiguous Pallaces to Earth. . . . . . . 347 M. EBIDE   II.2   311
Osmyn-Alph: Or Earth, it rests, and rots to silent Dust.   . . .   351 M. EBIDE   III.1   62
Osmyn-Alph: Or this vile Earth, an Altar for such Off'rings? . . 357 M. EBIDE   III.1   326
Osmyn-Alph: 'Till gorg'd with suffocating Earth. . . . . . .   358 M. EBIDE   III.1 V356
Almeria: But prone, and dumb, rot the firm Face of Earth   . . 358 M. EBIDE   III.1   373
Almeria: O Earth, behcld, I kneel upon thy Bosom, ... 368 M. EBIDE   IV.1   273
Almeria: Stooping to raise frcm Earth the filial Reverence; . . 369 M. BRIDE   IV.1   324
Almeria: O hear me then, thus crawling on the Earth-- . . .   369 M. EBIDE   IV.1   327
Almeria: Drag me, harrow the Earth with my bare Bosom.   . . . 369 M. EBIDE   IV.1   337
Perez: He lies supine on earth; as easily . . . . 372 M. BRIDE   V.1   8
Perez: He lies supine on earth; with as much ease . . . . 372 M. BRIDE   V.1 V   8
Perez: She might remove the Centre of this Earth, ... 372 M. BRIDE   V.1 V   9
Zara: Would, like the raging Dog-star, scorch the Earth,   . . 375 M. BBIDE   V.1   95
Garcia: The Earth already groans to bear this Deed; . . . . 378 M. BBIDE   V.2   75
Earth-quake (1)
Manuel: That like a sudden Earth-quake, shakes my Frame; . . 367 M. EBIDE   IV.1   233
Earthly (1)
Bellmour: his Glass. Let low and earthly Souls grovel 'till they have 37 OLD BATCH I.1 V 25
Earthquake (1)
Foresight: 'Tis nc Earthquake! . . . . 266 FOR LCVE   III.1   491
Earthy (1)
Bellmour: his Glass. Let low and earthy Souls grovel till they have 37 OLD BATCH I.1   25
Ease (9)
Araminta: Person, for his ease, sometimes confesses Secrets his . . 58 OLD BATCH II.2   137
Laetitia: still cn your Stomach; lying on your Stomach, will ease . 91 OLD BATCH IV.4   86
Heartwell: And Adam, sure, cou'd with more Ease abide . . . . 108 OLD BATCH   V.2   14
Almeria: And Beds of Ease, to thinking me thy Wife? . . . . 357 M. EBIDE   III.1   313
Osmyn-Alph: Are they not soothing Softness, sinking Ease, . . .   358 M. EBIDE   III.1   363
Perez: He lies supine on earth; with as much ease . . . . 372 M. BRIDE   V.1 V   8
Manuel: One mcment's Ease? Hear my Command; and look . . .   374 M. EBIDE   V.1   72
Fainall: I do not--'Twas for my ease to oversee and . . . . 413 WAY WORLD II.1   143
Millamant: bestow, if I were reduc'd to an Inglorious ease; and free'd 449 WAY WORLD IV.1   168
Easie (16)
Bellmour: Faith I don't know, he's of a temper the most easie . . 42 OLD BATCH I.1   210
Vainlove: peace--I should not esteem a Pardon if too easie won. . . 63 OLD EATCH III.1   101
Lucy: easie Nature.--Well, For once I'll venture to serve . . 98 OLD BATCH V.1   75
Bellmour: humble, pliant, easie thing, a Lover, so guess at Plagues in 106 OLD BATCH V.1   382
Lady Ply: unaffected, so easie, so free, so particular, so agreeable-- 160 DOUEL DLR III.1   364
Maskwell: of mine, I have told 'em in plain terms, how easie 'tis for 194 DOUEL DLR V.1   263
Valentine: I am of my self, a plain easie simple Creature; and . . 244 FOR LCVE   II.1   345
Angelica: Fortune enough to make any Man easie that I can like; If . 299 FOR LCVE   V.1   61
Angelica: will make it easie to you. . . . . 310 FOR LCVE   V.1   482
Tattle: Easie! Pox on't, I don't believe I shall sleep to Night. . 310 FOR LCVE   V.1   483
Zara: Most easie and inevitable Death. . . . . 375 M. BRIDE   V.1   134
Gonsalez: How much Report has wrong'd your easie Faith. . . .   377 M. EBIDE   V.2   46
Mirabell: easie as to know when a Visit began to be troublesome; . 396 WAY WORLD I.1   39
Marwood: profess'd a Friendship to her; and could not see her easie 414 WAY WORLD II.1   163
Fainall: love you and be easie in my Doubts--Pray forbear . . . 416 WAY WORLD II.1   241
Millamant: Natural, easie Suckling! . . . . 447 WAY WCBLD IV.1   106
Easily (12)
Sharper: So-h, O Sir I am easily pacify'd, the acknowledgment . . 49 OLD EATCH II.1   62
Vainlove: peace--I should not esteem a Pardon if too easily won. . 63 OLD BATCH III.1 V101

Easily   (continued)
Heartwell: will more easily be thrust forward than drawn back.   .   .   73   OLD BATCH III.2   73
Maskwell: easily and pleasantly is that dissembled before Fruition!   155   DOUEL DLR III.1   184
Careless: Why, methinks that might be easily remedied--my   .   .   .   161   DOUEL DLR III.1   419
Maskwell: when we are together, and you not easily get in to surprize   181   DOUEL DLR IV.1   518
Valentine: was easily turn'd another way; and at least look'd well on   246   FOR LCVE II.1   409
Valentine: Acquaint Jeremy with it, he may easily bring it   292   FOR LCVE IV.1   616
Perez: He lies supine on earth; as easily   372   M. BRIDE   V.1   8
Fainall: Women do not easily forgive Omissions of that Nature.   .   .   397   WAY WCRLD I.1   84
Marwood: you might as easily put off Petulant and Witwoud, as your   433   WAY WCRLD III.1   315
Mirabell: live Easily together.   478   WAY WCBLD V.1   619
Easiness (2)
Araminta: upon the easiness of my Temper, has much deceiv'd you,   .   87   OLD BATCH IV.3   158
Mirabell: bestowing on your easiness that time, which is the   .   .   421   WAY WORLD III.1   435
East (1)   see North-East
Scandal: Wise Men of the East ow'd their Instruction to a Star,   .   267   FOR LCVE III.1   535
Eastern (2)
Sr Sampson: Eastern Empire under my Feet; it would make me only a   .   .   300   FCR LCVE   V.1   99
Garcia: The Eastern Gate is to the Foe betray'd, ...   377   M. BRIDE   V.2   32
Easy (2)
Bellmour: Does it sit easy on me?   75   OLD BATCH IV.1   4
Bellmour: See the great Blessing of an easy Faith; Opinion   .   .   .   96   OLD BATCH IV.4   271
Eat (10)
Sir Joseph: Let me but tell Mr. Sharper a little, how you eat   .   .   .   53   OLD BATCH II.1   218
Heartwell: Awake; Sigh much, Drink little, Eat less, court Solitude,   .   73   OLD BATCH III.2   81
Sir Paul: Nilus in his Belly, he will eat thee up alive.   .   .   .   145   DOUBL DLR II.1   248
Sir Paul: Nilus is in his Belly, he will eat thee up alive.   .   .   145   DOUBL DLR II.1 V248
Lady Touch: what I said to you, or you had better eat your own Horns,   192   DCUEL DLR V.1   192
Sr Sampson: rather eat a Pheasant, than a piece of poor John; and smell,   245   FCR LCVE II.1   369
Ben: Thus we live at Sea; eat Bisket, and drink Flip; put on a   275   FOR LCVE III.1   800
Almeria: And eat into thy Flesh, festring thy Limbs   356   M. BRIDE III.1   268
Lady Wish: murder'd. I'll have him poyson'd. Where does he eat? I'll   427   WAY WCBLD III.1   103
Lady Wish: before you eat? Dinner's almcst ready.   441   WAY WCBLD IV.1   600
Eaten (2)
Jeremy: there is nothing to be eaten.   216   FOR LCVE   I.1   22
Fainall: with a little Loss, than to be quite eaten up, with being   400   WAY WCRLD I.1   208
Eater (0)   see Beef-eater
Eating-house (1)
Marwood: in an Eating-house.   467   WAY WCRLD V.1   227
Ebb (2)
Heartwell: that noble passion, Lust, should ebb tc this degree--No   .   72   OLD BATCH III.2   48
Brisk: Like an Oyster at low Ebb, I'gad--ha, ha, ha.   165   DOUEL DLR III.1   576
Ebbing (1)
Manuel: But wearing now a-pace with ebbing Sand, ...   364   M. BRIDE IV.1   107
Eccho (4)
Millamant: one's Wit to an Eccho: They can but reflect what we look   .   420   WAY WORLD II.1   410
Mirabell: selves prais'd; and to an Eccho the pleasure of hearing your   421   WAY WCRLD II.1   417
Witwoud: she won't give an Eccho fair play; she has that everlasting   421   WAY WCRLD II.1   420
Witwoud: Rotaticn of Tongue, that an Eccho must wait till she dies,   421   WAY WORLD II.1   421
Eccles (3)
              (Set by Mr. John Eccles.)   .   .   .   258   FOR LCVE III.1   199
              (Set by Mr. John Eccles.)   .   .   274   FOR LCVE III.1   757
              (Set by Mr. John Eccles, ...   434   WAY WCRLD III.1   374
Echo's (2)
Almeria: My own affrights me with its Echo's.   339   M. BRIDE II.1   69
Almeria: Thy Voice--my own affrights me with its Echo's.   .   .   .   339   M. BRIDE II.1 V 69
Echoes (1)
Osmyn-Alph: When broken Echoes of a distant Voice, ...   343   M. BRIDE II.2   160
Eclips'd (2)
Brisk: O Jesu! Madam, you have Eclips'd me quite, let me   .   .   201   DOUBL DLR V.1   534
Brisk: Madam, you have Eclips'd me quite, let me   201   DOUEL DLR V.1 V534
Eclipse (2)
Angelica: last Invisible Eclipse, laying in Provision as 'twere for a   237   FOR LOVE II.1   80
Foresight: Really, Sir Sampson, this is a sudden Eclipse--   .   .   .   313   FCR LCVE   V.1   582
Ecstacies (1)   see Extacies
Lady Wish: Trances, and the Tremblings, the Ardors and the Ecstacies,   458   WAY WCRLD IV.1   514
Ecstasie (1)
Maskwell: dissemble Ardour and Ecstasie, that's resolv'd: How   .   .   155   DOUEL DLR III.1   183
Eden (1)
              It seems like Eden, fruitful of its own accord.   .   .   .   213   FOR LOVE PRO.   17
Edg'd (1)
Maskwell: --a Son and Heir, would have edg'd Young   137   DOUBL DLB I.1   377
Edge (2)
Heartwell: edge cf your puny Stomacks. Your love is like your   .   .   43   OLD BATCH I.1   245
Fainall: and t'other set your Teeth on edge; one is all Pulp, and   .   401   WAY WCRLD I.1   214
Edge-Tools (1)
              And are afraid to use their own Edge-Tools.   214   FOR LCVE PRO.   38
Edges (1)
Sir Wilful: round the Edges, no broader than a Subpoena. I might expect   439   WAY WORLD III.1   542
Education (4)
Cynthia: 'em; for these have Quality and Education, Wit and fine   .   167   DOUEL DLR III.1   627
Mrs Frail: Account I have heard of his Education can be no Conjurer: .   248   FOR LCVE II.1   493
Tattle: University: But the Education is a little too pedantick for   302   FOR LCVE   V.1   187
Lady Wish: and I promise you, her Education has been unexceptionable   466   WAY WORLD   V.1   182
Edward (1)
Fainall: Languish Widdow in trust to Edward Mirabell. Confusion!   .   476   WAY WCRLD   V.1   552
Ee (3)
Fondlewife: Nykin, ee, ee, ee,--Here will be the good Man anon, to   .   79   OLD BATCH IV.1   136
Eel (1)
Ben: But an he comes near me, may-hap I may giv'n a Salt Eel   .   264   FOR LOVE III.1   421
Effect (16)
Sharper: upon reflection, seems only an effect of a too powerful
              passion.   79   OLD BATCH IV.1   157
Mellefont: express; which when she saw had no effect; but still I   .   130   DOUBL DLR I.1   111
Mellefont: esteem, that he may be able to effect it.   131   DOUBL DLR I.1   157
Lady Touch: effect made you Lord of all, of me, and of my Lord?   .   .   136   DOUEL DLR I.1   349

'em (continued)

Speaker	Text	PAGE	TITLE	ACT.SC	LINE
Mirabell:	she who does not refuse 'em every thing, can refuse 'em	397	WAY WORLD	I.1	88
Mirabell:	and separated her Failings; I study'd 'em, and got 'em by	399	WAY WORLD	I.1	165
Mirabell:	end I so us'd my self to think of 'em, that at length, contrary	399	WAY WORLD	I.1	168
Mirabell:	habitual to me, to remember 'em without being displeas'd.	399	WAY WORLD	I.1	171
Mirabell:	and in all probability in a little time longer I shall like 'em	399	WAY WORLD	I.1	173
Witwoud:	You shall see he won't go to 'em because there's nc	405	WAY WORLD	I.1	363
Petulant:	Places. Pox on 'em I won't come.--Dee hear, tell 'em	405	WAY WORLD	I.1	386
Petulant:	I won't come.--Let 'em snivel and cry their Hearts	405	WAY WORLD	I.1	387
Petulant:	Enough, let 'em trundle. Anger helps Complexion,	406	WAY WORLD	I.1	416
Petulant:	What, what? Then let 'em either shew their Innocence	409	WAY WORLD	I.1	529
Marwood:	I have done hating 'em; and am now come to	411	WAY WORLD	II.1	45
Marwood:	despise 'em; the next thing I have to do, is eternally to	411	WAY WORLD	II.1	46
Marwood:	forget 'em.	411	WAY WORLD	II.1	47
Marwood:	Will you not follow 'em?	413	WAY WORLD	II.1	118
Marwood:	Hands, do--I'd leave 'em to get loose.	416	WAY WORLD	II.1	226
Millamant:	For I am as sick of 'em--	419	WAY WORLD	II.1	338
Millamant:	how to write Letters; and yet one has 'em, one does not	419	WAY WORLD	II.1	361
Lady Wish:	entertain 'em. I'll make all imaginable haste. Dear Friend	432	WAY WORLD	III.1	280
Millamant:	I could consent to wear 'em, if they wou'd wear	433	WAY WORLD	III.1	304
Millamant:	Things! without one cou'd give 'em to one's	433	WAY WORLD	III.1	306
Servant-W:	hard to know 'em all.	437	WAY WORLD	III.1	471
Painall:	Encrease of fortune,--I cou'd have worn 'em tipt with	442	WAY WORLD	III.1	646
Painall:	and will herd no more with 'em. True, I wear the Badge;	444	WAY WORLD	III.1	720
Painall:	but I'll disown the Order. And since I take my leave of 'em,	444	WAY WORLD	III.1	721
Painall:	I care not if I leave 'em a common Motto, to their common	444	WAY WORLD	III.1	722
Sir Wilful:	shou'd hate 'em both! Hah 'tis like you may; there are	448	WAY WORLD	IV.1	128
Mirabell:	Wou'd you have 'em both before Marriage? Or	449	WAY WORLD	IV.1	182
Mrs Pain:	'em?	453	WAY WORLD	IV.1	324
Witwoud:	Left 'em? I cou'd stay no longer--I have laugh'd	453	WAY WORLD	IV.1	325
Witwoud:	neither of 'em speak for rage; And so fell a sputt'ring at	453	WAY WORLD	IV.1	333
Witwoud:	If there had been words enow between 'em to have	454	WAY WORLD	IV.1	361
Sir Wilful:	Head and drink a Health to 'em--A Match or no Match,	456	WAY WORLD	IV.1	426
Foible:	friends together, than set 'em at distance. But Mrs. Marwood	464	WAY WORLD	V.1	88
Mrs Pain:	me. I defie 'em all. Let 'em prove their aspersions: I know	466	WAY WORLD	V.1	177
Sir Wilful:	Cozen, will cross 'em once again, only to bear me Company,	471	WAY WORLD	V.1	350
Painall:	If it must all come out, why let 'em know it, 'tis but	474	WAY WORLD	V.1	475
	In shoals, I've mark'd 'em judging in the Pit;	479	WAY WORLD	EPI.	11

'ems (0)   see What-dee-call-'ems

Embark'd (1)

Zara:	About the time our Arms embark'd for Spain.	364	M. BRIDE	IV.1	121

Embarking (1)

Heartwell:	purpose, ever embarking in Adventures, yet never comes	42	OLD BATCH	I.1	199

Embers (2)

Lady Wish:	Chafeing-dish of starv'd Embers and Dining behind a	462	WAY WORLD	V.1	6
Lady Wish:	rakes the Embers which have so long layn smother'd in	472	WAY WORLD	V.1	411

Embrac'd (1)

Manuel:	Divinity embrac'd; to Whips and Prisons,	349	M. BRIDE	II.2	373

Embrace (5)

Sharper:	let me embrace you.	49	OLD BATCH	II.1	74
Sir Joseph:	Pray Mr. Sharper Embrace my Back--very	52	OLD BATCH	II.1	174
Heartwell:	--Oh Sharper! let me embrace thee.--But art	111	DOUBL DLR	IV.1	360
	(Embrace.)				
Zara:	Such Liberty as I embrace my self,	376	M. BRIDE	V.1	137

Embraces (6)

Musician:	But admitting their Embraces,	60	OLD BATCH	II.2	199
Heartwell:	the envenom'd Shirt, to run into the Embraces of a Fever,	62	OLD BATCH	III.1	67
Laetitia:	of your Embraces again, my Dear, if ever I saw his face	93	OLD BATCH	IV.4	151
Lady Ply:	Embraces--Say thou dear dying Man, when, where,	170	DOUBL DLR	IV.1	125
Maskwell:	lov'd Embraces, could e're be fond of an inferiour Slavery.	198	DOUBL DLR	V.1	426
Jeremy:	lying in the Arms of a needy Wit, before the Embraces of	219	FOR LOVE	I.1	114

Embrio (2)

Witwoud:	being in Embrio; and if it shou'd come to Life; poor	408	WAY WORLD	I.1	488
Painall:	a Cuckold in Embrio? Sure I was born with	442	WAY WORLD	III.1	632

Emergency (1)

Lady Wish:	Health, or some such Emergency--	468	WAY WORLD	V.1	264

Eminent (1)

Mrs Frail:	an Admiral and an eminent Justice of the Peace to be the	231	FOR LOVE	I.1	578

Emperour (3)

Valentine:	Emperour.	216	FOR LOVE	I.1	9
Sr Sampson:	I know the length of the Emperour of China's	241	FOR LOVE	II.1	219
Sr Sampson:	--Why nothing under an Emperour should be born	245	FOR LOVE	II.1	351

Empire (7)

Sr Sampson:	Eastern Empire under my Feet; it would make me only a	300	FOR LOVE	V.1	99
Zara:	For Fame, for Honour, and for Empire lost?	345	M. BRIDE	II.2	236
Zara:	But what is Loss of Honour, Fame and Empire?	345	M. BRIDE	II.2	237
Zara:	Look on me now, from Empire fall'n to Slavery;	347	M. BRIDE	II.2	303
Zara:	A Queen; for what are Riches, Empire, Power,	347	M. BRIDE	II.2	315
Alonzo:	Tho' for the Crown of Universal Empire.	379	M. BRIDE	V.2	112
Marwood:	Natures long to persevere. Love will resume his Empire	410	WAY WORLD	II.1	25

Employ (2)

Maskwell:	What, to Rebuild, will a whole Age Employ.	138	DOUBL DLR	I.1	422
Maskwell:	Conditions,--if not, here take this; you may employ it better,	199	DOUBL DLR	V.1	450

Employ'd (7)

Sharper:	You were well employ'd.--I think there is no	99	OLD BATCH	V.1	123
Setter:	do condescend to be scandalously employ'd in the	105	OLD BATCH	V.1	338
Maskwell:	What d'e think of my being employ'd in the	149	DOUBL DLR	II.1	397
Maskwell:	What d'ye think of my being employ'd in the	149	DOUBL DLR	II.1	V397
Maskwell:	be otherwhere employ'd--do you procure her Night-Gown,	199	DOUBL DLR	V.1	444
Scandal:	employ'd when the Match is so much mended. Valentine,	313	FOR LOVE	V.1	600
Gonsalez:	I wish her Mutes are meant to be employ'd	366	M. BRIDE	IV.1	205

Employ'st (1)

Millamant:	Tho' thou do'st thine, employ'st the Power and Art.	447	WAY WORLD	IV.1	105

Enemy (continued)
Maskwell:	greatest Enemy, and she does but Journey-Work under	.	148	DOUEL DLR	II.1	394
Maskwell:	bears an Enemy in his Breast: For your honest man, as I	.	150	DOUEL DLR	II.1	452
Lady Touch:	with you for ever,--nay, I'll be your Enemy, and pursue	.	192	DOUEL DLR	V.1	182
Scandal:	Why, Honour is a publick Enemy; and Conscience a	.	271	FOR LOVE	III.1	675
Angelica:	would no more be his Wife, than his Enemy. For his	.	299	FOR LOVE	V.1	76
Angelica:	that is an Enemy to Valentine.	.	312	FOR LOVE	V.1	556
Almeria:	Why did he not use me like an Enemy?	.	327	M. BRIDE	I.1	67
Almeria:	Why not ill treated, like an Enemy?	.	327	M. BRIDE	I.1 V 67
Zara:	Your Enemy; I have discover'd Osmyn,	.	364	M. BRIDE	IV.1	138
Fainall:	What should provoke her to be your Enemy, without	.	397	WAY WORLD	I.1	82
Fainall:	What should provoke her to be your Enemy, unless	.	397	WAY WORLD	I.1 V 82
Witwoud:	Petulant's an Enemy to Learning; he relies	.	436	WAY WORLD	III.1	416
Petulant:	No, I'm no Enemy to Learning; it hurts not me.	.	436	WAY WORLD	III.1	418
Marwood:	That's a Sign indeed its no Enemy to you.	.	436	WAY WORLD	III.1	419
Petulant:	No, no, it's no Enemy to any Body, but them that	.	436	WAY WORLD	III.1	420

Enforce (1)   see Re-inforce
Gonsalez:	And cling, as if with Claws they did enforce	.	332	M. BRIDE	I.1	239

Engag'd (6)   see Ingaged, Pre-engag'd
Osmyn-Alph:	For which I stand engag'd to this All-excellence:	.	343	M. BRIDE	II.2	139
Mirabell:	Ay; I have been engag'd in a Matter of some sort	.	399	WAY WORLD	I.1	136
Fainall:	Faith, I am not Jealous. Besides, most who are engag'd	.	399	WAY WORLD	I.1	141
Fainall:	that by permitting her to be engag'd, I might continue	.	414	WAY WORLD	II.1	145
Mirabell:	You saw I was engag'd.	.	421	WAY WORLD	II.1	432
Mirabell:	has had compassion upon Lovers and generously engag'd a	.	477	WAY WORLD	V.1	579

Engage (5)
Sharper:	trivial a Sum, will wholly acquit you and doubly engage	.	50	OLD BATCH	II.1	90
Mellefont:	will be a Pleasure to your self; I must get you to engage	.	130	DOUEL DLR	I.1	125
Mellefont:	to engage her more irresistably. 'Tis only an inhancing the	.	158	DOUEL DLR	III.1	301
Scandal:	to engage your Sister.	.	234	FOR LOVE	I.1	672
Almeria:	Yet, one Thing more, I would engage from thee.	.	330	M. BRIDE	I.1	194

Engaged (4)
Lady Touch:	which once was paid me, and everlastingly engaged?	.	136	DOUEL DLR	I.1	351
Maskwell:	of some farther design of yours, and has engaged	.	154	DOUEL DLR	III.1	137
Maskwell:	him to what you please; your Guests are so engaged in	.	155	DOUEL DLR	III.1	167
Scandal:	And you, like a true great Man, having engaged their	.	221	FOR LOVE	I.1	193

Engagements (2)
Zara:	The present Form of our Engagements rests,	.	355	M. BRIDE	III.1	217
Zara:	So does the present Form of our Engagements rest,	.	355	M. BRIDE	III.1 V217

Engaging (1)
Brisk:	engaging Creature, if she were not so fond of that damn'd		175	DOUEL DLR	IV.1	292

Engendred (2)
Mellefont:	malice can be engendred no where else.	.	145	DOUEL DLR	II.1	271
Sr Sampson:	you engendred, Muckworm?	.	245	FOR LOVE	II.1	378

Engine (2)
Mellefont:	flash, the priming of her Engine; destruction follows hard,		148	DOUEL DLR	II.1	378
Marwood:	Indeed Mrs. Engine, is it thus with you?	.	431	WAY WORLD	III.1	225

Engineer (1)
Vainlove:	Well, I'le leave you with your Engineer.	.	64	OLD BATCH	III.1	120

Engines (1)
Osmyn-Alph:	That strain my cracking Nerves; Engines and Wheels	.	356	M. BRIDE	III.1	292

England (3)
Heartwell:	illustrious Whore in England.	.	45	OLD BATCH	I.1	313
Sir Paul:	England.	.	145	DOUEL DLR	II.1	262
Fainall:	No matter for that; 'tis for the Honour of England,	.	400	WAY WORLD	I.1	201

English (3)
Sharper:	Oh Madam! He was our English Horace.	.	87	OLD BATCH	IV.3	147
Jeremy:	now to tell 'em in plain downright English--	.	220	FOR LOVE	I.1	173
Sir Wilful:	plain English.	.	447	WAY WORLD	IV.1	112

Enjoin'd (1)
Millamant:	enjoin'd it him, to be so coy--If I had the Vanity to	.	433	WAY WORLD	III.1	338

Enjoy (5)
Bellmour:	him, that she will enjoy him in Effigie.	.	39	OLD BATCH	I.1	65
Maskwell:	Compose your self, You shall Enjoy and Ruin	.	137	DOUEL DLR	I.1	402
Lord Touch:	Thou shalt enjoy it--if all I'm worth in	.	189	DOUEL DLR	V.1	74
Maskwell:	thank you--What, enjoy my Love! Forgive the	.	189	DOUEL DLR	V.1	80
Fainall:	content you shall enjoy your own proper Estate during	.	468	WAY WORLD	V.1	252

Enjoy'd (2)
Vainlove:	enjoy'd her.	.	38	OLD BATCH	I.1	46
	And be enjoy'd, tho' sure to be undone;	.	113	OLD BATCH	EPI.	2

Enjoying (1)
Bellmour:	place, and the pleasure of enjoying some half a score	.	41	OLD BATCH	I.1	139

Enjoyment (3)
Belinda:	enjoyment of that Conversation you admire.	.	57	OLD BATCH	II.2	89
Sir Paul:	deny'd my self the enjoyment of lawful Domestick	.	179	DOUEL DLR	IV.1	428
Witwoud:	Love without Enjoyment, or Wine without Toasting; but	.	404	WAY WORLD	I.1	358

Enjoys (1)
Lucy:	That Woman sure enjoys a blessed Night,	.	75	OLD BATCH	III.2	162

Enlarg'd (2)
Almeria:	My Soul, enlarg'd from its vile Bonds will mount,	.	340	M. BRIDE	II.2	25
Mirabell:	Measure enlarg'd into a Husband?	.	450	WAY WORLD	IV.1	231

Enmity (1)
Manuel:	When my first Foe was laid in Earth, such Enmity,	.	333	M. BRIDE	I.1	308

Enough (95)   see Enow
Bellmour:	Why faith I think it will do well enough--If the	.	38	OLD BATCH	I.1	55
Vainlove:	and peevish: But I have seen him pleasant enough in his	.	40	OLD BATCH	I.1	107
Heartwell:	think it time enough to be lew'd, after I have had the	.	43	OLD BATCH	I.1	233
Bellmour:	Time enough, ay too soon, I should rather have	.	43	OLD BATCH	I.1	235
Capt Bluff:	Enough.	.	54	OLD BATCH	II.1	245
Bellmour:	I could be well enough pleas'd to drive on a Love-bargain		60	OLD BATCH	II.2	220
Lucy:	doubt will be eager enough to day, to swallow the	.	61	OLD BATCH	III.1	12
Setter:	To be Men perhaps; nay faith like enough; I often	.	65	OLD BATCH	III.1	174
Laetitia:	it not affliction enough that you are to leave me, but you		77	OLD BATCH	IV.1	88
Sir Joseph:	Say: Pooh, Pox, I've enough to say,--never	.	85	OLD BATCH	IV.3	72
Araminta:	(aside). I hope my Fool has not Confidence enough	.	85	OLD BATCH	IV.3	92
Araminta:	Base Man! Was it not enough to affront me with	.	87	OLD BATCH	IV.3	162

Enough   (continued)

		PAGE	TITLE	ACT.SC	LINE
Laetitia:	think that I have nothing to do but excuse him; 'tis enough,	93	OLD BATCH	IV.4	168
Fondlewife:	enough. No thanks to you Sir, for her Vertue.--But,	96	OLD BATCH	IV.4	268
Sharper:	In my Conscience, like enough.	99	OLD BATCH	V.1	102
Araminta:	Hang me, if I pity you; you are right enough	109	OLD BATCH	V.2	61
Brisk:	pretty and Metaphorical enough: I' Gad I could not have	128	DOUBL DLR	I.1	38
Brisk:	Enough, enough; Careless, bring your Apprehension	129	DOUBL DLR	I.1	61
Lady Ply:	am her Father's Wife; and that's near enough to make it	146	DOUBL DLR	II.1	310
Lady Touch:	Or, may be, he thought he was not enough	153	DOUBL DLR	III.1	87
Maskwell:	enough. Pox I have lost all Appetite to her ; yet she's a fine	155	DOUBL DLR	III.1	175
Mellefont:	her, till he has been fool enough to think of her out of her	159	DOUBL DLR	III.1	317
Brisk:	That's well enough; let me perish, ha ha ha. O Miraculous,	177	DOUBL DLR	IV.1	356
Lady Froth:	We shall have whispering time enough, you	177	DOUBL DLR	IV.1	386
Lord Touch:	Enough--You are my Friend; I know	181	DOUBL DLR	IV.1	540
Lady Touch:	Married? Is there not reward enough in raising his low	191	DOUBL DLR	V.1	126
Sir Paul:	O, if she be with Mr. Careless, 'tis well enough.	192	DOUBL DLR	V.1	190
Mellefont:	you have Love enough to run the venture.	193	DOUBL DLR	V.1	201
Cynthia:	I don't know whether I have Love enough,--	193	DOUBL DLR	V.1	202
Cynthia:	but I find I have obstinacy enough to pursue whatever I	193	DOUBL DLR	V.1	203
Jeremy:	help me, I'm poor enough to be a Wit--But I was	217	FOR LOVE	I.1	41
Scandal:	enough? Must you needs shew your Wit to get more?	219	FOR LOVE	I.1	128
Valentine:	Whore, she knows my Condition well enough, and might	221	FOR LOVE	I.1	211
Mrs Frail:	Pooh, No I thank you, I have enough to do to	232	FOR LOVE	I.1	596
Scandal:	have Paintings too, some pleasant enough.	233	FOR LOVE	I.1	634
Sr Sampson:	Haste, ay, ay; haste enough, my Son Ben will	240	FOR LOVE	II.1	192
Sr Sampson:	and so forth, large enough for the inside of a Cardinal, this	245	FOR LOVE	II.1	387
Valentine:	Fortune was provident enough to supply all the	246	FOR LOVE	II.1	394
Sr Sampson:	Now let's see, if you have Wit enough to keep your self?--	246	FOR LOVE	II.1	401
Mrs Fore:	enough; my awkard Daughter-in-Law, who you know	248	FOR LOVE	II.1	499
Mrs Frail:	sure enough.	250	FOR LOVE	II.1	572
Angelica:	had Concern enough to ask my self the Question.	254	FOR LOVE	III.1	32
Scandal:	Nor good Nature enough to answer him that did	254	FOR LOVE	III.1	33
Ben:	So, so, enough Father--Mess, I'de rather kiss these	260	FOR LOVE	III.1	276
Ben:	Ey, ey, been! Been far enough, an that be all--well	261	FOR LOVE	III.1	289
Ben:	tho'f they love a man well enough, yet they don't care to	263	FOR LOVE	III.1	392
Ben:	--Sea-calf? I an't Calf enough to lick your Chalk'd face,	264	FOR LOVE	III.1	424
Scandal:	scrupulous enough, Mr. Foresight--He has been	267	FOR LOVE	III.1	521
Scandal:	when you had Charity enough to give me your Attention,	269	FOR LOVE	III.1	588
Mrs Fore:	is well enough, and your Understanding is not a-miss.	272	FOR LOVE	III.1	689
Jeremy:	Like enough, Sir, for I told her Maid this morning,	276	FOR LOVE	IV.1	14
Jeremy:	No, no, Sir; he's safe enough, Sir, an he were but as	279	FOR LOVE	IV.1	124
Sr Sampson:	Pocket.) There Val: it's safe enough, Boy--But thou	282	FOR LOVE	IV.1	233
Valentine:	scratch'd--My Nails are not long enough--Let	282	FOR LOVE	IV.1	239
Ben:	No, I'm pleas'd well enough, now I have found you,--	285	FOR LOVE	IV.1	359
Mrs Frail:	No, no, I am not mad, Monster, I am wise enough	286	FOR LOVE	IV.1	406
Valentine:	It is enough. Ha! Who's here?	291	FOR LOVE	IV.1	589
Jeremy:	Mad encugh to own it?	295	FOR LOVE	IV.1	744
Angelica:	I did not think you had Apprehension enough to be	296	FOR LOVE	IV.1	762
Angelica:	Fortune enough to make any Man easie that I can like; If	299	FOR LOVE	V.1	61
Tattle:	Ay; 'tis well enough for a Servant to be bred at an	302	FOR LOVE	V.1	186
Sr Sampson:	and we'll beget Sons and Daughters enough to put the	308	FOR LOVE	V.1	398
Ben:	enough to hold her, and if she can't drag her Anchor	310	FOR LOVE	V.1	493
Sr Sampson:	the Stars are Lyars; and if I had Breath enough, I'd curse	313	FOR LOVE	V.1	V584
Valentine:	never distinguish it self enough, to be taken notice of. If	313	FOR LOVE	V.1	610
Valentine:	can't love enough.	313	FOR LOVE	V.1	612
Almeria:	I will, for I should never look enough.	343	M. BRIDE	II.2	125
Osmyn-Alph:	Then, then 'twill be enough--I shall be Old.	343	M. BRIDE	II.2	142
Manuel:	Enough; his Punishment be what you please.	349	M. BRIDE	II.2	381
Selim:	The King, and were alone enough to urge	361	M. BRIDE	IV.1	5
Selim:	Your own Request's enough.	362	M. BRIDE	IV.1	49
Fainall:	have Cruelty enough, not to satisfie a Lady's longing; you	397	WAY WORLD	I.1	91
Mirabell:	She has Beauty enough to make any Man think so;	399	WAY WORLD	I.1	153
Mirabell:	and Complaisance enough not to contradict him who shall	399	WAY WORLD	I.1	154
Mirabell:	because he has not Wit enough to invent an Evasion.	404	WAY WORLD	I.1	338
Petulant:	Enough, let 'em trundle. Anger helps Complexion,	406	WAY WORLD	I.1	416
Petulant:	Why that's enough--You and he are not	407	WAY WORLD	I.1	438
Petulant:	Enough, I'm in a Humour to be severe.	409	WAY WORLD	I.1	522
Mirabell:	But hast not thou then Sense enough to know that	409	WAY WORLD	I.1	533
Mirabell:	Reputation with the Town, enough to make that Woman	417	WAY WORLD	II.1	273
Waitwell:	Day! 'Tis enough to make any Man forget himself. The	424	WAY WORLD	II.1	556
Lady Wish:	young. It will be time enough when he comes back, and	432	WAY WORLD	III.1	264
Sir Wilful:	Enough, enough, Cozen, Yes, yes, all a case--	448	WAY WORLD	IV.1	142
Mrs Fain:	wou'd fall into fits, and maybe not recover time enough to	452	WAY WORLD	IV.1	301
Lady Wish:	get thee but far enough, to the Saracens or the Tartars, or	456	WAY WORLD	IV.1	439
Waitwell:	Enough, his date is short.	461	WAY WORLD	IV.1	621
Foible:	cou'd have told you long enough since, but I love to keep	464	WAY WORLD	V.1	86
Lady Wish:	frailties of my Daughter. Well Friend, you are enough to	465	WAY WORLD	V.1	131
Lady Wish:	Jewells and ruine my Neice, and all little enough--	466	WAY WORLD	V.1	152
Mirabell:	enough, that I have lost what in my heart I hold most dear,	472	WAY WORLD	V.1	388
Sir Wilful:	S'heart you'll have time enough to toy after	477	WAY WORLD	V.1	V599
Sir Wilful:	S'heart you'll have him time enough to toy after	477	WAY WORLD	V.1	599
	And furnish Fool enough to entertain.	479	WAY WORLD	EPI.	27

Enow (1)

Witwoud:	If there had been words enow between 'em to have	454	WAY WORLD	IV.1	361

Enquir'd (3)

Leonora:	Have softly whisper'd, and enquir'd his Health;	327	M. BRIDE	I.1	27
Millamant:	enquir'd after you, as after a new Fashion.	419	WAY WORLD	II.1	348
Foible:	put upon his Clergy--Yes indeed, I enquir'd of the	463	WAY WORLD	V.1	44

Enquire (8)

Araminta:	for a Venture, Sir, that you enquire?	85	OLD BATCH	IV.3	96
	Enquire if Characters are nicely bred;	204	DOUBL DLR	EPI.	22
Scandal:	enquire.	228	FOR LOVE	I.1	451
Valentine:	and go and enquire when Angelica will return.	246	FOR LOVE	II.1	412
Tattle:	enquire for me, than ever went to see the Hermaphrodite,	257	FOR LOVE	III.1	161

Ever   (continued)

		PAGE	TITLE	ACT.SC	LINE
Laetitia:	or ever will have.	77	OLD BATCH	IV.1	82
Bellmour:	--'till just now, (the first time I ever look'd upon the	82	OLD BATCH	IV.2	55
Bellmour:	to mine,--and seal 'em up for ever.	82	OLD BATCH	IV.2	74
Laetitia:	of your Embraces again, my Dear, if ever I saw his face	93	OLD BATCH	IV.4	151
Heartwell:	with you and bauk'd it? Did you ever offer me the Favour	109	OLD BATCH	V.2	57
Careless:	Was there ever such a Fury! 'tis well Nature has not	130	DOUBL DLR	I.1	100
Cynthia:	Then neither my Lord and you would ever have	139	DOUBL DLR	II.1	25
Cynthia:	Then neither my Lord nor you would ever have	139	DOUBL DLR	II.1 V	25
Lord Froth:	a Captive first, and ever since 't has been in Love with	140	DOUBL DLR	II.1	69
Lady Froth:	you're a Judge; was ever any thing so well-bred as my	140	DOUBL DLR	II.1	82
Sir Paul:	my Lady Froth says; was ever the like read of in Story?	143	DOUBL DLR	II.1	196
Sir Paul:	Heart--I'm sure if ever I should have Horns, they	146	DOUBL DLR	II.1	281
Maskwell:	must ever after be in awe of you.	157	DOUBL DLR	III.1	256
Mellefont:	Good Fortune ever go along with thee.	157	DOUBL DLR	III.1	262
Mellefont:	hands and sprawling in his Sleep; and ever since she has	158	DOUBL DLR	III.1	289
Careless:	Lady Plyant is not thought of--if that can ever be.	160	DOUBL DLR	III.1	377
Lady Ply:	should ever be wanting in a respectful acknowledgment	169	DOUBL DLR	IV.1	80
Careless:	ever from your sight, and drown me in my Tomb.	170	DOUBL DLR	IV.1	117
Careless:	I thank Heav'n, they are the saddest that I ever	170	DOUBL DLR	IV.1	122
Sir Paul:	pound a Year upon the Rogue as soon as ever he looks me	173	DOUBL DLR	IV.1	225
Maskwell:	Gratitude, and my own Inclination, to be ever your	181	DOUBL DLR	IV.1	538
Maskwell:	Guilt is ever at a loss and confusion waits upon it,	184	DOUBL DLR	IV.2	19
Maskwell:	Lips be ever clos'd. (Kisses her.) And thus--Oh who	184	DOUBL DLR	IV.2	25
Lady Touch:	let me not hope forgiveness, 'twill ever be in your power	185	DOUBL DLR	IV.2	83
Mellefont:	Upon such terms I will be ever yours in every	185	DOUBL DLR	IV.2	87
Maskwell:	ever must; no, let it prey upon my Heart; for I would	188	DOUBL DLR	V.1	36
Lady Touch:	with you for ever,--nay, I'll be your Enemy, and pursue	192	DOUBL DLR	V.1	182
Lady Ply:	who would ever trust a man? O my heart akes for fear	202	DOUBL DLR	V.1	546
Valentine:	then ever, and appear more notoriously her Admirer in	217	FOR LOVE	I.1	51
Scandal:	Attendance, and promis'd more than ever you intend to	221	FOR LOVE	I.1	194
Scandal:	Attendance, and promis'd more than ever you intended to	221	FOR LOVE	I.1 V194	
Tattle:	lose my Reputation of Secresie for ever--I shall never	230	FOR LOVE	I.1	515
Tattle:	No Man but the Painter and my self was ever blest	232	FOR LOVE	I.1	610
Nurse:	and swear now, ha, ha, ha, Marry and did you ever see the	235	FOR LOVE	II.1	23
Angelica:	we were ever after to live under Ground, or at least making	237	FOR LOVE	II.1	83
Foresight:	How Hussie! was there ever such a provoking	237	FOR LOVE	II.1	93
Nurse:	ever hear the like now--Sir, did ever I do any thing	238	FOR LOVE	II.1	101
Sr Sampson:	Did you ever hear the like! Did you ever hear the like!	244	FOR LOVE	II.1	319
Mrs Fore:	Why, was I ever in any of these places?	247	FOR LOVE	II.1	441
Mrs Fore:	Why, was I ever in any of those places?	247	FOR LOVE	II.1 V441	
Mrs Fore:	spoil'd already--d'ee think shee'll ever endure a	250	FOR LOVE	II.1	561
Tattle:	more complying; and as soon as ever I make you say	252	FOR LOVE	II.1	622
Tattle:	enquire for me, than ever went to see the Hermaphrodite,	257	FOR LOVE	III.1	161
Angelica:	I'm pretty even with him, Sir Sampson; for if ever I	260	FOR LOVE	III.1	245
Scandal:	and the Uneasiness that has attended me ever since, brings	269	FOR LOVE	III.1	591
Mrs Fore:	Was there ever such Impudence, to make Love	269	FOR LOVE	III.1	593
Mrs Fore:	this Project? You don't think, that you are ever like to	271	FOR LOVE	III.1	660
Mrs Fore:	Did you ever hear such a Toad--heark'ee	271	FOR LOVE	III.1	664
Scandal:	(aside). That ever I shou'd suspect such a Heathen of	281	FOR LOVE	IV.1	212
Sr Sampson:	What the Devil had I to do, ever to beget Sons?	282	FOR LOVE	IV.1	260
Sr Sampson:	Why did I ever marry?	282	FOR LOVE	IV.1	261
Jeremy:	O Lord, Madam, did you ever know any Madman	295	FOR LOVE	IV.1	743
Sr Sampson:	None of old Foresight's Sybills ever utter'd such a	299	FOR LOVE	V.1	79
Jeremy:	could ever find out his Head-Quarters.	302	FOR LOVE	V.1	195
Tattle:	The Devil take me if ever I was so much concern'd at any	309	FOR LOVE	V.1	460
Valentine:	ever you seem to love too much, it must be only when I	313	FOR LOVE	V.1	611
Almeria:	Thy dear Resemblance is for ever fixt;	328	M. BRIDE	I.1	75
Almeria:	For which I mourn, and will for ever mourn;	329	M. BRIDE	I.1	144
Almeria:	Or ever dry these swoll'n, and watry Eyes;	329	M. BRIDE	I.1	146
Almeria:	Or, ever taste content, or peace of Heart,	329	M. BRIDE	I.1	147
Almeria:	If ever I do yield, or give consent,	330	M. BRIDE	I.1	185
Garcia:	But to devote, and yield my self for ever	334	M. BRIDE	I.1	336
Almeria:	For these thy Chains, or Death shall join us ever.	355	M. BRIDE	III.1	248
Osmyn-Alph:	That ever I should think, beholding thee,	355	M. BRIDE	III.1	250
Osmyn-Alph:	But knowing Heav'n, to know it lost for ever.	358	M. BRIDE	III.1	366
Zara:	When he is dead, I must despair for ever.	362	M. BRIDE	IV.1	30
Zara:	For ever! that's Despair--it was Distrust	362	M. BRIDE	IV.1	31
Zara:	Before; Distrust will ever be in Love,	362	M. BRIDE	IV.1	32
Almeria:	Did ever Father curse his kneeling Child!	369	M. BRIDE	IV.1	321
Almeria:	He shall be mine, still and for ever mine.	370	M. BRIDE	IV.1	353
Selim:	Avert it, Heav'n, that you should ever suffer	375	M. BRIDE	V.1	113
Zara:	And ever and anon, the Sight was dash'd	379	M. BRIDE	V.2	139
Almeria:	What dead at last, quite, quite, for ever dead?	382	M. BRIDE	V.2	233
Osmyn-Alph:	Nor ever wake to less substantial Joys.	383	M. BRIDE	V.2	290
Osmyn-Alph:	For Blessings ever wait on vertuous Deeds;	384	M. BRIDE	V.2	321
Mirabell:	other will be rotten without ever being ripe at all.	401	WAY WORLD	I.1	217
Mrs Fain:	Men are ever in Extreams; either doating or averse.	410	WAY WORLD	II.1	3
Marwood:	that Love shou'd ever die before us; and that the Man so	410	WAY WORLD	II.1	10
Marwood:	O if he shou'd ever discover it, he wou'd	411	WAY WORLD	II.1	61
Marwood:	have him ever to continue upon the Rack of Fear and	411	WAY WORLD	II.1	63
Marwood:	--I hate you, and shall for ever.	415	WAY WORLD	II.1	217
Millamant:	melancholly as a Watch-light. Well Mirabell, If ever you	422	WAY WORLD	II.1	477
Lady Wish:	--Frippery! old Frippery! Was there ever such a foul-mouth'd	428	WAY WORLD	III.1	118
Petulant:	Why shou'd a Man be ever the further from being	436	WAY WORLD	III.1	428
Petulant:	S'life, Witwoud, were you ever an Attorney's Clerk?	440	WAY WORLD	III.1	554
Millamant:	for ever After. Let us never Visit together, nor go to a	450	WAY WORLD	IV.1	206
Millamant:	ever After. Let us never Visit together, nor go to a	450	WAY WORLD	IV.1 V206	
Millamant:	lastly, where ever I am, you shall always knock at the door	450	WAY WORLD	IV.1	224
Lady Wish:	will ever endure such a Borachio! you're an absolute	455	WAY WORLD	IV.1	389
Foible:	O that ever I was Born, O that I was ever Married,	463	WAY WORLD	V.1	58
Foible:	and He are nearer related than ever their Parents	464	WAY WORLD	V.1	89
Mirabell:	ever been accounted Venial. At least think it is Punishment	472	WAY WORLD	V.1	387

Ever-during (1)

		PAGE	TITLE	ACT.SC	LINE
Zara:	But in Despair, and ever-during Death,	362	M. BRIDE	IV.1	34

Ever-kindling (1)
  Osmyn-Alph: Gladness, and Warmth of ever-kindling Love, ... 345   M. BRIDE   II.2   211
Ever-living (1)
  Gonsalez: Loaden with Spoils, and ever-living Laurel, ... 331   M. BRIDE   I.1   225
Everlasting (3)
  Maskwell: profess'd an everlasting Friendship to him.   182   DOUBL DLR   IV.1   567
  Osmyn-Alph: My All of Bliss, my everlasting Life, ... 357   M. BRIDE   III.1   304
  Witwoud: she won't give an Eccho fair play; she has that everlasting 421   WAY WORLD   II.1   420
Everlastingly (2)
  Lady Touch: which once was paid me, and everlastingly engaged?   . . . 136   DOUBL DLR   I.1   351
  Brisk: I'm everlastingly your humble Servant, Deuce take   . . . 140   DOUBL DLR   II.1   93
Every (69)   see Ev'ry
  Heartwell: I am for having every body be what they pretend   . . . 43   OLD BATCH   I.1   253
  Capt Bluff: abroad? for every Cock will fight upon his own Dunghil.   . 51   OLD BATCH   II.1   153
  Capt Bluff: went every day to Coffee-houses to read the Gazette my   . 53   OLD BATCH   II.1   208
  Belinda: obvious to every Stander by.   55   OLD BATCH   II.2   35
  Araminta: --Every Man, now, changes his Mistress and his   . . . 58   OLD BATCH   II.2   148
  Musician: Every Woman is the same.   60   OLD BATCH   II.2   202
  Heartwell: Why every Man plays the Fool once in his Life: But to   . 74   OLD BATCH   III.2   117
  Heartwell: me in every thing, so like my Wife, the World shall   . . 74   OLD BATCH   III.2   121
  Bellmour: every thing but your Unkindness.   81   OLD BATCH   IV.2   32
  Belinda: Ah so fine! So extreamly fine! So every thing in the   . . 87   OLD BATCH   IV.3   148
  Araminta: There's poison in every thing you touch.--   88   OLD BATCH   IV.3   181
  Fondlewife: inclining to believe every word you say.   94   OLD BATCH   IV.4   186
  Heartwell: Oh! Any thing, every thing, a Leg or two, or an   . . . 109   OLD BATCH   V.2   75
  Lord Froth: 'tis such a Vulgar Expression of the Passion! every body can 132   DOUBL DLR   I.1   200
  Lady Touch: in my Temper, Passions in my Soul, apt to every provocation; 135   DOUBL DLR   I.1   326
  Sir Paul: with Lambs, and every Creature couple with its Foe, as   . 144   DOUBL DLR   II.1   225
  Lady Ply: every thing in the World, but give me Mathemacular   . . . 146   DOUBL DLR   II.1   302
  Lady Ply: guilt of deceiving every body; Marrying the Daughter,   . . 147   DOUBL DLR   II.1   315
  Lord Touch: Plyant has a large Eye, and wou'd centre every thing in   . 151   DOUBL DLR   III.1   6
  Lady Froth: For as the Sun shines every day, ... 164   DOUBL DLR   III.1   515
  Brisk: because you say the Sun shines every day.   164   DOUBL DLR   III.1   518
  Lady Froth: For as the Sun shines every day, ... 164   DOUBL DLR   III.1   529
  Sir Paul: every inch of him that resembles me; ah this Eye, this   . . 173   DOUBL DLR   IV.1   234
  Lady Ply: dare swear every Circumstance of me trembles.--O your   . 178   DOUBL DLR   IV.1   398
  Mellefont: Upon such terms I will be ever yours in every   185   DOUBL DLR   IV.2   87
  Maskwell: every look you cheaply throw away on any other Object   . 199   DOUBL DLR   V.1   435
  Lady Touch: Thou can'st deceive every body,--nay, ... 199   DOUBL DLR   V.1   453
     For every one's both Judge and Jury here;   204   DOUBL DLR   EPI.   13
     'Tis hard that they must every one admit;   204   DOUBL DLR   EPI.   31
  Tattle: No matter for that--Yes, yes, every body knows   . . . 227   FOR LOVE   I.1   427
  Tattle: --No doubt on't, every body knows my Secrets--   . . . 227   FOR LOVE   I.1   428
  Tattle: one and t'other, and every thing in the World; and, says I, 227   FOR LOVE   I.1   432
  Scandal: She'll be here by and by, she sees Valentine every   . . 229   FOR LOVE   I.1   483
  Mrs Frail: here too? Oh Mr. Tattle, every thing is safe with you, we 230   FOR LOVE   I.1   548
  Mrs Frail: Bodkin?--Oh Sister, Sister!--Sister every way.   . . . 248   FOR LOVE   II.1   470
  Tattle: for it's whisper'd every where.   254   FOR LOVE   III.1   48
  Angelica: was whisper'd every where.   254   FOR LOVE   III.1   51
  Valentine: Westminster-Hall the first Day of every Term--Let me see   . 280   FOR LOVE   IV.1   173
  Valentine: behind Counters, as if Religion were to be sold in every   . 289   FOR LOVE   IV.1   502
  Valentine: and blotted by every Goose's Quill. I know you; for I   . 292   FOR LOVE   IV.1   639
  Jeremy: care every thing shall be ready.   293   FOR LOVE   IV.1   672
  Valentine: Mad, and will be Mad to every Body but this Lady.   . . . 296   FOR LOVE   IV.1   774
  Tattle: must think of a new Man every Morning, and forget him   . 303   FOR LOVE   V.1   244
  Tattle: every Night--No, no, to marry, is to be a Child again,   . 303   FOR LOVE   V.1   245
  Angelica: No, I have it; and I'll use it, as I would every thing   . 312   FOR LOVE   V.1   555
  Sr Sampson: them and you, my self and every Body--Cons, Cully'd,   . 313   FOR LOVE   V.1   V585
  Valentine: Any thing, my Friend, every thing that looks like   . . . 313   FOR LOVE   V.1   602
     For still in every Storm, they all run hither, ... 315   FOR LOVE   EPI.   3
  Leonora: In Tears, when Joy appears in every other Face.   . . . 330   M. BRIDE   I.1   168
  Leonora: when Joy appears in every other Face.   330   M. BRIDE   I.1   V168
  Almeria: And Joy he brings to every other Heart, ... 330   M. BRIDE   I.1   169
  Gonsalez: Be every Day of your long Life like this.   331   M. BRIDE   I.1   220
  Gonsalez: The swarming Populace, spread every Wall, ... 332   M. BRIDE   I.1   238
  Gonsalez: As they were all of Eyes, and every Limb   332   M. BRIDE   I.1   241
  Gonsalez: As if they were all Eyes, and every Limb   332   M. BRIDE   I.1   V241
  Perez: And every Look of his and hers confess it.   338   M. BRIDE   II.1   46
  Perez: And every Look from him and her confirms it.   338   M. BRIDE   II.1   V 46
  Manuel: Is manifest from every Circumstance.   366   M. BRIDE   IV.1   214
  Mirabell: she who does not refuse 'em every thing, can refuse 'em   . 397   WAY WORLD   I.1   88
  Mirabell: to my Design and Expectation, they gave me every   . . 399   WAY WORLD   I.1   169
  Marwood: in our Breasts, and every Heart, or soon or late, receive
     and   410   WAY WORLD   II.1   26
  Fainall: and any way, every way will make amends:--I'll   . . . 416   WAY WORLD   II.1   243
  Millamant: have ask'd every living Thing I met for you; I have   . . 419   WAY WORLD   II.1   347
  Marwood: very Master-Key to every Bodies strong Box. My Friend   . 431   WAY WORLD   III.1   228
  Lady Wish: expect my Nephew Sir Wilfull every moment too--Why   . . 431   WAY WORLD   III.1   257
  Millamant: every Thing that has been said. For my part, I thought   . 432   WAY WORLD   III.1   293
  Millamant: loath the Country and every thing that relates to it.   . . 448   WAY WORLD   IV.1   122
  Sir Wilful: For he's drunk every Night, ... 455   WAY WORLD   IV.1   419
  Mrs Fain: Ay, all's out, My affair with Mirabell, every   464   WAY WORLD   V.1   81
Everybody (1)
  Heartwell: informed) very troublesome to everybody else. If this be   . 73   OLD BATCH   III.2   83
Everything (1)
  Lady Wish: thing, everything for Composition.   468   WAY WORLD   V.1   240
Evident (1)
  Cynthia: Money, He should give me a very evident demonstration   . . 168   DOUBL DLR   IV.1   46
Evil (3)
  Belinda: my Sol, I'm afraid you'l follow evil Courses.   55   OLD BATCH   II.2   52
  Foresight: are mad to day--It is of evil portent, and bodes Mischief   236   FOR LOVE   II.1   47
  Mirabell: Aunt, your Wife's Mother, my evil Genius; or to sum up   . 395   WAY WORLD   I.1   23
Evils (1)
  Mellefont: importunities of her Love; and of two evils, I thought my   129   DOUBL DLR   I.1   93
Exaltation (1)
  Scandal: his Exaltation of madness into the road of common Sense,   . 278   FOR LOVE   IV.1   106

Excus'd (1)
| | | | | |
| Mirabell: | stand excus'd, who has suffer'd herself to be won by his | . 417 | WAY WORLD | II.1 274 |

Excuse (29)
	O Lord, for Heavens sake excuse the Play, ...	. 35	OLD BATCH	PRO. 23
Sharper:	He has need of such an excuse, considering the present	. 44	OLD BATCH	I.1 288
Capt Bluff:	Oh excuse me Sir; have you serv'd abroad Sir?	. 52	OLD BATCH	II.1 185
Bellmour:	very honourably, to excuse her, and very impudently . .	. 93	OLD BATCH	IV.4 148
Laetitia:	think that I have nothing to do but excuse him; 'tis enough,	. 93	OLD BATCH	IV.4 168
Bellmour:	Fit of the Cholick, to excuse my lying down upon your . .	. 94	OLD BATCH	IV.4 211
Sharper:	Objection to the Excuse.	. 99	OLD BATCH	V.1 124
Mellefont:	excuse me, I have a little business.	. 128	DOUBL DLR	I.1 44
Lady Touch:	temperately bad, what excuse can clear?	. 136	DOUBL DLR	I.1 329
Lady Touch:	your Temper. I'll make an excuse of sudden Business to	. 153	DOUBL DLR	III.1 117
Lord Touch:	Nay, I excuse your Friendship to my	. 182	DOUBL DLR	IV.1 544
Lord Touch:	I know you would excuse him--and I	. 182	DOUBL DLR	IV.1 555
Lady Touch:	You can excuse a fault too well, not to have	. 183	DOUBL DLR	IV.2 16
Maskwell:	excuse. My Lord is thoughtful--I'le be so too; yet he shall	. 188	DOUBL DLR	V.1 13
Maskwell:	Mellefont. I'll urge haste, to excuse your silence. . .	. 195	DOUBL DLR	V.1 295
	He offers but this one Excuse, 'twas writ	. 214	FOR LOVE	PRO. 46
Scandal:	Others excuse him, and blame you: only the Ladies are . .	. 220	FOR LOVE	I.1 161
Valentine:	I would have an excuse for your Barbarity and	. 244	FOR LOVE	II.1 321
Sr Sampson:	Excuse! Impudence! why Sirrah, mayn't I do	. 244	FOR LOVE	II.1 323
Sr Sampson:	Sham-sickness shan't excuse him--O, here's his . . .	. 278	FOR LOVE	IV.1 117
Scandal:	You must excuse his Passion, Mr. Foresight; for he . .	. 283	FOR LOVE	IV.1 297
Manuel:	It shall be your Excuse that I command it.	. 334	M. BRIDE	I.1 V326
Manuel:	She does excuse him; 'tis as I suspected.	. 337	M. BRIDE	I.1 441
Witwoud:	No, but prithee excuse me,--my Memory is	. 402	WAY WORLD	I.1 273
Witwoud:	upon him, you are, faith. Let me excuse him;--I can .	. 403	WAY WORLD	I.1 309
Witwoud:	Friend.--No, my Dear, excuse me there.	. 403	WAY WORLD	I.1 315
Witwoud:	Wit will excuse that: A Wit shou'd no more be sincere,	. 403	WAY WORLD	I.1 319
Lady Wish:	excuse me.	. 432	WAY WORLD	III.1 281
Sir Wilful:	my leave--If so be you'll be so kind to make my Excuse,	. 446	WAY WORLD	IV.1 78

Excused (2)
Laetitia:	not guilty, or he has handsomly excused him.	. 82	OLD BATCH	IV.2 60
Manuel:	You stand excused that I command it.	. 334	M. BRIDE	I.1 326

Excuses (1)
| | | | | |
| Lady Touch: | black!--O I have Excuses, Thousands for my Faults; Fire | . 135 | DOUBL DLR | I.1 325 |

Executes (1)
| | | | | |
| | As one Thief scapes, that executes another. . . . . . | . 323 | M. BRIDE | PRO. 32 |

Executing (1)
| | | | | |
| Zara: | In executing, puzzled, lame and lost. . . . . . . | . 375 | M. BRIDE | V.1 112 |

Execution (10)
Maskwell:	execution of all her Plots? Ha, ha, ha, by Heaven it's true;	149	DOUBL DLR	II.1 398
Sir Paul:	Execution in its time Girl; why thou hast my Leer			
	Hussey, just	. 173	DOUBL DLR	IV.1 236
Lord Touch:	we don't presently prevent the Execution of their plots;--	200	DOUBL DLR	V.1 477
Scandal:	He begs Pardon like a Hangman at an Execution. . . .	. 225	FOR LOVE	I.1 328
Selim:	And Order given for publick Execution.	. 361	M. BRIDE	IV.1 16
Selim:	That Execution may be done in private.	. 362	M. BRIDE	IV.1 47
Selim:	Who at the Place of Execution, will	. 362	M. BRIDE	IV.1 53
Gonsalez:	Their Execution better were deferr'd, ...	. 363	M. BRIDE	IV.1 69
Manuel:	We will our self behold the Execution.	. 364	M. BRIDE	IV.1 V128
Gonsalez:	I've seen thy Sword do noble Execution.	. 372	M. BRIDE	IV.1 430

Execution's (1)
| | | | | |
| Heartwell: | When Execution's over, you offer a Reprieve. . . . . | . 109 | OLD BATCH | V.2 73 |

Executioner (2)
Lucy:	An Executioner qualified to do your Business. He has . .	. 97	OLD BATCH	V.1 18
	Nay, and what's worse, an Executioner.	. 204	DOUBL DLR	EPI. 14

Executioners (1)
| | | | | |
| Zara: | Of grim and gashly Executioners. . . . . | . 379 | M. BRIDE | V.2 141 |

Exemplary (2)
Heartwell:	Effigie, pasted up for the exemplary Ornament of necessary	63	OLD BATCH	III.1 83
Scandal:	Well, Madam, You have done Exemplary Justice, ...	. 313	FOR LOVE	V.1 619

Exerts (2)
Almeria:	Exerts my Spirits; and my present Fears	. 339	M. BRIDE	II.1 79
Lady Wish:	Neice exerts a lawfull claim, having Match'd her self by	. 472	WAY WORLD	V.1 417

Exeunt (69)
	(Exeunt.)	. 47	OLD BATCH	I.1 389
	(Exeunt.)	. 54	OLD BATCH	II.1 250
	(Exeunt Omnes.)	. 60	OLD BATCH	II.2 227
	(Exeunt.)	. 62	OLD BATCH	III.1 58
	(Exeunt.)	. 70	OLD BATCH	III.1 365
	(Exeunt.)	. 75	OLD BATCH	III.2 164
	(Exeunt.)	. 75	OLD BATCH	IV.1 12
	(Exeunt.)	. 80	OLD BATCH	IV.1 192
	(Exeunt.)	. 83	OLD BATCH	IV.2 94
	(Exeunt Sir Joseph and Bluffe.) . . .	. 86	OLD BATCH	IV.3 125
	(Exeunt Belinda and Sharper.) . . .	. 87	OLD BATCH	IV.3 151
	(Exeunt.)	. 88	OLD BATCH	IV.3 211
	(Exeunt.)	. 96	OLD BATCH	IV.4 275
	(Exeunt.)	. 98	OLD BATCH	V.1 80
	(Exeunt.)	. 104	OLD BATCH	V.1 V282
	(Exeunt.)	. 106	OLD BATCH	V.1 354
	(Exeunt.)	. 107	OLD BATCH	V.1 404
	(Exeunt Omnes.)	. 112	OLD BATCH	V.2 196
	(Exeunt.)	. 135	DOUBL DLR	I.1 297
	(Exeunt.)	. 138	DOUBL DLR	I.1 423
	(Exeunt.)	. 167	DOUBL DLR	III.1 623
	(Exeunt.)	. 169	DOUBL DLR	IV.1 67
	(Exeunt.)	. 177	DOUBL DLR	IV.1 388
	(Exeunt.)	. 178	DOUBL DLR	IV.1 404
	(Exeunt.)	. 181	DOUBL DLR	IV.1 V511
	(Exeunt, severally.) . . .	. 183	DOUBL DLR	IV.1 592
	(Exeunt.)	. 187	DOUBL DLR	IV.2 140
	(Exeunt.)	. 190	DOUBL DLR	V.1 120
	(Exeunt.)	. 196	DOUBL DLR	V.1 331

Exeunt   (continued)

			PAGE	TITLE	ACT.SC	LINE
	(Exeunt Mellefont and Careless.)	. .	197	DOUBL DLR	V.1	355
	(Exeunt.)	.	200	DOUBL DLR	V.1	490
	(Exeunt Omnes.)	.	203	DOUBL DLR	V.1	597
	(Exeunt Steward, Trapland and Jeremy.)	.	225	FOR LOVE	I.1	327
	(Exeunt.)	.	234	FOR LOVE	I.1	682
	(Exeunt Sir Sampson and Foresight.)	.	246	FOR LOVE	II.1	405
	(Exeunt.)	.	246	FOR LOVE	II.1	413
	(Exeunt Mrs. Foresight and Mrs. Frail.)	.	251	FOR LOVE	II.1	580
	(Exeunt all but Ben and Miss Prue.)	.	263	FOR LOVE	III.1	359
	(Exeunt.)	.	265	FOR LOVE	III.1	454
	(Exeunt.)	.	275	FOR LOVE	III.1	821
(Exeunt Foresight, Mrs. Foresight and Scandal.)		.	285	FOR LOVE	IV.1	354
(Exeunt Foresight, Mrs. Foresight, Tattle, Mrs. Frail, and			293	FOR LOVE	IV.1	683
	(Exeunt Angelica and Jenny.)	. .	296	FOR LOVE	IV.1	794
	(Exeunt.)	.	297	FOR LOVE	IV.1	817
	(Exeunt.)	.	301	FOR LOVE	V.1	163
	(Exeunt Nurse and Miss Prue.)	. .	306	FOR LOVE	V.1	V329
	(Exeunt Omnes.)	.	314	FOR LOVE	V.1	638
	(Exeunt Omnes.)	.	337	M. BRIDE	I.1	462
	(Exeunt.)	.	339	M. BRIDE	II.1	50
	(Exeunt.)	.	339	M. BRIDE	II.1	85
	(Exeunt Omnes.)	.	349	M. BRIDE	II.2	392
	(Exeunt Omnes.)	.	361	M. BRIDE	III.1	459
	(Exeunt Garcia, Perez, and Attendants.)	.	364	M. BRIDE	IV.1	135
	(Exeunt Zara and Selim.)	.	366	M. BRIDE	IV.1	193
	(Exeunt.)	.	374	M. BRIDE	V.1	89
	(Exeunt.)	.	376	M. BRIDE	V.1	140
	(Exeunt.)	.	379	M. BRIDE	V.2	129
	(Exeunt.)	.	384	M. BRIDE	V.2	323
	(Exeunt.)	.	409	WAY WORLD	I.1	543
	(Exeunt Mrs. Fainall and Mirabell.)	.	412	WAY WORLD	II.1	108
	(Exeunt.)	.	416	WAY WORLD	II.1	250
	(Exeunt.)	.	424	WAY WORLD	II.1	564
	(Exeunt.)	.	430	WAY WORLD	III.1	223
	(Exeunt Millamant and Mincing.)	. .	436	WAY WORLD	III.1	436
	(Exeunt.)	.	444	WAY WORLD	III.1	726
	(Exeunt Millamant and Mrs. Fainall.)	.	456	WAY WORLD	IV.1	435
	(Exeunt.)	.	462	WAY WORLD	IV.1	649
	(Exeunt Mincing and Foible.) . . .	.	465	WAY WORLD	V.1	123
	(Exeunt Omnes.)	.	478	WAY WORLD	V.1	624

Exit (141)

			PAGE	TITLE	ACT.SC	LINE
Vainlove:		(Exit.)	40	OLD BATCH	I.1	136
Heartwell:		(Exit.)	46	OLD BATCH	I.1	337
		(Exit Betty.)	56	OLD BATCH	II.2	V 71
		(Exit Footman.)	57	OLD BATCH	II.2	84
	(Exit Betty with the Things.)	. .	57	OLD BATCH	II.2	V100
Footman:		(Exit.)	58	OLD BATCH	II.2	159
Vainlove:		(Exit.)	64	OLD BATCH	III.1	121
		(Exit Bellmour.) . . .	64	OLD BATCH	III.1	136
Lucy:	now--I'me not 'ith humour. (Exit.) . . .		67	OLD BATCH	III.1	237
Setter:		(Exit after her.) . . .	67	OLD BATCH	III.1	240
	(Exit Bellmour, Sharper.)	. .	70	OLD BATCH	III.1	330
Heartwell:		(Exit.)	74	OLD BATCH	III.2	142
		(Exit Barnaby.)	76	OLD BATCH	IV.1	48
Fondlewife:		(Exit.)	79	OLD BATCH	IV.1	151
		(Exit Servant.)	80	OLD BATCH	IV.2	3
Vainlove:		(Exit.)	88	OLD BATCH	IV.3	190
Araminta:	(Takes up the Letter, and Exit.)	. .	88	OLD BATCH	IV.3	193
Sir Joseph:		(Exit.)	91	OLD BATCH	IV.4	69
Bellmour:	quickly, I'll follow you:--I wou'd not be known. (Exit	.	97	OLD BATCH	V.1	11
Heartwell:		(Exit Heartwell.) . . .	97	OLD BATCH	V.1	22
Vainlove:		(Exit.)	100	OLD BATCH	V.1	128
Bellmour:		(Exit.)	100	OLD BATCH	V.1	161
Sharper:		(Exit.)	102	OLD BATCH	V.1	220
Heartwell:		(Exit.)	105	OLD BATCH	V.1	325
Sharper:		(Exit.)	107	OLD BATCH	V.1	394
		(Exit Boy.)	107	OLD BATCH	V.2	8
Sharper:		(Exit.)	110	OLD BATCH	V.2	92
Brisk:		(Exit.)	129	DOUBL DLR	I.1	63
	(Exit Lord Touchwood and Sir Paul.)		133	DOUBL DLR	I.1	221
	(Exit Lady Froth and Brisk.)	. .	142	DOUBL DLR	II.1	146
Lord Froth:		(Exit.)	142	DOUBL DLR	II.1	148
	(Exit Sir Paul, and Cynthia.)	. .	146	DOUBL DLR	II.1	288
Lady Ply:		(Exit.)	148	DOUBL DLR	II.1	373
Mellefont:		(Exit.)	149	DOUBL DLR	II.1	438
Maskwell:		(Exit.)	150	DOUBL DLR	II.1	V469
	(Exit Lord Touchwood.)	. .	154	DOUBL DLR	III.1	125
	(Exit Lady Touchwood.)	. .	155	DOUBL DLR	III.1	173
Maskwell:	. . .	(Exit.)	157	DOUBL DLR	III.1	V261
Mellefont:		(Exit.)	159	DOUBL DLR	III.1	319
	(Carries the Letter to my Lady and Exit.)	. .	161	DOUBL DLR	III.1	V401
	(Exit Careless and Lady Plyant.)	. .	163	DOUBL DLR	III.1	496
	(Exit Sir Paul.)		163	DOUBL DLR	III.1	500
Cynthia:		(Exit.)	167	DOUBL DLR	III.1	635
Careless:		(Exit.)	171	DOUBL DLR	IV.1	131
	(Exit Cynthia.)		175	DOUBL DLR	IV.1	283
Lady Ply:		(Exit.)	175	DOUBL DLR	IV.1	285
Sir Paul:		(Exit.)	175	DOUBL DLR	IV.1	289
Lady Ply:		(Exit.)	180	DOUBL DLR	IV.1	489
Mellefont:		(Exit.)	181	DOUBL DLR	IV.1	526
Maskwell:		(Exit.)	185	DOUBL DLR	IV.2	92
Mellefont:		(Exit.)	187	DOUBL DLR	IV.2	156
Lady Touch:		(Exit.)	188	DOUBL DLR	V.1	9
Lord Touch:		(Exit.)	189	DOUBL DLR	V.1	84
Lord Touch:		(Exit.)	191	DOUBL DLR	V.1	141

Eyes (continued)

		PAGE	TITLE	ACT.SC	LINE
Gonsalez:	My Eyes with more Delight, than they can hold.	332	M. BRIDE	I.1	274
Manuel:	How is it Almeria, that you meet our Eyes	333	M. BRIDE	I.1	279
Manuel:	Why is't, Almeria, that you meet our Eyes	333	M. BRIDE	I.1	V279
Manuel:	Who with such Lustre, strike admiring Eyes,	335	M. BRIDE	I.1	388
Manuel:	If not in Words, I bid it by my Eyes.	336	M. BRIDE	I.1	409
Manuel:	If not in Words, I bid it by my Eyes.	336	M. BRIDE	I.1	V409
Manuel:	Her Eyes, did more than bid--free her and hers,	336	M. BRIDE	I.1	410
Manuel:	All Eyes, so by Preheminence of Soul	336	M. BRIDE	I.1	422
Manuel:	And sullen Port, glooms downward with his Eyes;	336	M. BRIDE	I.1	426
Manuel:	But rules with settled Sway in Zara's Eyes.	337	M. BRIDE	I.1	461
Heli:	And to revisit with my long-clos'd Eyes	337	M. BRIDE	II.1	6
Perez:	And striding with distemper'd Haste: his Eyes	338	M. BRIDE	II.1	20
Leonora:	What do I see? O Heav'n! either my Eyes	340	M. BRIDE	II.2	9
Almeria:	And from my Eyes.	341	M. BRIDE	II.2	45
Leonora:	Alas, she stirs not yet, nor lifts her Eyes;	341	M. BRIDE	II.2	59
Osmyn-Alph:	Look up Almeria, bless me with thy Eyes;	341	M. BRIDE	II.2	71
Osmyn-Alph:	Hast thou thy Eyes, yet can'st not see Alphonso?	342	M. BRIDE	II.2	79
Osmyn-Alph:	And gaze upon thy Eyes, is so much Joy;	342	M. BRIDE	II.2	97
Almeria:	Nor I, nor could I, for my Eyes were yours.	344	M. BRIDE	II.2	184
Osmyn-Alph:	Should come and see the straining of my Eyes	345	M. BRIDE	II.2	203
Osmyn-Alph:	Turn your Lights inward, Eyes, and look	345	M. BRIDE	II.2	215
Osmyn-Alph:	Turn your Lights inward, Eyes, and view my Thought,	345	M. BRIDE	II.2	V215
Osmyn-Alph:	Thus, do our Eyes, like common Mirrours	345	M. BRIDE	II.2	221
Osmyn-Alph:	Thus, do our Eyes, as do all common Mirrours	345	M. BRIDE	II.2	V221
Zara:	Why dost thou leave my Eyes, and fly my Arms,	345	M. BRIDE	II.2	239
Zara:	But with such dumb, and thankless Eyes you look;	346	M. BRIDE	II.2	256
Zara:	When I beheld the Day-break of thy Eyes,	347	M. BRIDE	II.2	286
Zara:	'Tis that, I know; for thou dost look, with Eyes	348	M. BRIDE	II.2	343
Manuel:	Or lift his Eyes to like, where I adore?	348	M. BRIDE	II.2	357
Zara:	That having seen it, thou do'st turn thy Eyes	353	M. BRIDE	III.1	149
Zara:	And Look again, with Wishes in thy Eyes.	353	M. BRIDE	III.1	155
Zara:	Forbidding rest; may stretch his Eyes awake	355	M. BRIDE	III.1	209
Osmyn-Alph:	That I cou'd almost turn my Eyes away,	356	M. BRIDE	III.1	253
Almeria:	One Cup, the common Stream of both our Eyes,	356	M. BRIDE	III.1	261
Almeria:	Thy Heart will burst, thy Eyes look red and start;	356	M. BRIDE	III.1	273
Osmyn-Alph:	But dash'd with Rain from Eyes, and swail'd with Sighs,	357	M. BRIDE	III.1	323
Osmyn-Alph:	Think how my Heart will heave, and Eyes will strain	358	M. BRIDE	III.1	345
Almeria:	Where levell'd low, no more we'll lift our Eyes,	358	M. BRIDE	III.1	372
Zara:	Strike, damp, deaden her Charms, and kill his Eyes;	359	M. BRIDE	III.1	401
Zara:	Forsake their down, to wake with wat'ry Eyes,	360	M. BRIDE	III.1	428
Manuel:	What mean those swollen and redfleck'd Eyes, that look	367	M. BRIDE	IV.1	248
Almeria:	And bend my flowing Eyes, to stream upon	368	M. BRIDE	IV.1	274
Almeria:	Turn not your Eyes away--look on me kneeling;	369	M. BRIDE	IV.1	319
Manuel:	Entring he met my Eyes, and started back,	373	M. BRIDE	V.1	15
Manuel:	And give her Eyes yet greater Disappointment.	374	M. BRIDE	V.1	82
Zara:	His Eyes like Meteors roll'd, then darted down	374	M. BRIDE	V.1	93
Selim:	His Eyes had err'd, he hastily recall'd	375	M. BRIDE	V.1	99
Gonsalez:	Enter that Chamber, and convince your Eyes,	377	M. BRIDE	V.2	45
Garcia:	Blasted my Eyes, and speechless be my Tongue,	377	M. BRIDE	V.2	55
Zara:	With haggar'd Eyes? why are your Arms a-cross	380	M. BRIDE	V.2	157
Zara:	Ha! prostrate! bloody! headless! O--start Eyes,	380	M. BRIDE	V.2	162
Zara:	Nor that I meant to fall before his Eyes,	381	M. BRIDE	V.2	192
Leonora:	But O forbear--lift up your Eyes no more;	381	M. BRIDE	V.2	226
Leonora:	Will stab the Sight, and make your Eyes rain Blood.	381	M. BRIDE	V.2	230
Leonora:	Ready to stab the Sight, and make your Eyes	381	M. BRIDE	V.2	V230
Almeria:	Had they or Hearts, or Eyes, that did this Deed?	382	M. BRIDE	V.2	236
Almeria:	Could Eyes endure to guide such cruel Hands?	382	M. BRIDE	V.2	237
Almeria:	Are not my Eyes guilty alike with theirs,	382	M. BRIDE	V.2	238
Osmyn-Alph:	Give a new Birth to thy long-shaded Eyes,	383	M. BRIDE	V.2	286
Fainall:	Cheeks, and sparkling from your Eyes,	413	WAY WORLD	EPI.	141
Lady Wish:	a--Ha Foible? A swimminess in the Eyes--Yes, I'll	429	WAY WORLD	III.1	169
Lady Wish:	a--Ha Foible? A swimmingness in the Eyes--Yes, I'll	429	WAY WORLD	III.1	V169
Singer:	When I insult a Rival's Eyes:	435	WAY WORLD	III.1	388
Millamant:	a New Chariot, to provoke Eyes and Whispers; And then	450	WAY WORLD	IV.1	203
Lady Wish:	his protesting Eyes! Oh no memory can Register.	458	WAY WORLD	IV.1	517
Lady Wish:	(apart). Oh, he has Witch-craft in his Eyes and	472	WAY WORLD	V.1	408
Lady Wish:	(aside). Oh, he has Witch-craft in his Eyes and	472	WAY WORLD	V.1	V408
Waitwell:	At hand Sir, rubbing their Eyes,--Just risen	475	WAY WORLD	V.1	515

Fable's (1)

	Unless the Fable's good, and Moral sound.	204	DOUBL DLR	EPI.	18

Fables (2)

Sir Joseph:	in Aesop's Fables, Bully? A-Gad there are good Morals to	101	OLD BATCH	V.1	175
Sir Joseph:	be pick'd out of Aesop's Fables, let me tell you that; and	101	OLD BATCH	V.1	176

Fac'd (2)   see Bare-fac'd, Bare-Faced, Out-fac'd, Shame-fac'd

Ben:	chitty fac'd thing, as he would have me marry,--so he	285	FOR LOVE	IV.1	364
Marwood:	you would but appear bare fac'd now, and own Mirabell;	433	WAY WORLD	III.1	314

Face (124)   see Sleek-face

Bellmour:	she own'd it to my Face; and blushing like the Virgin Morn	38	OLD BATCH	I.1	48
Bellmour:	perswading that the Face she had been making all the	42	OLD BATCH	I.1	184
Heartwell:	like his Grace, has just his smile and air of's Face. Then	45	OLD BATCH	I.1	321
Sir Joseph:	because I never saw your face before, agad. Ha, ha, ha.	48	OLD BATCH	II.1	41
Lucy:	his Face--Receive it! why he receiv'd it, as I would one	61	OLD BATCH	III.1	20
Lucy:	your Face in Innocence and Smiles; and dissemble the very	62	OLD BATCH	III.1	49
Setter:	Face and produce your natural Vizor.	65	OLD BATCH	III.1	180
Lucy:	Face.	66	OLD BATCH	III.1	203
Lucy:	penitent Face.	67	OLD BATCH	III.1	233
Capt Bluff:	for the Mony, and if you would look me in the Face again	67	OLD BATCH	III.1	249
Bellmour:	the Knight of the sorrowful Face.	68	OLD BATCH	III.1	288
Capt Bluff:	Face.	70	OLD BATCH	III.1	354
Sir Joseph:	To that Face I grant you Captain--No, no,	70	OLD BATCH	III.1	356
Sir Joseph:	I grant you--Not to that Face by the Lord Harry--If	70	OLD BATCH	III.1	357
Sir Joseph:	you had put on your fighting Face before, you had done	70	OLD BATCH	III.1	358
Sir Joseph:	you to your Face--But a Man can no more help what's	70	OLD BATCH	III.1	360
Silvia:	Frowns, and make calm an angry Face; will soften a	72	OLD BATCH	III.2	66
Laetitia:	(aside). Vainlove's Friend! I know his Face, and he has	81	OLD BATCH	IV.2	18

Face (continued)

		PAGE	TITLE	ACT.SC	LINE
Bellmour:	And more Love; or my Face is a False-Witness, and	82	OLD BATCH	IV.2	66
Araminta:	--Well, Sir Joseph, you shall see my Face.--But,	86	OLD BATCH	IV.3	103
Capt Bluff:	Nay, by the World, I'll see your face.	86	OLD BATCH	IV.3	111
Araminta:	find fools, have the same advantage, over a Face in a Mask;	86	OLD BATCH	IV.3	117
Fondlewife:	Ravish my Wife before my face! I warrant he's a Papist in	91	OLD BATCH	IV.4	74
Laetitia:	Sure, when he does not see his face, he won't discover	91	OLD BATCH	IV.4	90
Laetitia:	of your Embraces again, my Dear, if ever I saw his face	93	OLD BATCH	IV.4	151
Fondlewife:	face to face before? Speak.	93	OLD BATCH	IV.4	156
Bellmour:	relentless face in your salt trickling Tears.--So, a few				
	scft	95	OLD BATCH	IV.4	238
Sharper:	Court: Not so much as wrinkle my Face with one Smile;	100	OLD BATCH	V.1	140
Sir Joseph:	Prithee, What do you see in my face, that looks as	101	OLD BATCH	V.1	191
Mellefont:	to him they have born the face of kindness; while her	129	DOUBL DLR	I.1	89
Careless:	Face, than a Jest.	132	DOUBL DLR	I.1	215
Lord Froth:	you, O Intemperate! I have a flushing in my Face already.	134	DOUBL DLR	I.1	289
Lady Touch:	Face; but walks unstartled from the Mirrour, and streight	136	DOUBL DLR	I.1	V331
Maskwell:	Conscience and Honour in my Face, to rebate my Inclinations.	136	DOUBL DLR	I.1	338
Lady Ply:	your face; for now Sir Paul's gone, you are Corum Nobus.	146	DOUBL DLR	II.1	299
Lady Ply:	have brought all the Blood into my face; I warrant, I am	147	DOUBL DLR	II.1	335
Maskwell:	any thing--Why, let me see, I have the same Pace, the	150	DOUBL DLR	II.1	460
Lady Ply:	privacy? I swear and declare in the face of the World I'm	159	DOUBL DLR	III.1	332
Lady Ply:	face of the World that no body is more sensible of Favours	159	DOUBL DLR	III.1	351
Brisk:	red face, and you comparing him to the Sun--and you	164	DOUBL DLR	III.1	508
Lady Froth:	He shows his drunken fiery Face,	164	DOUBL DLR	III.1	531
Lady Ply:	declare in the face of the World, never any body gain'd so	169	DOUBL DLR	IV.1	72
Careless:	overspreads my face, a cold deadly dew already vents	170	DOUBL DLR	IV.1	115
Sir Paul:	in the Face, I will Gads-bud. I'm overjoy'd to think I have	173	DOUBL DLR	IV.1	226
Brisk:	can hardly hold Laughing in his Face.	177	DOUBL DLR	IV.1	380
Lady Ply:	I do, see my Face no more;	179	DOUBL DLR	IV.1	457
Lord Touch:	to my Name; when next I see that Face, I'le write Villain	186	DOUBL DLR	IV.2	119
Lady Touch:	meanings lurk in each corner of that various face. O! that	198	DOUBL DLR	V.1	395
Maskwell:	and with your Hoods tied over your face, meet	199	DOUBL DLR	V.1	445
Mellefont:	your Chaplain, look in the Face cf your injur'd Friend;	202	DOUBL DLR	V.1	570
Valentine:	my Sins in my Face: Here, give her this,	221	FOR LOVE	I.1	208
Valentine:	serve his Friend in Distress, tho' I say it to his face.				
	Come,	223	FOR LCVE	I.1	262
Scandal:	with a hundred Hands, two Heads, and but one Face; a	233	FOR LOVE	I.1	643
Sr Sampson:	go up Holborn-hill,--Has he not a Rogues face?--Speak,	243	FOR LOVE	II.1	304
Sr Sampson:	damn'd Tyburn face, without the benefit o' the Clergy.	243	FOR LOVE	II.1	307
Foresight:	Man,--he has a violent death in his face; but I hope no	243	FOR LOVE	II.1	309
Sr Sampson:	erect with that audacious face, hah? Answer me that?	244	FOR LOVE	II.1	329
Mrs Fore:	You deny it positively to my Face.	247	FOR LOVE	II.1	458
Mrs Frail:	Your Face, what's Your Face?	247	FCB LCVE	II.1	459
Mrs Fore:	No matter for that, it's as good a Face as yours.	247	FOR LOVE	II.1	460
Mrs Frail:	deny it positively to Your Face then.	247	FOR LOVE	II.1	462
Mrs Fore:	Face;--for I'll swear your impudence has put me out of	248	FOR LCVE	II.1	464
Ben:	tell'n so to's face: If that's the Case, why silence gives	263	FOR LOVE	III.1	393
Ben:	--Sea-calf? I an't Calf enough tc lick your Chalk'd face,	264	FOR LCVE	III.1	424
Mrs Fore:	to me before my Husband's Face? I'll Swear I'll tell him.	269	FOR LOVE	III.1	594
Ben:	fair a Face, as a Citizen cr a Courtier; but for all				
	that, I've	273	FOR LCVE	III.1	735
Angelica:	I don't like Raillery from a serious Face--pray	276	FCR LOVE	IV.1	27
Sr Sampson:	the Nose in one's face: What, are my Eyes better than	281	FOR LCVE	IV.1	225
Mrs Fore:	Did nct! with that face can you ask the	284	FOR LOVE	IV.1	331
Scandal:	to a man's face in the morning, that she had layn with him	284	FOR LOVE	IV.1	335
Mrs Frail:	that lurk beneath that faithless smiling face.	286	FOR LOVE	IV.1	395
Valentine:	upon, and look Matrimony in the face. Ha, ha, ha! That a	289	FOR LOVE	IV.1	526
Foresight:	How! I cannot Read that knowledge in ycur Face,	291	FOR LCVE	IV.1	610
Tattle:	Why de'e think I'll tell you, Sir! Read it in my Face?	292	FOR LCVE	IV.1	612
Valentine:	an Old Acquaintance with a new Face.	292	FOR LCVE	IV.1	620
Angelica:	Beaus, that set a good Face upon Fifty, Fifty! I have	298	FOR LCVE	V.1	30
	And scme here know I have a begging Face.	316	FCR LCVE	EPI.	42
Leonora:	In Tears, when Jcy appears in every other Face.	330	M. FRIDE	I.1	168
Leonora:	when Jcy appears in every other Face.	330	M. BRIDE	I.1	V168
Almeria:	How rev'rend is the Face of this tall Pile,	339	M. BRIDE	II.2	59
Osmyn-Alph:	'Tis she; shew me her Face, and let me feel	341	M. BRIDE	II.2	68
Almeria:	It is, it is Alphonso, 'tis his Face,	342	M. BRIDE	II.2	82
Almeria:	I know not, 'tis to see thy Face I think--	342	M. BRIDE	II.2	104
Almeria:	'Tis more than Recompence, to see thy Face:	343	M. FRIDE	II.2	147
Zara:	And like the Morn vermilion'd o'er thy Face.	347	M. BRIDE	II.2	284
Manuel:	Drag him with speed, and rid me of his Face.	349	M. BRIDE	II.2	374
Zara:	What, does my Face displease thee?	353	M. FRIDE	III.1	148
Osmyn-Alph:	Disfigur'd Face, and rive my clotted Hair,	358	M. BRIDE	III.1	351
Osmyn-Alph:	And dash my Face, and rive my clotted Hair,	358	M. BRIDE	III.1	V351
Almeria:	But prone, and dumb, rot the firm Face of Earth	358	M. BBIDE	III.1	373
Zara:	Confusion in his Face, and Grief in hers!	359	M. BRIDE	III.1	397
Almeria:	Thy Face, imploring thee that thou wilt yield;	368	M. ERIDE	IV.1	275
Manuel:	What dar'st thou to my Pace avow thy Guilt?	369	M. BRIDE	IV.1	315
Manuel:	I shall convict her to her Face of Falshood.	374	M. EBIDE	V.1	V86C
Zara:	The Face of thy Design; alone disguising	375	M. BRIDE	V.1	104
Gonsalez:	By fits reveals--his Pace seems turn'd to favour	376	M. BRIDE	V.2	8
Garcia:	What means this Blood? and why this Face of Horror?	377	M. BRIDE	V.2	29
Garcia:	Oppress her not, nor think to stain her Face	378	M. BRIDE	V.2	76
Zara:	That hither lead, nor Humane Face, nor Voice	379	M. BRIDE	V.2	134
Zara:	Still further from me; look, he hides his Face,	381	M. BRIDE	V.2	209
Almeria:	Horrour! a headless Trunk! nor Lips nor Face,	382	M. BRIDE	V.2	270
Fainall:	--'Sdeath they ccme, hide your Face, your Tears--	416	WAY WORLD	II.1	247
Mirabell:	rather than your Face.	420	WAY WCRLD	II.1	398
Millamant:	violent and inflexible wise Face, like Solomon at the				
	dividing	422	WAY WORLD	II.1	468
Millamant:	What, with that Face? No, if you keep your	422	WAY WORLD	II.1	472
Millamant:	Face. Ha, ha, ha--Well I won't laugh, don't be	422	WAY WORLD	II.1	475
Lady Wish:	Face, with mentioning that Traytor. She durst not have the	426	WAY WCRLD	III.1	50
Lady Wish:	Face. This Wretch has fretted me that I am absolutely	428	WAY WCRLD	III.1	142
Mrs Fain:	Nay, nay, put not on that strange Face. I am	430	WAY WCRLD	III.1	188

Face   (continued)
    Marwood: Face, that goodly Face, which in defiance of her   . . 433   WAY WORLD III.1 321
    Servant-W: Why truly Sir, I cannot safely swear to her Face in a   . 437   WAY WORLD III.1 461
    Mirabell: Face, as long as I shall. And while it passes Current with 451   WAY WORLD IV.1   246
    Petulant: have my Reward, say so; if not, fight for your Face the . 454   WAY WORLD IV.1   369
    Sir Wilful: Till it laugh in my Face, ... 455   WAY WORLD IV.1   398
    Foible: and would have hid his face. 461   WAY WORLD IV.1   614
    Lady Wish: shou'd be kill'd I must never shew my face; or hang'd,--O 461   WAY WORLD IV.1   627
    Lady Wish: --O, she never look'd a Man in the Face but her own   . 467   WAY WORLD V.1   191
    Sir Wilful: frown desperately, because her face is none of her own; . 471   WAY WORLD V.1   362
    Mirabell: had a Face of guiltiness,--it was at most an Artifice which 472   WAY WORLD V.1   385
                  Yet each pretends to know the Copy'd Face. 479   WAY WORLD EPI.   20
                  For, as when Painters form a matchless Face, ... 479   WAY WORLD EPI.   31
Faced (0)   see Fair-faced, Bare-faced
Faces (19)
    Musician: Nothing's new besides our Faces, ...   60   OLD BATCH II.2   201
    Singer: Joining Faces, mingling Kisses, ...   71   OLD BATCH III.2   4
    Setter: --They have indeed, very perswading faces. But--   . . . 103   OLD BATCH V.1   248
    Careless: disguises their Inclinations as much as their Faces.   . 158   DOUBL DLR III.1 309
    Lord Froth: She her self makes her own Faces, ... 166   DOUEL DLR III.1 599
                  Methinks I see some Faces in the Pit, ... 204   DOUEL DLR EPI.   32
    Scandal: Divine with two Faces, and one Head; and I have a Soldier 233   FOR LOVE   I.1   644
    Scandal: Coats, Steinkirk Cravats, and terrible Faces; with Cat-calls 234 FOR LOVE   I.1   655
    Sr Sampson: shall know one another's Faces without the help of a   . 240   FOR LOVE   II.1   200
    Valentine: the usual Hours. Yet you will see such Zealous Faces   . 289   FOR LOVE   IV.1   501
    Valentine: one anothers Faces, till we have done something to be   . 290   FOR LOVE   IV.1   563
    Angelica: a Masquerade is done, when we come to shew Faces;   . . 296   FOR LOVE   IV.1   790
    Angelica: a Masquerade is done, when we come to shew our Faces;   . 296   FOR LOVE   IV.1 V790
    Tattle: I fancy you have a wrong Notion of Faces. 304   FOR LOVE   V.1   265
    Zara: With frightful Faces, and the meagre Looks   379   M. BRIDE   V.2   140
                  I've leisure, now, to mark your sev'ral Faces, ... 385   M. BRIDE   EPI.   5
    Mirabell: grave Faces, whisper'd one another; then complain'd   . 396   WAY WORLD I.1   30
    Millamant: without Interrogatories or wry Faces on your part. To   . 450   WAY WORLD IV.1   214
Facetious (2)
    Sir Paul: most facetious Person.--and the best Company.--   . . . 132   DOUBL DLR I.1   182
    Sir Paul: Good strange! Mr. Brisk is such a Merry Facetious   . . 174   DOUEL DLR IV.1   274
Fact (6)
    Mellefont: grant it; and next to the Villany of such a fact, is the . 146   DOUEL DLR II.1   294
    Sir Paul: from him to treat with you about the very matter of Fact.-- 178   DOUBL DLR IV.1   410
    Sir Paul: Matter of Fact! Very pretty; it seems then I am conducing . 178   DOUBL DLR IV.1   411
    Sir Paul: Gads-bud, would that were Matter of Fact too. Die and   . 178   DOUBL DLR IV.1   417
    Lady Ply: Why is not here Matter of Fact? 180   DOUBL DLR IV.1   475
    Sir Paul: matter of Fact is all his own doing.--I confess I had a   . 180   DOUBL DLR IV.1   477
Faculties (1)
    Zara: Benumb the living Faculties, and give 375   M. BRIDE   V.1   133
Faculty (5)
    Bellmour: to Fools; they have need of 'em: Wit, be my Faculty;   . .   37   OLD BATCH I.1   23
    Gonsalez: Would feed his Faculty of Admiration. 332   M. BRIDE   I.1   242
    Gonsalez: Would feed its Faculty of Admiration. 332   M. BRIDE   I.1 V242
    Osmyn-Alph: Which to exterior Objects ow'st thy Faculty, ... 345   M. BRIDE   II.2   218
    Osmyn-Alph: Owest thy Faculty-- 345   M. BRIDE   II.2   219
Faddle (1)
    Lady Ply: Fiddle, faddle, don't tell me of this and that, and   . 146   DOUBL DLR II.1   301
Fadler (1)
    Millamant: or fond, nor kiss before folks, like my Lady Fadler and Sr. 450   WAY WORLD IV.1   201
Fail (14)
    Vainlove: thinks her Vertuous; that's one reason why I fail her: .   40   OLD BATCH I.1   119
    Fondlewife: a warm-hand, rather than fail. What Book's this?   . . .   91   OLD BATCH IV.4   98
    Maskwell: I will not fail. 155   DOUEL DLR III.1 172
    Maskwell: head that cannot fail: Where's Cynthia? 190   DOUBL DLR V.1   116
    Cynthia: I will not fail. 194   DOUEL DLR V.1   260
    Scandal: fail me. 230   FOR LOVE   I.1   545
    Heli: Occasion will not fail to point out Ways 352   M. BRIDE   III.1   97
    Gonsalez: So, this can hardly fail. Alphonso slain, ... 372   M. BRIDE   IV.1   444
    Selim: I needs must fail; impute not as a Crime, ... 375   M. BRIDE   V.1   118
    Lady Wish: But art thou sure Sir Rowland will not fail to   429   WAY WORLD III.1 155
    Lady Wish: come? Or will a not fail when he does come? Will he be   . 429   WAY WORLD III.1 156
    Lady Wish: come? Or will he not fail when he does come? Will he be   . 429   WAY WORLD III.1 V156
    Marwood: Flag in her part, I will not fail to prompt her.   . . . 443   WAY WORLD III.1 666
    Waitwell: break my heart--or if that should fail, I shall be   . . 458   WAY WORLD IV.1   499
Fail'd (3)
    Bellmour: When Wit and Reason, both, have fail'd to move;   . . .   60   OLD BATCH II.2   224
    Selim: If I have fail'd in what, as being a Man, ... 375   M. BRIDE   V.1   117
    Servant-M: afraid his Lungs would have fail'd before it came to our . 398   WAY WORLD I.1   117
Failing (3)
    Laetitia: privy to a weak Woman's Failing, won't turn it to the   .   82   OLD BATCH IV.2   63
    Araminta: and, to confess my Failing, I am willing to give him an   .   85   OLD BATCH IV.3   78
    Angelica: Failing, which I must own to you--I fear my Happiness   . 277   FOR LOVE   IV.1   55
Failings (4)
    Lady Touch: your Bride--Do but conceal my failings, and forgive--   . 185   DOUBL DLR IV.2   86
    Fainall: somewhat too discerning in the Failings of your Mistress.   399   WAY WORLD I.1   157
    Mirabell: and separated her Failings; I study'd 'em, and got 'em by 399   WAY WORLD I.1   165
    Witwoud: speaks:--We have all our Failings; you're too hard   . . 403   WAY WORLD I.1   308
Fails (3)
    Selim: My Tongue faulters, and my Voice fails-- 380   M. BRIDE   V.2   183
    Selim: My Tongue faulters, and my Voice fails--I sink--   . . . 380   M. BRIDE   V.2 V183
    Mirabell: Not always; but as often as his Memory fails him,   . . 401   WAY WORLD I.1   223
Fain (3)
    Araminta: entertaining-- (aside) I know she'd fain be persuaded to
                  stay.   57   OLD BATCH II.2   87
    Sir Paul: For I would fain have some resemblance of my self in   . 173   DOUBL DLR IV.1   228
    Mrs Fain: pleasant Relation last Night: I wou'd fain hear it out.   . 412   WAY WORLD II.1   99
Fainall (50)
                  Mirabell and Fainall Rising from Cards. Betty waiting.   . 395   WAY WORLD I.1
    Mirabell: You are a fortunate Man, Mr. Fainall. 395   WAY WORLD I.1   1
                           (Re-Enter Fainall.)   398   WAY WORLD I.1   134

Fair   (continued)

		PAGE	TITLE	ACT.SC	LINE
Scandal:	So, why this is fair, here's Demonstration with a	257	FOR LOVE	III.1	147
Ben:	words however. I spoke you fair d'ee see, and civil.--As	264	FOR LOVE	III.1	403
Ben:	fair a Face, as a Citizen or a Courtier; but for all				
	that, I've	273	FOR LOVE	III.1	735
Ben:	That won this Fair Maids Heart.	274	FOR LOVE	III.1	789
Ben:	then put off with the next fair wind. How de'e like us?	275	FOR LOVE	III.1	803
Ben:	after all your fair speeches, and stroaking my Cheeks,	286	FOR LOVE	IV.1	417
Sr Sampson:	a fair Lady, a great while--Odd, Madam, you have	298	FOR LOVE	V.1	14
Leonora:	The Memory of that brave Prince stands fair	328	M. BRIDE	I.1	104
Manuel:	At this fair Shrine, to lay my Laurels down,	337	M. BRIDE	I.1	450
Osmyn-Alph:	Esteem; to this she's fair, few more can boast	355	M. BRIDE	III.1	225
Manuel:	Pardon, fair Excellence, this long Neglect:	363	M. BRIDE	IV.1	104
Manuel:	Are we not much indebted to this fair one.	366	M. BRIDE	IV.1	199
	And therefore to the Fair commends his Cause.	385	M. BRIDE	EPI.	28
Fainall:	after I left you; my fair Cousin has some Humours, that	395	WAY WORLD	I.1	18
Mirabell:	one whose Wit and outward fair Behaviour have gain'd a	417	WAY WORLD	II.1	272
Witwoud:	she won't give an Eccho fair play; she has that everlasting	421	WAY WORLD	II.1	420
Witwoud:	In the Name of Bartlemew and his Fair, what have	436	WAY WORLD	III.1	437
Mrs Fain:	return to Sir Rowland, who as Foible tells me is in a fair	452	WAY WORLD	IV.1	302
Waitwell:	I do not, fair shrine of Vertue.	459	WAY WORLD	IV.1	542
Foible:	we have had many a fair word from Madam Marwood, to	464	WAY WORLD	V.1	93
	They from each Fair One catch some different Grace,	479	WAY WORLD	EPI.	32

Fair-faced (1)

Maskwell:	Hypocrisie; oh 'tis such a pleasure, to angle for fair-faced	150	DOUBL DLR	II.1	458

Fair-Weather (1)

Ben:	What, do you mean that fair-Weather Spark that was	264	FOR LOVE	III.1	419

Fairer (2)

Mellefont:	Imagination cannot form a fairer and more plausible	187	DOUBL DLR	IV.2	150
Sir Wilful:	fairer? If I have broke any thing, I'll pay for't, an it				
	cost a	470	WAY WORLD	V.1	318

Fairest (1)

Manuel:	Why does the Fairest of her Kind, withdraw	348	M. BRIDE	II.2	352

Fairly (4)

Lucy:	Hook, Age will come; he nibbled fairly yesterday, and no	61	OLD BATCH	III.1	11
Sharper:	No, I'll deal fairly with you.--'Tis a full and	110	OLD BATCH	V.2	85
Scandal:	have fair Play for your Life. If you can't be fairly run				
	down	220	FOR LOVE	I.1	142
Mirabell:	You wrong him, his name is fairly written as shall	476	WAY WORLD	V.1	527

Fairy (1)

Lady Wish:	brought! Dost thou take me for a Fairy, to drink out of an	425	WAY WORLD	III.1	29

Faith (93)   see I'faith

Bellmour:	No faith Frank you wrong her; she has been just	38	OLD BATCH	I.1	43	
Bellmour:	Why faith I think it will do well enough--If the	38	OLD BATCH	I.1	55	
Vainlove:	Faith I hate Love when 'tis forced upon a Man; as	39	OLD BATCH	I.1	94	
Bellmour:	No faith, not for that--But there's a Business of	41	OLD BATCH	I.1	151	
Sharper:	Faith e'en give her over for good-and-all; you can	41	OLD BATCH	I.1	161	
Bellmour:	faith upon second Thoughts, she does not appear to be so	41	OLD BATCH	I.1	171	
Bellmour:	Faith I don't know, he's of a temper the most easie	42	OLD BATCH	I.1	210	
Sharper:	Say you so? faith I am as poor as a Chymist and	46	OLD BATCH	I.1	347	
Capt Bluff:	Undoubtedly he did Sir; faith Hannibal was a very	52	OLD BATCH	II.1	178	
Bellmour:	Faith, Madam, I dare not speak to her, but I'll	60	OLD BATCH	II.2	210	
Setter:	To be Men perhaps; nay faith like enough; I often	65	OLD BATCH	III.1	174	
Lucy:	Ay, the Breach of Faith, which he has begun: Thou	65	OLD BATCH	III.1	177	
Setter:	Nay faith Lucy I'me sorry, I'le own my self to blame,	66	OLD BATCH	III.1	212	
Bellmour:	Nay, 'Faith, Madam, 'tis a pleasant one; and worth	82	OLD BATCH	IV.2	48	
Sharper:	Faith, Madam, the Talent was born with me:--I	88	OLD BATCH	IV.3	198	
Bellmour:	Why, Faith I must confess, so I design'd you.--	94	OLD BATCH	IV.4	187	
Bellmour:	of your absence, by my Spy, (for Faith, honest Isaac, I	94	OLD BATCH	IV.4	206	
Bellmour:	That you may, Faith, and I hope you won't believe	95	OLD BATCH	IV.4	219	
Bellmour:	Heart of a Mountain-Tyger. By the faith of a sincere	95	OLD BATCH	IV.4	235	
Bellmour:	See the great Blessing of an easy Faith; Opinion	96	OLD BATCH	IV.4	271	
Sharper:	No, Faith; I believe not.--Few Women, but	104	OLD BATCH	V.1	303	
Vainlove:	Faith, that's a sure way.--But here's one can	109	OLD BATCH	V.2	79	
Careless:	No faith, but your Fools grow noisy--and if a	127	DOUBL DLR	I.1	7	
Careless:	No faith, but your Fools grow noisie--and if a	127	DOUBL DLR	I.1 V	7	
Mellefont:	Faith 'tis a good natur'd Cox-Comb, and has very	129	DOUBL DLR	I.1	65	
Careless:	Faith I cannot help it, you know I never lik'd him;	131	DOUBL DLR	I.1	147	
Cynthia:	Why Faith, Madam, he that won't take my Word,	139	DOUBL DLR	II.1	43	
Careless:	Why faith I have in my time known Honest Gentlemen	180	DOUBL DLR	IV.1	496	
Sir Paul:	That's a jest with all my heart, faith and troth,--	192	DOUBL DLR	V.1	171	
Jeremy:	No, faith Sir; I have put 'em off so long with patience	220	FOR LOVE	I.1	171	
Valentine:	Faith and Troth, I am heartily glad to see you--	222	FOR LOVE	I.1	242	
Valentine:	No faith, we'll mind the Widow's business, fill	223	FOR LOVE	I.1	283	
Valentine:	Nay faith, I'm apt to believe him--Except	227	FOR LOVE	I.1	414	
Tattle:	me, and I told her something or other, faith--I know	228	FOR LOVE	I.1	447	
Scandal:	Yes Faith. Ask Valentine else.	228	FOR LOVE	I.1	472	
Scandal:	Nor I faith--But Tattle does not use to bely a	229	FOR LOVE	I.1	489	
Scandal:	Yes Faith, I can shew you your Picture, and I	232	FOR LOVE	I.1	617	
Foresight:	Ha, How? Faith and troth I'm glad of it, and so I	236	FOR LOVE	II.1	29	
Foresight:	Faith and troth you shall--Does my Wife complain?	239	FOR LOVE	II.1	149	
Foresight:	faith and troth, here 'tis, if it will but hold--I wish	240	FOR LOVE	II.1	187	
Valentine:	Faith, I hope not.	244	FOR LOVE	II.1	317	
Mrs Frail:	Come, Faith let us be gone--If my Brother	250	FOR LOVE	II.1	570	
Scandal:	So faith, your Business is done here; now you may	255	FOR LOVE	III.1	91	
Tattle:	Faith, Madam, you're in the right; no more I have, as	256	FOR LOVE	III.1	100	
Sr Sampson:	Faith and Troth you're a wise Woman, and I'm	260	FOR LOVE	III.1	257	
Sr Sampson:	Support, like Ivy round a dead Oak: Faith I do; I love to	260	FOR LOVE	III.1	264	
Ben:	not for dropping Anchor here; About Ship i' faith--	261	FOR LOVE	III.1	281	
Sr Sampson:	own Son, faith, he'll touzle her, and mouzle her: The	265	FOR LOVE	III.1	458	
Scandal:	Yes, Faith.I do; I have a better Opinion both of you	271	FOR LOVE	III.1	662	
Scandal:	Yes, Faith, I believe some Women are Vertuous too;	271	FOR LOVE	III.1	669	
Scandal:	Yes Faith, I think so; I love to speak my mind.	272	FOR LOVE	III.1	685	
Scandal:	Faith, I'm sound.	272	FOR LOVE	III.1	704	
Scandal:	Why Faith, I have a good lively Imagination; and	275	FOR LOVE	III.1	813	
Jeremy:	Why faith, Madam, he's mad for want of his Wits,	276	FOR LOVE	IV.1	33	

223

Family   (continued)

		PAGE	TITLE	ACT.SC	LINE
Bellmour:	What not to make your family Man! and provide	45	OLD BATCH	I.1	314
Araminta:	Family.--	84	OLD BATCH	IV.3	37
Sir Paul:	Sons nor Grandsons? Must the Family of the Plyants be .	171	DOUBL DLR	IV.1	137
Sir Paul:	any of my Family that will bring Children into the World.	173	DOUBL DLR	IV.1	227
Sir Paul:	our Family Thy; our House is distinguished by a Languishing	173	DOUBL DLR	IV.1	239
Lord Touch:	in any thing that has concern'd me or my Family. . . .	181	DOUBL DLR	IV.1	536
Lord Touch:	our ancient Family; him I thus blow away, and constitute	189	DOUBL DLR	V.1	58
Sir Paul:	say truth, all our Family are Cholerick; I am the only .	192	DOUBL DLR	V.1	196
Sir Paul:	No, no, I mean the Family,--your Lady's	200	DOUBL DLR	V.1	505
	If in our larger Family we grieve	213	FCR LCVE	PRO.	21
Foresight:	Hey day! What are all the Women cf my Family	235	FOB LCVE	II.1	1
Foresight:	to the Master of a Family--I remember an old	236	FOB LCVE	II.1	48
Sr Sampson:	Hopes of my Family--I han't seen him these Three . . .	259	FOR LCVE	III.1	213
Valentine:	Occupy the Family. Coffee-Houses will be full of Smoak .	289	FOR LCVE	IV.1	507
Sr Sampson:	a long liv'd Race, and inherit Vigour, none of my Family	298	FCR LCVE	V.1	37
Mirabell:	What, is the Chief of that noble Family in Town, . .	400	WAY WCRLD	I.1	187
Petulant:	Of the Family of the Furnivals. Ha, ha, ha!	440	WAY WCRLD	III.1	555
Lady Wish:	and his Family. Beastly Creature, I know not what to do .	456	WAY WORLD	V.1	437
Lady Wish:	my self, and made you Governante of my whole Family. .	462	WAY WCRLD	V.1	21
Marwood:	Family, shou'd admit of Misconstruction, or make me .	466	WAY WCRLD	V.1	163

Famine (1)

Jeremy:	Spirit of Famine appears to me; scmetimes like a decay'd .	218	FCR LCVE	I.1	95

Famous (1)

Tattle:	answer'd, I was the famous Tattle, who had ruin'd so . .	257	FOR LCVE	III.1	164

Fan (4)

Sharper:	Or omit playing with her Fan, and cooling her if . .	44	OLD BATCH	I.1	263
Mirabell:	Here she comes i'faith full sail, with her Fan spread . .	418	WAY WCRLD	III.1	323
Millamant:	a Flame--I have broke my Fan--Mincing, lend me yours; .	432	WAY WCRLD	III.1	288
Marwood:	Indeed my Dear, you'll tear another Fan, if	433	WAY WCRLD	III.1	333

Fanatick (9)

Bellmour:	the Fanatick one-ey'd Parson!	39	OLD BATCH	I.1	85
Bellmour:	Well in this Fanatick Fathers habit, will I confess .	64	OLD BATCH	III.1	130
	(The Street Enter Bellmour in Fanatick habit, Setter.) .	75	OLD BATCH	IV.1	
	A Servant introducing Bellmour in Fanatick Habit, with a .	80	OLD BATCH	IV.2	
	(Enter Bellmour in Fanatick Habit, and Setter.) . . .	96	OLD BATCH	V.1	
Heartwell:	O Pox; He's a Fanatick.	97	OLD BATCH	V.1	17
Heartwell:	O ay; He's a Fanatick.	97	OLD BATCH	V.1 V	17
Sharper:	real Fanatick can look better pleas'd after a successful .	100	OLD BATCH	V.1	133
Jeremy:	Bethlehem; Nay, he's as Mad as any Projector, Fanatick, .	295	FOR LCVE	IV.1	739

Fancies (1)

Sir Paul:	little fancies--But as I was telling you, Mr. Careless,				
	if it	161	DOUEL DLR	III.1	403

Fancy (18)

Bellmour:	help out with her own Fancy.	38	OLD BATCH	I.1	59
Belinda:	Fancy--This Love is the Devil, and sure to be in Love .	54	OLD BATCH	II.2	12
Belinda:	O I love your hideous Fancy! Ha, ha, ha, love a . . .	55	OLD BATCH	II.2	22
Belinda:	O Gad I hate your hideous Fancy--You said that . . .	59	OLD BATCH	II.2	167
Maskwell:	Fancy. You had best go to my Lord, keep him as long as .	155	DOUEL DLR	III.1	165
Scandal:	of any Body that I know: you fancy that parting with .	234	FOR LCVE	I.1	677
Mrs Fore:	Soul, I shall fancy my self Old indeed, to have this great	249	FCR LCVE	II.1	512
Mrs Frail:	know, but I fancy, if I were a Man--	250	FOR LCVE	II.1	558
Angelica:	Ha! I saw him wink and smile--I fancy 'tis a	277	FOR LCVE	IV.1	53
Scandal:	be occasion; for I fancy his Presence provokes him more. .	280	FCR LCVE	IV.1	190
Valentine:	fancy I begin to come to my self.	294	FOR LCVE	IV.1	698
Tattle:	I fancy you have a wrong Notion of Faces.	304	FOR LCVE	V.1	265
Gonsalez:	Your too excessive Grief, works cn your Fancy, . . .	370	M. ERIDE	IV.1	375
Millamant:	. . . I fancy ones Hair wou'd nct	419	WAY WCRLD	II.1 V366	
Millamant:	that, I fancy one's Old and Ugly.	420	WAY WORLD	II.1	388
Marwood:	'Tis ycur Brother, I fancy. Don't you know	436	WAY WORLD	III.1	439
Marwood:	Hand in forgetfulness--I fancy he has forgot you too. .	437	WAY WORLD	III.1	476
Mrs Fain:	Confederacy? I fancy Marwood has not told her, tho' she .	464	WAY WCRLD	V.1	76

Fancy'd (1)

Almeria:	It was a fancy'd Noise; for all is hush'd.	339	M. EBIDE	II.1	52

Fans (1)

Mirabell:	of Muslin, China, Fans, Atlases, &c.--Item when you shall .	451	WAY WCRLD	IV.1	254

Fansied (1)

Belinda:	And t'cther did so stare and gape,--I fansied her like the	84	OLD BATCH	IV.3	45

Fantoms (1)

Almeria:	With Apparitions and affrighting Fantoms:	383	M. EBIDE	V.2	296

Far (43)

Sir Joseph:	Fondlewife, as far as two hundred Pound, and this Afternoon	51	OLD BATCH	I.1	133
Belinda:	Heav'n knows how far you may be tempted: I am tender . .	57	OLD EATCH	II.2	107
Fondlewife:	(aside). Verily I fear I have carry'd the Jest, too far .	77	OLD EATCH	IV.1	97
Laetitia:	Jest tco far indeed.	78	OLD EATCH	IV.1	120
Sir Paul:	far as Passion will permit.	145	DOUEL DLR	II.1	240
Mellefont:	that's sinking; tho' ne'er so far off.	148	DOUEL DLR	II.1	390
Mellefont:	as far as she betrays her self. No tragical design upon my	156	DOUEL DLR	III.1	210
Maskwell:	No, no--so far you are right, and I am, as an . . .	156	DOUEL DLR	III.1	228
Sir Paul:	am her Husband, as I may say, though far unworthy of .	162	DOUEL DLR	III.1	437
Lady Ply:	far upon me as your self, with Blushes I must own it, you	169	DOUEL DLR	IV.1	73
Lady Ply:	far you have gain'd upon me; I assure you if Sir Paul .	170	DOUEL DLR	IV.1	110
Lord Touch:	unnatural Nephew thus far--but I know you have been . .	182	DOUEL DLR	IV.1	545
Maskwell:	Leave it to my care; that shall be so far from being .	193	DOUEL DLR	V.1	210
Maskwell:	of your Love; yet so far I prize your Pleasures o're my own,	199	DOUEL DLR	V.1	436
	But Poets run much greater hazards far, ...	204	DOUEL DLR	EPI.	8
Sr Sampson:	Body o' me, I have gone too far;--I must not . . .	242	FOB LOVE	II.1	241
Tattle:	O pox, Scandal, that was too far put--Never have . .	256	FOR LCVE	III.1	116
Ben:	Ey, ey, been! Been far enough, an that be all--well . .	261	FOR LCVE	III.1	289
Ben:	heard as far as another,--I'll heave off to please you. .	263	FOR LCVE	III.1	367
Ben:	That he had brought from far, Sir.	274	FOR LCVE	III.1	772
Valentine:	Pray let me see it, Sir. Ycu hold it so far off, that .	281	FOB LCVE	IV.1	217
Sr Sampson:	(Stretches his Arm as far as he can.) .	281	FOR LCVE	IV.1	227
Ben:	neither--But I'll sail as far as Ligorn, and back again, .	306	FOR LCVE	V.1	352
Ben:	as if so be you should sail so far as the Streights without	308	FOR LCVE	V.1	415
	Thus far, alone does to the Wits relate;	323	M. EBIDE	PRO.	33

Far (continued)

		PAGE	TITLE	ACT.SC	LINE
Leonora:	Alas you search too far, and think too deeply.	327	M. BRIDE	I.1	64
Almeria:	And saw her Rate so far exceeding ours;	329	M. BRIDE	I.1	135
Almeria:	Unheard of Curses on me, greater far	330	M. BRIDE	I.1	188
Garcia:	(kneeling). Your Pardon, Sir, if I presume so far,	334	M. BRIDE	I.1	327
Garcia:	Far be it from me, officiously to pry	338	M. BRIDE	II.1	36
Osmyn-Alph:	Far be the Guilt of such Reproaches, from me;	346	M. BRIDE	II.2	252
Heli:	Where not far off some Male-Contents hold Counsel	352	M. BRIDE	III.1	100
Heli:	Where not far off some Male-Contents hold Council	352	M. BRIDE	III.1	V100
Zara:	So far to visit him, at his request.	365	M. BRIDE	IV.1	182
Gonsalez:	Is far from hence, beyond your Father's Power.	370	M. BRIDE	IV.1	377
Garcia:	And bathe it to the Hilt, in far less damnable	378	M. BRIDE	V.2	79
Mirabell:	Fellow, which I carry'd so far, that I told her the malicious	397	WAY WORLD	I.1	73
Mirabell:	to betray me by trusting him too far. If your Mother, in	417	WAY WORLD	II.1	292
Fainall:	much to hope. Thus far concerning my repose. Now for	443	WAY WORLD	III.1	683
Lady Wish:	get thee but far enough, to the Saracens or the Tartars, or	456	WAY WORLD	IV.1	439
Waitwell:	Far be it from me--	458	WAY WORLD	IV.1	533
Foible:	stifl'd the Letter before she read so far. Has that	464	WAY WORLD	V.1	79
Marwood:	Not far Madam; I'll return immediately.	471	WAY WORLD	V.1	357

Farce (2)

Valentine:	Why you Thick-Skull'd Rascal, I tell you the Farce	295	FOR LOVE	IV.1	749
	Some Humour too, no Farce; but that's a Fault.	393	WAY WORLD	PRO.	30

Fare (8)

Lady Froth:	His fare is paid him, and he sets in Milk.	164	DOUBL DLR	III.1	541
Brisk:	good Rhime) but don't you think bilk and fare too like a	165	DOUBL DLR	III.1	545
	And tho' of Homely Fare we make the Feast,	213	FOR LOVE	PRO.	27
Jeremy:	some great Fortune; and his Fare to be paid him like the	218	FOR LOVE	I.1	100
	Sure scribbling Fools, call'd Poets, fare the worst.	393	WAY WORLD	PRO.	2
Millamant:	fare you well;--I see they are walking away.	422	WAY WORLD	II.1	479
Mirabell:	Your bill of fare is something advanc'd in this latter	450	WAY WORLD	IV.1	228
Waitwell:	fare the worse for't--I shall have no appetite to	459	WAY WORLD	IV.1	561

Fare-thee-well (1)

Setter:	--Well, honest Lucy, Fare-thee-well.--I	111	OLD BATCH	V.2	141

Fares (1)

	So fares it with our Poet; and I'm sent	113	OLD BATCH	EPI.	5

Farewell (5)

Heartwell:	Well, farewell then--if I can get out of her sight I	74	OLD BATCH	III.2	129
Heartwell:	Well, farewell then--if I can get out of sight I	74	OLD BATCH	III.2	V129
Barnaby:	I have done Sir, then farewell 500 Pound.	76	OLD BATCH	IV.1	18
Osmyn-Alph:	Farewell,	352	M. BRIDE	III.1	122
Marwood:	scorn you most. Farewell.	415	WAY WORLD	II.1	221

Farm (1)

Mirabell:	Foible--The Lease shall be made good and the Farm	424	WAY WORLD	II.1	539

Farr (1)

Waitwell:	sign'd this Night? May I hope so farr?	461	WAY WORLD	IV.1	639

Farther (14)

Laetitia:	there needs no farther Apology.	81	OLD BATCH	IV.2	47
Vainlove:	Madam, will admit of no farther reasoning.--But	88	OLD BATCH	IV.3	177
Fondlewife:	Speculation! No, no; something went farther	92	OLD BATCH	IV.4	116
Maskwell:	of some farther design of yours, and has engaged	154	DOUBL DLR	III.1	137
Careless:	to you has carried me a little farther in this matter--	180	DOUBL DLR	IV.1	493
Lord Touch:	farther proceedings in it, till you have consider'd it, but	191	DOUBL DLR	V.1	139
Maskwell:	our farther Security, I would have you Disguis'd like a	193	DOUBL DLR	V.1	231
Miss Prue:	to say, I can hear you farther off, I an't deaf.	263	FOR LOVE	III.1	365
Scandal:	Passion. But come a little farther this way, and I'll tell you	269	FOR LOVE	III.1	596
Sr Sampson:	thine? I believe I can read it farther off yet--let me see.	281	FOR LOVE	IV.1	226
Foresight:	presently, till farther Orders from me--not a Word	306	FOR LOVE	V.1	325
Manuel:	--Stay thee--I've farther thought--I'll add to	374	M. BRIDE	V.1	80
Leonora:	Alas, a little farther, and behold	381	M. BRIDE	V.2	222
Mirabell:	and adjourn the Consummation till farther Order; bid	398	WAY WORLD	I.1	128

Farthest (1)

Mellefont:	and sometimes the Two farthest are together, but the	143	DOUBL DLR	II.1	166

Farthing (3)

Sir Paul:	--gadsbud he does not care a Farthing for any thing	146	DOUBL DLR	II.1	277
Jeremy:	that did not care a Farthing for you in your Prosperity;	217	FOR LOVE	I.1	45
Tattle:	a Farthing for you then in a twinckling.	251	FOR LOVE	II.1	605

Farthings (1)

Foible:	into Black Friers for Brass Farthings, with an old Mitten.	428	WAY WORLD	III.1	138

Fashion (8) see O'fashion

Heartwell:	lov'd; but that fashion is chang'd, Child.	73	OLD BATCH	III.2	104
Belinda:	to the Fashion, or any thing in practice! I had not patience	84	OLD BATCH	IV.3	32
Mrs Fore:	fond of it, as of being first in the Fashion, or of seeing a new	250	FOR LOVE	II.1	549
Witwoud:	And for my part--But that it is almost a Fashion to admire	407	WAY WORLD	I.1	466
Millamant:	enquir'd after you, as after a new Fashion.	419	WAY WORLD	II.1	348
Mirabell:	after an old Fashion, to ask a Husband for his Wife.	419	WAY WORLD	II.1	352
Witwoud:	Serjeants--'Tis not the fashion here; 'tis not indeed,	439	WAY WORLD	III.1	536
Sir Wilful:	you wou'd have been in the fashion too, and have remember'd	441	WAY WORLD	III.1	603

Fashion'd (1)

Miss Prue:	our old fashion'd Country way of speaking ones mind;--	252	FOR LOVE	II.1	625

Fashion's (1)

Sir Wilful:	The Fashion's a Fool; and you're a Fop, dear	439	WAY WORLD	III.1	538

Fashionable (1)

Angelica:	Fifty a contemptible Age! Not at all, a very fashionable	298	FOR LOVE	V.1	28

Fashioning (1)

Zara:	Long fashioning within thy labouring Mind,	354	M. BRIDE	III.1	195

Fashions (1)

Mirabell:	Fashions, spoiling Reputations, railing at absent Friends, and	451	WAY WORLD	IV.1	268

Fast (7)

Mellefont:	Ned, Ned, whither so fast? What, turn'd flincher!	127	DOUBL DLR	I.1	1
Tattle:	You shall not fly so fast, as I'll pursue.	253	FOR LOVE	II.1	662
Valentine:	Ha, ha, ha; you need not run so fast, Honesty will	282	FOR LOVE	IV.1	246
Osmyn-Alph:	My Arms which ake to fold thee fast, and grow	343	M. BRIDE	II.2	123

Fathers   (continued)
  Valentine: upon all alike--There are Fathers that have many Children;   280 FOR LCVE IV.1 162
  Valentine: and there are Children that have many Fathers--'tis   . 280 FOR LCVE IV.1 163
  Leonora: The distant Shouts, proclaim your Fathers Triumph; . . 330 M. EBIDE I.1 163
Fatigue (1)
  Lady Wish: to sink under the fatigue; and I cannot but have some fears 478 WAY WCRLD V.1 610
Fatigues (1)
  Millamant: from the Agreeable fatigues of sollicitation. . . . . 449 WAY WCRLD IV.1 169
Fatten (1)
      And fatten on the Spoils of Providence: . . . . . 385 M. EBIDE EPI. 24
Fault (19)
  Setter: Adsbud who's in fault, Mistress Mine? who flung the . . 66 OLD EATCH III.1 204
  Setter: though we were both in fault as to our Offices-- . . 66 OLD BATCH III.1 213
  Sharper: (reads). Hum hum--And what then appear'd a fault, . . 79 OLD EATCH IV.1 156
  Sharper: Fault: This Letter, that sc sticks in thy Maw, is
      Counterfeit, ... 99 OLD BATCH V.1 108
  Lady Ply: his passion: 'Tis not your fault; nor I swear it is not
      mine,-- . . . . 148 DOUBL DLR II.1 357
  Lady Ply: should be a fault,--but my honour--well, but . . . . 148 DOUEL DLR II.1 360
  Lady Touch: You can excuse a fault too well, not to have . . . 183 DOUBL DLR IV.2 16
  Maskwell: Why, qui vult decipi decipiatur.--'Tis nc fault . . . 194 DOUBL DLR V.1 262
      Forbear your Wonder, and the Fault forgive, ... 213 FCR LCVE PRO. 20
  Mrs Pore: I'll allow you now to find fault with my . . . . . 248 FOR LCVE II.1 463
  Tattle: not find fault with her pretty simplicity, it becomes her 249 FCR LCVE II.1 535
  Zara: So kindly of my Fault, to call it Madness; . . . 354 M. EBIDE III.1 179
      Some Humour too, no Farce; but that's a Fault. . . 393 WAY WCRLD PBO. 30
  Witwoud: Porter. Now that is a Fault. . . . . 404 WAY WCRLD I.1 342
  Mrs Fain: wou'd think it dissembl'd; for you have laid a Fault to . 412 WAY WCRLD II.1 75
  Waitwell: That she did indeed, Sir. It was my Fault that she . . 423 WAY WCRLD II.1 516
  Foible: met that confident Thing? Was I in Fault? If you had . 427 WAY WCRLD III.1 86
  Sir Wilful: but he spits after a Bumper, and that's a Fault. . . 455 WAY WCRLD IV.1 414
      Set up for Spys on Plays and finding Fault. . . . . 479 WAY WCRLD EPI. 15
Faulters (2)
  Selim: My Tongue faulters, and my Voice fails-- . . . . . 380 M. EBIDE V.2 183
  Selim: My Tongue faulters, and my Voice fails--I sink-- . . 380 M. EBIDE V.2 V183
Faults (9)
  Lucy: not to affect his Masters faults; and consequently . . 64 OLD EATCH III.1 147
  Lady Touch: black!--O I have Excuses, Thousands for my Faults; Fire . 135 DOUBL DLR I.1 325
  Lady Touch: to forgive the faults I have imagined, but never put in . 185 DOUEL DLR IV.2 73
  Scandal: Expence, have been your greatest faults. . . . . . 220 FCR LCVE I.1 163
  Angelica: Faults than he has Virtues; and 'tis hardly more Pleasure 312 FCR LCVE V.1 576
  Mirabell: a Lover; for I like her with all her Faults; nay, like
      her for . . . . 399 WAY WCRLD I.1 159
  Mirabell: her Faults. Her Follies are so natural, cr so artful,
      that they . . . . 399 WAY WCRLD I.1 160
  Witwoud: defend most of his Faults, except cne cr two; one he has, 403 WAY WCRLD I.1 310
  Millamant: Faults--I can't bear it. Well, I won't have you Mirabell . 422 WAY WCRLD II.1 456
Faux pas (1)
  Lady Ply: made one Trip, not one faux pas; O consider it, what would 147 DOUEL DLR II.1 319
Fav'rite (1)
  Manuel: None, say you, none? what not the Fav'rite Eunuch? . . . 372 M. EBIDE V.1 2
Favour (29)
      He's very civil, and entreats your Favour. . . . . 35 OLD EATCH PBO. 13
  Sir Joseph: your favour.   (Bcws.) . . . . . 49 OLD BATCH II.1 61
  Bellmour: then pursues it for the Favour. . . . . 58 OLD BATCH II.2 134
  Bellmour: the Favour. . . . . 68 OLD BATCH III.1 283
  Bellmour: have a long time designed thee this favour) I knew Spin-text 94 OLD EATCH IV.4 207
  Sir Joseph: I'm in the Lady's favour?--No matter, I'll make your . 103 OLD BATCH V.1 V261
  Heartwell: with you and bauk'd it? Did you ever offer me the Favour . 100 OLD BAICH V.2 57
  Mellefont: Pray let us have the Favour of you, to practice the Song, . 143 DOUEL DLR II.1 175
  Mellefont: She is most gracious in her Favour,--well, and . . 149 DOUBL DLR II.1 430
  Careless: and that the first Favour he receiv'd from her, was a . 157 DOUEL DLR III.1 275
  Sir Paul: are mightily in her favour. . . . . 162 DOUBL DLR III.1 445
  Careless: your favour--I feel my Spirits faint, a general dampness . 170 DOUBL DLR IV.1 114
  Maskwell: of a Girl. No--yet tho' I doat on each last Favour . . 199 DOUBL DLR V.1 433
  Maskwell: in his Uncle's favour, if he'll comply with your desires; . 199 DOUBL DLR V.1 448
      Thus poor Poets the Favour are deny'd, ... 204 DOUBL DLR EPI. 29
      Poor Poets thus the Favour are deny'd, ... 204 DOUBL DLR EPI. V 29
  Jeremy: Favour? Why Sir Sampson will be irreconcilable. If your . 218 FOR LCVE I.1 83
  Scandal: favour, as a Doctor says, No, to a Bishoprick, only that it . 226 FOR LCVE I.1 377
  Valentine: She dces me the favour--I mean of a Visit . . . 229 FOR LOVE I.1 486
  Scandal: which is rightly cbserv'd by Gregory the Great in favour of 267 FOR LCVE III.1 536
  Scandal: to allow some other Men the last Favour; you mistake, . . 272 FCB LCVE III.1 696
  Jeremy: Yes, Sir; he says he'll favour it, and mistake her for . 288 FOR LCVE IV.1 482
  Sr Sampson: I have a Proviso in the Obligation in favour of my self . 300 FCR LCVE V.1 126
  Angelica: But I believe Mr. Tattle meant the Favour to me, I . . 309 FOR LCVE V.1 455
      For a clear Stage won't do, without your Favour. . . 316 FOR LCVE EPI. 44
  Gonsalez: By fits reveals--his Pace seems turn'd to favour . . 376 M. EBIDE V.2 8
      With whom, he hopes, this Play will Favour find, . . 385 M. BRIDE EPI. 30
      This Author, heretofore, has found your Favour, . . 393 WAY WCRLD PRO. 16
  Mirabell: plead for favour;--Nay not for Pardon, I am a . . . 471 WAY WCRLD V.1 373
Favour'd (2)
  Mellefont: self favour'd in her aversion: But whether urged by her . 129 DOUBL DLR I.1 94
  Maskwell: had never favour'd, but through Revenge and Policy. . 136 DOUBL DLR I.1 357
Favourable (5)
  Belinda: and in this favourable disposition of your Mind, . . 57 OLD BATCH II.2 106
  Sharper: not what, forced me. I only beg a favourable Censure of this 79 OLD BATCH IV.3 160
  Araminta: my Fame.--No, I have not err'd in one favourable . . 87 OLD EATCH IV.3 169
  Marwood: O then it seems you are one of his favourable . . . 412 WAY WORLD II.1 77
  Mrs Fain: Nay, I'll swear you shall never lose so favourable . . 447 WAY WCRLD IV.1 87
Favourably (2)
  Lady Touch: I am willing to believe as favourably of my Nephew as I . 151 DOUBL DLR III.1 24
  Lady Wish: favourably, Judge Candidly and conclude you have found . 459 WAY WCRLD IV.1 552
Favourite (5)
  Zara: You're grown a Favourite since last we parted; . . . 359 M. EBIDE III.1 412
  Zara: I did not know the Princess Favourite; . . . . . 359 M. EBIDE III.1 415

Favourite   (continued)
    Mirabell: I thought you had been the greatest Favourite.   408   WAY WORLD   I.1   499
    Witwoud: As a Favourite in disgrace; and with as few   418   WAY WORLD   II.1 335
    Witwoud: As a Favourite just disgrac'd; and with as few   418   WAY WORLD   II.1 V335
Favours (18)
    Araminta: Favours that are got by Impudence and Importunity,   . . . 58   OLD BATCH   II.2 135
    Vainlove: I should rather think Favours, so gain'd, to be due   . . 58   OLD BATCH   II.2 139
    Sharper: of some favours lately receiv'd; I would not have you draw 69   OLD BATCH   III.1 303
    Sir Joseph: I'm in the Ladies favours?--No matter, I'll make your . . 103 OLD BATCH   V.1   261
    Sir Paul: me and my Wife, with continual Favours.   . . . . . . 159 DOUBL DLR   III.1 326
    Lady Ply: face of the World that no body is more sensible of Favours 159 DOUBL DLR   III.1 351
    Scandal: Yes, all that have done him Favours, if you will   . . . 232 FOR LOVE   I.1   606
    Valentine: Pictures of all that have granted him favours, he has the 233 FOR LOVE   I.1   623
    Tattle: some Favours, as to conceal others.   . . . . 255 FOR LOVE   III.1 86
    Tattle: confess I have had Favours from Persons--But as the . . 257 FOR LOVE   III.1 150
    Tattle: Favours are numberless, so the Persons are nameless. . . 257 FOR LOVE   III.1 151
    Scandal: all night, and denying favours with more impudence, than . 284 FOR LOVE   IV.1 336
    Scandal: . . . favours with more impudence, than   . . . . . . 284 FOR LOVE   IV.1 V336
    Scandal: Favours, either on those who do not merit, or who do not . 314 FOR LOVE   V.1   625
    Zara: Favours conferr'd, tho' when unsought, deserve   . . . 336 M. BRIDE   I.1   415
    Zara: Such Favours so conferr'd, tho' when unsought, ... 336 M. BRIDE   I.1   V415
                   For Fortune favours all her Idiot-Race: . . . . . . 393 WAY WORLD   PRO. 6
    Mirabell: But do not you know, that when favours are conferr'd . . 449 WAY WORLD   IV.1 170
Fawn (1)
    Heartwell: that will fawn upon me again, and entertain any Puppy . . 42   OLD BATCH   I.1   190
Fawning (2)
    Heartwell: nauseous Flattery, fawning upon a little tawdry Whore, . . 42   OLD BATCH   I.1   189
    Scandal: more servile, timorous, and fawning, than any I have . . 220 FOR LOVE   I.1   147
Fear (58)
    Sir Joseph: I am quite another thing, when I am with him: I don't fear 50   OLD BATCH   II.1 122
    Capt Bluff: How how, my young Knight? Not for fear I hope; he   . . . 51   OLD BATCH   II.1 142
    Capt Bluff: How now, my young Knight? Not for fear I hope; he   . . . 51   OLD BATCH   II.1 V142
    Capt Bluff: that knows me must be a stranger to fear.   51   OLD BATCH   II.1 143
    Sir Joseph: Nay agad I hate fear ever since I had like to have   . . 51   OLD BATCH   II.1 144
    Silvia: but I'le do my weak endeavour, though I fear I have not . 62   OLD BATCH   III.1 52
    Capt Bluff: Composition; I believe you gave it him out of fear, pure . 68   OLD BATCH   III.1 269
    Capt Bluff: paultry fear--confess.   68   OLD BATCH   III.1 270
    Sir Joseph: that it was altogether out of fear, but partly to prevent 68   OLD BATCH   III.1 273
    Fondlewife: who will tempt her Isaac?--I fear it much--But   . . . 76   OLD BATCH   IV.1 57
    Fondlewife: (aside). Verily I fear I have carry'd the Jest, too far . 77   OLD BATCH   IV.1 97
    Sir Joseph: fear it;--that is, if I can but think on't: Truth is, I . 85   OLD BATCH   IV.3 73
    Capt Bluff: Fear him not,--I am prepar'd for him now; and he   . . . 101 OLD BATCH   V.1   167
    Sir Joseph: No, no, Never fear, Man, the Lady's business shall   . . 103 OLD BATCH   V.1   242
    Setter: No, no; never fear me, Sir.--I privately inform'd   . . 106 OLD BATCH   V.1   347
    Sharper: fear.--A fine Lady, and a Lady of very good Quality. . . 111 OLD BATCH   V.2   135
    Bellmour: O my Conscience she dares not consent, for fear   . . . 112 OLD BATCH   V.2   175
                   For 'tis our way (you know) for fear o'th' worst,   . . 113 OLD BATCH   EPI. 21
    Careless: I thought your fear of her had been over--is not   . . 129 DOUBL DLR   I.1   79
    Mellefont: Consideration or the fear of Repentance. Pox o'Fortune, . 168 DOUBL DLR   IV.1 29
    Lord Touch: Fear not his Displeasure; I will put you out   . . . . 182 DOUBL DLR   IV.1 570
    Mellefont: shapes in shining day, then fear shews Cowards in the . . 186 DOUBL DLR   IV.2 V125
    Lord Touch: I fear he's mad indeed--Let's send Maskwell   . . . . 187 DOUBL DLR   IV.2 135
    Cynthia: How's this! now I fear indeed.   . . . . 197 DOUBL DLR   V.1   361
    Lady Ply: who would ever trust a man? O my heart akes for fear . . 202 DOUBL DLR   V.1   546
    Careless: You need not fear, Madam, you have Charms to   . . . . 202 DOUBL DLR   V.1   548
                   And dare not bite, for fear of being bit.   . . . . . 214 FOR LOVE   PRO. 36
    Mrs Fore: they're in perpetual fear of being seen and censur'd?-- . 247 FOR LOVE   I.1   433
    Ben: What I said was in Obedience to Father; Gad I fear a . . 264 FOR LOVE   III.1 406
    Scandal: I thank my Stars that have inclin'd me--But I fear . . 268 FOR LOVE   III.1 543
    Scandal: Violence--I fear he does not act wholly from himself; . . 268 FOR LOVE   III.1 549
    Scandal: but 'tis as I believe some Men are Valiant, thro' fear--For 271 FOR LOVE   III.1 670
    Angelica: Failing, which I must own to you--I fear my Happiness . . 277 FOR LOVE   IV.1 55
    Scandal: work a Cure; as the fear of your Aversion occasion'd his . 277 FOR LOVE   IV.1 64
    Foresight: Scandal, Heav'n keep us all in our Senses--I fear   . . 306 FOR LOVE   V.1   332
    Ben: Mess, I fear his Fire's little better than Tinder; may hap 308 FOR LOVE   V.1   410
                   But we can't fear, since you're so good to save us, . . 315 FOR LOVE   EPI. 38
    Leonora: This Torrent of your Grief; for, much I fear   . . . . 330 M. BRIDE   I.1   166
    Leonora: Alas! I fear some fatal Resolution.   . . . . 331 M. BRIDE   I.1   200
    Manuel: A Fit of Bridal Fear; How is't, Almeria?   . . . . . 334 M. BRIDE   I.1   V348
    Almeria: It was thy Fear; or else some transient Wind   . . . . 339 M. BRIDE   II.1 54
    Almeria: Thou hast wept much Alphonso; and I fear, ... 342 M. BRIDE   II.2 117
    Zara: Dost fear so much, thou dar'st not wish. The King! . . 348 M. BRIDE   II.2 347
    Osmyn-Alph: She'll come; 'tis what I wish, yet what I fear.   . . . 351 M. BRIDE   III.1 51
    Osmyn-Alph: The Sea. I fear when she shall know the truth,   . . . 355 M. BRIDE   III.1 230
    Osmyn-Alph: For whom I fear, to shield me from my Fears.   . . . . 355 M. BRIDE   III.1 233
    Selim: Have Cause to fear his Guards may be corrupted,   . . . 362 M. BRIDE   IV.1 51
    Gonsalez: If what I fear be true, she'll be concern'd   . . . . 367 M. BRIDE   IV.1 239
    Zara: Shun me when seen! I fear thou hast undone me.   . . . 375 M. BRIDE   V.1   101
    Garcia: Granada's lost; and to confirm this Fear, ... 377 M. BRIDE   V.2   37
    Garcia: Were it a Truth, I fear 'tis now too late.   . . . . . 379 M. BRIDE   V.2   105
    Marwood: have him ever to continue upon the Rack of Fear and . . 411 WAY WORLD   II.1 63
    Fainall: But he, I fear, is too Insensible.   . . . . 413 WAY WORLD   II.1 130
    Foible: is so impatient, I fear she'll come for me, if I stay. . 430 WAY WORLD   III.1 220
    Sir Wilful: Tony, belike, I may'nt call him Brother for fear of offence. 441 WAY WORLD   III.1 605
    Lady Wish: Traytor,--I fear I cannot fortifie my self to support his 470 WAY WORLD   V.1   335
    Lady Wish: I fear I shall turn to Stone, petrifie Incessantly. . . 470 WAY WORLD   V.1   337
    Mirabell: grant I love you not too well, that's all my fear. . . . 477 WAY WORLD   V.1   598
Fear'd (5)
    Mellefont: then came the Storm I fear'd at first: For starting from my 130 DOUBL DLR   I.1   113
    Maskwell: (aside). This I fear'd. Did not your Lordship tell . . 195 DOUBL DLR   V.1   312
    Perez: As to some Object frightful, yet not fear'd.   . . . . 338 M. BRIDE   II.1 23
    Gonsalez: She fear'd her stronger Charms, might cause the Moor's . 366 M. BRIDE   IV.1 224
    Mirabell: Tho' 'twere a Man whom he fear'd, or a Woman   . . . . 403 WAY WORLD   I.1   305
Fearful (5)
    Singer: The fearful Nymph reply'd--Forbear;   71   OLD BATCH   III.2 V 10
    Angelica: upon one fearful of Affliction, to tell me what I   . . 277 FOR LOVE   IV.1 58

Fearful   (ccntinued)
  Foresight: O fearful! I think the Girl's influenc'd too,-- . . . . . 305 FOR LCVE   V.1   313
  Leonora: But fearful to renew your Troubles past, ... 328 M. EBIDE   I.1   107
  Mincing: He swears, and my old Lady cry's. There's a fearful
                Hurricane . . . . 465 WAY WCBLD   V.1   109
Fears (13)
  Bellmour: but your fears. . . . . 89 OLD BATCH   IV.4   2
                Why that's some Comfort, to an Author's fears, ... 113 OLD EATCH   EPI.   15
  Singer: Much she fears I should undo her, ... 143 DOUBL DLB   II.1 181
  Cynthia: but our fears. . . . . 168 DOUEL DLR   IV.1   26
  Maskwell: and she fears it; though chance brought my Lord, 'twas . 187 DOUEL DLR   V.1   4
  Careless: her, confirm me in my fears. Where's Mellefont? . . . . 196 DOUEL DLR   V.1   338
  Manuel: This idle Vow hangs on her Woman's Fears. . . . . . 334 M. EBIDE   I.1   353
  Almeria: It may my Fears, but cannot add to that. . . . . . . 339 M. BRIDE   II.1   72
  Almeria: Exerts my Spirits; and my present Fears . . . . . 339 M. EBIDE   II.1   79
  Zara: O Heav'n! my Fears interpret . . . . 354 M. EFIDE   III.1 193
  Osmyn-Alph: For whom I fear, to shield me frcm my Fears. . . . 355 M. BBIDE   III.1 233
  Almeria: I chatter, shake, and faint with thrilling Fears. . . . 358 M. EBIDE   III.1 369
  Lady Wish: to sink under the fatigue; and I cannot but have some fears 478 WAY WCRLD   V.1   610
Feast (6)
  Careless: feast upon that hand; O let me press it to my heart, my . 170 DOUBL DLR   IV.1   92
                And tho' of Homely Fare we make the Feast, ... 213 FOR LCVE   PRC.   27
  Valentine: Page dcubled down in Epictetus, that is a Feast for an . 216 FCB LCVE   I.1   8
  Valentine: to live upon Instruction; feast your Mind, and mortifie . 216 FOR LCVE   I.1   13
  Jeremy: Humph, and so he has made a very fine Feast, where . . 216 FOR LCVE   I.1   21
  Almeria: There, we will feast; and smile on past Distress, . . 358 M. EFIDE   III.1 339
Feasted (1)
  Manuel: I tell thee she's to blame, not to have feasted . . . 333 M. EFIDE   I.1   307
Feasts (1)
                Grave solemn Things, as Graces are to Feasts; . . . . 35 OLD EATCH   PRO.   3
Feather'd (1)
  Lady Wish: You have forgot this, have you, ncw you have feather'd . 462 WAY WCBLD   V.1   22
Feathers (2)
  Belinda: with their Feathers growing the wrong way.--C such . . 84 OLD EATCH   IV.3   30
  Mirabell: Feathers, and meet me at One a Clcck by Rosamond's Pond. . 398 WAY WCRLD   I.1   130
Features (4)
  Tattle: In the way of Art: I have some taking Features, and . . 304 FOR LCVE   V.1   267
  Lady Wish: my Features, to receive Sir Rowland with any Oeconcmy of . 428 WAY WORLD III.1 141
  Lady Wish: look so--My Niece affects it; but she wants Features. Is . 429 WAY WCRLD III.1 170
                And shining Features in cne Portrait blend, ... 479 WAY WCRLD   EPI.   33
Fed (4)   see High-fed
  Jeremy: Appetite to be fed with your Commands a great while; . . 301 FOR LCVE   V.1   172
  Gonsalez: With Hopes, and fed with Expectation of . . . . . 378 M. EBIDE   V.2   103
  Gonsalez: And in the meantime fed with Expectation . . . . . 378 M. BBIDE   V.2 V103
  Singer: A sickly Flame, which if not fed expires; . . . . . 435 WAY WCBLD III.1 379
Fee (1)
  Maskwell: Aunt has given me a retaining Fee;--nay, I am your . . 148 DOUBL DLR   II.1 393
Feeble (3)
  Lady Ply: frailty? Alas! Humanity is feeble, Heaven knows! very . . 147 DOUEL DLR   II.1 321
  Lady Ply: feeble, and unable tc support it self. . . . . . . 147 DOUBL DLR   II.1 322
  Manuel: Away begon thou feeble Boy, fond Love, ... 374 M. EBIDE   V.1   62
Feebly (1)
  Gonsalez: A Lamp that feebly lifts a sickly Flame, ... 376 M. EBIDE   V.2   7
Feed (17)
  Araminta: avert the cure: Let me have Oil to feed that Flame and . 54 OLD EATCH   II.2   9
  Singer: O let me feed as well as taste, ... 71 OLD EATCH III.2   7
  Vainlove: Yes, when I feed my self--Eut I hate to be cram'd . . . 80 OLD BATCH   IV.1 174
  Belinda: --But when we come to feed, 'tis all Froth, . . . 106 OLD EATCH   V.1   374
                And feed like Sharks, upon an Infant Play. . . . . 125 DOUBL DLR   PRO.   13
                When what should feed the Tree, devours the Root: . . 213 FOR LCVE   PRO.   4
  Sr Sampson: feed thee out of my own Vitals?--'S'heart, live by . . 246 FOR LCVE   II.1 399
  Gonsalez: Would feed his Faculty of Admiration. . . . . . 332 M. BRIDE   I.1   242
  Gonsalez: Would feed its Faculty of Admiration. . . . . . 332 M. BRIDE   I.1 V242
  Almeria: Feed on each others Heart, devour our Woes . . . . 356 M. EBIDE   III.1 259
  Almeria: That still is left us, and on that we'll feed, . . . 358 M. BBIDE   III.1 337
  Lady Wish: Desarts and Solitudes; and feed harmless Sheep by Groves . 465 WAY WCBLD   V.1   133
                These with false Glosses, feed their own Ill-nature, . 479 WAY WORLD   EPI.   21
Feeding (2)
  Jeremy: this fine Feeding: But if you please, I had rather be at . 217 FOR LCVE   I.1   25
  Singer: And feeding, wastes in Self-consuming Fires. . . . . 435 WAY WORLD III.1 380
Feel (17)
  Silvia: Methinks I feel the Woman strong within me, and . . 61 OLD BATCH III.1   33
  Bellmour: Oh, a Convulsion.--I feel the Symptoms. . . . . . 83 OLD BATCH   IV.2   89
  Laetitia: --I swear, I was heartily frightned.--Feel how my . . 89 OLD BATCH   IV.4   4
  Fondlewife: Ay, I feel it here; I sprout, I bud, I blossom, I am . . 92 OLD EATCH   IV.4 126
  Careless: your favour--I feel my Spirits faint, a general dampness . 170 DOUEL DLR   IV.1 114
  Nurse: thing; feel, feel here, if I have any thing but like . . 238 FOR LCVE   II.1 124
  Sr Sampson: Val: Hcw do'st thou do? let me feel thy Pulse--Oh, . . 281 FOR LCVE   IV.1 201
  Sr Sampson: Let me feel thy Hand again, Val: it does not . . . . 281 FCB LCVE   IV.1 206
  Almeria: I feel I'm more at large, ... 331 M. BRIDE   I.1   202
  Almeria: Nor Violence.--I feel my self more light, ... 331 M. BRIDE   I.1 V202
  Zara: With usual Homage wait. But when I feel . . . . . 336 M. BRIDE   I.1   399
  Heli: I feel, to hear of Osmyn's Name; to hear . . . . . 338 M. BRIDE   II.1   10
  Osmyn-Alph: 'Tis she; shew me her Face, and let me feel . . . . 341 M. EBIDE   II.2   68
  Almeria: Thy second self should feel each other Wound, . . . 356 M. BBIDE   III.1 287
  Zara: I cannot feel it--quite beyond my reach. . . . . 381 M. BRIDE   V.2   210
  Mrs Fain: live to be Old and feel the craving of a false Appetite when 418 WAY WCBLD   II.1 315
Feeling (1)   see Fellow-feeling
  Leonora: Feeling Remorse too late, for what they've done. . . . 381 M. BRIDE   V.2   225
Fees (1)
  Bellmour: Lawyer, between two Fees. . . . . 63 OLD EATCH III.1   92
Feet (19)
  Musician: While wishing at your Feet they lie: . . . . . . 60 OLD BATCH   II.2 198
  Heartwell: Well, Why do you not move? Feet do your . . . . . 62 OLD EATCH III.1   73
  Mellefont: Feet like a gull'd Bassa that has married a Relaticn of the 158 DOUBL DLR III.1 282
  Mellefont: him swaddled up in Blankets, and his hands and feet . . 158 DOUBL DLR III.1 290

Fellows   (continued)
Sr Sampson:	your Antideluvian Families, Fellows, that the Flood could	.	298	FOR LCVE	V.1	40
Mirabell:	fellows; for prevention of which; I banish all Foreign	.	451	WAY WCRLD	IV.1	271
Millamant:	fellows, Odious Men! I hate your Odious prcviso's. . . .	.	452	WAY WCRLD	IV.1	279
Sir Wilful:	Fellows--If I had a Bumper I'd stand upon my	.	456	WAY WCRLD	IV.1	425

Felt (6)
Sharper:	Ay thou inimitable Coward and to be felt--As	.	69	OLD EATCH	III.1	324
Zara:	And felt the Balm of thy respiring Lips!	.	347	M. EBIDE	II.2	287
Almeria:	Then knowing thou hast felt it. Tell it me.	.	356	M. EBIDE	III.1	279
Almeria:	Than knowing thou hast felt it. Tell it me.	.	356	M. EBIDE	III.1	V279
Witwoud:	have been bound Prentice tc a Felt maker in Shrewsbury;	.	440	WAY WOBLD	III.1	561
Lady Wish:	that he has sworn, the Palpitations that he has felt, the	.	458	WAY WCBLD	IV.1	513

Felts (1)
Witwoud:	this Fellow wou'd have bound me tc a Maker of Felts. .	.	440	WAY WCBLD	III.1	562

Female (3)
Cynthia:	have once resolved; and a true Female courage to oppose	.	193	DOUBL DLR	V.1	204
Fainall:	O the pious Friendships of the Female Sex!	.	414	WAY WCBLD	II.1	166
Mrs Fain:	Female Frailty! We must all come to it, if we	.	418	WAY WCBLD	II.1	314

Females (1)
Foresight:	What, wou'd you be gadding too? Sure all Females . . .	.	236	FOR LCVE	II.1	46

Feminine (1)
Lady Wish:	Coats; Nay her very Babies were of the Feminine Gender,	.	467	WAY WCRLD	V.1	190

Fencing (1)
Mrs Frail:	take great care when one makes a thrust in Fencing, not to		248	FOR LCVE	II.1	474

Ferdinand (1)
Foresight:	Ferdinand Mendez Pinto was but a Type of thee, thou Lyar	.	241	FOR LCVE	II.1	236

Permentation (1)
Sir Paul:	Gads bud! I am provoked into a Fermentation, as . . .	.	143	DOUBL DLR	II.1	195

Ferret (1)
Fondlewife:	is this Apocryphal Elder? I'll ferret him.	.	92	OLD BATCH	IV.4	118

Ferreting (1)
Foible:	are sc early abroad, or Catering (says he) ferreting for	.	427	WAY WCBLD	III.1	96

Festring (1)
Almeria:	And eat into thy Flesh, festring thy Limbs	.	356	M. EBIDE	III.1	268

Fetch (8)
Fondlewife:	If you will tarry a Moment, till I fetch my Papers, I'll wait	.	90	OLD BATCH	IV.4	43
Jeremy:	it may concern; That the Bearer hereof, Jeremy Fetch by	.	218	FOR LCVE	I.1	66
Scandal:	refund the Sack; Jeremy fetch him some warm water, or	.	224	FCR LCVE	I.1	310
Tattle:	Letters writ in Juice of Lemon, for no Fire can fetch it out.	.	292	FCB LCVE	IV.1	614
Lady Wish:	Fetch me the Red--The Red, do you hear, Sweet-heart?	.	425	WAY WCRLD	III.1	5
Lady Wish:	Wench stirs! Why dost thcu not fetch me a little Red?	.	425	WAY WCRLD	III.1	7
Lady Wish:	A Pox take you both--Fetch me the Cherry-Brandy . .	.	425	WAY WCRLD	III.1	20
Sir Wilful:	fetch a walk this Evening, if so be that I might nct be	.	448	WAY WCBLD	IV.1	116

Fetch'd (1)
Boy:	There was a Man too that fetch'd 'em out:--Setter, I	.	107	OLD BATCH	V.2	2

Fetter'd (1)
Fainall:	Imprison'd, Fetter'd? Have I not a Wife? Nay a Wife	.	415	WAY WORLD	II.1	210

Fetters (3)
Belinda:	Prisoner, make much of your Fetters.	.	112	OLD BATCH	V.2	168
Gonsalez:	Prisoners of War in shining Fetters, follow; . . .	.	331	M. EFIDE	I.1	234
Osmyn-Alph:	How run into thy Arms with-held by Fetters, . . .	.	355	M. EBIDE	III.1	239

Feud (1)
Leonora:	Revenge, and that Hereditary Feud	.	327	M. BBIDE	I.1	43

Fever (4)
Belinda:	Man--you don't know what you said, your Fever has . .	.	54	OLD BATCH	II.2	6
Belinda:	Man--you don't know what you've said, your Fever has . .	.	54	OLD BATCH	II.2	V 6
Araminta:	If Love be the Fever which you mean; kind Heav'n . .	.	54	OLD BATCH	II.2	8
Heartwell:	the envenom'd Shirt, to run into the Embraces of a Fever,	.	62	OLD BATCH	III.1	67

Few (20)
Bellmour:	enrich'd himself with the plunder of a few Oaths;--and	.	47	OLD BATCH	I.1	370
Araminta:	Nature well, for there are few Men, but do more silly	.	60	OLD BATCH	II.2	216
Bellmour:	relentless face in your salt trickling Tears.--So, a few soft	.	95	OLD BATCH	IV.4	238
Sharper:	No, Faith; I believe not.--Few Women, but	.	104	OLD BATCH	V.1	303
Maskwell:	(aside). By Heav'n, he meets my wishes. Few . . .	.	196	DOUEL DLR	V.1	322
Maskwell:	No more,--there want but a few Minutes of	.	199	DOUEL DLB	V.1	456
Maskwell:	No more,--it wants but a few Minutes of	.	199	DOUEL DLB	V.1	V456
Foresight:	you had been read in these matters--Few Young Men .	.	267	FOR LOVE	III.1	541
Valentine:	few Acquaintance.	.	280	FOR LCVE	IV.1	179
Angelica:	but few have the Constancy to stay till it becomes your	.	314	FCR LCVE	V.1	630
Angelica:	How few, like Valentine, would persevere even unto	.	314	FOR LCVE	V.1	633
Angelica:	How few, like Valentine, wculd persevere even to	.	314	FOR LOVE	V.1	V633
Zara:	Some News, few Minutes past arriv'd, which seem'd .	.	354	M. EBIDE	III.1	204
Osmyn-Alph:	Esteem; to this she's fair, few more can boast . .	.	355	M. EBIDE	III.1	225
Garcia:	The few remaining Soldiers with Despair, ...	.	378	M. EBIDE	V.2	94
Mirabell:	Of thcse few Fools, who with ill Stars are curs'd, .	.	393	WAY WOBLD	PRO.	1
	Hour less and less disturbance; 'till in a few Days it became	.	399	WAY WORLD	I.1	170
Mirabell:	a good Memory, and some few Scraps of cther Folks Wit.	.	401	WAY WORLD	I.1	225
Witwoud:	As a Favourite in disgrace; and with as few . . .	.	418	WAY WCRLD	II.1	335
Witwoud:	As a Favourite just disgrac'd; and with as few . . .	.	418	WAY WORLD	II.1	V335

Fez (1)
Zara:	When he receiv'd you as the Prince of Fez;	.	347	M. BBIDE	II.2	295

Fib (1)
Sir Paul:	Pshaw, Pshaw, you fib you Baggage, ycu do	.	174	DOUEL DLR	IV.1	246

Fickle (1)
Manuel:	Fickle in Fields, unsteadily she flyes, ...	.	337	M. EBIDE	I.1	460

Fiction (1)
Millamant:	O Fiction; Painall, let us leave these Men.	.	421	WAY WORLD	II.1	423

Fictions (1)
Lady Touch:	and sooth me to a fond belief of all your fictions; .	.	197	DOUBL DLR	V.1	380

Fiddle (4)
Lady Ply:	Fiddle, faddle, don't tell me of this and that, and .	.	146	DOUBL DLR	II.1	301
Cynthia:	As dancing without a Fiddle.	.	163	DOUBL DLB	III.1	479

234

Figure   (continued)

Jeremy:	lying is a Figure in Speech, that interlards the greatest	296	FOR LCVE	IV.1	776
Lady Wish:	figure shall I give his Heart the first Impression?				
	There is a	445	WAY WCRLD	IV.1	18
Petulant:	Thou art (without a figure) Just one half of an Ass; .	454	WAY WCRLD	IV.1	350

Figures (1)

Sr Sampson:	Figures of St. Dunstan's Clock, and Consummatum est shall .	266	FOR LCVE	III.1	477

Files (1)

	Garcia and several Officers. Files of Prisoners in Chains,	332	M. BEIDE	I.1	266

Filial (3)

Sr Sampson:	No doubt of it, sweet Sir, but your filial Piety, . . .	243	FOR LOVE	II.1	293
Manuel:	In Filial Duty, had aton'd and giv'n	333	M. BEIDE	I.1	291
Almeria:	Stooping to raise from Earth the filial Reverence; . .	369	M. BEIDE	IV.1	324

Fill (13)

Lord Touch:	sign'd, and have his name inserted--yours will fill the .	189	DOUEL DLR	V.1	63
Valentine:	my Service tc you,--fill, fill, tc honest Mr. Trapland, .	222	FCR LOVE	I.1	243
Valentine:	T'other Glass, and then we'll talk. Fill, Jeremy. . . .	222	FCR LOVE	I.1	248
Valentine:	Sirrah, fill when I bid you.--And how do's	222	FCR LOVE	I.1	250
Valentine:	fill each Man his Glass.	223	FCR LOVE	I.1	263
Valentine:	No faith, we'll mind the Widow's business, fill . . .	223	FOR LOVE	I.1	283
Almeria:	To fill my Ears, with Garcia's valiant Deeds;	331	M. EBIDE	I.1	214
Manuel:	Th' ignoble Currs, that yelp to fill the Cry,-- . . .	362	M. EEIDE	IV.1	63
Lady Wish:	of Nutmeg? I warrant thee. Come, fill, fill.--So--again .	425	WAY WCRLD	III.1	32
Foible:	best Liveries, with the Coach-man and Postilion to fill up	444	WAY WCRLD	IV.1	5
Sir Wilful:	Prithee fill me the Glass	455	WAY WCRLD	IV.1	397

Fill'd (6)

	These Walls but t'other Day were fill'd with Noise . . .	315	FCR LCVE	EPI.	28
	And ncw they're fill'd with Jests, and Flights, and Bombast!	315	FCR LCVE	EPI.	31
Gonsalez:	But Tears of Joy. To see you thus, has fill'd . . .	332	M. EBIDE	I.1	273
Gonsalez:	But Tears of Joy. Believe me, Sir, tc see you thus,				
	has fill'd	332	M. EBIDE	I.1 V273
Almeria:	O thanks the liberal Hand that fill'd thee thus; . . .	382	M. EBIDE	V.2	259
Almeria:	Thanks to the liberal Hand that fill'd thee thus; . . .	382	M. EBIDE	V.2 V259

Filthy (12)

Belinda:	Commendation of that filthy, awkward, two-leg'd Creature,	54	OLD BATCH	II.2	5
Belinda:	Filthy Fellow! I wonder Cousin--	55	OLD BATCH	II.2	19
Lucy:	Beast, filthy Toad, I can hold no longer, look and . .	66	OLD EATCH	III.1	198
Belinda:	O monstrous filthy Fellow! Good slovenly Captain . . .	85	OLD BATCH	IV.3	86
Belinda:	O the filthy rude Beast!	107	OLD BATCH	V.1	398
Lady Froth:	--Ay my Dear--were you? Oh filthy Mr. Sneer;	165	DOUEL DLR	III.1	561
Mrs Frail:	O' my Soul, I'm afraid not--eh!--filthy	250	FOR LCVE	II.1	564
Lady Wish:	Me? What did the filthy Fellow say?	427	WAY WCRLD	III.1	92
Millamant:	He? Ay, and filthy Verses--So I am.	446	WAY WCRLD	IV.1	57
Millamant:	O horrid proviso's! filthy strong Waters! I toste . .	452	WAY WCRLD	IV.1	278
Millamant:	Eh! filthy creature--what was the quarrel?	454	WAY WCRLD	IV.1	358
Lady Wish:	and gcing to filthy Flays; and Profane Musick-meetings,	467	WAY WCRLD	V.1	199

Filthy-fellow (1)

Belinda:	Oh foh! What does the filthy-fellow mean? Lard, ...	109	OLD EATCH	V.2	59

Find (122)

Bellmour:	our Afternoon Service to our Mistresses; I find I am . .	40	OLD EATCH	I.1	132
Bellmour:	our Afternoon Services to our Mistresses; I find I am . .	40	OLD EATCH	I.1 V132
Capt Bluff:	O Lord I beg your pardon Sir, I find you are not of . .	51	OLD BATCH	II.1	162
Bellmour:	So Fortune be prais'd! To find you both within, ...	57	OLD BATCH	II.2	114
Araminta:	Nay ccme, I find we are growing serious, and	58	OLD BATCH	II.2	151
Bellmour:	Well, I find my Apishness has paid the Ransome	60	OLD BATCH	II.2	218
Bellmour:	Laughter; the ill-natur'd Town will find the Jest just where	63	OLD BATCH	III.1	90
Capt Bluff:	Husht, 'tis not so convenient ncw--I shall find a . . .	69	OLD BATCH	III.1	313
Heartwell:	I am--However, I find I am pretty sure of her consent, if .	73	OLD EATCH	III.2	97
Silvia:	Midwife, some nine Months hence--Well, I find dissembling,	75	OLD BATCH	III.2	150
Laetitia:	to find the meaning of it--	77	OLD BATCH	IV.1	86
Bellmour:	find it directed to Mr. Vainlove. Gad, Madam, I ask you a .	82	OLD BATCH	IV.2	57
Araminta:	to find me in discourse with you.--Be discreet.-- . . .	86	OLD BATCH	IV.3	105
Araminta:	find fcols, have the same advantage, over a Face in a Mask;	86	OLD BATCH	IV.3	117
Vainlove:	('tis true) where they find most Goodness to forgive.--	87	OLD BATCH	IV.3	138
Vainlove:	I find, Madam, the Fcrmality of the Law must be . . .	87	OLD BATCH	IV.3	152
Araminta:	and so you shall find.	87	OLD EATCH	IV.3	159
Araminta:	Still mystically senceless and impudent.--I find . . .	88	OLD BATCH	IV.3	185
Fondlewife:	Nay, I find you are both in a Story; that, I must . . .	93	OLD BATCH	IV.4	161
Vainlove:	--And why did you not find me out, to tell me this . .	99	OLD BATCH	V.1	120
Capt Bluff:	shall find he might have safer rous'd a sleeping Lion. . .	101	OLD EATCH	V.1	168
Setter:	Some by Experience find those Words misplac'd:	105	OLD BATCH	V.1	330
Belinda:	(to Bellmour). O my Conscience, I cou'd find in my . . .	106	OLD BATCH	V.1	364
Heartwell:	the Lcad of Life!--We hope to find	108	OLD BATCH	V.2	10
Belinda:	at the Month's End, you shall hardly find a Married-man, .	108	OLD BATCH	V.2	29
Heartwell:	you, Sir, I shall find a time; but take off your Wasp here, .	108	OLD BATCH	V.2	34
Sir Joseph:	Pray, Madam, Who are you? For I find, you and I . . .	111	OLD EATCH	V.2	131
Capt Bluff:	I plant Laurels for my Head abroad, I may find the Branches	111	OLD BATCH	V.2	148
Bellmour:	But there is a fatality in Marriage.--For I find I'm . .	111	OLD BATCH	V.2	155
	The Pcet's sure he shall some comfort find:	125	DOUEL DLR	PRO.	32
Lord Froth:	find Champagne is powerful. I assure you, Sir Paul, I . .	132	DOUEL DLR	I.1	191
Careless:	I find a Quibble bears more sway in your Lordships . .	132	DOUEL DLR	I.1	214
Brisk:	O Lord, why can't you find it out?--Why there	133	DOUEL DLR	I.1	248
Lady Froth:	Etymology.--But I'm the more amazed, to find you . . .	139	DOUEL DLR	II.1	40
Cynthia:	Then I find its like Cards, if either of us have a good .	142	DOUEL DLR	II.1	162
Singer:	Then too late, desire will find you, ...	143	DOUEL DLR	II.1	188
Sir Paul:	find Passion coming upon me by inspiration, and I cannot .	144	DOUEL DLR	II.1	207
Sir Paul:	find Passion coming upon me by inflation, and I cannot .	144	DOUEL DLR	II.1 V207
Maskwell:	May so much Fraud and Power of Baseness find? . . .	150	DOUEL DLR	II.1	468
Lord Touch:	find you so cold in his Defence.	151	DOUEL DLR	III.1	30
Lady Touch:	disadvantage; besides, I find, my Lord, you are prepared .	151	DOUEL DLR	III.1	36
Careless:	reason to complain of my Reception; but I find women are .	158	DOUBL DLR	III.1	307
Cynthia:	(aside). Well, I find there are no Fools so inconsiderable .	165	DOUEL DLR	III.1	577
Cynthia:	was the Devil, I'll allow for irresistable odds. But if				
	I find	169	DOUBL DLR	IV.1	59
Sir Paul:	so, I'm of that Opinion again; but I can neither find my .	171	DOUBL DLR	IV.1	157
Cynthia:	(aside). I'm amazed to find her of our side, for I'm .	171	DOUBL DLR	IV.1	161

Find   (continued)

Fine   (continued)
  Sir Joseph: fine weather.   90   OLD BATCH IV.4   37
  Sharper: fear.--A fine Lady, and a Lady of very good Quality. . . 111   OLD BATCH V.2   135
  Lady Froth: say'st right--for sure my Lord Froth is as fine a Gentleman, 139   DOUBL DLR II.1   28
  Maskwell: enough. Pox I have lost all Appetite to her; yet she's a
                   fine 155   DCUBL DLR III.1 175
  Maskwell: she smoke my design upon Cynthia, I were in a fine pickle. 155   DOUBL DLR III.1 180
  Lady Ply: Critick and so fine a Gentleman, that it is impossible for 159   DOUEL DLR III.1 344
  Sir Paul: Gad's bud, she's a fine person-- 159   DOUBL DLR III.1 347
  Lady Ply: So gay, so graceful, so good teeth, so fine shape, . . . 160   DCUBL DLR III.1 367
  Lady Ply: so fine limbs, so fine linen, and I don't doubt but you have 160   DOUEL DLR III.1 368
  Sir Paul: fine way of living, as I may say, peacefully and happily, 160   DOUEL DLR III.1 384
  Sir Paul: Blessing, a fine, discreet, well-spoken woman as you shall 160   DOUEL DLR III.1 387
  Sir Paul: Daughter, and a fine dutiful Child she is, though I say it, 161   DOUBL DLR III.1 412
  Careless: Lady's a fine likely Woman-- 161   DOUBL DLR III.1 420
  Sir Paul: Oh, a fine likely Woman as you shall see in a 161   DOUEL DLR III.1 421
  Cynthia: 'em; for these have Quality and Education, Wit and fine 167   DOUBL DLR III.1 627
  Lady Ply: And say so many fine things, and nothing is so moving to . 169   DOUBL DLR IV.1   70
  Lady Ply: me as a fine thing. Well, I must do you this justice, and 169   DOUBL DLR IV.1   71
  Lady Ply: Ah! Very fine. 170   DOUBL DLR IV.1   89
  Lady Ply: O that's so passionate and fine, I cannot hear it . . . 170   DOUBL DLR IV.1   97
  Maskwell: then were fine work indeed! her fury wou'd spare nothing, 190   DOUBL DLR V.1   93
  Jeremy: Humph, and so he has made a very fine Feast, where . . 216   FOR LCVE   I.1   21
  Jeremy: this fine Feeding: But if you please, I had rather be at 217   FOR LCVE   I.1   25
  Tattle: Upon my Soul Angelica's a fine Woman--And 228   FOR LCVE   I.1   456
  Scandal: Yes, Mrs. Frail is a very fine Woman, we all know . . . 228   FCB LCVE   I.1   458
  Valentine: have a fine time, whose Reputations are in your keeping. 229   FOR LCVE   I.1   503
  Mrs Frail: Hey day! I shall get a fine Reputation by coming . . . 230   FCR LCVE   I.1   546
  Mrs Frail: I shall get a fine Reputation by coming 230   FOR LCVE   I.1 V546
  Nurse: Miss I say, God's my Life, here's fine dcings towards-- 253   FCR LCVE   III.1   9
  Miss Prue: fine Gentleman, and a sweet Gentleman, that was here . . 264   FCR LCVE   III.1 415
  Sr Sampson: a Man that admires a fine Woman, as much as I do. . . 298   FCR LCVE   V.1   19
  Jeremy: 'Tis an Act of Charity, Sir, to save a fine Woman . . . 302   FOR LCVE   V.1   209
  Witwoud: I; fine Ladies I say. 406   WAY WCRLD I.1   405
  Petulant: A fine Gentleman, but he's silly withal. 408   WAY WCRLD I.1   506
  Mirabell: of gay fine Perrukes hovering round you. 418   WAY WCRLD II.1   330
  Marwood: one Suit, tho' never so fine. A Fool and a Doily Stuff . . 433   WAY WCRLD III.1 301
  Marwood: of the Play-house? A fine gay glossy Fool, shou'd be given 433   WAY WCRLD III.1 309
  Marwood: What pity 'tis, so much fine Raillery, and 434   WAY WCRLD III.1 345
  Foible: quarter of an hours lying and swearing to a fine Lady? 459   WAY WORLD IV.1   559
  Lady Wish: this Exceeds all precedent; I am brought to fine uses, to 463   WAY WCRLD V.1   50
  Sir Wilful: Cozen's a Fine Lady, and the Gentleman loves her and she 477   WAY WCRLD V.1   583
Finely (4)
  Lady Froth: O finely taken! I swear, now you are even with 202   DOUBL DLR V.1   541
  Mrs Frail: Wife? I should have been finely fobb'd indeed, very finely 286   FCR LCVE   IV.1   411
  Ben: senses, d'ee see; for ought as I perceive I'm like to be
                   finely 286   FCR LCVE   IV.1   414
Finery (1)
  Sir Joseph: Finery. 70   OLD BATCH III.1 335
Finest (1)
  Brisk: the finest night! 201   DCUEL ELB V.1   518
Finger (3)
  Maskwell: one of 'em have a finger in't, he promised me to be within 194   DOUBL DLR V.1   269
  Maskwell: one of them has a finger in't, he promised me to be within 194   DOUEL DIB V.1 V269
                                              (Set by Mr. Finger.) . . . 293   FCR LCVE   IV.1   651
Fingers (3)
  Mellefont: out Cuckoldom with her Fingers, and you're running . . . 187   DOUBL DLR IV.2   132
  Mincing: 'Till I had the Cremp in my Fingers I'll vow Mem. . . . 419   WAY WCRLD II.1   371
  Mincing: 'Till I had the Cramp in my Fingers I'll vow Mem. . . . 419   WAY WCRLD II.1 V371
Finish (1)
  Fainall: If you have a mind to finish his Picture, you have an . . 401   WAY WCRLD I.1   232
Finish'd (2)
  Fondlewife: --Heh! You have finish'd the matter, Heh? And I am, . . 94   OLD BATCH IV.4   183
  Scandal: Make Blest the Ripen'd Maid, and Finish'd Man. 275   FCR LCVE   III.1 820
Finishing (2)
  Bellmour: the finishing of an Alderman; it seems I must put the last 41   OLD EATCH I.1   157
  Maskwell: you please, defer the finishing of your Wit, and let us talk 194   DOUEL DLR V.1   278
Finns (1)
  Mrs Frail: whistled to by Winds; and thou art come forth with Finns . 286   FCR LCVE   IV.1   400
Fir'd (1)
  Almeria: And Heat of War, and dire Revenge, he fir'd. 329   M. EPIDE   I.1   114
Fircu (1)
  Sr Sampson: you, I have travel'd old Fircu, and know the Globe. I have 241   FOR LCVE   II.1   207
Fire (24)
  Sir Joseph: fire once out of the mouth of a Canon--agad he did; those 53   OLD BATCH II.1   219
  Belinda: endure the sight of a Fire this Twelvemonth. 59   OLD EATCH II.2   165
  Heartwell: more Consuming Fire, a Womans Arms. Ha! well 62   OLD BATCH III.1 69
  Lady Touch: For, by the Eternal Fire, you shall not scape my Vengance. 135   DOUEL DLR I.1   322
  Lady Touch: black!--O I have Excuses, Thousands for my Faults; Fire . 135   DOUEL DLR I.1   325
  Lady Touch: not met your Love with forward Fire? 137   DOUEL DLR I.1   373
  Maskwell: same Fire? Do you not Love him still? How have I this . . 137   DOUEL DLR I.1   387
  Mellefont: fire; but I shall counter-work her Spells, and ride the . 167   DOUEL DLR IV.1   4
  Lady Touch: the love of you, was the first wandring fire that e're
                   misled 185   DOUEL DLR IV.2   76
  Lady Touch: wild with this suprize of Treachery: Hell and Fire, it is 191   DOUBL DLR V.1   144
  Lady Touch: anothers Arms; oh! that I were Fire indeed, that I might . 191   DOUBL DLR V.1   151
  Lady Touch: Damnation proof, a Devil already, and Fire is his Element. 191   DOUEL DLR V.1 V153
  Angelica: Siege? What a World of Fire and Candle, Matches and . . 237   FCR LCVE   II.1   81
  Tattle: Letters writ in Juice of Lemon, for no Fire can fetch
                   it out. 292   FOR LCVE   IV.1   614
  Mrs Fore: I'm glad to hear you have so much Fire in 308   FOR LCVE   V.1   408
  Almeria: Thro' all Impediments, of purging Fire, ... 330   M. EBIDE   I.1   182
  Osmyn-Alph: O my Antonio, I am all on Fire, ... 351   M. EBIDE   III.1 80
  Mirabell: Rudeness and ill Language, Satyr and Fire. 401   WAY WORLD I.1   231
  Witwoud: Fellow has Fire and Life. 403   WAY WCBLD I.1   300
  Witwoud: O rare Petulant; thou art as quick as a Fire in a . . . 409   WAY WORLD I.1   519

First   (continued)

Speaker	Text	PAGE	TITLE	ACT.SC	LINE
Sr Sampson:	Sir, you must ask me leave first; that Lady, No,	311	FOR LCVE	V.1	V517
	Sure Providence at first, design'd this Place	315	FOR LCVE	EPI.	1
	Grant Heaven, we don't return tc our first Station.	315	FCR LCVE	EPI.	34
Almeria:	No, it shall never be; for I will die first,	330	M. BRIDE	I.1	175
Manuel:	When my first Foe was laid in Earth, such Enmity,	333	M. BRIDE	I.1	308
Zara:	For saving thee, when I beheld thee first,	346	M. BRIDE	II.2	275
Zara:	Think cn my Suff'ring first, then, look on me;	347	M. BRIDE	II.2	304
Selim:	The Heads of those who first began the Mutiny.	361	M. BRIDE	IV.1	14
Selim:	With them who first began the Mutiny.	361	M. BRIDE	IV.1	V 14
Gonsalez:	No matter--give me first to know the Cause	377	M. BRIDE	V.2	30
	Suffer'd at first some trifling Stakes to win:	393	WAY WCRLD	PRO.	12
Lady Wish:	first. Here, here, under the Table--What wou'dst	426	WAY WORLD	III.1	34
Foible:	He! I hope to see him lodge in Ludgate first, and Angle	428	WAY WORLD	III.1	137
Witwoud:	first, I say.	437	WAY WCRLD	III.1	478
Sir Wilful:	matter in Town, to learn somewhat of your Lingo first,	440	WAY WCRLD	III.1	582
Marwood:	an opportunity to part;--and now you have it. But first	442	WAY WCBLD	III.1	640
Marwood:	--But let the Mine be sprung first, and then I care not if	444	WAY WCRLD	III.1	706
Lady Wish:	figure shall I give his Heart the first Impression?	444			
	There is a	445	WAY WCRLD	IV.1	18
Lady Wish:	great deal in the first Impressicn. Shall I sit?--No I	445	WAY WORLD	IV.1	19
Lady Wish:	Yes, yes, I'll give the first Impression on a Couch--I wont	445	WAY WCRLD	IV.1	24
Sir Wilful:	somewhat wary at first, before I am acquainted;--But I	446	WAY WCRLD	IV.1	75
Millamant:	an Air. Ah! I'll never marry, unless I am first	449	WAY WCRLD	IV.1	180
Mirabell:	will ycu be contented with the first now, and stay for the	449	WAY WCBLD	IV.1	183
Millamant:	Francis: Nor goe to Hide-Park together the first Sunday in	450	WAY WCRLD	IV.1	202
Millamant:	of one another the first Week, and asham'd of one another	450	WAY WCRLD	IV.1	205
Millamant:	presume to approach without first asking leave. And	450	WAY WCRLD	IV.1	223
Waitwell:	I told you at first I knew the hand--A Womans	460	WAY WORLD	IV.1	600
Foible:	me; I am not the first that he has wheadl'd with his	463	WAY WCRLD	V.1	26
Foible:	first, to secure your Lady-ship. He cou'd not have bedded	463	WAY WCRLD	V.1	41
Marwood:	Let us first dispatch the affair in hand Madam,	465	WAY WCRLD	V.1	136
Lady Wish:	not out.--Ah! her first Husband my Son Languish,	469	WAY WCRLD	V.1	304
Mirabell:	Let me be pitied first; and afterwards forgotten,	471	WAY WCRLD	V.1	378
Fainall:	Insist upon my first proposal. You shall submit your own	473	WAY WCRLD	V.1	434
Lady Wish:	--and I must perform mine.--First I pardcn for	477	WAY WORLD	V.1	573

First-fruit (1)

	The First-fruit Offering, of a Virgin Play.	213	FOR LCVE	PRO.	25

Fish (6)

Setter:	Ay, I know her, Sir: At least, I'm sure I can fish it out	99	OLD BATCH	V.1	103
	Criticks avaunt; for you are Fish of Prey,	125	DOUBL DLR	PRO.	12
Mrs Frail:	Fish cf prey.	286	FOR LCVE	IV.1	402
Sr Sampson:	your Element, Fish, be mute, Fish, and to Sea, rule your	308	FOR LCVE	V.1	418
Witwoud:	as drunk and as mute as a Fish.	453	WAY WCRLD	IV.1	338

Fishing (0)   see Whale-fishing

Fishmcnger (1)

Witwoud:	a Quaker hates a Parrot, or than a Fishmonger hates a	408	WAY WORLD	I.1	485

Fists (1)

Belinda:	Hold off your Fists, and see that he gets a Chair with	57	OLD BATCH	II.2	95

Fit (39)

Bellmour:	A very even Temper and fit for my purpose. I must	40	OLD BATCH	I.1	111
Vainlove:	will, for you have made him fit for no Body else--Well--	40	OLD BATCH	I.1	114
Sharper:	that's all thou art fit for now.	43	OLD BATCH	I.1	228
Capt Bluff:	your Jesuits Powder for a shaking fit--But who hast thou	51	OLD BATCH	I.1	147
Heartwell:	and in some raving fit, be led tc plunge my self into that	62	OLD BATCH	III.1	68
Bellmour:	Well and how Setter hae, does my Hypocrisy fit me hae?	75	OLD BATCH	IV.1	3
Vainlove:	'Tis fit Men should be coy, when Women woo.	80	OLD BATCH	IV.1	191
Bellmour:	may lie down;--quickly, for I'm afraid I shall have a Fit.	82	OLD BATCH	IV.2	87
Laetitia:	Bless me! What Fit?	82	OLD BATCH	IV.2	88
Bellmour:	Fit will be soon over.	83	OLD BATCH	IV.2	93
Laetitia:	Spin-text, has a sad Fit of the Cholick, and is forced				
	to lie	91	OLD BATCH	IV.4	78
Bellmour:	Fit of the Cholick, to excuse my lying down upon your	94	OLD BATCH	IV.4	211
Sir Joseph:	Ay; Do, do, Captain, if you think fit.--You	101	OLD BATCH	V.1	183
Bellmour:	That they are fit for no Ccmpany but their Wives.	108	OLD BATCH	V.2	27
Lady Touch:	think fit.	137	DOUBL DLR	I.1	409
Lady Ply:	and uncontroulable? Is it fit a Woman of my Spirit, and	144	DOUBL DLR	II.1	217
Sir Paul:	fit for nothing but to be a Stalking-Horse, to stand before	145	DOUBL DLR	II.1	266
Lady Touch:	not fit to be tcld you.	151	DOUBL DLB	III.1	43
Lord Touch:	Not fit to be told me, Madam? Ycu can have no Interests,	152	DOUBL DLR	III.1	46
Maskwell:	here before me; but 'tis fit I should be still behind hand,	183	DOUEL DLR	IV.2	14
Foresight:	I'm so perplex'd and vex'd, I am not fit to receive	239	FOR LCVE	II.1	164
Sr Sampson:	and my Fatherly fondness wcu'd fit like two Tallies.--	243	FCB LCVE	II.1	294
Tattle:	Quality that shall be nameless, in a raging Fit of				
	Jealousie,	258	FCR LCVE	III.1	175
Angelica:	(aside). Aye, but if I don't fit you, I'll be hang'd.	294	FOR LCVE	IV.1	699
Manuel:	A Fit cf Bridal Fear; How is't, Almeria?	334	M. BRIDE	I.1	V348
Manuel:	Fit restitution here--Thus, I release you,	336	M. BRIDE	I.1	413
Osmyn-Alph:	My Friend and Counsellour; as thou think'st fit,	352	M. BRIDE	III.1	104
Zara:	I think it fit to tell you that your Guards	364	M. BRIDE	IV.1	142
Zara:	Of that hereafter; but, mean time, 'tis fit	365	M. BRIDE	IV.1	161
Zara:	Think fit, I'll leave thee my Command to die.	375	M. BRIDE	V.1	127
Gonsalez:	'Twere fit the Soldiers were amuz'd, mean time,	378	M. BRIDE	V.2	102
Gonsalez:	'Twere fit the Soldiers were amus'd, with Hopes;	378	M. BRIDE	V.2	V102
Osmyn-Alph:	Nay, I must grant, 'tis fit you shou'd be thus--	383	M. BRIDE	V.2	309
Mirabell:	Where Modesty's ill Manners, 'tis but fit	409	WAY WCRLD	I.1	541
Foible:	but (says he) I'll fit you for that, I warrant you (says he)	428	WAY WORLD	III.1	114
Marwood:	a very fit Match. He may Travel afterwards. 'Tis a Thing	432	WAY WCBLD	III.1	267
Mincing:	I vow Mem, I thought once they wou'd have fit.	432	WAY WCBLD	III.1	295
Lady Wish:	the Turks--for thou are not fit to live in a Christian	456	WAY WORLD	IV.1	440
	Tho' they're on no pretence for Judgment fit	479	WAY WORLD	EPI.	12

Fits (4)

Bellmour:	Truth on't is she fits his temper best, is a kind of	42	OLD BATCH	I.1	205
Mrs Fore:	if in cne of his mad fits he will bring you to him in her	288	FOR LCVE	IV.1	471
Gonsalez:	By fits reveals--his Face seems turn'd to favour	376	M. BRIDE	V.2	8
Mrs Fain:	wou'd fall into fits, and maybe not recover time enough to	452	WAY WORLD	IV.1	301

Fled (8)
Singer:	The hasty Joy, in strugling fled.	71	OLD BATCH	III.2 V	16
Sharper:	see, the Owls are fled, as at the break of Day.	86	OLD BATCH	IV.3	128
Selim:	'Tis certain Heli too is fled, and with him	361	M. BRIDE	IV.1	8
Gonsalez:	In Roderigo's House, who fled with him.	363	M. BRIDE	IV.1	76
Gonsalez:	They who are fled have that way bent their course. . . .	363	M. BRIDE	IV.1	80
Manuel:	This Tumult, and the Lords who fled with Heli, . . .	366	M. BRIDE	IV.1	215
Garcia:	Are through a Postern fled, and join the Foe.	377	M. BRIDE	V.2	39
Alonzo:	My Lord, for certain truth, Perez is fled;	377	M. BRIDE	V.2	48

Fleece (1)
| Fondlewife: | Fleece here!--You don't love Mutton?--you Magdalen . . . | 93 | OLD BATCH | IV.4 | 145 |

Fleecy (1)
| Gonsalez: | White as the fleecy Rain on Alpine Hills; . . . . . | 331 | M. BRIDE | I.1 | 231 |

Fleering (1)
| Heartwell: | fleering Coxcomb scoff and cry, Mr. your Son's mighty . . | 45 | OLD BATCH | I.1 | 320 |

Fleers (1)
| Foible: | With his Taunts and his Fleers, tossing up his Nose. Humh . | 427 | WAY WORLD | III.1 | 94 |

Fleet (3)
Sr Sampson:	but a new Tax, and the loss of the Canary Fleet. . . .	266	FOR LOVE	III.1	486
Sr Sampson:	but a new Tax, or the loss of the Canary Fleet. . . .	266	FOR LOVE	III.1 V	486
Sr Sampson:	French Fleet were at Anchor at Blackwall.	266	FOR LOVE	III.1	488

Flesh (1b)   see Womans-flesh
Bellmour:	Flesh and Blood cannot bear it always.	41	OLD BATCH	I.1	145
Fondlewife:	I'm afraid, 'tis the Flesh, thou Harlot. Deare, with				
	the Pox.	92	OLD BATCH	IV.4	136
Sir Joseph:	may dispose of your own Flesh as you think fitting, d'ye .	101	OLD BATCH	V.1	184
Careless:	wanton. Maskwell is Flesh and Blood at best, and				
	opportunities	131	DOUBL DLR	I.1	162
Cynthia:	Wife One Flesh, it leaves 'em still Two Fools; and they .	142	DOUBL DLR	I.1	151
	But since in Paradise frail Flesh gave way, ...	213	FOR LOVE	PRO.	18
Valentine:	your Flesh; Read, and take your Nourishment in at your .	216	FOR LOVE	I.1	14
Ben:	o' Nine-tails laid cross your Shoulders. Flesh! who are .	264	FOR LOVE	III.1	409
Ben:	break her Cable in a storm, as well as I love her.				
	Flesh, you	273	FOR LOVE	III.1	731
Ben:	All mad, I think--Flesh, I believe all the Calentures of .	285	FOR LOVE	IV.1	356
Almeria:	And eat into thy Flesh, festring thy Limbs	356	M. BRIDE	III.1	268
Almeria:	This weak and tender Flesh, to have been bruis'd . . .	369	M. BRIDE	IV.1	312
Almeria:	And cloath their Nakedness with my own Flesh; . . .	370	M. BRIDE	IV.1	350
Almeria:	But spouting Veins, and mangled Flesh! O, O. . . .	382	M. BRIDE	V.2	272
Lady Wish:	shoud'st be my Child, Bone of my Bone, and Flesh of .	465	WAY WORLD	V.1	140
Lady Wish:	my Flesh, and as I may say, another Me, and yet transgress	465	WAY WORLD	V.1	141

Flesh-wounds (1)
| Mrs Frail: | With all my heart, ours are but slight Flesh-wounds, . | 248 | FOR LOVE | II.1 | 480 |

Flew (1)
| Mellefont: | Bed-side like a Fury, she flew to my Sword, and with . | 130 | DOUBL DLR | I.1 | 114 |

Flies (1)
| Belinda: | kept open, for the Entertainment of travelling Flies. . . | 84 | OLD BATCH | IV.3 | 48 |

Flight (4)
Mellefont:	heavy and retard your flight.	184	DOUBL DLR	IV.2	56
Almeria:	Who knew our Flight, we closely were pursu'd, . . .	329	M. BRIDE	I.1	123
Almeria:	And all the Damps of Grief, that did retard their Flight; .	330	M. BRIDE	I.1	158
Zara:	Soul of my Love, and I will wait thy flight.	381	M. BRIDE	V.2	201

Flights (1)
| | And now they're fill'd with Jests, and Flights, and Bombast! | 315 | FOR LOVE | EPI. | 31 |

Flincher (1)
| Mellefont: | Ned, Ned, whither so fast? What, turn'd flincher! . . . | 127 | DOUBL DLR | I.1 | 1 |

Fling (3)
Bellmour:	Sinner, she's innocent, for me. Go to him, Madam, fling .	95	OLD BATCH	IV.4	236
Valentine:	Pox on her, cou'd she find no other time to fling .	221	FOR LOVE	I.1	207
Foible:	had a Fling at your Ladyship too; and then I could not .	427	WAY WORLD	III.1	90

Flinging (1)
| Maskwell: | Rogue still, to do you Service; and you are flinging . | 136 | DOUBL DLR | I.1 | 337 |

Flings (1)
| Vainlove: | have a Lure may make you stoop. (Flings a Letter.) . | 38 | OLD BATCH | I.1 | 31 |

Flint (3)
Almeria:	Than Trees, or Flint? O Force of constant Woe! . . .	326	M. BRIDE	I.1	7
Zara:	This Heart of Flint, 'till it shall bleed; and thou .	353	M. BRIDE	III.1	167
Osmyn-Alph:	Thy Errour then is plain: but I were Flint	383	M. BRIDE	V.2	313

Flinty (2)
| Osmyn-Alph: | Break on the flinty Ground my throbbing Breast, . . . | 358 | M. BRIDE | III.1 | 352 |
| Osmyn-Alph: | Break on the flinty Floor my throbbing Breast, . . . | 358 | M. BRIDE | III.1 V | 352 |

Flip (1)
| Ben: | Thus we live at Sea; eat Bisket, and drink Flip; put on a . | 275 | FOR LOVE | III.1 | 800 |

Flirt (0)   see Jill-flirt

Float (1)
| Almeria: | In liquid Light, and float on Seas of Bliss . . . . . | 340 | M. BRIDE | II.2 | 28 |

Floating (3)
Bellmour:	floating Island; sometimes seems in reach, then vanishes .	42	OLD BATCH	I.1	206
Sir Joseph:	the recollection of my errour, and leave me floating .	49	OLD BATCH	II.1	58
Almeria:	The Shoal, and save me floating on the Waves, . . .	329	M. BRIDE	I.1	130

Flock (1)
| Mirabell: | us'd to have the Beau-mond Throng after you; and a Flock . | 418 | WAY WORLD | II.1 | 329 |

Flocks (1)
| Scandal: | of my Love. And d'ee hear, bid Margery put more Flocks . | 222 | FOR LOVE | I.1 | 218 |

Flood (1)   see Flouds
| Sr Sampson: | your Antideluvian Families, Fellows, that the Flood could . | 298 | FOR LOVE | V.1 | 40 |

Floor (1)
| Osmyn-Alph: | Break on the flinty Floor my throbbing Breast, ... | 358 | M. BRIDE | III.1 V | 352 |

Flouds (1)
| | What Crops of Coxcombs, or what Flouds of Fools. . . . | 323 | M. BRIDE | PRO. | 12 |

Flounder (1)
| Mellefont: | flounder your self a weary, and be nevertheless my Prisoner. | 184 | DOUBL DLR | IV.2 | 52 |

Flounder-man's (1)
| Marwood: | loud Flounder-man's . . . . | 468 | WAY WORLD | V.1 | 234 |

Flourish (4)
| | (Flourish.) . . . . | 332 | M. BRIDE | I.1 | 262 |

Fond   (continued)
Lady Touch:	punish your fond, rash Contempt! Again smile!	198	DOUBL DLR	V.1	392
Maskwell:	lov'd Embraces, could e're be fond of an inferiour Slavery.	198	DOUBL DLR	V.1	426
Nurse:	home yet: Poor Child, I warrant she's fond o'seeing the	235	FOR LOVE	II.1	20
Foresight:	Ne marl, if it be fruitful fond.	236	FOR LOVE	II.1	56
Sr Sampson:	your Wits,--You were always fond of the Wits,--	246	FOR LOVE	II.1	400
Mrs Fore:	is design'd for his Wife, is grown fond of Mr. Tattle;	248	FOR LOVE	II.1	500
Mrs Fore:	is design'd to be his Wife, is grown fond of Mr. Tattle;	248	FOR LOVE	II.1	V500
Mrs Fore:	fond of it, as of being first in the Fashion, or of seeing				
	a new	250	FOR LOVE	II.1	549
Manuel:	Away begon thou feeble Boy, fond Love,	374	M. BRIDE	V.1	62
Fainall:	that fond discovery--that had been forfeited, had they been	442	WAY WORLD	III.1	644
Mrs Fain:	You are very fond of Sir John Suckling to day,	446	WAY WORLD	IV.1	55
Millamant:	or fond, nor kiss before folks, like my Lady Fadler and Sr.	450	WAY WORLD	IV.1	201

Ponder (1)
Fondlewife:	Yes--Why then!--Ay, but to say truth, She's fonder of	77	OLD BATCH	IV.1	59

Fondest (1)
Fondlewife:	--Nay look you now if she does not weep--'tis the fondest	78	OLD BATCH	IV.1	98

Fondlewife (14)
Vainlove:	if you can make Alderman Fondlewife of your Perswasion,	39	OLD BATCH	I.1	69
Vainlove:	for me, this Evening; when Fondlewife will be gone out	39	OLD BATCH	I.1	79
Bellmour:	Prithee, what sort of Fellow is Fondlewife?	40	OLD BATCH	I.1	105
Sir Joseph:	Fondlewife, as far as two hundred Pound, and this Afternoon	51	OLD BATCH	II.1	133
Capt Bluff:	You have given him a note upon Fondlewife for a	67	OLD BATCH	III.1	245
Setter:	S'bud Sir, away quickly, there's Fondlewife just turn'd	75	OLD BATCH	IV.1	9
	(Enter Fondlewife and Barnaby.)	75	OLD BATCH	IV.1	13
Sir Joseph:	Night on't.--I'll go to Alderman Fondlewife by-and-by,	85	OLD BATCH	IV.3	62
	(Enter Fondlewife, and Sir Joseph.)	89	OLD BATCH	IV.4	22
	(Enter Fondlewife.)	90	OLD BATCH	IV.4	41
	(As Fondlewife is going into the Chamber, she runs to Sir	90	OLD BATCH	IV.4	49
Laetitia:	'Tis no body but Mr. Fondlewife, Mr. Spin-text, lie	91	OLD BATCH	IV.4	85
	(Fondlewife returns with Papers.)	91	OLD BATCH	IV.4	93
	(Fondlewife haling out Bellmour.)	92	OLD BATCH	IV.4	120

Fondlewife's (3)
	(Scene changes to a chamber in Fondlewife's House.	80	OLD BATCH	IV.2	
	(Scene changes to a Chamber in Fondlewife's House.	89	OLD BATCH	IV.4	
	kisses her hand, behind Fondlewife's back.)	95	OLD BATCH	IV.4	242

Fondly (1)
	And fondly hopes for rich and generous Fruit,	213	FOR LOVE	PRO.	3

Fondness (11)
Bellmour:	Fondness and Impatience of his Absence, by choosing a	38	OLD BATCH	I.1	57
Vainlove:	way; much addicted to Jealousie, but more to Fondness:	40	OLD BATCH	I.1	108
Laetitia:	Well--well--You know my Fondness, and you love to	77	OLD BATCH	IV.1	90
Mellefont:	Cynthia has such a share in his Fatherly fondness, he would	130	DOUBL DLR	I.1	139
Valentine:	you, cut of Fatherly fondness, will be pleas'd to add, shall	243	FOR LOVE	II.1	291
Sr Sampson:	and my Fatherly fondness wou'd fit like two Tallies.--	243	FOR LOVE	II.1	294
Angelica:	turn to an extream Fondness, you must not suspect it.	313	FOR LOVE	V.1	607
Valentine:	doat on at that immoderate rate, that your Fondness shall	313	FOR LOVE	V.1	609
Valentine:	doat on at that immoderate Degree, that your Fondness shall	313	FOR LOVE	V.1	V609
Gonsalez:	Of a Father's Fondness, these Ills arose;	378	M. BRIDE	V.2	82
Mirabell:	partial Opinion and fondness of you, she cou'd never have	476	WAY WORLD	V.1	543

Fool (74)
Heartwell:	And proves that Vainlove plays the Fool with	42	OLD BATCH	I.1	216
Heartwell:	No, besides my Business, I see a Fool coming this	46	OLD BATCH	I.1	335
Bellmour:	Why a Fool.	46	OLD BATCH	I.1	342
Sir Joseph:	Well I am a Fool sometimes--But I'm sorry.	54	OLD BATCH	II.1	244
Heartwell:	(aside). That a Fool should ask such a malicious	73	OLD BATCH	III.2	95
Silvia:	No, no, I'm not such a Fool neither but I can keep my	73	OLD BATCH	III.2	109
Heartwell:	Why every Man plays the Fool once in his Life: But to	74	OLD BATCH	III.2	117
Heartwell:	Marry, is playing the Fool all ones Life long.	74	OLD BATCH	III.2	118
Fondlewife:	Fool--	78	OLD BATCH	IV.1	99
Laetitia:	would get another Wife--Another fond Fool, to break her	78	OLD BATCH	IV.1	107
Fondlewife:	He, he, he, wilt thou poor Fool? Then I will go,	79	OLD BATCH	IV.1	134
Belinda:	Oh Gad, here comes the Fool that din'd at my Lady	84	OLD BATCH	IV.3	55
Araminta:	(aside). I hope my Fool has not Confidence enough	85	OLD BATCH	IV.3	92
Araminta:	Vainlove to know us, I'll be rid of my Fool by fair means	86	OLD BATCH	IV.3	102
Laetitia:	Ha! This fool may be of use. Stand off, rude Ruffian.	90	OLD BATCH	IV.4	46
Sharper:	Heh! Sure, Fortune has sent this Fool hither on	101	OLD BATCH	V.1	163
Sharper:	Impossible! Araminta take a liking to a Fool!	102	OLD BATCH	V.1	196
Heartwell:	hold:--If he shou'd not, I were a Fool to discover it.--	104	OLD BATCH	V.1	299
	--That deserves a Fool with a better Title.--	111	OLD BATCH	V.2	137
Vainlove:	Now that's at stake--No fool, 'tis out o'fashion.	113	OLD BATCH	EPI.	12
	To be before-hand still, and cry Fool first.	113	OLD BATCH	EPI.	22
Mellefont:	to have Wit, that thou may'st seem a Fool.	129	DOUBL DLR	I.1	72
Lord Froth:	Barbarous! I'd as lieve you call'd me Fool.	132	DOUBL DLR	I.1	186
Maskwell:	will be made a Fool of by no body, but himself: Ha, ha, ha.	150	DOUBL DLR	II.1	456
Mellefont:	her, till he has been fool enough to think of her out of her	159	DOUBL DLR	III.1	317
Cynthia:	Yes, my Lord--(aside) I must humour this Fool.	162	DOUBL DLR	III.1	468
Lady Froth:	can't hit her Name; the old fat Fool that Paints so	166	DOUBL DLR	III.1	581
Lady Touch:	that you're a Fool, Brother?	192	DOUBL DLR	V.1	166
Sir Paul:	A Fool; he, he, he, you're merry--no, no, not	192	DOUBL DLR	V.1	167
Sir Paul:	a Fool.	192	DOUBL DLR	V.1	178
Lady Touch:	Fool, Sot, insensible Ox! but remember	192	DOUBL DLR	V.1	191
Valentine:	Sense, and you are a Fool.	217	FOR LOVE	I.1	39
Jeremy:	Aye, Sir, I am a Fool, I know it: And yet, Heav'n	217	FOR LOVE	I.1	40
Jeremy:	always a Fool, when I told you what your Expences would	217	FOR LOVE	I.1	42
Jeremy:	a wealthy Fool.	219	FOR LOVE	I.1	115
Scandal:	Fortunes either expect another great Fortune, or a Fool.	225	FOR LOVE	I.1	354
Mrs Frail:	Old Fool! He would have perswaded me, that this was an	231	FOR LOVE	I.1	580
Valentine:	Weatherheaded fool, I know how to laugh at him; but	244	FOR LOVE	II.1	312
Tattle:	Foresight mean by this Civility? Is it to make a Fool of me?	251	FOR LOVE	II.1	592
Scandal:	neither Deform'd, nor a Fool.	272	FOR LOVE	III.1	691
Jeremy:	playing the Madman, won't make her play the Fool, and	276	FOR LOVE	IV.1	9
Scandal:	and be content only to be made a Fool with other reasonable	278	FOR LOVE	IV.1	107
Valentine:	I make a Fool of my Father.	283	FOR LOVE	IV.1	272
Ben:	marry himself. Gad, says I, an you play the fool and marry	286	FOR LOVE	IV.1	382

Fool   (continued)

Speaker	Text		PAGE	TITLE	ACT.SC	LINE
Ben:	d'ee mean all this while, to make a fool of me?	. . . .	287	FOR LOVE	IV.1	427
Mrs Frail:	Any fool, but a Husband.		287	FOR LOVE	IV.1	428
Angelica:	the Fool you take me for; and you are Mad and don't	.	296	FOR LOVE	IV.1	792
Angelica:	would neither have an absolute Wit, nor a Fool. . .	.	299	FOR LOVE	V.1	64
Sr Sampson:	Fool in the Eye of the World, is a very hard Task. But,		299	FOR LOVE	V.1	67
Sr Sampson:	Wit and a Fool.		299	FOR LOVE	V.1	69
Angelica:	She that marries a Fool, Sir Sampson, commits the	. .	299	FOR LOVE	V.1	70
Angelica:	She that marries a Fool, Sir Sampson, forfeits the	.	299	FOR LOVE	V.1 V	70
Valentine:	No; here's the Fool; and if occasion be, I'll give it	.	310	FOR LOVE	V.1	497
Sr Sampson:	You're an illiterate Fool, and I'm another, and	. . .	313	FOR LOVE	V.1	583
Sr Sampson:	You're an illiterate Fool, and I'm another,	. . . .	313	FOR LOVE	V.1 V583	
Gonsalez:	O Wretch! O curs'd, and rash, deluded Fool!	. . . .	378	M. BRIDE	V.2	68
	Should he by chance a Knave or Fool expose,	. . . .	393	WAY WORLD	PRO.	35
Mirabell:	Fool, can have but one Reason for associating with a	.	399	WAY WORLD	I.1	146
Mirabell:	and his common place of Comparisons. He is a Fool with	.	401	WAY WORLD	I.1	224
Witwoud:	from the Fool my Brother, as heavy as a Panegyrick in a	.	401	WAY WORLD	I.1	245
Mirabell:	A Fool, and your Brother, Witwoud!	.	402	WAY WORLD	I.1	249
Mirabell:	Then 'tis possible he may be but half a Fool. . .	.	402	WAY WORLD	I.1	252
Mirabell:	I never knew a Fool but he affected to complain, either of	.	402	WAY WORLD	I.1	276
Witwoud:	do with the Fool?	.	409	WAY WORLD	I.1	516
Mirabell:	as a Mortification; for sure to please a Fool is some degree		421	WAY WORLD	II.1	439
Mirabell:	Dictates of Reason, and yet persevere to play the Fool by		423	WAY WORLD	II.1	500
Lady Wish:	Ratifia, Fool? No Fool. Not the Ratifia Fool--	.	425	WAY WORLD	III.1	11
Marwood:	one Suit, tho' never so fine. A Fool and a Doily Stuff	.	433	WAY WORLD	III.1	301
Marwood:	of the Play-house? A fine gay glossy Fool, shou'd be given		433	WAY WORLD	III.1	309
Sir Wilful:	The Fashion's a Fool; and you're a Fop, dear	. . .	439	WAY WORLD	III.1	538
Millamant:	to undergo a Fool, thou art Married and hast Patience--I	.	446	WAY WORLD	IV.1	65
	And furnish Fool enough to entertain.	.	479	WAY WORLD	EPI.	27

Fool'd (1)

Fainall:	Madam, I'll be fool'd no longer.		475	WAY WORLD	V.1	503

Fool's (1)

Marwood:	over, and we have done with the Disguise. For a Fool's	.	433	WAY WORLD	III.1	311

Fooling (2)

Osmyn-Alph:	Fooling the Follower, betwixt Shade and Shining.	. . .	350	M. BRIDE	III.1	38
Marwood:	This is precious Fooling, if it wou'd pass, but . .		471	WAY WORLD	V.1	354

Foolish (6)

Setter:	above it. So that Reputation is e'en as foolish	. . .	102	OLD BATCH	V.1	232
Lord Froth:	when any of their foolish Wit prevails upon the side	. .	133	DOUBL DLR	I.1	229
Careless:	Excessively foolish--But that which gives me most	. .	158	DOUBL DLR	III.1	295
Tattle:	(aside). O Pox, how shall I get rid of this foolish Girl?	.	303	FOR LOVE	V.1	225
Tattle:	one another now--Fshaw, that would be a foolish	. . .	303	FOR LOVE	V.1	242
Millamant:	--That foolish trifle of a heart--Sir Wilfull! . .		447	WAY WORLD	IV.1	101

Fools (37)   see April-fools

Bellmour:	to Fools; they have need of 'em: Wit, be my Faculty;	. .	37	OLD BATCH	I.1	23
Heartwell:	of thy Sex, if their Fools are not known by this					
	Party-coloured		73	OLD BATCH	III.2	77
Araminta:	find fools, have the same advantage, over a Face in a Mask;		86	OLD BATCH	IV.3	117
Careless:	No faith, but your Fools grow noisy--and if a	. . .	127	DOUBL DLR	I.1	7
Careless:	No faith, but your Fools grow noisie--and if a	. . .	127	DOUBL DLR	I.1 V	7
Cynthia:	Wife One Flesh, it leaves 'em still Two Fools; and they	.	142	DOUBL DLR	II.1	151
Mellefont:	That's only when Two Fools meet, and their	. . .	142	DOUBL DLR	II.1	153
Cynthia:	as Fools. 'Tis an odd Game we're going to Play at: What	.	142	DOUBL DLR	II.1	157
Maskwell:	Fools! then that hungry Gudgeon Credulity, will bite at	.	150	DOUBL DLR	II.1	459
Maskwell:	Why will Mankind be Fools, and be deceiv'd?	. . .	150	DOUBL DLR	II.1	465
Cynthia:	(aside). Well, I find there are no Fools so inconsiderable		165	DOUBL DLR	III.1	577
Cynthia:	Affliction, as to dissemble Mirth in Company of Fools--		167	DOUBL DLR	III.1	625
Cynthia:	Why should I call 'em Fools? The World thinks better of	.	167	DOUBL DLR	III.1	626
Cynthia:	The Wise are Wretched, and Fools only Bless'd.		167	DOUBL DLR	III.1	634
	They hold their Pens, as Swords are held by Fools,	. .	214	FOR LOVE	PRO.	37
Sr Sampson:	the matter is with him, or I'll crack your Fools Skull.	.	279	FOR LOVE	IV.1	136
Sr Sampson:	we are Fools as we use to be--Oons, that you cou'd	. .	283	FOR LOVE	IV.1	280
Valentine:	morrow, Knaves will thrive thro' craft, and Fools thro'		288	FOR LOVE	IV.1	492
	What Crops of Coxcombs, or what Flouds of Fools.	. .	323	M. BRIDE	PRO.	12
Zara:	O Fate of Fools! officious in Contriving;	.	375	M. BRIDE	V.1	111
	Of those few Fools, who with ill Stars are curs'd,	. . .	393	WAY WORLD	PRO.	1
	Sure scribbling Fools, call'd Poets, fare the worst.	. .	393	WAY WORLD	PRO.	2
	For they're a sort of Fools which Fortune makes,	. . .	393	WAY WORLD	PRO.	3
	And after she has made 'em Fools, forsakes. . . .	.	393	WAY WORLD	PRO.	4
Mirabell:	Fools.		400	WAY WORLD	I.1	206
Mirabell:	and her Streamers out, and a shoal of Fools for Tenders	.	418	WAY WORLD	II.1	324
Mirabell:	and Streamers out, and a shoal of Fools for Tenders	.	418	WAY WORLD	II.1 V324	
Mirabell:	Fools; Things who visit you from their excessive Idleness;		421	WAY WORLD	II.1	434
Millamant:	converse with Fools, is for my Health.	.	421	WAY WORLD	II.1	442
Mirabell:	Conversation of Fools?		421	WAY WORLD	II.1	444
Millamant:	Yes, the Vapours; Fools are Physicks for it, next	. . .	421	WAY WORLD	II.1	445
Mirabell:	You are not in a Course of Fools?		421	WAY WORLD	II.1	447
Millamant:	alike; but Fools never wear out--they are such Drap-du-berry	433	WAY WORLD	III.1	305
Fainall:	The Wise too Jealous are, Fools too secure.	. . .	444	WAY WORLD	III.1	725
Millamant:	acquaintance; or to be intimate with Fools, because they	.	450	WAY WORLD	IV.1	218
Sir Wilful:	Let Mahometan Fools		456	WAY WORLD	IV.1	452
	To think themselves alone the Fools design'd:	. . .	479	WAY WORLD	EPI.	24

Foot (11)   see Bare-foot

Bellmour:	work'd themselves six foot deep into a Grave--	. . .	38	OLD BATCH	I.1	26
Lucy:	Here's some Villany a Foot he's so thoughtful; may be I	.	65	OLD BATCH	III.1	154
Valentine:	And the prettiest Foot! Oh if a Man could but fasten his	.	223	FOR LOVE	I.1	286
Sr Sampson:	Foot; have kiss'd the Great Mogul's Slipper, and rid a	.	241	FOR LOVE	II.1	220
Sir Wilful:	And a Hare's Foot, and a Hare's Scut for your Service, Sir;		439	WAY WORLD	III.1	524
Lady Wish:	lie neither but loll and lean upon one Elbow; with one Foot		445	WAY WORLD	IV.1	25
Lady Wish:	some Confusion.--It shows the Foot to advantage, and	.	445	WAY WORLD	IV.1	30
Millamant:	were wavering at the grate of a Monastery, with one foot	.	449	WAY WORLD	IV.1	163
Lady Wish:	Amour and put your best foot foremost--		455	WAY WORLD	IV.1	393
Lady Wish:	her foot within the door of a Play-house. O my dear	.	467	WAY WORLD	V.1	205
Lady Wish:	her foot within the door of a Play-house. O dear	.	467	WAY WORLD	V.1 V205	

Foot-men (1)

Foible:	and plac'd the Foot-men in a Row in the Hall, in their	.	444	WAY WORLD	IV.1	4

Force   (continued)
    Laetitia: kiss from me by main force.   90   OLD BATCH IV.4   54
    Vainlove: force, I'll win her, or weary her into a Forgiveness. . . 100   OLD BATCH V.1   127
    Cynthia: Touchwood, as you boasted, and force her to give her   .   169   DOUEL DLR IV.1   48
    Scandal: the force of open honest Satire.   220   FOR LCVE   I.1   150
    Valentine: of Confinement, and absence frcm Angelica, force me to   . 225   FOR LOVE   I.1   341
    Foresight: Prophesie is not in full Force.   237   FOR LCVE   II.1   65
    Angelica: But my Inclinations are in force, I have a mind to go   . 237   FOR LCVE   II.1   66
                   To start a Jest, or force a little Sense.   323   M. ERIDE   PRO.   20
    Almeria: Than Trees, or Flint? O Force of constant Woe!   326   M. BRIDE   I.1   7
    Almeria: Is it of Force?   327   M. ERIDE   I.1 V 56
    Gonsalez: The Force and Influence of your matchless Charms.   .   . 332   M. ERIDE   I.1   258
    Manuel: Fix'd her by Force, and snatch'd the doubtful Day.   .   . 337   M. ERIDE   I.1   457
    Almeria: I've sworn I'll not wed Garcia; why d'ye force me?   . .   . 341   M. ERIDE   II.2   74
    Zara: And fcrce their Balls abroad, at this dead Hour.   . .   . 355   M. EBIDE   III.1   210
    Almeria: O that thy Words had force to break those Bonds,   . .   . 357   M. EBIDE   III.1   300
    Selim: Attempt to force his way for an Escape.   362   M. EBIDE   IV.1   54
    Zara: And try the Force of yet more Obligations.   363   M. EBIDE   IV.1   98
    Garcia: Or to repell their Force, cr bravely die.   379   M. EBIDE   V.2   107
    Marwood: those insipid dry Discourses, with which our Sex of force 410   WAY WCRLD II.1   21
    Mirabell: the force of Instinct--here ccme my pair of Turtles   . 423   WAY WCRLD II.1   501
    Mirabell: force comply. For my part I will Contribute all that in   . 478   WAY WCRLD V.1   615
Forced (9)
    Vainlove: Faith I hate Love when 'tis forced upon a Man; as   . .   . 39   OLD EATCH I.1   94
    Heartwell: burdens, are forced to undergo Dressing, Dancing, Singing,   44 OLD EATCH I.1   273
    Setter: in disgrace at present about a Kiss which he forced. You   . 67 OLD BATCH III.1   225
    Barnaby: House, and yet be forced to let Lcdgings, to help pay the   76 OLD BATCH IV.1   43
    Sharper: not what, forced me. I only beg a favourable Censure of this 79 OLD BATCH IV.1   160
    Araminta: --So were forced to draw, in our own defence.   86   OLD BATCH IV.3   119
    Laetitia: Spin-text, has a sad Fit of the Cholick, and is forced
                                               to lie   91   OLD BATCH IV.4   78
    Brisk: coxcomly Lord of hers; and yet I am forced to allow him   . 175 DOUEL DLR IV.1   293
    Brisk: forced to examine their Stock, and forecast the Charges of   175 DOUEL DLR IV.1   302
Forces (1)
    Mirabell: Forces, all Auxiliaries to the Tea-Table, as Orange-Brandy, 451 WAY WCRLD IV.1   272
Forcing (2)
    Lady Touch: him once from forcing me.   155   DOUEL DLR III.1   163
    Lord Touch: though you have once actually hindered him from forcing   . 182 DOUEL DLR IV.1   550
Fore (0)   see A-fore
Fore-castle (1)
    Sr Sampson: bring your Fore-castle Jests upon your Father? But I shall   308 FOR LCVE   V.1   423
Fore-see (1)
    Almeria: O I fore-see that Object in my Mind.   382   M. EBIDE   V.2   231
Forecast (2)
    Brisk: forced to examine their Stock, and forecast the Charges of   175 DOUBL DLR IV.1   302
    Valentine: any forecast in her.   221   FOR LOVE   I.1   213
Foregad (1)
    Heartwell: Office--Not one Inch; no, Foregad I'me caught--   62   OLD BATCH III.1 V 74
Foregod (1)
    Heartwell: Office--Not one Inch; no, Foregod I'me caught--   62   OLD EATCH III.1   74
Forehead (3)
    Fainall: Gold, tho' my forehead had been furnish'd like a   442   WAY WCRLD III.1   647
    Sir Wilful: 'Sheart an she shou'd her forehead wou'd wrinkle like the   471 WAY WCRLD V.1   363
    Sir Wilful: 'Sheart and she shou'd her forehead wou'd wrinkle like the   471 WAY WCRLD V.1 V363
Foreign (8)
    Sir Paul: polluted by Foreign Iniquity? O my Lady Plyant, you were   . 179 DOUBL DLR IV.1   430
    Manuel: Swear thou hast never seen that foreign Dog, ... 368   M. EBIDE   IV.1   287
    Witwoud: Pleasure, and the Town, a Question at once so Foreign and   . 402 WAY WCRLD I.1   257
    Sir Wilful: I may say now, and am minded to see Foreign Parts. If an   . 440 WAY WORLD III.1   574
    Sir Wilful: French as they say, whereby to hcld discourse in Foreign   . 440 WAY WCRLD III.1   584
    Mirabell: fellows; for prevention of which; I banish all Foreign   . 451 WAY WCRLD IV.1   271
    Sir Wilful: He is to be my Interpreter in foreign Parts. He has been   . 471 WAY WCRLD V.1   380
    Sir Wilful: to see Foreign Parts--I have set on't--And when I'm set   . 477 WAY WCRLD V.1   585
Foreigners (3)
    Belinda: Out-landish Creatures! Such Tramontanae, and Foreigners   . 84   OLD BATCH IV.3   31
    Valentine: (whispers). Scandal, who are all these? Foreigners?   .   . 291   FOR LCVE   IV.1   593
    Valentine: (whispers). Scandal, who are these? Foreigners?   291   FOR LCVE   IV.1 V593
Foreknow (1)
    Almeria: O I foreknow, foresee that Object.   382   M. BRIDE   V.2 V231
Foremost (1)
    Lady Wish: Amour and put your best foot foremost--   455   WAY WCRLD IV.1   393
Forerunner (2)
    Silvia: He's gcing for a Farson, Girl, the forerunner of a   . .   . 75   OLD BATCH III.2   149
    Witwoud: forerunner of the Author, as an Epistle Dedicatory.   . .   401   WAY WCRLD I.1   248
Foresaw (1)
    Almeria: Alphonso, who foresaw my Father's Cruelty, ... 329   M. EBIDE   I.1   119
Foresee (4)   see Forsee, Fore-see
    Sr Sampson: not foresee that the Moon wou'd predominate, and my   . .   . 283   FOR LCVE   IV.1   281
    Foresight: Wherein was I mistaken, not to foresee this?   284   FOR LCVE   IV.1   309
    Scandal: he did not foresee, and more particularly relating to his   284 FOR LOVE   IV.1   312
    Almeria: O I fcreknow, foresee that Object.   382   M. EBIDE   V.2 V231
Foreseen (2)
    Angelica: knows I pitie you; and could I have foreseen the sad   .   . 294   FOR LCVE   IV.1   712
    Angelica: knows I pitie you; and could I have foreseen the bad   .   . 294   FOR LCVE   IV.1 V712
Foresight (54)
    Mellefont: foresight, I am caught, caught in my security,--yet this was 148 DOUBL DLR II.1   375
    Tattle: her Unkle Old Foresight: I think your Father lies at   .   . 228   FOR LOVE   I.1   453
    Tattle: so is Mrs. Foresight, and her Sister Mrs. Frail.   .   . 228   FOR LOVE   I.1   457
    Mrs Frail: Foresight has cast both their Nativities, and prognosticates 231 FOR LOVE   I.1   577
    Mrs Frail: Exchange, I must call my Sister Foresight there.   . .   . 234   FOR LOVE   I.1   665
                   (A Rocm in Foresight's House. Foresight and Servant.)   . 235   FOR LOVE   II.1
    Sr Sampson: Brother Foresight, leave Superstition--Pox o'th' time;   .   240 FOR LCVE   II.1   196
    Sr Sampson: Money, Brother Foresight.   243   FOR LCVE   II.1   276
    Sr Sampson: Here's a Rogue, Brother Foresight, makes a Bargain under   . 243 FOR LCVE   II.1   295
    Sr Sampson: your Friend and Servant--Come Brother Foresight.   .   . 246   FOR LCVE   II.1   404
                               (Exeunt Sir Sampson and Foresight.)   . 246   FOR LCVE   II.1   405

Forgive   (continued)

		PAGE	TITLE	ACT.SC	LINE
Vainlove:	('tis true) where they find most Goodness to forgive.--	87	OLD BATCH	IV.3	138
Vainlove:	(to Araminta). Oh, 'twas Frenzy all: Cannot you forgive	106	OLD BATCH	V.1	356
Araminta:	no need to forgive what is not worth my Anger.	106	OLD BATCH	V.1	363
Sharper:	to forgive the loss of his Mistress.--I know not how	111	OLD BATCH	V.2	122
Lady Touch:	to forgive the faults I have imagined, but never put in	185	DOUBL DLR	IV.2	73
Lady Touch:	your Bride--Do but conceal my failings, and forgive--	185	DOUBL DLR	IV.2	86
Lady Touch:	forgive all that's past--O Heaven, you will not ravish	186	DOUBL DLR	IV.2	103
Maskwell:	thank you--What, enjoy my Love! Forgive the	189	DOUBL DLR	V.1	80
	Forbear your Wonder, and the Fault forgive,	213	FOR LOVE	PRO.	20
Trapland:	I hope you forgive me, my business requires--	225	FOR LOVE	I.1	326
Foresight:	something; tell me, and I'll forgive you; do, good Neice	239	FOR LOVE	II.1	147
	Good Wits, forgive this Liberty we take,	323	M. BRIDE	PRO.	27
Almeria:	Forgive me, Sir, if I offend.	333	M. BRIDE	I.1	283
Almeria:	Forgive me, Sir, if I in this offend.	333	M. BRIDE	I.1	V283
Zara:	Can'st thou forgive me then! wilt thou believe	354	M. BRIDE	III.1	178
Zara:	Forgive my Rage; I know thy Love and Truth.	362	M. BRIDE	IV.1	41
Fainall:	Women do not easily forgive Omissions of that Nature.	397	WAY WORLD	I.1	84
Marwood:	'Twas spoke in scorn, and I never will forgive it.	414	WAY WORLD	II.1	183
Fainall:	If yet you lov'd, you could forgive a Jealousy: But you are	415	WAY WORLD	II.1	185
Sir Wilful:	you nothing, Aunt--Come, come, Forgive and Forget	471	WAY WORLD	V.1	381
Sir Wilful:	take Shipping--Aunt, if you don't forgive quickly; I shall	472	WAY WORLD	V.1	395
Lady Wish:	from Ruine, from Want, I'll forgive all that's past; Nay	473	WAY WORLD	V.1	454

Forgiven (2)

Sir Joseph:	whom I have got--now, but all's forgiven.	110	OLD BATCH	V.2	114
Selim:	But to be punish'd and forgiven. Here, strike;	375	M. BRIDE	V.1	121

Forgiveness (3)

Vainlove:	force, I'll win her, or weary her into a Forgiveness.	100	OLD BATCH	V.1	127
Lady Touch:	let me not hope forgiveness, 'twill ever be in your power	185	DOUBL DLR	IV.2	83
Sr Sampson:	belong'd to a Father, but Forgiveness and Affection; no	240	FOR LOVE	II.1	176

Forgiving (1)

Bellmour:	have the pleasure of forgiving 'em.	63	OLD BATCH	III.1	99

Forgivness (1)

Lord Touch:	I do him fresh wrong to question his forgivness;	200	DOUBL DLR	V.1	481

Forgot (19)

	Well, the Deuce take me, if I han't forgot it.	35	OLD BATCH	PRO.	22
Capt Bluff:	Pish you have put me out, I have forgot what I was	53	OLD BATCH	II.1	224
Laetitia:	been in such a fright, that I forgot to tell you, poor Mr.	91	OLD BATCH	IV.4	77
Fondlewife:	(Sees the Book that Bellmour forgot.)	91	OLD BATCH	IV.4	99
Lady Touch:	have forgot it; and so has he, I hope--for I have not	153	DOUBL DLR	III.1	97
Angelica:	little Nutmeg-Grater, which she had forgot in the Caudle-Cup	238	FOR LOVE	I.1	110
Ben:	Mess, and that's true: marry I had forgot. Dick's dead	261	FOR LOVE	III.1	294
Ben:	Mess, that's true: marry I had forgot. Dick's dead	261	FOR LOVE	III.1	V294
Scandal:	Dear, too considerable to be forgot so soon.	284	FOR LOVE	IV.1	317
Manuel:	Rise, Garcia--I forgot. Yet stay, Almeria.	334	M. BRIDE	I.1	329
Osmyn-Alph:	Wilt thou not know me? Hast thou then forgot me?	342	M. BRIDE	II.2	78
Witwoud:	have forgot what I was going to say to you.	402	WAY WORLD	I.1	271
Lady Wish:	Come, come Foible--I had forgot my Nephew will be	432	WAY WORLD	III.1	274
Witwoud:	forgot him; I have not seen him since the Revolution.	436	WAY WORLD	III.1	442
Marwood:	Hand in forgetfulness--I fancy he has forgot you too.	437	WAY WORLD	III.1	476
Sir Wilful:	to have forgot your Relations. Here's your Cousin	441	WAY WORLD	III.1	604
Sir Wilful:	Nay, nay Cozen,--I have forgot my Gloves,--	447	WAY WORLD	IV.1	91
Sir Wilful:	Wilfull will do't, that's my Crest--my Motto I have forgot.	455	WAY WORLD	IV.1	405
Lady Wish:	You have forgot this, have you, now you have feather'd	462	WAY WORLD	V.1	22

Forgotten (2)

Mirabell:	it be forgotten--I confess I have deservedly forfeited the	471	WAY WORLD	V.1	370
Mirabell:	Let me be pitied first; and afterwards forgotten,	471	WAY WORLD	V.1	378

Forks (1)

Mellefont:	Heaven she laughs, grins, points to your Back, she forks	186	DOUBL DLR	IV.2	131

Forlorn (1)

Almeria:	Into thy Womb the last and most forlorn	368	M. BRIDE	IV.1	277

Form (10)

Lucy:	Form of Godliness?	97	OLD BATCH	V.1	16
Bellmour:	--But you timorous Virgins, form a dreadful Chimaera	106	OLD BATCH	V.1	380
Lady Touch:	forgets the hideous form.	136	DOUBL DLR	I.1	V332
Mellefont:	But the greatest Villain imagination can form, I	146	DOUBL DLR	II.1	293
Mellefont:	Imagination cannot form a fairer and more plausible	187	DOUBL DLR	IV.2	150
Jeremy:	In the Form of a worn-out Punk, with Verses in her Hand,	219	FOR LOVE	I.1	108
Osmyn-Alph:	That tender, lovely Form of painted Air	341	M. BRIDE	II.2	51
Zara:	The present Form of our Engagements rests,	355	M. BRIDE	III.1	217
Zara:	So does the present Form of our Engagements rest,	355	M. BRIDE	III.1	V217
	For, as when Painters form a matchless Face,	479	WAY WORLD	EPI.	31

Form'd (1)

Tattle:	Ladyship's good Judgment, I form'd the Ballance of a	255	FOR LOVE	III.1	71

Forma Pauperis (1)

Valentine:	out to be in Forma Pauperis presently.	282	FOR LOVE	IV.1	248

Formality (2)

Vainlove:	I find, Madam, the Formality of the Law must be	87	OLD BATCH	IV.3	152
Cynthia:	formality; for which I like him: Here he comes.	139	DOUBL DLR	II.1	54

Former (8)

	How this vile World is chang'd! In former days,	35	OLD BATCH	PRO.	1
Angelica:	now you have restor'd me to my former Opinion and	296	FOR LOVE	IV.1	767
Jeremy:	--And now, Sir, my former Master, having much	301	FOR LOVE	V.1	173
Zara:	Whose former Faith had merited much more:	349	M. BRIDE	II.2	377
Fainall:	Yes; he is half Brother to this Witwoud by a former	400	WAY WORLD	I.1	192
Mrs Fain:	by producing a Certificate of her Gallants former	417	WAY WORLD	II.1	298
Waitwell:	Familiarity with my former self; and fall from my				
	Transformation	424	WAY WORLD	II.1	558
Foible:	thought the former good Correspondence between your	430	WAY WORLD	III.1	197

Formerly (2)

Sir Paul:	submit as formerly, therefore give way.	144	DOUBL DLR	II.1	208
Brisk:	asterism, and say,--Jehu was formerly a Hackney	165	DOUBL DLR	III.1	552

Forming (3)

Maskwell:	the forming of another Plot that I have in my head--	154	DOUBL DLR	III.1	160
Maskwell:	the forming another Plot that I have in my head--	154	DOUBL DLR	III.1	V160

Found (continued)

		PAGE	TITLE	ACT.SC	LINE
Sir Joseph:	You have found it Sir then it seems; I profess I'me	49	OLD BATCH	II.1	85
Sir Joseph:	Sum--But han't you found it Sir!	50	OLD BATCH	II.1	93
Capt Bluff:	Mr. Sharper, the matter is plain--Sir Joseph has found	69	OLD BATCH	III.1	296
Lucy:	Vainlove, I have found out a picque she has taken at him;	75	OLD BATCH	III.2	156
Bellmour:	Upon the Perusal I found the Contents so charming, that	82	OLD BATCH	IV.2	53
Setter:	found me, and over-heard all they said. Mr. Bellmour is to	98	OLD BATCH	V.1	84
Setter:	were tc be found at that time: And such like.	99	OLD BATCH	V.1	116
Sharper:	that had found his Wife Knowing the first Night.	104	OLD BATCH	V.1	297
Lord Froth:	found out the Wit.	133	DOUEL DLR	I.1	245
Maskwell:	Nephew, when I first Sigh'd for you; I quickly found it	136	DOUEL DLR	I.1	361
Lady Touch:	will be found so: but that will require some time; for in	151	DOUEL DLR	III.1	17
Sir Paul:	year; I'm sure I have found it sc; and alas, what's once a	162	DOUEL DLR	III.1	434
Lady Ply:	found out that contrivance to let you see this Letter; which	179	DCUEL DLR	IV.1	455
Lord Touch:	I have always found you prudent and careful	181	DOUEL DLB	IV.1	535
Lady Touch:	found him here. Who does not prevent the Hcur of Love;	183	DOUEL DIR	IV.2	9
Lady Touch:	Thou hast, thou hast found the cnly way to turn my Rage;	198	DOUEL DLR	V.1	398
	So, the poor Husbands of the Stage, whc found	213	FOR LCVE	PRO.	7
Valentine:	provide for me, I desire you wou'd leave me as you found	244	FCR LCVE	II.1	335
Valentine:	to you. For you found her Vertue, upon the Backwardness	256	FCR LCVE	III.1	131
Angelica:	fruitless he has fcund his Endeavours, and to confess all	257	FCR LCVE	III.1	143
Valentine:	not overtake you--Ha, ha, ha, the Rogue found me	282	FOR LCVE	IV.1	247
Ben:	No, I'm pleas'd well enough, now I have found you,--	285	FOR LCVE	IV.1	359
Ben:	Why, Father came and found me squabling with ycn	285	FCR LCVE	IV.1	363
Valentine:	lov'd a Woman, and lov'd her so long, that I found out a	292	FOR LCVE	IV.1	640
Valentine:	strange thing: I found out what a Woman was good for.	292	FCR LCVE	IV.1	641
Jeremy:	to be mad: And I think I have not found him very quiet	295	FOR LCVE	IV.1	755
Miss Prue:	O Mr. Tattle, are you here! I'm glad I have found	303	FCR LCVE	V.1	222
Sr Sampson:	What, have ycu fcund your Senses at last then?	310	FCB LCVE	V.1	502
Manuel:	Receive this Lord, as one whom I have found	334	M. BBIDE	I.1	333
Osmyn-Alph:	Affliction is nc more, now thou art found.	343	M. EBIDE	II.2	121
Zara:	Thou and thy Friend; till my Compassion found thee,	346	M. EBIDE	II.2	278
Osmyn-Alph:	In a dark Corner of my Cell, I found	350	M. BRIDE	III.1	6
Osmyn-Alph:	Within I found it, by my Father's Hand	352	M. EBIDE	III.1	111
Manuel:	Not tc be found? in an ill hour he's absent.	372	M. EBIDE	V.1	1
Selim:	Be found--	380	M. EBIDE	V.2	174
Selim:	I found the dead and bloody Body strip'd--	380	M. EBIDE	V.2	182
	This Author, heretofore, has found your Favour,	393	WAY WCRLD	PRC.	16
	If that be fcund a forfeited Estate.	393	WAY WCRLD	PRO.	21
Witwoud:	found out this way, I have known him call for	405	WAY WORLD	I.1	366
Marwood:	found it: The secret is grown too big for the Pretence:	433	WAY WCRLD	III.1	317
Millamant:	the Town has found it. (Exit Mincing.) What has it found?	433	WAY WCRLD	III.1	327
Mirabell:	shall be found out.--And rail at me for missing the	451	WAY WORLD	IV.1	241
Lady Wish:	favourably, Judge Candidly and ccnclude you have found	459	WAY WORLD	IV.1	552
Mincing:	found you and Mr. Fainall in the Blew garret; by the same	474	WAY WCRLD	V.1	487

Foundation (4)

		PAGE	TITLE	ACT.SC	LINE
Careless:	I confess a very fair Foundation, for a Lover to	130	DOUEL DLR	I.1	131
Lady Ply:	have shaken, as I may say, the very foundation of my	169	DOUEL DLR	IV.1	74
Mellefont:	away the very root and foundation of his hopes; What	187	DOUEL DLR	IV.2	147
Perez:	She might remove the fix'd foundation, as	372	M. EBIDE	V.1	9

Foundations (1)

		PAGE	TITLE	ACT.SC	LINE
Maskwell:	Foundations.	150	DOUEL DLR	II.1	445

Foundress (1)

		PAGE	TITLE	ACT.SC	LINE
Mirabell:	And whc may have been the Foundress of this	396	WAY WORLD	I.1	59

Fountain (1)

		PAGE	TITLE	ACT.SC	LINE
Jeremy:	troubled the Fountain of his Understanding; it is a very	302	FOR LCVE	V.1	174

Four (7)

		PAGE	TITLE	ACT.SC	LINE
Jeremy:	mean, to mew your self up here with Three cr Four	217	FOR LCVE	I.1	32
Valentine:	will immediately furnish me with Four thousand Pound to	225	FOR LCVE	I.1	337
Tattle:	three or four places, that I said this and that, and writ to	227	FOR LCVE	I.1	420
Sr Sampson:	day in a Bill of Four thousand Pound: A great deal of	243	FCR LCVE	II.1	275
Sr Sampson:	Again! 'Ouns han't you four thousand Pound	246	FCR LCVE	II.1	396
Mirabell:	Yes, and Mrs. Marwood and three cr four more,	396	WAY WCRLD	I.1	28
Petulant:	of Asses split, would make just four of you.	454	WAY WCRLD	IV.1	352

Fourscore (2)

		PAGE	TITLE	ACT.SC	LINE
Sr Sampson:	Cadua of Fourscore for Sustenance. Odd, I love to see a	260	FOR LCVE	III.1	262
Sr Sampscn:	Fourscore. I am of your Patriarchs, I, a Branch of one of	298	FCB LCVE	V.1	39

Fourty (1)

		PAGE	TITLE	ACT.SC	LINE
Waitwell:	iteration of Nuptials--this eight and fourty Hours	459	WAY WCRLD	IV.1	562

Fowl (0) see Barn-docr-Fowl

Fox (6)

		PAGE	TITLE	ACT.SC	LINE
Silvia:	Ha, ha, ha, an cld Fox trapt--	74	OLD BATCH	III.2	143
Sir Joseph:	Reynard the Fox too.	101	OLD BATCH	V.1	177
Mrs Fore:	Oh hang him old Fox, he's too cunning,	288	FCB LCVE	IV.1	462
Mirabell:	Uncle, he might like Mosca in the Fox, stand upon Terms;	417	WAY WCRLD	II.1	294
Sir Wilful:	you talk of an Instrument Sir, I have an old Fox by my	473	WAY WCRLD	V.1	425
Fainall:	your Fox if you please Sir, and make a Bear-Garden flourish	473	WAY WCRLD	V.1	440

Foy (4)

		PAGE	TITLE	ACT.SC	LINE
Lord Froth:	O foy, Sir Paul, what do you mean? Merry! O	132	DOUEL DLR	I.1	185
Lord Froth:	O foy, don't misapprehend me, I don't say so, for	132	DOUEL DLR	I.1	197
Lord Froth:	O foy, Mr. Careless, all the World allcw Mr.	134	DOUEL DLR	I.1	273
Lord Froth:	O foy, Mr. Careless, all the World allows Mr.	134	DOUEL DLR	I.1	V273

Frail (24)

		PAGE	TITLE	ACT.SC	LINE
Maskwell:	I have been frail, I confess, Madam, fcr your	135	DOUEL DLR	I.1	301
	But since in Paradise frail Flesh gave way,	213	FOR LCVE	PRO.	18
Tattle:	so is Mrs. Foresight, and her Sister Mrs. Frail.	228	FOR LCVE	I.1	457
Scandal:	Yes, Mrs. Frail is a very fine Woman, we all know	228	FOR LCVE	I.1	458
Scandal:	Frail?	228	FCB LCVE	I.1	464
Jeremy:	Sir, Mrs. Frail has sent tc know if you are stirring.	229	FCR LCVE	I.1	505
	(Enter Mrs. Frail.)	230	FOR LCVE	I.1	541
Valentine:	my side: What's here? Mrs. Foresight and Mrs. Prail, they	246	FOR LCVE	II.1	410
	(Enter Mrs. Foresight and Mrs. Prail.)	246	FCB LCVE	II.1	414
	(Exeunt Mrs. Foresight and Mrs. Frail.)	251	FOR LCVE	II.1	580
	(Enter Sir Sampson, Mrs. Frail, Miss Prue, and Servant.)	259	FOR LCVE	III.1	209
Sr Sampson:	Frail, you shall see my Son Ben--Body o' me, he's the	259	FOR LOVE	III.1	212
Miss Prue:	(aside to Mrs. Frail). Pish, he shall be none of my	259	FOR LOVE	III.1	218

Frail   (continued)

Ben:	(Kisses Mrs. Frail.) . . .	261	FOR LOVE	III.1 282
	(Enter Mrs. Foresight, and Mrs. Frail.)	264	FOR LOVE	III.1 432
	(Enter Mrs. Frail, and Ben.)	272	FOR LOVE	III.1 712
	(Enter Foresight, Mrs. Foresight, and Mrs. Frail.) . .	283	FOR LOVE	IV.1 273
Scandal:	is of a piece with Mrs. Frail. He Courts Angelica, if			
	we cou'd	291	FOR LOVE	IV.1 598
Jeremy:	(to Mrs. Frail). You'll meet, Madam;--I'll take . .	293	FOR LOVE	IV.1 671
	(Exeunt Foresight, Mrs. Foresight, Tattle, Mrs. Frail, and	293	FOR LOVE	IV.1 683
	(Enter Tattle and Mrs. Frail.) . .	309	FOR LOVE	V.1 439
Tattle:	Nor I--But poor Mrs. Frail and I are--	309	FOR LOVE	V.1 447
Mrs Fore:	(aside to Mrs. Frail). He's better than no Husband . .	310	FOR LOVE	V.1 469
Osmyn-Alph:	Frail life, to be entirely bless'd. Even now, ...	383	M. BRIDE	V.2 301

Frailties (2)

Mirabell:	They are now grown as familiar to me as my own Frailties;	399	WAY WORLD	I.1 172
Lady Wish:	frailties of my Daughter. Well Friend, you are enough to .	465	WAY WORLD	V.1 131

Frailty (6)

Setter:	the frailty of his Wife.	64	OLD BATCH	III.1 129
Lady Ply:	frailty? Alas! Humanity is feeble, Heaven knows! very . .	147	DOUBL DLR	II.1 321
Maskwell:	I'm afraid my frailty leans that way--but I don't . . .	156	DOUBL DLR	III.1 207
Heli:	To be surpriz'd by Strangers in its Frailty.	338	M. BRIDE	II.1 34
Mrs Fain:	Female Frailty! We must all come to it, if we	418	WAY WORLD	II.1 314
Singer:	Love's but the frailty of the Mind, ...	435	WAY WORLD	III.1 377

Fram'd (1)

Lucy:	and have fram'd a Letter, that makes her sue for			
	Reconciliation	75	OLD BATCH	III.2 157

Frame (2)

Osmyn-Alph:	In Bonds, the Frame of this exalted Mind?	347	M. BRIDE	II.2 323
Manuel:	That like a sudden Earth-quake, shakes my Frame; . . .	367	M. BRIDE	IV.1 233

France (1)

Marwood:	I thought you had design'd for France at all	440	WAY WORLD	III.1 576

Francis (1)

Millamant:	Francis: Nor goe to Hide-Park together the first Sunday in	450	WAY WORLD	IV.1 202

Frank (9)

Bellmour:	No faith Frank you wrong her; she has been just	38	OLD BATCH	I.1 43
Bellmour:	Frank thou art the truest Friend in the World.	39	OLD BATCH	I.1 74
Bellmour:	the deeper the Sin the sweeter. Frank I'm amaz'd at thy good	39	OLD BATCH	I.1 92
Sharper:	Never leave this damn'd illnatur'd whimsey Frank? . . .	79	OLD BATCH	IV.1 171
Sharper:	Heartwell when I see him. Prithee, Frank, let's teaze him;	99	OLD BATCH	V.1 87
Sharper:	Here, Frank; your Blood-Hound has made out the	99	OLD BATCH	V.1 107
Bellmour:	Frank, Will you keep us in Countenance.	112	OLD BATCH	V.2 170
Tattle:	(aside). Frank, I Gad at least. What a Pox does Mrs. .	251	FOR LOVE	II.1 591
Lady Wish:	a return, by a frank Communication--You shall see . .	460	WAY WORLD	IV.1 582

Frankincense (1)

Waitwell:	Frankincense, all Chastity and Odour.	459	WAY WORLD	IV.1 546

Frankly (1)

	Affront to none, but frankly speaks his mind.	214	FOR LOVE	PRO. 44

Fraud (2)

Maskwell:	May so much Fraud and Power of Baseness find?	150	DOUBL DLR	II.1 468
Almeria:	And Fraud, to find the fatal Secret out, ...	370	M. BRIDE	IV.1 381

Frauds (1)

Mirabell:	That marriage frauds too oft are paid in kind. . . .	478	WAY WORLD	V.1 623

Fray (2)

Mrs Fain:	So, Is the fray made up, that you have left	453	WAY WORLD	IV.1 323
Witwoud:	yes the fray is compos'd; my Lady came in like a . .	453	WAY WORLD	IV.1 329

Free (32)

Belinda:	I shall oblige you, in leaving you to the full and free .	57	OLD BATCH	II.2 88
Bellmour:	Actions free to--Quicken your Apprehension--And I-gad . .	59	OLD BATCH	II.2 182
Sharper:	free Discharge to Sir Joseph Wittoll and Captain Bluffe; for	110	OLD BATCH	V.2 86
Maskwell:	earnest of that Bargain, to have full and free possession of	156	DOUBL DLR	III.1 229
Lady Ply:	unaffected, so easie, so free, so particular, so agreeable--	160	DOUBL DLR	III.1 364
Lady Touch:	I'le hold my breath and die, but I'le be free.	184	DOUBL DLR	IV.2 53
Maskwell:	for those free discourses which I have had with my self. .	189	DOUBL DLR	V.1 51
Tattle:	To be free with you, I have--I don't care if I own . .	227	FOR LOVE	I.1 409
Ben:	man, than a Galley-slave is like one of us free Sailors,			
	he is	262	FOR LOVE	III.1 316
Ben:	forsooth you may be as free with me.	262	FOR LOVE	III.1 343
Mrs Fore:	And so you think we are free for one another?	272	FOR LOVE	III.1 684
Singer-V:	Then never let us chain what should be free, ...	293	FOR LOVE	IV.1 662
Scandal:	your Ladyship to the free Confession of your Inclinations. .	294	FOR LOVE	IV.1 692
Manuel:	Those Bonds! 'twas my Command you should be free: . . .	336	M. BRIDE	I.1 403
Manuel:	'Tis false; 'twas more; I bad she should be free: . . .	336	M. BRIDE	I.1 408
Manuel:	'Tis false; 'twas more; I bid she should be free: . .	336	M. BRIDE	I.1 V408
Manuel:	Her Eyes, did more than bid--free her and hers, . . .	336	M. BRIDE	I.1 410
Heli:	And as your self made free, hither I came	344	M. BRIDE	II.2 177
Zara:	We may be free; the Conquerour is mine;	348	M. BRIDE	II.2 324
Osmyn-Alph:	What neither can bestow. Set free your self, ...	348	M. BRIDE	II.2 329
Zara:	A Slave, not daring to be free! nor dares	348	M. BRIDE	II.2 341
Zara:	You free: But shall return much better pleas'd, . . .	360	M. BRIDE	III.1 418
Almeria:	And free of all bad Purposes. So Heav'ns	368	M. BRIDE	IV.1 290
Gonsalez:	To set him free? Ay, now 'tis plain; O well	371	M. BRIDE	IV.1 413
Manuel:	free--	374	M. BRIDE	V.1 53
Manuel:	Thee free, Alphonso--Hell! curs'd, curs'd Alphonso! .	374	M. BRIDE	V.1 60
Manuel:	'Tis well--that when she comes to set him free, . . .	374	M. BRIDE	V.1 77
Zara:	I'll give thee Freedom, if thou dar'st be free: . . .	376	M. BRIDE	V.1 136
Mirabell:	You are very free with your Friends Acquaintance. . .	404	WAY WORLD	I.1 356
Marwood:	Certainly. To be free; I have no Taste of	410	WAY WORLD	II.1 20
Lady Wish:	Marwood shall I be free with you again, and beg you to .	432	WAY WORLD	III.1 279
Millamant:	You have free leave; propose your utmost, speak . . .	450	WAY WORLD	IV.1 232

Free-love's (1)

Belinda:	Free-love's t'other Day.	84	OLD BATCH	IV.3 56

Free-loves (1)

Sir Joseph:	Free-loves! Sir Joseph, thou art a Mad-man. Agad, I'm in .	86	OLD BATCH	IV.3 109

Free'd (1)

Millamant:	bestow, if I were reduc'd to an Inglorious ease; and free'd	449	WAY WORLD	IV.1 168

Freed (1)

		PAGE	TITLE	ACT.SC	LINE
	But tho' he cannot Write, let him be freed	204	DOUBL DLR	EPI.	35

Freedom (12)

Bellmour:	Freedom of his Bed: He not coming home all Night, a	82	OLD BATCH	IV.2	51
Vainlove:	sell you freedom better cheap.	109	OLD BATCH	V.2	80
	The Freedom Man was born to, you've restor'd,	213	FOR LOVE	PRO.	15
	But as with Freedom, judge with Candour too.	324	M. BRIDE	PRO.	40
Zara:	And through my Hopes in you, I promis'd Freedom	349	M. BRIDE	II.2	378
Zara:	wake thee to Freedom. Now, 'tis late; and yet	354	M. BRIDE	III.1	203
Zara:	Somewhat of weight to me, requires his Freedom.	358	M. BRIDE	III.1	376
Zara:	I'll give thee Freedom, if thou dar'st be free:	376	M. BRIDE	V.1	136
Witwoud:	Ay, ay, Friendship without Freedom is as dull as	404	WAY WORLD	I.1	357
Marwood:	You see my Friendship by my Freedom.	410	WAY WORLD	II.1	30
Millamant:	Mirabell, If you persist in this offensive Freedom	422	WAY WORLD	II.1	448
Lady Wish:	may examine her with more freedom--You'll pardon	426	WAY WORLD	III.1	63

Freeholder (1)

Jeremy:	absolutely and substantially Mad, as any Freeholder in	295	FOR LOVE	IV.1	738

Freely (2)

Angelica:	Am I? Well, I freely confess I have resisted a great	257	FOR LOVE	III.1	137
	Then freely judge the Scenes that shall ensue,	324	M. BRIDE	PRO.	39

French (4)

Belinda:	Marriage a mere French Dish.	106	OLD BATCH	V.1	370
Bellmour:	(aside). I hope there's no French Sawce.	106	OLD BATCH	V.1	371
Sr Sampson:	French Fleet were at Anchor at Blackwall.	266	FOR LOVE	III.1	488
Sir Wilful:	French as they say, whereby to hold discourse in Foreign	440	WAY WORLD	III.1	584

French-man (1)

Fondlewife:	his heart, at least, if not a French-man.	91	OLD BATCH	IV.4	75

Frenzy (5)

Vainlove:	(to Araminta). Oh, 'twas Frenzy all: Cannot you forgive	106	OLD BATCH	V.1	356
Maskwell:	express my Concern; for I think his Frenzy increases daily.	182	DOUBL DLR	IV.1	561
Foresight:	His Frenzy is very high now, Mr. Scandal.	289	FOR LOVE	IV.1	529
Foresight:	there is a contagious Frenzy abroad. How does Valentine?	306	FOR LOVE	V.1	333
Fainall:	Frenzy!	415	WAY WORLD	II.1	193

Frequent (2)

Careless:	between them are frequent. His Affection to you,	131	DOUBL DLR	I.1	163
Lady Ply:	Conveniency of frequent Opportunities,--I'll never	147	DOUBL DLR	II.1	351

Fresh (8)

Bellmour:	Lucy.--Here's my Hand, I will; with a fresh Assurance.	98	OLD BATCH	V.1	72
Lord Touch:	These two days! Is it so fresh? Unnatural	153	DOUBL DLR	III.1	99
Lady Touch:	and fresh cause of fury from unthought of	191	DOUBL DLR	V.1	156
Lady Touch:	You want but leasure to invert fresh falshood,	197	DOUBL DLR	V.1	379
Lord Touch:	I do him fresh wrong to question his forgivness;	200	DOUBL DLR	V.1	481
Mrs Fore:	fresh harmless Creature; and left us, Sister, presently.	250	FOR LOVE	II.1	545
Leonora:	Yet fresh and unconsum'd by Time, or Worms.	340	M. BRIDE	II.2	8
Selim:	The Fate of Osmyn: but to that, fresh News	361	M. BRIDE	IV.1	6

Fret (2)

Vainlove:	I would have her fret her self out of conceit with me, that	40	OLD BATCH	I.1	120
Sharper:	make him fret till he foam at the Mouth, and disgorge his	59	OLD BATCH	V.1	88

Fretted (3)

Sharper:	haste to Silvia's Lodgings, before Heartwell has fretted	107	OLD BATCH	V.1	391
Lady Wish:	I have no more patience--If I have not fretted	425	WAY WORLD	III.1	3
Lady Wish:	Face. This wretch has fretted me that I am absolutely	428	WAY WORLD	III.1	142

Friar (1)

Tattle:	like a Nun; and I must be hooded like a Friar; ha, Jeremy?	302	FOR LOVE	V.1	198

Friend (111)

Bellmour:	Friend, be close pursued, or lost. Business is the rub of Life,	37	OLD BATCH	I.1	10
Bellmour:	Frank thou art the truest Friend in the World.	39	OLD BATCH	I.1	74
Bellmour:	Oh, 'tis Sir Joseph Wittoll with his friend;	46	OLD BATCH	I.1	339
Sir Joseph:	of knowing me--I only mean a Friend of mine whom I	50	OLD BATCH	II.1	118
Sharper:	unless it be to serve my particular Friend, as Sir Joseph here,	51	OLD BATCH	II.1	159
Capt Bluff:	you my Friend; Abus'd and Cuff'd and Kick'd.	70	OLD BATCH	III.1	349
Heartwell:	Friend or gain a Mistress.	72	OLD BATCH	III.2	60
Laetitia:	(aside). Vainlove's Friend! I know his Face, and he has	81	OLD BATCH	IV.2	18
Bellmour:	your bearing. Expecting a Friend, last Night, at his Lodgings,	82	OLD BATCH	IV.2	49
Bellmour:	Money). Look you, Heartwell is my Friend; and tho' he be	98	OLD BATCH	V.1	60
Capt Bluff:	Prodigious! What, will you forsake your Friend in his	101	OLD BATCH	V.1	187
Capt Bluff:	Prodigious! What, will you forsake your Friend in	101	OLD BATCH	V.1	V187
Vainlove:	No signing to a Blank, friend.	110	OLD BATCH	V.2	84
Lady Touch:	known betray his Friend!	135	DOUBL DLR	I.1	304
Maskwell:	What Friend have I betray'd? Or to Whom?	135	DOUBL DLR	I.1	305
Lady Touch:	Your fond Friend Mellefont, and to me; can	135	DOUBL DLR	I.1	306
Lady Froth:	Friend,--but really, as you say, I wonder too,--but	138	DOUBL DLR	II.1	9
Cynthia:	Here's my Mother-in-Law, and your Friend Careless,	169	DOUBL DLR	IV.1	65
Sir Paul:	Well, 'tis a rare thing to have an ingenious Friend. Well,	172	DOUBL DLR	IV.1	202
Sir Paul:	no Man make a Friend that would not be a Cuckold: For	178	DOUBL DLR	IV.1	420
Sir Paul:	no Man make a Friend that would not be Cuckold; For	178	DOUBL DLR	IV.1	V420
Lady Ply:	now, Sir Paul, what do you think of your Friend Careless?	179	DOUBL DLR	IV.1	438
Sir Paul:	to my Lady, I can't contain my self; come my dear Friend.	181	DOUBL DLR	IV.1	509
Lord Touch:	Enough--You are my Friend; I know	181	DOUBL DLR	IV.1	540
Lord Touch:	He is your Friend, and what am I?	182	DOUBL DLR	IV.1	568
Maskwell:	But should it be known! then I have lost a Friend!	188	DOUBL DLR	V.1	22
Mellefont:	your Chaplain, look in the Face of your injur'd Friend;	202	DOUBL DLR	V.1	570
Jeremy:	won't have a Friend left in the World, if you turn Poet	218	FOR LOVE	I.1	86
Valentine:	one day bring a Confinement on your Body, my Friend.	221	FOR LOVE	I.1	200
Valentine:	O Mr. Trapland! my old Friend! Welcome. Jeremy, a	222	FOR LOVE	I.1	228
Valentine:	doing good.--Scandal, Drink to me, my Friend Trapland's	223	FOR LOVE	I.1	260
Valentine:	serve his Friend in Distress, tho' I say it to his face. Come,	223	FOR LOVE	I.1	262
Foresight:	World too, Friend.	245	FOR LOVE	II.1	384
Sr Sampson:	your Friend and Servant--Come Brother Foresight.	246	FOR LOVE	II.1	404
Mrs Frail:	a turn with one's Friend.	246	FOR LOVE	II.1	420

Friends (continued)
Maskwell:	And why are Friends and Lovers Oaths believ'd; . . .	150	DOUEL DLR	II.1	466
	There's Humour, which for chearful Friends we got, . .	213	FOR LOVE	PRO.	29
Valentine:	Scandal, learn to spare your Friends, and do not . .	221	FOR LOVE	I.1	198
Mrs Fore:	better Friends than before.	248	FOR LOVE	II.1	479
Tattle:	find: For sure my intimate Friends wou'd have known-- .	256	FOR LOVE	III.1	113
Garcia:	The Friends perhaps are met; let us avoid 'em. . . .	339	M. BRIDE	II.1	49
Mirabell:	You are very free with your Friends Acquaintance. . .	404	WAY WORLD	I.1	356
Petulant:	Friends; and if he shou'd marry and have a Child, you may	407	WAY WORLD	I.1	439
Witwoud:	no further--Between Friends, I shall never break my .	407	WAY WORLD	I.1	468
Marwood:	Thing amiss from your Friends, Sir. You are among your .	438	WAY WORLD	III.1	507
Marwood:	Friends here, tho' it may be you don't know it--If I .	438	WAY WORLD	III.1	508
Sir Wilful:	your Friends and your Relations, your Elders, and your .	439	WAY WORLD	III.1	529
Sir Wilful:	then to your Friends round the Rekin. We cou'd have .	439	WAY WORLD	III.1	551
Lady Wish:	Wit. And your great Wits always rally their best Friends	441	WAY WORLD	III.1	607
Mirabell:	Fashions, spoiling Reputations, railing at absent				
	Friends, and	451	WAY WORLD	IV.1	268
Foible:	friends together, than set 'em at distance. But Mrs. Marwood	464	WAY WORLD	V.1	88
Sir Wilful:	willing to marry my Cozen. So pray let's all be Friends, .	470	WAY WORLD	V.1	321
Mirabell:	Friends and of Sages learned in the Laws of this Land, .	476	WAY WORLD	V.1	545

Friendship (16)
Sharper:	since it has purchas'd me the friendship and acquaintance of	49	OLD BATCH	II.1	77
Heartwell:	esteem my Friendship, or your own Safety,--come	105	OLD BATCH	V.1	322
Maskwell:	Ponds of Friendship, and sets Men right upon their first .	150	DOUEL DLR	II.1	444
Maskwell:	dissuade him: Tho' my Friendship and Love to him has .	154	DOUEL DLR	III.1	152
Sir Paul:	friendship! What art thou but a Name! Henceforward, let .	178	DOUEL DLR	IV.1	419
Careless:	said all I could, but can't prevail--Then my Friendship .	180	DOUEL DLR	IV.1	492
Lord Touch:	Nay, I excuse your Friendship to my	182	DOUEL DLR	IV.1	544
Maskwell:	profess'd an everlasting Friendship to him.	182	DOUEL DLR	IV.1	567
Maskwell:	Friendship to my Lord, and base Self-interest. Let me . .	188	DOUEL DLR	V.1	40
Mrs Frail:	Well, as an earnest of Friendship and Confidence; . . .	248	FOR LOVE	II.1	485
Garcia:	I've heard with Admiration, of your Friendship;	338	M. BRIDE	II.1	13
Zara:	Of strictest Friendship, was profess'd between	364	M. BRIDE	IV.1	123
Witwoud:	Ay, ay, Friendship without Freedom is as dull as . . .	404	WAY WORLD	I.1	357
Marwood:	You see my Friendship by my Freedom.	410	WAY WORLD	II.1	30
Marwood:	profess'd a Friendship to her; and could not see her easie	414	WAY WORLD	II.1	163
Fainall:	What, was it Conscience then! profess'd a Friendship! . .	414	WAY WORLD	II.1	165
Marwood:	Fidelity to you, and sacrific'd my Friendship to keep my .	414	WAY WORLD	II.1	173

Friendships (2)
Marwood:	affect Endearments to each other, profess eternal				
	Friendships, ...	410	WAY WORLD	II.1	23
Fainall:	O the pious Friendships of the Female Sex!	414	WAY WORLD	II.1	166

Friers (1)
| Foible: | into Black Friers for Brass Farthings, with an old Mitten. | 428 | WAY WORLD | III.1 | 138 |

Friezland-Hens (1)
| Belinda: | so bedeck'd, you wou'd have taken 'em for Friezland-Hens, | 84 | OLD BATCH | IV.3 | 29 |

Frigat (1)
| Ben: | you will go to Sea in a Hen-peck'd Frigat.--I believe that, | 287 | FOR LOVE | IV.1 | 439 |

Fright (9)
Sir Joseph:	dy'd of a fright. But--	51	OLD BATCH	II.1	145
Silvia:	You lock ready to fright one, and talk as if your Passion	72	OLD BATCH	III.2	68
Laetitia:	Oh! I am sick with the fright; won't you take him . .	90	OLD BATCH	IV.4	57
Laetitia:	been in such a fright, that I forgot to tell you, poor Mr.	91	OLD BATCH	IV.4	77
Lady Ply:	I'm in such a fright; the strangest Quandary	178	DOUEL DLR	IV.1	396
Zara:	And fright him from my Arms--See, see, he slides . .	381	M. BRIDE	V.2	209
Mrs Fain:	O Foible, I have been in a Fright, least I shou'd . .	430	WAY WORLD	III.1	184
Mirabell:	bring you home in a pretended fright, when you think you .	451	WAY WORLD	IV.1	240
Millamant:	fright--Fainall, I shall never say it--well--I think-- .	452	WAY WORLD	IV.1	289

Frighted (7)
Sir Joseph:	Purpose, if he han't frighted it out of my memory. Hem! .	49	OLD BATCH	II.1	53
Silvia:	Bless me! you frighted me, I thought he had been come .	74	OLD BATCH	III.2	145
Laetitia:	(aside). Oh then alls safe. I was terrible frighted-- . .	78	OLD BATCH	IV.1	102
Laetitia:	(aside). Oh then alls safe. I was terribly frighted-- . .	78	OLD BATCH	IV.1	V102
Lady Touch:	you have frighted me. Nay, look pleas'd, I'll tell you. .	152	DOUEL DLR	III.1	70
Miss Prue:	Lies--but they frighted me, and said it was a sin. . . .	252	FOR LOVE	II.1	630
Manuel:	Frighted, and tumbling one hand in his Bosom, . . .	373	M. BRIDE	V.1	16

Frightful (6)
Belinda:	A little! O frightful! What a furious Fiz I have! O . .	83	OLD BATCH	IV.3	8
Belinda:	me now? Hideous, ha? Frightful still? Or how? . . .	83	OLD BATCH	IV.3	17
Belinda:	O frightful! Cousin, What shall we do? These things . .	85	OLD BATCH	IV.3	75
Perez:	As to some Object frightful, yet not fear'd.	338	M. BRIDE	II.1	23
Zara:	With frightful Faces, and the meagre Looks	379	M. BRIDE	V.2	140
Leonora:	Zara all pale and dead! two frightful Men, ...	381	M. BRIDE	V.2	223

Frightn'd (1)
| Sir Joseph: | and frightn'd 'em away--but agad I durst not stay to give | 47 | OLD BATCH | II.1 | 9 |

Frightned (3)
Bellmour:	though I believe he was heartily frightned, for as soon as	46	OLD BATCH	I.1	362
Capt Bluff:	By these Hilts I believe he frightned you into this . .	68	OLD BATCH	III.1	268
Laetitia:	--I swear, I was heartily frightned.--Feel how my . . .	89	OLD BATCH	IV.4	4

Frippery (7)
Foible:	I'll hamper you for that (says he) you and your old Frippery	428	WAY WORLD	III.1	115
Lady Wish:	--Frippery? old Frippery! Was there ever such a foul-mouth'd	428	WAY WORLD	III.1	118
Lady Wish:	Frippery? Superannuated Frippery! I'll	428	WAY WORLD	III.1	128
Lady Wish:	Frippery the Villain; I'll reduce him to Frippery and Rags.	428	WAY WORLD	III.1	129

Frisoneer-gorget (1)
| Lady Wish: | Go hang out an old Frisoneer-gorget, with a yard of . . | 462 | WAY WORLD | V.1 | 14 |

Frivolous (1)
| Marwood: | Deceit and frivolous Pretence. . . . . | 415 | WAY WORLD | II.1 | 208 |

Frolick (3)
Sr Sampson:	'tis as they commit Murder; out of a Frolick: And are .	299	FOR LOVE	V.1	57
Valentine:	counterfeited Madness; I don't know but the Frolick may .	311	FOR LOVE	V.1	525
Mirabell:	Play, and disappointing the Frolick which you had to pick	451	WAY WORLD	IV.1	242

Frollick (1)
| Mellefont: | you wont baulk the Frollick? . . . . | 168 | DOUEL DLR | IV.1 | 42 |

From (275)

Front (1)
| Belinda: | Front of her Father's Hall; her Eyes were the two . . | 84 | OLD BATCH | IV.3 | 46 |

Full   (continued)
		PAGE	TITLE	ACT.SC	LINE
Sharper:	No, I'll deal fairly with you.--'Tis a full and	110	OLD BATCH	V.2	85
Mellefont:	How now, Jack? What, so full of Contemplation	155	DOUBL DLR	III.1	198
Maskwell:	earnest of that Bargain, to have full and free possession of	156	DOUEL DLR	III.1	229
Mellefont:	Industry grown full and ripe, ready to drop into his mouth,	187	DOUBL DLR	IV.2	144
Mellefont:	Industry grow full and ripe, ready to drop into his mouth,	187	DOUBL DLR	IV.2	V144
Maskwell:	full fruition of my Love, I'll bear the railings of a losing	190	DOUEL DLR	V.1	87
Brisk:	the Man in't already, I'm so full of the Wounds which	201	DOUBL DLR	V.1	539
Scandal:	while; but when the full Cry is against you, you won't	219	FOR LOVE	I.1	141
Scandal:	while; but when the full Cry is against you, you shan't	219	FOR LOVE	I.1	V141
Foresight:	Prophesie is not in full Force.	237	FOR LOVE	II.1	65
Ben:	indeed, and full in my Teeth. Lock you forsooth, I am as	263	FOR LOVE	III.1	371
Valentine:	is full--There are People that we do know, and	280	FOR LOVE	IV.1	160
Valentine:	Occupy the Family. Coffee-Houses will be full of Smoak	289	FOR LOVE	IV.1	507
Selim:	The King, in full belief of all you told him,	361	M. BBIDE	IV.1	12
Perez:	Fast bound in double chains, and at full length	372	M. BRIDE	V.1	7
Almeria:	Ha! point again? 'tis there, and full I hope.	382	M. BRIDE	V.2	258
Mirabell:	Detestation of Mankind; and full of the Vigour of Fifty	396	WAY WCRLD	I.1	61
Fainall:	opportunity to do it at full length. Behcld the Original.	401	WAY WORLD	I.1	233
Fainall:	Arms in full Security. But cou'd you think because the	414	WAY WORLD	II.1	147
Mirabell:	Here she comes i'faith full sail, with her Fan spread	418	WAY WORLD	II.1	323
Marwood:	panting ripe; with a Heart full cf Hope, and a Head full of	431	WAY WORLD	III.1	247
Lady Wish:	entrance; and then turn full upon him--No, that will	445	WAY WORLD	IV.1	21
Mrs Fain:	drop off when she's full. Madam you sha'not pawn a	466	WAY WORLD	V.1	175
Mrs Fain:	drop off when she's full. Madam you shan't pawn a	466	WAY WORLD	V.1	V175
Full-blown (1)					
Manuel:	That wait to be full-blown at ycur Approach,	349	M. BRIDE	II.2	385
Fuller (1)					
Valentine:	fuller.	222	FOR LOVE	I.1	244
Fully (1)					
Zara:	Against your State: and fully to discharge	364	M. BBIDE	IV.1	140
Fulsamick (1)					
Lady Froth:	he's a nauseous figure, a most fulsamick Fop, Foh--he	165	DOUEL DLR	III.1	562
Fulsome (1)					
Heartwell:	I confess I have not been sneering fulsome Lies and	42	OLD BATCH	I.1	188
Fulsomely (1)					
Millamant:	Men and their Wives are so fulscmely familiar,--I shall	450	WAY WCRLD	IV.1	199
Fumbling (2)					
Manuel:	Frighted, and fumbling one hand in his Bosom,	373	M. BRIDE	V.1	16
Marwood:	have your Case open'd by an old fumbling Leacher in a	467	WAY WCBLD	V.1	212
Fumes (1)					
Osmyn-Alph:	Like Fumes of Sacred Incense, c'er the Clouds,	353	M. BBIDE	III.1	130
Function (2)					
Setter:	first Stone? who undervalued my Function? and who the	66	OLD BATCH	III.1	205
Setter:	somewhat fall'n from the Dignity cf my Function; and	105	OLD BATCH	V.1	337
Funeral (2)					
Witwoud:	Funeral Sermon, or a Copy of Commendatory Verses	401	WAY WORLD	I.1	246
Waitwell:	For decency of Funeral, Madam. The delay will	458	WAY WCRLD	IV.1	498
Furies (2)					
Heartwell:	Not Fiends or Furies could have added to my	108	OLD BATCH	V.2	39
Mellefont:	Death and Furies, will you not hear me--Why by	186	DOUBL DLR	IV.2	130
Furious (1)					
Belinda:	A little! O frightful! What a furious Fiz I have! O	83	OLD BATCH	IV.3	8
Furnace (1)					
Mellefont:	By Heav'n into a hot Furnace sooner.	157	DOUEL DLR	III.1	238
Furnish (2)					
Valentine:	will immediately furnish me with Four thousand Pound to	225	FOR LOVE	I.1	337
	And furnish Focl enough to entertain.	479	WAY WCRLD	EPI.	27
Furnish'd (1)					
Fainall:	Gold, tho' my forehead had been furnish'd like a	442	WAY WORLD	III.1	647
Furnishes (1)					
Lady Wish:	furnishes with Blushes, and re-composing Airs beyond	445	WAY WCRLD	IV.1	31
Furnival's (1)					
Sir Wilful:	of Furnival's Inn--Ycu cou'd intreat to be remember'd	439	WAY WORLD	III.1	550
Furnivals (1)					
Petulant:	Of the Family of the Furrivals. Ha, ha, ha!	440	WAY WCRLD	III.1	555
Further (16)					
Heartwell:	Debts, which by the time you have pay'd, yields no further	44	OLD BATCH	I.1	279
Ben:	(Sits further off.)	263	FOR LOVE	III.1	368
Valentine:	further; You look suspiciously. Are you a Husband?	289	FOR LCVE	IV.1	514
Osmyn-Alph:	Essaying further to Futurity;	345	M. BBIDE	II.2	227
Zara:	Still further frcm me; look, he hides his Face,	381	M. BBIDE	V.2	209
Mirabell:	is to be flatter'd further, unless a Man shou'd endeavour	397	WAY WCRLD	I.1	77
Witwoud:	no further--Between Friends, I shall never break my	407	WAY WCBLD	I.1	468
Marwood:	my Aversion further.	411	WAY WORLD	II.1	51
Petulant:	Why shou'd a Man be ever the further frcm being	436	WAY WORLD	III.1	428
Petulant:	Why shou'd a Man be any further from being	436	WAY WCRLD	III.1	V428
Sir Wilful:	step to the Stable, you may enquire further of my Horse,	438	WAY WOBLD	III.1	500
Sir Wilful:	further acquaintance,--So for the present Cozen, I'll take	446	WAY WCBLD	IV.1	77
Sir Wilful:	present, 'tis sufficient till further acquaintance, that's				
	all--	447	WAY WCBLD	IV.1	85
Millamant:	further to say to me?	448	WAY WCRLD	IV.1	133
Mirabell:	for ycu can fly no further.--	449	WAY WCRLD	IV.1	159
Sir Wilful:	melt, I can tell you that. My contract went no further	472	WAY WCRLD	V.1	396
Fury (13)					
Careless:	Was there ever such a Fury! 'tis well Nature has not	130	DOUBL DLR	I.1	100
Mellefont:	Bed-side like a Fury, she flew to my Sword, and with	130	DOUBL DLR	I.1	114
Sir Paul:	provoked to fury, I cannot incorporate with Patience and	144	DOUEL DLR	II.1	223
Mellefont:	Ha, ha, ha, I, a very Fury; but I was most afraid	149	DOUBL DLR	II.1	416
Mellefont:	Ha, ha, ha, ay, a very Fury; but I was most afraid	149	DOUBL DLR	II.1	V416
Maskwell:	then were fine work indeed! her fury wou'd spare nothing,	190	DOUBL DLR	V.1	93
Lady Touch:	and fresh cause of fury from unthought of	191	DOUBL DLR	V.1	156
Maskwell:	So, 'tis well--let your wild fury have a vent;	198	DOUEL DLR	V.1	408
	The Law provides a curb for 'its own Fury,	204	DOUBL DLR	EPI.	10
Valentine:	Marriage indeed may qualifie the Fury of his	231	FOR LOVE	I.1	560
Zara:	Nor Hell a Fury, like a Woman scorn'd.	361	M. BBIDE	III.1	458

Gather'd (1)
    Foresight: Cheeks have been gather'd many Years;--ha! I do not   . . 269   FOR LOVE   III.1 603
Gathering (2)
    Bellmour: (Looking about, and gathering up his things.)   89   OLD BATCH IV.4   14
    Ben: has been gathering foul weather in her Mouth, and now it . 265   FOR LOVE   III.1 442
Gause (1)
    Lady Wish: begon, go go,--that I took from Washing of old Gause   . . 462   WAY WORLD   V.1   4
Gav'n (1)
    Ben: gav'n that wipe--He had'nt a word to say, and so I left 'n, 286 FOR LOVE   IV.1 385
Gave (28)
    Lucy: Hum'd it over, gave you his Respects, and said, he   . . . 61   OLD BATCH III.1   26
    Sir Joseph: the Guts for a hundred Pound--Why I gave that   67   OLD BATCH III.1 254
    Capt Bluff: Composition; I believe you gave it him out of fear, pure . 68   OLD BATCH III.1 269
    Heartwell: Why 'twas I Sung and Danc'd; I gave Musick to   72   OLD BATCH III.2   32
    Bellmour: till 'twas late; my Intimacy with him gave me the   . . . 82   OLD BATCH IV.2   50
    Belinda: of it; for she thank'd me, and gave me two Apples, piping . 84 OLD BATCH IV.3   43
    Mellefont: where it was directed. Still it gave me less perplexity to 129 DOUBL DLR   I.1   91
    Lady Froth: Whymsies and Vapours, but I gave them vent.   . . . . . 138 DOUBL DLR II.1   11
    Lady Froth: gave you my Picture, here suppose this my Picture--   . . 140 DOUBL DLR II.1   74
    Maskwell: Conscience are my Witnesses, I never gave one working   . 188 DOUBL DLR   V.1   34
                    As Nature gave the World to Man's first Age, ... 213 FOR LOVE   PRO. 13
                    But since in Paradise frail Flesh gave way, ... 213 FOR LOVE   PRO. 18
    Valentine: You know her temper; she never gave me any great . . . 225 FOR LOVE   I.1 346
    Valentine: to be kept at small expence; but the Retinue that you gave 244 FOR LOVE   II.1 346
    Miss Prue: --Smell him Mother, Madam, I mean--He gave . . . . . 249 FOR LOVE   II.1 521
    Valentine: gave Beauty, when it grafted Roses on a Briar. You are   . 292 FOR LOVE   IV.1 635
    Scandal: Reason, which you gave to Mr. Tattle; for his impertinence 294 FOR LOVE   IV.1 688
    Sr Sampson: Who gave you Authority to speak, Sirrah? To . . . . . 308 FOR LOVE   V.1 417
    Leonora: My Love of you, my Royal Mistress, gave me   . . . . . 327 M. BRIDE   I.1   35
    Leonora: Love of my Royal Mistress, gave me   . . . . 327 M. BRIDE   I.1 V 35
    Almeria: And Vows I gave my Dear Alphonso, basely   . . . . . . 330 M. BRIDE   I.1 173
    Almeria: I gave my Dear Alphonso, basely broken.   . . . . . . 330 M. BRIDE   I.1 V173
    Manuel: Yet something too is due to me, who gave   . . . . . . 333 M. BRIDE   I.1 289
    Manuel: He answers well, the Character you gave him.   . . . . 336 M. BRIDE   I.1 429
    Heli: Gave order to the Guards for my Admittance.   . . . . 351 M. BRIDE III.1   44
    Mirabell: to my Design and Expectation, they gave me every   . . 399 WAY WORLD   I.1 169
    Millamant: I gave you some Pain.   . . . . 420 WAY WORLD II.1 380
    Foible: hold; But i'faith I gave him his own.   . . . . 427 WAY WORLD III.1   91
Gavot (3)
    Araminta: Is Mr. Gavot gone?   58   OLD BATCH II.2 157
    Araminta: If Mr. Gavot will walk with us in the Garden, we'll have . 60 OLD BATCH II.2 207
    Araminta: If Mr. Gavot will walk with us into the Garden, we'll have 60 OLD BATCH II.2 V207
Gawdy (1)
    Heartwell: With gawdy Plumes and gingling Bells made proud,   . . 112 OLD BATCH   V.2 186
Gay (4)
    Lady Ply: So gay, so graceful, so good teeth, so fine shape,   . . 160 DOUBL DLR III.1 367
    Mirabell: gay; that's all.   . . . . 395 WAY WORLD   I.1   16
    Mirabell: of gay fine Perrukes hovering round you.   . . . . . 418 WAY WORLD II.1 330
    Marwood: of the Play-house? A fine gay glossy Fool, shou'd be given 433 WAY WORLD III.1 309
Gaze (6)
    Almeria: One Moment, cease to gaze on perfect Bliss, ... 330 M. BRIDE   I.1 V179
    Gonsalez: The Multitude should gaze) in Absence of your Eyes.   . 332 M. BRIDE   I.1 245
    Osmyn-Alph: And gaze upon thy Eyes, is so much Joy;   . . . . . 342 M. BRIDE   II.2   97
    Osmyn-Alph: Why? what dost thou mean? why dost thou gaze so?   . 342 M. BRIDE   II.2 103
    Osmyn-Alph: And why? what dost thou mean? why dost thou gaze so? . 342 M. BRIDE   II.2 V103
    Almeria: That thus can gaze, and yet not turn to Stone? . . . 382 M. BRIDE   V.2 239
Gazer (0)   see Star-Gazer
Gazette (3)
    Capt Bluff: Gazette! Why there again now--Why, Sir, there are   . . 52   OLD BATCH II.1 192
    Capt Bluff: Gazette--I'll tell you a strange thing now as to that--   . 52   OLD BATCH II.1 194
    Capt Bluff: went every day to Coffee-houses to read the Gazette my . 53   OLD BATCH II.1 208
Gazette-writer (1)
    Capt Bluff: Gazette-writer never so much as once mention'd me--Not once 53 OLD BATCH II.1 203
Gazettes (1)
    Sharper: Not I, Sir, no more than publick Letters, or Gazettes . . 52   OLD BATCH II.1 190
Gazetts (1)
    Sir Wilful: Gazetts then, and Dawks's Letter, and the weekly Bill, 'till 440 WAY WORLD III.1 552
Gazing (0)   see Star-gazing
Gemini (5)
    Silvia: them--O Gemini, I hope you don't mean so--For I   . . . 73   OLD BATCH III.2   88
    Lady Ply: nay you shan't ask me, I swear I'll deny it. O Gemini, you 147 DOUBL DLR II.1 334
    Foresight: under Gemini, which may incline her to Society; she has a 239 FOR LOVE   II.1 152
    Miss Prue: O Gemini! well, I always had a great mind to tell . . . 252 FOR LOVE   II.1 629
    Petulant: and Baldwin yonder, thy half Brother is the rest--A gemini 454 WAY WORLD IV.1 351
Gems (1)
    Gonsalez: Chariots of War, adorn'd with glittering Gems, ... 331 M. BRIDE   I.1 229
Gen'rous (1)
    Garcia: Go Gen'rous Heli, and relieve your Friend.   . . . . 338 M. BRIDE   II.1   35
Gender (1)
    Lady Wish: Coats; Nay her very Babies were of the Feminine Gender, . 467 WAY WORLD   V.1 190
General (11)
    Bellmour: here vents 'em against the General, who slighting Men of . 47   OLD BATCH   I.1 371
    Sharper: greater General breathing.   52   OLD BATCH II.1 184
    Sir Joseph: he would put in for't he might be made General himself . 53   OLD BATCH II.1 215
    Sharper: general Release.   . . . . 110 OLD BATCH   V.2 101
    Maskwell: general acquittance--Rival is equal, and Love like Death . 150 DOUBL DLR II.1 449
    Careless: your favour--I feel my Spirits faint, a general dampness . 170 DOUBL DLR IV.1 114
    Scandal: say in general Terms, He only is Secret who never was   . 256 FOR LOVE III.1 125
    Almeria: Thou hadst no Cause, but general Compassion.   . . . . 327 M. BRIDE   I.1   34
    Almeria: Are busied in the General Joy, that thou   . . . . . 331 M. BRIDE   I.1 197
    Almeria: Are wrap'd and busied in the general Joy, ... 331 M. BRIDE   I.1 V197
    Mirabell: acquaintance be General; that you admit no sworn Confident, 451 WAY WORLD IV.1 235
Generally (3)
    Heartwell: generally Masters in it: But I'm so newly entred, you   . 72   OLD BATCH III.2   57
    Maskwell: And whereas pleasure is generally paid with . . . . . 156 DOUBL DLR III.1 218
    Angelica: due. Men are generally Hypocrites and Infidels, they   . 314 FOR LOVE   V.1 631

264

Gentlewoman   (continued)
| Ben: | No, I hope the Gentlewoman is not angry; I mean all in | 262 | FOR LOVE | III.1 | 341 |
| Mirabell: | with the Gentlewoman in what-de-call-it-Court. Item, I shut | 451 | WAY WORLD | IV.1 | 252 |

Gentlewomen (4)
Araminta:	body so? They might be Gentlewomen of a very good	84	OLD BATCH	IV.3	36
Ben:	Gentlewomen.	260	FOR LOVE	III.1	277
Coachman:	Three Gentlewomen in the Coach would speak	404	WAY WORLD	I.1	346
Coachman:	Three Gentlewomen in a Coach would speak	404	WAY WORLD	I.1	V346

Gently (3)
Scandal:	For Heav'ns sake softly, Sir, and gently; don't	279	FOR LOVE	IV.1	152
Sr Sampson:	I'll speak gently--Val, Val, do'st thou not	279	FOR LOVE	IV.1	156
Osmyn-Alph:	But gently take thy self away, lest she	345	M. BRIDE	II.2	202

Genuine (1)
| Mirabell: | drinks, as Tea, Chocolate and Coffee. As likewise to Genuine | 451 | WAY WORLD | IV.1 | 266 |

George (13)
Bellmour:	How now George, where hast thou been snarling odious	42	OLD BATCH	I.1	180
Sharper:	Not till you had Mouth'd a little George, I think	43	OLD BATCH	I.1	227
Bellmour:	George, you must not quarrel with little Gallantries of	44	OLD BATCH	I.1	259
Bellmour:	Well come off George, if at any time you should be	44	OLD BATCH	I.1	286
Bellmour:	How George, do's the Wind blow there?	44	OLD BATCH	I.1	293
Bellmour:	Well but George I have one Question to ask you--	45	OLD BATCH	I.1	330
Bellmour:	Nay prithee George--	46	OLD BATCH	I.1	334
Bellmour:	poor George, thou art i'th right, thou hast sold thy self to	63	OLD BATCH	III.1	89
Sharper:	me, or I'll go and have the Lady to my self. B'w'y' George.	104	OLD BATCH	V.1	306
Bellmour:	Now George, What Rhyming! I thought the	108	OLD BATCH	V.2	17
Vainlove:	George,--	109	OLD BATCH	V.2	65
Bellmour:	I thank thee, George, for thy good intention.--	111	OLD BATCH	V.2	154
Bellmour:	Come, take your Fellow-Travellers. Old George, I'm sorry	112	OLD BATCH	V.2	183

Gesture (1)
| Marwood: | deliver'd with so significant Gesture, shou'd be so | 434 | WAY WORLD | III.1 | 346 |

Get (70)
Bellmour:	get your Man Setter to provide my Disguise.	40	OLD BATCH	I.1	112
Sir Joseph:	him, till I can get out of his sight; but out o'sight out	48	OLD BATCH	II.1	45
	c'mind	48	OLD BATCH	II.1	45
Belinda:	Get my Hoods and Tippet, and bid the Footman call	56	OLD BATCH	II.2	69
Belinda:	What will you get by that? To make such Signs as	59	OLD BATCH	II.2	179
Lucy:	Go get you in Madam, receive him pleasantly, dress up	62	OLD BATCH	III.1	48
Bellmour:	But how the Devil dost thou expect to get her if	63	OLD BATCH	III.1	110
Bellmour:	other way to get himself a heat.	70	OLD BATCH	III.1	329
Heartwell:	Well, farewell then--if I can get out of her sight I	74	OLD BATCH	III.2	129
Heartwell:	Well, farewell then--if I can get out of sight I	74	OLD BATCH	III.2	V129
Heartwell:	may get the better of my self.	74	OLD BATCH	III.2	130
Laetitia:	would get another Wife--Another fond Fool, to break her	78	OLD BATCH	IV.1	107
Fondlewife:	more, and then get you in--So--Get you in,	79	OLD BATCH	IV.1	144
Fondlewife:	get you in, By, by.	79	OLD BATCH	IV.1	145
Sir Joseph:	and get 50 Pieces more from him. Adslidikins, Bully, we'll	85	OLD BATCH	IV.3	63
Belinda:	you're a pure Man; Where did you get this excellent	88	OLD BATCH	IV.3	196
Bellmour:	to Church in the Morning?--May be it may get	112	OLD BATCH	V.2	177
Careless:	Prithee get thee gone; thou seest we are serious.	128	DOUBL DLR	I.1	45
Careless:	think thou hast no more Sense, than to get an Heir upon her	130	DOUBL DLR	I.1	120
Mellefont:	will be a Pleasure to your self; I must get you to engage	130	DOUBL DLR	I.1	125
Maskwell:	New Song, we'll get 'em to give it us by the way.	143	DOUBL DLR	II.1	173
Mellefont:	to make your Uncle Disinherit you, to get you turn'd out	149	DOUBL DLR	II.1	400
Mellefont:	get into her Confidence.--Ha! How But was it her	149	DOUBL DLR	II.1	409
Careless:	Mellefont, get out o'th' way, my Lady Plyant's	157	DOUBL DLR	III.1	264
Careless:	'Pox I can't get an Answer from her, that does not	157	DOUBL DLR	III.1	270
Careless:	I can't get an Answer from her, that does not	157	DOUBL DLR	III.1	V270
Sir Paul:	Go, go Child, go, get you gone and Dance and be	175	DOUBL DLR	IV.1	280
Maskwell:	when we are together, and you not easily get in to surprize	181	DOUBL DLR	IV.1	518
Maskwell:	get my Lord to consent to my private management. He	190	DOUBL DLR	V.1	96
Maskwell:	Well, get your selves ready, and meet me in half	194	DOUBL DLR	V.1	238
Mellefont:	No; my Dear, will you get ready--the things	196	DOUBL DLR	V.1	343
Valentine:	ends of Acts: d'ye hear, get the Maids to Crambo in an	218	FOR LOVE	I.1	78
Jeremy:	sit at the Door, that I don't get double the Stomach that	218	FOR LOVE	I.1	92
Scandal:	enough? Must you needs shew your Wit to get more?	219	FOR LOVE	I.1	128
Mrs Frail:	Hey day! I shall get a fine Reputation by coming	230	FOR LOVE	I.1	546
Mrs Frail:	I shall get a fine Reputation by coming	230	FOR LOVE	I.1	V546
Sr Sampson:	'Oons, what had I to do to get Children,--	245	FOR LOVE	II.1	349
Valentine:	thee this Lesson of Fustian to get by Rote?	255	FOR LOVE	III.1	74
Ben:	and may hap may'nt get 'em out again when he wou'd.	261	FOR LOVE	III.1	313
Scandal:	two. I can get nothing out of him but Sighs. He desires	266	FOR LOVE	III.1	501
Sr Sampson:	Black-Guard or his shall get the better of the Day.	267	FOR LOVE	III.1	511
Scandal:	what Project I had to get him out of the way; that I might	269	FOR LOVE	III.1	597
Ben:	our Landladies once a Year, get rid of a little Mony; and	275	FOR LOVE	III.1	802
Valentine:	Thou liest, for I am Truth. 'Tis hard I cannot get a	280	FOR LOVE	IV.1	171
Ben:	and if so be that he cou'd get a Woman to his mind, he'd	286	FOR LOVE	IV.1	381
Ben:	Graceless, why did he beget me so? I did not get my self.	286	FOR LOVE	IV.1	391
Mrs Fore:	stead, and get you married together, and put to Bed	288	FOR LOVE	IV.1	472
Valentine:	shake off Age; get thee Medea's Kettle, and be boil'd a-new,	289	FOR LOVE	IV.1	522
Valentine:	Get me a Coul and Beads, that I may play my part,--	290	FOR LOVE	IV.1	560
Valentine:	If they are, I'll tell you what I think--get away all the	291	FOR LOVE	IV.1	594
Tattle:	(aside). O Pox, how shall I get rid of this foolish Girl?	303	FOR LOVE	V.1	225
Miss Prue:	won't get me one, I'll get one for my self: I'll marry our	305	FOR LOVE	V.1	316
Angelica:	be a good Father, or you'll never get a second Wife. I	312	FOR LOVE	V.1	572
Selim:	In secret, by your Mutes; and get an Order,	362	M. BRIDE	IV.1	57
Zara:	Get thee to Hell, and seek him there.	380	M. BRIDE	V.2	175
Witwoud:	Lady? Gad, I say any thing in the World to get this Fellow	402	WAY WORLD	I.1	255
Marwood:	Hands, do--I'd leave 'em to get loose.	416	WAY WORLD	II.1	226
Mrs Fain:	I believe my Lady will do any thing to get a Husband; and	418	WAY WORLD	II.1	308
Mrs Fain:	suppose she will submit to any thing to get rid of him.	418	WAY WORLD	II.1	310
Foible:	him Madam, starve him, marry Sir Rowland and get him	427	WAY WORLD	III.1	107
Mirabell:	Then I'll get up in a morning as early as I please.	449	WAY WORLD	IV.1	192
Millamant:	Ah! Idle Creature, get up when you will--	450	WAY WORLD	IV.1	193
Witwoud:	A plot, a plot, to get rid of the Knight,--your	454	WAY WORLD	IV.1	381
Lady Wish:	with him--Travel quoth a; Ay travel, travel, get thee gone,	456	WAY WORLD	IV.1	438
Lady Wish:	get thee but far enough, to the Saracens or the Tartars, or	456	WAY WORLD	IV.1	439

Get   (continued)

Give   (continued)

		PAGE	TITLE	ACT.SC	LINE
Sir Joseph:	Ah, honest Setter.--Sirrah, I'll give thee any	104	OLD BATCH	V.1	281
Bellmour:	But give your selves the trouble to walk to that	107	OLD BATCH	V.1	401
Belinda:	Joy, Joy Mr. Bride-groom; I give you Joy, Sir.	108	OLD BATCH	V.2	22
Heartwell:	'Tis not in thy Nature to give me Joy--A	108	OLD BATCH	V.2	23
Heartwell:	Woman can as soon give Immortality.	108	OLD BATCH	V.2	24
Vainlove:	Bellmour, Give it over; you vex him too much; 'tis	109	OLD BATCH	V.2	47
Vainlove:	What would you give?	109	OLD BATCH	V.2	74
	Would give the World she could her Icy recover:	113	OLD BATCH	EPI.	4
Brisk:	Boys, Boys, Lads, where are you? What, do you give	128	DOUBL DLR	I.1	20
Mellefont:	narrowly, and give me notice upon any Suspicion. As for	130	DOUBL DLR	I.1	137
Mellefont:	New Song, we'll get 'em to give it us by the way.	143	DOUBL DLR	II.1	173
Singer:	Yet she's vext if I give over;	143	DOUBL DLR	II.1	180
Sir Paul:	Pray your Ladyship give me leave to be Angry--	144	DOUBL DLR	II.1	199
Sir Paul:	submit as formerly, therefore give way.	144	DOUBL DLR	II.1	208
Lady Ply:	every thing in the World, but give me Mathemacular	146	DOUBL DLR	II.1	302
Mellefont:	Madam, pray give me leave to ask you one	147	DOUBL DLR	II.1	330
Maskwell:	Well for Wisdom and Honesty, give me Cunning and	150	DOUBL DLR	II.1	457
Maskwell:	self any longer: and was just going to give vent to a				
	Secret.	156	DOUBL DLR	III.1	201
Maskwell:	and give you notice.	157	DOUBL DLR	III.1	261
Lady Ply:	at the same time you must give me leave to declare in the	159	DOUBL DLR	III.1	350
Cynthia:	Within reach; for example, give me your hand;	168	DOUBL DLR	IV.1	23
Cynthia:	a Ditch--Here then, I give you my promise, in spight of	168	DOUBL DLR	IV.1	35
Cynthia:	Money, He should give me a very evident demonstration	168	DOUBL DLR	IV.1	46
Cynthia:	Touchwood, as you boasted, and force her to give her	169	DOUBL DLR	IV.1	48
Cynthia:	Why if you give me very clear demonstration that it	169	DOUBL DLR	IV.1	58
Sir Paul:	Gads bud, I am transported! give me leave to kiss	172	DOUBL DLR	IV.1	192
Sir Paul:	Merry, Gads-bud I'm serious, I'll give thee 500 [Pound] for	173	DOUBL DLR	IV.1	233
Lady Ply:	Has he been Treacherous, or did you give his insolence a	179	DOUBL DLR	IV.1	439
Sir Paul:	did you give me this Letter on purpose he? Did you?	179	DOUBL DLR	IV.1	461
Lord Touch:	How! give me but Proof of it, Ocular	182	DOUBL DLR	IV.1	562
Lord Touch:	honest, I will secure thy Fidelity to him, and give	182	DOUBL DLR	IV.1	572
Lord Touch:	make me. Can you give me a demonstrative Proof?	182	DOUBL DLR	IV.1	574
Lord Touch:	shalt have due reward of all thy worth. Give me thy hand	189	DOUBL DLR	V.1	56
Lord Touch:	should Command: my very Slaves will shortly give me	195	DOUBL DLR	V.1	303
Cynthia:	immediately to follow you, and give you notice.	196	DOUBL DLR	V.1	349
Cynthia:	and listen; perhaps this chance may give you proof of	197	DOUBL DLR	V.1	375
Maskwell:	more than all the rest; though I would give a Limb for	199	DOUBL DLR	V.1	434
Jeremy:	Hem!--Sir, if you please to give me a small	217	FOR LOVE	I.1	64
Valentine:	my Sins in my Face: Here, give her this,	221	FOR LOVE	I.1	208
Valentine:	If I can give that Cerberus a Sop, I shall be at rest				
	for one	222	FOR LOVE	I.1	225
Valentine:	What, the Widows Health; give it him--off	223	FOR LOVE	I.1	275
Trapland:	Verily, give me a Glass,--you're a Wag,--	224	FOR LOVE	I.1	289
Scandal:	before they act, so they rarely give us any light to guess				
	at	225	FOR LOVE	I.1	349
Valentine:	give Scandal such an Advantage; why, your running away	229	FOR LOVE	I.1	512
Mrs Frail:	to give place to his Manners.	231	FOR LOVE	I.1	557
Mrs Frail:	you give me now? Come, I must have something.	231	FOR LOVE	I.1	584
Valentine:	Step into the next Room--and I'll give you	231	FOR LOVE	I.1	585
Scandal:	Ay, we'll all give you something.	231	FOR LOVE	I.1	587
Mrs Frail:	Well, what will you all give me?	232	FOR LOVE	I.1	588
Mrs Frail:	I thought you would give me something, that	232	FOR LOVE	I.1	590
Valentine:	And Scandal shall give you a good Name.	232	FOR LOVE	I.1	592
Mrs Frail:	you give me, Mr. Tattle?	232	FOR LOVE	I.1	594
Valentine:	I'll come to him--will you give me leave, I'll	234	FOR LOVE	I.1	662
Scandal:	I'll give an account of you, and your Proceedings. If	234	FOR LOVE	I.1	675
Foresight:	How, how? Sir Sampson, that all? Give me leave to	240	FOR LOVE	II.1	202
Jeremy:	Sola's or Sonata's, they give me the Spleen.	245	FOR LOVE	II.1	375
Sr Sampson:	--If I had it again, I wou'd not give thee a Groat,	246	FOR LOVE	II.1	397
Mrs Frail:	Well, give me your Hand in token of sisterly secresie and	248	FOR LOVE	II.1	482
Miss Prue:	give me something to make me smell so--Oh pray	249	FOR LOVE	II.1	525
Miss Prue:	he'll give me something that will make my Smocks smell	249	FOR LOVE	II.1	527
Ben:	good part: For if I give a Jest, I'll take a Jest: And so	262	FOR LOVE	III.1	342
Ben:	Look you Young Woman, You may learn to give good	264	FOR LOVE	III.1	402
Ben:	if you shou'd give such Language at Sea, you'd have a Cat	264	FOR LOVE	III.1	408
Scandal:	when you had Charity enough to give me your Attention,	269	FOR LOVE	III.1	588
Scandal:	Well; You'll give me leave to wait upon you to	273	FOR LOVE	III.1	745
Valentine:	strange! But I am Truth, and come to give the World	280	FOR LOVE	IV.1	164
Valentine:	Prophecy comes, Truth must give place.	283	FOR LOVE	IV.1	275
Mrs Frail:	Lover, and give him his discharge, and come to you.	285	FOR LOVE	IV.1	352
Valentine:	that it may be secret; and Juno shall give her Peacock	290	FOR LOVE	IV.1	550
Singer-V:	To you I should my earliest Off'ring give;	293	FOR LOVE	IV.1	654
Angelica:	Aunt, Mr. Tattle desires you would give him leave to wait	293	FOR LOVE	IV.1	677
Angelica:	and if I find what you propose practicable; I'll give	301	FOR LOVE	V.1	135
Sr Sampson:	--Odd, I think we are very well met;--Give me	301	FOR LOVE	V.1	144
Sr Sampson:	--as what?--Odd, as t'other Hand--give me	301	FOR LOVE	V.1	146
Sr Sampson:	No, no, only give you a Rent-roll of my	301	FOR LOVE	V.1	152
Foresight:	Robin make ready to give an Account of his Plate and	306	FOR LOVE	V.1	327
Ben:	Nay, I'll give you leave to guess--I'll undertake to make	306	FOR LOVE	V.1	350
Angelica:	Father, and give me.	307	FOR LOVE	V.1	394
Sr Sampson:	be even with you, I won't give you a Groat. Mr. Buckram is	308	FOR LOVE	V.1	424
Valentine:	No; here's the Fool; and if occasion be, I'll give it	310	FOR LOVE	V.1	497
Valentine:	Give me the Paper.	312	FOR LOVE	V.1	549
Angelica:	(to Valentine). Had I the World to give you, it	312	FOR LOVE	V.1	560
	I'm sure 'tis some such Latin Name they give 'em,	315	FOR LOVE	EPI.	13
Almeria:	If ever I do yield, or give consent,	330	M. BRIDE	I.1	185
Manuel:	Draw near, and give your hand; and, Garcia, yours:	334	M. BRIDE	I.1	332
Manuel:	A King and Conquerour can give, are yours.	335	M. BRIDE	I.1	386
Almeria:	Give my Hand, and speak to me, nay, speak,	339	M. BRIDE	II.1	67
Almeria:	Give me thy Hand, and let me hear thy Voice;	339	M. BRIDE	II.1 V	67
Zara:	And give thee in Exchange, my Love.	346	M. BRIDE	II.2	269
Zara:	And give thee, for 'em, in Exchange, my Love.	346	M. BRIDE	II.2 V	269
Osmyn-Alph:	I have not wheresithal to give again.	346	M. BRIDE	II.2	271
Zara:	Give it me as it is; I ask no more	346	M. BRIDE	II.2	273

Give   (continued)

Given   (continued)
  Almeria: To the remorseless Rack I would have given 369   M. BRIDE   IV.1   311
  Osmyn-Alph: O my Heart's Comfort; 'tis not given to this 383   M. BRIDE   V.2   300
  Lady Wish: corrupt Integrity it self. If she has given him an
                Opportunity, ... 426   WAY WORLD   III.1   58
  Marwood: of the Play-house? A fine gay glossy Fool, shou'd be given 433 WAY WORLD III.1 309
  Marwood: worse than when you had her--I dare swear she had given 442 WAY WORLD III.1 651
  Millamant: Sir, I have given my consent. 473   WAY WORLD   V.1   421
Giver (1)
  Mirabell: diminish in their value, and that both the giver loses the 449 WAY WORLD IV.1 172
Gives (32)
  Bellmour: all My Heart--It adds a Gusto to an Amour; gives it the . 39   OLD BATCH   I.1   90
  Vainlove: (Gives a letter.) 79   OLD BATCH   IV.1   155
  Laetitia: (She gives him the Key, goes to the Chamber-door, and speaks 91 OLD BATCH IV.4 83
  Bellmour: Intentions for thee too: Let this mollifie.--(Gives her 98   OLD BATCH   V.1   59
  Bellmour: (Gives her more Money.) 98   OLD BATCH   V.1   61
  Sir Joseph: (Gives him Gold.) 103   OLD BATCH   V.1   246
  Capt Bluff: time, here's Earnest. (Gives him Money). Come, Knight; . 104   OLD BATCH   V.1   279
  Brisk: judged by Mellefont here, who gives and takes Raillery . 128   DOUBL DLR   I.1   27
  Maskwell: One Minute, gives Invention to Destroy, ... 138   DOUBL DLR   I.1   421
                           (Gives him a Pocket-glass.) 140   DOUBL DLR   II.1   75
  Careless: Excessively foolish--But that which gives me most . 158   DOUBL DLR III.1   295
                            (Gives him the Letter.) 162   DOUBL DLR III.1   453
  Cynthia: My Mind gives me it wont--because we are 168   DOUBL DLR   IV.1   11
  Careless: you. (Gives her a Note) 171   DOUBL DLR   IV.1   130
  Sir Paul: (Bows and gives the Letter.) . . . 173   DOUBL DLR   IV.1   219
  Lady Ply: both Letters.-- (Puts the wrong Letter hastily up, and
                gives him 174   DOUBL DLR   IV.1   263
  Lady Touch: (Gives the Dagger.) . . . 198   DOUBL DLR   V.1   405
  Maskwell: (Gives the Dagger.) 199   DOUBL DLR   V.1   452
  Valentine: (Gives Money.) 221   FOR LOVE   I.1   209
  Scandal: (Gives Money.) 222   FOR LOVE   I.1   217
  Scandal: a Whisper; and deny a Woman's name, while he gives you . 226 FOR LOVE I.1 371
  Ben: tell'n so to's face: If that's the Case, why silence gives 263 FOR LOVE III.1 393
  Scandal: with you--But my Mind gives me, these things cannot . 267   FOR LOVE   III.1   523
  Scandal: reason. (She gives him the Glass: Scandal and she whisper.) 269 FOR LOVE III.1 585
  Scandal: Since Custome gives the Losers leave to speak. 323   M. BRIDE   PRO.   28
  Almeria: O no! Time gives Encrease to my Afflictions. 330   M. BRIDE   I.1   152
  Heli: And when his Soul gives all her Passions Way, . . . 338   M. BRIDE   II.1   31
                       (A Mute kneels and gives one of the
                Bowls.) 381   M. BRIDE   V.2   199
  Witwoud: Learning, gives him the more opportunities to shew his . 404 WAY WORLD I.1 327
  Witwoud: Words gives me the pleasure very often to explain his . 404   WAY WORLD   I.1   331
  Mirabell: (Gives Mony.) 424   WAY WORLD   II.1   535
  Singer: Or am'rous Youth, that gives the Joy; 435   WAY WORLD III.1   383
Giving (7)
  Belinda: (Giving her Hand.) 112   OLD BATCH   V.2   169
  Lord Froth: avoid giving them encouragement. 133   DOUBL DLR   I.1   232
  Cynthia: think you of drawing Stakes, and giving over in time? . 142   DOUBL DLR   II.1   158
  Tattle: by giving me a Kiss? 252   FOR LOVE   II.1   632
  Angelica: Husband, and you are giving me your Consent--I . . . 300   FOR LOVE   V.1   106
  Mrs Fain: one scandalous Story, to avoid giving an occasion to make 412 WAY WORLD II.1 105
  Millamant: without giving a reason. To have my Closet Inviolate; to . 450 WAY WORLD IV.1 221
Glad (32)
  Bellmour: Sharper, I'm glad to see thee. 41   OLD BATCH   I.1   149
  Sir Joseph: heartily glad-- 49   OLD BATCH   II.1   86
  Araminta: O I am glad we shall have a Song to divert the . . . 59   OLD BATCH II.2   186
  Laetitia: Husband ought to behave himself--I shall be glad to . 79   OLD BATCH   IV.1   140
  Belinda: Lard, my Dear! I am glad I have met you;--I 83   OLD BATCH IV.3   1
  Careless: Well, I shall be glad to be mistaken; but, your . . . 131   DOUBL DLR   I.1   158
  Maskwell: I'm glad you're come, for I could not contain my . . . 156   DOUBL DLR III.1   200
  Cynthia: I'm glad to see you so merry, Sir. 173   DOUBL DLR   IV.1   232
  Brisk: tell whether I am glad or sorry that your Ladiship has made 176 DOUBL DLR IV.1 339
  Careless: Sir Paul, I'm glad I've met with you, 'gad I have . . . 180 DOUBL DLR IV.1 491
  Valentine: Faith and Troth, I am heartily glad to see you-- . . . 222   FOR LOVE   I.1   242
  Foresight: Ha, How? Faith and troth I'm glad of it, and so I . . . 236   FOR LOVE   II.1   29
  Sr Sampson: be--hah! old Merlin! body o' me, I'm so glad I'm . . . 240   FOR LOVE   II.1   184
  Sr Sampson: I'm glad on't: Where is he? I long to see him. Now, Mrs. . 259 FOR LOVE III.1 211
  Sr Sampson: glad to hear you say so; I was afraid you were in Love . 260   FOR LOVE III.1 258
  Ben: Thank you Father, and I'm glad to see you. 260   FOR LOVE III.1   272
  Sr Sampson: Odsbud, and I'm glad to see thee, kiss me Boy, . . . 260   FOR LOVE III.1   273
  Sr Sampson: indisposed: But I'm glad thou'rt better, honest Val. . 281   FOR LOVE   IV.1   203
  Ben: --I'm glad you shew your self, Mistress:--Let . . . 287   FOR LOVE   IV.1   436
  Mrs Fore: glad at least to make you a good Settlement.--Here they . 288 FOR LOVE IV.1 475
  Foresight: --Mr. Scandal, I shall be very glad to confer with you . 289   FOR LOVE IV.1   532
  Scandal: Madam, I am very glad that I overheard a better . . . 294   FOR LOVE IV.1   687
  Valentine: Go see, you Sot. I'm very glad that I can move your . . . 295   FOR LOVE IV.1   759
  Angelica: How! I'm glad on't--If he has a mind I should . . . 297   FOR LOVE   V.1   5
  Miss Prue: O Mr. Tattle, are you here! I'm glad I have found . . . 303   FOR LOVE   V.1   222
  Tattle: and I have a Secret in my Heart, which you wou'd be glad 305 FOR LOVE V.1 289
  Mrs Fore: I'm glad to hear you have so much Fire in 308   FOR LOVE   V.1   408
  Almeria: I'll drink my glad Acknowledgment-- 382   M. BRIDE   V.2   260
  Mirabell: of Mirth, which is not yet ripe for discovery. I am glad . 399 WAY WORLD I.1 137
  Lady Wish: O I'm glad he's a brisk Man. Let my 429   WAY WORLD III.1   180
  Witwoud: and this Fellow was my Guardian; ay, ay, I was glad . 440   WAY WORLD III.1   558
  Marwood: to huddle up all in Silence, I shall be glad. You must . 468 WAY WORLD V.1 244
Gladly (4)
  Sir Wilful: before I cross the Seas. I'd gladly have a spice of your . 440 WAY WORLD III.1 583
  Sir Wilful: Yes; my Aunt would have it so,--I would gladly . . . . 446 WAY WORLD IV.1   73
  Sir Wilful: Yes; my Aunt will have it so,--I would gladly . . . . 446 WAY WORLD IV.1 V 73
  Waitwell: before I die--I wou'd gladly go out of the World with . 458 WAY WORLD IV.1 502
Gladness (3)
  Osmyn-Alph: Gladness, and Warmth of ever-kindling Love, ... 345 M. BRIDE II.2 211
  Osmyn-Alph: Yet look for Gaiety and Gladness there. . . . . . . 346 M. BRIDE II.2 263
  Osmyn-Alph: Warm her to Life, and wake her into Gladness. . . . . 383 M. BRIDE V.2 279

274

Gonsalez   (continued)
Manuel: Let all except Gonsalez leave the Room.   364   M. EBIDE   IV.1 V131
Manuel: What dost thou think, Gonsalez;   366   M. EBIDE   IV.1   198
Alonzo: 'Twill quit me of my Promise to Gonsalez.   373   M. EBIDE   V.1   30
             Enter Gonsalez, disguis'd like a Mute, with a Dagger.)   . 376   M. EBIDE   V.2
             Gonsalez alone, disguis'd like a Mute, with a Dagger.)   . 376   M. EBIDE   V.2   V
Alonzo: My Lord, My Lord, what, hoa? My Lord Gonsalez?   376   M. EBICE   V.2   22
             (Enter Gonsalez, bloody.)   . 376   M. EBIDE   V.2   23
Osmyn-Alph: Gonsalez and Alonzo, both of Wounds   383   M. EBIDE   V.2   305
Good (242)
             So, standing only on his good Behaviour, ... 35   OLD BATCH PRO.   12
Bellmour: Vainlove, and abroad so early! good Morrow; I   37   OLD BATCH I.1   1
Vainlove: Bellmour, good Morrow--Why truth on't is, these   . . . 37   OLD BATCH I.1   5
Bellmour: I'le take care, he shall not be at home. Good! Spintext! Ch 39   OLD EATCH I.1   84
Bellmour: the Servants. Very good! Then I must be disguised--With   . 39   OLD BATCH I.1   89
Bellmour: the deeper the Sin the sweeter. Frank I'm amaz'd at thy good 39   OLD BATCH I.1   92
Vainlove: Well good Morrow, let's dine together, I'l meet at   . . 40   OLD BATCH I.1   129
Sharper: She had need have a good share of sense, to manage.   . . 42   OLD BATCH I.1   208
Sharper: An argument of very little Passion, very good   42   OLD BATCH I.1   214
Heartwell: Good Mr. Young-fellow, you're mistaken; as   43   OLD EATCH I.1   229
Bellmour: Thou art an old Fornicator of a singular good   43   OLD EATCH I.1   250
Sharper: ill Wind that blows no body good: well, you may rejoyce   . 48   OLD BATCH II.1   33
Sir Joseph: Ha, ha, ha, a very good Jest I Profess, ha, ba, ha, a   . . 50   OLD BATCH II.1 114
Sir Joseph: very good Jest, and I did not know that I had say'd it, and 50   OLD BATCH II.1 115
Sir Joseph: been long acquainted; you have lost a good Jest for want   . 50   OLD BATCH II.1 117
Capt Bluff: Good Mr. Sharper speak to him; I dare not look   54   OLD BATCH II.1 238
Belinda: Ay! nay Dear--prithee good, dear sweet Cousin no   . . . 54   OLD BATCH II.2   1
Bellmour: heartily? I'de do a little more good in my generation first, 63   OLD BATCH III.1 107
Bellmour: A good hearing, Setter. 64   OLD BATCH III.1 119
Setter: Good words, Damsel, or I shall--But how dost   65   OLD BATCH III.1 171
Sir Joseph: And good Nature, Eack; I am good Natur'd and   67   OLD BATCH III.1 243
Silvia: rugged Temper, and make ill-humoured People good: . . . 72   OLD EATCH III.2 67
Heartwell: Damn her let her go, and a good riddance--Yet so   . . . 74   OLD EATCH III.2 114
Silvia: Well--good by. 74   OLD BATCH III.2 131
Fondlewife: Good lack! I profess the Spirit of contradiction   . . . 75   OLD EATCH IV.1   16
Fondlewife: while her good Husband is deluded by his Godly appearance   . 76   OLD BATCH IV.1   30
Fondlewife: Good lack, good lack--I profess it is a very sufficient   . 76   OLD BATCH IV.1   39
Fondlewife: Good lack, good lack, she would melt a Heart of   78   OLD BATCH IV.1 114
Fondlewife: Nykin, ee, ee, ee,--Here will be the good Man anon, to   . 79   OLD BATCH IV.1 136
Fondlewife: That's my good Dear--Come Kiss Nykin once   79   OLD BATCH IV.1 143
Belinda: like one of 'em:--Good Dear, pin this, and I'll tell you.   . 83   OLD BATCH IV.3   13
Araminta: body so? They might be Gentlewomen of a very good   . . . 84   OLD BATCH IV.3   36
Belinda: O monstrous filthy Fellow! Good slovenly Captain   . . . 85   OLD BATCH IV.3   86
Belinda: shall I be bound for your good Behaviour for the future?   . 86   OLD BATCH IV.3 135
Sir Joseph: Pray, first let me have 50 Pounds, good Alderman.   . . . 89   OLD BATCH IV.4   27
Fondlewife: Good Lack! Good Lack!--I profess, the poor   91   OLD BATCH IV.4   94
Fondlewife: Good Man! I warrant he dropp'd it on purpose, ... 91   OLD BATCH IV.4 102
Laetitia: Dear Husband, I'm amaz'd:--Sure it's a good   92   OLD BATCH IV.4 114
Laetitia: In the Name of the--Oh! Good, my Dear, don't   92   OLD BATCH IV.4 132
Fondlewife: Good again--A very civil Person this, and, I   94   OLD BATCH IV.4 179
Bellmour: Well, since I see thou art a good honest Fellow, I'll   . . 94   OLD BATCH IV.4 198
Bellmour: Bed, hoping that when she heard of it, her good Nature   . 94   OLD BATCH IV.4 212
Bellmour: Words, and a Kiss; and the good Man melts. See, how   . 95   OLD BATCH IV.4 239
Setter: Joy of your Return, Sir. Have you made a good   96   OLD EATCH V.1   9
Lucy: in good earnest, you kiss so devoutly.   97   OLD BATCH V.1   38
Bellmour: fitter Husband for her.--Come, Here's Earnest of my good   . 98   OLD BATCH V.1   58
Bellmour: good Quality.--But to the purpose, if you will give   . 98   OLD BATCH V.1   65
Sir Joseph: in Aesop's Fables, Bully? A-Gad there are good Morals to   . 101 OLD BATCH V.1   175
Sir Joseph: How's this! Good Bully, hold your breath, and   . . . . 102 OLD EATCH V.1   203
Sir Joseph: And how, and how, good Setter, did the little   . . . . 103 OLD BATCH V.1   253
Sir Joseph: I warrant, I'll bring you into the Ladies good Graces.   . 103 OLD BATCH V.1   263
Vainlove: But have a good heart, I heard of your Misfortune, and   . 109 OLD BATCH V.2   71
Sharper: fear.--A fine Lady, and a Lady of very good Quality.   . . 111 OLD BATCH V.2   135
Bellmour: I thank thee, George, for thy good intention.--   . . . . 111 OLD BATCH V.2   154
Heartwell: Then good Councel will be thrown away upon   . . . . . 112 OLD BATCH V.2   157
             How nearly some Good Men might have scap'd Sinking.   . 125 DOUEL DLR PRO.   24
             I'th' Good Man's Arms, the Chopping Bastard thrives,   . 125 DOUEL DLR PRO.   29
Brisk: of Wine,--the Deuce take me if there were three good   . 128 DOUEL DLR I.1   35
Mellefont: keep up good Humour and Sense in the Company, prithee   . 128 DOUEL DLR I.1   47
Brisk: But the Deuce take me if I say a good thing till you come.-- 128 DOUEL DLR I.1   51
Mellefont: Faith 'tis a good natur'd Cox-Comb, and has very   . . 129 DOUEL DLR I.1   65
Sir Paul: good, strange! I swear I'm almost Tipsy--t'other   . . 131 DOUBL DLR I.1   178
Sir Paul: good, strange! I swear I'm almost Tipsie--t'other   . . 131 DOUBL DLR I.1   V178
Brisk: Well then, you tell me, some good Jest, or very Witty   . 134 DOUEL DLR I.1   267
Lady Froth: then your Bow! Good my Lord, bow as you did when I   . . 140 DOUEL DLR II.1   73
Lord Froth: I hope Mellefont will make a good Husband too.   . . . 141 DOUEL DLR II.1 100
Cynthia: Then I find its like Cards, if either of us have a good   . 142 DOUEL DLR II.1 162
Lady Ply: --to wrong so good, so fair a Creature, and one that   . 146 DOUEL DLR II.1 290
Lady Ply: Nay, nay, rise up, come you shall see my good   . . . 148 DOUEL DLR II.1 355
Lady Touch: willing to have remote from your hearing. Good my Lord,   . 152 DOUEL DLR III.1 51
Lady Touch: the Company, and come to you. Pray, good dear my Lord,   . 153 DOUEL DLR III.1 118
Mellefont: Good Fortune ever go along with thee.   . . . . 157 DOUEL DLR III.1 262
Lady Ply: So gay, so graceful, so good teeth, so fine shape,   . . 160 DOUEL DLR III.1 367
Lady Ply: a very good skin, Sir.   . . . . 160 DOUEL DLR III.1 369
Sir Paul: Fortune, a good Estate in the Country, some houses in   . 161 DOUEL DLR III.1 408
Sir Paul: year to an Old Man, who would do good in his Generation?   . 162 DOUEL DLR III.1 435
Cynthia: think they are all in good nature with the World, and only 163 DOUEL DLR III.1 482
Sir Paul: O ho, I wish you good success, I wish you good   . . . 163 DOUEL DLR III.1 497
Brisk: good Rhime) but don't you think bilk and fare too like a   . 165 DOUEL DLR III.1 545
Cynthia: O good my Lord let's hear it.   . . . . 166 DOUEL DLR III.1 590
Sir Paul: Good strange! Mr. Brisk is such a Merry Facetious   . . 174 DOUBL DLR IV.1 274
Brisk: (aside). That's good I'gad, that's good, Deuce take me I   . 177 DOUEL DLR IV.1 379
Sir Paul: speak a good word only just for me, Gads-bud only for   . 180 DOUEL DLR IV.1 472
Lord Touch: she has told me all: Her good Nature conceal'd it as long   . 182 DOUEL DLR IV.1 547
Mellefont: turn to good account.   . . . . 185 DOUEL DLR IV.2   63
Lady Touch: Moderate your rage good my Lord! he's   . . . . 186 DOUBL DLR IV.2 112

Good (continued)

Speaker		Page	Title	Act.Sc	Line
Lady Touch:	Come, come, good my Lord, my Heart	187	DOUBL DLR	IV.2	138
Lord Touch:	and my good Genius led me hither--mine, in that I . . .	189	DOUBL DLR	V.1	54
Sir Paul:	Why, what's the matter now? Good Lord, what's . . .	192	DOUBL DLR	V.1	185
Maskwell:	Nay, good Mr. Saygrace do not prolong the time, ...	194	DOUBL DLR	V.1	276
Maskwell:	Good, let them be carried to him,--have you	195	DOUBL DLR	V.1	287
Cynthia:	Nay, good my Lord, forbear Resentment, let us . . .	198	DOUBL DLR	V.1	428
Sir Paul:	Affairs may be in a very good posture; I saw her go into .	200	DOUBL DLR	V.1	506
Mellefont:	Good Heavens! how I believ'd and Lov'd this	202	DOUBL DLR	V.1	573
	Unless the Fable's good, and Moral sound.	204	DOUBL DLR	EPI.	18
Jeremy:	Young Maids, not to prefer Poetry to good Sense; or .	219	FOR LOVE	I.1	113
Trapland:	A good Morning to you Mr. Valentine, and to you . . .	222	FOR LOVE	I.1	231
Scandal:	The Morning's a very good Morning, if you don't . .	222	FOR LOVE	I.1	233
Valentine:	your handsome Daughter--Come a good Husband to . .	222	FOR LOVE	I.1	251
Valentine:	doing good.--Scandal, Drink to me, my Friend Trapland's	223	FOR LOVE	I.1	260
Valentine:	No Apology, good Mr. Scrivener, you shall be . . .	224	FOR LOVE	I.1	324
Tattle:	Valentine good Morrow, Scandal I am Yours.-- . .	226	FOR LOVE	I.1	382
Valentine:	play at Losing Loadum; you must lose a good Name to .	226	FOR LOVE	I.1	389
Scandal:	Come then, sacrifice half a Dozen Women of good . .	230	FOR LOVE	I.1	526
Mrs Frail:	good Breeding, for it begets his Civility to other People.	231	FOR LOVE	I.1	565
Valentine:	Pox take 'em, their Conjunction bodes no good, . . .	231	FOR LOVE	I.1	574
Valentine:	Pox take 'em, their Conjunction bodes me no good, .	231	FOR LOVE	I.1	V574
Valentine:	And Scandal shall give you a good Name.	232	FOR LOVE	I.1	592
Tattle:	I have a pretty good Collection at your Service, some .	232	FOR LOVE	I.1	599
Nurse:	Dinner--good lack-a-day, ha, ha, ha, O strange; I'll vow .	235	FOR LOVE	II.1	22
Nurse:	Pray Heav'n send your Worship good Luck, Marry . .	235	FOR LOVE	II.1	26
Foresight:	have, that may be good Luck in troth, in troth it may, .	236	FOR LOVE	II.1	30
Foresight:	very good Luck: Nay, I have had some Omens; I got out .	236	FOR LOVE	II.1	31
Foresight:	pretty good that too; but then I stumbl'd coming . .	236	FOR LOVE	II.1	33
Foresight:	bad, some good, our lives are chequer'd, Mirth and . .	236	FOR LOVE	II.1	35
Foresight:	he's at leisure--'tis now Three a Clock, a very good hour	236	FOR LOVE	II.1	41
Angelica:	Is not it a good hour for Pleasure too? Uncle, pray .	236	FOR LOVE	II.1	44
Foresight:	And leave good Man to Brew and Bake, ...	236	FOR LOVE	II.1	52
Foresight:	something; tell me, and I'll forgive you: do, good Neice .	239	FOR LOVE	II.1	147
Foresight:	But come, be a good Girl, don't perplex your poor Uncle, .	239	FOR LOVE	II.1	157
Angelica:	Good bu'y Uncle--Call me a Chair--I'll find	239	FOR LOVE	II.1	161
Sr Sampson:	Candle, and that's all the Stars are good for. . . .	240	FOR LOVE	II.1	201
Sr Sampson:	What, thou art not angry for a Jest, my good Haly--I .	242	FOR LOVE	II.1	246
Jeremy:	Yes, I have a reasonable good Ear, Sir, as to Jiggs and .	245	FOR LOVE	II.1	373
Mrs Fore:	No matter for that, it's as good a Face as yours. . .	247	FOR LOVE	II.1	460
Miss Prue:	Oh good! how sweet it is--Mr. Tattle is all over sweet, .	249	FOR LOVE	II.1	518
Tattle:	Or does she leave us together out of good Morality, and .	251	FOR LOVE	II.1	593
Scandal:	Nor good Nature enough to answer him that did . . .	254	FOR LOVE	III.1	33
Angelica:	What, are you setting up for good Nature?	254	FOR LOVE	III.1	35
Tattle:	Ladyship's good Judgment, I form'd the Ballance of a .	255	FOR LOVE	III.1	71
Tattle:	good Fortune to be trusted once with a Lady's Secret, not	256	FOR LOVE	III.1	105
Valentine:	Good.	257	FOR LOVE	III.1	141
Valentine:	I don't know but my Father in good Nature may press me .	259	FOR LOVE	III.1	225
Angelica:	If I marry, Sir Sampson, I'm for a good Estate with . .	260	FOR LOVE	III.1	253
Angelica:	any Man, and for any Man with a good Estate: Therefore .	260	FOR LOVE	III.1	254
Ben:	good part: For if I give a Jest, I'll take a Jest: And so .	262	FOR LOVE	III.1	342
Ben:	Look you Young Woman, You may learn to give good . .	264	FOR LOVE	III.1	402
Foresight:	Ah, good Mr. Scandal--	267	FOR LOVE	III.1	518
Foresight:	hem! faintish. My Heart is pretty good; yet it beats; and .	269	FOR LOVE	III.1	605
Foresight:	great Comfort to me. Hem, hem! good Night. . . .	271	FOR LOVE	III.1	654
Scandal:	Good Night, good Mr. Foresight;--and I hope Mars . .	271	FOR LOVE	III.1	656
Mrs Frail:	And tho' I have a good Portion; you know one	273	FOR LOVE	III.1	723
Ben:	as good Blood in my Veins, and a Heart as sound as a .	273	FOR LOVE	III.1	736
Scandal:	Why Faith, I have a good lively Imagination; and . .	275	FOR LOVE	III.1	813
Angelica:	deluded with vain Hopes. Good Nature and Humanity . .	277	FOR LOVE	IV.1	72
Scandal:	So, faith good Nature works a-pace; you were . . .	278	FOR LOVE	IV.1	84
Jeremy:	Good lack! What's the matter now? Are any more of .	278	FOR LOVE	IV.1	98
Jeremy:	is almost mad in good earnest, with the Joyful News of .	278	FOR LOVE	IV.1	100
Buckram:	Good, Sir. And the Conveyance is ready drawn in . .	278	FOR LOVE	IV.1	114
Buckram:	it is not good in Law.	279	FOR LOVE	IV.1	144
Foresight:	You speak with singular good Judgment, Mr. . . .	285	FOR LOVE	IV.1	347
Ben:	it's an ill Wind blows no body good,--may-hap I have .	287	FOR LOVE	IV.1	425
Ben:	it's an ill Wind blows no body good,--may-hap I have a .	287	FOR LOVE	IV.1	V425
Ben:	good riddance on you, if these be your Tricks,--What .	287	FOR LOVE	IV.1	426
Mrs Fore:	project in my head for you, and I have gone a good way .	288	FOR LOVE	IV.1	464
Mrs Fore:	glad at least to make you a good Settlement.--Here they .	288	FOR LOVE	IV.1	475
Tattle:	Hah! A good open Speaker, and not to be trusted . .	292	FOR LOVE	IV.1	629
Valentine:	strange thing: I found out what a Woman was good for. .	292	FOR LOVE	IV.1	641
Valentine:	O exceeding good to keep a Secret: For tho' she . . .	292	FOR LOVE	IV.1	645
Tattle:	Hah! good again, faith.	292	FOR LOVE	IV.1	647
Angelica:	Beaus, that set a good Face upon Fifty, Fifty! I have .	298	FOR LOVE	V.1	30
Sr Sampson:	devilish Handsom.--Madam, you deserve a good Husband, .	298	FOR LOVE	V.1	51
Angelica:	reasonable Stock of good Nature and Sense--For I .	299	FOR LOVE	V.1	63
Sr Sampson:	had a Son that was spoil'd among 'em; a good hopeful .	299	FOR LOVE	V.1	81
Sr Sampson:	live; and leave you a good Jointure when I die. . .	300	FOR LOVE	V.1	120
Sr Sampson:	little Sampson: Odd, Sampson's a very good Name for an .	301	FOR LOVE	V.1	154
Tattle:	pretty soft kind of Phrase, and with a good perswading .	302	FOR LOVE	V.1	182
Tattle:	Close Dog! A good Whoremaster, I warrant him . . .	302	FOR LOVE	V.1	196
Tattle:	Ay faith, so she will, Jeremy: You're a good Friend to .	302	FOR LOVE	V.1	206
Tattle:	turn of good Fortune, in the Lottery of Wives; and promise	304	FOR LOVE	V.1	269
Tattle:	were good--But this is the most cruel thing, to marry .	309	FOR LOVE	V.1	458
Sr Sampson:	In good time, Sir.	310	FOR LOVE	V.1	503
Sr Sampson:	Very good, Sir--Mr. Buckram, are you	311	FOR LOVE	V.1	513
Angelica:	be a good Father, or you'll never get a second Wife. I .	312	FOR LOVE	V.1	572
Scandal:	Lover: But there is a Third good Work, which I, in particular,	314	FOR LOVE	V.1	621
	But we can't fear, since you're so good to save us, .	315	FOR LOVE	EPI.	38
	Good Wits, forgive this Liberty we take, ...	323	M. BRIDE	PRO.	27
Almeria:	The silent Tomb receiv'd the good old King; . . .	326	M. BRIDE	I.1	10
Almeria:	Whilst the good King, to shun approaching Flames, . .	329	M. BRIDE	I.1	115
Almeria:	The good King flying to avoid the Flames, ...	329	M. BRIDE	I.1	V115

Good   (continued)
Almeria: While the good Queen and my Alphonso perish'd. 329   M. BRIDE   I.1   131
Leonora: Look down good Heav'n, with Pity on her 329   M. BRIDE   I.1   149
Almeria: Steal forth, and visit good Anselmo's Tomb. 331   M. BRIDE   I.1   199
Manuel: What Tears! my good old Friend.-- 332   M. BRIDE   I.1   272
Leonora: The poor Remains of good Anselmo rest; 340   M. BRIDE   II.2   7
Osmyn-Alph: Grant me but Life, good Heaven, but length of 343   M. BRIDE   II.2 135
Osmyn-Alph: That thus with open Hand it scatters good, ... 344   M. BRIDE   II.2 186
Osmyn-Alph: It scatters good, as in a Waste of Mercy? 344   M. BRIDE   II.2 V187
Osmyn-Alph: On high; and of good Men, the very best 350   M. BRIDE   III.1   29
Osmyn-Alph: My Friend, the Good thou dost deserve attend thee. . . 352   M. BRIDE   III.1 123
Gonsalez: I'm not i'th' Way at Present, good Alonzo. 371   M. BRIDE   IV.1 421
Gonsalez: Away, I've not been seen--haste good Alonzo. . . . 372   M. BRIDE   IV.1 442
Gonsalez: And say, I've not been seen--haste good Alonzo. . . . 372   M. BRIDE   IV.1 V442
Gonsalez: I shall make good, and shelter his Retreat. 379   M. BRIDE   V.2 128
Mirabell: good old Lady broke thro' her painful Taciturnity, with an   396   WAY WORLD   I.1   35
Mirabell: Woman's good Manners to her Prejudice; and think that . . 397   WAY WORLD   I.1   87
Fainall: To give the t'other his due; he has something of good . . 401   WAY WORLD   I.1 221
Fainall: To give t'other his due; he has something of good . . 401   WAY WORLD   I.1 V221
Mirabell: a good Memory, and some few Scraps of other Folks Wit. . 401   WAY WORLD   I.1 225
Mirabell: it is now and then to be endur'd. He has indeed one good . 401   WAY WORLD   I.1 227
Witwoud: Good, good Mirabell, le Drole! Good, good, hang . . . 402   WAY WORLD   I.1 253
Petulant: Well, well; I come--Sbud, a Man had as good 405   WAY WORLD   I.1 383
Mirabell: me; if thou hadst but good Nature equal to thy Wit . . 407   WAY WORLD   I.1 452
Mrs Fain: Why, had not you as good do it? 411   WAY WORLD   II.1   60
Mirabell: Yes, I think the good Lady wou'd marry any 418   WAY WORLD   II.1 311
Witwoud: As a Phisician of a good Air--I cannot help it . . . 419   WAY WORLD   II.1 339
Mirabell: Foible--The Lease shall be made good and the Farm . . 424   WAY WORLD   II.1 539
Lady Wish: O Marwood, let her come in. Come in good 426   WAY WORLD   III.1   40
Lady Wish: she has as good as put her Integrity into his Hands. . . 426   WAY WORLD   III.1   59
Foible: Poyson him? Poysoning's too good for him. Starve . . 427   WAY WORLD   III.1 106
Lady Wish: Things be remov'd, good Foible. 429   WAY WORLD   III.1 181
Foible: thought the former good Correspondence between your . . 430   WAY WORLD   III.1 197
Foible: Generosity.--Sweet Lady, to be so good! Mr. Mirabell . . 430   WAY WORLD   III.1 203
Marwood: now I'll have none of him. Here comes the good Lady, . 431   WAY WORLD   III.1 246
Marwood: of one Set of Acquaintance, tho' never so good, as we are of   432   WAY WORLD   III.1 300
Sir Wilful: you are in good Health, and so forth--To begin with . 439   WAY WORLD   III.1 544
Millamant: never bear that,--Good Mirabell don't let us be familiar . . 450   WAY WORLD   IV.1 200
Millamant: Well, If Mirabell shou'd not make a good Husband, . . 453   WAY WORLD   IV.1 315
Sir Wilful: the Sun's a good Pimple, an honest Soaker, he has a Cellar   456   WAY WORLD   IV.1 422
Sir Wilful: Antipodes--your Antipodes are a good rascally sort of
                topsy-turvy 456   WAY WORLD   IV.1 424
Lady Wish: Sir Rowland impatient? Good lack! what shall . . . 457   WAY WORLD   IV.1 460
Foible: No, good Sir Rowland, don't incurr the Law. . . . 461   WAY WORLD   IV.1 622
Waitwell: a good cause--my Lady shall be satisfied of my Truth . 461   WAY WORLD   IV.1 624
Foible: shou'd not have brib'd me to conspire against so Good, so   463   WAY WORLD   V.1   32
Mrs Fain: Have a good heart Foible, Mirabell's gone to . . . 464   WAY WORLD   V.1   65
Foible: Peace and Quietness by my good will: I had rather bring . 464   WAY WORLD   V.1   87
Lady Wish: good Genius. 466   WAY WORLD   V.1 172
Marwood: in more Naughty Law Latin; while the good Judge . . 467   WAY WORLD   V.1 219
Mirabell: so good a Lady, with a sincere remorse, and a hearty . 471   WAY WORLD   V.1 367
Sir Wilful: be O' the Quorum--an it were not as good a deed as to . 472   WAY WORLD   V.1 393
Millamant: Good Sir Wilfull, respite your valour. 473   WAY WORLD   V.1 431
Mirabell: O in good time--Your leave for the other Offender . . 475   WAY WORLD   V.1 506
Good-and-all (2)
Vainlove: Ay, you may take him for good-and-all if you . . . 40   OLD BATCH   I.1 113
Sharper: Faith e'en give her over for good-and-all; you can . . 41   OLD BATCH   I.1 161
Goodly (2)
Setter: dispose of! A goodly Pinnace, richly laden, and to launch   102   OLD BATCH   V.1 222
Marwood: Face, that goodly Face, which in defiance of her . . 433   WAY WORLD III.1 321
Goodness (14)
Sir Joseph: intire dependance Sir, upon the superfluity of your
                goodness, ... 49   OLD BATCH   II.1   56
Vainlove: ('tis true) where they find most Goodness to forgive.-- . 87   OLD BATCH   IV.3 138
Laetitia: Oh, Goodness keep us! Who's this? Who are you? . . . 92   OLD BATCH   IV.4 129
Lucy: Now, Goodness have Mercy upon me! Mr. Bellmour! . . 97   OLD BATCH   V.1   29
Maskwell: still to be more and more indebted to your goodness. . . 183   DOUBL DLR   IV.2   15
Lord Touch: for I know him to be all goodness,--yet my 200   DOUBL DLR   V.1 482
Leonora: His most industrious Goodness could invent; . . . 327   M. BRIDE   I.1   47
Gonsalez: What she has done, was in excess of Goodness: . . . 334   M. BRIDE   I.1 318
Osmyn-Alph: This exquisite, amazing Goodness, ... 343   M. BRIDE   II.2 145
Osmyn-Alph: This exquisite, this most amazing Goodness, . . . 343   M. BRIDE   II.2 V145
Zara: O thou dost wound me now, with this thy Goodness, . . 354   M. BRIDE   III.1 185
Lady Wish: forgetfulness--But my dear Friend is all Goodness. . . 431   WAY WORLD III.1 251
Lady Wish: benefits that I have receiv'd from your goodness? To you I   465   WAY WORLD   V.1 126
Mirabell: with all acknowledgments for your transcendent goodness. . 472   WAY WORLD   V.1 407
Goods (1)
Foresight: Undertakings successful; or Goods stoll'n recover'd, I . 241   FOR LOVE   II.1 217
Goose's (1)
Valentine: and blotted by every Goose's Quill. I know you; for I . 292   FOR LOVE   IV.1 639
Gore (1)
Manuel: With reeking Gore, from Traytors on the Back: . . . 367   M. BRIDE   IV.1 253
Gorg'd (1)
Osmyn-Alph: 'Till gorg'd with suffocating Earth. 358   M. BRIDE   III.1 V356
Gorge (1)
Manuel: And planted here to see me gorge this Bait, ... 373   M. BRIDE   V.1   43
Gorget (0)   see Frisoneer-gorget
Gorgon (1)
Lady Wish: appearance. He is as terrible to me as a Gorgon; if I
                see him, ... 470   WAY WORLD   V.1 336
Got (19)
Capt Bluff: got with thee, is he of mettle? 51   OLD BATCH   II.1 148
Araminta: Favours that are got by Impudence and Importunity, . . 58   OLD BATCH   II.2 135
Bellmour: --I got an Opportunity (after I had marry'd 'em) of . 100   OLD BATCH   V.2 149
Sir Joseph: whom I have got--now, but all's forgiven. 110   OLD BATCH   V.2 114
Vainlove: I know whom you have not got; pray Ladies 110   OLD BATCH   V.2 115

Grant   (continued)
Osmyn-Alph: Grant me but Life, good Heaven, but length of   .   .   .   343   M. BRIDE   II.2   135
Selim: This Grant--and I'll acquaint you with the rest.   .   .   .   362   M. BRIDE   IV.1   60
Gonsalez: I grant it, Sir, and doubt not, but in Rage   .   .   .   366   M. BRIDE   IV.1   218
Almeria: 'Till you are mov'd, and grant that he may live.   .   .   369   M. BRIDE   IV.1   331
Osmyn-Alph: Nay, I must grant, 'tis fit you shou'd be thus--   .   .   .   383   M. BRIDE   V.2   309
Witwoud: Bum-baily, that I grant you,--'Tis Pity faith; the   .   .   403   WAY WORLD   I.1   299
Witwoud: Bum-baily, that I grant you,--'Tis Pity; the   403   WAY WORLD   I.1 V299
Petulant: If I do, will you grant me common Sense then, for   .   .   407   WAY WORLD   I.1   458
Mirabell: Heav'n may grant it thee in the mean time.   407   WAY WORLD   I.1   461
Lady Wish: Grant me patience! I mean the Spanish Paper Idiot,
Complexion   425   WAY WORLD   III.1   12
Millamant: ha, ha; tho' I grant you 'tis a little barbarous, Ha, ha,
ha.   434   WAY WORLD   III.1   344
Lady Wish: You will grant me time to Consider.   469   WAY WORLD   V.1   290
Mirabell: grant I love you not too well, that's all my fear.   .   .   477   WAY WORLD   V.1   598
Granted (6)
Capt Bluff: be granted--But Alas Sir! were he alive now, he would   .   .   52   OLD BATCH   II.1   181
Scandal: may be granted him--In Short, he is a publick Professor of   226   FOR LOVE   I.1   378
Valentine: sometimes. I did not think she had granted more to any   .   229   FOR LOVE   I.1   487
Valentine: Pictures of all that have granted him favours, he has the   233   FOR LOVE   I.1   623
Almeria: The Queen too, did assist his Suit--I granted,   .   .   .   329   M. BRIDE   I.1   140
Petulant: I have a Humour to prove it, it must be granted.   .   .   435   WAY WORLD   III.1   406
Granting (1)
Osmyn-Alph: Granting you had, from you I have deserv'd it.   .   .   .   354   M. BRIDE   III.1   177
Grants (1)
Should Grants to Poets made, admit Resumption: .   .   .   393   WAY WORLD   PRO.   19
Grape (1)
Sir Wilful: Infidels, and believe not in the Grape. Your Mahometan,   .   456   WAY WORLD   IV.1   443
Grapple (1)
Ben: stand a stern a that'n, we shall never grapple together,--   263   FOR LOVE   III.1   361
Grasp (2)
Osmyn-Alph: I'll catch it 'ere it goes, and grasp her Shade.   .   .   341   M. BRIDE   II.2   53
Osmyn-Alph: To grasp and reach what is deny'd my Hands;   .   .   .   358   M. BRIDE   III.1   346
Grass (2)
Zara: To hide, the rustling Leaves, and bended Grass   .   .   .   375   M. BRIDE   V.1   109
Fainall: Wife to Grass--I have already a deed of Settlement of the   .   444   WAY WORLD   III.1   709
Grasshopper (1)
Sir Joseph: has made me as light as a Grasshopper.--Hist, hist,   .   .   85   OLD BATCH   IV.3   65
Grate (3)
Leonora: Where, while his Gaoler slept, I thro' the Grate   .   .   326   M. BRIDE   I.1   26
Zara: To grate the Sense, when entred here; from Groans,   .   .   379   M. BRIDE   V.2   136
Millamant: were wavering at the grate of a Monastery, with one foot   .   449   WAY WORLD   IV.1   163
Grateful (2)
Osmyn-Alph: Yet lighted up, his last most grateful Sacrifice;   .   .   .   357   M. BRIDE   III.1   322
Foible: cannot chuse but be grateful. I find your Ladyship has his   430   WAY WORLD   III.1   204
Gratefully (1)
We who remain, would gratefully repay   213   FOR LOVE   PRO.   23
Grater (0)   see Nutmeg-Grater
Grates (1)
Leonora: Unclos'd; the Iron Grates that lead to Death   340   M. BRIDE   II.2   11
Gratifie (3)
Maskwell: gratifie your taste, and cheat the World, to prove a
faithful   199   DOUBL DLR   V.1   438
We've something too, to gratifie ill Nature, ...   213   FOR LOVE   PRO.   31
Zara: But larger Means to gratifie the Will?   347   M. BRIDE   II.2   316
Gratifying (1)
Scandal: and gratifying your Creditors.   221   FOR LOVE   I.1   197
Gratitude (11)
Sharper: You Bellmour are bound in gratitude to stickle for   .   .   43   OLD BATCH   I.1   218
Sir Joseph: and gratitude of your superabundant humble Servant   .   .   49   OLD BATCH   II.1   68
Sharper: your gratitude and generosity. Since the refunding so   .   .   50   OLD BATCH   II.1   89
Sharper: your Gratitude and Generosity. Since the paying so   .   .   50   OLD BATCH   II.1 V 89
Heartwell: --And I cannot in gratitude (for I see which way thou   .   111   OLD BATCH   V.2   151
Mellefont: He has Obligations of Gratitude, to bind him to   .   .   .   131   DOUBL DLR   I.1   149
Lady Touch: Necessity, Impudence! Can no Gratitude   136   DOUBL DLR   I.1   345
Maskwell: Duty to Kings, Piety to Parents, Gratitude to Benefactors,   150   DOUBL DLR   II.1   446
Lady Ply: now you make me swear--O Gratitude forbid, that I   .   .   169   DOUBL DLR   IV.1   79
Maskwell: Gratitude, and my own Inclination, to be ever your   .   .   181   DOUBL DLR   IV.1   538
Maskwell: You oppress me with Bounty; my Gratitude is   189   DOUBL DLR   V.1   78
Grave (16)
Grave solemn Things, as Graces are to Feasts;   35   OLD BATCH   PRO.   3
Bellmour: work'd themselves six foot deep into a Grave--   .   .   .   38   OLD BATCH   I.1   26
Laetitia: to lie at peace in my cold Grave--Since it will   .   .   .   78   OLD BATCH   IV.1   111
Brisk: your self--I look grave, and ask the cause of this   .   .   134   DOUBL DLR   I.1   256
Brisk: to tell me--still I look grave, not so much as   .   .   .   134   DOUBL DLR   I.1   258
Almeria: Shall rest; shews me the Grave where Nature wearied,   .   .   340   M. BRIDE   II.2   17
Almeria: Shall rest; shews me the Grave where Nature weary   .   .   340   M. BRIDE   II.2 V 17
Osmyn-Alph: Grave, ...   341   M. BRIDE   II.2   38
Zara: Am I more loathsome to thee, than the Grave?   345   M. BRIDE   II.2   241
Zara: My Love. But to the Grave I'll follow thee--   346   M. BRIDE   II.2   243
Osmyn-Alph: And grovel with gash'd Hands to scratch a Grave,   .   .   .   358   M. BRIDE   III.1   353
Almeria: I'll dig a Grave, and tear up Death; I will;   370   M. BRIDE   IV.1   348
Gonsalez: And tho' I know he hates beyond the Grave   371   M. BRIDE   IV.1   409
Mirabell: Not at all: I happen to be grave to day; and you are   .   395   WAY WORLD   I.1   15
Mirabell: grave Faces, whisper'd one another; then complain'd   .   .   396   WAY WORLD   I.1   30
Millamant: Come, don't look grave then. Well, what do you   .   .   422   WAY WORLD   II.1   462
Gravely (1)
Maskwell: Ha, ha, ha, how gravely he looks--Come, come, I   .   .   .   157   DOUBL DLR   III.1   243
Gravity (3)
Bellmour: expected, from a person of your gravity.   43   OLD BATCH   I.1   236
Sharper: Gravity as a Bishop hears Venereal Causes in the Spiritual   100   OLD BATCH   V.1   139
Marwood: gravity of the Bench, and provoke Naughty Interrogatories,   467   WAY WORLD   V.1   218
Gray (1)   see Grey
Valentine: That Gray Hairs shou'd cover a Green Head--and   .   .   .   283   FOR LOVE   IV.1   271

Grazing (1)

		PAGE	TITLE	ACT.SC	LINE
Maskwell:	Grazing, and to--ha, ha, ha, Marry Cynthia my self;	149	DOUEL DLR	II.1	403

Great (108)

		PAGE	TITLE	ACT.SC	LINE
Bellmour:	Husband: For 'tis an Argument of her great Zeal towards	39	OLD BATCH	I.1	64
Heartwell:	the hatred of all the great Families in Town.	45	OLD BATCH	I.1	305
Sir Joseph:	have all my ready Mony to redeem his great Sword from	51	OLD BATCH	II.1	131
Sharper:	(aside). That you are Ile be sworn. Why that's great	51	OLD BATCH	II.1	136
Sir Joseph:	Ah, well said my Hero; was not that great Sir?	52	OLD BATCH	II.1	166
Araminta:	then we are in great danger of being dull--If my Musick-master	58	OLD BATCH	II.2	152
Setter:	Why if I were known, I might come to be a great	65	OLD BATCH	III.1	158
Capt Bluff:	By the immortal Thunder of great Guns, 'tis false	70	OLD BATCH	III.1	352
Sharper:	I'me afraid I give too great a Proof of my own at this time--	79	OLD BATCH	IV.1	158
Sharper:	great a Brute as to slight her.	80	OLD BATCH	IV.1	187
Belinda:	Jut-Windows, and her Mouth the great Door, most hospitably	84	OLD BATCH	IV.3	47
Belinda:	Almanack, and a Comb-Case; the Mother, a great Fruz-Towr,	84	OLD BATCH	IV.3	52
Sir Joseph:	(aside). The great Fortune, that dined at my Lady	86	OLD BATCH	IV.3	108
Belinda:	and laugh at the Vulgar.--Both the great Vulgar and the	87	OLD BATCH	IV.3	144
Belinda:	small.--Oh Gad! I have a great Passion for Cowley.	87	OLD BATCH	IV.3	145
Sir Joseph:	has been so a great while.	90	OLD BATCH	IV.4	40
Fondlewife:	Man is in great torment, he lies as flat--Dear, you	91	OLD BATCH	IV.4	95
Bellmour:	See the great Blessing of an easy Faith; Opinion	96	OLD BATCH	IV.4	271
Capt Bluff:	Husband--But here, both these are from Persons of great	103	OLD BATCH	V.1	269
Sir Joseph:	They are either from Persons of great Quality, or	103	OLD BATCH	V.1	271
Vainlove:	May I presume to hope so great a Blessing?	112	OLD BATCH	V.2	171
Brisk:	a great while first.	134	DOUEL DLR	I.1	264
Careless:	Well, but prithee don't let it be a great while, because	134	DOUEL DLR	I.1	265
Lord Froth:	Brisk to have Wit; my Wife says, he has a great deal. I	134	DOUEL DLR	I.1	274
Maskwell:	not to be heard. I have been a very great Rogue for your	136	DOUEL DLR	I.1	335
Lady Froth:	a great deal of Wit: Mr. Mellefont, don't you think Mr.	140	DOUEL DLR	II.1	86
Lady Touch:	Nay, no great matter, only--well I have	152	DOUEL DLR	III.1	81
Maskwell:	have been in a great measure kept by her, the case is alter'd;	155	DOUEL DLR	III.1	177
Careless:	tho' she begins to tack about; but I made Love a great	157	DOUEL DLR	III.1	266
Mellefont:	great Beard, like a Russian Bear upon a drift of Snow. You	158	DOUEL DLR	III.1	292
Mellefont:	are very great with him, I wonder he never told you his	158	DOUEL DLR	III.1	293
Lady Ply:	rather. (Curtesies). But I know Mr. Careless is so great a	159	DOUEL DLR	III.1	343
Sir Paul:	be Providence--ay, truly, Mr. Careless, my Lady is a great	160	DOUEL DLR	III.1	386
Sir Paul:	and it is a great grief to me, indeed it is Mr. Careless, that I	161	DOUEL DLR	III.1	410
Lord Froth:	'tis such a sight to see some teeth--sure you're a great	162	DOUEL DLR	III.1	460
Brisk:	sounds great; besides your Ladyship's Coach-man having a	163	DOUEL DLR	III.1	507
Lady Froth:	Then that t'other great strapping Lady--I	166	DOUEL DLR	III.1	580
Brisk:	great Beard that bristles through it, and makes her look as	166	DOUEL DLR	III.1	586
Sir Paul:	Person that I have a great value for not only for that, but	172	DOUEL DLR	IV.1	179
Sir Paul:	because he has a great veneration for your Ladiship.	172	DOUEL DLR	IV.1	180
Sir Paul:	great desire to have some Honours Conferr'd upon me,	180	DOUEL DLR	IV.1	478
Lady Touch:	But this is a thing of too great moment, to	191	DOUEL DLR	V.1	124
Cynthia:	My Lord, have patience, and be sensible how great	200	DOUEL DLR	V.1	474
	(A great shriek from the corner of the Stage. Lady Touchwood	202	DOUEL DLR	V.1	556
Jeremy:	some great Fortune; and his Fare to be paid him like the	218	FOR LOVE	I.1	100
Scandal:	worthless great Men, and dull rich Rogues, avoid a witty	219	FOR LOVE	I.1	132
Valentine:	By this, Scandal, you may see what it is to be great;	221	FOR LOVE	I.1	167
Scandal:	And you, like a true great Man, having engaged their	221	FOR LOVE	I.1	193
Valentine:	You know her temper; she never gave me any great	225	FOR LOVE	I.1	346
Scandal:	besides, Angelica has a great Fortune of her own; and great	225	FOR LOVE	I.1	353
Scandal:	Fortunes either expect another great Fortune, or a Fool.	225	FOR LOVE	I.1	354
Mrs Frail:	if he be but as great a Sea-Beast, as she is a Land-Monster,	231	FOR LOVE	I.1	570
Mrs Frail:	of these Mornings: I hear you have a great many Pictures.	232	FOR LOVE	I.1	598
Angelica:	great unnatural Teat under your Left Arm, and he another;	238	FOR LOVE	II.1	120
Angelica:	and the Goat. Bless me! there are a great many Horn'd	239	FOR LOVE	II.1	138
Sr Sampson:	Foot; have kiss'd the Great Mogul's Slipper, and rid a	241	FOR LOVE	II.1	220
Sr Sampson:	day in a Bill of Four thousand Pound: A great deal of	243	FOR LOVE	II.1	275
Foresight:	Aye indeed, Sir Sampson, a great deal of Money for	243	FOR LOVE	II.1	277
Mrs Frail:	Yes marry will I--A great piece of business to	246	FOR LOVE	II.1	418
Mrs Frail:	I'll swear you have a great deal of Impudence, and	247	FOR LOVE	II.1	453
Mrs Frail:	I'll swear you have a great deal of Confidence, and	247	FOR LOVE	II.1	V453
Mrs Frail:	take great care when one makes a thrust in Fencing, not to	248	FOR LOVE	II.1	474
Mrs Frail:	a loss, and have no great Stock either of Fortune or Reputation;	248	FOR LOVE	II.1	490
Mrs Fore:	for the Booby, it may go a great way towards his	249	FOR LOVE	II.1	502
Mrs Fore:	Soul, I shall fancy my self Old indeed, to have this great	249	FOR LOVE	II.1	512
Mrs Fore:	great lubberly Tarpawlin--Gad I warrant you, she	250	FOR LOVE	II.1	562
Miss Prue:	O Gemini! well, I always had a great mind to tell	252	FOR LOVE	II.1	629
Angelica:	Am I? Well, I freely confess I have resisted a great	257	FOR LOVE	III.1	137
Valentine:	the Great Turk.	257	FOR LOVE	III.1	167
Tattle:	whom I mean; for there were a great many Ladies raffled	258	FOR LOVE	III.1	188
Tattle:	whom I mean; for there was a great many Ladies raffled	258	FOR LOVE	III.1	V188
Miss Prue:	great Sea-calf.	264	FOR LOVE	III.1	418
Scandal:	it is with a great deal of Consideration, and Discretion, and	267	FOR LOVE	III.1	516
Scandal:	which is rightly observ'd by Gregory the Great in favour of	267	FOR LOVE	III.1	536
Foresight:	great Comfort to me. Hem, hem! good Night.	271	FOR LOVE	III.1	654
Scandal:	I have no great Opinion of my self; yet I think, I'm	272	FOR LOVE	III.1	690
Scandal:	I have no great Opinion of my self; but I think, I'm	272	FOR LOVE	III.1	V690
Mrs Fore:	--that I'm afraid you have a great many Confederates.	272	FOR LOVE	III.1	703
Jeremy:	Yes, Sir; you need make no great doubt of that; he	276	FOR LOVE	IV.1	3
Jeremy:	all: I suppose your Ladyship has thought him so a great	276	FOR LOVE	IV.1	30
Sr Sampson:	VALENTINE LEGEND, in great Letters.	281	FOR LOVE	IV.1	224
Jenny:	He's at the great Glass in the Dining-Room, Madam,	297	FOR LOVE	V.1	3
Sr Sampson:	a fair Lady, a great while--Odd, Madam, you have	298	FOR LOVE	V.1	14
Angelica:	Why you have no great reason to complain, Sir	298	FOR LOVE	V.1	16
Sr Sampson:	Zooks, but it is, Madam, a very great while; to	298	FOR LOVE	V.1	18
Jeremy:	Appetite to be fed with your Commands a great while;	301	FOR LOVE	V.1	172
Jeremy:	great Beauty and Fortune into your Arms, whom I have	302	FOR LOVE	V.1	178

Grief   (continued)
Osmyn-Alph:	O that's the greatest Grief--I am so poor,	. . . .	. 346	M. BRIDE	II.2 270
Osmyn-Alph:	With Grief, as wou'd draw Tears from Inhumanity.	. . .	. 352	M. BRIDE	III.1 115
Osmyn-Alph:	More Anxious Grief. This shou'd have better taught me;	. .	. 353	M. BRIDE	III.1 127
Osmyn-Alph:	Grief wou'd not double thus, his Darts against me.	. . .	. 356	M. BRIDE	III.1 283
Osmyn-Alph:	Grief cou'd not double thus, his Darts against me.	. . .	. 356	M. BRIDE	III.1 V283
Almeria:	Thou dost me Wrong, and Grief too robs my	. . . . .	. 356	M. BRIDE	III.1 284
Zara:	Confusion in his Face, and Grief in hers!	. . . .	. 359	M. BRIDE	III.1 397
Zara:	O 'tis more Grief but to suppose his Death,	. . . .	. 362	M. BRIDE	IV.1 27
Manuel:	Whence is thy Grief? give me to know the Cause,	. . .	. 367	M. BRIDE	IV.1 262
Almeria:	What means these Tears, but Grief unutterable?	. . .	. 368	M. BRIDE	IV.1 268
Gonsalez:	Your too excessive Grief, works on your Fancy,	. . .	. 370	M. BRIDE	IV.1 375
Almeria:	Their Heads in Sign of Grief and Innocence!	. . .	. 382	M. BRIDE	V.2 251
Waitwell:	Ay there's the Grief; that's the sad change of Life;	.	. 424	WAY WORLD	II.1 562

Griefs (8)
Almeria:	'Tis not in Harmony to calm my Griefs.	. . . . .	. 326	M. BRIDE	I.1 8
Leonora:	Your Griefs, there is no Cause--	. . .	. 326	M. BRIDE	I.1 16
Leonora:	Or moderate your Griefs; there is no Cause--	. . .	. 326	M. BRIDE	I.1 V 16
Almeria:	My Griefs? Thou dost already know 'em;	. . .	. 328	M. BRIDE	I.1 99
Almeria:	No, no, thy Griefs have done this to thee.	. . .	. 342	M. BRIDE	II.2 116
Almeria:	No, no, thy Griefs, I know, have done this to thee.	. . .	. 342	M. BRIDE	II.2 V116
Zara:	I come to mourn with thee; to share thy Griefs,	. . .	. 346	M. BRIDE	II.2 268
Almeria:	Why do'st thou heave, and stifle in thy Griefs?	. . .	. 356	M. BRIDE	III.1 272

Griev'd (2)
	Were you not griev'd, as often as you saw	. . . .	. 323	M. BRIDE	PRO. 17
Gonsalez:	She's greatly griev'd; nor am I less surpriz'd.	. . .	. 371	M. BRIDE	IV.1 396

Grievance (1)
Sr Sampson:	Body o' me, I don't know any universal Grievance,	. . .	. 266	FOR LOVE	III.1 485

Grievances (1)
Mellefont:	Grievances, he will I warrant you.	. . . . .	. 158	DOUBL DLR	III.1 294

Grieve (3)
	'Twould grieve your hearts to see him; shall I call him?	.	. 113	OLD BATCH	EPI. 25
	If in our larger Family we grieve	. . . . . .	. 213	FOR LOVE	PRO. 21
Manuel:	Then, then, to weep, and pray, and grieve? By Heav'n,	. .	. 333	M. BRIDE	I.1 314

Grievous (1)
Heli:	With Tyranny and grievous Impositions,	. . . . . .	. 351	M. BRIDE	III.1 69

Grim (3)
Almeria:	Of Eternal Peace. Death, grim Death, will fold	. . .	. 340	M. BRIDE	II.2 20
Almeria:	Of Peace Eternal. Death, grim Death, will fold	. . .	. 340	M. BRIDE	II.2 V 20
Zara:	Of grim and gashly Executioners.	. . . . .	. 379	M. BRIDE	V.2 141

Grimaces (1)
	And know each Critick by his sowre Grimaces.	. . . .	. 385	M. BRIDE	EPI. 6

Grin (3)
Lord Froth:	upon the broad grin, all laugh and no Company; ah, then	. 162	DOUBL DLR	III.1 459
	Tho Satire scarce dares grin, 'tis grown so mild;	. .	. 213	FOR LOVE	PRO. 33
Manuel:	His Teeth may grin, and mock at her Remorse,	. . . .	. 374	M. BRIDE	V.1 78

Grind (2)
Gonsalez:	Sweat by his Chariot Wheel, and lick, and grind	. . .	. 332	M. BRIDE	I.1 236
Osmyn-Alph:	That Piece-meal grind, are Beds of Down and Balm	. .	. 357	M. BRIDE	III.1 293

Grinn (1)
Belinda:	You think the malicious Grinn becomes you--The	. . .	. 56	OLD BATCH	II.2 56

Grinning (1)
Heartwell:	Sighing, Whining, Rhyming, Flattering, Lying, Grinning,	. 44	OLD BATCH	I.1 274

Grins (1)
Mellefont:	Heaven she laughs, grins, points to your Back, she forks	. 186	DOUBL DLR	IV.2 131

Gripings (0)   see Hand-Gripings

Grizled (1)
Almeria:	See, see, look yonder! where a grizled, pale	. . . .	. 371	M. BRIDE	IV.1 387

Groan (1)
Gonsalez:	Which groan beneath the Weight of Moorish Wealth.	. . .	. 331	M. BRIDE	I.1 228

Groans (4)
Almeria:	The Sighs, the Tears, the Groans, the restless Cares,	.	. 330	M. BRIDE	I.1 157
Almeria:	Or dying Groans from my Alphonso's Breast?	. . . .	. 371	M. BRIDE	IV.1 386
Garcia:	The Earth already groans to bear this Deed;	. . . .	. 378	M. BRIDE	V.2 75
Zara:	To grate the Sense, when entred here; from Groans,	. . .	. 379	M. BRIDE	V.2 136

Groat (5)
Valentine:	A very rich Man.--Not worth a Groat.	. . . . . .	. 216	FOR LOVE	I.1 20
Sr Sampson:	but a Groat in his Pocket, may have a Stomach capable	.	. 245	FOR LOVE	II.1 353
Sr Sampson:	--If I had it again, I wou'd not give thee a Groat,	. .	. 246	FOR LOVE	II.1 397
Sr Sampson:	be even with you, I won't give you a Groat. Mr. Buckram is	. 308	FOR LOVE	V.1 424
Fainall:	Not while you are worth a Groat, indeed my dear.	. . .	. 475	WAY WORLD	V.1 502

Grond (1)
Foresight:	And when the Head is set in Grond,	. . . . . .	. 236	FOR LOVE	II.1 55

Groom (0)   see Bride-groom

Gross (3)
Araminta:	Fie, this is gross Affectation--A little of Bellmour's	. 55	OLD BATCH	II.2 17
Fainall:	wilfully neglect the gross advances made him by my Wife;	. 413	WAY WORLD	II.1 144
Fainall:	That sham is too gross to pass on me,--tho 'tis	. . .	. 472	WAY WORLD	V.1 419

Ground (14)
Brisk:	ground? Mortgage for a Bottle, ha? Careless, this is your	128	DOUBL DLR	I.1 21
Lord Touch:	Father-in-Law, and me, to maintain our ground against	. 131	DOUBL DLR	I.1 173
Careless:	bewitching Fair? O let me grow to the ground here, and	. 170	DOUBL DLR	IV.1 91
Sir Paul:	whether I fly on Ground, or walk in Air--Gads bud, she	. 172	DOUBL DLR	IV.1 198
Lady Touch:	Ground, be buried quick beneath it, e're I be consenting to	. 186	DOUBL DLR	IV.2 99
Lady Touch:	Ground, be buried quick beneath it, e're I'll be			
	consenting to	. . . .	. 186	DOUBL DLR	IV.2 V 99
	Their Labours lost upon the ungrateful Ground,	. . .	. 213	FOR LOVE	PRO. 8
	Their Labours lost upon ungratefull Ground,	. . .	. 213	FOR LOVE	PRO. V 8
Angelica:	we were ever after to live under Ground, or at least making	. 237	FOR LOVE	II.1 83
Sr Sampson:	up old Star-Gazer. Now is he poring upon the Ground for	. 265	FOR LOVE	III.1 466
Heli:	I saw you on the Ground, and rais'd you up.	. . .	. 344	M. BRIDE	II.2 181
Osmyn-Alph:	Break on the flinty Ground my throbbing Breast,	. . .	. 358	M. BRIDE	III.1 352
Osmyn-Alph:	. . . where I will bite the Ground	. . . . .	. 358	M. BRIDE	III.1 V355
	(They point at the Bowl on the Ground.)	382	M. BRIDE	V.2 252

Grounded (1)
Careless:	you have confessed, is grounded upon his Interest, that,	. 131	DOUBL DLR	I.1 164

Groundless (1)
Marwood:	that can confirm your groundless Accusation. I hate him.	. 414	WAY WORLD	II.1	154

Grovel (3)
Bellmour:	his Glass. Let low and earthy Souls grovel till they have	37	OLD BATCH	I.1	25
Bellmour:	his Glass. Let low and earthly Souls grovel 'till they have	37	OLD BATCH	I.1 V	25
Osmyn-Alph:	And grovel with gash'd Hands to scratch a Grave, . .	358	M. BRIDE	III.1	353

Groveling (1)
| Zara: | This groveling Baseness--Thou say'st true, I know . . | 348 | M. BRIDE | II.2 | 335 |

Groves (1)
| Lady Wish: | Desarts and Solitudes; and feed harmless Sheep by Groves | . 465 | WAY WORLD | V.1 | 133 |

Grow (17)
	You think that strange--no matter, he'll out grow it. . .	35	OLD BATCH	PRO.	16
Belinda:	Ha, ha, ha, O Gad, Men grow such Clowns when	108	OLD BATCH	V.2	25
Heartwell:	or the Clown may grow boistrous, I have a Fly-flap. .	108	OLD BATCH	V.2	35
Careless:	No faith, but your Fools grow noisy--and if a . . .	127	DOUBL DLR	I.1	7
Careless:	No faith, but your Fools grow noisie--and if a . . .	127	DOUBL DLR	I.1 V	7
Lord Froth:	and mortify the Poets; the Fellows grow so Conceited, .	133	DOUBL DLR	I.1	228
Lord Froth:	and mortifie the Poets; the Fellows grow so Conceited, .	133	DOUBL DLR	I.1 V	228
Lady Froth:	Lord you sha'n't kiss it so much; I shall grow jealous, I	140	DOUBL DLR	II.1	77
Lady Froth:	Lord you shan't kiss it so much; I shall grow jealous, I	140	DOUBL DLR	II.1 V	77
Careless:	bewitching Fair? O let me grow to the ground here, and	170	DOUBL DLR	IV.1	91
Lady Touch:	(aloud). Never, never! I'le grow to the	186	DOUBL DLR	IV.2	98
Mellefont:	Industry grow full and ripe, ready to drop into his mouth,	187	DOUBL DLR	IV.2 V	144
Jeremy:	You'll grow Devilish fat upon this Paper-Diet. . . .	216	FOR LOVE	I.1	5
Mrs Fore:	often done in Duels, take care of one another, and grow	248	FOR LOVE	II.1	478
Scandal:	Mr. Foresight, we had best leave him. He may grow .	293	FOR LOVE	IV.1	668
Osmyn-Alph:	My Arms which ake to fold thee fast, and grow . . .	343	M. BRIDE	II.2	123
Fainall:	Fie, fie Friend, if you grow Censorious I must leave .	397	WAY WORLD	I.1	99

Growing (7)
Araminta:	Nay come, I find we are growing serious, and	58	OLD BATCH	II.2	151
Belinda:	with their Feathers growing the wrong way.--O such . .	84	OLD BATCH	IV.3	30
Araminta:	young, and your early baseness has prevented its growing	87	OLD BATCH	IV.3	172
Scandal:	Girls, and growing Boys.	275	FOR LOVE	III.1	818
Osmyn-Alph:	And growing to his dead Father's Shrowd, roots up .	341	M. BRIDE	II.2	39
Osmyn-Alph:	And growing to his Father's Shrowd, roots up	341	M. BRIDE	II.2 V	39
Servant-M:	dispatch, besides, the Parson growing hoarse, we were .	398	WAY WORLD	I.1	116

Grown (15)
Heartwell:	am grown very entertaining to my self, and (as I am .	73	OLD BATCH	III.2	82
Lady Touch:	grown together when I told you--almost a Twelvemonth .	153	DOUBL DLR	III.1	110
Mellefont:	Industry grown full and ripe, ready to drop into his mouth,	187	DOUBL DLR	IV.2	144
	Tho Satire scarce dares grin, 'tis grown so mild; .	213	FOR LOVE	PRO.	33
Mrs Fore:	is design'd for his Wife, is grown fond of Mr. Tattle;	248	FOR LOVE	II.1	500
Mrs Fore:	is design'd to be his Wife, is grown fond of Mr. Tattle;	248	FOR LOVE	II.1 V	500
Sr Sampson:	Years--I warrant he's grown--Call him in, bid .	259	FOR LOVE	III.1	214
Scandal:	My Passion for you is grown so violent--that I am no .	269	FOR LOVE	III.1	586
Almeria:	What then am I? Am I more senseless grown	326	M. BRIDE	I.1	6
Almeria:	Lead me, for I am bolder grown: Lead me	339	M. BRIDE	II.1	81
Almeria:	Lead me, for I am bolder grown: Lead on	339	M. BRIDE	II.1 V	81
Zara:	You're grown a Favourite since last we parted; . . .	359	M. BRIDE	III.1	412
Mirabell:	Town took notice that she was grown fat of a suddain; .	397	WAY WORLD	I.1	74
Mirabell:	They are now grown as familiar to me as my own Frailties;	399	WAY WORLD	I.1	172
Marwood:	found it: The secret is grown too big for the Pretence: .	433	WAY WORLD	III.1	317

Grows (6)
Bellmour:	Amour as he cares for, and quits it when it grows stale, or	42	OLD BATCH	I.1	212
Mrs Frail:	time he grows only rude to his Wife, and that is the highest	231	FOR LOVE	I.1	564
Foresight:	and hem! and my hem!--breath, hem!--grows short; .	269	FOR LOVE	III.1	610
Scandal:	(aside). Miracle! the Monster grows loving. . .	281	FOR LOVE	IV.1	205
Fainall:	Not at all; Witwoud grows by the Knight, like a . . .	401	WAY WORLD	I.1	212
Millamant:	Wilfull grows very powerful, Egh! how he smells! I shall	456	WAY WORLD	IV.1	432

Grudging (1)
| Careless: | Nay, I don't despair--but still she has a grudging . . | 158 | DOUBL DLR | III.1 | 304 |

Grutch (1)
| Sir Wilful: | 'Sheart, an you grutch me your Liquor, make a . . . | 455 | WAY WORLD | IV.1 | 394 |

Guard (5) see Black-Guard
Careless:	may not have the weakest Guard, where the Enemy is . .	131	DOUBL DLR	I.1	143
	Perez and a Guard, and attended by Selim, and several .	335	M. BRIDE	I.1	383
Gonsalez:	Nor Centinel, nor Guard! the Doors unbarr'd!	376	M. BRIDE	V.2	1
Fainall:	Indeed? are you provided of a Guard, with your . . .	473	WAY WORLD	V.1	432
Fainall:	Indeed? are you provided of your Guard, with your . .	473	WAY WORLD	V.1 V	432

Guardian (1)
| Witwoud: | and this Fellow was my Guardian; ay, ay, I was glad . | 440 | WAY WORLD | III.1 | 558 |

Guardians (1)
| Mellefont: | Like any two Guardians to an Orphan Heiress-- . . . | 156 | DOUBL DLR | III.1 | 216 |

Guards (11)
	and Guards, who are ranged in Order, round the Stage. .	332	M. BRIDE	I.1	267
	(Guards carry off Osmyn.)	349	M. BRIDE	II.2	375
Heli:	Gave order to the Guards for my Admittance.	351	M. BRIDE	III.1	44
Selim:	Have Cause to fear his Guards may be corrupted, . . .	362	M. BRIDE	IV.1	51
Manuel:	For doubling all our Guards; Command that our . . .	364	M. BRIDE	IV.1 V	132
Zara:	I think it fit to tell you that your Guards	364	M. BRIDE	IV.1	142
Manuel:	Is Treason then so near us as our Guards!	364	M. BRIDE	IV.1	145
Gonsalez:	As she pretends--I doubt it now--Your Guards . . .	366	M. BRIDE	IV.1	206
Manuel:	O'er them that are thy Guards--Mark that thou . . .	374	M. BRIDE	V.1	55
Alonzo:	Which may be still mistaken by the Guards, ...	379	M. BRIDE	V.2	119
	Guards and Attendants.)	382	M. BRIDE	V.2	274

Gudgeon (1)
| Maskwell: | Fools! then that hungry Gudgeon Credulity, will bite at | 150 | DOUBL DLR | II.1 | 459 |

Guess (13) see Other-guess-toys
Vainlove:	Pleasure, I guess you mean.	37	OLD BATCH	I.1	13
Heartwell:	over. For such I guess may have been your late . . .	42	OLD BATCH	I.1	192
Bellmour:	humble, pliant, easie thing, a Lover, so guess at Plagues in	106	OLD BATCH	V.1	382
Scandal:	before they act, so they rarely give us any light to guess at	225	FOR LOVE	I.1	349
Tattle:	Yes, my Dear--I think I can guess--But	251	FOR LOVE	II.1	583
Tattle:	For Heaven's sake, if you do guess, say nothing; Gad, .	258	FOR LOVE	III.1	194
Scandal:	Can't you guess at what ought to afflict you and . .	266	FOR LOVE	III.1	483

Ha   (continued)

		PAGE	TITLE	ACT.SC	LINE
Fondlewife:	Ha, how's that? Stay stay, did you leave word . . .	76	OLD BATCH	IV.1	19
Belinda:	most rueful! Ha, ha, ha: O Gad, I hope no-body will . .	83	OLD BATCH	IV.3	9
Belinda:	my Dear,--I have seen such unhewn Creatures since,--Ha,	83	OLD BATCH	IV.3	11
Belinda:	ha, ha, I can't for my Soul help thinking that I look just	83	OLD BATCH	IV.3	12
Belinda:	me now? Hideous, ha? Frightful still? Or how?	83	OLD BATCH	IV.3	17
Belinda:	hot, out of her Under-Petticoat-Pocket,--Ha, ha, ha:	84	OLD BATCH	IV.3	44
Belinda:	ha, ha, ha.--Well, a Lover in the state of separation from	86	OLD BATCH	IV.3	133
Laetitia:	Ha! This fool may be of use. Stand off, rude Ruffian.	90	OLD BATCH	IV.4	46
Sir Joseph:	O Lord! Oh terrible! Ha, ha, ha, Is your Wife	90	OLD BATCH	IV.4	55
Laetitia:	Ha!	92	OLD BATCH	IV.4	123
Fondlewife:	Ha! This is Apocryphal; I may chuse whether I	95	OLD BATCH	IV.4	217
Bellmour:	Ha! Is not that Heartwell at Sylvia's Door; be gone . .	97	OLD BATCH	V.1	10
Bellmour:	marry 'em.--Ha? Are not Matters in this posture? . . .	97	OLD BATCH	V.1	44
Sharper:	Ha, ha; 'Twill be a pleasant Cheat.--I'll plague . . .	99	OLD BATCH	V.1	86
Vainlove:	Ha! It has a Colour.--But how do you know	99	OLD BATCH	V.1	110
Setter:	under Hatches.--Ha! All this committed to my Care! . .	102	OLD BATCH	V.1	225
Heartwell:	I'll dissemble, and try him.--Ha, ha, ha. Why, Tom; Is	104	OLD BATCH	V.1	300
Sharper:	My old Batchelor married! That were a Jest. Ha, . . .	105	OLD BATCH	V.1	319
Sharper:	ha, ha.	105	OLD BATCH	V.1	320
Belinda:	Ha, ha, ha, O Gad, Men grow such Clowns when	108	OLD BATCH	V.2	25
Belinda:	any body else. Jesus! how he looks already. Ha, ha, ha.	108	OLD BATCH	V.2	31
Belinda:	any body else. How he looks already. Ha, ha, ha. . .	108	OLD BATCH	V.2 V 31	
Bellmour:	Ha, ha, ha.	108	OLD BATCH	V.2	32
Capt Bluff:	--That you are over-reach'd too, ha, ha, ha, only . . .	110	OLD BATCH	V.2	107
Brisk:	ground? Mortgage for a Bottle, ha? Careless, this is your	128	DOUEL DLR	I.1	21
Brisk:	Pooh, ha, ha, ha, I know you envy me. Spite, proud . .	128	DOUEL DLR	I.1	25
Brisk:	to Laugh at. I think there I was with you, ha? Mellefont.	128	DOUEL DLR	I.1	30
Brisk:	said it out of thy Company.--Careless, ha?	128	DOUEL DLR	I.1	39
Brisk:	I'gad, ha, ha, ha.	132	DOUEL DLR	I.1	207
Lady Touch:	Ha!	136	DOUEL DLR	I.1	358
Lady Froth:	leap, I vow I sigh when I think on't: my dear Lord! ha,	140	DOUEL DLR	II.1	63
Lady Froth:	ha, ha, do you remember, my Lord?	140	DOUEL DLR	II.1	64
Lady Froth:	ha, ha, ha.	141	DOUEL DLR	II.1	123
Brisk:	Because my Lord's Title's Froth, I'gad, ha, ha, ha, . .	141	DOUEL DLR	II.1	124
Brisk:	Deuce take me very a-Propos and Surprizing, ha, ha, ha.	141	DOUEL DLR	II.1	125
Mellefont:	Ha! how's this?	148	DOUEL DLR	II.1	396
Maskwell:	execution of all her Plots? Ha, ha, ha, by Heaven it's true;	149	DOUEL DLR	II.1	398
Maskwell:	of Doors; and to--ha, ha, ha, I can't tell ycu for Laughing,	149	DOUEL DLR	II.1	401
Maskwell:	Grazing, and to--ha, ha, ha, Marry Cynthia my self; . .	149	DOUEL DLR	II.1	403
Mellefont:	Ha! O I see, I see my Rising Sun! Light breaks . . .	149	DOUEL DLR	II.1	405
Mellefont:	Ha! O see, I see my Rising Sun! Light breaks	149	DOUEL DLR	II.1 V405	
Mellefont:	get into her Confidence.--Ha! How But was it her . .	149	DOUEL DLR	II.1	409
Mellefont:	Ha, ha, ha, I, a very Fury; but I was most afraid . .	149	DOUEL DLR	II.1	416
Mellefont:	Ha, ha, ha, ay, a very Fury; but I was most afraid . .	149	DOUEL DLR	II.1 V416	
Maskwell:	Ha, ha, ha, I know her temper,--well, you must . . .	149	DOUEL DLR	II.1	419
Maskwell:	an universal Leveller of Mankind. Ha! but is there not such	150	DOUEL DLR	II.1	450
Maskwell:	will be made a Fool of by no body, but himself: Ha, ha, ha.	150	DOUEL DLR	II.1	456
Lady Touch:	Lord--Ha, ha, ha. Well but that's all--now you have . .	153	DOUEL DLR	III.1	90
Maskwell:	Thirst. Ha! yonder comes Mellefont thoughtful. Let me .	155	DOUEL DLR	III.1	186
Maskwell:	think: Meet her at eight--hum--ha! by Heaven I . . .	155	DOUEL DLR	III.1	187
Mellefont:	ha?	156	DOUEL DLR	III.1	206
Mellefont:	Ha!--Pho, you trifle.	156	DOUEL DLR	III.1	231
Maskwell:	Ha, ha, ha, how gravely he looks--Come, come, I . . .	157	DOUEL DLR	III.1	243
Brisk:	Like an Oyster at low Ebb, I'gad--ha, ha, ha.	165	DOUEL DLR	III.1	576
Sir Paul:	did you swear, did that sweet Creature swear! ha? How .	171	DOUEL DLR	IV.1	139
Sir Paul:	durst you swear without my Consent, ha? Gads—bud, who .	171	DOUEL DLR	IV.1	140
Brisk:	(sings). I'm sick with Love, ha ha, prithee come (walking	175	DOUEL DLR	IV.1	306
Lady Froth:	thought Mr. Brisk could have been in Love, ha ha ha. O	176	DOUEL DLR	IV.1	333
Lady Froth:	in Love! Ha ha ha	176	DOUEL DLR	IV.1	342
Brisk:	O barbarous, to turn me into ridicule! Yet, ha ha ha. .	176	DOUEL DLR	IV.1	343
Brisk:	ha ha ha; yet by Heavens I have a violent passion for your	176	DOUEL DLR	IV.1	345
Lady Froth:	Seriously? Ha ha ha.	176	DOUEL DLR	IV.1	347
Brisk:	Seriously, ha ha ha. Gad, I have, for all I Laugh. . .	176	DOUEL DLR	IV.1	348
Lady Froth:	Ha ha ha! What d'e think I Laugh at? Ha ha ha. . . .	176	DOUEL DLR	IV.1	349
Brisk:	Me I'gad, ha ha.	176	DOUEL DLR	IV.1	350
Lady Froth:	Brisk, ha ha ha.	176	DOUEL DLR	IV.1	353
Lady Froth:	Seriously, ha ha ha.	176	DOUEL DLR	IV.1	355
Brisk:	That's well enough; let me perish, ha ha ha. O Miraculous,	177	DOUEL DLR	IV.1	356
Lady Touch:	(Aside.) Ha! my Lord listning! O Fortune has o'repaid me	186	DOUEL DLR	IV.2	95
Mellefont:	Ha!	186	DOUEL DLR	IV.2	101
Lord Touch:	Ha!	188	DOUEL DLR	V.1	32
Maskwell:	and, if I can, all thought of that pernicious Beauty. Ha!	188	DOUEL DLR	V.1	42
Mellefont:	No, no; ha, ha, I dare swear thou wilt not.	193	DOUEL DLR	V.1	229
Lady Touch:	Ha! a steady Villain to the last!	197	DOUEL DLR	V.1	384
Maskwell:	Ha, ha, ha.	198	DOUEL DLR	V.1	390
Lady Touch:	Ha! do you mock my Rage? then this shall	198	DOUEL DLR	V.1	391
Lord Touch:	Ha! O poison to my Ears! what do I hear!	198	DOUEL DLR	V.1	427
Lord Touch:	ha, I'll do't, where's Mellefont, my poor injured Nephew.	200	DOUEL DLR	V.1	478
Tattle:	Ha, ha, ha; nay, now you make a Jest of it indeed. . .	227	FOR LOVE	I.1	403
Valentine:	Ha, ha, ha.	227	FOR LOVE	I.1	436
Scandal:	and ha, ha, ha, well, go on, and what did you say to her	227	FOR LOVE	I.1	439
Scandal:	no? You have had her? Ha?	228	FOR LOVE	I.1	477
Nurse:	Dinner--good lack-a-day, ha, ha, ha, O strange; I'll vow	235	FOR LOVE	II.1	22
Nurse:	and swear now, ha, ha, ha, Marry and did you ever see the	235	FOR LOVE	II.1	23
Foresight:	Ha, How? Faith and troth I'm glad of it, and so I . .	236	FOR LOVE	II.1	29
Angelica:	Ascendant, ha, ha, ha.	237	FOR LOVE	II.1	73
Angelica:	Ha, ha, ha.	239	FOR LOVE	II.1	155
Sr Sampson:	How now, who sent for you? Ha! what wou'd you . . .	242	FOR LOVE	II.1	261
Sr Sampson:	Oh Sir, I understand you,--that's all, ha?--	243	FOR LOVE	II.1	289
Sr Sampson:	The Spleen, ha, ha, ha, a Pox confound you---	245	FOR LOVE	II.1	376
Mrs Frail:	Now if I cou'd wheedle him, Sister, ha? You understand	248	FOR LOVE	II.1	495
Miss Prue:	any more Lavender among my Smocks--ha, Cousin? . . .	249	FOR LOVE	II.1	530
Scandal:	Ha, ha, ha.	254	FOR LOVE	III.1	49
Sr Sampson:	help of a Parson, ha? Odd if he should I cou'd not be angry	265	FOR LOVE	III.1	461
Sr Sampson:	Ha! thou'rt melancholly old Prognostication; As melancholly	265	FOR LOVE	III.1	463

Ha (continued)

Speaker	Line	PAGE	TITLE	ACT.SC	LINE
Sr Sampson:	Ha! thou'rt melancholick old Prognostication; As melancholick	265	FOR LOVE	III.1	V463
Foresight:	Cheeks have been gather'd many Years;--ha! I do not	269	FOR LOVE	III.1	603
Foresight:	my Pulses ha!--I have none--Mercy on me--hum--Yes,	269	FOR LOVE	III.1	606
Angelica:	Ha! I saw him wink and smile--I fancy 'tis a	277	FOR LOVE	IV.1	53
Sr Sampson:	What, is he gone out of Town, run away, ha!	279	FOR LOVE	IV.1	122
Valentine:	(starting). Ha! who's that?	279	FOR LOVE	IV.1	151
Sr Sampson:	shake--I believe thou can'st write, Val: Ha, boy? Thou	281	FOR LOVE	IV.1	207
Valentine:	Ha, ha, ha; you need not run so fast, Honesty will	282	FOR LOVE	IV.1	246
Valentine:	not overtake you--Ha, ha, ha, the Rogue found me	282	FOR LOVE	IV.1	247
Valentine:	A ha! Old Truepenny, say'st thou so? thou hast	282	FOR LOVE	IV.1	268
Foresight:	What says he? What, did he prophesie? Ha, Sir	283	FOR LOVE	IV.1	277
Foresight:	Ha! say you so?	283	FOR LOVE	IV.1	301
Mrs Frail:	Ha, ha, ha, no doubt on't.--	287	FOR LOVE	IV.1	445
Valentine:	upon, and look Matrimony in the face. Ha, ha, ha! That a	289	FOR LOVE	IV.1	526
Valentine:	the Pidgeons ought rather to be laid to his feet, ha, ha, ha.	289	FOR LOVE	IV.1	528
Valentine:	Argo's hundred Eyes be shut, ha? No body shall know,	290	FOR LOVE	IV.1	552
Valentine:	It is enough. Ha! Who's here?	291	FOR LOVE	IV.1	589
Angelica:	Ha, ha, ha, you see he denies it.	295	FOR LOVE	IV.1	742
Angelica:	Ha, ha, ha, is he mad, or no, Jeremy?	295	FOR LOVE	IV.1	752
Tattle:	close, ha?	302	FOR LOVE	V.1	189
Tattle:	like a Nun; and I must be hooded like a Friar; ha, Jeremy?	302	FOR LOVE	V.1	198
Foresight:	to try if I could discover it by my Art--hum, ha! I	304	FOR LOVE	V.1	259
Sr Sampson:	mine elect? a ha, Old Foresight, Uncle Foresight, wish me	307	FOR LOVE	V.1	377
Valentine:	Ha!	312	FOR LOVE	V.1	559
Manuel:	Ha! what? thou dost not weep to think of that?	333	M. BRIDE	I.1	302
Osmyn-Alph:	Osmyn-Alph. Ha! it sinks, it falls,	341	M. BRIDE	II.2	52
Heli:	By Heav'n 'tis he, and with--ha! Almeria!	341	M. BRIDE	II.2	63
Heli:	Ha! 'tis he! and with--Almeria!	341	M. BRIDE	II.2	V 63
Almeria:	But still, how camest thou hither? how thus?--Ha!	344	M. BRIDE	II.2	166
Almeria:	But still, how camest thou hither? how thus?--Ha!	344	M. BRIDE	II.2	V166
Osmyn-Alph:	Where? ha! what do I see? Antonio here!	344	M. BRIDE	II.2	169
Osmyn-Alph:	Where? ha! what do I see? Antonio!	344	M. BRIDE	II.2	V169
Osmyn-Alph:	Ha, Zara!	346	M. BRIDE	II.2	247
Osmyn-Alph:	Ha, 'tis Zara!	346	M. BRIDE	II.2	V247
Manuel:	Of Death and Night? Ha! what Disorder's this?	348	M. BRIDE	II.2	354
Osmyn-Alph:	If my Alphonso--Ha!	350	M. BRIDE	III.1	9
Osmyn-Alph:	Where is Alphonso? ha! where? where indeed?	352	M. BRIDE	III.1	86
Zara:	Ha!	359	M. BRIDE	III.1	384
Zara:	Ha!	360	M. BRIDE	III.1	V444
Zara:	Ha! haste thee! fly, prevent his Fate and mine;	361	M. BRIDE	IV.1	17
Zara:	(aside to Selim). Ha! hear'st thou that? Is Osmyn then	363	M. BRIDE	IV.1	90
Gonsalez:	Ha!	365	M. BRIDE	IV.1	183
Manuel:	Ha! who may live? take heed, no more of that.	369	M. BRIDE	IV.1	332
Manuel:	Ha! what say'st thou? Husband! Husband!	369	M. BRIDE	IV.1	339
Gonsalez:	Ha!	370	M. BRIDE	IV.1	383
Gonsalez:	Her husband too! Ha! where is Garcia then?	371	M. BRIDE	IV.1	400
Manuel:	Ha! seize that Mute; Alonzo, follow him.	373	M. BRIDE	V.1	13
Manuel:	Ha! stop and seize that Mute; Alonzo, follow him.	373	M. BRIDE	V.1	V 13
Manuel:	And treble Fury--Ha! who's there?	373	M. BRIDE	V.1	37
Manuel:	And trebled Fury--Ha! who's there?	373	M. BRIDE	V.1	V 37
Manuel:	Ha! stir not, on thy Life: For thou wert fix'd,	373	M. BRIDE	V.1	42
Zara:	The Mute not yet return'd! 'tis strange. 'twas	374	M. BRIDE	V.1	91
Zara:	The Mute not yet return'd! ha! 'twas the King!	374	M. BRIDE	V.1	V 91
Gonsalez:	Ha! sure he sleeps--all's dark within, save what	376	M. BRIDE	V.2	6
Gonsalez:	What says my Son? what Ruine? ha? what	377	M. BRIDE	V.2	53
Garcia:	Ha! what? atone this Murther with a greater!	378	M. BRIDE	V.2	73
Zara:	What have you seen? Ha! wherefore stare you thus,	380	M. BRIDE	V.2	155
Zara:	Ha! prostrate! bloody! headless! O--start Eyes,	380	M. BRIDE	V.2	162
Zara:	Ha! prostrate! bloody! headless! O--I'm lost,	380	M. BRIDE	V.2	V162
Almeria:	And point! what mean they; Ha! a Cup. O well	382	M. BRIDE	V.2	253
Almeria:	Ha! point again? 'tis there, and full I hope.	382	M. BRIDE	V.2	258
Osmyn-Alph:	Ill-fated Zara! Ha! a Cup? alas!	383	M. BRIDE	V.2	312
Mirabell:	How pertinently the Jade answers me! Ha? almost	398	WAY WORLD	I.1	108
Witwoud:	Truths! Ha, ha, ha! No, no, since you will have it,	404	WAY WORLD	I.1	339
Witwoud:	Ha, ha, ha; I had a Mind to see how the Rogue	406	WAY WORLD	I.1	409
Witwoud:	wou'd come off--Ha, ha, ha; Gad I can't be angry	406	WAY WORLD	I.1	410
Petulant:	be disinherited, ha?	407	WAY WORLD	I.1	440
Marwood:	Ha, ha, ha; he comes opportunely for you.	412	WAY WORLD	II.1	85
Fainall:	Ha, ha, ha; you are my Wife's Friend too.	414	WAY WORLD	II.1	170
Mirabell:	--Ha, no, I cry her Mercy.	418	WAY WORLD	II.1	325
Millamant:	Ha, ha, ha. What wou'd you give, that you cou'd help	422	WAY WORLD	II.1	458
Millamant:	Face. Ha, ha, ha--Well I won't laugh, don't be	422	WAY WORLD	II.1	475
Lady Wish:	a--Ha Foible? A swimminess in the Eyes--Yes, I'll	429	WAY WORLD	III.1	169
Lady Wish:	a--Ha Foible? A swimmingness in the Eyes--Yes, I'll	429	WAY WORLD	III.1	V169
Millamant:	O silly! Ha, ha, ha. I cou'd laugh immoderately.	433	WAY WORLD	III.1	335
Millamant:	Ha, ha, ha. Pardon me, dear Creature, I must laugh, Ha,	434	WAY WORLD	III.1	343
Millamant:	ha; tho' I grant you 'tis a little barbarous, Ha, ha, ha.	434	WAY WORLD	III.1	344
Millamant:	it--Ha, ha, ha.	434	WAY WORLD	III.1	353
Millamant:	loves me, Ha, ha, ha. How can one forbear laughing to	434	WAY WORLD	III.1	356
Witwoud:	and Base. Ha, Petulant!	435	WAY WORLD	III.1	397
Sir Wilful:	my Aunt han't din'd yet--Ha, Friend?	437	WAY WORLD	III.1	450
Sir Wilful:	Fellow, ha!	437	WAY WORLD	III.1	456
Sir Wilful:	if thou see'st her, ha Friend?	437	WAY WORLD	III.1	460
Witwoud:	Ha, ha, ha, to him; to him Petulant, smoke him.	438	WAY WORLD	III.1	488
Witwoud:	Ha, ha, ha.	438	WAY WORLD	III.1	495
Petulant:	Of the Family of the Furnivals. Ha, ha, ha!	440	WAY WORLD	III.1	555
Millamant:	Ha, ha, ha. Yes, 'tis like I may.--You have nothing	448	WAY WORLD	IV.1	132
Millamant:	Ay, ay, ha, ha, ha.	448	WAY WORLD	IV.1	152
Lady Wish:	be wrong'd after all, ha? I don't know what to think,--	466	WAY WORLD	V.1	181

Ha' (4)

Speaker	Line	PAGE	TITLE	ACT.SC	LINE
Nurse:	Town,--Marry, pray Heav'n they ha' given her any	235	FOR LOVE	II.1	21
Ben:	afore I ha' done with 'en.	265	FOR LOVE	III.1	438

Ha' (continued)
    Sir Wilful: We'll drink and we'll never ha' done Boys 455   WAY WORLD IV.1 416
    Lady Wish: wou'd ha' shriek'd, If she had but seen a Man, till she was 466 WAY WORLD V.1   187
Ha'n't (1)
    Sir Joseph: that's a better Jest than tother. 'Tis a sign you and I
                   ha'n't 50   OLD BATCH II.1 116
Habit (15)
    Bellmour: much more agreeable, if you can counterfeit his Habit to
                   blind 39   OLD BATCH I.1   88
    Bellmour: No, But is a pretender, and wears the habit of a . . . 46   OLD EATCH I.1   366
    Bellmour: Well in this Fanatick Fathers habit, will I confess . 64   OLD BATCH III.1 130
                   (The Street Enter Bellmour in Fanatick habit, Setter.) 75   OLD BATCH IV.1
                   A Servant introducing Bellmour in Fanatick Habit, with a 80 OLD BATCH IV.2
    Laetitia: Appearance promised: The Piety of your Habit was . . . 81   OLD BATCH IV.2   25
    Bellmour: for him, and procured his Habit; in which, I pass'd upon 94 OLD BATCH IV.4 209
                   (Enter Bellmour in Fanatick Habit, and Setter.) . . . 96   OLD BATCH V.1
    Bellmour: I'll leave him with you, and go shift my Habit. . . . . 100 OLD BATCH V.1   160
    Maskwell: the business in hand--have you provided a Habit for . 195   DOUEL DLR V.1   283
    Mellefont: are all in my Chamber; I want nothing but the Habit. . 196 DOUEL DLR V.1   344
    Maskwell: the Chaplain's habit, wait for Cynthia in your
                   Dressing-Room: 199   DOUEL DLB V.1   442
                   (Mellefont disguis'd in a Parson's Habit . . . . 202 DOUBL DLB V.1 V566
    Marwood: there, like a new masking Habit, after the Masquerade is 433 WAY WCBLD III.1 310
                   (Enter Sir Wilfull Witwoud in a Country Riding Habit, and 436 WAY WCBLD III.1 443
Habitation (2)
    Sr Sampson: t'other spins his Habitation out of his Entrails. . . . 246 FOR LCVE   II.1 393
    Sr Sampson: t'other spins his Habitation out of his own Entrails, . 246 FOR LCVE   II.1 V393
Habits (1)
    Leonora: Of two in shining Habits, cross the Ile, ... 344 M. BRIDE   II.2 192
Habitual (1)
    Mirabell: habitual to me, to remember 'em without being displeas'd. 399 WAY WCBLD I.1   171
Hack (1)
    Sir Wilful: Thigh shall hack your Instrument of Ram Vellum to shreds, . 473 WAY WCBLD V.1   426
Hackney (5)
    Brisk: Hackney Coach-man? . . . . 165 DOUEL DLB III.1 546
    Lady Froth: Jehu was a Hackney Coach-man, when my Lord took him. . 165 DOUEL DLR III.1 548
    Brisk: Was that he then, I'm answered, if Jehu was a Hackney . 165 DOUEL DLR III.1 549
    Brisk: Was he? I'm answered, if Jehu was a Hackney . . . . . 165 DOUEL DLR III.1 V549
    Angelica: Hackney, or a Chair, and leave you to erect a Scheme, and 237 FOR LOVE   II.1 68
Hackney-Coach (4)
    Belinda: Oh the most inhumane, barbarous Hackney-Coach! . . . . 83 OLD BATCH IV.3 4
    Mrs Frail: go to Covent-Garden Square in a Hackney-Coach, and take . 246 FOR LCVE   II.1 419
    Mrs Fore: publick, and to be seen with a man in a Hackney-Coach . 247 FOR LCVE   II.1 430
    Mrs Frail: your self happy in a Hackney-Coach before now.--If I . 247 FOR LCVE   II.1 437
Hackney-Coachman (2)
    Scandal: with a Hackney-Coachman. . . . . 233 FOR LCVE   I.1   640
    Witwoud: and Mask, slap into a Hackney-Coach, and drive hither . 405 WAY WORLD I.1   373
Had (309)
Had'nt (1)
    Ben: gav'n that wipe--He had'nt a word to say, and so I left 'n, 286 FOR LOVE   IV.1 385
Had'st (2)
    Mrs Frail: to find you out.--Had'st thou the Impudence to aspire . 286 FOR LOVE   IV.1 407
    Lady Wish: me to that faithless Mirabell?--What had'st thou to . 427 WAY WORLD III.1 81
Hadn't (1)
    Sir Joseph: An it hadn't been for a civil Gentleman as came by . . . 47 OLD BATCH II.1 8
Hadst (8)
    Bellmour: Would thou hadst come a little sooner, Vainlove . . . 42 OLD BATCH I.1   194
    Araminta: my Honour.--But tho' thou hadst all the Treachery . . . 87 OLD BATCH IV.3 167
    Scandal: Not knew 'em? Why, thou never hadst to do with . . . . 226 FOR LOVE   I.1   401
    Sr Sampson: as if thou hadst spilt the Salt, or par'd thy Nails of a . 265 FOR LCVE   III.1 464
    Sr Sampson: as if thou hadst spilt the Salt, or par'd thy Nails on a . 265 FCB LCVE   III.1 V464
    Almeria: O Leonora, hadst thou known Anselmo, ... 327 M. BRIDE   I.1   32
    Almeria: Thou hadst no Cause, but general Compassion. . . . . . 327 M. EBIDE   I.1   34
    Mirabell: me; if thou hadst but good Nature equal to thy Wit . . 407 WAY WORLD I.1   452
Hae (3)
    Bellmour: Well and how Setter hae, does my Hypocrisy fit me hae? . 75   OLD BATCH IV.1 3
    Millamant: Hae? Dear Creature I ask your Pardon--I . . . . 434 WAY WORLD III.1 348
Haggar'd (1)
    Zara: With haggar'd Eyes? why are your Arms a-cross . . . . 380 M. EBIDE   V.2   157
Hah (9)
    Scandal: 20000 [Pounds] in Money. A hah! Old Trap. . . . . . . 223 FOR LOVE   I.1   270
    Valentine: hah! . . . . 223 FOR LOVE   I.1   280
    Sr Sampson: be--hah! old Merlin! body o' me, I'm so glad I'm . . . 240 FOR LOVE   II.1 184
    Sr Sampson: erect with that audacious face, hah? Answer me that? . 244 FOR LOVE   II.1 329
    Tattle: Hah! A good open Speaker, and not to be trusted . . . 292 FOR LOVE   IV.1 629
    Tattle: Hah! good again, faith. . . . . 292 FOR LOVE   IV.1 647
    Sir Wilful: Indeed! Hah! Look ye, look ye, you do? Nay, ... 448 WAY WORLD IV.1 123
    Sir Wilful: Dear Heart, that's much--Hah! that you . . . . 448 WAY WORLD IV.1 127
    Sir Wilful: shou'd hate 'em both! Hah 'tis like you may; there are . 448 WAY WCBLD IV.1 128
Hainous (1)
    Fondlewife: detestable, how hainous, and how Crying a Sin, the Sin . 77 OLD BATCH IV.1 68
Hair (12)
    Sir Joseph: Nay, now I must speak; it will split a Hair by the . . 53 OLD BATCH II.1 232
    Brisk: if she were plaistred with Lime and Hair, let me perish. . 166 DOUEL DLB III.1 587
    Zara: Ev'n then. Kneeling on Earth, I loos'd my Hair, . . . 346 M. BRIDE   II.2 281
    Osmyn-Alph: Let ev'ry Hair, which Sorrow by the Roots, ... 350 M. EBIDE   III.1 16
    Osmyn-Alph: Disfigur'd Face, and rive my clotted Hair, ... 358 M. BRIDE   III.1 351
    Osmyn-Alph: And dash my Face, and rive my clotted Hair, ... 358 M. BRIDE   III.1 V351
    Millamant: know why--They serve one to pin up one's Hair. . . . 419 WAY WORLD II.1 362
    Witwoud: Hair with all your Letters? I find I must keep Copies. . 419 WAY WORLD II.1 364
    Millamant: pin up my Hair with Prose. . . . . 419 WAY WORLD II.1 366
    Millamant: . . . I fancy ones Hair wou'd not . . . . 419 WAY WOBLD II.1 V366
    Millamant: --Is not all the Powder out of my Hair? . . . . 432 WAY WOBLD III.1 289
    Lady Wish: and Weaving of dead Hair, with a bleak blew Nose, over a . 462 WAY WORLD V.1   5
Hairs (1)
    Valentine: That Gray Hairs shou'd cover a Green Head--and . . . . 283 FOR LOVE   IV.1 271

Hale (1)
  Sr Sampson: --Come, don't despise Fifty; odd Fifty, in a hale . . . 298   FOR LCVE   V.1   26
Half (39)
  Bellmour: place, and the pleasure of enjoying some half a score . . 41   OLD BATCH I.1 139
  Sharper: came half despairing to recover; but thanks to my better . 49   OLD BATCH II.1 83
  Bellmour: Or as you did to day, when half afraid you snatch'd . 63   OLD BATCH III.1 95
  Lord Touch: (half aside). I don't know that. . . . . 151 DOUBL DLR III.1 26
  Lady Ply: your next half year. 162 DOUBL DLR III.1 452
  Lady Ply: the next half year. 162 DOUBL DLR III.1 V452
  Lady Froth: to you for the hint, stay we'll read over those half a score 164 DOUEL DLR III.1 511
  Lady Froth: I have seen her take 'em half chew'd out of her . . . 165 DOUBL DLR III.1 570
  Maskwell: He was an ill Man, and I have gain'd; for half my self
          I lent . 188 DOUBL DLR V.1 23
  Lady Touch: Why then you don't know half your . . . 192 DOUBL DLR V.1 169
  Maskwell: Well, get your selves ready, and meet me in half . 194 DOUBL DLR V.1 238
  Maskwell: Meet me in half an Hour, here in your own . . 195 DOUBL DLR V.1 292
  Jeremy: would have been an Alderman by this time with half the . 218 FCR LCVE I.1 90
  Jeremy: sake. Now like a thin Chairman, melted down to half . 218 FOR LOVE I.1 98
  Scandal: by Heav'n to seize the better half. . . . . . . 219 FOR LOVE I.1 135
  Jeremy: Nothing new, Sir; I have dispatch'd some half a . 220 FOR LOVE I.1 166
  Snap: must dc our Office, tell us.--We have half a dozen . . 224 FOR LCVE I.1 296
  Scandal: Come then, sacrifice half a Dozen Women cf good . . . 230 FOR LOVE I.1 526
  Tattle: at home, and the Parson had not half his Congregation. . 258 FOR LOVE III.1 170
  Angelica: is over, methinks I am not half so sorry for him as I was-- 277 FOR LCVE IV.1 83
  Angelica: is over, methinks I am not half so sorry as I was-- . 277 FOR LOVE IV.1 V 83
  Mrs Frail: --O' my life I am half vex'd at the insensibility of a . 287 FOR LOVE IV.1 452
  Angelica: by over acting Sobriety; I was half inclining to believe . 296 FOR LOVE IV.1 765
  Angelica: like him, it's a sign he likes me; and that's more than half 297 FOR LCVE V.1 6
  Jeremy: and meet you in half a quarter of an hour, with your . 303 FOR LOVE V.1 216
  Tattle: know of it half an Hour ago; and the Lady stays for me, . 305 FOR LCVE V.1 294
  Almeria: O no, thou know'st not half--thou know'st . . . . 328 M. BRIDE I.1 88
  Almeria: O no, thou know'st not half, ... 328 M. BRIDE I.1 V 88
  Fainall: What? tho' half her Fortune depends upon her . . . 396 WAY WCRLD I.1 45
  Fainall: Marry her, marry her; be half as well acquainted . . 400 WAY WCRLD I.1 175
  Fainall: Yes; he is half Brother to this Witwoud by a former . 400 WAY WCRLD I.1 192
  Witwoud: Ay, ay, my half Brother. My half Brother he is, . 402 WAY WCRLD I.1 250
  Mirabell: Then 'tis possible he may be but half a Fool. . . . 402 WAY WCRLD I.1 252
  Poible: some distanded Officer I warrant--Half Pay is but . 427 WAY WORLD III.1 97
  Marwood: prevent their Plot,--the half of Millamant's Fortune is . 442 WAY WORLD III.1 641
  Poible: Mirabell has waited this half hour for an Opportunity to 445 WAY WORLD IV.1 44
  Petulant: Thou art (without a figure) Just one half of an Ass; . 454 WAY WORLD IV.1 350
  Petulant: and Baldwin yonder, thy half Brother is the rest--A gemini 454 WAY WORLD IV.1 351
Half-way (1)
  Almeria: Nature inclines, and half-way meets that Duty, ... 369 M. BRIDE IV.1 323
Haling (1)
        (Fondlewife haling out Bellmour.) . . 92 OLD BATCH IV.4 120
Hall (6)   see Westminster-Hall, Wittoll-hall
  Belinda: Front of her Father's Hall; her Eyes were the two . . 84 OLD BATCH IV.3 46
  Brisk: The Fiddles have stay'd this hour in the Hall; and my . 174 DOUBL DLR IV.1 277
  Brisk: Sir Paul, will you send Careless into the Hall if you . 175 DOUBL DLR IV.1 286
  Lady Wish: Boots here--Go down into the Hall--Dinner . . . . 441 WAY WCRLD III.1 621
  Fainall: Deputy-Lieutenant's Hall. . . . . 442 WAY WORLD III.1 648
  Foible: and plac'd the Foot-men in a Row in the Hall, in their . 444 WAY WORLD IV.1 4
Halves (2)
  Scandal: must pay a Tribute to one, and go halves with the t'other. 271 FOR LOVE III.1 677
  Scandal: must pay a Tribute to one, and go halves with t'other. . 271 FOR LCVE III.1 V677
Haly (1)
  Sr Sampson: What, thou art not angry for a Jest, my good Haly--I . 242 FOR LOVE II.1 246
Hammock (1)
  Ben: chance to swing in a Hammock together. . . . . . . 263 FOR LCVE III.1 377
Hamper (3)
  Foresight: reveng'd on you, Cockatrice; I'll hamper you--You . . 238 FOR LOVE II.1 114
  Sr Sampson: wou'd she wou'd like me, then I shou'd hamper my young . 298 FOR LCVE V.1 49
  Foible: I'll hamper you for that (says he) you and your old Frippery 428 WAY WCRLD IV.1 115
Han't (9)
        Well, the Deuce take me, if I han't forgot it. . 35 OLD BATCH PRO. 22
  Sir Joseph: Purpose, if he han't frighted it out of my memory. Hem! . 49 OLD BATCH II.1 53
  Sir Joseph: Sum--But han't you found it Sir! . . . . . 50 OLD BATCH II.1 93
  Lady Froth: O-law, I swear it's but the sixth,--and I han't . . . 166 DOUEL DLR III.1 612
  Nurse: . . . or any Teats, but two that han't . . . . . 238 FOR LOVE II.1 V125
  Sr Sampson: Again! 'Ouns han't you four thousand Pound . . . 246 FOR LOVE II.1 396
  Sr Sampson: Hopes of my Family--I han't seen him these Three . . 259 FOR LCVE III.1 213
  Ben: We're merry Folk, we Sailors, we han't much to care for. . 275 FOR LCVE III.1 799
  Sir Wilful: my Aunt han't din'd yet--Ha, Friend? . . . . . 437 WAY WORLD III.1 450
Hand (106)   see Before-hand, Short-hand, Warm-hand
  Bellmour: I marry Sir, I have a Hawks Eye at a Womans hand . . . 38 OLD BATCH I.1 32
  Bellmour: hand to it, and dub him Cuckold, that he may be of equal . 41 OLD BATCH I.1 158
        (Laying his Hand upon his
          Sword.) . . . . 51 OLD BATCH II.1 149
        Patch upon one Eye, and a Book in his Hand.) . . . . 80 OLD BATCH IV.2
        kisses her hand, behind Fondlewife's back.) . . . . 95 OLD BATCH IV.4 242
  Bellmour: Lucy.--Here's my Hand, I will; with a fresh Assurance. . 98 OLD BATCH V.1 72
  Setter: of Gold in his Hand, I'll dispose of mine to the best . 102 OLD BATCH V.1 234
  Sir Joseph: no Quality at all, 'tis such a Damn'd ugly Hand. . 103 OLD BATCH V.1 272
  Capt Bluff: I'll give't you under my Hand.--In the mean . 104 OLD BATCH V.1 278
  Belinda: (Giving her Hand.) . . . 112 OLD BATCH V.2 169
  Cynthia: shall never have it under my Hand. . . . . . . 139 DOUBL DLR II.1 44
  Cynthia: (Squeezes him by the hand, looks kindly on him, sighs, and 140 DOUBL DLR II.1 65
        Hand, it is an Accident of Fortune. . . . . . 142 DOUBL DLR II.1 163
  Mellefont: There's comfort in a hand stretch'd out, to one . . . 148 DOUBL DLR II.1 389
  Mellefont: hand: For a woman never thinks a man truly in love with . 159 DOUBL DLR III.1 316
  Cynthia: People walk hand in hand, there's neither overtaking nor . 168 DOUBL DLR IV.1 15
  Cynthia: Within reach; for example, give me your hand; . . . 168 DOUBL DLR IV.1 23
  Careless: feast that hand; O let me press it to my heart, my . 170 DOUBL DLR IV.1 92
  Sir Paul: your Ladiships Hand. . . . . . . 172 DOUBL DLR IV.1 193
  Sir Paul: Why now as I hope to be saved, I had no hand in . . . 180 DOUBL DLR IV.1 468

289

Handl'd   (continued)
Marwood: and very learnedly handl'd. . . . . 436 WAY WORLD III.1 413
Handle (5)
Saygrace: But pithy, and I will handle it with Discretion. . . . 195 DOUBL DLR   V.1 298
Tattle: a part of my Character, to handle the Reputation of others 226 FOR LOVE   I.1 394
Tattle: a part of my Character, to handle the Reputations of others 226 FOR LOVE   I.1 V394
Foible: too (says he) I'll handle you-- . . . . 428 WAY WORLD III.1 116
Lady Wish: Audacious Villain! handle me, wou'd he durst . . . . . 428 WAY WORLD III.1 117
Hands (38)
Bellmour: Business upon my hands, because it lay too heavy upon his: 41 OLD BATCH   I.1 141
Bellmour: hands cf some Nightwalkers, who I suppose would have . . 46 OLD BATCH   I.1 360
Sir Joseph: But I profess, 'tis a Dirt I have wash'd my Hands of . 50 OLD BATCH   I.1 111
Vainlove: That Tongue, which denies what the Hands have . . . . 88 OLD BATCH IV.3 183
              and Sword in his Hands; as just risen from Table: . . 127 DOUBL DLR   I.1
Mellefont: hands and sprawling in his Sleep; and ever since she has 158 DOUBL DLR III.1 289
Mellefont: him swaddled up in Blankets, and his hands and feet . 158 DOUBL DLR III.1 290
Lady Froth: then joyn hands again; I could teach my Lord this Dance . 177 DOUBL DLR IV.1 367
Lord Touch: joyn your hands.--Unwearied Nights, and wishing . . . 203 DOUBL DLR   V.1 587
Valentine: I'll take some of their Trade out of their Hands. . . 217 FOR LOVE   I.1   60
Scandal: with a hundred Hands, two Heads, and but one Face; a . 233 FOR LOVE   I.1 643
Scandal: in their Hands, and Horn-Books about their Necks. . . 234 FOR LOVE   I.1 656
Foresight: have your Fortune in your own Hands--But I'll find . . 238 FOR LOVE II.1 115
Sr Sampson: Spiders; the one has its Nutriment in his own hands; and 246 FOR LOVE II.1 392
Mrs Fore: world to answer for, remember I wash my Hands of it, . 251 FOR LOVE II.1 578
Miss Prue: Ah, but I'll hold the Door with both Hands, and . . . 252 FOR LOVE II.1 651
Valentine: Alas, poor Man; his Eyes are sunk, and his Hands . . 289 FOR LOVE IV.1 519
Valentine: come forth with lab'ring Callous Hands, a Chine of Steel, 289 FOR LOVE IV.1 523
Angelica: No, Sir Sampson, I have no Quarrel upon my Hands . . 298 FOR LOVE   V.1   44
Almeria: That Day, that fatal Day, our Hands were joyn'd: . . 329 M. BRIDE   I.1 133
Manuel: With speed--yet stay--my Hands alone can . . . . . 336 M. BRIDE   I.1 411
Manuel: Shifting the Prize in unresolving Hands: . . . . . 337 M. BRIDE   I.1 455
Osmyn-Alph: To grasp and reach what is deny'd my Hands; . . . . 358 M. BRIDE III.1 346
Osmyn-Alph: And grovel with gash'd Hands to scratch a Grave, . . 358 M. BRIDE III.1 353
Almeria: Curst these weak Hands, that cou'd not hold him here; . 370 M. BRIDE IV.1 373
Almeria: Could Eyes endure to guide such cruel Hands? . . . . 382 M. BRIDE   V.2 237
Almeria: Behold me well; your bloody Hands have err'd, . . . 382 M. BRIDE   V.2 247
              Devoutly praying, with up-lifted Hands, ... 385 M. BRIDE EPI.   21
Messenger: Wilfull, which I am charg'd to deliver into his own Hands. 400 WAY WORLD   I.1 184
Marwood: Hands, do--I'd leave 'em to get loose. . . . . . . 416 WAY WORLD II.1 226
Lady Wish: that, Changeling, dangling thy Hands like Bobbins before 425 WAY WORLD III.1   14
Lady Wish: she has as good as put her Integrity into his Hands. . 426 WAY WORLD III.1   59
Foible: of kissing your Ladyship's Hands after Dinner. . . . 428 WAY WORLD III.1 127
Foible: Letter, who must deliver it into your own hands. . . 459 WAY WORLD IV.1 550
Waitwell: that into your hands. . . . . 461 WAY WORLD IV.1 635
Marwood: be transferr'd to the hands, nay into the Throats and . 468 WAY WORLD   V.1 232
Mirabell: my hands--I own I have not deserv'd you shou'd owe . . 473 WAY WORLD   V.1 451
Mirabell: your hands as Witnesses to a certain Parchment. . . . 475 WAY WORLD   V.1 524
Handsom (7)
Laetitia: be mistaken after all this.--A handsom Fellow if he had . 81 OLD BATCH IV.2   43
Tattle: I was reveng'd upon him, for he had a handsom Daughter . 258 FOR LOVE III.1 172
Sr Sampson: devilish Handsom.--Madam, you deserve a good Husband, . 298 FOR LOVE   V.1   51
Sr Sampson: Odd, you're devilish Handsom; Faith and Troth, you're . 301 FOR LOVE   V.1 141
Sr Sampson: very Handsom, and I'm very Young, and very Lusty-- . . 301 FOR LOVE   V.1 142
Ben: The Young Woman's a Handsom Young Woman, I . . . . . 308 FOR LOVE   V.1 412
Petulant: matters conclude Premises,--If you are not handsom, . 454 WAY WORLD IV.1 367
Handsome (24)
Bellmour: What, the old Banker with the handsome Wife? . . . . 39 OLD BATCH   I.1   71
Sharper: too handsome for a Wife. . . . . 41 OLD BATCH   I.1 164
Fondlewife: vexation, for a Man to have a handsome Wife. . . . . 76 OLD BATCH IV.1   40
Mellefont: handsome, and knows it; is very silly, and thinks she has 130 DOUBL DLR   I.1 129
Careless: you. She is Handsome and cunning, and naturally . . . 131 DOUBL DLR   I.1 161
Valentine: your handsome Daughter--Come a good Husband to . . . 222 FOR LOVE   I.1 251
Tattle: Handsome, you must deny it, and say I flatter you-- . 252 FOR LOVE II.1 616
Mrs Frail: That wou'd be pity, such a Handsome Young . . . . . 261 FOR LOVE III.1 304
Ben: Handsome! he, he, he, nay forsooth, an you be for . . 261 FOR LOVE III.1 306
Ben: handsome Gentlewoman for a Bed-fellow hugely, how say . 262 FOR LOVE III.1 325
Ben: you? You heard t'other handsome Young Woman speak . . 264 FOR LOVE III.1 410
Miss Prue: Well, and there's a handsome Gentleman, and a . . . 264 FOR LOVE III.1 414
Scandal: I'll Swear you're Handsome. . . . . 272 FOR LOVE III.1 706
Miss Prue: Robin the Butler, he says he loves me, and he's a Handsome 305 FOR LOVE   V.1 317
Ben: And there's the handsome young Woman, she, as they . . 306 FOR LOVE   V.1 345
Witwoud: She's handsome; but she's a sort of an uncertain . . 408 WAY WORLD   I.1 471
Witwoud: Now, Demme, I shou'd hate that, if she were as handsome 408 WAY WORLD   I.1 477
Mirabell: you have made a handsome Woman blush, then you think . 409 WAY WORLD   I.1 527
Fainall: that was a Widow, a young Widow, a handsome Widow; . . 415 WAY WORLD II.1 211
Mirabell: longer handsome when you've lost your Lover; your . . 420 WAY WORLD II.1 392
Millamant: If they did not commend us, we were not handsome! . . 420 WAY WORLD II.1 400
Millamant: one was not handsome. Beauty the Lover's Gift-- . . . 420 WAY WORLD II.1 402
Lady Wish: Sir Rowland handsome? Let my Toilet be remov'd--I'll . 429 WAY WORLD III.1 171
Lady Wish: dress above. I'll receive Sir Rowland here. Is he handsome? 429 WAY WORLD III.1 172
Handsomer (1)
Millamant: handsomer--And within a Year or two as young. . . . . 434 WAY WORLD III.1 359
Handsomest (1)
Vainlove: handsomest Woman in Company, so consequently apply'd . . 39 OLD BATCH   I.1   97
Handsomly (1)
Laetitia: not guilty, or he has handsomly excused him. . . . . 82 OLD BATCH IV.2   60
Hang (24)
              Hang me if I know what he prays, or how! . . . . . 35 OLD BATCH PRO.   20
Bellmour: Hang him, no, he a Draggon! if he be 'tis a very . . 46 OLD BATCH   I.1 351
Lucy: Hang Art, Madam, and trust to Nature for . . . . . 62 OLD BATCH III.1   54
Lucy: Hang thee--Beggars Curr--Thy Master is but . . . . 66 OLD BATCH III.1 192
Araminta: Hang me, if I pity you; you are right enough . . . 109 OLD BATCH   V.2   61
Mellefont: No, no, hang him, he has no tast.--but dear Brisk . . 128 DOUBL DLR   I.1   43
Mellefont: No, no, hang him, he has no taste.--but dear Brisk . . 128 DOUBL DLR   I.1 V 43
Lady Froth: self; for hang me if I have not a violent Passion for Mr. 176 DOUBL DLR IV.1 352
Mellefont: doubt you have some unrepented Sins that may hang . . 184 DOUBL DLR IV.2   55

Hang (continued)

		PAGE	TITLE	ACT.SC	LINE
Scandal:	Hang him, let him alone, he has a mind we should	228	FOR LOVE	I.1	450
Scandal:	Hang him, he has nothing but the Seasons and the	232	FOR LOVE	I.1	601
Mrs Frail:	O hang you; who'll believe you?--You'd be	250	FOR LOVE	II.1	554
Mrs Fore:	will hang us--He'll think we brought 'em acquainted.	250	FOR LOVE	II.1	569
Tattle:	hang me if I know the reason of it.	251	FOR LOVE	II.1	584
Sr Sampson:	Heart: Hang him, Mungrel; cast him off; you shall see the	260	FOR LOVE	III.1	260
Mrs Fore:	Oh hang him old Fox, he's too cunning,	288	FOR LOVE	IV.1	462
Sr Sampson:	outsides. Hang your side-Box Beaus; no, I'm none of those,	298	FOR LOVE	V.1	34
Sr Sampson:	ready to hang themselves, or to be hang'd by the Law,	299	FOR LOVE	V.1	58
Manuel:	Her Chains hang heavier on him than his own.	335	M. BRIDE	I.1	381
Witwoud:	Good, good Mirabell, le Drole! Good, good, hang	402	WAY WORLD	I.1	253
Witwoud:	No, no, hang him, the Rogue has no Manners at	403	WAY WORLD	I.1	297
Waitwell:	am tantaliz'd on a rack; And do but hang Madam, on the	457	WAY WORLD	IV.1	492
Waitwell:	am tantaliz'd on the rack; And do but hang Madam, on the	457	WAY WORLD	IV.1	V492
Lady Wish:	Go hang out an old Prisoneer-gorget, with a yard of	462	WAY WORLD	V.1	14

Hang-Dog (1)

Lucy:	Ther's the Hang-Dog his Man--I had a power over	64	OLD BATCH	III.1	145

Hang'd (10)   see Hung

	I shall be hang'd for wanting what to say.	35	OLD BATCH	PRO.	25
Heartwell:	Batchelors Fall; and upon the third, I shall be hang'd in	63	OLD BATCH	III.1	82
Lucy:	You could know my Office by instinct, and be hang'd,	66	OLD BATCH	III.1	207
Sr Sampson:	Sirrah, you'l be hang'd; I shall live to see you	243	FOR LOVE	II.1	303
Mrs Frail:	hang'd before you'd confess--we know you--	250	FOR LOVE	II.1	555
Angelica:	(aside). Aye, but if I don't fit you, I'll be hang'd.	294	FOR LOVE	IV.1	699
Sr Sampson:	ready to hang themselves, or to be hang'd by the Law,	299	FOR LOVE	V.1	58
Petulant:	Hang'd. The Ordinary's paid for setting the Psalm, and	436	WAY WORLD	III.1	430
Fainall:	but I'le be hang'd if she did not put Pam in her Pocket.	442	WAY WORLD	III.1	V654
Lady Wish:	shou'd be kill'd I must never shew my face; or hang'd,--O	461	WAY WORLD	IV.1	627

Hang't (2)

Sir Joseph:	No, no, hang't I was not afraid neither--Tho' I	68	OLD BATCH	III.1	271
Mellefont:	No, hang't, that's not endeavouring to Win,	142	DOUEL DLR	II.1	159

Hanging (6)   see Tapestry-hanging

Mellefont:	Hanging, with the Expectation of what I shall see--Hist,	183	DOUBL DLR	IV.2	3
Mellefont:	(Goes behind the Hanging.)	183	DOUBL DLR	IV.2	6
Sr Sampson:	Brother, you understand Physiognomy, a hanging look	243	FOR LOVE	II.1	305
Foresight:	danger of Hanging.	243	FOR LOVE	II.1	310
Sr Sampson:	ne're a young Fellow worth hanging--that's a very	299	FOR LOVE	V.1	54
Sr Sampson:	ne're a young Fellow worth hanging--that is a very	299	FOR LOVE	V.1	V 54

Hangings (1)

Mellefont:	(Goes behind the Hangings.)	183	DOUEL DLR	IV.2	V 6

Hangman (1)

Scandal:	He begs Pardon like a Hangman at an Execution.	225	FOR LOVE	I.1	328

Hangs (3)

	(She goes and hangs upon his neck, and kisses him. Bellmour	95	OLD BATCH	IV.4	241
	(They carry out Maskwell, who hangs down his head.)	203	DOUBL DLR	V.1	577
Manuel:	This idle Vow hangs on her Woman's Fears.	334	M. BRIDE	I.1	353

Hannibal (3)

Sharper:	Hannibal I believe you mean Sir Joseph.	52	OLD BATCH	II.1	177
Capt Bluff:	Undoubtedly he did Sir; faith Hannibal was a very	52	OLD BATCH	II.1	178
Capt Bluff:	Hannibal was a very pretty Fellow in those Days, it must	52	OLD BATCH	II.1	180

Hap (3)   see May-hap

Ben:	and may hap may'nt get 'em out again when he wou'd.	261	FOR LOVE	III.1	313
Ben:	and the Green Girl together;--May hap the Bee may bite,	286	FOR LOVE	IV.1	386
Ben:	Mess, I fear his Fire's little better than Tinder; may hap	308	FOR LOVE	V.1	410

Hapned (1)

Vainlove:	only hapned to be once or twice, where, Laetitia was the	39	OLD BATCH	I.1	96

Happen (5)

Lady Ply:	happen together,--to my thinking, now I could	147	DOUEL DLR	II.1	326
Scandal:	any body's else, that will never happen.	226	FOR LOVE	I.1	385
Sr Sampson:	said of what's past, and all that is to come will happen.	240	FOR LOVE	II.1	198
Valentine:	come;--Dost thou know what will happen to morrow?	288	FOR LOVE	IV.1	490
Mirabell:	Not at all: I happen to be grave to day; and you are	395	WAY WORLD	I.1	15

Happens (1)

Bellmour:	That only happens sometimes, where the Dog has	44	OLD BATCH	I.1	257

Happiest (4)

Cynthia:	I vow, my Lord, I think you the happiest Couple in	141	DOUEL DLR	II.1	96
Careless:	O, Sir Paul, you are the happiest man alive. Such a	160	DOUBL DLR	III.1	380
Sir Paul:	were not for one thing, I should think my self the happiest	161	DOUBL DLR	III.1	404
Mrs Frail:	O' you are the happiest, merriest Men alive.	275	FOR LOVE	III.1	804

Happily (3)

Sir Paul:	fine way of living, as I may say, peacefully and happily,	160	DOUBL DLR	III.1	384
Heli:	Most happily, in finding you thus bless'd.	344	M. BRIDE	II.2	171
Zara:	Who would not be thus happily confin'd,	360	M. BRIDE	III.1	425

Happiness (14)   see Happyness

Mellefont:	happiness that your Lordship has, I shall think my self	141	DOUBL DLR	II.1	112
Cynthia:	not that true Wisdom, for 'tis Happiness: And for ought I	167	DOUBL DLR	III.1	630
Cynthia:	If Happiness in Self-content is plac'd,	167	DOUBL DLR	III.1	633
Lady Touch:	self create your Happiness, and Cynthia shall be this night	185	DOUEL DLR	IV.2	85
Cynthia:	our happiness is, that this discovery was not made too late.	200	DOUBL DLR	V.1	475
Mrs Frail:	the happiness of conversing where we like.	246	FOR LOVE	II.1	425
Mrs Fore:	it, I think there's no happiness like conversing with an	247	FOR LOVE	II.1	427
Angelica:	Failing, which I must own to you--I fear my Happiness	277	FOR LOVE	IV.1	55
Valentine:	If my happiness cou'd receive Addition, this Kind	312	FOR LOVE	V.1	579
Tattle:	I'm indebted to you for my Happiness.	313	FOR LOVE	V.1	591
Heli:	Almeria! O Miracle of Happiness!	341	M. BRIDE	II.2	64
Heli:	O Miracle of Happiness!	341	M. BRIDE	II.2	V 64
Almeria:	If Heaven is greater Joy, it is no Happiness,	343	M. BRIDE	II.2	148
Witwoud:	That! that's his Happiness--His want of	404	WAY WORLD	I.1	326

Happy (27)

Sharper:	Is it possible! Then I am happy to have obliged the	49	OLD BATCH	II.1	72
Lucy:	it you. Come Madam, you're like to have a happy time	75	OLD BATCH	III.2	159
Mellefont:	scarce make her a Moment uneasy, to have her happy	131	DOUBL DLR	I.1	140
Maskwell:	Indignation; your Disposition, my Arguments, and happy	136	DOUBL DLR	I.1	368
Lord Froth:	happy Slavery.	140	DOUBL DLR	II.1	70
Lord Froth:	Don't you think us a happy Couple?	140	DOUBL DLR	II.1	95

Happy (continued)

			PAGE	TITLE	ACT.SC	LINE
Cynthia:	the World, for you are not only happy in one another, and		141	DOUBL DLR	II.1	97
Cynthia:	when you are together, but happy in your selves, and by	.	141	DOUBL DLR	II.1	98
Lord Froth:	well, Mellefont, you'll be a happy Creature.	. . . .	141	DOUBL DLR	II.1	110
Mellefont:	happy.	. . . .	141	DOUBL DLR	II.1	113
Brisk:	in the World,--I hope you'll make me happy in		142	DOUBL DLR	II.1	132
Brisk:	what a happy Discovery. Ah my dear charming	. . . .	177	DOUBL DLR	IV.1	357
Maskwell:	I am happy to be in the way of your Lordships		181	DOUBL DLR	IV.1	533
Maskwell:	--But could you think that I who had been happy in your	.	198	DOUBL DLR	V.1	425
Lord Touch:	Circling Joys, tread round each happy Year of your long	.	203	DOUBL DLR	V.1	589
Foresight:	or short, Happy or Unhappy; whether Diseases are	. .	241	FOR LOVE	II.1	215
Mrs Fore:	alight as I did?--How can any Body be happy, while	. .	247	FOR LOVE	II.1	432
Mrs Frail:	your self happy in a Hackney-Coach before now.--If I	. .	247	FOR LOVE	II.1	437
Tattle:	Well, my pretty Creature; will you make me happy	. .	252	FOR LOVE	II.1	631
Mrs Frail:	O I am happy to have discover'd the Shelves and Quicksands	286	FOR LOVE	IV.1	394
Sr Sampson:	and I a happy Man. Odd, Madam, I'll love you as long as I	.	300	FOR LOVE	V.1	119
Jeremy:	what a happy Exchange has she made, between a Madman	.	302	FOR LOVE	V.1	204
Angelica:	to me, that I can make him and my self happy, than that I		312	FOR LOVE	V.1	577
Osmyn-Alph:	Been happy; why, why was that Heav'nly Creature	. . .	351	M. BRIDE	III.1	55
Mrs Fain:	Ay, ay, dear Marwood, if we will be happy, we	. . .	410	WAY WORLD	II.1	1
Lady Wish:	come alive. O this is a happy discovery.	. . . .	461	WAY WORLD	IV.1	641
Mirabell:	I am too Happy,--Ah Madam, there was a time--but let	. .	471	WAY WORLD	V.1	369

Happyness (1)

Lady Touch:	happyness?	. . . .	192	DOUBL DLR	V.1	170

Harbour (3)

Heartwell:	to harbour.	. . . .	42	OLD BATCH	I.1	200
Ben:	your Harbour. How say you Mistress? the short of the	.	263	FOR LOVE	III.1	375
Osmyn-Alph:	Harbour no Thought, that may disturb thy Peace;	. . .	345	M. BRIDE	II.2	201

Hard (33)

Silvia:	'Tis as hard to Counterfeit Love, as it is to conceal it:		62	OLD BATCH	III.1	51
Lady Froth:	those Two hard Words? If you don't, I'll explain	. . .	139	DOUBL DLR	II.1	33
Mellefont:	flash, the priming of her Engine; destruction follows hard,		148	DOUBL DLR	II.1	378
Maskwell:	as your wise man, who is too hard for all the World, and	.	150	DOUBL DLR	II.1	455
Maskwell:	open: 'twill be hard, if then you can't bring her to any	.	157	DOUBL DLR	III.1	253
Cynthia:	'Tis not so hard to counterfeit Joy in the depth of	. . .	167	DOUBL DLR	III.1	624
Maskwell:	O my Lord! consider that is hard: besides, time	. . .	182	DOUBL DLR	IV.1	565
	'Tis hard that they must every one admit;	. . . . . .	204	DOUEL DLR	EPI.	31
Scandal:	in her Bed, shift twice a Week, and not work so hard, that		222	FOR LOVE	I.1	219
Valentine:	they are very hard, but my Necessity is very pressing:		224	FOR LOVE	I.1	318
Tattle:	'Tis very hard--Won't a Baronet's Lady pass?	. . .	230	FOR LOVE	I.1	530
Valentine:	Tell Angelica, I am about making hard Conditions	. . .	234	FOR LOVE	I.1	673
Valentine:	those hard Conditions, which my necessity Sign'd to.	. .	243	FOR LOVE	II.1	284
Valentine:	A couple of very civil Proverbs, truly: 'Tis hard to	.	256	FOR LOVE	III.1	129
Valentine:	Thou liest, for I am Truth. 'Tis hard I cannot get a	.	280	FOR LOVE	IV.1	171
Jeremy:	I have heard 'em say, Sir, they read hard Hebrew	. .	297	FOR LOVE	IV.1	805
Sr Sampson:	Odd, you are hard to please, Madam; to find a	. .	299	FOR LOVE	V.1	65
Sr Sampson:	Fool in the Eye of the World, is a very hard Task. But,	.	299	FOB LOVE	V.1	67
Angelica:	and struggl'd very hard to make this utmost Tryal of your		312	FOR LOVE	V.1	563
	Hard Fate for us! still harder in th' Event;	. . . .	323	M. BRIDE	PRO.	21
Osmyn-Alph:	Hard Means, to ratifie that Word!--O Cruelty!	. . .	355	M. BRIDE	III.1	249
Gonsalez:	That were too hard a Thought--but see she comes.	. . .	367	M. BRIDE	IV.1	236
Witwoud:	That's hard, that's very hard;--A Messenger,	. . .	401	WAY WORLD	I.1	243
Fainall:	for you are sure to be too hard for him at Repartee: since		402	WAY WORLD	I.1	282
Witwoud:	speaks;--We have all our Failings; you're too hard	. .	403	WAY WORLD	I.1	308
Witwoud:	hard Frost. Whether this Uncle has seen Mrs. Millamant or		408	WAY WORLD	I.1	486
Servant-W:	hard to know 'em all.	. . . . . .	437	WAY WORLD	III.1	471
Millamant:	That's hard!	. . . .	446	WAY WORLD	IV.1	54
Sir Wilful:	Cozen, with the hard Name,--Aunt, Wilfull will do't, If		456	WAY WORLD	IV.1	427
Sir Wilful:	hard Word, Aunt, and (hiccup) Greek for Claret.	. . .	456	WAY WORLD	IV.1	448
Lady Wish:	O, 'tis very hard!	. . . . . .	467	WAY WORLD	V.1	223
	How hard a thing 'twould be, to please you all.	. . .	479	WAY WORLD	EPI.	4

Harder (3)

Bellmour:	'em, but must also undertake the harder Task, of obliging		41	OLD BATCH	I.1	143
Valentine:	Understood! She is harder to be understood than a	. .	297	FOR LOVE	IV.1	801
	Hard Fate for us! still harder in th' Event;	. . . .	323	M. BRIDE	PRO.	21

Hardest (1)

Valentine:	No; He has sent me the hardest Conditions in the	. . .	225	FOR LOVE	I.1	331

Hardly (16)

Belinda:	at the Month's End, you shall hardly find a Married-man,		108	OLD BATCH	V.2	29
	Thus hardly to be prov'd Legitimate!	. . . . .	125	DOUBL DLR	PRO.	20
Lady Touch:	You censure hardly, my Lord; my Sister's	. . .	151	DOUBL DLR	III.1	11
Maskwell:	me to watch you. I believe he will hardly be able to	. .	154	DOUBL DLR	III.1	138
Brisk:	can hardly hold Laughing in his Face.	. . . . .	177	DOUBL DLR	IV.1	380
Lady Ply:	. . . there has hardly been		179	DOUBL DLR	IV.1	V457
Tattle:	her, poor Creature--I swear I do it hardly so much in	.	302	FOR LOVE	V.1	207
Angelica:	Faults than he has Virtues; and 'tis hardly more Pleasure		312	FOR LOVE	V.1	576
Manuel:	So hardly can endure Captivity;	. . . . . .	336	M. BRIDE	I.1	V432
Gonsalez:	That last restraint; you hardly can suspect	. . .	365	M. BRIDE	IV.1	179
Gonsalez:	So, this can hardly fail. Alphonso slain,	. . . .	372	M. BRIDE	IV.1	444
Alonzo:	And hardly wrench'd his Hand to wring it from him;	. .	373	M. BRIDE	V.1	25
Witwoud:	'Tis what she will hardly allow any Body else;--	. .	408	WAY WORLD	I.1	476
Millamant:	more Gallantry--'Tis hardly well bred to be so particular		434	WAY WORLD	III.1	340
Millamant:	Ah! to marry an Ignorant! that can hardly Read	. .	436	WAY WORLD	III.1	426
Sir Wilful:	than a little Mouth-Glew, and that's hardly dry;--One	.	472	WAY WORLD	V.1	397

Hare (1)

Vainlove:	dull and unnatural to have a Hare run full in the Hounds	.	80	OLD BATCH	IV.1	178

Hare's (2)

Sir Wilful:	And a Hare's Foot, and a Hare's Scut for your Service, Sir;	439	WAY WORLD	III.1	524

Hare's-gall (1)

Mirabell:	--Hog's-bones, Hare's-gall, Pig-water, and the	. . . .	451	WAY WORLD	IV.1	250

Hares (1)

Vainlove:	Ay, am I not? To be continually starting of Hares	. . .	39	OLD BATCH	I.1	75

Hark (11)   see Heark

Heartwell:	--hark! (pulling out a Purse and chinking it) how sweetly		72	OLD BATCH	III.2	35
Lord Touch:	--hark! what noise!	. . . .	197	DOUBL DLR	V.1	370
Leonora:	Hark!	. . . .	339	M. BRIDE	II.1	57

Hark   (continued)
Heli:	Yet cannot find him--Hark! sure 'tis the Voice	. . . .	340	M. BRIDE	II.2	2
Almeria:	I'll catch it--hark! a Voice cries Murder! 'tis	. . .	371	M. BRIDE	IV.1	391
Almeria:	I'll catch it--hark! a Voice cries Murder! ah!	. . .	371	M. BRIDE	IV.1	V391
Manuel:	Hark thee, Villain, Traitor--answer me Slave.	. . .	374	M. BRIDE	V.1	67
Garcia:	Fatal Ambition! Hark! the Foe is enter'd:	. . . .	378	M. BRIDE	V.2	88
Lady Wish:	--Hark! I hear her--Go you Thing and send her	. . .	426	WAY WORLD	III.1	61
Lady Wish:	--Hark! I hear her--(To Peg.) Go you Thing and send her	.	426	WAY WORLD	III.1	V 61
Lady Wish:	Comparison. Hark! There's a Coach.	. . . . . .	445	WAY WORLD	IV.1	32

Hark-ye (1)   see Heark-ye
| Sharper: | Hark-ye. | . . . . | 101 | OLD BATCH | V.1 | 165 |

Harkee (2)   see Heark'ee, Hearkee
| Brisk: | harkee,--you understand me. Somewhat heavy, a | . . . | 133 | DOUBL DLR | I.1 | 251 |
| Careless: | Sir Paul, harkee, I'm reasoning the matter you know; | . . | 163 | DOUBL DLR | III.1 | 493 |

Harlot (1)
| Fondlewife: | I'm afraid, 'tis the Flesh, thou Harlot. Deare, with | | | | | |
| | the Pox. | . . . . | 92 | OLD BATCH | IV.4 | 136 |

Harlotry (1)
| Nurse: | O Lord, We're all undone--O you young Harlotry | . . . . | 253 | FOR LOVE | III.1 | 10 |

Harm (2)
| Lord Froth: | (aside). --Oh I see there's no harm yet--But I | . . . | 177 | DOUBL DLR | IV.1 | 372 |
| Ben: | ben't as willing as I, say so a God's name, there's no harm | 263 | FOR LOVE | III.1 | 390 |

Harmless (4)
Singer:	And exchanging harmless Blisses;	. . . .	71	OLD BATCH	III.2	5
Lady Touch:	harmless mirth--only misplac'd that's all--but if it	.	153	DOUBL DLR	III.1	95
Mrs Fore:	fresh harmless Creature; and left us, Sister, presently.		250	FOR LOVE	II.1	545
Lady Wish:	Desarts and Solitudes; and feed harmless Sheep by Groves		465	WAY WORLD	V.1	133

Harmony (4)
Cynthia:	without any harmony; for sure, my Lord, to laugh out of	.	163	DOUBL DLR	III.1	472
Sr Sampson:	your Harmony of Chiromancy with Astrology. Ah!	. . . .	283	FOR LOVE	IV.1	285
Almeria:	'Tis not in Harmony to calm my Griefs.	. . . .	326	M. BRIDE	I.1	8
Manuel:	And shook his Chains in Transport, and rude Harmony.	. .	333	M. BRIDE	I.1	317

Harness (1)
| Heartwell: | A Morning-Sun his Tinsell'd Harness gilds, | . . . . . | 112 | OLD BATCH | V.2 | 188 |

Harrow (1)
| Almeria: | Drag me, harrow the Earth with my bare Bosom. | . . . . | 369 | M. BRIDE | IV.1 | 337 |

Harrows (1)
| Osmyn-Alph: | But thou wilt know, what harrows up my Heart. | . . . . | 357 | M. BRIDE | III.1 | 317 |

Harry (7)   see Lord-Harry
Sir Joseph:	Poor Gentleman--by the Lord Harry I'le stay no	. . .	48	OLD BATCH	II.1	25
Sir Joseph:	by the Lord Harry he says true; Fighting, is Meat, Drink	.	52	OLD BATCH	II.1	167
Sir Joseph:	well--Ey the Lord Harry Mr. Sharper he's as brave a	. .	52	OLD BATCH	II.1	175
Capt Bluff:	Yet by the Lord Harry 'tis true Mr. Sharper, for I	. .	53	OLD BATCH	II.1	207
Sir Joseph:	Lord Harry, I have seen it.	. . . .	53	OLD BATCH	II.1	233
Sir Joseph:	I grant you--Not to that Face by the Lord Harry--If	.	70	OLD BATCH	III.1	357
Sir Joseph:	see:--But, by the Lord Harry, I'll leave you.	. . . .	101	OLD BATCH	V.1	185

Hartshorn (1)
| Lady Froth: | Snuff some of my Spirit of Hartshorn. | . . . . . . | 201 | DOUBL DLR | V.1 | 526 |

Has (457)
Hast (78)
Haste (45)
Heartwell:	in no haste for an Answer--for I shan't stay now.	. . .	46	OLD BATCH	I.1	332
Lucy:	would take time to peruse it--But then he was in haste.	.	61	OLD BATCH	III.1	27
Singer:	He trembling, cry'd, with eager haste,	. . . . . .	71	OLD BATCH	III.2	6
Lucy:	Lord, Madam, I met your Lover in as much haste, as	. .	74	OLD BATCH	III.2	147
Laetitia:	Ah! There he is. Make haste, gather up your things.	.	89	OLD BATCH	IV.4	10
Fondlewife:	Nay, prithee, Dear, Ifeck I'm in haste.	. . . . .	89	OLD BATCH	IV.4	19
Sir Joseph:	for I'm in haste.	. . . .	89	OLD BATCH	IV.4	28
Sharper:	press her to make all the haste imaginable.	. . . .	102	OLD BATCH	V.1	219
Sharper:	Marry'd in haste, we may repent at leisure.	. . .	105	OLD BATCH	V.1	328
Setter:	At leisure marry'd, they repent in haste.	. . . .	105	OLD BATCH	V.1	331
Sharper:	haste to Silvia's Lodgings, before Heartwell has fretted		107	OLD BATCH	V.1	391
Sharper:	I'm in haste now, but I'll come in at the Catastrophe.	.	107	OLD BATCH	V.1	V393
Brisk:	But prithee dear Rogue, make haste, prithee make haste,	.	128	DOUBL DLR	I.1	52
Maskwell:	You had best make haste, for she's but gone to	. . .	181	DOUBL DLR	IV.1	521
Maskwell:	You had best make haste, for after she has	. . .	181	DOUBL DLR	IV.1	V521
Maskwell:	Mellefont. I'll urge haste, to excuse your silence.	. .	195	DOUBL DLR	IV.1	295
Lord Touch:	I'll add to my Plot too,--let us haste to find out, and		200	DOUBL DLR	V.1	486
Snap:	if we don't make haste, the Chairmen will be abroad, and		224	FOR LOVE	I.1	298
Foresight:	haste--	. . . .	240	FOR LOVE	II.1	191
Sr Sampson:	Haste, ay, ay; haste enough, my Son Ben will	. . .	240	FOR LOVE	II.1	192
Miss Prue:	Well, now I'll run and make more haste than you.	. . .	253	FOR LOVE	II.1	660
Sr Sampson:	him make haste--I'm ready to cry for Joy.	. . .	259	FOR LOVE	III.1	215
Sr Sampson:	Mr. Buckram, bid him make haste back with the	. . .	281	FOR LOVE	IV.1	209
Tattle:	Sir, I beg your Pardon, I'm in haste--	. . . . .	304	FOR LOVE	V.1	276
Foresight:	haste to be married.	. . . .	309	FOR LOVE	V.1	454
Perez:	And striding with distemper'd Haste: his Eyes	. . .	338	M. BRIDE	II.1	20
Garcia:	Let's haste to follow him, and know the Cause.	. . .	338	M. BRIDE	II.1	24
Zara:	Haste me to know it, what?	. . . .	354	M. BRIDE	III.1	189
Zara:	Ha! haste thee! fly, prevent his Fate and mine;	. .	361	M. BRIDE	IV.1	17
Gonsalez:	Away, I've not been seen--haste good Alonzo.	. . .	372	M. BRIDE	IV.1	442
Gonsalez:	And say, I've not been seen--haste good Alonzo.	. . .	372	M. BRIDE	IV.1	V442
Alonzo:	With rash and greedy haste, at once to cram	. . .	373	M. BRIDE	V.1	23
Garcia:	But I'll omit no Care, nor Haste; and try	. . .	379	M. BRIDE	V.2	106
Gonsalez:	Repent. Haste thee, Alonzo, hence, with speed,	. . .	379	M. BRIDE	V.2	125
Gonsalez:	Haste thee, Alonzo, haste thee hence with Speed,	. .	379	M. BRIDE	V.2	V125
Leonora:	But haste away, fly from this Fatal Place,	. . .	381	M. BRIDE	V.2	227
Millamant:	Long! Lord, have I not made violent haste? I	. . . .	419	WAY WORLD	II.1	346
Foible:	Sir, I made as much haste as I could.	. . . .	423	WAY WORLD	II.1	515
Foible:	haste home and prevent her. Your Servant Sir. B'w'y	.	424	WAY WORLD	II.1	547
Lady Wish:	here before Dinner--I must make haste.	. . . .	432	WAY WORLD	III.1	275
Lady Wish:	entertain 'em. I'll make all imaginable haste. Dear Friend	432	WAY WORLD	III.1	280
Sir Wilful:	there's no haste; it will keep cold as they say,--Cozen,	.	448	WAY WORLD	IV.1	146

Hasten (1)
| Lord Touch: | let me hasten to do Justice, in rewarding Virtue and wrong'd | 203 | DOUBL DLR | V.1 | 582 |

Hastily (2)
  Lady Ply: both Letters.--(Puts the wrong Letter hastily up, and
              gives him   174   DOUBL DLR   IV.1   263
  Selim: His Eyes had err'd, he hastily recall'd   375   M. BRIDE   V.1   99
Hasty (4)
  Singer: The hasty Joy, in strugling fled.   71   OLD BATCH   III.2 V 16
  Sir Paul: together; she's a little hasty sometimes, and so am   . 160   DOUBL DLR   III.1   389
  Scandal: Sir Sampson is hasty, very hasty;--I'm afraid he is not   . 267   FOR LOVE   III.1   520
Hat (3)
  Setter: All, all Sir; the large sanctified Hat, and the little   . 64   OLD BATCH   III.1   123
            Enter Laetitia and Bellmour, his Cloak, Hat, &c. lying   . 89   OLD BATCH   IV.4
            (Enter Careless, Crossing the Stage, with his Hat, Gloves,   127   DOUBL DLR   I.1
Hatch (1)
            O'er which she broods to hatch the Changling-Kind. . . .   393   WAY WORLD   PRO.   8
Hatch'd (1)
  Brisk: an Old Hen, as if she were not well hatch'd, I'gad, he?   . 174   DOUBL DLR   IV.1   273
Hatches (2)
  Setter: under Hatches.--Ha! All this committed to my Care!   . . . 102   OLD BATCH   V.1   225
  Ben: not for keeping any thing under Hatches,--so that if you   . 263   FOR LOVE   III.1   389
Hatching (1)
  Foible: (says he) what you are a hatching some Plot (says he) you   . 427   WAY WORLD   III.1   95
Hate (40)
  Vainlove: Faith I hate Love when 'tis forced upon a Man; as   . . . 39   OLD BATCH   I.1   94
  Heartwell: So I hate Physick too--yet I may love to take it   . . . 44   OLD BATCH   I.1   284
  Sharper: And you in return of Spleen hate them: But could   . . . 45   OLD BATCH   I.1   306
  Sir Joseph: Nay agad I hate fear ever since I had like to have   . . . 51   OLD BATCH   II.1   144
  Capt Bluff: Oh fy no Sir Joseph--You know I hate this.   53   OLD BATCH   II.1   217
  Belinda: There was a Whine--O Gad I hate your horrid   54   OLD BATCH   II.2   11
  Belinda: O Gad I hate your hideous Fancy--You said that   59   OLD BATCH   II.2   167
  Silvia: (Throws the Purse) I hate you now, and I'll never see you   . 74   OLD BATCH   III.2   111
  Vainlove: Yes, when I feed my self--But I hate to be cram'd   . .   80   OLD BATCH   IV.1   174
  Lady Touch: knows I hate him too: Let him but once be mine, and next   . 137   DOUBL DLR   I.1   400
  Valentine: hate, for just such another Reason; because they abound in   217   FOR LOVE   I.1   38
  Jeremy: but your Prosperity; and now when you are poor, hate you   . 217   FOR LOVE   I.1   47
  Valentine: I must be plain. (Coming up to them.) I am Truth, and hate   292   FOR LOVE   IV.1   619
  Valentine: sides alike. Yet while she does not seem to hate me, I will   297   FOR LOVE   IV.1   812
  Sr Sampson: faith and troth you speak very discreetly; For I hate both a   299   FOR LOVE   V.1   68
  Sr Sampson: Truth. Odsbud, you have won my Heart: I hate a Wit; I   . 299   FOR LOVE   V.1   80
  Tattle: reason to hate her neither; but I believe I shall lead her a 309   FOR LOVE   V.1   467
  Leonora: Of his Success; that then, in spite of Hate, ...   327   M. BRIDE   I.1   42
  Osmyn-Alph: I hate her not, nor can dissemble Love: 352   M. BRIDE   III.1   107
  Gonsalez: As if she'd rather that she did not hate him.   366   M. BRIDE   IV.1   204
  Manuel: Fell hate, within my breast, Revenge and Gall.   374   M. BRIDE   V.1   65
  Mirabell: hopes, one Day or other to hate her heartily: To which   . 399   WAY WORLD   I.1   167
  Witwoud: Now, Demme, I shou'd hate that, if she were as handsome   . 408   WAY WORLD   II.1   477
  Marwood: You hate Mankind?   410   WAY WORLD   II.1   34
  Mrs Fain: Is it possible? Dost thou hate those Vipers   411   WAY WORLD   II.1   43
  Marwood: Because I hate him.   411   WAY WORLD   II.1   69
  Mrs Fain: Reason have you to hate him in particular?   411   WAY WORLD   II.1   71
  Marwood: I think she do's not hate him to that degree   413   WAY WORLD   II.1   128
  Marwood: that can confirm your groundless Accusation. I hate him.   . 414   WAY WORLD   II.1   154
  Fainall: And wherefore do you hate him? He is Insensible, . . .   414   WAY WORLD   II.1   155
  Marwood: --I hate you, and shall for ever.   415   WAY WORLD   II.1   217
  Fainall: hate my Wife yet more, Dam her, I'll part with her, rob   . 416   WAY WORLD   II.1   244
  Mirabell: O you should Hate with Prudence.   416   WAY WORLD   II.1   256
  Millamant: persecuted with Letters--I hate Letters--No Body knows   . 419   WAY WORLD   II.1   360
  Marwood: That I detest him, hate him, Madam.   434   WAY WORLD   III.1   354
  Marwood: I hope you are convinc'd that I hate Mirabell, ...   444   WAY WORLD   III.1   712
  Millamant: Ah l'etourdie! I hate the Town too.   448   WAY WORLD   IV.1   126
  Sir Wilful: shou'd hate 'em both! Hah 'tis like you may; there are   . 448   WAY WORLD   IV.1   128
  Millamant: never sure in Love. O, I hate a Lover, that can dare to
              think, ...   449   WAY WORLD   IV.1   175
  Millamant: fellows, Odious Men! I hate your Odious proviso's.   . . . 452   WAY WORLD   IV.1   279
Hated (5)
  Angelica: always lov'd your Son, and hated your unforgiving   . . . 312   FOR LOVE   V.1   573
  Manuel: Hated Anselmo, was interr'd--By Heav'n, ...   333   M. BRIDE   I.1   297
  Zara: You hated Manuel, I urg'd my Husband   347   M. BRIDE   II.2   300
  Almeria: One hated Line of more extended Woe.   367   M. BRIDE   IV.1   261
  Mrs Fain: While I only hated my Husband, I could bear   416   WAY WORLD   II.1   254
Hater (0)   see Woman-hater
Hates (8)
  Sharper: And here comes one who Swears as heartily he hates   . . . 41   OLD BATCH   I.1   176
  Sharper: He! he hates the Sex.   44   OLD BATCH   I.1   283
  Mrs Fore: besides he hates both you and me.--But I have a   288   FOR LOVE   IV.1   463
  Singer-V: Love hates to center in a Point assign'd, ...   293   FOR LOVE   IV.1   660
  Gonsalez: And tho' I know he hates beyond the Grave   371   M. BRIDE   IV.1   409
  Witwoud: has been told; and you know she hates Mirabell, worse than   408   WAY WORLD   I.1   484
  Witwoud: a Quaker hates a Parrot, or than a Fishmonger hates a   . . 408   WAY WORLD   I.1   485
Hath (2)
  Fondlewife: hath possess'd the Lad--I say I will tarry at home--Varlet.   75   OLD BATCH   IV.1   17
  Fondlewife: hath already defiled the Tabernacle of our Sister Comfort;   76   OLD BATCH   IV.1   29
Hating (5)
  Zara: As one hating to be oblig'd--   336   M. BRIDE   I.1   417
  Zara: Such Thanks as one hating to be oblig'd--   336   M. BRIDE   I.1 V417
  Zara: Yet hating more, Ingratitude, can pay, ...   336   M. BRIDE   I.1   418
  Heli: Nightly; hating this Tyrant; some, who love   352   M. BRIDE   III.1   101
  Marwood: I have done hating 'em; and am now come to   411   WAY WORLD   II.1   45
Hatred (4)
  Heartwell: the hatred of all the great Families in Town.   45   OLD BATCH   I.1   305
  Zara: No, no, it must be Hatred, dire Revenge, ...   353   M. BRIDE   III.1   162
  Zara: Heav'n has no Rage, like Love to Hatred turn'd, ...   361   M. BRIDE   III.1   457
  Gonsalez: Methinks this Lady's Hatred to the Moor, ...   366   M. BRIDE   IV.1   202
Haughty (1)
  Garcia: And with a haughty Mien, and stern Civility   335   M. BRIDE   I.1   370
Haule (1)
  Ben: Come, I'll haule a Chair; there, an you please to sit, I'll 263   FOR LOVE   III.1   362

Have (1331)	see Ha'				
Having (19)					
Bellmour:	damnably in Love; I'm so uneasie for not having seen Belinda	40	OLD BATCH	I.1	V133
Heartwell:	I am for having every body be what they pretend	43	OLD BATCH	I.1	253
Sir Joseph:	my transgression of ingratitude and omission; having my	49	OLD BATCH	II.1	55
Bellmour:	your Wife, and there will be some hopes of having her	95	OLD BATCH	IV.4	225
Mellefont:	having disarm'd her; in a gust of Passion she left me, and	130	DOUBL DLR	I.1	116
Maskwell:	To my Lord, as having been privy to Mellefont's	154	DOUBL DLR	III.1	150
Mellefont:	And having trusted thee with the Secrets of her	156	DOUBL DLR	III.1	204
Brisk:	sounds great; besides your Ladyship's Coach-man having a	163	DOUEL DLR	III.1	507
Sir Paul:	but in having the honour, to appertain in some measure, to	172	DOUEL DLR	IV.1	183
Lady Ply:	(Having read the Letter). O dear Mr. Careless, I	174	DOUBL DLR	IV.1	258
Scandal:	And you, like a true great Man, having engaged their	221	FOR LOVE	I.1	193
Jeremy:	--And now, Sir, my former Master, having much	301	FOR LOVE	V.1	173
Almeria:	Methinks my Heart has some Relief: Having	330	M. BRIDE	I.1	192
Almeria:	My Heart has some Relief: having so well	330	M. BRIDE	I.1	V192
Zara:	That having seen it, thou do'st turn thy Eyes	353	M. BRIDE	III.1	149
Manuel:	(Having read the Letter.)	373	M. BRIDE	V.1	34
Fainall:	For having only that one Hope, the accomplishment	413	WAY WORLD	II.1	112
Lady Wish:	Neice exerts a lawfull claim, having Match'd her self by	472	WAY WORLD	V.1	417
Mirabell:	having it seems receiv'd some Cautions respecting your	476	WAY WORLD	V.1	541
Hawk (1)					
Jeremy:	Aye, Sir, hooded like a Hawk, to seize at first sight	302	FOR LOVE	V.1	199
Hawkers (1)					
Marwood:	Lungs of Hawkers, with Voices more Licentious than the	468	WAY WORLD	V.1	233
Hawks (1)					
Bellmour:	I marry Sir, I have a Hawks Eye at a Womans hand	38	OLD BATCH	I.1	32
Hazard (4)					
Barnaby:	And run the hazard to lose your affair so!	76	OLD BATCH	IV.1	38
Barnaby:	And run the hazard to lose your affair, Sir!	76	OLD BATCH	IV.1	V 38
Maskwell:	and run the hazard along with you.	193	DOUBL DLR	V.1	207
	But that late knowledge, does much hazard cost,	204	DOUBL DLR	EPI.	4
Hazards (3)					
	As a rash Girl, who will all Hazards run,	113	OLD BATCH	EPI.	1
	But Poets run much greater hazards far,	204	DOUEL DLR	EPI.	8
	But what unequal Hazards do they run!	393	WAY WORLD	PRO.	13
Hazle (1)					
Foresight:	young and sanguine, has a wanton Hazle Eye, and was born	239	FOR LOVE	II.1	151
He (887)	see A'				
He'd (6)					
Sir Joseph:	he shou'd hear the Lion roar, he'd cudgel him into an Ass,	101	OLD BATCH	V.1	173
Jeremy:	Younger Brother shou'd come from Sea, he'd never look	218	FOR LOVE	I.1	84
Sr Sampson:	he do with a distinguishing taste?--I warrant now he'd	245	FOR LOVE	II.1	368
Mrs Frail:	Foresight shou'd find us with them;--He'd think so,	250	FOR LOVE	II.1	571
Ben:	tell him so much.--So he said he'd make my heart ake;	285	FOR LOVE	IV.1	380
Ben:	and if so be that he cou'd get a Woman to his mind, he'd	286	FOR LOVE	IV.1	381
He'l (3)					
Sir Joseph:	Look you now, I tell you he's so modest he'l own	53	OLD BATCH	II.1	222
Setter:	He'l be in the Piaza presently.	67	OLD BATCH	III.1	231
Scandal:	He begins to Chuckle;--ply him close, or he'l	224	FOR LOVE	I.1	292
He'll (27)					
	You think that strange--no matter, he'll out grow it.	35	OLD BATCH	PRO.	16
Brisk:	Touchwood swears, he'll Disinherit you, and Sir Paul Plyant	128	DOUBL DLR	I.1	54
Lord Froth:	D'e think he'll Love you as well as I do my	141	DOUEL DLR	II.1	102
Cynthia:	I believe he'll Love me better.	141	DOUEL DLR	II.1	104
Lady Touch:	sake away my Lord, he'll either tempt you to extravagance,	186	DOUEL DLR	IV.2	128
Maskwell:	in his Uncle's favour, if he'll comply with your desires;	199	DOUBL DLR	V.1	448
Maskwell:	his Case is desperate, and I believe he'll yield to any	199	DOUBL DLR	V.1	449
Valentine:	Scandal; have pity on him; he'll yield to any	230	FOR LOVE	I.1	523
Miss Prue:	Yes; I may tell my Mother--And he says he'll	249	FOR LOVE	II.1	524
Miss Prue:	he'll give me something that will make my Smocks smell	249	FOR LOVE	II.1	527
Mrs Fore:	will hang us--He'll think we brought 'em acquainted.	250	FOR LOVE	II.1	569
Mrs Fore:	together is as bad--And he's such a sly Devil, he'll never	250	FOR LOVE	II.1	574
Miss Prue:	any more, he'll thrash your Jacket for you, he will, you	264	FCB LOVE	III.1	417
Ben:	Tar-barrel? Let your Sweet-heart there call me so, if he'll	264	FOR LOVE	III.1	434
Sr Sampson:	own Son, faith, he'll touzle her, and mouzle her: The	265	FOR LOVE	III.1	458
Ben:	and he'll marry her himself, with all my heart.	286	FOR LOVE	IV.1	387
Mrs Fore:	revoking. And if he should recover his Senses, he'll be	288	FOR LOVE	IV.1	474
Jeremy:	Yes, Sir; he says he'll favour it, and mistake her for	288	FOR LOVE	IV.1	482
Miss Prue:	Man, and shall be my Husband: I warrant he'll be my	305	FOR LOVE	V.1	318
Gonsalez:	Her Mutes alone must strangle him or he'll	366	M. BRIDE	IV.1	211
Gonsalez:	No body? sure he'll wait without--I would	376	M. BRIDE	V.2	11
	He swears he'll not resent one hiss'd-off Scene,	393	WAY WORLD	PRO.	26
	He'll not instruct, lest it should give Offence.	393	WAY WORLD	PRO.	34
Witwoud:	as to that.--Yes, Faith, in a Controversie he'll	403	WAY WORLD	I.1	303
Lady Wish:	Is he! O then he'll Importune, if he's a brisk	429	WAY WORLD	III.1	176
Mincing:	I vow. He says Mem, how that he'll have my Lady's	465	WAY WORLD	V.1	110
Mincing:	Fortune made over to him, or he'll be divorc'd.	465	WAY WORLD	V.1	111
He's (88)					
	He's very civil, and entreats your Favour.	35	OLD BATCH	PRO.	13
	But on my Conscience he's a bashful Poet;	35	OLD BATCH	PRO.	15
Vainlove:	a Venture which he's in danger of losing. Read, read.	39	OLD BATCH	I.1	81
Vainlove:	So that as he is often Jealous without a Cause, he's as often	40	OLD BATCH	I.1	109
Bellmour:	Faith I don't know, he's of a temper the most easie	42	OLD BATCH	I.1	210
Bellmour:	He's of another opinion, and says I do the drudgery	43	OLD BATCH	I.1	222
Sir Joseph:	Stay, stay Sir, let me recollect--(aside) he's a	48	OLD BATCH	II.1	43
Sir Joseph:	as it were to me--agad he's a brave Fellow--Pauh,	50	OLD BATCH	II.1	121
Sir Joseph:	well--By the Lord Harry Mr. Sharper he's as brave a	52	OLD BATCH	II.1	175
Sir Joseph:	Look you now, I tell you he's so modest he'l own	53	OLD BATCH	II.1	222
Silvia:	Respects, and peruse it! He's gone, and Araminta	61	OLD BATCH	III.1	28
Vainlove:	He's talking to himself, I think; Prithee lets try if	62	OLD BATCH	III.1	61
Lucy:	Here's some Villany a Foot he's so thoughtful; may be I	65	OLD BATCH	III.1	154
Lucy:	Masters employment. For he's the head Pimp to Mr.	65	OLD BATCH	III.1	169
Setter:	Too forward to be turn'd back--Though he's a little	67	OLD BATCH	III.1	224
Lucy:	Stand off--He's a precious Jewel.	67	OLD BATCH	III.1	227

He's   (continued)

		PAGE	TITLE	ACT.SC	LINE
Sir Joseph:	dear Captain, don't be in Passion now, he's gone--	70	OLD BATCH	III.1	340
Silvia:	He's going for a Parson, Girl, the forerunner of a	75	OLD BATCH	III.2	149
Fondlewife:	Ravish my Wife before my face! I warrant he's a Papist in	91	OLD BATCH	IV.4	74
Heartwell:	O Pox; He's a Fanatick.	97	OLD BATCH	V.1	17
Heartwell:	O ay; He's a Fanatick.	97	OLD BATCH	V.1 V	17
	If he's an Ass, he will be Try'd by's Peers.	113	OLD BATCH	EPI.	16
Sir Paul:	but Mr. Brisk--where is he? I swear and vow, he's a	132	DOUBL DLR	I.1	181
Lady Ply:	He's hot-headed still! 'Tis in vain to talk to you;	144	DOUBL DLR	II.1	227
Cynthia:	Pray, Sir, stay, hear him, I dare affirm he's innocent.	146	DOUBL DLR	II.1	274
Sir Paul:	of thee, but thy Portion, why he's in Love with my Wife;	146	DOUBL DLR	II.1	278
Lady Touch:	--I dare swear he's sorry--and were it to do again, would	152	DOUBL DLR	III.1	77
Lady Froth:	There he's secure from danger of a bilk,	164	DOUBL DLR	III.1	540
Lady Froth:	he's a nauseous figure, a most fulsamick Fop, Foh--he	165	DOUBL DLR	III.1	562
Maskwell:	I have kept my word, he's here, but I must not be	185	DOUBL DLR	IV.2	90
Lady Touch:	Moderate your rage good my Lord! he's	186	DOUBL DLR	IV.2	112
Lady Touch:	mad, alas he's mad--indeed he is my Lord, and knows not	186	DOUBL DLR	IV.2	113
Lord Touch:	I fear he's mad indeed--Let's send Maskwell	187	DOUBL DLR	IV.2	135
Lady Touch:	yonders my Lord, I believe he's coming to find you, I'le	188	DOUBL DLR	V.1	7
Maskwell:	this dotage, I know not; but he's gone to Sir Paul about my	190	DOUBL DLR	V.1	111
Lord Touch:	know he's no way to be rewarded but in her. I'll defer my	191	DOUBL DLR	V.1	138
Lady Touch:	. . . to a Hell of Torments,--but he's	191	DOUBL DLR	V.1 V152	
Mellefont:	Man!--Take him hence, for he's a Disease to my Sight.	202	DOUBL DLR	V.1	574
Scandal:	Intelligence.--He's here.	226	FOR LOVE	I.1	380
Foresight:	he's at leisure--'tis now Three a Clock, a very good hour	236	FOR LOVE	II.1	41
Foresight:	there's no more to be said--he's here already	239	FOR LOVE	II.1 V170	
Mrs Frail:	Ah Devil, sly Devil--He's as close, Sister, as	250	FOR LOVE	II.1	542
Mrs Fore:	together is as bad--And he's such a sly Devil, he'll never	250	FOR LOVE	II.1	574
Sr Sampson:	Frail, you shall see my Son Ben--Body c' me, he's the	259	FOR LOVE	III.1	212
Sr Sampson:	Years--I warrant he's grown--Call him in, bid	259	FOR LOVE	III.1	214
Sr Sampson:	all Interest; he's an undone Scoundrel, and courts your	260	FOR LOVE	III.1	242
Scandal:	He's gone to Bed upon't, and very ill--He speaks	266	FOR LOVE	III.1	497
Jeremy:	Why faith, Madam, he's mad for want of his Wits,	276	FOR LOVE	IV.1	33
Jeremy:	Ah, Sir, he's quite gone.	278	FOR LOVE	IV.1	119
Jeremy:	No, no, Sir; he's safe enough, Sir, an he were but as	279	FOR LOVE	IV.1	124
Jeremy:	his Skull's crack'd, poor Gentleman; he's stark mad, Sir.	279	FOR LOVE	IV.1	138
Buckram:	Sir, I can do you no Service while he's in this	280	FOR LOVE	IV.1	183
Valentine:	the Lawyer with an itching Palm; and he's come to be	282	FOR LOVE	IV.1	238
Mrs Frail:	foul Weather--He's us'd to an inconstant Element,	284	FOR LOVE	IV.1	307
Mrs Fore:	Not much,--he's superstitious; and you	284	FOR LOVE	IV.1	323
Mrs Fore:	Oh hang him old Fox, he's too cunning,	288	FOR LOVE	IV.1	462
Jeremy:	Bethlehem; Nay, he's as Mad as any Projector, Fanatick,	295	FOR LOVE	IV.1	739
Jenny:	He's at the great Glass in the Dining-Room, Madam,	297	FOR LOVE	V.1	3
Angelica:	are very much abus'd in that Matter; He's no more Mad	299	FOR LOVE	V.1	87
Foresight:	Alas! he's Mad, Child, stark Wild.	305	FOR LOVE	V.1	303
Miss Prue:	Robin the Butler, he says he loves me, and he's a Handsome	305	FOR LOVE	V.1	317
Ben:	Who, Father? ay, he's come home with a Vengeance.	306	FOR LOVE	V.1	341
Ben:	Matter! Why he's Mad.	306	FOR LOVE	V.1	343
Ben:	she's mad for a Husband, and he's Horn-mad, I think, or	307	FOR LOVE	V.1	373
Mrs Fore:	(aside to Mrs. Frail). He's better than no Husband	310	FOR LOVE	V.1	469
Mrs Fore:	at all--tho he's a Coxcomb.	310	FOR LOVE	V.1	470
Gonsalez:	For Osmyn's Death, as he's Alphonso's Friend.	367	M. BRIDE	IV.1	240
Almeria:	I would to Heav'n I were--he's gone!	370	M. BRIDE	IV.1	369
Manuel:	Not to be found? in an ill hour he's absent.	372	M. BRIDE	V.1	1
Zara:	Insensible of this last Proof he's gone.	381	M. BRIDE	V.2	194
Zara:	O now he's gone, and all is dark--	381	M. BRIDE	V.2	211
Betty:	He's in the next Room, Friend--That way.	400	WAY WORLD	I.1	185
Fainall:	Obstinacy--But when he's drunk, he's as loving as	401	WAY WORLD	I.1	219
Witwoud:	He's reckoning his Mony,--my Mony it was,	402	WAY WORLD	I.1	279
Fainall:	What I warrant he's unsincere, or 'tis some such	403	WAY WORLD	I.1	316
Fainall:	He's Impudent.	404	WAY WORLD	I.1	333
Petulant:	Ay, ay, pox I'm malicious, Man. Now he's soft	408	WAY WORLD	I.1	503
Petulant:	well bred, he's what you call a--What-dee-call-'em.	408	WAY WORLD	I.1	505
Petulant:	A fine Gentleman, but he's silly withal.	408	WAY WORLD	I.1	506
Mrs Fain:	to see him; but since I have despis'd him, he's too				
	offensive.	416	WAY WORLD	II.1	255
Lady Wish:	Is he! O then he'll Importune, if he's a brisk	429	WAY WORLD	III.1	176
Lady Wish:	O I'm glad he's a brisk Man. Let my	429	WAY WORLD	III.1	180
Lady Wish:	O he's in less Danger of being spoil'd by his	431	WAY WORLD	III.1	262
Lady Wish:	O he's a Rallier, Nephew--My Cousin's a	441	WAY WORLD	III.1	606
Mrs Fain:	He's horridly drunk--how came you all in	454	WAY WORLD	IV.1	379
Sir Wilful:	For he's drunk every Night,	455	WAY WORLD	IV.1	419
Sir Wilful:	That he's able next Morning to light us.	455	WAY WORLD	IV.1	421

Head (60)   see Maiden-head, Block-head

Heartwell:	punish'd with a Wife of Birth--be a Stag of the first Head	45	OLD BATCH	I.1	310
Belinda:	is to be possess'd--Tis in the Head, the Heart, the	54	OLD BATCH	II.2	13
Lucy:	I have that in my Head may make Mischief.	61	OLD BATCH	III.1	35
Lucy:	Trouble not your Head. Let me alone--I will	62	OLD BATCH	III.1	44
Lucy:	Masters employment. For he's the head Pimp to Mr.	65	OLD BATCH	III.1	169
Fondlewife:	will fall upon his Head.	77	OLD BATCH	IV.1	72
Laetitia:	does not think, that ever I had any such thing in my Head,	77	OLD BATCH	IV.1	81
Fondlewife:	No no, I tell you I shall have it in my Head--	77	OLD BATCH	IV.1	83
Setter:	Her head runs on nothing else, nor she can talk of	102	OLD BATCH	V.1	198
Capt Bluff:	I plant Laurels for my Head abroad, I may find the Branches	111	OLD BATCH	V.2	148
Mellefont:	keep my Lady Touchwood's Head from Working: For	129	DOUBL DLR	I.1	76
Sir Paul:	won't be a Brute, and have my Head fortifi'd, that I am thus	144	DOUBL DLR	II.1	231
Maskwell:	Come, trouble not your head, I'll joyn you together e're	148	DOUBL DLR	II.1	386
Maskwell:	the forming of another Plot that I have in my head--	154	DOUBL DLR	III.1	160
Maskwell:	the forming another Plot that I have in my head--	154	DOUBL DLR	III.1 V160	
Maskwell:	She has a damn'd penetrating head, and knows how to	155	DOUBL DLR	III.1	181
Maskwell:	No matter, Sir, don't trouble your head, all's in	190	DOUBL DLR	V.1	106
Maskwell:	head that cannot fail: Where's Cynthia?	190	DOUBL DLR	V.1	116
Mellefont:	your hand;--do you hold down your head? Yes, I am	202	DOUBL DLR	V.1	569
	(They carry out Maskwell, who hangs down his head.)	203	DOUBL DLR	V.1	577
Scandal:	upon the outside of his Head, than the Lining. Why,	219	FOR LOVE	I.1	126
Scandal:	Divine with two Faces, and one Head; and I have a Soldier	233	FOR LOVE	I.1	644

Head   (continued)
Scandal:	with his Brains in his Belly, and his Heart where his Head	233	FOR LOVE	I.1	645
Mrs Frail:	And no Head?	233	FOR LOVE	I.1	647
Scandal:	No Head.	233	FOR LOVE	I.1	648
Foresight:	That House doth stond upon its Head;	236	FOR LOVE	II.1	54
Foresight:	And when the Head is set in Grond, ...	236	FOR LOVE	II.1	55
Foresight:	Fruitful, the Head fruitful, that bodes Horns; the Fruit	236	FOR LOVE	II.1	57
Foresight:	of the Head is Horns--Dear Neice, stay at home--	236	FOR LOVE	II.1	58
Foresight:	For by the Head of the House is meant the Husband; the	236	FOR LOVE	II.1	59
Scandal:	my Head to communicate to you.	259	FOR LOVE	III.1	232
Ben:	Sail o' your Head--Top and Top-gallant by the Mess. .	262	FOR LOVE	III.1	332
Sr Sampson:	a crooked Pin, or an old Horse-nail, with the head towards	265	FOR LOVE	III.1	467
Jeremy:	just as he was poor for want of Money; his Head is e'en as	276	FOR LOVE	IV.1	34
Valentine:	That Gray Hairs shou'd cover a Green Head--and . .	283	FOR LOVE	IV.1	271
Foresight:	Ah, Sir Sampson, Heav'n help your Head-- . . .	283	FOR LOVE	IV.1	293
Mrs Fore:	project in my head for you, and I have gone a good way	288	FOR LOVE	IV.1	464
Angelica:	pull'd an old House over his Head at last. . . .	301	FOR LOVE	V.1	159
Jeremy:	my Head--I have been at Cambridge.	302	FOR LOVE	V.1	185
Jeremy:	as the Head of Nilus.	302	FOR LOVE	V.1	191
Almeria:	The dire collected Dews, on my poor Head; . . .	330	M. BRIDE	I.1	160
Osmyn-Alph:	In Murmurs round my Head. I rose and listened; .	344	M. BRIDE	II.2	162
Osmyn-Alph:	Tears from my hoary and devoted Head;	350	M. BRIDE	III.1	17
Heli:	Are risen in Arms, and call for Chiefs to head . .	351	M. BRIDE	III.1	70
Manuel:	Though on the Head that wears it, were too little. .	365	M. BRIDE	IV.1	160
Almeria:	And ghastly Head, glares by, all smear'd with Blood,	371	M. BRIDE	IV.1	388
Gonsalez:	And I yet fix the Crown on Garcia's Head. . . .	372	M. BRIDE	IV.1	447
Manuel:	That thou obey, or Horrour on thy Head. . . .	374	M. BRIDE	V.1	73
Gonsalez:	The King's immediate Presence at their Head. . .	378	M. BRIDE	V.2	104
Gonsalez:	To see the King in Person at their Head. . . .	378	M. BRIDE	V.2	V104
Alonzo:	Sever'd the Head; and in a Corner of	379	M. BRIDE	V.2	115
Alonzo:	Sever'd the Head; and in an obscure Corner . . .	379	M. BRIDE	V.2	V115
Zara:	The blazing Torrent on the Tyrant's Head; . . .	380	M. BRIDE	V.2	V170
Witwoud:	out of my Head. I beg Pardon that I shou'd ask a Man of	402	WAY WORLD	I.1	256
Marwood:	Man shcu'd have his Head and Horns, and Woman the .	431	WAY WORLD	III.1	238
Marwood:	panting ripe; with a Heart full of Hope, and a Head full of	431	WAY WORLD	III.1	247
Mirabell:	a Shape, till you mold my boy's head like a Sugar-loaf; and	451	WAY WORLD	IV.1	261
Witwoud:	Now Petulant, all's over, all's well; Gad my head begins	453	WAY WORLD	IV.1	336
Sir Wilful:	Head and drink a Health to 'em--A Match or no Match,	456	WAY WORLD	IV.1	426
Waitwell:	his head, and then go out in a stink like a Candle's end	458	WAY WORLD	IV.1	524

Head-Quarters (1)
Jeremy:	could ever find cut his Head-Quarters.	302	FOR LOVE	V.1	195

Head's (2)
Araminta:	Your Head's a little out of Order.	83	OLD BATCH	IV.3	7
Ben:	at these years, there's more danger of your head's aking .	286	FOR LOVE	IV.1	383

Headed (1)   see Hot-headed
Sr Sampson:	Body o' me, what a many headed Monster have . . .	244	FOR LOVE	II.1	343

Headless (3)
Zara:	Ha! prostrate! bloody! headless! O--start Eyes, . .	380	M. BRIDE	V.2	162
Zara:	Ha! prostrate! bloody! headless! O--I'm lost, . .	380	M. BRIDE	V.2	V162
Almeria:	Horrour! a headless Trunk! nor Lips nor Face, . .	382	M. BRIDE	V.2	270

Headpiece (1)
Sir Joseph:	through all dangers--he is indeed Back, Breast and Headpiece	50	OLD BATCH	II.1	120

Heads (9)
Lord Touch:	Ladys, and Drink a Dish of Tea, to settle our Heads. .	132	DOUBL DLR	I.1	217
Lord Touch:	Ladies, and Drink a Dish of Tea, to settle our Heads. .	132	DOUBL DLR	I.1	V217
Sir Paul:	I suppose they have been laying their heads . . .	201	DOUBL DLR	V.1	509
Scandal:	with a hundred Hands, two Heads, and but one Face; a .	233	FOR LOVE	I.1	643
Almeria:	Whose antient Pillars rear their Marble Heads, . .	339	M. BRIDE	II.1	60
Selim:	The Heads of those who first began the Mutiny. . .	361	M. BRIDE	IV.1	14
Zara:	Your heavy and desponding Heads hung down? . . .	380	M. BRIDE	V.2	158
Zara:	And curl their Crimson Heads, to kiss the Clouds! . .	380	M. BRIDE	V.2	V167
Almeria:	Their Heads in Sign of Grief and Innocence! . . .	382	M. BRIDE	V.2	251

Headstrong (2)
Lady Ply:	disobedient, headstrong Brute.	144	DOUBL DLR	II.1	229
Sir Paul:	No, 'tis because I won't be headstrong, because I . .	144	DOUBL DLR	II.1	230

Healing (1)
Bellmour:	by those healing Lips.--Oh! press the soft Charm close .	82	OLD BATCH	IV.2	73

Health (18)
Heartwell:	for my health.	44	OLD BATCH	I.1	285
Sir Joseph:	by night, or by day, in sickness, or in health, Winter, or	49	OLD BATCH	II.1	66
Lord Touch:	Days attend you both; mutual Love, lasting Health, and .	203	DOUBL DLR	V.1	588
Valentine:	Health. An honester Man lives not, nor one more ready to	223	FOR LOVE	I.1	261
Valentine:	What, the Widows Health; give it him--off	223	FOR LOVE	I.1	275
Foresight:	I am in Health, I think.	268	FOR LOVE	III.1	569
Valentine:	Health, and Liberty at once, to a despairing, starving, and	290	FOR LOVE	IV.1	542
Tattle:	Figure, with Youth and Health, and all his five Senses in .	291	FOR LOVE	IV.1	582
Leonora:	Have softly whisper'd, and enquir'd his Health; . .	327	M. BRIDE	I.1	27
Osmyn-Alph:	My Life, my Health, my Liberty, my All.	355	M. BRIDE	III.1	236
Millamant:	converse with Fools, is for my Health.	421	WAY WORLD	II.1	442
Mirabell:	Your Health! Is there a worse Disease than the . .	421	WAY WORLD	II.1	443
Sir Wilful:	you are in good Health, and so forth--To begin with .	439	WAY WORLD	III.1	544
Lady Wish:	'tis with drinking your Health--O' my Word you are .	455	WAY WORLD	IV.1	407
Sir Wilful:	In vino veritas Aunt,--If I drunk your Health to . .	455	WAY WORLD	IV.1	409
Sir Wilful:	Head and drink a Health to 'em--A Match or no Match,	456	WAY WORLD	IV.1	426
Sir Wilful:	Crown a Health to the King, ...	456	WAY WORLD	IV.1	456
Lady Wish:	Health, or some such Emergency--	468	WAY WORLD	V.1	264

Healths (1)
Mirabell:	mens prerogative, and presume to drink healths, or toste	451	WAY WORLD	IV.1	270

Heaps (1)
Garcia:	Who but for heaps of Slain, that choak the Passage, .	377	M. BRIDE	V.2	33

Hear (123)   see Over-hear
	I cannot stay to hear your Resolution.	35	OLD BATCH	PRO.	27
Belinda:	more. Oh Gad, I swear you'd make one sick to hear you. .	54	OLD BATCH	II.2	2
Araminta:	What, before you hear it?	55	OLD BATCH	II.2	49
Bellmour:	Why, you wont hear me with Patience.	59	OLD BATCH	II.2	160
Belinda:	Devil, wrapt in Flames--I'll not hear a Sentence	59	OLD BATCH	II.2	170

Hear   (continued)

Hear   (continued)
Lady Wish:	Did'st thou not hear me, Mopus?	425	WAY WORLD	III.1	8
Lady Wish:	--Hark! I hear her--Go you Thing and send her	426	WAY WORLD	III.1	61
Lady Wish:	--Hark! I hear her--(To Peg.) Go you Thing and send her	426	WAY WORLD	III.1 V	61
Foible:	disinherited. O you would bless your self, to hear what he	428	WAY WORLD	III.1	108
Foible:	Humh (says he) I hear you are laying Designs against	428	WAY WORLD	III.1	111
Marwood:	Marrying than Travelling at his Years. I hear he is turn'd	431	WAY WORLD	III.1	260
Millamant:	O Dear, what? for it is the same thing, if I hear	434	WAY WORLD	III.1	352
Millamant:	hear it Madam--Not that there's any great matter in	434	WAY WORLD	III.1	372
Millamant:	Dee hear the Creature? Lord, here's Company,	436	WAY WORLD	III.1	434
Sir Wilful:	can'st not guess, enquire her out, do'st hear Fellow? And	437	WAY WORLD	III.1	465
Sir Wilful:	Hold ye, hear me Friend; a Word with you in	437	WAY WORLD	III.1	468
Millamant:	and dee hear, I won't be call'd names after I'm Married;	450	WAY WORLD	IV.1	194
Witwoud:	Revenge--and hear me, if thou canst learn to write	454	WAY WORLD	IV.1	372
Foible:	No, no, dear Madam. Do but hear me, have but a	462	WAY WORLD	V.1	24
Foible:	Pray do but hear me Madam, he cou'd not marry	463	WAY WORLD	V.1	38
Mincing:	six thousand Pound. O, come Mrs. Foible, I hear my old	465	WAY WORLD	V.1	116
Marwood:	and this you must hear till you are stunn'd; Nay you must	468	WAY WORLD	V.1	235
Marwood:	hear nothing else for some days.	468	WAY WORLD	V.1	236
Fainall:	I come to make demands,--I'll hear no	469	WAY WORLD	V.1	288
Fainall:	Mirabell, You shall hear of this Sir, be sure you shall,	476	WAY WORLD	V.1	560

Hear'st (2)
Zara:	(aside to Selim). Ha! hear'st thou that? Is Osmyn then	363	M. BRIDE	IV.1	90
Zara:	Hast stung the Traveller; and, after, hear'st	375	M. BRIDE	V.1	107

Heard (44)   see Over-heard
Bellmour:	loves thee intirely--I have heard her breath such Raptures	38	OLD BATCH	I.1	40
Silvia:	again, and had heard me.	74	OLD BATCH	III.2	146
Laetitia:	I durst have sworn, I had heard my Monster's Voice.	89	OLD BATCH	IV.4	3
Bellmour:	Bed, hoping that when she heard of it, her good Nature	94	OLD BATCH	IV.4	212
Vainlove:	But have a good heart, I heard of your Misfortune, and	109	OLD BATCH	V.2	71
Maskwell:	not to be heard. I have been a very great Rogue for your	136	DOUBL DLR	I.1	335
Lady Touch:	heard any thing from him these two days.	153	DOUBL DLR	III.1	98
Cynthia:	I heard him loud as I came by the Closet-Door, and	167	DOUBL DLR	IV.1	1
Lady Touch:	Cold indifference; Love has no Language to be heard.	184	DOUBL DLR	IV.2	23
Lord Touch:	incense her--something she has heard of you which carries	195	DOUBL DLR	V.1	310
Jeremy:	O Lord! I have heard much of him, when I waited	216	FOR LOVE	I.1	17
Valentine:	World: You have heard of a Booby-Brother of mine, that	225	FOR LOVE	I.1	332
Mrs Frail:	I have heard Gentlemen say, Sister; that one should	248	FOR LOVE	II.1	473
Mrs Frail:	Account I have heard of his Education can be no Conjurer:	248	FOR LOVE	II.1	493
Angelica:	What is, Mr. Tattle? I heard you say something	254	FOR LOVE	III.1	50
Tattle:	take me, I beg your Pardon--for I never heard a	254	FOR LOVE	III.1	55
Angelica:	O barbarous! I never heard so insolent a piece of	258	FOR LOVE	III.1	182
Ben:	heard as far as another,--I'll heave off to please you.	263	FOR LOVE	III.1	367
Ben:	you? You heard t'other handsome Young Woman speak	264	FOR LOVE	III.1	410
Scandal:	I have heard of her.	273	FOR LOVE	III.1	754
Scandal:	think I heard her bid the Coach-man drive hither.	276	FOR LOVE	IV.1	13
Scandal:	This I have heard of before, but never believ'd. I	284	FOR LOVE	IV.1	333
Jeremy:	I have heard 'em say, Sir, they read hard Hebrew	297	FOR LOVE	V.1	805
Jeremy:	heard you Sigh for.	302	FOR LOVE	V.1	179
Valentine:	I have heard as much, Sir; but I wou'd have it from	311	FOR LOVE	V.1	520
	It's like what I have heard our Poets tell us:	315	FOR LOVE	EPI.	6
Leonora:	For I had heard, that when the Chance of War	327	M. BRIDE	I.1	38
Leonora:	And I have heard imperfectly his Loss;	328	M. BRIDE	I.1	106
Garcia:	I've heard with Admiration, of your Friendship;	338	M. BRIDE	II.1	13
Almeria:	And thou hast heard my Prayer; for thou art come	343	M. BRIDE	II.2	132
Osmyn-Alph:	And thought, I heard thy Spirit call Alphonso.	344	M. BRIDE	II.2	163
Zara:	Not heard! Ungrateful Osmyn.	346	M. BRIDE	II.2	246
Manuel:	Somewhat I heard of King and Rival mention'd.	348	M. BRIDE	II.2	355
Osmyn-Alph:	But Heav'n was deaf, Heav'n heard him not; but thus,	350	M. BRIDE	III.1	24
Heli:	Was never heard in vain: Heav'n has in Store	352	M. BRIDE	III.1	118
Zara:	'Tis well. By what I heard upon your Entrance,	364	M. BRIDE	IV.1	114
Zara:	I've heard, her Charity did once extend	365	M. BRIDE	IV.1	181
Zara:	Is seen, or heard. A dreadful Din was wont	379	M. BRIDE	V.2	135
Mirabell:	thou heard of my Uncle?	407	WAY WORLD	I.1	445
Witwoud:	We staid pretty late there last Night; and heard	408	WAY WORLD	I.1	480
Lady Wish:	Morning, and never heard of since.	426	WAY WORLD	III.1	46
Foible:	heard how he us'd me, and all upon your Ladyship's	427	WAY WORLD	III.1	87
Lady Wish:	How, how!--I heard the Villain was in the	461	WAY WORLD	IV.1	615
Lady Wish:	to have been Catechis'd by him; and have heard his long	467	WAY WORLD	V.1	197

Hearing (13)
Araminta:	hearing. You'l bring my Cousin.	60	OLD BATCH	II.2	209
Bellmour:	A good hearing, Setter.	64	OLD BATCH	III.1	119
Bellmour:	your hearing. Expecting a Friend, last Night, at his				
	Lodgings,	82	OLD BATCH	IV.2	49
Lady Ply:	change upon bearing--hearing is one of the Senses,	147	DOUBL DLR	II.1	340
Lady Touch:	willing to have remote from your hearing. Good my Lord,	152	DOUBL DLR	III.1	51
Lord Touch:	worth your hearing.	197	DOUBL DLR	V.1	366
Cynthia:	be worth your hearing.	197	DOUBL DLR	V.1	368
Ben:	I warrant that brings 'em, an' they be within hearing.	274	FOR LOVE	III.1	794
Petulant:	their Discretion by not hearing what they would not be	409	WAY WORLD	I.1	531
Mrs Fain:	Curiosity, and will willingly dispence with the hearing of	412	WAY WORLD	II.1	104
Mirabell:	To your Lover you owe the pleasure of hearing your	421	WAY WORLD	II.1	416
Mirabell:	selves prais'd; and to an Eccho the pleasure of hearing your	421	WAY WORLD	II.1	417

Heark (2)
Sr Sampson:	Body o' me, so do I.--Heark ye, Valentine,	243	FOR LOVE	II.1	279
Leonora:	Heark!	330	M. BRIDE	I.1	162

Heark-ye (1)
Heartwell:	Death: D'ye mock me? Heark-ye: If either you	105	OLD BATCH	V.1	321

Heark'ee (7)
Sir Paul:	Innocent! why heark'ee, come hither Thy,	146	DOUBL DLR	II.1	275
Sir Paul:	heark'ee, I had it from his Aunt, my Sister Touchwood,	146	DOUBL DLR	II.1	276
Lady Froth:	No matter,--heark'ee, shall you and I make	201	DOUBL DLR	V.1	536
Mrs Fore:	Heark'ee, Sister--by my Soul the Girl is	250	FOR LOVE	II.1	560
Mrs Fore:	Did you ever hear such a Toad--heark'ee	271	FOR LOVE	III.1	664
Valentine:	Heark'ee;--I have a Secret to tell you--	290	FOR LOVE	IV.1	546
Scandal:	contrive to couple 'em together--Heark'ee--.	291	FOR LOVE	IV.1	599

Hearkee (10)
   Sharper: Hearkee, Sir Joseph, a word with ye--In consideration . . 69   OLD BATCH III.1 302
   Sir Paul: but hearkee, my Lord told me something of a Revolution . 192 DOUEL DLR V.1 172
   Valentine: and can set him right--Hearkee, Friend, the straight . 282 FOR LCVE IV.1 252
   Ben: Hearkee forsooth; If so be that you are in your right . 286 FOR LCVE IV.1 413
   Petulant: Pass cn, Witwoud--Hearkee, by this Light his . . . . 406 WAY WCRLD I.1 406
   Mirabell: How! hearkee Petulant, come hither--Explain, ... 406 WAY WCRLD I.1 432
   Petulant: Well, hearkee. . . . . 407 WAY WCRLD I.1 462
   Witwoud: her, I shou'd--Hearkee--To tell you a Secret, but let it go 407 WAY WCRLD I.1 467
   Sir Wilful: frown, she can't kill you;--besides--Hearkee she dare not 471 WAY WCRLD V.1 361
   Lady Wish: generous at last! But it is not possible. Hearkee. I'll
          break . . . . 474 WAY WORLD V.1 463
Hearken (2)
   Sir Joseph: let's hearken. A-gad, this must be I.-- . . . . . 102 OLD BATCH V.1 204
   Fainall: 'Tis impossible Millamant should hearken to it. . . . 408 WAY WCRLD I.1 491
Hears (4)
   Sharper: Gravity as a Bishop hears Venereal Causes in the Spiritual 100 OLD BATCH V.1 139
   Valentine: hears is Landed; whereupcn he very affectionately sends . 225 FOR LCVE I.1 334
   Jeremy: would not see her, till he hears how she takes it. . . 276 FOR LCVE IV.1 17
   Zara: He Looks not, minds not, hears not; barbarous Man! . 346 M. BBIDE II.2 244
Heart (153)   see Sweet-Heart, Sweet-heart
   Bellmour: all My Heart--It adds a Gusto to an Amour; gives it the . 39 OLD BATCH I.1 90
   Bellmour: With all my Heart, it lies convenient for us, to pay . 40 OLD BATCH I.1 131
   Heartwell: Devil--Oh the Pride and Joy of Heart 'twould be to me, . 45 OLD BATCH I.1 318
   Sir Joseph: with all my Heart, Blood and Guts Sir; and if you did but 48 OLD BATCH II.1 36
   Sir Joseph: my Bully, my Back; agad my heart has gcne a pit . . . 51 OLD BATCH II.1 140
   Belinda: is to be possess'd--Tis in the Head, the Heart, the . . 54 OLD EATCH II.2 13
   Belinda: Not I; witness my Heart I stay cut of pure Affection. . 57 OLD EATCH II.2 111
   Araminta: Heart knows nothing cf. . . . . 58 OLD EATCH II.2 138
   Bellmour: Yet all can't melt that cruel frozen Heart. . . . . 59 OLD EATCH II.2 166
   Lucy: as his Love. Therefore e'n set your Heart at rest, and . 61 OLD EATCH III.1 8
   Laetitia: poor Heart, while it holds; which cannot be long, with . 77 OLD EATCH IV.1 92
   Laetitia: Heart--Well, be as cruel as you can to me, I'le pray for . 78 OLD BATCH IV.1 108
   Fondlewife: Good lack, good lack, she would melt a Heart of . . 78 OLD BATCH IV.1 114
   Fondlewife: Ifeck you'l break my Heart--Ifeck you will--See you have . 78 OLD BATCH IV.1 116
   Laetitia: heart beats. . . . . 89 OLD BATCH IV.4 5
   Fondlewife: his heart, at least, if not a French-man. . . . . . 91 OLD BATCH IV.4 75
   Laetitia: (aside). How my heart akes! All my comfort lies in . . 94 OLD BATCH IV.4 202
   Laetitia: break my heart, if you talk of parting. . . . . . 95 OLD BATCH IV.4 231
   Bellmour: Heart of a Mountain-Tyger. By the faith of a sincere . 95 OLD EATCH IV.4 235
   Laetitia: Oh, my heart will break! . . . . 96 OLD BATCH IV.4 257
   Heartwell: How my Heart akes.) . . . . 104 OLD EATCH V.1 290
   Belinda: Heart to marry thee, purely to be rid of thee.--At . 106 OLD BATCH V.1 365
   Vainlove: But have a good heart, I heard of your Misfortune, and . 109 OLD BATCH V.2 71
   Sir Joseph: Ah! O Lord, my heart akes--Ah! Setter, a . . . . 110 OLD EATCH V.2 118
   Sir Paul: With all my heart.--Mr. Brisk you'll come to . . . 133 DOUBL DLR I.1 218
   Lord Froth: With all my heart, methinks we are a Sclitude . . . 134 DOUEL DLR I.1 284
   Maskwell: Fix'd, Rooted in my Heart, whence nothing can . . . 136 DOUEL DLR I.1 352
   Lady Froth: I'm not asham'd to own it now; ah! it makes my heart . 140 DOUBL DLR II.1 62
   Lord Froth: ay, there it is; who could resist! 'twas sc my heart was
          made . . . . 140 DOUBL DLR II.1 68
   Sir Paul: Heart--I'm sure if ever I should have Horns, they . . 146 DOUBL DLR II.1 281
   Lady Ply: Heart? May be you don't think it a sin,--they say . . 147 DOUBL DLR II.1 346
   Maskwell: --oh she has open'd her heart to me,--I am to turn you a 149 DOUBL DLR II.1 402
   Maskwell: that belief, told me the Secrets of her heart. At length we 149 DOUBL DLR II.1 426
   Lady Touch: make me lay my heart before you, but don't be thus . . 152 DOUBL DLR III.1 65
   Sir Paul: indeed it's true, Mr. Careless, it breaks my heart--I . 162 DOUBL DLR III.1 436
   Brisk: With all my Heart and Soul, and proud of the vast . . 165 DOUEL DLR III.1 556
   Careless: feast upon that hand; O let me press it to my heart, my . 170 DOUBL DLR IV.1 92
   Careless: aking trembling heart, the nimble movement shall instruct 170 DOUBL DLR IV.1 93
   Careless: trembling heart, the nimble movement shall instruct . 170 DOUBL DLR IV.1 V 93
   Lady Ply: the Palpitation of the Heart. . . . . 170 DOUBL DLR IV.1 105
   Lady Ply: Sir, you have Conquered--What heart of Marble . . . 170 DOUBL DLR IV.1 119
   Sir Paul: all my hopes lost--My Heart would break, and my . . 174 DOUBL DLR IV.1 253
   Brisk: Froth! Heigho! Break Heart; God's I thank you. . . 175 DOUBL DLR IV.1 310
   Lady Froth: With all my heart. . . . . 177 DOUBL DLR IV.1 383
   Sir Paul: were not for Providence, sure poor Sir Paul thy Heart . 179 DOUBL DLR IV.1 434
   Lady Touch: Heart, and gnaw it piece-meal, for not boding to me this . 184 DOUBL DLR IV.2 47
   Lady Touch: little thou swelling Heart; let me have some intermission 185 DOUBL DLR IV.2 65
   Lady Touch: Come, come, good my Lord, my Heart . . . . . 187 DOUBL DLR IV.2 138
   Maskwell: ever must; no, let it prey upon my Heart; for I would . 188 DOUBL DLR V.1 36
   Sir Paul: That's a jest with all my heart, faith and troth,-- . 192 DOUBL DLR V.1 171
   Lady Touch: but I will stab the Lie that's forming in your heart, and
          save . . . . 197 DOUBL DLR V.1 381
   Lady Touch: they were written in thy heart, That I, with this, might lay 198 DOUBL DLR V.1 396
   Maskwell: than in the Heart of one who is nothing when not yours. . 199 DOUBL DLR V.1 451
   Lady Ply: who would ever trust a man? O my heart akes for fear . 202 DOUBL DLR V.1 546
   Scandal: with his Brains in his Belly, and his Heart where his Head 233 FOR LOVE I.1 645
   Nurse: Wee'st heart, I know not, they're none of 'em come . . 235 FOR LOVE II.1 19
   Nurse: and Amen with all my heart, for you have put on one . . 235 FOR LOVE II.1 27
   Sr Sampson: Reverence the Sun, Moon and Stars with all my heart. . 242 FOR LOVE II.1 247
   Sr Sampson: With all my heart: Ccme, Uncase, Strip, and . . . 244 FOR LOVE II.1 337
   Mrs Frail: With all my heart, ours are but slight Flesh-wounds, . 248 FOR LOVE II.1 480
   Mrs Fore: Here 'tis with all my heart. . . . . 248 FOR LOVE II.1 484
   Mrs Fore: Heart, to think that any body else shou'd be before-hand . 250 FOR LOVE II.1 551
   Tattle: With all my heart,--Now then my little Angel. . . . 252 FOR LOVE II.1 638
   Tattle: Heart--You know whom I mean--You know . . . 258 FOR LOVE III.1 178
   Sr Sampson: Heart: Hang him, Mungrel; cast him off; you shall see the 260 FOR LOVE III.1 260
   Sr Sampson: With all my Heart. . . . . 265 FOR LOVE III.1 471
   Foresight: hem! faintish. My Heart is pretty good; yet it beats; and 269 FOR LOVE III.1 605
   Mrs Frail: break my Heart. . . . . 273 FOR LOVE III.1 729
   Ben: Break your Heart? I'de rather the Mary-gold shou'd . 273 FOR LOVE III.1 730
   Ben: as good Blood in my Veins, and a Heart as sound as a . 273 FOR LOVE III.1 736
   Ben: That won this Fair Maids Heart. . . . . . . 274 FOR LOVE III.1 789
   Jeremy: Sir, I have a most broke my Heart about him--I can't . 279 FOR LOVE IV.1 131
   Jeremy: Sir, I have almost broke my Heart about him--I can't . 279 FOR LOVE IV.1 V131

Heart   (continued)

Speaker	Text	PAGE	TITLE	ACT.SC	LINE
Sr Sampson:	my Heart--What matter is it who holds it? What	281	FOR LOVE	IV.1	230
Ben:	tell him so much.--So he said he'd make my heart ake;	285	FOR LOVE	IV.1	380
Ben:	than my heart.--He was woundy angry when I	286	FOR LOVE	IV.1	384
Ben:	and he'll marry her himself, with all my heart.	286	FOR LOVE	IV.1	387
Mrs Frail:	inhumane merciless Creature have I set my heart upon?	286	FOR LOVE	IV.1	393
Tattle:	ventur'd to declare the very inmost Passion of my Heart.	291	FOR LOVE	IV.1	579
Tattle:	No, Sir, 'tis written in my Heart. And safer there,	292	FOR LOVE	IV.1	613
	Sir, than	292	FOR LOVE	IV.1	613
Singer-V:	I know my Eyes would lead my Heart to you,	293	FOR LOVE	IV.1	655
Sr Sampson:	Truth. Odsbud, you have won my Heart: I hate a Wit; I	299	FOR LOVE	V.1	80
Sr Sampson:	With all my Heart;--Come in with me, and	301	FOR LOVE	V.1	137
Sr Sampson:	in my time; but i'Gad I could never find in my Heart to	303	FOR LOVE	V.1	213
Tattle:	and I have a Secret in my Heart, which you wou'd be glad	305	FOR LOVE	V.1	289
Ben:	Heart. Look you, Friend, if I may advise you, when she's	310	FOR LOVE	V.1	490
Valentine:	With all my Heart, Sir.	311	FOR LOVE	V.1	540
Angelica:	Passion: Here's my Hand, my Heart was always yours,	312	FOR LOVE	V.1	562
	I can't reflect without an aking Heart,	315	FOR LOVE	EPI.	36
	For only Nature can affect the Heart.	324	M. BRIDE	PRO.	38
Almeria:	How would thy Heart have bled to see his Suff'rings!	327	M. BRIDE	I.1	33
Almeria:	They must to me bring Curses, Grief of Heart,	327	M. BRIDE	I.1	62
Almeria:	But in my Heart thou art interr'd, there, there,	328	M. BRIDE	I.1	74
Almeria:	If for my swelling Heart I can, I'll tell thee.	329	M. BRIDE	I.1	109
Almeria:	Or, ever taste content, or peace of Heart,	329	M. BRIDE	I.1	147
Almeria:	And Joy he brings to every other Heart,	330	M. BRIDE	I.1	169
Almeria:	Methinks my Heart has some Relief: Having	330	M. BRIDE	I.1	192
Almeria:	My Heart has some Relief: having so well	330	M. BRIDE	I.1	V192
Leonora:	My Heart, my Life and Will, are only yours.	330	M. BRIDE	I.1	195
Almeria:	But I am arm'd, with Ice around my Heart,	331	M. BRIDE	I.1	217
Almeria:	O my boding Heart--What is your Pleasure,	334	M. BRIDE	I.1	330
Almeria:	my boding Heart--What is your Pleasure,	334	M. BRIDE	I.1	V330
Heli:	I know his Noble Heart would burst with Shame	338	M. BRIDE	II.1	33
Almeria:	And shoot a Chilness to my trembling Heart.	339	M. BRIDE	II.1	66
Almeria:	O my strain'd Heart--let me behold thee,	342	M. BRIDE	II.2	112
Almeria:	O my strain'd Heart--let me again behold thee,	342	M. BRIDE	II.2	V112
Osmyn-Alph:	To thee with twining? Come, come to my Heart.	343	M. BRIDE	II.2	124
Osmyn-Alph:	Dwell with thee, and revive the Heart in Absence.	345	M. BRIDE	II.2	212
Zara:	Thou hast a Heart, though 'tis a savage one;	346	M. BRIDE	II.2	272
Zara:	O Heav'n! how did my Heart rejoice and ake,	347	M. BRIDE	II.2	285
Zara:	In Chains unseen, I hold him by the Heart,	348	M. BRIDE	II.2	325
Zara:	O that thy Heart, had taught	353	M. BRIDE	III.1	143
Zara:	This Heart of Flint, 'till it shall bleed; and thou	353	M. BRIDE	III.1	167
Zara:	Thy Anger cou'd not pierce thus, to my Heart.	354	M. BRIDE	III.1	187
Osmyn-Alph:	The Cause and Comfort of my boding Heart.	355	M. BRIDE	III.1	235
Osmyn-Alph:	Of my Heart, to see thy Sufferings--O Heav'n!	356	M. BRIDE	III.1	252
Almeria:	Feed on each others Heart, devour our Woes	356	M. BRIDE	III.1	259
Almeria:	Thy Heart will burst, thy Eyes look red and start;	356	M. BRIDE	III.1	273
Osmyn-Alph:	With such a Dagger, as then stuck my Heart.	356	M. BRIDE	III.1	277
Almeria:	Heart,	356	M. BRIDE	III.1	285
Almeria:	That sucks thy warm Life-Blood, and gnaws thy Heart?	357	M. BRIDE	III.1	299
Almeria:	As they have Strength to tear this Heart in sunder;	357	M. BRIDE	III.1	301
Osmyn-Alph:	But thou wilt know, what harrows up my Heart.	357	M. BRIDE	III.1	317
Osmyn-Alph:	Is this to call thee mine? O hold my Heart;	357	M. BRIDE	III.1	329
Osmyn-Alph:	Think how my Heart will heave, and Eyes will strain	358	M. BRIDE	III.1	345
Almeria:	And cleaves my Heart; I would have born it all,	369	M. BRIDE	IV.1	309
Manuel:	Drench me thy Dagger in Alphonso's Heart.	374	M. BRIDE	V.1	74
Gonsalez:	'Twere done--I'll crawl and sting him to the Heart;	376	M. BRIDE	V.2	12
Zara:	Or does my Heart bode more? what can it more	380	M. BRIDE	V.2	147
Zara:	Split Heart, burst ev'ry Vein, at this dire Object:	380	M. BRIDE	V.2	V163
Zara:	He dy'd unknowing in my Heart.	381	M. BRIDE	V.2	190
Zara:	But Oh, he dy'd unknowing in my Heart.	381	M. BRIDE	V.2	V190
Zara:	O friendly Draught, already in my Heart!	381	M. BRIDE	V.2	204
Almeria:	Yes, yes, I know to mourn; I'll sluce this Heart,	382	M. BRIDE	V.2	243
Osmyn-Alph:	Save her from Death, and snatch her to my Heart.	383	M. BRIDE	V.2	276
Witwoud:	Heart for her.	407	WAY WORLD	I.1	469
Marwood:	in our Breasts, and every Heart, or soon or late, receive	410	WAY WORLD	II.1	26
	and	410	WAY WORLD	II.1	26
Fainall:	and would be again a Widow, but that I have a Heart of	415	WAY WORLD	II.1	212
Mirabell:	Heart of a Man that is lodg'd in a Woman. There is no	423	WAY WORLD	II.1	495
Foible:	Heart still. Now, Madam, I can safely tell your Ladyship	430	WAY WORLD	III.1	205
Marwood:	panting ripe; with a Heart full of Hope, and a Head full of	431	WAY WORLD	III.1	247
Singer:	That Heart which others bleed for, bleed for me.	435	WAY WORLD	III.1	390
Sir Wilful:	--O'ds heart, and then tell a familiar Tale of a Cock	439	WAY WORLD	III.1	546
Lady Wish:	figure shall I give his Heart the first Impression?	445	WAY WORLD	IV.1	18
	There is a	445	WAY WORLD	IV.1	18
Millamant:	--That foolish trifle of a heart--Sir Wilfull!	447	WAY WORLD	IV.1	101
Sir Wilful:	Dear Heart, that's much--Hah! that you	448	WAY WORLD	IV.1	127
Millamant:	Sweet heart and the rest of that Nauseous Cant, in which	450	WAY WORLD	IV.1	198
Sir Wilful:	Tony, Ods heart where's Tony--Tony's an honest fellow,	455	WAY WORLD	IV.1	413
Waitwell:	break my heart--or if that should fail, I shall be	458	WAY WORLD	IV.1	499
Foible:	my heart akes--get it from her--	460	WAY WORLD	IV.1	576
Mrs Fain:	Have a good heart Foible, Mirabell's gone to	464	WAY WORLD	V.1	65
Mirabell:	enough, that I have lost what in my heart I hold most dear,	472	WAY WORLD	V.1	388
Mirabell:	With all my heart dear Sir Wilfull, what shall we	477	WAY WORLD	V.1	603

Heart-breaking (1)
| Almeria: | O dismal Cruelty! heart-breaking Horrour! | 358 | M. BRIDE | III.1 | V357 |

Heart-heavings (1)
| Lady Wish: | the Kneelings and the Riseings, the Heart-heavings, and the | 458 | WAY WORLD | IV.1 | 515 |

Heart-wounding (1)
| Garcia: | (returning). Ruine and Horrour! O heart-wounding | 377 | M. BRIDE | V.2 | 51 |

Heart's (2)
| Fondlewife: | Ah! No, no, I cannot speak; my heart's so full--I | 95 | OLD BATCH | IV.4 | 248 |
| Osmyn-Alph: | O my Heart's Comfort; 'tis not given to this | 383 | M. BRIDE | V.2 | 300 |

Hearted (1)
  see Tender-hearted, False-hearted
| Ben: | What, are you false hearted then? | 287 | FOR LOVE | IV.1 | 422 |

Heav'n (continued)

Valentine:	between me and Heav'n; but Providence laid Purgatory	313	FOR LOVE	V.1	596
Almeria:	Is it of Moment to the Peace of Heav'n	327	M. BRIDE	I.1	58
Almeria:	But Heav'n spared me for yet more Affliction!	329	M. BRIDE	I.1	128
Leonora:	Look down good Heav'n, with Pity on her	329	M. BRIDE	I.1	149
Almeria:	To that bright Heav'n, where my Alphonso reigns,	330	M. BRIDE	I.1	183
Almeria:	Another Lord; may then just Heav'n show'r down	330	M. BRIDE	I.1	187
Almeria:	I bend to Heav'n with Thanks and Humble Praise.	332	M. BRIDE	I.1	251
Almeria:	I bend to Heav'n with Thanks.	332	M. BRIDE	I.1 V251
Manuel:	By Heav'n thou lov'st me, and I'm pleas'd thou do'st:	333	M. BRIDE	I.1	275
Almeria:	The Year, which I have vow'd to pay to Heav'n,	333	M. BRIDE	I.1	284
Manuel:	Your Zeal to Heav'n is great; so is your Debt:	333	M. BRIDE	I.1	288
Manuel:	That Life, which Heav'n preserv'd. A Day bestow'd	333	M. BRIDE	I.1	290
Manuel:	Hated Anselmo, was interr'd--By Heav'n,	333	M. BRIDE	I.1	297
Manuel:	Then, then, to weep, and pray, and grieve? By Heav'n,	333	M. BRIDE	I.1	314
Heli:	Let Heav'n with Thunder to the Centre strike me,	337	M. BRIDE	II.1	4
Almeria:	To him, to Heav'n and my Alphonso's Soul.	339	M. BRIDE	II.1	83
Leonora:	I go; but Heav'n can tell with what Regret.	339	M. BRIDE	II.1	84
Leonora:	What do I see? O Heav'n! either my Eyes	340	M. BRIDE	II.2	9
Leonora:	O Heav'n unfold these Wonders!	341	M. BRIDE	II.2 V 58
Heli:	By Heav'n 'tis he, and with--ha! Almeria!	341	M. BRIDE	II.2	63
Osmyn-Alph:	Thou Excellence, thou Joy, thou Heav'n of Love!	342	M. BRIDE	II.2	109
Almeria:	How is all this? All-powerful Heav'n, what are we!	342	M. BRIDE	II.2	111
Almeria:	To Heav'n and thee; and sooner wou'd have dy'd--	343	M. BRIDE	II.2	127
Almeria:	To my Distress, to my Despair, which Heav'n	343	M. BRIDE	II.2	133
Osmyn-Alph:	What means the Bounty of All-gracious Heav'n,	344	M. BRIDE	II.2	185
Osmyn-Alph:	Where will this end! but Heav'n is Infinite	344	M. BRIDE	II.2	188
Zara:	O Heav'n! how did my Heart rejoice and ake,	347	M. BRIDE	II.2	285
Zara:	As I could wish; by Heav'n I'll be reveng'd.	348	M. BRIDE	II.2	350
Manuel:	Better for him, to tempt the Rage of Heav'n,	349	M. BRIDE	II.2	368
Osmyn-Alph:	Sure 'tis the Hand of Heav'n, that leads me thus,	350	M. BRIDE	III.1	4
Osmyn-Alph:	If my Alphonso live, restore him, Heav'n,	350	M. BRIDE	III.1	10
Osmyn-Alph:	'Tis wanting what should follow--Heav'n, Heav'n shou'd	350	M. BRIDE	III.1	20
Osmyn-Alph:	'Tis wanting what should follow--Heav'n, shou'd	350	M. BRIDE	III.1 V 20
Osmyn-Alph:	Be torn from his Petition? 'Twas to Heav'n.	350	M. BRIDE	III.1	23
Osmyn-Alph:	But Heav'n was deaf, Heav'n heard him not; but thus,	350	M. BRIDE	III.1	24
Osmyn-Alph:	Thus as the Name of Heav'n from this is torn,	350	M. BRIDE	III.1	25
Osmyn-Alph:	She'll come, but whither, and to whom? O Heav'n!	351	M. BRIDE	III.1	52
Osmyn-Alph:	Abandon'd o'er to love what Heav'n forsakes?	351	M. BRIDE	III.1	56
Osmyn-Alph:	By Heav'n thou'st rous'd me from my Lethargy.	351	M. BRIDE	III.1	73
Heli:	Was never heard in vain: Heav'n has in Store	352	M. BRIDE	III.1	118
Osmyn-Alph:	The Care of Heav'n. Not so, my Father bore	352	M. BRIDE	III.1	126
Zara:	O Heav'n! my Fears interpret	354	M. BRIDE	III.1	193
Osmyn-Alph:	Of my Heart, to see thy Sufferings--O Heav'n!	356	M. BRIDE	III.1	252
Osmyn-Alph:	But knowing Heav'n, to know it lost for ever.	358	M. BRIDE	III.1	366
Osmyn-Alph:	Distress, Heav'n will repay; all Thanks are poor.	359	M. BRIDE	III.1	404
Osmyn-Alph:	Distress'd, Heav'n will repay; all Thanks are poor.	359	M. BRIDE	III.1 V404
Zara:	Heav'n has no Rage, like Love to Hatred turn'd,	361	M. BRIDE	III.1	457
Zara:	Quick; or, by Heav'n, this Dagger drinks thy Blood.	362	M. BRIDE	IV.1	38
Zara:	O Heav'n! a thousand things occur	363	M. BRIDE	IV.1	92
Zara:	O Heav'n! a thousand things occur at once	363	M. BRIDE	IV.1 V 92
Manuel:	Say'st thou? by Heav'n thou hast arous'd a Thought,	367	M. BRIDE	IV.1	232
Manuel:	Confesses it. By Heav'n I'll have him rack'd,	368	M. BRIDE	IV.1	294
Almeria:	And yet alone would I have dy'd, Heav'n knows,	368	M. BRIDE	IV.1	305
Almeria:	And wedded Husband--Heav'n, and Air, and Seas;	370	M. BRIDE	IV.1	359
Almeria:	I would to Heav'n I were--he's gone!	370	M. BRIDE	IV.1	369
Manuel:	And lash against the Hook--by Heav'n you're all	373	M. BRIDE	V.1	44
Manuel:	By Heav'n I'll meet, and counterwork this Treachery.	374	M. BRIDE	V.1	66
Selim:	Avert it, Heav'n, that you should ever suffer	375	M. BRIDE	V.1	113
Almeria:	Where am I? Heav'n! what does this Dream intend?	383	M. BRIDE	V.2	288
Osmyn-Alph:	The just Decrees of Heav'n, in turning on	383	M. BRIDE	V.2	307
Osmyn-Alph:	The just Decrees of Heav'n, which on themselves	383	M. BRIDE	V.2 V307
Osmyn-Alph:	Seest thou, how just the Hand of Heav'n has been?	383	M. BRIDE	V.2	317
Mirabell:	Heav'n may grant it thee in the mean time.	407	WAY WORLD	I.1	461
Sir Wilful:	Cozen, nor Stripling: I thank Heav'n, I'm no Minor.	447	WAY WORLD	IV.1	108
Mirabell:	as often as possibly I can. (Kisses her hand). Well, heav'n	477	WAY WORLD	V.1	597

Heav'nly (2)

Osmyn-Alph:	Been happy; why, why was that Heav'nly Creature	351	M. BRIDE	III.1	55
Osmyn-Alph:	The Heav'nly Powers allot me; no, not you,	354	M. BRIDE	III.1	174

Heav'ns (13)

Belinda:	once before--If you must talk impertinently, for Heav'ns	59	OLD BATCH	II.2	168
Brisk:	O Heav'ns, Madam--	140	DOUBL DLR	III.1 V 91
Brisk:	know the Sun is call'd Heav'ns Charioteer.	164	DOUBL DLR	III.1	509
Brisk:	Then too like Heav'ns Charioteer, the Sun:	164	DOUBL DLR	III.1	536
Lady Froth:	Never to Marry! Heav'ns forbid: must I neither have	171	DOUBL DLR	IV.1 V136
Sir Paul:	Brag! O Heav'ns! Why, did I name any body?	255	FOR LOVE	III.1	93
Tattle:	For Heav'ns sake softly, Sir, and gently; don't	279	FOR LOVE	IV.1	152
Scandal:	Husband! O heav'ns!	328	M. BRIDE	I.1	77
Leonora:	(If such there be in angry Heav'ns Vengeance)	330	M. BRIDE	I.1	189
Almeria:	My Ears, and reach the Heav'ns; where is the King?	352	M. BRIDE	III.1	85
Osmyn-Alph:	And free of all bad Purposes. So Heav'ns	368	M. BRIDE	IV.1	290
Almeria:	Prescience is Heav'ns alone, not giv'n to Man.	375	M. BRIDE	V.1	116
Selim:	Heav'ns! what dismal Scene	381	M. BRIDE	V.2	218

Heave (3)

Ben:	heard as far as another,--I'll heave off to please you.	263	FOR LOVE	III.1	367
Almeria:	Why do'st thou heave, and stifle in thy Griefs?	356	M. BRIDE	III.1	272
Osmyn-Alph:	Think how my Heart will heave, and Eyes will strain	358	M. BRIDE	III.1	345

Heaven (39)

Bellmour:	Never--Her Affections, 'tis true by Heaven,	38	OLD BATCH	I.1	47
Heartwell:	quotha! I hope in Heaven I have a greater portion of Grace,	44	OLD BATCH	I.1	295
Heartwell:	Quality--I thank Heaven, I have very honestly purchas'd	45	OLD BATCH	I.1	304
Vainlove:	Could you be content to go to Heaven?	63	OLD BATCH	III.1	105
Heartwell:	Heaven she kisses sweeter than Liberty--I will Marry	74	OLD BATCH	III.2	134
Heartwell:	Heaven her kiss is sweeter than Liberty--I will Marry	74	OLD BATCH	III.2 V134
Sharper:	Lost! Pray Heaven thou hast not lost thy Wits.	79	OLD BATCH	IV.1	163
Bellmour:	deserves to be pillory'd.--No, by Heaven, I	82	OLD BATCH	IV.2	67

303

Heaven   (continued)

Heeds (1)
Gonsalez: The King is blinded by his Love, and heeds . . . . . 365 M. BRIDE IV.1 177
Heels (1)
Sharper: Thus Grief still treads upon the Heels of Pleasure: . . 105 OLD BATCH V.1 327
Heh (16)
Fondlewife: --Heh! You have finish'd the matter, Heh? And I am, . . 94 OLD BATCH IV.4 183
Fondlewife: called a Cuckold, Heh. Is it not so? Come, I'm . . . . 94 OLD BATCH IV.4 185
Fondlewife: the Philistines have been upon thee. Heh! Art thou not vile 95 OLD BATCH IV.4 251
Fondlewife: the Philistines--Heh! Art thou not vile . . . . . 95 OLD BATCH IV.4 V251
Fondlewife: and unclean, Heh? Speak. . . . . . . 95 OLD BATCH IV.4 252
Fondlewife: Heh. How? No, stay, stay, I will believe thee, I . . 96 OLD BATCH IV.4 259
Sharper: Heh! Sure, Fortune has sent this Fool hither on . . . 101 OLD BATCH V.1 163
Sir Joseph: Heh, heh, heh: Here 'tis for you, i'Faith, Mr. . . . 103 OLD BATCH V.1 236
Sir Joseph: Garter, when she was thinking of her Love. Heh, Setter. . 103 OLD BATCH V.1 258
Sir Joseph: No, no, Captain, you need not own, Heh, heh, . . . 110 OLD BATCH V.2 105
Sir Joseph: heh. 'Tis I must own-- . . . . 110 OLD BATCH V.2 106
Sir Paul: Girl? Do gads-bud, think on thy old Father; Heh? Make . 173 DOUBL DLR IV.1 230
Heigh (1)
Valentine: about without going together by the Ears--heigh ho! . 280 FOR LOVE IV.1 192
Heigho (2)
Brisk: Froth! Heigho! Break Heart; God's I thank you. . . . 175 DOUBL DLR IV.1 310
Millamant: peevish--Heigho! Now I'll be melancholly, as . . . . . 422 WAY WORLD II.1 476
Height (2)
Valentine: at the height of a Song, sent by an unknown Hand, or a . 218 FOR LOVE I.1 80
Zara: He knew I lov'd, but knew not to what height: . . . 381 M. BRIDE V.2 191
Heir (8)
Heartwell: to have my Son and heir resemble such a Duke--to have a . 45 OLD BATCH I.1 319
Careless: think thou hast no more Sense, than to get an Heir upon her 130 DOUBL DLR I.1 120
Maskwell: --a Son and Heir, would have edg'd Young . . . . 137 DOUBL DLR I.1 377
Lord Touch: thee in his room to be my Heir-- . . . . . . 189 DOUBL DLR V.1 59
Maskwell: Marriage with Cynthia, and has appointed me his Heir. . 190 DOUBL DLR V.1 112
Lady Touch: Maskwell your Heir, and Marry Cynthia! . . . . . . 191 DOUBL DLR V.1 122
As if indeed a Widow, or an Heir. . . . . . . 385 M. BRIDE EPI. 4
Waitwell: in spight of treachery; Ay and get an Heir that shall defeat 461 WAY WORLD IV.1 643
Heiress (1)
Mellefont: Like any two Guardians to an Orphan Heiress-- . . . . 156 DOUBL DLR III.1 216
Held (5) see With-held
Sir Paul: held fifty to one, I could have drawn my own Picture . 174 DOUBL DLR IV.1 242
(Draws, and runs at Mellefont, is held by Lady Touchwood.) 186 DOUBL DLR IV.2 108
They hold their Pens, as Swords are held by Fools, . . 214 FOR LOVE PRO. 37
Mirabell: high Place I once held, of sighing at your Feet; nay kill 471 WAY WORLD V.1 371
Mincing: shou'd have held our Tongues; You wou'd have brib'd . 474 WAY WORLD V.1 490
Heli (15)
Zara: Heli . . . . 337 M. BRIDE I.1 447
Enter Garcia, Heli and Perez.) . . . . 337 M. BRIDE II.1
Garcia: To mourn, brave Heli, thy mistaken Fate. . . . . 337 M. BRIDE II.1 3
Garcia: Go Gen'rous Heli, and relieve your Friend. . . . . 338 M. BRIDE II.1 35
Monument fronting the View, greater than the rest. Enter
Heli.) . . . . 340 M. BRIDE II.2
(Enter Heli.) . . . . . 341 M. BRIDE II.2 57
Osmyn-Alph: And he Heli. All, all he will unfold. . . . . 345 M. BRIDE II.2 208
(Exit Almeria, Leonora, and Heli.) . 345 M. BRIDE II.2 213
(Enter Heli.) . . . . . 350 M. BRIDE III.1 41
(Exit Heli.) . . . . . 352 M. BRIDE III.1 124
Selim: 'Tis certain Heli too is fled, and with him . . . 361 M. BRIDE IV.1 8
Manuel: Are none return'd of those who follow'd Heli? . . 363 M. BRIDE IV.1 74
Zara: Alphonso, Heli, and the Traytour Osmyn. . . . . 364 M. BRIDE IV.1 124
Manuel: This Tumult, and the Lords who fled with Heli, . . 366 M. BRIDE IV.1 215
(Enter Alphonso, Heli, Perez, with Garcia Prisoner, 382 M. BRIDE V.2 273
Hell (29)
Sharper: to me is Hell; nothing to be found, but the despair of what 48 OLD BATCH II.1 23
Capt Bluff: Death and Hell to be affronted thus! I'll die before . . 70 OLD BATCH III.1 336
Heartwell: (aside). Death, and Hell, and Marriage! My Wife! . . . 104 OLD BATCH V.1 295
Heartwell: (aside). Hell, and the Devil! Does he know it? But, . . 104 OLD BATCH V.1 298
Mellefont: Hell is not more busie than her Brain, nor contains more . 129 DOUBL DLR I.1 77
Mellefont: (aside). Hell and Damnation! this is my Aunt; such . . 145 DOUBL DLR II.1 270
Lord Touch: Confusion and Hell, what do I hear! . . . . . . 153 DOUBL DLR III.1 86
Mellefont: Hell and the Devil, she abandon'd of all Grace-- . . 156 DOUBL DLR III.1 235
Mellefont: Ay, Hell thank her, as gentle breezes moderate a . . 167 DOUBL DLR IV.1 3
Lady Touch: turn? has Hell no remedy? . . . . 185 DOUBL DLR IV.2 58
Mellefont: None, Hell has served you even as Heaven has . . . . 185 DOUBL DLR IV.2 59
Lady Touch: Hell and Amazement, she's in Tears. . . . . . . 185 DOUBL DLR IV.2 93
Mellefont: Host of Hell her Servants; . . . . 186 DOUBL DLR IV.2 124
Lady Touch: wild with this surprize of Treachery: Hell and Fire, it is 191 DOUBL DLR V.1 144
Lady Touch: . . . to a Hell of Torments,--but he's . . . . 191 DOUBL DLR V.1 V152
Lord Touch: Hell. . . . . 200 DOUBL DLR V.1 473
Scandal: Death and Hell! Where's Valentine? . . . . . . 308 FOR LOVE V.1 400
That after Death, ne're went to Hell, nor Heaven, . . 315 FOR LOVE EPI. 16
Osmyn-Alph: No no, nor should the subtlest Pains that Hell, . . . 357 M. BRIDE III.1 314
Osmyn-Alph: Hell, Hell! have I not Cause to rage and rave? . . 358 M. BRIDE III.1 361
Zara: Hell ! Hell! . . . . 360 M. BRIDE III.1 438
Zara: Nor Hell a Fury, like a Woman scorn'd. . . . . 361 M. BRIDE III.1 458
Manuel: Hell, Hell! do I hear this, and yet endure! . . . 369 M. BRIDE IV.1 314
Manuel: Thee free, Alphonso--Hell! curs'd, curs'd Alphonso! . 374 M. BRIDE V.1 60
Zara: Get thee to Hell, and seek him there. . . . 380 M. BRIDE V.2 175
Mrs Fain: a false accusation, as false as Hell, as false as your
Friend . . . . 466 WAY WORLD V.1 154
Hell-born (1)
Osmyn-Alph: Or hell-born Malice can invent; extort . . . . 357 M. BRIDE III.1 315
Hellish (3)
Lady Touch: (within). No, Monster! Hellish Traitor! no. . . . 197 DOUBL DLR V.1 372
Manuel: And plots in Private with this hellish Moor. . . . 367 M. BRIDE IV.1 235
Zara: His hellish Rage had wanted Means to act, ... 380 M. BRIDE V.2 177
Helm (2)
Sr Sampson: Helm, Sirrah, don't direct me. . . . . 308 FOR LOVE V.1 419
Ben: Well, well, take you care of your own Helm, or you . . 308 FOR LOVE V.1 420

Hen-peck'd (1)
		PAGE	TITLE	ACT.SC	LINE
Ben:	you will go to Sea in a Hen-peck'd Frigat.--I believe that,	287	FOR LOVE	IV.1	439

Hence (21)
Silvia:	Midwife, some nine Months hence--Well, I find dissembling,	75	OLD BATCH	III.2	150
Maskwell:	this Gallery an hour hence, by that time I imagine our	149	DOUBL DLR	II.1	435
Maskwell:	just gone from hence.	156	DOUBL DLR	III.1	203
Maskwell:	Lordship will meet me a quarter of an Hour hence there,	183	DOUBL DLR	IV.1	584
Lord Touch:	Hence from my sight, thou living infamy	186	DOUBL DLR	IV.2	118
Mellefont:	Man!--Take him hence, for he's a Disease to my Sight.	202	DOUBL DLR	V.1	574
Lord Touch:	Let secret Villany from hence be warn'd;	203	DOUBL DLR	V.1	591
Valentine:	For she'll meet me Two Hours hence in black and white,	290	FOR LOVE	IV.1	561
Foresight:	Why, you told me just now, you went hence in	309	FOR LOVE	V.1	453
Manuel:	Bear hence these Prisoners. Garcia, which is he,	335	M. BRIDE	I.1	363
Almeria:	O take me to thy Arms, and bear me hence,	342	M. BRIDE	II.2	84
Manuel:	'Tis daring for a God. Hence, to the Wheel	349	M. BRIDE	II.2	371
Zara:	Thou hast the Wrong, 'till I redeem thee hence;	355	M. BRIDE	III.1	218
Manuel:	Hence, e'er I curse--fly my just Rage with speed;	369	M. BRIDE	IV.1	316
Gonsalez:	Is far from hence, beyond your Father's Power.	370	M. BRIDE	IV.1	377
Almeria:	Hence, thou detested, ill-tim'd Flatterer;	370	M. BRIDE	IV.1	378
Manuel:	Hence, Slave, how dar'st thou bide, to watch and pry	373	M. BRIDE	V.1	39
Zara:	The King that parted hence; frowning he went;	374	M. BRIDE	V.1	92
Gonsalez:	Repent. Haste thee, Alonzo, hence, with speed,	379	M. BRIDE	V.2	125
Gonsalez:	Haste thee, Alonzo, haste thee hence with Speed,	379	M. BRIDE	V.2	V125
Mirabell:	From hence let those be warn'd, who mean to wed;	478	WAY WORLD	V.1	620

Henceforth (1)
Almeria:	Henceforth are equal; this the Day of Death,	367	M. BRIDE	IV.1	258

Henceforward (1)
Sir Paul:	friendship! What art thou but a Name! Henceforward, let	178	DOUBL DLR	IV.1	419

Hens (0) see Friezland-Hens

Her (784)

Her's (1)
Lady Wish:	this is her's; she is match'd now with a Witness--I	470	WAY WORLD	V.1	306

Hercules (1)
Setter:	wary and soforth--And to all this valiant as Hercules	65	OLD BATCH	III.1	151

Herd (3)
Valentine:	Clocks will strike Twelve at Noon, and the Horn'd Herd	289	FOR LOVE	IV.1	504
Mirabell:	Unkind. You had the leisure to entertain a Herd of	421	WAY WORLD	II.1	433
Fainall:	and will herd no more with 'em. True, I wear the badge;	444	WAY WORLD	III.1	720

Here (220)

Here's (54)
Capt Bluff:	But? Look you here Boy, here's your antidote, here's	51	OLD BATCH	II.1	146
Lucy:	Here's some Villany a Foot he's so thoughtful; may be I	65	OLD BATCH	III.1	154
Servant:	Here's a Chair, Sir, if you please to repose your self.	80	OLD BATCH	IV.2	1
Vainlove:	(aside). Hey day! Which way now? Here's fine	87	OLD BATCH	IV.3	160
Vainlove:	here's a silent Witness of your acquaintance.--	88	OLD BATCH	IV.3	V178
Bellmour:	Here's no body, nor no noise;--'twas nothing	89	OLD BATCH	IV.4	1
Fondlewife:	Adultery, and innocent! O Lord! Here's Doctrine!	92	OLD BATCH	IV.4	112
Fondlewife:	Ay, here's Discipline!	92	OLD BATCH	IV.4	113
Bellmour:	fitter Husband for her.--Come, Here's Earnest of my good	98	OLD BATCH	V.1	58
Bellmour:	Lucy.--Here's my Hand, I will; with a fresh Assurance.	98	OLD BATCH	V.1	72
Capt Bluff:	Quality. Here, here's from a Countess too. Hum--No	103	OLD BATCH	V.1	267
Capt Bluff:	time, here's Earnest. (Gives him Money). Come, Knight;	104	OLD BATCH	V.1	279
Setter:	mine. Here's Company coming, if you'll walk this way,	106	OLD BATCH	V.1	352
Vainlove:	Faith, that's a sure way.--But here's one can	109	OLD BATCH	V.2	79
Careless:	And here's this Cox-Comb most Critically come to	128	DOUBL DLR	I.1	17
Lady Ply:	necessity--O Lord, here's some body coming, I dare	148	DOUBL DLR	II.1	362
Lady Touch:	Well but go now, here's some body coming.	153	DOUBL DLR	III.1	122
Lady Ply:	Here, Sir Paul, it's from your Steward, here's a	162	DOUBL DLR	III.1	450
Cynthia:	Here's my Mother-in-Law, and your Friend Careless,	169	DOUBL DLR	IV.1	65
Lady Ply:	her own), Sir Paul, here's your Letter, to Morrow Morning	174	DOUBL DLR	IV.1	264
Lady Froth:	near any other Man. Oh here's my Lord, now you shall	177	DOUBL DLR	IV.1	369
Sir Paul:	all this for? Pooh, here's a joke, indeed--why, where's	192	DOUBL DLR	V.1	186
Lord Touch:	Here's Company--come this way and tell	196	DOUBL DLR	V.1	329
Sir Paul:	but here's the strangest Revolution, all turn'd topsie	200	DOUBL DLR	V.1	497
Trapland:	and here's to the Widow.	224	FOR LOVE	I.1	290
Scandal:	Here's a Dog now, a Traytor in his Wine, Sirrah	224	FOR LOVE	I.1	309
Jeremy:	Sir, here's the Steward again from your Father.	234	FOR LOVE	I.1	661
Foresight:	well pleas'd at my Stocking--Oh here's my Neice!--	236	FOR LOVE	II.1	38
Sr Sampson:	Here's a Rogue, Brother Foresight, makes a Bargain under	243	FOR LOVE	II.1	295
Sr Sampson:	from it in the Afternoon; here's a Rogue, Dog, here's	243	FOR LOVE	II.1	297
Sr Sampson:	Here's a Cormorant too,--'S'heart this	245	FOR LOVE	II.1	357
Mrs Frail:	Pooh, here's a Clutter--why should it reflect	247	FOR LOVE	II.1	435
Miss Prue:	giv'n me--Look you here Cousin, here's a Snuff-box;	249	FOR LOVE	II.1	516
Nurse:	Miss I say, God's my Life, here's fine doings towards--	253	FOR LOVE	III.1	9
Scandal:	So, why this is fair, here's Demonstration with a	257	FOR LOVE	III.1	147
Mrs Fore:	Hold, here's my Sister coming toward us.	273	FOR LOVE	III.1	747
Sr Sampson:	D'ye see, Mr. Buckram, here's the Paper sign'd	278	FOR LOVE	IV.1	112
Sr Sampson:	Sham-sickness shan't excuse him--O, here's his	278	FOR LOVE	IV.1	117
Buckram:	Condition: Here's your Paper, Sir--He may do me a	280	FOR LOVE	IV.1	184
Angelica:	Oh here's a reasonable Creature--sure he will	295	FOR LOVE	IV.1	733
Sr Sampson:	Odso, here's some body coming.	301	FOR LOVE	V.1	162
Miss Prue:	But here's my Father, and he knows my Mind.	304	FOR LOVE	V.1	254
Mrs Fore:	Here's Mr. Benjamin, he can tell us if his Father	306	FOR LOVE	V.1	339
Sr Sampson:	here's a Conjunction that was not foretold in all	307	FOR LOVE	V.1	379
Valentine:	No; here's the Fool; and if occasion be, I'll give it	310	FOR LOVE	V.1	497
Angelica:	Passion: Here's my Hand, my Heart was always yours,	312	FOR LOVE	V.1	562
Ben:	Mess, here's the Wind chang'd again. Father, you and I	312	FOR LOVE	V.1	568
Mrs Fain:	Here's your Mistress.	418	WAY WORLD	II.1	321
Millamant:	Dee hear the Creature? Lord, here's Company,	436	WAY WORLD	III.1	434
Servant-W:	Sir, my Lady's dressing. Here's Company; if you	437	WAY WORLD	III.1	445
Sir Wilful:	to have forgot your Relations. Here's your Cousin	441	WAY WORLD	III.1	604
Waitwell:	Here's a Villain! Madam, don't you perceive it,	460	WAY WORLD	IV.1	597

Hereafter (3)
Mellefont:	hereafter.	131	DOUBL DLR	I.1	141
Lord Touch:	Authority--hereafter, you shall rule where I have Power.	189	DOUBL DLR	V.1	66
Zara:	Of that hereafter; but, mean time, 'tis fit	365	M. BRIDE	IV.1	161

Hereditary (1)
  Leonora: Revenge, and that Hereditary Feud . . . . 327 M. BRIDE   I.1   43
Hereof (2)
  Sharper: present Date hereof.--How say you? . . . . 110 OLD BATCH   V.2   88
  Jeremy: it may concern; That the Bearer hereof, Jeremy Fetch by . 218 FOR LOVE   I.1   66
Heretofore (2)
  Setter: we have dallied with heretofore--And art come   . . . . 65 OLD BATCH III.1 184
               This Author, heretofore, has found your Favour, . . . 393 WAY WORLD PRO.   16
Hermaphrodite (1)
  Tattle: enquire for me, than ever went to see the Hermaphrodite, . 257 FOR LOVE III.1 161
Hero (1)
  Sir Joseph: Ah, well said my Hero; was not that great Sir? . . . . 52 OLD BATCH   II.1 166
Heroically (1)
  Mrs Fore: What then, he bore it most Heroically? . . . . 287 FOR LOVE   IV.1 454
Heroick (3)
  Lady Froth: Lampoons, Plays, or Heroick Poems. . . . . 138 DOUBL DLR   II.1   17
  Brisk: an Heroick Poem. . . . . 141 DOUBL DLR   II.1 119
  Brisk: Incomparable, let me perish--but then being an Heroick . 163 DOUBL DLR   II.1 505
Hers (9)
  Lucy: keeps him hers-- . . . . 61 OLD BATCH III.1   38
  Vainlove: Now must I pretend ignorance equal to hers, cf . . . . 87 OLD BATCH IV.3 136
  Maskwell: I might be trusted; since it was as much my interest as hers 149 DOUBL DLR   II.1 423
  Brisk: coxcomly Lord of hers; and yet I am forced to allow him . 175 DOUBL DLR   IV.1 293
  Scandal: of hers. . . . . 225 FOR LOVE   I.1 345
  Manuel: Her Eyes, did more than bid--free her and hers, . . . 336 M. BRIDE   I.1 410
  Perez: And every Look of his and hers confess it. . . . . . 338 M. BRIDE   II.1   46
  Zara: Confusion in his Face, and Grief in hers! . . . . . 359 M. BRIDE   III.1 397
  Fainall: Wife's--Why she had parted with hers before; so bringing . 443 WAY WORLD III.1 686
Herself (1)
  Mirabell: stand excus'd, who has suffer'd herself to be won by his . 417 WAY WORLD II.1 274
Hey (10)
  Sharper: Hey day! Captain, what's the matter? You can tell. . . . 69 OLD BATCH III.1 295
  Vainlove: (aside). Hey day! Which way now? Here's fine . . . . 87 OLD BATCH IV.3 160
  Mrs Frail: Hey day! I shall get a fine Reputation by coming . . . 230 FOR LOVE   I.1 546
  Foresight: Hey day! What are all the Women of my Family . . . . 235 FOR LOVE   II.1   1
  Foresight: gallop, hey! Whither will they hurry me?--Now they're . 269 FOR LOVE   III.1 608
  Scandal: Hey, brave Woman, i' faith--Won't you see . . . . . 277 FOR LOVE   IV.1   77
  Sr Sampson: Hey day, Rascal, do you banter me? Sirrah, ... 279 FOR LOVE   IV.1 127
  Ben: Hey toss! what's the matter now? why you ben't . . . 286 FOR LOVE   IV.1 396
  Foresight: Hey day! What time of the Moon is this? . . . . 305 FOR LOVE   V.1 286
  Witwoud: Hey day! what are you all got together like Players . 475 WAY WORLD   V.1 521
Hey-day (1)
  Sir Joseph: Hey-day! Traytor yourself.--By the Lord-Harry, . . . 90 OLD BATCH IV.4   61
Hiccup (2)
  Petulant: he (hiccup) rises upon my stomack like a Radish. . . . . 454 WAY WORLD   IV.1 357
  Sir Wilful: hard Word, Aunt, and (hiccup) Greek for Claret. . . . 456 WAY WORLD   IV.1 448
Hid (3)
  Bellmour: Nature, Night, had hid, confess'd her Soul was true to . 38 OLD BATCH   I.1   50
  Zara: And scorn vile Slavery, tho' doubly hid . . . . . 336 M. BRIDE   I.1 401
  Foible: and would have hid his face. . . . . 461 WAY WORLD   IV.1 614
Hide (7)
  Miss Prue: No, indeed won't I: But I'll run there, and hide . . . 252 FOR LOVE   II.1 648
  Almeria: Comfort me, help me, hold me, hide me, hide me, . . . 341 M. BRIDE   II.2   43
  Zara: To hide, the rustling Leaves, and bended Grass . . . 375 M. BRIDE   V.1 109
  Fainall: --'Sdeath they come, hide your Face, your Tears-- . . 416 WAY WORLD   II.1 247
  Mincing: Foible; and wou'd have you hide your self in my Lady's . 465 WAY WORLD   V.1 106
  Fainall: to hide thy Shame; Your Body shall be Naked as . . . 475 WAY WORLD   V.1 496
Hide-Park (2)
  Millamant: Francis: Nor goe to Hide-Park together the first Sunday in 450 WAY WORLD   IV.1 202
  Foible: when you were at Hide-Park;--And we were thought to . 464 WAY WORLD   V.1   95
Hideous (5)
  Belinda: O I love your hideous Fancy! Ha, ha, ha, love a . . . 55 OLD BATCH   II.2   22
  Belinda: O Gad I hate your hideous Fancy--You said that . . . 59 OLD BATCH   II.2 167
  Belinda: me now? Hideous, ha? Frightful still? Or how? . . . 83 OLD BATCH   IV.3   17
  Belinda: Huffe, Bluffe, (What's your hideous Name?) be gone: . . 85 OLD BATCH   IV.3   87
  Lady Touch: forgets the hideous form. . . . . 136 DOUBL DLR   I.1 V332
Hides (1)
  Zara: Still further from me; look, he hides his Face, ... 381 M. BRIDE   V.2 209
Hieroglyphical (1)
  Foresight: are very Mysterious and Hieroglyphical. . . . . . . 289 FOR LOVE   IV.1 534
Hieroglyphick (1)
  Sr Sampson: an Illustrious Creature, my trusty Hieroglyphick; and may 242 FOR LOVE   II.1 243
Hieroglyphicks (3)
  Scandal: I have some Hieroglyphicks too; I have a Lawyer . . . 233 FOR LOVE   I.1 642
  Sr Sampson: with Hieroglyphicks, thou shalt have it sent home to thy 242 FOR LOVE   II.1 251
  Sr Sampson: with Hieroglyphicks, thou shalt have it brought home to thy 242 FOR LOVE   II.1 V251
High (17)
  Vainlove: Element Ned--Well as high as a Flyer as you are, I . . . 38 OLD BATCH   I.1   30
  Belinda: a high Roof, or a very low Seat--Stay, Come back here . 57 OLD BATCH   II.2   96
  Setter: opened for all Comers. In Fine thou art the high Road to . 66 OLD BATCH III.1 196
  Sir Paul: Gad'sbud, I can't find her high nor low; where can . . . 192 DOUBL DLR   V.1 162
  Maskwell: 'Tis that; you know my Lady has a high Spirit, . . . 195 DOUBL DLR   V.1 315
  Ben: high Wind, or that Lady.--You mayn't carry so much . 262 FOR LOVE   III.1 331
  Ben: Discourse with you, an 'twere not a main high Wind . 263 FOR LOVE   III.1 370
  Foresight: His Frenzy is very high now, Mr. Scandal. . . . . . 289 FOR LOVE   IV.1 529
  Almeria: Led on his conqu'ring Troops, high as the Gates . . . 329 M. BRIDE   I.1 112
  Manuel: And all this high and ample Roof to ring . . . . . 333 M. BRIDE   I.1 312
  Gonsalez: For this high Honour. . . . . 334 M. BRIDE   I.1 V339
  Osmyn-Alph: On high; and of good Men, the very best . . . . . 350 M. BRIDE   III.1   29
  Zara: This thy Silence; somewhat of high Concern, ... 354 M. BRIDE   III.1 194
  Selim: Who bore high Offices of Weight and Trust, ... 361 M. BRIDE   IV.1   10
  Zara: Than your high Courage suffers you to see; . . . . 364 M. BRIDE   IV.1 110
  Zara: A Forfeit as thy Life: Somewhat of high . . . . . 375 M. BRIDE   V.1 124
  Mirabell: high Place I once held, of sighing at your Feet; nay kill 471 WAY WORLD   V.1 371
High-fed (1)
  Fondlewife: trust my Wife, with a Lords high-fed Chaplain. . . . . 76 OLD BATCH   IV.1   33

Higher (1)
Bellmour:	Business is not my Element--I rowl in a higher Orb	38	OLD BATCH	I.1	27

Highest (2)
Lady Touch:	have you not wrong'd him in the highest manner, in his	135	DOUBL DLR	I.1	311
Mrs Frail:	time he grows only rude to his Wife, and that is the highest	231	FOR LOVE	I.1	564

Highly (2)
Lady Ply:	all--and highly honoured in that Title.	172	DOUBL DLR	IV.1	191
Selim:	Your Accusation highly has incens'd	361	M. BRIDE	IV.1	4

Highness (1)
Alonzo:	The Lord Gonsalez comes to tell your Highness	331	M. BRIDE	I.1	209

Hill (0) see Down-hill, Holborn-hill

Hills (1)
Gonsalez:	White as the fleecy Rain on Alpine Hills;	331	M. BRIDE	I.1	231

Hilt (1)
Garcia:	And bathe it to the Hilt, in far less damnable	378	M. BRIDE	V.2	79

Hilts (3)
Capt Bluff:	Fighting, Sir I Kiss your Hilts.	51	OLD BATCH	II.1	157
Capt Bluff:	By these Hilts I believe he frightned you into this	68	OLD BATCH	III.1	268
Capt Bluff:	Ladies, by these Hilts you are well met.	85	OLD BATCH	IV.3	82

Him (732)

Himself (60)
Bellmour:	himself, to see what pains he will take, and how he will	40	OLD BATCH	I.1	126
Bellmour:	to himself in the World; he takes as much always of an	42	OLD BATCH	I.1	211
Bellmour:	enrich'd himself with the plunder of a few Oaths;--and	47	OLD BATCH	I.1	370
Sir Joseph:	he would put in for't he might be made General himself	53	OLD BATCH	II.1	215
Lucy:	on him, himself--Contrive a kind Letter as from her,	62	OLD BATCH	III.1	41
Vainlove:	He's talking to himself, I think; Prithee lets try if	62	OLD BATCH	III.1	61
Bellmour:	other way to get himself a heat.	70	OLD BATCH	III.1	329
Fondlewife:	pampereth himself up with Dainties, that he may look	76	OLD BATCH	IV.1	27
Fondlewife:	himself--	77	OLD BATCH	IV.1	76
Laetitia:	Husband ought to behave himself--I shall be glad to	79	OLD BATCH	IV.1	140
Laetitia:	Let the wicked Man answer for himself; does he	93	OLD BATCH	IV.4	167
Bellmour:	(Discovers himself.)	97	OLD BATCH	V.1	28
Sharper:	Hugging himself in his prosperous Mischief--No	100	OLD BATCH	V.1	132
Sharper:	himself out of breath.--	107	OLD BATCH	V.1	392
Cynthia:	himself.	141	DOUBL DLR	II.1	108
Lady Ply:	Sir Paul himself?	145	DOUBL DLR	II.1	256
Maskwell:	will cheat no body but himself; such another Coxcomb,	150	DOUBL DLR	II.1	454
Maskwell:	will be made a Fool of by no body, but himself: Ha, ha, ha.	150	DOUBL DLR	II.1	456
Lady Touch:	a mind to amuse himself, sometimes with a little Gallantry	153	DOUBL DLR	III.1	83
	speaks as it were to himself.)	155	DOUBL DLR	III.1	193
Lady Ply:	breeding to think Mr. Careless did not apply himself to me.	159	DOUBL DLR	III.1	330
Lady Ply:	respect--That he has own'd himself to be my Admirer	172	DOUBL DLR	IV.1	166
Lady Touch:	or commit some himself.	186	DOUBL DLR	IV.2	129
Lord Touch:	Talking to himself!	188	DOUBL DLR	V.1	17
Lady Touch:	or she? nay, he himself perhaps may have Affections	191	DOUBL DLR	V.1	129
Lady Touch:	My Lord himself surpriz'd me with the	198	DOUBL DLR	V.1	416
Jeremy:	himself, or were resolv'd to turn Author, and bring the	219	FOR LOVE	I.1	106
Jeremy:	has more Wit than himself?	219	FOR LOVE	I.1	130
Mrs Frail:	That's more than he has for himself. And what will	232	FOR LOVE	I.1	593
Scandal:	represented as they are in himself: And he himself is the	232	FOR LOVE	I.1	603
Sr Sampson:	Rogue shew himself, and make Love to some desponding	260	FOR LOVE	III.1	261
Scandal:	Violence--I fear he does not act wholly from himself;	268	FOR LOVE	III.1	549
Angelica:	more than he has done by himself: and now the Surprize	277	FOR LOVE	IV.1	82
Jeremy:	Would you could, Sir; for he has lost himself. Indeed,	279	FOR LOVE	IV.1	130
Ben:	marry himself. Gad, says I, an you play the fool and marry	286	FOR LOVE	IV.1	382
Ben:	and he'll marry her himself, with all my heart.	286	FOR LOVE	IV.1	387
Mrs Frail:	committing Matrimony himself.--If he has a mind to	287	FOR LOVE	IV.1	459
Mrs Frail:	throw himself away, he can't do it more effectually than	287	FOR LOVE	IV.1	460
Angelica:	when Valentine confesses himself in his Senses; he must	300	FOR LOVE	V.1	122
Leonora:	He did endear himself to your Affection,	327	M. BRIDE	I.1	45
Heli:	To act some Violence upon himself,	338	M. BRIDE	II.1	29
Zara:	Attempt no Means to make himself away;	360	M. BRIDE	III.1	V448
Zara:	Himself. I've been deceiv'd. The publick Safety	360	M. BRIDE	III.1	449
Gonsalez:	He there disclos'd himself to Albucacim,	363	M. BRIDE	IV.1	85
Gonsalez:	While he himself, returning to Valentia	363	M. BRIDE	IV.1	88
Zara:	You more. One that did call himself Alphonso,	364	M. BRIDE	IV.1	116
Zara:	You more. One who did call himself Alphonso,	364	M. BRIDE	IV.1	V116
Fainall:	He comes to Town in order to Equip himself for	400	WAY WORLD	I.1	197
Witwoud:	himself--	405	WAY WORLD	I.1	367
Fainall:	Call for himself? What dost thou mean?	405	WAY WORLD	I.1	368
Witwoud:	himself, that I mean, call for himself, wait for himself,	405	WAY WORLD	I.1	375
	nay				
Witwoud:	and what's more, not finding himself, sometimes leave a	405	WAY WORLD	I.1	376
Witwoud:	Letter for himself.	405	WAY WORLD	I.1	377
Mirabell:	he waits for himself now, he is so long a coming; O I ask	405	WAY WORLD	I.1	379
Waitwell:	Day! 'Tis enough to make any Man forget himself. The	424	WAY WORLD	II.1	556
Marwood:	oblig'd me to that, with those Excesses of himself; and	431	WAY WORLD	III.1	245
Lady Wish:	has acquir'd Discretion to choose for himself.	432	WAY WORLD	III.1	265

Hinder (4)
Cynthia:	and hinder one another in the Race; I swear it never do's	168	DOUBL DLR	IV.1	13
Angelica:	his Mistress. Mr. Tattle, we must not hinder Lovers.	262	FOR LOVE	III.1	346
Almeria:	The extremest Malice of our Fate can hinder:	358	M. BRIDE	III.1	336
Sir Wilful:	once, he shall come in; and see who'll hinder him.	471	WAY WORLD	V.1	352

Hinder'd (1)
Foible:	Ladyship and Mr. Mirabell, might have hinder'd his	430	WAY WORLD	III.1	198

Hindered (1)
Lord Touch:	though you have once actually hindered him from forcing	182	DOUBL DLR	IV.1	550

Hindrance (1)
Ben:	that be all--Pray don't let me be your hindrance; e'en	261	FOR LOVE	III.1	301

Hindred (2)
Bellmour:	hindred the making of your own Fortune.	94	OLD BATCH	IV.4	189
Lady Touch:	I'll do it--I'll tell him you hindred	155	DOUBL DLR	III.1	162

Hinge (1)
Leonora:	Beneath, are still wide stretch'd upon their Hinge,	340	M. BRIDE	II.2	12

Hoity (1)

Sr Sampson:	Hoity toity, What have I to do with his Dreams . . .	267	FOR LOVE	III.1	504

Holborn-hill (1)

| Sr Sampson: | go up Holborn-hill,--Has he not a Rogues face?--Speak, | 243 | FOR LOVE | II.1 | 304 |

Hold (94)

Vainlove:	Hold hold, 'slife that's the wrong.	38	OLD BATCH	I.1	37
Bellmour:	their Mistresses--I must take up, or I shall never hold out;	41	OLD BATCH	I.1	144
Capt Bluff:	about, Pray hold your Tongue, and give me leave. . . .	53	OLD BATCH	II.1	225
Belinda:	Let me see; hold the Glass--Lard I look wretchedly . .	57	OLD BATCH	II.2	91
Belinda:	Hold off your Fists, and see that he gets a Chair with	57	OLD BATCH	II.2	95
Belinda:	Prithee hold thy Tongue--Lard, he has so	59	OLD BATCH	II.2	163
Lucy:	about it streight--Hold, I'me mistaken, or that's . .	62	OLD BATCH	III.1	46
Lucy:	Beast, filthy Toad, I can hold no longer, look and . .	66	OLD BATCH	III.1	198
Fondlewife:	Oak--I profess I can hold no longer--Nay dear Cocky--	78	OLD BATCH	IV.1	115
Bellmour:	If we part so I'm mistaken.--Hold, hold, ...	81	OLD BATCH	IV.2	37
Laetitia:	Does it hold you long? I'm afraid to carry you into .	83	OLD BATCH	IV.2	90
Fondlewife:	Devil's Pater-noster. Hold, let me see: The Innocent Adultery.	92	OLD BATCH	IV.4	107
Sir Joseph:	How's this! Good Bully, hold your breath, and . . .	102	OLD BATCH	V.1	203
Capt Bluff:	hold--That's from a Knight's Wife, she sent it me by her	103	OLD BATCH	V.1	268
Heartwell:	hold:--If he shou'd not, I were a Fool to discover it.--	104	OLD BATCH	V.1	299
Sharper:	(Now hold Spleen.) Married!	105	OLD BATCH	V.1	314
Heartwell:	self on her Wedding-Day! Not hold out till Night! . .	107	OLD BATCH	V.2	6
Bellmour:	Hold, hold. What the Devil, thou wilt not draw . . .	108	OLD BATCH	V.2	42
Lucy:	Hold your prating.--I'm thinking what Vocation . . .	111	OLD BATCH	V.2	144
	But hold--I am exceeding my Commission;	113	OLD BATCH	EPI.	17
Lady Ply:	hold you Contented.	144	DOUBL DLR	II.1	203
Sir Paul:	Hold your self Contented, my Lady Plyant,--I	144	DOUBL DLR	II.1	206
Cynthia:	Hold--Never to Marry any Body else.	168	DOUBL DLR	IV.1	40
Brisk:	can hardly hold Laughing in his Face.	177	DOUBL DLR	IV.1	380
Sir Paul:	Hold, stay, I beseech your Ladiship--I'm so	179	DOUBL DLR	IV.1	465
Lady Touch:	Hold, let me Lock the Door first.	184	DOUBL DLR	IV.2	28
Mellefont:	Hold, Madam, you have no more holes to your Burrough, .	184	DOUBL DLR	IV.2	42
Lady Touch:	I'le hold my breath and die, but I'le be free. . . .	184	DOUBL DLR	IV.2	53
Lady Touch:	(aside). Hold in my passion, and fall, fall, a . . .	185	DOUBL DLR	IV.2	64
Lady Touch:	O Heavens my Lord! hold, hold, for	186	DOUBL DLR	IV.2	109
Lady Touch:	Spirits faint, and I want strength to hold it, thou hast	198	DOUBL DLR	V.1	403
Mellefont:	your hand;--do you hold down your head? Yes, I am .	202	DOUBL DLR	V.1	569
	They hold their Pens, as Swords are held by Fools, .	214	FOR LOVE	PRO.	37
Trapland:	Hold, Sweet-heart.--This is not to our Business: . .	222	FOR LOVE	I.1	245
Foresight:	faith and troth, here 'tis, if it will but hold--I wish	240	FOR LOVE	II.1	187
Tattle:	you'l cry out, you must be sure to hold your Tongue. .	252	FOR LOVE	II.1	623
Tattle:	Hold, hold, that's pretty well,--but you should not .	252	FOR LOVE	II.1	635
Miss Prue:	Ah, but I'll hold the Door with both Hands, and . .	252	FOR LOVE	II.1	651
Miss Prue:	Oh but you sha'nt, for I'll hold my Tongue.-- . .	253	FOR LOVE	II.1	658
Ben:	An we were a League asunder, I'de undertake to hold .	263	FOR LOVE	III.1	369
Mrs Frail:	Hold, there's my Sister, I'll call her to hear it. .	273	FOR LOVE	III.1	741
Mrs Fore:	Hold, here's my Sister coming toward us.	273	FOR LOVE	III.1	747
Sr Sampson:	Hold, hold, don't you go yet.	280	FOR LOVE	IV.1	188
Valentine:	Pray let me see it, Sir. You hold it so far off, that	281	FOR LOVE	IV.1	217
Valentine:	Will you please to let me hold it, Sir?	281	FOR LOVE	IV.1	228
Sr Sampson:	Let thee hold it, say'st thou--Aye, with all . . .	281	FOR LOVE	IV.1	229
Sr Sampson:	need any body hold it?--I'll put it up in my Pocket. .	281	FOR LOVE	IV.1	231
Sr Sampson:	Val: And then no body need hold it (puts the Paper in his	281	FOR LOVE	IV.1	232
Valentine:	their Necks. But hold, I must examine you before I go .	289	FOR LOVE	IV.1	513
Angelica:	O fie for shame, hold your Tongue, A passionate . .	291	FOR LOVE	IV.1	585
Tattle:	But in short, de'e see, I will hold you a Hundred Pound	291	FOR LOVE	IV.1	608
Angelica:	Hold, hold, Sir Sampson. I ask'd your Advice for a . .	300	FOR LOVE	V.1	105
Angelica:	Hold, Sir Sampson--You're profuse of your	301	FOR LOVE	V.1	149
Ben:	a Voyage to Antegoa--No, hold, I maynt say so . . .	306	FOR LOVE	V.1	351
Ben:	Hold. They say a Witch will sail in a Sieve--But I .	309	FOR LOVE	V.1	434
Sr Sampson:	Hold your Tongue, Sirrah. How now, who's	309	FOR LOVE	V.1	437
Ben:	enough to hold her, and if she can't drag her Anchor .	310	FOR LOVE	V.1	493
Gonsalez:	Their Hold, thro' clifted Stones; stretching, and staring,	332	M. BRIDE	I.1	240
Gonsalez:	My Eyes with more Delight, than they can hold. . . .	332	M. BRIDE	I.1	274
Almeria:	Comfort me, help me, hold me, hide me, hide me, . .	341	M. BRIDE	II.2	43
Osmyn-Alph:	Why dost thou weep, and hold thee from my Arms, . .	343	M. BRIDE	II.2	122
Zara:	In Chains unseen, I hold him by the Heart, . . .	348	M. BRIDE	II.2	325
Manuel:	With that Ixion, who aspires to hold	349	M. BRIDE	II.2	372
Heli:	Where not far off some Male-Contents hold Counsel . .	352	M. BRIDE	III.1	100
Heli:	Where not far off some Male-Contents hold Council . .	352	M. BRIDE	III.1	V100
Osmyn-Alph:	Would hold thee here, and clog thy Expedition. . .	352	M. BRIDE	III.1	110
Osmyn-Alph:	Is this to call thee mine? O hold my Heart; . . .	357	M. BRIDE	III.1	329
Almeria:	No, hold me not--O, let us not support, . . .	358	M. BRIDE	III.1	370
Zara:	O Curse! I cannot hold--	360	M. BRIDE	III.1	430
Almeria:	No, never will I rise, nor loose this Hold, . . .	369	M. BRIDE	IV.1	330
Almeria:	Curst these weak Hands, that cou'd not hold him here; .	370	M. BRIDE	IV.1	373
Gonsalez:	Hold, let me think--if I shou'd tell the King-- . .	371	M. BRIDE	IV.1	403
Leonora:	O hold	382	M. BRIDE	V.2	261
Osmyn-Alph:	Forbear; my Arms alone shall hold her up: . . .	383	M. BRIDE	V.2	278
Fainall:	other Hold to keep you here?	416	WAY WORLD	II.1	228
Millamant:	Countenance, 'tis impossible I shou'd hold mine. Well,	422	WAY WORLD	II.1	473
Foible:	hold; But i'faith I gave him his own. . . .	427	WAY WORLD	III.1	91
Sir Wilful:	Hold ye, hear me Friend; a Word with you in . . .	437	WAY WORLD	III.1	468
Sir Wilful:	the salt Seas, if my Mind hold.	440	WAY WORLD	III.1	568
Sir Wilful:	French as they say, whereby to hold discourse in Foreign	440	WAY WORLD	III.1	584
Sir Wilful:	Why then let him hold his Tongue in the mean . .	441	WAY WORLD	III.1	611
Millamant:	thank'd--here kiss my hand tho'--so hold your tongue .	452	WAY WORLD	IV.1	296
Mirabell:	enough, that I have lost what in my heart I hold most dear,	472	WAY WORLD	V.1	388
Lady Wish:	Hold Nephew, hold.	473	WAY WORLD	V.1	430
Sir Wilful:	Hold Sir, now you may make your Bear-Garden . .	476	WAY WORLD	V.1	558
Lady Wish:	As I am a person I can hold out no longer;--I . . .	478	WAY WORLD	V.1	608

Holding (4)

Brisk:	holding your sides, and Laughing as if you would bepiss	134	DOUBL DLR	I.1	255
Brisk:	holding your sides, and Laughing as if you would--well--	134	DOUBL DLR	I.1	V255
Scandal:	What, Jeremy holding forth?	219	FOR LOVE	I.1	117

Holding   (continued)
   Mirabell: --(holding out the Parchment.) tho perhaps what is   . . . 476   WAY WORLD   V.1   548
Holds (7)
   Laetitia: poor Heart, while it holds; which cannot be long, with   .   77   OLD BATCH   IV.1   92
   Mellefont: and just when he holds out his hand to gather it, to have a 187   DOUBL DLR   IV.2   145
   Scandal: Secresie, and makes Proclamation that he holds private . 226   FOR LOVE   I.1   379
   Sr Sampson: (Shews him the Paper, but holds it out of his reach.) . . 281   FOR LOVE   IV.1   216
   Sr Sampson: my Heart--What matter is it who holds it? What   . . . 281   FOR LOVE   IV.1   230
   Osmyn-Alph: That holds my Father's Ashes; and but now, ... 349   M. BRIDE   III.1   2
   Sir Wilful: how that the Peace holds, whereby that is, Taxes abate. . 440   WAY WORLD   III.1 575
Hole (0)   see Key-hole
Holes (1)
   Mellefont: Hold, Madam, you have no more holes to your Burrough,   . . 184   DOUBL DLR   IV.2   42
Holla (1)
   Ben: it as you will, may-hap you may holla after me when I   . . 287   FOR LOVE   IV.1   442
Hollow (2)
   Almeria: My Father's Voice; hollow it sounds, and from   371   M. BRIDE   IV.1   392
   Almeria: My Father's Voice; hollow it sounds, and calls   371   M. BRIDE   IV.1 V392
Hollows (1)
   Almeria: Whistling thro' Hollows of this vaulted Isle.   339   M. BRIDE   II.1   55
Holy (1)
   Perez: By all that's holy, I'm amaz'd-- 373   M. BRIDE   V.1   49
Homage (1)
   Zara: With usual Homage wait. But when I feel   336   M. BRIDE   I.1   399
Home (34)
   Bellmour: I'le take care, he shall not be at home. Good! Spintext! Oh 39   OLD BATCH   I.1   84
   Footman: at home. 56   OLD BATCH   II.2   80
   Lucy: Strike Heartwell home, before the Bait's worn off the   . . 61   OLD BATCH   III.1   10
   Fondlewife: I say I will tarry at home. 75   OLD BATCH   IV.1   14
   Fondlewife: hath possess'd the Lad--I say I will tarry at home--Varlet. 75   OLD BATCH   IV.1   17
   Barnaby: as ever he comes home--I could have brought young   . . . 76   OLD BATCH   IV.1   22
   Bellmour: Freedom of his Bed: He not coming home all Night, a   . . . 82   OLD BATCH   IV.2   51
   Fondlewife: I'm come home. 89   OLD BATCH   IV.4   9
   Bellmour: That's home. 108   OLD BATCH   V.2   38
   Capt Bluff: sprout at home. 111   OLD BATCH   V.2   149
   Mellefont: O' my word, Brisk, that was a home thrust; you   128   DOUBL DLR   I.1   31
   Foresight: abroad? Is not my Wife come home? Nor my Sister, nor   . . 235   FOR LOVE   II.1   2
   Foresight: home? 235   FOR LOVE   II.1   7
   Nurse: home yet: Poor Child, I warrant she's fond o'seeing the   . 235   FOR LOVE   II.1   20
   Foresight: of the Head is Horns--Dear Neice, stay at home--   . . . 236   FOR LOVE   II.1   58
   Angelica: staying at home. 237   FOR LOVE   II.1   63
   Angelica: you keep her at Home, if you're Jealous when she's abroad? 237   FOR LOVE   II.1   70
   Angelica: you keep her at Home, if you're Jealous of her when she's
                  abroad? 237   FOR LOVE   II.1 V 70
   Angelica: come home--You'll have a Letter for Alimony to   239   FOR LOVE   II.1   134
   Angelica: out my Aunt, and tell her, she must not come home. . . . 239   FOR LOVE   II.1   162
   Sr Sampson: with Hieroglyphicks, thou shalt have it sent home to thy . 242   FOR LOVE   II.1   251
   Sr Sampson: with Hieroglyphicks, thou shalt have it brought home to thy 242   FOR LOVE   II.1 V251
   Mrs Fore: But can't you converse at home?--I own   247   FOR LOVE   II.1   426
   Tattle: at home, and the Parson had not half his Congregation. . 258   FOR LOVE   III.1   170
   Ben: Father, and how do all at home? How do's Brother Dick,   . 261   FOR LOVE   III.1   290
   Ben: me alone as soon as I come home, with such a dirty dowdy . 264   FOR LOVE   III.1   423
   Ben: clean Shirt once a Quarter--Come home and lie with   . . 275   FOR LOVE   III.1   801
   Mrs Fore: be come home. 306   FOR LOVE   V.1   340
   Ben: Who, Father? ay, he's come home with a Vengeance.   . . . 306   FOR LOVE   V.1   341
   Mirabell: Has the Taylor brought Waitwell's Cloaths home, ... 398   WAY WORLD   I.1   124
   Mirabell: That's well. Do you go home again, d'ee hear, ... 398   WAY WORLD   I.1   127
   Mirabell: That's well. Do you go home again, d'ye hear, ... 398   WAY WORLD   I.1   V127
   Foible: haste home and prevent her. Your Servant Sir. B'w'y   . . 424   WAY WORLD   II.1   547
   Mirabell: bring you home in a pretended fright, when you think you . 451   WAY WORLD   IV.1   240
Homely (1)
                  And tho' of Homely Fare we make the Feast, ... 213   FOR LOVE   PRO.   27
Honest (45)
   Silvia: self--honest--Here, I won't keep any thing that's yours, . 73   OLD BATCH   III.2   110
   Heartwell: (aside). A Woman, and Ignorant, may be honest, ... 74   OLD BATCH   III.2   126
   Bellmour: Well, since I see thou art a good honest Fellow, I'll   . . 94   OLD BATCH   IV.4   198
   Fondlewife: Oh, I am a very honest Fellow--You never   94   OLD BATCH   IV.4   200
   Bellmour: of your absence, by my Spy, (for Faith, honest Isaac, I   . 94   OLD BATCH   IV.4   206
   Sharper: Experiment. But honest Setter, here, over-heard you with . 100   OLD BATCH   V.1   145
   Setter: honest. Reputed honest! Hum: Is that all? Ay: For, to be . 102   OLD BATCH   V.1   228
   Setter: honest is nothing; the Reputation of it is all. Reputation! 102   OLD BATCH   V.1   229
   Sir Joseph: Ah, honest Setter.--Sirrah, I'll give thee any   104   OLD BATCH   V.1   281
   Heartwell: been honest. 109   OLD BATCH   V.2   68
   Setter: --Well, honest Lucy, Fare-thee-well.--I   111   OLD BATCH   V.2   141
   Brisk: --My Lord, Careless, is a very honest Fellow, but   . . . 133   DOUBL DLR   I.1   250
   Maskwell: bears an Enemy in his Breast: For your honest man, as I   . 150   DOUBL DLR   II.1   452
   Careless: Why faith I have in my time known Honest Gentlemen   . . . 180   DOUBL DLR   IV.1   496
   Lord Touch: honest, I will secure thy Fidelity to him, and give   . . 182   DOUBL DLR   IV.1   572
   Mellefont: honest way. 185   DOUBL DLR   IV.2   88
   Maskwell: 'Twas honest--And shall I be rewarded for it?   188   DOUBL DLR   V.1   18
   Maskwell: No, 'twas honest, therefore I shan't;--Nay, rather,
                  therefore   188   DOUBL DLR   V.1   19
   Maskwell: ruine all, consume my honest Character, and brand me   . . 188   DOUBL DLR   V.1   30
   Lord Touch: you, and yet it shall not need--Honest Maskwell! thy   . . 189   DOUBL DLR   V.1   53
   Mellefont: a Statesman or a Jesuite, but that thou'rt too honest for 193   DOUBL DLR   V.1   236
   Mellefont: a Statesman or a Jesuite, but thou art too honest for   . . 193   DOUBL DLR   V.1   V236
   Scandal: the force of open honest Satire. 220   FOR LOVE   I.1   150
   Scandal: would be to invent the honest means of keeping your word, 221   FOR LOVE   I.1   196
   Valentine: my Service to you,--fill, fill, to honest Mr. Trapland,   . 222   FOR LOVE   I.1   243
   Scandal: that was not an honest Fellow. 223   FOR LOVE   I.1   266
   Sr Sampson: provoke honest Albumazar--an Egyptian Mummy is   242   FOR LOVE   II.1   242
   Mrs Frail: and honest, I shou'd like such a humour in a Husband   . . 262   FOR LOVE   III.1   322
   Mrs Fore: Devil; do you think any Woman Honest?   271   FOR LOVE   III.1   665
   Scandal: Yes, several, very honest;--they'll cheat a little at   . . 271   FOR LOVE   III.1   666
   Ben: will be honest, tho'f may-hap he has never a Penny of   . . 273   FOR LOVE   III.1   733
   Sr Sampson: thy own Father, and this is honest Brief Buckram the Lawyer. 279   FOR LOVE   IV.1   158

Honest   (continued)
Sr Sampson:	No, no, come, come, sit you down, honest	281	FOR LCVE	IV.1 200
Sr Sampson:	No, no, come, come, sit thee down, honest	281	FOR LCVE	IV.1 V200
Sr Sampson:	indisposed: But I'm glad thou'rt better, honest Val. .	281	FOR LOVE	IV.1 203
Sr Sampson:	thou'rt honest, and wilt perform Articles. . . .	281	FOR LOVE	IV.1 215
Mrs Frail:	have seen the Resolution of a Lover,--Honest Tarr and .	287	FCR LOVE	IV.1 450
Witwoud:	honest Fellow, and a very pretty Fellow, and has a smattering	403	WAY WORLD	I.1 289
Witwoud:	pretty Fellow, and a very honest Fellow, and has a smattering	403	WAY WCRLD	I.1 V289
Mirabell:	Come, thou art an honest Fellow, Petulant, and shalt .	407	WAY WORLD	I.1 443
Sir Wilful:	Time, when you liv'd with honest Pumple Nose the Attorney	439	WAY WORLD	III.1 549
Sir Wilful:	Tony, Cds heart where's Tony--Tcny's an honest fellow,	455	WAY WORLD	IV.1 413
Sir Wilful:	the Sun's a good Pimple, an honest Soaker, he has a Cellar	456	WAY WCRLD	IV.1 422
Sir Wilful:	Map says that your Turk is not so honest a Man as your .	456	WAY WCRLD	IV.1 445
Honester (2)				
Fondlewife:	lay with an honester Man's Wife in your life.	94	OLD BATCH	IV.4 201
Valentine:	Health. An honester Man lives not, nor one more ready to .	223	FOR LCVE	I.1 261
Honestly (1)				
Heartwell:	Quality--I thank Heaven, I have very honestly purchas'd	45	OLD BATCH	I.1 304
Honesty (15)				
Heartwell:	much Tenderness and Beauty--and Honesty together . .	74	OLD BATCH	III.2 115
Setter:	. . . as honesty.	102	OLD BATCH	V.1 232
Setter:	. . . a thing as Honesty.	102	OLD BATCH	V.1 V232
Setter:	O Lord, Sir, What d'ye mean? Corrupt my honesty. . .	103	OLD BATCH	V.1 247
Maskwell:	Honesty, because you know I am a Rascal: But I would .	136	DOUBL DLR	I.1 343
Maskwell:	a thing as Honesty? Yes, and whosoever has it about him,	150	DOUEL DLR	II.1 451
Maskwell:	Well for Wisdcm and Honesty, give me Cunning and . .	150	DOUEL DLR	II.1 457
Maskwell:	and Hcnesty, and create in him a new Confidence in me, .	154	DOUBL DLR	III.1 158
Lord Touch:	I will be secret, and reward your Honesty	183	DOUBL DLR	IV.1 590
Lord Touch:	think so--Honesty to me is true Nobility. However, 'tis .	196	DOUEL DLR	V.1 318
Sr Sampson:	Conscience and Honesty; this is your Wit now, this is the	243	FOR LCVE	I.1 298
Valentine:	Ha, ha, ha; you need not run so fast, Honesty will . .	282	FCR LCVE	IV.1 246
Valentine:	Fortune; and Honesty will go as it did, Frost-nip't in a .	288	FOR LCVE	IV.1 493
Angelica:	Reputation of her Honesty or Understanding to the . .	299	FOR LCVE	V.1 71
Mirabell:	Wit, cr a Fortune by his Hcnesty, as win a Woman . .	422	WAY WCRLD	II.1 465
Honour (65)				
Sharper:	honour of Sir Joseph Wittoll.	50	OLD EATCH	II.1 98
Capt Bluff:	Say ycu so? then I honour him--But has he been . .	51	OLD BATCH	II.1 152
Capt Bluff:	I'le recommend my self--Sir I honour you; I understand .	51	OLD BATCH	II.1 155
Capt Bluff:	Ay! Then I honour him again--Sir may I crave your . .	52	OLD BATCH	II.1 171
Capt Bluff:	Man cf Honour.	69	OLD BATCH	III.1 298
Sir Joseph:	Man of Honour Sir, and so Sir--	69	OLD BATCH	III.1 301
Laetitia:	more Honour.--	82	OLD BATCH	IV.2 65
Araminta:	my Honour.--But tho' thou hadst all the Treachery . .	87	OLD BATCH	IV.3 167
Capt Bluff:	to my Honour.	101	OLD BATCH	V.1 181
Capt Bluff:	extremity! You can't, in honour, refuse to carry him a .	101	OLD BATCH	V.1 188
Sir Joseph:	if I wculd carry a Challenge? Honour is your Province, .	101	OLD BATCH	V.1 192
Heartwell:	impair'd the Honour of your House, promis'd your . .	109	OLD BATCH	V.2 52
Mellefont:	pleaded Honour and nearness of Blood to my Uncle; . .	130	DOUBL DLR	I.1 112
Maskwell:	Conscience and Honour in my Pace, to rebate my Inclinations.	136	DOUBL DLR	I.1 338
Sir Paul:	exasperated,--but I will protect my Honour, and yonder .	144	DOUBL DLR	II.1 232
Lady Ply:	'Tis my Honour that is concern'd, and the violation . .	144	DOUBL DLR	II.1 234
Lady Ply:	was intended to me. Your Honour! You have none, . . .	144	DOUBL DLR	II.1 235
Lady Ply:	preserved my Honour as it were in a Snow-House for . .	145	DOUBL DLR	II.1 254
Lady Ply:	and all the Senses are fallible; I won't trust my Honour, I	147	DOUBL DLR	II.1 341
Lady Ply:	assure you; my Honour is infallible and uncomatible. .	147	DOUBL DLR	II.1 342
Lady Ply:	I did not think it a sin,--but still my honour, if it were	147	DOUBL DLR	II.1 349
Lady Ply:	should be a fault,--but my honour--well, but	148	DOUBL DLR	II.1 360
Lady Ply:	your honour too--but the sin!--well but the	148	DOUBL DLR	II.1 361
Lady Touch:	Honour is very well known.	151	DOUBL DLR	III.1 12
Lady Touch:	Consider your own and my Honour--nay, I told you . .	153	DOUBL DLR	III.1 105
Maskwell:	It will confirm my Lord's opinion of my Honour . . .	154	DOUBL DLR	III.1 157
Maskwell:	know whether I can in honour discover all.	156	DOUBL DLR	III.1 208
Maskwell:	know whether I can in honour discover 'em all . . .	156	DOUBL DLR	III.1 V208
Mellefont:	All, all man, what you may in honour betray her . . .	156	DOUBL DLR	III.1 209
Careless:	begin with her Hcnour, or her Vertue, her Religion, or .	157	DOUBL DLR	III.1 271
Lady Ply:	and Things; for with the Reserve of my Hcnour, I assure	159	DOUBL DLR	III.1 352
Sir Paul:	that honour, yet I am her Husband; but alas-a-day, I have	162	DOUBL DLR	III.1 438
Lord Froth:	True, as I'm a Person of Honour--for Heaven's . . .	163	DOUBL DLR	III.1 486
Brisk:	honour, let me perish.	165	DOUBL DLR	III.1 557
Lady Ply:	Honour--Well, sure if I escape your Importunities, I .	169	DOUBL DLR	IV.1 75
Lady Ply:	Honour! Whither is it going? I protest you have given me	170	DOUBL DLR	IV.1 104
Lady Ply:	Conscience, or Honour, or any thing in the World.-- .	172	DOUBL DLR	IV.1 170
Lady Ply:	most extraordinary respect and hcnour for you, Sir Paul.	172	DOUBL DLR	IV.1 175
Sir Paul:	but in having the honour, to appertain in some measure, to	172	DOUBL DLR	IV.1 183
Lady Ply:	my Honour; your guilty Cheeks confess it; Oh where . .	179	DOUBL DLR	IV.1 445
Lord Touch:	my Hcnour never to own any Discovery that you shall .	182	DOUBL DLR	IV.1 573
Maskwell:	Honour was not of my seeking, nor would I build my . .	189	DOUBL DLR	V.1 72
Tattle:	Who I? Upon Honour I don't know whether she be . .	228	FCB LOVE	I.1 465
Tattle:	Tho' I have more Honour than to tell first; I have more .	229	FOR LCVE	I.1 478
Tattle:	Mum--O Madam, you do me too much Honour.	231	FOR LOVE	I.1 551
Foresight:	I protest I honour you, Mr. Scandal--I did not think .	267	FOR LOVE	III.1 540
Mrs Fore:	Honour?	271	FOR LOVE	III.1 674
Scandal:	Why, Honour is a publick Enemy; and Conscience a . .	271	FOR LOVE	III.1 675
Scandal:	As for Honour, that you have secur'd, for you have . .	271	FCR LOVE	III.1 678
Scandal:	Pleasure, so you have taken care of Honour, and 'tis the .	271	FCR LCVE	III.1 682
Scandal:	and honour you.--You look pretty well, Mr. Foresight;-- .	284	FOR LOVE	IV.1 338
Tattle:	that--Madam, will you do me the Honour?	293	FOR LCVE	IV.1 680
Gonsalez:	For this high Honour.	334	M. BRIDE	I.1 V339
Zara:	For Fame, for Honour, and for Empire lost?	345	M. BBIDE	II.2 236
Zara:	But what is Loss of Honour, Fame and Empire?	345	M. BBIDE	II.2 237
Osmyn-Alph:	Still in the Paths of Honour persevere;	384	M. BBIDE	V.2 319
Fainall:	have too much Generosity, not to be tender of her Honour.	397	WAY WORLD	I.1 92
Mirabell:	Person; I think you have the Honour to be related to him.	400	WAY WORLD	I.1 191
Fainall:	No matter for that; 'tis for the Honour of England, .	400	WAY WORLD	I.1 201

Honour   (continued)

		PAGE	TITLE	ACT.SC	LINE
Witwoud:	no nearer upon Honour.	402	WAY WORLD	I.1	251
Marwood:	that I am tender of your Honour?	413	WAY WORLD	II.1	125
Marwood:	in Honour, as indigent of Wealth.	415	WAY WORLD	II.1	197
Lady Wish:	from no body that I know)--I have that honour for	460	WAY WORLD	IV.1	585
Lady Wish:	save the Honour of my House, and Compound for the	465	WAY WORLD	V.1	130
Lady Wish:	Ay, ay, Sir, upon my honour.	476	WAY WORLD	V.1	534

Honour'd (3)

Sr Sampson:	I have not been honour'd with the Commands of	298	FOR LOVE	V.1	13
Zara:	And as my Kinsman, honour'd and advanc'd you.	347	M. BRIDE	II.2	296
Sir Wilful:	this, when you left off Honour'd Brother; and hoping	439	WAY WORLD	III.1	543

Honour's (2)

Jeremy:	extraordinary Passion for your Honour's Service.	301	FOR LOVE	V.1	169
Lady Wish:	a Person who wou'd suffer racks in honour's cause, dear	459	WAY WORLD	IV.1	553

Honourable (7)

Bellmour:	contented with the slavery of honourable Love in one	40	OLD BATCH	I.1	138
Setter:	that's much the more honourable employment--by all	64	OLD BATCH	III.1	141
Scandal:	No, nothing under a Right Honourable.	230	FOR LOVE	I.1	531
Marwood:	Besides you forget, Marriage is honourable.	443	WAY WORLD	III.1	690
Fainall:	honourable as you say; and if so, Wherefore should	443	WAY WORLD	III.1	692
Fainall:	honourable a root?	443	WAY WORLD	III.1	694
Marwood:	Nay I know not; if the root be Honourable,	443	WAY WORLD	III.1	695

Honourably (1)

Bellmour:	very honourably, to excuse her, and very impudently	93	OLD BATCH	IV.4	148

Honoured (1)

Lady Ply:	all--and highly honoured in that Title.	172	DOUBL DLR	IV.1	191

Honours (6)

Sir Paul:	great desire to have some Honours Conferr'd upon me,	180	DOUBL DLR	IV.1	478
Maskwell:	her of the Honours you designed me?	195	DOUBL DLR	V.1	313
Scandal:	nam'd: Without you could retrieve the Ancient Honours	220	FOR LOVE	I.1	148
Almeria:	The gilded Trophies of exterior Honours.	332	M. BRIDE	I.1	247
Manuel:	What Welcome, and what Honours, beauteous Zara,	335	M. BRIDE	I.1	385
Zara:	To like Captivity, or think those Honours,	335	M. BRIDE	I.1	394

Hood (2)   see Knight-hood, Widdow-hood

Witwoud:	--Then trip to his Lodging, clap on a Hood and Scarf,	405	WAY WORLD	I.1	372
Marwood:	Hood and Scarf. And indeed 'tis time, for the Town has	433	WAY WORLD	III.1	316

Hooded (2)

Tattle:	like a Nun; and I must be hooded like a Friar; ha, Jeremy?	302	FOR LOVE	V.1	198
Jeremy:	Aye, Sir, hooded like a Hawk, to seize at first sight	302	FOR LOVE	V.1	199

Hoods (4)

Belinda:	Get my Hoods and Tippet, and bid the Footman call	56	OLD BATCH	II.2	69
	(Enter Betty, with Hoods and				
	Looking-glass.)	57	OLD BATCH	II.2	90
	(Putting on her Hoods.)	57	OLD BATCH	II.2	94
Maskwell:	and with your Hoods tied over your face, meet	199	DOUBL DLR	V.1	445

Hoofs (1)

Laetitia:	come near it, I'm afraid 'tis the Devil; indeed it has				
	hoofs,	92	OLD BATCH	IV.4	133

Hook (6)

Heartwell:	Hook your selves have baited, but you are cloy'd with the	43	OLD BATCH	I.1	243
Lucy:	Hook, Age will come; he nibbled fairly yesterday, and no	61	OLD BATCH	III.1	11
Mellefont:	Consider I have you on the hook; you will but	184	DOUBL DLR	IV.2	51
Angelica:	naked Hook appears.	260	FOR LOVE	III.1	248
Sr Sampson:	Hook.	260	FOR LOVE	III.1	252
Manuel:	And lash against the Hook--by Heav'n you're all	373	M. BRIDE	V.1	44

Hoot (1)

Heartwell:	S'death how the young Fellows will hoot me! I shall be	63	OLD BATCH	III.1	78

Hope (114)

Heartwell:	quotha! I hope in Heaven I have a greater portion of Grace,	44	OLD BATCH	I.1	295
Sharper:	you hope to be receiv'd into the Alliance of a noble	45	OLD BATCH	I.1	307
Heartwell:	No, I hope I shall never merit that affliction--to be	45	OLD BATCH	I.1	309
Heartwell:	Pox I have pratled away my time--I hope you are	46	OLD BATCH	I.1	331
Sir Joseph:	which, like an innundation will I hope totally immerge	49	OLD BATCH	II.1	57
Sir Joseph:	by the help of which, I shall once more hope to swim into	49	OLD BATCH	II.1	60
Sir Joseph:	hundred Pound--I meant innocently as I hope to be sav'd	51	OLD BATCH	II.1	129
Capt Bluff:	How how, my young Knight? Not for fear I hope; he	51	OLD BATCH	II.1	142
Capt Bluff:	How now, my young Knight? Not for fear I hope; he	51	OLD BATCH	II.1	V142
Capt Bluff:	this time--as I hope for a Truncheon--this rascally	53	OLD BATCH	II.1	202
Araminta:	I hope you are not going out in dudgeon, Cousin.	56	OLD BATCH	II.2	72
Araminta:	No Miracle, I hope.	57	OLD BATCH	II.2	116
Lucy:	You may as soon hope, to recover your own Maiden-head,	61	OLD BATCH	III.1	7
Sharper:	and refuse my Thanks--But I hope you are not offended	68	OLD BATCH	III.1	290
Sir Joseph:	am both Sir; what then? I hope I may be offended, without	68	OLD BATCH	III.1	293
Silvia:	them--O Gemini, I hope you don't mean so--For I	73	OLD BATCH	III.2	88
Laetitia:	I hope my dearest Jewel, is not going to leave me--	77	OLD BATCH	IV.1	65
Laetitia:	Who has wrong'd me to my Dearest? I hope my Jewel	77	OLD BATCH	IV.1	80
Laetitia:	(aside). I hope to have one that will shew me how a	79	OLD BATCH	IV.1	139
Sharper:	However I hope you don't mean to forsake it, that	80	OLD BATCH	IV.1	181
Laetitia:	I hope you are a Gentleman;--and since you are	82	OLD BATCH	IV.2	62
Belinda:	most rueful! Ha, ha, ha: O Gad, I hope no-body will	83	OLD BATCH	IV.3	9
Araminta:	(aside). I hope my Fool has not Confidence enough	85	OLD BATCH	IV.3	92
Vainlove:	But, Madam, I hope I shall prove of a Temper, not to	87	OLD BATCH	IV.3	139
Bellmour:	That you may, Faith, and I hope you won't believe	95	OLD BATCH	IV.4	219
Sharper:	O Rogue! Well, but I hope--	105	OLD BATCH	V.1	346
Bellmour:	(aside). I hope there's no French Sawce.	106	OLD BATCH	V.1	371
Heartwell:	the Load of Life!--We hope to find	108	OLD BATCH	V.2	10
Vainlove:	May I presume to hope so great a Blessing?	112	OLD BATCH	V.2	171
Lord Froth:	hope you think her a Judge?	134	DOUBL DLR	I.1	275
Lord Froth:	I hope Mellefont will make a good Husband too.	141	DOUBL DLR	II.1	100
Brisk:	in the World,--I hope you'll make me happy in	142	DOUBL DLR	II.1	132
Lady Ply:	must not Love you,--therefore don't hope,--but don't	148	DOUBL DLR	II.1	371
Lady Touch:	Nay, my Lord, it may be so, and I hope it	151	DOUBL DLR	III.1	16
Lady Touch:	have forgot it; and so has he, I hope--for I have not	153	DOUBL DLR	III.1	97
Mellefont:	Person I hope.	156	DOUBL DLR	III.1	211
Mellefont:	there's hope.	169	DOUBL DLR	IV.1	64
Sir Paul:	Estate would be left to the wide World, he? I hope you	174	DOUBL DLR	IV.1	254

Hopes   (continued)

		PAGE	TITLE	ACT.SC	LINE
Sir Paul:	all my hopes lost--My Heart would break, and my	174	DOUBL DLR	IV.1	253
Maskwell:	Indeed I was in hopes 'thad been a youthful Heat	182	DOUBL DLR	IV.1	557
Lord Touch:	beyond your Hopes.	183	DOUBL DLR	IV.1	591
Mellefont:	away the very root and foundation of his hopes; What	187	DOUBL DLR	IV.2	147
Mellefont:	O Maskwell, what hopes? I am confounded in a	190	DOUBL DLR	V.1	103
Maskwell:	way, but in the hopes of her Marrying you.--	193	DOUBL DLR	V.1	220
	And fondly hopes for rich and generous Fruit,	213	FOR LOVE	PRO.	3
	Yet hopes there's no ill-manners in his Play:	214	FOR LOVE	PRO.	42
Scandal:	the Hand too; and sworn to a truth; but he hopes	226	FOR LOVE	I.1	375
Scandal:	Who hopes to purchase Wealth, by selling Land;	234	FOR LOVE	I.1	680
Sr Sampson:	Hopes of my Family--I han't seen him these Three	259	FOR LOVE	III.1	213
Scandal:	and I had Hopes of finding another opportunity of	269	FOR LOVE	III.1	589
Angelica:	deluded with vain Hopes. Good Nature and Humanity	277	FOR LOVE	IV.1	72
Osmyn-Alph:	Which shews me Bankrupt even in my Hopes.	347	M. BRIDE	II.2	290
Osmyn-Alph:	Which shews me poor and Bankrupt even in Hopes.	347	M. BRIDE	II.2	V290
Manuel:	(aside). How? better than my Hopes; does she accuse	348	M. BRIDE	II.2	359
Zara:	And build bold Hopes, on my dejected Fate?	349	M. BRIDE	II.2	367
Zara:	And through my Hopes in you, I promis'd Freedom	349	M. BRIDE	II.2	378
Zara:	And through my Hopes in you, I undertook	349	M. BRIDE	II.2	V378
Heli:	Have Hopes, and hear the Voice of better Fate.	351	M. BRIDE	III.1	63
Gonsalez:	'Twere fit the Soldiers were amus'd, with Hopes;	378	M. BRIDE	V.2	V102
Gonsalez:	With Hopes, and fed with Expectation of	378	M. BRIDE	V.2	103
	With whom, he hopes, this Play will Favour find,	385	M. BRIDE	EPI.	30
Servant-M:	was the last Couple to lead up; and no hopes appearing of	398	WAY WORLD	I.1	115
Mirabell:	hopes, one Day or other to hate her heartily: To which	399	WAY WORLD	I.1	167
Fainall:	of it, of Consequence must put an end to all my hopes;	413	WAY WORLD	II.1	113
Fainall:	and what a Wretch is he who must survive his hopes!	413	WAY WORLD	II.1	114
Mirabell:	hopes to ruin me, shou'd consent to marry my pretended	417	WAY WORLD	II.1	293
Mirabell:	hopes of future Comfort.	472	WAY WORLD	V.1	391

Hoping (2)

Bellmour:	Bed, hoping that when she heard of it, her good Nature	94	OLD BATCH	IV.4	212
Sir Wilful:	this, when you left off Honour'd Brother; and hoping	439	WAY WORLD	III.1	543

Horace (2)

Sharper:	Oh Madam! He was our English Horace.	87	OLD BATCH	IV.3	147
Lady Froth:	and Horace.--My Lord you must not be Jealous, I'm	142	DOUBL DLR	II.1	139

Horis (0)   see Nemo omnibus horis
Horn (1)   see Ripe-horn-mad, Powder-Horn

Mellefont:	Horn mad after your Fortune.	187	DOUBL DLR	IV.2	133

Horn-Books (1)

Scandal:	in their Hands, and Horn-Books about their Necks.	234	FOR LOVE	I.1	656

Horn-mad (1)

Ben:	she's mad for a Husband, and he's Horn-mad, I think, or	307	FOR LOVE	V.1	373

Horn'd (2)

Angelica:	and the Goat. Bless me! there are a great many Horn'd	239	FOR LOVE	II.1	138
Valentine:	Clocks will strike Twelve at Noon, and the Horn'd Herd	289	FOR LOVE	IV.1	504

Horns (11)

Heartwell:	and bear my Horns aloft, like one of the supporters of my	45	OLD BATCH	I.1	311
Bellmour:	Pox choak him, would his Horns were in his	89	OLD BATCH	IV.4	12
Fondlewife:	Indeed, and I have Horns, Deare. The Devil, no.	92	OLD BATCH	IV.4	135
Sir Paul:	Heart--I'm sure if ever I should have Horns, they	146	DOUBL DLR	II.1	281
Lady Touch:	what I said to you, or you had better eat your own Horns,	192	DOUBL DLR	V.1	192
Foresight:	Fruitful, the Head fruitful, that bodes Horns; the Fruit	236	FOR LOVE	II.1	57
Foresight:	of the Head is Horns--Dear Neice, stay at home--	236	FOR LOVE	II.1	58
Sr Sampson:	By the Horns of the Moon, you wou'd say,	241	FOR LOVE	II.1	233
Marwood:	Man shou'd have his Head and Horns, and Woman the	431	WAY WORLD	III.1	238
Fainall:	'twere somewhat,--but to crawl after, with my Horns	442	WAY WORLD	III.1	636
Fainall:	Married. My Wife had added Lustre to my Horns, by that	442	WAY WORLD	III.1	645

Horrible (1)

Witwoud:	Horrible! He has a breath like a Bagpipe--ay, ay,	457	WAY WORLD	IV.1	474

Horrid (9)

Belinda:	There was a Whine--O Gad I hate your horrid	54	OLD BATCH	II.2	11
Almeria:	But brands my Innocence with horrid Crimes,	368	M. BRIDE	IV.1	282
Gonsalez:	Should make atonement by a Death as horrid;	378	M. BRIDE	V.2	71
Almeria:	O let me seek him in this horrid Cell;	381	M. BRIDE	V.2	215
Foible:	Lady that Mr. Mirabell rail'd at her. I laid horrid Things	430	WAY WORLD	III.1	208
Millamant:	That horrid Fellow Petulant, has provok'd me into	432	WAY WORLD	III.1	287
Millamant:	O horrid proviso's! filthy strong Waters! I toste	452	WAY WORLD	IV.1	278
Millamant:	Well then--I'll take my death I'm in a horrid	452	WAY WORLD	IV.1	288
Millamant:	Are you? I think I have--and the horrid Man	452	WAY WORLD	IV.1	293

Horridly (2)

Belinda:	I am jolted to a Jelly.--Am I not horridly touz'd?	83	OLD BATCH	IV.3	5
Mrs Fain:	He's horridly drunk--how came you all in	454	WAY WORLD	IV.1	379

Horror (2)

Lady Ply:	O reflect upon the horror of that, and then the	147	DOUBL DLR	II.1	314
Mrs Fain:	with Horror and Distaste; they meet us like the Ghosts	410	WAY WORLD	II.1	7

Horrors (1)

Zara:	Than did that Scene of complicated Horrors.	379	M. BRIDE	V.2	143

Horrour (11)

Leonora:	Let us return; the Horrour of this Place	339	M. BRIDE	II.1	70
Zara:	To find this Place of Horrour and Obscurity?	345	M. BRIDE	II.2	240
Zara:	Away, as from Deformity and Horrour.	353	M. BRIDE	III.1	150
Almeria:	O dismal Cruelty! heart-breaking Horrour!	358	M. BRIDE	III.1	V357
Manuel:	That thou obey, nor Horrour on thy Head.	374	M. BRIDE	V.1	73
Garcia:	What means this Blood? and why this Face of Horrour?	377	M. BRIDE	V.2	29
Garcia:	(returning). Ruine and Horrour! O heart-wounding	377	M. BRIDE	V.2	51
Gonsalez:	Horrour?	377	M. BRIDE	V.2	54
Garcia:	The Horrour of that Thought, has damp'd my Rage.	378	M. BRIDE	V.2	74
Gonsalez:	'Twas an Act of Horrour;	379	M. BRIDE	V.2	122
Almeria:	Horrour! a headless Trunk! nor Lips nor Face,	382	M. BRIDE	V.2	270

Horrours (1)

Manuel:	Nor shall the guilty Horrours of this Day	367	M. BRIDE	IV.1	255

Horse (7)   see Stalking-Horse

Jeremy:	for him as a Passing-Bell, Sir; or a Horse in a Pound.	279	FOR LOVE	IV.1	133
Garcia:	Osmyn, who led the Moorish Horse; he does,	335	M. BRIDE	I.1	366
Garcia:	Osmyn, who led the Moorish Horse; but he	335	M. BRIDE	I.1	V366

Horse (continued)

		PAGE	TITLE	ACT.SC	LINE
Sir Wilful:	step to the Stable, you may enquire further of my Horse,	438	WAY WORLD	III.1	500
Petulant:	Your Horse, Sir! Your Horse is an Ass, Sir!	438	WAY WORLD	III.1	502
Marwood:	S'life, we shall have a Quarrel betwixt an Horse and an Ass,	438	WAY WORLD	III.1	505

Horse-nail (1)

Sr Sampson:	a crocked Pin, or an old Horse-nail, with the head towards	265	FOR LOVE	III.1	467

Horse-Race (1)

Jeremy:	I do at a Horse-Race. The Air upon Banstead-Downs is	218	FOR LOVE	I.1	93

Horses (4)

Cynthia:	But how can the Coach and six Horses be got ready	193	DOUBL DLR	V.1	208
Foresight:	--Come, you shall have my Coach and Horses--	239	FOR LOVE	II.1	148
Tattle:	came down in her Coach and Six Horses, and expos'd her	258	FOR LOVE	III.1	176
Sir Wilful:	pair of Slippers?--My Man's with his Horses, I	441	WAY WORLD	III.1	618

Hospitable (1)

Almeria:	Within it's cold, but hospitable Bosom.	326	M. BRIDE	I.1	12

Hospitably (1)

Belinda:	Jut-Windows, and her Mouth the great Door, most hospitably	84	OLD BATCH	IV.3	47

Hospital (1)

Lady Wish:	Hospital for a decay'd Pimp? No damage? O thou frontless	463	WAY WORLD	V.1	36

Host (2)

Mellefont:	Host of Hell her Servants;	186	DOUBL DLR	IV.2	124
Almeria:	Angels, and all the Host of heaven support me!	340	M. BRIDE	II.2	36

Hot (6)

Sharper:	she were hot, when it might entitle him to the office of	44	OLD BATCH	I.1	264
Sir Joseph:	Sir--a damn'd hot Fellow--only as I was saying, I let him	51	OLD BATCH	II.1	130
Belinda:	hot, out of her Under-Petticoat-Pocket,--Ha, ha, ha:	84	OLD BATCH	IV.3	44
Heartwell:	hot Brothel. Ask no Questions.	105	OLD BATCH	V.1	324
Mellefont:	By Heav'n into a hot Furnace sooner.	157	DOUBL DLR	III.1	238
Valentine:	me have a Pair of Red hot Tongues quickly, quickly,	282	FOR LOVE	IV.1	240

Hot-headed (1)

Lady Ply:	He's hot-headed still! 'Tis in vain to talk to you;	144	DOUBL DLR	II.1	227

Hound (0)   see Blood-Hound

Hounds (2)

Vainlove:	dull and unnatural to have a Hare run full in the Hounds	80	OLD BATCH	IV.1	178
Scandal:	by the Hounds, you will be treacherously shot by the	220	FOR LOVE	I.1	143

Hour (44)

Bellmour:	Poor Rogue. Any hour of the day or night will serve her--	40	OLD BATCH	I.1	116
Bellmour:	'Tis pretty near the Hour--	75	OLD BATCH	IV.1	1
Barnaby:	Sir, the Hour draws nigh--And nothing will be	76	OLD BATCH	IV.1	34
Setter:	This afternoon, Sir, about an Hour before my Master	99	OLD BATCH	V.1	100
Maskwell:	this Gallery an hour hence, by that time I imagine our	149	DOUBL DLR	II.1	435
Lady Touch:	toy away an hour in mirth.	155	DOUBL DLR	III.1	171
Maskwell:	I know what she means by toying away an hour well	155	DOUBL DLR	III.1	174
Mellefont:	This very next ensuing hour of Eight a Clock, is	169	DOUBL DLR	IV.1	52
Brisk:	The Fiddles have stay'd this hour in the Hall; and my	174	DOUBL DLR	IV.1	277
Maskwell:	Lordship will meet me a quarter of an Hour hence there,	183	DOUBL DLR	IV.1	584
Lady Touch:	found him here. Who does not prevent the Hour of Love;	183	DOUBL DLR	IV.2	9
Maskwell:	perish first, and from this hour avoid all sight and speech,	188	DOUBL DLR	V.1	41
Maskwell:	an hour, yonder in my Lady's Dressing-Room; go by the	194	DOUBL DLR	V.1	239
Maskwell:	at this hour,--Mr. Saygrace, Mr. Saygrace.	194	DOUBL DLR	V.1	270
Maskwell:	Meet me in half an Hour, here in your own	195	DOUBL DLR	V.1	292
Maskwell:	his hour.	199	DOUBL DLR	V.1	458
Foresight:	he's at leisure--'tis now Three a Clock, a very good hour	236	FOR LOVE	II.1	41
Foresight:	for Business, Mercury governs this hour.	236	FOR LOVE	II.1	42
Angelica:	Is not it a good hour for Pleasure too? Uncle, pray	236	FOR LOVE	II.1	44
Foresight:	him; I shall scarce recover my self before the Hour be	239	FOR LOVE	II.1	165
Foresight:	When was this Sign'd, what Hour? Odso, you should	240	FOR LOVE	II.1	189
Scandal:	me now hither at this unseasonable hour--	269	FOR LOVE	III.1	592
Sr Sampson:	in Expectation of a lucky Hour. When, body o' me,	283	FOR LOVE	IV.1	290
Sr Sampson:	there never was a lucky Hour after the first opportunity.	283	FOR LOVE	IV.1	291
Foresight:	This is none of your lucky Hour; Nemo omnibus horis sapit.	283	FOR LOVE	IV.1	294
Jeremy:	and meet you in half a quarter of an hour, with your	303	FOR LOVE	V.1	216
Tattle:	know of it half an Hour ago; and the Lady stays for me,	305	FOR LOVE	V.1	294
Tattle:	you can't solve this; stay here a Quarter of an Hour, and	305	FOR LOVE	V.1	297
Manuel:	Not from that Hour, wherein thou wert preserv'd,	333	M. BRIDE	I.1	300
Gonsalez:	One 'pointed Hour should be Alphonso's Loss,	333	M. BRIDE	I.1	305
Manuel:	But should have smil'd that Hour, through all his Care,	333	M. BRIDE	I.1	316
Heli:	So to be caught in an unguarded Hour,	338	M. BRIDE	II.1	30
Manuel:	Where, ev'ry Hour shall roll in circling Joys;	349	M. BRIDE	II.2	387
Osmyn-Alph:	This Lesson, in some Hour of Inspiration,	353	M. BRIDE	III.1	128
Osmyn-Alph:	Time may have still one fated Hour to come,	354	M. BRIDE	III.1	198
Zara:	And force their Balls abroad, at this dead Hour.	355	M. BRIDE	III.1	210
Manuel:	An unforeseen, unwelcome Hour of Business,	363	M. BRIDE	IV.1	105
Manuel:	Not to be found? in an ill hour he's absent.	372	M. BRIDE	V.1	1
Manuel:	This hour I throw ye off, and entertain	374	M. BRIDE	V.1	64
Alonzo:	As but an hour ago, I'd not have done,	379	M. BRIDE	V.2	111
Betty:	Turn'd of the last Canonical Hour, Sir.	398	WAY WORLD	I.1	106
Mirabell:	Hour less and less disturbance; 'till in a few Days it became	399	WAY WORLD	I.1	170
Foible:	Impatience in which Sir Rowland burns for the dear hour	428	WAY WORLD	III.1	126
Foible:	Mirabell has waited this half hour for an Opportunity to	445	WAY WORLD	IV.1	44

Hours (17)

Singer:	Melting the Hours, in gentle Play;	71	OLD BATCH	III.2	3
Heartwell:	two Hours?	105	OLD BATCH	V.1	318
Maskwell:	needs this? I say nothing but what your self, in open hours	137	DOUBL DLR	I.1	384
Maskwell:	needs this? I say nothing but what you your self, in open hours	137	DOUBL DLR	I.1	V384
Lady Froth:	seen her these two hours.--The poor dear Creature	166	DOUBL DLR	III.1	613
Scandal:	two Hours ago.	268	FOR LOVE	III.1	573
Scandal:	I must work her into the Project. You keep early Hours,	269	FOR LOVE	III.1	579
Valentine:	the usual Hours. Yet you will see such Zealous Faces	289	FOR LOVE	IV.1	501
Valentine:	For she'll meet me Two Hours hence in black and white,	290	FOR LOVE	IV.1	561
Jeremy:	Two Hours--I'm sure I left him just now, in a Humour	295	FOR LOVE	IV.1	754
Jeremy:	Two Hours--I'm sure I left him just now, in the Humour	295	FOR LOVE	IV.1	V754
Almeria:	The circling Hours, that gather all the Woes,	330	M. BRIDE	I.1	153
Zara:	And watch like Tapers o'er your Hours of Rest.	360	M. BRIDE	III.1	429

Hours (continued)
```
     Petulant:    rate; to be knock'd up and rais'd at all Hours and in all   405   WAY WORLD   I.1    385
     Lady Wish:   O Sir Rowland, the hours that he has dy'd  . . . . .         458   WAY WORLD   IV.1   511
     Foible:      quarter of an hours lying and swearing to a fine Lady?       459   WAY WORLD   IV.1   559
     Waitwell:    iteration of Nuptials--this eight and fourty Hours  . . .    459   WAY WORLD   IV.1   562
House (40)         see Chocolate-House, Coffee-House, Corner-House, Eating-house,
                   Corner-house, Play-House, Play-house, Snow-House
     Heartwell:   Hum--Let me think--Is not this Silvia's House, the  . . .     62   OLD BATCH   III.1   64
     Lucy:        presume to enter the House.                                   66   OLD BATCH   III.1  194
     Barnaby:     House, and yet be forced to let Lodgings, to help pay the     76   OLD BATCH   IV.1    43
                  (Scene changes to a chamber in Fondlewife's House. . . .      80   OLD BATCH   IV.2
     Laetitia:    Who are you, Sir? You have mistaken the House  . . . . .      81   OLD BATCH   IV.2    29
                  (Scene changes to a Chamber in Fondlewife's House. . . .      89   OLD BATCH   IV.4
     Fondlewife:  of my house, thou Son of the Whore of Babylon; Off-spring     90   OLD BATCH   IV.4    65
     Fondlewife:  I'll show you the way out of my house, if you please. Come,   96   OLD BATCH   IV.4   269
     Heartwell:   not near that House,--that Corner-house,--that  . . . .      105   OLD BATCH   V.1    323
     Setter:      Shifting Cloaths for the purpose at a Friend's House of      106   OLD BATCH   V.1    351
     Araminta:    our House since.  . . . . . . . . . . . . . .                107   OLD BATCH   V.1    400
     Heartwell:   impair'd the Honour of your House, promis'd your  . . .      109   OLD BATCH   V.2     52
                  (A Gallery in the Lord Touchwood's House,  . . . . .         127   DOUBL DLR   I.1
     Mellefont:   House this moment and Marry one another, without  . . .      168   DOUBL DLR   IV.1    28
     Sir Paul:    our Family Thy; our House is distinguished by a Languishing  173   DOUBL DLR   IV.1   239
     Sir Paul:    Eye, as the House of Austria is by a thick Lip. . . . .      173   DOUBL DLR   IV.1   240
     Jeremy:      Nothing thrives that belongs to't. The Man of the House .    218   FOR LOVE    I.1     89
                  (A Room in Foresight's House. Foresight and Servant.)  .     235   FOR LOVE    II.1
     Foresight:   When Housewifes all the House forsake,  . . . . . .          236   FOR LOVE    II.1    51
     Foresight:   That House doth stand upon its Head;  . . . . . .            236   FOR LOVE    II.1    54
     Foresight:   For by the Head of the House is meant the Husband; the  .    236   FOR LOVE    II.1    59
     Foresight:   House of my Nativity; there the Curse of Kindred was  .      238   FOR LOVE    II.1   130
     Foresight:   I'll punish you, not a Man shall enter my House.  . . .      238   FOR LOVE    II.1   132
     Angelica:    let no Mankind come near the House, but Converse with  .     239   FOR LOVE    II.1   136
     Sr Sampson:  House, and make an Entertainment for all the Philomaths,     242   FOR LOVE    II.1   252
     Scandal:     House.                                                       271   FOR LOVE    III.1  652
                  (A Room in Foresight's House. Enter Angelica and Jenny.)     297   FOR LOVE    V.1
     Angelica:    pull'd an old House over his Head at last. . . . . .         301   FOR LOVE    V.1    159
                  Or in this very House, for ought we know,  . . . . .         315   FOR LOVE    EPI.    23
     Zara:        What is't to me, this House of Misery? . . . . .             346   M. BRIDE    II.2   266
     Gonsalez:    In Roderigo's House, who fled with him. . . . . .            363   M. BRIDE    IV.1    76
                  (A Room in Lady Wishfort's House.  . . . . . . .             425   WAY WORLD   III.1
     Servant-W:   A Week, Sir; longer than any Body in the House,  . . .       437   WAY WORLD   III.1  457
     Servant-W:   A Week, Sir; longer than any in the House,  . . . .          437   WAY WORLD   III.1 V457
     Sir Wilful:  tell her, her Nephew, Sir Wilfull Witwoud is in the House.   437   WAY WORLD   III.1  466
     Lady Wish:   house indeed, and now I remember, my Niece went away  .      461   WAY WORLD   IV.1   616
     Lady Wish:   Out of my house, out of my house, thou  . . . . .            462   WAY WORLD   V.1      1
     Lady Wish:   dealt in when I took you into my house, plac'd you next  .    462   WAY WORLD   V.1     20
     Lady Wish:   save the Honour of my House, and Compound for the  . .       465   WAY WORLD   V.1    130
Houses (4)         see Chocolate-Houses, Coffee-Houses, Coffee-houses
     Heartwell:   Houses and Coblers Stalls--Death, I can't think  . . .        63   OLD BATCH   III.1   84
     Sir Paul:    Fortune, a good Estate in the Country, some houses in  .     161   DOUBL DLR   III.1  408
     Foresight:   Houses. Can judge of Motions Direct and Retrograde, of  .    241   FOR LOVE    II.1   212
                  That, does from Bodies, we from Houses strole. . . . .       315   FOR LOVE    EPI.    20
Housewifes (1)
     Foresight:   When Housewifes all the House forsake,  . . . . . . .        236   FOR LOVE    II.1    51
Hover (1)
     Zara:        Hover a Moment, yet, thou gentle Spirit,  . . . . . .        381   M. BRIDE    V.2    200
Hovering (1)
     Mirabell:    of gay fine Perrukes hovering round you.  . . . . . .        418   WAY WORLD   II.1   330
How (373)
How's (9)
     Sharper:     How's this!  . . . . . . . . . . . . . .                      47   OLD BATCH   II.1     7
     Fondlewife:  Ha, how's that? Stay stay, did you leave word  . . . .        76   OLD BATCH   IV.1    19
     Sir Joseph:  How's this! Good Bully, hold your breath, and  . . . .       102   OLD BATCH   IV.1   203
     Mellefont:   Ha! how's this?                                             148   DOUBL DLR   II.1   396
     Lady Touch:  (aside). Confusion! how's this!  . . . . . . .              191   DOUBL DLR   V.1    134
     Cynthia:     How's this! now I fear indeed.  . . . . . . .               197   DOUBL DLR   V.1    361
     Scandal:     How's this! Tattle making Love to Angelica!  . . . .        291   FOR LOVE    IV.1   574
     Manuel:      How's this? my mortal Foe beneath my Roof!  . . . .         373   M. BRIDE    V.1     33
     Lady Wish:   How's this dear Neice? Have I any comfort?  . . . .         470   WAY WORLD   V.1    323
Howe'er (1)
     Gonsalez:    And try howe'er, if I've divin'd aright.  . . . . .         367   M. BRIDE    IV.1   238
Howe're (1)
     Lord Touch:  Howe're in private, Mischiefs are conceiv'd,  . . . .       203   DOUBL DLR   V.1    592
However (7)
     Heartwell:   I am--However, I find I am pretty sure of her consent, if .   73   OLD BATCH   III.2   97
     Sharper:     However I hope you don't mean to forsake it, that  . . .      80   OLD BATCH   IV.1   181
     Lord Touch:  think so--Honesty to me is true Nobility. However, 'tis .    196   DOUBL DLR   V.1    318
     Ben:         words however. I spoke you fair d'ee see, and civil.--As     264   FOR LOVE    III.1  403
     Selim:       However, for a Colour, tell him, you  . . . . . .            362   M. BRIDE    IV.1    50
     Sir Wilful:  I'm very well I thank you Aunt--However,  . . . . .          441   WAY WORLD   III.1  601
     Sir Wilful:  However that's as time shall try,--But spare to speak and    448   WAY WORLD   IV.1   137
Howls (1)
     Zara:        And Howls of Slaves condemn'd; from Clink of Chains,  . .    379   M. BRIDE    V.2    137
Huddle (1)
     Marwood:     to huddle up all in Silence, I shall be glad. You must  .    468   WAY WORLD   V.1    244
Huffe (1)
     Belinda:     Huffe, Bluffe, (What's your hideous Name?) be gone:  . .      85   OLD BATCH   IV.3    87
Hug (2)
     Sr Sampson:  see 'em hug and cotten together, like Down upon a  . . .     260   FOR LOVE    III.1  265
     Almeria:     And hug in scorn of it, our mutual Ruine.  . . . . .         358   M. BRIDE    III.1  340
Huge (3)
     Scandal:     are huge Proportion'd Criticks, with long Wigs, Lac'd  .     233   FOR LOVE    I.1    654
     Valentine:   Affections, Appetites, Senses, and the huge Train of  .      244   FOR LOVE    II.1   341
     Osmyn-Alph:  A fatal Wretch--a huge stupendous Ruine,  . . . . .          347   M. BRIDE    II.2   309
Hugely (1)
     Ben:         handsome Gentlewoman for a Bed-fellow hugely, how say  .     262   FOR LOVE    III.1  325
```

Hugging (2)

Sharper: Hugging himself in his prosperous Mischief--No . . . 100 OLD BATCH V.1 132
Ben: and Kissing and Hugging, what wou'd you sheer off so? . . 286 FOR LOVE IV.1 418

Hulk (1)

Fainall: turn'd a drift, like a Leaky hulk to Sink or Swim, as she   473 WAY WORLD V.1 443

Hum (27)

Bellmour: (Reads). Hum, Hum--Out of Town this Evening, and . . . 39 OLD BATCH I.1 82
Bellmour: (Reads). Hum, Hum--That your Conversation will be . . . 39 OLD BATCH I.1 87
Bellmour: told you there's twelve thousand Pound--Hum--Why . . . 41 OLD BATCH I.1 170
Heartwell: Hum--Let me think--Is not this Silvia's House, the . . . 62 OLD BATCH III.1 64
Bellmour: Hum, not immediately, in my conscience not . . . . . 63 OLD BATCH III.1 106
Sharper: (reads). Hum hum--And what then appear'd a fault, . . . 79 OLD BATCH IV.1 156
Setter: honest. Reputed honest! Hum: Is that all? Ay: For, to be . 102 OLD BATCH V.1 228
Capt Bluff: Quality. Here, here's from a Countess too. Hum--No . . 103 OLD BATCH V.1 267
Careless: Hum, ay, what is't? . . . . 128 DOUEL DLR I.1 40
Brisk: was in the Lid of my Snuff-Box. Hum! Deuce take me, I . 135 DOUBL DLR I.1 292
Sir Paul: Hum, gads bud she says true,--well, my Lady, ... 145 DOUBL DLR II.1 238
Maskwell: think: Meet her at eight--hum--ha! by Heaven I . . . 155 DOUBL DLR III.1 187
Mellefont: Hum, 'gad I believe there's something in't;-- . . . 168 DOUBL DLR IV.1 19
Sir Paul: (Reads) Hum--After Supper in the Wardrobe by the . . 178 DOUBL DLR IV.1 408
Foresight: Hum--truly I don't care to discourage a young . . . 243 FOR LOVE II.1 308
Tattle: Hum--Yes--But you must believe I speak . . . . . . 252 FOR LOVE II.1 627
Foresight: my Pulses ha!--I have none--Mercy on me--hum--Yes, . . 269 FOR LOVE III.1 606
Foresight: Hum, not so well as I thought I was. Lend me your . . 269 FOR LOVE III.1 614
Foresight: to try if I could discover it by my Art--hum, ha! I . 304 FOR LOVE V.1 259
Witwoud: Hum, faith I don't know as to that,--I can't say . . 403 WAY WORLD I.1 302
Witwoud: Hum, a hit, a hit, a palpable hit, I confess it. . . 419 WAY WORLD II.1 353
Sir Wilful: Hum! What sure 'tis not--Yea by'r Lady, ... 438 WAY WORLD III.1 514
Fainall: Hum! That may be-- . . . . 442 WAY WORLD III.1 653
Fainall: Hum! Faith and that's well thought on; Marriage is . . 443 WAY WORLD III.1 691

Hum'd (1)

Lucy: Hum'd it over, gave you his Respects, and said, he . . . 61 OLD BATCH III.1 26

Humane (4)

Mellefont: Entertaining follies--you must be more humane to him; at . 129 DOUBL DLR I.1 66
Leonora: It bore the Accent of a Humane Voice. . . . . 339 M. BRIDE II.1 53
Almeria: Of Humane Bodies; for I'll mix with them, ... 339 M. BRIDE II.1 75
Zara: That hither lead, nor Humane Face, nor Voice . . . . 379 M. BRIDE V.2 134

Humanity (2)

Lady Ply: frailty? Alas! Humanity is feeble, Heaven knows! very . . 147 DOUBL DLR II.1 321
Angelica: deluded with vain Hopes. Good Nature and Humanity . . 277 FOR LOVE IV.1 72

Humanum est errare(1)

Foresight: Alas Mr. Scandal--Humanum est errare. . . . . 267 FOR LOVE III.1 526

Humble (17)

Sir Joseph: and gratitude of your superabundant humble Servant . . . 49 OLD BATCH II.1 68
Sharper: Sir your humble Servant--I don't question but you . . . 49 OLD BATCH II.1 87
Capt Bluff: done but an humble Servant of yours, that shall be nameless, . 52 OLD BATCH II.1 198
Sharper: Ladies, your humble Servant.--We were . . . . 86 OLD BATCH IV.3 114
Bellmour: humble, pliant, easie thing, a Lover, so guess at Plagues in 106 OLD BATCH V.1 382
Lady Touch: Where is that humble Love, the Languishing, that Adoration, . 136 DOUBL DLR I.1 350
Brisk: I'm everlastingly your humble Servant, Deuce take . . 140 DOUBL DLR II.1 93
Lord Froth: O your humble Servant for that, dear Madam; . . . . 141 DOUBL DLR II.1 109
Brisk: I'm your Humble Servant, let me perish.--I . . . . 142 DOUBL DLR II.1 136
Sir Paul: O, sweet Sir, you load your humble Servants, both . . 159 DOUBL DLR III.1 325
Sir Paul: Your humble Servant, I am I thank Heaven in a . . . 160 DOUBL DLR III.1 383
Brisk: My Lady Froth! Your Ladyships most humble Servant; . . 175 DOUBL DLR IV.1 313
Brisk: My Lord, your humble Servant; Sir Paul yours,-- . . . 201 DOUBL DLR V.1 517
Scandal: she cou'd grant 'em.--Madam, I'm your humble Servant, . 284 FOR LOVE IV.1 337
Almeria: I bend to Heav'n with Thanks and Humble Praise. . . . 332 M. BRIDE I.1 251
Mrs Fain: He is an humble Servant to Foible my Mothers . . . . 417 WAY WORLD II.1 286
Foible: O dear Sir, your humble Servant. . . . . 424 WAY WORLD II.1 536

Humbly (4)

            My Business here, was humbly to petition: . . . . . 113 OLD BATCH EPI. 18
Sir Paul: I humbly thank your Ladiship--I don't know . . . . 172 DOUBL DLR IV.1 197
Maskwell: I humbly would petition-- . . . . 189 DOUBL DLR V.1 67
            (Enter Gonsalez, Bowing very humbly.) . 331 M. BRIDE I.1 219

Humh (3)

Scandal: Humh!--An admirable Composition, faith, this . . . . 278 FOR LOVE IV.1 92
Foible: With his Taunts and his Fleers, tossing up his Nose. Humh . 427 WAY WORLD III.1 94
Foible: Humh (says he) I hear you are laying Designs against . 428 WAY WORLD III.1 111

Humility (1)

Lord Touch: His humility long stifled his Passion: And his . . . 191 DOUBL DLR V.1 135

Humorist (1)

Witwoud: kind of a Humorist. . . . . 408 WAY WORLD I.1 493

Humour (34)

Araminta: But if you continue your Humour, it won't be very . . . 57 OLD BATCH II.2 86
Araminta: Religion, as his Humour varies or his Interest. . . . . 58 OLD BATCH II.2 149
Lucy: now--I'me not 'ith humour. (Exit.) . . . . 67 OLD BATCH III.1 237
Setter: the humour. . . . . 67 OLD BATCH III.1 239
Mellefont: keep up good Humour and Sense in the Company, prithee . 128 DOUBL DLR I.1 47
Brisk: particular and novel in the Humour; 'tis true, it makes . 133 DOUBL DLR I.1 238
Brisk: particular in the Humour; 'tis true, it makes . . . 133 DOUEL DLR I.1 V238
Sir Paul: A humour of my wife's, you know women have . . . . 161 DOUBL DLR III.1 402
Cynthia: Yes, my Lord-- (aside) I must humour this Fool. . . . 162 DOUBL DLR III.1 468
            There's Humour, which for chearful Friends we got, . . 213 FOR LOVE PRO. 29
Valentine: he is perfectly thy reverse both in humour and
            understanding; . . . . 226 FOR LOVE I.1 365
Mrs Frail: Not at all; I like his humour mightily, it's plain . . 262 FOR LOVE III.1 321
Mrs Frail: and honest, I shou'd like such a humour in a Husband . 262 FOR LOVE III.1 322
Scandal: Humour him, Madam, by all means. . . . . 290 FOR LOVE IV.1 540
Jeremy: Two Hours--I'm sure I left him just now, in a Humour . 295 FOR LOVE IV.1 754
Jeremy: Two Hours--I'm sure I left him just now, in the Humour . 295 FOR LOVE IV.1 V754
            Some Humour too, no Farce; but that's a Fault. . . . 393 WAY WORLD PRO. 30
Fainall: of Humour. . . . . 395 WAY WORLD I.1 14
Mirabell: I was then in such a Humour, that I shou'd have been . 396 WAY WORLD I.1 47
Petulant: All's one, let it pass--I have a Humour to be . . . 405 WAY WORLD I.1 390
Petulant: Humour--By this Hand, if they were your--a--a--your . 405 WAY WORLD I.1 395

Humour (continued)

		PAGE	TITLE	ACT.SC	LINE
Petulant:	Enough, I'm in a Humour to be severe.	409	WAY WORLD	I.1	522
Mrs Fain:	Mankind, only in compliance with my Mothers Humour.	410	WAY WORLD	II.1	19
Mrs Fain:	Mankind, only in compliance to my Mothers Humour.	410	WAY WORLD	II.1 V	19
Mrs Fain:	He has a Humour more prevailing than his	412	WAY WORLD	II.1	103
Millamant:	it--But 'tis agreeable to my Humour.	434	WAY WORLD	III.1	373
Petulant:	Ay in the main--But when I have a Humour to	435	WAY WORLD	III.1	398
Witwoud:	Ay, when he has a Humour to contradict, then I	435	WAY WORLD	III.1	400
Petulant:	If he says Black's Black--If I have a Humour to	435	WAY WORLD	III.1	404
Petulant:	I have a Humour to prove it, it must be granted.	435	WAY WORLD	III.1	406
Millamant:	dine in my dressing room when I'm out of humour	450	WAY WORLD	IV.1	220
Petulant:	kiss'd your twin yonder in a humour of reconciliation, till	454	WAY WORLD	IV.1	356
Petulant:	If I have a humour to Quarrel, I can make less	454	WAY WORLD	IV.1	366
Petulant:	what then? If I have a humour to prove it.--If I shall	454	WAY WORLD	IV.1	368

Humoured (0)   see Ill-humoured

Humours (1)

		PAGE	TITLE	ACT.SC	LINE
Fainall:	after I left you; my fair Cousin has some Humours, that	395	WAY WORLD	I.1	18

Humph (6)

		PAGE	TITLE	ACT.SC	LINE
Sir Joseph:	Humph.	50	OLD BATCH	II.1	96
Bellmour:	Humph, I thought so, that you might have all the	59	OLD BATCH	II.2	176
Fondlewife:	Humph.	93	OLD BATCH	IV.4	159
Fondlewife:	Humph, Nay, if you mince the matter once, and	94	OLD BATCH	IV.4	190
Bellmour:	Humph, Sits the Wind there?--What a lucky	97	OLD BATCH	V.1	23
Jeremy:	Humph, and so he has made a very fine Feast, where	216	FOR LOVE	I.1	21

Hums (1)

		PAGE	TITLE	ACT.SC	LINE
Tattle:	(Hums a Song.)	228	FOR LOVE	I.1	449

Hundred (15)

		PAGE	TITLE	ACT.SC	LINE
Sharper:	only dropt a Bill of a hundred Pound, which I confess, I	49	OLD BATCH	II.1	82
Sharper:	Pshaw you can't want a hundred Pound. Your	50	OLD BATCH	II.1	107
Sharper:	hundred Pound to lose? (Angrily.)	50	OLD BATCH	II.1	127
Sir Joseph:	hundred Pound--I meant innocently as I hope to be sav'd	51	OLD BATCH	II.1	129
Sir Joseph:	Fondlewife, as far as two hundred Pound, and this Afternoon	51	OLD BATCH	II.1	133
Capt Bluff:	hundred Pound.	67	OLD BATCH	III.1	246
Sir Joseph:	the Guts for a hundred Pound--Why I gave that	67	OLD BATCH	III.1	254
Sir Joseph:	hundred Pound for being saved, and d'ee think, an there	67	OLD BATCH	III.1	255
Sir Joseph:	by, I would as soon have let him a' had a hundred of my	68	OLD BATCH	III.1	277
Fondlewife:	A Hundred has already been paid, by your Order,	89	OLD BATCH	IV.4	29
Scandal:	with a hundred Hands, two Heads, and but one Face; a	233	FOR LOVE	I.1	643
Valentine:	Argo's hundred Eyes be shut, ha? No body shall know,	290	FOR LOVE	IV.1	552
Tattle:	But in short, de'e see, I will hold you a Hundred Pound	291	FOR LOVE	IV.1	608
Gonsalez:	Five Hundred Mules, precede his solemn March,	331	M. BRIDE	I.1	227
Gonsalez:	Succeed; and next, a Hundred neighing Steeds,	331	M. BRIDE	I.1	230

Hung (2)

		PAGE	TITLE	ACT.SC	LINE
Zara:	Your heavy and desponding Heads hung down?	380	M. BRIDE	V.2	158
Lady Wish:	A Tatterdemallion--I hope to see him hung with	428	WAY WORLD	III.1	130

Hungry (3)

		PAGE	TITLE	ACT.SC	LINE
Maskwell:	Fools! then that hungry Gudgeon Credulity, will bite at	150	DOUBL DLR	II.1	459
	To cultivate each Year a hungry Soil;	213	FOR LOVE	PRO.	2
Jeremy:	Dozen Duns with as much Dexterity, as a hungry Judge	220	FOR LOVE	I.1	167

Hunt (2)

		PAGE	TITLE	ACT.SC	LINE
Cynthia:	meeting: We Hunt in Couples where we both pursue the	168	DOUBL DLR	IV.1	16
Mellefont:	Marriage is the Game that we Hunt, and while we think	168	DOUBL DLR	IV.1	20

Hunter (1)   see Omen-hunter

		PAGE	TITLE	ACT.SC	LINE
Vainlove:	Mouth; and would distaste the keenest Hunter--I	80	OLD BATCH	IV.1	179

Hunting (1)

		PAGE	TITLE	ACT.SC	LINE
Sr Sampson:	Hunting upon an Elephant with the Cham of Tartary--	241	FOR LOVE	II.1	221

Huntsmen (1)

		PAGE	TITLE	ACT.SC	LINE
Scandal:	Huntsmen.--No, turn Pimp, Flatterer, Quack, Lawyer,	220	FOR LOVE	I.1	144

Hurricane (2)

		PAGE	TITLE	ACT.SC	LINE
Ben:	Mess, I've had such a Hurricane upon your account	285	FOR LOVE	IV.1	360
Mincing:	He swears, and my old Lady cry's. There's a fearful Hurricane	465	WAY WORLD	V.1	109

Hurries (2)

		PAGE	TITLE	ACT.SC	LINE
Almeria:	As hurries all my Soul, and dozes my weak Sense.	343	M. BRIDE	II.2	155
Almeria:	It hurries all my Soul, and stuns my Sense.	343	M. BRIDE	II.2 V155	

Hurry (1)

		PAGE	TITLE	ACT.SC	LINE
Foresight:	gallop, hey! Whither will they hurry me?--Now they're	269	FOR LOVE	III.1	608

Hurry'd (3)

		PAGE	TITLE	ACT.SC	LINE
Tattle:	Discretion, as the Heat of the Lady's Passion hurry'd her	258	FOR LOVE	III.1	186
Scandal:	Cause of that? And Sir Sampson is hurry'd on by an unusual	268	FOR LOVE	III.1	548
Almeria:	My Grief has hurry'd me beyond all Thought.	328	M. BRIDE	I.1	79

Hurt (4)

		PAGE	TITLE	ACT.SC	LINE
Heartwell:	I'll have my Beard shav'd, it shan't hurt thee, and	73	OLD BATCH	III.2	107
Osmyn-Alph:	Shall I not hurt and bruise thy tender Body,	355	M. BRIDE	III.1	242
Osmyn-Alph:	Shall I not hurt or bruise thy tender Body,	355	M. BRIDE	III.1 V242	
Fainall:	I would not hurt you for the World. Have I no	416	WAY WORLD	II.1	227

Hurts (2)

		PAGE	TITLE	ACT.SC	LINE
	That hurts none here, sure here are none of those.	393	WAY WORLD	PRO.	36
Petulant:	No, I'm no Enemy to Learning; it hurts not me.	436	WAY WORLD	III.1	418

Husband (99)   see Moor-Husband, Rank-Husband

		PAGE	TITLE	ACT.SC	LINE
Bellmour:	Husband be out of the way, for the Wife to shew her	38	OLD BATCH	I.1	56
Vainlove:	For she only stalks under him to take aim at her Husband.	38	OLD BATCH	I.1 V	62
Bellmour:	Husband: For 'tis an Argument of her great Zeal towards	39	OLD BATCH	I.1	64
Fondlewife:	while her good Husband is deluded by his Godly appearance	76	OLD BATCH	IV.1	30
Barnaby:	Husband. 'Tis then indeed, like the vanity of taking a fine	76	OLD BATCH	IV.1	42
Fondlewife:	yet thy Husband must also bear his part: For thy iniquity	77	OLD BATCH	IV.1	71
Fondlewife:	your Husband?	77	OLD BATCH	IV.1	78
Laetitia:	Husband ought to behave himself--I shall be glad to	79	OLD BATCH	IV.1	140
Laetitia:	Dear Husband, I'm amaz'd:--Sure it's a good	92	OLD BATCH	IV.4	114
Fondlewife:	have been a tender Husband, a tender Yoke-fellow; you	95	OLD BATCH	IV.4	249
Bellmour:	No Husband, by his Wife, can be deceiv'd:	96	OLD BATCH	IV.4	273
Lucy:	Husband?	98	OLD BATCH	V.1	50
Bellmour:	fitter Husband for her.--Come, Here's Earnest of my good	98	OLD BATCH	V.1	58
Bellmour:	help your Mistress to a Husband.--Nay, and thee too,	98	OLD BATCH	V.1	71
Bellmour:	Husband, somewhat pacify'd her.	100	OLD BATCH	V.1	153
Capt Bluff:	Husband--But here, both these are from Persons of great	103	OLD BATCH	V.1	269

Husbands   (continued)
Speaker	Quotation	PAGE	TITLE	ACT.SC	LINE
Fainall:	Jealous no,--by this Kiss--let Husbands be Jealous;	444	WAY WORLD	III.1	714
Fainall:	when he proves his Mistress true; but let Husbands doubts	444	WAY WORLD	III.1	717
Fainall:	All Husbands must, or pain, or shame, endure;	444	WAY WORLD	III.1	724

Hush (5)   see Hist, Hust, 'st
Vainlove:	Hush--	62	OLD BATCH	III.1 V	72
Sir Joseph:	Hush, hush: Don't you see him?	101	OLD BATCH	V.1	169
Mrs Frail:	Hush: Well he shan't, leave that to me--I'll	259	FOR LOVE	III.1	220
Scandal:	Hush, softly--the Pleasures of last Night, my	284	FOR LOVE	IV.1	316

Hush'd (3)
Mellefont:	hush'd into a Sigh. It was long before either of us spoke,	130	DOUBL DLR	I.1	107
Almeria:	It was a fancy'd Noise; for all is hush'd.	339	M. BRIDE	II.1	52
Almeria:	No, all is hush'd, and still as Death--'Tis dreadful!	339	M. BRIDE	II.1	58

Husht (4)
Capt Bluff:	Husht, 'tis not so convenient now--I shall find a	69	OLD BATCH	III.1	313
Sir Joseph:	Love, up to the Ears. But I'll be discreet, and husht.	86	OLD BATCH	III.3	110
Nurse:	cry husht--O Lord, who's there? (peeps) What's here	253	FOR LOVE	III.1	7
Valentine:	Husht--Interrupt me not--I'll whisper	288	FOR LOVE	IV.1	486

Hussey (1)
Sir Paul:	Execution in its time Girl; why thou hast my Leer Hussey, just	173	DOUBL DLR	IV.1	236

Hussie (2)
Foresight:	How Hussie! was there ever such a provoking	237	FOR LOVE	II.1	93
Foresight:	I defie you, Hussie; but I'll remember this, I'll be	238	FOR LOVE	II.1	113

Hussy (5)
Sir Paul:	--Ah! when I was of your Age Hussy, I would have	174	DOUBL DLR	IV.1	241
Sr Sampson:	Odsbud, Hussy, you know how to chuse, and so do I;	301	FOR LOVE	V.1	143
Sr Sampson:	Say you so, Hussy?--Come lets go then;	301	FOR LOVE	V.1	160
Foresight:	Hussy you shall have a Rod.	305	FOR LOVE	V.1	314
Foresight:	Hussy--Do what I bid you, no Reply, away. And bid	306	FOR LOVE	V.1	326

Hust (1)
Vainlove:	Hust--	62	OLD BATCH	III.1	72

Hymen (2)
Bellmour:	How never like! marry Hymen forbid. But this it	58	OLD BATCH	II.2	121
Valentine:	not a word. Hymen shall put his Torch into a dark Lanthorn,	290	FOR LOVE	IV.1	549

Hymenial (1)
Osmyn-Alph:	Delay'd: nor has our Hymenial Torch	357	M. BRIDE	III.1	321

Hypocrisie (4)
Laetitia:	welcome, but not the Hypocrisie.	81	OLD BATCH	IV.2	26
Bellmour:	(aside). Rather the Hypocrisie was welcome, but not	81	OLD BATCH	IV.2	27
Maskwell:	Hypocrisie; oh 'tis such a pleasure, to angle for fair-faced	150	DOUBL DLR	II.1	458
Valentine:	Hypocrisie apart,--The Comedy draws toward an	294	FOR LOVE	IV.1	707

Hypocrisy (1)
Bellmour:	Well and how Setter hae, does my Hypocrisy fit me hae?	75	OLD BATCH	IV.1	3

Hypocrite (1)
Bellmour:	the Hypoorite.	81	OLD BATCH	IV.2	28

Hypocrites (2)
Bellmour:	Hypocrites.--Oh! she comes.	80	OLD BATCH	IV.2	8
Angelica:	due. Men are generally Hypocrites and Infidels, they	314	FOR LOVE	V.1	631

I (4109)

I'd (24)
Sir Joseph:	angry, I'd tell him--Mum.	68	OLD BATCH	III.1	279
Sir Joseph:	--I'd rather go plain all my Life, than wear such	70	OLD BATCH	III.1	334
Lucy:	Whore! I'd have you know, my Mistress scorns--	98	OLD BATCH	V.1	63
Lucy:	Whore! I'd have you to know, my Mistress scorns--	98	OLD BATCH	V.1 V	63
Lord Froth:	Barbarous! as lieve you call'd me Fool.	132	DOUBL DLR	I.1	186
Lady Ply:	should die, of all Mankind there's none I'd sooner make	170	DOUBL DLR	IV.1	111
Angelica:	if I were obliged to make a Choice, I declare I'd rather	260	FOR LOVE	III.1	255
Tattle:	and be sorry for't afterwards. I'd have you to know, Sir,	305	FOR LOVE	V.1	291
Miss Prue:	I don't know for what--And I'd rather be always a	305	FOR LOVE	V.1	311
Miss Prue:	I don't know for what--And I'd rather be always	305	FOR LOVE	V.1 V311	
Sr Sampson:	the Stars are Lyars; and if I had Breath enough, I'd curse	313	FOR LOVE	V.1 V584	
Manuel:	Which I'd have broken.	334	M. BRIDE	I.1	356
Manuel:	Begets a Doubt. I'd have 'em watch'd: perhaps	335	M. BRIDE	I.1	380
Osmyn-Alph:	Then you may know for whom I'd die.	360	M. BRIDE	III.1	437
Gonsalez:	Of those, tho' purchas'd by his Death; I'd give	372	M. BRIDE	IV.1	438
Alonzo:	As but an hour ago, I'd not have done,	379	M. BRIDE	V.2	111
Fainall:	losing Gamester lessens the Pleasure of the Winner: I'd no	395	WAY WORLD	I.1	7
Fainall:	I'd make Love to a Woman who undervalu'd the Loss of	395	WAY WORLD	I.1	9
Marwood:	No; but I'd make him believe I did, and that's	411	WAY WORLD	II.1	58
Marwood:	Hands, do--I'd leave 'em to get loose.	416	WAY WORLD	II.1	226
Sir Wilful:	before I cross the Seas. I'd gladly have a spice of your	440	WAY WORLD	III.1	583
Sir Wilful:	Fellows--If I had a Bumper I'd stand upon my	456	WAY WORLD	IV.1	425
Waitwell:	--by this hand I'd rather be a Chair-man in the Dog-days	459	WAY WORLD	IV.1	563
Waitwell:	If he were my Son as he is my Nephew I'd Pistoll him--	460	WAY WORLD	IV.1	603

I'de (5)
Bellmour:	heartily? I'de do a little more good in my generation first,	63	OLD BATCH	III.1	107
Ben:	So, so, enough Father--Mess, I'de rather kiss these	260	FOR LOVE	III.1	276
Ben:	An we were a League asunder, I'de undertake to hold	263	FOR LOVE	III.1	369
Ben:	Break your Heart? I'de rather the Mary-gold shou'd	273	FOR LOVE	III.1	730
Ben:	told 'n in plain terms, if I were minded to marry, I'de	285	FOR LOVE	IV.1	371

I'faith (12)
Bellmour:	--Confess.--Come, I'll be faithful: I will I-faith.	97	OLD BATCH	V.1	45
Sir Joseph:	Heh, heh, heh: Here 'tis for you, i'Faith, Mr.	103	OLD BATCH	V.1	236
Careless:	be told on't; she must i'faith, Sir Paul; 'tis an injury to the	162	DOUBL DLR	III.1	442
Lord Froth:	Just 'ifaith, that was at my tongues end.	163	DOUBL DLR	III.1	480
Valentine:	Say you so, I'faith: Come, we'll remember the	223	FOR LOVE	I.1	271
Valentine:	A Lovely Girl, I'faith, black sparkling Eyes, soft pouting	223	FOR LOVE	I.1	278
Ben:	not for dropping Anchor here; About Ship i' faith--	261	FOR LOVE	III.1	281
Scandal:	Hey, brave Woman, i' faith--Won't you see	277	FOR LOVE	IV.1	77
Witwoud:	i'faith.	408	WAY WORLD	I.1	490
Mirabell:	Here she comes i'faith full sail, with her Fan spread	418	WAY WORLD	II.1	323
Foible:	hold; But i'faith I gave him his own.	427	WAY WORLD	III.1	91
Sir Wilful:	i'faith! What do'st thou not know me? By'r Lady nor I	439	WAY WORLD	III.1	517

I'gad (20)

		PAGE	TITLE	ACT.SC	LINE
Bellmour:	Actions free to--Quicken your Apprehension--And I-gad	59	OLD BATCH	II.2	182
Brisk:	pretty and Metaphorical enough: I' Gad I could not have	128	DOUBL DLR	I.1	38
Brisk:	I'gad so they will--well I will, I will, Gad you	128	DOUBL DLR	I.1	49
Brisk:	I'gad, ha, ha, ha.	132	DOUBL DLR	I.1	207
Brisk:	Write, but--I'gad, I love to be malicious.--Nay,	133	DOUBL DLR	I.1	240
Brisk:	no other way, I'gad.	133	DOUBL DLR	I.1	243
Brisk:	(to Lady Froth). Your Ladyship is in the right; but I'gad	141	DOUBL DLR	II.1	115
Brisk:	but when I do--keen Iambicks I'gad. But my Lord	141	DOUBL DLR	II.1	117
Brisk:	Because my Lord's Title's Froth, I'gad, ha, ha, ha,	141	DOUBL DLR	II.1	124
Brisk:	Biddy! I'gad very pretty--Deuce take me if your	142	DOUBL DLR	II.1	130
Brisk:	Incomparable well and proper, Igad--but I have one	164	DOUBL DLR	III.1	543
Brisk:	Like an Oyster at low Ebb, I'gad--ha, ha, ha.	165	DOUBL DLR	III.1	576
Brisk:	Short, but there's Salt in't, my way of writing I'gad.	166	DOUBL DLR	III.1	602
Brisk:	an Old Hen, as if she were not well hatch'd, I'gad, he?	174	DOUBL DLR	IV.1	273
Brisk:	Woman of parts, and I'gad parts will carry her. She said	175	DOUBL DLR	IV.1	295
Brisk:	all I'gad. I was fallen into the most agreeable amusement in	175	DOUBL DLR	IV.1	315
Brisk:	No more I have I'gad, for I adore 'em all in your	176	DOUBL DLR	IV.1	336
Brisk:	Me I'gad, ha ha.	176	DOUBL DLR	IV.1	350
Brisk:	(aside). That's good I'gad, that's good, Deuce take me I	177	DOUBL DLR	IV.1	379
Tattle:	in my time; but i'Gad I could never find in my Heart to	303	FOR LOVE	V.1	213

I'l (2)

Vainlove:	Well good Morrow, let's dine together, I'l meet at	40	OLD BATCH	I.1	129
Capt Bluff:	--This Sword I'l maintain to be the best Divine,	53	OLD BATCH	II.2	229

I'le (31)

Bellmour:	I'le take care, he shall not be at home. Good! Spintext! Oh	39	OLD BATCH	I.1	84
Sir Joseph:	Poor Gentleman--by the Lord Harry I'le stay no	48	OLD BATCH	II.1	25
Sir Joseph:	I don't know, but I'le present you--	51	OLD BATCH	II.1	154
Capt Bluff:	I'le recommend my self--Sir I honour you; I understand	51	OLD BATCH	II.1	155
Silvia:	but I'le do my weak endeavour, though I fear I have not	62	OLD BATCH	III.1	52
Heartwell:	on't--I'le run into the danger to lose the	63	OLD BATCH	III.1	85
Vainlove:	Well, I'le leave you with your Engineer.	64	OLD BATCH	III.1	120
Lucy:	No Sirrah, I'le keep it cn to abuse thee and leave thee	65	OLD BATCH	III.1	181
Setter:	Nay faith Lucy I'me sorry, I'le own my self to blame,	66	OLD BATCH	III.1	212
Setter:	Come I'le make you any reparation.	66	OLD BATCH	III.1	214
Lucy:	No no, avaunt--I'le not be slabber'd and kiss'd	67	OLD BATCH	III.1	236
Setter:	I'le not quit you so--I'le Follow and put you into	67	OLD BATCH	III.1	238
Capt Bluff:	go--and bring it me hither. I'le stay here for you.	67	OLD BATCH	III.1	251
Sir Joseph:	were no danger, I'le be so ungrateful to take it from the	67	OLD BATCH	III.1	256
Lucy:	first. I know that will do--walk in and I'le shew	75	OLD BATCH	III.1	158
Fondlewife:	I'le tarry, d'ee see.	76	OLD BATCH	IV.1	37
Laetitia:	Heart--Well, be as cruel as you can to me, I'le pray for	78	OLD BATCH	IV.1	108
Fondlewife:	buss poor Nykin--And I wont leave thee--I'le lose all first.	78	OLD BATCH	IV.1	118
Fondlewife:	And so thou shalt say, for I'le leave it to stay with thee.	78	OLD BATCH	IV.1	130
Laetitia:	indeed you sant. Nykin--if you don't go, I'le think	78	OLD BATCH	IV.1	132
Brisk:	spite, by the Gods! and burning envy.--I'le be	128	DOUBL DLR	I.1	26
Mellefont:	Gallantry, as they call it. I'le observe my Uncle my self;	130	DOUBL DLR	I.1	135
Lady Touch:	I'le hold my breath and die, but I'le be free.	184	DOUBL DLR	IV.2	53
Lady Touch:	(aloud). Never, never! I'le grow to the	186	DOUBL DLR	IV.2	98
Lady Touch:	O cruel Man, will you not let me go--I'le	186	DOUBL DLR	IV.2	102
Lord Touch:	to my Name; when next I see that Face, I'le write Villain	186	DOUBL DLR	IV.2	119
Lady Touch:	yonders my Lord, I believe he's coming to find you, I'le	188	DOUBL DLR	V.1	7
Maskwell:	excuse. My Lord is thoughtful--I'le be so too; yet he shall	188	DOUBL DLR	V.1	13
Fainall:	but I'le be hang'd if she did not put Pam in her Pocket.	442	WAY WORLD	III.1	V654

I'll (489)

Capt Bluff:	Gazette--I'll tell you a strange thing now as to that--	52	OLD BATCH	II.1	194
Belinda:	that in his Breast. Araminta, come I'll talk seriously	55	OLD BATCH	II.2	30
	to you	55	OLD BATCH	II.2	30
Araminta:	be not gone, I'll entertain you with a new Song,	58	OLD BATCH	II.2	153
Footman:	Only to the next door, Madam; I'll call him.	58	OLD BATCH	II.2	158
Belinda:	Devil, wrapt in Flames--I'll not hear a Sentence	59	OLD BATCH	II.2	170
Bellmour:	Faith, Madam, I dare not speak to her, but I'll	60	OLD BATCH	II.2	210
Capt Bluff:	him--I'll pink his Soul--but whisper that softly	68	OLD BATCH	III.1	261
Sir Joseph:	self--I'll give him the Lie if you'll stand to it.	69	OLD BATCH	III.1	307
Sharper:	Nay then I'll be beforehand with you, take that--	69	OLD BATCH	III.1	308
Capt Bluff:	Death and Hell to be affronted thus! I'll die before	70	OLD BATCH	III.1	336
Capt Bluff:	I'll suffer it.	70	OLD BATCH	III.1	337
Capt Bluff:	I'll call a Council of War within to consider of my	70	OLD BATCH	III.1	363
Heartwell:	Marry you? no, no, I'll love you.	73	OLD BATCH	III.2	99
Heartwell:	I'll have my Beard shav'd, it shan't hurt thee, and	73	OLD BATCH	III.2	107
Silvia:	(Throws the Purse) I hate you now, and I'll never see you	74	OLD BATCH	III.2	111
Heartwell:	I'll give thee all I have: And thou shalt live with	74	OLD BATCH	III.2	120
Silvia:	No, I'll die before I'll be your Whore--as well as I	74	OLD BATCH	III.2	124
Servant:	I'll call my Mistress.	80	OLD BATCH	IV.2	2
Belinda:	like one of 'em:--Good Dear, pin this, and I'll tell you.	83	OLD BATCH	IV.3	13
Sir Joseph:	Nay, gad, I'll pick up; I'm resolv'd to make a	85	OLD BATCH	IV.3	61
Sir Joseph:	Night on't.--I'll go to Alderman Fondlewife by-and-by,	85	OLD BATCH	IV.3	62
Araminta:	Vainlove to know us, I'll be rid of my Fool by fair means	86	OLD BATCH	IV.3	102
Sir Joseph:	Love, up to the Ears. But I'll be discreet, and husht.	86	OLD BATCH	IV.3	110
Capt Bluff:	Nay, by the World, I'll see your face.	86	OLD BATCH	IV.3	111
Belinda:	see a couple, I'll give you their History.	87	OLD BATCH	IV.3	150
Belinda:	O Lord, No, I'll go along with her. Come, Mr.	88	OLD BATCH	IV.3	209
Laetitia:	Then, I'll let you in.	89	OLD BATCH	IV.4	20
Sir Joseph:	Agad, it's a curious, fine, pretty Rogue; I'll speak	89	OLD BATCH	IV.4	32
Fondlewife:	If you will tarry a Moment, till I fetch my Papers,				
	I'll wait	90	OLD BATCH	IV.4	43
Fondlewife:	I'll shut this Door, to secure him from coming	91	OLD BATCH	IV.4	72
Laetitia:	him. Dear Fortune, help me but this once, and I'll never	91	OLD BATCH	IV.4	91
Fondlewife:	is this Apocryphal Elder? I'll ferret him.	92	OLD BATCH	IV.4	118
Bellmour:	Well, since I see thou art a good honest Fellow, I'll	94	OLD BATCH	IV.4	198
Laetitia:	won't you speak to me, cruel Nykin? Indeed, I'll die, if	95	OLD BATCH	IV.4	246
Bellmour:	Turtle to you, that I'll go and sollicite Matrimony with all	96	OLD BATCH	IV.4	265
Fondlewife:	I'll show you the way out of my house, if you please. Come,	96	OLD BATCH	IV.4	269
Bellmour:	quickly, I'll follow you--I wou'd not be known. (Exit	97	OLD BATCH	V.1	11
Heartwell:	I'll pay him well, if you'll break the Matter to him.	97	OLD BATCH	V.1	20
Bellmour:	--Confess.--Come, I'll be faithful: I will I-faith.	97	OLD BATCH	V.1	45

I'll   (continued)

Maskwell:	full fruition of my Love, I'll bear the railings of a losing	190	DOUEL DLR	V.1	87
Lord Touch:	know he's no way to be rewarded but in her. I'll defer my	191	DOUEL DLR	V.1	138
Lady Touch:	me, and I'll renounce all Blood, all relation and concern	192	DOUEL DLR	V.1	181
Lady Touch:	with you for ever,--nay, I'll be your Enemy, and pursue	192	DOUEL DLR	V.1	182
Lady Touch:	you to Destruction, I'll tear your Eyes out, and tread	192	DOUEL DLR	V.1	183
Maskwell:	That's right,--well, I'll secure the Writings;	193	DOUEL DLR	V.1	206
Maskwell:	Why, I'll tell my Lord, I laid this Plot with you,	193	DOUEL DLR	V.1	217
Maskwell:	self ready, I'll wheedle her intc the Coach; and instead of	193	DOUEL DLR	V.1	223
Maskwell:	observ'd.--I'll send the Chaplain to you with his Robes;	194	DOUEL DLR	V.1	241
Maskwell:	No, no, I'll after him immediately, and tell him.	194	DOUEL DLR	V.1	259
Maskwell:	Mellefont. I'll urge haste, to excuse your silence.	195	DOUEL DLR	V.1	295
Lord Touch:	her as much as reason--by Heav'n, I'll not be Wife-ridden;	196	DOUEL DLR	V.1	320
Maskwell:	Cynthia, and my Chaplain will be ready, I'll prepare for	199	DOUEL DLR	V.1	463
Lord Touch:	ha, I'll do't, where's Mellefont, my poor injured Nephew,--	200	DOUEL DLR	V.1	478
Lord Touch:	I'll add to my Plot too,--let us haste to find out, and	200	DOUEL DLR	V.1	486
Lord Touch:	all the Company into this Gallery,--I'll expose the Strumpet,	200	DOUEL DLR	V.1	488
Valentine:	Here, take away; I'll walk a turn, and digest what	216	FOR LCVE	I.1	3
Valentine:	be reveng'd on 'em all; I'll pursue Angelica with more Love	217	FOR LCVE	I.1	50
Valentine:	I'll take some of their Trade out of their Hands.	217	FOR LCVE	I.1	60
Valentine:	Yes, I do; I'll write a Play.	217	FOR LCVE	I.1	63
Valentine:	--I'll have you learn to make Couplets, to tag the	218	FOR LCVE	I.1	77
Scandal:	I'll rip up his Stomach, and go the shortest way to his	224	FOR LCVE	I.1	311
Scandal:	Pox on him, I'll be gone.	225	FOR LCVE	I.1	362
Scandal:	I'm resolv'd I'll ask her.	229	FOR LOVE	I.1	493
Tattle:	I'll be gone.	229	FOR LCVE	I.1	508
Tattle:	Titles; I'll describe their Persons.	230	FCB LCVE	I.1	535
Tattle:	till another time--I'll double the number.	230	FOR LCVE	I.1	543
Mrs Frail:	No, I'll allow a Lover present with his Mistress to	231	FCB LCVE	I.1	555
Mrs Frail:	Well, I'll tell you News; but I suppose you hear your	231	FOR LCVE	I.1	566
Valentine:	Step into the next Room--and I'll give you	231	FOR LCVE	I.1	585
Mrs Frail:	take care of my own. Well; but I'll come and see ycu one	232	FCB LCVE	I.1	597
Mrs Frail:	Well, I'll come, if it be only to disprove you.	234	FOR LOVE	I.1	659
Mrs Frail:	Well, I'll come, if it be but to disprove you.	234	FOR LCVE	I.1 V659	
Valentine:	I'll come to him--will you give me leave, I'll	234	FOR LCVE	I.1	662
Mrs Frail:	No, I'll be gone. Come, who Squires me to the	234	FOR LCVE	I.1	664
Scandal:	I'll give an account of you, and your Proceedings. If	234	FOR LCVE	I.1	675
Nurse:	Dinner--good lack-a-day, ha, ha, ha, O strange; I'll vow	235	FOR LOVE	II.1	22
Foresight:	Sirrah, go tell Sir Sampson Legend I'll wait on him, if	236	FOR LOVE	II.1	40
Angelica:	abroad; and if you won't lend me your Coach, I'll take a	237	FCB LCVE	II.1	67
Angelica:	Nay Uncle, don't be angry--If you are, I'll	237	FCB LCVE	II.1	76
Angelica:	idle Divinations. I'll secure your Nusance to the	237	FOR LCVE	II.1	78
Angelica:	Will ycu lend me your Coach, or I'll go on--	237	FOR LCVE	II.1	87
Angelica:	Nay, I'll declare how you prophecy'd Popery was coming,	237	FOR LCVE	II.1	88
Angelica:	and Spoon-meat together--Indeed, Uncle, I'll indite you	237	FOR LCVE	II.1	91
Foresight:	I defie you, Hussie; but I'll remember this, I'll be	238	FCB LCVE	II.1	113
Foresight:	reveng'd on you, Cockatrice; I'll hamper you--You	238	FCB LCVE	II.1	114
Foresight:	have your Fortune in your own Hands--But I'll find	238	FCB LCVE	II.1	115
Foresight:	I'll punish you, not a Man shall enter my House.	238	FCB LCVE	II.1	132
Foresight:	something; tell me, and I'll forgive ycu; do, good Neice	239	FCB LCVE	II.1	147
Foresight:	Do you laugh?--Well Gentlewoman, I'll--	239	FCB LCVE	II.1	156
Foresight:	tell me--won't you speak? Odd I'll--	239	FOR LCVE	II.1	158
Angelica:	Good bu'y Uncle--Call me a Chair--I'll find	239	FOR LCVE	II.1	161
Sr Sampson:	here 'tis, I have it in my Hand, Old Ptolomee; I'll make the	240	FOR LCVE	II.1	173
Foresight:	send your Son to Sea again. I'll wed my Daughter to an	241	FCB LCVE	II.1	238
Sr Sampson:	--What, I'll make thee a Present of a Mummy: Now	242	FOR LCVE	II.1	248
Jeremy:	Nay, that's as clear as the Sun; I'll make Oath of it	245	FOR LCVE	II.1	355
Sr Sampson:	Why look you there now,--I'll maintain	245	FOR LCVE	II.1	365
Valentine:	are earnest,--I'll avoid 'em,--Come this way,	246	FOR LCVE	II.1	411
Mrs Frail:	What have you to do to watch me?--'S'life I'll	246	FOR LCVE	II.1	415
Mrs Fore:	Nay, two or three Turns, I'll take my Oath.	246	FOR LOVE	II.1	421
Mrs Frail:	place call'd the World's-End? I'll swear you can keep your	247	FOR LOVE	II.1	451
Mrs Frail:	I'll swear you have a great deal of Impudence, and	247	FOR LOVE	II.1	453
Mrs Frail:	I'll swear you have a great deal of Confidence, and	247	FOR LOVE	II.1 V453	
Mrs Fore:	I'll allow you now to find fault with my	248	FOR LOVE	II.1	463
Mrs Fore:	Face;--for I'll swear your impudence has put me out of	248	FOR LOVE	II.1	464
Mrs Frail:	I'll acquaint you with a design that I have: To tell Truth,	248	FOR LOVE	II.1	486
Tattle:	do as she would be done by--Gad I'll understand it so.	251	FOR LCVE	II.1	594
Miss Prue:	No, indeed won't I: But I'll run there, and hide	252	FOR LOVE	II.1	648
Tattle:	I'll follow you.	252	FOR LOVE	II.1	650
Miss Prue:	Ah, but I'll hold the Door with both Hands, and	252	FOR LOVE	II.1	651
Tattle:	No, I'll come in first, and push you down afterwards.	253	FOR LOVE	II.1	654
Miss Prue:	Will you? then I'll be more angry, and more	253	FOR LOVE	II.1	655
Tattle:	Then I'll make you cry out.	253	FOR LCVE	II.1	657
Miss Prue:	Oh but you sha'nt, for I'll hold my Tongue.--	253	FOR LOVE	II.1	658
Miss Prue:	Well, now I'll run and make more haste than you.	253	FOR LOVE	II.1	660
Tattle:	You shall not fly so fast, as I'll pursue.	253	FOR LOVE	II.1	662
Nurse:	(knocks) Ods my Life, won't you open the Door? I'll	253	FOR LOVE	III.1	11
Tattle:	say nothing, I think. I hear her--I'll leave you together,	254	FOR LCVE	III.1	23
Scandal:	ask you: I'll say that for you, Madam.	254	FOR LOVE	III.1	34
Tattle:	You say true, I beg your Pardon;--I'll bring all off--	255	FOR LOVE	III.1	65
Scandal:	And I'll answer for him; for I'm sure if he had, he	256	FOR LOVE	III.1	109
Angelica:	Vanity--Fie, Mr. Tattle--I'll swear I could not	258	FOR LOVE	III.1	183
Scandal:	No don't; for then you'l tell us no more--Come, I'll	258	FOR LOVE	III.1	190
Mrs Frail:	Hush: Well he shan't, leave that to me--I'll	259	FOR LOVE	III.1	220
Valentine:	Estate, and I'll defer it as long as I can--Well, you'll come	259	FOR LOVE	III.1	227
Scandal:	Come, Valentine, I'll go with you; I've something in	259	FOR LOVE	III.1	231
Ben:	Why then, I'll go to Sea again, so there's one for t'other, an	261	FOR LOVE	III.1	300
Ben:	Joking, I'll Joke with you, for I love my jest, an the Ship	261	FOR LOVE	III.1	307
Ben:	were sinking, as we sayn at Sea. But I'll tell you why I	261	FOR LOVE	III.1	308
Ben:	But I'll tell you one thing, and you come to Sea in a	262	FOR LOVE	III.1	330
Ben:	good part: For if I give a Jest, I'll take a Jest: And so	262	FOR LOVE	III.1	342
Sr Sampson:	I'll venture that.	263	FOR LOVE	III.1	358

Ben:	Come, I'll haule a Chair; there, an you please to sit, I'll	263	FOR LOVE	III.1	362
Ben:	heard as far as another,--I'll heave off to please you.	263	FOR LOVE	III.1	367
Miss Prue:	But I'm sure it is not so, for I'll speak sooner than .	264	FOR LOVE	III.1	395
Miss Prue:	you should believe that; and I'll speak truth, tho' one				
	should	264	FOR LOVE	III.1	396
Miss Prue:	do what he will; I'm too big to be whipt, so I'll tell you	264	FOR LOVE	III.1	398
Ben:	You Cheese-curd you,--Marry thee! Oons I'll Marry a .	264	FOR LOVE	III.1	425
Ben:	take your part, Your Tom Essence, and I'll say something to	265	FOR LOVE	III.1	435
Ben:	him; Gad I'll lace his Musk-Doublet for him, I'll make him	265	FOR LOVE	III.1	436
Mrs Frail:	down into the Parlour, and I'll carry Mr. Benjamin into .	265	FOR LOVE	III.1	448
Sr Sampson:	But I'll bring him a Parson to tell him, that the Devil's a	267	FOR LOVE	III.1	508
Sr Sampson:	Liar--Or if that won't do, I'll bring a Lawyer that .	267	FOR LOVE	III.1	509
Sr Sampson:	shall out-lie the Devil. And so I'll try whether my .	267	FOR LOVE	III.1	510
Scandal:	Pray lend it him, Madam--I'll tell you the	269	FOR LOVE	III.1	584
Mrs Fore:	to me before my Husband's Face? I'll Swear I'll tell him.	269	FOR LOVE	III.1	594
Scandal:	Do, I'll dye a Martyr, rather than disclaim my . . .	269	FOR LOVE	III.1	595
Scandal:	Passion. But come a little farther this way, and I'll				
	tell you	269	FOR LOVE	III.1	596
Mrs Fore:	Why then I'll speak my mind. Now as to	272	FOR LOVE	III.1	686
Mrs Fore:	me; why, I'll confess it does not displease me. Your Person	272	FOR LOVE	III.1	688
Mrs Fore:	O, fie--I'll Swear you're Impudent.	272	FOR LOVE	III.1	705
Scandal:	I'll Swear you're Handsome.	272	FOR LOVE	III.1	706
Ben:	Nay, an I love once, I'll stick like pitch; I'll tell				
	you that.	273	FOR LOVE	III.1	739
Ben:	Come, I'll sing you a Song of a Sailor.	273	FOR LOVE	III.1	740
Mrs Frail:	Hold, there's my Sister, I'll call her to hear it. . .	273	FOR LOVE	III.1	741
Mrs Frail:	Night; because I'll retire to my own Chamber, and think .	273	FOR LOVE	III.1	743
Mrs Frail:	If it won't interrupt you, I'll entertain you with a .	273	FOR LOVE	III.1	748
Ben:	come, my Lads, let's have a round, and I'll make one. .	275	FOR LOVE	III.1	797
Scandal:	Well, I'll try her--'tis she, here she comes.	276	FOR LOVE	IV.1	14
Angelica:	trick--I'll try--I would disguise to all the World a .	277	FOR LOVE	IV.1	58
Scandal:	for I can't resolve you; but I'll inform your Master. In .	278	FOR LOVE	IV.1	103
Scandal:	People. I hear Sir Sampson, you know your Cue; I'll .	278	FOR LOVE	IV.1	108
Sr Sampson:	the matter is with him, or I'll crack your Fools Skull. .	279	FOR LOVE	IV.1	136
Sr Sampson:	--Mad, I'll make him find his Senses.	279	FOR LOVE	IV.1	146
Jeremy:	Mr. Scandal is with him, Sir; I'll knock at the Door. .	279	FOR LOVE	IV.1	147
Sr Sampson:	I'll speak gently--Val, Val, do'st thou not	279	FOR LOVE	IV.1	156
Valentine:	--No matter how long--But I'll tell you one	280	FOR LOVE	IV.1	174
Sr Sampson:	need any body hold it?--I'll put it up in my Pocket, .	281	FOR LOVE	IV.1	231
Buckram:	O Lord, let me be gone; I'll not venture my self . .	282	FOR LOVE	IV.1	243
Mrs Frail:	Sister, do you stay with them; I'll find out my . . .	285	FOR LOVE	IV.1	351
Mrs Frail:	No, I'll leave you a-drift, and go which way you . .	286	FOR LOVE	IV.1	420
Mrs Frail:	on the Shore. But I'll tell you a hint that he has given	287	FOR LOVE	IV.1	457
Valentine:	Hush!--Interrupt me not--I'll whisper	288	FOR LOVE	IV.1	486
Valentine:	have told thee what's past,--Now I'll tell what's to .	208	FOR LOVE	IV.1	V489
Jeremy:	I'll take care, and--	290	FOR LOVE	IV.1	566
Angelica:	Mad as Valentine, I'll believe you love me, and the maddest	291	FOR LOVE	IV.1	587
Valentine:	If they are, I'll tell you what I think--get away all the	291	FOR LOVE	IV.1	594
Tattle:	Why de'e think I'll tell you, Sir! Read it in my Face? .	292	FOR LOVE	IV.1	612
Valentine:	about,--They are welcome, and I'll tell 'em so my self. (To	292	FOR LOVE	IV.1	617
Jeremy:	(to Scandal). I'll do't, Sir.	293	FOR LOVE	IV.1	667
Jeremy:	(to Mrs. Frail). You'll meet, Madam;--I'll take . .	293	FOR LOVE	IV.1	671
Angelica:	No, I'll stay with him--Mr. Scandal will protect me. .	293	FOR LOVE	IV.1	676
Scandal:	So I'll leave him to make use of the Discovery; and .	294	FOR LOVE	IV.1	691
Angelica:	(aside). Aye, but if I don't fit you, I'll be hang'd. .	294	FOR LOVE	IV.1	699
Jeremy:	Counterfeit, Madam! I'll maintain him to be as . . .	295	FOR LOVE	IV.1	737
Angelica:	But I'll tell you two things before I leave you; I am not	296	FOR LOVE	IV.1	791
Sr Sampson:	and I a happy Man. Odd, Madam, I'll love you as long as I	300	FOR LOVE	V.1	119
Sr Sampson:	let us find Children, and I'll find an Estate. . . .	300	FOR LOVE	V.1	129
Sr Sampson:	O Rogue! But I'll trust you. And will you	300	FOR LOVE	V.1	132
Angelica:	and if I find what you propose practicable; I'll give .	301	FOR LOVE	V.1	135
Sr Sampson:	I'll lend you the Bond,--You shall consult your Lawyer, .	301	FOR LOVE	V.1	138
Sr Sampson:	and I'll consult a Parson; Odzooks I'm a young Man: .	301	FOR LOVE	V.1	139
Sr Sampson:	Odzooks I'm a young Man, and I'll make it appear-- . .	301	FOR LOVE	V.1	140
Sr Sampson:	t'other Hand, and I'll mumble 'em, and kiss 'em till they	301	FOR LOVE	V.1	147
Tattle:	I'll make thy Fortune; say no more--Thou art a . . .	302	FOR LOVE	V.1	180
Jeremy:	Well, Sir, I'll go and tell her my Master's coming; .	303	FOR LOVE	V.1	215
Tattle:	No, no, let me alone for a Counterfeit;--I'll be . .	303	FOR LOVE	V.1	219
Tattle:	(aside) what do's the Old Prig mean? I'll banter him, and	304	FOR LOVE	V.1	263
Tattle:	I'll come and explain it to you.	305	FOR LOVE	V.1	298
Miss Prue:	A Fiddle of a Rod, I'll have a Husband; and if you . .	305	FOR LOVE	V.1	315
Miss Prue:	won't get me one, I'll get one for my self: I'll marry our	305	FOR LOVE	V.1	316
Foresight:	Did he so--I'll dispatch him for't presently; . . .	305	FOR LOVE	V.1	321
Ben:	Nay, I'll give you leave to guess--I'll undertake to make	306	FOR LOVE	V.1	350
Ben:	neither--But I'll sail as far as Ligorn, and back again, .	306	FOR LOVE	V.1	352
Ben:	Why then I'll tell you, There's a new wedding upon the .	307	FOR LOVE	V.1	358
Sr Sampson:	That he shall, or I'll burn his Globes--Body	308	FOR LOVE	V.1	395
Sr Sampson:	o' me, he shall be thy Father, I'll make him thy Father, and	308	FOR LOVE	V.1	396
Sr Sampson:	thou shalt make me a Father, and I'll make thee a Mother,	308	FOR LOVE	V.1	397
Valentine:	No; here's the Fool; and if occasion be, I'll give it .	310	FOR LOVE	V.1	497
Angelica:	No, I have it; and I'll use it, as I would every thing .	312	FOR LOVE	V.1	555
Angelica:	I'll advise you, how you may avoid such another. Learn to	312	FOR LOVE	V.1	571
Valentine:	I'll prevent that suspicion--For I intend to	313	FOR LOVE	V.1	608
Almeria:	If for my swelling Heart I can, I'll tell thee. . . .	329	M. BRIDE	I.1	109
Manuel:	I'll have a Priest shall preach her from her Faith, .	334	M. BRIDE	I.1	354
Manuel:	I'll have Enquiry made; his Friend may be	337	M. BRIDE	I.1	445
Manuel:	I'll have Enquiry made; perhaps his Friend	337	M. BRIDE	I.1	V445
Almeria:	Of Humane Bodies; for I'll mix with them, ...	339	M. BRIDE	II.1	75
Heli:	Of one complaining--There it sounds--I'll follow it. .	340	M. BRIDE	II.2	3
Osmyn-Alph:	I'll catch it 'ere it goes, and grasp her Shade. . . .	341	M. BRIDE	II.2	53
Almeria:	I've sworn I'll not wed Garcia; why d'ye force me? . .	341	M. BRIDE	II.2	74
Osmyn-Alph:	O I'll not ask, nor answer how, or why, ...	342	M. BRIDE	II.2	91
Osmyn-Alph:	To follow thee. I'll think, how we may meet	345	M. BRIDE	II.2	204
Osmyn-Alph:	I'll muse on that, lest I exceed in thinking. . . .	345	M. BRIDE	II.2	V230
Zara:	My Love. But to the Grave I'll follow thee--	346	M. BRIDE	II.2	243

I'll (continued)

Speaker	Quotation	PAGE	TITLE	ACT.SC	LINE
Zara:	Give me thy Love, I'll give thee Liberty.	348	M. BRIDE	II.2	327
Zara:	As I could wish; by Heav'n I'll be reveng'd.	348	M. BRIDE	II.2	350
Osmyn-Alph:	But as I may, I'll do. I have a Paper	352	M. BRIDE	III.1	108
Osmyn-Alph:	I'll treasure as more worth than Diadems,	353	M. BRIDE	III.1	V137
Zara:	Tell me, and thou shall see how I'll revenge	353	M. BRIDE	III.1	165
Zara:	Tell me, and thou shalt see how I'll revenge	353	M. BRIDE	III.1	V165
Zara:	Thee on this false one, how I'll stab and tear	353	M. BRIDE	III.1	166
Zara:	I'll try.	355	M. BRIDE	III.1	211
Zara:	Yet I'll be calm--Dark and unknown Betrayer!	360	M. BRIDE	III.1	439
Zara:	Confer with him. I'll quit you to the King.	360	M. BRIDE	III.1	452
Zara:	Or speak with him. I'll quit you to the King.	360	M. BRIDE	III.1	V452
Selim:	This Grant--and I'll acquaint you with the rest.	362	M. BRIDE	IV.1	60
Manuel:	Confesses it. By Heav'n I'll have him rack'd,	368	M. BRIDE	IV.1	294
Almeria:	I'll not let go, 'till you have spar'd my Husband.	369	M. BRIDE	IV.1	338
Almeria:	Let me go, let me fall, sink deep--I'll dig,	370	M. BRIDE	IV.1	347
Almeria:	I'll dig a Grave, and tear up Death; I will;	370	M. BRIDE	IV.1	348
Almeria:	I'll scrape 'till I collect his rotten Bones.	370	M. BRIDE	IV.1	349
Manuel:	Which I'll not hear, 'till I am more at peace.	370	M. BRIDE	IV.1	364
Almeria:	I'll catch it--hark! a Voice cries Murder! 'tis	371	M. BRIDE	IV.1	391
Almeria:	I'll catch it--hark! a Voice cries Murder! ah!	371	M. BRIDE	IV.1	V391
Almeria:	The Tomb it calls--I'll follow it, for there	371	M. BRIDE	IV.1	393
Almeria:	Me from the Tombs--I'll follow it, for there	371	M. BRIDE	IV.1	V393
Alonzo:	If't please your Lordship, I'll return, and say	371	M. BRIDE	IV.1	422
Alonzo:	I'll be so bold to borrow his Attire;	373	M. BRIDE	V.1	29
Manuel:	By Heav'n I'll meet, and counterwork this Treachery.	374	M. BRIDE	V.1	66
Manuel:	--Stay thee--I've farther thought--I'll add to	374	M. BRIDE	V.1	80
Manuel:	I'll be conducted thither--	374	M. BRIDE	V.1	86
Manuel:	I'll be conducted thither--mark me well--	374	M. BRIDE	V.1	V 86
Manuel:	Sudden I'll start, and dash her with her Guilt.	374	M. BRIDE	V.1	V86F
Manuel:	But see she comes; I'll shun th' Encounter; do	374	M. BRIDE	V.1	87
Manuel:	But see she comes; I'll shun th' Encounter; thou	374	M. BRIDE	V.1	V 87
Zara:	Think fit, I'll leave thee my Command to die.	375	M. BRIDE	V.1	127
Zara:	I'll give thee Freedom, if thou dar'st be free:	376	M. BRIDE	V.1	136
Gonsalez:	Th' Attempt: I'll steal, and do it unperceiv'd.	376	M. BRIDE	V.2	9
Gonsalez:	'Twere done--I'll crawl and sting him to the Heart;	376	M. BRIDE	V.2	12
Garcia:	But I'll omit no Care, nor Haste; and try	379	M. BRIDE	V.2	106
Gonsalez:	To aid my Son. I'll follow with the last	379	M. BRIDE	V.2	126
Zara:	I'll creep into his Bosom, lay me there;	381	M. BRIDE	V.2	206
Almeria:	Yes, yes, I know to mourn; I'll sluce this Heart,	382	M. BRIDE	V.2	243
Almeria:	I'll drink my glad Acknowledgment--	382	M. BRIDE	V.2	260
Almeria:	From his pale Lips; I'll kiss him e'er I drink,	382	M. BRIDE	V.2	267
Mirabell:	What you please. I'll play on to entertain you.	395	WAY WORLD	I.1	3
Fainall:	No, I'll give you your Revenge another time, when	395	WAY WORLD	I.1	4
Fainall:	you;--I'll look upon the Gamesters in the next Room.	397	WAY WORLD	I.1	100
Mirabell:	agreeable. I'll tell thee, Fainall, she once us'd me with that	399	WAY WORLD	I.1	163
Witwoud:	Wit: Nay, I'll do him Justice. I'm his Friend, I won't	403	WAY WORLD	I.1	291
Betty:	I'll tell him.	404	WAY WORLD	I.1	349
Mirabell:	Faith I'll do what I can for thee; and I'll pray that	407	WAY WORLD	I.1	460
Fainall:	Ay, I'll take a turn before Dinner.	409	WAY WORLD	I.1	509
Marwood:	By all my Wrongs I'll do't--I'll publish to	415	WAY WORLD	II.1	194
Fainall:	and any way, every way will make amends;--I'll	416	WAY WORLD	II.1	243
Fainall:	hate my Wife yet more, Dam her, I'll part with her, rob	416	WAY WORLD	II.1	244
Fainall:	where to another World. I'll marry thee--Be pacify'd	416	WAY WORLD	II.1	246
Mincing:	'Till I had the Cremp in my Fingers I'll vow Mem.	419	WAY WORLD	II.1	371
Mincing:	'Till I had the Cramp in my Fingers I'll vow Mem.	419	WAY WORLD	II.1	V371
Millamant:	peevish--Heigho! Now I'll be melancholly, as	422	WAY WORLD	II.1	476
Foible:	him; which I'll be sure to say has made him so enamour'd	423	WAY WORLD	II.1	522
Foible:	I'll be gone; I'm sure my Lady is at her Toilet, and can't	424	WAY WORLD	II.1	543
Foible:	seen me with you I'm sure she'll tell my Lady. I'll make	424	WAY WORLD	II.1	546
Lady Wish:	Ods my Life, I'll have him, I'll have him	427	WAY WORLD	III.1	102
Lady Wish:	murder'd. I'll have him poyson'd. Where does he eat? I'll	427	WAY WORLD	III.1	103
Lady Wish:	marry a Drawer to have him poyson'd in his Wine. I'll	427	WAY WORLD	III.1	104
Foible:	but (says he) I'll fit you for that, I warrant you (says he)	428	WAY WORLD	III.1	114
Foible:	I'll hamper you for that (says he) you and your old Frippery	428	WAY WORLD	III.1	115
Foible:	too (says he) I'll handle you--	428	WAY WORLD	III.1	116
Lady Wish:	Fellow? I'll be married to Morrow, I'll be	428	WAY WORLD	III.1	119
Lady Wish:	Frippery? Superannuated Frippery! I'll	428	WAY WORLD	III.1	128
Lady Wish:	Frippery the Villain; I'll reduce him to Frippery and Rags.	428	WAY WORLD	III.1	129
Lady Wish:	whole Court upon a Birth day. I'll spoil his Credit with his	428	WAY WORLD	III.1	134
Lady Wish:	a--Ha Foible? A swimminess in the Eyes--Yes, I'll	429	WAY WORLD	III.1	169
Lady Wish:	a--Ha Foible? A swimmingness in the Eyes--Yes, I'll	429	WAY WORLD	III.1	V169
Lady Wish:	Sir Rowland handsome? Let my Toilet be remov'd--I'll	429	WAY WORLD	III.1	171
Lady Wish:	dress above. I'll receive Sir Rowland here. Is he handsome?	429	WAY WORLD	III.1	172
Lady Wish:	Don't answer me. I won't know: I'll be surpriz'd. I'll be	429	WAY WORLD	III.1	173
Foible:	to his charge, I'll vow; and my Lady is so incens'd, that	430	WAY WORLD	III.1	209
Mrs Fain:	I'll go with you up the back Stairs, lest I shou'd	430	WAY WORLD	III.1	221
Marwood:	now I'll have none of him. Here comes the good Lady,	431	WAY WORLD	III.1	246
Lady Wish:	since 'tis your Judgment, I'll think on't again. I assure you	432	WAY WORLD	III.1	270
Lady Wish:	I'll propose it.	432	WAY WORLD	III.1	272
Lady Wish:	entertain 'em. I'll make all imaginable haste. Dear Friend	432	WAY WORLD	III.1	280
Millamant:	Well, 'tis a lamentable thing I'll swear, that one	432	WAY WORLD	III.1	296
Millamant:	I'll take my Death, Marwood, you are more Censorious,	433	WAY WORLD	III.1	323
Millamant:	what he can see in me. I'll take my Death, I think you are	434	WAY WORLD	III.1	358
Millamant:	me Melancholly--Now I'll be sad.	434	WAY WORLD	III.1	362
Millamant:	me Melancholick--Now I'll be sad.	434	WAY WORLD	III.1	V362
Millamant:	Dee say so? Then I'm resolv'd I'll have a Song to	434	WAY WORLD	III.1	365
Millamant:	I'll be gone.	436	WAY WORLD	III.1	435
Sir Wilful:	then; if I say't, I'll do't: But I	440	WAY WORLD	III.1	581
Marwood:	I'll follow you, Madam--Before Sir Wilfull	441	WAY WORLD	III.1	625
Fainall:	O, for that matter leave me to manage him; I'll	443	WAY WORLD	III.1	671
Fainall:	I'll set his hand in.	443	WAY WORLD	III.1	673
Fainall:	If the worst come to the worst,--I'll turn my	444	WAY WORLD	III.1	708
Fainall:	but I'll disown the Order. And since I take my leave of 'em,	444	WAY WORLD	III.1	721

I'll (continued)
Lady Wish:	won't sit--I'll walk--aye I'll walk from the door upon his	445	WAY WORLD	IV.1	20
Lady Wish:	be too sudden. I'll lie--aye, I'll lie down--I'll	445	WAY WORLD	IV.1	22
Lady Wish:	Yes, yes, I'll give the first Impression on a Couch--I wont	445	WAY WORLD	IV.1	24
Lady Wish:	Ods my life, I'll send him to her. Call her down,	445	WAY WORLD	IV.1	37
Lady Wish:	Foible; bring her hither. I'll send him as I go--When	445	WAY WORLD	IV.1	38
Millamant:	him hither,--just as you will Dear Foible.--I think I'll see	446	WAY WORLD	IV.1	61
Sir Wilful:	further acquaintance,--So for the present Cozen, I'll take	446	WAY WORLD	IV.1	77
Sir Wilful:	I'll return to my Company--	446	WAY WORLD	IV.1	79
Sir Wilful:	that--for if so be that I set on't, I'll do't. But only				
	for the	447	WAY WORLD	IV.1	84
Mrs Fain:	Nay, I'll swear you shall never lose so favourable	447	WAY WORLD	IV.1	87
Mrs Fain:	an opportunity, if I can help it. I'll leave you together				
	and	447	WAY WORLD	IV.1	88
Sir Wilful:	Your Servant, then with your leave I'll return	448	WAY WORLD	IV.1	149
Millamant:	Vanity! No--I'll fly and be follow'd to the	449	WAY WORLD	IV.1	160
Millamant:	over the threshold. I'll be solicited to the very last,				
	nay and	449	WAY WORLD	IV.1	164
Millamant:	an Air. Ah! I'll never marry, unless I am first	449	WAY WORLD	IV.1	180
Millamant:	more than Impossible--positively Mirabell, I'll lie a Bed in	449	WAY WORLD	IV.1	190
Mirabell:	Then I'll get up in a morning as early as I please.	449	WAY WORLD	IV.1	192
Millamant:	Well then--I'll take my death I'm in a horrid	452	WAY WORLD	IV.1	288
Millamant:	I'll endure you.	452	WAY WORLD	IV.1	290
Millamant:	thing you, I'll have you,--I won't be kiss'd, nor I won't be	452	WAY WORLD	IV.1	295
Petulant:	Stand off--I'll kiss no more Males,--I have	454	WAY WORLD	IV.1	355
Petulant:	next time your self--I'll go sleep.	454	WAY WORLD	IV.1	370
Witwoud:	by to morrow Morning, Pen me a Challenge--I'll carry it	454	WAY WORLD	IV.1	373
Petulant:	Dogs, and read Romances--I'll go to bed to my	454	WAY WORLD	IV.1	376
Sir Wilful:	Word, and I'll do't--Wilfull will do't, that's the Word--	455	WAY WORLD	IV.1	404
Lady Wish:	sleep, you Sot--Or as I'm a person, I'll have you				
	bastinado'd	457	WAY WORLD	IV.1	462
Sir Wilful:	Lead on little Tony--I'll follow thee my Anthony,	457	WAY WORLD	IV.1	476
Sir Wilful:	My Tantony, Sirrah thou sha't be my Tantony; and I'll	457	WAY WORLD	IV.1	477
Waitwell:	I'll do't. In three weeks he shall be bare-foot; in a	458	WAY WORLD	IV.1	521
Lady Wish:	your Passion by your Jealousie, I promise you I'll make you	460	WAY WORLD	IV.1	581
Lady Wish:	your Passion by your Jealousie, I promise you I'll make	460	WAY WORLD	IV.1	V581
Lady Wish:	fight,--I'll go in and Examine my Niece; I'll make her	461	WAY WORLD	IV.1	629
Waitwell:	must let me give you;--I'll go for a black box, which	461	WAY WORLD	IV.1	633
Waitwell:	Dead or Alive I'll come--and married we will be	461	WAY WORLD	IV.1	642
Foible:	Dear Madam, I'll beg pardon on my knees.	462	WAY WORLD	V.1	9
Foible:	Moment's patience--I'll Confess all. Mr. Mirabell seduc'd	462	WAY WORLD	V.1	25
Lady Wish:	Abigails and Andrews! I'll couple you, Yes, I'll baste you	463	WAY WORLD	V.1	52
Lady Wish:	together, you Pander--I'll Dukes-Place you, as	463	WAY WORLD	V.1	53
Mincing:	O yes Mem, I'll vouch any thing for your Ladyship's	465	WAY WORLD	V.1	121
Lady Wish:	make it up, Madam; ay, ay, I'll Compound. I'll give	468	WAY WORLD	V.1	238
Fainall:	I come to make demands,--I'll hear no	469	WAY WORLD	V.1	288
Sir Wilful:	fairer? If I have broke any thing, I'll pay for't, an it				
	cost a	470	WAY WORLD	V.1	318
Lady Wish:	Well, I'll swear I am something reviv'd at this	470	WAY WORLD	V.1	333
Sir Wilful:	--'Sheart, I'll call him in,--an I set on't	471	WAY WORLD	V.1	351
Marwood:	I'll know the bottom of it.	471	WAY WORLD	V.1	355
Marwood:	Not far Madam; I'll return immediately.	471	WAY WORLD	V.1	357
Sir Wilful:	Look up Man, I'll stand by you, 'sbud an she do	471	WAY WORLD	V.1	360
Fainall:	I'll answer you when I have the rest of it in my	473	WAY WORLD	V.1	448
Lady Wish:	from Ruine, from Want, I'll forgive all that's past; Nay	473	WAY WORLD	V.1	454
Lady Wish:	I'll consent to any thing to come, to be deliver'd from this	473	WAY WORLD	V.1	455
Mirabell:	be it as it may. I am resolv'd I'll serve you, may not	474	WAY WORLD	V.1	460
Lady Wish:	generous at last! But it is not possible. Hearkee. I'll				
	break	474	WAY WORLD	V.1	463
Foible:	Yes indeed Madam; I'll take my Bible-oath of it.	474	WAY WORLD	V.1	478
Fainall:	I'll be put off no longer--You thing that was	475	WAY WORLD	V.1	494
Fainall:	Madam, I'll be fool'd no longer.	475	WAY WORLD	V.1	503
Fainall:	S'death what's this to me? I'll not wait your private	475	WAY WORLD	V.1	517
Fainall:	Perfidious Fiend! then thus I'll be reveng'd.--(offers	476	WAY WORLD	V.1	556
Marwood:	Confusion, or I'll perish in the attempt.	477	WAY WORLD	V.1	566

I'm (287)
	Well, I'm his Advocate--by me he prays you,	35	OLD BATCH	PRO.	17
	For my sake then--but I'm in such Confusion,	35	OLD BATCH	PRO.	26
Bellmour:	the deeper the Sin the sweeter. Frank I'm amaz'd at thy good	39	OLD BATCH	I.1	92
Bellmour:	damnably in Love; I'm so uneasie for not seeing Belinda	40	OLD BATCH	I.1	133
Bellmour:	damnably in Love; I'm so uneasie for not having seen Belinda	40	OLD BATCH	I.1	V133
Sharper:	I'm sorry to see this, Ned: Once a Man comes to his	41	OLD BATCH	I.1	147
Bellmour:	Sharper, I'm glad to see thee.	41	OLD BATCH	I.1	149
Bellmour:	Woman's a Woman, and that's all. As such I'm sure I shall	41	OLD BATCH	I.1	173
Sir Joseph:	Well I am a Fool sometimes--But I'm sorry.	54	OLD BATCH	II.1	244
Belinda:	my Sol, I'm afraid you'l follow evil Courses.	55	OLD BATCH	II.2	52
Bellmour:	Ay, but if I'm Tongue-ty'd, I must have all my	59	OLD BATCH	II.2	181
Setter:	which Tribulation Spintext wears as I'm inform'd, upon	64	OLD BATCH	III.1	126
Sir Joseph:	mad? Or de'e think I'm mad? Agad for my part, I don't	68	OLD BATCH	III.1	265
Sir Joseph:	Teeth. Adsheart if he should come just now when I'm	68	OLD BATCH	III.1	278
Sharper:	Mony paid at sight: I'm come to return my Thanks--	68	OLD BATCH	III.1	285
Singer:	I die, if I'm not wholly blest.	71	OLD BATCH	III.2	8
Silvia:	I dare not speak till I believe you, and indeed I'm	72	OLD BATCH	III.2	53
Heartwell:	generally Masters in it: But I'm so newly entred, you	72	OLD BATCH	III.2	57
Heartwell:	a naked Truth, which I'm ashamed to discover.	72	OLD BATCH	III.2	66
Silvia:	No, no, I'm not such a Fool neither but I can keep my	73	OLD BATCH	III.2	109
Heartwell:	I'm impatient till it be done; I will not give my	74	OLD BATCH	III.2	138
Bellmour:	If we part so I'm mistaken.--Hold, hold,	81	OLD BATCH	IV.2	37
Bellmour:	may lie down;--quickly, for I'm afraid I shall have a Fit.	82	OLD BATCH	IV.2	87
Laetitia:	Does it hold you long? I'm afraid to carry you into	83	OLD BATCH	IV.2	90
Sir Joseph:	Nay, gad, I'll pick up; I'm resolv'd to make a	85	OLD BATCH	IV.3	61
Sir Joseph:	(aside). Nay, now I'm in--I can prattle like a	85	OLD BATCH	IV.3	97
Belinda:	Dear Araminta, I'm tir'd.	86	OLD BATCH	IV.3	100
Sir Joseph:	Free-loves! Sir Joseph, thou art a Mad-man. Agad, I'm in	86	OLD BATCH	IV.3	109
Araminta:	I'm amaz'd! This Insolence exceeds t'other;--	87	OLD BATCH	IV.3	156
Araminta:	I'm amaz'd! This Insolence exceeds t'other;--	87	OLD BATCH	IV.3	V156

I'm (continued)

Speaker	Text	PAGE	TITLE	ACT.SC	LINE
Vainlove:	No, Madam, I'm gone.--She knows her	88	OLD BATCH	IV.3	187
Fondlewife:	I'm come home.	89	OLD BATCH	IV.4	9
Fondlewife:	Nay, prithee, Dear, Ifeck I'm in haste.	89	OLD BATCH	IV.4	19
Laetitia:	(aside). Oh, I'm undone!	89	OLD BATCH	IV.4	26
Sir Joseph:	for I'm in haste.	89	OLD BATCH	IV.4	28
Fondlewife:	Oh Traytor! I'm astonished. Oh bloody-minded . . .	90	OLD BATCH	IV.4	59
Laetitia:	Dear Husband, I'm amaz'd:--Sure it's a good . . .	92	OLD BATCH	IV.4	114
Laetitia:	(aside). I'm so distracted, I can't think of a Lye. .	92	OLD BATCH	IV.4	119
Laetitia:	come near it, I'm afraid 'tis the Devil; indeed it has hoofs, . . .	92	OLD BATCH	IV.4	133
Fondlewife:	I'm afraid, 'tis the Flesh, thou Harlot. Deare, with the Pox. . . .	92	OLD BATCH	IV.4	136
Fondlewife:	called a Cuckold, Heh. Is it not so? Come, I'm .	94	OLD BATCH	IV.4	185
Heartwell:	I'm impatient till it be done.	97	OLD BATCH	V.1	13
Vainlove:	I'm sure he tells me Truth;--but I am not sure she told .	99	OLD BATCH	V.1	94
Setter:	Ay, I know her, Sir: At least, I'm sure I can fish it out .	99	OLD BATCH	V.1	103
Setter:	I warrant you, Sir, I'm instructed.	101	OLD BATCH	V.1	195
Setter:	Sir Joseph and the Captain too! undone, undone! I'm .	103	OLD BATCH	V.1	239
Sir Joseph:	her little Bubbies? And--A-gad, I'm so over-joy'd--And .	103	OLD BATCH	V.1	256
Sir Joseph:	I'm in the Ladies favours?--No matter, I'll make your .	103	OLD BATCH	V.1	261
Sir Joseph:	I'm in the Lady's favour?--No matter, I'll make your .	103	OLD BATCH	V.1 V261	
Capt Bluff:	--I'm capitulating with Mr. Setter for you. . .	104	OLD BATCH	V.1	280
Sharper:	I'm in haste now, but I'll come in at the Catastrophe. .	107	OLD BATCH	V.1 V393	
Lucy:	Hold your prating.--I'm thinking what Vocation . .	111	OLD BATCH	V.2	144
Bellmour:	But there is a fatality in Marriage.--For I find I'm .	111	OLD BATCH	V.2	155
Bellmour:	Come, take your Fellow-Travellers. Old George, I'm sorry	112	OLD BATCH	V.2	183
	So fares it with our Poet; and I'm sent	113	OLD BATCH	EPI.	5
Careless:	Where are the Women? Pox I'm weary of guzling, . .	127	DOUBL DLR	I.1	3
Careless:	Where are the Women? i'm weary of guzling, . .	127	DOUBL DLR	I.1 V	3
Careless:	I'm mistaken if there be not a Familiarity between . .	131	DOUBL DLR	I.1	153
Sir Paul:	good, strange! I swear I'm almost Tipsy--t'other .	131	DOUBL DLR	I.1	178
Sir Paul:	good, strange! I swear I'm almost Tipsy--t'other .	131	DOUBL DLR	I.1 V178	
Brisk:	against Wit, and I'm sorry for some Friends of mine that .	133	DOUBL DLR	I.1	239
Brisk:	I'm sorry for him, Deuce take me.	134	DOUBL DLR	I.1	282
Maskwell:	Nay, Madam, I'm gone, if you Relapse,--what . .	137	DOUBL DLR	I.1	383
Cynthia:	O Lord, not I, Madam; I'm content to be a . . .	139	DOUBL DLR	II.1	18
Cynthia:	Yes, yes, Madam, I'm not so Ignorant.-- . .	139	DOUBL DLR	II.1	35
Lady Froth:	Etymology.--But I'm the more amazed, to find you .	139	DOUBL DLR	II.1	40
Lady Froth:	I'm not asham'd to own it now; ah! it makes my heart .	140	DOUBL DLR	II.1	62
Brisk:	I'm everlastingly your humble Servant, Deuce take . .	140	DOUBL DLR	II.1	93
Lord Froth:	Wife? I'm afraid not.	141	DOUBL DLR	II.1	103
Brisk:	I'm wholly turn'd into Satyr. I confess I Write but seldom,	141	DOUBL DLR	II.1	116
Brisk:	I'm wholly turn'd into Satire. I confess I write but seldom,	141	DOUBL DLR	II.1 V116	
Brisk:	I'm your Humble Servant, let me perish.--I . .	142	DOUBL DLR	II.1	136
Lady Froth:	and Horace.--My Lord you must not be Jealous, I'm .	142	DOUBL DLR	II.1	139
Cynthia:	I'm thinking, that tho' Marriage makes Man and . .	142	DOUBL DLR	II.1	150
Cynthia:	I'm thinking, tho' Marriage makes Man and . .	142	DOUBL DLR	II.1 V150	
Sir Paul:	It concerns me, and only me;--besides, I'm not to .	144	DOUBL DLR	II.1	220
Sir Paul:	Heart--I'm sure if ever I should have Horns, they .	146	DOUBL DLR	II.1	281
Lord Touch:	(aside). I'm amaz'd, here must be something . .	152	DOUBL DLR	III.1	44
Maskwell:	I'm glad you're come, for I could not contain my . .	156	DOUBL DLR	III.1	200
Maskwell:	I'm afraid my frailty leans that way--but I don't .	156	DOUBL DLR	III.1	207
Maskwell:	By this Light, I'm serious; all raillery apart-- . .	156	DOUBL DLR	III.1	232
Careless:	Masquerade, when I'm satisfied she knew me, and I had no .	158	DOUBL DLR	III.1	306
Lady Ply:	privacy? I swear and declare in the face of the World I'm	159	DOUBL DLR	III.1	332
Lady Ply:	qualified in all those Circumstances, I'm sure I should .	159	DOUBL DLR	III.1	340
Lady Ply:	for I'm sure there's nothing in the World that I would .	159	DOUBL DLR	III.1	342
Careless:	For Heaven's sake, Madam--I'm quite out of . .	160	DOUBL DLR	III.1	370
Sir Paul:	I; but mine's soon over, and then I'm so sorry--O, Mr. .	160	DOUBL DLR	III.1	390
Sir Paul:	year; I'm sure I have found it so; and alas, what's once a	162	DOUBL DLR	III.1	434
Lord Froth:	True, as I'm a Person of Honour--for Heaven's . .	163	DOUBL DLR	III.1	486
Lady Ply:	I'm busie, Sir Paul, I wonder at your . . .	163	DOUBL DLR	III.1	491
Careless:	Sir Paul, harkee, I'm reasoning the matter you know; .	163	DOUBL DLR	III.1	493
Lady Froth:	Oh, infinitely better; I'm extremely beholding . .	164	DOUBL DLR	III.1	510
Lady Froth:	Oh, infinitely better; I'm extremely beholden . .	164	DOUBL DLR	III.1 V510	
Brisk:	I'm afraid that simile wont do in wet Weather-- . .	164	DOUBL DLR	III.1	517
Lady Froth:	I swear and vow I'm afraid so--And yet our . .	165	DOUBL DLR	III.1	547
Brisk:	Was that he then, I'm answered, if Jehu was a Hackney .	165	DOUBL DLR	III.1	549
Brisk:	Was he? I'm answered, if Jehu was a Hackney . .	165	DOUBL DLR	III.1 V549	
Cynthia:	thing but the very Devil, I'm inexorable: Only still I'll	169	DOUBL DLR	IV.1	61
Lady Ply:	challenges much more, I'm sure, than my illiterate Praises	169	DOUBL DLR	IV.1	83
Careless:	I'm almost at the end of my Cant, if she does not yield .	170	DOUBL DLR	IV.1	95
Sir Paul:	'Slife yonder's Sir Paul, but if he were not come, I'm .	171	DOUBL DLR	IV.1	128
Sir Paul:	so, I'm of that Opinion again; but I can neither find my .	171	DOUBL DLR	IV.1	157
Lady Ply:	I'm satisfied that my Cousin Mellefont has been . .	171	DOUBL DLR	IV.1	159
Cynthia:	(aside). I'm amazed to find her of our side, for I'm .	171	DOUBL DLR	IV.1	161
Sir Paul:	in the Case, I will Gads-bud. I'm overjoy'd to think I have	173	DOUBL DLR	IV.1	226
Cynthia:	I'm glad to see you so merry, Sir.	173	DOUBL DLR	IV.1	232
Sir Paul:	Merry, Gads-bud I'm serious, I'll give thee 500 [Pound] for	173	DOUBL DLR	IV.1	233
Cynthia:	I'm all Obedience, Sir, to your Commands. . . .	174	DOUBL DLR	IV.1	257
Brisk:	(sings). I'm sick with Love, ha ha ha, prithee come (walking	175	DOUBL DLR	IV.1	306
Brisk:	I'm sick with, &c.	175	DOUBL DLR	IV.1	308
Lady Ply:	O Mr. Careless, Mr. Careless, I'm ruin'd, I'm . .	177	DOUBL DLR	IV.1	390
Lady Ply:	O the unlucki'st Accident, I'm afraid I shan't . .	178	DOUBL DLR	IV.1	393
Lady Ply:	I'm in such a fright; the strangest Quandary . . .	178	DOUBL DLR	IV.1	396
Lady Ply:	and Premunire! I'm all over in a Universal Agitation, I .	178	DOUBL DLR	IV.1	397
Sir Paul:	O strange, what will become of me!--I'm so . .	179	DOUBL DLR	IV.1	459
Sir Paul:	Hold, stay, I beseech your Ladiship--I'm so . .	179	DOUBL DLR	IV.1	465
Sir Paul:	poor Sir Paul, I'm an Anabaptist, or a Jew, or what you	180	DOUBL DLR	IV.1	473
Careless:	Sir Paul, I'm glad I've met with you, 'gad I have . .	180	DOUBL DLR	IV.1	491
Sir Paul:	I can't tell you I'm so overjoy'd; come along with me .	181	DOUBL DLR	IV.1	508
Lord Touch:	Thou shalt enjoy it--if all I'm worth in . . .	189	DOUBL DLR	V.1	74
Lord Touch:	I'm sure Sir Paul's Consent will follow Fortune; I'll .	189	DOUBL DLR	V.1	76
Lord Froth:	No, my dear; I'm but just awake.-- . . .	201	DOUBL DLR	V.1	525
Brisk:	the Man in't already, I'm so full of the Wounds which .	201	DOUBL DLR	V.1	539

329

I'm   (continued)

		PAGE	TITLE	ACT.SC	LINE
Lady Touch:	O I'm betray'd,--save me, help me.	202	DOUEL DLR	V.1	558
Jeremy:	help me, I'm poor enough to be a Wit--Eut I was	217	FOR LOVE	I.1	41
Valentine:	of Fortune. And for the Wits, I'm sure I'm in a Condition	217	FOR LOVE	I.1	56
Valentine:	of Fortune. And for the Wits, I'm sure I am in a Condition	217	FOR LOVE	I.1 V	56
Scandal:	Aye? Why then I'm afraid Jeremy has Wit: For	219	FOR LOVE	I.1	120
Tattle:	that--Nay more (I'm going to say a bold Word now) I	227	FOR LOVE	I.1	410
Valentine:	Nay faith, I'm apt to believe him--Except	227	FOR LOVE	I.1	414
Scandal:	I'm resolv'd I'll ask her.	229	FOR LOVE	I.1	493
Valentine:	I'm sure.	231	FOR LOVE	I.1	575
Foresight:	Ha, How? Faith and troth I'm glad of it, and so I	236	FOR LOVE	II.1	29
Angelica:	her Nature. Uncle, I'm afraid you are not Lord of the	237	FOR LOVE	II.1	72
Foresight:	I'm sc perplex'd and vex'd, I am not fit to receive	239	FOR LOVE	II.1	164
Foresight:	past: Go Nurse, tell Sir Sampson I'm ready to wait on him.	239	FOR LOVE	II.1	166
Sr Sampson:	be--hah! old Merlin! body o' me, I'm so glad I'm	240	FOR LOVE	II.1	184
Mrs Frail:	and speak openly one to another; I'm afraid the World	248	FOR LOVE	II.1	487
Miss Prue:	Lavender mun--I'm resolv'd I won't let Nurse put	249	FOR LOVE	II.1	529
Mrs Frail:	O' my Soul, I'm afraid not--eh!--filthy	250	FOR LOVE	II.1	564
Mrs Fore:	I'm thoroughly Innocent.	251	FOR LOVE	II.1	579
Miss Prue:	No, indeed; I'm angry at you.--	252	FOR LOVE	II.1	633
Tattle:	Yes, I vow and swear I have: Lord, Madam, I'm the	255	FOR LOVE	III.1	81
Scandal:	And I'll answer for him; for I'm sure if he had, he	256	FOR LOVE	III.1	109
Tattle:	I'm very unfortunate.	258	FOR LOVE	III.1	195
Sr Sampson:	I'm glad on't: Where is he? I long to see him. Now, Mrs.	259	FOR LOVE	III.1	211
Sr Sampson:	him make haste--I'm ready to cry for Jcy.	259	FOR LOVE	III.1	215
Angelica:	I'm pretty even with him, Sir Sampson; for if ever I	260	FOR LOVE	III.1	245
Angelica:	If I marry, Sir Sampson, I'm for a good Estate with	260	FOR LOVE	III.1	253
Sr Sampson:	Faith and Troth you're a wise Wcman, and I'm	260	FOR LOVE	III.1	257
Ben:	Thank you Father, and I'm glad to see you.	260	FOR LOVE	III.1	272
Sr Sampson:	Odsbud, and I'm glad to see thee, kiss me Boy,	260	FOR LOVE	III.1	273
Ben:	Forsooth an you please--(Salutes her.) Nay Mistress, I'm	261	FOR LOVE	III.1	280
Ben:	Forsooth if you please--(Salutes her.) Nay Mistress, I'm	261	FOR LOVE	III.1 V280	
Ben:	No, I'm sorry for that.--But pray why are you so	263	FOR LOVE	III.1	380
Ben:	part d'ee see, I'm for carrying things above Board, I'm	263	FOR LOVE	III.1	388
Miss Prue:	But I'm sure it is nct so, for I'll speak scooner than	264	FOR LOVE	III.1	395
Miss Prue:	do what he will; I'm too big to be whipt, so I'll tell you	264	FOR LOVE	III.1	398
Scandal:	Alas, Mr. Foresight, I'm afraid all is not right--	267	FOR LOVE	III.1	513
Scandal:	Sir Sampson is hasty, very hasty;--I'm afraid he is not	267	FCR LOVE	III.1	520
Foresight:	gone again--And now I'm faint again; and pale again,	269	FOR LOVE	III.1	609
Scandal:	I have no great Opinion of my self; yet I think, I'm	272	FOR LOVE	III.1	690
Scandal:	I have no great Opinion of my self; but I think, I'm	272	FOR LOVE	III.1 V690	
Mrs Fore:	--that I'm afraid you have a great many Confederates.	272	FOR LOVE	III.1	703
Scandal:	Faith, I'm sound.	272	FOR LOVE	III.1	704
Ben:	don't think I'm false-hearted, like a Land-man. A Sailor	273	FOR LOVE	III.1	732
Scandal:	I'm afraid the Physician is not willing you shou'd	277	FOR LOVE	IV.1	50
Angelica:	(aside). Say you so; nay, then I'm convinc'd: And if I	277	FOR LOVE	IV.1	66
Angelica:	without I suck the Poyson from his Wounds, I'm	277	FOR LOVE	IV.1	75
Jeremy:	refrain Tears when I think of him, Sir; I'm as melancholy	279	FOR LOVE	IV.1	132
Sr Sampson:	indispcsed: But I'm glad thou'rt better, honest Val.	281	FOR LOVE	IV.1	203
Scandal:	she cou'd grant 'em.--Madam, I'm your humble Servant,	284	FOR LOVE	IV.1	337
Scandal:	I'm apt to believe there is something mysterious in his	285	FCR LOVE	IV.1	344
Ben:	No, I'm pleas'd well enough, now I have found you,--	285	FOR LOVE	IV.1	359
Ben:	senses, d'ee see; for ought as I perceive I'm like to be				
	finely	286	FOR LOVE	IV.1	414
Ben:	--I'm glad you shew your self, Mistress:--Let	287	FOR LOVE	IV.1	436
Jeremy:	Two Hours--I'm sure I left him just now, in a Humour	295	FOR LOVE	IV.1	754
Jeremy:	Two Hours--I'm sure I left him just now, in the Humour	295	FOR LOVE	IV.1 V754	
Valentine:	Go see, you Sot. I'm very glad that I can move your	295	FOR LOVE	IV.1	759
Valentine:	Stupidity! You know the Penalty of all I'm	296	FOR LOVE	IV.1	772
Valentine:	worth must pay for the Confession of my Senses; I'm	296	FOR LOVE	IV.1	773
Angelica:	How! I'm glad on't--If he has a mind I should	297	FCR LOVE	V.1	5
Sr Sampson:	outsides. Hang your side-Box Beaus; no, I'm none of those,	298	FOR LOVE	V.1	34
Angelica:	Courage at this time. To tell you the Truth, I'm weary of	298	FOR LOVE	V.1	46
Sr Sampson:	and I'll consult a Parson; Odzooks I'm a Young Man;	301	FOR LOVE	V.1	139
Sr Sampson:	Odzooks I'm a young Man, and I'll make it appear--	301	FOR LOVE	V.1	140
Sr Sampson:	very Handsom, and I'm very Young, and very Lusty--	301	FOR LOVE	V.1	142
Jeremy:	O Sir, for that Sir, 'tis my chief Talent; I'm as secret	302	FCB LOVE	V.1	190
Jeremy:	comply with any thing to please him. Poor Lady, I'm	302	FOR LOVE	V.1	202
Miss Prue:	O Mr. Tattle, are you here! I'm glad I have found	303	FOB LOVE	V.1	222
Miss Prue:	thing, till I'm as tired as any thing in the World.	303	FOR LOVE	V.1	224
Tattle:	Sir, I beg your Pardon, I'm in haste--	304	FOR LOVE	V.1	276
Tattle:	Who I, Sir? I'm an absolute Stranger to you and your	305	FOR LOVE	V.1	284
Tattle:	--And I'm going to be Married just now, yet did not	305	FOR LOVE	V.1	293
Miss Prue:	way or other. Oh! methinks I'm sick when I think of a	305	FOB LOVE	V.1	308
Miss Prue:	Life: For when I'm awake, it makes me wish and long, and	305	FOR LOVE	V.1	310
Ben:	That may be--but I'm sure it is as I tell you.	307	FOR LOVE	V.1	366
Sr Sampson:	and I'm Lord of the Ascendant. Odd, you're an old Fellow,	307	FOB LOVE	V.1	382
Foresight:	I'm Thunder-strook! You are not married to my	307	FOR LOVE	V.1	388
Mrs Fore:	I'm glad to hear you have so much Fire in	308	FOB LOVE	V.1	408
Tattle:	Poor Woman! Gad I'm sorry for her too; for I have no	309	FOR LOVE	V.1	466
Sr Sampson:	your Wedding Night? I'm an older Fellow than you, and	310	FOB LOVE	V.1	485
Ben:	one another. I'm sorry for the Young Man with all my	310	FOR LOVE	V.1	489
Valentine:	Sir, I'm come to acknowledge my Errors, and ask	310	FOR LOVE	V.1	500
Scandal:	No really, Sir; I'm his Witness, it was all Counterfeit.	311	FOR LOVE	V.1	506
Sr Sampson:	You're an illiterate Fool, and I'm another, and	313	FOB LOVE	V.1	583
Sr Sampson:	You're an illiterate Fool, and I'm another,	313	FOR LOVE	V.1 V583	
Tattle:	I'm indebted to you for my Happiness.	313	FOB LOVE	V.1	591
	I'm sure 'tis some such Latin Name they give 'em,	315	FOR LOVE	EPI.	13
Almeria:	I feel I'm more at large,	331	M. BRIDE	I.1	202
Manuel:	By Heav'n thou lov'st me, and I'm pleas'd thou do'st:	333	M. BRIDE	I.1	275
Osmyn-Alph:	Her Lips with mine--'Tis she, I'm not deceiv'd;	341	M. BRIDE	II.2	69
Osmyn-Alph:	I'm fortunate indeed--my Friend too safe!	344	M. BRIDE	II.2 V170	
Leonora:	Or I'm deceiv'd, or I beheld the Glimpse	344	M. BRIDE	II.2	191
Osmyn-Alph:	How I'm not call'd Alphonso, now, but Osmyn;	345	M. BRIDE	II.2	207
Osmyn-Alph:	Zara! I'm betray'd	353	M. BRIDE	III.1	146
Osmyn-Alph:	Or take thee into mine, while I'm thus manacled	355	M. BRIDE	III.1 V240	

330

I've   (continued)
   Scandal: Come, Valentine, I'll go with you; I've something in   . . 259 FOR LOVE   III.1 231
   Ben: fair a Face, as a Citizen or a Courtier; but for all
                   that, I've . . . . 273 FOR LOVE   III.1 735
   Ben: Mess, I've had such a Hurricane upon your account   . . 285 FOR LOVE   IV.1   360
   Almeria: I've read, that things inanimate have mov'd, ... 326 M. BRIDE   I.1   3
   Garcia: I've heard with Admiration, of your Friendship;   . . . 338 M. BRIDE   II.1   13
   Almeria: I've sworn I'll not wed Garcia; why d'ye force me? . . 341 M. BRIDE   II.2   74
   Zara: For all I've done, and all I have endur'd, ... 346 M. BRIDE   II.2   274
   Heli: I've learn'd, there are Disorders ripe for Mutiny   . . 351 M. BRIDE   III.1 64
   Heli: For your Escape. Mean time, I've thought already   . . . 352 M. BRIDE   III.1 98
   Osmyn-Alph: I've been to blame, and question'd with Impiety   . . . 352 M. BRIDE   III.1 125
   Zara: To give, than I've already lost. But as   . . . . . 355 M. BRIDE   III.1 216
   Zara: To give, than I've already lost. But now   . . . . . 355 M. BRIDE   III.1 V216
   Zara: 'Tis plain, I've been abus'd--Death and Destruction! . 359 M. BRIDE   III.1 398
   Zara: Himself. I've been deceiv'd. The publick Safety   . . . 360 M. BRIDE   III.1 449
   Zara: I've been deceiv'd. The publick Safety now   . . . . . 360 M. BRIDE   III.1 V449
   Zara: My self of what I've undertaken; now, ... 364 M. BRIDE   IV.1   141
   Zara: I've heard, her Charity did once extend   . . . . . 365 M. BRIDE   IV.1   181
   Gonsalez: And try howe'er, if I've divin'd aright.   . . . . . 367 M. BRIDE   IV.1   238
   Gonsalez: I've seen thy Sword do noble Execution.   . . . . . 372 M. BRIDE   IV.1   430
   Gonsalez: Away, I've not been seen--haste good Alonzo.   . . . . 372 M. BRIDE   IV.1   442
   Gonsalez: And say, I've not been seen--haste good Alonzo.   . . 372 M. BRIDE   IV.1 V442
   Manuel: --Stay thee--I've farther thought--I'll add to   . . . 374 M. BRIDE   V.1   80
   Zara: When I've concluded on my self, if I   . . . . . . 375 M. BRIDE   V.1   126
   Gonsalez: For thee I've been ambitious, base, and bloody: . . . 378 M. BRIDE   V.2   83
   Gonsalez: For thee I've plung'd into this Sea of Sin;   . . . . 378 M. BRIDE   V.2   84
   Alonzo: My Lord, I've thought how to conceal the Body;   . . . 378 M. BRIDE   V.2   96
   Alonzo: Or who can wound the Dead?--I've from the Body,   . . . 379 M. BRIDE   V.2   114
   Zara: The King; tell him, what he requir'd, I've done: . . 380 M. BRIDE   V.2   152
   Selim: I've sought in vain, the King is no where, to   . . . 380 M. BRIDE   V.2   173
   Selim: I've sought in vain, for no where can the King   . . . 380 M. BRIDE   V.2 V173
   Almeria: And living? yes, I will; I've been abus'd   . . . . . 383 M. BRIDE   V.2   295
   Almeria: I've leisure, now, to mark your sev'ral Paces,   . . . 385 M. BRIDE   EPI.   5
   Fainall: --I believe you; I'm convinc'd I've done you wrong;   . 416 WAY WORLD II.1   242
   Witwoud: Not I--Yes, I think it is he--I've almost   . . . . . 436 WAY WORLD III.1 441
   Sir Wilful: Brother. 'Sheart, I've suspected this--By'r Lady I   . 439 WAY WORLD III.1 539
                 In shoals, I've mark'd 'em judging in the Pit;   . . . 479 WAY WORLD EPI.   11
Iambicks (1)
   Brisk: but when I do--keen Iambicks I'gad. But my Lord   . . . 141 DOUBL DLR II.1   117
Ice (4)
   Belinda: I have broke the ice for you, Mr. Vainlove, and so I   . . 87   OLD BATCH IV.3   142
   Sir Paul: Chaste as Ice, but you are melted now, and false as Water. . 179 DOUBL DLR IV.1   431
   Almeria: But I am arm'd, with Ice around my Heart, ... 331 M. BRIDE   I.1   217
   Almeria: O, I am struck; thy Words are Bolts of Ice,   .✓ . . . 358 M. BRIDE   III.1 367
Icicles (1)
   Zara: Cold, cold; my Veins are Icicles and Frost.   . . . . 381 M. BRIDE   V.2   205
Ideot (1)
   Sharper: Death, it can't be--An Oaf, an Ideot, a Wittal.   . . . 102 OLD BATCH V.1   205
Idiot (2)
   Lady Wish: Grant me patience! I mean the Spanish Paper Idiot,
                   Complexion . . . . 425 WAY WORLD III.1 12
   Marwood: draw him like an Idiot, a Driveler, with a Bib and Bells. . 431 WAY WORLD III.1 237
Idiot-Race (1)
                 For Fortune favours all her Idiot-Race: . . . . . 393 WAY WORLD PRO.   6
Idle (6)
   Angelica: idle Divinations. I'll swear you are a Nusance to the   . 237 FOR LOVE   II.1   78
   Sr Sampson: of these young idle Rogues about the Town. Odd, there's   . 299 FOR LOVE   V.1   53
   Almeria: Not to be warm'd with Words, nor idle Eloquence.   . . 331 M. BRIDE   I.1   218
   Almeria: Not to be warm'd with Words, nor idle Eloquence.   . . . 331 M. BRIDE   I.1 V218
   Manuel: This idle Vow hangs on her Woman's Fears.   . . . . 334 M. BRIDE   I.1   353
   Millamant: Ah! Idle Creature, get up when you will--   . . . . 450 WAY WORLD IV.1   193
Idleness (1)
   Mirabell: Fools; Things who visit you from their excessive Idleness; 421 WAY WORLD II.1   434
Idlers (1)
   Bellmour: nothing. Come come, leave Business to Idlers, and Wisdom   . 37   OLD BATCH I.1   22
Idly (2)
   Belinda: Oh you have raved, talked idly, and all in   54   OLD BATCH I.2   4
   Lady Touch: My Lord, you hear him--he talks Idly.   . . . . . . 186 DOUBL DLR IV.2   117
Idol (2)
   Maskwell: there was Revenge in view; that Womans Idol had defil'd   . 137 DOUBL DLR I.1   375
   Mirabell: Actions? To save that Idol Reputation. If the   . . . 417 WAY WORLD II.1   266
Idolatry (1)
   Vainlove: by all our Protestant Husbands for flat Idolatry--But   . 39   OLD BATCH I.1   68
Idols (2)
   Araminta: Rather poor silly Idols of your own making, which,   . . 58   OLD BATCH II.2   146
If (670)

                 Hang me if I know what he prays, or how!   35   OLD BATCH PRO.   20
                 Well, the Deuce take me, if I han't forgot it.   . . . 35   OLD BATCH PRO.   22
                 Because, you know, if it be damn'd to day, ... 35   OLD BATCH PRO.   24
   Bellmour: Why faith I think it will do well enough--If the   . . 38   OLD BATCH I.1   55
   Vainlove: if you can make Alderman Fondlewife of your Perswasion,   . 39   OLD BATCH I.1   69
   Bellmour: much more agreeable, if you can counterfeit his Habit to
                   blind 39   OLD BATCH I.1   88
   Vainlove: Never doubt it; for if the Spirit of Cuckoldom be   . . 40   OLD BATCH I.1   102
   Vainlove: Ay, you may take him for good-and-all if you   . . . 40   OLD BATCH I.1   113
   Bellmour: like her; for the Devil take me if I don't love all the   . 41   OLD BATCH I.1   174
   Bellmour: refuse to kiss a Lap-Dog, if it were preliminary to the Lips 44   OLD BATCH I.1   261
   Sharper: Or omit playing with her Fan, and cooling her if   . . 44   OLD BATCH I.1   263
   Bellmour: Well come off George, if at any time you should be   . . 44   OLD BATCH I.1   286
   Sharper: Why if whoring be purging--as you call it--then I   . . 44   OLD BATCH I.1   291
   Bellmour: Hang him, no, he a Draggon! if he be 'tis a very   . . 46   OLD BATCH I.1   351
   Sir Joseph: with all my Heart, Blood and Guts Sir; and if you did but . 48   OLD BATCH II.1   36
   Sir Joseph: Purpose, if he han't frighted it out of my memory. Hem!   . 49   OLD BATCH II.1   53
   Sir Joseph: You are only pleas'd to say so Sir--But pray if I   . . 49   OLD BATCH II.1   79
   Sir Joseph: the Devil--God bless us--almost if he be by. Ah--had he   . 50   OLD BATCH II.1   123

If   (continued)

Speaker	Text	PAGE	TITLE	ACT.SC	LINE
Sir Joseph:	the Devil--bless us--almost if he be by. Ah--had he	50	OLD BATCH	II.1	V123
Sharper:	If he had Sir, what then? he could have done no	50	OLD BATCH	II.1	125
Sharper:	How Sir! I make a doubt, if there be at this Day a	52	OLD BATCH	II.1	183
Capt Bluff:	by the Wars--Took no more notice, than as if Nol. Bluffe	53	OLD BATCH	II.1	204
Sir Joseph:	Ay, this damn'd Modesty of yours--Agad if	53	OLD BATCH	II.1	214
Araminta:	If Love be the Fever which you mean; kind Heav'n	54	OLD BATCH	II.2	8
Araminta:	--Sure if I had not pinch'd you till you wak'd, you	55	OLD BATCH	II.2	43
Footman:	No, Madam, they sent before, to know if you were	56	OLD BATCH	II.2	79
Araminta:	But if you continue your Humour, it won't be very	57	OLD BATCH	II.2	86
Araminta:	then we are in great danger of being dull--If my Musick-master	58	OLD BATCH	II.2	152
Belinda:	once before--If you must talk impertinently, for Heav'ns	59	OLD BATCH	II.2	168
Bellmour:	Talk to your self--You had better let me speak; for if my	59	OLD BATCH	II.2	177
Bellmour:	Ay, but if I'm Tongue-ty'd, I must have all my	59	OLD BATCH	II.2	181
Araminta:	If Mr. Gavot will walk with us in the Garden, we'll have	60	OLD BATCH	II.2	207
Araminta:	If Mr. Gavot will walk with us into the Garden, we'll have	60	OLD BATCH	II.2	V207
Lucy:	Yes Yes, come, I warrant him, if you will go in and be	60	OLD BATCH	III.1	2
Lucy:	--a' receiv'd it, as if 'thad been a Letter from his	61	OLD BATCH	III.1	23
Vainlove:	He's talking to himself, I think; Prithee lets try if	62	OLD BATCH	III.1	61
Vainlove:	peace--I should not esteem a Pardon if too easie won.	63	OLD BATCH	III.1	101
Vainlove:	peace--I should not esteem a Pardon if too easily won.	63	OLD BATCH	III.1	V101
Bellmour:	But how the Devil dost thou expect to get her if	63	OLD BATCH	III.1	110
Setter:	Why if I were known, I might come to be a great	65	OLD BATCH	III.1	158
Capt Bluff:	for the Mony, and if you would look me in the Face again	67	OLD BATCH	III.1	249
Capt Bluff:	ensue--If he refuse, tell him---But whisper that--Tell	68	OLD BATCH	III.1	260
Sir Joseph:	mischief--For he was a devilish cholerick Fellow: And if	68	OLD BATCH	III.1	274
Sir Joseph:	mischief done, that's flat. And yet I believe if you had been	68	OLD BATCH	III.1	276
Sir Joseph:	Teeth. Adsheart if he should come just now when I'm	68	OLD BATCH	III.1	278
Sir Joseph:	self--I'll give him the Lie if you'll stand to it.	69	OLD BATCH	III.1	307
Sir Joseph:	I grant you--Not to that Face by the Lord Harry--If	70	OLD BATCH	III.1	357
Singer:	I die, if I'm not wholly blest.	71	OLD BATCH	III.2	8
Singer:	Do not--do not--if you Love me	71	OLD BATCH	III.2	V 13
Silvia:	If you could Sing and Dance so, I should love to look	72	OLD BATCH	III.2	30
Silvia:	Must you lie then, if you say you Love me?	72	OLD BATCH	III.2	61
Silvia:	You look ready to fright one, and talk as if your Passion	72	OLD BATCH	III.2	68
Silvia:	Indeed if I were well assur'd you lov'd; but how can I	73	OLD BATCH	III.2	74
Heartwell:	of thy Sex, if their Fools are not known by this Party-coloured	73	OLD BATCH	III.2	77
Heartwell:	informed) very troublesome to everybody else. If this be	73	OLD BATCH	III.2	83
Silvia:	Nay if you would Marry me, you should not come to	73	OLD BATCH	III.2	92
Heartwell:	I am--However, I find I am pretty sure of her consent, if	73	OLD BATCH	III.2	97
Silvia:	Nay, but if you love me, you must Marry me; what	73	OLD BATCH	III.2	100
Heartwell:	Well, farewell then--if I can get out of her sight I	74	OLD BATCH	III.2	129
Heartwell:	Well, farewell then--if I can get out of sight I	74	OLD BATCH	III.2	V129
Lucy:	if he had been going for a Midwife.	74	OLD BATCH	III.2	148
Fondlewife:	--Nay look you now if she does not weep--'tis the fondest	78	OLD BATCH	IV.1	98
Laetitia:	indeed you sant. Nykin--if you don't go, I'le think	78	OLD BATCH	IV.1	132
Vainlove:	I should disappoint her if I did not--By her	80	OLD BATCH	IV.1	188
Servant:	Here's a Chair, Sir, if you please to repose your self.	80	OLD BATCH	IV.2	1
Bellmour:	If we part so I'm mistaken.--Hold, hold,	81	OLD BATCH	IV.2	37
Laetitia:	be mistaken after all this.--A handsome Fellow if he had	81	OLD BATCH	IV.2	43
Laetitia:	We are all liable to Mistakes, Sir: If you own it to be so,	81	OLD BATCH	IV.2	46
Laetitia:	prejudice of her Reputation--You look as if you had	82	OLD BATCH	IV.2	64
Laetitia:	Nay, don't swear if you'd have me believe you; but	82	OLD BATCH	IV.2	69
Belinda:	Creature, I warrant, was as full of Courtesies, as if I had	84	OLD BATCH	IV.3	40
Belinda:	Creature, I warrant, was as full of Curtsies, as if I had	84	OLD BATCH	IV.3	V 40
Sir Joseph:	fear it;--that is, if I can but think on't: Truth is, I	85	OLD BATCH	IV.3	73
Belinda:	rubb'd his Eyes, since break of Day neither, he looks as if	86	OLD BATCH	IV.3	130
Footman:	if your Ladiship would have the Coach come again for	88	OLD BATCH	IV.3	207
Fondlewife:	If you will tarry a Moment, till I fetch my Papers, I'll wait	90	OLD BATCH	IV.4	43
Sir Joseph:	I was in most danger of being ravish'd, if you go	90	OLD BATCH	IV.4	62
Fondlewife:	his heart, at least, if not a French-man.	91	OLD BATCH	IV.4	75
Bellmour:	(peeping). Damn'd Chance! If I had gone a-Whoring	92	OLD BATCH	IV.4	109
Laetitia:	of your Embraces again, my Dear, if ever I saw his face	93	OLD BATCH	IV.4	151
Laetitia:	if I can clear my own innocence to my own Deare.	93	OLD BATCH	IV.4	169
Fondlewife:	Humph, Nay, if you mince the matter once, and	94	OLD BATCH	IV.4	190
Laetitia:	break my heart, if you talk of parting.	95	OLD BATCH	IV.4	231
Laetitia:	won't you speak to me, cruel Nykin? Indeed, I'll die, if	95	OLD BATCH	IV.4	246
Fondlewife:	I'll show you the way out of my house, if you please. Come,	96	OLD BATCH	IV.4	269
Bellmour:	She still is Vertuous, if she's so believ'd.	96	OLD BATCH	IV.4	274
Heartwell:	I'll pay him well, if you'll break the Matter to him.	97	OLD BATCH	V.1	20
Bellmour:	Rogue am I! Oh, what Sport will be here, if I can persuade	97	OLD BATCH	V.1	24
Lucy:	Reputation; And can you blame her if she stop it up with a	98	OLD BATCH	V.1	49
Lucy:	Reputation; And can you blame her if she make it up with a	98	OLD BATCH	V.1	V 49
Bellmour:	good Quality.--But to the purpose, if you will give	98	OLD BATCH	V.1	65
Bellmour:	--If you do, I'll spoil all.--I have some private	98	OLD BATCH	V.1	68
Lucy:	you; but if you do deceive me, the Curse of all kind,	98	OLD BATCH	V.1	76
Vainlove:	And so I remember in the Park.--She had reason, if I	99	OLD BATCH	V.1	97
Vainlove:	Pox o' my sawcy Credulity.--If I have lost	100	OLD BATCH	V.1	125
Vainlove:	her, I deserve it. But if Confession and Repentance be of	100	OLD BATCH	V.1	126
Vainlove:	did a little while ago.--Look yonder.--A-gad, if	100	OLD BATCH	V.1	172
Sir Joseph:	Ay; Do, do, Captain, if you think fit.--You	101	OLD BATCH	V.1	183
Sir Joseph:	Ay; Do, do, Captain, if you think fitting.--You	101	OLD BATCH	V.1	V183
Sir Joseph:	if I would carry a Challenge? Honour is your Province,	101	OLD BATCH	V.1	192
Setter:	--And, for my part, if I meet Sir Joseph with a Purse	102	OLD BATCH	V.1	233
Sir Joseph:	and to speak, is but loss of time; but if there be occasion,	103	OLD BATCH	V.1	244
Heartwell:	hold:--If he shou'd not, I were a Fool to discover it.--	104	OLD BATCH	V.1	299
Heartwell:	Death: D'ye mock me? Heark-ye: If either you	105	OLD BATCH	V.1	321
Setter:	Sublimate, if you please, Sir: I think my Atchievments	105	OLD BATCH	V.1	334
Setter:	mine. Here's Company coming, if you'll walk this way,	106	OLD BATCH	V.1	352
Sharper:	Hist,--Bellmour: If you'll bring the Ladies, make	107	OLD BATCH	V.1	390
Araminta:	Hang me, if I pity you; you are right enough	109	OLD BATCH	V.2	61
Heartwell:	If Sylvia had not been your Whore, my Wife might have	109	OLD BATCH	V.2	67

If   (continued)

Speaker	Text	PAGE	TITLE	ACT.SC	LINE
Heartwell:	If Sylvia had not been your Mistress, my Wife might have	109	OLD BATCH	V.2 V	67
Vainlove:	And if Sylvia had not been your Wife, my Whore	109	OLD BATCH	V.2	69
Vainlove:	And if Sylvia had not been your Wife, my Mistress	109	OLD BATCH	V.2 V	69
	If loss of that should follow want of Wit,	113	OLD BATCH	EPI.	13
	If he's an Ass, he will be Try'd by's Peers.	113	OLD BATCH	EPI.	16
	A Barbarous Device, to try if Spouse,	125	DOUBL DLR	PRO.	5
	To know, if it be truly born of Wit.	125	DOUBL DLR	PRO.	11
	For if his Muse has play'd him false, the worst	125	DOUBL DLR	PRO.	33
	You Husbands Judge, if that, be to be Curs'd.	125	DOUBL DLR	PRO.	35
Careless:	No faith, but your Fools grow noisy--and if a	127	DOUBL DLR	I.1	7
Careless:	No faith, but your Fools grow noisie--and if a	127	DOUBL DLR	I.1 V	7
Brisk:	Oh, my dear Mellefont, let me perish, if thou art not the	128	DOUBL DLR	I.1	33
Brisk:	of Wine,--the Deuce take me if there were three good	128	DOUBL DLR	I.1	35
Brisk:	want of Apprehension: The Deuce take me if I tell you.	128	DOUBL DLR	I.1	42
Mellefont:	We'll come immediately, if you'll but go in, and	128	DOUBL DLR	I.1	46
Brisk:	But the Deuce take me if I say a good thing till you come.--	128	DOUBL DLR	I.1	51
Mellefont:	may not work her to her Interest. And if you chance to	130	DOUBL DLR	I.1	127
Careless:	I'm mistaken if there be not a Familiarity between	131	DOUBL DLR	I.1	153
Brisk:	Ay, my Lord, it's a sign I hit you in the Teeth, if you	132	DOUBL DLR	I.1	210
Lord Touch:	Sir Paul, if you please we'll retire to the	132	DOUBL DLR	I.1	216
Brisk:	holding your sides, and Laughing as if you would bepiss	134	DOUBL DLR	I.1	255
Brisk:	holding your sides, and Laughing as if you would--well--	134	DOUBL DLR	I.1 V255	
Brisk:	thing, Laughing all the while as if you were ready to die	134	DOUBL DLR	I.1	268
Careless:	No; for if it were a witty thing, I should not expect	134	DOUBL DLR	I.1	271
Maskwell:	Nay, Madam, I'm gone, if you Relapse,--what	137	DOUBL DLR	I.1	383
Maskwell:	lay a stronger Plot: if I gain a little time, I shall not want	138	DOUBL DLR	I.1	419
Lady Froth:	O Inconsistent! In Love, and not Write! if my	139	DOUBL DLR	II.1	20
Lady Froth:	would that have been, if my Lord and I should never	139	DOUBL DLR	II.1	23
Lady Froth:	those Two hard Words? If you don't, I'll explain	139	DOUBL DLR	II.1	33
Brisk:	Biddy! I'gad very pretty--Deuce take me if your	142	DOUBL DLR	II.1	130
Cynthia:	Then I find its like Cards, if either of us have a good	142	DOUBL DLR	II.1	162
Singer:	Yet she's vext if I give over;	143	DOUBL DLR	II.1	180
Sir Paul:	Heart--I'm sure if ever I should have Horns, they	146	DOUBL DLR	II.1	281
Lady Ply:	you have to answer for, if you should provoke me to	147	DOUBL DLR	II.1	320
Lady Ply:	it is no sin to them that don't think it so;--indeed, If	147	DOUBL DLR	II.1	348
Lady Ply:	I did not think it a sin,--but still my honour, if it were	147	DOUBL DLR	II.1	349
Lady Ply:	how can I help it, if I have Charms? And how can you	148	DOUBL DLR	II.1	358
Lady Ply:	help it, if you are made a Captive? I swear it's pity it	148	DOUBL DLR	II.1	359
Mellefont:	if not most presently prevented.	148	DOUBL DLR	II.1	379
Mellefont:	of her violence at last,--if you had not come as you did;	149	DOUBL DLR	II.1	417
Maskwell:	made this agreement, if I accomplish her designs (as I told	149	DOUBL DLR	II.1	427
Lady Touch:	Pliant, if he refuse his Daughter upon this Provocation?	150	DOUBL DLR	III.1	2
Lady Touch:	and can believe any thing worse, if it were laid to his charge	151	DOUBL DLR	III.1	41
Lady Touch:	What if you can't.	152	DOUBL DLR	III.1	60
Lady Touch:	harmless mirth--only misplac'd that's all--but if it	153	DOUBL DLR	III.1	95
Lady Touch:	me if you take such publick notice of it, it will be a Town-talk.	153	DOUBL DLR	III.1	104
Maskwell:	little stomach to her now as if I were her Husband. Should	155	DOUBL DLR	III.1	179
Maskwell:	have it--if I can speak to my Lord before--Was	155	DOUBL DLR	III.1	188
Maskwell:	open: 'twill be hard, if then you can't bring her to any	157	DOUBL DLR	III.1	253
Lady Ply:	Mr. Careless, If a person that is wholly illiterate	159	DOUBL DLR	III.1	336
Careless:	Lady Plyant is not thought of--if that can ever be.	160	DOUBL DLR	III.1	377
Sir Paul:	see--if it becomes me to say so; and we live very comfortably	160	DOUBL DLR	III.1	388
Sir Paul:	Careless, if it were not for one thing--	160	DOUBL DLR	III.1	391
Sir Paul:	little fancies--But as I was telling you, Mr. Careless, if it	161	DOUBL DLR	III.1	403
Sir Paul:	unworthy Sinner--But if I had a Son, ah, that's my	161	DOUBL DLR	III.1	415
Sir Paul:	Indeed, I should be mightily bound to you, if you	162	DOUBL DLR	III.1	448
Careless:	Madam,--if your Ladyship please, we'll discourse of this in	163	DOUBL DLR	III.1	494
Brisk:	Was that he then, I'm answered, if Jehu was a Hackney	165	DOUBL DLR	III.1	549
Brisk:	Was he? I'm answered, if Jehu was a Hackney	165	DOUBL DLR	III.1 V549	
Lord Froth:	O silly! yet his Aunt is as fond of him, as if she	165	DOUBL DLR	III.1	565
Brisk:	if she were plaistred with Lime and Hair, let me perish.	166	DOUBL DLR	III.1	587
Cynthia:	If not, they like and admire themselves--And why is	167	DOUBL DLR	III.1	629
Cynthia:	If Happiness in Self-content is plac'd,	167	DOUBL DLR	III.1	633
Cynthia:	If you had not been so assured of your own Conduct	168	DOUBL DLR	IV.1	43
Cynthia:	Well, if the Devil should assist her, and your Plot	169	DOUBL DLR	IV.1	55
Cynthia:	Why if you give me very clear demonstration that it	169	DOUBL DLR	IV.1	58
Cynthia:	was the Devil, I'll allow for irresistable odds. But if I find	169	DOUBL DLR	IV.1	59
Lady Ply:	Honour--Well, sure if I escape your Importunities, I	169	DOUBL DLR	IV.1	75
Careless:	I'm almost at the end of my Cant, if she does not yield	170	DOUBL DLR	IV.1	95
Lady Ply:	--I am not safe if I stay, and must leave you.	170	DOUBL DLR	IV.1	98
Lady Ply:	far you have gain'd upon me; I assure you if Sir Paul	170	DOUBL DLR	IV.1	110
Careless:	'Slife yonder's Sir Paul, but if he were not come, I'm	171	DOUBL DLR	IV.1	128
Cynthia:	I would obey you to my power, Sir; but if I have	171	DOUBL DLR	IV.1	134
Lady Ply:	Ay, but Sir Paul, I conceive if she has sworn,	171	DOUBL DLR	IV.1	150
Lady Ply:	d'ye mark me, if she has once sworn: It is most unchristian	171	DOUBL DLR	IV.1	151
Sir Paul:	that Opinion once too--Nay if your Ladiship conceives	171	DOUBL DLR	IV.1	156
Lady Ply:	any dishonourable Notions of things; so that if this be	172	DOUBL DLR	IV.1	168
Sir Paul:	Indeed if this be made plain, as my Lady your	172	DOUBL DLR	IV.1	171
Sir Paul:	her Example, that would spoil all indeed. Bless us, if you	174	DOUBL DLR	IV.1	250
Brisk:	an Old Hen, as if she were not well hatch'd, I'gad, he?	174	DOUBL DLR	IV.1	273
Brisk:	Sir Paul, will you send Careless into the Hall if you	175	DOUBL DLR	IV.1	286
Brisk:	engaging Creature, if she were not so fond of that damn'd	175	DOUBL DLR	IV.1	292
Brisk:	be splenatick, or airy upon't; the Deuce take me if I can	176	DOUBL DLR	IV.1	338
Lady Froth:	No the Deuce take me if I don't Laugh at my	176	DOUBL DLR	IV.1	351
Lady Froth:	self; for hang me if I have not a violent Passion for Mr.	176	DOUBL DLR	IV.1	352
Sir Paul:	Gallery. If Sir Paul should surprize us, I have a Commission	178	DOUBL DLR	IV.1	409
Sir Paul:	this Conspiracy; still I am beholden to Providence, if it	179	DOUBL DLR	IV.1	433
Lady Ply:	anger.) Gad's my Life if I thought it were so, I would this	179	DOUBL DLR	IV.1	442
Sir Paul:	The Devil take me now if he did not go beyond my	180	DOUBL DLR	IV.1	470

If   (continued)

Speaker	Text	PAGE	TITLE	ACT.SC	LINE
Sir Paul:	Commission--If I desired him to do any more than · · ·	180	DOUBL DLR	IV.1	471
Sir Paul:	Nay but Madam, I shall offend again if you don't · · ·	180	DOUBL DLR	IV.1	V485
Maskwell:	disswade him from a Design, which I suspect; and if I had	182	DOUBL DLR	IV.1	578
Maskwell:	mean now, is only a bare Suspicion of my own. If your ·	183	DOUBL DLR	IV.1	583
Mellefont:	Paradice; yet if you please you may make it a Purgatory;	185	DOUBL DLR	IV.2	61
Lady Touch:	Eye o're all my future Conduct; and if I once relapse, ·	185	DOUBL DLR	IV.2	82
Mellefont:	which (if possible) are greater--Though she has all the ·	186	DOUBL DLR	IV.2	123
Lady Touch:	akes so, I shall faint if I stay. · · · · · · · ·	187	DOUBL DLR	IV.2	139
Maskwell:	and, if I can, all thought of that pernicious Beauty. Ha!	188	DOUBL DLR	V.1	42
Lord Touch:	Thou shalt enjoy it--if all I'm worth in · · · · · ·	189	DOUBL DLR	V.1	74
Lady Touch:	indebted to him, if you knew all, damn'd Villain! oh, I am	191	DOUBL DLR	V.1	143
Lady Touch:	indebted to him, if you knew all, Villain! oh, I am · ·	191	DOUBL DLR	V.1	V143
Sir Paul:	O, if she be with Mr. Careless, 'tis well enough. · ·	192	DOUBL DLR	V.1	190
Mellefont:	I know no other way but this he has proposed; If · ·	193	DOUBL DLR	V.1	200
Maskwell:	Parson, that if my Lord should have Curiosity to peep, he	193	DOUBL DLR	V.1	232
Maskwell:	me to cheat 'em; and if they will not hear the Serpent's	194	DOUBL DLR	V.1	264
Maskwell:	by describing to me the shortness of your stay; rather if	194	DOUBL DLR	V.1	277
Lord Touch:	He has a quick invention, if this were · · · · · ·	197	DOUBL DLR	V.1	358
Lady Touch:	If this were true--but how can it be? · · · · · ·	199	DOUBL DLR	V.1	440
Maskwell:	in his Uncle's favour, if he'll comply with your desires;	199	DOUBL DLR	V.1	448
Maskwell:	Conditions,--if not, here take this; you may employ it better,	199	DOUBL DLR	V.1	450
Lord Touch:	I thank you, yet it may be still too late, if · · ·	200	DOUBL DLR	V.1	476
	Enquire if Characters are nicely bred; · · · · · ·	204	DOUBL DLR	EPI.	22
	If the soft things are Penn'd and spoke with grace; ·	204	DOUBL DLR	EPI.	23
	If in our larger Family we grieve · · · · · · ·	213	FOR LOVE	PRO.	21
	(If there be any here) and that is Satire. · · · ·	213	FOR LOVE	PRO.	32
	Or only shews its Teeth, as if it smil'd. · · · · ·	213	FOR LOVE	PRO.	34
Jeremy:	this fine Feeding: But if you please, I had rather be at	217	FOR LOVE	I.1	25
Jeremy:	Hem!--Sir, if you please to give me a small · · · ·	217	FOR LOVE	I.1	64
Jeremy:	Favour? Why Sir Sampson will be irreconcilable. If ·	218	FOR LOVE	I.1	83
Jeremy:	won't have a Friend left in the World, if you turn Poet	218	FOR LOVE	I.1	86
Jeremy:	Trade, if he had set up in the City--For my part, I never ·	218	FOR LOVE	I.1	91
Jeremy:	terrify'd Countenance, that looks as if he had written for	219	FOR LOVE	I.1	105
Jeremy:	Muses; or as if she were carrying her Linnen to the Paper-Mill, · · · · · · · · · · · · · · ·	219	FOR LOVE	I.1	111
Jeremy:	Scandal, for Heaven's sake, Sir, try if you can disswade ·	219	FOR LOVE	I.1	123
Scandal:	have fair Play for your Life. If you can't be fairly run down · · · · · · · · · · · · · · · ·	220	FOR LOVE	I.1	142
Valentine:	You are as inveterate against our Poets, as if your ·	220	FOR LOVE	I.1	151
Jeremy:	if you don't like my Negotiation, will you be pleas'd to ·	221	FOR LOVE	I.1	183
Valentine:	have overlaid the Child a Fortnight ago, if she had had ·	221	FOR LOVE	I.1	212
Valentine:	If I can give that Cerberus a Sop, I shall be at rest for one · · · · · · · · · · · · · · · ·	222	FOR LOVE	I.1	225
Scandal:	The Morning's a very good Morning, if you don't · · ·	222	FOR LOVE	I.1	233
Valentine:	And the prettiest Foot! Oh if a Man could but fasten his ·	223	FOR LOVE	I.1	286
Snap:	By your leave, Gentlemen,--Mr. Trapland, if we · · ·	224	FOR LOVE	I.1	295
Snap:	if we don't make haste, the Chairmen will be abroad, and ·	224	FOR LOVE	I.1	298
Valentine:	me word; If I will make a Deed of Conveyance of my Right	225	FOR LOVE	I.1	335
Tattle:	To be free with you, I have--I don't care if I own · ·	227	FOR LOVE	I.1	409
Tattle:	if your Grace--	227	FOR LOVE	I.1	433
Tattle:	I am strangely surpriz'd! Yes, yes, I can't deny't, if	229	FOR LOVE	I.1	481
Valentine:	Nay, if you have known Scandal thus long, and · · ·	229	FOR LOVE	I.1	501
Jeremy:	Sir, Mrs. Frail has sent to know if you are stirring. ·	229	FOR LOVE	I.1	505
Valentine:	If there were, you have more Discretion, than to · ·	229	FOR LOVE	I.1	511
Scandal:	Well, begin then: But take notice, if you are so ill a ·	230	FOR LOVE	I.1	536
Valentine:	But what if he have more Passion than Manners? · ·	231	FOR LOVE	I.1	558
Valentine:	But what if he has more Passion than Manners? · · ·	231	FOR LOVE	I.1	V558
Mrs Frail:	if he be but as great a Sea-Beast, as she is a Land-Monster,	231	FOR LOVE	I.1	570
Scandal:	Yes, all that have done him Favours, if you will · ·	232	FOR LOVE	I.1	606
Scandal:	No, no; come to me if you wou'd see Pictures. · · · ·	232	FOR LOVE	I.1	615
Valentine:	Pictures of all that have refus'd him: If Satyrs, Descriptions, · · · · · · · · · · · · ·	233	FOR LOVE	I.1	624
Mrs Frail:	Well, I'll come, if it be only to disprove you. · · ·	234	FOR LOVE	I.1	659
Mrs Frail:	Well, I'll come, if it be but to disprove you. · · ·	234	FOR LOVE	I.1	V659
Scandal:	Well, if Tattle entertains you, I have the better opportunity · · · · · · · · · · · · · ·	234	FOR LOVE	I.1	671
Scandal:	I'll give an account of you, and your Proceedings. If ·	234	FOR LOVE	I.1	675
Foresight:	Sirrah, go tell Sir Sampson Legend I'll wait on him, if ·	236	FOR LOVE	II.1	40
Foresight:	Ne mar!, if it be fruitful fond. · · · · · · · ·	236	FOR LOVE	II.1	56
Angelica:	abroad; and if you won't lend me your Coach, I'll take a ·	237	FOR LOVE	II.1	67
Angelica:	you keep her at Home, if you're Jealous when she's abroad?	237	FOR LOVE	II.1	70
Angelica:	you keep her at Home, if you're Jealous of her when she's abroad? · · · · · · · · · · · · ·	237	FOR LOVE	II.1	V 70
Angelica:	Nay Uncle, don't be angry--If you are, I'll · · · ·	237	FOR LOVE	II.1	76
Angelica:	--Nay, I know something worse, if I would · · · ·	238	FOR LOVE	II.1	111
Nurse:	thing; feel, feel here, if I have any thing but like ·	238	FOR LOVE	II.1	124
Angelica:	Nor there had not been that one, if she had had to · ·	239	FOR LOVE	II.1	143
Foresight:	Well--Why, if I was born to be a Cuckold, · · · ·	239	FOR LOVE	II.1	169
Sr Sampson:	warrant you, if he danc'd till Doomsday, he thought I ·	240	FOR LOVE	II.1	179
Foresight:	faith and troth, here 'tis, if it will but hold--I wish ·	240	FOR LOVE	II.1	187
Sr Sampson:	If the Sun shine by Day, and the Stars by Night, why, we	240	FOR LOVE	II.1	199
Foresight:	Cureable or Incureable. If Journeys shall be prosperous, ·	241	FOR LOVE	II.1	216
Foresight:	Nay, if you were but in Jest.--Who's that · · · ·	242	FOR LOVE	II.1	263
Sr Sampson:	if there is too much, refund the Superfluity; Do'st hear	243	FOR LOVE	II.1	280
Sr Sampson:	if there be too much, refund the Superfluity; Do'st hear	243	FOR LOVE	II.1	V280
Valentine:	you call'd me. But here I am, and if you don't mean to ·	244	FOR LOVE	II.1	334
Sr Sampson:	And if this Rogue were Anatomiz'd now, and · · · ·	245	FOR LOVE	II.1	385
Valentine:	Necessities of my Nature; if I had my right of Inheritance.	246	FOR LOVE	II.1	395
Sr Sampson:	--If I had it again, I wou'd not give thee a Groat, · ·	246	FOR LOVE	II.1	397
Sr Sampson:	Now let's see, if you have Wit enough to keep your self?--	246	FOR LOVE	II.1	401
Mrs Frail:	Well, what if I took twenty--I warrant if · · · ·	246	FOR LOVE	II.1	422
Mrs Frail:	--Lord, where's the comfort of this Life, if we can't have	246	FOR LOVE	II.1	424
Mrs Fore:	is scandalous: What if any Body else shou'd have seen you	247	FOR LOVE	II.1	431
Mrs Frail:	your self happy in a Hackney-Coach before now.--If I ·	247	FOR LOVE	II.1	437

335

If (continued)

If   (continued)

Angelica:	Leave me, and d'ye hear, if Valentine shou'd come,	297	FOR LOVE	V.1	9
Sr Sampson:	of any thing;--And if they commit Matrimony,	299	FOR LOVE	V.1	56
Angelica:	Fortune enough to make any Man easie that I can like; If	299	FOR LOVE	V.1	61
Sr Sampson:	Lady of your inccmparable Beauty and Merit.--If I	300	FOR LOVE	V.1	97
Sr Sampson:	Odd, Madam, I love you--And if you	300	FOR LOVE	V.1	103
Angelica:	to satisfie you about Valentine: For if a Match were				
	seemingly	300	FOR LOVE	V.1	108
Sr Sampson:	If we were to gc through with it. But why must the Match	300	FCR LOVE	V.1	114
Angelica:	and if I find what you propose practicable; I'll give	301	FOR LOVE	V.1	135
Angelica:	Have a care, and don't over-act your Part--If	301	FOR LOVE	V.1	157
Jeremy:	Ah Sir, if you are not very faithful and close in this				
	Business,	301	FOR LOVE	V.1	167
Miss Prue:	my Husband now if you please.	303	FOR LOVE	V.1	230
Foresight:	to try if I could discover it by my Art--hum, ha! I	304	FOR LOVE	V.1	259
Tattle:	you,--I know you love to untie Difficulties--Or if	305	FOR LOVE	V.1	296
Miss Prue:	Man; and if I can't have one, I wou'd go to sleep all my	305	FOR LOVE	V.1	309
Miss Prue:	A Fiddle of a Rod, I'll have a Husband; and if you	305	FOR LOVE	V.1	315
Mrs Fore:	Here's Mr. Benjamin, he can tell us if his Father	306	FOR LOVE	V.1	339
Ben:	can't deny it: But, Father, if I might be your Pilot in this	308	FCR LOVE	V.1	413
Ben:	as if so be you should sail so far as the Streights without	308	FOR LOVE	V.1	415
Ben:	in your Conscience--If so be that one had a	309	FOR LOVE	V.1	432
Tattle:	The Devil take me if ever I was so much concern'd at any	309	FOR LOVE	V.1	460
Angelica:	'Tis very unhappy, if you don't care for one another.	309	FOR LOVE	V.1	462
Ben:	Heart. Look you, Friend, if I may advise you, when she's	310	FCB LOVE	V.1	490
Ben:	enough to hold her, and if she can't drag her Anchor	310	FOR LOVE	V.1	493
Valentine:	No; here's the Fool; and if occasion be, I'll give it	310	FOR LOVE	V.1	497
Valentine:	If you please, Sir; but first I would ask this Lady	311	FOR LOVE	V.1	515
Angelica:	to me; nay, what if you were sincere? still you must	311	FOR LOVE	V.1	532
Angelica:	pardon me, if I think my own Inclinations have a better	311	FOR LOVE	V.1	533
Valentine:	If my happiness cou'd receive Addition, this Kind	312	FOR LOVE	V.1	579
Sr Sampson:	the Stars are Lyars; and if I had Breath enough, I'd curse	313	FOR LOVE	V.1 V584	
Tattle:	If the Gentleman is in this discrder for want of a Wife,	313	FCB LOVE	V.1	589
Angelica:	I have done dissembling now, Valentine; and if that	313	FOR LOVE	V.1	605
Valentine:	never distinguish it self enough, to be taken notice of. If	313	FOR LOVE	V.1	610
	'Twere some Amends if they could reimburse:	323	M. EFIDE	PRO.	24
	But if, provok'd, your dreadful Wrath remains,	323	M. EFIDE	PRO.	29
Almeria:	That I should be afflicted thus?--if not,	327	M. EFIDE	I.1	59
Almeria:	--If thou didst!--	328	M. EBIDE	I.1	90
Almeria:	If I should tell thee, wouldst thou pity me?	328	M. EBIDE	I.1	91
Almeria:	If for my swelling Heart I can, I'll tell thee.	329	M. EBIDE	I.1	109
Almeria:	And thou Anselmo, if yet thou art arriv'd	330	M. EBIDE	I.1	181
Almeria:	If ever I do yield, or give consent,	330	M. EBIDE	I.1	185
Almeria:	(If such there be in angry Heav'ns Vengeance)	330	M. EBIDE	I.1	189
Gonsalez:	And cling, as if with Claws they did enforce	332	M. EBIDE	I.1	239
Gonsalez:	As if they were all Eyes, and every Limb	332	M. EBIDE	I.1 V241	
Almeria:	Forgive me, Sir, if I offend.	333	M. EBIDE	I.1	283
Almeria:	Forgive me, Sir, if I in this offend.	333	M. EBIDE	I.1 V283	
Gonsalez:	To have offended you. If Fate decreed,	333	M. EBIDE	I.1	304
Gonsalez:	As if she had offended.	334	M. EBIDE	I.1	320
Gonsalez:	As if she had offended.--Sure, nc more,	334	M. EBIDE	I.1 V320	
Garcia:	(kneeling). Your Pardon, Sir, if I presume so far,	334	M. EBIDE	I.1	327
Alonzo:	And with a Train, as if she still were Wife	335	M. EBIDE	I.1	360
Garcia:	Dumbly declines all Offers: if he speak	335	M. EBIDE	I.1	371
Zara:	If I cn any Terms could condescend	335	M. EBIDE	I.1	393
Manuel:	If not in Words, I had it by my Eyes.	336	M. EBIDE	I.1	409
Manuel:	If not in Words, I bid it by my Eyes.	336	M. EBIDE	I.1 V409	
Heli:	If to arise in very deed from Death,	337	M. BBIDE	II.1	5
Garcia:	If so, Unhappiness attends their Love	339	M. EBIDE	II.1	47
Almeria:	If I cou'd speak; how I have mourn'd and pray'd,	343	M. BBIDE	II.2	130
Almeria:	If Heaven is greater Joy, it is no Happiness,	343	M. EBIDE	II.2	148
Almeria:	Sure I have dreamt, if we must part so soon.	344	M. EBIDE	II.2	194
Zara:	What Joy do I require? if thou dost mourn,	346	M. EBIDE	II.2	267
Zara:	If I have gain'd thy Love, 'tis Glorious Ruine;	347	M. EBIDE	II.2	313
Osmyn-Alph:	If my Alphonso--Ha!	350	M. BBIDE	III.1	9
Osmyn-Alph:	If my Alphonso live, restore him, Heav'n,	350	M. BBIDE	III.1	10
Osmyn-Alph:	If Piety be thus debarr'd Access	350	M. BBIDE	III.1	28
Zara:	If so, this Sable Curtain shall again	353	M. BBIDE	III.1	151
Almeria:	If there, he shoot not ev'ry other Shaft;	356	M. EBIDE	III.1	286
Almeria:	Indeed; if that be so, if I'm thy Torment,	357	M. EBIDE	III.1	296
Osmyn-Alph:	If possible--	359	M. EBIDE	III.1	391
Gonsalez:	Which seem to intimate, as if Alphonso,	363	M. EBIDE	IV.1	77
Zara:	For me, if it be known--If not, what Hope	363	M. BBIDE	IV.1	95
Gonsalez:	If such a one, so 'scaping, was receiv'd	363	M. EBIDE	IV.1	102
Manuel:	Is pass'd; if you revoke it not, he dies.	364	M. EBIDE	IV.1	113
Gonsalez:	As if she'd rather that she did not hate him.	366	M. EBIDE	IV.1	204
Gonsalez:	What if she had seen Osmyn? tho' 'twere strange.	366	M. BBIDE	IV.1	222
Gonsalez:	But if she had, what was't to her? unless	366	M. BRIDE	IV.1	223
Gonsalez:	If Osmyn be, as Zara has related,	367	M. EBIDE	IV.1	229
Gonsalez:	And try howe'er, if I were divin'd aright.	367	M. EBIDE	IV.1	238
Gonsalez:	If what I fear be true, she'll be concern'd	367	M. EBIDE	IV.1	239
Gonsalez:	Urge that, to try if she'll sollicite for him.	367	M. EBIDE	IV.1	241
Manuel:	Rise, I command thee rise--and if thou would'st	368	M. EBIDE	IV.1	285
Manuel:	Hear me; then, if thou canst, reply, know Traitress,	368	M. EBIDE	IV.1	300
Almeria:	Now curse me if you can, now spurn me off.	369	M. EBIDE	IV.1	320
Gonsalez:	And deludes your Sense. Alphonso, if living,	370	M. EBIDE	IV.1	376
Gonsalez:	Hold, let me think--if I shou'd tell the King--	371	M. EBIDE	IV.1	403
Gonsalez:	Wedded already--what if he should yield?	371	M. EBIDE	IV.1	405
Gonsalez:	Anselmo's Race; yet if--that If concludes me.	371	M. EBIDE	IV.1	410
Gonsalez:	If I delay--'twill do--or better so.	371	M. EBIDE	IV.1	416
Zara:	Their red and angry Beams; as if his Sight	375	M. BBIDE	V.1	94
Selim:	He did: But then as if	375	M. BBIDE	V.1	98
Selim:	Yes: But then, as if he thought	375	M. BBIDE	V.1 V 98	
Selim:	If I have fail'd in what, as being a Man,	375	M. BBIDE	V.1	117
Zara:	When I've concluded on my self, if I	375	M. BBIDE	V.1	126
Zara:	I'll give thee Freedom, if thou dar'st be free:	376	M. BBIDE	V.1	136

337

		PAGE	TITLE	ACT.SC	LINE
Alonzo:	For Osmyn, if in seeking for the King,	379	M. BRIDE	V.2	120
Almeria:	And of a suddain I am calm, as if	382	M. BRIDE	V.2	241
	As if indeed a Widow, or an Heir.	385	M. BRIDE	EPI.	4
	But if he 'scape, with what Regret they're seiz'd!	385	M. BRIDE	EPI.	13
	And how they're disappointed if they're pleas'd!	385	M. BRIDE	EPI.	14
	If that be found a forfeited Estate.	393	WAY WORLD	PRO.	21
	But if they're naught ne're spare him for his Pains:	393	WAY WORLD	PRO.	23
Mirabell:	better pleas'd if she had been less discreet.	396	WAY WORLD	I.1	48
Mirabell:	reported to be in Labour. The Devil's in't, if an old woman	397	WAY WORLD	I.1	76
Fainall:	Fie, fie Friend, if you grow Censorious I must leave	397	WAY WORLD	I.1	99
Mirabell:	Of her Understanding I am, if not of her Person.	399	WAY WORLD	I.1	150
Fainall:	Mother. If you marry Millamant you must call Cousins	400	WAY WORLD	I.1	194
Fainall:	If you have a mind to finish his Picture, you have an	401	WAY WORLD	I.1	232
Mirabell:	You had better step and ask his Wife; if you wou'd	402	WAY WORLD	I.1	266
Witwoud:	wrong him neither--And if he had but any Judgment	403	WAY WORLD	I.1	292
Witwoud:	wrong him.--And if he had any Judgment	403	WAY WORLD	I.1	V292
Witwoud:	that's the Truth on't, if he were my Brother, I cou'd not	403	WAY WORLD	I.1	311
Witwoud:	No, no, what if he be? 'Tis no matter for that, his	403	WAY WORLD	I.1	318
Petulant:	Condition, Condition's a dry'd Fig, if I am not in	405	WAY WORLD	I.1	394
Petulant:	Humour--By this Hand, if they were your--a--a--your	405	WAY WORLD	I.1	395
Petulant:	off, if I want Appetite.	405	WAY WORLD	I.1	397
Witwoud:	with him; if he said they were my Mother and my Sisters.	406	WAY WORLD	I.1	411
Witwoud:	with him; if he had said they were my Mother and my Sisters.	406	WAY WORLD	I.1	V411
Petulant:	Friends; and if he shou'd marry and have a Child, you may	407	WAY WORLD	I.1	439
Petulant:	I, nothing I. If Throats are to be cut, let Swords	407	WAY WORLD	I.1	446
Mirabell:	me; if thou hadst but good Nature equal to thy Wit	407	WAY WORLD	I.1	452
Petulant:	If I do, will you grant me common Sense then, for	407	WAY WORLD	I.1	458
Witwoud:	Now, Demme, I shou'd hate that, if she were as handsome	408	WAY WORLD	I.1	477
Witwoud:	being in Embrio; and if it shou'd come to Life; poor	408	WAY WORLD	I.1	488
Mrs Fain:	Ay, ay, dear Marwood, if we will be happy, we	410	WAY WORLD	II.1	1
Mrs Fain:	While they are Lovers, if they have Fire and Sense, their	410	WAY WORLD	II.1	4
Marwood:	Faith by Marrying; if I cou'd but find one	411	WAY WORLD	II.1	53
Marwood:	O if he shou'd ever discover it, he wou'd	411	WAY WORLD	II.1	61
Fainall:	Excellent Creature! Well sure if I shou'd live to be	413	WAY WORLD	II.1	109
Marwood:	If I am, is it inconsistent with my Love to you	413	WAY WORLD	II.1	124
Fainall:	You wou'd intimate then, as if there were a	413	WAY WORLD	II.1	126
Fainall:	If yet you lov'd, you could forgive a Jealousy: But you are	415	WAY WORLD	II.1	185
Marwood:	discover'd; be sure you shall. I can but be expos'd--If I	415	WAY WORLD	II.1	188
Mirabell:	Actions? To save that Idol Reputation. If the	417	WAY WORLD	II.1	266
Mirabell:	to betray me by trusting him too far. If your Mother, in	417	WAY WORLD	II.1	292
Mrs Fain:	So, if my poor Mother is caught in a Contract,	417	WAY WORLD	II.1	296
Mrs Fain:	Female Frailty! We must all come to it, if we	418	WAY WORLD	II.1	314
Millamant:	curl if it were pinn'd up with Prose.	419	WAY WORLD	II.1	V367
Millamant:	If they did not commend us, we were not handsome!	420	WAY WORLD	II.1	400
Millamant:	Now you must know they could not commend one, if	420	WAY WORLD	II.1	401
Millamant:	pleases, and they die as soon as one pleases: And then if	420	WAY WORLD	II.1	405
Millamant:	and say; vain empty Things if we are silent or unseen, and	421	WAY WORLD	II.1	411
Mirabell:	they are not capable: Or if they were, it shou'd be to you	421	WAY WORLD	II.1	438
Millamant:	Mirabell, If you persist in this offensive Freedom	422	WAY WORLD	II.1	448
Millamant:	What, with that Face? No, if you keep your	422	WAY WORLD	II.1	472
Millamant:	melancholly as a Watch-light. Well Mirabell, If ever you	422	WAY WORLD	II.1	477
Millamant:	will win me woo me now--Nay, if you are so tedious,	422	WAY WORLD	II.1	478
Waitwell:	to Business, Sir. I have instructed her as well as I cou'd.	423	WAY WORLD	II.1	509
Mirabell:	stock'd, if we succeed.	424	WAY WORLD	II.1	540
Foible:	not doubt of Success. If you have no more Commands Sir,	424	WAY WORLD	II.1	542
Foible:	that was Mrs. Marwood that went by in a Mask; if she has	424	WAY WORLD	II.1	545
Waitwell:	Sir Rowland if you please. The Jade's so pert upon	424	WAY WORLD	II.1	550
Lady Wish:	I have no more patience--If I have not fretted	425	WAY WORLD	III.1	3
Lady Wish:	Confidence. I sent her to Negotiate an Affair, in which if	426	WAY WORLD	III.1	51
Lady Wish:	I'm detected I'm undone. If that wheadling Villain has	426	WAY WORLD	III.1	52
Lady Wish:	Friend, I'm a Wretch of Wretches if I'm detected.	426	WAY WORLD	III.1	54
Lady Wish:	corrupt Integrity it self. If she has given him an Opportunity,	426	WAY WORLD	III.1	58
Foible:	Well, if worshipping of Pictures be a Sin	427	WAY WORLD	III.1	77
Foible:	what shall I say?--Alas, Madam, cou'd I help it, if I	427	WAY WORLD	III.1	85
Foible:	met that confident Thing? Was I in Fault? If you had	427	WAY WORLD	III.1	86
Foible:	Nay, if that had been the worst I cou'd have born: But he	427	WAY WORLD	III.1	89
Lady Wish:	Importunate Foible, and push? For if he shou'd not be	429	WAY WORLD	III.1	157
Lady Wish:	shall die with Confusion, if I am forc'd to advance--Oh	429	WAY WORLD	III.1	159
Lady Wish:	no, I can never advance--I shall swoon if he shou'd	429	WAY WORLD	III.1	160
Lady Wish:	Is he! O then he'll Importune, if he's a brisk	429	WAY WORLD	III.1	176
Lady Wish:	Man. I shall save Decorums if Sir Rowland importunes. I	429	WAY WORLD	III.1	177
Foible:	is so impatient, I fear she'll come for me, if I stay.	430	WAY WORLD	III.1	220
Marwood:	Woman! The Devil's an Ass: If I were a Painter, I wou'd	431	WAY WORLD	III.1	236
Marwood:	If we had the liberty, we shou'd be as weary	432	WAY WORLD	III.1	299
Marwood:	If we had that liberty, we shou'd be as weary	432	WAY WORLD	III.1	V299
Millamant:	I could consent to wear 'em, if they wou'd wear	433	WAY WORLD	III.1	304
Marwood:	of Wit, which to blind her Affair with a Lover of Sense. If	433	WAY WORLD	III.1	313
Marwood:	Indeed my Dear, you'll tear another Fan, if	433	WAY WORLD	III.1	333
Millamant:	enjoin'd it him, to be so coy--If I had the Vanity to	433	WAY WORLD	III.1	338
Millamant:	O Dear, what? for it is the same thing, if I hear	434	WAY WORLD	III.1	352
Millamant:	think of it--I am a Sybil if I am not amaz'd to think	434	WAY WORLD	III.1	357
Millamant:	--If you cou'd but stay for me, I shou'd overtake you	434	WAY WORLD	III.1	360
Singer:	A sickly Flame, which if not fed expires;	435	WAY WORLD	III.1	379
Singer:	If there's Delight in Love, 'tis when I see	435	WAY WORLD	III.1	389
Petulant:	If he says Black's Black--If I have a Humour to	435	WAY WORLD	III.1	404
Petulant:	say 'tis Blue--Let that pass--All's one for that. If	435	WAY WORLD	III.1	405
Servant-W:	Sir, my Lady's dressing. Here's Company; if you	437	WAY WORLD	III.1	445
Sir Wilful:	if thou see'st her, ha Friend?	437	WAY WORLD	III.1	460
Sir Wilful:	Well prithee try what thou can'st do; if thou	437	WAY WORLD	III.1	464
Petulant:	It seems as if you had come a Journey, Sir;	438	WAY WORLD	III.1	489
Sir Wilful:	Why, 'tis like you may, Sir: If you are not	438	WAY WORLD	III.1	498
Sir Wilful:	satisfy'd with the Information of my Boots, Sir, if you will	438	WAY WORLD	III.1	499
Marwood:	Friends here, tho' it may be you don't know it--If I	438	WAY WORLD	III.1	508

Ill-natur'd   (continued)
  Vainlove: --Ill-natur'd, as an old Maid.-- . . . . 112 OLD EATCH   V.2 161
  Sr Sampson: Unnatural Whelp! There's an ill-natur'd Dog! What, . . 259 FOR LOVE   III.1 236
Ill-nature (1)
                 These with false Glosses, feed their own Ill-nature, . 479 WAY WORLD   EPI.   21
Ill-tim'd (2)
  Almeria: Hence, thou detested, ill-tim'd Flatterer; . . . . . 370 M. BRIDE   IV.1 378
  Gonsalez: Of these your rash and ill-tim'd Exclamations. . . . . 377 M. BRIDE   V.2   31
Illiterate (7)
  Lady Ply: Mr. Careless, If a person that is wholly illiterate . . 159 DOUBL DLR III.1 336
  Lady Ply: challenges much more, I'm sure, than my illiterate Praises 169 DOUBL DLR IV.1   83
  Sr Sampson: You're an illiterate Fool, and I'm another, and . . . . 313 FOR LOVE   V.1 583
  Sr Sampson: You're an illiterate Fool, and I'm another, ... 313 FOR LOVE   V.1 V583
  Fainall: Too Illiterate. . . . . 404 WAY WORLD   I.1 325
  Millamant: Well, an illiterate Man's my Aversion. I wonder . . . 436 WAY WORLD III.1 422
  Millamant: at the Impudence of any Illiterate Man, to offer to make . 436 WAY WORLD III.1 423
Ills (4)
  Heartwell: You are the principal Cause of all my present Ills. . . 109 OLD BATCH   V.2   66
  Zara: And all those Ills, which thou so long hast mourn'd; . 361 M. BRIDE   III.1 456
  Gonsalez: Of a Father's Fondness, these Ills arose; . . . . . 378 M. BRIDE   V.2   82
  Osmyn-Alph: And not from past or present Ills Despair: . . . . 384 M. BRIDE   V.2 320
Illusion (2)
  Osmyn-Alph: Amazement and Illusion! Rivet me . . . . 341 M. BRIDE   II.2   46
  Osmyn-Alph: Amazement and Illusion! . . . . 341 M. BRIDE   II.2 V 46
Illustrious (3)
  Heartwell: illustrious Whore in England. . . . . 45 OLD EATCH   I.1 313
  Sr Sampson: an Illustrious Creature, my trusty Hieroglyphick; and may 242 FOR LOVE   II.1 243
  Sr Sampson: more Illustrious than the Moon; for she has her Chastity 242 FOR LOVE   II.1 258
Image (2)
  Sharper: stamp your image on the Gold. . . . . 43 OLD BATCH   I.1 221
  Bellmour: image cf Valour. He calls him his Back, and indeed they 46 OLD BATCH   I.1 357
Images (1)
  Osmyn-Alph: Successively reflect succeeding Images; . . . . . 345 M. BRIDE   II.2 222
Imaginable (2)
  Sharper: press her to make all the haste imaginable. . . . . 102 OLD BATCH   V.1 219
  Lady Wish: entertain 'em. I'll make all imaginable haste. Dear Friend 432 WAY WORLD III.1 280
Imagination (7)
  Vainlove: So was true as Turtle--in imagination Ned, ha? . . 38 OLD EATCH   I.1   52
  Setter: to tickle thy Imagination with remembrance of iniquity 65 OLD EATCH III.1 185
  Mellefont: But the greatest Villain imagination can form, I . . 146 DOUBL DLR   II.2 293
  Sir Paul: Rogue by the help of imagination; why, 'tis the mark of 173 DOUBL DLR   IV.1 238
  Brisk: Object to my imagination, but--But did I indeed?--To . 176 DOUBL DLR   IV.1 328
  Mellefont: Imagination cannot form a fairer and more plausible . 187 DOUBL DLR   IV.2 150
  Scandal: Why Faith, I have a good lively Imagination; and . 275 FOR LOVE   III.1 813
Imaginations (1)
  Mellefont: Devils, than that Imaginations. . . . . 129 DOUBL DLR   I.1   78
Imagine (5)
  Araminta: I wonder Cousin you should imagine, I don't . . . 55 OLD BATCH   II.2   20
  Maskwell: this Gallery an hour hence, by that time I imagine our 149 DOUBL DLR   II.1 435
  Tattle: It was impossible, Madam, for me to imagine, that a Person 255 FOR LOVE III.1   66
  Millamant: Unless by the help of the Devil you can't imagine; . . 423 WAY WORLD   II.1 485
  Millamant: Without the help of the Devil you can't imagine; . . 423 WAY WORLD   II.1 V485
Imagined (1)
  Lady Touch: to forgive the faults I have imagined, but never put in . 185 DOUBL DLR   IV.2   73
Immediate (4)
  Lady Touch: immediate Ruin seize him. . . . . 137 DOUBL DLR   I.1 401
  Lady Touch: immediate Lightning blast thee, me and the whole World . 184 DOUBL DLR   IV.2   45
  Valentine: to the immediate Signing the Deed of Conveyance of my . 259 FOR LOVE   III.1 226
  Gonsalez: The King's immediate Presence at their Head. . . . . 378 M. BRIDE   V.2 104
Immediately (11)
  Bellmour: Hum, not immediately, in my conscience not . . . 63 OLD BATCH III.1 106
  Araminta: be gone immediately.--I see one that will be Jealous, . . 86 OLD BATCH   IV.3 104
  Mellefont: We'll come immediately, if you'll but go in, and . . 128 DOUBL DLR   I.1   46
  Lady Touch: let me beg you do now: I'll come immediately, and tell . 153 DOUBL DLR III.1 119
  Maskwell: No, no, I'll after him immediately, and tell him. . . 194 DOUBL DLR   V.1 259
  Cynthia: immediately to follow you, and give you notice. . . . 196 DOUBL DLR   V.1 349
  Valentine: will immediately furnish me with Four thousand Pound to . 225 FOR LOVE   I.1 337
  Mrs Fain: Immediately; I have a Word or two for Mr. . . . . . 421 WAY WORLD   II.1 425
  Lady Wish: send for Robin from Lockets--Immediately. . . . . . 427 WAY WORLD III.1 105
  Marwood: Not far Madam; I'll return immediately. . . . . 471 WAY WORLD   V.1 357
  Lady Wish: resign the Contract with my Neice Immediately. . . . 472 WAY WORLD   V.1 404
Immerge (1)
  Sir Joseph: which, like an innundation will I hope totally immerge . 49 OLD BATCH   II.1   57
Imminent (2)
  Zara: You're too secure: The Danger is more imminent . . . 364 M. BRIDE   IV.1 109
  Lady Wish: her fortune; if you can but save me from this imminent . 474 WAY WORLD   V.1 465
Immoderate (3)
  Brisk: Immoderate Mirth.--You Laugh on still, and are not able . 134 DOUBL DLR   I.1 257
  Valentine: doat on at that immoderate rate, that your Fondness shall 313 FOR LOVE   V.1 609
  Valentine: doat on at that immoderate Degree, that your Fondness shall 313 FOR LOVE   V.1 V609
Immoderately (1)
  Millamant: O silly! Ha, ha, ha. I cou'd laugh immoderately. . . . 433 WAY WORLD III.1 335
Immortal (1)
  Capt Bluff: By the immortal Thunder of great Guns, 'tis false . . . 70 OLD BATCH III.1 352
Immortality (1)
  Heartwell: Woman can as soon give Immortality. . . . . . . 108 OLD BATCH   V.2   24
Immoveable (1)
  Almeria: By its own Weight, made stedfast, and immoveable, . . 339 M. BRIDE   II.1   62
Impair'd (1)
  Heartwell: impair'd the Honour of your House, promis'd your . . 109 OLD BATCH   V.2   52
Impal'd (1)
  Manuel: Torn, mangl'd, flay'd, impal'd--all Pains and . . . 368 M. BRIDE   IV.1 295
Impart (2)   see T'impart
  Scandal: Ghost of Lilly. He has Secrets to impart I suppose to you . 266 FOR LOVE   III.1 500
  Mirabell: knew I came to impart a Secret to you, that concern'd my . 421 WAY WORLD   II.1 430

Indeed (128)

Speaker	Text	PAGE	TITLE	ACT.SC	LINE
Heartwell:	so much Mercury in my Limbs; 'tis true indeed, I don't	43	OLD BATCH	I.1	231
Bellmour:	principle indeed! and art for encouraging Youth, that they	43	OLD BATCH	I.1	251
Bellmour:	image of Valour. He calls him his Back, and indeed they	46	OLD BATCH	I.1	357
Sir Joseph:	through all dangers--he is indeed Back, Breast and Headpiece	50	OLD BATCH	II.1	120
Silvia:	Indeed it is very fine--I could look upon 'em all	71	OLD BATCH	III.2	26
Silvia:	I dare not speak till I believe you, and indeed I'm	72	OLD BATCH	III.2	53
Heartwell:	Lying, Child, is indeed the Art of Love; and Men are	72	OLD BATCH	III.2	56
Silvia:	Indeed if I were well assur'd you lov'd; but how can I	73	OLD BATCH	III.2	74
Barnaby:	Husband. 'Tis then indeed, like the vanity of taking a fine	76	OLD BATCH	IV.1	42
Laetitia:	Jest too far indeed.	78	OLD BATCH	IV.1	120
Laetitia:	indeed you sant. Nykin--if you don't go, I'le think	78	OLD BATCH	IV.1	132
Sharper:	The second-best;--indeed I think.	88	OLD BATCH	IV.3	203
Laetitia:	come near it, I'm afraid 'tis the Devil; indeed it has hoofs,	92	OLD BATCH	IV.4	133
Fondlewife:	Indeed, and I have Horns, Deare. The Devil, no.	92	OLD BATCH	IV.4	135
Laetitia:	Indeed, and indeed, now my dear Nykin--I never	93	OLD BATCH	IV.4	139
Laetitia:	No, indeed Dear.	93	OLD BATCH	IV.4	160
Laetitia:	Indeed, my Dear, I was but just coming down stairs,	95	OLD BATCH	IV.4	243
Laetitia:	Indeed, my Dear, I was but just come down stairs,	95	OLD BATCH	IV.4	V243
Laetitia:	won't you speak to me, cruel Nykin? Indeed, I'll die, if	95	OLD BATCH	IV.4	246
Setter:	--They have indeed, very perswading faces. But--	103	OLD BATCH	V.1	248
Bellmour:	That were a miserable Wretch indeed, who cou'd	106	OLD BATCH	V.1	378
Lord Froth:	Oh, no.--Never Laugh indeed, Sir.	133	DOUEL DLR	I.1	225
Careless:	Then I shall be disappointed indeed.	134	DOUEL DLR	I.1	279
Cynthia:	Indeed, Madam! Is it Possible your Ladyship could	138	DOUEL DLR	II.1	1
Cynthia:	He does not indeed affect either pertness, or	139	DOUEL DLR	II.1	53
Mellefont:	Fortune indeed makes the match, and the Two nearest,	143	DOUEL DLR	II.1	165
Sir Paul:	I should, indeed, Thy,--therefore come away; but	146	DOUEL DLR	II.1	284
Lady Ply:	it is no sin to them that don't think it so;--indeed, If	147	DOUEL DLR	II.1	348
Lady Touch:	make you lose one minutes temper. 'Tis not indeed, my	152	DOUEL DLR	III.1	67
Lady Touch:	wish I had not told you any thing.--Indeed, my Lord,	152	DOUEL DLR	III.1	69
Lady Touch:	Nay, but will you be calm--indeed it's	152	DOUEL DLR	III.1	72
Lady Touch:	Expedition indeed; for all we do, must be	154	DOUEL DLR	III.1	141
Sir Paul:	man in the World: indeed that touches me near, very near.	161	DOUEL DLR	III.1	405
Sir Paul:	and it is a great grief to me, indeed it is Mr. Careless, that I	161	DOUEL DLR	III.1	410
Sir Paul:	blessed be Providence I may say; for indeed, Mr. Careless,	161	DOUEL DLR	III.1	413
Sir Paul:	affliction, and my only afflicticn; indeed I cannot refrain	161	DOUEL DLR	III.1	416
Sir Paul:	Summers-day--indeed she is, Mr. Careless, in all	161	DOUEL DLR	III.1	422
Sir Paul:	no, no, you shoot wide of the mark a mile; indeed you do,	161	DOUEL DLR	III.1	427
Sir Paul:	indeed it's true, Mr. Careless, it breaks my heart--I	162	DOUEL DLR	III.1	436
Sir Paul:	than with my own Mother--no indeed.	162	DOUEL DLR	III.1	440
Sir Paul:	Indeed, I should be mightily bound to you, if you	162	DOUEL DLR	III.1	448
Sir Paul:	Indeed if this be made plain, as my Lady your	172	DOUEL DLR	IV.1	171
Lady Ply:	O las, no indeed, Sir Paul, 'tis upon your account.	172	DOUEL DLR	IV.1	181
Lady Ply:	My Lip indeed, Sir Paul, I swear you shall.	172	DOUEL DLR	IV.1	195
Sir Paul:	her Example, that would spoil all indeed. Bless us, if you	174	DOUEL DLR	IV.1	250
Brisk:	Object to my imagination, but--But did I indeed?--To	176	DOUEL DLR	IV.1	328
Sir Paul:	Indeed--Well Sir--(aside) I'll dissemble with him	180	DOUEL DLR	IV.1	494
Maskwell:	Indeed I was in hopes 'thad been a youthful Heat	182	DOUEL DLR	IV.1	557
Lady Touch:	mad, alas he's mad--indeed he is my Lord, and knows not	186	DOUEL DLR	IV.2	113
Lord Touch:	I fear he's mad indeed--Let's send Maskwell	187	DOUEL DLR	IV.2	135
Maskwell:	This is prosperous indeed--Why let him find	190	DOUEL DLR	V.1	85
Maskwell:	then were fine work indeed! her fury wou'd spare nothing,	190	DOUEL DLR	V.1	93
Lady Touch:	anothers Arms; oh! that I were Fire indeed, that I might	191	DOUEL DLR	V.1	151
Sir Paul:	all this for? Pooh, here's a joke, indeed--why, where's	192	DOUEL DLR	V.1	186
Cynthia:	How's this! now I fear indeed.	197	DOUEL DLR	V.1	361
Maskwell:	So, this was a pinch indeed, my invention was	199	DOUEL DLR	V.1	461
Jeremy:	Ay, more indeed; for who cares for any Body that	219	FOR LOVE	I.1	129
Trapland:	No more indeed.	223	FOR LOVE	I.1	274
Scandal:	with, are to be handl'd tenderly indeed.	226	FOR LOVE	I.1	397
Tattle:	Ha, ha, ha; nay, now you make a Jest of it indeed.	227	FOR LOVE	I.1	403
Valentine:	Marriage indeed may qualifie the Fury of his	231	FOR LOVE	I.1	560
Valentine:	No indeed, he speaks truth now: For as Tattle has	233	FOR LOVE	I.1	622
Servant:	I can't tell indeed, Sir.	235	FOR LOVE	II.1	14
Angelica:	and Spoon-meat together--Indeed, Uncle, I'll indite you	237	FOR LOVE	II.1	91
Foresight:	Aye indeed, Sir Sampson, a great deal of Money for	243	FOR LOVE	II.1	277
Mrs Fore:	Soul, I shall fancy my self Old indeed, to have this great	249	FOR LOVE	II.1	512
Miss Prue:	No, indeed; I'm angry at you.--	252	FOR LOVE	II.1	633
Miss Prue:	No, indeed won't I: But I'll run there, and hide	252	FOR LOVE	II.1	648
Tattle:	O Lord! yes indeed, Madam, several times.	255	FOR LOVE	III.1	79
Tattle:	No indeed, Madam, you don't know me at all, I	256	FCR LCVE	III.1	112
Ben:	indeed, and full in my Teeth. Look you forsooth, I am as	263	FOR LCVE	III.1	371
Foresight:	Indeed! bless me.	268	FOR LOVE	III.1	574
Foresight:	I thank you, Mr. Scandal, indeed that wou'd be a	271	FOR LOVE	III.1	653
Ben:	is indeed, as like as two Cable Ropes.	273	FOR LOVE	III.1	722
Ben:	spring a Leak. You have hit it indeed, Mess you've nick'd	273	FOR LOVE	III.1	726
Jeremy:	sound, poor Gentleman. He is indeed here, Sir, and not	279	FOR LOVE	IV.1	125
Jeremy:	Would you could, Sir; for he has lost himself. Indeed,	279	FOR LOVE	IV.1	130
Mrs Frail:	Wife? I should have been fobb'd indeed, very finely	286	FOR LOVE	IV.1	411
Angelica:	was indeed thinking to propose something like it in a Jest,	300	FOR LOVE	V.1	107
Tattle:	thing indeed--Fie, fie, you're a Woman now, and	303	FOR LOVE	V.1	243
Miss Prue:	long as she's an Old Woman? Indeed but I won't: For	305	FOR LCVE	V.1	306
Angelica:	'Tis very true indeed, Uncle; I hope you'll be my	308	FOR LCVE	V.1	393
Valentine:	Indeed, I thought, Sir, when the Father endeavoured	311	FOR LOVE	V.1	511
Scandal:	'S'death, you are not mad indeed, to ruine your	311	FOR LOVE	V.1	541
Almeria:	Thou canst not tell--thou hast indeed no Cause.	326	M. BRIDE	I.1	19
Almeria:	Indeed thou hast a soft and gentle Nature,	327	M. BRIDE	I.1	30
Leonora:	Indeed I knew not this.	328	M. BRIDE	I.1	87
Almeria:	I thank thee--indeed I do--	328	M. BRIDE	I.1	94
Almeria:	Indeed, I do, for pitying thy sad Mistress;	328	M. BRIDE	I.1	V 95
Leonora:	Indeed 'twas mournful--	329	M. BRIDE	I.1	142
Gonsalez:	This Sight, which is ir ed not seen (tho' twice	332	M. BRIDE	I.1	244
Manuel:	A Conquerour indeed, w e you are won;	335	M. BRIDE	I.1	387
Almeria:	Indeed I wou'd--Nay, I ou'd tell thee all	343	M. BRIDE	II.2	129

Indeed   (continued)

Speaker	Text	PAGE	TITLE	ACT.SC	LINE
Osmyn-Alph:	I indeed shou'd see thee--	344	M. BRIDE	II.2	165
Osmyn-Alph:	That I indeed shou'd be so blest to see thee. . . .	344	M. BRIDE	II.2	V165
Osmyn-Alph:	I'm fortunate indeed--my Friend too safe! . . .	344	M. BRIDE	II.2	V170
Osmyn-Alph:	Where is Alphonso? ha! where? where indeed? . . .	352	M. BRIDE	III.1	86
Almeria:	Indeed; if that be so, if I'm thy Torment, . . .	357	M. BRIDE	III.1	296
Gonsalez:	Which wears indeed this Colour of a Truth; . . .	363	M. BRIDE	IV.1	79
Zara:	Indeed? Then 'twas a Whisper spread by some . . .	366	M. BRIDE	IV.1	189
	As if indeed a Widow, or an Heir.	385	M. BRIDE	EPI.	4
Mirabell:	it is now and then to be endur'd. He has indeed one good .	401	WAY WORLD	I.1	227
Witwoud:	acquit him--That indeed I cou'd wish were otherwise. . .	403	WAY WORLD	I.1	312
Witwoud:	Indeed, so crips?	420	WAY WORLD	II.1	375
Waitwell:	Your Pardon, Sir. With Submission, we have indeed . .	423	WAY WORLD	II.1	507
Waitwell:	That she did indeed, Sir. It was my Fault that she . .	423	WAY WORLD	II.1	516
Foible:	Your Ladyship has frown'd a little too rashly, indeed .	429	WAY WORLD	III.1	144
Marwood:	Indeed Mrs. Engine, is it thus with you?	431	WAY WORLD	III.1	225
Marwood:	'Twere better so indeed. Or what think you	433	WAY WORLD	III.1	308
Marwood:	Hood and Scarf. And indeed 'tis time, for the Town has	433	WAY WORLD	III.1	316
Marwood:	before, but it burnishes on her Hips. Indeed, Millamant, you	433	WAY WORLD	III.1	319
Marwood:	Indeed my Dear, you'll tear another Fan, if . . .	433	WAY WORLD	III.1	333
Marwood:	That's a Sign indeed its no Enemy to you. . . .	436	WAY WORLD	III.1	419
Witwoud:	Serjeants--'Tis not the fashion here; 'tis not indeed, . .	439	WAY WORLD	III.1	536
Sir Wilful:	What dee do? 'Shart a'has lock'd the Door indeed I . .	447	WAY WORLD	IV.1	92
Sir Wilful:	Indeed! Hah! Look ye, look ye, you do? Nay, ...	448	WAY WORLD	IV.1	123
Sir Wilful:	Town, as Plays and the like that must be confess'd indeed.	448	WAY WORLD	IV.1	125
Lady Wish:	Indeed you do.	459	WAY WORLD	IV.1	541
Lady Wish:	house indeed, and now I remember, my Niece went away .	461	WAY WORLD	IV.1	616
Foible:	your Lady-ship, Madam--No indeed his Marriage . . .	463	WAY WORLD	V.1	39
Foible:	put upon his Clergy--Yes indeed, I enquir'd of the . .	463	WAY WORLD	V.1	44
Foible:	Indeed Madam, and so 'tis a Comfort if you knew all, .	464	WAY WORLD	V.1	84
Marwood:	'Tis severe indeed Madam, that you shou'd	469	WAY WORLD	V.1	300
Fainall:	Indeed? are you provided of a Guard, with your . . .	473	WAY WORLD	V.1	432
Fainall:	Indeed? are you provided of your Guard, with your . .	473	WAY WORLD	V.1	V432
Foible:	Yes indeed Madam; I'll take my Bible-oath of it. . .	474	WAY WORLD	V.1	478
Fainall:	Not while you are worth a Groat, indeed my dear. . .	475	WAY WORLD	V.1	502

Indefatigable (1)

Vainlove:	Rewards to indefatigable Devotion--For as Love is a . .	58	OLD BATCH	II.2	140

Independent (1)

Millamant:	he draws a moments air, Independent on the Bounty of his .	449	WAY WORLD	IV.1	176

India (1)

Waitwell:	India? I have twenty Letters in my Pocket from him, in .	461	WAY WORLD	IV.1	607

Indications (1)

Tattle:	obvious to Vulgar Eyes; that are Indications of a sudden .	304	FOR LOVE	V.1	268

Indies (1)

Foible:	come to no damage--Or else the Wealth of the Indies . .	463	WAY WORLD	V.1	31

Indifference (8)

Lucy:	senseless indifference. By this Light I could have spit in	61	OLD BATCH	III.1	19
Lady Touch:	Cold indifference; Love has no Language to be heard. . .	184	DOUBL DLR	IV.2	23
Scandal:	a Woman of this Age, who has had an indifference for you .	225	FOR LOVE	I.1	351
Angelica:	You mistake Indifference for Uncertainty; I never . . .	254	FOR LOVE	III.1	31
Mrs Frail:	I are parted;--and with the same indifference that we met.	287	FOR LOVE	IV.1	451
Valentine:	without a Reverse or Inscription; for Indifference has both	297	FOR LOVE	IV.1	811
Fainall:	Yet you speak with an Indifference which seems to be .	397	WAY WORLD	I.1	93
Marwood:	pass our Youth in dull Indifference, to refuse the Sweets	410	WAY WORLD	II.1	13

Indifferent (3)

Sir Joseph:	Indifferent, agad in my opinion very indifferent . . .	70	OLD BATCH	III.1	333
Fainall:	you are not so indifferent; you are thinking of something	395	WAY WORLD	I.1	5

Indigent (1)

Marwood:	in Honour, as indigent of Wealth.	415	WAY WORLD	II.1	197

Indigestion (1)

Lady Wish:	or Indigestion of Widdow-hood; Nor Impute my Complacency,	458	WAY WORLD	IV.1	530

Indignation (2)

Maskwell:	Indignation; your Disposition, my Arguments, and happy .	136	DOUBL DLR	I.1	368
Mirabell:	that to your cruel Indignation, I have offer'd up this .	472	WAY WORLD	V.1	389

Indiscreet (1)

Capt Bluff:	'twas indiscreet, when you know what will provoke me-- .	54	OLD BATCH	II.1	242

Indiscretion (2)

Scandal:	Indiscretion be a sign of Love, you are the most a Lover .	234	FOR LOVE	I.1	676
Mrs Fain:	Yes, for I have Lov'd with Indiscretion.	416	WAY WORLD	II.1	257

Indisposed (1)

Sr Sampson:	indisposed: But I'm glad thou'rt better, honest Val. . .	281	FOR LOVE	IV.1	203

Indite (1)

Angelica:	and Spoon-meat together--Indeed, Uncle, I'll indite you .	237	FOR LOVE	II.1	91

Inditing (1)

Lady Ply:	now I find was of your own inditing--I do Heathen, . . .	179	DOUBL DLR	IV.1	456

Individual (1)

Sir Joseph:	Ay, now it's out; 'tis I, my own individual Person. . .	102	OLD BATCH	V.1	206

Indolent (1)

Millamant:	morning thoughts, agreeable wakings, indolent slumbers, .	449	WAY WORLD	IV.1	188

Indued (1)

Saygrace:	I have; the Gown will not be indued without	195	DOUBL DLR	V.1	290

Indulge (1)

Zara:	And will indulge it now. What Miseries?	360	M. BRIDE	III.1	424

Indulgence (3)

Lady Touch:	own'd your Love to him, and his indulgence would assist .	198	DOUBL DLR	V.1	418
Valentine:	hope you will have more Indulgence, than to oblige me to .	243	FOR LOVE	II.1	283
Sr Sampson:	to intimate, concerning Indulgence?	243	FOR LOVE	II.1	286

Indulgent (1)

Leonora:	By all the worthy and indulgent ways, ...	327	M. BRIDE	I.1	46

Industrious (2)

Sharper:	would be as industrious. But what was he that follow'd .	46	OLD BATCH	I.1	348
Leonora:	His most industrious Goodness could invent;	327	M. BRIDE	I.1	47

Industry (2)

Mellefont:	Industry grown full and ripe, ready to drop into his mouth,	187	DOUBL DLR	IV.2	144
Mellefont:	Industry grow full and ripe, ready to drop into his mouth,	187	DOUBL DLR	IV.2	V144

Insolence (continued)
Zara:	He should be set at large; thence sprung his Insolence,	.	349	M. BRIDE	II.2 V379
Mirabell:	Insolence, that in Revenge I tock her to pieces; sifted her		399	WAY WORLD	I.1 164
Lady Wish:	This Insolence is beyond all Precedent, all		469	WAY WORLD	V.1 298

Insolent (5)
Araminta:	how insolent wou'd a real Pardon make you? But there's		106	OLD BATCH	V.1 362
Lady Touch:	Insolent Devil! But have a care,--provoke me not; . .		135	DOUEL DLR	I.1 321
Angelica:	O barbarous! I never heard so insolent a piece of . .		258	FOR LOVE	III.1 182
Angelica:	Man, submits both to the Severity and insolent Conduct of		299	FOR LOVE	V.1 73
Angelica:	Man is a Slave to the Severity and insolent Conduct of		299	FOR LOVE	V.1 V 73

Inspir'd (2)
Scandal:	Discourses, and sometimes rather think him inspir'd than		285	FOR LOVE	IV.1 345
Millamant:	(Repeating.) Thyrsis a Youth of the Inspir'd train--	.	446	WAY WORLD	IV.1 63

Inspiration (2)
Sir Paul:	find Passion coming upon me by inspiration, and I cannot		144	DOUBL DLR	II.1 207
Osmyn-Alph:	This Lesson, in some Hour of Inspiration, ...		353	M. BRIDE	III.1 128

Inspire (0)   see Re-inspire

Instance (3)
	Give you one Instance of a Passive Poet.		393	WAY WORLD	PRO. 38
Marwood:	'Tis false. I challenge you to shew an Instance . . .		414	WAY WORLD	II.1 153
Fainall:	and your Resentment fcllows his Neglect. An Instance?		414	WAY WORLD	II.1 156

Instant (8)
Vainlove:	Ay, ay, to this instant Moment.--I have past		110	OLD BATCH	V.2 102
Lady Ply:	this instant.		179	DOUEL DLR	IV.1 447
Tattle:	Word of your Ladyships Passion, till this instant. .		254	FOR LOVE	III.1 56
Alonzo:	And on the instant, flung'd it in his Breast.		373	M. BRIDE	V.1 27
Almeria:	That Sense, which in one Instant shews him dead . . .		383	M. BRIDE	V.2 294
Mirabell:	Beauty dies upon the Instant: For Beauty is the Lover's		420	WAY WORLD	II.1 393
Mrs Fain:	O Sir Wilfull; you are come at the Critical Instant. There's		446	WAY WORLD	IV.1 70
Mirabell:	upon Instant and tedious Sollicitation, that they . .		449	WAY WORLD	IV.1 171

Instantly (5)
Lady Touch:	I follow instantly--So.		154	DOUEL DLR	III.1 126
Lady Ply:	him instantly.--		179	DOUEL DLR	IV.1 464
Maskwell:	instantly.		181	DOUEL DLR	IV.1 524
Zara:	I will retire, and instantly prepare		366	M. BRIDE	IV.1 191
Zara:	Attend me instantly, with each a Bowl		375	M. BRIDE	V.1 131

Instead (4)
Lady Ply:	given Sir Paul your Letter instead of his own. . . .		178	DOUBL DLR	IV.1 400
Maskwell:	self ready, I'll wheedle her intc the Coach; and instead of		193	DOUEL DLR	V.1 223
Mirabell:	instead of a Man-child, make me the Father to a Crooked-billet.		451	WAY WORLD	IV.1 262
Mirabell:	instead of a Man-child, make me Father to a Crooked-billet.		451	WAY WORLD	IV.1 V262

Instinct (4)
Setter:	Devil could know you by instinct?		66	OLD BATCH	III.1 206
Lucy:	You could know my Office by instinct, and be hang'd, .		66	OLD BATCH	III.1 207
	There, as instinct directs, to Swim, or Drown. . . .		125	DOUEL DLR	PRO. 4
Mirabell:	the force of Instinct--O here come my pair of Turtles .		423	WAY WORLD	II.1 501

Instruct (6)
Careless:	aking trembling heart, the nimble movement shall instruct		170	DOUEL DLR	IV.1 93
Careless:	trembling heart, the nimble movement shall instruct .		170	DOUEL DLR	IV.1 V 93
Maskwell:	But first I must instruct my little Levite, there is no Plot, ...		194	DOUEL DLR	V.1 267
Lord Touch:	Instruct me how this may be done, you shall		196	DOUBL DLR	V.1 324
Zara:	Instruct the two remaining Mutes, that they		375	M. BRIDE	V.1 130
	He'll not instruct, lest it should give Cffence. . .		393	WAY WORLD	PRO. 34

Instructed (7)
Setter:	I warrant you, Sir, I'm instructed.		101	OLD BATCH	V.1 195
Brisk:	instructed. Suppose, as I was saying, you come up to me,		134	DOUEL DLR	I.1 254
Mellefont:	be instructed.		134	DOUEL DLR	I.1 281
Mrs Fain:	Whom have you instructed to represent your		417	WAY WORLD	II.1 283
Millamant:	endure to be reprimanded, nor instructed; 'tis so dull to		422	WAY WORLD	II.1 454
Waitwell:	to Business, Sir. I have instructed her as well as I cou'd. If		423	WAY WORLD	II.1 509
Poible:	But I told my Lady as you instructed me, Sir. That I .		423	WAY WORLD	II.1 519

Instruction (5)
Valentine:	to live upon Instruction; feast your Mind, and mortifie		216	FOR LOVE	I.1 13
Scandal:	Wise Men of the East ow'd their Instruction to a Star,		267	FOR LOVE	III.1 535
Valentine:	Riddle. There's my Instruction, and the Moral of my .		296	FOR LOVE	IV.1 796
Zara:	Instruction, for my Ministers of Death.		366	M. BRIDE	IV.1 192
Mirabell:	That was by Poible's Direction, and my Instruction, .		418	WAY WORLD	II.1 305

Instructions (4)
Fondlewife:	instructions, I will reason with her before I go. . .		76	OLD BATCH	IV.1 47
Cynthia:	Instructions.		139	DOUEL DLR	I.1 37
Scandal:	your Chamber-door; and leave you my last Instructions?		273	FOR LOVE	III.1 746
Waitwell:	she can take your Directions as readily as my Instructions,		423	WAY WORLD	II.1 510

Instrument (8)
Osmyn-Alph:	Why was I made the Instrument, tc throw		347	M. BRIDE	II.2 322
Fainall:	Yes, while the Instrument is drawing, to which you . .		469	WAY WORLD	V.1 291
Fainall:	Instrument, and till my return, you may Ballance this .		469	WAY WORLD	V.1 295
Fainall:	the Instrument, are you prepar'd to sign?		472	WAY WORLD	V.1 415
Sir Wilful:	in defiance of you Sir, and of your Instrument. S'heart an		473	WAY WORLD	V.1 424
Sir Wilful:	you talk of an Instrument Sir, I have an old Fox by my		473	WAY WORLD	V.1 425
Sir Wilful:	Thigh shall hack your Instrument of Ram Vellum to shreds,		473	WAY WORLD	V.1 426
Sir Wilful:	measure; therefore withdraw your Instrument Sir, or .		473	WAY WORLD	V.1 428

Insufferably (1)
Marwood:	insufferably proud.		412	WAY WORLD	II.1 73

Insufficient (1)
Barnaby:	Never Sir, but when the Man is an insufficient . . .		76	OLD BATCH	IV.1 41

Insult (2)
Scandal:	comes Tyrannically to insult a ruin'd Lover, and make .		276	FOR LOVE	IV.1 24
Singer:	When I insult a Rival's Eyes:		435	WAY WORLD	III.1 388

Insupportable (4)
Laetitia:	Oh, insupportable Impudence!		94	OLD BATCH	IV.4 181
Heartwell:	and whore my Wife? No, That's insupportable.-- . . .		104	OLD BATCH	V.1 310
Mrs Fain:	Jealousies are insupportable: And when they cease to Love,		410	WAY WORLD	II.1 5
Lady Wish:	O, 'tis Insupportable. No, no, dear Friend		468	WAY WORLD	V.1 237

Int'rest (2)
Selim: And as to your Revenge, not his own Int'rest, ... 361 M. BRIDE IV.1 21
Selim: And some of them bought off to Osmyn's Int'rest, . . . 362 M. BRIDE IV.1 52
Integrity (4)
Marwood: Integrity. . . . . 426 WAY WORLD III.1 56
Lady Wish: corrupt Integrity it self. If she has given him an
          Opportunity, ... 426 WAY WORLD III.1 58
Lady Wish: she has as good as put her Integrity into his Hands. . . 426 WAY WORLD III.1 59
Lady Wish: Ah dear Marwood, what's Integrity to an Opportunity? . 426 WAY WORLD III.1 60
Intelligence (1)
Scandal: Intelligence.--He's here. . . . . 226 FOR LOVE I.1 380
Intemperate (1)
Lord Froth: you, O Intemperate! I have a flushing in my Face already. . 134 DOUBL DLR I.1 289
Intend (11)
Silvia: one. But do you intend to Marry me? . . . . 73 OLD BATCH III.2 94
Sir Paul: Lord nor my Lady to know what they intend. . . . . . 171 DOUBL DLR IV.1 158
Brisk: Deuce take me I believe you intend to Marry your . . . 174 DOUBL DLR IV.1 271
Maskwell: Why, I intend to tell my Lord the whole matter of . . 193 DOUBL DLR V.1 214
Scandal: Attendance, and promis'd more than ever you intend to . 221 FOR LOVE I.1 194
Sr Sampson: No, I intend you shall Marry, Ben; I would not . . . 261 FOR LOVE III.1 297
Mrs Frail: So then you intend to go to Sea again? . . . . . . 285 FOR LOVE IV.1 378
Angelica: my design, for I intend to make you my Confident. . . 290 FOR LOVE IV.1 V569
Valentine: I'll prevent that suspicion--For I intend to . . . . 313 FOR LOVE V.1 608
Almeria: Where am I? Heav'n! what does this Dream intend? . . 383 M. BRIDE V.2 288
Marwood: You intend to Travel, Sir, as I'm inform'd. . . . . 440 WAY WORLD III.1 566
Intended (10)
Bellmour: short of the intended Mark. . . . . 37 OLD BATCH I.1 12
Setter: --Our Stratagem succeeding as you intended, ... 105 OLD BATCH V.1 342
Setter: --Our Stratagem succeeded as you intended, ... 105 OLD BATCH V.1 V342
Lady Ply: was intended to me. Your Honour! You have none, . . . 144 DOUBL DLR II.1 235
Lady Ply: strike him with the remorse of his intended Crime. . . 145 DOUBL DLR II.1 273
Maskwell: intended this Evening to have try'd all Arguments to . 182 DOUBL DLR IV.1 577
Scandal: Attendance, and promis'd more than ever you intended to . 221 FOR LOVE I.1 V194
Ben: When she no more intended, ... 274 FOR LOVE III.1 764
Angelica: my design, for I intended to make you my Confident. . . 290 FOR LOVE IV.1 569
Marwood: why should you not keep her longer than you intended? . 442 WAY WORLD III.1 657
Intent (2)
Singer-F: Their Intent was to try if his Oracle knew . . . . 258 FOR LOVE III.1 202
Such, who watch Plays, with scurrilous intent . . . . 479 WAY WORLD EPI. 17
Intention (2)
Heartwell: of the intention, and none of the pleasure of the practice-- 43 OLD BATCH I.1 239
Bellmour: I thank thee, George, for thy good intention.-- . . . 111 OLD BATCH V.2 154
Intentions (3)
Bellmour: Intentions for thee too: Let this mollifie.--(Gives her . 98 OLD BATCH V.1 59
Bellmour: I have no such Intentions at present.--Prithee, . . . 100 OLD BATCH V.1 156
Tattle: I did, as I hope to be sav'd, Madam, my Intentions . . . 309 FOR LOVE V.1 457
Intercede (2)
Sir Joseph: let these worthy Gentlemen intercede for me. . . . . 103 OLD BATCH V.1 245
Sir Paul: spoken Man, I desired him to intercede for me.-- . . . 180 DOUBL DLR IV.1 480
Interceding (1)
Osmyn-Alph: Of interceding for me with the King; . . . . . . 359 M. BRIDE III.1 389
Intercepted (1)
Mirabell: Ay Madam; but that is too late, my reward is intercepted. 473 WAY WORLD V.1 457
Intercessor (1)
Lady Wish: you are become an Intercessor with my Son-in-Law, to . 465 WAY WORLD V.1 129
Interdiction (1)
Gonsalez: That Interdiction so particular, ... 365 M. BRIDE IV.1 174
Interest (20)   see Int'rest, Self-interest
Bellmour: Merit, and preferring only those of interest, has made him 47 OLD BATCH I.1 372
Sharper: My loss, I esteem as a trifle repay'd with interest, . . 49 OLD BATCH II.1 76
Bellmour: importunity at Court; first creates its own Interest, and 58 OLD BATCH II.2 133
Araminta: Religion, as his Humour varies or his Interest. . . . . 58 OLD BATCH II.2 149
Sharper: Matrimonial Oath with Interest.--Come, thou'rt . . . 99 OLD BATCH V.1 89
Mellefont: may not work her to her Interest. And if you chance to . 130 DOUBL DLR I.1 127
Careless: you have confessed, is grounded upon his Interest, that, . 131 DOUBL DLR I.1 164
Cynthia: 'Tis my Interest to believe he will, my Lord. . . . . 141 DOUBL DLR II.1 101
Maskwell: I might be trusted; since it was as much my interest as hers 149 DOUBL DLR II.1 423
Sir Paul: to his Bed, and there return his Caresses with interest
          to his . . . . 178 DOUBL DLR IV.1 422
Maskwell: Lucky! Fortune is your own, and 'tis her interest . . 187 DOUBL DLR V.1 2
Lord Touch: Wealth or Interest can purchase Cynthia, she is thine.-- 189 DOUBL DLR V.1 75
Sr Sampson: not a Drachm of Generous Love about him: All Interest, . 260 FOR LOVE III.1 241
Sr Sampson: all Interest; he's an undone Scoundrel, and courts your . 260 FOR LOVE III.1 242
Angelica: for mercenary Ends and sordid Interest. . . . . . . 294 FOR LOVE IV.1 724
Angelica: for by mercenary Ends and sordid Interest . . . . . 294 FOR LOVE IV.1 V724
Valentine: Nay, now you do me Wrong; for if any Interest . . . 295 FOR LOVE IV.1 725
Angelica: Martyrdom, and sacrifice their Interest to their Constancy! 314 FOR LOVE V.1 634
Zara: To find you have an Interest superiour. . . . . . 360 M. BRIDE III.1 419
Mrs Fain: Woman; and may win her to your Interest. . . . . 417 WAY WORLD II.1 287
Interested (1)
Mirabell: knew Fainall to be a Man lavish of his Morals, an interested 417 WAY WORLD II.1 270
Interests (1)
Lord Touch: Not fit to be told me, Madam? You can have no Interests, . 152 DOUBL DLR III.1 46
Interlards (1)
Jeremy: lying is a Figure in Speech, that interlards the greatest 296 FOR LOVE IV.1 776
Intermission (1)
Lady Touch: little thou swelling Heart; let me have some intermission 185 DOUBL DLR IV.2 65
Interposed (1)
Valentine: Tattle, I thank you, you would have interposed . . . . 313 FOR LOVE V.1 595
Interposing (1)
Fainall: The Injuries you have done him are a proof: Your interposing 414 WAY WORLD II.1 157
Interpret (3)
Maskwell: interpret a Coldness the right way; therefore I must . 155 DOUBL DLR III.1 182
Zara: O Heav'n! my Fears interpret . . . . 354 M. BRIDE III.1 193
Mirabell: am not one of those Coxcombs who are apt to interpret a . 397 WAY WORLD I.1 86

```
Interpretation (1)
  Mrs Frail:      . . . Artimedorus for Interpretation,   . . . . . .  231  FOR LCVE    I.1  582
Interpreter (2)
  Mirabell:       or I shall call your Interpreter.   . . . . . . . .  406  WAY WCRLD   I.1  433
  Sir Wilful:     He is to be my Interpreter in foreign Parts. He has been  .  471  WAY WORLD   V.1  348
Interr'd (4)
  Almeria:        But in my Heart thou art interr'd, there, there,   . . .  328  M. ERIDE    I.1   74
  Manuel:         Hated Anselmo, was interr'd--By Heav'n,   . . . . .  333  M. EBIDE    I.1  297
  Osmyn-Alph:     She shall be Royally interr'd. O Garcia,   . . . . .  383  M. ERIDE    V.2  315
  Osmyn-Alph:     She shall be Royally interr'd.   . . . . . . . . .  383  M. ERIDE    V.2 V315
Interrogatories (2)
  Millamant:      without Interrogatories or wry Faces on your part. To  . .  450  WAY WCRLD  IV.1  214
  Marwood:        gravity of the Bench, and provoke Naughty Interrogatories,  467  WAY WCBLD   V.1  218
Interrupt (6)
  Lucy:           Not to interrupt your meditation--   . . . . . . .   65  OLD EATCH III.1  160
  Careless:       interrupt you.   . . . . . . . . . . . . . . . .  128  DOUEL DLR   I.1   18
  Brisk:          Pshaw, pshaw, prithee don't interrupt me.--But I   . . .  134  DOUBL DLR   I.1  262
  Lady Ply:       Nay, not to interrupt you my Dear--only   . . . . .  173  DOUEL DLR  IV.1  214
  Mrs Frail:      If it won't interrupt you, I'll entertain you with a  . .  273  FOR LCVE  III.1  748
  Valentine:      Husht--Interrupt me not--I'll whisper   . . . . . .  288  FOR LCVE   IV.1  486
Interrupted (5)
  Bellmour:       Though you should be now and then interrupted in a  . . .   44  OLD BATCH   I.1  268
  Capt Bluff:     Death, had any cther Man interrupted me--   . . . .   54  OLD EATCH   I.1  237
  Scandal:        Pox on her, she has interrupted my Design--But   . . .  269  FOR LCVE  III.1  578
  Scandal:        longer Master of my self--I was interrupted in the morning,  269  FOR LCVE  III.1  587
  Mrs Pain:       Mr. Mirabell; my Mother interrupted you in a   . . . .  412  WAY WCRLD  II.1   98
Interval (1)
  Angelica:       am I deluded by this Interval of Sense, to reason with a  .  295  FOR LCVE   IV.1  729
Intervals (2)
  Sr Sampson:     Has he no Intervals?   . . . . . . . . . . . .  280  FCR LOVE   IV.1  181
  Jeremy:         Yes, Madam; He has Intervals: But you see he begins   .  295  FCB LCVE   IV.1  747
Intimacy (1)
  Bellmour:       till 'twas late; my Intimacy with him gave me the   . .   82  OLD EATCH  IV.2   50
Intimate (6)
  Sr Sampson:     to intimate, concerning Indulgence?   . . . . . . .  243  FOR LCVE   II.1  286
  Tattle:         find: For sure my intimate Friends wou'd have known--  .  256  FCR LCVE  III.1  113
  Gonsalez:       Which seem to intimate, as if Alphonso,   . . . . .  363  M. ERIDE   IV.1   77
  Fainall:        You wcu'd intimate then, as if there were a   . . . .  413  WAY WCRLD  II.1  126
  Millamant:      acquaintance; or to be intimate with Fools, because they  .  450  WAY WCRLD  IV.1  218
  Mirabell:       or Intimate of your own Sex; No she friend to skreen  .  451  WAY WCBLD  IV.1  236
Intire (2)
  Sir Joseph:     intire dependance Sir, upon the superfluity of your
                      goodness,  . . . . . . . . . . . . . . . .   49  OLD EATCH  II.1   56
  Lady Ply:       of an intire resignation of all my best Wishes, for the  .  169  DOUEL DLR  IV.1   81
Intirely (1)
  Bellmour:       loves thee intirely--I have heard her breath such Raptures   38  OLD BATCH   I.1   40
Into (126)
Into't (2)
  Careless:       into't.   . . . . . . . . . . . . . . . . .  128  DOUBL DLR   I.1   24
  Sr Sampson:     go naked out of the World as you came into't.   . . .  244  FCB LCVE   II.1  338
Intreat (1)
  Sir Wilful:     of Furnival's Inn--You cou'd intreat to be remember'd  .  439  WAY WCRLD III.1  550
Intrepid (1)
  Osmyn-Alph:     Of God-like Mould, intrepid and ccmmanding,   . . . .  355  M. EBIDE  III.1  223
Intriegue (1)
  Tattle:         a private Intriegue of Destiny, kept secret from the
                      piercing  . . . . . . . . . . . . . . . .  304  FCB LCVE    V.1  271
Intrigue (1)
  Bellmour:       Come, I know the Intrigue between Heartwell and your  . .   97  OLD EATCH   V.1   42
Intrigues (1)
  Maskwell:       their own Follies and Intrigues, they'll miss neither of
                      you.  . . . . . . . . . . . . . . . . . .  155  DOUEL CLR III.1  168
Introduc'd (1)
  Tattle:         Third Person--or have introduc'd an Amour of my   . . .  256  FOR LCVE  III.1  118
Introducing (2)
                  A Servant introducing Bellmour in Fanatick Habit, with a  .   80  OLD BATCH  IV.2
  Maskwell:       So; I durst not cwn my introducing my Lord,   . . . .  188  DOUEL DLR    V.1   10
Intruding (1)
  Zara:           Perhaps I'm sawcy and Intruding--   . . . . . . .  359  M. ERIDE  III.1  413
Invades (1)
  Lady Wish:      that invades me with scme precipitation--You will oblige  .  457  WAY WORLD  IV.1  468
Invasion (4)
  Zara:           On to this Invasion; where he was lost,   . . . . .  347  M. EBIDE   II.2  301
  Zara:           To this Invasion; where he late was lost,   . . . .  347  M. EBIDE   II.2 V301
  Gonsalez:       Open'd the Way to this Invasion;   . . . . . . . .  363  M. EBIDE   IV.1   87
  Gonsalez:       Open'd and urg'd the Way to this Invasion;   . . . .  363  M. EBIDE   IV.1  V 87
Invective (1)
  Mirabell:       Invective against long Visits. I would not have understood  396  WAY WOBLD   I.1   36
Invent (6)
  Lady Touch:     You want but leasure to invent fresh falshood,   . . .  197  DOUEL DLR    V.1  379
  Scandal:        would be to invent the honest means of keeping your word,  221  FOR LCVE    I.1  196
  Leonora:        His most industrious Goodness could invent;   . . . .  327  M. EBIDE    I.1   47
  Osmyn-Alph:     Or hell-born Malice can invent; extort   . . . . .  357  M. EBIDE  III.1  315
  Zara:           What shall I say? Invent, contrive, advise   . . . .  361  M. EBIDE   IV.1   23
  Mirabell:       because he has not Wit enough to invent an Evasion.   .  404  WAY WCRLD   I.1  338
Invented (2)
  Mrs Frail:      invented a Dream, and sent him to   . . . . . . .  231  FOR LOVE    I.1  582
  Gonsalez:       Invented Tale! he was Alphonso's Friend.   . . . .  371  M. ERIDE   IV.1  414
Inventing (1)
  Maskwell:       will be inventing) which I thought to communicate to   .  196  DOUEL DLR    V.1  327
Invention (7)
  Maskwell:       One Minute, gives Invention to Destroy,   . . . . .  138  DOUEL DLB    I.1  421
  Brisk:          to win her with a new airy invention of my own, hem!   .  175  DOUEL DLB   IV.1  304
  Lord Touch:     He has a quick invention, if this were   . . . . .  197  DOUEL DLB    V.1  358
  Maskwell:       (aside). Thanks, my invention; and now I have it   . .  198  DOUEL DLB    V.1  412
  Maskwell:       So, this was a pinch indeed, my invention was   . . .  199  DOUBL DLR    V.1  '461
```

353

Invention   (continued)
  Mrs Frail: Pooh, this is all Invention. Have you ne're a   233   FOR LOVE   I.1   649
  Witwoud: No; the Rogue's Wit and Readiness of Invention   406   WAY WORLD   I.1   413
Inveterate (1)
  Valentine: You are as inveterate against our Poets, as if your   . . 220   FOR LOVE   I.1   151
Inveterately (1)
  Mrs Fain: Heartily, Inveterately. 410   WAY WORLD   II.1   35
Invincible (2)
  Sir Paul: Nay, she has been an invincible Wife, even to   145   DOUBL DLR   II.1 V257
  Valentine: me are craving and invincible; they are so many Devils . 244   FOR LOVE   II.1 347
Inviolably (1)
  Lady Wish: will bind me to you inviolably. I have an Affair of moment 457 WAY WORLD   IV.1 467
Inviolate (2)
  Marwood: Love inviolate? And have you the baseness to charge me   . 414 WAY WORLD   II.1 174
  Millamant: without giving a reason. To have my Closet Inviolate; to . 450 WAY WORLD   IV.1 221
Invisible (1)
  Angelica: last Invisible Eclipse, laying in Provision as 'twere for a 237 FOR LOVE   II.1   80
Invite (1)
  Sir Wilful: Let Apollo's Example invite us;   455   WAY WORLD   IV.1 418
Invites (1)
  Almeria: Invites me to the Bed, where I alone   . . . . 340 M. BRIDE   II.2   16
Inviting (1)
  Lord Froth: Lady's is the most inviting Couch; and a slumber there, is 200 DOUBL DLR   V.1   494
Involuntary (1)
  Angelica: and involuntary; if he loves, he can't help it; and if I
                  don't   . . . . 278 FOR LOVE   IV.1   87
Involv'd (1)
  Maskwell: tho' she involv'd her self in ruine. No, it must be by   . 190 DOUBL DLR   V.1   94
Involve (1)
  Mrs Fain: Mirabell's Uncle, and as such winning my Lady, to involve 430 WAY WORLD III.1 191
Inward (3)
  Almeria: Some small reserve of near and inward Woe, ... 328 M. BRIDE   I.1   83
  Osmyn-Alph: Turn your Lights inward, Eyes, and look   . . . . . . 345 M. BRIDE   II.2 215
  Osmyn-Alph: Turn your Lights inward, Eyes, and view my Thought,   . 345 M. BRIDE   II.2 V215
Irish (1)
  Valentine: Piece of Aegyptian Antiquity, or an Irish Manuscript; you . 297 FOR LOVE IV.1 802
Iron (2)
  Leonora: Unclos'd; the Iron Grates that lead to Death   . . . . . 340 M. BRIDE   II.2   11
  Zara: Thro' all the Gloomy Ways, and Iron Doors   . . . . . . 379 M. BRIDE   V.2   133
Irons (2)
  Zara: Has leaden thee with Chains and galling Irons: . . . 353 M. BRIDE   III.1 159
  Osmyn-Alph: Rude Irons? Must I meet thee thus, Almeria?   . . . . . 355 M. BRIDE   III.1 244
Irreconcilable (1)
  Jeremy: Favour? Why Sir Sampson will be irreconcilable. If your . 218 FOR LOVE   I.1   83
Irrecoverably (1)
  Heartwell: Certainly, irrecoverably married.   . . . . 105 OLD BATCH   V.1   315
Irresistable (1)
  Cynthia: was the Devil, I'll allow for irresistable odds. But if
                  I find   . . . . 169 DOUBL DLR   IV.1   59
Irresistably (1)
  Mellefont: to engage her more irresistably. 'Tis only an inhancing the 158 DOUBL DLR III.1 301
Is (1064)
Is't (11)
  Careless: Hum, ay, what is't?   . . . . 128 DOUBL DLR   I.1   40
  Brisk: O, Mon Coeur! What is't! nay gad I'll punish you for   . 128 DOUBL DLR   I.1   41
  Lord Touch: Is't for your self?--I'll hear of nought for   . . . . 189 DOUBL DLR   V.1   69
  Lord Froth: what a Clock is't? past Eight, on my Conscience; my   . 200 DOUBL DLR   V.1   493
  Valentine: What a Clock is't? My Father here! Your Blessing, Sir? . 280 FOR LOVE   IV.1 193
  Manuel: Why is't, Almeria, that you meet our Eyes   . . . . . . 333 M. BRIDE   I.1 V279
  Manuel: A Bridal Qualm; soon off. How is't, Almeria?   . . . . 334 M. BRIDE   I.1   348
  Manuel: A Fit of Bridal Fear; How is't, Almeria?   . . . . . . 334 M. BRIDE   I.1 V348
  Zara: What is't to me, this House of Misery?   . . . . 346 M. BRIDE   II.2 266
  Zara: Why is't you more than speak in these sad Signs?   . . 380 M. BRIDE   V.2   159
  Zara: We both should die. Nor is't that I survive;   . . . . 380 M. BRIDE   V.2   188
Isaac (6)
  Fondlewife: Tell me Isaac, why art thee Jealous? Why art thee
                  distrustful   . . . . 76 OLD BATCH   IV.1   50
  Fondlewife: thee marry Isaac?--Because she was beautiful and tempting, 76 OLD BATCH IV.1   53
  Fondlewife: who will tempt her Isaac?--I fear it much--But   . . . 76 OLD BATCH   IV.1   57
  Fondlewife: canst reach, th' hast experimented Isaac--But Mum. . . 77 OLD BATCH   IV.1   63
  Bellmour: of your absence, by my Spy, (for Faith, honest Isaac, I . 94 OLD BATCH   IV.4 206
  Bellmour: How canst thou be so cruel, Isaac? Thou hast the   . . 95 OLD BATCH   IV.4 234
Iscariot (1)
  Sir Paul: be Damn'd for a Judas Maccabeus, and Iscariot both. O . 178 DOUBL DLR   IV.1 418
Island (2)
  Bellmour: floating Island; sometimes seems in reach, then vanishes . 42 OLD BATCH I.1   206
  Sharper: For Love's Island: I, for the Golden Coast.   . . . . . 47 OLD BATCH   I.1   387
Isle (1)   see Ile
  Almeria: Whistling thro' Hollows of this vaulted Isle.   . . . 339 M. BRIDE   II.2   55
Issue (3)
  Sir Paul: utterly extinct for want of Issue Male. Oh Impiety! But . 171 DOUBL DLR IV.1 138
  Sr Sampson: present Majesty of Bantam is the Issue of these Loyns. . 241 FOR LOVE   II.1 223
  Sr Sampson: upon the Issue Male of our Two Bodies begotten. Odsbud, . 300 FOR LOVE   V.1   128
Issue-Male (1)
  Mrs Frail: Issue-Male of their two Bodies; 'tis the most superstitious 231 FOR LOVE I.1   579
It (1163)   see What-de-call-it-Court
It's (49)
  Capt Bluff: Zoons Sir, it's a Lie, you have not seen it, nor shant . 53 OLD BATCH II.1 234
  Belinda: Prithee tell it all the World, it's false. Betty. (Calls) . 56 OLD BATCH II.2   61
  Sir Joseph: Agad, it's a curious, fine, pretty Rogue; I'll speak   . . 89 OLD BATCH IV.4   32
  Laetitia: Dear Husband, I'm amaz'd:--Sure it's a good   . . . . . 92 OLD BATCH   IV.4 114
  Sir Joseph: Ay, now it's out; 'tis I, my own individual Person. . . 102 OLD BATCH V.1   206
  Brisk: Ay, my Lord, it's a sign I hit you in the Teeth, if you . 132 DOUBL DLR I.1   210
  Mellefont: because it's possible we may lose; since we have Shuffled 142 DOUBL DLR II.1   160
  Lady Ply: help it, if you are made a Captive? I swear it's pity it . 148 DOUBL DLR II.1   359
  Maskwell: execution of all her Plots? Ha, ha, ha, by Heaven it's true; 149 DOUBL DLR II.1 398

It's   (continued)
Lady Touch:	Nay, but will you be calm--indeed it's	152	DOUBL DLR	III.1	72
Maskwell:	No, but it's a Comical design upon mine.	156	DOUBL DLR	III.1	212
Sir Paul:	my Lady is so nice--it's very strange, but it's true: too	161	DOUBL DLR	III.1	431
Sir Paul:	indeed it's true, Mr. Careless, it breaks my heart--I	162	DOUBL DLR	III.1	436
Lady Ply:	Here, Sir Paul, it's from your Steward, here's a	162	DOUBL DLR	III.1	450
Brisk:	'Tis not a Song neither--it's a sort of an Epigram, or	166	DOUBL DLR	III.1	591
Brisk:	call it, but it's Satyr.--Sing it my Lord.	166	DOUBL DLR	III.1	593
Lady Froth:	O-law, I swear it's but the sixth,--and I han't	166	DOUBL DLR	III.1	612
Cynthia:	It's impossible; she'll cast beyond you still--I'll	167	DOUBL DLR	IV.1	6
Maskwell:	I have it, it must be by Stratagem; for it's in vain	190	DOUBL DLR	V.1	114
Jeremy:	Sir, it's impossible--I may die with you, starve with	218	FOR LOVE	I.1	72
Scandal:	where-ever it is, it's always contriving it's own Ruine.	219	FOR LOVE	I.1	121
Mrs Fore:	No matter for that, it's as good a Face as yours.	247	FOR LOVE	II.1	460
Mrs Fore:	It's very true, Sister: Well since all's out, and	248	FOR LOVE	II.1	476
Miss Prue:	this way--Is not it pure?--It's better than	249	FOR LOVE	II.1	528
Tattle:	for it's whisper'd every where.	254	FOR LOVE	III.1	48
Valentine:	There, now it's out.	255	FOR LOVE	III.1	87
Tattle:	Gad, it's very true, Madam, I think we are oblig'd to	257	FOR LOVE	III.1	134
Mrs Frail:	Not at all; I like his humour mightily, it's plain	262	FOR LOVE	III.1	321
Ben:	Nay, You say true in that, it's but a folly to lie: For to	263	FOR LOVE	III.1	385
Sr Sampson:	Watch, and the Bridegroom shall observe it's Motions;	266	FOR LOVE	III.1	474
Mrs Fore:	Husband, will you go to Bed? It's Ten a	268	FOR LOVE	III.1	576
Mrs Fore:	Entertainment. I believe it's late.	275	FOR LOVE	III.1	806
Valentine:	thing; it's a Question that would puzzle an Arithmetician,	280	FOR LOVE	IV.1	175
Sr Sampson:	Pocket.) There Val: it's safe enough, Boy--But thou	282	FOR LOVE	IV.1	233
Ben:	it's an ill Wind blows no body good,--may-hap I have	287	FOR LOVE	IV.1	425
Ben:	it's an ill Wind blows no body good,--may-hap I have a	287	FOR LOVE	IV.1	V425
Angelica:	like him, it's a sign he likes me; and that's more than half	297	FOR LOVE	V.1	6
Scandal:	'S'death it's a Jest. I can't believe it.	307	FOR LOVE	V.1	367
Ben:	Look you, Friend, it's nothing to me, whether you	307	FOR LOVE	V.1	368
Sr Sampson:	in Winter? Not at all--It's a Plot to undermine Cold	308	FOR LOVE	V.1	405
Ben:	Case, you should not marry her. It's just the same thing,	308	FOR LOVE	V.1	414
Mrs Frail:	(to her). Aye, aye, it's well it's no worse--Nay,	310	FOR LOVE	V.1	471
	It's like what I have heard our Poets tell us:	315	FOR LOVE	EPI.	6
Marwood:	was something in it; but it seems it's over with you. Your	431	WAY WORLD	III.1	230
Petulant:	No, no, it's no Enemy to any Body, but them that	436	WAY WORLD	III.1	420
Sir Wilful:	Dressing! What it's but Morning here I warrant	437	WAY WORLD	III.1	447

Itch (0)   see Cow-Itch

Itches (1)
Silvia:	Vengeance itches in the room of Love.	61	OLD BATCH	III.1	34

Itching (1)
Valentine:	the Lawyer with an itching Palm; and he's come to be	282	FOR LOVE	IV.1	238

Item (3)
Mirabell:	Item, I Article, that you continue to like your own	451	WAY WORLD	IV.1	245
Mirabell:	with the Gentlewoman in what-de-call-it-Court. Item, I shut	451	WAY WORLD	IV.1	252
Mirabell:	of Muslin, China, Fans, Atlases, &c.--Item when you shall	451	WAY WORLD	IV.1	254

Items (1)
Witwoud:	not, I cannot say; but there were Items of such a Treaty	408	WAY WORLD	I.1	487

Iteration (2)
Lady Wish:	you do not think me prone to any iteration of Nuptials.--	458	WAY WORLD	IV.1	532
Waitwell:	iteration of Nuptials--this eight and fourty Hours	459	WAY WORLD	IV.1	562

Its (32)
Capt Bluff:	War in Flanders, with all its particulars.	52	OLD BATCH	II.1	189
Bellmour:	importunity at Court; first creates its own Interest, and	58	OLD BATCH	II.2	133
Araminta:	young, and your early baseness has prevented its growing	87	OLD BATCH	IV.3	172
Cynthia:	Then I find its like Cards, if either of us have a good	142	DOUBL DLR	III.1	162
Sir Paul:	with Lambs, and every Creature couple with its Foe, as	144	DOUBL DLR	III.1	225
Brisk:	exception to make--don't you think bilk (I know its	164	DOUBL DLR	III.1	544
Sir Paul:	Execution in its time Girl; why thou hast my Leer				
	Hussey, just	173	DOUBL DLR	IV.1	236
Sir Paul:	Pleasures to preserve its Purity, and must I now find it	179	DOUBL DLR	IV.1	429
	It seems like Eden, fruitful of its own accord.	213	FOR LOVE	PRO.	17
	Or only shews its Teeth, as if it smil'd.	213	FOR LOVE	PRO.	34
Foresight:	That House doth stand upon its Head;	236	FOR LOVE	II.1	54
Sr Sampson:	Spiders; the one has its Nutriment in his own hands; and	246	FOR LOVE	II.1	392
Valentine:	nick'd it--But its wonderful strange, Jeremy!	282	FOR LOVE	IV.1	269
Almeria:	Within its cold, but hospitable Bosom.	326	M. BRIDE	I.1	12
Gonsalez:	Would feed its Faculty of Admiration.	332	M. BRIDE	I.1	V242
Manuel:	Thy senseless Vow appear'd to bear its Date,	333	M. BRIDE	I.1	299
Heli:	To be surpriz'd by Strangers in its Frailty.	338	M. BRIDE	II.1	34
Almeria:	To bear aloft its arch'd and pond'rous Roof,	339	M. BRIDE	II.1	61
Almeria:	By its own Weight, made stedfast, and immoveable,	339	M. BRIDE	II.1	62
Almeria:	My own affrights me with its Echo's.	339	M. BRIDE	II.1	69
Almeria:	Thy Voice--my own affrights me with its Echo's.	339	M. BRIDE	II.1	V 69
Almeria:	My Soul, enlarg'd from its vile Bonds will mount,	340	M. BRIDE	II.2	25
Osmyn-Alph:	You have pursu'd Misfortune, to its Dwelling;	346	M. BRIDE	II.2	262
Osmyn-Alph:	That tumbling on its Prop, crush'd all beneath,	347	M. BRIDE	II.2	310
Zara:	From my Despair, my Anger had its source;	362	M. BRIDE	IV.1	29
Zara:	And kindle Ruine in its Course. Think'st thou	375	M. BRIDE	V.1	96
Zara:	And kindle Ruine in its Course. Dost think	375	M. BRIDE	V.1	V 96
Marwood:	readmit him as its lawful Tyrant.	410	WAY WORLD	II.1	27
Marwood:	That's a Sign indeed its no Enemy to you.	436	WAY WORLD	III.1	419
Millamant:	I swear it will not do its part,	447	WAY WORLD	IV.1	104
Sir Wilful:	For a Bumper has not its Fellow.	455	WAY WORLD	IV.1	402
	But pray consider, ere you doom its fall,	479	WAY WORLD	EPI.	3

'its (1)
	The Law provides a curb for 'its own Fury,	204	DOUBL DLR	EPI.	10

Ivy (1)
Sr Sampson:	Support, like Ivy round a dead Oak: Faith I do; I love to	260	FOR LOVE	III.1	264

Ixion (1)
Manuel:	With that Ixion, who aspires to hold	349	M. BRIDE	II.2	372

Jack (4)
Mellefont:	and Jack Maskwell has promised me, to watch my Aunt	130	DOUBL DLR	I.1	136
Mellefont:	dear Jack, how hast thou Contrived?	149	DOUBL DLR	II.1	431
Mellefont:	How now, Jack? What, so full of Contemplation	155	DOUBL DLR	III.1	198

Jeremy (continued)

Joseph   (continued)
		PAGE	TITLE	ACT.SC	LINE
Sharper:	Are you so extravagant in Cloaths Sir Joseph?	50	OLD BATCH	II.1	113
Sharper:	unless it be to serve my particular Friend, as Sir				
	Joseph here,	51	OLD BATCH	II.1	159
Sharper:	Hannibal I believe you mean Sir Joseph.	52	OLD BATCH	II.1	177
Capt Bluff:	pretty Fellow--but Sir Joseph, comparisons are odious--	52	OLD BATCH	II.1	179
Capt Bluff:	Oh fy no Sir Joseph--You know I hate this.	53	OLD BATCH	II.1	217
Capt Bluff:	Death, what do you mean Sir Joseph?	53	OLD BATCH	II.1	221
Capt Bluff:	Nay come Sir Joseph, you know my Heat's soon over.	54	OLD BATCH	II.1	243
	(Enter Sir Joseph Wittoll, Bluffe.)	67	OLD BATCH	III.1	241
Sharper:	Sir Joseph--Your Note was accepted, and the	68	OLD BATCH	III.1	284
Capt Bluff:	Mr. Sharper, the matter is plain--Sir Joseph has found	69	OLD BATCH	III.1	296
Sharper:	Hearkee, Sir Joseph, a word with ye--In consideration	69	OLD BATCH	III.1	302
Capt Bluff:	Is not this fine, Sir Joseph?	70	OLD BATCH	III.1	332
Sir Joseph:	Put up, put up, dear Back, 'tis your Sir Joseph begs, come	70	OLD BATCH	III.1	341
Capt Bluff:	Well, Sir Joseph, at your entreaty--But were not	70	OLD BATCH	III.1	348
	(Enter Sir Joseph and Bluffe.)	84	OLD BATCH	IV.3	57
Araminta:	--Well, Sir Joseph, you shall see my Face.--But,	86	OLD BATCH	IV.3	103
Sir Joseph:	Free-loves! Sir Joseph, thou art a Mad-man. Agad, I'm in	86	OLD BATCH	IV.3	109
Capt Bluff:	(To Sir Joseph.)	86	OLD BATCH	IV.3	122
	(Exeunt Sir Joseph and Bluffe.)	86	OLD BATCH	IV.3	125
	(Enter Fondlewife, and Sir Joseph.)	89	OLD BATCH	IV.4	22
Fondlewife:	Here are fifty Pieces in this Purse, Sir Joseph--	90	OLD BATCH	IV.4	42
	Joseph, almost pushes him down, and Cries out.)	90	OLD BATCH	IV.4	50
	(Enter Sir Joseph and Bluffe.)	101	OLD BATCH	V.1	162
	(Bluffe frowns upon Sir Joseph.)	102	OLD BATCH	V.1	211
Setter:	--And, for my part, if I meet Sir Joseph with a Purse	102	OLD BATCH	V.1	233
Setter:	Sir Joseph and the Captain too! undone, undone! I'm	103	OLD BATCH	V.1	239
Setter:	Well, Sir Joseph, you have such a winning way with	103	OLD BATCH	V.1	251
Sir Joseph:	Rogue look, when she talk'd of Sir Joseph? Did not her	103	OLD BATCH	V.1	254
	(While Sir Joseph reads, Bluffe whispers Setter.)	103	OLD BATCH	V.1	273
Setter:	Sham-Settlement upon Sir Joseph.	105	OLD BATCH	V.1	345
Sharper:	free Discharge to Sir Joseph Wittoll and Captain Bluffe; for	110	OLD BATCH	V.2	86
	(Re-enter Sharper, with Sir Joseph, Bluffe, Sylvia, Lucy,	110	OLD BATCH	V.2	95
Sharper:	Sir Joseph, you had better have pre-engag'd this	111	OLD BATCH	V.2	120
Sharper:	Come, Sir Joseph, your Fortune is not so bad as you	111	OLD BATCH	V.2	134

Joseph's (2)
		PAGE	TITLE	ACT.SC	LINE
Sharper:	Captain, Sir Joseph's penitent.	54	OLD BATCH	II.1	240
Sharper:	Sir Joseph's Back.	54	OLD BATCH	II.1	249

Journey (3)
Bellmour:	Now set we forward on a Journey for Life:--	112	OLD BATCH	V.2	182
Petulant:	It seems as if you had come a Journey, Sir;	438	WAY WORLD	III.1	489
Lady Wish:	Will you drink any Thing after your Journey, Nephew,	441	WAY WORLD	III.1	599

Journey-Work (1)
Maskwell:	greatest Enemy, and she does but Journey-Work under	148	DOUBL DLR	II.1	394

Journeys (1)
Foresight:	Cureable or Incureable. If Journeys shall be prosperous,	241	FOR LOVE	II.1	216

Joy (45)
Heartwell:	Devil--Oh the Pride and Joy of Heart 'twould be to me,	45	OLD BATCH	I.1	318
Singer:	The hasty Joy, in strugling fled.	71	OLD BATCH	III.2	V 16
Setter:	Joy of your Return, Sir. Have you made a good	96	OLD BATCH	V.1	2
Belinda:	Joy, Joy Mr. Bride-groom; I give you Joy, Sir.	108	OLD BATCH	V.2	22
Heartwell:	'Tis not in thy Nature to give me Joy--A	108	OLD BATCH	V.2	23
Cynthia:	'Tis not so hard to counterfeit Joy in the depth of	167	DOUBL DLR	III.1	624
Maskwell:	Excess of Joy had made me stupid! Thus may my	184	DOUBL DLR	IV.2	24
Maskwell:	Excess of Joy has made me stupid! Thus may my	184	DOUBL DLR	IV.2	V 24
Sr Sampson:	him make haste--I'm ready to cry for Joy.	259	FOR LOVE	III.1	215
Singer-V:	But runs with Joy the Circle of the Mind.	293	FOR LOVE	IV.1	661
Sr Sampson:	Joy Uncle Foresight, double Joy, both as Uncle and				
	Astrologer;	307	FOR LOVE	V.1	378
Valentine:	Joy and Transport.	313	FOR LOVE	V.1	603
Almeria:	Then fly with Joy and Swiftness from me.	330	M. BRIDE	I.1	161
Leonora:	In Tears, when Joy appears in every other Face.	330	M. BRIDE	I.1	168
Leonora:	when Joy appears in every other Face.	330	M. BRIDE	I.1	V168
Almeria:	And Joy he brings to every other Heart,	330	M. BRIDE	I.1	169
Almeria:	Are busied in the General Joy, that thou	331	M. BRIDE	I.1	197
Almeria:	Are wrap'd and busied in the general Joy,	331	M. BRIDE	I.1	V197
Gonsalez:	But Tears of Joy. To see you thus, has fill'd	332	M. BRIDE	I.1	273
Gonsalez:	But Tears of Joy. Believe me, Sir, to see you thus,				
	has fill'd	332	M. BRIDE	I.1	V273
Heli:	Afford a Thought, or Glimpse of Joy,	338	M. BRIDE	II.1	8
Heli:	Afford a Thought, or show a Glimpse of Joy,	338	M. BRIDE	II.1	V 8
Garcia:	And could with equal Joy and Envy, view	338	M. BRIDE	II.1	V 14
Almeria:	To my Alphonso's Soul. O Joy too great!	340	M. BRIDE	II.2	29
Heli:	O Joy unhop'd for, does Almeria live!	341	M. BRIDE	II.2	65
Osmyn-Alph:	And gaze upon thy Eyes, is so much Joy;	342	M. BRIDE	II.2	97
Almeria:	Of Joy, of Bliss--I cannot bear--I must	342	M. BRIDE	II.2	V107
Osmyn-Alph:	Thou Excellence, thou Joy, thou Heav'n of Love!	342	M. BRIDE	II.2	109
Almeria:	If Heaven is greater Joy, it is no Happiness,	343	M. BRIDE	II.2	148
Osmyn-Alph:	Look round; Joy is not here, nor Cheerfulness.	346	M. BRIDE	II.2	261
Zara:	What Joy do I require? if thou dost mourn,	346	M. BRIDE	II.2	267
Osmyn-Alph:	How speak to thee the Words of Joy and Transport?	355	M. BRIDE	III.1	238
Osmyn-Alph:	Thee mine, were Comfort, Joy, extremest Exstacy.	357	M. BRIDE	III.1	331
Osmyn-Alph:	The Words of Joy and Peace; warm thy cold Beauties,	383	M. BRIDE	V.2	281
Osmyn-Alph:	In this extreamest Joy my Soul can taste,	383	M. BRIDE	V.2	302
	O with what Joy they run, to spread the News	385	M. BRIDE	EPI.	11
Fainall:	Joy of your Success, Mirabell; you look pleas'd.	399	WAY WORLD	I.1	135
Mirabell:	Give you Joy, Mrs. Foible.	423	WAY WORLD	II.1	512
Singer:	Or am'rous Youth, that gives the Joy;	435	WAY WORLD	III.1	383
Fainall:	to endear his pleasure, and prepare the Joy that follows,	444	WAY WORLD	III.1	716
Millamant:	Ay as Wife, Spouse, My dear, Joy, Jewel, Love,	450	WAY WORLD	IV.1	197
Lady Wish:	Well Sir, take her, and with her all the Joy I	477	WAY WORLD	V.1	592

Joy'd (0)   see Over-joy'd
Joyful (1)
Jeremy:	is almost mad in good earnest, with the Joyful News of	278	FOR LOVE	IV.1	100

Just   (continued)
Belinda: ha, ha, I can't for my Soul help thinking that I look just   83   OLD BATCH   IV.3   12
Laetitia: Indeed, my Dear, I was but just coming down stairs,   .   .   95   OLD BATCH   IV.4   243
Laetitia: Indeed, my Dear, I was but just come down stairs,   .   .   .   95   OLD BATCH   IV.4 V243
Bellmour: Setter.) Pox take 'em, they stand just in my Way.   .   .   .   97   OLD BATCH   V.1   12
Sharper: Just now, say you, gone in with Lucy?   98   OLD BATCH   V.1   82
Vainlove: might have been just.--There, we are even.--   109   OLD BATCH   V.2   70
                But how?--Just as the Devil does a Sinner.   113   OLD BATCH   EPI.   28
                and Sword in his Hands; as just risen from Table: .   .   . 127   DOUBL DLR   I.1
Mellefont: suspicions just,--but see the Company is broke up,   .   .   . 131   DOUBL DLR   I.1   168
Mellefont: I beg your Lordships Pardon--We were just   131   DOUBL DLR   I.1   175
Maskwell: just Repulsed by him, warm at once with Love and   .   .   . 136   DOUBL DLR   I.1   367
Lady Froth: Biddy, that's all; just my own Name.   141   DOUBL DLR   II.1   129
Maskwell: self any longer: and was just going to give vent to a
                Secret, ... 156   DOUBL DLR III.1   201
Maskwell: just gone from hence.   156   DOUBL DLR III.1   203
Lord Froth: Just 'ifaith, that was at my tongues end.   163   DOUBL DLR III.1   480
Lady Froth: Just as the Sun does, more or less.   164   DOUBL DLR III.1   532
Sir Paul: Execution in its time Girl; why thou hast my Leer
                Hussey, just   173   DOUBL DLR   IV.1   236
Lady Froth: Just now as I came in, bless me, why don't you   .   .   . 176   DOUBL DLR   IV.1   323
Sir Paul: speak a good word only just for me, Gads-bud only for   .   . 180   DOUBL DLR   IV.1   472
Maskwell: My Lady is just gone down from my Lords Closet,   .   .   . 181   DOUBL DLR   IV.1   515
Maskwell: My Lady is just gone into my Lords Closet, ... 181   DOUBL DLR   IV.1 V515
Mellefont: she comes--Little does she think what a Mine is just ready 183   DOUBL DLR   IV.2   4
Mellefont: and just when he holds out his hand to gather it, to have a 187   DOUBL DLR   IV.2   145
Lord Froth: No, my dear; I'm but just awake.--   201   DOUBL DLR   V.1   525
Valentine: hate, for just such another Reason; because they abound in 217   FOR LOVE   I.1   38
Valentine: an Army lead just such a life as I do; have just such Crowds 221   FOR LOVE   I.1   189
Scandal: A mender of Reputations! aye, just as he is a keeper   .   . 226   FOR LOVE   I.1   368
Tattle: pardon me, if from a just weight of his Merit, with your   . 255   FOR LOVE   III.1   70
Ben: speak one thing, and to think just the contrary way; is as
                it   263   FOR LOVE   III.1   386
Ben: here just now? Will he thrash my Jacket?--Let'n, let'n,--   . 264   FOR LOVE   III.1   420
Mrs Fore: They have quarrel'd just as we cou'd wish.   264   FOR LOVE   III.1   433
Scandal: So was Valentine this Morning; and look'd just so.   .   .   . 268   FOR LOVE   III.1   570
Foresight: within a quarter of Twelve--hem--he, hem!--just upon   .   . 270   FOR LOVE   III.1   646
Ben: He, he, he; why that's true; just so for all the World it   . 273   FOR LOVE   III.1   721
Ben: And just e'en as he meant, Sir, ... 274   FOR LOVE   III.1   785
Scandal: I saw her take Coach just now with her Maid; and   .   .   . 276   FOR LOVE   IV.1   12
Jeremy: just as he was poor for want of Money; his Head is e'en as 276   FOR LOVE   IV.1   34
Scandal: confessing just now an Obligation to his Love.   278   FOR LOVE   IV.1   85
Angelica: Why he talk'd very sensibly just now.   295   FOR LOVE   IV.1   746
Jeremy: Two Hours--I'm sure I left him just now, in a Humour   .   . 295   FOR LOVE   IV.1   754
Jeremy: Two Hours--I'm sure I left him just now, in the Humour   .   . 295   FOR LOVE   IV.1 V754
Jeremy: So--Just the very backside of Truth,--But   296   FOR LOVE   IV.1   775
Tattle: Is not that she, gone out just now?   301   FOR LOVE   V.1   165
Jeremy: Aye, Sir, she's just going to the Place of appointment.   .   . 301   FOR LOVE   V.1   166
Tattle: --And I'm going to be Married just now, yet did not   .   .   . 305   FOR LOVE   V.1   293
Ben: married, or just going to be married, I know not which.   .   . 307   FOR LOVE   V.1   370
Ben: Case, you should not marry her. It's just the same thing,   . 308   FOR LOVE   V.1   414
Foresight: Why, you told me just now, you went hence in   309   FOR LOVE   V.1   453
                For just as one prognosticates the Weather, ... 323   M. BRIDE   PRO.   8
                Prepar'd, by just Decrees to stand, or fall.   324   M. BRIDE   PRO.   44
Almeria: Another Lord; may then just Heav'n show'r down   330   M. BRIDE   I.1   187
Alonzo: The King is just arriv'd.   331   M. BRIDE   I.1   V210
Manuel: It looks as thou didst mourn for him: Just as   333   M. BRIDE   I.1   298
Osmyn-Alph: Because Captivity has robb'd me of a just Revenge.   .   .   . 336   M. BRIDE   I.1   434
Osmyn-Alph: Just as the Hand of Chance administers.   345   M. BRIDE   II.2   224
Zara: And now just ripe for Birth, my Rage has ruin'd.   354   M. BRIDE III.1   196
Zara: Alphonso, privately departed, just   364   M. BRIDE   IV.1   120
Zara: Alphonso, secretly departed, just   364   M. BRIDE   IV.1 V120
Manuel: Hence, e'er I curse--fly my just Rage with speed;   .   .   . 369   M. BRIDE   IV.1   316
Selim: I bare my Breast to meet your just Revenge.   375   M. BRIDE   V.1   122
Osmyn-Alph: The just Decrees of Heav'n, in turning on   383   M. BRIDE   V.2   307
Osmyn-Alph: The just Decrees of Heav'n, which on themselves   383   M. BRIDE   V.2   V307
Osmyn-Alph: Seest thou, how just the Hand of Heav'n has been?   .   .   . 383   M. BRIDE   V.2   317
Witwoud: just when you had been talking to him--As   405   WAY WORLD   I.1   370
Mirabell: You shou'd have just so much disgust for your   416   WAY WORLD   II.1   258
Witwoud: As a Favourite just disgrac'd; and with as few   418   WAY WORLD   II.1 V335
Marwood: the opportunity of breaking it, just upon the discovery of   . 442   WAY WORLD III.1   662
Millamant: him hither,--just as you will Dear Foible.--I think I'll see 446   WAY WORLD   IV.1   61
Millamant: will oblige me to leave me: I have just now a little   .   .   . 448   WAY WORLD   IV.1   140
Petulant: Thou art (without a figure) Just one half of an Ass;   .   .   . 454   WAY WORLD   IV.1   350
Petulant: of Asses split, would make just four of you.   454   WAY WORLD   IV.1   352
Lady Wish: my just resentment at my Nephew's request.--I will   .   .   . 472   WAY WORLD   V.1   402
Waitwell: At hand Sir, rubbing their Eyes,--Just risen   475   WAY WORLD   V.1   515
Justice (13)
Bellmour: to speak the truth in justice to your Wife.--No.   .   .   .   93   OLD BATCH   IV.4   158
Lady Ply: me as a fine thing. Well, I must do you this justice, and   . 169   DOUBL DLR   IV.1   71
Maskwell: Piece of Justice--   183   DOUBL DLR   IV.1   589
Lord Touch: let me hasten to do Justice, in rewarding Virtue and wrong'd 203   DOUBL DLR   V.1   582
Mrs Frail: an Admiral and an eminent Justice of the Peace to be the   . 231   FOR LOVE   I.1   578
Jeremy: before any Justice in Middlesex.   245   FOR LOVE   II.1   356
Valentine: in your way--You have but Justice.   313   FOR LOVE   V.1   597
Scandal: Well, Madam, You have done Exemplary Justice, ... 313   FOR LOVE   V.1   619
Osmyn-Alph: But who shall dare to tax Eternal Justice!   350   M. BRIDE III.1   32
Zara: That done, I leave thy Justice to return   355   M. BRIDE III.1   219
Witwoud: Wit: Nay, I'll do him Justice. I'm his Friend, I won't   .   . 403   WAY WORLD   I.1   291
Mirabell: In Justice to you, I have made you privy to my   417   WAY WORLD   II.1   280
Foible: be had to a Justice, and put to Bridewell to beat Hemp, poor 463   WAY WORLD   V.1   63
Justifiable (1)
Sharper: my Country, or my Religion, or in some very Justifiable   .   51   OLD BATCH   II.1   160
Justifie (2)
Sir Joseph: O Lord, O Lord, Captain, come justifie your   69   OLD BATCH III.1   306
Lord Touch: Proof, that I may justifie my Dealing with him to the   .   . 182   DOUBL DLR   IV.1   563

Kept (continued)
   Tattle: a private Intriegue of Destiny, kept secret from the
                    piercing . . . . 304 FOR LOVE   V.1   271
   Leonora: Your Father kept in Chains his Fellow-King: . . . . . 326 M. BRIDE   I.1   23
   Almeria: I would have kept that Secret; though I know . . . . . 328 M. BRIDE   I.1   80
   Marwood: without you cou'd have kept his Counsel closer. I shall . 431 WAY WORLD   III.1 242
   Fainall: Out-Matrimony'd,--If I had kept my speed like a Stag, . . 442 WAY WORLD   III.1 635
   Lady Wish: Well Mr. Mirabell, you have kept your promise, ... 477 WAY WORLD   V.1   572
Kettle (2)
   Ben: Said he could mend her Kettle, ... 274 FOR LOVE   III.1 777
   Valentine: shake off Age; get thee Medea's Kettle, and be boil'd a-new, 289 FOR LOVE   IV.1   522
Key (4)   see Master-Key
   Fondlewife: back.--Give me the Key of your Cabinet, Cocky-- . . . . 91 OLD BATCH   IV.4   73
   Fondlewife: Papers.--I won't disturb him; Give me the Key. . . . . 91 OLD BATCH   IV.4   82
   Laetitia: (She gives him the Key, goes to the Chamber-door, and speaks 91 OLD BATCH   IV.4   83
   Peg: and carry'd the Key with her. . . . . 425 WAY WORLD   III.1   19
Key-hole (1)
   Angelica: Yes, I saw you together, through the Key-hole of . . . 238 FOR LOVE   II.1   106
Kick (2)
   Bellmour: kick this Puppy without a Man were cold, and had no . . 70 OLD BATCH   III.1 328
   Bellmour: kick this Puppy unless a Man were cold, and had no . . . 70 OLD BATCH   III.1 V328
Kick'd (2)
   Capt Bluff: you my Friend; Abus'd and Cuff'd and Kick'd. . . . . . 70 OLD BATCH   III.1 349
   Sir Joseph: his Business--He durst as soon have kiss'd you, as kick'd 70 OLD BATCH   III.1 359
Kicks (3)
   Sharper: (Kicks him.) . . . . . 69 OLD BATCH   III.1 318
   Sharper: (Kicks him.) . . . . . 69 OLD BATCH   III.1 321
   Sharper: (Kicks him.) . . . . . 69 OLD BATCH   III.1 326
Kid-Gloves (1)
   Belinda: tore two Pair of Kid-Gloves, with trying 'em on.-- . . . 84 OLD BATCH   IV.3   54
Kid-leather (1)
   Belinda: tore two Pair of Kid-leather Gloves, with trying 'em on.-- 84 OLD BATCH   IV.3 V 54
Kidney (1)
   Sharper: Ay, Is he of that kidney? . . . . 46 OLD BATCH   I.1   355
Kill (8)
   Sir Paul: would kill me; they would never come kindly, I should . . 146 DOUBL DLR   II.1   282
   Almeria: Kill me, kill me then, dash me with thy Chains; . . . . 357 M. BRIDE   III.1 297
   Zara: Strike, damp, deaden her Charms, and kill his Eyes; . . 359 M. BRIDE   III.1 401
   Almeria: I will be Death; then tho' you kill my Husband, ... 370 M. BRIDE   IV.1   352
   Lady Wish: No, don't kill him at once Sir Rowland, starve . . . . 458 WAY WORLD   IV.1   519
   Sir Wilful: frown, she can't kill you;--besides--Hearkee she dare not 471 WAY WORLD   V.1   361
   Mirabell: high Place I once held, of sighing at your Feet; nay kill 471 WAY WORLD   V.1   371
Kill'd (1)
   Lady Wish: shou'd be kill'd I must never shew my face; or hang'd,--O 461 WAY WORLD   IV.1   627
Killed (1)
   Lady Touch: been to me, you have already killed the quiet of this Life, 185 DOUBL DLR   IV.2   75
Killing (5)
   Bellmour: Give me leave to swear--by those Eyes, those killing Eyes; 82 OLD BATCH   IV.2   72
   Osmyn-Alph: O could'st thou be less killing, soft or kind, ... 356 M. BRIDE   III.1 282
   Osmyn-Alph: O would'st thou be less killing, soft or kind, ... 356 M. BRIDE   III.1 V282
   Zara: Cruel, cruel, O more than killing Object! . . . . . . 380 M. BRIDE   V.2 V164
   Foible: Most killing well, Madam. . . . . 445 WAY WORLD   IV.1   16
Kin (0)   see A-kin
Kind (30)   see Changling-Kind, Woman-kind
   Vainlove: A kind of Mungril Zealot, sometimes very precise . . . 40 OLD BATCH   I.1   106
   Bellmour: Truth on't is she fits his temper best, is a kind of . . 42 OLD BATCH   I.1   205
   Araminta: If Love be the Fever which you mean; kind Heav'n . . . 54 OLD BATCH   II.2   8
   Bellmour: Kind Looks and Actions(from Success)do prove, ... 60 OLD BATCH   II.2   225
   Lucy: on him, himself--Contrive a kind Letter as from her, . . 62 OLD BATCH   III.1   41
   Sharper: will be but a kind of a Mungril Curs trick. Well, are you 80 OLD BATCH   IV.1   182
   Bellmour: kind Nature works, and boils over in him. . . . . . . 95 OLD BATCH   IV.4   240
   Lucy: you; but if you do deceive me, the Curse of all kind, . . 98 OLD BATCH   V.1   76
   Sharper: Vainlove, I have been a kind of a God-father to you, . . 109 OLD BATCH   V.2   81
                 Alone to the Offspring of the Muses kind: . . . . . . 125 DOUBL DLR   PRO.   26
   Maskwell: time he attempted any thing of that kind, to discover it to 154 DOUBL DLR   III.1 154
   Mellefont: That's but a kind of Negative Consent.--Why, ... 168 DOUBL DLR   IV.1   41
   Mellefont: done, left you to your self.--You're in a kind of Erasmus 185 DOUBL DLR   IV.2   60
   Mellefont: and hope they are of the purest kind--Penitential Tears. . 185 DOUBL DLR   IV.2   69
                 For that's a kind of Assignation Learning. . . . . . . 204 DOUBL DLR   EPI.   26
   Scandal: I have many more of this kind, very well Painted, as you . 234 FOR LOVE   I.1   657
   Scandal: Not upon a kind occasion, Madam. But when a Lady . . . 276 FOR LOVE   IV.1   23
   Tattle: pretty soft kind of Phrase, and with a good perswading . 302 FOR LOVE   V.1   182
   Valentine: If my happiness cou'd receive Addition, this Kind . . . 312 FOR LOVE   V.1   579
   Angelica: A Lover true: Not that a Woman's Kind. . . . . 314 FOR LOVE   V.1   637
                 Then pray continue this your kind behaviour, ... 316 FOR LOVE   EPI.   43
   Manuel: Why does the Fairest of her Kind, withdraw . . . . . . 348 M. BRIDE   II.2   352
   Zara: And call it Passion; then, be still more kind, ... 354 M. BRIDE   III.1 181
   Osmyn-Alph: O could'st thou be less killing, soft or kind, ... 356 M. BRIDE   III.1 282
   Osmyn-Alph: O would'st thou be less killing, soft or kind, ... 356 M. BRIDE   III.1 V282
   Fainall: Kind too Contemptible to give Scandal. . . . . 399 WAY WORLD   I.1   143
   Witwoud: kind of a Humorist. . . . . 408 WAY WORLD   I.1   493
   Sir Wilful: my leave--If so be you'll be so kind to make my Excuse, . 446 WAY WORLD   IV.1   78
   Foible: Sweet, so kind a Lady as you have been to me. . . . . 463 WAY WORLD   V.1   33
   Mirabell: That marriage frauds too oft are paid in kind. . . . . 478 WAY WORLD   V.1   623
Kinder (1)
   Vainlove: You have given that Passion a much kinder Epithet . . . 87 OLD BATCH   IV.3   164
Kindle (2)
   Zara: And kindle Ruine in its Course. Think'st thou . . . . 375 M. BRIDE   V.1   96
   Zara: And kindle Ruine in its Course. Dost think . . . . . 375 M. BRIDE   V.1 V 96
Kindled (1)
   Lady Touch: To be kindled to a flame, only to light him to . . . . 191 DOUBL DLR   V.1   150
Kindles (1)
   Silvia: Vengeance kindles in the room of Love. . . . . 61 OLD BATCH   III.1 V 34
Kindling (0)   see Ever-kindling
Kindly (7)
   Bellmour: Madam? Those Eyes shone kindly on my first Appearance, . 81 OLD BATCH   IV.2   21

Kindly   (continued)

		PAGE	TITLE	ACT.SC	LINE
Sir Paul:	(Squeezes him by the hand, looks kindly on him, sighs, and would kill me; they would never come kindly, I should	140	DOUBL DLR	II.1	65
	would kill me; they would never come kindly, I should	146	DOUBL DLR	II.1	282
	Unless transplanted to more kindly Earth.	213	FOR LCVE	PRO.	6
	Well may they hope, when ycu sc kindly aid,	213	FCR LCVE	PRO.	11
Mrs Frail:	(Looks kindly on him.)	265	FCR LCVE	III.1	451
Zara:	So kindly of my Fault, to call it Madness;	354	M. BRIDE	III.1	179
Kindness (8)					
Sharper:	This is a double Generosity--Do me a Kindness	68	OLD BATCH	III.1	289
Mellefont:	to him they have born the face cf kindness; while her	129	DOUEL DLR	I.1	89
Lady Touch:	Kindness--but will you go into your Closet, and recover	153	DOUEL DLR	III.1	116
Careless:	ruine me with Kindness; your Charming Tongue pursues	169	DOUBL DLR	IV.1	86
Lady Ply:	I know my Lady Touchwood has no kindness for	171	DOUEL CLR	IV.1	163
Scandal:	forc'd you tc acknowledge a Kindness for Valentine,	294	FCR LCVE	IV.1	689
Tattle:	serious Kindness--I never lik'd any body less in my Life.	309	FCR LCVE	V.1	465
Garcia:	I would oblige him, but he shuns my Kindness;	335	M. BRIDE	I.1	369
Kindred (1)					
Foresight:	House of my Nativity; there the Curse of Kindred was	238	FOR LCVE	II.1	130
King (62) see Fellow-King					
Sr Sampson:	Body o' me, I have made a Cuckold of a King, and the	241	FOR LCVE	II.1	222
Foresight:	King of Bantam, yet by the Bcdy cf the Sun--	241	FCR LCVE	II.1	232
Sr Sampson:	King, that I purloyn'd from one of the Pyramids, pcwder'd	242	FOR LCVE	II.1	250
Almeria:	The silent Tcmb receiv'd the good old King;	326	M. BRIDE	I.1	10
Almeria:	Of King Anselmo's Pallace; which in Rage	329	M. BRIDE	I.1	113
Almeria:	Whilst the good King, to shun approaching Flames,	329	M. BRIDE	I.1	115
Almeria:	The good King flying to avoid the Flames,	329	M. BRIDE	I.1	V115
Alonzo:	The King is just arriv'd.	331	M. BRIDE	I.1	V210
Leonora:	Madam, the King.	332	M. BRIDE	I.1	261
	(Symphcny of Warlike Musick. Enter the King, attended by	332	M. BRIDE	I.1	265
	Almeria meets the King and kneels: afterwards Gonsalez	332	M. BRIDE	I.1	268
Manuel:	A King and Ccnquerour can give, are yours.	335	M. BRIDE	I.1	386
Garcia:	Perez, the King expects from our return,	338	M. BRIDE	II.1	40
Zara:	You know how I abus'd the credulcus King;	347	M. BRIDE	II.2	293
Zara:	Dost fear so much, thou dar'st nct wish. The King!	348	M. BRIDE	II.2	347
Selim:	Madam, the King is here.	348	M. BRIDE	II.2	349
Selim:	Madam, the King is here, and entring ncw.	348	M. BRIDE	II.2	V349
	(Enter the King, Perez, and Attendants.)	348	M. BRIDE	II.2	351
Manuel:	Somewhat I heard of King and Rival mention'd.	348	M. BRIDE	II.2	355
Manuel:	What's he that dares be Rival tc the King?	348	M. BRIDE	II.2	356
Heli:	You may; anon, at Midnight, when the King	351	M. BRIDE	III.1	47
Osmyn-Alph:	My Ears, and reach the Heav'ns; where is the King?	352	M. BRIDE	III.1	85
Zara:	To shake the Temper of the King--who knows	354	M. BRIDE	III.1	205
Osmyn-Alph:	Of interceding for me with the King;	359	M. BRIDE	III.1	389
Zara:	Confer with him. I'll quit you to the King.	360	M. BRIDE	III.1	452
Zara:	Or speak with him. I'll quit you to the King.	360	M. BRIDE	III.1	V452
Selim:	Tho King, and were alone enough to urge	361	M. BRIDE	IV.1	5
Selim:	The King, in full belief of all you told him,	361	M. BRIDE	IV.1	12
Zara:	Find out the King, tell him I have of Weight	361	M. BRIDE	IV.1	18
Selim:	It needs not, for the King will strait be here,	361	M. BRIDE	IV.1	20
Zara:	Somewhat, to blind the King, and save his Life	361	M. BRIDE	IV.1	24
Selim:	Then offer to the King to have him strangl'd	362	M. BRIDE	IV.1	56
Selim:	I can no more, the King is here. Obtain	362	M. BRIDE	IV.1	59
	(Enter King, Gonsalez, Garcia, Perez.)	362	M. BRIDE	IV.1	61
Zara:	And oft had private Conference with the King;	364	M. BRIDE	IV.1	118
Gonsalez:	The King is blinded by his Love, and heeds	365	M. BRIDE	IV.1	177
Gonsalez:	Dear Madam, speak, or you'll incense the King.	367	M. BRIDE	IV.1	266
	(Exit King.)	370	M. BRIDE	IV.1	367
Gonsalez:	Hold, let me think--if I shou'd tell the King--	371	M. BRIDE	IV.1	403
Gonsalez:	This subtle Wcman will amuze the King,	371	M. BRIDE	IV.1	415
Alonzo:	The King expects your Lordship.	371	M. BRIDE	IV.1	419
	(A Room of State. Enter King, Perez, and Alonzo.)	372	M. BRIDE	V.1	
	(A Mute appears, and seeing the King retires.)	373	M. BRIDE	V.1	12
Manuel:	Into hcw poor and mean a thing, a King descends;	373	M. BRIDE	V.1	40
Manuel:	Into how poor a thing, a King decends;	373	M. BRIDE	V.1	V 40
Zara:	The Mute nct yet return'd! ha! 'twas the King!	374	M. BRIDE	V.1	V 91
Zara:	The King that parted hence; frowning he went;	374	M. BRIDE	V.1	92
Garcia:	The King? Confusion, all is on the Rout!	376	M. BRIDE	V.2	17
Garcia:	Are entring now our Doors. Where is the King?	377	M. BRIDE	V.2	28
Garcia:	The King in Person animate our Men,	377	M. BRIDE	V.2	36
Alonzo:	Was to Revenge a Blow the King had giv'n him.	377	M. BRIDE	V.2	50
Garcia:	The King--	377	M. BRIDE	V.2	58
Gonsalez:	The King!	377	M. BRIDE	V.2	59
Alonzo:	The King!	377	M. BRIDE	V.2	59
Gonsalez:	To see the King in Person at their Head.	378	M. BRIDE	V.2	V104
Alonzo:	For Osmyn, if in seeking for the King,	379	M. BRIDE	V.2	120
Zara:	The King; tell him, what he requir'd, I've done:	380	M. BRIDE	V.2	152
Zara:	O this accurs'd, this base, this treach'rous King!	380	M. BRIDE	V.2	V168
Zara:	Scorch and consume the curst perfidious King.	380	M. BRIDE	V.2	V171
Selim:	I've scught in vain, the King is no where, to	380	M. BRIDE	V.2	173
Selim:	I've sought in vain, for no where can the King	380	M. BRIDE	V.2	V173
Sir Wilful:	Crown a Health to the King,	456	WAY WORLD	IV.1	456
King's (7)					
Alonzo:	Of the King's approach.	331	M. BRIDE	I.1	210
	kneels and kisses the King's Hand, while Garcia does the	332	M. BRIDE	I.1	269
Zara:	There, there's the dreadful Sound, the King's thy Rival!	348	M. BRIDE	II.2	348
Zara:	Dare you dispute the King's Command? Behold	359	M. BRIDE	III.1	377
Perez:	Whate'er it is the King's Complexion turns.	373	M. BRIDE	IV.1	32
Garcia:	What's to be done? the King's Death known, will strike	378	M. BRIDE	V.2	93
Gonsalez:	The King's immediate Presence at their Head.	378	M. BRIDE	V.2	104
Kings (5)					
Maskwell:	Duty to Kings, Piety to Parents, Gratitude to Benefactors,	150	DOUBL DLR	II.1	446
Leonora:	Entail'd between Valentia's and Granada's Kings;	327	M. BRIDE	I.1	44
Leonora:	Between Valentia's and Granada's Kings;	327	M. BRIDE	I.1	V 44
Osmyn-Alph:	Might hope to captivate the Hearts of Kings.	355	M. BRIDE	III.1	227
Alonzo:	But what are Kings reduc'd to ccmmon Clay?	379	M. BRIDE	V.2	113

Kinsman (1)
  Zara: And as my Kinsman, honour'd and advanc'd you. . . . . 347 M. BRIDE   II.2 296

Kiss (50)
  Heartwell: Vainlove, kiss a Lap-Dog with passion, when it would . . 43 OLD BATCH   I.1 255
  Bellmour: refuse to kiss a Lap-Dog, if it were preliminary to the Lips 44 OLD BATCH   I.1 261
  Capt Bluff: Fighting, Sir I Kiss your Hilts. . . . . 51 OLD BATCH   II.1 157
  Araminta: Come then, Kiss and Friends. . . . . . . 56 OLD BATCH   II.2   62
  Bellmour: a kiss from Araminta. . . . . 63 OLD BATCH III.1   96
  Setter: in disgrace at present about a Kiss which he forced. You . 67 OLD BATCH III.1 225
  Setter: and I can Kiss Lucy withcut all that. . . . . 67 OLD BATCH III.1 226
  Sir Joseph: let me kiss thee, so so, put up, put up. . . . 70 OLD BATCH III.1 342
  Heartwell: Ha! Nay come, we'll kiss at parting (kisses her) by . 74 OLD BATCH III.2 133
  Heartwell: Heaven her kiss is sweeter than Liberty--I will Marry . 74 OLD BATCH III.2 V134
  Heartwell: that Kiss--one more. . . . . 74 OLD BATCH III.2 136
  Heartwell: Licence streight--in the Evening expect me--One Kiss . 74 OLD BATCH III.2 140
  Fondlewife: made me weep--made poor Nykin weep--Nay come Kiss, . . 78 OLD BATCH   IV.1 117
  Fondlewife: Wcnt you Kiss Nykin? . . . . 78 OLD BATCH   IV.1 121
  Fondlewife: Kiss kiss, ifeck I do. . . . . 78 OLD BATCH   IV.1 123
  Fondlewife: I wont be dealous--Poor Cocky, Kiss Nykin, Kiss . . 79 OLD BATCH   IV.1 135
                 (Kiss.) . . 79 OLD BATCH   IV.1 142
  Fondlewife: That's my good Dear--Come Kiss Nykin once . . . . 79 OLD BATCH   IV.1 143
                 (Kiss.) . . 82 OLD BATCH   IV.2   82
  Fondlewife: Kiss, Dear,--I met the Master of the Ship . . . 89 OLD BATCH   IV.4   23
  Laetitia: kiss from me by main force. . . . . 90 OLD BATCH   IV.4   54
  Bellmour: Words, and a Kiss; and the good Man melts. See, how . 95 OLD BATCH   IV.4 239
  Lucy: in good earnest, you kiss so devcutly. . . . . . 97 OLD BATCH   V.1   38
  Lady Froth: Lord you sha'n't kiss it so much; I shall grow jealous, I 140 DOUBL DLR   II.1   77
  Lady Froth: Lord you shan't kiss it so much; I shall grow jealous, I 140 DOUBL DLR   II.1 V 77
  Lady Touch: Dear. Nay, by this kiss you shan't be angry. O Lord, I . 152 DOUBL DLR III.1   68
  Sir Paul: Gads bud, I am transported! give me leave to kiss . . 172 DOUBL DLR   IV.1 192
  Sir Paul: and kiss Papa. . . . . 173 DOUBL DLR   IV.1 208
  Maskwell: this kiss-- . . . . 184 DOUBL DLR   IV.2   34
  Miss Prue: me this Ring for a kiss. . . . . 249 FOR LOVE   II.1 522
  Tattle: O fie Miss, you must not kiss and tell. . . . . 249 FOR LOVE   II.1 523
  Tattle: Kiss me, you must be angry, but you must not refuse me. 252 FOR LOVE   II.1 620
  Tattle: by giving me a Kiss? . . . . 252 FOR LOVE   II.1 632
  Sr Sampson: Odsbud, and I'm glad to see thee, kiss me Boy, . . 260 FOR LOVE III.1 273
  Sr Sampson: kiss me again and again, dear Ben. . . . . . 260 FOR LOVE III.1 274
  Ben: So, so, enough Father--Mess, I'de rather kiss these . 260 FOR LOVE III.1 276
  Sr Sampson: your Hand, Odd let me kiss it; 'tis as warm and as soft . 301 FOR LOVE   V.1 145
  Sr Sampson: t'other Hand, and I'll mumble 'em, and kiss 'em till they 301 FOR LOVE   V.1 147
  Sr Sampson: within a Kiss of the matter, as you see. . . . 307 FOR LOVE   V.1 391
  Zara: And curl their Crimson Heads, to kiss the Clcuds! . . 380 M. BRIDE   V.2 V167
  Almeria: From his pale Lips; I'll kiss him e'er I drink, . . 382 M. BRIDE   V.2 267
  Witwoud: slabber and kiss one another when they meet, like a Call of 439 WAY WORLD III.1 535
  Fainall: Jealous no,--by this Kiss--let Husbands be Jealous; . 444 WAY WORLD III.1 714
  Millamant: or fond, nor kiss before folks, like my Lady Fadler and Sr. 450 WAY WCRLD   IV.1 201
  Mirabell: Then wee're agreed. Shall I kiss your hand upon the . 452 WAY WORLD   IV.1 280
  Millamant: thank'd--here kiss my hand tho'--so hold your tongue . 452 WAY WORLD   IV.1 296
  Witwoud: Thou dcst bite my dear Mustard-seed; kiss me for . . 454 WAY WORLD   IV.1 353
  Petulant: Stand off--I'll kiss no more Males,--I have . . . 454 WAY WORLD   IV.1 355

Kiss'd (7)
  Lucy: No no, avaunt--I'le not be slabber'd and kiss'd . . . 67 OLD BATCH III.1 236
  Sir Joseph: his Business--He durst as soon have kiss'd you, as kick'd 70 OLD BATCH III.1 359
  Singer: She frown'd and blush'd, then sigh'd and kiss'd, . . 71 OLD BATCH III.2 V 19
  Sr Sampson: Foot; have kiss'd the Great Mogul's Slipper, and rid a . 241 FOR LOVE   II.1 220
  Foible: Well, here it is, all that is left; all that is not kiss'd
        away-- . . . . 427 WAY WORLD III.1 V 76
  Millamant: thing you, I'll have you,--I wcn't be kiss'd, nor I won't be 452 WAY WORLD   IV.1 295
  Petulant: kiss'd your twin yonder in a humour of reconciliation, till 454 WAY WCRLD   IV.1 356

Kissed (1)
  Lord Froth: I saw my self there, and kissed it for your sake. . . . 140 DOUBL DLR   II.1   80

Kisses (21)
  Araminta: had stifled me with Kisses. . . . . 55 OLD BATCH   II.2   44
  Singer: Joining Faces, mingling Kisses, ... 71 OLD BATCH III.2   4
  Heartwell: Ha! Nay come, we'll kiss at parting (kisses her) by . 74 OLD BATCH III.2 133
  Heartwell: Heaven her kisses sweeter than Liberty--I will Marry . . 74 OLD BATCH III.2 134
  Laetitia: (She kisses him.) . . . 78 OLD BATCH   IV.1 125
  Bellmour: (He kisses her.) . . . 82 OLD BATCH   IV.2   75
      (She goes and hangs upon his neck, and kisses him. Bellmour 95 OLD BATCH   IV.4 241
      kisses her hand, behind Fondlewife's back.) . . . 95 OLD BATCH   IV.4 242
  Bellmour: (Kisses her.) . . 97 OLD BATCH   V.1   36
      (He bows profoundly low, then kisses the Glass.) . 140 DOUBL DLR   II.1   79
      (He kisses her, and bows very low.) . 172 DOUBL DLR   IV.1 196
  Maskwell: Lips be ever clos'd. (Kisses her.) And thus--Oh who . 184 DOUBL DLR   IV.2   25
  Miss Prue: (Buns and Kisses him.) . . 252 FOR LOVE   II.1 634
  Tattle: (Kisses her.) . . . 252 FOR LOVE   II.1 639
  Tattle: (Kisses again.) . . . 252 FOR LOVE   II.1 642
  Sr Sampson: (Kisses him.) . . . 260 FOR LOVE III.1 275
  Ben: (Kisses Mrs. Frail.) . . 261 FOR LOVE III.1 282
  Ben: (Kisses Miss Prue.) . . 261 FOR LOVE III.1 284
  Sr Sampson: (Kisses Angelica.) . . 307 FOR LOVE   V.1 392
      kneels and kisses the King's Hand, while Garcia does the . 332 M. BRIDE   I.1 269
  Mirabell: as often as possibly I can. (Kisses her hand). Well, heav'n 477 WAY WORLD   V.1 597

Kissing (3)
  Ben: and Kissing and Hugging, what wou'd you sheer off so? . 286 FOR LOVE   IV.1 418
  Foible: of kissing your Ladyship's Hands after Dinner. . . . 428 WAY WORLD III.1 127
  Foible: of kissing your Ladyship's Hand after Dinner. . . . 428 WAY WCRLD III.1 V127

Knack (1)
  Valentine: Evening, and learn the knack of Rhiming, ycu may arrive . 218 FOR LOVE   I.1   79

Knapsack-Carrier (1)
  Capt Bluff: What says my little Knapsack-Carrier? . . . . . 85 OLD BATCH   IV.3   84

Knave (2)
      Should he by chance a Knave or Fcol expose, ... 393 WAY WORLD PRO.   35
  Foible: Or arrant Knave. . . . . 462 WAY WORLD   IV.1 648

Knighted (1)
Waitwell: my self--Married, Knighted and attended all in one   .   .   .   424   WAY WORLD   II.1   555

Knighthood (2)
Sharper: Mirrour of Knighthood and Pink cf Courtesie in the Age,   .   49   OLD BATCH   II.1   73
Foible: the return of her Husband after Knighthood, with that   .   .   428   WAY WORLD   III.1   125

Knights-bridge (1)
Mrs Frail: had gcne to Knights-bridge, or to Chelsey, or to
         Spring-Garden, ...   247   FOR LOVE   II.1   438

Knock (3)
Jeremy: suspicious Fellows like lawful Pads, that wou'd knock   .   .   221   FOR LOVE   I.1   203
Jeremy: Mr. Scandal is with him, Sir; I'll knock at the Door.   .   .   279   FOR LOVE   IV.1   147
Millamant: lastly, where ever I am, you shall always knock at the door   450   WAY WORLD   IV.1   224

Knock'd (3)
Bellmour: like an uncivil Person, you kncck'd at the Door, before   .   95   OLD BATCH   IV.4   215
Laetitia: when ycu knock'd at the door; and the Maid told me,   .   95   OLD BATCH   IV.4   244
Petulant: rate; to be knock'd up and rais'd at all Hours and in all   .   405   WAY WORLD   I.1   385

Knocking (1)
Jeremy: body be surpriz'd at the Matter--(Knocking)--Again! Sir,   .   221   FOR LOVE   I.1   182

Knocks (5)
Maskwell: (Goes to the Chamber Door and knocks.)   194   DOUBL DLR   V.1   271
             (One Knocks.)   .   .   .   220   FOR LOVE   I.1   154
Nurse: (knocks) Ods my Life, won't you open the Door? I'll   .   253   FOR LOVE   III.1   11
             (One Knocks.)   .   .   .   295   FOR LOVE   IV.1   757
Lady Wish: See who that is--(One knocks.) Set down the Bottle   .   .   425   WAY WORLD   III.1   33

Knotted (1)
Almeria: To soften Rocks, or bend a knotted Oak.   326   M. BRIDE   I.1   2

Know (428)

   (I don't know whether I shall speak to please you)   .   .   35   OLD BATCH   PRO.   18
   Hang me if I know what he prays, or how!   35   OLD BATCH   PRO.   20
   Because, you know, if it be damn'd to day,   .   .   .   35   OLD BATCH   PRO.   24
Bellmour: know and believe more than really we do. You read of but   .   37   OLD BATCH   I.1   20
Bellmour: But dc you know nothing of a new Rival there?   .   .   .   40   OLD BATCH   I.1   117
Vainlove: she may entertain scme Thoughts of him. I know he   .   .   40   OLD BATCH   I.1   121
Bellmour: Why you must know, 'tis a piece cf Work toward   .   .   .   41   OLD BATCH   I.1   156
Bellmour: morning was none of her own? for I know thou art as   .   42   OLD BATCH   I.1   185
Bellmour: Faith I don't know, he's of a temper the most easie   .   .   42   OLD BATCH   I.1   210
Bellmour: are never asunder--yet last night, I know not by what   .   .   46   OLD BATCH   I.1   358
Bellmour: Black Gown does Atheism--You must know he has been   .   .   47   OLD BATCH   I.1   368
Sir Joseph: know me, you'd nere say I were so ill natur'd.   .   .   .   48   OLD BATCH   II.1   37
Sharper: Know you! why can you be so ungrateful, to forget   .   .   48   OLD BATCH   II.1   38
Sir Joseph: very good Jest, and I did not know that I had say'd it, and   50   OLD BATCH   II.1   115
Sir Joseph: I don't know, but I'le present ycu--   51   OLD BATCH   II.1   154
Sir Joseph: Night--You know I told you.   52   OLD BATCH   II.1   170
Capt Bluff: Oh I thought so--Why then you can know nothing   .   .   52   OLD BATCH   II.1   187
Capt Bluff: Sir: I'me afraid you scarce know the History of the Late   .   52   OLD BATCH   II.1   188
Capt Bluff: You must know, Sir, I was resident in Flanders the last   .   52   OLD BATCH   II.1   195
Capt Bluff: you know--Well, Mr. Sharper, would you think it? In all   .   53   OLD BATCH   II.1   201
Capt Bluff: Oh fy no Sir Joseph--You know I hate this.   53   OLD BATCH   II.1   217
Capt Bluff: 'twas indiscreet, when you know what will provoke me--   .   54   OLD BATCH   II.1   242
Capt Bluff: Nay ccme Sir Joseph, you know my Heat's soon over.   .   .   54   OLD BATCH   II.1   243
Belinda: Man--ycu don't know what you said, your Fever has   .   .   54   OLD BATCH   II.2   6
Belinda: Man--ycu don't know what you've said, your Fever has   .   54   OLD BATCH   II.2 V   6
Araminta: Bellmour meet. You don't know that you dreamt of   .   .   55   OLD BATCH   II.2   37
Footman: No, Madam, they sent before, to know if you were   .   .   56   OLD BATCH   II.2   79
Araminta: entertaining--(aside) I know she'd fain be persuaded to
         stay.   57   OLD BATCH   II.2   87
Belinda: Then know, I would be Ador'd in Silence.   59   OLD BATCH   II.2   175
Silvia: For I would know, though to the anguish of my Soul;   .   .   61   OLD BATCH   III.1   15
Lucy: You knew Aramintas dissembled Coyness has won, and   .   .   61   OLD BATCH   III.1   37
Lucy: want of Dissimulation--You know what will take him.   .   .   62   OLD BATCH   III.1   50
Bellmour: Thou dost not know what thou would'st be at;   .   .   .   63   OLD BATCH   III.1   102
Setter: thou know my Master or me?   65   OLD BATCH   III.1   172
Lucy: Yes, I know both Master and Man to be--   .   .   .   65   OLD BATCH   III.1   173
Setter: Devil could kncw you by instinct?   66   OLD BATCH   III.1   206
Lucy: You could know my Office by instinct, and be hang'd,   .   66   OLD BATCH   III.1   207
Sir Joseph: Lord-Harry. I know better things than to be run through   .   67   OLD BATCH   III.1   253
Heartwell: Questicn! Death, I shall be drawn in, before I know where   .   73   OLD BATCH   III.2   96
Silvia: dont I know my Father lov'd my Mcther, and was married   .   73   OLD BATCH   III.2   101
Silvia: Never tell me that, I know it is not chang'd by my   .   .   73   OLD BATCH   III.2   105
Lucy: first. I know that will do--walk in and I'le shew   .   .   75   OLD BATCH   III.2   158
Laetitia: (aside). I know not what to think. But I'me resolv'd   .   77   OLD BATCH   IV.1   85
Laetitia: Well--Well--You know my Fondness, and you love to   .   .   77   OLD BATCH   IV.1   90
Sharper: I am in disorder for what I have written. But something,
         I know   79   OLD BATCH   IV.1   159
Laetitia: (aside). Vainlove's Friend! I know his Face, and he has   .   81   OLD BATCH   IV.2   18
Araminta: May be he may not kncw us again.   84   OLD BATCH   IV.3   58
Capt Bluff: Come cn then, Knight.--But d'ye know what to   .   .   .   85   OLD BATCH   IV.3   70
Araminta: Vainlove to know us, I'll be rid of my Fool by fair means   .   86   OLD BATCH   IV.3   102
Sharper: afraid, you would not have given us leave to know you.   .   86   OLD BATCH   IV.3   115
Sir Joseph: I wish I durst stay to let her know my   86   OLD BATCH   IV.3   123
Araminta: deceiv'd me in you, I know not; my Opinion was but   .   .   87   OLD BATCH   IV.3   171
Footman: She's not very well, Madam, and has sent to know,   .   .   88   OLD BATCH   IV.3   206
Fondlewife: Alack poor Man.--No, no,--you don't kncw the   .   .   .   91   OLD BATCH   IV.4   81
Fondlewife: Wcmans-flesh. What, you know nothing of him, but his   .   93   OLD BATCH   IV.4   144
Bellmour: (aside). Well, now I know my Cue.--That is   .   .   .   93   OLD BATCH   IV.4   147
Fondlewife: you know your Patient, Mrs. Quack? Oh, lie upon your   .   93   OLD BATCH   IV.4   163
Fondlewife: think I don't kncw how to behave my self in the Employment   94   OLD BATCH   IV.4   195
Bellmour: --You know what might have fcllow'd.--But   .   .   .   95   OLD BATCH   IV.4   248
Fondlewife: know I have--But thou hast been a faithless Dallilah, and   .   95   OLD BATCH   IV.4   250
Bellmour: Come, I know the Intrigue between Heartwell and your   .   97   OLD BATCH   V.1   42
Lucy: Whore! I'd have you know, my Mistress scorns--   .   .   98   OLD BATCH   V.1   63
Lucy: Whore! I'd have you to know, my Mistress scorns--   .   .   98   OLD BATCH   V.1 V   63
Lucy: Ah, the Devil is not so cunning.--You know my   .   .   98   OLD BATCH   V.1   74
Setter: Ay, I know her, Sir: At least, I'm sure I can fish it out   .   99   OLD BATCH   V.1   103
Vainlove: Ha! It has a Colour.--But how do you know   .   .   .   99   OLD BATCH   V.1   110
Bellmour: Countenance. But, to tell you scmething you don't know.   .   100   OLD BATCH   V.1   '48

Know   (continued)

Speaker	Text	PAGE	TITLE	ACT.SC	LINE
Sir Joseph:	Captain: Take it--All the World know me to be a Knight,	101	OLD BATCH	V.1	193
Sharper:	I know, she commended him all the while we were	102	OLD BATCH	V.1	200
Sir Joseph:	peace.--I know, they were a little smart upon you--But,	103	OLD BATCH	V.1	262
Capt Bluff:	Not at all. Don't I know him?	104	OLD BATCH	V.1	276
Heartwell:	(aside). Hell, and the Devil! Does he know it? But,	104	OLD BATCH	V.1	298
Belinda:	have been I know not how many times warm'd for other	106	OLD BATCH	V.1	376
Sir Joseph:	countermin'd, or so--Mr. Vainlove, I suppose you know	110	OLD BATCH	V.2	113
Vainlove:	I know whom you have not got; pray Ladies	110	OLD BATCH	V.2	115
Sharper:	to forgive the loss of his Mistress.--I know not how	111	OLD BATCH	V.2	122
	For 'tis our way (you know) for fear o'th' worst,	113	OLD BATCH	EPI.	21
	Moors, have this way (as Story tells) to know	125	DOUBL DLR	PRO.	1
	To know, if it be truly born of Wit.	125	DOUBL DLR	PRO.	11
	I know not one Moor-Husband in the City.	125	DOUBL DLR	PRO.	28
Brisk:	Pooh, ha, ha, ha, I know you envy me. Spite, proud	128	DOUBL DLR	I.1	25
Mellefont:	with Cynthia, I know not; but this Morning she surpriz'd	130	DOUBL DLR	I.1	98
Careless:	Faith I cannot help it, you know I never lik'd him;	131	DOUBL DLR	I.1	147
Lady Touch:	Ungrateful; come, I know you false.	135	DOUBL DLR	I.1	300
Maskwell:	How am I to behave my self? You know I am your	136	DOUBL DLR	I.1	339
Maskwell:	Honesty, because you know I am a Rascal: But I would	136	DOUBL DLR	I.1	343
Maskwell:	your self, and hear me. You know you Lov'd your	136	DOUBL DLR	I.1	360
Maskwell:	I know it.--I don't depend upon it.--	138	DOUBL DLR	I.1	417
Mellefont:	I am so amazed, I know not what to speak.	145	DOUBL DLR	II.1	263
Mellefont:	I am so amazed, I know not what to say.	145	DOUBL DLR	II.1	V263
Lady Ply:	resist the strongest Temptation,--but yet I know, 'tis	147	DOUBL DLR	II.1	327
Lady Ply:	impossible for me to know whether I could or no, there	147	DOUBL DLR	II.1	328
Lady Ply:	impossible for me to know whether I could or not, there	147	DOUBL DLR	II.1	V328
Lady Ply:	you afterwards: For one does not know how ones mind may	147	DOUBL DLR	II.1	339
Lady Ply:	Nature. I know Love is powerful, and no body can help	148	DOUBL DLR	II.1	356
Lady Ply:	I know you don't Love Cynthia, only as a blind for your	148	DOUBL DLR	II.1	368
Maskwell:	I know it; I met Sir Paul towing away Cynthia:	148	DOUBL DLR	II.1	385
Maskwell:	why you don't know, that while I plead for you, your	148	DOUBL DLR	II.1	392
Mellefont:	I don't know what she might have attempted.	149	DOUBL DLR	II.1	418
Maskwell:	Ha, ha, ha, I know her temper,--well, you must	149	DOUBL DLR	II.1	419
Maskwell:	know then, that all my Contrivances were but Bubbles; till	149	DOUBL DLR	II.1	420
Maskwell:	don't know, but she may come this way; I am to meet her	149	DOUBL DLR	II.1	433
Lord Touch:	--Pho, 'tis nonsense. Come, come; I know my Lady	150	DOUBL DLR	III.1	5
Lord Touch:	Yes, I believe I know some that have been	151	DOUBL DLR	III.1	13
Lord Touch:	(half aside). I don't know that.	151	DOUBL DLR	III.1	26
Lady Touch:	I don't know; I am very unwilling to speak	151	DOUBL DLR	III.1	34
Lord Touch:	How? Then I must know, nay I will: No	152	DOUBL DLR	III.1	61
Lady Touch:	a nearer relation on his own; a Lover you know, my	153	DOUBL DLR	III.1	89
Lady Touch:	Lord, I don't know: I wish my Lips had	153	DOUBL DLR	III.1	109
Maskwell:	I know what she means by toying away an hour well	155	DOUBL DLR	III.1	174
Maskwell:	Woman, and I lov'd her once. But I don't know, since I	155	DOUBL DLR	III.1	176
Maskwell:	Woman, I lov'd her once. But I don't know, since I	155	DOUBL DLR	III.1	V176
Maskwell:	know whether I can in honour discover all.	156	DOUBL DLR	III.1	208
Maskwell:	know whether I can in honour discover 'em all	156	DOUBL DLR	III.1	V208
Lady Ply:	rather. (Curtesies). But I know Mr. Careless is so great a	159	DOUBL DLR	III.1	343
Lady Ply:	those Advantages: I know my own Imperfections--but	159	DOUBL DLR	III.1	349
Lady Ply:	you, Mr. Careless I don't know any thing in the World I	159	DOUBL DLR	III.1	353
Sir Paul:	A humour of my wife's, you know women have	161	DOUBL DLR	III.1	402
Lord Froth:	then, what do they laugh at? For you know laughing	163	DOUBL DLR	III.1	477
Careless:	Sir Paul, harkee, I'm reasoning the matter you know;	163	DOUBL DLR	III.1	493
Lady Froth:	Dairymaid, and our Coach-man is not amiss; you know,	163	DOUBL DLR	III.1	503
Brisk:	know the Sun is call'd Heav'ns Charioteer.	164	DOUBL DLR	III.1	509
Lady Froth:	lines again (pulls out a Paper.) Let me see here, you know	164	DOUBL DLR	III.1	512
Lady Froth:	what goes before, the comparison, you know.	164	DOUBL DLR	III.1	513
Lady Froth:	Coachman, for you know there's most occasion for a	164	DOUBL DLR	III.1	520
Lady Froth:	too, you know, tho' we don't see him.	164	DOUBL DLR	III.1	525
Lady Froth:	For Susan, you know, is Thetis, and so--	164	DOUBL DLR	III.1	542
Brisk:	exception to make--don't you think bilk (I know its	164	DOUBL DLR	III.1	544
Brisk:	I know whom you mean--But Deuce take me,	166	DOUBL DLR	III.1	583
Brisk:	rather an Epigrammatick Sonnet; I don't know what to	166	DOUBL DLR	III.1	592
Cynthia:	know, we have misapply'd the Name all this while, and	167	DOUBL DLR	III.1	631
Mellefont:	I don't know why we should not steal out of the	168	DOUBL DLR	IV.1	27
Cynthia:	Ay, ay, what have we to do with 'em; you know we	168	DOUBL DLR	IV.1	31
Sir Paul:	Lord nor my Lady to know what they intend.	171	DOUBL DLR	IV.1	158
Lady Ply:	I know my Lady Touchwood has no kindness for	171	DOUBL DLR	IV.1	163
Sir Paul:	I humbly thank your Ladiship--I don't know	172	DOUBL DLR	IV.1	197
Lady Ply:	I'll send him to them, I know where he is--	175	DOUBL DLR	IV.1	284
Lady Froth:	know it?	176	DOUBL DLR	IV.1	324
Brisk:	Ladiship--Let me perish, I don't know whether to	176	DOUBL DLR	IV.1	337
Lady Froth:	know, since we are Partners.	177	DOUBL DLR	IV.1	387
Sir Paul:	Surprize! Why I don't know any thing at all, nor I don't	179	DOUBL DLR	IV.1	449
Sir Paul:	know whether there be any thing at all in the World, or	179	DOUBL DLR	IV.1	450
Careless:	Subject: Then I writ a Letter to her; I don't know what	180	DOUBL DLR	IV.1	501
Lord Touch:	Enough--You are my Friend; I know	181	DOUBL DLR	IV.1	540
Lord Touch:	unnatural Nephew thus far--but I know you have been	182	DOUBL DLR	IV.1	545
Lord Touch:	I know you would excuse him--and I	182	DOUBL DLR	IV.1	555
Lord Touch:	know as well than you can't.	182	DOUBL DLR	IV.1	556
Maskwell:	know my thoughts; or think he does--	188	DOUBL DLR	V.1	14
Maskwell:	It must not be; nay, shou'd my Lady know it--ay,	190	DOUBL DLR	V.1	92
Maskwell:	this dotage, I know not; but he's gone to Sir Paul about my	190	DOUBL DLR	V.1	111
Lady Touch:	my Niece? how know you that my Brother will consent,	191	DOUBL DLR	V.1	128
Lord Touch:	know he's no way to be rewarded but in her. I'll defer my	191	DOUBL DLR	V.1	138
Lady Touch:	ought to be served; making you a Beast. Don't you know	192	DOUBL DLR	V.1	165
Sir Paul:	I, I know no such matter.	192	DOUBL DLR	V.1	168
Lady Touch:	Why then you don't know half your	192	DOUBL DLR	V.1	169
Sir Paul:	of things; I don't know what to make on't,--gad'sbud	192	DOUBL DLR	V.1	173
Sir Paul:	Nephew; and I don't know what,--look you, Sister,	192	DOUBL DLR	V.1	175
Sir Paul:	I must know my Girl has to trust to; or not a syllable	192	DOUBL DLR	V.1	176
Mellefont:	I know no other way but this he has proposed; If	193	DOUBL DLR	V.1	200
Cynthia:	I don't know whether I have Love enough,--	193	DOUBL DLR	V.1	202
Maskwell:	'Tis that; you know my Lady has a high Spirit,	195	DOUBL DLR	V.1	315
Lady Touch:	not Courage; no, I know thee well: but thou shalt miss	197	DOUBL DLR	V.1	388

Know   (continued)

Lady Touch:	thee open to my sight! But then 'twill be too late to know--	198	DOUBL DLR	V.1	397
Lord Touch:	for I know him to be all goodness,--yet my	200	DOUEL DLE	V.1	482
Sir Paul:	The Ccmpany, gad'sbud, I don't know, my Lord,	200	DOUEL DLR	V.1	496
Lady Froth:	I don't know how long.	201	DOUEI DLR	V.1	520
Lord Touch:	but too soon you'll know mine, and that Woman's shame.	202	DOUEL DLR	V.1	565
Lady Froth:	You know I told you Saturn lock'd a little more	203	DOUBL DLR	V.1	579
	So till the Thief has stcll'n, he cannot know	204	DOUEL DLR	EPI.	6
Valentine:	Why, Sirrah, I have no Money, you know it; and	217	FOR LCVE	I.1	34
Jeremy:	Aye, Sir, I am a Fccl, I know it: And yet, Heav'n	217	FCR LCVE	I.1	40
Valentine:	Come sit you down, you know his way.	222	FCR LCVE	I.1	235
Trapland:	And I desire to know what Course you have taken	222	FCR LCVE	I.1	240
Scandal:	What, I know Trapland has been a Whoremaster,	223	FOR LCVE	I.1	264
Scandal:	What dcn't I know?--I know the Buxom black	223	FOR LCVE	I.1	268
Valentine:	Widow: I know where abouts you are: Come, to the	223	FOB LCVE	I.1	272
Valentine:	draw the Writing--Mr. Trapland, you know this Man,	224	FCR LCVE	I.1	320
Valentine:	You know her temper; she never gave me any great	225	FOR LCVE	I.1	346
Tattle:	when you know not the persons of whom you speak?	226	FCR LCVE	I.1	399
Scandal:	Not krcw 'em? Why, thou never hadst to do with	226	FCR LCVE	I.1	401
Tattle:	Pooh, I know Madam Drab has made her Brags in	227	FOR LCVE	I.1	419
Tattle:	her, and did I know not what--But, upon my Reputation,	227	FOR LCVE	I.1	421
Tattle:	Malice--But I know the bottom of it. She was brib'd	227	FOR LCVE	I.1	423
Tattle:	to that by one that we all know--A Man too. Only tc	227	FOR LCVE	I.1	424
Scandal:	Whom we all know.	227	FOR LCVE	I.1	426
Tattle:	me, and I told her scmething or cther, faith--I kncw	228	FOR LCVE	I.1	447
Scandal:	Yes, Mrs. Frail is a very fine Wcman, we all know	228	FOR LCVE	I.1	458
Scandal:	To tell what? Why, what do you know of Mrs.	228	FCB LCVE	I.1	463
Tattle:	Who I? Upon Honour I don't know whether she be	228	FOR LCVE	I.1	465
Jeremy:	Sir, Mrs. Frail has sent tc know if you are stirring.	229	FOR LCVE	I.1	505
Scandal:	Painter, that I cannot know the Person by your Picture of	230	FOR LCVE	I.1	537
Mrs Frail:	know.	230	FCB LCVE	I.1	549
Scandal:	of any Body that I know: you fancy that parting with	234	FOR LCVE	I.1	677
Foresight:	No, I know you can't, Sir: But I can tell, Sir, and	235	FOR LCVE	II.1	15
Foresight:	No, I know you can't, Sir: But I can tell and	235	FOR LCVE	II.1 V	15
Nurse:	Wee'st heart, I know not, they're none of 'em come	235	FOR LCVE	II.1	19
Angelica:	You kncw my Aunt is a little Retrograde (as you call it) in	237	FOR LCVE	II.1	71
Angelica:	--Nay, I know something worse, if I would	238	FCR LCVE	II.1	111
Foresight:	How? how? is that the reason? Come, you know	239	FOR LCVE	II.1	146
Foresight:	Come, I know Wcmen tell one ancther--She is	239	FOR LCVE	II.1	150
Sr Sampson:	ungracious Prodigal know who begat him; I will, old	240	FOR LCVE	II.1	174
Sr Sampson:	shall know one ancther's Faces without the help of a	240	FOR LCVE	II.1	200
Sr Sampson:	you, I have travel'd old Fircu, and kncw the Globe. I have	241	FOR LCVE	II.1	207
Foresight:	Coelestial Spheres, know the Signs and the Planets, and				
	their	241	FOR LCVE	II.1	211
Foresight:	and Aquatical Trigons. Know whether Life shall be long	241	FOR LCVE	II.1	214
Foresight:	know--	241	FOR LCVE	II.1	218
Sr Sampson:	I know the length of the Emperour of China's	241	FOR LCVE	II.1	219
Foresight:	I know when Travellers lie or speak Truth, when	241	FOR LCVE	II.1	224
Foresight:	they don't know it themselves.	241	FOR LCVE	II.1	225
Foresight:	But what do you know of my Wife, Sir Sampson?	242	FCR LCVE	II.1	255
Valentine:	Weatherheaded fool, I know how to laugh at him; but	244	FOR LCVE	II.1	312
Sr Sampson:	That's more than I know, Sir, and I believe not.	244	FOB LCVE	II.1	316
Valentine:	I know no more why I came, than you do why	244	FCR LCVE	II.1	333
Mrs Fore:	Poor innocent! you don't know that there's a	247	FOR LCVE	II.1	450
Mrs Frail:	The Estate You know is to be made over to him:--	248	FOR LCVE	II.1	494
Mrs Fore:	enough; my awkard Daughter-in-Law, who you know	248	FOR LCVE	II.1	499
Tattle:	have such a thought--sure you don't know me?	250	FOR LCVE	II.1	541
Mrs Frail:	hang'd before you'd confess--we know you--	250	FOR LCVE	II.1	555
Mrs Frail:	know, but I fancy, if I were a Man--	250	FOR LCVE	II.1	558
Miss Prue:	they mean, do you know?	251	FCR LCVE	II.1	582
Tattle:	hang me if I know the reason of it.	251	FOR LCVE	II.1	584
Valentine:	I know no effectual Difference between continued	254	FOR LCVE	III.1	40
Tattle:	No, nc, not a Syllable--I know that's a Secret,	254	FOR LCVE	III.1	47
Scandal:	wou'd have told me; I find, Madam, you don't know	256	FOR LCVE	III.1	110
Tattle:	No indeed, Madam, you don't know me at all, I	256	FOR LCVE	III.1	112
Tattle:	Heart--I know whom I mean--You know	258	FOR LCVE	III.1	178
Tattle:	beyond her Reputation--But I hope you don't know	258	FOR LCVE	III.1	187
Valentine:	I don't know but my Father in good Nature may press me	259	FCR LCVE	III.1	225
Miss Prue:	I don't know what to say to you, nor I don't care	263	FOR LCVE	III.1	378
Mrs Frail:	my Chamber, for they must not know that they are fall'n	265	FOR LCVE	III.1	449
Sr Sampson:	Body c' me, I don't know any universal Grievance,	266	FCR LCVE	III.1	485
Scandal:	No, not yet; nor Whirlwind. But we don't know	266	FOR LCVE	III.1	492
Scandal:	you dc not know your self.	268	FOR LCVE	III.1	564
Scandal:	Come, I know what you wou'd say,--you think	272	FOR LCVE	III.1	694
Scandal:	And now I think we know one another pretty well.	272	FOR LCVE	III.1	710
Mrs Frail:	the Estate be setled; for you know, Marrying without an	273	FOR LCVE	III.1	719
Mrs Frail:	And tho' I have a good Portion; you know one	273	FOR LCVE	III.1	723
Ben:	know her, Sir. Before she was Marry'd, she was call'd	273	FOR LOVE	III.1	752
Angelica:	(aside). I know not what to think--Yet I shou'd	277	FOR LOVE	IV.1	47
Angelica:	tell me, for you know what I wou'd ask?	277	FOR LOVE	IV.1	60
Scandal:	nor I don't know her if I see her; nor you neither.	278	FOR LOVE	IV.1	97
Scandal:	People. I hear Sir Sampson, you know your Cue; I'll	278	FOR LOVE	IV.1	108
Sr Sampson:	Gads bobs, does he not know me? Is he mischievous?	279	FOR LOVE	IV.1	155
Sr Sampson:	know me, Boy? Not know thy own Father, Val? I am	279	FOR LOVE	IV.1	157
Valentine:	It may be so--I did not know you--the World	280	FOR LOVE	IV.1	159
Valentine:	is full--There are People that we do know, and	280	FOB LOVE	IV.1	160
Valentine:	People that we do not know; and yet the Sun shines	280	FOR LOVE	IV.1	161
Sr Sampson:	Body o' me, I kncw not what to say to him.	280	FOR LOVE	IV.1	166
Valentine:	thou? Dost thou know me?	280	FOR LOVE	IV.1	169
Sr Sampson:	Do'st thou know this Paper, Val: I know	281	FOR LOVE	IV.1	214
Valentine:	I can't tell whether I know it cr no.	281	FOR LOVE	IV.1	218
Sr Sampson:	Oons! What a Vexation is here! I know not	282	FOR LOVE	IV.1	249
Sr Sampson:	pox on't, that I that know the World, and Men and	283	FOR LOVE	IV.1	286
Ben:	put'n into a passion; but what did I know that, what's that	285	FOR LOVE	IV.1	367
Mrs Frail:	temper?--You that know not how to submit to a Father,	286	FOR LOVE	IV.1	409
Ben:	wou'd have me; now I know your mind, tho'f you had	287	FOB LOVE	IV.1	430

Know (continued)

		PAGE	TITLE	ACT.SC	LINE
Ben:	them marry you, as don't know you:--Gad I know	287	FOR LOVE	IV.1	437
Valentine:	come;--Dost thou know what will happen to morrow?	288	FOR LOVE	IV.1	490
Valentine:	Argo's hundred Eyes be shut, ha? No body shall know,	290	FOR LOVE	IV.1	552
Tattle:	Tell, Madam! alas you don't know me--I have	291	FOR LOVE	IV.1	575
Jeremy:	No, no, Madam, he won't know her, if he shou'd, I	291	FOR LOVE	IV.1	591
Mrs Fore:	He won't know you, Cousin, he knows no	291	FOR LOVE	IV.1	601
Tattle:	now, that I know more Secrets than he.	291	FOR LOVE	IV.1	609
Foresight:	Mr. Tattle--Pray, what do you know?	291	FOR LOVE	IV.1	611
Tattle:	Do you know me, Valentine?	292	FOR LOVE	IV.1	622
Angelica:	Do you know me, Valentine?	292	FOR LOVE	IV.1	631
Valentine:	and blotted by every Goose's Quill. I know you; for I	292	FOR LOVE	IV.1	639
Singer-V:	I know my Eyes would lead my Heart to you,	293	FOR LOVE	IV.1	655
Jeremy:	O Lord, Madam, did you ever know any Madman	295	FOR LOVE	IV.1	743
Jeremy:	Partly I think--for he does not know his Mind	295	FOR LOVE	IV.1	753
Jeremy:	Partly I think--for he does not know his own Mind	295	FOR LOVE	IV.1	V753
Valentine:	Sir, your Father has sent to know if you are any	296	FOR LOVE	IV.1	770
Valentine:	Stupidity! You knew the Penalty of all I'm	296	FOR LOVE	IV.1	772
Angelica:	Never let us know one another better; for the Pleasure of	296	FOR LOVE	IV.1	789
Angelica:	know it.	296	FOR LOVE	IV.1	793
Valentine:	pursue her, and know her if it be possible, in spight of the	297	FOR LOVE	IV.1	813
Angelica:	Age I think--I assure you I know very considerable	298	FOR LOVE	V.1	29
Angelica:	of losing me: For you know he has long pretended a	300	FOR LOVE	V.1	111
Sr Sampson:	Odsbud, Hussy, you know how to chuse, and so do I;	301	FOR LOVE	V.1	143
Miss Prue:	and you won't be my Husband. And I know you may be	303	FOR LOVE	V.1	229
Tattle:	you're a Woman, and don't know your own mind.	304	FOR LOVE	V.1	253
Tattle:	to know, and shan't know; and yet you shall know it too,	305	FOR LOVE	V.1	290
Tattle:	and be sorry for't afterwards. I'd have you to know, Sir,	305	FOR LOVE	V.1	291
Tattle:	know of it half an Hour ago; and the Lady stays for me,	305	FOR LOVE	V.1	294
Tattle:	and does not know of it yet--There's a Mystery for	305	FOR LOVE	V.1	295
Tattle:	you,--I know your love to untie Difficulties--Or if	305	FOR LOVE	V.1	296
Miss Prue:	I don't know for what--And I'd rather be always a	305	FOR LOVE	V.1	311
Miss Prue:	I don't know for what--And I'd rather be always	305	FOR LOVE	V.1	V311
Ben:	married, or just going to be married, I know not which.	307	FOR LOVE	V.1	370
Ben:	I don't know what you may call Madness--But	307	FOR LOVE	V.1	372
Tattle:	one does not know how, nor why, nor wherefore--	309	FOR LOVE	V.1	459
Valentine:	counterfeited Madness; I don't know but the Frolick may	311	FOR LOVE	V.1	525
Angelica:	try'd you too, and know you both. You have not more	312	FOR LOVE	V.1	575
Angelica:	Have a care of large Promises; You know you are	313	FOR LOVE	V.1	613
Angelica:	Have a care of Promises; You know you are	313	FOR LOVE	V.1	V613
	And we, who know no better, must believe 'em.	315	FOR LOVE	EPI.	14
	But liv'd, I know not how, in Beasts; and then	315	FOR LOVE	EPI.	17
	Or in this very House, for ought we know,	315	FOR LOVE	EPI.	23
	I know not what these think, but for my Part,	315	FOR LOVE	EPI.	35
	And some here know I have a begging Face.	316	FOR LOVE	EPI.	42
Almeria:	I would have kept that Secret; though I know	328	M. BRIDE	I.1	80
Almeria:	Tell me? I know thou wouldst, thou art compassionate.	328	M. BRIDE	I.1	92
Almeria:	My Griefs? Thou dost already know 'em:	328	M. BRIDE	I.1	99
Almeria:	My Miseries? Thou dost already know 'em:	328	M. BRIDE	I.1	V 99
Almeria:	And when I said thou didst know nothing,	328	M. BRIDE	I.1	100
Almeria:	And when I told thee thou didst nothing know,	328	M. BRIDE	I.1	V100
Almeria:	It was because thou didst not know Alphonso:	328	M. BRIDE	I.1	101
Almeria:	That's his Pretence. I know his Errand is	331	M. BRIDE	I.1	213
Garcia:	Let's haste to follow him, and know the Cause.	338	M. BRIDE	II.1	24
Heli:	I know his Melancholy, and such Starts	338	M. BRIDE	II.1	27
Heli:	I know his Noble Heart would burst with Shame	338	M. BRIDE	II.1	33
Osmyn-Alph:	Wilt thou not know me? Hast thou then forgot me?	342	M. BRIDE	II.2	78
Almeria:	His Voice, I know him now, I know him all.	342	M. BRIDE	II.2	83
Osmyn-Alph:	To meet again in Life, to know I have thee,	342	M. BRIDE	II.2	93
Osmyn-Alph:	I have not Leisure to reflect, or know,	342	M. BRIDE	II.2	98
Almeria:	I know not, 'tis to see thy Face I think--	342	M. BRIDE	II.2	104
Almeria:	No, no, thy Griefs, I know, have done this to thee.	342	M. BRIDE	II.2	V116
Almeria:	I have a thousand Things to know, and ask,	343	M. BRIDE	II.2	150
Heli:	Zara with Selim, Sir, I saw and know 'em:	344	M. BRIDE	II.2	197
Zara:	The faithful Selim, and my Women know	347	M. BRIDE	II.2	291
Zara:	You know how I abus'd the credulous King;	347	M. BRIDE	II.2	293
Osmyn-Alph:	Alas, you know me not.	348	M. BRIDE	II.2	332
Zara:	This groveling Baseness--Thou say'st true, I know	348	M. BRIDE	II.2	335
Zara:	'Tis that, I know; for thou dost look, with Eyes	348	M. BRIDE	II.2	343
Zara:	I know, my Charms have reach'd thy very Soul,	348	M. BRIDE	II.2	345
Osmyn-Alph:	How does Almeria? But I know; she is	351	M. BRIDE	III.1	45
Heli:	When they shall know you live, assist your Cause.	352	M. BRIDE	III.1	103
Zara:	Haste me to know it, what?	354	M. BRIDE	III.1	189
Osmyn-Alph:	The Sea. I fear when she shall know the truth,	355	M. BRIDE	III.1	230
Almeria:	Why? why? to know it, cannot wound me more,	356	M. BRIDE	III.1	278
Osmyn-Alph:	But thou wilt know, what harrows up my Heart.	357	M. BRIDE	III.1	317
Osmyn-Alph:	But knowing Heav'n, to know it lost for ever.	358	M. BRIDE	III.1	366
Zara:	Choak in my Rage, and know the utmost depth	359	M. BRIDE	III.1	407
Zara:	I did not know the Princess Favourite;	359	M. BRIDE	III.1	415
Zara:	I know thou could'st; but I'm not often pleas'd,	360	M. BRIDE	III.1	423
Zara:	Thou ly'st; for now I know for whom thou'dst live.	360	M. BRIDE	III.1	436
Osmyn-Alph:	Then you may know for whom I'd die.	360	M. BRIDE	III.1	437
Zara:	Yes, thou shalt know, spite of thy past Distress,	361	M. BRIDE	III.1	455
Zara:	Forgive my Rage; I know thy Love and Truth.	362	M. BRIDE	IV.1	41
Zara:	What I know more, is, That a tripple League	364	M. BRIDE	IV.1	122
Manuel:	Whence is thy Grief? give me to know the Cause,	367	M. BRIDE	IV.1	262
Manuel:	And look thou answer me with truth: for know,	367	M. BRIDE	IV.1	264
Manuel:	Hear me; then, if thou canst, reply, know Traitress,	368	M. BRIDE	IV.1	300
Almeria:	And know that Osmyn was Alphonso.	370	M. BRIDE	IV.1	382
Gonsalez:	And tho' I know he hates beyond the Grave	371	M. BRIDE	IV.1	409
Gonsalez:	No matter--give me first to know the Cause	377	M. BRIDE	V.2	30
Almeria:	Yes, yes, I know to mourn; I'll sluce this Heart,	382	M. BRIDE	V.2	243
	The Tragedy thus done, I am, you know,	385	M. BRIDE	EPI.	1
	And know each Critick by his sowre Grimaces.	385	M. BRIDE	EPI.	6
Mirabell:	easie as to know when a Visit began to be troublesome;	396	WAY WORLD	I.1	39
Painall:	He is expected to Day. Do you know him?	400	WAY WORLD	I.1	189

370

Know (continued)

		PAGE	TITLE	ACT.SC	LINE
Fainall:	that all Europe should know we have Blockheads of all	400	WAY WORLD	I.1	202
Witwoud:	don't know what I say: But she's the best Woman in the	402	WAY WORLD	I.1	259
Witwoud:	don't know what I say: she's the best Woman in the	402	WAY WORLD	I.1	V259
Fainall:	'Tis well you don't know what you say, or else your	402	WAY WORLD	I.1	261
Witwoud:	Hum, faith I don't know as to that,--I can't say	403	WAY WORLD	I.1	302
Witwoud:	Bawd troubl'd with Wind. Now you may know what the	404	WAY WORLD	I.1	354
Petulant:	Not I--I mean no Body--I know nothing	406	WAY WORLD	I.1	428
Petulant:	Explain, I know nothing--Why you have an	407	WAY WORLD	I.1	434
Petulant:	All's one for that; why then say I know something.	407	WAY WORLD	I.1	442
Mirabell:	O Raillery, Raillery. Come, I know thou art in	407	WAY WORLD	I.1	448
Mirabell:	know you staid at Millamant's last Night, after I went.	407	WAY WORLD	I.1	450
Witwoud:	has been told; and you know she hates Mirabell, worse than	408	WAY WORLD	I.1	484
Petulant:	you know, they are not in awe of him--The Fellow's	408	WAY WORLD	I.1	504
Mirabell:	I thank you, I know as much as my Curiosity	409	WAY WORLD	I.1	507
Mirabell:	But hast not thou then Sense enough to know that	409	WAY WORLD	I.1	533
Marwood:	then know the worst; and be out of his Pain; but I wou'd	411	WAY WORLD	II.1	62
Fainall:	O my Dear I am satisfy'd of your Tenderness; I know	412	WAY WORLD	II.1	95
Fainall:	To let you know I see through all your little Arts--	413	WAY WORLD	II.1	136
Fainall:	You know I love you.	416	WAY WORLD	II.1	230
Mirabell:	When you are weary of him, you know your Remedy.	417	WAY WORLD	II.1	277
Millamant:	know why--They serve one to pin up one's Hair.	419	WAY WORLD	II.1	362
Millamant:	Now you must know they could not commend one, if	420	WAY WORLD	II.1	401
Witwoud:	But I know a Lady that loves talking so incessantly,	421	WAY WORLD	II.1	419
Mirabell:	I would give something that you did not know, I	422	WAY WORLD	II.1	460
Mirabell:	But how you came to know it--	422	WAY WORLD	II.1	484
Mirabell:	for Motion not Method is their Occupation. To know this,	423	WAY WORLD	II.1	498
Foible:	I told her Sir, because I did not know that you might	424	WAY WORLD	II.1	530
Lady Wish:	Sipping? Tasting? Save thee, dost thou not know the	425	WAY WORLD	III.1	24
Lady Wish:	Don't answer me. I won't know: I'll be surpriz'd. I'll be	429	WAY WORLD	III.1	173
Mrs Fain:	privy to the whole Design, and know that Waitwell, to	430	WAY WORLD	III.1	189
Foible:	me.--She has a Month's mind; but I know Mr.	430	WAY WORLD	III.1	217
Lady Wish:	Affairs really I know not what to do--(Calls)--Foible--I	431	WAY WORLD	III.1	256
Witwoud:	contradict too. What, I know my Cue. Then we contradict	435	WAY WORLD	III.1	401
Marwood:	'Tis your Brother, I fancy. Don't you know	436	WAY WORLD	III.1	439
Sir Wilful:	thou not know me, Friend? Why then send Somebody	437	WAY WORLD	III.1	454
Sir Wilful:	Why then belike thou dost not know thy Lady,	437	WAY WORLD	III.1	459
Servant-W:	hard to know 'em all.	437	WAY WORLD	III.1	471
Marwood:	Friends here, tho' it may be you don't know it--If I	438	WAY WORLD	III.1	508
Marwood:	Don't you know this Gentleman, Sir?	438	WAY WORLD	III.1	513
Sir Wilful:	but 'tis--'Sheart I know not whether 'tis or no--	438	WAY WORLD	III.1	515
Sir Wilful:	i'faith! What do'st thou not know me? By'r Lady nor I	439	WAY WORLD	III.1	517
Sir Wilful:	A pox, is this your Inns o' Court breeding, not to know	439	WAY WORLD	III.1	528
Witwoud:	you, 'tis not modish to know Relations in Town. You	439	WAY WORLD	III.1	533
Marwood:	Nay I know not; if the root be Honourable,	443	WAY WORLD	III.1	695
Marwood:	unknown hand--for the less I appear to know of the truth	443	WAY WORLD	III.1	702
Marwood:	have Foible provok'd if I cou'd help it,--because you know	443	WAY WORLD	III.1	704
Sir Wilful:	see, to come and know if that how you were dispos'd to	447	WAY WORLD	IV.1	115
Mirabell:	But do not you know, that when favours are conferr'd	449	WAY WORLD	IV.1	170
Mirabell:	for the Night, made of oil'd skins and I know not what	451	WAY WORLD	IV.1	249
Mrs Fain:	--what they have done by this time I know not. But	452	WAY WORLD	IV.1	313
Mrs Fain:	--what they may have done by this time I know not. But	452	WAY WORLD	IV.1	V313
Lady Wish:	and his Family. Beastly Creature, I know not what to do	456	WAY WORLD	IV.1	437
Witwoud:	Come Knight--Pox on him. I don't know what to	457	WAY WORLD	IV.1	470
Foible:	(to him). By Heaven! Mrs. Marwood's, I know it,--	460	WAY WORLD	IV.1	575
Lady Wish:	from no body that I know)--I have that honour for	460	WAY WORLD	IV.1	585
Lady Wish:	know you are abus'd. He who pretends to be Sir Rowland	460	WAY WORLD	IV.1	587
Foible:	Yes, yes; I know it Madam; she was in my Lady's	464	WAY WORLD	V.1	68
Mrs Fain:	Do's your Lady and Mirabell know that?	465	WAY WORLD	V.1	112
Mrs Fain:	Does your Lady or Mirabell know that?	465	WAY WORLD	V.1	V112
Mrs Fain:	I know what I mean Madam, and so do you; and	466	WAY WORLD	V.1	158
Mrs Fain:	me. I defie 'em all. Let 'em prove their aspersions: I know	466	WAY WORLD	V.1	177
Lady Wish:	be wrong'd after all, ha? I don't know what to think,--	466	WAY WORLD	V.1	181
Lady Wish:	Out Caterpillar, Call not me Aunt, I know thee	470	WAY WORLD	V.1	312
Marwood:	I'll know the bottom of it.	471	WAY WORLD	V.1	355
Fainall:	If it must all come out, why let 'em know it, 'tis but	474	WAY WORLD	V.1	475
Mirabell:	Very well, now you shall know--Madam, your	476	WAY WORLD	V.1	532
Mirabell:	Mr. Fainall, it is now time that you shou'd know,	476	WAY WORLD	V.1	535
	Yet each pretends to know the Copy'd Face.	479	WAY WORLD	EPI.	20
	For well the Learn'd and the Judicious know,	479	WAY WORLD	EPI.	28

Know'st (8)

		PAGE	TITLE	ACT.SC	LINE
Bellmour:	True. But to convince thee who I am, thou know'st	97	OLD BATCH	V.1	34
Lady Touch:	thee, thou know'st me, know'st the very inmost Windings	137	DOUBL DLR	I.1	397
Lady Touch:	Too well thou know'st my jealous Soul cou'd never bear	198	DOUBL DLR	V.1	399
Almeria:	O no, thou know'st not half--thou know'st	328	M. BRIDE	I.1	88
Almeria:	O no, thou know'st not half,	328	M. BRIDE	I.1	V 88
Almeria:	Know'st nothing of my Sorrows	328	M. BRIDE	I.1	V 89

Knowing (10)

		PAGE	TITLE	ACT.SC	LINE
Sir Joseph:	of knowing me--I only mean a Friend of mine whom I	50	OLD BATCH	II.1	118
Sharper:	that had found his Wife Knowing the first Night.	104	OLD BATCH	V.1	297
Tattle:	that I am as knowing as the Stars, and as secret as the Night.	305	FOR LOVE	V.1	292
Osmyn-Alph:	Is knowing more than any Circumstance,	342	M. BRIDE	II.2	94
Zara:	Commenc'd? not knowing who you were, nor why	347	M. BRIDE	II.2	299
Almeria:	Then knowing thou hast felt it. Tell it me.	356	M. BRIDE	III.1	279
Almeria:	Than knowing thou hast felt it. Tell it me.	356	M. BRIDE	III.1	V279
Osmyn-Alph:	Because not knowing Danger. But look forward;	358	M. BRIDE	III.1	342
Osmyn-Alph:	But knowing Heav'n, to know it lost for ever.	358	M. BRIDE	III.1	366
Gonsalez:	Knowing no Remedy, for what is past;	371	M. BRIDE	IV.1	406

Knowledge (8)

		PAGE	TITLE	ACT.SC	LINE
Lord Touch:	it: Yet there has been a thing in your Knowledge, which	181	DOUBL DLR	IV.1	541
	But that late knowledge, does much hazard cost,	204	DOUBL DLR	EPI.	4
Foresight:	How! I cannot Read that knowledge in your Face,	291	FOR LOVE	IV.1	610
Valentine:	Knowledge.	297	FOR LOVE	IV.1	804
Zara:	Most certain; though my Knowledge is not yet	364	M. BRIDE	IV.1	146
Zara:	Give me more ample Knowledge of this Mourning.	380	M. BRIDE	V.2	160

Lack-a-day (1)
Nurse:	Dinner--good lack-a-day, ha, ha, ha, O strange; I'll vow	.	235	FOR LOVE	II.1	22

Lactea (0) see Via Lactea

Lactilla (1)
| Brisk: | Lactilla may be,--'gad I cannot tell. | . . . . . . | 141 | DOUBL DLR | II.1 | 128 |

Lad (2)
| Fondlewife: | hath possess'd the Lad--I say I will tarry at home--Varlet. | | 75 | OLD BATCH | IV.1 | 17 |
| Sr Sampson: | Lad, till he learn'd to be a Wit--And might have | . . . | 299 | FOR LOVE | V.1 | 82 |

Laden (1) see Heavy-laden, Well-laden
| Setter: | dispose of! A goodly Pinnace, richly laden, and to launch | | 102 | OLD BATCH | V.1 | 222 |

Ladies (22)
Bellmour:	Ladies, is--		57	OLD BATCH	II.2	115
Setter:	And therefore you'd have him to set in your Ladies	. . .	67	OLD BATCH	III.1	228
Capt Bluff:	Ladies, by these Hilts you are well met.	. . . . .	85	OLD BATCH	IV.3	82
Sharper:	Ladies, your humble Servant.--We were	. . . . .	86	OLD BATCH	IV.3	114
Sharper:	the society of Ladies.	. . . .	88	OLD BATCH	IV.3	200
Sir Joseph:	I'm in the Ladies favours?--No matter, I'll make your	.	103	OLD BATCH	V.1	261
Sir Joseph:	I warrant, I'll bring you into the Ladies good Graces.		103	OLD BATCH	V.1	263
Sharper:	Hist,--Bellmour: If you'll bring the Ladies, make	. .	107	OLD BATCH	V.1	390
Sharper:	Then, let me beg these Ladies to wear their Masks, a	.	110	OLD BATCH	V.2	90
Vainlove:	I know whom you have not got; pray Ladies	. . . . .	110	OLD BATCH	V.2	115
Lord Touch:	Ladies, and Drink a Dish of Tea, to settle our Heads.	. .	132	DOUBL DLR	I.1	V217
Mellefont:	Shall we go to the Ladies, my Lord?	. . . .	134	DOUBL DLR	I.1	283
Careless:	I had a mind to try my Ladies Vertue--And when I could	.	180	DOUBL DLR	IV.1	498
Scandal:	Others excuse him, and blame you: only the Ladies are	.	220	FOR LOVE	I.1	161
Scandal:	not to be believ'd; and refuses the reputation of a Ladies		226	FOR LOVE	I.1	376
Valentine:	cannot avoid such a palpable Decoy as this was; the Ladies		229	FOR LOVE	I.1	502
Tattle:	us'd by the Ladies.	. . . .	255	FOR LOVE	III.1	83
Tattle:	whom I mean; for there were a great many Ladies raffled	.	258	FOR LOVE	III.1	188
Tattle:	whom I mean; for there was a great many Ladies raffled	.	258	FOR LOVE	III.1	V188
Witwoud:	I; fine Ladies I say.	. . . .	406	WAY WORLD	I.1	405
Witwoud:	Ay, we'll all walk in the Park, the Ladies talk'd of	.	409	WAY WORLD	I.1	510
Mirabell:	not us be accessary to your putting the Ladies out of	.	409	WAY WORLD	I.1	524

Lading (1)
| Setter: | Voyage. Or have you brought your own Lading back? | . . . | 96 | OLD BATCH | V.1 | 3 |

Ladiship (15)
Footman:	if your Ladiship would have the Coach come again for	. .	88	OLD BATCH	IV.3	207
Cynthia:	I'll wait upon your Ladiship.	. . . .	167	DOUBL DLR	III.1	617
Sir Paul:	Does your Ladiship conceive so--Why I was of	. . . .	171	DOUBL DLR	IV.1	155
Sir Paul:	that Opinion once too--Nay if your Ladiship conceives	.	171	DOUBL DLR	IV.1	156
Cynthia:	(aside). And for your Ladiship too, I believe, or else	.	172	DOUBL DLR	IV.1	176
Sir Paul:	because he has a great veneration for your Ladiship.	. .	172	DOUBL DLR	IV.1	180
Sir Paul:	I humbly thank your Ladiship--I don't know	. . . .	172	DOUBL DLR	IV.1	197
Sir Paul:	your Ladiship is of opinion that the Match may go forward.		172	DOUBL DLR	IV.1	203
Sir Paul:	Did your Ladiship call?	. . . .	173	DOUBL DLR	IV.1	213
Brisk:	Ladiship--Let me perish, I don't know whether to	. . .	176	DOUBL DLR	IV.1	337
Brisk:	tell whether I am glad or sorry that your Ladiship has made		176	DOUBL DLR	IV.1	339
Brisk:	Ladiship, seriously.	. . . .	176	DOUBL DLR	IV.1	346
Sir Paul:	Hold, stay, I beseech your Ladiship--I'm so	. . . .	179	DOUBL DLR	IV.1	465
Sir Paul:	this Letter--Nay hear me, I beseech your Ladiship:	. .	180	DOUBL DLR	IV.1	469
Tattle:	I will; because I have a tender for your Ladiship.	. .	234	FOR LOVE	I.1	668

Ladiships (3)
Footman:	Your Ladiships Chair is come.	. . . .	166	DOUBL DLR	III.1	605
Sir Paul:	your Ladiships Hand.	. . . .	172	DOUBL DLR	IV.1	193
Sir Paul:	which lie all in your Ladiships Breast, and he being a well		180	DOUBL DLR	IV.1	479

Lads (3)
Brisk:	Boys, Boys, Lads, where are you? What, do you give	. . .	128	DOUBL DLR	I.1	20
Ben:	come, my Lads, let's have a round, and I'll make one.	. .	275	FOR LOVE	III.1	797
Sir Wilful:	But let British Lads sing,	. . . .	456	WAY WORLD	IV.1	455

Lady (209)
Bellmour:	discourse of their diseases and infirmities? What fine Lady		42	OLD BATCH	I.1	182
Bellmour:	of his Lady?	. . . .	44	OLD BATCH	I.1	262
Belinda:	Oh Gad, here comes the Fool that din'd at my Lady	. . .	84	OLD BATCH	IV.3	55
Sir Joseph:	(aside). The great Fortune, that dined at my Lady	. .	86	OLD BATCH	IV.3	108
Sharper:	me, or I'll go and have the Lady to my self. B'w'y' George.		104	OLD BATCH	V.1	306
Setter:	private Conveyance of the Lady to him, and put a	. .	105	OLD BATCH	V.1	344
Sharper:	fear.--A fine Lady, and a Lady of very good Quality.	. .	111	OLD BATCH	V.2	135
Sir Joseph:	Thanks to my Knight-hood, she's a Lady--	. . . .	111	OLD BATCH	V.2	136
Mellefont:	keep my Lady Touchwood's Head from Working: For	. . .	129	DOUBL DLR	I.1	76
Mellefont:	my Lady Plyant all this Evening, that my Pious Aunt	. .	130	DOUBL DLR	I.1	126
Careless:	Lady, I don't see what you can expect from the Fruit.	. .	131	DOUBL DLR	I.1	166
	(Enter Lady Touchwood, and Maskwell.)	. . .	135	DOUBL DLR	I.1	298
Maskwell:	You have already been tampering with my Lady	. . . .	137	DOUBL DLR	I.1	406
	(Enter Lady Froth and Cynthia.)	. .	138	DOUBL DLR	II.1	
Brisk:	(to Lady Froth). Your Ladyship is in the right; but I'gad		141	DOUBL DLR	II.1	115
	(Exit Lady Froth and Brisk.)	. .	142	DOUBL DLR	II.1	146
	(Enter Sir Paul Plyant and Lady Plyant.)		143	DOUBL DLR	II.1	194
Sir Paul:	my Lady Froth says; was ever the like read of in Story?	.	143	DOUBL DLR	II.1	196
Sir Paul:	Hold your self Contented, my Lady Plyant,--I	. . .	144	DOUBL DLR	II.1	206
Sir Paul:	Lady Plyant shall Command Sir Paul; but when I am	. .	144	DOUBL DLR	II.1	222
Sir Paul:	Hum, gads bud she says true,--well, my Lady,	. . .	145	DOUBL DLR	II.1	238
	(Lady Plyant and Sir Paul come up to Mellefont.)	.	145	DOUBL DLR	II.1	241
Mellefont:	Contrivance to perswade my Lady Plyant to this	. . .	149	DOUBL DLR	II.1	410
	(Enter Lord Touchwood, and Lady Touchwood.)	. . .	150	DOUBL DLR	III.1	
Lord Touch:	--Pho, 'tis nonsense. Come, come; I know my Lady	. .	150	DOUBL DLR	III.1	5
	(Exit Lady Touchwood.)	. . .	155	DOUBL DLR	III.1	173
Maskwell:	Mean? Not to disappoint the Lady I assure you--	. .	157	DOUBL DLR	III.1	242
Careless:	Mellefont, get out o'th' way, my Lady Plyant's	. . .	157	DOUBL DLR	III.1	264
	(Enter Sir Paul and Lady Plyant.)	. . .	159	DOUBL DLR	III.1	320
Sir Paul:	(aside to her). I acquiesce, my Lady; but don't snub so	.	159	DOUBL DLR	III.1	334
Sir Paul:	So, now, now; now my Lady.	. . . .	160	DOUBL DLR	III.1	360
Sir Paul:	should hear--Gad's bud, you may talk of my Lady	. .	160	DOUBL DLR	III.1	373
Careless:	O fie, fie, not to be named of a day--my Lady Froth	. .	160	DOUBL DLR	III.1	375
Careless:	Lady Plyant is not thought of--if that can ever be.	.	160	DOUBL DLR	III.1	377
Careless:	Lady! that is the envy of her Sex, and the admiration of	.	160	DOUBL DLR	III.1	381
Careless:	Lady! that is the envy of her own Sex, and the admiration of	160	DOUBL DLR	III.1	V381

Lady   (continued)

Speaker	Text	PAGE	TITLE	ACT.SC	LINE
Sir Paul:	be Prcvidence--ay, truly, Mr. Careless, my Lady is a great	160	DOUBL DLR	III.1	386
Sir Paul:	Gad so, gad's bud--Tim, carry it to my Lady, you	161	DCUEL DLR	III.1	395
Sir Paul:	should have carry'd it to my Lady first.	161	DOUBL DLR	III.1	396
Sir Paul:	Well, well, my Lady reads all Letters first--Child,	161	DOUBL DLR	III.1	398
	(Carries the Letter to my Lady and Exit.)	161	DOUBL DLR	III.1	V401
Sir Paul:	my Lady is so nice--it's very strange, but it's true: too	161	DOUBL DLR	III.1	431
Careless:	Alas-a-day, this is a lamentable story; my Lady must	162	DOUBL DLR	III.1	441
Lord Froth:	admirer of my Lady Whitler, Mr. Sneer, and Sir Laurence	162	DOUBL DLR	III.1	461
Lord Froth:	Woman of Quality--you have been at my Lady Whifler's	162	DOUBL DLR	III.1	466
Lord Froth:	Hee, hee, hee, right; and then my Lady Whifler is	163	DOUBL DLR	III.1	475
Sir Paul:	'Gads so--Wife, Wife, my Lady Plyant, I have a	163	DOUBL DLR	III.1	489
	(Exit Careless and Lady Plyant.)	163	DOUBL DLR	III.1	496
Sir Paul:	success. Boy, tell my Lady, when she has done, I would	163	DOUBL DLR	III.1	498
	(Enter Lady Froth and Brisk.)	163	DOUBL DLR	III.1	501
Lord Froth:	wont you joyn with us, we were laughing at my Lady	165	DOUBL DLR	III.1	559
Brisk:	Who, my Lady Toothless; O, she's a mortifying	165	DOUBL DLR	III.1	567
Lady Froth:	Then that t'other great strapping Lady--I	166	DOUBL DLR	III.1	580
Brisk:	Pray, Madam, how old is Lady Sapho?	167	DOUBL DLR	III.1	618
Cyntaia:	my Lady with him, but she seem'd to moderate his Passion.	167	DOUBL DLR	IV.1	2
Cynthia:	of his Wit: Therefore let me see you undermine my Lady	168	DOUBL DLR	IV.1	47
	(Enter Careless and Lady Plyant.)	169	DOUBL DLR	IV.1	68
Sir Paul:	Lord nor my Lady to know what they intend.	171	DOUBL DLR	IV.1	158
Lady Ply:	I know my Lady Touchwood has no kindness for	171	DOUBL DLR	IV.1	163
Sir Paul:	Indeed if this be made plain, as my Lady your	172	DOUBL DLR	IV.1	171
Sir Paul:	Lady here: Marry Heaven forbid that you should follow	174	DOUBL DLR	IV.1	249
Brisk:	practice.--Ah! My dear Lady Froth! She's a mcst	175	DOUBL DLR	IV.1	291
	(Enter Lady Froth.)	175	DOUBL DLR	IV.1	305
Brisk:	O ye Powers! O my Lady Froth, my Lady Froth! My Lady	175	DOUBL DLR	IV.1	309
Brisk:	My Lady Froth! Your Ladyships most humble Servant;	175	DOUBL DLR	IV.1	313
Brisk:	my Lady Froth?	176	DOUBL DLR	IV.1	330
Brisk:	Lady Froth.	177	DOUEL DLR	IV.1	358
	(Enter Lady Plyant, and Careless.)	177	DOUBL DLR	IV.1	389
Sir Paul:	polluted by Foreign Iniquity? O my Lady Plyant, you were	179	DOUBL DLR	IV.1	430
	(Enter Lady Plyant.)	179	DOUBL DLR	IV.1	436
Sir Paul:	to my Lady, I can't ccntain my self; come my dear Friend.	181	DOUBL DLR	IV.1	509
Maskwell:	My Lady is just gone down from my Lords Closet,	181	DOUBL DLR	IV.1	515
Maskwell:	My Lady is just gone into my Lords Closet,	181	DOUBL DLR	IV.1	V515
	(Scene opening, shews Lady Touchwood's Chamber.)	183	DOUBL DLR	IV.2	
	(Enter Lady Touchwood.)	183	DOUBL DLR	IV.2	7
	(Draws, and runs at Mellefont, is held by Lady Touchwood.)	186	DOUBL DLR	IV.2	108
	(Enter Lady Touchwood and Maskwell.)	187	DOUBL DLR	V.1	
Maskwell:	It must not be; nay, shou'd my Lady know it--ay,	190	DOUBL DLR	V.1	92
	(Enter Lord Touchwood, Lady Touchwood.)	190	DOUBL DLR	V.1	121
Sir Paul:	Madam, Sister, my Lady Sister, did you see my	191	DOUBL DLR	V.1	159
Sir Paul:	Lady my Wife!	191	DOUBL DLR	V.1	160
Maskwell:	was, the finding it impossible to gain the Lady any other	193	DOUBL DLR	V.1	219
Maskwell:	'Tis that; you know my Lady has a high Spirit,	195	DOUBL DLR	V.1	315
Careless:	that I saw your Father in, my Lady Touchwood's Passion,	196	DOUBL DLR	V.1	336
Cynthia:	My Lady and Maskwell! this may be lucky--	197	DOUBL DLR	V.1	373
	(Enter Lady Touchwood with a Dagger, Maskwell.)	197	DOUBL DLR	V.1	378
	(Enter Lady Froth, Brisk.)	201	DOUBL DLR	V.1	516
	(Enter Lady Plyant, Careless, Cynthia.)	202	DOUBL DLR	V.1	544
Lord Froth:	and Lady?	202	DOUBL DLR	V.1	552
	(A great shriek from the ccrner cf the Stage. Lady Touchwood	202	DOUEL DLR	V.1	556
	The Lady Criticks, who are better Read,	204	DOUBL DLR	EPI.	21
Jeremy:	Treats and your Balls; your being in Love with a Lady,	217	FOR LCVE	I.1	44
Tattle:	But I soon satisfy'd the Lady of my Innocence; for I told	227	FOR LCVE	I.1	429
Tattle:	Manners to contradict what a Lady has declar'd.	229	FOR LOVE	I.1	479
Scandal:	Lady; it is contrary to his Character--How one may	229	FCR LOVE	I.1	490
Tattle:	'Tis very hard--Won't a Baronet's Lady pass?	230	FOR LOVE	I.1	530
Valentine:	Well Lady Galloper, how does Angelica?	231	FCR LOVE	I.1	552
Scandal:	Then I have a Lady burning of Brandy in a Cellar	233	FCR LOVE	I.1	639
Scandal:	Then I have a Lady burning Brandy in a Cellar	233	FCR LOVE	I.1	V639
Angelica:	never ask'd any thing, but what a Lady might modestly	255	FCR LOVE	III.1	89
Valentine:	tell whether the Lady or Mr. Tattle be the more obliged	256	FOR LOVE	III.1	130
Tattle:	afterwards, for it was talk'd of in Town--And a Lady of	258	FOR LOVE	III.1	174
Ben:	high Wind, or that Lady.--You mayn't carry sc much	262	FCR LOVE	III.1	331
Scandal:	Look you there now--Your Lady says your	269	FOR LOVE	III.1	616
Scandal:	Not upon a kind occasion, Madam. But when a Lady	276	FOR LCVE	IV.1	23
Valentine:	Mad, and will be Mad to every Body but this Lady.	296	FOR LOVE	IV.1	774
Jeremy:	What, is the Lady gone again, Sir? I hope you	296	FOR LOVE	IV.1	799
Sr Sampson:	a fair Lady, a great while--Odd, Madam, you have	298	FCR LCVE	V.1	14
Sr Sampson:	a Lady any way--Come, come, let me tell you, you	298	FCR LOVE	V.1	24
Sr Sampson:	Lady of your incomparable Beauty and Merit.--If I	300	FOR LCVE	V.1	97
Tattle:	pretty Fellow, and can'st carry a Message to a Lady, in a	302	FCR LOVE	V.1	181
Jeremy:	comply with any thing to please him. Poor Lady, I'm	302	FCR LOVE	V.1	202
Tattle:	know of it half an Hour ago; and the Lady stays for me,	305	FCR LOVE	V.1	294
Valentine:	If you please, Sir; but first I would ask this Lady	311	FCR LOVE	V.1	515
Sr Sampson:	Sir, you must ask my leave first; that Lady, No,	311	FOR LOVE	V.1	517
Sr Sampson:	Sir, you must ask me leave first; that Lady, No,	311	FOR LCVE	V.1	V517
Sr Sampson:	Sir; you shall ask that Lady no Questions, till you have	311	FOR LOVE	V.1	518
Sr Sampson:	ask'd her Blessing, Sir; that Lady is to be my Wife.	311	FOR LCVE	V.1	519
Valentine:	only Pleasure was to please this Lady: I have made many	312	FCR LOVE	V.1	546
Mirabell:	all in her own Name, my old Lady Wishfort came in.--	395	WAY WORLD	I.1	24
Mirabell:	good cld Lady broke thro' her painful Taciturnity, with an	396	WAY WORLD	I.1	35
Mirabell:	Sect? My Lady Wishfort, I warrant, who publishes her	396	WAY WCRLD	I.1	60
Mirabell:	Concern for which the Lady is more indebted to you, than	397	WAY WCRLD	I.1	97
Mirabell:	Concern for which the Lady is more indebted to you, than is	397	WAY WORLD	I.1	V 97
Mirabell:	That I may see her before she returns to her Lady; and as	398	WAY WORLD	I.1	131
Painall:	Wife, who was Sister to my Lady Wishfort, my Wife's	400	WAY WORLD	I.1	193
Witwoud:	Lady? Gad, I say any thing in the World to get this Fellow	402	WAY WCRLD	I.1	255
Petulant:	my Lady Wishfort's?	407	WAY WCRLD	I.1	436
Witwoud:	Mirabell and he are at some distance, as my Lady Wishfort	408	WAY WORLD	I.1	483
Witwoud:	No, no, he comes to his Aunts, my Lady Wishfort;	409	WAY WORLD	I.1	514
Marwood:	My Obligaticns to my Lady urg'd me: I had	414	WAY WORLD	II.1	162

Lady   (continued)

Speaker	Text	PAGE	TITLE	ACT.SC	LINE
Fainall:	Marriage, my Lady had been incens'd beyond all means of	415	WAY WORLD	II.1	203
Mrs Fain:	I believe my Lady will do any thing to get a Husband; and	418	WAY WORLD	II.1	308
Mirabell:	Yes, I think the good Lady wou'd marry any	418	WAY WORLD	II.1	311
Witwoud:	But I know a Lady that loves talking so incessantly,	421	WAY WORLD	II.1	419
Foible:	O las Sir, I'm so asham'd--I'm afraid my Lady	423	WAY WORLD	II.1	513
Foible:	But I told my Lady as you instructed me, Sir. That I	423	WAY WORLD	II.1	519
Foible:	I'll be gone; I'm sure my Lady is at her Toilet, and can't	424	WAY WORLD	II.1	543
Foible:	seen me with you I'm sure she'll tell my Lady. I'll make	424	WAY WORLD	II.1	546
	(A Room in Lady Wishfort's House.	425	WAY WORLD	III.1	
	Lady Wishfort at her Toilet, Peg waiting.)	425	WAY WORLD	III.1	
Foible:	your Lady propose? Let me see (says he) what she must	427	WAY WORLD	III.1	99
Lady Wish:	than to put a Lady to the necessity of breaking her Forms.	429	WAY WORLD	III.1	162
Mrs Fain:	with Mirabell, and I'm afraid will discover it to my Lady.	430	WAY WORLD	III.1	186
Mrs Fain:	Mirabell's Uncle, and as such winning my Lady, to involve	430	WAY WORLD	III.1	191
Foible:	Generosity.--Sweet Lady, to be so good! Mr. Mirabell	430	WAY WORLD	III.1	203
Foible:	our success, Mrs. Marwood had told my Lady; but I warrant	430	WAY WORLD	III.1	206
Foible:	Lady that Mr. Mirabell rail'd at her. I laid horrid Things	430	WAY WORLD	III.1	208
Foible:	to his charge, I'll vow; and my Lady is so incens'd, that	430	WAY WORLD	III.1	209
Foible:	remove my Lady's Toilet. Madam your Servant. My Lady	430	WAY WORLD	III.1	219
Marwood:	now I'll have none of him. Here comes the good Lady,	431	WAY WORLD	III.1	246
	(Enter Lady Wishfort.)	431	WAY WORLD	III.1	249
	(Exit Lady and Foible.)	432	WAY WORLD	III.1	282
Marwood:	can no more conceal it, than my Lady Strammel can her	433	WAY WORLD	III.1	320
	Servant to Lady Wishfort.)	436	WAY WORLD	III.1	444
Sir Wilful:	My Aunt Sir, yes my Aunt Sir, and your Lady	437	WAY WORLD	III.1	452
Sir Wilful:	Sir; your Lady is my Aunt, Sir--Why, what do'st	437	WAY WORLD	III.1	453
Sir Wilful:	here that does. How long hast thou liv'd with thy Lady,	437	WAY WORLD	III.1	455
Sir Wilful:	hither that does. How long hast thou liv'd with thy Lady,	437	WAY WORLD	III.1	V455
Sir Wilful:	Why then belike thou dost not know thy Lady,	437	WAY WORLD	III.1	459
Sir Wilful:	Save you Gentlemen and Lady.	437	WAY WORLD	III.1	479
Sir Wilful:	Right Lady; I am Sir Wilfull Witwoud, so I	438	WAY WORLD	III.1	510
Sir Wilful:	to the Lady Wishfort, of this Mansion.	438	WAY WORLD	III.1	512
Sir Wilful:	Hum! What sure 'tis not--Yea by'r Lady,	438	WAY WORLD	III.1	514
Sir Wilful:	i'faith! What do'st thou not know me? Ey'r Lady nor I	439	WAY WORLD	III.1	517
Sir Wilful:	Brother. 'Sheart, I've suspected this--By'r Lady I	439	WAY WORLD	III.1	539
Sir Wilful:	Discourse to the Lady, Sir: 'Tis like my Aunt may have	440	WAY WORLD	III.1	572
	(Enter Lady Wishfort and Fainall.)	441	WAY WORLD	III.1	592
Marwood:	Discover to my Lady your Wife's conduct;	442	WAY WORLD	III.1	659
Marwood:	threaten to part with her--My Lady loves her, and	442	WAY WORLD	III.1	660
Marwood:	this imposture. My Lady will be enraged beyond bounds,	442	WAY WORLD	III.1	663
Marwood:	I'm sorry I hinted to my Lady to endeavour a	443	WAY WORLD	III.1	668
Marwood:	your Lady?	443	WAY WORLD	III.1	675
Marwood:	to my Lady at the time when that Rascal who is	443	WAY WORLD	III.1	700
	(Scene Continues. Enter Lady Wishfort and Foible.)	444	WAY WORLD	IV.1	
Millamant:	or fond, nor kiss before folks, like my Lady Fadler and Sr.	450	WAY WORLD	IV.1	201
Witwoud:	yes the fray is compos'd; my Lady came in like a	453	WAY WORLD	IV.1	329
	(Enter Lady Wishfort and Sir Wilfull drunk.)	454	WAY WORLD	IV.1	383
	(Enter Foible, and whispers Lady Wishfort.)	456	WAY WORLD	IV.1	459
Foible:	quarter of an hours lying and swearing to a fine Lady?	459	WAY WORLD	IV.1	559
	(Enter Lady Wishfort with a Letter.)	459	WAY WORLD	IV.1	565
Waitwell:	a good cause--my Lady shall be satisfied of my Truth	461	WAY WORLD	IV.1	624
	(Scene Continues. Enter Lady Wishfort and Foible.)	462	WAY WORLD	V.1	
Foible:	Sweet, so kind a Lady as you have been to me.	463	WAY WORLD	V.1	33
Foible:	Dinner. She sent the Letter to my Lady, and that missing	464	WAY WORLD	V.1	70
Foible:	Marwood declar'd all to my Lady.	464	WAY WORLD	V.1	73
Foible:	Yes Madam; but my Lady did not see that part; We	464	WAY WORLD	V.1	78
Mincing:	My Lady wou'd speak with Mrs. Foible, Mem. Mr.	464	WAY WORLD	V.1	104
Mincing:	Closet, till my old Lady's anger is abated. O, my old Lady	465	WAY WORLD	V.1	107
Mincing:	He swears, and my old Lady cry's. There's a fearful	465	WAY WORLD	V.1	109
	Hurricane	465	WAY WORLD	V.1	112
Mrs Fain:	Do's your Lady and Mirabell know that?	465	WAY WORLD	V.1	V112
Mrs Fain:	Does your Lady or Mirabell know that?	465	WAY WORLD	V.1	114
Mincing:	sober, and to bring him to them. My Lady is resolv'd to	465	WAY WORLD	V.1	117
Mincing:	Lady.	465	WAY WORLD	V.1	124
	(Enter Lady Wishfort and Marwood.)	465	WAY WORLD	V.1	251
Fainall:	by the Importunity of this Lady your Friend; and am	468	WAY WORLD	V.1	258
Marwood:	That condition I dare answer, my Lady will	468	WAY WORLD	V.1	367
Mirabell:	so good a Lady, with a sincere remorse, and a hearty	471	WAY WORLD	V.1	380
Sir Wilful:	By'r Lady a very reasonable request; and will cost	471	WAY WORLD	V.1	429
Sir Wilful:	by'r Lady I shall draw mine.	473	WAY WORLD	V.1	441
Fainall:	somewhere else; For here it will not avail. This, my Lady	473	WAY WORLD	V.1	472
Marwood:	(to Fainall) O my shame! (Mirabell and Lady	474	WAY WORLD	V.1	536
Mirabell:	that your Lady while she was at her own disposal, and	476	WAY WORLD	V.1	540
Mirabell:	Yes Sir. I say that this Lady while a Widow,	476	WAY WORLD	V.1	555
Mirabell:	Elder Date than what you have obtain'd from your Lady.	476	WAY WORLD	V.1	583
Sir Wilful:	Cozen's a Fine Lady, and the Gentleman loves her and she	477	WAY WORLD	V.1	

Lady-ship (4)

Speaker	Text	PAGE	TITLE	ACT.SC	LINE
Foible:	Chamber, but I wou'd not tell your Lady-ship to	461	WAY WORLD	IV.1	619
Foible:	your Lady-ship, Madam--No indeed his Marriage	463	WAY WORLD	V.1	39
Foible:	first, to secure your Lady-ship. He cou'd not have bedded	463	WAY WORLD	V.1	41
Foible:	your Lady-ship: for if he had Consummated with your	463	WAY WORLD	V.1	42

Lady-ship's (2)

Speaker	Text	PAGE	TITLE	ACT.SC	LINE
Foible:	dissembling Tongue; Your Lady-ship's own Wisdom has	463	WAY WORLD	V.1	27
Millamant:	to make a Resignation of it, in your Lady-ship's presence;	470	WAY WORLD	V.1	331

Lady's (28)

Speaker	Text	PAGE	TITLE	ACT.SC	LINE
Heartwell:	disgust him from the Lady's own Lips.	43	OLD BATCH	I.1	256
Bellmour:	when it may be the means of getting into a fair Lady's				
	Books?	44	OLD BATCH	I.1	V267
Setter:	of her. She's the very Sluce to her Lady's Secrets:--	99	OLD BATCH	V.1	104
Setter:	undone, my Master's undone, my Lady's undone, and all	103	OLD BATCH	V.1	240
Sir Joseph:	No, no, Never fear, Man, the Lady's business shall	103	OLD BATCH	V.1	242
Sir Joseph:	I'm in the Lady's favour?--No matter, I'll make your	103	OLD BATCH	V.1	V261
Lord Froth:	Laugh at no bodies Jest but my own, or a Lady's; I assure	132	DOUBL DLR	I.1	192
Sir Paul:	And my Lady's quite out of Breath; or else you	160	DOUBL DLR	III.1	372
Careless:	Lady's a fine likely Woman--	161	DOUBL DLR	III.1	420

Lady's (continued)
Maskwell:	in that Lobby by my Lady's Bed-Chamber, I shall be able	.	183	DOUBL DLR	IV.1	585
Maskwell:	an hour, yonder in my Lady's Dressing-Room; go by the	. .	194	DOUBL DLR	V.1	239
Lord Froth:	Lady's is the most inviting Couch; and a slumber there, is		200	DOUBL DLR	V.1	494
Sir Paul:	No, no, I mean the Family,--your Lady's	. . . .	200	DOUBL DLR	V.1	505
Tattle:	thing to a Lady's Prejudice in my Life--For as I was	.	256	FOR LOVE	III.1	102
Tattle:	good Fortune to be trusted once with a Lady's Secret, not		256	FOR LOVE	III.1	105
Tattle:	Discretion, as the Heat of the Lady's Passion hurry'd her		258	FOR LOVE	III.1	186
Gonsalez:	Methirks this Lady's Hatred to the Moor, ...		366	M. BRIDE	IV.1	202
Fainall:	marrying with my Lady's Approbation?		396	WAY WORLD	I.1	46
Fainall:	have Cruelty enough, not to satisfie a Lady's longing; you		397	WAY WORLD	I.1	91
Foible:	remove my Lady's Toilet. Madam your Servant. My Lady		430	WAY WORLD	III.1	219
Servant-W:	Sir, my Lady's dressing. Here's Company; if you . . .		437	WAY WORLD	III.1	445
Servant-W:	except my Lady's Woman.		437	WAY WORLD	III.1	458
Foible:	talk with you. Tho' my Lady's Orders were to leave you		445	WAY WORLD	IV.1	45
Foible:	O Madam, my Lady's gone for a Constable; I shall . .		463	WAY WORLD	V.1	62
Foible:	Yes, yes; I know it Madam; she was in my Lady's . . .		464	WAY WORLD	V.1	68
Mincing:	Foible; and wou'd have you hide your self in my Lady's		465	WAY WORLD	V.1	106
Mincing:	Closet, till my old Lady's anger is abated. O, my old Lady		465	WAY WORLD	V.1	107
Mincing:	I vow. He says Mem, how that he'll have my Lady's . .		465	WAY WORLD	V.1	110

Ladys (1)
| Lord Touch: | Ladys, and Drink a Dish of Tea, to settle our Heads. . | | 132 | DOUBL DLR | I.1 | 217 |

Ladyship (52)
see Ladiship, Lady-ship, Laship
Betty:	Did your Ladyship call, Madam?		56	OLD BATCH	II.2	68
Footman:	Vainlove to wait upon your Ladyship.		56	OLD BATCH	II.2	77
Cynthia:	Indeed, Madam! Is it Possible your Ladyship could . .		138	DOUBL DLR	II.1	1
Cynthia:	Love, and so much Wit as your Ladyship has, did not . .		138	DOUBL DLR	II.1	6
Brisk:	Never any thing; but your Ladyship, let me perish. . .		140	DOUBL DLR	II.1	84
Brisk:	(to Lady Froth). Your Ladyship is in the right; but I'gad		141	DOUBL DLR	II.1	115
Brisk:	was telling me, your Ladyship has made an Essay toward		141	DOUBL DLR	II.1	118
Brisk:	Ladyship has not the Art of Surprizing the most Naturally		142	DOUBL DLR	II.1	131
Brisk:	presume your Ladyship has Read Bossu?		142	DOUBL DLR	II.1	137
Sir Paul:	Pray your Ladyship give me leave to be Angry--		144	DOUBL DLR	II.1	199
Maskwell:	Excellent! your Ladyship has a most improving		155	DOUBL DLR	III.1	164
Careless:	O your Ladyship is abounding in all Excellence, . . .		160	DOUBL DLR	III.1	356
Careless:	Your Ladyship is so charming.		160	DOUBL DLR	III.1	359
Careless:	Madam,--if your Ladyship please, we'll discourse of this in		163	DOUBL DLR	III.1	494
Sir Paul:	your Ladyship, that's all.		172	DOUBL DLR	IV.1	184
Brisk:	O Lord I Madam! I beseech your Ladyship--		176	DOUBL DLR	IV.1	321
Brisk:	your Ladyship was in my Thoughts; and I was in a sort of		176	DOUBL DLR	IV.1	326
Sir Paul:	Does it not tire your Ladyship? are not you weary . .		201	DOUBL DLR	V.1	521
Brisk:	Not comparable to your Ladyship; you are the very . .		201	DOUBL DLR	V.1	530
Brisk:	Not comparably to your Ladyship; you are the very . .		201	DOUBL DLR	V.1 V	530
Brisk:	With all my Soul,--your Ladyship has made me . . .		201	DOUBL DLR	V.1	538
Sir Paul:	So he has, gad'sbud, and so has your Ladyship. . .		202	DOUBL DLR	V.1	543
Tattle:	Who I, Madam?--Oh Lord, how can your Ladyship . .		250	FOR LOVE	II.1	540
Tattle:	No, Madam, his Love for your Ladyship--Gad . . .		254	FOR LOVE	III.1	54
Tattle:	Not in my Power, Madam! What does your Ladyship . . .		256	FOR LOVE	III.1	96
Tattle:	Ladyship is to speak first--		257	FOR LOVE	III.1	136
Jeremy:	all: I suppose your Ladyship has thought him so a great		276	FOR LOVE	IV.1	30
Tattle:	much ado to tell your Ladyship, how long I have been in		291	FOR LOVE	IV.1	576
Scandal:	your Ladyship to the free Confession of your Inclinations.		294	FOR LOVE	IV.1	692
Peg:	The red Ratifia does your Ladyship mean, or the Cherry		425	WAY WORLD	III.1	9
Peg:	Lord, Madam, your Ladyship is so impatient--I cannot .		425	WAY WORLD	III.1	17
Marwood:	I'm surpriz'd to find your Ladyship in dishabilie . .		426	WAY WORLD	III.1	43
Foible:	Nay, 'tis your Ladyship has done, and are to do; I . .		427	WAY WORLD	III.1	74
Foible:	had a Fling at your Ladyship too; and then I could not		427	WAY WORLD	III.1	90
Foible:	Uncle; (he does not suspect a Word of your Ladyship;)		428	WAY WORLD	III.1	113
Foible:	Your Ladyship has frown'd a little too rashly, indeed .		429	WAY WORLD	III.1	144
Foible:	A little Scorn becomes your Ladyship.		429	WAY WORLD	III.1	166
Foible:	Confidence in your Ladyship that was deficient; but I .		430	WAY WORLD	III.1	196
Foible:	Ladyship and Mr. Mirabell, might have hinder'd his . .		430	WAY WORLD	III.1	198
Foible:	Gentleman--But your Ladyship is the Pattern of . . .		430	WAY WORLD	III.1	202
Foible:	cannot chuse but be grateful. I find your Ladyship has his		430	WAY WORLD	III.1	204
Foible:	Heart still. Now, Madam, I can safely tell your Ladyship		430	WAY WORLD	III.1	205
Foible:	Madam, I beg your Ladyship to acquaint Mr. Mirabell .		430	WAY WORLD	III.1	214
Foible:	your Ladyship.		432	WAY WORLD	III.1	277
Foible:	Madam, I stay'd here, to tell your Ladyship that Mr. .		445	WAY WORLD	IV.1	43
Foible:	me; and how he assur'd me your Ladyship shou'd . . .		463	WAY WORLD	V.1	30
Foible:	Ladyship, he must have run the risque of the Law, and been		463	WAY WORLD	V.1	43
Foible:	mischeivous Devil told Mr. Fainall of your Ladyship then?		464	WAY WORLD	V.1	80
Foible:	--he has been even with your Ladyship; which I . . .		464	WAY WORLD	V.1	85
Mrs Fain:	I don't understand your Ladyship.		466	WAY WORLD	V.1	147
Marwood:	done. I am sorry my Zeal to serve your Ladyship and .		466	WAY WORLD	V.1	162
Waitwell:	What your Ladyship pleases.--I have brought the . . .		475	WAY WORLD	V.1	510

Ladyship's (9)
see Ladiships, Lady-ship's, Ladyships
Brisk:	sounds great; besides your Ladyship's Coach-man having a		163	DOUBL DLR	III.1	507
Tattle:	of your Ladyship's Wit and Gallantry, could have so .		255	FOR LOVE	III.1	67
Tattle:	Ladyship's good Judgment, I form'd the Ballance of a .		255	FOR LOVE	III.1	71
Foible:	I wou'd put her Ladyship's Picture in my Pocket to shew		423	WAY WORLD	II.1	521
Foible:	Ladyship's Feet and worship the Original.		423	WAY WORLD	II.1	524
Foible:	heard how he us'd me, and all upon your Ladyship's .		427	WAY WORLD	III.1	87
Foible:	of kissing your Ladyship's Hands after Dinner. . . .		428	WAY WORLD	III.1	127
Foible:	of kissing your Ladyship's Hand after Dinner. . . .		428	WAY WORLD	III.1 V	127
Mincing:	O yes Mem, I'll vouch any thing for your Ladyship's .		465	WAY WORLD	V.1	121

Ladyships (5)
Maskwell:	Ladyships Service.		135	DOUBL DLR	I.1	302
Maskwell:	With your Ladyships help, and for your Service, . . .		135	DOUBL DLR	I.1	313
Brisk:	My Lady Froth! Your Ladyships most humble Servant; .		175	DOUBL DLR	IV.1	313
Tattle:	Word of your Ladyships Passion, till this instant. . .		254	FOR LOVE	III.1	56
Jeremy:	part of my Conversation--Madam, your Ladyships . .		296	FOR LOVE	IV.1	777

Laetitia (6)
Bellmour:	Let me see, Laetitia! Oh 'tis a delicious Morsel. Dear		39	OLD BATCH	I.1	73
Vainlove:	only hapned to be once or twice, where, Laetitia was the		39	OLD BATCH	I.1	96
Bellmour:	Laetitia.		64	OLD BATCH	III.1	131
	(Enter Laetitia)		77	OLD BATCH	IV.1	64

Languishing (2)
Lady Touch: Where is that humble Love, the Languishing, that Adoration,   136   DOUBL DLR   I.1   350
Sir Paul: our Family Thy; our House is distinguished by a Languishing   173   DOUEL DLR   IV.1   239
Lanthorn (3)
Mellefont: Malice, like a Dark Lanthorn, cnely shcne upon me,   . . .   129   DOUEL DLR   I.1   90
Mellefont: Malice, like a Dark Lanthorn, only shone upon me,   . . .   129   DOUEL DLR   I.1 V 90
Valentine: not a word. Hymen shall put his Torch into a dark Lanthorn,   290   FCR LCVE   IV.1   549
Lap-Dog (2)
Heartwell: Vainlove, kiss a Lap-Dog with passion, when it would   .   43   OLD BATCH   I.1   255
Bellmour: refuse to kiss a Lap-Dog, if it were preliminary to the Lips   44   OLD EATCH   I.1   261
Lapland-Witch (2)
Ben: Lapland-Witch as soon, and live upon selling of contrary   . 264   FOR LCVE   III.1   426
Ben: Lapland-Witch as soon, and live ufon selling contrary   . . 264   FCR LCVE   III.1 V426
Lapsus Linguae (1)
Tattle: Not a word as I hope to be sav'd; an errant Lapsus Linguae   228   FOR LCVE   I.1   442
Lard (7)
Belinda: Vainlove--Lard I have seen an Ass look so Chagrin,   . . . 55   OLD BATCH   II.2   26
Belinda: My Denyal is premeditated like your Malice--Lard,   . . . 55   OLD EATCH   II.2   50
Belinda: Let me see; hold the Glass--Lard I look wretchedly   . . . 57   OLD BATCH   II.2   91
Belinda: Prithee hold thy Tongue--Lard, he has so   59   OLD EATCH   II.2   163
Belinda: Lard, my Dear! I am glad I have met you;--I   83   OLD BATCH   IV.3   1
Lucy: Nay, Mr. Bellmour: O Lard! I believe you are a Parson   . . 97   OLD BATCH   V.1   37
Belinda: Oh foh! What does the filthy-fellow mean? Lard, ... 109   OLD BATCH   V.2   59
Large (12)
Sharper: Dirt, you have large Acres and can soon repay it--   . . . 50   OLD BATCH   II.1   109
Setter: All, all Sir; the large sanctified Hat, and the little   . . 64   OLD EATCH III.1   123
Lord Touch: Plyant has a large Eye, and wou'd centre every thing in   . 151   DOUBL DLR III.1   6
Scandal: another large Piece too, representing a School; where there   233   FOR LCVE   I.1   653
Sr Sampscn: and sc forth, large enough for the inside of a Cardinal,
    this   245   FOR LCVE   II.1   387
Angelica: Have a care of large Promises; You know you are   . . . 313   FOR LCVE   V.1   613
Almeria: I feel I'm more at large, ... 331   M. BEIDE   I.1   202
Almeria: And more at large, since I have made this Vow.   . . . 331   M. BBIDE   I.1 V203
Zara: He shculd be set at large; thence sprung his Insolence,   . 349   M. EEIDE   II.2 V379
Almeria: So should'st thou be at large frcm all Oppression.   . . . 357   M. BRIDE   III.1   302
Mirabell: rote. The Catalogue was so large, that I was not without   . 399   WAY WCRLD   I.1   166
Waitwell: hand? the Rascal writes a sort of a large hand; your   . 460   WAY WCBLD   IV.1   601
Larger (2)
    If in our larger Family we grieve   213   FOR LCVE   PRO.   21
Zara: But larger Means to gratifie the Will?   347   M. EBIDE   II.2   316
Larum (1)
Lady Touch: a Larum, only to rouse my own still'd Soul for your   . 137   DOUBL DLR   I.1   381
Las (2)
Lady Ply: O las, no indeed, Sir Paul, 'tis upon your account.   . . 172   DOUBL DLR   IV.1   181
Foible: O las Sir, I'm so asham'd--I'm afraid my Lady   . . . 423   WAY WCRLD   II.1   513
Lash (2)
    Not one has dar'd to lash this Crying Age.   214   FOR LCVE   PEO.   40
Manuel: And lash against the Hook--by Heav'n you're all   . . . 373   M. BRIDE   V.1   44
Lashing (1)
Bellmour: seem to rouse, 'tis but well lashing him, and he will sleep   46   OLD BATCH   I.1   353
Laship (5)
Mincing: O Mem, your Iaship staid to peruse a Pecquet of   . . . 419   WAY WCRLD   II.1   357
Mincing: O Mem, your Iaship staid to peruse a Pacquet of   . . . 419   WAY WCRLD   II.1 V357
Mincing: And all to nc purpose. But when your Laship pins it up   . 419   WAY WCRLD   II.1   372
Mincing: Mem, I come to acquaint your Laship that Dinner   . . . 441   WAY WCBLD III.1   614
Mincing: Mem, I am come to acquaint ycur Laship that Dinner   . . 441   WAY WCBLD III.1 V614
Lass (1)
Sir Wilful: He that Whines for a Lass, ... 455   WAY WCBLD   IV.1   400
Last (86)
Bellmour: the finishing of an Alderman; it seems I must put the last   41   OLD BATCH   I.1   157
Bellmour: are never asunder--yet last night, I know not by what   . 46   OLD EATCH   I.1   358
Sir Joseph: have Eutcher'd me last night: No doubt, they would   . . 47   OLD EATCH   II.1   4
Sharper: Methought the service I did you last night Sir, in   . . . 48   OLD EATCH   II.1   47
Sharper: O term it no longer so Sir. In the Scuffle last Night I   . 49   OLD EATCH   II.1   81
Sir Joseph: been with me last night--   50   OLD EATCH   II.1   124
Sir Joseph: best Friends I have in the World and saved my Life last   . 52   OLD EATCH   II.1   169
Capt Bluff: You must know, Sir, I was resident in Flanders the last   . 52   OLD EATCH   II.1   195
Araminta: Bellmour last Night, and call'd him alcud in your sleep.   . 55   OLD BATCH   II.2   38
Araminta: Discourse--Pray oblige us with the last new Song.   . . . 59   OLD EATCH   II.2   187
Bellmour: your hearing. Expecting a Friend, last Night, at his
    Lodgings, ... 82   OLD BATCH   IV.2   49
Setter: her last; When you were to see her next; And, Where you   . 99   OLD BATCH   V.1   115
Belinda: Company, and at last serv'd up cold to the Wife.   . . . 106   OLD BATCH   V.1   377
Capt Bluff: Oh, the Devil, cheated at last!   110   OLD BATCH   V.2   110
Brisk: tell you, you shall tell me--at last.--But it shall be   . 134   DOUBL DLR   I.1   263
Lady Froth: Ah! Gallantry to the last degree--Mr. Erisk, ... 140   DOUBL DLR   II.1   81
Mellefont: of her violence at last,--if you had nct ccme as you did;   . 149   DOUBL DLR   II.1   417
Maskwell: at last I pretended to have been long Secretly in Love with   149   DOUBL DLR   II.1   421
Mellefont: the last Minute of her Reign, unless the Devil assist her in   169   DOUBL DLR   IV.1   53
Lady Ply: The last of any Man in the World, by my purity;   169   DOUBL DLB   IV.1   78
Lord Touch: command this time; for 'tis the last, in which I will assume   189   DOUBL DLR   V.1   65
Saygrace: (looking out). Sweet Sir, I will but pen the last Line   . 194   DOUBL DLB   V.1   272
Lady Touch: Ha! a steady Villain to the last!   197   DOUBL DLE   V.1   384
Maskwell: of a Girl. No--yet tho' I doat on each last Favour   . . 199   DOUBL DLR   V.1   433
Maskwell: upon the Rack; and made discov'ry of her last Plot: I hope   199   DOUBL DLR   V.1   462
    This last and only Remedy have prov'd;   213   FOR LCVE   PRO.   9
Tattle: Valentine, I Supp'd last Night with your Mistress, and   . 228   FOR LCVE   I.1   452
Angelica: last Invisible Eclipse, laying in Provision as 'twere for a   237   FOR LCVE   II.1   80
Scandal: Pray sing the first Song in the last new Play.   258   FOR LCVE   III.1   197
Scandal: to allow some other Men the last Favour; you mistake,   . . 272   FOR LCVE   III.1   696
Scandal: your Chamber-door; and leave you my last Instructions?   . 273   FOR LCVE   III.1   746
Scandal: and imperfect Lover; 'tis the last glimpse of Love to
    wornout   275   FOR LOVE   III.1   816
Scandal: Hush, softly--the Pleasures of last Night, my   284   FOR LOVE   IV.1   316
Mrs Fore: Last Night! and what wou'd your Impudence   284   FCR LCVE   IV.1   318
Mrs Fore: infer from last night? last Night was like the Night before, 284   FCR LOVE   IV.1   319

Last   (continued)

Speaker	Quotation	PAGE	TITLE	ACT.SC	LINE
Scandal:	How did you rest last night?	284	FOR LOVE	IV.1	339
Angelica:	pull'd an old House over his Head at last. . . .	301	FOR LOVE	V.1	159
Miss Prue:	last Night then?	304	FOR LOVE	V.1	249
Sr Sampson:	What, have you found your Senses at last then? .	310	FOR LOVE	V.1	502
Valentine:	vain Attempts, and find at last, that nothing but my Ruine	312	FOR LOVE	V.1	547
Sr Sampson:	Bubbl'd, Jilted, Woman-bobb'd at last--I have not . .	313	FOR LOVE	V.1 V586	
	But thinking of this change which last befel us, . .	315	FOR LOVE	EPI.	5
Almeria:	Anselmo sleeps, and is at Peace; last Night, ...	326	M. BRIDE	I.1	9
Almeria:	The last Distress of Life, and sure Despair. . . .	327	M. BRIDE	I.1	63
Zara:	But what, this last Ingratitude declares, ...	348	M. BRIDE	II.2	334
Osmyn-Alph:	This his last Legacy to me, which I	353	M. BRIDE	III.1	136
Osmyn-Alph:	This his last Legacy to me, which here	353	M. BRIDE	III.1 V136	
Osmyn-Alph:	Yet lighted up, his last most grateful Sacrifice; .	357	M. BRIDE	III.1	322
Zara:	You're grown a Favourite since last we parted; . .	359	M. BRIDE	III.1	412
Gonsalez:	That last restraint; you hardly can suspect . . .	365	M. BRIDE	IV.1	179
Almeria:	Into thy Womb the last and most forlorn	368	M. BRIDE	IV.1	277
Gonsalez:	To aid my Son. I'll follow with the last	379	M. BRIDE	V.2	126
Zara:	Insensible of this last Proof he's gone.	381	M. BRIDE	V.2	194
Almeria:	Is it at last then so? is he then dead?	382	M. BRIDE	V.2	232
Almeria:	What dead at last, quite, quite, for ever dead? . .	382	M. BRIDE	V.2	233
Almeria:	And stain the Colour of my last Adieu.	382	M. BRIDE	V.2	269
Osmyn-Alph:	Expiring, have with their last Breath, confess'd . .	383	M. BRIDE	V.2	306
Fainall:	Confess, Millamant you quarrell'd last Night, . .	395	WAY WORLD	I.1	17
Mirabell:	For which Reason I resolv'd not to stir. At last the .	396	WAY WORLD	I.1	34
Fainall:	of you; last Night was one of their Cabal-nights; they .	396	WAY WORLD	I.1	50
Mirabell:	Conscience; I proceeded to the very last Act of Flattery .	397	WAY WORLD	I.1	69
Betty:	Turn'd of the last Canonical Hour, Sir.	398	WAY WORLD	I.1	106
Servant-M:	was the last Couple to lead up; and no hopes appearing of	398	WAY WORLD	I.1	115
Mirabell:	know you staid at Millamant's last Night, after I went.	407	WAY WORLD	I.1	450
Witwoud:	We staid pretty late there last Night; and heard . .	408	WAY WORLD	I.1	480
Mirabell:	And this is the Sum of what you cou'd collect last . .	408	WAY WORLD	I.1	494
Mrs Fain:	pleasant Relation last Night: I wou'd fain hear it out.	412	WAY WORLD	II.1	99
Mrs Fain:	She talk'd last Night of endeavouring at a . . .	418	WAY WORLD	II.1	303
Millamant:	Mirabell, Did not you take Exceptions last Night? .	420	WAY WORLD	II.1	377
Millamant:	Mirabell, Did you take Exceptions last Night? . .	420	WAY WORLD	II.1 V377	
Witwoud:	before it can catch her last Words.	421	WAY WORLD	II.1	422
Mirabell:	You had the Tyranny to deny me last Night; tho' you .	421	WAY WORLD	II.1	429
Foible:	find an Opportunity; she had so much Company last .	424	WAY WORLD	II.1	531
Sir Wilful:	a Rat me, Knight, I'm so sick of a last Nights debauch	439	WAY WORLD	III.1	545
Millamant:	last moment, tho' I am upon the very Verge of Matrimony,	449	WAY WORLD	IV.1	161
Millamant:	over the threshold. I'll be solicited to the very last,				
	nay and	449	WAY WORLD	IV.1	164
Mirabell:	What, after the last?	449	WAY WORLD	IV.1	166
Waitwell:	the last remaining glimpse of hope in my abandon'd .	461	WAY WORLD	IV.1	644
Mrs Fain:	thing discover'd. This is the last day of our living				
	together, ...	464	WAY WORLD	V.1	82
Fainall:	appear by the last Will and Testament of your deceas'd .	469	WAY WORLD	V.1	281
Millamant:	and insist upon the contract still. Then 'tis the last				
	time he	470	WAY WORLD	V.1	339
Lady Wish:	Are you sure it will be the last time?--if I . . .	470	WAY WORLD	V.1	341
Lady Wish:	generous at last! But it is not possible. Hearkee. I'll				
	break	474	WAY WORLD	V.1	463
Waitwell:	Black box at last, Madam.	475	WAY WORLD	V.1	511
Witwoud:	at the end of the last Act?	475	WAY WORLD	V.1	522

Lasting (4)

Speaker	Quotation	PAGE	TITLE	ACT.SC	LINE
Araminta:	'Tis a lasting Quarrel: I think he has never been at .	107	OLD BATCH	V.1	399
Bellmour:	commit my self to lasting Durance.	112	OLD BATCH	V.2	167
Lord Touch:	Days attend you both; mutual Love, lasting Health, and .	203	DOUBL DLR	V.1	588
Fainall:	O there it is then--She has a lasting Passion for .	396	WAY WORLD	I.1	25

Lastly (3)

Speaker	Quotation	PAGE	TITLE	ACT.SC	LINE
Jeremy:	rest of his Brethren into the same Condition. And Lastly,	219	FOR LOVE	I.1	107
Millamant:	lastly, where ever I am, you shall always knock at the door	450	WAY WORLD	IV.1	224
Mirabell:	Lastly to the Dominion of the Tea-Table, I submit.--	451	WAY WORLD	IV.1	263
Fainall:	must be agreed unto, and that positively. Lastly, I will be	469	WAY WORLD	V.1	277

Late (36)

Speaker	Quotation	PAGE	TITLE	ACT.SC	LINE
Heartwell:	over. For such I guess may have been your late . . .	42	OLD BATCH	I.1	192
Heartwell:	Yet it is oftentimes too late with some of you . . .	43	OLD BATCH	I.1	237
Capt Bluff:	Sir: I'me afraid you scarce know the History of the Late .	52	OLD BATCH	II.1	188
Laetitia:	(aside). My Letter! Base Vainlove! Then 'tis too late .	81	OLD BATCH	IV.2	34
Bellmour:	till 'twas late; my Intimacy with him gave me the . .	82	OLD BATCH	IV.2	50
Singer:	Then too late, desire will find you, ...	143	DOUBL DLR	II.1	188
Maskwell:	He has own'd nothing to me of late, and what I . .	183	DOUBL DLR	IV.1	582
Lady Touch:	thee open to my sight! But then 'twill be too late to know--	198	DOUBL DLR	V.1	397
Cynthia:	our happiness is, that this discovery was not made too late.	200	DOUBL DLR	V.1	475
Lord Touch:	I thank you, yet it may be still too late, if . . .	200	DOUBL DLR	V.1	476
	But that late knowledge, does much hazard cost, . .	204	DOUBL DLR	EPI.	4
	Before your late Encouragement of Wit.	214	FOR LOVE	PRO.	47
Scandal:	Sleep has been unquiet of late.	269	FOR LOVE	III.1	617
Mrs Fore:	Entertainment. I believe it's late.	275	FOR LOVE	III.1	806
Angelica:	Effects, I wou'd have striven; but that's too late. .	294	FOR LOVE	IV.1	713
Valentine:	What sad Effects?--What's too late? my seeming . .	294	FOR LOVE	IV.1	715
	Tho' they are more like Almanacks of late;	323	M. BRIDE	PRO.	5
Manuel:	But late, I find, that War is but her Sport; . . .	337	M. BRIDE	I.1	458
Manuel:	Now late, I find, that War is but her Sport; . . .	337	M. BRIDE	I.1	458
Zara:	To this Invasion; where he late was lost, ...	347	M. BRIDE	II.2 V301	
Heli:	(Who takes the Privilege to visit late, ...	351	M. BRIDE	III.1	49
Osmyn-Alph:	And Chaff, the Sport of adverse Winds; till late . .	351	M. BRIDE	III.1	60
Zara:	Wake thee to Freedom. Now, 'tis late; and yet . .	354	M. BRIDE	III.1	203
Zara:	Or Love, that late at Night still lights his Camp, . .	354	M. BRIDE	III.1	207
Zara:	Vile and ingrate! too late thou shalt repent . . .	360	M. BRIDE	III.1	453
Garcia:	Were it a Truth, I fear 'tis now too late. . . .	379	M. BRIDE	V.2	105
Leonora:	Feeling Remorse too late, for what they've done. . .	381	M. BRIDE	V.2	225
Osmyn-Alph:	And tho' a late, a sure Reward succeeds.	384	M. BRIDE	V.2	322
Mirabell:	She was always civil to me, till of late; I confess I .	397	WAY WORLD	I.1	85
Witwoud:	We staid pretty late there last Night; and heard . .	408	WAY WORLD	I.1	480

Late   (continued)

Marwood:	in our Breasts, and every Heart, or soon or late, receive and	410	WAY WORLD	II.1	26
Fainall:	yet too late--	416	WAY WORLD	II.1	234
Marwood:	No, it is not yet too late--I have that Comfort. . .	416	WAY WORLD	II.1	235
Mrs Fain:	come too late. That Devil Marwood saw you in the Park .	430	WAY WORLD	III.1	185
Sir Wilful:	of late Days.	440	WAY WORLD	III.1	553
Mirabell:	Ay Madam; but that is too late, my reward is intercepted.	473	WAY WORLD	V.1	457

Lately (6)

Sharper:	of some favours lately receiv'd; I would not have you draw	69	OLD BATCH	III.1	303
Lord Touch:	Have you seen my Wife lately, or	195	DOUEL DLR	V.1	306
Valentine:	Character had been lately expos'd upon the Stage.--Nay, I	220	FOR LOVE	I.1	152
Valentine:	Pardon me, Sir. But I reflect that I very lately . .	311	FOR LOVE	V.1	524
Petulant:	Uncle, have you not, lately come to Town, and lodges by .	407	WAY WORLD	I.1	435
Witwoud:	something of an Uncle to Mirabell, who is lately come to .	408	WAY WORLD	I.1	481

Latin (3)

Sr Sampson:	there's Latin for you to prove it, and an Argument . .	240	FOR LOVE	II.1	205
	I'm sure 'tis some such Latin Name they give 'em, . .	315	FOR LOVE	EPI.	13
Marwood:	in more Naughty Law Latin; while the good Judge . . .	467	WAY WORLD	V.1	219

Latmos (1)

Valentine:	Endymion and the Moon shall meet us upon Mount Latmos, .	290	FOR LOVE	IV.1	547

Latter (2)

Mirabell:	and like the faint Offer of a latter Spring, serves but to	418	WAY WORLD	II.1	319
Mirabell:	Your bill of fare is something advanc'd in this latter .	450	WAY WORLD	IV.1	228

Laugh (36)

Belinda:	You may laugh, but--	56	OLD BATCH	II.2	54
Belinda:	and laugh at the Vulgar.--Both the great Vulgar and the .	87	OLD BATCH	IV.3	144
Sharper:	but let thee look simply, and laugh by thy self. . .	100	OLD BATCH	V.1	141
Brisk:	to Laugh at. I think there I was with you, ha? Mellefont.	128	DOUEL DLR	I.1	30
Sir Paul:	Brisk Jokes, your Lordships Laugh does so become you, .	132	DOUEL DLR	I.1	188
Lord Froth:	Laugh at no bodies Jest but my own, or a Lady's; I assure	132	DOUEL DLR	I.1	192
Lord Froth:	more unbecoming a Man of Quality, than to Laugh; Jesu, .	132	DOUEL DLR	I.1	199
Lord Froth:	more unbecoming a Man of Quality, than to Laugh; . .	132	DOUEL DLR	I.1	V199
Lord Froth:	Laugh. Then especially to Laugh at the Jest of an Inferiour	132	DOUEL DLR	I.1	201
Lord Froth:	not Laugh with him. Ridiculous! To be pleased with what .	132	DOUEL DLR	I.1	203
Lord Froth:	not Laugh with one. Ridiculous! To be pleased with what .	132	DOUEL DLR	I.1	203
Lord Froth:	pleases the Croud! Now when I Laugh, I always Laugh .	132	DOUEL DLR	I.1	204
Brisk:	I suppose that's because you Laugh at your own Jests, .	132	DOUEL DLR	I.1	206
Sir Paul:	Laugh incontinently.	133	DOUEL DLR	I.1	220
Lord Froth:	O yes, sometimes,--but I never Laugh.	133	DOUEL DLR	I.1	223
Lord Froth:	Oh, no.--Never Laugh indeed, Sir.	133	DOUEL DLR	I.1	225
Lord Froth:	constrained my Inclinations to Laugh.--He, he, he, to .	133	DOUEL DLR	I.1	231
Brisk:	Immoderate Mirth.--You Laugh on still, and are not able .	134	DOUEL DLR	I.1	257
Lord Froth:	upon the broad grin, all laugh and no Company; ah, then .	162	DOUEL DLR	III.1	459
Cynthia:	without any harmony; for sure, my Lord, to laugh out of .	163	DOUEL DLR	III.1	472
Lord Froth:	then, what do they laugh at? For you know laughing .	163	DOUEL DLR	III.1	477
Cynthia:	laugh at one another; and you must allow they have all .	163	DOUEL DLR	III.1	483
Lady Froth:	Mouth, to Laugh, and then put 'em in again--Foh. . .	165	DOUEL DLR	III.1	571
Lady Froth:	Then she's always ready to Laugh when Sneer	165	DOUEL DLR	III.1	573
Brisk:	Seriously, ha, ha ha. Gad, I have, for all I Laugh. .	176	DOUEL DLR	IV.1	348
Lady Froth:	Ha ha ha! What d'e think I Laugh at? Ha ha ha. . .	176	DOUEL DLR	IV.1	349
Lady Froth:	No the Deuce take me if I don't Laugh at my . . .	176	DOUEL DLR	IV.1	351
Foresight:	Do you laugh?--Well Gentlewoman, I'll--	239	FOR LOVE	II.1	156
Valentine:	Weatherheaded fool, I know how to laugh at him; but .	244	FOR LOVE	II.1	312
Tattle:	laugh at him, and leave him.	304	FOR LOVE	V.1	264
Millamant:	Face. Ha, ha, ha--Well I won't laugh, don't be . .	422	WAY WORLD	II.1	475
Millamant:	O silly! Ha, ha, ha. I cou'd laugh immoderately. . .	433	WAY WORLD	III.1	335
Millamant:	Ha, ha, ha. Pardon me, dear Creature, I must laugh, Ha, .	434	WAY WORLD	III.1	343
Sir Wilful:	Till it laugh in my Face, ...	455	WAY WORLD	IV.1	398

Laugh'd (3)

Brisk:	me perish, do I never say any thing worthy to be Laugh'd .	132	DOUBL DLR	I.1	195
Maskwell:	afflicted, but rather laugh'd at the shallow Artifice, which	154	DOUBL DLR	III.1	135
Witwoud:	Left 'em? I cou'd stay no longer--I have laugh'd . .	453	WAY WORLD	IV.1	325

Laughing (15)

Belinda:	Ha, ha, ha, (you must pardon me I can't help Laughing) .	55	OLD BATCH	II.2	27
Careless:	Laughing when a Man has a mind to't.	133	DOUBL DLR	I.1	247
Brisk:	'tis, in the not Laughing--don't you Apprehend me? . .	133	DOUBL DLR	I.1	249
Brisk:	holding your sides, and Laughing as if you would bepiss .	134	DOUBL DLR	I.1	255
Brisk:	holding your sides, and Laughing as if you would--well-- .	134	DOUBL DLR	I.1	V255
Brisk:	thing, Laughing all the while as if you were ready to die	134	DOUEL DLR	I.1	268
Maskwell:	of Doors; and to--ha, ha, ha, I can't tell you for Laughing,	149	DOUEL DLR	II.1	401
Cynthia:	O most ridiculous, a perpetual consort of laughing . .	163	DOUBL DLR	III.1	471
Lord Froth:	then, what do they laugh at? For you know laughing .	163	DOUBL DLR	III.1	477
Lord Froth:	wont you joyn with us, we were laughing at my Lady . .	165	DOUBL DLR	III.1	559
Brisk:	The Deuce take me, I can't help laughing my self neither,	176	DOUBL DLR	IV.1	344
Brisk:	The Deuce take me, I can't help laughing my self, . .	176	DOUBL DLR	IV.1	V344
Brisk:	can hardly hold Laughing in his Face.	177	DOUBL DLR	IV.1	380
Millamant:	loves me, Ha, ha, ha. How can one forbear laughing to .	434	WAY WORLD	III.1	356
Witwoud:	like ten Christnings--I am tipsy with laughing--If I had .	453	WAY WORLD	IV.1	326

Laughing-stock (1)

Heartwell:	Death, Am I made your Laughing-stock? For	108	OLD BATCH	V.2	33

Laughs (4)

	then laughs out.)	140	DOUBL DLR	IV.1	66
Sir Paul:	I think she laughs a little too much.	162	DOUBL DLR	III.1	464
Mellefont:	Heaven she laughs, grins, points to your Back, she forks .	186	DOUBL DLR	IV.2	131
Witwoud:	Pshaw, pshaw, that she laughs at Petulant is plain. .	407	WAY WORLD	I.1	465

Laughter (3)

Bellmour:	witty Scene, and she perhaps preserve her Laughter, till .	44	OLD BATCH	I.1	269
Bellmour:	Laughter; the ill-natur'd Town will find the Jest just where	63	OLD BATCH	III.1	90
Careless:	said--Oh! (Aside.) I shall never contain Laughter. . .	170	DOUEL DLR	IV.1	123

Launch (1)

Setter:	dispose of! A goodly Pinnace, richly laden, and to launch	102	OLD BATCH	V.1	222

Laurels (3)   see Laurel

Lucy:	I shall follow, while my Spouse is planting Laurels in the	111	OLD BATCH	V.2	145
Capt Bluff:	I plant Laurels for my Head abroad, I may find the Branches	111	OLD BATCH	V.2	148
Manuel:	At this fair Shrine, to lay my Laurels down, ...	337	M. BRIDE	I.1	450

383

Led   (continued)

Garcia:	Osmyn, who led the Moorish Horse; but he	. 335	M. BRIDE	I.1	V366
Manuel:	In Triumph led; your Beauty's Slave.	. 335	M. BRIDE	I.1	392
Manuel:	In pleasing Triumph led; your Beauty's Slave. . . .	. 335	M. BRIDE	I.1	V392
Zara:	Compassion led me to bemoan his State, ...	. 349	M. BRIDE	II.2	376
Manuel:	Let 'em be led away to present Death.	. 362	M. BRIDE	IV.1	66

Leer (2)

Sir Paul:	Execution in its time Girl; why thou hast my Leer				
	Hussey, just	. 173	DOUBL DLR	IV.1	236
Sir Paul:	thy Father's Leer.--Let it be transmitted to the young	. 173	DOUBL DLR	IV.1	237

Left (33)

Araminta:	but you left off before you began.	. 83	OLD BATCH	IV.3	22
Mellefont:	having disarm'd her; in a gust of Passion she left me, and	. 130	DOUBL DLR	I.1	116
Maskwell:	Mellefont upon the brink of Ruin, and left him nought	. 137	DOUBL DLR	I.1	378
Maskwell:	Mellefont upon the brink of Ruin, and left him none	. 137	DOUBL DLR	I.1	V378
Sir Paul:	Left Eye! A 1000 [Pound] for this Left Eye. This has done	. 173	DOUBL DLR	IV.1	235
Sir Paul:	Estate would be left to the wide World, he? I hope you	. 174	DOUBL DLR	IV.1	254
Maskwell:	(aside). That I believ'd; 'twas well I left the private	. 184	DOUBL DLR	IV.2	30
Mellefont:	done, left you to your self.--You're in a kind of Erasmus	. 185	DOUBL DLR	IV.2	60
Jeremy:	won't have a Friend left in the World, if you turn Poet	. 218	FOR LOVE	I.1	86
Foresight:	Yes, yes; while there's one Woman left, the	. 237	FOR LOVE	II.1	64
Angelica:	great unnatural Teat under your Left Arm, and he another;	. 238	FOR LOVE	II.1	120
Mrs Fore:	fresh harmless Creature; and left us, Sister, presently.	. 250	FOR LOVE	II.1	545
Miss Prue:	I can't abide to be left alone, mayn't my Cousin . .	. 262	FOR LOVE	III.1	352
Sr Sampson:	I left 'em together here; What are they gone? . . .	. 265	FOR LOVE	III.1	456
Ben:	gav'n that wipe--He had'nt a word to say, and so I left 'n,	. 286	FOR LOVE	IV.1	385
Mrs Frail:	start of me; and I the poor forsaken Maid am left				
	complaining	. 287	FOR LOVE	IV.1	456
Jeremy:	Two Hours--I'm sure I left him just now, in a Humour .	. 295	FOR LOVE	IV.1	754
Jeremy:	Two Hours--I'm sure I left him just now, in the Humour	. 295	FOR LOVE	IV.1	V754
Zara:	And are like Lumber, to be left and scorn'd. . . .	. 347	M. BRIDE	II.2	321
Heli:	The Care of Providence, sure left it there, ...	. 352	M. BRIDE	III.1	116
Osmyn-Alph:	Left this Example of his Resignation, ...	. 353	M. BRIDE	III.1	135
Almeria:	That still is left us, and on that we'll feed, . . .	. 358	M. BRIDE	III.1	337
Almeria:	--Those Men have left to weep; and look on me! . . .	. 382	M. BRIDE	V.2	245
Almeria:	--Those Men have left to weep; they lock on me! . . .	. 382	M. BRIDE	V.2	V245
Fainall:	after I left you; my fair Cousin has some Humours, that	. 395	WAY WORLD	I.1	18
Mirabell:	Have you not left off your impudent Pretensions . . .	. 406	WAY WORLD	I.1	422
Marwood:	'tis better to be left, than never to have been lov'd. To	. 410	WAY WORLD	II.1	12
Foible:	Well, here it is, all that is left; all that is not kiss'd				
	away--	. 427	WAY WORLD	III.1	V 76
Mrs Fain:	Cousin and her Fortune left to her own disposal. . .	. 430	WAY WORLD	III.1	194
Sir Wilful:	this, when you left off Honour'd Brother; and hoping .	. 439	WAY WORLD	III.1	543
Mrs Fain:	So, Is the fray made up, that you have left	. 453	WAY WORLD	IV.1	323
Witwoud:	Left 'em? I cou'd stay no longer--I have laugh'd . .	. 453	WAY WORLD	IV.1	325

Leg (1)

Heartwell:	Oh! Any thing, every thing, a Leg or two, or an . . .	. 109	OLD BATCH	V.2	75

Leg'd (0)   see Two-leg'd

Legacy (2)

Osmyn-Alph:	This his last Legacy to me, which I	. 353	M. BRIDE	III.1	136
Osmyn-Alph:	This his last Legacy to me, which here	. 353	M. BRIDE	III.1	V136

Legal (1)

Marwood:	Infamy to light, to be a Theme for legal Punsters, and	. 467	WAY WORLD	V.1	214

Legend (6)

Jeremy:	serv'd Valentine Legend Esq; and that he is not now turn'd	. 218	FOR LOVE	I.1	68
Foresight:	Sirrah, go tell Sir Sampson Legend I'll wait on him, if	. 236	FOR LOVE	II.1	40
	(Enter Sir Sampson Legend with a Paper.)	. 240	FOR LOVE	II.1	171
	(Enter Ben. Legend and Servant.)	. 260	FOR LOVE	III.1	267
	(Enter Sir Sampson Legend with a Lawyer.) . .	. 278	FOR LOVE	IV.1	111
Sr Sampson:	VALENTINE LEGEND, in great Letters.	. 281	FOR LOVE	IV.1	224

Leggs (1)

Sr Sampson:	Sir? Here, to stand here, upon those two Leggs, and look	. 244	FOR LOVE	II.1	328

Legitimate (1)

	Thus hardly to be prov'd Legitimate!	. 125	DOUBL DLR	PRO.	20

Legorne (1)

Sr Sampson:	Years; I writ you word, when you were at Legorne. . .	. 261	FOR LOVE	III.1	293

Legs (2)   see Leggs

Valentine:	Legs at liberty, and Tame Cuckolds, with Chains about	. 289	FOR LOVE	IV.1	512
Valentine:	shrivell'd; his Legs dwindl'd, and his back bow'd, Pray,	. 289	FOR LOVE	IV.1	520

Leisure (9)   see Leasure

Sharper:	Marry'd in haste, we may repent at leisure.	. 105	OLD BATCH	V.1	328
Setter:	At leisure marry'd, they repent in haste.	. 105	OLD BATCH	V.1	331
Foresight:	he's at leisure--'tis now Three a Clock, a very good hour	. 236	FOR LOVE	II.1	41
Osmyn-Alph:	I have not Leisure to reflect, or know, ...	. 342	M. BRIDE	II.2	98
Zara:	I have not leisure, now, to take so poor	. 375	M. BRIDE	V.1	123
	I've leisure, now, to mark your sev'ral Faces, . . .	. 385	M. BRIDE	EPI.	5
Mirabell:	Unkind. You had the leisure to entertain a Herd of . .	. 421	WAY WORLD	II.1	433
Foible:	are at leisure?	. 445	WAY WORLD	IV.1	47
Marwood:	we shall have leisure to think of Retirement afterwards.	. 465	WAY WORLD	V.1	137

Lemon (1)

Tattle:	Letters writ in Juice of Lemon, for no Fire can fetch				
	it out.	. 292	FOR LOVE	IV.1	614

Lend (12)

Lady Ply:	lend me your Letter, which you had from your Steward to	. 173	DOUBL DLR	IV.1	215
Angelica:	lend me your Coach, mine's out of Order.	. 236	FOR LOVE	II.1	45
Angelica:	abroad; and if you won't lend me your Coach, I'll take a	. 237	FOR LOVE	II.1	67
Angelica:	Will you lend me your Coach, or I'll go on--	. 237	FOR LOVE	II.1	87
Miss Prue:	lend me your Handkerchief--Smell Cousin; he says, . .	. 249	FOR LOVE	II.1	526
Foresight:	My Dear, pray lend me your Glass, your little . . .	. 269	FOR LOVE	III.1	582
Scandal:	Pray lend it him, Madam--I'll tell you the	. 269	FOR LOVE	III.1	584
Foresight:	Hum, not so well as I thought I was. Lend me your . .	. 269	FOR LOVE	III.1	614
Sr Sampson:	I'll lend you the Bond,--You shall consult your Lawyer,	. 301	FOR LOVE	V.1	138
Leonora:	Who 'ere thou art, and lend thy Hand to raise . . .	. 341	M. BRIDE	II.2	61
Heli:	You must be quick, for Love will lend her Wings. . .	. 344	M. BRIDE	II.2	198
Millamant:	a Flame--I have broke my Fan--Mincing, lend me yours; .	. 432	WAY WORLD	III.1	288

Length (9)
Maskwell:	that belief, told me the Secrets of her heart. At length we	149	DOUBL DLR	II.1	426
Sr Sampson:	I know the length of the Emperour of China's	241	FOR LOVE	II.1	219
Singer-F:	But sagely at length he this Secret disclos'd:	259	FOR LOVE	III.1	206
Valentine:	length deserv'd you shou'd confess it.	294	FOR LOVE	IV.1	710
Osmyn-Alph:	Grant me but Life, good Heaven, but length of	343	M. BRIDE	II.2	135
Osmyn-Alph:	At length, imprison'd in some Cleft of Rock, ...	351	M. BRIDE	III.1	61
Perez:	Fast bound in double chains, and at full length	372	M. BRIDE	V.1	7
Mirabell:	end I so us'd my self to think of 'em, that at length, contrary	399	WAY WORLD	I.1	168
Fainall:	opportunity to do it at full length. Behold the Original.	401	WAY WORLD	I.1	233

Lent (3)
Sharper:	much lent you--And you scorn, 'Ile say that for you-- . .	50	OLD BATCH	II.1	103
	Would you were all as forward, to keep Lent. . . .	113	OLD BATCH	EPI.	7
Maskwell:	He was an ill Man, and I have gain'd; for half my self I lent	188	DOUBL DLR	V.1	7

Leonora (10)
Almeria:	O Leonora, hadst thou known Anselmo, ...	327	M. BRIDE	I.1	32
Almeria:	I thank thee, Leonora, ...	328	M. BRIDE	I.1 V	94
	(Enter Almeria and Leonora.) . .	339	M. BRIDE	II.1	51
	(Re-Enter, Almeria and Leonora.) . .	340	M. BRIDE	II.2	5
Almeria:	Leonora, in thy Bosom, from the Light, ...	341	M. BRIDE	II.2	44
	(Exit Almeria, Leonora, and Heli.) . .	345	M. BRIDE	II.2	213
	(Enter Almeria and Leonora.) . . .	367	M. BRIDE	IV.1	242
	(Exit Leonora.) . . .	367	M. BRIDE	IV.1	246
	(Enter Leonora and Attendants.)	369	M. BRIDE	IV.1	336
	(Enter Almeria and Leonora.)	381	M. BRIDE	V.2	214

Less (28)
Heartwell:	Awake; Sigh much, Drink little, Eat less, court Solitude, .	73	OLD BATCH	III.2	81
Mellefont:	where it was directed. Still it gave me less perplexity to	129	DOUBL DLR	I.1	91
Lady Froth:	Just as the Sun does, more or less. . . .	164	DOUBL DLR	III.1	532
Brisk:	. . . More or Less. . . .	164	DOUBL DLR	III.1 V533
Lady Ply:	Drink the less you Sot, and do't before you	180	DOUBL DLR	IV.1 V487
Ben:	Let her cry: The more she cries, the less she'll--she . .	265	FOR LOVE	III.1	441
Mrs Fore:	Mr. Tattle might have us'd less Ceremony.	293	FOR LOVE	IV.1	681
Tattle:	serious Kindness--I never lik'd any body less in my Life.	309	FOR LOVE	V.1	465
Mrs Frail:	like him less.	310	FOR LOVE	V.1	474
	And a less Number New, would well content ye. . . .	323	M. BRIDE	PRO.	2
Osmyn-Alph:	Of Personal Charms, or with less Vanity	355	M. BRIDE	III.1	226
Osmyn-Alph:	O could'st thou be less killing, soft or kind, ...	356	M. BRIDE	III.1	282
Osmyn-Alph:	O would'st thou be less killing, soft or kind, ...	356	M. BRIDE	III.1 V282
Gonsalez:	She's greatly griev'd; nor am I less surpriz'd. . . .	371	M. BRIDE	IV.1	396
Garcia:	And bathe it to the Hilt, in far less damnable . . .	378	M. BRIDE	V.2	79
Osmyn-Alph:	O may'st thou never dream of less Delight; . . .	383	M. BRIDE	V.2	289
Osmyn-Alph:	Nor ever wake to less substantial Joys.	383	M. BRIDE	V.2	290
Mirabell:	better pleas'd if she had been less discreet. . . .	396	WAY WORLD	I.1	48
Mirabell:	Hour less and less disturbance; 'till in a few Days it became	399	WAY WORLD	I.1	170
Lady Wish:	O he's in less Danger of being spoil'd by his . . .	431	WAY WORLD	III.1	262
Millamant:	dressing; their Folly is less provoking than your Mallice,	433	WAY WORLD	III.1	326
Millamant:	dressing; their Folly is less provoking than your Mallice, ...	433	WAY WORLD	III.1 V326
Sir Wilful:	Oons this Fellow knows less than a Starling; I	437	WAY WORLD	III.1	473
Marwood:	unknown hand--for the less I appear to know of the truth .	443	WAY WORLD	III.1	702
Millamant:	Like Phoebus sung the no less am'rous Boy.	448	WAY WORLD	IV.1	153
Witwoud:	Thou hast utter'd Volumes, Folio's, in less than . . .	453	WAY WORLD	IV.1	342
Petulant:	If I have a humour to Quarrel, I can make less	454	WAY WORLD	V.1	366

Lessen (2)
Angelica:	Concern for him may lessen--If I forget him, 'tis no . .	277	FOR LOVE	IV.1	81
Zara:	And do your Arms so lessen, what they conquer, ...	348	M. BRIDE	II.2	362

Lessens (2)
Fainall:	losing Gamester lessens the Pleasure of the Winner: I'd no	395	WAY WORLD	I.1	7
Mirabell:	grace, and the receiver lessens his Pleasure?	449	WAY WORLD	IV.1	173

Lesson (3)
Valentine:	thee this Lesson of Fustian to get by Rote?	255	FOR LOVE	III.1	74
Valentine:	Lesson.	296	FOR LOVE	IV.1	797
Osmyn-Alph:	This Lesson, in some Hour of Inspiration, ...	353	M. BRIDE	III.1	128

Lest (11)
Heartwell:	self liberty to think, lest I should cool--I will about a	74	OLD BATCH	III.2	139
Lady Touch:	the Company break up; lest my Lord should cool, and .	154	DOUBL DLR	III.1	143
Osmyn-Alph:	Let me not stir, nor breath, lest I disolve	341	M. BRIDE	II.2	50
Osmyn-Alph:	But gently take thy self away, lest she	345	M. BRIDE	II.2	202
Osmyn-Alph:	I'll muse on that, lest I exceed in thinking. . . .	345	M. BRIDE	II.2 V230
Manuel:	Lest I forget us both, and spurn thee from me.	369	M. BRIDE	IV.1	317
Alonzo:	Lest you forbid; what then you may approve.	378	M. BRIDE	V.2	98
Almeria:	Lest the rank Juice should blister on my Mouth, . . .	382	M. BRIDE	V.2	268
	He'll not instruct, lest it should give Offence. . . .	393	WAY WORLD	PRO.	34
Mrs Fain:	I'll go with you up the back Stairs, lest I shou'd . .	430	WAY WORLD	III.1	221
Mirabell:	Lest mutual falsehood stain the Bridal-Bed:	478	WAY WORLD	V.1	621

Let (283)
Bellmour:	and Pleasure, my Occupation; and let Father Time shake .	37	OLD BATCH	I.1	24
Bellmour:	his Glass. Let low and earthy Souls grovel till they have .	37	OLD BATCH	I.1	25
Bellmour:	his Glass. Let low and earthly Souls grovel 'till they have .	37	OLD BATCH	I.1 V 25
Bellmour:	Let me see--How now! Dear perfidious Vainlove.	38	OLD BATCH	I.1	35
Bellmour:	Let me see, Laetitia! Oh 'tis a delicious Morsel. Dear .	39	OLD BATCH	I.1	73
Heartwell:	And it should be mine to let 'em go again.	43	OLD BATCH	I.1	226
Bellmour:	Oh here he comes, stand close let 'em pass.	46	OLD BATCH	I.1 V339
Sir Joseph:	Stay, stay Sir, let me recollect--(aside) he's a . . .	48	OLD BATCH	II.1	43
Sharper:	let me embrace you.	49	OLD BATCH	II.1	74
Sir Joseph:	Sir--a damn'd hot Fellow--only as I was saying, I let him .	51	OLD BATCH	II.1	130
Sir Joseph:	Let me but tell Mr. Sharper a little, how you eat . .	53	OLD BATCH	II.1	218
Araminta:	avert the cure: Let me have Oil to feed that Flame and .	54	OLD BATCH	II.2	9
Araminta:	never let it be extinct, till I my self am Ashes. . . .	54	OLD BATCH	II.2	10
Belinda:	Let me see; hold the Glass--Lard I look wretchedly . .	57	OLD BATCH	II.2	91
Araminta:	then, Cousin, and let me have all the Company to my . .	57	OLD BATCH	II.2	102
Belinda:	let us alone.	58	OLD BATCH	II.2	143

Let   (continued)
Belinda: sake let it be with variety; don't come always, like the .   59   OLD BATCH   II.2   169
Bellmour: Talk to your self--You had better let me speak; for if my   59   OLD BATCH   II.2   177
Bellmour: let me tell you, my standing Argument is depress'd in   .   .   59   OLD BATCH   II.2   183
Bellmour: let me tell you, my most prevailing Argument is express'd in   59   OLD BATCH   II.2 V183
Musician: Never let him all discover, ...   59   OLD BATCH   II.2   194
Musician: Never let him much obtain.   59   OLD BATCH   II.2   195
Lucy: Trouble not your Head. Let me alone--I will   62   OLD BATCH   III.1   44
Heartwell: Hum--Let me think--Is not this Silvia's House, the   .   .   .   62   OLD BATCH   III.1   64
Lucy: Remember to Days behaviour--Let me see you with a   .   .   .   67   OLD BATCH   III.1   232
Sir Joseph: by, I would as soon have let him a' had a hundred of my   .   68   OLD BATCH   III.1   277
Sir Joseph: let me kiss thee, so so, put up, put up.   70   OLD BATCH   III.1   342
Singer: O let me feed as well as taste, ...   71   OLD BATCH   III.2   7
Singer: O let me--still the Shepherd said;   71   OLD BATCH   III.2 V 14
Heartwell: Damn her let her go, and a good riddance--Yet so   .   .   .   74   OLD BATCH   III.2   114
Heartwell: believe it: Nay, thou shalt think so thy self--Only let me   74   OLD BATCH   III.2   122
Fondlewife: How how, say Varlet! I say let him not come   76   OLD BATCH   IV.1   25
Barnaby: House, and yet be forced to let Lodgings, to help pay the   76   OLD BATCH   IV.1   43
Bellmour: Oh, No: Let me lie down upon the Bed;--the   83   OLD BATCH   IV.2   92
Sir Joseph: I wish I durst stay to let her know my   86   OLD BATCH   IV.3   123
Bellmour: let us--   89   OLD BATCH   IV.4   7
Laetitia: Then, I'll let you in.   89   OLD BATCH   IV.4   20
Sir Joseph: Pray, first let me have 50 Pounds, good Alderman,   .   .   89   OLD BATCH   IV.4   27
Fondlewife: Ay, ay, lie still, lie still; don't let me disturb you.   .   91   OLD BATCH   IV.4   88
Fondlewife: Let her clap a warm thing to his Stomach, or chafe it with   91   OLD BATCH   IV.4   97
Fondlewife: Let her clap some warm thing to his Stomach, or chafe it
                with   91   OLD BATCH   IV.4 V 97
Fondlewife: Devil's Pater-noster. Hold, let me see: The Innocent
                Adultery.   92   OLD BATCH   IV.4   107
Fondlewife: than Speculation when I was not to be let in.--Where   .   92   OLD BATCH   IV.4   117
Laetitia: Let the wicked Man answer for himself; does he   .   .   .   93   OLD BATCH   IV.4   167
Bellmour: Intentions for thee too: Let this mollifie.--(Gives her   .   98   OLD BATCH   V.1   59
Sharper: but let thee look simply, and laugh by thy self.   .   .   100   OLD BATCH   V.1   141
Sir Joseph: be pick'd out of Aesop's Fables, let me tell you that; and   101   OLD BATCH   V.1   176
Sir Joseph: let these worthy Gentlemen intercede for me.   .   .   .   103   OLD BATCH   V.1   245
Heartwell: Death! Shall I own my Shame, or wittingly let him go   .   104   OLD BATCH   V.1   309
Heartwell: Damn your pity. But let me be calm a little.--   .   .   .   109   OLD BATCH   V.2   50
Belinda: let me begone.   109   OLD BATCH   V.2   60
Sharper: Then, let me beg these Ladies to wear their Masks, a   .   110   OLD BATCH   V.2   90
Heartwell: --Oh Sharper! Let me embrace thee.--But art   .   .   .   111   OLD BATCH   V.2   126
Setter: And my Relation; pray let her be respected accordingly.   111   OLD BATCH   V.2   140
                Let Nature work, and do not Damn too soon, ...   125   DOUBL DLR   PRO.   16
                Let it at least rise thrice, before it Drown.   .   .   .   125   DOUBL DLR   PRO.   18
                Let us consider, had it been our Fate, ...   125   DOUBL DLR   PRO.   19
Brisk: Oh, my dear Mellefont, let me perish, if thou art not the   128   DOUBL DLR   I.1   33
Brisk: How? how, my Lord? What, affront my Wit! Let   .   .   .   132   DOUBL DLR   I.1   194
Brisk: Let me perish, my Lord, but there is something very   .   .   133   DOUBL DLR   I.1   237
Careless: Well, but prithee don't let it be a great while, because   134   DOUBL DLR   I.1   265
Mellefont: Let him alone, Brisk, he is obstinately bent not to   .   .   134   DOUBL DLR   I.1   280
Brisk: Let me see, let me see, my Lord, I broke my Glass that   135   DOUBL DLR   I.1   291
Lady Touch: knows I hate him too: Let him but once be mine, and next   137   DOUBL DLR   I.1   400
Brisk: Never any thing; but your Ladyship, let me perish.   .   .   140   DOUBL DLR   II.1   84
Lady Froth: O prettily turn'd again; let me die, but you have   .   .   140   DOUBL DLR   II.1   85
Brisk: I'm your Humble Servant, let me perish.--I   142   DOUBL DLR   II.1   136
Mellefont: Pray let us have the Favour of you, to practice the Song,   143   DOUBL DLR   II.1   175
Lady Ply: Sir Paul have patience, let me alone to rattle him   .   .   143   DOUBL DLR   II.1   197
Maskwell: you, I meet the only Obstacle to my Fortune. Cynthia, let   150   DOUBL DLR   II.1   440
Maskwell: any thing--Why, let me see, I have the same Face, the   .   150   DOUBL DLR   II.1   460
Lady Touch: to be unknown which cannot be prevented; therefore let   152   DOUBL DLR   III.1   55
Lord Touch: of my doors this moment, and let him rot and perish,   .   153   DOUBL DLR   III.1   101
Lady Touch: self. Pray, my Lord, don't let the Company see you in this   153   DOUBL DLR   III.1   112
Lady Touch: let me beg you do now: I'll come immediately, and tell   153   DOUBL DLR   III.1   119
Maskwell: Thirst. Ha! yonder comes Mellefont thoughtful. Let me   .   155   DOUBL DLR   III.1   186
Mellefont: Let me adore thee, my better Genius! By Heav'n I   .   .   157   DOUBL DLR   III.1   257
Lord Froth: sake let us sacrifice 'em to mirth a little.   .   .   .   163   DOUBL DLR   III.1   487
Brisk: Incomparable, let me perish--but then being an Heroick   163   DOUBL DLR   III.1   505
Lady Froth: lines again (pulls out a Paper.) Let me see here, you know   164   DOUBL DLR   III.1   512
Lady Froth: Well you shall hear--let me see.   164   DOUBL DLR   III.1   527
Brisk: honour, let me perish.   165   DOUBL DLR   III.1   557
Brisk: if she were plaistred with Lime and Hair, let me perish.   166   DOUBL DLR   III.1   587
Cynthia: of his Wit: Therefore let me see you undermine my Lady   168   DOUBL DLR   IV.1   47
Careless: bewitching Fair? O let me grow to the ground here, and   170   DOUBL DLR   IV.1   91
Careless: feast upon that hand; O let me press it to my heart, my   170   DOUBL DLR   IV.1   92
Careless: And must you leave me! Rather let me Languish   .   .   .   170   DOUBL DLR   IV.1   99
Sir Paul: thy Father's Leer.--Let it be transmitted to the young   173   DOUBL DLR   IV.1   237
Brisk: Sir Paul, Gads-bud you're an uncivil Person, let me tell   174   DOUBL DLR   IV.1   267
Brisk: Not I, let me perish--But did I! Strange! I confess   .   176   DOUBL DLR   IV.1   325
Brisk: Ladiship--Let me perish, I don't know whether to   .   .   176   DOUBL DLR   IV.1   337
Brisk: That's well enough; let me perish, ha ha ha. O Miraculous,   177   DOUBL DLR   IV.1   356
Sir Paul: discover'd--But let me see to make an end on't.--   .   .   178   DOUBL DLR   IV.1   407
Sir Paul: Person! Well, let me see--Till then I Languish a   .   .   178   DOUBL DLR   IV.1   414
Sir Paul: friendship! What art thou but a Name! Henceforward, let   178   DOUBL DLR   IV.1   419
Lady Ply: found out that contrivance to let you see this Letter; which   179   DOUBL DLR   IV.1   455
Lady Touch: Hold, let me Lock the Door first.   184   DOUBL DLR   IV.2   28
Lady Touch: little thou swelling Heart; let me have some intermission   185   DOUBL DLR   IV.2   65
Lady Touch: let me not hope forgiveness, 'twill ever be in your power   185   DOUBL DLR   IV.2   83
Lady Touch: O cruel Man, will you not let me go--I'le   186   DOUBL DLR   IV.2   102
Maskwell: ever must; no, let it prey upon my Heart; for I would   .   188   DOUBL DLR   V.1   36
Maskwell: Friendship to my Lord, and base Self-interest. Let me   .   188   DOUBL DLR   V.1   40
Lord Touch: Start not--let guilty and dishonest Souls   189   DOUBL DLR   V.1   47
Lord Touch: Blank as well--I will have no reply--Let me   .   .   .   189   DOUBL DLR   V.1   64
Maskwell: This is prosperous indeed--Why let him find   .   .   .   190   DOUBL DLR   V.1   85
Maskwell: to delay--let me think--shou'd my Lord proceed   .   .   190   DOUBL DLR   V.1   89
Maskwell: Let us go and consult her, my life for yours, I   .   .   .   190   DOUBL DLR   V.1   118
Maskwell: you please, defer the finishing of your Wit, and let us talk   194   DOUBL DLR   V.1   278
Maskwell: Good, let them be carried to him,--have you   195   DOUBL DLR   V.1   287

		PAGE	TITLE	ACT.SC	LINE
Maskwell:	Chamber. When Cynthia comes, let there be no Light, and	195	DOUBL DLR	V.1	293
Cynthia:	My Lord, let me entreat you to stand behind this Skreen,	197	DOUBL DLR	V.1	374
Maskwell:	So, 'tis well--let your wild fury have a vent;	198	DOUBL DLR	V.1	408
Lord Touch:	and let us hear the rest.	198	DOUBL DLR	V.1	422
Cynthia:	Nay, good my Lord, forbear Resentment, let us	198	DOUBL DLR	V.1	428
Lord Touch:	I'll add to my Plot too,--let us haste to find out, and	200	DOUBL DLR	V.1	486
Brisk:	O Jesu! Madam, you have Eclips'd me quite, let me	201	DOUBL DLR	V.1	534
Brisk:	Madam, you have Eclips'd me quite, let me	201	DOUBL DLR	V.1 V534
Lady Touch:	Stand off, let me go,	202	DOUBL DLR	V.1	560
Brisk:	This is all very surprizing, let me perish.	203	DOUBL DLR	V.1	578
Lord Touch:	let me hasten to do Justice, in rewarding Virtue and wrong'd	203	DOUBL DLR	V.1	582
Lord Touch:	And be each others comfort;--let me	203	DOUBL DLR	V.1	586
Lord Touch:	Let secret Villany from hence be warn'd;	203	DOUBL DLR	V.1	591
	But tho' he cannot Write, let him be freed	204	DOUBL DLR	EPI.	35
Valentine:	I agree to 'em, take Mr. Trapland with you, and let him	224	FOR LOVE	I.1	319
Scandal:	Hang him, let him alone, he has a mind we should	228	FOR LOVE	I.1	450
Mrs Frail:	Then let him Marry and reform.	231	FOR LOVE	I.1	559
Mrs Frail:	Unlucky Day, and wou'd not let me come abroad: But I	231	FOR LOVE	I.1	581
Mrs Frail:	Ay, let me see those, Mr. Tattle.	232	FOR LOVE	I.1	608
Angelica:	morrow morning--But let me be gone first, and then	239	FOR LOVE	II.1	135
Angelica:	let no Mankind come near the House, but Converse with	239	FOR LOVE	II.1	136
Foresight:	Odso, let me see; Let me see the Paper--Ay,	240	FOR LOVE	II.1	186
Mrs Fore:	as you say, since we are both Wounded, let us do that is	248	FOR LOVE	II.1	477
Mrs Fore:	as you say, since we are both Wounded, let us do what is	248	FOR LOVE	II.1 V477
Mrs Fore:	liking of you. Here they come together; and let us contrive	249	FOR LOVE	II.1	503
Mrs Fore:	liking you. Here they come together; and let us contrive	249	FOR LOVE	II.1 V503
Miss Prue:	Lavender mun--I'm resolv'd I won't let Nurse put	249	FOR LOVE	II.1	529
Tattle:	strangely--pretty Miss, don't let 'em perswade you	249	FOR LOVE	II.1	536
Mrs Fore:	won't let him come near her, after Mr. Tattle.	250	FOR LOVE	II.1	563
Mrs Fore:	Nay, why did we let him--my Husband	250	FOR LOVE	II.1	568
Mrs Frail:	Come, Faith let us be gone--If my Brother	250	FOR LOVE	II.1	570
Tattle:	I must make Love to you, pretty Miss; will you let	251	FOR LOVE	II.1	588
Tattle:	You must let me speak Miss, you must not speak first;	251	FOR LOVE	II.1	598
Ben:	that be all--Pray don't let me be your hindrance; e'en	261	FOR LOVE	III.1	301
Miss Prue:	always tell a lie to a man; and I don't care, let my Father	264	FOR LOVE	III.1	397
Ben:	Tar-barrel? Let your Sweet-heart there call me so, if he'll	264	FOR LOVE	III.1	434
Ben:	Let her cry: The more she cries, the less she'll--she	265	FOR LOVE	III.1	441
Scandal:	Come, come, Mr. Foresight, let not the Prospect of	268	FOR LOVE	III.1	554
Foresight:	I thank you Mr. Scandal, I will--Nurse, let me have	270	FOR LOVE	III.1	640
Foresight:	Do I? And d'ye hear--bring me, let me see--	270	FOR LOVE	III.1	645
Ben:	And then he let fly at her,	274	FOR LOVE	III.1	787
Sr Sampson:	Oons, I won't believe it; let me see him, Sir	279	FOR LOVE	IV.1	145
Valentine:	Westminster-Hall the first Day of every Term--Let me see	280	FOR LOVE	IV.1	173
Scandal:	You'd better let him go, Sir; and send for him if there	280	FOR LOVE	IV.1	189
Sr Sampson:	Val: How do'st thou do? let me feel thy Pulse--Oh,	281	FOR LOVE	IV.1	201
Sr Sampson:	Let me feel thy Hand again, Val: it does not	281	FOR LOVE	IV.1	206
Valentine:	Pray let me see it, Sir. You hold it so far off, that	281	FOR LOVE	IV.1	217
Sr Sampson:	'tis thy own Hand, Val. Why, let me see, I can read it as	281	FOR LOVE	IV.1	220
Sr Sampson:	thine? I believe I can read it farther off yet--let me see.	281	FOR LOVE	IV.1	226
Valentine:	Will you please to let me hold it, Sir?	281	FOR LOVE	IV.1	228
Sr Sampson:	Let thee hold it, say'st thou--Aye, with all	281	FOR LOVE	IV.1	229
Valentine:	scratch'd--My Nails are not long enough--Let	282	FOR LOVE	IV.1	239
Buckram:	O Lord, let me be gone; I'll not venture my self	282	FOR LOVE	IV.1	243
Foresight:	vulgar think mad. Let us go in to him.	285	FOR LOVE	IV.1	350
Foresight:	vulgar think mad. Let us go to him.	285	FOR LOVE	IV.1 V350
Ben:	man.--I had another Voyage to make, let him take	285	FOR LOVE	IV.1	376
Ben:	--I'm glad you shew your self, Mistress:--Let	287	FOR LOVE	IV.1	436
Valentine:	and Atlas' Shoulders. Let Taliacotius trim the Calves of	289	FOR LOVE	IV.1	524
Singer-V:	Then never let us chain what should be free,	293	FOR LOVE	IV.1	662
Valentine:	Nay faith, now let us understand one another,	294	FOR LOVE	IV.1	706
Valentine:	end, and let us think of leaving acting, and be our selves;	294	FOR LOVE	IV.1	708
Angelica:	Never let us know one another better; for the Pleasure of	296	FOR LOVE	IV.1	789
Sr Sampson:	a Lady any way--Come, come, let me tell you, you	298	FOR LOVE	V.1	24
Sr Sampson:	only be seemingly carried on?--Odd, let it be a real	300	FOR LOVE	V.1	115
Sr Sampson:	let us find Children, and I'll find an Estate.	300	FOR LOVE	V.1	129
Angelica:	Let me consult my Lawyer concerning this Obligation;	301	FOR LOVE	V.1	134
Sr Sampson:	your Hand, Odd let me kiss it; 'tis as warm and as soft	301	FOR LOVE	V.1	145
Tattle:	No, no, let me alone for a Counterfeit;--I'll be	303	FOR LOVE	V.1	219
Miss Prue:	O Father, why will you let him go? Won't you	305	FOR LOVE	V.1	300
Ben:	when she's going, let her go. For no Matrimony is tough	310	FOR LOVE	V.1	492
Garcia:	Thus let me kneel to take--O not to take,	334	M. BRIDE	I.1	335
Gonsalez:	O let me prostrate, pay my worthless Thanks	334	M. BRIDE	I.1	338
Heli:	Let Heav'n with Thunder to the Centre strike me,	337	M. BRIDE	II.1	4
Heli:	My Lord, let me entreat you to forbear:	338	M. BRIDE	II.1	25
Garcia:	The Friends perhaps are met; let us avoid 'em.	339	M. BRIDE	II.1	49
Almeria:	Give me thy Hand, and let me hear thy Voice;	339	M. BRIDE	II.1 V 67
Almeria:	And let me hear thy Voice;	339	M. BRIDE	II.1	68
Almeria:	Nay, quickly speak to me, and let me hear	339	M. BRIDE	II.1 V 68
Leonora:	Let us return; the Horrour of this Place	339	M. BRIDE	II.1	70
Osmyn-Alph:	Let me not stir, nor breath, lest I disolve	341	M. BRIDE	II.2	50
Osmyn-Alph:	Let me behold and touch her, and be sure	341	M. BRIDE	II.2	67
Osmyn-Alph:	'Tis she; shew me her Face, and let me feel	341	M. BRIDE	II.2	68
Almeria:	Let me look on thee, yet a little more.	342	M. BRIDE	II.2	100
Almeria:	O my strain'd Heart--let me behold thee,	342	M. BRIDE	II.2	112
Almeria:	O my strain'd Heart--let me again behold thee,	342	M. BRIDE	II.2 V112
Manuel:	But let me lead you from this Place of Sorrow,	349	M. BRIDE	II.2	382
Osmyn-Alph:	Let ev'ry Hair, which Sorrow by the Roots,	350	M. BRIDE	III.1	16
Almeria:	No, hold me not--O, let us not support,	358	M. BRIDE	III.1	370
Osmyn-Alph:	Speak of Compassion, let her hear you speak	359	M. BRIDE	III.1	388
Osmyn-Alph:	Let me	359	M. BRIDE	III.1	393
Manuel:	Let 'em be led away to present Death.	362	M. BRIDE	IV.1	66
Manuel:	Let all else void the Room. Garcia, give Order	364	M. BRIDE	IV.1	131
Manuel:	Let all except Gonsalez leave the Room.	364	M. BRIDE	IV.1 V131
Manuel:	Let your Attendant be dismiss'd; I have	367	M. BRIDE	IV.1	245
Manuel:	Be thou advis'd, and let me go while yet	369	M. BRIDE	IV.1	328

Let   (continued)

Manuel:	Away, off, let me go,--Call her Attendants.	369	M. BRIDE	IV.1	335
Almeria:	I'll not let go, 'till you have spar'd my Husband.	369	M. BRIDE	IV.1	338
Almeria:	Let me go, let me fall, sink deep--I'll dig,	370	M. BRIDE	IV.1	347
Gonsalez:	Hold, let me think--if I shou'd tell the King--	371	M. BRIDE	IV.1	403
Manuel:	And let the Cell where she'll expect to see him,	374	M. BRIDE	V.1	84
Zara:	Let 'em set down the Bowls, and warn Alphonso	380	M. BRIDE	V.2	149
Almeria:	O let me seek him in this horrid Cell;	381	M. BRIDE	V.2	215
Almeria:	The Source of Woe, and let the Torrent loose.	382	M. BRIDE	V.2	244
Osmyn-Alph:	Away, stand off, where is she? let me fly,	383	M. BRIDE	V.2	275
Osmyn-Alph:	O let me talk to thy reviving Sense,	383	M. BRIDE	V.2	280
Osmyn-Alph:	Let 'em remove the Body from her Sight.	383	M. BRIDE	V.2	311
Osmyn-Alph:	Let us that thro' our Innocence survive,	384	M. BRIDE	V.2	318
Osmyn-Alph:	Let us who thro' our Innocence survive,	384	M. BRIDE	V.2	V318
Mirabell:	five, declares for a Friend and Ratifia; and let Posterity shift	397	WAY WORLD	I.1	62
Witwoud:	upon him, you are, faith. Let me excuse him;--I can	403	WAY WORLD	I.1	309
Petulant:	I won't come.--Let 'em snivel and cry their Hearts	405	WAY WORLD	I.1	387
Petulant:	All's one, let it pass--I have a Humour to be	405	WAY WORLD	I.1	390
Petulant:	Enough, let 'em trundle. Anger helps Complexion,	406	WAY WORLD	I.1	416
Petulant:	Ay, ay, let that pass--There are other Throats	406	WAY WORLD	I.1	425
Petulant:	I, nothing I. If Throats are to be cut, let Swords	407	WAY WORLD	I.1	446
Witwoud:	her, I shou'd--Hearkee--To tell you a Secret, but let it go	407	WAY WORLD	I.1	467
Mirabell:	Are you? Pray then walk by your selves,--Let	409	WAY WORLD	I.1	523
Petulant:	What, what? Then let 'em either shew their Innocence	409	WAY WORLD	I.1	529
Marwood:	Pray let us; I have a Reason.	413	WAY WORLD	II.1	120
Fainall:	To let you know I see through all your little Arts--	413	WAY WORLD	II.1	136
Marwood:	Let me go.	416	WAY WORLD	II.1	223
Marwood:	I care not--Let me go--Break my	416	WAY WORLD	II.1	225
Millamant:	O Fiction; Fainall, let us leave these Men.	421	WAY WORLD	II.1	423
Lady Wish:	O Marwood, let her come in. Come in good	426	WAY WORLD	III.1	40
Foible:	your Lady propose? Let me see (says he) what she must	427	WAY WORLD	III.1	99
Lady Wish:	Let me see the Glass--Cracks, say'st thou?	429	WAY WORLD	III.1	147
Lady Wish:	Sir Rowland handsome? Let my Toilet be remov'd--I'll	429	WAY WORLD	III.1	171
Lady Wish:	O I'm glad he's a brisk Man. Let my	429	WAY WORLD	III.1	180
Millamant:	despair to prevail, and so let him follow his own way.	434	WAY WORLD	III.1	342
Petulant:	say 'tis Blue--Let that pass--All's one for that. If	435	WAY WORLD	III.1	405
Sir Wilful:	Why then let him hold his Tongue in the mean	441	WAY WORLD	III.1	611
Marwood:	And let me alone to keep her warm, if she should	443	WAY WORLD	III.1	665
Fainall:	Why faith I'm thinking of it.--Let me see--	443	WAY WORLD	III.1	676
Marwood:	--But let the Mine be sprung first, and then I care not if	444	WAY WORLD	III.1	706
Fainall:	Jealous no,--by this Kiss--let Husbands be Jealous;	444	WAY WORLD	III.1	714
Fainall:	But let the Lover still believe. Or if he doubt, let it be only	444	WAY WORLD	III.1	715
Fainall:	when he proves his Mistress true; but let Husbands doubts	444	WAY WORLD	III.1	717
Fainall:	Convert to endless Jealousie; or if they have belief, let it	444	WAY WORLD	III.1	718
Millamant:	him--Shall I? Ay, let the Wretch come.	446	WAY WORLD	IV.1	62
Millamant:	never bear that,--Good Mirabell don't let us be familiar	450	WAY WORLD	IV.1	200
Millamant:	for ever After. Let us never Visit together, nor go to a	450	WAY WORLD	IV.1	206
Millamant:	ever After. Let us never Visit together, nor go to a	450	WAY WORLD	IV.1	V206
Millamant:	Play together, But let us be very strange and well bred:	450	WAY WORLD	IV.1	207
Millamant:	let us be as strange as if we had been married a great while;	450	WAY WORLD	IV.1	208
Witwoud:	staid any longer I shou'd have burst,--I must have been let	453	WAY WORLD	IV.1	327
Sir Wilful:	Let Apollo's Example invite us;	455	WAY WORLD	IV.1	418
Sir Wilful:	she has her Maidenhead let her look to't,--if she has not,	456	WAY WORLD	IV.1	428
Sir Wilful:	let her keep her own Counsel in the mean time, and cry	456	WAY WORLD	IV.1	429
Sir Wilful:	Let Mahometan Fools	456	WAY WORLD	IV.1	452
Sir Wilful:	But let British Lads sing,	456	WAY WORLD	IV.1	455
Sir Wilful:	let me bite your Cheek for that.	457	WAY WORLD	IV.1	473
Lady Wish:	your Character, that I think my self oblig'd to let you	460	WAY WORLD	IV.1	586
Waitwell:	How, how, Let me see, let me see--(reading) A	460	WAY WORLD	IV.1	591
Waitwell:	must let me give you;--I'll go for a black box, which	461	WAY WORLD	IV.1	633
Lady Wish:	and Purling Streams. Dear Marwood, let us leave the World,	465	WAY WORLD	V.1	134
Marwood:	Let us first dispatch the affair in hand Madam,	465	WAY WORLD	V.1	136
Mrs Fain:	me. I defie 'em all. Let 'em prove their aspersions: I know	466	WAY WORLD	V.1	177
Lady Wish:	friend, I can't believe it, No, no; as she says, let him prove	467	WAY WORLD	V.1	206
Lady Wish:	it, let him prove it.	467	WAY WORLD	V.1	207
Sir Wilful:	Pound. And so let that content for what's past, and make	470	WAY WORLD	V.1	319
Sir Wilful:	let him come in; why we are sworn Brothers and fellow	471	WAY WORLD	V.1	346
Mirabell:	I am too Happy,--Ah Madam, there was a time--but let	471	WAY WORLD	V.1	369
Mirabell:	Let me be pitied first; and afterwards forgotten,	471	WAY WORLD	V.1	378
Fainall:	If it must all come out, why let 'em know it, 'tis but	474	WAY WORLD	V.1	475
Fainall:	let me pass Oafe.	476	WAY WORLD	V.1	561
Mirabell:	For that Madam, give your self no trouble--let	477	WAY WORLD	V.1	577
Sir Wilful:	you're married; or if you will toy now; Let us have a	477	WAY WORLD	V.1	600
Mirabell:	Madam, let me before these Witnesses, restore to you this	478	WAY WORLD	V.1	617
Mirabell:	From hence let those be warn'd, who mean to wed;	478	WAY WORLD	V.1	620

Let'n   (2)

Ben:	here just now? Will he thrash my Jacket?--Let'n, let'n,--	264	FOR LOVE	III.1	420

Let's   (20)

Bellmour:	Nay let's see the Name (Silvia!) how can'st thou be	38	OLD BATCH	I.1	38
Vainlove:	Well good Morrow, let's dine together, I'l meet at	40	OLD BATCH	I.1	129
Sharper:	Heartwell when I see him. Prithee, Frank, let's teaze him;	99	OLD BATCH	V.1	87
Sir Joseph:	let's hearken. A-gad, this must be I.--	102	OLD BATCH	V.1	204
	Let's have a fair Tryal, and a clear Sea.	125	DOUBL DLR	PRO.	15
Mellefont:	let's meet 'em.	131	DOUBL DLR	I.1	169
Mellefont:	and Cutt, let's e'en turn up Trump now.	142	DOUBL DLR	II.1	161
Cynthia:	O good my Lord let's hear it.	166	DOUBL DLR	III.1	590
Lady Froth:	O the dear Creature! Let's go see it.	166	DOUBL DLR	III.1	608
Lord Touch:	I fear he's mad indeed--Let's send Maskwell	187	DOUBL DLR	IV.2	135
Careless:	use his Chamber; let's follow and examine him.	196	DOUBL DLR	V.1	353
Tattle:	--Come, let's talk of something else.	228	FOR LOVE	I.1	443
Tattle:	not what--Come, let's talk of something else.	228	FOR LOVE	I.1	448
Mrs Frail:	Come, let's hear 'em.	233	FOR LOVE	I.1	635

390

Lie   (continued)

		PAGE	TITLE	ACT.SC	LINE
Laetitia:	Spin-text, has a sad Fit of the Cholick, and is forced				
	to lie	91	OLD BATCH	IV.4	78
Laetitia:	'Tis no body but Mr. Fondlewife, Mr. Spin-text, lie	91	OLD BATCH	IV.4	85
Fondlewife:	Ay, ay, lie still, lie still; don't let me disturb you.	91	OLD BATCH	IV.4	88
Fondlewife:	you know your Patient, Mrs. Quack? Oh, lie upon your	93	OLD BATCH	IV.4	163
Bellmour:	To lie with your Wife.	94	OLD BATCH	IV.4	178
Lady Ply:	ought to lie upon me: That you should have so little	159	DOUEL DLR	III.1	329
Sir Paul:	which lie all in your Ladiships Breast, and he being a well	180	DOUEL DLR	IV.1	479
Maskwell:	lie conceal'd there; otherwise she may Lock the Door	181	DOUEL DLR	IV.1	517
Lady Touch:	but I will stab the Lie that's forming in your heart, and				
	save	197	DOUEL DLR	V.1	381
Foresight:	I believe you lie, Sir.	235	FOR LCVE	II.1	9
Foresight:	I say you lie, Sir. It is impossible that any thing	235	FOR LCVE	II.1	11
Foresight:	I know when Travellers lie or speak Truth, when	241	FCR LCVE	II.1	224
Miss Prue:	Why, must I tell a Lie then?	251	FOR LCVE	II.1	609
Tattle:	Lie--Besides, you are a Woman, ycu must never	251	FCB LCVE	II.1	611
Miss Prue:	and must not you lie too?	252	FCR LCVE	II.1	626
Miss Prue:	me a Lie.	253	FCR LCVE	III.1	20
Tattle:	There's no occasion for a Lie; I cou'd never tell a Lie	253	FOR LCVE	III.1	21
Miss Prue:	better not speak at all, I think, and truly I won't tell				
	a lie	263	FOR ICVE	III.1	383
Ben:	Nay, You say true in that, it's but a folly to lie: For to	263	FOR LCVE	III.1	385
Miss Prue:	always tell a lie to a man; and I don't care, let my Father	264	FCR LCVE	III.1	397
Ben:	And lie o' Nights alone.	274	FCR LCVE	III.1	767
Ben:	clean Shirt once a Quarter--Come home and lie with	275	FCR LCVE	III.1	801
Scandal:	Faith, Madam, I wish telling a Lie would mend the	277	FOR LCVE	IV.1	45
Valentine:	the Lie.	280	FCR LCVE	IV.1	165
Valentine:	thou can'st not lie with my Wife? I am very poor, and	292	FCR LCVE	IV.1	626
Valentine:	Sirrah, you lie; I am not Mad.	295	FCR LCVE	IV.1	741
Sr Sampson:	That's as much as to say, I lie, Sir, and you don't	311	FCR LCVE	V.1	522
Osmyn-Alph:	Then Garcia shall lie panting on thy Bosom,	358	M. BRIDE	III.1	358
Witwoud:	will lie like a Chambermaid, or a Woman of Quality's	404	WAY WCRLD	I.1	341
Marwood:	reflect that Guilt upon me, which should lie buried in your	414	WAY WORLD	II.1	177
Foible:	of her Beauty, that he burns with Impatience to lie at her	423	WAY WCRLD	II.1	523
Lady Wish:	be too sudden. I'll lie--aye, I'll lie down--I'll	445	WAY WCRLD	IV.1	22
Lady Wish:	lie neither but loll and lean upcn one Elbow; with one Foot	445	WAY WCRLD	IV.1	25
Millamant:	more than Impossible--positively Mirabell, I'll lie a Bed in	449	WAY WORLD	IV.1	190
Lady Wish:	I do with this beastly Tumbril?--Go lie down and	457	WAY WORLD	IV.1	461

Lies (19)   see Lyes

Bellmour:	With all my Heart, it lies convenient for us, to pay	40	OLD BATCH	I.1	131
Heartwell:	I confess I have not been sneering fulsome Lies and	42	OLD BATCH	I.1	188
Lucy:	a Mumper in Love, lies Canting at the Gate; but never dare	66	OLD BATCH	III.1	193
Fondlewife:	Man is in great torment, he lies as flat--Dear, you	91	OLD BATCH	IV.4	95
Laetitia:	(aside). How my heart akes! All my ccmfort lies in	94	OLD BATCH	IV.4	202
Setter:	Pounds, and all her Rigging; besides what lies conceal'd	102	OLD DATCH	V.1	224
Mellefont:	swath'd down, and so put to bed; and there he lies with a	158	DOUEL DLR	III.1	291
Maskwell:	No Mask like open Truth to cover Lies,	190	DOUEL DLR	V.1	100
Lord Touch:	Like Vipers in the Womb, base Treach'ry lies,	203	DOUEL DLR	V.1	594
Tattle:	her Unkle Old Foresight: I think your Father lies at	228	FOR LOVE	I.1	453
Miss Prue:	Lies--but they frighted me, and said it was a sin.	252	FOR LOVE	II.1	630
Perez:	He lies supine on earth; as easily	372	M. BRIDE	V.1	8
Perez:	He lies supine on earth; with as much ease	372	M. BRIDE	V.1 V	8
Manuel:	And laid along as he now lies supine,	374	M. FBIDE	V.1	V86B
Gonsalez:	There lies my way, that Door is too unlock'd.	376	M. BRIDE	V.2	4
Garcia:	See, see, attir'd like Osmyn, where he lies.	377	M. EBIDE	V.2	61
Almeria:	There, there I see him; there he lies, the Blood	382	M. BRIDE	V.2	234
Almeria:	Seest thou not there, whc prostrate lies;	362	M. BRIDE	V.2	264
Mirabell:	me lies to a Reunion, (To Mrs. Fainall) in the mean time,	478	WAY WCRLD	V.1	616

Liest (1)   see Ly'st, Lyest

Valentine:	Thou liest, for I am Truth. 'Tis hard I cannot get a	280	FOR LOVE	IV.1	171

Lieutenant (0)   see Deputy-Lieutenant

Lieve (1)

Lord Froth:	Barbarous! I'd as lieve you call'd me Fool.	132	DOUEL DLR	I.1	186

Life (100)

Bellmour:	Friend, be close pursued, or lost. Business is the rub of				
	Life,	37	OLD BATCH	I.1	10
Sir Joseph:	best Friends I have in the World and saved my Life last	52	OLD BATCH	II.1	169
Sir Joseph:	--I'd rather go plain all my Life, than wear such	70	OLD BATCH	III.1	334
Heartwell:	the Voice, and Life to their Measures--Look you	72	OLD BATCH	III.2	33
Heartwell:	Why every Man plays the Fool once in his Life: But to	74	OLD BATCH	III.2	117
Heartwell:	Marry, is playing the Fool all ones Life long.	74	OLD BATCH	III.2	118
Fondlewife:	lay with an honester Man's Wife in your life.	94	OLD BATCH	IV.4	201
Bellmour:	life.	95	OLD BATCH	IV.4	221
Heartwell:	the Load of Life!--We hope to find	108	OLD BATCH	V.2	10
Heartwell:	expiring, and endeavour to prolong his life, and you	109	OLD BATCH	V.2	55
Bellmour:	Now set we forward on a Journey for Life:--	112	OLD BATCH	V.2	182
Heartwell:	What rugged Ways attend the Noon of Life!	112	OLD BATCH	V.2	191
	For Life will struggle lcng, 'ere it sink down:	125	DOUEL DLR	PRO.	17
Maskwell:	No, that I deny; for I never told in all my Life:	135	DOUEL DLR	I.1	318
Maskwell:	Creature, my Life and Fortune in your power; to disoblige	136	DOUEL DLR	I.1	340
Lady Ply:	Gads my life, the man's Distracted, why how	144	DOUEL DLR	II.1	214
Sir Paul:	never angry before in my Life, and I'll never be appeased	145	DOUEL DLR	II.1	268
Lady Ply:	Why, gads my life, Cousin Mellefont, you cannot	146	DOUEL DLR	II.1	297
Mellefont:	By Heaven, I love her more than life,--	146	DOUEL DLR	II.1	300
Lady Ply:	is no certainty in the things of this life.	147	DOUEL DLR	II.1	329
Lord Touch:	By my Life, my Dear, I will.	152	DOUEL DLR	III.1	59
Lady Touch:	was never so surpriz'd in my Life--Who would have	153	DOUEL DLR	III.1	114
Cynthia:	lay my Life it will never be a Match.	167	DOUEL DLR	IV.1	7
Careless:	out a Wretched Life, and breath my Soul beneath your	170	DOUEL DLR	IV.1	100
Lady Ply:	anger.) Gad's my Life if I thought it were so, I would this	179	DOUEL DLR	IV.1	442
Lady Ply:	never dissembled in my Life. Yet to make tryal of you,	179	DOUEL DLR	IV.1	453
Lady Touch:	been to me, you have already killed the quiet of this Life,	185	DOUEL DLR	IV.2	75
Lord Touch:	Monster, Dog! your Life shall answer	186	DOUEL DLR	IV.2	106
Mellefont:	Causes and Accidents of Fortune in this Life! but to what	187	DOUEL DLR	IV.2	142
Maskwell:	Let us go and consult her, my life for yours, I	190	DOUEL DLR	V.1	118

394

Like   (continued)

		PAGE	TITLE	ACT.SC	LINE
Mellefont:	Malice, like a Dark Lanthorn, only shone upon me,	129	DOUBL DLR	I.1 V	90
Mellefont:	Bed-side like a Fury, she flew tc my Sword, and with	130	DOUBL DLR	I.1	114
Lady Touch:	Again, provoke me! Do you wind me like	137	DOUBL DLR	I.1	380
Cynthia:	formality; for which I like him: Here he comes.	139	DOUBL DLR	II.1	54
Cynthia:	Then I find its like Cards, if either of us have a good	142	DOUBL DLR	II.1	162
Mellefont:	No, Marriage is rather like a Game at Bowls,	143	DOUBL DLR	II.1	164
Sir Paul:	my Lady Froth says; was ever the like read of in Story?	143	DOUBL DLR	II.1	196
Lady Ply:	Have I, I say, preserv'd my self, like a fair Sheet	145	DOUBL DLR	II.1	259
Sir Paul:	dye of 'em, like any Child, that were cutting his Teeth--	146	DOUBL DLR	II.1	283
Sir Paul:	die of 'em, like a Child, that was cutting his Teeth--	146	DOUBL DLR	II.1	V283
Maskwell:	general acquittance--Rival is equal, and Love like Death	150	DOUBL DLR	II.1	449
Lady Ply:	like to be suspected in the end, and 'tis a pain any longer	151	DOUBL DLR	III.1	39
Mellefont:	Like any two Guardians to an Orphan Heiress--	156	DOUBL DLR	III.1	216
Mellefont:	Feet like a gull'd Bassa that has married a Relation of the	158	DOUBL DLR	III.1	282
Mellefont:	great Beard, like a Russian Bear upon a drift of Snow. You	158	DOUBL DLR	III.1	292
Lady Froth:	Then too like Heav'ns Charioteer, the Sun:	164	DOUBL DLR	III.1	536
Brisk:	good Rhime) but don't you think bilk and fare too like a	165	DOUBL DLR	III.1	545
Brisk:	Spectacle; she's always chewing the Cud like an old Yew.	165	DOUBL DLR	III.1	568
Brisk:	Like an Oyster at low Ebb, I'gad--ha, ha, ha.	165	DOUBL DLR	III.1	576
Cynthia:	If not, they like and admire themselves--And why is	167	DOUBL DLR	III.1	629
Cynthia:	consent to like a Man without the vile Consideration of	168	DOUBL DLR	IV.1	45
Sir Paul:	the young Rogue as like as you can.	173	DOUBL DLR	IV.1	231
Brisk:	Daughter your self; you're always brooding over her like	174	DOUBL DLR	IV.1	272
Brisk:	Men like rich Fellows, are always ready for all Expences;	175	DOUBL DLR	IV.1	300
Brisk:	while your Blockheads, like poor needy Scoundrels, are	175	DOUBL DLR	IV.1	301
Brisk:	like Respect.	175	DOUBL DLR	IV.1	318
Lord Froth:	don't like this familiarity.	177	DOUBL DLR	IV.1	373
Lady Ply:	pretended to like that Monster of Iniquity, Careless, and	179	DOUBL DLR	IV.1	454
Mellefont:	You have been to blame--I like those Tears,	185	DOUBL DLR	IV.2	68
Mellefont:	Women like flames have a destroying pow'r,	187	DOUBL DLR	IV.2	154
Maskwell:	that I have done, would look like Rivals Malice, false	188	DOUBL DLR	V.1	39
Maskwell:	No Mask like open Truth to cover Lies,	190	DOUBL DLR	V.1	100
Maskwell:	our farther Security, I would have you Disguis'd like a	193	DOUBL DLR	V.1	231
Lady Froth:	Astronomy like an old Egyptian.	201	DOUBL DLR	V.1	529
	runs out affrighted, my Lord after her, like a Parson.)	202	DOUBL DLR	V.1	557
	of the Stage, Mellefont like a Parson.)	202	DOUBL DLR	V.1	567
Lord Touch:	Like Vipers in the Womb, base Treach'ry lies,	203	DOUBL DLR	V.1	594
	It seems like Eden, fruitful of its own accord.	213	FOR LOVE	PRO.	17
Jeremy:	Spirit of Famine appears to me; sometimes like a decay'd	218	FOR LOVE	I.1	95
Jeremy:	and Songs; not like other Porters for Hire, but for the Jests	218	FOR LOVE	I.1	97
Jeremy:	sake. Now like a thin Chairman, melted down to half	218	FOR LOVE	I.1	98
Jeremy:	some great Fortune; and his Fare to be paid him like the	218	FOR LOVE	I.1	100
Jeremy:	Sometimes like a bilk'd Bookseller, with a meagre	219	FOR LOVE	I.1	104
Scandal:	Jeremy speaks like an Oracle. Don't you see how	219	FOR LOVE	I.1	131
Scandal:	Man of small Fortune? Why, he looks like a Writ of Enquiry	219	FOR LOVE	I.1	133
Jeremy:	if you don't like my Negotiation, will you be pleas'd to	221	FOR LOVE	I.1	183
Scandal:	And you, like a true great Man, having engaged their	221	FOR LOVE	I.1	193
Jeremy:	suspicious Fellows like lawful Pads, that wou'd knock	221	FOR LOVE	I.1	203
Scandal:	He begs Pardon like a Hangman at an Execution.	225	FOR LOVE	I.1	328
Scandal:	her, you must be condemned, like other bad Painters, to	230	FOR LOVE	I.1	538
Scandal:	most of your Acquaintance to the Life, and as like as at	232	FOR LOVE	I.1	618
Nurse:	like!	235	FOR LOVE	II.1	24
Nurse:	ever hear the like now--Sir, did ever I do any thing	238	FOR LOVE	II.1	101
Angelica:	the Closet, one Night, like Saul and the Witch of Endor,	238	FOR LOVE	II.1	107
Nurse:	thing; feel, feel here, if I have any thing but like	238	FOR LOVE	II.1	124
Foresight:	Fellow? I don't like his Physiognomy.	242	FOR LOVE	II.1	264
Sr Sampson:	and my Fatherly fondness wou'd fit like two Tallies.--	243	FOR LOVE	II.1	294
Sr Sampson:	Did you ever hear the like! Did you ever hear the like!	244	FOR LOVE	II.1	319
Jeremy:	Country Dances; and the like; I don't much matter your	245	FOR LOVE	II.1	374
Mrs Frail:	the happiness of conversing where we like.	246	FOR LOVE	II.1	425
Mrs Fore:	it, I think there's no happiness like conversing with an	247	FOR LOVE	II.1	427
Miss Prue:	What, is it like the Catechisme?--Come then	251	FOR LOVE	II.1	600
Tattle:	speak you:--And like me, for the Beauty which I say	252	FOR LOVE	II.1	618
Miss Prue:	O Lord, I swear this is pure,--I like it better than	252	FOR LOVE	II.1	624
Singer-F:	Apollo was mute, and had like t' have been pos'd,	259	FOR LOVE	III.1	205
Sr Sampson:	Support, like Ivy round a dead Oak: Faith I do; I love to	260	FOR LOVE	III.1	264
Sr Sampson:	see 'em hug and cotter together, like Down upon a	260	FOR LOVE	III.1	265
Ben:	A man that is marri'd, d'ee see, is no more like another	262	FOR LOVE	III.1	315
Ben:	man, than a Galley-slave is like one of us free Sailors, he is	262	FOR LOVE	III.1	316
Mrs Frail:	Not at all; I like his humour mightily, it's plain	262	FOR LOVE	III.1	321
Mrs Frail:	and honest, I shou'd like such a humour in a Husband	262	FOR LOVE	III.1	322
Ben:	Say'n you so forsooth: Marry and I shou'd like such a	262	FOR LOVE	III.1	324
Ben:	you Mistress, wou'd you like going to Sea? Mess you're a	262	FOR LOVE	III.1	326
Ben:	by Father, and if you like of it, may-hap I may steer into	263	FOR LOVE	III.1	374
Ben:	thing is this, that if you like me, and I like you, we may	263	FOR LOVE	III.1	376
Ben:	thing is that if you like me, and I like you, we may	263	FOR LOVE	III.1	V376
Miss Prue:	plainly, I don't like you, nor love you at all, nor never will,	264	FOR LOVE	III.1	399
Ben:	end;--And may-hap I like you as little as you do me:--	264	FOR LOVE	III.1	405
Ben:	stink; he shall smell more like a Weasel than a Civet-Cat,	265	FOR LOVE	III.1	437
Sr Sampson:	with him; twould be but like me, A Chip of the Old Block.	265	FOR LOVE	III.1	462
Sr Sampson:	and when the Alarm strikes, they shall keep time like the	266	FOR LOVE	III.1	476
Foresight:	like that suddain flushing--gone already!--hem, hem,	269	FOR LOVE	III.1	604
Mrs Fore:	this Project? You don't think, that you are ever like to	271	FOR LOVE	III.1	660
Mrs Frail:	Estate, is like Sailing in a Ship without Ballast.	273	FOR LOVE	III.1	720
Ben:	is indeed, as like as two Cable Ropes.	273	FOR LOVE	III.1	722
Ben:	don't think I'm false-hearted, like a Land-man. A Sailor	273	FOR LOVE	III.1	732
Ben:	Nay, an I love once, I'll stick like pitch; I'll tell you that.	273	FOR LOVE	III.1	739
Ben:	The Souldier Swore like Thunder,	274	FOR LOVE	III.1	769
Ben:	then put off with the next fair wind. How de'e like us?	275	FOR LOVE	III.1	803
Jeremy:	Like enough, Sir, for I told her Maid this morning,	276	FOR LOVE	IV.1	14
Angelica:	I don't like Raillery from a serious Face--pray	276	FOR LOVE	IV.1	27

Like   (continued)

Speaker	Text	PAGE	TITLE	ACT.SC	LINE
Valentine:	There's a couple of Topicks for you, no more like one	282	FOR LOVE	IV.1	256
Mrs Fore:	infer from last night? last Night was like the Night before,	284	FOR LOVE	IV.1	319
Ben:	senses, d'ee see; for ought as I perceive I'm like to be				
	finely	286	FOR LOVE	IV.1	414
Mrs Fore:	come, stand aside a little, and tell me how you like the	288	FOR LOVE	IV.1	476
Valentine:	Where is she? Oh I see her--she comes, like Riches,	290	FOR LOVE	IV.1	541
Valentine:	like--	292	FOR LOVE	IV.1	649
Valentine:	That Women are like Tricks by slight of Hand,	297	FOR LOVE	IV.1	815
Angelica:	like him, it's a sign he likes me; and that's more than half	297	FOR LOVE	V.1	6
Sr Sampson:	wou'd she wou'd like me, then I shou'd hamper my young	298	FOR LOVE	V.1	49
Angelica:	Fortune enough to make any Man easie that I can like; If	299	FOR LOVE	V.1	61
Angelica:	her Husband. I should like a Man of Wit for a Lover,	299	FOR LOVE	V.1	74
Angelica:	was indeed thinking to propose something like it in a Jest,	300	FOR LOVE	V.1	107
Sr Sampson:	and Troth I like you the better--But, I warrant you,	300	FOR LOVE	V.1	125
Tattle:	like a Nun; and I must be hooded like a Friar; ha, Jeremy?	302	FOR LOVE	V.1	198
Jeremy:	Aye, Sir, hooded like a Hawk, to seize at first sight	302	FOR LOVE	V.1	199
Miss Prue:	you; I have been looking up and down for you like any	303	FOR LOVE	V.1	223
Foresight:	resemblance of her; and the Girl is like me.	304	FOR LOVE	V.1	261
Mrs Frail:	like him less.	310	FOR LOVE	V.1	474
Jeremy:	any thing like it--Then how could it be otherwise?	313	FOR LOVE	V.1	594
Valentine:	Any thing, my Friend, every thing that looks like	313	FOR LOVE	V.1	602
Scandal:	that all Women are not like Fortune, blind in bestowing	314	FOR LOVE	V.1	624
Angelica:	How few, like Valentine, would persevere even unto	314	FOR LOVE	V.1	633
Angelica:	How few, like Valentine, would persevere even to	314	FOR LOVE	V.1 V633
	It's like what I have heard our Poets tell us:	315	FOR LOVE	EPI.	6
	I vow, I don't much like this Transmigration,	315	FOR LOVE	EPI.	32
	New Plays did then like Almanacks appear;	323	M. BRIDE	PRO.	3
	Tho' they are more like Almanacks of late;	323	M. BRIDE	PRO.	5
	In such like Prophecies were Poets skill'd,	323	M. BRIDE	PRO.	13
Almeria:	Why did he not use me like an Enemy?	327	M. BRIDE	I.1	67
Almeria:	Why not ill treated, like an Enemy?	327	M. BRIDE	I.1 V 67
Gonsalez:	Be every Day of your long Life like this.	331	M. BRIDE	I.1	220
Manuel:	To my Brightness, like Daughters of Affliction.	333	M. BRIDE	I.1	282
Manuel:	And yours are all like Daughters of Affliction.	333	M. BRIDE	I.1 V282
Zara:	To like Captivity, or think those Honours,	335	M. BRIDE	I.1	394
Garcia:	I saw him not, nor any like him.	338	M. BRIDE	II.1 V 18
Osmyn-Alph:	So like Almeria. Ha! it sinks, it falls,	341	M. BRIDE	II.2	52
Almeria:	What's he, that like thy self, is started here	344	M. BRIDE	II.2	167
Almeria:	What's he, who like thy self, is started here	344	M. BRIDE	II.2 V167
Osmyn-Alph:	Thus, do our Eyes, like common Mirrours	345	M. BRIDE	II.2	221
Zara:	And like the Morn vermilion'd o'er thy Face.	347	M. BRIDE	II.2	284
Zara:	And are like Lumber, to be left and scorn'd.	347	M. BRIDE	II.2	321
Manuel:	Or lift his Eyes to like, where I adore?	348	M. BRIDE	II.2	357
Manuel:	And spread like Roses to the Morning Sun.	349	M. BRIDE	II.2	386
Osmyn-Alph:	One, driv'n about the World like blasted Leaves	351	M. BRIDE	III.1	59
Osmyn-Alph:	Like Fumes of Sacred Incense, o'er the Clouds,	353	M. BRIDE	III.1	130
Osmyn-Alph:	And pinion'd like a Thief or Murderer?	355	M. BRIDE	III.1	241
Zara:	And watch like Tapers o'er your Hours of Rest.	360	M. BRIDE	III.1	429
Zara:	Heav'n has no Rage, like Love to Hatred turn'd,	361	M. BRIDE	III.1	457
Zara:	Nor Hell a Fury, like a Woman scorn'd.	361	M. BRIDE	III.1	458
Gonsalez:	I like it not.	366	M. BRIDE	IV.1	197
Manuel:	That like a sudden Earth-quake, shakes my Frame;	367	M. BRIDE	IV.1	233
Manuel:	How like thy self when Passion treads him down?	373	M. BRIDE	V.1	41
Zara:	His Eyes like Meteors roll'd, then darted down	374	M. BRIDE	V.1	93
Zara:	Would, like the raging Dog-star, scorch the Earth,	375	M. BRIDE	V.1	95
Zara:	And, like a Cobweb-Veil, but thinly shades	375	M. BRIDE	V.1	103
Zara:	Thou like the Adder, venomous and deaf,	375	M. BRIDE	V.1	106
	Enter Gonsalez, disguis'd like a Mute, with a Dagger.)	376	M. BRIDE	V.2	
	Gonsalez alone, disguis'd like a Mute, with a Dagger.)	376	M. BRIDE	V.2 V
Garcia:	See, see, attir'd like Osmyn, where he lies.	377	M. BRIDE	V.2	61
	Scatter'd, like Rats-bane, up and down the Pit;	385	M. BRIDE	EPI.	8
	While others watch like Parish-Searchers, hir'd	385	M. BRIDE	EPI.	9
	Nor, like those peevish Wits, his Play maintain,	393	WAY WORLD	PRO.	27
Fainall:	another's Apartments, where they come together like the	396	WAY WORLD	I.1	52
Mirabell:	a Lover, for I like her with all her Faults; nay, like				
	her for	399	WAY WORLD	I.1	159
Mirabell:	and in all probability in a little time longer I shall				
	like 'em	399	WAY WORLD	I.1	173
Fainall:	Not at all; Witwoud grows by the Knight, like a	401	WAY WORLD	I.1	212
Witwoud:	Domestick. But I talk like an old Maid at a Marriage, I	402	WAY WORLD	I.1	258
Witwoud:	Ay; but I like him for that now; for his want of	404	WAY WORLD	I.1	330
Witwoud:	will lie like a Chambermaid, or a Woman of Quality's	404	WAY WORLD	I.1	341
Mrs Fain:	with Horror and Distaste; they meet us like the Ghosts	410	WAY WORLD	II.1	7
Marwood:	and seem to doat like Lovers; but 'tis not in our	410	WAY WORLD	II.1	24
Fainall:	and weep like Alexander, when he wanted other Worlds to	413	WAY WORLD	II.1	116
Mirabell:	Uncle, he might like Mosca in the Fox, stand upon Terms;	417	WAY WORLD	II.1	294
Mirabell:	An old Woman's Appetite is deprav'd like that of	418	WAY WORLD	II.1	317
Mirabell:	and like the faint Offer of a latter Spring, serves but to	418	WAY WORLD	II.1	319
Witwoud:	Like Moths about a Candle--I had like to have	418	WAY WORLD	II.1	331
Witwoud:	Do Mrs. Mincing, like a Skreen before a great Fire.	419	WAY WORLD	II.1	343
Mirabell:	By your leave Witwoud, that were like enquiring	419	WAY WORLD	II.1	351
Millamant:	violent and inflexible wise Face, like Solomon at the				
	dividing	422	WAY WORLD	II.1	468
Millamant:	Plot to speed?--No.	422	WAY WORLD	II.1	483
Lady Wish:	that, Changeling, dangling thy Hands like Bobbins before	425	WAY WORLD	III.1	14
Lady Wish:	then--(Exit Peg). I'm as pale and as faint, I look like	425	WAY WORLD	III.1	21
Lady Wish:	thou go with the Bottle in thy Hand like a Tapster. As I'm	426	WAY WORLD	III.1	35
Lady Wish:	before she came to me, like Maritornes the Asturian in Don	426	WAY WORLD	III.1	37
Lady Wish:	The Miniature has been counted like--But	427	WAY WORLD	III.1	79
Lady Wish:	Tatters, like a long Lane Pent-house, or a Gibbet-thief.	428	WAY WORLD	III.1	131
Lady Wish:	Why I am arrantly flea'd--I look like an old peel'd Wall.	429	WAY WORLD	III.1	148
Foible:	Picture like you; and now a little of the same Art, must	429	WAY WORLD	III.1	152
Foible:	make you like your Picture. Your Picture must sit for you,	429	WAY WORLD	III.1	153
Marwood:	draw him like an Idiot, a Driveler, with a Bib and Bells.	431	WAY WORLD	III.1	237
Marwood:	Care, like any Chymist upon the Day of Projection.	431	WAY WORLD	III.1	248

Like (continued)
Marwood:	there, like a new masking Habit, after the Masquerade is	433	WAY WORLD III.1 310
Marwood:	'Tis like Mrs. Primly's great Belly; she may lace it down	433	WAY WORLD III.1 318
Witwoud:	Animosity--The falling out of Wits is like the falling	435	WAY WORLD III.1 395
Witwoud:	out of Lovers--We agree in the main, like Treble	435	WAY WORLD III.1 396
Witwoud:	one another like two Battle-dores: For	435	WAY WORLD III.1 402
Witwoud:	Contradictions beget one another like Jews.	435	WAY WORLD III.1 403
Servant-W:	Morning, before she is dress'd. 'Tis like I may give a	437	WAY WORLD III.1 462
Sir Wilful:	Why, 'tis like you may, Sir: If you are not	438	WAY WORLD III.1 498
Witwoud:	slabber and kiss one another when they meet, like a Call of	439	WAY WORLD III.1 535
Sir Wilful:	Discourse to the Lady, Sir: 'Tis like my Aunt may have	440	WAY WORLD III.1 572
Sir Wilful:	I can't tell that; 'tis like I may, and 'tis like I may	440	WAY WORLD III.1 578
Sir Wilful:	There is? 'Tis like there may.	440	WAY WORLD III.1 587
Witwoud:	Yes, refin'd, like a Dutch Skipper from a	441	WAY WORLD III.1 590
Fainall:	budding Antlers like a young Satyre, or a Citizens Child.	442	WAY WORLD III.1 633
Fainall:	Out-Matrimony'd,--If I had kept my speed like a Stag,	442	WAY WORLD III.1 635
Fainall:	like a Snail, and out-strip'd by my Wife--'tis Scurvy	442	WAY WORLD III.1 637
Fainall:	like a Snail, and be out-stripp'd by my Wife--'tis Scurvy	442	WAY WORLD III.1 V637
Fainall:	Gold, tho' my forehead had been furnish'd like a	442	WAY WORLD III.1 647
Fainall:	disable him for that, he will drink like a Dane: after		
	dinner,	443	WAY WORLD III.1 672
Sir Wilful:	'tis like you may--Here are choice of Pastimes here in	448	WAY WORLD IV.1 124
Sir Wilful:	Town, as Plays and the like that must be confess'd indeed.	448	WAY WORLD IV.1 125
Sir Wilful:	shou'd hate 'em both! Hah 'tis like you may; there are	448	WAY WORLD IV.1 128
Sir Wilful:	the Ccuntry,--'tis like you may be one of those,	448	WAY WORLD IV.1 130
Millamant:	Ha, ha, ha. Yes, 'tis like I may.--You have nothing	448	WAY WORLD IV.1 132
Sir Wilful:	Not at present, Cozen.--'tis like when I have	448	WAY WORLD IV.1 134
Millamant:	Like Phoebus sung the no less am'rous Boy.	448	WAY WORLD IV.1 153
Mirabell:	--Like Daphne she as lovely and as Coy. Do you	449	WAY WORLD IV.1 155
Millamant:	or fond, nor kiss before folks, like my Lady Fadler and Sr.	450	WAY WORLD IV.1 201
Millamant:	converse with Wits that I don't like, because they are your	450	WAY WORLD IV.1 217
Mirabell:	Item, I Article, that you continue to like your own	451	WAY WORLD IV.1 245
Mirabell:	a Shape, till you mold my boy's head like a Sugar-loaf; and	451	WAY WORLD IV.1 261
Witwoud:	like ten Christmings--I am tipsy with laughing--If I had	453	WAY WORLD IV.1 326
Witwoud:	out and piec'd in the sides like an unsiz'd Camlet,--Yes,	453	WAY WORLD IV.1 328
Witwoud:	yes the fray is compos'd; my Lady came in like a	453	WAY WORLD IV.1 329
Witwoud:	one another like two roasting Apples.	453	WAY WORLD IV.1 334
Witwoud:	Remnants of Remnants, like a maker of Pincushions--thou	453	WAY WORLD IV.1 347
Petulant:	he (hiccup) rises upon my stomack like a Radish.	454	WAY WORLD IV.1 357
Witwoud:	Ears like a pair of Castanets.	454	WAY WORLD IV.1 363
Witwoud:	Do, rap thy self up like a Wood-louse and dream	454	WAY WORLD IV.1 371
Witwoud:	Horrible! He has a breath like a Bagpipe--ay, ay,	457	WAY WORLD IV.1 474
Waitwell:	his head, and then go out in a stink like a Candle's end	458	WAY WORLD IV.1 524
Lady Wish:	you may see by the Superscription it is like a Woman's	460	WAY WORLD IV.1 573
Lady Wish:	you may see, the Superscription is like a Woman's	460	WAY WORLD IV.1 V573
Marwood:	More Temper wou'd look more like Innocence. But I have	466	WAY WORLD V.1 161
Mrs Fain:	you? ay, like a Leach, to suck your best Blood--she'll	466	WAY WORLD V.1 174
Marwood:	Quoif like a Man Midwife to bring your Daughter's	467	WAY WORLD V.1 213
Marwood:	Temple, take Notes like Prentices at a Conventicle; and	467	WAY WORLD V.1 225
Fainall:	which you like a careful Aunt had provided for her.	469	WAY WORLD V.1 285
Sir Wilful:	'Sheart an she shou'd her forehead wou'd wrinkle like the	471	WAY WORLD V.1 363
Sir Wilful:	'Sheart and she shou'd her forehead wou'd wrinkle like the	471	WAY WORLD V.1 V363
Fainall:	turn'd a drift, like a Leaky hulk to Sink or Swim, as she	473	WAY WORLD V.1 443
Witwoud:	Hey day! what are you all got together like Players	475	WAY WORLD V.1 521
Witwoud:	in a maze yet, like a Dog in a Dancing School.	477	WAY WORLD V.1 591

Likelihood (1)
Millamant:	And yet our Distemper in all likelihood will be	422	WAY WORLD II.1 452

Likely (7)
Careless:	Lady's a fine likely Woman--	161	DOUBL DLR III.1 420
Sir Paul:	Oh, a fine likely Woman as you shall see in a	161	DOUBL DLR III.1 421
Foresight:	Very likely.	270	FOR LOVE III.1 618
Foresight:	Very likely truly; You understand these Matters	289	FOR LOVE IV.1 531
Sir Wilful:	Very likely, Sir, that it may seem so.	438	WAY WORLD III.1 492
Lady Wish:	Jubilee. But I hope where there is likely to be so near an	457	WAY WORLD IV.1 487
Fainall:	Very likely Sir, What's here? Damnation! (Reads) A	476	WAY WORLD V.1 550

Likeness (2)
Tattle:	more love for your Daughter, than I have likeness of you;	305	FOR LOVE V.1 288
	And tho' no perfect likeness they can Trace;	479	WAY WORLD EPI. 19

Likes (4)
Bellmour:	that which he likes best; 'tis his diversion to Set, 'tis		
	mine	43	OLD BATCH I.1 224
Lady Touch:	likes him so well, that she will believe it faster than I		
	can	138	DOUBL DLR I.1 413
Angelica:	like him, it's a sign he likes me; and that's more than half	297	FOR LOVE V.1 6
Sr Sampson:	(aside). Odsbud I believe she likes me--Ah,	299	FOR LOVE V.1 93

Likewise (1)
Mirabell:	drinks, as Tea, Chocolate and Coffee. As likewise to Genuine	451	WAY WORLD IV.1 266

Liking (5)
Sharper:	Impossible! Araminta take a liking to a Fool!	102	OLD BATCH V.1 196
Mrs Fore:	liking of you. Here they come together; and let us contrive	249	FOR LOVE II.1 503
Mrs Fore:	liking you. Here they come together; and let us contrive	249	FOR LOVE II.1 V503
Ben:	take a liking to me.--	263	FOR LOVE III.1 356
Ben:	for your Love or your liking, I don't value it of a Rope's	264	FOR LOVE III.1 404

Lilly (2)
Scandal:	Ghost of Lilly. He has Secrets to impart I suppose to you	266	FOR LOVE III.1 500
Sr Sampson:	for thee, old Lilly, that we will, and thou shalt lead up a	307	FOR LOVE V.1 386

Limb (3)
Maskwell:	more than all the rest; though I would give a Limb for	199	DOUBL DLR V.1 434
Gonsalez:	As they were all of Eyes, and every Limb	332	M. BRIDE I.1 241
Gonsalez:	As if they were all Eyes, and every Limb	332	M. BRIDE I.1 V241

Limbo (1)
Sir Joseph:	Limbo--But Sir I have a Letter of Credit to Alderman	51	OLD BATCH II.1 132

Limbs (3)
Heartwell:	so much Mercury in my Limbs; 'tis true indeed, I don't	43	OLD BATCH I.1 231
Lady Ply:	so fine limbs, so fine linen, and I don't doubt but you have	160	DOUBL DLR III.1 368
Almeria:	And eat into thy Flesh, festring thy Limbs	356	M. BRIDE III.1 268

398

Little   (continued)
Foible:	of his success. I wou'd be seen as little as possible to				
	speak	430	WAY WORLD	III.1	215
Millamant:	ha, ha; tho' I grant you 'tis a little barbarous, Ha, ha,				
	ha.	434	WAY WORLD	III.1	344
Witwoud:	--We hit off a little Wit now and then, but no . . .	435	WAY WORLD	III.1	394
Lady Wish:	shall stay for you--My Nephew's a little unbred, . . .	441	WAY WORLD	III.1	622
Lady Wish:	receive him in my little dressing Room, there's a Couch--	445	WAY WORLD	IV.1	23
Lady Wish:	a little dangling off, Jogging in a thoughtful way--Yes--	445	WAY WORLD	IV.1	26
Millamant:	will oblige me to leave me: I have just now a little .	448	WAY WORLD	IV.1	140
Millamant:	to endure you a little longer, I may by degrees dwindle into	450	WAY WORLD	IV.1	226
Lady Wish:	My Nephew's a little overtaken Cozen--but	455	WAY WORLD	IV.1	406
Sir Wilful:	Lead on little Tony--I'll follow thee my Anthony, . .	457	WAY WORLD	IV.1	476
Lady Wish:	--and dispence with a little Ceremony.	457	WAY WORLD	IV.1	489
Lady Wish:	Jewells and ruine my Neice, and all little enough-- .	466	WAY WORLD	V.1	152
Sir Wilful:	I confess I have been a little in disguise as they say, .	470	WAY WORLD	V.1	314
Sir Wilful:	than a little Mouth-Glew, and that's hardly dry;--One .	472	WAY WORLD	V.1	397
Petulant:	For my part, I say little--I think things are best . .	477	WAY WORLD	V.1	588

Liv'd (10)   see Short-liv'd
Jeremy:	Diogenes, because he understands Confinement, and liv'd .	217	FOR LOVE	I.1	30
Sr Sampson:	Bear? that my Cubs might have liv'd upon sucking their .	246	FOR LOVE	II.1	390
Sr Sampson:	a long liv'd Race, and inherit Vigour, none of my Family .	298	FOR LOVE	V.1	37
Sr Sampson:	a long liv'd Race, and inherit Vigour, none of my Ancestors	298	FOR LOVE	V.1 V	37
	But liv'd, I know not how, in Beasts; and then . .	315	FOR LOVE	EPI.	17
Osmyn-Alph:	I shall have liv'd beyond all Aera's then, ...	343	M. BRIDE	II.2	143
Lady Wish:	a Person, this Wench has liv'd in an Inn upon the Road, .	426	WAY WORLD	III.1	36
Sir Wilful:	here that does. How long hast thou liv'd with thy Lady, .	437	WAY WORLD	III.1	455
Sir Wilful:	hither that does. How long hast thou liv'd with thy Lady,	437	WAY WORLD	III.1 V455	
Sir Wilful:	Time, when you liv'd with honest Pumple Nose the Attorney	439	WAY WORLD	III.1	549

Live (43)   see Out-live
Capt Bluff:	I am content to retire--Live a private Person--	53	OLD BATCH	II.1	211
Capt Bluff:	and live, go, and force him, to redeliver you the Note-- .	67	OLD BATCH	III.1	250
Heartwell:	I'll give thee all I have: And thou shalt live with .	74	OLD BATCH	III.2	120
Mellefont:	thro' Clouds upon me, and I shall live in Day--O my .	149	DOUBL DLR	II.1	406
Sir Paul:	see--if it becomes me to say so; and we live very				
	comfortably	160	DOUBL DLR	III.1	388
Cynthia:	And he that can't live upon Love, deserves to die in .	168	DOUBL DLR	IV.1	34
Cynthia:	keep my word, and live a Maid for your sake. . . .	169	DOUBL DLR	IV.1	62
Lady Ply:	shall value my self as long as I live, I swear. . . .	169	DOUBL DLR	IV.1	76
Lady Ply:	live to tell it you.	178	DOUBL DLR	IV.1	394
Valentine:	to live upon Instruction; feast your Mind, and mortifie .	216	FOR LOVE	I.1	13
Valentine:	No, Sirrah, you shall live with me still.	218	FOR LOVE	I.1	71
Jeremy:	you, or be damn'd with your Works: But to live even .	218	FOR LOVE	I.1	73
Angelica:	we were ever after to live under Ground, or at least making	237	FOR LOVE	II.1	83
Sr Sampson:	Sirrah, you'l be hang'd; I shall live to see you . .	243	FOR LOVE	II.1	303
Sr Sampson:	feed thee out of my own Vitals?--'S'heart, live by . .	246	FOR LOVE	II.1	399
Ben:	Lapland-Witch as soon, and live upon selling of contrary .	264	FOR LOVE	III.1	426
Ben:	Lapland-Witch as soon, and live upon selling contrary .	264	FOR LOVE	III.1 V426	
Ben:	Thus we live at Sea; eat Bisket, and drink Flip; put on a .	275	FOR LOVE	III.1	800
Singer-V:	And could again begin to Love and Live, ...	293	FOR LOVE	IV.1	653
Sr Sampson:	live; and leave you a good Jointure when I die. . . .	300	FOR LOVE	V.1	120
Sr Sampson:	and yet you shall live to dance at my Wedding; faith and .	307	FOR LOVE	V.1	384
Almeria:	Why do I live to say you are no more?	327	M. BRIDE	I.1	55
Almeria:	No, I will live to be thy Monument;	328	M. BRIDE	I.1	72
Heli:	O Joy unhop'd for, does Almeria live!	341	M. BRIDE	II.2	65
Almeria:	It is too much! too much to bear and live!	342	M. BRIDE	II.2	105
Manuel:	And then, then only, when we love, we live. . . .	349	M. BRIDE	II.2	391
Osmyn-Alph:	If my Alphonso live, restore him, Heav'n, ...	350	M. BRIDE	III.1	10
Heli:	When they shall know you live, assist your Cause. . .	352	M. BRIDE	III.1	103
Heli:	In that Assurance live; which Time, I hope, ...	352	M. BRIDE	III.1	120
Zara:	Thou ly'st; for now I know for whom thou'dst live. . .	360	M. BRIDE	III.1	436
Zara:	In whom I live. Spite of my Rage, and Pride, ...	361	M. BRIDE	IV.1	25
Almeria:	'Till you are mov'd, and grant that he may live. . . .	369	M. BRIDE	IV.1	331
Manuel:	Ha! who may live? take heed, no more of that. . . .	369	M. BRIDE	IV.1	332
Selim:	I plead not for a Pardon, and to live, ...	375	M. BRIDE	V.1	120
Fainall:	Excellent Creature! Well sure if I shou'd live to be . .	413	WAY WORLD	II.1	109
Mrs Fain:	live to be Old and feel the craving of a false Appetite when	418	WAY WORLD	II.1	315
Millamant:	Lovers as fast as one pleases, and they live as long as one	420	WAY WORLD	II.1	404
Lady Wish:	the Turks--for thou are not fit to live in a Christian .	456	WAY WORLD	IV.1	440
Sir Wilful:	Live by Heathenish Rules, ...	456	WAY WORLD	IV.1	453
Waitwell:	me, If I cou'd but live so long as to be reveng'd on that	458	WAY WORLD	IV.1	504
Waitwell:	Sure? am I here? do I live? do I love this Pearl of .	461	WAY WORLD	IV.1	606
Lady Wish:	Must I live to be confiscated at this Rebel-rate?--Here .	470	WAY WORLD	V.1	308
Mirabell:	live Easily together.	478	WAY WORLD	V.1	619

Lively (2)
Scandal:	Why Faith, I have a good lively Imagination; and . .	275	FOR LOVE	III.1	813
Tattle:	of a poor decay'd Creature--Here, a compleat and lively .	291	FOR LOVE	IV.1	581

Livelyhood (1)
Valentine:	Livelyhood amongst you. I have been sworn out of . .	280	FOR LOVE	IV.1	172

Liveries (3)
Jeremy:	bring you to; your Coaches and your Liveries; your . .	217	FOR LOVE	I.1	43
Mirabell:	and the new Liveries?	398	WAY WORLD	I.1	125
Foible:	best Liveries, with the Coach-man and Postilion to fill up	444	WAY WORLD	IV.1	5

Livery (3)
Heartwell:	Livery--I am Melancholy when thou art absent;	73	OLD BATCH	III.2	78
Heartwell:	Livery--I am Melancholy when thou art absent;	73	OLD BATCH	III.2 V	78
Valentine:	Mask of Madness, and this motly Livery, only as the Slave	294	FOR LOVE	IV.1	703

Lives (12)
Lord Touch:	Lives.	203	DOUBL DLR	V.1	590
Valentine:	Health. An honester Man lives not, nor one more ready to .	223	FOR LOVE	I.1	261
Foresight:	bad, some good, our lives are chequer'd, Mirth and .	236	FOR LOVE	II.1	35
Manuel:	Yet lives, and is a Prisoner. His Name?	337	M. BRIDE	I.1 V446	
Heli:	That Osmyn lives, and I again shall see him. . . .	338	M. BRIDE	II.1	11
Osmyn-Alph:	Precedes the Will to think; and Errour lives . . .	350	M. BRIDE	III.1	34
Zara:	While Osmyn lives, you are not safe.	364	M. BRIDE	IV.1	111
Manuel:	Are Confirmation.--That Alphonso lives, ...	366	M. BRIDE	IV.1	216

Look   (continued)

Speaker	Text	PAGE	TITLE	ACT.SC	LINE
Singer:	Prithee Cynthia look behind you, ...	143	DOUBL DLR	II.1	186
Lady Touch:	you have frighted me. Nay, look pleas'd, I'll tell you.	152	DOUBL DLR	III.1	70
Brisk:	great Beard that bristles through it, and makes her look as	166	DOUBL DLR	III.1	586
Lady Ply:	day: I would look upon the Account again; and may be	173	DOUBL DLR	IV.1	216
Sir Paul:	Merry, I'll come and look at you by and by--Where's	175	DOUBL DLR	IV.1	281
Sir Paul:	I will, I will, I'll go and look for him on purpose.	175	DOUBL DLR	IV.1	288
Brisk:	(Aside.) I'll seem to conceal my Passion, and that will look	175	DOUBL DLR	IV.1	317
Lady Ply:	De'e see here? Lock, read it? (Snatches the Letter as in	179	DOUBL DLR	IV.1	441
Maskwell:	that I have done, would look like Rivals Malice, false	188	DOUBL DLR	V.1	39
Sir Paul:	Nephew; and I don't know what,--look you, Sister,	192	DOUBL DLR	V.1	175
Maskwell:	every look you cheaply throw away on any other Object	199	DOUBL DLR	V.1	435
Lord Touch:	has this discover'd! I am confounded when I look back,	200	DOUBL DLR	V.1	470
Mellefont:	your Chaplain, look in the Face of your injur'd Friend;	202	DOUBL DLR	V.1	570
Jeremy:	Younger Brother shou'd come from Sea, he'd never look	218	FOR LOVE	I.1	84
Angelica:	Look to it, Nurse; I can bring Witness that you have a	238	FOR LOVE	II.1	119
Sr Sampson:	Brother, you understand Physiognomy, a hanging look	243	FOR LOVE	II.1	305
Sr Sampson:	Sir? Here, to stand here, upon those two Leggs, and look	244	FOR LOVE	II.1	328
Sr Sampson:	Why look you there now,--I'll maintain	245	FOR LOVE	II.1	365
Sr Sampson:	morning, and then look you perform Covenants, and so	246	FOR LOVE	II.1	403
Mrs Fore:	Countenance:--But look you here now,--where did	248	FOR LOVE	II.1	465
Mrs Fore:	Nay, 'tis Yours, look at it.	248	FOR LOVE	II.1	468
Mrs Frail:	and therefore must look sharply about me. Sir	248	FOR LOVE	II.1	491
Miss Prue:	Mother, Mother, Mother, look you here.	249	FOR LOVE	II.1	506
Miss Prue:	Look you here, Madam then, what Mr. Tattle has	249	FOR LOVE	II.1	515
Miss Prue:	giv'n me--Look you here Cousin, here's a Snuff-box;	249	FOR LOVE	II.1	516
Sr Sampson:	Body o' me, Madam, you say true:--Look	262	FOR LOVE	III.1	349
Ben:	Look you Father, may-hap the young Woman mayn't	263	FOR LOVE	III.1	355
Ben:	indeed, and full in my Teeth. Look you forsooth, I am as	263	FOR LOVE	III.1	371
Ben:	were, to look one way, and to row another. Now, for my	263	FOR LOVE	III.1	387
Ben:	Look you Young Woman, You may learn to give good	264	FOR LOVE	III.1	402
Sr Sampson:	Sunday:--Come, Cheer up, look about thee: Look	265	FOR LOVE	III.1	465
Scandal:	methinks he does not look as he used to do.	268	FOR LOVE	III.1	550
Scandal:	Are you certain? You do not look so.	268	FOR LOVE	III.1	568
Foresight:	here;--Methinks I look with a serene and benign	269	FOR LOVE	III.1	601
Scandal:	Look you there now--Your Lady says your	269	FOR LOVE	III.1	616
Scandal:	No, no, you look much better.	270	FOR LOVE	III.1	644
Scandal:	Well, Is your Master ready; do's he look madly, and	275	FOR LOVE	IV.1	1
Sr Sampson:	plain as can be: Look you here (reads) The Condition of this	281	FOR LOVE	IV.1	221
Sr Sampson:	Obligation--Look you, as plain as can be, so it begins--	281	FOR LOVE	IV.1	222
Scandal:	and honour you.--You look pretty well, Mr. Foresight;--	284	FOR LOVE	IV.1	338
Ben:	look after a Husband; for my part I was none of her	285	FOR LOVE	IV.1	375
Valentine:	further; You look suspiciously. Are you a Husband?	289	FOR LOVE	IV.1	514
Valentine:	upon, and look Matrimony in the face. ha, ha, ha! That a	289	FOR LOVE	IV.1	526
Tattle:	Oh, Madam, look upon us both. There you see the ruins	291	FOR LOVE	IV.1	580
Tattle:	Look you, Mr. Foresight, It is not my way to make	291	FOR LOVE	IV.1	606
Valentine:	Scandal) What, do you look strange upon me?--Then	292	FOR LOVE	IV.1	618
Jeremy:	to look wild again now.	295	FOR LOVE	IV.1	748
Ben:	Look you, Friend, it's nothing to me, whether you	307	FOR LOVE	V.1	368
Tattle:	Look you there, I thought as much--pox on't, I	310	FOR LOVE	V.1	475
Ben:	Heart. Look you, Friend, if I may advise you, when she's	310	FOR LOVE	V.1	490
Leonora:	Look down good Heav'n, with Pity on her	329	M. BRIDE	I.1	149
Almeria:	Die ten thousand Deaths--Lock down, look down	330	M. BRIDE	I.1	176
Zara:	These Bonds, I look with loathing on my self;	336	M. BRIDE	I.1	400
Perez:	And every Look of his and hers confess it.	338	M. BRIDE	II.1	46
Perez:	And every Look from him and her confirms it.	338	M. BRIDE	II.1 V	46
Almeria:	And Monumental Caves of Death, look Cold,	339	M. BRIDE	II.1	65
Osmyn-Alph:	Look up Almeria, bless me with thy Eyes;	341	M. BRIDE	II.2	71
Osmyn-Alph:	Look on thy Love, thy Lover, and thy Husband,	341	M. BRIDE	II.2	72
Osmyn-Alph:	Look on Alphonso.	341	M. BRIDE	II.2 V	73
Osmyn-Alph:	Look on thy Alphonso.	341	M. BRIDE	II.2 V	76
Almeria:	Let me look on thee, yet a little more.	342	M. BRIDE	II.2	100
Almeria:	I will, for I should never look enough.	343	M. BRIDE	II.2	125
Osmyn-Alph:	Turn your Lights inward, Eyes, and look	345	M. BRIDE	II.2	215
Zara:	Disdains to listen now, or look on Zara.	346	M. BRIDE	II.2	251
Zara:	But with such dumb, and thankless Eyes you look;	346	M. BRIDE	II.2	256
Osmyn-Alph:	Look round; Joy is not here, nor Cheerfulness.	346	M. BRIDE	II.2	261
Osmyn-Alph:	Yet look for Gaiety and Gladness there.	346	M. BRIDE	II.2	263
Zara:	Look on me now, from Empire fall'n to Slavery;	347	M. BRIDE	II.2	303
Zara:	Think on my Suff'ring first, then, look on me;	347	M. BRIDE	II.2	304
Zara:	Reflect on Osmyn, and then look on Zara,	347	M. BRIDE	II.2	306
Zara:	'Tis that, I know; for thou dost look, with Eyes	348	M. BRIDE	II.2	343
Almeria:	And Look again, with Wishes in thy Eyes.	353	M. BRIDE	III.1	155
Almeria:	What dost thou think? Look not so tenderly	356	M. BRIDE	III.1	264
Almeria:	Thy Heart will burst, thy Eyes look red and start;	356	M. BRIDE	III.1	273
Osmyn-Alph:	Because not knowing Danger. But look forward;	358	M. BRIDE	III.1	342
Zara:	As you'll answer it, look, this Slave	360	M. BRIDE	III.1 V	447
Manuel:	What mean those swollen and redfleck'd Eyes, that look	367	M. BRIDE	IV.1	248
Manuel:	And lock thou answer me with truth: for know,	367	M. BRIDE	IV.1	263
Almeria:	Turn not your Eyes away--look on me kneeling;	369	M. BRIDE	IV.1	319
Manuel:	And look that she attempt not on her Life.	370	M. BRIDE	IV.1	366
Almeria:	See, see, look yonder! where a grizled, pale	371	M. BRIDE	IV.1	387
Manuel:	One moment's Ease? Hear my Command; and look	374	M. BRIDE	V.1	72
Selim:	Th' imperfect Look, and sternly turn'd away.	375	M. BRIDE	V.1	100
	(The Mutes return and look affrighted.)	380	M. BRIDE	V.2	156
Zara:	Still further from me; look, he hides his Face,	381	M. BRIDE	V.2	209
Leonora:	And look not on; for there's a Dagger that	381	M. BRIDE	V.2	229
Leonora:	Return and look not on; for there's a Dagger	381	M. BRIDE	V.2 V	229
Almeria:	--Those Men have left to weep; and look on me!	382	M. BRIDE	V.2	245
Almeria:	--Those Men have left to weep; they look on me!	382	M. BRIDE	V.2 V	245
Almeria:	I hope they murder all on whom they look.	382	M. BRIDE	V.2	246
	Look out when Storms arise, and Billows roar,	385	M. BRIDE	EPI.	20
Fainall:	you;--I'll look upon the Gamesters in the next Room.	397	WAY WORLD	I.1	100
Fainall:	Joy of your Success, Mirabell; you look pleas'd.	399	WAY WORLD	I.1	135
Mrs Fain:	(we ought to think at least) they loath; they look upon us	410	WAY WORLD	II.1	6
Marwood:	Enemies. Methinks you look a little pale, and now you	412	WAY WORLD	II.1	78

Look   (continued)
		PAGE	TITLE	ACT.SC	LINE
Fainall:	You don't look well to Day, Child.	412	WAY WORLD	II.1	89
Millamant:	one's Wit to an Eccho: They can but reflect what we look	420	WAY WORLD	II.1	410
Millamant:	Come, don't look grave then. Well, what do you	422	WAY WORLD	II.1	462
Millamant:	Sententious Mirabell! Prithee don't look with that	422	WAY WORLD	II.1	467
Lady Wish:	An errant Ash colour, as I'm a Person. Look you how this	425	WAY WORLD	III.1	6
Lady Wish:	then--(Exit Peg). I'm as pale and as faint, I look like	425	WAY WORLD	III.1	21
Lady Wish:	decay'd. Look Foible.	428	WAY WORLD	III.1	143
Lady Wish:	Why I am arrantly flea'd--I look like an old peel'd Wall.	429	WAY WORLD	III.1	148
Lady Wish:	look so--My Niece affects it; but she wants Features. Is	429	WAY WORLD	III.1	170
Lady Wish:	And--well--and how do I look, Foible?	445	WAY WORLD	IV.1	15
Sir Wilful:	Indeed! Hah! Look ye, look ye, you do? Nay,	448	WAY WORLD	IV.1	123
Millamant:	sawcy look of an assured man, Confident of Success. The	449	WAY WORLD	IV.1	178
Petulant:	Look you Mrs. Millamant,--If you can love me dear	453	WAY WORLD	IV.1	339
Sir Wilful:	she has her Maidenhead let her look to't,--if she has not,	456	WAY WORLD	IV.1	428
Sir Wilful:	it--wee'll open it together--look you here.	460	WAY WORLD	IV.1	583
Lady Wish:	(Reads)--Madam, tho' unknown to you (Look you there 'tis	460	WAY WORLD	IV.1	584
Marwood:	More Temper wou'd look more like Innocence. But I have	466	WAY WORLD	V.1	161
Sir Wilful:	Look up Man, I'll stand by you, 'sbud an she do	471	WAY WORLD	V.1	360

Look'd (9)
		PAGE	TITLE	ACT.SC	LINE
Bellmour:	--'till just now, (the first time I ever look'd upon the	82	OLD BATCH	IV.2	55
Mellefont:	What at first amaz'd me; for I lock'd to have seen	130	DOUBL DLR	I.1	103
Lady Touch:	seriously, but methought it look'd odly.	153	DOUBL DLR	III.1	85
Cynthia:	why have you look'd through the wrong end of the	168	DOUBL DLR	IV.1	24
Cynthia:	you have look'd through the wrong end of the	168	DOUBL DLR	IV.1 V	24
Lady Froth:	You know I told you Saturn look'd a little more	203	DOUBL DLR	V.1	579
Valentine:	was easily turn'd another way; and at least look'd well on	246	FOR LOVE	II.1	409
Scandal:	So was Valentine this Morning; and look'd just so.	268	FOR LOVE	III.1	570
Lady Wish:	--O, she never look'd a Man in the Face but her own	467	WAY WORLD	V.1	191

Looking (16)
		PAGE	TITLE	ACT.SC	LINE
Bellmour:	unmannerly and as unwelcome to a Woman, as a Looking	42	OLD BATCH	I.1	186
Heartwell:	(Looking on his Watch.)	46	OLD BATCH	I.1	333
Sharper:	I've lost. (Looking about as in search.)	48	OLD BATCH	II.1	24
Bellmour:	(Looking on his Watch.)	75	OLD BATCH	IV.1	2
Bellmour:	(Looking about, and gathering up his things.)	89	OLD BATCH	IV.4	14
Mellefont:	Maskwell! I have been looking for you--'tis	181	DOUBL DLR	IV.1	513
Saygrace:	(looking out). Sweet Sir, I will but pen the last Line	194	DOUBL DLR	V.1	272
Sir Paul:	with looking up?	201	DOUBL DLR	V.1	522
Foresight:	(looking in the Glass). I do not see any Revolution	269	FOR LOVE	III.1	600
Miss Prue:	you; I have been looking up and down for you like any	303	FOR LOVE	V.1	223
Ben:	Privateers were looking for a Prize, and should fall foul of	310	FOR LOVE	V.1	488
Almeria:	Looking Tranquility. It strikes an Awe	339	M. BRIDE	II.1	63
Mirabell:	One a Clock! (looking on his Watch) O y'are come--	398	WAY WORLD	I.1	109
Foible:	dress till I come--(Looking out.) O Dear, I'm sure	424	WAY WORLD	II.1	544
Peg:	Madam, I was looking for a Cup.	425	WAY WORLD	III.1	27
Sir Wilful:	have some other employment, besides looking on.	477	WAY WORLD	V.1	602

Looking-glass (3)
		PAGE	TITLE	ACT.SC	LINE
	(Enter Betty, with Hoods and				
	Looking-glass.)	57	OLD BATCH	II.2	90
Foresight:	Looking-glass.	269	FOR LOVE	III.1	583
Mirabell:	Cheat. The Ugly and the Old, whom the Looking-glass	420	WAY WORLD	II.1	395

Looks (29)
		PAGE	TITLE	ACT.SC	LINE
Bellmour:	Kind Looks and Actions(from Success)do prove,	60	OLD BATCH	II.2	225
Bellmour:	I doubt the Knight repents, Tom--He looks like	68	OLD BATCH	III.1	287
Capt Bluff:	(Looks big.)	70	OLD BATCH	III.1	355
Belinda:	rubb'd his Eyes, since break of Day neither, he looks as if	86	OLD BATCH	IV.3	130
Belinda:	friends with him.--I swear, he looks so very simply,	86	OLD BATCH	IV.3	130
Sir Joseph:	Prithee, What do you see in my face, that looks as	101	OLD BATCH	V.1	191
Belinda:	any body else. Jesus! how he looks already. Ha, ha, ha.	108	OLD BATCH	V.2	31
Belinda:	any body else. How he looks already. Ha, ha, ha.	108	OLD BATCH	V.2 V	31
	(Takes out a Pocket-Glass, and looks in it.)	134	DOUBL DLR	I.1	290
	(Takes the Glass and looks.	135	DOUBL DLR	I.1	294
	(Squeezes him by the hand, looks kindly on him, sighs, and	140	DOUBL DLR	II.1	65
Maskwell:	Ha, ha, ha, how gravely he looks--Come, come, I	157	DOUBL DLR	III.1	243
Sir Paul:	pound a Year upon the Rogue as soon as ever he looks me	173	DOUBL DLR	IV.1	225
Lady Ply:	and he looks charmingly, and he has charm'd me, as much as I	174	DOUBL DLR	IV.1	260
Lady Touch:	what he does--see how wild he looks.	186	DOUBL DLR	IV.2	114
Jeremy:	terrify'd Countenance, that looks as if he had written for	219	FOR LOVE	I.1	105
Scandal:	Man of small Fortune? Why, he looks like a Writ of Enquiry	219	FOR LOVE	I.1	133
Foresight:	By your Looks, you shou'd go up Stairs out of the	245	FOR LOVE	II.1	383
Mrs Frail:	--she looks so wholsome;--ne're stir, I don't	250	FOR LOVE	II.1	557
Mrs Frail:	(Looks kindly on him.)	265	FOR LOVE	III.1	451
Scandal:	looks better than he did.	270	FOR LOVE	III.1	627
Valentine:	Any thing, my Friend, every thing that looks like	313	FOR LOVE	V.1	602
Manuel:	It looks as thou didst mourn for him: Just as	333	M. BRIDE	I.1	298
Gonsalez:	Of his Arrogance yet; she looks concern'd.	337	M. BRIDE	I.1	444
Gonsalez:	His arrogant Reply; she looks concern'd.	337	M. BRIDE	I.1 V444	
Zara:	He Looks not, minds not, hears not; barbarous Man!	346	M. BRIDE	II.2	244
Gonsalez:	(Looks in.)	376	M. BRIDE	V.2	5
Zara:	With frightful Faces, and the meagre Looks	379	M. BRIDE	V.2	140
Millamant:	looks as if he thought so too--Well, you ridiculous	452	WAY WORLD	IV.1	294

Loos'd (1)
		PAGE	TITLE	ACT.SC	LINE
Zara:	Ev'n then. Kneeling on Earth, I loos'd my Hair,	346	M. BRIDE	II.2	281

Loose (8)
		PAGE	TITLE	ACT.SC	LINE
Bellmour:	ever he was loose, he ran away, without staying to see who	46	OLD BATCH	I.1	363
	loose about the Chamber.)	89	OLD BATCH	IV.4	
Heli:	Secure and loose in friendly Solitude.	338	M. BRIDE	II.1	32
Almeria:	No, never will I rise, nor loose this Hold,	369	M. BRIDE	IV.1	330
Perez:	As loose the rivets of his bonds.	372	M. BRIDE	V.1 V 10	
Almeria:	The Source of Woe, and let the Torrent loose.	382	M. BRIDE	V.2	244
Marwood:	Hands, do--I'd leave 'em to get loose.	416	WAY WORLD	II.1	226
Mincing:	have him I think, rather than loose such a vast Summ as	465	WAY WORLD	V.1	115

Lord (240)
		PAGE	TITLE	ACT.SC	LINE
	O Lord, for Heavens sake excuse the Play,	35	OLD BATCH	PRO.	23
Heartwell:	Lord what d'ee-cals Mouth to a Tittle--Then I to put it	45	OLD BATCH	I.1	324
Sir Joseph:	Poor Gentleman--by the Lord Harry I'le stay no	48	OLD BATCH	II.1	25

Lord   (continued)

Sir Joseph:	O Lord forget him! No no Sir, I don't forget you-- . . .	48	OLD BATCH	II.1	40
Sir Joseph:	O Lord Sir!	49	OLD BATCH	II.1	75
Sir Joseph:	O Lord Sir.	50	OLD BATCH	II.1	99
Sir Joseph:	O Lord Sir by no means--but I might have sav'd a . .	51	OLD BATCH	II.1	128
Capt Bluff:	O Lord I beg ycur pardon Sir, I find you are not of . .	51	OLD BATCH	II.1	162
Sir Joseph:	by the Lord Harry he says true; Fighting, is Meat, Drink	52	OLD BATCH	II.1	167
Sir Joseph:	well--Ey the Lord Harry Mr. Sharper he's as brave a .	52	OLD EATCH	II.1	175
Capt Bluff:	Yet by the Lord Harry 'tis true Mr. Sharper, for I .	53	OLD BATCH	II.1	207
Sir Joseph:	Lord Harry, I have seen it.	53	OLD BATCH	II.1	233
Lucy:	Lord does his Mercers Bill, or a begging Dedication; .	61	OLD EATCH	III.1	22
Sir Joseph:	O Lord, O Lord, Captain, come justifie your	69	OLD BATCH	III.1	306
Sir Joseph:	O Lord his Anger was not raised before--Nay, . . .	70	OLD BATCH	III.1	339
Sir Joseph:	I grant you--Not to that Face by the Lord Harry--If .	70	OLD BATCH	III.1	357
Lucy:	Lord, Madam, I met your Lover in as much haste, as . .	74	OLD BATCH	III.2	147
Belinda:	World that I like.--Oh Lord, walk this way.--I . .	87	OLD BATCH	IV.3	149
Belinda:	O Lord, No, I'll go along with her. Come, Mr. . . .	88	OLD BATCH	IV.3	209
Sir Joseph:	O Lord! Oh terrible! Ha, ha, ha, Is your Wife . . .	90	OLD BATCH	IV.4	55
Fondlewife:	Adultery, and innocent! O Lord! Here's Doctrine! .	92	OLD BATCH	IV.4	112
Fondlewife:	O Lord! O strange! I am in admiration of your . . .	93	OLD BATCH	IV.4	153
Lucy:	How! O Lord!--	98	OLD BATCH	V.1	56
Setter:	O Lord, Sir!	100	OLD BATCH	V.1	159
Sir Joseph:	see:--But, by the Lord Harry, I'll leave you. . . .	101	OLD BATCH	V.1	185
Setter:	O Lord, Sir, What d'ye mean? Corrupt my honesty. .	103	OLD EATCH	V.1	247
Sir Joseph:	Ah! O Lord, my heart akes--Ah! Setter, a	110	OLD EATCH	V.2	118
	(A Gallery in the Lord Touchwood's House, ...	127	DOUBL DLR	I.1	
Brisk:	I shall burst else.--And yonder your Uncle my Lord .	128	DOUEL DLR	I.1	53
Brisk:	threatens to disclaim you for a Son-in-Law, and my Lord	128	DOUEL DLR	I.1	55
Mellefont:	For my Lord Froth, he and his Wife will be sufficiently	130	DOUEL DLR	I.1	133
	(Enter Lord Touchwood, Lord Froth, Sir Paul Plyant, .	131	DOUEL DLR	I.1	170
Sir Paul:	And, my Lord Froth, your Lordship is so merry a Man, .	132	DOUBL DLR	I.1	183
Brisk:	How? how, my Lord? What, affront my Wit! Let . .	132	DOUBL DLR	I.1	194
Brisk:	Ay, my Lord, it's a sign I hit you in the Teeth, if you	132	DOUBL DLR	I.1	210
	(Exit Lord Touchwood and Sir Paul.)	133	DOUEL DLR	I.1	221
Mellefont:	You are Cruel to your self, my Lord, as well as . .	133	DOUEL DLR	I.1	233
Brisk:	Let me perish, my Lord, but there is something very .	133	DOUEL DLR	I.1	237
Brisk:	O Lord, why can't you find it out?--Why there . .	133	DOUEL DLR	I.1	248
Brisk:	--My Lcrd, Careless, is a very honest Fellow, but . .	133	DCUEL DLR	I.1	250
Brisk:	Pooh, my Lord, his Voice goes fcr nothing.--I . .	134	DOUEL DLR	I.1	276
Mellefont:	Shall we go to the Ladies, my Lord?	134	DCUEL DLR	I.1	283
Brisk:	Let me see, let me see, my Lord, I broke my Glass that	135	DOUEL DLR	I.1	291
Lady Touch:	Have you not wrcng'd my Lord, who has	135	DOUEL DLR	I.1	309
Lady Touch:	effect made you Lcrd of all, of me, and of my Lord? .	136	DOUEL DLR	I.1	349
Cynthia:	O Lord, not I, Madam; I'm content to be a	139	DOUBL DLR	II.1	18
Lady Froth:	Lord and I had been both of your Temper, we had never .	139	DOUEL DLR	II.1	21
Lady Froth:	would that have been, if my Lord and I should never .	139	DOUEL DLR	II.1	23
Cynthia:	Then neither my Lord and ycu would ever have . . .	139	DOUEL DLR	II.1	25
Cynthia:	Then neither my Lord nor you would ever have . . .	139	DOUEL DLR	II.1 V	25
Lady Froth:	say'st right--for sure my Lord Froth is as fine a Gentleman,	139	DOUBL DLR	II.1	28
Lady Froth:	Complaisance of my Lord, or something of his own, that should	139	DOUEL DLR	II.1	50
Lady Froth:	And my Lord with him: pray observe the	139	DOUEL DLR	II.1	55
	(Enter Lord Froth, Mellefont, Brisk.) . . .	139	DOUEL DLR	II.1	57
Lady Froth:	My Lord, I have been telling my dear Cynthia, . . .	140	DOUBL DLR	II.1	60
Lady Froth:	My Lord, I have been telling Cynthia, ...	140	DOUBL DLR	II.1 V	60
Lady Froth:	leap, I vow I sigh when I think on't: my dear Lord! ha,	140	DOUBL DLR	II.1	63
Lady Froth:	ha, ha, do you remember, my Lord?	140	DOUBL DLR	II.1	64
Lady Froth:	then your Bow! Good my Lord, bow as you did when I .	140	DOUBL DLR	II.1	73
Lady Froth:	Pray mind, my Lord; ah! he bows Charmingly; nay, my .	140	DOUBL DLR	II.1	76
Lady Froth:	Lord you sha'n't kiss it so much; I shall grcw jealous,	140	DOUBL DLR	II.1	77
Lady Froth:	Lord you shan't kiss it so much; I shall grow jealous, I	140	DOUBL DLR	II.1 V	77
Lady Froth:	Lord?	140	DOUBL DLR	II.1	83
Brisk:	O Lord, Madam--	140	DOUEL DLR	II.1	89
Cynthia:	I vow, my Lord, I think you the happiest Couple in .	141	DOUBL DLR	II.1	96
Cynthia:	'Tis my Interest to believe he will, my Lord. . .	141	DOUBL DLR	II.1	101
Mellefont:	Ay, my Lord, I shall have the same reason for my . .	141	DOUBL DLR	II.1	111
Brisk:	but when I do--keen Iambicks I'gad. But my Lord . .	141	DOUBL DLR	II.1	117
Lady Froth:	Did my Lord tell you? Yes I vow, and the Subject . .	141	DOUBL DLR	II.1	120
Lady Froth:	He, Ay, is not it?--and then I call my Lord . . .	141	DOUBL DLR	II.1	126
Lady Froth:	and Horace.--My Lord you must not be Jealous, I'm .	142	DOUBL DLR	II.1	139
Mellefont:	Musick!--Oh, my Lord has promised the Company a . .	143	DOUBL DLR	II.1	172
Lady Ply:	O Lord, ask me the question, I'll swear I'll . . .	147	DOUBL DLR	II.1	332
Lady Ply:	necessity--O Lord, here's some body coming, I dare . .	148	DOUBL DLR	II.1	362
Lady Ply:	think that I'll grant you any thing; O Lord, no,--but .	148	DOUBL DLR	II.1	366
Lady Ply:	Passion to me; yet it will make me jealous,--O Lord, .	148	DOUBL DLR	II.1	369
	(Enter Lord Touchwood, and Lady Touchwcod.) . . .	150	DOUBL DLR	III.1	
Lady Touch:	My Lord, can you blame my Brother	150	DOUBL DLR	III.1	1
Lady Touch:	You censure hardly, my Lord; my Sister's	151	DOUBL DLR	III.1	11
Lady Touch:	Nay, my Lord, it may be so, and I hope it	151	DOUBL DLR	III.1	16
Lady Touch:	Lord?	151	DOUBL DLR	III.1	28
Lady Touch:	disadvantage; besides, I find, my Lord, you are prepared	151	DOUBL DLR	III.1	36
Lady Touch:	--Don't ask me my Reasons, my Lord, for they are . .	151	DOUBL DLR	III.1	42
Lady Touch:	willing to have remote from your hearing. Good my Lord,	152	DOUBL DLR	III.1	51
Lady Touch:	Nay, my Lord, you need say no more, to	152	DOUBL DLR	III.1	64
Lady Touch:	Dear. Nay, by this kiss you shan't be angry. O Lord, I	152	DOUBL DLR	III.1	68
Lady Touch:	wish I had not tcld you any thing.--Indeed, my Lord, .	152	DOUBL DLR	III.1	69
Lady Touch:	Lord--Ha, ha, ha. Well but that's all--now you have .	153	DOUBL DLR	III.1	90
Lady Touch:	it; well remember your promise, my Lord, and don't .	153	DOUBL DLR	III.1	91
Lady Touch:	O for Heaven's sake, my Lord, you'll ruine . . .	153	DOUBL DLR	III.1	103
Lady Touch:	Lord, I don't know: I wish my Lips had	153	DOUBL DLR	III.1	109
Lady Touch:	self. Pray, my Lord, don't let the Company see you in this	153	DOUBL DLR	III.1	112
Lady Touch:	the Ccmpany, and come to you. Pray, good dear my Lord,	153	DOUBL DLR	III.1	118
Lady Touch:	you all; will you, my Lord?	153	DOUBL DLR	III.1	120
	(Exit Lord Touchwood.) . .	154	DOUBL DLR	III.1	125
Lady Touch:	the Ccmpany break up; lest my Lord should cool, and .	154	DOUBL DLR	III.1	143
Lady Touch:	Lord must not see him again.	154	DOUBL DLR	III.1	145

Lord   (continued)

Lord (continued)

		PAGE	TITLE	ACT.SC	LINE
Nurse:	cry husht--O Lord, who's there? (peeps) What's here	253	FOR LOVE	III.1	7
Nurse:	O Lord, We're all undone--O you young Harlotry	253	FOR LOVE	III.1	10
Miss Prue:	O Lord, she's coming--and she'll tell my	253	FOR LOVE	III.1	15
Tattle:	O Lord! yes indeed, Madam, several times.	255	FOR LOVE	III.1	79
Tattle:	Yes, I vow and swear I have: Lord, Madam, I'm the	255	FOR LOVE	III.1	81
Mrs Frail:	Lord, what shall we do, there's my Brother	265	FOR LOVE	III.1	446
Foresight:	hope, neither the Lord of my Ascendant, nor the Moon	270	FOR LOVE	III.1	648
Mrs Fore:	O Lord, who's here?	272	FOR LOVE	III.1	711
Buckram:	O Lord, what must I say?--Yes, Sir.	280	FOR LOVE	IV.1	170
Buckram:	O Lord, let me be gone; I'll not venture my self	282	FOR LOVE	IV.1	243
Ben:	O Lord, O Lord, she's mad, poor Young Woman, Love	286	FOR LOVE	IV.1	403
Mrs Frail:	O Lord, what must I say?	290	FOR LOVE	IV.1	539
Mrs Frail:	(to Jeremy). O Lord, her coming will spoil all.	291	FOR LOVE	IV.1	590
Tattle:	O Lord!	292	FOR LOVE	IV.1	644
Jeremy:	O Lord, Madam, did you ever know any Madman	295	FOR LOVE	IV.1	743
Sr Sampson:	and I'm Lord of the Ascendant. Odd, you're an old Fellow,	307	FOR LOVE	V.1	382
Almeria:	My Love, my Lord, my Husband still, though lost.	328	M. BRIDE	I.1	76
Almeria:	For when my Lord beheld the Ship pursuing,	329	M. BRIDE	I.1	134
Almeria:	Another Lord; may then just Heav'n show'r down	330	M. BRIDE	I.1	187
Alonzo:	The Lord Gonsalez comes to tell your Highness	331	M. BRIDE	I.1	209
Gonsalez:	Your Royal Father, my Victorious Lord,	331	M. BRIDE	I.1	224
Almeria:	My Lord, my Eyes ungratefully behold	332	M. BRIDE	I.1	246
Manuel:	Receive this Lord, as one whom I have found	334	M. BRIDE	I.1	333
Garcia:	My Lord, she did.	335	M. BRIDE	I.1	378
Perez:	Yonder, my Lord, behold the Noble Moor.	338	M. BRIDE	II.1	16
Heli:	My Lord, let me entreat you to forbear:	338	M. BRIDE	II.1	25
Zara:	Waiting my Nod, the Creature of my Lord,	349	M. BRIDE	II.2	365
Heli:	My Lord, require you should compose your self,	352	M. BRIDE	III.1	93
Gonsalez:	My Lord, the Queen advises well.	365	M. BRIDE	IV.1	156
Alonzo:	I have, my Lord.	372	M. BRIDE	IV.1	435
Perez:	None, my Lord.	372	M. BRIDE	V.1	5
Perez:	My Lord.	373	M. BRIDE	V.1	38
Perez:	My Lord, I will.	374	M. BRIDE	V.1	76
Alonzo:	My Lord, he enter'd, but a moment since,	376	M. BRIDE	V.2	20
Alonzo:	My Lord, My Lord, what, hoa? My Lord Gonsalez?	376	M. BRIDE	V.2	22
Alonzo:	My Lord, for certain truth, Perez is fled;	377	M. BRIDE	V.2	48
Alonzo:	My Lord, I've thought how to conceal the Body;	378	M. BRIDE	V.2	96
Almeria:	This is my Lord, my Life, my only Husband.	383	M. BRIDE	V.2	297
Millamant:	Long! Lord, have I not made violent haste? I	419	WAY WORLD	II.1	346
Millamant:	Lord, what is a Lover, that it can give? Why one makes	420	WAY WORLD	II.1	403
Peg:	Lord, Madam, your Ladyship is so impatient--I cannot	425	WAY WORLD	III.1	17
Millamant:	Dee hear the Creature? Lord, here's Company,	436	WAY WORLD	IV.1	434

Lord-Harry (2)

		PAGE	TITLE	ACT.SC	LINE
Sir Joseph:	Lord-Harry. I know better things than to be run through	67	OLD BATCH	III.1	253
Sir Joseph:	Hey-day! Traytor yourself.--By the Lord-Harry,	90	OLD BATCH	IV.4	61

Lord's (5)

		PAGE	TITLE	ACT.SC	LINE
Lady Froth:	is my Lord's Love to me. And what do you think I	141	DOUBL DLR	II.1	121
Brisk:	Because my Lord's Title's Froth, I'gad, ha, ha, ha,	141	DOUBL DLR	II.1	124
Maskwell:	Lord's Displeasure to a degree that will admit of no	154	DOUBL DLR	III.1	147
Maskwell:	It will confirm my Lord's opinion of my Honour	154	DOUBL DLR	III.1	157
Maskwell:	suspected, that it shall be got ready by my Lord's own	193	DOUBL DLR	V.1	211

Lords (7)

		PAGE	TITLE	ACT.SC	LINE
Fondlewife:	trust my Wife, with a Lords high-fed Chaplain.	76	OLD BATCH	IV.1	33
Maskwell:	My Lady is just gone down from my Lords Closet,	181	DOUBL DLR	IV.1	515
Maskwell:	My Lady is just gone into my Lords Closet,	181	DOUBL DLR	IV.1	V515
Maskwell:	my Lords absence all this while, and will to her Chamber	181	DOUBL DLR	IV.1	523
Maskwell:	my Lords absence all this while, she'll retire to her Chamber	181	DOUBL DLR	IV.1	V523
Maskwell:	you, Borrow my Lords Chaplain, and so run away with	193	DOUBL DLR	V.1	224
Manuel:	This Tumult, and the Lords who fled with Heli,	366	M. BRIDE	IV.1	215

Lordship (15)

		PAGE	TITLE	ACT.SC	LINE
Sir Paul:	And, my Lord Froth, your Lordship is so merry a Man,	132	DOUBL DLR	I.1	183
Mellefont:	But does your Lordship never see Comedies?	133	DOUBL DLR	I.1	222
Mellefont:	happiness that your Lordship has, I shall think my self	141	DOUBL DLR	II.1	112
Maskwell:	not succeeded, to have informed your Lordship of what I	182	DOUBL DLR	IV.1	579
Maskwell:	Lordship will meet me a quarter of an Hour hence there,	183	DOUBL DLR	IV.1	584
Maskwell:	My Duty to your Lordship, makes me do a severe	183	DOUBL DLR	IV.1	588
Maskwell:	I am concern'd to see your Lordship discomposed--	195	DOUBL DLR	V.1	305
Maskwell:	(aside). This I fear'd. Did not your Lordship tell	195	DOUBL DLR	V.1	312
Maskwell:	your Lordship--but it may be as well done to night.	196	DOUBL DLR	V.1	328
Cynthia:	Your Lordship was thoughtful.	197	DOUBL DLR	V.1	364
Cynthia:	They'll wait upon your Lordship presently.	202	DOUBL DLR	V.1	553
Alonzo:	The King expects your Lordship.	371	M. BRIDE	IV.1	419
Alonzo:	If't please your Lordship, I'll return, and say	371	M. BRIDE	IV.1	422
Alonzo:	All that it can, your Lordship shall command.	372	M. BRIDE	IV.1	431
Alonzo:	Conclude it done. Where shall I wait your Lordship?	372	M. BRIDE	IV.1	440

Lordship's (2)

		PAGE	TITLE	ACT.SC	LINE
Maskwell:	Lordship's Servant.	181	DOUBL DLR	IV.1	539
Maskwell:	I am confounded, and beg your Lordship's pardon	189	DOUBL DLR	V.1	50

Lordships (5)

		PAGE	TITLE	ACT.SC	LINE
Mellefont:	I beg your Lordships Pardon--We were just	131	DOUBL DLR	I.1	175
Sir Paul:	Brisk Jokes, your Lordships Laugh does so become you,	132	DOUBL DLR	I.1	188
Careless:	I find a Quibble bears more sway in your Lordships	132	DOUBL DLR	I.1	214
Maskwell:	I am happy to be in the way of your Lordships	181	DOUBL DLR	IV.1	533
Mellefont:	We are your Lordships Creatures.	203	DOUBL DLR	V.1	585

Lose (20)

		PAGE	TITLE	ACT.SC	LINE
Sharper:	me to lose what was ventur'd in your service; Nay 'twas	50	OLD BATCH	II.1	101
Sharper:	hundred Pound to lose? (Angrily.)	50	OLD BATCH	II.1	127
Heartwell:	on't--I'le run into the danger to lose the	63	OLD BATCH	III.1	85
Barnaby:	And run the hazard to lose your affair so!	76	OLD BATCH	IV.1	38
Barnaby:	And run the hazard to lose your affair, Sir!	76	OLD BATCH	IV.1	V 38
Fondlewife:	buss poor Nykin--And I wont leave thee--I'le lose all first.	78	OLD BATCH	IV.1	118
Mellefont:	because it's possible we may lose; since we have Shuffled	142	DOUBL DLR	II.1	160
Singer:	But much more, to lose her Lover:	143	DOUBL DLR	II.1	182
Lady Touch:	make you lose one minutes temper. 'Tis not indeed, my	152	DOUBL DLR	III.1	67

Lose   (continued)
  Mellefont: sight, and to lose so much time as to write to her.   . . 159 DOUBL DLR III.1 318
  Maskwell: would not lose his Speech, upon condition to have Joys . 184 DOUBL DLR IV.2   26
  Valentine: play at Losing Loadum; you must lose a good Name to . 226 FOR LOVE   I.1 389
  Tattle: lose my Reputation of Secresie for ever--I shall never . 230 FOR LOVE   I.1 515
  Mrs Fore: you lose this Gold Bodkin?--Oh Sister, Sister! . . . 248 FOR LOVE II.1 466
  Angelica: he won't recover his Senses till I lose mine. . . 277 FOR LOVE IV.1   76
             He wou'd not lose thro' Prejudice his Cause; . . . . 324 M. BRIDE   PRO.   41
             And in Parnassus he must lose his Seat, ... 393 WAY WORLD PRO.   20
  Waitwell: To lose my Title, and yet keep my Wife. . . . . 424 WAY WORLD III.1 563
  Fainall: of Play, that I should lose to one, who has not . . 443 WAY WORLD III.1 688
  Mrs Fain: Nay, I'll swear you shall never lose so favourable . . 447 WAY WORLD IV.1   87

Loser (1)
  Cynthia: be a Loser. . . . . 143 DOUBL DLR II.1 169

Losers (1)
             Since Custome gives the Losers leave to speak. . . . 323 M. BRIDE   PRO.   28

Loses (3)
  Singer: And not Winning, thus she loses. . . . . 143 DOUBL DLR II.1 184
  Valentine: that loses hope may part with any thing. I never valu'd . 312 FOR LOVE   V.1 544
  Mirabell: diminish in their value, and that both the giver loses the 449 WAY WORLD IV.1 172

Losing (5)
  Vainlove: a Venture which he's in danger of losing. Read, read. . 39 OLD BATCH I.1   81
  Maskwell: full fruition of my Love, I'll bear the railings of a losing 190 DOUBL DLR V.1   87
  Scandal: Or win a Mistress, with a losing hand. . . . . 234 FOR LOVE   I.1 681
  Angelica: of losing me: For you know he has long pretended a . . 300 FOR LOVE   V.1 111
  Fainall: losing Gamester lessens the Pleasure of the Winner: I'd no 395 WAY WORLD I.1   7

Losing Loadum (1)
  Valentine: play at Losing Loadum; you must lose a good Name to . 226 FOR LOVE   I.1 389

Loss (22)
  Sir Joseph: found nothing but what has been to my loss, as I may say,   48 OLD BATCH II.1   30
  Sir Joseph: I rejoyce! agad not I Sir; I'me sorry for your loss,   . 48 OLD BATCH II.1   35
  Sir Joseph: I rejoyce! agad not I Sir; I'me very sorry for your loss, 48 OLD BATCH II.1 V 35
  Sharper: My loss, I esteem as a trifle repay'd with interest,   . 49 OLD BATCH II.1   76
  Sir Joseph: may be so bold, what is that loss you mention? . . 49 OLD BATCH II.1   80
  Sharper: Were it not Loss of Time, you should make the . . . 100 OLD BATCH V.1 144
  Sir Joseph: and to speak, is but loss of time; but if there be occasion, 103 OLD BATCH V.1 244
  Sharper: to forgive the loss of his Mistress.--I know not how . 111 OLD BATCH V.2 122
  Sharper: Heartwell may take the loss of his Wife. . . . . 111 OLD BATCH V.2 123
             If loss of that should follow want of Wit, . . . 113 OLD BATCH EPI.   13
  Maskwell: Guilt is ever at a loss and confusion waits upon it, . 184 DOUBL DLR IV.2   19
  Mellefont: 'Tis loss of time--I cannot think him false. . . 197 DOUBL DLR V.1 354
  Mrs Frail: a loss, and have no great Stock either of Fortune or
             Reputation; . . . . 248 FOR LOVE II.1 490
  Sr Sampson: but a new Tax, and the loss of the Canary Fleet. . . 266 FOR LOVE III.1 486
  Sr Sampson: but a new Tax, or the loss of the Canary Fleet. . . 266 FOR LOVE III.1 V486
  Almeria: For to have known my Loss, thou must have known . . 328 M. BRIDE   I.1 102
  Leonora: And I have heard imperfectly his Loss; . . . . . 328 M. BRIDE   I.1 106
  Gonsalez: One 'pointed Hour should be Alphonso's Loss, . . . 333 M. BRIDE   I.1 305
  Zara: Of not revenging on his Foes, that Loss, ... 337 M. BRIDE   I.1 439
  Zara: But what is Loss of Honour, Fame and Empire? . . . 345 M. BRIDE II.2 237
  Fainall: I'd make Love to a Woman who undervalu'd the Loss of . 395 WAY WORLD I.1   9
  Fainall: with a little Loss, than to be quite eaten up, with being 400 WAY WORLD I.1 208

Lost (53)
  Vainlove: or be lost. . . . .   37 OLD BATCH I.1   8
  Bellmour: Friend, be close pursued, or lost. Business is the rub of
             Life, ...   37 OLD BATCH I.1   10
  Sharper: No, 'tis gone, 'tis lost--ten thousand Devils on that .   48 OLD BATCH II.1   21
  Sharper: I've lost.   (Looking about as in search.)   48 OLD BATCH II.1   24
  Sir Joseph: been long acquainted; you have lost a good Jest for want . 50 OLD BATCH II.1 117
  Bellmour: thou hast lost it. Ha, ha, how a' strugled, like an Old . 63 OLD BATCH III.1 91
  Bellmour: thou hast lost it. Ha, ha, how he strugled, like an Old . 63 OLD BATCH III.1 V 91
  Setter: Setter what a treasure is here lost for want of being known. 65 OLD BATCH III.1 153
  Sharper: How! Araminta lost! . . . . 79 OLD BATCH IV.1 153
  Sharper: Lost! Pray Heaven thou hast not lost thy Wits. . . . 79 OLD BATCH IV.1 163
  Vainlove: Pox o' my sawcy Credulity.--If I have lost . . . 100 OLD BATCH V.1 125
  Maskwell: enough. Pox I have lost all Appetite to her; yet she's a
             fine . . . . 155 DOUBL DLR III.1 175
  Sir Paul: all my hopes lost--My Heart would break, and my . . 174 DOUBL DLR IV.1 253
  Maskwell: But should it be known! then I have lost a Friend! . . 188 DOUBL DLR V.1   22
  Lady Touch: my designs are lost, my Love unsated, my Revenge unfinished, 191 DOUBL DLR V.1 155
             Till Dice are thrown, there's nothing won, nor lost. . 204 DOUBL DLR EPI.   5
             Their Labours lost upon the ungrateful Ground, . . 213 FOR LOVE PRO.   8
             Their Labours lost upon ungratefull Ground, . . . 213 FOR LOVE PRO. V 8
  Snap: block up the Chocolate-Houses, and then our labour's lost. 224 FOR LOVE   I.1 299
  Angelica: Spoons, and thought they were lost. Away went Religion . 237 FOR LOVE II.1   90
  Jeremy: Would you could, Sir; for he has lost himself. Indeed, . 279 FOR LOVE IV.1 130
  Mrs Frail: What, has my Sea-Lover lost his Anchor of Hope . . . 283 FOR LOVE IV.1 302
  Valentine: Between Pleasure and Amazement, I am lost-- . . . 312 FOR LOVE   V.1 565
             But there's the Devil, tho' their Cause is lost, . . 323 M. BRIDE   PRO.   25
  Almeria: My Love, my Lord, my Husband still, though lost. . . 328 M. BRIDE   I.1   76
  Zara: That Gallant Moor, in Battle lost a Friend . . . 337 M. BRIDE   I.1 437
  Almeria: Are lost in dread of greater Ill. Shew me, . . . 339 M. BRIDE II.1   80
  Almeria: Are lost in dread of greater Ill. Then shew me, . 339 M. BRIDE II.1 V 80
  Zara: For Fame, for Honour, and for Empire lost? . . . 345 M. BRIDE II.2 236
  Zara: Yes, Traytor, Zara; lost, abandon'd Zara, . . . 346 M. BRIDE II.2 248
  Osmyn-Alph: Lost in my self, and blinded by my Thoughts, . . . 346 M. BRIDE II.2 253
  Zara: On to this Invasion; where he was lost, ... 347 M. BRIDE II.2 301
  Zara: To this Invasion; where he late was lost, . . . 347 M. BRIDE II.2 V301
  Zara: Where all is lost, and I am made a Slave. . . . 347 M. BRIDE II.2 302
  Zara: The fall'n, the lost, the Captive Zara. . . . 347 M. BRIDE II.2 307
  Zara: The fall'n, the lost, and now the Captive Zara. . 347 M. BRIDE II.2 V307
  Zara: That to have lov'd thee, makes me yet more lost . . 348 M. BRIDE II.2 338
  Zara: To give, than I've already lost. But as . . . 355 M. BRIDE III.1 216
  Zara: To give, than I've already lost. But now . . . 355 M. BRIDE III.1 V216
  Osmyn-Alph: But knowing Heav'n, to know it lost for ever. . . 358 M. BRIDE III.1 366
  Osmyn-Alph: We are lost! undone! discover'd! . . . . 359 M. BRIDE III.1 386

Lost (continued)

Almeria:	Oh I am lost--there, Fate begins to wound.	368	M. BRIDE	IV.1	299
Zara:	In executing, puzzled, lame and lost.	375	M. BRIDE	V.1	112
Garcia:	All's lost, all ruin'd by Surprize and Treachery.	376	M. BRIDE	V.2	18
Garcia:	Granada's lost; and to confirm this Fear,	377	M. BRIDE	V.2	37
Zara:	Ha! prostrate! bloody! headless! O--I'm lost,	380	M. BRIDE	V.2	V162
Witwoud:	lost my Comparison for want of Breath.	418	WAY WORLD	II.1	332
Mirabell:	vain how lost a Thing you'll be! Nay, 'tis true: You are no	420	WAY WORLD	II.1	391
Mirabell:	longer handsome when you've lost your Lover; your	420	WAY WORLD	II.1	392
Lady Wish:	Foible's a lost Thing; has been abroad since	426	WAY WORLD	III.1	45
Millamant:	I am a lost thing;--for I find I love him violently.	453	WAY WORLD	IV.1	316
Mirabell:	enough, that I have lost what in my heart I hold most dear,	472	WAY WORLD	V.1	388

Loth (1)

Trapland:	Sincerely, I am loth to be thus pressing, but my	224	FOR LOVE	I.1	322

Lottery (3)

Jeremy:	ruin'd more Young Men than the Royal Oak Lottery--	218	FOR LOVE	I.1	88
Tattle:	turn of good Fortune, in the Lottery of Wives; and promise	304	FOR LOVE	V.1	269
Lady Wish:	Prodigal's in Debt as much as the Million Lottery, or the	428	WAY WORLD	III.1	133

Loud (8)

Sir Joseph:	Nay, Don't speak so loud.--I don't jest, as I	101	OLD BATCH	V.1	171
Sir Joseph:	Prithee, don't speak so loud.	101	OLD BATCH	V.1	179
Sir Paul:	loud.	159	DOUBL DLR	III.1	335
Lord Froth:	Loud, and that gang.	162	DOUBL DLR	III.1	462
Cynthia:	I heard him loud as I came by the Closet-Door, and	167	DOUBL DLR	IV.1	1
Lady Froth:	loud?--	176	DOUBL DLR	IV.1	320
Osmyn-Alph:	Deaf to revenge, and the loud Crys of my	351	M. BRIDE	III.1	75
Marwood:	loud Flounder-man's	468	WAY WORLD	V.1	234

Louse (0)   see Wood-louse

Lov'd (39)

Silvia:	Indeed if I were well assur'd you lov'd; but how can I	73	OLD BATCH	III.2	74
Silvia:	dont I know my Father lov'd my Mother, and was married	73	OLD BATCH	III.2	101
Heartwell:	lov'd; but that fashion is chang'd, Child.	73	OLD BATCH	III.2	104
Maskwell:	your self, and hear me. You know you Lov'd your	136	DOUBL DLR	I.1	360
Maskwell:	an Argument that I Lov'd; for with that Art you veil'd	136	DOUBL DLR	I.1	362
Maskwell:	Minute, and was blest. How I have Lov'd you since,	137	DOUBL DLR	I.1	370
Lady Ply:	lov'd you tenderly--'tis a barbarity of barbarities, and	146	DOUBL DLR	II.1	291
Maskwell:	Woman, and I lov'd her once. But I don't know, since I	155	DOUBL DLR	III.1	176
Maskwell:	Woman, I lov'd her once. But I don't know, since I	155	DOUBL DLR	III.1	V176
Cynthia:	sure she lov'd him.	171	DOUBL DLR	IV.1	162
Maskwell:	thought a vent; which might discover that I lov'd, nor	188	DOUBL DLR	V.1	35
Maskwell:	lov'd Embraces, could e're be fond of an inferiour Slavery.	198	DOUBL DLR	V.1	426
Mellefont:	Good Heavens! how I believ'd and Lov'd this	202	DOUBL DLR	V.1	573
Angelica:	you, that I lov'd you.	254	FOR LOVE	III.1	28
Ben:	He lov'd her more than Plunder;	274	FOR LOVE	III.1	770
Jeremy:	fall in Love with him: or at least own that she has lov'd	276	FOR LOVE	IV.1	10
Ben:	your weight in Gold and Jewels, and tho'f I lov'd you	287	FOR LOVE	IV.1	431
Angelica:	I never lov'd him till he was Mad; but don't tell	291	FOR LOVE	IV.1	572
Valentine:	lov'd a Woman, and lov'd her so long, that I found out a	292	FOR LOVE	IV.1	640
Valentine:	and since you have lov'd me, you must own I have at	294	FOR LOVE	IV.1	709
Angelica:	(sighs). I would I had lov'd you--for Heaven	294	FOR LOVE	IV.1	711
Miss Prue:	Why, my Father--I told him that you lov'd me.	303	FOR LOVE	V.1	232
Angelica:	always lov'd your Son, and hated your unforgiving	312	FOR LOVE	V.1	573
Zara:	Whom more than Life he lov'd; and the Regret,	337	M. BRIDE	I.1	438
Zara:	That to have lov'd thee, makes me yet more lost	348	M. BRIDE	II.2	338
Zara:	Cou'd one that lov'd, thus torture what she lov'd?	353	M. BRIDE	III.1	161
Zara:	Cou'd one who lov'd, thus torture whom she lov'd?	353	M. BRIDE	III.1	V161
Zara:	He knew I lov'd, but knew not to what height:	381	M. BRIDE	V.2	191
Mirabell:	whom he lov'd.	403	WAY WORLD	I.1	306
Marwood:	'tis better to be left, than never to have been lov'd. To	410	WAY WORLD	II.1	12
Marwood:	that lov'd me very well, and would be throughly sensible	411	WAY WORLD	II.1	54
Marwood:	I never lov'd him; he is, and always was	412	WAY WORLD	II.1	72
Fainall:	If yet you lov'd, you could forgive a Jealousy: But you are	415	WAY WORLD	II.1	185
Mrs Fain:	Yes, for I have Lov'd with Indiscretion.	416	WAY WORLD	II.1	257
Mrs Fain:	You have been the cause that I have lov'd	417	WAY WORLD	II.1	261
Fainall:	never lov'd her, or if I had, why that wou'd have been over	443	WAY WORLD	III.1	679

Lov'st (2)

Manuel:	By Heav'n thou lov'st me, and I'm pleas'd thou do'st:	333	M. BRIDE	I.1	275
Almeria:	Tho' 'tis because thou lov'st me. Do not say	356	M. BRIDE	III.1	256

Love (328)

Vainlove:	Faith I hate Love when 'tis forced upon a Man; as	39	OLD BATCH	I.1	94
Bellmour:	Yet rails on still, and thinks his Love unknown to us;	40	OLD BATCH	I.1	123
Bellmour:	damnally in Love; I'm so uneasie for not seeing Belinda	40	OLD BATCH	I.1	133
Bellmour:	damnally in Love; I'm so uneasie for not having seen Belinda	40	OLD BATCH	I.1	V133
Bellmour:	Why what a Cormorant in Love am I! who not	40	OLD BATCH	I.1	137
Bellmour:	contented with the slavery of honourable Love in one	40	OLD BATCH	I.1	138
Bellmour:	like her; for the Devil take me if I don't love all the	41	OLD BATCH	I.1	174
Heartwell:	edge of your puny Stomacks. Your love is like your	43	OLD BATCH	I.1	245
Heartwell:	Ay, why to come to Love through all these	44	OLD BATCH	I.1	277
Bellmour:	Prithee how dost thou love?	44	OLD BATCH	I.1	282
Heartwell:	So I hate Physick too--yet I may love to take it	44	OLD BATCH	I.1	284
Capt Bluff:	you love Fighting, I reverence a Man that loves	51	OLD BATCH	II.1	156
Araminta:	If Love be the Fever which you mean; kind Heav'n	54	OLD BATCH	II.2	8
Belinda:	Fancy--This Love is the Devil, and sure to be in Love	54	OLD BATCH	II.2	12
Araminta:	perceive you love him.	55	OLD BATCH	II.2	21
Belinda:	O I love your hideous Fancy! Ha, ha, ha, love a	55	OLD BATCH	II.2	22
Araminta:	Love a Man! yes, you would not love a Beast.	55	OLD BATCH	II.2	24
Belinda:	would you from thence infer I love him?	55	OLD BATCH	II.2	40
Araminta:	you love him. I tell no Body else Cousin--I have not	56	OLD BATCH	II.2	59
Bellmour:	world of Love in your Service, that you think you can	58	OLD BATCH	II.2	123
Belinda:	But a Dun for Love is an eternal Torment that never	58	OLD BATCH	II.2	129
Bellmour:	Till he has created Love where there was none, and	58	OLD BATCH	II.2	131
Bellmour:	then gets it from his pains. For importunity in Love, like	58	OLD BATCH	II.2	132
Vainlove:	Rewards to indefatigable Devotion--For as Love is a	58	OLD BATCH	II.2	140
Belinda:	O Gad, would you would all pray to Love then, and	58	OLD BATCH	II.2	142
Vainlove:	You are the Temples of Love, and 'tis through you,	58	OLD BATCH	II.2	144
Araminta:	which comes pretty near my own Opinion of Love and	58	OLD BATCH	II.2	154

Love   (continued)

Speaker	Text	PAGE	TITLE	ACT.SC LINE
Bellmour:	Ev'n Silence may be Eloquent in Love.	60	OLD BATCH	II.2 226
Lucy:	as his Love. Therefore e'n set your Heart at rest, and	61	OLD BATCH	III.1 8
Silvia:	Jealousie attend her Love; and Disappointment meet his	61	OLD BATCH	III.1 31
Silvia:	Vengeance itches in the rccm of Love.	61	OLD BATCH	III.1 34
Silvia:	Vengeance kindles in the room of Love.	61	OLD BATCH	III.1 V 34
Silvia:	'Tis as hard to Counterfeit Love, as it is to conceal it:	62	OLD BATCH	III.1 51
Vainlove:	And I love to have the pleasure cf making my	63	OLD BATCH	III.1 100
Lucy:	a Bumper in Love, lies Canting at the Gate; but never dare	66	OLD BATCH	III.1 193
Sir Joseph:	love to be the Messenger of ill News; 'tis an ungrateful	68	OLD BATCH	III.1 266
Singer:	Do not--do not--if you Love me	71	OLD BATCH	III.2 V 13
Silvia:	If you could Sing and Dance so, I should love to look	72	OLD BATCH	III.2 30
Heartwell:	worth for the purchase of thy Love--Say, is it mine then,	72	OLD BATCH	III.2 39
Heartwell:	reflux of vigorous Blood: But milky Love, supplies the	72	OLD BATCH	III.2 49
Heartwell:	love me Silvia? speak.	72	OLD BATCH	III.2 52
Heartwell:	Lying, Child, is indeed the Art of Love; and Men are	72	OLD BATCH	III.2 56
Silvia:	Must you lie then, if you say you Love me?	72	OLD BATCH	III.2 61
Heartwell:	--I tell thee I do love thee, and tell it for a Truth,	72	OLD BATCH	III.2 63
Silvia:	But Love, they say, is a tender thing, that will smooth	72	OLD BATCH	III.2 65
Silvia:	were not Love, but Anger.	72	OLD BATCH	III.2 69
Heartwell:	not Lcve, it is Madness, and then it is pardonable--Nay	73	OLD BATCH	III.2 84
Heartwell:	Marry you? no, no, I'll love you.	73	OLD BATCH	III.2 99
Silvia:	Nay, but if you love me, you must Marry me; what	73	OLD BATCH	III.2 100
Silvia:	self; for I love you, and would Marry you.	73	OLD BATCH	III.2 106
Silvia:	love you.	74	OLD BATCH	III.2 125
Lucy:	on't, both your Love and Anger satisfied!--All that can	75	OLD BATCH	III.2 160
Lucy:	Whom Love and Vengeance do at once delight.	75	OLD BATCH	III.2 163
Lucy:	Whom Love and Vengeance both at cnce delight.	75	OLD BATCH	III.2 V163
Fondlewife:	does not thy Wife love thee, nay doat upon thee?--	77	OLD BATCH	IV.1 58
Laetitia:	Well--Well--You know my Fondness, and you love to	77	OLD BATCH	IV.1 90
Laetitia:	that I should love to this degree! yet--	78	OLD BATCH	IV.1 104
Laetitia:	that will love you as well as I have done: I shall be contented	78	OLD BATCH	IV.1 110
Laetitia:	Go naughty Nykin, you don't love me.	78	OLD BATCH	IV.1 122
Fondlewife:	What not love Cocky!	78	OLD BATCH	IV.1 126
Fondlewife:	I profess I do love thee better, than 500 Pound--	78	OLD BATCH	IV.1 129
Sharper:	breeding Love to thee all this while, and just now she is	79	OLD BATCH	IV.1 167
Vainlove:	her Lcve.	79	OLD BATCH	IV.1 170
Sharper:	Thou hast a sickly peevish Appetite; only chew Love and	80	OLD BATCH	IV.1 172
Bellmour:	And more Love; or my Face is a False-Witness, and	82	OLD BATCH	IV.2 66
Sir Joseph:	Love, up to the Ears. But I'll be discreet, and husht.	86	OLD BATCH	IV.3 110
Bellmour:	'Tis an alarm to love.--Come in again, and	89	OLD BATCH	IV.4 6
Fondlewife:	Fleece here!--You don't love Mutton?--you Magdalen	93	OLD BATCH	IV.4 145
Fondlewife:	of your Profession.--Confess, ccnfess, I shall love thee	94	OLD BATCH	IV.4 193
Bellmour:	For my part, I am so charm'd with the Love of your	96	OLD BATCH	IV.4 264
Sir Joseph:	Garter, when she was thinking of her Love. Heh, Setter.	103	OLD BATCH	V.1 258
Mellefont:	importunities of her Love; and of two evils, I thought my	129	DOUBL DLR	I.1 93
Mellefont:	or of her Love, terminated in the view of this my Marriage	129	DOUBL DLR	I.1 97
Mellefont:	that the most vielent Love could urge, or tender words	130	DOUBL DLR	I.1 110
Brisk:	Write, but--I'gad, I love to be malicious.--Nay,	133	DOUBL DLR	I.1 240
Lady Touch:	oppressed at once with Love, and with Despair. But	135	DOUBL DLR	I.1 327
Lady Touch:	Where is that humble Love, the Languishing, that Adoration,	136	DOUBL DLR	I.1 350
Maskwell:	just Repulsed by him, warm at once with Love and	136	DOUBL DLR	I.1 367
Lady Touch:	not met your Love with forward Fire?	137	DOUBL DLR	I.1 373
Maskwell:	the Temple of the God, and Love was made a Mock-Worship,	137	DOUBL DLR	I.1 376
Maskwell:	of Love, have told me. Why should you deny it? Nay,	137	DOUBL DLR	I.1 385
Maskwell:	same Fire? Do ycu not Love him still? How have I this	137	DOUBL DLR	I.1 387
Cynthia:	have been so much in Love?	138	DOUBL DLR	II.1 2
Cynthia:	Love, and so much Wit as your Ladyship has, did not	138	DOUBL DLR	II.1 6
Lady Froth:	O Inconsistent! In Love, and not Write! if my	139	DOUBL DLR	II.1 20
Lady Froth:	Mellefcnt believe you Love him?	139	DOUBL DLR	II.1 42
Lady Froth:	how much I have been in Love with you; I swear I have;	140	DOUBL DLR	II.1 61
Lord Froth:	a Captive first, and ever since 't has been in Love with	140	DOUBL DLR	II.1 69
Lord Froth:	D'e think he'll Love you as well as I do my	141	DOUBL DLR	II.1 102
Cynthia:	I believe he'll Love me better.	141	DOUBL DLR	II.1 104
Lady Froth:	is my Lord's Love to me. And what do you think I	141	DOUBL DLR	II.1 121
Sir Paul:	of thee, but thy Portion, why he's in Love with my Wife;	146	DOUBL DLR	II.1 278
Mellefont:	By Heaven, I love her more than life, or--	146	DOUBL DLR	II.1 300
Lady Ply:	Nature. I know Love is powerful, and no body can help	148	DOUBL DLR	II.1 356
Lady Ply:	I know you don't Love Cynthia, cnly as a blind for your	148	DOUBL DLR	II.1 368
Lady Ply:	must nct Love you,--therefore don't hope,--but don't	148	DOUBL DLR	II.1 371
Maskwell:	at last I pretended to have been long Secretly in Love with	149	DOUBL DLR	II.1 421
Maskwell:	--Treachery, what Treachery? Love cancels all the	150	DOUBL DLR	II.1 443
Maskwell:	general acquittance--Rival is equal, and Love like Death	150	DOUBL DLR	II.1 449
Lord Touch:	Respect for Love, and made Sir Paul jealous of the Civility	151	DOUBL DLR	III.1 8
Maskwell:	dissuade him: Tho' my Friendship and Love to him has	154	DOUBL DLR	III.1 152
Careless:	tho' she begins to tack about; but I made Love a great	157	DOUBL DLR	III.1 266
Mellefont:	hand: For a woman never thinks a man truly in love with	159	DOUBL DLR	III.1 316
Lady Froth:	--I swear, my Lord, you don't Love poor little Sapho	167	DOUBL DLR	III.1 614
Cynthia:	Marry for Love.	168	DOUBL DLR	IV.1 32
Mellefont:	Love, Love, down right very Villanous Love.	168	DOUBL DLR	IV.1 33
Cynthia:	And he that can't live upon Love, deserves to die in	168	DOUBL DLR	IV.1 34
Brisk:	(sings). I'm sick with Love, ha ha ha, prithee come (walking	175	DOUBL DLR	IV.1 306
Brisk:	see hcw Love and Murder will out. But did I really name	176	DOUBL DLR	IV.1 329
Lady Froth:	Three times aloud, as I love Letters--But	176	DOUBL DLR	IV.1 331
Lady Froth:	did you talk of Love? O Parnassus! Who would have	176	DOUBL DLR	IV.1 332
Lady Froth:	thought Mr. Brisk could have been in Love, ha ha ha. O	176	DOUBL DLR	IV.1 333
Lady Froth:	in Love! Ha ha ha.	176	DOUBL DLR	IV.1 342
Careless:	not prevail for you, 'gad I pretended to be in Love my self	180	DOUBL DLR	IV.1 499
Lady Touch:	found him here. Who does not prevent the Hour of Love;	183	DOUBL DLR	IV.2 9
Lady Touch:	Not in Love, Words are the weak support of	184	DOUBL DLR	IV.2 22
Lady Touch:	Cold indifference; Love has no Language to be heard.	184	DOUBL DLR	IV.2 23
Lady Touch:	the love of you, was the first wandring fire that e're misled	185	DOUBL DLR	IV.2 76
Maskwell:	Why do I love! yet Heaven and my waking	188	DOUBL DLR	V.1 33
Maskwell:	O, should it once be known I love fair Cynthia, all this	188	DOUBL DLR	V.1 38

Love   (continued)

Lovers (10)
  Lucy: of your Lovers that should come empty-handed; as a Court . 61   OLD BATCH III.1   21
  Maskwell: And why are Friends and Lovers Oaths believ'd; 150   DOUBL DLR II.1   466
  Angelica: his Mistress. Mr. Tattle, we must not hinder Lovers. .   262   FOR LOVE   III.1 346
  Mrs Fain: While they are Lovers, if they have Fire and Sense, their 410 WAY WORLD II.1   4
  Marwood: and seem to doat like Lovers; but 'tis not in cur . .   410   WAY WORLD II.1   24
  Millamant: Lovers as fast as one pleases, and they live as long as one 420 WAY WORLD II.1   404
  Witwoud: of Lovers, Madam, than of making so many Card-matches. . 420 WAY WORLD II.1   408
  Witwoud: out of Lovers--We agree in the main, like Treble . . . 435   WAY WORLD III.1 396
  Mirabell: has had compassion upon Lovers and generously engag'd a . 477 WAY WORLD V.1   579
  Sir Wilful: Dance in the mean time, that we who are not Lovers, may . 477 WAY WORLD V.1   601
Loves (26)   see Free-loves
  Bellmour: loves thee intirely--I have heard her breath such Raptures 38 OLD BATCH I.1   40
  Bellmour: Baggage loves me, for she never speaks well of me her . . 41 OLD BATCH I.1   168
  Heartwell: What, has he been here? that's one of Loves . . . . . 42 OLD BATCH I.1   197
  Sharper: loves to buffet with the Winds, meet the Tide and sail in . 42 OLD BATCH I.1   202
  Capt Bluff: you love Fighting, I reverence a Man that loves . . .   51 OLD BATCH II.1   156
  Silvia: Could we perswade him, that she Loves another-- . . .   61 OLD BATCH III.1   39
  Singer: For Thyrsis deaf to Loves allarms, ...   71 OLD BATCH III.2 V 23
  Maskwell: Loves her. . . . . 138 DOUBL DLR I.1   411
  Lady Ply: loves you tenderly--'tis a barbarity of barbarities, and . 146 DOUBL DLR II.1 V291
  Lord Touch: No, I am convinced he loves her. . . . . 191 DOUBL DLR V.1   131
  Scandal: and loves a Wench still. You never knew a Whoremaster, . 223 FOR LOVE   I.1   265
  Sr Sampson: now, why I warrant he can smell, and loves Perfumes .   245 FOR LOVE   II.1   370
  Miss Prue: that loves me, and I love him; and if he sees you speak to
                 me . . . . 264 FOR LOVE   III.1 416
  Scandal: She's concern'd, and loves him. . . . .   276 FOR LOVE   IV.1   40
  Angelica: and involuntary; if he loves, he can't help it; and if I
                 don't . . . . 278 FOR LOVE   IV.1   87
  Miss Prue: Robin the Butler, he says he loves me, and he's a Handsome 305 FOR LOVE   V.1   317
  Osmyn-Alph: Say somewhat quickly to conceal our Loves, ...   359 M. BRIDE   III.1 390
  Petulant: Aunt, that loves Catterwauling better than a Conventicle. 406 WAY WORLD I.1   408
  Petulant: Aunt, who loves Catterwauling better than a Conventicle. 406 WAY WORLD I.1   V408
  Mirabell: familiarities of our Loves had produc'd that Consequence, 417 WAY WORLD II.1   267
  Witwoud: But I know a Lady that loves talking so incessantly, .   421 WAY WORLD II.1   419
  Millamant: That Mirabell loves me is no more a Secret, than it is a . 433 WAY WORLD III.1 328
  Millamant: loves me, Ha, ha, ha. How can one forbear laughing to . 434 WAY WORLD III.1 356
  Marwood: threaten to part with her--My Lady loves her, and . .   442 WAY WORLD III.1 660
  Sir Wilful: Cozen's a Fine Lady, and the Gentleman loves her and she 477 WAY WORLD V.1   583
  Sir Wilful: loves him, and they deserve one another; my resolution is 477 WAY WORLD V.1   584
Loving (9)
  Heartwell: Cringing, and the drudgery of loving to boot. . . .   44 OLD BATCH I.1   275
  Bellmour: O Brute, the drudgery of loving! . . . . 44 OLD BATCH I.1   276
  Heartwell: pleased with you--And a Pox upon me for loving thee so . 73 OLD BATCH III.2   71
  Scandal: (aside). Miracle! the Monster grows loving. . . . . 281 FOR LOVE   IV.1   205
  Painall: Obstinacy--But when he's drunk, he's as loving as . . 401 WAY WORLD I.1   219
  Fainall: With Infidelity, with loving of another, with love of . 414 WAY WORLD II.1   151
  Fainall: With Infidelity, with loving another, with love of . . 414 WAY WORLD II.1 V151
  Fainall: For loving you? . . . . 415 WAY WORLD II.1   218
  Millamant: loving me? . . . . 422 WAY WORLD II.1   459
Low (15)
  Bellmour: his Glass. Let low and earthy Souls grovel till they have 37 OLD BATCH I.1   25
  Bellmour: his Glass. Let low and earthly Souls grovel 'till they have 37 OLD BATCH I.1 V 25
  Sharper: You are above--I'me sure--a thought so low, to suffer .   50 OLD BATCH II.1   100
  Belinda: a high Roof, or a very low Seat--Stay, Come back here .   57 OLD BATCH II.2   96
  Capt Bluff: (In a low Voice.) . . . . 101 OLD BATCH V.1   182
                 (He bows profoundly low, then kisses the Glass.) . . 140 DOUBL DLR II.1   79
  Brisk: Like an Oyster at low Ebb, I'gad--ha, ha. . . . . . 165 DOUBL DLR III.1 576
                 (He kisses her, and bows very low.) . . . . . . 172 DOUBL DLR IV.1   196
  Lady Touch: Married? Is there not reward enough in raising his low . 191 DOUBL DLR V.1   126
  Sir Paul: Gad'sbud, I can't find her high nor low; where can . . 192 DOUBL DLR V.1   162
  Zara: Am I become so low, by my Captivity; . . . . . .   348 M. BRIDE   II.2   361
  Osmyn-Alph: I bear my Fortunes with so low a Mind, ... 354 M. BRIDE   III.1 170
  Osmyn-Alph: Have cast me down to this low Being: or, ... 354 M. BRIDE   III.1 176
  Almeria: Where levell'd low, no more we'll lift our Eyes, . .   358 M. BRIDE   III.1 372
               That Satire scorns to stoop so meanly low, ...   479 WAY WORLD EPI.   29
Lower (2)
  Lady Froth: cast off, and meet me at the lower end of the Room, and . 177 DOUBL DLR IV.1   366
  Almeria: But sink each other, lower yet, down, down, ... 358 M. BRIDE   III.1 371
Lowest (3)
  Sharper: A Wretch, that has flown for shelter to the lowest . . 102 OLD BATCH V.1   207
  Gonsalez: Garcia, my Son, your Beauties lowest Slave, ... 332 M. BRIDE   I.1   255
  Zara: Have I? Yet 'twere the lowest Baseness, now, ... 363 M. BRIDE   IV.1   96
Lowness (2)
  Valentine: that Love, which has principally reduc'd me to this Lowness 217 FOR LOVE   I.1   55
  Valentine: the Love, which has principally reduc'd me to this Lowness 217 FOR LOVE   I.1 V 55
Loyalty (1)
  Manuel: No more; my Promise long since pass'd, thy Loyalty, . . 334 M. BRIDE   I.1   340
Loyns (1)
  Sr Sampson: present Majesty of Bantam is the Issue of these Loyns. . 241 FOR LOVE   II.1   223
Lubber (1)
  Millamant: How can you name that super-annuated Lubber, ... 453 WAY WORLD IV.1   320
Lubberly (2)
  Mrs Fore: great lubberly Tarpawlin--Gad I warrant you, she . .   250 FOR LOVE   II.1   562
  Witwoud: think you're in the Country, where great lubberly Brothers 439 WAY WORLD III.1 534
Luck (6)
  Sharper: now luck!--curs'd fortune! this must be the place, this . 48 OLD BATCH II.1   17
  Nurse: Pray Heav'n send your Worship good Luck, Marry . . . 235 FOR LOVE   II.1   26
  Foresight: have, that may be good Luck in troth, in troth it may, . 236 FOR LOVE   II.1   30
  Foresight: very good Luck: Nay, I have had some Omens; I got out . 236 FOR LOVE   II.1   31
  Witwoud: --I have no Luck to Day. . . . . 402 WAY WORLD I.1   280
  Foible: O what luck it is Sir Rowland, that you were present .   461 WAY WORLD IV.1   610
Luckily (1)
  Mrs Fore: power--And I can tell you one thing that falls out luckily 248 FOR LOVE   II.1   498
Lucky (9)
  Bellmour: Thou'rt a lucky Rogue; there's your Benefactor, . . . 68 OLD BATCH III.1 281

Lying (continued)
```
  Osmyn-Alph:  I was, and lying on my Father's Lead;  . . . . . .  . 343  M. BRIDE   II.2  159
  Foible:      quarter of an hours lying and swearing to a fine Lady?  . 459  WAY WORLD  IV.1  559
Maccabeus (1)
  Sir Paul:    be Damn'd for a Judas Maccabeus, and Iscariot both. O  .  . 178  DOUBL DLR  IV.1  418
Mad (59)   see Horn-mad, Ripe-horn-mad
  Sir Joseph:  mad? Or de'e think I'm mad? Agad for my part, I don't  . .  . 68  OLD BATCH  III.1  265
  Heartwell:   more to confirm me mad; so.  . . . . . . . . . .  . 74  OLD BATCH  III.2  141
  Sir Joseph:  mad, Alderman? . . . . . . . . . . . .  . 90  OLD BATCH  IV.4   56
  Sharper:     Mad, by this Light.  . . . . . . . . . . . .  . 105  OLD BATCH  V.1   326
  Lady Touch:  mad, alas he's mad--indeed he is my Lord, and knows not  . 186  DOUBL DLR  IV.2  113
  Mellefont:   By Heaven 'twere senceless not to be mad, and see  . .  . 186  DOUBL DLR  IV.2  115
  Mellefont:   Horn mad after your Fortune.  . . . . . . . .  . 187  DOUBL DLR  IV.2  133
  Lord Touch:  I fear he's mad indeed--Let's send Maskwell  . . . .  . 187  DOUBL DLR  IV.2  135
  Foresight:   are mad to day--It is of evil portent, and bodes Mischief  . 236  FOR LOVE   II.1   47
  Jeremy:      my Master was run stark mad only for Love of her Mistress;  . 276  FOR LOVE   IV.1   15
  Jeremy:      No strange matter, Madam; my Master's mad, that's  . .  . 276  FOR LOVE   IV.1   29
  Angelica:    How d'ye mean, mad?  . . . . . . . . . .  . 276  FOR LOVE   IV.1   32
  Jeremy:      Why faith, Madam, he's mad for want of his Wits,  . .  . 276  FOR LOVE   IV.1   33
  Jeremy:      us to be mad? Why, Sir, my Master longs to see her; and  . 278  FOR LOVE   IV.1   99
  Jeremy:      is almost mad in good earnest, with the Joyful News of  . 278  FOR LOVE   IV.1  100
  Jeremy:      his Skull's crack'd, poor Gentleman; he's stark mad, Sir.  . 279  FOR LOVE   IV.1  138
  Sr Sampson:  Mad! . . . . . . . . . . . . . . .  . 279  FOR LOVE   IV.1  139
  Sr Sampson:  --Mad, I'll make him find his Senses.  . . . . . .  . 279  FOR LOVE   IV.1  146
  Sr Sampson:  Son be mad--Where's your Oppositions, your Trines, and  . 283  FOR LOVE   IV.1  282
  Mrs Fore:    are mad in my opinion.  . . . . . . . . . .  . 284  FOR LOVE   IV.1  324
  Scandal:     You make me mad--You are not serious--  . . . . .  . 284  FOR LOVE   IV.1  325
  Scandal:     mad. . . . . . . . . . . . . . . . .  . 285  FOR LOVE   IV.1  346
  Foresight:   vulgar think mad. Let us go in to him.  . . . . .  . 285  FOR LOVE   IV.1  350
  Foresight:   vulgar think mad. Let us go to him.  . . . . . .  . 285  FOR LOVE   IV.1 V350
  Ben:         All mad, I think--Flesh, I believe all the Calentures of  . 285  FOR LOVE   IV.1  356
  Ben:         way--(It seems Brother Val is gone mad, and so that  . .  . 285  FOR LOVE   IV.1  366
  Ben:         O Lord, O Lord, she's mad, poor Young Woman, Love  . .  . 286  FOR LOVE   IV.1  403
  Mrs Frail:   No, no, I am not mad, Monster, I am wise enough  . . .  . 286  FOR LOVE   IV.1  406
  Mrs Fore:    if in one of his mad fits he will bring you to him in her  . 288  FOR LOVE   IV.1  471
  Angelica:    I never lov'd him till he was Mad; but don't tell  . .  . 291  FOR LOVE   IV.1  572
  Angelica:    Mad as Valentine, I'll believe you love me, and the maddest  . 291  FOR LOVE   IV.1  587
  Jeremy:      absolutely and substantially Mad, as any Freeholder in  .  . 295  FOR LOVE   IV.1  738
  Jeremy:      Bethlehem; Nay, he's as Mad as any Projector, Fanatick,  . 295  FOR LOVE   IV.1  739
  Valentine:   Sirrah, you lie; I am not Mad.  . . . . . . . .  . 295  FOR LOVE   IV.1  741
  Jeremy:      Mad enough to own it?  . . . . . . . . . .  . 295  FOR LOVE   IV.1  744
  Valentine:   is done, and I will be Mad no longer.  . . . . . .  . 295  FOR LOVE   IV.1  750
  Angelica:    Ha, ha, ha, is he mad, or no, Jeremy?  . . . . .  . 295  FOR LOVE   IV.1  752
  Jeremy:      to be mad: And I think I have not found him very quiet  . 295  FOR LOVE   IV.1  755
  Jeremy:      better yet--Will you please to be Mad, Sir, or how?  . .  . 296  FOR LOVE   IV.1  771
  Valentine:   Mad, and will be Mad to every Body but this Lady.  . .  . 296  FOR LOVE   IV.1  774
  Angelica:    the Fool you take me for; and you are Mad and don't  . .  . 296  FOR LOVE   IV.1  792
  Angelica:    are very much abus'd in that Matter; He's no more Mad  . 299  FOR LOVE   V.1   87
  Foresight:   Alas! he's Mad, Child, stark Wild.  . . . . . . .  . 305  FOR LOVE   V.1   303
  Ben:         Matter! Why he's Mad.  . . . . . . . . . .  . 306  FOR LOVE   V.1   343
  Ben:         say, Brother Val. went mad for, she's mad too, I think.  . 306  FOR LOVE   V.1   346
  Foresight:   Well, I shall run mad next.  . . . . . . . . .  . 306  FOR LOVE   V.1   348
  Mrs Fore:    Well, but how mad? how d'ee mean?  . . . . . . .  . 306  FOR LOVE   V.1   349
  Foresight:   Well, but they are not Mad, that is, not Lunatick?  . .  . 307  FOR LOVE   V.1   371
  Ben:         she's mad for a Husband, and he's Horn-mad, I think, or  . 307  FOR LOVE   V.1   373
  Foresight:   How! Not Mad! Mr. Scandal.  . . . . . . . . .  . 310  FOR LOVE   V.1   505
  Scandal:     'S'death, you are not mad indeed, to ruine your  . . .  . 311  FOR LOVE   V.1   541
  Jeremy:      mistake--You see, Sir, my Master was never mad, nor  . .  . 313  FOR LOVE   V.1   593
  Almeria:     Be mad--I cannot be transported thus.  . . . . . .  . 342  M. BRIDE   II.2  108
  Almeria:     O stay, yet stay, hear me, I am not mad.  . . . . .  . 370  M. BRIDE   IV.1  368
  Lady Wish:   shall be mad, Dear Friend is there no Comfort for me?  .  . 470  WAY WORLD  V.1   307
Madam (274)
  Betty:       Did your Ladyship call, Madam?  . . . . . . . .  . 56  OLD BATCH  II.2   68
  Footman:     Madam, there are--  . . . . . . . . . . .  . 56  OLD BATCH  II.2   74
  Footman:     No, Madam, there are Mr. Bellmour and Mr.  . . . . .  . 56  OLD BATCH  II.2   76
  Footman:     No, Madam, they sent before, to know if you were  . .  . 56  OLD BATCH  II.2   79
  Bellmour:    Not o' your side, Madam, I confess--But my  . . . .  . 57  OLD BATCH  II.2  117
  Vainlove:    O Madam--  . . . . . . . . . . . . . .  . 58  OLD BATCH  II.2  150
  Footman:     Only to the next door, Madam; I'll call him.  . . . .  . 58  OLD BATCH  II.2  158
  Bellmour:    Nothing, Madam, only--  . . . . . . . . . .  . 59  OLD BATCH  II.2  162
  Belinda:     you, Madam.  . . . . . . . . . . . . .  . 59  OLD BATCH  II.2  172
  Bellmour:    Faith, Madam, I dare not speak to her, but I'll  . . .  . 60  OLD BATCH  II.2  210
  Lucy:        Go get you in Madam, receive him pleasantly, dress up  . 62  OLD BATCH  III.1   48
  Lucy:        Hang Art, Madam, and trust to Nature for  . . . . .  . 62  OLD BATCH  III.1   54
  Lucy:        Lord, Madam, I met your Lover in as much haste, as  . .  . 74  OLD BATCH  III.2  147
  Lucy:        it you. Come Madam, you're like to have a happy time  . 75  OLD BATCH  III.2  159
  Bellmour:    Madam? Those Eyes shone kindly on my first Appearance,  . 81  OLD BATCH  IV.2   21
  Bellmour:    Madam;--I confess I have run into an Errour:--I beg your  . 81  OLD BATCH  IV.2   38
  Bellmour:    Nay, 'Faith, Madam, 'tis a pleasant one; and worth  . .  . 82  OLD BATCH  IV.2   48
  Bellmour:    find it directed to Mr. Vainlove. Gad, Madam, I ask you a  . 82  OLD BATCH  IV.2   57
  Bellmour:    You appear concern'd, Madam.  . . . . . . . .  . 82  OLD BATCH  IV.2   61
  Sir Joseph:  Hem! Pray Madam, Which Way's the Wind?  . . . . .  . 85  OLD BATCH  IV.3   94
  Vainlove:    But, Madam, I hope I shall prove of a Temper, not to  . 87  OLD BATCH  IV.3  139
  Sharper:     Oh Madam! He was our English Horace.  . . . . . .  . 87  OLD BATCH  IV.3  147
  Vainlove:    I find, Madam, the Formality of the Law must be  . . .  . 87  OLD BATCH  IV.3  152
  Vainlove:    Madam, will admit of no farther reasoning.--But  . . .  . 88  OLD BATCH  IV.3  177
  Vainlove:    No, Madam, I'm gone.--She knows her  . . . . . .  . 88  OLD BATCH  IV.3  187
  Sharper:     Faith, Madam, the Talent was born with me:--I  . . .  . 88  OLD BATCH  IV.3  198
  Footman:     She's not very well, Madam, and has sent to know,  . .  . 88  OLD BATCH  IV.3  206
  Sir Joseph:  to her,--Pray, Madam, what News d'ye hear?  . . . .  . 89  OLD BATCH  IV.4   33
  Sir Joseph:  I wonder at that, Madam, for 'tis most curious  . . .  . 90  OLD BATCH  IV.4   36
  Sir Joseph:  As you say, Madam, 'tis pretty bad Weather, and  . . .  . 90  OLD BATCH  IV.4   39
  Bellmour:    Sinner, she's innocent, for me. Go to him, Madam, fling  . 95  OLD BATCH  IV.4  236
  Bellmour:    Madam.  . . . . . . . . . . . . . . .  . 97  OLD BATCH  V.1   27
  Setter:      stood towards Madam Araminta. As, When you had seen  . 99  OLD BATCH  V.1   114
  Bellmour:    You have an Opportunity now, Madam, to revenge  . . .  . 107  OLD BATCH  V.1   395
```

Madam   (continued)

		PAGE	TITLE	ACT.SC	LINE
Scandal:	Madam, I am very glad that I overheard a better . . .	294	FOR LOVE	IV.1	687
Scandal:	No, Madam; I only leave a Madman to his Remedy. . . .	294	FOR LOVE	IV.1	695
Valentine:	Madam, you need not be very much afraid, for I . . .	294	FOR LOVE	IV.1	697
Jeremy:	Counterfeit, Madam! I'll maintain him to be as . . .	295	FOR LOVE	IV.1	737
Jeremy:	O Lord, Madam, did you ever know any Madman . . .	295	FOR LOVE	IV.1	743
Jeremy:	Yes, Madam; He has Intervals: But you see he begins .	295	FOR LOVE	IV.1	747
Jeremy:	part of my Conversation--Madam, your Ladyships . .	296	FOR LOVE	IV.1	777
Jenny:	(aside to Angelica) Yes, Madam, Sir Sampson will wait	296	FOR LOVE	IV.1	782
Jenny:	He's at the great Glass in the Dining-Room, Madam, . .	297	FOR LOVE	V.1	3
Jenny:	I hear him, Madam.	297	FOR LOVE	V.1	8
Sr Sampson:	a fair Lady, a great while--Odd, Madam, you have . .	298	FOR LOVE	V.1	14
Sr Sampson:	Zooks, but it is, Madam, a very great while; to . .	298	FOR LOVE	V.1	18
Sr Sampson:	Not at all, Madam: Odsbud you wrong me; I . . .	298	FOR LOVE	V.1	21
Sr Sampson:	not wash away. Well, Madam, what are your Commands? .	298	FOR LOVE	V.1	41
Sr Sampson:	devilish Handsom.--Madam, you deserve a good Husband,	298	FOR LOVE	V.1	51
Sr Sampson:	the next Morning.--Odso, have a care, Madam. . .	299	FOR LOVE	V.1	59
Sr Sampson:	Odd, you are hard to please, Madam; to find a . .	299	FOR LOVE	V.1	65
Sr Sampson:	How, Madam! Wou'd I cou'd prove it.	299	FOR LOVE	V.1	89
Sr Sampson:	Madam, all my Affairs are scarce worthy to be laid at .	299	FOR LOVE	V.1	94
Sr Sampson:	your Feet; And I wish, Madam, they stood in a better .	300	FOR LOVE	V.1	95
Sr Sampson:	your Feet; And I wish, Madam, they were in a better .	300	FOR LOVE	V.1 V	95
Sr Sampson:	Odd, Madam, I love you--And if you	300	FOR LOVE	V.1	103
Sr Sampson:	and I a happy Man. Odd, Madam, I'll love you as long as I	300	FOR LOVE	V.1	119
Tattle:	I did, as I hope to be sav'd, Madam, my Intentions .	309	FOR LOVE	V.1	457
Scandal:	Well, Madam, You have done Exemplary Justice, . .	313	FOR LOVE	V.1	619
Leonora:	For Heaven's sake, dear Madam, moderate . . .	326	M. BRIDE	I.1	15
Leonora:	For Heaven's sake, dear Madam, cease	326	M. BRIDE	I.1 V	15
Leonora:	Believe me, Madam, I lament Anselmo, . . .	326	M. BRIDE	I.1	20
Leonora:	Madam, the King.	332	M. BRIDE	I.1	261
Selim:	Madam, the King is here.	348	M. BRIDE	II.2	349
Selim:	Madam, the King is here, and entring now. . . .	348	M. BRIDE	II.2 V	349
Osmyn-Alph:	--Madam!	359	M. BRIDE	III.1	414
Osmyn-Alph:	How, Madam!	360	M. BRIDE	III.1	433
Selim:	Madam, take heed; or you have ruin'd all. . . .	366	M. BRIDE	IV.1	185
Gonsalez:	Dear Madam, speak, or you'll incense the King. . .	367	M. BRIDE	IV.1	266
Mirabell:	He is the only Man that do's, Madam.	412	WAY WORLD	II.1	91
Fainall:	That I have been deceiv'd Madam, and you are false. .	413	WAY WORLD	II.1	134
Mirabell:	You seem to be unattended, Madam--You . . .	418	WAY WORLD	II.1	328
Witwoud:	Madam, tho' 'tis against my self.	419	WAY WORLD	II.1	340
Witwoud:	Madam, truce with your Similitudes--No, . . .	419	WAY WORLD	II.1	349
Witwoud:	Is that the way? Pray Madam, do you pin up your . .	419	WAY WORLD	II.1	363
Witwoud:	of Lovers, Madam, than of making so many Card-matches.	420	WAY WORLD	II.1	408
Mirabell:	You are merry, Madam, but I wou'd perswade you . .	422	WAY WORLD	II.1	470
Foible:	You have seen Madam Millamant, Sir? . . .	424	WAY WORLD	II.1	528
Peg:	No, Madam.	425	WAY WORLD	III.1	2
Peg:	Lord, Madam, your Ladyship is so impatient--I cannot .	425	WAY WORLD	III.1	17
Peg:	come at the Paint, Madam; Mrs. Foible has lock'd it up,	425	WAY WORLD	III.1	18
Peg:	Madam, I was looking for a Cup.	425	WAY WORLD	III.1	27
Peg:	No Madam, Mrs. Marwood.	426	WAY WORLD	III.1	39
Marwood:	O Madam, you cannot suspect Mrs. Foible's . .	426	WAY WORLD	III.1	55
Foible:	Madam, I have seen the Party.	427	WAY WORLD	III.1	72
Foible:	what shall I say?--Alas, Madam, cou'd I help it, if I .	427	WAY WORLD	III.1	85
Foible:	O Madam; 'tis a shame to say what he said-- . .	427	WAY WORLD	III.1	93
Foible:	him Madam, starve him, marry Sir Rowland and get him .	427	WAY WORLD	III.1	107
Foible:	The sooner the better, Madam.	428	WAY WORLD	III.1	121
Foible:	Incontinently, Madam. No new Sheriff's Wife expects .	428	WAY WORLD	III.1	124
Foible:	Madam. There are some Cracks discernable in the white .	429	WAY WORLD	III.1	145
Foible:	I warrant you, Madam; a little Art once made your . .	429	WAY WORLD	III.1	151
Foible:	Madam.	429	WAY WORLD	III.1	154
Foible:	By Storm, Madam. Sir Rowland's a brisk Man. . .	429	WAY WORLD	III.1	175
Foible:	Discover what, Madam?	430	WAY WORLD	III.1	187
Foible:	O dear Madam, I beg your Pardon. It was not my . .	430	WAY WORLD	III.1	195
Foible:	O dear Madam, Mr. Mirabell is such a sweet winning .	430	WAY WORLD	III.1	201
Foible:	Heart still. Now, Madam, I can safely tell your Ladyship	430	WAY WORLD	III.1	205
Foible:	Madam, I beg your Ladyship to acquaint Mr. Mirabell .	430	WAY WORLD	III.1	214
Foible:	to him,--besides, I believe Madam Marwood watches .	430	WAY WORLD	III.1	216
Foible:	remove my Lady's Toilet. Madam your Servant. My Lady .	430	WAY WORLD	III.1	219
Marwood:	rest of him. Poor simple Fiend! Madam Marwood has a .	431	WAY WORLD	III.1	239
Marwood:	No Apologies, dear Madam. I have been very . .	431	WAY WORLD	III.1	252
Marwood:	That I detest him, hate him, Madam. . . .	434	WAY WORLD	III.1	354
Millamant:	O Madam, why so do I--And yet the Creature . .	434	WAY WORLD	III.1	355
Mincing:	The Gentlemen stay but to Comb, Madam; and . .	434	WAY WORLD	III.1	368
Millamant:	hear it Madam--Not that there's any great matter in .	434	WAY WORLD	III.1	372
Witwoud:	Raillery, Raillery, Madam, we have no Animosity . .	435	WAY WORLD	III.1	393
Witwoud:	Madam.	435	WAY WORLD	III.1	411
Sir Wilful:	Belike I may Madam. I may chance to sail upon . .	440	WAY WORLD	III.1	567
Sir Wilful:	told you, Madam--Yes, I have settl'd my Concerns, .	440	WAY WORLD	III.1	573
Lady Wish:	you'll pardon him, Madam--Gentlemen will you . .	441	WAY WORLD	III.1	623
Marwood:	I'll follow you, Madam--Before Sir Wilfull . .	441	WAY WORLD	III.1	625
Foible:	Yes, Madam. I have put Wax-Lights in the Sconces; .	444	WAY WORLD	IV.1	3
Foible:	Yes, Madam.	445	WAY WORLD	IV.1	10
Foible:	All is ready, Madam.	445	WAY WORLD	IV.1	14
Foible:	Most killing well, Madam.	445	WAY WORLD	IV.1	16
Foible:	'Tis he, Madam.	445	WAY WORLD	IV.1	33
Foible:	Sir Wilfull is set in to Drinking, Madam, in the Parlour.	445	WAY WORLD	IV.1	36
Foible:	Madam, I stay'd here, to tell your Ladyship that Mr. .	445	WAY WORLD	IV.1	43
Foible:	Sir Wilfull is coming, Madam. Shall I send Mr. Mirabell	446	WAY WORLD	IV.1	58
Millamant:	Your Pardon Madam, I can stay no longer--Sir . .	456	WAY WORLD	IV.1	431
Waitwell:	My Impatience Madam, is the effect of my transport; .	457	WAY WORLD	IV.1	490
Waitwell:	am tantaliz'd on a rack; And do but hang Madam, on the	457	WAY WORLD	IV.1	492
Waitwell:	am tantaliz'd on the rack; And do but hang Madam, on the	457	WAY WORLD	IV.1 V	492
Waitwell:	For decency of Funeral. The delay will . . .	458	WAY WORLD	IV.1	498
Waitwell:	Dear Madam, no. You are all Camphire and . .	459	WAY WORLD	IV.1	545
Foible:	Madam, the Dancers are ready, and there's one with a .	459	WAY WORLD	IV.1	549
Waitwell:	A Woman's hand? No Madam, that's no Woman's . .	460	WAY WORLD	IV.1	577

Madam   (continued)

		PAGE	TITLE	ACT.SC	LINE
Lady Wish:	(Reads)--Madam, tho' unknown to you (Look you there 'tis	460	WAY WORLD	IV.1	584
Waitwell:	Here's a Villain! Madam, don't you perceive it,	460	WAY WORLD	IV.1	597
Foible:	Mirabell disguis'd to Madam Millamant this Afternoon. I	461	WAY WORLD	IV.1	612
Foible:	Then, then Madam, Mr. Mirabell waited for her in her	461	WAY WORLD	IV.1	618
Waitwell:	I am Charm'd Madam, I obey. But some proof you	461	WAY WORLD	IV.1	632
Foible:	Dear Madam, I'll beg pardon on my knees.	462	WAY WORLD	V.1	9
Foible:	No, no, dear Madam. Do but hear me, have but a	462	WAY WORLD	V.1	24
Foible:	defend my self? O Madam, if you knew but what he promis'd	463	WAY WORLD	V.1	29
Foible:	Pray do but hear me Madam, he cou'd not marry	463	WAY WORLD	V.1	38
Foible:	your Lady-ship, Madam--No indeed his Marriage	463	WAY WORLD	V.1	39
Foible:	O Madam, my Lady's gone for a Constable; I shall	463	WAY WORLD	V.1	62
Foible:	Yes, yes; I know it Madam; she was in my Lady's	464	WAY WORLD	V.1	68
Foible:	Yes Madam; but my Lady did not see that part; We	464	WAY WORLD	V.1	78
Foible:	Indeed Madam, and so 'tis a Comfort if you knew all,	464	WAY WORLD	V.1	84
Foible:	I can take my Oath of it Madam, so can Mrs. Mincing;	464	WAY WORLD	V.1	92
Foible:	we have had many a fair word from Madam Marwood, to	464	WAY WORLD	V.1	93
Foible:	we were sworn to secresie too; Madam Marwood took a	464	WAY WORLD	V.1	97
Foible:	Yes, yes Madam.	465	WAY WORLD	V.1	120
Marwood:	Let us first dispatch the affair in hand Madam,	465	WAY WORLD	V.1	136
Mrs Fain:	I know what I mean Madam, and so do you; and	466	WAY WORLD	V.1	158
Marwood:	I am sorry to see you so passionate, Madam.	466	WAY WORLD	V.1	160
Marwood:	liable to affronts. You will pardon me, Madam, If I meddle	466	WAY WORLD	V.1	164
Mrs Fain:	I tell you Madam you're abus'd--stick to	466	WAY WORLD	V.1	173
Mrs Fain:	drop off when she's full. Madam you sha'not pawn a	466	WAY WORLD	V.1	175
Mrs Fain:	drop off when she's full. Madam you shan't pawn a	466	WAY WORLD	V.1	V175
Marwood:	Prove it Madam? What, and have your name	467	WAY WORLD	V.1	208
Marwood:	Nay Madam, I advise nothing, I only lay before	468	WAY WORLD	V.1	241
Fainall:	Well Madam; I have suffer'd my self to be overcome	468	WAY WORLD	V.1	250
Marwood:	Madam, when we retire to our pastoral Solitude we shall	468	WAY WORLD	V.1	261
Marwood:	'Tis severe indeed Madam, that you shou'd	469	WAY WORLD	V.1	300
Millamant:	Madam, and to Convince you that I had no hand in the	470	WAY WORLD	V.1	326
Marwood:	Not far Madam; I'll return immediately.	471	WAY WORLD	V.1	357
Mirabell:	I am too Happy,--Ah Madam, there was a time--but let	471	WAY WORLD	V.1	369
Mirabell:	Consider Madam, in reality; You cou'd not receive	472	WAY WORLD	V.1	383
Fainall:	Your date of deliberation Madam, is expir'd. Here is	472	WAY WORLD	V.1	414
Fainall:	Impos'd on you, Madam.	472	WAY WORLD	V.1	420
Fainall:	Tenor of this other Covenant,--I suppose Madam, your	473	WAY WORLD	V.1	437
Mirabell:	Ay Madam; but that is too late, my reward is intercepted.	473	WAY WORLD	V.1	457
Foible:	Yes indeed Madam; I'll take my Bible-oath of it.	474	WAY WORLD	V.1	478
Fainall:	Madam, I'll be fool'd no longer.	475	WAY WORLD	V.1	503
Mirabell:	and Penitent to appear, Madam.	475	WAY WORLD	V.1	507
Waitwell:	Black box at last, Madam.	475	WAY WORLD	V.1	511
Mirabell:	Give it me. Madam, you remember your promise.	475	WAY WORLD	V.1	512
Mirabell:	Very well, now you shall know--Madam, your	476	WAY WORLD	V.1	532
Mrs Fain:	Madam, you seem to stifle your Resentment:	476	WAY WORLD	V.1	563
Mirabell:	For that Madam, give your self no trouble--let	477	WAY WORLD	V.1	577
Mirabell:	Madam, disquiet not your self on that account, to	478	WAY WORLD	V.1	613
Mirabell:	Madam, let me before these Witnesses, restore to you this	478	WAY WORLD	V.1	617

Maddest (1)

Angelica:	Mad as Valentine, I'll believe you love me, and the maddest	291	FOR LOVE	IV.1	587

Made (128)

Vainlove:	But is it not an Abuse to the Lover to be made a	38	OLD BATCH	I.1	60
Vainlove:	will, for you have made him fit for no Body else--Well--	40	OLD BATCH	I.1	114
Bellmour:	Merit, and preferring only those of interest, has made him	47	OLD BATCH	I.1	372
Sir Joseph:	he would put in for't he might be made General himself	53	OLD BATCH	II.1	215
Lucy:	Man, was by Nature Womans Cully made:	62	OLD BATCH	III.1	56
Vainlove:	She has made a quarrel on't.	63	OLD BATCH	III.1	97
Setter:	which he was made.	65	OLD BATCH	III.1	176
Lucy:	thou Maukin made up of the Shreds and Pairings of his	66	OLD BATCH	III.1	188
Singer:	But while she fond Resistance made,	71	OLD BATCH	III.2	V 15
Fondlewife:	made me weep--made poor Nykin weep--Nay come Kiss,	78	OLD BATCH	IV.1	117
Bellmour:	--But it is a Mistake which any Body might have made.	81	OLD BATCH	IV.2	41
Sir Joseph:	has made me as light as a Grasshopper.--Hist, hist,	85	OLD BATCH	IV.3	65
Araminta:	Woman's Obstinacy made me blind to what	88	OLD BATCH	IV.3	191
Setter:	Joy of your Return, Sir. Have you made a good	96	OLD BATCH	V.1	2
Bellmour:	made a delicious Voyage, Setter; and might have rode at	96	OLD BATCH	V.1	5
Lucy:	ruin'd my poor Mistress: You have made a Gap in her	98	OLD BATCH	V.1	48
Sharper:	Here, Frank; your Blood-Hound has made out the	99	OLD BATCH	V.1	107
Belinda:	Yes: You flattering Men of the Mode have made	106	OLD BATCH	V.1	369
Belinda:	Yes: You fluttering Men of the Mode have made	106	OLD BATCH	V.1	V369
Heartwell:	The Bone when broken, than when made a Bride.	108	OLD BATCH	V.2	15
Heartwell:	Death, Am I made your Laughing-stock? For	108	OLD BATCH	V.2	33
Heartwell:	With gawdy Plumes and gingling Bells made proud,	112	OLD BATCH	V.2	186
Mellefont:	Custome, after Dinner.--But I made a pretence	127	DOUBL DLR	I.1	13
Lady Touch:	effect made you Lord of all, of me, and of my Lord?	136	DOUBL DLR	I.1	349
Maskwell:	This discovery made me bold; I confess it; for by it, I	136	DOUBL DLR	I.1	364
Maskwell:	the Temple of the God, and Love was made a Mock-Worship,	137	DOUBL DLR	I.1	376
Lord Froth:	ay, there it is; who could resist! 'twas so my heart was made	140	DOUBL DLR	II.1	68
Brisk:	was telling me, your Ladyship has made an Essay toward	141	DOUBL DLR	II.1	118
Sir Paul:	he would have tantalized thee, and made a Cuckold of thy	146	DOUBL DLR	II.1	279
Lady Ply:	made one Trip, not one faux pas; O consider it, what would	147	DOUBL DLR	II.1	319
Lady Ply:	help it, if you are made a Captive? I swear it's pity it	148	DOUBL DLR	II.1	359
Maskwell:	your diversion: Tho it made you a little uneasy for the	149	DOUBL DLR	II.1	413
Maskwell:	made this agreement, if I accomplish her designs (as I told	149	DOUBL DLR	II.1	427
Maskwell:	will be made a Fool of by no body, but himself: Ha, ha, ha.	150	DOUBL DLR	II.1	456
Lord Touch:	Respect for Love, and made Sir Paul jealous of the Civility	151	DOUBL DLR	III.1	8
Maskwell:	made me conceal it; yet you may say, I threatned the next	154	DOUBL DLR	III.1	153
Careless:	tho' she begins to tack about; but I made Love a great	157	DOUBL DLR	III.1	266
Lady Froth:	Oh you made a Song upon her, Mr. Brisk.	166	DOUBL DLR	III.1	588
Lady Ply:	made plain--I don't see how my Daughter can in	172	DOUBL DLR	IV.1	169
Sir Paul:	Indeed if this be made plain, as my Lady your	172	DOUBL DLR	IV.1	171
Sir Paul:	It becomes me, when there is any comparison made,	172	DOUBL DLR	IV.1	187
Brisk:	tell whether I am glad or sorry that your Ladiship has made	176	DOUBL DLR	IV.1	339
Sir Paul:	here made? Why, this is better and more Miraculous than	180	DOUBL DLR	IV.1	505

Made (continued)

		PAGE	TITLE	ACT.SC	LINE
Maskwell:	made some Apology to the Ccmpany for her own, and	181	DOUBL DLR	IV.1	V522
Maskwell:	Excess of Joy had made me stupid! Thus may my	184	DOUEL DLR	IV.2	24
Maskwell:	Excess of Joy has made me stupid! Thus may my	184	DOUBL DLR	IV.2	V 24
Mellefont:	Now, by my Soul, I will not go till I have made	186	DOUBL DLR	IV.2	121
Mellefont:	known my wrongs--Nay, till I have made known yours,	186	DOUBL DLR	IV.2	122
Lord Touch:	Love of Mellefont would have made him still conceal it,--	191	DOUBL DLR	V.1	136
Lady Touch:	made him false to Mellefont,--Shame and Destruction!	191	DOUBL DLR	V.1	148
Lady Touch:	made him false to Mellefont,--Shame and Distraction!	191	DOUBL DLR	V.1	V148
Maskwell:	I have made him my own,--and ordered him to meet	194	DOUBL DLR	V.1	242
Maskwell:	upon the Rack; and made discov'ry of her last Plot: I hope	199	DOUBL DLR	V.1	462
Cynthia:	our happiness is, that this discovery was not made too late.	200	DOUBL DLR	V.1	475
Brisk:	With all my Soul,--your Ladyship has made me	201	DOUBL DLR	V.1	538
	And plant a Soil which you so rich have made.	213	FOR LOVE	PRO.	12
	Well plant a Soil which you so rich have made;	213	FOR LCVE	PRO.	V 12
	And when but two were made, both went astray;	213	FCR LOVE	PRO.	19
Jeremy:	Humph, and so he has made a very fine Feast, where	216	FOR LOVE	I.1	21
Valentine:	that made Court to her; so shall my Poverty be a				
	Mortification	217	FOR LOVE	I.1	53
Scandal:	what the Devil has not your Poverty made you Enemies	219	FOR LOVE	I.1	127
Tattle:	Pooh, I know Madam Drab has made her Brags in	227	FCR LOVE	I.1	419
Foresight:	things were done, and the Conveyance made--	240	FOR LOVE	II.1	188
Sr Sampson:	Body o' me, I have made a Cuckcld of a King, and the	241	FOR LCVE	II.1	222
Sr Sampson:	I have known an Astrologer made a Cuckold in	241	FOR LOVE	II.1	226
Foresight:	Wife, Sir Sampson? Tho' you made a Cuckcld of the	241	FOR LCVE	II.1	231
Jeremy:	By the Provision that's made for me, you might have	245	FCR LCVE	II.1	360
Mrs Frail:	The Estate You know is to be made over to him:--	248	FOR LOVE	II.1	494
Tattle:	Church, once, an Enquiry being made, who I was, it was	257	FOR LCVE	III.1	163
Ben:	The Song was made upon one of our Ships-Crew's	273	FCR LOVE	III.1	750
Ben:	Wife; our Boat-swain made the Song, may-hap you may	273	FOR LCVE	III.1	751
Scandal:	and be content orly to be made a Fool with other reasonable	278	FOR LCVE	IV.1	107
Mrs Fore:	towards it. I have almost made a Bargain with Jeremy,	288	FOR LCVE	IV.1	465
Jeremy:	what a happy Exchange she has made, between a Madman	302	FOR LCVE	V.1	204
Mrs Frail:	nothing but his being my Husband could have made me	310	FOR LCVE	V.1	473
Valentine:	only Pleasure was to please this Lady: I have made many	312	FOR LCVE	V.1	546
Leonora:	The Glory of the whole, were made the Prey	327	M. BRIDE	I.1	41
Almeria:	Started amidst his Foes, and made Captivity his Refuge;	329	M. BRIDE	I.1	116
Almeria:	Started amidst his Foes, and made Captivity	329	M. BRIDE	I.1	V116
Almeria:	Since I have made this Vow:	331	M. BRIDE	I.1	203
Almeria:	And more at large, since I have made this Vow.	331	M. BRIDE	I.1	V203
Manuel:	She should have made these Pallace Walls to shake,	333	M. BRIDE	I.1	311
Manuel:	I'll have Enquiry made; his Friend may be	337	M. BRIDE	I.1	445
Manuel:	I'll have Enquiry made; perhaps his Friend	337	M. BRIDE	I.1	V445
Almeria:	By its own Weight, made stedfast, and immoveable,	339	M. BRIDE	II.1	62
Osmyn-Alph:	Of yet unmeasur'd Time; when I have made	343	M. BRIDE	II.2	144
Heli:	And as your self made free, hither I came	344	M. BRIDE	II.2	177
Zara:	Where all is lost, and I am made a Slave.	347	M. BRIDE	II.2	302
Osmyn-Alph:	Why was I made the Instrument, to throw	347	M. BRIDE	II.2	322
Zara:	That Zara must be made the Sport of Slaves?	348	M. BRIDE	II.2	363
Osmyn-Alph:	Has made perforce subservient to that End	354	M. BRIDE	III.1	173
Gonsalez:	And by a secret Compact made with him,	363	M. BRIDE	IV.1	86
Manuel:	The light Impression thou hast made, remains.	369	M. BRIDE	IV.1	329
	And after she has made 'em Fools, forsakes.	393	WAY WORLD	PRO.	4
	Should Grants to Poets made, admit Resumption:	393	WAY WORLD	PRO.	19
Fainall:	she has made you Advances, which you have slighted?	397	WAY WORLD	I.1	83
Mirabell:	Was there any mention made of my Uncle, or me? Tell	407	WAY WORLD	I.1	451
Mirabell:	you have made a handsome Woman blush, then you think	409	WAY WORLD	I.1	527
Fainall:	another, have made you clash till you have both struck	413	WAY WORLD	II.1	139
Fainall:	wilfully neglect the gross advances made him by my Wife;	413	WAY WORLD	II.1	144
Mirabell:	In Justice to you, I have made you privy to my	417	WAY WORLD	II.1	280
Mirabell:	so I made him sure before-hand.	417	WAY WORLD	II.1	295
Millamant:	Long! Lord, have I not made violent haste? I	419	WAY WORLD	II.1	346
Mirabell:	and yet continue to be in Love, is to be made wise from the	423	WAY WORLD	II.1	499
Foible:	Sir, I made as much haste as I could.	423	WAY WORLD	II.1	515
Foible:	him; which I'll be sure to say has made him so enamour'd	423	WAY WORLD	II.1	522
Mirabell:	Excellent Foible! Matrimony has made you	424	WAY WORLD	II.1	525
Mirabell:	Foible--The Lease shall be made good and the Farm	424	WAY WORLD	II.1	539
Foible:	I warrant you, Madam; a little Art once made your	429	WAY WORLD	III.1	151
Fainall:	Dam him, that had been mine--had you not made	442	WAY WORLD	III.1	643
Lady Wish:	O dear, has my Nephew made his Addresses	445	WAY WORLD	IV.1	34
Millamant:	There never yet was Woman made,	446	WAY WORLD	IV.1	52
Sir Wilful:	Cozen, I made bold to pass thro' as it were,--I think this	447	WAY WORLD	IV.1	95
Sir Wilful:	Not at present Cozen,--Yes, I made bold to	447	WAY WORLD	IV.1	114
Millamant:	made sure of my will and pleasure.	449	WAY WORLD	IV.1	181
Mirabell:	for the Night, made of oil'd skins and I know not what	451	WAY WORLD	IV.1	249
Mrs Pain:	So, Is the fray made up, that you have left	453	WAY WORLD	IV.1	323
Lady Wish:	think that I have made a prostitution of decorums, but in	459	WAY WORLD	IV.1	535
Lady Wish:	abruptly, when Sir Wilfull was to have made his addresses.	461	WAY WORLD	IV.1	617
Lady Wish:	my self, and made you Governante of my whole Family.	462	WAY WORLD	V.1	21
Lady Wish:	you? What, have you made a passive Bawd of me?--	463	WAY WORLD	V.1	49
Mrs Pain:	Was there no mention made of me in the	464	WAY WORLD	V.1	74
Mincing:	Fortune made over to him, or he'll be divorc'd.	465	WAY WORLD	V.1	111
Lady Wish:	--I may say it; for I chiefly made it my own Care to	466	WAY WORLD	V.1	183
Lady Wish:	Father, or the Chaplain, and him we made a shift to put	467	WAY WORLD	V.1	192
Fainall:	remainder of her Fortune, not made over already; And for	469	WAY WORLD	V.1	269
Mirabell:	made me a Compensation for all my Services;--But	474	WAY WORLD	V.1	459

Madera (1)

| Sir Joseph: | --A-Gad, t'other Glass of Madera, and I durst have attack'd | 85 | OLD BATCH | IV.3 | 68 |

Madera-Wine (1)

| Sir Joseph: | wallow in Wine and Women. Why, this same Madera-Wine | 85 | OLD BATCH | IV.3 | 64 |

Madly (3)

Scandal:	Well, Is your Master ready; do's he look madly, and	275	FOR LOVE	IV.1	1
Scandal:	talk madly?	275	FOR LOVE	IV.1	2
Jeremy:	madly, she won't distinguish the Tone of your Voice.	303	FOR LOVE	V.1	218

Madman (12)

| Sir Joseph: | Free-loves! Sir Joseph, thou art a Mad-man. Agad, I'm in | 86 | OLD BATCH | IV.3 | 109 |

Make   (continued)

		PAGE	TITLE	ACT.SC	LINE
Valentine:	--I'll have you learn to make Couplets, to tag the . . .	218	FOR LOVE	I.1	77
Snap:	if we don't make haste, the Chairmen will be abroad, and .	224	FOR LOVE	I.1	298
Jeremy:	Sir, your Father's Steward says he comes to make . . .	224	FOR LOVE	I.1	302
Valentine:	me word; If I will make a Deed of Conveyance of my Right .	225	FOR LOVE	I.1	335
Valentine:	pay my Debts, and make my Fortune. This was once . . .	225	FOR LOVE	I.1	338
Tattle:	Ha, ha, ha; nay, now you make a Jest of it indeed. . . .	227	FOR LOVE	I.1	403
Tattle:	her--Madam, says I, there are some Persons who make . .	227	FOR LOVE	I.1	430
Foresight:	Sorrow, Want and Plenty, Night and Day, make up our . .	236	FOR LOVE	II.1	36
Angelica:	Well, but I can neither make you a Cuckold, Uncle, . . .	236	FOR LOVE	II.1	61
Angelica:	Yes, I can make Oath of your unlawful Midnight	237	FOR LOVE	II.1	96
Foresight:	a way to make your Lover, your Prodigal Spendthrift . .	238	FOR LOVE	II.1	116
Sr Sampson:	here 'tis, I have it in my Hand, Old Ptolomee; I'll make the	240	FOR LOVE	II.1	173
Sr Sampson:	as my Son Benjamin is arriv'd, he is to make over to him .	240	FOR LOVE	II.1	182
Foresight:	have consulted me for the time. Well, but we'll make . .	240	FOR LOVE	II.1	190
Sr Sampson:	--What, I'll make thee a Present of a Mummy: Now . . .	242	FOR LOVE	II.1	248
Sr Sampson:	House, and make an Entertainment for all the Philomaths, .	242	FOR LOVE	II.1	252
Jeremy:	Nay, that's as clear as the Sun; I'll make Oath of it .	245	FOR LOVE	II.1	355
Mrs Fore:	Countenance purely, you'd make an Admirable Player. . .	247	FOR LOVE	II.1	452
Mrs Fore:	now if we can improve that, and make her have an Aversion .	248	FOR LOVE	II.1	501
Miss Prue:	give me something to make me smell so--Oh pray	249	FOR LOVE	II.1	525
Miss Prue:	he'll give me something that will make my Smocks smell . .	249	FOR LOVE	II.1	527
Tattle:	I must make Love to you, pretty Miss; will you let . . .	251	FOR LOVE	II.1	588
Tattle:	me make Love to you?	251	FOR LOVE	II.1	589
Tattle:	Foresight mean by this Civility? Is it to make a Fool of me?	251	FOR LOVE	II.1	592
Miss Prue:	Well, and how will you make Love to me--	251	FOR LOVE	II.1	595
Miss Prue:	Come, I long to have you begin;--must I make Love . . .	251	FOR LOVE	II.1	596
Tattle:	more complying; and as soon as ever I make you say . . .	252	FOR LOVE	II.1	622
Tattle:	Well, my pretty Creature; will you make me happy . . .	252	FOR LOVE	II.1	631
Tattle:	Then I'll make you cry out.	253	FOR LOVE	II.1	657
Miss Prue:	Well, now I'll run and make more haste than you. . . .	253	FOR LOVE	II.1	660
Tattle:	shall make Oath, that I receive more Letters than the . .	257	FOR LOVE	III.1	159
Sr Sampson:	him make haste--I'm ready to cry for Joy.	259	FOR LOVE	III.1	215
Angelica:	if I were obliged to make a Choice, I declare I'd rather .	260	FOR LOVE	III.1	255
Sr Sampson:	Rogue shew himself, and make Love to some desponding . .	260	FOR LOVE	III.1	261
Ben:	him; Gad I'll lace his Musk-Doublet for him, I'll make him .	265	FOR LOVE	III.1	436
Mrs Fore:	Was there ever such Impudence, to make Love	269	FOR LOVE	III.1	593
Mrs Fore:	Well; and what use do you hope to make of	271	FOR LOVE	III.1	659
Mrs Fore:	this Affair between you and me. Here you make love to . .	272	FOR LOVE	III.1	687
Ben:	To make a Maid a Wife, Sir, ...	274	FOR LOVE	III.1	761
Ben:	come, my Lads, let's have a round, and I'll make one. . .	275	FOR LOVE	III.1	797
Scandal:	Make Blest the Ripen'd Maid, and Finish'd Man.	275	FOR LOVE	III.1	820
Jeremy:	Yes, Sir; you need make no great doubt of that; he . . .	276	FOR LOVE	IV.1	3
Jeremy:	playing the Madman, won't make her play the Fool, and . .	276	FOR LOVE	IV.1	9
Scandal:	comes Tyrannically to insult a ruin'd Lover, and make . .	276	FOR LOVE	IV.1	24
Angelica:	make me uneasie--If I don't see him, perhaps my	277	FOR LOVE	IV.1	80
Sr Sampson:	--Mad, I'll make him find his Senses.	279	FOR LOVE	IV.1	146
Sr Sampson:	Mr. Buckram, bid him make haste back with the	281	FOR LOVE	IV.1	209
Valentine:	together by a State-Cook, make Sauce for the whole . . .	282	FOR LOVE	IV.1	258
Sr Sampson:	join'd together, make yet a greater, that's a Man and his .	282	FOR LOVE	IV.1	266
Valentine:	I make a Fool of my Father.	283	FOR LOVE	IV.1	272
Scandal:	'S'death do you make no difference between me and . . .	284	FOR LOVE	IV.1	321
Scandal:	You make me mad--You are not serious--	284	FOR LOVE	IV.1	325
Ben:	for her to learn her Sampler, and make Dirt-pies, than to .	285	FOR LOVE	IV.1	374
Ben:	man.--I had another Voyage to make, let him take . . .	285	FOR LOVE	IV.1	376
Ben:	tell him so much.--So he said he'd make my heart ake; . .	285	FOR LOVE	IV.1	380
Ben:	d'ee mean all this while, to make a fool of me?	287	FOR LOVE	IV.1	427
Mrs Fore:	glad at least to make you a good Settlement.--Here they .	288	FOR LOVE	IV.1	475
Scandal:	It may make sport.	288	FOR LOVE	IV.1	484
Scandal:	It may make us sport.	288	FOR LOVE	IV.1	V484
Valentine:	Twenty Chairmen, and make thee Pedestals to stand erect .	289	FOR LOVE	IV.1	525
Angelica:	Nay, Mr. Tattle, If you make Love to me, you spoil . .	290	FOR LOVE	IV.1	568
Angelica:	my design, for I intended to make you my Confident. . .	290	FOR LOVE	IV.1	569
Angelica:	my design, for I intend to make you my Confident. . . .	290	FOR LOVE	IV.1	V569
Tattle:	Look you, Mr. Foresight, It is not my way to make . . .	291	FOR LOVE	IV.1	606
Scandal:	So I'll leave him to make use of the Discovery; and . . .	294	FOR LOVE	IV.1	691
Valentine:	more than Love, to make me worthy of you.	295	FOR LOVE	IV.1	727
Angelica:	Fortune enough to make any Man easie that I can like; If .	299	FOR LOVE	V.1	61
Angelica:	thing that wou'd make me appear to be too much concern'd .	299	FOR LOVE	V.1	91
Sr Sampson:	Posture, that I might make a more becoming Offer to a . .	300	FOR LOVE	V.1	96
Sr Sampson:	Eastern Empire under my Feet; it would make me only a .	300	FOR LOVE	V.1	99
Angelica:	make over his Inheritance to his younger Brother. . . .	300	FOR LOVE	V.1	123
Sr Sampson:	Odzooks I'm a young Man, and I'll make it appear-- . . .	301	FOR LOVE	V.1	140
Tattle:	I'll make thy Fortune; say no more--Thou art a . . .	302	FOR LOVE	V.1	180
Foresight:	How! I will make it appear that what you say is	304	FOR LOVE	V.1	274
Tattle:	No, Sir; 'tis to be done Privately--I never make . . .	304	FOR LOVE	V.1	280
Miss Prue:	make him be my Husband?	305	FOR LOVE	V.1	301
Miss Prue:	make him to be my husband?	305	FOR LOVE	V.1	V301
Foresight:	Robin make ready to give an Account of his Plate and . .	306	FOR LOVE	V.1	327
Ben:	Nay, I'll give you leave to guess--I'll undertake to make .	306	FOR LOVE	V.1	350
Ben:	they'd ne're make a Match together--Here they come. . .	307	FOR LOVE	V.1	374
Sr Sampson:	o' me, he shall be thy Father, I'll make him thy Father, and	308	FOR LOVE	V.1	396
Sr Sampson:	thou shalt make me a Father, and I'll make thee a Mother, .	308	FOR LOVE	V.1	397
Sr Sampson:	Aunt? Not at all, for a young Couple to make a Match . .	308	FOR LOVE	V.1	404
Angelica:	will make it easie to you.	310	FOR LOVE	V.1	482
Angelica:	cou'd not make me worthy of so generous and faithful a .	312	FOR LOVE	V.1	561
Angelica:	and struggl'd very hard to make this utmost Tryal of your .	312	FOR LOVE	V.1	563
Ben:	may make a Voyage together now.	312	FOR LOVE	V.1	569
Angelica:	to me, that I can make him and my self happy, than that I .	312	FOR LOVE	V.1	577
Valentine:	surprize would make it double.	312	FOR LOVE	V.1	580
Valentine:	make your best on't.	313	FOR LOVE	V.1	616
Almeria:	I would consent the Priest might make us one;	329	M. BRIDE	I.1	137
Almeria:	I would consent the Priest shou'd make us one;	329	M. BRIDE	I.1	V137
Almeria:	Alphonso, hear the Sacred Vow I make;	330	M. BRIDE	I.1	178
Manuel:	And make it Sin, not to renounce that Vow, ...	334	M. BRIDE	I.1	355
Manuel:	make	336	M. BRIDE	I.1	412

424

Makes   (continued)

Mrs Frail:	take great care when one makes a thrust in Fencing, not to	248	FOR LCVE	II.1	474
Miss Prue:	What makes 'em go away, Mr. Tattle? What do	251	FOR LCVE	II.1	581
Scandal:	Astrology! And Albertus Magnus makes it the most valuable .	267	FOR LCVE	III.1	537
Valentine:	You see what disguises Love makes us put on;	294	FOR LCVE	IV.1	700
Miss Prue:	Life: For when I'm awake, it makes me wish and long, and .	305	FOR LCVE	V.1	310
Zara:	That to have lov'd thee, makes me yet more lost . . .	348	M. BRIDE	II.2	338
Gonsalez:	Disquiets her too much; which makes it seem	366	M. ERIDE	IV.1	203
	For they're a sort of Fools which Fortune makes, . . .	393	WAY WORLD	PRO.	3
Fainall:	have something to brag of the next time he makes Court .	406	WAY WORLD	I.1	419
Millamant:	Lord, what is a Lover, that it can give? Why one makes .	420	WAY WORLD	II.1	403
Millamant:	one pleases, one makes more.	420	WAY WORLD	II.1	406
Millamant:	--But that cannot be--Well, that Thought makes . . .	434	WAY WORLD	III.1	361
Sir Wilful:	And that makes him so bright, ...	455	WAY WORLD	IV.1	420

Making (20)

Bellmour:	perswading that the Face she had been making all the . .	42	OLD BATCH	I.1	184
Araminta:	Rather poor silly Idols of your own making, which, . .	58	OLD BATCH	II.2	146
Vainlove:	And I love to have the pleasure of making my	63	OLD BATCH	III.1	100
Araminta:	Opportunity of making his Peace with me;--and to . .	85	OLD BATCH	IV.3	79
Bellmour:	hindred the making of your own Fortune.	94	OLD BATCH	IV.4	189
Lady Ply:	be making Answers, and taking that upon you, which . .	159	DOUBL DLR	III.1	328
Sir Paul:	but have a care of making rash Vows; Come hither to me, .	173	DOUBL DLR	IV.1	207
Lady Touch:	ought to be served; making you a Beast. Don't you know .	192	DOUBL DLR	V.1	165
Maskwell:	So, why so, while you are busied in making your . . .	193	DOUEL DLR	V.1	222
Sir Paul:	making Couplets.	201	DOUBL DLR	V.1	513
Valentine:	Tell Angelica, I am about making hard Conditions . .	234	FCR LCVE	I.1	673
Angelica:	we were ever after to live under Ground, or at least making	237	FOR LCVE	II.1	83
Scandal:	this Marriage and making over this Estate, this transferring	268	FCR LCVE	III.1	544
Scandal:	thereby incapable of making any Conveyance in Law; so .	283	FCR LCVE	IV.1	299
Scandal:	How's this! Tattle making Love to Angelica!	291	FOR LCVE	IV.1	574
Tattle:	of Valentine's making any more Addresses to you, I have .	291	FCR LCVE	IV.1	578
Witwoud:	Very pretty. Why you make no more of making	420	WAY WCBLD	II.1	407
Witwoud:	of Lovers, Madam, than of making so many Card-matches. .	420	WAY WORLD	II.1	408
Mrs Fain:	release her, by his making his Conditions to have my .	430	WAY WORLD	III.1	193
Sir Wilful:	not. I am somewhat dainty in making a Resolution,-- .	440	WAY WORLD	III.1	579

Malapert (1)

Foresight:	Why, you malapert Slut--	237	FOR LOVE	II.1	86

Male (3)   see Issue-Male

Sir Paul:	utterly extinct for want of Issue Male. Oh Impiety! But .	171	DOUBL DLR	IV.1	138
Sr Sampson:	upon the Issue Male of our Two Bodies begotten. Odsbud, .	300	FCR LOVE	V.1	128
Fainall:	that all the Male Sex shou'd be excepted; but somebody .	396	WAY WORLD	I.1	55

Male-Child (1)

Lady Wish:	never suffer'd to play with a Male-Child, tho' but in .	467	WAY WORLD	V.1	189

Male-Contents (2)

Heli:	Where not far off some Male-Contents hold Counsel . .	352	M. BBIDE	III.1	100
Heli:	Where not far off some Male-Contents hold Council . .	352	M. BBIDE	III.1	V100

Males (1)

Petulant:	Stand off--I'll kiss no more Males,--I have	454	WAY WORLD	IV.1	355

Malice (17)   see Mallice

	Not but the Man has Malice, would he show it, . . .	35	OLD BATCH	PRO.	14
Belinda:	My Denyal is premeditated like your Malice--Lard, . .	55	OLD BATCH	II.2	50
Araminta:	and Malice of thy Sex, thou canst not lay a Blemish on .	87	OLD BATCH	IV.3	168
Mellefont:	Malice, like a Dark Lanthorn, onely shone upon me, . .	129	DOUBL DLR	I.1	90
Mellefont:	Malice, like a Dark Lanthorn, only shone upon me, . .	129	DOUBL DLR	I.1	V 90
Mellefont:	malice can be engendred no where else.	145	DOUBL DLR	II.1	271
Maskwell:	that I have done, would look like Rivals Malice, false .	188	DOUBL DLR	V.1	39
Tattle:	Malice--But I know the bottom of it. She was brib'd .	227	FOR LOVE	I.1	423
Scandal:	Inconstancy, Covetousness, Dissimulation, Malice, and .	233	FOR LOVE	I.1	629
Angelica:	Malice is not a more terrible Consequence of his Aversion,	299	FOR LCVE	V.1	77
Zara:	Than all the Malice of my other Fate.	348	M. EBIDE	II.2	339
Osmyn-Alph:	Or hell-born Malice can invent; extort	357	M. BRIDE	III.1	315
Almeria:	The extremest Malice of our Fate can hinder: . . .	358	M. BÉIDE	III.1	336
Mirabell:	That Impudence and Malice, pass for Wit.	409	WAY WORLD	I.1	542
Marwood:	'Tis false, you urg'd it with deliberate Malice-- . .	414	WAY WORLD	II.1	182
Mrs Fain:	I despise you and defie your Malice--You	475	WAY WORLD	V.1	498
	Others there are whose Malice we'd prevent;	479	WAY WCRLD	EPI.	16

Malicious (11)

Belinda:	You think the malicious Grinn becomes you--The . . .	56	OLD BATCH	II.2	56
Araminta:	I am oblig'd to you--But who's malicious now, . . .	57	OLD BATCH	II.2	109
Heartwell:	(aside). That a Fool should ask such a malicious . .	73	OLD BATCH	III.2	95
Mellefont:	Malicious to them.	133	DOUBL DLR	I.1	234
Brisk:	Write, but--I'gad, I love to be malicious.--Nay, . .	133	DOUBL DLR	I.1	240
Maskwell:	self, and some ill Chance might have directed malicious .	189	DOUBL DLR	V.1	44
Foresight:	malicious Conjunctions and Oppositions in the Third .	238	FOR LCVE	II.1	129
Mirabell:	Fellow, which I carry'd so far, that I told her the				
	malicious	397	WAY WORLD	I.1	73
Witwoud:	Come, come, you are malicious now, and wou'd . . .	403	WAY WORLD	I.1	287
Petulant:	Ay, ay, pox I'm malicious, Man. Now he's soft . . .	408	WAY WORLD	I.1	503
	May such malicious Fops this Fortune find, ...	479	WAY WORLD	EPI.	23

Maliciously (1)

Setter:	Ha! what art, who thus maliciously hast awakned me, . .	65	OLD BATCH	III.1	165

Mall (3)   see Pall-Mall

Sharper:	for the Mall?	80	OLD BATCH	IV.1	183
Mirabell:	requires. Fainall, are you for the Mall?	409	WAY WORLD	I.1	508
Witwoud:	frosty Morning; thou shalt to the Mall with us; and we'll	409	WAY WORLD	I.1	520

Mallice (2)

Millamant:	dressing; their Folly is less provoking than your Mallice,	433	WAY WORLD	III.1	326
Millamant:	dressing here; their Folly is less provoking than your				
	Mallice, ...	433	WAY WORLD	III.1	V326

Man (224)   see Cast-serving-man, Chair-man, Coach-man, French-man, Land-man,
            Madman, Married-man

	Not but the Man has Malice, would he show it, . . .	35	OLD BATCH	PRO.	14
Vainlove:	How how, Ned, a wise Man say more than he	37	OLD BATCH	I.1	17
Bellmour:	one wise Man, and all that he knew was, that he knew .	37	OLD BATCH	I.1	21
Vainlove:	Faith I hate Love when 'tis forced upon a Man; as . .	39	OLD BATCH	I.1	94
Bellmour:	get your Man Setter to provide my Disguise.	40	OLD BATCH	I.1	112

Man   (continued)

Speaker	Text	PAGE	TITLE	ACT.SC	LINE
Valentine:	fill each Man his Glass.	223	FOR LOVE	I.1	263
Valentine:	And the prettiest Foot! Oh if a Man could but fasten his	223	FOR LOVE	I.1	286
Valentine:	draw the Writing--Mr. Trapland, you know this Man,	224	FOR LOVE	I.1	320
Tattle:	to that by one that we all know--A Man too. Only to	227	FOR LOVE	I.1	424
Tattle:	Man or Woman; but by the smoothness of her Chin,	228	FOR LOVE	I.1	466
Tattle:	only obliges a Man to Secresie, that she may have the	228	FOR LOVE	I.1	474
Tattle:	No Man but the Painter and my self was ever blest	232	FOR LOVE	I.1	610
Foresight:	And leave good Man to Brew and Bake,	236	FOR LOVE	II.1	52
Foresight:	I'll punish you, not a Man shall enter my House.	238	FOR LOVE	II.1	132
Sr Sampson:	Moon, and thou art the Man in the Moon: Nay, she is	242	FOR LOVE	II.1	257
Foresight:	a young Man, I wonder what he can do with it!	243	FOR LOVE	II.1	278
Foresight:	Man,--he has a violent death in his face; but I hope no	243	FOR LOVE	II.1	309
Sr Sampson:	can't a private man be born without all these followers:	245	FOR LOVE	II.1	350
Mrs Fore:	agreeable man; I don't quarrel at that, nor I don't think	247	FOR LOVE	II.1	428
Mrs Fore:	publick, and to be seen with a man in a Hackney-Coach	247	FOR LOVE	II.1	430
Mrs Frail:	or Barn-Elms with a man alone--something	247	FOR LOVE	II.1	439
Mrs Frail:	I at a worse place, and with a man!	247	FOR LOVE	II.1	445
Mrs Frail:	know, but I fancy, if I were a man	250	FOR LOVE	II.1	558
Nurse:	to do?--O the Father! a Man with her!--Why,	253	FOR LOVE	III.1	8
Tattle:	most unfortunate Man in the World, and the most cruelly	255	FOR LOVE	III.1	82
Angelica:	any Man, and for any Man with a good Estate: Therefore	260	FOR LOVE	III.1	254
Ben:	never abide to be Portbound as we call it: Now a man that	261	FOR LOVE	III.1	311
Ben:	A man that is marri'd, d'ee see, is no more like another	262	FOR LOVE	III.1	315
Ben:	man, than a Galley-slave is like one of us free Sailors, he is	262	FOR LOVE	III.1	316
Ben:	tho'f they love a man well enough, yet they don't care to	263	FOR LOVE	III.1	392
Miss Prue:	always tell a lie to a man; and I don't care, let my Father	264	FOR LOVE	III.1	397
Miss Prue:	thus, so I won't.--If I were a man,--(Crys.)--You durst not	264	FOR LOVE	III.1	429
Scandal:	You are a Wise Man, and a Conscientious Man; a Searcher	267	FOR LOVE	III.1	514
Scandal:	You say true, Man will err; meer Man will err--	267	FOR LOVE	III.1	527
Scandal:	why shou'd a Man court Danger, or a Woman shun	271	FOR LOVE	III.1	671
Scandal:	Make Blest the Ripen'd Maid, and Finish'd Man.	275	FOR LOVE	III.1	820
Angelica:	to see a Woman visit a Man at his own Lodgings in a	276	FOR LOVE	IV.1	21
Angelica:	Inhumanity, as not to be concern'd for a Man I must own	277	FOR LOVE	IV.1	43
Angelica:	Man, or I my being a Woman; or no more than I can help	278	FOR LOVE	IV.1	89
Valentine:	two greatest Monsters in the World are a Man and a	282	FOR LOVE	IV.1	263
Sr Sampson:	join'd together, make yet a greater, that's a Man and his	282	FOR LOVE	IV.1	266
Foresight:	opinion in this matter, and do reverence a man whom the	285	FOR LOVE	IV.1	349
Ben:	man.--I had another Voyage to make, let him take	285	FOR LOVE	IV.1	376
Mrs Fore:	Valentine's man, to sell his Master to us.	288	FOR LOVE	IV.1	466
Valentine:	Alas, poor Man; his Eyes are sunk, and his Hands	289	FOR LOVE	IV.1	519
Valentine:	Man shou'd have a Stomach to a Wedding Supper, when	289	FOR LOVE	IV.1	527
Valentine:	My Friend, what to do? I am no Married Man, and	292	FOR LOVE	IV.1	625
Sr Sampson:	a Man that admires a fine Woman, as much as I do.	298	FOR LOVE	V.1	19
Sr Sampson:	am not so old neither, to be a bare Courtier, only a Man of	298	FOR LOVE	V.1	22
Sr Sampson:	Women think a Man old too soon, faith and troth you do	298	FOR LOVE	V.1	25
Angelica:	Fortune enough to make any Man easie that I can like; If	299	FOR LOVE	V.1	61
Angelica:	there were such a thing as a young agreeable Man, with a	299	FOR LOVE	V.1	62
Angelica:	Man, submits both to the Severity and insolent Conduct of	299	FOR LOVE	V.1	73
Angelica:	Man is a Slave to the Severity and insolent Conduct of	299	FOR LOVE	V.1 V	73
Angelica:	her Husband. I should like a Man of Wit for a Lover,	299	FOR LOVE	V.1	74
Sr Sampson:	and I a happy Man. Odd, Madam, I'll love you as long as I	300	FOR LOVE	V.1	119
Sr Sampson:	and I'll consult a Parson; Odzooks I'm a Young Man:	301	FOR LOVE	V.1	139
Sr Sampson:	Odzooks I'm a young Man, and I'll make it appear--	301	FOR LOVE	V.1	140
Tattle:	must think of a new Man every Morning, and forget him	303	FOR LOVE	V.1	244
Foresight:	O, Mr. Tattle, your Servant, you are a close Man;	304	FOR LOVE	V.1	256
Miss Prue:	now my Mind is set upon a Man, I will have a Man some	305	FOR LOVE	V.1	307
Miss Prue:	Man; and if I can't have one, I wou'd go to sleep all my	305	FOR LOVE	V.1	309
Miss Prue:	Man, and shall be my Husband: I warrant he'll be my	305	FOR LOVE	V.1	318
Ben:	one another. I'm sorry for the Young Man with all my	310	FOR LOVE	V.1	489
Manuel:	Take it for Thanks, Old Man, that I rejoice	333	M. BRIDE	I.1	276
Manuel:	Such sullenness, and in a Man so brave,	335	M. BRIDE	I.1	375
Manuel:	Whence comes it, valiant Osmyn, that a Man	336	M. BRIDE	I.1	430
Zara:	He Looks not, minds not, hears not; barbarous Man!	346	M. BRIDE	II.2	244
Manuel:	That Wit of Man, and dire Revenge can think,	368	M. BRIDE	IV.1	297
Alonzo:	Soon as I seiz'd the Man,	373	M. BRIDE	V.1	21
Selim:	Prescience is Heav'ns alone, not giv'n to Man.	375	M. BRIDE	V.1	116
Selim:	If I have fail'd in what, as being a Man,	375	M. BRIDE	V.1	117
Mirabell:	You are a fortunate Man, Mr. Fainall.	395	WAY WORLD	I.1	1
Fainall:	more play with a Man that slighted his ill Fortune, than	395	WAY WORLD	I.1	8
Fainall:	mov'd that to avoid Scandal there might be one Man	396	WAY WORLD	I.1	56
Mirabell:	I did as much as Man cou'd, with any reasonable	397	WAY WORLD	I.1	68
Mirabell:	is to be flatter'd further, unless a Man shou'd endeavour	397	WAY WORLD	I.1	77
Fainall:	You are a gallant Man, Mirabell; and tho' you may	397	WAY WORLD	I.1	90
Mirabell:	Man that is.	399	WAY WORLD	I.1	147
Mirabell:	Man who is one.	399	WAY WORLD	I.1 V147	
Mirabell:	She has Beauty enough to make any Man think so;	399	WAY WORLD	I.1	153
Fainall:	For a passionate Lover, methinks you are a Man	399	WAY WORLD	I.1	156
Mirabell:	And for a discerning Man, somewhat too passionate	399	WAY WORLD	I.1	158
Fainall:	Life on't, you are your own Man again.	400	WAY WORLD	I.1	177
Mirabell:	For Travel! Why the Man that I mean is above	400	WAY WORLD	I.1	199
Witwoud:	out of my Head. I beg Pardon that I shou'd ask a Man of	402	WAY WORLD	I.1	256
Witwoud:	No Man in Town lives well with a Wife but	402	WAY WORLD	I.1	264
Mirabell:	Tho' 'twere a Man whom he fear'd, or a Woman	403	WAY WORLD	I.1	305
Petulant:	Well, well; I come--Sbud, a Man had as good	405	WAY WORLD	I.1	383
Petulant:	Ay, ay, pox I'm malicious, Man. Now he's soft	408	WAY WORLD	I.1	503
Marwood:	that Love shou'd ever die before us; and that the Man so	410	WAY WORLD	II.1	10
Mirabell:	He is the only Man that do's, Madam.	412	WAY WORLD	II.1	91
Mrs Fain:	The only Man that would tell me so at least;	412	WAY WORLD	II.1	92
Mrs Fain:	and the only Man from whom I could hear it without	412	WAY WORLD	II.1	93
Fainall:	rid of my Wife, I shou'd be a miserable Man.	413	WAY WORLD	II.1	110
Mrs Fain:	make me marry this Man?	417	WAY WORLD	II.1	264
Mirabell:	knew Fainall to be a Man lavish of his Morals, an interested	417	WAY WORLD	II.1	270
Mirabell:	Addresses. A better Man ought not to have been sacrific'd	417	WAY WORLD	II.1	275
Mirabell:	Thing that resembl'd a Man, tho' 'twere no more than	418	WAY WORLD	II.1	312

Manner   (continued)
Manners (10)
Mansion (3)
Manuel (3)
Manuring (1)
Manuscript (1)
Many (31)
Map (2)
Marble (3)
March (4)
Margery (3)
Marginal (2)
Mariage (1)
Maritornes (1)
Mark (13)

431

Married   (continued)

		PAGE	TITLE	ACT.SC	LINE
Mrs Fain:	Ingenious Mischief! Wou'd thou wert married	411	WAY WCRLD	II.1	65
Fainall:	Death, am I not married? what's pretence? Am I not	415	WAY WCRLD	II.1	209
Mirabell:	by this time. They were married this morning.	417	WAY WCRLD	II.1	289
Millamant:	To hear you tell me that Fcible's married, and your	422	WAY WCRLD	II.1	482
Millamant:	To hear you tell me Foible's married, and your	422	WAY WCRLD	II.1	V482
Mirabell:	Sirrah, Waitwell, why sure you think ycu were married	423	WAY WCRLD	II.1	505
Waitwell:	my self--Married, Knighted and attended all in one	424	WAY WCRLD	II.1	555
Waitwell:	me, I am married, and can't be my own Man again.	424	WAY WCRLD	II.1	561
Waitwell:	me, I'm married, and can't be my cwn Man again.	424	WAY WCRLD	II.1	V561
Lady Wish:	Fellow? I'll be married to Morrow, I'll be	428	WAY WCRLD	III.1	119
Mrs Fain:	whom thou wert this morning Married, is to personate	430	WAY WCRLD	III.1	190
Petulant:	married tho' he can't Read, any more than he is from being	436	WAY WCRLD	III.1	429
Petulant:	married tho' he can't Read, than he is frcm being	436	WAY WCRLD	III.1	V429
Fainall:	Married. My Wife had added Lustre to my Horns, by that	442	WAY WCRLD	III.1	645
Marwood:	You Married her to keep you; and if you	442	WAY WCRLD	III.1	655
Fainall:	I am married already; so that's over,--my Wife has	443	WAY WCRLD	III.1	677
Fainall:	my Reputation,--As tc my own, I married not for it; so	443	WAY WCRLD	III.1	684
Millamant:	to undergo a Fool, thou art Married and hast Patience--I	446	WAY WCRLD	IV.1	65
Millamant:	and dee hear, I won't be call'd names after I'm Married;	450	WAY WCRLD	IV.1	194
Millamant:	let us be as strange as if we had been married a great while;	450	WAY WORLD	IV.1	208
Waitwell:	Dead or Alive I'll ccme--and married we will be	461	WAY WCRLD	IV.1	642
Foible:	was tc have been void in Law; for he was married tc me	463	WAY WCRLD	V.1	40
Foible:	O that ever I was Born, O that I was ever Married,	463	WAY WCRLD	V.1	58
Lady Wish:	'Twas against my Consent that she Married	469	WAY WCRLD	V.1	302
Sir Wilful:	you're married; or if you will toy now; Let us have a	477	WAY WCRLD	V.1	600

Married-man (1)

Belinda:	at the Month's End, you shall hardly find a Married-man,	108	OLD BATCH	V.2	29

Marries (4)

Ben:	you too well, by sad experience;--I believe he that marries	287	FCR LCVE	IV.1	438
Angelica:	She that marries a Fool, Sir Sampson, commits the	299	FOR LCVE	V.1	70
Angelica:	She that marries a Fool, Sir Sampson, forfeits the	299	FOR LCVE	V.1	V 70
Angelica:	Censure of the World: And she that marries a very Witty	299	FCR LCVE	V.1	72

Marrow (1)

Mirabell:	marrow of a roasted Cat. In short, I forbid all Commerce	451	WAY WCRLD	IV.1	251

Marry (95)

Bellmour:	I marry Sir, I have a Hawks Eye at a Womans hand	38	OLD BATCH	I.1	32
Heartwell:	It will as soon blow North and by South--marry	44	OLD BATCH	I.1	294
Bellmour:	How never like? marry Hymen forbid. But this it	58	OLD BATCH	II.2	121
Bellmour:	thou be content to marry Araminta?	63	OLD BATCH	III.1	104
Vainlove:	Nor I to marry Araminta till I merit her.	63	OLD EATCH	III.1	109
Bellmour:	Marry her without her Consent; thou'rt a Riddle	64	OLD BATCH	III.1	113
Silvia:	Nay if you would Marry me, you should not ccme to	73	OLD BATCH	III.2	92
Silvia:	one. But do you intend to Marry me?	73	OLD BATCH	III.2	94
Heartwell:	Marry you? no, no, I'll love you.	73	OLD BATCH	III.2	99
Silvia:	Nay, but if you love me, you must Marry me; what	73	OLD EATCH	III.2	100
Silvia:	self; for I love you, and would Marry you.	73	OLD EATCH	III.2	106
Heartwell:	is a Jewel--Stay Silvia--But then to Marry--	74	OLD BATCH	III.2	116
Heartwell:	Marry, is playing the Fool all ones Life long.	74	OLD BATCH	III.2	118
Heartwell:	Heaven she kisses sweeter than Liberty--I will Marry	74	OLD BATCH	III.2	134
Heartwell:	Heaven her kiss is sweeter than Liberty--I will Marry	74	OLD BATCH	III.2	V134
Fondlewife:	thee marry Isaac?--Because she was beautiful and tempting,	76	OLD BATCH	IV.1	53
Bellmour:	marry 'em.--Ha? Are not Matters in this posture?	97	OLD BATCH	V.1	44
Bellmour:	marry Heartwell, Lucy.	98	OLD EATCH	V.1	55
Bellmour:	unwittingly marry a Whore.	98	OLD BATCH	V.1	62
Bellmour:	the Mistake of me: I'll marry 'em.--Nay, don't pause:	98	OLD BATCH	V.1	67
Setter:	marry 'em.	98	OLD BATCH	V.1	85
Sharper:	of your Promise? Will you marry her your self?	100	OLD BATCH	V.1	155
Sharper:	She has given Vainlove her Promise, to marry him	102	OLD BATCH	V.1	212
Belinda:	Heart to marry thee, purely to be rid of thee.--At	106	OLD BATCH	V.1	365
Sir Paul:	No marry will I not be pleased, I am pleased to be	144	DOUEL DLR	II.1	211
Lady Ply:	you? What did I Marry you for? Am I not to be absolute	144	DOUBL DLR	II.1	216
Sir Paul:	no sin,--but then, to Marry my Daughter, for the	147	DOUEL DLR	II.1	350
Maskwell:	Grazing, and to--ha, ha, ha, Marry Cynthia my self;	149	DOUEL DLR	II.1	403
Mellefont:	House this mcment and Marry one another, without	168	DOUEL DLR	IV.1	28
Cynthia:	Marry for Love.	168	DOUEL DLR	IV.1	32
Cynthia:	Hold--Never to Marry any Body else.	168	DOUEL DLR	IV.1	40
Cynthia:	not him, I have sworn never to Marry.	171	DOUEL DLR	IV.1	135
Sir Paul:	Never to Marry! Heav'ns forbid; must I neither have	171	DOUEL DLR	IV.1	136
Sir Paul:	Never to Marry! Heav'ns forbid; must I neither have	171	DOUEL DLR	IV.1	V136
Sir Paul:	Lady here: Marry Heaven forbid that you should follow	174	DOUEL DLR	IV.1	249
Brisk:	Deuce take me I believe you intend to Marry your	174	DOUEL DLR	IV.1	271
Lady Touch:	Maskwell your Heir, and Marry Cynthia!	191	DOUBL DLR	V.1	122
Lady Touch:	News, You were to marry Cynthia--that you had	198	DOUEL DLR	V.1	417
Mrs Frail:	Then let him Marry and reform.	231	FOR LCVE	I.1	559
Nurse:	Town,--Marry, pray Heav'n they ha' given her any	235	FOR LCVE	II.1	21
Nurse:	and swear now, ha, ha, ha, Marry and did you ever see the	235	FOR LCVE	II.1	23
Nurse:	Pray Heav'n send your Worship good Luck, Marry	235	FOR LCVE	II.1	26
Nurse:	Marry Heav'n defend--I at Midnight Practices	238	FOR LCVE	II.1	98
Mrs Frail:	Yes marry will I--A great piece cf business to	246	FOR LCVE	II.1	418
Nurse:	Miss, Miss, Miss Frue--Mercy on me, marry and	253	FOR LCVE	III.1	1
Angelica:	If I marry, Sir Sampson, I'm for a good Estate with	260	FOR LCVE	III.1	253
Ben:	Mess, and that's true: marry I had forgot. Dick's dead	261	FOR LCVE	III.1	294
Ben:	Mess, that's true: marry I had forgot. Dick's dead	261	FOR LCVE	III.1	V294
Sr Sampson:	No, I intend you shall Marry, Ben; I would not	261	FOR LCVE	III.1	297
Sr Sampson:	Marry for thy sake.	261	FOR LCVE	III.1	298
Ben:	Nay, what do's that signifie?--an you Marry again--	261	FOR LCVE	III.1	299
Ben:	Marry a God's Name an the wind sit that way. As for my	261	FOR LCVE	III.1	302
Ben:	part, may-hap I have no mind to Marry.	261	FOR LCVE	III.1	303
Ben:	Say'n you so forsooth: Marry and I shou'd like such a	262	FOR LCVE	III.1	324
Ben:	You Cheese-curd you,--Marry thee! Oons I'll Marry a	264	FOR LCVE	III.1	425
Sr Sampson:	Why did I ever marry?	282	FOR LCVE	IV.1	261
Ben:	chitty fac'd thing, as he would have me marry,--so he	285	FOR LCVE	IV.1	364
Ben:	told 'n in plain terms, if I were minded to marry, I'de	285	FOR LCVE	IV.1	371
Ben:	marry to please my self, not him; and for the Young	285	FOR LOVE	IV.1	372

Marry   (continued)

		PAGE	TITLE	ACT.SC	LINE
Ben:	marry himself. Gad, says I, an you play the fool and marry	286	FOR LOVE	IV.1	382
Ben:	and he'll marry her himself, with all my heart.	286	FOR LOVE	IV.1	387
Ben:	them marry you, as don't know you:--Gad I know	287	FOR LOVE	IV.1	437
Valentine:	and yet we'll Marry one another in spite of the Pope--	290	FOR LOVE	IV.1	559
Tattle:	Marry any body before.	303	FOR LOVE	V.1	214
Miss Prue:	must not marry the Seaman now--my Father says so.	303	FOR LOVE	V.1	227
Tattle:	every Night--No, no, to marry, is to be a Child again,	303	FOR LOVE	V.1	245
Foresight:	marry my Daughter without my Consent?	304	FOR LOVE	V.1	283
Miss Prue:	won't get me one, I'll get one for my self: I'll marry our	305	FOR LOVE	V.1	316
Ben:	Case, you should not marry her. It's just the same thing,	308	FOR LOVE	V.1	414
Tattle:	were good--But this is the most cruel thing, to marry	309	FOR LOVE	V.1	458
Fainall:	Marry her, marry her; be half as well acquainted	400	WAY WORLD	I.1	175
Fainall:	Mother. If you marry Millamant you must call Cousins	400	WAY WORLD	I.1	194
Mirabell:	Ay marry, what's that, Witwoud?	403	WAY WORLD	I.1	313
Petulant:	Friends; and if he shou'd marry and have a Child, you may	407	WAY WORLD	I.1	439
Fainall:	And wherefore did I marry, but to make lawful Prize of a	415	WAY WORLD	II.1	206
Fainall:	where to another World. I'll marry thee--Be pacify'd	416	WAY WORLD	II.1	246
Mrs Fain:	make me marry this Man?	417	WAY WORLD	II.1	264
Mirabell:	hopes to ruin me, shou'd consent to marry my pretended	417	WAY WORLD	II.1	293
Mirabell:	Yes, I think the good Lady wou'd marry any	418	WAY WORLD	II.1	311
Lady Wish:	marry a Drawer to have him poyson'd in his Wine. I'll	427	WAY WORLD	III.1	104
Foible:	him Madam, starve him, marry Sir Rowland and get him	427	WAY WORLD	III.1	107
Foible:	me too (says he), and Mrs. Millamant is to marry my	428	WAY WORLD	III.1	112
Millamant:	Ah! to marry an Ignorant! that can hardly Read	436	WAY WORLD	III.1	426
Millamant:	an Air. Ah! I'll never marry, unless I am first	449	WAY WORLD	IV.1	180
Sir Wilful:	but if you wou'd have me Marry my Cozen,--say the	455	WAY WORLD	IV.1	403
Lady Wish:	No damage? What to Betray me, tc Marry me	463	WAY WORLD	V.1	34
Foible:	Pray do but hear me Madam, he ccu'd not marry	463	WAY WORLD	V.1	38
Fainall:	Life; on condition you oblige your self never to Marry,	468	WAY WORLD	V.1	253
Lady Wish:	Never to Marry?	468	WAY WORLD	V.1	255
Sir Wilful:	willing to marry my Cozen. So pray lets all be Friends,	470	WAY WORLD	V.1	321
Sir Wilful:	Over-sea's once already; and with provisc that I Marry my	471	WAY WORLD	V.1	349
Sir Wilful:	S'heart Aunt, I have no mind to marry. My	477	WAY WORLD	V.1	582

Marry'd (11)

Bellmour:	--I got an Opportunity (after I had marry'd 'em) of	100	OLD BATCH	V.1	149
Sharper:	Marry'd in haste, we may repent at leisure.	105	OLD BATCH	V.1	328
Setter:	At leisure marry'd, they repent in haste.	105	OLD BATCH	V.1	331
Ben:	to ask you; well, you be'nt Marry'd again, Father, be you?	261	FOR LOVE	III.1	296
Ben:	is marry'd, has as it were, d'ee see, his feet in the	261	FOR LOVE	III.1	312
	Bilboes,				
Mrs Fore:	have been Marry'd.	270	FOR LOVE	III.1	624
Ben:	know her, Sir. Before she was Marry'd, she was call'd	273	FOR LOVE	III.1	752
Valentine:	and we'll be Marry'd in the dead of Night.--But say	290	FOR LOVE	IV.1	548
Almeria:	They wou'd have marry'd me; but I had sworn	343	M. BRIDE	II.2	126
Marwood:	up her Game, before she was Marry'd.	442	WAY WORLD	III.1	652
Sir Wilful:	Marry'd, say the Word, and send for the Piper, Wilfull	455	WAY WORLD	IV.1	411

Marrying (8)

Lady Ply:	guilt of deceiving every body; Marrying the Daughter,	147	DOUBL DLR	II.1	315
Maskwell:	way, but in the hopes of her Marrying you.--	193	DOUBL DLR	V.1	220
Mrs Frail:	the Estate be setled; for you know, Marrying without an	273	FOR LOVE	III.1	719
Tattle:	and play with the same Rattle always: O fie, marrying is a	303	FOR LOVE	V.1	246
Fainall:	marrying with my Lady's Approbation?	396	WAY WORLD	I.1	46
Marwood:	Faith by Marrying; if I cou'd but find one	411	WAY WORLD	II.1	53
Marwood:	Marrying than Travelling at his Years. I hear he is turn'd	431	WAY WORLD	III.1	260
Lady Wish:	Travels--I am against my Nephews marrying too	431	WAY WORLD	III.1	263

Mars (1)

Scandal:	Good Night, good Mr. Foresight;--and I hope Mars	271	FOR LOVE	III.1	656

Martial (1)

Gonsalez:	Is entring now, in Martial Pomp the Pallace.	331	M. BRIDE	I.1	226

Martins (1)

Foresight:	No; St. Martins in the Fields.	289	FOR LOVE	IV.1	518

Martyr (3)

Scandal:	vain! Who would die a Martyr to Sense in a Country	219	FOR LOVE	I.1	139
Scandal:	Do, I'll dye a Martyr, rather than disclaim my	269	FOR LOVE	III.1	595
Zara:	A Martyr and a victim to my Vows:	381	M. BRIDE	V.2	193

Martyrdom (1)

Angelica:	Martyrdom, and sacrifice their Interest to their Constancy!	314	FOR LOVE	V.1	634

Marwood (36)

Mirabell:	Yes, and Mrs. Marwood and three or four more,	396	WAY WORLD	I.1	28
Mirabell:	Marwood.	397	WAY WORLD	I.1	81
	(St. James's Park. Enter Mrs. Fainall and Mrs. Marwood.)	410	WAY WORLD	II.1	
Mrs Fain:	Ay, ay, dear Marwood, if we will be happy, we	410	WAY WORLD	II.1	1
Foible:	that was Mrs. Marwood that went by in a Mask; if she has	424	WAY WORLD	II.1	545
Peg:	No Madam, Mrs. Marwood.	426	WAY WORLD	III.1	39
Lady Wish:	O Marwood, let her come in. Come in good	426	WAY WORLD	III.1	40
Lady Wish:	Marwood.	426	WAY WORLD	III.1	41
	(Enter Mrs. Marwood.)	426	WAY WORLD	III.1	42
Lady Wish:	Ah dear Marwood, what's Integrity to an Opportunity?	426	WAY WORLD	III.1	60
	(Exit Marwood.)	426	WAY WORLD	III.1	68
Mrs Fain:	come too late. That Devil Marwood saw you in the Park	430	WAY WORLD	III.1	185
Foible:	our success, Mrs. Marwood had told my Lady; but I warrant	430	WAY WORLD	III.1	206
Foible:	to him,--besides, I believe Madam Marwood watches	430	WAY WORLD	III.1	216
	(Enter Mrs. Marwood.)	431	WAY WORLD	III.1	224
Marwood:	rest of him. Poor simple Fiend! Madam Marwood has a	431	WAY WORLD	III.1	239
Lady Wish:	O dear Marwood what shall I say, for this rude	431	WAY WORLD	III.1	250
Lady Wish:	Marwood shall I be free with you again, and beg you to	432	WAY WORLD	III.1	279
Millamant:	Man--Marwood, your Servant.	432	WAY WORLD	III.1	285
Millamant:	I'll take my Death, Marwood, you are more Censorious,	433	WAY WORLD	III.1	323
Sir Wilful:	(Salutes Mrs. Marwood.)	438	WAY WORLD	III.1	485
	(Fainall and Mrs. Marwood talk a-part.)	441	WAY WORLD	III.1	610
Lady Wish:	walk? Marwood--	441	WAY WORLD	III.1	624
	(Manent Mrs. Marwood and Fainall.)	441	WAY WORLD	III.1	627
Foible:	Marwood declar'd all to my Lady.	464	WAY WORLD	V.1	73
Mrs Fain:	Confederacy? I fancy Marwood has not told her, tho' she	464	WAY WORLD	V.1	76
Foible:	friends together, than set 'em at distance. But Mrs. Marwood	464	WAY WORLD	V.1	88

Master   (continued)

		PAGE	TITLE	ACT.SC	LINE
Lucy:	To be brief then; what is the reason your Master did	66	OLD BATCH	III.1	217
Fondlewife:	Kiss, Dear,--I met the Master of the Ship	89	OLD BATCH	IV.4	23
Setter:	This afternoon, Sir, about an Hour before my Master	99	OLD BATCH	V.1	100
Sharper:	Well, I'll go and inform your Master; and do you	102	OLD BATCH	V.1	218
Setter:	As I suppose my Master Heartwell.	105	OLD BATCH	V.1	332
Jeremy:	his Master from any future Authority over him--	218	FOR LOVE	I.1	70
Jeremy:	Why so I have been telling my Master, Sir: Mr.	219	FOR LOVE	I.1	122
Foresight:	to the Master of a Family--I remember an old	236	FOR LOVE	II.1	48
Jeremy:	No, Sir, Mr. Valentine, my master,--'tis the first	242	FOR LOVE	II.1	267
Jeremy:	those same Whoreson Appetites too; that my Master	245	FOR LOVE	II.1	363
Mrs Frail:	I shou'd not doubt that, if you were Master of me.	262	FOR LOVE	III.1	329
Scandal:	longer Master of my self--I was interrupted in the morning,	269	FOR LOVE	III.1	587
Mrs Fore:	Nurse; your Master is not well; put him to	270	FOR LOVE	III.1	635
Scandal:	Well, Is your Master ready; do's he look madly, and	275	FOR LOVE	IV.1	1
Jeremy:	my Master was run stark mad only for Love of her Mistress;	276	FOR LOVE	IV.1	15
Jeremy:	us to be mad? Why, Sir, my Master longs to see her; and	278	FOR LOVE	IV.1	99
Scandal:	for I can't resolve you; but I'll inform your Master. In	278	FOR LOVE	IV.1	103
Scandal:	to your Master.	278	FOR LOVE	IV.1	109
Sr Sampson:	Scoundrel. Sirrah, where's your Master?	278	FOR LOVE	IV.1	118
Mrs Fore:	Valentine's man, to sell his Master to us.	288	FOR LOVE	IV.1	466
Scandal:	And have you given your Master a hint of their Plot	288	FOR LOVE	IV.1	479
Jeremy:	--And now, Sir, my former Master, having much	301	FOR LOVE	V.1	173
Jeremy:	mistake--You see, Sir, my Master was never mad, nor	313	FOR LOVE	V.1	593
Coachman:	Is Master Petulant here, Mistress?	404	WAY WORLD	I.1	344

Master-Key (1)

| Marwood: | very Master-Key to every Bodies strong Box. My Friend | 431 | WAY WORLD | III.1 | 228 |

Master-piece (1)

| Maskwell: | This was a Master-piece, and did not need my | 154 | DOUBL DLR | III.1 | 128 |

Master's (7)

Setter:	undone, my Master's undone, my Lady's undone, and all	103	OLD BATCH	V.1	240
Jeremy:	No strange matter, Madam; my Master's mad, that's	276	FOR LOVE	IV.1	29
Valentine:	Master's Shop in the morning, may ten to one, dirty his	289	FOR LOVE	IV.1	509
Angelica:	acknowledge your Trick, and confess your Master's	295	FOR LOVE	IV.1	735
Jeremy:	upon the Quarry. It is the Whim of my Master's Madness	302	FOR LOVE	V.1	200
Jeremy:	Well, Sir, I'll go and tell her my Master's coming;	303	FOR LOVE	V.1	215
Gonsalez:	I who have spilt my Royal Master's Blood,	378	M. BRIDE	V.2	70

Masters (6)

Bellmour:	Be at your Masters Lodging in the Evening--I	64	OLD BATCH	III.1	134
Lucy:	not to affect his Masters faults; and consequently	64	OLD BATCH	III.1	147
Lucy:	Masters employment. For he's the head Fimp to Mr.	65	OLD BATCH	III.1	169
Lucy:	No thou pitiful Flatterer of thy Masters imperfections;	66	OLD BATCH	III.1	187
Heartwell:	generally Masters in it: But I'm so newly entred, you	72	OLD BATCH	III.2	57
Nurse:	Doings with my Masters Worship--Why, did you	238	FOR LOVE	II.1	100

Match (31)   see Cock-match

Maskwell:	day Offended you, but in not breaking off his Match with	137	DOUBL DLR	I.1	388
Cynthia:	met with your Match, on my Conscience.	139	DOUBL DLR	II.1	26
Mellefont:	Fortune indeed makes the match, and the Two nearest,	143	DOUBL DLR	II.1	165
Sir Paul:	Reason,--as soon may Tygers Match with Tygers, Lambs	144	DOUBL DLR	II.1	224
Lady Ply:	consent to that, as sure as can be, I'll break the Match.	147	DOUBL DLR	II.1	352
Maskwell:	I have undertaken to break the Match, I have undertaken	149	DOUBL DLR	II.1	399
Maskwell:	to break the Match: Then she thought my Jealousie might	149	DOUBL DLR	II.1	424
Cynthia:	lay my Life it will never be a Match.	167	DOUBL DLR	IV.1	7
Lady Ply:	make up this Match again, because Mr. Careless said it	171	DOUBL DLR	IV.1	153
Lady Ply:	make up the Match again, because Mr. Careless said it	171	DOUBL DLR	IV.1	V153
Sir Paul:	your Ladiship is of opinion that the Match may go forward.	172	DOUBL DLR	IV.1	203
Mrs Frail:	there's a Match talk'd of by the Old People--Well,	231	FOR LOVE	I.1	569
Angelica:	to satisfie you about Valentine: For if a Match were seemingly	300	FOR LOVE	V.1	108
Sr Sampson:	If we were to go through with it. But why must the Match	300	FOR LOVE	V.1	114
Sr Sampson:	consent? Is it a Match then?	300	FOR LOVE	V.1	133
Ben:	they'd ne're make a Match together--Here they come.	307	FOR LOVE	V.1	374
Sr Sampson:	Aunt? Not at all, for a young Couple to make a Match	308	FOR LOVE	V.1	404
Ben:	it will only serve to light up a Match for some body else.	308	FOR LOVE	V.1	411
Ben:	Why there's another Match now, as tho'f a couple of	310	FOR LOVE	V.1	487
Scandal:	employ'd when the Match is so much mended. Valentine,	313	FOR LOVE	V.1	600
Leonora:	Proposing by a Match between Alphonso	327	M. BRIDE	I.1	48
Fainall:	Aunt, and be the officious Obstacle of his Match with	414	WAY WORLD	II.1	160
Mrs Fain:	Match between Millamant and your Uncle.	418	WAY WORLD	II.1	304
Marwood:	met with your Match.--O Man, Man! Woman,	431	WAY WORLD	III.1	235
Marwood:	a very fit Match. He may Travel afterwards. 'Tis a Thing	432	WAY WORLD	III.1	267
Marwood:	match between Millamant and Sir Wilfull, that may be an	443	WAY WORLD	III.1	669
Sir Wilful:	Head and drink a Health to 'em--A Match or no Match,	456	WAY WORLD	IV.1	426
Lady Wish:	This will never do. It will never make a Match.	457	WAY WORLD	IV.1	481
Fainall:	and by refusing the offer'd Match with Sir Wilfull Witwoud,	469	WAY WORLD	V.1	284
Lady Wish:	my Nephews Match, you shall have my Niece yet, and all	474	WAY WORLD	V.1	464

Match'd (2)

| Lady Wish: | this is her's; she is match'd now with a Witness--I | 470 | WAY WORLD | V.1 | 306 |
| Lady Wish: | Neice exerts a lawfull claim, having Match'd her self by | 472 | WAY WORLD | V.1 | 417 |

Matches (1)   see Card-matches

| Angelica: | Siege? What a World of Fire and Candle, Matches and | 237 | FOR LOVE | II.1 | 81 |

Matchiavilian (1)

| Mellefont: | but a shallow artifice, unworthy of my Matchiavilian | 148 | DOUBL DLR | II.1 | 376 |

Matchless (3)

Gonsalez:	The Force and Influence of your matchless Charms.	332	M. BRIDE	I.1	258
Osmyn-Alph:	Some Recompence of Love and matchless Truth.	343	M. BRIDE	II.2	146
	For, as when Painters form a matchless Face,	479	WAY WORLD	EPI.	31

Matchmaking (1)

| Fainall: | Why then Foible's a Bawd, an Errant, Rank, Matchmaking | 442 | WAY WORLD | III.1 | 628 |

Mathemacular (1)

| Lady Ply: | every thing in the World, but give me Mathemacular | 146 | DOUBL DLR | II.1 | 302 |

Matin (0)   see Someils du Matin

Matrimonial (1)

| Sharper: | Matrimonial Oath with Interest.--Come, thou'rt | 99 | OLD BATCH | V.1 | 89 |

Matrimonie (1)

| Ben: | don't much stand towards Matrimonie. I love to roam | 261 | FOR LOVE | III.1 | 309 |

435

Matrimony (12)

		PAGE	TITLE	ACT.SC	LINE
Fondlewife:	to Matrimony? Come, come, plain-dealing is a Jewel.	94	OLD BATCH	IV.4	197
Bellmour:	Turtle to you, that I'll go and sollicite Matrimony with all	96	OLD BATCH	IV.4	265
Setter:	Promotion of Vulgar Matrimony.	105	OLD BATCH	V.1	339
Bellmour:	Matrimony, in Opposition to the Pleasures of Courtship.	107	OLD BATCH	V.1	383
Ben:	it were, bound for the Land of Matrimony; 'tis a Voyage	263	FOR LOVE	III.1	372
Mrs Frail:	committing Matrimony himself.--If he has a mind to	287	FOR LOVE	IV.1	459
Valentine:	upon, and look Matrimony in the face. Ha, ha, ha! That a	289	FOR LOVE	IV.1	526
Sr Sampson:	of any thing;--And if they commit Matrimony,	299	FOR LOVE	V.1	56
Ben:	when she's going, let her go. For no Matrimony is tough	310	FOR LOVE	V.1	492
Mirabell:	Excellent Foible! Matrimony has made you	424	WAY WORLD	II.1	525
Millamant:	last moment, tho' I am upon the very Verge of Matrimony,	449	WAY WORLD	IV.1	161
Fainall:	amongst other secrets of Matrimony and Policy, as they are	469	WAY WORLD	V.1	275

Matrimony'd (0) see Out-Matrimony'd

Matter (99)

		PAGE	TITLE	ACT.SC	LINE
	You think that strange--no matter, he'll out grow it.	35	OLD BATCH	PRO.	16
Capt Bluff:	Campagn, had a small Post there; but no matter for that--	52	OLD BATCH	II.1	196
Capt Bluff:	Ay, ay, no matter--You see Mr. Sharper after all	53	OLD BATCH	II.1	210
Belinda:	Cousin, you talk odly--What ever the Matter is, O	55	OLD BATCH	II.2	51
Araminta:	What's the Matter, Cousin.	59	OLD BATCH	II.2	161
Sir Joseph:	you--Why what a Devil's the Matter, Bully, are you	68	OLD BATCH	III.1	264
Sharper:	Hey day! Captain, what's the matter? You can tell.	69	OLD BATCH	III.1	295
Capt Bluff:	Mr. Sharper, the matter is plain--Sir Joseph has found	69	OLD BATCH	III.1	296
Capt Bluff:	Very well--Very fine--But 'tis no matter--	70	OLD BATCH	III.1	331
Sir Joseph:	Ay, ay, so were you too; no matter, 'tis past.	70	OLD BATCH	III.1	351
Araminta:	Why, What's the matter?	83	OLD BATCH	IV.3	3
Araminta:	No matter,--I see Vainlove coming this way,--	85	OLD BATCH	IV.3	77
Laetitia:	My Jewel, Art thou there? No matter for your	89	OLD BATCH	IV.4	15
Fondlewife:	Bless us! What's the matter? What's the matter?	90	OLD BATCH	IV.4	51
Fondlewife:	--Heh! You have finish'd the matter, Heh? And I am,	94	OLD BATCH	IV.4	183
Fondlewife:	Humph, Nay, if you mince the matter once, and	94	OLD BATCH	IV.4	190
Bellmour:	confess the whole matter to thee.	94	OLD BATCH	IV.4	199
Fondlewife:	No, no, for that matter--when she and I part,	95	OLD BATCH	IV.4	228
Heartwell:	I'll pay him well, if you'll break the Matter to him.	97	OLD BATCH	V.1	20
Sir Joseph:	I'm in the Ladies favours?--No matter, I'll make your	103	OLD BATCH	V.1	261
Sir Joseph:	I'm in the Lady's favour?--No matter, I'll make your	103	OLD BATCH	V.1	V261
Vainlove:	What's the Matter?	108	OLD BATCH	V.2	44
Lady Ply:	Conduct, should be contradicted in a matter of this	144	DOUBL DLR	II.1	218
Maskwell:	anon, after that I'll tell you the whole matter; be here in	149	DOUBL DLR	II.1	434
Lady Touch:	Nay, no great matter, only--well I have	152	DOUBL DLR	III.1	81
Maskwell:	it my Brain or Providence? No Matter which--I will	155	DOUBL DLR	III.1	189
Mellefont:	Why, what's the Matter? She's convinc'd that I	157	DOUBL DLR	III.1	268
Careless:	No, what can be the matter then?	161	DOUBL DLR	III.1	429
Sir Paul:	no more familiarity with her Person--as to that matter--	162	DOUBL DLR	III.1	439
Careless:	Sir Paul, harkee, I'm reasoning the matter you know;	163	DOUBL DLR	III.1	493
Sir Paul:	Gads-bud no matter for that, Conscience and Law	171	DOUBL DLR	IV.1	148
Lady Ply:	the matter.	173	DOUBL DLR	IV.1	205
Sir Paul:	O Law, what's the matter now? I hope you are not	174	DOUBL DLR	IV.1	269
Brisk:	Wit too, to keep in with him--No matter, she's a	175	DOUBL DLR	IV.1	294
Lady Froth:	O Heavens Mr. Brisk! What's the matter?	175	DOUBL DLR	IV.1	312
Brisk:	--The matter Madam? Nothing, Madam, nothing at	175	DOUBL DLR	IV.1	314
Careless:	What's the matter, Madam?	178	DOUBL DLR	IV.1	392
Sir Paul:	from him to treat with you about the very matter of Fact.--	178	DOUBL DLR	IV.1	410
Sir Paul:	Matter of Fact? Very pretty; it seems then I am conducing	178	DOUBL DLR	IV.1	411
Sir Paul:	Gads-bud, would that were Matter of Fact too. Die and	178	DOUBL DLR	IV.1	417
Lady Ply:	Why is not here Matter of Fact?	180	DOUBL DLR	IV.1	475
Sir Paul:	matter of Fact is all his own doing.--I confess I had a	180	DOUBL DLR	IV.1	477
Careless:	to you has carried me a little farther in this matter--	180	DOUBL DLR	IV.1	493
Maskwell:	discover the whole and real truth of the matter to him,	190	DOUBL DLR	V.1	98
Maskwell:	No matter, Sir, don't trouble your head, all's in	190	DOUBL DLR	V.1	106
Sir Paul:	I, I know no such matter.	192	DOUBL DLR	V.1	168
Sir Paul:	Why, what's the matter now? Good Lord, what's	192	DOUBL DLR	V.1	185
Maskwell:	Why, I intend to tell my Lord the whole matter of	193	DOUBL DLR	V.1	214
Lord Froth:	O Heaven's, what's the matter? Where's my	200	DOUBL DLR	V.1	499
Lady Froth:	No matter,--heark'ee, shall you and I make	201	DOUBL DLR	V.1	536
All:	What's the matter?	202	DOUBL DLR	V.1	555
Jeremy:	body be surpriz'd at the Matter--(Knocking)--Again! Sir,	221	FOR LOVE	I.1	182
Tattle:	No matter for that--Yes, yes, every body knows	227	FOR LOVE	I.1	427
Foresight:	Why how now, what's the matter?	235	FOR LOVE	II.1	25
Sr Sampson:	be done to Night--No matter for the time; prithee,	240	FOR LOVE	II.1	195
Jeremy:	Country Dances; and the like; I don't much matter your	245	FOR LOVE	II.1	374
Mrs Fore:	No matter for that, it's as good a Face as yours.	247	FOR LOVE	II.1	460
Miss Prue:	for the matter.	263	FOR LOVE	III.1	384
Mrs Fore:	Bless me, what's the matter? Miss, what do's	265	FOR LOVE	III.1	439
Sr Sampson:	Why, what's the matter?	266	FOR LOVE	III.1	482
Angelica:	tell me what is the matter.	276	FOR LOVE	IV.1	28
Jeremy:	No strange matter, Madam; my Master's mad, that's	276	FOR LOVE	IV.1	29
Scandal:	matter. But this is no new effect of an unsuccessful Passion.	277	FOR LOVE	IV.1	46
Jeremy:	Good lack! What's the matter now? Are any more of	278	FOR LOVE	IV.1	98
Sr Sampson:	the matter is with him, or I'll crack your Fools Skull.	279	FOR LOVE	IV.1	136
Jeremy:	Ah, you've hit it, Sir; that's the matter with him, Sir;	279	FOR LOVE	IV.1	137
Valentine:	--No matter how long--But I'll tell you one	280	FOR LOVE	IV.1	174
Sr Sampson:	my Heart--What matter is it who holds it? What	281	FOR LOVE	IV.1	230
Foresight:	opinion in this matter, and do reverence a man whom the	285	FOR LOVE	IV.1	349
Mrs Frail:	My account, pray what's the matter?	285	FOR LOVE	IV.1	362
Ben:	ask'd what was the matter.--He ask'd in a surly sort of a	285	FOR LOVE	IV.1	365
Ben:	Hey toss! what's the matter now? why you ben't	286	FOR LOVE	IV.1	396
Ben:	No matter what I can do? don't call Names,--I	287	FOR LOVE	IV.1	434
Angelica:	are very much abus'd in that Matter; He's no more Mad	299	FOR LOVE	V.1	87
Angelica:	Bless me, Sir Sampson, what's the matter?	300	FOR LOVE	V.1	102
Tattle:	Night, and did not so much as dream of the matter.	303	FOR LOVE	V.1	238
Mrs Fore:	What's the Matter, Husband?	306	FOR LOVE	V.1	330
Mrs Fore:	Why, What's the Matter?	306	FOR LOVE	V.1	342
Ben:	Matter! Why he's Mad.	306	FOR LOVE	V.1	343
Ben:	before you shall guess at the matter, and do nothing else;	306	FOR LOVE	V.1	353

Matter   (continued)

Matters (7)

Mature (1)

Maukin (1)

Maul (1)

Maw (1)

Maxim (1)

May (354)
May-hap (16)

May'st (2)

Maybe (1)

Mayn't (11)

Maze (3)

Mazes (1)

Me (1387)
Me's (1)

Meagre (2)

Meal (0)   see Piece-meal
Mean (114)

Mean (continued)

Speaker	Line	PAGE	TITLE	ACT.SC	LINE
Araminta:	If Love be the Fever which you mean; kind Heav'n	54	OLD BATCH	II.2	8
Silvia:	Why did you not tell me?--Whom mean you?	61	OLD BATCH	III.1	4
Lucy:	Whom you should mean, Heartwell.	61	OLD BATCH	III.1	5
Sir Joseph:	thy Sword I mean.	70	OLD BATCH	III.1	347
Silvia:	them--O Gemini, I hope you don't mean so--For I	73	OLD BATCH	III.2	88
Barnaby:	Mr. Prig, to have kept my Mistress Company in the mean	76	OLD BATCH	IV.1	23
Fondlewife:	And in the mean time, I will reason with my self--	76	OLD BATCH	IV.1	49
Sharper:	However I hope you don't mean to forsake it, that	80	OLD BATCH	IV.1	181
Laetitia:	(aside). What can this mean! 'Tis impossible he should	81	OLD BATCH	IV.2	42
Bellmour:	the mean time, I promise,--and rely upon me,--to	98	OLD BATCH	V.1	70
Setter:	O Lord, Sir, What d'ye mean? Corrupt my honesty.	103	OLD BATCH	V.1	247
Capt Bluff:	I'll give't you under my Hand.--In the mean	104	OLD BATCH	V.1	278
Belinda:	Oh foh! What does the filthy-fellow mean? Lard,	109	OLD BATCH	V.2	59
Brisk:	by leaving it, I mean you leave No body for the Company	128	DOUBL DLR	I.1	29
Mellefont:	Maskwell, you mean; prithee why should you	131	DOUBL DLR	I.1	145
Careless:	Upon your Aunt, you mean.	131	DOUBL DLR	I.1	151
Lord Froth:	O foy, Sir Paul, what do you mean? Merry! O	132	DOUBL DLR	I.1	185
Mellefont:	What can this mean!	144	DOUBL DLR	II.1	213
Cynthia:	Bless me! Sir; Madam; what mean you?	145	DOUBL DLR	II.1	244
Mellefont:	Nay, Madam, hear me; I mean--	147	DOUBL DLR	II.1	337
Mellefont:	What dost thou mean?	156	DOUBL DLR	III.1	213
Mellefont:	What d'ye mean?	157	DOUBL DLR	III.1	241
Maskwell:	Mean? Not to disappoint the Lady I assure you--	157	DOUBL DLR	III.1	242
Brisk:	I know whom you mean--But Deuce take me,	166	DOUBL DLR	III.1	583
Careless:	What do you mean?	181	DOUBL DLR	IV.1	507
Maskwell:	mean now, is only a bare Suspicion of my own. If your	183	DOUBL DLR	IV.1	583
Maskwell:	Tell him so! Ay, why you don't think I mean to	193	DOUBL DLR	V.1	227
Maskwell:	No, my Lord. (Aside.) What can this mean?	195	DOUBL DLR	V.1	308
Lord Froth:	How do you mean? My Wife!	200	DOUBL DLR	V.1	502
Sir Paul:	No, no, I mean the Family,--your Lady's	200	DOUBL DLR	V.1	505
Jeremy:	mean, to mew your self up here with Three or Four	217	FOR LOVE	I.1	32
Jeremy:	Paper; you don't mean to write!	217	FOR LOVE	I.1	62
Valentine:	And how the Devil do you mean to keep your	221	FOR LOVE	I.1	178
Scandal:	what they mean: But you have little reason to believe that	225	FOR LOVE	I.1	350
Valentine:	She does me the favour--I mean of a Visit	229	FOR LOVE	I.1	486
Tattle:	Nay, what do you mean, Gentlemen?	229	FOR LOVE	I.1	492
Foresight:	be better inform'd of this--(Aside)--Do you mean my	241	FOR LOVE	II.1	230
Valentine:	you call'd me. But here I am, and if you don't mean to	244	FOR LOVE	II.1	334
Mrs Fore:	What do you mean Sister?	247	FOR LOVE	II.1	442
Mrs Frail:	Was I? what do you mean?	247	FOR LOVE	II.1	443
Mrs Frail:	The World's end! What, do you mean to banter	247	FOR LOVE	II.1	448
Miss Prue:	--Smell him Mother, Madam, I mean--He gave	249	FOR LOVE	II.1	521
Miss Prue:	they mean, do you know?	251	FOR LOVE	II.1	582
Tattle:	No, no, they don't mean that.	251	FOR LOVE	II.1	586
Tattle:	Foresight mean by this Civility? Is it to make a Fool of me?	251	FOR LOVE	II.1	592
Tattle:	mean, that I have no Womans Reputation in my	256	FOR LOVE	III.1	97
Tattle:	Heart--You know whom I mean--You know	258	FOR LOVE	III.1	178
Tattle:	whom I mean; for there were a great many Ladies raffled	258	FOR LOVE	III.1	188
Tattle:	whom I mean; for there was a great many Ladies raffled	258	FOR LOVE	III.1	V188
Ben:	No, I hope the Gentlewoman is not angry; I mean all in	262	FOR LOVE	III.1	341
Ben:	What, do you mean that fair-Weather Spark that was	264	FOR LOVE	III.1	419
Ben:	for's Supper, for all that. What do's Father mean to leave	264	FOR LOVE	III.1	422
Scandal:	wicked, and Heav'n grant he may mean well in his Affair	267	FOR LOVE	III.1	522
Mrs Fore:	Pshaw! but Vertuous, I mean.	271	FOR LOVE	III.1	668
Ben:	For my part, I mean to toss a Can, and remember my	275	FOR LOVE	III.1	808
Angelica:	How d'ye mean, mad?	276	FOR LOVE	IV.1	32
Scandal:	the mean time, if our Project succeed no better with his	278	FOR LOVE	IV.1	104
Mrs Fore:	What do you mean? I don't understand you.	284	FOR LOVE	IV.1	315
Ben:	and you are tack'd about already.--What d'ee mean,	286	FOR LOVE	IV.1	416
Ben:	d'ee mean all this while, to make a fool of me?	287	FOR LOVE	IV.1	427
Tattle:	(aside) what do's the Old Prig mean? I'll banter him, and	304	FOR LOVE	V.1	263
Foresight:	Well; but my Consent I mean--You won't	304	FOR LOVE	V.1	282
Mrs Fore:	Well, but how mad? how d'ee mean?	306	FOR LOVE	V.1	349
Sr Sampson:	Foresight; Uncle I mean, a very old Fellow, Uncle Foresight;	307	FOR LOVE	V.1	383
Sr Sampson:	don't mean to sleep.	310	FOR LOVE	V.1	486
Almeria:	No, on my Life, my Faith, I mean no Violence.	331	M. BRIDE	I.1	201
Almeria:	No, on my Life, my Faith, I mean no Ill,	331	M. BRIDE	I.1	V201
Osmyn-Alph:	Why? what dost thou mean? why dost thou gaze so?	342	M. BRIDE	II.2	103
Osmyn-Alph:	And why? what dost thou mean? why dost thou gaze so?	342	M. BRIDE	II.2	V103
Zara:	Thou canst not mean so poorly, as thou talk'st.	348	M. BRIDE	II.2	331
Heli:	For your Escape. Mean time, I've thought already	352	M. BRIDE	III.1	98
Gonsalez:	Till Osmyn die. Mean time we may learn more	363	M. BRIDE	IV.1	70
Zara:	Of that hereafter; but, mean time, 'tis fit	365	M. BRIDE	IV.1	161
Manuel:	What mean those swollen and redfleck'd Eyes, that look	367	M. BRIDE	IV.1	248
Manuel:	They mean thy Guilt; and say thou wert Confederate	368	M. BRIDE	IV.1	V270
Manuel:	What Husband? who? whom do'st thou mean?	370	M. BRIDE	IV.1	354
Manuel:	Yet somewhat she must mean of dire Import,	370	M. BRIDE	IV.1	363
Manuel:	What dost thou mean?	373	M. BRIDE	V.1	20
Manuel:	Into how poor and mean a thing, a King descends;	373	M. BRIDE	V.1	40
Gonsalez:	'Twere fit the Soldiers were amuz'd, mean time,	378	M. BRIDE	V.2	102
Almeria:	And point! what mean they; Ha! a Cup. O well	382	M. BRIDE	V.2	253
Almeria:	--Oh, for another Draught of Death--What mean they?	382	M. BRIDE	V.2	V256
Mirabell:	For Travel! Why the Man that I mean is above	400	WAY WORLD	I.1	199
Witwoud:	--I mean he never speaks Truth at all,--that's all. He	404	WAY WORLD	I.1	340
Fainall:	Call for himself? What dost thou mean?	405	WAY WORLD	I.1	368
Witwoud:	Mean, why he wou'd slip you out of this Chocolate-house,	405	WAY WORLD	I.1	369
Witwoud:	himself, that I mean, call for himself, wait for himself, nay	405	WAY WORLD	I.1	375
Petulant:	Not I--I mean no Body--I know nothing	406	WAY WORLD	I.1	428
Mirabell:	Heav'n may grant it thee in the mean time.	407	WAY WORLD	I.1	461
Marwood:	That I am false! What mean you?	413	WAY WORLD	II.1	135
Mirabell:	Your Diligence will merit more--In the mean	424	WAY WORLD	II.1	533
Peg:	The red Ratifia does your Ladyship mean, or the Cherry	425	WAY WORLD	III.1	9
Lady Wish:	Grant me patience! I mean the Spanish Paper Idiot, Complexion	425	WAY WORLD	III.1	12

Mean   (continued)

Servant-W:	please to walk in, in the mean time.	437	WAY WORLD	III.1	446
Sir Wilful:	Why then let him hold his Tongue in the mean	441	WAY WORLD	III.1	611
Sir Wilful:	these days, Cozen, in the mean while, I must answer in	447	WAY WORLD	IV.1	111
Millamant:	Ay, go, go. In the mean time I suppose you have	452	WAY WORLD	IV.1	306
Sir Wilful:	let her keep her own Counsel in the mean time, and cry	456	WAY WORLD	IV.1	429
Foible:	pretended to go for the Papers; and in the mean time Mrs.	464	WAY WORLD	V.1	72
Marwood:	Friend, what do you mean?	466	WAY WORLD	V.1	157
Mrs Fain:	I know what I mean Madam, and so do you; and	466	WAY WORLD	V.1	158
Fainall:	possible speed. In the mean while, I will go for the said	469	WAY WORLD	V.1	294
Sir Wilful:	Dance in the mean time, that we who are not Lovers, may	477	WAY WORLD	V.1	601
Mirabell:	me lies to a Reunion, (To Mrs. Fainall) in the mean time,	478	WAY WORLD	V.1	616
Mirabell:	From hence let those be warn'd, who mean to wed;	478	WAY WORLD	V.1	620

Meaning (9)

Bellmour:	Ay, what else has meaning?	37	OLD BATCH	I.1	14
Laetitia:	to find the meaning of it--	77	OLD BATCH	IV.1	86
Foresight:	Mercy on us, what can be the meaning of it? Sure	235	FOR LOVE	II.1	5
Sr Sampson:	Oons, what is the meaning of this?	312	FOR LOVE	V.1	567
Gonsalez:	Should have more Meaning than appears bare-fac'd.	365	M. BRIDE	IV.1	176
Gonsalez:	Dumb Men, that make their Meaning known by Signs.	372	M. BRIDE	IV.1	434
Gonsalez:	Dumb Men, who make their Meaning known by Signs.	372	M. BRIDE	IV.1	V434
Witwoud:	meaning.	404	WAY WORLD	I.1	332
Mirabell:	Meaning mine, Sir?	406	WAY WORLD	I.1	427

Meanings (1)

Lady Touch:	meanings lurk in each corner of that various face. O! that	198	DOUBL DLR	V.1	395

Meanly (1)

	That Satire scorns to stoop so meanly low,	479	WAY WORLD	EPI.	29

Means (40)

Bellmour:	when it may be the means of getting into a fair Lady's Books?	44	OLD BATCH	I.1	V267
Sharper:	This must be Bellmour he means--ha! I have a	48	OLD BATCH	II.1	11
Sir Joseph:	O Lord Sir by no means--but I might have sav'd a	51	OLD BATCH	II.1	128
Setter:	means--I follow one as my Master, but the tother	64	OLD BATCH	III.1	142
Setter:	means--I follow one as my Master, t'other	64	OLD BATCH	III.1	V142
Laetitia:	Bless me, what means my Dear!	77	OLD BATCH	IV.1	73
Araminta:	Vainlove to know us, I'll be rid of my Fool by fair means	86	OLD BATCH	IV.3	102
Mellefont:	me; his Dependance upon my Uncle is through my means.	131	DOUBL DLR	I.1	150
Lady Ply:	means of procuring the Mother?	146	DOUBL DLR	II.1	307
Maskwell:	By no means; therefore you must aggravate my	154	DOUBL DLR	III.1	146
Maskwell:	I know what she means by toying away an hour well	155	DOUBL DLR	III.1	174
Lady Ply:	By all means--Mr. Careless has satisfied me of	173	DOUBL DLR	IV.1	204
Lady Froth:	O be merry by all means--Prince Volscius	176	DOUBL DLR	IV.1	341
Careless:	Arm--he cannot be ignorant that Maskwell means to	196	DOUBL DLR	V.1	352
Scandal:	would be to invent the honest means of keeping your word,	221	FOR LOVE	I.1	196
Scandal:	Humour him, Madam, by all means.	290	FOR LOVE	IV.1	540
Valentine:	think of means to reconcile me to him; and preserve the	294	FOR LOVE	IV.1	717
Osmyn-Alph:	Or Means by which I have thee--	342	M. BRIDE	II.2	95
Osmyn-Alph:	What means the Bounty of All-gracious Heav'n,	344	M. BRIDE	II.2	185
Zara:	But larger Means to gratifie the Will?	347	M. BRIDE	II.2	316
Heli:	The Means of Liberty restor'd. That, gain'd;	352	M. BRIDE	III.1	96
Osmyn-Alph:	Hard Means, to ratifie that Word!--O Cruelty!	355	M. BRIDE	III.1	249
Zara:	Attempt no Means to make himself away;	360	M. BRIDE	III.1	V448
Zara:	Not to be born--devise the means to shun it,	362	M. BRIDE	IV.1	37
Almeria:	What means these Tears, but Grief unutterable?	368	M. BRIDE	IV.1	268
Gonsalez:	But how prevent the Captive Queen, who means	371	M. BRIDE	IV.1	412
Selim:	For my Defect; or that the Means which I	375	M. BRIDE	V.1	114
Garcia:	What means this Blood? and why this Face of Horrour?	377	M. BRIDE	V.2	29
Alonzo:	Require me not to tell the Means, till done,	378	M. BRIDE	V.2	97
Gonsalez:	They shout again! Whate'er he means to do	378	M. BRIDE	V.2	100
Zara:	His hellish Rage had wanted Means to act,	380	M. BRIDE	V.2	177
Fainall:	By no means, 'tis better as 'tis; 'tis better to Trade	400	WAY WORLD	I.1	207
Witwoud:	he means Sultana Queens.	406	WAY WORLD	I.1	400
Mrs Fain:	must find the means in our selves, and among our selves.	410	WAY WORLD	II.1	2
Fainall:	Marriage, my Lady had been incens'd beyond all means of	415	WAY WORLD	II.1	203
Lady Wish:	Foible--He means to Travel for Improvement.	431	WAY WORLD	III.1	258
Fainall:	The means, the means.	442	WAY WORLD	III.1	658
Lady Wish:	Is there no means, no Remedy, to stop my	473	WAY WORLD	V.1	445
Mirabell:	deed of trust. It may be a means well manag'd to make you	478	WAY WORLD	V.1	618

Meant (15)

Sir Joseph:	hundred Pound--I meant innocently as I hope to be sav'd	51	OLD BATCH	II.1	129
Silvia:	Senseless Creature, I meant my Vainlove.	61	OLD BATCH	III.1	6
Belinda:	Courtship, one wou'd think you meant a noble Entertainment:	106	OLD BATCH	V.1	373
Heartwell:	That Help which Nature meant in Woman-kind,	108	OLD BATCH	V.2	11
Lady Touch:	towards me. Nay, I can't think he meant any thing	153	DOUBL DLR	III.1	84
Mellefont:	Excellent Maskwell, thou wer't certainly meant for	193	DOUBL DLR	V.1	235
Foresight:	For by the Head of the House is meant the Husband; the	236	FOR LOVE	II.1	59
Ben:	And just e'en as he meant, Sir,	274	FOR LOVE	III.1	785
Angelica:	But I believe Mr. Tattle meant the Favour to me, I	309	FOR LOVE	V.1	455
Gonsalez:	I wish her Mutes are meant to be employ'd	366	M. BRIDE	IV.1	205
Zara:	Nor that I meant to fall before his Eyes,	381	M. BRIDE	V.2	192
Fainall:	You misinterpret my Reproof. I meant but to remind	414	WAY WORLD	II.1	179
Sir Wilful:	May be not, Sir; thereafter as 'tis meant, Sir.	438	WAY WORLD	III.1	496
	To mark out who by Characters are meant.	479	WAY WORLD	EPI.	18
	And turn to Libel, what was meant a Satire.	479	WAY WORLD	EPI.	22

Meantime (1)

Gonsalez:	And in the meantime fed with Expectation	378	M. BRIDE	V.2	V103

Measure (6)

Maskwell:	have been in a great measure kept by her, the case is alter'd;	155	DOUBL DLR	III.1	177
Sir Paul:	but in having the honour, to appertain in some measure, to	172	DOUBL DLR	IV.1	183
Ben:	With off'ring her his Measure.	274	FOR LOVE	III.1	775
Sir Wilful:	mind in some measure,--I conjecture you partly guess--	448	WAY WORLD	IV.1	136
Mirabell:	Measure enlarg'd into a Husband?	450	WAY WORLD	IV.1	231
Sir Wilful:	measure; therefore withdraw your Instrument Sir, or	473	WAY WORLD	V.1	428

Measures (2)

Heartwell:	the Voice, and Life to their Measures--Look you	72	OLD BATCH	III.2	33

Melt   (continued)
    Sr Sampson: melt in my Mouth. 301   FOR LOVE   V.1   148
    Almeria: That thus couldst melt to see a Stranger's Wrongs. . . 327   M. BRIDE   I.1   31
    Osmyn-Alph: And melt me down to mingle with thy Weepings? . . . 357   M. BRIDE   III.1 307
    Almeria: Which shot into my Breast, now melt and chill me. . . 358   M. BRIDE   III.1 369
    Fainall: Medlar grafted on a Crab. One will melt in your Mouth, . 401   WAY WORLD I.1   213
    Sir Wilful: melt, I can tell you that. My contract went no further . 472   WAY WORLD V.1   396
Melted (5)
    Heartwell: thee--There thou hast don't, all my Resolve melted in . . 74   OLD BATCH III.2 135
    Heartwell: thee--There thou hast don't, all my Resolves melted in . 74   OLD BATCH III.2 V135
    Mellefont: Lightning in her Eyes; I saw her melted into Tears, and . 130   DOUBL DLR I.1   106
    Sir Paul: Chaste as Ice, but you are melted now, and false as Water. 179   DOUBL DLR IV.1 431
    Jeremy: sake. Now like a thin Chairman, melted down to half . 218   FOR LOVE   V.1   98
Melting (2)
    Singer: Melting the Hours, in gentle Play; 71   OLD BATCH III.2 3
    Lady Ply: O you have Conquered, sweet, melting, moving 170   DOUBL DLR IV.1 118
Melts (2)
    Bellmour: Words, and a Kiss; and the good Man melts. See, how . . 95   OLD BATCH IV.4 239
    Lady Touch: Anger melts. (weeps) Here, take this Ponyard, for my very 198   DOUBL DLR V.1   402
Mem (14)
    Mincing: O Mem, your Laship staid to peruse a Pacquet of . . . 419   WAY WORLD II.1 357
    Mincing: O Mem, your Laship staid to peruse a Pacquet of . . . 419   WAY WORLD II.1 V357
    Mincing: O Mem, I shall never forget it. 419   WAY WORLD II.1 369
    Mincing: 'Till I had the Cremp in my Fingers I'll vow Mem. . . 419   WAY WORLD II.1 371
    Mincing: 'Till I had the Cramp in my Fingers I'll vow Mem. . . 419   WAY WORLD II.1 V371
    Mincing: I vow Mem, I thought once they wou'd have fit. . . . 432   WAY WORLD III.1 295
    Mincing: Mem, I come to acquaint your Laship that Dinner . . . 441   WAY WORLD III.1 614
    Mincing: Mem, I am come to acquaint your Laship that Dinner . . 441   WAY WORLD III.1 V614
    Mincing: My Lady wou'd speak with Mrs. Fcible, Mem. Mr. . . . 464   WAY WORLD V.1   104
    Mincing: I vow. He says Mem, how that he'll have my Lady's . . 465   WAY WORLD V.1   110
    Mincing: Yes Mem, they have sent me to see if Sir Wilfull be . . 465   WAY WORLD V.1   113
    Mincing: O yes Mem, I'll vouch any thing for your Ladyship's . . 465   WAY WORLD V.1   121
    Mincing: And so will I, Mem. 474   WAY WORLD V.1   479
    Mincing: Mercenary, Mem? I scorn your words. 'Tis true we . . 474   WAY WORLD V.1   486
Members (2)
    Sir Joseph: my Members. 47   OLD BATCH II.1 V 6
    Fainall: Petulant were enroll'd Members. 396   WAY WORLD I.1   58
Memorandum (1)
    Sharper: your time--A Memorandum. 69   OLD BATCH III.1 317
Memory (16)
    Sharper: better root in your shallow memory. 48   OLD BATCH II.1 49
    Sir Joseph: Purpose, if he han't frighted it out of my memory. Hem! . 49   OLD BATCH II.1 53
    Sir Joseph: have but a treacherous Memory. 85   OLD BATCH IV.3 74
    Almeria: But there's no time shall rase thee from my Memory. . 328   M. BRIDE   I.1   71
    Almeria: No Time shall rase thee from my Memory. 328   M. BRIDE   I.1 V 71
    Leonora: The Memory of that brave Prince stands fair 328   M. BRIDE   I.1   104
    Almeria: While I have Life, or Memory of my Alphonso. 329   M. BRIDE   I.1   148
    Heli: Anselmo's Memory, and will, no doubt, ... 352   M. BRIDE   III.1 102
    Heli: Anselmo's Memory, and will, for certain 352   M. BRIDE   III.1 V102
    Osmyn-Alph: Not to o'er-flow in Tribute to thy Memory. 383   M. BRIDE   V.2   314
    Mirabell: Not always; but as often as his Memory fails him, . . 401   WAY WORLD I.1   223
    Mirabell: a good Memory, and some few Scraps of other Folks Wit. . 401   WAY WORLD I.1   225
    Witwoud: No, but prithee excuse me,--my Memory is 402   WAY WORLD I.1   273
    Witwoud: such a Memory. 402   WAY WORLD I.1   274
    Mirabell: the Spleen or his Memory. 402   WAY WORLD I.1   277
    Lady Wish: his protesting Eyes! Oh no memory can Register. . . . 458   WAY WORLD IV.1 517
Men (57)   see Foot-men
    Bellmour: here vents 'em against the General, who slighting Men of . 47   OLD BATCH I.1   371
    Musician: Men will admire, adore and die, ... 60   OLD BATCH II.2 197
    Araminta: Nature well, for there are few Men, but do more silly . . 60   OLD BATCH II.2 216
    Setter: To be Men perhaps; nay faith like enough; I often . . . 65   OLD BATCH III.1 174
    Heartwell: Lying, Child, is indeed the Art of Love; and Men are . . 72   OLD BATCH III.2 56
    Vainlove: 'Tis Men should be coy, when Women woo. 80   OLD BATCH IV.1 191
    Vainlove: what she knows as well as I. (Aside). Men are apt to offend 87   OLD BATCH IV.3 137
    Setter: --'Tis above us:--And, for Men of Quality, they are . . 102   OLD BATCH V.1   231
    Vainlove: it?--Men in Madness have a Title to your Pity. . . . 106   OLD BATCH V.1   357
    Belinda: Yes: You flattering Men of the Mode have made . . . 106   OLD BATCH V.1   369
    Belinda: Yes: You fluttering Men of the Mode have made . . . 106   OLD BATCH V.1 V369
    Belinda: Ha, ha, ha, O Gad, Men grow such Clowns when . . . 108   OLD BATCH V.2   25
                   How many Undone Men were in the Pit! 113   OLD BATCH EPI.   14
                   How nearly some Good Men might have scap'd Sinking. . 125   DOUBL DLR PRO.   24
    Maskwell: Bonds of Friendship, and sets Men right upon their first . 150   DOUBL DLR II.1 444
    Brisk: Men like rich Fellows, are always ready for all Expences; 175   DOUBL DLR IV.1 300
                   The dreadful men of Learning, all Confound, ... 204   DOUBL DLR EPI.   17
    Valentine: follow the Examples of the wisest and wittiest Men in all 217   FOR LOVE   I.1   36
    Jeremy: ruin'd more Young Men than the Royal Oak Lottery-- . . 218   FOR LOVE   I.1   88
    Scandal: worthless great Men, and dull rich Rogues, avoid a witty . 219   FOR LOVE   I.1   132
    Scandal: there are some set out in their true Colours, both Men and 233   FOR LOVE   I.1   627
    Mrs Fore: They're all so, Sister, these Men--they 250   FOR LOVE   II.1 547
    Valentine: of the Men; and his Secresie, upon the mistrust of the . 256   FOR LOVE   III.1 132
    Scandal: Men; but they were such as you--Men who consulted . . 267   FOR LOVE   III.1 529
    Scandal: Wise Men of the East ow'd their Instruction to a Star, . 267   FOR LOVE   III.1 535
    Foresight: you had been read in these matters--Few Young Men . . 267   FOR LOVE   III.1 541
    Scandal: but 'tis as I believe some Men are Valiant, thro' fear--For 271   FOR LOVE   III.1 670
    Scandal: to allow some other Men the last Favour; you mistake, . . 272   FOR LOVE   III.1 696
    Ben: To lick her Lips at Men, Sir, ... 274   FOR LOVE   III.1 765
    Mrs Frail: O' you are the happiest, merriest Men alive. 275   FOR LOVE   III.1 804
    Sr Sampson: pox on't, that I that know the World, and Men and . . 283   FOR LOVE   IV.1 286
    Angelica: pretending to a sound Understanding; as Drunken men do . 296   FOR LOVE   IV.1 764
    Angelica: due. Men are generally Hypocrites and Infidels, they . . 314   FOR LOVE   V.1   631
                   Now to these Men (say they) such Souls were given, . . 315   FOR LOVE   EPI.   15
                   When many Years were past, in Men again. 315   FOR LOVE   EPI.   18
    Osmyn-Alph: On high; and of good Men, the very best 350   M. BRIDE   III.1 29
    Zara: So ripe, to point at the particular Men. 364   M. BRIDE   IV.1 147
    Gonsalez: Dumb Men, that make their Meaning known by Signs. . . 372   M. BRIDE   IV.1 434
    Gonsalez: Dumb Men, who make their Meaning known by Signs. . . 372   M. BRIDE   IV.1 V434

443

Met (22)
Sir Joseph:	wish to have met with.	51	OLD BATCH	II.1	135
Lucy:	Lord, Madam, I met your Lover in as much haste, as	74	OLD EATCH	III.2	147
Vainlove:	would have overtaken, not have met my Game.	80	OLD EATCH	IV.1	180
Belinda:	Lard, my Dear! I am glad I have met you:--I	83	OLD BATCH	IV.3	1
Capt Bluff:	Ladies, by these Hilts you are well met.	85	OLD EATCH	IV.3	82
Fondlewife:	Kiss, Dear,--I met the Master of the Ship	89	OLD BATCH	IV.4	23
Lady Touch:	not met your Love with forward Fire?	137	DOUBL DLR	I.1	373
Lady Froth:	have met!	139	DOUBL DLR	II.1	24
Cynthia:	met with your Match, on my Conscience.	139	DOUBL DLR	II.1	26
Maskwell:	I know it; I met Sir Paul towing away Cynthia:	148	DOUBL DLR	II.1	385
Careless:	Sir Paul, I'm glad I've met with you, 'gad I have	180	DOUBL DLR	IV.1	491
Foresight:	down Stairs, and met a Weasel; bad Omens those: some	236	FOR LOVE	II.1	34
Mrs Frail:	I are parted;--and with the same indifference that we met.	287	FOR LOVE	IV.1	451
Sr Sampson:	--Odd, I think we are very well met;--Give me	301	FOR LCVE	V.1	144
Garcia:	The Friends perhaps are met; let us avcid 'em.	339	M. BRIDE	II.1	49
Osmyn-Alph:	Could sleep till we again were met.	344	M. BRIDE	II.2	196
Osmyn-Alph:	Or we could sleep till we again were met.	344	M. BRIDE	II.2	V196
Manuel:	Entring he met my Eyes, and started back,	373	M. BRIDE	V.1	15
Millamant:	have ask'd every living Thing I met for you; I have	419	WAY WORLD	II.1	347
Witwoud:	you met her Husband and did not ask him for her.	419	WAY WORLD	II.1	350
Foible:	met that confident Thing? Was I in Fault? If you had	427	WAY WORLD	III.1	86
Marwood:	met with your Match.--O Man, Man! Woman,	431	WAY WORLD	III.1	235

Metamorphosis (1)
Valentine:	pray, for a Metamorphosis--Change thy Shape, and	289	FOR LCVE	IV.1	521

Metaphorical (1)
Brisk:	pretty and Metaphorical enough: I' Gad I could not have	128	DOUEL DLR	I.1	38

Metaphorically (1)
Witwoud:	art in truth (Metaphorically speaking) A speaker of	453	WAY WORLD	IV.1	348

Meteors (1)
Zara:	His Eyes like Meteors roll'd, then darted down	374	M. BRIDE	V.1	93

Methink (1)
Heartwell:	replies another--methink he has more of the Marquess of	45	OLD BATCH	I.1	322

Methinks (27)
Silvia:	Methinks I feel the Woman strong within me, and	61	OLD BATCH	III.1	33
Bellmour:	Methinks I am the very Picture cf Montufar in the	80	OLD EATCH	IV.2	7
Laetitia:	not surpriz'd me: Methinks, now I look on him again,	81	OLD BATCH	IV.2	44
Laetitia:	Methinks, 't has been very ill Weather.	90	OLD BATCH	IV.4	38
Sharper:	Methinks I long to see Bellmour come forth.	100	OLD EATCH	V.1	129
	Methinks I hear him in Consideration!	113	OLD BATCH	EPI.	10
Lord Froth:	With all my heart, methinks we are a Solitude	134	DOUEL DLR	I.1	284
Lady Froth:	Methinks he wants a Manner.	139	DOUEL DLR	II.1	46
Careless:	Why, methinks that might be easily remedied--my	161	DOUBL DLR	III.1	419
Lady Touch:	'Tis Fight a Clock: Methinks I should have	183	DOUBL DLR	IV.2	8
	Methinks I see some Faces in the Pit,	204	DOUBL DLR	EPI.	32
Angelica:	methinks Sir Sampson, You shou'd leave him alone with	262	FOR LOVE	III.1	345
Scandal:	over-reach'd, methinks you shou'd not--	267	FOR LCVE	III.1	525
Scandal:	methinks he does not look as he used to do.	268	FOR LCVE	III.1	550
Foresight:	here;--Methinks I lock with a serene and benign	269	FOR LCVE	III.1	601
Angelica:	is over, methinks I am not half so sorry for him as I was--	277	FOR LCVE	IV.1	83
Angelica:	is over, methinks I am not half sc sorry as I was--	277	FOR LOVE	IV.1	V 83
Foresight:	but methinks your Love to my Daughter was a Secret I	304	FOR LCVE	V.1	257
Miss Prue:	way or other. Oh! methinks I'm sick when I think of a	305	FOR LCVE	V.1	308
Scandal:	own Wedding; methinks 'tis pity they should not be	313	FOR LOVE	V.1	599
	Methinks, we Players resemble such a Soul,	315	FOR LCVE	EPI.	19
Almeria:	Methinks my Heart has some Relief: Having	330	M. BRIDE	I.1	192
Gonsalez:	Methinks this Lady's Hatred to the Moor,	366	M. EBIDE	IV.1	202
Fainall:	For a passionate lover, methinks you are a Man	399	WAY WORLD	I.1	156
Marwood:	Enemies. Methinks you look a little pale, and now you	412	WAY WORLD	II.1	78
Marwood:	Methinks Sir Wilfull should rather think of	431	WAY WCRLD	III.1	259
Marwood:	Methinks Mrs. Millamant and he wou'd make	432	WAY WCRLD	III.1	266

Method (2)
Valentine:	there's Regularity and Method in that; she is a Medal	297	FOR LOVE	IV.1	810
Mirabell:	for Motion not Method is their Occupation. To know this,	423	WAY WORLD	II.1	498

Methodically (1)
Valentine:	Shop. Oh things will go methodically in the City, the	289	FOR LOVE	IV.1	503

Methought (2)
Sharper:	Methought the service I did you last night Sir, in	48	OLD BATCH	II.1	47
Lady Touch:	seriously, but methought it lock'd odly.	153	DOUBL DLR	III.1	85

Mettle (2)
Capt Bluff:	got with thee, is he of mettle?	51	OLD BATCH	II.1	148
Ben:	The Tinker too with Mettle,	274	FOR LOVE	III.1	776

Mew (1)
Jeremy:	mean, to mew your self up here with Three or Four	217	FOR LCVE	I.1	32

Mexico (1)
Sr Sampson:	had Peru in one Hand, and Mexico in t'other, and the	300	FOR LOVE	V.1	98

Middle (2)
Saygrace:	middle of a Sermon to do you pleasure.	195	DOUEL DLR	V.1	281
Saygrace:	middle of a Sermon to do you a pleasure.	195	DOUBL DLR	V.1	V281

Middlesex (1)
Jeremy:	before any Justice in Middlesex.	245	FOR LOVE	II.1	356

Midnight (6)
Angelica:	Yes, I can make Oath of your unlawful Midnight	237	FOR LOVE	II.1	96
Nurse:	Marry Heav'n defend--I at Midnight Practices	238	FOR LOVE	II.1	98
Nurse:	of your Midnight Concerns--but warm your Bed,	238	FOR LCVE	II.1	102
Sr Sampson:	seen the Antipodes, where the Sun rises at Midnight, and	241	FOR LOVE	II.1	208
Heli:	You may; anon, at Midnight, when the King	351	M. BRIDE	III.1	47
Gonsalez:	I'th' Evening Osmyn was to die; at Mid-night	366	M. EBIDE	IV.1	208

'Midst (1)
Bellmour:	Well; 'Midst of these dreadful Denunciations, and	112	OLD BATCH	V.2	165

Midwife (4)
Lucy:	if he had been going for a Midwife.	74	OLD BATCH	III.2	148
Silvia:	Midwife, some nine Months hence--Well, I find dissembling,	75	OLD BATCH	III.2	150
Petulant:	be a profess'd Midwife as a profest Whoremaster, at this	405	WAY WORLD	I.1	384
Marwood:	Quoif like a Man Midwife to bring your Daughter's	467	WAY WORLD	V.1	213

445

Mirabell   (continued)

Mirth   (continued)

		PAGE	TITLE	ACT.SC	LINE
Lady Touch:	harmless mirth--only misplac'd that's all--but if it	153	DOUBL DLR	III.1	95
Lady Touch:	toy away an hour in mirth.	155	DOUBL DLR	III.1	171
Lord Froth:	sake let us sacrifice 'em to mirth a little.	163	DOUBL DLR	III.1	487
Cynthia:	Affliction, as to dissemble Mirth in Company of Fools--	167	DOUBL DLR	III.1	625
Trapland:	'Udso that's true, Mr. Valentine I love Mirth, but	224	FOR LOVE	I.1	300
Foresight:	bad, some good, our lives are checquer'd, Mirth and	236	FOR LOVE	II.1	35
Valentine:	Mirth, tho' not your Compassion.	295	FOR LOVE	IV.1	760
Osmyn-Alph:	I could at this time spare your Mirth.	360	M. BRIDE	III.1	422
Mirabell:	of Mirth, which is not yet ripe for discovery. I am glad	399	WAY WORLD	I.1	137

Misapply'd (1)

Cynthia:	know, we have misapply'd the Name all this while, and	167	DOUBL DLR	III.1	631

Misapprehend (1)

Lord Froth:	O foy, don't misapprehend me, I don't say so, for	132	DOUBL DLR	I.1	197

Miscarriage (1)

Singer:	The sad miscarriage of their Wooing:	71	OLD BATCH	III.2 V	21

Miscarriages (1)

Belinda:	play the Game, and consequently can't see the Miscarriages	55	OLD BATCH	II.2	34

Miscarried (3)

Bellmour:	strein to be deliver'd of a Secret, when he has miscarried	40	OLD BATCH	I.1	127
Vainlove:	'Tis an untimely Fruit, and she has miscarried of	79	OLD BATCH	IV.1	169
Mellefont:	design than this of his which has miscarried.--O my	187	DOUBL DLR	IV.1	151

Miscarry (3)

Maskwell:	which (should this design miscarry) will be necessary to	154	DOUBL DLR	III.1	159
Cynthia:	miscarry--	169	DOUBL DLR	IV.1	56
Marwood:	unhappily directed to miscarry.	434	WAY WORLD	III.1	347

Mischance (2)

Bellmour:	mischance, the Knight was alone, and had fallen into the	46	OLD BATCH	I.1	359
Selim:	The Mute you sent, by some Mischance was seen,	380	M. BRIDE	V.2	180

Mischeivous (1)

Foible:	mischeivous Devil told Mr. Fainall of your Ladyship then?	464	WAY WORLD	V.1	80

Mischief (16)

Sir Joseph:	mischief done I perceive.	48	OLD BATCH	II.1	20
Lucy:	I have that in my Head may make Mischief.	61	OLD BATCH	III.1	35
Sir Joseph:	mischief--For he was a devilish cholerick Fellow: And if	68	OLD BATCH	III.1	274
Sir Joseph:	mischief done, that's flat. And yet I believe if you had been	68	OLD BATCH	III.1	276
Sharper:	Hugging himself in his prosperous Mischief--No	100	OLD BATCH	V.1	132
Heartwell:	uncommon Mischief?	104	OLD BATCH	V.1	302
Mellefont:	much ado I prevented her doing me or her self a mischief:	130	DOUBL DLR	I.1	115
Maskwell:	mischief, what mischief I shall do, is to be paid with	156	DOUBL DLR	III.1	219
Maskwell:	mischief, what mischief I do, is to be paid with	156	DOUBL DLR	III.1 V	219
Foresight:	are mad to day--It is of evil portent, and bodes Mischief	236	FOR LOVE	II.1	47
Buckram:	mischief if I stay--The Conveyance is ready, Sir. If	280	FOR LOVE	IV.1	185
Scandal:	outragious, and do mischief.	293	FOR LOVE	IV.1	669
Zara:	What should have ne'er been seen; imperfect Mischief!	375	M. BRIDE	V.1	105
Mrs Fain:	Ingenious Mischief! Wou'd thou wert married	411	WAY WORLD	II.1	65

Mischiefs (1)

Lord Touch:	Howe're in private, Mischiefs are conceiv'd,	203	DOUBL DLR	V.1	592

Mischievous (1)

Sr Sampson:	Gads bobs, does he not know me? Is he mischievous?	279	FOR LOVE	IV.1	155

Misconceive (1)

Maskwell:	Nay, Misconceive me not, Madam, when I say	136	DOUBL DLR	I.1	355

Misconstruction (1)

Marwood:	Family, shou'd admit of Misconstruction, or make me	466	WAY WORLD	V.1	163

Misconstrued (1)

Lady Touch:	thought my Nephew could have so misconstrued my	153	DOUBL DLR	III.1	115

Misdeeds (1)

Gonsalez:	And of a piece with this Day's dire Misdeeds.	379	M. BRIDE	V.2	123

Misdemeanour (1)

Jeremy:	away for any Misdemeanour; but does voluntarily dismiss	218	FOR LOVE	I.1	69

Miserable (3)

Bellmour:	That were a miserable Wretch indeed, who cou'd	106	OLD BATCH	V.1	378
Almeria:	Is there necessity I must be miserable?	327	M. BRIDE	I.1	57
Fainall:	rid of my Wife, I shou'd be a miserable Man.	413	WAY WORLD	II.1	110

Miseries (6)

Almeria:	My Miseries? Thou dost already know 'em:	328	M. BRIDE	I.1 V	99
Zara:	Shalt weep for mine, forgetting thy own Miseries.	353	M. BRIDE	III.1	168
Osmyn-Alph:	And thou dost speak of Miseries impossible.	357	M. BRIDE	III.1	310
Osmyn-Alph:	You do not come to mock my Miseries?	360	M. BRIDE	III.1	420
Zara:	And will indulge it now. What Miseries?	360	M. BRIDE	III.1	424
Leonora:	Where Miseries are multiply'd; return	381	M. BRIDE	V.2	228

Misery (3)

Almeria:	And Misery Eternal will succeed.	326	M. BRIDE	I.1	18
Zara:	What is't to me, this House of Misery?	346	M. BRIDE	II.2	266
Osmyn-Alph:	But O thou art not mine, not ev'n in misery;	357	M. BRIDE	III.1	332

Misfortune (5)

Laetitia:	(aside). Misfortune! Now all's ruin'd again.	92	OLD BATCH	IV.4	108
Vainlove:	But have a good heart, I heard of your Misfortune, and	109	OLD BATCH	V.2	71
Lady Touch:	misfortune.	184	DOUBL DLR	IV.2	48
Osmyn-Alph:	You have pursu'd Misfortune, to its Dwelling;	346	M. BRIDE	II.2	262
Osmyn-Alph:	One, who has tir'd Misfortune with pursuing?	351	M. BRIDE	III.1	58

Misfortunes (1)

Jeremy:	More Misfortunes, Sir.	225	FOR LOVE	I.1	356

Misinform'd (3)

Sharper:	Sir your Servant, but you are misinform'd, for	51	OLD BATCH	II.1	158
Manuel:	Never. You have been mis-inform'd.	366	M. BRIDE	IV.1	188
Millamant:	Plot, as you were misinform'd; I have laid my commands	470	WAY WORLD	V.1	327

Misinterpret (1)

Fainall:	You misinterpret my Reproof. I meant but to remind	414	WAY WORLD	II.1	179

Mislaid (2)

Angelica:	only because the Butler had mislaid some of the Apostle's	237	FOR LOVE	II.1	89
Angelica:	only because the Butler had mislaid some of the Apostle	237	FOR LOVE	II.1 V	89

Mislead (1)

Garcia:	Where, where is he? Why dost thou thus mislead me?	376	M. BRIDE	V.2	19

Misled (1)
   Lady Touch: the love of you, was the first wandring fire that e're
               misled . . . . 185 DOUBL DLR IV.2   76
Misplac'd (3)
   Setter: Some by Experience find those Words misplac'd: . . . 105 OLD BATCH V.1   330
   Maskwell: Your Zeal I grant was Ardent, but misplac'd; . . . . 137 DOUBL DLR I.1   374
   Lady Touch: harmless mirth--only misplac'd that's all--but if it . 153 DOUBL DLR III.1   95
Misplace (1)
   Angelica: In admiring me, you misplace the Novelty. . . . . . 314 FOR LOVE   V.1   635
Miss (40)   see A-miss
   Maskwell: their own Follies and Intrigues, they'll miss neither of
               you. . . . . 155 DOUBL DLR III.1 168
   Lady Touch: not Courage; no, I know thee well: but thou shalt miss . 197 DOUBL DLR V.1   388
               (Enter Tattle, and Miss Prue.) . . 249 FOR LOVE   II.1   505
   Mrs Fore: Fie, fie, Miss, how you bawl--besides, I   . . . . 249 FOR LOVE   II.1   507
   Mrs Fore: Girl call me Mother--Well, but Miss, what are you   . . 249 FOR LOVE   II.1   513
   Tattle: O fie Miss, you must not kiss and tell. . . . . 249 FOR LOVE   II.1   523
   Mrs Frail: Fie, Miss; amongst your Linnen, you must say . . . 249 FOR LOVE   II.1   531
   Tattle: Oh Madam; you are too severe upon Miss; you must   . 249 FOR LOVE   II.1   534
   Tattle: strangely--pretty Miss, don't let 'em perswade you . . 249 FOR LOVE   II.1   536
   Mrs Fore: miss an opportunity. . . . . 250 FOR LOVE   II.1   575
   Tattle: I must make Love to you, pretty Miss; will you let . . 251 FOR LOVE   II.1   588
   Tattle: You must let me speak Miss, you must not speak first;   . 251 FOR LOVE   II.1   598
   Tattle: And won't you shew me, pretty Miss, where your   . . 252 FOR LOVE   II.1   646
               (Exit Miss Prue.)   . . . . 253 FOR LOVE   II.1   661
   Nurse: Miss, Miss, Miss Prue--Mercy on me, marry and   . . . 253 FOR LOVE   III.1   1
   Nurse: Amen: Why, what's become of the Child?--Why Miss,   . . 253 FOR LOVE   III.1   2
   Nurse: Miss Foresight--Sure she has not lock'd her self up   . 253 FOR LOVE   III.1   3
   Nurse: Miss Foresight--Sure she has lock'd her self up . . 253 FOR LOVE   III.1 V 3
   Nurse: in her Chamber, and gone to sleep, or to Prayers; Miss, . 253 FOR LOVE   III.1   4
   Nurse: Miss, I hear her--Come to your Father, Child: . . . 253 FOR LOVE   III.1   5
   Nurse: Open the Door--Open the Door Miss--I hear you   . . 253 FOR LOVE   III.1   6
   Nurse: Miss I say, God's my Life, here's fine doings towards--   . 253 FOR LOVE   III.1   9
               (Tattle and Miss Prue at the Door.) . 253 FOR LOVE   III.1 V 14
          (Enter Sir Sampson, Mrs. Frail, Miss Prue, and Servant.)   . 259 FOR LOVE   III.1 209
   Mrs Frail: Now Miss, you shall see your Husband. . . . . . 259 FOR LOVE   III.1 217
   Ben: (Kisses Miss Prue.) . . . 261 FOR LOVE   III.1 284
   Tattle: Well Miss, I have your promise. . . . . . 262 FOR LOVE   III.1 347
   Tattle: (Aside to Miss Prue.) . . 262 FOR LOVE   III.1 348
   Sr Sampson: you Ben; this is your Mistress,--Come Miss, you must . 262 FOR LOVE   III.1 350
          (Exeunt all but Ben and Miss Prue.) . 263 FOR LOVE   III.1 359
   Mrs Fore: Bless me, what's the matter? Miss, what do's . . . . 265 FOR LOVE   III.1 439
   Mrs Fore: Come, Miss, come along with me, and tell . . . . 265 FOR LOVE   III.1 444
   Mrs Frail: Foresight, and Sir Sampson coming. Sister, do you take Miss 265 FOR LOVE   III.1 447
               (Enter Miss Prue.) . . . 303 FOR LOVE   V.1   221
   Tattle: O fie, Miss: Who told you so, Child? . . . . . 303 FOR LOVE   V.1   231
   Tattle: O fie, Miss, why did you do so? and who told you so, . 303 FOR LOVE   V.1   233
   Tattle: O Pox, that was Yesterday, Miss, that was a great . . 303 FOR LOVE   V.1   236
               (Exeunt Nurse and Miss Prue.) . . 306 FOR LOVE   V.1 V329
Miss'd (2)
   Singer: Vex'd at the Pleasure she had miss'd, ... 71 OLD BATCH III.2 V 18
           And Nature miss'd, in vain he boasts his Art, . . . 324 M. BRIDE   PRO.   37
Missing (2)
   Mirabell: shall be found out.--And rail at me for missing the . 451 WAY WORLD IV.1   241
   Foible: Dinner. She sent the Letter to my Lady, and that missing . 464 WAY WORLD V.1   70
Mistake (15)
   Bellmour: --But it is a Mistake which any Body might have made. . . 81 OLD BATCH IV.2   41
   Lucy: I had none, but through Mistake. . . . . 97 OLD BATCH V.1   40
   Bellmour: Which Mistake you must go through with, Lucy.-- . . 97 OLD BATCH V.1   41
   Bellmour: the Mistake of me: I'll marry 'em.--Nay, don't pause: . 98 OLD BATCH V.1   67
   Mellefont: 'Tis a mistake, for women may most properly be . . . 158 DOUBL DLR III.1 310
   Lady Ply: Letter, your Letter! By an Unfortunate Mistake, I have . 178 DOUBL DLR IV.1   399
   Cynthia: mistake. . . . . 194 DOUBL DLR V.1   258
   Angelica: You mistake Indifference for Uncertainty; I never . . 254 FOR LOVE   III.1   31
   Scandal: to allow some other Men the last Favour; you mistake, . . 272 FOR LOVE   III.1 696
   Scandal: We are all under a mistake--Ask no Questions, . . . 278 FOR LOVE   IV.1   102
   Jeremy: Yes, Sir; he says he'll favour it, and mistake her for . 288 FOR LOVE   IV.1   482
   Jeremy: mistake--You see, Sir, my Master was never mad, nor . . 313 FOR LOVE   V.1   593
   Zara: Your Pardon, Sir--mistake me not; you think . . . 359 M. BRIDE   III.1 416
   Gonsalez: Nor now had known it, but from her mistake. . . . 371 M. BRIDE   IV.1   399
   Garcia: This Deed--O dire Mistake! O fatal Blow! . . . . 377 M. BRIDE   V.2   57
Mistaken (21)
   Heartwell: Good Mr. Young-fellow, you're mistaken; as . . . 43 OLD BATCH I.1   229
   Lucy: about it streight--Hold, I'me mistaken, or that's . . 62 OLD BATCH III.1   46
   Laetitia: Who are you, Sir? You have mistaken the House . . . 81 OLD BATCH IV.2   29
   Laetitia: to dissemble. 'Tis plain then you have mistaken the Person. 81 OLD BATCH IV.2   35
   Bellmour: If we part so I'm mistaken.--Hold, hold, ... 81 OLD BATCH IV.2   37
   Laetitia: be mistaken after all this.--A handsom Fellow if he had . 81 OLD BATCH IV.2   43
   Laetitia: I would not have him mistaken. . . . . 81 OLD BATCH IV.2   45
   Belinda: --Affront! Pshaw, how you're mistaken! The poor . . 84 OLD BATCH IV.3   39
   Careless: I'm mistaken if there be not a Familiarity between . . 131 DOUBL DLR I.1   153
   Careless: Well, I shall be glad to be mistaken; but, your . . . 131 DOUBL DLR I.1   158
   Lord Froth: Ridiculous! Sir Paul you're strangely mistaken, I . . 132 DOUBL DLR I.1   190
   Lord Touch: her own Circle; 'tis not the first time she has mistaken . 151 DOUBL DLR III.1   7
   Cynthia: mistaken the thing: Since . . . . 167 DOUBL DLR III.1 632
   Mrs Frail: You are the most mistaken in the World; there is . . 231 FOR LOVE   I.1   562
   Angelica: have mistaken my Compassion, and think me guilty of a . 277 FOR LOVE   IV.1   69
   Foresight: Wherein was I mistaken, not to foresee this? . . . 284 FOR LOVE   IV.1   309
   Mrs Frail: O Impiety! how have I been mistaken! what an . . . 286 FOR LOVE   IV.1   392
   Garcia: To mourn, brave Heli, thy mistaken Fate. . . . . 337 M. BRIDE   II.1   3
   Alonzo: Which may be still mistaken by the Guards, . . . 379 M. BRIDE   V.2   119
   Millamant: You're mistaken. Ridiculous! . . . . 433 WAY WORLD III.1 332
   Marwood: am not mistaken, you are Sir Wilfull Witwoud. . . . 438 WAY WORLD III.1 509
Mistakes (1)
   Laetitia: We are all liable to Mistakes, Sir: If you own it to be so, 81 OLD BATCH IV.2   46

Mistook (1)

Speaker	Text	PAGE	TITLE	ACT.SC	LINE
Bellmour:	Mistress; and you mistook me for Tribulation Spin-text, to	97	OLD BATCH	V.1	43

Mistress (49)

Speaker	Text	PAGE	TITLE	ACT.SC	LINE
Sharper:	have no hopes of getting her for a Mistress, and she is too	41	OLD BATCH	I.1	162
Araminta:	--Every Man, now, changes his Mistress and his	58	OLD BATCH	II.2	148
Lucy:	him in the Reign of my Mistress;	64	OLD BATCH	III.1	146
Setter:	thy Mistress,	66	OLD BATCH	III.1	197
Setter:	Adsbud who's in fault, Mistress Mine? who flung the	66	OLD BATCH	III.1	204
Heartwell:	Friend or gain a Mistress.	72	OLD BATCH	III.2	60
Barnaby:	Mr. Prig, to have kept my Mistress Company in the mean	76	OLD BATCH	IV.1	23
Servant:	I'll call my Mistress.	80	OLD BATCH	IV.2	2
Servant:	My Mistress is coming, Sir.	80	OLD BATCH	IV.2 V	2
Belinda:	his Mistress, is like a Body without a Soul. Mr. Vainlove,	86	OLD BATCH	IV.3	134
Bellmour:	Mistress; and you mistook me for Tribulation Spin-text, to	97	OLD BATCH	V.1	43
Lucy:	ruin'd my poor Mistress: You have made a Gap in her	98	OLD BATCH	V.1	48
Bellmour:	trust me with another Secret. Your Mistress must not	98	OLD BATCH	V.1	54
Lucy:	Whore! I'd have you know, my Mistress scorns--	98	OLD BATCH	V.1	63
Lucy:	Whore! I'd have you to know, my Mistress scorns--	98	OLD BATCH	V.1 V 63
Bellmour:	help your Mistress to a Husband.--Nay, and thee too,	98	OLD BATCH	V.1	71
Heartwell:	If Sylvia had not been your Mistress, my Wife might have	109	OLD BATCH	V.2 V 67
Vainlove:	And if Sylvia had not been your Wife, my Mistress	109	OLD BATCH	V.2 V 69
Sharper:	to forgive the loss of his Mistress.--I know not how	111	OLD BATCH	V.2	122
Lady Proth:	Heaven's I thought you cou'd have no Mistress but the	176	DOUBL DLR	IV.1	334
Tattle:	Valentine, I Supp'd last Night with your Mistress, and	228	FOR LOVE	I.1	452
Mrs Frail:	No, I'll allow a Lover present with his Mistress to	231	FOR LOVE	I.1	555
Scandal:	your Estate, will help you to your Mistress.--In my mind	234	FOR LOVE	I.1	678
Scandal:	Or win a Mistress, with a losing hand.	234	FOR LOVE	I.1	681
Foresight:	Nurse, Where's your young Mistress?	235	FOR LOVE	II.1	18
Ben:	Forsooth an you please--(Salutes her.) Nay Mistress, I'm	261	FOR LOVE	III.1	280
Ben:	Forsooth if you please--(Salutes her.) Nay Mistress, I'm	261	FOR LOVE	III.1 V280
Ben:	you Mistress, wou'd you like going to Sea? Mess you're a	262	FOR LOVE	III.1	326
Angelica:	his Mistress. Mr. Tattle, we must not hinder Lovers.	262	FOR LOVE	III.1	346
Sr Sampson:	you Ben; this is your Mistress,--Come Miss, you must	262	FOR LOVE	III.1	350
Ben:	Come Mistress, will you please to sit down, for an you	263	FOR LOVE	III.1	360
Ben:	your Harbour. How say you Mistress? the short of the	263	FOR LOVE	III.1	375
Jeremy:	my Master was run stark mad only for Love of her Mistress;	276	FOR LOVE	IV.1	15
Scandal:	Father, than it does with his Mistress, he may descend from	278	FOR LOVE	IV.1	105
Ben:	--I'm glad you shew your self, Mistress:--Let	287	FOR LOVE	IV.1	436
Foresight:	Here, take your young Mistress, and lock her up	306	FOR LOVE	V.1	324
Leonora:	My Love of you, my Royal Mistress, gave me	327	M. BRIDE	I.1	35
Leonora:	Love of my Royal Mistress, gave me	327	M. BRIDE	I.1 V 35
Almeria:	I thank thee, that thou'lt pity thy sad Mistress;	328	M. BRIDE	I.1	95
Almeria:	Indeed, I do, for pitying thy sad Mistress;	328	M. BRIDE	I.1 V 95
Garcia:	The Slave and Creature of my Royal Mistress.	334	M. BRIDE	I.1	337
Mirabell:	She is more Mistress of her self, than to be under	396	WAY WORLD	I.1	43
Fainall:	somewhat too discerning in the Failings of your Mistress.	399	WAY WORLD	I.1	157
Coachman:	Is Master Petulant here, Mistress?	404	WAY WORLD	I.1	344
Mirabell:	make Love to my Mistress, thou sha't, Faith. What hast	407	WAY WORLD	I.1	444
Mrs Fain:	Here's your Mistress.	418	WAY WORLD	II.1	321
Fainall:	when he proves his Mistress true; but let Husbands doubts	444	WAY WORLD	III.1	717
Mrs Fain:	your Mistress up to the Ears in Love and Contemplation,	446	WAY WORLD	IV.1	71
Millamant:	Mistress. There is not so Impudent a thing in Nature, as the	449	WAY WORLD	IV.1	177

Mistresses (7)

Speaker	Text	PAGE	TITLE	ACT.SC	LINE
Bellmour:	our Afternoon Service to our Mistresses; I find I am	40	OLD BATCH	I.1	132
Bellmour:	our Afternoon Services to our Mistresses; I find I am	40	OLD BATCH	I.1 V132
Bellmour:	Mistresses of my own acquiring; must yet take Vainlove's	41	OLD BATCH	I.1	140
Bellmour:	their Mistresses--I must take up, or I shall never hold out;	41	OLD BATCH	I.1	144
Setter:	Thou are thy Mistresses foul self, Composed of her	66	OLD BATCH	III.1	190
Setter:	Thou art the Wicket to thy Mistresses Gate, to be	66	OLD BATCH	III.1	195
Petulant:	Carry your Mistresses Monkey a Spider,--go flea	454	WAY WORLD	IV.1	375

Mistrust (1)

Speaker	Text	PAGE	TITLE	ACT.SC	LINE
Valentine:	of the Men; and his Secresie, upon the mistrust of the	256	FOR LOVE	III.1	132

Misunderstand (1)

Speaker	Text	PAGE	TITLE	ACT.SC	LINE
Valentine:	Oh, 'tis barbarous to misunderstand me longer.	295	FOR LOVE	IV.1	731

Mitigate (1)

Speaker	Text	PAGE	TITLE	ACT.SC	LINE
Marwood:	you don't mitigate those violent Airs.	433	WAY WORLD	III.1	334

Mitten (1)

Speaker	Text	PAGE	TITLE	ACT.SC	LINE
Foible:	into Black Friers for Brass Farthings, with an old Mitten.	428	WAY WORLD	III.1	138

Mittimus (1)

Speaker	Text	PAGE	TITLE	ACT.SC	LINE
Sir Wilful:	Sir. It shall not be sufficient for a Mittimus or a Taylor's	473	WAY WORLD	V.1	427

Mix (2)

Speaker	Text	PAGE	TITLE	ACT.SC	LINE
Lady Touch:	Fortune, but he must mix his Blood with mine, and Wed	191	DOUBL DLR	V.1	127
Almeria:	Of Humane Bodies; for I'll mix with them,	339	M. BRIDE	II.1	75

Mix'd (3)

Speaker	Text	PAGE	TITLE	ACT.SC	LINE
Osmyn-Alph:	Such Sanctity, such Tenderness, so mix'd	352	M. BRIDE	III.1	114
Zara:	Of those Ingredients mix'd, as will with speed	375	M. BRIDE	V.1	132
Zara:	Of such Ingredients mix'd, as will with speed	375	M. BRIDE	V.1 V132

Mixture (1)

Speaker	Text	PAGE	TITLE	ACT.SC	LINE
Fainall:	Sir Wilfull is an odd mixture of Bashfulness and	401	WAY WORLD	I.1	218

Moan (1)

Speaker	Text	PAGE	TITLE	ACT.SC	LINE
Singer:	And seem'd to moan, in sullen Cooing,	71	OLD BATCH	III.2 V 20

Mock (4)

Speaker	Text	PAGE	TITLE	ACT.SC	LINE
Heartwell:	Death: D'ye mock me? Heark-ye: If either you	105	OLD BATCH	V.1	321
Lady Touch:	Ha! do you mock my Rage? then this shall	198	DOUBL DLR	V.1	391
Osmyn-Alph:	You do not come to mock my Miseries?	360	M. BRIDE	III.1	420
Manuel:	His Teeth may grin, and mock at her Remorse.	374	M. BRIDE	V.1	78

Mock-Praises (1)

Speaker	Text	PAGE	TITLE	ACT.SC	LINE
Zara:	Beneath Mock-Praises, and dissembled State.	336	M. BRIDE	I.1	402

Mock-Worship (1)

Speaker	Text	PAGE	TITLE	ACT.SC	LINE
Maskwell:	the Temple of the God, and Love was made a Mock-Worship,	137	DOUBL DLR	I.1	376

Mode (2)

Speaker	Text	PAGE	TITLE	ACT.SC	LINE
Belinda:	Yes: You flattering Men of the Mode have made	106	OLD BATCH	V.1	369
Belinda:	Yes: You fluttering Men of the Mode have made	106	OLD BATCH	V.1 V369

Model (1)

Speaker	Text	PAGE	TITLE	ACT.SC	LINE
Lady Wish:	but a Pattern for you, and a Model for you, after you were	465	WAY WORLD	V.1	145

Money (continued)

		PAGE	TITLE	ACT.SC	LINE
Scandal:	And how do you expect to have your Money again,	224	FOR LOVE	I.1	315
Valentine:	of my Creditors for their Money, and my own impatience	225	FOR LOVE	I.1	340
Sr Sampson:	Money, Brother Foresight.	243	FOR LOVE	II.1	276
Foresight:	Aye indeed, Sir Sampson, a great deal of Money for	243	FOR LOVE	II.1	277
Jeremy:	just as he was poor for want of Money; his Head is e'en as	276	FOR LOVE	IV.1	34
Valentine:	thou can'st not borrow Money of me; Then what	292	FOR LOVE	IV.1	627
Sr Sampson:	out of his Money, and now his Poverty has run him out of	299	FOR LOVE	V.1	84

Monger (0)   see Ballad-monger
Monkey (1)

Petulant:	Carry your Mistresses Monkey a Spider,--go flea	454	WAY WORLD	IV.1	375

Monopolize (1)

Fainall:	you monopolize the Wit that is between you, the Fortune	402	WAY WORLD	I.1	283

Monster (15)   see Land-Monster

	Be ev'ry Monster of the Deep away;	125	DOUBL DLR	PRO.	14
Lord Touch:	Ungrateful Monster, how long?--	153	DOUBL DLR	III.1	108
Lady Ply:	Ungrateful Monster! He? Is it so? Ay, I see it, a Plot upon	179	DOUBL DLR	IV.1	444
Lady Ply:	pretended to like that Monster of Iniquity, Careless, and	179	DOUBL DLR	IV.1	454
Lady Touch:	I had not time to think--I was surprised to see a Monster in	185	DOUBL DLR	IV.2	71
Lord Touch:	Monster, Dog! your Life shall answer	186	DOUBL DLR	IV.2	106
Lady Touch:	(within). No, Monster! Hellish Traitor! no.	197	DOUBL DLR	V.1	372
Lady Touch:	(within). No, Monster! Traitor! no.	197	DOUBL DLR	V.1 V372	
Lord Touch:	Are you silent, Monster?	202	DOUBL DLR	V.1	572
Sr Sampson:	Body o' me, what a many headed Monster have	244	FOR LOVE	II.1	343
Scandal:	(aside). Miracle! the Monster grows loving.	281	FOR LOVE	IV.1	205
Valentine:	Because thou wer't a Monster; old Boy:--The	282	FOR LOVE	IV.1	262
Mrs Frail:	No, no, I am not mad, Monster, I am wise enough	286	FOR LOVE	IV.1	406
Zara:	Traytour, Monster, cold and perfidious Slave;	348	M. BRIDE	II.2	340
Fainall:	the Monster in the Tempest; and much after the same manner.	401	WAY WORLD	I.1	220

Monster's (1)

Laetitia:	I durst have sworn, I had heard my Monster's Voice.	89	OLD BATCH	IV.4	3

Monsters (2)

Valentine:	two greatest Monsters in the World are a Man and a	282	FOR LOVE	IV.1	263
Sr Sampson:	Why, my Opinion is, that those two Monsters	282	FOR LOVE	IV.1	265

Monstrous (3)

Belinda:	O monstrous filthy Fellow! Good slovenly Captain	85	OLD BATCH	IV.3	86
Fondlewife:	O bless me! O monstrous! A Prayer-Book? Ay, this is the	92	OLD BATCH	IV.4	106
Mrs Fore:	O Monstrous! What are Conscience and	271	FOR LOVE	III.1	673

Month (1)

Waitwell:	month out at knees with begging an Alms,--he shall	458	WAY WORLD	IV.1	522

Month's (2)

Belinda:	at the Month's End, you shall hardly find a Married-man,	108	OLD BATCH	V.2	29
Foible:	me.--She has a Month's mind; but I know Mr.	430	WAY WORLD	III.1	217

Months (4)

Silvia:	Midwife, some nine Months hence--well, I find dissembling,	75	OLD BATCH	III.2	150
Sir Paul:	He? And wilt thou bring a Grandson at 9 Months	173	DOUBL DLR	IV.1	223
Marwood:	Months Mind, but he can't abide her--'Twere better	431	WAY WORLD	III.1	240
Sir Wilful:	out at the nine Months end.	456	WAY WORLD	IV.1	430

Montufar (1)

Bellmour:	Methinks I am the very Picture of Montufar in the	80	OLD BATCH	IV.2	7

Monument (2)

Almeria:	No, I will live to be thy Monument;	328	M. BRIDE	I.1	72
	Monument fronting the View, greater than the rest. Enter Heli.)	340	M. BRIDE	II.2	

Monumental (1)

Almeria:	And Monumental Caves of Death, look Cold,	339	M. BRIDE	II.1	65

Monuments (1)

Heli:	I wander thro' this Maze of Monuments,	340	M. BRIDE	II.2	1

Mony (13)

Bellmour:	But she can't have too much Mony--There's	41	OLD BATCH	I.1	165
Sharper:	Mony is but Dirt Sir Joseph--Mere Dirt.	50	OLD BATCH	II.1	110
Sir Joseph:	have all my ready Mony to redeem his great Sword from	51	OLD BATCH	II.1	131
Belinda:	troublesome of Duns--A Dun for Mony will be	58	OLD BATCH	II.2	127
Capt Bluff:	for the Mony, and if you would look me in the Face again	67	OLD BATCH	III.1	249
Sharper:	Mony paid at sight! I'm come to return my Thanks--	68	OLD BATCH	III.1	285
Heartwell:	yet a more certain Sign than all this; I give thee my Mony.	73	OLD BATCH	III.2	85
Silvia:	give Mony to any naughty Woman to come to Bed to	73	OLD BATCH	III.2	87
Ben:	Mony in his Pocket--May-hap I may not have so	273	FOR LOVE	III.1	734
Ben:	our Landladies once a Year, get rid of a little Mony; and	275	FOR LOVE	III.1	802
Witwoud:	He's reckoning his Mony,--my Mony it was,	402	WAY WORLD	I.1	279
Mirabell:	(Gives Mony.)	424	WAY WORLD	II.1	535

Moon (10)

Foresight:	the Moon is in all her Fortitudes; Is my Neice Angelica at	235	FOR LOVE	II.1	6
Sr Sampson:	By the Horns of the Moon, you wou'd say,	241	FOR LOVE	II.1	233
Sr Sampson:	Reverence the Sun, Moon and Stars with all my heart.	242	FOR LOVE	II.1	247
Sr Sampson:	Moon, and thou art the Man in the Moon: Nay, she is	242	FOR LOVE	II.1	257
Sr Sampson:	more Illustrious than the Moon; for she has her Chastity	242	FOR LOVE	II.1	258
Foresight:	hope, neither the Lord of my Ascendant, nor the Moon	270	FOR LOVE	III.1	648
Sr Sampson:	not foresee that the Moon wou'd predominate, and my	283	FOR LOVE	IV.1	281
Valentine:	Endymion and the Moon shall meet us upon Mount Latmos,	290	FOR LOVE	IV.1	547
Foresight:	Hey day! What time of the Moon is this?	305	FOR LOVE	V.1	286

Moor (11)

Alonzo:	To Albucacim; and the Moor had conquer'd.	335	M. BRIDE	I.1	361
Zara:	That Gallant Moor, in Battle lost a Friend	337	M. BRIDE	I.1	437
Perez:	Yonder, my Lord, behold the Noble Moor.	338	M. BRIDE	II.1	16
Manuel:	Stay, Soldier; they shall suffer with the Moor.	363	M. BRIDE	IV.1	73
Manuel:	Her Warrant, have Admittance to the Moor.	365	M. BRIDE	IV.1	169
Gonsalez:	The Princess is Confederate with the Moor.	365	M. BRIDE	IV.1	180
Gonsalez:	Methinks this Lady's Hatred to the Moor,	366	M. BRIDE	IV.1	202
Manuel:	But think'st thou that my Daughter saw this Moor?	367	M. BRIDE	IV.1	228
Manuel:	And plots in Private with this hellish Moor.	367	M. BRIDE	IV.1	235
Garcia:	The Traytor Perez, and the Captive Moor,	377	M. BRIDE	V.2	38
Gonsalez:	The Moor, is dead. That Osmyn was Alphonso;	377	M. BRIDE	V.2	41

Moor-Husband (1)

	I know not one Moor-Husband in the City.	125	DOUBL DLR	PRO.	28

More   (continued)

Speaker	Text	PAGE	TITLE	ACT.SC	LINE
Lady Touch:	Nay, my Lord, you need say no more, to	152	DOUBL DLR	III.1	64
Lady Touch:	were more, 'tis over now, and all's well. For my part I	153	DOUBL DLR	III.1	96
Lady Touch:	--nay, I won't tell you any more, till ycu are your	153	DOUBL DLR	III.1	111
Lord Touch:	would hear more of this.	154	DOUBL DLR	III.1	124
Mellefont:	to engage her more irresistably. 'Tis only an inhancing the	158	DOUBL DLR	III.1	301
Lady Ply:	face of the World that no body is more sensible of Favours	159	DOUBL DLR	III.1	351
Sir Paul:	do so no more; d'ye hear, Tim?	161	DOUBL DLR	III.1	399
Sir Paul:	no more familiarity with her Person--as to that matter--	162	DOUBL DLR	III.1	439
Lady Froth:	Just as the Sun does, more or less.	164	DOUBL DLR	III.1	532
Brisk:	. . . More or Less.	164	DOUBL DLR	III.1	V533
Lady Ply:	challenges much more, I'm sure, than my illiterate Praises	169	DOUBL DLR	IV.1	83
Lady Ply:	O rise I beseech you, say no more till you rise	170	DOUBL DLR	IV.1	107
Lady Ply:	that Mellefont had never any thing more than a profound	171	DOUBL DLR	IV.1	165
Brisk:	No more I have I'gad, for I adore 'em all in your	176	DOUBL DLR	IV.1	336
Lady Ply:	I do, see my Face no more;	179	DOUBL DLR	IV.1	457
Sir Paul:	Commission--If I desired him to do any more than	180	DOUBL DLR	IV.1	471
Sir Paul:	here made? Why, this is better and more Miraculous than	180	DOUBL DLR	IV.1	505
Maskwell:	I have nothing more to say, my Lord--but to	182	DOUBL DLR	IV.1	560
Maskwell:	to tell you more.	183	DOUBL DLR	IV.1	586
Maskwell:	still to be more and more indebted to your goodness.	183	DOUBL DLR	IV.2	15
Mellefont:	Hold, Madam, you have no more hcles to your Burrough,	184	DOUBL DLR	IV.2	42
Mellefont:	. . . Though she can wear more	186	DOUBL DLR	IV.2	V124
Mellefont:	me; I never had more need cf him--But what can he do?	187	DOUBL DLR	IV.2	149
Mellefont:	Imagination cannot form a fairer and more plausible	187	DOUBL DLR	IV.2	150
Lord Touch:	No more--I have resolv'd--The	189	DOUBL DLR	V.1	61
Maskwell:	Stratagem--I must deceive Mellefcnt once more, and	190	DOUBL DLR	V.1	95
Maskwell:	Stables--it will be more convenient.	194	DOUBL DLR	V.1	256
Saygrace:	You have no more Commands?	195	DOUBL DLR	V.1	296
Maskwell:	more than all the rest; though I would give a Limb for	199	DOUBL DLR	V.1	434
Maskwell:	No more,--there want but a few Minutes of	199	DOUBL DLR	V.1	456
Maskwell:	No more,--it wants but a few Minutes of	199	DOUBL DLR	V.1	V456
Lady Froth:	You know I told you Saturn look'd a little more	203	DOUBL DLR	V.1	579
	Unless transplanted to more kindly Earth.	213	FOR LCVE	PRO.	6
Valentine:	be reveng'd on 'em all; I'll pursue Angelica with more Love	217	FOR LCVE	I.1	50
Valentine:	then ever, and appear more notoriously her Admirer in	217	FOR LCVE	I.1	51
Jeremy:	Three days, the Life of a Play, I no more expect it, than to	218	FOR LCVE	I.1	74
Jeremy:	ruin'd more Young Men than the Royal Oak Lottery--	218	FOR LCVE	I.1	88
Scandal:	enough? Must you needs shew your Wit to get more?	219	FOR LCVE	I.1	128
Jeremy:	Ay, more indeed; for who cares fcr any Bcdy that	219	FOR LCVE	I.1	129
Jeremy:	has more Wit than himself?	219	FOR LCVE	I.1	130
Scandal:	more servile, timorous, and fawning, than any I have	220	FOR LCVE	I.1	147
Scandal:	Attendance, and promis'd more than ever you intend to	221	FOR LCVE	I.1	194
Scandal:	Attendance, and promis'd more than ever you intended to	221	FOR LCVE	I.1	V194
Scandal:	perform; are more perplex'd to find Evasions, than you	221	FOR LCVE	I.1	195
Valentine:	and bid her trouble me no more; a thoughtless two handed	221	FOR LCVE	I.1	210
Scandal:	of my Love. And d'ee hear, bid Margery put more Flocks	222	FCR LCVE	I.1	218
Trapland:	No more, in truth.--I have forborn, I say--	222	FCR LCVE	I.1	249
Valentine:	Health. An honester Man lives not, nor one more ready to	223	FOR LCVE	I.1	261
Trapland:	No more indeed.	223	FOR LCVE	I.1	274
Valentine:	You need say no more, I understand the Conditions;	224	FOR LCVE	I.1	317
Jeremy:	More Misfortunes, Sir.	225	FOR LCVE	I.1	356
Tattle:	For there is nothing more known, than that no body	227	FCB LCVE	I.1	404
Tattle:	that--Nay more (I'm going to say a bold Word now) I	227	FOR LCVE	I.1	410
Scandal:	Why, Tattle, thou hast more Impudence than one	227	FOR LCVE	I.1	437
Tattle:	Tho' I have more Honour than to tell first; I have more	229	FCR LCVE	I.1	478
Valentine:	sometimes. I did not think she had granted more to any	229	FCR LCVE	I.1	487
Valentine:	If there were, you have more Discretion, than to	229	FOR LCVE	I.1	511
Tattle:	Name cf Trusty Mr. Tattle more--You will not be so	230	FOR LCVE	I.1	521
Valentine:	But what if he have more Passion than Manners?	231	FOR LCVE	I.1	558
Valentine:	But what if he has more Passion than Manners?	231	FOR LCVE	I.1	V558
Mrs Frail:	That's more than he has for himself. And what will	232	FOR LCVE	I.1	593
Scandal:	I have many more of this kind, very well Painted, as you	234	FOR LCVE	I.1	657
Foresight:	there's no more to be said--	239	FOR LCVE	II.1	170
Foresight:	there's no more to be said--he's there already	239	FOR LCVE	II.1	V170
Sr Sampson:	Nor no more to be done, Old Boy; that's plain--	240	FOR LCVE	II.1	172
Sr Sampson:	there's no time but the time present, there's no more to be	240	FOR LCVE	II.1	197
Sr Sampson:	more Illustrious than the Moon; for she has her Chastity	242	FOR LCVE	II.1	258
Valentine:	hope you will have more Indulgence, than to oblige me to	243	FOR LCVE	II.1	283
Sr Sampson:	That's more than I know, Sir, and I believe not.	244	FOR LCVE	II.1	316
Valentine:	I know no more why I came, than you do why	244	FOR LCVE	II.1	333
Mrs Frail:	have observ'd us more than we have observ'd one another.	248	FOR LCVE	III.1	488
Miss Prue:	any more Lavender among my Smocks--ha, Cousin?	249	FOR LCVE	III.1	530
Tattle:	But you must think your self more Charming than I	252	FOR LCVE	II.1	617
Tattle:	If I ask you for more, you must be more angry,--but	252	FOR LCVE	II.1	621
Tattle:	more complying; and as soon as ever I make you say	252	FOR LCVE	II.1	622
Miss Prue:	Will ycu? then I'll be more angry, and more	253	FOR LCVE	II.1	655
Miss Prue:	Well, now I'll run and make more haste than you.	253	FOR LCVE	II.1	660
Tattle:	Faith, Madam, you're in the right; no more I have, as	256	FOR LCVE	III.1	100
Valentine:	tell whether the Lady or Mr. Tattle be the more obliged	256	FCR LCVE	III.1	130
Tattle:	shall make Oath, that I receive more Letters than the	257	FOR LCVE	III.1	159
Tattle:	Secretary's Office; and that I have more Vizor-Masks to	257	FOR LCVE	III.1	160
Scandal:	No don't; for then you'l tell us no more--Come, I'll	258	FOR LCVE	III.1	190
Sr Sampson:	oblige him. Odsbud, Madam, have no more to say to	259	FOR LCVE	III.1	239
Ben:	A man that is marri'd, d'ee see, is no more like another	262	FOR LCVE	III.1	315
Miss Prue:	that's more: So, there's your answer for you; and don't	264	FOR LCVE	III.1	400
Miss Prue:	trouble me no more, you ugly thing.	264	FOR LCVE	III.1	401
Ben:	Whipping no more than you do. But I tell you one thing,	264	FOR LCVE	III.1	407
Ben:	your self, Gad I don't think you are any more to compare	264	FOR LCVE	III.1	412
Miss Prue:	any more, he'll thrash your Jacket for you, he will, you	264	FOR LCVE	III.1	417
Ben:	stink; he shall smell more like a Weasel than a Civet-Cat,	265	FOR LCVE	III.1	437
Ben:	Let her cry: The more she cries, the less she'll--	265	FOR LCVE	III.1	441
Scandal:	him, and all of us, more than any thing else?	266	FOR LCVE	III.1	484
Scandal:	but you are something more--There have been wise	267	FOR LCVE	III.1	528
Scandal:	it more dangerous to be seen in Conversation with me, than	272	FOR LCVE	III.1	695
Ben:	When she no more intended,	274	FOR LCVE	III.1	764

Speaker	Text	PAGE	TITLE	ACT.SC LINE
Ben:	He lov'd her more than Plunder;	274	FOR LOVE	III.1 770
Angelica:	more than he has done by himself: and now the Surprize	277	FOR LOVE	IV.1 82
Angelica:	love, I can't help it; no more than he can help his being a	278	FOR LOVE	IV.1 88
Angelica:	Man, or I my being a Woman; or no more than I can help	278	FOR LOVE	IV.1 89
Jeremy:	Good lack! What's the matter now? Are any more of	278	FOR LOVE	IV.1 98
Valentine:	if you should ask him, whether the Bible saves more	280	FOR LOVE	IV.1 176
Valentine:	Souls in Westminster-Abby, or damns more in			
	Westminster-Hall:	280	FOR LOVE	IV.1 177
Scandal:	be occasion; for I fancy his Presence provokes him more.	280	FOR LOVE	IV.1 190
Valentine:	There's a couple of Topicks for you, no more like one	282	FOR LOVE	IV.1 256
Scandal:	he did not foresee, and more particularly relating to his	284	FOR LOVE	IV.1 312
Scandal:	all night, and denying favours with more impudence, than	284	FOR LOVE	IV.1 336
Scandal:	. . . favours with more impudence, than	284	FOR LOVE	IV.1 V336
Ben:	Woman that she provided for me, I thought it more fitting	285	FOR LOVE	IV.1 373
Ben:	at these years, there's some danger of your head's aking	286	FOR LOVE	IV.1 383
Mrs Frail:	O see me no more,--for thou wert born amongst	286	FOR LOVE	IV.1 398
Ben:	More shame for you,--the Wind's chang'd?--	287	FOR LOVE	IV.1 424
Mrs Frail:	throw himself away, he can't do it more effectually than	287	FOR LOVE	IV.1 460
Tattle:	of Valentine's making any more Addresses to you, I have	291	FOR LOVE	IV.1 578
Foresight:	But he knows more than any body,--Oh	291	FOR LOVE	IV.1 603
Tattle:	now, that I knew more Secrets than he.	291	FOR LOVE	IV.1 609
Valentine:	No more, for I am melancholly.	293	FOR LOVE	IV.1 665
Valentine:	more than Love, to make me worthy of you.	295	FOR LOVE	IV.1 727
Angelica:	like him, it's a sign he likes me; and that's more than half	297	FOR LOVE	V.1 6
Angelica:	--I have more Occasion for your Conduct than your	298	FOR LOVE	V.1 45
Angelica:	would no more be his Wife, than his Enemy. For his	299	FOR LOVE	V.1 76
Angelica:	Malice is not a more terrible Consequence of his Aversion,	299	FOR LOVE	V.1 77
Angelica:	are very much abus'd in that Matter; He's no more Mad	299	FOR LOVE	V.1 87
Sr Sampson:	Posture, that I might make a more becoming Offer to a	300	FOR LOVE	V.1 96
Sr Sampson:	more glorious Victim to be offer'd at the Shrine of your	300	FOR LOVE	V.1 100
Tattle:	I'll make thy Fortune; say no more--Thou art a	302	FOR LOVE	V.1 180
Tattle:	more love for your Daughter, than I have likeness of you;	305	FOR LOVE	V.1 288
Angelica:	try'd you too, and know you both. You have not more	312	FOR LOVE	V.1 575
Angelica:	Faults than he has Virtues; and 'tis hardly more Pleasure	312	FOR LOVE	V.1 576
Angelica:	apt to run more in Debt than you are able to pay.	313	FOR LOVE	V.1 614
	Tho' they are more like Almanacks of late;	323	M. BRIDE	PRO. 5
Almeria:	What then am I? Am I more senseless grown	326	M. BRIDE	I.1 6
Almeria:	At Peace; Father and Son are now no more--	327	M. BRIDE	I.1 53
Almeria:	Both, both--Father and Son are now no more.	327	M. BRIDE	I.1 V 53
Almeria:	Why do I live to say you are no more?	327	M. BRIDE	I.1 55
Almeria:	The cruel Ocean is no more thy Tomb,	328	M. BRIDE	I.1 V 73
Almeria:	But Heav'n spared me for yet more Affliction!	329	M. BRIDE	I.1 128
Almeria:	Yet, one Thing more, I would engage from thee.	330	M. BRIDE	I.1 194
Almeria:	I feel I'm more at large,	331	M. BRIDE	I.1 202
Almeria:	Nor Violence.--I feel my self more light,	331	M. BRIDE	I.1 V202
Almeria:	And more at large, since I have made this Vow.	331	M. BRIDE	I.1 V203
Almeria:	Perhaps I would repeat it there more solemnly.	331	M. BRIDE	I.1 204
Almeria:	Upon my Word no more,	331	M. BRIDE	I.1 206
Gonsalez:	My Eyes with more Delight, than they can hold.	332	M. BRIDE	I.1 274
Manuel:	A Dispensation to your Vow--No more.	333	M. BRIDE	I.1 292
Gonsalez:	As if she had offended.--Sure, no more,	334	M. BRIDE	I.1 V320
Manuel:	No more; my Promise long since pass'd, thy Loyalty,	334	M. BRIDE	I.1 340
Manuel:	No more; my Promise long since pass'd, thy Services,	334	M. BRIDE	I.1 V340
Manuel:	'Tis false; 'twas more; I bad she should be free:	336	M. BRIDE	I.1 408
Manuel:	'Tis false; 'twas more; I bid she should be free:	336	M. BRIDE	I.1 V408
Manuel:	Her Eyes, did more than bid--free her and hers,	336	M. BRIDE	I.1 410
Zara:	Yet hating more, Ingratitude, can pay,	336	M. BRIDE	I.1 418
Zara:	Whom more than Life he lov'd; and the Regret,	337	M. BRIDE	I.1 438
Manuel:	Conquest and Triumph, now, are mine no more;	337	M. BRIDE	I.1 452
Almeria:	Of Garcia's more detested Bed. That Thought,	339	M. BRIDE	II.1 78
Osmyn-Alph:	Is knowing more than any Circumstance,	342	M. BRIDE	II.2 94
Almeria:	Let me look on thee, yet a little more.	342	M. BRIDE	II.2 100
Osmyn-Alph:	No more, my Life; talk not of Tears or Grief;	343	M. BRIDE	II.2 120
Osmyn-Alph:	Affliction is no more, now thou art found.	343	M. BRIDE	II.2 121
Almeria:	'Tis more than Recompence, to see thy Face;	343	M. BRIDE	II.2 147
Almeria:	More Miracles! Antonio too escap'd!	344	M. BRIDE	II.2 172
Osmyn-Alph:	To part no more; my Friend will tell thee all;	345	M. BRIDE	II.2 205
Osmyn-Alph:	Yet I behold her--Now no more.	345	M. BRIDE	II.2 214
Zara:	Am I more loathsome to thee, than the Grave?	345	M. BRIDE	II.2 241
Zara:	Give it me as it is; I ask no more	346	M. BRIDE	II.2 273
Zara:	Ruine, 'tis still to reign, and to be more	347	M. BRIDE	II.2 314
Zara:	That to have lov'd thee, makes me yet more lost	348	M. BRIDE	II.2 338
Zara:	Whose former Faith had merited much more:	349	M. BRIDE	II.2 377
Osmyn-Alph:	Give me more Weight, crush my declining Years	350	M. BRIDE	III.1 11
Osmyn-Alph:	It is his Hand; this was his Pray'r--yet more.	350	M. BRIDE	III.1 14
Osmyn-Alph:	More Anxious Grief. This shou'd have better taught me;	353	M. BRIDE	III.1 127
Osmyn-Alph:	Will treasure here; more worth than Diadems,	353	M. BRIDE	III.1 137
Osmyn-Alph:	I'll treasure as more worth than Diadems,	353	M. BRIDE	III.1 V137
Zara:	And call it Passion; then, be still more kind,	354	M. BRIDE	III.1 181
Zara:	Thou canst not owe me more, nor have I more	355	M. BRIDE	III.1 215
Osmyn-Alph:	Esteem; to this she's fair, few more can boast	355	M. BRIDE	III.1 225
Almeria:	To part no more--Now we will part no more,	355	M. BRIDE	III.1 247
Almeria:	Why? why? to know it, cannot wound me more,	356	M. BRIDE	III.1 278
Almeria:	Where levell'd low, no more we'll lift our Eyes,	358	M. BRIDE	III.1 372
Zara:	Requires he should be more confin'd; and none,	360	M. BRIDE	III.1 450
Selim:	Is since arrived, of more revolted Troops.	361	M. BRIDE	IV.1 7
Zara:	More than his Crown, t'impart 'ere Osmyn die.	361	M. BRIDE	IV.1 19
Zara:	O 'tis more Grief but to suppose his Death,	362	M. BRIDE	IV.1 27
Selim:	I can no more, the King is here. Obtain	362	M. BRIDE	IV.1 59
Gonsalez:	Till Osmyn die. Mean time we may learn more	363	M. BRIDE	IV.1 70
Zara:	And try the Force of yet more Obligations.	363	M. BRIDE	IV.1 98
Zara:	You're too secure: The Danger is more imminent	364	M. BRIDE	IV.1 109
Zara:	You more. One that did call himself Alphonso,	364	M. BRIDE	IV.1 116
Zara:	You more. One who did call himself Alphonso,	364	M. BRIDE	IV.1 V116
Zara:	What I know more, is, That a tripple League	364	M. BRIDE	IV.1 122

More (continued)

Zara:	Forbear a Moment; somewhat more I have	. . . . . .	364	M. BRIDE	IV.1	129
Gonsalez:	Should have more Meaning than appears bare-fac'd.	. . .	365	M. BRIDE	IV.1	176
Almeria:	One hated Line of more extended Woe.	. . . . . .	367	M. BRIDE	IV.1	261
Almeria:	That was—that was, but is no more a Father.	. . . .	368	M. BRIDE	IV.1	281
Almeria:	Who was—who was, but is no more a Father.	. . . .	368	M. BRIDE	IV.1	V281
Manuel:	Ha! who may live? take heed, no more of that.	. . .	369	M. BRIDE	IV.1	332
Manuel:	Should I hear more; I too should catch thy Madness.	. .	370	M. BRIDE	IV.1	362
Manuel:	Which I'll not hear, 'till I am more at peace.	. . .	370	M. BRIDE	IV.1	364
Zara:	And more important Fate, requires my Thought.	. . .	375	M. BRIDE	V.1	125
Zara:	Thou shalt partake. Since Fates no more afford;	. . .	376	M. BRIDE	V.1	138
Garcia:	With more unnatural Blood. Murder my Father!	. . .	378	M. BRIDE	V.2	77
Zara:	Yet, more, this Stilness terrifies my Soul,	. . . .	379	M. BRIDE	V.2	142
Zara:	Or does my Heart bode more? what can it more	. . .	380	M. BRIDE	V.2	147
Zara:	Why is't you more than speak in these sad Signs?	. .	380	M. BRIDE	V.2	159
Zara:	Give me more ample Knowledge of this Mourning.	. .	380	M. BRIDE	V.2	160
Zara:	Cruel, cruel, O more than killing Object!	. . . .	380	M. BRIDE	V.2	V164
Leonora:	But O forbear—lift up your Eyes no more;	. . . .	381	M. BRIDE	V.2	226
Almeria:	Yet bubling from his Wounds—O more than savage!	. .	382	M. BRIDE	V.2	235
Almeria:	I have him now, and we no more will part.	. . . .	383	M. BRIDE	V.2	298
	No more a Princess, but in statu quo:	. . . . . .	385	M. BRIDE	EPI.	2
	Damn him the more; have no Commiseration	. . .	393	WAY WORLD	PRO.	24
Fainall:	more play with a Man that slighted his ill Fortune, than	.	395	WAY WORLD	I.1	8
Mirabell:	Yes, and Mrs. Marwood and three or four more,	. .	396	WAY WORLD	I.1	28
Mirabell:	She is more Mistress of her self, than to be under	. . .	396	WAY WORLD	I.1	43
Mirabell:	for it self, she'll breed no more.	. . . . . .	397	WAY WORLD	I.1	63
Mirabell:	Concern for which the Lady is more indebted to you, than	.	397	WAY WORLD	I.1	97
Mirabell:	Concern for which the Lady is more indebted to you, than is	397	WAY WORLD	I.1	V 97
Mirabell:	always the more the Scandal: For a Woman who is not a	.	399	WAY WORLD	I.1	145
Mirabell:	Woman wou'd be odious, serve but to make her more	. .	399	WAY WORLD	I.1	162
Witwoud:	all, that I must own—No more breeding than a	. . .	403	WAY WORLD	I.1	298
Witwoud:	Wit will excuse that: A Wit shou'd no more be sincere,	. .	403	WAY WORLD	I.1	319
Witwoud:	Learning, gives him the more opportunities to shew his	.	404	WAY WORLD	I.1	327
Witwoud:	and something more by the Week, to call on him	. . .	405	WAY WORLD	I.1	360
Witwoud:	more Company here to take notice of him—Why	. . . .	405	WAY WORLD	I.1	364
Witwoud:	and what's more, not finding himself, sometimes leave a	.	405	WAY WORLD	I.1	376
Mirabell:	Eye, by a Pearl of Orient; he wou'd no more be seen by	.	407	WAY WORLD	I.1	455
Petulant:	The Quintessence. May be Witwoud knows more, he	. .	408	WAY WORLD	I.1	496
Mrs Fain:	He has a Humour more prevailing than his	. . . . .	412	WAY WORLD	II.1	103
Marwood:	More tender, more sincere, and more enduring,	. . .	414	WAY WORLD	II.1	167
Fainall:	hate my Wife yet more, Dam her, I'll part with her, rob	.	416	WAY WORLD	II.1	244
Mirabell:	that she might seem to carry it more privately.	. . .	418	WAY WORLD	II.1	306
Mirabell:	Thing that resembl'd a Man, tho' 'twere no more than	.	418	WAY WORLD	II.1	312
Millamant:	one pleases, one makes more.	. . . .	420	WAY WORLD	II.1	406
Witwoud:	Very pretty. Why you make no more of making	. . .	420	WAY WORLD	II.1	407
Millamant:	One no more owes one's Beauty to a Lover, than	. . .	420	WAY WORLD	II.1	409
Mirabell:	I have something more—Gone—Think of	. . . .	423	WAY WORLD	II.1	490
Mirabell:	were a Case of more steady Contemplation; a very tranquility	423	WAY WORLD	II.1	492
Mirabell:	Windmill, has not a more whimsical Dwelling than the	.	423	WAY WORLD	II.1	494
Waitwell:	did not make more.	. . . .	423	WAY WORLD	II.1	517
Mirabell:	Your Diligence will merit more—In the mean	. . .	424	WAY WORLD	II.1	533
Foible:	not doubt of Success. If you have no more Commands Sir,	424	WAY WORLD	II.1	542
Lady Wish:	I have no more patience—If I have not fretted	. . . .	425	WAY WORLD	III.1	3
Lady Wish:	may examine her with more freedom—You'll pardon	. .	426	WAY WORLD	III.1	51
Marwood:	can no more conceal it, than my Lady Strammel can her	.	433	WAY WORLD	III.1	320
Millamant:	I'll take my Death, Marwood, you are more Censorious,	.	433	WAY WORLD	III.1	323
Millamant:	That Mirabell loves me is no more a Secret, than it is a	.	433	WAY WORLD	III.1	328
Millamant:	more Gallantry—'Tis hardly well bred to be so particular	434	WAY WORLD	III.1	340
Petulant:	married tho' he can't Read, any more than he is from being	436	WAY WORLD	III.1	429
Marwood:	now you'll be no more Jealous.	. . . .	444	WAY WORLD	III.1	713
Fainall:	and will herd no more with 'em. True, I wear the badge;	.	444	WAY WORLD	III.1	720
Lady Wish:	nothing is more alluring than a Levee from a Couch in	.	445	WAY WORLD	IV.1	29
Millamant:	Press me no more for that slight Toy.	. . . . .	447	WAY WORLD	IV.1	99
Sir Wilful:	an Opportunity to be more private,—I may break my	. .	448	WAY WORLD	IV.1	135
Mirabell:	lock your self up from me, to make my search more	. .	449	WAY WORLD	IV.1	156
Millamant:	more than Impossible—positively Mirabell, I'll lie a Bed in	449	WAY WORLD	IV.1	190
Mirabell:	Have you any more Conditions to offer? Hitherto	. . .	450	WAY WORLD	IV.1	210
Petulant:	Stand off—I'll kiss no more Males,—I have	. . . .	454	WAY WORLD	IV.1	355
Sir Wilful:	Bill—Give me more drink and take my Purse.	. . .	455	WAY WORLD	IV.1	395
Lady Wish:	the Retrospection of my own rudeness,—I have more	. .	457	WAY WORLD	IV.1	485
Lady Wish:	Impudence, more than a big-Belly'd Actress.	. . . .	463	WAY WORLD	V.1	37
Marwood:	More Temper wou'd look more like Innocence. But I have	466	WAY WORLD	V.1	161
Marwood:	no more with an affair, in which I am not Personally	.	466	WAY WORLD	V.1	165
Lady Wish:	more from you than all your life can accomplish—O don't	.	466	WAY WORLD	V.1	170
Marwood:	in more Naughty Law Latin; while the good Judge	. . .	467	WAY WORLD	V.1	219
Marwood:	Lungs of Hawkers, with Voices more Licentious than the	.	468	WAY WORLD	V.1	233
Fainall:	No more Sir Rowlands,—the next Imposture	. . . .	468	WAY WORLD	V.1	256
Fainall:	must set your Hand till more sufficient Deeds can be	. .	469	WAY WORLD	V.1	292
Lady Wish:	come two more of my Egyptian Plagues too.	. . . .	470	WAY WORLD	V.1	309
Sir Wilful:	no more words. For what's to come to pleasure you I'm	.	470	WAY WORLD	V.1	320
Mirabell:	never shall behold you more—	. . . .	471	WAY WORLD	V.1	375
Mirabell:	—I ask no more.	. . . .	471	WAY WORLD	V.1	379
Sir Wilful:	dolefull Sigh more from my fellow Traveller and 'tis	. .	472	WAY WORLD	V.1	398
Mirabell:	Will you? I take you at your word. I ask no more.	. .	474	WAY WORLD	V.1	467
Fainall:	or abate one tittle of my Terms, no, I will insist the more.	474	WAY WORLD	V.1	477
	And sure he must have more than mortal Skill,	. . . .	479	WAY WORLD	EPI.	7

Morn (3)

Bellmour:	she own'd it to my Face; and blushing like the Virgin Morn	38	OLD BATCH	I.1	48
Zara:	And like the Morn vermilion'd o'er thy Face.	. . . .	347	M. BRIDE	II.2	284
Zara:	My self will fly; and earlier than the Morn,	. . . .	354	M. BRIDE	III.1	202

Morning (50)

Bellmour:	parted with his Bed in a Morning, than a' could have slept	37	OLD BATCH	I.1	V 3
Bellmour:	parted with his Bed in a Morning, than he could have slept	37	OLD BATCH	I.1	V 3
Bellmour:	morning was none of her own? for I know thou art as	.	42	OLD BATCH	I.1	185
Bellmour:	Letter was deliver'd to me by a Servant, in the Morning:	.	82	OLD BATCH	IV.2	52
Sharper:	before to Morrow Morning.—Has she not?	. . . .	102	OLD BATCH	V.1	213

Morning   (continued)
		PAGE	TITLE	ACT.SC	LINE
Capt Bluff:	than she. Look here: These were sent me this Morning--	103	OLD BATCH	V.1	265
Bellmour:	to Church in the Morning?--May be it may get	112	OLD BATCH	V.2	177
Mellefont:	with Cynthia, I know not; but this Morning she surpriz'd	130	DOUEL DLR	I.1	98
Maskwell:	to Morrow Morning, or drown between you in the	148	DOUEL DLR	II.1	387
Lord Proth:	And each Morning wears a new one;	166	DOUEL DLR	III.1	600
Lady Ply:	her own), Sir Paul, here's your Letter, to Morrow Morning	174	DOUEL DLR	IV.1	264
Maskwell:	us to Morrow Morning at St. Albans; there we will Sum	194	DOUEL DLR	V.1	243
Valentine:	of Visitants in a morning, all scliciting cf past promises;	221	FOR LCVE	I.1	190
Trapland:	A good Morning to you Mr. Valentine, and to you	222	FCR LCVE	I.1	231
Scandal:	The Morning's a very good Morning, if you don't	222	FCB LCVE	I.1	233
Scandal:	Morning.	229	FCB LCVE	I.1	484
Mrs Frail:	to see Fellows in a Morning. Scandal, you Devil, are you	230	FCB LCVE	I.1	547
Foresight:	of Bed backwards too this morning, without Premeditation;	236	FCB LCVE	II.1	32
Angelica:	morrow morning--But let me be gone first, and then	239	FCB LCVE	II.1	135
Sr Sampson:	Hand and Seal in the Morning, and would be releas'd	243	FOR LCVE	II.1	296
Sr Sampson:	morning, and then look you perform Covenants, and so	246	FCR LCVE	II.1	403
Foresight:	morning.	265	FCB LCVE	III.1	470
Scandal:	he may see you in the Morning, but would not be disturb'd	266	FCR LCVE	III.1	502
Scandal:	So was Valentine this Morning; and look'd just so.	268	FCR LCVE	III.1	570
Scandal:	longer Master of my self--I was interrupted in the morning,	269	FCB LCVE	III.1	587
Scandal:	Yes, yes, I hope this will be gone by Morning, taking	270	FCB LCVE	III.1	631
Scandal:	I hope you will be able to see Valentine in the Morning,	270	FCB LCVE	III.1	637
Jeremy:	that was so near turning Poet yesterday morning, can't be	276	FCR LCVE	IV.1	4
Jeremy:	Like enough, Sir, for I told her Maid this morning,	276	FCR LCVE	IV.1	14
Angelica:	morning.	276	FCR LCVE	IV.1	22
Scandal:	to a man's face in the morning, that she had layn with him	284	FCR LCVE	IV.1	335
Valentine:	Master's Shop in the morning, may ten to one, dirty his	289	FCR LCVE	IV.1	509
Valentine:	Articles, I must this Morning have resign'd: And this I	294	FOR LCVE	IV.1	719
Sr Sampson:	the next Morning.--Odso, have a care, Madam.	299	FCB LCVE	V.1	59
Tattle:	must think of a new Man every Morning, and forget him	303	FOR LCVE	V.1	244
Scandal:	tho' it be Morning, we may have a Dance.	313	FOR LCVE	V.1	601
Manuel:	And spread like Roses to the Morning Sun.	349	M. EBIDE	II.2	386
Gonsalez:	I'th' Morning he must die again; e're Noon	366	M. BRIDE	IV.1	210
Witwoud:	frosty Morning; thou shalt tc the Mall with us; and we'll	409	WAY WCRLD	I.1	520
Mirabell:	by this time. They were married this morning.	417	WAY WCRLD	II.1	289
Millamant:	Ay, poor Mincing tift and tift all the morning.	419	WAY WCRLD	II.1	370
Lady Wish:	Morning, and never heard of since.	426	WAY WCRLD	III.1	46
Mrs Fain:	whom thou wert this morning Married, is to personate	430	WAY WCRLD	III.1	190
Sir Wilful:	Dressing! What it's but Morning here I warrant	437	WAY WCRLD	III.1	447
Servant-W:	Morning, before she is dress'd. 'Tis like I may give a	437	WAY WCRLD	III.1	462
Millamant:	morning thoughts, agreeable wakings, indolent slumbers,	449	WAY WORLD	IV.1	188
Millamant:	a morning as long as I please.	449	WAY WCRLD	IV.1	191
Mirabell:	Then I'll get up in a morning as early as I please.	449	WAY WCRLD	IV.1	192
Witwoud:	by to morrow Morning, Pen me a Challenge--I'll carry it	454	WAY WCRLD	IV.1	373
Sir Wilful:	That he's able next Morning to light us.	455	WAY WCRLD	IV.1	421

Morning-Sun (1)
		PAGE	TITLE	ACT.SC	LINE
Heartwell:	A Morning-Sun his Tinsell'd Harness gilds,	112	OLD BATCH	V.2	188

Morning's (1)
		PAGE	TITLE	ACT.SC	LINE
Scandal:	The Morning's a very good Morning, if you don't	222	FOR LCVE	I.1	233

Mornings (1)
		PAGE	TITLE	ACT.SC	LINE
Mrs Frail:	of these Mornings: I hear you have a great many Pictures.	232	FOR LCVE	I.1	598

Morrow (27)
		PAGE	TITLE	ACT.SC	LINE
Bellmour:	Vainlove, and abroad so early! good Morrow; I	37	OLD BATCH	I.1	1
Vainlove:	Bellmour, good Morrow--Why truth on't is, these	37	OLD BATCH	I.1	5
Vainlove:	Well good Morrow, let's dine together, I'l meet at	40	OLD BATCH	I.1	129
Sharper:	before to Morrow Morning.--Has she not?	102	OLD BATCH	V.1	213
Brisk:	Froth won't Dance at your Wedding to Morrow; nor	129	DOUEL DLR	I.1	56
Careless:	to Morrow appointed for your Marriage with Cynthia, and	129	DOUEL DLR	I.1	80
Maskwell:	Cynthia? Which e're to Morrow shall be done,--had	137	DOUEL DLR	I.1	389
Lady Touch:	Married to Morrow! Despair strikes me. Yet my Soul	137	DOUEL DLR	I.1	399
Maskwell:	to Morrow Morning, or drown between you in the	148	DOUEL DLR	II.1	387
Careless:	through all my Pores, and will to Morrow wash me for	170	DOUEL DLR	IV.1	116
Lady Ply:	her own), Sir Paul, here's your Letter, to Morrow Morning	174	DOUEL DLR	IV.1	264
Maskwell:	us to Morrow Morning at St. Albans; there we will Sum	194	DOUEL DLR	V.1	243
Maskwell:	I had laid a small design for to morrow (as Love	196	DOUEL DLR	V.1	326
Jeremy:	To morrow.	221	FOR LCVE	I.1	177
Jeremy:	that I reckon it will break of course by to morrow, and no	221	FOR LCVE	I.1	181
Tattle:	Valentine good Morrow, Scandal I am Yours.--	226	FOR LOVE	I.1	382
Angelica:	morrow morning--But let me be gone first, and then	239	FCR LOVE	II.1	135
Sr Sampson:	Your Brother will be in Town to Night, or to morrow	246	FCR LCVE	II.1	402
Foresight:	Sir Sampson, we'll have the Wedding to morrow	265	FOR LCVE	III.1	469
Valentine:	come;--Dost thou know what will happen to morrow?	288	FCR LCVE	IV.1	490
Valentine:	morrow, Knaves will thrive thro' craft, and Fools thro'	288	FCR LCVE	IV.1	492
Valentine:	Summer suit. Ask me Questions concerning to morrow?	288	FCR LCVE	IV.1	494
Osmyn-Alph:	Think cn to Morrow, when thou shalt be torn	358	M. EBIDE	III.1	343
Almeria:	To Morrow, and the next, and each that follows,	367	M. EBIDE	IV.1	259
Lady Wish:	Fellow? I'll be married to Morrow, I'll be	428	WAY WORLD	III.1	119
Witwoud:	by to morrow Morning, Pen me a Challenge--I'll carry it	454	WAY WCRLD	IV.1	373
Waitwell:	--than Act Sir Rcwland, till this time to morrow.	459	WAY WCRLD	IV.1	564

Morrow's (1)
		PAGE	TITLE	ACT.SC	LINE
Manuel:	This Day we triumph; but to morrow's Sun	334	M. BRIDE	I.1	342

Morsel (2)
		PAGE	TITLE	ACT.SC	LINE
Bellmour:	Let me see, Laetitia! Oh 'tis a delicious Morsel. Dear	39	OLD BATCH	I.1	73
Alonzo:	The Morsel down his throat. I catch'd his Arm,	373	M. BRIDE	V.1	24

Mortal (5)
		PAGE	TITLE	ACT.SC	LINE
Osmyn-Alph:	And waking to the World and mortal Sense,	353	M. BRIDE	III.1	134
Manuel:	How's this? my mortal Foe beneath my Roof!	373	M. EBIDE	V.1	33
Zara:	Yet Fate, alone can rob his mortal Part	381	M. EBIDE	V.2	195
Lady Wish:	have a mortal Terror at the apprehension of cffending	429	WAY WCRLD	III.1	178
	And sure he must have more than mortal Skill,	479	WAY WCRLD	EPI.	7

Mortals (1)
		PAGE	TITLE	ACT.SC	LINE
Bellmour:	greater resemblance of Theft; and among us lewd Mortals,	39	OLD BATCH	I.1	91

Mortgage (1)
		PAGE	TITLE	ACT.SC	LINE
Brisk:	ground? Mortgage for a Bottle, ha? Careless, this is your	128	DOUBL DLR	I.1	21

Mortification (3)
Valentine:	that made Court to her; so shall my Poverty be a				
	Mortification	217	FOR LOVE	I.1	53
Mrs Fain:	Mortification.	412	WAY WORLD	II.1	94
Mirabell:	as a Mortification; for sure to please a Fool is some degree	421	WAY WORLD	II.1	439

Mortifie (3)
Lord Froth:	and mortifie the Poets; the Fellows grow so Conceited,	133	DOUEL DLR	I.1	V228
Lord Froth:	Then you must mortifie him, with a Patch; my . .	135	DOUEL DLR	I.1	295
Valentine:	to live upon Instruction; feast your Mind, and mortifie	216	FOR LOVE	I.1	13

Mortifies (1)
| Mirabell: | mortifies, yet after Commendation can be flatter'd by it, | 420 | WAY WORLD | II.1 | 396 |

Mortify (1)
| Lord Froth: | and mortify the Poets; the Fellows grow so Conceited, . . | 133 | DOUEL DLR | I.1 | 228 |

Mortifying (1)
| Brisk: | Who, my Lady Toothless; O, she's a mortifying . . . . | 165 | DOUEL DLR | III.1 | 567 |

Mosca (1)
| Mirabell: | Uncle, he might like Mosca in the Fox, stand upon Terms; . | 417 | WAY WORLD | II.1 | 294 |

Most (99)
Bellmour:	Faith I don't know, he's of a temper the most easie . .	42	OLD BATCH	I.1	210
Sharper:	May each succeed in what he wishes most.	47	OLD BATCH	I.1	388
Sir Joseph:	hem! Sir, I most submissively implore your pardon for . .	49	OLD BATCH	II.1	V 54
Belinda:	Ay, on my Conscience, and the most impertinent and . .	58	OLD BATCH	II.2	126
Bellmour:	let me tell you, my most prevailing Argument is express'd in	59	OLD BATCH	II.2	V183
Setter:	Gentlemen I do most properly appertain--The one	64	OLD BATCH	III.1	138
Lucy:	Of thy most vile Cogitations--Thou poor, Conceited . .	65	OLD BATCH	III.1	167
Lucy:	which you have slander'd most abominably. It vexes me . .	66	OLD BATCH	III.1	208
Setter:	O most religiously well Sir.	75	OLD BATCH	IV.1	5
Bellmour:	Superscription,) I am the most surpriz'd in the World to .	82	OLD BATCH	IV.2	56
Belinda:	Oh the most inhumane, barbarous Hackney-Coach! . . .	83	OLD BATCH	IV.3	4
Belinda:	most rueful! Ha, ha, ha: O Gad, I hope no-body will . .	83	OLD BATCH	IV.3	9
Belinda:	Oh; a most Comical Sight: A Country-Squire, with . .	84	OLD BATCH	IV.3	23
Belinda:	Jut-Windows, and her Mouth the great Door, most hospitably	84	OLD BATCH	IV.3	47
Belinda:	You stink of Brandy and Tobacco, most Soldier-like. Foh. .	85	OLD BATCH	IV.3	88
Vainlove:	('tis true) where they find most Goodness to forgive.--	87	OLD BATCH	IV.3	138
Sir Joseph:	I wonder at that, Madam, for 'tis most curious . . .	90	OLD BATCH	IV.4	36
Sir Joseph:	I was in most danger of being ravish'd, if you go . .	90	OLD BATCH	IV.4	62
Careless:	And here's this Cox-Comb most Critically come to . .	128	DOUBL DLR	I.1	17
Mellefont:	that the most violent Love could urge, or tender words .	130	DOUBL DLR	I.1	110
Sir Paul:	most facetious Person.--and the best Company.-- . . .	132	DOUEL DLB	I.1	182
Lady Touch:	most my Shame,--have you not Dishonoured me?	135	DOUEL DLB	I.1	317
Brisk:	Ladyship has not the Art of Surprizing the most Naturally .	142	DOUEL DLB	II.1	131
Mellefont:	if not most presently prevented.	148	DOUEL DLB	II.1	379
Mellefont:	Ha, ha, ha, I, a very Fury; but I was most afraid . .	149	DOUEL DLB	II.1	416
Mellefont:	Ha, ha, ha, ay, a very Fury; but I was most afraid . .	149	DOUEL DLB	II.1	V416
Mellefont:	She is most gracious in her Favour,--well, and . .	149	DOUBL DLB	II.1	430
Maskwell:	Excellent! your Ladyship has a most improving . .	155	DOUEL DLR	III.1	164
Careless:	Excessively foolish--But that which gives me most . .	158	DOUEL DLB	III.1	295
Mellefont:	'Tis a mistake, for women may most properly be . . .	158	DOUEL DLB	III.1	310
Mellefont:	and next to being in the dark, or alone, they are most truly	158	DOUEL DLR	III.1	313
Cynthia:	O most ridiculous, a perpetual consort of laughing . .	163	DOUBL DLR	III.1	471
Lady Froth:	Coachman, for you know there's most occasion for a . .	164	DOUBL DLR	III.1	520
Lady Froth:	he's a nauseous figure, a most fulsamick Pop, Poh--he . .	165	DOUBL DLR	III.1	562
Mellefont:	To run most wilfully and unreasonably away with . . .	168	DOUEL DLR	IV.1	38
Lady Ply:	d'ye mark me, if she has once sworn: It is most unchristian	171	DOUBL DLB	IV.1	151
Lady Ply:	most extraordinary respect and honour for you, Sir Paul. .	172	DOUBL DLB	IV.1	175
Sir Paul:	the most beholden to Mr. Careless--As sure as can . . .	172	DOUEL DLR	IV.1	200
Brisk:	practice.--Ah! My dear Lady Froth! She's a most . .	175	DOUEL DLR	IV.1	291
Brisk:	My Lady Froth! Your Ladyships most humble Servant; . . .	175	DOUEL DLR	IV.1	313
Brisk:	all I'gad. I was fallen into the most agreeable amusement in	175	DOUEL DLR	IV.1	315
Lord Froth:	Lady's is the most inviting Couch; and a slumber there, is	200	DOUEL DLR	V.1	494
Lady Ply:	You tell me most surprizing things; bless me	202	DOUEL DLR	V.1	545
	Whether to thank, or blame their Audience, most: . . .	204	DOUEL DLR	EPI.	3
	Each chusing that, in which he has most Art.	204	DOUEL DLR	EPI.	16
Tattle:	But, Gentlemen, this is the most inhumane . . .	229	FOR LOVE	I.1	499
Mrs Frail:	You are the most mistaken in the World; there is . .	231	FOR LOVE	I.1	562
Mrs Frail:	we shall have a most Amphibious Breed--The Progeny . .	231	FOR LOVE	I.1	571
Mrs Frail:	Issue-Male of their two Bodies; 'tis the most superstitious	231	FOR LOVE	I.1	579
Scandal:	most of your Acquaintance to the Life, and as like as at .	232	FOR LOVE	I.1	618
Scandal:	Yes, mine are most in black and white.--And yet . .	233	FOR LOVE	I.1	626
Scandal:	Indiscretion is a sign of Love, you are the most a Lover .	234	FOR LOVE	I.1	676
Sr Sampson:	to me;--of all my Boys the most unlike me; a has a . .	243	FOR LOVE	II.1	306
Sr Sampson:	to me;--of all my Boys the most unlike me; he has a . .	243	FOR LOVE	II.1	V306
Mrs Fore:	Very well, that will appear who has most, ...	247	FOR LOVE	II.1	455
Tattle:	most unfortunate Man in the World, and the most cruelly .	255	FOR LOVE	III.1	82
Tattle:	telling you Madam, I have been the most unsuccessful . .	256	FOR LOVE	III.1	103
Sr Sampson:	Woman than I thought you were: For most young . . .	260	FOR LOVE	III.1	250
Scandal:	Astrology! And Albertus Magnus makes it the most valuable	267	FOR LOVE	III.1	537
Jeremy:	Sir, I have a most broke my Heart about him--I can't .	279	FOR LOVE	IV.1	131
Mrs Frail:	and Scales, and three rows of Teeth, a most outrageous .	286	FOR LOVE	IV.1	401
Mrs Fore:	What then, he bore it most Heroically?	287	FOR LOVE	IV.1	454
Mrs Frail:	Most Tyranically,--for you see he has got the . . .	287	FOR LOVE	IV.1	455
Tattle:	perfection, Madam, and to all this, the most passionate .	291	FOR LOVE	IV.1	583
Angelica:	exceptious: But Madmen shew themselves most, by over .	296	FOR LOVE	IV.1	763
Sr Sampson:	Gadzooks, a most ingenious Contrivance--	300	FOR LOVE	V.1	113
Jeremy:	you'll certainly be the Death of a Person that has a most	301	FOR LOVE	V.1	168
Mrs Frail:	O, Sister, the most unlucky Accident!	309	FOR LOVE	V.1	440
Tattle:	O, the Two most unfortunate poor Creatures in the . .	309	FOR LOVE	V.1	442
Tattle:	were good--But this is the most cruel thing, to marry .	309	FOR LOVE	V.1	458
Leonora:	His most industrious Goodness could invent; . . .	327	M. BRIDE	I.1	47
Gonsalez:	And bless this Day with most unequal Lustre. . . .	331	M. BRIDE	I.1	223
Gonsalez:	And bless this Day with most unequal'd Lustre.	331	M. BRIDE	I.1	V223
Osmyn-Alph:	This exquisite, this most amazing Goodness, . . .	343	M. BRIDE	II.2	V145
Heli:	Most happily, in finding you thus bless'd.	344	M. BRIDE	II.2	171
Osmyn-Alph:	Yet lighted up, his last most grateful Sacrifice; . .	357	M. BRIDE	III.1	322
Selim:	You must still seem most resolute and fix'd . . .	362	M. BRIDE	IV.1	44
Zara:	Most certain; though my Knowledge is not yet	364	M. BRIDE	IV.1	146

Most   (continued)

Almeria:	Into thy Womb the last and most forlorn	. . . . .	368	M. BRIDE	IV.1 277
Manuel:	Now doom'd to die, that most accursed Osmyn.	. . . .	368	M. BRIDE	IV.1 288
Zara:	Most easie and inevitable Death.		375	M. BRIDE	V.1 134
Garcia:	Of this surprizing and most fatal Errour.	. . . . .	378	M. BRIDE	V.2 92
Osmyn-Alph:	Themselves, their own most bloody Purposes.	. . . .	383	M. BRIDE	V.2 308
Osmyn-Alph:	Has turn'd their own most bloody Purposes.	. . . .	383	M. BRIDE	V.2 V308
Fainall:	Faith, I am not Jealous. Besides, most who are engag'd	.	399	WAY WORLD	I.1 141
Witwoud:	defend most of his Faults, except one or two; one he has,		403	WAY WORLD	I.1 310
Mirabell:	thou ought'st to be most asham'd thy Self, when thou hast		409	WAY WORLD	I.1 534
Mrs Fain:	Most transcendantly; ay, tho' I say it,	. . . . .	411	WAY WORLD	II.1 37
Marwood:	scorn you most. Farewell.		415	WAY WORLD	II.1 221
Fainall:	Sir Wilfull, your most faithful Servant.		441	WAY WORLD	III.1 595
Foible:	Most killing well, Madam.		445	WAY WORLD	IV.1 16
Mirabell:	with Ratifia and the most noble Spirit of Clary,--but	.	451	WAY WORLD	IV.1 274
Lady Wish:	press things to a Conclusion, with a most prevailing	.	458	WAY WORLD	IV.1 495
Mrs Fain:	This discovery is the most opportune thing		464	WAY WORLD	V.1 101
Lady Wish:	the most minute Particle of severe Vertue? Is it possible		465	WAY WORLD	V.1 142
Lady Wish:	This is most inhumanly Savage; exceeding the		469	WAY WORLD	V.1 271
Mirabell:	had a Face of guiltiness,--it was at most an Artifice which		472	WAY WORLD	V.1 385
Mirabell:	enough, that I have lost what in my heart I hold most dear,		472	WAY WORLD	V.1 388

Mother (29)

Silvia:	dont I know my Father lov'd my Mother, and was married	.	73	OLD BATCH	III.2 101
Belinda:	Almanack, and a Comb-Case; the Mother, a great Fruz-Towr,	.	84	OLD BATCH	IV.3 52
Lady Ply:	means of procuring the Mother?		146	DOUBL DLR	II.1 307
Mellefont:	The Daughter procure the Mother!		146	DOUBL DLR	II.1 308
Mellefont:	The Daughter to procure the Mother!		146	DOUBL DLR	II.1 V308
Lady Ply:	Ay, for tho' I am not Cynthia's own Mother, I . . .		146	DOUBL DLR	II.1 309
Sir Paul:	than with my own Mother--no indeed.		162	DOUBL DLR	III.1 440
Sir Paul:	Mother says Child--		172	DOUBL DLR	IV.1 172
Sr Sampson:	What, wou'd you have your Mother a Whore!		244	FOR LOVE	II.1 318
Jeremy:	Mother sold Oysters in Winter, and Cucumbers in Summer;	.	245	FOR LOVE	II.1 380
Miss Prue:	Mother, Mother, Mother, look you here.		249	FOR LOVE	II.1 506
Mrs Fore:	have told you, you must not call me Mother.		249	FOR LOVE	II.1 508
Mrs Fore:	Girl call me Mother--Well, but Miss, what are you . .		249	FOR LOVE	II.1 513
Miss Prue:	--Smell him Mother, Madam, I mean--He gave		249	FOR LOVE	II.1 521
Miss Prue:	Yes; I may tell my Mother--And he says he'll		249	FOR LOVE	II.1 524
Sr Sampson:	thou shalt make me a Father, and I'll make thee a Mother,		308	FOR LOVE	V.1 397
Almeria:	--I have no Parent else--be thou a Mother, ...		368	M. BRIDE	IV.1 279
Mirabell:	Aunt, your Wife's Mother, my evil Genius; or to sum up	.	395	WAY WORLD	I.1 23
Fainall:	Mother. If you marry Millamant you must call Cousins .		400	WAY WORLD	I.1 194
Witwoud:	with him; if he said they were my Mother and my Sisters.	.	406	WAY WORLD	I.1 411
Witwoud:	with him; if he had said they were my Mother and my Sisters.		406	WAY WORLD	I.1 V411
Mrs Fain:	Mr. Mirabell; my Mother interrupted you in a . . .		412	WAY WORLD	II.1 98
Mirabell:	to betray me by trusting him too far. If your Mother, in	.	417	WAY WORLD	II.1 292
Mrs Fain:	So, if my poor Mother is caught in a Contract, . . .		417	WAY WORLD	II.1 296
Mrs Fain:	--You have neither time to talk nor stay. My Mother .		452	WAY WORLD	IV.1 299
Mrs Fain:	my Mother has been forc'd to leave Sir Rowland to appease		452	WAY WORLD	IV.1 311
Mrs Fain:	Letter?--My Mother do's not suspect my being in the .	.	464	WAY WORLD	V.1 75

Mother-in-Law (2)

Cynthia:	Here's my Mother-in-Law, and your Friend Careless, . . .		169	DOUBL DLR	IV.1 65
Sir Paul:	nice, Gads-bud don't learn after your Mother-in-Law my	.	174	DOUBL DLR	IV.1 248

Mother's (1)

Lady Wish:	inherited thy Mother's prudence.		477	WAY WORLD	V.1 569

Mothers (5)

Heartwell:	force a smile and cry, ay, the Boy takes after his Mothers		45	OLD BATCH	I.1 326
	Were each to suffer for his Mothers Sin:		125	DOUBL DLR	PRO. 22
Mrs Fain:	Mankind, only in compliance with my Mothers Humour.	. .	410	WAY WORLD	II.1 19
Mrs Fain:	Mankind, only in compliance to my Mothers Humour.	. .	410	WAY WORLD	II.1 V 19
Mrs Fain:	He is an humble Servant to Foible my Mothers		417	WAY WORLD	II.1 286

Moths (1)

Witwoud:	Like Moths about a Candle--I had like to have . . .		418	WAY WORLD	II.1 331

Motion (4)

Sir Paul:	have even been depriv'd of motion, ...		178	DOUBL DLR	IV.1 425
Sir Paul:	have been even depriv'd of motion, ...		178	DOUBL DLR	IV.1 V425
Fainall:	of the Community; upon which Motion Witwoud and . .		396	WAY WORLD	I.1 57
Mirabell:	for Motion not Method is their Occupation. To know this,		423	WAY WORLD	II.1 498

Motionless (1)

Osmyn-Alph:	That motionless, I may be still deceiv'd.		341	M. BRIDE	II.2 49

Motions (2)

Foresight:	Houses. Can judge of Motions Direct and Retrograde, of	.	241	FOR LOVE	II.1 212
Sr Sampson:	Watch, and the Bridegroom shall observe it's Motions;	. .	266	FOR LOVE	III.1 474

Motly (1)

Valentine:	Mask of Madness, and this motly Livery, only as the Slave		294	FOR LOVE	IV.1 703

Motto (2)

Fainall:	I care not if I leave 'em a common Motto, to their common		444	WAY WORLD	III.1 722
Sir Wilful:	Wilfull will do't, that's my Crest--my Motto I have forgot.		455	WAY WORLD	IV.1 405

Mould (2)

Maskwell:	you can in his Closet, and I doubt not but you will mould		155	DOUBL DLR	III.1 166
Osmyn-Alph:	Of God-like Mould, intrepid and commanding, ...		355	M. BRIDE	III.1 223

Mouldring (1)

Almeria:	Lead me o'er Bones and Skulls, and mouldring Earth . .		339	M. BRIDE	II.1 74

Mount (3)

Foresight:	Liberality on the Mount of Venus.		239	FOR LOVE	II.1 154
Valentine:	Endymion and the Moon shall meet us upon Mount Latmos,	.	290	FOR LOVE	IV.1 547
Almeria:	My Soul, enlarg'd from its vile Bonds will mount, . .		340	M. BRIDE	II.2 25

Mountain-Tyger (1)

Bellmour:	Heart of a Mountain-Tyger. By the faith of a sincere . .		95	OLD BATCH	IV.4 235

Mountains (1)

Mrs Fore:	imposes on him.--Now I have promis'd him Mountains; .		288	FOR LOVE	IV.1 470

Mourn (12)

Almeria:	Which they unseen, may wail, and weep, and mourn, . .		328	M. BRIDE	I.1 85
Almeria:	For which I mourn, and will for ever mourn;		329	M. BRIDE	I.1 144
Manuel:	Here are we seem to mourn at our Success!		333	M. BRIDE	I.1 278
Manuel:	It looks as thou didst mourn for him: Just as . . .		333	M. BRIDE	I.1 298
Manuel:	With her Rejoicings. What, to mourn, and weep; . . .		333	M. BRIDE	I.1 313

Mourn (continued)

Garcia:	To mourn, brave Heli, thy mistaken Fate.	337	M. BRIDE	II.1	3
Osmyn-Alph:	mourn;	346	M. BRIDE	II.2	259
Zara:	What Joy do I require? if thou dost mourn,	346	M. BRIDE	II.2	267
Zara:	I come to mourn with thee; to share thy Griefs,	346	M. BRIDE	II.2	268
	(The Mutes kneel and mourn over her.)	381	M. BRIDE	V.2	213
Almeria:	Yes, yes, I know to mourn; I'll sluce this Heart,	382	M. BRIDE	V.2	243

Mourn'd (2)

| Almeria: | If I cou'd speak; how I have mourn'd and pray'd, | 343 | M. BRIDE | II.2 | 130 |
| Zara: | And all those Ills, which thou so long hast mourn'd; | 361 | M. BRIDE | III.1 | 456 |

Mournful (1)

| Leonora: | Indeed 'twas mournful-- | 329 | M. BRIDE | I.1 | 142 |

Mourning (5)

Setter:	one Eye, as a penal Mourning for the ogling Offences of	64	OLD BATCH	III.1	127
	(Attendants to Almeria enter in				
	Mourning.)	332	M. BRIDE	I.1	264
Almeria:	In Mourning, and strict Life, for my Deliverance	333	M. BRIDE	I.1	285
Zara:	Give me more ample Knowledge of this Mourning.	380	M. BRIDE	V.2	160
	And now as unconcern'd this Mourning wear,	385	M. BRIDE	EPI.	3

Mouth (19)

Heartwell:	Lord what d'ee-cals Mouth to a Tittle--Then I to put it	45	OLD BATCH	I.1	324
Sir Joseph:	fire once out of the mouth of a Canon--agad he did; those	53	OLD BATCH	II.1	219
Vainlove:	Mouth; and would distaste the keenest Hunter--I	80	OLD BATCH	IV.1	179
Belinda:	Jut-Windows, and her Mouth the great Door, most hospitably	84	OLD BATCH	IV.3	47
Sir Joseph:	(aside). Now am I slap-dash down in the Mouth,	85	OLD BATCH	IV.3	90
Sharper:	make him fret till he foam at the Mouth, and disgorge his	99	OLD BATCH	V.1	88
Sir Joseph:	Eyes twinkle, and her Mouth water? Did not she pull up	103	OLD BATCH	V.1	255
Mellefont:	your mouth with a plumb.	156	DOUBL DLR	III.1	222
Lady Froth:	Mouth, to Laugh, and then put 'em in again--Foh.	165	DOUBL DLR	III.1	571
Lady Froth:	her Gums bare, and her Mouth open.--	165	DOUBL DLR	III.1	575
Mellefont:	Industry grown full and ripe, ready to drop into his mouth,	187	DOUBL DLR	IV.2	144
Mellefont:	Industry grow full and ripe, ready to drop into his mouth,	187	DOUBL DLR	IV.2	V144
Valentine:	Eyes; shut up your Mouth, and chew the Cud of	216	FOR LCVE	I.1	15
Ben:	has been gathering foul weather in her Mouth, and now it	265	FOR LCVE	III.1	442
Sr Sampson:	melt in my Mouth.	301	FOR LCVE	V.1	148
Valentine:	her own Mouth.	311	FOR LCVE	V.1	521
Almeria:	And that dumb Mouth, significant in Show,	340	M. BRIDE	II.2	15
Almeria:	Lest the rank Juice should blister on my Mouth,	382	M. BRIDE	V.2	268
Fainall:	Medlar grafted on a Crab. One will melt in your Mouth,	401	WAY WCBLD	I.1	213

Mouth-Glew (1)

| Sir Wilful: | than a little Mouth-Glew, and that's hardly dry;--One | 472 | WAY WORLD | V.1 | 397 |

Mouth'd (2)

see Foul-mouth'd, Slander-mouth'd

| Sharper: | Not till you had Mouth'd a little George, I think | 43 | OLD BATCH | I.1 | 227 |
| Laetitia: | came open mouth'd upon me, and would have ravished a | 90 | OLD BATCH | IV.4 | 53 |

Mouths (2)

| Jeremy: | Mouths of your Creditors? Will Plato be Bail for you? Or | 217 | FOR LCVE | I.1 | 29 |
| Manuel: | And spend their Mouths in barking Tyranny. | 362 | M. BRIDE | IV.1 | 64 |

Mouzle (1)

| Sr Sampson: | own Son, faith, he'll touzle her, and mouzle her: The | 265 | FOR LOVE | III.1 | 458 |

Mov'd (3)

Almeria:	I've read, that things inanimate have mov'd,	326	M. BRIDE	I.1	3
Almeria:	'Till you are mov'd, and grant that he may live.	369	M. BRIDE	IV.1	331
Fainall:	mov'd that to avoid Scandal there might be one Man	396	WAY WCBLD	I.1	56

Move (9)

Araminta:	Bless me! what have I said to move you thus?	54	OLD BATCH	II.2	3
Bellmour:	When Wit and Reason, both, have fail'd to move;	60	OLD BATCH	II.2	224
Heartwell:	Well, Why do ycu not move? Feet do your	62	OLD BATCH	III.1	73
Singer:	Dearest Thyrsis, do not move me,	71	OLD BATCH	III.2	V 12
Valentine:	Go see, you Sot. I'm very glad that I can move your	295	FOR LCVE	IV.1	759
	To please and move, has been our Poets Theme,	323	M. BRIDE	PRO.	35
Almeria:	Curst my own Tongue, that cou'd not move his Pity.	370	M. BRIDE	IV.1	372
Sir Wilful:	An he do's not move me, I might never	472	WAY WCBLD	V.1	392
Sir Wilful:	An he do's not move me, wou'd I may never	472	WAY WCBLD	V.1	V392

Moved (1)

| Lady Touch: | more moved with the reflection of his Crimes, than of his | 136 | DOUEL DLR | I.1 | V330 |

Movement (2)

| Careless: | aking trembling heart, the nimble movement shall instruct | 170 | DOUBL DLR | IV.1 | 93 |
| Careless: | trembling heart, the nimble movement shall instruct | 170 | DOUEL DLR | IV.1 | V 93 |

Moving (3)

Lady Ply:	And say so many fine things, and nothing is so moving to	169	DOUBL DLR	IV.1	70
Lady Ply:	O you have Conquered, sweet, melting, moving	170	DOUBL DLB	IV.1	118
Millamant:	after all, there is something very moving in a love-sick	422	WAY WORLD	II.1	474

Mr (254)

Bellmour:	talks of sending for Mr. Spintext to keep me Company; but	39	OLD BATCH	I.1	83
Heartwell:	Good Mr. Young-fellow, you're mistaken; as	43	OLD BATCH	I.1	229
Heartwell:	fleering Coxcomb scoff and cry, Mr. your Son's mighty	45	OLD BATCH	I.1	320
Sir Joseph:	Pray Mr. Sharper Embrace my Back--very	52	OLD BATCH	II.1	174
Sir Joseph:	well--By the Lord Harry Mr. Sharper he's as brave a	52	OLD BATCH	II.1	175
Capt Bluff:	you know--Well, Mr. Sharper, would you think it? In all	53	OLD BATCH	II.1	201
Capt Bluff:	Yet by the Lord Harry 'tis true Mr. Sharper, for I	53	OLD BATCH	II.1	207
Capt Bluff:	Ay, ay, no matter--You see Mr. Sharper after all	53	OLD BATCH	II.1	210
Sir Joseph:	Let me but tell Mr. Sharper a little, how you eat	53	OLD BATCH	II.1	218
Capt Bluff:	This Sword I think I was telling you of Mr. Sharper	53	OLD BATCH	II.1	228
Capt Bluff:	Good Mr. Sharper speak to him; I dare not look	54	OLD BATCH	II.1	238
Sir Joseph:	Mr. Sharper will you partake?	54	OLD BATCH	II.1	247
Footman:	No, Madam, there are Mr. Bellmour and Mr.	56	OLD BATCH	II.2	76
Araminta:	Is Mr. Gavot gone?	58	OLD BATCH	II.2	157
Araminta:	If Mr. Gavot will walk with us in the Garden, we'll have	60	OLD BATCH	II.2	207
Araminta:	If Mr. Gavot will walk with us into the Garden, we'll have	60	OLD BATCH	II.2	V207
Lucy:	Masters employment. For he's the head Pimp to Mr.	65	OLD BATCH	III.1	169
Capt Bluff:	Mr. Sharper, the matter is plain--Sir Joseph has found	69	OLD BATCH	III.1	296
Barnaby:	Mr. Prig, to have kept my Mistress Company in the mean	76	OLD BATCH	IV.1	23
Bellmour:	find it directed to Mr. Vainlove. Gad, Madam, I ask you a	82	OLD BATCH	IV.2	57
Belinda:	Very courtly.--I believe, Mr. Vainlove has not	86	OLD BATCH	IV.3	129
Belinda:	his Mistress, is like a Body without a Soul. Mr. Vainlove,	86	OLD BATCH	IV.3	134
Belinda:	I have broke the ice for you, Mr. Vainlove, and so I	87	OLD BATCH	IV.3	142

Mr (continued)

Mr   (continued)

		PAGE	TITLE	ACT.SC	LINE
Millamant:	Only with those in Verse, Mr. Witwoud. I never	419	WAY WORLD	II.1	365
Mincing:	You're such a Critick, Mr. Witwoud.	420	WAY WORLD	II.1	376
Mrs Fain:	Immediately; I have a Word or two for Mr.	421	WAY WORLD	II.1	425
Foible:	Ladyship and Mr. Mirabell, might have hinder'd his . .	430	WAY WORLD	III.1	198
Foible:	O dear Madam, Mr. Mirabell is such a sweet winning . .	430	WAY WORLD	III.1	201
Foible:	Generosity.--Sweet Lady, to be so good! Mr. Mirabell .	430	WAY WORLD	III.1	203
Foible:	Lady that Mr. Mirabell rail'd at her. I laid horrid Things	430	WAY WORLD	III.1	208
Foible:	Madam, I beg your Ladyship to acquaint Mr. Mirabell . .	430	WAY WORLD	III.1	214
Foible:	me.--She has a Month's mind; but I know Mr.	430	WAY WORLD	III.1	217
Marwood:	of Generosity, that I confess. Well, Mr. Fainall, you have	431	WAY WORLD	III.1	234
Foible:	Mr. Witwoud and Mr. Petulant, are come to Dine with . .	432	WAY WORLD	III.1	276
Marwood:	Mr. Mirabell and you both, may think it a	434	WAY WORLD	III.1	350
	(Set by Mr. John Eccles, ...	434	WAY WORLD	III.1	374
Marwood:	Mr. Witwoud, your Brother is not behind	437	WAY WORLD	III.1	475
Marwood:	For shame Mr. Witwoud; why won't you	437	WAY WORLD	III.1	480
Lady Wish:	Cousin Witwoud, your Servant; Mr. Petulant, ...	441	WAY WORLD	III.1	597
Foible:	Madam, I stay'd here, to tell your Ladyship that Mr. . . '	445	WAY WORLD	IV.1	43
Foible:	and Sir Wilfull together. Shall I tell Mr. Mirabell that you	445	WAY WORLD	IV.1	46
Foible:	Sir Wilfull is coming, Madam. Shall I send Mr. Mirabell .	446	WAY WORLD	IV.1	58
Foible:	at this Juncture! this was the business that brought Mr. .	461	WAY WORLD	IV.1	611
Foible:	Then, then Madam, Mr. Mirabell waited for her in her .	461	WAY WORLD	IV.1	618
Foible:	Moment's patience--I'll Confess all. Mr. Mirabell seduc'd .	462	WAY WORLD	V.1	25
Foible:	Effect, Mr. Fainall laid this Plot to arrest Waitwell,				
	when he	464	WAY WORLD	V.1	71
Foible:	mischeivous Devil told Mr. Fainall of your Ladyship then? .	464	WAY WORLD	V.1	80
Mincing:	My Lady wou'd speak with Mrs. Foible, Mem. Mr.	464	WAY WORLD	V.1	104
Mincing:	is in a perilous passion, at something Mr. Fainall has said.	465	WAY WORLD	V.1	108
Marwood:	have Overseen. Here comes Mr. Fainall. If he will be				
	satisfi'd	468	WAY WORLD	V.1	243
Fainall:	Consent is not requisite in this Case; nor Mr.				
	Mirabell, your	473	WAY WORLD	V.1	438
Lady Wish:	How! dear Mr. Mirabell, can you be so	474	WAY WORLD	V.1	462
Mincing:	found you and Mr. Fainall in the Blew garret; by the same	474	WAY WORLD	V.1	487
Fainall:	are you the better for this? Is this Mr. Mirabell's				
	Expedient?	475	WAY WORLD	V.1	493
Lady Wish:	Ah Mr. Mirabell, this is small comfort, the	475	WAY WORLD	V.1	504
Mirabell:	Mr. Fainall, it is now time that you shou'd know, . . .	476	WAY WORLD	V.1	535
Mrs Fain:	Thank Mr. Mirabell, a Cautious Friend, to whose . . .	477	WAY WORLD	V.1	570
Lady Wish:	Well Mr. Mirabell, you have kept your promise, ...	477	WAY WORLD	V.1	572

Mrs (92)

		PAGE	TITLE	ACT.SC	LINE
Belinda:	you Mrs. Fidget--You are so ready to go to the	57	OLD BATCH	II.2	97
Setter:	How, Mrs. Lucy!	66	OLD BATCH	III.1	201
Belinda:	the Equipage of a Wife and two Daughters, came to Mrs. .	84	OLD BATCH	IV.3	24
Fondlewife:	you know your Patient, Mrs. Quack? Oh, lie upon your .	93	OLD BATCH	IV.4	163
Scandal:	What think you of that Noble Commoner, Mrs.	227	FOR LOVE	I.1	417
Tattle:	so is Mrs. Foresight, and her Sister Frail.	228	FOR LOVE	I.1	457
Scandal:	Yes, Mrs. Frail is a very fine Woman, we all know . .	228	FOR LOVE	I.1	458
Scandal:	To tell what? Why, what do you know of Mrs.	228	FOR LOVE	I.1	463
Jeremy:	Sir, Mrs. Frail has sent to know if you are stirring. .	229	FOR LOVE	I.1	505
	(Enter Mrs. Frail.)	230	FOR LOVE	I.1	541
Valentine:	my side: What's here? Mrs. Foresight and Mrs. Frail, they	246	FOR LOVE	II.1	410
	(Enter Mrs. Foresight and Mrs. Frail.)	246	FOR LOVE	II.1	414
	(Exeunt Mrs. Foresight and Mrs. Frail.)	251	FOR LOVE	II.1	580
Tattle:	(aside). Frank, I Gad at least. What a Pox does Mrs. .	251	FOR LOVE	II.1	591
	(Enter Sir Sampson, Mrs. Frail, Miss Prue, and Servant.)	259	FOR LOVE	III.1	209
Sr Sampson:	I'm glad on't: Where is he? I long to see him. Now, Mrs.	259	FOR LOVE	III.1	211
Miss Prue:	(aside to Mrs. Frail). Pish, he shall be none of my .	259	FOR LOVE	III.1	218
Sr Sampson:	And so thou shalt,--Mrs. Angelica, my	261	FOR LOVE	III.1	278
	(Kisses Mrs. Frail.)	261	FOR LOVE	III.1	282
Ben:	(Enter Mrs. Foresight, and Mrs. Frail.) . . .	264	FOR LOVE	III.1	432
	(Enter Mrs. Foresight.)	268	FOR LOVE	III.1	575
	(Enter Mrs. Frail, and Ben.)	272	FOR LOVE	III.1	712
	(Enter Foresight, Mrs. Foresight, and Mrs. Frail.)	283	FOR LOVE	IV.1	273
Mrs Frail:	(Aside to Mrs. Foresight.)	283	FOR LOVE	IV.1	304
Scandal:	(Aside to Mrs. Foresight.)	284	FOR LOVE	IV.1	314
	(Exeunt Foresight, Mrs. Foresight and Scandal.) . .	285	FOR LOVE	IV.1	354
	(Enter Mrs. Foresight.)	287	FOR LOVE	IV.1	448
Scandal:	is of a piece with Mrs. Frail. He Courts Angelica, if				
	we cou'd	291	FOR LOVE	IV.1	598
Jeremy:	(to Mrs. Frail). You'll meet, Madam;--I'll take . . .	293	FOR LOVE	IV.1	671
	(Exeunt Foresight, Mrs. Foresight, Tattle, Mrs. Frail, and	293	FOR LOVE	IV.1	683
	(Enter Scandal, Mrs. Foresight, and Nurse.) . .	305	FOR LOVE	V.1	320
	(Enter Tattle and Mrs. Frail.)	309	FOR LOVE	V.1	439
Tattle:	Nor I--But poor Mrs. Frail and I are--	309	FOR LOVE	V.1	447
Mrs Fore:	(aside to Mrs. Frail). He's better than no Husband . .	310	FOR LOVE	V.1	469
Mirabell:	Yes, and Mrs. Marwood and three or four more, ...	396	WAY WORLD	I.1	28
Mirabell:	Indebted to your Friend, or your Wife's Friend, Mrs. .	397	WAY WORLD	I.1	80
Witwoud:	hard Frost. Whether this Uncle has seen Mrs. Millamant or	408	WAY WORLD	I.1	486
	(St. James's Park. Enter Mrs. Fainall and Mrs. Marwood.)	410	WAY WORLD	II.1	
	(Exeunt Mrs. Fainall and Mirabell.)	412	WAY WORLD	II.1	108
	(Enter Mirabell and Mrs. Fainall.)	416	WAY WORLD	II.1	251
	(Enter Mrs. Millamant, Witwoud, and Mincing.) .	418	WAY WORLD	II.1	322
Witwoud:	Do Mrs. Millamant, like a Skreen before a great Fire. .	419	WAY WORLD	II.1	343
Mirabell:	(aside to Mrs. Fainall). Draw off Witwoud.	421	WAY WORLD	II.1	424
	(Exit Witwoud and Mrs. Fainall.)	421	WAY WORLD	II.1	428
Mirabell:	Give you Joy, Mrs. Foible.	423	WAY WORLD	II.1	512
Foible:	that was Mrs. Marwood that went by in a Mask; if she has	424	WAY WORLD	II.1	545
Peg:	come at the Paint, Madam; Mrs. Foible has lock'd it up, .	425	WAY WORLD	III.1	18
Lady Wish:	Mrs. Qualmsick the Curate's Wife, that's always breeding .	425	WAY WORLD	III.1	22
Peg:	No Madam, Mrs. Marwood.	426	WAY WORLD	III.1	39
	(Enter Mrs. Marwood.)	426	WAY WORLD	III.1	42
Marwood:	O Madam, you cannot suspect Mrs. Foible's	426	WAY WORLD	III.1	55
Foible:	me too (says he), and Mrs. Millamant is to marry my .	428	WAY WORLD	III.1	112
	(Enter Mrs. Fainall.)	429	WAY WORLD	III.1	183
Foible:	our success, Mrs. Marwood had told my Lady; but I warrant .	430	WAY WORLD	III.1	206

Mrs   (continued)

Speaker	Text	PAGE	TITLE	ACT.SC	LINE
	(Enter Mrs. Marwood.)	431	WAY WORLD	III.1	224
Marwood:	Indeed Mrs. Engine, is it thus with you?	431	WAY WORLD	III.1	225
Marwood:	Methinks Mrs. Millamant and he wou'd make	432	WAY WORLD	III.1	266
	(Enter Mrs. Millamant and Mincing.)	432	WAY WORLD	III.1	283
Marwood:	'Tis like Mrs. Primly's great Belly; she may lace it down	433	WAY WORLD	III.1	318
Millamant:	Desire Mrs.--that is in the next Room to	434	WAY WORLD	III.1	370
	. . . and Sung by Mrs. Hodgson.)	434	WAY WORLD	III.1	V374
Sir Wilful:	(Salutes Mrs. Marwood.)	438	WAY WORLD	III.1	485
	(Fainall and Mrs. Marwood talk a-part.)	441	WAY WORLD	III.1	610
	(Manent Mrs. Marwood and Fainall.)	441	WAY WORLD	III.1	627
	(Enter Mrs. Millamant, and Mrs. Fainall.)	445	WAY WORLD	IV.1	42
	(Enter Mrs. Fainall.)	452	WAY WORLD	IV.1	283
Petulant:	Look you Mrs. Millamant,--If you can love me dear	453	WAY WORLD	IV.1	339
	(Exeunt Millamant and Mrs. Fainall.)	456	WAY WORLD	IV.1	435
Foible:	(to him). By Heaven! Mrs. Marwood's, I know it,--	460	WAY WORLD	IV.1	575
	(Enter Mrs. Fainall.)	463	WAY WORLD	V.1	60
Foible:	pretended to go for the Papers; and in the mean time Mrs.	464	WAY WORLD	V.1	72
Foible:	friends together, than set 'em at distance. But Mrs. Marwood	464	WAY WORLD	V.1	88
Foible:	I can take my Oath of it Madam, so can Mrs. Mincing;	464	WAY WORLD	V.1	92
Mincing:	My Lady wou'd speak with Mrs. Foible, Mem. Mr.	464	WAY WORLD	V.1	104
Mincing:	Mirabell is with her, he has set your Spouse at liberty Mrs.	464	WAY WORLD	V.1	105
Mincing:	six thousand Pound. O, come Mrs. Foible, I hear my old	465	WAY WORLD	V.1	116
Marwood:	My Friend, Mrs. Fainall? Your Husband my	466	WAY WORLD	V.1	156
Fainall:	Pound, which is the Moiety of Mrs. Millamant's Fortune	469	WAY WORLD	V.1	279
	(Enter Fainall and Mrs. Marwood.)	472	WAY WORLD	V.1	413
	(Enter Mrs. Fainall, Foible, and Mincing.)	474	WAY WORLD	V.1	471
Marwood:	Wishfort go to Mrs. Fainall and Foible). These Corrupt	474	WAY WORLD	V.1	473
Fainall:	to run at Mrs. Fainall.)	476	WAY WORLD	V.1	557
Mirabell:	me lies to a Reunion, (To Mrs. Fainall) in the mean time,	478	WAY WORLD	V.1	616

Much (157)

Speaker	Text	PAGE	TITLE	ACT.SC	LINE
Bellmour:	much more agreeable, if you can counterfeit his Habit to blind	39	OLD BATCH	I.1	88
Vainlove:	way; much addicted to Jealousie, but more to Fondness:	40	OLD BATCH	I.1	108
Bellmour:	But she can't have too much Mony--There's	41	OLD BATCH	I.1	165
Bellmour:	to himself in the World; he takes as much always of an	42	OLD BATCH	I.1	211
Heartwell:	so much Mercury in my Limbs; 'tis true indeed, I don't	43	OLD BATCH	I.1	231
Sharper:	much lent you--And you scorn, 'Ile say that for you--	50	OLD BATCH	II.1	103
Sharper:	Word is sufficient any where: 'Tis but borrowing so much	50	OLD BATCH	II.1	108
Sharper:	more, nor perhaps have suffer'd so much--had he a	50	OLD BATCH	II.1	126
Capt Bluff:	Gazette-writer never so much as once mention'd me--Not once	53	OLD BATCH	II.1	203
Belinda:	No; upon deliberation, I have too much Charity	57	OLD BATCH	II.2	104
Musician:	Never let him much obtain.	59	OLD BATCH	II.2	195
Bellmour:	O very well perform'd--But I don't much	60	OLD BATCH	II.2	204
Araminta:	I expected it--there's too much Truth in 'em:	60	OLD BATCH	II.2	206
Belinda:	than your talking Impertinence; an an Ape is a much more	60	OLD BATCH	II.2	213
Setter:	that's much the more honourable employment--by all	64	OLD BATCH	III.1	141
Heartwell:	Awake; Sigh much, Drink little, Eat less, court Solitude,	73	OLD BATCH	III.2	81
Heartwell:	much Tenderness and Beauty--and Honesty together	74	OLD BATCH	III.2	115
Lucy:	Lord, Madam, I met your Lover in as much haste, as	74	OLD BATCH	III.2	147
Bellmour:	in an opinion of Atheism; when they may be so much	75	OLD BATCH	IV.1	7
Fondlewife:	who will tempt her Isaac?--I fear it much--But	76	OLD BATCH	IV.1	57
Araminta:	upon the easiness of my Temper, hast much deceiv'd you,	87	OLD BATCH	IV.3	158
Vainlove:	You have given that Passion a much kinder Epithet	87	OLD BATCH	IV.3	164
Bellmour:	That's as much as to say, The Pox take me.--Well	98	OLD BATCH	V.1	78
Setter:	I do suspect as much;--because why, Sir:--	99	OLD BATCH	V.1	112
Sharper:	thy Mirth: Hear thee tell thy mighty Jest, with as much	100	OLD BATCH	V.1	138
Sharper:	Court: Not so much as wrinkle my Face with one Smile;	100	OLD BATCH	V.1	140
Vainlove:	Bellmour, Give it over; you vex him too much; 'tis	109	OLD BATCH	V.2	47
Belinda:	Prisoner, make much of your Fetters.	112	OLD BATCH	V.2	168
	Women and Wits are used e'en much at one;	113	OLD BATCH	EPI.	29
Mellefont:	much ado I prevented her doing me or her self a mischief:	130	DOUBL DLR	I.1	115
Sir Paul:	Were you, Son? Gadsbud much better as it is--	131	DOUBL DLR	I.1	177
Brisk:	to tell me--still I look grave, not so much as	134	DOUBL DLR	I.1	258
Cynthia:	have been so much in Love?	138	DOUBL DLR	II.1	2
Cynthia:	Prodigious! I wonder, want of sleep, and so much	138	DOUBL DLR	II.1	5
Cynthia:	Love, and so much Wit as your Ladyship has, did not	138	DOUBL DLR	II.1	6
Lady Froth:	and as much a Man of Quality! Ah! Nothing at all	139	DOUBL DLR	II.1	29
Lady Froth:	look a little Je-ne-scay-quoysh; he is too much a Mediocrity,	139	DOUBL DLR	II.1	51
Lady Froth:	how much I have been in Love with you; I swear I have;	140	DOUBL DLR	II.1	61
Lady Froth:	Lord you sha'n't kiss it so much; I shall grow jealous, I	140	DOUBL DLR	II.1	77
Lady Froth:	Lord you shan't kiss it so much; I shall grow jealous, I	140	DOUBL DLR	II.1	V 77
Cynthia:	Because he has not so much reason to be fond of	141	DOUBL DLR	II.1	107
Singer:	Much she fears I should undo her,	143	DOUBL DLR	II.1	181
Singer:	But much more, to lose her Lover:	143	DOUBL DLR	II.1	182
Lady Ply:	you talk of Heaven! and have so much wickedness in your	147	DOUBL DLR	II.1	345
Lady Ply:	strive as much as can be against it,--strive be sure--but	148	DOUBL DLR	II.1	364
Maskwell:	I might be trusted; since it was as much my interest as hers	149	DOUBL DLR	II.1	423
Maskwell:	May so much Fraud and Power of Baseness find?	150	DOUBL DLR	II.1	468
Maskwell:	Secure in my Assistance, he seem'd not much	154	DOUBL DLR	III.1	134
Careless:	with much Solemnity on his anniversary Wedding-night.	158	DOUBL DLR	III.1	279
Careless:	disguises their Inclinations as much as their Faces.	158	DOUBL DLR	III.1	309
Mellefont:	sight, and so much time as to write to her.	159	DOUBL DLR	III.1	318
Sir Paul:	I think she laughs a little too much.	162	DOUBL DLR	III.1	464
Lady Ply:	challenges much more, I'm sure, than my illiterate Praises	169	DOUBL DLR	IV.1	83
Lady Ply:	much wrong'd.	171	DOUBL DLR	IV.1	160
Sir Paul:	I am much obliged to Mr. Careless really, he is a	172	DOUBL DLR	IV.1	178
Sir Paul:	--Gads-bud I could have done--not so much as you	174	DOUBL DLR	IV.1	243
Lady Ply:	and he looks charmingly, and he has charm'd me, as much as I	174	DOUBL DLR	IV.1	260
Lord Touch:	have discovered so much Manly Vertue; thine, in that thou	189	DOUBL DLR	V.1	55
Lord Touch:	I cannot do too much, for so much merit.	191	DOUBL DLR	V.1	123
Lord Touch:	want you by this time, as much as you want her.	192	DOUBL DLR	V.1	189
Lord Touch:	her as much as reason--by Heav'n, I'll not be Wife-ridden;	196	DOUBL DLR	V.1	320
	But that late knowledge, does much hazard cost,	204	DOUBL DLR	EPI.	4
	But Poets run much greater hazards far,	204	DOUBL DLR	EPI.	8

Much   (continued)

		PAGE	TITLE	ACT.SC LINE
Jeremy:	O Lord! I have heard much of him, when I waited	216	FOR LOVE	I.1 17
Jeremy:	as much as they do one another.	217	FOR LOVE	I.1 48
Jeremy:	Dozen Duns with as much Dexterity, as a hungry Judge . .	220	FOR LOVE	I.1 167
Jeremy:	Keep it? Not at all; it has been so very much stretch'd,	221	FOR LOVE	I.1 180
Valentine:	I was much oblig'd to you for your Supply: It did . . .	223	FOR LOVE	I.1 258
Valentine:	Why Tattle, you need not be much concern'd at . . .	226	FOR LOVE	I.1 387
Tattle:	Mum--O Madam, you do me too much Honour.	231	FOR LOVE	I.1 551
Sr Sampson:	if there is too much, refund the Superfluity; Do'st hear .	243	FOR LOVE	II.1 280
Sr Sampson:	if there be too much, refund the Superfluity; Do'st hear .	243	FOR LOVE	II.1 V280
Jeremy:	Country Dances; and the like; I don't much matter your .	245	FOR LOVE	II.1 374
Valentine:	'Tis as much as I expected--I did not come to see . . .	246	FOR LOVE	II.1 407
Mrs Frail:	in my mind too much for the Stage.	247	FOR LOVE	II.1 454
Tattle:	you have, as much as if I had it my self--If I ask you to	252	FOR LOVE	II.1 619
Tattle:	No, I hope not 'tis as much ingratitude to own . . .	255	FOR LOVE	III.1 85
Ben:	don't much stand towards Matrimonie. I love to roam . .	261	FOR LOVE	III.1 309
Ben:	high Wind, or that Lady.--You mayn't carry so much . .	262	FOR LOVE	III.1 331
Scandal:	No, no, you look much better.	270	FOR LOVE	III.1 644
Ben:	We're merry Folk, we Sailors, we han't much to care for. .	275	FOR LOVE	III.1 799
Scandal:	can Dream as much to the purpose as another, if I set about	275	FOR LOVE	III.1 814
Jeremy:	much to seek in playing the Madman to day.	276	FOR LOVE	IV.1 5
Angelica:	Mr. Scandal, you can't think me guilty of so much . .	277	FOR LOVE	IV.1 42
Scandal:	So, this is pretty plain--Be not too much	277	FOR LOVE	IV.1 61
Angelica:	Weakness I am a Stranger to. But I have too much Sincerity	277	FOR LOVE	IV.1 70
Angelica:	to deceive you, and too much Charity to suffer him to be .	277	FOR LOVE	IV.1 71
Mrs Fore:	Not much,--he's superstitious; and you	284	FOR LOVE	IV.1 323
Ben:	tell him so much.--So he said he'd make my heart ake; .	285	FOR LOVE	IV.1 380
Tattle:	much ado to tell your Ladyship, how long I have been in .	291	FOR LOVE	IV.1 576
Tattle:	many words of Matters, and so I shan't say much,-- . .	291	FOR LOVE	IV.1 607
Valentine:	Madam, you need not be very much afraid, for I . . .	294	FOR LOVE	IV.1 697
Sr Sampson:	a Man that admires a fine Woman, as much as I do. . .	298	FOR LOVE	V.1 19
Angelica:	are very much abus'd in that Matter; He's no more Mad .	299	FOR LOVE	V.1 87
Angelica:	thing that wou'd make me appear to be too much concern'd	299	FOR LOVE	V.1 91
Jeremy:	--And now, Sir, my former Master, having much . . .	301	FOR LOVE	V.1 173
Tattle:	her, poor Creature--I swear I do it hardly so much in .	302	FOR LOVE	V.1 207
Tattle:	Night, and did not so much as dream of the matter. . .	303	FOR LOVE	V.1 238
Mrs Fore:	Your Experiment will take up a little too much . . .	306	FOR LOVE	V.1 356
Mrs Fore:	I'm glad to hear you have so much Fire in	308	FOR LOVE	V.1 408
Sr Sampson:	descend to this Scoundrel? I would not so much as have .	308	FOR LOVE	V.1 426
Tattle:	The Devil take me if ever I was so much concern'd at any .	309	FOR LOVE	V.1 460
Tattle:	Look you there, I thought as much--pox on't, I . . .	310	FOR LOVE	V.1 475
Valentine:	I have heard as much, Sir; but I wou'd have it from . .	311	FOR LOVE	V.1 520
Sr Sampson:	That's as much as to say, I lie, Sir, and you don't . .	311	FOR LOVE	V.1 522
Scandal:	employ'd when the Match is so much mended. Valentine, .	313	FOR LOVE	V.1 600
Valentine:	ever you seem to love too much, it must be only when I .	313	FOR LOVE	V.1 611
Valentine:	I vow, I don't much like this Transmigration, ...	315	FOR LOVE	EPI. 32
Leonora:	This Torrent of your Grief; for, much I fear	330	M. BRIDE	I.1 166
Gonsalez:	Betray'd by too much Piety, to seem	334	M. BRIDE	I.1 319
Osmyn-Alph:	And gaze upon thy Eyes, is so much Joy;	342	M. BRIDE	II.2 97
Almeria:	It is too much! too much to bear and live!	342	M. BRIDE	II.2 105
Almeria:	Much, much, alas; how, thou art chang'd!	342	M. BRIDE	II.2 114
Almeria:	Much, much; how, thou art chang'd!	342	M. BRIDE	II.2 V114
Almeria:	Thou hast wept much Alphonso; and I fear, ...	342	M. BRIDE	II.2 117
Almeria:	Too much lamented me.	342	M. BRIDE	II.2 118
Almeria:	Too much, too tenderly lamented me.	342	M. BRIDE	II.2 V118
Osmyn-Alph:	Wrong not my Love, to say too much.	343	M. BRIDE	II.2 119
Zara:	Dost fear so much, thou dar'st not wish. The King! . .	348	M. BRIDE	II.2 347
Zara:	Whose former Faith had merited much more:	349	M. BRIDE	II.2 377
Almeria:	--Thou giv'st me Pain, with too much Tenderness! . .	356	M. BRIDE	III.1 280
Zara:	Of this Deceiver--you seem much surpriz'd.	359	M. BRIDE	III.1 408
Zara:	You free: But shall return much better pleas'd, . . .	360	M. BRIDE	III.1 418
Osmyn-Alph:	Come, 'tis much.	360	M. BRIDE	III.1 431
Osmyn-Alph:	Come, 'tis too much.	360	M. BRIDE	III.1 V431
Manuel:	Are we not much indebted to this fair one.	366	M. BRIDE	IV.1 199
Gonsalez:	Disquiets her too much; which makes it seem	366	M. BRIDE	IV.1 203
Perez:	He lies supine on earth; with as much ease	372	M. BRIDE	V.1 V 8
Manuel:	Thou art Accomplice too much with Zara; here . . .	373	M. BRIDE	V.1 51
Gonsalez:	How much Report has wrong'd your easie Faith. . . .	377	M. BRIDE	V.2 46
	So much she doats on her adopted Care.	393	WAY WORLD	PRO. 10
Mirabell:	I did as much as Man cou'd, with any reasonable . . .	397	WAY WORLD	I.1 68
Fainall:	have too much Generosity, not to be tender of her Honour.	397	WAY WORLD	I.1 92
Fainall:	the Monster in the Tempest; and much after the same manner.	401	WAY WORLD	I.1 220
Mirabell:	I thank you, I know as much as my Curiosity	409	WAY WORLD	I.1 507
Mirabell:	You shou'd have just so much disgust for your . . .	416	WAY WORLD	II.1 258
Foible:	Sir, I made as much haste as I could.	423	WAY WORLD	II.1 515
Foible:	find an Opportunity; she had so much Company last . .	424	WAY WORLD	II.1 531
Lady Wish:	Prodigal's in Debt as much as the Million Lottery, or the	428	WAY WORLD	III.1 133
Marwood:	What pity 'tis, so much fine Raillery, and	434	WAY WORLD	III.1 345
Sir Wilful:	'Sheart, Sir, but there is, and much offence.-- . . .	439	WAY WORLD	III.1 527
Marwood:	No doubt you will return very much	440	WAY WORLD	III.1 588
Fainall:	much to hope. Thus far concerning my repose. Now for .	443	WAY WORLD	III.1 683
Sir Wilful:	Daunted, No, that's not it, it is not so much for . . .	447	WAY WORLD	IV.1 83
Sir Wilful:	Dear Heart, that's much--Hah! that you	448	WAY WORLD	IV.1 127
Millamant:	I expect you shou'd solicite me as much as if I . . .	449	WAY WORLD	IV.1 162
Lady Wish:	Contribute much both to the saving of your Life; and the	458	WAY WORLD	IV.1 507
Lady Wish:	Person of so much Importance--	459	WAY WORLD	IV.1 537
Lady Wish:	Too well, too well. I have seen too much.	460	WAY WORLD	IV.1 599
Marwood:	Twas much she shou'd be deceiv'd so long.	467	WAY WORLD	V.1 195
Marwood:	much experienc'd the perfidiousness of Men. Besides .	468	WAY WORLD	V.1 260
Mirabell:	much prejudice; it was an Innocent device; tho' I confess it	472	WAY WORLD	V.1 384
Marwood:	Have you so much Ingratitude and Injustice, ...	474	WAY WORLD	V.1 483

Muckworm (1)

| Sr Sampson: | you engendred, Muckworm?   .   .   .   . | 245 | FOR LOVE | II.1   378 |

Muffled (2)

| Alonzo: | The Boom, dispos'd it muffled in the Mute's   .   .   .   . | 379 | M. BRIDE | V.2   116 |
| Alonzo: | Dispos'd it, muffled in the Mute's Attire, ... | 379 | M. BRIDE | V.2 V116 |

Mufti (1)
  Sir Wilful: Christian--I cannot find by the Map that your Mufti is . 456 WAY WORLD IV.1 446
Mule (1)
  Witwoud: a Mule, a Beast of Burden, he has brought me a Letter . . 401 WAY WORLD I.1 244
Mules (1)
  Gonsalez: Five Hundred Mules, precede his solemn March, ... 331 M. BRIDE I.1 227
Multiply'd (1)
  Leonora: Where Miseries are multiply'd; return . . . . 381 M. BRIDE V.2 228
Multitude (1)
  Gonsalez: The Multitude should gaze) in Absence of your Eyes. . . 332 M. BRIDE I.1 245
Mum (5)
  Sir Joseph: angry, I'd tell him--Mum. . . . . 68 OLD BATCH III.1 279
  Fondlewife: canst reach, th' hast experimented Isaac--But Mum. . . . 77 OLD BATCH IV.1 63
  Tattle: Mum--O Madam, you do me too much Honour. . . . . . . 231 FOR LOVE I.1 551
  Scandal: Mum, Tattle. . . . . 258 FOR LOVE III.1 180
  Sir Wilful: Coat of a Cream-cheese, but mum for that, fellow . . . 471 WAY WORLD V.1 364
Mumble (1)
   As Asses Thistles, Poets mumble Wit, ... 214 FOR LOVE PRO. 35
  Sr Sampson: t'other Hand, and I'll mumble 'em, and kiss 'em till they 301 FOR LOVE V.1 147
Mummy (4)
  Foresight: Egyptian Mummy, e're she shall Incorporate with a . . 241 FOR LOVE II.1 239
  Sr Sampson: provoke honest Albumazar--an Egyptian Mummy is . . . 242 FOR LOVE II.1 242
  Sr Sampson: wou'd my Son were an Egyptian Mummy for thy sake. . . 242 FOR LOVE II.1 245
  Sr Sampson: --What, I'll make thee a Present of a Mummy: Now . . . 242 FOR LOVE II.1 248
Mumper (1)
  Lucy: a Mumper in Love, lies Canting at the Gate; but never dare 66 OLD BATCH III.1 193
Mun (1)
  Miss Prue: Lavender mun--I'm resolv'd I won't let Nurse put . . . 249 FOR LOVE II.1 529
Mungrel (1)
  Sr Sampson: Heart: Hang him, Mungrel; cast him off; you shall see the 260 FOR LOVE III.1 260
Mungril (2)
  Vainlove: A kind of Mungril Zealot, sometimes very precise . . . 40 OLD BATCH I.1 106
  Sharper: will be but a kind of a Mungril Curs trick. Well, are you 80 OLD BATCH IV.1 182
Murder (6) see Murther, Self-Murder
  Brisk: see how Love and Murder will out. But did I really name . 176 DOUBL DLR IV.1 329
  Sr Sampson: 'tis as they commit Murder; out of a Frolick: And are . . 299 FOR LOVE V.1 57
  Almeria: I'll catch it--hark! a Voice cries Murder! 'tis . . . 371 M. BRIDE IV.1 391
  Almeria: I'll catch it--hark! a Voice cries Murder! ah! . . . . 371 M. BRIDE IV.1 V391
  Garcia: With more unnatural Blood. Murder my Father! . . . . . 378 M. BRIDE V.2 77
  Almeria: I hope they murder all on whom they look. . . . . . . 382 M. BRIDE V.2 246
Murder'd (3)
  Almeria: All things were well: and yet my Husband's murder'd! . . 382 M. BRIDE V.2 242
  Fainall: Coroner's Inquest, to sit upon the murder'd Reputations of 396 WAY WORLD I.1 53
  Lady Wish: murder'd. I'll have him poyson'd. Where does he eat? I'll 427 WAY WORLD III.1 103
Murderer (2)
  Osmyn-Alph: And pinion'd like a Thief or Murderer? . . . . 355 M. BRIDE III.1 241
  Almeria: Now calls me Murderer, and Parricide. . . . . 368 M. BRIDE IV.1 284
Murderers (1)
  Leonora: Who seem the Murderers, kneel weeping by: . . . . . . 381 M. BRIDE V.2 224
Murmurs (2)
  Osmyn-Alph: In Murmurs round my Head. I rose and listened; . . . . 344 M. BRIDE II.2 162
  Osmyn-Alph: The Piercing Sighs, and Murmurs of my Love . . . . . 351 M. BRIDE III.1 77
Murther (1)
  Garcia: Ha! what? atone this Murther with a greater! . . . . . 378 M. BRIDE V.2 73
Muscovite (1)
  Lady Wish: Barbarity of a Muscovite Husband. . . . . 469 WAY WORLD V.1 272
Muse (4)
   For if his Muse has play'd him false, the worst . . . . 125 DOUBL DLR PRO. 33
  Jeremy: be Canoniz'd for a Muse after my Decease. . . . . . . 218 FOR LOVE I.1 75
  Osmyn-Alph: I'll muse on that, lest I exceed in thinking. . . . . . 345 M. BRIDE II.2 V230
   Of a damn'd Poet, and departed Muse! . . . . 385 M. BRIDE EPI. 12
Muses (3)
   Alone to the Offspring of the Muses kind: . . . . . . 125 DOUBL DLR PRO. 26
  Lady Froth: Nine Muses. . . . . 176 DOUBL DLR IV.1 335
  Jeremy: Muses; or as if she were carrying her Linnen to the
   Paper-Mill, ... 219 FOR LOVE I.1 111
Musical (2)
  Careless: the Women have the more Musical Voices, and become . . . 127 DOUBL DLR I.1 9
  Careless: the Women have more Musical Voices, and become . . . . 127 DOUBL DLR I.1 V 9
Musicians (1)
   (Musicians crossing the Stage.) . . . 143 DOUBL DLR II.1 174
Musick (15)
  Heartwell: Why 'twas I Sung and Danc'd; I gave Musick to . . . . 72 OLD BATCH III.2 32
  Heartwell: here Silvia, here are Songs and Dances, Poetry and Musick . 72 OLD BATCH III.2 34
  Heartwell: to the Musick of their own Chink. This buys all the 'tother 72 OLD BATCH III.2 37
  Bellmour: Alas! Courtship to Marriage, is but as the Musick in the . 107 OLD BATCH V.1 384
  Mellefont: Musick!--Oh, my Lord has promised the Company a . . . 143 DOUBL DLR II.1 172
   (To the Musick, they go out.) 143 DOUBL DLR II.1 193
  Sr Sampson: above a stink.--Why there's it; and Musick, don't you . 245 FOR LOVE II.1 371
  Sr Sampson: love Musick, Scoundrel? . . . . 245 FOR LOVE II.1 372
  Valentine: I would have Musick--Sing me the Song that I . . . . 292 FOR LOVE IV.1 648
  Sr Sampson: troth you shall. Odd we'll have the Musick of the Spheres 307 FOR LOVE V.1 385
  Scandal: The Musick stays for you. . . . . 313 FOR LOVE V.1 617
  Almeria: Musick has Charms to sooth a savage Breast, ... 326 M. BRIDE I.1 1
   (Symphony of Warlike Musick. Enter the King, attended by . 332 M. BRIDE I.1 265
  Lady Wish: And are the Dancers and the Musick ready, ... 445 WAY WORLD IV.1 11
  Mirabell: do for Musick? . . . . 477 WAY WORLD V.1 604
Musick-master (2)
  Araminta: then we are in great danger of being dull--If my
   Musick-master . . . . 58 OLD BATCH II.2 152
   (Enter Musick-master.) . . 59 OLD BATCH II.2 185
Musick-meetings (1)
  Lady Wish: and going to filthy Plays; and Profane Musick-meetings, . 467 WAY WORLD V.1 199
Musing (4)
   (Enter Mellefont musing.) . 155 DOUBL DLR III.1 195
  Brisk: (Stands musing with his Arms a-cross.) 175 DOUBL DLR IV.1 311

Nails (4)
Sr Sampson:	as if thou hadst spilt the Salt, or par'd thy Nails of a	. 265	FOR LOVE	III.1 464
Sr Sampson:	as if thou hadst spilt the Salt, or par'd thy Nails on a	. 265	FOR lCVE	III.1 V464
Valentine:	scratch'd--My Nails are not long enough--Let	. 282	FOR LCVE	IV.1 239
Osmyn-Alph:	Stripping my Nails, to tear this Pavement up	. 358	M. BRIDE	III.1 354

Naked (9)
Heartwell:	a naked Truth, which I'm ashamed to discover. . . .	. 72	OLD BATCH	III.2 64
Lord Touch:	Villain! 'Death I'll have him stripp'd and turn'd naked out	153	DOUBL DLR	III.1 100
Maskwell:	As to go naked is the best disguise.	. 190	DOUEL DLR	V.1 101
Sr Sampson:	go naked out of the World as you came into't. . .	. 244	FOR LCVE	III.1 338
Tattle:	or the Naked Prince. And it is notorious, that in a Country	257	FOR LCVE	III.1 162
Angelica:	naked Hook appears.	. 260	FOR LCVE	III.1 248
Sr Sampson:	Women now-a-days are to be tempted with a naked	. 260	FOR LOVE	III.1 251
Zara:	Thee bare, the naked Mark cf Publick View.	. 360	M. BRIDE	III.1 442
Fainall:	to hide thy Shame; Your Body shall be Naked as . .	. 475	WAY WORLD	V.1 496

Nakedness (1)
| Almeria: | And cloath their Nakedness with my own Flesh; . . . | . 370 | M. EBIDE | IV.1 350 |

Nam'd (2)
| Scandal: | nam'd: Without you could retrieve the Ancient Honours . | . 220 | FOR LOVE | I.1 148 |
| Mrs Fain: | So do I; but I can hear him nam'd. But what . . . | . 411 | WAY WCBLD | II.1 70 |

Name (64)   see Nick-Name
Bellmour:	Nay let's see the Name (Silvia!) how can'st thou be . .	. 38	OLD BATCH	I.1 38
Sharper:	What in the name of wonder is it?	. 46	OLD BATCH	I.1 341
Sharper:	His name, and I have done.	. 47	OLD BAICH	I.1 382
Capt Bluff:	name?	. 52	OLD EATCH	II.1 172
Capt Bluff:	share in't. Tho' I might say that too, since I name no Body	53	OLD BATCH	II.1 V200
Lucy:	in the name of opportunity mind your own Business. . .	. 61	OLD BATCH III.1	9
Silvia:	has bewitch'd him from me--Oh how the name of . .	. 61	OLD BATCH III.1	29
Heartwell:	Why whither in the Devils name am I going now? . .	. 62	OLD BATCH III.1	63
Heartwell:	Why whither in the Devils name am I a-going now? . .	. 62	OLD BATCH III.1 V	63
Belinda:	Huffe, Bluffe, (What's your hideous Name?) be gone:	. 85	OLD BATCH	IV.3 87
Fondlewife:	ripe-horn-mad. But who, in the Devil's name, are you?			
	Mercy on	. 92	OLD BATCH	IV.4 127
Laetitia:	In the Name of the--Oh! Good, my Dear, don't . . .	. 92	OLD BATCH	IV.4 132
Sharper:	Name, which I think you are bound to perform. . . .	. 109	OLD BATCH	V.2 83
Lady Froth:	Biddy, that's all; just my own Name.	. 141	DOUBL DLR	II.1 129
Lady Ply:	O name it no more--bless me, how can	. 147	DOUEL DLR	II.1 344
Maskwell:	Ties: But the Name of Rival cuts 'em all asunder, and is a	. 150	DOUEL DLR	II.1 448
Lady Froth:	can't hit of her Name; the old fat Fool that Paints so	. 166	DOUBL DLR	III.1 581
Brisk:	I can't hit of her Name neither--Paints de'e say? . .	. 166	DOUEL DLR	III.1 584
Cynthia:	know, we have misapply'd the Name all this while, and .	. 167	DOUBL DLR	III.1 631
Brisk:	see how Love and Murder will out. But did I really name	. 176	DOUBL DLR	IV.1 329
Sir Paul:	friendship! What art thou but a Name! Henceforward, let	. 178	DOUBL DLR	IV.1 419
Lord Touch:	to my Name; when next I see that Face, I'le write Villain	. 186	DOUBL DLR	IV.2 119
Maskwell:	with the name of Villain.	. 188	DOUEL DLR	V.1 31
Lord Touch:	sign'd, and have his name inserted--yours will fill the	. 189	DOUBL DLR	V.1 63
Jeremy:	Name, has for the space of Sev'n Years truly and faithfully	218	FOR LOVE	I.1 67
Scandal:	of the Name, recall the Stage of Athens, and be allow'd	. 220	FOB LOVE	I.1 149
Scandal:	a Whisper; and deny a Woman's name, while he gives you	. 226	FOR LOVE	I.1 371
Valentine:	play at Losing Loadum; you must lose a good Name to	. 226	FOR LOVE	I.1 389
Tattle:	Name cf Trusty Mr. Tattle more--You will not be so .	. 230	FOR LOVE	I.1 521
Scandal:	write the Name at the bottcm.	. 230	FOR LOVE	I.1 539
Valentine:	And Scandal shall give you a gocd Name.	. 232	FOR LOVE	I.1 592
Tattle:	Brag! O Heav'ns! Why, did I name any body? . . .	. 255	FOR LOVE	III.1 93
Ben:	Marry a God's Name an the wind sit that way. As for my	. 261	FOR LOVE	III.1 302
Ben:	ben't as willing as I, say so a God's name, there's no harm	263	FCR LOVE	III.1 390
Scandal:	It takes, pursue it in the name of Love and Pleasure. .	. 269	FOR LOVE	III.1 612
Ben:	Whose Name was Buxom Joan.	. 274	FOR LOVE	III.1 762
Sr Sampson:	can'st write thy Name, Val?--Jeremy, step and overtake	. 281	FOR LOVE	IV.1 208
Sr Sampson:	little Sampson: Odd, Sampson's a very good Name for an	. 301	FOR LOVE	V.1 154
Angelica:	you remember, the strongest Sampson of your Name, .	. 301	FCR LCVE	V.1 158
Angelica:	you remember, Sampson, the strongest of the Name .	. 301	FCR LCVE	V.1 V158
Ben:	of her Name.	. 307	FOR LOVE	V.1 362
	I'm sure 'tis some such Latin Name they give 'em, .	. 315	FCB LOVE	EPI. 13
Manuel:	A Priscner. His Name?	. 337	M. EBIDE	I.1 446
Manuel:	Yet lives, and is a Prisoner. His Name?	. 337	M. EBIDE	I.1 V446
Heli:	I feel, to hear of Osmyn's Name; to hear . . .	. 338	M. EBIDE	II.1 10
Zara:	Compassion, scarce will't own that Name sc soon, . .	. 346	M. BBIDE	II.2 279
Zara:	Compassion, scarce will't own that Name so soon, . .	. 346	M. EBIDE	II.2 V279
Zara:	Thee nct, for what thou art, yet wants a Name: . .	. 348	M. BRIDE	II.2 336
Osmyn-Alph:	Thus as the Name of Heav'n from this is torn, . .	. 350	M. EBIDE	III.1 25
Zara:	O, give that Madness yet a milder Name, . . .	. 354	M. BRIDE	III.1 180
Osmyn-Alph:	Give it a Name, ...	. 354	M. EBIDE	III.1 183
Gonsalez:	That some Impostor has usurp'd his Name. . . .	. 363	M. EBIDE	IV.1 100
Mirabell:	all in her own Name, my old Lady Wishfort came in.--	. 395	WAY WCBLD	I.1 24
Marwood:	I loath the name of Love after such usage; . . .	. 415	WAY WORLD	II.1 219
Mirabell:	fix'd a Father's Name with Credit, but on a Husband? I	. 417	WAY WCRLD	II.1 269
Witwoud:	In the Name of Bartlemew and his Fair, what have .	. 436	WAY WORLD	III.1 437
Sir Wilful:	don't think a' knows his own Name.	. 437	WAY WCRLD	III.1 474
Millamant:	Ah! Name it not.	. 451	WAY WORLD	IV.1 256
Millamant:	How can you name that super-annuated Lubber, . .	. 453	WAY WORLD	IV.1 320
Sir Wilful:	Cozen, with the hard Name,--Aunt, Wilfull will do't, If	. 456	WAY WCRLD	IV.1 427
Lady Wish:	the sight or name of an obscene Play-Book--and can I	. 467	WAY WORLD	V.1 202
Marwood:	Prove it Madam? What, and have your name . . .	. 467	WAY WCRLD	V.1 208
Mrs Fain:	not name it, but starve together--perish. . . .	. 475	WAY WCRLD	V.1 501
Mirabell:	You wrong him, his name is fairly written as shall . .	. 476	WAY WORLD	V.1 527

Name's (2)
| Sharper: | Ay Sir, my name's Sharper. . . . . | . 52 | OLD.BATCH | II.1 173 |
| Vainlove: | Name's to it, which she will be unwilling to expose to the | 88 | OLD BATCH | IV.3 188 |

Named (2)
| Araminta: | when you named him, and press'd me to your Bosom . | . 55 | OLD BATCH | II.2 42 |
| Careless: | O fie, fie, not to be named of a day--my Lady Froth . | . 160 | DOUBL DLR | III.1 375 |

Nameless (3)
| Capt Bluff: | done but an humble Servant of yours, that shall be nameless. | . 52 | OLD BATCH | II.1 198 |
| Tattle: | Favours are numberless, so the Persons are nameless. . | . 257 | FCR LCVE | III.1 151 |

Nameless (continued)

| Tattle: | Quality that shall be nameless, in a raging Fit of Jealousie, ... | 258 | FOR LOVE | III.1 | 175 |

Names (10)

Tattle:	O inhumane! You don't expect their Names.	230	FOR LOVE	I.1	532
Tattle:	O inhuman! You don't expect their Names.	230	FOR LOVE	I.1	V532
Angelica:	to write poor innocent Servants Names in Blood, about a	238	FOR LOVE	II.1	109
Miss Prue:	I won't be call'd Names, nor I won't be abus'd . . .	264	FOR LOVE	III.1	428
Ben:	No matter what I can do? don't call Names,--I . . .	287	FOR LOVE	IV.1	434
Almeria:	And for the tender Names of Child and Daughter, . . .	368	M. BRIDE	IV.1	283
Manuel:	Acquit thy self of those detested Names, ...	368	M. BRIDE	IV.1	286
Millamant:	and dee hear, I won't be call'd names after I'm Married;	450	WAY WORLD	IV.1	194
Millamant:	positively I won't be call'd Names.	450	WAY WORLD	IV.1	195
Mirabell:	Names!	450	WAY WORLD	IV.1	196

Napes (0)   see Tankard--napem

Napkin (2)

| Fondlewife: | should heat a Trencher, or a Napkin.--Where's Deborah? | 91 | OLD BATCH | IV.4 | 96 |
| Mirabell: | what a Butler cou'd pinch out of a Napkin. . . . . | 418 | WAY WORLD | II.1 | 313 |

Narrow (2)

| Sharper: | which narrow Souls cannot dare to admire.--And . . . | 86 | OLD BATCH | IV.3 | 127 |
| Sharper: | the narrow Joys of Wedlock. But prithee come along with | 104 | OLD BATCH | V.1 | 305 |

Narrowly (1)

| Mellefont: | narrowly, and give me notice upon any Suspicion. As for | 130 | DOUBL DLR | I.1 | 137 |

Nation (2)

| Valentine: | Nation. . . . . | 282 | FOR LOVE | IV.1 | 259 |
| Mirabell: | the Credit of the Nation, and prohibit the Exportation of | 400 | WAY WORLD | I.1 | 205 |

Native (3)

Zara:	And Native Right to Arbitrary Sway;	336	M. BRIDE	I.1	397
Heli:	And Native Rights.	351	M. BRIDE	III.1	V 72
Mirabell:	but restrain your self to Native and Simple Tea-Table	451	WAY WORLD	IV.1	265

Nativities (1)

| Mrs Frail: | Foresight has cast both their Nativities, and prognosticates | 231 | FOR LOVE | I.1 | 577 |

Nativity (1)

| Foresight: | House of my Nativity; there the Curse of Kindred was . | 238 | FOR LOVE | II.1 | 130 |

Natur'd (3)   see Ill-natur'd

Sir Joseph:	know me, you'd nere say I were so ill natur'd. . . .	48	OLD BATCH	II.1	37
Sir Joseph:	And good Nature, Back; I am good Natur'd and	67	OLD BATCH	III.1	243
Mellefont:	Faith 'tis a good natur'd Cox-Comb, and has very . .	129	DOUBL DLR	I.1	65

Natural (7)

Heartwell:	force Appetite, but wait the natural call of my Lust, and	43	OLD BATCH	I.1	232
Setter:	Face and produce your natural Vizor.	65	OLD BATCH	III.1	180
Silvia:	to our Sex is as natural as swimming to a Negro; we .	75	OLD BATCH	III.2	151
Sr Sampson:	Cou'd neither Love, nor Duty, nor Natural Affection .	259	FOR LOVE	III.1	238
Mirabell:	her Faults. Her Follies are so natural, or so artful,	399	WAY WORLD	I.1	160
	that they				
Witwoud:	natural Parts.	404	WAY WORLD	I.1	328
Millamant:	Natural, easie Suckling!	447	WAY WORLD	IV.1	106

Naturally (5)

Vainlove:	All Naturally fly what does pursue:	80	OLD BATCH	IV.1	190
Careless:	you. She is Handsome and cunning, and naturally . .	131	DOUBL DLR	I.1	161
Lady Touch:	She is so Credulous that way naturally, and	138	DOUBL DLR	I.1	412
Brisk:	Ladyship has not the Art of Surprizing the most Naturally	142	DOUBL DLR	II.1	131
Valentine:	Ages; these Poets and Philosophers whom you naturally .	217	FOR LOVE	I.1	37

Nature (59)   see Ill-nature

Bellmour:	Nature, Night, had hid, confess'd her Soul was true to .	38	OLD BATCH	I.1	50
Bellmour:	Nature--	39	OLD BATCH	I.1	93
Sharper:	Understanding, and very ill Nature.	42	OLD BATCH	I.1	215
Bellmour:	this nature; Women are often won by 'em: who would . .	44	OLD BATCH	I.1	260
Araminta:	Nature well, for there are few Men, but do more silly .	60	OLD BATCH	II.2	216
Lucy:	Hang Art, Madam, and trust to Nature for	62	OLD BATCH	III.1	54
Lucy:	Man, was by Nature Womans Cully made:	62	OLD BATCH	III.1	56
Sir Joseph:	And good Nature, Back; I am good Natur'd and	67	OLD BATCH	III.1	243
Bellmour:	Bed, hoping that when she heard of it, her good Nature	94	OLD BATCH	IV.4	212
Bellmour:	kind Nature works, and boils over in him.	95	OLD BATCH	IV.4	240
Lucy:	easie Nature.--Well, For once I'll venture to serve .	98	OLD BATCH	V.1	75
Heartwell:	That Help which Nature meant in Woman-kind, ...	108	OLD BATCH	V.2	11
Heartwell:	'Tis not in thy Nature to give me Joy--A	108	OLD BATCH	V.2	23
	Let Nature work, and do not Damn too soon, ...	125	DOUBL DLR	PRO.	16
Careless:	Was there ever such a Fury! 'tis well Nature has not .	130	DOUBL DLR	I.1	100
Lady Touch:	Were you not in the nature of a Servant, and have not I in	136	DOUBL DLR	I.1	348
Lady Ply:	you think to reverse Nature so, to make the Daughter the	146	DOUBL DLR	II.1	306
Lady Ply:	Nature. I know Love is powerful, and no body can help .	148	DOUBL DLR	II.1	356
Maskwell:	from Nature.	150	DOUBL DLR	II.1	464
Cynthia:	think they are all in good nature with the World, and only	163	DOUBL DLR	III.1	482
Sir Paul:	of using the common benefits of Nature?	178	DOUBL DLR	IV.1	V426
Lord Touch:	she has told me all: Her good Nature conceal'd it as long	182	DOUBL DLR	IV.1	547
	As Nature gave the World to Man's first Age, ...	213	FOR LOVE	PRO.	13
	We've something too, to gratifie ill Nature, ...	213	FOR LOVE	PRO.	31
Tattle:	knows any thing of that nature of me: As I hope to be .	227	FOR LOVE	I.1	405
Angelica:	her Nature. Uncle, I'm afraid you are not Lord of the .	237	FOR LOVE	II.1	72
Sr Sampson:	Paws; Nature has been provident only to Bears and . .	246	FOR LOVE	II.1	391
Valentine:	Necessities of my Nature; if I had my right of Inheritance.	246	FOR LOVE	II.1	395
Scandal:	Nor good Nature enough to answer him that did . . .	254	FOR LOVE	III.1	33
Angelica:	What, are you setting up for good Nature?	254	FOR LOVE	III.1	35
Scandal:	ill Nature.	254	FOR LOVE	III.1	37
Tattle:	Creature living, in things of that nature; and never had the	256	FOR LOVE	III.1	104
Valentine:	I don't know but my Father in good Nature may press me	259	FOR LOVE	III.1	225
Angelica:	I swear, Mr. Benjamin is the verriest Wag in nature; .	262	FOR LOVE	III.1	336
Foresight:	He was always of an impetuous Nature--But	268	FOR LOVE	III.1	551
Angelica:	deluded with vain Hopes. Good Nature and Humanity . .	277	FOR LOVE	IV.1	72
Scandal:	So, faith good Nature works a-pace; you were . . .	278	FOR LOVE	IV.1	84
Angelica:	reasonable Stock of good Nature and Sense--For I . .	299	FOR LOVE	V.1	63
Tattle:	a Gentleman. I hope you are secret in your Nature, private,	302	FOR LOVE	V.1	188
Valentine:	to undo the Son, it was a reasonable return of Nature. .	311	FOR LOVE	V.1	512
Angelica:	Nature. I was resolv'd to try him to the utmost; I have .	312	FOR LOVE	V.1	574
	Art may direct, but Nature is his aim;	324	M. BRIDE	PRO.	36

			PAGE	TITLE	ACT.SC	LINE
Necessaries (1)						
Bellmour:	And hast thou provided necessaries?		64	OLD BATCH	III.1	122
Necessary (3)						
Heartwell:	Effigie, pasted up for the exemplary Ornament of necessary		63	OLD BATCH	III.1	83
Lady Touch:	such a Case as this, demonstration is necessary. . . .		151	DOUBL DLR	III.1	18
Maskwell:	which (should this design miscarry) will be necessary to		154	DOUEL DLR	III.1	159
Necessities (1)						
Valentine:	Necessities of my Nature; if I had my right of Inheritance.		246	FOR LOVE	II.1	395
Necessity (16)						
Maskwell:	convince you, from the necessity of my being firm to you.		136	DOUEL DLR	I.1	344
Lady Touch:	Necessity, Impudence! Can no Gratitude		136	DOUEL DLR	I.1	345
Lady Ply:	necessity--O Lord, here's some body coming, I dare . .		148	DOUBL DLR	II.1	362
Maskwell:	so little time must of necessity discover. Yet he is					
	apprehensive		154	DOUEL DLR	III.1	136
Maskwell:	either to my Inclination or your own necessity-- . .		157	DOUEL DLR	III.1	246
Valentine:	me Signal Service in my necessity. But you delight in .		223	FOR LOVE	I.1	259
Valentine:	they are very hard, but my Necessity is very pressing:		224	FOR LOVE	I.1	318
Trapland:	necessity.		224	FOR LOVE	I.1	323
Valentine:	those hard Conditions, which my necessity Sign'd to. .		243	FOR LOVE	II.1	284
Almeria:	Is there necessity I must be miserable?		327	M. BRIDE	I.1	57
Osmyn-Alph:	Not seeing of Election, but Necessity.		345	M. BRIDE	II.2	220
Zara:	And Osmyn's Death requir'd of strong necessity. . . .		364	M. BRIDE	IV.1	126
Mirabell:	the necessity of such a resignation.		396	WAY WORLD	I.1	44
Lady Wish:	than to put a Lady to the necessity of breaking her Forms.		429	WAY WORLD	III.1	162
Mrs Fain:	Mirabell, there's a Necessity for your obedience, . .		452	WAY WORLD	IV.1	298
Lady Wish:	Aye that's true; but in Case of Necessity; as of . .		468	WAY WORLD	V.1	263
Neck (2)						
Bellmour:	your snowy Arms about his stubborn Neck; bathe his . . .		95	OLD BATCH	IV.4	237
	(She goes and hangs upon his neck, and kisses him. Bellmour		95	OLD BATCH	IV.4	241
Necklace (1)						
	see Fat-Amber-Necklace					
Lady Wish:	rowes of Pins and a Childs Fiddle; A Glass Necklace with the		462	WAY WORLD	V.1	16
Necks (2)						
Scandal:	in their Hands, and Horn-Books about their Necks. . .		234	FOR LOVE	I.1	656
Valentine:	their Necks. But hold, I must examine you before I go .		289	FOR LOVE	IV.1	513
Ned (7)						
Vainlove:	How how, Ned, a wise Man say more than he		37	OLD BATCH	I.1	17
Vainlove:	Element Ned--Well as high as a Flyer as you are, I . .		38	OLD BATCH	I.1	30
Vainlove:	So was true as Turtle--in imagination Ned, ha? . . .		38	OLD BATCH	I.1	52
Sharper:	I'm sorry to see this, Ned: Once a Man comes to his .		41	OLD BATCH	I.1	147
Mellefont:	Ned, Ned, whither so fast? What, turn'd flincher! . .		127	DOUBL DLR	I.1	1
Sir Paul:	Dying Ned. Careless.		178	DOUEL DLR	IV.1	416
Need (21)						
Bellmour:	to Fools; they have need of 'em: Wit, be my Faculty; .		37	OLD BATCH	I.1	23
Sharper:	She had need have a good share of sense, to manage. .		42	OLD BATCH	I.1	208
Sharper:	He has need of such an excuse, considering the present .		44	OLD BATCH	I.1	288
Araminta:	no need to forgive what is not worth my Anger. . . .		106	OLD BATCH	V.1	363
Sir Joseph:	No, no, Captain, you need not own, Heh, heh, ...		110	OLD BATCH	V.2	105
Lady Touch:	Nay, my Lord, you need say no more, to		152	DOUBL DLR	III.1	64
Maskwell:	This was a Master-piece, and did not need my		154	DOUBL DLR	III.1	128
Sir Paul:	and I think need not envy any of my Neighbours, blessed		160	DOUEL DLR	III.1	385
Mellefont:	me; I never had more need of him--But what can he do? .		187	DOUBL DLR	IV.2	149
Lord Touch:	you, and yet it shall not need--Honest Maskwell! thy .		189	DOUBL DLR	V.1	53
Maskwell:	way into it, so that you need not come thro' this Door .		194	DOUBL DLR	V.1	254
Careless:	You need not fear, Madam, you have Charms to		202	DOUBL DLR	V.1	548
Valentine:	You need say no more, I understand the Conditions; . .		224	FOR LOVE	I.1	317
Valentine:	Why Tattle, you need not be much concern'd at . . .		226	FOR LOVE	I.1	387
Miss Prue:	You need not sit so near one, if you have any thing . .		263	FOR LOVE	III.1	364
Jeremy:	Yes, Sir; you need make no great doubt of that; he . .		276	FOR LOVE	IV.1	3
Sr Sampson:	need any body hold it?--I'll put it up in my Pocket, .		281	FOR LOVE	IV.1	231
Sr Sampson:	Val: And then no body need hold it (puts the Paper in his		281	FOR LOVE	IV.1	232
Valentine:	Ha, ha, ha; you need not run so fast, Honesty will . .		282	FOR LOVE	IV.1	246
Valentine:	Madam, you need not be very much afraid, for I . . .		294	FOR LOVE	IV.1	697
Foible:	I don't question your Generosity, Sir: And you need .		424	WAY WORLD	II.1	541
Needle (1)						
Heartwell:	There stands my North, and thither my Needle points . .		63	OLD BATCH	III.1	75
Needless (2)						
Vainlove:	this Letter will be needless.		39	OLD BATCH	I.1	70
Gonsalez:	But why that needless Caution of the Princess? . . .		366	M. BRIDE	IV.1	221
Needs (10)						
Bellmour:	birth, and the discovery must needs be very pleasant from		40	OLD BATCH	I.1	125
Laetitia:	there needs no farther Apology.		81	OLD BATCH	IV.2	47
Capt Bluff:	'Tis very generous, Sir, since I needs must own-- . .		110	OLD BATCH	V.2	104
Maskwell:	needs this? I say nothing but what your self, in open hours		137	DOUEL DLR	I.1	384
Maskwell:	needs this? I say nothing but what you your self, in open					
	hours		137	DOUBL DLR	I.1 V384	
Maskwell:	present, yet the reflection of it must needs be					
	entertaining.		149	DOUBL DLR	II.1	414
Scandal:	enough? Must you needs shew your Wit to get more? . .		219	FOR LOVE	I.1	128
Foresight:	Prophecy needs no Explanation.		236	FOR LOVE	II.1	60
Selim:	It needs not, for the King will strait be here, . . .		361	M. BRIDE	IV.1	20
Selim:	I needs must fail; impute not as a Crime, ...		375	M. BRIDE	V.1	118
Needy (2)						
Brisk:	while your Blockheads, like poor needy Scoundrels, are		175	DOUBL DLR	IV.1	301
Jeremy:	lying in the Arms of a needy Wit, before the Embraces of		219	FOR LOVE	I.1	114
Negative (1)						
Mellefont:	That's but a kind of Negative Consent.--Why, ...		168	DOUBL DLR	IV.1	41
Neglect (5)						
Laetitia:	No you shan't neglect your business for me--No . . .		78	OLD BATCH	IV.1	131
Lady Touch:	--I was accusing you of Neglect.		183	DOUBL DLR	IV.2	11
Manuel:	Pardon, fair Excellence, this long Neglect:		363	M. BRIDE	IV.1	104
Fainall:	wilfully neglect the gross advances made him by my Wife;		413	WAY WORLD	II.1	144
Fainall:	and your Resentment follows his Neglect. An Instance? .		414	WAY WORLD	II.1	156
Neglected (1)						
Zara:	Am I neglected thus? Am I despised?		346	M. BRIDE	II.2	245
Negligence (1)						
Fainall:	affected; and confesses you are conscious of a Negligence.		397	WAY WORLD	I.1	94

Negligently (1)
```
  Fainall:      else now, and play too negligently; the Coldness of a  .  . 395  WAY WORLD   I.1     6
Negotiate (1)
  Lady Wish:    Confidence. I sent her to Negotiate an Affair, in which if    426  WAY WORLD III.1    51
Negotiation (1)
  Jeremy:       if you don't like my Negotiation, will you be pleas'd to  . 221  FOR LOVE    I.1   183
Negro (1)
  Silvia:       to our Sex is as natural as swimming to a Negro; we   .  .   75  OLD BATCH III.2   151
Neice (12)
  Foresight:    the Moon is in all her Fortitudes; Is my Neice Angelica at   235  FOR LOVE   II.1     6
  Foresight:    well pleas'd at my Stocking--Oh here's my Neice!--   .  .  . 236  FOR LOVE   II.1    38
  Foresight:    of the Head is Horns--Dear Neice, stay at home--   .  .  . . 236  FOR LOVE   II.1    58
  Foresight:    something; tell me, and I'll forgive you; do, good Neice   . 239  FOR LOVE   II.1   147
  Foresight:    Neice, he knows things past and to come, and all the   .  . 291  FOR LOVE   IV.1   604
  Marwood:      and Sacrifice Neice, and Fortune, and all at that
                Conjuncture.  .  .  .  .  .  .  .  .  .  .  .  .  .  .  .  . 442  WAY WORLD III.1   664
  Lady Wish:    --Fogh! how you stink of Wine! Dee think my Neice   .  .  . 455  WAY WORLD  IV.1   388
  Lady Wish:    Jewells and ruine my Neice, and all little enough--   .  .  . 466  WAY WORLD   V.1   152
  Lady Wish:    up all, my self and my all, my Neice and her all,--any   .  . 468  WAY WORLD   V.1   239
  Lady Wish:    How's this dear Neice? Have I any comfort?   .  .  .  . .  . 470  WAY WORLD   V.1   323
  Lady Wish:    resign the Contract with my Neice Immediately.   .  .  . .  472  WAY WORLD   V.1   404
  Lady Wish:    Neice exerts a lawfull claim, having Match'd her self by  . 472  WAY WORLD   V.1   417
Neighbourhood (1)
  Angelica:     Neighbourhood--What a Bustle did you keep against the   .  . 237  FOR LOVE   II.1    79
Neighbours (1)
  Sir Paul:     and I think need not envy any of my Neighbours, blessed   . 160  DOUEL DLR III.1   385
Neighing (1)
  Gonsalez:     Succeed; and next, a Hundred neighing Steeds,   .  .  .  . 331  M. BRIDE    I.1   230
Neighs (1)
  Heartwell:    The youthful Beast sets forth, and neighs aloud.   .  .  . 112  OLD BATCH   V.2   187
Neither (42)
Nemo omnibus horis (1)
  Foresight:    This is none of your lucky Hour; Nemo omnibus horis sapit.   283  FOR LOVE   IV.1   294
Nephew (29)
  Lord Touch:   Out upon't, Nephew--leave your   .  .  .  .  .  .  .  .  . 131  DOUEL DLR   I.1   172
  Maskwell:     Nephew, when I first Sigh'd for you; I quickly found it   . 136  DOUEL DLR   I.1   361
  Lady Touch:   I am willing to believe as favourably of my Nephew as I   . 151  DOUEL DLR III.1    24
  Lady Touch:   your promise--Pho, why nothing, only your Nephew had   .  . 152  DOUEL DLR III.1    82
  Lady Touch:   thought my Nephew could have so misconstrued my   .  .  . . 153  DOUEL DLR III.1   115
  Lord Touch:   unnatural Nephew thus far--but I know you have been   .  . 182  DOUEL DLR  IV.1   545
  Lord Touch:   --my Nephew is the alone remaining Branch of all   .  .  . 189  DOUEL DLR   V.1    57
  Sir Paul:     Nephew; and I don't know what,--look you, Sister,   .  .  . 192  DOUEL DLR   V.1   175
  Lord Touch:   ha, I'll do't, where's Mellefont, my poor injured Nephew,-- 200  DOUEL DLR   V.1   478
  Lord Touch:   inform my Nephew, and do you quickly as you can, bring   . 200  DOUEL DLR   V.1   487
  Lord Touch:   Innocence.--Nephew, I hope I have your pardon, and   .  .  . 203  DOUEL DLR   V.1   583
  Lady Wish:    expect my Nephew Sir Wilfull every moment too--Why   .  .  . 431  WAY WORLD III.1   257
  Lady Wish:    Come, come Foible--I had forgot my Nephew will be   .  .  . 432  WAY WORLD III.1   274
  Sir Wilful:   tell her, her Nephew, Sir Wilfull Witwoud is in the House.  437  WAY WORLD III.1   466
  Sir Wilful:   write my self; no offence to any Body, I hope; and Nephew   438  WAY WORLD III.1   511
  Lady Wish:    Nephew, you are welcome.   .  .  .  .  .  .  .  .  .  .  . 441  WAY WORLD III.1   593
  Lady Wish:    your Servant.--Nephew, you are welcome again.   .  .  .  . 441  WAY WORLD III.1   598
  Lady Wish:    Will you drink any Thing after your Journey, Nephew,   .  . 441  WAY WORLD III.1   599
  Lady Wish:    O he's a Rallier, Nephew--My Cousin's a   .  .  .  .  .  . 441  WAY WORLD III.1   606
  Lady Wish:    to chuse. When you have been abroad, Nephew, you'll   .  . 441  WAY WORLD III.1   608
  Lady Wish:    Fie, fie, Nephew, you wou'd not pull off your   .  .  .  . 441  WAY WORLD III.1   620
  Lady Wish:    O dear, has my Nephew made his Addresses   .  .  .  .  .  . 445  WAY WORLD  IV.1    34
  Waitwell:     Poyscn'd. My Nephew will get an irkling of my Designs   . 458  WAY WORLD  IV.1   500
  Waitwell:     If he were my Son as he is my Nephew I'd Pistoll him--   . 460  WAY WORLD  IV.1   603
  Waitwell:     Nephew. Come my Buxom Widdow.  .  .  .  .  .  .  .  .  .  . 461  WAY WORLD  IV.1   645
  Lady Wish:    My Nephew was non Compos; and cou'd not   .  .  .  .  .  . 469  WAY WORLD   V.1   286
  Lady Wish:    Well Nephew, upon your account--ah,   .  .  .  .  .  .  . 472  WAY WORLD   V.1   400
  Lady Wish:    Hold Nephew, hold.  .  .  .  .  .  .  .  .  .  .  .  .  . 473  WAY WORLD   V.1   430
  Lady Wish:    thing is to break the Matter to my Nephew--and how   .  . 477  WAY WORLD   V.1   575
Nephew's (6)
  Maskwell:     thought you in my Power. Your Nephew's Scorn of you,   .  . 136  DOUEL DLR   I.1   365
  Lord Touch:   by some pitiful Contriver, envious of my Nephew's Merit.   . 151  DOUEL DLR III.1    15
  Lady Wish:    shall stay for you--My Nephew's a little unbred,   .  .  . 441  WAY WORLD III.1   622
  Lady Wish:    My Nephew's a little overtaken Cozen--but   .  .  .  .  . 455  WAY WORLD  IV.1   406
  Foible:       (to him). Say 'tis your Nephew's hand.--quickly, his   . 460  WAY WORLD  IV.1   595
  Lady Wish:    my just resentment at my Nephew's request.--I will   .  . 472  WAY WORLD   V.1   402
Nephews (3)
  Petulant:     --But there are Uncles and Nephews in the World   .  .  . 406  WAY WORLD   I.1   429
  Lady Wish:    Travels--I am against my Nephews marrying too   .  .  .  . 431  WAY WORLD III.1   263
  Lady Wish:    my Nephews Match, you shall have my Niece yet, and all   . 474  WAY WORLD   V.1   464
Nere (1)
  Sir Joseph:   know me, you'd nere say I were so ill natur'd.   .  .  .  .  48  OLD BATCH  II.1    37
Nerves (1)
  Osmyn-Alph:   That strain my cracking Nerves; Engines and Wheels   .  .  . 356  M. BRIDE  III.1   292
Nest (2)
                In her own Nest the Cuckow-Eggs we find,   .  .  .  .  . . 393  WAY WORLD  PRO.     7
  Lady Wish:    your Nest?  .  .  .  .  .  .  .  .  .  .  .  .  .  .  .  . 462  WAY WORLD   V.1    23
Nettl'd (1)
  Marwood:      You are nettl'd.  .  .  .  .  .  .  .  .  .  .  .  .  .  . 433  WAY WORLD III.1   331
Never (221)     see Ne'er, Ne're, Nere
Never-slacking (1)
  Almeria:      Drink bitter Draughts, with never-slacking Thirst.   .  . 356  M. BRIDE  III.1   262
Nevertheless (1)
  Mellefont:    flounder your self a weary, and be nevertheless my Prisoner. 184  DOUEL DLR  IV.2    52
New (36)         see A-new
  Bellmour:     But do you know nothing of a new Rival there?   .  .  .  .  40  OLD BATCH   I.1   117
  Araminta:     upon the least displeasure you forsake, and set up new   .  58  OLD BATCH  II.2   147
  Araminta:     be not gone, I'll entertain you with a new Song,   .  .  .  58  OLD BATCH  II.2   153
  Araminta:     Discourse--Pray oblige us with the last new Song.   .  .  .  59  OLD BATCH  II.2   187
  Musician:     Nothing's new besides our Faces,  .  .  .  .  .  .  .  .   60  OLD BATCH  II.2   201
  Laetitia:     they are both new to me.--You are not what your first   .  .  81  OLD BATCH  IV.2    24
  Vainlove:     abuse Mercy, by committing new Offences.   .  .  .  .  .  .  87  OLD BATCH  IV.3   140
```

New   (continued)
Mellefont:	New Song, we'll get 'em to give it us by the way. . .	. 143	DOUEL DLR	II.1	173
Maskwell:	and Honesty, and create in him a new Confidence in me,	. 154	DOUEL DLR	III.1	158
Lord Froth:	And each Morning wears a new one;	. 166	DOUEL DLR	III.1	60C
Brisk:	to win her with a new airy invention of my own, hem! .	. 175	DOUEL DLR	IV.1	304
	And hope new Fruit from ancient Stocks remov'd.	. 213	FOR LCVE	PRO.	10
Jeremy:	Nothing new, Sir; I have dispatch'd some half a . . .	. 220	FCR LCVE	I.1	166
Mrs Fore:	fond cf it, as of being first in the Fashion, cr of seeing				
	a new	. 250	FOR LCVE	II.1	549
Scandal:	Pray sing the first Song in the last new Play. . . .	. 258	FOR LCVE	III.1	197
Sr Sampson:	but a new Tax, and the loss of the Canary Fleet. . .	. 266	FOR LCVE	III.1	486
Sr Sampson:	but a new Tax, or the loss of the Canary Fleet. . . .	. 266	FOR LCVE	III.1	V486
Scandal:	matter. But this is no new effect of an unsuccessful				
	Passion.	. 277	FCR LCVE	IV.1	46
Valentine:	Truth, and can teach thy Tongue a new Trick,--I . . .	. 288	FOR LCVE	IV.1	488
Valentine:	an Old Acquaintance with a new Face.	. 292	FCR LCVE	IV.1	620
Tattle:	must think of a new Man every Morning, and forget him .	. 303	FCR LCVE	V.1	244
Ben:	Why then I'll tell you, There's a new wedding upon the .	. 307	FOR LCVE	V.1	358
Ben:	mayn't keep your new Vessel steddy.	. 308	FCR LCVE	V.1	V421
	And a less Number New, would well content ye. . . .	. 323	M. ERIDE	PRC.	2
	New Plays did then like Almanacks appear;	. 323	M. ERIDE	PRO.	3
Manuel:	Yet new, unborn and blooming in the Bud, ...	. 349	M. ERIDE	II.2	384
Manuel:	Give me new Rage, implacable Revenge, ...	. 373	M. ERIDE	V.1	V 36
Osmyn-Alph:	Give a new Birth to thy long-shaded Eyes, ...	. 383	M. ERIDE	V.2	286
	So Criticks throng to see a New Play split, ...	. 385	M. ERIDE	EPI.	25
	Some Plot we think he has, and some new Thought; . . .	. 393	WAY WCRLD	PRC.	29
Mirabell:	and the new Liveries?	. 398	WAY WCRLD	I.1	125
Millamant:	enquir'd after you, as after a new Fashion.	. 419	WAY WCRLD	II.1	348
Foible:	Incontinently, Madam. No new Sheriff's Wife expects .	. 428	WAY WCRLD	III.1	124
Marwood:	there, like a new masking Habit, after the Masquerade is .	. 433	WAY WCRLD	III.1	310
Millamant:	a New Chariot, to provoke Eyes and Whispers; And then .	. 450	WAY WCRLD	IV.1	203
Mirabell:	me, that you endeavour not to new Coin it. To which end, .	. 451	WAY WCRLD	IV.1	247

New-born (2)
Bellmour:	And ev'ry Eye receives a new-born Sight.	. 81	OLD BATCH	IV.2	12
	Into the sea, the New-born Babe is thrown, ...	. 125	DOUEL DLR	PRC.	3

New-flushing (1)
Osmyn-Alph:	With the new-flushing Ardour of my Cheek;	. 383	M. ERIDE	V.2	282

New-married (1)
Sharper:	Why, thou art as musty as a New-married Man, ...	. 104	OLD BATCH	V.1	296

Newly (1)
Heartwell:	generally Masters in it: But I'm so newly entred, you . .	. 72	OLD EATCH	III.2	57

News (16)
Sir Joseph:	love to be the Messenger of ill News; 'tis an ungrateful .	. 68	OLD EATCH	III.1	266
Sir Joseph:	to her,--Pray, Madam, what News d'ye hear?	. 89	OLD BATCH	IV.4	33
Lady Touch:	News, You were to marry Cynthia--that you had . . .	. 198	DOUEL DLR	V.1	417
Mrs Frail:	Well, I'll tell you News; but I suppose you hear your .	. 231	FCR LCVE	I.1	566
Scandal:	Sir Sampson, sad News.	. 266	FOR LCVE	III.1	48C
Jeremy:	is almost mad in good earnest, with the Joyful News of .	. 278	FCR LCVE	IV.1	100
Valentine:	News;--Angelica is turn'd Nun; and I am turning Fryar, .	. 290	FCR LCVE	IV.1	558
Miss Prue:	O I have pure News, I can tell you pure News--I . . .	. 303	FCR LCVE	V.1	226
Almeria:	Ready to sail, and when this News was brought, . . .	. 329	M. ERIDE	I.1	121
Heli:	Converts. This News has reach'd Valentia's Frontiers; .	. 351	M. ERIDE	III.1	67
Zara:	Some News, few Minutes past arriv'd, which seem'd . .	. 354	M. ERIDE	III.1	204
Selim:	The Fate of Osmyn: but to that, fresh News	. 361	M. ERIDE	IV.1	6
	O with what Joy they run, to spread the News	. 385	M. ERIDE	EPI.	11
Lady Wish:	Merciful, no News of Foible yet?	. 425	WAY WCRLD	III.1	1
Sir Wilful:	--You cou'd write News before you were out of your . .	. 439	WAY WCRLD	III.1	548

Next (39)
Footman:	Only to the next door, Madam; I'll call him. . . .	. 58	OLD BATCH	II.2	158
Setter:	her last; When you were to see her next; And, Where you .	. 99	OLD BATCH	V.1	115
Maskwell:	So that Accusation's Answer'd; cn to the next. . . .	. 135	DOUEL DLR	I.1	319
Lady Touch:	knows I hate him too: Let him but once be mine, and next .	. 137	DOUEL DLR	I.1	400
Lady Froth:	you go into the next Room? and there I'll shew you all .	. 142	DOUEL DLR	II.1	144
Lady Froth:	you gc into the next Room? and there I'll shew you what .	. 142	DOUEL DLR	II.1	V144
Mellefont:	grant it; and next to the Villany of such a fact, is the .	. 146	DOUEL DLR	II.1	294
Maskwell:	made me conceal it; yet you may say, I threatned the next .	. 154	DOUEL DLR	III.1	153
Mellefont:	and next to being in the dark, or alone, they are most truly	. 158	DOUEL DLR	III.1	313
Lady Ply:	your next half year.	. 162	DOUEL DLR	III.1	452
Lady Ply:	the next half year.	. 162	DOUEL DLR	III.1	V452
Careless:	the next Room.	. 163	DOUEL DLR	III.1	495
Mellefont:	This very next ensuing hour of Eight a Clock, is . .	. 169	DOUEL DLR	IV.1	52
Lord Touch:	to my Name; when next I see that Face, I'le write Villain .	. 186	DOUEL DLR	IV.2	119
Valentine:	Step into the next Rccm--and I'll give you	. 231	FOR LCVE	I.1	585
Tattle:	The next Sunday all the Old Women kept their Daughters .	. 258	FOR LCVE	III.1	169
Scandal:	Proverbs, and I see one in the next Room that will sing it. .	. 258	FOR LCVE	III.1	192
Ben:	then put off with the next fair wind. How de'e like us? .	. 275	FOR LCVE	III.1	803
Mrs Frail:	Do with him, send him to Sea again in the next . . .	. 284	FOR LCVE	IV.1	306
Sr Sampson:	the next Morning.--Odso, have a care, Madam. . . .	. 299	FCR LCVE	V.1	59
Foresight:	Well, I shall run mad next.	. 306	FCR LCVE	V.1	348
Gonsalez:	Succeed; and next, a Hundred neighing Steeds, . . .	. 331	M. ERIDE	I.1	230
Almeria:	E'er next we meet--	. 345	M. ERIDE	II.2	V209
Heli:	And our next meeting will confirm.	. 352	M. ERIDE	III.1	121
Almeria:	To Morrow, and the next, and each that follows, . . .	. 367	M. ERIDE	IV.1	259
Fainall:	you;--I'll look upon the Gamesters in the next Room. .	. 397	WAY WCRLD	I.1	100
Betty:	He's in the next Room, Friend--That way.	. 400	WAY WORLD	I.1	185
Fainall:	have something to brag of the next time he makes Court .	. 406	WAY WORLD	I.1	419
Marwood:	despise 'em; the next thing I have to do, is eternally to .	. 411	WAY WCRLD	II.1	46
Marwood:	and next to the Guilt with which you wou'd asperse me, I .	. 415	WAY WORLD	II.1	220
Mincing:	with Poetry, it sits so pleasant the next Day as any Thing,	. 420	WAY WORLD	II.1	373
Millamant:	Yes, the Vapours; Fools are Physicks for it, next . .	. 421	WAY WORLD	II.1	445
Millamant:	Desire Mrs.--that is in the next Room to	. 434	WAY WORLD	III.1	370
Petulant:	next time your self--I'll go sleep.	. 454	WAY WORLD	IV.1	370
Sir Wilful:	That he's able next Morning to light us.	. 455	WAY WORLD	IV.1	421
Lady Wish:	dealt in when I took you into my house, plac'd you next .	. 462	WAY WORLD	V.1	20
Fainall:	No more Sir Rowlands,--the next Imposture	. 468	WAY WORLD	V.1	256
Fainall:	is your Apothecary. Next, my Wife shall settle on me the .	. 469	WAY WORLD	V.1	268

Night   (continued)
		PAGE	TITLE	ACT.SC	LINE
Sr Sampson:	your Wedding Night? I'm an older Fellow than you, and	310	FOR LCVE	V.1	485
Almeria:	Anselmo sleeps, and is at Peace; last Night,	326	M. BRIDE	I.1	9
Leonora:	And oft at Night, when all have been retir'd,	326	M. BRIDE	I.1	24
Manuel:	Of Death and Night? Ha! what Disorder's this?	348	M. BRIDE	II.2	354
Zara:	Or Love, that late at Night still lights his Camp,	354	M. BRIDE	III.1	207
Zara:	To have contending Queens, at dead of Night	360	M. BRIDE	III.1	427
Manuel:	As they had wept in Blood, and worn the Night	367	M. BRIDE	IV.1	249
Gonsalez:	And all as still, as at the Noon of Night!	376	M. BRIDE	V.2	2
Fainall:	Confess, Millamant and you quarrell'd last Night,	395	WAY WCRLD	I.1	17
Fainall:	of you; last Night was one of their Cabal-nights; they	396	WAY WCRLD	I.1	50
Mirabell:	know you staid at Millamant's last Night, after I went.	407	WAY WORLD	I.1	450
Witwoud:	We staid pretty late there last Night; and heard	408	WAY WORLD	I.1	480
Mirabell:	Night.	4C8	WAY WCRLD	I.1	495
Mrs Fain:	pleasant Relation last Night: I wou'd fain hear it out.	412	WAY WCRLD	II.1	99
Mrs Fain:	She talk'd last Night of endeavouring at a	418	WAY WORLD	II.1	303
Millamant:	Mirabell, Did not you take Exceptions last Night?	420	WAY WCRLD	II.1	377
Millamant:	Mirabell, Did you take Exceptions last Night?	420	WAY WCRLD	II.1 V377	
Mirabell:	You had the Tyranny to deny me last Night; tho' you	421	WAY WCRLD	II.1	429
Foible:	Night.	424	WAY WCRLD	II.1	532
Lady Wish:	contracted to Night.	428	WAY WCRLD	III.1	120
Foible:	she'll be contracted to Sir Rowland to Night, she says;--	430	WAY WCRLD	III.1	210
Mirabell:	for the Night, made of oil'd skins and I know not what	451	WAY WCRLD	IV.1	249
Sir Wilful:	For he's drunk every Night,	455	WAY WCRLD	IV.1	419
Waitwell:	sign'd this Night? May I hope sc farr?	461	WAY WCRLD	IV.1	639

Night-Cap (1)
Careless:	Gallantry, converted into a Night-Cap, and wears it still	158	DOUEL DLR	III.1	278

Night-cap (1)
Lady Wish:	Beads troken, and a Quilted Night-cap with one Ear. Go,	462	WAY WCRLD	V.1	17

Night-Gown (1)
Maskwell:	be otherwhere employ'd--do you procure her Night-Gown,	199	DOUEL DLR	V.1	444

Night's (1)
Sir Joseph:	thing but a Night's Lodging.	104	OLD BATCH	V.1	282

Nightly (1)
Heli:	Nightly; hating this Tyrant; some, who love	352	M. BRIDE	III.1	101

Nights (5)   see Cabal-nights, O'nights
Careless:	whole nights together upon the Stairs, before her Chamber-door;	157	DOUBL DLR	III.1	274
Lord Touch:	joyn your hands.--Unwearied Nights, and wishing	203	DOUBL DLR	V.1	587
Mrs Fore:	Never, never; till within these three Nights;	270	FCR LCVE	III.1	622
Ben:	And lie o' Nights alone.	274	FCR LOVE	III.1	767
Sir Wilful:	a Rat me, Knight, I'm so sick of a last Nights debauch	439	WAY WCRLD	III.1	545

Nightwalkers (1)
Bellmour:	hands of some Nightwalkers, who I suppcse would have	46	OLD BATCH	I.1	360

Nilus (3)
Sir Paul:	Nilus in his Belly, he will eat thee up alive.	145	DOUBL DLR	II.1	248
Sir Paul:	Nilus is in his Belly, he will eat thee up alive.	145	DOUEL DLR	II.1 V248	
Jeremy:	as the Head of Nilus.	302	FCR LCVE	V.1	191

Nimble (3)
Heartwell:	able as your self and as nimble too, though I mayn't have	43	OLD BATCH	I.1	230
Careless:	aking trembling heart, the nimble movement shall instruct	170	DOUBL DLR	IV.1	93
Careless:	trembling heart, the nimble movement shall instruct	170	DOUEL DLR	IV.1 V 93	

Nine (4)
Silvia:	Midwife, some nine Months hence--Well, I find dissembling,	75	OLD BATCH	III.2	150
Careless:	Sir Paul's nine years Courtship; how he has lain for	157	DOUEL DLR	III.1	273
Lady Froth:	Nine Muses.	176	DOUBL DLR	IV.1	335
Sir Wilful:	out at the nine Months end.	456	WAY WCBLD	IV.1	430

Nine-tails (1)
Ben:	o' Nine-tails laid cross your Shoulders. Flesh! who are	264	FOR LCVE	III.1	409

Nip't (0)   see Prost-nip't

No (767)

No-body (2)
Belinda:	most rueful! Ha, ha, ha: O Gad, I hope no-body will	83	OLD BATCH	IV.3	9
Belinda:	Nay, we have spared No-body, I swear. Mr. Sharper,	88	OLD BATCH	IV.3	195

No-h (2)
Laetitia:	No-h	78	OLD BATCH	IV.1	127
Laetitia:	No-h.	96	OLD BATCH	IV.4	254

Nobility (2)
Heartwell:	Compound of the whole Body of Nobility.	45	OLD BATCH	I.1	328
Lord Touch:	think so--Honesty to me is true Nobility. However, 'tis	196	DOUEL DLR	V.1	318

Noble (16)
Sharper:	you hope to be receiv'd into the Alliance of a noble	45	OLD BATCH	I.1	307
Heartwell:	that noble passion, Lust, should ebb to this degree--No	72	OLD BATCH	III.2	48
Setter:	Were I a Rogue now, what a noble Prize could I	102	OLD BATCH	V.1	221
Belinda:	Courtship, one wou'd think you meant a noble Entertainment:	106	OLD BATCH	V.1	373
Scandal:	What think you of that Noble Commoner, Mrs.	227	FOR LOVE	I.1	417
Zara:	Acknowledgment frcm Noble Minds. Such Thanks	336	M. BRIDE	I.1	416
Zara:	Deserve acknowledgment from Noble Minds.	336	M. BRIDE	I.1 V416	
Perez:	Yonder, my Lord, behold the Noble Moor.	338	M. BRIDE	II.1	16
Heli:	I know his Noble Heart would burst with Shame	338	M. BRIDE	II.1	33
Heli:	Y'are truly Noble.	338	M. BRIDE	II.1 V 38	
Perez:	From visiting the Noble Prisoner.	359	M. BRIDE	III.1	382
Gonsalez:	I've seen thy Sword do noble Execution.	372	M. BRIDE	IV.1	430
Almeria:	O noble Thirst! and yet too greedy to	382	M. BRIDE	V.2	255
Almeria:	O noble Thirst! yet greedy, to drink all--	382	M. BRIDE	V.2 V255	
Mirabell:	What, is the Chief of that noble Family in Town,	400	WAY WOBLD	I.1	187
Mirabell:	with Ratifia and the most noble Spirit of Clary,--but	451	WAY WORLD	IV.1	274

Noblest (1)
Gonsalez:	And Captains of the Noblest Blood of Affrick,	331	M. BRIDE	I.1	235

Nobly (1)
Zara:	I am your Captive, and you've us'd me Nobly;	364	M. BRIDE	IV.1	136

Nobus (0)   see Corum Nobus

Nod (2)
Zara:	Waiting my Nod, the Creature of my Lord,	349	M. BRIDE	II.2	365
Zara:	Waiting my Nod, the Creature of my Pow'r,	349	M. BRIDE	II.2 V365	

Nodding (1)

| Fainall: | nodding Husband would not wake, that e'er the watchful | . 414 | WAY WORLD | II.1 148 |

Noise (11)

Bellmour:	being full of blustring noise and emptiness--	. . 47	OLD BATCH	I.1 378
Bellmour:	take a drubbing with as little noise as a Pulpit Cushion.	. 47	OLD BATCH	I.1 381
Bellmour:	Here's no body, nor no noise;--'twas nothing	 89	OLD BATCH	IV.4 1
Careless:	man must endure the noise of words without Sence, I think	. 127	DOUEL DLR	I.1 8
Mellefont:	Patience purchase folly, and Attention be paid with noise:	. 129	DOUBL DLR	I.1 69
Mellefont:	am Jealous of a Plot. I would have Noise and Impertinence	. 129	DOUEL DLR	I.1 75
Lord Touch:	--hark! what noise!	. 197	DOUEL DLR	V.1 370
	These Walls but t'other Day were fill'd with Ncise	. . 315	FOR LOVE	EPI. 28
Almeria:	It was a fancy'd Noise; for all is hush'd.	 339	M. BRIDE	II.1 52
Osmyn-Alph:	What Ncise! Who's there? My Friend, how cam'st	. . 350	M. ERIDE	III.1 39
Gonsalez:	What Noise! some body coming? 'st, Alonzo?	 376	M. ERIDE	V.2 10

Noisie (1)

| Careless: | No faith, but your Fools grow noisie--and if a | . . . 127 | DOUEL DLR | I.1 V 7 |

Noisy (2)

| Careless: | No faith, but your Fools grow noisy--and if a | . . . . 127 | DOUEL DLR | I.1 7 |
| Mrs Fain: | Yonder Sir Wilfull's Drunk; and so noisy that | . . . 452 | WAY WORLD | IV.1 310 |

Nol (1)

| Capt Bluff: | by the Wars--Took no more notice, than as if Nol. Bluffe | . 53 | OLD BATCH | II.1 204 |

Noli prosequi (2)

| Witwoud: | Noli prosequi and stop't their proceedings. | . . . . 453 | WAY WORLD | IV.1 330 |
| Witwoud: | Noli prosequi and stop't the Proceedings. | . . . . 453 | WAY WORLD | IV.1 V330 |

Non Compos (3)

Buckram:	What, is he Non Ccmpos?	. 279	FCR LOVE	IV.1 140
Jeremy:	Quite Ncn Compos, Sir.	. 279	FOR LOVE	IV.1 141
Lady Wish:	My Nephew was non Compos; and cou'd not	 469	WAY WORLD	V.1 286

Non Compos mentis (1)

| Buckram: | Non Ccmpos mentis, his Act and Deed will be of no effect, | . 279 | FOR LOVE | IV.1 143 |

Non compos mentis (1)

| Scandal: | has been heartily vex'd--His Son is Non compos mentis, and | 283 | FOR LOVE | IV.1 298 |

None (44)

Vainlove:	I do Wine--And this Business is none of my seeking; I	. . 39	OLD BATCH	I.1 95
Bellmour:	morning was none of her own? for I know thou art as	. - 42	OLD BATCH	I.1 185
Heartwell:	of the intention, and none of the pleasure of the practice--	. 43	OLD BATCH	I.1 239
Bellmour:	Till he has created Love where there was none, and	. - 58	OLD BATCH	II.2 131
Lucy:	I had none, but through Mistake.	. 97	OLD BATCH	V.1 40
Mellefont:	Truth. Prithee do thou wear none to day; but allow Brisk	. 129	DOUEL DLR	I.1 71
Mellefont:	to be allarm'd. None besides you, and Maskwell, are	. 129	DOUBL DLR	I.1 84
Maskwell:	Mellefont upcn the brink of Ruin, and left him ncne	. 137	DOUBL DLR	I.1 V378
Lady Ply:	was intended to me. Your Honour! You have none, . .	. 144	DOUEL DLR	II.1 235
Cynthia:	jests in their Persons, though they have none in their	. 163	DOUBL DLR	III.1 484
Lady Ply:	should die, cf all Mankind there's none I'd sooner make	. 170	DOUEL DLR	IV.1 111
Sir Paul:	make cf none effect your Oath: So you may unswear it	. 171	DOUEL DLR	IV.1 145
Brisk:	thinking what to say? None but dull Rogues think; witty	. 175	DOUEL DLR	IV.1 299
Mellefont:	None, Hell has served you even as Heaven has	. . . 185	DOUEL DLR	IV.2 59
Maskwell:	None, your Text is short.	. 195	DOUEL DLR	V.1 297
	Affront to none, but frankly speaks his mind.	 214	FOR LOVE	PRO. 44
Nurse:	Wee'st heart, I know not, they're none of 'em come	. . 235	FOR LCVE	II.1 19
Singer-F:	He alone won't Betray in whom none will Confide,	. . . 259	FOR LCVE	III.1 207
Miss Prue:	(aside to Mrs. Frail). Pish, he shall be none of my	. . 259	FOR LCVE	III.1 218
Ben:	d'ee see that was none of my seeking, I was commanded	. 263	FOR LCVE	III.1 373
Foresight:	my Pulses ha!--I have none--Mercy on me--hum--Yes,	. . 269	FOR LCVE	III.1 606
Foresight:	This is none of your lucky Hour; Nemo omnibus horis sapit.	. 283	FOR LCVE	IV.1 294
Ben:	look after a Husband; for my part I was none of her	. . 285	FOR LCVE	IV.1 375
Valentine:	closer--that none may over-hear us;--Jeremy, I can tell you	290	FOR LCVE	IV.1 557
Sr Sampson:	outsides. Hang your side-Box Beaus; no, I'm none of those,	. 298	FOR LOVE	V.1 34
Sr Sampson:	none of your forc'd Trees, that pretend to Blossom in the	. 298	FOR LCVE	V.1 35
Sr Sampson:	a long liv'd Race, and inherit Vigour, none of my Family	. 298	FOR LCVE	V.1 37
Sr Sampson:	a long liv'd Race, and inherit Vigour, none of my Ancestors	298	FOR LCVE	V.1 V 37
Sr Sampson:	None of old Foresight's Sybills ever utter'd such a	. . 299	FOR LOVE	V.1 79
Zara:	Requires he should be more confin'd; and none,	. . . 360	M. ERIDE	III.1 450
Selim:	That none but Mutes may have Admittance to him.	. . . 362	M. EBIDE	IV.1 58
Manuel:	Are none return'd of those who fcllow'd Heli?	 363	M. EBIDE	IV.1 74
Gonsalez:	None, Sir. Scme Papers have been since discover'd,	. . . 363	M. EBIDE	IV.1 75
Zara:	You order none may have Admittance to	. 365	M. EBIDE	IV.1 162
Zara:	You give strict Charge, that none may be admitted	. . . 365	M. EBIDE	IV.1 V162
Manuel:	None, say you, none? what not the Fav'rite Eunuch?	. . 372	M. EBIDE	V.1 2
Perez:	None, my Lord.	. 372	M. EBIDE	V.1 5
	That hurts none here, sure here are none of those.	. . 393	WAY WORLD	PRO. 36
Marwood:	now I'll have none of him. Here comes the good Lady,	. . 431	WAY WCRLD	III.1 246
Fainall:	none to me, she can take none frcm me, 'tis against all rule	443	WAY WCRLD	III.1 687
Sir Wilful:	frown desperately, because her face is none of her own;	. 471	WAY WORLD	V.1 362

Nonsence (1)

| Careless: | Nonsence better. . . . . | . 127 | DOUEL DLR | I.1 10 |

Nonsense (1)

| Lord Touch: | --Pho, 'tis nonsense. Come, come; I know my Lady | . . 150 | DOUEL DLR | III.1 5 |

Noon (4)

Heartwell:	What rugged Ways attend the Noon of Life!	 112	OLD BATCH	V.2 191
Valentine:	Clocks will strike Twelve at Noon, and the Horn'd Herd	. 289	FOR LOVE	IV.1 504
Gonsalez:	I'th' Morning he must die again; e're Ncon	 366	M. BRIDE	IV.1 210
Gonsalez:	And all as still, as at the Noon of Night!	 376	M. EBIDE	V.2 2

Noon-day (1)

| Sr Sampson: | sets at Noon-day. . . . . | . 241 | FOR LOVE | II.1 209 |

Nor (122)

North (2)

| Heartwell: | It will as soon blow North and by South--marry | . . . . 44 | OLD BATCH | I.1 294 |
| Heartwell: | There stands my North, and thither my Needle points | . . 63 | OLD BATCH | III.1 75 |

North-East (1)

| Sr Sampson: | way to come to it, but by the North-East Passage. | . . . 308 | FOR LOVE | V.1 428 |

Northern (1)

| Fainall: | at present Practis'd in the Northern Hemisphere. But this | . 469 | WAY WORLD | V.1 276 |

Nose (8)

| Heartwell: | such a place, about his Nose and Eyes; though a' has my | . 45 | OLD BATCH | I.1 323 |
| Heartwell: | such a place, about his Nose and Eyes; though he has my | . 45 | OLD BATCH | I.1 V323 |

```
Nose  (continued)
  Sr Sampson:   the Nose in one's Face: What, are my Eyes better than  .  .  281  FOR LOVE  IV.1  225
  Valentine:    by the Nose. .  .  .  .  .  .  .  .  .  .  .  .  .  .  .  282  FOR LOVE  IV.1  242
  Valentine:    his Nose always, will very often be led into a Stink.  .  282  FOR LOVE  IV.1  254
  Foible:       With his Taunts and his Fleers, tossing up his Nose. Humh  427  WAY WORLD III.1  94
  Sir Wilful:   Time, when you liv'd with honest Pumple Nose the Attorney  .  439  WAY WORLD III.1  549
  Lady Wish:    and Weaving of dead Hair, with a bleak blew Nose, over a  .  462  WAY WORLD  V.1   5
Noster (0)       see Pater-noster
Nostrodamus (1)
  Sr Sampson:   Nostrodamus. What, I warrant my Son thought nothing  .  .  240  FOR LOVE  II.1  175
Not (1193)
Note (6)
  Capt Bluff:   You have given him a note upon Fondlewife for a  .  .  .  67  OLD BATCH III.1  245
  Capt Bluff:   and live, go, and force him, to redeliver you the Note--  .  67  OLD BATCH III.1  250
  Sharper:      Sir Joseph--Your Note was accepted, and the  .  .  .  .  68  OLD BATCH III.1  284
  Careless:     so transported I cannot speak--This Note will inform  .  171  DOUBL DLR  IV.1  129
  Careless:     you. (Gives her a Note)  .  .  .  .  .  .  .  .  .  .  171  DOUBL DLR  IV.1  130
  Marwood:      Your merry Note may be chang'd sooner  .  .  .  .  .  434  WAY WORLD III.1  363
Notes (5)
  Brisk:        Coach-man--you may put that into the marginal Notes,  .  .  165  DOUBL DLR III.1  550
  Brisk:        Coach-man--you may put that in the marginal Notes,  .  .  165  DOUBL DLR III.1 V550
  Lady Froth:   I will; you'd oblige me extremely to write Notes  .  .  165  DOUBL DLR III.1  554
  Gonsalez:     Of the same Nature, divers Notes have been  .  .  .  363  M. BRIDE  IV.1  81
  Marwood:      Temple, take Notes like Prentices at a Conventicle; and  .  467  WAY WORLD  V.1  225
Nothing (108)
  Bellmour:     Ay ay, pox Wisdom's nothing but a pretending to  .  .  .  .  37  OLD BATCH  I.1  19
  Bellmour:     Ay, ay, Wisdom's nothing but a pretending to  .  .  .  .  37  OLD BATCH  I.1 V 19
  Bellmour:     nothing. Come come, leave Business to Idlers, and Wisdom  .  37  OLD BATCH  I.1  22
  Bellmour:     But do you know nothing of a new Rival there?  .  .  .  .  40  OLD BATCH  I.1  117
  Sharper:      to me is Hell; nothing to be found, but the despair of what  .  48  OLD BATCH  II.1  23
  Sir Joseph:   found nothing but what has been to my loss, as I may say,  .  48  OLD BATCH  II.1  30
  Capt Bluff:   be nothing, Nothing in the Earth.  .  .  .  .  .  .  .  52  OLD BATCH  II.1  182
  Capt Bluff:   Oh I thought so--Why then you can know nothing  .  .  .  52  OLD BATCH  II.1  187
  Sir Joseph:   nothing. .  .  .  .  .  .  .  .  .  .  .  .  .  .  .  53  OLD BATCH  II.1  223
  Araminta:     Heart knows nothing of.  .  .  .  .  .  .  .  .  .  58  OLD BATCH  II.2  138
  Bellmour:     Nothing, Madam, only--  .  .  .  .  .  .  .  {  .  .  59  OLD BATCH  II.2  162
  Barnaby:      Sir, the Hour draws nigh--And nothing will be  .  .  .  76  OLD BATCH  IV.1  34
  Fondlewife:   And nothing can be done here till I go--So that  .  .  .  76  OLD BATCH  IV.1  36
  Laetitia:     (aside). I'me amaz'd; sure he has discover'd nothing--  .  77  OLD BATCH  IV.1  79
  Bellmour:     I cou'd think of nothing all Day but putting 'em in practice  82  OLD BATCH  IV.2  54
  Bellmour:     Here's no body, nor no noise;--'twas nothing  .  .  .  89  OLD BATCH  IV.4  1
  Fondlewife:   Womans-flesh. What, you know nothing of him, but his  .  93  OLD BATCH  IV.4  144
  Laetitia:     think that I have nothing to do but excuse him; 'tis enough,  93  OLD BATCH  IV.4  168
  Bellmour:     No, I have brought nothing but Ballast back,--  .  .  .  96  OLD BATCH  V.1  4
  Setter:       Her head runs on nothing else, nor she can talk of  .  .  102  OLD BATCH  V.1  198
  Setter:       nothing else. .  .  .  .  .  .  .  .  .  .  .  .  .  102  OLD BATCH  V.1  199
  Setter:       honest is nothing; the Reputation of it is all. Reputation!  102  OLD BATCH  V.1  229
  Mellefont:    In short, the Consequence was thus, she omitted nothing,  .  130  DOUBL DLR  I.1  109
  Mellefont:    Pooh, pooh, nothing in the World but his design  .  .  .  131  DOUBL DLR  I.1  155
  Lord Froth:   I often smile at your Conceptions, But there is nothing  .  132  DOUBL DLR  I.1  198
  Brisk:        Pooh, my Lord, his Voice goes for nothing.--I  .  .  .  134  DOUBL DLR  I.1  276
  Maskwell:     Fix'd, Rooted in my Heart, whence nothing can  .  .  .  136  DOUBL DLR  I.1  352
  Maskwell:     needs this? I say nothing but what your self, in open hours  137  DOUBL DLR  I.1  384
  Maskwell:     needs this? I say nothing but what you your self, in open
                hours  .  .  .  .  .  .  .  .  .  .  .  .  .  .  137  DOUBL DLR  I.1 V384
  Lady Froth:   and as much a Man of Quality! Ah! Nothing at all  .  .  139  DOUBL DLR  II.1  29
  Lady Froth:   nothing, but a Blue Ribbon and a Star, to make him Shine,  .  139  DOUBL DLR  II.1  31
  Lord Froth:   No, no, I'll allow Mr. Brisk; have you nothing  .  .  .  142  DOUBL DLR  II.1  141
  Sir Paul:     hither Girl, go not near him, there's nothing but deceit  .  145  DOUBL DLR  II.1  246
  Sir Paul:     fit for nothing but to be a Stalking-Horse, to stand before  145  DOUBL DLR  II.1  266
  Lady Ply:     nothing could be guilty of it--  .  .  .  .  .  .  146  DOUBL DLR  II.1  292
  Lady Touch:   nothing but--  .  .  .  .  .  .  .  .  .  .  .  .  152  DOUBL DLR III.1  73
  Lady Touch:   your promise--Pho, why nothing, only your Nephew had  .  152  DOUBL DLR III.1  82
  Lady Ply:     for I'm sure there's nothing in the World that I would  .  159  DOUBL DLR III.1  342
  Cynthia:      Perspective all this while; for nothing has been between us  168  DOUBL DLR  IV.1  25
  Lady Ply:     And say so many fine things, and nothing is so moving to  .  169  DOUBL DLR  IV.1  70
  Lady Ply:     No, no, nothing else I thank you, Sir Paul,--  .  .  .  173  DOUBL DLR  IV.1  220
  Brisk:        --The matter Madam? Nothing, Madam, nothing at  .  .  175  DOUBL DLR  IV.1  314
  Maskwell:     I have nothing more to say, my Lord--but to  .  .  .  182  DOUBL DLR  IV.1  560
  Maskwell:     He has own'd nothing to me of late, and what I  .  .  .  183  DOUBL DLR  IV.1  582
  Lord Touch:   Writings are ready drawn, and wanted nothing but to be  .  189  DOUBL DLR  V.1  62
  Maskwell:     then were fine work indeed! her fury wou'd spare nothing,  .  190  DOUBL DLR  V.1  93
  Mellefont:    are all in my Chamber; I want nothing but the Habit.  .  .  196  DOUBL DLR  V.1  344
  Maskwell:     than in the Death of one who is nothing when not yours.  .  199  DOUBL DLR  V.1  451
  Maskwell:     than in the Heart of one who is nothing when not yours.  .  199  DOUBL DLR  V.1  451
                Till Dice are thrown, there's nothing won, nor lost.  .  .  204  DOUBL DLR  EPI.  5
  Jeremy:       there is nothing to be eaten. .  .  .  .  .  .  .  216  FOR LOVE  I.1  22
  Jeremy:       and keeping Company with Wits, that car'd for nothing  .  217  FOR LOVE  I.1  46
  Jeremy:       Nothing thrives that belongs to't. The Man of the House  .  218  FOR LOVE  I.1  89
  Jeremy:       nothing to it for a Whetter; yet I never see it, but the  .  218  FOR LOVE  I.1  94
  Jeremy:       Nothing new, Sir; I have dispatch'd some half a  .  .  .  220  FOR LOVE  I.1  166
  Tattle:       For there is nothing more known, than that no body  .  .  227  FOR LOVE  I.1  404
  Tattle:       Pooh, pooh, nothing at all, I only rally'd with you  .  .  228  FOR LOVE  I.1  445
  Scandal:      No, nothing under a Right Honourable.  .  .  .  .  .  230  FOR LOVE  I.1  531
  Scandal:      Hang him, he has nothing but the Seasons and the  .  .  232  FOR LOVE  I.1  601
  Sr Sampson:   Nostrodamus. What, I warrant my Son thought nothing  .  .  240  FOR LOVE  II.1  175
  Sr Sampson:   Authority, no Correction, no Arbitrary Power; nothing  .  240  FOR LOVE  II.1  177
  Sr Sampson:   --Why nothing under an Emperour should be born  .  .  245  FOR LOVE  II.1  351
  Tattle:       to no purpose--But since we have done nothing, we must  .  253  FOR LOVE III.1  22
  Tattle:       say nothing, I think. I hear her--I'll leave you together,  .  254  FOR LOVE III.1  23
  Scandal:      Pooh, pox, this proves nothing.  .  .  .  .  .  .  257  FOR LOVE III.1  152
  Scandal:      Pooh, this proves nothing.  .  .  .  .  .  .  .  .  257  FOR LOVE III.1 V152
  Tattle:       For Heaven's sake, if you do guess, say nothing; Gad,  .  258  FOR LOVE III.1  194
  Scandal:      two. I can get nothing out of him but Sighs. He desires  .  266  FOR LOVE III.1  501
  Scandal:      Cards, sometimes, but that's nothing.  .  .  .  .  .  271  FOR LOVE III.1  667
  Ben:          Mess, I love to speak my mind--Father has nothing  .  .  272  FOR LOVE III.1  713
```

Nothing   (continued)

Speaker	Text	PAGE	TITLE	ACT.SC	LINE
Mrs Frail:	in short, I will deny thee nothing.	293	FOR LOVE	IV.1	674
Valentine:	From a Riddle, you can expect nothing but a	296	FOR LOVE	IV.1	795
Ben:	before you shall guess at the matter, and do nothing else;	306	FOR LOVE	V.1	353
Ben:	Look you, Friend, it's nothing to me, whether you	307	FOR LOVE	V.1	368
Sr Sampson:	the Conveyance so worded, that nothing can possibly	308	FOR LOVE	V.1	425
Mrs Frail:	nothing but his being my Husband could have made me	310	FOR LOVE	V.1	473
Valentine:	vain Attempts, and find at last, that nothing but my Ruine	312	FOR LOVE	V.1	547
Almeria:	nothing	328	M. BRIDE	I.1	89
Almeria:	Know'st nothing of my Sorrows	328	M. BRIDE	I.1	V 89
Almeria:	And when I said thou didst know nothing,	328	M. BRIDE	I.1	100
Almeria:	And when I told thee thou didst nothing know,	328	M. BRIDE	I.1	V100
Garcia:	Nothing remains to do, or to require,	377	M. BRIDE	V.2	65
Mirabell:	with a constrain'd Smile told her, I thought nothing was so	396	WAY WORLD	I.1	38
Mirabell:	nothing.	397	WAY WORLD	I.1	89
Witwoud:	this is nothing to what he us'd to do;--Before he	405	WAY WORLD	I.1	365
Petulant:	Not I--I mean no Body--I know nothing	406	WAY WORLD	I.1	428
Petulant:	Explain, I know nothing--Why you have an	407	WAY WORLD	I.1	434
Petulant:	I, nothing I. If Throats are to be cut, let Swords	407	WAY WORLD	I.1	446
Fainall:	Nothing remains when that Day comes, but to sit down	413	WAY WORLD	II.1	115
Lady Wish:	do with him in the Park? Answer me, has he got nothing	427	WAY WORLD	III.1	82
Lady Wish:	. . . Nothing but Importunity can surmount Decorums.	429	WAY WORLD	III.1	V179
Millamant:	Nay, he has done nothing; he has only talk'd--	432	WAY WORLD	III.1	291
Millamant:	Nay, he has said nothing neither; but he has contradicted	432	WAY WORLD	III.1	292
Lady Wish:	nothing is more alluring than a Levee from a Couch in	445	WAY WORLD	IV.1	29
Sir Wilful:	Nay nothing--Only for the walks sake, that's	448	WAY WORLD	IV.1	119
Millamant:	Ha, ha, ha. Yes, 'tis like I may.--You have nothing	448	WAY WORLD	IV.1	132
Millamant:	O, I should think I was poor and had nothing to	449	WAY WORLD	IV.1	167
Waitwell:	starve upward and upward, till he has nothing living but	458	WAY WORLD	IV.1	523
Lady Wish:	traytress, that I rais'd from nothing--begon, begon,	462	WAY WORLD	V.1	3
Lady Wish:	where the Leud Trebles squeek nothing but Bawdy, and	467	WAY WORLD	V.1	200
Marwood:	Nay this is nothing; if it wou'd end here,	468	WAY WORLD	V.1	229
Marwood:	hear nothing else for some days.	468	WAY WORLD	V.1	236
Marwood:	Nay Madam, I advise nothing, I only lay before	468	WAY WORLD	V.1	241
Sir Wilful:	you nothing, Aunt--Come, come, Forgive and Forget	471	WAY WORLD	V.1	381
Petulant:	Not I. I writ. I read nothing.	476	WAY WORLD	V.1	531
Witwoud:	I Gad I understand nothing of the matter,--I'm	477	WAY WORLD	V.1	590

Nothing's (1)

Speaker	Text	PAGE	TITLE	ACT.SC	LINE
Musician:	Nothing's new besides our Faces,	60	OLD BATCH	II.2	201

Notice (12)

Speaker	Text	PAGE	TITLE	ACT.SC	LINE
Capt Bluff:	by the Wars--Took no more notice, than as if Nol. Bluffe	53	OLD BATCH	II.1	204
Mellefont:	narrowly, and give me notice upon any Suspicion. As for	130	DOUBL DLR	I.1	137
Lady Touch:	take any notice of it to him.	153	DOUBL DLR	III.1	92
Lady Touch:	me if you take such publick notice of it, it will be a	153	DOUBL DLR	III.1	104
	Town-talk:				
Maskwell:	you shall have notice at the critical minute to come and	157	DOUBL DLR	III.1	249
Maskwell:	and give you notice.	157	DOUBL DLR	III.1	261
Lady Froth:	Take no notice--But observe me--Now	177	DOUBL DLR	IV.1	365
Cynthia:	immediately to follow you, and give you notice.	196	DOUBL DLR	V.1	349
Scandal:	Well, begin then: But take notice, if you are so ill a	230	FOR LOVE	I.1	536
Valentine:	never distinguish it self enough, to be taken notice of. If	313	FOR LOVE	V.1	610
Mirabell:	Town took notice that she was grown fat of a suddain;	397	WAY WORLD	I.1	74
Witwoud:	more Company here to take notice of him--Why	405	WAY WORLD	I.1	364

Notion (2)

Speaker	Text	PAGE	TITLE	ACT.SC	LINE
Tattle:	I fancy you have a wrong Notion of Faces.	304	FOR LOVE	V.1	265
Foresight:	How? What? A wrong Notion! How so?	304	FOR LOVE	V.1	266

Notions (1)

Speaker	Text	PAGE	TITLE	ACT.SC	LINE
Lady Ply:	any dishonourable Notions of things; so that if this be	172	DOUBL DLR	IV.1	168

Notorious (1)

Speaker	Text	PAGE	TITLE	ACT.SC	LINE
Tattle:	or the Naked Prince. And it is notorious, that in a Country	257	FOR LOVE	III.1	162

Notoriously (1)

Speaker	Text	PAGE	TITLE	ACT.SC	LINE
Valentine:	then ever, and appear more notoriously her Admirer in	217	FOR LOVE	I.1	51

Notwithstanding (2)

Speaker	Text	PAGE	TITLE	ACT.SC	LINE
Bellmour:	notwithstanding the Warning and Example before me, I	112	OLD BATCH	V.2	166
Careless:	them, you do not suspect: Notwithstanding her Passion for				
	you.	131	DOUBL DLR	I.1	V154

Nought (3)

Speaker	Text	PAGE	TITLE	ACT.SC	LINE
Maskwell:	Mellefont upon the brink of Ruin, and left him nought	137	DOUBL DLR	I.1	378
Lord Touch:	Is't for your self?--I'll hear of nought for	189	DOUBL DLR	V.1	69
Scandal:	There's nought but willing, waking Love, that can	275	FOR LOVE	III.1	819

Nourishment (1)

Speaker	Text	PAGE	TITLE	ACT.SC	LINE
Valentine:	your Flesh; Read, and take your Nourishment in at your	216	FOR LOVE	I.1	14

Novel (2)

Speaker	Text	PAGE	TITLE	ACT.SC	LINE
Brisk:	particular and novel in the Humour; 'tis true, it makes	133	DOUBL DLR	I.1	238
Tattle:	own, in Conversation, by way of Novel: but never have	256	FOR LOVE	III.1	119

Novels (1)

Speaker	Text	PAGE	TITLE	ACT.SC	LINE
Bellmour:	and trusty Scarron's Novels my Prayer-Book.--	80	OLD BATCH	IV.2	6

Novelty (2)

Speaker	Text	PAGE	TITLE	ACT.SC	LINE
Angelica:	Mr. Scandal, I suppose you don't think it a Novelty,	276	FOR LOVE	IV.1	20
Angelica:	In admiring me, you misplace the Novelty.	314	FOR LOVE	V.1	635

Novice (1)

Speaker	Text	PAGE	TITLE	ACT.SC	LINE
Lady Wish:	You are no Novice in the Labyrinth of Love--You	458	WAY WORLD	IV.1	527

Now (359)

Speaker	Text	PAGE	TITLE	ACT.SC	LINE
	But now, no more like Suppliants, we come;	35	OLD BATCH	PRO.	5
	He prays--O bless me! what shall I do now!	35	OLD BATCH	PRO.	19
Bellmour:	Let me see--How now! Dear perfidious Vainlove.	38	OLD BATCH	I.1	35
Bellmour:	How now George, where hast thou been snarling odious	42	OLD BATCH	I.1	180
Sharper:	that's all thou art fit for now.	43	OLD BATCH	I.1	228
Bellmour:	Though you should be now and then interrupted in a	44	OLD BATCH	I.1	268
Heartwell:	in no haste for an Answer--for I shan't stay now.	46	OLD BATCH	I.1	332
Bellmour:	Soldier, which now a'days as often cloaks Cowardice, as a	46	OLD BATCH	I.1	367
Sharper:	now luck!--curs'd fortune! this must be the place, this	48	OLD BATCH	II.1	17
Capt Bluff:	How now, my young Knight? Not for fear I hope; he	51	OLD BATCH	II.1	V142
Capt Bluff:	Sweet Sauce. Now I think--Fighting, for Fighting sake's	52	OLD BATCH	II.1	164
Capt Bluff:	be granted--But Alas Sir! were he alive now, he would	52	OLD BATCH	II.1	181
Capt Bluff:	Gazette! Why there again now--Why, Sir, there are	52	OLD BATCH	II.1	192

Now   (continued)

		PAGE	TITLE	ACT.SC	LINE
Capt Bluff:	Gazette--I'll tell you a strange thing now as to that--	52	OLD BATCH	II.1	194
Sir Joseph:	Look you now, I tell you he's so modest he'l own	53	OLD BATCH	II.1	222
Sir Joseph:	Nay, now I must speak; it will split a Hair by the	53	OLD BATCH	II.1	232
Capt Bluff:	see it; Sir I say you can't see; what de'e say to that now?	53	OLD BATCH	II.1	235
Belinda:	now; could you but see with my Eyes, the buffoonry of	55	OLD BATCH	II.2	31
Araminta:	Oh is it come out--Now you are angry, I am sure	56	OLD BATCH	II.2	58
Araminta:	I am oblig'd to you--But who's malicious now,	57	OLD BATCH	II.2	109
Araminta:	--Every Man, now, changes his Mistress and his	58	OLD BATCH	II.2	148
Heartwell:	Why whither in the Devils name am I going now?	62	OLD BATCH	III.1	63
Heartwell:	Why whither in the Devils name am I a-going now?	62	OLD BATCH	III.1 V	63
Bellmour:	Now Venus forbid!	62	OLD BATCH	III.1	71
Heartwell:	--Now could I curse my self, yet cannot repent. O	63	OLD BATCH	III.1	76
Lucy:	Now Poverty and the Pox light upon thee, for a	65	OLD BATCH	III.1	163
Setter:	Why how now! prithee who art? lay by that Worldly	65	OLD BATCH	III.1	179
Lucy:	Where is he now?	67	OLD BATCH	III.1	230
Lucy:	now--I'me not 'ith humour. (Exit.)	67	OLD BATCH	III.1	237
Sir Joseph:	Teeth. Adsheart if he should come just now when I'm	68	OLD BATCH	III.1	278
Bellmour:	you ought to return him Thanks now you have receiv'd	68	OLD BATCH	III.1	282
Capt Bluff:	Husht, 'tis not so convenient now--I shall find a	69	OLD BATCH	III.1	313
Sir Joseph:	dear Captain, don't be in Passion now, he's gone--	70	OLD BATCH	III.1	340
Heartwell:	Now by my Soul, I cannot lie, though it were to serve a	72	OLD BATCH	III.2	59
Silvia:	(Throws the Purse) I hate you now, and I'll never see you	74	OLD BATCH	III.2	111
Fondlewife:	--Nay look you now if she does not weep--'tis the fondest	78	OLD BATCH	IV.1	98
Sharper:	breeding Love to thee all this while, and just now she is	79	OLD BATCH	IV.1	167
Bellmour:	tho' now they are o'er-cast.	81	OLD BATCH	IV.2	22
Laetitia:	not surpriz'd me: Methinks, now I look on him again,	81	OLD BATCH	IV.2	44
Bellmour:	--'till just now, (the first time I ever look'd upon the	82	OLD BATCH	IV.2	55
Laetitia:	Nay, now--- (aside) I never saw any thing so agreeably	82	OLD BATCH	IV.2	79
Laetitia:	Impudent. Won't you censure me for this, now;--but 'tis	82	OLD BATCH	IV.2	80
Belinda:	me now? Hideous, ha? Frightful still? Or how?	83	OLD BATCH	IV.3	17
Sir Joseph:	(aside). Now am I slap-dash down in the Mouth,	85	OLD BATCH	IV.3	90
Sir Joseph:	(aside). Nay, now I'm in--I can prattle like a	85	OLD BATCH	IV.3	97
Vainlove:	Now must I pretend ignorance equal to hers, of	87	OLD BATCH	IV.3	136
Vainlove:	(aside). Hey day! Which way now? Here's fine	87	OLD BATCH	IV.3	160
Araminta:	Woman's Curiosity now tempts me to see.	88	OLD BATCH	IV.3	191
Belinda:	How now, Pace? Where's my Cousin?	88	OLD BATCH	IV.3	205
Laetitia:	(aside). What can I do now! Oh! my Dear, I have	91	OLD BATCH	IV.4	76
Laetitia:	(aside). Misfortune! Now all's ruin'd again.	92	OLD BATCH	IV.4	108
Fondlewife:	Who, how now! Who have we here?	92	OLD BATCH	IV.4	122
Laetitia:	Indeed, and indeed, now my dear Nykin--I never	93	OLD BATCH	IV.4	139
Bellmour:	(aside). Well, now I know my Cue.--That is	93	OLD BATCH	IV.4	147
Lucy:	Now, Goodness have Mercy upon me! Mr. Bellmour!	97	OLD BATCH	V.1	29
Sharper:	Just now, say you, gone in with Lucy?	98	OLD BATCH	V.1	82
Sharper:	Now, were I ill-natur'd, wou'd I utterly disappoint	100	OLD BATCH	V.1	137
Capt Bluff:	Fear him not,--I am prepar'd for him now; and he	101	OLD BATCH	V.1	167
Sir Joseph:	Ay, now it's out; 'tis I, my own individual Person.	102	OLD BATCH	V.1	206
Setter:	Were I a Rogue now, what a noble Prize could I	102	OLD BATCH	V.1	221
Sir Joseph:	Now--	103	OLD BATCH	V.1	250
Sir Joseph:	How now, Bully? What, melancholy because	103	OLD BATCH	V.1	260
Sharper:	How now?	105	OLD BATCH	V.1	312
Sharper:	(Now hold Spleen.) Married!	105	OLD BATCH	V.1	314
Sharper:	I'm in haste now, but I'll come in at the Catastrophe.	107	OLD BATCH	V.1 V	393
Bellmour:	You have an Opportunity now, Madam, to revenge	107	OLD BATCH	V.1	395
Bellmour:	Now George, What Rhyming! I thought the	108	OLD BATCH	V.2	17
Sir Joseph:	whom I have got--now, but all's forgiven.	110	OLD BATCH	V.2	114
Bellmour:	Now set we forward on a Journey for Life:--	112	OLD BATCH	V.2	182
	Now the Deed's done, the Giddy-thing has leasure	113	OLD BATCH	EPI.	8
	Now that's at stake--No fool, 'tis out o'fashion.	113	OLD BATCH	EPI.	12
Careless:	Why, how now, why this extravagant proposition?	129	DOUBL DLR	I.1	73
Sir Paul:	Nay, I protest and vow now, 'tis true; when Mr.	132	DOUBL DLR	I.1	187
Lord Froth:	pleases the Croud! Now when I Laugh, I always Laugh	132	DOUBL DLR	I.1	204
Lord Froth:	now I think I have Conquer'd it.	133	DOUBL DLR	I.1	236
Brisk:	little shallow, or so.--Why I'll tell you now, suppose	133	DOUBL DLR	I.1	252
Brisk:	now, you come up to me--nay, prithee Careless be	133	DOUBL DLR	I.1	253
Cynthia:	with her now.	140	DOUBL DLR	II.1	59
Lady Froth:	I'm not asham'd to own it now; ah! it makes my heart	140	DOUBL DLR	II.1	62
Lady Froth:	vow now.	140	DOUBL DLR	II.1	78
Mellefont:	and Cutt, let's e'en turn up Trump now.	142	DOUBL DLR	II.1	161
Lady Ply:	How now! will you be pleased to retire,	144	DOUBL DLR	II.1	209
Lady Ply:	now, who are you? What am I? 'Slidikins can't I govern	144	DOUBL DLR	II.1	215
Lady Ply:	your face; for now Sir Paul's gone, you are Corum Nobus.	146	DOUBL DLR	II.1	299
Lady Ply:	happen together,--to my thinking, now I could	147	DOUBL DLR	II.1	326
Maskwell:	I would not have you stay to hear it now; for I	149	DOUBL DLR	II.1	432
Lady Touch:	Lord--Ha, ha, ha. Well but that's all--now you have	153	DOUBL DLR	III.1	90
Lady Touch:	were more, 'tis over now, and all's well. For my part I	153	DOUBL DLR	III.1	96
Lady Touch:	let me beg you do now: I'll come immediately, and tell	153	DOUBL DLR	III.1	119
Lady Touch:	Well but go now, here's some body coming.	153	DOUBL DLR	III.1	122
Maskwell:	little stomach to her now as if I were her Husband. Should	155	DOUBL DLR	III.1	179
Maskwell:	Here he comes, now for me--	155	DOUBL DLR	III.1	194
Mellefont:	How now, Jack? What, so full of Contemplation	155	DOUBL DLR	III.1	198
Sir Paul:	So, now, now; now my Lady.	160	DOUBL DLR	III.1	360
Lady Froth:	that he peeps now and then, yet he does shine all the day	164	DOUBL DLR	III.1	524
Lord Froth:	Shall I tell you now?	166	DOUBL DLR	III.1	598
Lord Froth:	Where's the Wonder now?	166	DOUBL DLR	III.1	601
Lady Froth:	How now?	166	DOUBL DLR	III.1	604
Lady Ply:	now you make me swear--O Gratitude forbid, that I	169	DOUBL DLR	IV.1	79
Cynthia:	you had not chang'd sides so soon; now I begin to find it.	172	DOUBL DLR	IV.1	177
Lady Ply:	O law now, I swear and declare, it shan't be so,	172	DOUBL DLR	IV.1	185
Lady Ply:	(Aside.) So now I can read my own Letter under the cover	173	DOUBL DLR	IV.1	221
Sir Paul:	O Law, what's the matter now? I hope you are not	174	DOUBL DLR	IV.1	269
Sir Paul:	done with her now.	174	DOUBL DLR	IV.1	276
Brisk:	So now they are all gone, and I have an opportunity to	175	DOUBL DLR	IV.1	290
Brisk:	she would follow me into the Gallery--Now to make	175	DOUBL DLR	IV.1	296
Lady Froth:	Just now as I came in, bless me, why don't you	176	DOUBL DLR	IV.1	323
Lord Froth:	The Company are all ready--How now!	177	DOUBL DLR	IV.1	362

481

Now   (continued)

Speaker	Text	Page	Title	Act.Sc	Line
Lady Froth:	Take no notice--Eut observe me--Now	177	DOUBL DLR	IV.1	365
Lady Froth:	near any other Man. Oh here's my Lord, now you shall .	177	DOUBL DLR	IV.1	369
Sir Paul:	Pleasures to preserve its Purity, and must I now find it	179	DOUBL DLR	IV.1	429
Sir Paul:	Chaste as Ice, but you are melted now, and false as Water.	179	DOUBL DLR	IV.1	431
Lady Ply:	now, Sir Paul, what do you think of your Friend Careless?	179	DOUBL DLR	IV.1	438
Lady Ply:	now I find was of your own inditing--I do Heathen, . . .	179	DOUBL DLR	IV.1	456
Sir Paul:	Why now as I hope to be saved, I had no hand in . . .	180	DOUBL DLR	IV.1	468
Sir Paul:	The Devil take me now if he did not go beyond my . .	180	DOUBL DLR	IV.1	470
Mellefont:	I go this moment: Now Fortune I defie thee.	181	DOUBL DLR	IV.1	525
Maskwell:	mean now, is only a bare Suspicion of my own. If your . .	183	DOUBL DLR	IV.1	583
Lady Touch:	the Glass, and now I find it it is my self; Can you have mercy	185	DOUBL DLR	IV.2	72
Lady Touch:	the Glass, and now I find 'tis my self; Can you have mercy	185	DOUBL DLR	IV.2 V	72
Mellefont:	Now, by my Soul, I will not go till I have made	186	DOUBL DLR	IV.2	121
Maskwell:	Now Heaven forbid--	189	DOUBL DLR	V.1	60
Maskwell:	comes opportunely--now will I, in my old way, . . .	190	DOUBL DLR	V.1	97
Lady Touch:	. . . now I see what	191	DOUBL DLR	V.1	147
Sir Paul:	Why, what's the matter now? Good Lord, what's . .	192	DOUBL DLR	V.1	185
Maskwell:	--Now to prepare my Lord to consent to this.-- . . .	194	DOUBL DLR	V.1	266
Careless:	Is not that he, now gone out with my Lord?	196	DOUBL DLR	V.1	333
Cynthia:	How's this! now I fear indeed.	197	DOUBL DLR	V.1	361
Lady Touch:	Now, now, now I am calm, and can hear	198	DOUBL DLR	V.1	410
Maskwell:	(aside). Thanks, my invention; and now I have it . .	198	DOUBL DLR	V.1	412
Cynthia:	Now, my Lord?	199	DOUBL DLR	V.1	467
Lady Froth:	O finely taken! I swear, now you are even with . . .	202	DOUBL DLR	V.1	541
Lord Touch:	Now what Evasion, Strumpet?	202	DOUBL DLR	V.1	559
Jeremy:	but your Prosperity; and now when you are poor, hate you .	217	FOR LOVE	I.1	47
Valentine:	Well; and now I am poor, I have an opportunity to . .	217	FOR LOVE	I.1	49
Jeremy:	Now Heav'n of Mercy continue the Tax upon	217	FOR LOVE	I.1	61
Jeremy:	serv'd Valentine Legend Esq; and that he is not now turn'd	218	FOR LOVE	I.1	68
Jeremy:	sake. Now like a thin Chairman, melted down to half .	218	FOR LOVE	I.1	98
Valentine:	How now?	220	FOR LOVE	I.1	165
Jeremy:	now to tell 'em in plain downright English--	220	FOR LOVE	I.1	173
Scandal:	Here's a Dog now, a Traytor in his Wine, Sirrah . . .	224	FOR LOVE	I.1	309
Tattle:	Ha, ha, ha; nay, now you make a Jest of it indeed. . .	227	FOR LOVE	I.1	403
Tattle:	that--Nay more (I'm going to say a bold Word now) I .	227	FOR LOVE	I.1	410
Mrs Frail:	Now you talk of Conjunction, my Brother	231	FOR LOVE	I.1	576
Mrs Frail:	you give me now? Come, I must have something. . .	231	FOR LOVE	I.1	584
Valentine:	No indeed, he speaks truth now: For as Tattle has . .	233	FOR LOVE	I.1	622
Nurse:	and swear now, ha, ha, ha, Marry and did you ever see the	235	FOR LOVE	II.1	23
Foresight:	Why how now, what's the matter?	235	FOR LOVE	II.1	25
Foresight:	he's at leisure--'tis now Three a Clock, a very good hour	236	FOR LOVE	II.1	41
Nurse:	ever hear the like now--Sir, did ever I do any thing . .	238	FOR LOVE	II.1	101
Nurse:	and your Urinal by you, and now and then rub the . .	238	FOR LOVE	II.1	104
Sr Sampson:	--What, I'll make thee a Present of a Mummy: Now .	242	FOR LOVE	II.1	248
Sr Sampson:	How now, who sent for you? Ha! what wou'd you . .	242	FOR LOVE	II.1	261
Sr Sampson:	Conscience and Honesty; this is your Wit now, this is the	243	FOR LOVE	II.1	298
Sr Sampson:	Why lock you there now,--I'll maintain	245	FOR LOVE	II.1	365
Sr Sampson:	he do with a distinguishing taste?--I warrant now he'd .	245	FOR LOVE	II.1	368
Sr Sampson:	now, why I warrant he can smell, and loves Perfumes .	245	FOR LOVE	II.1	370
Sr Sampson:	And if this Rogue were Anatomiz'd now, and	245	FOR LOVE	II.1	385
Sr Sampson:	Now let's see, if you have Wit enough to keep your self?--	246	FOR LOVE	II.1	401
Mrs Frail:	your self happy in a Hackney-Coach before now.--If I .	247	FOR LOVE	II.1	437
Mrs Fore:	I'll allow you now to find fault with my	248	FOR LOVE	II.1	463
Mrs Fore:	Countenance:--But look you here now,--where did . .	248	FOR LOVE	II.1	465
Mrs Frail:	Now if I cou'd wheedle him, Sister, ha? You understand .	248	FOR LOVE	II.1	495
Mrs Fore:	now if we can improve that, and make her have an Aversion	248	FOR LOVE	II.1	501
Tattle:	With all my heart,--Now then my little Angel. . . .	252	FOR LOVE	II.1	638
Miss Prue:	O fie, now I can't abide you.	252	FOR LOVE	II.1	643
Miss Prue:	Well, now I'll run and make more haste than you. . .	253	FOR LOVE	II.1	660
Miss Prue:	Father, what shall I do now?	253	FOR LOVE	III.1	16
Angelica:	Nay, now you're ungrateful.	255	FOR LOVE	III.1	84
Valentine:	There, now it's out.	255	FOR LOVE	III.1	87
Angelica:	I don't understand you now. I thought you had . .	255	FOR LOVE	III.1	88
Scandal:	So faith, your Business is done here; now you may . .	255	FOR LOVE	III.1	91
Tattle:	--Pox on't, now could I bite off my Tongue.	258	FOR LOVE	III.1	189
Sr Sampson:	I'm glad on't: Where is he? I long to see him. Now, Mrs.	259	FOR LOVE	III.1	211
Mrs Frail:	Now Miss, you shall see your Husband.	259	FOR LOVE	III.1	217
Ben:	never abide to be Portbound as we call it: Now a man that	261	FOR LOVE	III.1	311
Ben:	were, to look one way, and to row another. Now, for my	263	FOR LOVE	III.1	387
Ben:	here just now! Will he thrash my Jacket?--Let'n, let'n,--	264	FOR LOVE	III.1	420
Ben:	has been gathering foul weather in her Mouth, and now it	265	FOR LOVE	III.1	442
Sr Sampson:	up old Star-Gazer. Now is he poring upon the Ground for	265	FOR LOVE	III.1	466
Scandal:	me now hither at this unseasonable hour--	269	FOR LOVE	III.1	592
Foresight:	gallop, hey! Whither will they hurry me?--Now they're .	269	FOR LOVE	III.1	608
Foresight:	gone again--And now I'm faint again; and pale again, .	269	FOR LOVE	III.1	609
Scandal:	Look you there now--Your Lady says your	269	FOR LOVE	III.1	616
Mrs Fore:	Why then I'll speak my mind. Now as to	272	FOR LOVE	III.1	686
Scandal:	And now I think we know one another pretty well. . .	272	FOR LOVE	III.1	710
Ben:	For now the time was ended, ...	274	FOR LOVE	III.1	763
Scandal:	I saw her take Coach just now with her Maid; and . .	276	FOR LOVE	IV.1	12
Angelica:	more than he has done by himself: and now the Surprize .	277	FOR LOVE	IV.1	82
Scandal:	confessing just now an Obligation to his Love. . . .	278	FOR LOVE	IV.1	85
Jeremy:	Good lack! What's the matter now? Are any more of . .	278	FOR LOVE	IV.1	98
Sr Sampson:	How now, what's here to do?--	279	FOR LOVE	IV.1	150
Sr Sampson:	pretty well now, Val: Body o' me, I was sorry to see thee	281	FOR LOVE	IV.1	202
Mrs Fore:	O yes, now I remember, you were very	284	FOR LOVE	IV.1	327
Ben:	No, I'm pleas'd well enough, now I have found you,-- .	285	FOR LOVE	IV.1	359
Ben:	Hey toss! what's the matter now? why you ben't . .	286	FOR LOVE	IV.1	396
Ben:	wou'd have me; now I know your mind, tho'f you had .	287	FOR LOVE	IV.1	430
Mrs Fore:	imposes on him.--Now I have promis'd him Mountains; .	288	FOR LOVE	IV.1	470
Valentine:	have told thee what's past,--Now I tell what's to . .	288	FOR LOVE	IV.1	489
Valentine:	have told thee what's past,--Now I'll tell what's to .	288	FOR LOVE	IV.1 V489	
Foresight:	His Frenzy is very high now, Mr. Scandal.	289	FOR LOVE	IV.1	529
Mrs Fore:	Now, Sister.	290	FOR LOVE	IV.1	538
Tattle:	now, that I know more Secrets than he.	291	FOR LOVE	IV.1	609

Now   (continued)

Tattle:	Pox on't, there's no coming off, now she has said	293	FOR LOVE	IV.1	679
Valentine:	Nay faith, now let us understand one another,	294	FOR LOVE	IV.1	706
Valentine:	Nay, now you do me Wrong; for if any Interest	295	FOR LOVE	IV.1	725
Angelica:	Why he talk'd very sensibly just now.	295	FOR LOVE	IV.1	746
Jeremy:	to lock wild again now.	295	FOR LOVE	IV.1	748
Jeremy:	Two Hours--I'm sure I left him just now, in a Humour	295	FOR LOVE	IV.1	754
Jeremy:	Two Hours--I'm sure I left him just now, in the Humour	295	FOR LOVE	IV.1	V754
Angelica:	now you have restor'd me to my former Opinion and	296	FOR LOVE	IV.1	767
Sr Sampson:	out of his Money, and now his Poverty has run him out of	299	FOR LOVE	V.1	84
Tattle:	Is not that she, gone out just now?	301	FOR LOVE	V.1	165
Jeremy:	--And now, Sir, my former Master, having much	301	FOR LOVE	V.1	173
Miss Prue:	must not marry the Seaman now--my Father says so.	303	FOR LOVE	V.1	227
Miss Prue:	my Husband now if you please.	303	FOR LOVE	V.1	230
Tattle:	one another now--Pshaw, that would be a foolish	303	FOR LOVE	V.1	242
Tattle:	thing indeed--Fie, fie, you're a Woman now, and	303	FOR LOVE	V.1	243
Tattle:	--And I'm going to be Married just now, yet did not	305	FOR LOVE	V.1	293
Miss Prue:	now my Mind is set upon a Man, I will have a Man some	305	FOR LOVE	V.1	307
Foresight:	'Tis not convenient to tell you now--Mr.	306	FOR LOVE	V.1	331
Sr Sampson:	Hold your Tongue, Sirrah. How now, who's	309	FOR LOVE	V.1	437
Foresight:	Why, you told me just now, you went hence in	309	FOR LOVE	V.1	453
Ben:	Why there's another Match now, as tho'f a couple of	310	FOR LOVE	V.1	487
Sr Sampson:	How now?	310	FOR LOVE	V.1	499
Sr Sampson:	Are you answer'd now, Sir?	311	FOR LOVE	V.1	535
Sr Sampson:	now, Sir? Will you sign, Sir? Come, will you sign and	311	FOR LOVE	V.1	538
Sr Sampson:	How now!	312	FOR LOVE	V.1	558
Ben:	may make a Voyage together now.	312	FOR LOVE	V.1	569
Angelica:	I have done dissembling now, Valentine, and if that	313	FOR LOVE	V.1	605
Scandal:	and you have converted me--For now I am convinc'd	314	FOR LOVE	V.1	623
	Now to these Men (say they) such Souls were given,	315	FOR LOVE	EPI.	15
	May now be damn'd to animate an Ass;	315	FOR LOVE	EPI.	22
	Now find us toss'd into a Tennis-Court.	315	FOR LOVE	EPI.	27
	And now they're fill'd with Jests, and Flights, and Bombast!	315	FOR LOVE	EPI.	31
	Which now they find in their own Tribe fulfill'd:	323	M. BRIDE	PRO.	14
Almeria:	He and his Sorrows now are safely lodg'd	326	M. BRIDE	I.1	11
Almeria:	At Peace; Father and Son are now no more--	327	M. BRIDE	I.1	53
Almeria:	Both, both--Father and Son are now no more.	327	M. BRIDE	I.1	V 53
Almeria:	Than any I have yet endur'd--and now	330	M. BRIDE	I.1	190
Gonsalez:	Is entring now, in Martial Pomp the Pallace.	331	M. BRIDE	I.1	226
Manuel:	Now, what would Alonzo?	335	M. BRIDE	I.1	V358
Manuel:	Conquest and Triumph, now, are mine no more;	337	M. BRIDE	I.1	452
Manuel:	Now late, I find, that War is but her Sport;	337	M. BRIDE	I.1	458
Almeria:	His Voice, I know him now, I know him all.	342	M. BRIDE	II.2	83
Osmyn-Alph:	Affliction is no more, now thou art found.	343	M. BRIDE	II.2	121
Osmyn-Alph:	How I'm not call'd Alphonso, now, but Osmyn;	345	M. BRIDE	II.2	207
Osmyn-Alph:	Yet I behold her--Now no more.	345	M. BRIDE	II.2	214
Osmyn-Alph:	Yet I behold her--yet--And now	345	M. BRIDE	II.2	V214
Zara:	Is a regardless Suppliant, now, to Osmyn.	346	M. BRIDE	II.2	249
Zara:	Disdains to listen now, or look on Zara.	346	M. BRIDE	II.2	251
Osmyn-Alph:	I saw you not, 'till now.	346	M. BRIDE	II.2	V254
Zara:	Now, then you see me--	346	M. BRIDE	II.2	255
Zara:	Look on me now, from Empire fall'n to Slavery;	347	M. BRIDE	II.2	303
Zara:	The fall'n, the lost, and now the Captive Zara.	347	M. BRIDE	II.2	V307
Zara:	And now abandon'd--say what then is Osmyn?	347	M. BRIDE	II.2	V308
Selim:	Madam, the King is here, and entring now.	348	M. BRIDE	II.2	V349
Osmyn-Alph:	But now, and I was clos'd within the Tomb	349	M. BRIDE	III.1	1
Osmyn-Alph:	That holds my Father's Ashes; and but now,	349	M. BRIDE	III.1	2
Zara:	O no, thou canst not, for thou seest me now,	353	M. BRIDE	III.1	156
Zara:	O thou dost wound me now, with this thy Goodness,	354	M. BRIDE	III.1	185
Zara:	And now just ripe for Birth, my Rage has ruin'd.	354	M. BRIDE	III.1	196
Zara:	Wake thee to Freedom. Now, 'tis late; and yet	354	M. BRIDE	III.1	203
Zara:	To give, than I've already lost. But now	355	M. BRIDE	III.1	V216
Almeria:	To part no more--Now we will part no more,	355	M. BRIDE	III.1	247
Almeria:	Which shot into my Breast, now melt and chill me.	358	M. BRIDE	III.1	368
Zara:	And will indulge it now. What Miseries?	360	M. BRIDE	III.1	424
Zara:	Thou ly'st; for now I know for whom thou'dst live.	360	M. BRIDE	III.1	436
Zara:	But now the Dawn begins, and the slow Hand	360	M. BRIDE	III.1	440
Zara:	I've been deceiv'd. The publick Safety now	360	M. BRIDE	III.1	V449
Zara:	To my Remembrance now, that make it plain.	363	M. BRIDE	IV.1	93
Zara:	Have I? Yet 'twere the lowest Baseness, now,	363	M. BRIDE	IV.1	96
Manuel:	But wearing now a-pace with ebbing Sand,	364	M. BRIDE	IV.1	107
Zara:	My self of what I've undertaken; now,	364	M. BRIDE	IV.1	141
Gonsalez:	As she pretends--I doubt it now--Your Guards	366	M. BRIDE	IV.1	206
Gonsalez:	She now repents. It may be I'm deceiv'd.	366	M. BRIDE	IV.1	220
Manuel:	O Impious Parricide! now canst thou speak?	368	M. BRIDE	IV.1	272
Almeria:	Now calls me Murderer, and Parricide.	368	M. BRIDE	IV.1	284
Manuel:	Now doom'd to die, that most accursed Osmyn.	368	M. BRIDE	IV.1	288
Almeria:	Now curse me if you can, now spurn me off.	369	M. BRIDE	IV.1	320
Gonsalez:	Nor now had known it, but from her mistake.	371	M. BRIDE	IV.1	399
Gonsalez:	To set him free? Ay, now 'tis plain; O well	371	M. BRIDE	IV.1	413
Manuel:	And laid along as he now lies supine,	374	M. BRIDE	V.1	V86B
Zara:	I have not leisure, now, to take so poor	375	M. BRIDE	V.1	123
Garcia:	Are entring now our Doors. Where is the King?	377	M. BRIDE	V.2	28
Garcia:	Had enter'd long 'ere now, and born down all	377	M. BRIDE	V.2	34
Garcia:	Were it a Truth, I fear 'tis now too late.	379	M. BRIDE	V.2	105
Zara:	As thou art now--And I shall quickly be.	380	M. BRIDE	V.2	186
Zara:	O now he's gone, and all is dark--	381	M. BRIDE	V.2	211
Almeria:	I have him now, and we no more will part.	383	M. BRIDE	V.2	298
Osmyn-Alph:	Frail Life, to be entirely bless'd. Even now,	383	M. BRIDE	V.2	301
	And now as unconcern'd this Mourning wear,	385	M. BRIDE	EPI.	3
	I've leisure, now, to mark your sev'ral Faces,	385	M. BRIDE	EPI.	5
Fainall:	else now, and play too negligently; the Coldness of a	395	WAY WORLD	I.1	6
Fainall:	Now I remember, I wonder not they were weary	396	WAY WORLD	I.1	49
Mirabell:	They are now grown as familiar to me as my own Frailties;	399	WAY WORLD	I.1	172
Mirabell:	it is now and then to be endur'd. He has indeed one good	401	WAY WORLD	I.1	227
Betty:	Did not the Messenger bring you one but now, Sir?	401	WAY WORLD	I.1	240

Nurse   (continued)
  Mrs Fore: Nurse, Nurse! . . . . 270 FOR LOVE III.1 628
                              (Enter Nurse.) . . . . . 270 FOR LOVE III.1 634
  Mrs Fore: Nurse; your Master is not well; put him to . . . . 270 FOR LOVE III.1 635
  Foresight: I thank you Mr. Scandal, I will--Nurse, let me have . 270 FOR LOVE III.1 640
  Miss Prue: What, must I go to Bed to Nurse again, and be a Child as . 305 FOR LOVE V.1 305
               (Enter Scandal, Mrs. Foresight, and Nurse.) . 305 FOR LOVE V.1 320
  Foresight: Rogue! Oh, Nurse, come hither. . . . . 305 FOR LOVE V.1 322
                (Exeunt Nurse and Miss Prue.) . . . 306 FOR LOVE V.1 V329
  Foresight: Nurse, why are you not gone? . . . . 306 FOR LOVE V.1 V337
Nusance (1)
  Angelica: idle Divinations. I'll swear you are a Nusance to the . . 237 FOR LOVE II.1 78
Nutmeg (1)
  Lady Wish: of Nutmeg? I warrant thee. Come, fill, fill.--So--again . 425 WAY WORLD III.1 32
Nutmeg-Grater (1)
  Angelica: little Nutmeg-Grater, which she had forgot in the Caudle-Cup 238 FOR LOVE II.1 110
Nutriment (1)
  Sr Sampson: Spiders; the one has its Nutriment in his own hands; and . 246 FOR LOVE II.1 392
Nykin (14)
  Laetitia: Are you Nykin? . . . . 77 OLD BATCH IV.1 66
  Fondlewife: made me weep--made poor Nykin weep--Nay come Kiss . . 78 OLD BATCH IV.1 117
  Fondlewife: buss poor Nykin--And I wont leave thee--I'le lose all first. 78 OLD BATCH IV.1 118
  Fondlewife: Wont you Kiss Nykin? . . . . 78 OLD BATCH IV.1 121
  Laetitia: Go naughty Nykin, you don't love me. . . . . 78 OLD BATCH IV.1 122
  Laetitia: indeed you sant. Nykin--if you don't go, I'le think . . 78 OLD BATCH IV.1 132
  Fondlewife: I wont be dealous--Poor Cocky, Kiss Nykin, Kiss . . . . 79 OLD BATCH IV.1 135
  Fondlewife: Nykin, ee, ee, ee,--Here will be the good Man anon, to . 79 OLD BATCH IV.1 136
  Fondlewife: That's my good Dear--Come Kiss Nykin once . . . . . 79 OLD BATCH IV.1 143
  Laetitia: By Nykin. . . . . 79 OLD BATCH IV.1 146
  Laetitia: By Nykin. . . . . 79 OLD BATCH IV.1 148
  Laetitia: Patch.--You s'an't turn in, Nykin.--Run into my . . . . 89 OLD BATCH IV.4 16
  Laetitia: Indeed, and indeed, now my dear Nykin--I never . . . . 93 OLD BATCH IV.4 139
  Laetitia: won't you speak to me, cruel Nykin? Indeed, I'll die, if . 95 OLD BATCH IV.4 246
Nymph (6)
  Singer: The fearful Nymph reply'd--Forbear; . . . . 71 OLD BATCH III.2 V 10
  Singer-F: A Nymph and a Swain to Apollo once pray'd, ... 258 FOR LOVE III.1 200
  Singer-F: The Swain had been Jilted, the Nymph been Betray'd; . . 258 FOR LOVE III.1 201
  Singer-F: E're a Nymph that was Chaste, or a Swain that was True. . 258 FOR LOVE III.1 203
  Singer-F: And the Nymph may be Chaste that has never been Try'd. . 259 FOR LOVE III.1 208
  Petulant: Nymph--say it--and that's the Conclusion--pass on, or . 453 WAY WORLD IV.1 340
O (468)   see Oh
            He prays--O bless me! what shall I do now! . . . . 35 OLD BATCH PRO. 19
            O Lord, for Heavens sake excuse the Play, ... 35 OLD BATCH PRO. 23
  Bellmour: O Brute, the drudgery of loving! . . . . . . 44 OLD BATCH I.1 276
  Sharper: O your Servant Sir, you are safe then it seems; 'tis an . 48 OLD BATCH II.1 32
  Sir Joseph: O Lord forget him! No no Sir, I don't forget you-- . . 48 OLD BATCH II.1 40
  Sharper: So-h, O Sir I am easily pacify'd, the acknowledgment . . 49 OLD BATCH II.1 62
  Sir Joseph: O Lord Sir! . . . . 49 OLD BATCH II.1 75
  Sharper: O term it no longer so Sir. In the Scuffle last Night I . 49 OLD BATCH II.1 81
  Sir Joseph: O Lord Sir. . . . . 50 OLD BATCH II.1 99
  Sir Joseph: O Lord Sir by no means--but I might have sav'd a . . . 51 OLD BATCH II.1 128
  Capt Bluff: O Lord I beg your pardon Sir, I find you are not of . . 51 OLD BATCH II.1 162
  Capt Bluff: O I am calm Sir, calm as a discharg'd Culverin--But . . 54 OLD BATCH II.1 241
  Belinda: There was a Whine--O Gad I hate your horrid . . . . 54 OLD BATCH II.2 11
  Belinda: Blood, the--All over--O Gad you are quite . . . . 54 OLD BATCH II.2 14
  Belinda: O I love your hideous Fancy! Ha, ha, ha, love a . . . . 55 OLD BATCH II.2 22
  Belinda: and Appurtenances; O Gad! sure you would--But you . . 55 OLD BATCH II.2 33
  Belinda: O barbarous Aspersion! . . . . 55 OLD BATCH II.2 45
  Belinda: Cousin, you talk odly--What ever the Matter is, O . . 55 OLD BATCH II.2 51
  Belinda: O Gad, would you would all pray to Love then, and . . 58 OLD BATCH II.2 142
  Vainlove: O Madam-- . . . . 58 OLD BATCH II.2 150
  Belinda: O Gad I hate your hideous Fancy--You said that . . . . 59 OLD BATCH II.2 167
  Araminta: O I am glad we shall have a Song to divert the . . . . 59 OLD BATCH II.2 186
  Bellmour: O very well perform'd--But I don't much . . . . 60 OLD BATCH II.2 204
  Belinda: O fogh, your dumb Rhetorick is more ridiculous, ... 60 OLD BATCH II.2 212
  Heartwell: --Now could I curse my self, yet cannot repent. O . . 63 OLD BATCH III.1 76
  Sir Joseph: O Lord, O Lord, Captain, come justifie your . . . . . 69 OLD BATCH III.1 306
  Capt Bluff: O this is your time Sir, you had best make use on't. . . 69 OLD BATCH III.1 319
  Sir Joseph: O Lord his Anger was not raised before--Nay, ... 70 OLD BATCH III.1 339
  Singer: O let me feed as well as taste, ... 71 OLD BATCH III.2 7
  Singer: O let me--still the Shepherd said; . . . . 71 OLD BATCH III.2 V 14
  Heartwell: Baby for a Girl to dandle. O dotage, dotage! That ever . 72 OLD BATCH III.2 47
  Silvia: them--O Gemini, I hope you don't mean so--For I . . . 73 OLD BATCH III.2 88
  Setter: O most religiously well Sir. . . . . 75 OLD BATCH IV.1 5
  Belinda: A little! O frightful! What a furious Fiz I have! O . . 83 OLD BATCH IV.3 8
  Belinda: most rueful! Ha, ha, ha: O Gad, I hope no-body will . . 83 OLD BATCH IV.3 9
  Belinda: Ay, O my Conscience; fat as Barn-door-Fowl: But . . . 84 OLD BATCH IV.3 28
  Belinda: with their Feathers growing the wrong way.--O such . . . 84 OLD BATCH IV.3 30
  Belinda: O frightful! Cousin, What shall we do? These things . . 85 OLD BATCH IV.3 75
  Belinda: O monstrous filthy Fellow! Good slovenly Captain . . . 85 OLD BATCH IV.3 86
  Belinda: O Lord, No, I'll go along with her. Come, Mr. . . . . 88 OLD BATCH IV.3 209
  Laetitia: Help me, my Dear,--O bless me! Why will you leave me . 90 OLD BATCH IV.4 47
  Sir Joseph: O Lord! Oh terrible! Ha, ha, ha, Is your Wife . . . . 90 OLD BATCH IV.4 55
  Fondlewife: O bless me! O monstrous! A Prayer-Book? Ay, this is the . 92 OLD BATCH IV.4 106
  Fondlewife: Adultery, and innocent! O Lord! Here's Doctrine! . . . 92 OLD BATCH IV.4 112
  Fondlewife: O Lord! O strange! I am in admiration of your . . . . 93 OLD BATCH IV.4 153
  Laetitia: O beastly, impudent Creature. . . . . 94 OLD BATCH IV.4 176
  Heartwell: O Pox; He's a Fanatick. . . . . 97 OLD BATCH V.1 17
  Heartwell: O ay; He's a Fanatick. . . . . 97 OLD BATCH V.1 V 17
  Lucy: Nay, Mr. Bellmour: O Lard! I believe you are a Parson . 97 OLD BATCH V.1 37
  Lucy: How! O Lord!-- . . . . 98 OLD BATCH V.1 56
  Setter: O Lord, Sir! . . . . 100 OLD BATCH V.1 159
  Setter: O Lord, Sir, What d'ye mean? Corrupt my honesty. . . . 103 OLD BATCH V.1 247
  Heartwell: O Torture! How he racks and tears me!-- . . . . 104 OLD BATCH V.1 308
  Sharper: O Rogue! Well, but I hope-- . . . . 105 OLD BATCH V.1 346
  Belinda: (to Bellmour). O my Conscience, I cou'd find in my . . . 106 OLD BATCH V.1 364

O   (continued)

Speaker	Text	PAGE	TITLE	ACT.SC	LINE
Belinda:	O the filthy rude Beast!	107	OLD BATCH	V.1	398
Heartwell:	O cursed State! How wide we err, when apprehensive of	108	OLD BATCH	V.2	9
Belinda:	Ha, ha, ha, O Gad, Men grow such Clowns when	108	OLD BATCH	V.2	25
Sir Joseph:	Ah! O Lord, my heart akes--Ah! Setter, a	110	OLD BATCH	V.2	118
Bellmour:	O my Conscience she dares not consent, for fear	112	OLD BATCH	V.2	175
Brisk:	O, Mon Coeur! What is't! nay gad I'll punish you for	128	DOUBL DLR	I.1	41
Mellefont:	O, I would have no room for serious design; for I	129	DOUBL DLR	I.1	74
Lord Froth:	O foy, Sir Paul, what do you mean? Merry! O	132	DOUBL DLR	I.1	185
Lord Froth:	O foy, don't misapprehend me, I don't say so, for	132	DOUBL DLR	I.1	197
Lord Froth:	O yes, sometimes,--but I never Laugh.	133	DOUBL DLR	I.1	223
Brisk:	O Lord, why can't you find it out?--Why there	133	DOUBL DLR	I.1	248
Lord Froth:	O foy, Mr. Careless, all the World allow Mr.	134	DOUBL DLR	I.1	273
Lord Froth:	O foy, Mr. Careless, all the World allows Mr.	134	DOUBL DLR	I.1	V273
Lord Froth:	O, for the Universe, not a drop more I beseech	134	DOUBL DLR	I.1	288
Lord Froth:	you, O Intemperate! I have a flushing in my Face already.	134	DOUBL DLR	I.1	289
Lady Touch:	More! Audacious Villain. O what's more, is	135	DOUBL DLR	I.1	316
Lady Touch:	black!--O I have Excuses, Thousands for my Faults; Fire	135	DOUBL DLR	I.1	325
Lady Froth:	O my Dear Cynthia, you must not rally your	138	DOUBL DLR	II.1	8
Lady Froth:	O I Writ, Writ abundantly,--do you never	138	DOUBL DLR	II.1	13
Cynthia:	O Lord, not I, Madam; I'm content to be a	139	DOUBL DLR	II.1	18
Lady Froth:	O Inconsistent! In Love, and not Write! if my	139	DOUBL DLR	II.1	20
Lady Froth:	come together,--O bless me! What a sad thing	139	DOUBL DLR	II.1	22
Lady Froth:	O that Tongue, that dear deceitful Tongue! that	140	DOUBL DLR	II.1	71
Lady Froth:	O prettily turn'd again; let me die, but you have	140	DOUBL DLR	II.1	85
Mellefont:	O, yes, Madam.	140	DOUBL DLR	II.1	88
Brisk:	O Lord, Madam--	140	DOUBL DLR	II.1	89
Brisk:	O dear, Madam--	140	DOUBL DLR	II.1	V 89
Brisk:	O Jesu, Madam--	140	DOUBL DLR	II.1	91
Brisk:	O Heav'ns, Madam--	140	DOUBL DLR	II.1	V 91
Lord Froth:	O your humble Servant for that, dear Madam;	141	DOUBL DLR	II.1	109
Lady Froth:	O, you must be my Confident, I must ask your	142	DOUBL DLR	II.1	134
Lady Froth:	O yes, and Rapine, and Dacier upon Aristotle	142	DOUBL DLR	II.1	138
Singer:	Think, O think o'th' sad Condition,	143	DOUBL DLR	II.1	190
Lady Ply:	O, such a thing! the Impiety of it startles me	146	DOUBL DLR	II.1	289
Lady Ply:	the unparallel'd wickedness! O merciful Father! how could	146	DOUBL DLR	II.1	305
Mellefont:	(aside). Incest! O my precious Aunt, and the Devil	146	DOUBL DLR	II.1	312
Lady Ply:	O reflect upon the horror of that, and then the	147	DOUBL DLR	II.1	314
Lady Ply:	made one Trip, not one faux pas; O consider it, what would	147	DOUBL DLR	II.1	319
Lady Ply:	O Lord, ask me the question, I'll swear I'll	147	DOUBL DLR	II.1	332
Lady Ply:	nay you shan't ask me, I swear I'll deny it. O Gemini, you	147	DOUBL DLR	II.1	334
Lady Ply:	as red as a Turky-Cock; O fie, Cousin Mellefont!	147	DOUBL DLR	II.1	336
Lady Ply:	O name it no more--bless me, how can	147	DOUBL DLR	II.1	344
Lady Ply:	necessity--O Lord, here's some body coming, I dare	148	DOUBL DLR	II.1	362
Lady Ply:	think that I'll grant you any thing; O Lord, no,--but	148	DOUBL DLR	II.1	366
Lady Ply:	Passion to me; yet it will make me jealous,--O Lord,	148	DOUBL DLR	II.1	369
Lady Ply:	despair neither,--O, they're coming, I must fly.	148	DOUBL DLR	II.1	372
Mellefont:	Ha! O I see, I see my Rising Sun! Light breaks	149	DOUBL DLR	II.1	405
Mellefont:	Ha! O see, I see my Rising Sun! Light breaks	149	DOUBL DLR	II.1	V405
Mellefont:	thro' Clouds upon me, and I shall live in Day--O my	149	DOUBL DLR	II.1	406
Lady Touch:	Dear. Nay, by this kiss you shan't be angry. O Lord, I	152	DOUBL DLR	III.1	68
Lady Touch:	O for Heaven's sake, my Lord, you'll ruine	153	DOUBL DLR	III.1	103
Sir Paul:	O, sweet Sir, you load your humble Servants, both	159	DOUBL DLR	III.1	325
Careless:	O Heavens! Madam, you confound me.	159	DOUBL DLR	III.1	346
Lady Ply:	O Lord! Sir, pardon me, we women have not	159	DOUBL DLR	III.1	348
Careless:	O your Ladyship is abounding in all Excellence,	160	DOUBL DLR	III.1	356
Careless:	O Lord, I beseech you, Madam, don't--	160	DOUBL DLR	III.1	366
Careless:	O fie, fie, not to be named of a day--my Lady Froth	160	DOUBL DLR	III.1	375
Lady Ply:	O you overcome me--that is so excessive--	160	DOUBL DLR	III.1	378
Careless:	O, Sir Paul, you are the happiest man alive. Such a	160	DOUBL DLR	III.1	380
Sir Paul:	I; but mine's soon over, and then I'm so sorry--O, Mr.	160	DOUBL DLR	III.1	390
Lord Froth:	Merry! O Lord, what a character that is of a	162	DOUBL DLR	III.1	465
Cynthia:	O most ridiculous, a perpetual consort of laughing	163	DOUBL DLR	III.1	471
Sir Paul:	O ho, I wish you good success, I wish you good	163	DOUBL DLR	III.1	497
Lord Froth:	O silly! yet his Aunt is as fond of him, as if she	165	DOUBL DLR	III.1	565
Brisk:	Who, my Lady Toothless; O, she's a mortifying	165	DOUBL DLR	III.1	567
Cynthia:	O good my Lord let's hear it.	166	DOUBL DLR	III.1	590
Lady Froth:	O the dear Creature! Let's go see it.	166	DOUBL DLR	III.1	608
Lady Ply:	now you make me swear--O Gratitude forbid, that I	169	DOUBL DLR	IV.1	79
Careless:	bewitching Fair? O let me grow to the ground here, and	170	DOUBL DLR	IV.1	91
Careless:	feast upon that hand; O let me press it to my heart, my	170	DOUBL DLR	IV.1	92
Lady Ply:	O that's so passionate and fine, I cannot hear it	170	DOUBL DLR	IV.1	97
Lady Ply:	I swear I am ready to Languish too--O my	170	DOUBL DLR	IV.1	103
Lady Ply:	O rise I beseech you, say no more till you rise	170	DOUBL DLR	IV.1	107
Careless:	O Heaven! I can't out-live this Night without	170	DOUBL DLR	IV.1	113
Lady Ply:	O you have Conquered, sweet, melting, moving	170	DOUBL DLR	IV.1	118
Lady Ply:	O las, no indeed, Sir Paul, 'tis upon your account.	172	DOUBL DLR	IV.1	181
Lady Ply:	O law now, I swear and declare, it shan't be so,	172	DOUBL DLR	IV.1	185
Lady Ply:	O fy, fy, Sir Paul, you'l put me out of Countenance	172	DOUBL DLR	IV.1	189
Lady Ply:	(Having read the Letter). O dear Mr. Careless, I	174	DOUBL DLR	IV.1	258
Lady Ply:	when 'tis Dark. O Crimine! I hope, Sir Paul has not seen	174	DOUBL DLR	IV.1	262
Sir Paul:	O Law, what's the matter now? I hope you are not	174	DOUBL DLR	IV.1	269
Brisk:	O ye Powers! O my Lady Froth, my Lady Froth! My Lady	175	DOUBL DLR	IV.1	309
Lady Froth:	O Heavens Mr. Brisk! What's the matter?	175	DOUBL DLR	IV.1	312
Brisk:	O Lord I Madam! I beseech your Ladyship--	176	DOUBL DLR	IV.1	321
Lady Froth:	did you talk of Love? O Parnassus! Who would have	176	DOUBL DLR	IV.1	332
Lady Froth:	thought Mr. Brisk could have been in Love, ha ha ha. O	176	DOUBL DLR	IV.1	333
Lady Froth:	O be merry by all means--Prince Volscius	176	DOUBL DLR	IV.1	341
Brisk:	O barbarous, to turn me into ridicule! Yet, ha ha ha.	176	DOUBL DLR	IV.1	343
Brisk:	That's well enough; let me perish, ha ha ha. O Miraculous,	177	DOUBL DLR	IV.1	356
Lady Ply:	O Mr. Careless, Mr. Careless, I'm ruin'd, I'm	177	DOUBL DLR	IV.1	390
Lady Ply:	O the unlucki'st Accident, I'm afraid I shan't	178	DOUBL DLR	IV.1	393
Lady Ply:	dare swear every Circumstance of me trembles.--O your	178	DOUBL DLR	IV.1	398
Lady Ply:	O yonder he comes reading of it, for Heavens	178	DOUBL DLR	IV.1	402
Sir Paul:	--O Providence, what a Conspiracy have I	178	DOUBL DLR	IV.1	406
Sir Paul:	be Damn'd for a Judas Maccabeus, and Iscariot both. O	178	DOUBL DLR	IV.1	418

		PAGE	TITLE	ACT.SC	LINE
0	(continued)				
Sir Paul:	polluted by Foreign Iniquity? O my Lady Plyant, you were	179	DOUBL DLR	IV.1	430
Sir Paul:	O strange, what will become of me!--I'm so	179	DOUBL DLR	IV.1	459
Sir Paul:	O Providence! Providence! What Discoveries are	180	DOUBL DLR	IV.1	504
Maskwell:	O my Lord! consider that is hard: besides, time	182	DOUBL DLR	IV.1	565
Mellefont:	O Madam, have a care of dying unprepared, I	184	DOUBL DLR	IV.2	54
Lady Touch:	O. What shall I do? say? whither shall I	185	DOUBL DLR	IV.2	57
Lady Touch:	O the Scene was shifted quick before me--	185	DOUBL DLR	IV.2	70
Lady Touch:	practice--O Consider, Consider, how fatal you have	185	DOUBL DLR	IV.2	74
Lady Touch:	O be not cruelly incredulous--How	185	DOUBL DLR	IV.2	80
Lady Touch:	(Aside.) Ha! my Lord listning! O Fortune has o'repaid me	186	DOUBL DLR	IV.2	95
Lady Touch:	O cruel Man, will you not let me go--I'le	186	DOUBL DLR	IV.2	102
Lady Touch:	forgive all that's past--O Heaven, you will not ravish	186	DOUBL DLR	IV.2	103
Lady Touch:	O Heavens my Lord! hold, hold, for	186	DOUBL DLR	IV.2	109
Mellefont:	Confusion, my Uncle! O the damn'd Sorceress.	186	DOUBL DLR	IV.2	111
Mellefont:	O I could curse my Stars, Fate, and Chance; all	187	DOUBL DLR	IV.2	141
Mellefont:	design than this of his which has miscarried.--O my	187	DOUBL DLR	IV.2	151
Maskwell:	Yet I am wretched--O there is a secret burns	188	DOUBL DLR	V.1	28
Maskwell:	O, should it once be known I love fair Cynthia, all this	188	DOUBL DLR	V.1	38
Mellefont:	O Maskwell, what hopes? I am confounded in a	190	DOUBL DLR	V.1	103
Sir Paul:	O, if she be with Mr. Careless, 'tis well enough.	192	DOUBL DLR	V.1	190
Mellefont:	O I conceive you, you'll tell him so?	193	DOUBL DLR	V.1	226
Lady Touch:	meanings lurk in each corner of that various face. O! that	198	DOUBL DLR	V.1	395
Lord Touch:	Ha! O poison to my Ears! what do I hear!	198	DOUBL DLR	V.1	427
Lord Froth:	O Heaven's, what's the matter? Where's my	200	DOUBL DLR	V.1	499
Sir Paul:	O, here they come.	201	DOUBL DLR	V.1	515
Brisk:	O Jesu! Madam, you have Eclips'd me quite, let me	201	DOUBL DLR	V.1	534
Lady Froth:	O finely taken! I swear, now you are even with	202	DOUBL DLR	V.1	541
Lady Froth:	me, O Parnassus, you have an infinite deal of Wit.	202	DOUBL DLR	V.1	542
Lady Ply:	who would ever trust a man? O my heart akes for fear	202	DOUBL DLR	V.1	546
Lady Ply:	O dear, you make me blush.	202	DOUBL DLR	V.1	550
Lady Touch:	O I'm betray'd,--save me, help me.	202	DOUBL DLR	V.1	558
Jeremy:	O Lord! I have heard much of him, when I waited	216	FOR LOVE	I.1	17
Jeremy:	O Sir, there's Trapland the Scrivener, with two	221	FOR LOVE	I.1	202
Valentine:	O Mr. Trapland! my old Friend! Welcome. Jeremy, a	222	FOR LOVE	I.1	228
Tattle:	O Lord, what have I said? my Unlucky Tongue!	227	FOR LOVE	I.1	435
Tattle:	O Barbarous! why did you not tell me--	229	FOR LOVE	I.1	494
Tattle:	Scandal, you will not be so ungenerous--O, I shall	230	FOR LOVE	I.1	514
Tattle:	O inhumane! You don't expect their Names.	230	FOR LOVE	I.1	532
Tattle:	O inhuman! You don't expect their Names.	230	FOR LOVE	I.1	V532
Tattle:	O unfortunate! she's come already; will you have Patience	230	FOR LOVE	I.1	542
Tattle:	Mum--O Madam, you do me too much Honour.	231	FOR LOVE	I.1	551
Mrs Frail:	O lying Creature--Valentine, does not he lye?	233	FOR LOVE	I.1	620
Mrs Frail:	O Devil! Well, but that Story is not true.	233	FOR LOVE	I.1	641
Nurse:	Dinner--good lack-a-day, ha, ha, ha, O strange; I'll vow	235	FOR LOVE	II.1	22
Nurse:	O merciful Father, how she talks!	237	FOR LOVE	II.1	95
Nurse:	--O Lord, what's here to do?--I in unlawful	238	FOR LOVE	II.1	99
Nurse:	Soles of your Feet?--O Lord, I!	238	FOR LOVE	II.1	105
Nurse:	A Teat, a Teat, I an unnatural Teat! O the false slanderous	238	FOR LOVE	II.1	123
Mrs Fore:	(aside). O Devil on't, that I cou'd not discover	248	FOR LOVE	II.1	471
Tattle:	O fie Miss, you must not kiss and tell.	249	FOR LOVE	II.1	523
Mrs Frail:	O hang you; who'll believe you?--You'd be	250	FOR LOVE	II.1	554
Miss Prue:	O Lord, I swear this is pure,--I like it better than	252	FOR LOVE	II.1	624
Miss Prue:	O Gemini! well, I always had a great mind to tell	252	FOR LOVE	II.1	629
Miss Prue:	O fie, now I can't abide you.	252	FOR LOVE	II.1	643
Nurse:	cry husht--O Lord, who's there? (peeps) What's here	253	FOR LOVE	III.1	7
Nurse:	to do?--O the Father! a Man with her!--Why,	253	FOR LOVE	III.1	8
Nurse:	O Lord, We're all undone--O you young Harlotry	253	FOR LOVE	III.1	10
Miss Prue:	O Lord, she's coming--and she'll tell my	253	FOR LOVE	III.1	15
Miss Prue:	O Dear, what shall I say? Tell me, Mr. Tattle, tell	253	FOR LOVE	III.1	19
Valentine:	O the Devil, what damn'd Costive Poet has given	255	FOR LOVE	III.1	73
Tattle:	O Lord! yes indeed, Madam, several times.	255	FOR LOVE	III.1	79
Tattle:	Brag! O Heav'ns! Why, did I name any body?	255	FOR LOVE	III.1	93
Tattle:	O pox, Scandal, that was too far put--Never have	256	FOR LOVE	III.1	116
Angelica:	O barbarous! I never heard so insolent a piece of	258	FOR LOVE	III.1	182
Mrs Fore:	O, mighty restless, but I was afraid to tell him	270	FOR LOVE	III.1	619
Mrs Fore:	O Monstrous! What are Conscience and	271	FOR LOVE	III.1	673
Mrs Fore:	O, fie--I'll Swear you're Impudent.	272	FOR LOVE	III.1	705
Mrs Fore:	O Lord, who's here?	272	FOR LOVE	III.1	711
Sr Sampson:	Sham-sickness shan't excuse him--O, here's his	278	FOR LOVE	IV.1	117
Buckram:	O Lord, what must I say?--Yes, Sir.	280	FOR LOVE	IV.1	170
Buckram:	O Lord, let me be gone; I'll not venture my self	282	FOR LOVE	IV.1	243
Mrs Fore:	O yes, now I remember, you were very	284	FOR LOVE	IV.1	327
Mrs Frail:	O Impiety! how have I been mistaken! what an	286	FOR LOVE	IV.1	392
Mrs Frail:	O I am happy to have discover'd the Shelves and Quicksands	286	FOR LOVE	IV.1	394
Mrs Frail:	O see me no more,--for thou wert born amongst	286	FOR LOVE	IV.1	398
Ben:	O Lord, O Lord, she's mad, poor Young Woman, Love	286	FOR LOVE	IV.1	403
Mrs Frail:	O Sister, had you come a minute sooner, you would	287	FOR LOVE	IV.1	449
Mrs Frail:	O Lord, what must I say?	290	FOR LOVE	IV.1	539
Angelica:	O fie for shame, hold your Tongue, A passionate	291	FOR LOVE	IV.1	585
Mrs Frail:	(to Jeremy). O Lord, her coming will spoil all.	291	FOR LOVE	IV.1	590
Tattle:	O Lord!	292	FOR LOVE	IV.1	644
Valentine:	O exceeding good to keep a Secret: For tho' she	292	FOR LOVE	IV.1	645
Jeremy:	O Lord, Madam, did you ever know any Madman	295	FOR LOVE	IV.1	743
Sr Sampson:	O Pox, outsides, outsides; a pize take 'em, meer	298	FOR LOVE	V.1	33
Angelica:	O fie, Sir Sampson, what would the World say?	300	FOR LOVE	V.1	117
Sr Sampson:	O Rogue! But I'll trust you. And will you	300	FOR LOVE	V.1	132
Jeremy:	O Sir, for that Sir, 'tis my chief Talent; I'm as secret	302	FOR LOVE	V.1	190
Jeremy:	O Ignorance! (aside). A cunning Aegyptian, Sir, that	302	FOR LOVE	V.1	193
Miss Prue:	O Mr. Tattle, are you here! I'm glad I have found	303	FOR LOVE	V.1	222
Tattle:	(aside). O Pox, how shall I get rid of this foolish Girl?	303	FOR LOVE	V.1	225
Miss Prue:	O I have pure News, I can tell you pure News--I	303	FOR LOVE	V.1	226
Tattle:	O fie, Miss: Who told you so, Child?	303	FOR LOVE	V.1	231
Tattle:	O fie, Miss, why did you do so? and who told you so,	303	FOR LOVE	V.1	233
Tattle:	O Pox, that was Yesterday, Miss, that was a great	303	FOR LOVE	V.1	236
Miss Prue:	Pshaw, O but I dream't that it was so tho.	303	FOR LOVE	V.1	239

O (continued)

Speaker	Line	Page	Title	Act.Sc	Line
Zara:	Cruel, cruel, O more than killing Object!	380	M. BRIDE	V.2	V164
Zara:	O this accurs'd, this base, this treach'rous King!	380	M. BRIDE	V.2	V168
Zara:	O friendly Draught, already in my Heart!	381	M. BRIDE	V.2	204
Zara:	O now he's gone, and all is dark--	381	M. BRIDE	V.2	211
Almeria:	O let me seek him in this horrid Cell;	381	M. BRIDE	V.2	215
Leonora:	But O forbear--lift up your Eyes no more;	381	M. BRIDE	V.2	226
Almeria:	O I fore-see that Object in my Mind.	382	M. BRIDE	V.2	231
Almeria:	O I foreknow, foresee that Object.	382	M. BRIDE	V.2	V231
Almeria:	Yet bubling from his Wounds--O more than savage!	382	M. BRIDE	V.2	235
Almeria:	And point! what mean they; Ha! a Cup. O well	382	M. BRIDE	V.2	253
Almeria:	O noble Thirst! and yet too greedy to	382	M. BRIDE	V.2	255
Almeria:	O noble Thirst! yet greedy, to drink all--	382	M. BRIDE	V.2	V255
Almeria:	Drink all--O for another Draught of Death,	382	M. BRIDE	V.2	256
Almeria:	O thanks the liberal Hand that fill'd thee thus;	382	M. BRIDE	V.2	259
Leonora:	O hold	382	M. BRIDE	V.2	261
Almeria:	But spouting Veins, and mangled Flesh! O, O.	382	M. BRIDE	V.2	272
Osmyn-Alph:	O let me talk to thy reviving Sense,	383	M. BRIDE	V.2	280
Osmyn-Alph:	O may'st thou never dream of less Delight;	383	M. BRIDE	V.2	289
Almeria:	Giv'n me again from Death! O all ye Powers	383	M. BRIDE	V.2	291
Osmyn-Alph:	O my Heart's Comfort; 'tis not given to this	383	M. BRIDE	V.2	300
Osmyn-Alph:	She shall be Royally interr'd. O Garcia,	383	M. BRIDE	V.2	315
Osmyn-Alph:	. . . O Garcia,	383	M. BRIDE	V.2	V 315
	O with what Joy they run, to spread the News	385	M. BRIDE	EPI.	11
Fainall:	O there it is then--She has a lasting Passion for	396	WAY WORLD	I.1	25
Mirabell:	One a Clock! (looking on his Watch) O y'are come--	398	WAY WORLD	I.1	109
Witwoud:	O pardon me--Expose the Infirmities of my	403	WAY WORLD	I.1	314
Fainall:	O brave Petulant, three!	404	WAY WORLD	I.1	348
Mirabell:	he waits for himself now, he is so long a coming; O I ask	405	WAY WORLD	I.1	379
Mirabell:	O Raillery, Raillery. Come, I know thou art in	407	WAY WORLD	I.1	448
Witwoud:	O rare Petulant; thou art as quick as a Fire in a	409	WAY WORLD	I.1	519
Witwoud:	O rare Petulant; thou art as quick as a Fire in a	409	WAY WORLD	I.1	V519
Marwood:	O if he shou'd ever discover it, he wou'd	411	WAY WORLD	II.1	61
Marwood:	O then it seems you are one of his favourable	412	WAY WORLD	II.1	77
Fainall:	O my Dear I am satisfy'd of your Tenderness; I know	412	WAY WORLD	II.1	95
Fainall:	O the pious Friendships of the Female Sex!	414	WAY WORLD	II.1	166
Marwood:	Poor dissembling!--O that--Well,	416	WAY WORLD	II.1	231
Mirabell:	O you should Hate with Prudence.	416	WAY WORLD	II.1	256
Millamant:	O I have deny'd my self Airs to Day. I have walk'd	418	WAY WORLD	II.1	333
Millamant:	Ay, that's true--O but then I had--	419	WAY WORLD	II.1	355
Mincing:	O Mem, your Laship staid to peruse a Pecquet of	419	WAY WORLD	II.1	357
Mincing:	O Mem, your Laship staid to peruse a Pacquet of	419	WAY WORLD	II.1	V357
Millamant:	O ay, Letters--I had Letters--I am	419	WAY WORLD	II.1	359
Mincing:	O Mem, I shall never forget it.	419	WAY WORLD	II.1	369
Millamant:	O ay, and went away--Now I think on't I'm angry	420	WAY WORLD	II.1	378
Millamant:	O I ask your Pardon for that--One's Cruelty	420	WAY WORLD	II.1	385
Millamant:	O the Vanity of these Men! Fainall, dee hear him?	420	WAY WORLD	II.1	399
Millamant:	O Fiction; Fainall, let us leave these Men.	421	WAY WORLD	II.1	423
Mirabell:	the force of Instinct--O here come my pair of Turtles	423	WAY WORLD	II.1	501
Foible:	O las Sir, I'm so asham'd--I'm afraid my Lady	423	WAY WORLD	II.1	513
Foible:	O dear Sir, your humble Servant.	424	WAY WORLD	II.1	536
Foible:	dress till I come--(Looking out.) O Dear, I'm sure	424	WAY WORLD	II.1	544
Lady Wish:	O Marwood, let her come in. Come in good	426	WAY WORLD	III.1	40
Marwood:	O Madam, you cannot suspect Mrs. Foible's	426	WAY WORLD	III.1	55
Lady Wish:	O, he carries Poyson in his Tongue that wou'd	426	WAY WORLD	III.1	57
Lady Wish:	O Foible; where hast thou been? What hast thou been	427	WAY WORLD	III.1	70
Foible:	O Madam; 'tis a shame to say what he said--	427	WAY WORLD	III.1	93
Foible:	disinherited. O you would bless your self, to hear what he	428	WAY WORLD	III.1	108
Lady Wish:	Is he! O then he'll Importune, if he's a brisk	429	WAY WORLD	III.1	176
Lady Wish:	O I'm glad he's a brisk Man. Let my	429	WAY WORLD	III.1	180
Mrs Fain:	O Foible, I have been in a Fright, least I shou'd	430	WAY WORLD	III.1	184
Foible:	O dear Madam, I beg your Pardon. It was not my	430	WAY WORLD	III.1	195
Foible:	O dear Madam, Mr. Mirabell is such a sweet winning	430	WAY WORLD	III.1	201
Mrs Fain:	O rare Foible!	430	WAY WORLD	III.1	213
Marwood:	met with your Match.--O Man, Man! Woman,	431	WAY WORLD	III.1	235
Lady Wish:	O dear Marwood what shall I say, for this rude	431	WAY WORLD	III.1	250
Lady Wish:	O he's in less Danger of being spoil'd by his	431	WAY WORLD	III.1	262
Lady Wish:	O Dear, I can't appear till I'm dress'd. Dear	432	WAY WORLD	III.1	278
Millamant:	O silly! Ha, ha, ha. I cou'd laugh immoderately.	433	WAY WORLD	III.1	335
Millamant:	O Dear, what? for it is the same thing, if I hear	434	WAY WORLD	III.1	352
Millamant:	O Madam, why so do I--And yet the Creature	434	WAY WORLD	III.1	355
Lady Wish:	O he's a Rallier, Nephew--My Cousin's a	441	WAY WORLD	III.1	606
Fainall:	O, for that matter leave me to manage him; I'll	443	WAY WORLD	III.1	671
Lady Wish:	and rise to meet him in a pretty disorder--Yes--O,	445	WAY WORLD	IV.1	28
Lady Wish:	O dear, has my Nephew made his Addresses	445	WAY WORLD	IV.1	34
Mrs Fain:	O Sir Wilfull; you are come at the Critical Instant. There's	446	WAY WORLD	IV.1	70
Mrs Fain:	O fie Sir Wilfull! What, you must not be	446	WAY WORLD	IV.1	81
Millamant:	O, I should think I was poor and had nothing to	449	WAY WORLD	IV.1	167
Millamant:	never sure in Love. O, I hate a Lover, that can dare to think,	449	WAY WORLD	IV.1	175
Millamant:	O horrid proviso's! filthy strong Waters! I toste	452	WAY WORLD	IV.1	278
Lady Wish:	O Sir Rowland, the hours that he has dy'd	458	WAY WORLD	IV.1	511
Waitwell:	O, she is the Antidote to desire. Spouse, thou will't	459	WAY WORLD	IV.1	560
Waitwell:	Rascal and disguis'd and subborn'd for that imposture,--O	460	WAY WORLD	IV.1	592
Waitwell:	villany, O villany!--by the Contrivance of--	460	WAY WORLD	IV.1	593
Foible:	O Treachery! But are you sure Sir Rowland, it is his	460	WAY WORLD	IV.1	604
Foible:	O what luck it is Sir Rowland, that you were present	461	WAY WORLD	IV.1	610
Lady Wish:	shou'd be kill'd I must never shew my face; or hang'd,--O	461	WAY WORLD	IV.1	627
Lady Wish:	come alive. O this is a happy discovery.	461	WAY WORLD	IV.1	641
Foible:	defend my self? O Madam, if you knew but what he promis'd	463	WAY WORLD	V.1	29
Lady Wish:	Hospital for a decay'd Pimp? No damage? O thou frontless	463	WAY WORLD	V.1	36
Foible:	O that ever I was Born, O that I was ever Married,	463	WAY WORLD	V.1	58
Foible:	O Madam, my Lady's gone for a Constable; I shall	463	WAY WORLD	V.1	62
Mincing:	Closet, till my old Lady's anger is abated. O, my old Lady	465	WAY WORLD	V.1	107
Mincing:	six thousand Pound. O, come Mrs. Foible, I hear my old	465	WAY WORLD	V.1	116
Mincing:	O yes Mem, I'll vouch any thing for your Ladyship's	465	WAY WORLD	V.1	121

O (continued)

		PAGE	TITLE	ACT.SC	LINE
Lady Wish:	O my dear Friend, how can I Enumerate the	465	WAY WORLD	V.1	125
Lady Wish:	O Daughter, Daughter, Is it possible thou	465	WAY WORLD	V.1	139
Lady Wish:	O dear Friend; I am so asham'd that you	466	WAY WORLD	V.1	167
Lady Wish:	more from you than all your life can accomplish--O don't	466	WAY WORLD	V.1	170
Lady Wish:	--O, she never lock'd a Man in the Face but her own	467	WAY WORLD	V.1	191
Lady Wish:	the Bases roar Blasphemy. O, she wou'd have swooned at	467	WAY WORLD	V.1	201
Lady Wish:	her foot within the door of a Play-house. O my dear	467	WAY WORLD	V.1	205
Lady Wish:	her foot within the door of a Play-house. O dear	467	WAY WORLD	V.1	V205
Marwood:	Lawyers? To be usherd in with an O Yez of Scandal; and	467	WAY WORLD	V.1	211
Marwood:	Lawyers? To be usherd in with an O Yes of Scandal; and	467	WAY WORLD	V.1	V211
Lady Wish:	O, 'tis very hard!	467	WAY WORLD	V.1	223
Lady Wish:	O, 'tis Insupportable. No, no, dear Friend	468	WAY WORLD	V.1	237
Fainall:	O, if you are prescrib'd Marriage, you shall be	468	WAY WORLD	V.1	265
Lady Wish:	O dear Marwood, you are not going?	471	WAY WORLD	V.1	356
Lady Wish:	O what? what? to save me and my Child	473	WAY WORLD	V.1	453
Marwood:	(to Fainall) O my shame! (Mirabell and Lady	474	WAY WORLD	V.1	472
Lady Wish:	O Marwood, Marwood art thou false? my friend	474	WAY WORLD	V.1	480
Mirabell:	O in good time--Your leave for the other Offender	475	WAY WORLD	V.1	506
Lady Wish:	O Sir Rowland--well Rascal.	475	WAY WORLD	V.1	509
Lady Wish:	O Daughter, Daughter, 'tis plain thou hast	477	WAY WORLD	V.1	568
Foible:	O Sir, Some that were provided for Sir Rowland's	478	WAY WORLD	V.1	605

O-law (1)

		PAGE	TITLE	ACT.SC	LINE
Lady Froth:	O-law, I swear it's but the sixth,--and I han't	166	DOUBL DLR	III.1	612

O' (44)

		PAGE	TITLE	ACT.SC	LINE
Bellmour:	Pox o' Business--And so must Time, my	37	OLD BATCH	I.1	9
Bellmour:	Not o' your side, Madam, I confess--But my	57	OLD BATCH	II.2	117
Vainlove:	Pox o' my sawcy Credulity.--If I have lost	100	OLD BATCH	V.1	125
Mellefont:	O' my word, Brisk, that was a home thrust; you	128	DOUBL DLR	I.1	31
Lady Touch:	O' Maskwell, in Vain I do disguise me from	137	DOUBL DLR	I.1	396
Lady Froth:	O' my Conscience no more we should; thou	139	DOUBL DLR	II.1	27
Sr Sampson:	be--hah! old Merlin! body o' me, I'm so glad I'm	240	FOR LOVE	II.1	184
Sr Sampson:	Body o' me, I have made a Cuckold of a King, and the	241	FOR LOVE	II.1	222
Sr Sampson:	Body o' me, I have gone too far;--I must not	242	FOR LOVE	II.1	241
Sr Sampson:	I think on't, Body o' me, I have a Shoulder of an Egyptian	242	FOR LOVE	II.1	249
Sr Sampson:	Body o' me, so do I.--Heark ye, Valentine.	243	FOR LOVE	II.1	279
Sr Sampson:	damn'd Tyburn face, without the benefit o' the Clergy.	243	FOR LOVE	II.1	307
Sr Sampson:	Body o' me--	244	FOR LOVE	II.1	320
Sr Sampson:	Body o' me, what a many headed Monster have	244	FOR LOVE	II.1	343
Sr Sampson:	and unreasonable,--Body o' me, why was not I a	246	FOR LOVE	II.1	389
Mrs Frail:	O' my Soul, I'm afraid not--eh!--filthy	250	FOR LOVE	II.1	564
Sr Sampson:	Frail, you shall see my Son Ben--Body o' me, he's the	259	FOR LOVE	III.1	212
Sr Sampson:	Estate: Body o' me, he does not care a Doit for your	260	FOR LOVE	III.1	243
Sr Sampson:	My Son Ben! bless thee my dear Boy; body o'	260	FOR LOVE	III.1	270
Sr Sampson:	Dick, body o' me, Dick has been dead these two	261	FOR LOVE	III.1	292
Ben:	Sail o' your Head--Top and Top-gallant by the Mess.	262	FOR LOVE	III.1	332
Sr Sampson:	Body o' me, Madam, you say true:--Look	262	FOR LOVE	III.1	349
Ben:	o' Nine-tails laid cross your Shoulders. Flesh! who are	264	FOR LOVE	III.1	409
Sr Sampson:	Body o' me, I don't know any universal Grievance,	266	FOR LOVE	III.1	485
Sr Sampson:	Why, body o' me, out with't.	266	FOR LOVE	III.1	495
Sr Sampson:	or his Divination--Body o' me, this is a Trick to	267	FOR LOVE	III.1	505
Ben:	And lie o' Nights alone.	274	FOR LOVE	III.1	767
Mrs Frail:	O' you are the happiest, merriest Men alive.	275	FOR LOVE	III.1	804
Sr Sampson:	Ready, body o' me, he must be ready; his	278	FOR LOVE	IV.1	116
Sr Sampson:	Body o' me, I know not what to say to him.	280	FOR LOVE	IV.1	166
Sr Sampson:	Body o' me, he talks sensibly in his madness--	280	FOR LOVE	IV.1	180
Sr Sampson:	pretty well now, Val: Body o' me, I was sorry to see thee	281	FOR LOVE	IV.1	202
Sr Sampson:	Are we? A Pox o' your Prognostication--Why,	283	FOR LOVE	IV.1	279
Sr Sampson:	in Expectation of a lucky Hour. When, body o' me,	283	FOR LOVE	IV.1	290
Mrs Frail:	O' my Conscience, here he comes.	285	FOR LOVE	IV.1	353
Mrs Frail:	--O' my life I am half vex'd at the insensibility of a	287	FOR LOVE	IV.1	452
Sr Sampson:	--Body o' me, I have a Trick to turn the Settlement	300	FOR LOVE	V.1	127
Sr Sampson:	o' me, he shall be thy Father, I'll make him thy Father, and	308	FOR LOVE	V.1	396
Ben:	believe the Devil wou'd not venture aboard o' your	309	FOR LOVE	V.1	435
Sr Sampson:	Sleep Quotha! No, why you would not sleep o'	310	FOR LOVE	V.1	484
Mrs Pain:	Do I? I think I am a little sick o' the suddain.	412	WAY WORLD	II.1	80
Sir Wilful:	A pox, is this your Inns o' Court breeding, not to know	439	WAY WORLD	III.1	528
Lady Wish:	'tis with drinking your Health--O' my Word you are	455	WAY WORLD	IV.1	407
Sir Wilful:	be O' the Quorum--an it were not as good a deed as to	472	WAY WORLD	V.1	393

O'ds (1)

		PAGE	TITLE	ACT.SC	LINE
Sir Wilful:	--O'ds heart, and then tell a familiar Tale of a Cock	439	WAY WORLD	III.1	546

O'er (8)

		PAGE	TITLE	ACT.SC	LINE
Almeria:	Lead me o'er Bones and Skulls, and mouldring Earth	339	M. BRIDE	II.1	74
Zara:	And like the Morn vermilion'd o'er thy Face.	347	M. BRIDE	II.2	284
Osmyn-Alph:	Abandon'd o'er to love what Heav'n forsakes?	351	M. BRIDE	III.1	56
Osmyn-Alph:	Paternal Love prevailing o'er his Sorrows;	352	M. BRIDE	III.1	113
Osmyn-Alph:	Like Fumes of Sacred Incense, o'er the Clouds,	353	M. BRIDE	III.1	130
Zara:	And watch like Tapers o'er your Hours of Rest.	360	M. BRIDE	III.1	429
Manuel:	O'er them that are thy Guards!--Mark that thou	374	M. BRIDE	V	55
	O'er which she broods to hatch the Changling-Kind.	393	WAY WORLD	PRO.	8

O'er-cast (1)

		PAGE	TITLE	ACT.SC	LINE
Bellmour:	tho' now they are o'er-cast.	81	OLD BATCH	IV.2	22

O'er-flow (1)

		PAGE	TITLE	ACT.SC	LINE
Osmyn-Alph:	Not to o'er-flow in Tribute to thy Memory.	383	M. BRIDE	V.2	314

O'er-joy'd (1)

		PAGE	TITLE	ACT.SC	LINE
Sir Wilful:	'Sheart why do'st not speak? Art thou o'er-joy'd?	439	WAY WORLD	III.1	519

O'fashion (1)

		PAGE	TITLE	ACT.SC	LINE
	Now that's at stake--No fool, 'tis out o'fashion.	113	OLD BATCH	EPI.	12

O'Fortune (1)

		PAGE	TITLE	ACT.SC	LINE
Mellefont:	Consideration or the fear of Repentance. Pox o'Fortune,	168	DOUBL DLR	IV.1	29

O'mind (1)

		PAGE	TITLE	ACT.SC	LINE
Sir Joseph:	him, till I can get out of his sight; but out o'sight out				
	o'mind	48	OLD BATCH	II.1	45

O'nights (1)

		PAGE	TITLE	ACT.SC	LINE
Scandal:	Do you sleep well o'nights?	268	FOR LOVE	III.1	566

Obligation   (continued)
```
   Sr Sampson:   Obligation--Look you, as plain as can be, so it begins--  . 281  FOR LCVE    IV.1   222
   Sr Sampson:   I have a Proviso in the Obligation in favour of my self     . 300  FOR LOVE     V.1   126
   Angelica:     Let me consult my Lawyer concerning this Obligation;    .  . 301  FOR LOVE     V.1   134
   Millamant:    only tc my own taste; to have no obligation upon me to    . 450  WAY WORLD   IV.1   216
   Mirabell:     any Obligation to me; or else perhaps I cou'd advise.--   . 473  WAY WORLD    V.1   452
```
Obligations (5)
```
   Mellefont:    He has Obligaticns of Gratitude, to bind him to  . .  . . 131  DOUBL DLR    I.1   149
   Lady Touch:   incline you, no Obligations touch you? Have not my  . .  . 136  DOUEL DLR    I.1   346
   Lady Ply:     a suitable return to those Obligations which you are pleased 159  DOUBL DLR  III.1   338
   Zara:         And try the Force of yet more Obligations.     .    . .  . 363  M. BRIDE    IV.1    98
   Marwood:      My Obligations to my Lady urg'd me: I had  . .  . .  . . 414  WAY WCRLD   II.1   162
```
Oblige (17)
```
   Belinda:      I shall oblige you, in leaving you to the full and free   . 57  OLD BATCH   II.2    88
   Araminta:     So, this I expected--You won't oblige me   .  . .  . .  . 57  OLD BATCH   II.2   101
   Araminta:     Discourse--Pray oblige us with the last new Song.  .   .  . 59  OLD BATCH   II.2   187
   Laetitia:     Yes it will break to oblige you.  . .  . . .  . . . .    . 77  OLD BATCH   IV.1    95
   Lord Touch:   Don't cblige me to press you. .  . . . .  . . . . . .   . 152  DOUBL DLR  III.1    53
   Lady Froth:   I will; you'd oblige me extremely to write Notes    .    . 165  DOUBL DLR  III.1   554
   Lady Ply:     would oblige him. . .  . .  . . . .  . . . . . .  .  .  . 171  DOUBL DLR   IV.1   154
   Valentine:    hope you will have more Indulgence, than to cblige me to  . 243  FOR LCVE    II.1   283
   Sr Sampson:   oblige him. Odsbud, Madam, have nc more to say to  .  .  . 259  FCR LCVE   III.1   239
   Angelica:     oblige me to be ccncern'd for him; but to Love is neither  . 277  FOR LOVE    IV.1    73
   Angelica:     carried on, between you and me, it would oblige   .  .  . 300  FOR LCVE     V.1   109
   Manuel:       And Garcia's well-try'd Valour, all oblige me.  .  .   . 334  M. BRIDE     I.1   341
   Garcia:       I would oblige him, but he shuns my Kindness;   .  .  . 335  M. BRIDE     I.1   369
   Mrs Fain:     Mirabell, and I dare promise you will oblige us both.  . 412  WAY WCRLD   II.1   107
   Millamant:    will cblige me to leave me: I have just now a little    . 448  WAY WORLD   IV.1   140
   Lady Wish:    that invades me with scme precipitation--You will oblige  . 457  WAY WORLD   IV.1   468
   Fainall:      Life; on condition you oblige your self never to Marry,   . 468  WAY WCRLD    V.1   253
```
Obliged (7)
```
   Sharper:      Is it possible! Then I am happy to have obliged the   .  . 49  OLD BATCH   II.1    72
   Bellmour:     Since all Artifice is vain--and I think my self oblig'd   . 93  OLD BATCH   IV.4   157
   Sir Paul:     I am much obliged to Mr. Careless really, he is a  .  . 172  DOUBL DLR   IV.1   178
   Tattle:       there too--for then she is obliged to keep the Secret.   . 232  FOR LCVE     I.1   614
   Tattle:       there too--for then she's obliged to keep the Secret.    . 232  FOR LOVE     I.1 V614
   Valentine:    tell whether the Lady or Mr. Tattle be the more obliged   . 256  FOR LCVE   III.1   130
   Angelica:     if I were obliged to make a Choice, I declare I'd rather   . 260  FCR LOVE   III.1   255
```
Obliges (1)
```
   Tattle:       only cbliges a Man to Secresie, that she may have the   . 228  FOR LCVE     I.1   474
```
Obliging (4)
```
   Bellmour:     'em, but must also undertake the harder Task, of obliging   41  OLD BATCH    I.1   143
   Capt Bluff:   You are obliging Sir, but this is too publick a Place   . 69  OLD BATCH  III.1   322
   Araminta:     'Tis but pulling off our Masks, and obliging  .  . .  . 86  OLD BATCH   IV.3   101
   Lady Ply:     You are so obliging, Sir.  . . . . . . . . . . .  .  . 160  DOUEL DLR  III.1   358
```
Obliterated (1)
```
   Buckram:      Why then all's obliterated, Sir Sampson, if he be   .  . 279  FOR LOVE    IV.1   142
```
Oblivion (1)
```
   Vainlove:     an Act of Oblivion.  . . . . . . . . . . . .  .  . . 110  OLD BATCH    V.2   103
```
Obscene (2)
```
   Lady Ply:     inhumane, and obscene that she should break it. (Aside.)
                 I'll                                                    . 171  DOUEL DLR   IV.1   152
   Lady Wish:    the sight or name of an obscene Play-Book--and can I    . 467  WAY WORLD    V.1   202
```
Obscure (2)
```
   Gonsalez:     Her Words and Actions are obscure and double,   . . .  . 366  M. BRIDE    IV.1   195
   Alonzo:       Sever'd the Head; and in an obscure Corner   .  . . .  . 379  M. BRIDE     V.2 V115
```
Obscurity (2)
```
   Scandal:      into Cbscurity and Futurity; and if you commit an Error,   . 267  FOR LOVE   III.1   515
   Zara:         To find this Place of Horrour and Obscurity?   . .  . . 345  M. BRIDE    II.2   240
```
Observ'd (5)
```
   Vainlove:     observ'd tho' the Penalty of it be dispens'd with; and an   . 87  OLD BATCH   IV.3   153
   Maskwell:     observ'd.--I'll send the Chaplain to you with his Robes;  . 194  DOUBL DLR    V.1   241
   Mrs Frail:    have cbserv'd us more than we have observ'd one another.  . 248  FCR LOVE    II.1   488
   Scandal:      which is rightly observ'd by Gregory the Great in favour of   . 267  FOR LCVE   III.1   536
```
Observe (7)
```
   Sharper:      purpose. Setter, stand close; seem not to observe 'em; and,  101  OLD BATCH    V.1   164
   Mellefont:    Gallantry, as they call it. I'le observe my Uncle my self;  130  DOUBL DLR    I.1   135
   Mellefont:    Gallantry, as they call it. I'll observe my Uncle my self;  130  DOUBL DLR    I.1 V135
   Lady Froth:   And my lord with him: pray observe the   .  . . . .  . 139  DOUBL DLR    II.1    55
   Lady Froth:   Take no notice--But observe me--Now   .  . . . . . .  . 177  DOUEL DLR   IV.1   365
   Mrs Frail:    a Confessor--He thinks we don't observe him.  . . . .  . 250  FOR LOVE    II.1   543
   Sr Sampson:   Watch, and the Bridegroom shall observe it's Motions;  . 266  FOR LCVE   III.1   474
```
Observers (1)
```
   Scandal:      the Stars, and were Observers of Omens--Solomon was   . 267  FOR LOVE   III.1   530
```
Obstacle (4)
```
   Maskwell:     you, I meet the only Obstacle to my Fortune. Cynthia, let  . 150  DOUBL DLR   II.1   440
   Gonsalez:     The greatest Obstacle is then remov'd.  . . . .  . .  . 372  M. BBIDE    IV.1   445
   Fainall:      Aunt, and be the officious Obstacle of his Match with   . 414  WAY WCRLD   II.1   160
   Marwood:      Obstacle.   .  . .  . . . . . . . . . .  . . . .  . . 443  WAY WORLD  III.1   670
```
Obstinacy (4)
```
   Heartwell:    when 'tis out of Obstinacy and Contradiction--But    .  . 74  OLD BATCH  III.2   127
   Araminta:     Woman's Obstinacy made me blind to what   .  .  . .  . 88  OLD BATCH   IV.3   191
   Cynthia:      but I find I have obstinacy enough to pursue whatever I  . 193  DOUEL DLR    V.1   203
   Fainall:      Obstinacy--But when he's drunk, he's as loving as   . .  . 401  WAY WORLD    I.1   219
```
Obstinate (2)
```
   Fondlewife:   and because I was obstinate and doating; sc that my   .  . 76  OLD BATCH   IV.1    54
   Alonzo:       O bloody Proof, of obstinate Fidelity!   . . . . .  . . 373  M. BRIDE     V.1    19
```
Obstinately (1)
```
   Mellefont:    Let him alone, Brisk, he is obstinately bent not to   .  . 134  DOUBL DLR    I.1   280
```
Obtain (4)
```
   Musician:     Never let him much obtain.  .  .  . . . . . .  . . .  . 59  OLD BATCH   II.2   195
                 Nor wou'd obtain precariously Applause.   . . .  . .   . 324  M. BRIDE    PRO.    42
   Selim:        I can no more, the King is here. Obtain   .  . . . .  . 362  M. BBIDE    IV.1    59
   Mirabell:     Contrition, can but obtain the least glance of Compassion  471  WAY WCRLD    V.1   368
```
Obtain'd (2)
```
   Zara:         Our Wish; and that obtain'd, down with the Scaffolding   . 347  M. BBIDE    II.2   318
```

Obtain'd (continued)
  Mirabell: Elder Date than what you have obtain'd from your Lady.   . 476 WAY WORLD V.1 555
Obvious (2)
  Belinda: obvious to every Stander by. . . . .   55 OLD BATCH II.2   35
  Tattle: obvious to Vulgar Eyes; that are Indications of a sudden . 304 FOR LOVE   V.1 268
Occasion (24)
  Capt Bluff: You have disoblig'd me in it--for I have occasion . .   67 OLD BATCH III.1 248
  Sir Joseph: and to speak, is but loss of time; but if there be occasion, 103 OLD BATCH III.1 244
  Heartwell: that such an Occasion of Melancholy? Is it such an . . 104 OLD BATCH V.1 301
  Belinda: You have occasion for't, your Wife has been blown . . 108 OLD BATCH V.2   36
  Maskwell: added to my hopes; I watch'd the Occasion, and took you, . 136 DOUBL DLR I.1 366
  Maskwell: confirm all, had there been occasion. . . . . . . 154 DOUBL DLR III.1 130
  Lady Froth: Coachman, for you know there's most occasion for a . . 164 DOUBL DLR III.1 520
  Maskwell: this is an Occasion in which I would not willingly be . 182 DOUBL DLR IV.1 553
  Tattle: There's no occasion for a Lie; I cou'd never tell a Lie . 253 FOR LOVE   III.1 21
  Tattle: and if there be occasion for Witnesses, I can summon the . 257 FOR LOVE   III.1 154
  Scandal: Not upon a kind occasion, Madam. But when a Lady . . 276 FOR LOVE   IV.1   23
  Scandal: be occasion; for I fancy his Presence provokes him more. . 280 FOR LOVE   IV.1 190
  Angelica: --I have more Occasion for your Conduct than your . . 298 FOR LOVE   V.1   45
  Jeremy: plausible Occasion for me to quench my Thirst at the . 302 FOR LOVE   V.1 175
  Valentine: No; here's the Fool; and if occasion be, I'll give it . 310 FOR LOVE   V.1 497
  Manuel: To see thee weep on this Occasion--But some . . . . 333 M. BRIDE   I.1 277
  Manuel: To see thee weep on this Occasion--some . . . . 333 M. BRIDE   I.1 V277
  Heli: Occasion will not fail to point out Ways . . . . 352 M. BRIDE   III.1 97
  Osmyn-Alph: Occasion past. . . . . 354 M. BRIDE   III.1 200
  Zara: Swift as Occasion, I . . . . 354 M. BRIDE   III.1 201
  Mrs Fain: one scandalous Story, to avoid giving an occasion to make . 412 WAY WORLD II.1 105
  Mrs Fain: of which you have been the occasion? Why did you . . 417 WAY WORLD II.1 263
  Mirabell: to the Occasion; a worse had not answer'd to the Purpose. . 417 WAY WORLD II.1 276
  Mrs Fain: occasion, and slip down the back-stairs, where Foible . 452 WAY WORLD IV.1 304
Occasion'd (1)
  Scandal: work a Cure; as the fear of your Aversion occasion'd his . 277 FOR LOVE   IV.1   64
Occasions (6)
  Heartwell: occasions; till in a little time, being disabled or
                  disarm'd, ...   43 OLD BATCH I.1 247
  Sir Joseph: Summer, all Seasons and occasions shall testify the reality 49 OLD BATCH II.1   67
                But we're so us'd to Rail on these Occasions, ... 113 OLD BATCH EPI.   19
  Scandal: Occasions; some pity you, and condemn your Father: . . 220 FOR LOVE   I.1 160
  Mirabell: inscrib'd on the back may serve your occasions. . . . 476 WAY WORLD V.1 549
  Mirabell: written on the back may serve your occasions. . . . . 476 WAY WORLD V.1 V549
Occupation (2)
  Bellmour: and Pleasure, my Occupation; and let Father Time shake . 37 OLD BATCH I.1   24
  Mirabell: for Motion not Method is their Occupation. To know this, . 423 WAY WORLD IV.1 498
Occupy (1)
  Valentine: Occupy the Family. Coffee-Houses will be full of Smoak . 289 FOR LOVE   IV.1 507
Occur (2)
  Zara: O Heav'n! a thousand things occur . . . . 363 M. BRIDE   IV.1   92
  Zara: O Heav'n! a thousand things occur at once . . . . 363 M. BRIDE   IV.1 V 92
Ocean (2)
  Almeria: The cruel Ocean would deprive thee of a Tomb, . . . 328 M. BRIDE   I.1   73
  Almeria: The cruel Ocean is no more thy Tomb, ... 328 M. BRIDE   I.1 V 73
Ocular (1)
  Lord Touch: How! give me but Proof of it, Ocular . . . . . . 182 DOUBL DLR IV.1 562
Odd (29)
  Cynthia: as Fools. 'Tis an odd Game we're going to Play at: What . 142 DOUBL DLR II.1 157
  Foresight: tell me--won't you speak? Odd I'll-- . . . . . . 239 FOR LOVE   II.1 158
  Sr Sampson: Is Ben come? Odso, my Son Ben come? Odd, ... 259 FOR LOVE   III.1 210
  Sr Sampson: with the Reprobate; Odd, I was sorry for you with all my . 260 FOR LOVE   III.1 259
  Sr Sampson: Cadua of Fourscore for Sustenance. Odd, I love to see a . 260 FOR LOVE   III.1 262
  Sr Sampson: help of a Parson, ha? Odd if he should I cou'd not be angry . 265 FOR LOVE   III.1 461
  Sr Sampson: a fair Lady, a great while--Odd, Madam, you have . . 298 FOR LOVE   V.1   14
  Sr Sampson: Words. Odd, I have warm Blood about me yet, I can serve . 298 FOR LOVE   V.1   23
  Sr Sampson: Words. Odd, I have warm Blood about me yet, and can serve . 298 FOR LOVE   V.1 V 23
  Sr Sampson: --Come, don't despise Fifty; odd Fifty, in a hale . . 298 FOR LOVE   V.1   26
  Sr Sampson: Odsbud, and 'tis pity you should--(Aside.) Odd, . . . 298 FOR LOVE   V.1   48
  Sr Sampson: Rogues: Odd, wou'd she wou'd; faith and troth she's . 298 FOR LOVE   V.1   50
  Sr Sampson: of these young idle Rogues about the Town. Odd, there's . 299 FOR LOVE   V.1   53
  Sr Sampson: Odd, you are hard to please, Madam; to find a . . . 299 FOR LOVE   V.1   65
  Sr Sampson: Odd, Madam, I love you--And if you . . . . . . 300 FOR LOVE   V.1 103
  Sr Sampson: only be seemingly carried on?--Odd, let it be a real . 300 FOR LOVE   V.1 115
  Sr Sampson: and I a happy Man. Odd, Madam, I'll love you as long as I . 300 FOR LOVE   V.1 119
  Sr Sampson: Odd, you're cunning, a wary Baggage! Faith . . . . 300 FOR LOVE   V.1 124
  Sr Sampson: Odd, you're devilish Handsome; Faith and Troth, you're . 301 FOR LOVE   V.1 141
  Sr Sampson: --Odd, I think we are very well met;--Give me . . . 301 FOR LOVE   V.1 144
  Sr Sampson: your Hand, Odd let me kiss it; 'tis as warm and as soft . 301 FOR LOVE   V.1 145
  Sr Sampson: --as what?--Odd, as t'other Hand--give me . . . . 301 FOR LOVE   V.1 146
  Sr Sampson: little Sampson: Odd, Sampson's a very good Name for an . 301 FOR LOVE   V.1 154
  Sr Sampson: Odd, I long to be pulling down too, come away-- . . 301 FOR LOVE   V.1 161
  Sr Sampson: Odd, I long to be pulling too, come away-- . . . . 301 FOR LOVE   V.1 V161
  Sr Sampson: and I'm Lord of the Ascendant. Odd, you're an old Fellow, . 307 FOR LOVE   V.1 382
  Sr Sampson: troth you shall. Odd we'll have the Musick of the Spheres . 307 FOR LOVE   V.1 385
  Fainall: Sir Wilfull is an odd mixture of Bashfulness and . . 401 WAY WORLD I.1 218
  Witwoud: --Faith and Troth a pretty deal of an odd sort of a small . 403 WAY WORLD I.1 290
Odds (1)
  Cynthia: was the Devil, I'll allow for irresistable odds. But if
                  I find . . . . 169 DOUBL DLR IV.1   59
Odious (7)
  Bellmour: How now George, where hast thou been snarling odious . . 42 OLD BATCH I.1 180
  Capt Bluff: pretty Fellow--but Sir Joseph, comparisons are odious-- . 52 OLD BATCH II.1 179
  Mirabell: Woman wou'd be odious, serve but to make her more . . 399 WAY WORLD I.1 162
  Millamant: Sure never any thing was so Unbred as that odious . . 432 WAY WORLD III.1 284
  Millamant: Odious endeavours? . . . . 451 WAY WORLD IV.1 259
  Millamant: fellows, Odious Men! I hate your Odious proviso's. . . 452 WAY WORLD IV.1 279
Odium (1)
  Lady Wish: to Impress upon her tender Years, a Young Odium and . . 466 WAY WORLD V.1 185

Odly (2)

Belinda:	Cousin, you talk odly--What ever the Matter is, O	. . .	55	OLD BATCH	II.2	51
Lady Touch:	seriously, but methought it look'd odly.	. . . . . .	153	DOUBL DLR	III.1	85

Odour (1)

Waitwell:	Frankincense, all Chastity and Odour.	. . . . .	459	WAY WORLD	IV.1	546

Ods (4)   see O'ds

Nurse:	(knocks) Ods my Life, won't you open the Door? I'll	. .	253	FOR LOVE	III.1	11
Lady Wish:	Ods my Life, I'll have him, I'll have him	. . . .	427	WAY WORLD	III.1	102
Lady Wish:	Ods my life, I'll send him to her. Call her down,	. .	445	WAY WORLD	IV.1	37
Sir Wilful:	Tony, Ods heart where's Tony--Tony's an honest fellow,	.	455	WAY WORLD	IV.1	413

Odsbud (10)

Sr Sampson:	have significations of futurity about him; Odsbud, I	. .	242	FOR LOVE	II.1	244
Sr Sampson:	oblige him. Odsbud, Madam, have no more to say to	.	259	FOR LOVE	III.1	239
Sr Sampson:	Odsbud, well spoken; and you are a Wiser	. . . .	260	FOR LOVE	III.1	249
Sr Sampson:	Odsbud, and I'm glad to see thee, kiss me Boy,	. .	260	FOR LOVE	III.1	273
Sr Sampson:	Not at all, Madam: Odsbud you wrong me; I	. . . .	298	FOR LOVE	V.1	21
Sr Sampson:	Odsbud, and 'tis pity you should--(Aside.) Odd,	. . .	298	FOR LOVE	V.1	48
Sr Sampson:	Truth. Odsbud, you have won my Heart: I hate a Wit; I	.	299	FOR LOVE	V.1	80
Sr Sampson:	(aside). Odsbud I believe she likes me--Ah,	. . . .	299	FOR LOVE	V.1	93
Sr Sampson:	upon the Issue Male of our Two Bodies begotten. Odsbud,	.	300	FOR LOVE	V.1	128
Sr Sampson:	Odsbud, Hussy, you know how to chuse, and so do I;	. .	301	FOR LOVE	V.1	143

Odso (6)

Foresight:	Odso, let me see; Let me see the Paper--Ay,	. . . .	240	FOR LOVE	II.1	186
Foresight:	When was this Sign'd, what Hour? Odso, you should	. .	240	FOR LOVE	II.1	189
Sr Sampson:	Is Ben come? Odso, my Son Ben come? Odd,	. . . .	259	FOR LOVE	III.1	210
Sr Sampson:	the next Morning.--Odso, have a care, Madam.	. . . .	299	FOR LOVE	V.1	59
Sr Sampson:	Odso, here's some body coming.	. . . .	301	FOR LOVE	V.1	162
Witwoud:	Odso Brother, is it you? Your Servant Brother.	. . .	439	WAY WORLD	III.1	520

Odzooks (2)

Sr Sampson:	and I'll consult a Parson; Odzooks I'm a Young Man:	.	301	FOR LOVE	V.1	139
Sr Sampson:	Odzooks I'm a young Man, and I'll make it appear--	. .	301	FOR LOVE	V.1	140

Oeconomy (1)

Lady Wish:	my Features, to receive Sir Rowland with any Oeconomy of	.	428	WAY WORLD	III.1	141

Of (2327)   see O', O'th, Oth'

Of's (2)

Heartwell:	like his Grace, has just his smile and air of's Face. Then		45	OLD BATCH	I.1	321

Off (76)   see Hiss'd-off

	(Runs off.)	. . . . . .	35	OLD BATCH	PRO.	28
Bellmour:	perverts our Aim, casts off the Bias, and leaves us wide and		37	OLD BATCH	I.1	11
Bellmour:	Well come off George, if at any time you should be	. .	44	OLD BATCH	I.1	286
Heartwell:	off as unconcern'd, come chuck the Infant under the chin,		45	OLD BATCH	I.1	325
Belinda:	Hold off your Fists, and see that he gets a Chair with	.	57	OLD BATCH	II.2	95
Lucy:	Strike Heartwell home, before the Bait's worn off the	. .	61	OLD BATCH	III.1	10
Lucy:	Stand off--He's a precious Jewel.	. . . .	67	OLD BATCH	III.1	227
Bellmour:	(Throwing off his Cloak, Patch, &c.)	. .	81	OLD BATCH	IV.2	13
Belinda:	And so--But where did I leave off, my Dear? I was	. .	83	OLD BATCH	IV.3	19
Araminta:	but you left off before you began.	. . . .	83	OLD BATCH	IV.3	22
Araminta:	'Tis but pulling off our Masks, and obliging	. . . .	86	OLD BATCH	IV.3	101
Laetitia:	Ha! This fool may be of use. Stand off, rude Ruffian.	. .	90	OLD BATCH	IV.4	46
Heartwell:	you, Sir, I shall find a time; but take off your Wasp here,		108	OLD BATCH	V.2	34
Maskwell:	day Offended you, but in not breaking off his Match with	.	137	DOUBL DLR	I.1	388
Cynthia:	become more Conspicuous by setting off one another.	.	142	DOUBL DLR	I.1	152
Mellefont:	that's sinking; tho' ne'er so far off.	. . . . . .	148	DOUBL DLR	II.1	390
Lady Froth:	cast off, and meet me at the lower end of the Room, and	.	177	DOUBL DLR	IV.1	366
Lady Touch:	Hear me; consent to the breaking off this	. . . . .	192	DOUBL DLR	V.1	179
Saygrace:	(enters). You shall prevail, I would break off in the	.	195	DOUBL DLR	V.1	280
Lady Touch:	Stand off, let me go,	. . . .	202	DOUBL DLR	V.1	560
Jeremy:	No, faith Sir; I have put 'em off so long with patience		220	FOR LOVE	I.1	171
Trapland:	And in short, I can be put off no longer.	. . . . .	223	FOR LOVE	I.1	257
Valentine:	What, the Widows Health; give it him--off	. . . .	223	FOR LOVE	I.1	275
Valentine:	My Cloaths are soon put off:--But you must	. . . .	244	FOR LOVE	II.1	339
Tattle:	and come off as you can.	. . . .	254	FOR LOVE	III.1	24
Tattle:	You say true, I beg your Pardon;--I'll bring all off--		255	FOR LOVE	III.1	65
Tattle:	--Pox on't, now could I bite off my Tongue.	. . . .	258	FOR LOVE	III.1	189
Sr Sampson:	sneak'd off, and would not see his Brother? There's an	.	259	FOR LOVE	III.1	235
Angelica:	Estate too: But since that's gone, the Bait's off, and the		260	FOR LOVE	III.1	247
Sr Sampson:	Heart: Hang him, Mungrel; cast him off; you shall see the		260	FOR LOVE	III.1	260
Miss Prue:	to say, I can hear you farther off, I an't deaf.	. . . .	263	FOR LOVE	III.1	365
Ben:	heard as far as another,--I'll heave off to please you.	. .	263	FOR LOVE	III.1	367
Ben:	(Sits further off.)	. .	263	FOR LOVE	III.1	368
Ben:	then put off with the next fair wind. How de'e like us?	.	275	FOR LOVE	III.1	803
Valentine:	Pray let me see it, Sir. You hold it so far off, that	.	281	FOR LOVE	IV.1	217
Sr Sampson:	thine? I believe I can read it farther off yet--let me see.		281	FOR LOVE	IV.1	226
Ben:	and Kissing and Hugging, what wou'd you sheer off so?	.	286	FOR LOVE	IV.1	418
Valentine:	shake off Care; get thee Medea's Kettle, and be boil'd a-new,		289	FOR LOVE	IV.1	522
Tattle:	Pox on't, there's no coming off, now she has said	. .	293	FOR LOVE	IV.1	679
Angelica:	him to throw off his Disguise of Madness, in Apprehension		300	FOR LOVE	V.1	110
Manuel:	A Bridal Qualm; soon off. How is't, Almeria?	. . . .	334	M. BRIDE	I.1	348
	(Prisoners led off.)	. . .	335	M. BRIDE	I.1	365
	(Guards carry off Osmyn.)	. .	349	M. BRIDE	II.2	375
Osmyn-Alph:	But 'tis torn off--why should that Word alone	. . .	350	M. BRIDE	III.1	22
Osmyn-Alph:	To break these Chains. Off, off, ye Stains of Royalty.	.	352	M. BRIDE	III.1	88
Osmyn-Alph:	Off Slavery. O curse! that I alone	. . . . . .	352	M. BRIDE	III.1	89
Heli:	Where not far off some Male-Contents hold Counsel	. .	352	M. BRIDE	III.1	100
Heli:	Where not far off some Male-Contents hold Council	. .	352	M. BRIDE	III.1	V100
Selim:	And some of them bought off to Osmyn's Int'rest,	. .	362	M. BRIDE	IV.1	52
Almeria:	Now curse me if you can, now spurn me off.	. . . .	369	M. BRIDE	IV.1	320
Manuel:	Away, off, let me go,--Call her Attendants.	. . . .	369	M. BRIDE	IV.1	335
Almeria:	Yes, I will strip off Life, and we will change:	. . . .	370	M. BRIDE	IV.1	351
Manuel:	This hour I throw ye off, and entertain	. . . . .	374	M. BRIDE	V.1	64
Osmyn-Alph:	Away, stand off, where is she? let me fly,	. . . .	383	M. BRIDE	V.2	275
Petulant:	off, if I want Appetite.	. . . .	405	WAY WORLD	I.1	397
Witwoud:	wou'd come off--Ha, ha, ha; Gad I can't be angry	. .	406	WAY WORLD	I.1	410
Mirabell:	Have you not left off your impudent Pretensions	. . .	406	WAY WORLD	I.1	422
Mirabell:	(aside to Mrs. Fainall). Draw off Witwoud.	. . .	421	WAY WORLD	II.1	424
Mirabell:	Stand off Sir, not a Penny--Go on and prosper,	. . .	424	WAY WORLD	II.1	538

Off   (continued)

Marwood:	you might as easily put off Petulant and Witwoud, as your	433	WAY WORLD	III.1	315
Witwoud:	--We hit off a little Wit now and then, but no . . .	435	WAY WORLD	III.1	394
Sir Wilful:	this, when you left off Honour'd Brother; and hoping .	439	WAY WORLD	III.1	543
Sir Wilful:	I pull off my Boots. Sweet-heart, can you help me to a .	441	WAY WORLD	III.1	617
Lady Wish:	Fie, fie, Nephew, you wou'd not pull off your . . .	441	WAY WORLD	III.1	620
Marwood:	Then shake it off, You have often wish'd for	442	WAY WORLD	III.1	639
Lady Wish:	a little dangling off, Jogging in a thoughtful way--Yes--	445	WAY WORLD	IV.1	26
Petulant:	pass off,--that's all.	453	WAY WORLD	IV.1	341
Petulant:	Stand off--I'll kiss no more Males,--I have	454	WAY WORLD	IV.1	355
Witwoud:	Husband's advice; but he sneak'd off.	454	WAY WORLD	IV.1	382
Mrs Fain:	drop off when she's full. Madam you sha'not pawn a . .	466	WAY WORLD	V.1	175
Mrs Fain:	drop off when she's full. Madam you shan't pawn a . .	466	WAY WORLD	V.1	V175
Marwood:	and fidges off and on his Cushion as if he had swallow'd .	467	WAY WORLD	V.1	221
Marwood:	and figes off and on his Cushion as if he had swallow'd .	467	WAY WORLD	V.1	V221
Fainall:	I'll be put off no longer--You thing that was . . .	475	WAY WORLD	V.1	494
Petulant:	off or on.	477	WAY WORLD	V.1	589

Off-and-on (1)

| Setter: | think, you and I have been Play-fellows off-and-on, any . | 111 | OLD BATCH | V.2 | 142 |

Off-spring (1)

| Fondlewife: | of my house, thou Son of the Whore of Babylon; Off-spring . | 90 | OLD BATCH | IV.4 | 65 |

Off'ring (4)

Ben:	With off'ring her his Measure.	274	FOR LOVE	III.1	775
Singer-V:	To you I should my earliest Off'ring give;	293	FOR LOVE	IV.1	654
Manuel:	What Off'ring, or what Recompence remains	365	M. BRIDE	IV.1	157
Manuel:	Which was an Off'ring to the Sex design'd.	385	M. BRIDE	EPI.	31

Off'rings (1)

| Osmyn-Alph: | Or this vile Earth, an Altar for such Off'rings? . . | 357 | M. BRIDE | III.1 | 326 |

Offence (15)

Sir Joseph:	any offence to you Sir.	68	OLD BATCH	III.1	294
	He'll not instruct, lest it should give Offence. . .	393	WAY WORLD	PRO.	34
Sir Wilful:	No Offence, I hope.	438	WAY WORLD	III.1	484
Witwoud:	This is a vile Dog, I see that already. No Offence! .	438	WAY WORLD	III.1	487
Petulant:	No Offence, I hope, Sir.	438	WAY WORLD	III.1	493
Sir Wilful:	Do you speak by way of Offence, Sir?	438	WAY WORLD	III.1	503
Sir Wilful:	write my self; no offence to any Body, I hope; and Nephew	438	WAY WORLD	III.1	511
Witwoud:	No offence, I hope, Brother.	439	WAY WORLD	III.1	526
Sir Wilful:	'Sheart, Sir, but there is, and much offence.-- . .	439	WAY WORLD	III.1	527
Sir Wilful:	Tony, belike, I may'nt call him Brother for fear of offence.	441	WAY WORLD	III.1	605
Sir Wilful:	Yes,--your Servant. No offence I hope, Cozen. . . .	447	WAY WORLD	IV.1	102
Sir Wilful:	No Offence Aunt.	455	WAY WORLD	IV.1	386
Lady Wish:	Offence? As I'm a Person, I'm asham'd of you, . . .	455	WAY WORLD	IV.1	387
Sir Wilful:	your Mussulman is a dry Stinkard--No Offence, Aunt. My .	456	WAY WORLD	IV.1	444
Sir Wilful:	I hope I committed no Offence Aunt--and if I did I .	470	WAY WORLD	V.1	316

Offences (4)

Bellmour:	Pauh, Women are only angry at such offences, to . . .	63	OLD BATCH	III.1	98
Setter:	one Eye, as a penal Mourning for the ogling Offences of .	64	OLD BATCH	III.1	127
Vainlove:	abuse Mercy, by committing new Offences.	87	OLD BATCH	IV.3	140
	Since when, they by their own offences taught . . .	479	WAY WORLD	EPI.	14

Offend (5)

Vainlove:	what she knows as well as I. (Aside). Men are apt to offend	87	OLD BATCH	IV.3	137
Sir Paul:	Nay but Madam, I shall offend again if you don't . .	180	DOUBL DLR	IV.1	V485
Sr Sampson:	to be done, but for him to offend, and me to pardon. I .	240	FOR LOVE	II.1	178
Almeria:	Forgive me, Sir, if I offend.	333	M. BRIDE	I.1	283
Almeria:	Forgive me, Sir, if I in this offend.	333	M. BRIDE	I.1	V283

Offended (7)

Sharper:	and refuse my Thanks--But I hope you are not offended .	68	OLD BATCH	III.1	290
Sir Joseph:	am both Sir; what then? I hope I may be offended, without	68	OLD BATCH	III.1	293
Maskwell:	day Offended you, but in not breaking off his Match with .	137	DOUBL DLR	I.1	388
Angelica:	I thank you, Sir, I am not at all offended;--but . .	262	FOR LOVE	III.1	344
Gonsalez:	To have offended you. If Fate decreed, ...	333	M. BRIDE	I.1	304
Gonsalez:	As if she had offended.	334	M. BRIDE	I.1	320
Gonsalez:	As if she had offended.--Sure, no more, ...	334	M. BRIDE	I.1	V320

Offender (3)

Vainlove:	Offender must Plead to his Arraignment, tho' he have his .	87	OLD BATCH	IV.3	154
Vainlove:	Offender must Plead to his Arraignment, tho' he has his .	87	OLD BATCH	IV.3	V154
Mirabell:	O in good time--Your leave for the other Offender . .	475	WAY WORLD	V.1	506

Offending (1)

| Lady Wish: | have a mortal Terror at the apprehension of offending . | 429 | WAY WORLD | III.1 | 178 |

Offensive (4)

Manuel:	Of that offensive black; on me be all	334	M. BRIDE	I.1	324
Mrs Fain:	to see him; but since I have despis'd him, he's too offensive.	416	WAY WORLD	II.1	255
Millamant:	Mirabell, If you persist in this offensive Freedom . .	422	WAY WORLD	II.1	448
Millamant:	will be offensive to you.	470	WAY WORLD	V.1	340

Offer (13)

Heartwell:	with you and bauk'd it? Did you ever offer me the Favour .	109	OLD BATCH	V.2	57
Heartwell:	When Execution's over, you offer a Reprieve. . . .	109	OLD BATCH	V.2	73
Sr Sampson:	Posture, that I might make a more becoming Offer to a .	300	FOR LOVE	V.1	96
Leonora:	For Sighs and Pray'rs were all that I could offer. . .	327	M. BRIDE	I.1	29
Gonsalez:	With dying Words, to offer at your Praise.	332	M. BRIDE	I.1	254
Zara:	I offer.	336	M. BRIDE	I.1	419
Osmyn-Alph:	In vain you offer, and in vain require	348	M. BRIDE	II.2	328
Selim:	Then offer to the King to have him strangl'd	362	M. BRIDE	IV.1	56
Mirabell:	and like the faint Offer of a latter Spring, serves but to	418	WAY WORLD	II.1	319
Millamant:	at the Impudence of any Illiterate Man, to offer to make .	436	WAY WORLD	III.1	423
Sir Wilful:	I thank you for your courteous Offer. 'Sheart, I was afraid	441	WAY WORLD	III.1	602
Mirabell:	Have you any more Conditions to offer? Hitherto . .	450	WAY WORLD	IV.1	210
Mirabell:	account. Well, have I Liberty to offer Conditions--that .	450	WAY WORLD	IV.1	229

Offer'd (5)

Sharper:	that I offer'd 'em.	68	OLD BATCH	III.1	291
Sr Sampson:	more glorious Victim to be offer'd at the Shrine of your .	300	FOR LOVE	V.1	100
Fainall:	and by refusing the offer'd Match with Sir Wilfull Witwoud,	469	WAY WORLD	V.1	284
Mirabell:	If a deep sense of the many Injuries I have offer'd to .	471	WAY WORLD	V.1	366
Mirabell:	that to your cruel Indignation, I have offer'd up this .	472	WAY WORLD	V.1	389

Offered (1)
Mellefont: that they were weakly offered, and a challenge to him . . 158 DOUEL DLR III.1 300
Offering (1)   see Off'ring, Off'rings
                The First-fruit Offering, of a Virgin Play. . . . . . 213 FOR LCVE PRO. 25
Offers (6)
                (Takes out the Letter, and offers it: She snatches it,
                  and throws . . . . 88 OLD EATCH IV.3 179
Lady Froth: offers to speak--And sits in expectation of his no Jest,
                  with . . . . 165 DOUEL DLR III.1 574
Mellefont: Villain! (Offers to Draw.) . . . . 184 DOUEL DLR IV.2 38
                He offers but this one Excuse, 'twas writ . . . . . 214 FOR LCVE PRO. 46
Garcia: Dumbly declines all Offers: if he speak . . . . . 335 M. ERIDE I.1 371
Fainall: Perfidious Fiend! then thus I'll be reveng'd.--(offers . 476 WAY WORLD V.1 556
Office (7)
Sharper: she were hot, when it might entitle him to the office of . 44 OLD BATCH I.1 264
Heartwell: Office--Not one Inch; no, Foregod I'me caught-- . . . . 62 OLD BATCH III.1 74
Heartwell: Office--Not one Inch; no, Foregad I'me caught-- . . . 62 OLD EATCH III.1 V 74
Lucy: You could know my Office by instinct, and be hang'd, . . 66 OLD BATCH III.1 207
Sir Joseph: Office--So tell him your self. . . . . 68 OLD BATCH III.1 267
Snap: must do our Office, tell us.--We have half a dozen . . 224 FCB LCVE I.1 296
Tattle: Secretary's Office; and that I have more Vizor-Masks to . 257 FOR LCVE III.1 160
Officer (4)
                (Enter Officer.) . . . . 224 FOR LCVE I.1 294
Valentine: Officer, You shall have an answer presently. . . . . 224 FOR LCVE I.1 305
                (Exit Officer.) . . . . 224 FCB LCVE I.1 307
Poible: some disbanded Officer I warrant--Half Pay is but . . 427 WAY WCRLD III.1 97
Officers (1)
                Garcia and several Officers. Files of Prisoners in Chains, 332 M. BRIDE I.1 266
Offices (3)
Setter: though we were both in fault as to our Offices-- . . . 66 OLD EATCH III.1 213
Mellefont: Addresses, she has endeavour'd to do me all ill Offices with 129 DOUEL DLR I.1 87
Selim: Who bore high Offices of Weight and Trust, ... 361 M. EBIDE IV.1 10
Officious (2)
Zara: O Fate of Fools! officious in Contriving; . . . . . . 375 M. EBIDE V.1 111
Fainall: Aunt, and be the officious Obstacle of his Match with . 414 WAY WCRLD II.1 160
Officiously (1)
Garcia: Far be it from me, officiously to pry . . . . 338 M. EFIDE II.1 36
Offspring (1)
                Alone to the Offspring of the Muses kind: . . . . . 125 DOUEL DLR PRO. 26
Oft (4)
Leonora: And oft at Night, when all have been retir'd, . . . 326 M. BRIDE I.1 24
Zara: And oft had private Conference with the King; . . . 364 M. EBIDE IV.1 118
Mirabell: That marriage frauds too oft are paid in kind. . . . 478 WAY WCRLD V.1 623
                So Poets oft, do in one Piece expose . . . . . . 479 WAY WCBLD EPI. 35
Often (28)
Vainlove: So that as he is often Jealous without a Cause, he's as
                  often . . . . 40 OLD BATCH I.1 109
Heartwell: so often drawn, is bound to the Peace for ever after. . . 43 OLD EATCH I.1 249
Bellmour: this nature; Women are often won by 'em: who would . . 44 OLD BATCH I.1 260
Bellmour: Soldier, which now a'days as often cloaks Cowardice, as a . 46 OLD BATCH I.1 367
Belinda: Nor are ever like--Yet we often meet and clash. . . . . 58 OLD BATCH II.2 120
Setter: To be Men perhaps; nay faith like enough; I often . . 65 OLD BATCH III.1 174
Vainlove: says; and often blush'd with Anger and Surprize:-- . . . 99 OLD BATCH V.1 96
Belinda: and now you, in show. Nay, often, only Remains, which . 106 OLD BATCH V.1 375
Lord Froth: I often smile at your Conceptions, But there is nothing . 132 DOUEL DLR I.1 198
Lord Froth: Boxes.--I swear, he, he, he, I have often . . . . . 133 DOUEL DLR I.1 230
Lady Ply: How often have you been told of that you . . . . . 161 DOUEL DLR III.1 393
Lord Froth: sending it to and again so often, this is the seventh time 166 DOUEL DLR III.1 610
Mrs Fore: often done in Duels, take care of one another, and grow . 248 FOR LCVE II.1 478
Scandal: often he that has stolen the Treasure. I am a Jugler,
                  that act . . . . 272 FCR LCVE III.1 699
Valentine: his Nose always, will very often be led into a Stink. . . 282 FOR LCVE IV.1 254
                Were you not griev'd, as often as you saw . . . . . 323 M. EBIDE PRO. 17
Leonora: Have often wept, to see how cruelly . . . . 326 M. BBIDE I.1 22
Osmyn-Alph: At once, as I have seen her often; . . . . 345 M. BRIDE II.2 229
Osmyn-Alph: At once, as I before have seen her often; . . . . . 345 M. EBIDE II.2 V229
Zara: I know thou could'st; but I'm not often pleas'd, . . . 360 M. BEIDE III.1 423
Fainall: Are you Jealous as often as you see Witwoud . . . . . 399 WAY WCBLD I.1 148
Mirabell: Not always; but as often as his Memory fails him, . . 401 WAY WORLD I.1 223
Witwoud: Words gives me the pleasure very often to explain his . 404 WAY WCRLD I.1 331
Mirabell: roar out aloud as often as they pass by you; and when . 409 WAY WCRLD I.1 526
Marwood: often shou'd out-live the Lover. But say what you will, . 410 WAY WORLD II.1 11
Marwood: Then shake it off, You have often wish'd for . . . . 442 WAY WORLD III.1 639
Mirabell: as often as possibly I can. (Kisses her hand). Well, heav'n 477 WAY WORLD V.1 597
Oftentimes (1)
Heartwell: Yet it is oftentimes too late with some of you . . . . 43 OLD EATCH I.1 237
Oftner (1)
Fainall: unsuspected in my Pleasures; and take you oftner to my . 414 WAY WORLD II.1 146
Ogling (2)
Setter: one Eye, as a penal Mourning for the ogling Offences of . 64 OLD BATCH III.1 127
Valentine: Poppy-water, that he may fold his Ogling Tail, and . . 290 FOR LCVE IV.1 551
Oh (148)   see O
Vainlove: Oh the Wise will tell you-- . . . . 37 OLD EATCH I.1 15
Bellmour: Let me see, Laetitia! Oh 'tis a delicious Morsel. Dear . 39 OLD BATCH I.1 73
Bellmour: I'le take care, he shall not be at home. Good! Spintext! Oh 39 OLD BATCH I.1 84
Heartwell: Devil--Oh the Pride and Joy of Heart 'twould be to me, . 45 OLD BATCH I.1 318
Bellmour: Oh here he comes, stand close let 'em pass. . . . . . 46 OLD BATCH I.1 V339
Bellmour: Oh, 'tis Sir Joseph Wittoll with his friend; . . . . 46 OLD EATCH I.1 V339
Sir Joseph: Oh here a' comes--Ah my Hector of Troy, welcome . . . 51 OLD BATCH II.1 139
Capt Bluff: Oh excuse me Sir; have you serv'd abroad Sir? . . . . 52 OLD EATCH II.1 185
Capt Bluff: Oh I thought so--Why then you can know nothing . . . 52 OLD BATCH II.1 187
Capt Bluff: Oh fy no Sir Joseph--You know I hate this. . . . . . 53 OLD BATCH II.1 217
Belinda: more. Oh Gad, I swear you'd make one sick to hear you. . 54 OLD BATCH II.2 2
Belinda: Oh you have raved, talked idly, and all in . . . . 54 OLD EATCH II.2 4
Araminta: Oh is it come out--Now you are angry, I am sure . . . 56 OLD BATCH II.2 58
Silvia: has bewitch'd him from me--Oh how the name of . . . 61 OLD BATCH III.1 29

496

Oh (continued)

Speaker	Text	PAGE	TITLE	ACT.SC	LINE
Silvia:	Lust. Oh that I could revenge the Torment he has caus'd--	61	OLD BATCH	III.1	32
Silvia:	Oh that I could revenge the Torment he has caus'd--	61	OLD BATCH	III.1 V	32
Setter:	Oh! I begin to smoak ye, thou art some forsaken Abigail,	65	OLD BATCH	III.1	183
Heartwell:	Oh Manhood, where art thou! What am I come	72	OLD BATCH	III.2	45
Laetitia:	(aside). Oh then alls safe. I was terrible frighted--	78	OLD BATCH	IV.1	102
Laetitia:	(aside). Oh then alls safe. I was terribly frighted--	78	OLD BATCH	IV.1	V102
Laetitia:	My affliction is always your Jest, barbarous Man! Oh	78	OLD BATCH	IV.1	103
Bellmour:	Hypocrites.--Oh! she comes.	80	OLD BATCH	IV.2	8
Bellmour:	by those healing Lips.--Oh! press the soft Charm close	82	OLD BATCH	IV.2	73
Laetitia:	Oh, but what am I doing!	82	OLD BATCH	IV.2	83
Bellmour:	Bliss:--Oh, for Love-sake, lead me any whither, where I	82	OLD BATCH	IV.2	86
Bellmour:	Oh, a Convulsion.--I feel the Symptons.	83	OLD BATCH	IV.2	89
Bellmour:	Oh, No: Let me lie down upon the Bed;--the	83	OLD BATCH	IV.2	92
Belinda:	Oh the most inhumane, barbarous Hackney-Coach!	83	OLD BATCH	IV.3	4
Belinda:	Oh; a most Comical Sight: A Country-Squire, with	84	OLD BATCH	IV.3	23
Belinda:	Snipwel's Shop while I was there.--But, Oh Gad!	84	OLD BATCH	IV.3	25
Belinda:	Oh Gad, here comes the Fool that din'd at my Lady	84	OLD BATCH	IV.3	55
Belinda:	small.--Oh Gad! I have a great Passion for Cowley.	87	OLD BATCH	IV.3	145
Sharper:	Oh Madam! He was our English Horace.	87	OLD BATCH	IV.3	147
Belinda:	World that I like.--Oh Lord, walk this way.--I	87	OLD BATCH	IV.3	149
Laetitia:	(aside). Oh, I'm undone!	89	OLD BATCH	IV.4	26
Sir Joseph:	O Lord! Oh terrible! Ha, ha, ha, Is your Wife	90	OLD BATCH	IV.4	55
Laetitia:	Oh! I am sick with the fright; won't you take him	90	OLD BATCH	IV.4	57
Fondlewife:	Oh Traytor! I'm astonished. Oh bloody-minded	90	OLD BATCH	IV.4	59
Fondlewife:	Oh, how the blasphemous Wretch swears! Out	90	OLD BATCH	IV.4	64
Fondlewife:	Wife! My Dinah! Oh Schechemite! Begone, I say.	90	OLD BATCH	IV.4	67
Laetitia:	Oh! Won't you follow, and see him out of Doors,	91	OLD BATCH	IV.4	70
Laetitia:	(aside). What can I do now! Oh! my Dear, I have	91	OLD BATCH	IV.4	76
Fondlewife:	Oh, thou salacious Woman! Am I then brutified?	92	OLD BATCH	IV.4	125
Laetitia:	Oh, Goodness keep us! Who's this? Who are you?	92	OLD BATCH	IV.4	129
Laetitia:	In the Name of the--Oh! Good, my Dear, don't	92	OLD BATCH	IV.4	132
Fondlewife:	Oh, it is a Man then, it seems.	93	OLD BATCH	IV.4	141
Fondlewife:	you know your Patient, Mrs. Quack? Oh, lie upon your	93	OLD BATCH	IV.4	163
Laetitia:	Oh, insupportable Impudence!	94	OLD BATCH	IV.4	181
Fondlewife:	Oh, I am a very honest Fellow--You never	94	OLD BATCH	IV.4	200
Fondlewife:	Oh, that I could believe thee!	96	OLD BATCH	IV.4	256
Laetitia:	Oh, my heart will break!	96	OLD BATCH	IV.4	257
Laetitia:	Oh! Oh! Where is my Dear.	96	OLD BATCH	IV.4	261
Bellmour:	Rogue am I! Oh, what Sport will be here, if I can persuade	97	OLD BATCH	V.1	24
Setter:	Oh, Yes, Sir.	103	OLD BATCH	V.1	259
Heartwell:	Oh, Sharper.	104	OLD BATCH	V.1	311
Heartwell:	Oh, I am--married.	105	OLD BATCH	V.1	313
Heartwell:	Oh, an Age, an Age: I have been married these	105	OLD BATCH	V.1	317
Vainlove:	(to Araminta). Oh, 'twas Frenzy all: Cannot you forgive	106	OLD BATCH	V.1	356
Belinda:	Oh, foh,--no: Rather, Courtship to Marriage,	107	OLD BATCH	V.1	387
Belinda:	Oh foh! What does the filthy-fellow mean? Lard,	109	OLD BATCH	V.2	59
Heartwell:	Oh! Any thing, every thing, a Leg or two, or an	109	OLD BATCH	V.2	75
Capt Bluff:	Oh, the Devil, cheated at last!	110	OLD BATCH	V.2	110
Heartwell:	But, Oh,--	112	OLD BATCH	V.2	126
Heartwell:	--Oh Sharper! Let me embrace thee.--But art	111	OLD BATCH	V.2	190
Brisk:	Oh, my dear Mellefont, let me perish, if thou art not the	128	DOUBL DLR	I.1	33
Lord Froth:	Oh, no.--Never Laugh indeed, Sir.	133	DOUBL DLR	I.1	225
Lord Froth:	Oh, I thought you would not be long, before you	133	DOUBL DLR	I.1	244
Lady Touch:	and Recesses of my Soul.--Oh Mellefont! I burn;	137	DOUBL DLR	I.1	398
Mellefont:	Musick!--Oh, my Lord has promised the Company a	143	DOUBL DLR	II.1	172
Lady Ply:	patience--oh! the Impiety of it, as I was saying, and	146	DOUBL DLR	II.1	304
Maskwell:	--oh she has open'd her heart to me,--I am to turn you a	149	DOUBL DLR	II.1	402
Maskwell:	Hypocrisie; oh 'tis such a pleasure, to angle for fair-faced	150	DOUBL DLR	II.1	458
Sir Paul:	Oh, a fine likely Woman as you shall see in a	161	DOUBL DLR	III.1	421
Lady Froth:	Oh, infinitely better; I'm extremely beholding	164	DOUBL DLR	III.1	510
Lady Froth:	Oh, infinitely better; I'm extremely beholden	164	DOUBL DLR	III.1	V510
Lady Ply:	--Ay my Dear--were you? Oh filthy Mr. Sneer;	165	DOUBL DLR	III.1	561
Lady Froth:	Oh you made a Song upon her, Mr. Brisk.	166	DOUBL DLR	III.1	588
Careless:	said--Oh! (Aside.) I shall never contain Laughter.	170	DOUBL DLR	IV.1	123
Lady Ply:	Oh, I yield my self all up to your uncontroulable	170	DOUBL DLR	IV.1	124
Sir Paul:	utterly extinct for want of Issue Male. Oh Impiety! But	171	DOUBL DLR	IV.1	138
Lady Froth:	Oh my adored Mr. Brisk!	177	DOUBL DLR	IV.1	359
Lady Froth:	near any other Man. Oh here's my Lord, now you shall	177	DOUBL DLR	IV.1	369
Lord Froth:	(aside). --Oh I see there's no harm yet--But I	177	DOUBL DLR	IV.1	372
Lady Ply:	my Honour; your guilty Cheeks confess it; Oh where	179	DOUBL DLR	IV.1	445
Mellefont:	--Oh that her Lord were but sweating behind this	183	DOUBL DLR	IV.2	2
Maskwell:	Lips be ever clos'd. (Kisses her.) And thus--Oh who	184	DOUBL DLR	IV.2	25
Lady Touch:	--Oh! I could rack my self, play the Vulture to my own	184	DOUBL DLR	IV.2	46
Lady Touch:	indebted to him, if you knew all, damn'd Villain! oh, I am	191	DOUBL DLR	V.1	143
Lady Touch:	indebted to him, if you knew all, Villain! oh, I am	191	DOUBL DLR	V.1	V143
Lady Touch:	I cannot bear it, oh! what Woman can bear to be a Property?	191	DOUBL DLR	V.1	149
Lady Touch:	anothers Arms; oh! that I were Fire indeed, that I might	191	DOUBL DLR	V.1	151
Lady Touch:	Oh! Torture!	192	DOUBL DLR	V.1	161
Lady Touch:	silent? Oh, I am wilder'd in all Passions! but thus my	198	DOUBL DLR	V.1	401
Lady Froth:	Oh, no, I love it violently,--my dear you're	201	DOUBL DLR	V.1	523
Valentine:	And the prettiest Foot! Oh if a Man could but fasten his	223	FOR LOVE	I.1	286
Tattle:	Oh that--	227	FOR LOVE	I.1	416
Tattle:	Oh that is not fair.	228	FOR LOVE	I.1	460
Mrs Frail:	here too? Oh Mr. Tattle, every thing is safe with you, we	230	FOR LOVE	I.1	548
Tattle:	Oh Madam, those are Sacred to Love and Contemplation.	232	FOR LOVE	I.1	609
Foresight:	well pleas'd at my Stocking--Oh here's my Neice!--	236	FOR LOVE	II.1	38
Sr Sampson:	Oh Sir, I understand you,--that's all, ha?	243	FOR LOVE	II.1	289
Mrs Fore:	you lose this Gold Bodkin?--Oh Sister, Sister!	248	FOR LOVE	II.1	466
Mrs Frail:	Bodkin?--Oh Sister, Sister!--Sister every way.	248	FOR LOVE	II.1	470
Miss Prue:	Oh good! how sweet it is--Mr. Tattle is all over sweet,	249	FOR LOVE	II.1	518
Miss Prue:	give me something to make me smell so--Oh pray	249	FOR LOVE	II.1	525
Tattle:	Oh Madam; you are too severe upon Miss; you must	249	FOR LOVE	II.1	534
Mrs Fore:	Oh, Demn you Toad--I wish you don't	249	FOR LOVE	II.1	538
Tattle:	Who I, Madam?--Oh Lord, how can your Ladyship	250	FOR LOVE	II.1	540
Tattle:	Oh Lord, I swear I wou'd not for the World--	250	FOR LOVE	II.1	553

Oh   (continued)

		PAGE	TITLE	ACT.SC	LINE
Miss Prue:	Oh but you sha'nt, for I'll hold my Tongue.--	253	FOR LOVE	II.1	658
Tattle:	Oh my Dear, apt Scholar.	253	FOR LOVE	II.1	659
Ben:	Oh here they be--And Fiddles along with 'em;	275	FOR LOVE	III.1	796
Sr Sampson:	Val: How do'st thou do? let me feel thy Pulse--Oh,	281	FOR LOVE	IV.1	201
Valentine:	What, is my bad Genius here again! Oh no, 'tis	282	FOR LOVE	IV.1	237
Mrs Fore:	Oh Sister, what will you do with him?	283	FOR LOVE	IV.1	305
Mrs Fore:	Oh hang him old Fox, he's too cunning,	288	FOR LOVE	IV.1	462
Valentine:	Oh, Prayers will be said in empty Churches, at	289	FOR LOVE	IV.1	500
Valentine:	Shop. Oh things will go methodically in the City, the	289	FOR LOVE	IV.1	503
Valentine:	Oh, why would Angelica be absent from my Eyes	289	FOR LOVE	IV.1	535
Valentine:	Where is she? Oh I see her--she comes, like Riches,	290	FOR LOVE	IV.1	541
Valentine:	Oh welcome, welcome.	290	FOR LOVE	IV.1	544
Tattle:	Oh, Madam, look upon us both. There you see the ruins	291	FOR LOVE	IV.1	580
Foresight:	But he knows more than any body,--Oh	291	FOR LOVE	IV.1	603
Valentine:	Oh very well.	292	FOR LOVE	IV.1	632
Angelica:	Oh Heavens! You wont leave me alone with a	294	FOR LOVE	IV.1	693
Valentine:	Oh, 'tis barbarous to misunderstand me longer.	295	FOR LOVE	IV.1	731
Angelica:	Oh here's a reasonable Creature--sure he will	295	FOR LOVE	IV.1	733
Miss Prue:	way or other. Oh! methinks I'm sick when I think of a	305	FOR LOVE	V.1	308
Foresight:	Rogue! Oh, Nurse, come hither.	305	FOR LOVE	V.1	322
Tattle:	I can spare him mine. (to Jeremy) Oh are you there, Sir?	313	FOR LOVE	V.1	590
Almeria:	Oh!--	334	M. BRIDE	I.1	344
Osmyn-Alph:	Oh! o--	356	M. BRIDE	III.1	270
Almeria:	Oh I am lost--there, Fate begins to wound.	368	M. BRIDE	IV.1	299
Zara:	I have a Remedy for that. But Oh,	381	M. BRIDE	V.2	189
Zara:	But Oh, he dy'd unknowing in my Heart.	381	M. BRIDE	V.2	V190
Almeria:	--Oh, for another Draught of Death--What mean they?	382	M. BRIDE	V.2	V256
Almeria:	Oh--	383	M. BRIDE	V.2	277
Lady Wish:	wrought upon Foible to detect me, I'm ruin'd. Oh my dear	426	WAY WORLD	III.1	53
Lady Wish:	shall die with Confusion, if I am forc'd to advance--Oh	429	WAY WORLD	III.1	159
Lady Wish:	his protesting Eyes! Oh no memory can Register.	458	WAY WORLD	IV.1	517
Lady Wish:	Oh Heavens! what's this?	460	WAY WORLD	IV.1	589
Lady Wish:	I shall faint, I shall die, I shall die, oh!	460	WAY WORLD	IV.1	594
Lady Wish:	I shall faint, I shall die, oh!	460	WAY WORLD	IV.1	V594
Foible:	--a Bride, ay I shall be a Bridewell-Bride. Oh!	463	WAY WORLD	V.1	59
Lady Wish:	(apart). Oh, he has Witch-craft in his Eyes and	472	WAY WORLD	V.1	408
Lady Wish:	(aside.) Oh, he has Witch-craft in his Eyes and	472	WAY WORLD	V.1	V408

Oil (1)   see Oyl

Araminta:	avert the cure: Let me have Oil to feed that Flame and	54	OLD BATCH	II.2	9

Oil'd (1)

Mirabell:	for the Night, made of oil'd skins and I know not what	451	WAY WORLD	IV.1	249

Old (97)

Bellmour:	What, the old Banker with the handsome Wife?	39	OLD BATCH	I.1	71
Vainlove:	Yes, Heartwell, that surly, old, pretended Woman-hater	40	OLD BATCH	I.1	118
Vainlove:	the old place.	40	OLD BATCH	I.1	130
Bellmour:	Thou art an old Fornicator of a singular good	43	OLD BATCH	I.1	250
Musician:	Poor, old, repenting Delia said,	59	OLD BATCH	II.2	191
Bellmour:	thou hast lost it. Ha, ha, how a' strugled, like an Old	63	OLD BATCH	III.1	91
Bellmour:	thou hast lost it. Ha, ha, how he strugled, like an Old	63	OLD BATCH	III.1	V 91
Heartwell:	Ay, ay, in old days People married where they	73	OLD BATCH	III.2	103
Silvia:	Ha, ha, ha, an old Fox trapt--	74	OLD BATCH	III.2	143
Fondlewife:	vigorous, and I am Old and impotent--Then why didst	76	OLD BATCH	IV.1	52
Bellmour:	my old Token.	97	OLD BATCH	V.1	35
Sharper:	My old Batchelor married! That were a Jest. Ha,	105	OLD BATCH	V.1	319
Heartwell:	when I wed again, may she be--Ugly, as an old	112	OLD BATCH	V.2	159
Vainlove:	--Ill-natur'd, as an old Maid.--	112	OLD BATCH	V.2	161
Bellmour:	Come, take your Fellow-Travellers. Old George, I'm sorry	112	OLD BATCH	V.2	183
Mellefont:	Sense, and has an old fond Husband.	130	DOUBL DLR	I.1	130
Careless:	piece of an old Scarlet Petticoat for a Stomacher; which,	157	DOUBL DLR	III.1	276
Careless:	old--	161	DOUBL DLR	III.1	425
Sir Paul:	year to an Old Man, who would do good in his Generation?	162	DOUBL DLR	III.1	435
Brisk:	Spectacle; she's always chewing the Cud like an old Yew.	165	DOUBL DLR	III.1	568
Lady Froth:	can't hit of her Name; the old fat Fool that Paints so	166	DOUBL DLR	III.1	581
Brisk:	Pray, Madam, how old is Lady Sapho?	167	DOUBL DLR	III.1	618
Sir Paul:	Girl? Do gads-bud, think on thy old Father; Heh? Make	173	DOUBL DLR	IV.1	230
Brisk:	an Old Hen, as if she were not well hatch'd, I'gad, he?	174	DOUBL DLR	IV.1	273
Maskwell:	comes opportunely--now will I, in my old way,	190	DOUBL DLR	V.1	97
Lady Froth:	Astronomy like an old Egyptian.	201	DOUBL DLR	V.1	529
Scandal:	Old Woman, any thing but Poet; a Modern Poet is worse,	220	FOR LOVE	I.1	146
Scandal:	Patience, I suppose, the old Receipt.	220	FOR LOVE	I.1	170
Valentine:	O Mr. Trapland! your old Friend! Welcome. Jeremy, a	222	FOR LOVE	I.1	228
Scandal:	20000 [Pounds] in Money. A ha!! Old Trap.--	223	FOR LOVE	I.1	270
Tattle:	her Unkle Old Foresight: I think your Father lies at	228	FOR LOVE	II.1	453
Mrs Frail:	there's a Match talk'd of by the Old People--Well,	231	FOR LOVE	I.1	569
Mrs Frail:	Old Fool! He would have perswaded me, that this was an	231	FOR LOVE	I.1	580
Foresight:	to the Master of a Family--I remember an old	236	FOR LOVE	II.1	48
Angelica:	Practices; you and the old Nurse there--	237	FOR LOVE	II.1	97
Sr Sampson:	Nor no more to be done, Old Boy; that's plain--	240	FOR LOVE	II.1	172
Sr Sampson:	here 'tis, I have it in my Hand, Old Ptolomee; I'll make the	240	FOR LOVE	II.1	173
Sr Sampson:	ungracious Prodigal know who begat him; I will, old	240	FOR LOVE	II.1	174
Sr Sampson:	be--hah! old Merlin! body o' me, I'm so glad I'm	240	FOR LOVE	II.1	184
Sr Sampson:	you, I have travel'd old Fircu, and know the Globe. I have	241	FOR LOVE	II.1	207
Valentine:	Sir, is this Usage for your Son?--for that old,	244	FOR LOVE	II.1	311
Mrs Fore:	Soul, I shall fancy my self Old indeed, to have this great	249	FOR LOVE	II.1	512
Miss Prue:	our old fashion'd Country way of speaking ones mind;--	252	FOR LOVE	II.1	625
Tattle:	The next Sunday all the Old Women kept their Daughters	258	FOR LOVE	III.1	169
Sr Sampson:	young Spendthrift forc'd to cling to an Old Woman for	260	FOR LOVE	III.1	263
Sr Sampson:	for saying Grace, old Foresight, but fall too without the	265	FOR LOVE	III.1	460
Sr Sampson:	with him; twould be but like me, A Chip of the Old Block.	265	FOR LOVE	III.1	462
Sr Sampson:	Ha! thou'rt melancholly old Prognostication; As melancholly	265	FOR LOVE	III.1	463
Sr Sampson:	Ha! thou'rt melancholick old Prognostication; As melancholick	265	FOR LOVE	III.1	V463
Sr Sampson:	up old Star-Gazer. Now is he poring upon the Ground for	265	FOR LOVE	III.1	466
Sr Sampson:	a crooked Pin, or an old Horse-nail, with the head towards	265	FOR LOVE	III.1	467
Valentine:	Because thou wer't a Monster; old Boy:--The	282	FOR LOVE	IV.1	262

On't (continued)

Speaker	Text	PAGE	TITLE	ACT.SC	LINE
Careless:	be told on't; she must i'faith, Sir Paul: 'tis an injury to the	162	DOUBL DLR	III.1	442
Brisk:	--Pox on't, why should I disparage my parts by	175	DOUBL DLR	IV.1	298
Sir Paul:	discover'd--But let me see to make an end on't.--	178	DOUBL DLR	IV.1	407
Maskwell:	that he may not suspect one word on't.	190	DOUBL DLR	V.1	99
Sir Paul:	of things; I don't know what to make on't,--gad'sbud	192	DOUBL DLR	V.1	173
Jeremy:	the truth on't.	217	FOR LOVE	I.1	59
Tattle:	--No doubt on't, every body knows my Secrets--	227	FOR LOVE	I.1	428
Scandal:	No doubt on't. Well, but has she done you wrong, or	228	FOR LOVE	I.1	476
Sr Sampson:	I think on't, Body o' me, I have a Shoulder of an Egyptian	242	FOR LOVE	II.1	249
Mrs Fore:	(aside). O Devil on't, that I cou'd not discover	248	FOR LOVE	II.1	471
Angelica:	wou'd if you cou'd, no doubt on't.	255	FOR LOVE	III.1	95
Tattle:	--Pox on't, now could I bite off my Tongue.	258	FOR LOVE	III.1	189
Sr Sampson:	I'm glad on't: Where is he? I long to see him. Now, Mrs.	259	FOR LOVE	III.1	211
Sr Sampson:	pox on't, that I that know the World, and Men and	283	FOR LOVE	IV.1	286
Mrs Frail:	Ha, ha, ha, no doubt on't.--	287	FOR LOVE	IV.1	445
Tattle:	Pox on't, there's no coming off, now she has said	293	FOR LOVE	IV.1	679
Angelica:	How! I'm glad on't--If he has a mind I should	297	FOR LOVE	V.1	5
Sr Sampson:	risen in the State--But, a pox on't, his Wit run him	299	FOR LOVE	V.1	83
Tattle:	Look you there, I thought as much--pox on't, I	310	FOR LOVE	V.1	475
Tattle:	Easie! Pox on't, I don't believe I shall sleep to Night.	310	FOR LOVE	V.1	483
Valentine:	make your best on't.	313	FOR LOVE	V.1	616
Fainall:	Life on't, you are your own Man again.	400	WAY WORLD	I.1	177
Witwoud:	that's the Truth on't, if he were my Brother, I cou'd not	403	WAY WORLD	I.1	311
Millamant:	O ay, and went away--Now I think on't I'm angry	420	WAY WORLD	II.1	378
Millamant:	--No, now I think on't I'm pleas'd--For I believe	420	WAY WORLD	II.1	379
Lady Wish:	I promise you I have thought on't--And	432	WAY WORLD	III.1	269
Lady Wish:	since 'tis your Judgment, I'll think on't again. I assure you	432	WAY WORLD	III.1	270
Sir Wilful:	that--for if so be that I set on't, I'll do't. But only for the	447	WAY WORLD	IV.1	84
Sir Wilful:	--'Sheart, I'll call him in,--an I set on't	471	WAY WORLD	V.1	351
Sir Wilful:	to see Foreign Parts--I have set on't--And when I'm set	477	WAY WORLD	V.1	585
Sir Wilful:	on't, I must do't. And if these two Gentlemen wou'd	477	WAY WORLD	V.1	586

Once (81)

Speaker	Text	PAGE	TITLE	ACT.SC	LINE
Vainlove:	only hapned to be once or twice, where, Laetitia was the	39	OLD BATCH	I.1	96
Vainlove:	once raised up in a Woman, the Devil can't lay it, till she	40	OLD BATCH	I.1	103
Sharper:	I'm sorry to see this, Ned: Once a Man comes to his	41	OLD BATCH	I.1	147
Sir Joseph:	by the help of which, I shall once more hope to swim into	49	OLD BATCH	II.1	60
Capt Bluff:	Gazette-writer never so much as once mention'd me--Not once	53	OLD BATCH	II.1	203
Sir Joseph:	fire once out of the mouth of a Canon--agad he did; those	53	OLD BATCH	II.1	219
Belinda:	once before--If you must talk impertinently, for Heav'ns	59	OLD BATCH	II.2	168
Araminta:	it once again--You may like it better at second	60	OLD BATCH	II.2	208
Heartwell:	Why every Man plays the Fool once in his Life: But to	74	OLD BATCH	III.2	117
Lucy:	Whom Love and Vengeance do at once delight.	75	OLD BATCH	III.2	163
Lucy:	Whom Love and Vengeance both at once delight.	75	OLD BATCH	III.2	V163
Fondlewife:	That's my good Dear--Come Kiss Nykin once	79	OLD BATCH	IV.1	143
Laetitia:	him. Dear Fortune, help me but this once, and I'll never	91	OLD BATCH	IV.4	91
Fondlewife:	Humph, Nay, if you mince the matter once, and	94	OLD BATCH	IV.4	190
Lucy:	easie Nature.--Well, For once I'll venture to serve	98	OLD BATCH	V.1	75
Bellmour:	Play-house, till the Curtain's drawn; but that once up,	107	OLD BATCH	V.1	385
Bellmour:	Chimes of Verse were past, when once the doleful	108	OLD BATCH	V.2	18
Heartwell:	you.--For my part, I have once escap'd--And	112	OLD BATCH	V.2	158
Lady Touch:	oppressed at once with Love, and with Despair. But	135	DOUBL DLR	I.1	327
Lady Touch:	which once was paid me, and everlastingly engaged?	136	DOUBL DLR	I.1	351
Maskwell:	just Repulsed by him, warm at once with Love and	136	DOUBL DLR	I.1	367
Lady Touch:	knows I hate him too: Let him but once be mine, and next	137	DOUBL DLR	I.1	400
Lady Touch:	him once from forcing me.	155	DOUBL DLR	III.1	163
Maskwell:	Woman, and I lov'd her once. But I don't know, since I	155	DOUBL DLR	III.1	176
Maskwell:	Woman, I lov'd her once. But I don't know, since I	155	DOUBL DLR	III.1	V176
Mellefont:	with his Wife. He was once given to scrambling with his	158	DOUBL DLR	III.1	288
Mellefont:	with a Wife. He was once given to scrambling with his	158	DOUBL DLR	III.1	V288
Sir Paul:	touch a Man for the World--at least not above once a	162	DOUBL DLR	III.1	433
Sir Paul:	year; I'm sure I have found it so; and alas, what's once a	162	DOUBL DLR	III.1	434
Lady Ply:	d'ye mark me, if she has once sworn: It is most unchristian	171	DOUBL DLR	IV.1	151
Sir Paul:	that Opinion once too--Nay if your Ladiship conceives	171	DOUBL DLR	IV.1	156
Lord Touch:	though you have once actually hindered him from forcing	182	DOUBL DLR	IV.1	550
Lady Touch:	Eye o're all my future Conduct; and if I once relapse,	185	DOUBL DLR	IV.2	82
Maskwell:	within this Breast, which should it once blaze forth, would	188	DOUBL DLR	V.1	29
Maskwell:	rather die, than seem once, barely seem, dishonest:--	188	DOUBL DLR	V.1	37
Maskwell:	O, should it once be known I love fair Cynthia, all this	188	DOUBL DLR	V.1	38
Maskwell:	Stratagem--I must deceive Mellefont once more, and	190	DOUBL DLR	V.1	95
Cynthia:	have once resolved; and a true Female courage to oppose	193	DOUBL DLR	V.1	204
Lord Touch:	expect you in the Chaplain's Chamber,--for once,	200	DOUBL DLR	V.1	485
Valentine:	pay my Debts, and make my Fortune. This was once	225	FOR LOVE	I.1	338
Tattle:	good Fortune to be trusted once with a Lady's Secret, not	256	FOR LOVE	III.1	105
Tattle:	once.	256	FOR LOVE	III.1	106
Valentine:	Not once, I dare answer for him.	256	FOR LOVE	III.1	108
Tattle:	Church, once, an Enquiry being made, who I was, it was	257	FOR LOVE	III.1	163
Singer-F:	A Nymph and a Swain to Apollo once pray'd,	258	FOR LOVE	III.1	200
Mrs Fore:	I cannot say that he has once broken my Rest, since we	270	FOR LOVE	III.1	623
Ben:	Nay, an I love once, I'll stick like pitch; I'll tell you.	273	FOR LOVE	III.1	739
Ben:	Had once a doubtful strife, Sir,	274	FOR LOVE	III.1	760
Ben:	clean Shirt once a Quarter--Come home and lie with	275	FOR LOVE	III.1	801
Ben:	our Landladies once a Year, get rid of a little Mony; and	275	FOR LOVE	III.1	802
Valentine:	Health, and Liberty at once, to a despairing, starving, and	290	FOR LOVE	IV.1	542
Valentine:	asham'd of; and then we'll blush once for all.	290	FOR LOVE	IV.1	564
	Once of Philosophers they told us Stories,	315	FOR LOVE	EPI.	11
	And this our Audience, which did once resort	315	FOR LOVE	EPI.	25
	And thus our Audience, which did once resort	315	FOR LOVE	EPI.	V 25
Manuel:	At once regardless of his Chains, or Liberty?	336	M. BRIDE	I.1	427
Almeria:	All Thought; that all at once, thou art before me,	343	M. BRIDE	II.2	152
Osmyn-Alph:	At once, as I have seen her often;	345	M. BRIDE	II.2	229
Osmyn-Alph:	At once, as I before have seen her often;	345	M. BRIDE	II.2	V229

One   (continued)

		PAGE	TITLE	ACT.SC	LINE
Mellefont:	House this moment and Marry one another, without . . .	168	DOUBL DLR	IV.1	28
Mellefont:	And you won't die one, for your own, so still . . .	169	DOUBL DLR	IV.1	63
Sir Paul:	held fifty to one, I could have drawn my own Picture . .	174	DOUEL DLR	IV.1	242
Maskwell:	Nay then, there's but one way.	184	DOUBL DIR	IV.2	39
Lady Touch:	of this rage, and one minutes coolness to dissemble. .	185	DOUBL DLR	IV.2	66
Maskwell:	Conscience are my Witnesses, I never gave one working .	188	DOUEL DLR	V.1	34
Maskwell:	Fortune on another's ruine: I had but one desire-- . .	189	DOUBL DLR	V.1	73
Maskwell:	that he may not suspect one word on't.	190	DOUBL DLR	V.1	99
Mellefont:	maze of thoughts, each leading into one another, and all .	190	DOUEL DLR	V.1	104
Mellefont:	one, and too pious for the other.	193	DOUBL DLR	V.1	237
Maskwell:	one of 'em have a finger in't, he promised me to be within	194	DOUBL DLR	V.1	269
Maskwell:	one of them has a finger in't, he promised me to be within	194	DOUBL DLR	V.1 V269	
Maskwell:	than in the Death of one who is nothing when nct yours. .	199	DOUBL DLR	V.1	451
Maskwell:	than in the Heart of one who is nothing when not yours. .	199	DOUBL DLR	V.1	451
	'Tis hard that they must every one admit;	204	DOUEL DLR	EPI.	31
	One falling Adam, and one tempted Eve.	213	FOR LCVE	PRO.	22
	Not cne has dar'd to lash this Crying Age.	214	FOR LCVE	PRO.	40
	He offers but this one Excuse, 'twas writ	214	FOR LCVE	PRO.	46
Jeremy:	as much as they do one another.	217	FOB LCVE	I.1	48
Jeremy:	whole Tatter to her Tail, but as ragged as cne of the .	219	FOR LCVE	I.1	110
	(One Knocks.)	220	FCB LCVE	I.1	154
Valentine:	one day bring a Confinement on your Body, my Friend. .	221	FOR LCVE	I.1	200
Jeremy:	your Father's Steward, and the Nurse with cne of your .	221	FOR LCVE	I.1	205
Valentine:	If I can give that Cerberus a Sop, I shall be at rest				
	for one	222	FOR LCVE	I.1	225
Valentine:	Health. An honester Man lives not, nor one more ready to .	223	FCR LCVE	I.1	261
Valentine:	asunder; you are light and shadow, and shew one another; .	225	FCR LCVE	I.1	364
Tattle:	to that by one that we all know--A Man too. Only to .	227	FCR LCVE	I.1	424
Tattle:	one and t'other, and every thing in the World; and, says I,	227	FCR LCVE	I.1	432
Scandal:	Why, Tattle, thou hast more Impudence than one . . .	227	FOR LCVE	I.1	437
Scandal:	Lady; it is contrary to his Character--How one may .	229	FCB LCVE	I.1	490
Mrs Frail:	take care of my own. Well; but I'll come and see you one .	232	FCR LCVE	I.1	597
Scandal:	Ignorance, all in one Piece. Then I can shew you Lying, .	233	FOR LCVE	I.1	630
Scandal:	Impotence and Ugliness in another Piece; and yet one of .	233	FCR LCVE	I.1	632
Scandal:	with a hundred Hands, two Heads, and but one Face; a .	233	FOR LCVE	I.1	643
Scandal:	Divine with two Faces, and one Head; and I have a Soldier .	233	FOR LCVE	I.1	644
Nurse:	and Amen with all my heart, for you have put on one . .	235	FOR LCVE	II.1	27
Angelica:	by going abroad; nor secure you from being one, by . .	237	FOR LCVE	II.1	62
Foresight:	Yes, yes; while there's one Woman left, the	237	FOR LCVE	II.1	64
Angelica:	Tinderboxes did you purchase! Cne would have thought .	237	FOR LCVE	II.1	82
Angelica:	the Closet, one Night, like Saul and the Witch of Endor, .	238	FCB LCVE	II.1	107
Foresight:	But there's but one Virgin among the Twelve Signs, . .	239	FCB LCVE	II.1	141
Foresight:	Spitfire, but one Virgin.	239	FCB LCVE	II.1	142
Angelica:	Nct there had not been that one, if she had had to . .	239	FCR LCVE	II.1	143
Foresight:	Ccme, I know Wcmen tell one another--She is	239	FOR LCVE	II.1	150
Sr Sampson:	shall know one another's Faces without the help of a .	240	FOR LCVE	II.1	200
Sr Sampson:	King, that I purloyn'd from one of the Pyramids, powder'd	242	FCR LCVE	II.1	250
Sr Sampson:	Spiders; the one has its Nutriment in his own hands; and .	246	FCR LCVE	II.1	392
Mrs Frail:	I have heard Gentlemen say, Sister; that one should . .	248	FOR LCVE	II.1	473
Mrs Frail:	take great care when one makes a thrust in Fencing, not to	248	FCR LCVE	II.1	474
Mrs Fore:	often done in Duels, take care of one ancther, and grow .	248	FCR LCVE	II.1	478
Mrs Frail:	and speak openly one to another; I'm afraid the World .	248	FCR LCVE	II.1	487
Mrs Frail:	have observ'd us more than we have observ'd one another. .	248	FCR LCVE	II.1	488
Mrs Fore:	power--And I can tell you one thing that falls out luckily	248	FOR LCVE	II.1	498
Miss Prue:	How ycu love to jear one, Cousin.	250	FCR LCVE	II.1	559
Scandal:	Proverbs, and I see one in the next Room that will sing it.	258	FOR LCVE	III.1	192
	(Re-enter Scandal, with one to Sing.) .	258	FCB LCVE	III.1 V196	
Valentine:	We are the Twin-Stars, and cannot shine in one . . .	259	FOR LCVE	III.1	223
Angelica:	never have one.	259	FOR LCVE	III.1	230
Ben:	Why then, I'll go to Sea again, so there's one for				
	t'other, an	261	FOR LOVE	III.1	300
Ben:	man, than a Galley-slave is like one of us free Sailors,				
	he is	262	FOR LCVE	III.1	316
Ben:	But I'll tell you one thing, and you come to Sea in a .	262	FOR LCVE	III.1	330
Miss Prue:	You need not sit so near one, if you have any thing . .	263	FCR LCVE	III.1	364
Miss Prue:	As long as one must not speak one's mind, one had . .	263	FOR LCVE	III.1	382
Ben:	speak one thing, and to think just the contrary way; is as				
	it	263	FOR LOVE	III.1	386
Ben:	were, to look one way, and to row another. Now, for my .	263	FOR LOVE	III.1	387
Miss Prue:	you shculd believe that; and I'll speak truth, tho' one				
	should	264	FOR LOVE	III.1	396
Ben:	Whipping no more than you do. But I tell you one thing, .	264	FCR LOVE	III.1	407
Scandal:	must pay a Tribute to one, and go halves with the t'other.	271	FOR LCVE	III.1	677
Scandal:	must pay a Tribute to one, and gc halves with t'other. .	271	FOR LOVE	III.1 V677	
Mrs Fore:	And sc you think we are free for one another? . . .	272	FCB LCVE	III.1	684
Scandal:	And now I think we know one another pretty well. . .	272	FOR LOVE	III.1	710
Mrs Frail:	And tho' I have a good Pcrtion; you know one . . .	273	FOR LOVE	III.1	723
Mrs Frail:	wou'd not venture all in one Bottom.	273	FOR LCVE	III.1	724
Ben:	Why that's true again; for may-hap one Bottom may . .	273	FOR LOVE	III.1	725
Ben:	The Scng was made upcn one of our Ships-Crew's . . .	273	FCR LCVE	III.1	750
Ben:	come, my Lads, let's have a round, and I'll make one. .	275	FOR LCVE	III.1	797
Angelica:	upon one fearful of Affliction, to tell me what I . .	277	FOR LOVE	IV.1	58
Valentine:	--No matter how long--But I'll tell you one	280	FOR LOVE	IV.1	174
Valentine:	There's a couple of Topicks for you, no more like one .	282	FOR LOVE	IV.1	256
Mrs Fore:	if in cne of his mad fits he will bring you to him in her	288	FOR LOVE	IV.1	471
Valentine:	Master's Shop in the morning, may ten to one, dirty his .	289	FOR LOVE	IV.1	509
Valentine:	and yet we'll Marry one another in spite of the Pope-- .	290	FOR LOVE	IV.1	559
Valentine:	one ancthers Faces, till we have done something to be .	290	FOR LOVE	IV.1	563
Valentine:	You're a Woman,--One to whom Heav'n	292	FOR LOVE	IV.1	634
Valentine:	Nay faith, now let us understand one another, . . .	294	FOR LOVE	IV.1	706
	(One Knocks.)	295	FOR LOVE	IV.1	757
Angelica:	Never let us know one another better; for the Pleasure of	296	FOR LOVE	IV.1	789
Jeremy:	understood one another before she went.	296	FOR LOVE	IV.1	800
Sr Sampson:	Fourscore. I am of your Patriarchs, I, a Branch of one of	298	FOR LOVE	V.1	39
Angelica:	because I would have such an one in my Power; but I .	299	FOR LOVE	V.1	75

One   (continued)

Speaker	Text	PAGE	TITLE	ACT.SC	LINE
Sr Sampson:	had Peru in one Hand, and Mexico in t'other, and the	300	FOR LOVE	V.1	98
Tattle:	one another now--Pshaw, that would be a foolish	303	FOR LOVE	V.1	242
Miss Prue:	Man; and if I can't have one, I wou'd go to sleep all my	305	FOR LOVE	V.1	309
Miss Prue:	won't get me one, I'll get one for my self: I'll marry our	305	FOR LOVE	V.1	316
Ben:	in your Conscience--If so be that one had a	309	FOR LOVE	V.1	432
Tattle:	one another.	309	FOR LOVE	V.1	452
Tattle:	one does not know how, nor why, nor wherefore--	309	FOR LOVE	V.1	459
Angelica:	'Tis very unhappy, if you don't care for one another.	309	FOR LOVE	V.1	462
Ben:	one another. I'm sorry for the Young Man with all my	310	FOR LOVE	V.1	489
Valentine:	one Question.	311	FOR LOVE	V.1	516
	And One was thought sufficient for a Year:	323	M. BRIDE	PRO.	4
	For in One Year, I think they're out of Date.	323	M. BRIDE	PRO.	6
	For just as one prognosticates the Weather,	323	M. BRIDE	PRO.	8
	As one Thief scapes, that executes another.	323	M. BRIDE	PRO.	32
Almeria:	I would consent the Priest might make us one;	329	M. BRIDE	I.1	137
Almeria:	I would consent the Priest shou'd make us one;	329	M. BRIDE	I.1	V137
Almeria:	And in one Day, was wedded, and a Widow.	329	M. BRIDE	I.1	141
Almeria:	One Moment, cease to gaze on perfect Bliss,	330	M. BRIDE	I.1	V179
Almeria:	Yet, one Thing more, I would engage from thee.	330	M. BRIDE	I.1	194
Gonsalez:	One 'pointed Hour should be Alphonso's Loss,	333	M. BRIDE	I.1	305
Manuel:	Receive this Lord, as one whom I have found	334	M. BRIDE	I.1	333
Zara:	As one hating to be oblig'd--	336	M. BRIDE	I.1	417
Zara:	Such Thanks as one hating to be oblig'd--	336	M. BRIDE	I.1	V417
	(The Scene opening discovers a Place of Tombs. One	340	M. BRIDE	II.2	
Heli:	Of one complaining--There it sounds--I'll follow it.	340	M. BRIDE	II.2	3
Zara:	Thou hast a Heart, though 'tis a savage one;	346	M. BRIDE	II.2	272
Manuel:	To one, where young Delights attend; and Joys	349	M. BRIDE	II.2	383
Osmyn-Alph:	To one, whom had she never known, she had	351	M. BRIDE	III.1	54
Osmyn-Alph:	One, who has tir'd Misfortune with pursuing?	351	M. BRIDE	III.1	58
Osmyn-Alph:	One, driv'n about the World like blasted Leaves	351	M. BRIDE	III.1	59
Zara:	Cou'd one that lov'd, thus torture what she lov'd?	353	M. BRIDE	III.1	161
Zara:	Cou'd one who lov'd, thus torture whom she lov'd?	353	M. BRIDE	III.1	V161
Zara:	Thee on this false one, how I'll stab and tear	353	M. BRIDE	III.1	166
Osmyn-Alph:	Time may have still one fated Hour to come,	354	M. BRIDE	III.1	198
Almeria:	One Cup, the common Stream of both our Eyes,	356	M. BRIDE	III.1	261
Osmyn-Alph:	O--thou dost talk, my Love, as one resolv'd,	358	M. BRIDE	III.1	341
Osmyn-Alph:	This Charity to one unknown, and in	359	M. BRIDE	III.1	403
Perez:	Your Majesty one Moment to defer	359	M. BRIDE	III.1	380
Osmyn-Alph:	This Charity to one unknown, and thus	359	M. BRIDE	III.1	V403
Gonsalez:	If such a one, so 'scaping, was receiv'd	363	M. BRIDE	IV.1	102
Zara:	You more. One that did call himself Alphonso,	364	M. BRIDE	IV.1	116
Zara:	You more. One who did call himself Alphonso,	364	M. BRIDE	IV.1	V116
Manuel:	Are we not much indebted to this fair one.	366	M. BRIDE	IV.1	199
Almeria:	One hated Line of more extended Woe.	367	M. BRIDE	IV.1	261
Gonsalez:	One to my Wish. Alonzo, thou art welcome.	371	M. BRIDE	IV.1	417
Gonsalez:	And privacy, the wearing Garb of one	372	M. BRIDE	IV.1	437
Manuel:	Frighted, and fumbling one hand in his Bosom,	373	M. BRIDE	V.1	16
Manuel:	One moment's Ease? Hear my Command; and look	374	M. BRIDE	V.1	72
Gonsalez:	Stemming the Tide, with one weak Hand, and bearing	378	M. BRIDE	V.2	85
Gonsalez:	Stemming the Tide, with only one weak Hand,	378	M. BRIDE	V.2	V 85
	(A Mute kneels and gives one of the Bowls.)	381	M. BRIDE	V.2	199
Almeria:	That Sense, which in one Instant shews him dead	383	M. BRIDE	V.2	294
	He swears he'll not resent one hiss'd-off Scene,	393	WAY WORLD	PRO.	26
	Give you one Instance of a Passive Poet.	393	WAY WORLD	PRO.	38
Mirabell:	grave Faces, whisper'd one another; then complain'd	396	WAY WORLD	I.1	30
Fainall:	of you; last Night was one of their Cabal-nights; they	396	WAY WORLD	I.1	50
Fainall:	have 'em three times a Week, and meet by turns, at one	396	WAY WORLD	I.1	51
Fainall:	mov'd that to avoid Scandal there might be one Man	396	WAY WORLD	I.1	56
Mirabell:	am not one of those Coxcombs who are apt to interpret a	397	WAY WORLD	I.1	86
Mirabell:	One a Clock! (looking on his Watch) O y'are come--	398	WAY WORLD	I.1	109
Servant-M:	behind one another, as 'twere in a Country Dance. Ours	398	WAY WORLD	I.1	114
Mirabell:	Feathers, and meet me at One a Clock by Rosamond's Pond.	398	WAY WORLD	I.1	130
Mirabell:	Fool, can have but one Reason for associating with a	399	WAY WORLD	I.1	146
Mirabell:	Man who is one.	399	WAY WORLD	I.1	V147
Mirabell:	hopes, one Day or other to hate her heartily: To which	399	WAY WORLD	I.1	167
Messenger:	Is one Squire Witwoud here?	400	WAY WORLD	I.1	181
Fainall:	Medlar grafted on a Crab. One will melt in your Mouth,	401	WAY WORLD	I.1	213
Fainall:	and t'other set your Teeth on edge; one is all Pulp, and	401	WAY WORLD	I.1	214
Mirabell:	So one will be rotten before he be ripe, and the	401	WAY WORLD	I.1	216
Mirabell:	He is one whose Conversation can never be approv'd, yet	401	WAY WORLD	I.1	226
Mirabell:	it is now and then to be endur'd. He has indeed one good	401	WAY WORLD	I.1	227
Betty:	Did not the Messenger bring you one but now, Sir?	401	WAY WORLD	I.1	240
Betty:	Did not a Messenger bring you one but now, Sir?	401	WAY WORLD	I.1	V240
Witwoud:	from one Poet to another. And what's worse, 'tis as sure a	401	WAY WORLD	I.1	247
Witwoud:	defend most of his Faults, except one or two; one he has,	403	WAY WORLD	I.1	310
Witwoud:	than a Woman constant; one argues a decay of Parts, as	403	WAY WORLD	I.1	320
Petulant:	All's one, let it pass--I have a Humour to be	405	WAY WORLD	I.1	390
Petulant:	one for that--	406	WAY WORLD	I.1	431
Petulant:	All's one for that; why then say I know something.	407	WAY WORLD	I.1	442
Petulant:	and so have but one Trouble with you both.	409	WAY WORLD	I.1	518
Marwood:	as to wish to have been born Old, because we one Day	410	WAY WORLD	II.1	15
Marwood:	Faith by Marrying; if I cou'd but find one	411	WAY WORLD	II.1	53
Mrs Fain:	By the Reason you give for your Aversion, one	412	WAY WORLD	II.1	74
Marwood:	O then it seems you are one of his favourable	412	WAY WORLD	II.1	77
Mrs Fain:	one scandalous Story, to avoid giving an occasion to make	412	WAY WORLD	II.1	105
Fainall:	For having only that one Hope, the accomplishment	413	WAY WORLD	II.1	112
Fainall:	dissembl'd your Aversion. Your mutual Jealousies of one	413	WAY WORLD	II.1	138
Marwood:	professing Love to us, or mutual Faith to one another.	414	WAY WORLD	II.1	169
Mirabell:	one whose Wit and outward fair Behaviour have gain'd a	417	WAY WORLD	II.1	272
Mrs Fain:	I see but one poor empty Sculler; and he tows	418	WAY WORLD	II.1	326
Millamant:	how to write Letters; and yet one has 'em, one does not	419	WAY WORLD	II.1	361
Millamant:	know why--They serve one to pin up one's Hair.	419	WAY WORLD	II.1	362
Millamant:	is one's Power, and when one parts with one's Cruelty,	420	WAY WORLD	II.1	386
Millamant:	one parts with one's Power; and when one has parted with	420	WAY WORLD	II.1	387

One   (continued)

Millamant:	Now you must know they could not commend one, if	. . .	420	WAY WORLD	II.1	401
Millamant:	one was not handsome. Beauty the Lover's Gift--	. .	420	WAY WORLD	II.1	402
Millamant:	Lord, what is a Lover, that it can give? Why one makes	.	420	WAY WORLD	II.1	403
Millamant:	Lovers as fast as one pleases, and they live as long as one		420	WAY WORLD	II.1	404
Millamant:	pleases, and they die as soon as one pleases: And then if		420	WAY WORLD	II.1	405
Millamant:	one pleases, one makes more.		420	WAY WORLD	II.1	406
Millamant:	One no more owes one's Beauty to a Lover, than	. . .	420	WAY WORLD	II.1	409
Millamant:	the same; for we shall be sick of one another. I shan't	.	422	WAY WORLD	II.1	453
Mirabell:	for one Moment to be serious.	.	422	WAY WORLD	II.1	471
Mirabell:	one Moment--	.	422	WAY WORLD	II.1	481
Mirabell:	which they are not turn'd; and by one as well as another;		423	WAY WORLD	II.1	497
Waitwell:	my self--Married, Knighted and attended all in one	. .	424	WAY WORLD	II.1	555
Lady Wish:	See who that is--(One knocks.) Set down the Bottle	. .	425	WAY WORLD	III.1	33
Millamant:	Well, 'tis a lamentable thing I'll swear, that one	. .	432	WAY WORLD	III.1	296
Millamant:	Well, 'tis a lamentable thing I swear, that one	. . .	432	WAY WORLD	III.1	V296
Millamant:	has not the liberty of choosing one's Acquaintance, as one		432	WAY WORLD	III.1	297
Marwood:	of one Set of Acquaintance, tho' never so good, as we are of		432	WAY WORLD	III.1	300
Marwood:	one Suit, tho' never so fine. A Fool and a Doily Stuff	.	433	WAY WORLD	III.1	301
Millamant:	Things! without one cou'd give 'em to one's	. . .	433	WAY WORLD	III.1	306
Millamant:	on one Hand, and so insensible on the other. But I	. .	434	WAY WORLD	III.1	341
Millamant:	loves me, Ha, ha, ha. How can one forbear laughing to	.	434	WAY WORLD	III.1	356
Witwoud:	one another like two Battle-dores: For		435	WAY WORLD	III.1	402
Witwoud:	Contradictions beget one another like Jews.		435	WAY WORLD	III.1	403
Petulant:	say 'tis Blue--Let that pass--All's one for that. If	.	435	WAY WORLD	III.1	405
Petulant:	Importance is one Thing, and Learning's another;	. .	436	WAY WORLD	III.1	414
Petulant:	without Book--So all's one for that.	.	436	WAY WORLD	III.1	433
Marwood:	before they find one another out. You must not take any	.	438	WAY WORLD	III.1	506
Witwoud:	slabber and kiss one another when they meet, like a Call of		439	WAY WORLD	III.1	535
Fainall:	of Play, that I should lose to one, who has not	. . . .	443	WAY WORLD	III.1	688
Lady Wish:	lie neither but loll and lean upon one Elbow: with one Foot		445	WAY WORLD	IV.1	25
Sir Wilful:	Well, Well, I shall understand your Lingo one of	. .	447	WAY WORLD	IV.1	110
Sir Wilful:	the Country,--'tis like you may be one of those,	. . .	448	WAY WORLD	IV.1	130
Sir Wilful:	All's one for that,--yes, yes, if your Concerns call you,		448	WAY WORLD	IV.1	145
Millamant:	were wavering at the grate of a Monastery, with one foot	.	449	WAY WORLD	IV.1	163
Millamant:	of one another the first Week, and asham'd of one another		450	WAY WORLD	IV.1	205
Mirabell:	Contract? and here comes one to be a witness to the	. .	452	WAY WORLD	IV.1	281
Witwoud:	one another like two roasting Apples.		453	WAY WORLD	IV.1	334
Petulant:	Thou art (without a figure) Just one half of an Ass;	. .	454	WAY WORLD	IV.1	350
Foible:	Madam, the Dancers are ready, and there's one with a	. .	459	WAY WORLD	IV.1	549
Lady Wish:	Beads broken, and a Quilted Night-cap with one Ear. Go,	.	462	WAY WORLD	V.1	17
Foible:	conceal something that pass'd in our Chamber one Evening	.	464	WAY WORLD	V.1	94
Marwood:	Here is one who is concern'd in the treaty.	.	465	WAY WORLD	V.1	138
Sir Wilful:	than a little Mouth-Glew, and that's hardly dry;--One	.	472	WAY WORLD	V.1	397
Mirabell:	Foible is one and a Penitent.	.	474	WAY WORLD	V.1	470
Fainall:	or abate one tittle of my Terms, no, I will insist the more.		474	WAY WORLD	V.1	477
Sir Wilful:	loves him, and they deserve one another; my resolution is		477	WAY WORLD	V.1	584
	Who pleases any one against his Will.	.	479	WAY WORLD	EPI.	8
	As any one abstracted Fop to shew.	.	479	WAY WORLD	EPI.	30
	They from each Fair One catch some different Grace,	.	479	WAY WORLD	EPI.	32
	And shining Features in one Portrait blend,	.	479	WAY WORLD	EPI.	33
	So Poets oft, do in one Piece expose	. . . . . .	.	479	WAY WORLD	EPI.	35

One-and-twenty (1)

| Heartwell: | One-and-twenty? Madam, have I had an Opportunity | . . . | 109 | OLD BATCH | V.2 | 56 |

One-ey'd (1)

| Bellmour: | the Fanatick one-ey'd Parson! . . . . | | 39 | OLD BATCH | I.1 | 85 |

One's (15)

	For every one's both Judge and Jury here;		204	DOUBL DLR	EPI.	13
Mrs Frail:	a turn with one's Friend.		246	FOR LOVE	II.1	420
Miss Prue:	As long as one must not speak one's mind, one had	. .	263	FOR LOVE	III.1	382
Sr Sampson:	the Nose in one's Face: What, are my Eyes better than	.	281	FOR LOVE	IV.1	225
Millamant:	know why--They serve one to pin up one's Hair. . . .		419	WAY WORLD	II.1	362
Millamant:	O I ask your Pardon for that--One's Cruelty	. . . .	420	WAY WORLD	II.1	385
Millamant:	is one's Power, and when one parts with one's Cruelty,	.	420	WAY WORLD	II.1	386
Millamant:	one parts with one's Power; and when one has parted with		420	WAY WORLD	II.1	387
Millamant:	that, I fancy one's Old and Ugly.		420	WAY WORLD	II.1	388
Millamant:	One no more owes one's Beauty to a Lover, than	. . .	420	WAY WORLD	II.1	409
Millamant:	one's Wit to an Eccho: They can but reflect what we look		420	WAY WORLD	II.1	410
Millamant:	has not the liberty of choosing one's Acquaintance, as one		432	WAY WORLD	III.1	297
Millamant:	does one's Cloaths.		432	WAY WORLD	III.1	298
Millamant:	Things! without one cou'd give 'em to one's	. . . .	433	WAY WORLD	III.1	306

Onely (1)

| Mellefont: | Malice, like a Dark Lanthorn, onely shone upon me, | . . . | 129 | DOUBL DLR | I.1 | 90 |

Ones (6)

Heartwell:	Marry, is playing the Fool all ones Life long. . . .	.	74	OLD BATCH	III.2	118
Lady Ply:	you afterwards: For one does not know how ones mind may	.	147	DOUBL DLR	II.1	339
Mrs Frail:	lye open ones self.	.	248	FOR LOVE	II.1	475
Miss Prue:	our old fashion'd Country way of speaking ones mind;--	.	252	FOR LOVE	II.1	625
Millamant:	. . . I fancy ones Hair wou'd not	.	419	WAY WORLD	II.1	V366
Millamant:	act always by Advice, and so tedious to be told of ones	.	422	WAY WORLD	II.1	455

Only (135)   see Onely

Vainlove:	So, standing only on his good Behaviour, ...		35	OLD BATCH	PRO.	12
Vainlove:	For she only stalks under him to take aim at her Husband.	.	38	OLD BATCH	I.1	V 62
Vainlove:	only hapned to be once or twice, where, Laetitia was the	.	39	OLD BATCH	I.1	96
Bellmour:	So am not only forc'd to lie with other Mens Wives for	.	41	OLD BATCH	I.1	142
Bellmour:	That only happens sometimes, where the Dog has	. . .	44	OLD BATCH	I.1	257
Bellmour:	Merit, and preferring only those of interest, has made him	.	47	OLD BATCH	I.1	372
Bellmour:	the only implement of a Soldier he resembles, like that,	.	47	OLD BATCH	I.1	377
Sir Joseph:	You are only pleas'd to say so Sir--But pray if I	. .	49	OLD BATCH	II.1	79
Sharper:	only dropt a Bill of a hundred Pound, which I confess, I	.	49	OLD BATCH	II.1	82
Sir Joseph:	of knowing me--I only mean a Friend of mine whom I	. . .	50	OLD BATCH	II.1	118
Sir Joseph:	Sir--a damn'd hot Fellow--only as I was saying, I let him	.	51	OLD BATCH	II.1	130
Footman:	Only to the next door, Madam; I'll call him. . . .	.	58	OLD BATCH	II.2	158
Bellmour:	Nothing, Madam, only--	.	59	OLD BATCH	II.2	162
Bellmour:	Pauh, Women are only angry at such offences, to	. . .	63	OLD BATCH	III.1	98
Heartwell:	believe it: Nay, thou shalt think so thy self--Only let me		74	OLD BATCH	III.2	122

Only   (continued)

Speaker	Text	PAGE	TITLE	ACT.SC	LINE
Sharper:	upon reflection, seems only an effect of a too powerful passion.	79	OLD BATCH	IV.1	157
Sharper:	not what, forced me. I only beg a favourable Censure of this	79	OLD BATCH	IV.1	160
Sharper:	ripe, and only waits thy Cutting up--She has been	79	OLD BATCH	IV.1	166
Sharper:	Thou hast a sickly peevish Appetite; only chew Love and	80	OLD BATCH	IV.1	172
Belinda:	and a Fat-Amber-Necklace; the Daughters only	84	OLD BATCH	IV.3	53
Laetitia:	Book, and only tends to the Speculation of Sin.	92	OLD BATCH	IV.4	115
Sharper:	only a Trick of Sylvia in Revenge; contriv'd by Lucy.	99	OLD BATCH	V.1	109
Sharper:	in the Park; but I thought it had been only to make	102	OLD BATCH	V.1	201
Belinda:	and poor, but in show. Nay, often, only Remains, which	106	OLD BATCH	V.1	375
Belinda:	Only touch'd a gall'd-beast till he winch'd.	109	OLD BATCH	V.2	46
Capt Bluff:	--That you are over-reach'd too, ha, ha, ha, only	110	OLD BATCH	V.2	107
Capt Bluff:	a little Art-military, used--only undermined, or so, as	110	OLD BATCH	V.2	108
Sir Joseph:	Only a little Art-military Trick, Captain, only	110	OLD BATCH	V.2	112
	Only they trust to more inconstant Seas;	125	DOUBL DLR	PRO.	8
Mellefont:	Malice, like a Dark Lanthorn, only shone upon me,	129	DOUBL DLR	I.1 V	90
Lady Touch:	a Larum, only to rouse my own still'd Soul for your	137	DOUBL DLR	I.1	381
Cynthia:	the World, for you are not only happy in one another, and	141	DOUBL DLR	II.1	97
Mellefont:	That's only when Two Fools meet, and their	142	DOUBL DLR	II.1	153
Mellefont:	Not at all; only a Friendly Tryal of Skill, and the	143	DOUBL DLR	II.1	170
Sir Paul:	It concerns me, and only me;--besides, I'm not to	144	DOUBL DLR	II.1	220
Lady Ply:	only to make a Cuckold of the Father; and then seducing	147	DOUBL DLR	II.1	316
Lady Ply:	I know you don't Love Cynthia, only as a blind for your	148	DOUBL DLR	II.1	368
Maskwell:	you, I meet the only Obstacle to my Fortune. Cynthia, let	150	DOUBL DLR	II.1	440
Maskwell:	and dear dissimulation is the only Art, not to be known	150	DOUBL DLR	II.1	463
Lady Touch:	Nay, no great matter, only--well I have	152	DOUBL DLR	III.1	81
Lady Touch:	your promise--Pho, why nothing, only your Nephew had	152	DOUBL DLR	III.1	82
Lady Touch:	harmless mirth--only misplac'd that's all--but if it	153	DOUBL DLR	III.1	95
Maskwell:	won't perplex you. 'Tis the only thing that Providence	157	DOUBL DLR	III.1	244
Mellefont:	to engage her more irresistably. 'Tis only an inhancing the	158	DOUBL DLR	III.1	301
Sir Paul:	affliction, and my only affliction; indeed I cannot refrain	161	DOUBL DLR	III.1	416
Cynthia:	think they are all in good nature with the World, and only	163	DOUBL DLR	III.1	482
Brisk:	tho' to prevent Criticisms--only mark it with a small	165	DOUBL DLR	III.1	551
Brisk:	tho' to prevent Criticism--only mark it with a small	165	DOUBL DLR	III.1 V551	
Cynthia:	The Wise are Wretched, and Fools only Bless'd.	167	DOUBL DLR	III.1	634
Mellefont:	that we only have it in view, I don't see but we have it in	168	DOUBL DLR	IV.1	21
Cynthia:	it to be only chance, or destiny, or unlucky Stars, or any	169	DOUBL DLR	IV.1	60
Cynthia:	thing but the very Devil, I'm inexorable: Only still I'll	169	DOUBL DLR	IV.1	61
Sir Paul:	Person that I have a great value for not only for that, but	172	DOUBL DLR	IV.1	179
Lady Ply:	Nay, not to interrupt you my Dear--only	173	DOUBL DLR	IV.1	214
Sir Paul:	speak a good word only just for me, Gads-bud only for	180	DOUBL DLR	IV.1	472
Maskwell:	mean now, is only a bare Suspicion of my own. If your	183	DOUBL DLR	IV.1	583
Lady Touch:	my steps, and while I had only that in view, I was betray'd	185	DOUBL DLR	IV.2	77
Lady Touch:	I been Bawd to his designs? his Property only, a baiting place	191	DOUBL DLR	V.1	146
Lady Touch:	To be kindled to a flame, only to light him to	191	DOUBL DLR	V.1	150
Sir Paul:	say truth, all our Family are Cholerick; I am the only	192	DOUBL DLR	V.1	196
Lady Touch:	Thou hast, thou hast found the only way to turn my Rage;	198	DOUBL DLR	V.1	398
Sir Paul:	Nay, only about Poetry, I suppose, my lord;	201	DOUBL DLR	V.1	512
	This last and only Remedy have prov'd;	213	FOR LOVE	PRO.	9
	Or only shews its Teeth, as if it smil'd.	213	FOR LOVE	PRO.	34
Jeremy:	Was Epictetus a real Cook, or did he only write	216	FOR LOVE	I.1	10
Jeremy:	Certificate of Three Lines--only to certifie those whom	217	FOR LOVE	I.1	65
Scandal:	Others excuse him, and blame you: only the Ladies are	220	FOR LOVE	I.1	161
Scandal:	favour, as a Doctor says, No, to a Bishoprick, only that it	226	FOR LOVE	I.1	377
Tattle:	to that by one that we all know--A Man too. Only to	227	FOR LOVE	I.1	424
Tattle:	Pooh, pooh, nothing at all, I only rally'd with you	228	FOR LOVE	I.1	445
Tattle:	only obliges a Man to Secresie, that she may have the	228	FOR LOVE	I.1	474
Mrs Frail:	time he grows only rude to his Wife, and that is the highest	231	FOR LOVE	I.1	564
Scandal:	only Original you will see there.	232	FOR LOVE	I.1	604
Mrs Frail:	Well, I'll come, if it be only to disprove you.	234	FOR LOVE	I.1	659
Angelica:	only because the Butler had mislaid some of the Apostle's	237	FOR LOVE	II.1	89
Angelica:	only because the Butler had mislaid some of the Apostle	237	FOR LOVE	II.1 V	89
Sr Sampson:	Paws; Nature has been provident only to Bears and	246	FOR LOVE	II.1	391
Mrs Frail:	you had been there, it had been only innocent Recreation.	246	FOR LOVE	II.1	423
Mrs Fore:	Besides, it wou'd not only reflect upon you, Sister, but me.	247	FOR LOVE	II.1	434
Scandal:	Only for the affectation of it, as the Women do for	254	FOR LOVE	III.1	36
Angelica:	Mr. Tattle only judges of the Success of others, from the	255	FOR LOVE	III.1	76
Scandal:	say in general Terms, He only is Secret who never was	256	FOR LOVE	III.1	125
Sr Sampson:	A very Wag, Ben's a very Wag; only a little	262	FOR LOVE	III.1	319
Jeremy:	my Master was run stark mad only for Love of her Mistress;	276	FOR LOVE	IV.1	15
Scandal:	and be content only to be made a Fool with other reasonable	278	FOR LOVE	IV.1	107
Mrs Frail:	Only the Wind's chang'd.	287	FOR LOVE	IV.1	423
Angelica:	Mr. Scandal, I only stay till my Maid comes, and	293	FOR LOVE	IV.1	685
Scandal:	No, Madam; I only leave a Madman to his Remedy.	294	FOR LOVE	IV.1	695
Valentine:	Mask of Madness, and this motly Livery, only as the Slave	294	FOR LOVE	IV.1	703
Angelica:	Transport in your Soul; which, it seems, you only counterfeited.	294	FOR LOVE	IV.1	723
Sr Sampson:	am not so old neither, nor to be a bare Courtier, only a Man of	298	FOR LOVE	V.1	22
Sr Sampson:	Eastern Empire under my Feet; it would make me only a	300	FOR LOVE	V.1	99
Sr Sampson:	only be seemingly carried on?--Odd, let it be a real	300	FOR LOVE	V.1	115
Sr Sampson:	No, no, only give you a Rent-roll of my	301	FOR LOVE	V.1	152
Ben:	it will only serve to light up a Match for some body else.	308	FOR LOVE	V.1	411
Valentine:	I have been disappointed of my only Hope; and he	312	FOR LOVE	V.1	543
Valentine:	only Pleasure was to please this Lady: I have made many	312	FOR LOVE	V.1	546
Valentine:	ever you seem to love too much, it must be only when I	313	FOR LOVE	V.1	611
Angelica:	our Sex: You tax us with Injustice, only to cover your own	314	FOR LOVE	V.1	628
	That you have only set us up, to leave us.	316	FOR LOVE	EPI.	39
	For only Nature can affect the Heart.	324	M. BRIDE	PRO.	38
Leonora:	My Heart, my Life and Will, are only yours.	330	M. BRIDE	I.1	195
Almeria:	Could only by restoring thee have cur'd.	343	M. BRIDE	II.2 V134	
Osmyn-Alph:	And only for his Sorrows chose this Solitude?	346	M. BRIDE	II.2	260
Manuel:	And then, then only, when we love, we live.	349	M. BRIDE	II.2	391
Manuel:	That only Zara's Mutes, or such who bring	365	M. BRIDE	IV.1	168
Gonsalez:	Stemming the Tide, with only one weak Hand,	378	M. BRIDE	V.2 V	85

Only   (continued)
Almeria: This is my Lord, my Life, my only Husband;   383   M. BRIDE   V.2   297
Fainall: You were to blame to resent what she spoke only in   . . . 396   WAY WORLD   I.1   41
Mrs Fain: Mankind, only in compliance with my Mothers Humour.   . . 410   WAY WORLD   II.1   19
Mrs Fain: Mankind, only in compliance to my Mothers Humour.   . . 410   WAY WORLD   II.1 V 19
Mirabell: He is the only Man that do's, Madam.   412   WAY WORLD   II.1   91
Mrs Fain: The only Man that would tell me so at least;   412   WAY WORLD   II.1   92
Mrs Fain: and the only Man from whom I could hear it without   . . . 412   WAY WORLD   II.1   93
Fainall: For having only that one Hope, the accomplishment   . . . 413   WAY WORLD   II.1   112
Mrs Fain: While I only hated my Husband, I could bear   416   WAY WORLD   II.1   254
Millamant: Only with those in Verse, Mr. Witwoud. I never   419   WAY WORLD   II.1   365
Foible: have only promis'd. But a Man so enamour'd--So transported! 427   WAY WORLD   III.1   75
Mrs Fain: her in those Difficulties, from which Mirabell only must   . 430   WAY WORLD   III.1   192
Millamant: Nay, he has done nothing; he has only talk'd--   . 432   WAY WORLD   III.1   291
Witwoud: presumptive it only may. That's a Logical Distinction now,   435   WAY WORLD   III.1   410
Fainall: But let the Lover still believe. Or if he doubt, let it
    be only   444   WAY WORLD   III.1   715
Sir Wilful: that--for if so be that I set on't, I'll do't. But only
    for my   . . . 447   WAY WORLD   IV.1   84
Sir Wilful: Nay nothing--Only for the walks sake, that's   448   WAY WORLD   IV.1   119
Millamant: only to my own taste; to have no obligation upon me to   . 450   WAY WORLD   IV.1   216
Mrs Fain: him; But he answers her only with Singing and Drinking   . 452   WAY WORLD   IV.1   312
Lady Wish: the direct Mold of Vertue? I have not only been a Mold   . 465   WAY WORLD   V.1   144
Marwood: Nay Madam, I advise nothing, I only lay before   . . . 468   WAY WORLD   V.1   241
Fainall: consider'd; I will only reserve to my self the Power to
    chuse   468   WAY WORLD   V.1   266
Sir Wilful: Cozen, will cross 'em once again, only to bear me Company, 471   WAY WORLD   V.1   350
Mirabell: Suppliant only for your pity--I am going where I   . . 471   WAY WORLD   V.1   374
Mirabell: Suppliant only for Pity--I am going where I   471   WAY WORLD   V.1 V374
Mirabell: You have dispos'd of her, who only cou'd have   473   WAY WORLD   V.1   458
Oons (12)   see Ouns
Heartwell: ha? Speak Syren--Oons why do I look on her!   72   OLD BATCH III.2   40
Heartwell: And who wou'd you visit there, say you? (O'ons, ... 104   OLD BATCH   V.1   289
Sr Sampson: 'Oons, what had I to do to get Children,--   245   FOR LOVE   II.1   349
Sr Sampson: Sola's and Sonata's? 'Oons whose Son are you? how were   . 245   FOR LOVE   II.1   377
Ben: You Cheese-curd you,--Marry thee! Oons I'll Marry a   . 264   FOR LOVE   III.1   425
Sr Sampson: Oons, I won't believe it; let me see him, Sir   279   FOR LOVE   IV.1   145
Sr Sampson: Oons! What a Vexation is here! I know not   282   FOR LOVE   IV.1   249
Sr Sampson: we are Fools as we use to be--Oons, that you cou'd   . . 283   FOR LOVE   IV.1   280
Sr Sampson: Oons, what is the meaning of this?   312   FOR LOVE   V.1   567
Sr Sampson: Oons you're a Crocodile.   312   FOR LOVE   V.1   581
Sr Sampson: them and you, my self and every Body--Oons, Cully'd,   . 313   FOR LOVE   V.1 V585
Sir Wilful: Oons this Fellow knows less than a Starling; I   . . . 437   WAY WORLD III.1   473
Open (24)
Belinda: kept open, for the Entertainment of travelling Flies.   . . 84   OLD BATCH   IV.3   48
Fondlewife: Cocky, Cocky, open the door   89   OLD BATCH   IV.4   11
Laetitia: came open mouth'd upon me, and would have ravished a   . 90   OLD BATCH   IV.4   53
Maskwell: needs this? I say nothing but what your self, in open hours   137   DOUBL DLR   I.1   384
Maskwell: needs this? I say nothing but what you your self, in open
    hours   137   DOUBL DLR   I.1 V384
Maskwell: open: 'twill be hard, if then you can't bring her to any   . 157   DOUBL DLR III.1   253
Lady Froth: her Gums bare, and her Mouth open.--   165   DOUBL DLR III.1   575
Maskwell: passage open.   184   DOUBL DLR   IV.2   31
Maskwell: No Mask like open Truth to cover Lies, ... 190   DOUBL DLR   V.1   100
Lady Touch: thee open to my sight! But then 'twill be too late to know--   198   DOUBL DLR   V.1   397
Lord Touch: Torture and shame attend their open Birth: 203   DOUBL DLR   V.1   593
Scandal: the force of open honest Satire.   220   FOR LOVE   I.1   150
Foresight: Mole upon her Lip, with a moist Palm, and an open   . . 239   FOR LOVE   II.1   153
Mrs Frail: lye open ones self.   248   FOR LOVE   II.1   475
Nurse: Open the Door--Open the Door Miss--I hear you   . . . 253   FOR LOVE   III.1   6
Nurse: (knocks) Ods my Life, won't you open the Door? I'll   . . 253   FOR LOVE   III.1   11
Tattle: Hah! A good open Speaker, and not to be trusted   . . . 292   FOR LOVE   IV.1   629
Osmyn-Alph: That thus with open Hand it scatters good, ... 344   M. BRIDE   II.2   186
Osmyn-Alph: That persevering still with open Hand, ... 344   M. BRIDE   II.2 V186
Almeria: Open thy Bowels of Compassion, take   368   M. BRIDE   IV.1   276
Sir Wilful: think--Nay Cozen Fainall, open the Door--Pshaw,   . . 447   WAY WORLD   IV.1   93
Lady Wish: Letter--I wou'd open it in your presence, because I   . . 460   WAY WORLD   IV.1   570
Lady Wish: it--wee'll open it together--look you here.   460   WAY WORLD   IV.1   583
Open'd (4)
Maskwell: --oh she has open'd her heart to me,--I am to turn you a   . 149   DOUBL DLR   II.1   402
Gonsalez: Open'd the Way to this Invasion;   363   M. BRIDE   IV.1   87
Gonsalez: Open'd and urg'd the Way to this Invasion;   363   M. BRIDE   IV.1 V 87
Marwood: have your Case open'd by an old fumbling Leacher in a   . 467   WAY WORLD   V.1   212
Opened (1)
Setter: opened for all Comers. In Fine thou art the high Road to   . 66   OLD BATCH III.1   196
Opening (3)
    (Scene opening, shews Lady Touchwood's Chamber.)   . . . 183   DOUBL DLR   IV.2
    (The Scene opening discovers a Place of Tombs. One   . . . 340   M. BRIDE   II.2
    (Scene opening shews the Prison.   376   M. BRIDE   V.2 V
Openly (3)
Maskwell: to treat openly of my Marriage with Cynthia, all must be   . 190   DOUBL DLR   V.1   90
Valentine: this Restraint, than when I openly rival'd the rich Fops,   . 217   FOR LOVE   I.1   52
Mrs Frail: and speak openly one to another; I'm afraid the World   . 248   FOR LOVE   II.1   487
Opens (4)
Laetitia: (Opens the Door.)   89   OLD BATCH   IV.4   21
Bellmour: then opens the Scene of Pleasure.   107   OLD BATCH   V.1   386
    (Goes to the Scene, which opens and discovers Valentine upon 279   FOR LOVE   IV.1   148
    (They go to the Scene which opens and shews the Body.)   . 380   M. BRIDE   V.2   161
Opinion (27)
Bellmour: He's of another opinion, and says I do the drudgery   . . 43   OLD BATCH   I.1   222
Araminta: which comes pretty near my own Opinion of Love and   . . . 58   OLD BATCH   II.2   154
Sir Joseph: Indifferent, agad in my opinion very indifferent   . . . 70   OLD BATCH III.1   333
Bellmour: in an opinion of Atheism; when they may be so much   . . 75   OLD BATCH   IV.1   7
Araminta: deceiv'd me in you, I know not; my Opinion was but   . . . 87   OLD BATCH   IV.3   171
Bellmour: See the great Blessing of an easy Faith; Opinion   . . . 96   OLD BATCH   IV.4   271
Bellmour: Pshaw, No: I have a better Opinion of thy Wit.   100   OLD BATCH   V.1   142

Opinion (continued)

Osmyn   (continued)

	(A Prison. Enter Osmyn alone, with a Paper.)	349	M. BRIDE	III.1	
Selim:	The Fate of Osmyn: but to that, fresh News	361	M. BRIDE	IV.1	6
Zara:	More than his Crown, t'impart 'ere Osmyn die.	361	M. BRIDE	IV.1	19
Selim:	Pretend to sacrifice the Life of Osmyn.	361	M. BRIDE	IV.1	22
Gonsalez:	Till Osmyn die. Mean time we may learn more	363	M. BRIDE	IV.1	70
Zara:	(aside to Selim). Ha! hear'st thou that? Is Osmyn then	363	M. BRIDE	IV.1	90
Zara:	While Osmyn lives, you are not safe.	364	M. BRIDE	IV.1	111
Zara:	Alphonso, Heli, and the Traytour Osmyn.	364	M. BRIDE	IV.1	124
Zara:	Your Enemy; I have discover'd Osmyn,	364	M. BRIDE	IV.1	138
Zara:	To rescue Osmyn at the Place of Death.	364	M. BRIDE	IV.1	144
Zara:	Osmyn.	365	M. BRIDE	IV.1	155
Manuel:	How? she visit Osmyn! What, my Daughter?	365	M. BRIDE	IV.1	184
Gonsalez:	I'th' Evening Osmyn was to die; at Mid-night	366	M. BRIDE	IV.1	208
Gonsalez:	What if she had seen Osmyn? tho' 'twere strange.	366	M. BRIDE	IV.1	222
Gonsalez:	If Osmyn be, as Zara has related,	367	M. BRIDE	IV.1	229
Manuel:	Now doom'd to die, that most accursed Osmyn.	368	M. BRIDE	IV.1	288
Manuel:	Nor am I Ignorant what Osmyn is--	368	M. BRIDE	IV.1	302
Almeria:	O that I did, Osmyn, he is my Husband.	370	M. BRIDE	IV.1	356
Manuel:	Osmyn!	370	M. BRIDE	IV.1	357
Almeria:	Not Osmyn, but Alphonso is my Dear,	370	M. BRIDE	IV.1	358
Almeria:	And know that Osmyn was Alphonso.	370	M. BRIDE	IV.1	382
Gonsalez:	Osmyn Alphonso! no; she over-rates	371	M. BRIDE	IV.1	397
Manuel:	Is Osmyn so dispos'd, as I commanded?	372	M. BRIDE	V.1	6
Manuel:	Thou knew'st that Osmyn was Alphonso, knew'st	373	M. BRIDE	V.1	46
Zara:	Yes, Osmyn, yes; be Osmyn or Alphonso,	376	M. BRIDE	V.1	135
Gonsalez:	The Moor, is dead. That Osmyn was Alphonso;	377	M. BRIDE	V.2	41
Garcia:	Impossible; for Osmyn flying, was	377	M. BRIDE	V.2	43
Garcia:	Impossible; for Osmyn was, while flying	377	M. BRIDE	V.2 V	43
Garcia:	See, see, attir'd like Osmyn, where he lies.	377	M. BRIDE	V.2	61
Alonzo:	For Osmyn, if in seeking for the King,	379	M. BRIDE	V.2	120
Zara:	O Osmyn! O Alphonso! Cruel Fate!	380	M. BRIDE	V.2 V163	
Zara:	But cannot bear to find thee thus, my Osmyn--	380	M. BRIDE	V.2 V167	

Osmyn's (7)

Heli:	I feel, to hear of Osmyn's Name; to hear	338	M. BRIDE	II.1	10
Selim:	Concerning Osmyn's corresponding with	361	M. BRIDE	IV.1	13
Selim:	Concerning Osmyn's and his Correspondence	361	M. BRIDE	IV.1 V	13
Selim:	On Osmyn's Death; too quick a Change of Mercy,	362	M. BRIDE	IV.1	45
Selim:	And some of them bought off to Osmyn's Int'rest,	362	M. BRIDE	IV.1	52
Zara:	And Osmyn's Death requir'd of strong necessity.	364	M. BRIDE	IV.1	126
Gonsalez:	For Osmyn's Death, as he's Alphonso's Friend.	367	M. BRIDE	IV.1	240

Oth' (1)

	To think oth' Sting, that's in the tail of Pleasure.	113	OLD BATCH	EPI.	9

Other (60)   see T'other

Bellmour:	So am not only forc'd to lie with other Mens Wives for	41	OLD BATCH	I.1	142
Capt Bluff:	Death, had any other Man interrupted me--	54	OLD BATCH	II.1	237
Setter:	uses me as his Attendant; the other (being the better	64	OLD BATCH	III.1	139
Bellmour:	other way to get himself a heat.	70	OLD BATCH	III.1	329
Belinda:	have been I know not how many times warm'd for other	106	OLD BATCH	V.1	376
Brisk:	no other way, I'gad.	133	DOUBL DLR	I.1	243
Careless:	or other.	162	DOUBL DLR	III.1	447
Cynthia:	in themselves, but they can render other People	165	DOUBL DLR	III.1	578
Lady Froth:	near any other Man. Oh here's my Lord, now you shall	177	DOUBL DLR	IV.1	369
Lord Froth:	Any other time, my Dear, or we'll Dance it	177	DOUBL DLR	IV.1	381
Lady Touch:	Marriage, and the promoting any other, without consulting	192	DOUBL DLR	V.1	180
Mellefont:	I know no other way but this he has proposed; If	193	DOUBL DLR	V.1	200
Maskwell:	was, the finding it impossible to gain the Lady any other	193	DOUBL DLR	V.1	219
Mellefont:	one, and too pious for the other.	193	DOUBL DLR	V.1	237
Maskwell:	every look you cheaply throw away on any other Object	199	DOUBL DLR	V.1	435
	(Enter Mellefont lugging in Maskwell from the other side	202	DOUBL DLR	V.1	566
Jeremy:	and Songs; not like other Porters for Hire, but for the Jests	218	FOR LOVE	I.1	97
Jeremy:	and forbearance, and other fair words; that I was forc'd	220	FOR LOVE	I.1	172
Valentine:	Pox on her, cou'd she find no other time to fling	221	FOR LOVE	I.1	207
Tattle:	me, and I told her something or other, faith--I know	228	FOR LOVE	I.1	447
Scandal:	her, you must be condemned, like other bad Painters, to	230	FOR LOVE	I.1	538
Mrs Frail:	good Breeding, for it begets his Civility to other People.	231	FOR LOVE	I.1	565
Mrs Fore:	some way or other to leave 'em together.	249	FOR LOVE	II.1	504
Scandal:	to allow some other Men the last Favour; you mistake,	272	FOR LOVE	III.1	696
Ben:	as other Folks.	274	FOR LOVE	III.1	792
Scandal:	and be content only to be made a Fool with other reasonable	278	FOR LOVE	IV.1	107
Miss Prue:	way or other. Oh! methinks I'm sick when I think of a	305	FOR LOVE	V.1	308
Leonora:	In Tears, when Joy appears in every other Face.	330	M. BRIDE	I.1	168
Leonora:	when Joy appears in every other Face.	330	M. BRIDE	I.1 V168	
Almeria:	And Joy he brings to every other Heart,	330	M. BRIDE	I.1	169
Manuel:	Must have some other Cause than his Captivity.	335	M. BRIDE	I.1	376
Garcia:	To Osmyn; but some other Opportunity	338	M. BRIDE	II.1	43
Zara:	Than all the Malice of my other Fate.	348	M. BRIDE	II.2	339
Almeria:	If there, he shoot not ev'ry other Shaft;	356	M. BRIDE	III.1	286
Almeria:	Thy second self should feel each other Wound,	356	M. BRIDE	III.1	287
Osmyn-Alph:	A wish or Thought from me, to have thee other.	357	M. BRIDE	III.1	316
Almeria:	But sink each other, lower yet, down, down,	358	M. BRIDE	III.1	371
Almeria:	But sink each other, deeper yet, down, down	358	M. BRIDE	III.1 V371	
Zara:	They and no other; not the Princess self.	365	M. BRIDE	IV.1	170
Gonsalez:	With the other, the Crown, to wreath thy Brow,	378	M. BRIDE	V.2	86
	(They point to the other Cup.)	382	M. BRIDE	V.2	257
Mirabell:	hopes, one Day or other to hate her heartily: To which	399	WAY WORLD	I.1	167
Fainall:	the other all Core.	401	WAY WORLD	I.1	215
Mirabell:	other will be rotten without ever being ripe at all.	401	WAY WORLD	I.1	217
Mirabell:	a good Memory, and some few Scraps of other Folks Wit.	401	WAY WORLD	I.1	225
Witwoud:	Ay, but no other?	401	WAY WORLD	I.1	241
Mirabell:	there yet? I shall cut your Throat, sometime or other,	406	WAY WORLD	I.1	423
Petulant:	Ay, ay, let that pass--There are other Throats	406	WAY WORLD	I.1	425
Marwood:	affect Endearments to each other, profess eternal Friendships,	410	WAY WORLD	II.1	23
Fainall:	and weep like Alexander, when he wanted other Worlds to	413	WAY WORLD	II.1	116

Out   (continued)

		PAGE	TITLE	ACT.SC	LINE
Sir Joseph:	Purpose, if he han't frighted it out of my memory. Hem!	49	OLD BATCH	II.1	53
Sir Joseph:	I do scorn a dirty thing. But agad 'Ime a little out of	50	OLD BATCH	II.1	105
Sir Joseph:	at present; I have lay'd it all out upon my Back.	50	OLD BATCH	II.1	112
Sir Joseph:	fire once out of the mouth of a Canon--agad he did; those	53	OLD BATCH	II.1	219
Capt Bluff:	Pish you have put me out, I have forgot what I was	53	OLD BATCH	II.1	224
Belinda:	one Scene of Address, a Lover, set out with all his Equipage	55	OLD BATCH	II.2	32
Araminta:	Oh is it come out--Now you are angry, I am sure	56	OLD BATCH	II.2	58
Araminta:	I hope you are not going out in dudgeon, Cousin.	56	OLD BATCH	II.2	72
Belinda:	Not I; witness my Heart I stay out of pure Affection.	57	OLD BATCH	II.2	111
Bellmour:	is to run so extravagantly in Debt; I have laid out such a	58	OLD BATCH	II.2	122
Lucy:	No, you're out; could we perswade him, that she doats	62	OLD BATCH	III.1	1
Capt Bluff:	And so out of your unwonted Generosity--	67	OLD BATCH	III.1	242
Capt Bluff:	Composition; I believe you gave it him out of fear, pure	68	OLD BATCH	III.1	269
Sir Joseph:	that it was altogether out of fear, but partly to prevent	68	OLD BATCH	III.1	273
Capt Bluff:	out your Trick, and does not care to be put upon; being a	69	OLD BATCH	III.1	297
Heartwell:	--hark! (pulling out a Purse and chinking it) how sweetly	72	OLD BATCH	III.2	35
Heartwell:	when 'tis out of Obstinacy and Contradiction--But	74	OLD BATCH	III.2	127
Heartwell:	Well, farewell then--if I can get out of her sight I	74	OLD BATCH	III.2	129
Heartwell:	Well, farewell then--if I can get out of sight I	74	OLD BATCH	III.2	V129
Lucy:	Vainlove, I have found out a picque she has taken at him;	75	OLD BATCH	III.2	156
Fondlewife:	and bid my Cocky come out to me, I will give her some	76	OLD BATCH	IV.1	46
Bellmour:	(Pulls out the letter.)	81	OLD BATCH	IV.2	33
Belinda:	(Pulls out a Pocket-Glass.)	83	OLD BATCH	IV.3	6
Araminta:	Your Head's a little out of Order.	83	OLD BATCH	IV.3	7
Belinda:	hot, out of her Under-Petticoat-Pocket,--Ha, ha, ha:	84	OLD BATCH	IV.3	44
	(Takes out the Letter, and offers it: She snatches it,				
	and throws	88	OLD BATCH	IV.3	179
Fondlewife:	out of your Cabinet.	89	OLD BATCH	IV.4	25
	Joseph, almost pushes him down, and Cries cut.)	90	OLD BATCH	IV.4	50
Laetitia:	out of my sight?	90	OLD BATCH	IV.4	58
Fondlewife:	Oh, how the blasphemous Wretch swears! Out	90	OLD BATCH	IV.4	64
Laetitia:	Oh! Won't you follow, and see him out of Doors,	91	OLD BATCH	IV.4	70
	(Fondlewife haling out Bellmour.)	92	OLD BATCH	IV.4	120
Fondlewife:	Come out here, thou Ananias incarnate.--	92	OLD BATCH	IV.4	121
Fondlewife:	I'll show you the way out of my house, if you please. Come,	96	OLD BATCH	IV.4	269
Bellmour:	Phuh, Secret, ay.--And to be out of thy Debt, I'll	98	OLD BATCH	V.1	53
Setter:	Ay, I know her, Sir: At least, I'm sure I can fish it out	99	OLD BATCH	V.1	103
Sharper:	Here, Frank; your Blood-Hound has made out the	99	OLD BATCH	V.1	107
Vainlove:	--And why did you not find me out, to tell me this	99	OLD BATCH	V.1	120
Bellmour:	Nay, then I thank thee for not putting me out of	100	OLD BATCH	V.1	147
Sir Joseph:	be pick'd out of Aesop's Fables, let me tell you that; and	101	OLD BATCH	V.1	176
Sir Joseph:	Ay, now it's out; 'tis I, my own individual Person.	102	OLD BATCH	V.1	206
Sharper:	himself out of breath.--	107	OLD BATCH	V.1	392
Boy:	There was a Man too that fetch'd 'em out:--Setter, I	107	OLD BATCH	V.2	2
Heartwell:	self on her Wedding-Day! Not hold out till Night!	107	OLD BATCH	V.2	6
Heartwell:	art going) see thee fall into the same snare, out of which	111	OLD BATCH	V.2	152
	Now that's at stake--No fool, 'tis out o'fashion.	113	OLD BATCH	EPI.	12
Brisk:	said it out of thy Company.--Careless, ha?	128	DOUBL DLR	I.1	39
Lord Touch:	Out upon't, Nephew--leave your	131	DOUBL DLR	I.1	172
Lord Froth:	found out the Wit.	133	DOUBL DLR	I.1	245
Brisk:	O Lord, why can't you find it out?--Why there	133	DOUBL DLR	I.1	248
	(Takes out a Pocket-Glass, and looks in it.)	134	DOUBL DLR	I.1	290
	then laughs out.)	140	DOUBL DLR	II.1	66
Mellefont:	Winnings to be laid out in an Entertainment.--What's	143	DOUBL DLR	II.1	V171
	here, the	143	DOUBL DLR	II.1	193
	(To the Musick, they go out.)	143			
Mellefont:	There's comfort in a hand stretch'd out, to one	148	DOUBL DLR	II.1	389
Maskwell:	to make your Uncle Disinherit you, to get you turn'd out	149	DOUBL DLR	II.1	400
Lord Touch:	Villain! 'Death I'll have him stripp'd and turn'd naked out	153	DOUBL DLR	III.1	100
Careless:	Mellefont, get out o'th' way, my Lady Plyant's	157	DOUBL DLR	III.1	264
Careless:	since the day of his Marriage, he has, out of a piece of	158	DOUBL DLR	III.1	277
Mellefont:	secures them from blushing, and being out of Countenance,	158	DOUBL DLR	III.1	312
Mellefont:	her, till he has been fool enough to think of her out of her	159	DOUBL DLR	III.1	317
Careless:	For Heaven's sake, Madam--I'm quite out of	160	DOUBL DLR	III.1	370
Sir Paul:	And my Lady's quite out of Breath; or else you	160	DOUBL DLR	III.1	372
Cynthia:	without any harmony; for sure, my Lord, to laugh out of	163	DOUBL DLR	III.1	472
Cynthia:	time, is as disagreeable as to sing out of time or out of	163	DOUBL DLR	III.1	473
Lady Froth:	lines again (pulls out a Paper.) Let me see here, you know	164	DOUBL DLR	III.1	512
Lady Froth:	I have seen her take 'em half chew'd out of her	165	DOUBL DLR	III.1	570
Mellefont:	I don't know why we should not steal out of the	168	DOUBL DLR	IV.1	27
Careless:	out a Wretched Life, and breath my Soul beneath your	170	DOUBL DLR	IV.1	100
Lady Ply:	O fy, fy, Sir Paul, you'l put me out of Countenance	172	DOUBL DLR	IV.1	189
Lady Froth:	Bless me, why did you call out upon me so	176	DOUBL DLR	IV.1	319
Brisk:	see how Love and Murder will out. But did I really name	176	DOUBL DLR	IV.1	329
Lady Froth:	out of the way.	177	DOUBL DLR	IV.1	378
Lady Ply:	found out that contrivance to let you see this Letter; which	179	DOUBL DLR	IV.1	455
Lord Touch:	Fear not his Displeasure; I will put you out	182	DOUBL DLR	IV.1	570
Mellefont:	(Leaps out.)	184	DOUBL DLR	IV.2	36
Maskwell:	(Runs out.)	184	DOUBL DLR	IV.2	40
Mellefont:	out Cuckoldom with her Fingers, and you're running	187	DOUBL DLR	IV.2	132
Mellefont:	and just when he holds out his hand to gather it, to have a	187	DOUBL DLR	IV.2	145
Maskwell:	me out a Villain, settled in possession of a fair Estate,				
	and	190	DOUBL DLR	V.1	86
Maskwell:	Gamester--but shou'd he find me out before! 'tis dangerous	190	DOUBL DLR	V.1	88
Lady Touch:	you to Destruction, I'll tear your Eyes out, and tread	192	DOUBL DLR	V.1	183
Saygrace:	(looking out). Sweet Sir, I will but pen the last Line	194	DOUBL DLR	V.1	272
Careless:	Is not that he, now gone out with my Lord?	196	DOUBL DLR	V.1	333
Cynthia:	hear it out.	198	DOUBL DLR	V.1	429
Lord Touch:	I'll add to my Plot too,--let us haste to find out, and	200	DOUBL DLR	V.1	486
	runs out affrighted, my Lord after her, like a Parson.)	202	DOUBL DLR	V.1	557
Lady Touch:	(Runs out.)	202	DOUBL DLR	V.1	562
	(They carry out Maskwell, who hangs down his head.)	203	DOUBL DLR	V.1	577
Valentine:	I'll take some of their Trade out of their Hands.	217	FOR LOVE	I.1	60
Jeremy:	Porter, worn out with pimping, and carrying Billet doux	218	FOR LOVE	I.1	96
Trapland:	Thank you--I have been out of this Money--	223	FOR LOVE	I.1	254

Valentine:	Eyes tc her Feet, as they steal in and out, and play at	. 223	FOR LOVE	I.1	287
Mrs Frail:	Daughter is ccme out of the Country--I assure you, . .	. 231	FOR LCVE	I.1	568
Mrs Frail:	never been out of the Country.	. 231	FCB LCVE	I.1	573
Mrs Frail:	and so stole out to see you. Well, and what will . .	. 231	FOR LCVE	I.1	583
Scandal:	there are some set out in their true Cclours, both Men and	. 233	FOR LOVE	I.1	627
Foresight:	very good Luck: Nay, I have had some Omens; I got out .	. 236	FCR LCVE	II.1	31
Angelica:	lend me your Coach, mine's out of Order.	. 236	FOR LCVE	II.1	45
Angelica:	Will ycu? I care not, but all shall out then-- . . .	. 238	FOR LCVE	II.1	118
Angelica:	out my Aunt, and tell her, she must not come home. . .	. 239	FOR LCVE	II.1	162
Sr Sampson:	not keep the Devil out of his Wives Circle.	. 241	FOR LCVE	II.1	228
Sr Sampson:	not keep the Devil out of his Wife's Circle.	. 241	FOR LCVE	II.1 V228
Valentine:	you, cut of Fatherly fondness, will be pleas'd to add, shall	243	FOR LOVE	II.1	291
Sr Sampson:	go naked out of the World as you came into't. . . .	. 244	FOR LCVE	II.1	338
Foresight:	By your Looks, you shou'd go up Stairs out of the . .	. 245	FCR LCVE	II.1	383
Sr Sampson:	t'other spins his Habitation out of his Entrails. . .	. 246	FOR LCVE	II.1	393
Sr Sampson:	t'other spins his Habitation out of his cwn Entrails, .	. 246	FOR LCVE	II.1 V393
Sr Sampson:	feed thee out of my own Vitals?--'S'heart, live by . .	. 246	FOR LCVE	II.1	399
Mrs Fore:	Face;--for I'll swear your impudence has put me out of	. 248	FOR LCVE	II.1	464
Mrs Fore:	It's very true, Sister: Well since all's out, and . .	. 248	FCB LCVE	II.1	476
Mrs Fore:	power--And I can tell you one thing that falls out luckily	248	FOR LCVE	II.1	498
Tattle:	out of your Innocency.	. 249	FOR LCVE	II.1	537
Mrs Fore:	perswade her out of her Innocency.	. 249	FOR LCVE	II.1	539
Mrs Fore:	A cunning Cur; how soon he cou'd find cut a	. 250	FOR LCVE	II.1	544
Tattle:	Or does she leave us together out of good Morality, and	. 251	FOR LCVE	II.1	593
Tattle:	you'l cry out, you must be sure to hold your Tongue. .	. 252	FOR LCVE	II.1	623
Tattle:	Then I'll make you cry out.	. 253	FOR LCVE	II.1	657
Valentine:	There, now it's out.	. 255	FOR LCVE	III.1	87
Ben:	and may hap may'nt get 'em out again when he wou'd. .	. 261	FOR LCVE	III.1	313
Ben:	rains out at her Eyes.	. 265	FOR LCVE	III.1	443
Mrs Frail:	out.--Come, Sir, will you venture your self with me? .	. 265	FOR LCVE	III.1	450
Sr Sampson:	Why, body o' me, cut with't.	. 266	FOR LCVE	III.1	495
Scandal:	two. I can get nothing out of him but Sighs. He desires	. 266	FCR LCVE	III.1	501
Scandal:	what Project I had to get him out of the way; that I might	269	FCR LCVE	III.1	597
Scandal:	Service of your Sex. He that first cries out stop Thief, is	272	FOR LCVE	III.1	698
Ben:	That they should all fall out, Sir:	. 274	FOR LCVE	III.1	783
Sr Sampson:	What, is he gone cut of Town, run away, ha!	. 279	FOR LCVE	IV.1	122
Valentine:	Livelyhood amongst you. I have been sworn cut cf . .	. 280	FCR LCVE	IV.1	172
Valentine:	little out of Order; won't you please to sit, Sir? . .	. 281	FOR LCVE	IV.1	197
Sr Sampson:	(Shews him the Paper, but holds it out of his reach.) .	. 281	FOR LCVE	IV.1	216
Valentine:	out to be in Forma Pauperis presently.	. 282	FOR LCVE	IV.1	248
Valentine:	Who's that, that's out of his Way?--I am Truth, . . .	. 282	FOR LCVE	IV.1	251
Mrs Frail:	Sister, do you stay with them; I'll find out my . . .	. 285	FOR LCVE	IV.1	351
Mrs Frail:	to find you out.--Had'st thou the Impudence to aspire .	. 286	FOR LCVE	IV.1	407
Tattle:	Letters writ in Juice of Lemon, for no Fire can fetch			
	it out.	. 292	FOB LCVE	IV.1	614
Valentine:	lov'd a Woman, and lov'd her so long, that I fcund out a	. 292	FCB LCVE	IV.1	640
Valentine:	strange thing: I found out what a Cwoman was good for. .	. 292	FCB LCVE	IV.1	641
Sr Sampson:	'tis as they commit Murder; out of a Frolick: And are .	. 299	FOR LCVE	V.1	57
Sr Sampson:	out of his Money, and now his Poverty has run him out cf	. 299	FOR LCVE	V.1	84
Tattle:	Is not that she, gone out just now?	. 301	FOR LCVE	V.1	165
Jeremy:	could ever find out his Head-Quarters.	. 302	FOR LCVE	V.1	195
Sr Sampson:	Weekly Bills out of Countenance.	. 308	FOB LCVE	V.1	399
Mrs Frail:	I can't speak it out.	. 309	FOR LCVE	V.1	446
	For in One Year, I think they're out of Date. . . .	. 323	M. BRIDE	PRO.	6
Osmyn-Alph:	And for some Purpose points out these Remembrances. . .	. 350	M. ERIDE	III.1	5
Osmyn-Alph:	Is singled out to bleed, and bear the Scourge; . . .	. 350	M. BRIDE	III.1	30
Heli:	Occasion will not fail to point out Ways	. 352	M. BRIDE	III.1	97
Zara:	Find out the King, tell him I have of Weight	. 361	M. BRIDE	IV.1	18
Almeria:	And Fraud, to find the fatal Secret out, ...	. 370	M. BRIDE	IV.1	381
Alonzo:	He snatch'd frcm out his Bosom this--and strove . . .	. 373	M. ERIDE	V.1	22
	Look out when Storms arise, and Billows roar, . . .	. 385	M. BRIDE	EPI.	20
Fainall:	Prithee, why so reserv'd? Something has put you out .	. 395	WAY WCRLD	I.1	13
Witwoud:	out of my Head. I beg Pardon that I shou'd ask a Man of	. 402	WAY WCRLD	I.1	256
Witwoud:	found out this way, I have known him call for . . .	. 405	WAY WCRLD	I.1	366
Witwoud:	Mean, why he wou'd slip you out of this Chocolate-house,	. 405	WAY WCRLD	I.1	369
Petulant:	out.	. 405	WAY WCRLD	I.1	388
Mirabell:	not us be accessary to your putting the Ladies out of .	. 409	WAY WCRLD	I.1	524
Mirabell:	roar out aloud as often as they pass by you; and when .	. 409	WAY WCRLD	I.1	526
Mirabell:	put ancther out of Countenance.	. 409	WAY WCRLD	I.1	535
Marwood:	then know the worst; and be out of his Pain; but I wou'd	. 411	WAY WCRLD	II.1	62
Mrs Fain:	pleasant Relation last Night: I wou'd fain hear it out.	. 412	WAY WCRLD	II.1	99
Mirabell:	what a Butler cou'd pinch out of a Napkin.	. 418	WAY WCRLD	II.1	313
Mirabell:	and her Streamers out, and a shcal of Fools for Tenders	. 418	WAY WCRLD	II.1	324
Mirabell:	and Streamers out, and a shoal of Fools for Tenders .	. 418	WAY WCRLD	II.1 V324
Foible:	dress till I come--(Looking out.) O Dear, I'm sure . .	. 424	WAY WCRLD	II.1	544
Lady Wish:	brought! Dost thou take me for a Fairy, to drink out of an	425	WAY WCRLD	III.1	29
Lady Wish:	out of thee?	. 427	WAY WORLD	III.1	83
Lady Wish:	He has put me out of all patience. I shall never recompose	428	WAY WCRLD	III.1	140
Millamant:	--Is not all the Powder out of my Hair?	. 432	WAY WCRLD	III.1	289
Millamant:	alike; but Fools never wear out--they are such Drap-du-berry	433	WAY WCRLD	III.1	305
Witwoud:	Animosity--The falling out of Wits is like the falling .	. 435	WAY WCRLD	III.1	395
Witwoud:	out of Lovers--We agree in the main, like Treble . .	. 435	WAY WCRLD	III.1	396
Sir Wilful:	can'st not guess, enquire her out, do'st hear Fellow? And	437	WAY WCRLD	III.1	465
Marwood:	before they find one another out. You must not take any .	438	WAY WCRLD	III.1	506
Sir Wilful:	--You cou'd write News before you were out of your . .	. 439	WAY WCRLD	III.1	548
Fainall:	that's out of the Question,--And as to my part in my .	. 443	WAY WORLD	III.1	685
Marwood:	she knows some passages--Nay I expect all will come out .	444	WAY WORLD	III.1	705
Fainall:	best part of her Estate; which I wheadl'd out of her; And	444	WAY WORLD	III.1	710
Millamant:	dine in my dressing room when I'm out of humour . . .	. 450	WAY WORLD	IV.1	220
Mirabell:	shall be found out.--And rail at me for missing the . .	. 451	WAY WCRLD	IV.1	241
Witwoud:	out and piec'd in the sides like an unsiz'd Camlet,--Yes,	. 453	WAY WCRLD	IV.1	328
Lady Wish:	Out upon't, out upon't, at years of Discretion, . . .	. 455	WAY WORLD	IV.1	384
Sir Wilful:	out at the nine Months end.	. 456	WAY WORLD	IV.1	430
Waitwell:	before I die--I wou'd gladly go out of the World with .	. 458	WAY WORLD	IV.1	502
Waitwell:	month out at knees with begging an Alms,--he shall . .	. 458	WAY WORLD	IV.1	522

Over   (continued)

Speaker	Text	PAGE	TITLE	ACT.SC	LINE
Sr Sampson:	ring all over the Parish.	266	FOR LOVE	III.1	478
Scandal:	this Marriage and making over this Estate, this transferring	268	FOR LOVE	III.1	544
Angelica:	is over, methinks I am not half so sorry for him as I was--	277	FOR LOVE	IV.1	83
Angelica:	is over, methinks I am not half so sorry as I was--	277	FOR LOVE	IV.1 V	83
Angelica:	exceptious: But Madmen shew themselves most, by over	296	FOR LOVE	IV.1	763
Angelica:	by over acting Sobriety; I was half inclining to believe	296	FOR LOVE	IV.1	765
Angelica:	make over his Inheritance to his younger Brother.	300	FOR LOVE	V.1	123
Angelica:	pull'd an old House over his Head at last.	301	FOR LOVE	V.1	159
	(The Mutes kneel and mourn over her.)	381	M. BRIDE	V.2	213
Mirabell:	Well, is the grand Affair over? You have been something	398	WAY WORLD	I.1	111
Mirabell:	--What, billing so sweetly! Is not Valentine's Day over	423	WAY WORLD	II.1	502
Lady Wish:	are Books over the Chimney--Quarles and Pryn, and the	426	WAY WORLD	III.1	65
Marwood:	was something in it; but it seems it's over with you. Your	431	WAY WORLD	III.1	230
Marwood:	over, and we have done with the Disguise. For a Fool's	433	WAY WORLD	III.1	311
Fainall:	I am married already; so that's over,--my Wife has	443	WAY WORLD	III.1	677
Fainall:	plaid the Jade with me--Well, that's over too--I	443	WAY WORLD	III.1	678
Fainall:	never lov'd her, or if I had, why that wou'd have been over	443	WAY WORLD	III.1	679
Millamant:	over the threshold. I'll be solicited to the very last, nay and	449	WAY WORLD	IV.1	164
Witwoud:	Now Petulant, all's over, all's well; Gad my head begins	453	WAY WORLD	IV.1	336
Sir Wilful:	And be damn'd over Tea-Cups and Coffee.	456	WAY WORLD	IV.1	454
Lady Wish:	and Weaving of dead Hair, with a bleak blew Nose, over a	462	WAY WORLD	V.1	5
Mincing:	Fortune made over to him, or he'll be divorc'd.	465	WAY WORLD	V.1	111
Marwood:	after, talk it all over again in Commons, or before Drawers	467	WAY WORLD	V.1	226
Marwood:	after, talk it over again in Commons, or before Drawers	467	WAY WORLD	V.1	V226
Fainall:	remainder of her Fortune, not made over already; And for	469	WAY WORLD	V.1	269
Fainall:	Winter Evenings Conference over Brandy and Pepper,	469	WAY WORLD	V.1	274
Fainall:	Estate to my management, And absolutely make over my	473	WAY WORLD	V.1	435
Millamant:	me give my self to you over again.	477	WAY WORLD	V.1	595
Mirabell:	Ay, and over and over again; for I wou'd have you	477	WAY WORLD	V.1	596
Mirabell:	Ay, and over and over again; I wou'd have you	477	WAY WORLD	V.1	V596

Over-act (1)

| Angelica: | Have a care, and don't over-act your Part--If | 301 | FOR LOVE | V.1 | 157 |

Over-hear (1)

| Valentine: | closer--that none may over-hear us;--Jeremy, I can tell you | 290 | FOR LOVE | IV.1 | 557 |

Over-heard (6)

Setter:	found me, and over-heard all they said. Mr. Bellmour is to	98	OLD BATCH	V.1	84
Sharper:	Experiment. But honest Setter, here, over-heard you with	100	OLD BATCH	V.1	145
Sir Joseph:	be done. What--Come, Mr. Setter, I have over-heard all,	103	OLD BATCH	V.1	243
Lord Touch:	Come, I beg your pardon that I over-heard	189	DOUBL DLR	V.1	52
Careless:	with what imperfectly I over-heard between my Lord and	196	DOUBL DLR	V.1	337
Foible:	Closet, and over-heard all that you said to me before	464	WAY WORLD	V.1	69

Over-joy'd (1)

| Sir Joseph: | her little Bubbies? And--A-qad, I'm so over-joy'd--And | 103 | OLD BATCH | V.1 | 256 |

Over-rates (1)

| Gonsalez: | Osmyn Alphonso! no; she over-rates | 371 | M. BRIDE | IV.1 | 397 |

Over-reach'd (2)

| Capt Bluff: | --That you are over-reach'd too, ha, ha, ha, only | 110 | OLD BATCH | V.2 | 107 |
| Scandal: | over-reach'd, methinks you shou'd not-- | 267 | FOR LOVE | III.1 | 525 |

Over-run (1)

| Jeremy: | with his Arms would over-run the Country, yet no body | 302 | FOR LOVE | V.1 | 194 |

Over-sea's (1)

| Sir Wilful: | Over-sea's once already; and with proviso that I Marry my | 471 | WAY WORLD | V.1 | 349 |

Overcharg'd (1)

| Heartwell: | incumbrances is like coming to an Estate overcharg'd with | 44 | OLD BATCH | I.1 | 278 |

Overcome (5)

Mellefont:	to a man that she has overcome Temptations, is an argument	158	DOUBL DLR	III.1	299
Lady Ply:	O you overcome me--that is so excessive--	160	DOUBL DLR	III.1	378
Mrs Fain:	short upon me unawares, and has almost overcome me.	412	WAY WORLD	II.1	83
Millamant:	be overcome if I stay.	456	WAY WORLD	IV.1	433
Fainall:	Well Madam; I have suffer'd my self to be overcome	468	WAY WORLD	V.1	250

Overheard (1)

| Scandal: | Madam, I am very glad that I overheard a better | 294 | FOR LOVE | IV.1 | 687 |

Overjoy'd (5) see Over-joy'd

Sir Paul:	in the Face, I will Gads-bud. I'm overjoy'd to think I have	173	DOUBL DLR	IV.1	226
Sir Paul:	amazed, and so overjoy'd, so afraid, and so sorry.--But	179	DOUBL DLR	IV.1	460
Sir Paul:	overjoy'd, stay I'll confess all.	179	DOUBL DLR	IV.1	466
Sir Paul:	I can't tell you I'm so overjoy'd; come along with me	181	DOUBL DLR	IV.1	508
Mrs Fore:	so overjoy'd at?	249	FOR LOVE	II.1	514

Overlaid (1)

| Valentine: | have overlaid the Child a Fortnight ago, if she had had | 221 | FOR LOVE | I.1 | 212 |

Overnicely (1)

| Fainall: | You don't take your Friend to be overnicely bred. | 403 | WAY WORLD | I.1 | 296 |

Oversee (1)

| Fainall: | I do not--'Twas for my ease to oversee and | 413 | WAY WORLD | II.1 | 143 |

Overseen (1)

| Marwood: | have Overseen. Here comes Mr. Fainall. If he will be satisfi'd | 468 | WAY WORLD | V.1 | 243 |

Overset (2)

| Ben: | Why an you do, You may run the risk to be overset, | 262 | FOR LOVE | III.1 | 334 |
| Ben: | has turn'd her senses, her Brain is quite overset. Well-a-day, | 286 | FOR LOVE | IV.1 | 404 |

Overspreads (1)

| Careless: | overspreads my face, a cold deadly dew already vents | 170 | DOUBL DLR | IV.1 | 115 |

Overstock'd (1)

| Fainall: | overstock'd. | 400 | WAY WORLD | I.1 | 209 |

Overtake (4) see O'retake

Sr Sampson:	can'st write thy Name, Val?--Jeremy, step and overtake	281	FOR LOVE	IV.1	208
Valentine:	not overtake you--Ha, ha, ha, the Rogue found me	282	FOR LOVE	IV.1	247
Osmyn-Alph:	Which wing'd with Liberty, might overtake	354	M. BRIDE	III.1	199
Millamant:	--If you cou'd but stay for me, I shou'd overtake you	434	WAY WORLD	III.1	360

Overtaken (2)

| Vainlove: | would have overtaken, not have met my Game. | 80 | OLD BATCH | IV.1 | 180 |
| Lady Wish: | My Nephew's a little overtaken Cozen--but | 455 | WAY WORLD | IV.1 | 406 |

Overtaking (2)

		PAGE	TITLE	ACT.SC	LINE
Cynthia:	People walk hand in hand, there's neither overtaking nor	168	DOUBL DLR	IV.1	15
Angelica:	Life. Security is an insipid thing, and the overtaking and	296	FOR LCVE	IV.1	787

Ow'd (1)

Scandal:	Wise Men of the East ow'd their Instruction to a Star,	267	FOR LCVE	III.1	535

Ow'st (1)

Osmyn-Alph:	Which to exterior Objects ow'st thy Faculty,	345	M. EBIDE	II.2	V218

Owe (8)

Maskwell:	whom I owe my self.	188	DOUBL DLR	V.1	26
Zara:	Thou canst not owe me more, nor have I more	355	M. EBIDE	III.1	215
Mirabell:	Yet to those two vain empty Things, you cwe two	421	WAY WORLD	II.1	413
Mirabell:	To your Lover you owe the pleasure of hearing your	421	WAY WCRLD	II.1	416
Lady Wish:	owe the timely discovery of the false vows of Mirabell; To	465	WAY WCRLD	V.1	127
Lady Wish:	you I owe the Detection of the Impcster Sir Rowland. And now	465	WAY WCRLD	V.1	V128
Lady Wish:	ruine? Ungrateful Wretch! dost thou not owe thy being,	473	WAY WCRLD	V.1	446
Mirabell:	my hands--I own I have not deserv'd you shou'd owe	473	WAY WCRLD	V.1	451

Owes (1)

Millamant:	One nc more owes one's Beauty to a Lover, than	420	WAY WCRLD	II.1	409

Owest (1)

Osmyn-Alph:	Owest thy Faculty--	345	M. EBIDE	II.2	219

Owing (2)

Maskwell:	how can you? Is not all this present Heat owing to the	137	DOUBL DLR	I.1	386
Mrs Fain:	advice all is owing.	477	WAY WCRLD	V.1	571

Owls (1)

Sharper:	see, the Owls are fled, as at the break of Day.	86	OLD BATCH	IV.3	128

Own (198)

Vainlove:	In Castles ith' Air of thy own building: That's thy	38	OLD EATCH	I.1	29
Bellmour:	help cut with her own Fancy.	38	OLD EATCH	I.1	59
Bellmour:	Mistresses of my own acquiring; must yet take Vainlove's	41	OLD BATCH	I.1	140
Bellmour:	morning was none of her own? for I know thou art as	42	OLD EATCH	I.1	185
Heartwell:	disgust him frcm the Lady's own Lips.	43	OLD EATCH	I.1	256
Heartwell:	will produce at the expense of your own Sweat.	44	OLD EATCH	I.1	281
Sharper:	Wherein no doubt he magnifies his own	47	OLD EATCH	I.1	374
Bellmour:	Speaks Miracles, is the Drum to his own praise--	47	OLD EATCH	I.1	376
Capt Bluff:	abroad? for every Cock will fight upon his own Dunghil.	51	OLD EATCH	II.1	153
Sir Joseph:	Look ycu now, I tell you he's so modest he'l own	53	OLD EATCH	II.1	222
Bellmour:	importunity at Court; first creates its own Interest, and	58	OLD EATCH	II.2	133
Araminta:	Rather poor silly Idols of your own making, which,	58	OLD EATCH	II.2	146
Araminta:	which comes pretty near my own Opinion of Love and	58	OLD EATCH	II.2	154
Lucy:	You may as soon hope, to recover your own Maiden-head,	61	OLD EATCH	III.1	7
Lucy:	in the name cf opportunity mind your own Business.	61	OLD EATCH	III.1	9
Setter:	Nay faith Lucy I'me sorry, I'le own my self to blame,	66	OLD EATCH	III.1	212
Heartwell:	to the Musick of their own Chink. This buys all the 'tother	72	OLD EATCH	III.2	37
Sharper:	I'me afraid I give too great a Froof of my own at this time--	79	OLD EATCH	IV.1	158
Sharper:	Here, here, she's thy own Man, sign'd and seal'd too--	79	OLD EATCH	IV.1	164
Laetitia:	We are all liable to Mistakes, Sir: If you own it to be so,	81	OLD EATCH	IV.2	46
Bellmour:	Doing! No Tongue can express it,--not thy own;	82	OLD EATCH	IV.2	84
Sir Joseph:	'em in my own proper Person, without your help.	85	OLD EATCH	IV.3	69
Araminta:	--So were forced to draw, in our cwn defence.	86	OLD EATCH	IV.3	119
Fondlewife:	. . . I wish he has lain upon no bodies stomach but his own.	93	OLD BATCH	IV.4	V165
Laetitia:	if I can clear my own innocence to my own Deare.	93	OLD EATCH	IV.4	169
Bellmour:	hindred the making of your own Fortune.	94	OLD EATCH	IV.4	189
Fondlewife:	believe my own Eyes.	96	OLD EATCH	IV.4	263
Setter:	Voyage. Or have you brought your cwn Lading back?	96	OLD BATCH	V.1	3
Sir Joseph:	may dispose of your own Flesh as you think fitting, d'ye	101	OLD EATCH	V.1	184
Sir Joseph:	Ay, ncw it's out; 'tis I, my own individual Person.	102	OLD BATCH	V.1	206
Heartwell:	Death! Shall I own my Shame, or wittingly let him go	104	OLD BATCH	V.1	309
Heartwell:	esteem my Friendship, or your own Safety,--come	105	OLD EATCH	V.1	322
Vainlove:	Nay, 'tis a Sore of your own scratching.--Well	109	OLD EATCH	V.2	64
Capt Bluff:	'Tis very generous, Sir, since I needs must own--	110	OLD EATCH	V.2	104
Sir Joseph:	No, nc, Captain, you need not own, Heh, heh,	110	OLD BATCH	V.2	105
Sir Joseph:	heh. 'Tis I must own--	110	OLD BATCH	V.2	106
	For he thinks all his own, that is his Wives.	125	DOUBL DLR	PRO.	30
Lord Froth:	Laugh at no bodies Jest but my own, or a Lady's; I assure	132	DOUBL DLR	I.1	192
Brisk:	I suppose that's because you Laugh at your own Jests,	132	DOUBL DLR	I.1	206
Lady Touch:	a Larum, only to rouse my own still'd Soul fcr your	137	DOUBL DLR	I.1	381
Cynthia:	(aside). At least I won't own it, to be troubled with your	139	DOUBL DLR	II.1	36
Lady Froth:	Complaisance of my Lord, or something of his own, that should	139	DOUBL DLR	II.1	50
Lady Froth:	I'm not asham'd to own it now; ah! it makes my heart	140	DOUEL DLR	II.1	62
Lady Froth:	Biddy, that's all; just my own Name.	141	DOUBL DLR	II.1	129
Lady Ply:	Ay, for tho' I am not Cynthia's own Mother, I	146	DOUBL DLR	II.1	309
Maskwell:	When each, who searches strictly his own mind,	150	DOUBL DLR	II.1	467
Lord Touch:	her own Circle; 'tis not the first time she has mistaken	151	DOUBL DLR	III.1	7
Lady Touch:	which is not consenting with your own: But since I am	151	DOUBL DLR	III.1	38
Lady Touch:	to dissemble: I own it to you; in short I do believe it, nay,	151	DOUBL DLR	III.1	40
Lady Touch:	a nearer relation on his own; a Lover you know, my	153	DOUBL DLR	III.1	89
Lady Touch:	Consider your own and my Honour--nay, I told you	153	DOUBL DLR	III.1	105
Maskwell:	their own Follies and Intrigues, they'll miss neither of you.	155	DCUEL DLR	III.1	168
Maskwell:	either to my Inclination or your own necessity--	157	DOUBL DLR	III.1	246
Lady Ply:	those Advantages: I know my own Imperfections--but	159	DOUBL DLR	III.1	349
Careless:	Lady! that is the envy of her own Sex, and the admiration of	160	DOUBL DLR	III.1	V381
Sir Paul:	than with my own Mother--no indeed.	162	DOUBL DLR	III.1	440
Lord Froth:	She her self makes her own Faces,	166	DOUBL DLR	III.1	599
Mellefont:	Witch in her own Bridle.	167	DOUBL DLR	IV.1	5
Cynthia:	my own inclination to change--	168	DOUBL DLR	IV.1	37
Cynthia:	If you had not been so assured of your own Conduct	168	DOUBL DLR	IV.1	43
Mellefont:	And you won't die one, for your own, so still	169	DOUBL DLR	IV.1	63
Lady Ply:	far upon me as your self, with Blushes I must own it, you	169	DOUBL DLR	IV.1	73
Sir Paul:	was never thus before--Well, I must own my self	172	DOUBL DLR	IV.1	199
Lady Ply:	(Aside.) So now I can read my own Letter under the cover	173	DOUBL DLR	IV.1	221
Sir Paul:	held fifty to one, I could have drawn my own Picture	174	DOUBL DLR	IV.1	242
Lady Ply:	her own), Sir Paul, here's your Letter, to Morrow Morning	174	DOUBL DLR	IV.1	264

Own (continued)

Speaker	Text	PAGE	TITLE	ACT.SC	LINE
Brisk:	to win her with a new airy invention of my own, hem!	175	DOUBL DLR	IV.1	304
Lady Ply:	given Sir Paul your Letter instead of his own.	178	DOUBL DLR	IV.1	400
Sir Paul:	to my own Cuckoldom; why this is the very traiterous	178	DOUBL DLR	IV.1	412
Lady Ply:	now I find was of your own inditing--I do Heathen,	179	DOUBL DLR	IV.1	456
Sir Paul:	Ay, but by your own Vertue and Continency that	180	DOUBL DLR	IV.1	476
Sir Paul:	matter of Fact is all his own doing.--I confess I had a	180	DOUBL DLR	IV.1	477
Maskwell:	make some Apology to the Company for her own, and	181	DOUBL DLR	IV.1	522
Maskwell:	made some Apology to the Company for her own, and	181	DOUBL DLR	IV.1 V522	
Maskwell:	own Opinion; the appearance is very fair, but I have an	181	DOUBL DLR	IV.1	528
Maskwell:	Gratitude, and my own Inclination, to be ever your	181	DOUBL DLR	IV.1	538
Lord Touch:	my Honour never to own any Discovery that you shall	182	DOUBL DLR	IV.1	573
Maskwell:	mean now, is only a bare Suspicion of my own. If your	183	DOUBL DLR	IV.1	583
Lady Ply:	--Oh! I could rack my self, play the Vulture to my own	184	DOUBL DLR	IV.2	46
Lady Touch:	all, all! all's my own!	186	DOUBL DLR	IV.2	96
Maskwell:	Lucky! Fortune is your own, and 'tis her interest	187	DOUEL DLR	V.1	2
Maskwell:	your own art that turned it to advantage.	187	DOUEL DLR	V.1	5
Maskwell:	So; I durst not own my introducing my Lord,	188	DOUEL DLR	V.1	10
Lady Touch:	what I said to you, or you had better eat your own Horns,	192	DOUEL DLR	V.1	192
Maskwell:	suspected, that it shall be got ready by my Lord's own	193	DOUEL DLR	V.1	211
Maskwell:	I have made him my own,--and ordered him to meet	194	DOUEL DLR	V.1	242
Maskwell:	Meet me in half an Hour, here in your own	195	DOUEL DLR	V.1	292
Maskwell:	of your Love; yet so far I prize your Pleasures o're my own,	199	DOUEL DLR	V.1	436
Lord Froth:	I've some of my own, thank you, my dear.	201	DOUEL DLR	V.1	527
Lord Touch:	Go, and thy own Infamy pursue thee,--	202	DOUEL DLR	V.1	563
	The Law provides a curb for 'its own Fury,	204	DOUEL DLR	EPI.	10
	It seems like Eden, fruitful of its own accord.	213	FOR LOVE	PRO.	17
	And are afraid to use their own Edge-Tools.	214	FCR LOVE	PRO.	38
Scandal:	where-ever it is, it's always contriving it's own Ruine.	219	FOR LOVE	I.1	121
Valentine:	of my Creditors for their Money, and my own impatience	225	FOR LOVE	I.1	340
Scandal:	besides, Angelica has a great Fortune of her own; and great	225	FOR LOVE	I.1	353
Scandal:	That is, when I am yours; for while I am my own, or	226	FOR LOVE	I.1	384
Tattle:	To be free with you, I have--I dcn't care if I own	227	FOR LOVE	I.1	409
Scandal:	Well, you own it?	229	FOR LOVE	I.1	480
Mrs Frail:	take care of my own. Well; but I'll come and see you one	232	FOR LOVE	I.1	597
Scandal:	Yes Faith, I can shew you your cwn Picture, and	232	FOR LOVE	I.1	617
Foresight:	have your Fortune in your own Hands--But I'll find	238	FOR LOVE	II.1	115
Sr Sampson:	Spiders; the one has its Nutriment in his own hands; and	246	FOR LOVE	II.1	392
Sr Sampson:	t'other spins his Habitation out of his own Entrails,	246	FOR LOVE	II.1 V393	
Sr Sampson:	feed thee out of my own Vitals?--'S'heart, live by	246	FOR LOVE	II.1	399
Mrs Fore:	But can't you converse at home?--I own	247	FOR LOVE	II.1	426
Tattle:	with her own Affairs.	255	FOR LOVE	III.1	62
Angelica:	I dare swear you wrong him, it is his own--And	255	FOR LOVE	III.1	75
Angelica:	Effects of his own Merit. For certainly Mr. Tattle was	255	FOR LOVE	III.1	77
Tattle:	No, I hope not--'tis as much Ingratitude to own	255	FOR LOVE	III.1	85
Scandal:	(aside). Ouns, why you wen't own it, will you?	256	FOR LOVE	III.1	99
Tattle:	own, in Conversation, by way of Novel: but never have	256	FOR LOVE	III.1	119
Tattle:	Garden; my own Landlady and Valet de Chambre; all who	257	FOR LOVE	III.1	158
Ben:	civilly to me, of her own accord: Whatever you think of	264	FOR LOVE	III.1	411
Sr Sampson:	own Scn, faith, he'll touzle her, and mouzle her: The	265	FOR LOVE	III.1	458
Mrs Fore:	Night; because I'll retire to my own Chamber, and think	273	FCR LOVE	III.1	743
Jeremy:	fall in Love with him; or at least own that she has lov'd	276	FOR LOVE	IV.1	10
Angelica:	to see a Woman visit a Man at his own Lodgings in a	276	FOR LOVE	IV.1	21
Angelica:	Inhumanity, as not to be concern'd for a Man I must own	277	FOR LOVE	IV.1	43
Angelica:	Failing, which I must own to you--I fear my Happiness	277	FOR LOVE	IV.1	55
Sr Sampson:	with his own Hand.	278	FOR LOVE	IV.1	113
Sr Sampson:	know me, Boy? Not know thy own Father, Val! I am	279	FOR LOVE	IV.1	157
Sr Sampson:	thy own Father, and this is honest Brief Buckram the Lawyer.	279	FOR LOVE	IV.1	158
Sr Sampson:	'tis thy own Hand, Val. Why, let me see, I can read it as	281	FOR LOVE	IV.1	220
Scandal:	own Fortune.	284	FCR LOVE	IV.1	313
Valentine:	and since you have lov'd me, you must own I have at	294	FOR LOVE	IV.1	709
Jeremy:	Mad enough to own it?	295	FOR LOVE	IV.1	744
Jeremy:	Partly I think--for he does not know his own Mind	295	FOR LOVE	IV.1 V753	
Sr Sampson:	young Fellow that is neither a Wit in his own Eye, nor a	299	FCR LOVE	V.1	66
Jeremy:	Disguise, at your own Lodgings. You must talk a little	303	FOR LOVE	V.1	217
Tattle:	you're a Woman, and don't know your own mind.	304	FOR LOVE	V.1	253
Ben:	Well, well, take you care of your own Helm, or you	308	FOR LOVE	V.1	420
Ben:	mayn't keep your own Vessel steddy.	308	FOR LOVE	V.1	421
Valentine:	her own Mouth.	311	FOR LOVE	V.1	521
Angelica:	pardon me, if I think my own Inclinations have a better	311	FOR LOVE	V.1	533
Scandal:	own Wedding; methinks 'tis pity they should not be	313	FOR LOVE	V.1	599
Angelica:	our Sex: You tax us with Injustice, only to cover your own	314	FCR LOVE	V.1	628
	Which now they find in their own Tribe fulfill'd:	323	M. BRIDE	PRO.	14
Manuel:	Her Chains hang heavier on him than his cwn.	335	M. BRIDE	I.1	381
Almeria:	By its own Weight, made stedfast, and immoveable,	339	M. BRIDE	II.1	62
Almeria:	My own affrights me with its Echo's.	339	M. BRIDE	II.1	69
Almeria:	Thy Voice--my own affrights me with its Echo's.	339	M. BRIDE	II.1 V 69	
Zara:	Compassion, scarce will it own that Name sc soon,	346	M. BRIDE	II.2	279
Zara:	Compassion, scarce will't own that Name so soon,	346	M. BRIDE	II.2 V279	
Heli:	Which Manuel to his own Use and Avarice,	351	M. BRIDE	III.1	66
Osmyn-Alph:	The Spirit which was deaf to my own Wrongs,	351	M. BRIDE	III.1	74
Zara:	Shalt weep for mine, forgetting thy own Miseries.	353	M. BRIDE	III.1	168
Selim:	And as to your Revenge, not his cwn Int'rest,	361	M. BRIDE	IV.1	21
Selim:	Your own Request's enough.	362	M. BRIDE	IV.1	49
Almeria:	And cloath their Nakedness with my own Flesh;	370	M. BRIDE	IV.1	350
Almeria:	Curst my own Tongue, that cou'd not move his Pity.	370	M. BRIDE	IV.1	372
Garcia:	Our selves, and expiate with our own his Blood.	378	M. BRIDE	V.2	67
Gonsalez:	And fall beneath the Hand of my own Son.	378	M. BRIDE	V.2	72
Garcia:	Better with this to rip up my own Bowels,	378	M. BRIDE	V.2	78
Osmyn-Alph:	Themselves, their own most bloody Purposes.	383	M. BRIDE	V.2	308
Osmyn-Alph:	Has turn'd their own most bloody Purposes.	383	M. BRIDE	V.2 V308	
	In her own Nest the Cuckow-Eggs we find,	393	WAY WORLD	PRO.	7
	No Portion for her own she has to spare,	393	WAY WORLD	PRO.	9
	So Save or Damn, after your own Discretion.	393	WAY WORLD	PRO.	40
Mirabell:	all in her own Name, my old Lady Wishfort came in.--	395	WAY WORLD	I.1	24
Mirabell:	They are now grown as familiar to me as my own Frailties;	399	WAY WORLD	I.1	172

Own   (continued)
Fainall:	Life cn't, ycu are your own Man again.	400	WAY WORLD	I.1	177
Messenger:	Wilfull, which I am charg'd to deliver into his own Hands.	400	WAY WORLD	I.1	184
Witwoud:	all, that I must own--No more breeding than a	403	WAY WORLD	I.1	298
Marwood:	Disclose it to your Wife; own what has past	415	WAY WORLD	II.1	191
Mirabell:	for your own Recreation, and not for my Conveniency. .	423	WAY WORLD	II.1	506
Waitwell:	me, I am married, and can't be my own Man again. . .	424	WAY WORLD	II.1	561
Waitwell:	me, I'm married, and can't be my cwn Man again. . .	424	WAY WORLD	II.1 V561	
Foible:	hold; But i'faith I gave him his own.	427	WAY WORLD	III.1	91
Mrs Fain:	Cousin and her Fortune left to her own disposal. . .	430	WAY WORLD	III.1	194
Marwood:	you wou'd but appear bare fac'd now, and own Mirabell;	433	WAY WORLD	III.1	314
Millamant:	despair to prevail, and so let him follow his own way.	434	WAY WORLD	III.1	342
Sir Wilful:	don't think a' knows his own Name.	437	WAY WORLD	III.1	474
Witwoud:	long; pshaw, I was not in my own Power then. An Orphan,	440	WAY WORLD	III.1	557
Fainall:	my Reputation,--As to my own, I married not for it; so	443	WAY WORLD	III.1	684
Millamant:	would confer with my own Thoughts.	446	WAY WORLD	IV.1	66
Mrs Fain:	your Proxy in this Affair; but I have business of my own.	446	WAY WORLD	IV.1	68
Millamant:	only to my own taste; to have no obligation upon me to	450	WAY WORLD	IV.1	216
Mirabell:	or Intimate of your own Sex; No she friend tc skreen .	451	WAY WORLD	IV.1	236
Mirabell:	Item, I Article, that you continue to like your own .	451	WAY WORLD	IV.1	245
Sir Wilful:	let her keep her own Counsel in the mean time, and cry	456	WAY WORLD	IV.1	429
Lady Wish:	the Retrospection of my own rudenes,--I have more . .	457	WAY WORLD	IV.1	485
Foible:	Letter, who must deliver it into your own hands. . .	459	WAY WORLD	IV.1	550
Foible:	dissembling Tongue; Your Lady-ship's own Wisdom has .	463	WAY WORLD	V.1	27
Mrs Fain:	my own Innocence, and dare stand by a tryall. . . .	466	WAY WORLD	V.1	178
Mrs Fain:	my own Innocence, and dare stand a tryall.	466	WAY WORLD	V.1 V178	
Lady Wish:	--I may say it; for I chiefly made it my own Care to .	466	WAY WORLD	V.1	183
Lady Wish:	--O, she never look'd a Man in the Face but her own .	467	WAY WORLD	V.1	191
Fainall:	content you shall enjoy your own proper Estate during .	468	WAY WORLD	V.1	252
Fainall:	Matter in your own Discretion.	469	WAY WORLD	V.1	296
Sir Wilful:	frown desperately, because her face is none of her own;	471	WAY WORLD	V.1	362
Fainall:	Insist upon my first proposal. You shall submit your own	473	WAY WORLD	V.1	434
Mirabell:	my hands--I own I have not deserv'd you shou'd owe . .	473	WAY WORLD	V.1	451
Mirabell:	that your Lady while she was at her own disposal, and .	476	WAY WORLD	V.1	536
Mirabell:	Inconstancy and Tyranny of temper, which from her own .	476	WAY WORLD	V.1	542
	Since when, they by their own offences taught . . .	479	WAY WORLD	EPI.	14
	These with false Glosses, feed their own Ill-nature, .	479	WAY WORLD	EPI.	21

Own'd (4)
Bellmour:	she own'd it to my Face; and blushing like the Virgin Morn	38	OLD BATCH	I.1	48
Lady Ply:	respect--That he has own'd himself to be my Admirer .	172	DOUBL DLR	IV.1	166
Maskwell:	He has own'd nothing to me of late, and what I . . .	183	DOUBL DLR	IV.1	582
Lady Touch:	own'd your Love to him, and his indulgence would assist	198	DOUBL DLR	V.1	418

Owns (3)
	This time, the Poet owns the bold Essay, ...	214	FOR LOVE	PRO.	41
Manuel:	With Innocence? O Patience, hear--she owns it! . . .	368	M. BRIDE	IV.1 V293	
	He owns, with Toil, he wrought the following Scenes, .	393	WAY WORLD	PRO.	22

Ox (1)
| Lady Touch: | Fool, Sot, insensible Ox! but remember . . . . . | 192 | DOUBL DLR | V.1 | 191 |

Oyl (1)
| Valentine: | another than Oyl and Vinegar; and yet those two beaten . | 282 | FOR LOVE | IV.1 | 257 |

Oyster (1)
| Brisk: | Like an Oyster at low Ebb, I'gad--ha, ha, ha. . . . | 165 | DOUBL DLR | III.1 | 576 |

Oyster-woman (1)
| Bellmour: | Oyster-woman, to propagate young Fry for Bilingsgate-- . | 45 | OLD BATCH | I.1 | 299 |

Oysters (1)
| Jeremy: | Mother sold Oysters in Winter, and Cucumbers in Summer; | 245 | FOR LOVE | II.1 | 380 |

Pace (1)   see A-pace
| Belinda: | How now, Pace? Where's my Cousin? . . . . . . | 88 | OLD BATCH | IV.3 | 205 |

Pacify'd (3)
Sharper:	So-h, O Sir I am easily pacify'd, the acknowledgment .	49	OLD BATCH	II.1	62
Bellmour:	Husband, somewhat pacify'd her.	100	OLD BATCH	V.1	153
Fainall:	where to another World. I'll marry thee--Be pacify'd .	416	WAY WORLD	II.1	246

Pack (1)
| Marwood: | reputation worry'd at the Barr by a pack of Bawling . | 467 | WAY WORLD | V.1 | 210 |

Packthread (1)
| Lady Wish: | of small Ware, flaunting upon a Packthread, under a . | 462 | WAY WORLD | V.1 | 12 |

Pacquet (1)
| Mincing: | O Mem, your Laship staid to peruse a Pacquet of . . . | 419 | WAY WORLD | II.1 V357 | |

Pads (1)
| Jeremy: | suspicious Fellows like lawful Pads, that wou'd knock . | 221 | FOR LOVE | I.1 | 203 |

Pagan (1)
| Lady Wish: | Commonwealth, thou beastly Pagan. . . . . . . | 456 | WAY WORLD | IV.1 | 441 |

Page (1)
| Valentine: | Page doubled down in Epictetus, that is a Feast for an . | 216 | FOR LOVE | I.1 | 8 |

Pageantry (1)
| Almeria: | Or pompous Phrase; the Pageantry of Souls. . . . . | 332 | M. BRIDE | I.1 | 249 |

Paid (15)   see O'repaid, Pay'd, Repaid, Repay'd
Bellmour:	Well, I find my Apishness has paid the Ransome . . .	60	OLD BATCH	II.2	218
Sharper:	Mony paid at sight: I'm come to return my Thanks-- . .	68	OLD BATCH	III.1	285
Fondlewife:	A Hundred has already been paid, by your Order, . . .	89	OLD BATCH	IV.4	29
Mellefont:	Patience purchase folly, and Attention be paid with noise:	129	DOUBL DLR	I.1	69
Lady Touch:	which once was paid me, and everlastingly engaged? . .	136	DOUBL DLR	I.1	351
Maskwell:	And whereas pleasure is generally paid with	156	DOUBL DLR	III.1	218
Maskwell:	mischief, what mischief I shall do, is to be paid with	156	DOUBL DLR	III.1	219
Maskwell:	mischief, what mischief I do, is to be paid with . .	156	DOUBL DLR	III.1 V219	
Maskwell:	In short, the price of your Banishment is to be paid .	156	DOUBL DLR	III.1	224
Lady Froth:	His fare is paid him, and he sets in Milk.	164	DOUBL DLR	III.1	541
Jeremy:	some great Fortune; and his Fare to be paid him like the	218	FOR LOVE	I.1	100
Jeremy:	That they should be paid.	220	FOR LOVE	I.1	175
Valentine:	paid.	224	FOR LOVE	I.1	325
Petulant:	Hang'd. The Ordinary's paid for setting the Psalm, and	436	WAY WORLD	III.1	430
Mirabell:	That marriage frauds too oft are paid in kind. . . .	478	WAY WORLD	V.1	623

Pain (7)
Heartwell:	What Pain we tug that galling Load, a Wife.	112	OLD BATCH	V.2	193
Lady Touch:	like to be suspected in the end, and 'tis a pain any longer	151	DOUBL DLR	III.1	39
Almeria:	--Thou giv'st me Pain, with too much Tenderness! . .	356	M. BRIDE	III.1	280

Pain   (continued)
Marwood:	then know the worst; and be out of his Pain; but I wou'd	. 411	WAY WORLD	II.1	62
Millamant:	I gave you some Pain.	. 420	WAY WORLD	II.1	380
Millamant:	Infinitely; I love to give Pain.	. 420	WAY WORLD	II.1	382
Fainall:	All Husbands must, or pain, or shame, endure;	. 444	WAY WORLD	III.1	724

Painful (2)
	Is doing painful Penance in some Beau,	. 315	FOR LOVE	EPI.	24
Mirabell:	good old Lady broke thro' her painful Taciturnity, with an	. 396	WAY WORLD	I.1	35

Pains (8)
Bellmour:	himself, to see what pains he will take, and how he will	. 40	OLD BATCH	I.1	126
Sharper:	pains to sow: he does the drudgery in the Mine, and you	. 43	OLD BATCH	I.1	220
Bellmour:	then gets it for his pains. For importunity in Love, like	. 58	OLD BATCH	II.2	132
Osmyn-Alph:	No no, nor should the subtlest Pains that Hell,	. 357	M. BRIDE	III.1	314
Zara:	And Anger in Distrust, both short-liv'd Pains.	. 362	M. BRIDE	IV.1	33
Manuel:	Torn, mangl'd, flay'd, impal'd--all Pains and	. 368	M. BRIDE	IV.1	295
Almeria:	Nay, all the Pains that are prepar'd for thee:	. 369	M. BRIDE	IV.1	310
	But if they're naught ne're spare him for his Pains:	. 393	WAY WORLD	PRO.	23

Paint (5)
Petulant:	saves Paint.	. 406	WAY WORLD	I.1	417
Lady Wish:	Darling. Paint, Paint, Paint, dost thou understand	. 425	WAY WORLD	III.1	13
Peg:	come at the Paint, Madam; Mrs. Foible has lock'd it up,	. 425	WAY WORLD	III.1	18

Painted (2)
Scandal:	I have many more of this kind, very well Painted, as you	. 234	FOR LOVE	I.1	657
Osmyn-Alph:	That tender, lovely Form of painted Air	. 341	M. BRIDE	II.2	51

Painter (3)
Scandal:	Painter, that I cannot know the Person by your Picture of	. 230	FOR LOVE	I.1	537
Tattle:	No Man but the Painter and my self was ever blest	. 232	FOR LOVE	I.1	610
Marwood:	Woman! The Devil's an Ass: If I were a Painter, I wou'd	. 431	WAY WORLD	III.1	236

Painters (2)
Scandal:	her, you must be condemned, like other bad Painters, to	. 230	FOR LOVE	I.1	538
	For, as when Painters form a matchless Face,	. 479	WAY WORLD	EPI.	31

Paintings (1)
Scandal:	have Paintings too, some pleasant enough.	. 233	FOR LOVE	I.1	634

Paints (2)
Lady Froth:	can't hit of her Name; the old fat Fool that Paints so	. 166	DOUBL DLR	III.1	581
Brisk:	I can't hit of her Name neither--Paints de'e say?	. 166	DOUBL DLR	III.1	584

Pair (8)
Belinda:	tore two Pair of Kid-Gloves, with trying 'em on.--	. 84	OLD BATCH	IV.3	54
Belinda:	tore two Pair of Kid-leather Gloves, with trying 'em on.--	. 84	OLD BATCH	IV.3 V	54
Maskwell:	--and a Pair of private Stairs leads down to the	. 194	DOUBL DLR	V.1	255
Maskwell:	--and a Pair of private Stairs leading down to the	. 194	DOUBL DLR	V.1	V255
Valentine:	me have a Pair of Red hot Tongues quickly, quickly,	. 282	FOR LOVE	IV.1	240
Mirabell:	the force of Instinct--O here come my pair of Turtles	. 423	WAY WORLD	II.1	501
Sir Wilful:	pair of Slippers?--My Man's with his Horses, I	. 441	WAY WORLD	III.1	618
Witwoud:	Ears like a pair of Castanets.	. 454	WAY WORLD	IV.1	363

Pairings (1)
Lucy:	thou Maukin made up of the Shreds and Pairings of his	. 66	OLD BATCH	III.1	188

Palate (2)
Valentine:	I cannot talk about Business with a Thirsty Palate.--	. 222	FOR LOVE	I.1	238
Sr Sampson:	have been born without a Palate.--'S'heart, what shou'd	. 245	FOR LOVE	II.1	367

Pale (12)
Foresight:	aspect--pale, a little pale--but the Roses of these	. 269	FOR LOVE	III.1	602
Foresight:	gone again--And now I'm faint again; and pale again,	. 269	FOR LOVE	III.1	609
Almeria:	Or wind me in the Shroud of some pale Coarse	. 339	M. BRIDE	II.1	76
Almeria:	Will fly my pale Deformity with loathing.	. 340	M. BRIDE	II.2	24
Zara:	Pale and expiring, drench'd in briny Waves	. 346	M. BRIDE	II.2	277
Almeria:	See, see, look yonder! where a grizled, pale	. 371	M. BRIDE	IV.1	387
Leonora:	Zara all pale and dead! two frightful Men,	. 381	M. BRIDE	V.2	223
Almeria:	From his pale Lips; I'll kiss him e'er I drink,	. 382	M. BRIDE	V.2	267
Marwood:	Enemies. Methinks you look a little pale, and now you	. 412	WAY WORLD	II.1	78
Lady Wish:	my self till I am pale again, there's no Veracity in me.	. 425	WAY WORLD	III.1	4
Lady Wish:	then--(Exit Peg). I'm as pale and as faint, I look like	. 425	WAY WORLD	III.1	21

Paler (1)
Almeria:	For I weep to see thee--Art thou not paler,	. 342	M. BRIDE	II.2	113

Pall-Mall (3)
Snap:	Gentlemen to Arrest in Pall-Mall and Covent-Garden; and	. 224	FOR LOVE	I.1	297
Tattle:	Maids at the Chocolate-Houses, all the Porters of Pall-Mall	257	FOR LOVE	III.1	155
Tattle:	Maids at the Chocolate-Houses, all the Porters at Pall-Mall	257	FOR LOVE	III.1	V155

Pallace (4)
Almeria:	Of King Anselmo's Pallace; which in Rage	. 329	M. BRIDE	I.1	113
Gonsalez:	Is entring now, in Martial Pomp the Pallace.	. 331	M. BRIDE	I.1	226
Manuel:	She should have made these Pallace Walls to shake,	. 333	M. BRIDE	I.1	311
Garcia:	Before 'em, to the Pallace Walls. Unless	. 377	M. BRIDE	V.2	35

Pallaces (1)
Osmyn-Alph:	And bore contiguous Pallaces to Earth.	. 347	M. BRIDE	II.2	311

Pallat (1)
Capt Bluff:	of my Pallat, you can't relish a Dish of Fighting without	51	OLD BATCH	II.1	163

Palm (2)
Foresight:	Mole upon her Lip, with a moist Palm, and an open	. 239	FOR LOVE	II.1	153
Valentine:	the Lawyer with an itching Palm; and he's come to be	. 282	FOR LOVE	IV.1	238

Palpable (3)
Valentine:	cannot avoid such a palpable Decoy as this was; the Ladies	229	FOR LOVE	I.1	502
Scandal:	discourage you--But it is palpable that you are not				
	satisfy'd.	. 268	FOR LOVE	III.1	560
Witwoud:	Hum, a hit, a hit, a palpable hit, I confess it.	. 419	WAY WORLD	II.1	353

Palpitation (1)
Lady Ply:	the Palpitation of the Heart.	. 170	DOUBL DLR	IV.1	105

Palpitations (1)
Lady Wish:	that he has sworn, the Palpitations that he has felt, the	458	WAY WORLD	IV.1	513

Pam (1)
Fainall:	but I'le be hang'd if she did not put Pam in her Pocket.	. 442	WAY WORLD	III.1	V654

Pampereth (1)
Fondlewife:	pampereth himself up with Dainties, that he may look	. 76	OLD BATCH	IV.1	27

Pan (0)   see Warming-Pan

Pancras (1)
Servant-M:	Sir, there's such Coupling at Pancras, that they stand	. 398	WAY WORLD	I.1	113

Pardon   (continued)
  Valentine: Pardon me, Sir. But I reflect that I very lately   . . . 311 FOR LOVE   V.1 524
  Angelica: pardon me, if I think my own Inclinations have a better   . 311 FOR LOVE   V.1 533
  Garcia: (kneeling). Your Pardon, Sir, if I presume sc far,   . . . 334 M. BRIDE   I.1 327
  Zara: Your Pardon, Sir--mistake me not; you think   . . . . . 359 M. BRIDE   III.1 416
  Manuel: Pardon, fair Excellence, this long Neglect: . . . . . 363 M. BRIDE   IV.1 104
  Selim: I plead not for a Pardon, and to live, ... 375 M. BRIDE   V.1 120
  Witwoud: out of my Head. I beg Pardon that I shou'd ask a Man of . 402 WAY WORLD   I.1 256
  Witwoud: O pardon me--Expose the Infirmities of my   . . . . . 403 WAY WORLD   I.1 314
  Mirabell: his Pardon. . . . . 405 WAY WORLD   I.1 380
  Fainall: Pardon--No Tears--I was to blame, I cou'd not   . . . . 416 WAY WORLD   II.1 240
  Millamant: O I ask your Pardon for that--One's Cruelty   . . . . . 420 WAY WORLD   II.1 385
  Waitwell: Your Pardon, Sir. With Submission, we have indeed   . . 423 WAY WORLD   II.1 507
  Lady Wish: may examine her with more freedom--You'll pardon   . . . 426 WAY WORLD   III.1 63
  Foible: O dear Madam, I beg your Pardon. It was not my   . . . 430 WAY WORLD   III.1 195
  Millamant: Ha, ha, ha. Pardon me, dear Creature, I must laugh, Ha, . 434 WAY WORLD   III.1 343
  Millamant: Hae? Dear Creature I ask your Pardon--I   . . . . . . 434 WAY WORLD   III.1 348
  Lady Wish: you'll pardon him, Madam--Gentlemen will you   . . . . 441 WAY WORLD   III.1 623
  Millamant: Your Pardon Madam, I can stay no longer--Sir   . . . . 456 WAY WORLD   IV.1 431
  Foible: Dear Madam, I'll beg pardon on my knees.   . . . . . . 462 WAY WORLD   V.1   9
  Marwood: liable to affronts. You will pardon me, Madam, If I meddle . 466 WAY WORLD   V.1 164
  Lady Wish: Pardon on your Knees, Ungrateful Creature; she deserves . 466 WAY WORLD   V.1 169
  Mirabell: plead for favour;--Nay not for Pardon, I am a   . . . . 471 WAY WORLD   V.1 373
  Lady Wish: --and I must perform mine.--First I pardon for   . . . . 477 WAY WORLD   V.1 573
Pardonable (1)
  Heartwell: not Love, it is Madness, and then it is pardonable--Nay   . 73 OLD BATCH   III.2 84
Pardons (4)
  Bellmour: Million of Pardons, and will make you any Satisfaction.   . 82 OLD BATCH   IV.2 58
  Jeremy: Sir, I ask you Ten Thousand Pardons, 'twas an errant   . 313 FOR LOVE   V.1 592
  Witwoud: My Dear, I ask ten thousand Pardons;--Gad I   . . . . . 402 WAY WORLD   I.1 270
  Lady Wish: pardons to ask than the Pope distributes in the Year of   . 457 WAY WORLD   IV.1 486
Parent (4)
  Lord Touch: No sooner born, but the Vile Parent dies.   . . . . . . 203 DOUBL DLR   V.1 596
  Sr Sampson: . . . with the lawful Authority of a Parent, ... 244 FOR LOVE   II.1 331
  Almeria: Of all thy Race. Hear me, thou common Parent;   . . . . 368 M. BRIDE   IV.1 278
  Almeria: --I have no Parent else--be thou a Mother, ... 368 M. BRIDE   IV.1 279
Parents (2)
  Maskwell: Duty to Kings, Piety to Parents, Gratitude to Benefactors, . 150 DOUBL DLR   II.1 446
  Foible: and He are nearer related than ever their Parents   . . 464 WAY WORLD   V.1   89
Parish (4)
  Tattle: True; I was call'd Turk-Tattle all over the Parish-- . 258 FOR LOVE   III.1 168
  Sr Sampson: ring all over the Parish. . . . . 266 FOR LOVE   III.1 478
  Valentine: Parish? . . . . 289 FOR LOVE   IV.1 517
  Lady Wish: in the Parish. . . . . 463 WAY WORLD   V.1   56
Parish-Priest (1)
  Petulant: the Parish-Priest for reading the Ceremony. And for the   . 436 WAY WORLD   III.1 431
Parish-Searchers (1)
                While others watch like Parish-Searchers, hir'd   . . . 385 M. BRIDE   EPI.   9
Park (9)   see Hide-Park
                (Scene changes to St. James's Park. . . . . 83 OLD BATCH   IV.3
  Capt Bluff: and I must not draw in the Park. . . . . 86 OLD BATCH   IV.3 121
  Vainlove: And so I remember in the Park.--She had reason, if I   . 99 OLD BATCH   V.1   97
  Sharper: in the Park; but I thought it had been only to make   . 102 OLD BATCH   V.1 201
  Witwoud: Ay, we'll all walk in the Park, the Ladies talk'd of   . 409 WAY WORLD   I.1 510
                (St. James's Park. Enter Mrs. Fainall and Mrs. Marwood.)   . 410 WAY WORLD   II.1
  Marwood: the Park, in Conference with Mirabell. . . . . . . 426 WAY WORLD   III.1 48
  Lady Wish: do with him in the Park? Answer me, has he got nothing   . 427 WAY WORLD   III.1 82
  Mrs Fain: come too late. That Devil Marwood saw you in the Park   . 430 WAY WORLD   III.1 185
Parliament (1)
  Mirabell: I wonder there is not an Act of Parliament to save   . . . 400 WAY WORLD   I.1 204
Parlour (2)
  Mrs Frail: down into the Parlour, and I'll carry Mr. Benjamin into   . 265 FOR LOVE   III.1 448
  Foible: Sir Wilfull is set in to Drinking, Madam, in the Parlour.   . 445 WAY WORLD   IV.1 36
Parnassus (3)
  Lady Froth: did you talk of Love? O Parnassus! Who would have   . . 176 DOUBL DLR   IV.1 332
  Lady Froth: me, O Parnassus, you have an infinite deal of Wit.   . . 202 DOUBL DLR   V.1 542
                And in Parnassus he must lose his Seat, ... 393 WAY WORLD   PRO. 20
Parricide (2)
  Manuel: O Impious Parricide! now canst thou speak?   . . . . . 368 M. BRIDE   IV.1 272
  Almeria: Now calls me Murderer, and Parricide.   . . . . 368 M. BRIDE   IV.1 284
Parrot (2)
  Belinda: troublesome Animal than a Parrot. . . . . 60 OLD BATCH   II.2 214
  Witwoud: a Quaker hates a Parrot, or than a Fishmonger hates a   . 408 WAY WORLD   I.1 485
Parson (13)
  Bellmour: the Fanatick one-ey'd Parson!   . . . . 39 OLD BATCH   I.1 85
  Silvia: He's going for a Parson, Girl, the forerunner of a   . . 75 OLD BATCH   III.2 149
  Lucy: Nay, Mr. Bellmour: O Lard! I believe you are a Parson   . 97 OLD BATCH   V.1 37
  Maskwell: Parson, that if my Lord should have Curiosity to peep, he . 193 DOUBL DLR   V.1 232
                runs out affrighted, my Lord after her, like a Parson.)   . 202 DOUBL DLR   V.1 557
                of the Stage, Mellefont like a Parson.)   . . . . . . 202 DOUBL DLR   V.1 567
  Scandal: Parson, be Chaplain to an Atheist, or Stallion to an   . 220 FOR LOVE   I.1 145
  Tattle: at home, and the Parson had not half his Congregation.   . 258 FOR LOVE   III.1 170
  Sr Sampson: help of a Parson, ha? Odd if he should I cou'd not be angry . 265 FOR LOVE   III.1 461
  Sr Sampson: But I'll bring him a Parson to tell him, that the Devil's a . 267 FOR LOVE   III.1 508
  Sr Sampson: and I'll consult a Parson; Odzocks I'm a Young Man: . 301 FOR LOVE   V.1 139
  Mrs Frail: But, my Dear, that's impossible; the Parson and   . . . 310 FOR LOVE   V.1 478
  Servant-M: dispatch, besides, the Parson growing hoarse, we were   . 398 WAY WORLD   I.1 116
Parson's (1)
                (Mellefont disguis'd in a Parson's Habit   . . . . . 202 DOUBL DLR   V.1 V566
Part (65)   see A-part
  Setter: to part with dry Lips. . . . . 67 OLD BATCH   III.1 235
  Sir Joseph: mad? Or de'e think I'm mad? Agad for my part, I don't   . 68 OLD BATCH   III.1 265
  Fondlewife: yet thy Husband must also bear his part: For thy iniquity . 77 OLD BATCH   IV.1 71
  Bellmour: If we part so I'm mistaken.--Hold, hold, ... 81 OLD BATCH   IV.2 37
  Bellmour: No, for then you must of consequence part with   . . . 95 OLD BATCH   IV.4 224
  Fondlewife: No, no, for that matter--when she and I part,   . . . 95 OLD BATCH   IV.4 228

Pattern (4)
  Foible: Gentleman--But your Ladyship is the Pattern of   430   WAY WORLD III.1 202
  Marwood: Principal to be an Assistant; to procure for him! A Pattern   431   WAY WORLD III.1 233
  Marwood: not prove another Pattern of Generosity;   431   WAY WORLD III.1 243
  Lady Wish: but a Pattern for you, and a Model for you, after you were   465   WAY WORLD V.1   145
Pauh (2)
  Sir Joseph: as it were to me--agad he's a brave Fellow--Pauh,   . . .   50   OLD BATCH II.1   121
  Bellmour: Pauh, Women are only angry at such offences, tc   63   OLD BATCH III.1   98
Paul (62)
  Brisk: Touchwood swears, he'll Disinherit you, and Sir Paul Plyant   128   DOUBL DLR I.1   54
  Careless: her Father Sir Paul Plyant, come to settle the
                 Writings, this   129   DOUBL DLR I.1   81
  Mellefont: Sir Paul, my wise Father-in-Law that is to be, my Dear   .   130   DOUBL DLR I.1   138
               (Enter Lord Touchwood, Lord Froth, Sir Paul Plyant,   . .   131   DOUBL DLR I.1   170
  Lord Froth: O foy, Sir Paul, what do you mean? Merry! O   132   DOUBL DLR I.1   185
  Lord Froth: Ridiculous! Sir Paul you're strangely mistaken, I   . . .   132   DOUBL DLR I.1   190
  Lord Froth: find Champagne is powerful. I assure you, Sir Paul, I   . .   132   DOUBL DLR I.1   191
  Lord Froth: you, Sir Paul.   132   DOUBL DLR I.1   193
  Lord Touch: Sir Paul, if you please we'll retire to the   132   DOUBL DLR I.1   216
               (Exit Lord Touchwood and Sir Paul.)   133   DOUBL DLR I.1   221
               (Enter Sir Paul Plyant and Lady Plyant.)   143   DOUBL DLR II.1   194
  Lady Ply: Sir Paul have patience, let me alone to rattle him   . . .   143   DOUBL DLR II.1   197
  Lady Ply: You firk him, I'll firk him my self; pray Sir Paul   . . .   144   DOUBL DLR II.1   202
  Sir Paul: Lady Plyant shall Command Sir Paul; but when I am   . . .   144   DOUBL DLR II.1   222
               (Lady Plyant and Sir Paul come up to Mellefont.)   . . .   145   DOUBL DLR II.1   241
  Lady Ply: Sir Paul himself?   145   DOUBL DLR II.1   256
  Lady Ply: Sir Paul, take Cynthia from his sight; leave me to   . . .   145   DOUBL DLR II.1   272
               (Exit Sir Paul, and Cynthia.)   . . .   146   DOUBL DLR II.1   288
  Maskwell: I know it; I met Sir Paul towing away Cynthia.   148   DOUBL DLR II.1   385
  Lord Touch: Respect for Love, and made Sir Paul jealous of the Civility   151   DOUBL DLR III.1   8
               (Enter Sir Paul and Lady Plyant.)   . . .   159   DOUBL DLR III.1 320
  Careless: You bring that along with you, Sir Paul, that shall   . .   159   DOUBL DLR III.1 323
  Lady Ply: Jesu, Sir Paul, what a Phrase was there? You will   . . .   159   DOUBL DLR III.1 327
  Lady Ply: Sir Paul, what a Phrase was there? You will   159   DOUBL DLR III.1 V327
  Careless: O, Sir Paul, you are the happiest man alive. Such a   . .   160   DOUBL DLR III.1 380
               . . . carries it to Sir Paul.)   160   DOUBL DLR III.1 V392
  Careless: What can that be, Sir Paul?   161   DOUBL DLR III.1 406
  Careless: be told on't; she must i'faith, Sir Paul; 'tis an injury
                 to the   162   DOUBL DLR III.1 442
  Lady Ply: Here, Sir Paul, it's from your Steward, here's a   . . .   162   DOUBL DLR III.1 450
  Lord Froth: Heav'n, Sir Paul, you amaze me, of all things in   . . .   162   DOUBL DLR III.1 457
               (Enter Boy and whispers Sir Paul.)   . . .   163   DOUBL DLR III.1 488
  Lady Ply: I'm busie, Sir Paul, I wonder at your   163   DOUBL DLR III.1 491
  Careless: Sir Paul, harkee, I'm reasoning the matter you know;   . .   163   DOUBL DLR III.1 493
               (Exit Sir Paul.)   . . .   163   DOUBL DLR III.1 500
  Lady Ply: far you have gain'd upon me; I assure you if Sir Paul   . .   170   DOUBL DLR IV.1   110
  Lady Ply: and how--Ah, there's Sir Paul.   170   DOUBL DLR IV.1   126
               (Enter Sir Paul and Cynthia.)   . . .   171   DOUBL DLR IV.1   127
  Careless: 'Slife yonder's Sir Paul, but if he were not come, I'm   .   171   DOUBL DLR IV.1   128
  Lady Ply: Ay, but Sir Paul, I conceive if she has sworn, ...   171   DOUBL DLR IV.1   150
  Lady Ply: most extraordinary respect and honour for you, Sir Paul.   .   172   DOUBL DLR IV.1   175
  Lady Ply: O las, no indeed, Sir Paul, 'tis upon your account.   . .   172   DOUBL DLR IV.1   181
  Lady Ply: you're too modest, Sir Paul.   172   DOUBL DLR IV.1   186
  Lady Ply: O fy, Sir Paul, you'l put me out of Countenance   172   DOUBL DLR IV.1   189
  Lady Ply: My Lip indeed, Sir Paul, I swear you shall.   172   DOUBL DLR IV.1   195
  Lady Ply: yet I'll be sure to be unsuspected this time.--Sir Paul.   .   173   DOUBL DLR IV.1   212
  Lady Ply: No, no, nothing else I thank you, Sir Paul,--   173   DOUBL DLR IV.1   220
  Lady Ply: when 'tis Dark. O Crimine! I hope, Sir Paul has not seen   .   174   DOUBL DLR IV.1   262
  Lady Ply: her own), Sir Paul, here's your Letter, to Morrow Morning   174   DOUBL DLR IV.1   264
  Brisk: Sir Paul, Gads-bud you're an uncivil Person, let me tell   174   DOUBL DLR IV.1   267
  Brisk: Sir Paul, will you send Careless into the Hall if you   .   175   DOUBL DLR IV.1   286
  Lady Ply: given Sir Paul your Letter instead of his own.   178   DOUBL DLR IV.1   400
               (Enter Sir Paul with the Letter.)   . . .   178   DOUBL DLR IV.1   405
  Sir Paul: Gallery. If Sir Paul should surprize us, I have a Commission   178   DOUBL DLR IV.1   409
  Sir Paul: were not for Providence, sure poor Sir Paul thy Heart   . .   179   DOUBL DLR IV.1   434
  Lady Ply: now, Sir Paul, what do you think of your Friend Careless?   179   DOUBL DLR IV.1   438
  Sir Paul: poor Sir Paul, I'm an Anabaptist, or a Jew, or what you   .   180   DOUBL DLR IV.1   473
  Careless: Sir Paul, I'm glad I've met with you, 'gad I have   . . .   180   DOUBL DLR IV.1   491
  Maskwell: this dotage, I know not; but he's gone to Sir Paul about my   190   DOUBL DLR V.1   111
               (Enter Sir Paul.)   . . .   191   DOUBL DLR V.1   158
               (Enter Lord Froth, and Sir Paul.)   . . .   200   DOUBL DLR V.1   491
  Lord Froth: By Heaven's, I have slept an Age,--Sir Paul, ...   200   DOUBL DLR V.1   492
  Brisk: My Lord, your humble Servant; Sir Paul yours,--   201   DOUBL DLR V.1   517
Paul's (4)
  Lady Ply: nicety, befitting the Person of Sir Paul's Wife? Have I   .   145   DOUBL DLR II.1   253
  Lady Ply: your face; for now Sir Paul's gone, you are Corum Nobus.   .   146   DOUBL DLR II.1   299
  Careless: Sir Paul's nine years Courtship; how he has lain for   . .   157   DOUBL DLR III.1 273
  Lord Touch: I'm sure Sir Paul's Consent will follow Fortune; I'll   . .   189   DOUBL DLR V.1   76
Paultry (2)
  Capt Bluff: paultry fear--confess.   68   OLD BATCH III.1 270
  Scandal: Twelve Caesars, paultry Copies; and the Five Senses, as ill   232   FOR LOVE   I.1   602
Pauperis (0) see Forma Pauperis
Pause (3)
  Bellmour: the Mistake of me: I'll marry 'em.--Nay, don't pause: . .   98   OLD BATCH V.1   67
  Mellefont: (after a pause). So then,--spight of my care and   . . .   148   DOUBL DLR II.1   374
  Zara: Then, wherefore do I pause?--give me the Bowl.   381   M. BRIDE   V.2   198
Pauses (1)
               (Maskwell pauses.)   189   DOUBL DLR V.1   68
Pavement (1)
  Osmyn-Alph: Stripping my Nails, to tear this Pavement up   358   M. BRIDE   III.1 354
Paw (1)
  Tattle: paw thing.   303   FOR LOVE   V.1   247
Pawn (3)
  Lady Wish: and your Cuckoldomes. I must pawn my Plate, and my   . . .   466   WAY WORLD V.1   151
  Mrs Fain: drop off when she's full. Madam you sha'not pawn a   . . .   466   WAY WORLD V.1   175
  Mrs Fain: drop off when she's full. Madam you shan't pawn a   . . .   466   WAY WORLD V.1   V175

Paws (1)

| Sr Sampson: | Paws; Nature has been provident only to Bears and | 246 | FOR LOVE | II.1 | 391 |

Pay (24)

Bellmour:	With all my Heart, it lies convenient for us, to pay	40	OLD BATCH	I.1	131
Bellmour:	never be able to pay me all: So shun me for the same	58	OLD BATCH	II.2	124
Barnaby:	House, and yet be forced to let Lodgings, to help pay the	76	OLD BATCH	IV.1	43
Heartwell:	I'll pay him well, if you'll break the Matter to him.	97	OLD BATCH	V.1	20
Jeremy:	or any of these poor rich Rogues, teach you how to pay	217	FOR LOVE	I.1	27
Valentine:	pay my Debts, and make my Fortune. This was once	225	FOR LOVE	I.1	338
Foresight:	Gallant, Valentine, pay for all, I will.	238	FOR LOVE	II.1	117
Sr Sampson:	was to pay the Piper. Well, but here it is under Black and	240	FOR LOVE	II.1	180
Jeremy:	comes to pay his Duty to you.	242	FOR LOVE	II.1	269
Valentine:	Superfluity, Sir, it will scarce pay my Debts,--I	243	FOR LOVE	II.1	282
Scandal:	must pay a Tribute to one, and go halves with the t'other.	271	FOR LOVE	III.1	677
Scandal:	must pay a Tribute to one, and go halves with t'other.	271	FOR LOVE	III.1	V677
Valentine:	worth must pay for the Confession of my Senses; I'm	296	FOR LOVE	IV.1	773
Angelica:	apt to run more in Debt than you are able to pay.	313	FOR LOVE	V.1	614
	And wanting ready Cash to pay for Hearts,	315	FOR LOVE	EPI.	9
Almeria:	The Year, which I have vow'd to pay to Heav'n,	333	M. BRIDE	I.1	284
Gonsalez:	O let me prostrate, pay my worthless Thanks	334	M. BRIDE	I.1	338
Zara:	Yet hating more, Ingratitude, can pay,	336	M. BRIDE	I.1	418
Manuel:	It shall be mine to pay Devotion here;	337	M. BRIDE	I.1	449
Almeria:	Where I may kneel and pay my Vows again	339	M. BRIDE	II.1	82
Osmyn-Alph:	To pay some Part, some little of this Debt;	343	M. BRIDE	II.2	137
Foible:	some disbanded Officer I warrant--Half Pay is but	427	WAY WORLD	III.1	97
Millamant:	Trifles,--As liberty to pay and receive visits	450	WAY WORLD	IV.1	212
Sir Wilful:	fairer? If I have broke any thing, I'll pay for't, an it cost a	470	WAY WORLD	V.1	318

Pay'd (3)

Heartwell:	Debts, which by the time you have pay'd, yields no further	44	OLD BATCH	I.1	279
Sharper:	over my ill fortune, since it pay'd the price of your ransome.	48	OLD BATCH	II.1	34
Sharper:	in a manner--Pay'd down for your deliverance; 'twas so	50	OLD BATCH	II.1	102

Paying (1)

| Sharper: | your Gratitude and Generosity. Since the paying so | 50 | OLD BATCH | II.1 | V 89 |

Payment (1)

| Trapland: | for the Payment? | 222 | FOR LOVE | I.1 | 241 |

Peace (28)

Heartwell:	so often drawn, is bound to the Peace for ever after.	43	OLD BATCH	I.1	249
Vainlove:	peace--I should not esteem a Pardon if too easie won.	63	OLD BATCH	III.1	101
Vainlove:	peace--I should not esteem a Pardon if too easily won.	63	OLD BATCH	III.1	V101
Laetitia:	to lie at peace in my cold Grave--Since it will	78	OLD BATCH	IV.1	111
Araminta:	Opportunity of making his Peace with me;--and to	85	OLD BATCH	IV.3	79
Sir Joseph:	peace.--I know, they were a little smart upon you--But,	103	OLD BATCH	V.1	262
Maskwell:	your Pleasures; and will not rest till I have given you peace,	137	DOUBL DLR	I.1	394
Lord Touch:	mutual Peace to come; upon your Duty--	152	DOUBL DLR	III.1	63
Mrs Frail:	an Admiral and an eminent Justice of the Peace to be the	231	FOR LOVE	I.1	578
Almeria:	Anselmo sleeps, and is at Peace; last Night,	326	M. BRIDE	I.1	9
Almeria:	Why am not I at Peace?	326	M. BRIDE	I.1	13
Almeria:	Peace--No Cause! yes, there is Eternal Cause.	326	M. BRIDE	I.1	17
Almeria:	No Cause! Peace, peace; there is Eternal Cause.	326	M. BRIDE	I.1	V 17
Almeria:	At Peace; Father and Son are now no more--	327	M. BRIDE	I.1	53
Almeria:	Is it of Moment to the Peace of Heav'n	327	M. BRIDE	I.1	58
Almeria:	Or, ever taste content, or peace of Heart,	329	M. BRIDE	I.1	147
Almeria:	Of Eternal Peace. Death, grim Death, will fold	340	M. BRIDE	II.2	20
Almeria:	Of Peace Eternal. Death, grim Death, will fold	340	M. BRIDE	II.2	V 20
Osmyn-Alph:	Harbour no Thought, that may disturb thy Peace;	345	M. BRIDE	II.2	201
Osmyn-Alph:	Thy Sorrows have disturb'd thy Peace of Mind,	357	M. BRIDE	III.1	309
Manuel:	Which I'll not hear, 'till I am more at peace.	370	M. BRIDE	IV.1	364
Osmyn-Alph:	The Words of Joy and Peace; warm thy cold Beauties,	383	M. BRIDE	V.2	281
Sir Wilful:	how that the Peace holds, whereby that is, Taxes abate.	440	WAY WORLD	III.1	575
Foible:	Peace and Quietness by my good will: I had rather bring	464	WAY WORLD	V.1	87
Mirabell:	Beauty, and with her my Peace and Quiet; Nay all my	472	WAY WORLD	V.1	390

Peaceable (1)

| Sir Paul: | peaceable Person amongst 'em. | 192 | DOUBL DLR | V.1 | 197 |

Peacefull (1)

| Bellmour: | peacefull one, I can ensure his Anger dormant; or should he | 46 | OLD BATCH | I.1 | 352 |

Peacefully (1)

| Sir Paul: | fine way of living, as I may say, peacefully and happily, | 160 | DOUBL DLR | III.1 | 384 |

Peacock (1)

| Valentine: | that it may be secret; and Juno shall give her Peacock | 290 | FOR LOVE | IV.1 | 550 |

Peals (1)

| | What Peals of Thunder, and what Show'rs of Rain; | 323 | M. BRIDE | PRO. | 10 |

Pearl (2)

| Mirabell: | Eye, by a Pearl of Orient; he wou'd no more be seen by | 407 | WAY WORLD | I.1 | 455 |
| Waitwell: | Sure? am I here? do I live? do I love this Pearl of | 461 | WAY WORLD | IV.1 | 606 |

Pease (0)   see Grey-pease

Peck'd (0)   see Hen-peck'd

Pecquet (1)

| Mincing: | O Mem, your Laship staid to peruse a Pecquet of | 419 | WAY WORLD | II.1 | 357 |

Pedantick (2)

| Tattle: | University: But the Education is a little too pedantick for | 302 | FOR LOVE | V.1 | 187 |
| Millamant: | Pedantick arrogance of a very Husband, has not so Pragmatical | 449 | WAY WORLD | IV.1 | 179 |

Pedestals (1)

| Valentine: | Twenty Chairmen, and make thee Pedestals to stand erect | 289 | FOR LOVE | IV.1 | 525 |

Peel'd (1)

| Lady Wish: | Why I am arrantly flea'd--I look like an old peel'd Wall. | 429 | WAY WORLD | III.1 | 148 |

Peep (1)   see Bo-peep

| Maskwell: | Parson, that if my Lord should have Curiosity to peep, he | 193 | DOUBL DLR | V.1 | 232 |

Peeping (1)

| Bellmour: | (peeping). Damn'd Chance! If I had gone a-Whoring | 92 | OLD BATCH | IV.4 | 109 |

Peeps (2)

| Lady Froth: | that he peeps now and then, yet he does shine all the day | 164 | DOUBL DLR | III.1 | 524 |
| Nurse: | cry husht--O Lord, who's there? (peeps) What's here | 253 | FOR LOVE | III.1 | 7 |

Perez   (continued)
               Enter Garcia, Heli and Perez.) 337   M. BRIDE   II.1
    Garcia: Perez, the King expects from our return, ... 338   M. BRIDE   II.1   40
                          (Enter the King, Perez, and Attendants.) 348   M. BRIDE   II.2   351
                          (Enter Zara, Perez, and Selim.) . . . 358   M. BRIDE   III.1 375
                                    (Exit Perez.) 359   M. BRIDE   III.1 383
                                   (Enter Perez.) 360   M. BRIDE   III.1 446
                          (Enter King, Gonsalez, Garcia, Perez.) 362   M. BRIDE   IV.1   61
    Manuel: Perez, see it perform'd. 362   M. BRIDE   IV.1   67
                          (Exeunt Garcia, Perez, and Attendants.) 364   M. BRIDE   IV.1   135
                                   (Enter Perez.) 365   M. BRIDE   IV.1   166
                                    (Exit Perez.) 365   M. BRIDE   IV.1   173
               (A Room of State. Enter King, Perez, and Alonzo.) . . 372   M. BRIDE   V.1
                                   (Perez going.) 374   M. BRIDE   V.1   79
    Garcia: The Traytor Perez, and the Captive Moor, ... 377   M. BRIDE   V.2   38
    Garcia: Proclaim'd aloud by Perez, for Alphonso. 377   M. BRIDE   V.2   44
    Garcia: Pronounc'd aloud by Perez, for Alphonso. . . . . ' 377   M. BRIDE   V.2 V 44
    Alonzo: My Lord, for certain truth, Perez is fled; 377   M. BRIDE   V.2   48
               (Enter Alphonso, Heli, Perez, with Garcia Prisoner, . 382   M. BRIDE   V.2   273
Perfect (2)
    Almeria: One Moment, cease to gaze on perfect Bliss, ... 330   M. BRIDE   I.1 V179
               And tho' no perfect likeness they can Trace; 479   WAY WORLD EPI.   19
Perfected (1)
    Fainall: perfected, which I will take care shall be done with all . 469   WAY WORLD V.1   293
Perfection (4)
    Tattle: perfection, Madam, and to all this, the most passionate . 291   FOR LOVE   IV.1 583
    Angelica: Lover, and five Senses in perfection! when you are as . 291   FOR LOVE   IV.1 586
    Osmyn-Alph: Perfection of all Truth! 343   M. BRIDE   II.2   128
    Osmyn-Alph: Perfection of all Faithfulness and Love! 343   M. BRIDE   II.2 V128
Perfectly (3)
    Lord Froth: Pleasant Creature! perfectly well, ah! that look, . . . 140   DOUBL DLR II.1   67
    Valentine: he is perfectly thy reverse both in humour and
               understanding; 226   FOR LOVE   I.1   365
    Mrs Frail: no Creature perfectly Civil, but a Husband. For in a little 231   FOR LOVE   I.1   563
Perfidious (7)
    Bellmour: Let me see--How now! Dear perfidious Vainlove. 38   OLD BATCH I.1   35
    Zara: Traytcur, Monster, cold and perfidious Slave; 348   M. BRIDE   II.2   340
    Manuel: False perfidious Zara! Strumpet Daughter! 374   M. BRIDE   V.1   61
    Zara: Scorch and consume the curst perfidious King. 380   M. BRIDE   V.2 V171
    Lady Wish: my self; tho' he has been a perfidious wretch to me. . . 458   WAY WORLD IV.1 509
    Waitwell: Perfidious to you! 458   WAY WORLD IV.1 510
    Fainall: Perfidious Fiend! then thus I'll be reveng'd.--(offers . 476   WAY WORLD V.1   556
Perfidiousness (1)
    Marwood: much experienc'd the perfidiousness of Men. Besides . . 468   WAY WORLD V.1   260
Perforce (2)
    Osmyn-Alph: Has made perforce subservient to that End 354   M. BRIDE   III.1 173
    Osmyn-Alph: And thou perforce must yield, and aid his Transport, . . 358   M. BRIDE   III.1 360
Perform (5)
    Sharper: Name, which I think you are bound to perform. 109   OLD BATCH V.2   83
    Scandal: perform; are more perplex'd to find Evasions, than you . 221   FOR LOVE   I.1   195
    Sr Sampson: morning, and then lock you perform Covenants, and so . . 246   FOR LOVE   II.1 403
    Sr Sampson: thou'rt honest, and wilt perform Articles. 281   FOR LOVE   IV.1 215
    Lady Wish: --and I must perform mine.--First I pardon for 477   WAY WORLD V.1   573
Perform'd (3)
    Bellmour: O very well perform'd--But I don't much 60   OLD BATCH II.2   204
    Lady Touch: perform'd in the remaining part of this Evening, and before 154   DOUBL DLR III.1 142
    Manuel: Perez, see it perform'd. 362   M. BRIDE   IV.1   67
Performance (1)
    Sharper: performance. 47   OLD BATCH I.1   375
Perfumes (1)
    Sr Sampson: now, why I warrant he can smell, and loves Perfumes . . 245   FOR LOVE   II.1 370
Perhaps (21)
    Bellmour: witty Scene, and she perhaps preserve her Laughter, till . 44   OLD BATCH I.1   269
    Sharper: more, nor perhaps have suffer'd so much--had he a . . . 50   OLD BATCH II.1 126
    Capt Bluff: Perhaps, Sir, there was a scarce any thing of moment . . 52   OLD BATCH II.1 197
    Setter: To be Men perhaps; nay faith like enough; I often . . . 65   OLD BATCH III.1 174
    Lady Touch: or she? nay, he himself perhaps may have Affections . . . 191   DOUBL DLR V.1   129
    Cynthia: and listen; perhaps this chance may give you proof of . . 197   DOUBL DLR V.1   375
    Valentine: to her Pride, and perhaps, make her compassionate . . . 217   FOR LOVE   I.1   54
    Scandal: upon the Superscription: And yet perhaps he has
               Counterfeited 226   FOR LOVE   I.1   374
    Scandal: in the Superscription: And yet perhaps he has Counterfeited 226   FOR LOVE   I.1 V374
    Tattle: told Particulars, Madam. Perhaps I might have talk'd as of a 256   FOR LOVE   III.1 117
    Scandal: An Acknowledgment of Love from you, perhaps, may . . . 277   FOR LOVE   IV.1   63
    Angelica: make me uneasie--If I don't see him, perhaps my 277   FOR LOVE   IV.1   80
    Scandal: talk with Valentine, perhaps you may understand him; . . 284   FOR LOVE   IV.1 343
    Almeria: Perhaps I would repeat it there more solemnly. 331   M. BRIDE   I.1   204
    Manuel: Begets a Doubt. I'd have 'em watch'd: perhaps 335   M. BRIDE   I.1   380
    Manuel: I'll have Enquiry made; perhaps his Friend 337   M. BRIDE   I.1 V445
    Garcia: The Friends perhaps are met; let us avoid 'em. 339   M. BRIDE   II.1   49
    Zara: Perhaps I'm sawcy and Intruding-- 359   M. BRIDE   III.1 413
    Marwood: you as a Friend the Inconveniencies which perhaps you . . 468   WAY WORLD V.1   242
    Mirabell: any Obligation to me; or else perhaps I cou'd advise.-- . 473   WAY WORLD V.1   452
    Mirabell: --(holding out the Parchment.) tho perhaps what is . . . 476   WAY WORLD V.1   548
Perilous (1)
    Mincing: is in a perilous passion, at something Mr. Fainall has said. 465   WAY WORLD V.1   108
Perish (17)
    Brisk: Oh, my dear Mellefont, let me perish, if thou art not the 128   DOUBL DLR I.1   33
    Brisk: me perish, do I never say any thing worthy to be Laugh'd . 132   DOUBL DLR I.1   195
    Brisk: Let me perish, my Lord, but there is something very . . 133   DOUBL DLR I.1   237
    Brisk: Never any thing; but your Ladyship, let me perish. . . . 140   DOUBL DLR II.1   84
    Brisk: I'm your Humble Servant, let me perish.--I 142   DOUBL DLR II.1 136
    Lord Touch: of my doors this moment, and let him rot and perish, . . 153   DOUBL DLR III.1 101
    Brisk: Incomparable, let me perish--but then being an Heroick . 163   DOUBL DLR III.1 505
    Brisk: honour, let me perish. 165   DOUBL DLR III.1 557
    Brisk: if she were plaistred with Lime and Hair, let me perish. . 166   DOUBL DLR III.1 587

528

Perish   (continued)

Brisk:	Not I, let me perish--But did I! Strange! I confess . .	176	DOUBL DLR	IV.1 325
Brisk:	Ladiship--Let me perish, I don't know whether to . . .	176	DOUBL DLR	IV.1 337
Brisk:	That's well enough; let me perish, ha ha ha. O Miraculous,	177	DOUBL DLR	IV.1 356
Maskwell:	perish first, and frcm this hour avoid all sight and speech,	188	DCUBL DLR	V.1 41
Brisk:	perish,--I can't answer that.	201	DOUBL DLR	V.1 535
Brisk:	This is all very surprizing, let me perish.	203	DOUBL DLR	V.1 578
Mrs Fain:	not name it, but starve together--perish.	475	WAY WCRLD	V.1 501
Marwood:	Confusion, or I'll perish in the attempt.	477	WAY WCRLD	V.1 566

Perish'd (3)

Almeria:	Would I had perish'd in those Flames--	329	M. EBIDE	I.1 117
Almeria:	While the good Queen and my Alphcnso perish'd.	329	M. EBIDE	I.1 131
Manuel:	But that, wherein the curs'd Alphonso perish'd.	333	M. EBIDE	I.1 301

Permission (2)

Capt Bluff:	shall appear by the fair Araminta, my Wife's permission.	110	OLD EATCH	V.2 109
Lady Wish:	Now with your permission Sir Rowland I will peruse my .	460	WAY WCRLD	IV.1 569

Permit (1)

Sir Paul:	far as Passion will permit.	145	DOUBL DLR	II.1 240

Permitted (2)

Zara:	No not the Princess self, permitted to	360	M. EBIDE	III.1 451
Fainall:	permitted Mirabell with Millamant to have stcll'n their .	415	WAY WCRLD	II.1 202

Permitting (1)

Fainall:	that ly permitting her to be engag'd, I might continue .	414	WAY WORLD	II.1 145

Pernicious (2)

Maskwell:	and, if I can, all thought of that pernicious Beauty. Ha!	188	DOUEL DLR	V.1 42
Zara:	But fcr thy fatal and pernicious Counsel.	380	M. EBIDE	V.2 178

Perpetual (3)

Cynthia:	O most ridiculous, a perpetual consort of laughing . .	163	DOUBL DLR	III.1 471
Mrs Fore:	they're in perpetual fear of being seen and censur'd?-- .	247	FCR LCVE	II.1 433
Scandal:	purchas'd a perpetual opportunity for Pleasure. . . .	271	FOR LCVE	III.1 679

Perplex (2)

Maskwell:	won't perplex you. 'Tis the only thing that Providence .	157	DOUBL DLR	III.1 244
Foresight:	But ccme, be a good Girl, don't perplex your poor Uncle,	239	FOR LCVE	II.1 157

Perplex'd (2)

Scandal:	perform; are more perplex'd to find Evasions, than you .	221	FOR LCVE	I.1 195
Foresight:	I'm sc perplex'd and vex'd, I am not fit to receive . .	239	FOR LCVE	II.1 164

Perplexity (4)

Mellefont:	where it was directed. Still it gave me less perplexity to	129	DOUEL DLR	I.1 91
Mellefont:	ending in perplexity. My uncle will not see, nor hear me.	190	DOUBL DLR	V.1 105
Saygrace:	perplexity.	195	DOUBL DLR	V.1 291
Lady Wish:	leave me destitute in this Perplexity;--No, stick to me my	466	WAY WCRLD	V.1 171

Perquisite (1)

Fondlewife:	as I should be, a sort of a civil Perquisite to a Whore-master, ...	94	OLD BATCH	IV.4 184

Perruke (1)

Miss Prue:	his Perruke is sweet, and his Gloves are sweet.--and his .	249	FOR LCVE	II.1 519

Perrukes (1)

Mirabell:	of gay fine Perrukes hovering round you.	418	WAY WORLD	II.1 330

Persecuted (1)

Millamant:	persecuted with Letters--I hate Letters--No Body knows .	419	WAY WCRLD	II.1 360

Persevere (6)

Angelica:	not have the Impudence to persevere--Come, Jeremy, . .	295	FOR LCVE	IV.1 734
Angelica:	How few, like Valentine, would persevere even unto . .	314	FCR LCVE	V.1 633
Angelica:	How few, like Valentine, would persevere even to . .	314	FOR LCVE	V.1 V633
Osmyn-Alph:	Still in the Paths of Honour persevere;	384	M. EBIDE	V.2 319
Marwood:	Natures long to persevere. Love will resume his Empire .	410	WAY WORLD	II.1 25
Mirabell:	Dictates of Reason, and yet persevere to play the Fool by	423	WAY WCRLD	II.1 500

Perseveres (1)

Lord Touch:	as was possible; but he perseveres so in Villany, that she	182	DOUEL DLR	IV.1 548

Persevering (1)

Osmyn-Alph:	That persevering still with open Hand, ...	344	M. EBIDE	II.2 V186

Persian (2)

Sir Wilful:	Unknown to the Turk and the Persian:	456	WAY WORLD	IV.1 451
Sir Wilful:	Unknown to the Turk or the Persian:	456	WAY WCRLD	IV.1 V451

Persist (1)

Millamant:	Mirabell, If you persist in this offensive Freedom . .	422	WAY WORLD	II.1 448

Persisting (1)

Zara:	And fix'd event of my persisting Faith.	381	M. EBIDE	V.2 197

Person (64)

Bellmour:	expected, from a person of your gravity.	43	OLD BATCH	I.1 236
Sharper:	the person in the World, whose Character I admire. . .	49	OLD BATCH	II.1 78
Sir Joseph:	you shall see I am a Person, such a one as you would .	51	OLD BATCH	II.1 134
Capt Bluff:	I am content to retire--Like a private Person-- . . .	53	OLD BATCH	II.1 211
Araminta:	Person, for his ease, sometimes confesses Secrets his .	58	OLD BATCH	II.2 137
Lucy:	not what you said of my Person; but that my innocent .	66	OLD BATCH	III.1 209
Laetitia:	I may well be surpriz'd at your Person and Impudence; .	81	OLD BATCH	IV.2 23
Laetitia:	to dissemble. 'Tis plain then you have mistaken the Person.	81	OLD BATCH	IV.2 35
Sir Joseph:	'em in my own proper Person, without your help. . . .	85	OLD BATCH	IV.3 69
Fondlewife:	Good again--A very civil Person this, and, I	94	OLD BATCH	IV.4 179
Fondlewife:	go back of your word; you are not the Person I took you .	94	OLD BATCH	IV.4 191
Bellmour:	like an uncivil Person, you knock'd at the Door, before .	95	OLD EATCH	IV.4 215
Sir Joseph:	Ay, ncw it's out; 'tis I, my own individual Person. . .	102	OLD BATCH	V.1 206
Setter:	Person of Worth; be true to thy Trust, and be reputed .	102	OLD EATCH	V.1 227
Sir Paul:	most facetious Person.--and the best Company.-- . . .	132	DOUBL DLR	I.1 182
Lord Froth:	Person, or when any body else of the same Quality does .	132	DOUBL DLR	I.1 202
Lady Touch:	Fortune, and my Person, been subjected to your Pleasure?	136	DOUEL DLR	I.1 347
Lady Ply:	nicely, befitting the Person of Sir Paul's Wife? Have I .	145	DOUBL DLR	II.1 253
Maskwell:	take it, is that nice, scrupulous, conscientious Person, who	150	DOUBL DLR	II.1 453
Lord Touch:	of an undesigning person, the better to bespeak his security	151	DOUBL DLR	III.1 9
Mellefont:	Person I hope.	156	DOUBL DLR	III.1 211
Maskwell:	with the Person of--	156	DOUEL DLR	III.1 225
Maskwell:	the person of--your Aunt.	156	DOUEL DLR	III.1 230
Lady Ply:	Mr. Careless, If a person that is wholly illiterate . .	159	DOUBL DLR	III.1 336
Sir Paul:	Gad's bud, she's a fine person--	159	DOUBL DLB	III.1 347
Lady Ply:	would refuse to a person so meritorious--you'll . . .	159	DOUBL DLB	III.1 354
Sir Paul:	no more familiarity with her Person--as to that matter--	162	DOUBL DLR	III.1 439

529

Person (continued)

		PAGE	TITLE	ACT.SC	LINE
Lord Froth:	True, as I'm a Person of Honour--for Heaven's . . .	163	DOUBL DLR	III.1	486
Lady Ply:	Person and Parts of so accomplish'd a Person, whose Merit	169	DOUEL DLR	IV.1	82
Lady Ply:	And I assure you Mr. Careless is a Person--that has a . .	172	DOUBL DLR	IV.1	174
Sir Paul:	Person that I have a great value for nct only for that, but	172	DOUEL DLR	IV.1	179
Brisk:	Sir Paul, Gads-bud you're an uncivil Person, let me tell .	174	DOUEL DLR	IV.1	267
Sir Paul:	Person, he, he, he. No, No, I have done with her. I have .	174	DOUEL DLR	IV.1	275
Sir Paul:	Person! Well, let me see--Till then I Languish in . . .	178	DOUEL DLR	IV.1	414
Sir Paul:	peaceable Person amongst 'em.	192	DOUBL DLR	V.1	197
Scandal:	the marks of her Person: He will forswear receiving a .	226	FOR LOVE	I.1	372
Tattle:	him, that the World shall think the better of any Person .	226	FOR LCVE	I.1	392
Scandal:	Painter, that I cannot know the Person by your Picture of .	230	FOR LCVE	I.1	537
Tattle:	It was impossible, Madam, for me to imagine, that a Person	255	FOR LCVE	III.1	66
Tattle:	Third Person--or have introduc'd an Amour of my	256	FOR LCVE	III.1	118
Sr Sampson:	Person.	260	FOR LCVE	III.1	244
Mrs Fore:	me; why, I'll confess it does not displease me. Your Person	272	FOR LCVE	III.1	688
Tattle:	But, Madam, to throw away your Person, such a	290	FOR LCVE	IV.1	570
Tattle:	Person! and such a Fortune, on a Madman!	290	FOR LCVE	IV.1	571
Jeremy:	you'll certainly be the Death of a Person that has a most	301	FOR LCVE	V.1	168
Angelica:	Right to dispose of my Person, than yours.	311	FOR LCVE	V.1	534
Garcia:	The King in Person animate our Men, ...	377	M. ERIDE	V.2	36
Gonsalez:	To see the King in Person at their Head.	378	M. BRIDE	V.2	V104
Mirabell:	Of her Understanding I am, if not of her Person.	399	WAY WORLD	I.1	150
Mirabell:	Person; I think you have the Honour to be related to him. .	400	WAY WORLD	I.1	191
Lady Wish:	An errant Ash colour, as I'm a Person. Look you how this .	425	WAY WCRLD	III.1	6
Lady Wish:	a Person, this Wench has liv'd in an Inn upon the Road, .	426	WAY WORLD	III.1	36
Lady Wish:	As I'm a Person I am in a very Chaos to think I	431	WAY WORLD	III.1	254
Lady Wish:	Offence? As I'm a Person, I'm asham'd of you, ...	455	WAY WORLD	IV.1	387
Lady Wish:	sleep, you Sot--Or as I'm a perscn, I'll have you bastinado'd	457	WAY WORLD	IV.1	462
Waitwell:	--and till I have the possession cf your adoreable Person, I	457	WAY WORLD	IV.1	491
Lady Wish:	have the Clue--But as I am a person, Sir Rowland, . . .	458	WAY WORLD	IV.1	528
Lady Wish:	Person of so much Importance--	459	WAY WCRLD	IV.1	537
Lady Wish:	a Person who wou'd suffer racks in honour's cause, dear .	459	WAY WCRLD	IV.1	553
Lady Wish:	I'm a Person. Your Turtle is in Custody already; You shall	463	WAY WORLD	V.1	54
Lady Wish:	in her Teens. As I'm a Person 'tis true--She was . . .	466	WAY WORLD	V.1	188
Millamant:	on Mirabell to come in Person, and be a Witness that I give	470	WAY WCRLD	V.1	328
Lady Wish:	As I am a person I can hold out no longer;--I	478	WAY WCRLD	V.1	608

Persona (0) see Propria persona
Personal (2)

Sir Paul:	Town, and some money, a pretty tolerable personal Estate;	161	DOUBL DLR	III.1	409
Osmyn-Alph:	Of Personal Charms, or with less Vanity	355	M. ERIDE	III.1	226

Personally (2)

Mirabell:	downright personally to debauch her; and that my Virtue .	397	WAY WORLD	I.1	78
Marwood:	no more with an affair, in which I am not Personally . .	466	WAY WCRLD	IV.1	165

Personate (1)

Mrs Fain:	whom thou wert this morning Married, is to personate . .	430	WAY WCRLD	III.1	190

Persons (11)

Capt Bluff:	Husband--But here, both these are from Persons of great .	103	OLD EATCH	V.1	269
Sir Joseph:	They are either from Persons of great Quality, or . . .	103	OLD EATCH	V.1	271
Cynthia:	jests in their Persons, though they have none in their .	163	DOUBL DLR	III.1	484
Tattle:	when you know not the persons of whom you speak? . .	226	FOB LCVE	I.1	399
Tattle:	her--Madam, says I, there are some Persons who make . .	227	FOR LCVE	I.1	430
Tattle:	Titles; I'll describe their Perscns.	230	FOR LCVE	I.1	535
Tattle:	Yes, if you would be well-bred. All well-bred Persons .	251	FOR LCVE	II.1	610
Tattle:	confess I have had Favours from Persons--But as the . .	257	FOR LOVE	III.1	150
Tattle:	Favours are numberless, so the Persons are nameless. . .	257	FOR LCVE	III.1	151
Mirabell:	I hope they are not Persons of Condition that you . . .	405	WAY WCRLD	I.1	392
Mirabell:	The Persons concern'd in that Affair, have yet a . . .	412	WAY WORLD	I.1	100

Perspective (1)

Cynthia:	Perspective all this while; for nothing has been between us	168	DOUBL DLR	IV.1	25

Perspicuity (1)

Tattle:	Eye of Perspicuity; from all Astrologers, and the Stars .	304	FOR LOVE	V.1	272

Persuade (1)

Bellmour:	Rogue am I! Oh, what Sport will be here, if I can persuade	97	OLD EATCH	V.1	24

Persuaded (3)

Araminta:	entertaining-- (aside) I know she'd fain be persuaded to stay.	57	OLD EATCH	II.2	87
Mirabell:	and when she lay in of a Dropsie, persuaded her she was .	397	WAY WORLD	I.1	75
Fainall:	be persuaded.	416	WAY WCRLD	II.1	249

Persuasive (1)

Almeria:	By Magick Numbers and persuasive Sound.	326	M. BRIDE	I.1	5

Perswade (9)

Silvia:	Could we perswade him, that she Loves another-- . . .	61	OLD BATCH	III.1	39
Lucy:	No, you're out; could we perswade him, that she doats . .	62	OLD BATCH	III.1	40
Lady Touch:	perswade her. But I don't see what you can propose from .	138	DOUBL DLR	I.1	414
Mellefont:	Contrivance to perswade my Lady Plyant to this	149	DOUBL DLR	II.1	410
Tattle:	strangely--pretty Miss, don't let 'em perswade you . .	249	FOB LCVE	II.1	536
Mrs Fore:	perswade her out of her Innocency.	249	FOR LOVE	II.1	539
Angelica:	Perswade your Friend, that it is all Affectation. . . .	254	FOR LCVE	III.1	38
Jeremy:	can perswade him.	291	FOR LCVE	IV.1	592
Mirabell:	You are merry, Madam, but I wou'd perswade you . . .	422	WAY WORLD	II.1	470

Perswaded (2)

Maskwell:	She must be throughly perswaded, that Mellefont . . .	138	DOUBL DLR	I.1	410
Mrs Frail:	Old Fool! He would have perswaded me, that this was an .	231	FOR LOVE	I.1	580

Perswading (3)

Bellmour:	perswading that the Face she had been making all the . .	42	OLD BATCH	I.1	184
Setter:	--They have indeed, very perswading faces. But-- . . .	103	OLD BATCH	V.1	248
Tattle:	pretty soft kind of Phrase, and with a good perswading .	302	FOR LOVE	V.1	182

Perswasion (1)

Vainlove:	if you can make Alderman Fondlewife of your Perswasion, .	39	OLD BATCH	I.1	69

Pert (3)

Careless:	Pert Cox-Comb.	129	DOUBL DLR	I.1	64
Foresight:	Well, Jill-flirt, you are very pert--and always . . .	237	FOR LOVE	II.1	74
Waitwell:	Sir Rowland if you please. The Jade's so pert upon . . .	424	WAY WORLD	II.1	550

Pertinently (1)
Mirabell: How pertinently the Jade answers me! Ha? almost   . . . . 398 WAY WORLD I.1   108

Pertness (1)
Cynthia: He does not indeed affect either pertness, or   . . . . 139 DOUBL DLR II.1   53

Peru (1)
Sr Sampson: had Peru in one Hand, and Mexico in t'other, and the   . . 300 FOR LOVE V.1   98

Peruke (1)
Sir Paul: about him; Snakes are in his Peruke, and the Crocodile of   145 DOUBL DLR II.1   247

Perusal (1)
Bellmour: Upon the Perusal I found the Contents so charming, that   . 82 OLD BATCH IV.2   53

Peruse (5)
Lucy: would take time to peruse it--But then he was in haste.   . . 61 OLD BATCH III.1   27
Silvia: Respects, and peruse it! He's gone, and Araminta   . .   . . 61 OLD BATCH III.1   28
Mincing: O Mem, your Laship staid to peruse a Pecquet of   . . . . 419 WAY WORLD II.1   357
Mincing: O Mem, your Laship staid to peruse a Pacquet of   . . . . 419 WAY WORLD II.1 V357
Lady Wish: Now with your permission Sir Rowland I will peruse my   . 460 WAY WORLD IV.1   569

Perverseness (1)
Zara: And with Perverseness, from the Purpose, answer?   . . . 346 M. BRIDE II.2   265

Perverting (1)
Lady Ply: me, debauching my purity, and perverting me from the   . . 147 DOUBL DLR II.1   317

Perverts (1)
Bellmour: perverts our Aim, casts off the Bias, and leaves us wide and 37 OLD BATCH I.1   11

Pester'd (1)
Belinda: pester'd me with Flames and Stuff--I think I shan't   . . 59 OLD BATCH II.2   164

Pestilential (1)
Zara: The bluest Blast of Pestilential Air, ... 359 M. BRIDE III.1   400

Petition (3)
              My Business here, was humbly to petition: . . . . . 113 OLD BATCH EPI.   18
Maskwell: I humbly would petition--   . . . . 189 DOUBL DLR V.1   67
Osmyn-Alph: Be torn from his Petition? 'Twas to Heav'n.   . . . . 350 M. BRIDE III.1   23

Petitions (1)
Capt Bluff: Pshaw, I have Petitions to show, from other-guess-toys   . 103 OLD BATCH V.1   264

Petrifie (1)
Lady Wish: I fear I shall turn to Stone, petrifie Incessantly.   . . 470 WAY WORLD V.1   337

Petticoat (1)
              see Under-Petticoat-Pocket
Careless: piece of an old Scarlet Petticoat for a Stomacher; which,   157 DOUBL DLR III.1   276

Petticoats (1)
Valentine: Bo-peep under her Petticoats, ah! Mr. Trapland?   . . . 223 FOR LOVE I.1   288

Petulant (33)
Mirabell: Witwoud and Petulant; and what was worse, her   . . . 395 WAY WORLD I.1   22
Fainall: Petulant were enroll'd Members.   . . . . 396 WAY WORLD I.1   58
Fainall: Petulant and Witwoud.--Bring me some   . . . . . 398 WAY WORLD I.1   102
Fainall: What have you done with Petulant?   . . . . . . 402 WAY WORLD I.1   278
Mirabell: I don't find that Petulant confesses the Superiority   . 402 WAY WORLD I.1   285
Coachman: Is Master Petulant here, Mistress?   . . . . 404 WAY WORLD I.1   344
Fainall: O brave Petulant, three!   . . . . 404 WAY WORLD I.1   348
                             (Enter Petulant.)   . . . . 405 WAY WORLD I.1   381
Fainall: You are very cruel, Petulant.   . . . . 405 WAY WORLD I.1   389
Witwoud: charm me, dear Petulant.   . . . . 406 WAY WORLD I.1   414
Mirabell: Petulant, about that Business.   . . . . 406 WAY WORLD I.1   424
Mirabell: How! hearkee Petulant, come hither--Explain,   . . . 406 WAY WORLD I.1   432
Mirabell: Come, thou art an honest Fellow, Petulant, and shalt   . 407 WAY WORLD I.1   443
Mirabell: Petulant, Tony Witwoud, who is now thy Competitor in   . 407 WAY WORLD I.1   453
Fainall: Petulant and you both will find Mirabell as warm a   . . 407 WAY WORLD I.1   463
Witwoud: Pshaw, pshaw, that she laughs at Petulant is plain.   . 407 WAY WORLD I.1   465
Witwoud: O rare Petulant; thou art as quick as a Fire in a   . . 409 WAY WORLD I.1   519
Witwoud: O rare Petulant; thou art as quick as a Fire in a   . . 409 WAY WORLD I.1 V519
Foible: Mr. Witwoud and Mr. Petulant, are come to Dine with   . 432 WAY WORLD III.1   276
Millamant: That horrid Fellow Petulant, has provok'd me into   . . 432 WAY WORLD III.1   287
Marwood: you might as easily put off Petulant and Witwoud, as your   433 WAY WORLD III.1   315
                             (Enter Petulant and Witwoud.)   . . 435 WAY WORLD III.1   391
Witwoud: and Base. Ha, Petulant!   . . . . 435 WAY WORLD III.1   397
Witwoud: Petulant speak.   . . . . 438 WAY WORLD III.1   482
Witwoud: Ha, ha, ha, to him; to him Petulant, smoke him.   . . . 438 WAY WORLD III.1   488
Witwoud: Smoke the Boots, the Boots; Petulant, the Boots;   . . 438 WAY WORLD III.1   494
Lady Wish: Cousin Witwoud, your Servant; Mr. Petulant,   . . . 441 WAY WORLD III.1   597
Mrs Fain: Petulant and he were upon quarrelling as I came by.   . 452 WAY WORLD IV.1   314
                             (Enter Petulant Drunk.)   . . . 453 WAY WORLD IV.1   335
Witwoud: Now Petulant, all's over, all's well; Gad my head begins   453 WAY WORLD IV.1   336
Witwoud: Decimo Sexto, my Dear Lacedemonian, Sirrah Petulant, thou 453 WAY WORLD IV.1   343
                             (Enter Petulant and Witwoud.)   . . 475 WAY WORLD V.1   519
Witwoud: Ay I do, my hand I remember--Petulant set his   . . . 475 WAY WORLD V.1   525

Petulant's (2)
Witwoud: breed Debates.--Petulant's my Friend, and a very   . . 403 WAY WORLD I.1   288
Witwoud: Petulant's an Enemy to Learning; he relies   . . . . 436 WAY WORLD III.1   416

Pheasant (1)
Sr Sampson: rather eat a Pheasant, than a piece of poor John; and smell, 245 FOR LOVE II.1   369

Philander (1)
Lady Wish: together, you and your Philander. I'll Dukes-Place you, as 463 WAY WORLD V.1   53

Philistines (2)
Fondlewife: the Philistines have been upon thee. Heh! Art thou not vile 95 OLD BATCH IV.4   251
Fondlewife: the Philistines--Heh! Art thou not vile   . . . . . 95 OLD BATCH IV.4 V251

Phillis (1)
Lord Froth: Ancient Phillis has young Graces, ... 166 DOUBL DLR III.1   596

Philomaths (1)
Sr Sampson: House, and make an Entertainment for all the Philomaths,   . 242 FOR LOVE II.1   252

Philosophers (2)
Valentine: Ages; these Poets and Philosophers whom you naturally   . 217 FOR LOVE I.1   37
              Once of Philosophers they told us Stories, ... 315 FOR LOVE EPI.   11

Philosophy (1)
Millamant: Dear Fainall, Entertain Sir Wilfull--Thou hast Philosophy . 446 WAY WORLD IV.1   64

Phisician (1)
Witwoud: As a Phisician of a good Air--I cannot help it   . . . 419 WAY WORLD II.1   339

Pho (3)
Lord Touch: --Pho, 'tis nonsense. Come, come; I know my Lady   . . 150 DOUBL DLR III.1   5
Lady Touch: your promise--Pho, why nothing, only your Nephew had   . . 152 DOUBL DLR III.1   82

Pho   (continued)
  Mellefont: Ha!--Pho, you trifle. . . . . 156 DOUBL DLR III.1 231
Phoebus (1)
  Millamant: Like Phoebus sung the no less am'rous Boy. . . . . 448 WAY WORLD IV.1 153
Phosphorus (1)
  Lady Froth: the very Phosphorus of our Hemisphere. Do you understand . 139 DOUBL DLR II.1   32
Phrase (5)
  Lady Ply: Jesu, Sir Paul, what a Phrase was there? You will . . 159 DOUBL DLR III.1 327
  Lady Ply: Sir Paul, what a Phrase was there? You will . . . . 159 DOUBL DLR III.1 V327
  Careless: particularly that of Phrase. . . . . 160 DOUBL DLR III.1 357
  Tattle: pretty soft kind of Phrase, and with a good perswading . 302 FOR LOVE V.1 182
  Almeria: Or pompous Phrase; the Pageantry of Souls. . . . . 332 M. BRIDE I.1 249
Phrases (1)
  Witwoud: Thou art a retailer of Phrases; and dost deal in . . 453 WAY WORLD IV.1 346
Phuh (1)
  Bellmour: Phuh, Secret, ay.--And to be out of thy Debt, I'll . . . 98 OLD BATCH V.1   53
Physician (3)
    see Phisician
  Bellmour: Truths, and entertaining company like a Physician, with . 42 OLD BATCH I.1 181
  Heartwell: you? Did I bring a Physician to your Father when he lay . 109 OLD BATCH V.2   54
  Scandal: I'm afraid the Physician is not willing you shou'd . . 277 FOR LOVE IV.1   50
Physick (5)
  Heartwell: So I hate Physick too--yet I may love to take it . . . 44 OLD BATCH I.1 284
  Sharper: may say Marriage is entring into a Course of Physick. . . 44 OLD BATCH I.1 292
  Sr Sampson: and Students in Physick and Astrology in and about . . 242 FOR LOVE II.1 253
  Mirabell: Not in our Physick it may be. . . . . 422 WAY WORLD II.1 451
  Painall: for you. If your Physick be wholesome, it matters not who 468 WAY WORLD V.1 267
Physicks (1)
  Millamant: Yes, the Vapours; Fools are Physicks for it, next . . 421 WAY WORLD II.1 445
Physiognomy (4)
    see Fiz
  Careless: I am a little Superstitious in Physiognomy. . . . . . 131 DOUBL DLR I.1 148
  Foresight: Fellow? I don't like his Physiognomy. . . . . . . 242 FOR LOVE II.1 264
  Sr Sampson: Brother, you understand Physiognomy, a hanging look . . 243 FOR LOVE II.1 305
  Foresight: think there is something in your Physiognomy, that has a . 304 FOR LOVE V.1 260
Piaza (1)
  Setter: He'l be in the Piaza presently. . . . . 67 OLD BATCH III.1 231
Piazza (1)
  Setter: In the Piazza. . . . . 99 OLD BATCH V.1 118
Pick (2)
  Sir Joseph: Nay, gad, I'll pick up; I'm resolv'd to make a . . . . 85 OLD BATCH IV.3   61
  Mirabell: Play, and disappointing the Frolick which you had to pick 451 WAY WORLD IV.1 242
Pick'd (1)
  Sir Joseph: be pick'd out of Aesop's Fables, let me tell you that; and 101 OLD BATCH V.1 176
Picking (1)
  Scandal: Praise for Praise, and a Critick picking his Pocket. I have 233 FOR LOVE I.1 652
Pickle (2)
  Maskwell: she smoke my design upon Cynthia, I were in a fine pickle. 155 DOUBL DLR III.1 180
  Mrs Fain: this pickle?-- . . . . 454 WAY WORLD IV.1 380
Picque (1)
  Lucy: Vainlove, I have found out a picque she has taken at him; 75 OLD BATCH III.2 156
Picture (14)
  Bellmour: Methinks I am the very Picture of Montufar in the . . 80 OLD BATCH IV.2   7
  Lady Froth: gave you my Picture, here suppose this my Picture-- . . 140 DOUBL DLR II.1   74
  Sir Paul: held fifty to one, I could have drawn my own Picture . . 174 DOUBL DLR IV.1 242
  Scandal: Painter, that I cannot know the Person by your Picture of . 230 FOR LOVE I.1 537
  Tattle: Nor Woman, till she consented to have her Picture . . 232 FOR LOVE I.1 613
  Scandal: Yes Faith, I can shew you your own Picture, and . . . 232 FOR LOVE I.1 617
  Painall: If you have a mind to finish his Picture, you have an . 401 WAY WORLD I.1 232
  Foible: I wou'd put her Ladyship's Picture in my Pocket to shew . 423 WAY WORLD II.1 521
  Lady Wish: I shall never keep up to my Picture. . . . . 429 WAY WORLD III.1 150
  Foible: Picture like you; and now a little of the same Art, must . 429 WAY WORLD III.1 152
  Foible: make you like your Picture. Your Picture must sit for you, 429 WAY WORLD III.1 153
  Lady Wish: sort of a dyingness--You see that Picture has a sort of . 429 WAY WORLD III.1 168
Pictures (7)
  Mrs Frail: of these Mornings: I hear you have a great many Pictures. 232 FOR LOVE I.1 598
  Scandal: No, no; come to me if you wou'd see Pictures. . . . . 232 FOR LOVE I.1 615
  Valentine: Pictures of all that have granted him favours, he has the 233 FOR LOVE I.1 623
  Valentine: Pictures of all that have refus'd him: If Satyrs,
    Descriptions, ... 233 FOR LOVE I.1 624
  Valentine: Characters and Lampoons are Pictures. . . . . . . 233 FOR LOVE I.1 625
  Tattle: No? I can shew Letters, Locketts, Pictures, and Rings, . 257 FOR LOVE III.1 153
  Foible: Well, if worshipping of Pictures be a Sin . . . . . 427 WAY WORLD III.1   77
Pidgeons (1)
  Valentine: the Pidgeons ought rather to be laid to his feet, ha, ha,
    ha. . . . . 289 FOR LOVE IV.1 528
Piec'd (1)
  Witwoud: out and piec'd in the sides like an unsiz'd Camlet,--Yes, 453 WAY WORLD IV.1 328
Piece (14)
    see Master-piece
  Bellmour: Why you must know, 'tis a piece of Work toward . . . 41 OLD BATCH I.1 156
  Careless: piece of an old Scarlet Petticoat for a Stomacher; which, 157 DOUBL DLR III.1 276
  Careless: since the day of his Marriage, he has, out of a piece of . 158 DOUBL DLR III.1 277
  Maskwell: Piece of Justice-- . . . . 183 DOUBL DLR IV.1 589
  Scandal: Ignorance, all in one Piece. Then I can shew you Lying, . 233 FOR LOVE I.1 630
  Scandal: Impotence and Ugliness in another Piece; and yet one of . 233 FOR LOVE I.1 632
  Scandal: another large Piece too, representing a School; where there 233 FOR LOVE I.1 653
  Sr Sampson: rather eat a Pheasant, than a piece of poor John; and smell, 245 FOR LOVE II.1 369
  Mrs Frail: Yes marry will I--A great piece of business to . . . 246 FOR LOVE II.1 418
  Angelica: O barbarous! I never heard so insolent a piece of . . 258 FOR LOVE III.1 182
  Scandal: is of a piece with Mrs. Frail. He Courts Angelica, if
    we cou'd . . . . 291 FOR LOVE IV.1 598
  Valentine: Piece of Aegyptian Antiquity, or an Irish Manuscript; you 297 FOR LOVE IV.1 802
  Gonsalez: And of a piece with this Day's dire Misdeeds. . . . 379 M. BRIDE V.2 123
  Scandal: So Poets oft, do in one Piece expose . . . . . . 479 WAY WORLD EPI.   35
Piece-meal (2)
  Lady Touch: Heart, and gnaw it piece-meal, for not boding to me this . 184 DOUBL DLR IV.2   47
  Osmyn-Alph: That Piece-meal grind, are Beds of Down and Balm . . . 357 M. BRIDE III.1 293

Pieces (5)
  Sir Joseph: and get 50 Pieces more from him. Adslidikins, Bully, we'll   85   OLD BATCH   IV.3   63
  Fondlewife: Here are fifty Pieces in this Purse, Sir Joseph--   . . .   90   OLD BATCH   IV.4   42
  Almeria: And bulging 'gainst a Rock, was dash'd in pieces. . . .   329   M. BRIDE   I.1   127
  Mirabell: Insolence, that in Revenge I took her to pieces; sifted her   399   WAY WORLD   I.1   164
                 I'm thinking how this Play'll be pull'd to Pieces.   . . .   479   WAY WORLD   EPI.   2

Pierc'd (1)
  Singer: But 'tis the Glory to have pierc'd a Swain, ...   435   WAY WORLD   III.1 384
Pierce (1)
  Zara: Thy Anger cou'd not pierce thus, to my Heart.   354   M. BRIDE   III.1 187
Piercing (2)
  Tattle: a private Intriegue of Destiny, kept secret from the
                   piercing   304   FOR LOVE   V.1   271
  Osmyn-Alph: The Piercing Sighs, and Murmurs of my Love   351   M. BRIDE   III.1   77
Piercingly (2)
  Osmyn-Alph: What dost thou ask? why dost thou talk thus piercingly?   .   357   M. BRIDE   III.1 308
  Osmyn-Alph: Why dost thou ask? why dost thou talk thus piercingly?   .   357   M. BRIDE   III.1 V308
Pies (0)   see Dirt-pies
Piety (7)
  Laetitia: Appearance promised: The Piety of your Habit was   81   OLD BATCH   IV.2   25
  Bellmour: with the Practice of Piety in my Pocket, I had never been .   92   OLD BATCH   IV.4   110
  Maskwell: Duty to Kings, Piety to Parents, Gratitude to Benefactors,   150   DOUBL DLR   II.1   446
  Sr Sampson: No doubt of it, sweet Sir, but your filial Piety,   . . .   243   FOR LOVE   II.1   293
  Gonsalez: Betray'd by too much Piety, to seem   334   M. BRIDE   I.1   319
  Osmyn-Alph: If Piety be thus debarr'd Access   350   M. BRIDE   III.1   28
  Heli: To arm your Mind with Hope. Such Piety   352   M. BRIDE   III.1 117
Pig (1)
  Sir Wilful: be thy Pig.   457   WAY WORLD   IV.1   478
Pig-water (1)
  Mirabell: --Hog's-bones, Hare's-gall, Pig-water, and the . . .   451   WAY WORLD   IV.1   250
Pile (1)
  Almeria: How rev'rend is the Face of this tall Pile, ...   339   M. BRIDE   II.1   59
Pillag'd (1)
  Bellmour: pillag'd him. But I chanc'd to come by and rescued him, .   46   OLD BATCH   I.1   361
Pillars (1)
  Almeria: Whose antient Pillars rear their Marble Heads, ...   339   M. BRIDE   II.1   60
Pillory'd (1)
  Bellmour: deserves to be pillory'd.--No, by Heaven, I   82   OLD BATCH   IV.2   67
Pilot (1)
  Ben: can't deny it: But, Father, if I might be your Pilot in this   308   FOR LOVE   V.1   413
Pimp (10)
  Setter: acquainted with my parts) employs me as a Pimp: why   . .   64   OLD BATCH   III.1 140
  Setter: Undoubtedly 'tis impossible to be a Pimp and not a   . .   65   OLD BATCH   III.1 149
  Lucy: Contemplative Pimp.   65   OLD BATCH   III.1 164
  Lucy: Masters employment. For he's the head Pimp to Mr.   . .   65   OLD BATCH   III.1 169
  Setter: do deserve the Epithet.--Mercury was a Pimp too;   . .   105   OLD BATCH   V.1   335
  Sharper: As how, dear dexterous Pimp?   105   OLD BATCH   V.1   340
  Heartwell: So-h,--That precious Pimp too.--   107   OLD BATCH   V.2   4
  Lady Touch: and Pimp for your living, ...   192   DOUBL DLR   V.1 V193
  Scandal: Huntsmen.--No, turn Pimp, Flatterer, Quack, Lawyer,   .   220   FOR LOVE   I.1   144
  Lady Wish: Hospital for a decay'd Pimp? No damage? O thou frontless   463   WAY WORLD   V.1   36
Pimping (3)
  Setter: greatness by Pimping.   65   OLD BATCH   III.1 162
  Setter: Sir, I was Pimping for Mr. Bellmour.   99   OLD BATCH   V.1   122
  Jeremy: Porter, worn out with pimping, and carrying Billet doux .   218   FOR LOVE   I.1   96
Pimple (2)
  Brisk: have encourag'd a Pimple here too.   135   DOUBL DLR   I.1   293
  Sir Wilful: the Sun's a good Pimple, an honest Soaker, he has a Cellar   456   WAY WORLD   IV.1   422
Pin (5)
  Belinda: like one of 'em:--Good Dear, pin this, and I'll tell you.   83   OLD BATCH   IV.3   13
  Sr Sampson: a crooked Pin, or an old Horse-nail, with the head towards   265   FOR LOVE   III.1 467
  Millamant: know why--They serve one to pin up one's Hair.   . . .   419   WAY WORLD   II.1   362
  Witwoud: Is that the way? Pray Madam, do you pin up your   . . .   419   WAY WORLD   II.1   363
  Millamant: pin up my Hair with Prose.   419   WAY WORLD   II.1   366
Pinch (2)
  Maskwell: So, this was a pinch indeed, my invention was   . . .   199   DOUBL DLR   V.1   461
  Mirabell: what a Butler cou'd pinch out of a Napkin.   418   WAY WORLD   II.1   313
Pinch'd (1)
  Araminta: --Sure if I had not pinch'd you till you wak'd, you   .   55   OLD BATCH   II.2   43
Pincushions (1)
  Witwoud: Remnants of Remnants, like a maker of Pincushions--thou   453   WAY WORLD   IV.1   347
Pineda (1)
  Scandal: So says Pineda in his Third Book and Eighth Chapter-- .   267   FOR LOVE   III.1 532
Pinion'd (2)
  Sir Paul: Wife. Have I for this been pinion'd Night after Night for   .   178   DOUBL DLR   IV.1   423
  Osmyn-Alph: And pinion'd like a Thief or Murderer?   355   M. BRIDE   III.1 241
Pink (3)
  Sharper: Mirrour of Knighthood and Pink of Courtesie in the Age,   49   OLD BATCH   II.1   73
  Capt Bluff: him--I'll pink his Soul--but whisper that softly   . .   68   OLD BATCH   III.1 261
  Sir Joseph: Captain, will you see this? Won't you pink his . . .   69   OLD BATCH   III.1 311
Pinn'd (1)
  Millamant: curl if it were pinn'd up with Prose.   419   WAY WORLD   II.1 V367
Pinnace (1)
  Setter: dispose of! A goodly Pinnace, richly laden, and to launch   102   OLD BATCH   V.1   222
Pins (2)
  Mincing: And all to no purpose. But when your Laship pins it up   .   419   WAY WORLD   II.1   372
  Lady Wish: rowes of Pins and a Childs Fiddle; A Glass Necklace with the   462   WAY WORLD   V.1   16
Pinto (1)
  Foresight: Ferdinand Mendez Pinto was but a Type of thee, thou Lyar .   241   FOR LOVE   II.1   236
Pious (4)
  Fondlewife: that you might take it up, and read some of the pious   . .   91   OLD BATCH   IV.4   103
  Mellefont: my Lady Plyant all this Evening, that my Pious Aunt   .   130   DOUBL DLR   I.1   126
  Mellefont: one, and too pious for the other.   193   DOUBL DLR   V.1   237
  Fainall: O the pious Friendships of the Female Sex!   414   WAY WORLD   II.1   166
Piper (2)
  Sr Sampson: was to pay the Piper. Well, but here it is under Black and   240   FOR LOVE   II.1   180

Piper   (continued)
Sir Wilful:	Marry'd, say the Word, and send for the Piper, Wilfull	.	455	WAY WORLD	IV.1	411

Piping (1)
| Belinda: | of it; for she thank'd me, and gave me two Apples, piping | | 84 | OLD BATCH | IV.3 | 43 |

Pippins (1)
| Sharper: | Pippins? . . . . | . | 46 | OLD BATCH | I.1 | 350 |

Pish (7)
Capt Bluff:	Pish you have put me out, I have forgot what I was . .	.	53	OLD BATCH	II.1	224
Belinda:	Pish, I can't help dreaming of the Devil sometimes;	.	55	OLD BATCH	II.2	39
Belinda:	Pish.	.	56	OLD BATCH	II.2	63
Belinda:	as I was telling you--Pish, this is the untoward'st	.	83	OLD BATCH	IV.3	15
Miss Prue:	Pish.	.	252	FOR LOVE	II.1	640
Miss Prue:	(aside to Mrs. Frail). Pish, he shall be none of my	.	259	FOR LOVE	III.1	218
Mrs Fore:	Pish, you'd tell me so, tho' you did not think . .	.	272	FOR LOVE	III.1	707

Pistoll (1)
| Waitwell: | If he were my Son as he is my Nephew I'd Pistoll him-- | . | 460 | WAY WORLD | IV.1 | 603 |

Pit (8)
	To save our Plays, or else we'll damn your Pit. . . .	.	35	OLD BATCH	PRO.	9
Sir Joseph:	my Bully, my Back; agad my heart has gone a pit . .	.	51	OLD BATCH	II.1	140
	How many Undone Men were in the Pit!	.	113	OLD BATCH	EPI.	14
	To the Tempestuous Mercy of the Pit, ...	.	125	DOUBL DLR	PRO.	10
	The Vizor-Masks, that are in Pit and Gallery, . . .	.	204	DOUBL DLR	EPI.	19
	Methinks I see some Faces in the Pit, ...	.	204	DOUBL DLR	EPI.	32
	Scatter'd, like Rats-bane, up and down the Pit; . .	.	385	M. BRIDE	EPI.	8
	In shoals, I've mark'd 'em judging in the Pit; . . .	.	479	WAY WORLD	EPI.	11

Pitch (3)
Bellmour:	Thoughts fly to any pitch, I shall make villainous Signs.		59	OLD BATCH	II.2	178
Mrs Frail:	Creature, that smells all of Pitch and Tarr--Devil . .		250	FOR LOVE	II.1	565
Ben:	Nay, an I love once, I'll stick like pitch; I'll tell					
	you that.	.	273	FOR LOVE	III.1	739

Pithy (2)
| Araminta: | A pithy Question.--Have you sent your Wits . . . . | . | 85 | OLD BATCH | IV.3 | 95 |
| Saygrace: | But pithy, and I will handle it with Discretion. . . | . | 195 | DOUBL DLR | V.1 | 298 |

Pitie (2)
| Angelica: | knows I pitie you; and could I have foreseen the sad . | . | 294 | FOR LOVE | IV.1 | 712 |
| Angelica: | knows I pitie you; and could I have foreseen the bad . | . | 294 | FOR LOVE | IV.1 | V712 |

Pitied (1)
| Mirabell: | Let me be pitied first; and afterwards forgotten, . . | . | 471 | WAY WORLD | V.1 | 378 |

Pitiful (2)
| Lucy: | No thou pitiful Flatterer of thy Masters imperfections, | . | 66 | OLD BATCH | III.1 | 187 |
| Lord Touch: | by some pitiful Contriver, envious of my Nephew's Merit. | . | 151 | DOUBL DLR | III.1 | 15 |

Pity (27)
Heartwell:	The more is the pity.	.	73	OLD BATCH	III.2	90
Vainlove:	it?--Men in Madness have a Title to your Pity. . . .	.	106	OLD BATCH	V.1	357
Belinda:	Nay, I swear, I begin to pity him, my self. . . .	.	109	OLD BATCH	V.2	49
Heartwell:	Damn your pity. But let me be calm a little.-- . . .	.	109	OLD BATCH	V.2	50
Araminta:	Hang me, if I pity you; you are right enough . . .	.	109	OLD BATCH	V.2	61
	Our Christian Cuckolds are more bent to pity; . . .	.	125	DOUBL DLR	PRO.	27
Lady Ply:	help it, if you are made a Captive? I swear it's pity it	.	148	DOUBL DLR	II.1	359
Lady Touch:	a Sin, in pity to your Soul.	.	197	DOUBL DLR	V.1	382
Scandal:	Occasions; some pity you, and condemn your Father: . .	.	220	FOR LOVE	I.1	160
Valentine:	Scandal, have pity on him; he'll begin to any . . .	.	230	FOR LOVE	I.1	523
Mrs Frail:	That wou'd be pity, such a Handsome Young	.	261	FOR LOVE	III.1	304
Sr Sampson:	Odsbud, and 'tis pity you should--(Aside.) Odd, . .	.	298	FOR LOVE	V.1	48
Sr Sampson:	and 'twere pity you shou'd be thrown away upon any . .	.	298	FOR LOVE	V.1	52
Scandal:	own Wedding; methinks 'tis pity they should not be . .	.	313	FOR LOVE	V.1	599
Almeria:	If I should tell thee, wouldst thou pity me? . . .	.	328	M. BRIDE	I.1	91
Almeria:	I thank thee, that thou'lt pity thy sad Mistress; . .	.	328	M. BRIDE	I.1	95
Leonora:	Look down good Heav'n, with Pity on her	.	329	M. BRIDE	I.1	149
Garcia:	And I cou'd pity 'em. I hear some coming, ...	.	339	M. BRIDE	II.1	48
Almeria:	Curst my own Tongue, that cou'd not move his Pity. . .	.	370	M. BRIDE	IV.1	372
Manuel:	All Nature, Softness, Pity and Compassion, ...	.	374	M. BRIDE	V.1	63
Witwoud:	Afford me your Compassion, my Dears; pity me, . . .	.	401	WAY WORLD	I.1	235
Witwoud:	Fainall, Mirabell, pity me.	.	401	WAY WORLD	I.1	236
Witwoud:	Bum-baily, that I grant you,--'Tis Pity faith; the . .	.	403	WAY WORLD	I.1	299
Witwoud:	Bum-baily, that I grant you,--'Tis Pity; the . . .	.	403	WAY WORLD	I.1	V299
Marwood:	What pity 'tis, so much fine Raillery, and . . .	.	434	WAY WORLD	III.1	345
Mirabell:	Suppliant only for your pity--I am going where I . .	.	471	WAY WORLD	V.1	374
Mirabell:	Suppliant only for Pity--I am going where I . . .	.	471	WAY WORLD	V.1	V374

Pitying (1)
| Almeria: | Indeed, I do, for pitying thy sad Mistress; . . . | . | 328 | M. BRIDE | I.1 | V 95 |

Pize (3)
Sr Sampson:	O Pox, outsides, outsides; a pize take 'em, meer . .	.	298	FOR LOVE	V.1	33
Sr Sampson:	outsides, outsides; a pize take 'em, meer	.	298	FOR LOVE	V.1	V 33
Sr Sampson:	young Fellow--Pize on 'em, they never think beforehand	.	299	FOR LOVE	V.1	55

Plac'd (3)
Cynthia:	If Happiness in Self-content is plac'd, ...	.	167	DOUBL DLR	III.1	633
Foible:	and plac'd the Foot-men in a Row in the Hall, in their	.	444	WAY WORLD	IV.1	4
Lady Wish:	dealt in when I took you into my house, plac'd you next	.	462	WAY WORLD	V.1	20

Place (38)   see Dukes-Place
Vainlove:	the old place.	.	40	OLD BATCH	I.1	130
Bellmour:	place, and the pleasure of enjoying some half a score .	.	41	OLD BATCH	I.1	139
Heartwell:	such a place, about his Nose and Eyes; though a' has my	.	45	OLD BATCH	I.1	323
Heartwell:	such a place, about his Nose and Eyes; though he has my	.	45	OLD BATCH	I.1	V323
Sir Joseph:	Um--Ay this, this is the very damn'd place; the . . .	.	47	OLD BATCH	II.1	2
Sir Joseph:	reconciled to this place heartily.	.	48	OLD BATCH	II.1	15
Sharper:	now luck!--curs'd fortune! this must be the place, this	.	48	OLD BATCH	II.1	17
Sharper:	damn'd unlucky place--	.	48	OLD BATCH	II.1	18
Capt Bluff:	You are obliging Sir, but this is too publick a Place .	.	69	OLD BATCH	III.1	322
Vainlove:	than Sawcy, in another place.	.	87	OLD BATCH	IV.3	165
Araminta:	Another place! Some villainous Design to blast . .	.	87	OLD BATCH	IV.3	166
Araminta:	I must leave the place.	.	88	OLD BATCH	IV.3	186
Fondlewife:	Come, Sir, Who are you, in the first place? And . .	.	93	OLD BATCH	IV.4	172
Setter:	her all this Evening, in order to conduct her to the Place	102	OLD BATCH	V.1	216
Lady Touch:	I been Bawd to his designs? his Property only, a baiting					
	place	.	191	DOUBL DLR	V.1	146

Plate   (continued)
| | | | | |
Lady Wish: | and your Cuckoldcmes. I must pawn my Plate, and my . . . 466 | WAY WORLD | V.1 | 151
Plato (1)
Jeremy: | Mouths of your Creditors? Will Plato be Bail for you? Or . 217 | FOR LOVE | I.1 | 29
Plausible (2)
Mellefont: | Imagination cannot form a fairer and more plausible . . 187 | DOUBL DLR | IV.2 | 150
Jeremy: | plausible Occasion for me to quench my Thirst at the . . 302 | FOR LCVE | V.1 | 175
Play (45)
| A Play makes War, and Prologue is the Drum: . . . . . 35 | OLD BATCH | PRO. | 6
| We've a young Author and his first born Play; . . . . 35 | OLD BATCH | PRO. | 11
| O Lord, for Heavens sake excuse the Play, ... 35 | OLD BATCH | PRO. | 23
Bellmour: | What is it to read a Play in a rainy day, ... 44 | OLD BATCH | I.1 | 266
Belinda: | play the Game, and consequently can't see the Miscarriages 55 | OLD BATCH | II.2 | 34
Singer: | Melting the Hours, in gentle Play; . . . . 71 | OLD BATCH | III.2 | 3
Belinda: | as a very witty Prologue to a very dull Play. . . . . 107 | OLD BATCH | V.1 | 388
| And feed like Sharks, upon an Infant Play. . . . . . 125 | DOUEL DLR | PRO. | 13
| Whatever Fate is for this Play design'd, ... 125 | DOUBL DLR | PRO. | 31
Cynthia: | as Fccls. 'Tis an odd Game we're going to Play at: What . 142 | DOUEL DLR | II.1 | 157
Maskwell: | After-Game to play that shall turn the Tables, and here . 181 | DOUBL DLR | IV.1 | 529
Lady Touch: | --Oh! I could rack my self, play the Vulture to my own . 184 | DOUBL DLR | IV.2 | 46
| The First-fruit Offering, of a Virgin Play. . . . . 213 | FOR LCVE | PRO. | 25
| Yet hopes there's no ill-manners in his Play: . . . . 214 | FCR LCVE | PRO. | 42
Valentine: | Yes, I do; I'll write a Play. . . . . 217 | FOR LCVE | I.1 | 63
Jeremy: | Three days, the Life of a Play, I no more expect it, than to 218 | FOR LCVE | I.1 | 74
Scandal: | have fair Play for your Life. If you can't be fairly run
| dcwn . . . . 220 | FCR LCVE | I.1 | 142
Valentine: | Eyes to her Feet, as they steal in and out, and play at . 223 | FOR LCVE | I.1 | 287
Valentine: | play at Losing Loadum; you must lose a good Name to . . 226 | FCR LCVE | I.1 | 389
Mrs Fore: | Play the first day,--I warrant it wou'd break Mr. Tattle's 250 | FOR LCVE | II.1 | 550
Scandal: | Pray sing the first Song in the last new Play. . . . . 258 | FOR LCVE | III.1 | 197
Ben: | He then might play his part. . . . . 274 | FCR LCVE | III.1 | 784
Jeremy: | playing the Madman, won't make her play the Fool, and . . 276 | FOR LCVE | IV.1 | 9
Angelica: | don't play Trick for Trick, may I never taste the Pleasure 277 | FCR LCVE | IV.1 | 67
Ben: | marry himself. Gad, says I, an you play the fool and marry 286 | FOR LOVE | IV.1 | 382
Valentine: | Get me a Coul and Beads, that I may play my part,-- . . 290 | FOR LCVE | IV.1 | 560
Tattle: | and play with the same Rattle always: O fie, marrying is a 303 | FCR LCVE | V.1 | 246
| To tell of what Disease the Play expir'd. . . . . . 385 | M. BRIDE | EPI. | 10
| So Criticks throng to see a New Play split, ... 385 | M. ERIDE | EPI. | 25
| With whcm, he hopes, this Play will Favour find, . . 385 | M. EBIDE | EPI. | 30
| Nor, like those peevish Wits, his Play maintain, . . . 393 | WAY WCRLD | PRO. | 27
| In short, our Play, shall (with your leave to shew it) . 393 | WAY WORLD | PRO. | 37
Mirabell: | What you please. I'll play on to entertain you. . . . 395 | WAY WCRLD | I.1 | 3
Fainall: | else now, and play too negligently; the Coldness of a . 395 | WAY WORLD | I.1 | 6
Fainall: | more play with a Man that slighted his ill Fortune, than . 395 | WAY WORLD | I.1 | 8
Fainalli | You may allow him to win of you at Play;-- . . . . . 402 | WAY WORLD | I.1 | 281
Witwoud: | she wcn't give an Eccho fair play; she has that everlasting 421 | WAY WORLD | II.1 | 420
Mirabell: | Dictates of Reascn, and yet persevere to play the Fool by . 423 | WAY WORLD | II.1 | 500
Fainall: | of Play, that I should lose to one, who has not . . . 443 | WAY WORLD | III.1 | 688
Marwood: | --the better I can play the Incendiary. Besides I would not 443 | WAY WORLD | III.1 | 703
Millamant: | Play together, But let us be very strange and well bred: . 450 | WAY WORLD | IV.1 | 207
Mirabell: | you a fop--scrambling to the Play in a Mask--then . . . 451 | WAY WORLD | IV.1 | 239
Mirabell: | Play, and disappointing the Frolick which you had to pick . 451 | WAY WORLD | IV.1 | 242
Millamant: | Detestable Inprimis! I go to the Play in a Mask! . . . 451 | WAY WORLD | IV.1 | 244
Lady Wish: | never suffer'd to play with a Male-Child, tho' but in . . 467 | WAY WCRLD | V.1 | 189
Play-Book (1)
Lady Wish: | the sight or name of an obscene Play-Book--and can I . . 467 | WAY WORLD | V.1 | 202
Play-fellows (1)
Setter: | think, you and I have been Play-fellows off-and-on, any . 111 | OLD BATCH | V.2 | 142
Play-House (1)
Tattle: | and Ccvent-Garden, the Door-keepers at the Play-House, . 257 | FCR LCVE | III.1 | 156
Play-house (4)
Bellmour: | Play-house, till the Curtain's drawn; but that once up, . 107 | OLD BATCH | V.1 | 385
Marwood: | of the Play-house? A fine gay glossy Fool, shou'd be given 433 | WAY WORLD | III.1 | 309
Lady Wish: | her foot within the door of a Play-house. O my dear . . 467 | WAY WORLD | V.1 | 205
Lady Wish: | her foot within the door of a Play-house. O dear . . . 467 | WAY WORLD | V.1 V205
Play'd (1) | see Plaid
Play'll (1)
| For if his Muse has play'd him false, the worst . . . 125 | DOUEL DLB | PRO. | 33
| I'm thinking how this Play'll be pull'd to Pieces. . . . 479 | WAY WORLD | EPI. | 2
Player (1)
Mrs Fore: | Countenance purely, you'd make an Admirable Player. . . 247 | FCR LCVE | II.1 | 452
Player's (1)
| To be the Player's Refuge in distress; . . . . 315 | FOR LOVE | EPI. | 2
Players (2)
| Methinks, we Players resemble such a Soul, ... 315 | FOR LCVE | EPI. | 19
Witwoud: | Hey day! what are you all gct together like Players . . 475 | WAY WORLD | V.1 | 521
Playing (4)
Sharper: | Or omit playing with her Fan, and cooling her if . . . 44 | OLD BATCH | I.1 | 263
Heartwell: | Marry, is playing the Focl all ones Life long. . . . 74 | OLD BATCH | III.2 | 118
Jeremy: | much to seek in playing the Madman to day. . . . . 276 | FOR LCVE | IV.1 | 5
Jeremy: | playing the Madman, won't make her play the Fool, and . . 276 | FOR LOVE | IV.1 | 9
Plays (15)
| Prologues, were serious Speeches, before Plays; . . . 35 | OLD BATCH | PRO. | 2
| To save our Plays, or else we'll damn your Pit. . . . 35 | OLD BATCH | PRO. | 9
Heartwell: | And proves that Vainlove plays the Fool with . . . . 42 | OLD BATCH | I.1 | 216
Heartwell: | Why every Man plays the Fool once in his Life: But to . . 74 | OLD BATCH | III.2 | 117
| Such are the Tryals, Poets make of Plays: . . . . . 125 | DOUEL DLR | PRO. | 7
Lady Froth: | Lampoons, Plays, or Heroick Poems. . . . . 138 | DOUBL DLR | II.1 | 17
| Could Poets but forsee how Plays would take, ... 204 | DOUBL DLR | EPI. | 1
| The Time has been when Plays were not so plenty, . . . 323 | M. BRIDE | PRO. | 1
| New Plays did then like Almanacks appear; . . . . . 323 | M. BBIDE | PRO. | 3
| To poison Plays, I see some where they sit, ... 385 | M. EBIDE | EPI. | 7
| Criticks to Plays for the same end resort, ... 385 | M. EBIDE | EPI. | 15
Sir Wilful: | Town, as Plays and the like that must be confess'd indeed. 448 | WAY WORLD | IV.1 | 125
Lady Wish: | and going to filthy Plays; and Profane Musick-meetings, . 467 | WAY WCRLD | V.1 | 199
| Set up for Spys on Plays and finding Fault. . . . . 479 | WAY WCRLD | EPI. | 15

Plays   (continued)

	Such, who watch Plays, with scurrilous intent	479	WAY WORLD	EPI. 17

Plead (9)

Vainlove:	Offender must Plead to his Arraignment, tho' he have his .	87	OLD BATCH	IV.3 154
Vainlove:	Offender must Plead to his Arraignment, tho' he has his .	87	OLD BATCH	IV.3 V154
Maskwell:	why you don't know, that while I plead for you, your .	148	DOUEL DLR	II.1 392
Valentine:	I am ready to plead, Not guilty for you; and Guilty, .	257	FCR LOVE	III.1 145
Zara:	And me; presume to day to plead audacious Love, ...	349	M. BRIDE	II.2 366
Zara:	Presume to day to plead audacious Love, ...	349	M. BRIDE	II.2 V366
Selim:	I plead not for a Pardon, and to live, ...	375	M. BRIDE	V.1 120
Mirabell:	right, that you may plead the error of your Judgment in .	409	WAY WCRLD	I.1 539
Mirabell:	plead for favour;--Nay not for Pardon, I am a	471	WAY WORLD	V.1 373

Pleaded (1)

Mellefont:	pleaded Honour and nearness of Elood to my Uncle; . . .	130	DOUEL DLR	I.1 112

Pleading (2)

	For when behind cur Scenes their Suits are pleading, . .	315	FOR LCVE	EPI. 7
Gonsalez:	And urg'd by Nature pleading for his Child, ...	371	M. BRIDE	IV.1 407

Pleads (2)

Almeria:	And pleads against thee? who shall then prevail? . . .	382	M. BRIDE	V.2 265
	But pleads no Merit from his past Eehaviour.	393	WAY WCRLD	PRO. 17

Pleas'd (21)

Sir Joseph:	You are only pleas'd to say so Sir--But pray if I . . .	49	OLD BATCH	II.1 79
Bellmour:	I could be well enough pleas'd to drive on a Love-bargain,	60	OLD BATCH	II.2 220
Bellmour:	whether thou wouldst have her angry or pleas'd. Couldst .	63	OLD BATCH	III.1 103
Sharper:	real Fanatick can look better pleas'd after a successful .	100	OLD BATCH	V.1 133
Lady Touch:	you have frighted me. Nay, look pleas'd, I'll tell you.	152	DOUEL DLR	III.1 70
Jeremy:	if you don't like my Negotiation, will you be pleas'd to	221	FCR LOVE	I.1 183
Foresight:	time,--But in troth I am pleas'd at my Stocking. Very .	236	FCR LOVE	II.1 37
Foresight:	well pleas'd at my Stocking--Oh here's my Neice!-- . . .	236	FCR LOVE	II.1 38
Sr Sampson:	Sir, how, I beseech you, what were you pleas'd	243	FCR LOVE	II.1 285
Valentine:	you, cut of Fatherly fondness, will be pleas'd to add, shall	243	FCR LOVE	II.1 291
Ben:	No, I'm pleas'd well enough, now I have found you,-- .	285	FOR LOVE	IV.1 359
Manuel:	By Heav'n thou lov'st me, and I'm pleas'd thou do'st: .	333	M. BRIDE	I.1 275
Zara:	I might be pleas'd when I behold this Train	336	M. BRIDE	I.1 398
Zara:	You free: But shall return much better pleas'd, . . .	360	M. BRIDE	III.1 418
Zara:	I know thou could'st; but I'm not often pleas'd, . . .	360	M. BRIDE	III.1 423
	And hcw they're disappointed if they're pleas'd! . . .	385	M. BRIDE	EPI. 14
	And how they're disappointed when they're pleas'd! . .	385	M. BRIDE	EPI. V 14
Mirabell:	better pleas'd if she had been less discreet.	396	WAY WORLD	I.1 48
Fainall:	Joy of your Success, Mirabell; you look pleas'd. . . .	399	WAY WORLD	I.1 135
Millamant:	--No, now I think on't I'm pleas'd--For I believe . .	420	WAY WORLD	II.1 379
	They scarcely come inclining to be Pleas'd:	479	WAY WCRLD	EPI. 6

Pleasant (10)

Vainlove:	That's pleasant, by my troth frcm thee, who hast . . .	38	OLD BATCH	I.1 45
Vainlove:	and peevish: But I have seen him pleasant enough in his .	40	OLD BATCH	I.1 107
Bellmour:	birth, and the discovery must needs be very pleasant from .	40	OLD BATCH	I.1 125
Araminta:	Ha, ha, ha, this is pleasant.	56	OLD BATCH	II.2 53
Bellmour:	Nay, 'Faith, Madam, 'tis a pleasant one; and worth . .	82	OLD BATCH	IV.2 48
Sharper:	Ha, ha; 'Twill be a pleasant Cheat.--I'll plague . . .	99	OLD BATCH	V.1 86
Lord Froth:	Pleasant Creature! perfectly well, ah! that look, . . .	140	DOUBL DLR	II.1 67
Scandal:	have Paintings tco, some pleasant enough.	233	FOR LCVE	I.1 634
Mrs Fain:	pleasant Relation last Night: I wou'd fain hear it out. .	412	WAY WORLD	II.1 99
Mincing:	with Poetry, it sits so pleasant the next Day as any Thing,	420	WAY WCRLD	II.1 373

Pleasantly (2)

Lucy:	Go get you in Madam, receive him pleasantly, dress up . .	62	OLD BATCH	III.1 48
Maskwell:	easily and pleasantly is that dissembled before Fruition!	155	DOUBL DLR	III.1 184

Please (63)

	(I don't know whether I shall speak to please you) . . .	35	OLD BATCH	PRO. 18
Lucy:	charm our Sex conspire to please you.	75	OLD BATCH	III.2 161
Laetitia:	please you.	78	OLD BATCH	IV.1 112
Laetitia:	learn, to please my Jewel.	79	OLD BATCH	IV.1 141
Servant:	Here's a Chair, Sir, if you please to repose your self. .	80	OLD BATCH	IV.2 1
Fondlewife:	I'll show you the way out of my house, if you please. Come,	96	OLD BATCH	IV.4 269
Setter:	Sublimate, if you please, Sir: I think my Atchievments .	105	OLD BATCH	V.1 334
Lord Touch:	Sir Paul, if you please we'll retire to take	132	DOUEL DLR	I.1 216
Maskwell:	him too,--Will that please you?	137	DOUEL DLR	I.1 403
Lady Ply:	please--therefore don't provoke me.	145	DOUEL DLR	II.1 237
Maskwell:	him tc what you please; your Guests are so engaged in . .	155	DOUEL DLR	III.1 167
Boy:	No, an please you.	161	DOUEL DLR	III.1 400
Careless:	Madam,--if your Ladyship please, we'll discourse of this in	163	DOUEL DLR	III.1 494
Sir Paul:	please to call me.	180	DOUEL DLR	IV.1 474
Mellefont:	Paradice; yet if you please you may make it a Purgatory; .	185	DOUEL DLR	IV.2 61
Maskwell:	you please, defer the finishing of your Wit, and let us talk	194	DOUBL DLR	V.1 278
	We hope there's something that may please each Taste, .	213	FOR LCVE	PRO. 26
Jeremy:	this fine Feeding: But if you please, I had rather be at .	217	FOR LCVE	I.1 25
Jeremy:	Hem!--Sir, if you please to give me a small	217	FOR LCVE	I.1 64
Sr Sampson:	what I please? Are not you my Slave? Did not I beget you? .	244	FOR LCVE	II.1 324
Mrs Frail:	do what I please.	246	FOR LCVE	II.1 416
Miss Prue:	Yes, if you please.	251	FCR LCVE	II.1 590
Ben:	Forsooth an you please--(Salutes her.) Nay Mistress, I'm .	261	FOR LCVE	III.1 358
Ben:	Forsooth if you please--(Salutes her.) Nay Mistress, I'm .	261	FOR LCVE	III.1 V280
Ben:	Come Mistress, will you please to sit down, for an you .	263	FOR LCVE	III.1 360
Ben:	Come, I'll haule a Chair; there, an you please to sit, I'll	263	FOR LCVE	III.1 362
Ben:	heard as far as another,--I'll heave off to please you. .	263	FOR LCVE	III.1 367
Scandal:	by Confederacy; and if you please, we'll put a Trick . .	272	FOR LCVE	III.1 700
Ben:	The Tailor thought to please her, ...	274	FOR LCVE	III.1 774
Valentine:	little out of Order; won't you please to sit, Sir? . . .	281	FOR LCVE	IV.1 197
Valentine:	Will you please to let me hold it, Sir?	281	FOR LCVE	IV.1 228
Ben:	marry to please my self, not him; and for the Young . .	285	FOR LCVE	IV.1 372
Jeremy:	better yet--Will you please to be Mad, Sir, or how? . .	296	FOR LCVE	IV.1 771
Sr Sampson:	Odd, you are hard to please, Madam; to find a	299	FOR LCVE	V.1 65
Jeremy:	comply with any thing to please him. Poor Lady, I'm . .	302	FOR LCVE	V.1 202
Miss Prue:	my Husband now if you please.	303	FOB LCVE	V.1 230
Valentine:	If you please, Sir; but first I would ask this Lady . .	311	FOR LOVE	V.1 515
Valentine:	only Pleasure was to please this Lady: I have made many .	312	FOR LOVE	V.1 546
	To please and move, has been our Poets Theme, ...	323	M. EBIDE	PRO. 35

Please   (continued)

		PAGE	TITLE	ACT.SC	LINE
Manuel:	He is your Prisoner, as you please dispose him.	335	M. BRIDE	I.1	368
Zara:	And can unwind, or strain him as I please.	348	M. BRIDE	II.2	326
Manuel:	Enough; his Punishment be what you please.	349	M. BRIDE	II.2	381
Osmyn-Alph:	Or Being as you please, such I will think it. . . .	354	M. BRIDE	III.1	184
Alonzo:	If't please your Lordship, I'll return, and say . . .	371	M. BRIDE	IV.1	422
	To please, this time, has been his sole Pretence, . . .	393	WAY WORLD	PRO.	33
Mirabell:	What ycu please. I'll play on to entertain you. . .	395	WAY WCRLD	I.1	3
Mirabell:	Do's that please you?	420	WAY WCRLD	II.1	381
Mirabell:	as a Mortification; for sure to please a Fool is some degree	421	WAY WCRLD	II.1	439
Millamant:	I please my self--Besides sometimes to	421	WAY WCRLD	II.1	441
Waitwell:	Sir Rowland if you please. The Jade's so pert upon . .	424	WAY WCRLD	II.1	550
Servant-W:	please to walk in, in the mean time.	437	WAY WORLD	III.1	446
Witwoud:	short as a Shrewsbury Cake, if you please. But I tell . .	439	WAY WCRLD	III.1	532
Millamant:	Ay, if you please Foible, send him away,--Cr send . . .	446	WAY WCRLD	IV.1	60
Millamant:	a morning as long as I please.	449	WAY WCRLD	IV.1	191
Mirabell:	Then I'll get up in a morning as early as I please. .	449	WAY WCRLD	IV.1	192
Millamant:	to and from whom I please, to write and receive Letters, .	450	WAY WCRLD	IV.1	213
Millamant:	wear what I please; and choose Conversation with regard .	450	WAY WCRLD	IV.1	215
Millamant:	may be your Relations. Come to Dinner when I please, .	450	WAY WCRLD	IV.1	219
Millamant:	said something to please me.	452	WAY WCRLD	IV.1	307
Lady Wish:	sit if you please, and see the Entertainment. . . .	459	WAY WCRLD	IV.1	567
Painall:	your Fox if you please Sir, and make a Bear-Garden flourish	473	WAY WCRLD	V.1	440
Mirabell:	to the uses within mention'd. You may read if you please .	476	WAY WCRLD	V.1	547
	How hard a thing 'twould be, to please you all. . . .	479	WAY WORLD	EPI.	4

Pleased (8)

Heartwell:	pleased with you--And a Pox upon me for loving thee so .	73	OLD EATCH	III.2	71
Lord Froth:	not Laugh with him. Ridiculous! To be pleased with what .	132	DOUEL DLR	I.1	203
Lord Froth:	not Laugh with one. Ridiculous! To be pleased with what .	132	DOUEL DLR	I.1	203
Lady Ply:	How now! will you be pleased to retire, ...	144	DOUEL DLR	II.1	209
Sir Paul:	No marry will I not be pleased, I am pleased to be . .	144	DOUBL DLR	II.1	211
Lady Ply:	a suitable return to those Obligations which you are pleased	159	DOUEL DLR	III.1	338
Lord Froth:	the World--you are never pleased but when we are all . .	162	DOUEL DLR	III.1	458

Pleases (9)

Heartwell:	Pox, how her Innocence torments and pleases me!	72	OLD BATCH	III.2	55
Heartwell:	Death, how her Innocence torments and pleases me! . . .	72	OLD BATCH	III.2 V	55
Lord Froth:	pleases the Croud! Now when I Laugh, I always Laugh . .	132	DOUEL DLR	I.1	204
Millamant:	Lovers as fast as one pleases, and they live as long as one	420	WAY WCRLD	II.1	404
Millamant:	pleases, and they die as soon as one pleases: And then if .	420	WAY WCRLD	II.1	405
Millamant:	one pleases, one makes more.	420	WAY WCRLD	II.1	406
Waitwell:	What your Ladyship pleases.--I have brought the	475	WAY WORLD	V.1	510
	Who pleases any one against his Will.	479	WAY WORLD	EPI.	8

Pleasing (3)

Brisk:	Dream that did in a manner represent a very pleasing . .	176	DOUEL DLR	IV.1	327
Manuel:	Iu pleasing Triumph led; your Beauty's Slave. . . .	335	M. EBIDE	I.1 V392	
Mirabell:	Nature; your true Vanity is in the power of pleasing. . .	420	WAY WCRLD	II.1	384

Pleasurable (1)

Scandal:	merciful, and wish you well, since Love and Pleasurable .	220	FOR LCVE	I.1	162

Pleasure (50)

Vainlove:	Pleasure, I guess you mean.	37	OLD EATCH	I.1	13
Bellmour:	and Pleasure, my Occupation; and let Father Time shake .	37	OLD BATCH	I.1	24
Bellmour:	place, and the pleasure of enjoying some half a score . .	41	OLD EATCH	I.1	139
Sharper:	him; you with pleasure reap that fruit, which he takes .	43	OLD EATCH	I.1	219
Heartwell:	of the intention, and none of the pleasure of the practice--	43	OLD BATCH	I.1	239
Vainlove:	Or a ycung Wench, betwixt pleasure and	63	OLD EATCH	III.1 V	93
Vainlove:	Or a ycung Wench, between pleasure and	63	OLD EATCH	III.1 V 93	
Bellmour:	have the pleasure of forgiving 'em.	63	OLD EATCH	III.1	99
Vainlove:	And I love to have the pleasure of making my	63	OLD EATCH	III.1	100
Singer:	Vex'd at the Pleasure she had miss'd, ...	71	OLD BATCH	III.2 V	18
Vainlove:	pleasure of a chase: My sport is always balkt or cut short	80	OLD BATCH	IV.1	176
Sharper:	Thus Grief still treads upon the Heels of Pleasure: . .	105	OLD EATCH	V.1	327
Bellmour:	then opens the Scene of Pleasure.	107	OLD BATCH	V.1	386
	To think oth' Sting, that's in the tail of Pleasure. . .	113	OLD EATCH	EPI.	9
Mellefont:	will be a Pleasure to your self; I must get you to engage .	130	DOUEL DLR	I.1	125
Lady Touch:	Fortune, and my Person, been subjected to your Pleasure? .	136	DOUEL DLR	I.1	347
Sir Paul:	angry, that's my pleasure at this time.	144	DOUEL DLR	II.1	212
Maskwell:	Hypocrisie; oh 'tis such a pleasure, to angle for fair-faced	150	DOUEL DLR	II.1	458
Maskwell:	what was my Pleasure is become my Duty: And I have as .	155	DOUEL DLR	III.1	178
Maskwell:	And whereas pleasure is generally paid with	156	DOUEL DLR	III.1	218
Maskwell:	Pleasure.	156	DOUEL DLR	III.1	220
Saygrace:	middle of a Sermon to do you pleasure.	195	DOUEL DLR	V.1	281
Saygrace:	middle of a Sermon to do you a pleasure.	195	DOUEL DLR	V.1 V281	
Tattle:	pleasure of telling her self.	228	FOR LCVE	I.1	475
Angelica:	Is not it a good hour for Pleasure too? Uncle, pray . .	236	FOR' LCVE	II.1	44
Scandal:	It takes, pursue it in the name of Love and Pleasure. .	269	FOR LCVE	III.1	612
Scandal:	Pleasure?	271	FOR LCVE	III.1	672
Scandal:	Domestick Thief; and he that wou'd secure his Pleasure, .	271	FOR LCVE	III.1	676
Scandal:	purchas'd a perpetual opportunity for Pleasure. . . .	271	FOR LCVE	III.1	679
Mrs Fore:	An Opportunity for Pleasure!	271	FOR LCVE	III.1	680
Scandal:	Pleasure, so you have taken care of Honour, and 'tis the .	271	FOR LCVE	III.1	682
Angelica:	don't play Trick for Trick, may I never taste the Pleasure	277	FOR LCVE	IV.1	67
Valentine:	drive distinct Trades, and Care and Pleasure separately .	289	FOR LOVE	IV.1	506
Angelica:	Never let us know one another better; for the Pleasure of .	296	FOR LCVE	IV.1	789
Nurse:	What is your Worship's Pleasure?	305	FOR LCVE	V.1	323
Valentine:	Fortune, but as it was subservient to my Pleasure; and my	312	FOR LOVE	V.1	545
Valentine:	only Pleasure was to please this Lady: I have made many .	312	FOR LCVE	V.1	546
Valentine:	Between Pleasure and Amazement, I am lost--	312	FOR LCVE	V.1	565
Angelica:	Faults than he has Virtues; and 'tis hardly more Pleasure	312	FOR LCVE	V.1	576
Almeria:	O my boding Heart--What is your Pleasure, ...	334	M. EBIDE	I.1	330
Almeria:	my boding Heart--What is your Pleasure, ...	334	M. BRIDE	I.1 V330	
Painall:	losing Gamester lessens the Pleasure of the Winner: I'd no	395	WAY WORLD	I.1	7
Witwoud:	Pleasure, and the Town, a Question at once so Foreign and .	402	WAY WCRLD	I.1	257
Witwoud:	Words gives me the pleasure very often to explain his . .	404	WAY WORLD	I.1	331
Mirabell:	To your Lover you owe the pleasure of hearing your . . .	421	WAY WCRLD	II.1	416
Mirabell:	selves prais'd; and to an Eccho the pleasure of hearing your	421	WAY WCRLD	II.1	417
Painall:	to endear his pleasure, and prepare the Joy that follows, .	444	WAY WCRLD	III.1	716

Pleasure   (continued)

		PAGE	TITLE	ACT.SC	LINE
Mirabell:	grace, and the receiver lessens his Pleasure?	449	WAY WORLD	IV.1	173
Millamant:	made sure of my will and pleasure.	449	WAY WORLD	IV.1	181
Sir Wilful:	no more words. For what's to come to pleasure you I'm	470	WAY WORLD	IV.1	320

Pleasures (11)

Bellmour:	Matrimony, in Opposition to the Pleasures of Courtship.	107	OLD BATCH	V.1	383
Maskwell:	your Pleasures; and will not rest till I have given you				
	peace,	137	DOUBL DLR	I.1	394
Lord Touch:	in her unfeigned Pleasures.	151	DOUBL DLR	III.1	10
Sir Paul:	Pleasures to preserve its Purity, and must I now find it	179	DOUBL DLR	IV.1	429
Maskwell:	And so may all your Pleasures be, and secret as	184	DOUBL DLR	IV.2	33
Maskwell:	of your Love; yet so far I prize your Pleasures o're my own,	199	DOUBL DLR	V.1	436
Scandal:	Hush, softly--the Pleasures of last Night, my	284	FOR LOVE	IV.1	316
Mirabell:	refining on your Pleasures.	395	WAY WORLD	I.1	12
Fainall:	unsuspected in my Pleasures; and take you oftner to my	414	WAY WORLD	II.1	146
Fainall:	in Pleasures which we both have shar'd. Yet had not you	415	WAY WORLD	II.1	200
Mirabell:	the greatest Pleasures of your Life.	421	WAY WORLD	II.1	414

Plentiful (2)

Sir Paul:	Why, I have, I thank Heaven, a very plentiful	161	DOUBL DLR	III.1	407
	How plentiful the Crop, or scarce the Grain,	323	M. BRIDE	PRO.	9

Plenty (3)

	And to our World, such Plenty you afford,	213	FOR LOVE	PRO.	16
Foresight:	Sorrow, Want and Plenty, Night and Day, make up our	236	FOR LOVE	II.1	36
	The Time has been when Plays were not so plenty,	323	M. BRIDE	PRO.	1

Pliant (1)

Bellmour:	humble, pliant, easie thing, a Lover, so guess at Plagues in	106	OLD BATCH	V.1	382

Plod (1)

Bellmour:	to see thee still plod on alone.	112	OLD BATCH	V.2	184

Plot (26)

Mellefont:	am Jealous of a Plot. I would have Noise and Impertinence	129	DOUBL DLR	I.1	75
Maskwell:	lay a stronger Plot: if I gain a little time, I shall				
	not want	138	DOUBL DLR	I.1	419
Maskwell:	there's a Plot for you.	149	DOUBL DLR	II.1	404
Maskwell:	prevent your Plot, yet I would have you use Caution and	154	DOUBL DLR	III.1	139
Maskwell:	the forming of another Plot that I have in my head--	154	DOUBL DLR	III.1	160
Maskwell:	the forming another Plot that I have in my head--	154	DOUBL DLR	III.1	V160
Cynthia:	Well, if the Devil should assist her, and your Plot	169	DOUBL DLR	IV.1	55
Lady Ply:	Ungrateful Monster! He? Is it so? Ay, I see it, a Plot upon	179	DOUBL DLR	IV.1	444
Maskwell:	Why, I'll tell my Lord, I laid this Plot with you,	193	DOUBL DLR	V.1	217
Maskwell:	But first I must instruct my little Levite, there is no				
	Plot,	194	DOUBL DLR	V.1	267
Maskwell:	that all this seeming Plot that I have laid, has been to	199	DOUBL DLR	V.1	437
Maskwell:	upon the Rack; and made discov'ry of her last Plot: I hope	199	DOUBL DLR	V.1	462
Lord Touch:	I'll add to my Plot too,--let us haste to find out, and	200	DOUBL DLR	V.1	486
	And for the thinking Party there's a Plot.	213	FOR LOVE	PRO.	30
Scandal:	And have you given your Master a hint of their Plot	288	FOR LOVE	IV.1	479
Sr Sampson:	in Winter? Not at all--It's a Plot to undermine Cold	308	FOR LOVE	V.1	405
Sr Sampson:	Where's your Plot, Sir? and your Contrivance	311	FOR LOVE	V.1	537
	Some Plot we think he has, and some new Thought;	393	WAY WORLD	PRO.	29
Millamant:	Plot like to speed--No.	422	WAY WORLD	II.1	483
Foible:	(says he) what you are a hatching some Plot (says he) you	427	WAY WORLD	III.1	95
Marwood:	prevent their Plot,--the half of Millamant's Fortune is	442	WAY WORLD	III.1	641
Witwoud:	A plot, a plot, to get rid of the Knight,--your	454	WAY WORLD	IV.1	381
Foible:	plot, swear, swear it.--	460	WAY WORLD	IV.1	596
Foible:	Effect, Mr. Fainall laid this Plot to arrest Waitwell,				
	when he	464	WAY WORLD	V.1	71
Millamant:	Plot, as you were misinform'd; I have laid my commands	470	WAY WORLD	V.1	327

Plots (3)

Maskwell:	execution of all her Plots? Ha, ha, ha, by Heaven it's true;	149	DOUBL DLR	II.1	398
Lord Touch:	we don't presently prevent the Execution of their plots;--	200	DOUBL DLR	V.1	477
Manuel:	And plots in Private with this hellish Moor.	367	M. BRIDE	IV.1	235

Plumb (1)

Mellefont:	your mouth with a plumb.	156	DOUBL DLR	III.1	222

Plumes (1)

Heartwell:	With gawdy Plumes and gingling Bells made proud,	112	OLD BATCH	V.2	186

Plump (1)

Araminta:	I warrant, plump, Cherry-cheek'd Country-Girls.	84	OLD BATCH	IV.3	27

Plunder (3)

Bellmour:	enrich'd himself with the plunder of a few Oaths;--and	47	OLD BATCH	I.1	370
Ben:	He lov'd her more than Plunder;	274	FOR LOVE	III.1	770
Heli:	Among the Troops who thought to share the Plunder,	351	M. BRIDE	III.1	65

Plung'd (2)

Alonzo:	And on the instant, plung'd it in his Breast.	373	M. BRIDE	V.1	27
Gonsalez:	For thee I've plung'd into this Sea of Sin;	378	M. BRIDE	V.2	84

Plunge (2)

Heartwell:	and in some raving fit, be led to plunge my self into that	62	OLD BATCH	III.1	68
Silvia:	may depend upon our skill to save us at a plunge, though	75	OLD BATCH	III.2	152

Ply (2)

Mellefont:	Ply her close, and by and by clap a Billet doux into her	158	DOUBL DLR	III.1	315
Scandal:	He begins to Chuckle;--ply him close, or he'l	224	FOR LOVE	I.1	292

Plyant (22)

Brisk:	Touchwood swears, he'll Disinherit you, and Sir Paul Plyant	128	DOUBL DLR	I.1	54
Careless:	her Father Sir Paul Plyant, come to settle the				
	Writings, this	129	DOUBL DLR	I.1	81
Mellefont:	my Lady Plyant all this Evening, that my Pious Aunt	130	DOUBL DLR	I.1	126
	(Enter Lord Touchwood, Lord Froth, Sir Paul Plyant,	131	DOUBL DLR	I.1	170
Maskwell:	Plyant?	137	DOUBL DLR	I.1	407
	(Enter Sir Paul Plyant and Lady Plyant.)	143	DOUBL DLR	II.1	194
Sir Paul:	Hold your self Contented, my Lady Plyant,--I	144	DOUBL DLR	II.1	206
Sir Paul:	Lady Plyant shall Command Sir Paul; but when I am	144	DOUBL DLR	II.1	222
	(Lady Plyant and Sir Paul come up to Mellefont.)	145	DOUBL DLR	II.1	241
Mellefont:	Contrivance to perswade my Lady Plyant to this	149	DOUBL DLR	II.1	410
Lady Touch:	Plyant, if he refuse his Daughter upon this Provocation?	150	DOUBL DLR	III.1	2
Lord Touch:	Plyant has a large Eye, and wou'd centre every thing in	151	DOUBL DLR	III.1	6
	(Enter Sir Paul and Lady Plyant.)	159	DOUBL DLR	III.1	320
Careless:	Lady Plyant is not thought of--if that can ever be.	160	DOUBL DLR	III.1	377

Plyant   (continued)
```
    Sir Paul:    'Gads so--Wife, Wife, my Lady Plyant, I have a   . . .   163   DOUBL DLR  III.1   489
                 (Exit Careless and Lady Plyant.)         .   163   DOUBL DLR  III.1   496
                 (Enter Careless and Lady Plyant.)        .   169   DOUBL DLR  IV.1     68
                 (Enter Lady Plyant, and Careless.)       .   177   DOUBL DLR  IV.1    389
    Sir Paul:    polluted by Foreign Iniquity? O my Lady Plyant, you were  .   179   DOUBL DLR  IV.1    430
                 (Enter Lady Plyant.)      . . .   179   DOUBL DLR  IV.1    436
                 (Enter Lady Plyant, Careless, Cynthia.)   . . . . .   202   DOUBL DLR   V.1    544
Plyant's (1)
    Careless:    Mellefont, get out o'th' way, my Lady Plyant's   . . . .   157   DOUBL DLR  III.1   264
Plyants (1)
    Sir Paul:    Sons nor Grandsons? Must the Family of the Plyants be   . .   171   DOUBL DLR  IV.1    137
Pocket (13)    see Under-Petticoat-Pocket
    Sir Joseph:  pocket at present.   . . . . . . . . . . . . . .    50   OLD BATCH  II.1    106
    Bellmour:    I have Directions in my Pocket, which agree with   . . .    81   OLD BATCH  IV.2     31
    Vainlove:    Pardon in his pocket.   . . . . . . . . . . . .    87   OLD BATCH  IV.3    155
    Bellmour:    with the Practice of Piety in my Pocket, I had never been  .   92   OLD BATCH  IV.4    110
    Scandal:     Praise for Praise, and a Critick picking his Pocket. I have   233   FOR LOVE   I.1    652
    Sr Sampson:  but a Groat in his Pocket, may have a Stomach capable   . .   245   FOR LOVE   II.1    353
    Ben:         Mony in his Pocket--May-hap I may not have so   . . . .   273   FOR LOVE  III.1    734
    Sr Sampson:  need any body hold it?--I'll put it up in my Pocket,   . .   281   FOR LOVE   IV.1    231
    Sr Sampson:  Pocket.) There Val: it's safe enough, Boy--But thou   .   282   FOR LOVE   IV.1    233
    Foible:      I wou'd put her Ladyship's Picture in my Pocket to shew   .   423   WAY WORLD  II.1    521
    Lady Wish:   ne'er a Brass-Thimble clinking in thy Pocket with a bit   .   425   WAY WORLD III.1     31
    Fainall:     but I'le be hang'd if she did not put Pam in her Pocket.   .   442   WAY WORLD III.1  V654
    Waitwell:    India? I have twenty Letters in my Pocket from him, in   .   461   WAY WORLD  IV.1    607
Pocket-Glass (2)
    Belinda:     (Pulls out a Pocket-Glass.)    . . . .    83   OLD BATCH  IV.3      6
                 (Takes out a Pocket-Glass, and locks in it.)   . . . . .   134   DOUBL DLR   I.1    290
Pocket-glass (1)
                 (Gives him a Pocket-glass.)    . . . .   140   DOUBL DLR  II.1     75
Pocket-Tipstaves (1)
    Jeremy:      a Man down with Pocket-Tipstaves,--And there's   . . .   221   FOR LOVE   I.1    204
Pockets (1)
    Jeremy:      light as his Pockets; and any body that has a mind to a   .   276   FOR LOVE   IV.1     35
Poem (4)
    Brisk:       an Hercick Poem.   . . . . . . . . . . . . . .   141   DOUBL DLR  II.1    119
    Brisk:       Communicating the Poem.   . . . . . . . . . . .   142   DOUBL DLR  II.1    133
    Brisk:       Poem, had not you better call him a Charioteer? Charioteer   163   DOUBL DLR  III.1   506
    Lady Froth:  to the whole Poem.   . . . . . . . . . . . . .   165   DOUBL DLR  III.1   555
Poems (4)
    Lady Froth:  Lampoons, Plays, or Heroick Poems.   . . . . . . .   138   DOUBL DLR  II.1     17
    Foible:      Verses and Poems,--So long as it was not a Bible-Oath,   .   464   WAY WORLD   V.1     99
    Foible:      Poems,--So long as it was not a Bible-Oath,    . . . .   464   WAY WORLD   V.1  V  99
    Mincing:     token, you swore us to Seorosie upon Messalinas's Poems.  .   474   WAY WORLD   V.1    488
Poet (19)
                 But on my Conscience he's a bashful Poet;   . . . . . .    35   OLD BATCH  PRO.    15
                 So fares it with our Poet; and I'm sent    . . . . . .   113   OLD BATCH  EPI.     5
    Sir Paul:    the Poet says.--    . . . . . . . . . . . . . .   144   DOUBL DLR  II.1    226
                 This time, the Poet owns the bold Essay,   . . . . . .   214   FOR LOVE   PRO.    41
    Jeremy:      won't have a Friend left in the World, if you turn Poet   .   218   FOR LOVE   I.1     86
    Jeremy:      his Proportion, with carrying a Poet upon Tick, to visit   .   218   FOR LOVE   I.1     99
    Jeremy:      him from turning Poet.   . . . . . . . . . . . .   219   FOR LOVE   I.1    124
    Scandal:     Poet! He shall turn Soldier first, and rather depend   .   219   FOR LOVE   I.1    125
    Scandal:     Old Woman, any thing but Poet; a Modern Poet is worse,   .   220   FOR LOVE   I.1    146
    Mrs Frail:   Poet?   . . . . . . . . . . . . . . . . . .   233   FOR LOVE   I.1    650
    Scandal:     Yes, I have a Poet weighing Words, and selling   . . . .   233   FOR LOVE   I.1    651
    Valentine:   O the Devil, what damn'd Costive Poet has given   . . . .   255   FOR LOVE  III.1    73
    Jeremy:      that was so near turning Poet yesterday morning, can't be   276   FOR LOVE   IV.1     4
    Jeremy:      Chymist, Lover, or Poet in Europe.   . . . . . . .   295   FOR LOVE   IV.1    740
                 Of a damn'd Poet, and departed Muse!   . . . . . .   385   M. BRIDE   EPI.    12
                 Small Hope our Poet from these Prospects draws;   . . . .   385   M. BRIDE   EPI.    27
                 Give you one Instance of a Passive Poet.   . . . . . .   393   WAY WORLD  PRO.    38
    Witwoud:     from one Poet to another. And what's worse, 'tis as sure a   401   WAY WORLD  I.1     247
Poet's (2)
                 The Poet's sure he shall some comfort find:   . . . .   125   DOUBL DLR  PRO.    32
                 For that damn'd Poet's spar'd who dams a Brother,   . .   323   M. BRIDE   PRO.    31
Poetry (5)
    Heartwell:   here Silvia, here are Songs and Dances, Poetry and Musick   .   72   OLD BATCH III.2    34
    Lady Touch:  Alas he raves! talks very Poetry! for Heavens   . . .   186   DOUBL DLR  IV.2    127
    Sir Paul:    Nay, only about Poetry, I suppose, my Lord;   . . . .   201   DOUBL DLR   V.1    512
    Jeremy:      Young Maids, not to prefer Poetry to good Sense; or   .   219   FOR LOVE   I.1    113
    Mincing:     with Poetry, it sits so pleasant the next Day as any Thing,   420   WAY WORLD  II.1    373
Poets (20)
                 Where, Poets beg'd a Blessing, from their Guests.   . . .    35   OLD BATCH  PRO.     4
                 Such are the Tryals, Poets make of Plays:   . . . . .   125   DOUBL DLR  PRO.     7
    Lord Froth:  and mortify the Poets; the Fellows grow so Conceited,   .   133   DOUBL DLR  I.1     228
    Lord Froth:  and mortifie the Poets; the Fellows grow so Conceited,   .   133   DOUBL DLR  I.1   V228
                 Could Poets but forsee how Plays would take,   . . . .   204   DOUBL DLR  EPI.     1
                 But Poets run much greater hazards far,   . . . . .   204   DOUBL DLR  EPI.     8
                 Thus poor Poets the Favour are deny'd,   . . . . . .   204   DOUBL DLR  EPI.    29
                 Poor Poets thus the Favour are deny'd,   . . . . . .   204   DOUBL DLR  EPI.  V 29
                 As Asses Thistles, Poets mumble Wit,   . . . . . .   214   FOR LOVE   PRO.    35
    Valentine:   Ages; these Poets and Philosophers whom you naturally   .   217   FOR LOVE   I.1     37
    Valentine:   You are as inveterate against our Poets, as if your   . .   220   FOR LOVE   I.1    151
                 It's like what I have heard our Poets tell us:   . . . .   315   FOR LOVE   EPI.     6
                 In such like Prophecies were Poets skill'd,   . . . .   323   M. BRIDE   PRO.    13
                 To please and move, has been our Poets Theme,   . . . .   323   M. BRIDE   PRO.    35
                 Sure scribbling Fools, call'd Poets, fare the worst.   . .   393   WAY WORLD  PRO.     2
                 Poets are Bubbles, by the Town drawn in,   . . . . .   393   WAY WORLD  PRO.    11
                 Should Grants to Poets made, admit Resumption:   . . . .   393   WAY WORLD  PRO.    19
    Mrs Fain:    Millamant, and the Poets.   . . . . . . . . . .   446   WAY WORLD  IV.1    56
                 Then, all bad Poets we are sure are Foes,   . . . . .   479   WAY WORLD  EPI.     9
                 So Poets oft, do in one Piece expose   . . . . . . .   479   WAY WORLD  EPI.    35
Point (11)    see Cuckolds-point
    Lord Touch:  in't with my Swords point.   . . . . . . . . . .   186   DOUBL DLR  IV.2    120
```

Point   (continued)
		PAGE	TITLE	ACT.SC	LINE
Singer-V:	Love hates to center in a Point assign'd,	293	FOR LOVE	IV.1	660
Heli:	Occasion will not fail to point out Ways	352	M. BRIDE	III.1	97
Zara:	So ripe, to point at the particular Men.	364	M. BRIDE	IV.1	147
Zara:	Confess, and point the Path which thou hast crept.	375	M. BRIDE	V.1	110
	(They point at the Bowl on the Ground.)	382	M. BRIDE	V.2	252
Almeria:	And point! what mean they; Ha! a Cup. O well	382	M. BRIDE	V.2	253
	(They point to the other Cup.)	382	M. BRIDE	V.2	257
Almeria:	Ha! point again? 'tis there, and full I hope.	382	M. BRIDE	V.2	258
Mirabell:	Point of the Compass to which they cannot turn, and by	423	WAY WORLD	II.1	496
Mrs Fain:	pursue your Point, now or never.	446	WAY WORLD	IV.1	72

Point's (1)
		PAGE	TITLE	ACT.SC	LINE
Fainall:	So, so, why this point's clear,--Well how do we	443	WAY WORLD	III.1	697

Pointed (1)
		PAGE	TITLE	ACT.SC	LINE
	Arm'd with keen Satyr, and with pointed Wit,	35	OLD BATCH	PRO.	7

'pointed (1)
		PAGE	TITLE	ACT.SC	LINE
Gonsalez:	One 'pointed Hour should be Alphonso's Loss,	333	M. BRIDE	I.1	305

Pointing (1)
		PAGE	TITLE	ACT.SC	LINE
Leonora:	Who by their pointing seem to mark this Place.	344	M. BRIDE	II.2	V193

Points (5)
		PAGE	TITLE	ACT.SC	LINE
Heartwell:	There stands my North, and thither my Needle points	63	OLD BATCH	III.1	75
Mellefont:	Heaven she laughs, grins, points to your Back, she forks	186	DOUBL DLR	IV.2	131
Ben:	Mess you take in all the Points of the Compass, and	306	FOR LOVE	V.1	354
Osmyn-Alph:	And for some Purpose points out these Remembrances.	350	M. BRIDE	III.1	5
Lady Wish:	that he may be entertain'd in all points with	445	WAY WORLD	IV.1	12

Poison (5)   see Poyson
		PAGE	TITLE	ACT.SC	LINE
Araminta:	There's poison in every thing you touch.--	88	OLD BATCH	IV.3	181
Lord Touch:	Ha! O poison to my Ears! what do I hear!	198	DOUBL DLR	V.1	427
	To poison Plays, I see some where they sit,	385	M. BRIDE	EPI.	7
Lady Wish:	Smells! he would poison a Tallow-Chandler	456	WAY WORLD	IV.1	436
Waitwell:	and Poison me,--and I wou'd willingly starve him	458	WAY WORLD	IV.1	501

Policy (4)
		PAGE	TITLE	ACT.SC	LINE
Maskwell:	had never favour'd, but through Revenge and Policy.	136	DOUBL DLR	I.1	357
Almeria:	But doubly thou, who could'st alone have Policy,	370	M. BRIDE	IV.1	380
Gonsalez:	My Policy, I ne'er suspected it:	371	M. BRIDE	IV.1	398
Fainall:	amongst other secrets of Matrimony and Policy, as they are	469	WAY WORLD	V.1	275

Polishing (2)
		PAGE	TITLE	ACT.SC	LINE
Sr Sampson:	rough, he wants a little Polishing.	262	FOR LOVE	III.1	320
Sr Sampson:	want a little Polishing: You must not take any thing ill,	262	FOR LOVE	III.1	339

Politick (1)
		PAGE	TITLE	ACT.SC	LINE
Setter:	Man of parts. That is without being politick, diligent, secret,	65	OLD BATCH	III.1	150

Politicks (1)
		PAGE	TITLE	ACT.SC	LINE
Valentine:	Probatum est. But what are you for? Religion or Politicks?	282	FOR LOVE	IV.1	255

Polluted (1)
		PAGE	TITLE	ACT.SC	LINE
Sir Paul:	polluted by Foreign Iniquity? O my Lady Plyant, you were	179	DOUBL DLR	IV.1	430

Pomp (2)
		PAGE	TITLE	ACT.SC	LINE
Gonsalez:	Is entring now, in Martial Pomp the Pallace.	331	M. BRIDE	I.1	226
Manuel:	That had our Pomp, been with your Presence grac'd,	335	M. BRIDE	I.1	389

Pompous (1)
		PAGE	TITLE	ACT.SC	LINE
Almeria:	Or pompous Phrase; the Pageantry of Souls.	332	M. BRIDE	I.1	249

Pond (2)
		PAGE	TITLE	ACT.SC	LINE
Valentine:	the reflection of Heav'n in a Pond, and he that leaps at	292	FOR LOVE	IV.1	636
Mirabell:	Feathers, and meet me at One a Clock by Rosamond's Pond.	398	WAY WORLD	I.1	130

Pond'rous (1)
		PAGE	TITLE	ACT.SC	LINE
Almeria:	To bear aloft its arch'd and pond'rous Roof,	339	M. BRIDE	II.1	61

Ponder (2)
		PAGE	TITLE	ACT.SC	LINE
Gonsalez:	But 'tis not yet the time to ponder, or	379	M. BRIDE	V.2	124
Gonsalez:	But 'tis no time to ponder, or	379	M. BRIDE	V.2	V124

Pontack's (1)
		PAGE	TITLE	ACT.SC	LINE
Tattle:	the Drawers at Locket's, Pontack's, the Rummer, Spring	257	FOR LOVE	III.1	157

Ponyard (3)
		PAGE	TITLE	ACT.SC	LINE
Lady Touch:	Anger melts. (weeps) Here, take this Ponyard, for my very	198	DOUBL DLR	V.1	402
Alonzo:	Which done, he drew a Ponyard from his side,	373	M. BRIDE	V.1	26
Gonsalez:	In whose Hearts Blood this Ponyard yet is warm.	377	M. BRIDE	V.2	42

Pooh (15)
		PAGE	TITLE	ACT.SC	LINE
Sir Joseph:	Say: Pooh, Pox, I've enough to say,--never	85	OLD BATCH	IV.3	72
Brisk:	Pooh, ha, ha, ha, I know you envy me. Spite, proud	128	DOUBL DLR	I.1	25
Mellefont:	Pooh, pooh, nothing in the World but his design	131	DOUBL DLR	I.1	155
Brisk:	Pooh, my Lord, his Voice goes for nothing.--I	134	DOUBL DLR	I.1	276
Sir Paul:	all this for? Pooh, here's a joke, indeed--why, where's	192	DOUBL DLR	V.1	186
Tattle:	Pooh, I know Madam Drab has made her Brags in	227	FOR LOVE	I.1	419
Tattle:	Pooh, pooh, nothing at all, I only rally'd with you	228	FOR LOVE	I.1	445
Mrs Frail:	Pooh, No I thank you, I have enough to do to	232	FOR LOVE	I.1	596
Mrs Frail:	Pooh, this is all Invention. Have you ne're a	233	FOR LOVE	I.1	649
Mrs Frail:	Pooh, here's a Clutter--why should it reflect	247	FOR LOVE	II.1	435
Tattle:	Pooh, Pox, you must not say yes already; I shan't care	251	FOR LOVE	II.1	604
Scandal:	Pooh, pox, this proves nothing.	257	FOR LOVE	III.1	152
Scandal:	Pooh, this proves nothing.	257	FOR LOVE	III.1	V152

Poor (91)
		PAGE	TITLE	ACT.SC	LINE
Bellmour:	Poor Rogue. Any hour of the day or night will serve her--	40	OLD BATCH	I.1	116
Sharper:	Say you so? faith I am as poor as a Chymist and	46	OLD BATCH	I.1	347
Sir Joseph:	Poor Gentleman--by the Lord Harry I'le stay no	48	OLD BATCH	II.1	25
Belinda:	that an absolute Lover would have concluded the poor	55	OLD BATCH	II.2	28
Araminta:	Rather poor silly Idols of your own making, which,	58	OLD BATCH	II.2	146
Musician:	Poor, old, repenting Delia said,	59	OLD BATCH	II.2	191
Bellmour:	poor George, thou art i'th right, thou hast sold thy self to	63	OLD BATCH	III.1	89
Lucy:	Of thy most vile Cogitations--Thou poor, Conceited	65	OLD BATCH	III.1	167
Sir Joseph:	Ay ay, poor Fellow, he ventur'd fair for't.	67	OLD BATCH	III.1	247
Laetitia:	poor Heart, while it holds; which cannot be long, with	77	OLD BATCH	IV.1	92
Fondlewife:	made me weep--made poor Nykin weep--Nay come Kiss,	78	OLD BATCH	IV.1	117
Fondlewife:	buss poor Nykin--And I wont leave thee--I'le lose all first.	78	OLD BATCH	IV.1	118
Fondlewife:	He, he, he, wilt thou poor Fool? Then I will go,	79	OLD BATCH	IV.1	134
Fondlewife:	I wont be dealous--Poor Cocky, Kiss Nykin, Kiss	79	OLD BATCH	IV.1	135
Belinda:	--Affront! Pshaw, how you're mistaken! The poor	84	OLD BATCH	IV.3	39
Laetitia:	been in such a fright, that I forgot to tell you, poor Mr.	91	OLD BATCH	IV.4	77

Poor   (continued)

		PAGE	TITLE	ACT.SC	LINE
Fondlewife:	Alack poor Man.--No, no,--you don't know the	91	OLD BATCH	IV.4	81
Fondlewife:	Good Lack! Good Lack!--I profess, the poor	91	OLD BATCH	IV.4	94
Lucy:	ruin'd my poor Mistress: You have made a Gap in her	98	OLD BATCH	V.1	48
Setter:	What have such poor Rogues as I to do with Reputation?	102	OLD BATCH	V.1	230
Belinda:	and poor, but in show. Nay, often, only Remains, which	106	OLD BATCH	V.1	375
Sir Paul:	poor Father,--and that would certainly have broke my	146	DOUBL DLR	II.1	280
Sir Paul:	I am mightily beholding to Providence--a poor	161	DOUBL DLR	III.1	414
Sir Paul:	I am mightily beholden to Providence--a poor	161	DOUBL DLR	III.1	V414
Sir Paul:	How does my Girl? come hither to thy Father, poor	162	DOUBL DLR	III.1	455
Lady Froth:	seen her these two hours.--The poor dear Creature	166	DOUBL DLR	III.1	613
Lady Froth:	--I swear, my Lord, you don't Love poor little Sapho	167	DOUBL DLR	III.1	614
Careless:	the Victory of your Eyes, while at your Feet your poor	170	DOUBL DLR	IV.1	87
Cynthia:	(aside). That my poor Father, should be so very silly.	172	DOUBL DLR	IV.1	194
Brisk:	while your Blockheads, like poor needy Scoundrels, are	175	DOUEL DLR	IV.1	301
Sir Paul:	were not for Providence, sure poor Sir Paul thy Heart	179	DOUBL DLR	IV.1	434
Sir Paul:	poor Sir Paul, I'm an Anabaptist, or a Jew, or what you	180	DOUBL DLR	IV.1	473
Lord Touch:	ha, I'll do't, where's Mellefont, my poor injured Nephew,--	200	DOUBL DLR	V.1	478
	Thus poor Poets the Favour are deny'd,	204	DOUBL DLR	EPI.	29
	Poor Poets thus the Favour are deny'd,	204	DOUBL DLR	EPI. V	29
	So, the poor Husbands of the Stage, who found	213	FOR LOVE	PRO.	7
Jeremy:	or any of these poor rich Rogues, teach you how to pay	217	FOR LOVE	I.1	27
Jeremy:	help me, I'm poor enough to be a Wit--But I was	217	FOR LOVE	I.1	41
Jeremy:	but your Prosperity; and now when you are poor, hate you	217	FOR LOVE	I.1	47
Valentine:	Well; and now I am poor, I have an opportunity to	217	FOR LOVE	I.1	49
Nurse:	home yet: Poor Child, I warrant she's fond o'seeing the	235	FOR LOVE	II.1	20
Angelica:	to write poor innocent Servants Names in Blood, about a	238	FOR LOVE	II.1	109
Foresight:	But come, be a good Girl, don't perplex your poor Uncle,	239	FOR LOVE	II.1	157
Sr Sampson:	rather eat a Pheasant, than a piece of poor John; and smell,	245	FOR LOVE	II.1	369
Mrs Fore:	Poor innocent! you don't know that there's a	247	FOR LOVE	II.1	450
Mrs Fore:	me, poor Child.	265	FOR LOVE	III.1	445
Scandal:	it: But Dreaming is the poor retreat of a lazy, hopeless,	275	FOR LOVE	III.1	815
Jeremy:	just as he was poor for want of Money; his Head is e'en as	276	FOR LOVE	IV.1	34
Jeremy:	sound, poor Gentleman. He is indeed here, Sir, and not	279	FOR LOVE	IV.1	125
Jeremy:	his Skull's crack'd, poor Gentleman; he's stark mad, Sir.	279	FOR LOVE	IV.1	138
Ben:	O Lord, O Lord, she's mad, poor Young Woman, Love	286	FOR LOVE	IV.1	403
Mrs Frail:	start of me; and I the poor forsaken Maid am left				
	complaining	287	FOR LOVE	IV.1	456
Valentine:	Poor Creature! Is your Wife of Covent-Garden	289	FOR LOVE	IV.1	516
Valentine:	Alas, poor Man; his Eyes are sunk, and his Hands	289	FOR LOVE	IV.1	519
Tattle:	of a poor decay'd Creature--Here, a compleat and lively	291	FOR LOVE	IV.1	581
Valentine:	thou can'st not lie with my Wife? I am very poor, and	292	FOR LOVE	IV.1	626
Angelica:	Mercy on me, how he talks! poor Valentine!	294	FOR LOVE	IV.1	705
Jeremy:	comply with any thing to please him. Poor Lady, I'm	302	FOR LOVE	V.1	202
Tattle:	her, poor Creature--I swear I do it hardly so much in	302	FOR LOVE	V.1	207
Foresight:	O my poor Niece, my poor Niece, is she gone too?	306	FOR LOVE	V.1	347
Tattle:	O, the Two most unfortunate poor Creatures in the	309	FOR LOVE	V.1	442
Mrs Frail:	Ah Mr. Tattle and I, poor Mr. Tattle and I are--	309	FOR LOVE	V.1	445
Tattle:	Nor I--But poor Mrs. Frail and I are--	309	FOR LOVE	V.1	447
Tattle:	Poor Woman! Gad I'm sorry for her too; for I have no	309	FOR LOVE	V.1	466
Valentine:	I thought I had Reasons--But it was a poor	311	FOR LOVE	V.1	507
	Poor Actors thresh such empty Sheafs of Straw?	323	M. BRIDE	PRO.	18
Almeria:	For 'tis the poor Prerogative of Greatness,	328	M. BRIDE	I.1	96
Almeria:	For 'tis, alas, the poor Prerogative of Greatness,	328	M. BRIDE	I.1 V	96
Almeria:	The dire collected Dews, on my poor Head;	330	M. BRIDE	I.1	160
Leonora:	The poor Remains of good Anselmo rest;	340	M. BRIDE	II.2	7
Osmyn-Alph:	O that's the greatest Grief--I am so poor,	346	M. BRIDE	II.2	270
Osmyn-Alph:	Which shews me poor and Bankrupt even in Hopes.	347	M. BRIDE	II.2	V290
Almeria:	Thou canst not! thy poor Arms are bound and strive	356	M. BRIDE	III.1	266
Osmyn-Alph:	Distress, Heav'n will repay; all Thanks are poor.	359	M. BRIDE	III.1	404
Osmyn-Alph:	Distress'd, Heav'n will repay; all Thanks are poor.	359	M. BRIDE	III.1	V404
Manuel:	Into how poor and mean a thing, a King descends;	373	M. BRIDE	V.1	40
Manuel:	Into how poor a thing, a King decends;	373	M. BRIDE	V.1 V	40
Zara:	I have not leisure, now, to take so poor	375	M. BRIDE	V.1	123
Witwoud:	being in Embrio; and if it shou'd come to Life; poor	408	WAY WORLD	I.1	488
Marwood:	Poor dissembling!--O that--Well,	416	WAY WORLD	II.1	231
Mrs Fain:	So, if my poor Mother is caught in a Contract,	417	WAY WORLD	II.1	296
Mrs Fain:	I see but one poor empty Sculler; and he tows	418	WAY WORLD	II.1	326
Millamant:	Ay, poor Mincing tift and tift all the morning.	419	WAY WORLD	II.1	370
Foible:	--Poor Sir Rowland, I say.	427	WAY WORLD	III.1	78
Marwood:	rest of him. Poor simple Fiend! Madam Marwood has a	431	WAY WORLD	III.1	239
Millamant:	Poor Mirabell! his Constancy to me has quite destroy'd his	433	WAY WORLD	III.1	336
Millamant:	O, I should think I was poor and had nothing to	449	WAY WORLD	IV.1	167
Foible:	been deluded by him, then how shou'd I a poor Ignorant,	463	WAY WORLD	V.1	28
Mrs Fain:	Poor Foible, what's the matter?	463	WAY WORLD	V.1	61
Foible:	be had to a Justice, and put to Bridewell to beat Hemp, poor	463	WAY WORLD	V.1	63

Poorly (1)

Zara:	Thou canst not mean so poorly, as thou talk'st.	348	M. BRIDE	II.2	331

Pope (2)

Valentine:	and yet we'll Marry one another in spite of the Pope--	290	FOR LOVE	IV.1	559
Lady Wish:	pardons to ask than the Pope distributes in the Year of	457	WAY WORLD	IV.1	486

Popery (3)

Angelica:	Nay, I'll declare how you prophecy'd Popery was coming,	237	FOR LOVE	II.1	88
Sr Sampson:	Without Popery shou'd be landed in the West, or the	266	FOR LOVE	III.1	487
Sr Sampson:	Unless Popery shou'd be landed in the West, or the	266	FOR LOVE	III.1	V487

Poppy-Water (1)

Mirabell:	for Couslip-Wine, Poppy-Water and all Dormitives, those I	452	WAY WORLD	IV.1	275

Poppy-water (1)

Valentine:	Poppy-water, that he may fold his Ogling Tail, and	290	FOR LOVE	IV.1	551

Populace (1)

Gonsalez:	The swarming Populace, spread every Wall,	332	M. BRIDE	I.1	238

Pore (1)

Valentine:	may pore till you spoil your Eyes, and not improve your	297	FOR LOVE	IV.1	803

Pores (1)

Careless:	through all my Pores, and will to Morrow wash me for	170	DOUEL DLR	IV.1	116

Poring (1)
  Sr Sampson: up old Star-Gazer. Now is he poring upon the Ground for . 265 FOR LOVE III.1 466
Porpoise (1)
  Mrs Frail: Why canst thou love, Porpoise? . . . . 287 FOB LOVE IV.1 433
Port (4) see Sally-Fort
  Bellmour: Anchor in the Port till this time, but the Enemy surpriz'd 96 OLD BATCH V.1 6
  Ben: about from Port to Port, and from Land to Land: I could . 261 FOR LOVE III.1 310
  Manuel: And sullen Port, glooms downward with his Eyes; . . . 336 M. BRIDE I.1 426
Portbound (1)
  Ben: never abide to be Portbound as we call it: Now a man that 261 FOR LOVE III.1 311
Portend (1)
  Foresight: Mercy on us, what do these Lunacies portend? . . . . 305 FOR LOVE V.1 302
Portent (1)
  Foresight: are mad to day--It is of evil portent, and bodes Mischief 236 FOR LOVE II.1 47
Porter (2)
  Jeremy: Porter, worn out with pimping, and carrying Billet doux . 218 FOR LOVE I.1 96
  Witwoud: Porter. Now that is a Fault. . . . . 404 WAY WORLD I.1 342
Porters (3)
  Jeremy: and Songs; not like other Porters for Hire, but for the
         Jests . . . . 218 FOR LOVE I.1 97
  Tattle: Maids at the Chocolate-Houses, all the Porters of Pall-Mall 257 FOR LOVE III.1 155
  Tattle: Maids at the Chocolate-Houses, all the Porters at Pall-Mall 257 FOB LOVE III.1 V155
Portion (6)
  Heartwell: quotha! I hope in Heaven I have a greater portion of Grace, 44 OLD BATCH I.1 295
  Laetitia: considerable Portion. . . . . 94 OLD BATCH IV.4 204
  Sir Paul: of thee, but thy Portion, why he's in Love with my Wife; . 146 DOUBL DLR II.1 278
  Mellefont: Portion, Settlements and Joyntures. . . . . . . 168 DOUEL DLR IV.1 30
  Mrs Frail: And tho' I have a good Portion; you know one . . . 273 FOR LOVE III.1 723
         No Portion for her own she has to spare, ... 393 WAY WORLD PRO. 9
Portions (1)
  Almeria: And Woe shou'd be in equal Portions dealt.   . . . . 356 M. BRIDE III.1 288
Portrait (1)
         And shining Features in one Portrait blend, ... 479 WAY WORLD EPI. 33
Pos'd (1)
  Singer-F: Apollo was mute, and had like t' have been pos'd, . . 259 FOR LOVE III.1 205
Position (1)
  Sir Paul: Position of taking up Arms by my Authority, against my . 178 DOUEL DLR IV.1 413
Positive (4)
  Mirabell: May be you think him too positive? . . . . 403 WAY WORLD I.1 322
  Witwoud: No, no, his being positive is an Incentive to Argument, . 403 WAY WORLD I.1 323
  Petulant: Yes, it positively must, upon Proof positive. . . . 435 WAY WORLD III.1 408
  Witwoud: Ay, upon Proof positive it must; but upon Proof . . . 435 WAY WORLD III.1 409
Positively (7)
  Mrs Fore: You deny it positively to my Face. . . . . 247 FOR LOVE II.1 458
  Mrs Frail: deny it positively to Your Face then. . . . . . . 247 FOB LOVE II.1 462
  Witwoud: Not positively must--But it may--It may. . . . . 435 WAY WORLD III.1 407
  Petulant: Yes, it positively must, upon Proof positive. . . . 435 WAY WORLD III.1 408
  Millamant: more than Impossible--positively Mirabell, I'll lie a Bed in 449 WAY WORLD IV.1 190
  Millamant: positively I won't be call'd Names. . . . . . . 450 WAY WORLD IV.1 195
  Fainall: must be agreed unto, and that positively. Lastly, I will be 469 WAY WORLD V.1 277
Possess (2)
  Maskwell: Compose your self, You shall possess and ruin . . . . 137 DOUEL DLR I.1 V402
  Zara: Sparkling Desire, and trembling to possess. . . . . 348 M. BRIDE II.2 344
Possess'd (3)
  Belinda: is to be possess'd--Tis in the Head, the Heart, the . . 54 OLD BATCH II.2 13
  Fondlewife: hath possess'd the Lad--I say I will tarry at home--Varlet. 75 OLD BATCH IV.1 17
  Mellefont: Why the Woman is possess'd-- . . . . 156 DOUBL DLR III.1 236
Possessing (1)
  Angelica: possessing of a Wish, discovers the Folly of the Chase. . 296 FOR LOVE IV.1 788
Possession (7)
  Maskwell: earnest of that Bargain, to have full and free possession of 156 DOUBL DLR III.1 229
  Maskwell: me out a Villain, settled in possession of a fair Estate,
         and . . . . 190 DOUEL DLR V.1 86
  Marwood: but it shall never rust in my Possession. . . . . . 410 WAY WORLD II.1 17
  Mirabell: in her Possession. . . . . 418 WAY WORLD II.1 302
  Waitwell: --and till I have the possession of your adoreable Person, I 457 WAY WORLD IV.1 491
  Fainall: in your Possession: And which she has forfeited (as will . 469 WAY WORLD V.1 280
  Fainall: possession. . . . . 473 WAY WORLD V.1 449
Possessions (1)
  Sr Sampson: Possessions--Ah! Baggage--I warrant you for . . . . 301 FOR LOVE V.1 153
Possible (16)
  Sharper: Is it possible! Then I am happy to have obliged the . . 49 OLD BATCH II.1 72
  Cynthia: Indeed, Madam! Is it Possible your Ladyship could . . 138 DOUBL DLR II.1 1
  Mellefont: because it's possible we may lose; since we have Shuffled 142 DOUBL DLR II.1 160
  Lord Touch: as was possible; but he perseveres so in Villany, that she 182 DOUEL DLR IV.1 548
  Mellefont: which (if possible) are greater--Though she has all the . 186 DOUBL DLR IV.2 123
  Lord Touch: were it possible it shou'd be done this night. . . . 196 DOUBL DLR V.1 321
  Angelica: I swear I don't think 'tis possible. . . . . . . 255 FOB LOVE III.1 80
  Valentine: pursue her, and know her if it be possible, in spight of the 297 FOR LOVE IV.1 813
  Osmyn-Alph: If possible-- . . . . 359 M. BRIDE III.1 391
  Mirabell: Then 'tis possible he may be but half a Fool. . . . 402 WAY WORLD I.1 252
  Mrs Fain: Is it possible? Dost thou hate those Vipers . . . . 411 WAY WORLD II.1 43
  Foible: of his success. I wou'd be seen as little as possible to
         speak . . . . 430 WAY WORLD III.1 215
  Lady Wish: O Daughter, Daughter, Is it possible thou . . . . 465 WAY WORLD V.1 139
  Lady Wish: the most minute Particle of severe Vertue? Is it possible 465 WAY WORLD V.1 142
  Fainall: possible speed. In the mean while, I will go for the said 469 WAY WORLD V.1 294
  Lady Wish: generous at last! But it is not possible. Hearkee. I'll
         break . . . . 474 WAY WORLD V.1 463
Possibly (2)
  Sr Sampson: the Conveyance so worded, that nothing can possibly . . 308 FOR LOVE V.1 425
  Mirabell: as often as possibly I can. (Kisses her hand). Well, heav'n 477 WAY WORLD V.1 597
Post (2)
  Capt Bluff: Campagn, had a small Post there; but no matter for that-- 52 OLD BATCH II.1 196
  Mellefont: to spring under her Feet. But to my Post. . . . . . 183 DOUBL DLR IV.2 5

544

Power   (continued)
Mellefont:	our power.	168	DOUBL DLR	IV.1	22
Cynthia:	I would obey you to my power, Sir; but if I have	171	DOUBL DLR	IV.1	134
Lord Touch:	of his, and Fortune's Power, and for that thou art scrupulously	182	DOUBL DLR	IV.1	571
Lady Touch:	let me not hope forgiveness, 'twill ever be in your power	185	DOUBL DLR	IV.2	83
Maskwell:	so to be; By Heaven I believe you can controul her power,	187	DOUBL DLR	V.1	3
Lord Touch:	Authority--hereafter, you shall rule where I have Power.	189	DOUBL DLR	V.1	66
Maskwell:	my power.	190	DOUBL DLR	V.1	107
Sr Sampson:	Authority, no Correction, no Arbitrary Power; nothing	240	FOR LOVE	II.1	177
Mrs Fore:	power--And I can tell you one thing that falls out luckily	248	FOR LOVE	II.1	498
Angelica:	No; I suppose that is not in your Power; but you	255	FOR LOVE	III.1	94
Tattle:	Not in my Power, Madam! What does your Ladyship	256	FOR LOVE	III.1	96
Tattle:	Power?	256	FOR LOVE	III.1	98
Tattle:	I hope to be sav'd; I never had it in my Power to say any	256	FOR LOVE	III.1	101
Angelica:	in my Power nor Inclination; and if he can't be cur'd	277	FOR LOVE	IV.1	74
Angelica:	because I would have such an one in my Power; but I	299	FOR LOVE	V.1	75
Angelica:	Aye; But that is not in your Power, Sir Sampson; for	300	FOR LOVE	V.1	121
Almeria:	I might be his, beyond the Power of future Fate:	329	M. BRIDE	I.1	139
Zara:	A Queen; for what are Riches, Empire, Power,	347	M. BRIDE	II.2	315
Osmyn-Alph:	Ere Reason can be born: Reason, the Power	350	M. BRIDE	III.1	35
Heli:	The Captain influenc'd by Almeria's Power,	351	M. BRIDE	III.1	43
Osmyn-Alph:	You may be still deceiv'd; 'tis in my Power.	360	M. BRIDE	III.1	443
Gonsalez:	Is far from hence, beyond your Father's Power.	370	M. BRIDE	IV.1	377
Manuel:	That somewhere is repeated--I have power	374	M. BRIDE	V.1	54
Mirabell:	whole Design, and put it in your Power to ruin or advance	417	WAY WORLD	II.1	281
Mirabell:	Nature; your true Vanity is in the power of pleasing.	420	WAY WORLD	II.1	384
Millamant:	is one's Power, and when one parts with one's Cruelty,	420	WAY WORLD	II.1	386
Millamant:	one parts with one's Power; and when one has parted with	420	WAY WORLD	II.1	387
Mirabell:	your Power, to destroy your Lover--And then how	420	WAY WORLD	II.1	390
Witwoud:	long; pshaw, I was not in my own Power then. An Orphan,	440	WAY WORLD	III.1	557
Millamant:	Tho' thou do'st thine, employ'st the Power and Art.	447	WAY WORLD	IV.1	105
Fainall:	consider'd; I will only reserve to my self the Power to chuse	468	WAY WORLD	V.1	266

Powerful (5) see All-powerful
Sharper:	upon reflection, seems only an effect of a too powerful passion.	79	OLD BATCH	IV.1	157
Sir Paul:	Bottle would have been too powerful for me,--as	132	DOUBL DLR	I.1	179
Lord Froth:	find Champagne is powerful. I assure you, Sir Paul, I	132	DOUBL DLR	I.1	191
Lady Ply:	Nature. I know Love is powerful, and no body can help	148	DOUBL DLR	II.1	356
Millamant:	Wilfull grows very powerful, Egh! how he smells! I shall	456	WAY WORLD	IV.1	432

Powers (6)
Brisk:	O ye Powers! O my Lady Froth, my Lady Froth! My Lady	175	DOUBL DLR	IV.1	309
Osmyn-Alph:	To Earth, and nail me, where I stand, ye Powers;	341	M. BRIDE	II.2	47
Osmyn-Alph:	Rivit and nail me, where I stand, ye Powers;	341	M. BRIDE	II.2 V	47
Osmyn-Alph:	The Heav'nly Powers allot me; no, not you,	354	M. BRIDE	III.1	174
Manuel:	O, give me Patience, all ye Powers! no, rather,	373	M. BRIDE	V.1	35
Almeria:	Giv'n me again from Death! O all ye Powers	383	M. BRIDE	V.2	291

Pox (51) see Small-pox
Bellmour:	Pox o' Business--And so must Time, my	37	OLD BATCH	I.1	9
Bellmour:	Ay ay, pox Wisdom's nothing but a pretending to	37	OLD BATCH	I.1	19
Heartwell:	Pox I have pratled away my time--I hope you are	46	OLD BATCH	I.1	331
Lucy:	Now Poverty and the Pox light upon thee, for a	65	OLD BATCH	III.1	163
Setter:	. . . as a Clap is to the Pox.	66	OLD BATCH	III.1	V197
Heartwell:	Pox, how her Innocence torments and pleases me!	72	OLD BATCH	III.2	55
Heartwell:	pleased with you--And a Pox upon me for loving thee so	73	OLD BATCH	III.2	71
Sir Joseph:	Say: Pooh, Pox, I've enough to say,--never	85	OLD BATCH	IV.3	72
Bellmour:	Pox choak him, would his Horns were in his	89	OLD BATCH	IV.4	12
Fondlewife:	I'm afraid, 'tis the Flesh, thou Harlot. Deare, with the Pox.	92	OLD BATCH	IV.4	136
Bellmour:	Setter.) Pox take 'em, they stand just in my Way.	97	OLD BATCH	V.1	12
Heartwell:	O Pox; He's a Fanatick.	97	OLD BATCH	V.1	17
Bellmour:	That's as much as to say, The Pox take me.--Well	98	OLD BATCH	V.1	78
Vainlove:	Pox o' my sawcy Credulity.--If I have lost	100	OLD BATCH	V.1	125
Careless:	Where are the Women? Pox I'm weary of guzling,	127	DOUBL DLR	I.1	3
Brisk:	better, you or I. Pox, Man, when I say you spoil Company	128	DOUBL DLR	I.1	28
Maskwell:	enough. Pox I have lost all Appetite to her; yet she's a fine	155	DOUBL DLR	III.1	175
Maskwell:	Pox on't that a Man can't drink without quenching his	155	DOUBL DLR	III.1	185
Careless:	'Pox I can't get an Answer from her, that does not	157	DOUBL DLR	III.1	270
Mellefont:	Consideration or the fear of Repentance. Pox o'Fortune,	168	DOUBL DLR	IV.1	29
Brisk:	--Pox on't, why should I disparage my parts by	175	DOUBL DLR	IV.1	298
Jeremy:	--Ah Pox confound that Will's Coffee-House, it has	218	FOR LOVE	I.1	87
Valentine:	Pox on her, cou'd she find no other time to fling	221	FOR LOVE	I.1	207
Scandal:	Pox on him, I'll be gone.	225	FOR LOVE	I.1	362
Valentine:	Pox take 'em, their Conjunction bodes no good,	231	FOR LOVE	I.1	574
Valentine:	Pox take 'em, their Conjunction bodes me no good,	231	FOR LOVE	I.1	V574
Sr Sampson:	Brother Foresight, leave Superstition--Pox o'th' time;	240	FOR LOVE	II.1	196
Sr Sampson:	The Spleen, ha, ha, ha, a Pox confound you--	245	FOR LOVE	II.1	376
Tattle:	(aside). Frank, I Gad at least. What a Pox does Mrs.	251	FOR LOVE	II.1	591
Tattle:	Pooh, Pox, you must not say yes already; I shan't care	251	FOR LOVE	II.1	604
Tattle:	Pox take her; if she had staid two Minutes longer, I	253	FOR LOVE	III.1	17
Tattle:	O pox, Scandal, that was too far put--Never have	256	FOR LOVE	III.1	116
Scandal:	Pooh, pox, this proves nothing.	257	FOR LOVE	III.1	152
Tattle:	--Pox on't, now could I bite off my Tongue.	258	FOR LOVE	III.1	189
Scandal:	Pox on her, she has interrupted my Design--But	269	FOR LOVE	III.1	578
Sr Sampson:	A Pox confound your Similitudes, Sir--	279	FOR LOVE	IV.1	134
Sr Sampson:	Are we? A Pox o' your Prognostication--Why,	283	FOR LOVE	IV.1	279
Sr Sampson:	pox on't, that I that know the World, and Men and	283	FOR LOVE	IV.1	286
Tattle:	Pox on't, there's no coming off, now she has said	293	FOR LOVE	IV.1	679
Sr Sampson:	O Pox, outsides, outsides; a pize take 'em, meer	298	FOR LOVE	V.1	33
Sr Sampson:	risen in the State--But, a pox on't, his Wit run him	299	FOR LOVE	V.1	83
Tattle:	(aside). O Pox, how shall I get rid of this foolish Girl?	303	FOR LOVE	V.1	225
Tattle:	O Pox, that was Yesterday, Miss, that was a great	303	FOR LOVE	V.1	236
Tattle:	Look you there, I thought as much--pox on't, I	310	FOR LOVE	V.1	475
Tattle:	Easie! Pox on't, I don't believe I shall sleep to Night.	310	FOR LOVE	V.1	483

Precious   (continued)
Mellefont:	(aside). Incest! C my precious Aunt, and the Devil	. . . 146	DOUBL DLR	II.1	312
Heli:	The time's tco precicus to be spent in telling;	. . . 351	M. BRIDE	III.1	42
Marwood:	This is precious Fooling, if it wou'd pass, but	. . . 471	WAY WCRLD	V.1	354

Precipitated (1)
| Zara: | Precipitated Fires, and pour in sheets, | . . . . . 380 | M. BRIDE | V.2 V169 |

Precipitation (1)
| Lady Wish: | that invades me with some precipitation--You will oblige | . 457 | WAY WORLD | IV.1 | 468 |

Precise (2)
| Vainlove: | A kind of Mungril Zealot, sometimes very precise | . . 40 | OLD BATCH | I.1 | 106 |
| Setter: | precise Band, with a swinging lcng Spiritual Cloak, to | . 64 | OLD BATCH | III.1 | 124 |

Prediction (1)
| Valentine: | Prediction to thee, and thou shalt Prophesie;--I am | . . 288 | FOR LOVE | IV.1 | 487 |

Predominate (1)
| Sr Sampson: | not foresee that the Moon wou'd predominate, and my | . . 283 | FOR LCVE | IV.1 | 281 |

Prefer (1)
| Jeremy: | Young Maids, not to prefer Poetry to good Sense; or | . . 219 | FOR LOVE | I.1 | 113 |

Preferment (1)
| Waitwell: | her Preferment she forgets her self. | . . . . . . 424 | WAY WCRLD | II.1 | 551 |

Preferr'd (1)
| Jeremy: | which her Vanity had preferr'd tc Settlements, without a | . 219 | FOR LCVE | I.1 | 109 |

Preferring (1)
| Bellmour: | Merit, and preferring only those of interest, has made him | 47 | OLD BATCH | I.1 | 372 |

Preheminence (1)
| Manuel: | All Eyes, so by Preheminence of Soul | . . . . . . 336 | M. BRIDE | I.1 | 422 |

Prejudice (5)
Laetitia:	prejudice of her Reputation--You look as if you had	. . 82	OLD BATCH	IV.2	64
Tattle:	thing to a Lady's Prejudice in my Life--For as I was	. 256	FOR LOVE	III.1	102
	He wou'd not lose thro' Prejudice his Cause;	 324	M. BRIDE	PRO.	41
Mirabell:	Wcman's good Manners to her Prejudice; and think that	. . 397	WAY WCRLD	I.1	87
Mirabell:	much prejudice; it was an Innocent device; tho' I confess it	472	WAY WCRLD	V.1	384

Preliminary (1)
| Bellmour: | refuse to kiss a Lap-Dog, if it were preliminary to the Lips | 44 | OLD BATCH | I.1 | 261 |

Premeditated (1)
| Belinda: | My Denyal is premeditated like your Malice--Lard, | . . . 55 | OLD BATCH | II.2 | 50 |

Premeditation (1)
| Foresight: | of Bed backwards too this morning, without Premeditation; | 236 | FOR LCVE | II.1 | 32 |

Premises (1)
| Petulant: | matters conclude Premises,--If you are not handscm, | . . 454 | WAY WCRLD | IV.1 | 367 |

Premunire (2)
| Sharper: | your self into a Premunire, by trusting to that sign of a | 69 | OLD BATCH | III.1 | 304 |
| Lady Ply: | and Premunire! I'm all over in a Universal Agitation, I | . 178 | DOUBL DLR | IV.1 | 397 |

Prentice (3)
Ben:	my Father, I an't bound Prentice tc 'en:--so faith I	. 285	FOR LCVE	IV.1	370
Valentine:	and Stratagem. And the crcpt Prentice, that sweeps his	. 289	FOR LCVE	IV.1	508
Witwoud:	have been bound Frentice tc a Felt maker in Shrewsbury;	. 440	WAY WCRLD	III.1	561

Prentices (1)
| Marwood: | Temple, take Notes like Prentices at a Conventicle; and | . 467 | WAY WCRLD | V.1 | 225 |

Prepar'd (11)
Capt Bluff:	Fear him not,--I am prepar'd for him now; and he	. . 101	OLD BATCH	V.1	167
Lady Touch:	prepar'd.	 183	DOUBL DLR	IV.2	18
Lord Touch:	suddenly design'd--yet he says he had prepar'd my	. . . 197	DOUBL DLR	V.1	359
	Prepar'd, by just Decrees to stand, or fall.	. . . 324	M. BRIDE	PRO.	44
Almeria:	Nay, all the Pains that are prepar'd for thee:	 369	M. BRIDE	IV.1	310
Zara:	I came prepar'd to die, and see thee die--	 380	M. BRIDE	V.2 V165
Zara:	Nay, came prepar'd my self to give thee Death--	. . . 380	M. BRIDE	V.2 V166
Almeria:	And come prepar'd to yield my Throat--they shake	. . 382	M. BRIDE	V.2	250
Fainall:	the Instrument, are you prepar'd to sign?	 472	WAY WCRLD	V.1	415
Lady Wish:	If I were prepar'd; I am not Impowr'd. My	 472	WAY WORLD	V.1	416
Fainall:	single Beef-eater there? but I'm prepar'd for you; and	. 473	WAY WORLD	V.1	433

Preparation (1)
| Belinda: | You are so curious in the Preparation, that is, your | . . 106 | OLD BATCH | V.1 | 372 |

Preparative (1)
| Heartwell: | preparative, and what you mean for a Whet, turns the | . . 43 | OLD BATCH | I.1 | 244 |

Prepare (8)
Setter:	Rather prepare her for Confession, Sir by helping her	. . 64	OLD BATCH	III.1	132
Lucy:	I warrant you--Do you go and prepare your Bride.	. . . 97	OLD BATCH	V.1	21
Maskwell:	But it will prepare some thing else; and gain us leasure to	138	DOUBL DLR	I.1	418
Maskwell:	--Now to prepare my Lord to consent to this.--	 194	DOUBL DLR	V.1	266
Maskwell:	Cynthia, and my Chaplain will be ready, I'll prepare for	. 199	DOUBL DLR	V.1	463
Zara:	I will retire, and instantly prepare	 366	M. BRIDE	IV.1	191
Fainall:	to endear his pleasure, and prepare the Joy that follows,	444	WAY WORLD	III.1	716
Mrs Fain:	prepare to vcuch when I call her.	 465	WAY WCRLD	V.1	119

Prepared (1)
| Lady Touch: | disadvantage; besides, I find, my Lord, you are prepared | . 151 | DOUBL DLR | III.1 | 36 |

Preposterous (1)
| Marwood: | of Life because they once must leave us; is as preposterous, | 410 | WAY WCRLD | II.1 | 14 |

Prerogative (4)
Lady Ply:	--but though I may read all Letters first by Prerogative,	173	DOUBL DLR	IV.1	211
Almeria:	For 'tis the poor Prerogative of Greatness,	 328	M. BRIDE	I.1	96
Almeria:	For 'tis, alas, the poor Prerogative of Greatness,	. . . 328	M. BRIDE	I.1 V 96
Mirabell:	mens prerogative, and presume tc drink healths, or toste	. 451	WAY WCRLD	IV.1	270

Presage (1)
| | The Dearth of Wit they did so lcng presage, | . . . . 323 | M. BRIDE | PRO. | 15 |

Prescience (3)
Osmyn-Alph:	The Book of Prescience, he beheld this Day;	 353	M. BRIDE	III.1	133
Osmyn-Alph:	He in the Book of Prescience, he saw this Day;	. . . 353	M. BRIDE	III.1 V133
Selim:	Prescience is Heav'ns alone, not giv'n to Man.	 375	M. BRIDE	V.1	116

Prescrib'd (1)
| Fainall: | O, if you are prescrib'd Marriage, you shall be | . . . 468 | WAY WORLD | V.1 | 265 |

Presence (6)
Mellefont:	Maskwell, welcome, thy presence is a view of Land,	. . 148	DOUBL DLR	II.1	381
Scandal:	be occasion; for I fancy his Presence provokes him more.	. 280	FOR LOVE	IV.1	190
Manuel:	That had our Pomp, been with your Presence grac'd,	. . 335	M. BRIDE	I.1	389
Gonsalez:	The King's immediate Presence at their Head.	 378	M. BRIDE	V.2	104
Lady Wish:	Letter--I wou'd open it in your presence, because I	. . 460	WAY WCRLD	IV.1	570

Presence (continued)
 Millamant: to make a Resignation of it, in your Lady-ship's presence; 470 WAY WORLD V.1 331
Present (33)
 Sharper: He has need of such an excuse, considering the present . 44 OLD BATCH I.1 288
 Sir Joseph: pocket at present. . . . . 50 OLD BATCH II.1 106
 Sir Joseph: at present; I have lay'd it all out upon my Back. . . . 50 OLD BATCH II.1 112
 Sir Joseph: I don't know, but I'le present you-- . 51 OLD BATCH II.1 154
 Setter: in disgrace at present about a Kiss which he forced. You . 67 OLD BATCH III.1 225
 Heartwell: look like an Ass when thou art present; Wake for you, . . 73 OLD BATCH III.2 79
 Heartwell: look like an Ass when thou art present; Wake for thee, . 73 OLD BATCH III.2 V 79
 Bellmour: I have no such Intentions at present.--Prithee, . . . 100 OLD BATCH V.1 156
 Heartwell: You are the principal Cause of all my present Ills. . 109 OLD BATCH V.2 66
 Sharper: present Date hereof.--How say you? . . . 110 OLD BATCH V.2 88
 Maskwell: how can you? Is not all this present Heat owing to the . 137 DOUBL DLR I.1 386
 Maskwell: present, yet the reflection of it must needs be
   entertaining. . . . . 149 DOUBL DLR II.1 414
 Valentine: propos'd before, and I refus'd it; but the present
   impatience . . . 225 FOR LOVE I.1 339
 Mrs Frail: No, I'll allow a Lover present with his Mistress to . . 231 FOR LOVE I.1 555
 Sr Sampson: there's no time but the time present, there's no more to be 240 FOR LOVE II.1 197
 Sr Sampson: present Majesty of Bantam is the Issue of these Loyns. . 241 FOR LOVE II.1 223
 Sr Sampson: --What, I'll make thee a Present of a Mummy: Now . . 242 FOR LOVE II.1 248
 Tattle: Well, my Witnesses are not present--But I . . 257 FOR LOVE III.1 149
 Jeremy: at this present. . . . . . 295 FOR LOVE IV.1 756
 Almeria: Exerts my Spirits; and my present Fears . . . . 339 M. BRIDE II.1 79
 Osmyn-Alph: Revolves, and to the present adds the past: . . . 345 M. BRIDE II.2 226
 Zara: The present Form of our Engagements rests, . . . 355 M. BRIDE III.1 217
 Zara: So does the present Form of our Engagements rest, . . 355 M. BRIDE III.1 V217
 Manuel: Let 'em be led away to present Death. . . . . 362 M. BRIDE IV.1 66
 Zara: A Present once, from the Sultana Queen, ... 365 M. BRIDE IV.1 151
 Gonsalez: I'm not i'th' Way at Present, good Alonzo. . . . . 371 M. BRIDE IV.1 421
 Osmyn-Alph: And not from past or present Ills Despair: . . . 384 M. BRIDE V.2 320
 Sir Wilful: further acquaintance,--So for the present Cozen, I'll take 446 WAY WORLD IV.1 77
 Sir Wilful: present, 'tis sufficient till further acquaintance, that's
   all-- . 447 WAY WORLD IV.1 85
 Sir Wilful: Not at present Cozen,--Yes, I made bold to . . . 447 WAY WORLD IV.1 114
 Sir Wilful: Not at present, Cozen.--'tis like when I have . . . 448 WAY WORLD IV.1 134
 Foible: O what luck it is Sir Rowland, that you were present . 461 WAY WORLD IV.1 610
 Fainall: at present Practis'd in the Northern Hemisphere. But this . 469 WAY WORLD V.1 276
Presently (16)
 Setter: He'l be in the Piaza presently. . . . . . 67 OLD BATCH III.1 231
 Mellefont: if not most presently prevented. . . . . 148 DOUBL DLR II.1 379
 Lady Ply: . . . I'll be Divorced presently. . . . . . 179 DOUBL DLR IV.1 458
 Maskwell: I have so contriv'd, that Mellefont will presently, in . 199 DOUBL DLR V.1 441
 Lord Touch: we don't presently prevent the Execution of their plots;-- 200 DOUBL DLR V.1 477
 Cynthia: They'll wait upon your Lordship presently. . . . 202 DOUBL DLR V.1 553
 Valentine: Officer, You shall have an answer presently. . . . 224 FOR LOVE I.1 305
 Scandal: Reputation to me presently--Come, where are you . . 230 FOR LOVE I.1 527
 Valentine: wait on you again presently. . . . . 234 FOR LOVE I.1 663
 Mrs Fore: fresh harmless Creature; and left us, Sister, presently. . 250 FOR LOVE II.1 545
 Valentine: out to be in Forma Pauperis presently. . . . . 282 FOR LOVE IV.1 248
 Mrs Frail: presently. . . . . 290 FOR LOVE IV.1 555
 Jenny: upon you presently. . . . . 296 FOR LOVE IV.1 783
 Foresight: Did he so--I'll dispatch him for't presently; . . . 305 FOR LOVE V.1 321
 Foresight: presently, till farther Orders from me--not a Word . . 306 FOR LOVE V.1 325
 Waitwell: Roman hand--I saw there was a throat to be cut presently. 460 WAY WORLD IV.1 602
Preserv'd (4)
 Lady Ply: Have I, I say, preserv'd my self, like a fair Sheet . 145 DOUBL DLR II.1 259
 Manuel: That Life, which Heav'n preserv'd. A Day bestow'd . 333 M. BRIDE I.1 290
 Manuel: Not from that Hour, wherein thou wert preserv'd, . . 333 M. BRIDE I.1 300
 Fainall: Your Fame I have preserv'd. Your Fortune has been . . 415 WAY WORLD II.1 198
Preserve (5)
 Bellmour: witty Scene, and she perhaps preserve her Laughter, till . 44 OLD BATCH I.1 269
 Musician: Would you long preserve your Lover? . . . . . 59 OLD BATCH I.2 192
 Sir Paul: Pleasures to preserve its Purity, and must I now find it . 179 DOUBL DLR IV.1 429
 Valentine: think of means to reconcile me to him; and preserve the . 294 FOR LOVE IV.1 717
 Selim: My Life is yours, nor wish I to preserve it, . . . 362 M. BRIDE IV.1 39
Preserved (1)
 Lady Ply: preserved my Honour as it were in a Snow-House for . . 145 DOUBL DLR II.1 254
Preserving (1)
 Sharper: preserving you from those Ruffians, might have taken . . 48 OLD BATCH II.1 48
Presidents (1)
 Valentine: Secretaries of State, Presidents of . . . . . 221 FOR LOVE I.1 188
Press (14)
 Bellmour: by those healing Lips.--Oh! press the soft Charm close . 82 OLD BATCH IV.2 73
 Sharper: press her to make all the haste imaginable. . . . 102 OLD BATCH V.1 219
 Lady Touch: don't press me. . . . . 152 DOUBL DLR III.1 52
 Lord Touch: Don't oblige me to press you. . . . . 152 DOUBL DLR III.1 53
 Careless: feast upon that hand; O let me press it to my heart, my . 170 DOUBL DLR V.1 92
 Sr Sampson: press you to the service? . . . . . . 244 FOR LOVE II.1 332
 Sr Sampson: and press you to the service? . . . . . . 244 FOR LOVE II.1 V332
 Valentine: I don't know but my Father in good Nature may press me . 259 FOR LOVE III.1 225
 Garcia: Or Press upon the Privacies of others. . . . . 338 M. BRIDE II.1 37
 Almeria: Me in his leaden Arms, and press me close . . . . 340 M. BRIDE II.2 21
 Osmyn-Alph: To fold these thus, to press thy balmy Lips, . . . 342 M. BRIDE II.2 96
 Millamant: Press me no more for that slight Toy. . . . . 447 WAY WORLD IV.1 99
 Lady Wish: press things to a Conclusion, with a most prevailing . 458 WAY WORLD IV.1 495
 Marwood: Short-hand Writers to the publick Press; and from thence . 468 WAY WORLD V.1 231
Press'd (1)
 Araminta: when you named him, and press'd me to your Bosom . . 55 OLD BATCH II.2 42
Pressing (2)
 Valentine: they are very hard, but my Necessity is very pressing: . 224 FOR LOVE I.1 318
 Trapland: Sincerely, I am loth to be thus pressing, but my . . 224 FOR LOVE I.1 322
Prest (1)
 Maskwell: Opportunity, accomplish'd my Design; I prest the yielding 136 DOUBL DLR I.1 369

Presum'd (1)

Mirabell:	Which may be presum'd, with a blessing on our	. . .	451	WAY WORLD IV.1 257

Presume (14)

Lucy:	presume to enter the House.	. . .	66	OLD BATCH III.1 194
Vainlove:	May I presume to hope so great a Blessing?	.	112	OLD BATCH V.2 171
Brisk:	presume your Ladyship has Read Bossu?	. . .	142	DOUBL DLR II.1 137
Valentine:	Yes, Sir, all that I presume to ask.--But what	. .	243	FOR LOVE II.1 290
Mrs Frail:	presume to have a sufficient stock of Duty to undergo a	.	286	FOR LOVE IV.1 410
Leonora:	I never did presume to ask the Story.	. .	328	M. BRIDE I.1 108
Garcia:	(kneeling). Your Pardon, Sir, if I presume so far,	. .	334	M. BRIDE I.1 327
Zara:	And me; presume to day to plead audacious Love,	. .	349	M. BRIDE II.2 366
Zara:	Presume to day to plead audacious Love,	. . .	349	M. BRIDE II.2 V366
Gonsalez:	Might I presume;	. . .	363	M. BRIDE IV.1 68
Petulant:	Sir, I presume upon the Information of your Boots.	. .	438	WAY WORLD III.1 497
Millamant:	presume to approach without first asking leave. And	.	450	WAY WORLD IV.1 223
Mirabell:	mens prerogative, and presume to drink healths, or toste	.	451	WAY WORLD IV.1 270
Waitwell:	And may I presume to bring a Contract to be	. . .	461	WAY WORLD IV.1 638

Presuming (3)

Araminta:	whoever has encourag'd you to this assurance--presuming	.	87	OLD BATCH IV.3 157
Vainlove:	I am not presuming beyond a Pardon,	.	106	OLD BATCH V.1 360
Heli:	Presuming on a Bridegroom's Right--) she'll come.	. .	351	M. BRIDE III.1 50

Presumption (2)

Lady Ply:	Did you so, Presumption!	. . .	180	DOUBL DLR IV.1 481
	To build on that might prove a vain Presumption,	. .	393	WAY WORLD PRO. 18

Presumptive (1)

Witwoud:	presumptive it only may. That's a Logical Distinction now,		435	WAY WORLD III.1 410

Presumptuous (1)

Lady Ply:	'tis true, but he never was so presumptuous to entertain	.	172	DOUBL DLR IV.1 167

Pretence (9)

Mellefont:	Custome, after Dinner.--But I made a pretence	. . .	127	DOUBL DLR I.1 13
Almeria:	That's his Pretence. I know his Errand is	. . .	331	M. BRIDE I.1 213
Zara:	On what Pretence?	. . .	362	M. BRIDE IV.1 48
	To whose Rich Cargo, they may make Pretence,	. .	385	M. BRIDE EPI. 23
	To please, this time, has been his sole Pretence,	. .	393	WAY WORLD PRO. 33
Marwood:	Deceit and frivolous Pretence.		415	WAY WORLD II.1 208
Fainall:	Death, am I not married? what's pretence? Am I not	. .	415	WAY WORLD II.1 209
Marwood:	found it: The secret is grown too big for the Pretence:	.	433	WAY WORLD III.1 317
	Tho' they're on no pretence for Judgment fit	. . . .	479	WAY WORLD EPI. 12

Pretend (8)

Heartwell:	I am for having every body be what they pretend	.	43	OLD BATCH I.1 253
Vainlove:	Now must I pretend ignorance equal to hers, of	. .	87	OLD BATCH IV.3 136
Maskwell:	I would not be a Traytor to my self: I don't pretend to	.	136	DOUBL DLR I.1 342
	(They pretend to practice part of a Country-Dance.)	.	177	DOUBL DLR IV.1 371
Sr Sampson:	none of your forc'd Trees, that pretend to Blossom in the		298	FOR LOVE V.1 35
Angelica:	pretend to Worship, but have neither Zeal nor Faith:	.	314	FOR LOVE V.1 632
Selim:	Pretend to sacrifice the Life of Osmyn.	. .	361	M. BRIDE IV.1 22
	To which no single Beauty must pretend:	. . . . .	479	WAY WORLD EPI. 34

Pretended (15)

Vainlove:	Yes, Heartwell, that surly, old, pretended Woman-hater	.	40	OLD BATCH I.1 118
Bellmour:	your Servants, and was conducted hither. I pretended a	.	94	OLD BATCH IV.4 210
Maskwell:	at last I pretended to have been long Secretly in Love with		149	DOUBL DLR II.1 421
Lady Ply:	pretended to like that Monster of Iniquity, Careless, and	.	179	DOUBL DLR IV.1 454
Careless:	abused by a pretended Coyness in their Wives, and	. .	180	DOUBL DLR IV.1 497
Careless:	not prevail for you, 'gad I pretended to be in Love my self		180	DOUBL DLR IV.1 499
Angelica:	of losing me: For you know he has long pretended a	. .	300	FOR LOVE V.1 111
Angelica:	'Tis true, you have a great while pretended Love	. .	311	FOR LOVE V.1 531
Fainall:	of his pretended Passion? To undeceive the credulous	.	414	WAY WORLD II.1 159
Mrs Fain:	pretended Uncle?	. . .	417	WAY WORLD II.1 284
Mirabell:	hopes to ruin me, shou'd consent to marry my pretended	.	417	WAY WORLD II.1 293
Mirabell:	bring you home in a pretended fright, when you think you	.	451	WAY WORLD IV.1 240
Foible:	pretended to go for the Papers; and in the mean time Mrs.		464	WAY WORLD V.1 72
Mirabell:	pretended Settlement of the greatest part of her fortune--		476	WAY WORLD V.1 538
Fainall:	Sir! pretended!	. . .	476	WAY WORLD V.1 539

Pretender (1)

Bellmour:	No, But is a pretender, and wears the habit of a	. . .	46	OLD BATCH I.1 366

Pretending (5)

Bellmour:	Ay ay, pox Wisdom's nothing but a pretending to	. . .	37	OLD BATCH I.1 19
Bellmour:	Ay, ay, Wisdom's nothing but a pretending to	. . . .	37	OLD BATCH I.1 V 19
	(Maskwell pretending not to see him, walks by him, and	.	155	DOUBL DLR III.1 192
Cynthia:	and bid me meet him in the Chaplain's Room, pretending	.	196	DOUBL DLR V.1 348
Angelica:	pretending to a scund Understanding; as Drunken men do	.	296	FOR LOVE IV.1 764

Pretends (3)

Gonsalez:	As she pretends--I doubt it now--Your Guards	. .	366	M. BRIDE IV.1 206
Lady Wish:	know you are abus'd. He who pretends to be Sir Rowland	.	460	WAY WORLD IV.1 587
	Yet each pretends to know the Copy'd Face.	. . . .	479	WAY WORLD EPI. 20

Pretensions (2)

Mirabell:	Have you not left off your impudent Pretensions	. . .	406	WAY WORLD I.1 422
Mirabell:	And Sir, I have resign'd my pretensions.	. . . .	473	WAY WORLD V.1 422

Pretious (1)

Mellefont:	Pretious Aunt, I shall never thrive without I deal with the		187	DOUBL DLR IV.2 152

Prettiest (3)

	And 'twas the prettiest Prologue, as he wrote it!	. .	35	OLD BATCH PRO. 21
Lord Froth:	the prettiest amusement! but where's all the Company?	.	200	DOUBL DLR V.1 495
Valentine:	And the prettiest Foot! Oh if a Man could but fasten his	.	223	FOR LOVE I.1 286

Prettily (1)

Lady Froth:	O prettily turn'd again; let me die, but you have	. . .	140	DOUBL DLR II.1 85

Pretty (48)

Bellmour:	ungrateful to that Creature? She's extreamly pretty and	.	38	OLD BATCH I.1 39
Sir Joseph:	to the greatness of his merit--I had a pretty thing to that		49	OLD BATCH II.1 52
Capt Bluff:	pretty Fellow--but Sir Joseph, comparisons are odious--	.	52	OLD BATCH II.1 179
Capt Bluff:	Hannibal was a very pretty Fellow in those Days, it must	.	52	OLD BATCH II.1 180
Araminta:	which comes pretty near my own Opinion of Love and	. .	58	OLD BATCH II.2 154
Heartwell:	I am--However, I find I am pretty sure of her consent, if		73	OLD BATCH III.2 97
Bellmour:	'Tis pretty near the Hour--	. . .	75	OLD BATCH IV.1 1
Capt Bluff:	What says my pretty little Knapsack-Carrier?	. . .	85	OLD BATCH IV.3 84
Sir Joseph:	Agad, it's a curious, fine, pretty Rogue; I'll speak	.	89	OLD BATCH IV.4 32

Pretty   (continued)
Sir Joseph:	As you say, Madam, 'tis pretty bad Weather, and	. 90	OLD BATCH	IV.4	39
Brisk:	pretty and Metaphorical enough: I' Gad I could not have	. 128	DOUBL DLR	I.1	38
Lord Froth:	He, he, he, I swear that's so very pretty, I can't . .	. 132	DOUBL DLR	I.1	212
Lady Froth:	I Vow Mellefont's a pretty Gentleman, but	. 139	DOUBL DLR	II.1	45
Brisk:	Biddy! I'gad very pretty--Deuce take me if your . .	. 142	DOUBL DLR	II.1	130
Sir Paul:	Do you think my Daughter, this pretty Creature; . . .	. 145	DOUBL DLR	II.1	264
Sir Paul:	Nay, I swear and vow that was pretty.	. 160	DOUBL DLR	III.1	379
Sir Paul:	Town, and some money, a pretty tolerable personal Estate;	. 161	DOUBL DLR	III.1	409
Sir Paul:	Matter of Fact! Very pretty; it seems then I am conducing	. 178	DOUBL DLR	IV.1	411
Jeremy:	Nay, your Condition is pretty even with theirs, that's	. 217	FOR LOVE	I.1	58
Trapland:	pretty long standing--	. 222	FOR LOVE	I.1	237
Valentine:	again.--Pretty round heaving Breasts,--a Barbary . .	. 223	FOR LOVE	I.1	284
Tattle:	I have a pretty good Collection at your Service, some .	. 232	FOR LOVE	I.1	599
Foresight:	pretty good that too; but then I stumbl'd coming . .	. 236	FOR LOVE	II.1	33
Tattle:	not find fault with her pretty simplicity, it becomes her	. 249	FOR LOVE	II.1	535
Tattle:	strangely--pretty Miss, don't let 'em perswade you .	. 249	FOR LOVE	II.1	536
Mrs Frail:	she's very pretty!--Lord, what pure red and white! . .	. 250	FOR LOVE	II.1	556
Tattle:	I must make Love to you, pretty Miss; will you let .	. 251	FOR LOVE	II.1	588
Tattle:	Well, my pretty Creature; will you make me happy . .	. 252	FOR LOVE	II.1	631
Tattle:	Hold, hold, that's pretty well,--but you should not .	. 252	FOR LOVE	II.1	635
Tattle:	And won't you shew me, pretty Miss, where your . . .	. 252	FOR LOVE	II.1	646
Angelica:	I'm pretty even with him, Sir Sampson; for if ever I .	. 260	FOR LOVE	III.1	245
Foresight:	hem! faintish. My Heart is pretty good; yet it beats; and	. 269	FOR LOVE	III.1	605
Scandal:	And now I think we know one another pretty well. . .	. 272	FOR LOVE	III.1	710
Scandal:	So, this is pretty plain--Be not too much	. 277	FOR LOVE	IV.1	61
Valentine:	Thank you, Sir, pretty well--I have been a	. 281	FOR LOVE	IV.1	196
Sr Sampson:	pretty well now, Val: Body o' me, I was sorry to see thee	. 281	FOR LOVE	IV.1	202
Scandal:	and honour you.--You look pretty well, Mr. Foresight;--	. 284	FOR LOVE	IV.1	338
Tattle:	pretty Fellow, and can'st carry a Message to a Lady, in a	. 302	FOR LOVE	V.1	181
Tattle:	pretty soft kind of Phrase, and with a good perswading	. 302	FOR LOVE	V.1	182
Witwoud:	honest Fellow, and a very pretty Fellow, and has a smattering	. 403	WAY WORLD	I.1	289
Witwoud:	pretty Fellow, and a very honest Fellow, and has a smattering	. 403	WAY WORLD	I.1	V289
Witwoud:	--Faith and Troth a pretty deal of an odd sort of a small	. 403	WAY WORLD	I.1	290
Witwoud:	We staid pretty late there last Night; and heard . .	. 408	WAY WORLD	I.1	480
Witwoud:	Very pretty. Why you make no more of making . . .	. 420	WAY WORLD	II.1	407
Foible:	come down pretty deep now, she's super-annuated (says .	. 427	WAY WORLD	III.1	100
Lady Wish:	and rise to meet him in a pretty disorder--Yes--O, . .	. 445	WAY WORLD	IV.1	28
Mirabell:	Curious? Or is this pretty Artifice Contriv'd, to Signifie	. 449	WAY WORLD	IV.1	157
Mirabell:	your demands are pretty reasonable.	. 450	WAY WORLD	IV.1	211

Prevail (5)
Careless:	said all I could, but can't prevail--Then my Friendship	. 180	DOUBL DLR	IV.1	492
Careless:	not prevail for you, 'gad I pretended to be in Love my self	. 180	DOUBL DLR	IV.1	499
Saygrace:	(enters). You shall prevail, I would break off in the .	. 195	DOUBL DLR	V.1	280
Almeria:	And pleads against thee? who shall then prevail? . .	. 382	M. BRIDE	V.2	265
Millamant:	despair to prevail, and so let him follow his own way. .	. 434	WAY WORLD	III.1	342

Prevail'd (1)
Heartwell:	Well, has this prevail'd for me, and will you look . . .	. 71	OLD BATCH	III.2	28

Prevailing (4)
Bellmour:	let me tell you, my most prevailing Argument is express'd in	. 59	OLD BATCH	II.2	V183
Osmyn-Alph:	Paternal Love prevailing o'er his Sorrows;	. 352	M. BRIDE	III.1	113
Mrs Fain:	He has a Humour more prevailing than his	. 412	WAY WORLD	II.1	103
Lady Wish:	press things to a Conclusion, with a most prevailing .	. 458	WAY WORLD	IV.1	495

Prevails (1)
Lord Froth:	when any of their foolish Wit prevails upon the side .	. 133	DOUBL DLR	I.1	229

Prevent (15)
Sir Joseph:	that it was altogether out of fear, but partly to prevent	. 68	OLD BATCH	III.1	273
Mellefont:	prevent the success of her displeasure, than to avoid the	. 129	DOUBL DLR	I.1	92
Maskwell:	prevent your Plot, yet I would have you use Caution and .	. 154	DOUBL DLR	III.1	139
Brisk:	tho' to prevent Criticisms--only mark it with a small .	. 165	DOUBL DLR	III.1	551
Brisk:	tho' to prevent Criticism--only mark it with a small .	. 165	DOUBL DLR	III.1	V551
Lady Touch:	found him here. Who does not prevent the Hour of Love; .	. 183	DOUBL DLR	IV.2	9
Lord Touch:	we don't presently prevent the Execution of their plots;--	. 200	DOUBL DLR	V.1	477
Valentine:	I'll prevent that suspicion--For I intend to	. 313	FOR LOVE	V.1	608
Zara:	Ha! haste thee! fly, prevent his Fate and mine; . . .	. 361	M. BRIDE	IV.1	17
Zara:	Shall I prevent, or stop th' approaching Danger? . . .	. 362	M. BRIDE	IV.1	43
Gonsalez:	But how prevent the Captive Queen, who means . . .	. 371	M. BRIDE	IV.1	412
Marwood:	do it my self I shall prevent your Baseness.	. 415	WAY WORLD	II.1	189
Foible:	haste home and prevent her. Your Servant Sir. B'w'y .	. 424	WAY WORLD	II.1	547
Marwood:	prevent their Plot,--the half of Millamant's Fortune is .	. 442	WAY WORLD	III.1	641
Marwood:	Others there are whose Malice we'd prevent;	. 479	WAY WORLD	EPI.	16

Prevented (7)
Araminta:	young, and your early baseness has prevented its growing	. 87	OLD BATCH	IV.3	172
Mellefont:	much ado I prevented her doing me or her self a mischief:	. 130	DOUBL DLR	I.1	115
Sir Paul:	providence has prevented all, therefore come away, when	. 146	DOUBL DLR	II.1	285
Mellefont:	if not most presently prevented.	. 148	DOUBL DLR	II.1	379
Lady Touch:	to be unknown which cannot be prevented; therefore let	. 152	DOUBL DLR	III.1	55
Scandal:	might have prevented it.	. 266	FOR LOVE	III.1	490
Manuel:	Your coming has prevented me Almeria;	. 367	M. BRIDE	IV.1	243

Prevention (2)
Maskwell:	but you to catch at for Prevention.	. 137	DOUBL DLR	I.1	379
Mirabell:	fellows; for prevention of which; I banish all Foreign	. 451	WAY WORLD	IV.1	271

Prevents (1)
Setter:	As all lew'd projects do Sir, where the Devil prevents	. 64	OLD BATCH	III.1	117

Prey (4)
	Criticks avaunt; for you are Fish of Prey, ...	. 125	DOUBL DLR	PRO.	12
Maskwell:	ever must; no, let it prey upon my Heart; for I would .	. 188	DOUBL DLR	V.1	36
Mrs Frail:	Fish of prey.	. 286	FOR LOVE	IV.1	402
Leonora:	The Glory of the whole, were made the Prey	. 327	M. BRIDE	I.1	41

Price (3)
Sharper:	over my ill fortune, since it pay'd the price of your ransome.	. 48	OLD BATCH	II.1	34
Maskwell:	In short, the price of your Banishment is to be paid .	. 156	DOUBL DLR	III.1	224
Mellefont:	price of the Commodity, by telling you how many . . .	. 158	DOUBL DLR	III.1	302

Pricking (1)
Angelica: turning the Sieve and Sheers, and pricking your Thumbs, . 238 FOR LOVE II.1 108
Prickle (1)
Silvia: Bed to me--You have such a Beard and would so prickle . . 73 OLD BATCH III.2 93
Pride (5)
Heartwell: Devil--Oh the Pride and Joy of Heart 'twould be to me, . 45 OLD BATCH I.1 318
Lord Touch: Unworthy! 'tis an ignorant Pride in her to . . . 196 DOUBL DLR V.1 317
Valentine: to her Pride, and perhaps, make her compassionate . . . 217 FOR LOVE I.1 54
Scandal: Women. I can shew you Pride, Folly, Affectation, Wantonness, 233 FOR LOVE I.1 628
Zara: In whom I live. Spite of my Rage, and Pride, ... 361 M. BRIDE IV.1 25
Priest (3) see Parish-Priest
Almeria: I would consent the Priest might make us one; . . . 329 M. BRIDE I.1 137
Almeria: I would consent the Priest shou'd make us one; . . . 329 M. BRIDE I.1 V137
Manuel: I'll have a Priest shall preach her from her Faith, . . 334 M. BRIDE I.1 354
Prig (2)
Barnaby: Mr. Prig, to have kept my Mistress Company in the mean . 76 OLD BATCH IV.1 23
Tattle: (aside) what do's the Old Prig mean? I'll banter him, and 304 FOR LOVE V.1 263
Priming (1)
Mellefont: flash, the priming of her Engine; destruction follows hard, 148 DOUBL DLR II.1 378
Primitive (1)
Sir Joseph: and his primitive Braying. Don't you remember the Story . 101 OLD BATCH V.1 174
Primly's (1)
Marwood: 'Tis like Mrs. Primly's great Belly; she may lace it down . 433 WAY WORLD III.1 318
Prince (5)
Lady Froth: O be merry by all means--Prince Volscius . . . . . 176 DOUBL DLR IV.1 341
Tattle: or the Naked Prince. And it is notorious, that in a Country 257 FOR LOVE III.1 162
Leonora: His Son, the brave Valentia Prince, and you, ... 327 M. BRIDE I.1 49
Leonora: The Memory of that brave Prince stands fair . . . . 328 M. BRIDE I.1 104
Zara: When he receiv'd you as the Prince of Fez; . . . . 347 M. BRIDE II.2 295
Princess (13)
Lucy: Traytor to thy lawful Princess. . . . . 65 OLD BATCH III.1 178
Gonsalez: Excellent Princess! . . . . 332 M. BRIDE I.1 252
  same to the Princess.) . . . . 332 M. BRIDE I.1 270
Gonsalez: Have patience, Royal Sir, the Princess weeps . . . . 333 M. BRIDE I.1 303
Perez: Your entring, till the Princess is return'd, ... 359 M. BRIDE III.1 381
Zara: I did not know the Princess Favourite; . . . . 359 M. BRIDE III.1 415
Zara: No not the Princess self, permitted to . . . . 360 M. BRIDE III.1 451
Zara: No not the Princess suffer'd or to see . . . . 360 M. BRIDE III.1 V451
Zara: They and no other; not the Princess self. . . . . 365 M. BRIDE IV.1 170
Gonsalez: Pronounc'd with Vehemence against the Princess, . . . 365 M. BRIDE IV.1 175
Gonsalez: The Princess is Confederate with the Moor. . . . . 365 M. BRIDE IV.1 180
Gonsalez: But why that needless Caution of the Princess? . . . 366 M. BRIDE IV.1 221
  No more a Princess, but in statu quo: . . . . . 365 M. BRIDE EPI. 2
Principal (2)
Heartwell: You are the principal Cause of all my present Ills. . . 109 OLD BATCH V.2 66
Marwood: Principal to be an Assistant; to procure for him! A Pattern 431 WAY WORLD III.1 233
Principally (2)
Valentine: that Love, which has principally reduc'd me to this Lowness 217 FOR LOVE I.1 55
Valentine: the Love, which has principally reduc'd me to this Lowness 217 FOR LOVE I.1 V 55
Principle (1)
Bellmour: principle indeed! and art for encouraging Youth, that they 43 OLD BATCH I.1 251
Principles (1)
Lord Touch: I don't believe it true; he has better Principles . . . 150 DOUBL DLR III.1 4
Pris'ner (3)
Osmyn-Alph: Where he was Pris'ner, I am too imprison'd. . . . . 349 M. BRIDE III.1 3
Zara: The Pris'ner, but such Messengers, as I . . . . 365 M. BRIDE IV.1 163
Zara: To see the Pris'ner, but such Mutes as I . . . . 365 M. BRIDE IV.1 V163
Pris'ners (1)
Manuel: Give Order strait, that all the Pris'ners die, ... 364 M. BRIDE IV.1 127
Prison (8)
Jeremy: in a Tub, go to Prison for you? 'Slife, Sir, what do you . 217 FOR LOVE I.1 31
Leonora: Have stoll'n from Bed, and to his Prison crept: . . . 326 M. BRIDE I.1 25
  (A Prison. Enter Osmyn alone, with a Paper.) . . . 349 M. BRIDE III.1
Osmyn-Alph: To a vile Prison, and a captiv'd Wretch; . . . . 351 M. BRIDE III.1 53
  (Scene changes to the Prison. . . . . . . 376 M. BRIDE V.2
  (Scene opening shews the Prison. . . . . . . 376 M. BRIDE V.2 V
Almeria: For in the Tomb or Prison, I alone . . . . . . 381 M. BRIDE V.2 216
Foible: Waitwell's gone to prison already. . . . . . . 463 WAY WORLD V.1 64
Prisoner (10)
Belinda: Prisoner, make much of your Fetters. . . . . . 112 OLD BATCH V.2 168
Mellefont: flounder your self a weary, and be nevertheless my Prisoner. 184 DOUBL DLR IV.2 52
Valentine: Therefore I yield my Body as your Prisoner, and . . . 313 FOR LOVE V.1 615
Manuel: He is your Prisoner, as you please, dispose him. . . . 335 M. BRIDE I.1 368
Manuel: A Prisoner. His Name? . . . . 337 M. BRIDE I.1 446
Manuel: Yet lives, and is a Prisoner. His Name? . . . . 337 M. BRIDE I.1 V446
Heli: But fell unhurt, a Prisoner as your self; . . . . 344 M. BRIDE II.2 176
Zara: There, he; your Prisoner, and that was my Slave. . . . 348 M. BRIDE II.2 358
Perez: From visiting the Noble Prisoner. . . . . . 359 M. BRIDE III.1 382
  (Enter Alphonso, Heli, Perez, with Garcia Prisoner, . 382 M. BRIDE V.2 273
Prisoners (4)
Gonsalez: Prisoners of War in shining Fetters, follow; . . . . 331 M. BRIDE I.1 234
  Garcia and several Officers. Files of Prisoners in Chains, 332 M. BRIDE I.1 266
Manuel: Bear hence these Prisoners. Garcia, which is he, . . . 335 M. BRIDE I.1 363
  (Prisoners led off.) . . . 335 M. BRIDE I.1 365
Prisons (1)
Manuel: Divinity embrac'd; to Whips and Prisons, ... 349 M. BRIDE II.2 373
Prithee (40)
Bellmour: Prithee, what sort of Fellow is Fondlewife? . . . . 40 OLD BATCH I.1 105
Sharper: Prithee what mighty Business of Consequence canst . . . 41 OLD BATCH I.1 154
Bellmour: Prithee how dost thou love? . . . . 44 OLD BATCH I.1 282
Bellmour: Nay prithee George-- . . . . 46 OLD BATCH I.1 334
Belinda: Ay! nay Dear--prithee good, dear sweet Cousin no . . . 54 OLD BATCH II.2 1
Belinda: Prithee tell it all the World, it's false. Betty. (Calls) 56 OLD BATCH II.2 61
Araminta: Prithee don't be so Peevish. . . . . 56 OLD BATCH II.2 64
Belinda: Prithee don't be so Impertinent. . . . . . . 56 OLD BATCH II.2 65
Belinda: Prithee hold thy Tongue--Lard, he has so . . . . 59 OLD BATCH II.2 163

Prithee   (continued)
  Vainlove: He's talking to himself, I think; Prithee lets try if . . 62 OLD BATCH III.1   61
  Setter: Why how now! prithee who art? lay by that Worldly . . . 65 OLD BATCH III.1 179
  Bellmour: Ha, ha, ha, prithee come away, 'tis scandalous to . . . 69 OLD BATCH III.1 327
  Fondlewife: Nay, prithee, Dear, Ifeck I'm in haste. . . . . 89 OLD BATCH IV.4   19
  Sharper: Heartwell when I see him. Prithee, Frank, let's teaze him; 99 OLD BATCH V.1   87
  Bellmour: I have no such Intentions at present.--Prithee, ... 100 OLD BATCH V.1   156
  Sir Joseph: Prithee, don't speak so loud. . . . . 101 OLD BATCH V.1   179
  Sir Joseph: Prithee, What do you see in my face, that looks as . . 101 OLD BATCH V.1   191
  Sharper: Nay, Prithee, leave Railing, and come along with . . 104 OLD BATCH V.1   284
  Sharper: the narrow Joys of Wedlock. But prithee come along with . 104 OLD BATCH V.1   305
  Careless: Prithee get thee gone; thou seest we are serious. . . . 128 DOUBL DLR I.1   45
  Mellefont: keep up good Humour and Sense in the Company, prithee . 128 DOUBL DLR I.1   47
  Brisk: But prithee dear Rogue, make haste, prithee make haste, . 128 DOUBL DLR I.1   52
  Mellefont: Truth. Prithee do thou wear none to day; but allow Brisk . 129 DOUBL DLR I.1   71
  Mellefont: Maskwell, you mean; prithee why should you . . . . . 131 DOUBL DLR I.1   145
  Brisk: now, you come up to me--nay, prithee Careless be . . 133 DOUBL DLR I.1   253
  Brisk: Pshaw, pshaw, prithee don't interrupt me.--But I . . . 134 DOUBL DLR I.1   262
  Careless: Well, but prithee don't let it be a great while, because . 134 DOUBL DLR I.1   265
  Singer: Prithee Cynthia look behind you, ... 143 DOUBL DLR II.1 186
  Brisk: (sings). I'm sick with Love, ha ha ha, prithee come (walking 175 DOUBL DLR IV.1 306
  Valentine: No, prithee stay: Tattle and you should never be . . . 225 FOR LOVE   I.1   363
  Sr Sampson: be done to Night--No matter for the time; prithee, . . . 240 FOR LOVE   II.1 195
  Tattle: Aye, prithee, what's that? . . . . 292 FOR LOVE   IV.1 642
  Fainall: Prithee, why so reserv'd? Something has put you out . . 395 WAY WORLD I.1   13
  Witwoud: No, but prithee excuse me,--my Memory is . . . . . . 402 WAY WORLD I.1   273
  Millamant: Sententious Mirabell! Prithee don't look with that . . 422 WAY WORLD II.1 467
  Sir Wilful: Well prithee try what thou can'st do; if thou . . . . 437 WAY WORLD III.1 464
  Sir Wilful: your Ear, prithee who are these Gallants? . . . . . . 437 WAY WORLD III.1 469
  Millamant: I prithee spare me gentle Boy, ... 447 WAY WORLD IV.1   98
  Sir Wilful: Prithee fill me the Glass . . . . 455 WAY WORLD IV.1 397
Privacies (1)
  Garcia: Or Press upon the Privacies of others. . . . . 338 M. BRIDE   II.1   37
Privacy (3)
  Careless: be always welcome to my privacy. . . . . 159 DOUBL DLR III.1 324
  Lady Ply: privacy? I swear and declare in the face of the World I'm 159 DOUBL DLR III.1 332
  Gonsalez: And privacy, the wearing Garb of one . . . . 372 M. BRIDE   IV.1   437
Private (28)
  Capt Bluff: I am content to retire--Live a private Person-- . . . . 53 OLD BATCH II.1   211
  Araminta: We thought to have been private.--But we . . . . . . 86 OLD BATCH IV.3   116
  Bellmour: --If you do, I'll spoil all.--I have some private . . . 98 OLD BATCH V.1   68
  Setter: private Conveyance of the Lady to him, and put a . . . 105 OLD BATCH V.1   344
  Mellefont: private, and I am not like to have many opportunities . . 127 DOUBL DLR I.1   15
  Maskwell: against me, and I'll make my escape through the private . 157 DOUBL DLR III.1 251
  Sir Paul: you wou'd be private? . . . . 159 DOUBL DLR III.1 322
  Maskwell: (aside). That I believ'd; 'twas well I left the private . 184 DOUBL DLR IV.2   30
  Maskwell: get my Lord to consent to my private management. He . . 190 DOUBL DLR V.1   96
  Maskwell: --and a Pair of private Stairs leads down to the . . . 194 DOUBL DLR V.1   255
  Maskwell: --and a Pair of private Stairs leading down to the . . 194 DOUBL DLR V.1 V255
  Maskwell: publick or private, that can expect to prosper without . 194 DOUBL DLR V.1   268
  Lord Touch: How're in private, Mischiefs are conceiv'd, ... 203 DOUBL DLR V.1   592
  Scandal: Secresie, and makes Proclamation that he holds private . 226 FOR LOVE   I.1   379
  Sr Sampson: can't a private man be born without all these followers: . 245 FOR LOVE   II.1 350
  Tattle: (coming up). Scandal, are you in private Discourse, any . 254 FOR LOVE   III.1   42
  Tattle: a Gentleman. I hope you are secret in your Nature, private, 302 FOR LOVE   V.1   188
  Tattle: a private Intriegue of Destiny, kept secret from the
                      piercing . . . . 304 FOR LOVE   V.1   271
  Selim: That Execution may be done in private. . . . . 362 M. BRIDE   IV.1   47
  Gonsalez: In private, undertook to raise this Tumult. . . . . . 363 M. BRIDE   IV.1   89
  Zara: And oft had private Conference with the King; . . . . 364 M. BRIDE   IV.1 118
  Zara: Worthy your private Ear, and this your Minister. . . . 364 M. BRIDE   IV.1 130
  Zara: His private Practice and Conspiracy . . . . 364 M. BRIDE   IV.1 139
  Zara: (As there the Custom is) in private strangle . . . . 365 M. BRIDE   IV.1 154
  Manuel: And plots in Private with this hellish Moor. . . . . 367 M. BRIDE   IV.1 235
  Mirabell: I wou'd beg a little private Audience too-- . . . . . 421 WAY WORLD II.1 427
  Sir Wilful: an Opportunity to be more private,--I may break my . . 448 WAY WORLD IV.1 135
  Fainall: S'death what's this to me? I'll not wait your private . . 475 WAY WORLD V.1   517
Privateers (1)
  Ben: Privateers were looking for a Prize, and should fall foul of 310 FOR LOVE   V.1   488
Privately (10)
  Setter: No, no; never fear me, Sir.--I privately inform'd . . . 106 OLD BATCH V.1   347
  Lady Touch: have an opportunity to talk with him privately--my . . 154 DOUBL DLR III.1 144
  Maskwell: him in her stead, you may go privately by the back Stairs, 199 DOUBL DLR V.1   446
  Tattle: No, Sir; 'tis to be done Privately--I never make . . . 304 FOR LOVE   V.1   280
  Almeria: Wilt privately with me, ... 331 M. BRIDE   I.1   198
  Almeria: Thou wilt withdraw, and privately with me . . . . . . 331 M. BRIDE   I.1 V198
  Zara: Alphonso, privately departed, just . . . . 364 M. BRIDE   IV.1 120
  Manuel: My Daughter privately conferr'd with him, ... 373 M. BRIDE   V.1   47
  Manuel: My Daughter privately with him conferr'd; . . . . . . 373 M. BRIDE   V.1 V 47
  Mirabell: that she might seem to carry it more privately. . . . . 418 WAY WORLD II.1 306
Privilege (2)
  Mellefont: has the privilege of using the familiarity of a Husband . 158 DOUBL DLR III.1 287
  Heli: (Who takes the Privilege to visit late, ... 351 M. BRIDE   III.1   49
Privy (6)
  Laetitia: privy to a weak Woman's Failing, won't turn it to the . . 82 OLD BATCH IV.2   63
  Maskwell: To my Lord, as having been privy to Mellefont's . . . 154 DOUBL DLR III.1 150
  Lord Touch: Privy to his impious Designs upon my Wife. This Evening . 182 DOUBL DLR IV.1 546
  Tattle: Aye? Who's he, tho? A Privy Counsellor? . . . . . . 302 FOR LOVE   V.1   192
  Mirabell: In Justice to you, I have made you privy to my . . . . 417 WAY WORLD II.1 280
  Mrs Fain: privy to the whole Design, and know that Waitwell, to . 430 WAY WORLD III.1 189
Prize (6)
  Setter: Were I a Rogue now, what a noble Prize could I . . . 102 OLD BATCH V.1   221
  Maskwell: of your Love; yet so far I prize your Pleasures o're my own, 199 DOUBL DLR V.1   436
  Ben: Privateers were looking for a Prize, and should fall foul of 310 FOR LOVE   V.1   488
  Manuel: Shifting the Prize in unresolving Hands: . . . . . . 337 M. BRIDE   I.1   455
  Fainall: And wherefore did I marry, but to make lawful Prize of a . 415 WAY WORLD II.1 206

Prize   (continued)
  Singer: Then I alone the Conquest prize . . . . 435 WAY WORLD III.1 387
Probability (1)
  Mirabell: and in all probability in a little time longer I shall
              like 'em . . . . 399 WAY WORLD   I.1 173
Probably (1)
  Jeremy: Sir, you're a Gentleman, and probably understand . . . 217 FOR LOVE   I.1   24
Probation (1)
  Sharper: have their Year of Probation, before they are cloister'd in 104 OLD BATCH   V.1 304
Probatum est (2)
  Bellmour: A very certain remedy, probatum est--Ha, ha, ha,   . . . 63 OLD BATCH III.1   88
  Valentine: Probatum est. But what are you for? Religion or Politicks? 282 FOR LOVE   IV.1 255
Probe (1)
  Maskwell: You are merry, Sir, but I shall probe your Constitution. . 156 DOUEL DLR III.1 223
Proceed (6)
  Careless: us! Proceed. What follow'd? . . . . 130 DOUEL DLR   I.1 102
  Maskwell: to delay--let me think--shou'd my Lord proceed   . . . . 190 DOUEL DLR   V.1   89
          You who can Judge, to Sentence may proceed; . . . . . 204 DOUEL DLR EPI.   34
  Valentine: Very well, Sir; can you proceed? . . . . 219 FOR LOVE   I.1 103
          Still they proceed, and, at our Charge, write worse; . . 323 M. BRIDE   PRO.   23
  Fainall: proceed? . . . . 443 WAY WORLD III.1 698
Proceeded (1)
  Mirabell: Conscience; I proceeded to the very last Act of Flattery . 397 WAY WORLD   I.1   69
Proceeding (2)
  Tattle: Proceeding-- . . . . 229 FOR LOVE   I.1 500
  Marwood: tickl'd with the proceeding, Simpers under a Grey beard, . 467 WAY WORLD   V.1 220
Proceedings (4)
  Lord Touch: farther proceedings in it, till you have consider'd it, but 191 DOUEL DLR IV.1 139
  Scandal: I'll give an account of you, and your Proceedings. If . . 234 FOR LOVE   I.1 675
  Witwoud: Noli prosequi and stop't their proceedings. . . . . . 453 WAY WORLD IV.1 330
  Witwoud: Noli prosequi and stop't the Proceedings. . . . . . . 453 WAY WORLD IV.1 V330
Proclaim (1)
  Leonora: The distant Shouts, proclaim your Fathers Triumph; . . . 330 M. BRIDE   I.1 163
Proclaim'd (1)
  Garcia: Proclaim'd aloud by Perez, for Alphonso. . . . . . . 377 M. BRIDE   V.2   44
Proclamation (1)
  Scandal: Secresie, and makes Proclamation that he holds private . 226 FOR LOVE   I.1 379
Proctor (1)
  Lady Ply: have a Cousin that's a Proctor in the Commons, I'll go to . 179 DOUEL DLR IV.1 463
Procur'd (2)
  Setter: And I should not be the first that has procur'd his . . 65 OLD BATCH III.1 161
  Valentine: Madness has deceiv'd my Father, and procur'd me time to . 294 FOR LOVE   IV.1 716
Procure (5)
  Mellefont: The Daughter procure the Mother! . . . . 146 DOUEL DLR II.1 308
  Mellefont: The Daughter to procure the Mother! . . . . 146 DOUEL DLR II.1 V308
  Maskwell: be otherwhere employ'd--do you procure her Night-Gown, . 199 DOUEL DLR   V.1 444
  Gonsalez: Could'st thou procure with speed, ... 372 M. BRIDE   IV.1 436
  Marwood: Principal to be an Assistant; to procure for him! A Pattern 431 WAY WORLD III.1 233
Procured (1)
  Bellmour: for him, and procured his Habit; in which, I pass'd upon . 94 OLD BATCH IV.4 209
Procuring (1)
  Lady Ply: means of procuring the Mother? . . . . 146 DOUEL DLR II.1 307
Prodigal (2)
  Foresight: a way to make your Lover, your Prodigal Spendthrift . . . 238 FOR LOVE   II.1 116
  Sr Sampson: ungracious Prodigal know who begat him; I will, old . . 240 FOR LOVE   II.1 174
Prodigal's (1)
  Lady Wish: Prodigal's in Debt as much as the Million Lottery, or the . 428 WAY WORLD III.1 133
Prodigality (1)
  Fainall: bestow'd as the prodigality of your Love would have it, . 415 WAY WORLD II.1 199
Prodigious (3)
  Capt Bluff: Prodigious! What, will you forsake your Friend in his . . 101 OLD BATCH   V.1 187
  Capt Bluff: Prodigious! What, will you forsake your Friend in . . . 101 OLD BATCH   V.1 V187
  Cynthia: Prodigious! I wonder, want of sleep, and so much . . . 138 DOUEL DLR II.1   5
Produc'd (1)
  Mirabell: familiarities of our Loves had produc'd that Consequence, 417 WAY WORLD II.1 267
Produce (2)
  Heartwell: will produce at the expense of your own Sweat. . . . . 44 OLD BATCH   I.1 281
  Setter: Face and produce your natural Vizor. . . . . 65 OLD BATCH III.1 180
Produces (1)
  Mirabell: Love Contriv'd--and errours which Love produces have . . 472 WAY WORLD   V.1 386
Producing (1)
  Mrs Fain: by producing a Certificate of her Gallants former . . . 417 WAY WORLD II.1 298
Profane (1)
  Lady Wish: see Prophane
          and going to filthy Plays; and Profane Musick-meetings, . 467 WAY WORLD   V.1 199
Profess (13)
  Sir Joseph: You have found it Sir then it seems; I profess I'me . . 49 OLD BATCH II.1   85
  Sir Joseph: But I profess, 'tis a Dirt I have wash'd my Hands of . . 50 OLD BATCH II.1 111
  Sir Joseph: Ha, ha, ha, a very good Jest I Profess, ha, ha, ha, a . . 50 OLD BATCH II.1 114
  Fondlewife: Good lack! I profess the Spirit of contradiction . . . 75 OLD BATCH IV.1   16
  Fondlewife: Good lack, good lack--I profess it is a very sufficient . 76 OLD BATCH IV.1   39
  Fondlewife: I profess a very apt Comparison, Varlet. Go in . . . . 76 OLD BATCH IV.1   45
  Fondlewife: I profess a very apt Comparison, Varlet. Go . . . . . 76 OLD BATCH IV.1 V 45
  Fondlewife: (aside). I profess she has an alluring Eye; I am . . . 77 OLD BATCH IV.1   74
  Fondlewife: Oak--I profess I can hold no longer--Nay dear Cocky-- . . 78 OLD BATCH IV.1 115
  Fondlewife: I profess I do love thee better, than 500 Pound-- . . . 78 OLD BATCH IV.1 129
  Fondlewife: Good Lack! Good Lack!--I profess, the poor . . . . . 91 OLD BATCH IV.4   94
  Marwood: affect Endearments to each other, profess eternal
            Friendships, ... 410 WAY WORLD II.1   23
  Mrs Fain: profess a Libertine. . . . . 410 WAY WORLD II.1   29
Profess'd (5)
  Maskwell: profess'd an everlasting Friendship to him. . . . . . 182 DOUEL DLR IV.1 567
  Zara: Of strictest Friendship, was profess'd between . . . . 364 M. BRIDE   IV.1 123
  Petulant: be a profess'd Midwife as a profest Whoremaster, at this . 405 WAY WORLD   I.1 384
  Marwood: profess'd a Friendship to her; and could not see her easie 414 WAY WORLD II.1 163
  Fainall: What, was it Conscience then! profess'd a Friendship! . . 414 WAY WORLD II.1 165

Professing (2)

| Marwood: | professing Love to us, or mutual Faith to one another. | 414 | WAY WORLD | II.1 | 169 |
| Mirabell: | and professing Friend, a false and a designing Lover; yet | 417 | WAY WORLD | II.1 | 271 |

Profession (1)

| Fondlewife: | of your Profession.--Confess, confess, I shall love thee | 94 | OLD BATCH | IV.4 | 193 |

Professor (1)

| Scandal: | may be granted him--In short, he is a publick Professor of | 226 | FOR LOVE | I.1 | 378 |

Profest (2)

| Scandal: | these is a celebrated Beauty, and t'other a profest Beau. I | 233 | FOR LOVE | I.1 | 633 |
| Petulant: | be a profess'd Midwife as a profest Whoremaster, at this | 405 | WAY WORLD | I.1 | 384 |

Profit (1)

| Heartwell: | profit than what the bare tillage and manuring of the Land | 44 | OLD BATCH | I.1 | 280 |

Profited (1)

| Waitwell: | I think she has profited, Sir. I think so. | 424 | WAY WORLD | II.1 | 527 |

Profligate (1)

| Lady Wish: | profligate man? | 474 | WAY WORLD | V.1 | 482 |

Profound (3)

Lady Ply:	that Mellefont had never any thing more than a profound	171	DOUBL DLR	IV.1	165
Foresight:	profound Secrets of Time.	291	FOR LOVE	IV.1	605
Mirabell:	aloud of the Vapours, and after fell into a profound	396	WAY WORLD	I.1	31

Profoundly (1)

| | (He bows profoundly low, then kisses the Glass.) | 140 | DOUBL DLR | II.1 | 79 |

Profuse (1)

| Angelica: | Hold, Sir Sampson--You're profuse of your | 301 | FOR LOVE | V.1 | 149 |

Profusion (1)

| Almeria: | To see him thus again, is such profusion | 342 | M. BRIDE | II.2 | 106 |

Progeny (1)

| Mrs Frail: | we shall have a most Amphibious Breed--The Progeny | 231 | FOR LOVE | I.1 | 571 |

Prognosticates (2)

| Mrs Frail: | Foresight has cast both their Nativities, and prognosticates | 231 | FOR LOVE | I.1 | 577 |
| | For just as one prognosticates the Weather, | 323 | M. BRIDE | PRO. | 8 |

Prognostication (3)

Sr Sampson:	Ha! thou'rt melancholly old Prognostication; As melancholly	265	FOR LOVE	III.1	463
Sr Sampson:	Ha! thou'rt melancholick old Prognostication; As melancholick	265	FOR LOVE	III.1	V463
Sr Sampson:	Are we? A Pox o' your Prognostication--Why,	283	FOR LOVE	IV.1	279

Prohibit (2)

| Mirabell: | the Credit of the Nation, and prohibit the Exportation of | 400 | WAY WORLD | I.1 | 205 |
| Mirabell: | together with all Vizards for the day, I prohibit all Masks | 451 | WAY WORLD | IV.1 | 248 |

Project (7)

Bellmour:	Trusty Setter what tidings? How goes the project?	64	OLD BATCH	III.1	116
Scandal:	I must work her into the Project. You keep early Hours,	269	FOR LOVE	III.1	579
Scandal:	what Project I had to get him out of the way; that I might	269	FOR LOVE	III.1	597
Mrs Fore:	this Project? You don't think, that you are ever like to	271	FOR LOVE	III.1	660
Scandal:	the mean time, if our Project succeed no better with his	278	FOR LOVE	IV.1	104
Mrs Fore:	project in my head for you, and I have gone a good way	288	FOR LOVE	IV.1	464
Valentine:	and a long Veil to cover the Project, and we won't see	290	FOR LOVE	IV.1	562

Projection (1)

| Marwood: | Care, like any Chymist upon the Day of Projection. | 431 | WAY WORLD | III.1 | 248 |

Projector (1)

| Jeremy: | Bethlehem; Nay, he's as Mad as any Projector, Fanatick, | 295 | FOR LOVE | IV.1 | 739 |

Projects (1)

| Setter: | As all lew'd projects do Sir, where the Devil prevents | 64 | OLD BATCH | III.1 | 117 |

Prologue (3)

	A Play makes War, and Prologue is the Drum:	35	OLD BATCH	PRO.	6
	And 'twas the prettiest Prologue, as he wrote it!	35	OLD BATCH	PRO.	21
Belinda:	as a very witty Prologue to a very dull Play.	107	OLD BATCH	V.1	388

Prologues (1)

| | Prologues, were serious Speeches, before Plays; | 35 | OLD BATCH | PRO. | 2 |

Prolong (3)

Heartwell:	expiring, and endeavour to prolong his life, and you	109	OLD BATCH	V.2	55
Maskwell:	Nay, good Mr. Saygrace do not prolong the time,	194	DOUBL DLR	V.1	276
Almeria:	Will undistinguish'd roll, and but prolong	367	M. BRIDE	IV.1	260

Promis'd (7)

Heartwell:	impair'd the Honour of your House, promis'd your	109	OLD BATCH	V.2	52
Scandal:	Attendance, and promis'd more than ever you intend to	221	FOR LOVE	I.1	194
Scandal:	Attendance, and promis'd more than ever you intended to	221	FOR LOVE	I.1	V194
Mrs Fore:	imposes on him.--Now I have promis'd him Mountains,	288	FOR LOVE	IV.1	470
Zara:	And through my Hopes in you, I promis'd Freedom	349	M. BRIDE	II.2	378
Foible:	have only promis'd. But a Man so enamour'd--So transported!	427	WAY WORLD	III.1	75
Foible:	defend my self? O Madam, if you knew but what he promis'd	463	WAY WORLD	V.1	29

Promiscuous (1)

| Gonsalez: | Have all conspir'd, to blaze promiscuous Light, | 331 | M. BRIDE | I.1 | 222 |

Promise (26)

Laetitia:	promise.--	82	OLD BATCH	IV.2	70
Bellmour:	Well, I promise.--A promise is so cold.--	82	OLD BATCH	IV.2	71
Bellmour:	the mean time, I promise,--and rely upon me,--to	98	OLD BATCH	V.1	70
Bellmour:	Promise to make her Amends quickly with another	100	OLD BATCH	V.1	152
Sharper:	of your Promise? Will you marry her your self?	100	OLD BATCH	V.1	155
Sharper:	She has given Vainlove her Promise, to marry him	102	OLD BATCH	V.1	212
Lady Touch:	But will you promise me not to be angry	152	DOUBL DLR	III.1	75
Lady Touch:	your promise--Pho, why nothing, only your Nephew had	152	DOUBL DLR	III.1	82
Lady Touch:	it; well remember your promise, my Lord, and don't	153	DOUBL DLR	III.1	91
Cynthia:	a Ditch--Here then, I give you my promise, in spight of	168	DOUBL DLR	IV.1	35
Tattle:	Well Miss, I have your promise.	262	FOR LOVE	III.1	347
Tattle:	turn of good Fortune, in the Lottery of Wives; and promise	304	FOR LOVE	V.1	269
Almeria:	But I did promise I would tell thee--What?	328	M. BRIDE	I.1	98
Garcia:	As to remind you of your gracious Promise.	334	M. BRIDE	I.1	328
Manuel:	No more; my Promise long since pass'd, thy Loyalty,	334	M. BRIDE	I.1	340
Manuel:	No more; my Promise long since pass'd, thy Services,	334	M. BRIDE	I.1	V340
Alonzo:	'Twill quit me of my Promise to Gonsalez.	373	M. BRIDE	V.1	30
Mrs Fain:	Mirabell, and I dare promise you will oblige us both.	412	WAY WORLD	II.1	107
Lady Wish:	I promise you I have thought on't--And	432	WAY WORLD	III.1	269
Lady Wish:	your Passion by your Jealousie, I promise you I'll make you	460	WAY WORLD	IV.1	581
Lady Wish:	your Passion by your Jealousie, I promise you I'll make	460	WAY WORLD	IV.1	V581
Lady Wish:	and I promise you, her Education has been unexceptionable	466	WAY WORLD	V.1	182

Prove   (continued)
Sr Sampson: How, Madam! Wou'd I cou'd prove it. . . . . 299 FOR LCVE V.1   89
               To build on that might prove a vain Presumption, . . 393 WAY WORLD PRO.   18
Marwood: not prove another Pattern of Generosity;   . . . . . 431 WAY WCRLD III.1   243
Petulant: I have a Humour to prove it, it must be granted. . . 435 WAY WORLD III.1   406
Marwood: They may prove a Cap of Maintenance to . . . . 442 WAY WORLD III.1   649
Mirabell: me up and prove my Constancy. . . . . 451 WAY WORLD IV.1   243
Mirabell: prove a tractable and complying Husband. . . . . . 452 WAY WORLD IV.1   277
Petulant: what then? If I have a humour tc prove it.--If I shall . 454 WAY WCRLD IV.1   368
Mrs Fain: Say'st thou so Foible? Canst thou prove this? . . . . 464 WAY WORLD V.1   91
Mrs Fain: me. I defie 'em all. Let 'em prove their aspersions: I know 466 WAY WCRLD V.1   177
Lady Wish: friend, I can't believe it, No, no; as she says, let him
               prove . . . . 467 WAY WORLD V.1   206
Lady Wish: it, let him prove it. . . . . 467 WAY.WORLD V.1   207
Marwood: Prove it Madam? What, and have your name   . . . . 467 WAY WORLD V.1   208
Proverb (1)
Scandal: trusted; a Satyrical Proverb upon our Sex--There's . . . 256 FOR LCVE III.1   126
Proverbially (1)
Scandal: Why thence it arises--The thing is proverbially . . . . 256 FOR LCVE III.1   123
Proverbs (2)
Valentine: A couple of very civil Proverbs, truly: 'Tis hard to . . 256 FOR LCVE III.1   129
Scandal: Proverbs, and I see one in the next Room that will sing it. 258 FOR LCVE III.1   192
Proves (5)
Heartwell: And proves that Vainlove plays the Fool with . . . . . 42 OLD BATCH I.1   216
Heartwell: But proves a burning Caustick when apply'd. . . . . . 108 OLD BATCH V.2   13
Scandal: Pooh, pox, this proves nothing. . . . . 257 FOR LCVE III.1   152
Scandal: Pooh, this proves nothing. . . . . 257 FOR LCVE III.1 V152
Fainall: when he proves his Mistress true; but let Husbands doubts 444 WAY WCRLD III.1   717
Provide (4)
Bellmour: get your Man Setter to provide my Disguise. . . . . . 40 OLD BATCH I.1   112
Bellmour: What not to make your family Man! and provide . . . . 45 OLD BATCH I.1   314
Bellmour: Nay, don't be in Passion, Lucy:--I'll provide a . . . 98 OLD BATCH V.1   57
Valentine: provide for me, I desire you wou'd leave me as you found . 244 FOR LCVE II.1   335
Provided (12)
Bellmour: And hast thou provided necessaries? . . . . 64 OLD BATCH III.1   122
Mellefont: Say you so, were you provided for an Escape? . . . . 184 DOUBL DLR IV.2   41
Maskwell: the business in hand--have you provided a Habit for . . 195 DOUEL DLR V.1   283
Mrs Frail: You have a Rich Husband, and are provided for, I am at . 248 FOR LOVE II.1   489
Ben: Woman that be provided for me, I thought it more fitting . 285 FOR LCVE IV.1   373
Scandal: I hear the Fiddles that Sir Sampson provided for his . . 313 FOR LCVE V.1   598
               Provided they've a Body to dissect. . . . . 385 M. BRIDE EPI.   18
Mrs Fain: when she has this, which you have provided for her, I . . 418 WAY WCRLD II.1   309
Fainall: which you like a careful Aunt had provided for her. . . 469 WAY WORLD V.1   285
Fainall: Indeed? are you provided of a Guard, with your . . . 473 WAY WORLD V.1   432
Fainall: Indeed? are you provided of your Guard, with your . . 473 WAY WORLD V.1 V432
Foible: O Sir, Some that were provided for Sir Rowland's . . 478 WAY WORLD V.1   605
Providence (20)
Sir Paul: providence has prevented all, therefore come away, when . 146 DOUBL DLR II.1   285
Maskwell: it my Brain or Providence? No Matter which--I will . . 155 DOUBL DLR III.1   189
Maskwell: won't perplex you. 'Tis the only thing that Providence . . 157 DOUEL DLR III.1   244
Sir Paul: be Providence--ay, truly, Mr. Careless, my Lady is a great 160 DOUBL DLR III.1   386
Sir Paul: blessed be Providence I may say; for indeed, Mr. Careless, 161 DOUBL DLR III.1   413
Sir Paul: I am mightily beholding to Providence--a poor . . . 161 DOUBL DLR III.1   414
Sir Paul: I am mightily beholden to Providence--a poor . . . 161 DOUBL DLR III.1 V414
Sir Paul: --O Providence, what a Conspiracy have I . . . . . 178 DOUBL DLR IV.1   406
Sir Paul: --But Providence has been constant to me in discovering . 179 DOUEL DLR IV.1   432
Sir Paul: this Conspiracy; still I am beholden to Providence, if it . 179 DOUEL DLR IV.1   433
Sir Paul: were not for Providence, sure poor Sir Paul thy Heart . 179 DOUEL DLR IV.1   434
Sir Paul: O Providence! Providence! What Discoveries are . . . 180 DOUEL DLR IV.1   504
Sir Paul: turvy; as I hope for Providence. . . . . 200 DOUBL DLB V.1   498
Valentine: between me and Heav'n; but Providence laid Purgatory . 313 FOR LCVE V.1   596
Almeria: Sure Providence at first, design'd this Place . . . 315 FOR LCVE EPI.   1
Almeria: Mercy and Providence! O speak to it, ... 341 M. BBIDE II.2   41
Almeria: Mercy and Providence! O speak . . . . 341 M. BRIDE II.2 V 41
Heli: The Care of Providence, sure left it there, ... 352 M. BBIDE III.1   116
               And fatten on the Spoils of Providence: . . . . . 385 M. EBIDE EPI.   24
Provident (2)
Sr Sampson: Paws; Nature has been provident only to Bears and . . 246 FOR LCVE II.1   391
Valentine: Fortune was provident enough to supply all the . . . 246 FOR LCVE II.1   394
Provides (1)
               The Law provides a curb for 'its own Fury, ... 204 DOUBL DLR EPI.   10
Province (4)
Sir Joseph: if I would carry a Challenge? Honour is your Province, . 101 OLD BATCH V.1   192
Brisk: the whole Province of Contemplation: That's all-- . . 175 DOUEL DLR IV.1   316
Maskwell: World of Love, cou'd be confin'd within the puny Province 199 DOUBL DLR V.1   432
Mirabell: But with proviso, that you exceed not in your province; . 451 WAY WCRLD IV.1   264
Proving (2)
Gonsalez: In proving with his Sword, upon your Foes . . . . . 332 M. EBIDE I.1   257
Gonsalez: Has better done; in proving with his Sword . . . . 332 M. EBIDE I.1 V257
Provision (3)
Angelica: last Invisible Eclipse, laying in Provision as 'twere for a 237 FOR LCVE II.1   80
Jeremy: By the Provision that's made for me, you might have . 245 FOR LCVE II.1   360
Ben: Provision. . . . . 308 FOR LCVE V.1   416
Proviso (5)
Careless: upon you, is, with a Proviso, that your Uncle have no . 130 DOUBL DLR I.1   122
Sr Sampson: I have a Proviso in the Obligation in favour of my self . 300 FOR LCVE V.1   126
Mirabell: But with proviso, that you exceed not in your province; . 451 WAY WCRLD IV.1   264
Sir Wilful: Over-sea's once already; and with proviso that I Marry my 471 WAY WORLD V.1   349
Lady Wish: endeavour what I can to forget,--but on proviso that you . 472 WAY WORLD V.1   403
Proviso's (3)
Mirabell: allow,--these proviso's admitted, in other things I may . 452 WAY WORLD IV.1   276
Millamant: O horrid proviso's! filthy strong Waters! I toste . . 452 WAY WORLD IV.1   278
Millamant: fellows, Odious Men! I hate your Odious proviso's. . . 452 WAY WCRLD IV.1   279
Provocation (3)
Lady Touch: in my Temper, Passions in my Soul, apt to every provocation; 135 DOUBL DLR I.1   326
Lady Touch: Plyant, if he refuse his Daughter upon this Provocation? . 150 DOUEL DLR III.1   2

Provocation   (continued)
  Witwoud: express'd provocation; they had gone together by the   .   . 454 WAY WORLD IV.1   362
Provok'd (4)
                 But if, provok'd, your dreadful Wrath remains,   .   .   . 323 M. BRIDE   PRO.   29
  Fainall: conceal your Love to her Niece, has provok'd this
                   Separation: . . . . 397 WAY WORLD I.1   65
  Millamant: That horrid Fellow Petulant, has provok'd me into   .   . 432 WAY WORLD III.1 287
  Marwood: have Fcible provck'd if I cou'd help it,--because you know 443 WAY WORLD III.1 704
Provoke (12)
  Capt Bluff: 'twas indiscreet, when you know what will provoke me--   54 OLD BATCH II.1   242
  Lady Touch: Insolent Devil! But have a care,--provoke me not;   .   . 135 DOUBL DLR I.1   321
  Lady Touch: Again, provoke me! Do you wind me like . . . . . . 137 DOUBL DLR I.1   380
  Lady Ply: please--therefore don't provcke me. .   .   .   .   .   . 145 DOUBL DLR II.1   237
  Lady Ply: you have to answer for, if you should provoke me to   .   . 147 DOUBL DLR II.1   320
  Valentine: provcke your Enemies; this liberty of your Tongue, will   . 221 FOR LOVE   I.1   199
  Sr Sampson: provoke honest Albumazar--an Egyptian Mummy is   .   .   . 242 FOR LOVE   II.1   242
  Scandal: provoke him.   .   .   .   . 279 FOR LOVE   IV.1   153
  Fainall: What should provoke her to be your Enemy, without   .   . 397 WAY WORLD I.1   82
  Fainall: What should provoke her to be your Enemy, unless   .   .   . 397 WAY WORLD I.1 V 82
  Millamant: a New Chariot, to provoke Eyes and Whispers; And then   . 450 WAY WORLD IV.1   203
  Marwood: gravity of the Bench, and provoke Naughty Interrogatories, 467 WAY WORLD V.1   218
Provoked (2)
  Sir Paul: Gads bud! I am provoked into a Fermentation, as   .   .   . 143 DOUBL DLR II.1   195
  Sir Paul: provoked to fury, I cannot incorporate with Patience and . 144 DOUBL DLR II.1   223
Provokes (2)
  Lord Froth: He, he, I swear tho', your Raillery provokes me   .   .   . 132 DOUBL DLR I.1   208
  Scandal: be occasion; for I fancy his Presence provokes him more.   . 280 FOR LOVE   IV.1   190
Provoking (3)
  Foresight: How Hussie! was there ever such a provoking   .   .   .   . 237 FOR LOVE   II.1   93
  Millamant: dressing; their Folly is less provoking than your Mallice, 433 WAY WORLD III.1 326
  Millamant: dressing here; their Folly is less provoking than your
                   Mallice, ... 433 WAY WORLD III.1 V326
Proxy (1)
  Mrs Fain: your Proxy in this Affair; but I have business of my own.   446 WAY WORLD IV.1   68
Prudence (2)
  Mirabell: O you should Hate with Prudence.   .   .   .   . 416 WAY WORLD II.1   256
  Lady Wish: inherited thy Mother's prudence.   .   .   .   . 477 WAY WORLD V.1   569
Prudent (1)
  Lord Touch: I have always found you prudent and careful   .   .   .   . 181 DOUBL DLR IV.1   535
Prue (10)
                                  (Enter Tattle, and Miss Prue.)   .   .   . 249 FOR LOVE   II.1   505
                                          (Exit Miss Prue.)   .   .   .   . 253 FOR LOVE   II.1   661
  Nurse: Miss, Miss, Miss Prue--Mercy on me, marry and   .   .   . 253 FOR LOVE   III.1   1
                              (Tattle and Miss Prue at the Door.)   .   .   . 253 FOR LOVE   III.1 V 14
                 (Enter Sir Sampson, Mrs. Frail, Miss Prue, and Servant.)   . 259 FOR LOVE   III.1 209
  Ben: (Kisses Miss Prue.)   .   .   .   . 261 FOR LOVE   III.1 284
  Tattle: (Aside to Miss Prue.)   .   .   .   . 262 FOR LOVE   III.1 348
                       (Exeunt all but Ben and Miss Prue.)   .   .   .   .   . 263 FOR LOVE   III.1 359
                                      (Enter Miss Prue.)   .   .   .   .   .   . 303 FOR LOVE   V.1   221
                       (Exeunt Nurse and Miss Prue.)   .   .   .   . 306 FOR LOVE   V.1 V329
Pry (2)
  Garcia: Far be it from me, officiously to pry   .   .   .   .   .   . 338 M. BRIDE   II.1   36
  Manuel: Hence, Slave, how dar'st thou bide, to watch and pry   .   . 373 M. BRIDE   V.1   39
Pryn (1)
  Lady Wish: are Bocks over the Chimney--Quarles and Pryn, and the   . 426 WAY WORLD III.1   65
Psalm (1)
  Petulant: Hang'd. The Ordinary's paid for setting the Psalm, and   . 436 WAY WORLD III.1 430
Pshaw (18)
  Sharper: Pshaw you can't want a hundred Pound. Your   .   .   .   .   50 OLD BATCH II.1   107
  Belinda: --Affront! Pshaw, how you're mistaken! The poor   .   .   .   84 OLD BATCH IV.3   39
  Bellmour: Pshaw, No: I have a better Opinicn of thy Wit.   .   .   . 100 OLD BATCH V.1   142
  Capt Bluff: Pshaw, I have Petitions to show, from other-guess-toys   . 103 OLD BATCH V.1   264
  Sharper: Pshaw: Thou'rt so troublesom and inquisitive.--   .   .   . 104 OLD BATCH V.1   291
  Brisk: better, you or I. Pshaw, Man, when I say you spoil Company 128 DOUBL DLR I.1 V 28
  Brisk: Pshaw, pshaw, prithee don't interrupt me.--But I   .   .   . 134 DOUBL DLR I.1   262
  Sir Paul: Pshaw, Pshaw, you fib you Baggage, you do .   .   .   .   . 174 DOUBL DLR IV.1   246
  Mrs Fore: Pshaw! but Vertuous, I mean.   .   .   .   . 271 FOR LOVE   III.1 668
  Miss Prue: Pshaw, O but I dream't that it was so tho.   .   .   .   .   . 303 FOR LOVE   V.1   239
  Tattle: one another now--Pshaw, that would be a foolish   .   .   . 303 FOR LOVE   V.1   242
  Tattle: Pshaw, but I tell you, you would not--You forget   .   .   . 304 FOR LOVE   V.1   252
  Witwoud: Pshaw, pshaw, that she laughs at Petulant is plain.   .   . 407 WAY WORLD I.1   465
  Witwoud: long; pshaw, I was not in my own Power then. An Orphan,   . 440 WAY WORLD III.1 557
  Sir Wilful: think--Nay Cozen Fainall, open the Door--Pshaw,   .   .   . 447 WAY WORLD IV.1   93
Ptolomee (2)
  Sr Sampson: here 'tis, I have it in my Hand, Old Ptolomee; I'll make the 240 FOR LOVE   II.1   173
  Sr Sampson: Ptolcmee tell you? Your Messahalah and your Longomontanus, 283 FOR LOVE   IV.1   284
Publick (19)
  Sharper: Not I, Sir, no more than publick Letters, or Gazettes   .   .   52 OLD BATCH II.1   190
  Capt Bluff: You are obliging Sir, but this is too publick a Place   .   .   69 OLD BATCH III.1 322
  Bellmour: upon the Publick; then the encouragement of a separate   .   95 OLD BATCH IV.4   226
  Lady Touch: me if you take such publick notice of it, it will be a
                   Town-talk: .   .   .   . 153 DOUBL DLR III.1 104
  Maskwell: publick or private, that can expect to prosper without   . 194 DOUBL DLR V.1   268
  Scandal: may be granted him--In short, he is a publick Professor of   . 226 FOR LOVE   I.1   378
  Tattle: be receiv'd but upon Publick Days; and my Visits will   .   . 230 FOR LOVE   I.1   516
  Mrs Fore: publick, and to be seen with a man in a Hackney-Coach   . 247 FOR LOVE   II.1   430
  Scandal: Why, Honour is a publick Enemy; and Conscience a   .   .   . 271 FOR LOVE   III.1 675
  Zara: Thee bare, the naked Mark of Publick View.   .   .   .   .   . 360 M. BRIDE   III.1 442
  Zara: Himself. I've been deceiv'd. The publick Safety   .   .   .   . 360 M. BRIDE   III.1 449
  Zara: I've been deceiv'd. The publick Safety now   .   .   .   .   . 360 M. BRIDE   III.1 V449
  Selim: And Order given for publick Execution.   .   .   .   .   .   . 361 M. BRIDE   IV.1   16
  Manuel: Publick Report, is ratify'd in this.   .   .   .   . 364 M. BRIDE   IV.1   125
  Witwoud: once a Day at publick Places.   .   .   .   . 405 WAY WORLD I.1   361
  Petulant: Ay teste a teste; But not in publick, because I make   .   . 408 WAY WORLD I.1   500
  Petulant: Ay tete a tete; But not in publick, because I make   .   .   . 408 WAY WORLD I.1 V500
  Marwood: prostituted in a publick Court; Yours and your Daughters   . 467 WAY WORLD V.1   209

Pure   (continued)
Belinda:	you're a pure Man; Where did you get this excellent	88	OLD BATCH	IV.3	196
Miss Prue:	Handkerchief is sweet, pure sweet, sweeter than Roses	249	FOR LOVE	II.1	520
Miss Prue:	this way--Is not it pure?--It's better than	249	FOR LOVE	II.1	528
Mrs Frail:	she's very pretty!--Lord, what pure red and white!	250	FOR LOVE	II.1	556
Miss Prue:	O Lord, I swear this is pure,--I like it better than	252	FOR LOVE	II.1	624
Miss Prue:	O I have pure News, I can tell you pure News--I	303	FOR LOVE	V.1	226
Osmyn-Alph:	By him set down; when his pure Thoughts were born	353	M. BRIDE	III.1	129
Mincing:	and is so pure and so crips.	420	WAY WORLD	II.1	374

Purely (5)
Bellmour:	abroad--went purely to run away from a Campagne;	47	OLD BATCH	I.1	369
Belinda:	Heart to marry thee, purely to be rid of thee.--At	106	OLD BATCH	I.1	365
Lady Froth:	purely, but I vow Mr. Brisk, I can't tell how to come so	177	DOUBL DLR	IV.1	368
Mrs Fore:	Countenance purely, you'd make an Admirable Player.	247	FOR LOVE	II.1	452
Scandal:	the liberty I take in Talking, is purely affected, for the	272	FOR LOVE	III.1	697

Purest (1)
Mellefont:	and hope they are of the purest kind--Penitential Tears.	185	DOUBL DLR	IV.2	69

Purgatory (2)
Mellefont:	Paradice; yet if you please you may make it a Purgatory;	185	DOUBL DLR	IV.2	61
Valentine:	between me and Heav'n; but Providence laid Purgatory	313	FOR LOVE	V.1	596

Purging (2)
Sharper:	Why if whoring be purging--as you call it--then I	44	OLD BATCH	I.1	291
Almeria:	Thro' all Impediments, of purging Fire,	330	M. BRIDE	I.1	182

Purity (3)
Lady Ply:	me, debauching my purity, and perverting me from the	147	DOUBL DLR	II.1	317
Lady Ply:	The last of any Man in the World, by my purity;	169	DOUBL DLR	IV.1	78
Sir Paul:	Pleasures to preserve its Purity, and must I now find it	179	DOUBL DLR	IV.1	429

Purling (1)
Lady Wish:	and Purling Streams. Dear Marwood, let us leave the World,	465	WAY WORLD	V.1	134

Purloyn'd (1)
Sr Sampson:	King, that I purloyn'd from one of the Pyramids, powder'd	242	FOR LOVE	II.1	250

Purport (1)
Fainall:	Wife's to my sole use; As pursuant to the Purport and	473	WAY WORLD	V.1	436

Purpose (24)
Bellmour:	A very even Temper and fit for my purpose. I must	40	OLD BATCH	I.1	111
Heartwell:	purpose, ever embarking in Adventures, yet never comes	42	OLD BATCH	I.1	199
Sir Joseph:	Purpose, if he han't frighted it out of my memory. Hem!	49	OLD BATCH	II.1	53
Fondlewife:	Good Man! I warrant he dropp'd it on purpose,	91	OLD BATCH	IV.4	102
Bellmour:	good Quality.--But to the purpose, if you will give	98	OLD BATCH	V.1	65
Sharper:	purpose. Setter, stand close; seem not to observe 'em; and,	101	OLD BATCH	V.1	164
Setter:	Shifting Cloaths for the purpose at a Friend's House of	106	OLD BATCH	V.1	351
Careless:	day, on purpose?	129	DOUBL DLR	I.1	82
Careless:	while to no purpose.	157	DOUBL DLR	III.1	267
Sir Paul:	I will, I will, I'll go and look for him on purpose.	175	DOUBL DLR	IV.1	288
Sir Paul:	did you give me this Letter on purpose he? Did you?	179	DOUBL DLR	IV.1	461
Lord Touch:	I thank you. What is the Villains Purpose?	182	DOUBL DLR	IV.1	581
Mellefont:	purpose? yet, 'sdeath, for a Man to have the fruit of all				
	his	187	DOUBL DLR	IV.2	143
Maskwell:	on purpose to betray you; and that which put me upon it,	193	DOUBL DLR	V.1	218
Tattle:	to no purpose--But since we have done nothing, we must	253	FOR LOVE	III.1	22
Scandal:	can Dream as much to the purpose as another, if I set about	275	FOR LOVE	III.1	814
Zara:	And with Perverseness, from the Purpose, answer?	346	M. BRIDE	II.2	265
Osmyn-Alph:	And for some Purpose points out these Remembrances.	350	M. BRIDE	III.1	5
Osmyn-Alph:	Nor, should my secret Purpose take Effect,	355	M. BRIDE	III.1	213
Zara:	It may be, that the Cause, and Purpose of	379	M. BRIDE	V.2	144
Zara:	And Purpose, being chang'd from Life to Death,	379	M. BRIDE	V.2	V145
Zara:	Of Sense: His Soul still sees, and knows each Purpose,	381	M. BRIDE	V.2	196
Mirabell:	to the Occasion; a worse had not answer'd to the Purpose.	417	WAY WORLD	II.1	276
Mincing:	And all to no purpose. But when your Laship pins it up	419	WAY WORLD	II.1	372

Purposes (3)
Almeria:	And free of all bad Purposes. So Heav'ns	368	M. BRIDE	IV.1	290
Osmyn-Alph:	Themselves, their own most bloody Purposes.	383	M. BRIDE	V.2	308
Osmyn-Alph:	Has turn'd their own most bloody Purposes.	383	M. BRIDE	V.2	V308

Purse (6)
Heartwell:	--hark! (pulling out a Purse and chinking it) how sweetly	72	OLD BATCH	III.2	35
Silvia:	(Throws the Purse) I hate you now, and I'll never see you	74	OLD BATCH	III.2	111
Fondlewife:	Here are fifty Pieces in this Purse, Sir Joseph--	90	OLD BATCH	IV.4	42
Setter:	--And, for my part, if I meet Sir Joseph with a Purse	102	OLD BATCH	V.1	233
Sir Joseph:	(Chinking a Purse.)	103	OLD BATCH	V.1	238
Sir Wilful:	Bill--Give me more drink and take my Purse.	455	WAY WORLD	IV.1	395

Pursu'd (3)
Almeria:	Who knew our Flight, we closely were pursu'd,	329	M. BRIDE	I.1	123
Perez:	Then forward shot their Fires, which he pursu'd,	338	M. BRIDE	II.1	22
Osmyn-Alph:	You have pursu'd Misfortune, to its Dwelling;	346	M. BRIDE	II.2	262

Pursuant (1)
Fainall:	Wife's to my sole use; As pursuant to the Purport and	473	WAY WORLD	V.1	436

Pursue (14)
Vainlove:	--I stumble ore the Game I would pursue.--'Tis	80	OLD BATCH	IV.1	177
Vainlove:	--I stumble over the Game I would pursue.--'Tis	80	OLD BATCH	IV.1	V177
Vainlove:	All Naturally fly what does pursue:	80	OLD BATCH	IV.1	190
Cynthia:	meeting: We Hunt in Couples where we both pursue the	168	DOUBL DLR	IV.1	16
Lady Touch:	with you for ever,--nay, I'll be your Enemy, and pursue	192	DOUBL DLR	V.1	182
Cynthia:	but I find I have obstinacy enough to pursue whatever I	193	DOUBL DLR	V.1	203
Lord Touch:	Go, and thy own Infamy pursue thee,--	202	DOUBL DLR	V.1	563
Valentine:	be reveng'd on 'em all; I'll pursue Angelica with more Love	217	FOR LOVE	I.1	50
Tattle:	You shall not fly so fast, as I'll pursue.	253	FOR LOVE	II.1	662
Scandal:	It takes, pursue it in the name of Love and Pleasure.	269	FOR LOVE	III.1	612
Valentine:	pursue her, and know her if it be possible, in spight of the	297	FOR LOVE	IV.1	813
Mirabell:	You pursue the Argument with a distrust that seems	397	WAY WORLD	I.1	95
Mrs Fain:	pursue your Point, now or never.	446	WAY WORLD	IV.1	72
Lady Wish:	upon me yet, that my Son Fainall will pursue some	478	WAY WORLD	V.1	611

Pursued (1)
Bellmour:	Friend, be close pursued, or lost. Business is the rub of				
	Life,	37	OLD BATCH	I.1	10

Pursues (2)
Bellmour:	then pursues it for the Favour.	58	OLD BATCH	II.2	134

Puts (3)
Lucy: (Puts on her Masque.) . . . 65   OLD BATCH III.1   157
Lady Ply: both Letters.--(Puts the wrong Letter hastily up, and
                        gives him 174   DOUBL DLR IV.1   263
Sr Sampson: Val: And then no body need hold it (puts the Paper in his 281 FOR LCVE IV.1 232
Putting (7)
Bellmour: hast thou been putting out of conceit with her self, and . 42 OLD BATCH I.1 183
                                        (Putting on her Hoods.) . . 57 OLD BATCH II.2   94
Capt Bluff: (Putting up his Sword.) . . . 70 OLD BATCH III.1 350
Bellmour: I cou'd think of nothing all Day but putting 'em in practice 82 OLD BATCH IV.2 54
Bellmour: Nay, then I thank thee for not putting me out of . . . 100 OLD BATCH V.1 147
Maskwell: time in putting it on? . . . . 195 DOUBL DLR V.1   289
Mirabell: not us be accessary to your putting the Ladies out of . . 409 WAY WORLD I.1 524
Puzled (1)
Maskwell: suspected a design which I should have been puzled to . . 188 DOUBL DLR V.1   12
Puzzle (1)
Valentine: thing; it's a Question that would puzzle an Arithmetician, 280 FOR LCVE IV.1 175
Puzzled (2)
Maskwell: stitch'd the Gown Sleeve, that he may be puzzled, and waste 195 DOUBL DLR V.1 288
Zara: In executing, puzzled, lame and lost. . . . . . . 375 M. BRIDE V.1 112
Py (1)
               Whom, as I think they call'd--Py--Pythagories, ... 315 FOR LCVE EPI. 12
Pylades (1)
Sir Wilful: Travellers.--We are to be Pylades and Orestes, he and I-- . 471 WAY WORLD V.1 347
Pyramids (1)
Sr Sampson: King, that I purloyn'd from one of the Pyramids, powder'd 242 FOR LCVE II.1 250
Pythagories (1)
               Whom, as I think they call'd--Py--Pythagories, ... 315 FOR LCVE EPI. 12

Quack (2)
Fondlewife: you know your Patient, Mrs. Quack? Oh, lie upon your . . 93 OLD BATCH IV.4 163
Scandal: Huntsmen.--No, turn Pimp, Flatterer, Quack, Lawyer, . . 220 FOR LCVE I.1 144
Quadrates (2)
Foresight: Sextiles, Quadrates, Trines and Oppositions, Fiery Trigons 241 FOR LCVE II.1 213
Sr Sampson: your Quadrates?--What did your Cardan and your . . . 283 FOR LCVE IV.1 283
Quake (1)   see Earth-quake
Sir Joseph: remembrance makes me quake; agad I shall never be . . . 48 OLD BATCH II.1 14
Quaker (1)
Witwoud: a Quaker hates a Parrot, or than a Fishmonger hates a . . 408 WAY WORLD I.1 485
Qualification (1)
Belinda: Nay, sure Railing is the best qualification in a . . . 88 OLD BATCH IV.3 201
Qualifie (2)
Maskwell: qualifie me to assist her in her Revenge. And, in short, in 149 DOUBL DLR II.1 425
Valentine: Marriage indeed may qualifie the Fury of his . . . . 231 FOR LCVE I.1 560
Qualified (3)
Lucy: An Executioner qualified to do your Business. He has . . 97 OLD BATCH V.1 18
Lady Ply: might be supposed to be capable of being qualified to make 159 DOUBL DLR III.1 337
Lady Ply: qualified in all those Circumstances, I'm sure I should . 159 DOUBL DLR III.1 340
Qualify (1)
Sharper: confess, I have taken care to improve it; to qualify me for 88 OLD BATCH IV.3 199
Quality (23)
Bellmour: better quality. . . . . 45 OLD BATCH I.1 301
Heartwell: Quality--I thank Heaven, I have very honestly purchas'd . 45 OLD BATCH I.1 304
Bellmour: good Quality.--But to the purpose, if you will give . . 98 OLD BATCH V.1 65
Setter: --'Tis above us:--And, for Men of Quality, they are . . 102 OLD BATCH V.1 231
Capt Bluff: Quality. Here, here's from a Countess too. Hum--No . . 103 OLD BATCH V.1 267
Capt Bluff: Quality. . . . . 103 OLD BATCH V.1 270
Sir Joseph: They are either from Persons of great Quality, or . . 103 OLD BATCH V.1 271
Sir Joseph: no Quality at all, 'tis such a Damn'd ugly Hand. . . 103 OLD BATCH V.1 272
Sharper: fear.--A fine Lady, and a Lady of very gccd Quality. . 111 OLD BATCH V.2 135
Capt Bluff: What, Are you a Woman of Quality too, Spouse? . . . 111 OLD BATCH V.2 139
Lord Froth: more unbecoming a Man of Quality, than to Laugh; Jesu, 132 DOUBL DLR I.1 199
Lord Froth: more unbecoming a Man of Quality, than to Laugh; . . 132 DOUBL DLR I.1 V199
Lord Froth: Person, or when any body else of the same Quality does . 132 DOUBL DLR I.1 202
Lady Froth: and as much a Man of Quality! Ah! Nothing at all . . 139 DOUBL DLR II.1 29
Lady Froth: Some distinguishing Quality, as for example, the . . 139 DOUBL DLR II.1 48
Lord Froth: Woman of Quality--you have been at my Lady Whifler's . 162 DOUBL DLR III.1 466
Cynthia: 'em; for these have Quality and Education, Wit and fine 167 DOUBL DLR III.1 627
Tattle: bring me into Disgrace with a certain Woman cf Quality-- 227 FOR LOVE I.1 425
Scandal: familiar--And see that they are Women of Quality too, . 230 FOR LOVE I.1 528
Scandal: the first Quality-- . . . . 230 FOR LOVE I.1 529
Tattle: Quality that shall be nameless, in a raging Fit of
                        Jealousie, ... 258 FOR LOVE III.1 175
Scandal: have been told she had that admirable quality of forgetting 284 FOR LOVE IV.1 334
Mirabell: Quality, he is not Exceptious; for he so passionately . . 401 WAY WORLD I.1 228
Quality's (1)
Witwoud: will lie like a Chambermaid, or a Woman of Quality's . . 404 WAY WORLD I.1 341
Qualm (1)
Manuel: A Bridal Qualm; soon off. How is't, Almeria? . . . . 334 M. BRIDE I.1 348
Qualmsick (1)
Lady Wish: Mrs. Qualmsick the Curate's Wife, that's always breeding . 425 WAY WORLD III.1 22
Quandary (1)
Lady Ply: I'm in such a fright; the strangest Quandary . . . . 178 DOUBL DLR IV.1 396
Quarles (1)
Lady Wish: are Books over the Chimney--Quarles and Pryn, and the . 426 WAY WORLD III.1 65
Quarrel (11)
Bellmour: George, you must not quarrel with little Gallantries of . 44 OLD BATCH I.1 259
Vainlove: She has made a quarrel on't. . . . . 63 OLD BATCH III.1 97
Araminta: 'Tis a lasting Quarrel: I think he has never been at . 107 OLD BATCH V.1 399
Mrs Fore: agreeable man; I don't quarrel at that, nor I don't think 247 FOR LOVE II.1 428
Angelica: No, Sir Sampson, I have no Quarrel upon my Hands . . . 298 FOR LOVE V.1 44
Marwood: S'life, we shall have a Quarrel betwixt an Horse and an Ass, 438 WAY WCRLD III.1 505
Millamant: Eh! filthy creature--what was the quarrel? . . . . 454 WAY WCRLD IV.1 358
Petulant: There was no quarrel--there might have been a . . . 454 WAY WORLD IV.1 359
Petulant: quarrel. . . . . 454 WAY WORLD IV.1 360
Petulant: You were the Quarrel. . . . . 454 WAY WORLD IV.1 364
Petulant: If I have a humour to Quarrel, I can make less . . . 454 WAY WORLD IV.1 366

563

PAGE TITLE ACT.SC LINE

Quarrel'd (1)
Mrs Fore: They have quarrel'd just as we cou'd wish. . . . . . 264 FOR LOVE III.1 433

Quarrell'd (2)
Fainall: Confess, Millamant and you quarrell'd last Night, . . 395 WAY WORLD I.1 17
Millamant: Witwoud and he wou'd have quarrell'd. . . . . . . 432 WAY WORLD III.1 294

Quarrelling (1)
Mrs Fain: Petulant and he were upon quarrelling as I came by. . 452 WAY WORLD IV.1 314

Quarry (1)
Jeremy: upon the Quarry. It is the Whim of my Master's Madness . 302 FOR LOVE V.1 200

Quarter (8)
Maskwell: Well, I'll meet you here, within a quarter of eight, . 157 DOUBL DLR III.1 260
Mellefont: within a Quarter of Eight. . . . . 181 DOUBL DLR IV.1 514
Maskwell: Lordship will meet me a quarter of an Hour hence there, . 183 DOUBL DLR IV.1 584
Foresight: within a quarter of Twelve--hem--he, hem!--just upon . 270 FOR LOVE III.1 646
Ben: clean Shirt cnce a Quarter--Come home and lie with . . 275 FOR LCVE III.1 801
Jeremy: and meet you in half a quarter of an hour, with your . 303 FOR LCVE V.1 216
Tattle: you can't solve this; stay here a Quarter of an Hour, and 305 FCR LCVE V.1 297
Foible: quarter of an hours lying and swearing to a fine Lady? . 459 WAY WCRLD IV.1 559

Quarters (1)
see Head-Quarters
Lady Froth: Three Quarters, but I swear she has a World of . . . . 167 DOUBL DLR III.1 619

Queen (9)
Brisk: Cynthia of the Skies, and Queen of Stars. . . . . 201 DOUBL DLR V.1 531
Almeria: Had born the Queen and me, on board a Ship . . . . 329 M. BRIDE I.1 120
Almeria: While the good Queen and my Alphonso perish'd. . . . 329 M. BRIDE I.1 131
Almeria: The Queen too, did assist his Suit--I granted, . . . 329 M. BRIDE I.1 140
Zara: A Queen; for what are Riches, Empire, Fower, ... 347 M. BRIDE II.2 315
Zara: A Present once, from the Sultana Queen, ... 365 M. BRIDE IV.1 151
Gonsalez: My Lord, the Queen advises well. . . . . . . 365 M. BRIDE IV.1 156
Gonsalez: But how prevent the Captive Queen, who means . . . 371 M. BRIDE IV.1 412
Gonsalez: Among the followers of the Captive Queen, ... 372 M. BRIDE IV.1 433

Queens (2)
Zara: To have contending Queens, at dead of Night . . . . 360 M. BRIDE III.1 427
Witwoud: he means Sultana Queens. . . . . 406 WAY WORLD I.1 400

Quench (1)
Jeremy: plausible Occasion for me to quench my Thirst at the . 302 FOR LOVE V.1 175

Quench'd (1)
Mellefont: Ne'er to be quench'd, till they themselves devour. . . 187 DOUBL DLR IV.2 155

Quenching (1)
Maskwell: Pox on't that a Man can't drink without quenching his . 155 DOUEL DLR III.1 185

Question (18)
Bellmour: Well but George I have one Question to ask you-- . . 45 OLD BATCH I.1 330
Sharper: Sir your humble Servant--I don't question but you . . 49 OLD BATCH II.1 87
Heartwell: Question! Death, I shall be drawn in, before I know where . 73 OLD BATCH III.2 96
Araminta: A pithy Question.--Have you sent your Wits . . . 85 OLD BATCH IV.3 141
Mellefont: question.-- . . . . 147 DOUBL DLR II.1 331
Lady Ply: O Lord, ask me the question, I'll swear I'll . . . 147 DOUBL DLR II.1 332
Lord Touch: I do him fresh wrong to question his forgivness; . . . 200 DOUBL DLR V.1 481
Valentine: confess an Answer, when you never ask'd me the Question. . 229 FOR LOVE I.1 498
Angelica: had Ccncern enough to ask my self the Question. . . . 254 FOR LCVE III.1 32
Scandal: ask'd the Question. That's all. . . . . . . 256 FOR LOVE III.1 128
Valentine: thing; it's a Question that would puzzle an Arithmetician, . 280 FOR LOVE IV.1 175
Mrs Fore: Questicn? . . . . 284 FCB LOVE IV.1 332
Valentine: one Question. . . . . 311 FOR LCVE V.1 516
Zara: That Cuestion, speak again in that soft Voice, . . . 353 M. BRIDE III.1 154
Gonsalez: 'Twere not amiss to question her a little, . . . 367 M. BRIDE IV.1 237
Witwoud: Pleasure, and the Town, a Question at once so Foreign and . 402 WAY WCRLD I.1 257
Foible: I don't question your Generosity, Sir: And you need . 424 WAY WORLD II.1 541
Fainall: that's out of the Question,--And as to my part in my . 443 WAY WCRLD III.1 685

Question'd (1)
Osmyn-Alph: I've been to blame, and question'd with Impiety . . . . 352 M. BRIDE III.1 125

Questions (6)
Heartwell: hot Brothel. Ask no Questions. . . . . . . 105 OLD BATCH V.1 324
Tattle: I must ask you Questions, and you must answer. . . . 251 FOR LCVE II.1 599
Ben: as you say--well, and how? I have a many Questions . . 261 FOR LOVE III.1 295
Scandal: We are all under a mistake--Ask no Questions, . . . 278 FOR LOVE IV.1 102
Valentine: Summer suit. Ask me Cuestions ccncerning to morrow? . 288 FOR LOVE IV.1 494
Sr Sampson: Sir; you shall ask that Lady no Questions, till you have . 311 FOR LCVE V.1 518

Qui vult decipi (1)
Maskwell: Why, qui vult decipi decipiatur.--'Tis no fault . . . 194 DOUBL DLR V.1 262

Quibble (1)
Careless: I find a Quibble bears more sway in your Lordships . . . 132 DOUBL DLR I.1 214

Quiblers (1)
Marwood: Quiblers by the Statute; and become a Jest, against a Rule 467 WAY WCRLD V.1 215

Quick (11)
Lady Touch: O the Scene was shifted quick before me-- . . . . 185 DOUBL DLR IV.2 70
Lady Touch: Ground, be buried quick beneath it, e're I be consenting to 186 DOUBL DLR IV.2 99
Lady Touch: Ground, be buried quick beneath it, e're I'll be
consenting to . . . . 186 DOUBL DLR IV.2 V 99
Lord Touch: He has a quick invention, if this were . . . . 197 DOUBL DLR V.1 358
Sr Sampson: Conveyance--quick--quick (In Whisper to Jeremy.) . . . 281 FCR LOVE IV.1 210
Heli: You must be quick, for Love will lend her Wings. . . 344 M. BRIDE II.2 198
Zara: Quick; or, by Heav'n, this Dagger drinks thy Blood. . . 362 M. BRIDE IV.1 38
Selim: On Osmyn's Death; too quick a Change of Mercy, . . 362 M. BRIDE IV.1 45
Witwoud: O rare Petulant; thou art as quick as a Fire in a . . 409 WAY WCRLD I.1 519
Witwoud: O rare Petulant; thou art as quick as Fire in a . . . 409 WAY WCRLD I.1 V519

Quicken (1)
Bellmour: Actions free to--Quicken your Apprehension--And I-gad . . 59 OLD BATCH II.2 182

Quickly (25)
Sharper: restore it quickly, or by-- . . . . 48 OLD BATCH II.1 28
Setter: S'bud Sir, away quickly, there's Fondlewife just turn'd . 75 OLD BATCH IV.1 9
Bellmour: may lie down;--quickly, for I'm afraid I shall have a Fit. . 82 OLD BATCH IV.2 87
Laetitia: Chamber, quickly, quickly. You s'an't tum in. . . . 89 OLD BATCH IV.4 17
Bellmour: quickly, I'll follow you;--I wou'd not be known. (Exit . 97 OLD BATCH V.1 11
Bellmour: Promise to make her Amends quickly with another . . 100 OLD BATCH V.1 152
Maskwell: Nephew, when I first Sigh'd for you; I quickly found it . 136 DOUBL DLR I.1 361
Careless: quickly. . . . . 170 DOUEL DLR IV.1 96

564

Quickly   (continued)

Lady Ply:	sake step in here and advise me quickly, before he sees.	178	DOUEL DLR	IV.1	403
Lord Touch:	quickly show him which way that is going.	189	DOUBL DLR	V.1	77
Lord Touch:	inform my Nephew, and do you quickly as you can, bring	200	DOUEL DLR	V.1	487
Valentine:	Chair quickly: A Bottle of Sack and a Toast--fly--a Chair	222	FOR LCVE	I.1	229
Angelica:	Do Uncle, lock 'em up quickly before my Aunt	239	FOR LCVE	II.1	133
Valentine:	me have a Pair of Red hot Tongues quickly, quickly,	282	FCR LCVE	IV.1	240
Almeria:	Nay, quickly speak to me, and let me hear	339	M. EBIDE	II.1 V	68
Almeria:	Speak to it quickly, quickly, speak to me.	341	M. EBIDE	II.2	42
Zara:	So quickly was it Love; for thou wert Godlike	346	M. BRIDE	II.2	280
Osmyn-Alph:	Say somewhat quickly to conceal our Loves,	359	M. BRIDE	III.1	390
Manuel:	Will quickly waste, and give again the Day.	364	M. EBIDE	IV.1	108
Zara:	As thou art now--And I shall quickly be.	380	M. BRIDE	V.2	186
Foible:	(to him). Say 'tis your Nephew's hand.--quickly, his	460	WAY WORLD	IV.1	595
Sir Wilful:	take Shipping--Aunt, if you don't forgive quickly; I shall	472	WAY WCRLD	V.1	395

Quicksands (1)

Mrs Frail:	O I am happy to have discover'd the Shelves and Quicksands	286	FOR LCVE	IV.1	394

Quiet (6)

Belinda:	quiet, when he sees his Debtor has not wherewithal--	58	OLD EATCH	II.2	128
Belinda:	make a more than ordinary quiet Husband.	106	OLD BATCH	IV.1	367
Lady Touch:	been to me, you have already killed the quiet of this Life,	185	DOUBL DLR	IV.2	75
Jeremy:	to be mad: And I think I have nct found him very quiet	295	FCR LCVE	IV.1	755
Almeria:	Thou tco art quiet--long hast been at Peace--	327	M. BRIDE	I.1 V	52
Mirabell:	Beauty, and with her my Peace and Quiet; Nay all my	472	WAY WORLD	V.1	390

Quietness (1)

Foible:	Peace and Quietness by my good will: I had rather bring	464	WAY WORLD	V.1	87

Quill (1)

Valentine:	and blotted by every Goose's Quill. I know you; for I	292	FCR LCVE	IV.1	639

Quilted (1)

Lady Wish:	Beads broken, and a Quilted Night-cap with one Ear. Go,	462	WAY WCRLD	V.1	17

Quintessence (1)

Petulant:	The Quintessence. May be Witwoud knows more, he	408	WAY WCRLD	I.1	496

Quit (5)

Bellmour:	quit the Service.	47	OLD BATCH	I.1	373
Setter:	I'le not quit you so--I'le Follow and put you into	67	OLD BATCH	III.1	238
Zara:	Confer with him. I'll quit you to the King.	360	M. BRIDE	III.1	452
Zara:	Or speak with him. I'll quit you to the King.	360	M. BRIDE	III.1 V452	
Alonzo:	'Twill quit me of my Promise to Gonsalez.	373	M. EBIDE	V.1	30

Quite (16)

Sir Joseph:	I am quite another thing, when I am with him: I don't fear	50	OLD BATCH	II.1	122
Belinda:	Blood, the--All over--O Gad you are quite	54	OLD BATCH	II.2	14
Careless:	For Heaven's sake, Madam--I'm quite out of	160	DOUEL DLR	III.1	370
Sir Paul:	And my Lady's quite cut of Breath; or else you	160	DOUBL DLR	III.1	372
Brisk:	O Jesu! Madam, you have Eclips'd me quite, let me	201	DOUEL DLR	V.1	534
Brisk:	Madam, you have Eclips'd me quite, let me	201	DOUEL DLR	V.1 V534	
Jeremy:	Ah, Sir, he's quite gone.	278	FOR LCVE	IV.1	119
Jeremy:	Quite Non Compos, Sir.	279	FCB LCVE	IV.1	141
Ben:	has turn'd her senses, her Brain is quite overset.				
	Well-a-day,	286	FOR LCVE	IV.1	404
Zara:	I cannot feel it--quite beyond my reach.	381	M. EBIDE	V.2	210
Almeria:	What dead at last, quite, quite, for ever dead?	382	M. EBIDE	V.2	233
	With Nature's Oafs 'tis quite a diff'rent Case,	393	WAY WCRLD	PRO.	5
Fainall:	with a little Loss, than to be quite eaten up, with being	400	WAY WCRLD	I.1	208
Waitwell:	be quite the same Waitwell neither--For now I remember	424	WAY WCRLD	II.1	560
Millamant:	Poor Mirabell! his Constancy to me has quite destroy'd his	433	WAY WCRLD	III.1	336

Quits (2)

Vainlove:	another; for my Temper quits an Amour, just where	39	OLD EATCH	I.1	77
Bellmour:	Amour as he cares for, and quits it when it grows stale, or	42	OLD BATCH	I.1	212

Quixote (1)

Lady Wish:	Quixote. No Foible yet?	426	WAY WORLD	III.1	38

Quo (0)   see In statu quo

Quoif (1)

Marwood:	Quoif like a Man Midwife to bring your Daughter's	467	WAY WORLD	V.1	213

Quorum (1)

Sir Wilful:	be O' the Quorum--an it were not as good a deed as to	472	WAY WCRLD	V.1	393

Quoth (1)

Lady Wish:	with him--Travel quoth a; Ay travel, travel, get thee gone,	456	WAY WCRLD	IV.1	438

Quotha (2)

Heartwell:	quotha! I hope in Heaven I have a greater portion cf Grace,	44	OLD BATCH	I.1	295
Sr Sampson:	Sleep Quotha! No, why you would not sleep o'	310	FOR LCVE	V.1	484

Quoysh (0)   see Je-ne-scay-quoysh

Race (7)   see Horse-Race, Idiot-Race

Heartwell:	But 'tis with Whip and Spur the Bace is won.	112	OLD BATCH	V.2	195
Cynthia:	and hinder one another in the Race; I swear it never do's	168	DOUBL DLR	IV.1	13
Sr Sampson:	a long liv'd Race, and inherit Vigour, none of my Family	298	FCR LCVE	V.1	37
Sr Sampson:	a long liv'd Race, and inherit Vigour, none of my Ancestors	298	FOR LCVE	V.1 V 37	
Almeria:	Of all thy Race. Hear me, thou ccmmon Parent;	368	M. EBIDE	IV.1	278
Almeria:	Source of my Woes: thou and thy Race be curs'd;	370	M. EBIDE	IV.1	379
Gonsalez:	Anselmo's Race; yet if--that If concludes me.	371	M. EBIDE	IV.1	410

Rack (11)

Araminta:	are like Discoveries from the Rack, when the afflicted	58	OLD EATCH	II.2	136
Heartwell:	not rack me in suspence.	72	OLD BATCH	III.2	42
Heartwell:	not rack me with suspence.	72	OLD BATCH	III.2 V 42	
Lord Touch:	Sorry, for what? 'Death you rack me with	152	DOUBL DLR	III.1	79
Lady Touch:	--Oh! I could rack my self, play the Vulture to my own	184	DOUBL DLR	IV.2	46
Maskwell:	upon the Rack; and made discov'ry of her last Plot: I hope	199	DOUBL DLR	V.1	462
Manuel:	With reeking Gore, from Traytors on the Rack:	367	M. EBIDE	IV.1	253
Almeria:	To the remorsless Rack I would have given	369	M. EBIDE	IV.1	311
Marwood:	have him ever to continue upon the Rack of Fear and	411	WAY WORLD	II.1	63
Waitwell:	am tantaliz'd on a rack; And do but hang Madam, on the	457	WAY WORLD	IV.1	492
Waitwell:	am tantaliz'd on the rack; And do but hang Madam, on the	457	WAY WORLD	IV.1 V492	

Rack'd (2)

Zara:	Thou hast already rack'd me with thy stay;	361	M. EBIDE	IV.1	1
Manuel:	Confesses it. By Heav'n I'll have him rack'd,	368	M. EBIDE	IV.1	294

Rackets (1)

	Then bounding Balls and Backets they encompass'd,	315	FOR LOVE	EPI.	30

Racking (1)   see Soul-racking
    Zara: What racking Cares disease a Monarch's Bed? . . . . . 354 M. BRIDE III.1 206
Racks (4)
    Heartwell: O Torture! How he racks and tears me!-- . . . . . . 104 OLD BATCH V.1 308
    Almeria: Did'st thou not say, that Racks and Wheels were . . . 357 M. BRIDE III.1 311
    Osmyn-Alph: What are all Racks, and Wheels, and Whips to this? . . 358 M. BRIDE III.1 362
    Lady Wish: a Person who wou'd suffer racks in honour's cause, dear . 459 WAY WORLD IV.1 553
Radish (1)
    Petulant: he (hiccup) rises upon my stomack like a Radish. . . . 454 WAY WORLD IV.1 357
Raffl'd (1)
    Tattle: where we raffl'd-- . . . . 258 FOR LOVE III.1 179
Raffled (2)
    Tattle: whom I mean; for there were a great many Ladies raffled . 258 FOR LOVE III.1 188
    Tattle: whom I mean; for there was a great many Ladies raffled . 258 FOR LOVE III.1 V188
Rag (1)
    Lady Wish: Traverse Rag, in a shop no bigger than a Bird-cage,-- . 462 WAY WORLD V.1   7
Rage (28)
    Maskwell: surprize your Aunt and me together: Counterfeit a rage . 157 DOUBL DLR III.1 250
    Lady Touch: of this rage, and one minutes coolness to dissemble. . . 185 DOUBL DLR IV.2   66
    Lady Touch: Moderate your rage good my Lord! he's . . . . . . 186 DOUBL DLR IV.2 112
    Lady Touch: Ha! do you mock my Rage? then this shall . . . . . 198 DOUBL DLR V.1 391
    Lady Touch: Thou hast, thou hast found the only way to turn my Rage; . 198 DOUBL DLR V.1 398
    Lord Touch: Astonishment binds up my rage! Villany . . . . . 199 DOUBL DLR V.1 468
                  Since the Plain-Dealers Scenes of Manly Rage, . . . 214 FOR LOVE PRO.   39
    Almeria: Of King Anselmo's Pallace; which in Rage . . . . . 329 M. BRIDE I.1 113
    Osmyn-Alph: And twice escap'd, both from the Rage of Seas . . . 344 M. BRIDE II.2 V173
    Osmyn-Alph: And Rage of War: For in the Fight, I saw . . . . 344 M. BRIDE II.2 174
    Manuel: Better for him, to tempt the Rage of Heav'n, ... 349 M. BRIDE II.2 368
    Zara: Of these thy Wrongs; as she, whose barbarous Rage . . 353 M. BRIDE III.1 158
    Zara: And now just ripe for Birth, my Rage has ruin'd. . . . 354 M. BRIDE III.1 196
    Osmyn-Alph: Some swift and dire event, of her blind Rage, . . . 355 M. BRIDE III.1 231
    Osmyn-Alph: Hell, Hell! have I not Cause to rage and rave? . . . 358 M. BRIDE III.1 361
    Zara: Choak in my Rage, and know the utmost depth . . . . 359 M. BRIDE III.1 407
    Zara: Heav'n has no Rage, like Love to Hatred turn'd, . . . 361 M. BRIDE III.1 457
    Zara: In whom I live. Spite of my Rage, and Pride, ... 361 M. BRIDE IV.1   25
    Zara: Forgive my Rage; I know thy Love and Truth. . . . . 362 M. BRIDE IV.1   41
    Gonsalez: I grant it, Sir, and doubt not, but in Rage . . . . 366 M. BRIDE IV.1 218
    Manuel: Hence, e'er I curse--fly my just Rage with speed; . . . 369 M. BRIDE IV.1 316
    Manuel: Give me Rage, Rage, implacable Revenge, ... 373 M. BRIDE V.1   36
    Manuel: Give me new Rage, implacable Revenge, ... 373 M. BRIDE V.1 V 36
    Garcia: The Horrour of that Thought, has damp'd my Rage. . . . 378 M. BRIDE V.2   74
    Zara: His hellish Rage had wanted Means to act, ... 380 M. BRIDE V.2 177
    Fainall: Your Guilt, not your Resentment, begets your Rage. . . . 415 WAY WORLD II.1 184
    Witwoud: neither of 'em speak for rage; And so fell a sputt'ring at 453 WAY WORLD IV.1 333
Ragged (1)
    Jeremy: whole Tatter to her Tail, but as ragged as one of the . 219 FOR LOVE I.1 110
Raging (2)
    Tattle: Quality that shall be nameless, in a raging Fit of
                      Jealousie, ... 258 FOR LOVE III.1 175
    Zara: Would, like the raging Dog-star, scorch the Earth, . . 375 M. BRIDE V.1   95
Rags (1)
    Lady Wish: Frippery the Villain; I'll reduce him to Frippery and Rags. 428 WAY WORLD III.1 129
Rail (7)
    Bellmour: self, nor suffers any Body else to rail at me. Then as I . 41 OLD BATCH I.1 169
                  But we're so us'd to Rail on these Occasions, . . . 113 OLD BATCH EPI. 19
    Valentine: therefore resolve to rail at all that have: And in that I
                      but . . . . 217 FOR LOVE I.1   35
    Valentine: Therefore I would rail in my Writings, and be . . . 219 FOR LOVE I.1 136
    Scandal: Rail? At whom? the whole World? Impotent and . . . 219 FOR LOVE I.1 138
    Sir Wilful: time; and rail when that day comes. . . . . . . 441 WAY WORLD III.1 612
    Mirabell: shall be found out.--And rail at me for missing the . . 451 WAY WORLD IV.1 241
Rail'd (1)
    Foible: Lady that Mr. Mirabell rail'd at her. I laid horrid Things 430 WAY WORLD III.1 208
Railer (1)
    Lady Wish: A slander-mouth'd Railer: I warrant the Spendthrift . 428 WAY WORLD III.1 132
Railing (4)
    Belinda: Talent of Railing? . . . . 88 OLD BATCH IV.3 197
    Belinda: Nay, sure Railing is the best qualification in a . . . 88 OLD BATCH IV.3 201
    Sharper: Nay, Prithee, leave Railing, and come along with . . 104 OLD BATCH V.1 284
    Mirabell: Fashions, spoiling Reputations, railing at absent
                      Friends, and . . . . 451 WAY WORLD IV.1 268
Railings (1)
    Maskwell: full fruition of my Love, I'll bear the railings of a losing 190 DOUBL DLR V.1   87
Raillery (11)
    Brisk: judged by Mellefont here, who gives and takes Raillery . 128 DOUBL DLR I.1   27
    Lord Froth: He, he, I swear tho', your Raillery provokes me . . . 132 DOUBL DLR I.1 208
    Maskwell: By this Light, I'm serious; all raillery apart-- . . . 156 DOUBL DLR III.1 232
    Angelica: I don't like Raillery from a serious Face--pray . . . 276 FOR LOVE IV.1   27
    Mirabell: affects the Reputation of understanding Raillery; that he . 401 WAY WORLD I.1 229
    Mirabell: O Raillery, Raillery. Come, I know thou art in . . . 407 WAY WORLD I.1 448
    Marwood: What pity 'tis, so much fine Raillery, and . . . . 434 WAY WORLD III.1 345
    Witwoud: Raillery, Raillery, Madam, we have no Animosity . . . 435 WAY WORLD III.1 393
    Lady Wish: understand Raillery better. . . . . 441 WAY WORLD III.1 609
Rails (1)
    Bellmour: Yet rails on still, and thinks his Love unknown to us; . 40 OLD BATCH I.1 123
Rain (8)
                  What Peals of Thunder, and what Show'rs of Rain; . . 323 M. BRIDE PRO.   10
    Gonsalez: White as the fleecy Rain on Alpine Hills; . . . . . 331 M. BRIDE I.1 231
    Osmyn-Alph: But dash'd with Rain from Eyes, and swail'd with Sighs, . 357 M. BRIDE III.1 323
    Almeria: With Rivers of incessant scalding Rain. . . . . . 358 M. BRIDE III.1 374
    Zara: --Rain, rain ye Stars, spout from your burning Orbs . 380 M. BRIDE V.2 V168
    Leonora: Will stab the Sight, and make your Eyes rain Blood. . . 381 M. BRIDE V.2 230
    Leonora: Rain Blood.-- . . . . 382 M. BRIDE V.2 V231
Rains (1)
    Ben: rains out at her Eyes. . . . . 265 FOR LOVE III.1 443

Reading   (continued)

Reality   (continued)
| Valentine: | Affectation and Reality. . . . . | 254 | FOR LOVE | III.1 | 41 |
| Mirabell: | Consider Madam, in reality; You cou'd not receive . . | 472 | WAY WORLD | V.1 | 383 |

Really (11)
Bellmour:	know and believe more than really we do. You read of but .	37	OLD BATCH	I.1	20
Sharper:	Not I really Sir.	52	OLD BATCH	II.1	186
Heartwell:	thou sure she is really married to him?	111	OLD BATCH	V.2	127
Setter:	Really and lawfully married, I am witness. . . .	111	OLD BATCH	V.2	128
Lady Froth:	Friend,--but really, as you say, I wonder too,--but .	138	DOUBL DLR	II.1	9
Sir Paul:	I am much obliged to Mr. Careless really, he is a .	172	DOUBL DLR	IV.1	178
Brisk:	see how Love and Murder will out. But did I really name	176	DOUBL DLR	IV.1	329
Scandal:	No really, Sir; I'm his Witness, it was all Counterfeit.	311	FOR LOVE	V.1	506
Foresight:	Really, Sir Sampson, this is a sudden Eclipse-- .	313	FOR LOVE	V.1	582
Lady Wish:	Affairs really I know not what to do--(Calls)--Foible--I .	431	WAY WORLD	III.1	256
Servant-W:	Really Sir, I can't tell; here come so many here, 'tis .	437	WAY WORLD	IV.1	470

Reap (2)
| Sharper: | him; you with pleasure reap that fruit, which he takes . | 43 | OLD BATCH | I.1 | 219 |
| Angelica: | reap up all your false Prophesies, ridiculous Dreams, and | 237 | FOR LOVE | II.1 | 77 |

Rear (2)
| Setter: | march in the rear of my Master, and enter the Breaches . | 65 | OLD BATCH | III.1 | 175 |
| Almeria: | Whose antient Pillars rear their Marble Heads, . . . | 339 | M. BRIDE | II.1 | 60 |

Reason (50)
Vainlove:	satisfied without Reason.	40	OLD BATCH	I.1	110
Vainlove:	thinks her Vertuous; that's one reason why I fail her:	40	OLD BATCH	I.1	119
Bellmour:	reason that you would a Dun.	58	OLD BATCH	II.2	125
Bellmour:	When Wit and Reason, both, have fail'd to move; . .	60	OLD BATCH	II.2	224
Heartwell:	recollected, I will recover my reason and be gone. .	62	OLD BATCH	III.1	70
Lucy:	To be brief then; what is the reason your Master did .	66	OLD BATCH	III.1	217
Fondlewife:	instructions, I will reason with her before I go. .	76	OLD BATCH	IV.1	47
Fondlewife:	And in the mean time, I will reason with my self-- .	76	OLD BATCH	IV.1	49
Fondlewife:	me, than she has reason to be; and in the way of Trade,	77	OLD BATCH	IV.1	60
Vainlove:	And so I remember in the Park.--She had reason, if I .	99	OLD BATCH	V.1	97
Mellefont:	Then thy Reason staggers, and thou'rt almost . . .	127	DOUBL DLR	I.1	5
Mellefont:	True, but you shall judge whether I have not reason .	129	DOUBL DLR	I.1	83
Cynthia:	Because he has not so much reason to be fond of . .	141	DOUBL DLR	II.1	107
Mellefont:	Ay, my Lord, I shall have the same reason for my .	141	DOUBL DLR	II.1	111
Sir Paul:	Reason,--as soon may Tygers Match with Tygers, Lambs .	144	DOUBL DLR	II.1	224
Careless:	reason to complain of my Reception; but I find women are	158	DOUBL DLR	III.1	307
Cynthia:	any thing that resists my will, tho' 'twere reason it self.	193	DOUBL DLR	V.1	205
Lord Touch:	her as much as reason--by Heav'n, I'll not be Wife-ridden;	196	DOUBL DLR	V.1	320
Valentine:	hate, for just such another Reason; because they abound in	217	FOR LOVE	I.1	38
Valentine:	reason either for hope or despair.	225	FOR LOVE	I.1	347
Scandal:	what they mean: But you have little reason to believe that	225	FOR LOVE	I.1	350
Scandal:	can in reason expect: I shall have an esteem for thee, well,	227	FOR LOVE	I.1	438
Mrs Frail:	That's somewhat the better reason, to my	234	FOR LOVE	I.1	669
Foresight:	How? how? is that the reason? Come, you know . . .	239	FOR LOVE	II.1	146
Valentine:	also deprive me of Reason, Thought, Passions, Inclinations,	244	FOR LOVE	II.1	340
Valentine:	also divest me of Reason, Thought, Passions, Inclinations .	244	FOR LOVE	II.1	V340
Sr Sampson:	it, that by the rule of right Reason, this fellow ought to	245	FOR LOVE	II.1	366
Tattle:	hang me if I know the reason of it.	251	FOR LOVE	II.1	584
Scandal:	reason. (She gives him the Glass: Scandal and she whisper.)	269	FOR LOVE	III.1	585
Scandal:	Would he have Angelica acquainted with the Reason . .	276	FOR LOVE	IV.1	6
Scandal:	Reason, which you gave to Mr. Tattle; for his impertinence	294	FOR LOVE	IV.1	688
Valentine:	Gods have been in counterfeited Shapes for the same Reason;	294	FOR LOVE	IV.1	701
Angelica:	am I deluded by this Interval of Sense, to reason with a .	295	FOR LOVE	IV.1	729
Angelica:	Why you have no great reason to complain, Sir . . .	298	FOR LOVE	V.1	16
Jeremy:	sure she'll have reason to pray for me, when she finds .	302	FOR LOVE	V.1	203
Tattle:	reason to hate her neither; but I believe I shall lead her a	309	FOR LOVE	V.1	467
Valentine:	can effect it: Which, for that Reason, I will sign to--- .	312	FOR LOVE	V.1	548
	Nor were they without Reason join'd together; . . .	323	M. BRIDE	PRO.	7
Osmyn-Alph:	Ere Reason can be born: Reason, the Power	350	M. BRIDE	III.1	35
Manuel:	There's Reason in thy Doubt, and I am warn'd. . . .	367	M. BRIDE	IV.1	227
Fainall:	you, and with Reason.--What, then my Wife was . . .	396	WAY WORLD	I.1	26
Mirabell:	For which Reason I resolv'd not to stir. At last the .	396	WAY WORLD	I.1	34
Mirabell:	Fool, can have but one Reason for associating with a .	399	WAY WORLD	I.1	146
Mrs Fain:	Reason have you to hate him in particular?	411	WAY WORLD	II.1	71
Mrs Fain:	By the Reason you give for your Aversion, one . . .	412	WAY WORLD	II.1	74
Marwood:	Pray let us; I have a Reason.	413	WAY WORLD	II.1	120
Mirabell:	Dictates of Reason, and yet persevere to play the Fool by	423	WAY WORLD	II.1	500
Millamant:	Reason why you discover'd it is a Secret.	433	WAY WORLD	III.1	330
Millamant:	without giving a reason. To have my Closet Inviolate; to .	450	WAY WORLD	IV.1	221

Reasonable (9)
Cynthia:	I would not--But 'tis but reasonable that since I . .	168	DOUBL DLR	IV.1	44
Jeremy:	Yes, I have a reasonable good Ear, Sir, as to Jiggs and .	245	FOR LOVE	II.1	373
Scandal:	and be content only to be made a Fool with other reasonable	278	FOR LOVE	IV.1	107
Angelica:	Oh here's a reasonable Creature--sure he will . . .	295	FOR LOVE	IV.1	733
Angelica:	reasonable Stock of good Nature and Sense--For I . .	299	FOR LOVE	V.1	63
Valentine:	to undo the Son, it was a reasonable return of Nature. .	311	FOR LOVE	V.1	512
Mirabell:	I did as much as Man cou'd, with any reasonable . .	397	WAY WORLD	I.1	68
Mirabell:	your demands are pretty reasonable.	450	WAY WORLD	IV.1	211
Sir Wilful:	By'r Lady a very reasonable request; and will cost .	471	WAY WORLD	V.1	380

Reasoning (2)
| Vainlove: | Madam, will admit of no farther reasoning.--But . . . | 88 | OLD BATCH | IV.3 | 177 |
| Careless: | Sir Paul, harkee, I'm reasoning the matter you know; . | 163 | DOUBL DLR | III.1 | 493 |

Reasons (4)
Bellmour:	Reasons for what I do, which I'll tell you within.--In .	98	OLD BATCH	V.1	69
Lady Touch:	--Don't ask me my Reasons, my Lord, for they are . .	151	DOUBL DLR	III.1	42
Lord Touch:	same Reasons ought to be convincing to me, which create .	152	DOUBL DLR	III.1	48
Valentine:	I thought I had Reasons--But it was a poor	311	FOR LOVE	V.1	507

Rebate (1)
| Maskwell: | Conscience and Honour in my Face, to rebate my Inclinations. | 136 | DOUBL DLR | I.1 | 338 |

Rebel-rate (1)
| Lady Wish: | Must I live to be confiscated at this Rebel-rate?--Here . | 470 | WAY WORLD | V.1 | 308 |

Rebell (1)
| Waitwell: | What, my Rival! is the Rebell my Rival? a'dies. . . . | 458 | WAY WORLD | IV.1 | 518 |

Rebellious (1)
Manuel: Bear to the Dungeon, those Rebellious Slaves;   . . . . . 362 M. BRIDE IV.1 62
Rebuild (1)
Maskwell: What, to Rebuild, will a whole Age Employ. . . . . . 138 DOUBL DLR I.1 422
Recall (1)
Scandal: of the Name, recall the Stage of Athens, and be allow'd . 220 FOR LOVE I.1 149
Recall'd (2)
Maskwell: him, and that, I have recall'd; so I have served my self, 188 DOUBL DLR V.1 24
Selim: His Eyes had err'd, he hastily recall'd . . . . . 375 M. BRIDE V.1 99
Recant (1)
Bellmour: he shou'd recant. (Aside.) Well, we shall have your Company 112 OLD BATCH V.2 176
Recede (1)
Lady Wish: If you do, I protest I must recede--or . . . . . . 459 WAY WORLD IV.1 534
Receipt (1)
Scandal: Patience, I suppose, the old Receipt. . . . . 220 FOR LOVE I.1 170
Receipts (1)
Jeremy: Receipts? . . . . 216 FOR LOVE I.1 11
Receiv'd (16)
Sharper: you hope to be receiv'd into the Alliance of a noble . . 45 OLD BATCH I.1 307
Lucy: his Face--Receive it! why he receiv'd it, as I would one . 61 OLD BATCH III.1 20
Lucy: --a' receiv'd it, as if 'thad been a Letter from his . . 61 OLD BATCH III.1 23
Bellmour: you ought to return him Thanks now you have receiv'd . . 68 OLD BATCH III.1 282
Sharper: of some favours lately receiv'd; I would not have you draw 69 OLD BATCH III.1 303
Vainlove: There I receiv'd the Letter--It must be so. . . . . 99 OLD BATCH V.1 119
Careless: and that the first Favour he receiv'd from her, was a . 157 DOUBL DLR III.1 275
Cynthia: Conversation are receiv'd and admir'd by the World-- . 167 DOUBL DLR III.1 628
Tattle: be receiv'd but upon Publick Days; and my Visits will . 230 FOR LOVE I.1 516
Tattle: long receiv'd the passionate Addresses of the accomplisht 255 FOR LOVE III.1 68
Almeria: The silent Tomb receiv'd the good old King; . . . . 326 M. BRIDE I.1 10
Zara: When he receiv'd you as the Prince of Fez; . . . . 347 M. BRIDE II.2 295
Gonsalez: If such a one, so 'scaping, was receiv'd . . . . . 363 M. BRIDE IV.1 102
Fainall: came in, and was well receiv'd by her, while you . . 395 WAY WORLD I.1 20
Lady Wish: benefits that I have receiv'd from your goodness? To you I 465 WAY WORLD V.1 126
Mirabell: having it seems receiv'd some Cautions respecting your . 476 WAY WORLD V.1 541
Receive (22)
Lucy: ready to receive him. . . . . 60 OLD BATCH III.1 3
Silvia: how did he refuse? Tell me--how did he receive my . . 61 OLD BATCH III.1 16
Lucy: his Face--Receive it! why he receiv'd it, as I would one . 61 OLD BATCH III.1 20
Lucy: Go get you in Madam, receive him pleasantly, dress up . 62 OLD BATCH III.1 48
Lady Touch: to receive an ill impression from any opinion of mine . 151 DOUBL DLR III.1 37
Maskwell: receive me in her Bed-Chamber. . . . . 156 DOUBL DLR III.1 234
  So from your Bounty, we receive this Stage; . . . . 213 FOR LOVE PRO. 14
Foresight: I'm so perplex'd and vex'd, I am not fit to receive . . 239 FOR LOVE II.1 164
Valentine: I shall receive no Benefit from the Opinion: For . . . 254 FOR LOVE III.1 39
Tattle: shall make Oath, that I receive more Letters than the . 257 FOR LOVE III.1 159
Valentine: If my happiness cou'd receive Addition, this Kind . . 312 FOR LOVE V.1 579
Manuel: Receive this Lord, as one whom I have found . . . . 334 M. BRIDE I.1 333
Marwood: in our Breasts, and every Heart, or soon or late, receive
  and . . . . 410 WAY WORLD II.1 26
Lady Wish: my Features, to receive Sir Rowland with any Oeconomy of . 428 WAY WORLD III.1 141
Lady Wish: dress above. I'll receive Sir Rowland here. Is he handsome? 429 WAY WORLD III.1 172
Lady Wish: Well, and how shall I receive him? In what . . . . 445 WAY WORLD IV.1 17
Lady Wish: receive him in my little dressing Room, there's a Couch-- . 445 WAY WORLD IV.1 23
Millamant: Trifles,--As liberty to pay and receive visits . . . 450 WAY WORLD IV.1 212
Millamant: to and from whom I please, to write and receive Letters, . 450 WAY WORLD IV.1 213
Poible: discompose you when you were to receive Sir Rowland. . . 461 WAY WORLD IV.1 620
Waitwell: Ere long you shall Substantial proof receive . . . . 462 WAY WORLD IV.1 646
Mirabell: Consider Madam, in reality; You cou'd not receive . . 472 WAY WORLD V.1 383
Received (1)
Setter: received the Letter. . . . . 99 OLD BATCH V.1 101
Receiver (1)
Mirabell: grace, and the receiver lessens his Pleasure? . . . . 449 WAY WORLD IV.1 173
Receives (2)
Bellmour: And ev'ry Eye receives a new-born Sight. . . . . . 81 OLD BATCH IV.2 12
Sir Paul: whomsoever he receives into his bosom, will find the way . 178 DOUBL DLR IV.1 421
Receiving (1)
Scandal: the marks of her Person: He will forswear receiving a . . 226 FOR LOVE I.1 372
Receptacle (1)
Lady Wish: to a Cast-serving-man; to make me a receptacle, an . . . 463 WAY WORLD V.1 35
Reception (1)
Careless: reason to complain of my Reception; but I find women are . 158 DOUBL DLR III.1 307
Recesses (1)
Lady Touch: and Recesses of my Soul.--Oh Mellefont! I burn; . . . 137 DOUBL DLR I.1 398
Reciprocal (1)
Tattle: reciprocal Affection. . . . . 255 FOR LOVE III.1 72
Reckon (1)
Jeremy: that I reckon it will break of course by to morrow, and no 221 FOR LOVE I.1 181
Reckoning (1)
Witwoud: He's reckoning his Mony,--my Mony it was, ... 402 WAY WORLD I.1 279
Reclaiming (1)
Lucy: As you would wish--Since there is no reclaiming . . . 75 OLD BATCH III.2 155
Recollect (2)
Sir Joseph: Stay, stay Sir, let me recollect-- (aside) he's a . . 48 OLD BATCH II.1 43
Scandal: Pray recollect your self. . . . . 284 FOR LOVE IV.1 326
Recollected (1)
Heartwell: recollected, I will recover my reason and be gone. . . 62 OLD BATCH III.1 70
Recollection (1)
Sir Joseph: the recollection of my errour, and leave me floating . . 49 OLD BATCH II.1 58
Recommend (5)
Bellmour: thy Talent will never recommend thee to any thing of . . 45 OLD BATCH I.1 300
Heartwell: don't expect should ever recommend me to People of . . 45 OLD BATCH I.1 303
Capt Bluff: I'le recommend my self--Sir I honour you; I understand . 51 OLD BATCH II.1 155
Scandal: recommend a Song to you upon the Hint of my two . . . 258 FOR LOVE III.1 191
Jeremy: Spring of your Bounty--I thought I could not recommend . 302 FOR LOVE V.1 176
Recompence (5)
Osmyn-Alph: Some Recompence of Love and matchless Truth. . . . . 343 M. BRIDE II.2 146

Recompence   (continued)
  Almeria: 'Tis more than Recompence, to see thy Face: 343   M. BRIDE   II.2   147
  Zara: Is this the Recompence of Love?   345   M. BRIDE   II.2   238
  Zara: Is this the Recompence reserv'd for Love?   345   M. BRIDE   II.2 V238
  Manuel: What Off'ring, or what Recompence remains   365   M. BRIDE   IV.1   157
Recompose   (1)
  Lady Wish: He has put me out of all patience. I shall never recompose   428   WAY WORLD   III.1   140
Reconcil'd   (1)
  Fainall: reconcil'd to Truth and me?   415   WAY WORLD   II.1   215
Reconcile   (2)
  Valentine: think of means to reconcile me to him; and preserve the   . 294   FOR LOVE   IV.1   717
  Lady Wish: reconcile me to the bad World, or else I wou'd retire to   . 465   WAY WORLD   V.1   132
Reconciled   (1)
  Sir Joseph: reconciled to this place heartily.   48   OLD BATCH   II.1   15
Reconcilement   (1)
  Fainall: reconcilement: Millamant had forfeited the Moiety of her   . 415   WAY WORLD   II.1   204
Reconciliation   (2)
  Lucy: and have fram'd a Letter, that makes her sue for
                    Reconciliation   75   OLD BATCH III.2   157
  Petulant: kiss'd your twin yonder in a humour of reconciliation, till   454   WAY WORLD   IV.1   356
Record   (1)
  Marwood: record; not even in Dooms-day-Book: to discompose the   . 467   WAY WORLD   V.1   217
Recov'ring   (1)
                There's no recov'ring Damages or Cost.   323   M. BRIDE   PRO.   26
Recover   (12)
  Sharper: came half despairing to recover; but thanks to my better   . 49   OLD BATCH   II.1   83
  Lucy: You may as soon hope, to recover your own Maiden-head,   . 61   OLD BATCH III.1   7
  Heartwell: recollected, I will recover my reason and be gone.   . .   . 62   OLD BATCH III.1   70
                Would give the World she could her Toy recover: . . .   113   OLD BATCH   EPI.   4
  Lady Touch: Kindness--but will you go into your Closet, and recover   . 153   DOUBL DLR III.1   116
  Jeremy: But Sir, Is this the way to recover your Father's   . .   218   FOR LOVE   I.1   82
  Foresight: him; I shall scarce recover my self before the Hour be   . 239   FOR LOVE   II.1   165
  Angelica: he won't recover his Senses till I lose mine.   . . .   277   FOR LOVE   IV.1   76
  Buckram: he recover his Senses.   280   FOR LOVE   IV.1   186
  Mrs Fore: revoking. And if he should recover his Senses, he'll be   . 288   FOR LOVE   IV.1   474
  Waitwell: Difficulty will be how to recover my Acquaintance and   . 424   WAY WORLD   II.1   557
  Mrs Fain: wou'd fall into fits, and maybe not recover time enough to   452   WAY WORLD   IV.1   301
Recover'd   (1)
  Foresight: Undertakings successful; or Goods stoll'n recover'd, I   . 241   FOR LOVE   II.1   217
Recovers   (2)
  Sr Sampson: He recovers--bless thee, Val--How do'st   281   FOR LOVE   IV.1   194
  Gonsalez: She recovers.   334   M. BRIDE   I.1   347
Recovery   (1)
  Angelica: depends upon the recovery of Valentine. Therefore I   . 277   FOR LOVE   IV.1   56
Recreation   (2)
  Mrs Frail: you had been there, it had been only innocent Recreation.   246   FOR LOVE   II.1   423
  Mirabell: for your own Recreation, and not for my Conveniency.   . 423   WAY WORLD   II.1   506
Red   (10)
  Lady Ply: as red as a Turky-Cock; O fie, Cousin Mellefont!   . .   147   DOUBL DLR   II.1   336
  Brisk: red face, and you comparing him to the Sun--and you   . 164   DOUBL DLR III.1   508
  Mrs Frail: she's very pretty!--Lord, what pure red and white!   . 250   FOR LOVE   II.1   556
  Valentine: me have a Pair of Red hot Tongues quickly, quickly,   . 282   FOR LOVE   IV.1   240
  Almeria: Thy Heart will burst, thy Eyes look red and start;   . 356   M. BRIDE   III.1   273
  Zara: Their red and angry Beams; as if his Sight   375   M. BRIDE   V.1   94
  Lady Wish: Fetch me the Red--The Red, do you hear, Sweet-heart?   . 425   WAY WORLD III.1   5
  Lady Wish: Wench stirs! Why dost thou not fetch me a little Red?   . 425   WAY WORLD III.1   7
  Peg: The red Ratifia does your Ladyship mean, or the Cherry   . 425   WAY WORLD III.1   9
Red-hissing   (1)
  Manuel: And wrench the Bolt red-hissing, from the Hand   . . .   349   M. BRIDE   II.2   369
Red'ning   (1)
  Fainall: Fire. I have seen the warm Confession red'ning on your   . 413   WAY WORLD   II.1   140
Redeem   (2)
  Sir Joseph: have all my ready Mony to redeem his great Sword from   . .   51   OLD BATCH   II.1   131
  Zara: Thou hast the Wrong, 'till I redeem thee hence;   . . .   355   M. BRIDE   III.1   218
Redeem'd   (1)
  Zara: The Slave, the Wretch that she redeem'd from Death,   . 346   M. BRIDE   II.2   250
Redeliver   (1)
  Capt Bluff: and live, go, and force him, to redeliver you the Note--   . 67   OLD BATCH III.1   250
Redemption   (1)
  Laetitia: (aside). Ruin'd, past redemption! What shall I do?   . . .   90   OLD BATCH   IV.4   45
Redfleck'd   (1)
  Manuel: What mean those swollen and redfleck'd Eyes, that look   . 367   M. BRIDE   IV.1   248
Redned   (1)
  Mirabell: she redned and I withdrew, without expecting her Reply.   . 396   WAY WORLD   I.1   40
Reduc'd   (4)
  Valentine: that Love, which has principally reduc'd me to this Lowness   217   FOR LOVE   I.1   55
  Valentine: the Love, which has principally reduc'd me to this Lowness   217   FOR LOVE   I.1 V 55
  Alonzo: But what are Kings reduc'd to common Clay?   379   M. BRIDE   V.2   113
  Millamant: bestow, if I were reduc'd to an Inglorious ease; and free'd   449   WAY WORLD   IV.1   168
Reduce   (2)
  Heli: And think on what we may reduce to Practise.   352   M. BRIDE   III.1   94
  Lady Wish: Frippery the Villain; I'll reduce him to Frippery and Rags.   428   WAY WORLD III.1   129
Reeking   (1)
  Manuel: With reeking Gore, from Traytors on the Rack: 367   M. BRIDE   IV.1   253
Refin'd   (1)
  Witwoud: Yes, refin'd, like a Dutch Skipper from a   441   WAY WORLD III.1   590
Refine   (1)
  Valentine: Read, read, Sirrah, and refine your Appetite; learn   . 216   FOR LOVE   I.1   12
Refining   (1)
  Mirabell: refining on your Pleasures.   395   WAY WORLD   I.1   12
Reflect   (10)
  Lady Ply: O reflect upon the horror of that, and then the   147   DOUBL DLR   II.1   314
  Mrs Fore: Besides, it wou'd not only reflect upon you, Sister, but me.   247   FOR LOVE   II.1   434
  Mrs Frail: Pooh, here's a Clutter--why should it reflect   . . .   247   FOR LOVE   II.1   435
  Valentine: Pardon me, Sir. But I reflect that I very lately   . .   311   FOR LOVE   V.1   524
                I can't reflect without an aking Heart, ...   315   FOR LOVE   EPI.   36

575

579

Resign'd (2)
    Valentine: Articles, I must this Morning have resign'd: And this I   . 294   FOR LOVE   IV.1   719
    Mirabell: And Sir, I have resign'd my pretensions.   473   WAY WORLD V.1   422
Resignation (6)
    Lady Ply: of an intire resignation of all my best Wishes, for the   . 169   DOUBL DLR IV.1   81
    Osmyn-Alph: Left this Example of his Resignation, ... 353   M. BRIDE   III.1 135
                    Who to your Judgments yields all Resignation;   393   WAY WORLD PRO.   39
    Mirabell: the necessity of such a resignation.   396   WAY WORLD I.1   44
    Millamant: to make a Resignation of it, in your Lady-ship's presence; . 470   WAY WORLD V.1   331
    Painall: resignation; nor Sir Wilfull, ycur right--You may draw   . 473   WAY WORLD V.1   439
Resist (2)
    Lord Froth: ay, there it is; who could resist! 'twas sc my heart was
                    made   140   DOUBL DLR II.1   68
    Lady Ply: resist the strongest Temptation,--but yet I know, 'tis   . 147   DOUBL DLR II.1   327
Resistance (1)
    Singer: But while she fond Resistance made, ... 71   OLD BATCH III.2 V 15
Resisted (3)
    Careless: she has resisted.   158   DOUBL DLR III.1 297
    Angelica: Am I? Well, I freely confess I have resisted a great   . 257   FOR LOVE   III.1 137
    Tattle: not been resisted.   257   FOR LOVE   III.1 140
Resists (1)
    Cynthia: any thing that resists my will, tho' 'twere reason it self. 193   DOUBL DLR V.1   205
Resolute (2)
    Bellmour: resolute.   111   OLD BATCH V.2   156
    Selim: You must still seem most resolute and fix'd   362   M. BRIDE   IV.1   44
Resolution (9)
                    I cannot stay to hear your Resolution.   35   OLD BATCH PRO.   27
    Mellefont: in a resolution, confirm'd by a Thousand Curses, not to   . 130   DOUBL DLR I.1   117
    Sir Paul: should take a Vagarie and make a rash Resclution on your   . 174   DOUBL DLR I.1   251
    Valentine: to a Resolution.   259   FOR LOVE   III.1 228
    Angelica: I can't. Resolution must come to me, or I shall   259   FOR LOVE   III.1 229
    Mrs Frail: have seen the Resolution of a Lover,--Honest Tarr and   . 287   FOR LOVE   IV.1   450
    Leonora: Alas! I fear some fatal Resolution.   331   M. BRIDE   I.1   200
    Sir Wilful: not. I am somewhat dainty in making a Resolution,--   . 440   WAY WORLD III.1 579
    Sir Wilful: loves him, and they deserve cne another; my resolution is . 477   WAY WORLD V.1   584
Resolv'd (17)
    Laetitia: (aside). I know not what to think. But I'me resolv'd   . . . 77   OLD BATCH IV.1   85
    Sir Joseph: Nay, gad, I'll pick up; I'm resolv'd to make a   85   OLD BATCH IV.3   61
    Maskwell: dissemble Ardour and Ecstasie, that's resolv'd: How   . . . 155   DOUBL DLR III.1 183
    Lord Touch: No more--I have resolv'd--   189   DOUBL DLR V.1   61
    Lady Touch: be so suddenly resolv'd. Why, Cynthia? Why must he be   . . 191   DOUBL DLR V.1   125
    Jeremy: himself, or were resolv'd to turn Authcr, and bring the   . 219   FOR LOVE   I.1   106
    Scandal: I'm resolv'd I'll ask her.   229   FOR LOVE   I.1   493
    Miss Prue: Lavender mun--I'm resolv'd I won't let Nurse put   249   FOR LOVE   II.1   529
    Angelica: Nature. I was resolv'd to try him to the utmost; I have   . 312   FOR LOVE   V.1   574
    Osmyn-Alph: O--thcu dost talk, my Love, as one resolv'd, ... 358   M. BRIDE   III.1 341
    Zara: Are tainted; scme among 'em have resolv'd   364   M. BRIDE   IV.1   143
    Zara: To what I give in Charge: for I'm resolv'd.   375   M. BRIDE   V.1   129
    Mirabell: For which Reason I resolv'd not to stir. At last the   . . . 396   WAY WORLD I.1   34
    Millamant: --I'm resolv'd--I think--You may go--   422   WAY WORLD II.1   457
    Millamant: Dee say so? Then I'm resolv'd I'll have a Song to   434   WAY WORLD III.1 365
    Mincing: sober, and to bring him to them. My Lady is resolv'd to   . 465   WAY WORLD V.1   114
    Mirabell: be it as it may. I am resolv'd I'll serve you, you shall not 474   WAY WORLD V.1   460
Resolve (6)
    Heartwell: thee--There thou hast don't, all my Resolve melted in   . . 74   OLD BATCH III.2 135
    Valentine: therefcre resolve to rail at all that have: And in that I
                    but   217   FOR LOVE   I.1   35
    Scandal: for I can't resolve you; but I'll inform your Master. In   . 278   FOR LOVE   IV.1   103
    Manuel: Why dost thou start? Resolve to do't, or else--   374   M. BRIDE   V.1   75
    Manuel: Why dost thou start? Resolve , or--   374   M. BRIDE   V.1 V 75
    Millamant: --You'll displease me--I think I must resolve   422   WAY WORLD II.1   449
Resolved (1)
    Cynthia: have once resolved; and a true Female courage to oppose   . 193   DOUBL DLR V.1   204
Resolves (1)
    Heartwell: thee--There thou hast don't, all my Resolves melted in   . 74   OLD BATCH III.2 V135
Resort (3)
                    And this our Audience, which did once resort   315   FOR LOVE   EPI.   25
                    And thus our Audience, which did once resort   315   FOR LOVE   EPI. V 25
                    Criticks to Plays for the same end resort, ... 385   M. BRIDE   EPI.   15
Respect (6)
    Lord Touch: Respect for Love, and made Sir Paul jealcus of the Civility 151   DOUBL DLR III.1   8
    Lady Ply: respect--That he has own'd himself to be my Admirer   .   . 172   DOUBL DLR IV.1   166
    Lady Ply: most extraordinary respect and hcnour for you, Sir Paul.   . 172   DOUBL DLR IV.1   175
    Brisk: like Respect.   175   DOUBL DLR IV.1   318
                    For Innocence condemn'd they've no Respect, ... 385   M. BRIDE   EPI.   17
    Lady Wish: accomplishment cf your revenge--Not that I respect   . .   . 458   WAY WORLD IV.1   508
Respected (1)
    Setter: And my Relation; pray let her be respected accordingly.   . 111   OLD BATCH V.2   140
Respectful (1)
    Lady Ply: should ever be wanting in a respectful acknowledgment   . 169   DOUBL DLR IV.1   80
Respecting (1)
    Mirabell: having it seems receiv'd some Cautions respecting your   . 476   WAY WORLD V.1   541
Respects (3)
    Lucy: Hum'd it over, gave you his Respects, and said, he   . .   . 61   OLD BATCH III.1   26
    Silvia: Respects, and peruse it! He's gone, and Araminta   61   OLD BATCH III.1   28
    Sir Paul: respects.   161   DOUBL DLR III.1   423
Respiring (1)
    Zara: And felt the Balm of thy respiring Lips!   347   M. BRIDE   II.2   287
Respite (1)
    Millamant: Good Sir Wilfull, respite your valour.   473   WAY WORLD V.1   431
Rest (30)
    Bellmour: Dignity with the rest of his Brethren. So I must beg   .   . 41   OLD BATCH I.1   159
    Lucy: as his Love. Therefore e'n set your Heart at rest, and   . 61   OLD BATCH III.1   8
    Maskwell: your Pleasures; and will not rest till I have given you
                    peace, ... 137   DOUBL DLR I.1   394
    Lady Touch: me beg you rest satisfied--   152   DOUBL DLR III.1   56

Rest (continued)

		PAGE	TITLE	ACT.SC	LINE
Lady Touch:	me beg you to rest satisfied--	152	DOUBL DLR	III.1	V 56
Maskwell:	(aside) to cheat you, as well as the rest.	154	DOUBL DLR	III.1	161
Sir Paul:	the rest.	180	DOUBL DLR	IV.1	506
Lord Touch:	and let us hear the rest.	198	DOUEL DLR	V.1	422
Maskwell:	more than all the rest; though I would give a Limb for	199	DOUEL DLR	V.1	434
Jeremy:	rest of his Brethren into the same Condition. And Lastly,	219	FOR LOVE	I.1	107
Valentine:	If I can give that Cerberus a Sop, I shall be at rest for one	222	FOR LOVE	I.1	225
Mrs Fore:	I cannot say that he has once brcken my Rest, since we	270	FOR LCVE	III.1	623
Scandal:	How did you rest last night?	284	FOR LCVE	IV.1	339
	But from the rest, we hope a better Fate.	323	M. BRIDE	PRC.	34
Almeria:	Then why am I? O when shall I have Rest?	327	M. BRIDE	I.1	54
	Monument fronting the View, greater than the rest. Enter Heli.)	340	M. BRIDE	II.2	
Leonora:	The poor Remains of good Anselmo rest;	340	M. BRIDE	II.2	7
Almeria:	Shall rest; shews me the Grave where Nature wearied,	340	M. BRIDE	II.2	17
Almeria:	Shall rest; shews me the Grave where Nature weary	340	M. BRIDE	II.2	V 17
Heli:	Is gone to rest, and Garcia is retir'd,	351	M. BRIDE	III.1	48
Zara:	Forbidding rest; may stretch his Eyes awake	355	M. BRIDE	III.1	209
Zara:	So does the present Form of our Engagements rest,	355	M. BRIDE	III.1	V217
Zara:	And watch like Tapers o'er your Hours of Rest.	360	M. BRIDE	III.1	429
Selim:	This Grant--and I'll acquaint you with the rest.	362	M. BRIDE	IV.1	60
Manuel:	Rank Traytors; thou art with the rest combin'd;	373	M. BRIDE	V.1	45
Marwood:	rest of him. Poor simple Fiend! Madam Marwood has a	431	WAY WORLD	III.1	239
Petulant:	rest which is to follow in both Cases, a Man may do it	436	WAY WCRLD	III.1	432
Millamant:	Sweet heart and the rest of that Nauseous Cant, in which	450	WAY WORLD	IV.1	198
Petulant:	and Baldwin yonder, thy half Brother is the rest--A gemini	454	WAY WCRLD	IV.1	351
Fainall:	I'll answer you when I have the rest of it in my	473	WAY WCRLD	V.1	448

Restitution (1)

Manuel:	Fit restitution here--Thus, I release you,	336	M. BRIDE	I.1	413

Restless (2)

Mrs Fore:	O, mighty restless, but I was afraid to tell him	270	FOR LCVE	III.1	619
Almeria:	The Sighs, the Tears, the Groans, the restless Cares,	330	M. BRIDE	I.1	157

Restor'd (4)

Araminta:	--Which they forfeit when they are restor'd	106	OLD BATCH	V.1	358
	The Freedom Man was born to, you've restor'd,	213	FOR LCVE	PRO.	15
Angelica:	now you have restor'd me to my fcrmer Opinion and	296	FOR LCVE	IV.1	767
Heli:	The Means of Liberty restor'd. That, gain'd;	352	M. BRIDE	III.1	96

Restore (3)

Sharper:	restore it quickly, or by--	48	OLD BATCH	II.1	28
Osmyn-Alph:	If my Alphonso live, restore him, Heav'n,	350	M. BRIDE	III.1	10
Mirabell:	Madam, let me before these Witnesses, restore to you this	478	WAY WORLD	V.1	617

Restoring (1)

Almeria:	Could only by restoring thee have cur'd.	343	M. BRIDE	II.2	V134

Restrain (1)

Mirabell:	but restrain your self to Native and Simple Tea-Table	451	WAY WORLD	IV.1	265

Restraint (3)

Valentine:	this Restraint, than when I openly rival'd the rich Fops,	217	FOR LCVE	V.1	52
Heli:	Zara the Cause of your restraint, may be	352	M. BRIDE	III.1	95
Gonsalez:	That last restraint; you hardly can suspect	365	M. BRIDE	IV.1	179

Rests (3)

Belinda:	rests--	58	OLD BATCH	II.2	130
Osmyn-Alph:	Or Earth, it rests, and rots to silent Dust.	351	M. BRIDE	III.1	62
Zara:	The present Form of our Engagements rests,	355	M. BRIDE	III.1	217

Resume (1)

Marwood:	Natures long to persevere. Love will resume his Empire	410	WAY WORLD	II.1	25

Resumption (1)

	Should Grants to Poets made, admit Resumption:	393	WAY WORLD	PRO.	19

Retailer (1)

Witwoud:	Thou art a retailer of Phrases; and dost deal in	453	WAY WCRLD	IV.1	346

Retaining (1)

Maskwell:	Aunt has given me a retaining Fee;--nay, I am your	148	DOUEL DLR	II.1	393

Retard (2)

Mellefont:	heavy and retard your flight.	184	DOUBL DLR	IV.2	56
Almeria:	And all the Damps of Grief, that did retard their Flight;	330	M. BRIDE	I.1	158

Retinue (2)

Valentine:	to be kept at small expence; but the Retinue that you gave	244	FOR LCVE	V.1	346
Fainall:	I learn'd it from his Czarish Majestie's Retinue, in a	469	WAY WORLD	V.1	273

Retir'd (2)

Leonora:	And oft at Night, when all have been retir'd,	326	M. BRIDE	I.1	24
Heli:	Is gone to rest, and Garcia is retir'd,	351	M. BRIDE	III.1	48

Retire (16)

Capt Bluff:	I am content to retire--Live a private Person--	53	OLD BATCH	II.1	211
Lord Touch:	Sir Paul, if you please we'll retire to the	132	DOUBL DLR	I.1	216
Lady Ply:	How now! will you be pleased to retire,	144	DOUEL DLR	II.1	209
Maskwell:	my Lords absence all this while, she'll retire to her Chamber	181	DOUBL DLR	IV.1	V523
Mrs Fore:	Night; because I'll retire to my own Chamber, and think	273	FOR LCVE	III.1	743
Gonsalez:	While you alcne retire, and shun this Sight;	332	M. BRIDE	I.1	243
Manuel:	To day--Retire, divest your self with speed	334	M. BRIDE	I.1	323
Almeria:	Your Leave, Sir, to retire.	334	M. BRIDE	I.1	350
Osmyn-Alph:	Retire, my Life, with speed--Alas, we're seen!	359	M. BRIDE	III.1	387
Manuel:	Retire.	365	M. BRIDE	IV.1	172
Zara:	I will retire, and instantly prepare	366	M. BRIDE	IV.1	191
Fainall:	her of all she's worth, and we'll retire somewhere, any	416	WAY WORLD	II.1	245
Lady Wish:	in. (Exit Peg.) Dear Friend retire into my Closet, that I	426	WAY WORLD	III.1	62
Lady Wish:	reconcile me to the bad World, or else I wou'd retire to	465	WAY WCRLD	V.1	132
Lady Wish:	and retire by our selves and be Shepherdesses.	465	WAY WCRLD	V.1	135
Marwood:	Madam, when we retire to our pastoral Solitude we shall	468	WAY WORLD	V.1	261

Retired (2)

Mellefont:	Why, they are at that end of the Gallery; retired	127	DOUBL DLR	I.1	11
Mellefont:	Why, they are at the end of the Gallery; retired	127	DOUBL DLR	I.1	V 11

Retirement (1)

Marwood:	we shall have leisure to think cf Retirement afterwards.	465	WAY WORLD	V.1	137

Retires (1)
                 (A Mute appears, and seeing the King retires.)   . . . . 373 M. BRIDE   V.1   12
Retreat (2)
  Scandal: it: But Dreaming is the poor retreat of a lazy, hopeless,   275 FOR LCVE III.1   815
  Gonsalez: I shall make good, and shelter his Retreat.   . . . . .   379 M. BRIDE   V.2   128
Retrieve (2)
  Scandal: nam'd: Without you could retrieve the Ancient Honours . . 220 FOR LCVE   I.1   148
  Singer-V: I tell thee, Charmion, could I Time retrieve,   . . .   293 FOR LCVE   IV.1   652
Retrograde (2)
  Angelica: You know my Aunt is a little Retrograde (as you call it) in 237 FOR LOVE   II.1   71
  Foresight: Houses. Can judge of Motions Direct and Retrograde, of   . 241 FOR LCVE   II.1   212
Retrospection (1)
  Lady Wish: the Retrospection of my own rudenes,--I have more   . . . 457 WAY WCRLD IV.1   485
Return (33)
  Vainlove: of Town, to meet the Master of a Ship about the return of   39 OLD BATCH   I.1   80
  Bellmour: You're going to visit in return of Silvia's Letter-- . .   40 OLD BATCH   I.1   115
  Sharper: And you in return of Spleen hate them: But could   . . .   45 OLD BATCH   I.1   306
  Sir Joseph: the very Gentleman! how shall I make him a return suitable 49 OLD BATCH II.1   51
  Bellmour: you ought to return him Thanks now you have receiv'd   . .   68 OLD BATCH III.1   282
  Sharper: Mony paid at sight: I'm come to return my Thanks--   . . .   68 OLD BATCH III.1   285
  Setter: Joy of your Return, Sir. Have you made a good . . . . .   96 OLD BATCH   V.1   2
  Lady Ply: a suitable return to those Obligations which you are pleased 159 DOUBL DLR III.1   338
  Lady Ply: return of 600 Pounds; you may take fifty cf it for   . . . 162 DOUBL DLR III.1   451
  Sir Paul: to his Bed, and there return his Caresses with interest
                   to his   . . . .   178 DOUEL DLR IV.1   422
  Valentine: and go and enquire when Angelica will return.   . . .   246 FOR LOVE   II.1   412
  Valentine: to undo the Son, it was a reasonable return of Nature. . 311 FOR LOVE   V.1   512
                 Grant Heaven, we don't return tc our first Station.   .   315 FOR LOVE   EPI.   34
  Garcia: Perez, the King expects from our return, ...   338 M. BRIDE   II.1   40
  Leonora: Let us return; the Horrour of this Place   . . . . .   339 M. BRIDE   II.1   70
  Zara: Is it well done? Is this then the Return   . . . . .   345 M. BRIDE   II.2   235
  Zara: That done, I leave thy Justice to return   . . . . .   355 M. BRIDE III.1   219
  Osmyn-Alph: At your return so soon and unexpected!   . . . . .   359 M. BRIDE III.1   409
  Zara: You free: But shall return much better pleas'd,   . . .   360 M. BRIDE III.1   418
  Zara: And in return of that, though otherwise   . . . . .   364 M. BRIDE   IV.1   137
  Alonzo: If't please your Lordship, I'll return, and say   . . .   371 M. BRIDE   IV.1   422
  Zara: That I am here--so. You return and find   . . . . .   380 M. BRIDE   V.2   150
                 (The Mutes return and look affrighted.)   380 M. BRIDE   V.2   156
  Leonora: Where Miseries are multiply'd; return   . . . . .   381 M. BRIDE   V.2   228
  Leonora: Return and look not on; for there's a Dagger   . . . .   381 M. BRIDE   V.2 V229
  Foible: the return of her Husband after Knighthood, with that .   428 WAY WORLD III.1   125
  Marwood: No doubt you will return very much   . . . .   440 WAY WORLD III.1   588
  Sir Wilful: I'll return to my Company--   . . . .   446 WAY WORLD IV.1   79
  Sir Wilful: Your Servant, then with your leave I'll return   . . .   448 WAY WORLD IV.1   149
  Mrs Fain: return to Sir Rowland, who as Poible tells me is in a fair 452 WAY WORLD IV.1   302
  Lady Wish: a return, by a frank Communication--You shall see   .   460 WAY WCRLD IV.1   582
  Fainall: Instrument, and till my return, you may Ballance this .   469 WAY WORLD   V.1   295
  Marwood: Not far Madam; I'll return immediately.   . . . . .   471 WAY WORLD   V.1   357
Return'd (7)
  Foresight: I think she has not return'd, since she went abroad   .   306 FOR LOVE   V.1   336
  Almeria: But that my Father is return'd in Safety, ...   332 M. BRIDE   I.1   250
  Almeria: O how hast thou return'd? How hast thou charm'd   . .   342 M. BRIDE   II.2   87
  Perez: Your entring, till the Princess is return'd, ...   359 M. BRIDE III.1   381
  Manuel: Are none return'd of those who fcllow'd Heli?   . . .   363 M. BRIDE   IV.1   74
  Zara: The Mute not yet return'd! 'tis strange. Ha! 'twas   . .   374 M. BRIDE   V.1   91
  Zara: The Mute not yet return'd! ha! 'twas the King!   . . .   374 M. BRIDE   V.1 V 91
Returning (5)
  Mellefont: returning.--   . . . .   131 DOUEL DLR   I.1   176
  Gonsalez: While he himself, returning to Valentia   . . . . .   363 M. BRIDE   IV.1   88
  Almeria: For bended Knees, returning folding Arms, ...   369 M. BRIDE   IV.1   325
  Manuel: Watch her returning Sense, and bring me Word: . . .   370 M. BRIDE   IV.1   365
  Garcia: (returning). Ruine and Horrour! O heart-wounding   . .   377 M. BRIDE   V.2   51
Returns (5)
                 (Fondlewife returns with Papers.)   . .   91 OLD BATCH IV.4   93
                 (Garcia leads Almeria to the Door, and returns.)   . . .   334 M. BRIDE   I.1   352
                 (Alonzo follows him, and returns with a Paper.)   . . .   373 M. BRIDE   V.1 V 18
  Mirabell: That I may see her before she returns to her Lady; and as 398 WAY WORLD   I.1   131
  Lady Wish: should meet with such returns;--you ought to ask   . .   466 WAY WORLD   V.1   168
Reunion (1)
  Mirabell: me lies to a Reunion, (To Mrs. Fainall) in the mean time,. 478 WAY WCRLD   V.1   616
Rev'rend (1)
  Almeria: How rev'rend is the Face of this tall Pile, ...   339 M. BRIDE   II.1   59
Reveal'd (2)
  Almeria: Since thou'rt reveal'd, alone thou shalt not die.   . .   368 M. BRIDE   IV.1   304
  Almeria: And torn, rather than have reveal'd thy being.   . . .   369 M. BRIDE   IV.1   313
Revealed (1)
  Almeria: Repeated Deaths, rather than have revealed thee.   . .   368 M. BRIDE   IV.1   306
Reveals (1)
  Gonsalez: By fits reveals--his Face seems turn'd to favour   . .   376 M. BRIDE   V.2   8
Revelation (1)
  Lord Touch: start at the revelation of their thoughts, but be thou
                   fix'd, ...   189 DOUEL DLR   V.1   48
Revell'd (1)
  Manuel: My Daughter should have revell'd at his Death.   . . .   333 M. BRIDE   I.1   310
Revellers (1)
  Marwood: And then to have my Young Revellers of the   . . . .   467 WAY WORLD   V.1   224
Revelling (1)
  Osmyn-Alph: Luxurious, revelling amidst thy Charms;   . . . . .   358 M. BRIDE III.1   359
Reveng'd (8)
  Valentine: be reveng'd on 'em all; I'll pursue Angelica with more Love 217 FOR LCVE   I.1   50
  Valentine: reveng'd.   . . . .   219 FOR LOVE   I.1   137
  Foresight: reveng'd on you, Cockatrice; I'll hamper you--You   . .   238 FOR LOVE   II.1   114
  Sr Sampson: reveng'd on this undutiful Rogue.   . . . . . .   240 FOR LOVE   II.1   185
  Tattle: I was reveng'd upon him, for he had a handsom Daughter .   258 FOR LOVE III.1   172
  Zara: As I could wish; by Heav'n I'll be reveng'd.   . . .   348 M. BRIDE   II.2   350
  Waitwell: me, If I cou'd but live so long as to be reveng'd on that 458 WAY WORLD IV.1   504

Rigg'd (1)
Ben: tight Vessel, and well rigg'd, and you were but as well . 262   FOR LOVE   III.1   327

Rigging (1)
Setter: Pounds, and all her Rigging; besides what lies conceal'd . 102   OLD BATCH   V.1   224

Right (39)
Bellmour: Right, but then the comparison breaks, for he will . . . 47   OLD BATCH   I.1   380
Bellmour: poor George, thou art i'th right, thou hast sold thy self to . 63   OLD BATCH   III.1   89
Araminta: Hang me, if I pity you; you are right enough 109   OLD BATCH   V.2   61
Lady Froth: say'st right--for sure my Lord Froth is as fine a Gentleman, 139   DOUBL DLR   II.1   28
Brisk: (to Lady Froth). Your Ladyship is in the right; but I'gad . 141   DOUBL DLR   II.1   115
Maskwell: Bonds of Friendship, and sets Men right upon their first . 150   DOUBL DLR   II.1   444
Maskwell: interpret a Coldness the right way; therefore I must . . 155   DOUBL DLR   III.1   182
Maskwell: No, no--so far you are right, and I am, as an 156   DOUBL DLR   III.1   228
Lord Froth: Hee, hee, hee, right; and then my Lady Whifler is . . . 163   DOUBL DLR   III.1   475
Brisk: Right, right, that saves all. 164   DOUBL DLR   III.1   522
Brisk: Right, but the vulgar will never comprehend that. . . . 164   DOUBL DLR   III.1   526
Brisk: That's right, all's well, all's well. 164   DOUBL DLR   III.1   533
Mellefont: Love, Love, down right very Villanous Love. 168   DOUBL DLR   IV.1   33
Lady Ply: this, your Right Hand shall be swathed down again to . 180   DOUBL DLR   IV.1   V482
Maskwell: That's right,--well, I'll secure the Writings; . . . 193   DOUBL DLR   V.1   206
  All have a Right and Title to some part, ... 204   DOUBL DLR   EPI.   15
  The Cuckoldom, of Ancient Right, to Cits belongs. . . 204   DOUBL DLR   EPI.   28
Valentine: me word; If I will make a Deed of Conveyance of my Right . 225   FOR LOVE   I.1   335
Scandal: No, nothing under a Right Honourable. 230   FOR LOVE   I.1   531
Sr Sampson: his Right of Inheritance. Where's my Daughter that is to . 240   FOR LOVE   II.1   183
Sr Sampson: it, that by the rule of right Reason, this fellow ought to . 245   FOR LOVE   II.1   366
Valentine: Necessities of my Nature; if I had my right of Inheritance. 246   FOR LOVE   II.1   395
Tattle: That's right,--again my Charmer. 252   FOR LOVE   II.1   641
Tattle: Faith, Madam, you're in the right; no more I have, as . . 256   FOR LOVE   III.1   100
Scandal: Alas, Mr. Foresight, I'm afraid all is not right-- . . 267   FOR LOVE   III.1   513
Valentine: and can set him right--Hearkee, Friend, the straight . . 282   FOR LOVE   IV.1   252
Ben: Hearkee forsooth; If so be that you are in your right . . 286   FOR LOVE   IV.1   413
Valentine: right of my Inheritance to his Estate; which otherwise by . 294   FOR LOVE   IV.1   718
Ben: not hit Right. 306   FOR LOVE   V.1   355
Angelica: Right to dispose of my Person, than yours. 311   FOR LOVE   V.1   534
Zara: And Native Right to Arbitrary Sway; 336   M. BRIDE   I.1   397
Osmyn-Alph: To guess at Right and Wrong; the twinkling Lamp . . . 350   M. BRIDE   III.1   36
Heli: Presuming on a Bridegroom's Right--) she'll come. . . . 351   M. BRIDE   III.1   50
Mirabell: right, that you may plead the error of your Judgment in . 409   WAY WORLD   I.1   539
Sir Wilful: Right Lady; I am Sir Wilfull Witwoud, so I 438   WAY WORLD   III.1   510
Fainall: endow'd in right of my Wife, with that six thousand . . 469   WAY WORLD   V.1   278
Sir Wilful: And Sir, I assert my right; and will maintain it . . 473   WAY WORLD   V.1   423
Fainall: resignation; nor Sir Wilfull, your right--You may draw . 473   WAY WORLD   V.1   439

Rightful (1)
Scandal: of a rightful Inheritance, will bring Judgments upon us. . 268   FOR LOVE   III.1   545

Rightly (1)
Scandal: which is rightly observ'd by Gregory the Great in favour of 267   FOR LOVE   III.1   536

Rights (4)
Ben: how shall I do to set her to rights. 286   FOR LOVE   IV.1   405
Ben: Stocks; and they two are a going to be married to rights. . 307   FOR LOVE   V.1   359
Heli: And lead 'em, to regain their Rights and Liberty. . . . 351   M. BRIDE   III.1   V 71
Heli: And Native Rights. 351   M. BRIDE   III.1   V 72

Rigour (1)
Zara: Than still to meet the Rigour of his Scorn. 362   M. BRIDE   IV.1   28

Ring (3)
Miss Prue: me this Ring for a kiss. 249   FOR LOVE   II.1   522
Sr Sampson: ring all over the Parish. 266   FOR LOVE   III.1   478
Manuel: And all this high and ample Roof to ring 333   M. BRIDE   I.1   312

Rings (1)
Tattle: No? I can shew Letters, Locketts, Pictures, and Rings, . 257   FOR LOVE   III.1   153

Rip (2)
Scandal: I'll rip up his Stomach, and go the shortest way to his . 224   FOR LOVE   I.1   311
Garcia: Better with this to rip up my own Bowels, ... 378   M. BRIDE   V.2   78

Ripe (11)
Musician: Thus, to a ripe, consenting Maid, ... 59   OLD BATCH   II.2   190
Sharper: ripe, and only waits thy Cutting up--She has been . . 79   OLD BATCH   IV.1   166
Mellefont: Industry grown full and ripe, ready to drop into his mouth, 187   DOUBL DLR   IV.2   144
Mellefont: Industry grow full and ripe, ready to drop into his mouth, 187   DOUBL DLR   IV.2   V144
Heli: I've learn'd, there are Disorders ripe for Mutiny . . . 351   M. BRIDE   III.1   64
Zara: And now just ripe for Birth, my Rage has ruin'd. . . . 354   M. BRIDE   III.1   196
Zara: So ripe, to point at the particular Men. 364   M. BRIDE   IV.1   147
Mirabell: of Mirth, which is not yet ripe for discovery. I am glad . 399   WAY WORLD   I.1   137
Mirabell: So one will be rotten before he be ripe, and the . . 401   WAY WORLD   I.1   216
Mirabell: other will be rotten without ever being ripe at all. . 401   WAY WORLD   I.1   217
Marwood: panting ripe; with a Heart full of Hope, and a Head full of 431   WAY WORLD   III.1   247

Ripe-horn-mad (1)
Fondlewife: ripe-horn-mad. But who, in the Devil's name, are you?
   Mercy on 92   OLD BATCH   IV.4   127

Ripen'd (1)
Scandal: Make Blest the Ripen'd Maid, and Finish'd Man. . . . 275   FOR LOVE   III.1   820

Rise (15)
  Let it at least rise thrice, before it Drown. . . . 125   DOUBL DLR   PRO.   18
Lady Ply: Nay, nay, rise up, come you shall see my good . . . 148   DOUBL DLR   II.1   355
Lady Ply: O rise I beseech you, say no more till you rise . . . 170   DOUBL DLR   IV.1   107
Mellefont: Nay, I beseech you rise. 186   DOUBL DLR   IV.2   97
Maskwell: weak, and shrinks beneath the weight, and cannot rise to . 189   DOUBL DLR   V.1   79
Manuel: Almeria, rise--My best Gonsalez rise. 332   M. BRIDE   I.1   271
Manuel: Rise, Garcia--I forgot. Yet stay, Almeria. 334   M. BRIDE   I.1   329
Zara: The Steps on which we tread, to rise and reach . . . 347   M. BRIDE   II.2   317
Manuel: Rise, I command thee rise--and if thou would'st . . 368   M. BRIDE   IV.1   285
Almeria: No, never will I rise, nor loose this Hold, ... 369   M. BRIDE   IV.1   330
Zara: 'Till Surges roll, and foaming Billows rise, ... 380   M. BRIDE   V.2   V166
Lady Wish: and rise to meet him in a pretty disorder--Yes--O, . . . 445   WAY WORLD   IV.1   28

Riseings (1)
Lady Wish: the Kneelings and the Riseings, the Heart-heavings, and the 458   WAY WORLD   IV.1   515

Risen (4)
```
                  and Sword in his Hands; as just risen from Table:    . . .  127   DOUEL DLR    I.1
  Sr Sampson:     risen in the State--But, a pox on't, his Wit run him   . .  299   FOR LOVE     V.1     83
  Heli:           Are risen in Arms, and call for Chiefs to head    . . .    351   M. BRIDE    III.1     70
  Waitwell:       At hand Sir, rubbing their Eyes,--Just risen   . . . .     475   WAY WORLD    V.1    515
```
Rises (4)
```
  Capt Bluff:     My Blood rises at that Fellow: I can't stay where he is;   .  86   OLD BATCH   IV.3    120
  Sr Sampson:     seen the Antipodes, where the Sun rises at Midnight, and   .  241   FOR LOVE    II.1    208
  Valentine:      Sphere: when he Rises I must set--Besides, if I shou'd stay, 259   FOR LOVE   III.1    224
  Petulant:       he (hiccup) rises upon my stomack like a Radish.   . . .    454   WAY WORLD   IV.1    357
```
Rising (4)
```
  Mellefont:      Ha! O I see, I see my Rising Sun! Light breaks    . . . .   149   DOUEL DLR    II.1    405
  Mellefont:      Ha! O see, I see my Rising Sun! Light breaks  . . . . .     149   DOUBL DLR    II.1   V405
                       (Rising.)   . . . . . . . . . . .                      330   M. BRIDE     I.1    191
                  Mirabell and Fainall Rising from Cards. Betty waiting.   .  395   WAY WORLD    I.1
```
Risk (1)
```
  Ben:            Why an you do, You may run the risk to be overset,   . . .  262   FOR LOVE    III.1    334
```
Risque (1)
```
  Foible:         Ladyship, he must have run the risque of the Law, and been  463  WAY WORLD    V.1     43
```
Rites (2)
```
  Osmyn-Alph:     Yet unaccomplish'd; his mysterious Rites   . . . . .       357   M. BRIDE    III.1    320
  Manuel:         Wherefore I have deferr'd the Mariage Rites,   . . . . .    367   M. BRIDE     IV.1    254
```
Rival (10)
```
  Bellmour:       But do you know nothing of a new Rival there?   . . . .      40   OLD BATCH    I.1    117
  Silvia:         Rival fires my Blood--I could curse 'em both; eternal   . .  61   OLD BATCH  III.1     30
  Maskwell:       Ties: But the Name of Rival cuts 'em all asunder, and is a  150   DOUEL DLR    II.1    448
  Maskwell:       general acquittance--Rival is equal, and Love like Death   .150   DOUEL DLR    II.1    449
  Zara:           There, there's the dreadful Sound, the King's thy Rival!   .348   M. BRIDE     II.2    348
  Manuel:         Somewhat I heard of King and Rival mention'd.    . . .      348   M. BRIDE     II.2    355
  Manuel:         What's he that dares be Rival to the King?   . . . . .      348   M. BRIDE     II.2    356
  Fainall:        Rival as a Lover.    . . . . . . . . . . .                  407   WAY WORLD    I.1    464
  Waitwell:       What, my Rival! is the Rebell my Rival? a'dies.   . . . .   458   WAY WORLD   IV.1    518
```
Rival'd (1)
```
  Valentine:      this Restraint, than when I openly rival'd the rich Fops,   217   FOR LOVE     I.1     52
```
Rival's (1)
```
  Singer:         When I insult a Rival's Eyes:   . . . . . . . . .          435   WAY WORLD  III.1    388
```
Rivals (2)
```
  Maskwell:       that I have done, would look like Rivals Malice, false   .  188   DOUEL DLR    V.1     39
  Petulant:       --And they may be Rivals--What then? All's   . . . . .      406   WAY WORLD    I.1    430
```
Rive (2)
```
  Osmyn-Alph:     Disfigur'd Face, and rive my clotted Hair,   . . . .        358   M. BRIDE    III.1    351
  Osmyn-Alph:     And dash my Face, and rive my clotted Hair,   . . . . .     358   M. BRIDE    III.1   V351
```
Rivers (1)
```
  Almeria:        With Rivers of incessant scalding Rain.   . . . . .         358   M. BRIDE    III.1    374
```
Rivet (2)
```
  Osmyn-Alph:     Amazement and Illusion! Rivet me   . . . . .                341   M. BRIDE     II.2     46
  Osmyn-Alph:     Rivet and nail me, where I stand, ye Powers;   . . . .      341   M. BRIDE     II.2   V 47
```
Riveted (1)
```
  Servant-M:      were riveted in a trice.   . . . . . . . .                  398   WAY WORLD    I.1    119
```
Rivets (2)
```
  Perez:          Unlock the rivets of his bonds.   . . . . . . .             372   M. BRIDE     V.1     10
  Perez:          As loose the rivets of his bonds.   . . . . .               372   M. BRIDE     V.1   V 10
```
Road (6)
```
  Setter:         opened for all Comers. In Fine thou art the high Road to    66   OLD BATCH  III.1    196
  Lady Ply:       road of Virtue, in which I have trod thus long, and never  147   DOUEL DLR    II.1    318
  Lady Touch:     to stay his stomach in the road to her;   . . . . .        191   DOUEL DLR    V.1   V147
  Scandal:        his Exaltation of madness into the road of common Sense,   278   FOR LOVE     IV.1    106
  Valentine:      Road is the worst way you can go--He that follows   . .    282   FOR LOVE     IV.1    253
  Lady Wish:      a Person, this Wench has liv'd in an Inn upon the Road,   . 426   WAY WORLD  III.1     36
```
Roam (1)
```
  Ben:            don't much stand towards Matrimonie. I love to roam   .    261   FOR LOVE    III.1    309
```
Roar (4)
```
  Sir Joseph:     he shou'd hear the Lion roar, he'd cudgel him into an Ass,  101  OLD BATCH    V.1    173
                  Look out when Storms arise, and Billows roar,   . . .      385   M. BRIDE     EPI.    20
  Mirabell:       roar out aloud as often as they pass by you; and when  .   409   WAY WORLD    I.1    526
  Lady Wish:      the Bases roar Blasphemy. O, she wou'd have swooned at   .  467   WAY WORLD    V.1    201
```
Roaring (1)
```
                  Of Roaring Gamesters, and your Damme Boys.   . . . . .     315   FOR LOVE     EPI.    29
```
Roasted (1)
```
  Mirabell:       marrow of a roasted Cat. In short, I forbid all Commerce  .451   WAY WORLD   IV.1    251
```
Roasting (1)
```
  Witwoud:        one another like two roasting Apples.   . . . . . .        453   WAY WORLD   IV.1    334
```
Rob (2)
```
  Zara:           Yet Fate, alone can rob his mortal Part   . . . . .        381   M. BRIDE     V.2    195
  Fainall:        hate my Wife yet more, Dam her, I'll part with her, rob  . 416   WAY WORLD   II.1    244
```
Robb'd (1)
```
  Osmyn-Alph:     Because Captivity has robb'd me of a just Revenge.   . .   336   M. BRIDE     I.1    434
```
Robe (2)
```
  Manuel:         When thou hast ended him, bring me his Robe;   . . . .     374   M. BRIDE     V.1     83
  Manuel:         There with his Turbant, and his Robe array'd   . . . .     374   M. BRIDE     V.1  V86A
```
Robes (3)
```
  Bellmour:       shall use the Robes.   . . . . . . . . . . .                64   OLD BATCH  III.1    135
  Maskwell:       observ'd.--I'll send the Chaplain to you with his Robes;   .194  DOUEL DLR    V.1    241
  Almeria:        Nor will I change these black and dismal Robes,   . . .    329   M. BRIDE     I.1    145
```
Robin (3)
```
  Miss Prue:      Robin the Butler, he says he loves me, and he's a Handsome 305  FOR LOVE     V.1    317
  Foresight:      Robin make ready to give an Account of his Plate and   .   306   FOR LOVE     V.1    327
  Lady Wish:      send for Robin from Lockets--Immediately.   . . . . .      427   WAY WORLD  III.1    105
```
Robs (1)
```
  Almeria:        Thou dost me Wrong, and Grief too robs my   . . . . .      356   M. BRIDE    III.1    284
```
Rock (2)
```
  Almeria:        And bulging 'gainst a Rock, was dash'd in pieces.   . .    329   M. BRIDE     I.1    127
  Osmyn-Alph:     At length, imprison'd in some Cleft of Rock,   . . . .     351   M. BRIDE    III.1     61
```
Rocks (2)
```
  Mrs Frail:      Rocks, suckl'd by Whales, Cradled in a Tempest, and   .    286   FOR LOVE     IV.1    399
  Almeria:        To soften Rocks, or bend a knotted Oak.   . . . . .        326   M. BRIDE     I.1      2
```

Rocks   (continued)
Almeria: The Wildness of the Waves and Rocks to this? 342   M. BRIDE   II.2   88
Rod (2)
Foresight: Hussy you shall have a Rod. 305   FOR LOVE   V.1   314
Miss Prue: A Fiddle of a Rod, I'll have a Husband; and if you . . 305   FOR LOVE   V.1   315
Rode (1)
Bellmour: made a delicious Voyage, Setter, and might have rode at 96   OLD BATCH   V.1   5
Roderigo's (1)
Gonsalez: In Roderigo's House, who fled with him. 363   M. BRIDE   IV.1   76
Rogue (33)
Bellmour: Poor Rogue. Any hour of the day or night will serve her-- 40   OLD BATCH   I.1   116
Sharper: (aside). Impudent Rogue. 53   OLD BATCH   II.1   213
Bellmour: Thou'rt a lucky Rogue; there's your Benefactor,   . . 68   OLD BATCH III.1   281
Sir Joseph: Agad, it's a curious, fine, pretty Rogue; I'll speak . . 89   OLD BATCH   IV.4   32
Bellmour: Rogue am I! Oh, what Sport will be here, if I can persuade 97   OLD BATCH   V.1   24
Setter: Were I a Rogue now, what a noble Prize could I . . . 102 OLD BATCH   V.1   221
Sir Joseph: Rogue look, when she talk'd of Sir Joseph? Did not her . 103 OLD BATCH   V.1   254
Sharper: O Rogue! Well, but I hope-- 105   OLD BATCH   V.1   346
Sir Joseph: Rogue of all sides. 110   OLD BATCH   V.2   119
Brisk: But prithee dear Rogue, make haste, prithee make haste, 128   DOUEL DLR   I.1   52
Maskwell: not to be heard. I have been a very great Rogue for your 136   DOUEL DLR   I.1   335
Maskwell: Rogue still, to do you Service; and you are flinging   . 136   DOUEL DLR   I.1   337
Sir Paul: pound a Year upon the Rogue as soon as ever he looks me 173   DOUEL DLR   IV.1   225
Sir Paul: the young Rogue as like as you can. 173   DOUEL DLR   IV.1   231
Sir Paul: Rogue by the help of imagination; why, 'tis the mark of 173   DOUEL DLR   IV.1   238
Maskwell: Rogue to you. 199   DOUEL DLR   V.1   439
Valentine: You are witty, you Rogue, I shall want your Help; . . 218   FOR LOVE   I.1   76
Valentine: The Rogue has (with all the Wit he could muster . . . 219   FOR LOVE   I.1   118
Scandal: manner. For the Rogue will speak aloud in the posture of 226   FOR LOVE   I.1   370
Sr Sampson: reveng'd on this undutiful Rogue. 240   FOR LOVE   II.1   185
Sr Sampson: Here's a Rogue, Brother Foresight, makes a Bargain under 243   FOR LOVE   II.1   295
Sr Sampson: from it in the Afternoon; here's a Rogue, Dog, here's . 243   FOR LOVE   II.1   297
Sr Sampson: And if this Rogue were Anatomiz'd now, and   245   FOR LOVE   II.1   385
Sr Sampson: him; he is not worth your Consideration. The Rogue has 259   FOR LOVE   III.1   240
Sr Sampson: Rogue shew himself, and make Love to some desponding . 260   FOR LOVE   III.1   261
Valentine: not overtake you--Ha, ha, ha, the Rogue found me   . . 282   FOR LOVE   IV.1   247
Sr Sampson: Has any young Rogue affronted you, and shall I cut his . 298   FOR LOVE   V.1   42
Sr Sampson: O Rogue! But I'll trust you. And will you 300   FOR LOVE   V.1   132
Foresight: Rogue! Oh, Nurse, come hither. 305   FOR LOVE   V.1   322
Mrs Frail: that Rogue Jeremy will publish it. 310   FOR LOVE   V.1   479
Witwoud: No, no, hang him, the Rogue has no Manners at . . . 403   WAY WORLD   I.1   297
Witwoud: Ha, ha, ha; I had a Mind to see how the Rogue   . . . 406   WAY WORLD   I.1   409
Foible: What a washy Rogue art thou, to pant thus for a . . . 459   WAY WORLD   IV.1   558
Rogue's (2)
Sr Sampson: Rogue's sharp set, coming from Sea, if he should not stay 265   FOR LOVE   III.1   459
Witwoud: No; the Rogue's Wit and Readiness of Invention   . . . 406   WAY WORLD   I.1   413
Rogues (7)
Setter: What have such poor Rogues as I to do with Reputation? . 102 OLD BATCH   V.1   230
Brisk: thinking what to say? None but dull Rogues think; witty 175   DOUEL DLR   IV.1   299
Jeremy: or any of these poor rich Rogues, teach you how to pay . 217   FOR LOVE   I.1   27
Scandal: worthless great Men, and dull rich Rogues, avoid a witty 219   FOR LOVE   I.1   132
Sr Sampson: go up Holborn-hill,--Has he not a Rogues face?--Speak, . 243   FOR LOVE   II.1   304
Sr Sampson: Rogues: Odd, wou'd she wou'd; faith and troth she's . . 298   FOR LOVE   V.1   50
Sr Sampson: of these young idle Rogues about the Town. Odd, there's 299   FOR LOVE   V.1   53
Roll-roll (1) see Rent-roll, Rowl
Manuel: Where, ev'ry Hour shall roll in circling Joys; 349   M. BRIDE   II.2   387
Almeria: Will undistinguish'd roll, and but prolong   367   M. BRIDE   IV.1   260
Zara: 'Till Surges roll, and foaming Billows rise, ... 380   M. BRIDE   V.2 V166
Roll'd (1)
Zara: His Eyes like Meteors roll'd, then darted down   . . . 374   M. BRIDE   V.1   93
Roman (1)
Waitwell: Roman hand--I saw there was a throat to be cut presently. 460   WAY WORLD   IV.1   602
Romances (1)
Petulant: Dogs, and read Romances--I'll go to bed to my   . . . 454   WAY WORLD   IV.1   376
Roof (4)
Belinda: a high Roof, or a very low Seat--Stay, Come back here . 57   OLD BATCH   II.2   96
Manuel: And all this high and ample Roof to ring 333   M. BRIDE   I.1   312
Almeria: To bear aloft its arch'd and pond'rous Roof, ... 339   M. BRIDE   II.2   61
Manuel: How's this? my mortal Foe beneath my Roof! 373   M. BRIDE   V.1   33
Room (24)   see Dressing-Room, Drawing-Room, Dining-Room
Silvia: Vengeance itches in the room of Love. 61   OLD BATCH III.1   34
Silvia: Vengeance kindles in the room of Love. 61   OLD BATCH III.1 V 34
Mellefont: O, I would have no room for serious design; for I . . 129   DOUEL DLR   I.1   74
Lady Froth: you go into the next Room? and there I'll shew you all . 142   DOUEL DLR   II.1   144
Lady Froth: you go into the next Room? and there I'll shew you what 142   DOUBL DLR   II.1 V144
Careless: the next Room. 163   DOUEL DLR III.1   495
Lady Froth: cast off, and meet me at the lower end of the Room, and 177   DOUEL DLR   IV.1   366
Lord Touch: thee in his room to be my Heir-- 189   DOUEL DLR   V.1   59
Cynthia: and bid me meet him in the Chaplain's Room, pretending 196   DOUEL DLR   V.1   348
Valentine: Step into the next Room--and I'll give you 231   FOR LOVE   I.1   585
              (A Room in Foresight's House. Foresight and Servant.) . 235   FOR LOVE   II.1
Scandal: Proverbs, and I see one in the next Room that will sing it. 258   FOR LOVE   III.1   192
              (A Room in Foresight's House. Enter Angelica and Jenny.) 297   FOR LOVE   V.1
              (A Room of State. Enter Zara, and Selim.) 361   M. BRIDE   IV.1
Manuel: Let all else void the Room. Garcia, give Order   . . . 364   M. BRIDE   IV.1   131
Manuel: Let all except Gonsalez leave the Room. 364   M. BRIDE   IV.1 V131
              (A Room of State. Enter King, Perez, and Alonzo.) . . 372   M. BRIDE   V.1
Alonzo: The Room, dispos'd it muffled in the Mute's   379   M. BRIDE   V.2   116
Painall: you;--I'll look upon the Gamesters in the next Room. . 397   WAY WORLD   I.1   100
Betty: He's in the next Room, Friend--That way. 400   WAY WORLD   I.1   185
              (A Room in Lady Wishfort's House. 425   WAY WORLD III.1
Millamant: Desire Mrs.--that is in the next Room to   434   WAY WORLD III.1   370
Lady Wish: receive him in my little dressing Room, there's a Couch-- 445   WAY WORLD   IV.1   23
Millamant: dine in my dressing room when I'm out of humour . . . 450   WAY WORLD   IV.1   220
Root (7)
Sharper: better root in your shallow memory. 48   OLD BATCH   II.1   49

587

Root   (continued)
  Careless: you have transplanted; and should it take Root in my   . 131   DOUBL DLR   I.1   165
  Mellefont: away the very root and foundation of his hopes; What   . 187   DOUBL DLR   IV.2   147
      When what should feed the Tree, devours the Root: .   . 213   FOR LOVE   PRO.   4
  Osmyn-Alph: And tear her Virtues up, as Tempests root   355   M. BRIDE   III.1   229
  Fainall: honourable a root?   443   WAY WORLD   III.1   694
  Marwood: Nay I know not; if the root be Honourable, ... 443   WAY WORLD   III.1   695
Rooted (1)
  Maskwell: Fix'd, Rooted in my Heart, whence nothing can   136   DOUBL DLR   I.1   352
Roots (3)
  Osmyn-Alph: And growing to his dead Father's Shrowd, roots up   . . 341   M. BRIDE   II.2   39
  Osmyn-Alph: And growing to his Father's Shrowd, roots up   341   M. BRIDE   II.2 V 39
  Osmyn-Alph: Let ev'ry Hair, which Sorrow by the Roots, ... 350   M. BRIDE   III.1   16
Rope's (1)
  Ben: for your Love or your liking, I don't value it of a Rope's   264   FOR LOVE   III.1   404
Ropes (1)
  Ben: is indeed, as like as two Cable Ropes.   273   FOR LOVE   III.1   722
Rosamond's (1)
  Mirabell: Feathers, and meet me at One a Clock by Rosamond's Pond.   . 398   WAY WORLD   I.1   130
Rose (2)
  Osmyn-Alph: In Murmurs round my Head. I rose and listened;   . . . 344   M. BRIDE   II.2   162
  Mirabell: her, but Millamant joining in the Argument, I rose and   . 396   WAY WRLD   I.1   37
Roses (4)
  Miss Prue: Handkerchief is sweet, pure sweet, sweeter than Roses   . 249   FOR LOVE   II.1   520
  Foresight: aspect--pale, a little pale--but the Roses of these   . 269   FOR LOVE   III.1   602
  Valentine: gave Beauty, when it grafted Roses on a Briar. You are   . 292   FOR LOVE   IV.1   635
  Manuel: And spread like Roses to the Morning Sun.   349   M. BRIDE   III.2   386
Rot (2)
  Lord Touch: of my doors this moment, and let him rot and perish,   . . 153   DOUBL DLR   III.1   101
  Almeria: But prone, and dumb, rot the firm Face of Earth   . . . 358   M. BRIDE   III.1   373
Rotation (1)
  Witwoud: Rotation of Tongue, that an Eccho must wait till she dies,   421   WAY WORLD   II.1   421
Rote (2)
  Valentine: thee this Lesson of Fustian to get by Rote?   255   FOR LOVE   III.1   74
  Mirabell: rote. The Catalogue was so large, that I was not without   . 399   WAY WRLD   I.1   166
Rots (1)
  Osmyn-Alph: Or Earth, it rests, and rots to silent Dust.   351   M. BRIDE   III.1   62
Rotten (6)
  Scandal: Aye, such rotten Reputations as you have to deal   . . 226   FOR LOVE   I.1   396
  Tattle: Nay, but why rotten? Why should you say rotten,   . . 226   FOR LOVE   I.1   398
  Almeria: I'll scrape 'till I collect his rotten Bones,   . . . 370   M. BRIDE   IV.1   349
  Mirabell: So one will be rotten before he be ripe, and the   . . 401   WAY WORLD   I.1   216
  Mirabell: other will be rotten without ever being ripe at all.   . 401   WAY WORLD   I.1   217
Rough (1)
  Sr Sampson: rough, he wants a little Polishing.   262   FOR LOVE   III.1   320
Round (15)
  Capt Bluff: not three words of Truth, the Year round, put into the   . 52   OLD BATCH   II.1   193
  Lord Touch: Circling Joys, tread round each happy Year of your long   . 203   DOUBL DLR   V.1   589
  Valentine: again.--Pretty round heaving Breasts,--a Barbary   . . 223   FOR LOVE   III.1   284
  Sr Sampson: Support, like Ivy round a dead Oak: Faith I do; I love to   . 260   FOR LOVE   III.1   264
  Ben: come, my Lads, let's have a round, and I'll make one.   . 275   FOR LOVE   III.1   797
  Valentine: go round.   311   FOR LOVE   V.1   526
      and Guards, who are ranged in Order, round the Stage.   . 332   M. BRIDE   I.1   267
  Osmyn-Alph: In Murmurs round my Head. I rose and listened;   . . . 344   M. BRIDE   II.2   162
  Osmyn-Alph: Look round; Joy is not here, nor Cheerfulness.   . . . 346   M. BRIDE   II.2   261
  Servant-M: turn; so we drove round to Duke's Place: and there they   . 398   WAY WORLD   I.1   118
  Mirabell: of gay fine Perrukes hovering round you.   418   WAY WORLD   II.1   330
  Petulant: (Surveying him round.)   . 438   WAY WORLD   III.1   491
  Sir Wilful: round the Edges, no broader than a Subpoena. I might expect   439   WAY WORLD   III.1   542
  Sir Wilful: then to your Friends round the Rekin. We cou'd have   . 439   WAY WORLD   III.1   551
  Sir Wilful: will do't. If not, dust it away, and let's have tother
      round--   . 455   WAY WORLD   IV.1   412
Roundness (2)
  Tattle: and roundness of her Lips.   228   FOR LOVE   I.1   467
  Tattle: and roundness of her Hips.   228   FOR LOVE   I.1 V467
Rous'd (2)
  Capt Bluff: shall find he might have safer rous'd a sleeping Lion.   . 101   OLD BATCH   V.1   168
  Osmyn-Alph: By Heav'n thou'st rous'd me from my Lethargy.   351   M. BRIDE   III.1   73
Rouse (2)
  Bellmour: seem to rouse, 'tis but well lashing him, and he will sleep   46   OLD BATCH   I.1   353
  Lady Touch: a Larum, only to rouse my own still'd Soul for your   . . 137   DOUBL DLR   I.1   381
Rout (1)
  Garcia: The King? Confusion, all is on the Rout!   376   M. BRIDE   V.2   17
Row (2)
  Ben: were, to look one way, and to row another. Now, for my   . 263   FOR LOVE   III.1   387
  Foible: and plac'd the Foot-men in a Row in the Hall, in their   . 444   WAY WORLD   IV.1   4
Rowes (1)
  Lady Wish: rowes of Pins and a Childs Fiddle; A Glass Necklace with the 462   WAY WORLD   V.1   16
Rowl (1)
  Bellmour: Business is not my Element--I rowl in a higher Orb   . . 38   OLD BATCH   I.1   27
Rowland (48)
  Foible: had a prospect of seeing Sir Rowland your Uncle; and that   423   WAY WORLD   II.1   520
  Waitwell: Sir Rowland if you please. The Jade's so pert upon   . . 424   WAY WORLD   II.1   550
  Mirabell: --And transform into Sir Rowland.   424   WAY WORLD   II.1   553
  Foible: --Poor Sir Rowland, I say.   427   WAY WORLD   III.1   78
  Foible: him Madam, starve him, marry Sir Rowland and get him   . 427   WAY WORLD   III.1   107
  Lady Wish: Will Sir Rowland be here, say'st thou? when   428   WAY WORLD   III.1   122
  Foible: Impatience in which Sir Rowland burns for the dear hour   . 428   WAY WORLD   III.1   126
  Lady Wish: my Features, to receive Sir Rowland with any Oeconomy of   . 428   WAY WORLD   III.1   141
  Lady Wish: Thou must repair me Foible, before Sir Rowland comes; or   . 429   WAY WORLD   III.1   149
  Lady Wish: But art thou sure Sir Rowland will not fail to   . . . 429   WAY WORLD   III.1   155
  Lady Wish: expect advances. No, I hope Sir Rowland is better bred,   . 429   WAY WORLD   III.1   161
  Lady Wish: Sir Rowland handsome? Let my Toilet be remov'd--I'll   . 429   WAY WORLD   III.1   171
  Lady Wish: dress above. I'll receive Sir Rowland here. Is he handsome?   429   WAY WORLD   III.1   172
  Lady Wish: Man. I shall save Decorums if Sir Rowland importunes. I   . 429   WAY WORLD   III.1   177
  Foible: she'll be contracted to Sir Rowland to Night, she says;--   430   WAY WORLD   III.1   210

Ruin   (continued)

		PAGE	TITLE	ACT.SC	LINE
Mellefont:	close her Eyes, till they had seen my ruin.	130	DOUBL DLR	I.1	V118
Maskwell:	you, brings me certain Ruin. Allow it, I would betray you,	136	DOUBL DLR	I.1	341
Maskwell:	Mellefont upon the brink of Ruin, and left him nought	137	DOUBL DLR	I.1	378
Maskwell:	Mellefont upon the brink of Ruin, and left him none	137	DOUBL DLR	I.1	V378
Lady Touch:	immediate Ruin seize him.	137	DOUBL DLR	I.1	401
Maskwell:	Compose your self, You shall Enjoy and Ruin	137	DOUBL DLR	I.1	402
Maskwell:	Compose your self, You shall possess and ruin	137	DOUBL DLR	I.1	V402
Lady Touch:	to ruin me--My Lord shall sign to your desires; I will my	185	DOUBL DLR	IV.2	84
Mirabell:	whole Design, and put it in your Power to ruin or advance	417	WAY WORLD	II.1	281
Mirabell:	hopes to ruin me, shou'd consent to marry my pretended	417	WAY WORLD	II.1	293
Mirabell:	Ay, ay, suffer your Cruelty to ruin the object of	420	WAY WORLD	II.1	389

Ruin'd (15)

Laetitia:	(aside). Ruin'd, past redemption! What shall I do?	90	OLD BATCH	IV.4	45
Laetitia:	(aside). Misfortune! Now all's ruin'd again.	92	OLD BATCH	IV.4	108
Lucy:	ruin'd my poor Mistress: You have made a Gap in her	98	OLD BATCH	V.1	48
Sir Paul:	Wedding Night, to die a Maid; as she did; all were ruin'd,	174	DOUBL DLR	IV.1	252
Lady Ply:	O Mr. Careless, Mr. Careless, I'm ruin'd, I'm	177	DOUBL DLR	IV.1	390
Jeremy:	upon you again. You're undone, Sir; you're ruin'd; you	218	FOR LOVE	I.1	85
Jeremy:	ruin'd more Young Men than the Royal Oak Lottery--	218	FOR LOVE	I.1	88
Tattle:	answer'd, I was the famous Tattle, who had ruin'd so	257	FOR LOVE	III.1	164
Scandal:	comes Tyrannically to insult a ruin'd Lover, and make	276	FOR LOVE	IV.1	24
Zara:	And now just ripe for Birth, my Rage has ruin'd.	354	M. BRIDE	III.1	196
Selim:	Madam, take heed; or you have ruin'd all.	366	M. BRIDE	IV.1	185
Garcia:	All's lost, all ruin'd by Surprize and Treachery.	376	M. BRIDE	V.2	18
Lady Wish:	wrought upon Foible to detect me, I'm ruin'd. Oh my dear	426	WAY WORLD	III.1	53
Foible:	Unfortunate, all's ruin'd.	460	WAY WORLD	IV.1	590
Lady Wish:	Here I am ruin'd to Compound for your Caprices	466	WAY WORLD	V.1	150

Ruine (24)

Lady Touch:	O for Heaven's sake, my Lord, you'll ruine	153	DOUBL DLR	III.1	103
Maskwell:	about the rate of your ruine--	156	DOUBL DLR	III.1	215
Careless:	ruine me with Kindness; your Charming Tongue pursues	169	DOUBL DLR	IV.1	86
Lady Touch:	into unthought of ways of ruine.	185	DOUBL DLR	IV.2	78
Lady Touch:	'Tis true it might have been my ruine--but	188	DOUBL DLR	V.1	6
Maskwell:	ruine all, consume my honest Character, and brand me	188	DOUBL DLR	V.1	30
Maskwell:	Fortune on another's ruine: I had but one desire--	189	DOUBL DLR	V.1	73
Maskwell:	tho' she involv'd her self in ruine. No, it must be by	190	DOUBL DLR	V.1	94
Scandal:	where-ever it is, it's always contriving it's own Ruine.	219	FOR LOVE	I.1	121
Scandal:	'S'death, you are not mad indeed, to ruine your	311	FOR LOVE	V.1	541
Valentine:	vain Attempts, and find at last, that nothing but my Ruine	312	FOR LOVE	V.1	547
Osmyn-Alph:	A fatal Wretch--a huge stupendous Ruine,	347	M. BRIDE	II.2	309
Zara:	If I have gain'd thy Love, 'tis Glorious Ruine;	347	M. BRIDE	II.2	313
Zara:	Ruine, 'tis still to reign, and to be more	347	M. BRIDE	II.2	314
Almeria:	And hug in scorn of it, our mutual Ruine.	358	M. BRIDE	III.1	340
Zara:	Perdition catch 'em both, and Ruine part 'em.	359	M. BRIDE	III.1	402
Zara:	And kindle Ruine in its Course. Think'st thou	375	M. BRIDE	V.1	96
Zara:	And kindle Ruine in its Course. Dost think	375	M. BRIDE	V.1	V 96
Selim:	Devis'd to serve, should ruine your Design!	375	M. BRIDE	V.1	115
Garcia:	(returning). Ruine and Horrour! O heart-wounding	377	M. BRIDE	V.2	51
Gonsalez:	What says my Son? what Ruine? ha? what	377	M. BRIDE	V.2	53
Lady Wish:	Jewells and ruine my Neice, and all little enough--	466	WAY WORLD	V.1	152
Lady Wish:	ruine? Ungrateful Wretch! dost thou not owe thy being,	473	WAY WORLD	V.1	446
Lady Wish:	from Ruine, from Want, I'll forgive all that's past; Nay	473	WAY WORLD	V.1	454

Ruins (1)

Tattle:	Oh, Madam, look upon us both. There you see the ruins	291	FOR LOVE	IV.1	580

Rule (9)

Lord Touch:	Authority--hereafter, you shall rule where I have Power.	189	DOUBL DLR	V.1	66
Sr Sampson:	it, that by the rule of right Reason, this fellow ought to	245	FOR LOVE	II.1	366
Sr Sampson:	your Element, Fish, be mute, Fish, and to Sea, rule your	308	FOR LOVE	V.1	418
Zara:	Of equal Value, with unborrow'd Rule,	335	M. BRIDE	I.1	396
Manuel:	To rule all Hearts.	336	M. BRIDE	I.1	423
Osmyn-Alph:	Or all extended Rule of regal Pow'r.	353	M. BRIDE	III.1	138
Osmyn-Alph:	For this World's Rule, I wou'd not wound thy	356	M. BRIDE	III.1	275
Painall:	none to me, she can take none from me, 'tis against all rule	443	WAY WORLD	III.1	687
Marwood:	Quiblers by the Statute; and become a Jest, against a Rule	467	WAY WORLD	V.1	215

Rules (4)

Lord Touch:	Rules but I shall govern them.	195	DOUBL DLR	V.1	304
	So t'other can foretel by certain Rules	323	M. BRIDE	PRO.	11
Manuel:	But rules with settled Sway in Zara's Eyes.	337	M. BRIDE	I.1	461
Sir Wilful:	Live by Heathenish Rules,	456	WAY WORLD	IV.1	453

Rummer (1)

Tattle:	the Drawers at Locket's, Pontack's, the Rummer, Spring	257	FOR LOVE	III.1	157

Rumour (1)

Gonsalez:	Some ready of Belief, have rais'd this Rumour:	363	M. BRIDE	IV.1	83

Run (38)   see Over-run

Bellmour:	abroad--went purely to run away from a Campagne;	47	OLD BATCH	I.1	369
Bellmour:	is to run so extravagantly in Debt; I have laid out such a	58	OLD BATCH	II.2	122
Heartwell:	the envenom'd Shirt, to run into the Embraces of a Fever,	62	OLD BATCH	III.1	67
Heartwell:	on't--I'le run into the danger to lose the	63	OLD BATCH	III.1	85
Sir Joseph:	Lord-Harry. I know better things than to be run through	67	OLD BATCH	III.1	253
Barnaby:	And run the hazard to lose your affair so!	76	OLD BATCH	IV.1	38
Barnaby:	And run the hazard to lose your affair, Sir!	76	OLD BATCH	IV.1	V 38
Vainlove:	dull and unnatural to have a Hare run full in the Hounds	80	OLD BATCH	IV.1	178
Bellmour:	Madam;--I confess I have run into an Errour:--I beg your	81	OLD BATCH	IV.2	38
Laetitia:	Patch.--You s'an't turn in, Nykin.--Run into my	89	OLD BATCH	IV.4	16
Laetitia:	run in thy debt again. But this Opportunity is the Devil.	91	OLD BATCH	IV.4	92
Heartwell:	All Coursers the first Heat with Vigour run;	112	OLD BATCH	V.2	194
	As a rash Girl, who will all Hazards run,	113	OLD BATCH	EPI.	1
Mellefont:	that you run over!	155	DOUBL DLR	III.1	199
Mellefont:	To run most wilfully and unreasonably away with	168	DOUBL DLR	IV.1	38
Mellefont:	you have Love enough to run the venture.	193	DOUBL DLR	V.1	201
Maskwell:	and run the hazard along with you.	193	DOUBL DLR	V.1	207
Maskwell:	you, Borrow my Lords Chaplain, and so run away with	193	DOUBL DLR	V.1	224
	But Poets run much greater hazards far,	204	DOUBL DLR	EPI.	8
Scandal:	have fair Play for your Life. If you can't be fairly run down	220	FOR LOVE	I.1	142

Run (continued)
		PAGE	TITLE	ACT.SC	LINE
Tattle:	Closet, nor run behind a Screen, cr under a Table; never	230	FOR LCVE	I.1	519
Miss Prue:	No, indeed won't I: But I'll run there, and hide	252	FCR LCVE	II.1	648
Miss Prue:	Well, now I'll run and make more haste than you.	253	FOR LCVE	II.1	660
Ben:	Why an you do, You may run the risk to be overset,	262	FOR LCVE	III.1	334
Jeremy:	my Master was run stark mad only for Love of her Mistress;	276	FCR LCVE	IV.1	15
Sr Sampson:	What, is he gone cut of Town, run away, ha!	279	FOR LCVE	IV.1	122
Valentine:	Ha, ha, ha; you need not run so fast, Honesty will	282	FCR LCVE	IV.1	246
Ben:	Nay, nay, my mind run upon you,--but I wou'd not	285	FOR LCVE	IV.1	379
Sr Sampson:	risen in the State--But, a pox cn't, his Wit run him	299	FOR LCVE	V.1	83
Sr Sampson:	out of his Money, and now his Poverty has run him out of	299	FOR LCVE	V.1	84
Foresight:	Well, I shall run mad next.	306	FOR LCVE	V.1	348
Angelica:	apt to run more in Debt than you are able to pay.	313	FCR LCVE	V.1	614
	For still in every Storm, they all run hither,	315	FOR LCVE	EPI.	3
Osmyn-Alph:	How run into thy Arms with-held by Fetters,	355	M. EBIDE	III.1	239
	O with what Joy they run, to spread the News	385	M. EBIDE	EPI.	11
	But what unequal Hazards do they run!	393	WAY WCBLD	PRO.	13
Foible:	Ladyship, he must have run the risque of the Law, and been	463	WAY WCBLD	V.1	43
Fainall:	to run at Mrs. Fainall.)	476	WAY WCBLD	V.1	557

Rung (1)
		PAGE	TITLE	ACT.SC	LINE
Bellmour:	Marriage-knell was rung.	108	OLD BATCH	V.2	19

Running (2)
		PAGE	TITLE	ACT.SC	LINE
Mellefont:	out Cuckoldom with her Fingers, and you're running	187	DOUEL DLR	IV.2	132
Valentine:	give Scandal such an Advantage; why, your running away	229	FOR LOVE	I.1	512

Runs (10)
		PAGE	TITLE	ACT.SC	LINE
	(Runs off.)	35	OLD BATCH	PRO.	28
	(As Fondlewife is going into the Chamber, she runs to Sir	90	OLD BATCH	IV.4	49
Setter:	Her head runs on nothing else, nor she can talk of	102	OLD BATCH	V.1	198
Lady Touch:	a sedate, a thinking Villain, whose Black Blood runs	135	DOUEL DLR	I.1	328
Maskwell:	(Runs out.)	184	DOUEL DLR	IV.2	40
	(Draws, and runs at Mellefont, is held by Lady Touchwood.)	186	DCUEL DLR	IV.2	108
	runs cut affrighted, my Lord after her, like a Parson.)	202	DOUBL DLR	V.1	557
Lady Touch:	(Runs out.)	202	DOUEL DLR	V.1	562
Miss Prue:	(Runs and Kisses him.)	252	FCR LOVE	II.1	634
Singer-V:	But runs with Joy the Circle of the Mind.	293	FOR LOVE	IV.1	661

Russian (1)
		PAGE	TITLE	ACT.SC	LINE
Mellefont:	great Beard, like a Russian Bear upon a drift of Snow. You	158	DOUBL DLR	III.1	292

Rust (3)
		PAGE	TITLE	ACT.SC	LINE
Osmyn-Alph:	And stain thy Bosom with the Rust of these	355	M. EBIDE	III.1	243
Almeria:	With rancling Rust.	356	M. EBIDE	III.1	269
Marwood:	but it shall never rust in my Possession.	410	WAY WCBLD	II.1	17

Rustick (1)
		PAGE	TITLE	ACT.SC	LINE
Millamant:	Ah Rustick! ruder than Gothick.	447	WAY WCBLD	IV.1	109

Rustle (1)
		PAGE	TITLE	ACT.SC	LINE
Mirabell:	Waitwell shake his Ears, and Dame Partlet rustle up her	398	WAY WCBLD	I.1	129

Rustling (1)
		PAGE	TITLE	ACT.SC	LINE
Zara:	To hide, the rustling Leaves, and bended Grass	375	M. EBIDE	V.1	109

Rusty (1)
		PAGE	TITLE	ACT.SC	LINE
Zara:	And Crash of rusty Bars, and creeking Hinges:	379	M. EBIDE	V.2	138

S'an't (2)
		PAGE	TITLE	ACT.SC	LINE
Laetitia:	Patch.--You s'an't tum in, Nykin.--Run intc my	89	OLD BATCH	IV.4	16
Laetitia:	Chamber, quickly, quickly. You s'an't tum in.	89	OLD BATCH	IV.4	17

S'bud (4)
		PAGE	TITLE	ACT.SC	LINE
Setter:	S'bud Sir, away quickly, there's Fondlewife just turn'd	75	OLD BATCH	IV.1	9
Sr Sampson:	without her Inconstancy. 'S'bud I was but in Jest.	242	FOR LCVE	II.1	259
Petulant:	Well, well; I come--Sbud, a Man had as good	405	WAY WCBLD	I.1	383
Sir Wilful:	Look up Man, I'll stand by you, 'sbud an she do	471	WAY WCBLD	V.1	360

S'death (12)   see 'Death
		PAGE	TITLE	ACT.SC	LINE
Heartwell:	Wives Coat. S'death I would not be a Cuckold to ere an	45	OLD BATCH	I.1	312
Heartwell:	S'death how the young Fellows will hoot me! I shall be	63	OLD BATCH	III.1	78
Heartwell:	S'death it is but a may be, and upon scurvy Terms--	74	OLD BATCH	III.2	128
Mellefont:	purpose? yet, 'sdeath, for a Man to have the fruit of all				
	his	187	DOUBL DLR	IV.2	143
Valentine:	'Sdeath, are not you asham'd?	258	FOR LCVE	III.1	181
Scandal:	'S'death do you make no difference between me and	284	FOR LCVE	IV.1	321
Scandal:	'S'death it's a Jest. I can't believe it.	307	FCR LCVE	V.1	367
Scandal:	'S'death, you are not mad indeed, to ruine your	311	FCR LCVE	V.1	541
Fainall:	--'Sdeath they come, hide your Face, your Tears--	416	WAY WCBLD	II.1	247
Fainall:	in the Way of the World. 'S death	442	WAY WCBLD	III.1	631
Fainall:	'S death to be Out-Witted, to be Out-Jilted--	442	WAY WCBLD	III.1	634
Fainall:	S'death what's this to me? I'll not wait your private	475	WAY WCBLD	V.1	517

S'heart (21)
		PAGE	TITLE	ACT.SC	LINE
Sr Sampson:	Here's a Cormorant too,--'S'heart this	245	FOR LCVE	II.1	357
Sr Sampson:	have been born without a Palate.--'S'heart, what shou'd	245	FOR LCVE	II.1	367
Sr Sampson:	feed thee out of my own Vitals?--'S'heart, live by	246	FOR LCVE	II.1	399
Sir Wilful:	but 'tis--'Sheart I know not whether 'tis or no--	438	WAY WORLD	III.1	515
Sir Wilful:	'Sheart why do'st not speak? Art thou o'er-joy'd?	439	WAY WCBLD	III.1	519
Sir Wilful:	again--'Sheart, and your Friend and Servant to that--	439	WAY WORLD	III.1	522
Sir Wilful:	'Sheart, Sir, but there is, and much offence--	439	WAY EBIDE	III.1	527
Sir Wilful:	Brother. 'Sheart, I've suspected this--By'r Lady I	439	WAY WCBLD	III.1	539
Sir Wilful:	'Sheart, and better than to be bound to a Maker of	440	WAY WCBLD	III.1	563
Sir Wilful:	I thank you for your courteous Offer. 'Sheart, I was afraid	441	WAY WCBLD	III.1	602
Sir Wilful:	What dee do? 'Shart a'has lock'd the Door indeed I	447	WAY WCBLD	IV.1	92
Sir Wilful:	'Sheart, an you grutch me your Liquor, make a	455	WAY WCBLD	IV.1	394
Sir Wilful:	--S'heart! and I'm sorry for't. What wou'd you have?	470	WAY WCBLD	V.1	315
Sir Wilful:	'Sheart the Gentleman's a civil Gentleman, Aunt,	471	WAY WCBLD	V.1	345
Sir Wilful:	--'Sheart, I'll call him in,--an I set on't	471	WAY WCBLD	V.1	351
Sir Wilful:	'Sheart an she shou'd her forehead wou'd wrinkle like the	471	WAY WCBLD	V.1	363
Sir Wilful:	'Sheart and she shou'd her forehead wou'd wrinkle like the	471	WAY WORLD	V.1 V363
Sir Wilful:	in defiance of you Sir, and of your Instrument. S'heart an	473	WAY WCBLD	V.1	424
Sir Wilful:	S'heart Aunt, I have no mind to marry. My	477	WAY WCBLD	V.1	582
Sir Wilful:	S'heart you'll have him time enough to toy after	477	WAY WORLD	V.1	599
Sir Wilful:	S'heart you'll have time enough to toy after	477	WAY WORLD	V.1 V599

S'life (6)
		PAGE	TITLE	ACT.SC	LINE
Vainlove:	Hold hold, 'slife that's the wrong.	38	OLD BATCH	I.1	37
Careless:	'Slife yonder's Sir Paul, but if he were not come, I'm	171	DOUEL DLR	IV.1	128

S'life   (continued)
Jeremy:	in a Tub, go to Prison for you? 'Slife, Sir, what do you	217	FOR LOVE	I.1	31
Mrs Frail:	What have you to do to watch me?--'S'life I'll	246	FOR LOVE	II.1	415
Marwood:	S'life, we shall have a Quarrel betwixt an Horse and an Ass,	438	WAY WORLD	III.1	505
Petulant:	S'life, Witwoud, were you ever an Attorney's Clerk?	440	WAY WORLD	III.1	554

Sable   (2)
| Manuel: | To see that Sable worn upon the Day | 333 | M. BRIDE | I.1 | 295 |
| Zara: | If so, this Sable Curtain shall again | 353 | M. BRIDE | III.1 | 151 |

Sack   (5)
Valentine:	Chair quickly: A Bottle of Sack and a Toast--fly--a Chair	222	FOR LOVE	I.1	229
Valentine:	Sirrah the Sack.--	222	FOR LOVE	I.1	239
Scandal:	refund the Sack: Jeremy fetch him some warm water, or	224	FOR LOVE	I.1	310
Trapland:	Sack; but you cannot expect it again, when I have drank it.	224	FOR LOVE	I.1	314
Trapland:	Sack; but you cannot expect it again, when I have drunk it.	224	FOR LOVE	I.1	V314

Sacred   (7)
Sir Paul:	the Marriage Bed with reverence as to a sacred shrine, and	178	DOUBL DLR	IV.1	427
Tattle:	Oh Madam, those are Sacred to Love and Contemplation.	232	FOR LOVE	I.1	609
Almeria:	Alphonso, hear the Sacred Vow I make;	330	M. BRIDE	I.1	178
Leonora:	Behold the Sacred Vault, within whose Womb,	340	M. BRIDE	II.2	6
Osmyn-Alph:	Disturb'd the Sacred Silence of the Vault,	344	M. BRIDE	II.2	161
Osmyn-Alph:	Like Fumes of Sacred Incense, o'er the Clouds,	353	M. BRIDE	III.1	130
Osmyn-Alph:	The Sacred Union of Connubial Love,	357	M. BRIDE	III.1	319

Sacrific'd   (4)
Almeria:	I must be sacrific'd, and all the Faith	330	M. BRIDE	I.1	172
Almeria:	I must be sacrific'd, and all the Vows	330	M. BRIDE	I.1	V172
Marwood:	Fidelity to you, and sacrific'd my Friendship to keep my	414	WAY WORLD	II.1	173
Mirabell:	Addresses. A better Man ought not to have been sacrific'd	417	WAY WORLD	II.1	275

Sacrifice   (8)
Lord Froth:	sake let us sacrifice 'em to mirth a little.	163	DOUBL DLR	III.1	487
Scandal:	Come then, sacrifice half a Dozen Women of good	230	FOR LOVE	I.1	526
Angelica:	Martyrdom, and sacrifice their Interest to their Constancy!	314	FOR LOVE	V.1	634
Osmyn-Alph:	Yet lighted up, his last most grateful Sacrifice;	357	M. BRIDE	III.1	322
Selim:	Pretend to sacrifice the Life of Osmyn.	361	M. BRIDE	IV.1	22
Almeria:	I am the Sacrifice design'd to bleed;	361	M. BRIDE	IV.1	22
Marwood:	and Sacrifice Neice, and Fortune, and all at that Conjuncture.	442	WAY WORLD	III.1	664
Millamant:	I am content to be a Sacrifice to your repose	470	WAY WORLD	V.1	325

Sad   (17)
Singer:	The sad miscarriage of their Wooing:	71	OLD BATCH	III.2	V 21
Laetitia:	Spin-text, has a sad Fit of the Cholick, and is forced to lie	91	OLD BATCH	IV.4	78
Lady Froth:	come together,--O bless me! What a sad thing	139	DOUBL DLR	II.1	22
Singer:	Think, O think o'th' sad Condition,	143	DOUBL DLR	II.1	190
Lady Ply:	can refrain to weep and yield to such sad Sayings.--	170	DOUBL DLR	IV.1	120
Scandal:	Sir Sampson, sad News.	266	FOR LOVE	III.1	480
Ben:	you too well, by sad experience;--I believe he that marries	287	FOR LOVE	IV.1	438
Angelica:	knows I pitie you; and could I have foreseen the sad	294	FOR LOVE	IV.1	712
Valentine:	What sad Effects?--What's too late? my seeming	294	FOR LOVE	IV.1	715
Almeria:	I thank thee, that thou'lt pity thy sad Mistress;	328	M. BRIDE	I.1	95
Almeria:	Indeed, I do, for pitying thy sad Mistress;	328	M. BRIDE	I.1	V 95
Manuel:	Upon this solemn Day, in these sad Weeds?	333	M. BRIDE	I.1	280
Osmyn-Alph:	How shall I welcome thee, to this sad Place?	355	M. BRIDE	III.1	237
Zara:	Why is't you more than speak in these sad Signs?	380	M. BRIDE	V.2	159
Waitwell:	Ay there's the Grief; that's the sad change of Life;	424	WAY WORLD	II.1	562
Millamant:	me Melancholly--Now I'll be sad.	434	WAY WORLD	III.1	362
Millamant:	me Melancholick--Now I'll be sad.	434	WAY WORLD	III.1	V362

Saddest   (1)
| Careless: | I thank Heav'n, they are the saddest that I ever | 170 | DOUBL DLR | IV.1 | 122 |

Safe   (12)
Sharper:	O your Servant Sir, you are safe then it seems; 'tis an	48	OLD BATCH	II.1	32
Laetitia:	(aside). Oh then alls safe. I was terrible frighted--	78	OLD BATCH	IV.1	102
Laetitia:	(aside). Oh then alls safe. I was terribly frighted--	78	OLD BATCH	IV.1	V102
Lady Ply:	--I am not safe if I stay, and must leave you.	170	DOUBL DLR	IV.1	98
Lady Touch:	So, that's safe.	184	DOUBL DLR	IV.2	32
Mrs Frail:	here too? Oh Mr. Tattle, every thing is safe with you, we	230	FOR LOVE	I.1	548
Jeremy:	No, no, Sir; he's safe enough, Sir, an he were but as	279	FOR LOVE	IV.1	124
Sr Sampson:	Pocket.) There Val: it's safe enough, Boy--But thou	282	FOR LOVE	IV.1	233
Osmyn-Alph:	My Friend too safe!	344	M. BRIDE	II.2	170
Osmyn-Alph:	I'm fortunate indeed!--my Friend too safe!	344	M. BRIDE	II.2	V170
Zara:	While Osmyn lives, you are not safe.	364	M. BRIDE	IV.1	111
Foible:	we may break it with a safe Conscience.	464	WAY WORLD	V.1	100

Safely   (3)
Almeria:	He and his Sorrows now are safely lodg'd	326	M. BRIDE	I.1	11
Foible:	Heart still. Now, Madam, I can safely tell your Ladyship	430	WAY WORLD	III.1	205
Servant-W:	Why truly Sir, I cannot safely swear to her Face in a	437	WAY WORLD	III.1	461

Safer   (2)
| Capt Bluff: | shall find he might have safer rous'd a sleeping Lion. | 101 | OLD BATCH | V.1 | 168 |
| Tattle: | No, Sir, 'tis written in my Heart. And safer there, Sir, than | 292 | FOR LOVE | IV.1 | 613 |

Safety   (5)
Heartwell:	esteem my Friendship, or your own Safety,--come	105	OLD BATCH	V.1	322
Almeria:	But that my Father is return'd in Safety,	332	M. BRIDE	I.1	250
Heli:	With Speed and Safety, to convey my self	352	M. BRIDE	III.1	99
Zara:	Himself. I've been deceiv'd. The publick Safety	360	M. BRIDE	III.1	449
Zara:	I've been deceiv'd. The publick Safety now	360	M. BRIDE	III.1	V449

Sagely   (1)
| Singer-F: | But sagely at length he this Secret disclos'd: | 259 | FOR LOVE | III.1 | 206 |

Sages   (1)
| Mirabell: | Friends and of Sages learned in the Laws of this Land, | 476 | WAY WORLD | V.1 | 545 |

Said   (57)   see Say'd
Sir Joseph:	Ah, well said my Hero; was not that great Sir?	52	OLD BATCH	II.1	166
Araminta:	Bless me! what have I said to move you thus?	54	OLD BATCH	II.2	3
Belinda:	Man--you don't know what you said, your Fever has	54	OLD BATCH	II.2	6
Belinda:	Man--you don't know what you've said, your Fever has	54	OLD BATCH	II.2	V 6
Belinda:	O Gad I hate your hideous Fancy--You said that	59	OLD BATCH	II.2	167
Musician:	Poor, old, repenting Delia said,	59	OLD BATCH	II.2	191

Said   (continued)

		PAGE	TITLE	ACT.SC	LINE
Lucy:	Hum'd it over, gave you his Respects, and said, he	61	OLD BATCH	III.1	26
Lucy:	not what you said of my Person; but that my innocent	66	OLD BATCH	III.1	209
Sir Joseph:	done behind his Back, than what's said--Come wee'l	70	OLD BATCH	III.1	361
Singer:	O let me--still the Shepherd said;	71	OLD BATCH	III.2 V	14
Vainlove:	To ccnfirm what I have said read this	79	OLD BATCH	IV.1	154
Setter:	found me, and over-heard all they said. Mr. Bellmour is to	98	OLD BATCH	V.1	84
Brisk:	things said; or cne, understood, since thy Amputation	128	DOUEL DLR	I.1	36
Brisk:	said it out of thy Company.--Careless, ha?	128	DCUEL DLR	I.1	39
Lady Touch:	How, what said you Maskwell--	137	DOUEL DLR	I.1	391
Mellefont:	said to be unmask'd when they wear Vizers; fcr that	158	DOUEL DLR	III.1	311
Cynthia:	But that cannot be properly said of them, for I	163	DOUBL DLR	III.1	481
Careless:	said--Oh! (Aside.) I shall never contain Laughter.	170	DOUEL DLR	IV.1	123
Lady Ply:	make up this Match again, because Mr. Careless said it	171	DOUEL DLR	IV.1	153
Lady Ply:	make up the Match again, because Mr. Careless said it	171	DOUEL DLR	IV.1 V	153
Sir Paul:	be this is all his doings--something that he has said;	172	DOUEL DLR	IV.1	201
Sir Paul:	be this is all his doing--something that he has said.	172	DOUEL DLR	IV.1 V	201
Brisk:	Woman of parts, and I'gad parts will carry her. She said	175	DOUEL DLR	IV.1	295
Careless:	said all I could, but can't prevail--Ther my Friendship	180	DOUEL DLR	IV.1	492
Lady Touch:	what I said to you, or you had better eat your own Horns,	192	DOUEL DLR	V.1	192
Cynthia:	When you were gone, he said his mind was chang'd,	196	DOUEL DLR	V.1	347
Tattle:	three or four places, that I said this and that, and writ to	227	FOR LCVE	I.1	420
Tattle:	O Lord, what have I said? my Unlucky Tongue!	227	FOR LCVE	I.1	435
Foresight:	Withouten Guile, then be it said,	236	FOR LCVE	II.1	53
Foresight:	there's no more to be said--	239	FOR LCVE	II.1	170
Foresight:	there's no more to be said--he's here already	239	FOR LCVE	II.1 V	170
Sr Sampson:	said of what's past, and all that is tc come will happen.	240	FCR LCVE	II.1	198
Mrs Frail:	might have been said.	247	FOR LCVE	II.1	440
Miss Prue:	Lies--but they frighted me, and said it was a sin.	252	FOR LCVE	II.1	630
Ben:	What I said was in Obedience to Father; Gad I fear a	264	FCR LCVE	III.1	406
Mrs Fore:	of what you have said.	273	FOR LCVE	III.1	744
Ben:	Said he could mend her Kettle,	274	FOR LCVE	III.1	777
Ben:	tell him so much.--So he said he'd make my heart ake;	285	FCR LOVE	IV.1	380
Valentine:	Oh, Prayers will be said in empty Churches, at	289	FOR LCVE	V.1	500
Tattle:	Pox on't, there's no coming off, now she has said	293	FOR LCVE	IV.1	679
Almeria:	What have I said?	328	M. EBIDE	I.1	78
Almeria:	Alas! What have I said?	328	M. EBIDE	I.1 V	78
Almeria:	And when I said thou didst know nothing,	328	M. EBIDE	I.1	100
Manuel:	So great in Arms, as thou art said to be,	336	M. EBIDE	I.1	431
Witwoud:	with him; if he said they were my Mother and my Sisters.	406	WAY WCBLD	I.1	411
Witwoud:	with him; if he had said they were my Mother and my Sisters.	406	WAY WCRLD	I.1 V	411
Marwood:	I join with you; what I have said, has been to	411	WAY WCRLD	II.1	41
Foible:	O Madam; 'tis a shame to say what he said--	427	WAY WCRLD	III.1	93
Foible:	said.	428	WAY WCRLD	III.1	109
Millamant:	Nay, he has said nothing neither; but he has contradicted	432	WAY WCBLD	III.1	292
Millamant:	every Thing that has been said. For my part, I thought	432	WAY WCBLD	III.1	293
Millamant:	said something to please me.	452	WAY WCRLD	IV.1	307
Mrs Fain:	So it seems, when you mind not what's said to	453	WAY WCRLD	IV.1	317
Mrs Fain:	So it seems, for you mind not what's said to	453	WAY WCBLD	IV.1 V	317
Foible:	Closet, and over-heard all that you said to me before	464	WAY WCRLD	V.1	69
Mincing:	is in a perilous passion, at something Mr. Fainall has said.	465	WAY WCRLD	V.1	108
Fainall:	possible speed. In the mean while, I will go for the said	469	WAY WCRLD	V.1	294

Sail (8)

Sharper:	loves to buffet with the Winds, meet the Tide and sail in	42	OLD BATCH	I.1	202
Ben:	Sail o' your Head--Top and Top-gallant by the Mess.	262	FOR LCVE	III.1	332
Ben:	neither--But I'll sail as far as Ligorn, and back again,	306	FOR LCVE	V.1	352
Ben:	as if so be you should sail so far as the Streights without	308	FOR LCVE	V.1	415
Ben:	Hold. They say a Witch will sail in a Sieve--But I	309	FOR LCVE	V.1	434
Almeria:	Ready to sail, and when this News was brought,	329	M. BRIDE	I.1	121
Mirabell:	Here she comes i'faith full sail, with her Fan spread	418	WAY WORLD	II.1	323
Sir Wilful:	Belike I may Madam. I may chance to sail upon	440	WAY WCRLD	III.1	567

Sailing (1)

Mrs Frail:	Estate, is like Sailing in a Ship without Ballast.	273	FOR LCVE	III.1	720

Sailor (4)

Ben:	don't think I'm false-hearted, like a Land-man. A Sailor	273	FCB LCVE	III.1	732
Ben:	Come, I'll sing you a Song of a Sailor.	273	FOR LCVE	III.1	740
Ben:	A Souldier and a Sailor,	274	FOR LCVE	III.1	758
Ben:	The Sailor slily waiting,	274	FOR LCVE	III.1	781

Sailors (3)

Ben:	man, than a Galley-slave is like cne of us free Sailors, he is	262	FCR LCVE	III.1	316
Ben:	you shall see, that we Sailors can Dance sometimes, as well	274	FOR LCVE	III.1	791
Ben:	We're merry Folk, we Sailors, we han't much to care for.	275	FOR LCVE	III.1	799

Saint (2)   see St

Heartwell:	Yet I must--Speak dear Angel, Devil, Saint, Witch; do	72	OLD EATCH	III.2	41
Almeria:	For I have pray'd to thee as to a Saint:	343	M. EBIDE	II.2	131

Saist (1)

Zara:	What saist thou?	359	M. EBIDE	III.1	385

Sake (32)   see Love-sake

	O Lord, for Heavens sake excuse the Play,	35	OLD BATCH	PRO.	23
	For my sake then--but I'm in such Confusion,	35	OLD BATCH	PRO.	26
Belinda:	sake.	55	OLD BATCH	II.2	16
Belinda:	sake let it be with variety; don't ccme always, like the	59	OLD BATCH	II.2	169
Maskwell:	sake, and you reproach me with it; I am ready to be a	136	DOUBL DLR	I.1	336
Lord Froth:	I saw my self there, and kissed it for your sake.	140	DOUEL DLR	II.1	80
Mellefont:	For Heaven's sake, Madam, to whom do you direct	145	DOUEL DLR	II.1	250
Mellefont:	For Heaven's sake, Madam.--	147	DOUEL DLR	II.1	343
Lady Touch:	O for Heaven's sake, my Lord, you'll ruine	153	DOUEL DLR	III.1	103
Mellefont:	How, how, for Heaven's sake, dear Maskwell?	157	DOUBL DLR	III.1	247
Careless:	For Heaven's sake, Madam--I'm quite out of	160	DOUEL DLR	III.1	370
Lord Froth:	sake let us sacrifice 'em to mirth a little.	163	DOUEL DLR	III.1	487
Cynthia:	keep my word, and live a Maid for your sake.	169	DOUEL DLR	IV.1	62
Lady Ply:	sake step in here and advise me quickly, before he sees.	178	DOUEL DLR	IV.1	403
Lady Touch:	Heavens sake.	186	DOUEL DLB	IV.2	110
Lady Touch:	sake away my Lord, he'll either tempt you to extravagance,	186	DOUEL DLB	IV.2	128
Mellefont:	How? for Heaven's sake?	190	DOUEL DLB	V.1	108

Satisfaction   (continued)
    Lord Touch: your satisfaction or disquiet. . . . . 152 DOUBL DLR III.1   49
    Lord Touch: how shall I make him ample satisfaction?-- . . . . 200 DOUBL DLR   V.1 479
    Waitwell: that Satisfaction.--That wou'd be some Comfort to   . 458 WAY WORLD IV.1 503
    Sir Wilful: am willing to make satisfaction; and what can a man say . 470 WAY WORLD   V.1 317
Satisfactions (1)
    Maskwell: up this Account, to all our satisfactions.   . . . . 194 DOUBL DLR   V.1 244
Satisfi'd (1)
    Marwood: have Overseen. Here comes Mr. Fainall. If he will be
                  satisfi'd . . . . 468 WAY WORLD   V.1 243
Satisfie (4)
    Valentine: he shall satisfie you. . . . . 224 FOR LOVE   I.1 321
    Angelica: to satisfie you about Valentine: For if a Match were
                  seemingly . . . . 300 FOR LOVE   V.1 108
    Sr Sampson: Come, Chuck, satisfie him, answer him;-- . . . . 311 FOR LOVE   V.1 527
    Fainall: have Cruelty enough, not to satisfie a Lady's longing; you 397 WAY WORLD   I.1   91
Satisfied (10)
    Vainlove: satisfied without Reason. . . . .   40 OLD BATCH   I.1 110
    Lucy: on't, both your Love and Anger satisfied!--All that can .   75 OLD BATCH III.2 160
    Lady Touch: me beg you rest satisfied-- . . . . 152 DOUBL DLR III.1   56
    Lady Touch: me beg you to rest satisfied-- . . . . 152 DOUBL DLR III.1 V 56
    Lady Touch: you would not be satisfied when you knew it. . . . 153 DOUBL DLR III.1 106
    Lord Touch: Before I've done, I will be satisfied. . . . . . 153 DOUBL DLR III.1 107
    Careless: Masquerade, when I'm satisfied she knew me, and I had no . 158 DOUBL DLR III.1 306
    Lady Ply: I'm satisfied that my Cousin Mellefont has been . . . 171 DOUBL DLR   IV.1 159
    Lady Ply: By all means--Mr. Careless has satisfied me of . . . . 173 DOUBL DLR   IV.1 204
    Waitwell: a good cause--my Lady shall be satisfied of my Truth . 461 WAY WORLD   IV.1 624
Satisfy'd (7)
    Tattle: But I soon satisfy'd the Lady of your Innocence; for I told . 227 FOR LOVE   I.1 429
    Scandal: against your Conscience--You are not satisfy'd that you . 268 FOR LOVE III.1 556
    Scandal: You are not satisfy'd, I say--I am loath to . . . . 268 FOR LOVE III.1 559
    Scandal: discourage you--But it is palpable that you are not
                  satisfy'd. . . . . 268 FOR LOVE III.1 560
    Foresight: well satisfy'd. . . . . 268 FOR LOVE III.1 562
    Fainall: O my Dear I am satisfy'd of your Tenderness; I know . . 412 WAY WORLD   II.1   95
    Sir Wilful: satisfy'd with the Information of my Boots, Sir, if you will 438 WAY WORLD III.1 499
Saturn (1)
    Lady Froth: You know I told you Saturn look'd a little more . . . . 203 DOUBL DLR   V.1 579
Satyr (5)
                  Arm'd with keen Satyr, and with pointed Wit, ...   35 OLD BATCH PRO.   7
    Laetitia: alone with such a Satyr? . . . .   90 OLD BATCH IV.4   48
    Brisk: I'm wholly turn'd into Satyr. I confess I Write but seldom, 141 DOUBL DLR   II.1 116
    Brisk: call it, but it's Satyr.--Sing it my Lord. . . . . . 166 DOUBL DLR III.1 593
    Mirabell: Rudeness and ill Language, Satyr and Fire. . . . . . 401 WAY WORLD   I.1 231
Satyre (1)
    Fainall: budding Antlers like a young Satyre, or a Citizens Child. . 442 WAY WORLD III.1 633
Satyrical (1)
    Scandal: trusted; a Satyrical Proverb upon our Sex--There's . . . 256 FOR LOVE III.1 126
Satyrs (2)
    Lady Froth: Songs, Elegies, Satyrs, Encomiums, Panegyricks, ... 138 DOUBL DLR   II.1   16
    Valentine: Pictures of all that have refus'd him: If Satyrs,
                  Descriptions, ... 233 FOR LOVE   I.1 624
Sauce (1)   see Sawce
    Valentine: together by a State-Cook, make Sauce for the whole . . . 282 FOR LOVE   IV.1 258
Saul (1)
    Angelica: the Closet, one Night, like Saul and the Witch of Endor, . 238 FOR LOVE   II.1 107
Sav'd (11)
    Sir Joseph: Not I Sir, not I, as I've a Soul to be sav'd, I have . .   48 OLD BATCH   II.1   29
    Sir Joseph: O Lord Sir by no means--but I might have sav'd a . .   51 OLD BATCH   II.1 128
    Sir Joseph: hundred Pound--I meant innocently as I hope to be sav'd .   51 OLD BATCH   II.1 129
    Tattle: sav'd, Valentine, I never expos'd a Woman, since I knew . 227 FOR LOVE   I.1 406
    Tattle: Not a word as I hope to be sav'd; an errant Lapsus Linguae 228 FOR LOVE   I.1 442
    Tattle: Why then, as I hope to be sav'd, I believe a Woman . . . 228 FOR LOVE   I.1 473
    Tattle: I hope to be sav'd; I never had it in my Power to say any 256 FOR LOVE III.1 101
    Tattle: So 'tis, faith--I might have sav'd several others . . . 303 FOR LOVE   V.1 212
    Tattle: I did, as I hope to be sav'd, Madam, my Intentions . . . 309 FOR LOVE   V.1 457
    Gonsalez: That being sav'd upon the Coast of Africk, ... 363 M. BRIDE   IV.1   84
    Manuel: To cast beneath your Feet the Crown you've sav'd, . . . 365 M. BRIDE   IV.1 159
Savage (6)
    Almeria: Musick has Charms to sooth a savage Breast, ... 326 M. BRIDE   I.1   1
    Zara: Thou hast a Heart, though 'tis a savage one; . . . . 346 M. BRIDE   II.2 272
    Zara: As she, whose savage Breast has been the Cause . . . . 353 M. BRIDE   III.1 157
    Almeria: Yet bubling from his Wounds--O more than savage! . . . 382 M. BRIDE   V.2 235
    Lady Wish: This is most inhumanly Savage; exceeding the . . . . 469 WAY WORLD   V.1 271
    Mirabell: be wrong'd in this Savage manner. . . . . 474 WAY WORLD   V.1 461
Save (24)
                  To save our Plays, or else we'll damn your Pit. . . . .   35 OLD BATCH PRO.   9
    Heartwell: you save the Devil the trouble of leading you into it: Nor .   43 OLD BATCH   I.1 241
    Bellmour: in that silent manner--'Twould save a Man a World . . .   60 OLD BATCH   II.2 221
    Silvia: may depend upon our skill to save us at a plunge, though .   75 OLD BATCH III.2 152
    Lady Touch: but I will stak the Lie that's forming in your heart, and
                  save . . . . 197 DOUBL DLR   V.1 381
    Lady Touch: O I'm betray'd,--save me, help me. . . . . 202 DOUBL DLR   V.1 558
    Jeremy: 'Tis an Act of Charity, Sir, to save a fine Woman . . . 302 FOR LOVE   V.1 209
                  But we can't fear, since you're so good to save us, . . 315 FOR LOVE   EPI.   38
    Almeria: The Shoal, and save me floating on the Waves, ... 329 M. BRIDE   I.1 130
    Zara: Somewhat, to blind the King, and save his Life . . . . 361 M. BRIDE   IV.1   24
    Gonsalez: Ha! sure he sleeps--all's dark within, save what . . . 376 M. BRIDE   V.2   6
    Osmyn-Alph: Save her from Death, and snatch her to my Heart. . . . 383 M. BRIDE   V.2 276
                  So Save or Damn, after your own Discretion. . . . . . 393 WAY WORLD PRO.   40
    Mirabell: I wonder there is not an Act of Parliament to save . . . 400 WAY WORLD   I.1 204
    Mirabell: Actions? To save that Idol Reputation. If the . . . . 417 WAY WORLD   II.1 266
    Lady Wish: Sipping? Tasting? Save thee, dost thou not know the . . 425 WAY WORLD III.1   24
    Lady Wish: A Cup, save thee, and what a Cup hast thou . . . . . 425 WAY WORLD III.1   28
    Lady Wish: Man. I shall save Decorums if Sir Rowland importunes. I . 429 WAY WORLD III.1 177
    Sir Wilful: Save you Gentlemen and Lady. . . . . 437 WAY WORLD III.1 479

Save   (continued)
Marwood:	will come to any Composition to save her reputation, take	442	WAY WORLD	III.1 661
Lady Wish:	the Vehemence of Compassion, and to save the life of a .	459	WAY WORLD	IV.1 536
Lady Wish:	save the Honour of my House, and Compound for the . . .	465	WAY WORLD	V.1 130
Lady Wish:	O what? what? to save me and my Child	473	WAY WORLD	V.1 453
Lady Wish:	her fortune; if you can but save me from this imminent .	474	WAY WORLD	V.1 465

Save-all (1)
Waitwell:	upon a Save-all.	458	WAY WORLD	IV.1 525

Saved (3)
Sir Joseph:	best Friends I have in the World and saved my Life last	52	OLD BATCH	II.1 169
Sir Joseph:	hundred Pound for being saved, and d'ee think, an there .	67	OLD BATCH	III.1 255
Sir Paul:	Why now as I hope to be saved, I had no hand in . . .	180	DOUBL DLR	IV.1 468

Saves (3)
Brisk:	Right, right, that saves all.	164	DOUBL DLR	III.1 522
Valentine:	if you should ask him, whether the Bible saves more . .	280	FOR LOVE	IV.1 176
Petulant:	saves Paint.	406	WAY WORLD	I.1 417

Saving (2)
Zara:	For saving thee, when I beheld thee first, ...	346	M. BRIDE	II.2 275
Lady Wish:	Contribute much both to the saving of your Life; and the .	458	WAY WORLD	IV.1 507

Saw (41)
Vainlove:	But I saw my Araminta, yet am as impatient.	40	OLD BATCH	I.1 135
Sir Joseph:	because I never saw your face before, agad. Ha, ha, ha.	48	OLD BATCH	II.1 41
Laetitia:	Nay, now.--(aside) I never saw any thing so agreeably .	82	OLD BATCH	IV.2 79
Laetitia:	saw this wicked Man before.	93	OLD BATCH	IV.4 140
Laetitia:	of your Embraces again, my Dear, if ever I saw his face .	93	OLD BATCH	IV.4 151
Setter:	I saw him, Sir; and stood at the Corner where you . .	98	OLD BATCH	V.1 83
Mellefont:	despair, and the short prospect of time she saw, to . .	129	DOUBL DLR	I.1 95
Mellefont:	Lightning in her Eyes; I saw her melted into Tears, and .	130	DOUBL DLR	I.1 106
Mellefont:	express; which when she saw had no effect; but still I .	130	DOUBL DLR	I.1 111
Lord Froth:	I saw my self there, and kissed it for your sake. . .	140	DOUBL DLR	II.1 80
Cynthia:	I never saw him thus before.	144	DOUBL DLR	II.1 205
Careless:	that I saw your Father in, my Lady Touchwood's Passion, .	196	DOUBL DLR	V.1 336
Sir Paul:	Affairs may be in a very good posture; I saw her go into .	200	DOUBL DLR	V.1 506
Angelica:	Yes, I saw you together, through the Key-hole of . .	238	FOR LOVE	II.1 106
Sr Sampson:	since I saw thee.	261	FOR LOVE	III.1 288
Scandal:	I saw her take Coach just now with her Maid; and . .	276	FOR LOVE	IV.1 12
Angelica:	Ha! I saw him wink and smile--I fancy 'tis a . . .	277	FOR LOVE	IV.1 53
	Were you not griev'd, as often as you saw	323	M. BRIDE	PRO. 17
Almeria:	And saw her Rate so far exceeding ours;	329	M. BRIDE	I.1 135
Garcia:	I saw him not, nor any like him.	338	M. BRIDE	II.1 V 18
Perez:	I saw him when I spoke, thwarting my View, ...	338	M. BRIDE	II.1 19
Osmyn-Alph:	I thought I saw thee too; but O, I thought not . . .	344	M. BRIDE	II.2 164
Osmyn-Alph:	And Rage of War: For in the Fight, I saw	344	M. BRIDE	II.2 174
Osmyn-Alph:	And War: For in the Fight I saw him fall.	344	M. BRIDE	II.2 V174
Heli:	I saw you on the Ground, and rais'd you up. . . .	344	M. BRIDE	II.2 181
Heli:	I saw Almeria--	344	M. BRIDE	II.2 182
Heli:	When with Astonishment I saw Almeria--	344	M. BRIDE	II.2 V182
Osmyn-Alph:	I saw her too, and therefore saw not thee.	344	M. BRIDE	II.2 183
Heli:	Zara with Selim, Sir, I saw and know 'em:	344	M. BRIDE	II.2 197
Osmyn-Alph:	I saw you not.	346	M. BRIDE	II.2 254
Osmyn-Alph:	I saw you not, 'till now.	346	M. BRIDE	II.2 V254
Osmyn-Alph:	He in the Book of Prescience, he saw this Day; . . .	353	M. BRIDE	III.1 V133
Manuel:	But think'st thou that my Daughter saw this Moor? . .	367	M. BRIDE	IV.1 228
Zara:	He saw me not?	375	M. BRIDE	V.1 97
Zara:	He saw me ?	375	M. BRIDE	V.1 V 97
Mirabell:	whom I never saw before; seeing me, they all put on their	396	WAY WORLD	I.1 29
Mirabell:	You saw I was engag'd.	421	WAY WORLD	II.1 432
Marwood:	I saw her but now, as I came mask'd through	426	WAY WORLD	III.1 47
Mrs Fain:	come too late. That Devil Marwood saw you in the Park .	430	WAY WORLD	III.1 185
Waitwell:	Roman hand--I saw there was a throat to be cut presently.	460	WAY WORLD	IV.1 602

Sawce (2)
Capt Bluff:	Sweet Sawce. Now I think--Fighting, for Fighting sake's .	52	OLD BATCH	II.1 164
Bellmour:	(aside). I hope there's no French Sawce.	106	OLD BATCH	V.1 371

Sawcy (5)
Araminta:	your sawcy Passion?	87	OLD BATCH	IV.3 163
Vainlove:	than Sawcy, in another place.	87	OLD BATCH	IV.3 165
Vainlove:	Pox o' my sawcy Credulity.--If I have lost	100	OLD BATCH	V.1 125
Zara:	Perhaps I'm sawcy and Intruding--	359	M. BRIDE	III.1 413
Millamant:	sawcy look of an assured man, Confident of Success. The .	449	WAY WORLD	IV.1 178

Say (253)
	I shall be hang'd for wanting what to say.	35	OLD BATCH	PRO. 25
Vainlove:	How now, Ned, a wise Man say more than he	37	OLD BATCH	I.1 17
Bellmour:	As you say the Abuse is to the Lover, not the . . .	39	OLD BATCH	I.1 63
Sharper:	may say Marriage is entring into a Course of Physick. . .	44	OLD BATCH	I.1 292
Sharper:	Say you so? faith I am as poor as a Chymist and . .	46	OLD BATCH	I.1 347
Sir Joseph:	found nothing but what has been to my loss, as I may say,	48	OLD BATCH	II.1 30
Sir Joseph:	know me, you'd nere say I were so ill natur'd. . . .	48	OLD BATCH	II.1 37
Sir Joseph:	You are only pleas'd to say so Sir--But pray if I . .	49	OLD BATCH	II.1 79
Sharper:	much lent you--And you scorn, 'Ile say that for you-- .	50	OLD BATCH	II.1 103
Sir Joseph:	Nay 'Ile say that for my self--with your leave Sir-- .	50	OLD BATCH	II.1 104
Capt Bluff:	Say you so? then I honour him--But has he been . . .	51	OLD BATCH	II.1 152
Capt Bluff:	was an Eye-witness of--I won't say had the greatest . .	52	OLD BATCH	II.1 199
Capt Bluff:	share in't. Tho' I might say that too, since I am no Body	53	OLD BATCH	II.1 200
Capt Bluff:	share in't. Tho' I might say that too, since I name no Body	53	OLD BATCH	II.1 V200
Capt Bluff:	see it; Sir I say you can't see; what de'e say to that now?	53	OLD BATCH	II.1 235
Araminta:	things, than they say.	60	OLD BATCH	II.2 217
Setter:	his Youth; and some say, with that Eye, he first discover'd	64	OLD BATCH	III.1 128
Capt Bluff:	Well, go to him from me--Tell him, I say, he . . .	68	OLD BATCH	III.1 258
Sir Joseph:	confess he did in a manner snap me up--Yet I can't say .	68	OLD BATCH	III.1 272
Heartwell:	worth for the purchase of thy Love--Say, is it mine then,	72	OLD BATCH	III.2 39
Silvia:	Must you lie then, if you say you Love me?	72	OLD BATCH	III.2 61
Silvia:	But Love, they say, is a tender thing, that will smooth .	72	OLD BATCH	III.2 65
Silvia:	Ay, but that is no Sign, for they say, Gentlemen will . .	73	OLD BATCH	III.2 86
Fondlewife:	I say I will tarry at home.	75	OLD BATCH	IV.1 14
Fondlewife:	hath possess'd the Lad--I say I will tarry at home--Varlet.	75	OLD BATCH	IV.1 17
Fondlewife:	say you with his Wife? With Comfort her self. . . .	76	OLD BATCH	IV.1 20

Say   (continued)

Speaker	Text	PAGE	TITLE	ACT.SC	LINE
Barnaby:	time: but you say--	76	OLD BATCH	IV.1	24
Fondlewife:	How how, say Varlet! I say let him not come	76	OLD BATCH	IV.1	25
Fondlewife:	near my Doors. I say, he is a wanton young Levite and	76	OLD BATCH	IV.1	26
Fondlewife:	--I say, that even Lust doth sparkle in his Eyes,	76	OLD BATCH	IV.1	31
Fondlewife:	Yes--Why then!--Ay, but to say truth, She's fonder of	77	OLD BATCH	IV.1	59
Fondlewife:	of Adultery is? have you weigh'd it I say? For it is a very	77	OLD BATCH	IV.1	69
Fondlewife:	Speak I say, have you consider'd, what it is to Cuckold	77	OLD BATCH	IV.1	77
Fondlewife:	And so thou shalt say, for I'le leave it to stay with thee.	78	OLD BATCH	IV.1	130
Capt Bluff:	say to 'em?	85	OLD BATCH	IV.3	71
Sir Joseph:	Say: Pooh, Pox, I've enough to say,--never	85	OLD BATCH	IV.3	72
Sir Joseph:	and have not one Word to say.	85	OLD BATCH	IV.3	91
Sir Joseph:	As you say, Madam, 'tis pretty bad Weather, and	90	OLD BATCH	IV.4	39
Fondlewife:	Wife! My Dinah! Oh Schechemite! Begone, I say.	90	OLD BATCH	IV.4	67
Fondlewife:	inclining to believe every word you say.	94	OLD BATCH	IV.4	186
Fondlewife:	How! Would not you have me believe you, say	95	OLD BATCH	IV.4	222
Bellmour:	Well, It is as I say?	98	OLD BATCH	V.1	51
Bellmour:	Well, is it as I say?	98	OLD BATCH	V.1 V	51
Bellmour:	That's as much as to say, The Pox take me.--Well	98	OLD BATCH	V.1	78
Sharper:	Just now, say you, gone in with Lucy?	98	OLD BATCH	V.1	82
Heartwell:	And who wou'd you visit there, say you? (O'ons,	104	OLD BATCH	V.1	289
Bellmour:	Say you so?--Is that a Maxim among ye?	106	OLD BATCH	V.1	368
Heartwell:	Gone forth, say you, with her Maid!	107	OLD BATCH	V.2	1
Belinda:	that will do a civil thing to his Wife, or say a civil thing to	108	OLD BATCH	V.2	30
Sharper:	present Date hereof.--How say you?	110	OLD BATCH	V.2	88
	What will the World say? Where's my Reputation?	113	OLD BATCH	EPI.	11
	How say you, Sparks? How do you stand affected?	113	OLD BATCH	EPI.	23
	I will not say, we'd all in danger been,	125	DOUBL DLR	PRO.	21
Mellefont:	of following you, because I had something to say to you in	127	DOUBL DLR	I.1	14
Mellefont:	to follow you, because I had something to say to you in	127	DOUBL DLR	I.1 V	14
Brisk:	better, you or I. Pox, Man, when I say you spoil Company	128	DOUBL DLR	I.1	28
Brisk:	better, you or I. Pshaw, Man, when I say you spoil Company	128	DOUBL DLR	I.1 V	28
Brisk:	But the Deuce take me if I say a good thing till you come.--	128	DOUBL DLR	I.1	51
Brisk:	me perish, do I never say any thing worthy to be Laugh'd	132	DOUBL DLR	I.1	195
Lord Froth:	O foy, don't misapprehend me, I don't say so, for	132	DOUBL DLR	I.1	197
Brisk:	t'other way. Suppose I say a witty thing to you?	134	DOUBL DLR	I.1	278
Mellefont:	Or, what say you, to another Bottle of	134	DOUBL DLR	I.1	286
Maskwell:	Nay, Misconceive me not, Madam, when I say	136	DOUBL DLR	I.1	355
Maskwell:	needs this? I say nothing but what your self, in open hours	137	DOUBL DLR	I.1	384
Maskwell:	needs this? I say nothing but what you your self, in open hours	137	DOUBL DLR	I.1 V	384
Lady Froth:	Friend,--but really, as you say, I wonder too,--but	138	DOUBL DLR	II.1	9
Lady Froth:	of the Common Air,--I think I may say he wants	139	DOUBL DLR	II.1	30
Lady Ply:	Have I, I say, preserv'd my self, like a fair Sheet	145	DOUBL DLR	II.1	259
Mellefont:	I am so amazed, I know not what to say.	145	DOUBL DLR	II.1	263
Lady Ply:	Heart? May be you don't think it a sin,--they say	147	DOUBL DLR	II.1	346
Lady Ply:	what did I say? Jealous! no, no, I can't be jealous, for I	148	DOUBL DLR	II.1	370
Lady Touch:	That I can't tell: nay, I don't say there was--	151	DOUBL DLR	III.1	23
Lady Touch:	How? Don't you believe that, say you, my	151	DOUBL DLR	III.1	27
Lord Touch:	No, I don't say so--I confess I am troubled to	151	DOUBL DLR	III.1	29
Lady Touch:	Nay, my Lord, you need say no more, to	152	DOUBL DLR	III.1	64
Maskwell:	made me conceal it; yet you may say, I threatned the next	154	DOUBL DLR	III.1	153
Sir Paul:	fine way of living, as I may say, peacefully and happily,	160	DOUBL DLR	III.1	384
Sir Paul:	see--if it becomes me to say so; and we live very comfortably	160	DOUBL DLR	III.1	388
Sir Paul:	Daughter, and a fine dutiful Child she is, though I say it,	161	DOUBL DLR	III.1	412
Sir Paul:	blessed be Providence I may say; for indeed, Mr. Careless,	161	DOUBL DLR	III.1	413
Sir Paul:	am her Husband, as I may say, though far unworthy of	162	DOUBL DLR	III.1	437
Lady Froth:	So of our Coach-man I may say.	164	DOUBL DLR	III.1	516
Brisk:	because you say the Sun shines every day.	164	DOUBL DLR	III.1	518
Lady Froth:	Then I don't say the Sun shines all the day, but,	164	DOUBL DLR	III.1	523
Lady Froth:	So, of our Coach-man I may say,	164	DOUBL DLR	III.1	530
Brisk:	asterism, and say,--Jehu was formerly a Hackney	165	DOUBL DLR	III.1	552
Brisk:	I can't hit of her Name neither--Paints de'e say?	166	DOUBL DLR	III.1	584
Lady Ply:	And say so many fine things, and nothing is so moving to	169	DOUBL DLR	IV.1	70
Lady Ply:	have shaken, as I may say, the very foundation of my	169	DOUBL DLR	IV.1	74
Careless:	Feet. (Aside.) I must say the same thing over again, and	170	DOUBL DLR	IV.1	101
Lady Ply:	O rise I beseech you, say no more till you rise	170	DOUBL DLR	IV.1	107
Lady Ply:	Embraces--Say thou dear dying Man, when, where,	170	DOUBL DLR	IV.1	125
Brisk:	thinking what to say? None but dull Rogues think; witty	175	DOUBL DLR	IV.1	299
Sir Paul:	Gads-bud, what shall I say? This is the strangest	179	DOUBL DLR	IV.1	448
Mellefont:	He? you say true.	181	DOUBL DLR	IV.1	520
Lord Touch:	Say on.	182	DOUBL DLR	IV.1	559
Maskwell:	I have nothing more to say, my Lord--but to	182	DOUBL DLR	IV.1	560
Mellefont:	Say you so, were you provided for an Escape?	184	DOUBL DLR	IV.2	41
Lady Touch:	O. What shall I do? say? whither shall I	185	DOUBL DLR	IV.2	57
Sir Paul:	She's a passionate Woman, gad'sbud,--but to say	192	DOUBL DLR	V.1	195
Sir Paul:	You're a passionate Woman, gad'sbud,--but to say	192	DOUBL DLR	V.1 V	195
Sir Paul:	say truth, all our Family are Cholerick; I am the only	192	DOUBL DLR	V.1	196
Valentine:	the World say of me, and of my forc'd Confinement?	220	FOR LOVE	I.1	158
Valentine:	the World say of me, and my forc'd Confinement?	220	FOR LOVE	I.1 V	158
Trapland:	No more, in truth.--I have forborn, I say--	222	FOR LOVE	I.1	249
Valentine:	serve his Friend in Distress, tho' I say it to his face. Come,	223	FOR LOVE	I.1	262
Valentine:	Say you so, I'faith: Come, we'll remember the	223	FOR LOVE	I.1	271
Valentine:	You need say no more, I understand the Conditions;	224	FOR LOVE	I.1	317
Tattle:	Nay, but why rotten? Why should you say rotten,	226	FOR LOVE	I.1	398
Tattle:	that--Nay more (I'm going to say a bold Word now) I	227	FOR LOVE	I.1	410
Tattle:	it their Business to tell Stories, and say this and that of	227	FOR LOVE	I.1	431
Scandal:	and ha, ha, well, go on, and what did you say to her	227	FOR LOVE	I.1	439
Valentine:	What did I say? I hope you won't bring me to	229	FOR LOVE	I.1	497
Foresight:	I say you lie, Sir. It is impossible that any thing	235	FOR LOVE	II.1	11
Sr Sampson:	By the Horns of the Moon, you wou'd say,	241	FOR LOVE	II.1	233
Mrs Frail:	I have heard Gentlemen say, Sister; that one should	248	FOR LOVE	II.1	473
Mrs Fore:	as you say, since we are both Wounded, let us do that is	248	FOR LOVE	II.1	477

Say   (continued)

		PAGE	TITLE	ACT.SC	LINE
Mrs Fore:	as you say, since we are both Wounded, let us do what is	248	FOR LOVE	II.1	V477
Mrs Fore:	Madam; you must say Madam--By my	249	FOR LOVE	II.1	511
Mrs Frail:	Fie, Miss; amongst your Linnen, you must say	249	FOR LOVE	II.1	531
Mrs Frail:	--You must never say Smock.	249	FOR LOVE	II.1	532
Tattle:	Pooh, Pox, you must not say yes already; I shan't care	251	FOR LOVE	II.1	604
Miss Prue:	What must I say then?	251	FOR LOVE	II.1	606
Tattle:	Why you must say no, or you believe not, or you	251	FOR LOVE	II.1	607
Tattle:	So, when I ask you, if you can Love me, you must say no,	252	FOR LOVE	II.1	614
Tattle:	Handsome, you must deny it, and say I flatter you--	252	FOR LOVE	II.1	616
Tattle:	speak you:--And like me, for the Beauty which I say	252	FOR LOVE	II.1	618
Tattle:	more complying; and as soon as ever I make you say	252	FOR LOVE	II.1	622
Nurse:	Miss I say, God's my Life, here's fine doings towards--	253	FOR LOVE	III.1	9
Miss Prue:	O Dear, what shall I say? Tell me, Mr. Tattle, tell	253	FOR LOVE	III.1	19
Tattle:	say nothing, I think. I hear her--I'll leave you together,	254	FOR LOVE	III.1	23
Scandal:	ask you: I'll say that for you, Madam.	254	FOR LOVE	III.1	34
Angelica:	What is, Mr. Tattle? I heard you say something	254	FOR LOVE	III.1	50
Tattle:	You say true, I beg your Pardon;--I'll bring all off--	255	FOR LOVE	III.1	65
Tattle:	I hope to be sav'd; I never had it in my Power to say any	256	FOR LOVE	III.1	101
Scandal:	say in general Terms, He only is Secret who never was	256	FOR LOVE	III.1	125
Tattle:	For Heaven's sake, if you do guess, say nothing; Gad,	258	FOR LOVE	III.1	194
Sr Sampson:	oblige him. Odsbud, Madam, have no more to say to	259	FOR LOVE	III.1	239
Sr Sampson:	glad to hear you say so; I was afraid you were in Love	260	FOR LOVE	III.1	258
Ben:	as you say--well, and how? I have a many Questions	261	FOR LOVE	III.1	295
Ben:	handsome Gentlewoman for a Bed-fellow hugely, how say	262	FOR LOVE	III.1	325
Sr Sampson:	Body o' me, Madam, you say true:--Look	262	FOR LOVE	III.1	349
Miss Prue:	to say, I can hear you farther off, I an't deaf.	263	FOR LOVE	III.1	365
Ben:	Why that's true as you say, not I an't dumb, I can be	263	FOR LOVE	III.1	366
Ben:	your Harbour. How say you Mistress? the short of the	263	FOR LOVE	III.1	375
Miss Prue:	I don't know what to say to you, nor I don't care	263	FOR LOVE	III.1	378
Ben:	Nay, You say true in that, it's but a folly to lie: For to	263	FOR LOVE	III.1	385
Ben:	ben't as willing as I, say so a God's name, there's no harm	263	FOR LOVE	III.1	390
Ben:	take your part, Your Tom Essence, and I'll say something to	265	FOR LOVE	III.1	435
Scandal:	little, yet says he has a World to say. Asks for his Father	266	FOR LOVE	III.1	498
Scandal:	You say true, Man will err: meer Man will err--	267	FOR LOVE	III.1	527
Scandal:	You are not satisfy'd, I say--I am loath to	268	FOR LOVE	III.1	559
Mrs Fore:	I cannot say that he has once broken my Rest, since we	270	FOR LOVE	III.1	623
Scandal:	Do so, Mr. Foresight, and say your Pray'rs;--He	270	FOR LOVE	III.1	626
Scandal:	Come, I know what you wou'd say,--you think	272	FOR LOVE	III.1	694
Ben:	to do with me--Nay, I can't say that neither; he has	272	FOR LOVE	III.1	714
Angelica:	(aside). Say you so; nay, then I'm convinc'd: And if I	277	FOR LOVE	IV.1	66
Sr Sampson:	Body o' me, I know not what to say to him.	280	FOR LOVE	IV.1	166
Buckram:	O Lord, what must I say?--Yes, Sir.	280	FOR LOVE	IV.1	170
Sr Sampson:	what to do, or say, nor which way to go.	282	FOR LOVE	IV.1	250
Foresight:	Ha! say you so?	283	FOR LOVE	IV.1	301
Ben:	gav'n that wipe--He had'nt a word to say, and so I left 'n,	286	FOR LOVE	IV.1	385
Mrs Frail:	O Lord, what must I say?	290	FOR LOVE	IV.1	539
Valentine:	and we'll be Marry'd in the dead of Night.--But say	290	FOR LOVE	IV.1	548
Tattle:	many words of Matters, and so I shan't say much,--	291	FOR LOVE	IV.1	607
Jeremy:	I have heard 'em say, Sir, they read hard Hebrew	297	FOR LOVE	IV.1	805
Valentine:	They say so of a Witches Pray'r, and Dreams and	297	FOR LOVE	IV.1	808
Angelica:	O fie, Sir Sampson, what would the World say?	300	FOR LOVE	V.1	117
Sr Sampson:	Say, they would say, you were a Wise Woman.	300	FOR LOVE	V.1	118
Sr Sampson:	Say you so, Hussy?--Come lets go then;	301	FOR LOVE	V.1	160
Tattle:	I'll make thy Fortune; say no more--Thou art a	302	FOR LOVE	V.1	180
Miss Prue:	Why won't you be my Husband? You say you love me,	303	FOR LOVE	V.1	228
Foresight:	How! I will make it appear that what you say is	304	FOR LOVE	V.1	274
Ben:	say, Brother Val. went mad for, she's mad too, I think.	306	FOR LOVE	V.1	346
Ben:	a Voyage to Antegoa--No, hold, I maynt say so	306	FOR LOVE	V.1	351
Ben:	believe it or no. What I say is true; d'ee see, they are	307	FOR LOVE	V.1	369
Sr Sampson:	How! What does my Aunt say? Surprizing,	308	FOR LOVE	V.1	403
Ben:	Hold. They say a Witch will sail in a Sieve--But I	309	FOR LOVE	V.1	434
Tattle:	Aye, my Dear, so they will as you say.	310	FOR LOVE	V.1	480
Sr Sampson:	That's as much as to say, I lie, Sir, and you don't	311	FOR LOVE	V.1	522
Sr Sampson:	believe what I say.	311	FOR LOVE	V.1	523
	Now to these Men (say they) such Souls were given,	315	FOR LOVE	EPI.	15
Almeria:	Why do I live to say you are no more?	327	M. BRIDE	I.1	55
Osmyn-Alph:	Wrong not my Love, to say too much.	343	M. BRIDE	II.2	119
Osmyn-Alph:	Wrong not my Love, to say too tenderly.	343	M. BRIDE	II.2	V119
Almeria:	For 'tis not to be born--What shall I say?	343	M. BRIDE	II.2	149
Zara:	And now abandon'd--say what then is Osmyn?	347	M. BRIDE	II.2	V308
Almeria:	O say not so;	356	M. BRIDE	III.1	255
Almeria:	Tho' 'tis because thou lov'st me. Do not say	356	M. BRIDE	III.1	256
Almeria:	Did'st thou not say, that Racks and Wheels were	357	M. BRIDE	III.1	311
Osmyn-Alph:	Say somewhat quickly to conceal our Loves,	359	M. BRIDE	III.1	390
Zara:	What shall I say? Invent, contrive, advise	361	M. BRIDE	IV.1	23
Zara:	But say, what's to be done? or when, or how	362	M. BRIDE	IV.1	42
Manuel:	Thy guilty Mind; and say thou wert Confederate	368	M. BRIDE	IV.1	270
Manuel:	They mean thy Guilt; and say thou wert Confederate	368	M. BRIDE	IV.1	V270
Alonzo:	If't please your Lordship, I'll return, and say	371	M. BRIDE	IV.1	422
Gonsalez:	Say thou art my Friend.	372	M. BRIDE	IV.1	429
Gonsalez:	And say, I've not been seen--haste good Alonzo.	372	M. BRIDE	IV.1	V442
Manuel:	None, say you, none? what not the Fav'rite Eunuch?	372	M. BRIDE	V.1	2
Mirabell:	Say you so?	400	WAY WORLD	I.1	178
Witwoud:	Lady? Gad, I say any thing in the World to get this Fellow	402	WAY WORLD	I.1	255
Witwoud:	don't know what I say: But she's the best Woman in the	402	WAY WORLD	I.1	259
Witwoud:	don't know what I say: she's the best Woman in the	402	WAY WORLD	I.1	V259
Fainall:	'Tis well you don't know what you say, or else your	402	WAY WORLD	I.1	261
Witwoud:	have forgot what I was going to say to you.	402	WAY WORLD	I.1	271
Witwoud:	Hum, faith I don't know as to that,--I can't say	403	WAY WORLD	I.1	302
Petulant:	What does he say th' are?	406	WAY WORLD	I.1	404
Witwoud:	I; fine Ladies I say.	406	WAY WORLD	I.1	405
Petulant:	All's one for that; why then say I know something.	407	WAY WORLD	I.1	442
Witwoud:	not, I cannot say; but there were Items of such a Treaty	408	WAY WORLD	I.1	487
Petulant:	stay'd longer--Besides they never mind him; they say	408	WAY WORLD	I.1	497
Marwood:	often shou'd out-live the Lover. But say what you will,	410	WAY WORLD	II.1	11

Say   (continued)

		PAGE	TITLE	ACT.SC	LINE
Mrs Fain:	Most transcendantly; ay, tho' I say it,	411	WAY WORLD	II.1	37
Millamant:	and say; vain empty Things if we are silent or unseen, and	421	WAY WORLD	II.1	411
Millamant:	say to me?	422	WAY WORLD	II.1	463
Mirabell:	I say that a Man may as soon make a Friend by his	422	WAY WORLD	II.1	464
Foible:	him; which I'll be sure to say has made him so enamour'd	423	WAY WORLD	II.1	522
Foible:	--Poor Sir Rowland, I say.	427	WAY WORLD	III.1	78
Foible:	what shall I say?--Alas, Madam, cou'd I help it, if I	427	WAY WORLD	III.1	85
Lady Wish:	Me? What did the filthy Fellow say?	427	WAY WORLD	III.1	92
Foible:	O Madam; 'tis a shame to say what he said--	427	WAY WORLD	III.1	93
Foible:	for, as they say of a Welch Maiden-head.	430	WAY WORLD	III.1	212
Lady Wish:	O dear Marwood what shall I say, for this rude	431	WAY WORLD	III.1	250
Millamant:	Dee say so? Then I'm resolv'd I'll have a Song to	434	WAY WORLD	III.1	365
Petulant:	say 'tis Blue--Let that pass--All's one for that. If	435	WAY WORLD	III.1	405
Witwoud:	first, I say.	437	WAY WORLD	III.1	478
Sir Wilful:	I may say now, and am minded to see Foreign Parts. If an	440	WAY WORLD	III.1	574
Sir Wilful:	French as they say, whereby to hold discourse in Foreign	440	WAY WORLD	III.1	584
Fainall:	honourable as you say; and if so, Wherefore should	443	WAY WORLD	III.1	692
Millamant:	further to say to me?	448	WAY WORLD	IV.1	133
Sir Wilful:	spare to speed, as they say.	448	WAY WORLD	IV.1	138
Sir Wilful:	there's no haste; it will keep cold as they say,--Cozen,	448	WAY WORLD	IV.1	146
Millamant:	fright--Fainall, I shall never say it--well--I think--	452	WAY WORLD	IV.1	289
Millamant:	now, and don't say a word.	452	WAY WORLD	IV.1	297
Millamant:	now, don't say a word.	452	WAY WORLD	IV.1	V297
Petulant:	Nymph--say it--and that's the Conclusion--pass on, or	453	WAY WORLD	IV.1	340
Petulant:	have my Reward, say so; if not, fight for your Face the	454	WAY WORLD	IV.1	369
Sir Wilful:	but if you wou'd have me Marry my Cozen,--say the	455	WAY WORLD	IV.1	403
Sir Wilful:	Marry'd, say the Word, and send for the Piper, Wilfull	455	WAY WORLD	IV.1	411
Witwoud:	say to him--will you go to a Cock-match?	457	WAY WORLD	IV.1	471
Lady Wish:	Is he so Unnatural say you? truely I wou'd	458	WAY WORLD	IV.1	506
Foible:	(to him). Say 'tis your Nephew's hand.--quickly, his	460	WAY WORLD	IV.1	595
Lady Wish:	my Flesh, and as I may say, another Me, and yet transgress	465	WAY WORLD	V.1	141
Lady Wish:	--I may say it; for I chiefly made it my own Care to	466	WAY WORLD	V.1	183
Sir Wilful:	I confess I have been a little in disguise as they say,	470	WAY WORLD	V.1	314
Sir Wilful:	am willing to make satisfaction; and what can a man say	470	WAY WORLD	V.1	317
Mirabell:	Yes Sir. I say that this Lady while a Widow,	476	WAY WORLD	V.1	540
Mirabell:	suspected--she did I say by the wholesome advice of	476	WAY WORLD	V.1	544
Petulant:	For my part, I say little--I think things are best	477	WAY WORLD	V.1	588

Say'd (1)

Sir Joseph:	very good Jest, and I did not know that I had say'd it, and	50	OLD BATCH	II.1	115

Say'n (1)

Ben:	Say'n you so forsooth! Marry and I shou'd like such a	262	FOR LOVE	III.1	324

Say'st (11)   see Saist

Sharper:	Say'st thou so!	99	OLD BATCH	V.1	99
Lady Froth:	say'st right--for sure my Lord Froth is as fine a Gentleman,	139	DOUBL DLR	II.1	28
Sr Sampson:	Let thee hold it, say'st thou--Aye, with all	281	FOR LOVE	IV.1	229
Valentine:	A ha! Old Truepenny, say'st thou so? thou hast	282	FOR LOVE	IV.1	268
Zara:	This groveling Baseness--Thou say'st true, I know	348	M. BRIDE	II.2	335
Manuel:	Say'st thou? by Heav'n thou hast arous'd a Thought,	367	M. BRIDE	IV.1	232
Manuel:	Ha! what say'st thou? Husband! Husband!	369	M. BRIDE	IV.1	339
Lady Wish:	Will Sir Rowland be here, say'st thou? when	428	WAY WORLD	III.1	122
Lady Wish:	Let me see the Glass--Cracks, say'st thou?	429	WAY WORLD	III.1	147
Lady Wish:	Is Sir Rowland coming say'st thou, Foible?	444	WAY WORLD	IV.1	1
Mrs Fain:	Say'st thou so Foible? Canst thou prove this?	464	WAY WORLD	V.1	91

Say't (1)

Sir Wilful:	then; if I say't, I'll do't: But I	440	WAY WORLD	III.1	581

Saygrace (4)

Maskwell:	at this hour,--Mr. Saygrace, Mr. Saygrace.	194	DOUBL DLR	V.1	270
Maskwell:	Nay, good Mr. Saygrace do not prolong the time,	194	DOUBL DLR	V.1	276
Careless:	There's Saygrace tripping by with a bundle under his	196	DOUBL DLR	V.1	351

Saying (6)

Sir Joseph:	and as you were saying Sir.	48	OLD BATCH	II.1	31
Sir Joseph:	Sir--a damn'd hot Fellow--only as I was saying, I let him	51	OLD BATCH	II.1	130
Brisk:	instructed. Suppose, as I was saying, you come up to me,	134	DOUBL DLR	I.1	254
Lady Ply:	patience--oh! the Impiety of it, as I was saying, and	146	DOUBL DLR	II.1	304
Sr Sampson:	for saying Grace, old Foresight, but fall too without an	265	FOR LOVE	IV.1	460
Zara:	Thy Tongue that Saying.	353	M. BRIDE	III.1	145

Sayings (2)

Lady Ply:	can refrain to weep and yield to such sad Sayings.--	170	DOUBL DLR	IV.1	120
Foresight:	about these things which he has utter'd.--His Sayings	289	FOR LOVE	IV.1	533

Sayn (1)

Ben:	were sinking, as we sayn at Sea. But I'll tell you why I	261	FOR LOVE	III.1	308

Says (50)

Bellmour:	He's of another opinion, and says I do the drudgery	43	OLD BATCH	I.1	222
Sir Joseph:	by the Lord Harry he says true; Fighting, is Meat, Drink	52	OLD BATCH	II.1	167
Capt Bluff:	What says my pretty little Knapsack-Carrier?	85	OLD BATCH	IV.3	84
Vainlove:	says; and often blush'd with Anger and Surprize:--	99	OLD BATCH	V.1	96
Lord Froth:	Brisk to have Wit; my Wife says, he has a great deal. I	134	DOUBL DLR	I.1	274
Sir Paul:	my Lady Froth says; was ever the like read of in Story?	143	DOUBL DLR	II.1	196
Sir Paul:	the Poet says.--	144	DOUBL DLR	II.1	226
Sir Paul:	Hum, gads bud she says true,--well, my Lady,	145	DOUBL DLR	II.1	238
Sir Paul:	Mother says Child--	172	DOUBL DLR	IV.1	172
Lord Touch:	suddenly design'd--yet he says he had prepar'd my	197	DOUBL DLR	V.1	359
Jeremy:	Sir, your Father's Steward says he comes to make	224	FOR LOVE	I.1	302
Scandal:	favour, as a Doctor says, No, to a Bishoprick, only that it	226	FOR LOVE	I.1	377
Valentine:	any thing that he says: For to converse with Scandal, is to	226	FOR LOVE	I.1	388
Tattle:	her--Madam, says I, there are some Persons who make	227	FOR LOVE	I.1	430
Tattle:	one and t'other, and every thing in the World; and, says I,	227	FOR LOVE	I.1	432
Scandal:	She says otherwise.	228	FOR LOVE	I.1	470
Mrs Frail:	--I can't believe a word he says.	233	FOR LOVE	I.1	621
Miss Prue:	Yes; I may tell my Mother--and he says he'll	249	FOR LOVE	II.1	524
Miss Prue:	lend me your Handkerchief--Smell Cousin; he says,	249	FOR LOVE	II.1	526
Scandal:	little, yet says he has a World to say. Asks for his Father	266	FOR LOVE	III.1	498
Scandal:	So says Pineda in his Third Book and Eighth Chapter--	267	FOR LOVE	III.1	532
Scandal:	Science, Because, says he, it teaches us to consider the	267	FOR LOVE	III.1	538
Scandal:	Look you there now--Your Lady says your	269	FOR LOVE	III.1	616

Says   (continued)

		PAGE	TITLE	ACT.SC	LINE
Foresight:	What says he? What, did he prophesie? Ha, Sir	283	FOR LCVE	IV.1	277
Ben:	marry himself. Gad, says I, an you play the fool and marry	286	FOR LCVE	IV.1	382
Mrs Fore:	her, and Jeremy says will take any body for her that he .	288	FOR LCVE	IV.1	469
Jeremy:	Yes, Sir; he says he'll favour it, and mistake her for .	288	FCR LCVE	IV.1	482
Valentine:	Opinion of my Satirical Friend, Scandal, who says, . .	297	FOR LOVE	IV.1	814
Miss Prue:	must not marry the Seaman now--my Father says so. . . .	303	FOR LOVE	V.1	227
Miss Prue:	Robin the Butler, he says he loves me, and he's a Handsome	305	FOR LCVE	V.1	317
Gonsalez:	What says my Son? what Ruine? ha? what	377	M. EBIDE	V.2	53
Mirabell:	Betty, what says your Clock?	398	WAY WCRLD	I.1	105
Fainall:	Witwoud says they are--	406	WAY WORLD	I.1	403
Foible:	(says he) what you are a hatching some Plot (says he) you	427	WAY WCRLD	III.1	95
Foible:	are sc early abroad, or Catering (says he) ferreting for .	427	WAY WCRLD	III.1	96
Foible:	thin Subsistance (says he)--Well, what Pension does .	427	WAY WCRLD	III.1	98
Foible:	your Lady propose? Let me see (says he) what she must .	427	WAY WCRLD	III.1	99
Foible:	come dcwn pretty deep now, she's super-annuated (says .	427	WAY WCRLD	III.1	100
Foible:	Humh (says he) I hear you are laying Designs against .	428	WAY WCRLD	III.1	111
Foible:	me too (says he), and Mrs. Millamant is to marry my .	428	WAY WCRLD	III.1	112
Foible:	but (says he) I'll fit you for that, I warrant you (says he)	428	WAY WCRLD	III.1	114
Foible:	I'll hamper you for that (says he) you and your old Frippery	428	WAY WCRLD	III.1	115
Foible:	too (says he) I'll handle you--	428	WAY WCRLD	III.1	116
Foible:	she'll be contracted to Sir Rowland to Night, she says;--	430	WAY WCRLD	III.1	210
Petulant:	If he says Black's Black--If I have a Humour to . .	435	WAY WCRLD	III.1	404
Sir Wilful:	Map says that your Turk is not so honest a Man as your .	456	WAY WCRLD	IV.1	445
Mincing:	I vow. He says Mem, how that he'll have my Lady's .	465	WAY WCBLD	V.1	110
Lady Wish:	friend, I can't believe it, No, no; as she says, let him				
	prove	467	WAY WCRLD	V.1	206

Scabbard (1)

Araminta:	that a Coward has, while the Sword is in the Scabbard . .	86	OLD BATCH	IV.3	118

Scabbards (1)

Sir Joseph:	Gads-Daggers-Belts-Blades-and Scabbards, this is . . .	49	OLD EATCH	II.1	50

Scaffolding (1)

Zara:	Our Wish; and that obtain'd, down with the Scaffolding .	347	M. EBIDE	II.2	318

Scalding (1)

Almeria:	With Rivers of incessant scalding Rain.	358	M. EFIDE	III.1	374

Scales (1)

Mrs Frail:	and Scales, and three rows of Teeth, a most outragious .	286	FOR LCVE	IV.1	401

Scandal (70)

Mellefont:	to their Tea, and Scandal; according to their Antient . .	127	DOUEL DLR	I.1	12
Mellefont:	to their Tea, and Scandal; according to their Ancient . .	127	DOUEL DLR	I.1 V	12
	(Enter Scandal.) . . .	219	FCR LCVE	I.1	116
Jeremy:	Scandal, for Heaven's sake, Sir, try if you can disswade .	219	FOR LCVE	I.1	123
Valentine:	By this, Scandal, you may see what it is to be great; .	221	FOR LCVE	I.1	187
Valentine:	Scandal, learn to spare your Friends, and do not . .	221	FOR LCVE	I.1	198
Valentine:	Scandal, don't spoil my Boy's Milk.--Bid	222	FOR LCVE	I.1	222
Trapland:	Mr. Scandal.	222	FOR LCVE	I.1	232
Trapland:	--my Service to you Mr. Scandal--(Drinks)--I	222	FOR LCVE	I.1	246
Valentine:	Drink first. Scandal, why do you not Drink? . . .	223	FCB LCVE	I.1	255
Valentine:	doing good.--Scandal, Drink to me, my Friend Trapland's .	223	FOR LCVE	I.1	260
Trapland:	Fie, Mr. Scandal, you never knew--	223	FOR LCVE	I.1	267
Trapland:	Mr. Scandal, you are Uncivil; I did not value your . .	224	FOR LCVE	I.1	313
Tattle:	Valentine good Morrow, Scandal I am Yours.-- . . .	226	FOR LCVE	I.1	382
Valentine:	any thing that he says: For to ccnverse with Scandal, is to	226	FOR LCVE	I.1	388
Valentine:	Nay, if you have known Scandal thus long, and . . .	229	FOR LCVE	I.1	501
Valentine:	give Scandal such an Advantage; why, your running away .	229	FOR LCVE	I.1	512
Tattle:	Scandal, you will not be so ungenerous--O, I shall . .	230	FCB LCVE	I.1	514
Valentine:	Scandal, have pity on him; he'll yield to any . . .	230	FOR LCVE	I.1	523
Mrs Frail:	to see Fellows in a Morning. Scandal, you Devil, are you	230	FOR LCVE	I.1	547
Valentine:	And Scandal shall give you a good Name.	232	FCB LCVE	I.1	592
	(Enter Valentine, Scandal, and Angelica.)	254	FOR LCVE	III.1	26
Tattle:	(coming up). Scandal, are you in private Discourse, any .	254	FCR LCVE	III.1	42
Tattle:	(Aside to Scandal.) . . .	254	FOR LCVE	III.1	44
Tattle:	O pox, Scandal, that was too far put--Never have . .	256	FOR LCVE	III.1	116
	(Re-enter Scandal, with one to Sing.) .	258	FOR LCVE	III.1 V196	
	(Exit Valentine and Scandal.) . .	259	FOR LCVE	III.1	233
	(Enter Scandal.) . . .	266	FOR LCVE	III.1	479
Foresight:	Ah, good Mr. Scandal--	267	FCB LCVE	III.1	518
Foresight:	Alas Mr. Scandal--Humanum est errare.	267	FOR LCVE	III.1	526
Foresight:	You are learn'd, Mr. Scandal--	267	FOR LCVE	III.1	533
Foresight:	I protest I honour you, Mr. Scandal--I did not think .	267	FCR LCVE	III.1	540
Foresight:	How does it appear, Mr. Scandal? I think I am very .	268	FOR LCVE	III.1	561
Mrs Fore:	Clock. Mr. Scandal, your Servant--	268	FOR LCVE	III.1	577
Scandal:	reason. (She gives him the Glass: Scandal and she whisper.)	269	FCR LCVE	III.1	585
Foresight:	Do you think so, Mr. Scandal?	270	FOR LCVE	III.1	630
Foresight:	I thank you Mr. Scandal, I will--Nurse, let me have .	270	FOR LCVE	III.1	640
Foresight:	I thank you, Mr. Scandal, indeed that wou'd be a . .	271	FOR LCVE	III.1	653
Mrs Fore:	Mr. Scandal, you had best go to Bed and	275	FCB LCVE	III.1	811
	(Valentine's Lodging. Enter Scandal, and Jeremy.)	275	FOR LCVE	IV.1	
Angelica:	Mr. Scandal, I suppose you don't think it a Novelty, .	276	FOR LCVE	IV.1	20
Angelica:	Mr. Scandal, you can't think me guilty of so much . .	277	FOR LCVE	IV.1	42
Jeremy:	Mr. Scandal is with him, Sir; I'll knock at the Door. .	279	FOR LCVE	IV.1	147
	a Couch disorderly dress'd, Scandal by him.) . . .	279	FOR LCVE	IV.1	149
Foresight:	Truly Mr. Scandal, I was so taken up with broken . .	284	FOR LOVE	IV.1	340
Foresight:	Scandal, truly,--I am inclining to your Turkish . . .	285	FOR LCVE	IV.1	348
	(Exeunt Foresight, Mrs. Foresight and Scandal.) .	285	FOB LCVE	IV.1	354
	(Enter Valentine, Scandal, Foresight, and Jeremy.)	288	FOR LCVE	IV.1	478
Valentine:	Scandal will tell you;--I am Truth, I never	288	FOR LCVE	IV.1	497
Foresight:	His Frenzy is very high now, Mr. Scandal.	289	FCB LCVE	IV.1	529
Foresight:	--Mr. Scandal, I shall be very glad to confer with you .	289	FOR LCVE	IV.1	532
Valentine:	(whispers). Scandal, who are all these? Foreigners? . .	291	FOR LCVE	IV.1	593
Valentine:	(whispers). Scandal, who are these? Foreigners? . . .	291	FOR LOVE	IV.1 V593	
Valentine:	Scandal) What, dc you look strange upon me?--Then . .	292	FOB LCVE	IV.1	618
	(Scandal goes aside with Jeremy.) .	292	FOR LCVE	IV.1	621
Jeremy:	(to Scandal). I'll do't, Sir.	293	FOR LCVE	IV.1	667
Angelica:	No, I'll stay with him--Mr. Scandal will protect me. .	293	FOR LCVE	IV.1	676
Angelica:	Mr. Scandal, I only stay till my Maid comes, and . .	293	FOR LCVE	IV.1	685

See (continued)

		PAGE	TITLE	ACT.SC	LINE
Bellmour:	See the great Blessing of an easy Faith; Opinion	96	OLD BATCH	IV.4	271
Lucy:	for your Brother's Chaplain. Don't you see that stalking	97	OLD BATCH	V.1	15
Bellmour:	blind, I must not see him fall into the Snare, and	98	OLD BATCH	V.1	61
Sharper:	Heartwell when I see him. Prithee, Frank, let's teaze him;	99	OLD BATCH	V.1	87
Setter:	her last; When you were to see her next; And, Where you	99	OLD BATCH	V.1	115
Sharper:	Methinks I long to see Bellmour come forth.	100	OLD BATCH	V.1	129
Setter:	Talk of the Devil--See where he comes.	100	OLD BATCH	V.1	131
Sir Joseph:	Hush, hush: Don't you see him?	101	OLD BATCH	V.1	169
Sir Joseph:	see:--But, by the Lord Harry, I'll leave you.	101	OLD BATCH	V.1	185
Sir Joseph:	Prithee, What do you see in my face, that looks as	101	OLD BATCH	V.1	191
Heartwell:	--And I cannot in gratitude (for I see which way thou	111	OLD BATCH	V.2	151
Heartwell:	art going) see thee fall into the same snare, out of which	111	OLD BATCH	V.2	152
Bellmour:	you an Appetite to see us fall to before ye. Setter, Did	112	OLD BATCH	V.2	178
Bellmour:	to see thee still plod on alone.	112	OLD BATCH	V.2	184
	'Twould grieve your hearts to see him; shall I call him?	113	OLD BATCH	EPI.	25
Brisk:	--and see what a condition you're like to be brought	129	DOUBL DLR	I.1	58
Careless:	Lady, I don't see what you can expect from the Fruit.	131	DOUBL DLR	I.1	166
Mellefont:	suspicions just,--but see the Company is broke up,	131	DOUBL DLR	I.1	168
Brisk:	But does your Lordship never see Comedies?	133	DOUBL DLR	I.1	222
Brisk:	Let me see, let me see, my Lord, I broke my Glass that	135	DOUBL DLR	I.1	291
Lady Touch:	perswade her. But I don't see what you can propose from	138	DOUBL DLR	I.1	414
Lady Ply:	Nay, nay, rise up, come you shall see my good	148	DOUBL DLR	II.1	355
Mellefont:	see the Vessels are parted.	148	DOUBL DLR	II.1	384
Mellefont:	Ha! O I see, I see my Rising Sun! Light breaks	149	DOUBL DLR	II.1	405
Mellefont:	Ha! O see, I see my Rising Sun! Light breaks	149	DCUBL DLR	II.1	V405
Maskwell:	any thing--Why, let me see, I have the same Face, the	150	DOUBL DLR	II.1	460
Lady Touch:	self. Pray, my Lord, don't let the Company see you in this	153	DOUBL DLR	III.1	112
Lady Touch:	Lord must not see him again.	154	DOUBL DLR	III.1	145
	(Maskwell pretending not to see him, walks by him, and	155	DOUBL DLR	III.1	192
Sir Paul:	see--if it becomes me to say so; and we live very comfortably	160	DOUBL DLR	III.1	388
Sir Paul:	Oh, a fine likely Woman as you shall see in a	161	DOUBL DLR	III.1	421
Lord Froth:	'tis such a sight to see some teeth--sure you're a great	162	DOUBL DLR	III.1	460
Lady Froth:	lines again (pulls out a Paper.) Let me see here, you know	164	DOUBL DLR	III.1	512
Lady Froth:	too, you know, tho' we don't see him.	164	DOUBL DLR	III.1	525
Lady Froth:	Well you shall hear--let me see.	164	DOUBL DLR	III.1	527
Lady Froth:	O the dear Creature! Let's go see it.	166	DOUBL DLR	III.1	608
Lady Froth:	--Come, my dear Cynthia, Mr. Brisk, we'll go see	167	DOUBL DLR	III.1	615
Lady Froth:	Wont you? What not to see Saph? Pray, My Lord, come	167	DOUBL DLR	III.1	621
Lady Froth:	see little Saph. I knew you cou'd not stay.	167	DOUBL DLR	III.1	622
Mellefont:	that we only have it in view, I don't see but we have it in	168	DOUBL DLR	IV.1	21
Cynthia:	of his Wit: Therefore let me see you undermine my Lady	168	DOUBL DLR	IV.1	47
Cynthia:	I would not have 'em see us together yet.	169	DOUBL DLR	IV.1	66
Lady Ply:	transported, I did not see it.--Well, to shew you how	170	DOUBL DLR	IV.1	109
Lady Ply:	made plain--I don't see how my Daughter can in	172	DOUBL DLR	IV.1	169
Cynthia:	I'm glad to see you so merry, Sir.	173	DOUBL DLR	IV.1	232
Brisk:	the Day. Here she comes, I'll seem not to see her, and try	175	DOUBL DLR	IV.1	303
Brisk:	see how Love and Murder will out. But did I really name	176	DOUBL DLR	IV.1	329
Lady Froth:	see me do it with him.	177	DOUBL DLR	IV.1	370
Lord Froth:	(aside). --Oh I see there's no harm yet--But I	177	DOUBL DLR	IV.1	372
Sir Paul:	discover'd--But let me see to make an end on't.--	178	DOUBL DLR	IV.1	407
Sir Paul:	Person! Well, let me see--Till then I Languish in	178	DOUBL DLR	IV.1	414
Lady Ply:	So Sir, I see you have read the Letter,--well	179	DOUBL DLR	IV.1	437
Lady Ply:	De'e see here? Look, read it? (Snatches the Letter as in	179	DOUBL DLR	IV.1	441
Lady Ply:	Ungrateful Monster! He? Is it so? Ay, I see it, a Plot upon	179	DOUBL DLR	IV.1	444
Lady Ply:	found out that contrivance to let you see this Letter; which	179	DOUBL DLR	IV.1	455
Lady Ply:	I do, see my Face no more;	179	DOUBL DLR	IV.1	457
Mellefont:	Hanging, with the Expectation of what I shall see--Hist,	183	DOUBL DLR	IV.2	3
Maskwell:	I confess you do Reproach me when I see you	183	DOUBL DLR	IV.2	13
Lady Touch:	I had not time to think--I was surprised to see a Monster in	185	DOUBL DLR	IV.2	71
Lady Touch:	what he does--see how wild he looks.	186	DCUBL DLR	IV.2	114
Mellefont:	By Heaven 'twere senceless not to be mad, and see	186	DOUBL DLR	IV.2	115
Lord Touch:	to my Name; when next I see that Face, I'le write Villain	186	DOUBL DLR	IV.2	119
Mellefont:	ending in perplexity. My uncle will not see, nor hear me.	190	DOUBL DLR	V.1	105
Lady Touch:	. . . now I see what	191	DOUBL DLR	V.1	147
Sir Paul:	Madam, Sister, my Lady Sister, did you see my	191	DOUBL DLR	V.1	159
Maskwell:	I am concern'd to see your Lordship discomposed--	195	DOUBL DLR	V.1	305
Lord Touch:	see I want no inclination.	196	DOUBL DLR	V.1	325
	Methinks I see some Faces in the Pit,	204	DOUBL DLR	EPI.	32
Jeremy:	nothing to it for a Whetter; yet I never see it, but the	218	FOR LOVE	I.1	94
Scandal:	Jeremy speaks like an Oracle. Don't you see how	219	FOR LOVE	I.1	131
Valentine:	Jeremy, see who's there.	220	FOR LOVE	I.1	155
Valentine:	See who they are.	221	FOR LOVE	I.1	185
Valentine:	By this, Scandal, you may see what it is to be great;	221	FOR LOVE	I.1	187
Valentine:	Faith and Troth, I am heartily glad to see you--	222	FOR LOVE	I.1	242
Tattle:	never see a Bed-Chamber again, never be lock't in a	230	FOR LOVE	I.1	518
Scandal:	familiar--And see that they are Women of Quality too,	230	FOR LOVE	I.1	528
Mrs Frail:	to see Fellows in a Morning. Scandal, you Devil, are you	230	FOR LOVE	I.1	547
Mrs Frail:	and so stole out to see you. Well, and what will	231	FOR LOVE	I.1	583
Mrs Frail:	take care of my own. Well; but I'll come and see you one	232	FOR LOVE	I.1	597
Scandal:	only Original you will see there.	232	FOR LOVE	I.1	604
Mrs Frail:	Ay, let me see those, Mr. Tattle.	232	FOR LOVE	I.1	608
Scandal:	No, no; come to me if you wou'd see Pictures.	232	FOR LOVE	I.1	615
Scandal:	shall see.	234	FOR LOVE	I.1	658
Valentine:	to come abroad, and be at Liberty to see her.	234	FOR LOVE	I.1	674
Nurse:	and swear now, ha, ha, ha, Marry and did you ever see the	235	FOR LOVE	II.1	23
Foresight:	Odso, let me see; Let me see the Paper--Ay,	240	FOR LOVE	II.1	186
Sr Sampson:	Sirrah, you'll be hang'd; I shall live to see you	243	FOR LOVE	II.1	303
Sr Sampson:	Now let's see, if you have Wit enough to keep your self?--	246	FOR LOVE	II.1	401
Valentine:	'Tis as much as I expected--I did not come to see	246	FOR LOVE	II.1	407
Mrs Frail:	take you, you confounded Toad--why did you see	250	FOR LOVE	II.1	566
Tattle:	enquire for me, than ever went to see the Hermaphrodite,	257	FOR LOVE	III.1	161
Scandal:	Proverbs, and I see one in the next Room that will sing it.	258	FOR LOVE	III.1	192
Sr Sampson:	I'm glad on't: Where is he? I long to see him. Now, Mrs.	259	FOR LOVE	III.1	211
Sr Sampson:	Frail, you shall see my Son Ben--Body o' me, he's the	259	FOR LOVE	III.1	212

608

See   (continued)

			PAGE	TITLE	ACT.SC	LINE
Manuel:	Remove the Body thence, 'ere Zara see it.		373	M. BRIDE	V.1	28
Manuel:	And planted here to see me gorge this Bait,		373	M. BRIDE	V.1	43
Manuel:	And let the Cell where she'll expect to see him,		374	M. BRIDE	V.1	84
Manuel:	But see she comes; I'll shun th' Encounter; do		374	M. BRIDE	V.1	87
Manuel:	But see she comes; I'll shun th' Encounter; thou		374	M. BRIDE	V.1	V 87
Garcia:	Rather than or to see, or to relate		377	M. BRIDE	V.2	56
Garcia:	See, see, attir'd like Osmyn, where he lies.		377	M. BRIDE	V.2	61
Gonsalez:	To see the King in Person at their Head.		378	M. BRIDE	V.2	V104
Zara:	I came prepar'd to die, and see thee die--		380	M. BRIDE	V.2	V165
Zara:	And fright him from my Arms--See, see, he slides		381	M. BRIDE	V.2	208
Almeria:	There, there I see him; there he lies, the Blood		382	M. BRIDE	V.2	234
	To poison Plays, I see some where they sit,		385	M. BRIDE	EPI.	7
	So Criticks throng to see a New Play split,		385	M. BRIDE	EPI.	25
Mirabell:	That I may see her before she returns to her Lady; and as		398	WAY WORLD	I.1	131
Fainall:	Are you Jealous as often as you see Witwoud		399	WAY WORLD	I.1	148
Witwoud:	You shall see he won't go to 'em because there's no		405	WAY WORLD	I.1	363
Witwoud:	Ha, ha, ha; I had a Mind to see how the Rogue		406	WAY WORLD	I.1	409
Marwood:	You see my Friendship by my Freedom.		410	WAY WORLD	II.1	30
Mrs Fain:	My Husband. Don't you see him? He turn'd		412	WAY WORLD	II.1	82
Fainall:	To let you know I see through all your little Arts--		413	WAY WORLD	II.1	136
Marwood:	profess'd a Friendship to her; and could not see her easie		414	WAY WORLD	II.1	163
Mrs Fain:	to see him; but since I have despis'd him, he's too					
	offensive.		416	WAY WORLD	II.1	255
Mrs Fain:	I see but one poor empty Sculler; and he tows		418	WAY WORLD	II.1	326
Millamant:	fare you well;--I see they are walking away.		422	WAY WORLD	II.1	479
Lady Wish:	See who that is--(One knocks.) Set down the Bottle		425	WAY WORLD	III.1	33
Foible:	your Lady propose? Let me see (says he) what she must		427	WAY WORLD	III.1	99
Lady Wish:	A Tatterdemallion--I hope to see him hung with		428	WAY WORLD	III.1	130
Foible:	He! I hope to see him lodge in Ludgate first, and Angle		428	WAY WORLD	III.1	137
Lady Wish:	Let me see the Glass--Cracks, say'st thou?		429	WAY WORLD	III.1	147
Lady Wish:	sort of a dyingness--You see that Picture has a sort of		429	WAY WORLD	III.1	168
Millamant:	what he can see in me. I'll take my Death, I think you are		434	WAY WORLD	III.1	358
Singer:	If there's Delight in Love, 'tis when I see		435	WAY WORLD	III.1	389
Witwoud:	This is a vile Dog, I see that already. No Offence!		438	WAY WORLD	III.1	487
Sir Wilful:	I may say now, and am minded to see Foreign Parts. If an		440	WAY WORLD	III.1	574
Fainall:	Why faith I'm thinking of it.--Let me see--		443	WAY WORLD	III.1	676
Millamant:	him hither,--just as you will Dear Foible.--I think I'll see		446	WAY WORLD	IV.1	61
Sir Wilful:	see, to come and know if that how you were dispos'd to		447	WAY WORLD	IV.1	115
Mrs Fain:	is coming; and in my Conscience if she should see you,		452	WAY WORLD	IV.1	300
Lady Wish:	sit if you please, and see the Entertainment.		459	WAY WORLD	IV.1	567
Lady Wish:	you may see by the Superscription it is like a Woman's		460	WAY WORLD	IV.1	573
Lady Wish:	you may see, the Superscription is like a Woman's		460	WAY WORLD	IV.1	V573
Waitwell:	hand I see that already. That's some body whose throat		460	WAY WORLD	IV.1	578
Lady Wish:	a return, by a frank Communication--You shall see		460	WAY WORLD	IV.1	582
Waitwell:	How, how, Let me see, let me see--(reading) A		460	WAY WORLD	IV.1	591
Waitwell:	don't you see it?		460	WAY WORLD	IV.1	598
Foible:	Yes Madam; but my Lady did not see that part; We		464	WAY WORLD	V.1	78
Mincing:	Yes Mem, they have sent me to see if Sir Wilfull be		465	WAY WORLD	V.1	113
Marwood:	I am sorry to see you so passionate, Madam.		466	WAY WORLD	V.1	160
Lady Wish:	appearance. He is as terrible to me as a Gorgon; if I					
	see him,		470	WAY WORLD	V.1	336
Lady Wish:	were sure of that--shall I never see him again?		470	WAY WORLD	V.1	342
Sir Wilful:	once, he shall come in; and see who'll hinder him.		471	WAY WORLD	V.1	352
Lady Wish:	Tongue;--When I did not see him I cou'd have		472	WAY WORLD	V.1	409
Sir Wilful:	to see Foreign Parts--I have set on't--And when I'm set		477	WAY WORLD	V.1	585

See'st (1)

Sir Wilful:	if thou see'st her, ha Friend?		437	WAY WORLD	III.1	460

Seed (0)   see Mustard-seed

Seeds (1)

Jeremy:	Sir, I have the Seeds of Rhetorick and Oratory in		302	FOR LOVE	V.1	184

Seeing (9)   see O'seeing

Bellmour:	damnably in Love; I'm so uneasie for not seeing Belinda		40	OLD BATCH	I.1	133
Maskwell:	(Seems to start, seeing my Lord.)		189	DOUEL DLR	V.1	46
Mrs Fore:	fond of it, as of being first in the Fashion, or of seeing					
	a new		250	FOR LOVE	II.1	549
Osmyn-Alph:	That seeing my Disguise, thou seest not me?		342	M. BRIDE	II.2	81
Osmyn-Alph:	Not seeing of Election, but Necessity.		345	M. BRIDE	II.2	220
Zara:	Be drawn, and I will stand before thee seeing,		353	M. BRIDE	III.1	152
	(A Mute appears, and seeing the King retires.)		373	M. BRIDE	V.1	12
Mirabell:	whom I never saw before; seeing me, they all put on their		396	WAY WORLD	I.1	29
Foible:	had a prospect of seeing Sir Rowland your Uncle; and that		423	WAY WORLD	II.1	520

Seek (6)

Jeremy:	much to seek in playing the Madman to day.		276	FOR LOVE	IV.1	5
Heli:	To seek you, where, I knew your Grief would lead you,		344	M. BRIDE	II.2	178
Heli:	Impatiently to seek you, where, I knew		344	M. BRIDE	II.2	V178
Zara:	That thou dost seek to shield thee there, and shun		346	M. BRIDE	II.2	242
Zara:	Get thee to Hell, and seek him there.		380	M. BRIDE	V.2	175
Almeria:	O let me seek him in this horrid Cell;		381	M. BRIDE	V.2	215

Seeking (4)

Vainlove:	I do Wine--And this Business is none of my seeking; I		39	OLD BATCH	I.1	95
Maskwell:	Honour was not of my seeking, nor would I build my		189	DOUEL DLR	V.1	72
Ben:	d'ee see that was none of my seeking, I was commanded		263	FOR LOVE	III.1	373
Alonzo:	For Osmyn, if in seeking for the King,		379	M. BRIDE	V.2	120

Seeks (1)

Sharper:	shrub of Mankind, and seeks Protection from a blasted		102	OLD BATCH	V.1	208

Seem (28)

Bellmour:	seem to rouse, 'tis but well lashing him, and he will sleep	46	OLD BATCH	I.1	353
Araminta:	rid me of these Coxcombs, when I seem oppress'd with		85	OLD BATCH	IV.3	80
Lucy:	you are not what you seem to be.		97	OLD BATCH	V.1	33
Sharper:	purpose. Setter, stand close; seem not to observe 'em; and,	101	OLD BATCH	V.1	164
Mellefont:	to have Wit, that thou may'st seem a Fool.		129	DOUBL DLR	I.1	72
Brisk:	the Day. Here she comes, I'll seem not to see her, and try	175	DOUBL DLR	IV.1	303
Brisk:	(Aside.) I'll seem to conceal my Passion, and that will look	175	DOUBL DLR	IV.1	317
Maskwell:	rather die, than seem once, barely seem, dishonest:--		188	DOUEL DLR	V.1	37
Valentine:	sides alike. Yet while she does not seem to hate me, I will	297	FOR LOVE	IV.1	812

Seen   (continued)
Mrs Frail: have seen the Resolution of a Lover,--Honest Tarr and . . 287 FOR LCVE   IV.1 450
Angelica: seen Fifty in a side Box by Candle-light, out-blossom Five 298 FOR LCVE   V.1   31
Gonsalez: This Sight, which is indeed not seen (tho' twice   . . . 332 M. ERIDE   I.1   244
Manuel: I wonnot have the seeming cf a Scrrow seen   . . . . . 334 M. ERIDE   I.1   322
Manuel: Th' expecting Crowd had been deceiv'd; and seen   . . . 335 M. ERIDE   I.1   390
Garcia: This Way, we're told, Osmyn was seen to walk;   . . . . 337 M. ERIDE   II.1   1
Almeria: Ere seen?   . . . . 344 M. ERIDE   II.2 168
Osmyn-Alph: At once, as I have seen her often;   . . . . 345 M. ERIDE   II.2 229
Osmyn-Alph: At once, as I before have seen her often;   . . . . . 345 M. ERIDE   II.2 V229
Zara: Better I was unseen, than seen thus coldly.   . . . . . 346 M. ERIDE   II.2 257
Zara: That having seen it, thou do'st turn thy Eyes   . . . . 353 M. ERIDE   III.1 149
Osmyn-Alph: Retire, my Life, with speed--Alas, we're seen!   . . . . 359 M. ERIDE   III.1 387
Gonsalez: What if she had seen Osmyn? tho' 'twere strange.   . . . 366 M. ERIDE   IV.1 222
Manuel: Swear thou hast never seen that foreign Dog, ... 368 M. ERIDE   IV.1 287
Alonzo: I have not seen you.   . . . . 371 M. ERIDE   IV.1 423
Gonsalez: I've seen thy Sword do noble Execution.   . . . . . . 372 M. ERIDE   IV.1 430
Gonsalez: Thanks; and I take thee at thy Wcrd. Thou'st seen   . . . 372 M. ERIDE   IV.1 432
Gonsalez: Away, I've not been seen--haste good Alonzo.   . . . . . 372 M. ERIDE   IV.1 442
Gonsalez: And say, I've not been seen--haste good Alonzo.   . . . . 372 M. ERIDE   IV.1 V442
Zara: Shun me when seen! I fear thou hast undone me.   . . . 375 M. ERIDE   V.1   101
Zara: What should have ne'er been seen; imperfect Mischief!   . . 375 M. ERIDE   V.1   105
Zara: Is seen, or heard. A dreadful Din was wont   . . . . . 379 M. ERIDE   V.2   135
Zara: What have you seen? Ha! wherefore stare you thus,   . . 380 M. ERIDE   V.2   155
Selim: The Mute you sent, by some Mischance was seen, ... 380 M. ERIDE   V.2   180
Mirabell: I have seen him, he promises to be an extraordinary   . . 400 WAY WCRLD I.1   190
Mirabell: Eye, by a Pearl of Orient; he wou'd no more be seen by   . 407 WAY WCRLD I.1   455
Witwoud: hard Frost. Whether this Uncle has seen Mrs. Millamant or . 408 WAY WCRLD I.1   486
Mrs Fain: another by being seen to walk with his Wife. This way Mr. 412 WAY WCRLD II.1 106
Painall: Fire. I have seen the warm Confession red'ning on your   . 413 WAY WCRLD II.1 140
Foible: You have seen Madam Millamant, Sir?   . . . . 424 WAY WCRLD II.1 528
Foible: seen me with you I'm sure she'll tell my Lady. I'll make . 424 WAY WCRLD II.1 546
Foible: Madam, I have seen the Party.   . . . . 427 WAY WCRLD III.1 72
Foible: of his success. I wou'd be seen as little as possible to
                 speak   . . . . 430 WAY WCRLD III.1 215
Witwoud: forgot him; I have not seen him since the Revolution.   . 436 WAY WCRLD III.1 442
Sir Wilful: What a Vixon trick is this?--Nay, now a'has seen me too-- . 447 WAY WCRLD IV.1   94
Millamant: never to be seen there together again; as if we were proud 450 WAY WCRLD IV.1 204
Millamant: never be seen there together again; as if we were proud . 450 WAY WCRLD IV.1 V204
Lady Wish: Too well, too well. I have seen too much.   . . . . . 460 WAY WCRLD IV.1 599
Lady Wish: wou'd ha' shriek'd, If she had but seen a Man, till she was 466 WAY WCRLD V.1   187
Sees (7)
Belinda: quiet, when he sees his Debtor has not wherewithal--   . . 58 OLD BATCH II.2 128
Fondlewife: (Sees the Book that Bellmour forgot.)   . 91 OLD BATCH IV.4   99
Lady Ply: sake step in here and advise me quickly, before he sees. . 178 DOUEL DLR IV.1 403
               Th' unladen Boughs, he sees, bode certain Dearth,   . . . 213 FOR LCVE   PRO.   5
Scandal: She'll be here by and by, she sees Valentine every   . . . 229 FCR LCVE   I.1   483
Miss Prue: that lcves me, and I love him; and if he sees you speak to
                 me   . . . . 264 FOR LCVE   III.1 416
Zara: Of Sense: His Soul still sees, and knows each Purpose,   . 381 M. ERIDE   V.2   196
Seest (6)   see See'st
Careless: Prithee get thee gone; thou seest we are serious.   . . . 128 DOUEL DLR I.1   45
Osmyn-Alph: That seeing my Disguise, thou seest not me?   . . . . . 342 M. ERIDE   II.2   81
Zara: O no, thou canst not, for thou seest me now, ... 353 M. ERIDE   III.1 156
Almeria: Seest thou not there, who prostrate lies;   . . . . . . 382 M. ERIDE   V.2   264
Almeria: Seest thou not there? behold who prostrate lies,   . . . 382 M. ERIDE   V.2 V264
Osmyn-Alph: Seest thou, how just the Hand of Heav'n has been?   . . . 383 M. ERIDE   V.2   317
Seiz'd (2)
Alonzo: Soon as I seiz'd the Man, ... 373 M. ERIDE   V.1   21
               But if he 'scape, with what Regret they're seiz'd!   . . . 385 M. ERIDE   EPI.   13
Seize (7)
Lady Touch: immediate Ruin seize him.   . . . . 137 DOUEL DLR I.1   401
Lady Touch: Curses seize you all.   . . . . 202 DOUEL DLR V.1 V561
               (Servants seize him.)   . . . . . . 203 DOUEL DLR V.1 V577
Scandal: by Heav'n to seize the better half.   . . . . 219 FOR LCVE   I.1   135
Jeremy: Aye, Sir, hooded like a Hawk, to seize at first sight   . 302 FOR LCVE   V.1   199
Manuel: Ha! seize that Mute; Alonzo, follow him.   . . . . . 373 M. ERIDE   V.1   13
Manuel: Ha! stop and seize that Mute; Alcnzo, follow him.   . . . 373 M. ERIDE   V.1 V 13
Seizes (1)
Almeria: A sudden Chilness seizes on my Spirits.   . . . . . . 334 M. ERIDE   I.1   349
Seldom (4)
Laetitia: Sir, I seldom stir abroad.   . . . . 90 OLD BATCH IV.4   34
Brisk: I'm wholly turn'd into Satyr. I confess I Write but seldom, 141 DOUBL DLR II.1 116
Brisk: I'm wholly turn'd into Satire. I confess I write but seldom, 141 DOUBL DLR II.1 V116
Scandal: Women of her airy temper, as they seldom think   . . . . 225 FOR LCVE   I.1   348
Self (251)
Vainlove: my self to her--And it seems she has taken me at my   . . 39 OLD BATCH I.1   98
Vainlove: I would have her fret her self out of conceit with me, that 40 OLD BATCH I.1   120
Bellmour: self, nor suffers any Body else to rail at me. Then as I . 41 OLD BATCH I.1   169
Bellmour: hast thou been putting out of conceit with her self, and . 42 OLD BATCH I.1   183
Heartwell: able as your self and as nimble too, though I mayn't have   43 OLD BATCH I.1   230
Heartwell: caught in one my self.   . . . . 45 OLD BATCH I.1   297
Sir Joseph: Nay 'Ile say that for my self--with your leave Sir--   . . 50 OLD BATCH II.1 104
Sharper: and like your self.   . . . . 51 OLD BATCH II.1 137
Capt Bluff: I'le recommend my self--Sir I honour you; I understand   . 51 OLD BATCH II.1 155
Capt Bluff: self.   . . . . 53 OLD BATCH II.1 209
Araminta: never let it be extinct, till I my self am Ashes.   . . . 54 OLD BATCH II.2   10
Araminta: self?   . . . . 57 OLD BATCH II.2 103
Belinda: to trust you to your self. The Devil watches all
                 opportunities;   . . . . 57 OLD BATCH II.2 105
Bellmour: Talk to your self--You had better let me speak; for if my   59 OLD BATCH II.2 177
Lucy: inform my self of what past between 'em to Day, and   . . 62 OLD BATCH III.1   45
Heartwell: and in some raving fit, be led to plunge my self into that   62 OLD BATCH III.1   68
Heartwell: --Now could I curse my self, yet cannot repent. O   . . . 63 OLD BATCH III.1   76
Bellmour: poor George, thou art i'th right, thou hast sold thy self to   63 OLD BATCH III.1   89
Lucy: Wretch, how, wer't thou valuing thy self, upon thy   . . 65 OLD BATCH III.1 168

Self   (continued)

		PAGE	TITLE	ACT.SC	LINE
Setter:	Thou are thy Mistresses foul self, Composed of her . . .	66	OLD BATCH	III.1	190
Setter:	Nay faith Lucy I'me sorry, I'le own my self to blame, . .	66	OLD BATCH	III.1	212
Sir Joseph:	Office--So tell him your self.	68	OLD BATCH	III.1	267
Sharper:	your self into a Premunire, by trusting to that sign of a	69	OLD BATCH	III.1	304
Sir Joseph:	self--I'll give him the Lie if you'll stand to it. . . .	69	OLD BATCH	III.1	307
Heartwell:	'Tis both; for I am angry with my self, when I am . . .	72	OLD BATCH	III.2	70
Heartwell:	am grown very entertaining to my self, and (as I am . .	73	OLD BATCH	III.2	82
Silvia:	self; for I love you, and would Marry you.	73	OLD BATCH	III.2	106
Silvia:	self--honest--Here, I won't keep any thing that's yours, .	73	OLD BATCH	III.2	110
Heartwell:	believe it: Nay, thou shalt think so thy self--Only let me .	74	OLD BATCH	III.2	122
Heartwell:	may get the better of my self.	74	OLD BATCH	III.2	130
Heartwell:	self liberty to think, lest I should cool--I will about a	74	OLD BATCH	III.2	139
Fondlewife:	say you with his Wife? With Comfort her self.	76	OLD BATCH	IV.1	20
Fondlewife:	And in the mean time, I will reason with my self-- . . .	76	OLD BATCH	IV.1	49
Fondlewife:	her self.	79	OLD BATCH	IV.1	138
Vainlove:	Yes, when I feed my self--But I hate to be cram'd . . .	80	OLD BATCH	IV.1	174
Servant:	Here's a Chair, Sir, if you please to repose your self. .	80	OLD BATCH	IV.2	1
Belinda:	come this Way, till I put my self a little in Repair,--Ah!	83	OLD BATCH	IV.3	10
Belinda:	come this Way, till I have put my self a little in				
	Repair,--Ah!	83	OLD BATCH	IV.3 V	10
Bellmour:	accuse my self.	93	OLD BATCH	IV.4	149
Bellmour:	Since all Artifice is vain--and I think my self obliged	93	OLD BATCH	IV.4	157
Fondlewife:	think I don't know how to behave my self in the Employment	94	OLD BATCH	IV.4	195
Lucy:	That may be, without troubling your self to go again . .	97	OLD BATCH	V.1	14
Sharper:	but let thee look simply, and laugh by thy self. . . .	100	OLD BATCH	V.1	141
Sharper:	But how the Devil do you think to acquit your self . . .	100	OLD BATCH	V.1	154
Sharper:	of your Promise? Will you marry her your self?	100	OLD BATCH	V.1	155
Setter:	--Avaunt Temptation.--Setter, shew thy self a	102	OLD BATCH	V.1	226
Sharper:	me, or I'll go and have the Lady to my self. B'w'y' George.	104	OLD BATCH	V.1	306
Bellmour:	your self upon Heartwell, for affronting your Squirrel. .	107	OLD BATCH	V.1	396
Heartwell:	self on her Wedding-Day! Not hold out till Night! . . .	107	OLD BATCH	V.2	6
Heartwell:	To Man that Supplemental Self design'd;	108	OLD BATCH	V.2	12
Belinda:	Nay, I swear, I begin to pity him, my self.	109	OLD BATCH	V.2	49
Bellmour:	commit my self to lasting Durance.	112	OLD BATCH	V.2	167
Mellefont:	self favour'd in her aversion: But whether urged by her	129	DOUBL DLR	I.1	94
Mellefont:	much ado I prevented her doing me or her self a mischief:	130	DOUBL DLR	I.1	115
Careless:	Body to Disinherit thy self: for as I take it this				
	Settlement	130	DOUBL DLR	I.1	121
Mellefont:	will be a Pleasure to your self; I must get you to engage	130	DOUBL DLR	I.1	125
Mellefont:	secure her to your self, you may incline her to mine. She's	130	DOUBL DLR	I.1	128
Mellefont:	Gallantry, as they call it. I'le observe my Uncle my self;	130	DOUBL DLR	I.1	135
Mellefont:	Gallantry, as they call it. I'll observe my Uncle my self;	130	DOUBL DLR	I.1 V135
Lord Froth:	To distinguish my self from the Commonalty, ...	133	DOUBL DLR	I.1	227
Mellefont:	You are Cruel to your self, my Lord, as well as . . .	133	DOUBL DLR	I.1	233
Lord Froth:	I confess, I did my self some violence at first, but . .	133	DOUBL DLR	I.1	235
Brisk:	your self--I look grave, and ask the cause of this . .	134	DOUBL DLR	I.1	256
Maskwell:	How am I to behave my self? You know I am your	136	DOUBL DLR	I.1	339
Maskwell:	I would not be a Traytor to my self: I don't pretend to .	136	DOUBL DLR	I.1	342
Maskwell:	your self, and hear me. You know you Lov'd your . . .	136	DOUBL DLR	I.1	360
Maskwell:	needs this? I say nothing but what your self, in open hours	137	DOUBL DLR	I.1	384
Maskwell:	needs this? I say nothing but what your self, in open				
	hours	137	DOUBL DLR	I.1 V384
Maskwell:	Compose your self, You shall Enjoy and Ruin	137	DOUBL DLR	I.1	402
Maskwell:	Compose your self, You shall possess and ruin	137	DOUBL DLR	I.1 V402
Lord Froth:	I saw my self there, and kissed it for your sake. . . .	140	DOUBL DLR	II.1	80
Mellefont:	happiness that your Lordship has, I shall think my self	141	DOUBL DLR	II.1	112
Lady Froth:	Spumoso; and my self, what d'e think I call my self? .	141	DOUBL DLR	II.1	127
Lady Ply:	You firk him, I'll firk him my self; pray Sir Paul . .	144	DOUBL DLR	II.1	202
Sir Paul:	Hold your self Contented, my Lady Plyant,--I	144	DOUBL DLR	II.1	206
Lady Ply:	Have I behaved my self with all the decorum, and . . .	145	DOUBL DLR	II.1	252
Lady Ply:	Have I, I say, preserv'd my self, like a fair Sheet . .	145	DOUBL DLR	II.1	259
Lady Ply:	feeble, and unable to support it self.	147	DOUBL DLR	II.1	322
Maskwell:	Grazing, and to--ha, ha, ha, Marry Cynthia my self; .	149	DOUBL DLR	II.1	403
Lady Touch:	transported; compose your self: It is not of Concern, to .	152	DOUBL DLR	III.1	66
Lady Touch:	self. Pray, my Lord, don't let the Company see you in this	153	DOUBL DLR	III.1	112
Maskwell:	deceive 'em all, and yet secure my self, 'twas a lucky .	155	DOUBL DLR	III.1	190
Maskwell:	self any longer: and was just going to give vent to a				
	Secret, ...	156	DOUBL DLR	III.1	201
Mellefont:	as far as she betrays her self. No tragical design upon my	156	DOUBL DLR	III.1	210
Sir Paul:	were not for one thing, I should think my self the happiest	161	DOUBL DLR	III.1	404
Lord Froth:	had brought the Ape into the World her self.	165	DOUBL DLR	III.1	566
Lord Froth:	She her self makes her own Faces, ...	166	DOUBL DLR	III.1	599
Lady Ply:	far upon me as your self, with Blushes I must own it, you	169	DOUBL DLR	IV.1	73
Lady Ply:	shall value my self as long as I live, I swear.	169	DOUBL DLR	IV.1	76
Lady Ply:	Oh, I yield my self all up to your uncontroulable . . .	170	DOUBL DLR	IV.1	124
Sir Paul:	was never thus before--Well, I must own my self	172	DOUBL DLR	IV.1	199
Sir Paul:	For I would fain have some resemblance of my self in . .	173	DOUBL DLR	IV.1	228
Brisk:	Daughter your self; you're always brooding over her like .	174	DOUBL DLR	IV.1	272
Brisk:	The Deuce take me, I can't help laughing my self neither, .	176	DOUBL DLR	IV.1	344
Brisk:	The Deuce take me, I can't help laughing my self, . .	176	DOUBL DLR	IV.1 V344
Lady Froth:	self; for hang me if I have not a violent Passion for Mr.	176	DOUBL DLR	IV.1	352
Sir Paul:	deny'd my self the enjoyment of lawful Domestick . . .	179	DOUBL DLR	IV.1	428
Careless:	not prevail for you, 'gad I pretended to be in Love my self	180	DOUBL DLR	IV.1	499
Sir Paul:	to my Lady, I can't contain my self; come my dear Friend.	181	DOUBL DLR	IV.1	509
Lady Touch:	--Oh! I could rack my self, play the Vulture to my own .	184	DOUBL DLR	IV.2	46
Mellefont:	flounder your self a weary, and be nevertheless my Prisoner.	184	DOUBL DLR	IV.2	52
Mellefont:	done, left you to your self.--You're in a kind of Erasmus	185	DOUBL DLR	IV.2	60
Lady Touch:	the Glass, and now I find it is my self; Can you have mercy	185	DOUBL DLR	IV.2	72
Lady Touch:	the Glass, and now I find 'tis my self; Can you have mercy	185	DOUBL DLR	IV.2 V 72
Lady Touch:	self create your Happiness, and Cynthia shall be this night	185	DOUBL DLR	IV.2	85
Maskwell:	I ought not; for it rewards it self.	188	DOUBL DLR	V.1	20
Maskwell:	He was an ill Man, and I have gain'd; for half my self				
	I lent	188	DOUBL DLR	V.1	23
Maskwell:	him, and that, I have recall'd; so I have served my self,	188	DOUBL DLR	V.1	24
Maskwell:	whom I owe my self.	188	DOUBL DLR	V.1	26

Self   (continued)

		PAGE	TITLE	ACT.SC	LINE
Maskwell:	self, and some ill Chance might have directed malicious	189	DOUEL DLR	V.1	44
Maskwell:	for those free discourses which I have had with my self.	189	DOUEL DLR	V.1	51
Lord Touch:	Is't for your self?--I'll hear of nought for	189	DOUEL DLR	V.1	69
Maskwell:	tho' she involv'd her self in ruine. No, it must be by	190	DOUEL DLR	V.1	94
Cynthia:	any thing that resists my will, tho' 'twere reason it self.	193	DOUEL DLR	V.1	205
Maskwell:	self ready, I'll wheedle her intc the Coach; and instead of	193	DOUEL DLR	V.1	223
Maskwell:	her my self.	193	DOUEL DLR	V.1	225
Careless:	fix Inconstancy it self.	202	DOUEL DLR	V.1	549
Jeremy:	mean, to mew your self up here with Three or Four	217	FOR LCVE	I.1	32
Scandal:	The World behaves it self, as it used to do on such	220	FCB LCVE	I.1	159
Scandal:	The World behaves it self, as it uses to do on such	220	FCB LCVE	I.1	V159
Jeremy:	answer these your self.	221	FCR LCVE	I.1	184
Valentine:	him, before you can win it for your self.	226	FCB LCVE	I.1	390
Valentine:	Well, but how did you acquit your self?	228	FCR LCVE	I.1	444
Tattle:	pleasure of telling her self.	228	FCB LCVE	I.1	475
Tattle:	No Man but the Painter and my self was ever blest	232	FOR LCVE	I.1	610
Foresight:	him; I shall scarce recover my self before the Hour be	239	FOR LCVE	II.1	165
Valentine:	I am of my self, a plain easie simple Creature; and	244	FOR LCVE	II.1	345
Sr Sampson:	Now let's see, if you have Wit enough to keep your self?--	246	FCR LCVE	II.1	401
Mrs Frail:	your self happy in a Hackney-Coach before now.--If I	247	FOR LCVE	II.1	437
Mrs Frail:	her, without betraying my self.	248	FOR LCVE	II.1	472
Mrs Frail:	lye open ones self.	248	FCR LCVE	II.1	475
Mrs Fore:	Soul, I shall fancy my self Old indeed, to have this great	249	FCR LCVE	II.1	512
Tattle:	But you must think your self more Charming than I	252	FCR LCVE	II.1	617
Tattle:	you have, as much as if I had it my self--If I ask you to	252	FCR LCVE	II.1	619
Miss Prue:	my self from you behind the Curtains.	252	FCR LCVE	II.1	649
Nurse:	Miss Foresight--Sure she has not lock'd her self up	253	FCR LCVE	III.1	3
Nurse:	Miss Foresight--Sure she has lock'd her self up	253	FCR LCVE	III.1	V 3
Angelica:	had Concern enough to ask my self the Question.	254	FOR LCVE	III.1	32
Scandal:	self?	255	FCR LCVE	III.1	64
Valentine:	for my self.	257	FCR LCVE	III.1	146
Tattle:	self upon my Account; Gad, I was sorry for it with all my	258	FCR LCVE	III.1	177
Ben:	your self, Gad I don't think you are any more to compare	264	FCR LCVE	III.1	412
Mrs Frail:	out.--Come, Sir, will you venture your self with me?	265	FCR LCVE	III.1	450
Scandal:	Either you suffer your self to deceive your self; or	268	FCR LCVE	III.1	563
Scandal:	you dc not know your self.	268	FCR LCVE	III.1	564
Foresight:	Pray explain your self.	268	FCR LCVE	III.1	565
Scandal:	longer Master of my self--I was interrupted in the morning,	269	FOR ICVE	III.1	587
Scandal:	explaining my self to you--but was disappointed all this day;	269	FOR LCVE	III.1	590
Scandal:	and my self, than to despair.	271	FOR LCVE	III.1	663
Scandal:	I have no great Opinion of my self; yet I think, I'm	272	FCB LCVE	III.1	690
Scandal:	I have no great Opinion of my self; but I think, I'm	272	FCR LCVE	III.1	V690
Angelica:	my self oblig'd to--pray tell me truth.	277	FCR LCVE	IV.1	44
Buckram:	O Lord, let me be gone; I'll not venture my self	282	FCR LCVE	IV.1	243
Scandal:	Pray recollect your self.	284	FCR LCVE	IV.1	326
Ben:	marry to please my self, not him; and for the Young	285	FOR LCVE	IV.1	372
Ben:	Graceless, why did he beget me so? I did not get my self.	286	FOR LCVE	IV.1	391
Ben:	--I'm glad you shew your self, Mistress:--Let	287	FOR LCVE	IV.1	436
Valentine:	about,--They are welcome, and I'll tell 'em so my self. (To	292	FOR LCVE	IV.1	617
Valentine:	fancy I begin to come to my self.	294	FOR LCVE	IV.1	698
Sr Sampson:	I have a Proviso in the Obligation in favour of my self	300	FOR LCVE	V.1	126
Jeremy:	Even my unworthy self, Sir--Sir, I have had an	301	FOR LCVE	V.1	171
Jeremy:	my self better to you, Sir, than by the delivery of a	302	FOR LCVE	V.1	177
Tattle:	consideration of my self, as Compassion to her.	302	FOR LCVE	V.1	208
Jeremy:	with Thirty Thousand Pound, from throwing her self	302	FOR LCVE	V.1	210
Miss Prue:	won't get me one, I'll get one for my self: I'll marry our	305	FCR LCVE	V.1	316
Tattle:	speak for my self. Gad, I never had the least thought of	309	FCR LCVE	V.1	464
Scandal:	self?	311	FCR LCVE	V.1	542
Angelica:	to me, that I can make him and my self happy, than that I	312	FCR LCVE	V.1	577
Sr Sampson:	them and you, my self and every Body--Oons, Cully'd,	313	FOR LCVE	V.1	V585
Valentine:	never distinguish it self enough, to be taken notice of. If	313	FOR LCVE	V.1	610
Almeria:	Nor Violence.--I feel my self more light,	331	M. BRIDE	I.1	V202
Manuel:	To day--Retire, divest your self with speed	334	M. BRIDE	I.1	323
Garcia:	But to devote, and yield my self for ever	334	M. BRIDE	I.1	336
Zara:	These Bonds, I look with loathing on my self;	336	M. BRIDE	I.1	400
Manuel:	And by releasing you enslave my self.	336	M. BRIDE	I.1	414
Gonsalez:	That Friend may be her self; show no Resentment	337	M. BRIDE	I.1	443
Gonsalez:	That Friend may be her self; seem not to heed	337	M. BRIDE	I.1	V443
Osmyn-Alph:	'Tis Life! 'tis warm! 'tis she! 'tis she her self!	341	M. BRIDE	II.2	54
Almeria:	What's he, that like thy self, is started here	344	M. BRIDE	II.2	167
Almeria:	What's he, who like thy self, is started here	344	M. BRIDE	II.2	V167
Heli:	But felt unhurt, a Prisoner as your self;	344	M. BRIDE	II.2	176
Heli:	And as your self made free, hither I came	344	M. BRIDE	II.2	177
Osmyn-Alph:	But gently take thy self away, lest she	345	M. BRIDE	II.2	202
Osmyn-Alph:	Lost in my self, and blinded by my Thoughts,	346	M. BRIDE	II.2	253
Zara:	Think cn the Cause of all, then, view thy self:	347	M. BRIDE	II.2	305
Osmyn-Alph:	What neither can bestow. Set free your self,	348	M. BRIDE	II.2	329
Osmyn-Alph:	Not for my self, but him, hear me, all-gracious--	350	M. BRIDE	III.1	19
Heli:	My Lord, require you should compose your self,	352	M. BRIDE	III.1	93
Heli:	With Speed and Safety, to convey my self	352	M. BRIDE	III.1	99
Zara:	My self will fly; and earlier than the Morn,	354	M. BRIDE	III.1	202
Almeria:	Thy second self should feel each cther Wound,	356	M. BRIDE	III.1	287
Zara:	(Aside.) Confusion! yet I will contain my self.	359	M. BRIDE	III.1	411
Zara:	No not the Princess self, permitted to	360	M. BRIDE	III.1	451
Manuel:	We will our self behold the Execution.	364	M. BRIDE	IV.1	V128
Zara:	My self of what I've undertaken; now,	364	M. BRIDE	IV.1	141
Zara:	They self and no other; not the Princess self.	365	M. BRIDE	IV.1	170
Manuel:	Acquit thy self of those detested Names,	368	M. BRIDE	IV.1	286
Manuel:	Wilder than Winds or Waves thy self do'st rave.	370	M. BRIDE	IV.1	361
Manuel:	Nor she her self, nor any of her Mutes	372	M. BBIDE	V.1	3
Manuel:	How like thy self when Passion treads him down?	373	M. BBIDE	V.1	41
Zara:	When I've concluded on my self, if I	375	M. BBIDE	V.1	126
Zara:	Such Liberty as I embrace my self,	376	M. BBIDE	V.1	137
Zara:	Nay, came prepar'd my self to give thee Death--	380	M. BBIDE	V.2	V166

Self   (continued)

			PAGE	TITLE	ACT.SC	LINE
Mirabell:	She is more Mistress of her self, than to be under		396	WAY WORLD	I.1	43
Mirabell:	for it self, she'll breed no more.		397	WAY WORLD	I.1	63
Mirabell:	end I so us'd my self to think of 'em, that at length, contrary		399	WAY WORLD	I.1	168
Mirabell:	thou ought'st to be most asham'd thy Self, when thou hast		409	WAY WORLD	I.1	534
Marwood:	of ill usage; I think I shou'd do my self the violence of		411	WAY WORLD	II.1	55
Marwood:	do it my self I shall prevent your Baseness.		415	WAY WORLD	II.1	189
Marwood:	self and the whole treacherous World.		416	WAY WORLD	II.1	238
Witwoud:	O I have deny'd my self Airs to Day. I have walk'd		418	WAY WORLD	II.1	333
Millamant:	Madam, tho' 'tis against my self.		419	WAY WORLD	II.1	340
Millamant:	I please my self--Besides sometimes to		421	WAY WORLD	II.1	441
Millamant:	unless she shou'd tell me her self. Which of the two it		423	WAY WORLD	II.1	486
Waitwell:	her Preferment she forgets her self.		424	WAY WORLD	II.1	551
Mirabell:	Come Sir, will you endeavour to forget your self		424	WAY WORLD	II.1	552
Waitwell:	my self--Married, Knighted and attended all in one		424	WAY WORLD	II.1	555
Waitwell:	Familiarity with my former self; and fall from my Transformation		424	WAY WORLD	II.1	558
Lady Wish:	my self till I am pale again, there's no Veracity in me.		425	WAY WORLD	III.1	4
Lady Wish:	corrupt Integrity it self. If she has given him an Opportunity,		426	WAY WORLD	III.1	58
Foible:	disinherited. O you would bless your self, to hear what he		428	WAY WORLD	III.1	108
Foible:	I manag'd my self. I turn'd it all for the better. I told my		430	WAY WORLD	III.1	207
Lady Wish:	shou'd so forget my self--But I have such an Olio of		431	WAY WORLD	III.1	255
Sir Wilful:	write my self; no offence to any Body, I hope; and Nephew		438	WAY WORLD	III.1	511
Sir Wilful:	now you may set up for your self.		440	WAY WORLD	III.1	565
Millamant:	thoughtfull and would amuse my self,--bid him		446	WAY WORLD	IV.1	49
	(This while Millamant walks about Repeating to her self.)		446	WAY WORLD	IV.1	80
Mirabell:	lock your self up from me, to make my search more		449	WAY WORLD	IV.1	156
Mirabell:	but restrain your self to Native and Simple Tea-Table		451	WAY WORLD	IV.1	265
Petulant:	next time your self--I'll go sleep.		454	WAY WORLD	IV.1	370
Witwoud:	Do, rap thy self up like a Wood-louse and dream		454	WAY WORLD	IV.1	371
Lady Wish:	and Comport your self at this Rantipole rate.		455	WAY WORLD	IV.1	385
Lady Wish:	my self; tho' he has been a perfidious wretch to me.		458	WAY WORLD	IV.1	509
Lady Wish:	your Character, that I think my self oblig'd to let you		460	WAY WORLD	IV.1	586
Lady Wish:	Away, out, out, go set up for your self again		462	WAY WORLD	V.1	10
Lady Wish:	my self, and made you Governante of my whole Family.		462	WAY WORLD	V.1	21
Foible:	defend my self? O Madam, if you knew but what he promis'd		463	WAY WORLD	V.1	29
Mincing:	Foible; and wou'd have you hide your self in my Lady's		465	WAY WORLD	V.1	106
Lady Wish:	up all, my self and my all, my Neice and her all,--any		468	WAY WORLD	V.1	239
Fainall:	Well Madam; I have suffer'd my self to be overcome		468	WAY WORLD	V.1	250
Fainall:	Life; on condition you oblige your self never to Marry,		468	WAY WORLD	V.1	253
Fainall:	consider'd; I will only reserve to my self the Power to chuse		468	WAY WORLD	V.1	266
Fainall:	Contracting her self against your Consent or Knowledge;		469	WAY WORLD	V.1	283
Lady Wish:	Traytor,--I fear I cannot fortifie my self to support his		470	WAY WORLD	V.1	335
Sir Wilful:	self then.		471	WAY WORLD	V.1	377
Lady Wish:	Neice exerts a lawfull claim, having Match'd her self by		472	WAY WORLD	V.1	417
Mirabell:	For that Madam, give your self no trouble--let		477	WAY WORLD	V.1	577
Millamant:	me give my self to you over again.		477	WAY WORLD	V.1	595
Mirabell:	Madam, disquiet not your self on that account, to		478	WAY WORLD	V.1	613

Self-consuming (1)

Singer:	And feeding, wastes in Self-consuming Fires.		435	WAY WORLD	III.1	380

Self-content (1)

Cynthia:	If Happiness in Self-content is plac'd,		167	DOUBL DLR	III.1	633

Self-interest (1)

Maskwell:	Friendship to my Lord, and base Self-interest. Let me		188	DOUBL DLR	V.1	40

Self-Murder (1)

Garcia:	Self-Murder.		378	M. BRIDE	V.2	80

Selim (13)

	Perez and a Guard, and attended by Selim, and several		335	M. BRIDE	I.1	383
Heli:	Zara with Selim, Sir, I saw and know 'em:		344	M. BRIDE	II.2	197
	(Enter Zara attended by Selim.)		345	M. BRIDE	II.2	231
Zara:	The faithful Selim, and my Women know		347	M. BRIDE	II.2	291
	(Enter Zara, Perez, and Selim.)		358	M. BRIDE	III.1	375
	(A Room of State. Enter Zara, and Selim.)		361	M. BRIDE	IV.1	
Zara:	(aside to Selim). Ha! hear'st thou that? Is Osmyn then		363	M. BRIDE	IV.1	90
	(Exeunt Zara and Selim.)		366	M. BRIDE	IV.1	193
	(Enter Zara, and Selim.)		374	M. BRIDE	V.1	90
	(Enter Zara, follow'd by Selim, and Two Mutes bearing		379	M. BRIDE	V.2	130
	(Exit Selim.)		380	M. BRIDE	V.2	154
	(Enter Selim.)		380	M. BRIDE	V.2	172
Leonora:	Of Death, is this? The Eunuch Selim slain!		381	M. BRIDE	V.2	219

Sell (3)

Vainlove:	sell you freedom better cheap.		109	OLD BATCH	V.2	80
Mrs Fore:	Valentine's man, to sell his Master to us.		288	FOR LOVE	IV.1	466
Mrs Frail:	Sell him, how?		288	FOR LOVE	IV.1	467

Sellers (0)   see Brandy-sellers

Selling (4)

Scandal:	Yes, I have a Poet weighing Words, and selling		233	FOR LOVE	I.1	651
Scandal:	Who hopes to purchase Wealth, by selling Land;		234	FOR LOVE	I.1	680
Ben:	Lapland-Witch as soon, and live upon selling of contrary		264	FOR LOVE	III.1	426
Ben:	Lapland-Witch as soon, and live upon selling contrary		264	FOR LOVE	III.1	V426

Selves (15)

Heartwell:	Hook your selves have baited, but you are cloy'd with the		43	OLD BATCH	I.1	243
Lucy:	We, never are but by our selves betray'd.		62	OLD BATCH	III.1	57
Bellmour:	But give your selves the trouble to walk to that		107	OLD BATCH	V.1	401
Cynthia:	when you are together, but happy in your selves, and by		141	DOUBL DLR	II.1	98
Cynthia:	your selves.		141	DOUBL DLR	II.1	99
Maskwell:	Well, get your selves ready, and meet me in half		194	DOUBL DLR	V.1	238
Tattle:	acquit our selves--And for my part--But your		257	FOR LOVE	III.1	135
Valentine:	end, and let us think of leaving acting, and be our selves;		294	FOR LOVE	IV.1	708
Garcia:	Our selves, and expiate with our own his Blood.		378	M. BRIDE	V.2	67
Mirabell:	Are you? Pray then walk by your selves,--Let		409	WAY WORLD	I.1	523
Mrs Fain:	must find the means in our selves, and among our selves.		410	WAY WORLD	II.1	2
Mirabell:	selves prais'd; and to an Eccho the pleasure of hearing your		421	WAY WORLD	II.1	417

Selves (continued)

		PAGE	TITLE	ACT.SC	LINE
Mirabell:	selves talk.	421	WAY WORLD	II.1	418
Lady Wish:	and retire by our selves and be Shepherdesses. . . .	465	WAY WORLD	V.1	135

Sence (1)

Careless:	man must endure the noise of words without Sence, I think	127	DOUBL DLR	I.1	8

Senceless (2)

Araminta:	Still mystically senceless and impudent.--I find . .	88	OLD BATCH	IV.3	185
Mellefont:	By Heaven 'twere senceless not to be mad, and see . .	186	DOUEL DLR	IV.2	115

Send (24)

Barnaby:	I did; and Comfort will send Tribulation hither as soon .	76	OLD BATCH	IV.1	21
Lady Ply:	I'll send him to them, I know where he is-- . .	175	DOUEL DLR	IV.1	284
Brisk:	Sir Paul, will you send Careless into the Hall if you . .	175	DOUBL DLR	IV.1	286
Lord Touch:	I fear he's mad indeed--Let's send Maskwell . . .	187	DOUEL DLR	IV.2	135
Mellefont:	Send him, to her.	187	DOUEL DLR	IV.2	137
Maskwell:	observ'd.--I'll send the Chaplain to you with his Robes;	194	DOUEL DLR	V.1	241
Valentine:	Bid him come in: Mr. Trapland, send away your . . .	224	FOR LOVE	I.1	304
Nurse:	Pray Heav'n send your Worship good Luck, Marry . .	235	FOR LCVE	II.1	26
Foresight:	send your Son to Sea again. I'll wed my Daughter to an .	241	FOR LCVE	II.1	238
Scandal:	You'd better let him go, Sir; and send for him if there .	280	FOR LCVE	IV.1	189
Mrs Frail:	Do with him, send him to Sea again in the next . .	284	FOR LCVE	IV.1	306
Angelica:	or send, I am not to be spoken with.	297	FCR LCVE	V.1	10
Zara:	Shall send.	365	M. BRIDE	IV.1	164
Witwoud:	to the Door again in a trice; where he wou'd send in for .	405	WAY WORLD	I.1	374
Lady Wish:	--Hark! I hear her--Go you Thing and send her . .	426	WAY WORLD	III.1	61
Lady Wish:	--Hark! I hear her--(To Peg.) Go you Thing and send her .	426	WAY WCRLD	III.1	V 61
Lady Wish:	send for Robin frcm Lockets--Immediately. . . .	427	WAY WORLD	III.1	105
Sir Wilful:	thou nct know me, Friend? Why then send Somebody .	437	WAY WORLD	III.1	454
Lady Wish:	Ods my life, I'll send him to her. Call her down, . .	445	WAY WORLD	IV.1	37
Lady Wish:	Foible; bring her hither. I'll send him as I gc--When . .	445	WAY WORLD	IV.1	38
Foible:	Sir Wilfull is ccming, Madam. Shall I send Mr. Mirabell .	446	WAY WORLD	IV.1	58
Millamant:	Ay, if you please Foible, send him away,--Or send . .	446	WAY WCRLD	IV.1	60
Sir Wilful:	Marry'd, say the Word, and send for the Piper, Wilfull .	455	WAY WCRLD	IV.1	411

Sending (3)

Bellmour:	talks of sending for Mr. Spintext to keep me Company; but	39	OLD BATCH	I.1	83
Lord Froth:	sending it to and again so often, this is the seventh time	166	DOUEL DLR	III.1	610
Mellefont:	temper can contain? They talk of sending Maskwell to . .	187	DOUEL DLR	IV.2	148

Sends (1)

Valentine:	hears is Landed; whereupon he very affectionately sends .	225	FCR LOVE	I.1	334

Seneca (1)

Jeremy:	Board-Wages. Does your Epictetus, or your Seneca here, .	217	FOR LCVE	I.1	26

Sense (33)   see Sence

Sharper:	She had need have a good share of sense, tc manage. . .	42	OLD BATCH	I.1	208
Mellefont:	keep up good Humcur and Sense in the Company, prithee .	128	DOUEL DLR	I.1	47
Mellefont:	There are times when Sense may be unseasonable, as well as	129	DOUEL DLR	I.1	70
Careless:	think thou hast no more Sense, than to get an Heir upon her	130	DOUEL DLR	I.1	120
Mellefont:	Sense, and has an old fond Husband.	130	DOUEL DLR	I.1	130
Lord Froth:	Well and how? hee! what is your sense of the	162	DOUEL DLR	III.1	469
Valentine:	Sense, and ycu are a Fool.	217	FOR LCVE	I.1	39
Jeremy:	Young Maids, nct to prefer Poetry to gcod Sense; or . .	219	FOR LCVE	I.1	113
Scandal:	vain! Who would die a Martyr to Sense in a Country . .	219	FOR LCVE	I.1	139
Scandal:	his Exaltation of madness into the road of ccmmon Sense, .	278	FOR LCVE	IV.1	106
Angelica:	am I deluded by this Interval of Sense, to reason with a .	295	FCB LCVE	IV.1	729
Angelica:	reascnable Stock of good Nature and Sense--For I . .	299	FOR LCVE	V.1	63
	To start a Jest, or force a little Sense.	323	M. BRIDE	PRO.	20
Heli:	This living Light, could to my Soul, or Sense	338	M. BRIDE	II.1	7
Almeria:	As hurries all my Soul, and dozes my weak Sense. . . .	343	M. BRIDE	II.2	155
Almeria:	It hurries all my Soul, and stuns my Sense.	343	M. BRIDE	II.2	V155
Osmyn-Alph:	O impotence of Sight! Mechanick Sense, ...	345	M. BRIDE	II.2	V217
Osmyn-Alph:	Mechanick Sense, which to exteriour Objects, ...	345	M. BRIDE	II.2	218
Osmyn-Alph:	And waking to the World and mortal Sense, ...	353	M. BRIDE	III.1	134
Osmyn-Alph:	And thy excessive Love distracts my Sense!	356	M. BRIDE	III.1	281
Manuel:	Watch her returning Sense, and bring me Word: . . .	370	M. BRIDE	IV.1	365
Gonsalez:	And deludes your Sense. Alphonso, if living, ...	370	M. BRIDE	IV.1	376
Zara:	To grate the Sense, when entred here; from Groans, . .	379	M. BRIDE	V.2	136
Zara:	Of Sense: His Soul still sees, and knows each Purpose, .	381	M. BRIDE	V.2	196
Osmyn-Alph:	O let me talk to thy reviving Sense, ...	383	M. BRIDE	V.2	280
Almeria:	That Sense, which in one Instant shews him dead . . .	383	M. BRIDE	V.2	294
	Who, to assert their Sense, your Taste arraign. . . .	393	WAY WORLD	PRO.	28
Petulant:	If I do, will you grant me common Sense then, for . .	407	WAY WORLD	I.1	458
Mirabell:	But hast not thou then Sense enough to know that . .	409	WAY WORLD	I.1	533
Mrs Fain:	While they are Lovers, if they have Fire and Sense, their .	410	WAY WORLD	II.1	4
Marwood:	of Wit, but to blind her Affair with a Lover of Sense. If .	433	WAY WORLD	III.1	313
Petulant:	Witwoud--You are an anihilator of sense.	453	WAY WORLD	IV.1	345
Mirabell:	If a deep sense of the many Injuries I have offer'd to .	471	WAY WCRLD	V.1	366

Senseless (6)   see Senceless

Silvia:	Senseless Creature, I meant my Vainlove.	61	OLD BATCH	III.1	6
Lucy:	senseless indifference. By this Light I could have spit in	61	OLD BATCH	III.1	19
Singer:	Baffled and senseless, tir'd her Arms.	71	OLD BATCH	III.2	V 24
Almeria:	What then am I? Am I more senseless grown	326	M. BRIDE	I.1	6
Manuel:	Thy senseless Vow appear'd to bear its Date, ...	333	M. BRIDE	I.1	299
Mirabell:	Countenance, with your senseless Ribaldry; which you .	409	WAY WORLD	I.1	525

Senses (17)

Araminta:	to their Senses.	106	OLD BATCH	V.1	359
Lady Ply:	change upon hearing--hearing is one of the Senses, .	147	DOUEL DLR	II.1	340
Lady Ply:	and all the Senses are fallible; I won't trust my Honour, I	147	DOUBL DLR	II.1	341
Scandal:	Twelve Caesars, paultry Copies; and the Five Senses, as ill	232	FCR LCVE	I.1	602
Valentine:	Affections, Appetites, Senses, and the huge Train of . .	244	FOR LOVE	II.1	341
Angelica:	he won't recover his Senses till I lose mine.	277	FOR LOVE	IV.1	76
Sr Sampson:	--Mad, I'll make him find his Senses.	279	FOR LCVE	IV.1	146
Buckram:	he recover his Senses.	280	FOR LCVE	IV.1	186
Ben:	has turn'd her senses, her Brain is quite overset. Well-a-day,	286	FOR LOVE	IV.1	404
Ben:	senses, d'ee see; for ought as I perceive I'm like to be finely	286	FOR LOVE	IV.1	414
Mrs Fore:	revoking. And if he should recover his Senses, he'll be .	288	FOR LOVE	IV.1	474
Tattle:	Figure, with Youth and Health, and all his five Senses in .	291	FOR LCVE	IV.1	582

Serpent's (1)

Maskwell:	me to cheat 'em; and if they will not hear the Serpent's	194	DOUEL DLR	V.1	264

Serv'd (8)

Capt Bluff:	Oh excuse me Sir; have you serv'd abroad Sir?	52	OLD BATCH	II.1	185
Vainlove:	Deity, he must be serv'd by Prayer.	58	OLD BATCH	II.2	141
Belinda:	Company, and at last serv'd up cold to the Wife.	106	OLD BATCH	V.1	377
Araminta:	serv'd.	109	OLD BATCH	V.2	62
Maskwell:	It will be the first you have so serv'd.	195	DOUEL DLR	V.1	300
Jeremy:	serv'd Valentine Legend Esq; and that he is not now turn'd	218	FOR LCVE	I.1	68
Zara:	Of Sceptres, Crowns, and Thrones; they've serv'd their	347	M. BRIDE	II.2	319
Sir Wilful:	Fops; where, I suppose, you have serv'd your Time; and	440	WAY WCRLD	III.1	564

Servant (55)

Sharper:	O your Servant Sir, you are safe then it seems; 'tis an	48	OLD BATCH	II.1	32
Sir Joseph:	and gratitude of your superabundant humble Servant	49	OLD BATCH	II.1	68
Sharper:	Sir ycur humble Servant--I don't question but you	49	OLD BATCH	II.1	87
Sharper:	Sir your Servant, but you are misinform'd, for	51	OLD BATCH	II.1	158
Capt Bluff:	done but an humble Servant of ycurs, that shall be nameless,	52	OLD BATCH	II.1	198
	A Servant introducing Bellmour in Fanatick Habit, with a	80	OLD BATCH	IV.2	
	(Exit Servant.)	80	OLD BATCH	IV.2	3
Bellmour:	Letter was deliver'd to me by a Servant, in the Morning:	82	OLD BATCH	IV.2	52
Sharper:	Ladies, your humble Servant.--We were	86	OLD BATCH	IV.3	114
Lady Touch:	Were you not in the nature of a Servant, and have not I in	136	DOUEL DLR	I.1	348
Brisk:	I'm everlastingly your humble Servant, Deuce take	140	DOUEL DLR	II.1	93
Lord Froth:	O your humble Servant for that, dear Madam;	141	DOUEL DLR	II.1	109
Brisk:	I'm your Humble Servant, let me perish.--I	142	DOUEL DLR	II.1	136
Sir Paul:	Your humble Servant, I am I thank Heaven in a	160	DOUEL DLR	III.1	383
Brisk:	My Lady Froth! Your Ladyships most humble Servant;	175	DOUEL DLR	IV.1	313
Maskwell:	Lordship's Servant.	181	DOUEL DLR	IV.1	539
Brisk:	My Lord, your humble Servant; Sir Paul yours,--	201	DOUEL DLR	V.1	517
	(A Roon in Foresight's House. Foresight and Servant.)	235	FOR LOVE	II.1	
	(Exit Servant.)	236	FOR LCVE	II.1	43
	(Enter Servant.)	239	FOR LCVE	II.1	159
	(Exit Angelica and Servant.)	239	FOR LCVE	II.1	163
Sr Sampson:	your Friend and Servant--Come Brother Foresight.	246	FOR LCVE	II.1	404
	(Enter Sir Sampson, Mrs. Frail, Miss Prue, and Servant.)	259	FOR LCVE	III.1	209
	(Exit Servant.)	259	FOR LCVE	III.1	216
	(Enter Ben. Legend and Servant.)	260	FOR LCVE	III.1	267
Mrs Fore:	Clock. Mr. Scandal, your Servant--	268	FOR LCVE	III.1	577
Scandal:	she cou'd grant 'em.--Madam, I'm your humble Servant,	284	FOR LCVE	IV.1	337
Tattle:	Ay; 'tis well enough for a Servant to be bred at an	302	FOR LCVE	V.1	186
Foresight:	O, Mr. Tattle, your Servant, you are a close Man;	304	FOR LCVE	V.1	256
	(Enter a Servant.)	398	WAY WORLD	I.1	110
	(Exit Servant.)	398	WAY WCRLD	I.1	133
Mirabell:	Waitwell, my Servant.	417	WAY WCRLD	II.1	285
Mrs Fain:	He is an humble Servant to Foible my Mcthers	417	WAY WCRLD	II.1	286
Mirabell:	Waitwell and Foible. I wou'd not tempt my Servant	417	WAY WCRLD	II.1	291
Foible:	O dear Sir, your humble Servant.	424	WAY WORLD	II.1	536
Foible:	haste home and prevent her. Your Servant Sir. B'w'y	424	WAY WORLD	II.1	547
Foible:	remove my Lady's Toilet. Madam your Servant. My Lady	430	WAY WORLD	III.1	219
Millamant:	Man--Marwood, your Servant.	432	WAY WCRLD	III.1	285
	Servant to Lady Wishfort.)	436	WAY WCRLD	III.1	444
	(Exit Servant.)	437	WAY WCRLD	III.1	472
Witwoud:	Odso Brother, is it you? Your Servant Brother.	439	WAY WORLD	III.1	520
Sir Wilful:	Your Servant! Why yours, Sir. Your Servant	439	WAY WORLD	III.1	521
Sir Wilful:	again--'Sheart, and your Friend and Servant to that--	439	WAY WORLD	III.1	522
Sir Wilful:	Aunt, your Servant.	441	WAY WORLD	III.1	594
Painall:	Sir Wilfull, your most faithful Servant.	441	WAY WORLD	III.1	595
Lady Wish:	Cousin Witwoud, your Servant; Mr. Petulant,	441	WAY WORLD	III.1	597
Lady Wish:	your Servant.--Nephew, you are welcome again.	441	WAY WORLD	III.1	598
Sir Wilful:	your Servant.	447	WAY WORLD	IV.1	86
Sir Wilful:	Anan? Cozen, your Servant.	447	WAY WORLD	IV.1	100
Sir Wilful:	Yes,--your Servant. No offence I hope, Cozen.	447	WAY WOBLD	IV.1	102
Sir Wilful:	your Servant--I think this door's lock'd.	448	WAY WORLD	IV.1	147
Sir Wilful:	Your Servant, then with your leave I'll return	448	WAY WORLD	IV.1	149
Sir Wilful:	Aunt, your Servant.	470	WAY WORLD	V.1	311
Mirabell:	I have sent my Servant for it, and will deliver it to you,	472	WAY WORLD	V.1	406

Servants (6)

Bellmour:	the Servants. Very good! Then I must be disguised--With	39	OLD BATCH	I.1	89
Bellmour:	your Servants, and was conducted hither. I pretended a	94	OLD BATCH	IV.4	210
Sir Paul:	O, sweet Sir, you load your humble Servants, both	159	DOUEL DLR	III.1	325
Mellefont:	Host of Hell her Servants;	186	DOUEL DLR	IV.2	124
	(Servants seize him.)	203	DOUEL DLR	V.1	V577
Angelica:	to write poor innocent Servants Names in Blood, about a	238	FOR LCVE	II.1	109

Serve (23)

Bellmour:	Poor Rogue. Any hour of the day or night will serve her--	40	OLD BATCH	I.1	116
Sharper:	unless it be to serve my particular Friend, as Sir				
	Jcseph here,	51	OLD EATCH	II.1	159
Heartwell:	Now by my Soul, I cannot lie, though it were to serve a	72	OLD EATCH	III.2	59
Lucy:	easie Nature.--Well, For once I'll venture tc serve	98	OLD EATCH	V.1	75
Setter:	Captain, I wou'd do any thing to serve you; but this	104	OLD BATCH	V.1	274
Valentine:	serve his Friend in Distress, tho' I say it to his face.				
	Come,	223	FOR LCVE	I.1	262
Scandal:	No, their Titles shall serve.	230	FOR LOVE	I.1	533
Mrs Frail:	How de'e you, Sir? Can I serve you?	290	FOR LCVE	IV.1	545
Sr Sampson:	Words. Odd, I have warm Blood about me yet, I can serve	298	FOR LOVE	V.1	23
Sr Sampson:	Words. Odd, I have warm Blood about me yet, and can serve	298	FOR LCVE	V.1	V 23
Ben:	it will only serve to light up a Match for some body else.	308	FOR LCVE	V.1	411
Selim:	But to serve you. I have already thought.	362	M. BRIDE	IV.1	40
Gonsalez:	Yet stay, I would--but go; anon will serve--	371	M. BRIDE	IV.1	425
Selim:	Devis'd to serve, should ruine your Design!	375	M. BRIDE	V.1	115
Mirabell:	Woman wou'd be odious, serve but to make her more	399	WAY WORLD	I.1	162
Millamant:	know why--They serve one to pin up one's Hair.	419	WAY WORLD	II.1	362
Petulant:	And the Wind serve.	440	WAY WOBLD	III.1	569
Sir Wilful:	Serve or not serve, I shant ask License of you, Sir;	440	WAY WORLD	III.1	570
Marwood:	done. I am sorry my Zeal to serve your Ladyship and	466	WAY WORLD	V.1	162
Mirabell:	be it as it may. I am resolv'd I'll serve you, you shall not	474	WAY WORLD	V.1	460

Serve (continued)
```
    Mirabell:    inscrib'd on the back may serve your occasions.  . . . .  476  WAY WORLD   V.1  549
    Mirabell:    written on the back may serve your occasions.   . . . .  476  WAY WORLD   V.1 V549
Served (4)      see Serv'd
    Mellefont:   None, Hell has served you even as Heaven has  . . . . .  185  DOUBL DLR  IV.2   59
    Maskwell:    him, and that, I have recall'd; so I have served my self,  188  DOUBL DLR   V.1   24
    Maskwell:    and what is yet better, I have served a worthy Lord to  .  188  DOUBL DLR   V.1   25
    Lady Touch:  ought to be served; making you a Beast. Don't you know  .  192  DOUBL DLR   V.1  165
Serves (1)
    Mirabell:    and like the faint Offer of a latter Spring, serves but to  418  WAY WORLD  II.1  319
Service (28)
    Bellmour:    our Afternoon Service to our Mistresses; I find I am  . .   40  OLD BATCH   I.1  132
    Bellmour:    quit the Service. . . . . . . . . . . . . . . . . . .   47  OLD BATCH   I.1  373
    Sharper:     Methought the service I did you last night Sir, in  . . .   48  OLD BATCH  II.1   47
    Sharper:     me to lose what was ventur'd in your service; Nay 'twas  .   50  OLD BATCH  II.1  101
    Bellmour:    world of Love in your Service, that you think you can  . .   58  OLD BATCH  II.2  123
    Mellefont:   this Juncture it will do me Service.--I'll tell you, I  . .  129  DOUBL DLR   I.1   67
    Mellefont:   It is so. Well, the Service that you are to do me,  . . .  130  DOUBL DLR   I.1  124
    Mellefont:   It is so. Well, the Service you are to do me,  . . . . .  130  DOUBL DLR   I.1 V124
    Mellefont:   to do me Service; and he endeavours to be well in her  . .  131  DOUBL DLR   I.1  156
    Maskwell:    Ladyships Service. . . . . . . . . . . . . . .  135  DOUBL DLR   I.1  302
    Maskwell:    With your Ladyships help, and for your Service,  . . . .  135  DOUBL DLR   I.1  313
    Maskwell:    Rogue still, to do you Service; and you are flinging  . .  136  DOUBL DLR   I.1  337
    Valentine:   my Service to you,--fill, fill, to honest Mr. Trapland,  .  222  FOR LOVE    I.1  243
    Trapland:    --my Service to you Mr. Scandal--(Drinks)--I  . . . . .  222  FOR LOVE    I.1  246
    Valentine:   me Signal Service in my necessity. But you delight in  . .  223  FOR LOVE    I.1  259
    Tattle:      I have a pretty good Collection at your Service, some  . .  232  FOR LOVE    I.1  599
    Sr Sampson:  press you to the service? . . . . . . . . . . . .  244  FOR LOVE   II.1  332
    Sr Sampson:  and press you to the service? . . . . . . . . . .  244  FOR LOVE   II.1 V332
    Scandal:     Service of your Sex. He that first cries out stop Thief, is  272  FOR LOVE  III.1  698
    Buckram:     Sir, I can do you no Service while he's in this  . . . .  280  FOR LOVE   IV.1  183
    Jeremy:      extraordinary Passion for your Honour's Service.  . . .  301  FOR LOVE    V.1  169
    Gonsalez:    I think thou would'st not stop to do me Service.  . . . .  371  M. BRIDE   IV.1  427
    Perez:       My Service has not merited those Titles. . . . . . . .  374  M. BRIDE    V.1   68
    Manuel:      Dar'st thou reply? Take that--thy Service? thine?  . . .  374  M. BRIDE    V.1   69
    Sir Wilful:  And a--(puff) and a flap Dragon for your Service, Sir:  .  439  WAY WORLD III.1  523
    Sir Wilful:  And a Hare's Foot, and a Hare's Scut for your Service, Sir;  439  WAY WORLD III.1  524
    Mincing:     service, be what it will. . . . . . . . . . . .  465  WAY WORLD   V.1  122
    Mirabell:    Volunteer in this Action, for our Service, and now designs  477  WAY WORLD   V.1  580
Services (4)
    Bellmour:    our Afternoon Services to our Mistresses; I find I am  . .   40  OLD BATCH   I.1 V132
    Manuel:      No more; my Promise long since pass'd, thy Services,  . .  334  M. BRIDE    I.1 V340
    Manuel:      In me, that can be worthy so great Services? . . . . .  365  M. BRIDE   IV.1  158
    Mirabell:    made me a Compensation for all my Services;--But  . . .  474  WAY WORLD   V.1  459
Servile (1)
    Scandal:     more servile, timorous, and fawning, than any I have  . .  220  FOR LOVE    I.1  147
Serving (2)      see Cast-serving-man
    Maskwell:    could have contriv'd to make me capable of serving you,  .  157  DOUBL DLR III.1  245
    Lady Touch:  Where she's serving you, as all your Sex  . . . . . .  192  DOUBL DLR   V.1  164
Set (56)
    Bellmour:    that which he likes best; 'tis his diversion to Set, 'tis
                 mine  . . . . . . . . . . . . . . . . . . .   43  OLD BATCH   I.1  224
    Belinda:     one Scene of Address, a Lover, set out with all his Equipage   55  OLD BATCH  II.2   32
    Araminta:    upon the least displeasure you forsake, and set up new  .   58  OLD BATCH  II.2  147
    Bellmour:    for my Speech, and set it at liberty--Tho' I, confess,  .   60  OLD BATCH  II.2  219
    Lucy:        as his Love. Therefore e'n set your Heart at rest, and  .   61  OLD BATCH III.1    8
    Setter:      And therefore you'd have him to set in your Ladies  . . .   67  OLD BATCH III.1  228
    Bellmour:    Now set we forward on a Journey for Life:--  . . . . .  112  OLD BATCH   V.2  182
    Lord Froth:  Mr. Brisk, my Coach shall set you down.  . . . . . .  202  DOUBL DLR   V.1  554
    Jeremy:      Trade, if he had set up in the City--For my part, I never  .  218  FOR LOVE    I.1   91
    Valentine:   and as you set up for Defamation, he is a mender  . . .  226  FOR LOVE    I.1  366
    Scandal:     there are some set out in their true Colours, both Men and  233  FOR LOVE    I.1  627
    Foresight:   And when the Head is set in Grond,  . . . . . . . .  236  FOR LOVE   II.1   55
    Nurse:       and tuck you up, and set the Candle, and your Tobacco-Box,  238  FOR LOVE   II.1  103
                          (Set by Mr. John Eccles.)  . . . . .  258  FOR LOVE  III.1  199
    Valentine:   Sphere: when he Rises I must set--Besides, if I shou'd stay,  259  FOR LOVE  III.1  224
    Sr Sampson:  Rogue's sharp set, coming from Sea, if he should not stay  .  265  FOR LOVE  III.1  459
    Sr Sampson:  To a Minute, to a Second; thou shalt set thy  . . . . .  266  FOR LOVE  III.1  473
                          (Set by Mr. John Eccles.)  . . . . .  274  FOR LOVE  III.1  757
    Scandal:     can Dream as much to the purpose as another, if I set about  275  FOR LOVE  III.1  814
    Sr Sampson:  shalt have it as soon as thou hast set thy Hand to another  282  FOR LOVE   IV.1  234
    Valentine:   and can set him right--Hearkee, Friend, the straight  . .  282  FOR LOVE   IV.1  252
    Mrs Frail:   inhumane merciless Creature have I set my heart upon?  . .  286  FOR LOVE   IV.1  393
    Ben:         how shall I do to set her to rights. . . . . . . . .  286  FOR LOVE   IV.1  405
                          (Set by Mr. Finger.)  . . . . . . .  293  FOR LOVE   IV.1  651
    Angelica:    Beaus, that set a good Face upon Fifty, Fifty! I have  . .  298  FOR LOVE    V.1   30
    Miss Prue:   now my Mind is set upon a Man, I will have a Man some  . .  305  FOR LOVE    V.1  307
                 That you have only set us up, to leave us.  . . . . .  316  FOR LOVE   EPI.   39
    Osmyn-Alph:  What neither can bestow. Set free your self,  . . . . .  348  M. BRIDE   II.2  329
    Zara:        He should be set at large; thence sprung his Insolence,  .  349  M. BRIDE   II.2 V379
    Osmyn-Alph:  By him set down; when his pure Thoughts were born  . . .  353  M. BRIDE  III.1  129
    Zara:        I'm angry: you're deceiv'd. I came to set  . . . . . .  360  M. BRIDE  III.1  417
    Gonsalez:    To set him free? Ay, now 'tis plain; O well  . . . . .  371  M. BRIDE   IV.1  413
    Manuel:      Where she sets down--(reading) still will I set thee  . .  374  M. BRIDE    V.1   52
    Manuel:      (reading).--And still will I set  . . . . . . . . .  374  M. BRIDE    V.1   59
    Manuel:      'Tis well--that when she comes to set him free,  . . . .  374  M. BRIDE    V.1   77
    Zara:        Let 'em set down the Bowls, and warn Alphonso  . . . .  380  M. BRIDE    V.2  149
    Fainall:     and t'other set your Teeth on edge; one is all Pulp, and  .  401  WAY WORLD   I.1  214
    Fainall:     Ties, when set in Competition with your Love to me.  . .  414  WAY WORLD  II.1  181
    Mrs Fain:    without Bounds, and wou'd you set Limits to that Aversion,  417  WAY WORLD  II.1  262
    Lady Wish:   See who that is-- (One knocks.) Set down the Bottle  . . .  425  WAY WORLD III.1   33
    Marwood:     of one Set of Acquaintance, tho' never so good, as we are of  432  WAY WORLD III.1  300
                          (Set by Mr. John Eccles,  . . . . .  434  WAY WORLD III.1  374
    Sir Wilful:  now you may set up for your self.  . . . . . . . . .  440  WAY WORLD III.1  565
    Fainall:     I'll set his hand in.  . . . . . . . . . . . . .  443  WAY WORLD III.1  673
    Foible:      Sir Wilfull is set in to Drinking, Madam, in the Parlour. .  445  WAY WORLD  IV.1   36
```

Set   (continued)
Sir Wilful:	that--for if so be that I set on't, I'll do't. But only				
	for the	447	WAY WORLD	IV.1	84
Lady Wish:	Away, out, out, go set up for your self again	462	WAY WORLD	V.1	10
Foible:	friends together, than set 'em at distance. But Mrs. Marwood	464	WAY WORLD	V.1	88
Mincing:	Mirabell is with her, he has set your Spouse at liberty Mrs.	464	WAY WORLD	V.1	105
Lady Wish:	What, a Whore? And thought it excommunication to set	467	WAY WORLD	V.1	204
Fainall:	must set your Hand till more sufficient Deeds can be	469	WAY WORLD	V.1	292
Sir Wilful:	--'Sheart, I'll call him in,--an I set on't	471	WAY WORLD	V.1	351
Witwoud:	Ay I do, my hand I remember--Petulant set his	475	WAY WORLD	V.1	525
Sir Wilful:	to see Foreign Parts--I have set on't--And when I'm set	477	WAY WORLD	V.1	585
	Set up for Spys on Plays and finding Fault.	479	WAY WORLD	EPI.	15

Setled (1)
Mrs Frail:	the Estate be setled; for you know, Marrying without an	273	FOR LOVE	III.1	719

Sets (8)
Sharper:	That's because he always sets out in foul Weather,	42	OLD BATCH	I.1	201
Heartwell:	The youthful Beast sets forth, and neighs aloud.	112	OLD BATCH	V.2	187
Maskwell:	Bonds of Friendship, and sets Men right upon their first	150	DOUBL DLR	II.1	444
Lady Froth:	His fare is paid him, and he sets in Milk.	164	DOUBL DLR	III.1	541
Scandal:	of secrets, another Vertue that he sets up for in the same	226	FOR LOVE	I.1	369
Sr Sampson:	sets at Noon-day.	241	FOR LOVE	II.1	209
Osmyn-Alph:	It sets a Debt of that Account before me,	347	M. BRIDE	II.2	289
Manuel:	Where she sets down--(reading) still will I set thee	374	M. BRIDE	V.1	52

Setter (29)
Bellmour:	get your Man Setter to provide my Disguise.	40	OLD BATCH	I.1	112
	(Enter Setter.)	64	OLD BATCH	III.1	115
Bellmour:	Trusty Setter what tidings? How goes the project?	64	OLD BATCH	III.1	116
Bellmour:	A good hearing, Setter.	64	OLD BATCH	III.1	119
Setter:	Setter what a treasure is here lost for want of being known.	65	OLD BATCH	III.1	153
	(The Street Enter Bellmour in Fanatick habit, Setter.)	75	OLD BATCH	IV.1	
Bellmour:	Well and how Setter hae, does my Hypocrisy fit me hae?	75	OLD BATCH	IV.1	3
	(Enter Bellmour in Fanatick Habit, and Setter.)	96	OLD BATCH	V.1	
Bellmour:	Setter! Well encounter'd.	96	OLD BATCH	V.1	1
Bellmour:	made a delicious Voyage, Setter; and might have rode at	96	OLD BATCH	V.1	5
Bellmour:	Setter.) Pox take 'em, they stand just in my Way.	97	OLD BATCH	V.1	12
	(Enter Vainlove, Sharper and Setter.)	98	OLD BATCH	V.1	81
Sharper:	Experiment. But honest Setter, here, over-heard you with	100	OLD BATCH	V.1	145
Bellmour:	Mr. Setter will assist--	100	OLD BATCH	V.1	158
Sharper:	purpose. Setter, stand close; seem not to observe 'em; and,	101	OLD BATCH	V.1	164
Sharper:	(To Setter.)	102	OLD BATCH	V.1	214
Setter:	--Avaunt Temptation.--Setter, shew thy self a	102	OLD BATCH	V.1	226
Sir Joseph:	Setter. Nay, I'll take you at your Word.	103	OLD BATCH	V.1	237
Sir Joseph:	be done. What--Come, Mr. Setter, I have over-heard all,	103	OLD BATCH	V.1	243
Sir Joseph:	And how, and how, good Setter, did the little	103	OLD BATCH	V.1	253
Sir Joseph:	Garter, when she was thinking of her Love. Heh, Setter.	103	OLD BATCH	V.1	258
	(While Sir Joseph reads, Bluffe whispers Setter.)	103	OLD BATCH	V.1	273
Capt Bluff:	--I'm capitulating with Mr. Setter for you.	104	OLD BATCH	V.1	280
Sir Joseph:	Ah, honest Setter.--Sirrah, I'll give thee any	104	OLD BATCH	V.1	281
	(Setter Entering.)	105	OLD BATCH	V.1	329
Boy:	There was a Man too that fetch'd 'em out:--Setter, I	107	OLD BATCH	V.2	2
	Setter.)	110	OLD BATCH	V.2	96
Sir Joseph:	Ah! O Lord, my heart akes--Ah! Setter, a	110	OLD BATCH	V.2	118
Bellmour:	you an Appetite to see us fall to before ye. Setter, Did	112	OLD BATCH	V.2	178

Setting (5)
Setter:	'Tis but setting her Mill a-going, and I can drein her of	99	OLD BATCH	V.1	105
Cynthia:	become more Conspicuous by setting off one another.	142	DOUBL DLR	II.1	152
Angelica:	What, are you setting up for good Nature?	254	FOR LOVE	III.1	35
Jenny:	setting his Cravat and Wig.	297	FOR LOVE	V.1	4
Petulant:	Hang'd. The Ordinary's paid for setting the Psalm, and	436	WAY WORLD	III.1	430

Settl'd (1)
Sir Wilful:	told you, Madam--Yes, I have settl'd my Concerns,	440	WAY WORLD	III.1	573

Settle (7)
Careless:	her Father Sir Paul Plyant, come to settle the				
	Writings, this	129	DOUBL DLR	I.1	81
Lord Touch:	Ladys, and Drink a Dish of Tea, to settle our Heads.	132	DOUBL DLR	I.1	217
Lord Touch:	Ladies, and Drink a Dish of Tea, to settle our Heads.	132	DOUBL DLR	I.1	V217
Sir Paul:	end--He? A brave Chopping Boy.--I'll settle a Thousand	173	DOUBL DLR	IV.1	224
Lady Ply:	I'll settle the Accounts to your Advantage.	174	DOUBL DLR	IV.1	265
Lady Ply:	I'll settle Accounts to your Advantage.	174	DOUBL DLR	IV.1	V265
Fainall:	is your Apothecary. Next, my Wife shall settle on me the	469	WAY WORLD	V.1	268

Settled (2)   see Setled, Settl'd
Maskwell:	me out a Villain, settled in possession of a fair Estate,				
	and	190	DOUBL DLR	V.1	86
Manuel:	But rules with settled Sway in Zara's Eyes.	337	M. BRIDE	I.1	461

Settlement (6)   see Sham-Settlement
Careless:	Body to Disinherit thy self: for as I take it this				
	Settlement	130	DOUBL DLR	I.1	121
Sr Sampson:	draw up Writings of Settlement and Joynture--All shall	240	FOR LOVE	II.1	194
Mrs Fore:	glad at least to make you a good Settlement.--Here they	288	FOR LOVE	IV.1	475
Sr Sampson:	--Body o' me, I have a Trick to turn the Settlement	300	FOR LOVE	V.1	127
Fainall:	Wife to Grass--I have already a deed of Settlement of the	444	WAY WORLD	III.1	709
Mirabell:	pretended Settlement of the greatest part of her fortune--	476	WAY WORLD	V.1	538

Settlements (2)
Mellefont:	Portion, Settlements and Joyntures.	168	DOUBL DLR	IV.1	30
Jeremy:	which her Vanity had preferr'd to Settlements, without a	219	FOR LOVE	I.1	109

Sev'n (1)
Jeremy:	Name, has for the space of Sev'n Years truly and faithfully	218	FOR LOVE	I.1	67

Sev'ral (1)
	I've leisure, now, to mark your sev'ral Faces,	385	M. BRIDE	EPI.	5

Seven (1)
Setter:	time this Seven Years.	111	OLD BATCH	V.2	143

Seventh (1)
Lord Froth:	sending it to and again so often, this is the seventh time	166	DOUBL DLR	III.1	610

Sever'd (2)
Alonzo:	Sever'd the Head; and in a Corner of	379	M. BRIDE	V.2	115
Alonzo:	Sever'd the Head; and in an obscure Corner	379	M. BRIDE	V.2	V115

		PAGE	TITLE	ACT.SC	LINE
Several (7)	see Sev'ral				
	Several Books upon the Table.)	216	FOR LOVE	I.1	
Valentine:	And yet you have convers'd with several.	227	FOR LOVE	I.1	408
Tattle:	O Lord! yes indeed, Madam, several times.	255	FOR LOVE	III.1	79
Scandal:	Yes, several, very honest;--they'll cheat a little at	271	FOR LOVE	III.1	666
Tattle:	So 'tis, faith--I might have sav'd several others	303	FOR LOVE	V.1	212
	Garcia and several Officers. Files of Prisoners in Chains,	332	M. BRIDE	I.1	266
	Perez and a Guard, and attended by Selim, and several	335	M. BRIDE	I.1	383
Severally (2)					
	(Enter Mellefont and Maskwell severally.)	181	DOUBL DLR	IV.1	512
	(Exeunt, severally.)	183	DOUBL DLR	IV.1	592
Severe (7)					
Maskwell:	My Duty to your Lordship, makes me do a severe	183	DOUBL DLR	IV.1	588
Tattle:	Oh Madam; you are too severe upon Miss; you must	249	FOR LOVE	II.1	534
Witwoud:	be very severe.	409	WAY WORLD	I.1	521
Petulant:	Enough, I'm in a Humour to be severe.	409	WAY WORLD	I.1	522
Mirabell:	you have been severe.	409	WAY WORLD	I.1	528
Lady Wish:	the most minute Particle of severe Vertue? Is it possible	465	WAY WORLD	V.1	142
Marwood:	'Tis severe indeed Madam, that you shou'd	469	WAY WORLD	V.1	300
Severest (1)					
Lady Touch:	can you doubt these streaming Eyes? Keep the severest	185	DOUBL DLR	IV.2	81
Severity (3)					
Angelica:	Man, submits both to the Severity and insolent Conduct of	299	FOR LOVE	V.1	73
Angelica:	Man is a Slave to the Severity and insolent Conduct of	299	FOR LOVE	V.1 V	73
Lady Wish:	alliance,--We may unbend the severity of Decorum	457	WAY WORLD	IV.1	488
Sex (22)					
Bellmour:	Sex.	41	OLD BATCH	I.1	175
Sharper:	all the Sex.	41	OLD BATCH	I.1	177
Sharper:	He! he hates the Sex.	44	OLD BATCH	I.1	283
Araminta:	your Sex--Who's there? (Calls.)	58	OLD BATCH	II.2	155
Heartwell:	of thy Sex, if their Fools are not known by this Party-coloured	73	OLD BATCH	III.2	77
Silvia:	to our Sex is as natural as swimming to a Negro; we	75	OLD BATCH	III.2	151
Lucy:	charm our Sex conspire to please you.	75	OLD BATCH	III.2	161
Araminta:	and Malice of thy Sex, thou canst not lay a Blemish on	87	OLD BATCH	IV.3	168
Careless:	Lady! that is the envy of her Sex, and the admiration of	160	DOUBL DLR	III.1	381
Careless:	Lady! that is the envy of her own Sex, and the admiration of	160	DOUBL DLR	III.1	V381
Lady Touch:	Where she's serving you, as all your Sex	192	DOUBL DLR	V.1	164
Scandal:	trusted; a Satyrical Proverb upon our Sex--There's	256	FOR LOVE	III.1	126
Scandal:	Service of your Sex. He that first cries out stop Thief, is	272	FOR LOVE	III.1	698
Singer-V:	But for relief of either Sex agree,	293	FOR LOVE	IV.1	663
Scandal:	must thank you for; I was an Infidel to your Sex;	314	FOR LOVE	V.1	622
Angelica:	our Sex: You tax us with Injustice, only to cover your own	314	FOR LOVE	V.1	628
	Which was an Off'ring to their Sex design'd.	385	M. BRIDE	EPI.	31
Fainall:	that all the Male Sex shou'd be excepted; but somebody	396	WAY WORLD	I.1	55
Fainall:	to Millamant, and swear he has abandon'd the whole Sex	406	WAY WORLD	I.1	420
Marwood:	those insipid dry Discourses, with which our Sex of force	410	WAY WORLD	II.1	21
Fainall:	O the pious Friendships of the Female Sex!	414	WAY WORLD	II.1	166
Mirabell:	or Intimate of your own Sex; No she friend to skreen	451	WAY WORLD	IV.1	236
Sexes (1)					
Careless:	put it into her Sexes power to Ravish.--Well, bless	130	DOUBL DLR	I.1	101
Sextiles (1)					
Foresight:	Sextiles, Quadrates, Trines and Oppositions, Fiery Trigons	241	FOR LOVE	II.1	213
Sexto (0)	see Decimo Sexto				
Sha'n't (1)					
Lady Froth:	Lord you sha'n't kiss it so much; I shall grow jealous, I	140	DOUBL DLR	II.1	77
Sha'not (1)					
Mrs Fain:	drop off when she's full. Madam you sha'not pawn a	466	WAY WORLD	V.1	175
Sha'nt (1)					
Miss Prue:	Oh but you sha'nt, for I'll hold my Tongue.--	253	FOR LOVE	II.1	658
Sha't (2)					
Mirabell:	make Love to my Mistress, thou sha't, Faith. What hast	407	WAY WORLD	I.1	444
Sir Wilful:	My Tantony, Sirrah thou sha't be my Tantony; and I'll	457	WAY WORLD	IV.1	477
Shackled (1)					
Manuel:	There's not a Slave, a shackled Slave of mine,	333	M. BRIDE	I.1	315
Shade (3)					
Osmyn-Alph:	I'll catch it 'ere it goes, and grasp her Shade.	341	M. BRIDE	II.2	53
Osmyn-Alph:	Nor Dead, nor Shade, but breathing and alive!	341	M. BRIDE	II.2	55
Osmyn-Alph:	Fooling the Follower, betwixt Shade and Shining.	350	M. BRIDE	III.1	38
Shaded (0)	see Long-shaded				
Shades (2)					
Osmyn-Alph:	What Brightness, breaks upon me, thus thro' Shades,	353	M. BRIDE	III.1	140
Zara:	And, like a Cobweb-Veil, but thinly shades	375	M. BRIDE	V.1	103
Shadow (1)					
Valentine:	asunder; you are light and shadow, and shew one another;	225	FOR LOVE	I.1	364
Shaft (1)					
Almeria:	If there, he shoot not ev'ry other Shaft;	356	M. BRIDE	III.1	286
Shake (11)					
Bellmour:	and Pleasure, my Occupation; and let Father Time shake	37	OLD BATCH	I.1	24
Sr Sampson:	shake--I believe thou can'st write, Val: Ha, boy? Thou	281	FOR LOVE	IV.1	207
Valentine:	shake off Age; get thee Medea's Kettle, and be boil'd a-new,	289	FOR LOVE	IV.1	522
Almeria:	They shake their downy Wings, and scatter all	330	M. BRIDE	I.1	159
Manuel:	She should have made these Pallace Walls to shake,	333	M. BRIDE	I.1	311
Zara:	To shake the Temper of the King--who knows	354	M. BRIDE	III.1	205
Almeria:	I chatter, shake, and faint with thrilling Fears.	358	M. BRIDE	III.1	369
Manuel:	To talk with you. Come near, why dost thou shake?	367	M. BRIDE	IV.1	247
Almeria:	And come prepar'd to yield my Throat--they shake	382	M. BRIDE	V.2	250
Mirabell:	Waitwell shake his Ears, and Dame Partlet rustle up her	398	WAY WORLD	I.1	129
Marwood:	Then shake it off, You have often wish'd for	442	WAY WORLD	III.1	639
Shake-bag (1)					
Sir Wilful:	With a Wench, Tony? Is she a shake-bag Sirrah?	457	WAY WORLD	IV.1	472
Shaken (2)					
Lady Ply:	have shaken, as I may say, the very foundation of my	169	DOUBL DLR	IV.1	74
Gonsalez:	With which he seems to be already shaken.	371	M. BRIDE	IV.1	408
Shakes (2)					
Lord Touch:	Amazement shakes me--where will	198	DOUBL DLR	V.1	406

Shakes   (continued)
Manuel:	That like a sudden Earth-quake, shakes my Frame;	367	M. BRIDE	IV.1 233

Shaking (1)
| Capt Bluff: | your Jesuits Powder for a shaking fit--But who hast thou | 51 | OLD BATCH | II.1 147 |

Shall (400)

Shallow (5)
Sharper:	better root in your shallow memory.	48	OLD BATCH	II.1 49
Brisk:	little shallow, or so.--Why I'll tell you now, suppose	133	DOUBL DLR	I.1 252
Mellefont:	but a shallow artifice, unworthy of my Matchiavilian	148	DOUEL DLR	II.1 376
Maskwell:	afflicted, but rather laugh'd at the shallow Artifice, which	154	DOUEL DLR	III.1 135
Zara:	Thy shallow Artifice begets Suspicion.	375	M. BRIDE	V.1 102

Shalt (28)   see Sha't
Heartwell:	--And this thou shalt have; this, and all that I am	72	OLD BATCH	III.2 38
Heartwell:	I'll give thee all I have: And thou shalt live with	74	OLD BATCH	III.2 120
Heartwell:	believe it: Nay, thou shalt think so thy self--Only let me	74	OLD BATCH	III.2 122
Fondlewife:	And so thou shalt say, for I'le leave it to stay with thee.	78	OLD BATCH	IV.1 130
Sir Paul:	Thou art my tender Lambkin, and shalt do what	171	DOUEL DLR	IV.1 132
Lord Touch:	shalt have due reward of all thy worth. Give me thy hand	189	DOUBL DLR	V.1 56
Lord Touch:	Thou shalt enjoy it--if all I'm worth in	189	DOUBL DLR	V.1 74
Lady Touch:	not Courage; no, I know thee well: but thou shalt miss	197	DOUEL DLR	V.1 388
Sr Sampson:	with Hieroglyphicks, thou shalt have it sent home to thy	242	FOR LOVE	II.1 251
Sr Sampson:	with Hieroglyphicks, thou shalt have it brought home to thy	242	FOR LOVE	II.1 V251
Sr Sampson:	And so thou shalt,--Mrs. Angelica, my	261	FOR LOVE	III.1 278
Sr Sampson:	Ay boy--Come, thou shalt sit down by me.	281	FOR LOVE	IV.1 198
Sr Sampson:	shalt have it as soon as thou hast set thy Hand to another	282	FOR LOVE	IV.1 234
Valentine:	Prediction to thee, and thou shalt Prophesie;--I am	288	FOR LOVE	IV.1 487
Mrs Frail:	Thou shalt do what thou wilt,	293	FOR LOVE	IV.1 673
Sr Sampson:	for thee, old Lilly, that we will, and thou shalt lead up a	307	FOR LOVE	V.1 386
Sr Sampson:	thou shalt make me a Father, and I'll make thee a Mother,	308	FOR LOVE	V.1 397
Zara:	Tell me, and thou shalt see how I'll revenge	353	M. BRIDE	III.1 V165
Zara:	Shalt weep for mine, forgetting thy own Miseries.	353	M. BRIDE	III.1 168
Osmyn-Alph:	Think on to Morrow, when thou shalt be torn	358	M. BRIDE	III.1 343
Osmyn-Alph:	Think how I am, when thou shalt wed with Garcia!	358	M. BRIDE	III.1 349
Zara:	Thou shalt die.	360	M. BRIDE	III.1 434
Zara:	Vile and ingrate! too late thou shalt repent	360	M. BRIDE	III.1 453
Zara:	Yes, thou shalt know, spite of thy past Distress,	361	M. BRIDE	III.1 455
Almeria:	Since thou'rt reveal'd, alone thou shalt not die.	368	M. BRIDE	IV.1 304
Zara:	Thou shalt partake. Since Fates no more afford;	376	M. BRIDE	V.1 138
Mirabell:	Come, thou art an honest Fellow, Petulant, and shalt	407	WAY WORLD	I.1 443
Witwoud:	frosty Morning; thou shalt to the Mall with us; and we'll	409	WAY WORLD	I.1 520

Sham (2)
| Painall: | The discovery of your sham Addresses to her, to | 397 | WAY WORLD | I.1 64 |
| Painall: | That sham is too gross to pass on me,--tho 'tis | 472 | WAY WORLD | V.1 419 |

Sham-Settlement (1)
| Setter: | Sham-Settlement upon Sir Joseph. | 105 | OLD BATCH | V.1 345 |

Sham-sickness (1)
| Sr Sampson: | Sham-sickness shan't excuse him--O, here's his | 278 | FOR LOVE | IV.1 117 |

Shame (16)
Heartwell:	Death! Shall I own my Shame, or wittingly let him go	104	OLD BATCH	V.1 309
Heartwell:	Shame and Confusion. I am exposed.	108	OLD BATCH	V.2 20
Lady Touch:	most my Shame,--have you not Dishonoured me?	135	DOUEL DLR	I.1 317
Lady Touch:	made him false to Mellefont,--Shame and Destruction!	191	DOUBL DLR	V.1 148
Lady Touch:	made him false to Mellefont,--Shame and Distraction!	191	DOUBL DLR	V.1 V148
Lord Touch:	but too soon you'll know mine, and that Woman's shame.	202	DOUBL DLR	V.1 565
Lord Touch:	Torture and shame attend their open Birth:	203	DOUBL DLR	V.1 593
Ben:	More shame for you,--the Wind's chang'd?--	287	FOR LOVE	IV.1 424
Angelica:	O fie for shame, hold your Tongue, A passionate	291	FOR LOVE	IV.1 585
Heli:	I know his Noble Heart would burst with Shame	338	M. BRIDE	II.1 33
Marwood:	Shame and Ingratitude! Do you reproach me?	414	WAY WORLD	II.1 171
Foible:	O Madam; 'tis a shame to say what he said--	427	WAY WORLD	III.1 93
Marwood:	For shame Mr. Witwoud; why won't you	437	WAY WORLD	III.1 480
Painall:	All Husbands must, or pain, or shame, endure;	444	WAY WORLD	III.1 724
Marwood:	(to Painall) O my shame! (Mirabell and Lady	474	WAY WORLD	V.1 472
Painall:	to hide thy Shame; Your Body shall be Naked as	475	WAY WORLD	V.1 496

Shame-fac'd (2)
| Sr Sampson: | not be shame-fac'd, we'll leave you together. | 262 | FOR LOVE | III.1 351 |
| Ben: | done; may-hap you may be shame-fac'd, some Maidens | 263 | FOR LOVE | III.1 391 |

Shan't (22)   see S'an't, Sant, Sha'n't, Sha'nt, Shant
Heartwell:	in no haste for an Answer--for I shan't stay now.	46	OLD BATCH	I.1 332
Belinda:	pester'd me with Flames and Stuff--I think I shan't	59	OLD BATCH	II.2 164
Heartwell:	I'll have my Beard shav'd, it shan't hurt thee, and	73	OLD BATCH	III.2 107
Laetitia:	No you shan't neglect your business for me--No	78	OLD BATCH	IV.1 131
Lady Froth:	Lord you shan't kiss it so much; I shall grow jealous, I	140	DOUBL DLR	II.1 V 77
Lady Ply:	nay you shan't ask me, I swear I'll deny it. O Gemini, you	147	DOUBL DLR	II.1 334
Lady Touch:	Dear. Nay, by this kiss you shan't be angry. O Lord, I	152	DOUBL DLR	III.1 68
Sir Paul:	Shan't we disturb your Meditation, Mr. Careless:	159	DOUBL DLR	III.1 321
Lady Ply:	O law now, I swear and declare, it shan't be so,	172	DOUBL DLR	IV.1 185
Lady Ply:	O the unlucki'st Accident, I'm afraid I shan't	178	DOUBL DLR	IV.1 393
Maskwell:	No, 'twas honest, therefore I shan't;--Nay, rather, therefore	188	DOUBL DLR	V.1 19
Scandal:	while; but when the full Cry is against you, you shan't	219	FOR LOVE	I.1 V141
Tattle:	Pooh, Pox, you must not say yes already; I shan't care	251	FOR LOVE	II.1 604
Mrs Frail:	Hush! Well he shan't, leave that to me--I'll	259	FOR LOVE	III.1 220
Sr Sampson:	Sham-sickness shan't excuse him--O, here's his	278	FOR LOVE	IV.1 117
Tattle:	many words of Matters, and so I shan't say much,--	291	FOR LOVE	IV.1 607
Tattle:	to know, and shan't know; and yet you shall know it too,	305	FOR LOVE	V.1 290
Millamant:	after all, not to have you--We shan't agree.	422	WAY WORLD	II.1 450
Millamant:	the same; for we shall be sick of one another. I shan't	422	WAY WORLD	II.1 453
Waitwell:	to a Reformation into Waitwell. Nay, I shan't	424	WAY WORLD	II.1 559
Lady Wish:	Consider my Reputation Sir Rowland--No you shan't	461	WAY WORLD	IV.1 628
Mrs Fain:	drop off when she's full. Madam you shan't pawn a	466	WAY WORLD	V.1 V175

Shant (2)
| Capt Bluff: | Zoons Sir, it's a Lie, you have not seen it, nor shant | 53 | OLD BATCH | II.1 234 |
| Sir Wilful: | Serve or not serve, I shant ask License of you, Sir; | 440 | WAY WORLD | III.1 570 |

Shape (6)
| Lady Ply: | So gay, so graceful, so good teeth, so fine shape, | 160 | DOUBL DLR | III.1 367 |

Shape   (continued)
Valentine:	shape, and a Jut with her Bum, would stir an Anchoret:	.	223	FOR LOVE	I.1	285
Scandal:	Complexion, and Sweating for a Shape.	.	233	FOR LOVE	I.1	637
Angelica:	and that you Suckle a Young Devil in the Shape of a	. .	238	FOR LOVE	II.1	121
Valentine:	pray, for a Metamorphosis--Change thy Shape, and	. .	289	FOR LOVE	IV.1	521
Mirabell:	a Shape, till you mold my boy's head like a Sugar-loaf; and		451	WAY WORLD	IV.1	261

Shapes (2)
Mellefont:	shapes in shining day, then fear shews Cowards in the	. .	186	DOUBL DLR	IV.2 V125
Valentine:	Gods have been in counterfeited Shapes for the same Reason;		294	FOR LOVE	IV.1	701

Shar'd (1)
Fainall:	in Pleasures which we both have shar'd. Yet had not you	.	415	WAY WORLD	II.1	200

Share (8)
Sharper:	She had need have a good share of sense, to manage.	. . .	42	OLD BATCH	I.1	208
Bellmour:	in the Mine; well, we have each our share of sport, and each		43	OLD BATCH	I.1	223
Capt Bluff:	share in't. Tho' I might say that too, since I am no Body	.	53	OLD BATCH	II.1	200
Capt Bluff:	share in't. Tho' I might say that too, since I name no Body	.	53	OLD BATCH	II.1 V200
Mellefont:	Cynthia has such a share in his Fatherly fondness, he would		130	DOUBL DLR	I.1	139
Lord Touch:	World, and share my Fortunes.	.	182	DOUBL DLR	IV.1	564
Zara:	I come to mourn with thee; to share thy Griefs,	. . . .	346	M. BRIDE	II.2	268
Heli:	Among the Troops who thought to share the Plunder,	. . .	351	M. BRIDE	III.1	65

Shared (1)
Mellefont:	Winnings to be Shared between us.--What's here, the	.	143	DOUBL DLR	II.1	171

Sharks (1)
	And feed like Sharks, upon an Infant Play.	.	125	DOUBL DLR	PRO.	13

Sharp (1)
Sr Sampson:	Rogue's sharp set, coming from Sea, if he should not stay		265	FOR LOVE	III.1	459

Sharper (35)
	(Enter Sharper.)	. . .	41	OLD BATCH	I.1	146
Bellmour:	Sharper, I'm glad to see thee.	.	41	OLD BATCH	I.1	149
	(Sir Joseph Wittoll, Sharper following.)	.	47	OLD BATCH	II.1	
Sharper:	Ay Sir, my name's Sharper.	. .	52	OLD BATCH	II.1	173
Sir Joseph:	Pray Mr. Sharper Embrace my Back--very	. . .	52	OLD BATCH	II.1	174
Sir Joseph:	well--By the Lord Harry Mr. Sharper he's as brave a	. .	52	OLD BATCH	II.1	175
Capt Bluff:	you know--Well, Mr. Sharper, would you think it? In all	.	53	OLD BATCH	II.1	201
Capt Bluff:	Yet by the Lord Harry 'tis true Mr. Sharper, for I	. .	53	OLD BATCH	II.1	207
Capt Bluff:	Ay, ay, no matter--You see Mr. Sharper after all	. .	53	OLD BATCH	II.1	210
Sir Joseph:	Let me but tell Mr. Sharper a little, how you eat	. .	53	OLD BATCH	II.1	218
Capt Bluff:	This Sword I think I was telling you of Mr. Sharper	. .	53	OLD BATCH	II.1	228
Capt Bluff:	Good Mr. Sharper speak to him; I dare not look	. .	54	OLD BATCH	II.1	238
Sir Joseph:	Mr. Sharper will you partake?	.	54	OLD BATCH	II.1	247
	(Enter Sharper, Bellmour.) . .	.	68	OLD BATCH	III.1	280
Capt Bluff:	Mr. Sharper, the matter is plain--Sir Joseph has found	.	69	OLD BATCH	III.1	296
	(Exit Bellmour, Sharper.)	.	70	OLD BATCH	III.1	330
	(Enter Vainlove, Sharper.) . . .	.	79	OLD BATCH	IV.1	152
	(Enter Sharper and Vainlove, at a Distance.) . .	.	86	OLD BATCH	IV.3	99
	(Enter Sharper and Vainlove, at some Distance.)	.	86	OLD BATCH	IV.3 V 99
Belinda:	leave you. Come, Mr. Sharper, you and I will take a turn,		87	OLD BATCH	IV.3	143
	(Exeunt Belinda and Sharper.)	.	87	OLD BATCH	IV.3	151
	(Enter Belinda, Sharper.)	.	88	OLD BATCH	IV.3	194
Belinda:	Nay, we have spared No-body, I swear. Mr. Sharper,	. .	88	OLD BATCH	IV.3	195
Belinda:	Sharper.	.	88	OLD BATCH	IV.3	210
	(Enter Vainlove, Sharper and Setter.)	.	98	OLD BATCH	V.1	81
Setter:	(to Sharper). Sir, A Word with you.	.	99	OLD BATCH	V.1	91
Vainlove:	Sharper swears, she has forsworn the Letter.-- . . .	.	99	OLD BATCH	V.1	93
Bellmour:	Sharper! Fortifie thy Spleen: Such a Jest! Speak	. .	100	OLD BATCH	V.1	135
	(Enter Sharper, tugging in Heartwell.)		104	OLD BATCH	V.1	283
Heartwell:	Oh, Sharper.	.	104	OLD BATCH	V.1	311
	(Enter Sharper.)	.	107	OLD BATCH	V.1	389
	(Enter Sharper.)	.	109	OLD BATCH	V.2	78
	(Re-enter Sharper, with Sir Joseph, Bluffe, Sylvia, Lucy,		110	OLD BATCH	V.2	95
Capt Bluff:	All Injuries whatsoever, Mr. Sharper.	.	110	OLD BATCH	V.2	97
Heartwell:	--Oh Sharper! Let me embrace thee.--But art	. . . .	111	OLD BATCH	V.2	126

Sharply (1)
Mrs Frail:	and therefore must look sharply about me. Sir	. . . .	248	FOR LOVE	II.1	491

Shav'd (1)
Heartwell:	I'll have my Beard shav'd, it shan't hurt thee, and	. .	73	OLD BATCH	III.2	107

She (449)

She'd (2)
Araminta:	entertaining--(aside) I know she'd fain be persuaded to				
	stay.	.	57	OLD BATCH	II.2	87
Gonsalez:	As if she'd rather that she did not hate him.	.	366	M. BRIDE	IV.4	204

She'll (22)   see Shee'll
Fondlewife:	she'll carry her separate-maintenance about her.	. .	95	OLD BATCH	IV.4	229
Cynthia:	It's impossible; she'll cast beyond you still--I'll	.	167	DOUBL DLR	IV.1	6
Maskwell:	my Lords absence all this while, she'll retire to her				
	Chamber	. .	181	DOUBL DLR	IV.1 V523
Lord Touch:	Wife! Dam her,--she'll think to meet him in that	. .	200	DOUBL DLR	V.1	483
Scandal:	She'll be here by and by, she sees Valentine every	. .	229	FOR LOVE	I.1	483
Miss Prue:	O Lord, she's coming--and she'll tell my	.	253	FOR LOVE	III.1	15
Ben:	Let her cry: The more she cries, the less she'll--she	.	265	FOR LOVE	III.1	441
Valentine:	For she'll meet me Two Hours hence in black and white,	.	290	FOR LOVE	IV.1	561
Jeremy:	to be so dress'd; and she is so in Love with him, she'll		302	FOR LOVE	V.1	201
Jeremy:	sure she'll have reason to pray for me, when she finds	.	302	FOR LOVE	V.1	203
Ben:	along with her, she'll break her Cable, I can tell you that.	310	FOR LOVE	V.1	494
Heli:	Presuming on a Bridegroom's Right--) she'll come.	. . .	351	M. BRIDE	III.1	50
Osmyn-Alph:	She'll come; 'tis what I wish, yet what I fear.		351	M. BRIDE	III.1	51
Osmyn-Alph:	She'll come, but whither, and to whom? O Heav'n!	. . .	351	M. BRIDE	III.1	52
Gonsalez:	If what I fear be true, she'll be concern'd	.	367	M. BRIDE	IV.4	239
Gonsalez:	Urge that, to try if she'll sollicite for him. . . .	.	367	M. BRIDE	IV.4	241
Manuel:	And let the Cell where she'll expect to see him, . . .	.	374	M. BRIDE	V.1	84
Mirabell:	for it self, she'll breed no more.	.	397	WAY WORLD	I.1	63
Foible:	seen me with you I'm sure she'll tell my Lady. I'll make	.	424	WAY WORLD	II.1	546
Foible:	she'll be contracted to Sir Rowland to Night, she says;--	.	430	WAY WORLD	III.1	210
Foible:	is so impatient, I fear she'll come for me, if I stay.	.	430	WAY WORLD	III.1	220
Mrs Fain:	you? ay, like a Leach, to suck your best Blood--she'll	.	466	WAY WORLD	V.1	174

She's (61)
Bellmour: ungrateful to that Creature? She's extreamly pretty and   . 38 OLD BATCH   I.1   39
Vainlove: Ay, or any Body that she's about-- . . . .   38 OLD BATCH   I.1   42
Fondlewife: Yes--Why then!--Ay, but to say truth, She's fonder of   . . 77 OLD BATCH   IV.1   59
Sharper: Here, here, she's thy own Man, sign'd and seal'd too--   .   79 OLD BATCH   IV.1 164
Footman: She's not very well, Madam, and has sent to know,   . .   88 OLD BATCH   IV.3 206
Bellmour: Sinner, she's innocent, for me. Go to him, Madam, fling   95 OLD BATCH   IV.4 236
Bellmour: She still is Vertuous, if she's so believ'd.   . . . .   96 OLD BATCH   IV.4 274
Setter: of her. She's the very Sluce to her Lady's Secrets:--   .   99 OLD BATCH   V.1   104
Sir Joseph: Thanks to my Knight-hood, she's a Lady--   . . . . . 111 OLD BATCH   V.2   136
Mellefont: secure her to your self, you may incline her to mine. She's 130 DOUBL DLR   I.1   128
Singer: Yet she's vext if I give over; . . . . 143 DOUBL DLR   II.1 180
Sir Paul: gads bud she's a Wife for a Cherubin! Do you think her   145 DOUBL DLR   II.1 265
Maskwell: enough. Pox I have lost all Appetite to her; yet she's a
                 fine   . . . . 155 DOUBL DLR   III.1 175
Mellefont: Why, what's the Matter? She's convinc'd that I   . . . 157 DOUBL DLR   III.1 268
Sir Paul: Gad's bud, she's a fine person--   . . . . 159 DOUBL DLR   III.1 347
Sir Paul: together; she's a little hasty sometimes, and so am   . 160 DOUBL DLR   III.1 389
Sir Paul: true--she's so very nice, that I don't believe she would   162 DOUBL DLR   III.1 432
Sir Paul: I vow and swear she's a very merry Woman, but   . . . . 162 DOUBL DLR   III.1 463
Brisk: Who, my Lady Toothless; O, she's a mortifying   . . . 165 DOUBL DLR   III.1 567
Brisk: Spectacle; she's always chewing the Cud like an old Yew. 165 DOUBL DLR   III.1 568
Lady Froth: Then she's always ready to Laugh when Sneer   . . . . 165 DOUBL DLR   III.1 573
Brisk: practice.--Ah! My dear Lady Froth! She's a most   . . 175 DOUBL DLR   IV.1 291
Brisk: Wit too, to keep in with him--No matter, she's a   . . 175 DOUBL DLR   IV.1 294
Maskwell: You had best make haste, for she's but gone to   . . . 181 DOUBL DLR   IV.1 521
Lord Touch: Hell and Amazement, she's in Tears. . . . . 185 DOUBL DLR   IV.2   93
Lady Touch: Where she's serving you, as all your Sex   . . . . . 192 DOUBL DLR   V.1   164
Sir Paul: She's a passionate Woman, gad'sbud,--but to say   . . . 192 DOUBL DLR   V.1   195
Tattle: O unfortunate! she's come already; will you have Patience 230 FOR LOVE   I.1   542
Tattle: there too--for then she's obliged to keep the Secret. . 232 FOR LOVE   I.1 V614
Nurse: home yet: Poor Child, I warrant she's fond o'seeing the   235 FOR LOVE   II.1   20
Angelica: you keep her at Home, if you're Jealous when she's abroad? 237 FOR LOVE   II.1   70
Angelica: you keep her at Home, if you're Jealous of her when she's
                 abroad? . . . . 237 FOR LOVE   II.1 V 70
Sr Sampson: Thy Wife is a Constellation of Vertues; she's the   . . 242 FOR LOVE   II.1 256
Mrs Frail: she's very pretty!--Lord, what pure red and white!   . . 250 FOR LOVE   II.1 556
Miss Prue: O Lord, she's coming--and she'll tell my   . . . . . 253 FOR LOVE   III.1   15
Scandal: She's concern'd, and loves him. . . . . 276 FOR LOVE   IV.1   40
Ben: O Lord, O Lord, she's mad, poor Young Woman, Love   . . 286 FOR LOVE   IV.1 403
Jeremy: She's here, Sir. . . . . 289 FOR LOVE   IV.1 537
Sr Sampson: Rogues: Odd, wou'd she wou'd; faith and troth she's   . 298 FOR LOVE   V.1   50
Jeremy: Aye, Sir, she's just going to the Place of appointment.   301 FOR LOVE   V.1 166
Miss Prue: long as she's an Old Woman? Indeed but I won't: For   . 305 FOR LOVE   V.1 306
Ben: say, Brother Val. went mad for, she's mad too, I think.   306 FOR LOVE   V.1 346
Ben: she's mad for a Husband, and he's Horn-mad, I think, or   307 FOR LOVE   V.1 373
Ben: Heart. Look you, Friend, if I may advise you, when she's 310 FOR LOVE   V.1 490
Ben: when she's going, let her go. For no Matrimony is tough   310 FOR LOVE   V.1 492
Manuel: I tell thee she's to blame, not to have feasted   . . . 333 M. BRIDE   I.1 307
Osmyn-Alph: She's the Reverse of thee; she's my Unhappiness.   . . . 345 M. BRIDE   II.2 200
Osmyn-Alph: Esteem; to this she's fair, few more can boast   . . . 355 M. BRIDE   III.1 225
Osmyn-Alph: But till she's gone; then bless me thus again. . . . . 359 M. BRIDE   III.1 395
Gonsalez: She's greatly griev'd; nor am I less surpriz'd.   . . . 371 M. BRIDE   IV.1 396
Witwoud: don't know what I say: But she's the best Woman in the   402 WAY WORLD   I.1 259
Witwoud: don't know what I say: she's the best Woman in the   . . 402 WAY WORLD   I.1 V259
Witwoud: She's handsome; but she's a sort of an uncertain   . . 408 WAY WORLD   I.1 471
Witwoud: Faith, my Dear, I can't tell; she's a Woman and a   . . 408 WAY WORLD   I.1 492
Fainall: her of all she's worth, and we'll retire somewhere, any   416 WAY WORLD   II.1 245
Foible: come down pretty deep now, she's super-annuated (says   . 427 WAY WORLD   III.1 100
Marwood: you still, if you can away with your Wife. And she's no   442 WAY WORLD   III.1 650
Mrs Fain: drop off when she's full. Madam you sha'not pawn a   . . 466 WAY WORLD   V.1 175
Mrs Fain: drop off when she's full. Madam you shan't pawn a   . . 466 WAY WORLD   V.1 V175
Sheafs (1)
              Poor Actors thresh such empty Sheafs of Straw?   . . . . 323 M. BRIDE   PRO.   18
Shed (2)
              As to a Shed, that shields 'em from the Weather.   . . 315 FOR LOVE   EPI.   4
Lady Wish: away at my Feet, the Tears that he has shed, the Oaths   . 458 WAY WORLD   IV.1 512
Shee'll (1)
Mrs Fore: spoil'd already--d'ee think shee'll ever endure a   . . 250 FOR LOVE   II.1 561
Sheep (2)
Laetitia: Rather, sure it is a Wolf in the cloathing of a Sheep.   . 93 OLD BATCH   IV.4 142
Lady Wish: Desarts and Solitudes; and feed harmless Sheep by Groves   465 WAY WORLD   V.1 133
Sheer (1)
Ben: and Kissing and Hugging, what wou'd you sheer off so?   . 286 FOR LOVE   IV.1 418
Sheers (1)
Angelica: turning the Sieve and Sheers, and pricking your Thumbs,   238 FOR LOVE   II.1 108
Sheet (2)
Lady Ply: Have I, I say, preserv'd my self, like a fair Sheet   . 145 DOUBL DLR   II.1 259
Valentine: you is sunk. You are all white, a sheet of lovely spotless 292 FOR LOVE   IV.1 637
Sheets (3)
Ben: And gnaw the Sheets in vain, Sir, ... 274 FOR LOVE   III.1 766
Valentine: Sheets before Night. But there are two things that you will 289 FOR LOVE   IV.1 510
Zara: Precipitated Fires, and pour in sheets, ... 380 M. BRIDE   V.2 V169
Shelter (2)
Sharper: A Wretch, that has flown for shelter to the lowest   . . 102 OLD BATCH   V.1 207
Gonsalez: I shall make good, and shelter his Retreat.   . . . . 379 M. BRIDE   V.2 128
Shelves (1)
Mrs Frail: O I am happy to have discover'd the Shelves and Quicksands 286 FOR LOVE   IV.1 394
Shepherd (1)
Singer: O let me--still the Shepherd said;   . . . . 71 OLD BATCH   III.2 V 14
Shepherdesses (1)
Lady Wish: and retire by our selves and be Shepherdesses.   . . . 465 WAY WORLD   V.1 135
Sheriff's (1)
Foible: Incontinently, Madam. No new Sheriff's Wife expects   . 428 WAY WORLD   III.1 124
Shew (46)
Bellmour: Husband be out of the way, for the Wife to shew her   . . 38 OLD BATCH   I.1   56

Shew (continued)

		PAGE	TITLE	ACT.SC	LINE
Heartwell:	courage, which you shew for the first year or two upon all	43	OLD BATCH	I.1	246
Sir Joseph:	and will not stick to shew it in the greatest extremity,	49	OLD BATCH	II.1	65
Araminta:	Be ready to shew 'em up.	57	OLD BATCH	II.2	83
Bellmour:	dumb shew.	59	OLD BATCH	II.2	184
Bellmour:	make Signs. (Addresses Belinda in dumb shew.)	60	OLD BATCH	II.2	211
Lucy:	first. I know that will do--walk in and I'le shew	75	OLD BATCH	III.1	158
Laetitia:	(aside). I hope to have one that will shew me how a	79	OLD BATCH	IV.1	139
Capt Bluff:	Shew him to me. Where is he?	101	OLD BATCH	V.1	170
Setter:	--Avaunt Temptation.--Setter, shew thy self a	102	OLD BATCH	V.1	226
Lord Froth:	about you to shew him, my Dear?	142	DOUBL DLR	II.1	142
Lady Froth:	you go into the next Room? and there I'll shew you all	142	DOUBL DLR	II.1	144
Lady Froth:	you go into the next Room? and there I'll shew you what	142	DOUBL DLR	II.1	V144
Lady Ply:	transported, I did not see it.--Well, to shew you how	170	DOUEL DLR	V.1	109
Sir Paul:	of a Wedding, gad'sbud--to shew you that I am not	192	DOUBL DLR	V.1	177
Scandal:	enough? Must you needs shew your Wit to get more?	219	FOR LOVE	I.1	128
Valentine:	asunder; you are light and shadow, and shew one another;	225	FOR LOVE	I.1	364
Scandal:	Letter from her, and at the same time, shew you her Hand	226	FOR LOVE	I.1	373
Valentine:	Shew her up, when she comes.	229	FOR LOVE	I.1	506
Scandal:	Yes Faith, I can shew you your own Picture, and	232	FOR LOVE	I.1	617
Scandal:	Women. I can shew you Pride, Polly, Affectation, Wantonness,	233	FCR LOVE	I.1	628
Scandal:	Ignorance, all in one Piece. Then I can shew you Lying,	233	FOR LOVE	I.1	630
Tattle:	And won't you shew me, pretty Miss, where your	252	FOR LOVE	II.1	646
Tattle:	No? I can shew Letters, Locketts, Pictures, and Rings,	257	FOR LOVE	III.1	153
Sr Sampson:	Rogue shew himself, and make Love to some desponding	260	FOR LOVE	III.1	261
Ben:	--I'm glad you shew your self, Mistress:--Let	287	FOR LOVE	IV.1	436
Angelica:	a Masquerade is done, when we come to shew Faces;	296	FCR LOVE	IV.1	790
Angelica:	exceptious: But Madmen shew themselves most, by over	296	FOR LOVE	IV.1	763
Almeria:	Are lost in dread of greater Ill. Shew me,	339	M. BRIDE	II.1	80
Almeria:	No, I will on: shew me Anselmo's Tomb,	339	M. BRIDE	II.1	73
Almeria:	Are lost in dread of greater Ill. Then shew me,	339	M. BRIDE	II.1	V 80
Osmyn-Alph:	'Tis she; shew me her Face, and let me feel	341	M. ERIDE	II.2	68
Osmyn-Alph:	Which I would shew the Friend, but that the Sight	352	M. BRIDE	III.1	109
Almeria:	Shew me, for I am come in search of Death;	381	M. BRIDE	V.2	220
	In short, our Play, shall (with your leave to shew it)	393	WAY WORLD	PRO.	37
Witwoud:	Learning, gives him the more opportunities to shew his	404	WAY WORLD	I.1	327
Mirabell:	Fame, wou'd shew as dim by thee as a dead Whiting's	407	WAY WORLD	I.1	454
Petulant:	What, what? Then let 'em either shew their Innocence	409	WAY WORLD	I.1	529
Petulant:	by not understanding what they hear, or else shew	409	WAY WORLD	I.1	530
Marwood:	'Tis false. I challenge you to shew an Instance	414	WAY WORLD	II.1	436
Foible:	I wou'd put her Ladyship's Picture in my Pocket to shew	423	WAY WORLD	II.1	521
Millamant:	think he wou'd obey me; I wou'd command him to shew	433	WAY WORLD	III.1	339
Lady Wish:	shou'd be kill'd I must never shew my face; or hang'd,--O	461	WAY WORLD	IV.1	627
	As any one abstracted Fop to shew.	479	WAY WORLD	EPI.	30

Show'd (1)

Ben:	And shew'd her many a Scar, Sir,	274	FOR LOVE	III.1	771

Shewing (1)

Vainlove:	Sir-- (Shewing Letters.) And Business must be follow'd,	37	OLD BATCH	I.1	7

Shewn (1)

Valentine:	Contrivance, the Effect has shewn it such.	311	FOR LOVE	V.1	508

Shews (12)

	(Scene opening, shews Lady Touchwood's Chamber.)	183	DOUBL DLR	IV.2	
Lady Touch:	been to blame--a ready Answer shews you were	183	DOUBL DLR	IV.2	17
Mellefont:	shapes in shining day, then fear shews Cowards in the	186	DOUBL DLR	IV.2	V125
	Or only shews its Teeth, as if it smil'd.	213	FOR LCVE	PRO.	34
Sr Sampson:	(Shews him the Paper, but holds it out of his reach.)	281	FOR LOVE	IV.1	216
Almeria:	Shall rest; shews me the Grave where Nature wearied,	340	M. BRIDE	II.2	17
Almeria:	Shall rest; shews me the Grave where Nature weary	340	M. BRIDE	II.2	V 17
Osmyn-Alph:	Which shews me Bankrupt even in my Hopes.	347	M. BRIDE	II.2	290
Osmyn-Alph:	Which shews me poor and Bankrupt even in Hopes.	347	M. BRIDE	II.2	V290
	(Scene opening shews the Prison.	376	M. BRIDE	V.2 V	
	(They go to the Scene which opens and shews the Body.)	380	M. BRIDE	V.2	161
Almeria:	That Sense, which in one Instant shews him dead	383	M. BRIDE	V.2	294

Shield (2)

Zara:	That thou dost seek to shield thee there, and shun	346	M. BRIDE	II.2	242
Osmyn-Alph:	For whom I fear, to shield me from my Fears.	355	M. BRIDE	III.1	233

Shields (1)

	As to a Shed, that shields 'em from the Weather.	315	FOR LOVE	EPI.	4

Shift (4)

Bellmour:	I'll leave him with you, and go shift my Habit.	100	OLD BATCH	V.1	160
Scandal:	in her Bed, shift twice a Week, and not work so hard, that	222	FOR LOVE	I.1	219
Mirabell:	five, declares for a Friend and Ratifia; and let Posterity shift	397	WAY WORLD	I.1	62
Lady Wish:	Father, or the Chaplain, and him we made a shift to put	467	WAY WORLD	V.1	192

Shifted (1)

Lady Touch:	O the Scene was shifted quick before me--	185	DOUBL DLR	IV.2	70

Shifting (2)

Setter:	Shifting Cloaths for the purpose at a Friend's House of	106	OLD BATCH	V.1	351
Manuel:	Shifting the Prize in unresolving Hands:	337	M. BRIDE	I.1	455

Shill (1)

Sir Wilful:	. . . I don't stand shill I, shall I,	440	WAY WORLD	III.1	580

Shilling (1)

Sr Sampson:	of a Ten Shilling Ordinary.	245	FOR LOVE	II.1	354

Shine (7)

Lady Froth:	nothing, but a Blue Ribbon and a Star, to make him Shine,	139	DOUBL DLR	II.1	31
Lady Froth:	that he peeps now and then, yet he does shine all the day	164	DOUBL DLR	III.1	524
Sr Sampson:	If the Sun shine by Day, and the Stars by Night, why, we	240	FOR LOVE	II.1	199
Valentine:	We are the Twin-Stars, and cannot shine in one	259	FOR LOVE	III.1	223
Manuel:	Shall shine on Garcia's Nuptials.	334	M. BRIDE	I.1	343
Manuel:	Garcia, shall shine to grace thy Nuptials--	334	M. BRIDE	I.1	V343
Osmyn-Alph:	With the Breath of Love. Shine, awake, Almeria,	383	M. BRIDE	V.2	285

Shines (5)

Lady Froth:	For as the Sun shines every day,	164	DOUBL DLR	III.1	515
Brisk:	because you say the Sun shines every day.	164	DOUBL DLR	III.1	518
Lady Froth:	Then I don't say the Sun shines all the day, but,	164	DOUBL DLR	III.1	523
Lady Froth:	For as the Sun shines every day,	164	DOUBL DLR	III.1	529

Shines (continued)
  Valentine: People that we do not know; and yet the Sun shines . . . 280   FOR LCVE   IV.1 161
Shining (7)
  Mellefont: shapes in shining day, then fear shews Cowards in the . . 186   DOUEL DLR   IV.2 V125
              To shiring Theatres to see our Sport,   315   EPI.   26
  Gonsalez: Prisoners of War in shining Fetters, follow;   331   M. BRIDE   I.1   234
  Leonora: Of two in shining Habits, cross the Ile, ... 344   M. ERIDE   II.2 192
  Manuel: Her shining from the Day, to gild this Scene   348   M. ERIDE   II.2 353
  Osmyn-Alph: Fooling the Follower, betwixt Shade and Shining.   . . . 350   M. ERIDE   III.1 38
              And shining Features in one Portrait blend, ... 479   WAY WORLD   EPI.   33
Ship (8)   see Lady-ship
  Vainlove: of Town, to meet the Master of a Ship about the return of   39   OLD EATCH   I.1   80
  Fondlewife: Kiss, Dear,--I met the Master of the Ship   89   OLD BATCH   IV.4   23
  Ben: not for dropping Anchor here; Abcut Ship i' faith--   261   FOR LCVE   III.1 281
  Ben: Joking, I'll Joke with you, for I love my jest, an the Ship 261   FOR LCVE   III.1 307
  Mrs Frail: Estate, is like Sailing in a Ship without Ballast. . . . 273   FOR LOVE   III.1 720
  Almeria: Had born the Queen and me, on board a Ship   329   M. ERIDE   I.1   120
  Almeria: For when my Lord beheld the Ship pursuing, ...   329   M. EBIDE   I.1   134
              That some well-laden Ship may strike the Sands;   . . . 385   M. EBIDE   EPI.   22
Ship's (0)   see Lady-ship's
Shipping (1)
  Sir Wilful: take Shipping--Aunt, if you don't forgive quickly; I shall 472   WAY WCRLD   V.1   395
Ships-Crew's (1)
  Ben: The Song was made upon one of our Ships-Crew's   273   FOR LOVE   III.1 750
Shipwrack'd (1)
  Mellefont: appearing to my Shipwrack'd hopes: The Witch has rais'd . 148   DOUBL DLR   II.1 382
Shirt (2)
  Heartwell: the envenom'd Shirt, to run into the Embraces of a Fever,   62   OLD BATCH   III.1 67
  Ben: clean Shirt once a Quarter--Come home and lie with . . . 275   FOR LCVE   III.1 801
Shoal (3)
  Almeria: The Shoal, and save me floating on the Waves,   . . .   329   M. EBIDE   I.1   130
  Mirabell: and her Streamers out, and a shcal of Fools for Tenders . 418   WAY WCRLD   II.1 324
  Mirabell: and Streamers out, and a shoal of Fools for Tenders . . 418   WAY WCRLD   II.1 V324
Shoals (1)
              In shoals, I've mark'd 'em judging in the Pit;   479   WAY WCRLD   EPI.   11
Shoar (1)
              As Sussex Men, that dwell upon the Shoar, ... 385   M. EBIDE   EPI.   19
Shocks (1)
  Lady Touch: Thy stubborn temper shocks me, and you   197   DOUBL DLR   V.1   386
Shone (3)
  Bellmour: Madam? Those Eyes shone kindly on my first Appearance,   . 81   OLD BATCH   IV.2   21
  Mellefont: Malice, like a Dark Lanthorn, onely shone upon me,   . . . 129   DOUEL DLR   I.1   90
  Mellefont: Malice, like a Dark Lanthorn, only shone upon me,   . .   129   DOUEL DLR   I.1 V 90
Shook (1)
  Manuel: And shook his Chains in Transport, and rude Harmony.   . 333   M. EBIDE   I.1   317
Shoot (3)
  Sir Paul: no, no, you shoot wide of the mark a mile; indeed you do, 161   DOUEL DLR   III.1 427
  Almeria: And shoot a Chilness to my trembling Heart.   339   M. EBIDE   II.1   66
  Almeria: If there, he shoot not ev'ry other Shaft;   356   M. BRIDE   III.1 286
Shop (4)
  Belinda: Snipwel's Shop while I was there.--But, Oh Gad!   . . .   84   OLD BATCH   IV.3   25
  Valentine: Shop. Oh things will go methodically in the City, the . 289   FOR LOVE   IV.1 503
  Valentine: Master's Shop in the morning, may ten to one, dirty his   289   FOR LCVE   IV.1 509
  Lady Wish: Traverse Rag, in a shop no bigger than a Bird-cage,-- . 462   WAY WORLD   V.1   7
Shore (3)   see A-shore, Shoar
  Mrs Frail: on the Shore. But I'll tell you a hint that he has given . 287   FOR LOVE   IV.1 457
  Almeria: Of Africk: There our Vessel struck the Shore, ... 329   M. EBIDE   I.1   126
  Gonsalez: Whose weight has sunk me 'ere I reach'd the Shore. . . . 378   M. EBIDE   V.2   87
Short (25)
  Bellmour: short of the intended Mark.   37   OLD BATCH   I.1   12
  Vainlove: pleasure of a chase: My sport is always balkt cr cut short 80   OLD BATCH   IV.1 176
  Bellmour: In short then, I was informed of the opportunity . . .   94   OLD BATCH   IV.4 205
  Mellefont: despair, and the short prospect of time she saw, to . . 129   DOUBL DLR   I.1   95
  Mellefont: In short, the Consequence was thus, she omitted nothing,   130   DOUBL DLR   I.1   109
  Maskwell: qualifie me to assist her in her Revenge. And, in short, in 149   DOUBL DLR   II.1 425
  Lady Touch: to dissemble: I own it to you; in short I do believe it,
              nay, ...   151   DOUBL DLR   III.1 40
  Maskwell: In short, the price of your Banishment is to be paid . . 156   DOUBL DLR   III.1 224
  Brisk: Short, but there's Salt in't, my way of writing I'gad.   . 166   DOUBL DLR   III.1 602
  Maskwell: None, your Text is short.   195   DOUBL DLR   V.1   297
  Trapland: And in short, I can be put off no longer.   223   FOR LOVE   I.1   257
  Scandal: may be granted him--In short, he is a publick Professor of 226   FOR LOVE   I.1   378
  Foresight: or short, Happy or Unhappy; whether Diseases are . . .   241   FOR LCVE   II.1 215
  Ben: your Harbour. How say you Mistress? the short of the . . 263   FOR LCVE   III.1 375
  Foresight: and hem! and my hem!--breath, hem!--grows short;   . . . 269   FOR LCVE   III.1 610
  Jeremy: Very short, Sir.   280   FOR LOVE   IV.1 182
  Tattle: But in short, de'e see, I will hold you a Hundred Pound   291   FOR LOVE   IV.1 608
  Mrs Frail: in short, I will deny thee nothing.   293   FOR LOVE   IV.1 674
  Osmyn-Alph: Snatch me from Life, and cut me short unwarn'd;   343   M. BRIDE   II.2 141
              In short, our Play, shall (with your leave to shew it) . 393   WAY WCRLD   PRO.   37
  Mrs Fain: short upon me unawares, and has almost overcome me. . .   412   WAY WORLD   II.1   83
  Lady Wish: Short View of the Stage, with Bunyan's Works to entertain 426   WAY WORLD   III.1 66
  Witwoud: short as a Shrewsbury Cake, if you please. But I tell .   439   WAY WORLD   III.1 532
  Mirabell: marrow of a roasted Cat. In short, I forbid all Commerce   451   WAY WORLD   IV.1 251
  Waitwell: Enough, his date is short.   461   WAY WORLD   IV.1 621
Short-hand (2)
  Witwoud: short-hand.   453   WAY WORLD   IV.1 349
  Marwood: Short-hand Writers to the publick Press; and from thence   468   WAY WORLD   V.1   231
Short-liv'd (1)
  Zara: And Anger in Distrust, both short-liv'd Pains.   362   M. BRIDE   IV.1   33
Shortest (1)
  Scandal: I'll rip up his Stomach, and go the shortest way to his   224   FOR LOVE   I.1   311
Shortly (2)
  Lord Touch: should Command: my very Slaves will shortly give me . .   195   DOUBL DLR   V.1   303
  Scandal: shortly.   222   FOR LOVE   I.1   221

Shortness (1)

Maskwell: by describing to me the shortness of your stay; rather if   194 DOUBL DLR V.1 277

Shot (5)

Scandal:	by the Hounds, you will be treacherously shot by the	. .	220	FOR LOVE	I.1	143
Ben:	A shot 'twixt wind and water, ...		274	FOR LOVE	III.1	788
Sr Sampson:	--is shot from above, in a Jelly of Love, and so forth;		307	FOR LOVE	V.1	381
Perez:	Then forward shot their Fires, which he pursu'd,	. .	338	M. BRIDE	II.1	22
Almeria:	Which shot into my Breast, now melt and chill me.	. .	358	M. BRIDE	III.1	368

Shou'd (113)

Lucy:	Think: That I shou'd not believe my Eyes, and that	. . .	97	OLD BATCH	V.1	32
Sir Joseph:	he shou'd hear the Lion roar, he'd cudgel him into an Ass,		101	OLD BATCH	V.1	173
Heartwell:	hold:--If he shou'd not, I were a Fool to discover it.--	.	104	OLD BATCH	V.1	299
Bellmour:	he shou'd recant. (Aside.) Well, we shall have your Company		112	OLD BATCH	V.2	176
Maskwell:	Gamester--but shou'd he find me out before! 'tis dangerous		190	DOUBL DLR	V.1	88
Maskwell:	to delay--let me think--shou'd my Lord proceed	. . .	190	DOUBL DLR	V.1	89
Maskwell:	It must not be; nay, shou'd my Lady know it--ay,	. . .	190	DOUBL DLR	V.1	92
Lord Touch:	my Will it should be so, and that shou'd be convincing to		196	DOUBL DLR	V.1	319
Lord Touch:	my Will it shall be so, and that shou'd be convincing to		196	DOUBL DLR	V.1	V319
Lord Touch:	were it possible it shou'd be done this night.	. . . .	196	DOUBL DLR	V.1	321
Jeremy:	And shou'd th' ensuing Scenes not chance to hit,	. . .	214	FOR LOVE	PRO.	45
Scandal:	Younger Brother shou'd come from Sea, he'd never look	.	218	FOR LOVE	I.1	84
	shou'd be.		233	FOR LOVE	I.1	646
Sr Sampson:	have been born without a Palate.--'S'heart, what shou'd	.	245	FOR LOVE	II.1	367
Foresight:	By your Looks, you shou'd go up Stairs out of the	. .	245	FOR LOVE	II.1	383
Mrs Fore:	is scandalous: What if any Body else shou'd have seen you		247	FOR LOVE	II.1	431
Mrs Fore:	Heart, to think that any body else shou'd be before-hand	.	250	FOR LOVE	II.1	551
Mrs Frail:	Foresight shou'd find us with them;--He'd think so,	. .	250	FOR LOVE	II.1	571
Tattle:	shou'd have wish'd for her coming.	. . . .	253	FOR LOVE	III.1	18
Scandal:	spoken; but may be apply'd to him--As if we shou'd	. . .	256	FOR LOVE	III.1	124
Valentine:	Sphere: when he Rises I must set--Besides, if I shou'd stay,	259	FOR LOVE	III.1	224
Angelica:	cou'd have lik'd any thing in him, it shou'd have been his		260	FOR LOVE	III.1	246
Mrs Frail:	and honest, I shou'd like such a humour in a Husband	. .	262	FOR LOVE	III.1	322
Ben:	Say'n you so forsooth: Marry and I shou'd like such a	. .	262	FOR LOVE	III.1	324
Mrs Frail:	I shou'd not doubt that, if you were Master of me. . .	262	FOR LOVE	III.1	329
Angelica:	methinks Sir Sampson, You shou'd leave him alone with	.	262	FOR LOVE	III.1	345
Ben:	if you shou'd give such Language at Sea, you'd have a Cat		264	FOR LOVE	III.1	408
Sr Sampson:	Without Popery shou'd be landed in the West, or the	.	266	FOR LOVE	III.1	487
Sr Sampson:	Unless Popery shou'd be landed in the West, or the	.	266	FOR LOVE	III.1	V487
Scandal:	be wholly insignificant. You are wise, and shou'd not be	.	267	FOR LOVE	III.1	524
Scandal:	over-reach'd, methinks you shou'd not--	. . . . .	267	FOR LOVE	III.1	525
Scandal:	why shou'd a Man court Danger, or a Woman shun	. . .	271	FOR LOVE	III.1	671
Mrs Frail:	Well, but if you shou'd forsake me after all, you'd	. .	273	FOR LOVE	III.1	728
Ben:	Break your Heart? I'de rather the Mary-gold shou'd	. .	273	FOR LOVE	III.1	730
Angelica:	(aside). I know not what to think--Yet I shou'd	. . .	277	FOR LOVE	IV.1	47
Scandal:	I'm afraid the Physician is not willing you shou'd	. . .	277	FOR LOVE	IV.1	50
Scandal:	(aside). That ever I shou'd suspect such a Heathen of	.	281	FOR LOVE	IV.1	212
Valentine:	That Gray Hairs shou'd cover a Green Head--and	. . .	283	FOR LOVE	IV.1	271
Valentine:	Man shou'd have a Stomach to a Wedding Supper, when	.	289	FOR LOVE	IV.1	527
Jeremy:	No, no, Madam, he won't know her, if he shou'd, I	. .	291	FOR LOVE	IV.1	591
Valentine:	length deserv'd you shou'd confess it.	294	FOR LOVE	IV.1	710
Angelica:	Leave me, and d'ye hear, if Valentine shou'd come,	. .	297	FOR LOVE	V.1	9
Sr Sampson:	wou'd she wou'd like me, then I shou'd hamper my young		298	FOR LOVE	V.1	49
Sr Sampson:	and 'twere pity you shou'd be thrown away upon any	. .	298	FOR LOVE	V.1	52
Ben:	Pump to your Bosom, I believe we shou'd discover a foul		309	FOR LOVE	V.1	433
	How we shou'd end in our Original, a Cart.	315	FOR LOVE	EPI.	37
Almeria:	I would consent the Priest shou'd make us one; . . .	329	M. BRIDE	I.1	V137
Osmyn-Alph:	I indeed shou'd see thee--	344	M. BRIDE	II.2	165
Osmyn-Alph:	That I indeed shou'd be so blest to see thee. . . .	344	M. BRIDE	II.2	V165
Osmyn-Alph:	'Tis wanting what should follow--Heav'n shou'd	. . .	350	M. BRIDE	III.1	20
Osmyn-Alph:	'Tis wanting what should follow--Heav'n, shou'd	. . .	350	M. BRIDE	III.1	V 20
Osmyn-Alph:	More Anxious Grief. Thou shou'd have better taught me;		353	M. BRIDE	III.1	127
Almeria:	And Woe shou'd be in equal Portions dealt.	356	M. BRIDE	III.1	288
Gonsalez:	And where the Crown that shou'd descend on him, . . .	371	M. BRIDE	IV.1	401
Gonsalez:	Hold, let me think--if I shou'd tell the King-- . .	371	M. BRIDE	IV.1	403
Osmyn-Alph:	Nay, I must grant, 'tis fit you shou'd be thus-- . .	383	M. BRIDE	V.2	309
Mirabell:	I was then in such a Humour, that I shou'd have been .	396	WAY WORLD	I.1	47
Fainall:	that all the Male Sex shou'd be excepted; but somebody	.	396	WAY WORLD	I.1	55
Mirabell:	is to be flatter'd further, unless a Man shou'd endeavour		397	WAY WORLD	I.1	77
Witwoud:	out of my Head. I beg Pardon that I shou'd ask a Man of		402	WAY WORLD	I.1	256
Witwoud:	Wit will excuse that: A Wit shou'd no more be sincere,	.	403	WAY WORLD	I.1	319
Petulant:	Friends; and if he shou'd marry and have a Child, you may		407	WAY WORLD	I.1	439
Witwoud:	her, I shou'd--Hearkee--To tell you a Secret, but let it go		407	WAY WORLD	I.1	467
Witwoud:	Now, Demme, I shou'd hate that, if she were as handsome	.	408	WAY WORLD	I.1	477
Witwoud:	being in Embrio; and if it shou'd come to Life; poor	.	408	WAY WORLD	I.1	488
Marwood:	that Love shou'd ever die before us; and that the Man so	.	410	WAY WORLD	II.1	10
Marwood:	often shou'd out-live the Lover. But say what you will,	.	410	WAY WORLD	II.1	11
Marwood:	of ill usage; I think I shou'd do my self the violence of		411	WAY WORLD	II.1	55
Marwood:	O if he shou'd ever discover it, he wou'd	411	WAY WORLD	II.1	61
Fainall:	Excellent Creature! Well sure if I shou'd live to be	.	413	WAY WORLD	II.1	109
Fainall:	rid of my Wife, I shou'd be a miserable Man. . . .	413	WAY WORLD	II.1	110
Marwood:	with the Guilt, unmindful of the Merit! To you it shou'd		414	WAY WORLD	II.1	175
Mirabell:	You shou'd have just so much disgust for your . . .	416	WAY WORLD	II.1	258
Mirabell:	hopes to ruin me, shou'd consent to marry my pretended		417	WAY WORLD	II.1	293
Mirabell:	they are not capable: Or if they were, it shou'd be to you		421	WAY WORLD	II.1	438
Millamant:	Countenance, 'tis impossible I shou'd hold mine. Well,		422	WAY WORLD	II.1	473
Millamant:	unless she shou'd tell me her self. Which of the two it	.	423	WAY WORLD	II.1	486
Waitwell:	Why Sir; it will be impossible I shou'd remember	. . .	424	WAY WORLD	II.1	554
Lady Wish:	Importunate Foible, and push? For if he shou'd not be	.	429	WAY WORLD	III.1	157
Lady Wish:	no, I can never advance--I shall swoon if he shou'd	. .	429	WAY WORLD	III.1	160
Mrs Fain:	O Foible, I have been in a Fright, least I shou'd	. .	430	WAY WORLD	III.1	184
Mrs Fain:	I'll go with you up the back Stairs, lest I shou'd	. .	430	WAY WORLD	III.1	221
Marwood:	Man shou'd have his Head and Horns, and Woman the	. .	431	WAY WORLD	III.1	238
Lady Wish:	shou'd so forget my self--But I have such an Olio of	. .	431	WAY WORLD	III.1	255
Marwood:	If we had the liberty, we shou'd be as weary	432	WAY WORLD	III.1	299
Marwood:	If we had that liberty, we shou'd be as weary	432	WAY WORLD	III.1	V299
Marwood:	of the Play-house? A fine gay glossy Fool, shou'd be given	433	WAY WORLD	III.1	309

Shrivell'd (1)
Valentine: shrivell'd; his Legs dwindl'd, and his back bow'd, Pray, . 289 FOR LOVE IV.1 520
Shropshire (1)
Sir Wilful: in our Parts, down in Shropshire--Why then belike . . . 437 WAY WORLD III.1 449
Shroud (1)
Almeria: Or wind me in the Shroud of some pale Coarse . . . . . 339 M. BRIDE II.1 76
Shrowd (2)
Osmyn-Alph: And growing to his dead Father's Shrowd, roots up . . . 341 M. BRIDE II.2 39
Osmyn-Alph: And growing to his Father's Shrowd, roots up . . . . 341 M. BRIDE II.2 V 39
Shrub (1)
Sharper: shrub of Mankind, and seeks Protection from a blasted . 102 OLD BATCH V.1 208
Shrug (1)
Petulant: clash; snugs the Word, I shrug and am silent. . . . . 407 WAY WORLD I.1 447
Shuffled (1)
Mellefont: because it's possible we may lose; since we have Shuffled 142 DOUBL DLR II.1 160
Shun (11)
Bellmour: never be able to pay me all: So shun me for the same . . 58 OLD BATCH II.2 124
Heartwell: to shun as I would infection? To enter here, is to put on . 62 OLD BATCH III.1 66
Scandal: why shou'd a Man court Danger, or a Woman shun . . . 271 FOR LOVE III.1 671
Almeria: Whilst the good King, to shun approaching Flames, . . . 329 M. BRIDE I.1 115
Almeria: Conducting them who follow'd us, to shun . . . . . 329 M. BRIDE I.1 129
Gonsalez: While you alone retire, and shun this Sight; . . . . 332 M. BRIDE I.1 243
Zara: That thou dost seek to shield thee there, and shun . . 346 M. BRIDE II.2 242
Zara: Not to be born--devise the means to shun it, ... 362 M. BRIDE IV.1 37
Manuel: But see she comes; I'll shun th' Encounter; do . . . 374 M. BRIDE V.1 87
Manuel: But see she comes; I'll shun th' Encounter; thou . . . 374 M. BRIDE V.1 V 87
Zara: Shun me when seen! I fear thou hast undone me. . . . 375 M. BRIDE V.1 101
Shuns (1)
Garcia: I would oblige him, but he shuns my Kindness; . . . . 335 M. BRIDE I.1 369
Shut (5)
Fondlewife: I'll shut this door, to secure him from coming . . . . 91 OLD BATCH IV.4 72
Valentine: Eyes; shut up your Mouth, and chew the Cud of . . . 216 FOR LOVE I.1 15
Jeremy: your Debts without Money? Will they shut up the . . . 217 FOR LOVE I.1 28
Valentine: Argo's hundred Eyes be shut, ha? No body shall know, . 290 FOR LOVE IV.1 552
Mirabell: with the Gentlewoman in what-de-call-it-Court. Item, I shut 451 WAY WORLD IV.1 252
Shuts (2)
   (Scene shuts.) . . . . 187 DOUBL DLR IV.2 157
Tattle: (Thrusts her in, and shuts the Door.) . . . . 254 FOR LOVE III.1 25
Shutting (1)
Osmyn-Alph: His Voice; shutting the Gates of Pray'r against him. . . 350 M. BRIDE III.1 27
Sick (11)   see Love-sick
Belinda: more. Oh Gad, I swear you'd make one sick to hear you. . 54 OLD BATCH II.2 2
Laetitia: Oh! I am sick with the fright; won't you take him . . . 90 OLD BATCH IV.4 57
Brisk: (sings). I'm sick with Love, ha ha ha, prithee come (walking 175 DOUBL DLR IV.1 306
Brisk: I'm sick with, &c. . . . . . . 175 DOUBL DLR IV.1 308
Miss Prue: way or other. Oh! methinks I'm sick when I think of a . . 305 FOR LOVE V.1 308
Miss Prue: sleeping, than sick with thinking. . . . . . . 305 FOR LOVE V.1 312
Miss Prue: asleep, than sick with thinking. . . . . . . 305 FOR LOVE V.1 V312
Mrs Fain: Do I? I think I am a little sick o' the suddain. . . . 412 WAY WORLD II.1 80
Millamant: For I am as sick of 'em-- . . . . 419 WAY WORLD II.1 338
Millamant: the same; for we shall be sick of one another. I shan't . 422 WAY WORLD II.1 453
Sir Wilful: a Rat me, Knight, I'm so sick of a last Nights debauch . 439 WAY WORLD III.1 545
Sickly (3)
Sharper: Thou hast a sickly peevish Appetite; only chew Love and . 80 OLD BATCH IV.1 172
Gonsalez: A Lamp that feebly lifts a sickly Flame, ... 376 M. BRIDE V.2 7
Singer: A sickly Flame, which if not fed expires; . . . . . 435 WAY WORLD III.1 379
Sickness (2)   see Sham-sickness
Sir Joseph: by night, or by day, in sickness, or in health, Winter, or . 49 OLD BATCH II.1 66
Mirabell: a Girl--'Tis the Green Sickness of a second Childhood; . 418 WAY WORLD II.1 318
Side (8)   see Bed-side
Bellmour: Not o' your side, Madam, I confess--But my . . . . 57 OLD BATCH II.2 117
Lord Froth: when any of their foolish Wit prevails upon the side . . 133 DOUBL DLR I.1 229
Cynthia: (aside). I'm amazed to find here of our side, for I'm . . 171 DOUBL DLR IV.1 161
   (Enter Mellefont lugging in Maskwell from the other side . 202 DOUBL DLR V.1 566
Nurse: Stocking with the wrong side outward. . . . . . 235 FOR LOVE II.1 28
Valentine: my side: What's here? Mrs. Foresight and Mrs. Frail, they . 246 FOR LOVE II.1 410
Angelica: seen Fifty in a side Box by Candle-light, out-blossom Five . 298 FOR LOVE V.1 31
Alonzo: Which done, he drew a Ponyard from his side, . . . 373 M. BRIDE V.1 26
Side-Box (1)
Sr Sampson: outsides. Hang your side-Box Beaus; no, I'm none of those, 298 FOR LOVE V.1 34
Sides (6)
Sir Joseph: Rogue of all sides. . . . . 110 OLD BATCH V.2 119
Brisk: holding your sides, and Laughing as if you would bepiss . 134 DOUBL DLR I.1 255
Brisk: holding your sides, and Laughing as if you would--well-- . 134 DOUBL DLR I.1 V255
Cynthia: you had not chang'd sides so soon; now I begin to find it. 172 DOUBL DLR IV.1 177
Valentine: sides alike. Yet while she does not seem to hate me, I will 297 FOR LOVE IV.1 812
Witwoud: out and piec'd in the sides like an unsiz'd Camlet,--Yes, 453 WAY WORLD IV.1 328
Siege (1)
Angelica: Siege? What a World of Fire and Candle, Matches and . . 237 FOR LOVE II.1 81
Sieve (2)
Angelica: turning the Sieve and Sheers, and pricking your Thumbs, . 238 FOR LOVE II.1 108
Ben: Hold. They say a Witch will sail in a Sieve--But I . . . 309 FOR LOVE V.1 434
Sifted (1)
Mirabell: Insolence, that in Revenge I took her to pieces; sifted her 399 WAY WORLD I.1 164
Sigh (6)
Heartwell: Awake; Sigh much, Drink little, Eat less, court Solitude, . 73 OLD BATCH III.2 81
Mellefont: hush'd into a Sigh. It was long before either of us spoke, . 130 DOUBL DLR I.1 107
Lady Froth: leap, I vow I sigh when I think on't: my dear Lord! ha, . 140 DOUBL DLR II.1 63
Jeremy: heard you Sigh for. . . . . 302 FOR LOVE V.1 179
Almeria: Give me that Sigh. . . . . 356 M. BRIDE III.1 271
Sir Wilful: doleful Sigh more from my fellow Traveller and 'tis . . 472 WAY WORLD V.1 398
Sigh'd (3)
Singer: She frown'd and blush'd, then sigh'd and kiss'd, . . . 71 OLD BATCH III.2 V 19
Maskwell: Nephew, when I first Sigh'd for you; I quickly found it . 136 DOUBL DLR I.1 361
Singer: For whom inferiour Beauties sigh'd in vain. . . . . 435 WAY WORLD III.1 385

Sighing (4)
Heartwell: Sighing, Whining, Rhyming, Flattering, Lying, Grinning,   . 44   OLD BATCH   I.1   274
Fondlewife: (Sighing.) 96   OLD BATCH   IV.4 255
Careless: (Sighing). And Despise me. 169   DOUBL DLR   IV.1   77
Mirabell: high Place I once held, of sighing at your Feet; nay kill 471   WAY WORLD   V.1   371
Sighs (14)
Laetitia: (Sighs.) 77   OLD BATCH   IV.1   96
Laetitia: (Sighs.) 78   OLD BATCH   IV.1 113
Laetitia: (Sighs) 78   OLD BATCH   IV.1 128
              (Squeezes him by the hand, looks kindly on him, sighs, and 140   DOUBL DLR   II.1   65
Scandal: two. I can get nothing out of him but Sighs. He desires . 266   FOR LOVE   III.1 501
Angelica: (sighs). I would I had lov'd you--for Heaven   .   . 294   FOR LOVE   IV.1   711
Angelica: (Sighs.) 294   FOR LOVE   IV.1   714
Leonora: Sent in my Sighs and Pray'rs for his Deliv'rance;   . . 327   M. BRIDE   I.1   28
Leonora: For Sighs and Pray'rs were all that I could offer. . . 327   M. BRIDE   I.1   29
Almeria: The Sighs, the Tears, the Groans, the restless Cares, . 330   M. BRIDE   I.1   157
Osmyn-Alph: The Piercing Sighs, and Murmurs of my Love   .   . 351   M. BRIDE   III.1   77
Osmyn-Alph: But dash'd with Rain from Eyes, and swail'd with Sighs, . 357   M. BRIDE   III.1 323
Manuel: And breath her Sighs upon my Lips for his,   .   . 374   M. BRIDE   V.1 V86E
Osmyn-Alph: Of cordial Sighs; and re-inspire thy Bosom   383   M. BRIDE   V.2   284
Sight (43)   see O'sight
Sir Joseph: him, till I can get out of his sight; but out o'sight out
              c'mind 48   OLD BATCH   II.1   45
Sir Joseph: in your sight, upon the full blown Bladders of repentance--
              spoil'd--I shall loath the sight of Mankind for your   . . 49   OLD BATCH   II.1   59
Belinda: spoil'd--I shall loath the sight of Mankind for your   . . 55   OLD BATCH   II.2   15
Belinda: endure the sight of a Fire this Twelvemonth. 59   OLD BATCH   II.2   165
Sharper: Mony paid at sight! I'm come to return my Thanks-- . . . 68   OLD BATCH   III.1 285
Heartwell: Well, farewell then--if I can get out of her sight I   . . 74   OLD BATCH   III.2 129
Heartwell: Well, farewell then--if I can get out of sight I   . . . 74   OLD BATCH   III.2 V129
Bellmour: And ev'ry Eye receives a new-born Sight. 81   OLD BATCH   IV.2   12
Belinda: Oh; a most Comical Sight: A Country-Squire, with   . . . 84   OLD BATCH   IV.3   23
Laetitia: out of my sight? 90   OLD BATCH   IV.4   58
Lady Ply: Sir Paul, take Cynthia from his sight; leave me to   . . . 145   DOUBL DLR   II.1   272
Careless: coming, and I shall never succeed while thou art in sight-- . 157   DOUBL DLR   III.1 265
Mellefont: sight, and to lose so much time as to write to her.   . 159   DOUBL DLR   III.1 318
Lord Froth: 'tis such a sight to see some teeth--sure you're a great . 162   DOUBL DLR   III.1 460
Careless: ever from your sight, and drown me in my Tomb. 170   DOUBL DLR   IV.1   117
Lord Touch: Hence from my sight, thou living infamy 186   DOUBL DLR   IV.2   118
Maskwell: perish first, and from this hour avoid all sight and speech, . 188   DOUBL DLR   V.1   41
Lady Touch: thee open to my sight! But then 'twill be too late to know-- . 198   DOUBL DLR   V.1   397
Mellefont: Man!--Take him hence, for he's a Disease to my Sight. . . 202   DOUBL DLR   V.1   574
Tattle: with the Sight. 232   FOR LOVE   I.1   611
Jeremy: Aye, Sir, hooded like a Hawk, to seize at first sight   . . 302   FOR LOVE   V.1   199
Almeria: Devouring Seas have wash'd thee from my sight,   .   . 328   M. BRIDE   I.1   70
Gonsalez: While you alone retire, and shun this Sight;   332   M. BRIDE   I.1   243
Gonsalez: This Sight, which is indeed not seen (tho' twice   . . . 332   M. BRIDE   I.1   244
Manuel: Yet--upon thought, it doubly wounds my sight,   . . . 333   M. BRIDE   I.1   294
Almeria: And Terror on my aking Sight; the Tombs 339   M. BRIDE   II.1   64
Almeria: And with such Suddenness, hast hit my Sight;   343   M. BRIDE   II.2   153
Osmyn-Alph: It wonnot be; O, impotence of Sight!   345   M. BRIDE   II.2   217
Osmyn-Alph: O impotence of Sight! Mechanick Sense, ... 345   M. BRIDE   II.2 V217
Osmyn-Alph: Which I would shew thee Friend, but that the Sight   . . . 352   M. BRIDE   III.1 109
Osmyn-Alph: Or wish thee from my Sight. 356   M. BRIDE   III.1 254
Manuel: Be dark'ned, so as to amuze the Sight. 374   M. BRIDE   V.1   85
Zara: Their red and angry Beams; as if his Sight   375   M. BRIDE   V.1   94
Garcia: sight! 377   M. BRIDE   V.2   52
Zara: And ever and anon, the Sight was dash'd 379   M. BRIDE   V.2   139
Almeria: But want a Guide: for Tears have dim'd my Sight. . . . 381   M. BRIDE   V.2   221
Leonora: Will stab the Sight, and make your Eyes rain Blood. . . 381   M. BRIDE   V.2   230
Leonora: Ready to stab the Sight, and make your Eyes 381   M. BRIDE   V.2 V230
Almeria: My Sight, against my Sight? and shall I trust   . . . 383   M. BRIDE   V.2   293
Osmyn-Alph: Let 'em remove the Body from her Sight.   383   M. BRIDE   V.2   311
Lady Wish: Aversion to the very sight of Men,--ay Friend, she   . . 466   WAY WORLD   V.1   186
Lady Wish: the sight or name of an obscene Play-Book--and can I   . 467   WAY WORLD   V.1   202
Sigillatum (1)
Sr Sampson: White, Signatum, Sigillatum, and Deliberatum; that as soon 240   FOR LOVE   II.1   181
Sign (19)
Sir Joseph: that's a better Jest than tother. 'Tis a sign you and I
              ha'n't 50   OLD BATCH   II.1   116
Araminta: Ay, Cousin, and 'tis a sign the Creatures mimick   . . . 60   OLD BATCH   II.2   215
Sharper: your self into a Premunire, by trusting to that sign of a 69   OLD BATCH   III.1 304
Heartwell: yet a more certain Sign than all this; I give thee my Mony. 73   OLD BATCH   III.2   85
Silvia: Ay, but that is no Sign, for they say, Gentlemen will   . . 73   OLD BATCH   III.2   86
Brisk: Ay, my Lord, it's a sign I hit you in the Teeth, if you   . 132   DOUBL DLR   I.1   210
Lady Touch: to ruin me--My Lord shall sign to your desires; I will my 185   DOUBL DLR   IV.2   84
Scandal: Indiscretion be a sign of Love, you are the most a Lover . 234   FOR LOVE   I.1   676
Buckram: this Box, if he be ready to sign and seal. 278   FOR LOVE   IV.1   115
Angelica: like him, it's a sign he likes me; and that's more than half 297   FOR LOVE   V.1   6
Sr Sampson: ready?--Come, Sir, will you sign and seal? 311   FOR LOVE   V.1   514
Sr Sampson: now, Sir? Will you sign, Sir? Come, will you sign and   . 311   FOR LOVE   V.1   538
Valentine: can effect it: Which, for that Reason, I will sign to-- . 312   FOR LOVE   V.1   548
Valentine: sign this? 312   FOR LOVE   V.1   553
Almeria: Their Heads in Sign of Grief and Innocence! 382   M. BRIDE   V.2   251
Petulant: either for a Sign of Guilt, or ill Breeding. 409   WAY WORLD   I.1   537
Marwood: That's a Sign indeed its no Enemy to you. 436   WAY WORLD   III.1 419
Fainall: the Instrument, are you prepar'd to sign?   472   WAY WORLD   V.1   415
Sign'd (7)
Sharper: Here, here, she's thy own Man, sign'd and seal'd too-- . 79   OLD BATCH   IV.1   164
Lord Touch: sign'd, and have his name inserted--yours will fill the   . 189   DOUBL DLR   V.1   63
Foresight: When was this Sign'd, what Hour? Odso, you should   . . 240   FOR LOVE   II.1   189
Valentine: those hard Conditions, which my necessity Sign'd to.   . . 243   FOR LOVE   II.1   284
Sr Sampson: D'ye see, Mr. Buckram, here's the Paper sign'd 278   FOR LOVE   IV.1   112
Selim: Wherefore a Warrant for his Death is sign'd; 361   M. BRIDE   IV.1   15
Waitwell: sign'd this Night? May I hope so farr?   461   WAY WORLD   IV.1   639
Signal (1)
Valentine: me Signal Service in my necessity. But you delight in   . . 223   FOR LOVE   I.1   259

Simple (3)

Speaker	Text	PAGE	TITLE	ACT.SC	LINE
Valentine:	I am of my self, a plain easie simple Creature; and	244	FOR LOVE	II.1	345
Marwood:	rest of him. Poor simple Fiend! Madam Marwood has a	431	WAY WORLD	III.1	239
Mirabell:	but restrain your self to Native and Simple Tea-Table	451	WAY WORLD	IV.1	265

Simplicity (1)

Speaker	Text	PAGE	TITLE	ACT.SC	LINE
Tattle:	not find fault with her pretty simplicity, it becomes her	249	FOR LOVE	II.1	535

Simply (2)

Speaker	Text	PAGE	TITLE	ACT.SC	LINE
Belinda:	friends with him.--I swear, he looks so very simply,	86	OLD BATCH	IV.3	132
Sharper:	but let thee look simply, and laugh by thy self.	100	OLD BATCH	V.1	141

Sin (21)

Speaker	Text	PAGE	TITLE	ACT.SC	LINE
Bellmour:	the deeper the Sin the sweeter. Frank I'm amaz'd at thy good	39	OLD BATCH	I.1	92
Setter:	to Sin.	64	OLD BATCH	III.1	133
Fondlewife:	detestable, how hainous, and how Crying a Sin, the Sin	77	OLD BATCH	IV.1	68
Fondlewife:	weighty Sin; and although it may lie heavy upon thee,	77	OLD BATCH	IV.1	70
Laetitia:	Book, and only tends to the Speculation of Sin.	92	OLD BATCH	IV.4	115
	Were each to suffer for his Mothers Sin:	125	DOUBL DLR	PRO.	36
Lady Ply:	Heart? May be you don't think it a sin,--they say	147	DOUBL DLR	II.1	346
Lady Ply:	some of you Gentlemen don't think it a sin,--may be	147	DOUBL DLR	II.1	347
Lady Ply:	it is no sin to them that don't think it so;--indeed, If	147	DOUBL DLR	II.1	348
Lady Ply:	I did not think it a sin,--but still my honour, if it were	147	DOUBL DLR	II.1	349
Lady Ply:	no sin,--but then, to Marry my Daughter, for the	147	DOUBL DLR	II.1	350
Lady Ply:	your honour too--but the sin!--well but the	148	DOUBL DLR	II.1	361
Lady Touch:	so damn'd a Sin as Incest! unnatural Incest!	186	DOUBL DLR	IV.2	100
Lady Touch:	a Sin, in pity to your Soul.	197	DOUBL DLR	V.1	382
Jeremy:	Wages of Sin, either at the Day of Marriage, or the Day	218	FOR LOVE	I.1	101
Miss Prue:	Lies--but they frighted me, and said it was a sin.	252	FOR LOVE	II.1	630
	Our Authors Sin, but we alone repent.	323	M. BRIDE	PRO.	22
Manuel:	And make it Sin, not to renounce that Vow,	334	M. BRIDE	I.1	355
Gonsalez:	For thee I've plung'd into this Sea of Sin;	378	M. BRIDE	V.2	84
Foible:	Well, if worshipping of Pictures be a Sin	427	WAY WORLD	III.1	77

Since (80)

Speaker	Text	PAGE	TITLE	ACT.SC	LINE
Sharper:	over my ill fortune, since it pay'd the price of your ransome.	48	OLD BATCH	II.1	34
Sharper:	since it has purchas'd me the friendship and acquaintance of	49	OLD BATCH	II.1	77
Sharper:	your gratitude and generosity. Since the refunding so	50	OLD BATCH	II.1	89
Sharper:	your Gratitude and Generosity. Since the paying so	50	OLD BATCH	II.1	V 89
Sir Joseph:	Nay agad I hate fear ever since I had like to have	51	OLD BATCH	II.1	144
Capt Bluff:	share in't. Tho' I might say that too, since I am no Body	53	OLD BATCH	II.1	200
Capt Bluff:	share in't. Tho' I might say that too, since I name no Body	53	OLD BATCH	II.1	V200
Silvia:	Well, since there's no remedy--Yet tell me--	61	OLD BATCH	III.1	14
Lucy:	As you would wish--Since there is no reclaiming	75	OLD BATCH	III.2	155
Laetitia:	to lie at peace in my cold Grave--Since it will	78	OLD BATCH	IV.1	111
Laetitia:	I hope you are a Gentleman;--and since you are	82	OLD BATCH	IV.2	62
Belinda:	have been at the Exchange since, and am so tir'd--	83	OLD BATCH	IV.3	2
Belinda:	my Dear,--I have seen such unhewn Creatures since,--Ha,	83	OLD BATCH	IV.3	11
Belinda:	rubb'd his Eyes, since break of Day neither, he looks as if	86	OLD BATCH	IV.3	130
Bellmour:	Since all Artifice is vain--and I think my self obliged	93	OLD BATCH	IV.4	157
Bellmour:	Well, since I see thou art a good honest Fellow, I'll	94	OLD BATCH	IV.4	198
Araminta:	our House since.	107	OLD BATCH	V.1	400
Capt Bluff:	'Tis very generous, Sir, since I needs must own--	110	OLD BATCH	V.2	104
Brisk:	things said; or one, understood, since thy Amputation	128	DOUBL DLR	I.1	36
Mellefont:	violent Passion for me. Since my first refusal of her	129	DOUBL DLR	I.1	86
Maskwell:	Minute, and was blest. How I have Lov'd you since,	137	DOUBL DLR	I.1	370
Lord Froth:	a Captive first, and ever since 't has been in Love with	140	DOUBL DLR	II.1	69
Mellefont:	because it's possible we may lose; since we have Shuffled	142	DOUBL DLR	II.1	160
Maskwell:	I might be trusted; since it was as much my interest as hers	149	DOUBL DLR	II.1	423
Lady Touch:	which is not consenting with your own: But since I am	151	DOUBL DLR	III.1	38
Maskwell:	Woman, and I lov'd her once. But I don't know, since I	155	DOUBL DLR	III.1	176
Maskwell:	Woman, I lov'd her once. But I don't know, since I	155	DOUBL DLR	III.1	V176
Careless:	since the day of his Marriage, he has, out of a piece of	158	DOUBL DLR	III.1	277
Mellefont:	hands and sprawling in his Sleep; and ever since she has	158	DOUBL DLR	III.1	289
Cynthia:	mistaken the thing: Since	167	DOUBL DLR	III.1	632
Cynthia:	I would not--But 'tis but reasonable that since I	168	DOUBL DLR	IV.1	44
Lady Froth:	know, since we are Partners.	177	DOUBL DLR	IV.1	387
Maskwell:	Strike then--Since you will have it so.	197	DOUBL DLR	V.1	383
	But since in Paradise frail Flesh gave way,	213	FOR LOVE	PRO.	18
	Since the Plain-Dealers Scenes of Manly Rage,	214	FOR LOVE	PRO.	39
Scandal:	merciful, and wish you well, since Love and Pleasurable	220	FOR LOVE	I.1	162
Tattle:	sav'd, Valentine, I never expos'd a Woman, since I knew	227	FOR LOVE	I.1	406
Foresight:	I will have Patience, since it is the Will of the Stars	238	FOR LOVE	II.1	127
Jeremy:	time he has been abroad since his Confinement, and he	242	FOR LOVE	II.1	268
Valentine:	him: I came to Angelica; but since she was gone abroad, it	246	FOR LOVE	II.1	408
Mrs Fore:	It's very true, Sister: Well since all's out, and	248	FOR LOVE	II.1	476
Mrs Fore:	as you say, since we are both Wounded, let us do that is	248	FOR LOVE	II.1	477
Mrs Fore:	as you say, since we are both Wounded, let us do what is	248	FOR LOVE	II.1	V477
Tattle:	to no purpose--But since we have done nothing, we must	253	FOR LOVE	III.1	22
Angelica:	Estate too: But since that's gone, the Bait's off, and the	260	FOR LOVE	III.1	247
Sr Sampson:	since I saw thee.	261	FOR LOVE	III.1	288
Scandal:	and the Uneasiness that has attended me ever since, brings	269	FOR LOVE	III.1	591
Mrs Fore:	I cannot say that he has once broken my Rest, since we	270	FOR LOVE	III.1	623
Singer-V:	Since Women love to change, and so do we.	293	FOR LOVE	IV.1	664
Valentine:	and since you have lov'd me, you must own I have at	294	FOR LOVE	IV.1	709
Valentine:	was considered, it was yours; since I thought I wanted	295	FOR LOVE	IV.1	726
Sr Sampson:	reviv'd me--Not since I was Five and Thirty.	298	FOR LOVE	V.1	15
Tattle:	while ago, Child. I have been asleep since; slept a whole	303	FOR LOVE	V.1	237
Foresight:	I think she has not return'd, since she went abroad	306	FOR LOVE	V.1	336
Angelica:	Well, Sir Sampson, since I have plaid you a Trick,	312	FOR LOVE	V.1	570
	But we can't fear, since you're so good to save us,	315	FOR LOVE	EPI.	38
	Since Custome gives the Losers leave to speak.	323	M. BRIDE	PRO.	28
Almeria:	Since I have made this Vow:	331	M. BRIDE	I.1	203
Almeria:	And more at large, since I have made this Vow.	331	M. BRIDE	I.1	V203
Manuel:	No more; my Promise long since pass'd, thy Loyalty,	334	M. BRIDE	I.1	340
Manuel:	No more; my Promise long since pass'd, thy Services,	334	M. BRIDE	I.1	V340
Perez:	To me 'twas long since plain.	338	M. BRIDE	II.1	45
Zara:	You're grown a Favourite since last we parted;	359	M. BRIDE	III.1	412
Selim:	Is since arrived, of more revolted Troops.	361	M. BRIDE	IV.1	7

Since   (continued)

Gonsalez:	None, Sir. Some Papers have been since discover'd, . .	363	M. BRIDE	IV.1	75
Almeria:	Since thou'rt reveal'd, alone thou shalt not die. . .	368	M. BRIDE	IV.1	304
Zara:	Thou shalt partake. Since Fates no more afford;	376	M. BRIDE	V.1	138
Alonzo:	My Lord, he enter'd, but a moment since, ...	376	M. BRIDE	V.2	20
Fainall:	for ycu are sure to be too hard for him at Repartee: since	402	WAY WORLD	I.1	282
Witwoud:	Truths! Ha, ha, ha! No, no, since you will have it, . .	404	WAY WORLD	I.1	339
Mrs Fain:	to see him; but since I have despis'd him, he's too offensive.	416	WAY WORLD	II.1	255
Lady Wish:	Foible's a lost Thing; has been abroad since	426	WAY WORLD	III.1	45
Lady Wish:	Morning, and never heard of since.	426	WAY WORLD	III.1	46
Lady Wish:	since 'tis your Judgment, I'll think on't again. I assure you	432	WAY WORLD	III.1	270
Witwoud:	forgot him; I have not seen him since the Revolution. .	436	WAY WORLD	III.1	442
Sir Wilful:	conjectur'd you were a Fop, since you began to change the	439	WAY WORLD	III.1	540
Fainall:	but I'll disown the Order. And since I take my leave of 'em,	444	WAY WORLD	III.1	721
Lady Wish:	Nay Sir Rowland, since you give me a proof of . . .	460	WAY WORLD	IV.1	580
Foible:	cou'd have tcld ycu long enough since, but I love to keep	464	WAY WORLD	V.1	86
	Since when, they by their own offences taught . . .	479	WAY WORLD	EPI.	14

Sincere (6)

Bellmour:	Heart of a Mountain-Tyger. By the faith of a sincere . .	95	OLD BATCH	IV.4	235
Angelica:	to me; nay, what if you were sincere? still you must . .	311	FOR LOVE	V.1	532
Witwoud:	Wit will excuse that: A Wit shou'd no more be sincere, .	403	WAY WORLD	I.1	319
Marwood:	Come, be as sincere, acknowledge that your Sentiments .	410	WAY WORLD	II.1	31
Marwood:	More tender, more sincere, and more enduring, ...	414	WAY WORLD	II.1	167
Mirabell:	so gocd a Lady, with a sincere remorse, and a hearty .	471	WAY WORLD	V.1	367

Sincerely (2)

Fondlewife:	lovely in the Eyes of Women--Sincerely I am afraid he . .	76	OLD BATCH	IV.1	28
Trapland:	Sincerely, I am loth to be thus pressing, but my . .	224	FOR LCVE	I.1	322

Sincerity (3)

Angelica:	Weakness I am a Stranger to. But I have too much Sincerity	277	FOR LCVE	IV.1	70
Gonsalez:	In the Sincerity of Womens Actions.	366	M. BRIDE	IV.1	201
Mirabell:	with plain Dealing and Sincerity.	422	WAY WORLD	II.1	466

Sing (12)

Silvia:	If you could Sing and Dance so, I should love to look . .	72	OLD BATCH	III.2	30
Cynthia:	time, is as disagreeable as to sing out cf time or out of	163	DOUEL DLR	III.1	473
Brisk:	He? e'gad, so I did--My Lord can sing it.	166	DOUEL DLR	III.1	589
Brisk:	call it, but it's Satyr.--Sing it my Lord.	166	DOUEL DLR	III.1	593
Lady Froth:	Wit, and can sing a Tune already. My Lord wont you go? .	167	DOUEL DLR	III.1	620
Scandal:	Proverbs, and I see one in the next Room that will sing it.	258	FOR LCVE	III.1	192
	(Re-enter Scandal, with one to Sing.)	258	FOR LCVE	III.1	V196
Scandal:	Pray sing the first Song in the last new Play.	258	FOR LOVE	III.1	197
Ben:	Come, I'll sing you a Song of a Sailor.	273	FOR LOVE	III.1	740
Valentine:	I would have Musick--Sing me the Song that I	292	FOR LOVE	IV.1	648
Millamant:	sing the Song, I wou'd have learnt Yesterday. You shall .	434	WAY WORLD	III.1	371
Sir Wilful:	But let British Lads sing, ...	456	WAY WORLD	IV.1	455

Singing (4)

Heartwell:	burdens, are forced to undergo Dressing, Dancing, Singing,	44	OLD BATCH	I.1	273
Mrs Fain:	him; But he answers her only with Singing and Drinking .	452	WAY WORLD	IV.1	312
Sir Wilful:	(Exit Singing with Witwoud.)	457	WAY WORLD	IV.1	480
Lady Wish:	lectures, against Singing and Dancing, and such Debaucheries;	467	WAY WORLD	V.1	198

Single (4)

Angelica:	living single, and want a Husband.	298	FOR LCVE	V.1	47
Fainall:	Corrupt to Superstition, and blind Credulity. I am single;	444	WAY WORLD	III.1	719
Fainall:	single Beef-eater there? but I'm prepar'd for you; and .	473	WAY WORLD	V.1	433
	To which no single Beauty must pretend:	479	WAY WORLD	EPI.	34

Singled (1)

Osmyn-Alph:	Is singled out to bleed, and bear the Scourge;	350	M. BRIDE	III.1	30

Singly (1)

	To think they singly can support a Scene, ...	479	WAY WORLD	EPI.	26

Sings (8)

Sir Joseph:	Bully, dost thou see those Tearers? (Sings.) Look you what	85	OLD BATCH	IV.3	66
Lord Froth:	(sings).	166	DOUEL DLR	III.1	595
Brisk:	(sings). I'm sick with Love, ha ha ha, prithee come (walking	175	DOUEL DLR	IV.1	306
	(Ben Sings.)	273	FOR LOVE	III.1	755
Mrs Frail:	(Sings.)	287	FOR LOVE	IV.1	446
Sir Wilful:	(Sings,)	455	WAY WORLD	IV.1	396
Sir Wilful:	(Sings,)	455	WAY WORLD	IV.1	415
Sir Wilful:	(Sings,)	456	WAY WORLD	IV.1	449

Singular (2)

Bellmour:	Thou art an old Fornicator of a singular good	43	OLD BATCH	I.1	250
Foresight:	You speak with singular good Judgment, Mr.	285	FOR LOVE	IV.1	347

Sinister (1)

Lady Wish:	You must not attribute my yielding to any sinister appetite,	458	WAY WORLD	IV.1	529

Sink (8)

	For Life will struggle long, 'ere it sink down:	125	DOUEL DLR	PRO.	17
Almeria:	May lay the Burden down, and sink in Slumbers	340	M. BRIDE	II.2	19
Almeria:	But sink each other, lower yet, down, down, ...	358	M. BRIDE	III.1	371
Almeria:	But sink each other, deeper yet, down, down	358	M. BRIDE	III.1	V371
Almeria:	Let me go, let me fall, sink deep--I'll dig, ...	370	M. BRIDE	IV.1	347
Selim:	My Tongue faulters, and my Voice fails--I sink-- . . .	380	M. BRIDE	V.2	V183
Fainall:	turn'd a drift, like a Leaky hulk to Sink or Swim, as she	473	WAY WORLD	V.1	443
Lady Wish:	to sink under the fatigue; and I cannot but have some fears	478	WAY WORLD	V.1	610

Sinking (5)

	How nearly some Good Men might have scap'd Sinking. .	125	DOUEL DLR	PRO.	24
Mellefont:	that's sinking; tho' ne'er so far off.	148	DOUEL DLR	II.1	390
Maskwell:	No sinking, nor no danger,--come, cheer up;	148	DOUEL DLR	II.1	391
Ben:	were sinking, as we sayn at Sea. But I'll tell you why I	261	FOR LOVE	III.1	308
Osmyn-Alph:	Are they not soothing Softness, sinking Ease, . . .	358	M. BRIDE	III.1	363

Sinks (1)

Osmyn-Alph:	So like Almeria. Ha! it sinks, it falls, ...	341	M. BRIDE	II.2	52

Sinner (3)

Bellmour:	Sinner, she's innocent, for me. Go to him, Madam, fling .	95	OLD BATCH	IV.4	236
	But how?--Just as the Devil does a Sinner.	113	OLD BATCH	EPI.	28
Sir Paul:	unworthy Sinner--But if I had a Son, ah, that's my . . .	161	DOUEL DLR	III.1	415

Sinners (2)
| Heartwell: | young, termagant flashy sinners--you have all the guilt | . 43 | OLD BATCH | I.1 | 238 |
| Scandal: | Sinners, and the faint dawning of a Bliss to wishing | . . 275 | FOR LCVE | III.1 | 817 |

Sins (2)
| Mellefont: | doubt you have some unrepented Sins that may hang | . . . 184 | DOUBL DLR | IV.2 | 55 |
| Valentine: | my Sins in my Face: Here, give her this, ... | . 221 | FOR LCVE | I.1 | 208 |

Sipping (1)
| Lady Wish: | Sipping? Tasting? Save thee, dost thou not know the | . . 425 | WAY WCBLD | III.1 | 24 |

Sir (662)   see Sr
Vainlove:	Sir--(Shewing Letters.) And Business must be follow'd,	. 37	OLD BATCH	I.1	7
Bellmour:	I marry Sir, I have a Hawks Eye at a Wcmans hand	. . . 38	OLD BATCH	I.1	32
Bellmour:	Oh, 'tis Sir Joseph Wittoll with his friend;	. 46	OLD BATCH	I.1	V339
	(Sir Joseph Wittcll and Capt. Bluffe, cross the Stage.)	. 46	OLD BATCH	I.1	340
	(Sir Joseph Wittcll, Sharper following.)	. 47	OLD BATCH	II.1	
Sir Joseph:	Not I Sir, not I, as I've a Soul to be sav'd, I have	. . 48	OLD BATCH	II.1	29
Sir Joseph:	and as you were saying Sir.	. . 48	OLD BATCH	II.1	31
Sharper:	O your Servant Sir, you are safe then it seems; 'tis an	. 48	OLD BATCH	II.1	32
Sir Joseph:	I rejoyce agad not I Sir; I'me sorry for your loss,	. . 48	OLD BATCH	II.1	35
Sir Joseph:	I rejcyce! agad not I Sir; I'me very scrry for your loss,	. 48	OLD BATCH	II.1	V 35
Sir Joseph:	with all my Heart, Blood and Guts Sir; and if you did but	. 48	OLD BATCH	II.1	36
Sir Joseph:	O Lord forget him! No no Sir, I don't forget you-- . .	. 48	OLD BATCH	II.1	40
Sir Joseph:	Stay, stay Sir, let me recollect--(aside) he's a . .	. 48	OLD BATCH	II.1	43
Sharper:	Methought the service I did you last night Sir, in . .	. 48	OLD BATCH	II.1	47
Sir Joseph:	hem! Sir, I must submissively implore your pardon for	. . 49	OLD BATCH	II.1	54
Sir Joseph:	hem! Sir, I most submissively implore your pardon for	. . 49	OLD BATCH	II.1	V 54
Sir Joseph:	intire dependance Sir, upcn the superfluity of your				
	goodness,	. . 49	OLD BATCH	II.1	56
Sharper:	So-h, C Sir I am easily pacify'd, the acknowledgment	. . 49	OLD BATCH	II.1	62
Sir Joseph:	Acknowledgment! Sir I am all over acknowledgment, . .	. 49	OLD BATCH	II.1	64
Sir Joseph:	Sir Joseph Wittoll Knight. Hem! hem!	. 49	OLD BATCH	II.1	69
Sharper:	Sir Joseph Wittoll!	. 49	OLD BATCH	II.1	70
Sir Joseph:	The same Sir, of Wittoll-hall in Comitatu Bucks. . .	. 49	OLD BATCH	II.1	71
Sir Joseph:	O Lord Sir!	. 49	OLD BATCH	II.1	75
Sir Joseph:	You are only pleas'd to say so Sir--But pray if I . . .	. 49	OLD BATCH	II.1	79
Sharper:	O term it no longer so Sir. In the Scuffle last Night I	. 49	OLD BATCH	II.1	81
Sharper:	You have found it Sir then it seems; I profess I'me . .	. 49	OLD BATCH	II.1	85
Sir Joseph:	Sir ycur humble Servant--I don't question but you . .	. 49	OLD BATCH	II.1	87
Sir Joseph:	Sum--But han't you found it Sir!	. 50	OLD BATCH	II.1	93
Sharper:	Sir.	. 50	OLD BATCH	II.1	95
Sharper:	honour of Sir Joseph Wittoll.	. 50	OLD BATCH	II.1	98
Sir Joseph:	O Lord Sir.	. 5C	OLD BATCH	II.1	99
Sir Joseph:	Nay 'Ile say that for my self--with your leave Sir-- .	. 50	OLD BATCH	II.1	104
Sharper:	Mony is but Dirt Sir Joseph--Mere Dirt.	. 50	OLD BATCH	II.1	110
Sharper:	Are ycu so extravagant in Cloaths Sir Joseph? . . .	. 50	OLD BATCH	II.1	113
Sharper:	If he had Sir, what then? he could have done no . . .	. 50	OLD BATCH	II.1	125
Sir Joseph:	O Lord Sir by no means--but I might have sav'd a . . .	. 51	OLD BATCH	II.1	128
Sir Joseph:	Sir--a damn'd hot Fellow--only as I was saying, I let him	. 51	OLD EATCH	II.1	130
Sir Joseph:	Limbo--But Sir I have a Letter of Credit to Alderman .	. 51	OLD BATCH	II.1	132
Capt Bluff:	I'le recommend my self--Sir I hcnour you; I understand	. 51	OLD BATCH	II.1	155
Capt Bluff:	Fighting, Sir I Kiss your Hilts.	. 51	OLD BATCH	II.1	157
Sharper:	Sir your Servant, but you are misinform'd, for . . .	. 51	OLD BATCH	II.1	158
Sharper:	unless it be tc serve my particular Friend, as Sir				
	Joseph here, ...	. 51	OLD BATCH	II.1	159
Capt Bluff:	O Lord I beg your pardon Sir, I find ycu are not of	. . 51	OLD BATCH	II.1	162
Sir Joseph:	Ah, well said my Hero; was not that great Sir? . . .	. 52	OLD BATCH	II.1	166
Capt Bluff:	Ay! Then I honour him again--Sir may I crave your . .	. 52	OLD BATCH	II.1	171
Sharper:	Ay Sir, my name's Sharper.	. 52	OLD BATCH	II.1	173
Sharper:	Hannibal I believe you mean Sir Joseph.	. 52	OLD BATCH	II.1	177
Capt Bluff:	Undoubtedly he did Sir; faith Hannibal was a very . .	. 52	OLD BATCH	II.1	178
Capt Bluff:	pretty Fellow--but Sir Joseph, ccmparisons are odious--	. 52	OLD BATCH	II.1	179
Capt Bluff:	be granted--But Alas Sir! were he alive now, he would .	. 52	OLD BATCH	II.1	181
Sharper:	How Sir! I make a doubt, if there be at this Day a . .	. 52	OLD BATCH	II.1	183
Capt Bluff:	Oh excuse me Sir; have you serv'd abroad Sir? . . .	. 52	OLD BATCH	II.1	185
Sharper:	Not I really Sir.	. 52	OLD BATCH	II.1	186
Capt Bluff:	Sir: I'me afraid you scarce know the History of the Late	. 52	OLD BATCH	II.1	188
Sharper:	Not I, Sir, no more than publick Letters, or Gazettes	. 52	OLD EATCH	II.1	190
Capt Bluff:	Gazette! Why there again now--Why, Sir, there are . .	. 52	OLD BATCH	II.1	192
Capt Bluff:	You must know, Sir, I was resident in Flanders the last	. 52	OLD EATCH	II.1	195
Capt Bluff:	Perhaps, Sir, there was a scarce any thing of moment .	. 52	OLD BATCH	II.1	197
Capt Bluff:	Oh fy no Sir Joseph--you know I hate this.	. 53	OLD BATCH	II.1	217
Capt Bluff:	Death, what do you mean Sir Joseph?	. 53	OLD BATCH	II.1	221
Capt Bluff:	Zoons Sir, it's a Lie, you have not seen it, nor shant	. 53	OLD BATCH	II.1	234
Capt Bluff:	see it; Sir I say you can't see; what de'e say to that now?	. 53	OLD BATCH	II.1	235
Sharper:	Captain, Sir Joseph's penitent.	. 54	OLD BATCH	II.1	240
Capt Bluff:	O I am calm Sir, calm as a discharg'd Culverin--But .	. 54	OLD BATCH	II.1	241
Capt Bluff:	Nay ccme Sir Joseph, you know my Heat's soon over. . .	. 54	OLD BATCH	II.1	243
Sharper:	I wait on you Sir; nay pray Captain--You are	. 54	OLD BATCH	II.1	248
Sharper:	Sir Joseph's Back.	. 54	OLD EATCH	II.1	249
Setter:	As all lew'd projects do Sir, where the Devil prevents	. 64	OLD BATCH	III.1	117
Setter:	All, all Sir; the large sanctified Hat, and the little	. 64	OLD BATCH	III.1	123
Setter:	Rather prepare her for Confession, Sir by helping her	. 64	OLD BATCH	III.1	132
Setter:	I shall Sir--I wonder to which of these two	. 64	OLD BATCH	III.1	137
Lucy:	may discover something in my Masque--Worthy Sir, a . .	. 65	OLD BATCH	III.1	155
	(Enter Sir Joseph Wittoll, Bluffe.)	. 67	OLD BATCH	III.1	241
Sir Joseph:	Sir Joseph--Your Note was accepted, and the	. 68	OLD BATCH	III.1	284
Sir Joseph:	They won't be accepted, so readily as the Bill, Sir. .	. 68	OLD BATCH	III.1	286
Sir Joseph:	May be I am Sir, may be I am not Sir, may be I . . .	. 68	OLD BATCH	III.1	292
Sir Joseph:	am both Sir; what then? I hope I may be offended, without	. 68	OLD BATCH	III.1	293
Sir Joseph:	any offence to you Sir.	. 68	OLD EATCH	III.1	294
Capt Bluff:	Mr. Sharper, the matter is plain--Sir Joseph has found	. 69	OLD BATCH	III.1	296
Sharper:	Trick, Sir.	. 69	OLD BATCH	III.1	299
Sir Joseph:	Ay Trick, Sir, and won't be put upon Sir, being a . .	. 69	OLD BATCH	III.1	300
Sir Joseph:	Man of Honour Sir, and so Sir--	. 69	OLD BATCH	III.1	301
Sharper:	Hearkee, Sir Joseph, a word with ye--In consideration	. 69	OLD BATCH	III.1	302
Capt Bluff:	O this is your time Sir, you had best make use on't. .	. 69	OLD BATCH	III.1	319
Capt Bluff:	You are obliging Sir, but this is too publick a Place .	. 69	OLD BATCH	III.1	322

Sir (continued)

		PAGE	TITLE	ACT.SC	LINE
Lady Ply:	Sir Paul, what a Phrase was there? You will	159	DOUBL DLR	III.1	V327
Lady Ply:	O Lord! Sir, pardon me, we women have not	159	DOUBL DLR	III.1	348
Lady Ply:	You are so obliging, Sir.	160	DOUBL DLR	III.1	358
Lady Ply:	a very good skin, Sir.	160	DOUBL DLR	III.1	369
Careless:	O, Sir Paul, you are the happiest man alive. Such a . .	160	DOUBL DLR	III.1	392
	. . . carries it to Sir Paul.)	160	DOUBL DLR	III.1	V392
Careless:	What can that be, Sir Paul?	161	DOUBL DLR	III.1	406
Careless:	be told on't; she must i'faith, Sir Paul; 'tis an injury				
	to the	162	DOUBL DLR	III.1	442
Lady Ply:	Here, Sir Paul, it's from your Steward, here's a . .	162	DOUBL DLR	III.1	450
Lord Froth:	Heav'n, Sir Paul, you amaze me, of all things in . .	162	DOUBL DLR	III.1	457
Lord Froth:	admirer of my Lady Whifler, Mr. Sneer, and Sir Laurence	162	DOUBL DLR	III.1	461
	(Enter Boy and whispers Sir Paul.) . .	163	DOUBL DLR	III.1	488
Lady Ply:	I'm busie, Sir Paul, I wonder at your	163	DOUBL DLR	III.1	491
Careless:	Sir Paul, harkee, I'm reasoning the matter you know; .	163	DOUBL DLR	III.1	493
	(Exit Sir Paul.) . . .	163	DOUBL DLR	III.1	500
Lady Ply:	far you have gain'd upon me; I assure you if Sir Paul .	170	DOUBL DLR	IV.1	110
Lady Ply:	Sir, you have Conquered--What heart of Marble . . .	170	DOUBL DLR	IV.1	119
Lady Ply:	and how--Ah, there's Sir Paul.	170	DOUBL DLR	IV.1	126
	(Enter Sir Paul and Cynthia.) . . .	171	DOUBL DLR	IV.1	127
Careless:	'Slife yonder's Sir Paul, but if he were not come, I'm .	171	DOUBL DLR	IV.1	128
Cynthia:	I would obey you to my power, Sir; but if I have . .	171	DOUBL DLR	IV.1	134
Cynthia:	Pray don't be angry, Sir, when I swore, I had your . .	171	DOUBL DLR	IV.1	142
Lady Ply:	Ay, but Sir Paul, I conceive if she has sworn, . . .	171	DOUBL DLR	IV.1	150
Lady Ply:	most extraordinary respect and honour for you, Sir Paul.	172	DOUBL DLR	IV.1	175
Lady Ply:	O las, no indeed, Sir Paul, 'tis upon your account. .	172	DOUBL DLR	IV.1	181
Lady Ply:	you're too modest, Sir Paul.	172	DOUBL DLR	IV.1	186
Lady Ply:	O fy, Sir Paul, you'l put me out of Countenance . .	172	DOUBL DLR	IV.1	189
Lady Ply:	My Lip indeed, Sir Paul, I swear you shall. . . .	172	DOUBL DLR	IV.1	195
Lady Ply:	yet I'll be sure to be unsuspected this time.--Sir Paul.	173	DOUBL DLR	IV.1	212
Lady Ply:	No, no, nothing else I thank you, Sir Paul,-- . . .	173	DOUBL DLR	IV.1	220
Cynthia:	I'm glad to see you so merry, Sir.	173	DOUBL DLR	IV.1	232
Cynthia:	I don't Blush Sir, for I vow I don't understand.-- . .	174	DOUBL DLR	IV.1	245
Cynthia:	I'm all Obedience, Sir, to your Commands.	174	DOUBL DLR	IV.1	257
Lady Ply:	when 'tis Dark. O Crimine! I hope, Sir Paul has not seen	174	DOUBL DLR	IV.1	262
Lady Ply:	her own), Sir Paul, here's your Letter, to Morrow Morning	174	DOUBL DLR	IV.1	264
Brisk:	Sir Paul, Gads-bud you're an uncivil Person, let me tell	174	DOUBL DLR	IV.1	267
Brisk:	Sir Paul, will you send Careless into the Hall if you .	175	DOUBL DLR	IV.1	286
Lady Ply:	given Sir Paul your Letter instead of his own. . . .	178	DOUBL DLR	IV.1	400
	(Enter Sir Paul with the Letter.) .	178	DOUBL DLR	IV.1	405
Sir Paul:	Gallery. If Sir Paul should surprize us, I have a Commission	178	DOUBL DLR	IV.1	409
Sir Paul:	were not for Providence, sure poor Sir Paul thy Heart .	179	DOUBL DLR	IV.1	434
Lady Ply:	So Sir, I see you have read the Letter,--well . . .	179	DOUBL DLR	IV.1	437
Lady Ply:	now, Sir Paul, what do you think of your Friend Careless?	179	DOUBL DLR	IV.1	438
Sir Paul:	poor Sir Paul, I'm an Anabaptist, or a Jew, or what you	180	DOUBL DLR	IV.1	473
Careless:	Sir Paul, I'm glad I've met with you, 'gad I have . .	180	DOUBL DLR	IV.1	491
Sir Paul:	Indeed--Well Sir--(aside) I'll dissemble with him . .	180	DOUBL DLR	IV.1	494
Lord Touch:	I'm sure Sir Paul's Consent will follow Fortune; I'll .	189	DOUBL DLR	V.1	76
Maskwell:	No matter, Sir, don't trouble your head, all's in . .	190	DOUBL DLR	V.1	106
Maskwell:	this dotage, I know not; but he's gone to Sir Paul about my	190	DOUBL DLR	V.1	111
	(Enter Sir Paul.)	191	DOUBL DLR	V.1	158
Saygrace:	(looking out). Sweet Sir, I will but pen the last Line .	194	DOUBL DLR	V.1	272
	(Enter Lord Froth, and Sir Paul.) .	200	DOUBL DLR	V.1	491
Lord Froth:	By Heaven's, I have slept an Age,--Sir Paul, . . .	200	DOUBL DLR	V.1	492
Brisk:	My Lord, your humble Servant; Sir Paul yours,-- . .	201	DOUBL DLR	V.1	517
Jeremy:	Sir.	216	FOR LOVE	I.1	2
Jeremy:	Sir, you're a Gentleman, and probably understand . .	217	FOR LOVE	I.1	24
Jeremy:	in a Tub, go to Prison for you? 'Slife, Sir, what do you	217	FOR LOVE	I.1	31
Jeremy:	Aye, Sir, I am a Fool, I know it: And yet, Heav'n . .	217	FOR LOVE	I.1	40
Jeremy:	Hem!--Sir, if you please to give me a small . . .	217	FOR LOVE	I.1	64
Jeremy:	Sir, it's impossible--I may die with you, starve with .	218	FOR LOVE	I.1	72
Jeremy:	But Sir, Is this the way to recover your Father's . .	218	FOR LOVE	I.1	82
Jeremy:	Favour? Why Sir Sampson will be irreconcilable. If your	218	FOR LOVE	I.1	83
Jeremy:	upon you again. You're undone, Sir; you're ruin'd; you	218	FOR LOVE	I.1	85
Valentine:	Very well, Sir; can you proceed?	219	FOR LOVE	I.1	103
Jeremy:	Why so I have been telling my Master, Sir: Mr. . .	219	FOR LOVE	I.1	122
Jeremy:	Scandal, for Heaven's sake, Sir, try if you can disswade	219	FOR LOVE	I.1	123
Jeremy:	Nothing new, Sir; I have dispatch'd some half a . .	220	FOR LOVE	I.1	166
Jeremy:	No, faith Sir; I have put 'em off so long with patience	220	FOR LOVE	I.1	171
Jeremy:	body be surpriz'd at the Matter--(Knocking)--Again! Sir,	221	FOR LOVE	I.1	182
Jeremy:	O Sir, there's Trapland the Scrivener, with two . .	221	FOR LOVE	I.1	202
Jeremy:	Yes, Sir.	222	FOR LOVE	I.1	215
Jeremy:	Sir, your Father's Steward says he comes to make . .	224	FOR LOVE	I.1	302
Jeremy:	More Misfortunes, Sir.	225	FOR LOVE	I.1	356
Jeremy:	No Sir, but Mr. Tattle is come to wait upon you. . .	225	FOR LOVE	I.1	358
Jeremy:	Sir, Mrs. Frail has sent to know if you are stirring. .	229	FOR LOVE	I.1	505
Jeremy:	Sir, here's the Steward again from your Father. . .	234	FOR LOVE	I.1	661
Servant:	No, Sir.	235	FOR LOVE	II.1	4
Servant:	Yes, Sir.	235	FOR LOVE	II.1	8
Foresight:	I believe you lie, Sir.	235	FOR LOVE	II.1	9
Servant:	Sir?	235	FOR LOVE	II.1	10
Foresight:	I say you lie, Sir. It is impossible that any thing .	235	FOR LOVE	II.1	11
Foresight:	should be as I would have it; for I was born, Sir, when the	235	FOR LOVE	II.1	12
Servant:	I can't tell indeed, Sir.	235	FOR LOVE	II.1	14
Foresight:	No, I know you can't, Sir: But I can tell, Sir, and .	235	FOR LOVE	II.1	15
Foresight:	No, I know you can't, Sir: But I can tell and . . .	235	FOR LOVE	II.1	V 15
Foresight:	foretell, Sir.	235	FOR LOVE	II.1	15
Foresight:	Sirrah, go tell Sir Sampson Legend I'll wait on him, if	236	FOR LOVE	II.1	40
Nurse:	ever hear the like now--Sir, did ever I do any thing .	238	FOR LOVE	II.1	101
Servant:	Sir Sampson is coming down to wait upon you-- . . .	239	FOR LOVE	II.1	160
Foresight:	past: Go Nurse, tell Sir Sampson I'm ready to wait on him.	239	FOR LOVE	II.1	166
Nurse:	Yes, Sir.	239	FOR LOVE	II.1	167
	(Enter Sir Sampson Legend with a Paper.) . .	240	FOR LOVE	II.1	171
Foresight:	How, how? Sir Sampson, that all? Give me leave to .	240	FOR LOVE	II.1	202
Foresight:	Wife, Sir Sampson? Tho' you made a Cuckold of the .	241	FOR LOVE	II.1	231

Sir   (continued)

Speaker	Text	PAGE	TITLE	ACT.SC	LINE
Foresight:	But what do you know of my Wife, Sir Sampson?	242	FOR LOVE	II.1	255
Sr Sampson:	My Son, Sir; what Son, Sir? My Son Benjamin,	242	FOR LOVE	II.1	265
Jeremy:	No, Sir, Mr. Valentine, my master,--'tis the first	242	FOR LOVE	II.1	267
Sr Sampson:	Well, Sir.	242	FOR LOVE	II.1	270
Jeremy:	He is here, Sir.	242	FOR LOVE	II.1	272
Valentine:	Your Blessing, Sir.	243	FOR LOVE	II.1	273
Sr Sampson:	You've had it already, Sir, I think I sent it you to	243	FOR LOVE	II.1	274
Foresight:	Aye indeed, Sir Sampson, a great deal of Money for	243	FOR LOVE	II.1	277
Valentine:	Superfluity, Sir, it will scarce pay my Debts,--I	243	FOR LOVE	II.1	282
Sr Sampson:	Sir, how, I beseech you, what were you pleas'd	243	FOR LOVE	II.1	285
Valentine:	Why, Sir, that you wou'd not go to the extremity	243	FOR LOVE	II.1	287
Sr Sampson:	Oh Sir, I understand you,--that's all, ha?	243	FOR LOVE	II.1	289
Valentine:	Yes, Sir, all that I presume to ask.--But what	243	FOR LOVE	II.1	290
Sr Sampson:	No doubt of it, sweet Sir, but your filial Piety,	243	FOR LOVE	II.1	293
Valentine:	Sir, I don't deny it.--	243	FOR LOVE	II.1	302
Valentine:	Sir, is this Usage for your Son?--for that old,	244	FOR LOVE	II.1	311
Valentine:	you, Sir--	244	FOR LOVE	II.1	313
Sr Sampson:	You Sir; and you Sir:--Why, who are you Sir?	244	FOR LOVE	II.1	314
Valentine:	Your Son, Sir.	244	FOR LOVE	II.1	315
Sr Sampson:	That's more than I know, Sir, and I believe not.	244	FOR LOVE	II.1	316
Sr Sampson:	Sir? Here, to stand here, upon those two Leggs, and look	244	FOR LOVE	II.1	328
Jeremy:	Yes, I have a reasonable good Ear, Sir, as to Jiggs and	245	FOR LOVE	II.1	373
	(Exeunt Sir Sampson and Foresight.)	246	FOR LOVE	II.1	405
Mrs Frail:	and therefore must look sharply about me. Sir	248	FOR LOVE	II.1	491
Angelica:	Sir?	254	FOR LOVE	III.1	58
	(Enter Sir Sampson, Mrs. Frail, Miss Prue, and Servant.)	259	FOR LOVE	III.1	209
Angelica:	I'm pretty even with him, Sir Sampson; for if ever I	260	FOR LOVE	III.1	245
Angelica:	If I marry, Sir Sampson, I'm for a good Estate with	260	FOR LOVE	III.1	253
Servant:	There, Sir, his back's toward you.	260	FOR LOVE	III.1	269
Tattle:	Sir, you're welcome a-shore.	261	FOR LOVE	III.1	285
Angelica:	I thank you, Sir, I am not at all offended;--but	262	FOR LOVE	III.1	344
Angelica:	methinks Sir Sampson, You shou'd leave him alone with	262	FOR LOVE	III.1	345
Mrs Frail:	Foresight, and Sir Sampson coming. Sister, do you take Miss	265	FOR LOVE	III.1	447
Mrs Frail:	out.--Come, Sir, will you venture your self with me?	265	FOR LOVE	III.1	450
	(Enter Sir Sampson and Foresight.)	265	FOR LOVE	III.1	455
Foresight:	Sir Sampson, we'll have the Wedding to morrow	265	FOR LOVE	III.1	469
Scandal:	Sir Sampson, sad News.	266	FOR LOVE	III.1	480
Scandal:	Sir Sampson is hasty, very hasty;--I'm afraid he is not	267	FOR LOVE	III.1	520
Scandal:	Cause of that? And Sir Sampson is hurry'd on by an unusual	268	FOR LOVE	III.1	548
Nurse:	Yes, Sir.	270	FOR LOVE	III.1	642
Ben:	know her, Sir. Before she was Marry'd, she was call'd	273	FOR LOVE	III.1	752
Ben:	Had once a doubtful strife, Sir,	274	FOR LOVE	III.1	760
Ben:	To make a Maid a Wife, Sir,	274	FOR LOVE	III.1	761
Ben:	To lick her Lips at Men, Sir,	274	FOR LOVE	III.1	765
Ben:	And gnaw the Sheets in vain, Sir,	274	FOR LOVE	III.1	766
Ben:	And shew'd her many a Scar, Sir,	274	FOR LOVE	III.1	771
Ben:	That he had brought from far, Sir.	274	FOR LOVE	III.1	772
Ben:	Thought if it came about, Sir,	274	FOR LOVE	III.1	782
Ben:	That they should all fall out, Sir:	274	FOR LOVE	III.1	783
Ben:	And just e'en as he meant, Sir,	274	FOR LOVE	III.1	785
Ben:	To Loggerheads they went, Sir,	274	FOR LOVE	III.1	786
Jeremy:	Yes, Sir; you need make no great doubt of that; he	276	FOR LOVE	IV.1	3
Jeremy:	No, Sir, not yet;--He has a mind to try, whether his	276	FOR LOVE	IV.1	8
Jeremy:	Like enough, Sir, if I told her Maid this morning,	276	FOR LOVE	IV.1	14
Jeremy:	I hear a Coach stop; if it should be she, Sir, I believe he	276	FOR LOVE	IV.1	16
Jeremy:	What, is she gone, Sir?	278	FOR LOVE	IV.1	95
Jeremy:	us to be mad? Why, Sir, my Master longs to see her; and	278	FOR LOVE	IV.1	99
Scandal:	People. I hear Sir Sampson, you know your Cue; I'll	278	FOR LOVE	IV.1	108
	(Enter Sir Sampson Legend with a Lawyer.)	278	FOR LOVE	IV.1	111
Buckram:	Good, Sir. And the Conveyance is ready drawn in	278	FOR LOVE	IV.1	114
Jeremy:	Ah, Sir, he's quite gone.	278	FOR LOVE	IV.1	119
Jeremy:	No, Sir, not dead.	278	FOR LOVE	IV.1	121
Jeremy:	No, no, Sir; he's safe enough, Sir, an he were but as	279	FOR LOVE	IV.1	124
Jeremy:	sound, poor Gentleman. He is indeed here, Sir, and not	279	FOR LOVE	IV.1	125
Jeremy:	here, Sir.	279	FOR LOVE	IV.1	126
Jeremy:	Would you could, Sir; for he has lost himself. Indeed,	279	FOR LOVE	IV.1	130
Jeremy:	Sir, I have a most broke my Heart about him--I can't	279	FOR LOVE	IV.1	131
Jeremy:	Sir, I have almost broke my Heart about him--I can't	279	FOR LOVE	IV.1 V131	
Jeremy:	refrain Tears when I think of him, Sir; I'm as melancholy	279	FOR LOVE	IV.1	132
Jeremy:	for him as a Passing-Bell, Sir; or a Horse in a Pound.	279	FOR LOVE	IV.1	133
Sr Sampson:	A Pox confound your Similitudes, Sir--	279	FOR LOVE	IV.1	134
Jeremy:	Ah, you've hit it, Sir; that's the matter with him, Sir;	279	FOR LOVE	IV.1	137
Jeremy:	his Skull's crack'd, poor Gentleman; he's stark mad, Sir.	279	FOR LOVE	IV.1	138
Jeremy:	Quite Non Compos, Sir.	279	FOR LOVE	IV.1	141
Buckram:	Why then all's obliterated, Sir Sampson, if he be	279	FOR LOVE	IV.1	142
Sr Sampson:	Oons, I won't believe it; let me see him, Sir	279	FOR LOVE	IV.1	145
Jeremy:	Mr. Scandal is with him, Sir; I'll knock at the Door.	279	FOR LOVE	IV.1	147
Scandal:	For Heav'ns sake softly, Sir, and gently; don't	279	FOR LOVE	IV.1	152
Buckram:	O Lord, what must I say?--Yes, Sir.	280	FOR LOVE	IV.1	170
Jeremy:	Very short, Sir.	280	FOR LOVE	IV.1	182
Buckram:	Sir, I can do you no Service while he's in this	280	FOR LOVE	IV.1	183
Buckram:	Condition: Here's your Paper, Sir--He may do me a	280	FOR LOVE	IV.1	184
Buckram:	mischief if I stay--The Conveyance is ready, Sir. If	280	FOR LOVE	IV.1	185
Scandal:	You'd better let him go, Sir; and send for him if there	280	FOR LOVE	IV.1	189
Valentine:	What a Clock is't? My Father here! Your Blessing, Sir?	280	FOR LOVE	IV.1	193
Valentine:	Thank you, Sir, pretty well--I have been a	281	FOR LOVE	IV.1	196
Valentine:	little out of Order; won't you please to sit, Sir?	281	FOR LOVE	IV.1	197
Valentine:	Sir, 'tis my Duty to wait.	281	FOR LOVE	IV.1	199
Valentine:	I thank you, Sir.	281	FOR LOVE	IV.1	204
Valentine:	Pray let me see it, Sir. You hold it so far off, that	281	FOR LOVE	IV.1	217
Valentine:	Will you please to let me hold it, Sir?	281	FOR LOVE	IV.1	228
Jeremy:	What is, Sir?	283	FOR LOVE	IV.1	270
Foresight:	What says he? What, did he prophesie? Ha, Sir	283	FOR LOVE	IV.1	277
	(Exit Sir Sampson.)	283	FOR LOVE	IV.1	292
Foresight:	Ah, Sir Sampson, Heav'n help your Head--	283	FOR LOVE	IV.1	293

637

Sir   (continued)

Speaker	Line	PAGE	TITLE	ACT.SC	LINE
Garcia:	That, Sir, is he of whom I spoke, that's Osmyn.	336	M. BRIDE	I.1	V428
Heli:	Zara with Selim, Sir, I saw and know 'em:	344	M. BRIDE	II.2	197
Zara:	Your Pardon, Sir--mistake me not; you think	359	M. BRIDE	III.1	416
Gonsalez:	None, Sir. Some Papers have been since discover'd,	363	M. BRIDE	IV.1	75
Gonsalez:	I am a little slow of Credit, Sir,	366	M. BRIDE	IV.1	200
Gonsalez:	I grant it, Sir, and doubt not, but in Rage	366	M. BRIDE	IV.1	218
Perez:	Sir, I will.	374	M. BRIDE	V.1	V 76
Betty:	Turn'd of the last Canonical Hour, Sir.	398	WAY WORLD	I.1	106
Servant-M:	Sir, there's such Coupling at Pancras, that they stand	398	WAY WORLD	I.1	113
Servant-M:	Married and Bedded, Sir: I am Witness.	398	WAY WORLD	I.1	121
Servant-M:	Here it is, Sir.	398	WAY WORLD	I.1	123
Servant-M:	Yes, Sir.	398	WAY WORLD	I.1	126
Messenger:	I have a Letter for him, from his Brother Sir	400	WAY WORLD	I.1	183
Mirabell:	Sir Wilfull Witwoud?	400	WAY WORLD	I.1	188
Fainall:	Sir Wilfull is an odd mixture of Bashfulness and	401	WAY WORLD	I.1	218
Betty:	Did not the Messenger bring you one but now, Sir?	401	WAY WORLD	I.1	240
Betty:	Did not a Messenger bring you one but now, Sir?	401	WAY WORLD	I.1	V240
Betty:	No, Sir.	401	WAY WORLD	I.1	242
Betty:	Sir, the Coach stays.	405	WAY WORLD	I.1	382
Betty:	They are gone Sir, in great Anger.	406	WAY WORLD	I.1	415
Mirabell:	Meaning mine, Sir?	406	WAY WORLD	I.1	427
Mirabell:	Brother Sir Wilfull's arrival.	409	WAY WORLD	I.1	513
Waitwell:	Your Pardon, Sir. With Submission, we have indeed	423	WAY WORLD	II.1	507
Waitwell:	to Business, Sir. I have instructed her as well as I				
	cou'd. If	423	WAY WORLD	II.1	509
Waitwell:	Sir, your Affairs are in a prosperous way.	423	WAY WORLD	II.1	511
Foible:	O las Sir, I'm so asham'd--I'm afraid my Lady	423	WAY WORLD	II.1	513
Foible:	Sir, I made as much haste as I could.	423	WAY WORLD	II.1	515
Waitwell:	That she did indeed, Sir. It was my Fault that she	423	WAY WORLD	II.1	516
Foible:	But I told my Lady as you instructed me, Sir. That I	423	WAY WORLD	II.1	519
Foible:	had a prospect of seeing Sir Rowland your Uncle; and that	423	WAY WORLD	II.1	520
Waitwell:	I think she has profited, Sir. I think so.	424	WAY WORLD	II.1	527
Foible:	You have seen Madam Millamant, Sir?	424	WAY WORLD	II.1	528
Foible:	I told her Sir, because I did not know that you might	424	WAY WORLD	II.1	530
Foible:	O dear Sir, your humble Servant.	424	WAY WORLD	II.1	536
Mirabell:	Stand off Sir, not a Penny--Go on and prosper,	424	WAY WORLD	II.1	538
Foible:	I don't question your Generosity, Sir: And you need	424	WAY WORLD	II.1	541
Foible:	not doubt of Success. If you have no more Commands Sir,	424	WAY WORLD	II.1	542
Foible:	haste home and prevent her. Your Servant Sir. B'w'y	424	WAY WORLD	II.1	547
Waitwell:	Sir Rowland if you please. The Jade's so pert upon	424	WAY WORLD	II.1	550
Mirabell:	Come Sir, will you endeavour to forget your self	424	WAY WORLD	II.1	552
Mirabell:	--And transform into Sir Rowland.	424	WAY WORLD	II.1	553
Waitwell:	Why Sir; it will be impossible I shou'd remember	424	WAY WORLD	II.1	554
Foible:	--Poor Sir Rowland, I say.	427	WAY WORLD	III.1	78
Foible:	him Madam, starve him, marry Sir Rowland and get him	427	WAY WORLD	III.1	107
Lady Wish:	Will Sir Rowland be here, say'st thou? when	428	WAY WORLD	III.1	122
Foible:	Impatience in which Sir Rowland burns for the dear hour	428	WAY WORLD	III.1	126
Lady Wish:	my Features, to receive Sir Rowland with any Oeconomy of	428	WAY WORLD	III.1	141
Lady Wish:	Thou must repair me Foible, before Sir Rowland comes; or	429	WAY WORLD	III.1	149
Lady Wish:	But art thou sure Sir Rowland will not fail to	429	WAY WORLD	III.1	155
Lady Wish:	expect advances. No, I hope Sir Rowland is better bred,	429	WAY WORLD	III.1	161
Lady Wish:	Sir Rowland handsome? Let my Toilet be remov'd--I'll	429	WAY WORLD	III.1	171
Lady Wish:	dress above. I'll receive Sir Rowland here. Is he handsome?	429	WAY WORLD	III.1	172
Foible:	By Storm, Madam. Sir Rowland's a brisk Man.	429	WAY WORLD	III.1	175
Lady Wish:	Man. I shall save Decorums if Sir Rowland importunes. I	429	WAY WORLD	III.1	177
Foible:	she'll be contracted to Sir Rowland to Night, she says;--	430	WAY WORLD	III.1	210
Lady Wish:	expect my Nephew Sir Wilfull every moment too--Why	431	WAY WORLD	III.1	257
Marwood:	Methinks Sir Wilfull should rather think of	431	WAY WORLD	III.1	259
	(Enter Sir Wilfull Witwoud in a Country Riding Habit, and	436	WAY WORLD	III.1	443
	(Sir Wilfull Witwoud in a riding Dress,	436	WAY WORLD	III.1	V443
Servant-W:	Sir, my Lady's dressing. Here's Company; if you	437	WAY WORLD	III.1	445
Servant-W:	Your Aunt, Sir?	437	WAY WORLD	III.1	451
Sir Wilful:	My Aunt Sir, yes my Aunt Sir, and your Lady	437	WAY WORLD	III.1	452
Sir Wilful:	Sir; your Lady is my Aunt, Sir--Why, what do'st	437	WAY WORLD	III.1	453
Servant-W:	A Week, Sir; longer than any Body in the House,	437	WAY WORLD	III.1	457
Servant-W:	A Week, Sir; longer than any in the House,	437	WAY WORLD	III.1	V457
Servant-W:	Why truly Sir, I cannot safely swear to her Face in a	437	WAY WORLD	III.1	461
Sir Wilful:	tell her, her Nephew, Sir Wilfull Witwoud is in the House.	437	WAY WORLD	III.1	466
Servant-W:	I shall, Sir.	437	WAY WORLD	III.1	467
Servant-W:	Really Sir, I can't tell; here come so many here, 'tis	437	WAY WORLD	III.1	470
Marwood:	speak to him?--And you, Sir.	437	WAY WORLD	III.1	481
Petulant:	And you, Sir.	438	WAY WORLD	III.1	483
Marwood:	No sure, Sir.	438	WAY WORLD	III.1	486
Petulant:	It seems as if you had come a Journey, Sir;	438	WAY WORLD	III.1	489
Sir Wilful:	Very likely, Sir, that it may seem so.	438	WAY WORLD	III.1	492
Petulant:	No Offence, I hope, Sir.	438	WAY WORLD	III.1	493
Sir Wilful:	May be not, Sir; thereafter as 'tis meant, Sir.	438	WAY WORLD	III.1	496
Petulant:	Sir, I presume upon the Information of your Boots.	438	WAY WORLD	III.1	497
Sir Wilful:	Why, 'tis like you may, Sir: If you are not	438	WAY WORLD	III.1	498
Sir Wilful:	satisfy'd with the Information of my Boots, Sir, if you will	438	WAY WORLD	III.1	499
Sir Wilful:	Sir.	438	WAY WORLD	III.1	501
Petulant:	Your Horse, Sir! Your Horse is an Ass, Sir!	438	WAY WORLD	III.1	502
Sir Wilful:	Do you speak by way of Offence, Sir?	438	WAY WORLD	III.1	503
Marwood:	The Gentleman's merry, that's all, Sir--	438	WAY WORLD	III.1	504
Marwood:	Thing amiss from your Friends, Sir. You are among your	438	WAY WORLD	III.1	507
Marwood:	am not mistaken, you are Sir Wilfull Witwoud.	438	WAY WORLD	III.1	509
Sir Wilful:	Right Lady; I am Sir Wilfull Witwoud, so I	438	WAY WORLD	III.1	510
Marwood:	Don't you know this Gentleman, Sir?	438	WAY WORLD	III.1	513
Sir Wilful:	Your Servant! Why yours, Sir. Your Servant	439	WAY WORLD	III.1	521
Sir Wilful:	And a--(puff) and a flap Dragon for your Service, Sir:	439	WAY WORLD	III.1	523
Sir Wilful:	And a Hare's Foot, and a Hare's Scut for your Service, Sir;	439	WAY WORLD	III.1	524
Sir Wilful:	'Sheart, Sir, but there is, and much offence.--	439	WAY WORLD	III.1	527
Marwood:	You intend to Travel, Sir, as I'm inform'd.	440	WAY WORLD	III.1	566
Sir Wilful:	Serve or not serve, I shant ask License of you, Sir;	440	WAY WORLD	III.1	570
Sir Wilful:	Discourse to the Lady, Sir: 'Tis like my Aunt may have	440	WAY WORLD	III.1	572

Sir   (continued)

Sirrah (26)

Sirrah   (continued)

Speaker	Text	PAGE	TITLE	ACT.SC	LINE
Valentine:	Sirrah, fill when I bid you.--And how do's	222	FOR LOVE	I.1	250
Scandal:	Here's a Dog now, a Traytor in his Wine, Sirrah	224	FOR LOVE	I.1	309
Foresight:	Sirrah, go tell Sir Sampson Legend I'll wait on him, if	236	FOR LOVE	II.1	40
Sr Sampson:	Beau, and may be a--Why, Sirrah, is it not here	243	FOR LOVE	II.1	300
Sr Sampson:	Sirrah, you'l be hang'd; I shall live to see you	243	FOR LOVE	II.1	303
Sr Sampson:	Excuse! Impudence! why Sirrah, mayn't I do	244	FOR LOVE	II.1	323
Sr Sampson:	Scoundrel. Sirrah, where's your Master?	278	FOR LOVE	IV.1	118
Sr Sampson:	Hey day, Rascal, do you banter me? Sirrah,	279	FOR LOVE	IV.1	127
Sr Sampson:	d'ye banter me--Speak Sirrah, where is he, for I	279	FOR LOVE	IV.1	128
Valentine:	Sirrah, you lie; I am not Mad.	295	FOR LOVE	IV.1	741
Sr Sampson:	Who gave you Authority to speak, Sirrah? To	308	FOR LOVE	V.1	417
Sr Sampson:	Helm, Sirrah, don't direct me.	308	FOR LOVE	V.1	419
Sr Sampson:	Why you impudent Tarpaulin! Sirrah, do you	308	FOR LOVE	V.1	422
Sr Sampson:	Hold your Tongue, Sirrah. How now, who's	309	FOR LOVE	V.1	437
Sr Sampson:	Father! Sirrah, could you hope to prosper?	311	FOR LOVE	V.1	510
Mirabell:	Sirrah, Waitwell, why sure you think you were married	423	WAY WORLD	II.1	505
Witwoud:	Decimo Sexto, my Dear Lacedemonian, Sirrah Petulant, thou	453	WAY WORLD	IV.1	343
Sir Wilful:	With a Wench, Tony? Is she a shake-bag Sirrah?	457	WAY WORLD	IV.1	472
Sir Wilful:	My Tantony, Sirrah thou sha't be my Tantony; and I'll	457	WAY WORLD	IV.1	477

Sister (34)

Speaker	Text	PAGE	TITLE	ACT.SC	LINE
Fondlewife:	hath already defiled the Tabernacle of our Sister Comfort;	76	OLD BATCH	IV.1	29
Heartwell:	Sister Marriage, and whor'd her? Wherein have I injured	109	OLD BATCH	V.2	53
Sir Paul:	heark'ee, I had it from his Aunt, my Sister Touchwood,	146	DOUBL DLR	II.1	276
Sir Paul:	Madam, Sister, my Lady Sister, did you see my	191	DOUBL DLR	V.1	159
Sir Paul:	Nephew; and I don't know what,--look you, Sister,	192	DOUBL DLR	V.1	175
Tattle:	so is Mrs. Foresight, and her Sister Mrs. Frail.	228	FOR LOVE	I.1	457
Mrs Frail:	Exchange, I must call my Sister Foresight there.	234	FOR LOVE	I.1	665
Scandal:	I will; I have a mind to your Sister.	234	FOR LOVE	I.1	666
Scandal:	to engage your Sister.	234	FOR LOVE	I.1	672
Foresight:	abroad? Is not my Wife come home? Nor my Sister, nor	235	FOR LOVE	II.1	2
Mrs Fore:	Besides, it wou'd not only reflect upon you, Sister, but me.	247	FOR LOVE	II.1	434
Mrs Fore:	What do you mean Sister?	247	FOR LOVE	II.1	442
Mrs Fore:	you lose this Gold Bodkin?--Oh Sister, Sister!	248	FOR LOVE	II.1	466
Mrs Frail:	Bodkin?--Oh Sister, Sister!--Sister every way.	248	FOR LOVE	II.1	470
Mrs Frail:	I have heard Gentlemen say, Sister; that one should	248	FOR LOVE	II.1	473
Mrs Fore:	It's very true, Sister: Well since all's out, and	248	FOR LOVE	II.1	476
Mrs Frail:	Now if I cou'd wheedle him, Sister, ha? You understand	248	FOR LOVE	II.1	495
Mrs Frail:	Ah Devil, sly Devil--He's as close, Sister, as	250	FOR LOVE	II.1	542
Mrs Fore:	fresh harmless Creature; and left us, Sister, presently.	250	FOR LOVE	II.1	545
Mrs Fore:	They're all so, Sister, these Men--they	250	FOR LOVE	II.1	547
Mrs Fore:	Heark'ee, Sister--by my Soul the Girl is	250	FOR LOVE	II.1	560
Mrs Frail:	Foresight, and Sir Sampson coming. Sister, do you take Miss	265	FOR LOVE	III.1	447
Mrs Frail:	Hold, there's my Sister, I'll call her to hear it.	273	FOR LOVE	III.1	741
Mrs Fore:	Hold, here's my Sister coming toward us.	273	FOR LOVE	III.1	747
Mrs Fore:	Oh Sister, what will you do with him?	283	FOR LOVE	IV.1	305
Mrs Frail:	Sister, do you stay with them; I'll find out my	285	FOR LOVE	IV.1	351
Mrs Frail:	O Sister, had you come a minute sooner, you would	287	FOR LOVE	IV.1	449
Mrs Fore:	Now, Sister.	290	FOR LOVE	IV.1	538
Mrs Frail:	O, Sister, the most unlucky Accident!	309	FOR LOVE	V.1	440
Painall:	Wife, who was Sister to my Lady Wishfort, my Wife's	400	WAY WORLD	I.1	193

Sister's (1)

Speaker	Text	PAGE	TITLE	ACT.SC	LINE
Lady Touch:	You censure hardly, my Lord; my Sister's	151	DOUBL DLR	III.1	11

Sisterly (1)

Speaker	Text	PAGE	TITLE	ACT.SC	LINE
Mrs Frail:	Well, give me your Hand in token of sisterly secresie and	248	FOR LOVE	II.1	482

Sisters (2)

Speaker	Text	PAGE	TITLE	ACT.SC	LINE
Witwoud:	with him; if he said they were my Mother and my Sisters.	406	WAY WORLD	I.1	411
Witwoud:	with him; if he had said they were my Mother and my Sisters.	406	WAY WORLD	I.1	V411

Sit (21)

Speaker	Text	PAGE	TITLE	ACT.SC	LINE
	We threaten you who do for Judges sit,	35	OLD BATCH	PRO.	8
Bellmour:	Does it sit easy on me?	75	OLD BATCH	IV.1	4
Jeremy:	sit at the Door, that I don't get double the Stomach that	218	FOR LOVE	I.1	92
Valentine:	Come sit you down, you know his way.	222	FOR LOVE	I.1	235
Ben:	Marry a God's Name an you sit it that way. As for my	261	FOR LOVE	III.1	302
Ben:	Come Mistress, will you please to sit down, for an you	263	FOR LOVE	III.1	360
Ben:	Come, I'll haule a Chair; there, an you please to sit, I'll	263	FOR LOVE	III.1	362
Ben:	sit by you.	263	FOR LOVE	III.1	363
Miss Prue:	You need not sit so near one, if you have any thing	263	FOR LOVE	III.1	364
Mrs Fore:	Mr. Foresight is punctual, we sit up after him.	269	FOR LOVE	III.1	581
Valentine:	little out of Order; won't you please to sit, Sir?	281	FOR LOVE	IV.1	197
Sr Sampson:	Ay boy--Come, thou shalt sit down by me.	281	FOR LOVE	IV.1	198
Sr Sampson:	No, no, come, come, sit you down, honest	281	FOR LOVE	IV.1	200
Sr Sampson:	No, no, come, come, sit thee down, honest	281	FOR LOVE	IV.1	V200
	To poison Plays, I see some where they sit,	385	M. BRIDE	EPI.	7
Painall:	Coroner's Inquest, to sit upon the murder'd Reputations of	396	WAY WORLD	I.1	53
Painall:	Nothing remains when that Day comes, but to sit down	413	WAY WORLD	II.1	115
Foible:	make you like your Picture. Your Picture must sit for you,	429	WAY WORLD	III.1	153
Lady Wish:	great deal in the first Impression. Shall I sit?--No I	445	WAY WORLD	IV.1	19
Lady Wish:	won't sit--I'll walk--aye I'll walk from the door upon his	445	WAY WORLD	IV.1	20
Lady Wish:	sit if you please, and see the Entertainment.	459	WAY WORLD	IV.1	567

Sits (5)

Speaker	Text	PAGE	TITLE	ACT.SC	LINE
Bellmour:	Humph, Sits the Wind there?--What a lucky	97	OLD BATCH	V.1	23
Lady Froth:	offers to speak--And sits in expectation of his no Jest, with	165	DOUBL DLR	III.1	574
Trapland:	(sits). There is a Debt, Mr. Valentine, of 1500 [Pounds] of	222	FOR LOVE	I.1	236
Ben:	(Sits further off.)	263	FOR LOVE	III.1	368
Mincing:	with Poetry, it sits so pleasant the next Day as any Thing,	420	WAY WORLD	II.1	373

Six (5)

Speaker	Text	PAGE	TITLE	ACT.SC	LINE
Bellmour:	work'd themselves six foot deep into a Grave--	38	OLD BATCH	I.1	26
Cynthia:	But how can the Coach and six Horses be got ready	193	DOUBL DLR	V.1	208
Tattle:	came down in her Coach and Six Horses, and expos'd her	258	FOR LOVE	III.1	176
Mincing:	six thousand Pound. O, come Mrs. Foible, I hear my old	465	WAY WORLD	V.1	116
Painall:	endow'd in right of my Wife, with that six thousand	469	WAY WORLD	V.1	278

Sixth (2)

Speaker	Text	PAGE	TITLE	ACT.SC	LINE
Lady Froth:	O-law, I swear it's but the sixth,--and I han't	166	DOUBL DLR	III.1	612
Scandal:	and I hope I shall find both Sol and Venus in the sixth	271	FOR LOVE	III.1	651

Skies (1)
  Brisk: Cynthia of the Skies, and Queen of Stars. . . . . . . 201 DOUBL DLR V.1 531
Skill (4)
  Heartwell: cannot distrust me of any skill in the treacherous Mystery-- 72 OLD BATCH III.2 58
  Silvia: may depend upon our skill to save us at a plunge, though . 75 OLD BATCH III.2 152
  Mellefont: Not at all; only a Friendly Tryal of Skill, and the . . 143 DOUEL DLR II.1 170
              And sure he must have more than mortal Skill, ... 479 WAY WORLD EPI.   7
Skill'd (1)
              In such like Prophecies were Poets skill'd, ... 323 M. BRIDE PRO. 13
Skin (4)
  Sir Joseph: have flead me alive, have sold my Skin, and devour'd . . 47 OLD EATCH II.1   5
  Sir Joseph: have flead me alive, have sold my Skin, and devour'd &c. . 47 OLD BATCH II.1 V 5
  Lady Ply: a very good skin, Sir. . . . . 160 DOUBL DLR III.1 369
  Gonsalez: Then cast my Skin, and leave it there to answer it. . 376 M. BRIDE V.2 13
Skins (1)
  Mirabell: for the Night, made of oil'd skins and I know not what . 451 WAY WCRLD IV.1 249
Skipper (1)
  Witwoud: Yes, refin'd, like a Dutch Skipper from a . . . . . 441 WAY WCBLD III.1 590
Skreen (3)
  Cynthia: My Lord, let me entreat you to stand behind this Skreen, . 197 DOUBL DLR V.1 374
  Witwoud: Do Mrs. Mincing, like a Skreen before a great Fire. . 419 WAY WCRLD II.1 343
  Mirabell: or Intimate cf your own Sex; No she friend to skreen . 451 WAY WCRLD IV.1 236
Skull (1)
  Sr Sampson: the matter is with him, or I'll crack your Fools Skull. . 279 FOR LCVE IV.1 136
Skull'd (0)   see Thick-Skull'd
Skull's (1)
  Jeremy: his Skull's crack'd, poor Gentleman; he's stark mad, Sir. 279 FOR LOVE IV.1 138
Skulls (1)
  Almeria: Lead me o'er Bones and Skulls, and mouldring Earth . . 339 M. BRIDE II.1 74
Sky (1)
  Sr Sampson: Manners, that don't believe a Syllable in the Sky and . 283 FOR LCVE IV.1 287
Slabber (1)
  Witwoud: slabber and kiss one another when they meet, like a Call of 439 WAY WCBLD III.1 535
Slabber'd (1)
  Lucy: No no, avaunt--I'le not be slabber'd and kiss'd . . . . 67 OLD BATCH III.1 236
Slacking (0)   see Never-slacking
Slain (4)
  Gonsalez: So, this can hardly fail. Alphonso slain, ... 372 M. EBIDE IV.1 444
  Garcia: Who but for heaps of Slain, that choak the Passage, . 377 M. EBIDE V.2 33
  Leonora: Of Death, is this? The Eunuch Selim slain! . . . . 381 M. EBIDE V.2 219
  Almeria: And wrongfully have slain those Innocents. . . 382 M. EBIDE V.2 V248
Slander-mouth'd (1)
  Lady Wish: A slander-mouth'd Railer: I warrant the Spendthrift . 428 WAY WCRLD III.1 132
Slander'd (1)
  Lucy: which you have slander'd most abcminably. It vexes me . . 66 OLD BATCH III.1 208
Slanderous (1)
  Nurse: A Teat, a Teat, I an unnatural Teat! O the false slanderous 238 FOR LCVE II.1 123
Slap (1)
  Witwoud: and Mask, slap into a Hackney-Coach, and drive hither . 405 WAY WORLD I.1 373
Slap-dash (1)
  Sir Joseph: (aside). Now am I slap-dash down in the Mouth, ... 85 OLD EATCH IV.3 90
Slaughter (1)
  Capt Bluff: must refund--or Bilbo's the Word, and Slaughter will . . 68 OLD EATCH III.1 259
Slave (22)   see Galley-slave
  Maskwell: By heaven, no; I am your Slave, the Slave of all . . 137 DOUBL DLR I.1 393
  Sr Sampson: what I please? Are not you my Slave? Did nct I beget you? 244 FOR LCVE I.1 324
  Valentine: Mask of Madness, and this motly Livery, only as the Slave . 294 FOR LOVE IV.1 703
  Angelica: Man is a Slave to the Severity and insolent Conduct of . 299 FOR LCVE V.1 V 73
  Gonsalez: Garcia, my Son, your Beauties lowest Slave, ... 332 M. BRIDE I.1 255
  Manuel: There's not a Slave, a shackled Slave of mine, ... 333 M. EBIDE I.1 315
  Garcia: The Slave and Creature of my Royal Mistress. . . . . 334 M. EBIDE I.1 337
  Manuel: In Triumph led; your Beauty's Slave. . . . . 335 M. EBIDE I.1 392
  Manuel: In pleasing Triumph led; your Beauty's Slave. . . 335 M. EBIDE I.1 V392
  Zara: The Slave, the Wretch that she redeem'd frcm Death, . 346 M. BRIDE II.2 250
  Zara: Where all is lost, and I am made a Slave. . . . . . 347 M. BRIDE II.2 302
  Osmyn-Alph: And leave a Slave the Wretch that would be so. . . . 348 M. BRIDE II.2 330
  Zara: Traytour, Monster, cold and perfidious Slave; . . . . 348 M. EBIDE II.2 340
  Zara: A Slave, not daring to be free! nor dares . . . . 348 M. EBIDE II.2 341
  Zara: There, he; your Prisoner, and that was my Slave. . . . 348 M. BRIDE II.2 358
  Osmyn-Alph: This Slave. . . . . 354 M. EBIDE III.1 192
  Zara: As you'll answer it, look, this Slave . . . . . . 360 M. BRIDE III.1 V447
  Zara: This Slave commit no Violence upcn . . . . 360 M. BRIDE III.1 448
  Manuel: Hence, Slave, how dar'st thou bide, to watch and pry . 373 M. BRIDE V.1 39
  Manuel: Hark thee, Villain, Traitor--answer me Slave. . . . 374 M. EBIDE V.1 67
Slavery (8)
  Bellmour: contented with the slavery of hcnourable Love in one . . 40 OLD BATCH I.1 138
  Lord Froth: happy Slavery. . . . . 140 DOUEL DLR II.1 70
  Maskwell: lov'd Embraces, could e're be fond of an inferiour Slavery. 198 DOUBL DLR V.1 426
  Zara: And scorn vile Slavery, tho' doubly hid . . . . . 336 M. EBIDE I.1 401
  Zara: Look cn me now, from Empire fall'n to Slavery; . . . 347 M. EBIDE II.2 303
  Osmyn-Alph: Off Slavery. O curse! that I alone . . . . 352 M. BRIDE III.1 89
  Garcia: Perdition, Slavery, and Death, ... 377 M. EBIDE V.2 27
  Waitwell: Fie, fie!--What a Slavery have I undergone; . . . . 459 WAY WORLD IV.1 556
Slaves (5)
  Lord Touch: should Command: my very Slaves will shortly give me . . 195 DOUEL DLR V.1 303
  Zara: That Zara must be made the Sport of Slaves? . . . . 348 M. BRIDE II.2 363
  Osmyn-Alph: This Den for Slaves, this Dungeon damp'd with Woes; . . 357 M. BBIDE III.1 327
  Manuel: Bear to the Dungeon, those Rebellious Slaves; . . . . 362 M. EBIDE IV.1 62
  Zara: And Howls of Slaves condemn'd; from Clink of Chains, . 379 M. EBIDE V.2 137
Sleek-face (1)
  Lady Wish: and his Sleek-face; till she was going in her fifteen. . 467 WAY WORLD V.1 194
Sleep (21)
  Bellmour: seem to rouse, 'tis but well lashing him, and he will sleep 46 OLD BATCH I.1 353
  Araminta: Bellmour last Night, and call'd him alcud in your sleep. . 55 OLD BATCH II.2 38
  Heartwell: when I should Sleep, and even Dream of you, when I am . 73 OLD BATCH III.2 80
  Heartwell: when I should Sleep, and even Dream of thee, when I am . 73 OLD BATCH III.2 V 80

Sleep   (continued)
		PAGE	TITLE	ACT.SC	LINE
Lady Froth:	I could not sleep; I did not sleep one wink for . . .	138	DOUBL DLR	II.1	3
Cynthia:	Prodigious! I wonder, want of sleep, and so much . . .	138	DOUBL DLR	II.1	5
Mellefont:	hands and sprawling in his Sleep; and ever since she has .	158	DOUBL DLR	III.1	289
Nurse:	in her Chamber, and gone to sleep, or to Prayers; Miss, .	253	FOR LCVE	III.1	4
Scandal:	Do you sleep well o'nights?	268	FOR LCVE	III.1	566
Scandal:	Sleep has been unquiet of late.	269	FOR LCVE	III.1	617
Miss Prue:	Man; and if I can't have one, I wou'd go to sleep all my .	305	FOR LCVE	V.1	309
Tattle:	Easie! Pox on't, I don't believe I shall sleep to Night. .	310	FOR LCVE	V.1	483
Sr Sampson:	Sleep Quotha! No, why you would not sleep o'	310	FOR LCVE	V.1	484
Sr Sampscn:	don't mean to sleep.	310	FOR LOVE	V.1	486
Osmyn-Alph:	Could sleep till we again were met.	344	M. EBRIDE	II.2	196
Osmyn-Alph:	Or we could sleep till we again were met.	344	M. EBRIDE	II.2	V196
Petulant:	next time your self--I'll go sleep.	454	WAY WORLD	IV.1	370
Lady Wish:	sleep, you Sot--Or as I'm a person, I'll have you bastinado'd	457	WAY WORLD	IV.1	462
Waitwell:	from Sleep.	475	WAY WORLD	V.1	516

Sleeping (2)
Capt Bluff:	shall find he might have safer rous'd a sleeping Lion. .	101	OLD BATCH	V.1	168
Miss Prue:	sleeping, than sick with thinking.	305	FCR LOVE	V.1	312

Sleeps (2)
Almeria:	Anselmo sleeps, and is at Peace; last Night, ...	326	M. EBRIDE	I.1	9
Gonsalez:	Ha! sure he sleeps--all's dark within, save what . . .	376	M. EBRIDE	V.2	6

Sleeve (1)
Maskwell:	stitch'd the Gown Sleeve, that he may be puzzled, and waste	195	DOUEL DLR	V.1	288

Slept (6)
Bellmour:	parted with his Bed in a Morning, than a' could have slept	37	OLD BATCH	I.1	3
Bellmour:	parted with his Bed in a Morning, than he could have slept	37	OLD BATCH	I.1	V 3
Lord Froth:	By Heaven's, I have slept an Age,--Sir Paul, ...	200	DOUBL DLR	V.1	492
Tattle:	while ago, Child. I have been asleep since; slept a whole	303	FCR LOVE	V.1	237
Leonora:	Where, while his Gaoler slept, I thro' the Grate . . .	326	M. BRIDE	I.1	26
Fainall:	Lover slept!	414	WAY WCRLD	II.1	149

Slides (1)
Zara:	And fright him from my Arms--See, see, he slides . . .	381	M. BRIDE	V.2	208

'Slidikins (1)
Lady Ply:	now, who are you? What am I? 'Slidikins can't I govern .	144	DOUEL DLR	II.1	215

Slight (5)
Sharper:	great a Brute as to slight her.	80	OLD BATCH	IV.1	187
Mrs Frail:	With all my heart, ours are but slight Flesh-wounds, . .	248	FOR LCVE	II.1	480
Valentine:	That Women are like Tricks by slight of Hand, . . .	297	FOR LOVE	IV.1	815
Fainall:	you of the slight Account you once could make of strictest	414	WAY WCRLD	II.1	180
Millamant:	Press me no more for that slight Toy.	447	WAY WORLD	IV.1	99

Slighted (3)
Mellefont:	her in all the Transports of a slighted and revengful Woman:	130	DOUBL DLR	I.1	104
Fainall:	more play with a Man that slighted his ill Fortune, than .	395	WAY WCRLD	I.1	8
Fainall:	she has made you Advances, which you have slighted? .	397	WAY WCRLD	I.1	83

Slighting (1)
Bellmour:	here vents 'em against the General, who slighting Men of .	47	OLD BATCH	I.1	371

Slily (1)
Ben:	The Sailor slily waiting, ...	274	FOR LOVE	III.1	781

Slip (3)
Maskwell:	back Stairs, and so we may slip down without being . .	194	DOUBL DLR	V.1	240
Witwoud:	Mean, why he wou'd slip you out of this Chocolate-house, .	405	WAY WCRLD	I.1	369
Mrs Fain:	occasion, and slip down the back-stairs, where Foible .	452	WAY WCRLD	IV.1	304

Slipper (1)
Sr Sampson:	Foot; have kiss'd the Great Mogul's Slipper, and rid a .	241	FOR LCVE	II.1	220

Slippers (1)
Sir Wilful:	pair of Slippers?--My Man's with his Horses, I	441	WAY WCRLD	III.1	618

Slovenly (1)
Belinda:	O monstrous filthy Fellow! Good slovenly Captain . . .	85	OLD BATCH	IV.3	86

Slow (3)
Lady Touch:	outstays the Time; for to be dully punctual, is too slow.	183	DOUBL DLR	IV.2	10
Zara:	But now the Dawn begins, and the slow Hand	360	M. EBRIDE	III.1	440
Gonsalez:	I am a little slow of Credit, Sir, ...	366	M. EBRIDE	IV.1	200

Sluce (2)
Setter:	of her. She's the very Sluce to her Lady's Secrets:-- . .	99	OLD BATCH	V.1	104
Almeria:	Yes, yes, I know to mourn; I'll sluce this Heart, . . .	382	M. EBIDE	V.2	243

Slumber (1)
Lord Froth:	Lady's is the most inviting Couch; and a slumber there, is	200	DOUEL DLR	V.1	494

Slumbers (2)
Almeria:	May lay the Burden down, and sink in Slumbers . . .	340	M. EBRIDE	II.2	19
Millamant:	morning thoughts, agreeable wakings, indolent slumbers, .	449	WAY WCRLD	IV.1	188

Slut (1)
Foresight:	Why, you malapert Slut--	237	FOR LCVE	II.1	86

Sly (2)
Mrs Frail:	Ah Devil, sly Devil--He's as close, Sister, as	250	FOR LOVE	II.1	542
Mrs Fore:	together is as bad--And he's such a sly Devil, he'll never	250	FOR LOVE	II.1	574

Small (14)
Capt Bluff:	Campagn, had a small Post there; but no matter for that--	52	OLD BATCH	II.1	196
Belinda:	small.--Oh Gad! I have a great Passion for Cowley. .	87	OLD BATCH	IV.3	145
Brisk:	tho' to prevent Criticisms--only mark it with a small .	165	DOUBL DLR	III.1	551
Brisk:	tho' to prevent Criticism--only mark it with a small .	165	DOUEL DLR	III.1	V551
Maskwell:	I had laid a small design for to morrow (as Love . .	196	DOUBL DLR	V.1	326
Jeremy:	Hem!--Sir, if you please to give me a small	217	FOR LOVE	I.1	64
Scandal:	Man of small Fortune? Why, he looks like a Writ of Enquiry	219	FOR LCVE	I.1	133
Valentine:	to be kept at small expence; but the Retinue that you gave	244	FOR LCVE	II.1	346
Almeria:	Some small reserve of near and inward Woe, ...	328	M. EBRIDE	I.1	83
	Small Hope our Poet from these Prospects draws; . . .	385	M. BRIDE	EPI.	27
Witwoud:	--Faith and Troth a pretty deal of an odd sort of a small	403	WAY WORLD	I.1	290
Sir Wilful:	. . . have Thoughts to tarry a small	440	WAY WOBLD	III.1	581
Lady Wish:	of small Ware, flaunting upon a Packthread, under a .	462	WAY WORLD	V.1	12
Lady Wish:	Ah Mr. Mirabell, this is small comfort, the	475	WAY WCRLD	V.1	504

Small-beer (1)
Ben:	to her, than a Cann of Small-beer to a Bowl of Punch. . .	264	FOR LCVE	III.1	413

Small-pox (1)
Bellmour:	glass after the Small-pox.	42	OLD BATCH	I.1	187

Snatches (continued)

		PAGE	TITLE	ACT.SC	LINE
Lady Ply:	De'e see here? Look, read it? (Snatches the Letter as in	179	DOUBL DLR	IV.1	441

Sneak'd (2)

| Sr Sampson: | sneak'd off, and would not see his Brother? There's an | 259 | FOR LOVE | III.1 | 235 |
| Witwoud: | Husband's advice; but he sneak'd off. | 454 | WAY WORLD | IV.1 | 382 |

Sneer (4)

Lord Froth:	admirer of my Lady Whifler, Mr. Sneer, and Sir Laurence	162	DOUBL DLR	III.1	461
Lord Froth:	Whifler, and Mr. Sneer.	165	DOUBL DLR	III.1	560
Lady Froth:	--Ay my Dear--were you? Oh filthy Mr. Sneer;	165	DOUBL DLR	III.1	561
Lady Froth:	Then she's always ready to Laugh when Sneer	165	DOUBL DLR	III.1	573

Sneering (1)

| Heartwell: | I confess I have not been sneering fulsome Lies and | 42 | OLD BATCH | I.1 | 188 |

Snipwel's (1)

| Belinda: | Snipwel's Shop while I was there.--But, Oh Gad! | 84 | OLD BATCH | IV.3 | 25 |

Snivel (1)

| Petulant: | I won't come.--Let 'em snivel and cry their Hearts | 405 | WAY WORLD | I.1 | 387 |

Snow (1)

| Mellefont: | great Beard, like a Russian Bear upon a drift of Snow. You | 158 | DOUBL DLR | III.1 | 292 |

Snow-House (1)

| Lady Ply: | preserved my Honour as it were in a Snow-House for | 145 | DOUBL DLR | II.1 | 254 |

Snowy (1)

| Bellmour: | your snowy Arms about his stubborn Neck; bathe his | 95 | OLD BATCH | IV.4 | 237 |

Snub (1)

| Sir Paul: | (aside to her). I acquiesce, my Lady; but don't snub so | 159 | DOUBL DLR | III.1 | 334 |

Snuff (2)

| Lady Froth: | Snuff some of my Spirit of Hartshorn. | 201 | DOUBL DLR | V.1 | 526 |
| Miss Prue: | nay, there's Snuff in't;--here, will you have any-- | 249 | FOR LOVE | II.1 | 517 |

Snuff-Box (1)

| Brisk: | was in the Lid of my Snuff-Box. Hum! Deuce take me, I | 135 | DOUBL DLR | I.1 | 292 |

Snuff-box (1)

| Miss Prue: | giv'n me--Look you here Cousin, here's a Snuff-box; | 249 | FOR LOVE | II.1 | 516 |

Snugs (1)

| Petulant: | clash; snugs the Word, I shrug and am silent. | 407 | WAY WORLD | I.1 | 447 |

So (749)

So-h (2)   see **Soh**

| Sharper: | So-h, O Sir I am easily pacify'd, the acknowledgment | 49 | OLD BATCH | II.1 | 62 |
| Heartwell: | So-h,--That precious Pimp too.-- | 107 | OLD BATCH | V.2 | 4 |

Soaker (1)

| Sir Wilful: | the Sun's a good Pimple, an honest Soaker, he has a Cellar | 456 | WAY WORLD | IV.1 | 422 |

Soar (1)

| Osmyn-Alph: | Would soar, and stoop at Victory beneath. | 352 | M. BRIDE | III.1 | 91 |

Sober (1)

| Mincing: | sober, and to bring him to them. My Lady is resolv'd to | 465 | WAY WORLD | V.1 | 114 |

Sobriety (1)

| Angelica: | by over acting Sobriety; I was half inclining to believe | 296 | FOR LOVE | IV.1 | 765 |

Society (4)

Sharper:	the society of Ladies.	88	OLD BATCH	IV.3	200
Brisk:	from the body of our Society.--He, I think that's	128	DOUBL DLR	I.1	37
Foresight:	under Gemini, which may incline her to Society; she has a	239	FOR LOVE	II.1	152
Mirabell:	such Society? It is impossible they should admire you,	421	WAY WORLD	II.1	437

Soforth (1)

| Setter: | wary and soforth--And to all this valiant as Hercules | 65 | OLD BATCH | III.1 | 151 |

Soft (13)

Bellmour:	by these healing Lips.--Oh! press the soft Charm close	82	OLD BATCH	IV.2	73
Bellmour:	relentless face in your salt trickling Tears.--So, a few soft	95	OLD BATCH	IV.4	238
Bellmour:	of a Husband, as of a Creature contrary to that soft,	106	OLD BATCH	V.1	381
	If the soft things are Penn'd and spoke with grace;	204	DOUBL DLR	EPI.	23
Valentine:	A Lovely Girl, I'faith, black sparkling Eyes, soft pouting	223	FOR LOVE	I.1	278
Sr Sampson:	your Hand, Odd let me kiss it; 'tis as warm and as soft	301	FOR LOVE	V.1	145
Tattle:	pretty soft kind of Phrase, and with a good perswading	302	FOR LOVE	V.1	182
Almeria:	Indeed thou hast a soft and gentle Nature,	327	M. BRIDE	I.1	30
Zara:	That Question, speak again in that soft Voice,	353	M. BRIDE	III.1	154
Osmyn-Alph:	O could'st thou be less killing, soft or kind,	356	M. BRIDE	III.1	282
Osmyn-Alph:	O would'st thou be less killing, soft or kind,	356	M. BRIDE	III.1	V282
Osmyn-Alph:	Into thy Lips, pour the soft trickling Balm	383	M. BRIDE	V.2	283
Petulant:	Ay, ay, pox I'm malicious, Man. Now he's soft	408	WAY WORLD	I.1	503

Soften (2)

| Silvia: | Frowns, and make calm an angry Face; will soften a | 72 | OLD BATCH | III.2 | 66 |
| Almeria: | To soften Rocks, or bend a knotted Oak. | 326 | M. BRIDE | I.1 | 2 |

Softlier (1)

| Laetitia: | softlier. | 91 | OLD BATCH | IV.4 | 80 |

Softly (8)

Capt Bluff:	him--I'll pink his Soul--but whisper that softly	68	OLD BATCH	III.1	261
Sir Joseph:	So softly, that he shall never hear on't I warrant	68	OLD BATCH	III.1	263
Capt Bluff:	(Almost whispering, and treading softly after him.)	101	OLD BATCH	V.1	190
	(Softly to her.)	177	DOUBL DLR	IV.1	364
	(Enter Lord Touchwood, Maskwell softly behind him.)	185	DOUBL DLR	IV.2	89
Scandal:	For Heav'ns sake softly, Sir, and gently; don't	279	FOR LOVE	IV.1	152
Scandal:	Hush, softly--the Pleasures of last Night, my	284	FOR LOVE	IV.1	316
Leonora:	Have softly whisper'd, and enquir'd his Health;	327	M. BRIDE	I.1	27

Softness (4)

Heartwell:	empty Channels; and prompts me to the softness of a	72	OLD BATCH	III.2	50
Lady Froth:	Charming Softness in your Mien and your Expression, and	140	DOUBL DLR	II.1	72
Osmyn-Alph:	Are they not soothing Softness, sinking Ease,	358	M. BRIDE	III.1	363
Manuel:	All Nature, Softness, Pity and Compassion,	374	M. BRIDE	V.1	63

Soh (1)

| Bellmour: | Soh. | 92 | OLD BATCH | IV.4 | 131 |

Soil (3)

	To cultivate each Year a hungry Soil;	213	FOR LOVE	PRO.	2
	And plant a Soil which you so rich have made.	213	FOR LOVE	PRO.	12
	Well plant a Soil which you so rich have made.	213	FOR LOVE	PRO.	V 12

Sol (2)

| Belinda: | my Sol, I'm afraid you'l follow evil Courses. | 55 | OLD BATCH | II.2 | 52 |
| Scandal: | and I hope I shall find both Sol and Venus in the sixth | 271 | FOR LOVE | III.1 | 651 |

Some   (continued)

Some   (continued)
Garcia:	To Osmyn; but some other Opportunity	. . . . . .	338	M. BRIDE	II.1	43
Garcia:	And I cou'd pity 'em. I hear some coming,	. . . . .	339	M. BRIDE	II.1	48
Almeria:	It was thy Fear; or else some transient Wind	. . . .	339	M. BRIDE	II.1	54
Almeria:	Or wind me in the Shroud of some pale Coarse	. . . .	339	M. BRIDE	II.1	76
Osmyn-Alph:	To pay some Part, some little of this Debt;	. . .	343	M. BRIDE	II.2	137
Osmyn-Alph:	Some Recompence of Love and matchless Truth.	. . . .	343	M. BRIDE	II.2	146
Osmyn-Alph:	And for some Purpose points out these Remembrances.	.	350	M. BRIDE	III.1	5
Osmyn-Alph:	At length, imprison'd in some Cleft of Rock,	. . . .	351	M. BRIDE	III.1	61
Heli:	Where not far off some Male-Contents hold Counsel	. .	352	M. BRIDE	III.1	100
Heli:	Where not far off some Male-Contents hold Council	. .	352	M. BRIDE	III.1	V100
Heli:	Nightly; hating this Tyrant; some, who love	. . .	352	M. BRIDE	III.1	101
Osmyn-Alph:	This Lesson, in some Hour of Inspiration,	. . . . .	353	M. BRIDE	III.1	128
Zara:	Some News, few Minutes past arriv'd, which seem'd	. .	354	M. BRIDE	III.1	204
Osmyn-Alph:	Some swift and dire event, of her blind Rage,	. . .	355	M. BRIDE	III.1	231
Selim:	(Which breeds Amazement and Distraction) some	. . .	361	M. BRIDE	IV.1	9
Selim:	And some of them bought off to Osmyn's Int'rest,	. .	362	M. BRIDE	IV.1	52
Gonsalez:	None, Sir. Some Papers have been since discover'd,	. .	363	M. BRIDE	IV.1	75
Gonsalez:	Some ready of Belief, have rais'd this Rumour:	. . .	363	M. BRIDE	IV.1	83
Gonsalez:	That some Impostor has usurp'd his Name.	. . . .	363	M. BRIDE	IV.1	100
Zara:	Are tainted; some among 'em have resolv'd	. . . . .	364	M. BRIDE	IV.1	143
Zara:	I have remaining in my Train, some Mutes,	. . . . .	365	M. BRIDE	IV.1	150
Zara:	Indeed? Then 'twas a Whisper spread by some	. . . .	366	M. BRIDE	IV.1	189
Gonsalez:	What Noise! some body coming? 'st, Alonzo?	. . . .	376	M. BRIDE	V.2	10
Selim:	The Mute you sent, by some Mischance was seen,	. . .	380	M. BRIDE	V.2	180
	To poison Plays, I see some where they sit,	. . .	385	M. BRIDE	EPI.	7
	That some well-laden Ship may strike the Sands;	. . .	385	M. BRIDE	EPI.	22
	Suffer'd at first some trifling Stakes to win:	. . .	393	WAY WORLD	PRO.	12
	Some Plot we think he has, and some new Thought;	. . .	393	WAY WORLD	PRO.	29
	Some Humour too, no Farce; but that's a Fault.	. . . .	393	WAY WORLD	PRO.	30
Fainall:	after I left you; my fair Cousin has some Humours, that	.	395	WAY WORLD	I.1	18
Fainall:	wou'd tempt the patience of a Stoick. What, some Coxcomb	.	395	WAY WORLD	I.1	19
Fainall:	Petulant and Witwoud.--Bring me some	. . . . . .	398	WAY WORLD	I.1	102
Mirabell:	Ay; I have been engag'd in a Matter of some sort	.	399	WAY WORLD	I.1	136
Mirabell:	a good Memory, and some few Scraps of other Folks Wit.	.	401	WAY WORLD	I.1	225
Fainall:	What I warrant he's unsincere, or 'tis some such	. . .	403	WAY WORLD	I.1	316
Witwoud:	Mirabell and he are at some distance, as my Lady Wishfort		408	WAY WORLD	I.1	483
Witwoud:	Mirabell wou'd be in some sort unfortunately fobb'd	.	408	WAY WORLD	I.1	489
Mrs Fain:	I ought to stand in some degree of Credit with	. . .	417	WAY WORLD	II.1	278
Millamant:	I gave you some Pain.	. . . .	420	WAY WORLD	II.1	380
Mirabell:	as a Mortification; for sure to please a Fool is some degree	421	WAY WORLD	II.1	439
Foible:	(says he) what you are a hatching some Plot (says he) you		427	WAY WORLD	III.1	95
Foible:	some disbanded Officer I warrant--Half Pay is but	.	427	WAY WORLD	III.1	97
Foible:	Madam. There are some Cracks discernable in the white	.	429	WAY WORLD	III.1	145
Marwood:	she knows some passages--Nay I expect all will come out	.	444	WAY WORLD	III.1	705
Lady Wish:	some Confusion.--It shows the Foot to advantage, and	.	445	WAY WORLD	IV.1	30
Sir Wilful:	some can't relish the Town, and others can't away with	.	448	WAY WORLD	IV.1	129
Sir Wilful:	mind in some measure,--I conjecture you partly guess--		448	WAY WORLD	IV.1	136
Lady Wish:	that invades me with some precipitation--You will oblige	.	457	WAY WORLD	IV.1	468
Waitwell:	that Satisfaction.--That wou'd be some Comfort to	. .	458	WAY WORLD	IV.1	503
Waitwell:	hand I see that already. That's some body whose throat	.	460	WAY WORLD	IV.1	578
Waitwell:	I am Charm'd Madam, I obey. But some proof you	.	461	WAY WORLD	IV.1	632
Lady Wish:	Ay dear Sir Rowland, that will be some	. . . . .	461	WAY WORLD	IV.1	636
Marwood:	hear nothing else for some days.	468	WAY WORLD	V.1	236
Lady Wish:	Health, or some such Emergency--	. . . . . .	468	WAY WORLD	V.1	264
Mirabell:	having it seems receiv'd some Cautions respecting your	.	476	WAY WORLD	V.1	541
Sir Wilful:	have some other employment, besides looking on.	. .	477	WAY WORLD	V.1	602
Foible:	O Sir, Some that were provided for Sir Rowland's	. .	478	WAY WORLD	V.1	605
Lady Wish:	to sink under the fatigue; and I cannot but have some fears	478	WAY WORLD	V.1	610
Lady Wish:	upon me yet, that my Son Fainall will pursue some	. .	478	WAY WORLD	V.1	611
	There are some Criticks so with Spleen diseas'd,	.	479	WAY WORLD	EPI.	5
	They from each Fair One catch some different Grace,	.	479	WAY WORLD	EPI.	32

Somebody (2)
Fainall:	that all the Male Sex shou'd be excepted; but somebody	.	396	WAY WORLD	I.1	55
Sir Wilful:	thou not know me, Friend? Why then send Somebody	. .	437	WAY WORLD	III.1	454

Someils du Matin (1)
Millamant:	all ye douceurs, ye Someils du Matin, adieu--I can't				
	do't, 'tis	. . . .	449	WAY WORLD	IV.1	189

Something (67)
Araminta:	Yes, yes, I can see something near it when you and	. .	55	OLD BATCH	II.2	36
Lucy:	may discover something in my Masque--Worthy Sir, a	. .	65	OLD BATCH	III.1	155
Sharper:	I am in disorder for what I have written. But something,				
	I know	. . . .	79	OLD BATCH	IV.1	159
Araminta:	You were about to tell me something, Child,--	. . . .	83	OLD BATCH	IV.3	21
Fondlewife:	Speculation? No, no; something went farther	. . . .	92	OLD BATCH	IV.4	116
Bellmour:	Countenance. But, to tell you something you don't know.	.	100	OLD BATCH	IV.4	148
Mellefont:	of following you, because I had something to say to you in		127	DOUBL DLR	I.1	14
Mellefont:	to follow you, because I had something to say to you in		127	DOUBL DLR	I.1	V 14
Brisk:	Let me perish, my Lord, but there is something very	.	133	DOUBL DLR	I.1	237
Lady Froth:	Complaisance of my Lord, or something of his own, that				
	should	. . . .	139	DOUBL DLR	II.1	50
Lord Touch:	(aside). I'm amaz'd, here must be something	. . .	152	DOUBL DLR	III.1	44
Mellefont:	Hum, 'gad I believe there's something in't;--	. . .	168	DOUBL DLR	IV.1	19
Sir Paul:	be this is all his doings--something that he has said;	. .	172	DOUBL DLR	IV.1	201
Sir Paul:	be this is all his doing--something that he has said;	.	172	DOUBL DLR	IV.1	V201
Sir Paul:	but hearkee, my Lord told me something of a Revolution	.	192	DOUBL DLR	V.1	172
Lord Touch:	incense her--something she has heard of you which carries		195	DOUBL DLR	V.1	310
	We hope there's something that may please each Taste,	. .	213	FOR LOVE	PRO.	26
	We've something too, to gratifie ill Nature,	. . . .	213	FOR LOVE	PRO.	31
Valentine:	I confess this is something extraordinary.	. . . .	227	FOR LOVE	I.1	441
Tattle:	--Come, let's talk of something else.	. . . . . .	228	FOR LOVE	I.1	443
Tattle:	me, and I told her something or other, faith--I know	. .	228	FOR LOVE	I.1	447
Tattle:	not what--Come, let's talk of something else.	. . .	228	FOR LOVE	I.1	448
Mrs Frail:	you give me now? Come, I must have something.	. . .	231	FOR LOVE	I.1	584
Valentine:	something.	. . . .	231	FOR LOVE	I.1	586
Scandal:	Ay, we'll all give you something.	. . . . . .	231	FOR LOVE	I.1	587

Something   (continued)

			PAGE	TITLE	ACT.SC	LINE
Mrs Prail:	I thought you would give me something, that	. . . . .	232	FOR LOVE	I.1	590
Angelica:	--Nay, I know something worse, if I would	. . . . .	238	FOR LOVE	II.1	111
Foresight:	something; tell me, and I'll forgive you; do, good Neice	.	239	FOR LOVE	II.1	147
Mrs Prail:	or Barn-Elms with a man alone--something	. . . . .	247	FOR LOVE	II.1	439
Miss Prue:	give me something to make me smell so--Oh pray	. . .	249	FOR LOVE	II.1	525
Miss Prue:	he'll give me something that will make my Smocks smell	.	249	FOR LOVE	II.1	527
Angelica:	What is, Mr. Tattle? I heard you say something	. . .	254	FOR LOVE	III.1	50
Scandal:	Come, Valentine, I'll go with you; I've something in	. .	259	FOR LOVE	III.1	231
Ben:	take your part, Your Tom Essence, and I'll say something to	265	FOR LOVE	III.1	435
Scandal:	Something has appear'd to your Son Valentine--	. . . .	266	FOR LOVE	III.1	496
Scandal:	but you are something more--There have been wise	. . .	267	FOR LOVE	III.1	528
Ben:	something to do with me. But what do's that signifie? If	.	272	FOR LOVE	III.1	715
Scandal:	of it, something surprizes me.	. . . .	276	FOR LOVE	IV.1	26
Scandal:	Madam, you and I can tell him something else, that	. .	284	FOR LOVE	IV.1	311
Scandal:	I'm apt to believe there is something mysterious in his	.	285	FOR LOVE	IV.1	344
Valentine:	one anothers Faces, till we have done something to be	.	290	FOR LOVE	IV.1	563
Scandal:	I will,--I have discover'd something of Tattle, that	.	291	FOR LOVE	IV.1	597
Angelica:	was indeed thinking to propose something like it in a Jest,	300	FOR LOVE	V.1	107
Foresight:	think there is something in your Physiognomy, that has a	.	304	FOR LOVE	V.1	260
Manuel:	Yet something too is due to me, who gave	. . . . .	333	M. BRIDE	I.1	289
Zara:	But something so unworthy, and so vile,	. . . . .	348	M. BRIDE	II.2	337
Fainall:	you are not so indifferent; you are thinking of something	395	WAY WORLD	I.1	5
Fainall:	Prithee, why so reserv'd? Something has put you out	. .	395	WAY WORLD	I.1	13
Mirabell:	Well, is the grand Affair over? You have been something	.	398	WAY WORLD	I.1	111
Fainall:	To give the t'other his due; he has something of good	.	401	WAY WORLD	I.1	221
Fainall:	To give t'other his due; he has something of good	. . .	401	WAY WORLD	I.1	V221
Witwoud:	and something more by the Week, to call on him	. . .	405	WAY WORLD	I.1	360
Mirabell:	I confess this is something extraordinary--I believe	.	405	WAY WORLD	I.1	378
Fainall:	have something to brag of the next time he makes Court	.	406	WAY WORLD	I.1	419
Petulant:	All's one for that; why then say I know something.	. .	407	WAY WORLD	I.1	442
Witwoud:	something of an Uncle to Mirabell, who is lately come to	.	408	WAY WORLD	I.1	481
Fainall:	Proof, and something of a Constitution to bustle thro' the	415	WAY WORLD	II.1	213
Mirabell:	I would give something that you did not know, I	. . .	422	WAY WORLD	II.1	460
Millamant:	after all, there is something very moving in a love-sick	.	422	WAY WORLD	II.1	474
Mirabell:	I have something more--Gone--Think of	. . . . . .	423	WAY WORLD	II.1	490
Marwood:	was something in it; but it seems it's over with you. Your	431	WAY WORLD	III.1	230
Mirabell:	Your bill of fare is something advanc'd in this latter	.	450	WAY WORLD	IV.1	228
Millamant:	said something to please me.	. . . .	452	WAY WORLD	IV.1	307
Foible:	thought something was contriving, when he stole by me	.	461	WAY WORLD	IV.1	613
Foible:	conceal something that pass'd in our Chamber one Evening	.	464	WAY WORLD	V.1	94
Mincing:	is in a perilous passion, at something Mr. Fainall has said.	465	WAY WORLD	V.1	108
Lady Wish:	Well, I'll swear I am something reviv'd at this	. . .	470	WAY WORLD	V.1	333

Sometime (2)

Gonsalez:	Sometimes concur, and sometime disagree;	. . . . .	366	M. BRIDE	IV.1	196
Mirabell:	there yet? I shall cut your Throat, sometime or other,	.	406	WAY WORLD	I.1	423

Sometimes (22)

Vainlove:	A kind of Mungril Zealot, sometimes very precise	. .	40	OLD BATCH	I.1	106
Bellmour:	floating Island; sometimes seems in reach, then vanishes	.	42	OLD BATCH	I.1	206
Bellmour:	That only happens sometimes, where the Dog has	. . .	44	OLD BATCH	I.1	257
Sir Joseph:	Well I am a Fool sometimes--But I'm sorry.	. . . .	54	OLD BATCH	II.1	244
Belinda:	Pish, I can't help dreaming of the Devil sometimes;	. .	55	OLD BATCH	II.2	39
Araminta:	Person, for his ease, sometimes confesses Secrets his	. .	58	OLD BATCH	II.2	137
Lord Froth:	O yes, sometimes,--but I never Laugh.	. . . . . .	133	DOUBL DLR	I.1	223
Mellefont:	and sometimes the Two farthest are together, but the	.	143	DOUBL DLR	II.1	166
Lady Touch:	a mind to amuse himself, sometimes with a little Gallantry	153	DOUBL DLR	III.1	83
Sir Paul:	together; she's a little hasty sometimes, and so am	. .	160	DOUBL DLR	III.1	389
Jeremy:	Spirit of Famine appears to me; sometimes like a decay'd	.	218	FOR LOVE	I.1	95
Jeremy:	Sometimes like a bilk'd Bookseller, with a meagre	. .	219	FOR LOVE	I.1	104
Valentine:	sometimes. I did not think she had granted more to any	.	229	FOR LOVE	I.1	487
Scandal:	Cards, sometimes, but that's nothing.	. . . . . .	271	FOR LOVE	III.1	667
Ben:	you shall see, that we Sailors can Dance sometimes, as well	274	FOR LOVE	III.1	791
Scandal:	Discourses, and sometimes rather think him inspir'd than	.	285	FOR LOVE	IV.1	345
	To help their Love, sometimes they show their Reading;	.	315	FOR LOVE	EPI.	8
Gonsalez:	Sometimes concur, and sometime disagree;	. . . . .	366	M. BRIDE	IV.1	196
Mirabell:	What, he speaks unseasonable Truths sometimes,	. . .	404	WAY WORLD	I.1	337
Witwoud:	and what's more, not finding himself, sometimes leave a	.	405	WAY WORLD	I.1	376
Marwood:	And yet I am thinking sometimes, to carry	. . . .	411	WAY WORLD	II.1	50
Millamant:	I please my self--Besides sometimes to	. . . . .	421	WAY WORLD	II.1	441

Somewhat (20)

Sharper:	There is in true Beauty, as in Courage, somewhat,	. .	86	OLD BATCH	IV.3	126
Bellmour:	Husband, somewhat pacify'd her.	. . . .	100	OLD BATCH	V.1	153
Setter:	somewhat fall'n from the Dignity of my Function; and	.	105	OLD BATCH	V.1	337
Brisk:	harkee,--you understand me. Somewhat heavy, a	. . .	133	DOUBL DLR	I.1	251
Mrs Prail:	That's somewhat the better reason, to my	. . . . .	234	FOR LOVE	I.1	669
Manuel:	Somewhat I heard of King and Rival mention'd.	. . .	348	M. BRIDE	II.2	355
Zara:	This thy Silence; somewhat of high Concern,	. . . .	354	M. BRIDE	III.1	194
Zara:	Somewhat of weight to me, requires his Freedom.	. . .	358	M. BRIDE	III.1	376
Osmyn-Alph:	Say somewhat quickly to conceal our Loves,	. . . .	359	M. BRIDE	III.1	390
Zara:	Somewhat, to blind the King, and save his Life	. . .	361	M. BRIDE	IV.1	24
Zara:	Forbear a Moment; somewhat more I have	. . . . .	364	M. BRIDE	IV.1	129
Gonsalez:	There's somewhat yet of Mystery in this;	. . . . .	366	M. BRIDE	IV.1	194
Manuel:	Yet somewhat she must mean of dire Import,	. . . .	370	M. BRIDE	IV.1	363
Zara:	A Forfeit as thy Life: Somewhat of high	. . . . .	375	M. BRIDE	V.1	124
Fainall:	somewhat too discerning in the Failings of your Mistress.	.	399	WAY WORLD	I.1	157
Mirabell:	And for a discerning Man, somewhat too passionate	. .	399	WAY WORLD	I.1	158
Sir Wilful:	not. I am somewhat dainty in making a Resolution,--	.	440	WAY WORLD	III.1	579
Sir Wilful:	matter in Town, to learn somewhat of your Lingo first,	.	440	WAY WORLD	III.1	582
Fainall:	'twere somewhat,--but to crawl after, with my Horns	.	442	WAY WORLD	III.1	636
Sir Wilful:	somewhat wary at first, before I am acquainted;--But I	.	446	WAY WORLD	IV.1	75

Somewhere (5)

Scandal:	go brag somewhere else.	. . . .	255	FOR LOVE	III.1	92
Manuel:	That somewhere is repeated--I have power	. . . .	374	M. BRIDE	V.1	54
Fainall:	her of all she's worth, and we'll retire somewhere, any	.	416	WAY WORLD	II.1	245
Fainall:	somewhere else; For here it will not avail. This, my Lady	.	473	WAY WORLD	V.1	441
Sir Wilful:	flourish somewhere else Sir.	. . . .	476	WAY WORLD	V.1	559

Son (49)

		PAGE	TITLE	ACT.SC	LINE
Heartwell:	to have my Son and heir resemble such a Duke--to have a	45	OLD BATCH	I.1	319
Fondlewife:	of my house, thou Son of the Whore of Babylon; Off-spring	90	OLD BATCH	IV.4	65
Sir Paul:	Were you, Son? Gadsbud much better as it is--	131	DOUBL DLR	I.1	177
Maskwell:	--a Son and Heir, would have edg'd Young	137	DOUBL DLR	I.1	377
Sir Paul:	have not a Son to inherit this--'Tis true I have a	161	DOUBL DLR	III.1	411
Sir Paul:	unworthy Sinner--But if I had a Son, ah, that's my	161	DOUBL DLR	III.1	415
Careless:	I warrant you, what we must have a Son some way	162	DOUBL DLR	III.1	446
Sir Paul:	my Son Mellefont?	175	DOUBL DLR	IV.1	282
Sr Sampson:	Nostrodamus. What, I warrant my Son thought nothing	240	FOR LOVE	II.1	175
Sr Sampson:	as my Son Benjamin is arriv'd, he is to make over to him	240	FOR LOVE	II.1	182
Sr Sampson:	Haste, ay, ay; haste enough, my Son Ben will	240	FOR LOVE	II.1	192
Foresight:	send your Son to Sea again. I'll wed my Daughter to an	241	FOR LOVE	II.1	238
Sr Sampson:	wou'd my Son were an Egyptian Mummy for thy sake.	242	FOR LOVE	II.1	245
Sr Sampson:	My Son, Sir; what Son, Sir? My Son Benjamin,	242	FOR LOVE	II.1	265
Valentine:	Sir, is this Usage for your Son?--for that old,	244	FOR LOVE	II.1	311
Valentine:	Your Son, Sir.	244	FOR LOVE	II.1	315
Sr Sampson:	Sola's and Sonata's? 'Oons whose Son are you? how were	245	FOR LOVE	II.1	377
Jeremy:	I am by my Father, the Son of a Chair-man, my	245	FOR LOVE	II.1	379
Sr Sampson:	Son of a Cucumber.--These things are unaccountable	246	FOR LOVE	II.1	388
Mrs Frail:	Sampson has a Son that is expected to Night; and by the	248	FOR LOVE	II.1	492
Sr Sampson:	Is Ben come? Odso, my Son Ben come? Odd,	259	FOR LOVE	III.1	210
Sr Sampson:	Frail, you shall see my Son Ben--Body c' me, he's the	259	FOR LOVE	III.1	212
Sr Sampson:	What, is my Son Valentine gone? What, is he	259	FOR LOVE	III.1	234
Angelica:	have you than your Son.	260	FOR LOVE	III.1	256
Sr Sampson:	My Son Ben! bless thee my dear Boy; body o'	260	FOR LOVE	III.1	270
Sr Sampson:	Son Ben.	261	FOR LOVE	III.1	279
Sr Sampson:	own Son, faith, he'll touzle her, and mouzle her: The	265	FOR LOVE	III.1	458
Scandal:	Something has appear'd to your Son Valentine--	266	FOR LOVE	III.1	496
Sr Sampson:	Son be mad--Where's your Oppositions, your Trines, and	283	FOR LOVE	IV.1	282
Scandal:	has been heartily vex'd--His Son is Non compos mentis, and	283	FOR LOVE	IV.1	298
Sr Sampson:	had a Son that was spoil'd among 'em; a good hopeful	299	FOR LOVE	V.1	81
Valentine:	to undo the Son, it was a reasonable return of Nature.	311	FOR LOVE	V.1	512
Angelica:	always lov'd your Son, and hated your unforgiving	312	FOR LOVE	V.1	573
Leonora:	His Son, the brave Valentia Prince, and you,	327	M. BRIDE	I.1	49
Almeria:	At Peace; Father and Son are now no more--	327	M. BRIDE	I.1	53
Almeria:	Both, both--Father and Son are now no more.	327	M. BRIDE	I.1 V	53
Gonsalez:	Garcia, my Son, your Beauties lowest Slave,	332	M. BRIDE	I.1	255
Manuel:	Worthy to be your Husband, and my Son.	334	M. BRIDE	I.1	334
Osmyn-Alph:	But bless my Son, visit not him for me.	350	M. BRIDE	III.1	13
Osmyn-Alph:	Be doubled in thy Mercies to my Son:	350	M. BRIDE	III.1	18
Gonsalez:	What says my Son? what Ruine? ha? what	377	M. BRIDE	V.2	53
Gonsalez:	And fall beneath the Hand of my own Son.	378	M. BRIDE	V.2	72
Gonsalez:	O my Son, from the blind Dotage	378	M. BRIDE	V.2	81
Gonsalez:	To aid my Son. I'll follow with the last	379	M. BRIDE	V.2	126
Waitwell:	If he were my Son as he is my Nephew I'd Pistoll him--	460	WAY WORLD	IV.1	603
Lady Wish:	not out.--Ah! her first Husband my Son Languish,	469	WAY WORLD	V.1	304
Lady Wish:	upon me yet, that my Son Fainall will pursue some	478	WAY WORLD	V.1	611

Son-in-Law (2)

Brisk:	threatens to disclaim you for a Son-in-Law, and my Lord	128	DOUBL DLR	I.1	55
Lady Wish:	you are become an Intercessor with my Son-in-Law, to	465	WAY WORLD	V.1	129

Son's (3)

Heartwell:	fleering Coxcomb scoff and cry, Mr. your Son's mighty	45	OLD BATCH	I.1	320
Almeria:	And gild and magnifie has Son's Exploits.	331	M. BRIDE	I.1	V215
Almeria:	His Son's Exploits.	331	M. BRIDE	I.1	216

Sonata's (2)

Jeremy:	Sola's or Sonata's, they give me the Spleen.	245	FOR LOVE	II.1	375
Sr Sampson:	Sola's and Sonata's? 'Oons whose Son are you? how were	245	FOR LOVE	II.1	377

Song (27)

Araminta:	be not gone, I'll entertain you with a new Song,	58	OLD BATCH	II.2	153
Araminta:	O I am glad we shall have a Song to divert the	59	OLD BATCH	II.2	186
Araminta:	Discourse--Pray oblige us with the last new Song.	59	OLD BATCH	II.2	187
	(SONG.)	59	OLD BATCH	II.2	188
Araminta:	So, how de'e like the Song, Gentlemen?	60	OLD BATCH	II.2	203
	(After the Song, a Dance of Antick.)	71	OLD BATCH	III.2	25
Mellefont:	New Song, we'll get 'em to give it us by the way.	143	DOUBL DLR	II.1	173
Mellefont:	Pray let us have the Favour of you, to practice the Song,	143	DOUBL DLR	II.1	175
	(SONG.)	143	DOUBL DLR	II.1	177
Lady Froth:	Oh you made a Song upon her, Mr. Brisk.	166	DOUBL DLR	III.1	588
Brisk:	'Tis not a Song neither--it's a sort of an Epigram, or	166	DOUBL DLR	III.1	591
	(SONG.)	166	DOUBL DLR	III.1	594
Valentine:	at the height of a Song, sent by an unknown Hand, or a	218	FOR LOVE	I.1	80
Tattle:	(Hums a Song.)	228	FOR LOVE	I.1	449
Scandal:	recommend a Song to you upon the Hint of my two	258	FOR LOVE	III.1	191
Scandal:	Pray sing the first Song in the last new Play.	258	FOR LOVE	III.1	197
	(SONG.)	258	FOR LOVE	III.1	198
Ben:	Come, I'll sing you a Song of a Sailor.	273	FOR LOVE	III.1	740
Mrs Frail:	Song.	273	FOR LOVE	III.1	749
Ben:	The Song was made upon one of our Ships-Crew's	273	FOR LOVE	III.1	750
Ben:	Wife; our Boat-swain made the Song, may-hap you may	273	FOR LOVE	III.1	751
Valentine:	I would have Musick--Sing me the Song that I	292	FOR LOVE	IV.1	648
	(SONG.)	293	FOR LOVE	IV.1	650
Mirabell:	with her, and was guilty of a Song in her Commendation:	397	WAY WORLD	I.1	70
Millamant:	Dee say so? Then I'm resolv'd I'll have a Song to	434	WAY WORLD	III.1	365
Millamant:	sing the Song, I wou'd have learnt Yesterday. You shall	434	WAY WORLD	III.1	371
	(SONG.)	435	WAY WORLD	III.1	375

Songs (4)

Heartwell:	here Silvia, here are Songs and Dances, Poetry and Musick	72	OLD BATCH	III.2	34
Lady Froth:	Songs, Elegies, Satyrs, Encomiums, Panegyricks,	138	DOUBL DLR	I.1	16
	Beaus Judge of Dress; the Witlings Judge of Songs;	204	DOUBL DLR	EPI.	27
Jeremy:	and Songs; not like other Porters for Hire, but for the Jests	218	FOR LOVE	I.1	97

Sonnet (1)

Brisk:	rather an Epigrammatick Sonnet; I don't know what to	166	DOUBL DLR	III.1	592

Sons (4)

Sir Paul:	Sons nor Grandsons? Must the Family of the Plyants be	171	DOUBL DLR	IV.1	137

Sons   (continued)
  Sr Sampson: What the Devil had I to do, ever to beget Sons?   282   FOR LOVE   IV.1   260
  Sr Sampson: married till Fifty; yet they begct Sons and Daughters till   .   298   FOR LOVE   V.1   38
  Sr Sampson: and we'll beget Sons and Daughters enough to put the   .   308   FOR LOVE   V.1   398
Soon (45)
  Bellmour: Time enough, ay tco soon, I should rather have   43   OLD BATCH   I.1   235
  Heartwell: It will as soon blow North and by South--marry   44   OLD BATCH   I.1   294
  Bellmour: though I believe he was heartily frightned, for as soon as   .   46   OLD BATCH   I.1   362
  Sharper: Dirt, you have large Acres and can soon repay it--   . . .   50   OLD BATCH   II.1   109
  Capt Bluff: Nay come Sir Joseph, you know my Heat's soon over.   . . .   54   OLD BATCH   II.1   243
  Lucy: You may as soon hope, to recover your cwn Maiden-head,   .   61   OLD BATCH   III.1   7
  Sir Joseph: by, I would as scon have let him a' had a hundred of my   .   68   OLD BATCH   III.1   277
  Sir Joseph: his Business--He durst as soon have kiss'd you, as kick'd   .   70   OLD BATCH   III.1   359
  Barnaby: I did; and Comfort will send Tribulation hither as soon   .   76   OLD BATCH   IV.1   21
  Fondlewife: and glow upon his Cheeks, and that I would as soon   . . .   76   OLD BATCH   IV.1   32
  Laetitia: You will have your ends soon--You will--You will--   . . .   77   OLD BATCH   IV.1   94
  Bellmour: Fit will be soon over.   83   OLD BATCH   IV.2   93
  Bellmour: But, you were a little unlucky in coming sc soon, and   .   94   OLD BATCH   IV.4   188
  Heartwell: Woman can as soon give Immortality.   108   OLD BATCH   V.2   24
                 Soon as her Curiosity is over, ...   113   OLD BATCH   EPI.   3
                 Let Nature work, and do not Damn too scon,   .   125   DOUBL DLR   PRO.   16
  Sir Paul: Reason,--as soon may Tygers Match with Tygers, Lambs   .   144   DOUBL DLR   II.1   224
  Sir Paul: I; but mine's scon over, and then I'm so sorry--O, Mr.   .   160   DOUBL DLR   III.1   390
  Lord Froth: so ready--she always comes in three bars too soon--and   .   163   DOUBL DLR   III.1   476
  Cynthia: you had not chang'd sides so soon; now I begin to find it.   172   DOUBL DLR   IV.1   177
  Sir Paul: pound a Year upon the Rogue as scon as ever he looks me   .   173   DOUBL DLR   IV.1   225
  Maskwell: that might have soon boil'd over; but--   .   182   DOUBL DLR   IV.1   558
  Lord Touch: but toc soon you'll know mine, and that Woman's shame.   .   202   DOUBL DLR   V.1   565
  Tattle: But I soon satisfy'd the Lady of my Innocence; for I told   .   227   FOR LOVE   I.1   429
  Sr Sampson: White, Signatum, Sigillatum, and Deliberatum; that as soon   240   FOR LOVE   II.1   181
  Valentine: My Cloaths are scon put off:--But you must   .   244   FOR LOVE   II.1   339
  Mrs Fore: A cunning Cur; how soon he cou'd find out a   250   FOR LOVE   II.1   544
  Tattle: more complying; and as soon as ever I make you say   . .   252   FOR LOVE   II.1   622
  Ben: me alone as soon as I come home, with such a dirty dowdy   .   264   FOR LOVE   III.1   423
  Ben: Lapland-Witch as soon, and live upon selling of contrary   .   264   FOR LOVE   III.1   426
  Ben: Lapland-Witch as soon, and live upon selling contrary   .   264   FOR LOVE   III.1 V426
  Sr Sampson: shalt have it as soon as thou hast set thy Hand to another   282   FOR LOVE   IV.1   234
  Scandal: Dear, too considerable to be forgot so soon.   284   FOR LOVE   IV.1   317
  Sr Sampson: Women think a Man old too soon, faith and troth you do   .   298   FOR LOVE   V.1   25
  Manuel: A Bridal Qualm; scon off. How is't, Almeria?   334   M. BRIDE   I.1   348
  Almeria: Sure I have dreamt, if we must part so soon.   344   M. BRIDE   II.2   194
  Zara: Compassion, scarce will it own that Name so soon,   . . .   346   M. BRIDE   II.2   279
  Zara: Compassion, scarce will't own that Name so scon,   . . .   346   M. BRIDE   II.2 V279
  Osmyn-Alph: At your return so soon and unexpected!   359   M. BRIDE   III.1   409
  Alonzo: Soon as I seiz'd the Man, ...   373   M. BRIDE   V.1   21
  Witwoud: soon as your Back was turn'd--whip he was gone;   . . .   405   WAY WORLD   I.1   371
  Marwood: in our Breasts, and every Heart, or socn or late, receive
                   and   410   WAY WORLD   II.1   26
  Millamant: pleases, and they die as soon as one pleases: And then if   .   420   WAY WORLD   II.1   405
  Mirabell: I say that a Man may as soon make a Friend by his   . . .   422   WAY WORLD   II.1   464
  Lady Wish: and then as soon as he appears, start, ay, start and be
                   surpriz'd, ...   445   WAY WORLD   IV.1   27
Sooner (11)
  Bellmour: Would thou hadst come a little sconer, Vainlove   . . .   42   OLD BATCH   I.1   194
  Laetitia: Your back was no sooner turn'd, but like a Lion, he   . . .   90   OLD BATCH   IV.4   52
  Mellefont: By Heav'n into a hot Furnace sooner.   157   DOUBL DLR   III.1   238
  Lady Ply: should die, of all Mankind there's none I'd sooner make   . .   170   DOUBL DLR   IV.1   111
  Lord Touch: No sconer born, but the Vile Parent dies.   203   DOUBL DLR   V.1   596
  Miss Prue: But I'm sure it is not so, for I'll speak sooner than   . . .   264   FOR LOVE   III.1   395
  Mrs Frail: O Sister, had you come a minute sconer, you would   . . .   287   FOR LOVE   IV.1   449
  Valentine: The sconer the better--Jeremy, come hither--   . . .   290   FOR LOVE   IV.1   556
  Almeria: To Heav'n and thee; and sconer wou'd have dy'd--   .   343   M. BRIDE   II.2   127
  Foible: The sooner the better, Madam.   428   WAY WORLD   III.1   121
  Marwood: Your merry Note may be chang'd sooner   434   WAY WORLD   IV.1   363
Sooth (2)
  Lady Touch: and sooth me to a fond belief of all your fictions;   . .   197   DOUBL DLR   V.1   380
  Almeria: Musick has Charms to sooth a savage Breast, ...   326   M. BRIDE   I.1   1
Soothing (1)
  Osmyn-Alph: Are they not soothing Softness, sinking Ease, ...   358   M. BRIDE   III.1   363
Soothsayer (1)
  Sr Sampson: Where is this old Soothsayer? This Uncle of   307   FOR LOVE   V.1   376
Sop (1)
  Valentine: If I can give that Cerberus a Sop, I shall be at rest
                   fcr one   222   FOR LOVE   I.1   225
Sophisticated (1)
  Lady Wish: Naught? Have you not been Sophisticated? Not understand?   .   466   WAY WORLD   V.1   149
Sophy (2)
  Sir Wilful: And a Fig for your Sultan and Sophy.   456   WAY WORLD   IV.1   457
  Sir Wilful: --and a fig for your Sultan and Sophy.   457   WAY WORLD   IV.1   479
Sorceress (1)
  Mellefont: Confusion, my Uncle! O the damn'd Sorceress.   186   DOUBL DLR   IV.2   111
Sordid (2)
  Angelica: for mercenary Ends and sordid Interest.   294   FOR LOVE   IV.1   724
  Angelica: for by mercenary Ends and sordid Interest.   294   FOR LOVE   IV.1 V724
Sore (1)
  Vainlove: Nay, 'tis a Sore of your own scratching.--Well   . . .   109   OLD BATCH   V.2   64
Sorrow (4)
  Foresight: Sorrow, Want and Plenty, Night and Day, make up our   .   236   FOR LOVE   II.1   36
  Manuel: I wonnot have the seeming cf a Sorrow seen   334   M. BRIDE   I.1   322
  Manuel: But let me lead you from this Place of Sorrow, ...   349   M. BRIDE   II.2   382
  Osmyn-Alph: Let ev'ry Hair, which Sorrow by the Roots, ...   350   M. BRIDE   III.1   16
Sorrowful (1)
  Bellmour: the Knight of the sorrowful Face.   68   OLD BATCH   III.1   288
Sorrows (6)
  Almeria: He and his Sorrows now are safely lodg'd   326   M. BRIDE   I.1   11
  Almeria: Know'st nothing of my Sorrows   328   M. BRIDE   I.1 V 89

Sorrows   (continued)
  Leonora: Sorrows, ... 329   M. BRIDE   I.1   150
  Osmyn-Alph: And only for his Sorrows chose this Solitude? 346   M. BRIDE   II.2 260
  Osmyn-Alph: Paternal Love prevailing o'er his Sorrows; 352   M. BRIDE   III.1 113
  Osmyn-Alph: Thy Sorrows have disturb'd thy Peace of Mind, ... 357   M. BRIDE   III.1 309
Sorry (29)
  Sharper: I'm sorry to see this, Ned: Once a Man comes to his . . 41   OLD BATCH I.1   147
  Sir Joseph: I rejoyce! agad not I Sir; I'me sorry for your loss, . . 48   OLD BATCH II.1 35
  Sir Joseph: I rejoyce! agad not I Sir; I'me very sorry for your loss, . 48   OLD BATCH II.1 V 35
  Sir Joseph: Well I am a Fool sometimes--But I'm sorry. . . 54   OLD BATCH II.1 244
  Setter: Nay faith Lucy I'me sorry, I'le own my self to blame, . . 66   OLD BATCH III.1 212
  Bellmour: Come, take your Fellow-Travellers. Old George, I'm sorry . 112   OLD BATCH V.2   183
  Brisk: against Wit, and I'm sorry for some Friends of mine that . 133   DOUBL DLR I.1   239
  Brisk: I'm sorry for him, Deuce take me. 134   DOUBL DLR I.1   282
  Lady Touch: --I dare swear he's sorry--and were it to do again, would . 152   DOUBL DLR III.1 77
  Lord Touch: Sorry, for what? 'Death you rack me with 152   DOUBL DLR III.1 79
  Sir Paul: I; but mine's seen over, and then I'm so sorry--O, Mr. . 160   DOUBL DLR III.1 390
  Brisk: tell whether I am glad or sorry that your Ladiship has made . 176   DOUBL DLR IV.1 339
  Sir Paul: amazed, and so overjoy'd, so afraid, and so sorry.--But . 179   DOUBL DLR IV.1 460
  Maskwell: I am sorry, my Lord, I can make you no Answer; 182   DOUBL DLR IV.1 552
  Maskwell: I am sorry, my Lord, I can't make you an answer; . . . 182   DOUBL DLR IV.1 V552
  Tattle: self upon my Account; Gad, I was sorry for it with all my . 258   FOR LOVE   III.1 177
  Sr Sampson: with the Reprobate; Odd, I was sorry for you with all my . 260   FOR LOVE   III.1 259
  Ben: No, I'm sorry for that.--But pray why are you so . . . 263   FOR LOVE   III.1 380
  Angelica: is over, methinks I am not half so sorry for him as I was-- . 277   FOR LOVE   IV.1 83
  Angelica: is over, methinks I am not half so sorry as I was-- . . . 277   FOR LOVE   IV.1 V 83
  Sr Sampson: pretty well now, Val: Body o' me, I was sorry to see thee . 281   FOR LOVE   IV.1 202
  Tattle: and be sorry for't afterwards. I'd have you to know, Sir, . 305   FOR LOVE   V.1   291
  Tattle: Poor woman! Gad I'm sorry for her too; for I have no . . 309   FOR LOVE   V.1   466
  Ben: one another. I'm sorry for the Young Man with all my . . 310   FOR LOVE   V.1   489
  Fainall: Come, I'm sorry, ... 416   WAY WORLD II.1 224
  Marwood: I'm sorry I hinted to my Lady to endeavour a 443   WAY WORLD III.1 668
  Marwood: I am sorry to see you so passionate, Madam. 466   WAY WORLD V.1   160
  Marwood: done. I am sorry my Zeal to serve your Ladyship and . . 466   WAY WORLD V.1   162
  Sir Wilful: --S'heart! and I'm sorry for't. What wou'd you have? . . 470   WAY WORLD V.1   315
Sort (17)
  Bellmour: Prithee, what sort of Fellow is Fondlewife? 40   OLD BATCH I.1   105
  Fondlewife: as I should be, a sort of a civil Perquisite to a
                  Whore-master, ... 94   OLD BATCH IV.4 184
  Brisk: 'Tis not a Song neither--it's a sort of an Epigram, or . 166   DOUBL DLR III.1 591
  Brisk: your Ladyship was in my Thoughts; and I was in a sort of . 176   DOUBL DLR IV.1 326
  Valentine: which are but a civiller sort of Duns, that lay claim to . 221   FOR LOVE   I.1   191
  Ben: ask'd what was the matter.--He ask'd in a surly sort of a . 285   FOR LOVE   IV.1 365
  Ben: to me?)--So he ask'd in a surly sort of manner,-- . . . 285   FOR LOVE   IV.1 368
  Tattle: damn'd sort of a Life. 309   FOR LOVE   V.1   468
                  For they're a sort of Fools which Fortune makes, . . . 393   WAY WORLD PRO.   3
  Mirabell: Ay; I have been engag'd in a Matter of some sort . . . 399   WAY WORLD I.1   136
  Witwoud: --Faith and Troth a pretty deal of an odd sort of a small . 403   WAY WORLD I.1   290
  Witwoud: She's handsome; but she's a sort of an uncertain . . . 408   WAY WORLD I.1   471
  Witwoud: Mirabell wou'd be in some sort unfortunately fobb'd . . 408   WAY WORLD I.1   489
  Lady Wish: sort of a dyingness--You see that Picture has a sort of . 429   WAY WORLD III.1 168
  Sir Wilful: Antipodes--your Antipodes are a good rascally sort of
                  topsy-turvy 456   WAY WORLD IV.1 424
  Waitwell: hand? the Rascal writes a sort of a large hand; your . . 460   WAY WORLD IV.1 601
Sot (6)
  Vainlove: before, Sot? 99   OLD BATCH V.1   121
  Lady Ply: Drink the less you Sot, and do't before you 180   DOUBL DLR IV.1 V487
  Lady Touch: Fool, Sot, insensible Ox! but remember 192   DOUBL DLR V.1   191
  Valentine: Sot, can't you apprehend? 295   FOR LOVE   IV.1 745
  Valentine: Go see, you Sot. I'm very glad that I can move your . . 295   FOR LOVE   IV.1 759
  Lady Wish: sleep, you Sot--Or as I'm a person, I'll have you
                  bastinado'd 457   WAY WORLD IV.1 462
Sought (3)
  Selim: I've sought in vain, the King is no where, to 380   M. BRIDE   V.2   173
  Selim: I've sought in vain, for no where can the King . . . 380   M. BRIDE   V.2 V173
  Sir Wilful: troublesome, I wou'd have sought a walk with you. . . . 448   WAY WORLD IV.1 117
Soul (52)
  Bellmour: Nature, Night, had hid, confess'd her Soul was true to . 38   OLD BATCH I.1   50
  Sir Joseph: Not I Sir, not I, as I've a Soul to be sav'd, I have . 48   OLD BATCH II.1 29
  Silvia: For I would know, though to the anguish of my Soul; . . 61   OLD BATCH III.1 15
  Capt Bluff: him--I'll pink his Soul--but whisper that softly . . . 68   OLD BATCH III.1 261
  Sir Joseph: Soul? 69   OLD BATCH III.1 312
  Heartwell: Now by my Soul, I cannot lie, though it were to serve a . 72   OLD BATCH III.2 59
  Belinda: ha, ha, I can't for my Soul help thinking that I look just . 83   OLD BATCH IV.3 12
  Belinda: his Mistress, is like a Body without a Soul. Mr. Vainlove, . 86   OLD BATCH IV.3 134
  Brisk: Soul of Conversation, the very Essence of Wit, and Spirit . 128   DOUBL DLR I.1   34
  Lady Touch: in my Temper, Passions in my Soul, apt to every provocation; 135   DOUBL DLR I.1   326
  Lady Touch: a Larum, only to rouse my own still'd Soul for your . . 137   DOUBL DLR I.1   381
  Lady Touch: and Recesses of my Soul.--Oh Mellefont! I burn; . . . 137   DOUBL DLR I.1   398
  Lady Touch: Married to Morrow! Despair strikes me. Yet my Soul . . 137   DOUBL DLR I.1   399
  Mellefont: Soul, thou art villainously bent to discover all to me, . 156   DOUBL DLR III.1 205
  Brisk: With all my Heart and Soul, and proud of the vast . . 165   DOUBL DLR III.1 556
  Careless: out a Wretched Life, and breath my Soul beneath your . . 170   DOUBL DLR IV.1 100
  Mellefont: Now, by my Soul, I will not go till I have made . . . 186   DOUBL DLR IV.2 121
  Lady Touch: a Sin, in pity to your Soul. 197   DOUBL DLR V.1   382
  Lady Touch: Too well thou know'st my jealous Soul cou'd never bear . 198   DOUBL DLR V.1   399
  Lady Touch: disarm'd my Soul. 198   DOUBL DLR V.1   404
  Brisk: With all my Soul,--your Ladyship has made me 201   DOUBL DLR V.1   538
  Tattle: Upon my Soul Angelica's a fine Woman--And 228   FOR LOVE   I.1   456
  Tattle: I? My Soul, Madam. 232   FOR LOVE   I.1   595
  Mrs Fore: Soul, I shall fancy my self Old indeed, to have this great . 249   FOR LOVE   II.1 512
  Mrs Fore: Heark'ee, Sister--by my Soul the Girl is 250   FOR LOVE   II.1 560
  Mrs Frail: O' my Soul, I'm afraid not--eh!--filthy 250   FOR LOVE   II.1 564
  Angelica: Transport in your Soul; which, it seems, you only
                  counterfeited, ... 294   FOR LOVE   IV.1 723
                  Methinks, we Players resemble such a Soul, ... 315   FOR LOVE   EPI.   19

Soul   (continued)
	Thus Aristotle's Soul, of old that was,	315	FOR LCVE	EPI.	21
Manuel:	All Eyes, so by Preheminence of Scul	336	M. EBIDE	I.1	422
Heli:	This living Light, could to my Soul, or Sense	338	M. EBIDE	II.1	7
Heli:	And when his Soul gives all her Passions Way,	338	M. EBIDE	II.1	31
Almeria:	To him, to Heav'n and my Alphonso's Soul.	339	M. EBIDE	II.1	83
Almeria:	My Soul, enlarg'd from its vile Bonds will mcunt,	340	M. EBIDE	II.2	25
Almeria:	To my Alphonso's Soul. O Joy too great!	340	M. EBIDE	II.2	29
Almeria:	As hurries all my Soul, and dozes my weak Sense.	343	M. EBIDE	II.2	155
Almeria:	It hurries all my Soul, and stuns my Sense.	343	M. EBIDE	II.2	V155
Zara:	I know, my Charms have reach'd thy very Soul,	348	M. EBIDE	II.2	345
Osmyn-Alph:	My Soul is up in Arms, ready to charge	351	M. BRIDE	III.1	81
Osmyn-Alph:	This Woman has a Soul,	355	M. EBIDE	III.1	222
Almeria:	Give thy Soul Way, and tell me thy dark Thought.	356	M. EBIDE	III.1	274
Osmyn-Alph:	Soul of my Soul, and End of all my Wishes.	357	M. EBIDE	III.1	305
Osmyn-Alph:	To fcllow thee my separating Scul.	358	M. EBIDE	III.1	348
Manuel:	For on my Soul he dies, tho' thou, and I,	369	M. BRIDE	IV.1	333
Manuel:	What's thy whole Life, thy Soul, thy All, to my	374	M. BRIDE	V.1	71
Zara:	Yet, more, this Stilness terrifies my Soul.	379	M. EBIDE	V.2	142
Zara:	Of Sense: His Soul still sees, and knows each Purpose,	381	M. EBIDE	V.2	196
Zara:	Soul cf my Love, and I will wait thy flight.	381	M. EBIDE	V.2	201
Osmyn-Alph:	In this extreamest Joy my Soul can taste,	383	M. EBIDE	V.2	302
Mirabell:	I do from my Soul.	401	WAY WCBLD	I.1	237
Mrs Fain:	My Soul.	412	WAY WCBLD	II.1	88

Soul-racking (1)
| Osmyn-Alph: | To that soul-racking Thought. | 357 | M. EBIDE | III.1 | 294 |

Souldier (2)
| Ben: | A Souldier and a Sailor, | 274 | FOR LCVE | III.1 | 758 |
| Ben: | The Souldier Swore like Thunder, | 274 | FOR LCVE | III.1 | 769 |

Souls (8)
Bellmour:	his Glass. Let low and earthy Souls grovel till they have	37	OLD BATCH	I.1	25
Bellmour:	his Glass. Let low and earthly Souls grovel 'till they have	37	OLD EATCH	I.1	V 25
Sharper:	which narrow Souls cannot dare to admire.--And	86	OLD BATCH	IV.3	127
Lord Touch:	Start not--let guilty and dishonest Souls	189	DOUEL DLR	V.1	47
Valentine:	Souls in Westminster-Abby, or damns more in Westminster-Hall:	280	FOR LCVE	IV.1	177
	Now to these Men (say they) such Souls were given,	315	FCR LCVE	EPI.	15
Almeria:	And, as with living Souls, have been inform'd,	326	M. BRIDE	I.1	4
Almeria:	Or pompous Phrase; the Pageantry of Souls.	332	M. EBIDE	I.1	249

Sound (7)
	Unless the Fable's good, and Moral sound.	204	DOUEL DLR	EPI.	18
Scandal:	Faith, I'm sound.	272	FOR LCVE	III.1	704
Ben:	as good Blood in my Veins, and a Heart as sound as a	273	FOR LCVE	III.1	736
Jeremy:	sound, poor Gentleman. He is indeed here, Sir, and not	279	FOR LCVE	IV.1	125
Angelica:	pretending to a sound Understanding; as Drunken men do	296	FOR LCVE	IV.1	764
Almeria:	By Magick Numbers and persuasive Sound.	326	M. EBIDE	I.1	5
Zara:	There, there's the dreadful Sound, the King's thy Rival!	348	M. EBIDE	II.2	348

Sounding (1)
| Almeria: | Nor will my Ears be charm'd with sounding Words, | 332 | M. EBIDE | I.1 | 248 |

Sounds (4)
Brisk:	sounds great; besides your Ladyship's Coach-man having a	163	DOUEL DLR	III.1	507
Heli:	Of one complaining--There it sounds--I'll follow it.	340	M. EBIDE	II.2	3
Almeria:	My Father's Voice; hollow it sounds, and from	371	M. EBIDE	IV.1	392
Almeria:	My Father's Voice; hollow it sounds, and calls	371	M. EBIDE	IV.1	V392

Source (5)
Osmyn-Alph:	Of Light, to the bright Source of all. There, in	353	M. EBIDE	III.1	132
Osmyn-Alph:	Of Light, to the bright Source of all. For there	353	M. EBIDE	III.1	V132
Zara:	From my Despair, my Anger had its source;	362	M. EBIDE	IV.1	29
Almeria:	Source of my Woes: thou and thy Race be curs'd;	370	M. BRIDE	IV.1	379
Almeria:	The Source of Woe, and let the Torrent loose.	382	M. EBIDE	V.2	244

South (1)
| Heartwell: | It will as soon blow North and by South--marry | 44 | OLD EATCH | I.1 | 294 |

Sow (1)
| Sharper: | pains to sow: he does the drudgery in the Mine, and you | 43 | OLD BATCH | I.1 | 220 |

Sowre (1)
| | And know each Critick by his sowre Grimaces. | 385 | M. EBIDE | EPI. | 6 |

Space (1)
| Jeremy: | Name, has for the space of Sev'n Years truly and faithfully | 218 | FOR LOVE | I.1 | 67 |

Spain (1)
| Zara: | About the time our Arms embark'd for Spain. | 364 | M. EBIDE | IV.1 | 121 |

Spanish (1)
| Lady Wish: | Grant me patience! I mean the Spanish Paper Idiot, Complexion | 425 | WAY WCBLD | III.1 | 12 |

Spar'd (3)
	For that damn'd Poet's spar'd who dams a Brother,	323	M. EBIDE	PRO.	31
Almeria:	I'll not let go, 'till you have spar'd my Husband.	369	M. EBIDE	IV.1	338
Sir Wilful:	Travel too, I think they may be spar'd.	477	WAY WORLD	V.1	587

Spare (12)
Maskwell:	then were fine work indeed! her fury wou'd spare nothing,	190	DOUEL DLR	V.1	93
Valentine:	Scandal, learn to spare your Friends, and do not	221	FOR LOVE	I.1	198
Tattle:	Alas, that's the same thing: Pray spare me their	230	FOR LOVE	I.1	534
Tattle:	I can spare mine. (to Jeremy) Oh are you there, Sir?	313	FOR LOVE	V.1	590
Osmyn-Alph:	I could at this time spare your Mirth.	360	M. EBIDE	III.1	422
	No Portion for her own she has to spare,	393	WAY WCBLD	PRO.	9
	But if they're naught ne're spare him for his Pains:	393	WAY WCBLD	PRO.	23
Millamant:	I prithee spare me gentle Boy,	447	WAY WORLD	IV.1	98
Sir Wilful:	However that's as time shall try,--But spare to speak and	448	WAY WORLD	IV.1	137
Sir Wilful:	spare to speed, as they say.	448	WAY WORLD	IV.1	138
Millamant:	and spare not.	450	WAY WORLD	IV.1	233
Mrs Fain:	way to succeed. Therefore spare your Extacies for another	452	WAY WORLD	IV.1	303

Spared (3)
Belinda:	Nay, we have spared No-body, I swear. Mr. Sharper,	88	OLD BATCH	IV.3	195
Almeria:	But Heav'n spared me for yet more Affliction!	329	M. EBIDE	I.1	128
Gonsalez:	It not. Your Majesty sure, might have spared	365	M. BRIDE	IV.1	178

Spark (1)
| Ben: | What, do you mean that fair-Weather Spark that was | 264 | FOR LOVE | III.1 | 419 |

Sparkle (1)

Fondlewife:	--I say, that even Lust doth sparkle in his Eyes, . . .	76	OLD BATCH	IV.1	31

Sparkling (3)

Valentine:	A Lovely Girl, I'faith, black sparkling Eyes, soft pouting	223	FOR LOVE	I.1	278
Zara:	Sparkling Desire, and trembling to possess.	348	M. BRIDE	II.2	344
Fainall:	Cheeks, and sparkling from your Eyes.	413	WAY WORLD	II.1	141

Sparks (1)

	How say you, Sparks? How do you stand affected?	113	OLD BATCH	EPI.	23

Speak (114)

	(I don't know whether I shall speak to please you) . . .	35	OLD BATCH	PRO.	18
Sir Joseph:	Nay, now I must speak; it will split a Hair by the . . .	53	OLD BATCH	II.1	232
Capt Bluff:	Good Mr. Sharper speak to him; I dare not look . . .	54	OLD BATCH	II.1	238
Bellmour:	Talk to your self--You had better let me speak; for if my	59	OLD BATCH	II.2	177
Bellmour:	Faith, Madam, I dare not speak to her, but I'll . . .	60	OLD BATCH	II.2	210
Setter:	from my Dream of Glory? speak thou vile Disturber-- . .	65	OLD BATCH	III.1	166
Heartwell:	ha? Speak Syren--Cons why do I look on her! . . .	72	OLD BATCH	III.2	40
Heartwell:	Yet I must--Speak dear Angel, Devil, Saint, Witch; do .	72	OLD BATCH	III.2	41
Heartwell:	love me Silvia? speak.	72	OLD BATCH	III.2	52
Silvia:	I dare not speak till I believe you, and indeed I'm . .	72	OLD BATCH	III.2	53
Fondlewife:	Speak I say, have you consider'd, what it is to Cuckold .	77	OLD BATCH	IV.1	77
Sir Joseph:	Agad, it's a curious, fine, pretty Rogue; I'll speak .	89	OLD BATCH	IV.4	32
Fondlewife:	Come Syren, speak, confess, who is this reverend, brawny	92	OLD BATCH	IV.4	137
Fondlewife:	face to face before? Speak.	93	OLD BATCH	IV.4	156
Bellmour:	to speak the truth in justice to your Wife.--No. . .	93	OLD BATCH	IV.4	158
Laetitia:	won't you speak to me, cruel Nykin? Indeed, I'll die, if	95	OLD BATCH	IV.4	246
Fondlewife:	Ah! No, no, I cannot speak; my heart's so full--I . .	95	OLD BATCH	IV.4	248
Fondlewife:	and unclean, Heh? Speak.	95	OLD BATCH	IV.4	252
Bellmour:	Sharper! Fortifie thy Spleen: Such a Jest! Speak . .	100	OLD BATCH	V.1	135
Sir Joseph:	Nay, Don't speak so loud.--I don't jest, as I . . .	101	OLD BATCH	V.1	171
Sir Joseph:	Prithee, don't speak so loud.	101	OLD BATCH	V.1	179
Sir Joseph:	and to speak, is but loss of time; but if there be occasion,	103	OLD BATCH	V.1	244
Mellefont:	Well, I'll speak but three words, and follow you. . .	129	DOUBL DLR	I.1	60
Mellefont:	I am so amazed, I know not what to speak.	145	DOUBL DLR	II.1	263
Maskwell:	same words and Accents, when I speak what I do think; .	150	DOUBL DLR	II.1	461
Maskwell:	and when I speak what I do not think--the very same-- .	150	DOUBL DLR	II.1	462
Lady Touch:	I don't know; I am very unwilling to speak	151	DOUBL DLR	III.1	34
Maskwell:	have it--if I can speak to my Lord before--Was . . .	155	DOUBL DLR	III.1	188
Sir Paul:	speak with her below.	163	DOUBL DLR	III.1	499
Lady Froth:	offers to speak--And sits in expectation of his no Jest, with	165	DOUBL DLR	III.1	574
Careless:	so transported I cannot speak--This Note will inform .	171	DOUBL DLR	IV.1	129
Sir Paul:	speak a good word only just for me, Gads-bud only for .	180	DOUBL DLR	IV.1	472
Lord Touch:	Speak.	182	DOUBL DLR	IV.1	575
Maskwell:	do not speak, that she may not distinguish you from .	195	DOUBL DLR	V.1	294
Lady Touch:	Uncertainty. Speak then, and tell me--yet are you . .	198	DOUBL DLR	V.1	400
Scandal:	manner. For the Rogue will speak aloud in the posture of	226	FOR LOVE	I.1	370
Tattle:	That is, when you speak well of me.	226	FOR LOVE	I.1	383
Tattle:	when you know not the persons of whom you speak? . .	226	FOR LOVE	I.1	399
Angelica:	speak of it--	238	FOR LOVE	II.1	112
Foresight:	tell me--won't you speak? Odd I'll--	239	FOR LOVE	II.1	158
Foresight:	I know when Travellers lie or speak Truth, when . . .	241	FOR LOVE	II.1	224
Sr Sampson:	go up Holborn-hill,--Has he not a Rogues face?--Speak,	243	FOR LOVE	II.1	304
Mrs Frail:	and speak openly one to another; I'm afraid the World .	248	FOR LOVE	II.1	487
Tattle:	You must let me speak Miss, you must not speak first; .	251	FOR LOVE	II.1	598
Tattle:	speak what you think: Your words must contradict your .	251	FOR LOVE	II.1	612
Tattle:	speak you:--And like me, for the Beauty which I say .	252	FOR LOVE	II.1	618
Tattle:	Hum--Yes--But you must believe I speak	252	FOR LOVE	II.1	627
Scandal:	Angelica's Love for Valentine; you won't speak of it. .	254	FOR LOVE	III.1	46
Scandal:	Angelica's Love to Valentine; you won't speak of it. .	254	FOR LOVE	III.1 V	46
Tattle:	Ladyship is to speak first--	257	FOR LOVE	III.1	136
Miss Prue:	to speak with you at all.	263	FOR LOVE	III.1	379
Miss Prue:	As long as one must not speak one's mind, one had . .	263	FOR LOVE	III.1	382
Miss Prue:	better not speak at all, I think, and truly I won't tell a lie	263	FOR LOVE	III.1	383
Ben:	speak one thing, and to think just the contrary way; is as it	263	FOR LOVE	III.1	386
Miss Prue:	But I'm sure it is not so, for I'll speak sooner than .	264	FOR LOVE	III.1	395
Miss Prue:	you should believe that; and I'll speak truth, tho' one should	264	FOR LOVE	III.1	396
Ben:	you? You heard t'other handsome Young Woman speak .	264	FOR LOVE	III.1	410
Miss Prue:	that loves me, and I love him; and if he sees you speak to me	264	FOR LOVE	III.1	416
Scandal:	Yes Faith, I think so; I love to speak my mind. . . .	272	FOR LOVE	III.1	685
Mrs Fore:	Why then I'll speak my mind. Now as to	272	FOR LOVE	III.1	686
Ben:	Mess, I love to speak my mind--Father has nothing . .	272	FOR LOVE	III.1	713
Angelica:	If you speak Truth, your endeavouring at Wit is . . .	276	FOR LOVE	IV.1	38
Angelica:	am to hope for--I cannot speak--But you may tell me, .	277	FOR LOVE	IV.1	59
Sr Sampson:	has he trick't me? speak, Varlet.	279	FOR LOVE	IV.1	123
Sr Sampson:	d'ye banter me--Speak Sirrah, where is he, for I . .	279	FOR LOVE	IV.1	128
Sr Sampson:	Speak to be understood, and tell me in plain Terms what	279	FOR LOVE	IV.1	135
Sr Sampson:	I'll speak gently--Val, Val, do'st thou not	279	FOR LOVE	IV.1	156
Foresight:	You speak with singular good Judgment, Mr.	285	FOR LOVE	IV.1	347
Sr Sampson:	faith and troth you speak very discreetly; For I hate both a	299	FOR LOVE	V.1	68
Sr Sampson:	Who gave you Authority to speak, Sirrah? To . . .	308	FOR LOVE	V.1	417
Mrs Frail:	I can't speak it out.	309	FOR LOVE	V.1	446
Tattle:	speak for my self. Gad, I never had the least thought of	309	FOR LOVE	V.1	464
Tattle:	this Company wou'd speak of it.	310	FOR LOVE	V.1	477
	Since Custome gives the Losers leave to speak. . . .	323	M. BRIDE	PRO.	28
Garcia:	Dumbly declines all Offers: if he speak	335	M. BRIDE	I.1	371
Almeria:	Give me thy Hand, and speak to me, nay, speak, . . .	339	M. BRIDE	II.1	67
Almeria:	Nay, quickly speak to me, and let me hear	339	M. BRIDE	II.1 V	68
Almeria:	Mercy and Providence! O speak to it, ...	341	M. BRIDE	II.2	41
Almeria:	Mercy and Providence! O speak	341	M. BRIDE	II.2 V	41
Almeria:	Speak to it quickly, quickly, speak to me.	341	M. BRIDE	II.2	42
Almeria:	If I cou'd speak; how I have mourn'd and pray'd, . .	343	M. BRIDE	II.2	130
Almeria:	And speak--That thou art here, beyond all Hope, . .	343	M. BRIDE	II.2	151

Spendthrift   (continued)
  Sr Sampson: young Spendthrift forc'd to cling to an Old Woman for   . . 260   FOR LCVE   III.1 263
  Lady Wish: A slander-mouth'd Railer: I warrant the Spendthrift   .   428   WAY WCRLD III.1 132
Spent (4)
  Lady Froth: spent two days together in going about Ccvent-Garden to .   165   DOUBL DLR III.1 563
  Scandal: when a Gentleman has spent it?   224   FCR LCVE   I.1   316
  Osmyn-Alph: When scanty Numbers shall be spent in telling.   344   M. BRIDE   II.2   190
  Heli: The time's tco precious to be spent in telling;   351   M. BRIDE   III.1 42
Sphere (1)
  Valentine: Sphere: when he Rises I must set--Besides, if I shou'd stay, 259 FCR LOVE   III.1 224
Spheres (2)
  Foresight: Coelestial Spheres, know the Signs and the Planets, and
                  their 241   FOR LCVE   II.1   211
  Sr Sampson: troth you shall. Cdd we'll have the Musick of the Spheres   307   FOR LCVE   V.1   385
Spice (1)
  Sir Wilful: before I cross the Seas. I'd gladly have a spice of your .   440   WAY WCRLD III.1 583
Spider (1)
  Petulant: Carry your Mistresses Monkey a Spider,--go flea   454   WAY WCRLD IV.1   375
Spiders (1)
  Sr Sampson: Spiders; the one has its Nutriment in his own hands; and .   246   FOR LOVE   II.1   392
Spight (5)
  Mellefont: (after a pause). So then,--spight of my care and   .   . . 148   DOUBL DLR II.1   374
  Cynthia: a Ditch--Here then, I give you my promise, in spight of .   168   DOUBL DLR IV.1   35
  Valentine: pursue her, and know her if it be possible, in spight of the 297 FCR LCVE   IV.1   813
  Osmyn-Alph: And challenges in spight of me my best   355   M. FRIDE   III.1 224
  Waitwell: in spight of treachery; Ay and get an Heir that shall defeat 461 WAY WCRLD IV.1   643
Spilt (3)
  Sr Sampson: as if thou hadst spilt the Salt, or par'd thy Nails of a .   265   FOR LCVE   III.1 464
  Sr Sampson: as if thou hadst spilt the Salt, or par'd thy Nails on a .   265   FCR LCVE   III.1 V464
  Gonsalez: I who have spilt my Royal Master's Blood, ... 378   M. BRIDE   V.2   70
Spin-text (5)
  Laetitia: Spin-text, has a sad Fit of the Cholick, and is forced
                  to lie 91   OLD BATCH IV.4   78
  Laetitia: 'Tis no body but Mr. Fondlewife, Mr. Spin-text, lie . . . 91   OLD EATCH IV.4   85
  Bellmour: have a long time designed thee this favour) I knew Spin-text 94   OLD EATCH IV.4   207
  Laetitia: Mr. Spin-text was ill of the Chclick, upon our bed. And   95   OLD EATCH IV.4   245
  Bellmour: Mistress; and you mistook me for Tribulation Spin-text, to   97   OLD EATCH V.1   43
Spins (2)
  Sr Sampson: t'other spins his Habitation out of his Entrails.   .   . . 246   FOR LCVE   II.1   393
  Sr Sampson: t'other spins his Habitation out of his own Entrails,   . . 246   FOR LCVE   II.1   V393
Spintext (3)
  Bellmour: talks of sending for Mr. Spintext to keep me Company; but   39   OLD BATCH I.1   83
  Bellmour: I'le take care, he shall not be at home. Good! Spintext! Oh   39   OLD BATCH I.1   84
  Setter: which Tribulaticn Spintext wears as I'm inform'd, upon   .   64   OLD EATCH III.1 126
Spintext's (1)
  Laetitia: Mr. Spintext's Prayer-Book, Dear.--(aside) Pray   91   OLD EATCH IV.4   100
Spirit (12)
  Vainlove: Never doubt it; for if the Spirit of Cuckoldom be   . . .   40   OLD BATCH I.1   102
  Fondlewife: Good lack! I profess the Spirit of contradiction   . . .   75   OLD EATCH IV.1   16
  Brisk: Soul cf Conversation, the very Essence of Wit, and Spirit . 128   DOUBL DLR I.1   34
  Lady Ply: and uncontroulable? Is it fit a Wcman of my Spirit, and   .   144   DOUBL DLR II.1   217
  Maskwell: 'Tis that; you know my Lady has a high Spirit, ...   195   DOUEL DLR V.1   315
  Lady Froth: Snuff some of my Spirit of Hartshorn.   201   DOUBL DLR V.1   526
  Jeremy: Spirit of Famine appears to me; scmetimes like a decay'd .   218   FCR LCVE   I.1   95
  Osmyn-Alph: And thought, I heard thy Spirit call Alphonso.   344   M. EFIDE   II.2   163
  Osmyn-Alph: The Spirit which was deaf to my own Wrongs, ...   351   M. EBIDE   III.1 74
  Zara: Hover a Moment, yet, thou gentle Spirit, ...   381   M. EBIDE   V.2   200
  Mrs Fain: There spoke the Spirit of an Amazon, a   411   WAY WCRLD II.1   48
  Mirabell: with Ratifia and the most noble Spirit of Clary,--but   . . 451   WAY WCRLD IV.1   274
Spirits (8)
  Careless: your favour--I feel my Spirits faint, a general dampness .   170   DOUBL DLR IV.1   114
  Lady Touch: Spirits faint, and I want strength to hold it, thou hast .   198   DOUEL DLR V.1   403
  Angelica: Spirits and the Celestial Signs, the Bull, and the Ram, .   239   FOR LCVE   II.1   137
  Almeria: A sudden Chilness seizes on my Spirits.   334   M. EBIDE   I.1   349
  Almeria: Exerts my Spirits; and my present Fears   339   M. EBIDE   II.1   79
  Millamant: keep up my Spirits.   434   WAY WCRLD III.1 366
  Waitwell: Spouse, hast thou any Cordial--I want Spirits.   459   WAY WCBLD IV.1   557
  Lady Wish: have wasted my spirits so to day already; that I am ready   478   WAY WCRLD V.1   609
Spiritual (3)
  Setter: precise Band, with a swinging long Spiritual Cloak, to   .   64   OLD EATCH III.1 124
  Sharper: Gravity as a Bishop hears Venereal Causes in the Spiritual   100   OLD BATCH V.1   139
  Tattle: He wou'd have brought me into the Spiritual Court, but   .   258   FOR LCVE   III.1 171
Spit (1)
  Lucy: senseless indifference. By this Light I could have spit in   61   OLD EATCH III.1 19
Spite (7)
  Brisk: Pooh, ha, ha, ha, I know you envy me. Spite, proud   . . . 128   DOUBL DLR I.1   25
  Brisk: spite, by the Gods! and burning envy.--I'le be   128   DOUEL DLR I.1   26
  Valentine: and yet we'll Marry one another in spite of the Pope--   .   290   FOR LCVE   IV.1   559
  Leonora: Of his Success; that then, in spite of Hate, ... 327   M. BRIDE   I.1   42
  Zara: Yes, thou shalt know, spite of thy past Distress,   . . .   361   M. EBIDE   III.1 455
  Zara: In whcm I live. Spite of my Rage, and Eride, ... 361   M. BRIDE   IV.1   25
Spitfire (1)
  Foresight: Spitfire, but one Virgin.   239   FOR LCVE   II.1   142
Spits (2)
  Belinda: (Spits.)   85   OLD EATCH IV.3   89
  Sir Wilful: but he spits after a Bumper, and that's a Fault.   . . .   455   WAY WORLD IV.1   414
Spleen (7)
  Sharper: And you in return of Spleen hate them: But could   . . .   45   OLD BATCH I.1   306
  Bellmour: Sharper! Fortifie thy Spleen: Such a Jest! Speak   . . .   100   OLD BATCH V.1   135
  Sharper: (Now hold Spleen.) Married!   105   OLD BATCH V.1   314
  Jeremy: Sola's or Sonata's, they give me the Spleen.   245   FOR LCVE   II.1   375
  Sr Sampson: The Spleen, ha, ha, ha, a Pox ccnfound you--   245   FCR LCVE   II.1   376
  Mirabell: the Spleen or his Memory.   402   WAY WCRLD I.1   277
              There are some Criticks so with Spleen diseas'd,   . . .   479   WAY WCRLD EPI.   5
Splenatick (1)
  Brisk: be splenatick, or airy upon't; the Deuce take me if I cam   176   DOUBL DLR IV.1   338

Split (5)
    Capt Bluff: Controversie or split a Cause--   53   OLD BATCH   II.1   231
    Sir Joseph: Nay, ncw I must speak; it will split a Hair by the . . .   53   OLD BATCH   II.1   232
    Zara: Split Heart, burst ev'ry Vein, at this dire Object: . .   380   M. BRIDE   V.2   V163
                   So Criticks throng to see a New Play split, ...   385   M. BRIDE   EPI.   25
    Petulant: of Asses split, would make just four of you.   454   WAY WCRLD   IV.1   352
Spoil (12)
    Bellmour: --If ycu do, I'll spoil all.--I have scme private . . .   98   OLD BATCH   V.1   68
    Brisk: better, you or I. Pox, Man, when I say you spoil Company . 128   DOUEL DLR   I.1   28
    Brisk: better, you or I. Pshaw, Man, when I say you spoil Company 128   DOUEL DLR   I.1 V 28
    Lord Froth: I swear, my Dear, you'll spoil that Child, with   166   DOUEL DLR   III.1   609
    Sir Paul: her Example, that would spoil all indeed. Bless us, if you   174   DOUBL DLR   IV.1   250
    Valentine: Scandal, don't spoil my Boy's Milk.--Bid   222   FOR LCVE   I.1   222
    Scandal: spoil it.   222   FCR LOVE   I.1   234
    Angelica: Nay, Mr. Tattle, If you make Love to me, you spoil . . .   290   FOR LOVE   IV.1   568
    Mrs Frail: (to Jeremy). O Lord, her ccming will spoil all.   291   FOR LOVE   IV.1   590
    Valentine: may pore till you spoil your Eyes, and not improve your .   297   FOR LCVE   IV.1   803
    Leonora: And the rich Spoil of all the Field, and you   327   M. BRIDE   I.1   40
    Lady Wish: whole Court upon a Birth day. I'll spoil his Credit with his   428   WAY WCRLD   III.1   134
Spoil'd (4)
    Belinda: spoil'd--I shall loath the sight of Mankind for your . .   55   OLD BATCH   II.2   15
    Mrs Fore: spoil'd already--d'ee think shee'll ever endure a . . .   250   FOR LCVE   II.1   561
    Sr Sampson: had a Son that was spoil'd among 'em; a good hopeful .   299   FOR LOVE   V.1   81
    Lady Wish: O he's in less Danger of being spoil'd by his   431   WAY WCRLD   III.1   262
Spoiling (4)
    Brisk: trick; you're always spoiling Ccmpany by leaving it. . .   128   DOUEL DLR   I.1   22
    Careless: And thou art always spoiling Company by coming   128   DOUEL DLR   I.1   23
    Mrs Fore: love to have the spoiling of a Young Thing, they are as .   250   FOR LCVE   II.1   548
    Mirabell: Fashions, spoiling Reputations, railing at absent
                   Friends, and   451   WAY WORLD   IV.1   268
Spoils (3)
    Gonsalez: Loaden with Spoils, and ever-living Lawrel, ...   331   M. BRIDE   I.1   225
    Manuel: And raise Love's Altar on the Spoils of War.   337   M. BRIDE   I.1   451
                   And fatten on the Spoils of Providence: 385   M. BRIDE   EPI.   24
Spoke (8)
    Mellefont: hush'd into a Sigh. It was long before either of us spoke,   130   DOUEL DLR   I.1   107
                   If the soft things were Penn'd and spoke with grace; . .   204   DOUEL DLR   EPI.   23
    Ben: words however. I spoke you fair d'ee see, and civil.--As .   264   FOR LCVE   III.1   403
    Garcia: That, Sir, is he of whom I spoke, that's Osmyn.   336   M. BRIDE   I.1 V428
    Perez: I saw him when I spoke, thwarting my View, ...   338   M. BRIDE   II.1   19
    Painall: You were to blame to resent what she spoke only in . . .   396   WAY WCRLD   I.1   41
    Mrs Fain: There spoke the Spirit of an Amazon, a   411   WAY WCRLD   II.1   48
    Marwood: 'Twas spoke in scorn, and I never will forgive it. . .   414   WAY WCRLD   II.1   183
Spoken (4)   see Well-spoken
    Sir Paul: spoken Man, I desired him to intercede for me.-- . . .   180   DOUBL DLR   IV.1   480
    Scandal: spoken; but may be apply'd to him--As if we shou'd . . .   256   FCR LOVE   III.1   124
    Sr Sampson: Odsbud, well spoken; and you are a Wiser   260   FOR LCVE   III.1   249
    Angelica: or send, I am not to be spoken with.   297   FOR LCVE   V.1   10
Spoon-meat (1)
    Angelica: and Spoon-meat together--Indeed, Uncle, I'll indite you .   237   FCR LOVE   II.1   91
Spoons (1)
    Angelica: Spoons, and thought they were lost. Away went Religion .   237   FOR LOVE   II.1   90
Sport (10)
    Bellmour: in the Mine; well, we have each our share of sport, and each   43   OLD BATCH   I.1   223
    Vainlove: pleasure of a chase: My sport is always balkt or cut short   80   OLD BATCH   IV.1   176
    Bellmour: Rogue am I! Oh, what Sport will be here, if I can persuade   97   OLD BATCH   V.1   24
    Scandal: It may make sport.   288   FCR LCVE   IV.1   484
    Scandal: It may make us sport.   288   FOR LCVE   IV.1 V484
                   To shining Theatres to see our Sport, ...   315   FOR LCVE   EPI.   26
    Manuel: But late, I find, that War is but her Sport;   337   M. BRIDE   I.1   458
    Manuel: Now late, I find, that War is but her Sport;   337   M. BRIDE   I.1   458
    Zara: That Zara must be made the Sport of Slaves?   348   M. BRIDE   II.2   363
    Osmyn-Alph: And Chaff, the Spcrt of adverse Winds; till late . . .   351   M. BRIDE   III.1   60
Spot (1)
    Sharper: chance which drew me hither; ay here, just here, this spot   48   OLD BATCH   II.1   22
Spotless (1)
    Valentine: you is sunk. You are all white, a sheet of lovely spotless   292   FCR LOVE   IV.1   637
Spouse (9)
    Capt Bluff: What, Are you a Woman of Quality too, Spcuse?   111   OLD BATCH   V.2   139
    Lucy: I shall follow, while my Spouse is planting Laurels in the   111   OLD BATCH   V.2   145
    Capt Bluff: No more Wars, Spouse, no more Wars.--While   111   OLD BATCH   V.2   147
                   A Barbarous Device, to try if Spouse, ...   125   DOUEL DLR   PRO.   5
    Waitwell: Spouse.   424   WAY WORLD   II.1   537
    Millamant: Ay as Wife, Spouse, My dear, Joy, Jewel, Love, ...   450   WAY WORLD   IV.1   197
    Waitwell: Spouse, hast thou any Cordial?--I want Spirits.   459   WAY WORLD   IV.1   557
    Waitwell: O, she is the Antidote to desire. Spouse, thou will't .   459   WAY WORLD   IV.1   560
    Mincing: Mirabell is with her, he has set your Spouse at liberty Mrs.   464   WAY WCRLD   V.1   105
Spout (1)
    Zara: --Rain, rain ye Stars, spout frcm your burning Orbs . .   380   M. BRIDE   V.2   V168
Spouting (1)
    Almeria: But spouting Veins, and mangled Flesh! O, O.   382   M. BRIDE   V.2   272
Sprawling (1)
    Mellefont: hands and sprawling in his Sleep; and ever since she has .   158   DOUEL DLR   III.1   289
Spread (5)
    Gonsalez: The swarming Populace, spread every Wall, ...   332   M. BRIDE   I.1   238
    Manuel: And spread like Roses to the Morning Sun.   349   M. BRIDE   II.2   386
    Zara: Indeed? Then 'twas a Whisper spread by some   366   M. BRIDE   IV.1   189
                   O with what Joy they run, to spread the News   385   M. BRIDE   EPI.   11
    Mirabell: Here she comes i'faith full sail, with her Fan spread .   418   WAY WORLD   II.1   323
Spring (6)   see Off-spring
    Mellefont: to spring under her Feet. But to my Post.   183   DOUBL DLR   IV.2   5
    Tattle: the Drawers at Locket's, Pontack's, the Rummer, Spring .   257   FOR LOVE   III.1   157
    Ben: spring a Leak. You have hit it indeed, Mess you've nick'd   273   FOR LOVE   III.1   726
    Scandal: I believe it is a Spring Tide.   289   FOR LCVE   IV.1   530
    Jeremy: Spring of your Bounty--I thought I could not recommend .   302   FCR LOVE   V.1   176
    Mirabell: and like the faint Offer of a latter Spring, serves but to   418   WAY WORLD   II.1   319

Spring-Garden (1)
  Mrs Frail: had gone to Knights-bridge, or to Chelsey, or to
                Spring-Garden, ... 247 FOR LOVE   II.1 438
Springs (1)
  Almeria: --I do not weep! The Springs of Tears are dry'd;   . . . 382 M. BRIDE   V.2 240
Sprout (2)
  Fondlewife: Ay, I feel it here; I sprout, I bud, I blossom, I am   . .   92 OLD BATCH IV.4 126
  Capt Bluff: sprout at home. . . . . 111 OLD BATCH   V.2 149
Sprung (3)
  Zara: From his Chains; thence sprung his Insolence, ... 349 M. BRIDE   II.2 379
  Zara: He should be set at large; thence sprung his Insolence, . 349 M. BRIDE   II.2 V379
  Marwood: --But let the Mine be sprung first, and then I care not if 444 WAY WORLD III.1 706
Spumoso (1)
  Lady Froth: Spumoso; and my self, what d'e think I call my self?   . 141 DOUBL DLR II.1 127
Spur (1)
  Heartwell: But 'tis with Whip and Spur the Race is won. . . . . . 112 OLD BATCH   V.2 195
Spurn (3)
  Almeria: Tread on me, spurn me, am I the bosom Snake   . . . . 357 M. BRIDE III.1 298
  Manuel: Lest I forget us both, and spurn thee from me. . . . . 369 M. BRIDE   IV.1 317
  Almeria: Now curse me if you can, now spurn me off. . . . . . 369 M. BRIDE   IV.1 320
Sputt'ring (1)
  Witwoud: neither of 'em speak for rage; And so fell a sputt'ring at 453 WAY WORLD IV.1 333
Spy (2)
  Bellmour: of your absence, by my Spy, (for Faith, honest Isaac, I   .   94 OLD BATCH IV.4 206
  Manuel: And wert the Spy and Pander to their Meeting.   . . . 373 M. BRIDE   V.1   48
Spys (1)
           Set up for Spys on Plays and finding Fault. . . . . . 479 WAY WORLD EPI.   15
Squabling (1)
  Ben: Why, Father came and found me squabling with yon   . . 285 FOR LOVE   IV.1 363
Squander (1)
  Fainall: rich Widow's Wealth, and squander it on Love and you?   . 415 WAY WORLD II.1 207
Square (1)
  Mrs Frail: go to Covent-Garden Square in a Hackney-Coach, and take . 246 FOR LOVE   II.1 419
Squeek (1)
  Lady Wish: where the Leud Trebles squeek nothing but Bawdy, and   . 467 WAY WORLD   V.1 200
Squeezes (1)
           (Squeezes him by the hand, looks kindly on him, sighs, and 140 DOUBL DLR II.1   65
Squeezing (1)
  Mirabell: I denounce against all strait-Laceing, Squeezing for   . 451 WAY WORLD IV.1 260
Squire (3)   see Country-Squire, Esq
           The 'Squire that's butter'd still, is sure to be undone. . 393 WAY WORLD PRO.   15
  Messenger: Is one Squire Witwoud here? . . . . 400 WAY WORLD   I.1 181
  Mirabell: of the Squire his Brother, any thing related? . . . . 400 WAY WORLD   I.1 211
Squires (1)
  Mrs Frail: No, I'll be gone. Come, who Squires me to the   . . . 234 FOR LOVE   I.1 664
Squirrel (1)
  Bellmour: your self upon Heartwell, for affronting your Squirrel.   . 107 OLD BATCH   V.1 396
Sr (2)
  Bellmour: Yet is ador'd by that Biggot Sr. Joseph Wittoll, as the   .   46 OLD BATCH   I.1 356
  Millamant: or fond, nor kiss before folks, like my Lady Fadler and Sr. 450 WAY WORLD IV.1 201
St (6)
           (Scene changes to St. James's Park. . . . .   83 OLD BATCH IV.3
  Maskwell: us to Morrow Morning at St. Albans; there we will Sum   . 194 DOUBL DLR   V.1 243
  Sr Sampson: Figures of St. Dunstan's Clock, and Consummatum est shall . 266 FOR LOVE III.1 477
  Valentine: and you shall see me act St. Dunstan, and lead the Devil   . 282 FOR LOVE   IV.1 241
  Foresight: No; St. Martins in the Fields. . . . . 289 FOR LOVE   IV.1 518
           (St. James's Park. Enter Mrs. Fainall and Mrs. Marwood.) . 410 WAY WORLD II.1
'st (1)
  Gonsalez: What Noise! some body coming? 'st, Alonzo? . . . . 376 M. BRIDE   V.2   10
Stab (4)
  Lady Touch: but I will stab the Lie that's forming in your heart, and
            save . . . . 197 DOUBL DLR   V.1 381
  Zara: Thee on this false one, how I'll stab and tear . . . . 353 M. BRIDE III.1 166
  Leonora: Will stab the Sight, and make your Eyes rain Blood. . . 381 M. BRIDE   V.2 230
  Leonora: Ready to stab the Sight, and make your Eyes   . . . . 381 M. BRIDE   V.2 V230
Stable (2)
  Sir Wilful: step to the Stable, you may enquire further of my Horse, . 438 WAY WORLD III.1 500
  Lady Wish: Postilion, that they may not stink of the Stable, when Sir 444 WAY WORLD IV.1   8
Stables (1)
  Maskwell: Stables--it will be more convenient. . . . . 194 DOUBL DLR   V.1 256
Stabs (1)
           (Stabs him.) . . . . . . 380 M. BRIDE   V.2 176
Stag (2)
  Heartwell: punish'd with a Wife of Birth--be a Stag of the first Head   45 OLD BATCH   I.1 310
  Fainall: Out-Matrimony'd,--If I had kept my speed like a Stag,   . 442 WAY WORLD III.1 635
Stage (15)
           (Sir Joseph Wittoll and Capt. Bluffe, cross the Stage.)   .   46 OLD BATCH   I.1 340
  Heartwell: And the first Stage a Down-hill Green-sword yields.   . . 112 OLD BATCH   V.2 189
           (Enter Careless, Crossing the Stage, with his Hat, Gloves, 127 DOUBL DLR   I.1
           (Musicians crossing the Stage.) . . . 143 DOUBL DLR II.1 174
           (A great shriek from the corner of the Stage. Lady Touchwood 202 DOUBL DLR   V.1 556
           of the Stage, Mellefont like a Parson.) . . . . . . 202 DOUBL DLR   V.1 567
           So, the poor Husbands of the Stage, who found   . . . 213 FOR LOVE   PRO.   7
           So from your Bounty, we receive this Stage; . . . . 213 FOR LOVE   PRO.   14
  Scandal: of the Name, recall the Stage of Athens, and be allow'd   . 220 FOR LOVE   I.1 149
  Valentine: Character had been lately expos'd upon the Stage.--Nay, I   . 220 FOR LOVE   I.1 152
  Mrs Frail: in my mind too much for the Stage. . . . . 247 FOR LOVE   II.1 454
           For a clear Stage won't do, without your Favour. . . 316 FOR LOVE   EPI.   44
           Is fall'n on us, and almost starves the Stage.   . . . 323 M. BRIDE   PRO.   16
           and Guards, who are ranged in Order, round the Stage. . 332 M. BRIDE   I.1 267
  Lady Wish: Short View of the Stage, with Bunyan's Works to entertain . 426 WAY WORLD III.1   66
Staggers (1)
  Mellefont: Then thy Reason staggers, and thou'rt almost . . . . 127 DOUBL DLR   I.1   5
Staid (2)
  Tattle: Pox take her; if she had staid two Minutes longer, I   . 253 FOR LOVE III.1   17
  Mirabell: know you staid at Millamant's last Night, after I went.   . 407 WAY WORLD   I.1 450

Staid   (continued)
    Witwoud: We staid pretty late there last Night; and heard   . . . 408   WAY WORLD   I.1   480
    Mincing: O Mem, your Laship staid to peruse a Pecquet of   419   WAY WORLD   II.1 357
    Mincing: O Mem, your laship staid to peruse a Pacquet of   419   WAY WORLD   II.1 V357
    Witwoud: staid any longer I shou'd have burst,--I must have been let 453   WAY WORLD   IV.1 327
Stain (4)
    Osmyn-Alph: And stain thy Bosom with the Rust of these   355   M. BRIDE   III.1 243
    Garcia: Oppress her not, nor think to stain her Face   378   M. BRIDE   V.2   76
    Almeria: And stain the Colour of my last Adieu. 382   M. BRIDE   V.2   269
    Mirabell: Lest mutual falsehood stain the Bridal-Bed: 478   WAY WORLD   V.1   621
Stain'd (1)
    Manuel: But that the Beams of Light, are to be stain'd   367   M. BRIDE   IV.1 252
Stains (1)
    Osmyn-Alph: To break these Chains. Off, off, ye Stains of Royalty.   . 352   M. BRIDE   III.1 88
Stairs (12)
    see Back-stairs
    Fondlewife: upon you down stairs.   90   OLD BATCH   IV.4 44
    Laetitia: Indeed, my Dear, I was but just coming down stairs,   . . 95   OLD BATCH   IV.4 243
    Laetitia: Indeed, my Dear, I was but just come down stairs,   . . . 95   OLD BATCH   IV.4 V243
    Careless: whole nights together upon the Stairs, before her
                   Chamber-door;   157   DOUBL DLR   III.1 274
    Maskwell: back Stairs, and so we may slip down without being   . . . 194   DOUBL DLR   V.1   240
    Maskwell: --and a Pair of private Stairs leads down to the   . . . 194   DOUBL DLR   V.1   255
    Maskwell: --and a Pair of private Stairs leading down to the   . . . 194   DOUBL DLR   V.1   V255
    Maskwell: him in her stead, you may go privately by the back Stairs, 199   DOUBL DLR   V.1   446
    Foresight: down Stairs, and met a Weasel; bad Omens those: some   . 236   FOR LOVE   II.1 34
    Jeremy: and I came up Stairs into the World; for I was born   . . 245   FOR LOVE   II.1 381
    Foresight: By your Looks, you shou'd go up Stairs out of the   . . . 245   FOR LOVE   II.1 383
    Mrs Fain: I'll go with you up the back Stairs, lest I shou'd   . . . 430   WAY WORLD   III.1 221
Stake (2)
                   Now that's at stake--No fool, 'tis out o'fashion.   . . . 113   OLD BATCH   EPI. 12
    Fainall: wherewithal to stake.   443   WAY WORLD   III.1 689
Stakes (2)
    Cynthia: think you of drawing Stakes, and giving over in time?   . . 142   DOUBL DLR   II.1 158
                   Suffer'd at first some trifling Stakes to win: 393   WAY WORLD   PRO. 12
Stale (1)
    Bellmour: Amour as he cares for, and quits it when it grows stale, or 42   OLD BATCH   I.1   212
Stalk (1)
    Marwood: . . . and stalk for   431   WAY WORLD   III.1 V243
Stalking (1)
    Lucy: for your Brother's Chaplain. Don't you see that stalking   . 97   OLD BATCH   V.1   15
Stalking-Horse (1)
    Sir Paul: fit for nothing but to be a Stalking-Horse, to stand before 145   DOUBL DLR   II.1 266
Stalks (1)
    Vainlove: For she only stalks under him to take aim at her Husband.   38   OLD BATCH   I.1   V 62
Stallion (1)
    Scandal: Parson, be Chaplain to an Atheist, or Stallion to an   . . 220   FOR LOVE   I.1   145
Stalls (1)
    Heartwell: Houses and Coblers Stalls--Death, I can't think   63   OLD BATCH   III.1 84
Stamp (1)
    Sharper: stamp your image on the Gold.   43   OLD BATCH   I.1   221
Stand (39)
    Bellmour: Oh here he comes, stand close let 'em pass.   46   OLD BATCH   I.1   V339
    Lucy: Stand off--He's a precious Jewel.   67   OLD BATCH   III.1 227
    Sir Joseph: self--I'll give him the Lie if you'll stand to it.   . . . 69   OLD BATCH   III.1 307
    Laetitia: Ha! This fool may be of use. Stand off, rude Ruffian.   . . 90   OLD BATCH   IV.4 46
    Bellmour: Setter.) Pox take 'em, they stand just in my Way.   . . . 97   OLD BATCH   V.1   12
    Sharper: purpose. Setter, stand close; seem not to observe 'em; and, 101   OLD BATCH   V.1   164
                   How say you, Sparks? How do you stand affected?   113   OLD BATCH   EPI. 23
    Sir Paul: fit for nothing but to be a Stalking-Horse, to stand before 145   DOUBL DLR   II.1 266
    Mellefont: I'll stand between you and this Sally-Port.   184   DOUBL DLR   IV.2 43
    Cynthia: My Lord, let me entreat you to stand behind this Skreen,   . 197   DOUBL DLR   V.1   374
    Lady Touch: Stand off, let me go, ... 202   DOUBL DLR   V.1   560
                   Than they who stand their Trials at the Barr;   204   DOUBL DLR   EPI. 9
    Scandal: where the Religion is Folly? You may stand at Bay for a   . 219   FOR LOVE   I.1   140
    Sr Sampson: Sir? Here, to stand here, upon those two Leggs, and look   . 244   FOR LOVE   II.1 328
    Ben: don't much stand towards Matrimonie. I love to roam   . . 261   FOR LOVE   III.1 309
    Ben: stand a stern a that'n, we shall never grapple together,--   263   FOR LOVE   III.1 361
    Mrs Fore: come, stand aside a little, and tell me how you like the   . 288   FOR LOVE   IV.1 476
    Valentine: Twenty Chairmen, and make thee Pedestals to stand erect   . 289   FOR LOVE   IV.1 525
                   Prepar'd, by just Decrees to stand, or fall.   324   M. BRIDE   PRO. 44
    Manuel: You stand excused that I command it.   334   M. BRIDE   I.1   326
    Osmyn-Alph: To Earth, and nail me, where I stand, ye Powers;   . . . 341   M. BRIDE   II.2 47
    Osmyn-Alph: Rivit and nail me, where I stand, ye Powers, ... 341   M. BRIDE   II.2 V 47
    Osmyn-Alph: For which I stand engag'd to this All-excellence: . . . 343   M. BRIDE   II.2 139
    Zara: Be drawn, and I will stand before thee seeing, ... 353   M. BRIDE   III.1 152
    Osmyn-Alph: Away, stand off, where is she? let me fly, ... 383   M. BRIDE   V.2   275
    Servant-M: Sir, there's such Coupling at Pancras, that they stand   . 398   WAY WORLD   I.1   113
    Mirabell: stand excus'd, who has suffer'd herself to be won by his   . 417   WAY WORLD   II.1 274
    Mrs Fain: I ought to stand in some degree of Credit with   . . . 417   WAY WORLD   II.1 278
    Mirabell: Uncle, he might like Mosca in the Fox, stand upon Terms;   . 417   WAY WORLD   II.1 294
    Millamant: Yet again! Mincing, stand between me and his   419   WAY WORLD   II.1 341
    Mirabell: Stand off Sir, not a Penny--Go on and prosper, ... 424   WAY WORLD   II.1 538
    Marwood: him, till he takes his Stand to aim at a Fortune,   . . . 431   WAY WORLD   III.1 V244
    Sir Wilful: . . . I don't stand shill I, shall I, ... 440   WAY WORLD   III.1 580
    Marwood: Well, how do you stand affected towards   443   WAY WORLD   III.1 674
    Petulant: Stand off--I'll kiss no more Males,--I have   454   WAY WORLD   IV.1 355
    Sir Wilful: Fellows--If I had a Bumper I'd stand upon my   456   WAY WORLD   IV.1 425
    Mrs Fain: my own Innocence, and dare stand by a tryall.   466   WAY WORLD   V.1   178
    Mrs Fain: my own Innocence, and dare stand a tryall.   466   WAY WORLD   V.1   V178
    Sir Wilful: Look up Man, I'll stand by you, 'sbud an she do   . . . 471   WAY WORLD   V.1   360
Stander (1)
    Belinda: obvious to every Stander by.   55   OLD BATCH   II.2 35
Standing (3)
                   So, standing only on his good Behaviour, ... 35   OLD BATCH   PRO. 12
    Bellmour: let me tell you, my standing Argument is depress'd in   . . 59   OLD BATCH   II.2 183
    Trapland: pretty long standing--   222   FOR LOVE   I.1   237

Stands (8)
Lucy: Heartwell, who stands talking at the Corner--'tis he--   . 62   OLD BATCH III.1   47
Heartwell: There stands my North, and thither my Needle points   . 63   OLD BATCH III.1   75
Lady Touch: --Calm Villain! How unconcern'd he stands, Confessing   . 135   DOUBL DLR   I.1   323
Brisk: (Stands musing with his Arms a-cross.)   175   DOUBL DLR   IV.1   311
Leonora: The Memory of that brave Prince stands fair   328   M. BRIDE   I.1   104
Manuel: For, ling'ring there, in long suspence she stands,   . . 337   M. BRIDE   I.1   454
Zara: See, where he stands, folded and fix'd to Earth,   . . 345   M. BRIDE   II.2   232
Manuel: Life without Love is Load; and Time stands still: . . 349   M. BRIDE   II.2   389
Star (5)   see Dog-star
Lady Froth: nothing, but a Blue Ribbon and a Star, to make him Shine, . 139   DOUBL DLR   II.1   31
Sr Sampson: the twinckling of a Star; and seen a Conjurer, that cou'd 241   FOR LOVE   II.1   227
Scandal: Wise Men of the East ow'd their Instruction to a Star,   . 267   FOR LOVE   III.1   535
Sr Sampson: your Ephemeris--The brightest Star in the blew Firmament . 307   FOR LOVE   V.1   380
Osmyn-Alph: Not what they would, but must; a Star, or Toad: .   . . 345   M. BRIDE   II.2   223
Star-Gazer (1)
Sr Sampson: up old Star-Gazer. Now is he poring upon the Ground for . 265   FOR LOVE   III.1   466
Star-gazing (1)
Lady Froth: My dear, Mr. Brisk and I have been Star-gazing,   .   . . 201   DOUBL DLR   V.1   519
Starch'd (1)
Saygrace: with a clean starch'd Band and Cuffs.   195   DOUBL DLR   V.1   286
Stare (4)
Silvia: Nay don't stare at me so--You make me blush   72   OLD BATCH III.2   43
Belinda: And t'other did so stare and gape,--I fansied her like the   84   OLD BATCH IV.3   45
Lord Touch: you stare as you were all amazed,--I don't wonder at it,-- 202   DOUBL DLR   V.1   564
Zara: What have you seen? Ha! wherefore stare you thus,   . . 380   M. BRIDE   V.2   155
Staring (2)
Gonsalez: Their Hold, thro' clifted Stones; stretching, and staring, 332   M. BRIDE   I.1   240
Leonora: And staring on us with unfolded Leaves.   340   M. BRIDE   II.2   13
Stark (3)
Jeremy: my Master was run stark mad only for Love of her Mistress; 276   FOR LOVE   IV.1   15
Jeremy: his Skull's crack'd, poor Gentleman; he's stark mad, Sir. 279   FOR LOVE   IV.1   138
Foresight: Alas! he's Mad, Child, stark Wild. 305   FOR LOVE   V.1   303
Starling (1)
Sir Wilful: Oons this Fellow knows less than a Starling; I   .   . . 437   WAY WORLD III.1   473
Starry (1)
Almeria: And range the Starry Orbs, and Milky Ways, ... 340   M. BRIDE   II.2   26
Stars (18)   see Twin-Stars
Cynthia: it to be only chance, or destiny, or unlucky Stars, or any 169   DOUBL DLR   IV.1   60
Mellefont: O I could curse my Stars, Fate, and Chance; all   .   . . 187   DOUBL DLR   IV.2   141
Brisk: Cynthia of the Skies, and Queen of Stars.   201   DOUBL DLR   V.1   531
Foresight: I will have Patience, since it is the Will of the Stars . 238   FOR LOVE   II.1   127
Sr Sampson: If the Sun shine by Day, and the Stars by Night, why, we   240   FOR LOVE   II.1   199
Sr Sampson: Candle, and that's all the Stars are good for.   .   . . 240   FOR LOVE   II.1   201
Sr Sampson: Reverence the Sun, Moon and Stars with all my heart.   .   242   FOR LOVE   II.1   247
Scandal: the Stars, and were Observers of Omens--Solomon was   . 267   FOR LOVE   III.1   530
Scandal: I thank my Stars that have inclin'd me--But I fear   . . 268   FOR LOVE   III.1   543
Foresight: as to this marriage I have consulted the Stars; and all . 268   FOR LOVE   III.1   552
Sr Sampson: Stars, and Sun and Almanacks, and Trash, should be   . . 283   FOR LOVE   IV.1   288
Foresight: What, is he gone, and in contempt of Science! Ill Stars . 283   FOR LOVE   IV.1   295
Tattle: Eye of Perspicuity; from all Astrologers, and the Stars . 304   FOR LOVE   V.1   272
Tattle: that I am as knowing as the Stars, and as secret as the
               Night.   305   FOR LOVE   V.1   292
Sr Sampson: the Stars are Lyars; and if I had Breath enough, I'd curse 313   FOR LOVE   V.1 V584
Osmyn-Alph: But Destiny and inauspicious Stars   354   M. BRIDE   III.1   175
Zara: --Rain, rain ye Stars, spout from your burning Orbs   .   380   M. BRIDE   V.2 V168
               Of those few Fools, who with ill Stars are curs'd,   . . 393   WAY WORLD   PRO.   1
Start (14)
Maskwell: (Seems to start, seeing my Lord.)   .   .   .   189   DOUBL DLR   V.1   46
Lord Touch: Start not--let guilty and dishonest Souls   189   DOUBL DLR   V.1   47
Lord Touch: start at the revelation of their thoughts, but be thou
               fix'd, ... 189   DOUBL DLR   V.1   48
Mrs Frail: start of me; and I the poor forsaken Maid am left
               complaining   287   FOR LOVE   IV.1   456
               To start a Jest, or force a little Sense.   323   M. BRIDE   PRO.   20
Almeria: Thy Heart will burst, thy Eyes look red and start;   . . 356   M. BRIDE   III.1   273
Osmyn-Alph: Think how the Blood will start, and Tears will gush   .   358   M. BRIDE   III.1   347
Almeria: Why dost thou start? what dost thou see, or hear?   . . 370   M. BRIDE   IV.1   384
Manuel: Why dost thou start? Resolve to do't, or else--   .   .   374   M. BRIDE   V.1   75
Manuel: Why dost thou start? Resolve , or--   374   M. BRIDE   V.1 V 75
Manuel: Sudden I'll start, and dash her with her Guilt.   .   . . 374   M. BRIDE   V.1 V86P
Zara: Ha! prostrate! bloody! headless! O--start Eyes,   .   .   380   M. BRIDE   V.2   162
Lady Wish: and then as soon as he appears, start, ay, start and be
               surpriz'd, ... 445   WAY WORLD   IV.1   27
Started (5)
Almeria: Started amidst his Foes, and made Captivity his Refuge;   329   M. BRIDE   I.1   116
Almeria: Started amidst his Foes, and made Captivity   329   M. BRIDE   I.1 V116
Almeria: What's he, that like thy self, is started here   .   . . 344   M. BRIDE   II.2   167
Almeria: What's he, who like thy self, is started here   .   .   . 344   M. BRIDE   II.2 V167
Manuel: Entring he met my Eyes, and started back, ... 373   M. BRIDE   V.1   15
Starting (4)
Vainlove: Ay, am I not? To be continually starting of Hares   . .   39   OLD BATCH   I.1   75
Mellefont: then came the Storm I fear'd at first: For starting from my 130   DOUBL DLR   I.1   113
Mrs Fore: so--He has been subject to Talking and Starting.   .   .   270   FOR LOVE   III.1   620
Valentine: (starting). Ha! who's that?   279   FOR LOVE   IV.1   151
Startles (1)
Lady Ply: O, such a thing! the Impiety of it startles me   .   . . 146   DOUBL DLR   II.1   289
Starts (3)
                            (discovering him, starts)   81   OLD BATCH IV.2   16
Heli: I know his Melancholy, and such Starts   338   M. BRIDE   II.1   27
Almeria: (Coming nearer the Body, starts and lets fall the Cup.) . 382   M. BRIDE   V.2   271
Starv'd (1)
Lady Wish: Chafeing-dish of starv'd Embers and Dining behind a   . . 462   WAY WORLD   V.1   6
Starve (8)
Jeremy: Sir, it's impossible--I may die with you, starve with   . 218   FOR LOVE   I.1   72
Foible: Poyson him? Poysoning's too good for him. Starve   .   .   427   WAY WORLD III.1   106

Starve   (continued)

Foible:	him Madam, starve him, marry Sir Rowland and get him	.	427	WAY WORLD	III.1	107
Waitwell:	and Poison me,--and I wou'd willingly starve him	. .	458	WAY WORLD	IV.1	501
Lady Wish:	No, don't kill him at once Sir Rowland, starve	. . .	458	WAY WORLD	IV.1	519
Waitwell:	starve upward and upward, till he has nothing living but	.	458	WAY WORLD	IV.1	523
Lady Wish:	go, go, starve again, do, do.	. . . . .	462	WAY WORLD	V.1	8
Mrs Fain:	not name it, but starve together--perish.		475	WAY WORLD	V.1	501

Starves (1)

	Is fall'n on us, and almost starves the Stage. . . .	.	323	M. BRIDE	PRO.	16

Starving (2)

Jeremy:	musty Books, in commendation of Starving and Poverty? . .	217	FOR LOVE	I.1	33
Valentine:	Health, and Liberty at once, to a despairing, starving, and	290	FOR LOVE	IV.1	542

State (13)

Sharper:	state of his Body.	44	OLD BATCH	I.1	289
Belinda:	ha, ha, ha.--Well, a Lover in the state of separation from	86	OLD BATCH	IV.3	133
Heartwell:	O cursed State! How wide we err, when apprehensive of . .	108	OLD BATCH	V.2	9
Valentine:	Secretaries of State, Presidents of	221	FOR LOVE	I.1	188
Sr Sampson:	risen in the State--But, a pox on't, his Wit run him . .	299	FOR LOVE	V.1	83
Zara:	Beneath Mock-Praises, and dissembled State.	336	M. BRIDE	I.1	402
Zara:	Compassion led me to bemoan his State, ...	349	M. BRIDE	II.2	376
	(A Room of State. Enter Zara, and Selim.)	361	M. BRIDE	IV.1	
Selim:	Both in the State and Army. This confirms	361	M. BRIDE	IV.1	11
Selim:	The State of things will countenance all Suspicions. . .	362	M. BRIDE	IV.1	55
Zara:	Against your State: and fully to discharge	364	M. BRIDE	IV.1	140
	(A Room of State. Enter King, Perez, and Alonzo.) . .	372	M. BRIDE	V.1	
Fainall:	in the state of Nature.	397	WAY WORLD	I.1	67

State-Cook (1)

Valentine:	together by a State-Cook, make Sauce for the whole . . .	282	FOR LOVE	IV.1	258

Statesman (2)

Mellefont:	a Statesman or a Jesuite, but that thou'rt too honest for	193	DOUBL DLR	V.1	236
Mellefont:	a Statesman or a Jesuite, but thou art too honest for . .	193	DOUBL DLR	V.1	V236

Station (1)

	Grant Heaven, we don't return to our first Station. . .	315	FOR LOVE	EPI.	34

Statu (0)   see In statu quo

Statue (1)

Zara:	Stiff'ning in Thought; a Statue amongst Statues. . . .	345	M. BRIDE	II.2	233

Statues (1)

Marwood:	Quiblers by the Statute; and become a Jest, against a Rule	467	WAY WORLD	V.1	215

Stay (65)

	I cannot stay to hear your Resolution.	35	OLD BATCH	PRO.	27
Heartwell:	in no haste for an Answer--for I shan't stay now. . . .	46	OLD BATCH	I.1	332
Sir Joseph:	and frightn'd 'em away--but agad I durst not stay to give	47	OLD BATCH	II.1	9
Sir Joseph:	Poor Gentleman--by the Lord Harry I'le stay no	48	OLD BATCH	II.1	25
Sir Joseph:	Stay, stay Sir, let me recollect--(aside) he's a . .	48	OLD BATCH	II.1	43
Araminta:	entertaining--(aside) I know she'd fain be persuaded to				
	stay.	57	OLD BATCH	II.2	87
Belinda:	a high Roof, or a very low Seat--Stay, Come back here . .	57	OLD BATCH	II.2	96
Belinda:	Not I; witness my Heart I stay out of pure Affection. . .	57	OLD BATCH	II.2	111
Capt Bluff:	go--and bring it me hither. I'le stay here for you. . .	67	OLD BATCH	III.1	251
Sir Joseph:	You may stay till the day of Judgment then, by the . . .	67	OLD BATCH	III.1	252
Heartwell:	is a Jewel--Stay Silvia--But then to Marry--	74	OLD BATCH	III.2	116
Fondlewife:	Ha, how's that? Stay stay, you please leave word . .	76	OLD BATCH	IV.1	19
Fondlewife:	And so thou shalt say, for I'le leave it to stay with thee.	78	OLD BATCH	IV.1	130
Capt Bluff:	My Blood rises at that Fellow: I can't stay where he is;	86	OLD BATCH	IV.3	120
Sir Joseph:	I wish I durst stay to let her know my	86	OLD BATCH	IV.3	123
Fondlewife:	Heh. How? No, stay, stay, I will believe thee, I . . .	96	OLD BATCH	IV.4	259
Cynthia:	Pray, Sir, stay, hear him, I dare affirm he's innocent. .	146	DOUBL DLR	II.1	274
Lady Ply:	not stay. Well, you must consider of your Crime; and . .	148	DOUBL DLR	II.1	363
Maskwell:	I would not have you stay to hear it now; for I	149	DOUBL DLR	II.1	432
Lord Touch:	Well I go--you won't stay, for I	154	DOUBL DLR	III.1	123
Lady Froth:	to you for the hint, stay we'll read over those half a score	164	DOUBL DLR	III.1	511
Lady Froth:	see little Saph. I knew you cou'd not stay.	167	DOUBL DLR	III.1	622
Lady Ply:	--I am not safe if I stay, and must leave you.	170	DOUBL DLR	IV.1	98
Sir Paul:	Hold, stay, I beseech your Ladiship--I'm so	179	DOUBL DLR	IV.1	465
Sir Paul:	overjoy'd, stay I'll confess all.	179	DOUBL DLR	IV.1	466
Lady Touch:	akes so, I shall faint if I stay.	187	DOUBL DLR	IV.2	139
Lady Touch:	to stay his stomach in the road to her;	191	DOUBL DLR	V.1	V147
Maskwell:	Stay, I have a doubt--upon second thoughts, ...	194	DOUBL DLR	V.1	251
Maskwell:	by describing to me the shortness of your stay; rather if	194	DOUBL DLR	V.1	277
Trapland:	Mr. Snap stay within Call.	224	FOR LOVE	I.1	306
Valentine:	No, prithee stay: Tattle and you should never be . . .	225	FOR LOVE	I.1	363
Foresight:	of the Head is Horns--Dear Neice, stay at home-- . . .	236	FOR LOVE	II.1	58
Angelica:	Won't you stay and see your Brother?	259	FOR LOVE	III.1	222
Valentine:	Sphere: when he Rises I must set--Besides, if I shou'd stay,	259	FOR LOVE	III.1	224
Miss Prue:	stay with me?	262	FOR LOVE	III.1	353
Sr Sampson:	Rogue's sharp set, coming from Sea, if he should not stay	265	FOR LOVE	III.1	459
Angelica:	my want of Inclination to stay longer here--Come, Jenny.	278	FOR LOVE	IV.1	90
Buckram:	mischief if I stay--The Conveyance is ready, Sir. If . .	280	FOR LOVE	IV.1	185
Mrs Frail:	Sister, do you stay with me; I'll find out my	285	FOR LOVE	IV.1	351
Angelica:	No, I'll stay with him--Mr. Scandal will protect me. . .	293	FOR LOVE	IV.1	676
Angelica:	Mr. Scandal, I only stay till my Maid comes, and . . .	293	FOR LOVE	IV.1	685
Tattle:	you can't solve this; stay here a Quarter of an Hour, and	305	FOR LOVE	V.1	297
Angelica:	but few have the Constancy to stay till it becomes your .	314	FOR LOVE	V.1	630
Manuel:	Rise, Garcia--I forgot. Yet stay, Almeria.	334	M. BRIDE	I.1	329
Manuel:	With speed--yet stay--my Hands alone can	336	M. BRIDE	I.1	411
Almeria:	Stay a while--	342	M. BRIDE	II.2	V 99
Zara:	Thou hast already rack'd me with thy stay;	361	M. BRIDE	IV.1	1
Manuel:	Stay, Soldier; they shall suffer with the Moor. . . .	363	M. BRIDE	IV.1	73
Almeria:	O stay, yet stay, hear me, I am not mad.	370	M. BRIDE	IV.1	368
Gonsalez:	Yet stay, I would--but go; anon will serve--	371	M. BRIDE	IV.1	425
Manuel:	--Stay thee--I've farther thought--I'll add to . . .	374	M. BRIDE	V.1	80
Foible:	is so impatient, I fear she'll come for me, if I stay. .	430	WAY WORLD	III.1	220
Millamant:	--If you cou'd but stay for me, I shou'd overtake you .	434	WAY WORLD	III.1	360
Mincing:	The Gentlemen stay but to Comb, Madam; and	434	WAY WORLD	III.1	368
Sir Wilful:	Impatient? Why then belike it won't stay, 'till . . .	441	WAY WORLD	III.1	616
Lady Wish:	shall stay for you--My Nephew's a little unbred, . . .	441	WAY WORLD	III.1	622

661

Still'd (1)
  Lady Touch: a Larum, only to rouse my own still'd Soul for your . . 137 DOUEL DLR I.1 381

Stilness (1)
  Zara: Yet, more, this Stilness terrifies my Soul, ... 379 M. ERIDE V.2 142

Sting (2)
    To think oth' Sting, that's in the tail of Pleasure. . . 113 OLD BATCH EPI. 9
  Gonsalez: 'Twere done--I'll crawl and sting him to the Heart; . . 376 M. ERIDE V.2 12

Stink (8)
  Belinda: You stink of Brandy and Tobacco, most Soldier-like. Foh. . 85 OLD BATCH IV.3 88
  Scandal: any body that did not stink to all the Town. . . . . . 226 FOR LCVE I.1 402
  Sr Sampson: above a stink.--Why there's it; and Musick, don't you . . 245 FCR LCVE II.1 371
  Ben: stink; he shall smell more like a Weasel than a Civet-Cat, . 265 FCR LCVE III.1 437
  Valentine: his Nose always, will very often be led into a Stink. . . 282 FOR LCVE IV.1 254
  Lady Wish: Postilion, that they may not stink of the Stable, when Sir . 444 WAY WCRLD IV.1 8
  Lady Wish: --Fogh! how you stink of Wine! Dee think my Neice . . . 455 WAY WCRLD IV.1 388
  Waitwell: his head, and then go out in a stink like a Candle's end . 458 WAY WCRLD IV.1 524

Stinkard (1)
  Sir Wilful: your Mussulman is a dry Stinkard--No Offence, Aunt. My . 456 WAY WORLD IV.1 444

Stinking (1)
  Miss Prue: talk at this rate--No you durst not, you stinking . . . 264 FOR LCVE III.1 430

Stir (7)
  Laetitia: Sir, I seldom stir abroad. . . . . 90 OLD BATCH IV.4 34
  Valentine: shape, and a Jut with her Bum, would stir an Anchoret: . 223 FOR LCVE I.1 285
  Mrs Frail: --she looks so wholscme;--ne're stir, I don't . . . . 250 FOR LCVE II.1 557
  Osmyn-Alph: Let me not stir, nor breath, lest I disolve . . . . . 341 M. ERIDE II.2 50
  Manuel: Ha! stir not, on thy Life: For thou wert fix'd, ... 373 M. ERIDE V.1 42
  Mirabell: For which Reason I resolv'd not to stir. At last the . . 396 WAY WCRLD I.1 34
  Lady Wish: thee. Why dost thou not stir Puppet? thou wooden Thing . 425 WAY WCRLD III.1 15

Stirring (1)
  Jeremy: Sir, Mrs. Frail has sent to know if you are stirring. . . 229 FCR LOVE I.1 505

Stirs (2)
  Leonora: Alas, she stirs not yet, nor lifts her Eyes; . . . . 341 M. ERIDE II.2 59
  Lady Wish: Wench stirs! Why dost thou not fetch me a little Red? . . 425 WAY WCRLD III.1 7

Stitch'd (1)
  Maskwell: stitch'd the Gown Sleeve, that he may be puzzled, and waste 195 DOUBL DLR V.1 288

Stock (4) see Laughing-stock
  Brisk: forced to examine their Stock, and forecast the Charges of 175 DOUBL DLR IV.1 302
  Mrs Frail: a loss, and have no great Stock either of Fortune or
    Reputation; . . . . 248 FCR LCVE II.1 490
  Mrs Frail: presume to have a sufficient stock of Euty to undergo a . 286 FCR LCVE IV.1 410
  Angelica: reasonable Stock cf good Nature and Sense--For I . . . 299 FOR LCVE V.1 63

Stock'd (1)
  Mirabell: stock'd, if we succeed. . . . . 424 WAY WCRLD II.1 540

Stocking (3)
  Nurse: Stocking with the wrong side outward. . . . . . 235 FCR LCVE II.1 28
  Foresight: time,--But in troth I am pleas'd at my Stocking. Very . 236 FCR LCVE II.1 37
  Foresight: well pleas'd at my Stocking--Oh here's my Neice!-- . . 236 FCR LCVE II.1 38

Stocks (2)
    And hope new Fruit from ancient Stocks remov'd. . . . 213 FOR LCVE PRO. 10
  Ben: Stocks; and they two are a going to be married to rights. . 307 FOR LCVE V.1 359

Stoick (1)
  Fainall: wou'd tempt the patience of a Stoick. What, some Coxcomb . 395 WAY WCRLD I.1 19

Stole (2)
  Mrs Frail: and so stole out to see you. Well, and what will . . . 231 FCR LCVE I.1 583
  Foible: thought something was contriving, when he stcle by me . . 461 WAY WCRLD IV.1 613

Stolen (1)
  Scandal: often he that has stolen the Treasure. I am a Jugler,
    that act . . . . 272 FOR LCVE III.1 699

Stoll'n (5)
  Bellmour: you; tho' I by treachery had stoll'n the Bliss-- . . . 38 OLD BATCH I.1 51
    So till the Thief has stoll'n, he cannot know . . . . 204 DOUEL DLR EPI. 6
  Foresight: Undertakings successful; or Goods stoll'n recover'd, I . . 241 FOR LCVE II.1 217
  Leonora: Have stoll'n frcm Bed, and to his Priscn crept: . . . 326 M. ERIDE I.1 25
  Fainall: permitted Mirabell with Millamant to have stcll'n their . 415 WAY WCRLD II.1 202

Stomach (14)
  Lucy: 'twould disgust his nicety, and take away his Stcmach. . 62 OLD BATCH III.1 42
  Laetitia: still on your Stomach; lying on your Stomach, will ease . 91 OLD BATCH IV.4 86
  Fondlewife: Let her clap a warm thing to his Stomach, or chafe it with 91 OLD BATCH IV.4 97
  Fondlewife: Let her clap some warm thing to his Stcmach, or chafe it
    with . . . . 91 OLD BATCH IV.4 V 97
  Fondlewife: Stomach; lying upon your Stomach will cure you of the . . 93 OLD BATCH IV.4 164
  Fondlewife: . . . I wish he has lain upon no bodies stomach but his own. 93 OLD EATCH IV.4 V165
  Maskwell: little stomach to her now as if I were her Husband. Should 155 DOUBL DLR III.1 179
  Lady Touch: to stay his stomach in the road to her; . . . . . 191 DOUEL DLR V.1 V147
  Jeremy: sit at the Door, that I don't get double the Stomach that . 218 FOR LCVE I.1 92
  Scandal: I'll rip up his Stcmach, and go the shortest way to his . 224 FOR LOVE I.1 311
  Sr Sampson: but a Groat in his Pocket, may have a Stomach capable . 245 FCR LCVE II.1 353
  Valentine: Man shcu'd have a Stomach to a Wedding Supper, when . 289 FOR LCVE V.1 527

Stomacher (1)
  Careless: piece of an old Scarlet Petticoat for a Stomacher; which, 157 DOUBL DLR III.1 276

Stomack (1)
  Petulant: he (hiccup) rises upon my stomack like a Radish. . . . 454 WAY WORLD IV.1 357

Stomacks (1)
  Heartwell: edge of your puny Stomacks. Your love is like your . . . 43 OLD EATCH I.1 245

Stond (1)
  Foresight: That House doth stond upon its Head; . . . . . . 236 FOR LOVE II.1 54

Stone (3)
  Setter: first Stone? who undervalued my Function? and who the . . 66 OLD BATCH III.1 205
  Almeria: That thus can gaze, and yet not turn tc Stone? . . . . 382 M. BRIDE V.2 239
  Lady Wish: I fear I shall turn to Stone, petrifie Incessantly. . . . 470 WAY WCRLD V.1 337

Stones (1)
  Gonsalez: Their Hold, thro' clifted Stones; stretching, and staring, 332 M. ERIDE I.1 240

Stood (4)
  Setter: I saw him, Sir; and stood at the Corner where you . . . 98 OLD BATCH V.1 83
  Setter: stood towards Madam Araminta. As, When you had seen . . 99 OLD EATCH V.1 114
  Maskwell: help--tho' I stood ready for a Cue to come in and . . . 154 DOUEL DLR III.1 129

Stood (continued)
    Sr Sampson: your Feet; And I wish, Madam, they stood in a better   .   . 300   FOR LOVE   V.1   95
Stoop (3)
    Vainlove: have a Lure may make you stoop. (Flings a Letter.)   .   . 38   OLD BATCH   I.1   31
    Osmyn-Alph: Would soar, and stoop at Victory beneath.   352   M. BRIDE   III.1   91
                   That Satire scorns to stoop so meanly low, ... 479   WAY WORLD   EPI.   29
Stooping (1)
    Almeria: Stooping to raise from Earth the filial Reverence;   .   . 369   M. BRIDE   IV.1   324
Stop (8)
    Lucy: Reputation; And can you blame her if she stop it up with a 98   OLD BATCH   V.1   49
    Scandal: Service of your Sex. He that first cries out stop Thief, is 272   FOR LOVE   III.1   698
    Ben: And stop up ev'ry leak.   274   FOR LOVE   III.1   778
    Jeremy: I hear a Coach stop; if it should be she, Sir, I believe he 276   FOR LOVE   IV.1   16
    Zara: Shall I prevent, or stop th' approaching Danger?   .   .   . 362   M. BRIDE   IV.1   43
    Gonsalez: I think thou would'st not stop to do me Service.   .   .   . 371   M. BRIDE   IV.1   427
    Manuel: Ha! stop and seize that Mute; Alonzo, follow him.   .   .   . 373   M. BRIDE   V.1 V 13
    Lady Wish: Is there no means, no Remedy, to stop my   473   WAY WORLD   V.1   445
Stop't (2)
    Witwoud: Noli prosequi and stop't their proceedings.   453   WAY WORLD   IV.1   330
    Witwoud: Noli prosequi and stop't the Proceedings.   453   WAY WORLD   IV.1 V330
Store (1)
    Heli: Was never heard in vain: Heav'n has in Store   352   M. BRIDE   III.1   118
Stories (2)
    Tattle: it their Business to tell Stories, and say this and that of 227   FOR LOVE   I.1   431
                   Once of Philosophers they told us Stories, ... 315   FOR LOVE   EPI.   11
Storm (7)
    Mellefont: then came the Storm I fear'd at first: For starting from my 130   DOUBL DLR   I.1   113
    Mellefont: the Storm, and her Ministers have done their Work; you   . 148   DOUBL DLR   II.1   383
    Ben: Storm.   265   FOR LOVE   III.1   453
    Ben: break her Cable in a storm, as well as I love her.
                     Flesh, you   273   FOR LOVE   III.1   731
                   For still in every Storm, they all run hither,   .   .   . 315   FOR LOVE   EPI.   3
    Almeria: And almost taken; when a sudden Storm, ... 329   M. BRIDE   I.1   124
    Foible: By Storm, Madam. Sir Rowland's a brisk Man.   429   WAY WORLD III.1   175
Storms (1)
                   Look out when Storms arise, and Billows roar,   .   .   . 385   M. BRIDE   EPI.   20
Story (9)
    Fondlewife: Nay, I find you are both in a Story; that, I must   .   . 93   OLD BATCH   IV.4   161
    Sir Joseph: and his primitive Braying. Don't you remember the Story   . 101   OLD BATCH   V.1   174
    Sir Paul: Moors, have this way (as Story tells) to know   .   .   . 125   DOUBL DLR   PRO.   1
    Sir Paul: my Lady Froth says; was ever the like read of in Story?   . 143   DOUBL DLR   II.1   196
    Careless: Alas-a-day, this is a lamentable story; my Lady must   .   . 162   DOUBL DLR III.1   441
    Mrs Frail: O Devil! Well, but that Story is not true.   233   FOR LOVE   I.1   641
    Tattle: Gad so, the Heat of my Story carry'd me beyond my   .   . 258   FOR LOVE   III.1   185
    Leonora: I never did presume to ask the Story.   328   M. BRIDE   I.1   108
    Mrs Fain: one scandalous Story, to avoid giving an occasion to make 412   WAY WORLD   II.1   105
Straight (1)   see Strait, Streight
    Valentine: and can set him right--Hearkee, Friend, the straight   .   . 282   FOR LOVE   IV.1   252
Strain (3)   see Strein
    Zara: And can unwind, or strain him as I please.   348   M. BRIDE   II.2   326
    Osmyn-Alph: That strain my cracking Nerves; Engines and Wheels   .   . 356   M. BRIDE   III.1   292
    Osmyn-Alph: Think how my Heart will heave, and Eyes will strain   . 358   M. BRIDE   III.1   345
Strain'd (2)
    Almeria: O my strain'd Heart--let me behold thee, ... 342   M. BRIDE   II.2   112
    Almeria: O my strain'd Heart--let me again behold thee,   .   .   . 342   M. BRIDE   II.2 V112
Straining (1)
    Osmyn-Alph: Should come and see the straining of my Eyes   .   .   . 345   M. BRIDE   II.2   203
Strait (2)
    Selim: It needs not, for the King will strait be here,   .   .   . 361   M. BRIDE   IV.1   20
    Manuel: Give Order strait, that all the Pris'ners die,   .   .   . 364   M. BRIDE   IV.1   127
Strait-Laceing (1)
    Mirabell: I denounce against all strait-Laceing, Squeezing for   .   . 451   WAY WORLD   IV.1   260
Strammel (1)
    Marwood: can no more conceal it, than my Lady Strammel can her   .   . 433   WAY WORLD III.1   320
Strange (23)
                   You think that strange--no matter, he'll out grow it.   .   . 35   OLD BATCH   PRO.   16
    Capt Bluff: Gazette--I'll tell you a strange thing now as to that--   . 52   OLD BATCH   II.1   194
    Sharper: Strange!   53   OLD BATCH   II.1   206
    Fondlewife: O Lord! O strange! I am in admiration of your   .   .   . 93   OLD BATCH   IV.4   153
    Sir Paul: good, strange! I swear I'm almost Tipsy--t'other   .   . 131   DOUBL DLR   I.1   178
    Sir Paul: good, strange! I swear I'm almost Tipsie--t'other   .   . 131   DOUBL DLR   I.1 V178
    Sir Paul: my Lady is so nice--it's very strange, but it's true: too 161   DOUBL DLR III.1   431
    Lord Froth: 'Tis a strange thing, but a true one;   166   DOUBL DLR III.1   597
    Sir Paul: Good strange! Mr. Brisk is such a Merry Facetious   .   . 174   DOUBL DLR   IV.1   274
    Brisk: Not I, let me perish--But did I! Strange! I confess   .   . 176   DOUBL DLR   IV.1   325
    Sir Paul: O strange, what will become of me!--I'm so   179   DOUBL DLR   IV.1   459
    Nurse: Dinner--good lack-a-day, ha, ha, ha, O strange; I'll vow   . 235   FOR LOVE   II.1   22
    Jeremy: No strange matter, Madam; my Master's mad, that's   .   . 276   FOR LOVE   IV.1   29
    Valentine: strange! But I am Truth, and come to give the World   .   . 280   FOR LOVE   IV.1   164
    Valentine: nick'd it--But its wonderful strange, Jeremy!   .   .   . 282   FOR LOVE   IV.1   269
    Valentine: see very strange; which are Wanton Wives, with their   .   . 289   FOR LOVE   IV.1   511
    Valentine: Scandal! What, do you look strange upon me?--Then   .   . 292   FOR LOVE   IV.1   618
    Valentine: strange thing: I found out what a Woman was good for.   .   . 292   FOR LOVE   IV.1   641
    Gonsalez: What if she had seen Osmyn? tho' 'twere strange.   .   . 366   M. BRIDE   IV.1   222
    Zara: The Mute not yet return'd! 'tis strange. Ha! 'twas   .   . 374   M. BRIDE   V.1   91
    Mrs Fain: Nay, nay, put not on that strange Face. I am   430   WAY WORLD III.1   188
    Millamant: Play together, But let us be very strange and well bred: . 450   WAY WORLD   IV.1   207
    Millamant: let us be as strange as if we had been married a great
                   while;   450   WAY WORLD   IV.1   208
Strangely (3)
    Lord Froth: Ridiculous! Sir Paul you're strangely mistaken, I   .   . 132   DOUBL DLR   I.1   190
    Tattle: I am strangely surpriz'd! Yes, yes, I can't deny't, if   .   . 229   FOR LOVE   I.1   481
    Tattle: strangely--pretty Miss, don't let 'em perswade you   .   . 249   FOR LOVE   II.1   536
Stranger (4)
    Capt Bluff: that knows me must be a stranger to fear.   51   OLD BATCH   II.1   143
    Angelica: Weakness I am a Stranger to. But I have too much Sincerity 277   FOR LOVE   IV.1   70

Strikes (5)
  Lady Touch: Married to Morrow! Despair strikes me. Yet my Soul . . . 137 DOUBL DLR I.1 399
  Sr Sampson: and when the Alarm strikes, they shall keep time like the 266 FOR LOVE III.1 476
  Almeria: Looking Tranquility. It strikes an Awe . . . 339 M. BRIDE II.1 63
  Zara: And strikes his Rays thro' dusk, and folded Lids, . . . 354 M. BRIDE III.1 208
      (Strikes him.) . . . . 374 M. BRIDE V.1 70
Strings (1)
  Osmyn-Alph: O I could tear and burst the Strings of Life, ... 352 M. BRIDE III.1 87
Strip (2)   see Out-strip
  Sr Sampson: With all my heart: Come, Uncase, Strip, and . . . . 244 FOR LOVE II.1 337
  Almeria: Yes, I will strip off Life, and we will change: . . . 370 M. BRIDE IV.1 351
Strip'd (1)   see Out-strip'd
  Selim: I found the dead and bloody Body strip'd-- . . . . 380 M. BRIDE V.2 182
Stripling (1)
  Sir Wilful: Cozen, nor Stripling: I thank Heav'n, I'm no Minor. . . 447 WAY WORLD IV.1 108
Stripp'd (1)   see Out-stripp'd
  Lord Touch: Villain! 'Death I'll have him stripp'd and turn'd naked out 153 DOUBL DLR III.1 100
Stripping (1)
  Osmyn-Alph: Stripping my Nails, to tear this Pavement up . . . 358 M. BRIDE III.1 354
Strive (6)
  Lady Ply: strive as much as can be against it,--strive be sure--but 148 DOUBL DLR I.1 364
  Cynthia: both so willing; we each of us strive to reach the Gole, . . 168 DOUBL DLR IV.1 12
  Cynthia: both willing; we each of us strive to reach the Gole, . 168 DOUBL DLR IV.1 V 12
  Ben: tho'f he should strive against Wind and Tyde. . 272 FOR LOVE III.1 717
  Almeria: Thou canst not! thy poor Arms are bound and strive . 356 M. BRIDE III.1 266
Striven (1)
  Angelica: Effects, I wou'd have striven; but that's too late. . 294 FOR LOVE IV.1 713
Stroaking (1)
  Ben: after all your fair speeches, and stroaking my Cheeks, . 286 FOR LOVE IV.1 417
Stroke (1)
  Sir Joseph: stroke down her Belly; and then step aside to tie her . 103 OLD BATCH V.1 257
Strole (1)
    That, does from Bodies, we from Houses strole. . . . . 315 FOR LOVE EPI. 20
Stroling (1)
    Stroling from Place to Place, by Circulation. . . . . 315 FOR LOVE EPI. 33
Strong (5)
  Silvia: Methinks I feel the Woman strong within me, and . . . 61 OLD BATCH III.1 33
  Sr Sampson: able Fellow: Your Sampsons were strong Dogs from the . 301 FOR LOVE V.1 155
  Zara: And Osmyn's Death requir'd of strong necessity. . . . 364 M. BRIDE IV.1 126
  Marwood: very Master-Key to every Bodies strong Box. My Friend . 431 WAY WORLD III.1 228
  Millamant: O horrid proviso's! filthy strong Waters! I toste . . . 452 WAY WORLD IV.1 278
Stronger (2)
  Maskwell: lay a stronger Plot: if I gain a little time, I shall
    not want . . . . 138 DOUBL DLR I.1 419
  Gonsalez: She fear'd her stronger Charms, might cause the Moor's . 366 M. BRIDE IV.1 224
Strongest (4)
  Careless: strongest. . . . . 131 DOUBL DLR I.1 144
  Lady Ply: resist the strongest Temptation,--but yet I know, 'tis . 147 DOUBL DLR II.1 327
  Angelica: you remember, the strongest Sampson of your Name, . . . 301 FOR LOVE V.1 158
  Angelica: you remember, Sampson, the strongest of the Name . . . 301 FOR LOVE V.1 V158
Strook (0)   see Thunder-strook
Strove (1)
  Alonzo: He snatch'd from out his Bosom this--and strove . . . 373 M. BRIDE V.1 22
Struck (4)
  Almeria: Of Africk: There our Vessel struck the Shore, . . . 329 M. BRIDE I.1 126
  Almeria: O, I am struck; thy Words are Bolts of Ice, ... 358 M. BRIDE III.1 367
  Fainall: another, have made you clash till you have both struck . 413 WAY WORLD IV.1 139
Structure (1)
  Belinda: Fronts, the more modern Structure.-- . . . . . 84 OLD BATCH IV.3 34
Struggl'd (1)
  Angelica: and struggl'd very hard to make this utmost Tryal of your 312 FOR LOVE V.1 563
Struggle (1)
    For Life will struggle long, 'ere it sink down: . . . . 125 DOUBL DLR PRO. 17
Strugled (2)
  Bellmour: thou hast lost it. Ha, ha, how a' strugled, like an Old . 63 OLD BATCH III.1 91
  Bellmour: thou hast lost it. Ha, ha, how he strugled, like an Old . 63 OLD BATCH III.1 V 91
Strugling (2)
  Singer: The hasty Joy, in strugling fled. . . . . . . 71 OLD BATCH III.2 V 16
  Osmyn-Alph: From these weak, strugling, unextended Arms; . . . . 358 M. BRIDE III.1 344
Strumpet (4)
  Heartwell: Damn'd, damn'd Strumpet! Cou'd she not contain her . . . 107 OLD BATCH V.2 5
  Lord Touch: all the Company into this Gallery,--I'll expose the
    Strumpet, ... 200 DOUBL DLR V.1 488
  Lord Touch: Now what Evasion, Strumpet? . . . . 202 DOUBL DLR V.1 559
  Manuel: False perfidious Zara! Strumpet Daughter! . . . . . 374 M. BRIDE V.1 61
Strumpets (1)
  Witwoud: That should be for two fasting Strumpets, and a . . . 404 WAY WORLD I.1 353
Stubborn (3)
  Bellmour: your snowy Arms about his stubborn Neck; bathe his . . 95 OLD BATCH IV.4 237
  Lady Touch: Thy stubborn temper shocks me, and you . . . . 197 DOUBL DLR V.1 386
  Mrs Frail: at being a Husband with that stubborn and disobedient . 286 FOR LOVE IV.1 408
Stuck (1)
  Osmyn-Alph: With such a Dagger, as then stuck my Heart. . . . . 356 M. BRIDE III.1 277
Students (1)
  Sr Sampson: and Students in Physick and Astrology in and about . . . 242 FOR LOVE II.1 253
Study (1)
  Laetitia: must study to encrease it by unjust suspicions? (Crying) . 77 OLD BATCH IV.1 89
Study'd (1)
  Mirabell: and separated her Failings; I study'd 'em, and got 'em by 399 WAY WORLD I.1 165
Stuff (2)
  Belinda: pester'd me with Flames and Stuff--I think I shan't . . 59 OLD BATCH II.2 164
  Marwood: one Suit, tho' never so fine. A Fool and a Doily Stuff . 433 WAY WORLD III.1 301
Stumbl'd (1)
  Foresight: pretty good that too; but then I stumbl'd coming . . . 236 FOR LOVE II.1 33
Stumble (2)
  Vainlove: --I stumble ore the Game I would pursue.--'Tis . . . . 80 OLD BATCH IV.1 177

Success   (ccntinued)
    Maskwell: Till then, Success will attend me; for when I meet   . . . 150   DOUBL DLR   II.1   439
    Lady Touch: Evening in my Chamber; there rejoice at cur success, and   . 155   DOUEL DLR   III.1 170
    Sir Paul: O ho, I wish you good success, I wish you good   163   DOUEL DLR   III.1 497
    Sir Paul: success. Boy, tell my Lady, when she has done, I would   . 163   DOUBL DLR   III.1 498
    Angelica: Mr. Tattle only judges of the Success of others, from the 255   FCR LCVE   III.1 76
    Leonora: Of his Success; that then, in spite of Hate, ... 327   M. BRIDE   I.1   42
    Manuel: Here are who seem to mourn at our Success!   333   M. BBIDE   I.1   278
    Painall: Joy of your Success, Mirabell; you look pleas'd.   . . . 399   WAY WCRLD   I.1   135
    Mrs Pain: Well, I have an Opinion of your Success; for   418   WAY WCRLD   II.1   307
    Foible: not doubt of Success. If you have no more Commands Sir,   . 424   WAY WORLD   II.1   542
    Foible: our success, Mrs. Marwood had told my Lady; but I warrant   . 430   WAY WCRLD   III.1 206
    Foible: of his success. I wou'd be seen as little as possible to
                 speak   430   WAY WORLD   III.1 215
    Millamant: sawcy look of an assured man, Confident of Success. The   . 449   WAY WCRLD   IV.1   178
Successful (2)
    Sharper: real Fanatick can look better pleas'd after a successful   . 100   OLD BATCH   V.1   133
    Foresight: Undertakings successful; or Goods stoll'n recover'd, I   . 241   FOR LCVE   II.1   217
Successively (2)
    Almeria: To me; with me, successively, they leave   330   M. BBIDE   I.1   156
    Osmyn-Alph: Successively reflect succeeding Images;   345   M. EBIDE   II.2   222
Such (162)
                 For my sake then--but I'm in such Confusion, ...   35   OLD BATCH   PRO.   26
    Bellmour: loves thee intirely--I have heard her breath such Raptures 38   OLD BATCH   I.1   40
    Vainlove: It must be a very superstitious Country, where such   . . 39   OLD BATCH   I.1   66
    Bellmour: Woman's a Woman, and that's all. As such I'm sure I shall   . 41   OLD BATCH   I.1   173
    Heartwell: over. For such I guess may have been your late   . . .   42   OLD BATCH   I.1   192
    Sharper: He has need of such an excuse, considering the present   . 44   OLD BATCH   I.1   288
    Heartwell: to have my Son and heir resemble such a Duke--to have a   . 45   OLD BATCH   I.1   319
    Heartwell: such a place, about his Nose and Eyes; though a' has my   . 45   OLD BATCH   I.1   323
    Heartwell: such a place, about his Nose and Eyes; though he has my   . 45   OLD BATCH   I.1 V323
    Sir Joseph: you shall see I am a Person, such a one as you would   . . 51   OLD EATCH   II.1   134
    Bellmour: is to run so extravagantly in Debt; I have laid out such a   . 58   OLD BATCH   II.2   122
    Belinda: What will you get by that? To make such Signs as   . .   59   OLD BATCH   II.2   179
    Bellmour: Pauh, Women are only angry at such offences, to   63   OLD BATCH   III.1 98
    Sir Joseph: --I'd rather go plain all my Life, than wear such   . .   70   OLD BATCH   III.1 334
    Silvia: Bed to me--You have such a Beard and would so prickle   . . 73   OLD EATCH   III.2 93
    Heartwell: (aside). That a Fool should ask such a malicious   . .   73   OLD BATCH   III.2 95
    Silvia: No, no, I'm not such a Fool neither but I can keep my   . 73   OLD BATCH   III.2 109
    Laetitia: does not think, that ever I had any such thing in my Head, 77   OLD BATCH   IV.1   81
    Belinda: my Dear,--I have seen such unhewn Creatures since,--Ha,   . 83   OLD BATCH   IV.3   11
    Belinda: Two such unlick'd Cubs!--   84   OLD BATCH   IV.3   26
    Belinda: with their Feathers growing the wrong way.--O such   . . 84   OLD BATCH   IV.3   30
    Belinda: Out-landish Creatures! Such Tramontanae, and Foreigners   . 84   OLD BATCH   IV.3   31
    Laetitia: alone with such a Satyr!   90   OLD BATCH   IV.4   48
    Laetitia: been in such a fright, that I forgot to tell you, poor Mr. 91   OLD BATCH   TV.4   77
    Setter: were to be found at that time: And such like.   . . .   99   OLD BATCH   V.1   116
    Bellmour: Sharper! Fortifie thy Spleen: Such a Jest! Speak   . .   100   OLD BATCH   V.1   135
    Bellmour: I have no such Intentions at present.--Prithee,   . . . 100   OLD BATCH   V.1   156
    Setter: What have such poor Rogues as I to do with Reputation?   . 102   OLD EATCH   V.1   230
    Setter: Well, Sir Joseph, you have such a winning way with   . . 103   OLD BATCH   V.1   251
    Sir Joseph: no Quality at all, 'tis such a Damn'd ugly Hand.   . .   103   OLD BATCH   V.1   272
    Heartwell: that such an Occasion of Melancholy? Is it such an   . . 104   OLD BATCH   V.1   301
    Belinda: Ha, ha, ha, O Gad, Men grow such Clowns when   108   OLD BATCH   V.2   25
                 Such are the Tryals, Poets make of Plays: 125   DCUEL DLR   PRO.   7
    Careless: Was there ever such a Fury! 'tis well Nature has not   . . 130   DOUBL DLR   I.1   100
    Mellefont: Cynthia has such a share in his Fatherly fondness, he would 130   DOUBL DLR   I.1   139
    Lord Froth: 'tis such a Vulgar Expression of the Passion! every body can 132   DOUEL DLR   I.1   200
    Lady Touch: such a trifling design; for her first Conversing with   . 138   DOUBL DLR   I.1   415
    Cynthia: Bless me, what makes my Father in such a Passion!--   . 144   DOUBL DLR   II.1   204
    Mellefont: (aside). Hell and Damnation! this is my Aunt; such   . . 145   DOUBL DLR   II.1   270
    Lady Ply: O, such a thing! the Impiety of it startles me   . . . 146   DOUBL DLR   II.1   289
    Mellefont: grant it; and next to the Villany of such a fact, is the   . 146   DOUBL DLR   II.1   294
    Maskwell: an universal Leveller of Mankind. Ha! but is there not such 150   DOUBL DLR   II.1   450
    Maskwell: will cheat no body but himself; such another Coxcomb,   . . 150   DOUEL DLR   II.1   454
    Maskwell: Hypocrisie; oh 'tis such a pleasure, to angle for fair-faced 150   DOUBL DLR   II.1   458
    Lady Touch: such a Case as this, demonstration is necessary.   . . . 151   DOUBL DLR   III.1 18
    Lady Touch: me if you take such publick notice of it, it will be a
                 Town-talk: 153   DOUBL DLR   III.1 104
    Careless: some such Cant. Then she has told me the whole History of   157   DOUBL DLR   III.1 272
    Careless: O, Sir Paul, you are the happiest man alive. Such a   . 160   DOUBL DLR   III.1 380
    Lord Froth: 'tis such a sight to see some teeth--sure you're a great   . 162   DOUBL DLR   III.1 460
    Lady Ply: can refrain to weep and yield to such sad Sayings.--   . 170   DOUEL DLR   IV.1   120
    Lady Ply: I swear and declare, I am in such a twitter to   173   DOUEL DLR   IV.1   209
    Sir Paul: Good strange! Mr. Brisk is such a Merry Facetious   . . 174   DOUBL DLR   IV.1   274
    Lady Ply: I'm in such a fright; the strangest Quandary   178   DOUEL DLR   IV.1   396
    Mellefont: Upon such terms I will be ever yours in every   185   DOUBL DLR   IV.2   87
    Mellefont: such Witchcraft.   186   DOUBL DLR   IV.2   116
    Sir Paul: I, I know no such matter.   192   DOUBL DLR   V.1   168
    Lady Touch: And such a smile as speaks in Ambiguity! Ten thousand   . 198   DOUBL DLR   V.1   394
    Maskwell: for your Passion broke in such imperfect terms, that yet   . 198   DOUEL DLR   V.1   414
                 And to our World, such Plenty you afford, ...   213   FOR LOVE   PRO.   16
    Valentine: hate, for just such another Reason; because they abound in 217   FOR LOVE   I.1   38
    Scandal: The World behaves it self, as it used to do on such   . 220   FOR LOVE   I.1   159
    Scandal: The World behaves it self, as it uses to do on such   . 220   FOR LOVE   I.1 V159
    Valentine: an Army lead just such a life as I do; have just such Crowds 221   FOR LOVE   I.1   189
    Trapland: No, no, there's no such thing, we'd better mind our   . 223   FOR LOVE   I.1   281
    Scandal: Aye, such rotten Reputations as you have to deal   . . . 226   FOR LOVE   I.1   396
    Valentine: cannot avoid such a palpable Decoy as this was; the Ladies 229   FOR LOVE   I.1   502
    Valentine: give Scandal such an Advantage; why, your running away   . 229   FOR LOVE   I.1   512
    Foresight: How Hussie! was there ever such a provoking   237   FOR LOVE   II.1   93
    Tattle: have such a thought--sure you don't know me?   250   FOR LOVE   II.1   541
    Mrs Fore: together is as bad--And he's such a sly Devil, he'll never 250   FOR LOVE   II.1   574
    Mrs Frail: That wou'd be pity, such a Handsome Young   261   FCR LOVE   III.1 304
    Mrs Frail: and honest, I shou'd like such a humour in a Husband   . 262   FOR LOVE   III.1 322
    Ben: Say'n you so forsooth: Marry and I shou'd like such a   . 262   FOR LOVE   III.1 324

Suckle (1)
  Angelica: and that you Suckle a Young Devil in the Shape of a   . 238   FOR LOVE   II.1   121
Suckling (4)
  Mrs Fain: You are very fond of Sir John Suckling to day,   . . . 446   WAY WORLD   IV.1   55
  Millamant: Natural, easie Suckling!   447   WAY WORLD   IV.1   106
  Sir Wilful: Anan? Suckling? No such Suckling neither,   . . 447   WAY WORLD   IV.1   107
Sucks (2)
  Capt Bluff: --He sucks not vital Air who dares affirm it to this   . 70   OLD BATCH   III.1   353
  Almeria: That sucks thy warm Life-Blood, and gnaws thy Heart?   . 357   M. BRIDE   III.1   299
Suddain (4)
  Foresight: like that suddain flushing--gone already!--hem, hem,   . 269   FOR LOVE   III.1   604
  Almeria: And of a suddain I am calm, as if   382   M. BRIDE   V.2   241
  Mirabell: Town took notice that she was grown fat of a suddain;   . 397   WAY WORLD   I.1   74
  Mrs Fain: Do I? I think I am a little sick o' the suddain.   . . 412   WAY WORLD   II.1   80
Suddainly (1)
  Tattle: Suddainly--before we knew where we were--   309   FOR LOVE   V.1   450
Sudden (9)
  Lady Touch: your Temper. I'll make an excuse of sudden Business to   . 153   DOUBL DLR   III.1   117
  Mellefont: sudden Whirlwind come, tear up Tree and all, and bear   . 187   DOUBL DLR   IV.2   146
  Tattle: obvious to Vulgar Eyes; that are Indications of a sudden   . 304   FOR LOVE   V.1   268
  Foresight: Really, Sir Sampson, this is a sudden Eclipse--   . . . 313   FOR LOVE   V.1   582
  Almeria: And almost taken; when a sudden Storm, ... 329   M. BRIDE   I.1   124
  Almeria: A sudden Chilness seizes on my Spirits.   . . . 334   M. BRIDE   I.1   349
  Manuel: That like a sudden Earth-quake, shakes my Frame;   . . 367   M. BRIDE   IV.1   233
  Manuel: Sudden I'll start, and dash her with her Guilt.   . . . 374   M. BRIDE   V.1 V86F
  Lady Wish: be too sudden. I'll lie--aye, I'll lie down--I'll   . . 445   WAY WORLD   IV.1   22
Suddenly (2)
  Lady Touch: be so suddenly resolv'd. Why, Cynthia? Why must he be   . 191   DOUBL DLR   V.1   125
  Lord Touch: suddenly design'd--yet he says he had prepar'd my   . . 197   DOUBL DLR   V.1   359
Suddenness (1)
  Almeria: And with such Suddenness, hast hit my Sight;   343   M. BRIDE   II.2   153
Sue (1)
  Lucy: and have fram'd a Letter, that makes her sue for
       Reconciliation   75   OLD BATCH   III.2   157
Suff'ring (1)
  Zara: Think on my Suff'ring first, then, look on me;   . . . 347   M. BRIDE   II.2   304
Suff'rings (1)
  Almeria: How would thy Heart have bled to see his Suff'rings!   . 327   M. BRIDE   I.1   33
Suffer (11)
  Sharper: You are above--I'me sure--a thought so low, to suffer   . 50   OLD BATCH   II.1   100
  Capt Bluff: I'll suffer it.   70   OLD BATCH   III.1   337
     Were each to suffer for his Mothers Sin: 125   DOUBL DLR   PRO.   22
  Maskwell: would you suffer me.   137   DOUBL DLR   I.1   395
  Scandal: Either you suffer your self to deceive your self; or   . 268   FOR LOVE   III.1   563
  Angelica: to deceive you, and too much Charity to suffer him to be   . 277   FOR LOVE   IV.1   71
  Manuel: Stay, Soldier; they shall suffer with the Moor.   . . . 363   M. BRIDE   IV.1   73
  Selim: Avert it, Heav'n, that you should ever suffer   . . . 375   M. BRIDE   V.1   113
  Mirabell: suffer your Wife to be of such a Party.   399   WAY WORLD   I.1   140
  Mirabell: Ay, ay, suffer your Cruelty to ruin the object of   . . 420   WAY WORLD   II.1   389
  Lady Wish: a Person who wou'd suffer racks in honour's cause, dear   . 459   WAY WORLD   IV.1   553
Suffer'd (8)
  Sharper: more, nor perhaps have suffer'd so much--had he a   . . 50   OLD BATCH   II.1   126
  Tattle: have given it me, but have suffer'd me to take it.   . . 252   FOR LOVE   II.1   636
  Tattle: have given it me, but have suffer'd me to have taken it.   . 252   FOR LOVE   II.1 V636
  Zara: No not the Princess suffer'd or to see   360   M. BRIDE   III.1 V451
     Suffer'd at first some trifling Stakes to win: . . . 393   WAY WORLD   PRO.   12
  Mirabell: stand excus'd, who has suffer'd herself to be won by his   . 417   WAY WORLD   II.1   274
  Lady Wish: never suffer'd to play with a Male-Child, tho' but in   . 467   WAY WORLD   V.1   189
  Fainall: Well Madam; I have suffer'd my self to be overcome   . . 468   WAY WORLD   V.1   250
Sufferings (2)
  Scandal: which you deny'd to all his Sufferings and my
       Sollicitations.   294   FOR LOVE   IV.1   690
  Osmyn-Alph: Of my Heart, to see thy Sufferings--O Heav'n!   . . . 356   M. BRIDE   III.1   252
Suffers (3)
  Bellmour: self, nor suffers any Body else to rail at me. Then as I   . 41   OLD BATCH   I.1   169
     And suffers Judges to direct the Jury.   204   DOUBL DLR   EPI.   11
  Zara: Than your high Courage suffers you to see;   364   M. BRIDE   IV.1   110
Sufficient (10)
  Sharper: But that's sufficient--'Twere injustice to doubt the   . 50   OLD BATCH   II.1   97
  Sharper: Word is sufficient any where: 'Tis but borrowing so much   . 50   OLD BATCH   II.1   108
  Capt Bluff: sufficient Cause; Fighting, to me's Religion and the Laws.   . 52   OLD BATCH   II.1   165
  Fondlewife: Good lack, good lack--I profess it is a very sufficient   . 76   OLD BATCH   IV.1   39
  Mrs Frail: presume to have a sufficient stock of Duty to undergo a   . 286   FOR LOVE   IV.1   410
     And One was thought sufficient for a Year: 323   M. BRIDE   PRO.   4
  Mirabell: Husband, as may be sufficient to make you relish your   . 416   WAY WORLD   II.1   259
  Sir Wilful: present, 'tis sufficient till further acquaintance, that's
       all--   447   WAY WORLD   IV.1   85
  Fainall: must set your Hand till more sufficient Deeds can be   . 469   WAY WORLD   V.1   292
  Sir Wilful: Sir. It shall not be sufficient for a Mittimus or a Taylor's 473   WAY WORLD   V.1   427
Sufficiently (2)
  Mellefont: For my Lord Froth, he and his Wife will be sufficiently   . 130   DOUBL DLR   I.1   133
  Mincing: us sufficiently.   474   WAY WORLD   V.1   491
Suffocating (1)
  Osmyn-Alph: 'Till gorg'd with suffocating Earth.   358   M. BRIDE   III.1 V356
Sugar-loaf (1)
  Mirabell: a Shape, till you mold my boy's head like a Sugar-loaf; and 451   WAY WORLD   IV.1   261
Suit (4)
  Lady Froth: suit the lining of his Coach with his complexion.   . . 165   DOUBL DLR   III.1   564
  Valentine: Summer suit. Ask me Questions concerning to morrow?   . 288   FOR LOVE   IV.1   494
  Almeria: The Queen too, did assist his Suit--I granted,   . . . 329   M. BRIDE   I.1   140
  Marwood: one Suit, tho' never so fine. A Fool and a Doily Stuff   . 433   WAY WORLD   III.1   301
Suitable (2)
  Sir Joseph: the very Gentleman! how shall I make him a return suitable   49   OLD BATCH   II.1   51
  Lady Ply: a suitable return to those Obligations which you are pleased 159   DOUBL DLR   III.1   338
Suits (2)
     For when behind our Scenes their Suits are pleading,   . . 315   FOR LOVE   EPI.   7

Superfluous (1)
| Lucy: | superfluous Fopperies. . . . . | 66 | OLD BATCH | III.1 | 189 |

Superiority (1)
| Mirabell: | I don't find that Petulant confesses the Superiority | . . | 402 | WAY WCRLD | I.1 | 285 |

Superiour (1)
| Zara: | To find you have an Interest superiour. . . . . . | 360 | M. BRIDE | III.1 | 419 |

Superscription (6)
Bellmour:	Superscription (Takes up the Letter.) than in all Cicero--		38	OLD BATCH	I.1	34
Bellmour:	Superscription,) I am the most surpriz'd in the World to	.	82	OLD BATCH	IV.2	56
Scandal:	upon the Superscription: And yet perhaps he has					
	Counterfeited	.	226	FOR LCVE	I.1	374
Scandal:	in the Superscription: And yet perhaps he has Counterfeited	226	FOR LCVE	I.1	V374
Lady Wish:	you may see by the Superscription it is like a Woman's	.	460	WAY WCRLD	IV.1	573
Lady Wish:	you may see, the Superscription is like a Woman's	. .	460	WAY WCRLD	IV.1	V573

Superstition (2)
| Sr Sampson: | Brother Foresight, leave Superstition--Pox o'th' time; | . | 240 | FOR LOVE | III.1 | 196 |
| Painall: | Corrupt to Superstition, and blind Credulity. I am single; | 444 | WAY WOBLD | III.1 | 719 |

Superstitious (4)
Vainlove:	It must be a very superstitious Country, where such	.	39	OLD BATCH	I.1	66
Careless:	I am a little Superstitious in Physiogncmy.	131	DOUBL DLR	I.1	148
Mrs Frail:	Issue-Male of their two Bodies; 'tis the most superstitious	231	FOR LCVE	I.1	579
Mrs Fore:	Not much,--he's superstitious; and you	284	FOR LCVE	IV.1	323

Supine (3)
Perez:	He lies supine on earth; as easily	372	M. BRIDE	V.1	8
Perez:	He lies supine on earth; with as much ease	372	M. BRIDE	V.1	V 8
Manuel:	And laid along as he now lies supine, ...	374	M. BRIDE	V.1	V86B

Supp'd (1)
| Tattle: | Valentine, I Supp'd last Night with your Mistress, and | . | 228 | FOR LCVE | I.1 | 452 |

Supper (3)
Sir Paul:	(Reads) Hum--After Supper in the Wardrcbe by the	.	178	DOUBL DLR	IV.1	408
Ben:	for's Supper, for all that. What do's Father mean to leave	264	FCR LCVE	III.1	422
Valentine:	Man shou'd have a Stomach to a Wedding Supper, when	.	289	FOR LCVE	IV.1	527

Supplemental (1)
| Heartwell: | To Man that Supplemental Self design'd; . . . . . | 108 | OLD BATCH | V.2 | 12 |

Suppliant (3)
Zara:	Is a regardless Suppliant, now, to Osmyn.	346	M. BRIDE	II.2	249
Mirabell:	Suppliant only for your pity--I am going where I .	471	WAY WCRLD	V.1	374
Mirabell:	Suppliant only for Pity--I am gcing where I	471	WAY WCRLD	V.1	V374

Suppliants (1)
| | But now, no more like Suppliants, we come; . . . . . | 35 | OLD BATCH | PRO. | 5 |

Supplies (1)
| Heartwell: | reflux of vigorous Blood: But milky Love, supplies the | . | 72 | OLD BATCH | III.2 | 49 |

Supply (3)
Lord Froth:	Wife shall supply you. Come, Gentlemen, allons. . . .	135	DOUBL DLR	I.1	296
Valentine:	I was much oblig'd tc you for your Supply: It did . .	223	FOR LCVE	I.1	258
Valentine:	Fortune was provident enough to supply all the . . .	246	FCR LOVE	II.1	394

Support (10)
Lady Ply:	feeble, and unable to support it self.	147	DOUBL DLR	II.1	322
Lady Touch:	Not in Love, Words are the weak support of	184	DOUBL DLR	IV.2	22
Sr Sampson:	Support, like Ivy round a dead Oak: Faith I do; I love to	260	FOR LOVE	III.1	264
Garcia:	Alas, she faints! help to support her.	334	M. BRIDE	I.1	346
Garcia:	She faints! help to support her.	334	M. BRIDE	I.1	V346
Almeria:	Angels, and all the Host of heaven support me! . . .	340	M. BRIDE	II.2	36
Almeria:	No, hcld me not--0, let us not support, ...	358	M. BRIDE	III.1	370
Gonsalez:	Help, support her.	369	M. BRIDE	IV.1	346
Lady Wish:	Traytor,--I fear I cannot fortifie my self tc support his	470	WAY WCRLD	V.1	335
	To think they singly can support a Scene, ...	479	WAY WCBLD	EPI.	26

Supporters (1)
| Heartwell: | and bear my Horns aloft, like one of the supporters of my | 45 | OLD BATCH | I.1 | 311 |

Suppose (29)
Bellmour:	hands cf some Nightwalkers, who I suppose would have	. .	46	OLD BATCH	I.1	360
Belinda:	The Visit's to you, Cousin, I suppose I am at my . .	56	OLD BATCH	II.2	81
Setter:	As I suppose my Master Heartwell.	105	OLD BATCH	V.1	332
Sir Joseph:	countermin'd, or so--Mr. Vainlove, I suppose you know .	110	OLD BATCH	V.2	113
Brisk:	I suppose that's because you Laugh at your own Jests, .	132	DOUBL DLR	I.1	206
Brisk:	little shallow, or so.--Why I'll tell you now, suppose .	133	DOUEL DLR	I.1	252
Brisk:	instructed. Suppose, as I was saying, you come up to me,	134	DOUBL DLR	I.1	254
Careless:	you suppose I can't tell you?	134	DOUBL DLR	I.1	261
Brisk:	t'other way. Suppose I say a witty thing to you? . .	134	DOUEL DLR	I.1	278
Lady Froth:	gave you my Picture, here suppose this my Picture-- .	140	DOUBL DLR	II.1	74
Lady Touch:	So I suppose there was.	151	DOUBL DLR	III.1	21
Mellefont:	suppose when she apprehends being with Child, he never .	158	DOUBL DLR	III.1	286
Lady Froth:	I may suppose the Dairy in Town, as well as in the Country.	163	DOUBL DLR	III.1	504
Sir Paul:	I suppose they have been laying their heads	201	DOUBL DLR	V.1	509
Sir Paul:	Nay, only about Poetry, I suppose, my Lord;	201	DOUBL DLR	V.1	512
Scandal:	Patience, I suppose, the old Receipt.	220	FOR LCVE	I.1	170
Mrs Frail:	Well, I'll tell you News; but I suppose you hear your .	231	FOR LOVE	I.1	566
Mrs Fore:	I suppose you would not go alone to the	247	FOR LCVE	II.1	446
Angelica:	No; I suppose that is not in your Power; but you . .	255	FOR LCVE	III.1	94
Valentine:	It was there, I suppose, you got the Nick-Name of . .	257	FOR LOVE	III.1	166
Scandal:	Ghost of Lilly. He has Secrets to impart I suppose to you	266	FOR LOVE	III.1	500
Angelica:	Mr. Scandal, I suppose you don't think it a Novelty, .	276	FOR LOVE	IV.1	20
Jeremy:	all: I suppose your Ladyship has thought him so a great	276	FOR LOVE	IV.1	30
Zara:	O 'tis more Grief but to suppose his Death, ...	362	M. BRIDE	IV.1	27
Mrs Fain:	suppose she will submit to any thing to get rid of him.	418	WAY WORLD	II.1	310
Sir Wilful:	Pops; where, I suppose, you have serv'd your Time; and	440	WAY WORLD	III.1	564
Millamant:	Ay, go, go. In the mean time I suppose you have . .	452	WAY WORLD	IV.1	306
Painall:	Tenor of this other Covenant,--I suppose Madam, your .	473	WAY WORLD	V.1	437
Mirabell:	Widdows of the World. I suppose this Deed may bear an .	476	WAY WORLD	V.1	554

Supposed (1)
| Lady Ply: | might be supposed to be capable of being qualified to make | 159 | DOUBL DLR | III.1 | 337 |

Sure (117)
Bellmour:	Woman's a Woman, and that's all. As such I'm sure I shall	.	41	OLD BATCH	I.1	173
Sharper:	Sure that's he and alone.	47	OLD BATCH	II.1	1
Sharper:	You are above--I'me sure--a thought so low, to suffer	. .	50	OLD BATCH	II.1	100
Belinda:	Fancy--This Love is the Devil, and sure to be in Love	. .	54	OLD BATCH	II.2	12

Sure   (continued)

Speaker	Text	PAGE	TITLE	ACT.SC	LINE
Belinda:	and Appurtenances; O Gad! sure you would--But you	55	OLD BATCH	II.2	33
Araminta:	--Sure if I had rot pinch'd you till you wak'd, you	55	OLD BATCH	II.2	43
Araminta:	Oh is it come out--Now ycu are angry, I am sure	56	OLD BATCH	II.2	58
Heartwell:	I am--However, I find I am pretty sure of her consent, if	73	OLD BATCH	III.2	97
Lucy:	That Woman sure enjoys a blessed Night,	75	OLD BATCH	III.2	162
Laetitia:	(aside). I'me amaz'd; sure he has discover'd nothing--	77	OLD BATCH	IV.1	79
Laetitia:	sure.	81	OLD BATCH	IV.2	30
Belinda:	Nay, sure Railing is the best qualification in a	88	OLD BATCH	IV.3	201
Laetitia:	Sure, when he does not see his face, he won't discover	91	OLD BATCH	IV.4	90
Laetitia:	Dear Husband, I'm amaz'd:--Sure it's a good	92	OLD BATCH	IV.4	114
Laetitia:	Rather, sure it is a Wolf in the cloathing of a Sheep.	93	OLD BATCH	IV.4	142
Vainlove:	I'm sure he tells me Truth;--but I am not sure she told	99	OLD BATCH	V.1	94
Setter:	Ay, I know her, Sir: At least, I'm sure I can fish it out	99	OLD BATCH	V.1	103
Bellmour:	wilt thou think a little for me? I am sure the ingenious	100	OLD BATCH	V.1	157
Sharper:	Heh! Sure, Fortune has sent this Fool hither on	101	OLD BATCH	V.1	163
Heartwell:	And Adam, sure, cou'd with more Ease abide	108	OLD BATCH	V.2	14
Vainlove:	Faith, that's a sure way.--But here's one can	109	OLD BATCH	V.2	79
Heartwell:	thou sure she is really married to him?	111	OLD BATCH	V.2	127
	And be enjoy'd, tho' sure to be undone;	113	OLD BATCH	EPI.	2
	The Poet's sure he shall some comfort find:	125	DOUBL DLR	PRO.	32
Sir Paul:	sure as can be it would.--we wanted your Company,	132	DOUBL DLR	I.1	180
Lady Froth:	say'st right--for sure my Lord Froth is as fine a Gentleman,	139	DOUBL DLR	II.1	28
Sir Paul:	Heart--I'm sure if ever I should have Horns, they	146	DOUBL DLR	II.1	281
Mellefont:	Where am I? sure, is it day? and am I awake,	147	DOUBL DLR	II.1	323
Lady Ply:	consent to that, as sure as can be, I'll break the Match.	147	DOUBL DLR	II.1	352
Lady Ply:	strive as much as can be against it,--strive be sure--but	148	DOUBL DLR	II.1	364
Lady Ply:	be sure you lay aside all thoughts of the Marriage, for tho'	148	DOUBL DLR	II.1	367
Lady Ply:	qualified in all those Circumstances, I'm sure I should	159	DOUBL DLR	III.1	340
Lady Ply:	for I'm sure there's nothing in the World that I would	159	DOUBL DLR	III.1	342
Sir Paul:	year; I'm sure I have found it sc; and alas, what's once a	162	DOUBL DLR	III.1	434
Lord Froth:	'tis such a sight to see some teeth--sure you're a great	162	DOUBL DLR	III.1	460
Cynthia:	without any harmony; for sure, my Lord, to laugh out of	163	DOUBL DLR	III.1	472
Lady Ply:	Honour--Well, sure if I escape your Importunities, I	169	DOUBL DLR	IV.1	75
Lady Ply:	challenges much more, I'm sure, than my illiterate Praises	169	DOUBL DLR	IV.1	83
Cynthia:	sure she lov'd him.	171	DOUBL DLR	IV.1	162
Sir Paul:	the most beholden to Mr. Careless--As sure as can	172	DOUBL DLR	IV.1	200
Lady Ply:	yet I'll be sure to be unsuspected this time.--Sir Paul.	173	DOUBL DLR	IV.1	212
Sir Paul:	were not for Providence, sure poor Sir Paul thy Heart	179	DOUBL DLR	IV.1	434
Careless:	effects that will have, but I'll be sure to tell you when I do,	180	DOUBL DLR	IV.1	502
Lord Touch:	I'm sure Sir Paul's Consent will follow Fortune; I'll	189	DOUBL DLR	V.1	76
Lord Touch:	Sure I was born to be controuled by these I	195	DOUBL DLR	V.1	302
Sir Paul:	All turn'd topsie turvey, as sure as a Gun.	200	DOUBL DLR	V.1	501
Valentine:	of Fortune. And for the Wits, I'm sure in a Condition	217	FOR LOVE	I.1	56
Valentine:	of Fortune. And for the Wits, I'm sure I am in a Condition	217	FOR LOVE	I.1 V	56
Valentine:	I'm sure.	231	FOR LOVE	I.1	575
Foresight:	Mercy on us, what can be the meaning of it? Sure	235	FOR LOVE	II.1	5
Foresight:	What, wou'd you be gadding too? Sure all Females	236	FOR LOVE	II.1	46
Tattle:	have such a thought--sure you don't know me?	250	FOR LOVE	II.1	541
Mrs Frail:	sure enough.	250	FOR LOVE	II.1	572
Tattle:	you'l cry out, you must be sure to hold your Tongue.	252	FOR LOVE	II.1	623
Nurse:	Miss Foresight--Sure she has not lock'd her self up	253	FOR LOVE	III.1	3
Nurse:	Miss Foresight--Sure she lock'd her self up	253	FOR LOVE	III.1 V	3
Scandal:	And I'll answer for him; for I'm sure if he had, he	256	FOR LOVE	III.1	109
Tattle:	find: For sure my intimate Friends wou'd have known--	256	FOR LOVE	III.1	113
Miss Prue:	But I'm sure it is not so, for I'll speak sooner than	264	FOR LOVE	III.1	395
Angelica:	Oh here's a reasonable Creature--sure he will	295	FOR LOVE	IV.1	733
Jeremy:	Two Hours--I'm sure I left him just now, in a Humour	295	FOR LOVE	IV.1	754
Jeremy:	Two Hours--I'm sure I left him just now, in the Humour	295	FOR LOVE	IV.1 V	754
Jeremy:	sure she'll have reason to pray for me, when she finds	302	FOR LOVE	V.1	203
Ben:	That may be--but I'm sure it is as I tell you.	307	FOR LOVE	V.1	366
	Sure Providence at first, design'd this Place	315	FOR LOVE	EPI.	1
	I'm sure 'tis some such Latin Name they give 'em,	315	FOR LOVE	EPI.	13
Almeria:	By some unseen Hand, so, as of sure consequence	327	M. BRIDE	I.1 V	61
Almeria:	The last Distress of Life, and sure Despair.	327	M. BRIDE	I.1	63
Gonsalez:	As if she had offended.--Sure, nc more,	334	M. BRIDE	I.1 V	320
Heli:	Yet cannot find her--Hark! sure 'tis the Voice	340	M. BRIDE	II.2	2
Almeria:	Sure, 'tis the Friendly Yawn of Death for me;	340	M. BRIDE	II.2	14
Osmyn-Alph:	Let me behold and touch her, and be sure	341	M. BRIDE	II.2	67
Almeria:	Sure, from thy Father's Tomb, thou didst arise!	343	M. BRIDE	II.2	156
Almeria:	Sure I have dreamt, if we must part so soon.	344	M. BRIDE	II.2	194
Almeria:	Sure we shall meet again.	345	M. BRIDE	II.2	209
Osmyn-Alph:	Sure 'tis the Hand of Heav'n, that leads me thus,	350	M. BRIDE	III.1	4
Heli:	The Care of Providence, sure left it there,	352	M. BRIDE	III.1	116
Zara:	O certain Death for him, as sure Despair.	363	M. BRIDE	IV.1	94
Gonsalez:	It not. Your Majesty sure, might have spared	365	M. BRIDE	IV.1	178
Gonsalez:	Sure Death already has been busie here.	376	M. BRIDE	V.2	3
Gonsalez:	Ha! sure he sleeps--all's dark within, save what	376	M. BRIDE	V.2	6
Gonsalez:	No body? sure he'll wait without--I would	376	M. BRIDE	V.2	11
Osmyn-Alph:	And tho' a late, a sure Reward succeeds.	384	M. BRIDE	V.2	322
	Sure scribbling Fools, call'd Poets, fare the worst.	393	WAY WORLD	PRO.	2
	The 'Squire that's butter'd still, is sure to be undone.	393	WAY WORLD	PRO.	15
	That hurts none here, sure here are none of those.	393	WAY WORLD	PRO.	36
Mirabell:	So, sc, you are sure they are Married.	398	WAY WORLD	I.1	120
Witwoud:	from one Poet to another. And what's worse, 'tis as sure a	401	WAY WORLD	I.1	247
Fainall:	for ycu are sure to be too hard for him at Repartee: since	402	WAY WORLD	I.1	282
Mirabell:	thee, then Mercury is by the Sun: Come, I'm sure thou	407	WAY WORLD	I.1	456
Witwoud:	as Cleopatra. Mirabell is not so sure of her as he thinks for.	408	WAY WORLD	I.1	478
Fainall:	Excellent Creature! Well sure if I shou'd live to be	413	WAY WORLD	II.1	109
Marwood:	discover'd; be sure you shall. I can but be expos'd--If I	415	WAY WORLD	II.1	188
Mirabell:	so I made him sure before-hand.	417	WAY WORLD	II.1	295
Mirabell:	as a Mortification; for sure to please a Fool is some degree	421	WAY WORLD	II.1	439
Mirabell:	Sirrah, Waitwell, why sure you think you were married	423	WAY WORLD	II.1	505
Poible:	him; which I'll be sure to say has made him so enamour'd	423	WAY WORLD	II.1	522

Susan (continued)
| Lady Froth: | For Susan, you know, is Thetis, and so-- | 164 | DOUEL DLR | III.1 | 542 |

Suspect (14)
Fondlewife:	we still suspect the smoothest Dealers of the deepest	77	OLD EATCH	IV.1	61
Setter:	I do suspect as much;--because why, Sir:--	99	OLD BATCH	V.1	112
Mellefont:	suspect him?	131	DOUEL DLR	I.1	146
Careless:	them, you do not suspect: For all her Fassion for you.	131	DOUEL DLR	I.1	154
Careless:	them, you do not suspect: Notwithstanding her Fassion for you.	131	DOUEL DLR	I.1 V154
Maskwell:	disswade him from a Design, which I suspect; and if I had	182	DOUEL DLR	IV.1	578
Maskwell:	that he may not suspect one word on't.	190	DOUEL DLR	V.1	99
Scandal:	(aside). That ever I shou'd suspect such a Heathen of	281	FCR LCVE	IV.1	212
Angelica:	turn tc an extream Fondness, you must not suspect it.	313	FCR LCVE	V.1	607
Gonsalez:	That last restraint; you hardly can suspect	365	M. BRIDE	IV.1	179
Marwood:	O Madam, you cannot suspect Mrs. Foible's	426	WAY WCRLD	III.1	55
Foible:	Account, I'm sure you wou'd not suspect my Fidelity.	427	WAY WCRLD	III.1	88
Foible:	Uncle; (he does not suspect a Word of your Ladyship;)	428	WAY WCRLD	III.1	113
Mrs Fain:	Letter?--My Mother do's not suspect my being in the	464	WAY WCRLD	V.1	75

Suspected (8)
Lady Touch:	like to be suspected in the end, and 'tis a pain any longer	151	DOUEL DLR	III.1	39
Lady Ply:	License to make trial of your Wifes suspected Vertue?	179	DOUEL DLR	IV.1	440
Maskwell:	suspected a design which I should have been puzled to	188	DOUEL DLR	V.1	12
Maskwell:	suspected, that it shall be got ready by my Lord's own	193	DOUEL DLR	V.1	211
Manuel:	She does excuse him; 'tis as I suspected.	337	M. BRIDE	I.1	441
Gonsalez:	My Policy, I ne'er suspected it:	371	M. BRIDE	IV.1	398
Sir Wilful:	Brother. 'Sheart, I've suspected this--By'r Lady I	439	WAY WCRLD	III.1	539
Mirabell:	suspected--she did I say by the wholescme advice of	476	WAY WCRLD	V.1	544

Suspence (3)
Heartwell:	not rack me in suspence.	72	OLD BATCH	III.2	42
Heartwell:	not rack me with suspence.	72	OLD EATCH	III.2 V 42
Manuel:	For, ling'ring there, in long suspense she stands,	337	M. BRIDE	I.1	454

Suspicion (7)
Bellmour:	Secure in my Disguise, I have out-fac'd Suspicion,	80	OLD BATCH	IV.2	4
Mellefont:	narrowly, and give me notice upon any Suspicion. As for	130	DOUEL DLR	I.1	137
Maskwell:	mean now, is only a bare Suspicicn of my own. If your	183	DOUEL DLR	IV.1	583
Cynthia:	without suspicicn?	193	DOUEL DLR	V.1	209
Valentine:	I'll prevent that suspicion--For I intend to	313	FOR LOVE	V.1	608
Selim:	Might breed Suspicion of the Cause. Advise,	362	M. EBIDE	IV.1	46
Zara:	Thy shallow Artifice begets Suspicion,	375	M. BRIDE	V.1	102

Suspicions (4)
Laetitia:	must study to encrease it by unjust suspicions? (Crying)	77	OLD BATCH	IV.1	89
Mellefont:	suspicions just,--but see the Ccmpany is broke up,	131	DOUEL DLR	I.1	168
Cynthia:	what you ne're could have believ'd from my suspicions.	197	DOUEL DLR	V.1	376
Selim:	The State of things will countenance all Suspicions.	362	M. EBIDE	IV.1	55

Suspicious (1)
| Jeremy: | suspicious Fellows like lawful Pads, that wou'd knock | 221 | FOR LOVE | I.1 | 203 |

Suspiciously (1)
| Valentine: | further; You look suspiciously. Are you a Husband? | 289 | FCR LCVE | IV.1 | 514 |

Sussex (1)
| | As Sussex Men, that dwell upon the Shoar, | 385 | M. EBIDE | EPI. | 19 |

Sustenance (1)
| Sr Sampson: | Cadua of Fourscore for Sustenance. Odd, I love to see a | 260 | FOR LCVE | III.1 | 262 |

Swaddled (1)
| Mellefont: | him swaddled up in Blankets, and his hands and feet | 158 | DOUEL DLR | III.1 | 290 |

Swail'd (1)
| Osmyn-Alph: | But dash'd with Rain from Eyes, and swail'd with Sighs, | 357 | M. EBIDE | III.1 | 323 |

Swain (4)   see Boat-swain
Singer-F:	A Nymph and a Swain to Apollo once pray'd,	258	FOR LCVE	III.1	200
Singer-F:	The Swain had been Jilted, the Nymph been Eetray'd;	258	PCR LCVE	III.1	201
Singer-F:	E're a Nymph that was Chaste, or a Swain that was True.	258	FCR LCVE	III.1	203
Singer:	But 'tis the Glory to have pierc'd a Swain,	435	WAY WCRLD	III.1	384

Swallow (2)
| Heartwell: | is it out of discretion, that you don't swallow that very | 43 | OLD BATCH | I.1 | 242 |
| Lucy: | doubt will be eager enough to day, to swallow the | 61 | OLD EATCH | I.1 | 12 |

Swallow'd (3)
Mellefont:	So when you've swallow'd the Potion, you sweeten	156	DOUEL DLR	III.1	221
Marwood:	and fidges off and on his Cushicn as if he had swallow'd	467	WAY WCRLD	V.1	221
Marwood:	and figes off and on his Cushicn as if he had swallow'd	467	WAY WCBLD	V.1 V221

Swarming (1)
| Gonsalez: | The swarming Populace, spread every Wall, | 332 | M. EBIDE | I.1 | 238 |

Swath'd (2)
| Mellefont: | swath'd down, and so put to bed; and there he lies with a | 158 | DOUEL DLR | III.1 | 291 |
| Sir Paul: | three Years past? Have I been swath'd in Blankets till I | 178 | DOUEL DLR | IV.1 | 424 |

Swathed (1)
| Lady Ply: | this, your Right Hand shall be swathed down again to | 180 | DOUEL DLR | IV.1 V482 |

Sway (3)
Careless:	I find a Quibble bears more sway in your Lordships	132	DOUEL DLR	I.1	214
Zara:	And Native Right to Arbitrary Sway;	336	M. EBIDE	I.1	397
Manuel:	But rules with settled Sway in Zara's Eyes.	337	M. EBIDE	I.1	461

Swear (83)
Belinda:	more. Oh Gad, I swear you'd make one sick to hear you.	54	OLD BATCH	II.2	2
Lucy:	Swear.	66	OLD EATCH	III.1	215
Setter:	I do swear to the utmost of my power.	66	OLD EATCH	III.1	216
Bellmour:	swear--	82	OLD BATCH	IV.2	68
Laetitia:	Nay, don't swear if you'd have me believe you; but	82	OLD BATCH	IV.2	69
Bellmour:	Give me leave to swear--by those Eyes, those killing Eyes;	82	OLD BATCH	IV.2	72
Belinda:	Of a very ancient one, I dare swear, by their Dress.	84	OLD BATCH	IV.3	38
Belinda:	friends with him.--I swear, he looks so very simply,	86	OLD BATCH	IV.3	132
Belinda:	Nay, we have spared No-body, I swear. Mr. Sharper,	88	OLD BATCH	IV.3	195
Laetitia:	--I swear, I was heartily frightned.--Feel how my	89	OLD BATCH	IV.4	4
Belinda:	Nor for them neither, in a little time--I swear,	108	OLD BATCH	V.2	28
Belinda:	Nay, I swear, I begin to pity him, my self.	109	OLD BATCH	V.2	49
	I swear, young Bays within, is so dejected,	113	OLD EATCH	EPI.	24
Sir Paul:	good, strange! I swear I'm almost Tipsy--t'other	131	DOUEL DLR	I.1	178
Sir Paul:	good, strange! I swear I'm almost Tipsie--t'other	131	DOUEL DLR	I.1 V178
Sir Paul:	but Mr. Brisk--where is he? I swear and vow, he's a	132	DOUEL DLR	I.1	181

Sweet   (continued)
Miss Prue:	his Perruke is sweet, and his Gloves are sweet.--and his	. 249	FOR LOVE	II.1	519
Miss Prue:	Handkerchief is sweet, pure sweet, sweeter than Roses .	. 249	FOR LOVE	II.1	520
Miss Prue:	fine Gentleman, and a sweet Gentleman, that was here	. 264	FOR LOVE	III.1	415
Foible:	O dear Madam, Mr. Mirabell is such a sweet winning . .	. 430	WAY WORLD	III.1	201
Foible:	Generosity.--Sweet Lady, to be so good! Mr. Mirabell .	. 430	WAY WORLD	III.1	203
Millamant:	Sweet heart and the rest of that Nauseous Cant, in which	. 450	WAY WORLD	IV.1	198
Foible:	Sweet, so kind a Lady as you have been to me. . . .	. 463	WAY WORLD	V.1	33

Sweet-Heart (1)
Ben:	Sweet-Heart, a-fore I turn in; may-hap I may dream of .	. 275	FOR LOVE	III.1	809

Sweet-heart (4)
Trapland:	Hold, Sweet-heart.--This is not to our Business: . .	. 222	FOR LOVE	I.1	245
Ben:	Tar-barrel? Let your Sweet-heart there call me so, if he'll	264	FOR LOVE	III.1	434
Lady Wish:	Fetch me the Red--The Red, do you hear, Sweet-heart? .	. 425	WAY WORLD	III.1	5
Sir Wilful:	I pull off my Boots. Sweet-heart, can you help me to a .	. 441	WAY WORLD	III.1	617

Sweeten (1)
Mellefont:	So when you've swallow'd the Poticn, ycu sweeten . .	. 156	DOUBL DLR	III.1	221

Sweeter (5)
Bellmour:	the deeper the Sin the sweeter. Frank I'm amaz'd at thy good	39	OLD BATCH	I.1	92
Bellmour:	the sweeter Breath, for the more cleanly conveyance. But	. 44	OLD BATCH	I.1	258
Heartwell:	Heaven she kisses sweeter than Liberty--I will Marry .	. 74	OLD BATCH	III.2	134
Heartwell:	Heaven her kiss is sweeter than Liberty--I will Marry .	. 74	OLD BATCH	III.2 V134
Miss Prue:	Handkerchief is sweet, pure sweet, sweeter than Roses .	. 249	FOR LOVE	II.1	520

Sweetly (2)
Heartwell:	--hark! (pulling out a Purse and chinking it) how sweetly	72	OLD BATCH	III.2	35
Mirabell:	--What, billing so sweetly! Is not Valentine's Day over	. 423	WAY WORLD	II.1	502

Sweets (1)
Marwood:	pass cur Youth in dull Indifference, to refuse the Sweets	410	WAY WORLD	II.1	13

Swell (1)
Bellmour:	a little time will swell him so, he must be forc'd to give				
	it	. 40	OLD BATCH	I.1	124

Swell'd (1)
	And how their Number's swell'd the Town well knows: .	. 479	WAY WORLD	EPI.	10

Swelling (2)
Lady Touch:	little thou swelling Heart; let me have scme intermission	185	DOUBL DLR	IV.2	65
Almeria:	If for my swelling Heart I can, I'll tell thee. . . .	. 329	M. BRIDE	I.1	109

Swift (2)
Zara:	Swift as Occasion, I	. 354	M. BRIDE	III.1	201
Osmyn-Alph:	Some swift and dire event, of her blind Rage, . . .	. 355	M. BRIDE	III.1	231

Swiftness (1)
Almeria:	Then fly with Joy and Swiftness from me.	. 330	M. BRIDE	I.1	161

Swim (4)
Sir Joseph:	by the help of which, I shall cnce more hope to swim into	49	OLD BATCH	II.1	60
	There, as instinct directs, to Swim, or Drown. . . .	. 125	DOUBL DLR	PRO.	4
Almeria:	Of that refulgent World, where I shall swim . . .	. 340	M. BRIDE	II.2	27
Fainall:	turn'd a drift, like a Leaky hulk to Sink cr Swim, as she	473	WAY WORLD	V.1	443

Swimminess (1)
Lady Wish:	a--Ha Foible? A swimminess in the Eyes--Yes, I'll . .	429	WAY WORLD	III.1	169

Swimming (1)
Silvia:	to our Sex is as natural as swimming to a Negro; we . .	75	OLD BATCH	III.2	151

Swimmingly (1)
Marwood:	Fainall, have you carried it so swimmingly? I thought there	431	WAY WORLD	III.1	229

Swimmingness (1)
Lady Wish:	a--Ha Foible? A swimmingness in the Eyes--Yes, I'll . .	429	WAY WORLD	III.1 V169

Swing (1)
Ben:	chance to swing in a Hammock together.	. 263	FOR LOVE	III.1	377

Swinging (1)
Setter:	precise Band, with a swinging long Spiritual Cloak, to	. 64	OLD BATCH	III.1	124

Swoll'n (1)
Almeria:	Or ever dry these swoll'n, and watry Eyes;	. 329	M. BRIDE	I.1	146

Swollen (1)
Manuel:	What mean those swcllen and redfleck'd Eyes, that look	. 367	M. BRIDE	IV.1	248

Swoon (1)
Lady Wish:	no, I can never advance--I shall swoon if he shou'd . .	429	WAY WORLD	III.1	160

Swooned (1)
Lady Wish:	the Bases roar Blasphemy. O, she wou'd have swooned at	. 467	WAY WORLD	V.1	201

Sword (14)   see Green-sword
Sir Joseph:	have all my ready Mony to redeem his great Sword from .	. 51	OLD BATCH	II.1	131
	(Laying his Hand upon his				
	Sword.)	. 51	OLD BATCH	II.1	149
Capt Bluff:	This Sword I think I was telling you of Mr. Sharper .	. 53	OLD BATCH	II.1	228
Capt Bluff:	--This Sword I'l maintain to be the best Divine, . .	. 53	OLD BATCH	II.1	229
Sir Joseph:	thy Sword I mean.	. 70	OLD BATCH	III.1	347
Capt Bluff:	(Putting up his Sword.)	. 70	OLD BATCH	III.1	350
Araminta:	that a Coward has, while the Sword is in the Scabbard .	. 86	OLD BATCH	IV.3	118
	and Sword in his Hands; as just risen from Table: . .	. 127	DOUBL DLR	I.1	
Mellefont:	Bed-side like a Fury, she flew to my Sword, and with .	. 130	DOUBL DLR	I.1	114
Gonsalez:	In prcving with his Sword, upon your Foes	. 332	M. BRIDE	I.1	257
Gonsalez:	Has better done; in proving with his Sword	. 332	M. BRIDE	I.1 V257
Almeria:	Reproach cuts deeper than the keenest Sword, . . .	. 369	M. BRIDE	IV.1	308
Gonsalez:	I've seen thy Sword do noble Execution.	. 372	M. BRIDE	IV.1	430
Gonsalez:	On me, on me, turn your avenging Sword.	. 378	M. BRIDE	V.2	69

Swords (4)
Lord Touch:	in't with my Swords point.	. 186	DOUBL DLR	IV.2	120
	They hold their Pens, as Swords are held by Fools, . .	. 214	FOR LOVE	PRO.	37
Garcia:	But that we all should turn our Swords, against . . .	. 378	M. BRIDE	V.2	66
Petulant:	I, nothing I. If Throats are to be cut, let Swords . .	. 407	WAY WORLD	I.1	446

Swore (5)
Cynthia:	Pray don't be angry, Sir, when I swore, I had your . .	. 171	DOUBL DLR	IV.1	142
Cynthia:	Consent; and therefore I swore.	. 171	DOUBL DLR	IV.1	143
Ben:	The Souldier Swore like Thunder, ...	. 274	FOR LOVE	III.1	769
Foible:	Book and swore us upon it: But it was but a Book of .	. 464	WAY WORLD	V.1	98
Mincing:	token, you swore us to Secresie upon Messalinas's Poems.	. 474	WAY WORLD	V.1	488

Sworn (13)
Sharper:	(aside). That you are Ile be sworn. Why that's great .	. 51	OLD BATCH	II.1	136
Laetitia:	I durst have sworn, I had heard my Monster's Voice. . .	. 89	OLD BATCH	IV.4	3

Sworn   (continued)
  Cynthia: not him, I have sworn never to Marry.   171   DOUEL DLR   IV.1   135
  Lady Ply: Ay, but Sir Paul, I conceive if she has sworn,   171   DOUBL DLR   IV.1   150
  Lady Ply: d'ye mark me, if she has once sworn: It is most unchristian   171   DOUBL DLR   IV.1   151
  Scandal: the Hand too; and sworn to a truth; but he hopes   . . .   226   FOR LOVE   I.1   375
  Valentine: Livelyhood amongst you. I have been sworn out of   . .   280   FOR LCVE   IV.1   172
  Almeria: I've sworn I'll not wed Garcia; why d'ye force me? . . .   341   M. BRIDE   II.2   74
  Almeria: They wou'd have marry'd me; but I had sworn   . . .   343   M. EBIDE   II.2   126
  Mirabell: acquaintance be General; that you admit no sworn Confident,   451   WAY WCRLD   IV.1   235
  Lady Wish: that he has sworn, the Palpitations that he has felt, the   458   WAY WCRLD   IV.1   513
  Foible: we were sworn to secresie too; Madam Marwood took a   . .   464   WAY WORLD   V.1   97
  Sir Wilful: let him come in; why we are sworn Brothers and fellow   .   471   WAY WCRLD   V.1   346
Sybil (2)
  Valentine: What's here! Erra Pater? or a bearded Sybil? If   283   FOR LOVE   IV.1   274
  Millamant: think of it--I am a Sybil if I am not amaz'd to think   . .   434   WAY WORLD   III.1   357
Sybills (1)
  Sr Sampson: None of old Foresight's Sybills ever utter'd such a   . .   299   FOR LCVE   V.1   79
Syllable (3)
  Sir Paul: I must know what my Girl has to trust to; or not a syllable   192   DOUBL DLR   V.1   176
  Tattle: No, no, not a Syllable--I know that's a Secret, ...   254   FCB LCVE   III.1   47
  Sr Sampson: Manners, that don't believe a Syllable in the Sky and . .   283   FOR LOVE   IV.1   287
Sylvia (9)
  Sharper: only a Trick of Sylvia in Revenge; contriv'd by Lucy. . .   99   OLD BATCH   V.1   109
  Bellmour: discovering the Cheat to Sylvia. She took it at first, as   100   OLD BATCH   V.1   150
  Sharper: chide him about Sylvia.   104   OLD EATCH   V.1   294
  Heartwell: If Sylvia had not been your Whore, my Wife might have . .   109   OLD BATCH   V.2   67
  Heartwell: If Sylvia had not been your Mistress, my Wife might have .   109   OLD BATCH   V.2 V 67
  Vainlove: And if Sylvia had not been your Wife, my Whore   109   OLD EATCH   V.2   69
  Vainlove: And if Sylvia had not been your Wife, my Mistress . . .   109   OLD BATCH   V.2 V 69
                (Re-enter Sharper, with Sir Joseph, Bluffe, Sylvia, Lucy,   110   OLD EATCH   V.2   95
                                          (Sylvia unmasks.)   111   OLD EATCH   V.2   124
Sylvia's (2)
                (Heartwell and Lucy appear at Sylvia's Door.)   96   OLD BATCH   V.1 V 9
  Bellmour: Ha! Is not that Heartwell at Sylvia's Door; be gone   . .   97   OLD BATCH   V.1   10
Symphony (1)
                (Symphcny of Warlike Musick. Enter the King, attended by   332   M. EBIDE   I.1   265
Symptoms (2)
  Heartwell: Take the Symptcms--And ask all the Tyrants   73   OLD BATCH   III.2   76
  Bellmour: Oh, a Convulsion.--I feel the Symptoms.   83   OLD EATCH   IV.2   89
Syren (2)
  Heartwell: ha? Speak Syren--Oons why do I look on her!   72   OLD BATCH   III.2   40
  Fondlewife: Come Syren, speak, confess, who is this reverend, brawny .   92   OLD BATCH   IV.4   137
T' (1)
  Singer-F: Apollo was mute, and had like t' have been pos'd, . . .   259   FOR LCVE   III.1   205
't (2)
  Laetitia: Methinks, 't has been very ill Weather.   90   OLD BATCH   IV.4   38
  Lord Proth: a Captive first, and ever since 't has been in Love with .   140   DOUBL DLR   II.1   69
T'amuze (1)
  Gonsalez: Dispers'd, t'amuze the People; whereupon   363   M. EBIDE   IV.1   82
'thad (3)
  Vainlove: word--Had you been there or any Eody 'thad been the   . .   39   OLD BATCH   I.1   99
  Lucy: --a' receiv'd it, as if 'thad been a Letter from his   . .   61   OLD BATCH   III.1   23
  Maskwell: Indeed I was in hopes 'thad been a youthful Heat . . .   182   DOUEL DLR   IV.1   557
T'impart (1)
  Zara: More than his Crown, t'impart 'ere Osmyn die.   361   M. BRIDE   IV.1   19
T'other (35)
  Sir Joseph: that's a better Jest than tother. 'Tis a sign you and I
                ba'n't   50   OLD BATCH   II.1   116
  Setter: means--I follow one as my Master, but the tother . . .   64   OLD BATCH   III.1   142
  Setter: means--I follow cne as my Master, t'other   64   OLD BATCH   III.1 V142
  Heartwell: to the Musick of their own Chink. This buys all the 'tother   72   OLD BATCH   III.2   37
  Belinda: And t'cther did so stare and gape,--I fansied her like the   84   OLD EATCH   IV.3   45
  Belinda: Free-love's t'cther Day.   84   OLD BATCH   IV.3   56
  Sir Joseph: --A-Gad, t'other Glass of Madera, and I durst have attack'd   85   OLD BATCH   IV.3   68
  Araminta: I'm amaz'd! This Insolence exceeds the t'other;-- . .   87   OLD BATCH   IV.3   156
  Araminta: I'm amaz'd! This Insclence exceeds t'other;--   87   OLD BATCH   IV.3 V156
  Sir Paul: good, strange! I swear I'm almost Tipsy--t'other . . .   131   DOUBL DLR   I.1   178
  Sir Paul: good, strange! I swear I'm almost Tipsie--t'cther . . .   131   DOUBL DLR   I.1 V178
  Brisk: t'other way. Suppose I say a witty thing to you? . . .   134   DOUBL DLR   I.1   278
  Careless: to you--I talk'd to her t'other night at my Lord Froth's   158   DOUBL DLR   III.1   305
  Lady Froth: Then that t'other great strapping Lady--I   166   DOUBL DLR   III.1   580
  Valentine: T'other Glass, and then we'll talk. Fill, Jeremy. . .   222   FOR LOVE   I.1   248
  Tattle: one and t'other, and every thing in the World; and, says I,   227   FOR LOVE   I.1   432
  Scandal: these is a celebrated Beauty, and t'other a profest Beau. I   233   FOB LOVE   I.1   633
  Sr Sampson: t'other spins his Habitation out of his Entrails. . . .   246   FOR LCVE   II.1   393
  Sr Sampson: t'other spins his Habitation out of his own Entrails, . .   246   FOR LOVE   II.1 V393
  Ben: Why then, I'll go to Sea again, so there's one for
                t'other, an   261   FOB LOVE   III.1   300
  Ben: you? You heard t'other handsome Young Woman speak . .   264   FOR LOVE   III.1   410
  Scandal: must pay a Tribute to one, and gc halves with the t'other.   271   FOR LOVE   III.1   677
  Scandal: must pay a Tribute to one, and go halves with t'other. .   271   FOB LCVE   III.1 V677
  Sr Sampson: had Peru in one Hand, and Mexico in t'other, and the . .   300   FOR LCVE   V.1   98
  Angelica: t'other to me--   300   FOR LOVE   V.1   131
  Sr Sampson: --as what?--Odd, as t'other Hand--give me   301   FOR LOVE   V.1   146
  Sr Sampson: t'other Hand, and I'll mumble 'em, and kiss 'em till they   301   FOR LOVE   V.1   147
                These Walls but t'other Day were fill'd with Noise . .   315   FOR LOVE   EPI.   28
                So t'other can foretel by certain Rules   323   M. BRIDE   PRO.   11
  Gonsalez: While t'other bore, the Crown, to wreath thy Brow, . .   378   M. BRIDE   V.2 V 86
  Fainall: and t'cther set your Teeth on edge; one is all Pulp, and .   401   WAY WORLD   I.1   214
  Fainall: To give t'cther his due; he has something of good . . .   401   WAY WORLD   I.1   221
  Fainall: To give t'other his due; he has something of good . .   401   WAY WCRLD   I.1 V221
  Witwoud: t'other of Beauty.   403   WAY WCRLD   I.1   321
  Sir Wilful: will do't. If not, dust it away, and let's have tother
                round--   455   WAY WCBLD   IV.1   412
Tabby-Cat (1)
  Angelica: Tabby-Cat, by turns, I can.   238   FOR LOVE   II.1   122

Take   (continued)

		PAGE	TITLE	ACT.SC	LINE
Maskwell:	Conditions,--if not, here take this; you may employ it better,	199	DOUEL DLR	V.1	450
Lord Froth:	Come my dear, shall we take leave of my Lord	202	DOUEL DLR	V.1	551
Mellefont:	Man!--Take him hence, for he's a Disease to my Sight.	202	DOUEL DLR	V.1	574
	Could Poets but forsee how Plays would take,	204	DOUEL DLR	EPI.	1
Valentine:	Here, take away; I'll walk a turn, and digest what	216	FOR LCVE	I.1	3
Valentine:	your Flesh; Read, and take your Nourishment in at your	216	FOR LCVE	I.1	14
Valentine:	I'll take some of their Trade out of their Hands.	217	FOR LCVE	I.1	60
Scandal:	she may not smell so vigorously.--I shall take the Air	222	FCR LCVE	I.1	220
Valentine:	I agree to 'em, take Mr. Trapland with you, and let him	224	FCR LCVE	I.1	319
Scandal:	Well, begin then: But take notice, if you are so ill a	230	FOR LCVE	I.1	536
Scandal:	Well, on that Condition--Take heed you dcn't	230	FOR LCVE	I.1	544
Valentine:	Pox take 'em, their Conjunction bodes no good,	231	FOR LCVE	I.1	574
Valentine:	Pox take 'em, their Conjunction bodes me no good,	231	FOR LCVE	I.1	V574
Mrs Frail:	take care of my own. Well; but I'll come and see you one	232	FOR LCVE	I.1	597
Angelica:	abroad; and if you won't lend me your Coach, I'll take a	237	FOR LCVE	II.1	67
Foresight:	of the first Magnitude. Take back your Paper of Inheritance;	241	FCR LCVE	II.1	237
Mrs Frail:	go to Covent-Garden Square in a Hackney-Coach, and take	246	FCR LCVE	II.1	419
Mrs Fore:	Nay, two or three Turns, I'll take my Cath.	246	FCR LCVE	II.1	421
Mrs Frail:	take great care when one makes a thrust in Fencing, not to	248	FOR LCVE	II.1	474
Mrs Fore:	often done in Duels, take care of one another, and grow	248	FOR LCVE	II.1	478
Mrs Frail:	take you, you confounded Toad--why did you see	250	FOR LCVE	II.1	566
Tattle:	have given it me, but have suffer'd me tc take it.	252	FOR LCVE	II.1	636
Tattle:	Pox take her; if she had staid two Minutes longer, I	253	FOR LCVE	III.1	17
Tattle:	take me, I beg your Pardon--for I never heard a	254	FOR LCVE	III.1	55
Sr Sampson:	want a little Polishing: You must not take any thing ill,	262	FCR LCVE	III.1	339
Ben:	good part: For if I give a Jest, I'll take a Jest: And so	262	FOR LCVE	III.1	342
Ben:	take a liking to me.--	263	FOR LCVE	III.1	356
Ben:	take your part, Your Tom Essence, and I'll say something to	265	FOR LCVE	III.1	435
Mrs Frail:	Foresight, and Sir Sampson ccming. Sister, do you take Miss	265	FOR LCVE	III.1	447
Scandal:	--you had best take a little Diacodicn and Cowslip	270	FCR LCVE	III.1	638
Scandal:	least I can do to take care of Conscience.	271	FOR LCVE	III.1	683
Scandal:	the liberty I take in Talking, is purely affected, for the	272	FOR LCVE	III.1	697
Scandal:	I saw her take Coach just now with her Maid; and	276	FCR LCVE	IV.1	17
Ben:	man.--I had another Voyage to make, let him take	265	FOR LCVE	IV.1	376
Ben:	Anchor at Cuckolds-point; so there's a dash for you, take	287	FOR LCVE	IV.1	441
Mrs Fore:	her, and Jeremy says will take any body for her that he	288	FOR LCVE	IV.1	469
Jeremy:	I'll take care, and--	290	FOR LCVE	IV.1	566
Angelica:	shall take me.	291	FCR LCVE	IV.1	588
Jeremy:	(to Mrs. Frail). You'll meet, Madam;--I'll take	293	FOR LCVE	IV.1	671
Angelica:	the Fool you take me for; and ycu are Mad and don't	296	FCR LCVE	IV.1	792
Sr Sampson:	O Pox, outsides, outsides; a pize take 'em, meer	298	FOR LCVE	V.1	33
Sr Sampson:	outsides, outsides; a pize take 'em, meer	298	FOR LCVE	V.1	V 33
Sr Sampson:	wou'd take my Advice in a Husband--	300	FCR LCVE	V.1	104
Foresight:	Aye, but pray take me along with you, Sir--	304	FOR LCVE	V.1	279
Foresight:	Here, take your ycung Mistress, and lock her up	306	FCR LCVE	V.1	324
Ben:	Mess you take in all the Points of the Compass, and	306	FOR LCVE	V.1	354
Mrs Fore:	Your Experiment will take up a little too much	306	FOR LCVE	V.1	356
Ben:	Well, well, take you care of your own Helm, cr you	308	FOR LCVE	V.1	420
Tattle:	The Devil take me if ever I was so much concern'd at any	309	FOR LCVE	V.1	460
Valentine:	But on my Knees I take the Blessing.	312	FOR LCVE	V.1	566
	Good Wits, forgive this Liberty we take,	323	M. ERIDE	PRO.	27
	Take your Revenge upon the coming Scenes:	323	M. ERIDE	PRO.	30
Manuel:	Take it for Thanks, Old Man, that I rejoice	333	M. ERIDE	I.1	276
Garcia:	Thus let me kneel to take--O not to take,	334	M. ERIDE	I.1	335
Almeria:	Help me Alphonso, take me, reach thy Hand;	340	M. ERIDE	II.2	31
Almeria:	O take me to thy Arms, and bear me hence,	342	M. ERICE	II.2	84
Osmyn-Alph:	But gently take thy self away, lest she	345	M. ERIDE	II.2	202
Osmyn-Alph:	Nor, should my secret Purpose take Effect,	355	M. ERIDE	III.1	213
Osmyn-Alph:	Or take thee into mine, thus manacled	355	M. ERIDE	III.1	240
Osmyn-Alph:	Or take thee into mine, while I'm thus manacled	355	M. ERIDE	III.1	V240
Almeria:	Upon me--speak, and take me in thy Arms--	356	M. ERIDE	III.1	265
Zara:	As you'll answer it, take heed	360	M. ERIDE	III.1	447
Manuel:	On your Life take heed,	365	M. ERIDE	IV.1	167
Selim:	Madam, take heed; or you have ruin'd all.	366	M. ERIDE	IV.1	185
Manuel:	With damn'd Conspirators, to take my Life.	368	M. ERIDE	IV.1	271
Almeria:	Open thy Bowels of Ccmpassion, take	368	M. ERIDE	IV.1	276
Manuel:	Ha! whc may live? take heed, no more of that.	369	M. ERIDE	IV.1	332
Gonsalez:	Thanks; and I take thee at thy Word. Thou'st seen	372	M. ERIDE	IV.1	432
Manuel:	Dar'st thou reply? Take that--thy Service? thine?	374	M. ERIDE	V.1	69
Manuel:	When for Alphonso's she shall take my Hand,	374	M. ERIDE	V.1	V86D
Zara:	I have not leisure, now, to take so poor	375	M. ERIDE	V.1	123
Almeria:	Yet I will take a cold and parting Leave,	382	M. ERIDE	V.2	266
Fainall:	You don't take your Friend to be overnicely bred.	403	WAY WCBLD	I.1	296
Witwoud:	more Company here to take notice of him--Why	405	WAY WCRLD	I.1	364
Fainall:	Ay, I'll take a turn before Dinner.	409	WAY WCBLD	I.1	509
Petulant:	Not I, by this Hand--I always take blushing	409	WAY WCBLD	I.1	536
Fainall:	unsuspected in my Pleasures; and take you oftner to my	414	WAY WCBLD	II.1	146
Millamant:	Mirabell, Did not you take Exceptions last Night?	420	WAY WCRLD	II.1	377
Millamant:	Mirabell, Did you take Exceptions last Night?	420	WAY WCRLD	II.1	V377
Waitwell:	she can take your Directions as readily as my Instructions,	423	WAY WCRLD	II.1	510
Lady Wish:	A Pox take you both--Fetch me the Cherry-Brandy	425	WAY WCRLD	III.1	20
Lady Wish:	brought! Dost thou take me for a Fairy, to drink out of an	425	WAY WCRLD	III.1	29
Millamant:	I'll take my Death, Marwood, you are more Censorious,	433	WAY WCRLD	III.1	323
Millamant:	what he can see in me. I'll take my Death, I think you are	434	WAY WCRLD	III.1	358
Witwoud:	I hope so--The Devil take him that remembers	437	WAY WCRLD	III.1	477
Marwood:	before they find one another out. You must not take any	438	WAY WCRLD	III.1	506
Marwood:	will come to any Composition to save her reputation, take	442	WAY WCRLD	III.1	661
Fainall:	none to me, she can take none from me, 'tis against all rule	443	WAY WCRLD	III.1	687
Fainall:	but I'll disown the Order. And since I take my leave of 'em,	444	WAY WCRLD	III.1	721
Sir Wilful:	further acquaintance,--So for the present Cozen, I'll take	446	WAY WCBLD	IV.1	77
Mrs Fain:	Ay, ay, take him, take him, what shou'd you	452	WAY WCRLD	IV.1	286
Millamant:	Well then--I'll take my death I'm in a horrid	452	WAY WCRLD	IV.1	288
Mrs Fain:	you,--If you doubt him, you had best take up with Sir	453	WAY WCRLD	IV.1	318
Sir Wilful:	Bill--Give me more drink and take my Purse.	455	WAY WCRLD	IV.1	395

Talk   (continued)

		PAGE	TITLE	ACT.SC	LINE
Osmyn-Alph:	Why dost thou ask? why dost thou talk thus piercingly?	357	M. BRIDE	III.1	V308
Osmyn-Alph:	O--thou dost talk, my Love, as one resolv'd,	358	M. BRIDE	III.1	341
Manuel:	To talk with you. Come near, why dost thou shake?	367	M. BRIDE	IV.1	247
Osmyn-Alph:	O let me talk to thy reviving Sense,	383	M. BRIDE	V.2	280
Witwoud:	him, don't let's talk of him;--Fainall, how does your	402	WAY WORLD	I.1	254
Witwoud:	Domestick. But I talk like an old Maid at a Marriage, I	402	WAY WORLD	I.1	258
Mirabell:	selves talk.	421	WAY WORLD	II.1	418
	(Fainall and Mrs. Marwood talk a-part.)	441	WAY WORLD	III.1	610
Foible:	talk with you. Tho' my Lady's Orders were to leave you	445	WAY WORLD	IV.1	45
Mirabell:	and, Authoriz'd Tea-Table talk,--such as mending of	451	WAY WORLD	IV.1	267
Mrs Fain:	--You have neither time to talk nor stay. My Mother	452	WAY WORLD	IV.1	299
Marwood:	after, talk it all over again in Commons, or before Drawers	467	WAY WORLD	V.1	226
Marwood:	after, talk it over again in Commons, or before Drawers	467	WAY WORLD	V.1	V226
Sir Wilful:	you talk of an Instrument Sir, I have an old Fox by my	473	WAY WORLD	V.1	425

Talk'd (9)

Sir Joseph:	Rogue look, when she talk'd of Sir Joseph? Did not her	103	OLD BATCH	V.1	254
Careless:	to you--I talk'd to her t'other night at my Lord Froth's	158	DOUBL DLR	III.1	305
Mrs Frail:	there's a Match talk'd of by the Old People--Well,	231	FOR LOVE	I.1	569
Tattle:	told Particulars, Madam. Perhaps I might have talk'd as of a	256	FOR LOVE	III.1	117
Tattle:	afterwards, for it was talk'd of in Town--And a Lady of	258	FOR LOVE	III.1	174
Angelica:	Why he talk'd very sensibly just now.	295	FOR LOVE	IV.1	746
Witwoud:	Ay, we'll all walk in the Park, the Ladies talk'd of	409	WAY WORLD	I.1	510
Mrs Fain:	She talk'd last Night of endeavouring at a	418	WAY WORLD	II.1	303
Millamant:	Nay, he has done nothing; he has only talk'd--	432	WAY WORLD	III.1	291

Talk'st (1)

Zara:	Thou canst not mean so poorly, as thou talk'st.	348	M. BRIDE	II.2	331

Talked (10)

Belinda:	Oh you have raved, talked idly, and all in	54	OLD BATCH	II.2	4

Talking (10)

Belinda:	than your talking Impertinence; as an Ape is a much more	60	OLD BATCH	II.2	213
Lucy:	Heartwell, who stands talking at the Corner--'tis he--	62	OLD BATCH	III.1	47
Vainlove:	He's talking to himself, I think; Prithee lets try if	62	OLD BATCH	III.1	61
Lord Touch:	Talking to himself!	188	DOUBL DLR	V.1	17
Maskwell:	but what is my distraction doing? I am wildly talking to my	188	DOUBL DLR	V.1	43
Scandal:	Yes, but I dare trust you; We were talking of	254	FOR LOVE	III.1	45
Mrs Fore:	so--He has been subject to Talking and Starting.	270	FOR LOVE	III.1	620
Scandal:	the liberty I take in Talking, is purely affected, for the	272	FOR LOVE	III.1	697
Witwoud:	just when you had been talking to him--As	405	WAY WORLD	I.1	370
Witwoud:	But I know a Lady that loves talking so incessantly,	421	WAY WORLD	II.1	419

Talks (10)

Bellmour:	talks of sending for Mr. Spintext to keep me Company; but	39	OLD BATCH	I.1	83
Lady Ply:	. . . and he talks charmingly,	174	DOUBL DLR	IV.1	V259
Lady Touch:	My Lord, you hear him--he talks Idly.	186	DOUBL DLR	IV.2	117
Lady Touch:	Alas he raves! talks very Poetry! for Heavens	186	DOUBL DLR	IV.2	127
Sir Paul:	I must consult my Wife,--he talks of disinheriting his	192	DOUBL DLR	V.1	174
Nurse:	O merciful Father, how she talks!	237	FOR LOVE	II.1	95
Scandal:	and the Wise Foresight; talks of Raymond Lully, and the	266	FOR LOVE	III.1	499
Sr Sampson:	Body o' me, he talks sensibly in his madness--	280	FOR LOVE	IV.1	180
Mrs Frail:	me; Sir Sampson is enrag'd, and talks desperately of	287	FOR LOVE	IV.1	458
Angelica:	Mercy on me, how he talks! poor Valentine!	294	FOR LOVE	IV.1	705

Tall (1)

Almeria:	How rev'rend is the Face of this tall Pile,	339	M. BRIDE	II.1	59

Tallies (1)

Sr Sampson:	and my Fatherly fondness wou'd fit like two Tallies.--	243	FOR LOVE	II.1	294

Tallow-Chandler (1)

Lady Wish:	Smells! he would poison a Tallow-Chandler	456	WAY WORLD	IV.1	436

Tame (1)

Valentine:	Legs at liberty, and Tame Cuckolds, with Chains about	289	FOR LOVE	IV.1	512

Tampering (1)

Maskwell:	You have already been tampering with my Lady	137	DOUBL DLR	I.1	406

Tantaliz'd (2)

Waitwell:	am tantaliz'd on a rack; And do but hang Madam, on the	457	WAY WORLD	IV.1	492
Waitwell:	am tantaliz'd on the rack; And do but hang Madam, on the	457	WAY WORLD	IV.1	V492

Tantalized (1)

Sir Paul:	he would have tantalized thee, and made a Cuckold of thy	146	DOUBL DLR	II.1	279

Tantony (2)

Sir Wilful:	My Tantony, Sirrah thou sha't be my Tantony; and I'll	457	WAY WORLD	IV.1	477

Tapers (1)

Zara:	And watch like Tapers o'er your Hours of Rest.	360	M. BRIDE	III.1	429

Tapestry-hanging (1)

Millamant:	of the Child in an old Tapestry-hanging.	422	WAY WORLD	II.1	469

Tapster (1)

Lady Wish:	thou go with the Bottle in thy Hand like a Tapster. As I'm	426	WAY WORLD	III.1	35

Tar-barrel (2)

Miss Prue:	Tar-barrel.	264	FOR LOVE	III.1	431
Ben:	Tar-barrel? Let your Sweet-heart there call me so, if he'll	264	FOR LOVE	III.1	434

Tarpaulin (1)

Sr Sampson:	Why you impudent Tarpaulin! Sirrah, do you	308	FOR LOVE	V.1	422

Tarpawlin (1)

Mrs Fore:	great lubberly Tarpawlin--Gad I warrant you, she	250	FOR LOVE	II.1	562

Tarr (2)

Mrs Frail:	Creature, that smells all of Pitch and Tarr--Devil	250	FOR LOVE	II.1	565
Mrs Frail:	have seen the Resolution of a Lover,--Honest Tarr and	287	FOR LOVE	IV.1	450

Tarry (5)

Fondlewife:	I say I will tarry at home.	75	OLD BATCH	IV.1	14
Fondlewife:	hath possess'd the Lad--I say I will tarry at home--Varlet.	75	OLD BATCH	IV.1	17
Fondlewife:	I'le tarry, d'ee see.	76	OLD BATCH	IV.1	37
Fondlewife:	If you will tarry a Moment, till I fetch my Papers, I'll wait	90	OLD BATCH	IV.4	43
Sir Wilful:	. . . have Thoughts to tarry a small	440	WAY WORLD	III.1	581

Tartars (1)

Lady Wish:	get thee but far enough, to the Saracens or the Tartars, or	456	WAY WORLD	IV.1	439

Tartary (1)

Sr Sampson:	Hunting upon an Elephant with the Cham of Tartary--	241	FOR LOVE	II.1	221

Tedious-wasting (1)
Manuel: And Love, shall wing the tedious-wasting Day.   . . . . 349 M. EBIDE   II.2   388
Teens (1)
Lady Wish: in her Teens. As I'm a Person 'tis true--She was   . . 466 WAY WORLD   V.1   188
Teeth (14)
Sharper: the Teeth of opposition.   . . . . 42 OLD BATCH   I.1   203
Sir Joseph: Teeth. Adsheart if he should come just now when I'm   . 68 OLD EATCH   III.1 278
Brisk: Ay, my Lord, it's a sign I hit you in the Teeth, if you   . 132 DOUEL DLR   I.1   210
Sir Paul: dye of 'em, like any Child, that were cutting his Teeth--   146 DOUEL DLR   II.1   283
Sir Paul: die of 'em, like a Child, that was cutting his Teeth--   146 DOUEL DLR   II.1 V283
Lady Ply: So gay, so graceful, so good teeth, so fine shape,   . 160 DOUEL DLR   III.1 367
Lord Froth: 'tis such a sight to see some teeth--sure you're a great   . 162 DOUEL DLR   III.1 460
               Or only shews its Teeth, as if it smil'd.   . . . . . 213 FOR LOVE   PRO.   34
Foresight: Capricorn in your Teeth, thou Modern Mandevil;   . 241 FOR LCVE   II.1   235
Ben: indeed, and full in my Teeth. Look you forsooth, I am as   . 263 FCB LCVE   III.1 371
Mrs Frail: and Scales, and three rows of Teeth, a most outragious   . 286 FOR LCVE   IV.1   401
Gonsalez: With gnashing Teeth, the Dust his Tryumphs raise.   . . . 332 M. EBIDE   I.1   237
Manuel: His Teeth may grin, and mock at her Remorse.   . . . . . 374 M. EBIDE   V.1   78
Fainall: and t'other set your Teeth on edge; one is all Pulp, and   . 401 WAY WCRLD   I.1   214
Tell (248)
Vainlove: Oh the Wise will tell you--   . . . . 37 OLD BATCH   I.1   15
Sharper: tell us.   . . . . 52 OLD BATCH   II.1   191
Capt Bluff: Gazette--I'll tell you a strange thing now as to that--   . 52 OLD EATCH   II.1   194
Sir Joseph: Let me but tell Mr. Sharper a little, how you eat   . 53 OLD BATCH   II.1   218
Sir Joseph: Look you now, I tell you he's so modest he'l own   . 53 OLD BATCH   II.1   222
Araminta: can tell you more.   . . . . 55 OLD BATCH   II.2   47
Belinda: Devil take Bellmour--Why do you tell me of him?   . . . 56 OLD BATCH   II.2   57
Araminta: you love him. I tell no Body else Cousin--I have not   . 56 OLD BATCH   II.2   59
Belinda: Prithee tell it all the World, it's false. Betty. (Calls)   . 56 OLD BATCH   II.2   61
Araminta: I can't tell, Cousin, I believe we are equally concern'd: 57 OLD BATCH   II.2   85
Bellmour: But tell me how you would be Ador'd--I am very   . . 59 OLD BATCH   II.2   173
Bellmour: let me tell you, my standing Argument is depress'd in   . 59 OLD BATCH   II.2   183
Bellmour: let me tell you, my most prevailing Argument is express'd in 59 OLD BATCH   II.2 V183
Silvia: Why did you not tell me?--Whom mean you?   . . . . . 61 OLD BATCH   III.1   4
Silvia: Well, since there's no remedy--Yet tell me--   . . . . 61 OLD BATCH   III.1   14
Silvia: how did he refuse? Tell me--how did he receive my   . 61 OLD BATCH   III.1   16
Lucy: Come tell me in plain Terms, how forward he is   . . . 66 OLD BATCH   III.1 222
Capt Bluff: Well, go to him from me--Tell him, I say, he   . . 68 OLD BATCH   III.1 258
Capt Bluff: ensue--If he refuse, tell him--But whisper that--Tell   . 68 OLD BATCH   III.1 260
Sir Joseph: Office--So tell him your self.   . . . . 68 OLD BATCH   III.1 267
Sir Joseph: angry, I'd tell him--Mum.   . . . . 68 OLD BATCH   III.1 279
Sharper: Hey day! Captain, what's the matter? You can tell.   . . 69 OLD BATCH   III.1 295
Heartwell: --I tell thee I do love thee, and tell it for a Truth,   . 72 OLD BATCH   III.2   63
Silvia: Never tell me that, I know it is not chang'd by my   . . 73 OLD BATCH   III.2 105
Fondlewife: Tell me Isaac, why art thee Jealous? Why art thee
                   distrustful   . . . . 76 OLD EATCH   IV.1   50
Fondlewife: No no, I tell you I shall have it in my Head--   . . . . 77 OLD BATCH   IV.1   83
Belinda: like one of 'em:--Good Dear, pin this, and I'll tell you.   83 OLD BATCH   IV.3   13
Araminta: You were about to tell me something, Child,--   . . . 83 OLD BATCH   IV.3   21
Laetitia: been in such a fright, that I forgot to tell you, poor Mr.   . 91 OLD BATCH   IV.4   77
Bellmour: Reasons for what I do, which I'll tell you within.--In   . 98 OLD EATCH   V.1   69
Vainlove: And where did you tell her?   . . . . 99 OLD BATCH   V.1   117
Vainlove: --And why did you not find me out, to tell me this   . . 99 OLD BATCH   V.1   120
Sharper: thy Mirth: Hear thee tell thy mighty Jest, with as much   . 100 OLD BATCH   V.1   138
Bellmour: Countenance. But, to tell you something you don't know.   . 100 OLD BATCH   V.1   148
Sir Joseph: be pick'd out of Aesop's Fables, let me tell you that; and 101 OLD EATCH   V.1   176
Sharper: Why, I'll tell you: 'Tis a young Creature that Vainlove 104 OLD BATCH   V.1   292
Setter: Sir, I'll tell you.   . . . . 106 OLD BATCH   V.1   353
Bellmour: Corner-House, and I'll tell you by the way what may   . 107 OLD BATCH   V.1   402
Bellmour: not you tell me?--   . . . . 112 OLD BATCH   V.2   179
               To tell you, he already does repent: . . . . . 113 OLD BATCH   EPI.   6
Brisk: want of Apprehension: The Deuce take me if I tell you.   . 128 DOUEL DLR   I.1   42
Mellefont: this Juncture it will do me Service.--I'll tell you, I   . 129 DOUEL DLR   I.1   67
Brisk: little shallow, or so.--Why I'll tell you now, suppose   . 133 DOUEL DLR   I.1   252
Brisk: to tell me--still I look grave, not so much as   . . . 134 DOUEL DLR   I.1   258
Careless: you suppose I can't tell you?   . . . . 134 DOUEL DLR   I.1   261
Brisk: tell you, you shall tell me--at last.--But it shall be   . 134 DOUEL DLR   I.1   263
Brisk: Well then, you tell me, some good Jest, or very Witty   . 134 DOUEL DLR   I.1   267
Brisk: can't tell how to make him Apprehend,--take it   . . . 134 DOUEL DLR   I.1   277
Lady Froth: Did my Lord tell you? Yes I vow, and the Subject   . . 141 DOUEL DLR   II.1   120
Brisk: Lactilla may be--'gad I cannot tell.   . . . . . . 141 DOUEL DLR   II.1   128
Lady Ply: Fiddle, faddle, don't tell me of this and that, and   . 146 DOUEL DLR   II.1   301
Maskwell: of Doors; and to--ha, ha, ha, I can't tell you for Laughing, 149 DOUEL DLR   II.1   401
Mellefont: outwitted Woman.--But tell me, how could'st thou thus   . 149 DOUEL DLR   II.1   408
Maskwell: It was, and to tell you the truth, I encouraged it for   . 149 DOUEL DLR   II.1   412
Maskwell: anon, after that I'll tell you the whole matter; be here in 149 DOUEL DLR   II.1   434
Lady Touch: That I can't tell: nay, I don't say there was--   . . . 151 DOUEL DLR   III.1   23
Lord Touch: more trifling--I charge you tell me--by all our   . . . 152 DOUEL DLR   III.1   62
Lady Touch: you have frighted me. Nay, look pleas'd, I'll tell you.   . 152 DOUEL DLR   III.1   70
Lady Touch: --nay, I won't tell you any more, till you are your   . 153 DOUEL DLR   III.1 111
Lady Touch: let me beg you do now: I'll come immediately, and tell   . 153 DOUEL DLR   III.1 119
Lady Touch: I'll do it--I'll tell him you hindred   . . . . . . 155 DOUEL DLR   III.1 162
Mellefont: Did not she tell you at what a distance she keeps him. He 158 DOUEL DLR   III.1 284
Sir Paul: You'll scarcely believe me, when I shall tell you why   . 161 DOUEL DLR   III.1 430
Sir Paul: You'll scarcely believe me, when I shall tell you--   . 161 DOUEL DLR   III.1 V430
Sir Paul: success. Boy, tell my Lady, when she has done, I would   . 163 DOUEL DLR   III.1 498
Lord Froth: Shall I tell you now?   . . . . 166 DOUEL DLR   III.1 598
Lady Ply: have charm'd him; and so I'll tell him in the Wardrobe   . 174 DOUEL DLR   IV.1 261
Brisk: Sir Paul, Gads-bud you're an uncivil Person, let me tell   . 174 DOUEL DLR   IV.1 267
Brisk: tell whether I am glad or sorry that your Ladiship has made 176 DOUEL DLR   IV.1 339
Lady Froth: purely, but I vow Mr. Brisk, I can't tell how to come so   . 177 DOUEL DLR   IV.1 368
Lady Ply: live to tell it you.   . . . . 178 DOUEL DLR   IV.1 394
Careless: effects that will have, but I'll be sure to tell you when
                   I do, ... 180 DOUEL DLR   IV.1 502
Sir Paul: I can't tell you I'm so overjoy'd; come along with me   . 181 DOUEL DLR   IV.1 508
Maskwell: to tell you more.   . . . . 183 DOUEL DLR   IV.1 586

Tell   (continued)

		PAGE	TITLE	ACT.SC	LINE
Lord Touch:	I tell you, he confess'd it to me.	191	DOUEL DLR	V.1	V133
Maskwell:	Why, I intend to tell my Lord the whole matter of .	193	DOUEL DLR	V.1	214
Maskwell:	Why, I'll tell my Lord, I laid this Plot with you, . .	193	DOUEL DLR	V.1	217
Mellefont:	O I conceive you, you'll tell him so?	193	DOUEL DLR	V.1	226
Maskwell:	Tell him so! Ay, why you don't think I mean to . .	193	DOUEL DLR	V.1	227
Maskwell:	No, nc, I'll after him immediately, and tell him. .	194	DOUEL DLR	V.1	259
Maskwell:	(aside). This I fear'd. Did not your Lordship tell .	195	DOUEL DLR	V.1	312
Lord Touch:	Here's Ccmpany--come this way and tell	196	DOUEL DLR	V.1	329
Cynthia:	Did Maskwell tell you any thing of the Chaplain's .	196	DOUEL DLR	V.1	341
Lady Touch:	Uncertainty. Speak then, and tell me--yet are you .	198	DOUEL DLR	V.1	400
Maskwell:	and when you have temper, tell me.	198	DOUEL DLR	V.1	409
Maskwell:	for you.--First tell me what urg'd you to this violence?	198	DOUEL DLR	V.1	413
Lady Ply:	You tell me most surprizing things; bless me	202	DOUEL DLR	V.1	545
	Then they could tell what Epilogues to make;	204	DOUEL DLR	EPI.	2
Valentine:	But tell me what you would have me do?--What do . . .	220	FOR LOVE	I.1	157
Valentine:	But tell me what you would have me do?--What does . .	220	FOR LOVE	I.1	V157
Jeremy:	now tc tell 'em in plain downright English--	220	FOR LOVE	I.1	173
Snap:	must dc our Office, tell us.--We have half a dozen . .	224	FOR LOVE	I.1	296
Tattle:	it their Business to tell Stories, and say this and that of	227	FOR LOVE	I.1	431
Tattle:	To tell.	228	FOR LOVE	I.1	462
Scandal:	To tell what? Why, what do ycu know of Mrs.	228	FOR LOVE	I.1	463
Tattle:	Tho' I have more Honour than to tell first; I have more .	229	FOR LOVE	I.1	478
Tattle:	O Barbarous! why did you not tell me--	229	FOR LOVE	I.1	494
Valentine:	will prove all that he can tell her.	229	FCR LOVE	I.1	513
Mrs Frail:	Well, I'll tell you News; but I suppose you hear your .	231	FOR LOVE	I.1	566
Valentine:	Tell Angelica, I am about making hard Conditions . .	234	FOR LOVE	I.1	673
Servant:	I can't tell indeed, Sir.	235	FCR LOVE	II.1	14
Foresight:	No, I know you can't, Sir: But I can tell, Sir, and .	235	FOR LOVE	II.1	15
Foresight:	No, I know you can't, Sir: But I can tell and . . .	235	FOR LOVE	II.1	V 15
Foresight:	Sirrah, go tell Sir Sampson Legend I'll wait on him, if .	236	FOR LOVE	II.1	40
Foresight:	something; tell me, and I'll forgive you; do, good Neice	239	FOR LOVE	II.1	147
Foresight:	Come, I know Women tell cne ancther--She is	239	FOR LOVE	II.1	150
Foresight:	tell me--won't you speak? Odd I'll--	239	FOR LOVE	II.1	158
Angelica:	out my Aunt, and tell her, she must not come home. . .	239	FOR LOVE	II.1	162
Foresight:	past: Go Nurse, tell Sir Sampson I'm ready to wait on him.	239	FCR LOVE	II.1	166
Foresight:	contradict you, and tell you, you are ignorant. . . .	240	FOR LOVE	II.1	203
Sr Sampson:	to confound your Ephemeris--Ignorant!--I tell . . .	240	FOR LOVE	II.1	206
Sr Sampson:	I tell you I am wise; and sapiens dominabitur astris; .	240	FOR LOVE	II.1	204
Foresight:	But I tell you, I have travell'd, and travell'd in the .	241	FOR LOVE	II.1	210
Jeremy:	begot me too:--Nay, and to tell your Worship	245	FCR LOVE	II.1	361
Mrs Frail:	I'll acquaint you with a design that I have: To tell Truth,	248	FOR LOVE	II.1	486
Mrs Fore:	power--And I can tell you one thing that falls out luckily	248	FOR LOVE	II.1	498
Tattle:	O fie Miss, you must not kiss and tell.	249	FOR LOVE	II.1	523
Miss Prue:	Yes, I may tell my Mother--And he says he'll . . .	249	FOR LOVE	II.1	524
Miss Prue:	too? You must tell me how.	251	FCB LOVE	II.1	597
Tattle:	can't tell--	251	FOR LOVE	II.1	608
Miss Prue:	Why, must I tell a Lie then?	251	FOR LOVE	II.1	609
Tattle:	but you must Love me too--If I tell you you are . . .	252	FOR LOVE	II.1	615
Miss Prue:	O Gemini! well, I always had a great mind to tell . .	252	FOR LOVE	II.1	629
Miss Prue:	O Lord, she's coming--and she'll tell my	253	FOR LOVE	III.1	15
Miss Prue:	O Dear, what shall I say? Tell me, Mr. Tattle, tell .	253	FOR LOVE	III.1	19
Tattle:	There's no occasion for a Lie; I cou'd never tell a Lie .	253	FOR LOVE	III.1	21
Scandal:	Why, is the Devil in you? Did not I tell it you for a .	255	FOR LOVE	III.1	59
Valentine:	tell whether the Lady or Mr. Tattle be the more obliged	256	FOR LOVE	III.1	130
Scandal:	No dcn't; for then you'l tell us no more--Ccme, I'll .	258	FOR LOVE	III.1	190
Ben:	were sinking, as we sayn at Sea. But I'll tell you why I .	261	FOR LOVE	III.1	308
Ben:	But I'll tell you one thing, and you come to Sea in a .	262	FCR LOVE	III.1	330
Miss Prue:	better not speak at all, I think, and truly I won't tell				
	a lie	263	FOR LOVE	III.1	383
Miss Prue:	always tell a lie to a man; and I don't care, let my Father	264	FOR LOVE	III.1	397
Miss Prue:	do what he will; I'm too big to be whipt, so I'll tell you	264	FOR LOVE	III.1	398
Ben:	Whipping no more than you do. But I tell you one thing, .	264	FOR LOVE	III.1	407
Mrs Fore:	Come, Miss, come along with me, and tell	265	FOR LOVE	III.1	444
Sr Sampson:	tell him in a Dream, that he must not part with his Estate:	267	FOR LOVE	III.1	507
Sr Sampson:	But I'll bring him a Parson to tell him, that the Devil's a	267	FOR LOVE	III.1	508
Scandal:	Pray lend it him, Madam--I'll tell you the	269	FOR LOVE	III.1	584
Mrs Fore:	to me before my Husband's Face? I'll Swear I'll tell him. .	269	FOR LOVE	III.1	594
Scandal:	Passion. But come a little farther this way, and I'll				
	tell you	269	FOB LOVE	III.1	596
Mrs Fore:	O, mighty restless, but I was afraid to tell him . . .	270	FOR LOVE	III.1	619
Mrs Fore:	Pish, you'd tell me so, tho' you did not think . . .	272	FCB LOVE	III.1	707
Scandal:	And you'd think so, tho' I should not tell you so: . .	272	FOR LOVE	III.1	709
Ben:	Nay, an I love once, I'll stick like pitch; I'll tell				
	you that.	273	FOR LOVE	III.1	739
Angelica:	tell me what is the matter.	276	FOR LOVE	IV.1	28
Angelica:	my self oblig'd to--pray tell me truth.	277	FOR LOVE	IV.1	44
Angelica:	upon one fearful of Affliction, to tell me what I . .	277	FOR LOVE	IV.1	58
Angelica:	am to hope for--I cannot speak--But you may tell me, .	277	FOR LOVE	IV.1	59
Angelica:	tell me, for you know what I wou'd ask?	277	FOR LOVE	IV.1	60
Sr Sampson:	Speak to be understood, and tell me in plain Terms what .	279	FOR LOVE	IV.1	135
Valentine:	--No matter how long--But I'll tell you one	280	FOR LOVE	IV.1	174
Valentine:	For my part, I am Truth, and can't tell; I have very .	280	FOR LOVE	IV.1	178
Valentine:	I can't tell whether I know it cr no.	281	FOR LOVE	IV.1	218
Sr Sampson:	Ptolcmee tell you? Your Messahalah and your Longomontanus,	283	FOR LOVE	IV.1	284
Scandal:	Madam, you and I can tell him something else, that . .	284	FOR LOVE	IV.1	311
Ben:	tell him so much.--So he said he'd make my heart ake, .	285	FOR LOVE	IV.1	380
Mrs Frail:	on the Shore. But I'll tell you a hint that he has given .	287	FOR LOVE	IV.1	457
Mrs Fore:	come, stand aside a little, and tell me how you like the .	288	FOR LOVE	IV.1	476
Valentine:	have told thee what's past,--Now I tell what's to . .	288	FOR LOVE	IV.1	489
Valentine:	have told thee what's past,--Now I'll tell what's to .	288	FOR LOVE	IV.1	V489
Valentine:	--Answer me not--for I will tell thee. To	288	FOR LOVE	IV.1	491
Valentine:	Scandal will tell you;--I am Truth, I never	288	FOR LOVE	IV.1	497
Valentine:	Heark'ee;--I have a Secret to tell you--	290	FOR LOVE	IV.1	546
Valentine:	closer--that none may over-hear us;--Jeremy, I can tell you	290	FOR LOVE	IV.1	557
Angelica:	I never lov'd him till he was Mad; but don't tell . . .	291	FOR LOVE	IV.1	572

Tell   (continued)

Tattle:	Tell, Madam! alas you don't know me--I have	. 291	FOR LOVE	IV.1	575
Tattle:	much ado to tell your Ladyship, how long I have been in .	. 291	FOR LOVE	IV.1	576
Valentine:	If they are, I'll tell you what I think--get away all the	. 291	FOR LOVE	IV.1	594
Tattle:	Why de'e think I'll tell you, Sir! Read it in my Face?	. 292	FOR LOVE	IV.1	612
Valentine:	about,--They are welcome, and I'll tell 'em so my self. (To	. 292	FOR LOVE	IV.1	617
Valentine:	should tell, yet she is not to be believ'd.	. 292	FOR LOVE	IV.1	646
Singer-V:	I tell thee, Charmion, could I Time retrieve, ...	. 293	FOR LOVE	IV.1	652
Valentine:	Why you Thick-Skull'd Rascal, I tell you the Farce . . .	. 295	FOR LOVE	IV.1	749
Angelica:	But I'll tell you two things before I leave you; I am not .	. 296	FOR LOVE	IV.1	791
Angelica:	Where is Sir Sampson? Did you not tell me, he	. 297	FOR LOVE	V.1	1
Sr Sampson:	a Lady any way--Come, come, let me tell you, you . . .	. 298	FOR LOVE	V.1	24
Angelica:	Courage at this time. To tell you the Truth, I'm weary of .	. 298	FOR LOVE	V.1	46
Angelica:	Sir Sampson, as your Friend, I must tell you, you . . .	. 299	FOR LOVE	V.1	86
Angelica:	I can tell you how that may be done--But it is a . . .	. 299	FOR LOVE	V.1	90
Jeremy:	Well, Sir, I'll go and tell her my Master's coming; . .	. 303	FOR LOVE	V.1	215
Miss Prue:	O I have pure News, I can tell you pure News--I . . .	. 303	FOR LOVE	V.1	226
Tattle:	Ay, but your Father will tell you that Dreams come . .	. 303	FOR LOVE	V.1	240
Tattle:	Pshaw, but I tell you, you would not--You forget . . .	. 304	FOR LOVE	V.1	252
Foresight:	'Tis not convenient to tell you now--Mr.	. 306	FOR LOVE	V.1	331
Mrs Fore:	Here's Mr. Benjamin, he can tell us if his Father . .	. 306	FOR LOVE	V.1	339
Ben:	Why then I'll tell you, There's a new wedding upon the .	. 307	FOR LOVE	V.1	358
Ben:	That may be--but I'm sure it is as I tell you.	. 307	FOR LOVE	V.1	366
Ben:	along with her, she'll break her Cable, I can tell you that.	. 310	FOR LOVE	V.1	494
	It's like what I have heard our Poets tell us: . . .	. 315	FOR LOVE	EPI.	6
Almeria:	Thou canst not tell--thou hast indeed no Cause. . . .	. 326	M. BRIDE	I.1	19
Almeria:	If I should tell thee, wouldst thou pity me?	. 328	M. BRIDE	I.1	91
Almeria:	Tell me? I know thou wouldst, thou art compassionate. .	. 328	M. BRIDE	I.1	92
Almeria:	But I did promise I would tell thee--What?	. 328	M. BRIDE	I.1	98
Almeria:	If for my swelling Heart I can, I'll tell thee. . . .	. 329	M. BRIDE	I.1	109
Alonzo:	The Lord Gonsalez comes to tell your Highness . . .	. 331	M. BRIDE	I.1	209
Manuel:	I tell thee she's to blame, not to have feasted . . .	. 333	M. BRIDE	I.1	307
Leonora:	I go; but Heav'n can tell with what Regret.	. 339	M. BRIDE	II.1	84
Almeria:	Indeed I wou'd--Nay, I wou'd tell thee all	. 343	M. BRIDE	II.2	129
Osmyn-Alph:	To part no more; my Friend will tell thee all; . . .	. 345	M. BRIDE	II.2	205
Osmyn-Alph:	As I am. Tell me, may I hope to see her?	. 351	M. BRIDE	III.1	46
Zara:	So thou dost think; then, do but tell me so; . . .	. 353	M. BRIDE	III.1	164
Zara:	Tell me, and thou shall see how I'll revenge . . .	. 353	M. BRIDE	III.1	165
Zara:	Tell me, and thou shalt see how I'll revenge . . .	. 353	M. BRIDE	III.1 V165
Zara:	Have I done this? tell me, am I so curs'd? . . .	. 354	M. BRIDE	III.1	197
Almeria:	Give thy Soul Way, and tell me thy dark Thought. . .	. 356	M. BRIDE	III.1	274
Almeria:	Then knowing thou hast felt it. Tell it me. . . .	. 356	M. BRIDE	III.1	279
Almeria:	Than knowing thou hast felt it. Tell it me. . . .	. 356	M. BRIDE	III.1 V279
Zara:	Find out the King, tell him I have of Weight . . .	. 361	M. BRIDE	IV.1	18
Selim:	However, for a Colour, tell him, you	. 362	M. BRIDE	IV.1	50
Zara:	I think it fit to tell you that your Guards . . .	. 364	M. BRIDE	IV.1	142
Gonsalez:	Hold, let me think--if I shou'd tell the King-- . .	. 371	M. BRIDE	IV.1	403
Alonzo:	Require me not to tell the Means, till done, . . .	. 378	M. BRIDE	V.2	97
Zara:	The King; tell him, what he requir'd, I've done: . .	. 380	M. BRIDE	V.2	152
	To tell of what Disease the Play expir'd.	. 385	M. BRIDE	EPI.	10
Mirabell:	tell her so.	. 399	WAY WORLD	I.1	155
Mirabell:	agreeable. I'll tell thee, Fainall, she once us'd me with				
	that	. 399	WAY WORLD	I.1	163
Betty:	I'll tell him.	. 404	WAY WORLD	I.1	349
Witwoud:	to tell you a Secret, these are Trulls	. 405	WAY WORLD	I.1	359
Petulant:	Places. Pox on 'em I won't come.--Dee hear, tell 'em .	. 405	WAY WORLD	I.1	386
Mirabell:	Was there any mention made of my Uncle, or me? Tell .	. 407	WAY WORLD	I.1	451
Mirabell:	wo't tell me.	. 407	WAY WORLD	I.1	457
Witwoud:	her, I shou'd--Hearkee--To tell you a Secret, but let it go	. 407	WAY WORLD	I.1	467
Witwoud:	Faith, my Dear, I can't tell; she's a Woman and a .	. 408	WAY WORLD	I.1	492
Mrs Fain:	The only Man that would tell me so at least; . . .	. 412	WAY WORLD	II.1	92
Millamant:	To hear you tell me that Foible's married, and your .	. 422	WAY WORLD	II.1	482
Millamant:	To hear you tell me Foible's married, and your . . .	. 422	WAY WORLD	II.1 V482
Millamant:	unless she shou'd tell me her self. Which of the two it	. 423	WAY WORLD	II.1	486
Foible:	seen me with you I'm sure she'll tell my Lady. I'll make	. 424	WAY WORLD	II.1	546
Foible:	Heart still. Now, Madam, I can safely tell your Ladyship	. 430	WAY WORLD	III.1	205
Millamant:	Mincing, tell the Men they may come up. My Aunt is not	. 433	WAY WORLD	III.1	325
Marwood:	Thing impossible, when I shall tell him, by telling you--	. 434	WAY WORLD	III.1	351
Sir Wilful:	tell her, her Nephew, Sir Wilfull Witwoud is in the House.	. 437	WAY WORLD	III.1	466
Servant-W:	Really Sir, I can't tell; here come so many here, 'tis .	. 437	WAY WORLD	III.1	470
Witwoud:	short as a Shrewsbury Cake, if you please. But I tell .	. 439	WAY WORLD	III.1	532
Sir Wilful:	--O'ds heart, and then tell a familiar Tale of a Cock .	. 439	WAY WORLD	III.1	546
Sir Wilful:	I can't tell; 'tis like I may, and 'tis like I may .	. 440	WAY WORLD	III.1	578
Foible:	Madam, I stay'd here, to tell your Ladyship that Mr. .	. 445	WAY WORLD	IV.1	43
Foible:	and Sir Wilfull together. Shall I tell Mr. Mirabell that you	. 445	WAY WORLD	IV.1	46
Mrs Fain:	Fy, fy, have him, have him, and tell him so in . . .	. 452	WAY WORLD	IV.1	291
Foible:	Chamber, but I wou'd not tell your Lady-ship to . .	. 461	WAY WORLD	IV.1	619
Mrs Fain:	Foible, you must tell Mincing, that she must . . .	. 465	WAY WORLD	V.1	118
Mrs Fain:	I tell you Madam you're abus'd--stick to	. 466	WAY WORLD	V.1	173
Sir Wilful:	melt, I can tell you that. My contract went no further .	. 472	WAY WORLD	V.1	396

Tell'n (1)

Ben:	tell'n so to's face: If that's the Case, why silence gives	263	FOR LOVE	III.1	393

Telling (19)

Capt Bluff:	This Sword I think I was telling you of Mr. Sharper . .	53	OLD BATCH	II.1	228
Belinda:	as I was telling you--Pish, this is the untoward'st . .	83	OLD BATCH	IV.3	15
Belinda:	Lock--So, as I was telling you--How d'ye like . . .	83	OLD BATCH	IV.3	16
Belinda:	telling you--	83	OLD BATCH	IV.3	20
Bellmour:	a word on't.--But I can't help telling the truth, for my	95	OLD BATCH	IV.4	220
Lady Froth:	My Lord, I have been telling my dear Cynthia, . . .	140	DOUBL DLR	II.1	60
Lady Froth:	My Lord, I have been telling Cynthia, ...	140	DOUBL DLR	II.1 V 60
Brisk:	was telling me, your Ladyship has made an Essay toward .	141	DOUBL DLR	II.1	118
Careless:	hopes of her, is her telling me of the many Temptations .	158	DOUBL DLR	III.1	296
Mellefont:	price of the Commodity, by telling you how many . . .	158	DOUBL DLR	III.1	302
Sir Paul:	little fancies--But as I was telling you, Mr. Careless,				
	if it	161	DOUBL DLR	III.1	403
Jeremy:	Why so I have been telling my Master, Sir: Mr. . . .	219	FOR LOVE	I.1	122

Ten   (continued)

		PAGE	TITLE	ACT.SC	LINE
Mrs Fore:	Husband, will you go to Bed? It's Ten a	268	FOR LCVE	III.1	576
Valentine:	Master's Shop in the morning, may ten to one, dirty his	289	FOR LCVE	IV.1	509
Jeremy:	Sir, I ask you Ten Thousand Pardons, 'twas an errant	313	FOR LCVE	V.1	592
Almeria:	Die ten thousand Deaths--Look down, lock down	330	M. BRIDE	I.1	176
Witwoud:	My Dear, I ask ten thousand Pardons;--Gad I	402	WAY WCRLD	I.1	270
Witwoud:	like ten Christnings--I am tipsy with laughing--If I had	453	WAY WCRLD	IV.1	326

Tender (19)

		PAGE	TITLE	ACT.SC	LINE
Belinda:	Heav'n knows how far you may be tempted: I am tender	57	OLD BATCH	II.2	107
Silvia:	But Love, they say, is a tender thing, that will smooth	72	OLD BATCH	III.2	65
Fondlewife:	have been a tender Husband, a tender Ycke-fellow; you	95	OLD BATCH	IV.4	249
Mellefont:	that the most violent Love could urge, or tender words	130	DOUBL DLR	I.1	110
Sir Paul:	Thou art my tender Lambkin, and shalt do what	171	DOUBL DLR	IV.1	132
Tattle:	I will; because I have a tender for your Ladiship.	234	FOR LCVE	I.1	668
Angelica:	you, till I accidentally touch'd upon your tender Part: But	296	FOR LCVE	IV.1	766
Osmyn-Alph:	That tender, lcvely Form of painted Air	341	M. BRIDE	II.2	51
Osmyn-Alph:	Shall I not hurt and bruise thy tender Body,	355	M. BRIDE	III.1	242
Osmyn-Alph:	Shall I not hurt or bruise thy tender Eody,	355	M. BRIDE	III.1	V242
Almeria:	And for the tender Names of Child and Daughter,	368	M. BRIDE	IV.1	283
Almeria:	This weak and tender Flesh, to have been bruis'd	369	M. BRIDE	IV.1	312
	Your tender Hearts to Mercy are inclin'd,	385	M. BRIDE	EPI.	29
Fainall:	have too much Generosity, not to be tender of her Honour.	397	WAY WCRLD	I.1	92
Mirabell:	you tender your Ears be secret.	398	WAY WCRLD	I.1	132
Marwood:	that I am tender of your Honour?	413	WAY WCRLD	II.1	125
Marwood:	More tender, more sincere, and more enduring,	414	WAY WCRLD	II.1	167
Lady Wish:	to Impress upon her tender Years, a Young Odium and	466	WAY WCRLD	V.1	185

Tender-hearted (1)

		PAGE	TITLE	ACT.SC	LINE
Lucy:	tender-hearted Women light upon you.	98	OLD BATCH	V.1	77

Tenderly (9)

		PAGE	TITLE	ACT.SC	LINE
Lady Ply:	lov'd you tenderly--'tis a barbarity of barbarities, and	146	DOUEL DLR	II.1	291
Lady Ply:	loves you tenderly--'tis a barbarity of barbarities, and	146	DOUEL DLR	II.1	V291
Tattle:	very tenderly.	226	FOR LCVE	I.1	395
Scandal:	with, are to be handl'd tenderly indeed.	226	FOR LCVE	I.1	397
Almeria:	Or, when there, why was I us'd so tenderly?	327	M. BRIDE	I.1	66
Almeria:	Or there, why was I us'd so tenderly?	327	M. BRIDE	I.1	V 66
Almeria:	Too much, too tenderly lamented me.	342	M. BRIDE	II.2	V118
Osmyn-Alph:	Wrong not my Love, to say too tenderly.	343	M. BRIDE	II.2	V119
Almeria:	What dost thou think? Look not so tenderly	356	M. BRIDE	III.1	264

Tenderness (7)

		PAGE	TITLE	ACT.SC	LINE
Heartwell:	much Tenderness and Beauty--and Honesty together	74	OLD BATCH	III.2	115
Almeria:	His Worth, his Truth, and Tenderness of Love.	328	M. BRIDE	I.1	103
Osmyn-Alph:	This countless Summ of Tenderness and Love,	343	M. BRIDE	II.2	138
Osmyn-Alph:	Such Sanctity, such Tenderness, so mix'd	352	M. BRIDE	III.1	114
Almeria:	--Thou giv'st me Pain, with too much Tenderness!	356	M. BRIDE	III.1	280
Fainall:	O my Dear I am satisfy'd of your Tenderness; I know	412	WAY WCRLD	II.1	95
Lady Wish:	Yes, but Tenderness becomes me best--A	429	WAY WCRLD	III.1	167

Tenders (2)

		PAGE	TITLE	ACT.SC	LINE
Mirabell:	and her Streamers out, and a shoal of Fools for Tenders	418	WAY WORLD	II.1	324
Mirabell:	and Streamers out, and a shoal of Fools for Tenders	418	WAY WORLD	II.1	V324

Tends (1)

		PAGE	TITLE	ACT.SC	LINE
Laetitia:	Book, and only tends to the Speculation of Sin.	92	OLD BATCH	IV.4	115

Tennis-Court (1)

		PAGE	TITLE	ACT.SC	LINE
	Now find us toss'd into a Tennis-Court.	315	FOR LCVE	EPI.	27

Tenor (1)

		PAGE	TITLE	ACT.SC	LINE
Fainall:	Tenor of this other Covenant,--I suppose Madam, your	473	WAY WCRLD	V.1	437

Tenter (1)

		PAGE	TITLE	ACT.SC	LINE
Waitwell:	tenter of Expectation.	457	WAY WCRLD	IV.1	493

Term (3)

		PAGE	TITLE	ACT.SC	LINE
Sharper:	O term it no longer so Sir. In the Scuffle last Night I	49	OLD BATCH	II.1	81
Valentine:	Westminster-Hall the first Day of every Term--Let me see	280	FOR LCVE	IV.1	173
Zara:	No Term, no Bound, but Infinite of Woe.	362	M. BRIDE	IV.1	35

Termagant (1)

		PAGE	TITLE	ACT.SC	LINE
Heartwell:	young, termagant flashy sinners--you have all the guilt	43	OLD BATCH	I.1	238

Terminated (1)

		PAGE	TITLE	ACT.SC	LINE
Mellefont:	or of her Love, terminated in the view of this my Marriage	129	DOUBL DLR	I.1	97

Terms (14)

		PAGE	TITLE	ACT.SC	LINE
Lucy:	Come tell me in plain Terms, how forward he is	66	OLD BATCH	III.2	222
Heartwell:	S'death it is but a may be, and upon scurvy Terms--	74	OLD BATCH	III.2	128
Mellefont:	Upon such terms I will be ever yours in every	185	DOUBL DLR	IV.2	87
Maskwell:	of mine, I have told 'em in plain terms, how easie 'tis for	194	DOUBL DLR	V.1	263
Maskwell:	for your Passion broke in such imperfect terms, that yet	198	DOUBL DLR	V.1	414
Tattle:	Any, any Terms.	230	FOR LCVE	I.1	525
Scandal:	say in general Terms, He only is Secret who never was	256	FOR LCVE	III.1	125
Sr Sampson:	Speak to be understood, and tell me in plain Terms what	279	FOR LCVE	IV.1	135
Ben:	told 'n in plain terms, if I were minded to marry, I'de	285	FOR LCVE	IV.1	371
Zara:	If I cn any Terms could condescend	335	M. BRIDE	I.1	393
Almeria:	On any Terms, that thou dost wish me from thee.	356	M. BRIDE	III.1	257
Mirabell:	Uncle, he might like Mosca in the Fox, stand upon Terms;	417	WAY WORLD	II.1	294
Mrs Fain:	plain terms: For I am sure you have a mind to him.	452	WAY WORLD	IV.1	292
Fainall:	or abate one tittle cf my Terms, no, I will insist the more.	474	WAY WORLD	V.1	477

Terrible (5)

		PAGE	TITLE	ACT.SC	LINE
Laetitia:	(aside). Oh then alls safe. I was terrible frighted--	78	OLD BATCH	IV.1	102
Sir Joseph:	O Lord! Oh terrible! Ha, ha, ha, Is your Wife	90	OLD BATCH	IV.4	55
Scandal:	Coats, Steinkirk Cravats, and terrible Faces; with Cat-calls	234	FOR LCVE	I.1	655
Angelica:	Malice is not a more terrible Consequence of his Aversion,	299	FOR LCVE	V.1	77
Lady Wish:	appearance. He is as terrible to me as a Gorgon; if I see him,	470	WAY WORLD	V.1	336

Terribly (1)

		PAGE	TITLE	ACT.SC	LINE
Laetitia:	(aside). Oh then alls safe. I was terribly frighted--	78	OLD BATCH	IV.1	V102

Terrifies (1)

		PAGE	TITLE	ACT.SC	LINE
Zara:	Yet, more, this Stilness terrifies my Soul,	379	M. BRIDE	V.2	142

Terrify'd (1)

		PAGE	TITLE	ACT.SC	LINE
Jeremy:	terrify'd Countenance, that looks as if he had written for	219	FOR LOVE	I.1	105

Terror (2)

		PAGE	TITLE	ACT.SC	LINE
Almeria:	And Terror on my aking Sight; the Tombs	339	M. BRIDE	II.1	64
Lady Wish:	have a mortal Terror at the apprehension of offending	429	WAY WORLD	III.1	178

Testament (1)					
Fainall:	appear by the last Will and Testament of your deceas'd	469	WAY WORLD	V.1	281
Teste a teste (1)					
Petulant:	Ay teste a teste; But not in publick, because I make	408	WAY WORLD	I.1	500
Testify (1)					
Sir Joseph:	Summer, all Seasons and occasions shall testify the reality	49	OLD BATCH	II.1	67
Testimony (1)					
Lady Wish:	Testimony of your Obedience; but I cannot admit that	470	WAY WCRLD	V.1	334
Tete a tete (1)					
Petulant:	Ay tete a tete; But not in publick, because I make	408	WAY WORLD	I.1 V500
Text (1) see Spin-text					
Maskwell:	None, your Text is short.	195	DOUEL DLR	V.1	297
Th' (15)					
Capt Bluff:	Th' Affront.	70	OLD BATCH	III.1	345
Fondlewife:	canst reach, th' hast experimented Isaac--But Mum.	77	OLD EATCH	IV.1	63
Capt Bluff:	Damn your Morals: I must revenge th' Affront done	101	OLD BATCH	V.1	180
	Th' unladen Boughs, he sees, bode certain Dearth,	213	FOR LCVE	PRO.	5
	And shou'd th' ensuing Scenes not chance to hit,	214	FOR LCVE	PRO.	45
	Hard Fate for us! still harder in th' Event;	323	M. BRIDE	PRO.	21
Manuel:	Th' expecting Crowd had been deceiv'd; and seen	335	M. EFIDE	I.1	390
Zara:	Shall I prevent, or stop th' approaching Danger?	362	M. EFIDE	IV.1	43
Manuel:	Th' ignoble Currs, that yelp to fill the Cry,	362	M. EBIDE	IV.1	63
Manuel:	As to conceal th' Importance of his Errand.	373	M. BRIDE	V.1	17
Manuel:	But see she comes; I'll shun th' Encounter; do	374	M. BRIDE	V.1	87
Manuel:	But see she comes; I'll shun th' Encounter; thou	374	M. EBIDE	V.1 V 87
Selim:	Th' imperfect Look, and sternly turn'd away.	375	M. EFIDE	V.1	100
Gonsalez:	Th' Attempt: I'll steal, and do it unperceiv'd.	376	M. EFIDE	V.2	9
Petulant:	What does he say th' are?	406	WAY WCRLD	I.1	404
Than (234)					
Bellmour:	parted with his Bed in a Morning, than a' could have slept	37	OLD BATCH	I.1	3
Bellmour:	parted with his Bed in a Morning, than he could have slept	37	OLD EATCH	I.1 V	3
Bellmour:	More than they believe--Or understand.	37	OLD BATCH	I.1	16
Vainlove:	How how, Ned, a wise Man say more than he	37	OLD EATCH	I.1	17
Bellmour:	know and believe more than really we do. You read of but	37	OLD BATCH	I.1	20
Bellmour:	Superscription (Takes up the Letter.) than in all Cicero--	38	OLD BATCH	I.1	34
Heartwell:	profit than what the bare tillage and manuring of the Land	44	OLD BATCH	I.1	280
Sir Joseph:	that's a better Jest than tother. 'Tis a sign you and I ha'n't	50	OLD BATCH	II.1	116
Sharper:	Not I, Sir, no more than publick Letters, or Gazettes	52	OLD BATCH	II.1	190
Capt Bluff:	by the Wars--Took no more notice, than as if Nol. Eluffe	53	OLD BATCH	II.1	204
Belinda:	than your talking Impertinence; as an Ape is a much more	60	OLD EATCH	II.2	213
Belinda:	troublesome Animal than a Parrot.	60	OLD BATCH	II.2	214
Araminta:	things, than they say.	60	OLD BATCH	II.2	217
Sir Joseph:	Lord-Harry. I know better things than to be run through	67	OLD BATCH	III.1	253
Sir Joseph:	--I'd rather go plain all my Life, than wear such	70	OLD BATCH	III.1	334
Sir Joseph:	done behind his Back, than what's said--Come wee'l	70	OLD EATCH	III.1	361
Heartwell:	will more easily be thrust forward than drawn back.	73	OLD BATCH	III.2	73
Heartwell:	yet a more certain Sign than all this; I give thee my Mony.	73	OLD BATCH	III.2	85
Heartwell:	Heaven she kisses sweeter than Liberty--I will Marry	74	OLD BATCH	III.2	134
Heartwell:	Heaven her kiss is sweeter than Liberty--I will Marry	74	OLD BATCH	III.2 V134
Fondlewife:	inclination was (and is still) greater than my power--	76	OLD BATCH	IV.1	55
Fondlewife:	me, than she has reason to be; and in the way of Trade,	77	OLD BATCH	IV.1	60
Fondlewife:	designs--And that she has some designs deeper than thou	77	OLD BATCH	IV.1	62
Fondlewife:	I profess I do love thee better, than 500 Pound--	78	OLD BATCH	IV.1	129
Vainlove:	than Sawcy, in another place.	87	OLD BATCH	IV.3	165
Fondlewife:	a warm-hand, rather than fail. What Bock's this?	91	OLD BATCH	IV.4	98
Fondlewife:	than Speculation that I was not to be let in.--Where	92	OLD BATCH	IV.4	117
Fondlewife:	I warrant you, than to deny it. Come, Were you two never	93	OLD BATCH	IV.4	155
Capt Bluff:	than she. Look here: These were sent me this Morning--	103	OLD BATCH	V.1	265
Belinda:	make a more than ordinary quiet Husband.	106	OLD BATCH	V.1	367
Heartwell:	The Bone when broken, than when made a Bride.	108	OLD BATCH	V.2	15
Mellefont:	Hell is not more busie than her Brain, ncr contains more	129	DOUEL DLR	I.1	77
Mellefont:	Devils, than that Imaginations.	129	DOUEL DLR	I.1	78
Mellefont:	prevent the success of her displeasure, than to avoid the	129	DOUEL DLR	I.1	92
Careless:	think thou hast no more Sense, than to get an Heir upon her	130	DOUEL DLR	I.1	120
Lord Froth:	more unbecoming a Man of Quality, than to Laugh; Jesu,	132	DOUEL DLR	I.1	199
Lord Froth:	more unbecoming a Man of Quality, than to Laugh;	132	DOUEL DLR	I.1 V199
Careless:	Face, than a Jest.	132	DOUEL DLR	I.1	215
Lady Touch:	more moved with the reflection of his Crimes, than of his	136	DOUEL DLR	I.1	413
Lady Touch:	likes him so well, that she will believe it faster than I can	138	DOUEL DLR	I.1 V330
Lady Froth:	More Wit than any Body.	140	DOUEL DLR	II.1	92
Mellefont:	By Heaven, I love her more than life, or--	146	DOUEL DLR	II.1	300
Lord Touch:	more than ordinary in this.	152	DOUEL DLR	III.1	45
Lady Ply:	rather attempt it than any thing in the World, (Curtesies)	159	DOUEL DLR	III.1	341
Sir Paul:	than with my own Mother--no indeed.	162	DOUEL DLR	III.1	440
Lady Ply:	challenges much more, I'm sure, than my illiterate Praises	169	DOUEL DLR	IV.1	83
Lady Ply:	that Mellefont had never any thing more than a profound	171	DOUEL DLR	IV.1	165
Sir Paul:	are a better Christian than to think of being a Nun; he?	174	DOUEL DLR	IV.1	255
Sir Paul:	are a better Christian than to think of living a Nun; he?	174	DOUEL DLR	IV.1 V255
Sir Paul:	Commission--If I desired him to do any more than	180	DOUEL DLR	IV.1	471
Sir Paul:	here made? Why, this is better and more Miraculous than	180	DOUEL DLR	IV.1	505
Mellefont:	design than this of his which has miscarried.--O my	187	DOUEL DLR	IV.2	151
Maskwell:	rather die, than seem once, barely seem, dishonest:--	188	DOUEL DLR	V.1	37
Maskwell:	more than all the rest; though I would give a Limb for	199	DOUEL DLR	V.1	434
Maskwell:	than in the Death of one who is nothing when not yours.	199	DOUEL DLR	V.1	451
Maskwell:	than in the Heart of one who is nothing when not yours.	199	DOUEL DLR	V.1	451
Lady Froth:	angry than usual.	203	DOUEL DLR	V.1	580
	Than they who stand their Trials at the Barr;	204	DOUEL DLR	EPI.	9
Valentine:	this Restraint, than when I openly rival'd the rich Fops,	217	FOR LOVE	I.1	52
Jeremy:	Three days, the Life of a Play, I no more expect it, than to	218	FOR LOVE	I.1	74
Jeremy:	ruin'd more Young Men than the Royal Oak Lottery--	218	FOR LOVE	I.1	88
Scandal:	upon the outside of his Head, than the Lining. Why,	219	FOR LOVE	I.1	126
Jeremy:	has more Wit than himself?	219	FOR LCVE	I.1	130

Than   (continued)

Speaker	Text	Page	Title	Act.Sc	Line
Scandal:	more servile, timorous, and fawning, than any I have	220	FOR LOVE	I.1	147
Scandal:	Attendance, and promis'd more than ever you intend to	221	FOR LOVE	I.1	194
Scandal:	Attendance, and promis'd more than ever you intended to	221	FOR LOVE	I.1	V194
Scandal:	perform; are more perplex'd to find Evasions, than you	221	FOR LOVE	I.1	195
Valentine:	Ruby-Lips! better sealing there, than a Bond for a Million,	223	FOR LOVE	I.1	279
Tattle:	For there is nothing more known, than that no body	227	FOR LOVE	I.1	404
Scandal:	Why, Tattle, thou hast more Impudence than one	227	FOR LOVE	I.1	437
Tattle:	Tho' I have more Honour than to tell first; I have more	229	FOR LOVE	I.1	478
Tattle:	Manners than to contradict what a Lady has declar'd.	229	FOR LOVE	I.1	479
Valentine:	If there were, you have more Discretion, than to	229	FOR LOVE	I.1	511
Valentine:	But what if he have more Passion than Manners?	231	FOR LOVE	I.1	558
Valentine:	But what if he has more Passion than Manners?	231	FOR LOVE	I.1	V558
Mrs Frail:	That's more than he has for himself. And what will	232	FOR LOVE	I.1	593
Sr Sampson:	more Illustrious than the Moon; for she has her Chastity	242	FOR LOVE	II.1	258
Valentine:	hope you will have more Indulgence, than to oblige me to	243	FOR LOVE	II.1	283
Sr Sampson:	That's more than I know, Sir, and I believe not.	244	FOR LOVE	II.1	316
Valentine:	I know no more why I came, than you do why	244	FOR LOVE	II.1	333
Sr Sampson:	rather eat a Pheasant, than a piece of poor John; and smell,	245	FOR LOVE	II.1	369
Mrs Fore:	better Friends than before.	248	FOR LOVE	II.1	479
Mrs Frail:	have observ'd us more than we have observ'd one another.	248	FOR LOVE	II.1	488
Miss Prue:	Handkerchief is sweet, pure sweet, sweeter than Roses	249	FOR LOVE	II.1	520
Miss Prue:	this way--Is not it pure?--It's better than	249	FOR LOVE	II.1	528
Tattle:	But you must think your self more Charming than I	252	FOR LOVE	II.1	617
Miss Prue:	O Lord, I swear this is pure,--I like it better than	252	FOR LOVE	II.1	624
Miss Prue:	Well, now I'll run and make more haste than you.	253	FOR LOVE	II.1	660
Tattle:	shall make Oath, that I receive more Letters than the	257	FOR LOVE	III.1	159
Tattle:	enquire for me, than ever went to see the Hermaphrodite,	257	FOR LOVE	III.1	161
Sr Sampson:	Woman than I thought you were: For most young	260	FOR LOVE	III.1	250
Angelica:	have you than your Son.	260	FOR LOVE	III.1	256
Ben:	man, than a Galley-slave is like one of us free Sailors, he is	262	FOR LOVE	III.1	316
Miss Prue:	But I'm sure it is not so, for I'll speak sooner than	264	FOR LOVE	III.1	395
Ben:	Whipping no more than you do. But I tell you one thing,	264	FOR LOVE	III.1	407
Ben:	to her, than a Cann of Small-beer to a Bowl of Punch.	264	FOR LOVE	III.1	413
Ben:	stink; he shall smell more like a Weasel than a Civet-Cat,	265	FOR LOVE	III.1	437
Scandal:	him, and all of us, more than any thing else?	266	FOR LOVE	III.1	484
Scandal:	That may be, but your Beard is longer than it was	268	FOR LOVE	III.1	572
Scandal:	Do, I'll dye a Martyr, rather than disclaim my	269	FOR LOVE	III.1	595
Scandal:	looks better than he did.	270	FOR LOVE	III.1	627
Scandal:	and my self, than to despair.	271	FOR LOVE	III.1	663
Scandal:	it more dangerous to be seen in Conversation with me, than	272	FOR LOVE	III.1	695
Ben:	He lov'd her more than Plunder;	274	FOR LOVE	III.1	770
Jeremy:	bad Bargain, can't do better than to beg him for his	276	FOR LOVE	IV.1	36
Angelica:	more than he has done by himself: and now the Surprize	277	FOR LOVE	IV.1	82
Angelica:	love, I can't help it; no more than he can help his being a	278	FOR LOVE	IV.1	88
Angelica:	Man, or I my being a Woman; or no more than I can help	278	FOR LOVE	IV.1	89
Scandal:	Father, than it does with his Mistress, he may descend from	278	FOR LOVE	IV.1	105
Sr Sampson:	the Nose in one's Face: What, are my Eyes better than	281	FOR LOVE	IV.1	225
Valentine:	another than Oyl and Vinegar; and yet those two beaten	282	FOR LOVE	IV.1	257
Scandal:	all night, and denying favours with more impudence, than	284	FOR LOVE	IV.1	336
Scandal:	. . . favours with more impudence, than	284	FOR LOVE	IV.1	V336
Scandal:	Discourses, and sometimes rather think him inspir'd than	285	FOR LOVE	IV.1	345
Ben:	for her to learn her Sampler, and make Dirt-pies, than to	285	FOR LOVE	IV.1	374
Ben:	than my heart.--He was woundy angry when I	286	FOR LOVE	IV.1	384
Mrs Frail:	throw himself away, he can't do it more effectually than	287	FOR LOVE	IV.1	460
Foresight:	But he knows more than any body,--Oh	291	FOR LOVE	IV.1	603
Tattle:	now, that I know more Secrets than he.	291	FOR LOVE	IV.1	609
Tattle:	No, Sir, 'tis written in my Heart. And safer there, Sir, than	292	FOR LOVE	IV.1	613
Valentine:	more than Love, to make me worthy of you.	295	FOR LOVE	IV.1	727
Valentine:	Understood! She is harder to be understood than a	297	FOR LOVE	IV.1	801
Angelica:	like him, it's a sign he likes me; and that's more than half	297	FOR LOVE	V.1	6
Angelica:	--I have more Occasion for your Conduct than your	298	FOR LOVE	V.1	45
Angelica:	would no more be his Wife, than his Enemy. For his	299	FOR LOVE	V.1	76
Angelica:	than his Jealousie is of his Love.	299	FOR LOVE	V.1	78
Angelica:	than you are.	299	FOR LOVE	V.1	88
Jeremy:	my self better to you, Sir, than by the delivery of a	302	FOR LOVE	V.1	177
Tattle:	more love for your Daughter, than I have likeness of you;	305	FOR LOVE	V.1	288
Miss Prue:	sleeping, than sick with thinking.	305	FOR LOVE	V.1	312
Miss Prue:	asleep, than sick with thinking.	305	FOR LOVE	V.1	V312
Ben:	Mess, I fear his Fire's little better than Tinder; may hap	308	FOR LOVE	V.1	410
Mrs Fore:	(aside to Mrs. Frail). He's better than no Husband	310	FOR LOVE	V.1	469
Sr Sampson:	your Wedding Night? I'm an older Fellow than you, and	310	FOR LOVE	V.1	485
Angelica:	Right to dispose of my Person, than yours.	311	FOR LOVE	V.1	534
Angelica:	Faults than he has Virtues; and 'tis hardly more Pleasure	312	FOR LOVE	V.1	576
Angelica:	to me, that I can make him and my self happy, than that I	312	FOR LOVE	V.1	577
Angelica:	apt to run more in Debt than you are able to pay.	313	FOR LOVE	V.1	614
Almeria:	Than Trees, or Flint? O Force of constant Woe!	326	M. BRIDE	I.1	7
Almeria:	Than any I have yet endur'd--and now	330	M. BRIDE	I.1	190
Gonsalez:	My Eyes with more Delight, than they can hold.	332	M. BRIDE	I.1	274
Manuel:	Must have some other Cause than his Captivity.	335	M. BRIDE	I.1	376
Manuel:	Her Chains hang heavier on him than his own.	335	M. BRIDE	I.1	381
Manuel:	Her Eyes, did more than bid--free her and hers,	336	M. BRIDE	I.1	410
Zara:	Whom more than Life he lov'd; and the Regret,	337	M. BRIDE	I.1	438
Almeria:	Yet green in Earth, rather than be the Bride	339	M. BRIDE	II.1	77
Almeria:	Monument fronting the View, greater than the rest. Enter Heli.)	340	M. BRIDE	II.2	
Osmyn-Alph:	Is knowing more than any Circumstance,	342	M. BRIDE	II.2	94
Almeria:	'Tis more than Recompence, to see thy Face:	343	M. BRIDE	II.2	147
Zara:	Am I more loathsome to thee, than the Grave?	345	M. BRIDE	II.2	241
Zara:	Better I was unseen, than seen thus coldly.	346	M. BRIDE	II.2	257
Zara:	Than all the Malice of my other Fate.	348	M. BRIDE	II.2	339
Manuel:	(aside). How? better than my Hopes; does she accuse	348	M. BRIDE	II.2	359
Manuel:	Of him that thunders, than but think that Insolence.	349	M. BRIDE	II.2	370
Osmyn-Alph:	Will treasure here; more worth than Diadems,	353	M. BRIDE	III.1	137

Than   (continued)

Osmyn-Alph:	I'll treasure as more worth than Diadems,	353	M. BRIDE	III.1 V137
Zara:	Than e'er thou could'st with bitterest Reproaches;	354	M. BRIDE	III.1 186
Zara:	My self will fly; and earlier than the Morn,	354	M. BRIDE	III.1 202
Zara:	To give, than I've already lost. But as	355	M. BRIDE	III.1 216
Zara:	To give, than I've already lost. But now	355	M. BRIDE	III.1 V216
Almeria:	Thus, better, than for any Cause to part.	356	M. BRIDE	III.1 263
Almeria:	Than knowing thou hast felt it. Tell it me.	356	M. BRIDE	III.1 V279
Zara:	More than his Crown, t'impart 'ere Osmyn die.	361	M. BRIDE	IV.1 19
Zara:	Than still to meet the Rigour of his Scorn.	362	M. BRIDE	IV.1 28
Zara:	Than your high Courage suffers you to see;	364	M. BRIDE	IV.1 110
Gonsalez:	Should have more Meaning than appears bare-fac'd.	365	M. BRIDE	IV.1 176
Almeria:	Repeated Deaths, rather than have revealed thee.	368	M. BRIDE	IV.1 306
Almeria:	Reproach cuts deeper than the keenest Sword,	369	M. BRIDE	IV.1 308
Almeria:	And torn, rather than have reveal'd thy being.	369	M. BRIDE	IV.1 313
Manuel:	Wilder than Winds or Waves thy self do'st rave.	370	M. BRIDE	IV.1 361
Garcia:	Rather than or to see, or to relate	377	M. BRIDE	V.2 56
Zara:	Than did that Scene of complicated Horrors.	379	M. BRIDE	V.2 143
Zara:	Than Death?--	380	M. BRIDE	V.2 148
Zara:	Why is't you more than speak in these sad Signs?	380	M. BRIDE	V.2 159
Zara:	Cruel, cruel, O more than killing Object!	380	M. BRIDE	V.2 V164
Almeria:	Yet bubling from his Wounds--O more than savage!	382	M. BRIDE	V.2 235
Fainall:	more play with a Man that slighted his ill Fortune, than	395	WAY WORLD	I.1 8
Mirabell:	She is more Mistress of her self, than to be under	396	WAY WORLD	I.1 43
Mirabell:	Concern for which the Lady is more indebted to you, than	397	WAY WORLD	I.1 97
Mirabell:	Concern for which the Lady is more indebted to you, than is	397	WAY WORLD	I.1 V 97
Fainall:	I had rather be his Relation than his Acquaintance.	400	WAY WORLD	I.1 196
Witwoud:	with a little Loss, than to be quite eaten up, with being	400	WAY WORLD	I.1 208
Witwoud:	all, that I must own--No more breeding than a	403	WAY WORLD	I.1 298
Petulant:	than a Woman constant; one argues a decay of Parts, as	403	WAY WORLD	I.1 320
Petulant:	Aunt, that loves Catterwauling better than a Conventicle.	406	WAY WORLD	I.1 408
Witwoud:	Aunt, who loves Catterwauling better than a Conventicle.	406	WAY WORLD	I.1 V408
Witwoud:	has been told; and you know she hates Mirabell, worse than	408	WAY WORLD	I.1 484
Marwood:	a Quaker hates a Parrot, or than a Fishmonger hates a	408	WAY WORLD	I.1 485
Mrs Fain:	'tis better to be left, than never to have been lov'd. To	410	WAY WORLD	II.1 12
Marwood:	He has a Humour more prevailing than his	412	WAY WORLD	II.1 103
Mirabell:	than all the vain and empty Vows of Men, whether	414	WAY WORLD	II.1 168
Mirabell:	Thing that resembl'd a Man, tho' 'twere no more than	418	WAY WORLD	II.1 312
Witwoud:	rather than your Face.	420	WAY WORLD	II.1 398
Millamant:	of Lovers, Madam, than of making so many Card-matches.	420	WAY WORLD	II.1 408
Mirabell:	One no more owes one's Beauty to a Lover, than	420	WAY WORLD	II.1 409
Mirabell:	Your Health! Is there a worse Disease than the	421	WAY WORLD	II.1 443
Lady Wish:	Windmill, has not a more whimsical Dwelling than the	423	WAY WORLD	II.1 494
Marwood:	than to put a Lady to the necessity of breaking her Forms.	429	WAY WORLD	III.1 162
Marwood:	Marrying than Travelling at his Years. I hear he is turn'd	431	WAY WORLD	III.1 260
Millamant:	can no more conceal it, than my Lady Strammel can her	433	WAY WORLD	III.1 320
Millamant:	than a decay'd Beauty, or a discarded Tost;	433	WAY WORLD	III.1 324
Millamant:	dressing; their Folly is less provoking than your Mallice,	433	WAY WORLD	III.1 326
Millamant:	dressing here; their Folly is less provoking than your Mallice,	433	WAY WORLD	III.1 V326
Millamant:	That Mirabell loves me is no more a Secret, than it is a	433	WAY WORLD	III.1 328
Marwood:	Secret that you discover'd it to my Aunt, or than the	433	WAY WORLD	III.1 329
Petulant:	than you think.	434	WAY WORLD	III.1 364
Petulant:	married tho' he can't Read, any more than he is from being	436	WAY WORLD	III.1 429
Servant-W:	married tho' he can't read, than he is from being	436	WAY WORLD	III.1 V429
Servant-W:	A Week, Sir; longer than any Body in the House,	437	WAY WORLD	III.1 457
Sir Wilful:	A Week, Sir; longer than any in the House,	437	WAY WORLD	III.1 V457
Sir Wilful:	Oons this Fellow knows less than a Starling; I	437	WAY WORLD	III.1 473
Sir Wilful:	round the Edges, no broader than a Subpoena. I might expect	439	WAY WORLD	III.1 542
Marwood:	'Sheart, and better than to be bound to a Maker of	440	WAY WORLD	III.1 563
Marwood:	worse than when you had her--I dare swear she had given	442	WAY WORLD	III.1 651
Marwood:	can contrive to have her keep you better than you expected;	442	WAY WORLD	III.1 656
Lady Wish:	why should you not keep her longer than you intended?	442	WAY WORLD	III.1 657
Millamant:	nothing is more alluring than a Levee from a Couch in	445	WAY WORLD	IV.1 29
Millamant:	Ah Rustick! ruder than Gothick.	447	WAY WORLD	IV.1 109
Witwoud:	more than Impossible--positively Mirabell, I'll lie a Bed in	449	WAY WORLD	IV.1 190
Lady Wish:	Thou hast utter'd Volumes, Folio's, in less than	453	WAY WORLD	IV.1 342
Waitwell:	pardons to ask than the Pope distributes in the Year of	457	WAY WORLD	IV.1 486
Lady Wish:	--than Act Sir Rowland, till this time to morrow.	459	WAY WORLD	IV.1 564
Lady Wish:	Traverse Rag, in a shop no bigger than a Bird-cage,--	462	WAY WORLD	V.1 7
Foible:	Impudence, more than a big-Belly'd Actress.	463	WAY WORLD	V.1 37
Foible:	friends together, than set 'em at distance. But Mrs. Marwood	464	WAY WORLD	V.1 88
Mincing:	and He are nearer related than ever their Parents	464	WAY WORLD	V.1 89
Lady Wish:	have him I think, rather than loose such a vast Summ as	465	WAY WORLD	V.1 115
Marwood:	more from you than all your life can accomplish--O don't	466	WAY WORLD	V.1 170
Marwood:	Lungs of Hawkers, with Voices more Licentious than the	468	WAY WORLD	V.1 233
Sir Wilful:	think I would rather Congratulate, than Condole with	468	WAY WORLD	V.1 245
Mirabell:	than a little Mouth-Glew, and that's hardly dry;--One	472	WAY WORLD	V.1 397
	Elder Date than what you have obtain'd from your Lady.	476	WAY WORLD	V.1 555
	And sure he must have more than mortal Skill,	479	WAY WORLD	EPI. 7

Thank (51)

Heartwell:	Quality--I thank Heaven, I have very honestly purchas'd	45	OLD BATCH	I.1 304
Capt Bluff:	to thank you in: But in your Ear, you are to be seen again.	69	OLD BATCH	III.1 323
Belinda:	--Very well.--So, thank you my Dear.--But	83	OLD BATCH	IV.3 14
Bellmour:	Nay, then I thank thee for not putting me out of	100	OLD BATCH	V.1 147
Heartwell:	Bellmour, I approve thy mirth, and thank thee.	111	OLD BATCH	V.2 150
Bellmour:	I thank thee, George, for thy good intention.--	111	OLD BATCH	V.2 154
Mellefont:	Maskwell! how shall I thank or praise thee; Thou hast	149	DOUEL DLR	II.1 407
Sir Paul:	Your humble Servant, I am I thank Heaven in a	160	DOUEL DLR	III.1 383
Sir Paul:	Why, I have, I thank Heaven, a very plentiful	161	DOUEL DLR	III.1 407
Mellefont:	Ay, Hell thank her, as gentle breezes moderate a	167	DOUEL DLR	IV.1 3
Careless:	I thank Heav'n, they are the saddest that I ever	170	DOUEL DLR	IV.1 122
Sir Paul:	I humbly thank your Ladiship--I don't know	172	DOUEL DLR	IV.1 197
Lady Ply:	No, no, nothing else I thank you, Sir Paul,--	173	DOUEL DLR	IV.1 220
Brisk:	Froth! Heigho! Break Heart; God's I thank you.	175	DOUEL DLR	IV.1 310
Lord Touch:	I thank you. What is the Villains Purpose?	182	DOUEL DLR	IV.1 581

Thank   (continued)

		PAGE	TITLE	ACT.SC	LINE
Lady Touch:	(kneeling). Eternal Blessings thank you--	186	DOUBL DLR	IV.2	94
Maskwell:	thank you--What, enjoy my Love! Forgive the	189	DOUBL DLR	V.1	80
Mellefont:	Should I begin to thank or praise thee, I should	194	DOUBL DLR	V.1	245
Lord Touch:	I thank you, yet it may be still too late, if	200	DOUBL DLR	V.1	476
Lord Froth:	I've some of my own, thank you, my dear.	201	DOUBL DLR	V.1	527
	Whether to thank, or blame their Audience, most:	204	DOUBL DLR	EPI.	3
Trapland:	Thank you--I have been out of this Money--	223	FOR LOVE	I.1	254
Tattle:	for his Calumniation!--I thank Heav'n, it has always been	226	FOR LOVE	I.1	393
Mrs Frail:	Pooh, No I thank you, I have enough to do to	232	FOR LOVE	I.1	596
Ben:	Thank you Father, and I'm glad to see you.	260	FOR LOVE	III.1	272
Ben:	Thank you, thank you Friend.	261	FOR LOVE	III.1	286
Angelica:	I thank you, Sir, I am not at all offended;--but	262	FOR LOVE	III.1	344
Scandal:	I thank my Stars that have inclin'd me--But I fear	268	FOR LOVE	III.1	543
Foresight:	I thank you Mr. Scandal, I will--Nurse, let me have	270	FOR LOVE	III.1	640
Foresight:	I thank you, Mr. Scandal, indeed that wou'd be a	271	FOR LOVE	III.1	653
Valentine:	Thank you, Sir, pretty well--I have been a	281	FOR LOVE	IV.1	196
Valentine:	I thank you, Sir.	281	FOR LOVE	IV.1	204
Miss Prue:	Husband and thank me too, for he told me so.	305	FOR LOVE	V.1	319
Angelica:	thank him.	309	FOR LOVE	V.1	456
Valentine:	Tattle, I thank you, you would have interposed	313	FOR LOVE	V.1	595
Scandal:	must thank you for; I was an Infidel to your Sex;	314	FOR LOVE	V.1	622
Almeria:	I thank thee--indeed I do--	328	M. BRIDE	I.1	94
Almeria:	I thank thee, Leonora,	328	M. BRIDE	I.1 V	94
Almeria:	I thank thee, that thou'lt pity thy sad Mistress;	328	M. BRIDE	I.1	95
Almeria:	I thank thee. 'Tis but this; anon, when all	331	M. BRIDE	I.1	196
Osmyn-Alph:	I thank you.	360	M. BRIDE	III.1	435
Manuel:	I thank thee Friend.	367	M. BRIDE	IV.1	226
Mirabell:	I thank you heartily, heartily.	402	WAY WORLD	I.1	272
Mirabell:	I thank you, I know as much as my Curiosity	409	WAY WORLD	I.1	507
Lady Wish:	Ay dear Foible; thank thee for that dear Foible.	428	WAY WORLD	III.1	139
Sir Wilful:	I'm very well I thank you Aunt--However,	441	WAY WORLD	III.1	601
Sir Wilful:	I thank you for your courteous Offer. 'Sheart, I was afraid	441	WAY WORLD	III.1	602
Sir Wilful:	Cozen, nor Stripling: I thank Heav'n, I'm no Minor.	447	WAY WORLD	IV.1	108
Mirabell:	I thank you. Inprimis then, I Covenant that your	451	WAY WORLD	IV.1	234
Mrs Fain:	Thank Mr. Mirabell, a Cautious Friend, to whose	477	WAY WORLD	V.1	570

Thank'd (2)

Belinda:	of it; for she thank'd me, and gave me two Apples, piping	84	OLD BATCH	IV.3	43
Millamant:	thank'd--here kiss my hand tho'--so hold your tongue	452	WAY WORLD	IV.1	296

Thankless (1)

Zara:	But with such dumb, and thankless Eyes you look;	346	M. BRIDE	II.2	256

Thanks (20)

Sir Joseph:	him thanks.	47	OLD BATCH	II.1	10
Sharper:	came half despairing to recover; but thanks to my better	49	OLD BATCH	II.1	83
Bellmour:	you ought to return him Thanks now you have receiv'd	68	OLD BATCH	III.1	282
Sharper:	Mony paid at sight: I'm come to return my Thanks--	68	OLD BATCH	III.1	285
Sharper:	and refuse my Thanks--But I hope you are not offended	68	OLD BATCH	III.1	290
Fondlewife:	enough. No Thanks to you Sir, for her Vertue.--But,	96	OLD BATCH	IV.4	268
Sir Joseph:	Thanks to my Knight-hood, she's a Lady--	111	OLD BATCH	V.2	136
Mellefont:	You shall have my thanks below.	143	DOUBL DLR	II.1	192
Maskwell:	(aside). Thanks, my invention; and now I have it	198	DOUBL DLR	V.1	412
Almeria:	I bend to Heav'n with Thanks and Humble Praise.	332	M. BRIDE	I.1	251
Almeria:	I bend to Heav'n with Thanks.	332	M. BRIDE	I.1 V	251
Manuel:	Take it for Thanks, Old Man, that I rejoice	333	M. BRIDE	I.1	276
Gonsalez:	O let me prostrate, pay my worthless Thanks	334	M. BRIDE	I.1	338
Zara:	Acknowledgment from Noble Minds. Such Thanks	336	M. BRIDE	I.1	416
Zara:	Such Thanks as one hating to be oblig'd--	336	M. BRIDE	I.1 V	417
Osmyn-Alph:	Distress'd, Heav'n will repay; all Thanks are poor.	359	M. BRIDE	III.1	404
Osmyn-Alph:	Distress'd, Heav'n will repay; all Thanks are poor.	359	M. BRIDE	III.1 V	404
Gonsalez:	Thanks; and I take thee at thy Word. Thou'st seen	372	M. BRIDE	IV.1	432
Almeria:	O thanks the liberal Hand that fill'd thee thus;	382	M. BRIDE	V.2	259
Almeria:	Thanks to the liberal Hand that fill'd thee thus;	382	M. BRIDE	V.2 V	259

That (1384)

That'n (1)

Ben:	stand a stern a that'n, we shall never grapple together,--	263	FOR LOVE	III.1	361

That's (153)

Vainlove:	In Castles ith' Air of thy own building: That's thy	38	OLD BATCH	I.1	29
Vainlove:	Hold hold, 'slife that's the wrong.	38	OLD BATCH	I.1	37
Vainlove:	That's pleasant, by my troth from thee, who hast	38	OLD BATCH	I.1	45
Vainlove:	thinks her Vertuous; that's one reason why I fail her:	40	OLD BATCH	I.1	119
Bellmour:	Woman's a Woman, and that's all. As such I'm sure I shall	41	OLD BATCH	I.1	173
Heartwell:	What, has he been here? that's one of Loves	42	OLD BATCH	I.1	197
Heartwell:	April-fools, is always upon some errand that's to no	42	OLD BATCH	I.1	198
Sharper:	That's because he always sets out in foul Weather,	42	OLD BATCH	I.1	201
Sharper:	that's all thou art fit for now.	43	OLD BATCH	I.1	228
Sharper:	Sure that's he and alone.	47	OLD BATCH	II.1	1
Sharper:	But that's sufficient--'Twere injustice to doubt the	50	OLD BATCH	II.1	97
Sir Joseph:	that's a better Jest than tother. 'Tis a sign you and I				
	ha'n't	50	OLD BATCH	II.1	116
Sharper:	(aside). That you are Ile be sworn. Why that's great	51	OLD BATCH	II.1	136
Araminta:	But that's not all; you caught me in your Arms	55	OLD BATCH	II.2	41
Lucy:	about it streight--Hold, I'me mistaken, or that's	62	OLD BATCH	III.1	46
Vainlove:	That's true; but I would--	63	OLD BATCH	III.1	112
Setter:	that's much the more honourable employment--by all	64	OLD BATCH	III.1	141
Sir Joseph:	mischief done, that's flat. And yet I believe if you had				
	been	68	OLD BATCH	III.1	276
Sir Joseph:	No agad no more 'tis, for that's put up already;	70	OLD BATCH	III.1	346
Silvia:	self--honest--Here, I won't keep any thing that's yours,	73	OLD BATCH	III.2	110
Laetitia:	this usage of yours--But that's what you want--Well--	77	OLD BATCH	IV.1	93
Laetitia:	No no, you are weary of me, that's it--That's all, you	78	OLD BATCH	IV.1	106
Fondlewife:	That's my good Dear--Come Kiss Nykin once	79	OLD BATCH	IV.1	143
Bellmour:	little too backward, that's the truth on't.	93	OLD BATCH	IV.4	171
Bellmour:	That's as much as to say, The Pox take me.--Well	98	OLD BATCH	V.1	78
Sir Joseph:	That's you, Bully Back.	102	OLD BATCH	V.1	210
Capt Bluff:	There, read. (Shows Letters.) That--That's a Scrawl of	103	OLD BATCH	V.1	266
Capt Bluff:	hold--That's from a Knight's Wife, she sent it me by her	103	OLD BATCH	V.1	268

That's   (continued)

		PAGE	TITLE	ACT.SC	LINE
Heartwell:	and whore my Wife? No, That's insupportable.--	104	OLD BATCH	V.1	310
Bellmour:	That's home.	108	OLD BATCH	V.2	38
Vainlove:	Faith, that's a sure way.--But here's one can	109	OLD BATCH	V.2	79
	To think oth' Sting, that's in the tail of Pleasure.	113	OLD BATCH	EPI.	9
	Now that's at stake--No fool, 'tis out o'fashion.	113	OLD BATCH	EPI.	12
	Why that's some Comfort, to an Author's fears,	113	OLD BATCH	EPI.	15
Brisk:	from the body of our Society.--He, I think that's	128	DOUBL DLR	I.1	37
Brisk:	I suppose that's because you Laugh at your own Jests,	132	DOUBL DLR	I.1	206
Lord Froth:	He, he, he, I swear that's so very pretty, I can't	132	DOUBL DLR	I.1	212
Lord Froth:	Ah, that's all.	141	DOUBL DLR	II.1	114
Lady Froth:	Biddy, that's all; just my own Name.	141	DOUBL DLR	II.1	129
Mellefont:	That's only when Two Fools meet, and their	142	DOUBL DLR	II.1	153
Mellefont:	No, hang't, that's not endeavouring to Win,	142	DOUBL DLR	II.1	159
Sir Paul:	angry, that's my pleasure at this time.	144	DOUBL DLR	II.1	212
Sir Paul:	me, that's the truth on't.	145	DOUBL DLR	II.1	258
Lady Ply:	am her Father's Wife; and that's near enough to make it	146	DOUBL DLR	II.1	310
Mellefont:	that's sinking; tho' ne'er so far off.	148	DOUBL DLR	II.1	390
Lady Touch:	Lord--Ha, ha, ha. Well but that's all--now you have	153	DOUBL DLR III.1		90
Lady Touch:	harmless mirth--only misplac'd that's all--but if it	153	DOUBL DLR III.1		95
Maskwell:	dissemble Ardour and Ecstasie, that's resolv'd: How	155	DOUBL DLR III.1		183
Sir Paul:	unworthy Sinner--But if I had a Son, ah, that's my	161	DOUBL DLR III.1		415
Sir Paul:	Alas, that's not it, Mr. Careless; ah! that's not it;	161	DOUBL DLR III.1		426
Sir Paul:	that's not it, Mr. Careless; no, no, that's not it.	161	DOUBL DLR III.1		428
Brisk:	That's right, all's well, all's well.	164	DOUBL DLR III.1		533
Mellefont:	That's but a kind of Negative Consent.--Why,	168	DOUBL DLR	IV.1	41
Lady Ply:	O that's so passionate and fine, I cannot hear it	170	DOUBL DLR	IV.1	97
Sir Paul:	your Ladyship, that's all.	172	DOUBL DLR	IV.1	184
Lady Ply:	--Your very obedient and affectionate Wife; that's	172	DOUBL DLR	IV.1	190
Brisk:	the whole Province of Contemplation: That's all--	175	DOUBL DLR	IV.1	316
Brisk:	That's well enough; let me perish, ha ha ha. O Miraculous,	177	DOUBL DLR	IV.1	356
Brisk:	(aside). That's good I'gad, that's good, Deuce take me I	177	DOUBL DLR	IV.1	379
Lady Ply:	have a Cousin that's a Proctor in the Commons, I'll go to	179	DOUBL DLR	IV.1	463
Lady Touch:	So, that's safe.	184	DOUBL DLR	IV.2	32
Lady Touch:	forgive all that's past--O Heaven, you will not ravish	186	DOUBL DLR	IV.2	103
Sir Paul:	That's a jest with all my heart, faith and troth,--	192	DOUBL DLR	V.1	171
Maskwell:	That's right,--well, I'll secure the Writings;	193	DOUBL DLR	V.1	206
Maskwell:	our Contrivance, that's my way.	193	DOUBL DLR	V.1	215
Lady Touch:	but I will stab the Lie that's forming in your heart, and				
	save	197	DOUBL DLR	V.1	381
Lady Froth:	That's because I've no light, but what's by	201	DOUBL DLR	V.1	532
	For that's a kind of Assignation Learning.	204	DOUBL DLR	EPI.	26
Jeremy:	Nay, your Condition is pretty even with theirs, that's	217	FOR LOVE	I.1	58
Trapland:	'Udso that's true, Mr. Valentine I love Mirth, but	224	FOR LOVE	I.1	300
Tattle:	Alas, that's the same thing: Pray spare me their	230	FOR LOVE	I.1	534
Mrs Frail:	That's more than he has for himself. And what will	232	FOR LOVE	I.1	593
Mrs Frail:	That's somewhat the better reason, to my	234	FOR LOVE	I.1	669
Sr Sampson:	Nor no more to be done, Old Boy; that's plain--	240	FOR LOVE	II.1	172
Sr Sampson:	Candle, and that's all the Stars are good for.	240	FOR LOVE	II.1	201
Sr Sampson:	Oh Sir, I understand you,--that's all, ha?	243	FOR LOVE	II.1	289
Sr Sampson:	That's more than I know, Sir, and I believe not.	244	FOR LOVE	II.1	316
Jeremy:	Nay, that's as clear as the Sun; I'll make Oath of it	245	FOR LOVE	II.1	355
Jeremy:	By the Provision that's made for me, you might have	245	FOR LOVE	II.1	360
Tattle:	Hold, hold, that's pretty well,--but you should not	252	FOR LOVE	II.1	635
Tattle:	That's right,--again my Charmer.	252	FOR LOVE	II.1	641
Tattle:	No, no, not a Syllable--I know that's a Secret,	254	FOR LOVE	III.1	47
Scandal:	ask'd the Question. That's all.	256	FOR LOVE	III.1	128
Angelica:	Estate too: But since that's gone, the Bait's off, and the	260	FOR LOVE	III.1	247
Ben:	Mess, and that's true: marry I had forgot. Dick's dead	261	FOR LOVE	III.1	294
Ben:	Mess, that's true: marry I had forgot. Dick's dead	261	FOR LOVE	III.1 V294	
Ben:	Why that's true as you say, nor I an't dumb, I can be	263	FOR LOVE	III.1	366
Ben:	tell'n so to's face: If that's the Case, why silence gives	263	FOR LOVE	III.1	393
Miss Prue:	that's more: So, there's your answer for you; and don't	264	FOR LOVE	III.1	400
Scandal:	Cards, sometimes, but that's nothing.	271	FOR LOVE	III.1	667
Ben:	He, he, he; why that's true: just so for all the World it	273	FOR LOVE	III.1	721
Ben:	Why that's true again; for may-hap one Bottom may	273	FOR LOVE	III.1	725
Jeremy:	No strange matter, Madam; my Master's mad, that's	276	FOR LOVE	IV.1	29
Jeremy:	Ah, you've hit it, Sir; that's the matter with him, Sir;	279	FOR LOVE	IV.1	137
Valentine:	Who's that, that's out of his Way?--I am Truth,	282	FOR LOVE	IV.1	251
Sr Sampson:	join'd together, make yet a greater, that's a Man and his	282	FOR LOVE	IV.1	266
Angelica:	Effects, I wou'd have striven; but that's too late.	294	FOR LOVE	IV.1	713
Angelica:	like him, it's a sign he likes me; and that's more than half	297	FOR LOVE	V.1	6
Sr Sampson:	ne're a young Fellow worth hanging--that's a very	299	FOR LOVE	V.1	54
Ben:	Conscience. And that's for you.	309	FOR LOVE	V.1	436
Mrs Frail:	But, my Dear, that's impossible; the Parson and	310	FOR LOVE	V.1	478
Sr Sampson:	That's as much as to say, I lie, Sir, and you don't	311	FOR LOVE	V.1	522
Almeria:	That's his Pretence. I know his Errand is	331	M. BRIDE	I.1	213
Garcia:	That, Sir, is he of whom I spoke, that's Osmyn.	336	M. BRIDE	I.1 V428	
Osmyn-Alph:	O that's the greatest Grief--I am so poor,	346	M. BRIDE	II.2	270
Zara:	For ever! that's Despair--it was Distrust	362	M. BRIDE	IV.1	31
Perez:	By all that's holy, I'm amaz'd--	373	M. BRIDE	V.1	49
	The 'Squire that's butter'd still, is sure to be undone.	393	WAY WORLD	PRO.	15
	Some Humour too, no Farce; but that's a Fault.	393	WAY WORLD	PRO.	30
Mirabell:	gay; that's all.	395	WAY WORLD	I.1	16
Mirabell:	That's well. Do you go home again, d'ee hear,	398	WAY WORLD	I.1	127
Mirabell:	That's well. Do you go home again, d'ye hear,	398	WAY WORLD	I.1 V127	
Witwoud:	That's hard, that's very hard;--A Messenger,	401	WAY WORLD	I.1	243
Witwoud:	that's the Truth on't, if he were my Brother, I cou'd not	403	WAY WORLD	I.1	311
Witwoud:	That! that's his Happiness--His want of	404	WAY WORLD	I.1	326
Witwoud:	No; that's not it.	404	WAY WORLD	I.1	334
Witwoud:	--I mean he never speaks Truth at all,--that's all. He	404	WAY WORLD	I.1	340
Petulant:	Why that's enough--You and he are not	407	WAY WORLD	I.1	438
Marwood:	No; but I'd make him believe I did, and that's	411	WAY WORLD	II.1	58
Millamant:	Ay, that's true--O but then I had--	419	WAY WORLD	II.1	355
Waitwell:	Ay there's the Grief; that's the sad change of Life;	424	WAY WORLD	II.1	562
Lady Wish:	Mrs. Qualmsick the Curate's Wife, that's always breeding	425	WAY WORLD III.1		22

That's   (continued)
Witwoud:	presumptive it only may. That's a Logical Distinction now,	435	WAY WORLD	III.1	410
Marwood:	That's a Sign indeed its no Enemy to you.	436	WAY WORLD	III.1	419
Marwood:	The Gentleman's merry, that's all, Sir--	438	WAY WORLD	III.1	504
Fainall:	I am married already; so that's over,--my Wife has	443	WAY WORLD	III.1	677
Fainall:	plaid the Jade with me--Well, that's over too--I	443	WAY WORLD	III.1	678
Fainall:	that's out of the Question,--And as to my part in my	443	WAY WORLD	III.1	685
Fainall:	Hum! Faith and that's well thought on; Marriage is	443	WAY WORLD	III.1	691
Millamant:	That's hard!	446	WAY WORLD	IV.1	54
Sir Wilful:	Daunted, No, that's not it, it is not so much for	447	WAY WORLD	IV.1	83
Sir Wilful:	present, 'tis sufficient till further acquaintance, that's				
	all--	447	WAY WORLD	IV.1	85
Sir Wilful:	Nay nothing--Only for the walks sake, that's	448	WAY WORLD	IV.1	119
Sir Wilful:	Dear Heart, that's much--Hah! that you	448	WAY WORLD	IV.1	127
Sir Wilful:	However that's as time shall try,--But spare to speak and	448	WAY WORLD	IV.1	137
Witwoud:	That's the Jest, there was no dispute, they cou'd	453	WAY WORLD	IV.1	332
Petulant:	Nymph--say it--and that's the Conclusion--pass on, or	453	WAY WORLD	IV.1	340
Petulant:	pass off,--that's all.	453	WAY WORLD	IV.1	341
Sir Wilful:	Word, and I'll do't--Wilfull will do't, that's the Word--	455	WAY WORLD	IV.1	404
Sir Wilful:	Wilfull will do't, that's my Crest--my Motto I have forgot.	455	WAY WORLD	IV.1	405
Sir Wilful:	but he spits after a Bumper, and that's a Fault.	455	WAY WORLD	IV.1	414
Waitwell:	A Woman's hand? No Madam, that's no Woman's	460	WAY WORLD	IV.1	577
Waitwell:	hand I see that already. That's some body whose throat	460	WAY WORLD	IV.1	578
Mrs Fain:	that's my Comfort.	464	WAY WORLD	V.1	83
Lady Wish:	Aye that's true; but in Case of Necessity; as of	468	WAY WORLD	V.1	263
Sir Wilful:	than a little Mouth-Glew, and that's hardly dry;--One	472	WAY WORLD	V.1	397
Lady Wish:	from Ruine, from Want, I'll forgive all that's past; Nay	473	WAY WORLD	V.1	454
Mirabell:	grant I love you not too well, that's all my fear.	477	WAY WORLD	V.1	598

The (3303)   see Th'
Theatres (1)
	To shining Theatres to see our Sport,	315	FOR LOVE	EPI.	26

Thee (243)   see Fare-thee-well
Theft (1)
Bellmour:	greater resemblance of Theft; and among us lewd Mortals,	39	OLD BATCH	I.1	91

Their (143)
Theirs (2)
Jeremy:	Nay, your Condition is pretty even with theirs, that's	217	FOR LOVE	I.1	58
Almeria:	Are not my Eyes guilty alike with theirs,	382	M. BRIDE	V.2	238

Them (31)
Theme (2)
	To please and move, has been our Poets Theme,	323	M. BRIDE	PRO.	35
Marwood:	Infamy to light, to be a Theme for legal Punsters, and	467	WAY WORLD	V.1	214

Themselves (16)
Bellmour:	work'd themselves six foot deep into a Grave--	38	OLD BATCH	I.1	26
Cynthia:	opposition of their Wits, render themselves as ridiculous	142	DOUBL DLR	II.1	156
Cynthia:	opposition of their Wit, render themselves as ridiculous	142	DOUBL DLR	II.1	V156
Mellefont:	themselves in a Vizor Mask. Here they come, I'll leave you.	158	DOUBL DLR	III.1	314
Cynthia:	in themselves, but they can render other People	165	DOUBL DLR	III.1	578
Cynthia:	If not, they like and admire themselves--And why is	167	DOUBL DLR	III.1	629
Mellefont:	Ne'er to be quench'd, till they themselves devour.	187	DOUBL DLR	IV.2	155
Foresight:	they don't know it themselves.	241	FOR LOVE	II.1	225
Angelica:	exceptious: But Madmen shew themselves most, by over	296	FOR LOVE	IV.1	763
Sr Sampson:	ready to hang themselves, or to be hang'd by the Law,	299	FOR LOVE	V.1	58
Tattle:	themselves.	304	FOR LOVE	V.1	273
Osmyn-Alph:	The just Decrees of Heav'n, which on themselves	383	M. BRIDE	V.2	V307
Osmyn-Alph:	Themselves, their own most bloody Purposes.	383	M. BRIDE	V.2	308
Petulant:	What-dee-call-'ems themselves, they must wait or rub	405	WAY WORLD	I.1	396
Marwood:	must entertain themselves, apart from Men. We may	410	WAY WORLD	II.1	22
Marwood:	To think themselves alone the Fools design'd:	479	WAY WORLD	EPI.	24

Then (345)
	For my sake then--but I'm in such Confusion,	35	OLD BATCH	PRO.	26
Bellmour:	the Servants. Very good! Then I must be disguised--With	39	OLD BATCH	I.1	89
Bellmour:	self, nor suffers any Body else to rail at me. Then as I	41	OLD BATCH	I.1	169
Bellmour:	floating Island; sometimes seems in reach, then vanishes	42	OLD BATCH	I.1	206
Bellmour:	Though you should be now and then interrupted in a	44	OLD BATCH	I.1	268
Sharper:	Why if whoring be purging--as you call it--then I	44	OLD BATCH	I.1	291
Heartwell:	like his Grace, has just his smile and air of's Face. Then	45	OLD BATCH	I.1	321
Heartwell:	Lord what d'ee-cals Mouth to a Tittle--Then I to put it	45	OLD BATCH	I.1	324
Bellmour:	Right, but then the comparison breaks, for he will	47	OLD BATCH	I.1	380
Sharper:	O your Servant Sir, you are safe then it seems; 'tis an	48	OLD BATCH	II.1	32
Sharper:	Is it possible! I am happy to have obliged the	49	OLD BATCH	II.1	72
Sir Joseph:	You have found it Sir then it seems; I profess I'me	49	OLD BATCH	II.1	85
Sharper:	If he had Sir, which then? he could have done no	50	OLD BATCH	II.1	125
Capt Bluff:	Say you so? then I honour him--But has he been	51	OLD BATCH	II.1	152
Capt Bluff:	Ay! Then I honour him again--Sir may I crave your	52	OLD BATCH	II.1	171
Capt Bluff:	Oh I thought so--Why then you can know nothing	52	OLD BATCH	II.1	187
Araminta:	Come then, Kiss and Friends.	56	OLD BATCH	II.2	62
Araminta:	then, Cousin, and let me have all the Company to my	57	OLD BATCH	II.2	102
Bellmour:	then gets it for his pains. For importunity in Love, like	58	OLD BATCH	II.2	132
Bellmour:	then pursues it for the Favour.	58	OLD BATCH	II.2	134
Belinda:	O Gad, would you would all pray to Love then, and	58	OLD BATCH	II.2	142
Araminta:	then we are in great danger of being dull--If my				
	Musick-master	58	OLD BATCH	II.2	152
Belinda:	Then know, I would be Ador'd in Silence.	59	OLD BATCH	II.2	175
Silvia:	Will a' not come then?	60	OLD BATCH	III.1	1
Silvia:	Will he not come then?	60	OLD BATCH	III.1	V 1
Lucy:	would take time to peruse it--But then he was in haste.	61	OLD BATCH	III.1	27
Lucy:	To be brief then; what is the reason your Master did	66	OLD BATCH	III.1	217
Sir Joseph:	You may stay till the day of Judgment then, by the	67	OLD BATCH	III.1	252
Sir Joseph:	am both Sir; what then? I hope I may be offended, without	68	OLD BATCH	III.1	293
Sharper:	Nay then I'll be beforehand with you, take that--	69	OLD BATCH	III.1	308
Singer:	She frown'd and blush'd, then sigh'd and kiss'd,	71	OLD BATCH	III.2	V 19
Heartwell:	worth for the purchase of thy Love--Say, is it mine then,	72	OLD BATCH	III.2	39
Silvia:	Must you lie then, if you say you Love me?	72	OLD BATCH	III.2	61
Heartwell:	not Love, it is Madness, and then it is pardonable--Nay	73	OLD BATCH	III.2	84
Heartwell:	is a Jewel--Stay Silvia--But then to Marry--	74	OLD BATCH	III.2	116

Then   (continued)

Speaker	Text	PAGE	TITLE	ACT.SC	LINE
Heartwell:	Well, farewell then--if I can get out of her sight I	74	OLD BATCH	III.2	129
Heartwell:	Well, farewell then--if I can get out of sight I	74	OLD BATCH	III.2	V129
Silvia:	till then we never make the experiment--But how hast	75	OLD BATCH	III.2	153
Barnaby:	I have done Sir, then farewell 500 Pound.	76	OLD BATCH	IV.1	18
Barnaby:	Husband. 'Tis then indeed, like the vanity of taking a fine	76	OLD BATCH	IV.1	42
Fondlewife:	vigorous, and I am Old and impotent--Then why didst	76	OLD BATCH	IV.1	52
Fondlewife:	Yes--Why then!--Ay, but to say truth, She's fonder of	77	OLD BATCH	IV.1	59
Laetitia:	(aside). Oh then alls safe. I was terrible frighted--	78	OLD BATCH	IV.1	102
Laetitia:	(aside). Oh then alls safe. I was terribly frighted--	78	OLD BATCH	IV.1	V102
Fondlewife:	He, he, he, wilt thou poor Fool? Then I will go,	79	OLD BATCH	IV.1	134
Fondlewife:	more, and then get you in--So--Get you in,	79	OLD BATCH	IV.1	144
Sharper:	(reads). Hum hum--And what then appear'd a fault,	79	OLD BATCH	IV.1	156
Laetitia:	(aside). My Letter! Base Vainlove! Then 'tis too late	81	OLD BATCH	IV.2	34
Laetitia:	to dissemble. 'Tis plain then you have mistaken the Person.	81	OLD BATCH	IV.2	35
Araminta:	So then; you have been diverted. What did they	84	OLD BATCH	IV.3	49
Capt Bluff:	Come on then, Knight.--But d'ye know what to	85	OLD BATCH	IV.3	70
Laetitia:	Then, I'll let you in.	89	OLD BATCH	IV.4	20
Fondlewife:	Oh, thou salacious Woman! Am I then brutified?	92	OLD BATCH	IV.4	125
Fondlewife:	Oh, it is a Man then, it seems.	93	OLD BATCH	IV.4	141
Laetitia:	Why then, I wish I may never enter into the Heaven	93	OLD BATCH	IV.4	150
Bellmour:	In short then, I was informed of the opportunity	94	OLD BATCH	IV.4	205
Bellmour:	No, for then you must of consequence part with	95	OLD BATCH	IV.4	224
Bellmour:	upon the Publick; then the encouragement of a separate	95	OLD BATCH	IV.4	226
Lucy:	Well, It is then: But you'll be secret?	98	OLD BATCH	V.1	52
Bellmour:	Nay, then I thank thee for not putting me out of	100	OLD BATCH	V.1	147
Sir Joseph:	stroke down her Belly; and then step aside to tie her	103	OLD BATCH	V.1	257
Bellmour:	then opens the Scene of Pleasure.	107	OLD BATCH	V.1	386
Sharper:	Then, let me beg these Ladies to wear their Masks, a	110	OLD BATCH	V.2	90
Heartwell:	Then good Councel will be thrown away upon	112	OLD BATCH	V.2	157
	But then you cruel Criticks would so maul him!	113	OLD BATCH	EPI.	26
Mellefont:	Then thy Reason staggers, and thou'rt almost	127	DOUBL DLR	I.1	5
Mellefont:	then came the Storm I fear'd at first: For starting from my	130	DOUBL DLR	I.1	113
Lord Froth:	Laugh. Then especially to Laugh the Jest of an Inferiour	132	DOUBL DLR	I.1	201
Brisk:	Well then, you tell me, some good Jest, or very Witty	134	DOUBL DLR	I.1	267
Careless:	Then I shall be disappointed indeed.	134	DOUBL DLR	I.1	279
Lord Froth:	Then you must mortifie him, with a Patch; my	135	DOUBL DLR	I.1	295
Maskwell:	Words have not shewn, then how should Words express.	137	DOUBL DLR	I.1	371
Lady Froth:	then I had a way.--For between you and I, I had	138	DOUBL DLR	II.1	10
Cynthia:	Then neither my Lord and you would ever have	139	DOUBL DLR	II.1	25
Cynthia:	Then neither my Lord nor you would ever have	139	DOUBL DLR	II.1	V 25
	then laughs out.)	140	DOUBL DLR	II.1	66
Lady Froth:	then your Bow! Good my Lord, bow as you did when I	140	DOUBL DLR	II.1	73
	(He bows profoundly low, then kisses the Glass.)	140	DOUBL DLR	II.1	79
Lady Froth:	He, Ay, is not it? and then I call my Lord	141	DOUBL DLR	II.1	126
Cynthia:	Then I find its like Cards, if either of us have a good	142	DOUBL DLR	II.1	162
Singer:	Then too late, desire will find you,	143	DOUBL DLR	II.1	188
Sir Paul:	March on, I will fight under you then: I am convinced, as	145	DOUBL DLR	II.1	239
Lady Ply:	O reflect upon the horror of that, and then the	147	DOUBL DLR	II.1	314
Lady Ply:	only to make a Cuckold of the Father; and then seducing	147	DOUBL DLR	II.1	316
Lady Ply:	no sin,--but then, to Marry my Daughter, for the	147	DOUBL DLR	II.1	350
Mellefont:	(after a pause). So then,--spight of my care and	148	DOUBL DLR	II.1	374
Maskwell:	know then, that all my Contrivances were but Bubbles; till	149	DOUBL DLR	II.1	420
Maskwell:	to break the Match: Then she thought my Jealousie might	149	DOUBL DLR	II.1	424
Mellefont:	I will; till then, success attend thee.	149	DOUBL DLR	II.1	437
Maskwell:	Till then, Success will attend me; for when I meet	150	DOUBL DLR	II.1	439
Maskwell:	Fools! then that hungry Gudgeon Credulity, will bite at	150	DOUBL DLR	II.1	459
Lord Touch:	You believe it then?	151	DOUBL DLR	III.1	33
Lord Touch:	How? Then I must know, nay I will: No	152	DOUBL DLR	III.1	61
Maskwell:	open: 'twill be hard, if then you can't bring her to any	157	DOUBL DLR	III.1	253
Careless:	some such Cant. Then she has told me the whole History of	157	DOUBL DLR	III.1	272
Mellefont:	Nay, then you have her; for a woman's bragging	158	DOUBL DLR	III.1	298
Sir Paul:	I; but mine's soon over, and then I'm so sorry--O, Mr.	160	DOUBL DLR	III.1	390
Careless:	No, what can be the matter then?	161	DOUBL DLR	III.1	429
Lord Froth:	upon the broad grin, all laugh and no Company; ah, then	162	DOUBL DLR	III.1	459
Lord Froth:	Hee, hee, hee, right; and then my Lady Whifler is	163	DOUBL DLR	III.1	475
Lord Froth:	then, what do they laugh at? For you know laughing	163	DOUBL DLR	III.1	477
Lady Froth:	Then you think that Episode between Susan, the	163	DOUBL DLR	III.1	502
Brisk:	Incomparable, let me perish!--but then being an Heroick	163	DOUBL DLR	III.1	505
Lady Froth:	Then I don't say the Sun shines all the day, but,	164	DOUBL DLR	III.1	523
Lady Froth:	that he peeps now and then, yet he does shine all the day	164	DOUBL DLR	III.1	524
Lady Froth:	Then too like Heav'ns Charioteer, the Sun:	164	DOUBL DLR	III.1	536
Brisk:	Was that he then, I'm answered, if Jehu was a Hackney	165	DOUBL DLR	III.1	549
Lady Froth:	Mouth, to Laugh, and then put 'em in again--Foh.	165	DOUBL DLR	III.1	571
Lady Froth:	Then she's always ready to Laugh when Sneer	165	DOUBL DLR	III.1	573
Lady Froth:	Then that t'other great strapping Lady--I	166	DOUBL DLR	III.1	580
Brisk:	Why she lays it on with a Trowel--Then she has a	166	DOUBL DLR	III.1	585
Cynthia:	a Ditch--Here then, I give you my promise, in spight of	168	DOUBL DLR	IV.1	35
Cynthia:	Consent, and then--	169	DOUBL DLR	IV.1	49
Mellefont:	Ay, what am I to trust to then?	169	DOUBL DLR	IV.1	57
Sir Paul:	Why then the revoking my Consent does annul, or	171	DOUBL DLR	IV.1	144
Sir Paul:	Well, why then Lamb you may keep your Oath,	173	DOUBL DLR	IV.1	206
Lady Froth:	then joyn hands again; I could teach my Lord this Dance	177	DOUBL DLR	IV.1	367
Sir Paul:	Person! Well, let me see--Till then I Languish in	178	DOUBL DLR	IV.1	414
Careless:	said all I could, but can't prevail--Then my Friendship	180	DOUBL DLR	IV.1	492
Careless:	Subject: Then I writ a Letter to her; I don't know what	180	DOUBL DLR	IV.1	501
Maskwell:	may work upon him: then, for me to do it! I have	182	DOUBL DLR	IV.1	566
Maskwell:	Nay then, there's but one way.	184	DOUBL DLR	IV.2	39
Mellefont:	shapes in shining day, then fear shews Cowards in the	186	DOUBL DLR	IV.2	V125
Maskwell:	But should it be known! then what I have lost a Friend!	188	DOUBL DLR	V.1	22
Maskwell:	Then witness Heaven for me, this Wealth and	189	DOUBL DLR	V.1	71
Maskwell:	then were fine work indeed! her fury wou'd spare nothing,	190	DOUBL DLR	V.1	93
Lady Touch:	Why then you don't know half your	192	DOUBL DLR	V.1	169
Lord Touch:	Then Mellefont has urg'd some body to	195	DOUBL DLR	V.1	309
Maskwell:	Strike then--Since you will have it so.	197	DOUBL DLR	V.1	383
Lady Touch:	Ha! do you mock my Rage? then this shall	198	DOUBL DLR	V.1	391

Then   (continued)

Speaker	Text	PAGE	TITLE	ACT.SC	LINE
Lady Touch:	thee cpen to my sight! But then 'twill be too late to know--	198	DOUEL DLR	V.1	397
Lady Touch:	Uncertainty. Speak then, and tell me--yet are you	198	DOUEL DLR	V.1	400
	Then they could tell what Epilogues to make;	204	DOUEL DLR	EPI.	2
Valentine:	then ever, and appear more notoriously her Admirer in	217	FOR LOVE	I.1	51
Scandal:	Aye? Why then I'm afraid Jeremy has Wit: For	219	FOR LCVE	I.1	120
Valentine:	T'other Glass, and then we'll talk. Fill, Jeremy.	222	FCR LCVE	I.1	248
Snap:	block up the Chocolate-Houses, and then our labour's lost.	224	FCR LCVE	I.1	299
Tattle:	Why then, as I hope to be sav'd, I believe a Woman	228	FOR LCVE	I.1	473
Scandal:	Come then, sacrifice half a Dozen Women cf good	230	FOR LCVE	I.1	526
Scandal:	Well, begin then: But take notice, if you are so ill a	230	FOR LCVE	I.1	536
Tattle:	Well, first then--	230	FOR LOVE	I.1	540
Mrs Frail:	Then let him Marry and reform.	231	FOR LCVE	I.1	559
Tattle:	there too--for then she is obliged to keep the Secret.	232	FOR LCVE	I.1	614
Tattle:	there too--for then she's obliged to keep the Secret.	232	FOR LCVE	I.1 V614	
Scandal:	Ignorance, all in one Piece. Then I can shew you Lying,	233	FCR LCVE	I.1	630
Scandal:	Then I have a Lady burning of Brandy in a Cellar	233	FOR LCVE	I.1	639
Scandal:	Then I have a Lady burning Brandy in a Cellar	233	FOR LCVE	I.1 V639	
Foresight:	pretty good that too; but then I stumbl'd coming	236	FCR LCVE	II.1	33
Foresight:	Withouten Guile, then be it said,	236	FOR LCVE	II.1	53
Nurse:	and ycur Urinal by you, and now and then rub the	238	FOR LCVE	II.1	104
Angelica:	Will ycu? I care not, but all shall out then--	238	FOR LCVE	II.1	118
Angelica:	morrow morning--But let me be gone first, and then	239	FOR LCVE	II.1	135
Sr Sampson:	morning, and then look you perform Covenants, and so	246	FOR LCVE	II.1	403
Mrs Frail:	deny it positively to Your Face then.	247	FOR LOVE	II.1	462
Miss Prue:	What must I call you then, are not you my Father's	249	FOR LCVE	II.1	509
Miss Prue:	What must I call you then, are you not my Father's	249	FOR LCVE	II.1 V509	
Miss Prue:	Look you here, Madam then, what Mr. Tattle has	249	FOR LCVE	II.1	515
Mrs Fore:	So he wou'd--but then leaving 'em	250	FOR LCVE	II.1	573
Miss Prue:	No! what then? what shall you and I do together?	251	FOR LOVE	II.1	587
Miss Prue:	What, is it like the Catechisme?--Come then	251	FCR LCVE	II.1	600
Tattle:	a Farthing for you then in a twinckling.	251	FOR LCVE	II.1	605
Miss Prue:	What must I say then?	251	FCR LCVE	II.1	606
Miss Prue:	Why, must I tell a Lie then?	251	FCR LCVE	II.1	609
Tattle:	With all my heart,--Now then my little Angel.	252	FOR LCVE	II.1	638
Miss Prue:	Will ycu? then I'll be more angry, and more	253	FOR LCVE	II.1	655
Tattle:	Then I'll make you cry out.	253	FOR LCVE	II.1	657
Angelica:	Then it seems you would have told, if you had been	256	FOR LCVE	III.1	114
Scandal:	No don't; for then you'l tell us no more--Come, I'll	258	FOR LCVE	III.1	190
Ben:	Why then, I'll go to Sea again, so there's one for t'other, an	261	FOR LCVE	III.1	300
Ben:	and then you'll carry your Keels above Water, he, he, he.	262	FCR LCVE	III.1	335
Foresight:	will be combust; and then I may do well.	270	FOR LCVE	III.1	649
Mrs Fore:	Why then I'll speak my mind. Now as to	272	FOR LCVE	III.1	686
Ben:	He then might play his part.	274	FOR LOVE	III.1	784
Ben:	And then he let fly at her,	274	FOR LOVE	III.1	787
Ben:	then put off with the next fair wind. How de'e like us?	275	FOR LCVE	III.1	803
Angelica:	(aside). Say you so; nay, then I'm convinc'd: And if I	277	FCR LCVE	IV.1	66
Scandal:	him then, if he desire it?	277	FOR LCVE	IV.1	78
Buckram:	Why then all's obliterated, Sir Sampson, if he be	279	FOR LCVE	IV.1	142
Valentine:	Is the Lawyer gone? 'tis well, then we may drink	280	FOR LCVE	IV.1	191
Sr Sampson:	And then at the bottom--As witness my Hand,	281	FOR LCVE	IV.1	223
Sr Sampson:	Val: And then no body need hold it (puts the Paper in his	281	FOR LCVE	IV.1	232
Mrs Frail:	then?	283	FOR LCVE	IV.1	303
Mrs Frail:	So then you intend to go to Sea again?	285	FOR LCVE	IV.1	378
Ben:	Then why was he graceless first,--if I am undutiful and	286	FOR LCVE	IV.1	390
Ben:	What, are you false hearted then?	287	FOR LCVE	IV.1	422
Mrs Fore:	What then, he bore it most Heroically?	287	FOR LCVE	IV.1	454
Valentine:	asham'd of; and then we'll blush once for all.	290	FOR LCVE	IV.1	564
Valentine:	Scandal) What, dc you look strange upon me?--Then	292	FOR LCVE	IV.1	618
Valentine:	thou can'st not borrow Money of me; Then what	292	FOR LCVE	IV.1	627
Singer-V:	Then never let us chain what should be free,	293	FOR LCVE	IV.1	662
Angelica:	Then you thought me mercenary--But how	295	FOR LCVE	IV.1	728
Sr Sampson:	wou'd she wou'd like me, then I shou'd hamper my young	298	FOR LCVE	V.1	49
Sr Sampson:	consent? Is it a Match then?	300	FCR LCVE	V.1	133
Sr Sampson:	Say you so, Hussy?--Come lets go then;	301	FOR LCVE	V.1	160
Miss Prue:	last Night then?	304	FOR LCVE	V.1	249
Miss Prue:	What, and must not I have e're a Husband then?	305	FOR LCVE	V.1	304
Ben:	Why then I'll tell you, There's a new wedding upon the	307	FOR LCVE	V.1	358
Sr Sampson:	What, have you found your Senses at last then?	310	FOR LCVE	V.1	502
Jeremy:	any thing like it--Then how could it be otherwise?	313	FOR LCVE	V.1	594
	But liv'd, I know not how, in Beasts; and then	315	FOR LOVE	EPI.	17
	Then bounding Balls and Rackets they encompass'd,	315	FCR LCVE	EPI.	30
	Then pray continue this your kind behaviour,	316	FOR LOVE	EPI.	43
	New Plays did then like Almanacks appear;	323	M. BBIDE	PRO.	3
	Then freely judge the Scenes that shall ensue,	324	M. BBIDE	PRO.	39
Almeria:	What then am I? Am I more senseless grown	326	M. BBIDE	I.1	6
Leonora:	Of his Success; that then, in spite of Hate,	327	M. BBIDE	I.1	42
Almeria:	Then why am I? O when shall I have Rest?	327	M. BBIDE	I.1	54
Leonora:	Alas! were you then wedded to Alphonso?	329	M. BBIDE	I.1	132
Almeria:	Then fly with Joy and Swiftness from me.	330	M. BBIDE	I.1	161
Almeria:	Another Lord; may then just Heav'n show'r down	330	M. BBIDE	I.1	187
Manuel:	Then, then, to weep, and pray, and grieve? By Heav'n,	333	M. BBIDE	I.1	314
Manuel:	Did Zara, then, request he might attend her?	335	M. BBIDE	I.1	377
Perez:	Then forward shot their Fires, which he pursu'd,	338	M. BBIDE	II.1	22
Almeria:	Are lost in dread of greater Ill. Then shew me,	339	M. BBIDE	II.1 V 80	
Almeria:	To his cold clayie Breast: my Father then,	340	M. BBIDE	II.2	22
Osmyn-Alph:	Wilt thou not know me? Hast thou then forgot me?	342	M. BBIDE	II.2	78
Osmyn-Alph:	Then, bear me in a Whirl-wind to my Fate;	343	M. BBIDE	II.2	140
Osmyn-Alph:	Then, then 'twill be enough--I shall be Old.	343	M. BBIDE	II.2	142
Osmyn-Alph:	I shall have liv'd beyond all Aera's then,	343	M. BBIDE	II.2	143
Zara:	Is it well done? Is this then the Return	345	M. BBIDE	II.2	235
Zara:	Now, then you see me--	346	M. BBIDE	II.2	255
Zara:	Ev'n then. Kneeling on Earth, I loos'd my Hair,	346	M. BBIDE	II.2	281
Zara:	And with it dry'd thy wat'ry Cheeks; then chaf'd	346	M. BBIDE	II.2 V282	
Zara:	Think on my Suff'ring first, then, look on me;	347	M. BBIDE	II.2	304

Then   (continued)

Then   (continued)

		PAGE	TITLE	ACT.SC	LINE
Lady Wish:	they are together, then come to me Foible, that I may not	445	WAY WORLD	IV.1	39
Millamant:	A walk? What then?	448	WAY WORLD	IV.1	118
Sir Wilful:	Your Servant, then with your leave I'll return	448	WAY WORLD	IV.1	149
Millamant:	Contemplation, must I bid you then Adieu? ay-h adieu.--my	449	WAY WORLD	IV.1	187
Mirabell:	Then I'll get up in a morning as early as I please.	449	WAY WORLD	IV.1	192
Millamant:	a New Chariot, to provoke Eyes and Whispers; And then	450	WAY WORLD	IV.1	203
Mirabell:	I thank you. Inprimis then, I Covenant that your	451	WAY WORLD	IV.1	234
Mirabell:	you a fop--scrambling to the Play in a Mask--then	451	WAY WORLD	IV.1	239
Mirabell:	Then wee're agreed. Shall I kiss your hand upon the	452	WAY WORLD	IV.1	280
Millamant:	Well then--I'll take my death I'm in a horrid	452	WAY WORLD	IV.1	288
Petulant:	what then? If I have a humour to prove it.--If I shall	454	WAY WORLD	IV.1	368
Sir Wilful:	Put the glass then around with the Sun Boys	455	WAY WORLD	IV.1	417
Waitwell:	his head, and then go out in a stink like a Candle's end	458	WAY WORLD	IV.1	524
Foible:	Then, then Madam, Mr. Mirabell waited for her in her	461	WAY WORLD	V.1	28
Foible:	been deluded by him, then how shou'd I a poor Ignorant,	463	WAY WORLD	V.1	28
Lady Wish:	What, that I have been your Property, have	463	WAY WORLD	V.1	46
Foible:	mischeivous Devil told Mr. Fainall of your Ladyship then?	464	WAY WORLD	V.1	80
Marwood:	And then to have my young Revellers of the	467	WAY WORLD	V.1	224
Millamant:	and insist upon the contract still. Then 'tis the last time he	470	WAY WORLD	V.1	339
Sir Wilful:	self then.	471	WAY WORLD	V.1	377
Fainall:	Perfidious Fiend! then thus I'll be reveng'd.--(offers	476	WAY WORLD	V.1	556
	Then, all bad Poets we are sure are Foes,	479	WAY WORLD	EPI.	9

Thence (7)

		PAGE	TITLE	ACT.SC	LINE
Belinda:	would you from thence infer I love him?	55	OLD BATCH	II.2	40
Scandal:	Why thence it arises--The thing is proverbially	256	FOR LOVE	III.1	123
Zara:	From his Chains; thence sprung his Insolence,	349	M. BRIDE	II.2	379
Zara:	He should be set at large; thence sprung his Insolence,	349	M. BRIDE	II.2	V379
Osmyn-Alph:	And wafted thence, on Angels Wings, thro' Ways	353	M. BRIDE	III.1	131
Manuel:	Remove the Body thence, 'ere Zara see it.	373	M. BRIDE	V.1	28
Marwood:	Short-hand Writers to the publick Press; and from thence	468	WAY WORLD	V.1	231

Ther's (1)

		PAGE	TITLE	ACT.SC	LINE
Lucy:	Ther's the Hang-Dog his Man--I had a power over	64	OLD BATCH	III.1	145

There (264)

		PAGE	TITLE	ACT.SC	LINE
Vainlove:	word--Had you been there or any Body 'thad been the	39	OLD BATCH	I.1	99
Bellmour:	But do you know nothing of a new Rival there?	40	OLD BATCH	I.1	117
Bellmour:	How George, do's the Wind blow there?	44	OLD BATCH	I.1	293
Heartwell:	Ay there you've nick't it--there's the Devil upon	45	OLD BATCH	I.1	317
Sharper:	How Sir! I make a doubt, if there be at this Day a	52	OLD BATCH	II.1	183
Capt Bluff:	Gazette! Why there again now--Why, Sir, there are	52	OLD BATCH	II.1	192
Capt Bluff:	Campagn, had a small Post there; but no matter for that--	52	OLD BATCH	II.1	196
Capt Bluff:	Perhaps, Sir, there was a scarce any thing of moment	52	OLD BATCH	II.1	197
Belinda:	There was a Whine--O Gad I hate your horrid	54	OLD BATCH	II.2	11
Footman:	Madam, there are--	56	OLD BATCH	II.2	74
Belinda:	Is there a Chair?	56	OLD BATCH	II.2	75
Footman:	No, Madam, there are Mr. Bellmour and Mr.	56	OLD BATCH	II.2	76
Bellmour:	Tyrant there and I, are two Buckets that can never come	57	OLD BATCH	II.2	118
Bellmour:	Till he has created Love where there was none, and	58	OLD BATCH	II.2	131
Araminta:	your Sex--Who's there? (Calls.)	58	OLD BATCH	II.2	155
Araminta:	Nature well, for there are few Men, but do more silly	60	OLD BATCH	II.2	216
Heartwell:	There stands my North, and thither my Needle points	63	OLD BATCH	III.1	75
Sir Joseph:	hundred Pound for being saved, and d'ee think, an there	67	OLD BATCH	III.1	255
Sir Joseph:	my Choller had been up too, agad there would have been	68	OLD BATCH	III.1	275
Sharper:	Man there--That Pot-gun charg'd with Wind.	69	OLD BATCH	III.1	305
Heartwell:	thee--There thou hast don't, all my Resolve melted in	74	OLD BATCH	III.2	135
Heartwell:	thee--There thou hast don't, all my Resolve melted in	74	OLD BATCH	III.2	V135
Lucy:	As you would wish--Since there is no reclaiming	75	OLD BATCH	III.2	155
Bellmour:	Gads so there he is, he must not see me.	75	OLD BATCH	IV.1	11
Barnaby:	done there till you come.	76	OLD BATCH	IV.1	35
Vainlove:	No, she will be there this evening--Yes I will	80	OLD BATCH	IV.1	184
Laetitia:	there needs no farther Apology.	81	OLD BATCH	IV.2	47
Belinda:	Snipwel's Shop while I was there.--But, Oh Gad!	84	OLD BATCH	IV.3	25
Sharper:	There is in true Beauty, as in Courage, somewhat,	86	OLD BATCH	IV.3	126
Laetitia:	Ah! There he is. Make haste, gather up your things.	89	OLD BATCH	IV.4	10
Laetitia:	My Jewel, Art thou there? No matter for your	89	OLD BATCH	IV.4	15
Bellmour:	your Wife, and there will be some hopes of having her	95	OLD BATCH	IV.4	225
Bellmour:	Humph, Sits the Wind there?--What a lucky	97	OLD BATCH	V.1	23
Bellmour:	Nay, nay: Look you, Lucy; there are Whores of as	98	OLD BATCH	V.1	64
Vainlove:	There I receiv'd the Letter--It must be so.	99	OLD BATCH	V.1	119
Sharper:	You were well employ'd.--I think there is no	99	OLD BATCH	V.1	123
Sir Joseph:	in Aesop's Fables, Bully? A-Gad there are good Morals to	101	OLD BATCH	V.1	175
Sir Joseph:	and to speak, is but loss of time; but if there be occasion,	103	OLD BATCH	V.1	244
Sir Joseph:	'Tis too little, there's more, Man. There, take all--	103	OLD BATCH	V.1	249
Capt Bluff:	There, read. (Shows Letters.) That--That's a Scrawl of	103	OLD BATCH	V.1	266
Sharper:	Why, there: The Two white Posts.	104	OLD BATCH	V.1	288
Heartwell:	And who wou'd you visit there, say you? (O'ons,	104	OLD BATCH	V.1	289
Boy:	There was a Man too that fetch'd 'em out:--Setter, I	107	OLD BATCH	V.2	2
Vainlove:	might have been just.--There, we are even.--	109	OLD BATCH	V.2	70
Bellmour:	But there is a fatality in Marriage.--For I find I'm	111	OLD BATCH	V.2	155
	There, as instinct directs, to Swim, or Drown.	125	DOUBL DLR	PRO.	4
Brisk:	to Laugh at. I think there I was with you, ha? Mellefont.	128	DOUBL DLR	I.1	30
Brisk:	of Wine,--the Deuce take me if there were three good	128	DOUBL DLR	I.1	35
Mellefont:	There are times when Sense may be unseasonable, as well as	129	DOUBL DLR	I.1	70
Careless:	Was there ever such a Fury! 'tis well Nature has not	130	DOUBL DLR	I.1	100
Careless:	I'm mistaken if there be not a Familiarity between	131	DOUBL DLR	I.1	153
Lord Froth:	I often smile at your Conceptions, But there is nothing	132	DOUBL DLR	I.1	198
Careless:	No, why what d'ee go there for?	133	DOUBL DLR	I.1	226
Careless:	No, why what d'ye go there for?	133	DOUBL DLR	I.1	V226
Brisk:	Let me perish, my Lord, but there is something very	133	DOUBL DLR	I.1	237
Brisk:	O Lord, why can't you find it out?--Why there	133	DOUBL DLR	I.1	248
Lady Touch:	Treachery and Ingratitude! Is there a Vice more	135	DOUBL DLR	I.1	324
Lady Touch:	Treachery and Ingratitude! Is there a Vice more	135	DOUBL DLR	I.1	V324
Maskwell:	there was Revenge in view; that Womans Idol had defil'd	137	DOUBL DLR	I.1	375
Lord Froth:	ay, there it is; who could resist! 'twas so my heart was made	140	DOUBL DLR	II.1	68

There   (continued)
    Lord Froth: I saw my self there, and kissed it for your sake. . . . 140   DOUBL DLR   II.1   80
    Lady Froth: you go into the next Room? and there I'll shew you all   . 142   DOUEL DLR   II.1 144
    Lady Froth: you go into the next Room? and there I'll shew you what   . 142   DOUEL DLR   II.1 V144
    Lady Ply: impossible for me to know whether I could or no, there   . 147   DOUEL DLR   II.1 328
    Lady Ply: impossible for me to know whether I could or not, there . 147   DOUEL DLR   II.1 V328
    Mellefont: Aunt: There must be more behind, this is but the first   . 148   DOUEL DLR   II.1 377
    Maskwell: an universal Leveller of Mankind. Ha! but is there not such 150   DOUEL DLR   II.1 450
    Lord Touch: There should have been demonstration of the 151   DOUEL DLR III.1   19
    Lady Touch: So I suppose there was. 151   DOUEL DLR III.1   21
    Lady Touch: That I can't tell: nay, I don't say there was-- 151   DOUEL DLR III.1   23
    Maskwell: confirm all, had there been occasion. 154   DOUEL DLR III.1 130
    Lady Touch: Evening in my Chamber; there rejoice at our success, and . 155   DOUEL DLR III.1 170
    Mellefont: swath'd down, and so put to bed; and there he lies with a . 158   DOUEL DLR III.1 291
    Lady Ply: Jesu, Sir Paul, what a Phrase was there? You will . . . 159   DOUEL DLR III.1 327
    Lady Ply: Sir Paul, what a Phrase was there? You will 159   DOUEL DLR III.1 V327
    Sir Paul: Ay, so so, there. 160   DCUEL DLR III.1 365
    Lord Froth: Conversation there? 162   DOUEL DLR III.1 470
    Lady Froth: And there his whipping and his driving ends; 164   DOUEL DLR III.1 539
    Lady Froth: There he's secure from danger of a bilk, ... 164   DOUEL DLR III.1 540
    Cynthia: (aside). Well, I find there are no Fools so inconsiderable 165   DOUEL DLR III.1 577
    Sir Paul: It becomes me, when there is any comparison made, . . . 172   DOUEL DLR   IV.1 187
    Sir Paul: There it is, Madam; Do you want a Pen and Ink? 173   DOUEL DLR   IV.1 218
    Sir Paul: to his Bed, and there return his Caresses with interest
                      to his 178   DOUEL DLR   IV.1 422
    Sir Paul: know whether there be any thing at all in the World, or   . 179   DOUEL DLR   IV.1 450
    Lady Ply: . . . there has hardly been 179   DOUEL DLR   IV.1 V457
    Maskwell: lie conceal'd there; otherwise she may Lock the Door   . 181   DOUEL DLR   IV.1 517
    Lord Touch: it: Yet there has been a thing in your Knowledge, which . 181   DOUEL DLR   IV.1 541
    Maskwell: Lordship will meet me a quarter of an Hour hence there,   . 183   DOUEL DLR   IV.1 584
    Maskwell: Yet I am wretched--O there is a secret burns 188   DOUEL DLR   V.1   28
    Lady Touch: Married? Is there not reward enough in raising his low   . 191   DOUEL DLR   V.1 126
    Maskwell: us to Morrow Morning at St. Albans; there we will Sum   . 194   DOUEL DLR   V.1 243
    Maskwell: corner Chamber at this end of the Gallery, there is a back 194   DOUEL DLR   V.1 253
    Maskwell: But first I must instruct my little Levite, there is no
                      Plot, ... 194   DOUEL DLR   V.1 267
    Maskwell: Chamber. When Cynthia comes, let there be no Light, and   . 195   DOUEL DLR   V.1 293
    Maskwell: and, unperceiv'd, there you may propose to reinstate him . 199   DOUEL DLR   V.1 447
    Maskwell: No more,--there want but a few Minutes of 199   DOUEL DLR   V.1 456
    Maskwell: the time; and Mellefont's Love will carry him there before 199   DOUEL DLR   V.1 457
    Lord Froth: Lady's is the most inviting Couch; and a slumber there, is 200   DOUEL DLR   V.1 494
                   (If there be any here) and that is Satire. 213   FOR LCVE   PRO.   32
    Jeremy: there is nothing to be eaten. 216   FOR LCVE   I.1   22
    Valentine: Jeremy, see who's there. 220   FOR LCVE   I.1 155
    Trapland: (sits). There is a Debt, Mr. Valentine, of 1500 [Pounds] of 222   FOR LOVE   I.1 236
    Valentine: Ruby-Lips! better sealing there, than a Bond for a Million, 223   FOR LOVE   I.1 279
    Tattle: For there is nothing more known, than that no body . . . 227   FCB LOVE   I.1 404
    Tattle: her--Madam, says I, there are some Persons who make . . 227   FOR LOVE   I.1 430
    Tattle: Is there not a back way? 229   FOR LOVE   I.1 V510
    Valentine: If there were, you have more Discretion, than to . . . 229   FOR LCVE   I.1 511
    Mrs Frail: You are the most mistaken in the World; there is . . . 231   FCB LOVE   I.1 562
    Scandal: only Original you will see there. 232   FOR LCVE   I.1 604
    Tattle: there too--for then she is obliged to keep the Secret.   . 232   FOR LCVE   I.1 614
    Tattle: there too--for then she's obliged to keep the Secret.   . 232   FOR LCVE   I.1 V614
    Scandal: there are some set out in their true Colours, both Men and 233   FOR LCVE   I.1 627
    Scandal: another large Piece too, representing a School; where there 233   FOR LCVE   I.1 653
    Mrs Frail: Exchange, I must call my Sister Foresight there. . . . 234   FOR LCVE   I.1 665
    Angelica: a Voyage to Greenland, to inhabit there all the dark   . 237   FOR LCVE   II.1   84
    Foresight: How Hussie! was there ever such a provoking 237   FOR LCVE   II.1   93
    Angelica: Practices; you and the old Nurse there-- 237   FOR LCVE   II.1   97
    Foresight: House of my Nativity; there the Curse of Kindred was   . 238   FOR LCVE   II.1 130
    Angelica: and the Goat. Bless me! there are a great many Horn'd   . 239   FOR LCVE   II.1 138
    Angelica: Nor there had not been that one, if she had had to . . 239   FOR LCVE   II.1 143
    Sr Sampson: if there is too much, refund the Superfluity; Do'st hear . 243   FOR LCVE   II.1 280
    Sr Sampson: if there be too much, refund the Superfluity; Do'st hear . 243   FOR LCVE   II.1 V280
    Sr Sampson: Why lock you there now,--I'll maintain 245   FOR LCVE   II.1 365
    Mrs Frail: you had been there, it had been only innocent Recreation. 246   FOR LCVE   II.1 423
    Miss Prue: No, indeed won't I: But I'll run there, and hide . . . 252   FOR LCVE   II.1 648
    Nurse: cry husht--O Lord, who's there? (peeps) What's here   . 253   FOR LCVE III.1   7
    Valentine: There, now it's out. 255   FOR LCVE III.1   87
    Tattle: and if there be occasion for Witnesses, I can summon the . 257   FOR LCVE III.1 154
    Valentine: It was there, I suppose, you got the Nick-Name of . . . 257   FOR LCVE III.1 166
    Tattle: whom I mean; for there were a great many Ladies raffled   . 258   FCR LOVE III.1 188
    Tattle: whom I mean; for there was a great many Ladies raffled   . 258   FOR LCVE III.1 V188
    Servant: There, Sir, his back's toward you. 260   FOR LOVE III.1 269
    Ben: Come, I'll haule a Chair; there, an you please to sit, I'll 263   FOR LCVE III.1 362
    Ben: Tar-barrel? Let your Sweet-heart there call me so, if he'll 264   FOR LCVE III.1 434
    Scandal: but you are something more--There have been wise   . 267   FOR LCVE III.1 528
    Mrs Fore: Was there ever such Impudence, to make Love 269   FOR LCVE III.1 593
    Scandal: Look you there now--Your Lady says your 269   FOR LCVE III.1 616
    Valentine: is full--There are People that we do know, and . . . 280   FOR LCVE   IV.1 160
    Valentine: upon all alike--There are Fathers that have many Children; 280   FOR LCVE   IV.1 162
    Valentine: and there are Children that have many Fathers--'tis   . 280   FOR LCVE   IV.1 163
    Scandal: You'd better let him go, Sir; and send for him if there   . 280   FOR LCVE   IV.1 189
    Sr Sampson: Pocket.) There Val: it's safe enough, Boy--But thou   . 282   FOR LCVE   IV.1 233
    Sr Sampson: there never was a lucky Hour after the first opportunity.   . 283   FOR LCVE   IV.1 291
    Scandal: I'm apt to believe there is something mysterious in his   . 285   FOR LCVE   IV.1 344
    Valentine: come there. 288   FOR LCVE   IV.1 498
    Valentine: Sheets before Night. But there are two things that you will 289   FOR LCVE   IV.1 510
    Tattle: Oh, Madam, look upon us both. There you see the ruins   . 291   FOR LOVE   IV.1 580
    Tattle: No, Sir, 'tis written in my Heart. And safer there,
                      Sir, than 292   FOR LOVE   IV.1 613
    Jeremy: Who's there? 295   FOR LOVE   IV.1 758
    Angelica: Well, have you been there?--Come hither. 296   FOR LOVE   IV.1 781
    Angelica: there were such a thing as a young agreeable Man, with a   . 299   FOR LOVE   V.1   62
    Foresight: think there is something in your Physiognomy, that has a   . 304   FOR LOVE   V.1 260

There   (continued)
Speaker	Text	Page	Title	ACT.SC	LINE
Foresight:	there is a contagious Frenzy abroad. How does Valentine?	306	FOR LOVE	V.1	333
Sr Sampson:	him have the Prospect of an Estate; tho' there were no	308	FOR LOVE	V.1	427
Buckram:	Sir, it is drawn according to your Directions; there	308	FOR LOVE	V.1	429
Sr Sampson:	there?	309	FOR LOVE	V.1	438
Tattle:	Look you there, I thought as much--pox on't, I	310	FOR LOVE	V.1	475
Tattle:	I can spare him mine. (to Jeremy) Oh are you there, Sir?	313	FOR LOVE	V.1	590
Scandal:	Lover: But there is a Third good Work, which I, in particular,	314	FOR LOVE	V.1	621
Leonora:	Your Griefs, there is no Cause--	326	M. BRIDE	I.1	16
Leonora:	Or moderate your Griefs; there is no Cause--	326	M. BRIDE	I.1 V	16
Almeria:	Peace--No Cause! yes, there is Eternal Cause.	326	M. BRIDE	I.1	17
Almeria:	No Cause! Peace, peace; there is Eternal Cause.	326	M. BRIDE	I.1 V	17
Almeria:	Or, when there, why was I us'd so tenderly?	327	M. BRIDE	I.1	66
Almeria:	Or there, why was I us'd so tenderly?	327	M. BRIDE	I.1 V	66
Almeria:	But in my Heart thou art interr'd, there, there,	328	M. BRIDE	I.1	74
Almeria:	Of Africk: There our Vessel struck the Shore,	329	M. BRIDE	I.1	126
Almeria:	(If such there be in angry Heav'ns Vengeance)	330	M. BRIDE	I.1	189
Almeria:	Perhaps I would repeat it there more solemnly.	331	M. BRIDE	I.1	204
Manuel:	For, ling'ring there, in long suspence she stands,	337	M. BRIDE	I.1	454
Heli:	Of one complaining--There it sounds--I'll follow it.	340	M. BRIDE	II.2	3
Almeria:	How camest thou there? wert thou alone?	343	M. BRIDE	II.2	158
Almeria:	True; but how cam'st thou there? wert thou alone?	343	M. BRIDE	II.2 V158	
Osmyn-Alph:	There are no Wonders, or else all is Wonder.	344	M. BRIDE	II.2	180
Zara:	That thou dost seek to shield thee there, and shun	346	M. BRIDE	II.2	242
Osmyn-Alph:	Yet look for Gaiety and Gladness there.	346	M. BRIDE	II.2	263
Zara:	There, there's the dreadful Sound, the King's thy Rival!	348	M. BRIDE	II.2	348
Zara:	There, he; your Prisoner, and that was my Slave.	348	M. BRIDE	II.2	358
Osmyn-Alph:	What Noise! Who's there? My Friend, how cam'st	350	M. BRIDE	III.1	39
Heli:	I've learn'd, there are Disorders ripe for Mutiny	351	M. BRIDE	III.1	64
Heli:	The Care of Providence, sure left it there,	352	M. BRIDE	III.1	116
Osmyn-Alph:	Of Light, to the bright Source of all. There, in	353	M. BRIDE	III.1	132
Osmyn-Alph:	Of Light, to the bright Source of all. For there	353	M. BRIDE	III.1 V132	
Almeria:	If there, he shoot not ev'ry other Shaft;	356	M. BRIDE	III.1	286
Osmyn-Alph:	There, there, I bleed; there pull the cruel Cords,	356	M. BRIDE	III.1	291
Almeria:	There, we will feast; and smile on past Distress,	358	M. BRIDE	III.1	339
Zara:	Who waits there?	360	M. BRIDE	III.1	445
Gonsalez:	He there disclos'd himself to Albucacim,	363	M. BRIDE	IV.1	85
Zara:	(As there the Custom is) in private strangle	365	M. BRIDE	IV.1	154
Manuel:	Who waits there?	365	M. BRIDE	IV.1	165
Almeria:	Oh I am lost--there, Fate begins to wound.	368	M. BRIDE	IV.1	299
Almeria:	The Tomb it calls--I'll follow it, for there	371	M. BRIDE	IV.1	393
Almeria:	Me from the Tombs--I'll follow it, for there	371	M. BRIDE	IV.1 V393	
Manuel:	And treble Fury--Ha! who's there?	373	M. BRIDE	V.1	37
Manuel:	And trebled Fury--Ha! who's there?	373	M. BRIDE	V.1 V 37	
Manuel:	There with his Turbant, and his Robe array'd	374	M. BRIDE	V.1 V86A	
Gonsalez:	There lies my way, that Door is too unlock'd.	376	M. BRIDE	V.2	4
Gonsalez:	Then cast my Skin, and leave it there to answer it.	376	M. BRIDE	V.2	13
Zara:	Get thee to Hell, and seek him there.	380	M. BRIDE	V.2	175
Zara:	I'll creep into his Bosom, lay me there;	381	M. BRIDE	V.2	206
Almeria:	There, there I see him; there he lies, the Blood	382	M. BRIDE	V.2	234
Almeria:	Ha! point again? 'tis there, and full I hope.	382	M. BRIDE	V.2	258
Almeria:	Seest thou not there, who prostrate lies;	382	M. BRIDE	V.2	264
Almeria:	Seest thou not there? behold who prostrate lyes,	382	M. BRIDE	V.2 V264	
Fainall:	O there it is then--She has a lasting Passion for	396	WAY WORLD	I.1	25
Fainall:	there?	396	WAY WORLD	I.1	27
Fainall:	mov'd that to avoid Scandal there might be one Man	396	WAY WORLD	I.1	56
Servant-M:	turn; so we drove round to Duke's Place; and there they	398	WAY WORLD	I.1	118
Mirabell:	I wonder there is not an Act of Parliament to save	400	WAY WORLD	I.1	204
Witwoud:	Friend.--No, my Dear, excuse me there.	403	WAY WORLD	I.1	315
Mirabell:	there yet? I shall cut your Throat, sometime or other,	406	WAY WORLD	I.1	423
Petulant:	Ay, ay, let that pass--There are other Throats	406	WAY WORLD	I.1	425
Petulant:	--But there are Uncles and Nephews in the World	406	WAY WORLD	I.1	429
Mirabell:	Was there any mention made of my Uncle, or me? Tell	407	WAY WORLD	I.1	451
Witwoud:	We staid pretty late there last Night; and heard	408	WAY WORLD	I.1	480
Witwoud:	not, I cannot say; but there were Items of such a Treaty	408	WAY WORLD	I.1	487
Witwoud:	being there.	409	WAY WORLD	I.1	511
Mrs Fain:	There.	411	WAY WORLD	II.1	40
Mrs Fain:	There spoke the Spirit of an Amazon, a	411	WAY WORLD	II.1	48
Fainall:	You wou'd intimate then, as if there were a	413	WAY WORLD	II.1	126
Mirabell:	Your Health! Is there a worse Disease than the	421	WAY WORLD	II.1	443
Millamant:	after all, there is something very moving in a love-sick	422	WAY WORLD	II.1	474
Mirabell:	Heart of a Man that is lodg'd in a Woman. There is no	423	WAY WORLD	II.1	495
Lady Wish:	me dear Friend, I can make bold with you--There	426	WAY WORLD	III.1	64
Lady Wish:	--Frippery? old Frippery! Was there ever such a foul-mouth'd	428	WAY WORLD	III.1	118
Foible:	Madam. There are some Cracks discernable in the white	429	WAY WORLD	III.1	145
Marwood:	Fainall, have you carried it so swimmingly? I thought there	431	WAY WORLD	III.1	229
Marwood:	there, like a new masking Habit, after the Masquerade is	433	WAY WORLD	III.1	310
Sir Wilful:	'Sheart, Sir, but there is, and much offence.--	439	WAY WORLD	III.1	527
Sir Wilful:	There is? 'Tis like there may.	440	WAY WORLD	III.1	587
Lady Wish:	figure shall I give his Heart the first Impression? There is a	445	WAY WORLD	IV.1	18
Millamant:	There never yet was Woman made,	446	WAY WORLD	IV.1	52
Sir Wilful:	shou'd hate 'em both! Hah 'tis like you may; there are	448	WAY WORLD	IV.1	128
Millamant:	Mistress. There is not so Impudent a thing in Nature, as the	449	WAY WORLD	IV.1	177
Millamant:	never to be seen there together again; as if we were proud	450	WAY WORLD	IV.1	204
Millamant:	never be seen there together again; as if we were proud	450	WAY WORLD	IV.1 V204	
Witwoud:	That's the Jest, there was no dispute, they cou'd	453	WAY WORLD	IV.1	332
Petulant:	There was no quarrel--there might have been a	454	WAY WORLD	IV.1	359
Witwoud:	If there had been words enow between 'em to have	454	WAY WORLD	IV.1	361
Lady Wish:	Jubilee. But I hope where there is likely to be so near an	457	WAY WORLD	IV.1	490
Lady Wish:	(Reads)--Madam, tho' unknown to you (Look you there 'tis	460	WAY WORLD	IV.1	584
Waitwell:	Roman hand--I saw there was a throat to be cut presently.	460	WAY WORLD	IV.1	602
Lady Wish:	Coo in the same Cage, if there be Constable or warrant	463	WAY WORLD	V.1	55
Lady Wish:	Coo in the same Cage, if there be a Constable or warrant	463	WAY WORLD	V.1 V 55	
Mrs Fain:	Was there no mention made of me in the	464	WAY WORLD	V.1	74

There   (continued)

Speaker	Text	PAGE	TITLE	ACT.SC	LINE
Mrs Fain:	there, ay or your Friend's Friend, my false Husband.	466	WAY WORLD	V.1	155
Marwood:	of Court, where there is no precedent for a Jest in any	467	WAY WORLD	V.1	216
Lady Wish:	shall be mad, Dear Friend is there no Comfort for me?	470	WAY WORLD	V.1	307
Mirabell:	I am too Happy,--Ah Madam, there was a time--but let	471	WAY WORLD	V.1	369
Fainall:	single Beef-eater there? but I'm prepar'd for you; and	473	WAY WORLD	V.1	433
Lady Wish:	Is there no means, no Remedy, to stop my	473	WAY WORLD	V.1	445
Lady Wish:	your sake, Sir Rowland there and Foible,--The next	477	WAY WORLD	V.1	574
	There are some Criticks so with Spleen diseas'd,	479	WAY WORLD	EPI.	5
	Others there are whose Malice we'd prevent;	479	WAY WORLD	EPI.	16

There's (104)   see Ther's

Speaker	Text	PAGE	TITLE	ACT.SC	LINE
Bellmour:	--There's more Elegancy in the false Spelling of this	38	OLD BATCH	I.1	33
Bellmour:	No faith, not for that--But there's a Business of	41	OLD BATCH	I.1	151
Bellmour:	But she can't have too much Mony--There's	41	OLD BATCH	I.1	165
Bellmour:	told you there's twelve thousand Pound--Hum--Why	41	OLD BATCH	I.1	170
Heartwell:	Ay there you've nick't it--there's the Devil upon	45	OLD BATCH	I.1	317
Araminta:	I expected it--there's too much Truth in 'em:	60	OLD BATCH	II.2	206
Silvia:	Well, since there's no remedy--Yet tell me--	61	OLD BATCH	III.1	14
Bellmour:	Thou'rt a lucky Rogue; there's your Benefactor,	68	OLD BATCH	III.1	281
Sharper:	were the Incendiary--There's to put you in mind of	69	OLD BATCH	III.1	316
Sharper:	I Gad and so I will: There's again for you.	69	OLD BATCH	III.1	320
Setter:	S'bud Sir, away quickly, there's Fondlewife just turn'd	75	OLD BATCH	IV.1	9
Vainlove:	--By Heav'n there's not a Woman, will give a Man the	80	OLD BATCH	IV.1	175
Araminta:	There's poison in every thing you touch.--	88	OLD BATCH	IV.3	181
Sir Joseph:	'Tis too little, there's more, Man. There, take all--	103	OLD BATCH	V.1	249
Araminta:	how insolent wou'd a real Pardon make you? But there's	106	OLD BATCH	V.1	362
Belinda:	least, Thou art so troublesome a Lover, there's Hopes thou'lt	106	OLD BATCH	V.1	366
Bellmour:	(aside). I hope there's no French Sawce.	106	OLD BATCH	V.1	371
Brisk:	Deuce take me, there's Wit in't too--and Wit	133	DOUBL DLR	I.1	241
Sir Paul:	hither Girl, go not near him, there's nothing but deceit	145	DOUBL DLR	II.1	246
Mellefont:	There's comfort in a hand stretch'd out, to one	148	DOUBL DLR	II.1	389
Maskwell:	there's a Plot for you.	149	DOUBL DLR	II.1	404
Lady Ply:	for I'm sure there's nothing in the World that I would	159	DOUBL DLR	III.1	342
Lady Froth:	Coachman, for you know there's most occasion for a	164	DOUBL DLR	III.1	520
Brisk:	Short, but there's Salt in't, my way of writing I'gad.	166	DOUBL DLR	III.1	602
Cynthia:	People walk hand in hand, there's neither overtaking nor	168	DOUBL DLR	IV.1	15
Mellefont:	Hum, 'gad I believe there's something in't;--	168	DOUBL DLR	IV.1	19
Mellefont:	there's hope.	169	DOUBL DLR	IV.1	64
Lady Ply:	should die, of all Mankind there's none I'd sooner make	170	DOUBL DLR	IV.1	111
Lady Ply:	and how--Ah, there's Sir Paul.	170	DOUBL DLR	IV.1	126
Brisk:	Zoons, Madam, there's my Lord.	177	DOUBL DLR	IV.1	363
Lord Froth:	(aside). --Oh I see there's no harm yet--But I	177	DOUBL DLR	IV.1	372
Maskwell:	Nay then, there's but one way.	184	DOUBL DLR	IV.2	39
Careless:	By Heaven there's Treachery--the Confusion	196	DOUBL DLR	V.1	335
Careless:	There's Saygrace tripping by with a bundle under his	196	DOUBL DLR	V.1	351
	Till Dice are thrown, there's nothing won, ncr lost.	204	DOUBL DLR	EPI.	5
	We hope there's something that may please each Taste,	213	FOR LOVE	PRO.	26
	There's Humour, which for chearful Friends we got,	213	FOR LOVE	PRO.	29
	And for the thinking Party there's a Plot.	213	FOR LOVE	PRO.	30
	Yet hopes there's no ill-manners in his Play:	214	FOR LOVE	PRO.	42
Valentine:	And d'ye hear, go your to Breakfast--There's a	216	FOR LOVE	I.1	7
Jeremy:	O Sir, there's Trapland the Scrivener, with two	221	FOR LOVE	I.1	202
Jeremy:	a Man down with Pocket-Tipstaves,--And there's	221	FOR LOVE	I.1	204
Trapland:	No, no, there's no such thing, we'd better mind our	223	FOR LOVE	I.1	281
Mrs Frail:	there's a Match talk'd of by the Old People--Well,	231	FOR LOVE	I.1	569
Foresight:	Yes, yes; while there's one Woman left, the	237	FOR LOVE	II.1	64
Foresight:	But there's but one Virgin among the Twelve Signs,	239	FOR LOVE	II.1	141
Foresight:	there's no more to be said--	239	FOR LOVE	II.1	170
Foresight:	there's no more to be said--he's here already	239	FOR LOVE	II.1	V170
Sr Sampson:	there's no time but the time present, there's no more to be	240	FOR LOVE	II.1	197
Sr Sampson:	there's Latin for you to prove it, and an Argument	240	FOR LOVE	II.1	205
Sr Sampson:	above a stink.--Why there's it; and Musick, don't you	245	FOR LOVE	II.1	371
Mrs Fore:	it, I think there's no happiness like conversing with an	247	FOR LOVE	II.1	427
Mrs Fore:	Poor innocent! you don't know that there's a	247	FOR LOVE	II.1	450
Miss Prue:	nay, there's Snuff in't;--here, will you have any--	249	FOR LOVE	II.1	517
Tattle:	There's no occasion for a Lie; I cou'd never tell a Lie	253	FOR LOVE	III.1	21
Scandal:	trusted; a Satyrical Proverb upon our Sex--There's	256	FOR LOVE	III.1	126
Sr Sampson:	sneak'd off, and would not see his Brother? There's an	259	FOR LOVE	III.1	235
Sr Sampson:	Unnatural Whelp! There's an ill-natur'd Dog! There,	259	FOR LOVE	III.1	236
Ben:	Why then, I'll go to Sea again, so there's one for t'other, an	261	FOR LOVE	III.1	300
Ben:	ben't as willing as I, say so a God's name, there's no harm	263	FOR LOVE	III.1	390
Miss Prue:	that's more: So, there's your answer for you; and don't	264	FOR LOVE	III.1	400
Miss Prue:	Well, and there's a handsome Gentleman, and a	264	FOR LOVE	III.1	414
Mrs Frail:	Lord, what shall we do, there's my Brother	265	FOR LOVE	III.1	446
Mrs Frail:	Hold, there's my Sister, I'll call her to hear it.	273	FOR LOVE	III.1	741
Scandal:	There's nought but willing, waking Love, that can	275	FOR LOVE	III.1	819
Valentine:	There's a couple of Topicks for you, no more like one	282	FOR LOVE	IV.1	256
Ben:	at these years, there's more danger of your head's aking	286	FOR LOVE	IV.1	383
Ben:	Anchor at Cuckolds-point; so there's a dash for you, take	287	FOR LOVE	IV.1	441
Mrs Fore:	together; and after Consummation, Girl, there's no	288	FOR LOVE	IV.1	473
Tattle:	Pox on't, there's no coming off, now she has said	293	FOR LOVE	IV.1	679
Valentine:	Riddle. There's my Instruction, and the Moral of my	296	FOR LOVE	IV.1	796
Valentine:	there's Regularity and Method in that; she is a Medal	297	FOR LOVE	IV.1	810
Sr Sampson:	of these young idle Rogues about the Town. Odd, there's	299	FOR LOVE	V.1	53
Tattle:	and does not know of it yet--There's a Mystery for	305	FOR LOVE	V.1	295
Ben:	And there's the handsome young Woman, she, as they	306	FOR LOVE	V.1	345
Ben:	Why then I'll tell you, There's a new wedding upon the	307	FOR LOVE	V.1	358
Ben:	Lawyer, I believe there's many a Cranny and Leak unstopt	309	FOR LOVE	V.1	431
Ben:	Why there's another Match now, as tho'f a couple of	310	FOR LOVE	V.1	487
	But there's the Devil, tho' their Cause is lost,	323	M. BRIDE	PRO.	25
	There's no recov'ring Damages or Cost.	323	M. BRIDE	PRO.	26
Almeria:	But there's no time shall rase thee from my Memory.	328	M. BRIDE	I.1	71
Manuel:	There's not a Slave, a shackled Slave of mine,	333	M. BRIDE	I.1	315
Zara:	There, there's the dreadful Sound, the King's thy Rival!	348	M. BRIDE	II.2	348

There's   (ccntinued)

Gonsalez:	There's somewhat yet of Mystery in this;	366	M. BRIDE	IV.1	194
Manuel:	Yet, that there's Truth in what she has discover'd, . .	366	M. BRIDE	IV.1	213
Manuel:	There's Reason in thy Doubt, and I am warn'd.	367	M. BRIDE	IV.1	227
Leonora:	And look not on; for there's a Dagger that	381	M. BRIDE	V.2	229
Leonora:	Return and look not on; for there's a Dagger	381	M. BRIDE	V.2	V229
Servant-M:	Sir, there's such Coupling at Pancras, that they stand .	398	WAY WCRLD	I.1	113
Witwoud:	You shall see he won't go to 'em because there's no .	405	WAY WCRLD	I.1	363
Waitwell:	Ay there's the Grief; that's the sad change cf Life; .	424	WAY WCRLD	II.1	562
Lady Wish:	my self till I am pale again, there's no Veracity in me.	425	WAY WCRLD	III.1	4
Millamant:	hear it Madam--Not that there's any great matter in .	434	WAY WORLD	III.1	372
Singer:	If there's Delight in Love, 'tis when I see	435	WAY WCRLD	III.1	389
Fainall:	so there's an end of Jealousie. Weary of her, I am, and shall	443	WAY WCRLD	III.1	681
Fainall:	be--No, there's no end of that; No, no, that were too .	443	WAY WCRLD	III.1	682
Lady Wish:	receive him in my little dressing Rccm, there's a Couch--	445	WAY WCRLD	IV.1	23
Lady Wish:	Comparison. Hark! There's a Coach.	445	WAY WCRLD	IV.1	32
Mrs Fain:	O Sir Wilfull; you are ccme at the Critical Instant. There's	446	WAY WCRLD	IV.1	70
Sir Wilful:	there's no haste; it will keep cold as they say,--Cozen,	448	WAY WCRLD	IV.1	146
Mrs Fain:	Mirabell, there's a Necessity for your otedience. . .	452	WAY WCRLD	IV.1	298
Foible:	Madam, the Dancers are ready, and there's one with a .	459	WAY WCRLD	IV.1	549
Mincing:	He swears, and my old Lady cry's. There's a fearful Hurricane . .	465	WAY WCRLD	V.1	109

Thereafter (1)

Sir Wilful:	May be not, Sir; thereafter as 'tis meant, Sir.	438	WAY WCRLD	III.1	496

Thereby (1)

Scandal:	thereby incapable of making any Conveyance in Law; so .	283	FOR LCVE	IV.1	299

Therefore (29)

Lucy:	as his Love. Therefore e'n set your Heart at rest, and .	61	OLD BATCH	III.1	8
Setter:	And therefore you'd have him to set in your Ladies . .	67	OLD BATCH	III.1	228
Sir Paul:	submit as formerly, therefore give way.	144	DOUEL DLR	II.1	208
Lady Ply:	please--therefore don't provoke me.	145	DOUEL DLR	II.1	237
Sir Paul:	I should, indeed, Thy--therefore come away; tut . . .	146	DOUEL DLR	II.1	284
Sir Paul:	providence has prevented all, therefore ccme away, when	146	DOUEL DLR	II.1	285
Lady Ply:	refuse it; I swear I'll deny it,--therefore don't ask me,	147	DOUEL DLR	II.1	333
Lady Ply:	must not Love you,--therefcre dcn't hope,--but don't .	148	DOUEL DLR	II.1	371
Lady Touch:	to be unknown which cannot be prevented; therefore let .	152	DOUEL DLR	III.1	55
Maskwell:	By no means; therefore you must aggravate my	154	DOUEL DLR	III.1	146
Maskwell:	interpret a Coldness the right way; therefore I must .	155	DOUEL DLR	III.1	182
Cynthia:	of his Wit: Therefore let me see you undermine my Lady .	168	DCUEL DLR	IV.1	47
Cynthia:	Consent; and therefore I swore.	171	DOUEL DLR	IV.1	143
Maskwell:	No, 'twas honest, therefore I shan't;--Nay, rather, therefore	188	DOUEL DLR	V.1	19
Maskwell:	. . . Therefore, for	193	DCUEL DLR	V.1	230
Valentine:	therefcre resolve to rail at all that have: And in that I tut	217	FOR LCVE	I.1	35
Valentine:	Therefore I would rail in my Writings, and be . . .	219	FOR LCVE	I.1	136
Mrs Frail:	and therefore must look sharply about me. Sir . . .	248	FOR LCVE	II.1	491
Tattle:	Valentine, and yet remain insensible; therefore you will	255	FCR LCVE	III.1	69
Angelica:	any Man, and for any Man with a good Estate: Therefore .	260	FCR LCVE	III.1	254
Angelica:	depends upon the recovery of Valentine. Therefore I .	277	FCR LCVE	IV.1	56
Angelica:	Therefcre I ask your Advice, Sir Sampson: I have . .	299	FCR LCVE	V.1	60
Valentine:	Therefore I yield my Body as your Prisoner, and . . .	313	FCR LCVE	V.1	615
Osmyn-Alph:	I saw her toc, and therefore saw nct thee.	344	M. BRIDE	II.2	183
Zara:	Therefcre require me not to ask thee twice;	361	M. BRIDE	IV.1	2
	And therefore to the Fair ccmmends his Cause. . . .	385	M. BRIDF	EPI.	28
Mrs Fain:	way to succeed. Therefore spare your Extacies for another	452	WAY WCRLD	IV.1	303
Sir Wilful:	measure; therefore withdraw your Instrument Sir, or .	473	WAY WCRLD	V.1	428

Thereunto (1)

Mellefont:	That I have seen, with the Ceremony thereunto	158	DOUEL DLR	III.1	280

These (88)

Thetis (1)

Lady Froth:	For Susan, you know, is Thetis, and so--	164	DOUBI DLR	III.1	542

They (293)

They'd (1)

Ben:	they'd ne're make a Match together--Here they come. . .	307	FOR LCVE	V.1	374

They'll (4)

Mellefont:	do, they'll fall asleep else.	128	DOUEL DLR	I.1	48
Maskwell:	their own Follies and Intrigues, they'll miss neither of you.	155	DOUBI DLR	III.1	168
Cynthia:	They'll wait upon your Lordship presently.	202	DOUBI DLR	V.1	553
Scandal:	Yes, several, very honest;--they'll cheat a little at .	271	FCR LCVE	III.1	666

They're (18)

Setter:	They're at the Door: I'll call 'em in.	112	OLD BATCH	V.2	180
Lady Ply:	despair neither,--O, they're coming, I must fly. . .	148	DOUEL DLR	II.1	372
	In which, we do not doubt but they're discerning, . .	204	DOUEL DLR	EPI.	25
	Even tc make exceptions, when they're Try'd. . . .	204	DOUEL DLR	EPI.	30
Nurse:	Wee'st heart, I know not, they're none of 'em come . .	235	FOR LCVE	II.1	19
Mrs Fore:	they're in perpetual fear of being seen and censur'd?--	247	FOR LCVE	II.1	433
Mrs Fore:	They're all so, Sister, these Men--they	250	FOR LCVE	II.1	547
Foresight:	gallop, hey! Whither will they hurry me?--Now they're .	269	FCR LCVE	III.1	608
	And now they're fill'd with Jests, and Flights, and Bombast!	315	FCR LCVE	EPI.	31
	For in One Year, I think they're out of Date. . . .	323	M. EFIDE	PRO.	6
	But if he 'scape, with what Regret they're seiz'd! . .	385	M. BRIDE	EPI.	13
	And hcw they're disappointed if they're pleas'd! . .	385	M. BRIDE	EPI.	14
	And hcw they're disappointed when they're pleas'd! . .	385	M. BRIDE	EPI.	V 14
	For they're a sort of Fools which Fortune makes, . .	393	WAY WORLD	PRO.	3
	But if they're naught ne're spare him for his Pains: . .	393	WAY WCRLD	PRO.	23
	Tho' they're on no pretence for Judgment fit	479	WAY WORLD	EPI.	12

They've (5)

Zara:	Of Sceptres, Crowns, and Thrones; they've serv'd their .	347	M. BRIDE	II.2	319
Leonora:	Feeling Remorse too late, for what they've done. . .	381	M. BRIDE	V.2	225
	For Innocence condemn'd they've no Respect, ...	385	M. EFIDE	EPI.	17
	Provided they've a Body to dissect.	385	M. EFIDE	EPI.	18
	Each time they write, they venture all they've wcn: . .	393	WAY WCRLD	PRO.	14

Thick (1)
    Sir Paul: Eye, as the House of Austria is by a thick Lip. . . . . 173 DOUBL DLR IV.1 240
Thick-Skull'd (1)
    Valentine: Why you Thick-Skull'd Rascal, I tell you the Farce . . . 295 FOR LOVE   IV.1 749
Thief (5)   see Gibbet-thief
                   So till the Thief has stoll'n, he cannot know   . . . . 204 DOUEL DLR EPI.   6
    Scandal: Domestick Thief; and he that wou'd secure his Pleasure, . 271 FOR LOVE   III.1 676
    Scandal: Service of your Sex. He that first cries out stop Thief, is 272 FOR LOVE   III.1 698
                   As one Thief scapes, that executes another. . . . . . 323 M. EBIDE   PRO.   32
    Osmyn-Alph: And pinion'd like a Thief or Murderer? . . . . 355 M. EBIDE   III.1 241
Thigh (1)
    Sir Wilful: Thigh shall hack your Instrument of Ram Vellum to shreds, . 473 WAY WORLD   V.1 426
Thimble (1)   see Brass-Thimble
    Lady Wish: Acorn? Why didst thou not bring thy Thimble? Hast thou . 425 WAY WORLD III.1   30
Thin (2)
    Jeremy: sake. Now like a thin Chairman, melted down to half . . 218 FOR LOVE   I.1   98
    Foible: thin Subsistance (says he)--Well, what Pension does . . 427 WAY WORLD III.1   98
Thine (6)
    Vainlove: thine takes it up--But read that, it is an Appointment . 39 OLD EATCH   I.1   78
    Lord Touch: have discovered so much Manly Vertue; thine, in that thou . 189 DOUBL DLR   V.1   55
    Lord Touch: Wealth or Interest can purchase Cynthia, she is thine.-- . 189 DOUBL DLR   V.1   75
    Sr Sampson: thine? I believe I can read it farther off yet--let me see. 281 FOR LOVE   IV.1 226
    Manuel: Dar'st thou reply? Take that--thy Service? thine? . . . 374 M. EBIDE   V.1   69
    Millamant: Tho' thou do'st thine, employ'st the Power and Art. . . 447 WAY WORLD   IV.1 105
Thing (171)   see Giddy-thing
    Bellmour: thy Talent will never recommend thee to any thing of . . 45 OLD EATCH   I.1 300
    Sir Joseph: to the greatness of his merit--I had a pretty thing to that 49 OLD EATCH   II.1   52
    Sir Joseph: I do scorn a dirty thing. But agad 'Ime a little out of . 50 OLD EATCH   II.1 105
    Sir Joseph: I am quite another thing, when I am with him: I don't fear 50 OLD EATCH   II.1 122
    Capt Bluff: Gazette--I'll tell you a strange thing now as to that-- . 52 OLD EATCH   II.1 194
    Capt Bluff: Perhaps, Sir, there was a scarce any thing of moment . . 52 OLD EATCH   II.1 197
    Silvia: But Love, they say, is a tender thing, that will smooth . 72 OLD EATCH III.2   65
    Silvia: self--honest--Here, I won't keep any thing that's yours, . 73 OLD EATCH III.2 110
    Heartwell: me in every thing, sc like my Wife, the World shall . . 74 OLD EATCH III.2 121
    Laetitia: does not think, that ever I had any such thing in my Head, 77 OLD EATCH   IV.1   81
    Bellmour: every thing but your Unkindness. . . . . 81 OLD EATCH   IV.2   32
    Laetitia: Nay, now.--(aside) I never saw any thing so agreeably . . 82 OLD EATCH   IV.2   79
    Bellmour: nor any thing, but thy Lips. I am faint with the Excess of 82 OLD EATCH   IV.2   85
    Belinda: to the Fashion, or any thing in practice! I had not patience 84 OLD EATCH   IV.3   32
    Belinda: Ah so fine! So extreamly fine! So every thing in the . . 87 OLD EATCH   IV.3 148
    Araminta: There's poison in every thing ycu touch.-- . . . . . 88 OLD EATCH   IV.3 181
    Fondlewife: Let her clap a warm thing to his Stomach, or chafe it with 91 OLD EATCH   IV.4   97
    Fondlewife: Let her clap some warm thing to his Stcmach, or chafe it
                   with . . . . 91 OLD EATCH IV.4 V 97
    Setter: . . . a thing as Honesty. . . . . 102 OLD BATCH V.1 V232
    Setter: Captain, I wou'd do any thing to serve you; but this . . 104 OLD BATCH   V.1 274
    Sir Joseph: thing but a Night's Lodging. . . . . 104 OLD BATCH   V.1 282
    Bellmour: humble, pliant, easie thing, a Lover, so guess at Plagues in 106 OLD BATCH   V.1 382
    Belinda: that will do a civil thing to his Wife, or say a civil
                   thing to . . . . 108 OLD BATCH   V.2   30
    Heartwell: vexation, or any thing, but another Woman.-- . . . . . 108 OLD BATCH   V.2   40
    Heartwell: Oh! Any thing, every thing, a Leg or two, or an . . . . 109 OLD BATCH   V.2   75
    Brisk: But the Deuce take me if I say a good thing till ycu come.-- 128 DOUBL DLR   I.1   51
    Brisk: me perish, do I never say any thing worthy to be Laugh'd . 132 DOUBL DLR   I.1 195
    Brisk: thing, Laughing all the while as if you were ready to die 134 DOUEL DLR   I.1 268
    Careless: No; for if it were a witty thing, I should not expect . . 134 DOUEL DLR   I.1 271
    Brisk: t'other way. Suppose I say a witty thing tc you? . . . 134 DOUBL DLR   I.1 278
    Maskwell: thing more, Madam? . . . . 135 DOUEL DLR   I.1 315
    Maskwell: But it will prepare some thing else; and gain us leasure to 138 DOUBL DLR   I.1 418
    Lady Froth: come together,--O bless me! What a sad thing . . . . . 139 DOUBL DLR   II.1   22
    Lady Froth: you're a Judge; was ever any thing so well-bred as my . . 140 DOUBL DLR   II.1   82
    Brisk: Never any thing; but your Ladyship, let me perish. . . . 140 DOUBL DLR   II.1   84
    Sir Paul: --gadsbud he does not care a Farthing for any thing . . . 146 DOUBL DLR   II.1 277
    Lady Ply: O, such a thing! the Impiety of it startles me . . . . 146 DOUBL DLR   II.1 289
    Lady Ply: every thing in the World, but give me Mathemacular . . . 146 DOUBL DLR   II.1 302
    Lady Ply: think that I'll grant you any thing; O Lord, no,--but . . 148 DOUBL DLR   II.1 366
    Maskwell: a thing as Hcnesty? Yes, and whosoever has it about him, . 150 DOUBL DLR   II.1 451
    Maskwell: any thing--Why, let me see, I have the same Face, the . . 150 DOUBL DLR   II.1 460
    Lord Touch: Plyant has a large Eye, and wou'd centre every thing in . 151 DOUBL DLR III.1   6
    Lady Touch: defend an ill thing? . . . . 151 DOUBL DLR III.1   32
    Lady Touch: my Thoughts in any thing that may be to my Cousin's . . . 151 DOUBL DLR III.1   35
    Lady Touch: and can believe any thing worse, if it were laid to his
                   charge . . . . 151 DOUEL DLR III.1   41
    Lady Touch: wish I had not tcld you any thing.--Indeed, my Lord, . . 152 DOUBL DLR III.1   69
    Lady Touch: towards me. Nay, I can't think he meant any thing . . . 153 DOUEL DLR III.1   84
    Lady Touch: heard any thing from him these two days. . . . . 153 DOUBL DLR III.1   98
    Maskwell: time he attempted any thing of that kind, to discover it to 154 DOUEL DLR III.1 154
    Maskwell: won't perplex you. 'Tis the only thing that Providence . . 157 DOUEL DLR III.1 244
    Lady Ply: rather attempt it than any thing in the World, (Curtesies) 159 DOUEL DLR III.1 341
    Lady Ply: you, Mr. Careless I don't know any thing in the World I . 159 DOUEL DLR III.1 353
    Sir Paul: Careless, if it were not for one thing-- . . . . . . 160 DOUEL DLR III.1 391
    Sir Paul: were not for one thing, I should think my self the happiest 161 DOUEL DLR III.1 404
    Lord Froth: 'Tis a strange thing, but a true one; . . . . 166 DOUEL DLR III.1 597
    Cynthia: mistaken the thing: Since . . . . 167 DOUEL DLR III.1 632
    Cynthia: thing but the very Devil, I'm inexorable: Only still I'll . 169 DOUEL DLR   IV.1   61
    Lady Ply: me as a fine thing. Well, I must do you this justice, and . 169 DOUEL DLR   IV.1   71
    Careless: Feet. (Aside.) I must say the same thing over again, and . 170 DOUEL DLR   IV.1 101
    Lady Ply: that Mellefont had never any thing more than a profound . 171 DOUEL DLR   IV.1 165
    Lady Ply: Conscience, or Honour, or any thing in the World.-- . . 172 DOUEL DLR   IV.1 170
    Sir Paul: Well, 'tis a rare thing to have an ingenious Friend. Well, 172 DOUEL DLR   IV.1 202
    Sir Paul: Surprize! Why I don't know any thing at all, nor I don't . 179 DOUEL DLR   IV.1 449
    Sir Paul: know whether there be any thing at all in the World, or . 179 DOUEL DLR   IV.1 450
    Lord Touch: in any thing that has concern'd me or my Family. . . . . 181 DOUEL DLR   IV.1 536
    Lord Touch: it: Yet there has been a thing in your Knowledge, which . 181 DOUEL DLR   IV.1 541
    Lady Touch: But this is a thing of too great moment, to . . . . . 191 DOUEL DLR   V.1 124
    Cynthia: any thing that resists my will, tho' 'twere reason it self. 193 DOUEL DLR   V.1 205

Thing (continued)

Cynthia:	Did Maskwell tell you any thing of the Chaplain's . .	196	DOUEL DLR	V.1	341
Scandal:	Old Woman, any thing but Poet; a Modern Poet is worse,	220	FOR LCVE	I.1	146
Trapland:	No, no, there's no such thing, we'd better mind our . .	223	FOR LCVE	I.1	281
Valentine:	any thing that he says: For to converse with Scandal, is to	226	FOR LCVE	I.1	388
Tattle:	knows any thing of that nature of me: As I hope to be . .	227	FOR LCVE	I.1	405
Tattle:	one and t'other, and every thing in the World; and, says I,	227	FOR LCVE	I.1	432
Tattle:	Alas, that's the same thing: Pray spare me their . .	230	FOR LCVE	I.1	534
Mrs Frail:	here too? Oh Mr. Tattle, every thing is safe with you, we	230	FOR LCVE	I.1	548
Foresight:	I say you lie, Sir. It is impossible that any thing .	235	FOR LCVE	II.1	11
Nurse:	ever hear the like now--Sir, did ever I do any thing .	238	FOR LCVE	II.1	101
Nurse:	thing; feel, feel here, if I have any thing but like .	238	FOR LCVE	II.1	124
Angelica:	do with any thing but Astrologers, Uncle. That makes my .	239	FOR LCVE	II.1	144
Mrs Fore:	power--And I can tell you one thing that falls out luckily	248	FOR LCVE	II.1	498
Mrs Fore:	love to have the spoiling of a Young Thing, they are as .	250	FOR LCVE	II.1	548
Tattle:	thing of Secresie?	254	FOR LCVE	III.1	43
Angelica:	never deny'd any thing in his Life.	255	FOR LCVE	III.1	78
Angelica:	never ask'd any thing, but what a Lady might modestly .	255	FOR LCVE	III.1	89
Tattle:	thing to a Lady's Prejudice in my Life--For as I was . .	256	FOR LCVE	III.1	102
Scandal:	Why thence it arises--The thing is proverbially	256	FOR LCVE	III.1	123
Angelica:	cou'd have lik'd any thing in him, it shou'd have been his	260	FOR LCVE	III.1	246
Ben:	But I'll tell you one thing, and you come to Sea in a .	262	FOR LCVE	III.1	330
Sr Sampson:	want a little Polishing: You must not take any thing ill,	262	FOR LCVE	III.1	339
Miss Prue:	You need not sit so near one, if you have any thing .	263	FOR LCVE	III.1	364
Ben:	thing is this, that if you like me, and I like you, we may	263	FOR LCVE	III.1	376
Ben:	thing is that if you like me, and I like you, we may .	263	FOR LCVE	III.1	V376
Ben:	speak one thing, and to think just the contrary way; is as				
	it	263	FOR LCVE	III.1	386
Ben:	not for keeping any thing under Hatches,--so that if you	263	FOR LCVE	III.1	389
Miss Prue:	trouble me no more, you ugly thing.	264	FOR LCVE	III.1	401
Ben:	Whipping no more than you do. But I tell you one thing,	264	FOR LCVE	III.1	407
Scandal:	him, and all of us, more than any thing else?	266	FOR LCVE	III.1	484
Valentine:	thing; it's a Question that would puzzle an Arithmetician,	280	FOR LOVE	IV.1	175
Ben:	chitty fac'd thing, as he would have me marry,--so he .	285	FOR LOVE	IV.1	364
Valentine:	strange thing: I found out what a Woman was good for. .	292	FOR LOVE	IV.1	641
Jeremy:	care every thing shall be ready.	293	FOR LOVE	IV.1	672
Angelica:	Wou'd any thing, but a Madman complain of	296	FOR LOVE	IV.1	785
Angelica:	Life. Security is an insipid thing, and the overtaking and	296	FOR LOVE	IV.1	787
Sr Sampson:	of any thing;--And if they commit Matrimony, ...	299	FOR LOVE	V.1	56
Angelica:	there were such a Thing as a young agreeable Man, with a .	299	FOR LOVE	V.1	62
Angelica:	thing that wou'd make me appear to be too much concern'd .	299	FOR LOVE	V.1	91
Jeremy:	comply with any thing to please him. Poor Lady, I'm .	302	FOR LOVE	V.1	202
Miss Prue:	thing, till I'm as tired as any thing in the World. .	303	FOR LOVE	V.1	224
Tattle:	thing indeed--Fie, fie, you're a Woman now, and . . .	303	FOR LOVE	V.1	243
Tattle:	paw thing.	303	FOR LOVE	V.1	247
Ben:	Case, you should not marry her. It's just the same thing,	308	FOR LOVE	V.1	414
Tattle:	were good--But this is the most cruel thing, to marry .	309	FOR LOVE	V.1	458
Tattle:	thing in my Life.	309	FOR LOVE	V.1	461
Valentine:	that loses hope may part with any thing. I never valu'd .	312	FCB LOVE	V.1	544
Angelica:	No, I have it; and I'll use it, as I would every thing .	312	FOR LOVE	V.1	555
Jeremy:	any thing like it--Then how could it be otherwise? . . .	313	FOR LOVE	V.1	594
Valentine:	Any thing, my Friend, every thing that looks like .	313	FCB LOVE	V.1	602
Almeria:	Yet, one Thing more, I would engage from thee.	330	M. BRIDE	I.1	194
Osmyn-Alph:	Who calls that wretched thing, that was Alphonso? . . .	340	M. BRIDE	II.2	35
Osmyn-Alph:	That at this Time, I had not been this Thing.	354	M. BRIDE	III.1	190
Zara:	What Thing?	354	M. BRIDE	III.1	191
Manuel:	Into how poor and mean a thing, a King descends; . . .	373	M. BRIDE	V.1	40
Manuel:	Into how poor a thing, a King decends;	373	M. BRIDE	V.1	V 40
Mirabell:	she who does not refuse 'em every thing, can refuse 'em .	397	WAY WORLD	I.1	88
Mirabell:	of the Squire his Brother, any thing related?	400	WAY WORLD	I.1	211
Witwoud:	Lady? Gad, I say any thing in the World to get this Fellow	402	WAY WORLD	I.1	255
Petulant:	any thing before him.	408	WAY WORLD	I.1	498
Marwood:	despise 'em; the next thing I have to do, is eternally to	411	WAY WORLD	II.1	46
Fainall:	you cannot resent any thing from me; especially what is .	412	WAY WORLD	II.1	96
Mrs Fain:	I believe my Lady will do any thing to get a Husband; and	418	WAY WORLD	II.1	308
Mrs Fain:	suppose she will submit to any thing to get rid of him. .	418	WAY WORLD	II.1	310
Mirabell:	Thing that resembl'd a Man, tho' 'twere no more than .	418	WAY WORLD	II.1	312
Millamant:	have ask'd every living Thing I met for you; I have . .	419	WAY WORLD	II.1	347
Mincing:	with Poetry, it sits so pleasant the next Day as any Thing,	420	WAY WORLD	II.1	373
Mirabell:	vain how lost a Thing you'll be! Nay, 'tis true: You are no	420	WAY WORLD	II.1	391
Lady Wish:	thee. Why dost thou not stir Puppet? thou wooden Thing .	425	WAY WORLD	III.1	15
Lady Wish:	Foible's a lost Thing; has been abroad since	426	WAY WORLD	III.1	45
Lady Wish:	--Hark! I hear her--Go you Thing and send her	426	WAY WORLD	III.1	61
Lady Wish:	--Hark! I hear her-- (To Peg.) Go you Thing and send her .	426	WAY WORLD	III.1	V 61
Foible:	met that confident Thing? Was I in Fault? If you had .	427	WAY WORLD	III.1	86
Marwood:	a very fit Match. He may Travel afterwards. 'Tis a Thing	432	WAY WORLD	III.1	267
Millamant:	Sure never any thing was so Unbred as that odious . .	432	WAY WORLD	III.1	284
Millamant:	every Thing that has been said. For my part, I thought .	432	WAY WORLD	III.1	293
Millamant:	Well, 'tis a lamentable thing I'll swear, that one . .	432	WAY WORLD	III.1	296
Millamant:	Well, 'tis a lamentable thing I swear, that one	432	WAY WORLD	III.1	V296
Marwood:	Thing impossible, when I shall tell him, by telling you--	434	WAY WORLD	III.1	351
Millamant:	O Dear, what? for it is the same thing, if I hear . .	434	WAY WORLD	III.1	352
Petulant:	Importance is one Thing, and Learning's another; . . .	436	WAY WORLD	III.1	414
Marwood:	Thing amiss from your Friends, Sir. You are among your .	438	WAY WORLD	III.1	507
Lady Wish:	Will you drink any Thing after your Journey, Nephew, .	441	WAY WORLD	III.1	599
Millamant:	loath the Country and every thing that relates to it. .	448	WAY WORLD	IV.1	122
Millamant:	Mistress. There is not so Impudent a thing in Nature, as the	449	WAY WORLD	IV.1	177
Millamant:	thing you, I'll have you,--I won't be kiss'd, nor I won't be	452	WAY WORLD	IV.1	295
Millamant:	I am a lost thing;--for I find I love him violently. . .	453	WAY WORLD	IV.1	316
Mrs Fain:	thing discover'd. This is the last day of our living				
	together, ...	464	WAY WORLD	V.1	82
Mrs Fain:	This discovery is the most opportune thing	464	WAY WORLD	V.1	101
Mincing:	O yes Mem, I'll vouch any thing for your Ladyship's .	465	WAY WORLD	V.1	121
Lady Wish:	thing, everything for Composition.	468	WAY WORLD	V.1	240
Sir Wilful:	fairer? If I have broke any thing, I'll pay for't, an it				
	cost a	470	WAY WORLD	V.1	318

Thing   (continued)
Lady Wish: I'll consent to any thing to come, to be deliver'd from this   473   WAY WORLD   V.1   455
Fainall: Go, ycu are an Insignificant thing,--Well, what   475   WAY WORLD   V.1   492
Fainall: I'll be put off no longer--You thing that was   475   WAY WORLD   V.1   494
Mirabell: appear--you do not remember Gentlemen, any thing of   . .   476   WAY WORLD   V.1   528
Lady Wish: thing is to break the Matter to my Nephew--and how   . .   477   WAY WORLD   V.1   575
              How hard a thing 'twould be, to please you all.   479   WAY WORLD   EPI.   4

Things (55)
              Grave solemn Things, as Graces are to Feasts;   35   OLD BATCH   PRO.   3
Bellmour: Who Heartwell! Ay, but he knows better things--   42   OLD EATCH   I.1   179
              (Exit Betty with the Things.)   .   57   OLD BATCH   II.2 V100
Araminta: things, than they say.   60   OLD EATCH   II.2 217
Sir Joseph: Lord-Harry. I know better things than to be run through   67   OLD BATCH   III.1 253
Belinda: O frightful! Cousin, What shall we do? These things   .   85   OLD BATCH   IV.3 75
Laetitia: Ah! There he is. Make haste, gather up your things.   .   89   OLD EATCH   IV.4 10
Bellmour: (Looking about, and gathering up his things.)   .   89   OLD BATCH   IV.4 14
Sharper: yonder. I have promised and vow'd some things in your   .   109   OLD BATCH   V.2   82
Brisk: things said; or one, understood, since thy Amputation   .   128   DOUBL DLR   I.1   36
Lady Ply: is no certainty in the things of this life.   147   DOUBL DLR   II.1 329
Lady Ply: and Things; for with the Reserve of my Honour, I assure   159   DOUEL DLR   III.1 352
Lord Froth: Heav'n, Sir Paul, you amaze me, of all things in   . .   162   DOUBL DLR   III.1 457
Lady Ply: And say so many fine things, and nothing is so moving to .   169   DOUBL DLR   IV.1 70
Lady Ply: any dishonourable Notions of things; so that if this be .   172   DOUBL DLR   IV.1 168
Sir Paul: of things; I don't know what to make on't,--gad'sbud   .   192   DOUBL DLR   V.1   173
Maskwell: things are impossible to willing minds.   196   DOUBL DLR   V.1   323
Mellefont: No; my Dear, will you get ready--the things   196   DOUBL DLR   V.1   343
Lady Ply: You tell me most surprizing things; bless me   202   DOUBL DLR   V.1   545
              If the soft things are Penn'd and spoke with grace.   .   204   DOUBL DLR   EPI. 23
Foresight: things were done, and the Conveyance made--   240   FOR LOVE   II.1 188
Sr Sampson: Son of a Cucumber.--These things are unaccountable   .   246   FOR LOVE   II.1 308
Tattle: Creature living, in things of that nature; and never had the 256   FCR LCVE   III.1 104
Ben: part d'ee see, I'm for carrying things above Board, I'm   .   263   FOR LOVE   III.1 388
Scandal: with ycu--But my Mind gives me, these things cannot   .   267   FOR LOVE   III.1 523
Scandal: Causation of Causes, in the Causes of things.   267   FCB LCVE   III.1 539
Valentine: Shop. Oh things will go methodically in the City, the   .   289   FOR LOVE   IV.1 503
Valentine: Sheets before Night. But there are two things that you will   289   FCB LCVE   IV.1 510
Foresight: about these things which he has utter'd.--His Sayings   .   289   FCR LOVE   IV.1 533
Foresight: Neice, he knows things past and to come, and all the   .   291   FOR LCVE   IV.1 604
Angelica: But I'll tell you two things before I leave you; I am not .   296   FCB LCVE   IV.1 791
Mrs Frail: for my part I always despised Mr. Tattle of all things;   .   310   FOR LCVE   V.1   472
Almeria: I've read, that things inanimate have mov'd, ...   326   M. EBIDE   I.1   3
Almeria: Why are all these things thus?--   327   M. EBIDE   I.1   56
Almeria: Why is it thus contriv'd? Why are things laid   327   M. BRIDE   I.1   60
Almeria: I have a thousand Things to know, and ask, ...   343   M. BRIDE   II.2 150
Selim: The State of things will countenance all Suspicions.   .   362   M. BRIDE   IV.1 55
Zara: O Heav'n! a thousand things occur   363   M. BRIDE   IV.1 92
Zara: O Heav'n! a thousand things occur at once   363   M. ERIDE   IV.1 V 92
Gonsalez: Things come to this Extremety? his Daughter   371   M. BRIDE   IV.1 404
Almeria: All things were well: and yet my Husband's murder'd!   .   382   M. EBIDE   V.2   242
Fainall: Had you dissembl'd better, Things might have continu'd   .   397   WAY WCBLD   I.1   66
Millamant: and say; vain empty Things if we are silent or unseen, and   421   WAY WCBLD   II.1 411
Mirabell: Yet tc those two vain empty Things, you owe two   . . .   421   WAY WCRLD   II.1 413
Mirabell: Fools; Things who visit you from their excessive Idleness;   421   WAY WCRLD   II.1 434
Lady Wish: Things be remov'd, good Foible.   429   WAY WCBLD   III.1 181
Foible: Lady that Mr. Mirabell rail'd at her. I laid horrid Things   430   WAY WORLD   III.1 208
Millamant: Things! without one cou'd give 'em to one's   433   WAY WCBLD   III.1 306
Lady Wish: and are things in Order?   444   WAY WCBLD   IV.1 2
Millamant: It may be in things of common Application; but   449   WAY WCRLD   IV.1 174
Mirabell: allow,--these proviso's admitted, in other things I may   .   452   WAY WORLD   IV.1 276
Lady Wish: press things to a Conclusion, with a most prevailing   .   458   WAY WCBLD   IV.1 495
Marwood: things are bought and brought hither to expose me--   .   474   WAY WCBLD   V.1   474
Marwood: things are brought hither to expose me--   474   WAY WCBLD   V.1 V474
Petulant: For my part, I say little--I think things are best   . .   477   WAY WCBLD   V.1   588

Think (302)
              You think that strange--no matter, he'll out grow it.   . .   35   OLD BATCH   PRO. 16
Bellmour: Why faith I think it will do well enough--If the   . .   38   OLD BATCH   I.1   55
Bellmour: very affected neither--Give her her due, I think the   .   41   OLD EATCH   I.1   172
Sharper: Not till you had Mouth'd a little George, I think   .   43   OLD BATCH   I.1   227
Heartwell: think it time enough to be lew'd, after I have had the   .   43   OLD BATCH   I.1   233
Heartwell: and I think I have baited too many of those Traps, to be   45   OLD BATCH   I.1   296
Capt Bluff: Sweet Sawce. Now I think--Fighting, for Fighting sake's   52   OLD BATCH   II.1 164
Capt Bluff: you know--Well, Mr. Sharper, would you think it? In all   53   OLD BATCH   II.1 201
Capt Bluff: This Sword I think I was telling you of Mr. Sharper   .   53   OLD BATCH   II.1 228
Belinda: You think the malicious Grinn becomes you--The   . .   56   OLD BATCH   II.2 56
Bellmour: world of Love in your Service, that you think you can   .   58   OLD BATCH   II.2 123
Vainlove: I should rather think Favours, so gain'd, to be due   .   58   OLD BATCH   II.2 139
Belinda: pester'd me with Flames and Stuff--I think I shan't   .   59   OLD BATCH   II.2 164
Vainlove: He's talking to himself, I think; Prithee lets try if   .   62   OLD BATCH   III.1 61
Heartwell: Hum--Let me think--Is not this Silvia's House, the   .   62   OLD BATCH   III.1 64
Heartwell: Houses and Coblers Stalls--Death, I can't think   . . .   63   OLD BATCH   III.1 84
Sir Joseph: hundred Pound for being saved, and d'ee think, an there   67   OLD BATCH   III.1 255
Sir Joseph: mad? Or de'e think I'm mad? Agad for my part, I don't   .   68   OLD BATCH   III.1 265
Sir Joseph: think no more of what's past.   70   OLD BATCH   III.1 362
Heartwell: believe it: Nay, thou shalt think so thy self--Only let me   74   OLD BATCH   III.2 122
Heartwell: not think so.   74   OLD BATCH   III.2 123
Heartwell: self liberty to think, lest I should cool--I will about a   74   OLD BATCH   III.2 139
Laetitia: does not think, that ever I had any such thing in my Head,   77   OLD BATCH   IV.1 81
Laetitia: (aside). I know not what to think. But I'me resolv'd   .   77   OLD EATCH   IV.1 85
Laetitia: indeed you sant. Nykin--if you don't go, I'le think   .   78   OLD BATCH   IV.1 132
Vainlove: management I should think she expects it.   80   OLD BATCH   IV.1 189
Bellmour: I cou'd think of nothing all Day but putting 'em in practice   82   OLD EATCH   IV.2 54
Sir Joseph: fear it;--that is, if I can but think on't: Truth is, I   .   85   OLD BATCH   IV.3 73
Sharper: The second-best;--indeed I think.   88   OLD BATCH   IV.3 203
Sir Joseph: Why, the Devil's in the People, I think.   91   OLD BATCH   IV.4 68
Laetitia: (aside). I'm so distracted, I can't think of a Lye.   .   92   OLD BATCH   IV.4 119
Bellmour: Since all Artifice is vain--and I think my self obliged   .   93   OLD BATCH   IV.4 157

Think   (continued)

Think   (continued)

		PAGE	TITLE	ACT.SC LINE
Valentine:	sometimes. I did not think she had granted more to any	. 229	FOR LOVE	I.1 487
Mrs Frail:	be particular--Eut otherwise I think his Passion ought	. 231	FOR LOVE	I.1 556
Sr Sampson:	I think on't, Body o' me, I have a Shoulder of an Egyptian	242	FOR LOVE	II.1 249
Sr Sampson:	You've had it already, Sir, I think I sent it you to	. 243	FOR LOVE	II.1 274
Mrs Fore:	it, I think there's no happiness like conversing with an	. 247	FOR LOVE	II.1 427
Mrs Fore:	agreeable man; I don't quarrel at that, nor I don't think	247	FOR LOVE	II.1 428
Mrs Fore:	Heart, to think that any body else shou'd be before-hand	. 250	FOR LOVE	II.1 551
Mrs Fore:	spoil'd already--d'ee think shee'll ever endure a . .	. 250	FOR LOVE	II.1 561
Mrs Fore:	will hang us--He'll think we brought 'em acquainted.	. 250	FOR LOVE	II.1 569
Mrs Frail:	Foresight shou'd find us with them;--He'd think so,	. 250	FOR LOVE	II.1 571
Tattle:	Yes, my Dear--I think I can guess--But	. 251	FOR LOVE	II.1 583
Tattle:	De'e ycu think you can Love me?	. 251	FOR LOVE	II.1 602
Tattle:	speak what you think: Your words must contradict your	. 251	FOR LOVE	II.1 612
Tattle:	But you must think your self more Charming than I .	. 252	FOR LOVE	II.1 617
Tattle:	say nothing, I think. I hear her--I'll leave you together,	254	FOR LOVE	III.1 23
Angelica:	I swear I don't think 'tis possible.	. 255	FOR LOVE	III.1 80
Tattle:	Gad, it's very true, Madam, I think we are oblig'd to	. 257	FOR LOVE	III.1 134
Miss Prue:	better not speak at all, I think, and truly I won't tell			
	a lie	. 263	FOR LOVE	III.1 383
Ben:	speak one thing, and to think just the contrary way; is as			
	it	. 263	FOR LOVE	III.1 386
Ben:	civilly to me, of her own accord: Whatever you think of	. 264	FOR LOVE	III.1 411
Ben:	your self, Gad I don't think you are any more to compare	. 264	FOR LOVE	III.1 412
Foresight:	I protest I honour you, Mr. Scandal--I did not think	. 267	FOR LOVE	III.1 540
Foresight:	How does it appear, Mr. Scandal? I think I am very . .	. 268	FOR LOVE	III.1 561
Foresight:	I am in Health, I think.	. 268	FOR LOVE	III.1 569
Foresight:	Do you think so, Mr. Scandal?	. 270	FOR LOVE	III.1 630
Mrs Fore:	this Project? You don't think, that you are ever like to	. 271	FOR LOVE	III.1 660
Mrs Fore:	Devil; do you think any Woman Honest?	. 271	FOR LOVE	III.1 665
Mrs Fore:	And so you think we are free for one another? . . .	. 272	FOR LOVE	III.1 684
Scandal:	Yes Faith, I think so; I love to speak my mind. . .	. 272	FOR LOVE	III.1 685
Scandal:	I have no great Opinion of my self; yet I think, I'm	. 272	FOR LOVE	III.1 690
Scandal:	I have no great Opinion of my self; but I think, I'm	. 272	FOR LOVE	III.1 V690
Scandal:	Come, I know what you wou'd say,--you think . . .	. 272	FOR LOVE	III.1 694
Mrs Fore:	Pish, you'd tell me so, tho' you did not think . .	. 272	FOR LOVE	III.1 707
Scandal:	And you'd think so, tho' I should not tell you so: . .	. 272	FOR LOVE	III.1 709
Scandal:	And now I think we know one another pretty well. . .	. 272	FOR LOVE	III.1 710
Ben:	don't think I'm false-hearted, like a Land-man. A Sailor	. 273	FOR LOVE	III.1 732
Mrs Fore:	Night; because I'll retire to my own Chamber, and think	. 273	FOR LOVE	III.1 743
Ben:	Why, forsooth, an you think so, you had best go to Bed.	. 275	FOR LOVE	III.1 807
Scandal:	think I heard her bid the Coach-man drive hither. . .	. 276	FOR LOVE	IV.1 13
Angelica:	Mr. Scandal, I suppose you don't think it a Novelty,	. 276	FOR LOVE	IV.1 20
Angelica:	Mr. Scandal, you can't think me guilty of so much . .	. 277	FOR LOVE	IV.1 42
Angelica:	(aside). I know not what to think--Yet I shou'd . .	. 277	FOR LOVE	IV.1 47
Angelica:	have mistaken my Compassion, and think me guilty of a	. 277	FOR LOVE	IV.1 69
Jeremy:	refrain Tears when I think of him, Sir; I'm as melancholy	. 279	FOR LOVE	IV.1 132
Mrs Fore:	I think.	. 284	FOR LOVE	IV.1 320
Scandal:	Discourses, and sometimes rather think him inspir'd than	. 285	FOR LOVE	IV.1 345
Foresight:	vulgar think mad. Let us go in to him.	. 285	FOR LOVE	IV.1 350
Foresight:	vulgar think mad. Let us go to him.	. 285	FOR LOVE	IV.1 V350
Ben:	All mad, I think--Flesh, I believe all the Calentures of	. 285	FOR LOVE	IV.1 356
Valentine:	If they are, I'll tell you what I think--get away all the	291	FOR LOVE	IV.1 594
Tattle:	Why de'e think I'll tell you, Sir! Read it in my Face?	. 292	FOR LOVE	IV.1 612
Valentine:	end, and let us think of leaving acting, and be our selves;	294	FOR LOVE	IV.1 708
Valentine:	think cf means to reconcile me to him; and preserve the	. 294	FOR LOVE	IV.1 717
Jeremy:	Partly I think--for he does not know his Mind . .	. 295	FOR LOVE	IV.1 753
Jeremy:	Partly I think--for he does not know his own Mind . .	. 295	FOR LOVE	IV.1 V753
Jeremy:	to be mad: And I think I have not found him very quiet	. 295	FOR LOVE	IV.1 755
Angelica:	I did not think you had Apprehension enough to be . .	. 296	FOR LOVE	IV.1 762
Sr Sampson:	Women think a Man old too soon, faith and troth you do	. 298	FOR LOVE	V.1 25
Angelica:	Age I think--I assure you I know very considerable . .	. 298	FOR LOVE	V.1 29
Sr Sampson:	young Fellow--Pize on 'em, they never think beforehand	. 299	FOR LOVE	V.1 55
Sr Sampson:	--Odd, I think we are very well met;--Give me . .	. 301	FOR LOVE	V.1 144
Tattle:	must think of a new Man every Morning, and forget him	. 303	FOR LOVE	V.1 244
Foresight:	think there is something in your Physiognomy, that has a	. 304	FOR LOVE	V.1 260
Miss Prue:	way or other. Oh! methinks I'm sick when I think of a	. 305	FOR LOVE	V.1 308
Foresight:	O fearful! I think the Girl's influenc'd too,-- . .	. 305	FOR LOVE	V.1 313
Foresight:	I think she has not return'd, since she went abroad .	. 306	FOR LOVE	V.1 336
Ben:	say, Brother Val. went mad for, she's mad too, I think.	. 306	FOR LOVE	V.1 346
Ben:	she's mad for a Husband, and he's Horn-mad, I think, or	. 307	FOR LOVE	V.1 373
Angelica:	pardon me, if I think my own Inclinations have a better	. 311	FOR LOVE	V.1 533
	Whom, as I think they call'd--Py--Pythagories, . . .	. 315	FOR LOVE	EPI. 12
	I know not what these think, but for my Part, . . .	. 315	FOR LOVE	EPI. 35
	For in One Year, I think they're out of Date. . . .	. 323	M. BRIDE	PRO. 6
Leonora:	Alas you search too far, and think too deeply. . . .	. 327	M. BRIDE	I.1 64
Manuel:	Ha! what? thou dost not weep to think of that? . . .	. 333	M. BRIDE	I.1 302
Zara:	To like Captivity, or think those Honours, ...	. 335	M. BRIDE	I.1 394
Almeria:	I know not, 'tis to see thy Face I think--	. 342	M. BRIDE	II.2 104
Osmyn-Alph:	To follow thee. I'll think, how we may meet . . .	. 345	M. BRIDE	II.2 204
Zara:	Think on my Suff'ring first, then, look on me; . . .	. 347	M. BRIDE	II.2 304
Zara:	Think on the Cause of all, then, view thy self: . . .	. 347	M. BRIDE	II.2 305
Manuel:	Of him that thunders, than but think that Insolence. .	. 349	M. BRIDE	II.2 370
Osmyn-Alph:	Yet I may think--I may? I must; for Thought . . .	. 350	M. BRIDE	III.1 33
Osmyn-Alph:	Precedes the Will to think; and Errour lives . . .	. 350	M. BRIDE	III.1 34
Heli:	And think on what we may reduce to Practise. . . .	. 352	M. BRIDE	III.1 94
Zara:	So thou dost think; then, do but tell me so; . . .	. 353	M. BRIDE	III.1 164
Osmyn-Alph:	Or Being as you please, such I will think it. . . .	. 354	M. BRIDE	III.1 184
Almeria:	Thou told'st me thou would'st think how we might meet	. 355	M. BRIDE	III.1 246
Osmyn-Alph:	That ever I should think, beholding thee, ...	. 355	M. BRIDE	III.1 250
Almeria:	What dost thou think? Lock not so tenderly . . .	. 356	M. BRIDE	III.1 264
Osmyn-Alph:	Think on to Morrow, when thou shalt be torn . . .	. 358	M. BRIDE	III.1 343
Osmyn-Alph:	Think how my Heart will heave, and Eyes will strain	. 358	M. BRIDE	III.1 345
Osmyn-Alph:	Think how the Blood will start, and Tears will gush .	. 358	M. BRIDE	III.1 347
Osmyn-Alph:	Think how I am, when thou shalt wed with Garcial . .	. 358	M. BRIDE	III.1 349
Zara:	Your Pardon, Sir--mistake me not; you think	. 359	M. BRIDE	III.1 416

Think   (continued)
Zara:	O Torment, but to think! what then to bear?	. . . . .	362	M. BRIDE	IV.1	36
Zara:	I think it fit to tell you that your Guards	. . . .	364	M. BRIDE	IV.1	142
Manuel:	What dost thou think, Gonsalez;	. . . .	366	M. BRIDE	IV.1	198
Manuel:	That Wit of Man, and dire Revenge can think,	. . . .	368	M. BRIDE	IV.1	297
Almeria:	And yet a Father! think I am your Child.	. . . .	369	M. BRIDE	IV.1	318
Gonsalez:	Hold, let me think--if I shou'd tell the King--	. . . .	371	M. BRIDE	IV.1	403
Gonsalez:	I think thou would'st not stop to do me Service.	. . . .	371	M. BRIDE	IV.1	427
Zara:	And kindle Ruine in its Course. Dost think	. . . .	375	M. BRIDE	V.1 V 96
Zara:	Think fit, I'll leave thee my Command to die.	. . . .	375	M. BRIDE	V.1	127
Garcia:	Oppress her not, nor think to stain her Face	. . . .	378	M. BRIDE	V.2	76
Osmyn-Alph:	Yet am I dash'd to think that thou must weep;	. . . .	383	M. BRIDE	V.2	303
	Some Plot we think he has, and some new Thought;	. .	393	WAY WORLD	PRO.	29
Mirabell:	Woman's good Manners to her Prejudice; and think that	.	397	WAY WORLD	I.1	87
Mirabell:	She has Beauty enough to make any Man think so;	. .	399	WAY WORLD	I.1	153
Mirabell:	end I so us'd my self to think of 'em, that at length, contrary	. . . .	399	WAY WORLD	I.1	168
Mirabell:	Person; I think you have the Honour to be related to him.	400	WAY WORLD	I.1	191
Witwoud:	Well, well, he does not always think before he	. . .	403	WAY WORLD	I.1	307
Mirabell:	May be you think him too positive?	. . . .	403	WAY WORLD	I.1	322
Fainall:	Why do you think so?	. . . .	408	WAY WORLD	I.1	479
Mirabell:	you have made a handsome Woman blush, then you think	. .	409	WAY WORLD	I.1	527
Mirabell:	I confess you ought to think so. You are in the	. . . .	409	WAY WORLD	I.1	538
Mrs Fain:	(we ought to think at least) they loath; they look upon us	410	WAY WORLD	II.1	6
Marwood:	of ill usage; I think I shou'd do my self the violence of	.	411	WAY WORLD	II.1	55
Mrs Fain:	wou'd think it dissembl'd; for you have laid a Fault to	. .	412	WAY WORLD	II.1	75
Mrs Fain:	Do I? I think I am a little sick o' the suddain.	. . .	412	WAY WORLD	II.1	80
Mrs Fain:	Dee think so?	. . . .	412	WAY WORLD	II.1	90
Fainall:	Faith, I think not.	. . . .	413	WAY WORLD	II.1	119
Marwood:	I think she do's not hate him to that degree	. . . .	413	WAY WORLD	II.1	128
Fainall:	Arms in full Security. But cou'd you think because the	. .	414	WAY WORLD	II.1	147
Mirabell:	Yes, I think the good Lady wou'd marry any	. . . .	418	WAY WORLD	II.1	311
Millamant:	. . . I think I try'd once	. . . .	419	WAY WORLD	II.1	367
Millamant:	O ay, and went away--Now I think on't I'm angry	. .	420	WAY WORLD	II.1	378
Millamant:	--No, now I think on't I'm pleas'd--For I believe	. .	420	WAY WORLD	II.1	379
Millamant:	--You'll displease me--I think I must resolve	. . .	422	WAY WORLD	II.1	449
Millamant:	--I'm resolv'd--I think--You may go--	. . . .	422	WAY WORLD	II.1	457
Millamant:	have done thinking of that; think of me.	. . . .	423	WAY WORLD	II.1	488
Mirabell:	I have something more--Gone--Think of	. . . .	423	WAY WORLD	II.1	490
Mirabell:	you! To think of a Whirlwind, tho' 'twere in a Whirlwind,	.	423	WAY WORLD	II.1	491
Mirabell:	Sirrah, Waitwell, why sure you think you were married	. .	423	WAY WORLD	II.1	505
Waitwell:	I think she has profited, Sir. I think so.	. . . .	424	WAY WORLD	II.1	527
Lady Wish:	As I'm a Person I am in a very Chaos to think I	. . . .	431	WAY WORLD	III.1	254
Marwood:	Methinks Sir Wilfull should rather think of	. . . .	431	WAY WORLD	III.1	259
Lady Wish:	since 'tis your Judgment, I'll think on't again. I assure you	. .	432	WAY WORLD	III.1	270
Marwood:	'Twere better so indeed. Or what think you	. . . .	433	WAY WORLD	III.1	308
Millamant:	think he wou'd obey me; I wou'd command him to shew	. .	433	WAY WORLD	III.1	339
Marwood:	Mr. Mirabell and you both, may think it a	. . . .	434	WAY WORLD	III.1	350
Millamant:	think of it--I am a Sybil if I am not amaz'd to think	. .	434	WAY WORLD	III.1	357
Millamant:	what he can see in me. I'll take my Death, I think you are	.	434	WAY WORLD	III.1	358
Marwood:	than you think.	. . . .	434	WAY WORLD	III.1	364
Witwoud:	Not I--Yes, I think it is he--I've almost	. . . .	436	WAY WORLD	III.1	441
Sir Wilful:	don't think a' knows his own Name.	. . . .	437	WAY WORLD	III.1	474
Witwoud:	think you're in the Country, where great lubberly Brothers	439	WAY WORLD	III.1	534
Millamant:	him hither,--just as you will Dear Foible.--I think I'll see	446	WAY WORLD	IV.1	61
Sir Wilful:	think--Nay Cozen Fainall, open the Door--Pshaw,	. . .	447	WAY WORLD	IV.1	93
Sir Wilful:	Cozen, I made bold to pass thro' as it were,--I think this	.	447	WAY WORLD	IV.1	95
Sir Wilful:	your Servant--I think this door's lock'd.	. . . . .	448	WAY WORLD	IV.1	147
Millamant:	O, I should think I was poor and had nothing to	. . .	449	WAY WORLD	IV.1	167
Millamant:	never sure in Love. O, I hate a Lover, that can dare to think.	. . .	449	WAY WORLD	IV.1	175
Mirabell:	bring you home in a pretended fright, when you think you	.	451	WAY WORLD	IV.1	240
Millamant:	Fainall, what shall I do? shall I have him? I think	. .	452	WAY WORLD	IV.1	284
Millamant:	fright--Fainall, I shall never say it--well--I think--		452	WAY WORLD	IV.1	289
Millamant:	Are you? I think I have--and the horrid Man	. . .	452	WAY WORLD	IV.1	293
Lady Wish:	--Fogh! how you stink of Wine! Dee think my Neice	. .	455	WAY WORLD	IV.1	388
Lady Wish:	you do not think me prone to any iteration of Nuptials.--	.	458	WAY WORLD	IV.1	532
Lady Wish:	think that I have made a prostitution of decorums, but in	.	459	WAY WORLD	IV.1	535
Lady Wish:	If you think the least scruple of Carnality was	. . .	459	WAY WORLD	IV.1	543
Lady Wish:	Sir Rowland, will you give me leave? think	. . . .	459	WAY WORLD	IV.1	551
Lady Wish:	your Character, that I think my self oblig'd to let you	. .	460	WAY WORLD	IV.1	586
Mincing:	have him I think, rather than loose such a vast Summ as	.	465	WAY WORLD	V.1	115
Marwood:	we shall have leisure to think of Retirement afterwards.	.	465	WAY WORLD	V.1	137
Lady Wish:	be wrong'd after all, ha? I don't know what to think,--	.	466	WAY WORLD	V.1	181
Lady Wish:	think after all this, that my Daughter can be Naught?	.	467	WAY WORLD	V.1	203
Marwood:	think I would rather Congratulate, than Condole with	.	468	WAY WORLD	V.1	245
Fainall:	under such penalty as I think convenient.	. . . .	468	WAY WORLD	V.1	254
Mirabell:	ever been accounted Venial. At least think it is Punishment	472	WAY WORLD	V.1	387
Sir Wilful:	Travel too, I think they may be spar'd.	. . . .	477	WAY WORLD	V.1	587
Petulant:	For my part, I say little--I think things are best	. .	477	WAY WORLD	V.1	588
	To think themselves alone the Fools design'd:	. . .	479	WAY WORLD	EPI.	24
	To think they singly can support a Scene,	. . . .	479	WAY WORLD	EPI.	26

Think'st (4)
Osmyn-Alph:	My Friend and Counsellour; as thou think'st fit,	. .	352	M. BRIDE	III.1	104
Manuel:	But think'st thou that my Daughter saw this Moor?	. .	367	M. BRIDE	IV.1	228
Zara:	And kindle Ruine in its Course. Think'st thou	. .	375	M. BRIDE	V.1	96
Zara:	Not his pursuing Voice: ev'n where thou think'st	. .	375	M. BRIDE	V.1	108

Thinking (22)
Belinda:	ha, ha, I can't for my Soul help thinking that I look just	83	OLD BATCH	IV.3	12
Sir Joseph:	Garter, when she was thinking of her Love. Heh, Setter.	.	103	OLD BATCH	V.1	258
Lucy:	Hold your prating.--I'm thinking what Vocation	. .	111	OLD BATCH	V.2	144
	But by my Troth I cannot avoid thinking,	. . . . .	125	DOUBL DLR	PRO.	23
Lady Touch:	a sedate, a thinking Villain, whose Black Blood runs	.	135	DOUBL DLR	I.1	328
Cynthia:	I'm thinking, that tho' Marriage makes Man and	. . .	142	DOUBL DLR	II.1	150
Cynthia:	I'm thinking, tho' Marriage makes Man and	. . . . .	142	DOUBL DLR	II.1 V150

Thinking   (continued)
Lady Ply:	happen together,--to my thinking, now I could	. . .	.	147	DOUBL DLR	II.1	326
Brisk:	thinking what to say? None but dull Rogues think; witty	.	175	DOUEL DLR	IV.1	299
	And fcr the thinking Party there's a Plot.	. . . . .	213	FOR LCVE	PRO.	30
Angelica:	was indeed thinking to propose scmething like it in a Jest,	3C0	FOR LCVE	V.1	107
Miss Prue:	sleeping, than sick with thinking.	. . . .	305	FCB LCVE	V.1	312
Miss Prue:	asleep, than sick with thinking.	. . . .	305	FOR LCVE	V.1	V312
	But thinking of this change which last befel us,	.	.	315	FOR LCVE	EPI.	5
Osmyn-Alph:	Or trifle time in thinking.	. . . .	342	M. BBIDE	II.2	99
Osmyn-Alph:	I'll muse on that, lest I exceed in thinking.	. . . .	345	M. BRIDE	II.2	V230
Almeria:	And Beds of Ease, to thinking me thy Wife?	. . . . .	357	M. FBIDE	III.1	313
Fainall:	you are not so indifferent; you are thinking of something	395	WAY WCRLD	I.1	5
Marwood:	And yet I am thinking sometimes, to carry	. . . . .	411	WAY WCBLD	II.1	50
Millamant:	have done thinking of that; think of me.	. . . . . .	423	WAY WCBLD	II.1	488
Fainall:	Why faith I'm thinking of it.--Let me see--	. . . .	443	WAY WORLD	III.1	676
	I'm thinking how this Play'll be pull'd to Pieces.	. .	479	WAY WCBLD	EPI.	2

Thinks (10)
Vainlove:	thinks her Vertuous; that's cne reason why I fail her:	.	40	OLD BATCH	I.1	119
Bellmour:	Yet rails on still, and thinks his Love unknown to us;	.	40	OLD BATCH	I.1	123
	For he thinks all his own, that is his Wives.	. . .	125	DOUBL DLR	PRO.	30
Mellefont:	handsome, and knows it; is very silly, and thinks she has	130	DOUFL DLR	I.1	129
Mellefont:	hand: For a woman never thinks a man truly in love with	159	DOUEL DLR	III.1	316
Cynthia:	Why should I call 'em Fools? The World thinks better of	167	DOUBL DLR	III.1	626
Maskwell:	she thinks I am unworthy.	. . . .	195	DCUEL DLR	IV.1	316
Mrs Frail:	a Confessor--He thinks we don't cbserve him.	. . . .	250	FOR LCVE	II.1	543
	Satire, he thinks, you ought not tc expect,	. . . .	393	WAY WCBLD	PBC.	31
Witwoud:	as Clecpatra. Mirabell is not so sure of her as he thinks				
	for.	. . . .	408	WAY WCBLD	I.1	478

Thinly (1)
| Zara: | And, like a Cobweb-Veil, but thinly shades | . . . . | 375 | M. BRIDE | V.1 | 103 |

Third (5)
Heartwell:	Batchelors Fall; and upon the third, I shall be hang'd in	63	OLD BATCH	III.1	82
Foresight:	malicious Conjunctions and Oppcsitions in the Third	.	238	FOR LCVE	II.1	129
Tattle:	Third Person--or have introduc'd an Amour of my	. . .	256	FCB LCVE	III.1	118
Scandal:	So says Pineda in his Third Book and Eighth Chapter--	.	267	FOB LCVE	III.1	532
Scandal:	Lover: But there is a Third good Work, which I, in				
	particular,	. . . .	314	FOR LOVE	V.1	621

Thirst (5)
Maskwell:	Thirst. Ha! yonder comes Mellefont thoughtful. Let me	.	155	DOUBL DLR	III.1	186
Jeremy:	plausible Occasion for me to quench my Thirst at the	.	302	FCB LCVE	V.1	175
Almeria:	Drink bitter Draughts, with never-slacking Thirst.	. .	356	M. FBIDE	III.1	262
Almeria:	O noble Thirst! and yet too greedy to	. . . . . .	382	M. BRIDE	V.2	255
Almeria:	O noble Thirst! yet greedy, to drink all--	. . . .	382	M. BRIDE	V.2	V255

Thirsty (1)
| Valentino: | I cannot talk about Business with a Thirsty Palate.-- | . | 222 | FOR LCVE | I.1 | 238 |

Thirty (3)
Nurse:	given Suck this Thirty Years.	. . . .	238	FOR LCVE	II.1	V126
Sr Sampson:	reviv'd me--Not since I was Five and Thirty.	. . . .	298	FOR LCVE	V.1	15
Jeremy:	with Thirty Thousand Pound, from throwing her self	.	.	302	FOR LCVE	V.1	210

This (746)

Thistle (1)
| Sr Sampson: | Thistle. | . . . . | 260 | FOR LCVE | III.1 | 266 |

Thistles (1)
| | As Asses Thistles, Poets mumble Wit, | . . . . . . | 214 | FOR LCVE | PRO. | 35 |

Thither (3)
Heartwell:	There stands my North, and thither my Needle points	.	.	63	OLD BATCH	III.1	75
Manuel:	I'll be conducted thither--	. . . .	374	M. BRIDE	V.1	86
Manuel:	I'll be conducted thither--mark me well--	. . . . .	374	M. FFIDE	V.1	V 86

Tho (8)
Maskwell:	your diversion: Tho it made you a little uneasy for the	.	149	DOUBL DLR	II.1	413
	Tho Satire scarce dares grin, 'tis grown so mild;	. .	213	FCB LCVE	PRO.	33
Tattle:	Aye? Who's he, tho? A Privy Counsellor?	. . . . .	302	FOR LCVE	V.1	192
Miss Prue:	Pshaw, O but I dream't that it was so tho.	. . . .	303	FOR LCVE	V.1	239
Miss Prue:	No? Yes but I would tho.	. . . .	304	FCB LCVE	V.1	251
Mrs Fore:	at all--tho he's a Coxcomb.	. . . .	310	FOR LCVE	V.1	470
Fainall:	That sham is too gross to pass cn me,--tho 'tis	. . .	472	WAY WCRLD	V.1	419
Mirabell:	--(holding out the Parchment.) tho perhaps what is	. .	476	WAY WCRLD	V.1	548

Tho' (92)
Bellmour:	you; tho' I by treachery had stoll'n the Bliss--	. . .	38	OLD BATCH	I.1	51
Capt Bluff:	share in't. Tho' I might say that too, since I am no Body	.	53	OLD BATCH	II.1	200
Capt Bluff:	share in't. Tho' I might say that too, since I name no Body	53	OLD BATCH	II.1	V200
Bellmour:	for my Speech, and set it at liberty--Tho', I confess,	.	60	OLD BATCH	II.2	219
Sir Joseph:	No, no, hang't I was not afraid neither--Tho' I	. . .	68	OLD BATCH	III.1	271
Bellmour:	tho' now they are o'er-cast.	. . . .	81	OLD BATCH	IV.2	22
Vainlove:	observ'd tho' the Penalty of it be dispens'd with; and an	87	OLD BATCH	IV.3	153
Vainlove:	Offender must Plead to his Arraignment, tho' he have his	.	87	OLD BATCH	IV.3	154
Vainlove:	Offender must Plead to his Arraignment, tho' he has his	.	87	OLD BATCH	IV.3	V154
Araminta:	my Honour.--But tho' thou hadst all the Treachery	. .	87	OLD BATCH	IV.3	167
Bellmour:	Money). Look you, Heartwell is my Friend; and tho' he be	.	98	OLD BATCH	V.1	60
Setter:	but, tho' I blush to won it at this time, I must confess				
	I am	. . . .	105	OLD BATCH	V.1	336
Bellmour:	This is a little scurrilous tho'.	. . . .	109	OLD BATCH	V.2	63
	And be enjoy'd, tho' sure to be undone;	. . . . .	113	OLD BATCH	EPI.	2
Mellefont:	would have mirth continued this day at any rate; tho'	.	129	DOUBL DLR	I.1	68
Lord Froth:	He, he, I swear tho', your Baillery provokes me	. .	132	DOUBL DLR	I.1	208
Cynthia:	I'm thinking, that tho' Marriage makes Man and	. . .	142	DOUEL DLR	II.1	150
Cynthia:	I'm thinking, tho' Marriage makes Man and	. . . .	142	DOUEL DLR	II.1	V150
Lady Ply:	Ay, for tho' I am not Cynthia's own Mother, I	. . .	146	DOUBL DLR	II.1	309
Lady Ply:	be sure you lay aside all thoughts of the Marriage, for tho'	148	DOUBL DLR	II.1	367
Mellefont:	that's sinking; tho' ne'er so far off.	. . . . .	148	DOUBL DLR	II.1	390
Maskwell:	help--tho' I stood ready for a Cue to come in and	. .	154	DOUBL DLR	III.1	129
Maskwell:	dissuade him: Tho' my Friendship and Love to him has	.	154	DOUBL DLR	III.1	152
Careless:	tho' she begins to tack about; but I made Love a great	.	157	DOUBL DLR	III.1	266
Lady Froth:	too, you know, tho' we don't see him.	. . . . .	164	DOUBL DLR	III.1	525
Brisk:	tho' to prevent Criticisms--only mark it with a small	. .	165	DOUBL DLR	III.1	551
Brisk:	tho' to prevent Criticism--only mark it with a small	. .	165	DOUBL DLR	III.1	V551

Tho' (continued)

Speaker	Text	PAGE	TITLE	ACT.SC	LINE
Lady Froth:	Sapho, tho' my Lord wont.	167	DOUBL DLR	III.1	616
Careless:	tho' by this Light I believe her Virtue is impregnable.	180	DOUBL DLR	IV.1	503
Maskwell:	tho' she inyclv'd her self in ruine. No, it must be by	190	DOUBL DLR	V.1	94
Cynthia:	any thing that resists my will, tho' 'twere reason it self.	193	DOUBL DLR	V.1	205
Lord Touch:	Yes, I will contain, tho' I cou'd burst.	199	DOUBL DLR	V.1	430
Maskwell:	of a Girl. No--yet tho' I doat on each last Favour	199	DOUBL DLR	V.1	433
	But tho' he cannot Write, let him be freed	204	DOUBL DLR	EPI.	35
	And tho' of Homely Fare we make the Feast,	213	FOR LOVE	PRO.	27
Valentine:	serve his Friend in Distress, tho' I say it to his face. Come,	223	FOR LOVE	I.1	262
Tattle:	Tho' I have more Honour than to tell first; I have more	229	FOR LOVE	I.1	478
Foresight:	Wife, Sir Sampson? Tho' you made a Cuckold of the	241	FOR LOVE	II.1	231
Miss Prue:	you should believe that; and I'll speak truth, tho' one should	264	FOR LOVE	III.1	396
Ben:	Venture, Mess, and that I will, tho' 'twere to Sea in a	265	FOR LOVE	III.1	452
Mrs Fore:	Pish, you'd tell me so, tho' you did not think	272	FOR LOVE	III.1	707
Scandal:	And you'd think so, tho' I should not tell you so:	272	FOR LOVE	III.1	709
Mrs Frail:	And tho' I have a good Portion; you know one	273	FOR LOVE	III.1	723
Valentine:	O exceeding good to keep a Secret: For tho' she	292	FOR LOVE	IV.1	645
Valentine:	Mirth, tho' not your Compassion.	295	FOR LOVE	IV.1	760
Sr Sampson:	him have the Prospect of an Estate; tho' there were no	308	FOR LOVE	V.1	427
Scandal:	tho' it be Morning, we may have a Dance.	313	FOR LOVE	V.1	601
	Tho' they are more like Almanacks of late;	323	M. BRIDE	PRO.	5
	But there's the Devil, tho' their Cause is lost,	323	M. BRIDE	PRO.	25
Gonsalez:	This Sight, which is indeed not seen (tho' twice	332	M. BRIDE	I.1	244
Almeria:	Which had been brave, tho' I had ne'er been born.	332	M. BRIDE	I.1	260
Zara:	And scorn vile Slavery, tho' doubly hid	336	M. BRIDE	I.1	401
Zara:	Favours conferr'd, tho' when unsought, deserve	336	M. BRIDE	I.1	415
Zara:	Such Favours so conferr'd, tho' when unsought,	336	M. BRIDE	I.1	V415
Almeria:	Tho' 'tis because thou lov'st me. Do not say	356	M. BRIDE	III.1	256
Gonsalez:	What if she had seen Osmyn? tho' 'twere strange.	366	M. BRIDE	IV.1	222
Almeria:	Yes, all my Father's wounding Wrath, tho' each	368	M. BRIDE	IV.1	307
Manuel:	For on my Soul he dies, tho' thou, and I,	369	M. BRIDE	IV.1	333
Almeria:	I will be Death; then tho' you kill my Husband,	370	M. BRIDE	IV.1	352
Gonsalez:	And tho' I know he hates beyond the Grave	371	M. BRIDE	IV.1	409
Gonsalez:	Of those, tho' purchas'd by his Death; I'd give	372	M. BRIDE	IV.1	438
Alonzo:	Tho' for the Crown of Universal Empire.	379	M. BRIDE	V.2	112
Osmyn-Alph:	And tho' a late, a sure Reward succeeds.	384	M. BRIDE	V.2	322
Fainall:	What? tho' half her Fortune depends upon her	396	WAY WORLD	I.1	45
Fainall:	You are a gallant Man, Mirabell; and tho' you may	397	WAY WORLD	I.1	90
Mirabell:	Tho' 'twere a Man whom he fear'd, or a Woman	403	WAY WORLD	I.1	305
Mrs Fain:	Most transcendantly; ay, tho' I say it,	411	WAY WORLD	II.1	37
Mirabell:	Thing that resembl'd a Man, tho' 'twere no more than	418	WAY WORLD	II.1	312
Witwoud:	Madam, tho' 'tis against my self.	419	WAY WORLD	II.1	340
Mirabell:	You had the Tyranny to deny me last Night; tho' you	421	WAY WORLD	II.1	429
Mirabell:	you! To think of a Whirlwind, tho' 'twere in a Whirlwind,	423	WAY WORLD	II.1	491
Marwood:	of one Set of Acquaintance, tho' never so good, as we are of	432	WAY WORLD	III.1	300
Marwood:	one Suit, tho' never so fine. A Fool and a Doily Stuff	433	WAY WORLD	III.1	301
Millamant:	ha, ha; tho' I grant you 'tis a little barbarous, Ha, ha, ha.	434	WAY WORLD	III.1	344
Petulant:	married tho' he can't Read, any more than he is from being	436	WAY WORLD	III.1	429
Petulant:	married tho' he can't read, than he is from being	436	WAY WORLD	III.1	V429
Marwood:	Friends here, tho' it may be you don't know it--If I	438	WAY WORLD	III.1	508
Fainall:	Gold, tho' my forehead had been furnish'd like a	442	WAY WORLD	III.1	647
Foible:	talk with you. Tho' my Lady's Orders were to leave you	445	WAY WORLD	IV.1	45
Millamant:	Tho' thou do'st thine, employ'st the Power and Art.	447	WAY WORLD	IV.1	105
Millamant:	last moment, tho' I am upon the very Verge of Matrimony,	449	WAY WORLD	IV.1	161
Millamant:	thank'd--here kiss my hand tho'--so hold your tongue	452	WAY WORLD	IV.1	296
Lady Wish:	my self; tho' he has been a perfidious wretch to me.	458	WAY WORLD	IV.1	509
Lady Wish:	(Reads)--Madam, tho' unknown to you (Look you there 'tis	460	WAY WORLD	IV.1	584
Waitwell:	and Innocence, tho' it cost me my life.	461	WAY WORLD	IV.1	625
Mrs Fain:	Confederacy? I fancy Marwood has not told her, tho' she	464	WAY WORLD	V.1	76
Foible:	have gone a Walking: But we went up unawares,--tho'	464	WAY WORLD	V.1	96
Lady Wish:	never suffer'd to play with a Male-Child, tho' but in	467	WAY WORLD	V.1	189
Lady Wish:	this Barbarian, But she wou'd have him, tho' her Year was	469	WAY WORLD	V.1	303
Mirabell:	much prejudice; it was an Innocent device; tho' I confess it	472	WAY WORLD	V.1	384
	Tho' they're on no pretence for Judgment fit	479	WAY WORLD	EPI.	12
	And tho' no perfect likeness they can Trace;	479	WAY WORLD	EPI.	19

Tho'f (7)

Speaker	Text	PAGE	TITLE	ACT.SC	LINE
Ben:	tho'f they love a man well enough, yet they don't care to	263	FOR LOVE	III.1	392
Ben:	tho'f he should strive against Wind and Tyde.	272	FOR LOVE	III.1	717
Ben:	will be honest, tho'f may-hap he has never a Penny of	273	FOR LOVE	III.1	733
Ben:	and Gad I answer'd 'n as surlily,--What tho'f he be	285	FOR LOVE	IV.1	369
Ben:	wou'd have me; now I know your mind, tho'f you had	287	FOR LOVE	IV.1	430
Ben:	your weight in Gold and Jewels, and tho'f I lov'd you	287	FOR LOVE	IV.1	431
Ben:	Why there's another Match now, as tho'f a couple of	310	FOR LOVE	V.1	487

Thoroughly (1) see Throughly

Speaker	Text	PAGE	TITLE	ACT.SC	LINE
Mrs Fore:	I'm thoroughly Innocent.	251	FOR LOVE	II.1	579

Those (70)

Thou (453)

Thou'dst (1)

Speaker	Text	PAGE	TITLE	ACT.SC	LINE
Zara:	Thou ly'st; for now I know for whom thou'dst live.	360	M. BRIDE	III.1	436

Thou'lt (2)

Speaker	Text	PAGE	TITLE	ACT.SC	LINE
Belinda:	least, Thou art so troublesome a Lover, there's Hopes thou'lt	106	OLD BATCH	V.1	366
Almeria:	I thank thee, that thou'lt pity thy sad Mistress;	328	M. BRIDE	I.1	95

Thou'rt (13)

Speaker	Text	PAGE	TITLE	ACT.SC	LINE
Bellmour:	Marry her without her Consent; thou'rt a Riddle	64	OLD BATCH	III.1	113
Bellmour:	Thou'rt a lucky Rogue; there's your Benefactor.	68	OLD BATCH	III.1	281
Sharper:	Matrimonial Oath with Interest.--Come, thou'rt	99	OLD BATCH	V.1	89
Sharper:	Pshaw: Thou'rt so troublesom and inquisitive.--	104	OLD BATCH	V.1	291
Mellefont:	Then thy Reason staggers, and thou'rt almost	127	DOUBL DLR	I.1	5
Sir Paul:	Lamb, thou'rt melancholy.	162	DOUBL DLR	III.1	456
Sir Paul:	Lamb, thou'rt melancholick.	162	DOUBL DLR	III.1	V456
Mellefont:	a Statesman or a Jesuite, but that thou'rt too honest for	193	DOUBL DLR	V.1	236

Thou'rt   (continued)

Sr Sampson:	Ha! thou'rt melancholly old Prognostication; As melancholly		265	FOR LOVE	III.1	463
Sr Sampson:	Ha! thou'rt melancholick old Prognostication; As					
	melancholick		265	FOR LOVE	III.1	V463
Sr Sampson:	indisposed: But I'm glad thou'rt better, honest Val. .	.	281	FOR LOVE	IV.1	203
Sr Sampson:	thou'rt honest, and wilt perform Articles.		281	FOR LOVE	IV.1	215
Almeria:	Since thou'rt reveal'd, alone thou shalt not die. .	.	368	M. BRIDE	IV.1	304

Thou'st (2)

Osmyn-Alph:	By Heav'n thou'st rous'd me from my Lethargy.	351	M. BRIDE	III.1	73
Gonsalez:	Thanks; and I take thee at thy Word. Thou'st seen . . .	372	M. BRIDE	IV.1	432

Though (28)   see Tho, Tho'

Heartwell:	able as your self and as nimble too, though I mayn't have	43	OLD BATCH	I.1	230
Bellmour:	Though you should be now and then interrupted in a . .	44	OLD BATCH	I.1	268
Heartwell:	such a place, about his Nose and Eyes; though a' has my	45	OLD BATCH	I.1	323
Heartwell:	such a place, about his Nose and Eyes; though he has my	45	OLD BATCH	I.1	V323
Bellmour:	though I believe he was heartily frightned, for as soon as	46	OLD BATCH	I.1	362
Silvia:	For I would know, though to the anguish of my Soul; .	61	OLD BATCH	III.1	15
Silvia:	but I'le do my weak endeavour, though I fear I have not	62	OLD BATCH	III.1	52
Setter:	though we were both in fault as to our Offices-- . .	66	OLD BATCH	III.1	213
Setter:	Too forward to be turn'd back--Though he's a little .	67	OLD BATCH	III.1	224
Heartwell:	Now by my Soul, I cannot lie, though it were to serve a .	72	OLD BATCH	III.2	59
Silvia:	may depend upon our skill to save us at a plunge, though	75	OLD BATCH	III.2	152
Sharper:	Gentleman's Pardon: For though Vainlove be so generous	111	OLD BATCH	V.2	121
Sir Paul:	Daughter, and a fine dutiful Child she is, though I say it,	161	DOUBL DLR	III.1	412
Sir Paul:	am her Husband, as I may say, though far unworthy of .	162	DOUBL DLR	III.1	437
Cynthia:	jests in their Persons, though they have none in their .	163	DOUBL DLR	III.1	484
Lady Ply:	--but though I may read all Letters first by Prerogative,	173	DOUBL DLR	IV.1	211
Lord Touch:	though you have once actually hindered him from forcing .	182	DOUBL DLR	IV.1	550
Mellefont:	which (if possible) are greater--Though she has all the .	186	DOUBL DLR	IV.2	123
Mellefont:	. . . Though she can wear more	186	DOUBL DLR	IV.2	V124
Maskwell:	and she fears it; though chance brought my Lord, 'twas .	187	DOUBL DLR	V.1	4
Maskwell:	though it succeeded well for her, for she would have .	188	DOUBL DLR	V.1	11
Maskwell:	more than all the rest; though I would give a limb for .	199	DOUBL DLR	V.1	434
Almeria:	My Love, my Lord, my Husband still, though lost. . .	328	M. BRIDE	I.1	76
Almeria:	I would have kept that Secret; though I know	328	M. BRIDE	I.1	80
Zara:	Thou hast a Heart, though 'tis a savage one;	346	M. BRIDE	II.2	272
Zara:	And in return of that, though otherwise	364	M. BRIDE	IV.1	137
Zara:	Most certain; though my Knowledge is not yet	364	M. BRIDE	IV.1	146
Manuel:	Though on the Head that wears it, were too little. . .	365	M. BRIDE	IV.1	160

Thought (107)

Bellmour:	thought a Contemplative Lover could no more have . . .	37	OLD BATCH	I.1	2
Sharper:	thought--	48	OLD BATCH	II.1	12
Sharper:	You are above--I'me sure--a thought so low, to suffer .	50	OLD BATCH	II.1	100
Capt Bluff:	Oh I thought so--Why then you can know nothing . . .	52	OLD BATCH	II.1	187
Bellmour:	Humph, I thought so, that you might have all the . . .	59	OLD BATCH	II.2	176
Silvia:	Bless me! you frighted me, I thought he had been come .	74	OLD BATCH	III.2	145
Araminta:	We thought to have been private.--But we	86	OLD BATCH	IV.3	116
Araminta:	Thought of Mankind.--How time might have	87	OLD BATCH	IV.3	170
Sharper:	in the Park; but I thought it had been only to make .	102	OLD BATCH	V.1	201
Bellmour:	Now George, What Rhyming! I thought the	108	OLD BATCH	V.2	17
Careless:	I thought your fear of her had been over--is not . .	129	DOUBL DLR	I.1	79
Mellefont:	importunities of your Love; and of two evils, I thought my	129	DOUBL DLR	I.1	93
Lord Froth:	Oh, I thought you would not be long, before you . .	133	DOUBL DLR	I.1	244
Maskwell:	thought you in my Power. Your Nephew's Scorn of you, .	136	DOUBL DLR	I.1	365
Lady Froth:	from the Greek, I thought you might have escap'd the .	139	DOUBL DLR	II.1	39
Maskwell:	to break the Match: Then she thought my Jealousie might	149	DOUBL DLR	II.1	424
Lady Touch:	Or, may be, he thought he was not enough	153	DOUBL DLR	III.1	87
Lady Touch:	thought my Nephew could have so misconstrued my . . .	153	DOUBL DLR	III.1	115
Maskwell:	thought! Well this Double-Dealing is a Jewel. . . .	155	DOUBL DLR	III.1	191
Careless:	Lady Plyant is not thought of--if that can ever be. .	160	DOUBL DLR	III.1	377
Lady Froth:	thought Mr. Brisk could have been in Love, ha ha ha. O .	176	DOUBL DLR	IV.1	333
Lady Froth:	Heaven's I thought you cou'd have no Mistress but the .	176	DOUBL DLR	IV.1	334
Lady Ply:	anger.) Gad's my Life if I thought it were so, I would this	179	DOUBL DLR	IV.1	442
Lady Ply:	I thought I should try you, false Man. I that	179	DOUBL DLR	IV.1	452
Lady Ply:	Night--and I thought to have always allow'd you . . .	180	DOUBL DLR	IV.1	V483
Maskwell:	thought a vent; which might discover that I lov'd, nor .	188	DOUBL DLR	V.1	35
Maskwell:	and, if I can, all thought of that pernicious Beauty. Ha!	188	DOUBL DLR	V.1	42
Maskwell:	will be inventing) which I thought to communicate to .	196	DOUBL DLR	V.1	327
Careless:	always thought him.	196	DOUBL DLR	V.1	346
Mrs Frail:	I thought you would give me something, that	232	FOR LOVE	I.1	590
Angelica:	Tinderboxes did you purchase! One would have thought .	237	FOR LOVE	II.1	82
Angelica:	Spoons, and thought they were lost. Away went Religion .	237	FOR LOVE	II.1	90
Sr Sampson:	Nostrodamus. What, I warrant my Son thought nothing .	240	FOR LOVE	II.1	175
Sr Sampson:	warrant you, if he danc'd till Doomsday, he thought I .	240	FOR LOVE	II.1	179
Valentine:	also deprive me of Reason, Thought, Passions, Inclinations,	244	FOR LOVE	II.1	340
Valentine:	also divest me of Reason, Thought, Passions, Inclinations	244	FOR LOVE	II.1	V340
Mrs Frail:	upon you?--I don't doubt but you have thought . . .	247	FOR LOVE	II.1	436
Tattle:	have such a thought--sure you don't know me?	250	FOR LOVE	II.1	541
Tattle:	Gadso; but I thought she might have been trusted . .	255	FOR LOVE	III.1	61
Angelica:	I don't understand you now. I thought you had . . .	255	FOR LOVE	III.1	88
Sr Sampson:	Woman than I thought you were: For most young . . .	260	FOR LOVE	III.1	250
Foresight:	Hum, not so well as I thought I was. Lend me your . .	269	FOR LOVE	III.1	614
Ben:	The Tailor thought to please her, ...	274	FOR LOVE	III.1	774
Ben:	Thought if it came about, Sir, ...	274	FOR LOVE	III.1	782
Jeremy:	all: I suppose your Ladyship has thought him so a great .	276	FOR LOVE	IV.1	30
Ben:	Woman that he provided for me, I thought it more fitting	285	FOR LOVE	IV.1	373
Angelica:	How! I thought your love of me had caus'd this . . .	294	FOR LOVE	IV.1	722
Valentine:	was considered, it was yours; since I thought I wanted .	295	FOR LOVE	IV.1	726
Angelica:	Then you thought me mercenary--But how	295	FOR LOVE	IV.1	728
Jeremy:	Spring of your Bounty--I thought I could not recommend .	302	FOR LOVE	V.1	176
Tattle:	speak for my self. Gad, I never had the least thought of .	309	FOR LOVE	V.1	464
Tattle:	Look you there, I thought as much--pox on't, I	310	FOR LOVE	V.1	475
Valentine:	I thought I had Reasons--But it was a poor	311	FOR LOVE	V.1	507
Valentine:	Indeed, I thought, Sir, when the Father endeavoured .	311	FOR LOVE	V.1	511
	And One was thought sufficient for a Year:	323	M. BRIDE	PRO.	4
Almeria:	My Grief has hurry'd me beyond all Thought.	328	M. BRIDE	I.1	79

Thought   (continued)
Almeria:	While I have Life, and Thought of my Alphonso.	329	M. BRIDE	I.1 V148
Almeria:	By any Action, Word or Thought, to wed	330	M. BRIDE	I.1 186
Almeria:	'Tis that, or some such Melancholy Thought, ...	331	M. BRIDE	I.1 205
Manuel:	Yet--upon thought, it doubly wounds my sight, . . .	333	M. BRIDE	I.1 294
Heli:	Afford a Thought, or Glimpse of Joy, ...	338	M. BRIDE	II.1 8
Heli:	Afford a Thought, or show a Glimpse of Joy, ...	338	M. BRIDE	II.1 V 8
Almeria:	Of Garcia's more detested Bed. That Thought, . . .	339	M. BRIDE	II.1 78
Almeria:	O Exstacy of Thought! help me Anselmo:	340	M. BRIDE	II.2 30
Almeria:	All Thought; that all at once, thou art before me, . .	343	M. BRIDE	II.2 152
Osmyn-Alph:	And thought, I heard thy Spirit call Alphonso. . .	344	M. BRIDE	II.2 163
Osmyn-Alph:	I thought I saw thee too; but O, I thought not . .	344	M. BRIDE	II.2 164
Osmyn-Alph:	Harbour no Thought, that may disturb thy Peace; . .	345	M. BRIDE	II.2 201
Osmyn-Alph:	Turn your Lights inward, Eyes, and view my Thought, .	345	M. BRIDE	II.2 V215
Osmyn-Alph:	Upon my Thought; so, shall you still behold her. . .	345	M. BRIDE	II.2 216
Zara:	Stiff'ning in Thought; a Statue amongst Statues. . .	345	M. BRIDE	II.2 233
Osmyn-Alph:	Yet I may think--I may? I must; for Thought	350	M. BRIDE	III.1 33
Heli:	Among the Troops who thought to share the Plunder, . .	351	M. BRIDE	III.1 65
Heli:	For your Escape. Mean time, I've thought already . .	352	M. BRIDE	III.1 98
Almeria:	Give thy Soul Way, and tell me thy dark Thought. . .	356	M. BRIDE	III.1 274
Osmyn-Alph:	To that soul-racking Thought.	357	M. BRIDE	III.1 294
Osmyn-Alph:	A wish or Thought from me, to have thee other. . . .	357	M. BRIDE	III.1 316
Selim:	But to serve you. I have already thought.	362	M. BRIDE	IV.1 40
Manuel:	Say'st thou? by Heav'n thou hast arous'd a Thought, .	367	M. BRIDE	IV.1 232
Gonsalez:	That were too hard a Thought--but see she comes. . .	367	M. BRIDE	IV.1 236
Manuel:	--Stay thee--I've farther thought--I'll add to . .	374	M. BRIDE	V.1 80
Selim:	Yes: But then, as if he thought	375	M. BRIDE	V.1 V 98
Zara:	And more important Fate, requires my Thought. . . .	375	M. BRIDE	V.1 125
Garcia:	The Horrour of that Thought, has damp'd my Rage. . .	378	M. BRIDE	V.2 74
Alonzo:	My Lord, I've thought how to conceal the Body; . .	378	M. BRIDE	V.2 96
Selim:	You thought it better then--but I rewarded. . . .	380	M. BRIDE	V.2 179
	Some Plot we think he has, and some new Thought; . .	393	WAY WORLD	PRO. 29
Mirabell:	with a constrain'd Smile told her, I thought nothing was so	396	WAY WORLD	I.1 38
Fainall:	I thought you had dy'd for her.	408	WAY WORLD	I.1 473
Mirabell:	I thought you had been the greatest Favourite. . . .	408	WAY WORLD	I.1 499
Mirabell:	I thought you were oblig'd to watch for your . . .	409	WAY WORLD	I.1 512
Petulant:	thought to understand.	409	WAY WORLD	I.1 532
Marwood:	she wou'd be thought.	413	WAY WORLD	II.1 129
Foible:	thought the former good Correspondence between your .	430	WAY WORLD	III.1 197
Marwood:	Fainall, have you carried it so swimmingly? I thought there	431	WAY WORLD	III.1 229
Lady Wish:	I promise you I have thought on't--And	432	WAY WORLD	III.1 269
Millamant:	every Thing that has been said. For my part, I thought	432	WAY WORLD	III.1 293
Mincing:	I vow Mem, I thought once they wou'd have fit. . . .	432	WAY WORLD	III.1 295
Millamant:	--But that cannot be--Well, that Thought makes . .	434	WAY WORLD	III.1 361
Marwood:	I thought you had design'd for France at all . . .	440	WAY WORLD	III.1 576
Fainall:	Hum! Faith and that's well thought on; Marriage is . .	443	WAY WORLD	III.1 691
Millamant:	looks as if he thought so too--Well, you ridiculous .	452	WAY WORLD	IV.1 294
Foible:	thought something was contriving, when he stole by me .	461	WAY WORLD	IV.1 613
Foible:	thought for.	464	WAY WORLD	V.1 90
Foible:	when you were at Hide-Park;--And we were thought to .	464	WAY WORLD	V.1 95
Lady Wish:	What, a Whore? And thought it exccmmunication to set .	467	WAY WORLD	V.1 204

Thoughtful (7)
Sharper:	What, is Belinda cruel, that you are so thoughtful? . .	41	OLD BATCH	I.1 150
Lucy:	Here's some Villany a Foot he's so thoughtful; may be I .	65	OLD BATCH	III.1 154
Mellefont:	You're thoughtful, Cynthia?	142	DOUBL DLR	II.1 149
Maskwell:	Thirst. Ha! yonder comes Mellefont thoughtful. Let me .	155	DOUBL DLR	III.1 186
Maskwell:	excuse. My Lord is thoughtful--I'le be so too; yet he shall	188	DOUBL DLR	V.1 13
Cynthia:	Your Lordship was thoughtful.	197	DOUBL DLR	V.1 364
Lady Wish:	a little dangling off, Jogging in a thoughtful way--Yes--	445	WAY WORLD	IV.1 26

Thoughtfull (1)
Millamant:	thoughtfull and would amuse my self,--bid him	446	WAY WORLD	IV.1 49

Thoughtless (2)
Valentine:	and bid her trouble me no more; a thoughtless two handed .	221	FOR LOVE	I.1 210
Scandal:	he is a thoughtless Adventurer, ...	234	FOR LOVE	I.1 679

Thoughts (18)
Vainlove:	she may entertain some Thoughts of him. I know he . .	40	OLD BATCH	I.1 121
Bellmour:	faith upon second Thoughts, she does not appear to be so .	41	OLD BATCH	I.1 171
Bellmour:	Thoughts fly to any pitch, I shall make villainous Signs.	59	OLD BATCH	II.2 178
Lady Ply:	be sure you lay aside all thoughts of the Marriage, for tho'	148	DOUBL DLR	II.1 367
Lady Touch:	my Thoughts in any thing that may be to my Cousin's .	151	DOUBL DLR	III.1 35
Brisk:	your Ladyship was in my Thoughts; and I was in a sort of	176	DOUBL DLR	IV.1 326
Maskwell:	know my thoughts; or think he does--	188	DOUBL DLR	V.1 14
Lord Touch:	start at the revelation of their thoughts, but be thou			
	fix'd, ...	189	DOUBL DLR	V.1 48
Mellefont:	maze of thoughts, each leading into one another, and all .	190	DOUBL DLR	V.1 104
Maskwell:	Stay, I have a doubt--upon second thoughts, ...	194	DOUBL DLR	V.1 251
Lord Touch:	My thoughts were on serious business, not	197	DOUBL DLR	V.1 365
Tattle:	thoughts; but your Actions may contradict your words. .	251	FOR LOVE	I.1 613
Osmyn-Alph:	Lost in my self, and blinded by my Thoughts, ...	346	M. BRIDE	II.2 253
Osmyn-Alph:	By him set down; when his pure Thoughts were born . .	353	M. BRIDE	III.1 129
Sir Wilful:	. . . have Thoughts to tarry a small	440	WAY WORLD	III.1 581
Millamant:	would confer with my own Thoughts.	446	WAY WORLD	IV.1 66
Millamant:	morning thoughts, agreeable wakings, indolent slumbers, .	449	WAY WORLD	IV.1 188
Marwood:	bid adieu to all other Thoughts.	468	WAY WORLD	V.1 262

Thousand (21)
Bellmour:	twelve thousand Pound Tom--'Tis true she is excessively .	41	OLD BATCH	I.1 166
Bellmour:	told you there's twelve thousand Pound--Hum--Why . .	41	OLD BATCH	I.1 170
Sharper:	No, 'tis gone, 'tis lost--ten thousand Devils on that .	48	OLD BATCH	II.1 21
Bellmour:	Pardon a thousand times.--What an eternal Block-head .	81	OLD BATCH	IV.2 39
Setter:	forth under my Auspicious Convoy. Twelve Thousand . .	102	OLD BATCH	V.1 223
Mellefont:	in a resolution, confirm'd by a Thousand Curses, not to .	130	DOUBL DLR	I.1 117
Sir Paul:	end--He? A brave Chopping Boy.--I'll settle a Thousand .	173	DOUBL DLR	IV.1 224
Lady Touch:	And such a smile as speaks in Ambiguity! Ten thousand .	198	DOUBL DLR	V.1 394
Valentine:	will immediately furnish me with Four thousand Pound to .	225	FOR LOVE	I.1 337
Sr Sampson:	day in a Bill of Four thousand Pound: A great deal of .	243	FOR LOVE	II.1 275
Sr Sampson:	Again! 'Ouns han't you four thousand Pound	246	FOR LOVE	II.1 396

713

Thousand (continued)

Speaker	Quotation	PAGE	TITLE	ACT.SC	LINE
Jeremy:	with Thirty Thousand Pound, from throwing her self	302	FOR LOVE	V.1	210
Jeremy:	Sir, I ask you Ten Thousand Pardons, 'twas an errant	313	FOR LOVE	V.1	592
Almeria:	Die ten thousand Deaths--Look down, look down	330	M. BRIDE	I.1	176
Almeria:	I have a thousand Things to know, and ask,	343	M. BRIDE	II.2	150
Zara:	O Heav'n! a thousand things occur	363	M. BRIDE	IV.!	92
Zara:	O Heav'n! a thousand things occur at once	363	M. BRIDE	IV.1 V	92
Witwoud:	My Dear, I ask ten thousand Pardons;--Gad I	402	WAY WORLD	I.1	270
Foible:	has been in a thousand Inquietudes for me. But I protest,	423	WAY WORLD	II.1	514
Mincing:	six thousand Pound. O, come Mrs. Foible, I hear my old	465	WAY WORLD	V.1	116
Fainall:	endow'd in right of my Wife, with that six thousand	469	WAY WORLD	V.1	278

Thousands (1)

Lady Touch:	black!--O I have Excuses, Thousands for my Faults; Fire	135	DOUBL DLR	I.1	325

Thrash (2)

Miss Prue:	any more, he'll thrash your Jacket for you, he will, you	264	FOR LOVE	III.1	417
Ben:	here just now? Will he thrash my Jacket?--Let'n, let'n,--	264	FOR LOVE	III.1	420

Threaten (2)

Marwood:	We threaten you who do for Judges sit,	35	OLD BATCH	PRO.	8
	threaten to part with her--My Lady loves her, and	442	WAY WORLD	III.1	660

Threatens (1)

Brisk:	threatens to disclaim you for a Son-in-Law, and my Lord	128	DOUBL DLR	I.1	55

Threatned (1)

Maskwell:	made me conceal it; yet you may say, I threatned the next	154	DOUBL DLR	III.1	153

Three (29)

Capt Bluff:	not three words of Truth, the Year round, put into the	52	OLD BATCH	II.1	193
Brisk:	of Wine,--the Deuce take me if there were three good	128	DOUBL DLR	I.1	35
Mellefont:	Well, I'll speak but three words, and follow you.	129	DOUBL DLR	I.1	60
Lady Froth:	Three Weeks together.	138	DOUBL DLR	II.1	4
Lady Ply:	this three year past? Have I been white and unsulli'd even by	145	DOUBL DLR	II.1	255
Lady Ply:	these three Years past? Have I been white and unsulli'd even by	145	DOUBL DLR	II.1 V255	
Lord Froth:	so ready--she always comes in three bars too soon--and	163	DOUBL DLR	III.1	476
Lady Froth:	Three Quarters, but I swear she has a World of	167	DOUBL DLR	III.1	619
Lady Froth:	Three times aloud, as I love Letters--But	176	DOUBL DLR	IV.1	331
Sir Paul:	three Years past? Have I been swath'd in Blankets till I	178	DOUBL DLR	IV.1	424
Jeremy:	mean, to mew your self up here with Three or Four	217	FOR LOVE	I.1	32
Jeremy:	Certificate of Three Lines--only to certifie those whom	217	FOR LOVE	I.1	65
Jeremy:	Three days, the Life of a Play, I no more expect it, than to	218	FOR LOVE	I.1	74
Valentine:	was sent to Sea three Years ago? This Brother, my Father	225	FOR LOVE	I.1	333
Tattle:	three or four places, that I said this and that, and writ to	227	FOR LOVE	I.1	420
Foresight:	he's at leisure--'tis now Three a Clock, a very good hour	236	FOR LOVE	II.1	41
Mrs Fore:	Nay, two or three Turns, I'll take my Oath.	246	FOR LOVE	II.1	421
Sr Sampson:	Hopes of my Family--I han't seen him these Three	259	FOR LOVE	III.1	213
Mrs Fore:	Never, never; till within these three Nights;	270	FOR LOVE	III.1	622
Ben:	But while these three were prating,	274	FOR LOVE	III.1	780
Mrs Frail:	and Scales, and three rows of Teeth, a most outragious	286	FOR LOVE	IV.1	401
Mirabell:	Yes, and Mrs. Marwood and three or four more,	396	WAY WORLD	I.1	28
Fainall:	have 'em three times a Week, and meet by turns, at one	396	WAY WORLD	I.1	51
Coachman:	Three Gentlewomen in the Coach would speak	404	WAY WORLD	I.1	346
Coachman:	Three Gentlewomen in a Coach would speak	404	WAY WORLD	I.1 V346	
Fainall:	O brave Petulant, three!	404	WAY WORLD	I.1	348
Witwoud:	three are.	404	WAY WORLD	I.1	355
Waitwell:	I'll do't. In three weeks he shall be bare-foot; in a	458	WAY WORLD	IV.1	521
Lady Wish:	--do, drive a Trade, do, with your three penny-worth	462	WAY WORLD	V.1	11

Thresh (1)

	Poor Actors thresh such empty Sheafs of Straw?	323	M. BRIDE	PRO.	18

Threshold (1)

Millamant:	over the threshold. I'll be solicited to the very last, nay and	449	WAY WORLD	IV.1	164

Thrice (1)

	Let it at least rise thrice, before it Drown.	125	DOUBL DLR	PRO.	18

Thrill'd (1)

Zara:	And thrill'd thee through with darted Fires; but thou	348	M. BRIDE	II.2	346

Thrilling (1)

Almeria:	I chatter, shake, and faint with thrilling Fears.	358	M. BRIDE	III.1	369

Thrive (3)

Mellefont:	Pretious Aunt, I shall never thrive without I deal with the	187	DOUBL DLR	IV.2	152
Valentine:	morrow, Knaves will thrive thro' craft, and Fools thro'	288	FOR LOVE	IV.1	492
	And thrive and prosper on the Wrecks of Wit.	385	M. BRIDE	EPI.	26

Thrives (2)

	I'th' Good Man's Arms, the Chopping Bastard thrives,	125	DOUBL DLR	PRO.	29
Jeremy:	Nothing thrives that belongs to't. The Man of the House	218	FOR LOVE	I.1	89

Thro' (22)

Mellefont:	thro' Clouds upon me, and I shall live in Day--O my	149	DOUBL DLR	II.1	406
Maskwell:	way into it, so that you need not come thro' this Door	194	DOUBL DLR	V.1	254
Scandal:	but 'tis as I believe some Men are Valiant, thro' fear--For	271	FOR LOVE	III.1	670
Valentine:	morrow, Knaves will thrive thro' craft, and Fools thro'	288	FOR LOVE	IV.1	492
	He wou'd not lose thro' Prejudice his Cause;	324	M. BRIDE	PRO.	41
Leonora:	Where, while his Gaoler slept, I thro' the Grate	326	M. BRIDE	I.1	26
Almeria:	Which are diffus'd thro' the revolving Year,	330	M. BRIDE	I.1	154
Almeria:	Thro' all Impediments, of purging Fire,	330	M. BRIDE	I.1	182
Gonsalez:	Their Hold, thro' clifted Stones; stretching, and staring,	332	M. BRIDE	I.1	240
Almeria:	Whistling thro' Hollows of this vaulted Isle.	339	M. BRIDE	II.2	55
Heli:	I wander thro' this Maze of Monuments,	340	M. BRIDE	II.2	1
Osmyn-Alph:	And wafted thence, on Angels Wings, thro' Ways	353	M. BRIDE	III.1	131
Osmyn-Alph:	What Brightness, breaks upon me, thus thro' Shades,	353	M. BRIDE	III.1	140
Zara:	And strikes his Rays thro' dusk, and folded Lids,	354	M. BRIDE	III.1	208
Zara:	Thro' all the Gloomy Ways, and Iron Doors	379	M. BRIDE	V.2	133
Osmyn-Alph:	Let us that thro' our Innocence survive,	384	M. BRIDE	V.2	318
Osmyn-Alph:	Let us who thro' our Innocence survive,	384	M. BRIDE	V.2 V318	
Mirabell:	good old Lady broke thro' her painful Taciturnity, with an	396	WAY WORLD	I.1	35
Marwood:	You, you upbraid me! Have I been false to her, thro' strict	414	WAY WORLD	II.1	172
Fainall:	Proof, and something of a Constitution to bustle thro' the	415	WAY WORLD	II.1	213
Sir Wilful:	Cozen, I made bold to pass thro' as it were,--I think this	447	WAY WORLD	IV.1	95

Throat (7)
Bellmour:	Throat. My Patch, my Patch.	89	OLD BATCH	IV.4	13
Sr Sampson:	Throat? or--	298	FOR LCVE	V.1	43
Alonzo:	The Morsel down his throat. I catch'd his Arm, . . .	373	M. BRIDE	V.1	24
Almeria:	And come prepar'd to yield my Throat--they shake . .	382	M. BRIDE	V.2	250
Mirabell:	there yet? I shall cut your Throat, sometime or other,	406	WAY WORLD	I.1	423
Waitwell:	hand I see that already. That's some body whose throat	460	WAY WORLD	IV.1	578
Waitwell:	Roman hand--I saw there was a throat to be cut presently.	460	WAY WORLD	V.1	602

Throats (3)
Petulant:	Ay, ay, let that pass--There are other Throats . .	406	WAY WORLD	I.1	425
Petulant:	I, nothing I. If Throats are to be cut, let Swords . .	407	WAY WORLD	I.1	446
Marwood:	be transferr'd to the hands, nay into the Throats and	468	WAY WORLD	V.1	232

Throbbing (2)
Osmyn-Alph:	Break on the flinty Ground my throbbing Breast, ...	358	M. BRIDE	III.1	352
Osmyn-Alph:	Break on the flinty Floor my throbbing Breast, ...	358	M. BRIDE	III.1	V352

Thrones (1)
Zara:	Of Sceptres, Crowns, and Thrones; they've serv'd their .	347	M. BRIDE	II.2	319

Throng (2)
	So Criticks throng to see a New Play split, ...	385	M. BRIDE	EPI.	25
Mirabell:	us'd to have the Beau-mond Throng after you; and a Flock	418	WAY WORLD	II.1	329

Through (26) see Thro'
Heartwell:	Ay, why to come to Love through all these	44	OLD BATCH	I.1	277
Sir Joseph:	through all dangers--he is indeed Back, Breast and Headpiece	50	OLD BATCH	II.1	120
Vainlove:	You are the Temples of Love, and 'tis through you, . .	58	OLD BATCH	II.2	144
Sir Joseph:	Lord-Harry. I know better things than to be run through	67	OLD BATCH	III.1	253
Bellmour:	So breaks Aurora through the Veil of Night;	81	OLD BATCH	IV.2	10
Lucy:	I had none, but through Mistake.	97	OLD BATCH	V.1	40
Bellmour:	Which Mistake you must go through with, Lucy.-- . . .	97	OLD BATCH	V.1	41
Mellefont:	me; his Dependance upon my Uncle is through my means. . .	131	DOUEL DLR	I.1	150
Maskwell:	had never favour'd, but through Revenge and Policy. . .	136	DOUEL DLR	I.1	357
Maskwell:	against me, and I'll make my escape through the private . .	157	DOUEL DLR	III.1	251
Brisk:	great Beard that bristles through it, and makes her look as	166	DOUEL DLR	III.1	586
Cynthia:	why have you look'd through the wrong end of the . .	168	DOUEL DLR	IV.1	24
Cynthia:	you have look'd through the wrong end of the	168	DOUEL DLR	IV.1	V 24
Careless:	through all my Pores, and will to Morrow wash me for . .	170	DOUEL DLR	IV.1	116
Lord Touch:	and want a Clue to guide me through the various mazes . .	200	DOUEL DLR	V.1	471
Angelica:	Yes, I saw you together, through the Key-hole of . . .	238	FOR LCVE	II.1	106
Sr Sampson:	If we were to go through with it. But why must the Match	300	FOR LCVE	V.1	114
Manuel:	But should have smil'd that Hour, through all his Care, .	333	M. BRIDE	I.1	316
Manuel:	Unus'd to wait, I broke through her Delay, ...	337	M. BRIDE	I.1	456
Zara:	And thrill'd thee through with darted Fires; but thou .	348	M. BRIDE	II.2	346
Zara:	And through my Hopes in you, I promis'd Freedom	349	M. BRIDE	II.2	378
Zara:	And through my Hopes in you, I undertook	349	M. BRIDE	II.2	V378
Garcia:	Are through a Postern fled, and join the Foe.	377	M. BRIDE	V.2	39
Fainall:	To let you know I see through all your little Arts-- .	413	WAY WORLD	II.1	136
Millamant:	as fast through the Crowd--	418	WAY WORLD	II.1	334
Marwood:	I saw her but now, as I came mask'd through	426	WAY WORLD	III.1	47

Throughly (3)
Fondlewife:	Wife--Have you throughly consider'd how	77	OLD BATCH	IV.1	67
Maskwell:	She must be throughly perswaded, that Mellefont . . .	138	DOUEL DLR	I.1	410
Marwood:	that lov'd me very well, and would be throughly sensible	411	WAY WORLD	II.1	54

Throw (7)
Maskwell:	every look you cheaply throw away on any other Object .	199	DOUEL DLR	V.1	435
Mrs Frail:	throw himself away, he can't do it more effectually than .	287	FOR LCVE	V.1	460
Tattle:	But, Madam, to throw away your Person, such a . . .	290	FOR LCVE	IV.1	570
Angelica:	him to throw off his Disguise of Madness, in Apprehension	300	FOR LCVE	V.1	110
Osmyn-Alph:	Why was I made the Instrument, to throw	347	M. BRIDE	II.2	322
Manuel:	This hour I throw ye off, and entertain	374	M. BRIDE	V.1	64
Fainall:	. . . She might throw up her Cards;	442	WAY WORLD	III.1	V653

Throwing (2)
Bellmour:	(Throwing off his Cloak, Patch, &c.) .	81	OLD BATCH	IV.2	13
Jeremy:	with Thirty Thousand Pound, from throwing her self . .	302	FOR LCVE	V.1	210

Thrown (4)
Heartwell:	Then good Councel will be thrown away upon	112	OLD BATCH	V.2	157
	Into the sea, the New-born Babe is thrown, ...	125	DOUEL DLR	PRO.	3
	Till Dice are thrown, there's nothing won, nor lost. . .	204	DOUEL DLB	EPI.	5
Sr Sampson:	and 'twere pity you shou'd be thrown away upon any . .	298	FOR LCVE	V.1	52

Throws (2)
Silvia:	(Throws the Purse) I hate you now, and I'll never see you .	74	OLD BATCH	III.2	111
	(Takes out the Letter, and offers it: She snatches it,				
	and throws	88	OLD BATCH	IV.3	179

Thrust (4)
Heartwell:	will more easily be thrust forward than drawn back. . .	73	OLD BATCH	III.2	73
Mellefont:	O' my word, Brisk, that was a home thrust; you . . .	128	DOUBL DLR	I.1	31
Mrs Frail:	take great care when one makes a thrust in Fencing, not to	248	FOR LCVE	II.1	474
Manuel:	Has thrust between us and our while of Love;	363	M. BRIDE	IV.1	106

Thrusts (1)
Tattle:	(Thrusts her in, and shuts the Door.) .	254	FOR LCVE	III.1	25

Thumbs (1)
Angelica:	turning the Sieve and Sheers, and pricking your Thumbs, .	238	FOR LCVE	II.1	108

Thunder (6)
Capt Bluff:	By the immortal Thunder of great Guns, 'tis false . . .	70	OLD BATCH	III.1	352
Mellefont:	But when I expected Thunder from her Voice, and . . .	130	DOUEL DLR	I.1	105
Lady Touch:	Thunder strike thee Dead for this Deceit, ...	184	DOUEL DLR	IV.2	44
Ben:	The Souldier Swore like Thunder, ...	274	FOR LCVE	III.1	769
	What Peals of Thunder, and what Show'rs of Rain; . .	323	M. BRIDE	PRO.	10
Heli:	Let Heav'n with Thunder to the Centre strike me, . . .	337	M. BRIDE	II.1	4

Thunder-strock (1)
Foresight:	I'm Thunder-strook! You are not married to my . . .	307	FOR LCVE	V.1	388

Thunders (1)
Manuel:	Of him that thunders, than but think that Insolence. . .	349	M. BRIDE	II.2	370

Thus (109)
Araminta:	Bless me! what have I said to move you thus?	54	OLD BATCH	II.2	3
Musician:	Thus, to a ripe, consenting Maid, ...	59	OLD BATCH	II.2	190
Setter:	Ha! what art, who thus maliciously hast awakned me, . .	65	OLD BATCH	III.1	165
Capt Bluff:	Death and Hell to be affronted thus! I'll die before . .	70	OLD BATCH	III.1	336

Thus (continued)

		PAGE	TITLE	ACT.SC	LINE
Bellmour:	Thus fly the Clouds, divided by her Light,	81	OLD BATCH	IV.2	11
Laetitia:	Thus strew'd with Blushes, like--	81	OLD BATCH	IV.2	14
Sharper:	Thus Grief still treads upon the Heels of Pleasure:	105	OLD BATCH	V.1	327
	Thus hardly to be prov'd Legitimate!	125	DOUEL DLR	PRO.	20
Mellefont:	In short, the Consequence was thus, she omitted nothing,	130	DOUEL DLR	I.1	109
Brisk:	--and I hear it, and look thus.--Would not you	134	DOUEL DLR	I.1	269
Singer:	Thus, in doubting, she refuses;	143	DOUEL DLR	II.1	183
Singer:	And not Winning, thus she loses.	143	DOUEL DLR	II.1	184
Cynthia:	I never saw him thus before.	144	DOUEL DLR	II.1	205
Sir Paul:	won't be a Brute, and have my Head fortifi'd, that I am thus	144	DOUEL DLR	II.1	231
Lady Ply:	road of Virtue, in which I have trod thus long, and never	147	DOUEL DLR	II.1	318
Mellefont:	outwitted Woman.--But tell me, how could'st thou thus	149	DOUEL DLR	II.1	408
Lady Touch:	make me lay my heart before you, but don't be thus	152	DOUEL DLR	III.1	65
Maskwell:	Why thus--I'll go according to Appointment;	157	DOUEL DLR	III.1	248
Sir Paul:	was never thus before--Well, I must own my self	172	DOUEL DLR	IV.1	199
Lord Touch:	unnatural Nephew thus far--but I know you have been	182	DOUEL DLR	IV.1	545
Maskwell:	Excess of Joy had made me stupid! Thus may my	184	DOUEL DLR	IV.2	24
Maskwell:	Excess of Joy has made me stupid! Thus may my	184	DOUEL DLR	IV.2 V	24
Maskwell:	Lips be ever clos'd. (Kisses her.) And thus--Oh who	184	DOUEL DLR	IV.2	25
Mellefont:	And may all Treachery be thus discovered.	184	DOUEL DLR	IV.2	35
Lord Touch:	our ancient Family; him I thus blow away, and constitute	189	DOUEL DLR	V.1	58
Maskwell:	Come, why do you dally with me thus?	197	DOUEL DLR	V.1	385
Lady Touch:	silent? Oh, I am wilder'd in all Passions! but thus my	198	DOUEL DLR	V.1	401
	Thus poor Poets the Favour are deny'd,	204	DOUEL DLR	EPI.	29
	Poor Poets thus the Favour are deny'd,	204	DOUEL DLR	EPI. V	29
Trapland:	Sincerely, I am loth to be thus pressing, but my	224	FOR LOVE	I.1	322
Valentine:	Nay, if you have known Scandal thus long, and	229	FOR LOVE	I.1	501
Foresight:	Prophesie written by Messehalah the Arabian, and thus	236	FOR LOVE	II.1	49
Foresight:	I should be thus tormented--This is the effect of the	238	FOR LOVE	II.1	128
Miss Prue:	thus, so I won't.--If I were a man,--(Crys.)--You durst not	264	FOR LOVE	III.1	429
Ben:	Thus we live at Sea; eat Bisket, and drink Flip; put on a	275	FOR LOVE	III.1	800
	Thus Aristotle's Soul, of old that was,	315	FOR LOVE	EPI.	21
	And thus our Audience, which did once resort	315	FOR LOVE	EPI. V	25
	Thus from the past, we hope for future Grace,	316	FOR LOVE	EPI.	40
	Thus far, alone does to the Wits relate;	323	M. BRIDE	PRO.	33
Almeria:	That thus couldst melt to see a Stranger's Wrongs.	327	M. BRIDE	I.1	31
Almeria:	Why are all these things thus?--	327	M. BRIDE	I.1	56
Almeria:	That I should be afflicted thus?--if not,	327	M. BRIDE	I.1	59
Almeria:	Why is it thus contriv'd? Why are things laid	327	M. BRIDE	I.1	60
Leonora:	It will incense him, thus to see you drown'd	330	M. BRIDE	I.1	167
Gonsalez:	But Tears of Joy. To see you thus, has fill'd	332	M. BRIDE	I.1	273
Gonsalez:	But Tears of Joy. Believe me, Sir, to see you thus, has fill'd	332	M. BRIDE	I.1 V	273
Garcia:	Thus let me kneel to take--O not to take,	334	M. BRIDE	I.1	335
Perez:	But at some distance follow, thus attended.	336	M. BRIDE	I.1	407
Manuel:	Fit restitution here--Thus, I release you,	336	M. BRIDE	I.1	413
Almeria:	That thus relenting, they have giv'n thee back	342	M. BRIDE	II.2	89
Osmyn-Alph:	To fold thee thus, to press thy balmy Lips,	342	M. BRIDE	II.2	96
Almeria:	To see him thus again, is such profusion	342	M. BRIDE	II.2	106
Almeria:	Be mad--I cannot be transported thus.	342	M. BRIDE	II.2	108
Almeria:	But still, how camest thee hither? how thus?--Ha!	344	M. BRIDE	II.2	166
Almeria:	But still, how camest thou hither? how thus?--Ha!	344	M. BRIDE	II.2 V	166
Heli:	Most happily, in finding you thus bless'd.	344	M. BRIDE	II.2	171
Osmyn-Alph:	That thus with open Hand it scatters good,	344	M. BRIDE	II.2	186
Osmyn-Alph:	How I escap'd, how I am here, and thus;	345	M. BRIDE	II.2	206
Osmyn-Alph:	Thus, do our Eyes, like common Mirrours	345	M. BRIDE	II.2	221
Osmyn-Alph:	Thus, do our Eyes, as do all common Mirrours	345	M. BRIDE	II.2 V	221
Zara:	Why, cruel Osmyn, dost thou fly me thus?	345	M. BRIDE	II.2	234
Zara:	Am I neglected thus? Am I despised?	346	M. BRIDE	II.2	245
Zara:	Better I was unseen, than seen thus coldly.	346	M. BRIDE	II.2	257
Zara:	Inhumane! why, why dost thou wrack me thus?	346	M. BRIDE	II.2	264
Zara:	Yet thus, thus fall'n, thus levell'd with the vilest;	347	M. BRIDE	II.2	312
Osmyn-Alph:	Sure 'tis the Hand of Heav'n, that leads me thus,	350	M. BRIDE	III.1	4
Osmyn-Alph:	But Heav'n was deaf, Heav'n heard him not; but thus,	350	M. BRIDE	III.1	24
Osmyn-Alph:	Thus as the Name of Heav'n from this is torn,	350	M. BRIDE	III.1	25
Osmyn-Alph:	If Piety be thus debarr'd Access	350	M. BRIDE	III.1	28
Osmyn-Alph:	What Brightness, breaks upon me, thus thro' Shades,	353	M. BRIDE	III.1	140
Zara:	Cou'd one that lov'd, thus torture what she lov'd?	353	M. BRIDE	III.1	161
Zara:	Cou'd one who lov'd, thus torture whom she lov'd?	353	M. BRIDE	III.1 V	161
Zara:	And Detestation, thus cou'd use thee thus.	353	M. BRIDE	III.1	163
Zara:	Thy Anger cou'd not pierce thus, to my Heart.	354	M. BRIDE	III.1	187
Osmyn-Alph:	Or take thee into mine, thus manacled	355	M. BRIDE	III.1	240
Osmyn-Alph:	Or take thee into mine, while I'm thus manacled	355	M. BRIDE	III.1 V	240
Osmyn-Alph:	Rude Irons! Must I meet thee thus, Almeria?	355	M. BRIDE	III.1	244
Almeria:	Thus, thus; we parted, thus to meet again.	355	M. BRIDE	III.1	245
Almeria:	No, no, 'tis better thus, that we together	356	M. BRIDE	III.1	258
Almeria:	Thus, better, than for any Cause to part.	356	M. BRIDE	III.1	263
Osmyn-Alph:	Grief wou'd not double thus, his Darts against me.	356	M. BRIDE	III.1	283
Osmyn-Alph:	Grief cou'd not double thus, his Darts against me.	356	M. BRIDE	III.1 V283
Osmyn-Alph:	Why dost thou thus unman me with thy Words,	357	M. BRIDE	III.1	306
Osmyn-Alph:	What dost thou ask? why dost thou talk thus piercingly?	357	M. BRIDE	III.1	308
Osmyn-Alph:	Why dost thou ask? why dost thou talk thus piercingly?	357	M. BRIDE	III.1 V308
Osmyn-Alph:	To call thee mine? yes, thus, ev'n thus, to call	357	M. BRIDE	III.1	330
Osmyn-Alph:	But till she's gone; then bless me thus again.	359	M. BRIDE	III.1	395
Osmyn-Alph:	This Charity to one unknown, and thus	359	M. BRIDE	III.1 V403
Zara:	Who would not be thus happily confin'd,	360	M. BRIDE	III.1	425
Almeria:	O hear me then, thus crawling on the Earth--	369	M. BRIDE	IV.1	327
Garcia:	Where, where is he? Why dost thou thus mislead me?	376	M. BRIDE	V.2	19
Zara:	What have you seen? Ha! wherefore stare you thus,	380	M. BRIDE	V.2	155
Zara:	But cannot bear to find thee thus, my Osmyn--	380	M. BRIDE	V.2 V167
Almeria:	That thus can gaze, and yet not turn to Stone?	382	M. BRIDE	V.2	239
Almeria:	O thanks the liberal Hand that fill'd thee thus;	382	M. BRIDE	V.2	259
Almeria:	Thanks to the liberal Hand that fill'd thee thus;	382	M. BRIDE	V.2 V259
Osmyn-Alph:	Nay, I must grant, 'tis fit you shou'd be thus--	383	M. BRIDE	V.2	309
	The Tragedy thus done, I am, you know,	385	M. BRIDE	EPI.	1

Thus   (continued)

Fainall:	Nay, we must not part thus.	415	WAY WORLD	II.1	222
Marwood:	Indeed Mrs. Engine, is it thus with you? . . .	431	WAY WORLD	III.1	225
Fainall:	much to hope. Thus far concerning my repose. Now for	443	WAY WORLD	III.1	683
Foible:	What a washy Rogue art thou, to pant thus for a . .	459	WAY WORLD	IV.1	558
Lady Wish:	would not have carry'd it thus. Well, that was my Choice,	469	WAY WORLD	V.1	305
Fainall:	Perfidious Fiend! then thus I'll be reveng'd.--(offers	476	WAY WORLD	V.1	556

Thwarting (1)

Perez:	I saw him when I spoke, thwarting my View, ...	338	M. BRIDE	II.1	19

Thy (272)

Thyrsis (4)

Singer:	As Amoret and Thyrsis, lay	71	OLD BATCH	III.2	2
Singer:	Dearest Thyrsis, do not move me, ...	71	OLD BATCH	III.2 V	12
Singer:	For Thyrsis deaf to Loves allarms, ...	71	OLD BATCH	III.2 V	23
Millamant:	(Repeating.) Thyrsis a Youth of the Inspir'd train--	446	WAY WORLD	IV.1	63

Tick (1)

Jeremy:	his Proportion, with carrying a Poet upon Tick, to visit	218	FOR LOVE	I.1	99

Tickl'd (1)

Marwood:	tickl'd with the proceeding, Simpers under a Grey beard,	467	WAY WORLD	V.1	220

Tickle (1)

Setter:	to tickle thy Imagination with remembrance of iniquity	65	OLD BATCH	III.1	185

Tide (7)   see Tyde

Sharper:	loves to buffet with the Winds, meet the Tide and sail in	42	OLD BATCH	I.1	202
Foresight:	the turning of the Tide, bring me the Urinal;--And I .	270	FOR LOVE	III.1	647
Mrs Frail:	and won't be surpriz'd to see the Tide turn'd. . . .	284	FOR LOVE	IV.1	308
Scandal:	I believe it is a Spring Tide.	289	FOR LOVE	IV.1	530
Zara:	Driv'n by the Tide upon my Country's Coast, ...	346	M. BRIDE	II.2	22
Gonsalez:	Stemming the Tide, with one weak Hand, and bearing . .	378	M. BRIDE	V.2	85
Gonsalez:	Stemming the Tide, with only one weak Hand, . . .	378	M. BRIDE	V.2 V	85

Tidings (1)

Bellmour:	Trusty Setter what tidings? How goes the project? . .	64	OLD BATCH	III.1	116

Tie (1)

Sir Joseph:	stroke down her Belly; and then step aside to tie her .	103	OLD BATCH	V.1	257

Tied (1)   see Ty'd

Maskwell:	and with your Hoods tied over your face, meet . . .	199	DOUEL DLR	V.1	445

Ties (2)

Maskwell:	Ties: But the Name of Rival cuts 'em all asunder, and is a	150	DOUEL DLR	II.1	448
Fainall:	Ties, when set in Competition with your Love to me. . .	414	WAY WORLD	II.1	181

Tift (2)

Millamant:	Ay, poor Mincing tift and tift all the morning. . . .	419	WAY WORLD	II.1	370

Tight (1)

Ben:	tight Vessel, and well rigg'd, and you were but as well	262	FOR LOVE	III.1	327

Till (96)

Bellmour:	his Glass. Let low and earthy Souls grovel till they have	37	OLD BATCH	I.1	25
Vainlove:	once raised up in a Woman, the Devil can't lay it, till she	40	OLD BATCH	I.1	103
Sharper:	Not till you had Mouth'd a little George, I think . .	43	OLD BATCH	I.1	227
Heartwell:	occasions; till in a little time, being disabled or		OLD BATCH	I.1	247
	disarm'd, ...	43	OLD BATCH	I.1	247
Bellmour:	witty Scene, and she perhaps preserve her Laughter, till .	44	OLD BATCH	I.1	269
Sir Joseph:	him, till I can get out of his sight; but out o'sight out				
	o'mind	48	OLD BATCH	II.1	45
Araminta:	never let it be extinct, till I my self am Ashes. . .	54	OLD BATCH	II.2	10
Araminta:	--Sure if I had not pinch'd you till you wak'd, you . .	55	OLD BATCH	II.2	43
Bellmour:	Till he has created Love where there was none, and . .	58	OLD BATCH	II.2	131
Vainlove:	Nor I to marry Araminta till I merit her. . . .	63	OLD BATCH	III.1	109
Sir Joseph:	You may stay till the day of Judgment then, by the . .	67	OLD BATCH	III.1	252
Silvia:	I dare not speak till I believe you, and indeed I'm . .	72	OLD BATCH	III.2	53
Heartwell:	I'm impatient till it be done; I will not give my . .	74	OLD BATCH	III.2	138
Silvia:	till then we never make the experiment--But how hast . .	75	OLD BATCH	III.2	153
Barnaby:	done there till you come.	76	OLD BATCH	IV.1	35
Fondlewife:	And nothing can be done here till I go--So that . . .	76	OLD BATCH	IV.1	36
Bellmour:	till 'twas late; my Intimacy with him gave me the . .	82	OLD BATCH	IV.2	50
Belinda:	come this Way, till I put my self a little in Repair,--Ah!	83	OLD BATCH	IV.3	10
Belinda:	come this Way, till I have put my self a little in				
	Repair,--Ah!	83	OLD BATCH	IV.3 V	10
Fondlewife:	If you will tarry a Moment, till I fetch my Papers,				
	I'll wait	90	OLD BATCH	IV.4	43
Bellmour:	Anchor in the Port till this time, but the Enemy surpriz'd	96	OLD BATCH	V.1	6
Heartwell:	I'm impatient till it be done.	97	OLD BATCH	V.1	13
Sharper:	make him fret till he foam at the Mouth, and disgorge his	99	OLD BATCH	V.1	88
Bellmour:	Play-house, till the Curtain's drawn; but that once up, .	107	OLD BATCH	V.1	385
Heartwell:	self on her Wedding-Day! Not hold out till Night! . .	107	OLD BATCH	V.2	6
Belinda:	Only touch'd a gall'd-beast till he winch'd. . . .	109	OLD BATCH	V.2	46
Brisk:	But the Deuce take me if I say a good thing till you come.--	128	DOUBL DLR	I.1	51
Mellefont:	close her Eyes, till she had seen my ruin.	130	DOUEL DLR	I.1	118
Mellefont:	close her Eyes, till they had seen my ruin.	130	DOUEL DLR	I.1 V	118
Maskwell:	your Pleasures; and will not rest till I have given you				
	peace, ...	137	DOUEL DLR	I.1	394
Maskwell:	know then, that all my Contrivances were but Bubbles; till	149	DOUEL DLR	II.1	420
Mellefont:	I will; till then, success attend thee.	149	DOUEL DLR	II.1	437
Maskwell:	Till then, Success will attend me; for when I meet . .	150	DOUEL DLR	II.1	439
Lady Touch:	--nay, I won't tell you any more, till you are your . .	153	DOUEL DLR	III.1	111
Mellefont:	her, till he has been fool enough to think of her out of her	159	DOUEL DLR	III.1	317
Lady Ply:	O rise I beseech you, say no more till you rise . . .	170	DOUEL DLR	IV.1	107
Sir Paul:	Person! Well, let me see--Till then I Languish in . .	178	DOUEL DLR	IV.1	414
Sir Paul:	three Years past? Have I been swath'd in Blankets till I	178	DOUEL DLR	IV.1	424
Mellefont:	Now, by my Soul, I will not go till I have made . . .	186	DOUEL DLR	IV.2	121
Mellefont:	known my wrongs--Nay, till I have made known yours, . .	186	DOUEL DLR	IV.2	122
Mellefont:	Ne'er to be quench'd, till they themselves devour. . .	187	DOUEL DLR	IV.2	155
Lord Touch:	farther proceedings in it, till you have consider'd it, but	191	DOUBL DLR	V.1	139
	Till Dice are thrown, there's nothing won, nor lost. . .	204	DOUEL DLR	EPI.	5
	So till the Thief has stoll'n, he cannot know . . .	204	DOUEL DLR	EPI.	6
Tattle:	till another time--I'll double the number.	230	FOR LOVE	I.1	543
Tattle:	Nor Woman, till she consented to have her Picture . .	232	FOR LOVE	I.1	613
Sr Sampson:	warrant you, if he danc'd till Doomsday, he thought I .	240	FOR LOVE	II.1	179
Tattle:	Word of your Ladyships Passion, till this instant. . .	254	FOR LOVE	III.1	56

Till   (continued)

Mrs Fore:	Never, never; till within these three Nights;	. . .	270	FOR LOVE	III.1 622
Mrs Frail:	Aye, but my Dear, we must keep it secret, till	. . .	273	FOR LOVE	III.1 718
Jeremy:	would not see her, till he hears how she takes it.	. . .	276	FOR LOVE	IV.1 17
Angelica:	he won't recover his Senses till I lose mine.	. . .	277	FOR LOVE	IV.1 76
Valentine:	one anothers Faces, till we have done something to be	. .	290	FOR LOVE	IV.1 563
Angelica:	I never lov'd him till he was Mad; but don't tell	. .	291	FOR LOVE	IV.1 572
Angelica:	Mr. Scandal, I only stay till my Maid comes, and	. .	293	FOR LOVE	IV.1 685
Angelica:	you, till I accidentally touch'd upon your tender Part: But		296	FOR LOVE	IV.1 766
Valentine:	may pore till you spoil your Eyes, and not improve your	. .	297	FOR LOVE	IV.1 803
Sr Sampson:	married till Fifty; yet they begot Sons and Daughters till		298	FOR LOVE	V.1 38
Sr Sampson:	Lad, till he learn'd to be a Wit--And might have	. .	299	FOR LOVE	V.1 82
Sr Sampson:	t'other Hand, and I'll mumble 'em, and kiss 'em till they		301	FOR LOVE	V.1 147
Miss Prue:	thing, till I'm as tired as any thing in the World.	. .	303	FOR LOVE	V.1 224
Foresight:	presently, till farther Orders from me--not a Word	. . .	306	FOR LOVE	V.1 325
Sr Sampson:	Sir; you shall ask that Lady no Questions, till you have	.	311	FOR LOVE	V.1 518
Angelica:	but few have the Constancy to stay till it becomes your	.	314	FOR LOVE	V.1 630
Osmyn-Alph:	Could sleep till we again were met.		344	M. BRIDE	II.2 196
Osmyn-Alph:	Or we could sleep till we again were met.	. . . .	344	M. BRIDE	II.2 V196
Zara:	Thou and thy Friend; till my Compassion found thee,	. .	346	M. BRIDE	II.2 278
Zara:	Thy Temples, till reviving Blood arose, ...		346	M. BRIDE	II.2 283
Osmyn-Alph:	And Chaff, the Sport of adverse Winds; till late	. . .	351	M. BRIDE	III.1 60
Perez:	Your entring, till the Princess is return'd, ...		359	M. BRIDE	III.1 381
Osmyn-Alph:	But till she's gone; then bless me thus again. . .		359	M. BRIDE	III.1 395
Gonsalez:	Till Osmyn die. Mean time we may learn more		363	M. BRIDE	IV.1 70
Alonzo:	Require me not to tell the Means, till done, ...		378	M. BRIDE	V.2 97
Mirabell:	She was always civil to me, till of late; I confess I	.	397	WAY WORLD	I.1 85
Mirabell:	and adjourn the Consummation till farther Order; bid	.	398	WAY WORLD	I.1 128
Fainall:	another, have made you clash till you have both struck	.	413	WAY WORLD	II.1 139
Witwoud:	Rotation of Tongue, that an Eccho must wait till she dies,		421	WAY WORLD	II.1 421
Foible:	dress till I come--(Looking out.) O Dear, I'm sure	. .	424	WAY WORLD	II.1 544
Lady Wish:	my self till I am pale again, there's no Veracity in me.	.	425	WAY WORLD	III.1 4
Marwood:	him, till he takes his Stand to aim at a Fortune,	. .	431	WAY WORLD	III.1 V244
Lady Wish:	O Dear, I can't appear till I'm dress'd. Dear	. . .	432	WAY WORLD	III.1 278
Sir Wilful:	present, 'tis sufficient till further acquaintance, that's all--		447	WAY WORLD	IV.1 85
Mirabell:	other till after grace?	. . . .	449	WAY WORLD	IV.1 184
Mirabell:	a Shape, till you mold my boy's head like a Sugar-loaf; and		451	WAY WORLD	IV.1 261
Petulant:	kiss'd your twin yonder in a humour of reconciliation, till		454	WAY WORLD	IV.1 356
Sir Wilful:	Till it laugh in my Face, ...		455	WAY WORLD	IV.1 398
Waitwell:	--and till I have the possession of your adoreable Person, I		457	WAY WORLD	IV.1 491
Waitwell:	starve upward and upward, till he has nothing living but	.	458	WAY WORLD	IV.1 523
Waitwell:	--than Act Sir Rowland, till this time to morrow.	. . .	459	WAY WORLD	IV.1 564
Mincing:	Closet, till my old Lady's anger is abated. O, my old Lady		465	WAY WORLD	V.1 107
Lady Wish:	wou'd ha' shriek'd, If she had but seen a Man, till she was		466	WAY WORLD	V.1 187
Lady Wish:	and his Sleek-face; till she was going in her fifteen.	. .	467	WAY WORLD	V.1 194
Marwood:	and this you must hear till you are stunn'd; Nay you must		468	WAY WORLD	V.1 235
Fainall:	must set your Hand till more sufficient Deeds can be	.	469	WAY WORLD	V.1 292
Fainall:	Instrument, and till my return, you may Ballance this	.	469	WAY WORLD	V.1 295

'Till (5)

Osmyn-Alph:	'Till gorg'd with suffocating Earth.		358	M. BRIDE	III.1 V356
Almeria:	'Till you are mov'd, and grant that he may live.	. . .	369	M. BRIDE	IV.1 331
Zara:	'Till Surges roll, and foaming Billows rise, ...		380	M. BRIDE	V.2 V166
Mincing:	'Till I had the Cremp in my Fingers I'll vow Mem.	. . .	419	WAY WORLD	II.1 371
Mincing:	'Till I had the Cramp in my Fingers I'll vow Mem.	. . .	419	WAY WORLD	II.1 V371

'till (11)

Bellmour:	his Glass. Let low and earthly Souls grovel 'till they have		37	OLD BATCH	I.1 V 25
Bellmour:	--'till just now, (the first time I ever look'd upon the	.	82	OLD BATCH	IV.2 55
Osmyn-Alph:	I saw you not, 'till now.		346	M. BRIDE	II.2 V254
Zara:	This Heart of Flint, 'till it shall bleed; and thou	. .	353	M. BRIDE	III.1 167
Zara:	Thou hast the Wrong, 'till I redeem thee hence;	. . .	355	M. BRIDE	III.1 218
Almeria:	I'll not let go, 'till you have spar'd my Husband.	. . .	369	M. BRIDE	IV.1 338
Almeria:	I'll scrape 'till I collect his rotten Bones, ...		370	M. BRIDE	IV.1 349
Manuel:	Which I'll not hear, 'till I am more at peace.	. . .	370	M. BRIDE	IV.1 364
Mirabell:	Hour less and less disturbance; 'till in a few Days it became		399	WAY WORLD	I.1 170
Sir Wilful:	Gazetts then, and Dawks's Letter, and the weekly Bill, 'till		440	WAY WORLD	III.1 552
Sir Wilful:	Impatient? Why then belike it won't stay, 'till	. . . .	441	WAY WORLD	III.1 616

Tillage (1)

Heartwell:	profit than what the bare tillage and manuring of the Land		44	OLD BATCH	I.1 280

Tim (2)

Sir Paul:	Gad so, gad's bud--Tim, carry it to my Lady, you	. . .	161	DOUBL DLR	III.1 395
Sir Paul:	do so no more; d'ye hear, Tim?		161	DOUBL DLR	III.1 399

Tim'd (0)   see Ill-tim'd

Time (162)

Bellmour:	Pox o' Business--And so must Time, my	. . .	37	OLD BATCH	I.1 9
Bellmour:	Business!--And so must Time, my	. . .	37	OLD BATCH	I.1 V 9
Bellmour:	and Pleasure, my Occupation; and let Father Time shake	.	37	OLD BATCH	I.1 24
Bellmour:	a little time will swell him so, he must be forc'd to give it		40	OLD BATCH	I.1 124
Heartwell:	think it time enough to be lew'd, after I have had the	.	43	OLD BATCH	I.1 233
Bellmour:	Time enough, ay too soon, I should rather have	. . . .	43	OLD BATCH	I.1 235
Heartwell:	occasions; till in a little time, being disabled or disarm'd,		43	OLD BATCH	I.1 247
Heartwell:	Debts, which by the time you have pay'd, yields no further		44	OLD BATCH	I.1 279
Bellmour:	Well come off George, if at any time you should be	. . .	44	OLD BATCH	I.1 286
Heartwell:	Pox I have pratled away my time--I hope you are	. . .	46	OLD BATCH	I.1 331
Capt Bluff:	this time--as I hope for a Truncheon--this rascally	.	53	OLD BATCH	II.1 202
Lucy:	would take time to peruse it--But then he was in haste.	.	61	OLD BATCH	III.1 27
Capt Bluff:	time.	. . . . .	69	OLD BATCH	III.1 314
Sharper:	What do you mutter about a time, Rascal--You	. . . .	69	OLD BATCH	III.1 315
Sharper:	your time--A Memorandum.	. . . . .	69	OLD BATCH	III.1 317
Capt Bluff:	O this is your time Sir, you had best make use on't.	. .	69	OLD BATCH	III.1 319
Lucy:	it you. Come Madam, you're like to have a happy time	. .	75	OLD BATCH	III.2 159
Barnaby:	time: but you say--	. . . . .	76	OLD BATCH	IV.1 24
Fondlewife:	And in the mean time, I will reason with my self--	. . .	76	OLD BATCH	IV.1 49

Time   (continued)
Sharper:	I'me afraid I give too great a Proof of my own at this time--	79	OLD BATCH	IV.1	158
Bellmour:	--'till just now, (the first time I ever lock'd upon the	82	OLD BATCH	IV.2	55
Araminta:	Thought of Mankind.--How time might have	87	OLD BATCH	IV.3	170
Bellmour:	have a long time designed thee this favour) I knew Spin-text	94	OLD BATCH	IV.4	207
Bellmour:	Anchor in the Port till this time, but the Enemy surpriz'd	96	OLD BATCH	V.1	6
Bellmour:	the mean time, I promise,--and rely upon me,--to	98	OLD BATCH	V.1	70
Setter:	were to be found at that time: And such like.	99	OLD BATCH	V.1	116
Sharper:	Were it not Loss of Time, you should make the	100	OLD BATCH	V.1	144
Sir Joseph:	and to speak, is but loss of time; but if there be occasion,	103	OLD BATCH	V.1	244
Capt Bluff:	time, here's Earnest. (Gives him Money). Come, Knight;	104	OLD BATCH	V.1	279
Setter:	but, tho' I blush to won it at this time, I must confess I am	105	OLD BATCH	V.1	336
Belinda:	Nor for them neither, in a little time--I swear,	108	OLD BATCH	V.2	28
Heartwell:	you, Sir, I shall find a time; but take off your Wasp here,	108	OLD BATCH	V.2	34
Setter:	time this Seven Years.	111	OLD BATCH	V.2	143
Mellefont:	despair, and the short prospect of time she saw, to	129	DOUBL DLR	I.1	95
Maskwell:	lay a stronger Plot: if I gain a little time, I shall not want	138	DOUBL DLR	I.1	419
Cynthia:	think you of drawing Stakes, and giving over in time?	142	DOUBL DLR	II.1	158
Sir Paul:	angry, that's my pleasure at this time.	144	DOUBL DLR	II.1	212
Maskwell:	this Gallery an hour hence, by that time I imagine our	149	DOUBL DLR	II.1	435
Lord Touch:	her own Circle; 'tis not the first time she has mistaken	151	DOUBL DLR	III.1	7
Lady Touch:	will be found so: but that will require some time; for in	151	DOUBL DLR	III.1	17
Maskwell:	I have; and am to meet him here about this time.	154	DOUBL DLR	III.1	132
Maskwell:	so little time must of necessity discover. Yet he is apprehensive	154	DOUBL DLR	III.1	136
Maskwell:	time he attempted any thing of that kind, to discover it to	154	DOUBL DLR	III.1	154
Mellefont:	sight, and to lose so much time as to write to her.	159	DOUBL DLR	III.1	318
Lady Ply:	at the same time you must give me leave to declare in the	159	DOUBL DLR	III.1	350
Cynthia:	time, is as disagreeable as to sing out of time or out of	163	DOUBL DLR	III.1	473
Lord Froth:	sending it to and again so often, this is the seventh time	166	DOUBL DLR	III.1	610
Lady Ply:	yet I'll be sure to be unsuspected this time.--Sir Paul.	173	DOUBL DLR	IV.1	212
Sir Paul:	Execution in its time Girl; why thou hast my Leer Hussey, just	173	DOUBL DLR	IV.1	236
Lord Froth:	Any other time, my Dear, or we'll Dance it	177	DOUBL DLR	IV.1	381
Lady Froth:	We shall have whispering time enough, you	177	DOUBL DLR	IV.1	386
Careless:	Why faith I have in my time known Honest Gentlemen	180	DOUBL DLR	IV.1	496
Maskwell:	O my Lord! consider that is hard: besides, time	182	DOUBL DLR	IV.1	565
Lady Touch:	outstays the Time; for to be dully punctual, is too slow.	183	DOUBL DLR	IV.2	10
Lady Touch:	I had not time to think--I was surprised to see a Monster in	185	DOUBL DLR	IV.2	71
Lord Touch:	command this time; for 'tis the last, in which I will assume	189	DOUBL DLR	V.1	65
Lady Touch:	want you by this time, as much as you want her.	192	DOUBL DLR	V.1	189
Mellefont:	waste the little time we have.	194	DOUBL DLR	V.1	246
Maskwell:	Nay, good Mr. Saygrace do not prolong the time,	194	DOUBL DLR	V.1	276
Maskwell:	time in putting it on?	195	DOUBL DLR	V.1	289
Mellefont:	'Tis loss of time--I cannot think him false.	197	DOUBL DLR	V.1	354
Maskwell:	the time; and Mellefont's Love will carry him there before	199	DOUBL DLR	V.1	457
	They Judge of Action too, and Time, and Place;	204	DOUBL DLR	EPI.	24
	This time, the Poet owns the bold Essay,	214	FOR LOVE	PRO.	41
Jeremy:	would have been an Alderman by this time with half the	218	FOR LOVE	I.1	90
Jeremy:	do's Causes at Dinner time.	220	FOR LOVE	I.1	168
Valentine:	Pox on her, cou'd she find no other time to fling	221	FOR LOVE	I.1	207
Scandal:	Letter from her, and at the same time, shew you her Hand	226	FOR LOVE	I.1	373
Valentine:	have a fine time, whose Reputations are in your keeping.	229	FOR LOVE	I.1	503
Tattle:	till another time--I'll double the number.	230	FOR LOVE	I.1	543
Mrs Frail:	time he grows only rude to his Wife, and that is the highest	231	FOR LOVE	I.1	564
Foresight:	time,--But in troth I am pleas'd at my Stocking. Very	236	FOR LOVE	II.1	37
Foresight:	have consulted me for the time. Well, but we'll make	240	FOR LOVE	II.1	190
Sr Sampson:	be done to Night--No matter for the time; prithee,	240	FOR LOVE	II.1	195
Sr Sampson:	Brother Foresight, leave Superstition--Pox o'th' time;	240	FOR LOVE	II.1	196
Sr Sampson:	there's no time but the time present, there's no more to be	240	FOR LOVE	II.1	197
Jeremy:	time he has been abroad since his Confinement, and he	242	FOR LOVE	II.1	268
Sr Sampson:	and when the Alarm strikes, they shall keep time like the	266	FOR LOVE	III.1	476
Scandal:	it in time--	270	FOR LOVE	III.1	632
Ben:	For now the time was ended,	274	FOR LOVE	III.1	763
Scandal:	the mean time, if our Project succeed no better with his	278	FOR LOVE	IV.1	104
Foresight:	profound Secrets of Time.	291	FOR LOVE	IV.1	605
Singer-V:	I tell thee, Charmion, could I Time retrieve,	293	FOR LOVE	IV.1	652
Valentine:	Madness has deceiv'd my Father, and procur'd me time to	294	FOR LOVE	IV.1	716
Angelica:	Courage at this time. To tell you the Truth, I'm weary of	298	FOR LOVE	V.1	46
Angelica:	Vigour before your time: You'll spend your Estate before	301	FOR LOVE	V.1	150
Tattle:	--the time draws nigh, Jeremy. Angelica will be veil'd	302	FOR LOVE	V.1	197
Tattle:	in my time; but i'Gad I could never find in my Heart to	303	FOR LOVE	V.1	213
Foresight:	Hey day! What time of the Moon is this?	305	FOR LOVE	V.1	286
Mrs Fore:	time.	306	FOR LOVE	V.1	357
Angelica:	O you'll agree very well in a little time; Custom	310	FOR LOVE	V.1	481
Sr Sampson:	In good time, Sir.	310	FOR LOVE	V.1	503
	The Time has been when Plays were not so plenty,	323	M. BRIDE	PRO.	1
Almeria:	But there's no time shall rase thee from my Memory.	328	M. BRIDE	I.1	71
Almeria:	No Time shall rase thee from my Memory.	328	M. BRIDE	I.1 V	71
Leonora:	And grant, that Time may bring her some Relief.	329	M. BRIDE	I.1	151
Almeria:	O no! Time gives Encrease to my Afflictions.	330	M. BRIDE	I.1	152
Leonora:	Yet fresh and unconsum'd by Time, or Worms.	340	M. BRIDE	II.2	8
Osmyn-Alph:	Or trifle time in thinking.	342	M. BRIDE	II.2	99
Osmyn-Alph:	Of yet unmeasur'd Time; when I have made	343	M. BRIDE	II.2	144
Manuel:	Life without Love is Load; and Time stands still:	349	M. BRIDE	II.2	389
Heli:	Our Posture of Affairs and scanty Time,	352	M. BRIDE	III.1	92
Heli:	For your Escape. Mean time, I've thought already	352	M. BRIDE	III.1	98
Heli:	In that Assurance live; which Time, I hope,	352	M. BRIDE	III.1	120
Osmyn-Alph:	That at this Time, I had not been this Thing.	354	M. BRIDE	III.1	190
Osmyn-Alph:	Time may have still one fated Hour to come,	354	M. BRIDE	III.1	198
Osmyn-Alph:	I could at this time spare your Mirth.	360	M. BRIDE	III.1	422
Gonsalez:	Till Osmyn die. Mean time we may learn more	363	M. BRIDE	IV.1	70
Gonsalez:	At any time, in Albucacim's Court.	363	M. BRIDE	IV.1	103

Tir'd   (continued)
Belinda:	have been at the Exchange since, and am so tir'd--	. . .	83	OLD BATCH	IV.3	2
Belinda:	Dear Araminta, I'm tir'd.	. . . .	86	OLD BATCH	IV.3	100
Osmyn-Alph:	One, who has tir'd Misfortune with pursuing?	. . . .	351	M. BRIDE	III.1	58

Tire (1)
| Sir Paul: | Does it not tire your Ladyship? are not you weary | . . . | 201 | DOUEL DLR | V.1 | 521 |

Tired (1)
| Miss Prue: | thing, till I'm as tired as any thing in the World. | . . | 303 | FOR LOVE | V.1 | 224 |

Tis (1)
| Belinda: | is to be possess'd--Tis in the Head, the Heart, the | . . | 54 | OLD BATCH | II.2 | 13 |

'Tis (108)
Bellmour:	twelve thousand Pound Tom--'Tis true she is excessively	.	41	OLD BATCH	I.1	166
Sharper:	'Tis a tawdry Outside.	.	46	OLD BATCH	I.1	343
Sharper:	'Tis but trying, and being where I am at worst,	.	48	OLD BATCH	II.1	16
Sharper:	Word is sufficient any where: 'Tis but borrowing so much	.	50	OLD BATCH	II.1	108
Sir Joseph:	that's a better Jest than tother. 'Tis a sign you and I					
	ha'n't	.	50	OLD BATCH	II.1	116
Silvia:	'Tis as hard to Counterfeit Love, as it is to conceal it:		62	OLD BATCH	III.1	51
Heartwell:	'Tis both; for I am angry with my self, when I am	. . .	72	OLD BATCH	III.2	70
Heartwell:	well--Yet I must on--'Tis a bearded Arrow, and	.	73	OLD BATCH	III.2	72
Bellmour:	'Tis pretty near the Hour--	. . . .	75	OLD BATCH	IV.1	1
Barnaby:	Husband. 'Tis then indeed, like the vanity of taking a fine		76	OLD BATCH	IV.1	42
Vainlove:	'Tis an untimely Fruit, and she has miscarried of	. . .	79	OLD BATCH	IV.1	169
Vainlove:	--I stumble ore the Game I would pursue.--'Tis	. . . .	80	OLD BATCH	IV.1	177
Vainlove:	--I stumble over the Game I would pursue.--'Tis	. . . .	80	OLD BATCH	IV.1	V177
Vainlove:	'Tis fit Men should be coy, when Women woo.	. . . . .	80	OLD BATCH	IV.1	191
Laetitia:	to dissemble. 'Tis plain then you have mistaken the Person.		81	OLD BATCH	IV.2	35
Laetitia:	(aside). What can this mean! 'Tis impossible he should	.	81	OLD BATCH	IV.2	42
Araminta:	'Tis but pulling off our Masks, and obliging	. . . . .	86	OLD BATCH	IV.3	101
Bellmour:	'Tis an alarm to love.--Come in again, and	. . . . .	89	OLD BATCH	IV.4	6
Laetitia:	'Tis no body but Mr. Fondlewife, Mr. Spin-text, lie	. .	91	OLD BATCH	IV.4	85
Setter:	'Tis but setting her Mill a-going, and I can drein her of		99	OLD BATCH	V.1	105
Setter:	--'Tis above us:--And, for Men of Quality, they are	. .	102	OLD BATCH	V.1	231
Sir Joseph:	'Tis too little, there's more, Man. There, take all--	.	103	OLD BATCH	V.1	249
Sharper:	me: May be she mayn't be within. 'Tis but to yond'	. .	104	OLD BATCH	V.1	285
Sharper:	Why, I'll tell you: 'Tis a young Creature that Vainlove	.	104	OLD BATCH	V.1	292
Araminta:	'Tis a lasting Quarrel: I think he has never been at	. .	107	OLD BATCH	V.1	399
Heartwell:	'Tis not in thy Nature to give me Joy--A	. . . . .	108	OLD BATCH	V.2	23
Sharper:	No, I'll deal fairly with you.--'Tis a full and	. . .	110	OLD BATCH	V.2	85
Sharper:	'Tis done, those Gentlemen are witnesses to the	. . .	110	OLD BATCH	V.2	100
Capt Bluff:	'Tis very generous, Sir, since I needs must own--	. .	110	OLD BATCH	V.2	104
Sir Joseph:	heh. 'Tis I must own--	. . . .	110	OLD BATCH	V.2	106
Cynthia:	'Tis my Interest to believe he will, my Lord.	. . . .	141	DOUEL DLR	II.1	101
Cynthia:	as Fools. 'Tis an odd Game we're going to Play at: What		142	DOUEL DLR	II.1	157
Lady Ply:	He's hot-headed still! 'Tis in vain to talk to you;	. .	144	DOUEL DLR	II.1	227
Lady Ply:	'Tis my Honour that is concern'd, and the violation	. .	144	DOUEL DLR	II.1	234
Lady Ply:	his passion: 'Tis not your fault; nor I swear it is not					
	mine,--	.	148	DOUEL DLR	II.1	357
Lady Touch:	make you lose one minutes temper. 'Tis not indeed, my	.	152	DOUEL DLR	III.1	67
Maskwell:	won't perplex you. 'Tis the only thing that Providence	.	157	DOUEL DLR	III.1	244
Mellefont:	to engage her more irresistably. 'Tis only an inhancing the		158	DOUEL DLR	III.1	301
Mellefont:	'Tis a mistake, for women may most properly be	. . .	158	DOUEL DLR	III.1	310
Boy:	'Tis directed to your Worship.	. . . .	161	DOUEL DLR	III.1	397
Sir Paul:	have not a Son to inherit this--'Tis true I have a	. .	161	DOUEL DLR	III.1	411
Brisk:	'Tis not a Song neither--it's a sort of an Epigram, or	.	166	DOUEL DLR	III.1	591
Lord Froth:	'Tis a strange thing, but a true one;	. . . . . .	166	DOUEL DLR	III.1	597
Cynthia:	'Tis not so hard to counterfeit Joy in the depth of	. .	167	DOUEL DLR	III.1	624
Lady Touch:	'Tis Eight a Clock. Methinks I should have	. . . .	183	DOUEL DLR	IV.2	8
Lady Touch:	'Tis true it might have been my ruine--but	. . . .	188	DOUEL DLR	V.1	16
Maskwell:	Why, qui vult decipi decipiatur.--'Tis no fault	. . .	194	DOUEL DLR	V.1	262
Maskwell:	'Tis that; you know my Lady has a high Spirit,	. . .	195	DOUEL DLR	V.1	315
Mellefont:	'Tis loss of time--I cannot think him false.	. . .	197	DOUEL DLR	V.1	354
	'Tis hard that they must every one admit;	. . . . .	204	DOUEL DLR	EPI.	31
Tattle:	'Tis very hard--Won't a Baronet's Lady pass?	. . . .	230	FOR LOVE	I.1	530
Valentine:	'Tis as much as I expected--I did not come to see	. .	246	FOR LOVE	II.1	407
Valentine:	A couple of very civil Proverbs, truly: 'Tis hard to	. .	256	FOR LOVE	III.1	129
Foresight:	'Tis no Earthquake!	. . . .	266	FOR LOVE	III.1	491
Valentine:	Thou liest, for I am Truth. 'Tis hard I cannot get a	.	280	FOR LOVE	IV.1	171
Jeremy:	'Tis an Act of Charity, Sir, to save a fine Woman	. .	302	FOR LOVE	V.1	209
Foresight:	'Tis not convenient to tell you now--Mr.	. . . . .	306	FOR LOVE	V.1	331
Angelica:	'Tis very true indeed, Uncle; I hope you'll be my	. .	308	FOR LOVE	V.1	393
Angelica:	'Tis very unhappy, if you don't care for one another.	.	309	FOR LOVE	V.1	462
Angelica:	'Tis true, you have a great while pretended Love	. .	311	FOR LOVE	V.1	531
Angelica:	'Tis an unreasonable Accusation, that you lay upon	. .	314	FOR LOVE	V.1	627
Almeria:	'Tis not in Harmony to calm my Griefs.	. . . . .	326	M. BRIDE	I.1	8
Almeria:	I thank thee. 'Tis but this; anon, when all	. . . .	331	M. BRIDE	I.1	196
Almeria:	'Tis that, or some such Melancholy Thought,	. . .	331	M. BRIDE	I.1	205
Garcia:	'Tis scarce above a word; as he were born	. . . .	335	M. BRIDE	I.1	372
Manuel:	'Tis false; 'twas more; I bad she should be free:	. .	336	M. BRIDE	I.1	408
Manuel:	'Tis false; 'twas more; I bid she should be free:	. .	336	M. BRIDE	I.1	V408
Almeria:	No, all is hush'd, and still as Death--'Tis dreadful!	. .	339	M. BRIDE	II.1	58
Osmyn-Alph:	'Tis Life! 'tis warm! 'tis she! 'tis she her self!	. .	341	M. BRIDE	II.2	54
Osmyn-Alph:	'Tis she; shew me her Face, and let me feel	. . .	341	M. BRIDE	II.2	68
Osmyn-Alph:	Her Lips with mine--'Tis she, I'm not deceiv'd;	. . .	341	M. BRIDE	II.2	69
Almeria:	'Tis more than Recompence, to see thy Face:	. . .	343	M. BRIDE	II.2	147
Zara:	'Tis that, I know; for thou dost look, with Eyes	. .	348	M. BRIDE	II.2	343
Manuel:	'Tis daring for a God. Hence, to the Wheel	. . .	349	M. BRIDE	II.2	371
Osmyn-Alph:	'Tis wanting what should follow--Heav'n, Heav'n shou'd	.	350	M. BRIDE	III.1	20
Osmyn-Alph:	'Tis wanting what should follow--Heav'n, shou'd	.	350	M. BRIDE	III.1	V 20
Zara:	'Tis plain, I've been abus'd--Death and Destruction!	. .	359	M. BRIDE	III.1	398
Selim:	'Tis certain Heli too is fled, and with him	. . . .	361	M. BRIDE	IV.1	8
Gonsalez:	'Tis not impossible. Yet, it may be,	. . . . .	363	M. BRIDE	IV.1	99
Zara:	'Tis well. By what I heard upon your Entrance,	. . .	364	M. BRIDE	IV.1	114
Gonsalez:	'Tis no matter.	. . . .	371	M. BRIDE	IV.1	420
Manuel:	'Tis well.	. . . .	373	M. BRIDE	V.1	11
Manuel:	'Tis well--that when she comes to set him free,	. . .	374	M. BRIDE	V.1	77

'Tis (continued)

		PAGE	TITLE	ACT.SC LINE
Zara:	'Tis not that he is dead; for 'twas decreed	380	M. BRIDE	V.2 187
Fainall:	'Tis well you don't know what you say, or else your .	402	WAY WORLD	I.1 261
Witwoud:	Bum-baily, that I grant you,--'Tis Pity faith; the . .	403	WAY WORLD	I.1 299
Witwoud:	Bum-baily, that I grant you,--'Tis Pity; the . . .	403	WAY WORLD	I.1 V299
Witwoud:	No, no, what if he be? 'Tis no matter for that, his .	403	WAY WORLD	I.1 318
Witwoud:	'Tis what she will hardly allow any Body else;-- . .	408	WAY WORLD	I.1 476
Fainall:	'Tis impossible Millamant should hearken to it. . . .	408	WAY WORLD	I.1 491
Marwood:	'Tis false. I challenge you to shew an Instance . . .	414	WAY WORLD	II.1 153
Marwood:	'Tis false, you urg'd it with deliberate Malice-- . .	414	WAY WORLD	II.1 182
Fainall:	been false, I had e'er this repaid it--'Tis true--Had you	415	WAY WORLD	II.1 201
Mirabell:	a Girl--'Tis the Green Sickness of a second Childhood; .	418	WAY WORLD	II.1 318
Waitwell:	Day! 'Tis enough to make any Man forget himself. The .	424	WAY WORLD	II.1 556
Marwood:	a very fit Match. He may Travel afterwards. 'Tis a Thing	432	WAY WORLD	III.1 267
Marwood:	'Tis like Mrs. Primly's great Belly; she may lace it down	433	WAY WORLD	III.1 318
Millamant:	more Gallantry--'Tis hardly well bred to be so particular	434	WAY WORLD	III.1 340
Singer:	'Tis not to wound a wanton Boy	435	WAY WORLD	III.1 382
Marwood:	'Tis your Brother, I fancy. Don't you know	436	WAY WORLD	III.1 439
Servant-W:	Morning, before she is dress'd. 'Tis like I may give a .	437	WAY WORLD	III.1 462
Witwoud:	Serjeants--'Tis not the fashion here; 'tis not indeed, .	439	WAY WORLD	III.1 536
Sir Wilful:	Discourse to the Lady, Sir: 'Tis like my Aunt may have .	440	WAY WORLD	III.1 572
Sir Wilful:	There is? 'Tis like there may.	440	WAY WORLD	III.1 587
Foible:	'Tis he, Madam.	445	WAY WORLD	IV.1 33
Mrs Fain:	I am wrong'd and abus'd, and so are you. 'Tis . . .	466	WAY WORLD	V.1 153
Marwood:	'Tis severe indeed Madam, that you shou'd	469	WAY WORLD	V.1 300
Mincing:	Mercenary, Mem? I scorn your words. 'Tis true we . .	474	WAY WORLD	V.1 486

'tis (243)

		PAGE	TITLE	ACT.SC LINE
Bellmour:	Never--Her Affections, 'tis true by Heaven, . . .	38	OLD BATCH	I.1 47
Bellmour:	Husband: For 'tis an Argument of her great Zeal towards .	39	OLD BATCH	I.1 64
Bellmour:	Let me see, Laetitia! Oh 'tis a delicious Morsel. Dear .	39	OLD BATCH	I.1 73
Vainlove:	Faith I hate Love when 'tis forced upon a Man; as . .	39	OLD BATCH	I.1 94
Bellmour:	Why you must know, 'tis a piece of Work toward . . .	41	OLD BATCH	I.1 156
Bellmour:	that which he likes best; 'tis his diversion to Set, 'tis			
	mine	43	OLD BATCH	I.1 224
Heartwell:	so much Mercury in my Limbs; 'tis true indeed, I don't .	43	OLD BATCH	I.1 231
Heartwell:	'tis true you are so eager in pursuit of the temptation,			
	that	43	OLD BATCH	I.1 240
Heartwell:	relations--when the Devil and she knows, 'tis a little .	45	OLD BATCH	I.1 327
Bellmour:	Oh, 'tis Sir Joseph Wittoll with his friend;	46	OLD BATCH	I.1 V339
Bellmour:	Hang him, no, he a Draggon! if he be 'tis a very . .	46	OLD BATCH	I.1 351
Bellmour:	seem to rouse, 'tis but well lashing him, and he will sleep	46	OLD BATCH	I.1 353
Sir Joseph:	Agad and so 'tis--why here has been more	48	OLD BATCH	II.1 19
Sharper:	No, 'tis gone, 'tis lost--ten thousand Devils on that .	48	OLD BATCH	II.1 21
Sharper:	O your Servant Sir, you are safe then it seems; 'tis an .	48	OLD BATCH	II.1 32
Sir Joseph:	But I profess, 'tis a Dirt I have wash'd my Hands of .	50	OLD BATCH	II.1 111
Capt Bluff:	Yet by the Lord Harry 'tis true Mr. Sharper, for I . .	53	OLD BATCH	II.1 207
Vainlove:	You are the Temples of Love, and 'tis through you, . .	58	OLD BATCH	II.2 144
Araminta:	Ay, Cousin, and 'tis a sign the Creatures mimick . .	60	OLD BATCH	II.2 215
Lucy:	Heartwell, who stands talking at the Corner--'tis he-- .	62	OLD BATCH	III.1 47
Setter:	Undoubtedly 'tis impossible to be a Pimp and not a . .	65	OLD BATCH	III.1 149
Sir Joseph:	love to be the Messenger of ill News; 'tis an ungrateful	68	OLD BATCH	III.1 266
Capt Bluff:	Husht, 'tis not so convenient now--I shall find a . .	69	OLD BATCH	III.1 313
Bellmour:	Ha, ha, ha, prithee come away, 'tis scandalous to . .	69	OLD BATCH	III.1 327
Capt Bluff:	Very well--Very fine--But 'tis no matter--	70	OLD BATCH	III.1 331
Sir Joseph:	Put up, put up, dear Back, 'tis your Sir Joseph begs, come	70	OLD BATCH	III.1 341
Capt Bluff:	By Heav'n 'tis not to be put up.	70	OLD BATCH	III.1 343
Sir Joseph:	No agad no more 'tis, for that's put up already; . .	70	OLD BATCH	III.1 346
Sir Joseph:	Ay, ay, so were you too; no matter, 'tis past. . . .	70	OLD BATCH	III.1 351
Capt Bluff:	By the immortal Thunder of great Guns, 'tis false . .	70	OLD BATCH	III.1 352
Heartwell:	when 'tis out of Obstinacy and Contradiction--But . .	74	OLD BATCH	III.2 127
Fondlewife:	--Nay look you now if she does not weep--'tis the fondest	78	OLD BATCH	IV.1 98
Laetitia:	(aside). My Letter! Ease Vainlove! Then 'tis too late . .	81	OLD BATCH	IV.2 34
Bellmour:	Nay, 'Faith, Madam, 'tis a pleasant one; and worth . .	82	OLD BATCH	IV.2 48
Laetitia:	Impudent. Won't you censure me for this, now;--but 'tis .	82	OLD BATCH	IV.2 80
Vainlove:	('tis true) where they find most Goodness to forgive.-- .	87	OLD BATCH	IV.3 138
Sir Joseph:	I wonder at that, Madam, for 'tis most curious . . .	90	OLD BATCH	IV.4 36
Sir Joseph:	As you say, Madam, 'tis pretty bad Weather, and . . .	90	OLD BATCH	IV.4 39
Laetitia:	come near it, I'm afraid 'tis the Devil; indeed it has			
	hoofs, ...	92	OLD BATCH	IV.4 133
Fondlewife:	I'm afraid, 'tis the Flesh, thou Harlot. Deare, with			
	the Pox.	92	OLD BATCH	IV.4 136
Laetitia:	think that I have nothing to do but excuse him; 'tis enough,	93	OLD BATCH	IV.4 168
Bellmour:	By my troth, and so 'tis.--(aside) I have been a . . .	93	OLD BATCH	IV.4 170
Fondlewife:	Well, well, Sir, as long as I believe it, 'tis well . .	96	OLD BATCH	IV.4 267
Sir Joseph:	Ay, now it's out; 'tis I, my own individual Person. . .	102	OLD BATCH	V.1 206
Sir Joseph:	Heh, heh, heh: Here 'tis for you, i'Faith, Mr. . . .	103	OLD BATCH	V.1 236
Sir Joseph:	no Quality at all, 'tis such a Damn'd ugly Hand. . . .	103	OLD BATCH	V.1 272
Belinda:	--But when we come to feed, 'tis all Froth, ...	106	OLD BATCH	V.1 374
Vainlove:	Bellmour, Give it over; you vex him too much; 'tis . .	109	OLD BATCH	V.2 47
Vainlove:	Nay, 'tis a Sore of your own scratching.--Well . . .	109	OLD BATCH	V.2 99
Heartwell:	My Wife! By this Light 'tis she, the very Cockatrice . .	111	OLD BATCH	V.2 125
Heartwell:	But 'tis with Whip and Spur the Race is won.	112	OLD BATCH	V.2 195
	Now that's at stake--No fool, 'tis out o'fashion. . . .	113	OLD BATCH	EPI. 12
	For 'tis our way (you know) for fear o'th' worst, . .	113	OLD BATCH	EPI. 21
Mellefont:	Faith 'tis a good natur'd Cox-Comb, and has very . .	129	DOUBL DLR	I.1 65
Careless:	Was there ever such a Fury! 'tis well Nature has not . .	130	DOUBL DLR	I.1 100
Sir Paul:	Nay, I protest and vow now, 'tis true; when Mr. . . .	132	DOUBL DLR	I.1 187
Lord Froth:	'tis such a Vulgar Expression of the Passion! every body can	132	DOUBL DLR	I.1 200
Brisk:	particular and novel in the Humour; 'tis true, it makes .	133	DOUBL DLR	I.1 238
Brisk:	particular in the Humour; 'tis true, it makes . . .	133	DOUBL DLR	I.1 V238
Brisk:	'tis, in the not Laughing--don't you Apprehend me? . .	133	DOUBL DLR	I.1 249
Sir Paul:	No, 'tis because I won't be headstrong, because I . . .	144	DOUBL DLR	II.1 230
Lady Ply:	lov'd you tenderly--'tis a barbarity of barbarities, and .	146	DOUBL DLR	II.1 291
Lady Ply:	loves you tenderly--'tis a barbarity of barbarities, and .	146	DOUBL DLR	II.1 V291
Lady Ply:	resist the strongest Temptation,--but yet I know, 'tis .	147	DOUBL DLR	II.1 327
Maskwell:	Hypocrisie; oh 'tis such a pleasure, to angle for fair-faced	150	DOUBL DLR	II.1 458

'tis   (continued)

			PAGE	TITLE	ACT.SC	LINE
Lord Touch:	--Pho, 'tis nonsense. Come, come; I know my Lady	. .	150	DOUEL DLR	III.1	5
Lord Touch:	her own Circle; 'tis not the first time she has mistaken	.	151	DOUEL DLR	III.1	7
Lady Touch:	like to be suspected in the end, and 'tis a pain any longer		151	DOUEL DLR	III.1	39
Lady Touch:	Whatever it was, 'tis past: And that is better	. . .	152	DOUEL DLR	III.1	54
Lady Touch:	were more, 'tis over now, and all's well. For my part I	.	153	DOUEL DLR	III.1	96
Careless:	be told on't; she must i'faith, Sir Paul; 'tis an injury					
	to the	. .	162	DOUEL DLR	III.1	442
Lord Froth:	'tis such a sight to see some teeth--sure you're a great	.	162	DOUEL DLR	III.1	460
Cynthia:	Fie Mr. Brisk, 'tis Eringo's for her Cough.		165	DOUEL DLR	III.1	569
Cynthia:	not that true Wisdom, for 'tis Happiness: And for ought I	.	167	DOUEL DLR	III.1	630
Cynthia:	same Game, but forget one another; and 'tis because we	.	168	DOUEL DLR	IV.1	17
Cynthia:	I would not--But 'tis but reasonable that since I	. .	168	DOUEL DLR	IV.1	44
Lady Ply:	'tis true, but he never was so presumptuous to entertain	.	172	DOUEL DLR	IV.1	167
Lady Ply:	O las, no indeed, Sir Paul, 'tis upon your account.	.	172	DOUEL DLR	IV.1	181
Sir Paul:	Well, 'tis a rare thing to have an ingenious Friend. Well,		172	DOUEL DLR	IV.1	202
Sir Paul:	Rogue by the help of imagination; why, 'tis the mark of	.	173	DOUEL DLR	IV.1	238
Lady Ply:	when 'tis Dark. O Crimine! I hope, Sir Paul has not seen	.	174	DOUEL DLR	IV.1	262
Mellefont:	Maskwell! I have been looking for you--'tis	. .	181	DOUEL DLR	IV.1	513
Maskwell:	here before me; but 'tis fit I should be still behind hand,		183	DOUEL DLR	IV.2	14
Lady Touch:	the Glass, and now I find 'tis my self; Can you have mercy		185	DOUEL DLR	IV.2 V	72
Maskwell:	Lucky! Fortune is your own, and 'tis her interest	. .	187	DOUEL DLR	V.1	2
Lord Touch:	command this time; for 'tis the last, in which I will assume	189	DOUEL DLR	V.1	65
Maskwell:	Gamester--but shou'd he find me cut before! 'tis dangerous		190	DOUEL DLR	V.1	88
Sir Paul:	O, if she be with Mr. Careless, 'tis well enough.	. . .	192	DOUEL DLR	V.1	190
Maskwell:	of mine, I have told 'em in plain terms, how easie 'tis for		194	DOUEL DLR	V.1	263
Lord Touch:	Unworthy! 'tis an ignorant Pride in her to	. . .	196	DOUEL DLR	V.1	317
Lord Touch:	think so--Honesty to me is true Nobility. However, 'tis		196	DOUEL DLR	V.1	318
Maskwell:	So, 'tis well--let your wild fury have a vent;	. . .	198	DOUEL DLR	V.1	408
Lady Touch:	thou hast deceiv'd me; but 'tis as I would wish,--	. . .	199	DOUEL DLR	V.1	454
	Tho Satire scarce dares grin, 'tis grown so mild;	.	213	FOR LCVE	PRO.	33
Mrs Frail:	Issue-Male of their two Bodies; 'tis the most superstitious	231	FOR LCVE	I.1	579
Foresight:	he's at leisure--'tis now Three a Clock, a very good hour	.	236	FCR LCVE	II.1	41
Sr Sampson:	here 'tis, I have it in my Hand, Old Ptolomee; I'll make the	240	FOR LCVE	II.1	173
Foresight:	faith and troth, here 'tis, if it will but hold--I wish	.	240	FOR LCVE	II.1	187
Jeremy:	No, Sir, Mr. Valentine, my master,--'tis the first	. .	242	FCR LCVE	II.1	267
Mrs Fore:	Nay, 'tis Yours, look at it.	. . . . .	248	FCR LCVE	II.1	468
Mrs Fore:	Here 'tis with all my heart.	. . .	248	FOR LCVE	II.1	484
Angelica:	I swear I don't think 'tis possible.	. . . . .	255	FOR LCVE	III.1	80
Tattle:	No, I hope not--'tis as much Ingratitude to own	. . .	255	FOR LCVE	III.1	85
Ben:	it were, bound for the Land of Matrimony; 'tis a Voyage	.	263	FCR LCVE	III.1	372
Scandal:	Nay, nay, 'tis manifest; I do not flatter you--But	. .	267	FCR LCVE	III.1	519
Scandal:	but 'tis as I believe some Men are Valiant, thro' fear--For	271	FCR LCVE	III.1	670
Scandal:	Pleasure, so you have taken care of Honour, and 'tis the	.	271	FOR LCVE	III.1	682
Ben:	so be, that I ben't minded to be steer'd by him; 'tis as	.	272	FCR LCVE	III.1	716
Scandal:	and imperfect Lover; 'tis the last glimpse of Love to					
	wornout	. . .	275	FOR LCVE	III.1	816
Scandal:	Well, I'll try her--'tis she, here she comes.	. .	276	FOR LCVE	IV.1	18
Angelica:	Ha! I saw him wink and smile--I fancy 'tis a	. . .	277	FCR LCVE	IV.1	53
Angelica:	Concern for him may lessen--If I forget him, 'tis no	.	277	FOR LCVE	IV.1	81
Valentine:	and there are Children that have many Fathers--'tis	.	280	FCR LCVE	IV.1	163
Valentine:	Is the Lawyer gone? 'tis well, then we may drink	. .	280	FOR LCVE	IV.1	191
Valentine:	Sir, 'tis my Duty to wait.	281	FOR LCVE	IV.1	199
Sr Sampson:	'tis thy own Hand, Val. Why, let me see, I can read it as		281	FOR LCVE	IV.1	220
Sr Sampson:	. . . Why, 'tis as plain as	. . .	281	FOR LCVE	IV.1	224
Valentine:	What, is my bad Genius here again! Oh no, 'tis	. . .	282	FOR LCVE	IV.1	237
Tattle:	No, Sir, 'tis written in my Heart. And safer there,					
	Sir, than	. . .	292	FOR LCVE	IV.1	613
Valentine:	Oh, 'tis barbarous to misunderstand me longer.	. . .	295	FOR LCVE	IV.1	731
Sr Sampson:	Odsbud, and 'tis pity you should--(Aside.) Odd,	. . .	298	FOR LCVE	V.1	48
Sr Sampson:	'tis as they commit Murder; out of a Frolick: And are	.	299	FOR LCVE	V.1	57
Sr Sampson:	your Hand, Odd let me kiss it; 'tis as warm and as soft	.	301	FOR LCVE	V.1	145
Tattle:	Ay; 'tis well enough for a Servant to be bred at an	. .	302	FCR LCVE	V.1	186
Jeremy:	O Sir, for that Sir, 'tis my chief Talent; I'm as secret	.	302	FOR LCVE	V.1	190
Tattle:	So 'tis, faith--I might have sav'd several others	. .	303	FOR LCVE	V.1	212
Tattle:	No, Sir; 'tis to be done Privately--I never make	. .	304	FOR LCVE	V.1	280
Angelica:	Faults than he has Virtues; and 'tis hardly more Pleasure		312	FOR LCVE	V.1	576
Scandal:	own Wedding; methinks 'tis pity they should not be	. .	313	FOR LCVE	V.1	599
	I'm sure 'tis some such Latin Name they give 'em,	. .	315	FCR LCVE	EPI.	13
Almeria:	But 'tis the Wretches Comfort still to have	. . . .	328	M. BRIDE	I.1	82
Almeria:	For 'tis the poor Prerogative of Greatness,	. . . .	328	M. BRIDE	I.1	96
Almeria:	For 'tis, alas, the poor Prerogative of Greatness,	. . .	328	M. BRIDE	I.1 V	96
Gonsalez:	But 'tis a Task unfit for my weak Age, ...	332	M. BRIDE	I.1	253
Manuel:	She does excuse him; 'tis as I suspected.	. . .	337	M. BRIDE	I.1	441
Heli:	Yet cannot find him--Hark! sure 'tis the Voice	. . .	340	M. BRIDE	II.2	2
Almeria:	Sure, 'tis the Friendly Yawn of Death for me;	. . .	340	M. BRIDE	II.2	14
Osmyn-Alph:	'Tis Life! 'tis warm! 'tis she! 'tis she her self!	. .	341	M. BRIDE	II.2	54
Osmyn-Alph:	It is Almeria! 'tis my Wife!	. . . .	341	M. BRIDE	II.2	56
Osmyn-Alph:	It is Almeria! 'tis, it is, my Wife!	. . . . .	341	M. BRIDE	II.2 V	56
Heli:	By Heav'n 'tis he, and with--ha! Almeria!	. . . .	341	M. BRIDE	II.2	63
Heli:	Ha! 'tis he! and with--Almeria!	. . . .	341	M. BRIDE	II.2 V	63
Almeria:	It is, it is Alphonso, 'tis his Face,	. . . .	342	M. BRIDE	II.2	82
Almeria:	I know not, 'tis to see thy Face I think--	. . . .	342	M. BRIDE	II.2	104
Almeria:	For 'tis not to be born--What shall I say?	. . . .	343	M. BRIDE	II.2	149
Osmyn-Alph:	Ha, 'tis Zara!	. . . . .	346	M. BRIDE	II.2 V247
Zara:	Thou hast a Heart, though 'tis a savage one;	. . .	346	M. BRIDE	II.2	272
Zara:	If I have gain'd thy Love, 'tis Glorious Ruine;	. . .	347	M. BRIDE	II.2	313
Zara:	Ruine, 'tis still to reign, and to be more	. . .	347	M. BRIDE	II.2	314
Zara:	To love above him, for 'tis dangerous:	. . . .	348	M. BRIDE	II.2	342
Osmyn-Alph:	Sure 'tis the Hand of Heav'n, that leads me thus,	. . .	350	M. BRIDE	III.1	4
Osmyn-Alph:	But 'tis torn off--why should that Word alone	. . .	350	M. BRIDE	III.1	22
Osmyn-Alph:	She'll come; 'tis what I wish, yet what I fear.	. . .	351	M. BRIDE	III.1	51
Zara:	Wake thee to Freedom. Now, 'tis late; and yet	. . .	354	M. BRIDE	III.1	203
Almeria:	Tho' 'tis because thou lov'st me. Do not say	. . .	356	M. BRIDE	III.1	256
Almeria:	No, no, 'tis better thus, that we together	. . .	356	M. BRIDE	III.1	258
Osmyn-Alph:	And 'tis deny'd to me, to be so bless'd,	. . .	357	M. BRIDE	III.1	333

Titles (4)
```
Scandal:    into their Titles and Estates; and seems Commission'd  .  . 219  FOR LCVE   I.1   134
Scandal:    No, their Titles shall serve. . . . . . . . . . .        230  FOR LCVE   I.1   533
Tattle:     Titles; I'll describe their Persons.  .  .  .  .  .  .   230  FOR LCVE   I.1   535
Perez:      My Service has not merited those Titles.  .  .  .  .  .  374  M. BRIDE   V.1    68
```
Tittle (2)
```
Heartwell:  Lord what d'ee-cals Mouth to a Tittle--Then I to put it  .  45  OLD BATCH  I.1   324
Fainall:    or abate one tittle cf my Terms, no, I will insist the more. 474  WAY WCRLD V.1   477
```
To (3352)   see T'
To's (1)
```
Ben:        tell'n so to's face: If that's the Case, why silence gives 263  FOR LCVE  III.1  393
```
To't (3)
```
Careless:   Laughing when a Man has a mind to't.  .  .  .  .  .  .   133  DOUEL DLR  I.1   247
Jeremy:     Nothing thrives that belongs to't. The Man of the House  . 218  FCR LCVE   I.1    89
Sir Wilful: she has her Maidenhead let her lcok to't,--if she has not, 456  WAY WORLD  IV.1  428
```
Toad (5)
```
Lucy:       Beast, filthy Toad, I can hold no longer, look and  .  .  66  OLD BATCH III.1  198
Mrs Fore:   Oh, Demm you Toad--I wish you dcn't . . . . . . .        249  FOR LCVE   II.1  538
Mrs Frail:  take you, you confounded Toad--why did you see  .  .  .  250  FOR LCVE   II.1  566
Mrs Fore:   Did you ever hear such a Toad--heark'ee  .  .  .  .  .   271  FOR LCVE  III.1  664
Osmyn-Alph: Not what they would, but must; a Star, or Toad:  .  .  . 345  M. BRIDE   II.2  223
```
Toast (1)   see Tost, Toste
```
Valentine:  Chair quickly: A Bottle of Sack and a Toast--fly--a Chair . 222  FOR LOVE   I.1   229
```
Toasting (1)
```
Witwoud:    Love without Enjoyment, or Wine without Toasting; but  . 404  WAY WCRLD  I.1   358
```
Tobacco (1)
```
Belinda:    You stink of Brandy and Tobacco, most Soldier-like. Poh.  . 85  OLD BATCH IV.3    88
```
Tobacco-Box (1)
```
Nurse:      and tuck you up, and set the Candle, and your Tobacco-Box, 238  FOR LCVE   II.1  103
```
Toes (0)   see Tip-toes
Together (69)
```
Vainlove:   Well good Morrow, let's dine together, I'l meet at  .  .  .  40  OLD BATCH  I.1   129
Bellmour:   together. . . . . . . . . . . . . . . . . . . .          57  OLD BATCH  II.2  119
Heartwell:  much Tenderness and Beauty--and Honesty together  .  .   74  OLD BATCH  II.2  115
Lady Froth: Three Weeks together.  .  .  .  .  .  .  .  .  .  .  .  138  DOUEL DLR  II.1    4
Lady Froth: come together,--O bless me! What a sad thing  .  .  .  . 139  DOUEL DLR  II.1   22
Cynthia:    when you are together, but happy in your selves, and by  . 141  DOUEL DLR  II.1   98
Mellefont:  and sometimes the Two farthest are together, but the  .  143  DOUEL DLR  II.1  166
Lady Ply:   happen together,--to my thinking, now I could  .  .  .  147  DOUEL DLR  II.1  326
Maskwell:   Come, trouble not your head, I'll joyn you together e're  . 148  DOUEL DLR  II.1  386
Lady Touch: grown together when I told you--almost a Twelvemcnth  .  153  DOUEL DLR III.1  110
Maskwell:   surprize your Aunt and me together: Counterfeit a rage  . 157  DOUBL DLR III.1  250
Careless:   whole nights together upon the Stairs, before her
            Chamber-door;  .  .  .  .  .  .  .  .  .  .  .  .  .  .  157  DOUEL DLR III.1  274
Sir Paul:   together; she's a little hasty scmetimes, and so am  .  . 160  DOUEL DLR III.1  389
Lady Froth: spent two days together in going about Ccvent-Garden to  . 165  DOUEL DLR III.1  563
Cynthia:    are so near that we don't think of coming together.  .   168  DOUEL DLR  IV.1   18
Cynthia:    I would not have 'em see us together yet.  .  .  .  .  . 169  DOUEL DLF  IV.1   66
Sir Paul:   never go together; you must not expect that.  .  .  .  . 171  DOUEL DLR  IV.1  149
Maskwell:   when we are together, and you not easily get in to surprize 181  DOUEL DLR  IV.1  518
Saygrace:   I have, they are ready in my Chamber, together  .  .  .  195  DOUEL DLB  V.1   285
Sir Paul:   together. . . . . . . . . . . . . . . . . . . . .        201  DOUEL DLB  V.1   510
Lady Froth: an Almanack together.  .  .  .  .  .  .  .  .  .  .  .   201  DOUEL DLB  V.1   537
Angelica:   and Spoon-meat together--Indeed, Uncle, I'll indite you  . 237  FOR LCVE   II.1   91
Angelica:   Yes, I saw you together, through the Key-hole of  .  .  . 238  FOR LCVE   II.1  106
Mrs Fore:   liking of you. Here they ccme together; and let us contrive 249  FOR LCVE   II.1  503
Mrs Fore:   liking of you. Here they come together; and let us contrive 249  FOR LCVE   II.1 V503
Mrs Fore:   some way or other to leave 'em tcgether.  .  .  .  .  .  249  FOR LCVE   II.1  504
Mrs Fore:   together is as bad--And he's such a sly Devil, he'll never 250  FOR LCVE   II.1  574
Miss Prue:  No! what then? what shall you and I do together?  .  .  251  FOR LCVE   II.1  587
Tattle:     Or does she leave us together out of good Morality, and  . 251  FOR LCVE   II.1  593
Tattle:     say nothing, I think. I hear her--I'll leave you together, 254  FOR LCVE  III.1   23
Sr Sampson: see 'em hug and cotten together, like Down upon a  .  .  260  FOR LCVE  III.1  265
Sr Sampson: not be shame-fac'd, we'll leave you together.  .  .  .   262  FOR LCVE  III.1  351
Ben:        stand a stern a that'n, we shall never grapple together,-- 263  FOR LCVE  III.1  361
Ben:        chance to swing in a Hammock together.  .  .  .  .  .  . 263  FOR LCVE  III.1  377
Sr Sampson: I left 'em together here; What are they gone?  .  .  .  265  FOR LCVE  III.1  456
Scandal:    I are together. . . . . . . . . . . . . . . .           271  FOR LCVE  III.1  658
Valentine:  about without going together by the Ears--heigh ho!  .   280  FOR LCVE   IV.1  192
Valentine:  together by a State-Cook, make Sauce for the whole  .  . 282  FCR LCVE   IV.1  258
Sr Sampson: join'd together, make yet a greater, that's a Man and his 282  FOR LCVE   IV.1  266
Ben:        and the Green Girl together;--May hap the Bee may bite,  . 286  FOR LCVE   IV.1  386
Mrs Fore:   stead, and get you married together, and put to Bed  .  288  FOR LCVE   IV.1  472
Mrs Fore:   together; and after Consumation, Girl, there's no  .  .  288  FOR LCVE   IV.1  473
Scandal:    contrive to couple 'em together--Heark'ee--.  .  .  .   291  FOR LCVE   IV.1  599
Ben:        they'd ne're make a Match together--Here they come.  .  307  FOR LCVE   V.1   374
Ben:        may make a Voyage together now.  .  .  .  .  .  .  .  .  312  FOR LCVE   V.1   569
            Nor were they without Reason join'd together;  .  .  .   323  M. BRIDE   PRO.    7
Almeria:    No, no, 'tis better thus, that we together  .  .  .  .  356  M. BRIDE  III.1  258
Gonsalez:   Escape. This put together, suits not well. . . . . .     366  M. EBIDE   IV.1  212
Fainall:    another's Apartments, where they come together like the  . 396  WAY WCRLD  I.1    52
Lady Wish:  they are together, then come to me Foible, that I may not 445  WAY WCRLD  IV.1   39
Foible:     and Sir Wilfull together. Shall I tell Mr. Mirabell that you 445  WAY WCRLD  IV.1   46
Mrs Fain:   an opportunity, if I can help it. I'll leave you together
            and  .  .  .  .  .  .  .  .  .  .  .  .  .  .  .  .  .  447  WAY WCRLD  IV.1   88
Millamant:  Francis: Nor goe to Hide-Park together the first Sunday in 450  WAY WCRLD  IV.1  202
Millamant:  never to be seen there together again; as if we were proud 450  WAY WCRLD  IV.1  204
Millamant:  never be seen there together again; as if we were proud  . 450  WAY WCRLD  IV.1 V204
Millamant:  for ever After. Let us never Visit together, ncr go to a  . 450  WAY WCRLD  IV.1  206
Millamant:  ever After. Let us never Visit together, nor go to a  .   450  WAY WCRLD  IV.1 V206
Millamant:  Play together, But let us be very strange and well bred:  . 450  WAY WCRLD  IV.1  207
Mirabell:   together with all Vizards for the day, I prohibit all Masks 451  WAY WCRLD  IV.1  248
Mirabell:   all Anniseed, Cinamon, Citron and Barbadc's-Waters, together 451  WAY WCRLD  IV.1  273
Witwoud:    express'd provocation; they had gone together by the  .  454  WAY WORLD  IV.1  362
Lady Wish:  it--wee'll open it together--lock you here.  .  .  .  .  460  WAY WCRLD  IV.1  583
Lady Wish:  together, you and your Philander. I'll Dukes-Place you, as 463  WAY WORLD  V.1    53
```

Together (continued)

Mrs Fain:	thing discover'd. This is the last day of our living together,	464	WAY WORLD	V.1	82
Poible:	friends together, than set 'em at distance. But Mrs. Marwood	464	WAY WORLD	V.1	88
Millamant:	Sir Wilfull, you and he are to Travel together, are	470	WAY WORLD	V.1	343
Mrs Fain:	not name it, but starve together--perish.	475	WAY WORLD	V.1	501
Witwoud:	Hey day! what are you all got together like Players	475	WAY WORLD	V.1	521
Mirabell:	live Easily together.	478	WAY WORLD	V.1	619

Toil (2)

	The Husbandman in vain renews his Toil,	213	FOR LOVE	PRO.	1
	He owns, with Toil, he wrought the following Scenes,	393	WAY WORLD	PRO.	22

Toilet (4)

Poible:	I'll be gone; I'm sure my Lady is at her Toilet, and can't	424	WAY WORLD	II.1	543
	Lady Wishfort at her Toilet, Peg waiting.)	425	WAY WORLD	III.1	
Lady Wish:	Sir Rowland handsome? Let my Toilet be remov'd--I'll	429	WAY WORLD	III.1	171
Poible:	remove my Lady's Toilet. Madam your Servant. My Lady	430	WAY WORLD	III.1	219

Toiling (1)

	Toiling and lab'ring at their Lungs Expence,	323	M. BRIDE	PRO.	19

Toity (1)

Sr Sampson:	Hoity toity, What have I to do with his Dreams	267	FOR LOVE	III.1	504

Token (5)

Setter:	What no Token of amity Lucy? you and I don't use	67	OLD BATCH	III.1	234
Bellmour:	my old Token.	97	OLD BATCH	V.1	35
Scandal:	My Blessing to the Boy, with this Token	222	FOR LOVE	I.1	216
Mrs Frail:	Well, give me your Hand in token of sisterly secresie and	248	FOR LOVE	II.1	482
Mincing:	token, you swore us to Secresie upon Messalinas's Poems.	474	WAY WORLD	V.1	488

Told (69)

Bellmour:	told you there's twelve thousand Pound--Hum--Why	41	OLD BATCH	I.1	170
Sir Joseph:	Night--You know I told you.	52	OLD BATCH	II.1	170
Laetitia:	when you knock'd at the door; and the Maid told me,	95	OLD BATCH	IV.4	244
Vainlove:	I'm sure he tells me Truth;--but I am not sure she told	99	OLD BATCH	V.1	94
Sharper:	Lucy, and has told me all.	100	OLD BATCH	V.1	146
Maskwell:	as I told you before. I can't deny that neither.--Any	135	DOUEL DLR	I.1	314
Maskwell:	No, that I deny; for I never told in all my Life:	135	DOUEL DLR	I.1	318
Maskwell:	of Love, have told me. Why should you deny it? Nay,	137	DOUEL DLR	I.1	385
Maskwell:	that belief, told me the Secrets of her heart. At length we	149	DOUEL DLR	II.1	426
Maskwell:	made this agreement, if I accomplish her designs (as I told	149	DOUEL DLR	II.1	427
Lady Touch:	not fit to be told you.	151	DOUEL DLR	III.1	43
Lord Touch:	Not fit to be told me, Madam? You can have no Interests,	152	DOUEL DLR	III.1	46
Lord Touch:	When you have told me, I will--	152	DOUEL DLR	III.1	57
Lady Touch:	wish I had not told you any thing.--Indeed, my Lord,	152	DOUEL DLR	III.1	69
Lady Touch:	Consider your own and my Honour--nay, I told you	153	DOUEL DLR	III.1	105
Lady Touch:	grown together when I told you--almost a Twelvemonth	153	DOUEL DLR	III.1	110
Mellefont:	forget you told me this before.	156	DOUEL DLR	III.1	227
Careless:	some such Cant. Then she has told me the whole History of	157	DOUEL DLR	III.1	272
Mellefont:	are very great with him, I wonder he never told you his	158	DOUEL DLR	III.1	293
Lady Ply:	How often have you been told of that you	161	DOUEL DLR	III.1	393
Careless:	be told on't; she must i'faith, Sir Paul; 'tis an injury to the	162	DOUEL DLR	III.1	442
Lord Touch:	she has told me all: Her good Nature conceal'd it as long	182	DOUEL DLR	IV.1	547
Lord Touch:	has told me even you were weary of disswading him,	182	DOUEL DLR	IV.1	549
Lord Touch:	I told you, he confess'd it to me.	191	DOUEL DLR	V.1	133
Sir Paul:	but hearkee, my Lord told me something of a Revolution	192	DOUEL DLR	V.1	172
Maskwell:	of mine, I have told 'em in plain terms, how easie 'tis for	194	DOUEL DLR	V.1	263
Lady Froth:	You know I told you Saturn look'd a little more	203	DOUEL DLR	V.1	579
Jeremy:	always a Fool, when I told you what your Expences would	217	FOR LOVE	I.1	42
Tattle:	But I soon satisfy'd the Lady of my Innocence; for I told	227	FOR LOVE	I.1	429
Tattle:	me, and I told her something or other, faith--I know	228	FOR LOVE	I.1	447
Scandal:	No, you told us.	229	FOR LOVE	I.1	495
Jeremy:	I told you what your Visit wou'd come to.	246	FOR LOVE	II.1	406
Mrs Fore:	have told you, you must not call me Mother.	249	FOR LOVE	II.1	508
Angelica:	You can't accuse me of Inconstancy; I never told	254	FOR LOVE	III.1	27
Angelica:	My Passion! And who told you of my Passion, pray	254	FOR LOVE	III.1	57
Scandal:	wou'd have told me; I find, Madam, you don't know	256	FOR LOVE	III.1	110
Angelica:	Then it seems you would have told, if you had been	256	FOR LOVE	III.1	114
Tattle:	told Particulars, Madam. Perhaps I might have talk'd as of a	256	FOR LOVE	III.1	117
Sr Sampson:	Nay, Ben has Parts, but as I told you before, they	262	FOR LOVE	III.1	338
Jeremy:	Like enough, Sir, for I told her Maid this morning,	276	FOR LOVE	IV.1	14
Scandal:	have been told she had that admirable quality of forgetting	284	FOR LOVE	IV.1	334
Ben:	told 'n in plain terms, if I were minded to marry, I'de	285	FOR LOVE	IV.1	371
Valentine:	have told thee what's past,--Now I tell what's to	288	FOR LOVE	IV.1	489
Valentine:	have told thee what's past,--Now I'll tell what's to	288	FOR LOVE	IV.1	V489
Tattle:	O fie, Miss: Who told you so, Child?	303	FOR LOVE	V.1	231
Miss Prue:	Why, my Father--I told him that you lov'd me.	303	FOR LOVE	V.1	232
Tattle:	O fie, Miss, why did you do so? and who told you so,	303	FOR LOVE	V.1	233
Miss Prue:	Husband and thank me too, for he told me so.	305	FOR LOVE	V.1	319
Foresight:	Why, you told me just now, you went hence in	309	FOR LOVE	V.1	453
	Once of Philosophers they told us Stories,	315	FOR LOVE	EPI.	11
Almeria:	And when I told thee thou didst nothing knew,	328	M. BRIDE	I.1	V100
Almeria:	'Twas--as I have told thee--	329	M. BRIDE	I.1	V143
Garcia:	This Way, we're told, Osmyn was seen to walk;	337	M. BRIDE	II.1	1
Selim:	The King, in full belief of all you told him,	361	M. BRIDE	IV.1	12
Gonsalez:	Corrupted; how? by whom? who told her so?	366	M. BRIDE	IV.1	207
Mirabell:	with a constrain'd Smile told her, I thought nothing was so	396	WAY WORLD	I.1	38
Mirabell:	Fellow, which I carry'd so far, that I told her the malicious	397	WAY WORLD	I.1	73
Witwoud:	has been told; and you know she hates Mirabell, worse than	408	WAY WORLD	I.1	484
Millamant:	act always by Advice, and so tedious to be told of ones	422	WAY WORLD	II.1	455
Foible:	But I told my Lady as you instructed me, Sir. That I	423	WAY WORLD	II.1	519
Foible:	I told her Sir, because I did not know that you might	424	WAY WORLD	II.1	530
Foible:	our success, Mrs. Marwood had told my Lady; but I warrant	430	WAY WORLD	III.1	206
Foible:	I manag'd my self. I turn'd it all for the better. I told my	430	WAY WORLD	III.1	207
Sir Wilful:	told you, Madam--Yes, I have settl'd my Concerns,	440	WAY WORLD	III.1	573
Waitwell:	I told you at first I knew the hand--A Womans	460	WAY WORLD	IV.1	600
Mrs Fain:	Confederacy? I fancy Marwood has not told her, tho' she	464	WAY WORLD	V.1	76
Mrs Fain:	has told my husband.	464	WAY WORLD	V.1	77

Told (continued)
   Foible: mischeivous Devil told Mr. Fainall of your Ladyship then? . 464 WAY WORLD V.1   80
   Foible: cou'd have told you long enough since, but I love to keep   464 WAY WORLD V.1   86
Told'st (1)
   Almeria: Thou told'st me thou would'st think how we might meet . 355 M. BRIDE   III.1 246
Tolerable (1)
   Sir Paul: Town, and some money, a pretty tolerable personal Estate;   161 DOUBL DLR III.1 409
Toling (1)
   Almeria: Was it the doleful Bell, toling for Death?   . . . . . 370 M. BRIDE   IV.1   385
Toll (2)
   Sir Joseph: here is,--Look you what here
                  is:--Toll--loll--dera--toll--loll.   . . . . . . 85 OLD BATCH IV.3   67
Tollerable (1)
   Mirabell: tollerable Reputation--I am afraid Mr. Fainall will be . 412 WAY WORLD II.1   101
Tom (5)
   Bellmour: twelve thousand Pound Tom--'Tis true she is excessively . 41 OLD BATCH I.1   166
   Bellmour: worth your acquaintance--a little of thy Chymistry Tom, . 46 OLD BATCH I.1   345
   Bellmour: I doubt the Knight repents, Tom--He looks like   . . . . 68 OLD BATCH III.1 287
   Heartwell: I'll dissemble, and try him.--Ha, ha, ha. Why, Tom; Is . 104 OLD BATCH V.1   300
   Ben: take your part, Your Tom Essence, and I'll say something to 265 FOR LOVE   III.1 435
Tomb (11)
   Careless: ever from your sight, and drown me in my Tomb.   . . . 170 DOUBL DLR IV.1   117
   Almeria: The silent Tomb receiv'd the good old King;   . . . . 326 M. BRIDE   I.1   10
   Almeria: The cruel Ocean would deprive thee of a Tomb,   . . . 328 M. BRIDE   I.1   73
   Almeria: The cruel Ocean is no more thy Tomb, ... 328 M. BRIDE   I.1 V 73
   Almeria: Steal forth, and visit good Anselmo's Tomb.   . . . . 331 M. BRIDE   I.1   199
   Almeria: No, I will on: shew me Anselmo's Tomb, ... 339 M. BRIDE   II.1   73
                  (Osmyn ascending from the Tomb.)   . . 340 M. BRIDE   II.2   34
   Almeria: Sure, from thy Father's Tomb, thou didst arise!   . . 343 M. BRIDE   II.2   156
   Osmyn-Alph: But now, and I was clos'd within the Tomb   . . . . . 349 M. BRIDE   III.1   1
   Almeria: The Tomb it calls--I'll follow it, for there   . . . 371 M. BRIDE   IV.1   393
   Almeria: For in the Tomb or Prison, I alone   . . . . 381 M. BRIDE   V.2   216
Tombs (3)
   Almeria: And Terror on my aking Sight; the Tombs   . . . . . 339 M. BRIDE   II.1   64
                  (The Scene opening discovers a Place of Tombs. One   . . 340 M. BRIDE   II.2
   Almeria: Me from the Tombs--I'll follow it, for there   . . . 371 M. BRIDE   IV.1 V393
Tone (2)
   Careless: (in a whining Tone). Ah Heavens, Madam, you   . . . . 169 DOUBL DLR IV.1   85
   Jeremy: madly, she won't distinguish the Tone of your Voice.   . 303 FOR LOVE   V.1   218
Tongue (30)
   Capt Bluff: about, Pray hold your Tongue, and give me leave.   . . . 53 OLD BATCH II.1   225
   Belinda: Prithee hold thy Tongue--Lard, he has so   . . . . . 59 OLD BATCH II.2   163
   Bellmour: Doing! No Tongue can express it,--not thy own;   . . . 82 OLD BATCH IV.2   84
   Vainlove: That Tongue, which denies what the Hands have   . . . . 88 OLD BATCH IV.3   183
   Mellefont: Passion had ty'd her Tongue, and Amazement mine.--   . . 130 DOUBL DLR I.1   108
   Lady Froth: O that Tongue, that dear deceitful Tongue! that   . . . 140 DOUBL DLR II.1   71
   Careless: ruine me with Kindness; your Charming Tongue pursues   . 169 DOUBL DLR IV.1   86
   Valentine: provoke your Enemies; this liberty of your Tongue, will . 221 FOR LOVE   I.1   199
   Tattle: O Lord, what have I said? my Unlucky Tongue!   . . . . 227 FOR LOVE   I.1   435
   Tattle: you'l cry out, you must be sure to hold your Tongue.   . 252 FOR LOVE   II.1   623
   Miss Prue: Oh but you sha'nt, for I'll hold my Tongue.--   . . . . 253 FOR LOVE   II.1   658
   Tattle: --Pox on't, now could I bite off my Tongue.   . . . . 258 FOR LOVE   III.1 189
   Valentine: Truth, and can teach thy Tongue a new Trick,--I   . . . 288 FOR LOVE   IV.1   488
   Angelica: O fie for shame, hold your Tongue, A passionate   . . . 291 FOR LOVE   IV.1   585
   Sr Sampson: Hold your Tongue, Sirrah. How now, who's   . . . . . 309 FOR LOVE   V.1   437
   Almeria: And with his Artful Tongue, to gild and magnifie   . . 331 M. BRIDE   I.1   215
   Zara: Thy Tongue that Saying.   . . . . 353 M. BRIDE   III.1 145
   Almeria: Curst be that Tongue, that bids me be of Comfort;   . . 370 M. BRIDE   IV.1   371
   Almeria: Curst my own Tongue, that cou'd not move his Pity.   . . 370 M. BRIDE   IV.1   372
   Garcia: Blasted my Eyes, and speechless be my Tongue, ... 377 M. BRIDE   V.2   55
   Selim: My Tongue faulters, and my Voice fails--   . . . . . 380 M. BRIDE   V.2   183
   Selim: My Tongue faulters, and my Voice fails--I sink--   . . 380 M. BRIDE   V.2 V183
   Witwoud: Rotation of Tongue, that an Eccho must wait till she dies, 421 WAY WORLD II.1   421
   Lady Wish: O, he carries Poyson in his Tongue that wou'd   . . . . 426 WAY WORLD III.1   57
   Sir Wilful: Why then let him hold his Tongue in the mean   . . . . 441 WAY WORLD III.1 611
   Millamant: thank'd--here kiss my hand tho'--so hold your tongue   . 452 WAY WORLD IV.1   296
   Foible: dissembling Tongue; Your Lady-ship's own Wisdom has   . 463 WAY WORLD V.1   27
   Lady Wish: he has a false Insinuating Tongue--Well Sir, I will stifle 472 WAY WORLD V.1   401
   Lady Wish: Tongue;--When I did not see him I cou'd have   . . . . 472 WAY WORLD V.1   409
Tongue-ty'd (1)
   Bellmour: Ay, but if I'm Tongue-ty'd, I must have all my   . . . 59 OLD BATCH II.2   181
Tongues (3)
   Lord Froth: Just 'ifaith, that was at my tongues end.   . . . . . 163 DOUBL DLR III.1 480
   Valentine: me have a Pair of Red hot Tongues quickly, quickly,   . 282 FOR LOVE   IV.1   240
   Mincing: shou'd have held our Tongues; You wou'd have brib'd   . 474 WAY WORLD V.1   490
Tony (9)
   Mirabell: Petulant, Tony Witwoud, who is now thy Competitor in   . 407 WAY WORLD I.1   453
   Sir Wilful: Yea but 'tis, by the Rekin. Brother Anthony! What Tony   438 WAY WORLD III.1 516
   Sir Wilful: Yea but 'tis, by the Rekin. Brother Antony! What Tony   438 WAY WORLD III.1 V516
   Sir Wilful: Tony, belike, I may'nt call him Brother for fear of offence. 441 WAY WORLD III.1 605
   Sir Wilful: Tony, Ods heart where's Tony--Tony's an honest fellow,   455 WAY WORLD IV.1   413
   Sir Wilful: Ah Tony!   . . . . 456 WAY WORLD IV.1   458
   Sir Wilful: With a Wench, Tony? Is she a shake-bag Sirrah?   . . . 457 WAY WORLD IV.1   472
   Sir Wilful: Lead on little Tony--I'll follow thee my Anthony,   . . 457 WAY WORLD IV.1   476
Tony's (1)
   Sir Wilful: Tony, Ods heart where's Tony--Tony's an honest fellow, . 455 WAY WORLD IV.1   413
Too (254)
   Bellmour: Business upon my hands, because it lay too heavy upon his: 41 OLD BATCH I.1   141
   Sharper: have no hopes of getting her for a Mistress, and she is too 41 OLD BATCH I.1   162
   Sharper: Proud, too Inconstant, too Affected and too Witty, and . 41 OLD BATCH I.1   163
   Sharper: too handsome for a Wife.   . . . . 41 OLD BATCH I.1   164
   Bellmour: But she can't have too much Mony--There's   . . . . . 41 OLD BATCH I.1   165
   Heartwell: able as your self and as nimble too, though I mayn't have 43 OLD BATCH I.1   230
   Bellmour: Time enough, ay too soon, I should rather have   . . . . 43 OLD BATCH I.1   235
   Heartwell: Yet it is oftentimes too late with some of you   . . . . 43 OLD BATCH I.1   237
   Heartwell: So I hate Physick too--yet I may love to take it   . . . 44 OLD BATCH I.1   284

Too   (continued)

Too   (continued)

		PAGE	TITLE	ACT.SC	LINE
Sr Sampson:	if there is too much, refund the Superfluity; Do'st hear	243	FOR LOVE	II.1	280
Sr Sampson:	if there be too much, refund the Superfluity; Do'st hear	243	FOR LOVE	II.1	V280
Sr Sampson:	Here's a Cormorant too,--'S'heart this	245	FOR LOVE	II.1	357
Jeremy:	begot me too:--Nay, and to tell your Worship	245	FOR LOVE	II.1	361
Jeremy:	those same Whoreson Appetites too; that my Master	245	FOR LOVE	II.1	363
Foresight:	World too, Friend.	245	FOR LOVE	II.1	384
Mrs Frail:	in my mind too much for the Stage.	247	FOR LOVE	II.1	454
Tattle:	Oh Madam; you are too severe upon Miss; you must	249	FOR LOVE	II.1	534
Miss Prue:	Come, must not we go too?	251	FOR LOVE	II.1	585
Miss Prue:	too? You must tell me how.	251	FOR LOVE	II.1	597
Tattle:	but you must Love me too--If I tell you you are	252	FOR LOVE	II.1	615
Miss Prue:	and must not you lie too?	252	FOR LOVE	II.1	626
Tattle:	O pox, Scandal, that was too far put--Never have	256	FOR LOVE	III.1	116
Sr Sampson:	were you here too, Madam, and could not keep him!	259	FOR LOVE	III.1	237
Angelica:	Estate too: But since that's gone, the Bait's off, and the	260	FOR LOVE	III.1	247
Ben:	Nay, and you too, my little Cock-boat--so--	261	FOR LOVE	III.1	283
Miss Prue:	do what he will; I'm too big to be whipt, so I'll tell you	264	FOR LOVE	III.1	398
Sr Sampson:	for saying Grace, old Foresight, but fall too without the	265	FOR LOVE	III.1	460
Scandal:	Yes, Faith, I believe some Women are Vertuous too;	271	FOR LOVE	III.1	669
Ben:	The Tinker too with Mettle,	274	FOR LOVE	III.1	776
Mrs Fore:	Dream too.	275	FOR LOVE	III.1	812
Scandal:	So, this is pretty plain--Ee not too much	277	FOR LOVE	IV.1	61
Angelica:	Weakness I am a Stranger to. But I have too much Sincerity	277	FOR LOVE	IV.1	70
Angelica:	to deceive you, and too much Charity to suffer him to be	277	FOR LOVE	IV.1	71
Scandal:	Dear, too considerable to be forgot so soon.	284	FOR LOVE	IV.1	317
Ben:	you too well, by sad experience;--I believe he that marries	287	FOR LOVE	IV.1	438
Ben:	won't come too.	287	FOR LOVE	IV.1	443
Mrs Fore:	Oh hang him old Fox, he's too cunning,	288	FOR LOVE	IV.1	462
Angelica:	Effects, I wou'd have striven; but that's too late.	294	FOR LOVE	IV.1	713
Valentine:	What sad Effects?--What's too late? my seeming	294	FOR LOVE	IV.1	715
Sr Sampson:	Women think a Man old too soon, faith and troth you do	298	FOR LOVE	V.1	25
Angelica:	thing that wou'd make me appear to be too much concern'd	299	FOR LOVE	V.1	91
Sr Sampson:	Odd, I long to be pulling down too, come away--	301	FOR LOVE	V.1	161
Sr Sampson:	Odd, I long to be pulling too, come away--	301	FOR LOVE	V.1	V161
Tattle:	University: But the Education is a little too pedantick for	302	FOR LOVE	V.1	187
Tattle:	to know, and shan't know; and yet you shall know it too,	305	FOR LOVE	V.1	290
Foresight:	O fearful! I think the Girl's influenc'd too,--	305	FOR LOVE	V.1	313
Miss Prue:	Husband and thank me too, for he told me so.	305	FOR LOVE	V.1	319
Ben:	say, Brother Val. went mad for, she's mad too, I think.	306	FOR LOVE	V.1	346
Foresight:	O my poor Niece, my poor Niece, is she gone too?	306	FOR LOVE	V.1	347
Mrs Fore:	Your Experiment will take up a little too much	306	FOR LOVE	V.1	356
Tattle:	Poor Woman! Gad I'm sorry for her too; for I have no	309	FOR LOVE	V.1	466
Angelica:	try'd you too, and know you both. You have not more	312	FOR LOVE	V.1	575
Valentine:	ever you seem to love too much, it must be only when I	313	FOR LOVE	V.1	611
	But as with Freedom, judge with Candour too.	324	M. BRIDE	PRO.	40
Almeria:	O Alphonso, Alphonso! thou art too	327	M. BRIDE	I.1	52
Almeria:	Thou too art quiet--long hast been at Peace--	327	M. BRIDE	I.1	V 52
Leonora:	Alas you search too far, and think too deeply.	327	M. BRIDE	I.1	64
Almeria:	The Queen too, did assist his Suit--I granted,	329	M. BRIDE	I.1	140
Manuel:	Yet something too is due to me, who gave	333	M. BRIDE	I.1	289
Gonsalez:	Betray'd by too much Piety, to seem	334	M. BRIDE	I.1	319
Almeria:	Will cease his Tyranny; and Garcia too	340	M. BRIDE	II.2	23
Almeria:	To my Alphonso's Soul. O Joy too great!	340	M. BRIDE	II.2	29
Leonora:	He too is fainting--help me, help me, Stranger,	341	M. BRIDE	II.2	60
Almeria:	It is too much! too much to bear and live!	342	M. BRIDE	II.2	105
Almeria:	Too much lamented me.	342	M. BRIDE	II.2	118
Almeria:	Too much, too tenderly lamented me.	342	M. BRIDE	II.2	V118
Osmyn-Alph:	Wrong not my Love, to say too much.	343	M. BRIDE	II.2	119
Osmyn-Alph:	Wrong not my Love, to say too tenderly.	343	M. BRIDE	II.2	V119
Osmyn-Alph:	I thought I saw thee too; but O, I thought not	344	M. BRIDE	II.2	164
Osmyn-Alph:	My Friend too safe!	344	M. BRIDE	II.2	170
Osmyn-Alph:	I'm fortunate indeed--my Friend too safe!	344	M. BRIDE	II.2	V170
Almeria:	More Miracles! Antonio too escap'd!	344	M. BRIDE	II.2	172
Osmyn-Alph:	I saw her too, and therefore saw not thee.	344	M. BRIDE	II.2	183
Osmyn-Alph:	What would you from a Wretch, who came too	346	M. BRIDE	II.2	V258
Osmyn-Alph:	Where he was Pris'ner, I am too imprison'd.	349	M. BRIDE	III.1	3
Heli:	The time's too precious to be spent in telling;	351	M. BRIDE	III.1	42
Almeria:	--Thou giv'st me Pain, with too much Tenderness!	356	M. BRIDE	III.1	280
Almeria:	Thou dost me Wrong, and Grief too robs my	356	M. BRIDE	III.1	284
Osmyn-Alph:	O thou hast search'd too deep.	356	M. BRIDE	III.1	290
Zara:	And so unwish'd, unwanted too it seems.	359	M. BRIDE	III.1	410
Osmyn-Alph:	Come, 'tis too much.	360	M. BRIDE	III.1	V431
Zara:	Vile and ingrate! too late thou shalt repent	360	M. BRIDE	III.1	453
Selim:	'Tis certain Heli too is fled, and with him	361	M. BRIDE	IV.1	8
Selim:	On Osmyn's Death; too quick a Change of Mercy,	362	M. BRIDE	IV.1	45
Zara:	You're too secure: The Danger is more imminent	364	M. BRIDE	IV.1	109
Zara:	That too I will advise.	365	M. BRIDE	IV.1	149
Manuel:	Though on the Head that wears it, were too little.	365	M. BRIDE	IV.1	160
Gonsalez:	Disquiets her too much; which makes it seem	366	M. BRIDE	IV.1	203
Manuel:	Agrees expressly too with her Report.	366	M. BRIDE	IV.1	217
Gonsalez:	That were too hard a Thought--but see she comes.	367	M. BRIDE	IV.1	236
Manuel:	Should I hear more; I too should catch thy Madness.	370	M. BRIDE	IV.1	362
Gonsalez:	Your excessive Grief, works on your Fancy,	370	M. BRIDE	IV.1	375
Gonsalez:	Her husband too! Ha! where is Garcia then?	371	M. BRIDE	IV.1	400
Manuel:	Thou art Accomplice too much with Zara; here	373	M. BRIDE	V.1	51
Gonsalez:	There lies my way, that Door is too unlock'd.	376	M. BRIDE	V.2	4
Garcia:	Were it a Truth, I fear 'tis now too late.	379	M. BRIDE	V.2	105
Leonora:	Feeling Remorse too late, for what they've done.	381	M. BRIDE	V.2	225
Almeria:	O noble Thirst! and yet too greedy to	382	M. BRIDE	V.2	255
Almeria:	My Father too shall have Compassion--	383	M. BRIDE	V.2	299
	Some Humour too, no Farce; but that's a Fault.	393	WAY WORLD	PRO.	30
Fainall:	else now, and play too negligently; the Coldness of a	395	WAY WORLD	I.1	6
Fainall:	have too much Generosity, not to be tender of her Honour.	397	WAY WORLD	I.1	92
Fainall:	Kind too Contemptible to give Scandal.	399	WAY WORLD	I.1	143
Fainall:	somewhat too discerning in the Failings of your Mistress.	399	WAY WORLD	I.1	157

Too   (continued)
Mirabell:	And for a discerning Man, somewhat too passionate	. . .	399	WAY WCRLD	I.1	158
Fainall:	too.	400	WAY WCRLD	I.1	195
Fainall:	for you are sure to be too hard for him at Repartee: since	402	WAY WCRLD	I.1	282
Witwoud:	speaks;--We have all our Failings; you're too hard . . .	403	WAY WCRLD	I.1	308
Mirabell:	May be you think him too positive?	403	WAY WCRLD	I.1	322
Fainall:	Too Illiterate.	404	WAY WCRLD	I.1	325
Witwoud:	pox on him, I shall be troubled with him too; what shall I	409	WAY WCRLD	I.1	515
Fainall:	But he, I fear, is too Insensible.	413	WAY WCRLD	II.1	130
Fainall:	Ha, ha, ha; you are my Wife's Friend too.	414	WAY WCRLD	II.1	170
Marwood:	It shall be all discover'd. You too shall be	415	WAY WCRLD	II.1	187
Fainall:	yet too late--	416	WAY WCRLD	II.1	234
Marwood:	No, it is not yet too late--I have that Comfort. . .	416	WAY WCRLD	II.1	235
Mrs Fain:	to see him; but since I have despis'd him, he's too offensive.	416	WAY WCRLD	II.1	255
Mirabell:	to betray me by trusting him too far. If your Mother, in .	417	WAY WCRLD	II.1	292
Witwoud:	I confess I do blaze to Day, I am too bright.	419	WAY WCRLD	II.1	344
Mirabell:	I wou'd beg a little private Audience too--	421	WAY WCRLD	II.1	427
Foible:	had a Fling at your Ladyship too; and then I could not .	427	WAY WCRLD	III.1	90
Foible:	Poyson him? Poysoning's too good for him. Starve .	427	WAY WCRLD	III.1	106
Foible:	me too (says he), and Mrs. Millamant is to marry my .	428	WAY WCRLD	III.1	112
Foible:	too (says he) I'll handle you--	428	WAY WCRLD	III.1	116
Foible:	Your Ladyship has frown'd a little too rashly, indeed .	429	WAY WCRLD	III.1	144
Lady Wish:	I won't be too coy neither.--I won't give him despair .	429	WAY WCRLD	III.1	163
Mrs Fain:	come too late. That Devil Marwood saw you in the Park .	430	WAY WCRLD	III.1	185
Lady Wish:	expect my Nephew Sir Wilfull every moment too--Why . .	431	WAY WCRLD	III.1	257
Lady Wish:	Travels--I am against my Nephews marrying too	431	WAY WCRLD	III.1	263
Marwood:	found it: The secret is grown too big for the Pretence: .	433	WAY WCRLD	III.1	317
Witwoud:	contradict too. What, I know my Cue. Then we contradict .	435	WAY WCRLD	III.1	401
Witwoud:	That I confess I wonder at too.	436	WAY WCRLD	III.1	425
Marwood:	Hand in forgetfulness--I fancy he has forgot you too. . .	437	WAY WCRLD	III.1	476
Sir Wilful:	you wou'd have been in the fashion too, and have remember'd	441	WAY WCRLD	III.1	603
Marwood:	too Considerable to be parted with, to a Foe, to Mirabell. .	442	WAY WCRLD	III.1	642
Fainall:	plaid the Jade with me--Well, that's over too--I .	443	WAY WCRLD	III.1	678
Fainall:	too by this time--Jealous of her I cannot be, for I am certain;	443	WAY WCRLD	III.1	680
Fainall:	be--No, there's no end of that; No, no, that were too .	443	WAY WCRLD	III.1	682
Fainall:	The Wise too Jealous are, Fools too secure.	444	WAY WCRLD	III.1	725
Lady Wish:	be too sudden. I'll lie--aye, I'll lie down--I'll .	445	WAY WCRLD	IV.1	22
Lady Wish:	be too long alone with Sir Rowland.	445	WAY WCRLD	IV.1	40
Sir Wilful:	What a Vixon trick is this?--Nay, now a'has seen me too-- .	447	WAY WCRLD	IV.1	94
Millamant:	Ah l'etourdie! I hate the Town too.	448	WAY WCRLD	IV.1	126
Millamant:	looks as if he thought so too--Well, you ridiculous .	452	WAY WCRLD	IV.1	294
Lady Wish:	Too well, too well. I have seen too much.	460	WAY WCRLD	IV.1	599
Foible:	we were sworn to secresie too; Madam Marwood took a .	464	WAY WCRLD	V.1	97
Marwood:	consent to, without difficulty; she has already but too .	468	WAY WCRLD	V.1	259
Lady Wish:	come two more of my Egyptian Plagues too.	470	WAY WCRLD	V.1	309
Mirabell:	I am too Happy,--Ah Madam, there was a time--but let .	471	WAY WCRLD	V.1	369
Fainall:	That sham is too gross to pass on me,--tho 'tis . .	472	WAY WCRLD	V.1	419
Mirabell:	Ay Madam; but that is too late, my reward is intercepted. .	473	WAY WCRLD	V.1	457
Sir Wilful:	Travel too, I think they may be spar'd.	477	WAY WCRLD	V.1	587
Mirabell:	grant I love you not too well, that's all my fear. .	477	WAY WCRLD	V.1	598
Mirabell:	That marriage frauds too oft are paid in kind. . . .	478	WAY WCRLD	V.1	623

Took (12)
Capt Bluff:	by the Wars--Took no more notice, than as if Nol. Bluffe	. 53	OLD BATCH	II.1	204
Fondlewife:	go back of your word; you are not the Person I took you	. 94	OLD BATCH	IV.4	191
Bellmour:	discovering the Cheat to Sylvia. She took it at first, as	100	OLD BATCH	IV.1	150
Maskwell:	added to my hopes; I watch'd the Occasion, and took you,	. 136	DOUEL DLR	I.1	366
Lady Froth:	Jehu was a Hackney Coach-man, when my Lord took him. .	165	DOUEL DLR	III.1	548
Mrs Frail:	Well, what if I took twenty--I warrant if	246	FOR LCVE	II.1	422
Mrs Fore:	Valentine raves upon Angelica, and took me for	288	FOR LCVE	IV.1	468
Mirabell:	Town took notice that she was grown fat of a suddain; .	397	WAY WCRLD	I.1	74
Mirabell:	Insolence, that in Revenge I took her to pieces; sifted her	399	WAY WCRLD	I.1	164
Lady Wish:	begon, go go,--that I took from Washing of old Gause .	462	WAY WCRLD	V.1	4
Lady Wish:	dealt in when I took you into my house, plac'd you next .	462	WAY WCRLD	V.1	20
Foible:	we were sworn to secresie too; Madam Marwood took a .	464	WAY WCRLD	V.1	97

Tools (0)   see Edge-Tools

Toothless (1)
| Brisk: | Who, my Lady Toothless; O, she's a mortifying . . . . | 165 | DOUEL DLR | III.1 | 567 |

Top (3)
Bellmour:	like a Top.	46	OLD BATCH	I.1	354
Ben:	Sail o' your Head--Top and Top-gallant by the Mess. .	262	FOR LCVE	III.1	332
	They top their Learning on us, and their Parts. . . .	315	FOR LCVE	EPI.	10

Top-gallant (1)
| Ben: | Sail o' your Head--Top and Top-gallant by the Mess. . | 262 | FOR LCVE | III.1 | 332 |

Topicks (1)
| Valentine: | There's a couple of Topicks for you, no more like one . | 282 | FOR LCVE | IV.1 | 256 |

Topsie (2)
| Sir Paul: | but here's the strangest Revolution, all turn'd topsie . | 200 | DOUEL DLR | V.1 | 497 |
| Sir Paul: | All turn'd topsie turvey, as sure as a Gun. . . . . | 200 | DOUEL DLR | V.1 | 501 |

Topsy-turvy (1)
| Sir Wilful: | Antipodes--your Antipodes are a good rascally sort of topsy-turvy . . . . | 456 | WAY WORLD | IV.1 | 424 |

Torch (2)
| Valentine: | not a word. Hymen shall put his Torch into a dark Lanthorn, | 290 | FOR LCVE | IV.1 | 549 |
| Osmyn-Alph: | Delay'd: nor has our Hymenial Torch . . . . . . | 357 | M. BRIDE | III.1 | 321 |

Tore (2)
| Belinda: | tore two Pair of Kid-Gloves, with trying 'em on.-- . . . | 84 | OLD BATCH | IV.3 | 54 |
| Belinda: | tore two Pair of Kid-leather Gloves, with trying 'em on.-- | 84 | OLD BATCH | IV.3 V | 54 |

Torment (6)
Belinda:	But a Dun for Love is an eternal Torment that never . .	58	OLD BATCH	II.2	129
Silvia:	Lust. Oh that I could revenge the Torment he has caus'd-- .	61	OLD BATCH	III.1	32
Silvia:	Oh that I could revenge the Torment he has caus'd-- .	61	OLD BATCH	III.1 V	32
Fondlewife:	Man is in great torment, he lies as flat--Dear, you .	91	OLD BATCH	IV.4	95
Almeria:	Indeed; if that be so, if I'm thy Torment, ...	357	M. BRIDE	III.1	296
Zara:	O Torment, but to think! what then to bear?	362	M. BRIDE	IV.1	36

Tormented (1)
  Foresight: I should be thus tormented--This is the effect of the . 238 FOR LCVE II.1 128
Torments (3)
  Heartwell: Pox, how her Innocence torments and pleases me! . . . . 72 OLD EATCH III.2 55
  Heartwell: Death, how her Innocence torments and pleases me! . . . 72 OLD EATCH III.2 V 55
  Lady Touch: ... to a Hell of Torments,--but he's . . . . . 191 DOUEL DLR   V152
Torn (6)
  Osmyn-Alph: But 'tis torn off--why should that Word alone . . . 350 M. ERIDE III.1 22
  Osmyn-Alph: Be torn from his Petition? 'Twas to Heav'n. . . . . 350 M. ERIDE III.1 23
  Osmyn-Alph: Thus as the Name of Heav'n from this is torn, . . . 350 M. ERIDE III.1 25
  Osmyn-Alph: Think on to Morrow, when thou shalt be torn . . . 358 M. ERIDE III.1 343
  Manuel: Torn, mangl'd, flay'd, impal'd--all Pains and . . 368 M. ERIDE IV.1 295
  Almeria: And torn, rather than have reveal'd thy teing. . . 369 M. ERIDE IV.1 313
Torrent (3)
  Leonora: This Torrent of your Grief; for, much I fear . . 330 M. ERIDE I.1 166
  Zara: The blazing Torrent on the Tyrant's Head; . . . 380 M. ERIDE V.2 V170
  Almeria: The Source of Woe, and let the Torrent loose. . . 382 M. ERIDE V.2 244
Torture (6)
  Heartwell: O Torture! How he racks and tears me!-- . . . 104 OLD EATCH V.1 308
  Lady Touch: Oh! Torture! . . . . 192 DOUEI DLR V.1 161
  Lord Touch: Torture and shame attend their open Eirth: . . 203 DOUEL DLR V.1 593
  Zara: Cou'd one that lov'd, thus torture what she lov'd? . . 353 M. ERIDE III.1 161
  Zara: Cou'd one who lov'd, thus torture whom she lov'd? . . 353 M. ERIDE III.1 V161
  Osmyn-Alph: A Torture--yet, such is the bleeding Anguish . . . 356 M. ERIDE III.1 251
Tortures (1)
  Manuel: Tortures . . . . 368 M. ERIDE IV.1 296
Toss (2)
  Ben: For my part, I mean to toss a Can, and remember my . . 275 FOR LCVE III.1 808
  Ben: Hey tcss! what's the matter now? why ycu ben't . . 286 FOR LCVE IV.1 396
Toss'd (1)
    Now find us toss'd into a Tennis-Court. . . . . . 315 FOR LCVE EPI. 27
Tossing (1)
  Foible: With his Taunts and his Fleers, tossing up his Nose. Humh . 427 WAY WCRLD III.1 94
Tost (1)
  Millamant: than a decay'd Beauty, or a discarded Tost; . . . 433 WAY WCRLD III.1 324
Toste (2)
  Mirabell: mens prerogative, and presume tc drink healths, or toste . 451 WAY WCRLD IV.1 270
  Millamant: O horrid proviso's! filthy strong Waters! I toste . . 452 WAY WCRLD IV.1 278
Totally (1)
  Sir Joseph: which, like an innundation will I hope tctally immerge . 49 OLD EATCH II.1 57
Touch (7)
  Araminta: There's poison in every thing ycu touch.-- . . . . 88 OLD EATCH IV.3 181
  Lady Touch: incline you, no Cbligations touch? Have not my . . 136 DOUEL DLR I.1 346
  Sir Paul: Thy, Thy, come away Thy, touch him not, come . . . 145 DOUBL DLR II.1 245
  Sir Paul: touch a Man for the World--at least not above once a . . 162 DOUBL DLR III.1 433
  Mellefont: Pray Heaven my Aunt keep touch with her Assignation . . 183 DOUBL DLR IV.2 1
  Osmyn-Alph: Let me behold and touch her, and be sure . . . . 341 M. ERIDE II.2 67
  Sir Wilful: at your Antipodes. If I travel Aunt, I touch at your . 456 WAY WCRLD IV.1 423
Touch'd (2)
  Belinda: Only touch'd a gall'd-beast till he winch'd. . . . 109 OLD EATCH V.2 46
  Angelica: you, till I accidentally touch'd upon your tender Part: But 296 FCR LCVE IV.1 766
Touches (2)
  Sir Paul: man in the World; indeed that touches me near, very near. 161 DCUBL DLR III.1 405
  Scandal: already that touches us all. . . . . 266 FOR LCVE III.1 494
Touchwood (24)
  Brisk: Touchwood swears, he'll Disinherit you, and Sir Paul Plyant 128 DOUEL DLR I.1 54
    (Enter Lord Touchwood, Lcrd Froth, Sir Paul Plyant, . 131 DOUEL DLR I.1 170
    (Exit Lord Touchwood and Sir Paul.) . . . . . 133 DCUEL DLR I.1 221
    (Enter Lord Touchwood and Maskwell.) . . 135 DOUEL DLR I.1 298
  Sir Paul: heark'ee, I had it frcm his Aunt, my Sister Touchwood, . 146 DOUEL DLR II.1 276
    (Enter Lord Touchwood, and Lady Touchwood.) . . 150 DOUEL DLR III.1
    (Exit Lord Touchwood.) . 154 DOUEL DLR III.1 125
    (Exit Lady Touchwcod.) . 155 DOUEL DLR III.1 173
  Cynthia: Touchwood, as you boasted, and force her to give her . 169 DOUEL DLR IV.1 48
  Lady Ply: I know my Lady Touchwood has no kindness for . . 171 DOUEL DLR IV.1 163
    (Enter Lord Touchwood.) . 181 DOUEL DLR IV.1 531
    (Enter Lady Touchwood.) . 183 DOUEL DLR IV.2 7
    (Enter Lord Touchwood, Maskwell softly behind him.) . 185 DOUEL DLR IV.2 89
    (Draws, and runs at Mellefont, is held by Lady Touchwood.) 186 DOUEL DLR IV.2 108
    (Enter Lady Touchwood and Maskwell.) . 187 DOUEL DLR V.1
    (Enter Lord Touchwood.) . 188 DOUEL DLR V.1 15
    (Enter Lord Touchwood, Lady Touchwood.) . . . 190 DOUEL DLR V.1 121
    (Enter Lord Touchwood.) . 195 DOUEL DLR V.1 301
    (Enter Lord Touchwood.) . 197 DOUEL DLR V.1 357
    (Enter Lady Touchwood with a Dagger, Maskwell.) . 197 DOUEL DLR V.1 378
    (Cynthia, and Lord Touchwood, ccme forward.) . . 199 DOUEL DLR V.1 466
    (A great shriek from the corner of the Stage. Lady Touchwood 202 DOUEL DLR V.1 556
Touchwood's (5)
    (A Gallery in the Lord Touchwood's House, ... 127 DOUEL DLR I.1
  Mellefont: keep my Lady Touchwood's Head from Working: For . . 129 DOUEL DLR I.1 76
  Mellefont: acquainted with the Secret of my Aunt Touchwood's . . 129 DOUEL DLR I.1 85
    (Scene opening, shews Lady Touchwood's Chamber.) . 183 DOUEL DLR IV.2
  Careless: that I saw your Father in, my Lady Touchwood's Passion, . 196 DOUEL DLR V.1 336
Tough (1)
  Ben: when she's going, let her go. For no Matrimony is tough . 310 FOR LCVE V.1 492
Tout (0)   see Pass par tout
Toute (0)   see Pass par toute
Touz'd (1)
  Belinda: I am jolted to a Jelly.--Am I not horridly tcuz'd? . . . 83 OLD EATCH IV.3 5
Touzle (1)
  Sr Sampson: own Son, faith, he'll touzle her, and mouzle her: The . 265 FOR LCVE III.1 458
Toward (6)
  Bellmour: Why you must know, 'tis a piece of Work toward . . . 41 OLD EATCH I.1 156
  Belinda: come toward us. . . . . 85 OLD EATCH IV.3 76
  Brisk: was telling me, your Ladyship has made an Essay toward . 141 DOUBL DLR II.1 118
  Servant: There, Sir, his back's toward you. . . . . . . 260 FOB LCVE III.1 269

Toward   (continued)
Mrs Fore:	Hold, here's my Sister coming toward us.	273	FOR LOVE	III.1	747
Valentine:	Hypocrisie apart,--The Comedy draws toward an	294	FOR LOVE	IV.1	707

Towards (10)
Bellmour:	Husband: For 'tis an Argument of her great Zeal towards	39	OLD BATCH	I.1	64
Setter:	stood towards Madam Araminta. As, When you had seen	99	OLD BATCH	V.1	114
Lady Touch:	towards me. Nay, I can't think he meant any thing	153	DOUBL DLR	III.1	84
Mrs Fore:	for the Booby, it may go a great way towards his	249	FOR LOVE	II.1	502
Nurse:	Miss I say, God's my Life, here's fine doings towards--	253	FOR LOVE	III.1	9
Ben:	don't much stand towards Matrimonie. I love to roam	261	FOR LOVE	III.1	309
Sr Sampson:	a crooked Pin, or an old Horse-nail, with the head towards	265	FOR LOVE	III.1	467
Mrs Fore:	towards it. I have almost made a Bargain with Jeremy,	288	FOR LOVE	IV.1	465
Sir Wilful:	with you in London; we shou'd count it towards Afternoon	437	WAY WORLD	III.1	448
Marwood:	Well, how do you stand affected towards	443	WAY WORLD	III.1	674

Towing (1)
Maskwell:	I know it; I met Sir Paul towing away Cynthia:	148	DOUBL DLR	II.1	385

Town (34)
Vainlove:	of Town, to meet the Master of a Ship about the return of	39	OLD BATCH	I.1	80
Bellmour:	(Reads). Hum, Hum--Out of Town this Evening, and	39	OLD BATCH	I.1	82
Heartwell:	the hatred of all the great Families in Town.	45	OLD BATCH	I.1	305
Heartwell:	the Jest of the Town: Nay in two Days, I expect to be	63	OLD BATCH	III.1	79
Bellmour:	Laughter; the ill-natur'd Town will find the Jest just where	63	OLD BATCH	III.1	90
Sir Paul:	Town, and some money, a pretty tolerable personal Estate;	161	DOUBL DLR	III.1	409
Lady Froth:	I may suppose the Dairy in Town, as well as in the Country.	163	DOUBL DLR	III.1	504
Scandal:	any body that did not stink to all the Town.	226	FOR LOVE	I.1	402
Nurse:	Town,--Marry, pray Heav'n they ha' given her any	235	FOR LOVE	II.1	21
Sr Sampson:	be in Town to night--I have order'd my Lawyer to	240	FOR LOVE	II.1	193
Sr Sampson:	Your Brother will be in Town to Night, or to morrow	246	FOR LOVE	II.1	402
Tattle:	afterwards, he was talk'd of in Town--And a Lady of	258	FOR LOVE	III.1	174
Sr Sampson:	What, is he gone out of Town, run away, ha!	279	FOR LOVE	IV.1	122
Sr Sampson:	of these young idle Rogues about the Town. Odd, there's	299	FOR LOVE	V.1	53
	Poets are Bubbles, by the Town drawn in,	393	WAY WORLD	PRO.	11
	For so Reform'd a Town, who dares Correct?	393	WAY WORLD	PRO.	32
Mirabell:	Town took notice that she was grown fat of a suddain:	397	WAY WORLD	I.1	74
Mirabell:	What, is the Chief of that noble Family in Town,	400	WAY WORLD	I.1	187
Fainall:	He comes to Town in order to Equip himself for	400	WAY WORLD	I.1	197
Witwoud:	Pleasure, and the Town, a Question at once so Foreign and	402	WAY WORLD	I.1	257
Witwoud:	No Man in Town lives well with a Wife but	402	WAY WORLD	I.1	264
Petulant:	Uncle, have you not, lately come to Town, and lodges by	407	WAY WORLD	I.1	435
Witwoud:	Town,--and is between him and the best part of his Estate;	408	WAY WORLD	I.1	482
Mirabell:	Reputation with the Town, enough to make that Woman	417	WAY WORLD	II.1	273
Marwood:	Hood and Scarf. And indeed 'tis time, for the Town has	433	WAY WORLD	III.1	316
Millamant:	the Town has found it. (Exit Mincing.) What has it found?	433	WAY WORLD	III.1	327
Witwoud:	you, 'tis not modish to know Relations in Town. You	439	WAY WORLD	III.1	533
Sir Wilful:	matter in Town, to learn somewhat of your Lingo first,	440	WAY WORLD	III.1	582
Marwood:	Here is an Academy in Town for that use.	440	WAY WORLD	III.1	586
Sir Wilful:	Town, as Plays and the like that must be confess'd indeed.	448	WAY WORLD	IV.1	125
Millamant:	Ah l'etourdie! I hate the Town too.	448	WAY WORLD	IV.1	126
Sir Wilful:	some can't relish the Town, and others can't away with	448	WAY WORLD	IV.1	129
Fainall:	and the Current of this Lewd Town can agree.	473	WAY WORLD	V.1	444
	And how their Number's swell'd the Town well knows:	479	WAY WORLD	EPI.	10

Town-talk (1)
Lady Touch:	me if you take such publick notice of it, it will be a				
	Town-talk:	153	DOUBL DLR	III.1	104

Towr (0)   see Fruz-Towr

Tows (1)
Mrs Fain:	I see but one poor empty Sculler; and he tows	418	WAY WORLD	II.1	326

Toy (7)
Heartwell:	to? A Womans Toy; at these years! Death, a bearded	72	OLD BATCH	III.2	46
	Would give the World she could her Toy recover:	113	OLD BATCH	EPI.	4
Lady Touch:	toy away an hour in mirth.	155	DOUBL DLR	III.1	171
Millamant:	Press me no more for that slight Toy.	447	WAY WORLD	IV.1	99
Sir Wilful:	S'heart you'll have time enough to toy after	477	WAY WORLD	V.1	V599
Sir Wilful:	S'heart you'll have him time enough to toy after	477	WAY WORLD	V.1	599
Sir Wilful:	you're married; or if you will toy now; Let us have a	477	WAY WORLD	V.1	600

Toying (1)
Maskwell:	I know what she means by toying away an hour well	155	DOUBL DLR	III.1	174

Toys (0)   see Other-guess-toys

Trace (1)
	And tho' no perfect likeness they can Trace;	479	WAY WORLD	EPI.	19

Track (1)
Lord Touch:	upon Villany! Heavens, what a long track of dark deceit	199	DOUBL DLR	V.1	469

Tractable (2)
Bellmour:	tractable.	59	OLD BATCH	II.2	174
Mirabell:	prove a tractable and complying Husband.	452	WAY WORLD	IV.1	277

Trade (8)
Fondlewife:	me, than she has reason to be; and in the way of Trade,	77	OLD BATCH	IV.1	60
Valentine:	I'll take some of their Trade out of their Hands.	217	FOR LOVE	I.1	60
Jeremy:	Trade, if he had set up in the City--For my part, I never	218	FOR LOVE	I.1	91
Valentine:	am not violently bent upon the Trade.--	220	FOR LOVE	I.1	153
Zara:	Are practis'd in the Trade of Death; and shall	365	M. BRIDE	IV.1	153
Fainall:	By no means, 'tis better as 'tis; 'tis better to Trade	400	WAY WORLD	I.1	207
Lady Wish:	--do, drive a Trade, do, with your three penny-worth	462	WAY WORLD	V.1	11
Lady Wish:	go, drive a trade,--these were your Commodities	462	WAY WORLD	V.1	18

Trades (1)
Valentine:	drive distinct Trades, and Care and Pleasure separately	289	FOR LOVE	IV.1	506

Tragedy (1)
	The Tragedy thus done, I am, you know,	385	M. BRIDE	EPI.	1

Tragical (1)
Mellefont:	as far as she betrays her self. No tragical design upon my	156	DOUBL DLR	III.1	210

Train (6)
Valentine:	Affections, Appetites, Senses, and the huge Train of	244	FOR LOVE	II.1	341
Alonzo:	And with a Train, as if she still were Wife	335	M. BRIDE	I.1	360
	Mutes and Eunuchs in a Train.)	335	M. BRIDE	I.1	384
Zara:	I might be pleas'd when I behold this Train	336	M. BRIDE	I.1	398
Zara:	I have remaining in my Train, some Mutes,	365	M. BRIDE	IV.1	150

Train   (continued)
| Millamant: | (Repeating.) Thyrsis a Youth of the Inspir'd train-- | . 446 | WAY WORLD | IV.1 | 63 |

Traiterous (1)
| Sir Paul: | to my own Cuckoldom; why this is the very traiterous | . 178 | DOUEL DLR | IV.1 | 412 |

Traitor (3)   see Traytor, Traytour
Lady Touch:	(within). No, Monster! Hellish Traitor! no.	. 197	DOUEL DLR	V.1	372
Lady Touch:	(within). No, Monster! Traitor! no.	. 197	DOUEL DLR	V.1	V372
Manuel:	Hark thee, Villain, Traitor--answer me Slave.	. 374	M. ERIDE	V.1	67

Traitress (1)   see Traytress
| Manuel: | Hear me; then, if thou canst, reply, know Traitress, | . 368 | M. EFIDE | IV.1 | 300 |

Tramontanae (1)
| Belinda: | Out-landish Creatures! Such Tramontanae, and Foreigners | . 84 | OLD EATCH | IV.3 | 31 |

Trances (1)
| Lady Wish: | Trances, and the Tremblings, the Ardors and the Ecstacies, | 458 | WAY WORLD | IV.1 | 514 |

Tranquility (3)
Sir Paul:	be govern'd at all times. When I am in Tranquility, my	. 144	DOUEL DLR	II.1	221
Almeria:	Looking Tranquility. It strikes an Awe	. 339	M. EBIDE	II.1	63
Mirabell:	were a Case of more steady Contemplation; a very tranquility	423	WAY WCBLD	II.1	492

Transcendantly (1)
| Mrs Fain: | Most transcendantly; ay, tho' I say it, | . 411 | WAY WOBLD | II.1 | 37 |

Transcendent (2)
| Manuel: | As by transcendent Beauty to attract | . 336 | M. EFIDE | I.1 | 421 |
| Mirabell: | with all acknowledgments for your transcendent goodness. | . 472 | WAY WCBLD | V.1 | 407 |

Transferr'd (1)
| Marwood: | be transferr'd to the hands, nay into the Throats and | . 468 | WAY WCBLD | V.1 | 232 |

Transferring (1)
| Scandal: | this Marriage and making over this Estate, this transferring | 268 | FCB LCVE | III.1 | 544 |

Transform (1)
| Mirabell: | --And transform into Sir Rowland. | . 424 | WAY WCBLD | II.1 | 553 |

Transformation (1)
| Waitwell: | Familiarity with my former self; and fall from my Transformation | . 424 | WAY WCBLD | II.1 | 558 |

Transgress (1)
| Lady Wish: | my Flesh, and as I may say, another Me, and yet transgress | 465 | WAY WORLD | V.1 | 141 |

Transgression (1)
| Sir Joseph: | my transgression of ingratitude and omission; having my | . 49 | OLD BATCH | II.1 | 55 |

Transient (1)
| Almeria: | It was thy Fear; or else some transient Wind | . 339 | M. EBIDE | II.1 | 54 |

Translated (1)
| Foresight: | translated by a Reverend Buckinghamshire Bard. | . 236 | FOR LCVE | II.1 | 50 |

Transmigraticn (1)
| | I vow, I don't much like this Transmigration, | . 315 | FCR LCVE | EPI. | 32 |

Transmitted (1)
| Sir Paul: | thy Father's Leer.--Let it be transmitted to the young | . 173 | DOUEL DLR | IV.1 | 237 |

Transplanted (2)
| Careless: | you have transplanted; and should it take Root in my | . 131 | DOUEL DLR | I.1 | 165 |
| | Unless transplanted to more kindly Earth. | . 213 | FOR LCVE | PRO. | 6 |

Transport (6)
Angelica:	Transport in your Soul; which, it seems, you only counterfeited,	. 294	FCB LCVE	IV.1	723
Valentine:	Joy and Transport.	. 313	FCR LCVE	V.1	603
Manuel:	And shook his Chains in Transport, and rude Harmony.	. 333	M. EBIDE	I.1	317
Osmyn-Alph:	How speak to thee the Words of Joy and Transport?	. 355	M. EBIDE	III.1	238
Osmyn-Alph:	And thou perforce must yield, and aid his Transport,	. 358	M. EBIDE	III.1	360
Waitwell:	My Impatience Madam, is the effect of my transport;	. 457	WAY WCBLD	IV.1	490

Transported (8)
Belinda:	transported you.	. 54	OLD BATCH	II.2	7
Lady Touch:	transported; compose your self: It is not of Concern, to	. 152	DOUEL DLR	III.1	66
Lady Ply:	transported, I did not see it.--Well, to shew you how	. 170	DOUBL DLR	IV.1	109
Careless:	so transported I cannot speak--This Note will inform	. 171	DOUEL DLR	IV.1	129
Sir Paul:	Gads bud, I am transported! give me leave to kiss	. 172	DOUEL DLR	IV.1	192
Maskwell:	consenting to my Lord; nay, transported with the Blessing	. 198	DOUEL DLR	V.1	424
Almeria:	Be mad--I cannot be transported thus.	. 342	M. EBIDE	II.2	108
Foible:	have cnly promis'd. But a Man so enamour'd--So transported!	427	WAY WCBLD	III.1	75

Transports (3)
Mellefont:	her in all the Transports of a slighted and revengful Woman:	130	DOUEL DLR	I.1	104
Maskwell:	Transports of a Blessing so unexpected, so unhop'd for, so	189	DOUEL DLR	V.1	81
Garcia:	The transports of your meeting.	. 338	M. EBIDE	II.1	V 15

Trap (2)
| Bellmour: | was to come by your direction.--But I laid a trap | . 94 | OLD EATCH | IV.4 | 208 |
| Scandal: | 20000 [Pounds] in Money. A hah! Old Trap. | . 223 | FOB LCVE | I.1 | 270 |

Trapland (12)
Jeremy:	O Sir, there's Trapland the Scrivener, with two	. 221	FOR LOVE	I.1	202
Valentine:	Trapland come in.	. 222	FOR LOVE	I.1	223
	(Enter Trapland and Jeremy.)	. 222	FOR LOVE	I.1	227
Valentine:	O Mr. Trapland! my old Friend! Welcome. Jeremy, a	. 222	FOR LOVE	I.1	228
Valentine:	my Service to you,--fill, fill, to honest Mr. Trapland,	. 222	FCB LCVE	I.1	243
Scandal:	What, I know Trapland has been a Whoremaster,	. 223	FOR LCVE	I.1	264
Valentine:	Bo-peep under her Petticoats, ah! Mr. Trapland?	. 223	FOR LOVE	I.1	288
Snap:	By your leave, Gentlemen,--Mr. Trapland, if we	. 224	FOR LOVE	I.1	295
Valentine:	Bid him come in: Mr. Trapland, send away your	. 224	FOR LOVE	I.1	304
Valentine:	I agree to 'em, take Mr. Trapland with you, and let him	. 224	FOR LOVE	I.1	319
Valentine:	draw the Writing--Mr. Trapland, you know this Man,	. 224	FOR LCVE	I.1	320
	(Exeunt Steward, Trapland and Jeremy.)	. 225	FOR LCVE	I.1	327

Trapland's (1)
| Valentine: | doing good.--Scandal, Drink to me, my Friend Trapland's | . 223 | FOR LCVE | I.1 | 260 |

Traps (1)
| Heartwell: | and I think I have baited too many of those Traps, to be | . 45 | OLD BATCH | I.1 | 296 |

Trapt (1)
| Silvia: | Ha, ha, ha, an cld Fox trapt-- | . 74 | OLD BATCH | III.2 | 143 |

Trash (1)
| Sr Sampson: | Stars, and Sun and Almanacks, and Trash, should be | . 283 | FOR LCVE | IV.1 | 288 |

Travel (11)
Fainall:	Travel.	. 400	WAY WCBLD	I.1	198
Mirabell:	For Travel! Why the Man that I mean is above	. 400	WAY WOBLD	I.1	199
Lady Wish:	Foible--He means to Travel for Improvement.	. 431	WAY WORLD	III.1	258

Travel   (continued)
```
Marwood:        a very fit Match. He may Travel afterwards. 'Tis a Thing  . 432  WAY WORLD  III.1   267
Marwood:        You intend to Travel, Sir, as I'm inform'd.  . . . . .  440  WAY WORLD  III.1   566
Sir Wilful:     at your Antipodes. If I travel Aunt, I touch at your   . . 456  WAY WORLD  IV.1    423
Lady Wish:      with him--Travel quoth a; Ay travel, travel, get thee gone, . 456  WAY WORLD  IV.1    438
Millamant:      Sir Wilfull, you and he are to Travel together, are    . . 470  WAY WORLD  V.1     343
Sir Wilful:     Travel too, I think they may be spar'd.  . . . . . .  477  WAY WORLD  V.1     587
```
Travel'd (1)
```
Sr Sampson:     you, I have travel'd old Firco, and know the Globe. I have  241  FOR LOVE   II.1    207
```
Travell'd (2)
```
Foresight:      But I tell you, I have travell'd, and travell'd in the  . 241  FOR LOVE   II.1    210
```
Traveller (4)
```
Zara:           Hast stung the Traveller; and, after, hear'st   . . . .  375  M. BRIDE   V.1     107
Sir Wilful:     Traveller.  . . . . . . . . . . . . . . . .  471  WAY WORLD  V.1     365
Sir Wilful:     How, fellow Traveller!--You shall go by your  . . . .  471  WAY WORLD  V.1     376
Sir Wilful:     dolefull Sigh more from my fellow Traveller and 'tis   . 472  WAY WORLD  V.1     398
```
Travellers (2)
          see Fellow-Travellers
```
Foresight:      I know when Travellers lie or speak Truth, when  . . .  241  FOR LOVE   II.1    224
Sir Wilful:     Travellers.--We are to be Pylades and Crestes, he and I--  471  WAY WORLD  V.1     347
```
Travelling (2)
```
Belinda:        kept open, for the Entertainment of travelling Flies.  . .  84  OLD BATCH  IV.3     48
Marwood:        Marrying than Travelling at his Years. I hear he is turn'd  431  WAY WORLD  III.1   260
```
Travells (1)
```
Mirabell:       to prosecute his Travells.  . . . . . . . . . . .  477  WAY WORLD  V.1     581
```
Travels (1)
```
Lady Wish:      Travels--I am against my Nephews marrying too   . . . .  431  WAY WORLD  III.1   263
```
Traverse (1)
```
Lady Wish:      Traverse Rag, in a shop no bigger than a Bird-cage,--  . .  462  WAY WORLD  V.1       7
```
Traytor (13)
```
Lucy:           Traytor to thy lawful Princess.  . . . . . . . . .  65  OLD BATCH  III.1   178
Fondlewife:     Oh Traytor! I'm astonished. Oh bloody-minded  . . . . .  90  OLD BATCH  IV.4     59
Fondlewife:     Traytor!  . . . . . . . . . . . . . . . . . .  90  OLD BATCH  IV.4     60
Sir Joseph:     Hey-day! Traytor yourself.--By the Lord-Harry,   . . . .  90  OLD BATCH  IV.4     61
Setter:         --Bluffe turns errant Traytor; bribes me to make a   . .  105  OLD BATCH  V.1     343
Maskwell:       I would not be a Traytor to my self: I don't pretend to   . 136  DOUBL DLR  I.1     342
Lady Touch:     burn the vile Traytor.  . . . . . . . . . . . .  191  DOUBL DLR  V.1     152
Scandal:        Here's a Dog now, a Traytor in his Wine, Sirrah  . . . .  224  FOR LOVE   I.1     309
Zara:           Yes, Traytor, Zara; lost, abandon'd Zara,  . . . . . .  346  M. BRIDE   II.2    248
Manuel:         Traytor.  . . . . . . . . . . . . . . . . . .  374  M. BRIDE   V.1      56
Garcia:         The Traytor Perez, and the Captive Moor,  . . . . . .  377  M. BRIDE   V.2      38
Lady Wish:      Face, with mentioning that Traytor. She durst not have the  426  WAY WORLD  III.1    50
Lady Wish:      Traytor,--I fear I cannot fortifie my self to support his  470  WAY WORLD  V.1     335
```
Traytors (2)
```
Manuel:         With reeking Gore, from Traytors on the Rack:   . . . .  367  M. BRIDE   IV.1    253
Manuel:         Rank Traytors; thou art with the rest combin'd;  . . . .  373  M. BRIDE   V.1      45
```
Traytour (2)
```
Zara:           Traytour, Monster, cold and perfidious Slave;  . . . .  348  M. BRIDE   II.2    340
Zara:           Alphonso, Heli, and the Traytour Osmyn.  . . . . . .  364  M. BRIDE   IV.1    124
```
Traytress (1)
```
Lady Wish:      traytress, that I rais'd from nothing--begon, begon,  . .  462  WAY WORLD  V.1       3
```
Treach'rous (1)
```
Zara:           O this accurs'd, this base, this treach'rous King!  . . .  380  M. BRIDE   V.2 V168
```
Treach'ry (1)
```
Lord Touch:     Like Vipers in the Womb, base Treach'ry lies,  . . . .  203  DOUBL DLR  V.1     594
```
Treacherous (8)
```
Heartwell:      cannot distrust me of any skill in the treacherous Mystery--  72  OLD BATCH  III.2    58
Sir Joseph:     have but a treacherous Memory.  . . . . . . . . .  85  OLD BATCH  IV.3     74
Lady Ply:       Inhuman and Treacherous.  . . . . . . . . . . .  145  DOUBL DLR  IV.1    242
Lady Ply:       Has he been Treacherous, or did you give his insolence a   . 179  DOUBL DLR  IV.1    439
Marwood:        self and the whole treacherous World.  . . . . . . .  416  WAY WORLD  II.1    238
Lady Wish:      you treacherous Trull, this was your Merchandize you   . .  462  WAY WORLD  V.1      19
Lady Wish:      you treacherous Trull, this was the Merchandize you   . .  462  WAY WORLD  V.1 V  19
Mrs Fain:       falsehood--Go you and your treacherous--I will  . . . .  475  WAY WORLD  V.1     500
```
Treacherously (1)
```
Scandal:        by the Hounds, you will be treacherously shot by the  . .  220  FOR LOVE   I.1     143
```
Treachery (19)
```
Bellmour:       you; tho' I by treachery had stoll'n the Bliss--  . . .  38  OLD BATCH  I.1      51
Araminta:       my Honour.--But tho' thou hadst all the Treachery  . . .  87  OLD BATCH  IV.3    167
Setter:         the Knight of the Treachery; who has agreed, seemingly  . .  106  OLD BATCH  V.1     348
Lady Touch:     Treachery and Ingratitude! Is there Vice more   . . . .  135  DOUBL DLR  I.1     324
Lady Touch:     Treachery and Ingratitude! Is there a Vice more   . . . .  135  DOUBL DLR  I.1 V324
Maskwell:       Treachery or Deceit, shall be imputed to me as a Merit  . .  150  DOUBL DLR  II.1    442
Maskwell:       --Treachery, what Treachery? Love cancels all the  . . .  150  DOUBL DLR  II.1    443
Mellefont:      And may all Treachery be thus discovered.  . . . . .  184  DOUBL DLR  IV.2     35
Lady Touch:     wild with this surprize of Treachery: Hell and Fire, it is  191  DOUBL DLR  V.1     144
Lady Touch:     wild with this surprize of Treachery: it is  . . . . .  191  DOUBL DLR  V.1 V144
Careless:       By Heaven there's Treachery--the Confusion  . . . . .  196  DOUBL DLR  V.1     335
Cynthia:        Mine were on Treachery concerning you, and may   . . . .  197  DOUBL DLR  V.1     367
Lord Touch:     Treachery concerning me! pray be plain   . . . . . .  197  DOUBL DLR  V.1     369
Lord Touch:     of unheard of Treachery. My Wife! Damnation! my  . . .  200  DOUBL DLR  V.1     472
Manuel:         By Heav'n I'll meet, and counterwork this Treachery.   . .  374  M. BRIDE   V.1      66
Garcia:         All's lost, all ruin'd by Surprize and Treachery.  . . .  376  M. BRIDE   V.2      18
Foible:         O Treachery! But are you sure Sir Rowland, it is his  . .  460  WAY WORLD  IV.1    604
Waitwell:       in spight of treachery; Ay and get an Heir that shall defeat  461  WAY WORLD  IV.1    643
```
Tread (6)
```
Laetitia:       down upon our bed.--You'll disturb him; I can tread   . .  91  OLD BATCH  IV.4     79
Lady Touch:     you to Destruction, I'll tear your Eyes out, and tread   . .  192  DOUBL DLR  V.1     183
Lord Touch:     Circling Joys, tread round each happy Year of your long   . 203  DOUBL DLR  V.1     589
Zara:           The Steps on which we tread, to rise and reach   . . . .  347  M. BRIDE   II.2    317
Almeria:        Tread on me, spurn me, am I the bosom Snake   . . . .  357  M. BRIDE   III.1   298
Almeria:        Tread on me: What, am I the bosom Snake   . . . . .  357  M. BRIDE   III.1 V298
```
Treading (1)
```
Capt Bluff:     (Almost whispering, and treading softly after him.)   . .  101  OLD BATCH  V.1     190
```
Treads (2)
```
Sharper:        Thus Grief still treads upon the Heels of Pleasure:   . .  105  OLD BATCH  V.1     327
Manuel:         How like thy self when Passion treads him down?   . . . .  373  M. BRIDE   V.1      41
```

Trickt   (continued)
		PAGE	TITLE	ACT.SC	LINE
Tattle:	that Villain Jeremy, by the help of Disguises, trickt us into	309	FOR LCVE	V.1	451

Trifle (5)
Sharper:	My loss, I esteem as a trifle repay'd with interest,	49	OLD BATCH	II.1	76
Mellefont:	Ha!--Pho, you trifle.	156	DOUEL DLR	III.1	231
Osmyn-Alph:	Or trifle time in thinking.	342	M. BRIDE	II.2	99
Fainall:	Trifle.	403	WAY WORLD	I.1	317
Millamant:	--That foolish trifle of a heart--Sir Wilfull!	447	WAY WORLD	IV.1	101

Trifler (1)
Scandal:	A Trifler--but a Lover of Art--And the	267	FOR LCVE	III.1	534

Trifles (1)
Millamant:	Trifles,--As liberty to pay and receive visits	450	WAY WORLD	IV.1	212

Trifling (3)
Lady Touch:	such a trifling design; for her first Ccnversing with	138	DOUBL DLR	I.1	415
Lord Touch:	more trifling--I charge you tell me--by all our	152	DOUEL DLR	III.1	62
	Suffer'd at first some trifling Stakes to win:	393	WAY WORLD	PRO.	12

Trigons (2)
Foresight:	Sextiles, Quadrates, Trines and Cppositions, Fiery Trigons	241	FOR LCVE	II.1	213
Foresight:	and Aquatical Trigons. Know whether Life shall be long	241	FOR LCVE	II.1	214

Trim (1)
Valentine:	and Atlas' Shoulders. Let Taliacotius trim the Calves of	289	FOR LCVE	IV.1	524

Trines (2)
Foresight:	Sextiles, Quadrates, Trines and Oppositions, Fiery Trigons	241	FOR LCVE	II.1	213
Sr Sampson:	Son be mad--Where's your Oppositions, your Trines, and	283	FOR LCVE	IV.1	282

Trip (2)
Lady Ply:	made one Trip, not one faux pas; O consider it, what would	147	DOUEL DLR	II.1	319
Witwoud:	--Then trip to his Lcdging, clap cn a Hoed and Scarf,	405	WAY WORLD	I.1	372

Tripping (1)
Careless:	There's Saygrace tripping by with a bundle under his	196	DOUEL DLR	V.1	351

Tripple (1)
Zara:	What I know more, is, That a tripple League	364	M. BRIDE	IV.1	122

Triumph (7)
Laetitia:	Tyrannize--Go on cruel Man, do, Triumph over my	77	OLD BATCH	IV.1	91
Leonora:	The distant Shouts, proclaim your Fathers Triumph;	330	M. BRIDE	I.1	163
Manuel:	This Day we triumph; but to morrow's Sun	334	M. BRIDE	I.1	342
Manuel:	In Triumph led; your Beauty's Slave.	335	M. BRIDE	I.1	392
Manuel:	In pleasing Triumph led; your Beauty's Slave.	335	M. BRIDE	I.1	V392
Perez:	Your Crder was, she should not wait your Triumph;	336	M. BRIDE	I.1	406
Manuel:	Conquest and Triumph, now, are mine no more;	337	M. BRIDE	I.1	452

Triumphant (1)
Manuel:	Their Monarch enter not Triumphant, but	335	M. BRIDE	I.1	391

Triumphs (1)
see Tryumphs
Scandal:	manifest the cruel Triumphs of her Beauty; the barbarity	276	FOR LOVE	IV.1	25

Trivial (2)
Sharper:	trivial a Sum, will wholly acquit you and doubly engage	50	OLD BATCH	II.1	90
Sir Joseph:	(aside). What a dickens do's he mean by a trivial	50	OLD BATCH	II.1	92

Trod (2)
Lady Ply:	road of Virtue, in which I have trod thus long, and never	147	DOUEL DLR	II.1	318
Osmyn-Alph:	We both have backward trod the paths of Fate,	342	M. BRIDE	II.2	92

Troops (5)
Almeria:	Led on his conqu'ring Troops, high as the Gates	329	M. BRIDE	I.1	112
Heli:	Among the Troops who thought to share the Plunder,	351	M. BRIDE	III.1	65
Osmyn-Alph:	And bear amidst the Foe, with conqu'ring Troops.	351	M. BRIDE	III.1	82
Selim:	Is since arrived, of more revolted Troops.	361	M. BRIDE	IV.1	7
Manuel:	Ride forth, and view the Order cf our Trcops.	364	M. BRIDE	IV.1	V134

Trophies (1)
Almeria:	The gilded Trophies of exterior Honcurs.	332	M. BRIDE	I.1	247

Troth (19)
Vainlove:	That's pleasant, by my troth from thee, who hast	38	OLD BATCH	I.1	45
Bellmour:	By my troth, and so 'tis.--(aside) I have been a	93	OLD BATCH	IV.4	170
	But by my Troth I cannot avoid thinking,	125	DOUEL DLB	PRO.	23
Sir Paul:	That's a jest with all my heart, faith and troth,--	192	DOUEL DLR	V.1	171
Valentine:	Faith and Troth, I am heartily glad to see you--	222	FCR LCVE	I.1	242
Foresight:	Ha, Hcw? Faith and troth I'm glad of it, and so I	236	FOR LCVE	II.1	29
Foresight:	have, that may be good Luck in troth, in troth it may,	236	FOR LCVE	II.1	30
Foresight:	time,--But in troth I am pleas'd at my Stocking. Very	236	FOR LCVE	II.1	37
Foresight:	Faith and Troth you shall--Does my Wife complain?	239	FOR LCVE	II.1	149
Foresight:	faith and troth, here 'tis, if it will but hold--I wish	240	FCR LCVE	II.1	187
Sr Sampson:	Faith and Trcth you're a wise Wcman, and I'm	260	FOR LCVE	III.1	257
Sr Sampson:	Women think a Man old too soon, faith and troth you do	298	FOR LCVE	V.1	25
Sr Sampson:	Rogues: Odd, wou'd she wou'd; faith and troth she's	298	FOR LCVE	V.1	50
Sr Sampson:	faith and troth you speak very discreetly; For I hate both a	299	FOR LCVE	V.1	68
Sr Sampson:	and Troth I like you the better--But, I warrant you,	300	FOR LCVE	V.1	125
Sr Sampson:	Odd, you're devilish Handsom; Faith and Troth, you're	301	FOR LCVE	V.1	141
Sr Sampson:	troth you shall. Cdd we'll have the Musick of the Spheres	307	FOR LCVE	V.1	385
Witwoud:	--Faith and Troth a pretty deal cf an cdd sort of a small	403	WAY WCRLD	I.1	290

Troubl'd (1)
Witwoud:	Bawd troubl'd with Wind. Ncw you may know what the	404	WAY WORLD	I.1	354

Trouble (10)
Heartwell:	you save the Devil the trouble of leading you into it: Nor	43	OLD BATCH	I.1	241
Lucy:	Trouble not your Head. Let me alcne--I will	62	OLD BATCH	III.1	44
Bellmour:	But give your selves the trouble to walk to that	107	OLD BATCH	V.1	401
Maskwell:	Come, trouble not your head, I'll joyn you tcgether e're	148	DOUEL DLR	II.1	386
Maskwell:	No matter, Sir, don't trouble your head, all's in	190	DOUEL DLR	V.1	106
Valentine:	and bid her trouble me no more; a thoughtless two handed	221	FOR LCVE	I.1	210
Mrs Frail:	would be a trouble to you to keep.	232	FOR LCVE	I.1	591
Miss Prue:	trouble me no more, you ugly thing.	264	FOR LCVE	III.1	401
Petulant:	and so have but cne Trouble with you both.--	409	WAY WCRLD	I.1	518
Mirabell:	For that Madam, give your self nc trouble--let	477	WAY WCRLD	V.1	577

Troubled (4)
Cynthia:	(aside). At least I won't own it, to be troubled with your	139	DOUEL DLR	II.1	36
Lord Touch:	No, I don't say sc--I confess I am troubled to	151	DOUEL DLR	III.1	29
Jeremy:	troubled the Fountain of his Understanding; it is a very	302	FOB LOVE	V.1	174
Witwoud:	pox cn him, I shall be troubled with him too; what shall I	409	WAY WCRLD	I.1	515

Troubles (1)
| Leonora: | But fearful to renew your Troubles past, | . . . . . . | 328 | M. BRIDE | I.1 107 |

Troublesom (2)
| Araminta: | to be troublesom. . . . . | . | 85 | OLD BATCH | IV.3 93 |
| Sharper: | Pshaw: Thou'rt so troublesom and inquisitive.-- | . . . | 104 | OLD BATCH | V.1 291 |

Troublesome (6)
Belinda:	troublesome of Duns--A Dun for Mony will be	. . . .	58	OLD BATCH	II.2 127
Belinda:	troublesome Animal than a Parrot.	.	60	OLD BATCH	II.2 214
Heartwell:	informed) very troublesome to everybody else. If this be	.	73	OLD BATCH	III.2 83
Belinda:	least, Thou art so troublesome a Lover, there's Hopes				
	thou'lt	.	106	OLD BATCH	V.1 366
Mirabell:	easie as to know when a Visit began to be troublesome;	.	396	WAY WORLD	I.1 39
Sir Wilful:	troublesome, I wou'd have sought a walk with you.	. .	448	WAY WORLD	IV.1 117

Troubling (1)
| Lucy: | That may be, without troubling your self to go again | . . | 97 | OLD BATCH | V.1 14 |

Trowel (1)
| Brisk: | Why she lays it on with a Trowel--Then she has a | . . . | 166 | DOUBL DLR | III.1 585 |

Troy (1)
| Sir Joseph: | Oh here a' comes--Ah my Hector of Troy, welcome | . . . . | 51 | OLD BATCH | II.1 139 |

Truce (2)
| Millamant: | Dear Mr. Witwoud, truce with your Similitudes: | . . . . | 419 | WAY WORLD | II.1 337 |
| Witwoud: | Madam, truce with your Similitudes--No, | . . . . . | 419 | WAY WORLD | II.1 349 |

True (77)
Bellmour:	Never--Her Affections, 'tis true by Heaven,	. . . .	38	OLD BATCH	I.1 47
Bellmour:	Nature, Night, had hid, confess'd her Soul was true to	.	38	OLD BATCH	I.1 50
Vainlove:	So was true as Turtle--in imagination Ned, ha?	. .	38	OLD BATCH	I.1 52
Vainlove:	Zeal passes for true Devotion. I doubt it will be damn'd	.	39	OLD BATCH	I.1 67
Bellmour:	twelve thousand Pound Tom--'Tis true she is excessively	.	41	OLD BATCH	I.1 166
Heartwell:	so much Mercury in my Limbs; 'tis true indeed, I don't	.	43	OLD BATCH	I.1 231
Heartwell:	'tis true you are so eager in pursuit of the temptation,				
	that	.	43	OLD BATCH	I.1 240
Sir Joseph:	by the Lord Harry he says true; Fighting, is Meat, Drink	.	52	OLD BATCH	II.1 167
Capt Bluff:	Yet by the Lord Harry 'tis true Mr. Sharper, for I	. .	53	OLD BATCH	II.1 207
Vainlove:	That's true; but I would--	. .	63	OLD BATCH	III.1 112
Lucy:	. . . but he is too true a Valet de chambre	. .	64	OLD BATCH	III.1 146
Sharper:	There is in true Beauty, as in Courage, somewhat,	. .	86	OLD BATCH	IV.3 126
Vainlove:	('tis true) where they find most Goodness to forgive.--	.	87	OLD BATCH	IV.3 138
Bellmour:	True. But to convince thee who I am, thou know'st	.	97	OLD BATCH	V.1 34
Setter:	Person of Worth; be true to the Trust, ard be reputed	.	102	OLD BATCH	V.1 227
Mellefont:	True, but you shall judge whether I have not reason	.	129	DOUBL DLR	I.1 83
Sir Paul:	Nay, I protest and vow now, 'tis true; when Mr.	. . .	132	DOUBL DLR	I.1 187
Brisk:	particular and novel in the Humour; 'tis true, it makes	.	133	DOUBL DLR	I.1 238
Brisk:	particular in the Humour; 'tis true, it makes	. . . .	133	DOUBL DLR	I.1 V238
Sir Paul:	Hum, gads bud she says true,--well, my Lady,	. . .	145	DOUBL DLR	II.1 238
Maskwell:	execution of all her Plots? Ha, ha, ha, by Heaven it's true;	149	DOUBL DLR	II.1 398
Lord Touch:	I don't believe it true; he has better Principles	. .	150	DOUBL DLR	III.1 4
Sir Paul:	have not a Son to inherit this--'Tis true I have a	. .	161	DOUBL DLR	III.1 411
Sir Paul:	my Lady is so nice--it's very strange, but it's true: too	.	161	DOUBL DLR	III.1 431
Sir Paul:	true--she's so very nice, that I don't believe she would	.	162	DOUBL DLR	III.1 432
Sir Paul:	indeed it's true, Mr. Careless, it breaks my heart--I	.	162	DOUBL DLR	III.1 436
Lord Froth:	True, as I'm a Person of Honour--for Heaven's	. . .	163	DOUBL DLR	III.1 486
Lord Froth:	'Tis a strange thing, but a true one;	166	DOUBL DLR	III.1 597
Cynthia:	not that true Wisdom, for 'tis Happiness: And for ought I	.	167	DOUBL DLR	III.1 630
Lady Ply:	'tis true, but he never was so presumptuous to entertain	.	172	DOUBL DLR	IV.1 167
Mellefont:	He? you say true.	181	DOUBL DLR	IV.1 520
Mellefont:	May I believe this true?	185	DOUBL DLR	IV.2 79
Lady Touch:	'Tis true it might have been my ruine--but	. . .	188	DOUBL DLR	V.1 6
Cynthia:	have once resolved; and a true Female courage to oppose	.	193	DOUBL DLR	V.1 204
Lord Touch:	think so--Honesty to me is true Nobility. However, 'tis		196	DOUBL DLR	V.1 318
Maskwell:	I grant you in appearance all is true; I seem'd	. . .	198	DOUBL DLR	V.1 423
Lady Touch:	If this were true--but how can it be?	199	DOUBL DLR	V.1 440
Scandal:	And you, like a true great Man, having engaged their	.	221	FOR LOVE	I.1 193
Trapland:	'Udso that's true, Mr. Valentine I love Mirth, but	. .	224	FOR LOVE	I.1 300
Scandal:	there are some set out in their true Colours, both Men and		233	FOR LOVE	I.1 627
Mrs Frail:	O Devil! Well, but that Story is not true. . . .	233	FOR LOVE	I.1 641
Mrs Fore:	It's very true, Sister: Well since all's out, and	. .	248	FOR LOVE	II.1 476
Tattle:	You say true, I beg your Pardon;--I'll bring all off--	.	255	FOR LOVE	III.1 65
Tattle:	Gad, it's very true, Madam, I think we are oblig'd to	.	257	FOR LOVE	III.1 134
Tattle:	True; I was call'd Turk-Tattle all over the Parish--	.	258	FOR LOVE	III.1 168
Singer-F:	E're a Nymph that was Chaste, or a Swain that was True.	.	258	FOR LOVE	III.1 203
Ben:	Mess, and that's true: marry I had forgot. Dick's dead	.	261	FOR LOVE	III.1 294
Ben:	Mess, that's true: marry I had forgot. Dick's dead	.	261	FOR LOVE	III.1 V294
Sr Sampson:	Body o' me, Madam, you say true:--Look	. . . . .	262	FOR LOVE	III.1 349
Ben:	Why that's true as you say, nor I an't dumb, I can be	.	263	FOR LOVE	III.1 366
Ben:	Nay, You say true in that, it's but a folly to lie: For to		263	FOR LOVE	III.1 385
Scandal:	You say true, Man will err; meer Man will err--	. .	267	FOR LOVE	III.1 527
Ben:	He, he, he; why that's true; just so for all the World it	.	273	FOR LOVE	III.1 721
Ben:	Why that's true again; for may-hap one Bottom may	. .	273	FOR LOVE	III.1 725
Mrs Frail:	My true Love is gone to Sea.--	. . . .	287	FOR LOVE	IV.1 447
Singer-V:	But to be plain, I never would be true.	. . . .	293	FOR LOVE	IV.1 657
Tattle:	Very true, Sir, and desire to continue so. I have no	. .	305	FOR LOVE	V.1 287
Ben:	believe it or no. What I say is true; d'ee see, they are	.	307	FOR LOVE	V.1 369
Angelica:	'Tis very true indeed, Uncle; I hope you'll be my	. .	308	FOR LOVE	V.1 393
Angelica:	'Tis true, you have a great while pretended Love	. .	311	FOR LOVE	V.1 531
Angelica:	A Lover true: Not that a Woman's Kind.	314	FOR LOVE	V.1 637
Almeria:	True; but how cam'st thou there? wert thou alone?	. .	343	M. BRIDE	II.2 V158
Zara:	This groveling Baseness--Thou say'st true, I know	. .	348	M. BRIDE	II.2 335
Gonsalez:	If what I fear be true, she'll be concern'd	. . . .	367	M. BRIDE	III.1 239
Mirabell:	True.	. . . .	407	WAY WORLD	I.1 437
Marwood:	True, 'tis an unhappy Circumstance of Life,	. . . .	410	WAY WORLD	II.1 9
Fainall:	been false, I had e'er this repaid it--'Tis true--Had you		415	WAY WORLD	II.1 201
Mrs Fain:	the true is decay'd.	. . . . . .	418	WAY WORLD	II.1 316
Millamant:	Ay, that's true--C but then I had--	. . . .	419	WAY WORLD	II.1 355
Mirabell:	Nature; your true Vanity is in the power of pleasing.	.	420	WAY WORLD	II.1 384
Mirabell:	vain how lost a Thing you'll be! Nay, 'tis true: You are no	420	WAY WORLD	II.1 391
Fainall:	when he proves his Mistress true; but let Husbands doubts		444	WAY WORLD	III.1 717

True (continued)
Fainall:	and will herd no more with 'em. True, I wear the badge;	444	WAY WORLD	III.1	720
Lady Wish:	in her Teens. As I'm a Person 'tis true--She was	466	WAY WORLD	V.1	188
Lady Wish:	Aye that's true; but in Case of Necessity; as of	468	WAY WORLD	V.1	263
Lady Wish:	Can this be true?	470	WAY WORLD	V.1	324
Mincing:	Mercenary, Mem? I scorn your words. 'Tis true we	474	WAY WORLD	V.1	486

Truely (1)
| Lady Wish: | Is he so Unnatural say you? truely I wou'd | 458 | WAY WORLD | IV.1 | 506 |

Truepenny (1)
| Valentine: | A ha! Old Truepenny, say'st thou so? thou hast | 282 | FOR LOVE | IV.1 | 268 |

Truest (1)
| Bellmour: | Frank thou art the truest Friend in the World. | 39 | OLD BATCH | I.1 | 74 |

Trull (2)
| Lady Wish: | you treacherous Trull, this was your Merchandize you | 462 | WAY WORLD | V.1 | 19 |
| Lady Wish: | you treacherous Trull, this was the Merchandize you | 462 | WAY WORLD | V.1 V | 19 |

Trulls (1)
| Witwoud: | to tell you a Secret, these are Trulls | 405 | WAY WORLD | I.1 | 359 |

Truls (1)
| Marwood: | two such Mercenary Truls? | 474 | WAY WORLD | V.1 | 485 |

Truly (14)   see Truely
	Whether their Brats are truly got, or no;	125	DOUEL DLR	PRO.	2
	To know, if it be truly born of Wit.	125	DOUEL DLR	PRO.	11
Mellefont:	and next to being in the dark, or alone, they are most truly	158	DOUEL DLR	III.1	313
Mellefont:	hand: For a woman never thinks a man truly in love with	159	DOUEL DLR	III.1	316
Sir Paul:	be Providence--ay, truly, Mr. Careless, my Lady is a great	160	DOUEL DLR	III.1	386
Jeremy:	Name, has for the space of Sev'n Years truly and faithfully	218	FOR LOVE	I.1	67
Foresight:	Hum--truly I don't care to discourage a young	243	FOR LOVE	II.1	308
Valentine:	A couple of very civil Proverbs, truly: 'Tis hard to	256	FOR LOVE	III.1	129
Miss Prue:	better not speak at all, I think, and truly I won't tell a lie	263	FOR LOVE	III.1	383
Foresight:	Truly Mr. Scandal, I was so taken up with broken	284	FOR LOVE	IV.1	340
Foresight:	Scandal, truly,--I am inclining to your Turkish	285	FOR LOVE	IV.1	348
Foresight:	Very likely truly; You understand these Matters	289	FOR LOVE	IV.1	531
Heli:	Y'are truly Noble.	338	M. BRIDE	II.1 V	38
Servant-W:	Why truly Sir, I cannot safely swear to her Face in a	437	WAY WORLD	III.1	461

Trump (1)
| Mellefont: | and Cutt, let's e'en turn up Trump now. | 142 | DOUEL DLR | II.1 | 161 |

Trumpets (1)
| | (Trumpets.) | 334 | M. BRIDE | I.1 | V357 |

Truncheon (1)
| Capt Bluff: | this time--as I hope for a Truncheon--this rascally | 53 | OLD BATCH | II.1 | 202 |

Trundle (1)
| Petulant: | Enough, let 'em trundle. Anger helps Complexion, | 406 | WAY WORLD | I.1 | 416 |

Trunk (3)
Alonzo:	Alone the undistinguishable Trunk:	379	M. BRIDE	V.2	V117
Alonzo:	And undistinguishable Trunk:	379	M. BRIDE	V.2	118
Almeria:	Horrour! a headless Trunk! nor Lips nor Face.	382	M. BRIDE	V.2	270

Trust (20)
Belinda:	to trust you to your self. The Devil watches all opportunities;	57	OLD BATCH	II.2	105
Lucy:	Hang Art, Madam, and trust to Nature for	62	OLD BATCH	III.1	54
Fondlewife:	trust my Wife, with a Lords high-fed Chaplain.	76	OLD BATCH	IV.1	33
Fondlewife:	doubtfull, whether I shall trust her, even with Tribulation	77	OLD BATCH	IV.1	75
Bellmour:	trust thee with another Secret. Your Mistress must not	98	OLD BATCH	V.1	54
Setter:	Person of Worth; be true to thy Trust, and be reputed	102	OLD BATCH	V.1	227
	Only they trust to more inconstant Seas;	125	DOUEL DLR	PRO.	8
Lady Touch:	That I should trust a Man, whom I had	135	DOUEL DLR	I.1	303
Lady Ply:	and all the Senses are fallible; I won't trust my Honour, I	147	DOUEL DLR	II.1	341
Mellefont:	Ay, what am I to trust to then?	169	DOUEL DLR	IV.1	57
Sir Paul:	I must know what my Girl has to trust to; or not a syllable	192	DOUEL DLR	V.1	176
Lady Ply:	who would ever trust a man? O my heart akes for fear	202	DOUEL DLR	V.1	546
Scandal:	Yes, but I dare trust you; We were talking of	254	FOR LOVE	III.1	45
Scandal:	Is that your Discretion? trust a Woman with her	255	FOR LOVE	III.1	63
Sr Sampson:	O Rogue! But I'll trust you. And will you	300	FOR LOVE	V.1	132
Selim:	Who bore high Offices of Weight and Trust,	361	M. BRIDE	IV.1	10
Almeria:	My Sight, against my Sight? and shall I trust	383	M. BRIDE	V.2	293
Mirabell:	deliver this same as her Act and Deed to me in trust, and	476	WAY WORLD	V.1	546
Fainall:	Languish Widdow in trust to Edward Mirabell. Confusion!	476	WAY WORLD	V.1	552
Mirabell:	deed of trust. It may be a means well manag'd to make you	478	WAY WORLD	V.1	618

Trusted (10)
Maskwell:	I might be trusted; since it was as much my interest as hers	149	DOUEL DLR	II.1	423
Mellefont:	And having trusted thee with the Secrets of her	156	DOUEL DLR	II.1	204
Tattle:	Gadso; but I thought she might have been trusted	255	FOR LOVE	III.1	61
Tattle:	good Fortune to be trusted once with a Lady's Secret, not	256	FOR LOVE	III.1	105
Angelica:	trusted.	256	FOR LOVE	III.1	115
Angelica:	Secresie, if he was never trusted?	256	FOR LOVE	III.1	122
Scandal:	trusted; a Satyrical Proverb upon our Sex--There's	256	FOR LOVE	III.1	126
Tattle:	Hah! A good open Speaker, and not to be trusted	292	FOR LOVE	IV.1	629
Foresight:	might have been trusted with,--Or had you a mind	304	FOR LOVE	V.1	258
Marwood:	Fame and Fortune: With both I trusted you, you Bankrupt	415	WAY WORLD	II.1	196

Trusting (2)
| Sharper: | your self into a Premunire, by trusting to that sign of a | 69 | OLD BATCH | III.1 | 304 |
| Mirabell: | to betray me by trusting him too far. If your Mother, in | 417 | WAY WORLD | II.1 | 292 |

Trusty (6)
Bellmour:	when it disclosed the Cheat, which, that trusty Bawd of	38	OLD BATCH	I.1	49
Bellmour:	Trusty Setter what tidings? How goes the project?	64	OLD BATCH	III.1	116
Bellmour:	and trusty Scarron's Novels my Prayer-Book.--	80	OLD BATCH	IV.2	6
Lady Touch:	trusty Villain! I could worship thee.--	199	DOUEL DLR	V.1	455
Tattle:	Name of Trusty Mr. Tattle more--You will not be so	230	FOR LOVE	I.1	521
Sr Sampson:	an Illustrious Creature, my trusty Hieroglyphick; and may	242	FOR LOVE	II.1	243

Truth (64)
Vainlove:	Bellmour, good Morrow--Why truth on't is, these	37	OLD BATCH	I.1	5
Bellmour:	Truth on't is she fits his temper best, is a kind of	42	OLD BATCH	I.1	205
Heartwell:	My Talent is chiefly that of speaking truth, which I	45	OLD BATCH	I.1	302
Capt Bluff:	not three words of Truth, the Year round, put into the	52	OLD BATCH	II.1	193
Araminta:	I expected it--there's too much Truth in 'em:	60	OLD BATCH	II.2	206

Truth   (continued)
Heartwell:	--I tell thee I do love thee, and tell it for a Truth,	.	72	OLD BATCH	III.2	63
Heartwell:	a naked Truth, which I'm ashamed to discover.	. . .	72	OLD BATCH	III.2	64
Fondlewife:	Yes--Why then!--Ay, but to say truth, She's fonder of	.	77	OLD BATCH	IV.1	59
Belinda:	been her Godmother: The Truth on't is, I did endeavour to	.	84	OLD BATCH	IV.3	41
Sir Joseph:	fear it;--that is, if I can but think on't: Truth is, I	.	85	OLD BATCH	IV.3	73
Bellmour:	to speak the truth in justice to your Wife.--No.	. .	93	OLD BATCH	IV.4	158
Bellmour:	little too backward, that's the truth on't.	. .	93	OLD BATCH	IV.4	171
Fondlewife:	believe speaks truth.	. . . . .	94	OLD BATCH	IV.4	180
Bellmour:	a word on't.--But I can't help telling the truth, for my	.	95	OLD BATCH	IV.4	220
Vainlove:	I'm sure he tells me Truth;--but I am not sure she told	.	99	OLD BATCH	V.1	94
Vainlove:	him Truth:--Yet she was unaffectedly concern'd, he	. .	99	OLD BATCH	V.1	95
Mellefont:	Truth. Prithee do thou wear none to day; but allow Brisk	.	129	DOUBL DLR	I.1	71
Sir Paul:	me, that's the truth on't.	. . . . .	145	DOUBL DLR	II.1	258
Maskwell:	It was, and to tell you the truth, I encouraged it for	.	149	DOUBL DLR	II.1	412
Maskwell:	when Innocence and bold Truth are always ready for	.	184	DOUBL DLR	IV.2	20
Maskwell:	discover the whole and real truth of the matter to him,	.	190	DOUBL DLR	V.1	98
Maskwell:	No Mask like open Truth to cover Lies,	. . .	190	DOUBL DLR	V.1	100
Sir Paul:	say truth, all our Family are Cholerick; I am the only	.	192	DOUBL DLR	V.1	196
Jeremy:	the truth on't.	. . . . . .	217	FOR LOVE	I.1	59
Trapland:	No more, in truth.--I have forborn, I say--	. . .	222	FOR LOVE	I.1	249
Scandal:	the Hand too; and sworn to a truth; but he hopes	.	226	FOR LOVE	I.1	375
Valentine:	No indeed, he speaks truth now: For as Tattle has	.	233	FOR LOVE	I.1	622
Foresight:	I know when Travellers lie or speak Truth, when	. .	241	FOR LOVE	II.1	224
Jeremy:	another truth, I believe you did, for I find I was born with	245	FOR LOVE	II.1	362
Mrs Frail:	I'll acquaint you with a design that I have: To tell Truth,	.	248	FOR LOVE	II.1	486
Tattle:	Truth.	. . . .	252	FOR LOVE	II.1	628
Miss Prue:	you should believe that; and I'll speak truth, tho' one should	. . . . . .	264	FOR LOVE	III.1	396
Angelica:	If you speak Truth, your endeavouring at Wit is	.	276	FOR LOVE	IV.1	38
Angelica:	my self oblig'd to--pray tell me truth.	. .	277	FOR LOVE	IV.1	44
Valentine:	strange! But I am Truth, and come to give the World	.	280	FOR LOVE	IV.1	164
Valentine:	Thou liest, for I am Truth. 'Tis hard I cannot get a	.	280	FOR LOVE	IV.1	171
Valentine:	For my part, I am Truth, and can't tell; I have very	.	280	FOR LOVE	IV.1	178
Valentine:	Who's that, that's out of his Way?--I am Truth,	. .	282	FOR LOVE	IV.1	251
Valentine:	Prophecy comes, Truth must give place.	.	283	FOR LOVE	IV.1	275
Valentine:	Truth, and can teach thy Tongue a new Trick,--I	.	288	FOR LOVE	IV.1	488
Valentine:	Scandal will tell you;--I am Truth, I never	.	288	FOR LOVE	IV.1	497
Valentine:	I must be plain. (Coming up to them.) I am Truth, and hate	292	FOR LOVE	IV.1	619
Singer-V:	For by our weak and weary Truth, I find,	. .	293	FOR LOVE	IV.1	659
Jeremy:	So--Just the very backside of Truth,--But	. .	296	FOR LOVE	IV.1	775
Angelica:	Courage at this time. To tell you the Truth, I'm weary of	.	298	FOR LOVE	V.1	46
Sr Sampson:	Truth. Odsbud, you have won my Heart: I hate a Wit; I	.	299	FOR LOVE	V.1	80
Almeria:	His Worth, his Truth, and Tenderness of Love.	.	328	M. BRIDE	I.1	103
Osmyn-Alph:	Perfection of all Truth!	. . . .	343	M. BRIDE	II.2	128
Osmyn-Alph:	Some Recompence of Love and matchless Truth.	.	343	M. BRIDE	II.2	146
Osmyn-Alph:	The Sea. I fear when she shall know the truth,	.	355	M. BRIDE	III.1	230
Zara:	Forgive my Rage; I know thy Love and Truth.	.	362	M. BRIDE	IV.1	41
Gonsalez:	Which wears indeed this Colour of a Truth.	.	363	M. BRIDE	IV.1	79
Manuel:	Yet, that there's Truth in what she has discover'd,	.	366	M. BRIDE	IV.1	213
Manuel:	And look thou answer me with truth: for know,	.	367	M. BRIDE	IV.1	263
Alonzo:	My Lord, for certain truth, Perez is fled;	. .	377	M. BRIDE	V.2	48
Garcia:	Were it a Truth, I fear 'tis now too late.	. .	379	M. BRIDE	V.2	105
Witwoud:	that's the Truth on't, if he were my Brother, I cou'd not	.	403	WAY WORLD	I.1	311
Witwoud:	--I mean he never speaks Truth at all,--that's all. He	.	404	WAY WORLD	I.1	340
Mirabell:	Where hast thou stumbled upon all this Truth?	. .	407	WAY WORLD	I.1	441
Fainall:	reconcil'd to Truth and me?	. . .	415	WAY WORLD	II.1	215
Marwood:	Impossible. Truth and you are inconsistent	.	415	WAY WORLD	II.1	216
Marwood:	unknown hand--for the less I appear to know of the truth	.	443	WAY WORLD	III.1	702
Witwoud:	art in truth (Metaphorically speaking) A speaker of	.	453	WAY WORLD	IV.1	348
Waitwell:	a good cause--my Lady shall be satisfied of my Truth	.	461	WAY WORLD	IV.1	624

Truths (3)
Bellmour:	Truths, and entertaining company like a Physician, with	.	42	OLD BATCH	I.1	181
Mirabell:	What, he speaks unseasonable Truths sometimes,	. . .	404	WAY WORLD	I.1	337
Witwoud:	Truths! Ha, ha, ha! No, no, since you will have it,	.	404	WAY WORLD	I.1	339

Try (22)
Vainlove:	He's talking to himself, I think; Prithee lets try if	.	62	OLD BATCH	III.2	61
Heartwell:	I'll dissemble, and try him.--Ha, ha, ha. Why, Tom; Is	.	104	OLD BATCH	V.1	300
	A Barbarous Device, to try if Spouse,	. . . .	125	DOUBL DLR	PRO.	5
Brisk:	the Day. Here she comes, I'll seem not to see her, and try	.	175	DOUBL DLR	IV.1	303
Lady Ply:	I thought I should try you, false Man. I that	. .	179	DOUBL DLR	IV.1	452
Careless:	I had a mind to try my Ladies Vertue--And when I could	.	180	DOUBL DLR	IV.1	498
Jeremy:	Scandal, for Heaven's sake, Sir, try if you can disswade	.	219	FOR LOVE	I.1	123
Singer-F:	Their Intent was to try if his Oracle knew	. .	258	FOR LOVE	III.1	202
Sr Sampson:	shall out-lie the Devil. And so I'll try whether my	.	267	FOR LOVE	III.1	510
Jeremy:	No, Sir, not yet;--He has a mind to try, whether his	.	276	FOR LOVE	IV.1	8
Scandal:	Well, I'll try her--'tis she, here she comes.	.	276	FOR LOVE	IV.1	18
Angelica:	trick--I'll try--I would disguise to all the World a	.	277	FOR LOVE	IV.1	54
Foresight:	to try if I could discover it by my Art--hum, ha! I	.	304	FOR LOVE	V.1	259
Angelica:	Nature. I was resolv'd to try him to the utmost; I have	.	312	FOR LOVE	V.1	574
Zara:	I'll try.	. . . . . .	355	M. BRIDE	III.1	211
Zara:	And try the Force of yet more Obligations.	.	363	M. BRIDE	IV.1	98
Gonsalez:	And try howe'er, if I've divin'd aright.	. .	367	M. BRIDE	IV.1	238
Gonsalez:	Urge that, to try if she'll sollicite for him.	.	367	M. BRIDE	IV.1	241
Garcia:	But I'll omit no Care, nor Haste; and try	. .	379	M. BRIDE	V.2	106
Marwood:	try you.	. . . . . .	411	WAY WORLD	II.1	42
Sir Wilful:	Well prithee try what thou can'st do; if thou	. .	437	WAY WORLD	III.1	464
Sir Wilful:	However that's as time shall try,--But spare to speak and	.	448	WAY WORLD	IV.1	137

Try'd (7)   see Well-try'd
Setter:	To answer you as briefly--He has a cause to be try'd	.	66	OLD BATCH	III.1	220
	If he's an Ass, he will be Try'd by's Peers.	. . .	113	OLD BATCH	EPI.	16
Maskwell:	intended this Evening to have try'd all Arguments to	.	182	DOUBL DLR	IV.1	577
	Even to make exceptions, when they're Try'd.	.	204	DOUBL DLR	EPI.	30
Singer-F:	And the Nymph may be Chaste that has never been Try'd.	.	259	FOR LOVE	III.1	208
Angelica:	try'd you too, and know you both. You have not more	.	312	FOR LOVE	V.1	575
Millamant:	. . . I think I try'd once	. . . . .	419	WAY WORLD	II.1	367

Tryal (6)

		PAGE	TITLE	ACT.SC	LINE
	I could not help one tryal of your Patience:	113	OLD BATCH	EPI.	20
	Let's have a fair Tryal, and a clear Sea.	125	DOUEL DLR	PRO.	15
Mellefont:	Not at all; cnly a Friendly Tryal of Skill, and the .	143	DOUEL DLR	II.1	170
Lady Ply:	never dissembled in my Life. Yet to make tryal of you,	179	DOUEL DLR	IV.1	453
Angelica:	and struggl'd very hard to make this utmost Tryal of your	312	FOR LCVE	V.1	563
Mirabell:	tryal of a Mutual Secresie. No Decoy-Duck to wheadle .	451	WAY WORLD	IV.1	238

Tryall (2)

Mrs Fain:	my own Innocence, and dare stand by a tryall.	466	WAY WORLD	V.1	178
Mrs Fain:	my own Innocence, and dare stand a tryall.	466	WAY WORLD	V.1	V178

Tryals (2)

	Such are the Tryals, Poets make of Plays:	125	DOUEL DLR	PRO.	7
	That Surgeons wait cn Tryals in a Court;	385	M. ERIDE	EPI.	16

Trying (3)

Sharper:	'Tis but trying, and being where I am at worst, ...	48	OLD BATCH	II.1	16
Belinda:	tore two Pair of Kid-Gloves, with trying 'em on.-- . .	84	OLD EATCH	IV.3	54
Belinda:	tore two Pair of Kid-leather Gloves, with trying 'em on.--	84	OLD EATCH	IV.3	V 54

Tryumphs (1)

Gonsalez:	With gnashing Teeth, the Dust his Tryumphs raise. . .	332	M. EFIDE	I.1	237

Tub (1)

Jeremy:	in a Tub, go to Prison for you? 'Slife, Sir, what do you .	217	FOR LCVE	I.1	31

Tuck (1)

Nurse:	and tuck you up, and set the Candle, and your Tobacco-Box,	238	FOR LCVE	II.1	103

Tug (2)

Heartwell:	What Pain we tug that galling Load, a Wife.	112	OLD BATCH	V.2	193
Ben:	chain'd to an Oar all his life; and may-hap forc'd to tug a	262	FOR LCVE	III.1	317

Tugging (1)

	(Enter Sharper, tugging in Heartwell.)	104	OLD BATCH	V.1	283

Tum (2)

Laetitia:	Patch.--You s'an't tum in, Nykin.--Run into my	89	OLD BATCH	IV.4	16
Laetitia:	Chamber, quickly, quickly. You s'an't tum in.	89	OLD BATCH	IV.4	17

Tumbler (1)

Heartwell:	that comes; like a Tumbler with the same tricks over and .	42	OLD BATCH	I.1	191

Tumbling (1)

Osmyn-Alph:	That tumbling cn its Prop, crush'd all beneath, ...	347	M. ERIDE	II.2	310

Tumbril (1)

Lady Wish:	I do with this beastly Tumbril?--Go lie down and . . .	457	WAY WORLD	IV.1	461

Tumult (2)

Gonsalez:	In private, undertook to raise this Tumult.	363	M. ERIDE	IV.1	89
Manuel:	This Tumult, and the Lords who fled with Heli, ...	366	M. EFIDE	IV.1	215

Tune (3)

Heartwell:	Tune cf the Superanuated Maidens Comfort, or the . . .	63	OLD EATCH	III.1	81
Cynthia:	tune.	163	DOUEL DLR	III.1	474
Lady Froth:	Wit, and can sing a Tune already. My Lord wont you go? .	167	DOUBL DLR	III.1	620

Turbant (1)

Manuel:	There with his Turbant, and his Robe array'd	374	M. BRIDE	V.1	V86A

Turk (5)

Lady Ply:	Did I? Do you doubt me, Turk, Sarazen? I	179	DOUEL DLR	IV.1	462
Valentine:	the Great Turk.	257	FOR LCVE	III.1	167
Sir Wilful:	Map says that your Turk is not so honest a Man as your .	456	WAY WORLD	IV.1	445
Sir Wilful:	Unknown to the Turk and the Persian:	456	WAY WORLD	IV.1	451
Sir Wilful:	Unknown to the Turk or the Persian:	456	WAY WORLD	IV.1	V451

Turk-Tattle (1)

Tattle:	True; I was call'd Turk-Tattle all over the Parish-- . .	258	FOR LCVE	III.1	168

Turkish (1)

Foresight:	Scandal, truly,--I am inclining to your Turkish . . .	285	FOR LCVE	IV.1	348

Turks (4)

Lady Wish:	the Turks--for thou are not fit to live in a Christian .	456	WAY WORLD	IV.1	440
Sir Wilful:	Turks, no; no Turks, Aunt: Your Turks are	456	WAY WORLD	IV.1	442

Turky-Cock (1)

Lady Ply:	as red as a Turky-Cock; O fie, Cousin Mellefont! . . .	147	DOUBL DLR	II.1	336

Turn (37)

Laetitia:	privy to a weak Wcman's Failing, won't turn it to the . .	82	OLD BATCH	IV.2	63
Belinda:	leave you. Come, Mr. Sharper, you and I will take a turn, .	87	OLD BATCH	IV.3	143
Cynthia:	turn your Brain.	138	DOUEL DLR	II.1	7
Lord Froth:	I'll walk a turn in the Garden, and come to you. . .	142	DOUEL DLR	II.1	147
Mellefont:	and Cutt, let's e'en turn up Trump now.	142	DOUEL DLR	II.1	161
Maskwell:	--oh she has open'd her heart tc me,--I am to turn you a .	149	DOUEL DLR	II.1	402
Brisk:	O barbarous, to turn me into ridicule! Yet, ha ha ha. .	176	DOUEL DLR	IV.1	343
Maskwell:	After-Game to play that shall turn the Tables, and here .	181	DOUEL DLR	IV.1	529
Lady Touch:	turn? has Hell no remedy?	185	DOUEL DLR	IV.2	58
Mellefont:	turn tc good acccunt.	185	DOUEL DLR	IV.2	63
Lady Touch:	Thou hast, thou hast found the only way to turn my Rage; .	198	DOUEL DLR	V.1	398
Valentine:	Here, take away; I'll walk a turn, and digest what . .	216	FOR LCVE	I.1	3
Jeremy:	won't have a Friend left in the World, if you turn Poet .	218	FOR LCVE	I.1	86
Jeremy:	himself, or were resolv'd to turn Author, and bring the .	219	FOR LCVE	I.1	106
Scandal:	Poet! He shall turn Soldier first, and rather depend .	219	FOR LCVE	I.1	125
Scandal:	Huntsmen.--No, turn Pimp, Flatterer, Quack, Lawyer, .	220	FOR LCVE	I.1	144
Sr Sampson:	--What, would'st thou have me turn Pelican, and . .	246	FOR LOVE	II.1	398
Mrs Frail:	a turn with one's Friend.	246	FOR LOVE	II.1	420
Ben:	Sweet-Heart, a-fore I turn in; may-hap I may dream of .	275	FOR LCVE	III.1	809
Sr Sampson:	--Body o' me, I have a Trick to turn the Settlement .	300	FOR LOVE	V.1	127
Tattle:	turn of good Fcrtune, in the Lottery of Wives; and promise	304	FOR LOVE	V.1	269
Angelica:	turn tc an extream Fondness, you must not suspect it. .	313	FOR LCVE	V.1	607
Osmyn-Alph:	Turn your Lights inward, Eyes, and look	345	M. BRIDE	II.2	215
Osmyn-Alph:	Turn your Lights inward, Eyes, and view my Thought, .	345	M. BRIDE	II.2	V215
Zara:	That having seen it, thou do'st turn thy Eyes	353	M. BRIDE	III.1	149
Osmyn-Alph:	That I cou'd almost turn my Eyes away, ...	356	M. BRIDE	III.1	253
Almeria:	Turn not your Eyes away--look on me kneeling;	369	M. EBIDE	IV.1	319
Garcia:	But that we all should turn our Swords, against . . .	378	M. BRIDE	V.2	66
Gonsalez:	On me, on me, turn your avenging Sword.	378	M. BBIDE	V.2	69
Almeria:	That thus can gaze, and yet not turn to Stone? . . .	382	M. BRIDE	V.2	239
Servant-M:	turn; so we drove round to Duke's Place; and there they .	398	WAY WORLD	I.1	118
Fainall:	Ay, I'll take a turn before Dinner.	409	WAY WORLD	I.1	509
Mirabell:	Point of the Compass to which they cannot turn, and by .	423	WAY WORLD	II.1	496
Fainall:	If the worst come to the worst,--I'll turn my	444	WAY WORLD	III.1	708

Turn   (continued)
  Lady Wish: entrance; and then turn full upon him--No, that will   . . 445 WAY WCRLD   IV.1   21
  Lady Wish: I fear I shall turn to Stone, petrifie Incessantly.   . . 470 WAY WCRLD   V.1 337
                 And turn to Libel, what was meant a Satire.   . . . .   479 WAY WCRLD   EPI. 22
Turn'd (28)
  Bellmour: but I see he has turn'd the Corner and goes another way. .   46 OLD EATCH   I.1 V340
  Setter: Too fcrward to be turn'd back--Though he's a little   .   67 OLD EATCH III.1 224
  Setter: S'bud Sir, away quickly, there's Fondlewife just turn'd .   75 OLD EATCH   IV.1   9
  Laetitia: Your back was no sooner turn'd, but like a Lion, he   .   90 OLD EATCH   IV.4   52
  Mellefont: Ned, Ned, whither so fast? What, turn'd flincher!   . . . 127 DOUEL DLR   I.1   1
  Lady Froth: O prettily turn'd again; let me die, but you have   .   140 DOUEL CLR   II.1   85
  Brisk: I'm whclly turn'd into Satyr. I confess I Write but seldom, 141 DOUEL DLR   II.1 116
  Brisk: I'm wholly turn'd into Satire. I confess I write but seldom, 141 DOUEL DLR   II.1 V116
  Maskwell: to make your Uncle Disinherit you, to get you turn'd out . 149 DOUEL DLR   II.1 400
  Lord Touch: Villain! 'Death I'll have him stripp'd and turn'd naked out 153 DOUEL DLR III.1 100
  Sir Paul: but here's the strangest Revclution, all turn'd topsie   .   200 DOUEL DLR   V.1 497
  Sir Paul: All turn'd topsie turvey, as sure as a Gun.   . . . .   200 DOUEL DLR   V.1 501
  Jeremy: serv'd Valentine Legend Esq; and that he is not now turn'd   218 FOR LCVE   I.1   68
  Valentine: was easily turn'd another way; and at least lock'd well on   246 FCB LCVE   II.1 409
  Mrs Frail: and wcn't be surpriz'd to see the Tide turn'd.   . . . .   284 FOR LCVE   IV.1 308
  Ben: has turn'd her senses, her Brain is quite overset.
                 well-a-day, ...   286 FCB LCVE   IV.1 404
  Valentine: News;--Angelica is turn'd Nun; and I am turning Fryar,   .   290 FOR LCVE   IV.1 558
  Zara: Heav'n has no Rage, like Love to Hatred turn'd,   . . .   361 M. EFIDE   III.1 457
  Selim: Th' imperfect Look, and sternly turn'd away.   . . . .   375 M. EFIDE   V.1 100
  Gonsalez: By fits reveals--his Face seems turn'd tc favour   . .   376 M. EFIDE   V.2   8
  Osmyn-Alph: Has turn'd their own most bloody Purposes.   . . . .   383 M. EFIDE   V.2 V308
  Betty: Turn'd of the last Canonical Hour, Sir.   . . . . . .   398 WAY WCRLD   I.1 106
  Witwoud: soon as your Back was turn'd--Whip he was gone; . . . .   405 WAY WCRLD   I.1 371
  Mrs Fain: My Husband. Don't you see him? He turn'd   . . . . .   412 WAY WCRLD   II.1   82
  Mirabell: which they are not turn'd; and by one as well as another;   423 WAY WCRLD   II.1 497
  Foible: I manag'd my self. I turn'd it all for the better. I told my 430 WAY WCRLD III.1 207
  Marwood: Marrying than Travelling at his Years. I hear he is turn'd   431 WAY WCRLD III.1 260
  Fainall: turn'd a drift, like a Leaky hulk tc Sink or Swim, as she   473 WAY WCRLD   V.1 443
Turned (1)
  Maskwell: your cwn art that turned it to advantage.   . . . . .   187 DOUBL DLR   V.1   5
Turning (8)
  Jeremy: him frcm turning Foet.   . . . .   219 FCB LCVE   I.1 124
  Angelica: turning the Sieve and Sheers, and pricking your Thumbs, .   238 FOR LCVE   II.1 108
  Foresight: the turning of the Tide, bring me the Urinal;--And I   .   270 FCB LCVE   III.1 647
  Jeremy: that was so near turning Poet yesterday morning, can't be   276 FCB LCVE   IV.1   4
  Valentine: News;--Angelica is turn'd Nun; and I am turning Fryar,   .   290 FCB LCVE   IV.1 558
  Osmyn-Alph: The just Decrees of Heav'n, in turning on   . . . . .   383 M. EFIDE   V.2 307
  Mirabell: They are turning into the other Walk.   . . . . . .   416 WAY WCRLD   II.1 253
  Mirabell: me not, by turning from me in disdain,--I come not to   .   471 WAY WCRLD   V.1 372
Turns (9)
  Heartwell: preparative, and what you mean for a Whet, turns the   . . 43 OLD EATCH   I.1 244
  Silvia: (Turns and Weeps.)   . . .   74 OLD EATCH III.2 132
  Setter: --Bluffe turns errant Traytor; tribes me tc make a   . . 105 OLD BATCH   I.1 343
                 (As she is going she turns back and smiles at him.)   . .   187 DCUEL DLR   IV.2 134
  Angelica: Tabby-Cat, by turns, I can.   . . . .   238 FOR LCVE   II.1 122
  Mrs Fore: Nay, two or three Turns, I'll take my Cath.   . . . .   246 FOR LCVE   II.1 421
  Osmyn-Alph: Of wand'ring Life, that winks and wakes by turns,   . .   350 M. EFIDE   III.1   37
  Perez: Whate'er it is the King's Complexion turns.   . . . .   373 M. EFIDE   V.1   32
  Fainall: have 'em three times a Week, and meet by turns, at one   396 WAY WCRLD   I.1   51
Turtle (3)
  Vainlove: So was true as Turtle--in imagination Ned, ha?   . . . .   38 OLD EATCH   I.1   52
  Bellmour: Turtle to you, that I'll go and sollicite Matrimony with all 96 OLD EATCH   IV.4 265
  Lady Wish: I'm a Person. Your Turtle is in Custody already; You shall   463 WAY WCRLD   V.1   54
Turtles (1)
  Mirabell: the force of Instinct--O here come my pair of Turtles   .   423 WAY WCRLD   II.1 501
Turvey (1)
  Sir Paul: All turn'd topsie turvey, as sure as a Gun.   . . . .   200 DCUEL DLR   V.1 501
Turvy (1)   see Topsy-turvy
  Sir Paul: turvy; as I hope for Providence.   . . . .   200 DOUEL DLR   V.1 498
Twas (1)
  Marwood: Twas much she shou'd be deceiv'd so long.   . . . . .   467 WAY WCRLD   V.1 195
'Twas (11)
  Maskwell: 'Twas honest--And shall I be rewarded for it?   . . . .   188 DOUBL DLR   V.1   18
  Scandal: 'Twas a very forgetting Night.--But would ycu not   . .   284 FCB LCVE   IV.1 342
  Almeria: 'Twas that, ...   329 M. EFIDE   I.1 143
  Almeria: 'Twas--as I have told thee--   . . . .   329 M. EFIDE   I.1 V143
  Manuel: 'Twas weak and wilful--and a Wcman's Errour.   . . . .   333 M. EFIDE   I.1 293
  Osmyn-Alph: Be torn from his Petition? 'Twas to Heav'n.   . . . .   350 M. EFIDE   III.1   23
  Osmyn-Alph: 'Twas writ; a Prayer for me, wherein appears   . . . .   352 M. EFIDE   III.1 112
  Gonsalez: 'Twas an Act of Horrour;   . . . .   379 M. EFIDE   V.2 122
  Fainall: I do not--'Twas for my ease to oversee and   . . . .   413 WAY WCRLD   II.1 143
  Marwood: 'Twas spoke in scorn, and I never will fcrgive it.   . .   414 WAY WCRLD   II.1 183
  Lady Wish: 'Twas against my Consent that she Married   . . . . .   469 WAY WORLD   V.1 302
'twas (27)
                 And 'twas the prettiest Prologue, as he wrote it!   . .   35 OLD EATCH   PRO.   21
  Sharper: me to lose what was ventur'd in your service; Nay 'twas   50 OLD EATCH   II.1 101
  Sharper: in a manner--Pay'd down for your deliverance; 'twas so   .   50 OLD EATCH   II.1 102
  Capt Bluff: 'twas indiscreet, when you know what will provoke me--   .   54 OLD BATCH   II.1 242
  Heartwell: Why 'twas I Sung and Danc'd; I gave Musick to   . . . .   72 OLD BATCH III.2   32
  Bellmour: till 'twas late; my Intimacy with him gave me the   . .   82 OLD EATCH   IV.2   50
  Bellmour: Here's no body, nor no noise;--'twas nothing   . . . .   89 OLD EATCH   IV.4   1
  Vainlove: (to Araminta). Oh, 'twas Frenzy all: Cannot you forgive   106 OLD BATCH   V.1 356
  Maskwell: your Passion, 'twas imperceptible to all but Jealous Eyes.   136 DOUEL DLR   I.1 363
  Lord Froth: ay, there it is; who could resist! 'twas sc my heart was
                 made   . . . .   140 DOUEL DLR   II.1   68
  Maskwell: deceive 'em all, and yet secure my self, 'twas a lucky   .   155 DOUEL DLR III.1 190
  Maskwell: (aside). That I believ'd; 'twas well I left the private   . 184 DOUEL DLR   IV.2   30
  Maskwell: and she fears it; though chance brought my Lord, 'twas   .   187 DOUEL DLR   V.1   4
  Maskwell: No, 'twas honest, therefore I shan't;--Nay, rather,
                 therefore   . . . .   188 DOUEL DLR   V.1   19

'twas   (continued)

		PAGE	TITLE	ACT.SC	LINE
	He offers but this one Excuse, 'twas writ	214	FOR LOVE	PRO.	46
Jeremy:	Sir, I ask you Ten Thousand Pardons, 'twas an errant . .	313	FOR LOVE	V.1	592
Almeria:	But 'twas not so decreed.	329	M. BRIDE	I.1	118
Almeria:	Amid those Flames--but 'twas not so decreed. . . .	329	M. BRIDE	I.1	V118
Leonora:	Indeed 'twas mournful--	329	M. BRIDE	I.1	142
Manuel:	Those Bonds! 'twas my Command you should be free: . .	336	M. BRIDE	I.1	403
Manuel:	'Tis false; 'twas more; I bad she should be free: . .	336	M. BRIDE	I.1	408
Manuel:	'Tis false; 'twas more; I bid she should be free: . .	336	M. BRIDE	I.1	V408
Perez:	To me 'twas long since plain.	338	M. BRIDE	II.1	45
Zara:	Indeed? Then 'twas a Whisper spread by some . . .	366	M. BRIDE	IV.1	189
Zara:	The Mute not yet return'd! 'tis strange. Ha! 'twas . .	374	M. BRIDE	V.1	91
Zara:	The Mute not yet return'd! ha! 'twas the King! . . .	374	M. BRIDE	V.1	V 91
Zara:	'Tis not that he is dead; for 'twas decreed . . .	380	M. BRIDE	V.2	187

Twelve (8)

Bellmour:	twelve thousand Pound Tom--'Tis true she is excessively .	41	OLD BATCH	I.1	166
Bellmour:	told you there's twelve thousand Pound--Hum--Why . . .	41	OLD BATCH	I.1	170
Setter:	forth under my Auspicious Convoy. Twelve Thousand . . .	102	OLD BATCH	V.1	223
Scandal:	Twelve Caesars, paultry Copies; and the Five Senses, as ill	232	FOR LOVE	I.1	602
Angelica:	Beasts among the Twelve Signs, Uncle. But Cuckolds go .	239	FOR LOVE	II.1	139
Foresight:	But there's but one Virgin among the Twelve Signs, . .	239	FOR LOVE	II.1	141
Foresight:	within a quarter of Twelve--hem--he, hem!--just upon .	270	FOR LOVE	III.1	646
Valentine:	Clocks will strike Twelve at Noon, and the Horn'd Herd .	289	FOR LOVE	IV.1	504

Twelvemonth (2)

Belinda:	endure the sight of a Fire this Twelvemonth.	59	OLD BATCH	II.2	165
Lady Touch:	grown together when I told you--almost a Twelvemonth .	153	DOUBL DLR	III.1	110

Twenty (4)   see One-and-twenty

Mrs Frail:	Well, what if I took twenty--I warrant if	246	FOR LOVE	II.1	422
Valentine:	Twenty Chairmen, and make thee Pedestals to stand erect	289	FOR LOVE	IV.1	525
Angelica:	and Twenty.	298	FOR LOVE	V.1	32
Waitwell:	India? I have twenty Letters in my Pocket from him, in .	461	WAY WORLD	IV.1	607

'Twere (8)

Sharper:	But that's sufficient--'Twere injustice to doubt the . .	50	OLD BATCH	II.1	97
	'Twere some Amends if they could reimburse:	323	M. BRIDE	PRO.	24
Gonsalez:	'Twere not amiss to question her a little, ...	367	M. BRIDE	IV.1	237
Gonsalez:	'Twere done--I'll crawl and sting him to the Heart; . .	376	M. BRIDE	V.2	12
Gonsalez:	'Twere fit the Soldiers were amuz'd, mean time, . . .	378	M. BRIDE	V.2	102
Gonsalez:	'Twere fit the Soldiers were amus'd, with Hopes; . . .	378	M. BRIDE	V.2	V102
Marwood:	Months Mind, but he can't abide her--'Twere better . .	431	WAY WORLD	III.1	240
Marwood:	'Twere better so indeed. Or what think you . . .	433	WAY WORLD	III.1	308

'twere (15)

Bellmour:	Who the Devil would have thee? unless 'twere an . . .	45	OLD BATCH	I.1	298
Mellefont:	By Heaven 'twere senceless not to be mad, and see . .	186	DOUBL DLR	IV.2	115
Cynthia:	any thing that resists my will, tho' 'twere reason it self.	193	DOUBL DLR	V.1	205
Angelica:	last Invisible Eclipse, laying in Provision as 'twere for a	237	FOR LOVE	II.1	80
Ben:	Discourse with you, an 'twere not a main high Wind . .	263	FOR LOVE	III.1	370
Ben:	Venture, Mess, and that I will, tho' 'twere to Sea in a .	265	FOR LOVE	III.1	452
Sr Sampson:	and 'twere pity she shou'd be thrown away upon any . .	298	FOR LOVE	V.1	52
Zara:	Have I? Yet 'twere the lowest Baseness, now, ...	363	M. BRIDE	IV.1	96
Gonsalez:	What if she had seen Osmyn? tho' 'twere strange. . .	366	M. BRIDE	IV.1	222
Servant-M:	behind one another, as 'twere in a Country Dance. Ours .	398	WAY WORLD	I.1	114
Mirabell:	Tho' 'twere a Man whom he fear'd, or a Woman . . .	403	WAY WORLD	I.1	305
Mirabell:	Thing that resembl'd a Man, tho' 'twere no more than .	418	WAY WORLD	II.1	312
Mirabell:	you! To think of a Whirlwind, tho' 'twere in a Whirlwind,	423	WAY WORLD	II.1	491
Fainall:	'twere somewhat,--but to crawl after, with my Horns .	442	WAY WORLD	III.1	636
Marwood:	'twere well. But it must after this be consign'd by the .	468	WAY WORLD	V.1	230

Twice (6)

Vainlove:	only hapned to be once or twice, where, Laetitia was the .	39	OLD BATCH	I.1	96
Scandal:	in her Bed, shift twice a Week, and not work so hard, that	222	FOR LOVE	I.1	219
Gonsalez:	This Sight, which is indeed not seen (tho' twice . .	332	M. BRIDE	I.1	244
Osmyn-Alph:	And twice escap'd, both from the Wreck of Seas, . . .	344	M. BRIDE	II.2	173
Osmyn-Alph:	And twice escap'd, both from the Rage of Seas, . . .	344	M. BRIDE	II.2	V173
Zara:	Therefore require me not to ask thee twice;	361	M. BRIDE	IV.1	2

'Twill (3)

Sharper:	Ha, ha; 'Twill be a pleasant Cheat.--I'll plague . .	99	OLD BATCH	V.1	86
Leonora:	'Twill urge his Wrath, to see you drown'd in Tears, . .	330	M. BRIDE	I.1	V167
Alonzo:	'Twill quit me of my Promise to Gonsalez.	373	M. BRIDE	V.1	30

'twill (7)

Silvia:	Impossible, 'twill never take.	62	OLD BATCH	III.1	43
Maskwell:	open; 'twill be hard, if then you can't bring her to any .	157	DOUBL DLR	III.1	253
Lady Touch:	let me not hope forgiveness, 'twill ever be in your power	185	DOUBL DLR	IV.2	83
Lady Touch:	thee open to my sight! But then 'twill be too late to know--	198	DOUBL DLR	V.1	397
Osmyn-Alph:	Then, then 'twill be enough--I shall be Old.	343	M. BRIDE	II.2	142
Osmyn-Alph:	So shall you still behold her--'twill not be. . . .	345	M. BRIDE	II.2	V216
Gonsalez:	If I delay--'twill do--or better so.	371	M. BRIDE	IV.1	416

Twin (1)

Petulant:	kiss'd your twin yonder in a humour of reconciliation, till	454	WAY WORLD	IV.1	356

Twin-Stars (1)

Valentine:	We are the Twin-Stars, and cannot shine in one . . .	259	FOR LOVE	III.1	223

Twinckling (3)

Saygrace:	of an Acrostick, and be with you in the twinckling of an .	194	DOUBL DLR	V.1	273
Sr Sampson:	the twinckling of a Star; and seen a Conjurer, that cou'd	241	FOR LOVE	II.1	227
Tattle:	a Farthing for you then in a twinckling.	251	FOR LOVE	II.1	605

Twining (1)

Osmyn-Alph:	To thee with twining? Come, come to my Heart. . . .	343	M. BRIDE	II.2	124

Twinkle (1)

Sir Joseph:	Eyes twinkle, and her Mouth water? Did not she pull up .	103	OLD BATCH	V.1	255

Twinkling (1)   see Twinckling

Osmyn-Alph:	To guess at Right and Wrong; the twinkling Lamp . . .	350	M. BRIDE	III.1	36

Twit (1)

Foresight:	What does he twit me with my Wife too, I must . . .	241	FOR LOVE	II.1	229

Twitnam (1)

Jeremy:	Children from Twitnam.	221	FOR LOVE	I.1	206

Twitter (1)

Lady Ply:	I swear and declare, I am in such a twitter to	173	DOUBL DLR	IV.1	209

'twixt (1)

Speaker	Text	Page	Title	Act.Sc	Line
Ben:	A shot 'twixt wind and water,	274	FOR LOVE	III.1	788

Two (80)

Speaker	Text	Page	Title	Act.Sc	Line
Heartwell:	courage, which you shew for the first year or two upon all	43	OLD BATCH	I.1	246
Sir Joseph:	Fondlewife, as far as two hundred Pound, and this Afternoon	51	OLD BATCH	II.1	133
Bellmour:	Tyrant there and I, are two Buckets that can never come	57	OLD BATCH	II.2	118
Heartwell:	the Jest of the Town: Nay in two Days, I expect to be	63	OLD BATCH	III.1	79
Bellmour:	Lawyer, between two Fees.	63	OLD BATCH	III.1	92
Setter:	I shall Sir--I wonder to which of these two	64	OLD BATCH	III.1	137
Belinda:	the Equipage of a Wife and two Daughters, came to Mrs.	84	OLD BATCH	IV.3	24
Belinda:	Two such unlick'd Cubs!--	84	OLD BATCH	IV.3	26
Belinda:	of it; for she thank'd me, and gave me two Apples, piping	84	OLD BATCH	IV.3	43
Belinda:	Front of her Father's Hall; her Eyes were the two	84	OLD BATCH	IV.3	46
Belinda:	tore two Pair of Kid-Gloves, with trying 'em on.--	84	OLD BATCH	IV.3	54
Belinda:	tore two Pair of Kid-leather Gloves, with trying 'em on.--	84	OLD BATCH	IV.3 V	54
Fondlewife:	I warrant you, than to deny it. Come, Were you two never	93	OLD BATCH	IV.4	155
Sharper:	Why, there: The Two white Posts.	104	OLD BATCH	V.1	288
Heartwell:	two Hours.	105	OLD BATCH	V.1	318
Heartwell:	Oh! Any thing, every thing, a Leg or two, or an	109	OLD BATCH	V.2	75
Mellefont:	importunities of her Love; and of two evils, I thought my	129	DOUBL DLR	II.1	93
Lady Froth:	those Two hard Words? If you don't, I'll explain	139	DOUBL DLR	II.1	33
Cynthia:	Wife One Flesh, it leaves 'em still Two Fools; and they	142	DOUBL DLR	II.1	151
Mellefont:	That's only when Two Fools meet, and their	142	DOUBL DLR	II.1	153
Cynthia:	Nay, I have known Two Wits meet, and by the	142	DOUBL DLR	II.1	155
Mellefont:	Fortune indeed makes the match, and the Two nearest,	143	DOUBL DLR	II.1	165
Mellefont:	and sometimes the Two farthest are together, but the	143	DOUBL DLR	II.1	166
Lady Touch:	heard any thing from him these two days.	153	DOUBL DLR	III.1	98
Lord Touch:	These two days! Is it so fresh? Unnatural	153	DOUBL DLR	III.1	99
Mellefont:	Like any two Guardians to an Orphan Heiress--	156	DOUBL DLR	III.1	216
Lady Froth:	spent two days together in going about Covent-Garden to	165	DOUBL DLR	III.1	563
Lady Froth:	seen her these two hours.--The poor dear Creature	166	DOUBL DLR	III.1	613
	And when but two were made, both went astray;	213	FOR LOVE	PRO.	19
Jeremy:	O Sir, there's Trapland the Scrivener, with two	221	FOR LOVE	I.1	202
Valentine:	and bid her trouble me no more; a thoughtless two handed	221	FOR LOVE	I.1	210
Mrs Frail:	Issue-Male of their two Bodies; 'tis the most superstitious	231	FOR LOVE	I.1	579
Scandal:	with a hundred Hands, two Heads, and but one Face; a	233	FOR LOVE	I.1	643
Scandal:	Divine with two Faces, and one Head; and I have a Soldier	233	FOR LOVE	I.1	644
Nurse:	. . . or any Teats, but two that han't	238	FOR LOVE	II.1	V125
Sr Sampson:	and my Fatherly fondness wou'd it like two Tallies.--	243	FOR LOVE	II.1	294
Sr Sampson:	Sir? Here, to stand here, upon those two Leggs, and look	244	FOR LOVE	II.1	328
Mrs Fore:	Nay, two or three Turns, I'll take my Cath.	246	FOR LOVE	II.1	421
Tattle:	Pox take her; if she had staid two Minutes longer, I	253	FOR LOVE	III.1	17
Scandal:	recommend a Song to you upon the Hint of my two	258	FOR LOVE	III.1	191
Sr Sampson:	Dick, body o' me, Dick has been dead these two	261	FOR LOVE	III.1	292
Scandal:	two. I can get nothing out of him but Sighs. He desires	266	FOR LOVE	III.1	501
Scandal:	two Hours ago.	268	FOR LOVE	III.1	573
Ben:	is indeed, as like as two Cable Ropes.	273	FOR LOVE	III.1	722
Valentine:	another than Oyl and Vinegar; and yet those two beaten	282	FOR LOVE	IV.1	257
Valentine:	two greatest Monsters in the World are a Man and a	282	FOR LOVE	IV.1	263
Sr Sampson:	Why, my Opinion is, that those two Monsters	282	FOR LOVE	IV.1	265
Valentine:	Buz in the Exchange at Two. Wives and Husbands will	289	FOR LOVE	IV.1	505
Valentine:	Sheets before Night. But there are two things that you will	289	FOR LOVE	IV.1	510
Valentine:	For she'll meet me Two Hours hence in black and white,	290	FOR LOVE	IV.1	561
Jeremy:	Two Hours--I'm sure I left him just now, in a Humour	295	FOR LOVE	IV.1	754
Jeremy:	Two Hours--I'm sure I left him just now, in the Humour	295	FOR LOVE	IV.1	V754
Angelica:	But I'll tell you two things before I leave you; I am not	296	FOR LOVE	IV.1	791
Sr Sampson:	upon the Issue Male of our Two Bodies begotten. Odsbud,	300	FOR LOVE	V.1	192
Ben:	Stocks; and they two are a going to be married to rights.	307	FOR LOVE	V.1	359
Tattle:	O, the Two most unfortunate poor Creatures in the	309	FOR LOVE	V.1	442
Leonora:	Of two in shining Habits, cross the Ile,	344	M. BRIDE	II.2	192
Zara:	Instruct the two remaining Mutes, that they	375	M. BRIDE	V.1	130
Zara:	Give Order, that the two remaining Mutes	375	M. BRIDE	V.1	V130
	(Enter Zara, follow'd by Selim, and Two Mutes bearing	379	M. BRIDE	V.2	130
Leonora:	Zara all pale and dead! two frightful Men,	381	M. BRIDE	V.2	223
Witwoud:	defend most of his Faults, except one or two; one he has,	403	WAY WORLD	I.1	310
Coachman:	You must bring two Dishes of Chocolate and a	404	WAY WORLD	I.1	350
Witwoud:	That should be for two fasting Strumpets, and a	404	WAY WORLD	I.1	353
Petulant:	Relations--Two Coheiresses his Cousins, and an old	406	WAY WORLD	I.1	407
Mirabell:	Yet to those two vain empty Things, you owe two	421	WAY WORLD	II.1	413
Mrs Fain:	Immediately; I have a Word or two for Mr.	421	WAY WORLD	II.1	425
Millamant:	unless she shou'd tell me her self. Which of the two it	423	WAY WORLD	II.1	486
Millamant:	Chambermaid after a day or two.	433	WAY WORLD	III.1	307
Millamant:	handsomer--And within a Year or two as young.	434	WAY WORLD	III.1	359
Witwoud:	one another like two Battle-dores: For	435	WAY WORLD	III.1	402
Sir Wilful:	have been encouraged with a Bottle or two, because I'm	446	WAY WORLD	IV.1	74
Witwoud:	one another like two roasting Apples.	453	WAY WORLD	IV.1	334
Lady Wish:	Vehemence.--But a day or two for decency of	458	WAY WORLD	IV.1	496
Lady Wish:	Yellow Colberteen again; do; an old gnaw'd Mask, two	462	WAY WORLD	V.1	15
Lady Wish:	come two more of my Egyptian Plagues too.	470	WAY WORLD	V.1	309
Mirabell:	I must have leave for two Criminals to appear.	474	WAY WORLD	V.1	468
Marwood:	two such Mercenary Truls?	474	WAY WORLD	V.1	485
Sir Wilful:	on't, I must do't. And if these two Gentlemen wou'd	477	WAY WORLD	V.1	586

Two-leg'd (1)

Speaker	Text	Page	Title	Act.Sc	Line
Belinda:	Commendation of that filthy, awkward, two-leg'd Creature,	54	OLD BATCH	II.2	5

Twould (8)

Speaker	Text	Page	Title	Act.Sc	Line
Heartwell:	Devil--Oh the Pride and Joy of Heart 'twould be to me,	45	OLD BATCH	I.1	318
Bellmour:	in that silent manner--'Twould save a Man a World	60	OLD BATCH	II.2	221
Lucy:	'twould disgust his nicety, and take away his Stomach.	62	OLD BATCH	III.1	42
	'Twould grieve your hearts to see him; shall I call him?	113	OLD BATCH	EPI.	25
Maskwell:	I knew 'twould stun you: This Evening at eight she will	156	DOUBL DLR	III.1	233
Sr Sampson:	with him; 'twould be but like me, A Chip of the Old Block.	265	FOR LOVE	III.1	462
Angelica:	What signifie a Madman's Desires? Besides, 'twou'd	277	FOR LOVE	IV.1	79
	How hard a thing 'twould be, to please you all.	479	WAY WORLD	EPI.	4

Ty'd (1)   see Tongue-ty'd

Speaker	Text	Page	Title	Act.Sc	Line
Mellefont:	Passion had ty'd her Tongue, and Amazement mine.--	130	DOUBL DLR	I.1	108

Tyburn (1)
    Sr Sampson: damn'd Tyburn face, without the benefit o' the Clergy. . 243 FOR LOVE II.1 307
Tyde (1)
    Ben: tho'f he should strive against Wind and Tyde. . . . . 272 FOR LOVE III.1 717
Tyger (0)   see Mountain-Tyger
Tygers (2)
    Sir Paul: Reason,--as soon may Tygers Match with Tygers, Lambs . 144 DOUBL DLR II.1 224
Type (1)
    Foresight: Ferdinand Mendez Pinto was but a Type of thee, thou Lyar . 241 FOR LOVE II.1 236
Tyranically (1)
    Mrs Frail: Most Tyranically,--for you see he has got the . . . 287 FOR LOVE IV.1 455
Tyrannically (1)
    Scandal: comes Tyrannically to insult a ruin'd Lover, and make . 276 FOR LOVE IV.1 24
Tyrannize (1)
    Laetitia: Tyrannize--Go on cruel Man, do, Triumph over my . . . 77 OLD BATCH IV.1 91
Tyranny (6)
    Almeria: Will cease his Tyranny; and Garcia too . . . . . . 340 M. BRIDE II.2 23
    Heli: With Tyranny and grievous Impositions, ... 351 M. BRIDE III.1 69
    Manuel: And spend their Mouths in barking Tyranny. . . . . 362 M. BRIDE IV.1 64
    Mirabell: You had the Tyranny to deny me last Night; tho' you . 421 WAY WORLD II.1 429
    Lady Wish: Tyranny. . . . . 473 WAY WORLD V.1 456
    Mirabell: Inconstancy and Tyranny of temper, which from her own . 476 WAY WORLD V.1 542
Tyrant (3)
    Bellmour: Tyrant there and I, are two Buckets that can never come . 57 OLD BATCH II.2 118
    Heli: Nightly; hating this Tyrant; some, who love . . . 352 M. BRIDE III.1 101
    Marwood: readmit him as its lawful Tyrant. . . . . . . 410 WAY WORLD II.1 27
Tyrant's (1)
    Zara: The blazing Torrent on the Tyrant's Head; . . . . . 380 M. BRIDE V.2 V170
Tyrants (1)
    Heartwell: Take the Symptoms--And ask all the Tyrants . . . 73 OLD BATCH III.2 76
'Udso (1)
    Trapland: 'Udso that's true, Mr. Valentine I love Mirth, but . . 224 FOR LOVE I.1 300
Ugliness (1)
    Scandal: Impotence and Ugliness in another Piece; and yet one of . 233 FOR LOVE I.1 632
Ugly (5)
    Sir Joseph: no Quality at all, 'tis such a Damn'd ugly Hand. . . 103 OLD BATCH V.1 272
    Heartwell: when I wed again, may she be--Ugly, as an old . . . 112 OLD BATCH V.2 159
    Miss Prue: trouble me no more, you ugly thing. . . . . 264 FOR LOVE III.1 401
    Millamant: that, I fancy one's Old and Ugly. . . . . . 420 WAY WORLD II.1 388
    Mirabell: Cheat. The Ugly and the Old, whom the Looking-glass . 420 WAY WORLD II.1 395
Um (1)
    Sir Joseph: Um--Ay this, this is the very damn'd place; the . . 47 OLD BATCH II.1 2
Umh (1)
    Witwoud: Umh--No-- . . . . 408 WAY WORLD I.1 474
Unable (1)
    Lady Ply: feeble, and unable to support it self. . . . . . 147 DOUBL DLR II.1 322
Unaccomplish'd (1)
    Osmyn-Alph: Yet unaccomplish'd; his mysterious Rites . . . . 357 M. BRIDE III.1 320
Unaccountable (1)
    Sr Sampson: Son of a Cucumber.--These things are unaccountable . . . 246 FOR LOVE II.1 388
Unacquainted (1)
    Manuel: I am not unacquainted with thy Falshood. . . . . . 367 M. BRIDE IV.1 264
Unaffected (2)
    Lady Ply: unaffected, so easie, so free, so particular, so agreeable-- 160 DOUBL DLR III.1 364
    Mirabell: to be unaffected, and confesses you are conscious of a . 397 WAY WORLD I.1 96
Unaffectedly (1)
    Vainlove: him Truth:--Yet she was unaffectedly concern'd, he . . . 99 OLD BATCH V.1 95
Unattended (1)
    Mirabell: You seem to be unattended, Madam--You . . . . . . 418 WAY WORLD II.1 328
Unawares (2)
    Mrs Fain: short upon me unawares, and has almost overcome me. . . 412 WAY WORLD II.1 83
    Foible: have gone a Walking: But we went up unawares,--tho' . . 464 WAY WORLD V.1 96
Unbarr'd (1)
    Gonsalez: Nor Centinel, nor Guard! the Doors unbarr'd! . . . . 376 M. BRIDE V.2 1
Unbecoming (2)
    Lord Froth: more unbecoming a Man of Quality, than to Laugh; Jesu, . 132 DOUBL DLR I.1 199
    Lord Froth: more unbecoming a Man of Quality, than to Laugh; . . . 132 DOUBL DLR I.1 V199
Unbend (1)
    Lady Wish: alliance,--We may unbend the severity of Decorum . . 457 WAY WORLD IV.1 488
Unbind (1)
    (Beholding Osmyn as they unbind him.) . 336 M. BRIDE I.1 425
Unborn (1)
    Manuel: Yet new, unborn and blooming in the Bud, ... 349 M. BRIDE II.2 384
Unborrow'd (1)
    Zara: Of equal Value, with unborrow'd Rule, ... 335 M. BRIDE I.1 396
Unbred (2)
    Millamant: Sure never any thing was so Unbred as that odious . . 432 WAY WORLD III.1 284
    Lady Wish: shall stay for you--My Nephew's a little unbred, . . 441 WAY WORLD III.1 622
Uncapable (1)
    Sir Paul: . . . and render'd uncapable . . . . 178 DOUBL DLR IV.1 V425 |
Uncase (1)
    Sr Sampson: With all my heart: Come, Uncase, Strip, and . . . . 244 FOR LOVE II.1 337
Uncertain (1)
    Witwoud: She's handsome; but she's a sort of an uncertain . . 408 WAY WORLD I.1 471
Uncertainty (6)
    Lady Touch: Uncertainty. Speak then, and tell me--yet are you . . 198 DOUBL DLR V.1 400
    Valentine: But I can accuse you of Uncertainty, for not telling . 254 FOR LOVE III.1 29
    Angelica: You mistake Indifference for Uncertainty; I never . . 254 FOR LOVE III.1 31
    Valentine: You are not leaving me in this Uncertainty? . . . . 296 FOR LOVE IV.1 784
    Angelica: Uncertainty? Uncertainty and Expectation are the Joys of . 296 FOR LOVE IV.1 786
Unchristian (1)
    Lady Ply: d'ye mark me, if she has once sworn: It is most unchristian 171 DOUBL DLR IV.1 151
Uncivil (3)
    Bellmour: like an uncivil Person, you knock'd at the Door, before . 95 OLD BATCH IV.4 215
    Brisk: Sir Paul, Gads-bud you're an uncivil Person, let me tell . 174 DOUBL DLR IV.1 267
    Trapland: Mr. Scandal, you are Uncivil; I did not value your . . 224 FOR LOVE I.1 313

Ungracious (1)
Sr Sampson: ungracious Prodigal know who begat him; I will, old   . . 240 FOR LOVE   II.1   174
Ungrateful (12)
Bellmour: ungrateful to that Creature? She's extreamly pretty and . 38 OLD BATCH I.1   39
Sharper: Know you! why can you be so ungrateful, to forget   . . . 48 OLD BATCH II.1   38
Sir Joseph: were no danger, I'le be so ungrateful to take it from the 67 OLD BATCH III.1 256
Sir Joseph: love to be the Messenger of ill News; 'tis an ungrateful . 68 OLD BATCH III.1 266
Araminta: to a wrong Belief.--Unworthy, and ungrateful! Be   . . .   87 OLD BATCH IV.3   173
Lady Touch: Ungrateful; come, I know you false. . . . . 135 DOUBL DLR I.1   300
Lord Touch: Ungrateful Monster, how long?-- . . . . 153 DOUBL DLR III.1 108
Lady Ply: Ungrateful Monster! He? Is it so? Ay, I see it, a Plot upon 179 DOUBL DLR IV.1   444
              Their Labours lost upon the ungrateful Ground, ... 213 FOR LOVE   PRO.   8
Angelica: Nay, now you're ungrateful. . . . . 255 FOR LOVE   III.1 84
Zara: Not heard! Ungrateful Osmyn. . . . . 346 M. BRIDE   II.2   246
Lady Wish: ruine? Ungrateful Wretch! dost thou not owe thy being, . 473 WAY WORLD V.1   446
Ungratefull (2)
              Their Labours lost upon ungratefull Ground, ... 213 FOR LOVE   PRO. V 8
Lady Wish: Pardon on your Knees, Ungratefull Creature; she deserves . 466 WAY WORLD V.1   169
Ungratefully (1)
Almeria: My Lord, my Eyes ungratefully behold   . . . . 332 M. BRIDE   I.1   246
Unguarded (1)
Heli: So to be caught in an unguarded Hour, ... 338 M. BRIDE   II.1   30
Unhappily (1)
Marwood: unhappily directed to miscarry. . . . . 434 WAY WORLD III.1 347
Unhappiness (2)
Garcia: If so, Unhappiness attends their Love   . . . . . . 339 M. BRIDE   II.1   47
Osmyn-Alph: She's the Reverse of thee; she's my Unhappiness.   . . 345 M. BRIDE   II.2   200
Unhappy (3)
Foresight: or short, Happy or Unhappy; whether Diseases are   . . 241 FOR LOVE   II.1   215
Angelica: 'Tis very unhappy, if you don't care for one another. . 309 FOR LOVE   V.1   462
Marwood: True, 'tis an unhappy Circumstance of Life, ... 410 WAY WORLD IV.1   9
Unheard (3)
Lady Touch: The Contract's void by this unheard of Impiety. . . . 150 DOUBL DLR III.1 3
Lord Touch: of unheard of Treachery. My Wife! Damnation! my . . . 200 DOUBL DLR V.1   472
Almeria: Unheard of Curses on me, greater far   . . . . . . 330 M. BRIDE   I.1   188
Unhewn (1)
Belinda: my Dear,--I have seen such unhewn Creatures since,--Ha, . 83 OLD BATCH IV.3   11
Unhop'd (2)
Maskwell: Transports of a Blessing so unexpected, so unhop'd for, so 189 DOUBL DLR V.1   81
Heli: O Joy unhop'd for, does Almeria live! . . . . . . 341 M. BRIDE   II.2   65
Unhurt (1)
Heli: But fell unhurt, a Prisoner as your self; . . . . . 344 M. BRIDE   II.2   176
Union (1)
Osmyn-Alph: The Sacred Union of Connubial Love, ... 357 M. BRIDE   III.1 319
Unite (1)
Leonora: To end the long Dissention, and unite . . . . . . 327 M. BRIDE   I.1   50
Universal (5)
Maskwell: an universal Leveller of Mankind. Ha! but is there not such 150 DOUBL DLR II.1   450
Lady Ply: and Premunire! I'm all over in a Universal Agitation, I . 178 DOUBL DLR IV.1   397
Sr Sampson: Body o' me, I don't know any universal Grievance, . . . 266 FOR LOVE   III.1 485
Mrs Fore: Aye; but you are such an universal Jugler, ... 272 FOR LOVE   III.1 702
Alonzo: Tho' for the Crown of Universal Empire. . . . . . 379 M. BRIDE   V.2   112
Universe (1)
Lord Froth: O, for the Universe, not a drop more I beseech . . . . 134 DOUBL DLR I.1   288
University (1)
Tattle: University: But the Education is a little too pedantick for 302 FOR LOVE   V.1   187
Unjust (1)
Laetitia: must study to encrease it by unjust suspicions? (Crying) . 77 OLD BATCH IV.1   89
Unkind (2)
Laetitia: Unkind Dear! Was it for this, you sent to call me? is . . 77 OLD BATCH IV.1   87
Mirabell: Unkind. You had the leisure to entertain a Herd of . . 421 WAY WORLD II.1   433
Unkindness (1)
Bellmour: every thing but your Unkindness. . . . . 81 OLD BATCH IV.2   32
Unkle (1)
Tattle: her Unkle Old Foresight: I think your Father lies at . . 228 FOR LOVE   I.1   453
Unknowing (2)
Zara: He dy'd unknowing in my Heart. . . . . 381 M. BRIDE   V.2   190
Zara: But Oh, he dy'd unknowing in my Heart. . . . . . 381 M. BRIDE   V.2 V190
Unknown (10)
Bellmour: Yet rails on still, and thinks his Love unknown to us; . 40 OLD BATCH I.1   123
Lady Touch: to be unknown which cannot be prevented; therefore let . 152 DOUBL DLR III.1 55
Valentine: at the height of a Song, sent by an unknown Hand, or a . 218 FOR LOVE   I.1   80
Osmyn-Alph: This Charity to one unknown, and in . . . . 359 M. BRIDE   III.1 403
Osmyn-Alph: This Charity to one unknown, and thus . . . . . . 359 M. BRIDE   III.1 V403
Zara: Yet I'll be calm--Dark and unknown Betrayer! . . . . 360 M. BRIDE   III.1 439
Marwood: unknown hand--for the less I appear to know of the truth . 443 WAY WORLD III.1 702
Sir Wilful: Unknown to the Turk and the Persian: . . . . . . 456 WAY WORLD IV.1   451
Sir Wilful: Unknown to the Turk or the Persian: . . . . . . 456 WAY WORLD IV.1 V451
Lady Wish: (Reads)--Madam, tho' unknown to you (Look you there 'tis . 460 WAY WORLD IV.1   584
Unladen (1)
              Th' unladen Boughs, he sees, bode certain Dearth, . . . 213 FOR LOVE   PRO.   5
Unlawful (2)
Angelica: Yes, I can make Oath of your unlawful Midnight . . . . 237 FOR LOVE   II.1   96
Nurse: --O Lord, what's here to do?--I in unlawful . . . . 238 FOR LOVE   II.1   99
Unless (14)
Bellmour: Who the Devil would have thee? unless 'twere an . . . 45 OLD BATCH I.1   298
Sharper: unless it be to serve my particular Friend, as Sir
                   Joseph here, ... 51 OLD BATCH II.1   159
Bellmour: kick this Puppy unless a Man were cold, and had no . . . 70 OLD BATCH III.1 V328
Mellefont: the last Minute of her Reign, unless the Devil assist her in 169 DOUBL DLR IV.1   53
              Unless the Fable's good, and Moral sound. . . . . . 204 DOUBL DLR EPI.   18
              Unless transplanted to more kindly Earth. . . . . . 213 FOR LOVE   PRO.   6
Sr Sampson: Unless Popery shou'd be landed in the West, or the . . . 266 FOR LOVE   III.1 V487
Gonsalez: But if she had, what was't to her? unless . . . . . 366 M. BRIDE   IV.1   223
Garcia: Before 'em, to the Pallace Walls. Unless . . . . . 377 M. BRIDE   V.2   35
Mirabell: is to be flatter'd further, unless a Man shou'd endeavour . 397 WAY WORLD I.1   77

Unseen   (continued)
```
   Almeria:    Which they unseen, may wail, and weep, and mourn,   . . . 328   M. BRIDE    I.1     85
   Zara:       Better I was unseen, than seen thus coldly.   . . . . . 346   M. BRIDE    II.2   257
   Zara:       In Chains unseen, I hold him by the Heart,   . . . . . 348   M. BRIDE    II.2   325
   Zara:       And unseen. Is it my Love? ask again   . . . . . . . 353   M. BRIDE    III.1   153
   Millamant:  and say; vain empty Things if we are silent or unseen, and  421   WAY WORLD   II.1   411
Unsincere (1)
   Fainall:    What I warrant he's unsincere, or 'tis some such   . . . 403   WAY WORLD   I.1    316
Unsiz'd (1)
   Witwoud:    out and piec'd in the sides like an unsiz'd Camlet,--Yes,  453   WAY WORLD   IV.1   328
Unsought (2)
   Zara:       Favours conferr'd, tho' when unsought, deserve   . . . . 336   M. BRIDE    I.1    415
   Zara:       Such Favours so conferr'd, tho' when unsought,   . . . . 336   M. BRIDE    I.1  V415
Unstartled (1)
   Lady Touch: Face; but walks unstartled from the Mirrour, and streight  136   DOUBL DLR   I.1  V331
Unsteadily (1)
   Manuel:     Fickle in Fields, unsteadily she flyes,   . . . . . . 337   M. BRIDE    I.1    460
Unstopt (2)
   Buckram:    is not the least Cranny of the Law unstopt.   . . . . . 308   FOR LOVE    V.1    430
   Ben:        Lawyer, I believe there's many a Cranny and Leak unstopt  309   FOR LOVE    V.1    431
Unsuccessful (2)
   Tattle:     telling you Madam, I have been the most unsuccessful   . . 256   FOR LOVE    III.1  103
   Scandal:    matter. But this is no new effect of an unsuccessful
                 Passion.   . . . . . . . . . . . . . . . . . 277   FOR LOVE    IV.1    46
Unsulli'd (2)
   Lady Ply:   this three year past? Have I been white and unsulli'd
                 even by   . . . . . . . . . . . . . . . 145   DOUBL DLR   II.1   255
   Lady Ply:   these three Years past? Have I been white and unsulli'd
                 even by   . . . . . . . . . . . . . . . 145   DOUBL DLR   II.1  V255
Unsuspected (3)
   Lady Ply:   yet I'll be sure to be unsuspected this time.--Sir Paul.  . 173   DOUBL DLR   IV.1   212
   Almeria:    Some unsuspected hoard of darling Grief,   . . . . . . 328   M. BRIDE    I.1     84
   Fainall:    unsuspected in my Pleasures; and take you oftner to my  . 414   WAY WORLD   II.1   146
Unswear (1)
   Sir Paul:   make of none effect your Oath: So you may unswear it   . . 171   DOUBL DLR   IV.1   145
Unthought (3)
   Lady Touch: into unthought of ways of ruine.   . . . . . . . . . 185   DOUBL DLR   IV.2    78
   Maskwell:   unthought of!   . . . . . . . . . . . . . . . 189   DOUBL DLR   V.1     82
   Lady Touch: and fresh cause of fury from unthought of   . . . . . . 191   DOUBL DLR   V.1    156
Untie (1)
   Tattle:     you,--I know you love to untie Difficulties--Or if   . . . 305   FOR LOVE    V.1    296
Until (1)
   Sharper:    all Injuries whatsoever, done unto you by them; until the  110   OLD BATCH   V.2     87
Untimely (1)
   Vainlove:   'Tis an untimely Fruit, and she has miscarried of   . . . 79   OLD BATCH   IV.1   169
Unto (3)
   Sharper:    all Injuries whatsoever, done unto you by them; until the  110   OLD BATCH   V.2     87
   Angelica:   How few, like Valentine, would persevere even unto   . . 314   FOR LOVE    V.1    633
   Fainall:    must be agreed unto, and that positively. Lastly, I will be  469   WAY WORLD   V.1    277
Untoward'st (1)
   Belinda:    as I was telling you--Pish, this is the untoward'st   . . 83   OLD BATCH   IV.3    15
Unus'd (1)
   Manuel:     Unus'd to wait, I broke through her Delay,   . . . . . 337   M. BRIDE    I.1    456
Unusual (1)
   Scandal:    Cause of that? And Sir Sampson is hurry'd on by an unusual  268   FOR LOVE    III.1  548
Unutterable (1)
   Almeria:    What means these Tears, but Grief unutterable?   . . . . 368   M. BRIDE    IV.1   268
Unwanted (1)
   Zara:       And so unwish'd, unwanted too it seems.   . . . . . . 359   M. BRIDE    III.1  410
Unwarn'd (1)
   Osmyn-Alph: Snatch me from Life, and cut me short unwarn'd:   . . . . 343   M. BRIDE    II.2   141
Unwearied (2)
   Lord Touch: joyn your hands.--Unwearied Nights, and wishing   . . . 203   DOUBL DLR   V.1    587
   Osmyn-Alph: Why does she follow with unwearied Steps,   . . . . . . 351   M. BRIDE    III.1   57
Unwelcome (2)
   Bellmour:   unmannerly and as unwelcome to a Woman, as a Looking   . . 42   OLD BATCH   I.1    186
   Manuel:     An unforeseen, unwelcome Hour of Business,   . . . . . 363   M. BRIDE    IV.1   105
Unwilling (2)
   Vainlove:   Name's to it, which she will be unwilling to expose to the  88   OLD BATCH   IV.3   188
   Lady Touch: I don't know; I am very unwilling to speak   . . . . . 151   DOUBL DLR   III.1   34
Unwind (2)
   Lady Touch: another Caprice, to unwind my temper.   . . . . . . . 137   DOUBL DLR   I.1    392
   Zara:       And can unwind, or strain him as I please.   . . . . . 348   M. BRIDE    II.2   326
Unwish'd (1)
   Zara:       And so unwish'd, unwanted too it seems.   . . . . . . 359   M. BRIDE    III.1  410
Unwittingly (1)
   Bellmour:   unwittingly marry a Whore.   . . . . . . . . . . . 98   OLD BATCH   V.1     62
Unwonted (1)
   Capt Bluff: And so out of your unwonted Generosity--   . . . . . . 67   OLD BATCH   III.1  242
Unworthy (8)
   Araminta:   to a wrong Belief.--Unworthy, and ungrateful! Be   . . . 87   OLD BATCH   IV.3   173
   Mellefont:  but a shallow artifice, unworthy of my Matchiavilian   . . 148   DOUBL DLR   II.1   376
   Sir Paul:   unworthy Sinner--But if I had a Son, ah, that's my   . . 161   DOUBL DLR   III.1  415
   Sir Paul:   am her Husband, as I may say, though far unworthy of   . . 162   DOUBL DLR   III.1  437
   Maskwell:   she thinks I am unworthy.   . . . . . . . . . . 195   DOUBL DLR   V.1    316
   Lord Touch: Unworthy! 'tis an ignorant Pride in her to   . . . . . 196   DOUBL DLR   V.1    317
   Jeremy:     Even my unworthy self, Sir--Sir, I have had an   . . . . 301   FOR LOVE    V.1    171
   Zara:       But something so unworthy, and so vile,   . . . . . . 348   M. BRIDE    II.2   337
Up (151)
Up-lifted (1)
               Devoutly praying, with up-lifted Hands,   . . . . . . 385   M. BRIDE    EPI.    21
Upbraid (2)
   Zara:       Well, dost thou scorn me, and upbraid my Falseness;   . . 353   M. BRIDE    III.1  160
   Marwood:    You, you upbraid me! Have I been false to her, thro' strict  414   WAY WORLD   II.1   172
Upon (288)
```

Upon't (5)

Lord Touch:	Out upon't, Nephew--leave your	131	DOUEL DLR	I.1	172
Brisk:	be splenatick, or airy upon't; the Deuce take me if I can	176	DOUBL DLR	IV.1	338
Scandal:	He's gone to Bed upon't, and very ill--He speaks	266	FOR LCVE	III.1	497
Lady Wish:	Out upon't, out upon't, at years of Discretion,	455	WAY WCRLD	IV.1	384

Upward (2)

| Waitwell: | starve upward and upward, till he has nothing living but | 458 | WAY WCRLD | IV.1 | 523 |

Urg'd (7)

Lord Touch:	Then Mellefont has urg'd some body to	195	DOUEL DLR	V.1	309
Maskwell:	for you.--First tell me what urg'd you to this violence?	198	DOUEL DLR	V.1	413
Zara:	You hated Manuel, I urg'd my Husband	347	M. BRIDE	II.2	300
Gonsalez:	Open'd and urg'd the Way to this Invasion;	363	M. EBIDE	IV.1	V 87
Gonsalez:	And urg'd by Nature pleading for his Child,	371	M. EBIDE	IV.1	407
Marwood:	My Obligations to my Lady urg'd me: I had	414	WAY WORLD	II.1	162
Marwood:	'Tis false, you urg'd it with deliberate Malice--	414	WAY WCRLD	II.1	182

Urge (6)

Mellefont:	that the most viclent Love could urge, or tender words	130	DOUBL DLR	I.1	110
Maskwell:	Mellefont. I'll urge haste, to excuse your silence.	195	DOUEL DLR	V.1	295
Leonora:	'Twill urge his Wrath, to see ycu drown'd in Tears,	330	M. EBIDE	I.1	V167
Selim:	The King, and were alone enough to urge	361	M. EBIDE	IV.1	5
Gonsalez:	Urge that, to try if she'll sollicite for him.	367	M. EBIDE	IV.1	241
Fainall:	the way of the World. That shall nct urge me to relinquish	474	WAY WCRLD	V.1	476

Urged (1)

| Mellefont: | self favour'd in her aversion: Eut whether urged by her | 129 | DOUBL DLR | I.1 | 94 |

Urinal (2)

| Nurse: | and your Urinal by you, and now and then rub the | 238 | FOR LCVE | II.1 | 104 |
| Foresight: | the turning of the Tide, bring me the Urinal;--And I | 270 | FOR LCVE | III.1 | 647 |

Us (154)

Us'd (14)

	But we're so us'd to Rail on these Occasions,	113	OLD EATCH	EPI.	19
Tattle:	us'd by the Ladies.	255	FCR LCVE	III.1	83
Mrs Frail:	foul Weather--He's us'd to an inconstant Element,	284	FOR LCVE	IV.1	307
Mrs Fore:	Mr. Tattle might have us'd less Ceremony.	293	FOR LCVE	IV.1	681
Almeria:	Or, when there, why was I us'd so tenderly?	327	M. EBIDE	I.1	66
Almeria:	Or there, why was I us'd so tenderly?	327	M. EBIDE	I.1	V 66
Almeria:	For so my Father would have us'd his Child.	328	M. BRIDE	I.1	68
Zara:	What Arts I us'd to make you pass on him,	347	M. EBRIDE	II.2	294
Zara:	I am your Captive, and you've us'd me Nobly;	364	M. EBIDE	IV.1	136
Mirabell:	agreeable. I'll tell thee, Fainall, she once us'd me with that	399	WAY WORLD	I.1	163
Mirabell:	end I so us'd my self to think of 'em, that at length, contrary	399	WAY WCRLD	I.1	168
Witwoud:	this is nothing to what he us'd to do;--Before he	405	WAY WCRLD	I.1	365
Mirabell:	us'd tc have the Eeau-mond Throng after you; and a Flock	418	WAY WCRLD	I.1	329
Foible:	heard how he us'd me, and all upcn your Ladyship's	427	WAY WCRLD	III.1	87

Usage (5)

Laetitia:	this usage of yours--But that's what you want--Well--	77	OLD BATCH	IV.1	93
Valentine:	Sir, is this Usage for your Son?--for that cld,	244	FOR LCVE	II.1	311
Valentine:	Unnatural Usage.	244	FOR LCVE	II.1	322
Marwood:	of ill usage; I think I shou'd dc my self the violence of	411	WAY WCRLD	II.1	55
Marwood:	I loath the name of Love after such usage;	415	WAY WCRLD	II.1	219

Use (22)

Sharper:	And like that, of no use but to be beaten.	47	OLD EATCH	I.1	379
Bellmour:	shall use the Robes.	64	OLD BATCH	III.1	135
Setter:	What no Token of amity Lucy? you and I don't use	67	OLD EATCH	III.1	234
Capt Bluff:	O this is your time Sir, you had best make use on't.	69	OLD EATCH	III.1	319
Laetitia:	Ha! This fool may be of use. Stand off, rude Ruffian.	90	OLD BATCH	IV.4	46
Vainlove:	Pray use her as my Relation, or you shall hear on't.	111	OLD EATCH	V.2	138
Maskwell:	prevent your Plot, yet I would have you use Caution and	154	DOUEL DLR	III.1	139
Careless:	use his Chamber; let's follow and examine him.	196	DOUBL DLR	V.1	353
	And are afraid to use their own Edge-Tools.	214	FCR LCVE	PRO.	38
Scandal:	Nor I faith--But Tattle does not use to bely a	229	FOR LCVE	I.1	489
Scandal:	And did not use to be so.	270	FOR LCVE	III.1	621
Mrs Fore:	Well; and what use do you hope to make of	271	FOR LCVE	III.1	659
Sr Sampson:	we are Fools as we use to be--Ocns, that you cou'd	283	FOR LCVE	IV.1	280
Scandal:	So I'll leave him to make use of the Discovery; and	294	FOR LCVE	IV.1	691
Angelica:	No, I have it; and I'll use it, as I would every thing	312	FOR LCVE	V.1	555
Almeria:	Why did he not use me like an Enemy?	327	M. EBIDE	I.1	67
Heli:	Which Manuel to his own Use and Avarice,	351	M. EBIDE	III.1	66
Zara:	And Detestation, that cou'd use thee thus.	353	M. EBIDE	III.1	163
Gonsalez:	At my Appartment. Use thy utmost Diligence;	372	M. EBIDE	IV.1	441
Mirabell:	use at this time.	405	WAY WORLD	I.1	393
Marwood:	Here is an Academy in Town for that use.	440	WAY WORLD	III.1	586
Fainall:	Wife's to my sole use; As pursuant to the Purport and	473	WAY WCRLD	V.1	436

Used (4)

Capt Bluff:	a little Art-military, used--only undermined, or so, as	110	OLD BATCH	V.2	108
	Women and Wits are used e'en much at one;	113	OLD BATCH	EPI.	29
Scandal:	The World behaves it self, as it used to do on such	220	FOR LCVE	I.1	159
Scandal:	methinks he does not look as he used to do.	268	FOR LCVE	III.1	550

Uses (4)

Setter:	uses me as his Attendant; the cther (being the better	64	OLD EATCH	III.1	139
Scandal:	The World behaves it self, as it uses to do on such	220	FOR LCVE	I.1	V159
Lady Wish:	this Exceeds all precedent; I am brought to fine uses, to	463	WAY WCRLD	V.1	50
Mirabell:	to the uses within mention'd. You may read if you please	476	WAY WCRLD	V.1	547

Usher (1)

| Mirabell: | usher in the Fall; and withers in an affected Bloom. | 418 | WAY WCRLD | II.1 | 320 |

Usherd (2)

| Marwood: | Lawyers? To be usherd in with an O Yez of Scandal; and | 467 | WAY WORLD | V.1 | 211 |
| Marwood: | Lawyers? To be usherd in with an O Yes of Scandal; and | 467 | WAY WCRLD | V.1 | V211 |

Using (3)

Maskwell:	design upon you, but still using my utmost Endeavours to	154	DOUEL DLR	III.1	151
Mellefont:	has the privilege of using the familiarity of a Husband	158	DOUBL DLR	III.1	287
Sir Paul:	of using the common benefits of Nature?	178	DOUBL DLR	IV.1	V426

Usual (6)

| Vainlove: | early Sallies are not usual to me; but Business as you see | 37 | OLD BATCH | I.1 | 6 |
| Lady Froth: | angry than usual. | 203 | DOUEL DLR | V.1 | 580 |

Usual (continued)

		PAGE	TITLE	ACT.SC	LINE
Valentine:	the usual Hours. Yet you will see such Zealous Faces	289	FOR LCVE	IV.1	501
Zara:	With usual Hcmage wait. But when I feel	336	M. EFIDE	I.1	399
Heli:	Are usual to his Temper. It might raise him	338	M. EBIDE	II.1	28
Marwood:	very usual with ycung Gentlemen.	432	WAY WCRLD	III.1	268

Usurp'd (1)

Gonsalez:	That scme Impostor has usurp'd his Name.	363	M. BRIDE	IV.1	100

Usurper (1)

Sr Sampson:	Weather; and destroy that Usurper of a Bed call'd a	308	FOR LCVE	V.1	406

Utmost (8)

Setter:	I do swear to the utmost of my power.	66	OLD EATCH	III.1	216
Maskwell:	design upon you, but still using my utmost Endeavours to	154	DOUEL DLR	III.1	151
Mrs Fore:	I do; and will help you to the utmost of my	248	FCB LCVE	II.1	497
Angelica:	and struggl'd very hard to make this utmost Tryal of your	312	FCB LCVE	V.1	563
Angelica:	Nature. I was resclv'd to try him to the utmost; I have	312	FOR LCVE	V.1	574
Zara:	Choak in my Rage, and know the utmost depth	359	M. EFIDE	III.1	407
Gonsalez:	At my Appartment. Use thy utmost Diligence;	372	M. EBIDE	IV.1	441
Millamant:	You have free leave; propose ycur utmost, speak	450	WAY WCBLD	IV.1	232

Utter'd (3)

Foresight:	about these things which he has utter'd.--His Sayings	289	FOR LCVE	IV.1	533
Sr Sampson:	None cf old Foresight's Sybills ever utter'd such a	299	FCB LCVE	V.1	79
Witwoud:	Thou hast utter'd Volumes, Folio's, in less than	453	WAY WORLD	IV.1	342

Utterly (2)

Sharper:	Now, were I ill-natur'd, wou'd I utterly disappoint	100	OLD EATCH	V.1	137
Sir Paul:	utterly extinct for want of Issue Male. Oh Impiety! But	171	DOUEL DLR	IV.1	138

Vagarie (1)

Sir Paul:	should take a Vagarie and make a rash Besolution on your	174	DOUEL DLR	IV.1	251

Vain (29)

Singer:	But vain alas! were all her Charms;	71	OLD EATCH	III.2 V	22
Bellmour:	Since all Artifice is vain--and I think my self obliged	93	OLD BATCH	IV.4	157
Lady Touch:	O' Maskwell, in Vain I do disguise me frcm	137	DOUEL DLR	I.1	396
Lady Ply:	He's hot-headed still! 'Tis in vain to talk to you;	144	DOUEL DLR	II.1	227
Careless:	--but all in vain, she would not hear a word upon that	180	DOUEL DLR	IV.1	500
Maskwell:	I have it, it must be by Stratagem; for it's in vain	190	DOUBL DLR	V.1	114
	The Husbandman in vain renews his Toil,	213	FOR LCVE	PRO.	1
Scandal:	vain! Who would die a Martyr to Sense in a Ccuntry	219	FCR LCVE	I.1	139
Ben:	And gnaw the Sheets in vain, Sir,	274	FOR LCVE	III.1	766
Angelica:	deluded with vain Hopes. Good Nature and Humanity	277	FCR LCVE	IV.1	72
Valentine:	vain Attempts, and find at last, that nothing Lut my Ruine	312	FOR LCVE	V.1	547
	And Nature miss'd, in vain he boasts his Art,	324	M. EBIDE	PRO.	37
Osmyn-Alph:	But that in vain. I have Almeria here.	345	M. EFIDE	II.2	228
Osmyn-Alph:	In vain you cffer, and in vain require	348	M. EBIDE	II.2	328
Heli:	Was never heard in vain: Heav'n has in Store	352	M. EBIDE	III.1	118
Almeria:	In vain with the remorseless Chains, which gnaw	356	M. EFIDE	III.1	267
Selim:	I've sought in vain, the King is no where, to	380	M. EBIDE	V.2	173
Selim:	I've sought in vain, for no where can the King	380	M. EFIDE	V.2 V	173
Almeria:	With Thee, the kneeling World should beg in vain	382	M. EBIDF	V.2	263
	To build on that might prove a vain Presumption,	393	WAY WCRLD	PRO.	18
Fainall:	Commendation wou'd go near to make me either Vain	402	WAY WCRLD	I.1	262
Mirabell:	Vain.	404	WAY WCRLD	I.1	335
Marwood:	than all the vain and empty Vows of Men, whether	414	WAY WCRLD	II.1	168
Mirabell:	vain how lost a Thing you'll be! Nay, 'tis true: You are no	420	WAY WCBLD	II.1	391
Millamant:	and say; vain empty Things if we are silent or unseen, and	421	WAY WCBLD	II.1	411
Mirabell:	Yet to those two vain empty Things, you cwe two	421	WAY WCBLD	II.1	413
Singer:	For whom inferiour Beauties sigh'd in vain.	435	WAY WCBLD	III.1	385
	If any are so arrcgantly Vain,	479	WAY WCRLD	EPI.	25

Vainlove (34)

	(The Street. Bellmour and Vainlove Meeting)	37	OLD BATCH	I.1	
Bellmour:	Vainlove, and abroad so early! gccd Morrow; I	37	OLD BATCH	I.1	1
Bellmour:	Let me see--How now! Dear perfidious Vainlove.	38	OLD BATCH	I.1	35
Bellmour:	Would thou hadst come a little sconer, Vainlove	42	OLD BATCH	I.1	194
Heartwell:	And proves that Vainlove plays the Fool with	42	OLD EATCH	I.1	216
Heartwell:	Vainlove, kiss a Lap-Dog with passion, when it would	43	OLD EATCH	I.1	255
Belinda:	Vainlove--Lard I have seen an Ass lcok so Chagrin,	55	OLD EATCH	II.2	26
Footman:	Vainlove to wait upon your Ladyship.	56	OLD EATCH	II.2	77
	(Enter Bellmour, Vainlove.)	57	OLD EATCH	II.2	113
Silvia:	Senseless Creature, I meant my Vainlove.	61	OLD BATCH	III.1	6
	(Enter Heartwell, Vainlove and Bellmour following.	62	OLD BATCH	III.1	59
Lucy:	Vainlove, I have found out a picque she has taken at him;	75	OLD BATCH	III.2	156
	(Enter Vainlove, Sharper.)	79	OLD BATCH	IV.1	152
Laetitia:	(aside). My Letter! Vainlove! Then 'tis too late	81	OLD EATCH	IV.2	34
Bellmour:	find it directed to Mr. Vainlove. Gad, Madam, I ask you a	82	OLD EATCH	IV.2	57
Laetitia:	(aside). I am discover'd:--And either Vainlove is	82	OLD EATCH	IV.2	59
Araminta:	No matter,--I saw Vainlove coming this way,--	85	OLD EATCH	IV.3	77
	(Enter Sharper and Vainlove, at a Distance.)	86	OLD EATCH	IV.3	99
	(Enter Sharper and Vainlove, at some Distance.)	86	OLD EATCH	IV.3 V	99
Araminta:	Vainlove to know us, I'll be rid of my Fool by fair means	86	OLD EATCH	IV.3	102
Belinda:	Very courtly.--I believe, Mr. Vainlove has not	86	OLD BATCH	IV.3	129
Belinda:	his Mistress, is like a Body without a Scul. Mr. Vainlove,	86	OLD BATCH	IV.3	134
Belinda:	I have broke the ice for you, Mr. Vainlove, and so I	87	OLD BATCH	IV.3	142
Lucy:	Alas-a-day! You and Mr. Vainlove, between you, have	98	OLD BATCH	V.1	47
	(Enter Vainlove, Sharper and Setter.)	98	OLD BATCH	V.1	81
Sharper:	Vainlove jealous.--	102	OLD BATCH	V.1	202
Sharper:	She has given Vainlove her Promise, to marry him	102	OLD BATCH	V.1	212
Sharper:	Why, I'll tell you: 'Tis a young Creature that Vainlove	104	OLD EATCH	V.1	292
	(Enter Bellmour, Belinda, Araminta and Vainlove.)	106	OLD EATCH	V.1	355
	(Enter Bellmour, Belinda, Vainlove, Araminta.)	108	OLD EATCH	V.2	16
	(Vainlove and Araminta talk a-part.)	108	OLD EATCH	V.2	21
Sharper:	Vainlcve, I have been a kind of a God-father to you,	109	OLD EATCH	V.2	81
Sir Joseph:	countermin'd, cr so--Mr. Vainlove, I suppose you know	110	OLD EATCH	V.2	113
Sharper:	Gentleman's Pardon: For though Vainlove be so generous	111	OLD EATCH	V.2	121

Vainlove's (2)

Bellmour:	Mistresses of my own acquiring; must yet take Vainlove's	41	OLD BATCH	I.1	140
Laetitia:	(aside). Vainlove's Friend! I know his Face, and he has	81	OLD BATCH	IV.2	18

Val (18)

Ben:	and Brother Val?	261	FOR LOVE	III.1	291

Val   (continued)
  Sr Sampson: I'll speak gently--Val, Val, do'st thou not   279   FOR LOVE   IV.1   156
  Sr Sampson: know me, Boy? Not know thy own Father, Val! I am   . . .   279   FOR LOVE   IV.1   157
  Sr Sampson: He recovers--bless thee, Val--Hcw do'st   281   FOR LOVE   IV.1   194
  Sr Sampson: Val: Hcw do'st thou do? let me feel thy Pulse--Oh,   . . .   281   FOR LOVE   IV.1   201
  Sr Sampson: pretty well now, Val: Body o' me, I was sorry to see thee   281   FCR LOVE   IV.1   202
  Sr Sampson: indisposed: But I'm glad thou'rt better, honest Val.   .   281   FOR LOVE   IV.1   203
  Sr Sampson: Let me feel thy Hand again, Val: it does not   281   FOR LOVE   IV.1   206
  Sr Sampson: shake--I believe thou can'st write, Val: Ha, boy? Thou   281   FOR LOVE   IV.1   207
  Sr Sampson: can'st write thy Name, Val?--Jeremy, step and overtake   281   FCR LOVE   IV.1   208
  Sr Sampson: Do'st thou know this Paper, Val: I know   281   FOR LCVE   IV.1   214
  Sr Sampson: 'tis thy own Hand, Val. Why, let me see, I can read it as   281   FOR LCVE   IV.1   220
  Sr Sampson: Val: And then no body need hold it (puts the Paper in his   281   FOR LOVE   IV.1   232
  Sr Sampson: Pocket.) There Val: it's safe enough, Eoy--But thou   .   282   FOR LCVE   IV.1   233
  Sr Sampson: Paper, little Val.   282   FOR LCVE   IV.1   235
  Ben: way--(It seems Brother Val is gone mad, and so that   .   285   FOR LCVE   IV.1   366
  Ben: say, Erother Val. went mad for, she's mad too, I think.   306   FOR LCVE   V.1   346
Valentia (5)
  Leonora: His Son, the brave Valentia Prince, and you, ...   327   M. ERIDE   I.1   49
  Almeria: I was a welcome Captive in Valentia, ...   329   M. ERIDE   I.1   110
  Gonsalez: Still alive, were arming in Valentia: 363   M. ERIDE   IV.1   78
  Gonsalez: Were still alive, and arming in Valentia: 363   M. ERIDE   IV.1 V 78
  Gonsalez: While he himself, returning to Valentia   363   M. ERIDE   IV.1   88
Valentia's (3)
  Leonora: Entail'd between Valentia's and Granada's Kings;   . . .   327   M. EFIDE   I.1   44
  Leonora: Between Valentia's and Granada's Kings;   327   M. EFIDE   I.1 V 44
  Heli: Converts. This News has reach'd Valentia's Frontiers;   . .   351   M. EFIDE   III.1   67
Valentine (56)   see Val
                (Valentine in his Chamber Reading. Jeremy waiting.   . .   216   FOR LCVE   I.1
  Jeremy: serv'd Valentine Legend Esq; and that he is not now turn'd   218   FOR LCVE   I.1   68
  Trapland: A good Morning to you Mr. Valentine, and to you   . . .   222   FCR LCVE   I.1   231
  Trapland: (sits). There is a Debt, Mr. Valentine, of 1500 [Pounds] of   222   FCR LCVE   I.1   236
  Trapland: 'Udso that's true, Mr. Valentine I love Mirth, but   . .   224   FCB LCVE   I.1   300
                (Enter Steward and Whispers Valentine.)   . . .   224   FOR LCVE   I.1   308
  Tattle: Valentine good Morrow, Scandal I am Yours.--   226   FOR LCVE   I.1   382
  Tattle: sav'd, Valentine, I never expos'd a Woman, since I knew   227   FOR LCVE   I.1   406
  Tattle: Valentine, I Supp'd last Night with your Mistress, and   .   228   FCR LCVE   I.1   452
  Scandal: Yes Faith. Ask Valentine else.   228   FOR LCVE   I.1   472
  Scandal: She'll be here by and by, she sees Valentine every   . .   229   FOR LCVE   I.1   483
  Scandal: be deceiv'd in a Woman, Valentine?   229   FOR LCVE   I.1   491
  Tattle: And bid me ask Valentine.   229   FOR LCVE   I.1   496
  Mrs Frail: O lying Creature--Valentine, does not he lye?   233   FCR LCVE   I.1   620
  Foresight: Gallant, Valentine, pay for all, I will.   238   FOR LCVE   II.1   117
  Jeremy: No, Sir, Mr. Valentine, my master,--'tis the first   . .   242   FCR LCVE   II.1   267
                        ,   (Enter Valentine.)   242   FCR LCVE   II.1   271
  Sr Sampson: Body o' me, so do I.--Heark ye, Valentine, ...   243   FCR LCVE   II.1   279
                (Enter Valentine, Scandal, and Angelica.)   254   FOR LCVE   III.1   26
  Scandal: Angelica's Love for Valentine; you won't speak of it.   . .   254   FOR LCVE   III.1   46
  Scandal: Angelica's Love to Valentine; you won't speak cf it.   . .   254   FOR LCVE   III.1 V 46
  Scandal: Your Love of Valentine.   254   FOR LCVE   III.1   52
  Tattle: Valentine, and yet remain insensible; therefore you will   255   FOR LCVE   III.1   69
  Angelica: I cite Valentine here, to declare to the Court, how   . .   257   FOR LCVE   III.1   142
  Scandal: Come, Valentine, I'll go with you; I've something in   .   259   FOR LCVE   III.1   231
                (Exit Valentine and Scandal.)   . . .   259   FOR LCVE   III.1   233
  Sr Sampson: What, is my Son Valentine gone? What, is he   259   FOR LCVE   III.1   234
  Scandal: Something has appear'd to your Son Valentine--   266   FCR LCVE   III.1   496
  Scandal: not to be believ'd. Valentine is disturb'd, what can be the   268   FOR LCVE   III.1   547
  Scandal: So was Valentine this Morning; and look'd just so.   . .   268   FOR LCVE   III.1   570
  Scandal: I hope you will be able to see Valentine in the Morning,   .   270   FCR LCVE   III.1   637
  Angelica: depends upon the recovery of Valentine. Therefore I   .   277   FCR LCVE   IV.1   56
                (Goes to the Scene, which opens and discovers Valentine upon   279   FOR LCVE   IV.1   148
  Sr Sampson: VALENTINE LEGEND, in great Letters.   281   FCR LCVE   IV.1   224
  Scandal: talk with Valentine, perhaps you may understand him;   . .   284   FCB LCVE   IV.1   343
  Mrs Fore: Valentine raves upon Angelica, and took me for   288   FOR LCVE   IV.1   468
                (Enter Valentine, Scandal, Foresight, and Jeremy.)   288   FOR LCVE   IV.1   478
  Angelica: Mad as Valentine, I'll believe you love me, and the maddest   291   FOR LCVE   IV.1   587
  Tattle: Do you know me, Valentine?   292   FOR LCVE   IV.1   622
  Angelica: Do you know me, Valentine?   292   FOR LCVE   IV.1   631
  Scandal: forc'd you to acknowledge a Kindness for Valentine,   . .   294   FOR LCVE   IV.1   689
  Angelica: Mercy cn me, how he talks! poor Valentine!   294   FOR LCVE   IV.1   705
  Angelica: Leave me, and d'ye hear, if Valentine shou'd come,   . .   297   FOR LCVE   V.1   9
  Angelica: to satisfie you about Valentine: For if a Match were
                seemingly   300   FOR LCVE   V.1   108
  Angelica: when Valentine confesses himself in his Senses; he must   .   300   FOR LCVE   V.1   122
  Foresight: there is a contagious Frenzy abroad. How does Valentine?   306   FCR LCVE   V.1   333
  Scandal: Death and Hell! Where's Valentine?   308   FOR LCVE   V.1   400
                (Enter Valentine dress'd, Scandal, and Jeremy.)   .   310   FCR LCVE   V.1   496
                (Valentine goes to Angelica.)   . . .   311   FCR LCVE   V.1   530
  Angelica: (aside). Generous Valentine!   312   FOR LCVE   V.1   550
  Angelica: that is an Enemy to Valentine.   312   FOR LCVE   V.1   556
  Angelica: (to Valentine). Had I the World to give you, it   312   FCR LCVE   V.1   560
  Scandal: employ'd when the Match is so much mended. Valentine,   .   313   FOR LCVE   V.1   600
  Angelica: I have done dissembling now, Valentine; and if that   . .   313   FOR LCVE   V.1   605
  Angelica: How few, like Valentine, would persevere even unto   . .   314   FOR LCVE   V.1   633
  Angelica: How few, like Valentine, would persevere even to   . .   314   FOR LCVE   V.1 V633
Valentine's (4)
                (Valentine's Lodging. Enter Scandal, and Jeremy.)   . .   275   FOR LOVE   IV.1
  Mrs Fore: Valentine's man, to sell his Master to us.   288   FOR LCVE   IV.1   466
  Tattle: of Valentine's making any more Addresses to you, I have   .   291   FCR LCVE   IV.1   578
  Mirabell: --What, billing so sweetly! Is nct Valentine's Day over   .   423   WAY WCRLD   II.1   502
Valet de Chambre (1)
  Tattle: Garden; my own Landlady and Valet de Chambre; all who   .   257   FOR LCVE   III.1   158
Valet de chambre (1)
  Lucy: . . . but he is too true a Valet de chambre   64   OLD BATCH   III.1   146
Valiant (5)
  Setter: wary and soforth--And to all this valiant as Hercules   . .   65   OLD EATCH   III.1   151

Valiant   (continued)
Setter:	--That is, passively valiant and actively obedient. Ah!	.	65	OLD EATCH	III.1	152
Scandal:	but 'tis as I believe some Men are Valiant, thro' fear--For		271	FOR LCVE	III.1	670
Almeria:	To fill my Ears, with Garcia's valiant Deeds;	. . . .	331	M. BRIDE	I.1	214
Manuel:	Whence comes it, valiant Osmyn, that a Man		336	M. ERIDE	I.1	430
Valour (4)
Bellmour:	image of Valour. He calls him his Back, and indeed they	.	46	OLD EATCH	I.1	357
Manuel:	And Garcia's well-try'd Valour, all oblige me.		334	M. EBIDE	I.1	341
Manuel:	Of whose mute Valcur you relate such Wcnders?	.	335	M. BRIDE	I.1	364
Millamant:	Good Sir Wilfull, respite your valour.		473	WAY WCRLD	V.1	431
Valu'd (1)
Valentine:	that loses hope may part with any thing. I never valu'd	.	312	FOR LCVE	V.1	544
Valuable (1)
Scandal:	Astrolcgy! And Albertus Magnus makes it the most valuable	.	267	FOR LCVE	III.1	537
Value (7)
Lady Ply:	shall value my self as long as I live, I swear. . . .		169	DOUEL DLR	IV.1	76
Sir Paul:	Person that I have a great value for nct only for that, but		172	DCUEL DLR	IV.1	179
Trapland:	Mr. Scandal, you are Uncivil; I did not value your . .		224	FOR LCVE	I.1	313
Ben:	for your Love or your liking, I don't value it of a Rope's		264	FOR LCVE	III.1	404
Zara:	Of equal Value, with unborrow'd Rule, ...		335	M. EBIDE	I.1	396
Lady Wish:	I will; I value your Judgment extreamly. On my Word	.	432	WAY WCRLD	III.1	271
Mirabell:	diminish in their value, and that both the giver lcses the		449	WAY WORLD	IV.1	172
Valuing (1)
Lucy:	Wretch, how, wer't thou valuing thy self, upcn thy . .		65	OLD BATCH	III.1	168
Vanishes (1)
Bellmour:	floating Island; sometimes seems in reach, then vanishes	.	42	OLD BATCH	I.1	206
Vanity (9)
Barnaby:	Husband. 'Tis then indeed, like the vanity of taking a fine		76	OLD BATCH	IV.1	42
Jeremy:	which her Vanity had preferr'd to Settlements, without a	.	219	FOR LCVE	I.1	109
Scandal:	Foppery, Vanity, Cowardise, Bragging, Lechery, . . .		233	FOR LCVE	I.1	631
Angelica:	Vanity--Fie, Mr. Tattle--I'll swear I could not		258	FOR LCVE	III.1	183
Osmyn-Alph:	Of Personal Charms, or with less Vanity		355	M. EBIDE	III.1	226
Mirabell:	Nature; your true Vanity is in the power of pleasing. .	.	420	WAY WCRLD	II.1	384
Millamant:	O the Vanity of these Men! Fainall, dee hear him? .	.	420	WAY WCRLD	II.1	399
Millamant:	enjoin'd it him, to be so coy--If I had the Vanity to	.	433	WAY WCRLD	III.1	338
Millamant:	Vanity! No--I'll fly and be follow'd to the		449	WAY WCRLD	IV.1	160
Vapours (3)
Lady Froth:	Whymsies and Vapours, but I gave them vent.		138	DOUEL DLR	II.1	11
Mirabell:	aloud of the Vapours, and after fell intc a profound	.	396	WAY WORLD	I.1	31
Millamant:	Yes, the Vapours; Fools are Physicks for it, next . .		421	WAY WCRLD	II.1	445
Varies (1)
Araminta:	Religicn, as his Humour varies or his Interest.		58	OLD EATCH	II.2	149
Variety (4)
Belinda:	sake let it be with variety; don't come always, like the	.	59	OLD BATCH	II.2	169
	Yet you will find variety at least.		213	FCR LCVE	PRO.	28
Mirabell:	Can you not find in the variety of your Disposition .	.	422	WAY WORLD	II.1	480
Marwood:	variety.		433	WAY WCRLD	III.1	303
Various (4)
Lady Touch:	meanings lurk in each corner of that various face. O! that		198	DOUBL DLR	V.1	395
Lord Touch:	and want a Clue to guide me through the various mazes	. .	200	DOUEL DLR	V.1	471
Varlet (5)
Fondlewife:	hath possess'd the Lad--I say I will tarry at home--Varlet.		75	OLD BATCH	IV.1	17
Fondlewife:	How hcw, say Varlet! I say let him not come		76	OLD BATCH	IV.1	25
Fondlewife:	I profess a very apt Comparison, Varlet. Go in . . .		76	OLD BATCH	IV.1	45
Fondlewife:	I profess a very apt Comparison, Varlet. Go	. . .	76	OLD BATCH	IV.1 V	45
Sr Sampson:	has he trick't me? speak, Varlet.		279	FOR LCVE	IV.1	123
Vast (3)
Brisk:	With all my Heart and Soul, and proud of the vast . .		165	DOUEL DLR	III.1	556
Heli:	In least Proportion to the vast Eelight		338	M. BRIDE	II.1	9
Mincing:	have him I think, rather than lccse such a vast Summ as	.	465	WAY WCRLD	V.1	115
Vault (2)
Leonora:	Behold the Sacred Vault, within whose Womb, . . .		340	M. BRIDE	II.2	6
Osmyn-Alph:	Disturb'd the Sacred Silence of the Vault, ...		344	M. EBIDE	II.2	161
Vaulted (1)
Almeria:	Whistling thro' Hollows of this vaulted Isle.		339	M. ERIDE	II.1	55
Vehemence (3)
Gonsalez:	Pronounc'd with Vehemence against the Princess, . . .		365	M. BRIDE	IV.1	175
Lady Wish:	Vehemence.--But a day or two for decency of		458	WAY WCRLD	IV.1	496
Lady Wish:	the Vehemence of Compassion, and to save the life of a		459	WAY WORLD	IV.1	536
Veil (4)   see Cobweb-Veil
Bellmour:	So breaks Aurora through the Veil of Night; . . .		81	OLD BATCH	IV.2	10
Valentine:	and a long Veil to cover the Project, and we won't see	.	290	FOR LCVE	IV.1	562
Zara:	(Lifting her Veil.)	.	353	M. EBIDE	III.1	144
Zara:	Of Fate, is stretch'd to draw the Veil, and leave . .		360	M. BRIDE	III.1	441
Veil'd (3)
Maskwell:	an Argument that I Lov'd; for with that Art you veil'd	.	136	DOUEL DLR	I.1	362
Tattle:	--the time draws nigh, Jeremy. Angelica will be veil'd	.	302	FCR LCVE	V.1	197
	(Enter Zara veil'd.) . .		353	M. EBIDE	III.1	139
Vein (1)
Zara:	Split Heart, burst ev'ry Vein, at this dire Object: . .		380	M. EBIDE	V.2 V163
Veins (3)
Ben:	as good Blood in my Veins, and a Heart as sound as a .		273	FOR LCVE	III.1	736
Zara:	Cold, cold; my Veins are Icicles and Frost.		381	M. EBIDE	V.2	205
Almeria:	But spouting Veins, and mangled Flesh! O, O.		382	M. BRIDE	V.2	272
Vellum (1)
Sir Wilful:	Thigh shall back your Instrument of Bam Vellum to shreds,		473	WAY WORLD	V.1	426
Veneration (1)
Sir Paul:	because he has a great veneration for your Ladiship. .	.	172	DOUBL DLR	IV.1	180
Venereal (1)
Sharper:	Gravity as a Bishop hears Venereal Causes in the Spiritual		100	OLD EATCH	V.1	139
Vengance (1)
Lady Touch:	For, by the Eternal Fire, you shall not scape my Vengance.		135	DOUBL DLR	I.1	322
Vengeance (6)
Silvia:	Vengeance itches in the room of Love.		61	OLD BATCH	III.1	34
Silvia:	Vengeance kindles in the room of Love.		61	OLD EATCH	III.1 V 34
Lucy:	Whom Love and Vengeance do at once delight.		75	OLD EATCH	III.2	163

Vengeance   (continued)
Lucy: Whom Love and Vengeance both at once delight.   75   OLD BATCH   III.2 V163
Ben: Who, Father? ay, he's come home with a Vengeance.   . . .   306   FOR LOVE   V.1   341
Almeria: (If such there be in angry Heav'ns Vengeance)   330   M. BRIDE   I.1   189
Venial (1)
Mirabell: ever been accounted Venial. At least think it is Punishment   472   WAY WORLD   V.1   387
Venomous (1)
Zara: Thou like the Adder, venomous and deaf, ...   375   M. BRIDE   V.1   106
Vent (6)
Lady Froth: Whymsies and Vapours, but I gave them vent.   138   DOUBL DLR   II.1   11
Maskwell: self any longer: and was just going to give vent to a
             Secret, ...   156   DOUBL DLR   III.1   201
Maskwell: thought a vent; which might discover that I lov'd, nor   .   188   DOUBL DLR   V.1   35
Maskwell: So, 'tis well--let your wild fury have a vent;   198   DOUBL DLR   V.1   408
Mrs Fain: You had better give it Vent.   476   WAY WORLD   V.1   564
Marwood: Yes it shall have Vent--and to your   477   WAY WORLD   V.1   565
Vents (2)
Bellmour: here vents 'em against the General, who slighting Men of   .   47   OLD BATCH   I.1   371
Careless: overspreads my face, a cold deadly dew already vents   .   170   DOUBL DLR   IV.1   115
Ventur'd (3)
Sharper: me to lose what was ventur'd in your service; Nay 'twas   .   50   OLD BATCH   II.1   101
Sir Joseph: Ay ay, poor Fellow, he ventur'd fair for't.   67   OLD BATCH   III.1   247
Tattle: ventur'd to declare the very inmost Passion of my Heart.   .   291   FOR LOVE   IV.1   579
Venture (11)
Vainlove: a Venture which he's in danger of losing. Read, read.   . .   39   OLD BATCH   I.1   81
Araminta: for a Venture, Sir, that you enquire?   85   OLD BATCH   IV.3   96
Lucy: easie Nature.--Well, For once I'll venture to serve   . .   98   OLD BATCH   V.1   75
Mellefont: you have Love enough to run the venture.   193   DOUBL DLR   V.1   201
Sr Sampson: I'll venture that.   263   FOR LOVE   III.1   358
Mrs Frail: out.--Come, Sir, will you venture your self with me?   . .   265   FOR LOVE   III.1   450
Ben: Venture, Mess, and that I will, tho' 'twere to Sea in a   .   265   FOR LOVE   III.1   452
Mrs Frail: wou'd not venture all in one Bottom.   273   FOR LOVE   III.1   724
Buckram: O Lord, let me be gone; I'll not venture my self   . . .   282   FOR LOVE   IV.1   243
Ben: believe the Devil wou'd not venture aboard o' your   . .   309   FOR LOVE   V.1   435
             Each time they write, they venture all they've won: . .   393   WAY WORLD   PRO.   14
Venus (4)
Bellmour: Now Venus forbid!   62   OLD BATCH   III.1   71
Foresight: Liberality on the Mount of Venus.   239   FOR LOVE   II.1   154
Scandal: and I hope I shall find both Sol and Venus in the sixth   .   271   FOR LOVE   III.1   651
Scandal: and Venus will be in Conjunction;--while your Wife and   .   271   FOR LOVE   III.1   657
Veracity (1)
Lady Wish: my self till I am pale again, there's no Veracity in me.   .   425   WAY WORLD   III.1   4
Verge (1)
Millamant: last moment, tho' I am upon the very Verge of Matrimony,   .   449   WAY WORLD   IV.1   161
Verily (2)
Fondlewife: (aside). Verily I fear I have carry'd the Jest, too far   .   77   OLD BATCH   IV.1   97
Trapland: Verily, give me a Glass,--you're a Wag,--   224   FOR LOVE   I.1   289
Veritas (0)   see In vino veritas
Vermilion'd (1)
Zara: And like the Morn vermilion'd o'er thy Face.   347   M. BRIDE   II.2   284
Vermin (1)
Fondlewife: Ah, dissembling Vermin!   95   OLD BATCH   IV.4   233
Vernish (1)
Foible: Vernish.   429   WAY WORLD   III.1   146
Verriest (1)
Angelica: I swear, Mr. Benjamin is the verriest Wag in nature;   . .   262   FOR LOVE   III.1   336
Verse (2)
Bellmour: Chimes of Verse were past, when once the doleful   . .   108   OLD BATCH   V.2   18
Millamant: Only with those in Verse, Mr. Witwoud. I never   . . .   419   WAY WORLD   II.1   365
Verses (4)
Jeremy: In the Form of a worn-out Punk, with Verses in her Hand,   .   219   FOR LOVE   I.1   108
Witwoud: Funeral Sermon, or a Copy of Commendatory Verses   . .   401   WAY WORLD   I.1   246
Millamant: He? Ay, and filthy Verses--So I am.   446   WAY WORLD   IV.1   57
Foible: Verses and Poems,--So as long as it was not a Bible-Oath;   .   464   WAY WORLD   V.1   99
Vertue (15)
Fondlewife: enough. No thanks to you Sir, for her Vertue.--But,   . .   96   OLD BATCH   IV.4   268
Careless: begin with her Honour, or her Vertue, her Religion, or   .   157   DOUBL DLR   III.1   271
Lady Ply: License to make trial of your Wifes suspected Vertue?   . .   179   DOUBL DLR   IV.1   440
Lady Ply: shall wrong'd Vertue fly for Reparation! I'll be Divorced   .   179   DOUBL DLR   IV.1   446
Sir Paul: Ay, but by your own Vertue and Continency that   . . .   180   DOUBL DLR   IV.1   476
Careless: I had a mind to try my Ladies Vertue--And when I could   .   180   DOUBL DLR   IV.1   498
Lord Touch: as is thy Vertue.   189   DOUBL DLR   V.1   49
Lord Touch: have discovered so much Manly Vertue; thine, in that thou   .   189   DOUBL DLR   V.1   55
Scandal: of secrets, another Vertue that he sets up for in the same   226   FOR LOVE   I.1   369
Foresight: Contemner of Sciences, and a defamer of Vertue.   . .   241   FOR LOVE   II.1   240
Valentine: to you. For you found her Vertue, upon the Backwardness   .   256   FOR LOVE   III.1   131
Waitwell: I do not, fair shrine of Vertue.   459   WAY WORLD   V.1   542
Lady Wish: the most minute Particle of severe Vertue? Is it possible   465   WAY WORLD   V.1   142
Lady Wish: the direct Mold of Vertue? I have not only been a Mold   .   465   WAY WORLD   V.1   144
Lady Wish: Initiate her very Infancy in the Rudiments of Vertue, and   .   466   WAY WORLD   V.1   184
Vertues (1)
Sr Sampson: Thy Wife is a Constellation of Vertues; she's the   . .   242   FOR LOVE   II.1   256
Vertuous (5)
Vainlove: thinks her Vertuous; that's one reason why I fail her: . .   40   OLD BATCH   I.1   119
Bellmour: She still is Vertuous, if she's so believ'd.   96   OLD BATCH   IV.4   274
Mrs Fore: Pshaw! but Vertuous, I mean.   271   FOR LOVE   III.1   668
Scandal: Yes, Faith, I believe some Women are Vertuous too;   . . .   271   FOR LOVE   III.1   669
Osmyn-Alph: For Blessings ever wait on vertuous Deeds;   384   M. BRIDE   V.2   321
Very (236)
             He's very civil, and entreats your Favour.   35   OLD BATCH   PRO.   13
Vainlove: It must be a very superstitious Country, where such   . .   39   OLD BATCH   I.1   66
Bellmour: the Servants. Very good! Then I must be disguised--With   .   39   OLD BATCH   I.1   89
Vainlove: A kind of Mungril Zealot, sometimes very precise   . .   40   OLD BATCH   I.1   106
Bellmour: A very even Temper and fit for my purpose. I must   . . .   40   OLD BATCH   I.1   111
Bellmour: birth, and the discovery must needs be very pleasant from   .   40   OLD BATCH   I.1   125
Bellmour: very affected neither--Give her her due, I think the   . .   41   OLD BATCH   I.1   172

Very   (continued)

Speaker	Text	PAGE	TITLE	ACT.SC	LINE
Sir Paul:	to my own Cuckoldom; why this is the very traiterous	178	DOUBL DLR	IV.1	412
Maskwell:	own Opinion; the appearance is very fair, but I have an	181	DOUBL DLR	IV.1	528
Lady Touch:	Alas he raves! talks very Poetry! for Heavens	186	DOUBL DLR	IV.2	127
Mellefont:	away the very root and foundation of his hopes; What	187	DOUBL DLR	IV.2	147
Lord Touch:	should Command: my very Slaves will shortly give me	195	DOUBL DLR	V.1	303
Lady Touch:	Anger melts. (weeps) Here, take this Ponyard, for my very	198	DOUBL DLR	V.1	402
Sir Paul:	Affairs may be in a very good posture; I saw her go into	200	DOUBL DLR	V.1	506
Brisk:	Not comparable to your Ladyship; you are the very	201	DOUBL DLR	V.1	530
Brisk:	Not comparably to your Ladyship; you are the very	201	DOUBL DLR	V.1	V530
Brisk:	This is all very surprizing, let me perish.	203	DOUBL DLR	V.1	578
Valentine:	A very rich Man.--Not worth a Groat.	216	FOR LOVE	I.1	20
Jeremy:	Humph, and so he has made a very fine Feast, where	216	FOR LOVE	I.1	21
Valentine:	Very well, Sir; can you proceed?	219	FOR LOVE	I.1	103
Jeremy:	Keep it? Not at all; it has been so very much stretch'd,	221	FOR LOVE	I.1	180
Scandal:	The Morning's a very good Morning, if you don't	222	FOR LOVE	I.1	233
Valentine:	they are very hard, but my Necessity is very pressing:	224	FOR LOVE	I.1	318
Valentine:	hears is Landed; whereupon he very affectionately sends	225	FOR LOVE	I.1	334
Scandal:	A very desperate demonstration of your love to	225	FOR LOVE	I.1	343
Tattle:	very tenderly.	226	FOR LOVE	I.1	395
Scandal:	Yes, Mrs. Frail is a very fine Woman, we all know	228	FOR LOVE	I.1	458
Tattle:	'Tis very hard--Won't a Baronet's Lady pass?	230	FOR LOVE	I.1	530
Valentine:	Passion, but it very rarely mends a Man's Manners.	231	FOR LOVE	I.1	561
Scandal:	I have many more of this kind, very well Painted, as you	234	FOR LOVE	I.1	657
Foresight:	very good Luck: Nay, I have had some Omens; I got out	236	FOR LOVE	II.1	31
Foresight:	time,--But in troth I am pleas'd at my Stocking. Very	236	FOR LOVE	II.1	37
Foresight:	he's at leisure--'tis now Three a Clock, a very good hour	236	FOR LOVE	II.1	41
Foresight:	Well, Jill-flirt, you are very pert--and always	237	FOR LOVE	II.1	74
Mrs Fore:	but your Conversation was very innocent; but the place is	247	FOR LOVE	II.1	429
Mrs Fore:	Very well, that will appear who has most,	247	FOR LOVE	II.1	455
Mrs Fore:	It's very true, Sister: Well since all's out, and	248	FOR LOVE	II.1	476
Mrs Frail:	she's very pretty!--Lord, what pure red and white!	250	FOR LOVE	II.1	556
Valentine:	A couple of very civil Proverbs, truly: 'Tis hard to	256	FOR LOVE	III.1	129
Tattle:	Gad, it's very true, Madam, I think we are oblig'd to	257	FOR LOVE	III.1	134
Tattle:	I'm very unfortunate.	258	FOR LOVE	III.1	195
Sr Sampson:	A very Wag, Ben's a very Wag; only a little	262	FOR LOVE	III.1	319
Scandal:	He's gone to Bed upon't, and very ill--He speaks	266	FOR LOVE	III.1	497
Scandal:	Sir Sampson is hasty, very hasty;--I'm afraid he is not	267	FOR LOVE	III.1	520
Foresight:	How does it appear, Mr. Scandal? I think I am very	268	FOR LOVE	III.1	561
Foresight:	Very well.	268	FOR LOVE	III.1	567
Foresight:	Very likely.	270	FOR LOVE	III.1	618
Foresight:	And--hem, hem! I am very faint.--	270	FOR LOVE	III.1	643
Scandal:	Yes, several, very honest;--they'll cheat a little at	271	FOR LOVE	III.1	666
Angelica:	very unseasonable--	276	FOR LOVE	IV.1	39
Valentine:	For my part, I am Truth, and can't tell; I have very	280	FOR LOVE	IV.1	178
Jeremy:	Very short, Sir.	280	FOR LOVE	IV.1	182
Valentine:	his Nose always, will very often be led into a Stink.	282	FOR LOVE	IV.1	254
Mrs Fore:	O yes, now I remember, you were very	284	FOR LOVE	IV.1	327
Scandal:	'Twas a very forgetting Night.--But would you not	284	FOR LOVE	IV.1	342
Mrs Frail:	Wife? I should have been finely fobb'd indeed, very finely	286	FOR LOVE	IV.1	411
Valentine:	see very strange; which are Wanton Wives, with their	289	FOR LOVE	IV.1	511
Foresight:	His Frenzy is very high now, Mr. Scandal.	289	FOR LOVE	IV.1	529
Foresight:	Very likely truly; You understand these Matters	289	FOR LOVE	IV.1	531
Foresight:	--Mr. Scandal, I shall be very glad to confer with you	289	FOR LOVE	IV.1	532
Foresight:	are very Mysterious and Hieroglyphical.	289	FOR LOVE	IV.1	534
Tattle:	ventur'd to declare the very inmost Passion of my Heart.	291	FOR LOVE	IV.1	579
Valentine:	thou can'st not lie with my Wife? I am very poor, and	292	FOR LOVE	IV.1	626
Valentine:	Oh very well.	292	FOR LOVE	IV.1	632
Scandal:	Madam, I am very glad that I overheard a better	294	FOR LOVE	IV.1	687
Valentine:	Madam, you need not be very much afraid, for I	294	FOR LOVE	IV.1	697
Angelica:	Why he talk'd very sensibly just now.	295	FOR LOVE	IV.1	746
Jeremy:	to be mad: And I think I have not found him very quiet	295	FOR LOVE	IV.1	755
Valentine:	Go see, you Sot. I'm very glad that I can move your	295	FOR LOVE	IV.1	759
Jeremy:	So--Just the very backside of Truth,--But	296	FOR LOVE	IV.1	775
Sr Sampson:	Zooks, but it is, Madam, a very great while; to	298	FOR LOVE	V.1	18
Angelica:	Fifty a contemptible Age! Not at all, a very fashionable	298	FOR LOVE	V.1	28
Angelica:	Age I think--I assure you I know very considerable	298	FOR LOVE	V.1	29
Sr Sampson:	ne're a young Fellow worth hanging--that's a very	299	FOR LOVE	V.1	54
Sr Sampson:	ne're a young Fellow worth hanging--that is a very	299	FOR LOVE	V.1	V 54
Sr Sampson:	Fool in the Eye of the World, is a very hard Task. But,	299	FOR LOVE	V.1	67
Sr Sampson:	faith and troth you speak very discreetly; For I hate both a	299	FOR LOVE	V.1	68
Angelica:	Censure of the World: And she that marries a very Witty	299	FOR LOVE	V.1	72
Angelica:	are very much abus'd in that Matter; He's no more Mad	299	FOR LOVE	V.1	87
Sr Sampson:	very Handsom, and I'm very Young, and very Lusty--	301	FOR LOVE	V.1	142
Sr Sampson:	--Odd, I think we are very well met;--Give me	301	FOR LOVE	V.1	144
Sr Sampson:	little Sampson: Odd, Sampson's a very good Name for an	301	FOR LOVE	V.1	154
Jeremy:	Ah Sir, if you are not very faithful and close in this Business,	301	FOR LOVE	V.1	167
Jeremy:	troubled the Fountain of his Understanding; it is a very	302	FOR LOVE	V.1	174
Tattle:	Very true, Sir, and desire to continue so. I have no	305	FOR LOVE	V.1	287
Sr Sampson:	Foresight; Uncle I mean, a very old Fellow, Uncle Foresight;	307	FOR LOVE	V.1	383
Sr Sampson:	Not absolutely married, Uncle; but very near it,	307	FOR LOVE	V.1	390
Angelica:	'Tis very true indeed, Uncle; I hope you'll be my	308	FOR LOVE	V.1	393
Angelica:	'Tis very unhappy, if you don't care for one another.	309	FOR LOVE	V.1	462
Angelica:	O you'll agree very well in a little time; Custom	310	FOR LOVE	V.1	481
Sr Sampson:	Very good, Sir--Mr. Buckram, are you	311	FOR LOVE	V.1	513
Valentine:	Pardon me, Sir. But I reflect that I very lately	311	FOR LOVE	V.1	524
Angelica:	and struggl'd very hard to make this utmost Tryal of your	312	FOR LOVE	V.1	563
	Or in this very House, for ought we know,	315	FOR LOVE	EPI.	23
	(Enter Gonsalez, Bowing very humbly.)	331	M. BRIDE	I.1	219
Heli:	If to arise in very deed from Death,	337	M. BRIDE	II.1	5
Zara:	I know, my Charms have reach'd thy very Soul,	348	M. BRIDE	II.2	345
Osmyn-Alph:	On high; and of good Men, the very best	350	M. BRIDE	III.1	29
Mirabell:	Conscience; I proceeded to the very last Act of Flattery	397	WAY WORLD	I.1	69
Witwoud:	That's hard, that's very hard;--A Messenger,	401	WAY WORLD	I.1	243
Witwoud:	breed Debates.--Petulant's my Friend, and a very	403	WAY WORLD	I.1	288

View   (continued)

Violater (1)
    Sir Paul: is the Violater of my Fame. . . . . 144 DOUBL DLR   II.1 233
Violation (3)
    Lady Ply: 'Tis my Honour that is concern'd, and the violation . . 144 DOUBL DLR   II.1 234
    Manuel: The Violation of your Vow. . . . . 334 M. BRIDE   I.1   325
    Manuel: The Violation of your Vow: For you, ... 334 M. BRIDE   I.1 V325
Violence (10)
    Lord Froth: I confess, I did my self some violence at first, but . 133 DOUBL DLR   I.1   235
    Mellefont: of her violence at last,--if you had not come as you did; 149 DOUBL DLR   II.1 417
    Maskwell: for you.--First tell me what urg'd you to this violence? . 198 DOUBL DLR   V.1   413
    Scandal: Violence--I fear he does not act wholly from himself; . 268 FOR LOVE   III.1 549
    Almeria: No, on my Life, my Faith, I mean no Violence. . . 331 M. BRIDE   I.1   201
    Almeria: Nor Violence.--I feel my.self more light, ... 331 M. BRIDE   I.1 V202
    Heli: To act some Violence upon himself, ... 338 M. BRIDE   II.1   29
    Zara: This Slave commit no Violence upon . . . . . . 360 M. BRIDE   III.1 448
    Zara: Dash your encountering Streams, with mutual Violence, . 380 M. BRIDE   V.2 V165
    Marwood: of ill usage; I think I shou'd do my self the violence of 411 WAY WORLD   I.1   55
Violent (10)
    Mellefont: violent Passion for me. Since my first refusal of her . 129 DOUBL DLR   I.1   86
    Mellefont: that the most violent Love could urge, or tender words . 130 DOUBL DLR   I.1   110
    Maskwell: --I warrant she was very Violent at first. . . . . . 149 DOUBL DLR   II.1 415
    Brisk: ha ha ha; yet by Heavens I have a violent passion for your 176 DOUBL DLR   IV.1 345
    Lady Froth: self; for hang me if I have not a violent Passion for Mr. 176 DOUBL DLR   IV.1 352
    Foresight: Man,--he has a violent death in his face; but I hope no . 243 FOR LOVE   II.1 309
    Scandal: My Passion for you is grown so violent--that I am no . 269 FOR LOVE   III.1 586
    Millamant: Long! Lord, have I not made violent haste? I . . . . 419 WAY WORLD   I.1   346
    Millamant: violent and inflexible wise Face, like Solomon at the
                   dividing . . . . 422 WAY WORLD   II.1 468
    Marwood: you don't mitigate those violent Airs. . . . . . . 433 WAY WORLD   III.1 334
Violently (3)
    Lady Froth: Oh, no, I love it violently,--my dear you're . . . . 201 DOUBL DLR   V.1   523
    Valentine: am not violently bent upon the Trade.-- . . . . . 220 FOR LOVE   I.1   153
    Millamant: I am a lost thing;--for I find I love him violently. . 453 WAY WORLD   IV.1 316
Viper (2)
    Waitwell: Unnatural Viper. . . . . 458 WAY WORLD   IV.1 505
    Lady Wish: Viper, thou Serpent, that I have foster'd, thou bosome . 462 WAY WORLD   V.1   2
Vipers (2)
    Lord Touch: Like Vipers in the Womb, base Treach'ry lies, ... 203 DOUBL DLR   V.1   594
    Mrs Fain: Is it possible? Dost thou hate those Vipers . . . . 411 WAY WORLD   II.1 43
Virgin (4)
    Bellmour: she own'd it to my Face; and blushing like the Virgin Morn 38 OLD BATCH   I.1   48
                   The First-fruit Offering, of a Virgin Play. . . . . 213 FOR LOVE   PRO. 25
    Foresight: But there's but one Virgin among the Twelve Signs, . . 239 FOR LOVE   II.1 141
    Foresight: Spitfire, but one Virgin. . . . . 239 FOR LOVE   II.1 142
Virgins (1)
    Bellmour: --But you timorous Virgins, form a dreadful Chimaera . 106 OLD BATCH   V.1   380
Virility (1)
    Heartwell: Arm; nay, I would be divorced from my Virility, to be . 109 OLD BATCH   V.2   76
Virtue (22)   see Vertue
    Lady Ply: road of Virtue, in which I have trod thus long, and never 147 DOUBL DLR   II.1 318
    Careless: tho' by this Light I believe her Virtue is impregnable. . 180 DOUBL DLR   IV.1 503
    Lord Touch: (aside). Unequall'd Virtue! . . . . 188 DOUBL DLR   V.1   21
    Lord Touch: let me hasten to do Justice, in rewarding Virtue and wrong'd 203 DOUBL DLR   V.1   582
    Angelica: Virtue. . . . . 312 FOR LOVE   V.1   564
    Osmyn-Alph: Whose Virtue has renounc'd thy Father's Crimes, . . . 383 M. BRIDE   V.2   316
    Mirabell: downright personally to debauch her; and that my Virtue . 397 WAY WORLD   I.1   78
Virtues (2)   see Vertues
    Angelica: Faults than he has Virtues; and 'tis hardly more Pleasure 312 FOR LOVE   V.1   576
    Osmyn-Alph: And tear her Virtues up, as Tempests root . . . . . 355 M. BRIDE   III.1 229
Visible (1)
    Mellefont: I confess the Consequence is visible, were your . . . 131 DOUBL DLR   I.1   167
Vision (1)
    Vainlove: Eyes, or Ears? The Vision is here still.--Your Passion, . 88 OLD BATCH   IV.3 176
Visions (1)
    Foresight: Dreams and distracted Visions, that I remember little. . 284 FOR LOVE   IV.1 341
Visit (16)
    Bellmour: You're going to visit in return of Silvia's Letter-- . 40 OLD BATCH   I.1   115
    Heartwell: And who wou'd you visit there, say you? (O'ons, . . . 104 OLD BATCH   V.1   289
    Jeremy: his Proportion, with carrying a Poet upon Tick, to visit . 218 FOR LOVE   I.1   99
    Valentine: She does me the favour--I mean of a Visit . . . . . 229 FOR LOVE   I.1   486
    Jeremy: I told you what your Visit wou'd come to. . . . . . 246 FOR LOVE   II.1 406
    Angelica: to see a Woman visit a Man at his own Lodgings in a . 276 FOR LOVE   IV.1 21
    Almeria: Steal forth, and visit good Anselmo's Tomb. . . . . 331 M. BRIDE   I.1   199
    Osmyn-Alph: But bless my Son, visit not him for me. . . . . . 350 M. BRIDE   III.1 13
    Heli: (Who takes the Privilege to visit late, ... 351 M. BRIDE   III.1 49
    Zara: So far to visit him, at his request. . . . . . . 365 M. BRIDE   IV.1 182
    Manuel: How? she visit Osmyn! What, my Daughter? . . . . 365 M. BRIDE   IV.1 184
    Mirabell: easie as to know when a Visit began to be troublesome; . 396 WAY WORLD   I.1   39
    Mirabell: Fools; Things who visit you from their excessive Idleness; 421 WAY WORLD   II.1 434
    Marwood: Visit is always a Disguise; and never admitted by a Woman 433 WAY WORLD   III.1 312
    Millamant: for ever After. Let us never Visit together, nor go to a . 450 WAY WORLD   IV.1 206
    Millamant: ever After. Let us never Visit together, nor go to a . 450 WAY WORLD   IV.1 V206
Visit's (1)
    Belinda: The Visit's to you, Cousin, I suppose I am at my . . . 56 OLD BATCH   II.2 81
Visitants (1)
    Valentine: of Visitants in a morning, all soliciting of past promises; 221 FOR LOVE   I.1   190
Visiting (1)
    Perez: From visiting the Noble Prisoner. . . . . 359 M. BRIDE   III.1 382
Visits (4)
    Vainlove: visits her ev'ry day. . . . . 40 OLD BATCH   I.1   122
    Tattle: be receiv'd but upon Publick Days; and my Visits will . 230 FOR LOVE   I.1   516
    Mirabell: Invective against long Visits. I would not have understood 396 WAY WORLD   I.1   36
    Millamant: Trifles,--As liberty to pay and receive visits . . . 450 WAY WORLD   IV.1 212
Vital (1)
    Capt Bluff: --He sucks not vital Air who dares affirm it to this . 70 OLD BATCH III.1 353

Waiting (8)
                    (Araminta, Belinda, Betty waiting, in Araminta's Apartment)   54   OLD BATCH   II.2 V
                    (Valentine in his Chamber Reading. Jeremy waiting.   .   .   . 216   FOR LCVE   I.1
     Scandal: have an opportunity of waiting upon you.   269   FOR LCVE   III.1 598
     Ben: The Sailor slily waiting, ...   274   FOR LCVE   III.1 781
     Zara: Waiting my Nod, the Creature of my Lord, ...   349   M. BRIDE   II.2   365
     Zara: Waiting my Nod, the Creature of my Pow'r, ...   349   M. BRIDE   II.2 V365
                    Mirabell and Fainall Rising from Cards. Betty waiting.   395   WAY WCRLD   I.1
                    Lady Wishfort at her Toilet, Peg waiting.)   425   WAY WCRLD   III.1
Waiting-Women (1)
     Tattle: be distinguish'd among the Waiting-Women by the   230   FCR LCVE   I.1   520
Waits (7)
     Sharper: ripe, and only waits thy Cutting up--She has been   . .   79   OLD EATCH   IV.1   166
     Maskwell: Guilt is ever at a loss and confusion waits upon it,   . . 184   DOUEL DLR   IV.2   19
     Zara: Who waits there?   360   M. BRIDE   III.1 445
     Manuel: Who waits there?   365   M. BRIDE   IV.1   165
     Mirabell: he waits for himself now, he is so long a coming; C I ask   405   WAY WCRLD   I.1   379
     Mrs Fain: waits to consult you.   452   WAY WCRLD   V.1   305
     Millamant: --He is without and waits your leave for admittance.   .   470   WAY WCRLD   V.1   332
Waitwell (12)
     Mirabell: Waitwell shake his Ears, and Dame Partlet rustle up her   .   398   WAY WORLD   I.1   129
     Mirabell: Waitwell, my Servant.   417   WAY WCRLD   II.1   285
     Mirabell: Waitwell and Foible. I wou'd not tempt my Servant   . .   417   WAY WCRLD   II.1   291
                          (Enter Waitwell and Fcible.)   423   WAY WCRLD   II.1   504
     Mirabell: Sirrah, Waitwell, why sure you think you were married   .   423   WAY WCRLD   II.1   505
     Foible: Waitwell.   424   WAY WCRLD   II.1   548
     Waitwell: to a Reformation into Waitwell. Nay, I shan't   . . .   424   WAY WCRLD   II.1   559
     Waitwell: be quite the same Waitwell neither--For now I remember   .   424   WAY WCRLD   II.1   560
     Mrs Fain: privy to the whole Design, and know that Waitwell, to   .   430   WAY WCRLD   III.1 189
                    (Enter Waitwell, disguis'd as for Sir Fowland.)   457   WAY WCRLD   IV.1   483
     Foible: Effect, Mr. Fainall laid this Plct tc arrest Waitwell,
                       when he   464   WAY WORLD   V.1   71
                          (Enter Waitwell with a Box cf Writings.)   475   WAY WCRLD   V.1   508
Waitwell's (2)
     Mirabell: Has the Taylor brought Waitwell's Cloaths home,   . . .   398   WAY WORLD   I.1   124
     Foible: Waitwell's gcne to prison already.   463   WAY WCRLD   V.1   64
Wak'd (1)
     Araminta: --Sure if I had not pinch'd you till ycu wak'd, you   .   55   OLD BATCH   II.2   43
Wak'ned (1)
     Osmyn-Alph: Revive, or raise, my Peoples Voice has wak'ned. . . .   351   M. BRIDE   III.1   79
Wake (7)
     Heartwell: look like an Ass when thcu art present; Wake for you,   .   73   OLD BATCH   III.2   79
     Heartwell: look like an Ass when thou art present; Wake for thee,   .   73   OLD BATCH   III.2 V 79
     Zara: Wake thee to Freedom. Now, 'tis late; and yet   . . .   354   M. BRIDE   III.1 203
     Zara: Forsake their down, to wake with wat'ry Eyes,   . . .   360   M. BRIDE   III.1 428
     Osmyn-Alph: Warm her to Life, and wake her into Gladness.   . . .   383   M. BRIDE   V.2   279
     Osmyn-Alph: Nor ever wake to less substantial Joys.   383   M. BRIDE   V.2   290
     Fainall: nodding Husband would not wake, that e'er the watchful   .   414   WAY WCRLD   II.1   148
Wakes (2)
     Musician: Wakes 'em from the golden Dream;   60   OLD BATCH   II.2   200
     Osmyn-Alph: Of wand'ring Life, that winks and wakes by turns,   . .   350   M. BRIDE   III.1   37
Waking (4)
     Maskwell: Why do I love! yet Heaven and my waking   188   DOUBL DLR   V.1   33
     Scandal: There's nought but willing, waking Love, that can   . .   275   FOR LCVE   III.1 819
     Osmyn-Alph: And waking tc the World and mortal Sense, ...   353   M. BRIDE   III.1 134
     Manuel: In waking Anguish? why this, on the Day   367   M. BRIDE   IV.1   250
Wakings (1)
     Millamant: morning thoughts, agreeable wakings, indclent slumbers,   .   449   WAY WCRLD   IV.1   188
Walk (22)
     Araminta: If Mr. Gavot will walk with us in the Garden, we'll have   .   60   OLD BATCH   II.2   207
     Araminta: If Mr. Gavot will walk with us into the Garden, we'll have   .   60   OLD EATCH   II.2 V207
     Lucy: first. I know that will do--walk in and I'le shew   . .   75   OLD BATCH   III.2 158
     Belinda: World that I like.--Oh Lord, walk this way.--I   . . .   87   OLD BATCH   IV.3 149
     Setter: mine. Here's Company coming, if you'll walk this way,   . .   106   OLD BATCH   V.1   352
     Bellmour: But give your selves the trouble to walk to that   . . .   107   OLD BATCH   V.1   401
     Lord Froth: I'll walk a turn in the Garden, and come to you.   . .   142   DOUEL DLR   IV.1   147
     Cynthia: People walk hand in hand, there's neither overtaking nor   .   168   DOUEL DLR   IV.1   15
     Sir Paul: whether I fly cn Ground, or walk in Air--Gads bud, she   .   172   DOUEL DLR   IV.1   198
     Valentine: Here, take away; I'll walk a turn, and digest what   . .   216   FOR LCVE   I.1   3
     Garcia: This way, we're told, Osmyn was seen to walk;   . . .   337   M. BRIDE   II.1   1
     Witwoud: Ay, we'll all walk in the Park, the Ladies talk'd of   . .   409   WAY WCRLD   I.1   510
     Mirabell: Are you? Pray then walk by your selves,--Let   409   WAY WCRLD   I.1   523
     Mrs Fain: another by being seen to walk with his Wife. This way Mr.   .   412   WAY WCRLD   II.1   106
     Mirabell: They are turning into the cther Walk.   416   WAY WCRLD   II.1   253
     Servant-W: please to walk in, in the mean time.   437   WAY WCBLD   III.1 446
     Lady Wish: walk? Marwood--   441   WAY WCRLD   III.1 624
     Lady Wish: won't sit--I'll walk--aye I'll walk frcm the door upon his   445   WAY WCRLD   IV.1   20
     Sir Wilful: fetch a walk this Evening, if so be that I might not be   .   448   WAY WCRLD   IV.1   116
     Sir Wilful: troublesome, I wcu'd have sought a walk with you.   . . .   448   WAY WCRLD   IV.1   117
     Millamant: A walk? What then?   448   WAY WCRLD   IV.1   118
Walk'd (1)
     Millamant: O I have deny'd my self Airs to Day. I have walk'd   . .   418   WAY WCRLD   II.1   333
Walking (5)
     Brisk: (sings). I'm sick with Love, ha ha ha, prithee come (walking   175   DOUEL DLR   IV.1   306
     Millamant: fare you well;--I see they are walking away.   422   WAY WCRLD   II.1   479
     Millamant: (Repeating and Walking about.)   446   WAY WCRLD   IV.1   51
     Millamant: I Nauseate walking; 'tis a Ccuntry diversion, I   . . .   448   WAY WCRLD   IV.1   121
     Foible: have gone a Walking: But we went up unawares,--tho'   .   464   WAY WORLD   V.1   96
Walks (7)
     Laetitia: (Walks about in disorder.)   .   90   OLD BATCH   IV.4   35
     Lady Touch: Face; but walks unstartled from the Mirrour, and streight   136   DOUEL DLR   I.1 V331
                    (She Walks abcut Disorder'd.)   136   DOUEL DLR   I.1   333
                    (Maskwell pretending not to see him, walks by him, and   .   155   DOUEL DLR   III.1 192
     Valentine: (Walks musing.)   293   FOR LCVE   IV.1   666
                    (This while Millamant walks about Repeating to her self.)   446   WAY WCRLD   IV.1   80
     Sir Wilful: Nay nothing--Only for the walks sake, that's   448   WAY WCRLD   IV.1   119

Wall (3)
			PAGE	TITLE	ACT.SC	LINE
Gonsalez:	The swarming Populace, spread every Wall,		332	M. BRIDE	I.1	238
Lady Wish:	Why I am arrantly flea'd--I look like an old peel'd Wall.		429	WAY WORLD	III.1	148
Lady Wish:	Brandy-sellers Bulk, or against a dead Wall by a					
	Ballad-monger.		462	WAY WORLD	V.1	13

Wallow (1)
Sir Joseph:	wallow in Wine and Women. Why, this same Madera-Wine		85	OLD BATCH	IV.3	64

Walls (5)
	These Walls but t'other Day were fill'd with Noise		315	FOR LOVE	EPI.	28
Manuel:	She should have made these Pallace Walls to shake,		333	M. BRIDE	I.1	311
Osmyn-Alph:	Then will I smear these Walls with Blood, dash my		358	M. BRIDE	III.1	350
Osmyn-Alph:	Then will I smear these Walls with Blood, disfigure		358	M. BRIDE	III.1 V	350
Garcia:	Before 'em, to the Pallace Walls. Unless		377	M. BRIDE	V.2	35

Wand'ring (1)
Osmyn-Alph:	Of wand'ring Life, that winks and wakes by turns,		350	M. BRIDE	III.1	37

Wander (1)
Heli:	I wander thro' this Maze of Monuments,		340	M. BRIDE	II.2	1

Wandring (1)
Lady Touch:	the love of you, was the first wandring fire that e're					
	misled		185	DOUEL DLR	IV.2	76

Want (43)
Sharper:	Pshaw you can't want a hundred Pound. Your		50	OLD BATCH	II.1	107
Sir Joseph:	been long acquainted; you have lost a good Jest for want		50	OLD BATCH	II.1	117
Lucy:	want of Dissimulation--You know what will take him.		62	OLD BATCH	III.1	50
Setter:	Setter what a treasure is here lost for want of being known.		65	OLD BATCH	III.1	153
Laetitia:	this usage of yours--But that's what you want--Well--		77	OLD BATCH	IV.1	93
	If loss of that should follow want of Wit,		113	OLD BATCH	EPI.	13
Brisk:	want of Apprehension: The Deuce take me if I tell you.		128	DOUEL DLR	I.1	42
Maskwell:	lay a stronger Plot: if I gain a little time, I shall					
	not want		138	DOUEL DLR	I.1	419
Cynthia:	Prodigious! I wonder, of sleep, and so much		138	DOUEL DLR	II.1	5
Lady Ply:	pardon my want of Expression--		159	DOUEL DLR	III.1	355
Sir Paul:	utterly extinct for want of Issue Male. Oh Impiety! But		171	DOUEL DLR	IV.1	138
Sir Paul:	There it is, Madam; Do you want a Pen and Ink?		173	DOUEL DLR	IV.1	218
Lady Touch:	want you by this time, as much as you want her.		192	DOUEL DLR	V.1	189
Lord Touch:	see I want no inclination.		196	DOUEL DLR	V.1	325
Mellefont:	are all in my Chamber; I want nothing but the Habit.		196	DOUEL DLR	V.1	344
Lady Touch:	You want but leasure to invent fresh falshood,		197	DOUEL DLR	V.1	379
Lady Touch:	Spirits faint, and I want strength to hold it, thou hast		198	DOUEL DLR	V.1	403
Maskwell:	No more,--there want but a few Minutes of		199	DOUEL DLR	V.1	456
Lord Touch:	and want a Clue to guide me through the various mazes		200	DOUEL DLR	V.1	471
Valentine:	You are witty, you Rogue, I shall want your Help;		218	FOR LOVE	I.1	76
Foresight:	Sorrow, Want and Plenty, Night and Day, make up our		236	FOR LOVE	II.1	36
Sr Sampson:	want a little Polishing: You must not take any thing ill,		262	FOR LOVE	III.1	339
Jeremy:	Why faith, Madam, he's mad for want of his Wits,		276	FOR LOVE	IV.1	33
Jeremy:	just as he was poor for want of Money: his Head is e'en as		276	FOR LOVE	IV.1	34
Angelica:	my want of Inclination to stay longer here--Come, Jenny.		278	FOR LOVE	IV.1	90
Angelica:	living single, and want a Husband.		298	FOR LOVE	V.1	47
Tattle:	If the Gentleman is in this disorder for want of a Wife,		313	FOR LOVE	V.1	589
Scandal:	want 'em.		314	FOR LOVE	V.1	626
Angelica:	want of Merit. You would all have the Reward of Love;		314	FOR LOVE	V.1	629
Osmyn-Alph:	With Bolts, with Chains, Imprisonment and Want;		350	M. BRIDE	III.1	12
Selim:	My Nature's want; but punish Nature in me:		375	M. BRIDE	V.1	119
Almeria:	But want a Guide: for Tears have dim'd my Sight.		381	M. BRIDE	V.2	221
Fainall:	Nature, and does not always want Wit.		401	WAY WORLD	I.1	222
Witwoud:	That! that's his Happiness--His want of		404	WAY WORLD	I.1	326
Witwoud:	Ay; but I like him for that now; for his want of		404	WAY WORLD	I.1	330
Petulant:	off, if I want Appetite.		405	WAY WORLD	I.1	397
Witwoud:	lost my Comparison for want of Breath.		418	WAY WORLD	II.1	332
Millamant:	want a being.		421	WAY WORLD	II.1	412
Marwood:	loathing is not from a want of Appetite then, but from a		431	WAY WORLD	III.1	231
Waitwell:	Spouse, hast thou any Cordial--I want Spirits.		459	WAY WORLD	IV.1	557
Lady Wish:	from Ruine, from Want, I'll forgive all that's past; Nay		473	WAY WORLD	V.1	454
	But that they have been Damn'd for want of wit.		479	WAY WORLD	EPI.	13

Wanted (5)
Sir Paul:	sure as can be it would.--we wanted your Company,		132	DOUEL DLR	I.1	180
Lord Touch:	Writings are ready drawn, and wanted nothing but to be		189	DOUEL DLR	V.1	62
Valentine:	was considered, it was yours; since I thought I wanted		295	FOR LOVE	IV.1	726
Zara:	His hellish Rage had wanted Means to act,		380	M. BRIDE	V.2	177
Fainall:	and weep like Alexander, when he wanted other Worlds to		413	WAY WORLD	II.1	116

Wanting (5)
	I shall be hang'd for wanting what to say.		35	OLD BATCH	PRO.	25
Lady Ply:	should ever be wanting in a respectful acknowledgment		169	DOUEL DLR	IV.1	80
	And wanting ready Cash to pay for Hearts,		315	FOR LOVE	EPI.	9
Osmyn-Alph:	'Tis wanting what should follow--Heav'n, Heav'n shou'd		350	M. BRIDE	III.1	20
Osmyn-Alph:	'Tis wanting what should follow--Heav'n, shou'd		350	M. BRIDE	III.1 V	20

Wanton (6)
Fondlewife:	near my Doors. I say, he is a wanton young Levite and		76	OLD BATCH	IV.1	26
Bellmour:	Wanton, as a Young-widow.--		112	OLD BATCH	V.2	162
Careless:	wanton. Maskwell is Flesh and Blood at best, and					
	opportunities		131	DOUEL DLR	I.1	162
Foresight:	young and sanguine, has a warm Hazle Eye, and was born		239	FOR LOVE	II.1	151
Valentine:	see very strange; which are Wanton Wives, with their		289	FOR LOVE	IV.1	511
Singer:	'Tis not to wound a wanton Boy		435	WAY WORLD	III.1	382

Wanton'd (2)
Maskwell:	I that had wanton'd in the wide Circle of your		199	DOUEL DLR	V.1	431
Maskwell:	I that had wanton'd in the rich Circle of your		199	DOUEL DLR	V.1 V	431

Wantonness (2)
Scandal:	Women. I can shew you Pride, Folly, Affectation, Wantonness,		233	FOR LOVE	I.1	628
Marwood:	smart for your Daughters wantonness.		469	WAY WORLD	V.1	301

Wants (11)
Lady Touch:	been a Father to you in your wants, and given you being?		135	DOUEL DLR	I.1	310
Lady Froth:	of the Common Air,--I think I may say he wants		139	DOUEL DLR	II.1	30
Lady Froth:	Methinks he wants a Manner.		139	DOUEL DLR	II.1	46
Brisk:	Lord Froth wants a Partner, we can never begin without		174	DOUEL DLR	IV.1	278
Maskwell:	No more,--it wants but a few Minutes of		199	DOUEL DLR	V.1 V	456

Wants   (continued)
Sr Sampson:	rough, he wants a little Polishing.	262	FOR LCVE	III.1	320
Almeria:	From Wreck and Death, wants yet to be expired.	333	M. ERIDE	I.1	V286
Almeria:	Wants yet to be expired.	333	M. ERIDE	I.1	287
Zara:	Thee not, for what thou art, yet wants a Name:	348	M. ERIDE	II.2	336
Mirabell:	He wants Words.	404	WAY WCRLD	I.1	329
Lady Wish:	look so--My Niece affects it; but she wants Features. Is	429	WAY WORLD	III.1	170

War (14)
	A Play makes War, and Prologue is the Drum:	35	OLD EATCH	PRO.	6
Capt Bluff:	War in Flanders, with all its particulars.	52	OLD EATCH	II.1	189
Capt Bluff:	I'll call a Council of War within to ccnsider of my	70	OLD EATCH	III.1	363
Leonora:	For I had heard, that when the Chance of War	327	M. BRIDE	I.1	38
Almeria:	And Heat of War, and dire Revenge, he fir'd.	329	M. BRIDE	I.1	114
Gonsalez:	Chariots of War, adorn'd with glittering Gems,	331	M. EFIDE	I.1	229
Gonsalez:	Prisoners of War in shining Fetters, follow;	331	M. ERIDE	I.1	234
Manuel:	The ccmmon Chance of War?	336	M. BRIDE	I.1	433
Manuel:	And raise Love's Altar on the Spoils of War.	337	M. EBIDE	I.1	451
Manuel:	But late, I find, that War is but her Sport;	337	M. BRIDE	I.1	458
Manuel:	Now late, I find, that War is but her Sport;	337	M. BRIDE	I.1	458
Osmyn-Alph:	And Rage of War: For in the Fight, I saw	344	M. BRIDE	II.2	174
Osmyn-Alph:	And War: For in the Fight I saw him fall.	344	M. BRIDE	II.2	V174
Zara:	What did I not? Was't not for you, this War	347	M. BRIDE	II.2	298

Wardrobe (2)
Lady Ply:	have charm'd him; and so I'll tell him in the Wardrobe	174	DOUEL DLR	IV.1	261
Sir Paul:	(Reads) Hum--After Supper in the Wardrobe by the	178	DOUBL DLR	IV.1	408

Ware (1)
Lady Wish:	of small Ware, flaunting upon a Packthread, under a	462	WAY WORLD	V.1	12

Warlike (1)
	(Symphony of Warlike Musick. Enter the King, attended by	332	M. EBIDE	I.1	265

Warm (17)
Fondlewife:	Let her clap a warm thing to his Stomach, or chafe it with	91	OLD EATCH	IV.4	97
Fondlewife:	Let her clap some warm thing to his Stomach, or chafe it with	91	OLD BATCH	IV.4	V 97
Bellmour:	not afford one warm Dish for the Wife of his Boscm.	106	OLD EATCH	V.1	379
Maskwell:	just Repulsed by him, warm at once with Love and	136	DOUEL DLR	I.1	367
Scandal:	refund the Sack: Jeremy fetch him some warm water, or	224	FOR LCVE	I.1	310
Nurse:	of your Midnight Concerns--but warm your Bed,	238	FOR LCVE	II.1	102
Sr Sampson:	Words. Odd, I have warm Blood about me yet, I can serve	298	FCB LCVE	V.1	23
Sr Sampson:	Words. Odd, I have warm Blood about me yet, and can serve	298	FOR LCVE	V.1	V 23
Sr Sampson:	your Hand, Odd let me kiss it; 'tis as warm and as soft	301	FOR LOVE	V.1	145
Osmyn-Alph:	'Tis Life! 'tis warm! 'tis she! 'tis she her self!	341	M. BRIDE	II.2	54
Almeria:	That sucks thy warm Life-Blood, and gnaws thy Heart?	357	M. BRIDE	III.1	299
Gonsalez:	In whose Hearts Blood this Ponyard yet is warm.	377	M. BRIDE	V.2	42
Osmyn-Alph:	Warm her to Life, and wake her into Gladness.	383	M. EFIDE	V.2	279
Osmyn-Alph:	The Words of Joy and Peace; warm thy cold Beauties,	383	M. BRIDE	V.2	281
Painall:	Petulant and you both will find Mirabell as warm a	407	WAY WCRLD	I.1	463
Painall:	Fire. I have seen the warm Confession red'ning on your	413	WAY WCRLD	II.1	140
Marwood:	And let me alone to keep her warm, if she should	443	WAY WORLD	III.1	665

Warm-hand (1)
Fondlewife:	a warm-hand, rather than fail. What Book's this?	91	OLD EATCH	IV.4	98

Warm'd (5)
Belinda:	have been I know not how many times warm'd for other	106	OLD EATCH	V.1	376
Almeria:	Not to be warm'd with Words, nor idle Eloquence.	331	M. BRIDE	I.1	218
Almeria:	Not to be warm'd with Words, or idle Eloquence.	331	M. BBIDE	I.1	V218
Osmyn-Alph:	I taste her Breath, I warm'd her and am warm'd.	341	M. EFIDE	II.2	70

Warming (1)
Sharper:	warming her when she should be cold?	44	OLD EATCH	I.1	265

Warming-Pan (1)
Sr Sampson:	Warming-Pan.	308	FOB LCVE	V.1	407

Warmth (1)
Osmyn-Alph:	Gladness, and Warmth of ever-kindling Love,	345	M. EBIDE	II.2	211

Warn (1)
Zara:	Let 'em set down the Bowls, and warn Alphonso	380	M. BRIDE	V.2	149

Warn'd (3)
Lord Touch:	Let secret Villany from hence be warn'd;	203	DOUEL DLR	V.1	591
Manuel:	There's Reason in thy Doubt, and I am warn'd.	367	M. BRIDE	IV.1	240
Mirabell:	From hence let those be warn'd, who mean to wed;	478	WAY WCRLD	V.1	620

Warning (2)
Bellmour:	notwithstanding the Warning and Example before me, I	112	OLD EATCH	V.2	166
Jeremy:	to be converted into Folio Books, of Warning to all	219	FOR LCVE	I.1	112

Warrant (48)
Lucy:	Yes Yes, come, I warrant him, if you will go in and be	60	OLD BATCH	III.1	2
Sir Joseph:	So softly, that he shall never hear on't I warrant	68	OLD BATCH	III.1	263
Araminta:	I warrant, plump, Cherry-cheek'd Country-Girls.	84	OLD BATCH	IV.3	27
Belinda:	Creature, I warrant, was as full of Courtesies, as if I had	84	OLD EATCH	IV.3	40
Belinda:	Creature, I warrant, was as full of Curtsies, as if I had	84	OLD BATCH	IV.3	V 40
Fondlewife:	Ravish my Wife before my face! I warrant he's a Papist in	91	OLD BATCH	IV.4	74
Fondlewife:	Good Man! I warrant he dropp'd it on purpose,	91	OLD BATCH	IV.4	102
Fondlewife:	I warrant you, than to deny it. Come, Were you two never	93	OLD BATCH	IV.4	155
Lucy:	I warrant you--Do you go and prepare your Bride.	97	OLD BATCH	V.1	21
Setter:	I warrant you, Sir, I'm instructed.	101	OLD BATCH	V.1	195
Sir Joseph:	I warrant, I'll bring you into the Ladies gocd Graces.	103	OLD BATCH	V.1	263
Sir Paul:	I'll rattle him up I Warrant you, I'll firk him with a	144	DOUEL DLR	II.1	200
Lady Ply:	have brought all the Blood into my face; I warrant, I am	147	DOUBL DLR	II.1	335
Maskwell:	--I warrant she was very Violent at first.	149	DOUEL DLR	II.1	415
Mellefont:	Grievances, he will I warrant you.	158	DOUBL DLR	III.1	294
Careless:	I warrant you, what we must have a Son some way	162	DOUBL DLR	III.1	446
Nurse:	home yet: Poor Child, I warrant she's fond o'seeing the	235	FOR LCVE	II.1	20
Sr Sampson:	Nostrodamus. What, I warrant my Son thought nothing	240	FOR LCVE	II.1	175
Sr Sampson:	warrant you, if he danc'd till Docmsday, he thought I	240	FOR LGVE	II.1	179
Sr Sampson:	he do with a distinguishing taste?--I warrant now he'd	245	FOR LCVE	II.1	368
Sr Sampson:	now, why I warrant he can smell, and loves Perfumes	245	FOR LOVE	II.1	370
Mrs Frail:	Well, what if I took twenty--I warrant if	246	FOR LOVE	II.1	422
Mrs Fore:	Play the first day,--I warrant it wou'd break Mr. Tattle's	250	FOR LOVE	II.1	550
Mrs Fore:	great lubberly Tarpawlin--Gad I warrant you, she	250	FOR LOVE	II.1	562
Sr Sampson:	Years--I warrant he's grown--Call him in, bid	259	FOB LOVE	III.1	214

Warrant   (continued)

		PAGE	TITLE	ACT.SC	LINE
Sr Sampson:	I warrant thee Boy, Come, come, we'll be gone;	263	FOR LOVE	III.1	357
Sr Sampson:	defer Signing the Conveyance. I warrant the Devil will	267	FOR LOVE	III.1	506
Ben:	I warrant that brings 'em, an' they be within hearing.	274	FOR LOVE	III.1	794
Sr Sampson:	and Troth I like you the better--But, I warrant you,	300	FOR LOVE	V.1	125
Sr Sampson:	Possessions--Ah! Baggage--I warrant you for	301	FOR LOVE	V.1	153
Tattle:	Close Dog! A good Whoremaster, I warrant him	302	FOR LOVE	V.1	196
Miss Prue:	Man, and shall be my Husband: I warrant he'll be my	305	FOR LOVE	V.1	318
Selim:	Wherefore a Warrant for his Death is sign'd;	361	M. BRIDE	IV.1	15
Manuel:	Her Warrant, have Admittance to the Moor.	365	M. BRIDE	IV.1	169
Mirabell:	Sect? My Lady Wishfort, I warrant, who publishes her	396	WAY WORLD	I.1	60
Fainall:	What I warrant he's unsincere, or 'tis some such	403	WAY WORLD	I.1	316
Lady Wish:	of Nutmeg? I warrant thee. Come, fill, fill.--So--again	425	WAY WORLD	III.1	32
Foible:	some disbanded Officer I warrant--Half Pay is but	427	WAY WORLD	III.1	97
Foible:	but (says he) I'll fit you for that, I warrant you (says he)	428	WAY WORLD	III.1	114
Lady Wish:	A slander-mouth'd Railer: I warrant the Spendthrift	428	WAY WORLD	III.1	132
Foible:	I warrant you, Madam; a little Art once made your	429	WAY WORLD	III.1	151
Foible:	our success, Mrs. Marwood had told my Lady; but I warrant	430	WAY WORLD	III.1	206
Foible:	I warrant I work'd her up, that he may have her for asking	430	WAY WORLD	III.1	211
Sir Wilful:	Dressing! What it's but Morning here I warrant	437	WAY WORLD	III.1	447
Sir Wilful:	warrant.	441	WAY WORLD	III.1	619
Lady Wish:	Coo in the same Cage, if there be Constable or warrant	463	WAY WORLD	V.1	55
Lady Wish:	Coo in the same Cage, if there be a Constable or warrant	463	WAY WORLD	V.1 V	55
Lady Wish:	I warrant you, or she wou'd never have born	467	WAY WORLD	V.1	196

Wars (4)

Capt Bluff:	by the Wars--Took no more notice, than as if Nol. Bluffe	53	OLD BATCH	II.1	204
Lucy:	Wars.	111	OLD BATCH	V.2	146
Capt Bluff:	No more Wars, Spouse, no more Wars.--While	111	OLD BATCH	V.2	147

Wary (3)

Setter:	wary and soforth--And to all this valiant as Hercules	65	OLD BATCH	III.1	151
Sr Sampson:	Odd, you're cunning, a wary Baggage! Faith	300	FOR LOVE	V.1	124
Sir Wilful:	somewhat wary at first, before I am acquainted;--But I	446	WAY WORLD	IV.1	75

Was (414)

Was't (3)   see Wast

Lord Touch:	Dressing-Room,--was't not so? And Maskwell will	200	DOUBL DLR	V.1	484
Zara:	What did I not? Was't not for you, this War	347	M. BRIDE	II.2	298
Gonsalez:	But if she had, what was't to her? unless	366	M. BRIDE	IV.1	223

Wash (3)

Careless:	through all my Pores, and will to Morrow wash me for	170	DOUBL DLR	IV.1	116
Mrs Fore:	world to answer for, remember I wash my Hands of it,	251	FOR LOVE	II.1	578
Sr Sampson:	not wash away. Well, Madam, what are your Commands?	298	FOR LOVE	V.1	41

Wash'd (2)

Sir Joseph:	But I profess, 'tis a Dirt I have wash'd my Hands of	50	OLD BATCH	II.1	111
Almeria:	Devouring Seas have wash'd thee from my sight,	328	M. BRIDE	I.1	70

Washing (1)

Lady Wish:	begon, go go,--that I took from Washing of old Gause	462	WAY WORLD	V.1	4

Washy (1)

Foible:	What a washy Rogue art thou, to pant thus for a	459	WAY WORLD	IV.1	558

Wasp (1)

Heartwell:	you, Sir, I shall find a time; but take off your Wasp here,	108	OLD BATCH	V.2	34

Wast (1)

Lady Touch:	Wast not Lucky?	187	DOUBL DLR	V.1	1

Waste (6)

Mellefont:	waste the little time we have.	194	DOUBL DLR	V.1	246
Maskwell:	stitch'd the Gown Sleeve, that he may be puzzled, and waste	195	DOUBL DLR	V.1	288
Osmyn-Alph:	As in a Waste of Mercy?	344	M. BRIDE	II.2	187
Osmyn-Alph:	It scatters good, as in a Waste of Mercy?	344	M. BRIDE	II.2 V	187
Manuel:	Will quickly waste, and give again the Day.	364	M. BRIDE	IV.1	108
Marwood:	must be Old. For my part, my Youth may wear and waste,	410	WAY WORLD	II.1	16

Wasted (1)

Lady Wish:	have wasted my spirits so to day already; that I am ready	478	WAY WORLD	V.1	609

Wastes (1)

Singer:	And feeding, wastes in Self-consuming Fires.	435	WAY WORLD	III.1	380

Wasting (0)   see Tedious-wasting

Wat'ry (3)

Zara:	And with it dry'd thy wat'ry Cheeks; chafing	346	M. BRIDE	II.2	282
Zara:	And with it dry'd thy wat'ry Cheeks; then chaf'd	346	M. BRIDE	II.2 V	282
Zara:	Forsake their down, to wake with wat'ry Eyes,	360	M. BRIDE	III.1	428

Watch (15)

Heartwell:	(Looking on his Watch.)	46	OLD BATCH	I.1	333
Bellmour:	(Looking on his Watch.)	75	OLD BATCH	IV.1	2
Mellefont:	and Jack Maskwell has promised me, to watch my Aunt	130	DOUBL DLR	I.1	136
Maskwell:	me to watch you. I believe he will hardly be able to	154	DOUBL DLR	III.1	138
Mrs Frail:	What have you to do to watch me?--'S'life I'll	246	FOR LOVE	II.1	415
Sr Sampson:	Watch, and the Bridegroom shall observe it's Motions;	266	FOR LOVE	III.1	474
Zara:	And watch like Tapers o'er your Hours of Rest.	360	M. BRIDE	III.1	429
Manuel:	Watch her returning Sense, and bring me Word:	370	M. BRIDE	IV.1	365
Manuel:	Hence, Slave, how dar'st thou bide, to watch and pry	373	M. BRIDE	V.1	39
	While others watch like Parish-Searchers, hir'd	385	M. BRIDE	EPI.	9
Mirabell:	One a Clock! (looking on his Watch) O y'are come--	398	WAY WORLD	I.1	109
Mirabell:	I thought you were oblig'd to watch for your	409	WAY WORLD	I.1	512
Marwood:	shall watch you. Why this Wench is the Pass par tout, a	431	WAY WORLD	III.1	227
Marwood:	shall watch you. Why this Wench is the Pass par toute, a	431	WAY WORLD	III.1 V	227
	Such, who watch Plays, with scurrilous intent	479	WAY WORLD	EPI.	17

Watch-light (2)

Foresight:	a Watch-light, and lay the Crums of Comfort by me.--	270	FOR LOVE	III.1	641
Millamant:	melancholly as a Watch-light. Well Mirabell, If ever you	422	WAY WORLD	IV.1	477

Watch'd (2)

Maskwell:	added to my hopes; I watch'd the Occasion, and took you,	136	DOUBL DLR	I.1	366
Manuel:	Begets a Doubt. I'd have 'em watch'd: perhaps	335	M. BRIDE	I.1	380

Watches (3)

Sharper:	him? is not he a Draggon that watches those Golden	46	OLD BATCH	I.1	349
Belinda:	to trust you to your self. The Devil watches all opportunities	57	OLD BATCH	II.2	105
Foible:	to him,--besides, I believe Madam Marwood watches	430	WAY WORLD	III.1	216

Watchful (1)
Fainall:	nodding Husband would not wake, that e'er the watchful	.	414	WAY WORLD	II.1	148

Water (6)   see Cinnamon-water, Fig-water, Poppy-Water, Poppy-water
Sir Joseph:	Eyes twinkle, and her Mouth water? Did not she pull up	.	103	OLD BATCH	V.1	255
Sir Paul:	Chaste as Ice, but you are melted now, and false as Water.	.	179	DOUBL DLR	IV.1	431
Scandal:	refund the Sack: Jeremy fetch him some warm water, or	.	224	FOR LOVE	I.1	310
Ben:	and then you'll carry your Keels above Water, he, he, he.	.	262	FOR LOVE	III.1	335
Scandal:	water, and lye upon your back, may be you may dream.	.	270	FOR LOVE	III.1	639
Ben:	A shot 'twixt wind and water, ...	.	274	FOR LOVE	III.1	788

Waters (1)   see Barbado's-Waters
Millamant:	O horrid proviso's! filthy strong Waters! I toste	. .	452	WAY WORLD	IV.1	278

Watry (1)   see Wat'ry
Almeria:	Or ever dry these swoll'n, and watry Eyes;	. . . .	329	M. BRIDE	I.1	146

Wavering (1)
Millamant:	were wavering at the grate of a Monastery, with one foot	.	449	WAY WORLD	IV.1	163

Waves (5)
Almeria:	The Shoal, and save me floating on the Waves,	. . .	329	M. BRIDE	I.1	130
Almeria:	The Wildness of the Waves and Rocks to this?	. . . .	342	M. BRIDE	II.2	88
Zara:	Pale and expiring, drench'd in briny Waves	. . . .	346	M. BRIDE	II.2	277
Almeria:	Ye Winds and Waves, I call ye all to witness.	. . . .	370	M. BRIDE	IV.1	360
Manuel:	Wilder than Winds or Waves thy self do'st rave.	. . . .	370	M. BRIDE	IV.1	361

Wax-Lights (1)
Foible:	Yes, Madam. I have put Wax-Lights in the Sconces;	. .	444	WAY WORLD	IV.1	3

Way (117)   see Half-way
Bellmour:	Husband be out of the way, for the Wife to shew her	. .	38	OLD BATCH	I.1	56
Vainlove:	way; much addicted to Jealousie, but more to Fondness:	.	40	OLD BATCH	I.1	108
Heartwell:	way. Adieu.	.	46	OLD BATCH	I.1	336
Bellmour:	but I see he has turn'd the Corner and goes another way.	.	46	OLD BATCH	I.1	V340
Capt Bluff:	that way.	.	54	OLD BATCH	II.1	239
Bellmour:	other way to get himself a heat.	.	70	OLD BATCH	III.1	329
Setter:	the Corner, and on's coming this way.	.	75	OLD BATCH	IV.1	10
Fondlewife:	me, than she has reason to be; and in the way of Trade,	.	77	OLD BATCH	IV.1	60
Belinda:	come this Way, till I put my self a little in Repair,--Ah!	.	83	OLD BATCH	IV.3	10
Belinda:	come this Way, till I have put my self a little in Repair,--Ah!	.	83	OLD BATCH	IV.3	V 10
Belinda:	with their Feathers growing the wrong way.--O such	. .	84	OLD BATCH	IV.3	30
Araminta:	No matter,--I see Vainlove coming this way,--	.	85	OLD BATCH	IV.3	77
Belinda:	World that I like.--Oh Lord, walk this way.--I	.	87	OLD BATCH	IV.3	149
Vainlove:	(aside). Hey day! Which way now? Here's fine	. . . .	87	OLD BATCH	IV.3	160
Fondlewife:	by the way,--and I must have my Papers of Accounts	.	89	OLD BATCH	IV.4	24
Fondlewife:	I'll show you the way out of my house, if you please. Come,	.	96	OLD BATCH	IV.4	269
Bellmour:	Setter.) Pox take 'em, they stand just in my Way. . . .	.	97	OLD BATCH	V.1	12
Setter:	Well, Sir Joseph, you have such a winning way with	.	103	OLD BATCH	V.1	251
Setter:	mine. Here's Company coming, if you'll walk this way,	.	106	OLD BATCH	V.1	352
Bellmour:	Corner-House, and I'll tell you by the way what may	.	107	OLD BATCH	V.1	402
Vainlove:	Faith, that's a sure way.--But here's one can	.	109	OLD BATCH	V.2	79
Heartwell:	--And I cannot in gratitude (for I see which way thou	.	111	OLD BATCH	V.2	151
	For 'tis our way (you know) for fear o'th' worst,	. .	113	OLD BATCH	EPI.	21
	Moors, have this way (as Story tells) to know	. . .	125	DOUBL DLR	PRO.	1
Careless:	Aunts Aversion in her Revenge, cannot be any way so	.	131	DOUBL DLR	I.1	159
Brisk:	no other way, I'gad.	.	133	DOUBL DLR	I.1	243
Brisk:	t'other way. Suppose I say a witty thing to you?	.	134	DOUBL DLR	I.1	278
Lady Touch:	She is so Credulous that way naturally, and	.	138	DOUBL DLR	I.1	412
Lady Froth:	then I had a way.--For between you and I, I had	.	138	DOUBL DLR	II.1	10
Mellefont:	New Song, we'll get 'em to give it us by the way.	.	143	DOUBL DLR	II.1	173
Sir Paul:	submit as formerly, therefore give way.	.	144	DOUBL DLR	II.1	208
Mellefont:	Villany of aspersing me with the guilt. How? which way	.	146	DOUBL DLR	II.1	295
Maskwell:	don't know, but she may come this way; I am to meet her	.	149	DOUBL DLR	II.1	433
Maskwell:	interpret a Coldness the right way; therefore I must	.	155	DOUBL DLR	III.1	182
Maskwell:	I'm afraid my frailty leans that way--but I don't	. .	156	DOUBL DLR	III.1	207
Careless:	Mellefont, get cut o'th' way, my Lady Plyant's	.	157	DOUBL DLR	III.1	264
Sir Paul:	fine way of living, as I may say, peacefully and happily,	.	160	DOUBL DLR	III.1	384
Careless:	I warrant you, what we must have a Son some way	. . .	162	DOUBL DLR	III.1	446
Brisk:	Short, but there's Salt in't, my way of writing I'gad.	.	166	DOUBL DLR	III.1	602
Lady Froth:	out of the way.	.	177	DOUBL DLR	IV.1	378
Sir Paul:	whomsoever he receives into his bosom, will find the way	.	178	DOUBL DLR	IV.1	421
Maskwell:	I am happy to be in the way of your Lordships	.	181	DOUBL DLR	IV.1	533
Maskwell:	Nay then, there's but one way.	.	184	DOUBL DLR	IV.2	39
Mellefont:	honest way.	.	185	DOUBL DLR	IV.2	88
Maskwell:	Ears this way.	.	189	DOUBL DLR	V.1	45
Lord Touch:	quickly show him which way that is going.	. . . .	189	DOUBL DLR	V.1	77
Maskwell:	comes opportunely--now will I, in my old way,	. . .	190	DOUBL DLR	V.1	97
Lord Touch:	know he's no way to be rewarded but in her. I'll defer my	.	191	DOUBL DLR	V.1	138
Mellefont:	I know no other way but this he has proposed; If	. .	193	DOUBL DLR	V.1	200
Maskwell:	our Contrivance, that's my way.	.	193	DOUBL DLR	V.1	215
Maskwell:	way, but in the hopes of her Marrying you.--	.	193	DOUBL DLR	V.1	220
Maskwell:	way into it, so that you need not come thro' this Door	.	194	DOUBL DLR	V.1	254
Maskwell:	about our business, it shall be Tithes in your way.	.	194	DOUBL DLR	V.1	279
Lord Touch:	Here's Company--come this way and tell	. . .	196	DOUBL DLR	V.1	329
Lady Touch:	Thou hast, thou hast found the only way to turn my Rage;	.	198	DOUBL DLR	V.1	398
	But since in Paradise frail Flesh gave way,	. .	213	FOR LOVE	PRO.	18
Jeremy:	But Sir, Is this the way to recover your Father's	. . .	218	FOR LOVE	I.1	82
Valentine:	Come sit you down, you know his way.	. . .	222	FOR LOVE	I.1	235
Scandal:	I'll rip up his Stomach, and go the shortest way to his	.	224	FOR LOVE	I.1	311
Tattle:	Have you not a back way?	.	229	FOR LOVE	I.1	510
Tattle:	Is there not a back way?	.	229	FOR LOVE	I.1	V510
Foresight:	a way to make your Lover, your Prodigal Spendthrift	.	238	FOR LOVE	II.1	116
Valentine:	was easily turn'd another way; and at least look'd well on	.	246	FOR LOVE	II.1	409
Valentine:	are earnest,--I'll avoid 'em,--Come this way,	. . .	246	FOR LOVE	II.1	411
Mrs Frail:	Bodkin?--Oh Sister, Sister!--Sister every way.	. . .	248	FOR LOVE	II.1	470
Mrs Fore:	for the Booby, it may go a great way towards his	. .	249	FOR LOVE	II.1	502
Mrs Fore:	some way or other to leave 'em together.	.	249	FOR LOVE	II.1	504
Miss Prue:	this way--Is not it pure?--It's better than	. . .	249	FOR LOVE	II.1	528
Miss Prue:	our old fashion'd Country way of speaking ones mind;--	.	252	FOR LOVE	II.1	625
Nurse:	come in the back way.	.	253	FOR LOVE	III.1	12
Tattle:	own, in Conversation, by way of Novel: but never have	.	256	FOR LOVE	III.1	119

Way   (continued)

Ben:	Marry a God's Name an the wind sit that way. As for my	. 261	FOR LCVE	III.1	302
Ben:	speak one thing, and to think just the contrary way; is as				
	it	. 263	FOR LCVE	III.1	386
Ben:	were, to look one way, and to row another. Now, for my	. 263	FOR LOVE	III.1	387
Foresight:	How! Am I alter'd any way? I don't perceive it. . . .	. 268	FOR LOVE	III.1	571
Scandal:	Passion. But come a little farther this way, and I'll				
	tell you	269	FOR LCVE	III.1	596
Scandal:	What Project I had to get him out of the way; that I might	269	FOR LOVE	III.1	597
Sr Sampson:	What to do, or say, nor which way to go.	. 282	FCR LCVE	IV.1	250
Valentine:	Who's that, that's out of his Way?--I am Truth, . . .	. 282	FOR LCVE	IV.1	251
Valentine:	Road is the worst way you can go--He that fcllows . .	. 282	FOR LOVE	IV.1	253
Ben:	way--(It seems Brother Val is gone mad, and so that .	. 285	FOR LOVE	IV.1	366
Mrs Frail:	No, I'll leave you a-drift, and go which way you . .	. 286	FCR LCVE	IV.1	420
Mrs Fore:	project in my head for you, and I have gcne a good way	. 288	FCR LCVE	IV.1	464
Tattle:	Look you, Mr. Foresight, It is not my way to make . .	. 291	FOR LCVE	IV.1	606
Sr Sampson:	a Lady any way--Come, come, let me tell you, you . .	. 298	FOR LOVE	V.1	24
Tattle:	In the way of Art: I have some taking Features, not .	. 304	FOR LCVE	V.1	267
Miss Prue:	way or other. Oh! methinks I'm sick when I think of a .	. 305	FOR LCVE	V.1	308
Sr Sampson:	way to come to it, but by the Ncrth-East Passage. . .	. 308	FCR LCVE	V.1	428
Valentine:	in your way--You have but Justice.	. 313	FOR LOVE	V.1	597
Garcia:	This Way, we're told, Osmyn was seen to walk; . . .	. 337	M. BRIDE	II.1	1
Heli:	And when his Soul gives all her Passions Way, . . .	. 338	M. BRIDE	II.1	31
Leonora:	And bending this way.	. 344	M. BRIDE	II.2	193
Almeria:	Give thy Soul Way, and tell me thy dark Thought. . .	. 356	M. BRIDE	III.1	274
Selim:	Attempt to force his way for an Escape.	. 362	M. BRIDE	IV.1	54
Gonsalez:	They who are fled have that way bent their course. . .	. 363	M. BRIDE	IV.1	80
Gonsalez:	Open'd the Way to this Invasion;	. 363	M. BRIDE	IV.1	87
Gonsalez:	Open'd and urg'd the Way to this Invasion; . . .	. 363	M. BRIDE	IV.1 V 87
Gonsalez:	I'm not i'th' Way at Present, gcod Alonzo. . . .	. 371	M. BRIDE	IV.1	421
Gonsalez:	There lies my way, that Door is too unlock'd. . . .	. 376	M. BRIDE	IV.2	4
Betty:	He's in the next Room, Friend--That way.	. 400	WAY WORLD	I.1	185
Witwoud:	found out this way, I have known him call for . . .	. 405	WAY WCRLD	I.1	366
Mrs Fain:	another by being seen to walk with his Wife. This way Mr.	412	WAY WCRLD	II.1	106
Fainall:	and any way, every way will make amends;--I'll . . .	. 416	WAY WCRLD	II.1	243
Fainall:	You have a Mask, wear it a Moment. This way, this way,	. 416	WAY WCRLD	II.1	248
Witwoud:	Is that the way? Pray Madam, do you pin up your . .	. 419	WAY WCRLD	II.1	363
Waitwell:	Sir, ycur Affairs are in a prosperous way. . . .	. 423	WAY WORLD	II.1	511
Millamant:	despair to prevail, and so let him follow his own way.	. 434	WAY WCRLD	III.1	342
Sir Wilful:	Do you speak by way of Offence, Sir?	. 438	WAY WORLD	III.1	503
Fainall:	in the Way of the World. 'S death	. 442	WAY WORLD	III.1	631
Lady Wish:	a little dangling off, Jogging in a thoughtful way--Yes--	445	WAY WCRLD	IV.1	26
Millamant:	You may go this way Sir.	. 448	WAY WCRLD	IV.1	148
Mrs Fain:	way to succeed. Therefore spare your Extacies for another	452	WAY WCRLD	IV.1	303
Lady Wish:	Well, Sir Rowland, you have the way,--	. 458	WAY WORLD	IV.1	526
Fainall:	the way of the World. That shall not urge me to relinquish	474	WAY WCRLD	V.1	476
Mirabell:	Even sc Sir, 'tis the way of the World, Sir: of the .	. 476	WAY WCRLD	V.1	553

Way's (1)

Sir Joseph:	Hem! Pray Madam, Which Way's the Wind?	. 85	OLD BATCH	IV.3	94

Ways (8)

Heartwell:	What rugged Ways attend the Nocn of Life!	. 112	OLD BATCH	V.2	191
Lady Touch:	into unthought of ways of ruine.	. 185	DOUEL DLR	IV.2	78
Leonora:	By all the worthy and indulgent ways, ...	. 327	M. BRIDE	I.1	46
Almeria:	And range the Starry Orbs, and Milky Ways, ...	. 340	M. EBIDE	II.2	26
Heli:	Occasicn will not fail to point out Ways	. 352	M. EBIDE	III.1	97
Osmyn-Alph:	And wafted thence, on Angels Wings, thro' Ways . . .	. 353	M. EBIDE	III.1	131
Zara:	Thro' all the Gloomy Ways, and Iron Doors	. 379	M. EBIDE	V.2	133
Fainall:	ways of Wedlock and this World. Will you yet be . .	. 415	WAY WORLD	II.1	214

We (290)

We'd (3)

	I will not say, we'd all in danger been, ...	. 125	DOUBL DLR	PRO.	21
Trapland:	No, no, there's no such thing, we'd better mind our .	. 223	FOR LCVE	I.1	281
	Others there are whose Malice we'd prevent;	. 479	WAY WCRLD	EPI.	16

We'l (1)

Heartwell:	we'l go to Bed--	. 73	OLD BATCH	III.2	108

We'll (40)   see We'l, Wee'l, Wee'll

	To save our Plays, or else we'll damn your Pit. . . .	. 35	OLD EATCH	PRO.	9
Sir Joseph:	Come we'll go take a Glass to drown Animosities. . .	. 54	OLD EATCH	II.1	246
Araminta:	If Mr. Gavot will walk with us in the Garden, we'll have	. 60	OLD EATCH	II.2	207
Araminta:	If Mr. Gavot will walk with us into the Garden, we'll have	60	OLD BATCH	II.2 V207
Heartwell:	Ha! Nay come, we'll kiss at parting (kisses her) by .	. 74	OLD BATCH	III.2	133
Belinda:	We'll put on our Masks to secure his Ignorance. . . .	. 84	OLD EATCH	IV.3	59
Sir Joseph:	and get 50 Pieces more from him. Adslidikins, Bully, we'll	85	OLD BATCH	IV.3	63
Mellefont:	We'll come immediately, if you'll but go in, and . .	. 128	DOUEL DLR	I.1	46
Lord Touch:	Sir Paul, if you please we'll retire to the	. 132	DOUBL DLR	I.1	216
Mellefont:	New Song, we'll get 'em to give it us by the way. . .	. 143	DOUEL DLR	II.1	173
Careless:	Madam,--if your Ladyship please, we'll discourse of this in	163	DOUEL DLR	III.1	494
Lady Froth:	to you for the hint, stay we'll read over those half a score	164	DOUBL DLR	III.1	511
Lady Froth:	--Come, my dear Cynthia, Mr. Brisk, we'll go see . .	. 167	DOUEL DLR	III.1	615
Lord Froth:	Any other time, my Dear, or we'll Dance it	. 177	DOUEL DLR	IV.1	381
Lord Touch:	We'll think of punishment at leasure, but	. 203	DOUBL DLR	V.1	581
Valentine:	T'other Glass, and then we'll talk. Fill, Jeremy. . .	. 222	FOR LCVE	I.1	248
Valentine:	Say ycu so, I'faith: Come, we'll remember the . . .	. 223	FOR LOVE	I.1	271
Valentine:	No faith, we'll mind the Widow's business, fill . . .	. 223	FOR LCVE	I.1	283
Scandal:	Ay, we'll all give you something.	. 231	FOR LCVE	I.1	587
Foresight:	have consulted me for the time. Well, but we'll make .	. 240	FOR LOVE	II.1	190
Miss Prue:	Well, we'll do it again.	. 252	FOR LOVE	II.1	637
Sr Sampson:	not be shame-fac'd, we'll leave you together. . . .	. 262	FOR LOVE	III.1	351
Sr Sampson:	I warrant thee Boy, Ccme, come, we'll be gone; . . .	. 263	FOR LOVE	III.1	357
Foresight:	Sir Sampson, we'll have the Wedding to morrow . . .	. 265	FOR LOVE	III.1	469
Scandal:	by Confederacy; and if you please, we'll put a Trick .	. 272	FOR LOVE	III.1	700
Valentine:	and we'll be Marry'd in the dead of Night.--But say .	. 290	FOR LOVE	IV.1	548
Mrs Frail:	No, no, we'll keep it secret, it shall be done . . .	. 290	FOR LOVE	IV.1	554
Valentine:	and yet we'll Marry one another in spite of the Pope-- .	. 290	FOR LOVE	IV.1	559
Valentine:	asham'd of; and then we'll blush once for all. . . .	. 290	FOR LOVE	IV.1	564
Sr Sampson:	troth you shall. Odd we'll have the Musick of the Spheres	307	FOR LOVE	V.1	385

Weary   (continued)
Fainall: so there's an end of Jealousie. Weary of her, I am, and
                shall . . . . 443 WAY WORLD III.1 681
Weasel (2)
Foresight: down Stairs, and met a Weasel; bad Omens those: some . . 236 FOR LOVE II.1 34
Ben: stink; he shall smell more like a Weasel than a Civet-Cat, 265 FOR LOVE III.1 437
Weather (11)   see Fair-Weather
Sharper: That's because he always sets out in foul Weather, . . . 42 OLD BATCH I.1 201
Sir Joseph: fine Weather. . . . . 90 OLD BATCH IV.4 37
Laetitia: Methinks, 't has been very ill Weather. . . . . . . 90 OLD BATCH IV.4 38
Sir Joseph: As you say, Madam, 'tis pretty bad Weather, and . . . 90 OLD BATCH IV.4 39
Brisk: I'm afraid that simile wont do in wet Weather-- . . . . 164 DOUBL DLR III.1 517
Lady Froth: Coach in wet Weather. . . . . 164 DOUBL DLR III.1 521
Ben: has been gathering foul weather in her Mouth, and now it . 265 FOR LOVE III.1 442
Mrs Frail: foul Weather--He's us'd to an inconstant Element, . . . 284 FOR LOVE IV.1 307
Sr Sampson: Weather; and destroy that Usurper of a Bed call'd a . . 308 FOR LOVE V.1 406
                As to a Shed, that shields 'em from the Weather. . . . 315 FOR LOVE EPI. 4
                For just as one prognosticates the Weather, ... 323 M. BRIDE PRO. 8
Weather-Cock (1)
Sir Wilful: nor the Weather-Cock your Companion. I direct my . . . 440 WAY WORLD III.1 571
Weatherheaded (1)
Valentine: Weatherheaded fool, I know how to laugh at him; but . . 244 FOR LOVE II.1 312
Weaving (1)
Lady Wish: and Weaving of dead Hair, with a bleak blew Nose, over a . 462 WAY WORLD V.1 5
Wed (8)
Heartwell: when I wed again, may she be--Ugly, as an old . . . 112 OLD BATCH V.2 159
Lady Touch: Fortune, but he must mix his Blood with mine, and Wed . . 191 DOUBL DLR V.1 127
Foresight: send your Son to Sea again. I'll wed my Daughter to an . 241 FOR LOVE II.1 238
Almeria: By any Action, Word or Thought, to wed . . . . . . 330 M. BRIDE I.1 186
Almeria: I've sworn I'll not wed Garcia; why d'ye force me? . . . 341 M. BRIDE II.2 74
Osmyn-Alph: Think how I am, when thou shalt wed with Garcia! . . . 358 M. BRIDE III.1 349
Gonsalez: Almeria widow'd, yet again may wed; . . . . 372 M. BRIDE IV.1 446
Mirabell: From hence let those be warn'd, who mean to wed; . . . 478 WAY WORLD V.1 620
Wedded (4)
Leonora: Alas! were you then wedded to Alphonso? . . . . . . 329 M. BRIDE I.1 132
Almeria: And in one Day, was wedded, and a Widow. . . . . . 329 M. BRIDE I.1 141
Almeria: And wedded Husband--Heav'n, and Air, and Seas; . . . 370 M. BRIDE IV.1 359
Gonsalez: Wedded already--what if he should yield? . . . . . 371 M. BRIDE IV.1 405
Wedding (9)
Brisk: Froth won't Dance at your Wedding to Morrow; nor . . . 129 DOUBL DLR I.1 56
Sir Paul: Wedding Night, to die a Maid; as she did; all were ruin'd, 174 DOUBL DLR IV.1 252
Sir Paul: of a Wedding, gad'sbud--to shew you that I am not . . . 192 DOUBL DLR V.1 177
Foresight: Sir Sampson, we'll have the Wedding to morrow . . . 265 FOR LOVE III.1 469
Valentine: Man shou'd have a Stomach to a Wedding Supper, when . . 289 FOR LOVE IV.1 527
Ben: Why then I'll tell you, There's a new wedding upon the . 307 FOR LOVE V.1 358
Sr Sampson: and yet you shall live to dance at my Wedding; faith and . 307 FOR LOVE V.1 384
Sr Sampson: your Wedding Night? I'm an older Fellow than you, and . . 310 FOR LOVE V.1 485
Scandal: own Wedding; methinks 'tis pity they should not be . . 313 FOR LOVE V.1 599
Wedding-Day (1)
Heartwell: self on her Wedding-Day! Not hold out till Night! . . . 107 OLD BATCH V.2 6
Wedding-night (1)
Careless: with much Solemnity on his anniversary Wedding-night. . . 158 DOUBL DLR III.1 279
Wedlock (3)
Sharper: the narrow Joys of Wedlock. But prithee come along with . 104 OLD BATCH V.1 305
Fainall: ways of Wedlock and this World. Will you yet be . . . 415 WAY WORLD II.1 214
Fainall: Wedlock. . . . . 442 WAY WORLD III.1 638
Wee'l (1)
Sir Joseph: done behind his Back, than what's said--Come wee'l . . . 70 OLD BATCH III.1 361
Wee'll (1)
Lady Wish: it--wee'll open it together--lock you here. . . . . . 460 WAY WORLD IV.1 583
Wee're (1)
Mirabell: Then wee're agreed. Shall I kiss your hand upon the . . 452 WAY WORLD IV.1 280
Wee'st (1)
Nurse: Wee'st heart, I know not, they're none of 'em come . . . 235 FOR LOVE II.1 19
Weeds (1)
Manuel: Upon this solemn Day, in these sad Weeds? . . . . . . 333 M. BRIDE I.1 280
Week (7)
Scandal: in her Bed, shift twice a Week, and not work so hard, that 222 FOR LOVE I.1 219
Fainall: have 'em three times a Week, and meet by turns, at one . 396 WAY WORLD I.1 51
Fainall: the Week. You and I are excluded; and it was once propos'd 396 WAY WORLD I.1 54
Witwoud: and something more by the Week, to call on him . . . 405 WAY WORLD I.1 360
Servant-W: A Week, Sir; longer than any Body in the House, ... 437 WAY WORLD III.1 457
Servant-W: A Week, Sir; longer than any in the House, ... 437 WAY WORLD III.1 V457
Millamant: of one another the first Week, and asham'd of one another 450 WAY WORLD IV.1 205
Weekly (2)
Sr Sampson: Weekly Bills out of Countenance. . . . . 308 FOR LOVE V.1 399
Sir Wilful: Gazetts then, and Dawks's Letter, and the weekly Bill, 'till 440 WAY WORLD III.1 552
Weeks (2)
Lady Froth: Three Weeks together. . . . . 138 DOUBL DLR II.1 4
Waitwell: I'll do't. In three weeks he shall be bare-foot; in a . 458 WAY WORLD IV.1 521
Weep (18)
Fondlewife: --Nay look you now if she does not weep--'tis the fondest 78 OLD BATCH IV.1 98
Fondlewife: made me weep--made poor Nykin weep--Nay come Kiss, . . . 78 OLD BATCH IV.1 117
Lady Ply: can refrain to weep and yield to such sad Sayings.-- . . 170 DOUBL DLR IV.1 120
Almeria: Which they unseen, may wail, and weep, and mourn, . . . 328 M. BRIDE I.1 85
Manuel: To see thee weep on this Occasion--But some . . . . 333 M. BRIDE I.1 277
Manuel: To see thee weep on this Occasion--some . . . . . 333 M. BRIDE I.1 V277
Manuel: Ha! what? thou dost not weep to think of that? . . . 333 M. BRIDE I.1 302
Manuel: With her Rejoicings. What, to mourn, and weep; . . . 333 M. BRIDE I.1 313
Manuel: Then, then, to weep, and pray, and grieve? By Heav'n, . 333 M. BRIDE I.1 314
Almeria: For I weep to see thee--Art thou not paler, ... 342 M. BRIDE II.2 113
Osmyn-Alph: Why dost thou weep, and hold thee from my Arms, . . . 343 M. BRIDE II.2 122
Zara: Shalt weep for mine, forgetting thy own Miseries. . . . 353 M. BRIDE III.1 168
Almeria: --I do not weep! The Springs of Tears are dry'd; . . . 382 M. BRIDE V.2 240
Almeria: --Those Men have left to weep; and look on me! . . . 382 M. BRIDE V.2 245
Almeria: --Those Men have left to weep; they look on me! . . . 382 M. BRIDE V.2 V245

Weep   (continued)
  Osmyn-Alph: Yet am I dash'd to think that thou must weep; . . . . 383 M. BRIDE V.2 303
  Fainall: and weep like Alexander, when he wanted other Worlds to . 413 WAY WCRLD II.1 116
Weeping (4)
  Fondlewife: (Weeping.) . . . . . 95 OLD BATCH IV.4 253
  Zara: Trembling and weeping as he leads her forth! . . . . . 359 M. BRIDE III.1 396
  Zara: To be the Care of weeping Majesty? . . . . . 360 M. BRIDE III.1 426
  Leonora: Who seem the Murderers, kneel weeping by: . . . . . . 381 M. BRIDE V.2 224
Weepings (1)
  Osmyn-Alph: And melt me down to mingle with thy Weepings? . . . . 357 M. BRIDE III.1 307
Weeps (6)
  Silvia: (Turns and Weeps.) . . . . 74 OLD BATCH III.2 132
  Lady Touch: (She Weeps.) . . . . . 185 DOUEL DLR IV.2 67
  Lady Touch: Anger melts. (weeps) Here, take this Ponyard, for my very 198 DOUEL DLR V.1 402
  Almeria: (Weeps.) . . . . . . 326 M. BRIDE I.1 14
  Gonsalez: Have patience, Royal Sir, the Princess weeps . . . . . 333 M. BRIDE I.1 303
  Almeria: (She weeps.) . . . . . 383 M. BRIDE V.2 310
Weigh'd (1)
  Fondlewife: of Adultery is? have you weigh'd it I say? For it is a very 77 OLD BATCH IV.1 69
Weighing (1)
  Scandal: Yes, I have a Poet weighing Words, and selling . . . . 233 FOR LCVE I.1 651
Weight (12)
  Maskwell: weak, and shrinks beneath the weight, and cannot rise to . 189 DOUEL DLR V.1 79
  Tattle: pardcn me, if from a just weight of his Merit, with your . 255 FOR LCVE III.1 70
  Ben: your weight in Gold and Jewels, and thc'f I lov'd you . . 287 FCR LCVE IV.1 431
  Almeria: Come, heavy-laden with the oppressing Weight . . . . 330 M. BRIDE I.1 155
  Almeria: But double, double Weight of Wce to mine; . . . . . 330 M. BRIDE I.1 170
  Gonsalez: Which groan beneath the Weight of Moorish Wealth. . . 331 M. BRIDE I.1 228
  Almeria: By its own Weight, made stedfast, and immoveable, . . 339 M. BRIDE II.1 62
  Osmyn-Alph: Give me more Weight, crush my declining Years . . . 350 M. BRIDE III.1 11
  Zara: Somewhat of weight tc me, requires his Freedom. . . . . 358 M. BRIDE III.1 376
  Selim: Who bcre high Offices of Weight and Trust, ... 361 M. BRIDE IV.1 10
  Zara: Find cut the King, tell him I have of Weight . . . . . 361 M. BRIDE IV.1 18
  Gonsalez: Whose weight has sunk me 'ere I reach'd the Shore. . . 378 M. BRIDE V.2 87
Weighty (2)
  Fondlewife: weighty Sin; and although it may lie heavy upon thee, . . 77 OLD BATCH IV.1 70
  Setter: Why, to be brief, for I have weighty Affairs depending: . 105 OLD BATCH V.1 341
Welch (1)
  Foible: for, as they say cf a Welch Maiden-head. . . . . . 430 WAY WCRLD III.1 212
Welcome (18)
  Sir Joseph: Oh here a' comes--Ah my Hector of Troy, welcome . . . 51 OLD BATCH II.1 139
  Laetitia: welccme, but not the Hypocrisie. . . . . . 81 OLD BATCH IV.2 26
  Bellmour: (aside) Rather the Hypocrisie was welcome, but not . . 81 OLD BATCH IV.2 27
  Mellefont: Maskwell, welcome, thy presence is a view cf Land, . . 148 DOUEL DLR II.1 381
  Careless: be always welccme to my privacy. . . . . . 159 DOUEL DLR III.1 324
  Valentine: O Mr. Trapland! my old Friend! Welcome. Jeremy, a . . 222 FOR LCVE I.1 228
  Valentine: be doutly welccme. . . . . . 243 FCR LCVE II.1 292
  Sr Sampson: me, thou art heartily welccme. . . . . . 260 FOR LCVE III.1 271
  Tattle: Sir, ycu're welccme a-shore. . . . . . 261 FOR LCVE III.1 285
  Valentine: Oh welcome, welccme. . . . . . 290 FOR LCVE IV.1 544
  Valentine: about,--They are welcome, and I'll tell 'em so my self. (To 292 FOR LCVE IV.1 617
  Almeria: I was a welcome Captive in Valentia, ... 329 M. BRIDE I.1 110
  Manuel: What Welcome, and what Honours, beauteous Zara, . . . 335 M. BRIDE I.1 385
  Osmyn-Alph: How shall I welcome thee, to this sad Place? . . . . 355 M. BRIDE III.1 237
  Gonsalez: One tc my Wish. Alonzo, thou art welcome. . . . . 371 M. BRIDE IV.1 417
  Lady Wish: Nephew, you are welcome. . . . . . 441 WAY WCRLD III.1 593
  Lady Wish: your Servant.--Nephew, you are welcome again. . . . . 441 WAY WCRLD III.1 598
Well (369) see Fare-thee-well
    Well, I'm his Advocate--by me he prays ycu, ... 35 OLD BATCH PRO. 17
    Well, the Deuce take me, if I han't forgot it. . . . . 35 OLD BATCH PRO. 22
  Vainlove: Element Ned--Well as high as a Flyer as you are, I . . . 38 OLD BATCH I.1 30
  Bellmour: Why faith I think it will do well enough--If the . . . 38 OLD BATCH I.1 55
  Vainlove: will, for you have made him fit for no Body else--Well-- . 40 OLD BATCH I.1 114
  Vainlove: Well good Morrow, let's dine together, I'l meet at . . . 40 OLD BATCH I.1 129
  Bellmour: Baggage loves me, for she never speaks well of me her . . 41 OLD BATCH I.1 168
  Bellmour: in the Mine; well, we have each our share of sport, and each 43 OLD BATCH I.1 223
  Bellmour: Well ccme off George, if at any time ycu should be . . . 44 OLD BATCH I.1 286
  Bellmour: Well but George I have one Question to ask you-- . . . 45 OLD BATCH I.1 330
  Bellmour: seem to rouse, 'tis but well lashing him, and he will sleep 46 OLD BATCH I.1 353
  Sharper: Well, Ile endeavour his acquaintance--you steer . . . . 47 OLD BATCH I.1 385
  Sharper: ill Wind that blows no body good: well, you may rejoyce . 48 OLD BATCH II.1 33
  Sir Joseph: Ah, well said my Hero; was not that great Sir? . . . . 52 OLD BATCH II.1 166
  Sir Joseph: well--Ey the Lord Harry Mr. Sharper he's as brave a . . 52 OLD BATCH II.1 175
  Capt Bluff: you know--Well, Mr. Sharper, would you think it? In all . 53 OLD BATCH II.1 201
  Sir Joseph: Well I am a Focl sometimes--But I'm sorry. . . . . . 54 OLD BATCH II.1 244
  Bellmour: O very well perform'd--But I don't much . . . . . 60 OLD BATCH II.2 204
  Araminta: Nature well, for there are few Men, but do more silly . . 60 OLD BATCH II.2 216
  Bellmour: Well, I find my Apishness has paid the Ransome . . . . 60 OLD BATCH II.2 218
  Bellmour: I could be well enough pleas'd to drive on a Love-bargain, 60 OLD BATCH II.2 220
  Silvia: Well, since there's no remedy--Yet tell me-- . . . . 61 OLD BATCH III.1 14
  Heartwell: more Ccnsuming Fire, a Womans Arms. Ha! well . . . . 62 OLD BATCH III.1 69
  Heartwell: Well, Why do you move? Feet do your . . . . . 62 OLD BATCH III.1 73
  Vainlove: Well, I'le leave you with your Engineer. . . . . . 64 OLD BATCH III.1 120
  Bellmour: Well in this Fanatick Fathers habit, will I confess . . 64 OLD BATCH III.1 130
  Capt Bluff: Well, go to him frcm me--Tell him, I say, he . . . . 68 OLD BATCH III.1 258
  Capt Bluff: Very well--Very fine--But 'tis no matter-- . . . . 70 OLD BATCH III.1 331
  Capt Bluff: Well, Sir Joseph, at your entreaty--Eut were not . . . 70 OLD BATCH III.1 348
  Singer: O let me feed as well as taste, ... 71 OLD BATCH III.2 7
  Heartwell: Well, has this prevail'd for me, and will you look . . 71 OLD BATCH III.2 28
  Heartwell: well--Yet I must on--'Tis a bearded Arrow, and . . . 73 OLD BATCH III.2 72
  Silvia: Indeed if I were well assur'd you lov'd; but how can I . 73 OLD BATCH III.2 74
  Silvia: be well assur'd? . . . . . 73 OLD BATCH III.2 75
  Silvia: No, I'll die before I'll be your Whore--as well as I . 74 OLD BATCH III.2 124
  Heartwell: Well, farewell then--if I can get out of her sight I . 74 OLD BATCH III.2 129
  Heartwell: Well, farewell then--if I can get out of sight I . . . 74 OLD BATCH III.2 V129
  Silvia: Well--good by. . . . . . 74 OLD BATCH III.2 131

Silvia:	Midwife, some nine Months hence--Well, I find dissembling,	75	OLD BATCH	III.2	150
Bellmour:	Well and how Setter hae, does my Hypocrisy fit me hae?	75	OLD BATCH	IV.1	3
Setter:	O most religiously well Sir.	75	OLD BATCH	IV.1	5
Laetitia:	Well--well--You know my Fondness, and you love to	77	OLD BATCH	IV.1	90
Laetitia:	this usage of yours--But that's what you want--Well--	77	OLD BATCH	IV.1	93
Laetitia:	Heart--Well, be as cruel as you can to me, I'le pray for	78	OLD BATCH	IV.1	108
Laetitia:	that will love you as well as I have done: I shall be	78	OLD BATCH	IV.1	110
	contented				
Sharper:	will be but a kind of a Mungril Curs trick. Well, are you	80	OLD BATCH	IV.1	182
Laetitia:	I may well be surpriz'd at your Person and Impudence; . .	81	OLD BATCH	IV.2	23
Bellmour:	Well, I promise.--A promise is so cold.--	82	OLD BATCH	IV.2	71
Belinda:	--Very well.--So, thank you my Dear.--But	83	OLD BATCH	IV.3	14
Araminta:	No, nc; you're very well as can be.	83	OLD BATCH	IV.3	18
Capt Bluff:	Ladies, by these Hilts you are well met.	85	OLD BATCH	IV.3	82
Araminta:	--Well, Sir Joseph, you shall see my Face.--But, . .	86	OLD BATCH	IV.3	103
Belinda:	ha, ha, ha.--Well, a Lover in the state of separation from	86	OLD BATCH	IV.3	133
Vainlove:	what she knows as well as I. (Aside). Men are apt to offend	87	OLD BATCH	IV.3	137
Footman:	She's not very well, Madam, and has sent to know, . . .	88	OLD BATCH	IV.3	206
Bellmour:	(aside). Well, now I know my Cue.--That is	93	OLD BATCH	IV.4	147
Fondlewife:	Well Sir, And what came you hither for?	94	OLD BATCH	IV.4	177
Fondlewife:	Well, Sir,--Pray be cover'd--and you have	94	OLD BATCH	IV.4	182
Bellmour:	Well, since I see thou art a good honest Fellow, I'll . .	94	OLD BATCH	IV.4	198
Fondlewife:	Well, well, Sir, as long as I believe it, 'tis well	96	OLD BATCH	IV.4	267
Bellmour:	Setter! Well encounter'd.	96	OLD BATCH	V.1	1
Heartwell:	I'll pay him well, if you'll break the Matter to him. . .	97	OLD BATCH	V.1	20
Bellmour:	Well, Your Business with me, Lucy?	97	OLD BATCH	V.1	39
Bellmour:	Well, It is as I say?	98	OLD BATCH	V.1	51
Bellmour:	Well, is it as I say?	98	OLD BATCH	V.1 V	51
Lucy:	Well, It is then: But you'll be secret?	98	OLD BATCH	V.1	52
Lucy:	easie Nature.--Well, For once I'll venture to serve	98	OLD BATCH	V.1	75
Bellmour:	That's as much as to say, The Pox take me.--Well	98	OLD BATCH	V.1	78
Sharper:	You were well employ'd.--I think there is no	99	OLD BATCH	V.1	123
Sharper:	Well, I'll go and infcrm your Master; and do you . . .	102	OLD BATCH	V.1	218
Setter:	Well, Sir Joseph, you have such a winning way with . .	103	OLD BATCH	V.1	251
Sharper:	O Rogue! Well, but I hope--	105	OLD BATCH	V.1	346
Vainlove:	Nay, 'tis a Sore of your own scratching.--Well . .	109	OLD BATCH	V.2	64
Setter:	--Well, honest Lucy, Fare-thee-well.--I	111	OLD BATCH	V.2	141
Bellmour:	Well; 'Midst of these dreadful Denunciations, and . .	112	OLD BATCH	V.2	165
Bellmour:	he shou'd recant. (Aside.) Well, we shall have your Company	112	OLD BATCH	V.2	176
Brisk:	I'gad so they will--well I will, I will, Gad you . .	128	DOUBL DLR	I.1	49
Mellefont:	Well, I'll speak but three words, and follow you. . .	129	DOUBL DLR	I.1	60
Mellefont:	There are times when Sense may be unseasonable, as well as	129	DOUBL DLR	I.1	70
Careless:	Was there ever such a Fury! 'tis well Nature has not . .	130	DOUBL DLR	I.1	100
Careless:	put it into her Sexes power to Ravish.--Well, bless . .	130	DOUBL DLR	I.1	101
Mellefont:	It is so. Well, the Service that you are to do me, . .	130	DOUBL DLR	I.1	124
Mellefont:	It is so. Well, the Service you are to do me, . . .	130	DOUBL DLR	I.1 V	124
Mellefont:	to do me Service; and he endeavours to be well in her .	131	DOUBL DLR	I.1	156
Careless:	Well, I shall be glad to be mistaken; but, your . . .	131	DOUBL DLR	I.1	158
Mellefont:	You are Cruel to your self, my Lord, as well as . . .	133	DOUBL DLR	I.1	233
Brisk:	holding your sides, and Laughing as if ycu would--well--	134	DOUBL DLR	I.1 V	255
Careless:	Well, but prittee don't let it be a great while, because	134	DOUBL DLR	I.1	265
Brisk:	Well then, you tell me, some good Jest, or very Witty .	134	DOUBL DLR	I.1	267
Lady Touch:	Well, mollifying Devil!--And have I	137	DOUBL DLR	I.1	372
Lady Touch:	likes him so well, that she will believe it faster than I	138	DOUBL DLR	I.1	413
	can				
Lord Froth:	Pleasant Creature! perfectly well, ah! that look, . . .	140	DOUBL DLR	II.1	67
Lord Froth:	D'e think he'll Love you as well as I do my	141	DOUBL DLR	II.1	102
Lord Froth:	well, Mellefont, you'll be a happy Creature.	141	DOUBL DLR	II.1	110
Sir Paul:	Hum, gads bud she says true,--well, my Lady, ...	145	DOUBL DLR	II.1	238
Lady Ply:	should be a fault,--but my honour--well, but	148	DOUBL DLR	II.1	360
Lady Ply:	your honour toc--but the sin!--well but the	148	DOUBL DLR	II.1	361
Lady Ply:	not stay. Well, you must consider of your Crime; and .	148	DOUBL DLR	II.1	363
Maskwell:	Ha, ha, ha, I know her temper,--well, you must . . .	149	DOUBL DLR	II.1	419
Mellefont:	She is most gracious in her Favour,--well, and . . .	149	DOUBL DLR	II.1	430
Maskwell:	Well for Wisdom and Honesty, give me Cunning and . .	150	DOUBL DLR	II.1	457
Lady Touch:	Honour is very well known.	151	DOUBL DLR	III.1	12
Lady Touch:	Well, well.	152	DOUBL DLR	III.1	71
Lady Touch:	Nay, no great matter, only--well I have	152	DOUBL DLR	III.1	81
Lady Touch:	Lord--Ha, ha, ha. Well but that's all--ncw you have . .	153	DOUBL DLR	III.1	90
Lady Touch:	it; well remember your promise, my Lord, and don't . .	153	DOUBL DLR	III.1	91
Lady Touch:	were over, 'tis over now, and all's well. For my part I	153	DOUBL DLR	III.1	96
Lady Touch:	Well but go now, here's some body coming.	153	DOUBL DLR	III.1	122
Lord Touch:	Well I go--you won't stay, for I	154	DOUBL DLR	III.1	123
Maskwell:	(aside) to cheat you, as well as the rest.	154	DOUBL DLR	III.1	161
Maskwell:	I know what she means by toying away an hour well . .	155	DOUBL DLR	III.1	174
Maskwell:	thought! Well this Double-Dealing is a Jewel. . . .	155	DOUBL DLR	III.1	191
Mellefont:	well.	156	DOUBL DLR	III.1	217
Maskwell:	Well, will you go in my stead?	156	DOUBL DLR	III.1	237
Maskwell:	Well, I'll meet you here, within a quarter of eight, .	157	DOUBL DLR	III.1	260
Lady Ply:	So well bred.	160	DOUBL DLR	III.1	361
Lady Ply:	So well drest, so bocn mein, so eloquent, so	160	DOUBL DLR	III.1	363
Lady Ply:	So well drest, so bonne mine, so eloquent, so	160	DOUBL DLR	III.1 V	363
Careless:	is very well in her Accomplisments--but it is when my .	160	DOUBL DLR	III.1	376
Sir Paul:	Well, well, my Lady reads all Letters first--Child, .	161	DOUBL DLR	III.1	398
Lord Froth:	Well and how? hee! what is your sense of the	162	DOUBL DLR	III.1	469
Lady Froth:	I may suppose the Dairy in Town, as well as in the Country.	163	DOUBL DLR	III.1	504
Lady Froth:	Well you shall hear--let me see.	164	DOUBL DLR	III.1	527
Brisk:	That's right, all's well, all's well.	164	DOUBL DLR	III.1	533
Brisk:	Incomparable well and proper, Igad--but I have one . .	164	DOUBL DLR	III.1	543
Cynthia:	(aside). Well, I find there are no Fools so inconsiderable	165	DOUBL DLR	III.1	577
Cynthia:	well when the Parties are so agreed--for when . . .	168	DOUBL DLR	IV.1	14
Cynthia:	Well, if the Devil should assist her, and your Plot . .	169	DOUBL DLR	IV.1	55
Lady Ply:	me as a fine thing. Well, I must do you this justice, and	169	DOUBL DLR	IV.1	71
Lady Ply:	Honour--Well, sure if I escape your Importunities, I .	169	DOUBL DLR	IV.1	75
Lady Ply:	transported, I did not see it.--Well, to shew you how . .	170	DOUBL DLR	IV.1	109

Well   (continued)

Well   (continued)

Speaker	Text	PAGE	TITLE	ACT.SC	LINE
Mrs Fore:	Nurse; your Master is not well; put him to	270	FOR LOVE	III.1	635
Foresight:	will be combust; and then I may do well.	270	FOR LOVE	III.1	649
Mrs Fore:	Well; and what use do you hope to make of	271	FOR LOVE	III.1	659
Mrs Fore:	is well enough, and your Understanding is not a-miss.	272	FOR LOVE	III.1	689
Mrs Fore:	Libertine in Speech, as well as Practice,	272	FOR LOVE	III.1	693
Scandal:	And now I think we know one another pretty well.	272	FOR LOVE	III.1	710
Mrs Frail:	Well, but if you shou'd forsake me after all, you'd	273	FOR LOVE	III.1	728
Ben:	break her Cable in a storm, as well as I love her.				
	Flesh, you	273	FOR LOVE	III.1	731
Mrs Fore:	Well; I won't go to Bed to my Husband to	273	FOR LOVE	III.1	742
Scandal:	Well; You'll give me leave to wait upon you to	273	FOR LOVE	III.1	745
Ben:	you shall see, that we Sailors can Dance sometimes, as well	274	FOR LOVE	III.1	791
Scandal:	Well, Is your Master ready; do's he look madly, and	275	FOR LOVE	IV.1	1
Scandal:	Well, I'll try her--'tis she, here she comes.	276	FOR LOVE	IV.1	18
Valentine:	Is the Lawyer gone? 'tis well, then we may drink	280	FOR LOVE	IV.1	191
Valentine:	Thank you, Sir, pretty well--I have been a	281	FOR LOVE	IV.1	196
Sr Sampson:	pretty well now, Val: Body o' me, I was sorry to see thee	281	FOR LOVE	IV.1	202
Scandal:	and honour you.--You lock pretty well, Mr. Foresight;--	284	FOR LOVE	IV.1	338
Ben:	No, I'm pleas'd well enough, now I have found you,--	285	FOR LOVE	IV.1	359
Ben:	never so well.	287	FOR LOVE	IV.1	432
Ben:	don't love You so well as to bear that, whatever I did,	287	FOR LOVE	IV.1	435
Ben:	you too well, by sad experience;--I believe he that marries	287	FOR LOVE	IV.1	438
Valentine:	Oh very well.	292	FOR LOVE	IV.1	632
Angelica:	Well, have you been there?--Come hither.	296	FOR LOVE	IV.1	781
Sr Sampson:	not wash away. Well, Madam, what are your Commands?	298	FOR LOVE	V.1	41
Angelica:	Will you? well, do you find the Estate, and leave the	300	FOR LOVE	V.1	130
Sr Sampson:	--Odd, I think we are very well met;--Give me	301	FOR LOVE	V.1	144
Tattle:	Ay; 'tis well enough for a Servant to be bred at an	302	FOR LOVE	V.1	186
Jeremy:	Well, Sir, I'll go and tell her my Master's coming;	303	FOR LOVE	V.1	215
Miss Prue:	Well, but don't you love me as well as you did	304	FOR LOVE	V.1	248
Foresight:	Well; but my Consent I mean--You won't	304	FOR LOVE	V.1	282
Scandal:	O I hope he will do well again--I have a Message	306	FOR LOVE	V.1	334
Foresight:	Well, I shall run mad next.	306	FOR LOVE	V.1	348
Mrs Fore:	Well, but how mad? how d'ee mean?	306	FOR LOVE	V.1	349
Foresight:	Well, but they are not Mad, that is, not Lunatick?	307	FOR LOVE	V.1	371
Ben:	Well, well, take you care of your own Helm, or you	308	FOR LOVE	V.1	420
Mrs Frail:	(to her). Aye, aye, it's well it's no worse--Nay,	310	FOR LOVE	V.1	471
Angelica:	O you'll agree very well in a little time: Custom	310	FOR LOVE	V.1	481
Angelica:	Well, Sir Sampson, since I have plaid you a Trick,	312	FOR LOVE	V.1	570
Scandal:	Well, Madam, You have done Exemplary Justice,	313	FOR LOVE	V.1	619
	And a less Number New, would well content ye.	323	M. BRIDE	PRO.	2
Almeria:	My Heart has some Relief: having so well	330	M. BRIDE	I.1	V192
Manuel:	He answers well, the Character you gave him.	336	M. BRIDE	I.1	429
Zara:	Is it well done? Is this then the Return	345	M. BRIDE	II.2	235
Zara:	Well, dost thou scorn me, and upbraid my Falseness;	353	M. BRIDE	III.1	160
Zara:	'Tis well. By what I heard upon your Entrance,	364	M. BRIDE	IV.1	114
Gonsalez:	My Lord, the Queen advises well.	365	M. BRIDE	IV.1	156
Gonsalez:	Escape. This put together, suits not well.	366	M. BRIDE	IV.1	212
Gonsalez:	To set him free? Ay, now 'tis plain; O well	371	M. BRIDE	IV.1	413
Manuel:	'Tis well.	373	M. BRIDE	V.1	11
Manuel:	'Tis well--that when she comes to set him free,	374	M. BRIDE	V.1	77
Manuel:	I'll be conducted thither--mark me well--	374	M. BRIDE	V.1	V 86
Zara:	Regard me well; and dare not to reply	375	M. BRIDE	V.1	128
Almeria:	All things were well: and yet my Husband's murder'd!	382	M. BRIDE	V.2	242
Almeria:	Behold me well: your bloody Hands have err'd,	382	M. BRIDE	V.2	247
Almeria:	And point! what mean they; Ha! a Cup. O well	382	M. BRIDE	V.2	253
Painall:	came in, and was well receiv'd by her, while you	395	WAY WORLD	I.1	20
Mirabell:	Well, is the grand Affair over? You have been something	398	WAY WORLD	I.1	111
Mirabell:	That's well. Do you go home again, d'ee hear,	398	WAY WORLD	I.1	127
Mirabell:	That's well. Do you go home again, d'ye hear,	398	WAY WORLD	I.1	V127
Mirabell:	as well.	399	WAY WORLD	I.1	174
Painall:	Marry her, marry her; be half as well acquainted	400	WAY WORLD	I.1	175
Painall:	'Tis well you don't know what you say, or else your	402	WAY WORLD	I.1	261
Witwoud:	No Man in Town lives well with a Wife but	402	WAY WORLD	I.1	264
Witwoud:	Well, well, he does not always think before he	403	WAY WORLD	I.1	307
Petulant:	Well, well; I come--Sbud, a Man had as good	405	WAY WORLD	I.1	383
Petulant:	Well, hearkee.	407	WAY WORLD	I.1	462
Petulant:	well bred, he's what you call a--what-dee-call-'em.	408	WAY WORLD	I.1	505
Marwood:	that lov'd me very well, and would be throughly sensible	411	WAY WORLD	II.1	54
Painall:	You don't look well to Day, Child.	412	WAY WORLD	II.1	89
Painall:	Excellent Creature! Well sure if I shou'd live to be	413	WAY WORLD	II.1	109
Marwood:	Well, I have deserv'd it all.	416	WAY WORLD	II.1	229
Marwood:	Poor dissembling!--O that--Well,	416	WAY WORLD	II.1	231
Mrs Fain:	Well, I have an Opinion of your Success; for	418	WAY WORLD	II.1	307
Millamant:	Faults--I can't bear it. Well, I won't have you Mirabell	422	WAY WORLD	II.1	456
Millamant:	Come, don't look grave then. Well, what do you	422	WAY WORLD	II.1	462
Millamant:	Countenance, 'tis impossible I shou'd hold mine. Well,	422	WAY WORLD	II.1	473
Millamant:	Face. Ha, ha, ha--Well I won't laugh, don't be	422	WAY WORLD	II.1	475
Millamant:	melancholly as a Watch-light. Well Mirabell, If ever you	422	WAY WORLD	II.1	477
Millamant:	fare you well;--I see they are walking away.	422	WAY WORLD	II.1	479
Mirabell:	which they are not turn'd; and by one as well as another;	423	WAY WORLD	II.1	497
Waitwell:	to Business, Sir. I have instructed her as well as I				
	cou'd. If	423	WAY WORLD	II.1	509
Foible:	Well, here it is, all that is left; all that is not kiss'd				
	away--	427	WAY WORLD	III.1	V 76
Foible:	Well, if worshipping of Pictures be a Sin	427	WAY WORLD	III.1	77
Foible:	thin Subsistance (says he)--Well, what Pension does	427	WAY WORLD	III.1	98
Marwood:	of Generosity, that I confess. Well, Mr. Fainall, you have	431	WAY WORLD	III.1	234
Marwood:	well entertained.	431	WAY WORLD	III.1	253
Millamant:	Well, 'tis a lamentable thing I'll swear, that one	432	WAY WORLD	III.1	296
Millamant:	Well, 'tis a lamentable thing I swear, that one	432	WAY WORLD	III.1	V296
Millamant:	more Gallantry--'Tis hardly well bred to be so particular	434	WAY WORLD	III.1	340
Millamant:	--But that cannot be--Well, that Thought makes	434	WAY WORLD	III.1	361
Millamant:	Well, an illiterate Man's my Aversion. I wonder	436	WAY WORLD	III.1	422
Sir Wilful:	Well prithee try what thou can'st do; if thou	437	WAY WORLD	III.1	464

Well   (continued)
Sir Wilful:	I'm very well I thank you Aunt--However,	. . . . .	441	WAY WORLD III.1 601
Marwood:	Well, how do you stand affected towards	. .	443	WAY WORLD III.1 674
Fainall:	plaid the Jade with me--Well, that's over too--I	. .	443	WAY WORLD III.1 678
Fainall:	Hum! Faith and that's well thought on; Marriage is	. .	443	WAY WORLD III.1 691
Fainall:	So, sc, why this point's clear,--Well how do we	. .	443	WAY WORLD III.1 697
Lady Wish:	And--well--and how do I look, Foible?	. . .	445	WAY WORLD IV.1 15
Foible:	Most killing well, Madam.	. . .	445	WAY WORLD IV.1 16
Lady Wish:	Well, and how shall I receive him? In what	. . . .	445	WAY WORLD IV.1 17
Sir Wilful:	Well, Well, I shall understand your Lingo one of	. .	447	WAY WORLD IV.1 110
Sir Wilful:	well as another time; and another time as well as now.	.	448	WAY WORLD IV.1 144
Millamant:	Play together, But let us be very strange and well bred:	.	450	WAY WORLD IV.1 207
Millamant:	and as well bred as if we were not marri'd at all.	. .	450	WAY WORLD IV.1 209
Mirabell:	account. Well, have I Liberty to offer Conditions--that	.	450	WAY WORLD IV.1 229
Millamant:	Well then--I'll take my death I'm in a horrid	.	452	WAY WORLD IV.1 288
Millamant:	fright--Fainall, I shall never say it--well--I think--	.	452	WAY WORLD IV.1 289
Millamant:	looks as if he thought sc too--Well, you ridiculous	.	452	WAY WORLD IV.1 294
Millamant:	Well, If Mirabell shou'd not make a good Husband,	. .	453	WAY WORLD IV.1 315
Witwoud:	Now Petulant, all's over, all's well; Gad my head begins	.	453	WAY WORLD IV.1 336
Lady Wish:	Well, Sir Rowland, you have the way,--	. . . . .	458	WAY WORLD IV.1 526
Lady Wish:	Too well, too well. I have seen too much.	. . . .	460	WAY WORLD IV.1 599
Lady Wish:	frailties of my Daughter. Well Friend, you are enough to	.	465	WAY WORLD V.1 131
Marwood:	'twere well. But it must after this be consign'd by the	.	468	WAY WORLD V.1 230
Fainall:	Well Madam; I have suffer'd my self to be overcome	. .	468	WAY WORLD V.1 250
Lady Wish:	would not have carry'd it thus. Well, that was my Choice,	.	469	WAY WORLD V.1 305
Lady Wish:	Well, I'll swear I am something reviv'd at this	. . .	470	WAY WORLD V.1 333
Lady Wish:	Well Nephew, upon your account--ah,	. . . .	472	WAY WORLD V.1 400
Lady Wish:	he has a false Insinuating Tongue--Well Sir, I will stifle	.	472	WAY WORLD V.1 401
Fainall:	Go, ycu are an Insignificant thing,--Well, what	. .	475	WAY WORLD V.1 492
Lady Wish:	O Sir Rowland--well Rascal.	. . . . .	475	WAY WORLD V.1 509
Mirabell:	Very well, now you shall know--Madam, your	. . .	476	WAY WORLD V.1 532
Lady Wish:	Well Mr. Mirabell, you have kept your promise,	. .	477	WAY WORLD V.1 572
Lady Wish:	Well Sir, take her, and with her all the Joy I	. .	477	WAY WORLD V.1 592
Mirabell:	as often as possibly I can. (Kisses her hand). Well, heav'n	.	477	WAY WORLD V.1 597
Mirabell:	grant I love you not too well, that's all my fear.	. . .	477	WAY WORLD V.1 598
Mirabell:	deed of trust. It may be a means well manag'd to make you	.	478	WAY WORLD V.1 618
	And how their Number's swell'd the Town well knows:	. .	479	WAY WORLD EPI. 10
	For well the Learn'd and the Judicious know,	. . . .	479	WAY WORLD EPI. 28

Well-a-day (1)
Ben:	has turn'd her senses, her Brain is quite overset.			
	Well-a-day,	. . . .	286	FOR LCVE IV.1 404

Well-bred (3)
Lady Froth:	you're a Judge; was ever any thing so well-bred as my	.	140	DOUBL DLR II.1 82
Tattle:	Yes, if you would be well-bred. All well-bred Persons	.	251	FOR LCVE II.1 610

Well-laden (1)
	That some well-laden Ship may strike the Sands;	. . .	385	M. BRIDE EPI. 22

Well-spoken (1)
Sir Paul:	Blessing, a fine, discreet, well-spoken woman as you shall		160	DOUBI DLR III.1 387

Well-try'd (1)
Manuel:	And Garcia's well-try'd Valour, all oblige me.	. . . .	334	M. BRIDE I.1 341

Welt'ring (1)
Garcia:	Dead, welt'ring, drown'd in Blood.	. . . .	377	M. BRIDE V.2 60

Wench (11)
Vainlove:	Or a young Wench, betwixt pleasure and	. . . . .	63	OLD BATCH III.1 93
Vainlove:	Or a ycung Wench, between pleasure and	. . . .	63	OLD BATCH III.1 V 93
Bellmour:	this Wench to Secresie! You never knew a Whoremaster,	.	97	OLD BATCH V.1 25
Scandal:	and lcves a Wench still. You never knew a Whoremaster,	.	223	FOR LCVE I.1 265
Lady Wish:	Wench stirs! Why dost thou not fetch me a little Red?	.	425	WAY WORLD III.1 7
Lady Wish:	--Wench, come, come, Wench, what art thou doing,	.	425	WAY WORLD III.1 23
Lady Wish:	a Person, this Wench has liv'd in an Inn upon the Road,	.	426	WAY WORLD III.1 36
Marwood:	shall watch you. Why this Wench is the Pass par tout, a	.	431	WAY WORLD III.1 227
Marwood:	shall watch you. Why this Wench is the Pass par toute, a	.	431	WAY WORLD III.1 V227
Sir Wilful:	With a Wench, Tony? Is she a shake-bag Sirrah?	. . .	457	WAY WORLD IV.1 472

Wenches (4)
Lady Wish:	with Broom-sticks. Call up the Wenches.	. . . . .	457	WAY WORLD IV.1 463
Lady Wish:	with Broom-sticks. Call up the Wenches with broom-sticks.	.	457	WAY WORLD IV.1 V463
Sir Wilful:	Ahey! Wenches, where are the Wenches?	. . . . .	457	WAY WORLD IV.1 465

Went (19)
Bellmour:	abroad--went purely to run away from a Campagne;	. .	47	OLD BATCH I.1 369
Capt Bluff:	went every day to Coffee-houses to read the Gazette my	.	53	OLD BATCH II.1 208
Fondlewife:	Speculation! No, no; something went farther	. . .	92	OLD BATCH IV.4 116
	And when but two were made, both went astray;	. .	213	FOR LCVE PRO. 19
Angelica:	Spoons, and thought they were lost. Away went Religion	.	237	FOR LCVE I.1 90
Tattle:	enquire for me, than ever went to see the Hermaphrodite,	.	257	FOR LCVE III.1 161
Ben:	To Loggerheads they went, Sir,	. . . . . .	274	FOR LCVE III.1 786
Jeremy:	understood one another before she went.	. . . . .	296	FOR LCVE IV.1 800
Foresight:	I think she has not return'd, since she went abroad	.	306	FOR LCVE V.1 336
Ben:	say, Brother Val. went mad for, she's mad too, I think.	.	306	FOR LCVE V.1 346
Foresight:	Why, you told me just now, you went hence in	.	309	FOR LCVE V.1 453
	That after Death, ne're went to Hell, nor Heaven,	. .	315	FOR LCVE EPI. 16
Zara:	The King that parted hence; frowning he went;	. . .	374	M. BRIDE V.1 92
Mirabell:	know you staid at Millamant's last Night, after I went.	.	407	WAY WORLD I.1 450
Millamant:	O ay, and went away--Now I think on't I'm angry	. .	420	WAY WORLD II.1 378
Foible:	that was Mrs. Marwood that went by in a Mask; if she has	.	424	WAY WORLD III.1 545
Lady Wish:	house indeed, and now I remember, my Niece went away	.	461	WAY WORLD IV.1 616
Foible:	have gone a Walking: But we went up unawares,--tho'	.	464	WAY WORLD V.1 96
Sir Wilful:	melt, I can tell you that. My contract went no further	.	472	WAY WORLD V.1 396

Wept (3)
Leonora:	Have often wept, to see how cruelly	. . . . .	326	M. BRIDE I.1 22
Almeria:	Thou hast much lov'd Alphonso, and I fear,	. . .	342	M. BRIDE II.2 117
Manuel:	As they had wept in Blood, and worn the Night	. . .	367	M. BRIDE IV.1 249

Wer't (3)
Lucy:	Wretch, how, wer't thou valuing thy self, upon thy	. .	65	OLD BATCH III.1 168
Mellefont:	Excellent Maskwell, thou wer't certainly meant for	. .	193	DOUBL DLR V.1 235
Valentine:	Because thou wer't a Monster; old Boy;--The	. . .	282	FOR LCVE IV.1 262

What's   (continued)
Garcia:	What's to be done? the King's Death known, will strike	.	378	M. BRIDE	V.2	93
Betty:	Yes; what's your Business?	.	400	WAY WORLD	I.1	182
Fainall:	Why, what's the Matter?	.	401	WAY WORLD	I.1	238
Witwoud:	from cne Poet to another. And what's worse, 'tis as sure a		401	WAY WORLD	I.1	247
Mirabell:	Ay marry, what's that, Witwoud? . . .	.	403	WAY WORLD	I.1	313
Witwoud:	and what's more, not finding himself, sometimes leave a		405	WAY WORLD	I.1	376
Fainall:	Death, am I not married? what's pretence? Am I not	.	415	WAY WORLD	II.1	209
Lady Wish:	Ah dear Marwood, what's Integrity to an Opportunity?	.	426	WAY WORLD	III.1	60
Marwood:	You have a Colour, what's the matter?	.	432	WAY WORLD	III.1	286
Mrs Fain:	So it seems, when you mind not what's said to	.	453	WAY WORLD	IV.1	317
Mrs Fain:	So it seems, for you mind not what's said to		453	WAY WORLD	IV.1	V317
Lady Wish:	Oh Heavens! what's this?	.	460	WAY WORLD	IV.1	589
Mrs Fain:	Poor Foible, what's the matter?	.	463	WAY WORLD	V.1	61
Sir Wilful:	Pound. And so let that content for what's past, and make	.	470	WAY WORLD	V.1	319
Sir Wilful:	no more words. For what's to come to pleasure you I'm	.	470	WAY WORLD	V.1	320
Fainall:	S'death what's this to me? I'll not wait your private	.	475	WAY WORLD	V.1	517
Petulant:	How now? what's the matter? who's hand's out?	.	475	WAY WORLD	V.1	520
Fainall:	Very likely Sir, what's here? Damnation! (Reads) A . .		476	WAY WORLD	V.1	550

Whate'er (2)
Perez:	Whate'er it is the King's Complexion turns.		373	M. BRIDE	V.1	32
Gonsalez:	They shout again! Whate'er he means to dc		378	M. BRIDE	V.2	100

Whatever (5)
	Whatever Fate is for this Play design'd, ...		125	DOUBL DLR	PRO.	31
Lady Touch:	Whatever it was, 'tis past: And that is better . . .		152	DOUBL DLR	III.1	54
Cynthia:	but I find I have obstinacy enough to pursue whatever I	.	193	DOUBL DLR	V.1	203
Ben:	civilly to me, of her own accord: Whatever you think of	.	264	FOR LCVE	III.1	411
Ben:	don't love You so well as to bear that, whatever I did,	.	287	FOR LCVE	IV.1	435

Whatsoever (5)
Sharper:	all Injuries whatsoever, done unto you by them; until the		110	OLD BATCH	V.2	87
Capt Bluff:	All Injuries whatsoever, Mr. Sharper.	.	110	OLD BATCH	V.2	97
Sir Joseph:	Ay, ay, whatsoever, Captain, stick to that; . . .	.	110	OLD BATCH	V.2	98
Sir Joseph:	whatscever.	.	110	OLD BATCH	V.2	99
Maskwell:	thy Beauty gild my Crimes; and whatsoever I commit of	.	150	DOUBL DLR	II.1	441

Wheadl'd (3)
Fainall:	best part of her Estate; which I wheadl'd out of her; And		444	WAY WORLD	III.1	710
Foible:	me; I am not the first that he has wheadl'd with his	.	463	WAY WORLD	V.1	26
Mirabell:	before you had by your Insinuations wheadl'd her out of a	.	476	WAY WORLD	V.1	537

Wheadle (1)
Mirabell:	tryal of a Mutual Secresie. No Decoy-Duck to wheadle	.	451	WAY WORLD	IV.1	238

Wheadling (1)
Lady Wish:	I'm detected I'm undone. If that wheadling Villain has	.	426	WAY WORLD	III.1	52

Wheedle (2)
Maskwell:	self ready, I'll wheedle her intc the Coach; and instead of		193	DOUBL DLR	V.1	223
Mrs Frail:	Now if I cou'd wheedle him, Sister, ha? You understand	.	248	FOR LCVE	II.1	495

Wheel (2)
Gonsalez:	Sweat by his Chariot Wheel, and lick, and grind		332	M. BRIDE	I.1	236
Manuel:	'Tis daring for a God. Hence, to the Wheel		349	M. BRIDE	II.2	371

Wheels (3)
Osmyn-Alph:	That strain my cracking Nerves; Engines and Wheels . .		356	M. BRIDE	III.1	292
Almeria:	Did'st thou not say, that Racks and Wheels were . . .		357	M. BRIDE	III.1	311
Osmyn-Alph:	What are all Racks, and Wheels, and Whips to this? . .		358	M. BRIDE	III.1	362

Whelp (1)
Sr Sampson:	Unnatural Whelp! There's an ill-natur'd Dog! What, . .		259	FOR LOVE	III.1	236

When (314)

Whence (9)
Maskwell:	Fix'd, Rooted in my Heart, whence nothing can . . .		136	DOUBL DLR	I.1	352
Lord Touch:	Still gnawing that, whence first it did arise;		203	DOUBL DLR	V.1	595
Sr Sampson:	you or no? Ouns who are you? Whence came you? . . .		244	FOR LOVE	II.1	326
Angelica:	But whence comes the Reputation cf Mr. Tattle's . . .		256	FOR LCVE	III.1	121
Manuel:	Whence comes it, valiant Osmyn, that a Man		336	M. BRIDE	I.1	430
Osmyn-Alph:	Whence is that Voice whose Shrilness from the . . .		341	M. BRIDE	II.2	37
Manuel:	Whence is thy Grief? give me to know the Cause, . . .		367	M. BRIDE	IV.1	262
Gonsalez:	Perdition choak your Clamours--whence this		376	M. BRIDE	V.2	24
Garcia:	O whence, or how, or wherefore was this done? . . .		377	M. BRIDE	V.2	63

Where (151)

Where-ever (1)
Scandal:	where-ever it is, it's always contriving it's own Ruine.	.	219	FOR LCVE	I.1	121

Where's (22)
Belinda:	How now, Pace? Where's my Cousin?		88	OLD BATCH	IV.3	205
Fondlewife:	should heat a Trencher, or a Napkin.--Where's Deborah?	.	91	OLD BATCH	IV.4	96
Sharper:	Where's the Bride?		106	OLD BATCH	V.1	350
	What will the World say? Where's my Reputation? . . .		113	OLD BATCH	EPI.	11
Lord Froth:	Where's the Wonder now?	.	166	DOUBL DLR	III.1	601
Sir Paul:	Merry, I'll come and look at you by and by--Where's	.	175	DOUBL DLR	IV.1	281
Maskwell:	head that cannot fail: Where's Cynthia?		190	DOUBL DLR	V.1	116
Sir Paul:	all this for? Pooh, here's a joke, indeed--why, where's	.	192	DOUBL DLR	V.1	186
Careless:	her, confirm me in my fears. Where's Mellefont? . . .		196	DOUBL DLR	V.1	338
Lord Touch:	ha, I'll do't, where's Mellefont, my poor injured Nephew,--		200	DOUBL DLR	V.1	478
Lord Froth:	the prettiest amusement! but where's all the Company? .		200	DOUBL DLR	V.1	495
Lord Froth:	O Heaven's, what's the matter? Where's my		200	DOUBL DLR	V.1	499
Foresight:	Nurse, Where's your young Mistress?		235	FOR LOVE	II.1	18
Sr Sampson:	his Right of Inheritance. Where's my Daughter that is to	.	240	FOR LOVE	II.1	183
Mrs Frail:	--Lord, where's the comfort of this Life, if we can't have		246	FOR LOVE	II.1	424
Ben:	Where's Father?		260	FOR LOVE	III.1	268
Sr Sampson:	Scoundrel. Sirrah, where's your Master?		278	FOR LOVE	IV.1	118
Sr Sampson:	Son be mad--Where's your Oppositions, your Trines, and	.	283	FOR LOVE	IV.1	282
Scandal:	Death and Hell! Where's Valentine?		308	FOR LCVE	V.1	400
Sr Sampson:	Where's your Plot, Sir? and your Contrivance		311	FOR LCVE	V.1	537
Garcia:	Where? where? Alonzo, where's my Father? where . .		376	M. BRIDE	V.2	16
Sir Wilful:	Tony, Ods heart where's Tony--Tony's an honest fellow,		455	WAY WORLD	IV.1	413

Whereas (1)
Maskwell:	And whereas pleasure is generally paid with		156	DOUBL DLR	III.1	218

Whereby (3)
Sir Wilful:	how that the Peace hclds, whereby that is, Taxes abate.	.	440	WAY WORLD	III.1	575
Sir Wilful:	French as they say, whereby to hcld discourse in Foreign	.	440	WAY WORLD	III.1	584

Whereby   (continued)
Sir Wilful:	Orthodox--Whereby it is a plain Case, that Orthodox is a	.	456	WAY WORLD	IV.1	447

Wherefore (10)
Tattle:	one does not know how, nor why, nor wherefore--	. . . .	309	FOR LOVE	V.1	459
Selim:	Wherefore a Warrant for his Death is sign'd;	. . . . .	361	M. BRIDE	IV.1	15
Manuel:	Wherefore I have deferr'd the Mariage Rites,	. . .	367	M. BRIDE	IV.1	254
Almeria:	What is to speak? or wherefore should I speak?	. . .	368	M. BRIDE	IV.1	267
Garcia:	O whence, or how, or wherefore was this done?	. . .	377	M. BRIDE	V.2	63
Zara:	What have you seen? Ha! wherefore stare you thus,	. .	380	M. BRIDE	V.2	155
Zara:	Then, wherefore do I pause?--give me the Bowl.	. . .	381	M. BRIDE	V.2	198
Fainall:	And wherefore do you hate him? He is Insensible,	. .	414	WAY WORLD	II.1	155
Fainall:	And wherefore did I marry, but to make lawful Prize of a	.	415	WAY WORLD	II.1	206
Fainall:	honourable as you say; and if so, Wherefore should	. .	443	WAY WORLD	III.1	692

Wherein (7)
Sharper:	Wherein no doubt he magnifies his own	. . . . .	47	OLD BATCH	I.1	374
Heartwell:	Sister Marriage, and whor'd her? Wherein have I injured	.	109	OLD BATCH	V.2	53
Lord Touch:	wherein I am not concern'd, and consequently the	. .	152	DOUBL DLR	III.1	47
Foresight:	Wherein was I mistaken, not to foresee this?	. . .	284	FOR LOVE	IV.1	309
Manuel:	Not from that Hour, wherein thou wert preserv'd,	. . .	333	M. BRIDE	I.1	300
Manuel:	But that, wherein the curs'd Alphonso perish'd.	. . .	333	M. BRIDE	I.1	301
Osmyn-Alph:	'Twas writ; a Prayer for me, wherein appears	. . . . .	352	M. BRIDE	III.1	112

Whereupon (2)
Valentine:	hears is Landed; whereupon he very affectionately sends	.	225	FOR LOVE	I.1	334
Gonsalez:	Dispers'd, t'amuze the People; whereupon	. . . . . .	363	M. BRIDE	IV.1	82

Wherewithal (4)
Belinda:	quiet, when he sees his Debtor has not wherewithal--	. .	58	OLD BATCH	II.2	128
Osmyn-Alph:	I have not wherewithal to give again.	. . . . . .	346	M. BRIDE	II.2	271
Marwood:	And wherewithal can you reproach me?	. . . . . .	414	WAY WORLD	II.1	150
Fainall:	wherewithal to stake.	. . . .	443	WAY WORLD	III.1	689

Wherewithall (1)
Fainall:	a Wife, shall smart for this. I will not leave thee				
	wherewithall	. . . .	475	WAY WORLD	V.1	495

Whet (1)
Heartwell:	preparative, and what you mean for a Whet, turns the	. .	43	OLD BATCH	I.1	244

Whether (36)
	(I don't know whether I shall speak to please you)	. .	35	OLD BATCH	PRO.	18
Bellmour:	whether thou wouldst have her angry or pleas'd. Couldst	.	63	OLD BATCH	III.1	103
Fondlewife:	doubtfull, whether I shall trust her, even with Tribulation	.	77	OLD BATCH	IV.1	75
Fondlewife:	Ha! This is Apocryphal; I may chuse whether I	. . . .	95	OLD BATCH	IV.4	217
	Whether their Brats are truly got, or no;	. . . . .	125	DOUBL DLR	PRO.	2
Mellefont:	True, but you shall judge whether I have not reason	.	129	DOUBL DLR	I.1	83
Mellefont:	self favour'd in her aversion: But whether urged by her	.	129	DOUBL DLR	I.1	94
Mellefont:	accomplish her designs; whether the hopes of her revenge,	.	129	DOUBL DLR	I.1	96
Mellefont:	accomplish her designs; whether the hopes of revenge,	.	129	DOUBL DLR	I.1 V	96
Lady Ply:	impossible for me to know whether I could or no, there	.	147	DOUBL DLR	II.1	328
Lady Ply:	impossible for me to know whether I could or not, there	.	147	DOUBL DLR	II.1	V328
Maskwell:	know whether I can in honour discover all.	. . . .	156	DOUBL DLR	III.1	208
Maskwell:	know whether I can in honour discover 'em all	. . .	156	DOUBL DLR	III.1	V208
Sir Paul:	whether I fly on Ground, or walk in Air--Gads bud, she	.	172	DOUBL DLR	IV.1	198
Brisk:	Ladiship--Let me perish, I don't know whether to	. . .	176	DOUBL DLR	IV.1	337
Brisk:	tell whether I am glad or sorry that your Ladiship has made	.	176	DOUBL DLR	IV.1	339
Sir Paul:	know whether there be any thing at all in the World, or	.	179	DOUBL DLR	IV.1	450
Cynthia:	I don't know whether I have Love enough,--	. . . .	193	DOUBL DLR	V.1	202
	Whether to thank, or blame their Audience, most:	. . .	204	DOUBL DLR	EPI.	3
	Whether he shall escape the Law, or no.	. . . . .	204	DOUBL DLR	EPI.	7
Tattle:	Who I? Upon Honour I don't know whether she be	. . .	228	FOR LOVE	I.1	465
Foresight:	and Aquatical Trigons. Know whether Life shall be long	.	241	FOR LOVE	II.1	214
Foresight:	or short, Happy or Unhappy; whether Diseases are	. .	241	FOR LOVE	II.1	215
Sr Sampson:	And might not I have chosen whether I would have begot	.	244	FOR LOVE	II.1	325
Valentine:	me whether you did or no.	. . . .	254	FOR LOVE	III.1	30
Valentine:	me whether you did or not.	. . . .	254	FOR LOVE	III.1 V	30
Valentine:	tell whether the Lady or Mr. Tattle be the more obliged	.	256	FOR LOVE	III.1	130
Sr Sampson:	shall out-lie the Devil. And so I'll try whether my	.	267	FOR LOVE	III.1	510
Jeremy:	No, Sir, not yet;--He has a mind to try, whether his	.	276	FOR LOVE	IV.1	8
Valentine:	if you should ask him, whether the Bible saves more	.	280	FOR LOVE	IV.1	176
Valentine:	I can't tell whether I know it or no.	. . . . .	281	FOR LOVE	IV.1	218
Ben:	Look you, Friend, it's nothing to me, whether you	. .	307	FOR LOVE	V.1	368
Almeria:	That whether Death, or Victory ensu'd,	. . . . . .	329	M. BRIDE	I.1	138
Witwoud:	hard Frost. Whether this Uncle has seen Mrs. Millamant or	.	408	WAY WORLD	I.1	486
Marwood:	than all the vain and empty Vows of Men, whether	. .	414	WAY WORLD	II.1	168
Sir Wilful:	but 'tis--'Sheart I know not whether 'tis or no--	. .	438	WAY WORLD	III.1	515

Whetter (1)
Jeremy:	nothing to it for a Whetter; yet I never see it, but the	.	218	FOR LOVE	I.1	94

Which (231)

Whifler (3)
Lord Proth:	admirer of my Lady Whifler, Mr. Sneer, and Sir Laurence	.	162	DOUBL DLR	III.1	461
Lord Proth:	Hee, hee, hee, right; and then my Lady Whifler is	. .	163	DOUBL DLR	III.1	475
Lord Proth:	Whifler, and Mr. Sneer.	. . . .	165	DOUBL DLR	III.1	560

Whifler's (1)
Lord Proth:	Woman of Quality--you have been at my Lady Whifler's	. .	162	DOUBL DLR	III.1	466

While (80)
Musician:	While wishing at your Feet they lie:	. . . . . .	60	OLD BATCH	II.2	198
Singer:	But while she fond Resistance made,	. . . . . .	71	OLD BATCH	III.2 V	15
Fondlewife:	while her good Husband is deluded by his Godly appearance	.	76	OLD BATCH	IV.1	30
Laetitia:	poor Heart, while it holds; which cannot be long, with	.	77	OLD BATCH	IV.1	92
Sharper:	breeding Love to thee all this while, and just now she is	.	79	OLD BATCH	IV.1	167
Belinda:	Snipwel's Shop while I was there.--But, Oh Gad!	. . .	84	OLD BATCH	IV.3	25
Araminta:	that a Coward has, while the Sword is in the Scabbard	. .	86	OLD BATCH	IV.3	118
Sir Joseph:	has been so a great while.	. . . .	90	OLD BATCH	IV.4	40
Sir Joseph:	did a little while ago.--Look yonder.--A-gad, if	. . .	101	OLD BATCH	V.1	172
Sharper:	I know, she commended him all the while we were	. . .	102	OLD BATCH	V.1	200
	(While Sir Joseph reads, Bluffe whispers Setter.)	. . .	103	OLD BATCH	V.1	273
Lucy:	I shall follow, while my Spouse is planting Laurels in the	.	111	OLD BATCH	V.2	145
Capt Bluff:	No more Wars, Spouse, no more Wars.--While	. . . .	111	OLD BATCH	V.2	147
Mellefont:	to him they have born the face of kindness; while her	. .	129	DOUBL DLR	I.1	89
Brisk:	a great while first.	. . . .	134	DOUBL DLR	I.1	264

Whirl-wind (1)
| Osmyn-Alph: | Then, bear me in a Whirl-wind to my Fate; . . . . . | 343 | M. BRIDE | II.2 140 |

Whirlwind (4)
Mellefont:	sudden Whirlwind come, tear up Tree and all, and bear . .	187	DOUBL DLR	IV.2 146
Scandal:	No, not yet; nor Whirlwind. But we don't know . . .	266	FOR LOVE	III.1 492
Mirabell:	you! To think of a Whirlwind, tho' 'twere in a Whirlwind,	423	WAY WORLD	II.1 491

Whiskers (1)
| Sir Joseph: | impenetrable Whiskers of his have confronted Flames-- . . | 53 | OLD BATCH | II.1 220 |

Whisper (10)
Capt Bluff:	ensue--If he refuse, tell him--But whisper that--Tell . .	68	OLD BATCH	III.1 260
Capt Bluff:	him--I'll pink his Soul--but whisper that softly . . .	68	OLD BATCH	III.1 261
Scandal:	a Whisper; and deny a Woman's name, while he gives you .	226	FOR LOVE	I.1 371
Scandal:	reason. (She gives him the Glass: Scandal and she whisper.)	269	FOR LOVE	III.1 585
	(Whisper.)	269	FOR LOVE	III.1 599
Sr Sampson:	Conveyance--quick--quick (In Whisper to Jeremy.) . .	281	FOR LOVE	IV.1 210
Valentine:	Husht--Interrupt me not--I'll whisper	288	FOR LOVE	IV.1 486
Valentine:	Whisper.	290	FOR LOVE	IV.1 567
	(Whisper.)	291	FOR LOVE	IV.1 600
Zara:	Indeed? Then 'twas a Whisper spread by some	366	M. BRIDE	IV.1 189

Whisper'd (4)
Tattle:	for it's whisper'd every where.	254	FOR LOVE	III.1 48
Angelica:	was whisper'd every where.	254	FOR LOVE	III.1 51
Leonora:	Have softly whisper'd, and enquir'd his Health; . . .	327	M. BRIDE	I.1 27
Mirabell:	grave Faces, whisper'd one another; then complain'd . .	396	WAY WORLD	I.1 30

Whispering (2)
| Capt Bluff: | (Almost whispering, and treading softly after him.) . . | 101 | OLD BATCH | V.1 190 |
| Lady Froth: | We shall have whispering time enough, you . . . . . | 177 | DOUBL DLR | IV.1 386 |

Whispers (10)
Setter:	(Whispers him.)	99	OLD BATCH	V.1 92
Sharper:	(Whispers.)	101	OLD BATCH	V.1 166
	(While Sir Joseph reads, Bluffe whispers Setter.) . .	103	OLD BATCH	V.1 273
	(Enter Boy and whispers Sir Paul.) . .	163	DOUBL DLR	III.1 488
	(Enter Steward and Whispers Valentine.)	224	FOR LOVE	I.1 308
	(Steward who whispers.) . .	224	FOR LOVE	I.1 V308
Valentine:	(whispers). Scandal, who are all these? Foreigners? .	291	FOR LOVE	IV.1 593
Valentine:	(whispers). Scandal, who are these? Foreigners? . .	291	FOR LOVE	IV.1 V593
Millamant:	a New Chariot, to provoke Eyes and Whispers; And then .	450	WAY WORLD	IV.1 203
	(Enter Foible, and whispers Lady Wishfort.) .	456	WAY WORLD	IV.1 459

Whistled (1)
| Mrs Frail: | whistled to by Winds; and thou art come forth with Finns . | 286 | FOR LOVE | IV.1 400 |

Whistles (1)
| Ben: | (Whistles.) . . . . . | 274 | FOR LOVE | III.1 793 |

Whistling (1)
| Almeria: | Whistling thro' Hollows of this vaulted Isle. . . . | 339 | M. BRIDE | II.1 55 |

White (10)
Sharper:	Why, there: The Two white Posts.	104	OLD BATCH	V.1 288
Lady Ply:	this three year past? Have I been white and unsulli'd even by	145	DOUBL DLR	II.1 255
Lady Ply:	these three Years past? Have I been white and unsulli'd even by	145	DOUBL DLR	II.1 V255
Scandal:	Yes, mine are most in black and white.--And yet . . .	233	FOR LOVE	I.1 626
Sr Sampson:	White, Signatum, Sigillatum, and Deliberatum; that as soon	240	FOR LOVE	II.1 181
Mrs Frail:	she's very pretty!--Lord, what pure red and white! . .	250	FOR LOVE	II.1 556
Valentine:	For she'll meet me Two Hours hence in black and white, .	290	FOR LOVE	IV.1 561
Valentine:	you is sunk. You are all white, a sheet of lovely spotless	292	FOR LOVE	IV.1 637
Gonsalez:	White as the fleecy Rain on Alpine Hills;	331	M. BRIDE	I.1 231
Foible:	Madam. There are some Cracks discernable in the white .	429	WAY WORLD	III.1 145

Whither (10)
Heartwell:	Why whither in the Devils name am I going now? . . .	62	OLD BATCH	III.1 63
Heartwell:	Why whither in the Devils name am I a-going now? . .	62	OLD BATCH	III.1 V 63
Bellmour:	Bliss:--Oh, for Love-sake, lead me any whither, where I .	82	OLD BATCH	IV.2 86
Heartwell:	Whither? Whither? Which Corner-House?	104	OLD BATCH	V.1 287
Mellefont:	Ned, Ned, whither so fast? What, turn'd flincher! . .	127	DOUBL DLR	I.1 1
Lady Ply:	Honour! Whither is it going? I protest you have given me .	170	DOUBL DLR	IV.1 104
Lady Touch:	O. What shall I do? say? whither shall I	185	DOUBL DLR	IV.2 57
Foresight:	gallop, hey! Whither will they hurry me?--Now they're .	269	FOR LOVE	III.1 608
Osmyn-Alph:	She'll come, but whither, and to whom? O Heav'n! . .	351	M. BRIDE	III.1 52

Whiting's (1)
| Mirabell: | Fame, wou'd shew as dim by thee as a dead Whiting's . . | 407 | WAY WORLD | I.1 454 |

Who (202)
	We threaten you who do for Judges sit, ...	35	OLD BATCH	PRO. 8
Vainlove:	That's pleasant, by my troth from thee, who hast . . .	38	OLD BATCH	I.1 45
Bellmour:	Why what a Cormorant in Love am I! who not	40	OLD BATCH	I.1 137
Sharper:	And here comes one who Swears as heartily he hates . .	41	OLD BATCH	I.1 176
Bellmour:	Who Heartwell! Ay, but he knows better things-- . . .	42	OLD BATCH	I.1 179
Bellmour:	this nature; Women are often won by 'em: who would . .	44	OLD BATCH	I.1 260
Bellmour:	Who the Devil would have thee? unless 'twere an . . .	45	OLD BATCH	I.1 298
Bellmour:	hands of some Nightwalkers, who I suppose would have . .	46	OLD BATCH	I.1 360
Bellmour:	ever he was loose, he ran away, without staying to see who	46	OLD BATCH	I.1 363
Bellmour:	here vents 'em against the General, who slighting Men of .	47	OLD BATCH	I.1 371
Capt Bluff:	your Jesuits Powder for a shaking fit--But who hast thou .	51	OLD BATCH	II.1 147
Lucy:	Heartwell, who stands talking at the Corner--'tis he-- .	62	OLD BATCH	III.1 47
Setter:	Ha! what art, who thus maliciously hast awakned me, . .	65	OLD BATCH	III.1 165
Setter:	Why how now! prithee who art? lay by that Worldly . .	65	OLD BATCH	III.1 179
Setter:	Adsbud who's in fault, Mistress Mine? who flung the . .	66	OLD BATCH	III.1 204
Setter:	first Stone? who undervalued my Function? and who the .	66	OLD BATCH	III.1 205
Capt Bluff:	--He sucks not vital Air who dares affirm it to this . .	70	OLD BATCH	III.1 353
Fondlewife:	who will tempt her Isaac?--I fear it much--But . . .	76	OLD BATCH	IV.1 57
Laetitia:	Who has wrong'd me to my Dearest? I hope my Jewel . .	77	OLD BATCH	IV.1 80
Laetitia:	Who are you, Sir? You have mistaken the House . . .	81	OLD BATCH	IV.2 29
Fondlewife:	Who, how now! Who have we here?	92	OLD BATCH	IV.4 122
Fondlewife:	ripe-horn-mad. But who, in the Devil's name, are you? Mercy on	92	OLD BATCH	IV.4 127
Laetitia:	Oh, Goodness keep us! Who's this? Who are you? . . .	92	OLD BATCH	IV.4 129
Fondlewife:	Come Syren, speak, confess, who is this reverend, brawny	92	OLD BATCH	IV.4 137
Fondlewife:	Come, Sir, Who are you, in the first place? And . . .	93	OLD BATCH	IV.4 172

Who (continued)

		PAGE	TITLE	ACT.SC	LINE
Bellmour:	True. But to convince thee who I am, thou know'st	97	OLD BATCH	V.1	34
Heartwell:	And who wou'd you visit there, say you? (O'ons,	104	OLD BATCH	V.1	289
Setter:	the Knight of the Treachery; who has agreed, seemingly	106	OLD BATCH	V.1	348
Araminta:	You who cou'd reproach me with one Counterfeit,	106	OLD BATCH	V.1	361
Bellmour:	That were a miserable Wretch indeed, who cou'd	106	OLD BATCH	V.1	378
Sir Joseph:	Pray, Madam, Who are you? For I find, you and I	111	OLD BATCH	V.2	131
	As a rash Girl, who will all Hazards run,	113	OLD BATCH	EPI.	1
Brisk:	judged by Mellefont here, who gives and takes Raillery	128	DOUBL DLR	I.1	27
Lady Touch:	Have you not wrong'd my Lord, who has	135	DOUBL DLR	I.1	309
Lady Touch:	. . . one, who is no	136	DOUBL DLR	I.1	V329
Lord Froth:	ay, there it is; who could resist! 'twas so my heart was made	140	DOUBL DLR	II.1	68
Lady Ply:	now, who are you? What am I? 'Slidikins can't I govern	144	DOUBL DLR	II.1	215
Maskwell:	take it, is that nice, scrupulous, conscientious Person, who	150	DOUBL DLR	II.1	453
Maskwell:	as your wise man, who is too hard for all the World, and	150	DOUBL DLR	II.1	455
Maskwell:	When each, who searches strictly his own mind,	150	DOUBL DLR	II.1	467
Lady Touch:	was never so surpriz'd in my Life--Who would have	153	DOUBL DLR	III.1	114
Sir Paul:	year to an Old Man, who would do good in his Generation?	162	DOUBL DLR	III.1	435
Brisk:	Who, my Lady Toothless; O, she's a mortifying	165	DOUBL DLR	III.1	567
Sir Paul:	durst you swear without my Consent, ha? Gads-bud, who	171	DOUBL DLR	IV.1	140
Lady Froth:	did you talk of Love? O Parnassus! Who would have	176	DOUBL DLR	IV.1	332
Lady Touch:	found him here. Who does not prevent the Hour of Love;	183	DOUBL DLR	IV.2	9
Maskwell:	Lips be ever clos'd. (Kisses her.) And thus--Oh who	184	DOUBL DLR	IV.2	25
Maskwell:	--but could you think that I who had been happy in your	198	DOUBL DLR	V.1	425
Maskwell:	than in the Death of one who is nothing when not yours.	199	DOUBL DLR	V.1	451
Maskwell:	than in the Heart of one who is nothing when not yours.	199	DOUBL DLR	V.1	451
Lady Froth:	Reflection from you, who are the Sun.	201	DOUBL DLR	V.1	533
Lady Ply:	who would ever trust a man? O my heart akes for fear	202	DOUBL DLR	V.1	546
	(They carry out Maskwell, who hangs down his head.)	203	DOUBL DLR	V.1	577
	Than they who stand their Trials at the Barr;	204	DOUBL DLR	EPI.	9
	The Lady Criticks, who are better Read,	204	DOUBL DLR	EPI.	21
	You who can Judge, to Sentence may proceed;	204	DOUBL DLR	EPI.	34
	At least from their Contempt, who cannot Read.	204	DOUBL DLR	EPI.	36
	So, the poor Husbands of the Stage, who found	213	FOR LOVE	PRO.	7
	We who remain, would gratefully repay	213	FOR LOVE	PRO.	23
Jeremy:	Ay, more indeed; for who cares for any Body that	219	FOR LOVE	I.1	129
Scandal:	vain! Who would die a Martyr to Sense in a Country	219	FOR LOVE	I.1	139
Valentine:	See who they are.	221	FOR LOVE	I.1	185
	(Steward who whispers.)	224	FOR LOVE	I.1	V308
Scandal:	a Woman of this Age, who has had an indifference for you	225	FOR LOVE	I.1	351
Tattle:	her--Madam, says I, there are some Persons who make	227	FOR LOVE	I.1	430
Tattle:	Who I? Upon Honour I don't know whether she be	228	FOR LOVE	I.1	465
Mrs Frail:	No, I'll be gone. Come, who Squires me to the	234	FOR LOVE	I.1	664
Scandal:	Who hopes to purchase Wealth, by selling Land;	234	FOR LOVE	I.1	680
Sr Sampson:	ungracious Prodigal know who begat him; I will, old	240	FOR LOVE	II.1	174
Sr Sampson:	How now, who sent for you? Ha! what wou'd you	242	FOR LOVE	II.1	261
Sr Sampson:	You Sir; and you Sir:--Why, who are you Sir?	244	FOR LOVE	II.1	314
Sr Sampson:	you or no? Ouns who are you? Whence came you?	244	FOR LOVE	II.1	326
Mrs Fore:	Very well, that will appear who has most,	247	FOR LOVE	II.1	455
Mrs Fore:	enough; my awkard Daughter-in-Law, who you know	248	FOR LOVE	II.1	499
Tattle:	Who I, Madam?--Oh Lord, how can your Ladyship	250	FOR LOVE	II.1	540
Angelica:	My Passion! And who told you of my Passion, pray	254	FOR LOVE	III.1	57
Scandal:	say in general Terms, He only is Secret who never was	256	FOR LOVE	III.1	125
Scandal:	another upon yours--As she is chaste, who was never	256	FOR LOVE	III.1	127
Tattle:	Garden; my own Landlady and Valet de Chambre; all who	257	FOR LOVE	III.1	158
Tattle:	Church, once, an Enquiry being made, who I was, it was	257	FOR LOVE	III.1	163
Tattle:	answer'd, I was the famous Tattle, who had ruin'd so	257	FOR LOVE	III.1	164
Ben:	o' Nine-tails laid cross your Shoulders. Flesh! who are	264	FOR LOVE	III.1	409
Scandal:	Men; but they were such as you--Men who consulted	267	FOR LOVE	III.1	529
Valentine:	Answer me; Who is that? and that?	279	FOR LOVE	IV.1	154
Sr Sampson:	my Heart--What matter is it who holds it? What	281	FOR LOVE	IV.1	230
Valentine:	(whispers). Scandal, who are all these? Foreigners?	291	FOR LOVE	IV.1	593
Valentine:	(whispers). Scandal, who are these? Foreigners?	291	FOR LOVE	IV.1	V593
Valentine:	You? Who are you? No, I hope not.	292	FOR LOVE	IV.1	623
Angelica:	Who am I?	292	FOR LOVE	IV.1	633
Valentine:	Opinion of my Satirical Friend, Scandal, who says,	297	FOR LOVE	IV.1	814
Tattle:	O fie, Miss: Who told you so, Child?	303	FOR LOVE	V.1	231
Tattle:	O fie, Miss, why did you do so? and who told you so,	303	FOR LOVE	V.1	233
Miss Prue:	Who? Why you did; did not you?	303	FOR LOVE	V.1	235
Tattle:	Who I, Sir? I'm an absolute Stranger to you and your	305	FOR LOVE	V.1	284
Ben:	Who, Father? ay, he's come home with a Vengeance.	306	FOR LOVE	V.1	341
Scandal:	Who?	307	FOR LOVE	V.1	360
Sr Sampson:	Who gave you Authority to speak, Sirrah? To	308	FOR LOVE	V.1	417
Scandal:	Favours, either on those who do not merit, or who do not	314	FOR LOVE	V.1	625
	And we, who know no better, must believe 'em.	315	FOR LOVE	EPI.	14
	For that damn'd Poet's spar'd who dams a Brother,	323	M. BRIDE	PRO.	31
Almeria:	Alphonso, who foresaw my Father's Cruelty,	329	M. BRIDE	I.1	119
Almeria:	Who knew our Flight, we closely were pursu'd,	329	M. BRIDE	I.1	123
Almeria:	Conducting them who follow'd us, to shun	329	M. BRIDE	I.1	129
	and Guards, who are ranged in Order, round the Stage.	332	M. BRIDE	I.1	267
Manuel:	Here are who seem to mourn at our Success!	333	M. BRIDE	I.1	278
Manuel:	Yet something too is due to me, who gave	333	M. BRIDE	I.1	289
Garcia:	Osmyn, who led the Moorish Horse; he does,	335	M. BRIDE	I.1	366
Garcia:	Osmyn, who led the Moorish Horse; but he	335	M. BRIDE	I.1	V366
Manuel:	Who with such Lustre, strike admiring Eyes,	335	M. BRIDE	I.1	388
Manuel:	Garcia, what's he, who with contracted Brow,	336	M. BRIDE	I.1	424
Osmyn-Alph:	Who calls that wretched thing, that was Alphonso?	340	M. BRIDE	II.2	35
Leonora:	Who 'ere thou art, and lend thy Hand to raise	341	M. BRIDE	II.2	61
Almeria:	What's he, who like thy self, is started here	344	M. BRIDE	II.2	V167
Leonora:	Who by their pointing seem to mark this Place.	344	M. BRIDE	II.2	V193
Almeria:	What Love? Who is she?	345	M. BRIDE	II.2	199
Almeria:	What Love? Who is she? Why are you alarm'd?	345	M. BRIDE	II.2	V199
Osmyn-Alph:	What would you from a Wretch, who came too	346	M. BRIDE	II.2	V258
Zara:	Commenc'd? not knowing who you were, nor why	347	M. BRIDE	II.2	299
Zara:	Not who thou art.	348	M. BRIDE	II.2	333

Who (continued)

		PAGE	TITLE	ACT.SC	LINE
Manuel:	With that Ixion, who aspires to hold	349	M. EBIDE	II.2	372
Osmyn-Alph:	But who shall dare to tax Eternal Justice!	350	M. EBIDE	III.1	32
Heli:	(Who takes the Privilege to visit late,	351	M. EBIDE	III.1	49
Osmyn-Alph:	One, who has tir'd Misfortune with pursuing?	351	M. EBIDE	III.1	58
Heli:	Among the Troops who thought to share the Plunder,	351	M. EBIDE	III.1	65
Heli:	Nightly; hating this Tyrant; scme, who love	352	M. EBIDE	III.1	101
Zara:	Cou'd one who lov'd, thus torture whom she lov'd?	353	M. EBIDE	III.1	V161
Zara:	To shake the Temper of the King--who knows	354	M. EBIDE	III.1	205
Zara:	Who would not be thus happily confin'd,	360	M. EBIDE	III.1	425
Zara:	Who waits there?	360	M. EBIDE	III.1	445
Selim:	Who bore high Cffices of Weight and Trust,	361	M. EBIDE	IV.1	10
Selim:	The Heads of those who first began the Mutiny.	361	M. EBIDE	IV.1	14
Selim:	With them who first began the Mutiny.	361	M. EBIDE	IV.1	V 14
Selim:	Who at the Place of Execution, will	362	M. EBIDE	IV.1	53
Manuel:	Are ncne return'd of those who follow'd Heli?	363	M. BRIDE	IV.1	74
Gonsalez:	In Roderigo's House, who fled with him.	363	M. EBIDE	IV.1	76
Gonsalez:	They who are fled have that way bent their course.	363	M. EBIDE	IV.1	80
Zara:	You more. One who did call himself Alphonso,	364	M. EBIDE	IV.1	V116
Manuel:	Who waits there?	365	M. EBIDE	IV.1	165
Manuel:	That cnly Zara's Mutes, or such who bring	365	M. EBIDE	IV.1	168
Zara:	Who wish'd it sc: a common Art in Courts.	366	M. EBIDE	IV.1	190
Gonsalez:	Corrupted; how? by whom? who tcld ber so?	366	M. EBIDE	IV.1	207
Manuel:	This Tumult, and the Lords who fled with Heli,	366	M. EBIDE	IV.1	215
Almeria:	Who was--who was, but is nc more a Father.	368	M. EBIDE	IV.1	V281
Manuel:	Ha! whc may live? take heed, no more of that.	369	M. EBIDE	IV.1	332
Manuel:	What Husband? which? who?	369	M. EBIDE	IV.1	341
Manuel:	Poyson and Daggers! who?	369	M. EBIDE	IV.1	343
Manuel:	What Husband? who? whcm do'st thou mean?	370	M. BRIDE	IV.1	354
Almeria:	But doubly thou, who could'st alone have Policy,	370	M. EBIDE	IV.1	380
Gonsalez:	But hcw prevent the Captive Queen, who means	371	M. EBIDE	IV.1	412
Gonsalez:	Dumb Men, who make their Meaning known by Signs.	372	M. EBIDE	IV.1	V434
Garcia:	Who but for heaps of Slain, that choak the Passage,	377	M. EBIDE	V.2	33
Gonsalez:	I whc have spilt my Royal Master's Blood,	378	M. EBIDE	V.2	70
Alonzo:	Or who can wound the Dead?--I've from the Body,	379	M. EBIDE	V.2	114
Leonora:	Who seem the Murderers, kneel weeping by:	381	M. EBIDE	V.2	224
Almeria:	Seest thou not there, who prostrate lies;	382	M. EBIDE	V.2	264
Almeria:	Seest thou not there? behold who prostrate lyes,	382	M. BRIDE	V.2	V264
Almeria:	And pleads against thee? who shall then prevail?	382	M. EBIDE	V.2	265
Osmyn-Alph:	Let us who thro' our Innocence survive,	384	M. EBIDE	V.2	V318
	Of those few Fools, who with ill Stars are curs'd,	393	WAY WCRLD	PRO.	1
	Who, to assert their Sense, your Taste arraign.	393	WAY WCRLD	PRO.	28
	For so Reform'd a Town, who dares Correct?	393	WAY WCRLD	PRO.	32
	Who tc your Judgments yields all Resignation;	393	WAY WCRLD	PRO.	39
Fainall:	I'd make Love to a Wcman who undervalu'd the Loss of	395	WAY WORLD	I.1	9
Mirabell:	And who may have been the Foundress of this	396	WAY WCRLD	I.1	59
Mirabell:	Sect? My Lady Wishfort, I warrant, who publishes her	396	WAY WCRLD	I.1	60
Mirabell:	am not one of those Coxcombs who are apt to interpret a	397	WAY WCRLD	I.1	86
Mirabell:	she who does not refuse 'em every thing, can refuse 'em	397	WAY WCRLD	I.1	88
Mirabell:	Who are they?	397	WAY WCRLD	I.1	101
Mirabell:	this is not a Cabal-night. I wonder, Fainall, that you who	399	WAY WCRLD	I.1	138
Fainall:	Faith, I am not Jealous. Besides, most who are engag'd	399	WAY WCRLD	I.1	141
Mirabell:	always the more the Scandal: For a Woman who is not a	399	WAY WCRLD	I.1	145
Mirabell:	Man who is one.	399	WAY WCRLD	I.1	V147
Mirabell:	and Complaisance enough not to contradict him who shall	399	WAY WCRLD	I.1	154
Fainall:	Wife, who was Sister to my Lady Wishfort, my Wife's	400	WAY WCRLD	I.1	193
Petulant:	Aunt, who loves Catterwauling better than a Conventicle.	406	WAY WCRLD	I.1	V408
Mirabell:	Petulant, Tony Witwoud, who is now thy Competitor in	407	WAY WCRLD	I.1	453
Witwoud:	something of an Uncle to Mirabell, who is lately come to	408	WAY WCRLD	I.1	481
Fainall:	and what a Wretch is he who must survive his hopes!	413	WAY WORLD	II.1	114
Mirabell:	stand excus'd, who has suffer'd herself to be won by his	417	WAY WCRLD	II.1	274
Mrs Fain:	Who?	417	WAY WCRLD	II.1	290
Mirabell:	Fools; Things who visit you from their excessive Idleness;	421	WAY WCRLD	II.1	434
Lady Wish:	See who that is-- (One knocks.) Set down the Bottle	425	WAY WORLD	III.1	33
Sir Wilful:	your Ear, prithee who are these Gallants?	437	WAY WCRLD	III.1	469
Fainall:	of Play, that I should lose to one, who has not	443	WAY WCRLD	III.1	688
Marwood:	to my Lady at the time when that Rascal who is	443	WAY WCRLD	III.1	700
Mrs Fain:	return to Sir Rowland, who as Foible tells me is in a fair	452	WAY WCRLD	IV.1	302
Foible:	Letter, who must deliver it into your own hands.	459	WAY WCRLD	IV.1	550
Lady Wish:	a Person who wou'd suffer racks in honour's cause, dear	459	WAY WCRLD	IV.1	553
Lady Wish:	know you are abus'd. He who pretends to be Sir Rowland	460	WAY WCRLD	IV.1	587
Marwood:	Here is one who is concern'd in the treaty.	465	WAY WORLD	V.1	138
Lady Wish:	you should lean aside to Iniquity who have been Cast in	465	WAY WCRLD	V.1	143
Fainall:	for ycu. If your Physick be wholesome, it matters not who	468	WAY WCRLD	V.1	267
Mirabell:	You have dispos'd of her, who cnly cou'd have	473	WAY WORLD	V.1	458
Sir Wilful:	Dance in the mean time, that we who are not Lovers, may	477	WAY WCRLD	V.1	601
Mirabell:	From hence let those be warn'd, who mean to wed;	478	WAY WCRLD	V.1	620
	Who pleases any one against his Will.	479	WAY WCRLD	EPI.	8
	Such, who watch Plays, with scurrilous intent	479	WAY WCRLD	EPI.	17
	To mark out who by Characters are meant.	479	WAY WORLD	EPI.	18

Who'll (2)

Mrs Frail:	O hang you; who'll believe you?--You'd be	250	FOR LCVE	II.1	554
Sir Wilful:	once, he shall come in: and see who'll hinder him.	471	WAY WCRLD	V.1	352

Who's (23)

Sharper:	Ha! who's that has found? what have you found?	48	OLD EATCH	II.1	27
Araminta:	I am oblig'd to you--But who's malicious now,	57	OLD BATCH	II.2	109
Araminta:	your Sex--Who's there? (Calls.)	58	OLD BATCH	II.2	155
Setter:	Adsbud who's in fault, Mistress Mine? who flung the	66	OLD EATCH	III.1	204
Laetitia:	Ah! Heav'n defend me! Who's this?	81	OLD BATCH	IV.2	15
Laetitia:	Oh, Goodness keep us! Who's this? Who are you?	92	OLD BATCH	IV.4	129
Valentine:	Jeremy, see who's there.	220	FOR LCVE	I.1	155
Angelica:	find who's in Conjunction with your Wife. Why don't	237	FOR LOVE	II.1	69
Foresight:	Nay, if you were but in Jest.--Who's that	242	FOR LOVE	II.1	263
Nurse:	cry husht--O Lord, who's there? (peeps) What's here	253	FOR LCVE	III.1	7
Mrs Fore:	O Lord, who's here?	272	FOR LOVE	III.1	711
Valentine:	(starting). Ha! who's that?	279	FOB LOVE	IV.1	151

Whose   (continued)
    Lady Ply: Person and Parts of so accomplish'd a Person, whose Merit . 169 DOUBL DLR IV.1   82
    Valentine: have a fine time, whose Reputaticns are in your keeping. . 229 FOR LCVE   I.1   503
    Sr Sampson: Sola's and Sonata's? 'Oons whose Son are you? how were . 245 FOR LCVE   II.1   377
    Ben: Whose Name was Buxom Joan.   . . . . . 274 FOR LCVE III.1   762
    Manuel: Of whose mute Valour you relate such Wcnders? . . 335 M. BRIDE   I.1   364
    Almeria: Whose antient Pillars rear their Marble Heads,   . . . 339 M. BRIDE   II.1   60
    Leonora: Behold the Sacred Vault, within whose Womb, ... 340 M. BRIDE   II.2   6
    Osmyn-Alph: Whence is that Voice whose Shrilness from the   . . . 341 M. BRIDE   II.2   37
    Osmyn-Alph: Not so the Mind, whose undetermin'd View   . . . . 345 M. BRIDE   II.2   225
    Zara: Whose former Faith had merited much more: . . . . . 349 M. BRIDE   II.2   377
    Zara: As she, whose savage Breast has been the Cause   . . 353 M. BRIDE III.1   157
    Zara: Of these thy Wrongs; as she, whose barbarous Rage   . 353 M. BRIDE III.1   158
    Gonsalez: In whcse Hearts Blood this Ponyard yet is warm.   . . 377 M. BRIDE   V.2   42
    Gonsalez: Whose weight has sunk me 'ere I reach'd the Shore.   . . 378 M. BRIDE   V.2   87
    Osmyn-Alph: Whose Virtue has renounc'd thy Father's Crimes,   . . . 383 M. BRIDE   V.2   316
                   To whose Rich Cargo, they may make Pretence, ... 385 M. BRIDE   EPI.   23
    Mirabell: He is one whcse Conversation can never be approv'd, yet . 401 WAY WORLD I.1   226
    Mirabell: one whose Wit and outward fair Behaviour have gain'd a . 417 WAY WORLD II.1   272
    Waitwell: hand I see that already. That's some body whose throat . 460 WAY WORLD IV.1   578
    Mrs Fain: Thank Mr. Mirabell, a Cautious Friend, to whose   . . . 477 WAY WORLD V.1   570
                   Others there are whose Malice we'd prevent;   . . . . 479 WAY WCRLD EPI.   16
Whosoever (1)
    Maskwell: a thing as Honesty? Yes, and whoscever has it about him, . 150 DOUBL DLR II.1   451
Why (336)
Whymsies (1)
    Lady Froth: Whymsies and Vapours, but I gave them vent.   . . . . 138 DOUBL DLR II.1   11
Wicked (5)
    Bellmour: may be as wicked as thou art at thy years.   . . . . 43 OLD BATCH   I.1   252
    Laetitia: saw this wicked Man before. . . . . 93 OLD BATCH IV.4   140
    Laetitia: Let the wicked Man answer for himself; does he   . . . 93 OLD BATCH IV.4   167
    Scandal: wicked, and Heav'n grant he may mean well in his Affair . 267 FOR LCVE III.1   522
    Lady Wish: deceive me? hast thou been a wicked accomplice with that . 474 WAY WORLD V.1   481
Wickedness (3)
    Lady Ply: the unparallel'd wickedness! O merciful Father! how could . 146 DOUBL DLR II.1   305
    Lady Ply: you talk of Heaven! and have so much wickedness in your . 147 DOUBL DLR II.1   345
    Maskwell: Mercy on us, What will the Wickedness of this World   . 155 DOUBL DLR III.1   196
Wicket (1)
    Setter: Thou art the Wicket to thy Mistresses Gate, to be   . . . 66 OLD BATCH III.1   195
Widdow (4)
    Scandal: Widdow in the Poultry--800 [Pounds] a Year Joynture, and . 223 FOR LCVE   I.1   269
    Waitwell: Nephew. Come my Buxcm Widdow. . . . . 461 WAY WCRLD IV.1   645
    Mirabell: Yes Sir. I say that this Lady while a Widdow, ... 476 WAY WCRLD V.1   540
    Fainall: Languish Widdow in trust to Edward Mirabell. Confusion! . 476 WAY WCRLD V.1   552
Widdow-hood (1)
    Lady Wish: or Indigestion of Widdow-hood; Nor Impute my Complacency, . 458 WAY WCRLD IV.1   530
Widdows (1)
    Mirabell: Widdows of the World. I suppose this Deed may bear an . 476 WAY WCRLD V.1   554
Wide (6)
    Bellmour: perverts our Aim, casts off the Bias, and leaves us wide and 37 OLD BATCH   I.1   11
    Heartwell: O cursed State! Hcw wide we err, when apprehensive of . . 108 OLD BATCH   V.2   9
    Sir Paul: no, no, you shoot wide of the mark a mile; indeed you do, . 161 DOUBL DLR III.1   427
    Sir Paul: Estate would be left to the wide World, he? I hope you . 174 DOUBL DLR IV.1   254
    Maskwell: I that had wanton'd in the wide Circle of your   . . . 199 DOUBL DLR   V.1   431
    Leonora: Beneath, are still wide stretch'd upon their Hinge,   . . 340 M. BRIDE   II.2   12
Widow (9)   see Widdow, Young-widow
    Valentine: Widow: I know where abouts you are: Come, to the   . . . 223 FOR LCVE   I.1   272
    Valentine: Widow--   . . . . 223 FOR LCVE   I.1   273
    Trapland: and here's to the Widow.   . . . . . . 224 FOR LCVE   I.1   290
    Almeria: And in one Day, was wedded, and a Widow.   . . . . . 329 M. BRIDE   I.1   141
                   As if indeed a Widow, or an Heir.   . . . . . 385 M. BRIDE   EPI.   4
    Fainall: that was a Widow, a young Widow, a handsome Widow;   . . 415 WAY WORLD II.1   211
    Fainall: and would be again a Widow, but that I have a Heart of . 415 WAY WORLD II.1   212
Widow'd (1)
    Gonsalez: Almeria widow'd, yet again may wed;   . . . . 372 M. BRIDE IV.1   446
Widow's (2)
    Valentine: No faith, we'll mind the Widow's business, fill   . . . 223 FOR LCVE   I.1   283
    Fainall: rich Widow's Wealth, and squander it on Love and you? . . 415 WAY WCRLD II.1   207
Widows (1)   see Widdows
    Valentine: What, the Widows Health; give it him--off   . . . . . 223 FOR LCVE   I.1   275
Wife (133)   see Rank-Wife
    Bellmour: Husband be out of the way, for the Wife to shew her   . . 38 OLD BATCH   I.1   56
    Bellmour: What, the old Banker with the handsome Wife?   . . . . 39 OLD BATCH   I.1   71
    Sharper: too handsome for a Wife.   . . . . . . 41 OLD BATCH   I.1   164
    Heartwell: punish'd with a Wife of Birth--be a Stag of the first Head . 45 OLD BATCH   I.1   310
    Lucy: Wife.   . . . . 61 OLD BATCH III.1   24
    Setter: the frailty of his Wife.   . . . . . . 64 OLD BATCH III.1   129
    Heartwell: me in every thing, so like my Wife, the World shall   . . 74 OLD BATCH III.2   121
    Fondlewife: say you with his Wife? With Comfort her self.   . . . 76 OLD BATCH IV.1   20
    Fondlewife: trust my Wife, with a Lords high-fed Chaplain.   . . . 76 OLD BATCH IV.1   33
    Fondlewife: vexation, for a Man to have a handsome Wife.   . . . . 76 OLD BATCH IV.1   40
    Fondlewife: of the Wife of thy Bosom?--Because she is young and   . . 76 OLD BATCH IV.1   51
    Fondlewife: does not thy Wife love thee, nay doat upon thee?--   . . 77 OLD BATCH IV.1   58
    Fondlewife: Wife--Have you throughly consider'd how   . . . . . 77 OLD BATCH IV.1   67
    Laetitia: would get another Wife--Another fond Fool, to break her . 78 OLD BATCH IV.1   107
    Fondlewife: talk to Cocky and teach her how a Wife ought to behave . 79 OLD BATCH IV.1   137
    Belinda: the Equipage of a Wife and two Daughters, came to Mrs. . 84 OLD BATCH IV.3   24
    Sir Joseph: O Lord! Oh terrible! Ha, ha, ha, Is your Wife   . . . 90 OLD BATCH IV.4   55
    Fondlewife: Wife! My Dinah! Oh Schechemite! Begone, I say.   . . . 90 OLD BATCH IV.4   67
    Fondlewife: Ravish my Wife before my face! I warrant he's a Papist in . 91 OLD BATCH IV.4   74
    Bellmour: to speak the truth in justice to your Wife.--No.   . . 93 OLD BATCH IV.4 158
    Bellmour: To lie with your Wife.   . . . . 94 OLD BATCH IV.4 178
    Fondlewife: lay with an honester Man's Wife in your life.   . . . 94 OLD BATCH IV.4 201
    Bellmour: your Wife was come to me.   . . . . . . 95 OLD BATCH IV.4 216
    Bellmour: your Wife, and there will be some hopes of having her . . 95 OLD BATCH IV.4 225
    Bellmour: No Husband, by his Wife, can be deceiv'd: . . . . . 96 OLD BATCH IV.4 273

Wife   (continued)

Wilfully (2)
		PAGE	TITLE	ACT.SC	LINE
Mellefont:	To run most wilfully and unreasonably away with	168	DOUBL DLR	IV.1	38
Fainall:	wilfully neglect the gross advances made him by my Wife;	413	WAY WCRLD	II.1	144

Will (582)   [usages as noun (9)]
Cynthia:	any thing that resists my will, tho' 'twere reason it self.	193	DOUBL DLR	V.1	205
Foresight:	I will have Patience, since it is the Will of the Stars	238	FOR LCVE	II.1	127
Leonora:	My Heart, my Life and Will, are cnly yours.	330	M. BRIDE	I.1	195
Manuel:	It is cur Will she should be so attended.	335	M. BRIDE	I.1	362
Zara:	But larger Means to gratifie the Will?	347	M. BRIDE	II.2	316
Osmyn-Alph:	Precedes the Will to think; and Errour lives	350	M. BRIDE	III.1	34
Millamant:	made sure of my will and pleasure.	449	WAY WORLD	IV.1	181
Foible:	Peace and Quietness by my good will: I had rather bring	464	WAY WCRLD	V.1	87
Fainall:	appear by the last Will and Testament of your deceas'd	469	WAY WCRLD	V.1	281

Will's (1)
Jeremy:	--Ah Pox confound that Will's Coffee-Hcuse, it has	218	FOR LCVE	I.1	87

Will't (2)
Zara:	Compassion, scarce will't own that Name so soon,	346	M. BRIDE	II.2	V279
Waitwell:	O, she is the Antidote to desire. Spouse, thou will't	459	WAY WCRLD	IV.1	560

Willing (11)
Araminta:	and, to confess my Failing, I am willing to give him an	85	OLD BATCH	IV.3	78
Lady Touch:	I am willing to believe as favourably of my Nephew as I	151	DOUBL DLR	III.1	24
Lady Touch:	willing to have remote frcm your hearing. Good my Lord,	152	DOUBL DLR	III.1	51
Cynthia:	both so willing; we each of us strive to reach the Gole,	168	DOUBL DLR	IV.1	12
Cynthia:	both willing; we each of us strive to reach the Gole,	168	DOUBL DLR	IV.1	V 12
Maskwell:	things are impossible to willing minds.	196	DOUBL DLR	V.1	323
Ben:	ben't as willing as I, say so a God's name, there's no harm	263	FOR LCVE	III.1	390
Scandal:	There's nought but willing, waking Love, that can	275	FOR LCVE	III.1	819
Scandal:	I'm afraid the Physician is not willing you shou'd	277	FOR LCVE	IV.1	50
Sir Wilful:	am willing to make satisfaction; and what can a man say	470	WAY WCRLD	V.1	317
Sir Wilful:	willing to marry my Cozen. So pray lets all be Friends,	470	WAY WCRLD	V.1	321

Willingly (3)
Maskwell:	this is an Occasion in which I would not willingly be	182	DOUBL DLR	IV.1	553
Mrs Fain:	Curicsity, and will willingly dispence with the hearing of	412	WAY WCRLD	II.1	104
Waitwell:	and Pcison me,--and I wou'd willingly starve him	458	WAY WCRLD	IV.1	501

Wilt (15)   see Will't, Wo't
Fondlewife:	He, he, he, wilt thou poor Fool? Then I will go,	79	OLD BATCH	IV.1	134
Bellmour:	wilt thou think a little for me? I am sure the ingenious	100	OLD BATCH	V.1	157
Bellmour:	Hold, hold. What the Devil, thou wilt not draw	108	OLD BATCH	V.2	42
Sir Paul:	thou wilt--But endeavour to forget this Mellefont.	171	DOUBL DLR	IV.1	133
Sir Paul:	He? And wilt thcu bring a Grandscn at 9 Months	173	DOUBL DLR	IV.1	223
Mellefont:	No, nc; ha, ha, I dare swear thou wilt not.	193	DOUBL DLR	V.1	229
Sr Sampson:	thou'rt honest, and wilt perform Articles.	281	FCR LCVE	IV.1	215
Mrs Frail:	Thou shalt do what thou wilt,	293	FCR LCVE	IV.1	673
Mrs Frail:	. . . have what thou wilt,	293	FOR LCVE	IV.1	V673
Almeria:	Wilt privately with me,	331	M. BRIDE	I.1	198
Almeria:	Thou wilt withdraw, and privately with me	331	M. BRIDE	I.1	V198
Osmyn-Alph:	Wilt thou not know me? Hast thou then forgot me?	342	M. BRIDE	II.2	78
Zara:	Can'st thou forgive me then! wilt thou believe	354	M. BRIDE	III.1	178
Osmyn-Alph:	But thou wilt know, what harrows up my Heart.	357	M. BRIDE	III.1	317
Almeria:	Thy Pace, imploring thee that thou wilt yield;	368	M. BRIDE	IV.1	275

Win (10)
Vainlove:	force, I'll win her, or weary her into a Forgiveness.	100	OLD BATCH	V.1	127
Mellefont:	No, hang't, that's not endeavouring to Win,	142	DOUBL DLR	II.1	159
Brisk:	to win her with a new airy invention of my own, hem!	175	DOUBL DLR	IV.1	304
Valentine:	him, before you can win it for your self.	226	FOR LCVE	I.1	390
Scandal:	Or win a Mistress, with a losing hand.	234	FOR LCVE	I.1	681
	Suffer'd at first some trifling Stakes to win:	393	WAY WCRLD	PRO.	12
Fainall:	You may allow him to win of you at Play;--	402	WAY WCRLD	II.1	281
Mrs Fain	Woman; and may win her to your Interest.	417	WAY WCRLD	II.1	287
Mirabell:	Wit, or a Fortune by his Honesty, as win a Woman	422	WAY WCRLD	II.1	465
Millamant:	will win me woo me now--Nay, if you are so tedious,	422	WAY WCRLD	II.1	478

Winch'd (1)
Belinda:	Only touch'd a gall'd-beast till he winch'd.	109	OLD BATCH	V.2	46

Wind (20)   see Whirl-wind
Bellmour:	How George, do's the Wind blow there?	44	OLD BATCH	I.1	293
Sharper:	ill Wind that blows no body good: well, you may rejoyce	48	OLD BATCH	I.1	33
Sharper:	Man there--That Pot-gun charg'd with Wind.	69	OLD BATCH	III.1	305
Sir Joseph:	Hem! Pray Madam, Which Way's the Wind?	85	OLD BATCH	IV.3	94
Bellmour:	Humph, Sits the Wind there?--What a lucky	97	OLD BATCH	V.1	23
Lady Touch:	Again, provoke me! Do you wind me like	137	DOUBL DLR	I.1	380
Ben:	Marry a God's Name an the wind sit that way. As for my	261	FOR LOVE	III.1	302
Ben:	high Wind, or that Lady.--You mayn't carry so much	262	FOR LOVE	III.1	331
Ben:	Discourse with you, an 'twere nct a main high Wind	263	FOR LOVE	III.1	370
Ben:	tho'f he should strive against Wind and Tyde.	272	FCR LOVE	III.1	717
Ben:	A shot 'twixt wind and water,	274	FOR LOVE	III.1	788
Ben:	then put off with the next fair wind. How de'e like us?	275	FOR LOVE	III.1	803
Ben:	it's an ill Wind blows no body good,--may-hap I have	287	FOR LOVE	IV.1	425
Ben:	it's an ill Wind blows no body good,--may-hap I have a	287	FOR LOVE	IV.1	V425
Ben:	Mess, here's the Wind chang'd again. Father, you and I	312	FCR LOVE	V.1	568
Almeria:	It was thy Fear; or else some transient Wind	339	M. BRIDE	II.1	54
Almeria:	Or wind me in the Shroud of some pale Coarse	339	M. BRIDE	II.1	76
Osmyn-Alph:	But she has Passions which out-strip the Wind,	355	M. BRIDE	III.1	228
Witwoud:	Bawd troubl'd with Wind. Now you may know what the	404	WAY WCRLD	I.1	354
Petulant:	And the Wind serve.	440	WAY WCRLD	III.1	569

Wind's (2)
Mrs Frail:	Only the Wind's chang'd.	287	FOR LCVE	IV.1	423
Ben:	More shame for you,--the Wind's chang'd?--	287	FOR LOVE	IV.1	424

Windings (1)
Lady Touch:	thee, thou know'st me, kncw'st the very inmost Windings	137	DOUBL DLR	I.1	397

Windmill (1)
Mirabell:	Windmill, has not a more whimsical Dwelling than the	423	WAY WCRLD	II.1	494

Windows (0)   see Jut-Windows

Winds (6)
Sharper:	loves to buffet with the Winds, meet the Tide and sail in	42	OLD BATCH	I.1	202
Ben:	Winds, and Wrack'd Vessels.	264	FOR LOVE	III.1	427
Mrs Frail:	whistled to by Winds; and thou art come forth with Finns	286	FCR LCVE	IV.1	400

787

788

Wish (continued)

		PAGE	TITLE	ACT.SC	LINE
Scandal:	Faith, Madam, I wish telling a Lie would mend the . . .	277	FOR LOVE	IV.1	45
Angelica:	possessing of a Wish, discovers the Folly of the Chase.	296	FOR LOVE	IV.1	788
Sr Sampson:	your Feet; And I wish, Madam, they stood in a better	300	FOR LCVE	V.1	95
Sr Sampson:	your Feet; And I wish, Madam, they were in a better	300	FOR LCVE	V.1 V	95
Miss Prue:	Life: For when I'm awake, it makes me wish and long, and	305	FOR LOVE	V.1	310
Sr Sampson:	mine elect? a ha, Old Foresight, Uncle Foresight, wish me	307	FOR LCVE	V.1	377
Tattle:	wish we could keep it secret, why I don't believe any of	310	FOR LCVE	V.1	476
Osmyn-Alph:	I wish our Parting were a Dream; or we	344	M. BRIDE	II.2	195
Osmyn-Alph:	I wish at least our Parting were a Dream, ...	344	M. BRIDE	II.2	V195
Zara:	Our Wish; and that obtain'd, down with the Scaffolding	347	M. BRIDE	II.2	318
Zara:	Dost fear so much, thou dar'st not wish. The King!	348	M. BRIDE	II.2	347
Zara:	As I could wish; by Heav'n I'll be reveng'd.	348	M. ERIDE	II.2	350
Osmyn-Alph:	She'll come; 'tis what I wish, yet what I fear. . .	351	M. BRIDE	III.1	51
Osmyn-Alph:	Yet I could wish--	354	M. BRIDE	III.1	188
Osmyn-Alph:	Or wish thee from my Sight.	354	M. BRIDE	III.1	188
Almeria:	On any Terms, that thou dost wish me from thee. . .	356	M. EBIDE	III.1	254
Osmyn-Alph:	A wish or Thought from me, to have thee other. . . .	356	M. BRIDE	III.1	257
Selim:	My Life is yours, nor wish I to preserve it, ...	357	M. EFIDE	III.1	316
Gonsalez:	I wish her Mutes are meant to be employ'd	362	M. BRIDE	IV.1	39
Gonsalez:	But she might wish on his Account to see him. . . .	366	M. EBIDE	IV.1	205
Gonsalez:	One to my Wish. Alonzo, thou art welcome.	367	M. EBIDE	IV.1	231
Gonsalez:	Thee such Reward, as should exceed thy Wish. . . .	371	M. BRIDE	IV.1	417
Witwoud:	acquit him--That indeed I cou'd wish were otherwise.	372	M. EFIDE	IV.1	439
Marwood:	as to wish to have been born Old, because we one Day	403	WAY WORLD	I.1	312
Mrs Fain:	I cou'd wish. Now Mincing?	410	WAY WCRLD	I.1	15
		464	WAY WCRLD	V.1	102

Wish'd (4)

		PAGE	TITLE	ACT.SC	LINE
Lord Touch:	Maskwell, you are the Man I wish'd to meet.	181	DOUEL DLR	IV.1	532
Tattle:	shou'd have wish'd for her coming.	253	FOR LCVE	III.1	18
Zara:	Who wish'd it so: a common Art in Courts.	366	FOR LCVE	IV.1	190
Marwood:	Then shake it off, You have often wish'd for	442	WAY WCRLD	III.1	639

Wishes (5)

		PAGE	TITLE	ACT.SC	LINE
Sharper:	May each succeed in what he wishes most.	47	OLD BATCH	I.1	388
Lady Ply:	of an intire resignation of all my best Wishes, for the	169	DOUEL DLR	IV.1	81
Maskwell:	(aside). By Heav'n, he meets my wishes. Few . . .	196	DOUEL DLR	IV.1	322
Zara:	And Look again, with Wishes in thy Eyes.	353	M. EBIDE	III.1	155
Osmyn-Alph:	Soul of my Soul, and End of all my Wishes.	357	M. EFIDE	III.1	305

Wishfort (19)

		PAGE	TITLE	ACT.SC	LINE
Mirabell:	all in her own Name, my old Lady Wishfort came in.--	395	WAY WORLD	I.1	24
Mirabell:	Sect? My Lady Wishfort, I warrant, who publishes her	396	WAY WCRLD	I.1	60
Fainall:	Wife, who was Sister to my Lady Wishfort, my Wife's	400	WAY WCRLD	I.1	193
Witwoud:	Mirabell and he are at some distance, as my Lady Wishfort	408	WAY WCRLD	I.1	483
Witwoud:	No, no, he comes to his Aunts, my Lady Wishfcrt; . .	409	WAY WCRLD	I.1	514
	Lady Wishfort at her Toilet, Peg waiting.) . . .	425	WAY WCBLD	III.1	
	(Enter Lady Wishfort.)	431	WAY WCRLD	III.1	249
	Servant to Lady Wishfort.)	436	WAY WCRLD	III.1	444
Sir Wilful:	to the Lady Wishfort, of this Mansion.	438	WAY WCRLD	III.1	512
	(Enter Lady Wishfcrt and Fainall.) . .	441	WAY WORLD	III.1	592
	(Scene Continues. Enter Lady Wishfcrt and Foible.) .	444	WAY WCRLD	IV.1	
	(Enter Lady Wishfort and Sir Wilfull drunk.)	454	WAY WCBLD	IV.1	383
	(Enter Foible, and whispers Lady Wishfort.)	456	WAY WCRLD	IV.1	459
	(Enter Lady Wishfort with a Letter.)	459	WAY WCRLD	IV.1	565
	(Scene Continues. Lady Wishfort and Foible.) . . .	462	WAY WCRLD	V.1	
	(Enter Lady Wishfort and Marwood.)	465	WAY WCRLD	V.1	124
Fainall:	Husband Sir Jonathan Wishfort) by her disobedience in	469	WAY WORLD	V.1	282
Fainall:	Wishfort, must be subscrib'd, or your Darling Daughter's	473	WAY WORLD	V.1	442
Marwood:	Wishfcrt go to Mrs. Fainall and Foible). These Corrupt	474	WAY WCRLD	V.1	473

Wishfort's (2)

		PAGE	TITLE	ACT.SC	LINE
Petulant:	my Lady Wishfort's?	407	WAY WCRLD	I.1	436
	(A Rocm in Lady Wishfort's House.	425	WAY WCRLD	III.1	

Wishing (3)

		PAGE	TITLE	ACT.SC	LINE
Musician:	While wishing at your Feet they lie:	60	OLD BATCH	II.2	198
Lord Touch:	joyn your hands.--Unwearied Nights, and wishing . .	203	DOUEL DLR	V.1	587
Scandal:	Sinners, and the faint dawning of a Bliss to wishing	275	FCB LOVE	III.1	817

Wit (75)   see Sea-wit

		PAGE	TITLE	ACT.SC	LINE
	Arm'd with keen Satyr, and with pointed Wit, . . .	35	OLD BnTCH	PRO.	7
Bellmour:	to Fools; they have need of 'em: Wit, be my Faculty; .	37	OLD EATCH	I.1	23
Bellmour:	When Wit and Reason, both, have fail'd to move; . .	60	OLD EATCH	II.2	224
Bellmour:	Pshaw, No: I have a better Opinion of thy Wit. . .	100	OLD EATCH	V.1	142
	If loss of that should follow want of Wit.	113	OLD EATCH	EPI.	13
	To know, if it be truly born of Wit.	125	DOUEL DLR	PRO.	11
Brisk:	Soul of Conversation, the very Essence of Wit, and Spirit	128	DOUEL DLR	I.1	34
Mellefont:	to have Wit, that thou may'st seem a Fool.	129	DOUEL DLR	I.1	72
Brisk:	How? how, my Lord? What, affront my Wit! Let . .	132	DOUEL DLR	I.1	194
Lord Froth:	when any of their foolish Wit prevails upon the side .	133	DOUEL DLR	I.1	229
Brisk:	against Wit, and I'm sorry for some Friends of mine that	133	DOUEL DLR	I.1	239
Brisk:	Deuce take me, there's Wit in't too--and Wit . . .	133	DOUEL DLR	I.1	241
Brisk:	must te foil'd by Wit; cut a Diamond with a Diamond; .	133	DOUEL DLR	I.1	242
Lord Froth:	found out the Wit.	133	DOUEL DLB	I.1	245
Careless:	Wit, In what? Where the Devil's the Wit, in not . .	133	DOUEL DLR	I.1	246
Lord Froth:	Brisk to have Wit; my Wife says, he has a great deal. I	134	DOUEL DLR	I.1	274
Cynthia:	Love, and so much Wit as your Ladyship has, did not .	138	DOUEL DLR	II.1	6
Lady Froth:	a great deal of Wit: Mr. Mellefont, don't you think Mr.	140	DOUEL DLR	II.1	86
Lady Froth:	Brisk has a World of Wit?	140	DOUEL DLB	II.1	87
Lady Froth:	More Wit than any Body.	140	DOUEL DLR	II.1	92
Cynthia:	opposition of their Wit, render themselves as ridiculous	142	DOUEL DLB	II.1	V156
Lady Froth:	Wit, and can sing a Tune already. My Lord wont you go?	167	DOUEL DLR	III.1	620
Cynthia:	'em; for these have Quality and Education, Wit and fine	167	DOUEL DLB	III.1	627
Cynthia:	of his Wit: Therefore let me see you undermine my Lady	168	DOUEL DLR	IV.1	47
Brisk:	Wit too, to keep in with him--No matter, she's a . .	175	DOUEL DLR	IV.1	294
Maskwell:	you please, defer the finishing of your Wit, and let us talk	194	DOUEL DLR	V.1	278
Lady Froth:	me, O Parnassus, you have an infinite deal of Wit. .	202	DOUEL DLR	V.1	542
	Which must of Consequence be Foes to Wit.	204	DOUEL DLB	EPI.	33
	As Asses Thistles, Poets mumble Wit.	214	FCB LOVE	PRO.	35
	Before your late Encouragement of Wit.--	214	FOR LOVE	PRO.	47
Jeremy:	help me, I'm poor enough to be a Wit--Eut I was .	217	FOR LOVE	I.1	41

Wit   (continued)

Jeremy:	lying in the Arms of a needy Wit, before the Embraces of	.	219	FOR LOVE	I.1	114
Valentine:	The Rogue has (with all the Wit he could muster	.	219	FOR LOVE	I.1	118
Valentine:	up) been declaiming against Wit.	.	219	FOR LOVE	I.1	119
Scandal:	Aye? Why then I'm afraid Jeremy has Wit: For	.	219	FOR LOVE	I.1	120
Scandal:	enough? Must you needs shew your Wit to get more?	.	219	FOR LOVE	I.1	128
Jeremy:	has more Wit than himself?	.	219	FOR LOVE	I.1	130
Sr Sampson:	Conscience and Honesty; this is your Wit now, this is the	.	243	FOR LOVE	II.1	298
Sr Sampson:	Morality of your Wits! You are a Wit, and have been a	.	243	FOR LOVE	II.1	299
Sr Sampson:	Now let's see, if you have Wit enough to keep your self?--	.	246	FOR LOVE	II.1	401
Tattle:	of your Ladyship's Wit and Gallantry, could have so	.	255	FOR LOVE	III.1	67
Angelica:	If you speak Truth, your endeavouring at Wit is	.	276	FOR LOVE	IV.1	38
Angelica:	would neither have an absolute Wit, nor a Fool.	.	299	FOR LOVE	V.1	64
Sr Sampson:	young Fellow that is neither a Wit in his own Eye, nor a	.	299	FOR LOVE	V.1	66
Sr Sampson:	Wit and a Fool.	.	299	FOR LOVE	V.1	69
Angelica:	her Husband. I should like a Man of Wit for a Lover,	.	299	FOR LOVE	V.1	74
Sr Sampson:	Truth. Odsbud, you have won my Heart: I hate a Wit; I	.	299	FOR LOVE	V.1	80
Sr Sampson:	Lad, till he learn'd to be a Wit--And might have	.	299	FOR LOVE	V.1	82
Sr Sampson:	risen in the State--But, a pox on't, his Wit run him	.	299	FOR LOVE	V.1	83
	The Dearth of Wit they did so long presage,	.	323	M. BRIDE	PRO.	15
Manuel:	That Wit of Man, and dire Revenge can think,	.	368	M. BRIDE	IV.1	297
	And thrive and prosper on the Wrecks of Wit.	.	385	M. BRIDE	EPI.	26
Fainall:	Wit.	.	399	WAY WORLD	I.1	152
Fainall:	Nature, and does not always want Wit.	.	401	WAY WORLD	I.1	222
Mirabell:	a good Memory, and some few Scraps of other Folks Wit.	.	401	WAY WORLD	I.1	225
Fainall:	you monopolize the Wit that is between you, the Fortune	.	402	WAY WORLD	I.1	283
Mirabell:	of Wit to be your Talent, Witwoud.	.	402	WAY WORLD	I.1	286
Witwoud:	Wit: Nay, I'll do him Justice. I'm his Friend, I won't	.	403	WAY WORLD	I.1	291
Witwoud:	Wit will excuse that: A Wit shou'd no more be sincere,	.	403	WAY WORLD	I.1	319
Mirabell:	because he has not Wit enough to invent an Evasion.	.	404	WAY WORLD	I.1	338
Witwoud:	No; the Rogue's Wit and Readiness of Invention	.	406	WAY WORLD	I.1	413
Mirabell:	me; if thou hadst but good Nature equal to thy Wit	.	407	WAY WORLD	I.1	452
Fainall:	She has Wit.	.	408	WAY WORLD	I.1	475
Mirabell:	That Impudence and Malice, pass for Wit.	.	409	WAY WORLD	I.1	542
Mirabell:	one whose Wit and outward fair Behaviour have gain'd a	.	417	WAY WORLD	II.1	272
Millamant:	Wit.	.	419	WAY WORLD	II.1	342
Millamant:	one's Wit to an Eccho: They can but reflect what we look	.	420	WAY WORLD	II.1	410
Mirabell:	Wit, or a Fortune by his Honesty, as win a Woman	.	422	WAY WORLD	II.1	465
Marwood:	of Wit, but to blind her Affair with a Lover of Sense. If	.	433	WAY WORLD	III.1	313
Witwoud:	--We hit off a little Wit now and then, but no	.	435	WAY WORLD	III.1	394
Lady Wish:	Wit. And your great Wits always rally their best Friends	.	441	WAY WORLD	III.1	607
	But that they have been Damn'd for want of wit.	.	479	WAY WORLD	EPI.	13

Witch (5)   see Lapland-Witch

Heartwell:	Yet I must--Speak dear Angel, Devil, Saint, Witch; do	.	72	OLD BATCH	III.2	41
Mellefont:	appearing to my Shipwrack'd hopes: The Witch has rais'd	.	148	DOUBL DLR	III.1	382
Mellefont:	Witch in her own Bridle.	.	167	DOUEL DLR	IV.1	5
Angelica:	the Closet, one Night, like Saul and the Witch of Endor,	.	238	FOR LOVE	II.1	107
Ben:	Hold. They say a Witch will sail in a Sieve--But I	.	309	FOR LOVE	V.1	434

Witch-craft (2)

Lady Wish:	(apart). Oh, he has Witch-craft in his Eyes and	.	472	WAY WORLD	V.1	408
Lady Wish:	(aside.) Oh, he has Witch-craft in his Eyes and	.	472	WAY WORLD	V.1	V408

Witchcraft (1)

Mellefont:	such Witchcraft.	.	186	DOUEL DLR	IV.2	116

Witches (1)

Valentine:	They say so of a Witches Pray'r, and Dreams and	.	297	FOR LOVE	IV.1	808

With (969)

With-held (2)

Heli:	For you, those Blessings it with-held from him.	.	352	M. BRIDE	III.1	119
Osmyn-Alph:	How run into thy Arms with-held by Fetters,	.	355	M. BRIDE	III.1	239

With't (1)

Sr Sampson:	Why, body o' me, out with't.	.	266	FOR LOVE	III.1	495

Withal (1)

Petulant:	A fine Gentleman, but he's silly withal.	.	408	WAY WORLD	I.1	506

Withdraw (3)

Almeria:	Thou wilt withdraw, and privately with me	.	331	M. BRIDE	I.1	V198
Manuel:	Why does the Fairest of her Kind, withdraw	.	348	M. BRIDE	II.2	352
Sir Wilful:	measure; therefore withdraw your Instrument Sir, or	.	473	WAY WORLD	V.1	428

Withdrew (1)

Mirabell:	she redned and I withdrew, without expecting her Reply.	.	396	WAY WORLD	I.1	40

Withers (1)

Mirabell:	usher in the Fall; and withers in an affected Bloom.	.	418	WAY WORLD	II.1	320

Within (33)

Bellmour:	So Fortune be prais'd! To find you both within,	.	57	OLD BATCH	II.2	114
Silvia:	Methinks I feel the Woman strong within me, and	.	61	OLD BATCH	III.1	33
Capt Bluff:	I'll call a Council of War within to consider of my	.	70	OLD BATCH	III.1	363
Bellmour:	Reasons for what I do, which I'll tell you within.--In	.	98	OLD BATCH	V.1	69
Sharper:	me: May be she mayn't be within. 'Tis but to yond'	.	104	OLD BATCH	V.1	285
	I swear, young Bays within, is so dejected,	.	113	OLD BATCH	EPI.	24
Maskwell:	Well, I'll meet you here, within a quarter of eight,	.	157	DOUBL DLR	III.1	260
Cynthia:	Within reach; for example, give me your hand;	.	168	DOUBL DLR	IV.1	23
Mellefont:	within a Quarter of Eight.	.	181	DOUEL DLR	IV.1	514
Maskwell:	within this Breast, which should it once blaze forth, would	.	188	DOUBL DLR	V.1	29
Maskwell:	one of 'em have a finger in't, he promised me to be within	.	194	DOUBL DLR	V.1	269
Maskwell:	one of them has a finger in't, he promised me to be within	.	194	DOUBL DLR	V.1	V269
Maskwell:	(within). Will you not hear me?	.	197	DOUBL DLR	V.1	371
Lady Touch:	(within). No, Monster! Hellish Traitor! no.	.	197	DOUBL DLR	V.1	372
Lady Touch:	(within). No, Monster! Traitor! no.	.	197	DOUBL DLR	V.1	V372
Maskwell:	World of Love, ccu'd be confin'd within the puny Province	.	199	DOUBL DLR	V.1	432
Trapland:	Mr. Snap stay within Call.	.	224	FOR LOVE	I.1	306
Mrs Fore:	Never, never; till within these three Nights;	.	270	FOR LOVE	III.1	622
Foresight:	within a quarter of Twelve--hem--he, hem!--just upon	.	270	FOR LOVE	III.1	646
Ben:	I warrant that brings 'em, an' they be within hearing.	.	274	FOR LOVE	III.1	794
Sr Sampson:	within a Kiss of the matter, as you see.	.	307	FOR LOVE	V.1	391
Almeria:	Within its cold, but hospitable Bosom.	.	326	M. BRIDE	I.1	12
Leonora:	Behold the Sacred Vault, within whose Womb,	.	340	M. BRIDE	II.2	6
Osmyn-Alph:	But now, and I was clos'd within the Tomb	.	349	M. BRIDE	III.1	1

Within   (continued)

		PAGE	TITLE	ACT.SC	LINE
Osmyn-Alph:	Within I found it, by my Father's Hand	352	M. BRIDE	III.1	111
Zara:	Long fashioning within thy labouring Mind, ...	354	M. BRIDE	III.1	195
Manuel:	Fell hate, within my breast, Revenge and Gall. . .	374	M. BRIDE	V.1	65
Gonsalez:	Ha! sure he sleeps--all's dark within, save what . .	376	M. BRIDE	V.2	6
Millamant:	handsomer--And within a Year or two as young. . .	434	WAY WORLD	III.1	359
Lady Wish:	her foot within the door of a Play-house. O my dear .	467	WAY WORLD	V.1	205
Lady Wish:	her foot within the door of a Play-house. O dear . .	467	WAY WORLD	V.1	V205
Mirabell:	to the uses within mention'd. You may read if you please	476	WAY WORLD	V.1	547
Foible:	Entertainment are yet within Call.	478	WAY WORLD	V.1	606

Without (76)

		PAGE	TITLE	ACT.SC	LINE
Vainlove:	So that as he is often Jealous without a Cause, he's as				
	often	40	OLD BATCH	I.1	109
Vainlove:	satisfied without Reason.	40	OLD BATCH	I.1	110
Bellmour:	ever he was loose, he ran away, without staying to see who	46	OLD BATCH	I.1	363
Capt Bluff:	of my Pallat, you can't relish a Dish of Fighting without	51	OLD BATCH	II.1	163
Bellmour:	Marry her without her Consent; thou'rt a Riddle . . .	64	OLD BATCH	III.1	113
Setter:	Man of parts. That is without being politick, diligent,				
	secret,	65	OLD BATCH	III.1	150
Lucy:	without hopes of revenge.	65	OLD BATCH	III.1	182
Setter:	and I can Kiss Lucy without all that.	67	OLD BATCH	III.1	226
Sir Joseph:	am both Sir; what then? I hope I may be offended, without	68	OLD BATCH	III.1	293
Bellmour:	kick this Puppy without a Man were cold, and had no . .	70	OLD BATCH	III.1	328
Sir Joseph:	'em in my own proper Person, without your help. . . .	85	OLD BATCH	IV.3	69
Belinda:	his Mistress, is like a Body without a Soul. Mr. Vainlove,	86	OLD BATCH	IV.3	134
Fondlewife:	(without). Cocky, Cocky, Where are you Cocky? . .	89	OLD BATCH	IV.4	8
Lucy:	That may be, without troubling your self to go again .	97	OLD BATCH	V	14
Careless:	man must endure the noise of words without Sence, I think	127	DOUBL DLR	I.1	8
Lord Froth:	without 'em.	134	DOUBL DLR	I.1	285
Maskwell:	Pox cn't that a Man can't drink without quenching his .	155	DOUBL DLR	III.1	185
Cynthia:	without any harmony; for sure, my Lord, to laugh out of	163	DOUBL DLR	III.1	472
Lord Froth:	without a jest is as impertinent; hee! as, as-- .	163	DOUBL DLR	III.1	478
Cynthia:	As dancing without a Fiddle.	163	DOUBL DLR	III.1	479
Mellefont:	House this moment and Marry one another, without . .	168	DOUBL DLR	IV.1	28
Cynthia:	consent to like a Man without the vile Consideration of	168	DOUBL DLR	IV.1	45
Careless:	O Heaven! I can't out-live this Night without . .	170	DOUBL DLR	IV.1	113
Sir Paul:	durst you swear without my Consent, ha? Gads-bud, who .	171	DOUBL DLR	IV.1	140
Brisk:	Lord Froth wants a Partner, we can never begin without .	174	DOUBL DLR	IV.1	278
Mellefont:	Pretious Aunt, I shall never thrive without I deal with the	187	DOUBL DLR	IV.2	152
Lady Touch:	Marriage, and the promoting any other, without consulting	192	DOUBL DLR	V.1	180
Cynthia:	without suspicion?	193	DOUBL DLR	V.1	209
Maskwell:	back Stairs, and so we may slip down without being . .	194	DOUBL DLR	V.1	240
Maskwell:	publick or private, that can expect to prosper without .	194	DOUBL DLR	V.1	268
Saygrace:	I have; the Gown will not be indued without	195	DOUBL DLR	V.1	290
Jeremy:	your Debts without Money? Will they shut up the . .	217	FOR LOVE	I.1	28
Jeremy:	which her Vanity had preferr'd to Settlements, without a	219	FOR LOVE	I.1	109
Scandal:	nam'd: Without you could retrieve the Ancient Honours .	220	FOR LOVE	I.1	148
Foresight:	of Bed backwards too this morning, without Premeditation;	236	FOR LOVE	II.1	32
Sr Sampson:	shall know one another's Faces without the help of a .	240	FOR LOVE	II.1	200
Sr Sampson:	without her Inconstancy. 'S'bud I was but in Jest. .	242	FOR LOVE	II.1	259
Sr Sampson:	damn'd Tyburn face, without the benefit o' the Clergy. .	243	FOR LOVE	II.1	307
Sr Sampson:	can't a private man be born without all these followers: .	245	FOR LOVE	II.1	350
Sr Sampson:	have been born without a Palate.--'S'heart, what shou'd .	245	FOR LOVE	II.1	367
Mrs Fore:	her, without betraying my self.	248	FOR LOVE	II.1	472
Sr Sampson:	for saying Grace, old Foresight, but fall too without the	265	FOR LOVE	III.1	460
Sr Sampson:	Without Popery shou'd be landed in the West, or the .	266	FOR LOVE	III.1	487
Mrs Frail:	the Estate be setled; for you know, Marrying without an .	273	FOR LOVE	III.1	719
Mrs Frail:	Estate, is like Sailing in a Ship without Ballast. . .	273	FOR LOVE	III.1	720
Angelica:	without I suck the Poyson from his Wounds, I'm afraid .	277	FOR LOVE	IV.1	75
Valentine:	about without going together by the Ears--heigh ho! .	280	FOR LOVE	IV.1	192
Valentine:	without a Reverse or Inscription; for Indifference has both	297	FOR LOVE	IV.1	811
Foresight:	marry my Daughter without my Consent?	304	FOR LOVE	V.1	283
Ben:	as if so be you should sail so far as the Streights without	308	FOR LOVE	V.1	415
	I can't reflect without an aking Heart, ...	315	FOR LOVE	EPI.	36
	For a clear Stage won't do, without your Favour. . .	316	FOR LOVE	EPI.	44
	Nor were they without Reason join'd together; . . .	323	M. BRIDE	PRO.	7
Almeria:	Without thee cou'd not cure.	343	M. BRIDE	II.2	134
Manuel:	Life without Love is Load; and Time stands still: . .	349	M. BRIDE	II.2	389
Gonsalez:	No body? sure he'll wait without--I would	376	M. BRIDE	V.2	11
Mirabell:	she redned and I withdrew, without expecting her Reply. .	396	WAY WORLD	I.1	40
Fainall:	What should provoke her to be your Enemy, without . .	397	WAY WORLD	I.1	82
Mirabell:	rote. The Catalogue was so large, that I was not without	399	WAY WORLD	I.1	166
Mirabell:	habitual to me, to remember 'em without being displeas'd.	399	WAY WORLD	I.1	171
Mirabell:	other will be rotten without ever being ripe at all. .	401	WAY WORLD	I.1	217
Witwoud:	Ay, ay, Friendship without Freedom is as dull as . .	404	WAY WORLD	I.1	357
Witwoud:	Love without Enjoyment, or Wine without Toasting; but .	404	WAY WORLD	I.1	358
Mrs Fain:	and the only Man from whom I could hear it without . .	412	WAY WORLD	II.1	93
Mrs Fain:	without Bounds, and wou'd you set Limits to that Aversion,	417	WAY WORLD	II.1	262
Millamant:	Without the help of the Devil you can't imagine; . .	423	WAY WORLD	II.1	V485
Marwood:	without you cou'd have kept his Counsel closer. I shall .	431	WAY WORLD	III.1	242
Millamant:	Things! without one cou'd give 'em to one's . . .	433	WAY WORLD	III.1	306
Petulant:	without Book--So all's one for that.	436	WAY WORLD	III.1	433
Millamant:	without Interrogatories or wry Faces on your part. To .	450	WAY WORLD	IV.1	214
Millamant:	without giving a reason. To have my Closet Inviolate; to	450	WAY WORLD	IV.1	221
Millamant:	presume to approach without first asking leave. And .	450	WAY WORLD	IV.1	223
Petulant:	Thou art (without a figure) Just one half of an Ass; .	454	WAY WORLD	IV.1	350
Marwood:	consent to, without difficulty; she has already but too	468	WAY WORLD	V.1	259
Millamant:	--He is without and waits your leave for admittance. .	470	WAY WORLD	V.1	332

Withouten (1)

		PAGE	TITLE	ACT.SC	LINE
Foresight:	Withouten Guile, then be it said, ...	236	FOR LOVE	II.1	53

Withoutside (1)

		PAGE	TITLE	ACT.SC	LINE
Valentine:	carry his Conscience withoutside?--Lawyer, what art	280	FOR LOVE	IV.1	168

Witlings (1)

		PAGE	TITLE	ACT.SC	LINE
	Beaus Judge of Dress; the Witlings Judge of Songs; . .	204	DOUBL DLR	EPI.	27

Witness (17)   see Eye-witness, False-Witness

		PAGE	TITLE	ACT.SC	LINE
Belinda:	Not I; witness my Heart I stay out of pure Affection. . .	57	OLD BATCH	II.2	111

Won't   (continued)

		PAGE	TITLE	ACT.SC	LINE
Laetitia:	privy to a weak Woman's Failing, won't turn it to the	82	OLD BATCH	IV.2	63
Laetitia:	Impudent. Won't you censure me for this, now;--but 'tis	82	OLD BATCH	IV.2	80
Laetitia:	Oh! I am sick with the fright; won't you take him	90	OLD BATCH	IV.4	57
Laetitia:	Oh! Won't you follow, and see him out of Doors,	91	OLD BATCH	IV.4	70
Fondlewife:	Papers.--I won't disturb him; Give me the Key.	91	OLD BATCH	IV.4	82
Laetitia:	Sure, when he does not see his face, he won't discover	91	OLD BATCH	IV.4	90
Bellmour:	That you may, Faith, and I hope you won't believe	95	OLD BATCH	IV.4	219
Laetitia:	won't you speak to me, cruel Nykin? Indeed, I'll die, if	95	OLD BATCH	IV.4	246
Fondlewife:	Here, here, I do believe thee.--I won't	96	OLD BATCH	IV.4	262
Brisk:	Froth won't Dance at your Wedding to Morrow; nor	129	DOUBL DLR	I.1	56
Brisk:	the Deuce take me, I won't Write your Epithalamium	129	DOUBL DLR	I.1	57
Cynthia:	(aside). At least I won't own it, to be troubled with your	139	DOUBL DLR	II.1	36
Cynthia:	Why Faith, Madam, he that won't take my Word,	139	DOUBL DLR	II.1	43
Lady Froth:	call it? I dare Swear you won't guesse--The Sillibub,	141	DOUBL DLR	II.1	122
Sir Paul:	No, 'tis because I won't be headstrong, because I	144	DOUBL DLR	II.1	230
Sir Paul:	won't be a Brute, and have my Head fortifi'd, that I am thus	144	DOUBL DLR	II.1	231
Lady Ply:	and all the Senses are fallible; I won't trust my Honour, I	147	DOUBL DLR	II.1	341
Lady Touch:	You won't.	152	DOUBL DLR	III.1	58
Lady Touch:	--nay, I won't tell you any more, till you are your	153	DOUBL DLR	III.1	111
Lord Touch:	Well I go--you won't stay, for I	154	DOUBL DLR	III.1	123
Maskwell:	won't perplex you. 'Tis the only thing that Providence	157	DOUBL DLR	III.1	244
Mellefont:	And you won't die one, for your own, so still	169	DOUBL DLR	IV.1	63
Jeremy:	won't have a Friend left in the World, if you turn Poet	218	FOR LOVE	I.1	86
Scandal:	while; but when the full Cry is against you, you won't	219	FOR LOVE	I.1	141
Valentine:	What did I say? I hope you won't bring me to	229	FOR LOVE	I.1	497
Tattle:	'Tis very hard--Won't a Baronet's Lady pass?	230	FOR LOVE	I.1	530
Angelica:	abroad; and if you won't lend me your Coach, I'll take a	237	FOR LOVE	II.1	67
Foresight:	tell me--won't you speak? Odd I'll--	239	FOR LOVE	II.1	158
Miss Prue:	Lavender mun--I'm resolv'd I won't let Nurse put	249	FOR LOVE	II.1	529
Mrs Fore:	won't let him come near her, after Mr. Tattle.	250	FOR LOVE	II.1	563
Mrs Frail:	I don't care; I won't be seen in't.	250	FOR LOVE	II.1	576
Tattle:	And won't you shew me, pretty Miss, where your	252	FOR LOVE	II.1	646
Miss Prue:	No, indeed won't I: But I'll run there, and hide	252	FOR LOVE	II.1	648
Nurse:	(knocks) Ods my Life, won't you open the Door? I'll	253	FOR LOVE	III.1	11
Scandal:	Angelica's Love for Valentine; you won't speak of it.	254	FOR LOVE	III.1	46
Scandal:	Angelica's Love to Valentine; you won't speak of it.	254	FOR LOVE	III.1 V	46
Scandal:	(aside). Ouns, why you won't own it, will you?	256	FOR LOVE	III.1	99
Singer-F:	He alone won't Betray in whom none will Confide,	259	FOR LOVE	III.1	207
Angelica:	Won't you stay and see your Brother?	259	FOR LOVE	III.1	222
Miss Prue:	better not speak at all, I think, and truly I won't tell				
	a lie	263	FOR LOVE	III.1	383
Miss Prue:	I won't be call'd Names, nor I won't be abus'd	264	FOR LOVE	III.1	428
Miss Prue:	thus, so I won't.--If I were a man,--(Crys.)--You durst not	264	FOR LOVE	III.1	429
Sr Sampson:	Liar--Or if that won't do, I'll bring a Lawyer that	267	FOR LOVE	III.1	509
Mrs Fore:	Well; I won't go to Bed to my Husband to	273	FOR LOVE	III.1	742
Mrs Frail:	If it won't interrupt you, I'll entertain you with a	273	FOR LOVE	III.1	748
Jeremy:	playing the Madman, won't make her play the Fool, and	276	FOR LOVE	IV.1	9
Angelica:	he won't recover his Senses till I lose mine.	277	FOR LOVE	IV.1	76
Scandal:	Hey, brave Woman, i' faith--Won't you see	277	FOR LOVE	IV.1	77
Sr Sampson:	Oons, I won't believe it; let me see him, Sir	279	FOR LOVE	IV.1	145
Valentine:	little out of Order; won't you please to sit, Sir?	281	FOR LOVE	IV.1	197
Mrs Frail:	and won't be surpriz'd to see the Tide turn'd.	284	FOR LOVE	IV.1	308
Ben:	won't come too.	287	FOR LOVE	IV.1	443
Valentine:	and a long Veil to cover the Project, and we won't see	290	FOR LOVE	IV.1	562
Jeremy:	No, no, Madam, he won't know her, if he shou'd, I	291	FOR LOVE	IV.1	591
Mrs Fore:	He won't know you, Cousin, he knows no	291	FOR LOVE	IV.1	601
Jeremy:	madly, she won't distinguish the Tone of your Voice.	303	FOR LOVE	V.1	218
Miss Prue:	Why won't you be my Husband? You say you love me,	303	FOR LOVE	V.1	228
Miss Prue:	and you won't be my Husband. And I know you may be	303	FOR LOVE	V.1	229
Foresight:	Well; but my Consent I mean--You won't	304	FOR LOVE	V.1	282
Miss Prue:	O Father, why will you let him go? Won't you	305	FOR LOVE	V.1	300
Miss Prue:	long as she's an Old Woman? Indeed but I won't: For	305	FOR LOVE	V.1	306
Miss Prue:	won't get me one, I'll get one for my self: I'll marry our	305	FOR LOVE	V.1	316
Sr Sampson:	be even with you, I won't give you a Groat. Mr. Buckram is	308	FOR LOVE	V.1	424
	For a clear Stage won't do, without your Favour.	316	FOR LOVE	EPI.	44
Witwoud:	Wit: Nay, I'll do him Justice. I'm his Friend, I won't	403	WAY WORLD	I.1	291
Witwoud:	You shall see he won't go to 'em because there's no	405	WAY WORLD	I.1	363
Petulant:	Places. Pox on 'em I won't come.--Dee hear, tell 'em	405	WAY WORLD	I.1	386
Petulant:	I won't come.--Let 'em snivel and cry their Hearts	405	WAY WORLD	I.1	387
Witwoud:	she won't give an Eccho fair play; she has that everlasting	421	WAY WORLD	II.1	420
Millamant:	Faults--I can't bear it. Well, I won't have you Mirabell	422	WAY WORLD	II.1	456
Millamant:	Face. Ha, ha, ha--Well I won't laugh, don't let me	422	WAY WORLD	II.1	475
Lady Wish:	I won't be too coy neither.--I won't give him despair	429	WAY WORLD	III.1	163
Lady Wish:	Don't answer me. I won't know: I'll be surpriz'd. I'll be	429	WAY WORLD	III.1	173
Marwood:	For shame Mr. Witwoud; why won't you	437	WAY WORLD	III.1	480
Sir Wilful:	Impatient? Why then belike it won't stay, 'till	441	WAY WORLD	III.1	616
Lady Wish:	won't sit--I'll walk--aye I'll walk from the door upon his	445	WAY WORLD	IV.1	20
Millamant:	and dee hear, I won't be call'd names after I'm Married;	450	WAY WORLD	IV.1	194
Millamant:	positively I won't be call'd Names.	450	WAY WORLD	IV.1	195
Millamant:	thing you, I'll have you,--I won't be kiss'd, nor I won't be	452	WAY WORLD	IV.1	295

Wonder (23)

		PAGE	TITLE	ACT.SC	LINE
Sharper:	What in the name of wonder is it?	46	OLD BATCH	I.1	341
Belinda:	Filthy Fellow! I wonder Cousin--	55	OLD BATCH	II.2	19
Araminta:	I wonder Cousin you should imagine, I don't	55	OLD BATCH	II.2	20
Setter:	I shall Sir--I wonder to which of these two	64	OLD BATCH	III.1	137
Lucy:	I wonder thou hast the impudence to lock me in the	66	OLD BATCH	III.1	202
Bellmour:	I wonder why all our young Fellows should glory	75	OLD BATCH	IV.1	6
Sir Joseph:	I wonder at that, Madam, for 'tis most curious	90	OLD BATCH	IV.4	36
Cynthia:	Prodigious! I wonder, want of sleep, and so much	138	DOUBL DLR	II.1	5
Lady Froth:	Friend,--but really, as you say, I wonder too,--but	138	DOUBL DLR	II.1	9
Lord Touch:	I will--I am mute with wonder.	153	DOUBL DLR	III.1	121
Mellefont:	are very great with him, I wonder he never told you his	158	DOUBL DLR	III.1	293
Lady Ply:	I'm busie, Sir Paul, I wonder at your	163	DOUBL DLR	III.1	491
Lord Froth:	Where's the Wonder now?	166	DOUBL DLR	III.1	601
Lord Touch:	you stare as you were all amazed,--I don't wonder at it,--	202	DOUBL DLR	V.1	564

			PAGE	TITLE	ACT.SC	LINE

Wonder (continued)

Mellefont:	thou wonder of all Falsehood.	202	DOUEL DLR	V.1	571
	Forbear your Wonder, and the Fault forgive,	213	FOR LCVE	PRO.	20
Foresight:	a young Man, I wonder what he can do with it!	243	FOR LCVE	II.1	278
Osmyn-Alph:	There are no Wcnders, or else all is Wonder.	344	M. ERIDE	II.2	180
Fainall:	Now I remember, I wonder not they were weary	396	WAY WCRLD	I.1	49
Mirabell:	this is not a Cabal-night. I wonder, Fainall, that you who	399	WAY WCRLD	I.1	138
Mirabell:	I wonder there is not an Act of Parliament to save	400	WAY WCRLD	I.1	204
Millamant:	Well, an illiterate Man's my Aversion. I wonder	436	WAY WCRLD	III.1	422
Witwoud:	That I confess I wonder at too.	436	WAY WCRLD	III.1	425

Wcnderful (1)

Valentine:	nick'd it--But its wonderful strange, Jeremy!	282	FOR LCVE	IV.1	269

Wonders (3)

Manuel:	Of whose mute Valcur you relate such Wonders?	335	M. ERIDE	I.1	364
Leonora:	O Heav'n unfold these Wonders!	341	M. ERIDE	II.2 V	58
Osmyn-Alph:	There are no Wcnders, or else all is Wonder.	344	M. BRIDE	II.2	180

Wonnot (2)

Manuel:	I wonnot have the seeming of a Sorrow seen	334	M. ERIDE	I.1	322
Osmyn-Alph:	It wonnot be; O, impotence of Sight!	345	M. BRIDE	II.2	217

Wont (15)

Bellmour:	Why, you wont hear me with Patience.	59	OLD BATCH	II.2	160
Fondlewife:	buss poor Nykin--And I wont leave thee--I'le lose all first.	78	OLD BATCH	IV.1	118
Fondlewife:	Wcnt you Kiss Nykin?	78	OLD BATCH	IV.1	121
Fondlewife:	I wont be dealous--Poor Cocky, Kiss Nykin, Kiss	79	OLD BATCH	IV.1	135
Brisk:	I'm afraid that simile wont do in wet Weather--	164	DOUEL DLR	III.1	517
Lady Froth:	No, for the Sun it wont, but it will dc for the	164	DOUBL DLR	III.1	519
Lord Froth:	wont you joyn with us, we were laughing at my Lady	165	DOUBL DLR	III.1	559
Lady Froth:	Sapho, tho' my Lord wont.	167	DOUEL DLR	III.1	616
Lady Froth:	Wit, and can sing a Tune already. My Lord wont you go?	167	DOUEL DLR	III.1	620
Lady Froth:	Wont you? What not to see Saph? Pray, My Lord, come	167	DOUEL DLR	III.1	621
Cynthia:	My Mind gives me will not--because we are	168	DOUEL DLR	IV.1	11
Mellefont:	you wont baulk the Frollick?	168	DOUEL DLR	IV.1	42
Angelica:	Oh Heavens! You wont leave me alone with a	294	FOR LCVE	IV.1	693
Zara:	Is seen, or heard. A dreadful Din was wont	379	M. ERIDE	V.2	135
Lady Wish:	Yes, yes, I'll give the first Impression on a Couch--I wont	445	WAY WCRLD	IV.1	24

Woo (3)

Vainlove:	'Tis fit Men should be coy, when Women woo.	80	OLD BATCH	IV.1	191
Singer:	Cynthia frowns when e're I Woo her,	143	DOUEL DLR	II.1	179
Millamant:	will win me woo me now--Nay, if you are so tedious,	422	WAY WORLD	II.1	478

Wood-louse (1)

Witwoud:	Do, rap thy self up like a Wood-louse and dream	454	WAY WCRLD	IV.1	371

Wooden (1)

Lady Wish:	thee. Why dost thou not stir Puppet? thou wooden Thing	425	WAY WORLD	III.1	15

Wooing (1)

Singer:	The sad miscarriage of their Wocing:	71	OLD EATCH	III.2 V	21

Word (54)

Vainlove:	word--Had you been there or any Body 'thad been the	39	OLD BATCH	I.1	99
Sharper:	Word is sufficient any where: 'Tis but borrowing so much	50	OLD BATCH	II.1	108
Lucy:	word with you.	65	OLD BATCH	III.1	156
Capt Bluff:	must refund--or Bilbo's the Word, and Slaughter will	68	OLD BATCH	III.1	259
Sharper:	Hearkee, Sir Joseph, a word with ye--In consideration	69	OLD BATCH	III.1	302
Fondlewife:	Ha, how's that? Stay stay, did you leave word	76	OLD BATCH	IV.1	19
Sir Joseph:	and have not one Word to say.	85	OLD BATCH	IV.3	91
Fondlewife:	inclining to believe every word you say.	94	OLD BATCH	IV.4	186
Fondlewife:	go back of your word; you are not the Person I took you	94	OLD BATCH	IV.4	191
Bellmour:	a word on't.--But I can't help telling the truth, for my	95	OLD BATCH	IV.4	220
Setter:	(to Sharper). Sir, A Word with you.	99	OLD EATCH	V.1	91
Sir Joseph:	Setter. Nay, I'll take you at your Word.	103	OLD BATCH	V.1	237
Mellefont:	O' my word, Brisk, that was a home thrust; you	128	DOUEL DLR	I.1	31
Cynthia:	Why Faith, Madam, he that won't take my Word,	139	DOUEL DLR	II.1	43
Sir Paul:	word.	163	DOUEL DLR	III.1	490
Cynthia:	keep my word, and live a Maid for your sake.	169	DOUEL DLR	IV.1	62
Sir Paul:	speak a good word only just for me, Gads-bud only for	180	DOUEL DLR	IV.1	472
Careless:	--but all in vain, she would not hear a word upon that	180	DOUEL DLR	IV.1	500
Maskwell:	I have kept my word, he's here, but I must not be	185	DOUEL DLR	IV.2	90
Maskwell:	that he may not suspect one word on't.	190	DOUBL DLR	V.1	99
Maskwell:	word,--how the Devil she wrought my Lord into	190	DOUEL DLR	V.1	110
Valentine:	word?	221	FOR LCVE	I.1	179
Scandal:	would be to invent the honest means of keeping your word,	221	FOR LCVE	I.1	196
Valentine:	me word; If I will make a Deed of Conveyance of my Right	225	FOR LCVE	I.1	335
Tattle:	that--Nay more (I'm going to say a bold Word now) I	227	FOR LCVE	I.1	410
Tattle:	Not a word as I hope to be sav'd; an errant Lapsus Linguae	228	FOR LCVE	I.1	442
Mrs Frail:	--I can't believe a word he says.	233	FOR LCVE	I.1	621
Tattle:	Word of your Ladyships Passion, till this instant.	254	FOR LCVE	III.1	56
Sr Sampson:	Years; I writ you word, when you were at Legorne.	261	FOR LCVE	III.1	293
Ben:	gav'n that wipe--He had'nt a word to say, and so I left 'n,	286	FOR LCVE	IV.1	385
Valentine:	not a word. Hymen shall put his Torch into a dark Lanthorn,	290	FCB LCVE	IV.1	549
Foresight:	presently, till farther Orders from me--not a Word	306	FOR LCVE	V.1	325
Almeria:	By any Action, Word or Thought, to wed	330	M. ERIDE	I.1	186
Almeria:	Upon my Word no more,	331	M. EBIDE	I.1	206
Garcia:	'Tis scarce above a word; as he were born	335	M. ERIDE	I.1	372
Osmyn-Alph:	But 'tis torn off--why should that Word alone	350	M. ERIDE	III.1	22
Osmyn-Alph:	Hard Means, to ratifie that Word!--O Cruelty!	355	M. ERIDE	III.1	249
Manuel:	Watch her returning Sense, and bring me Word:	370	M. ERIDE	IV.1	365
Gonsalez:	Thanks; and I take thee at thy Word. Thou'st seen	372	M. BRIDE	IV.1	432
Zara:	I can but die with thee to keep my Word.	376	M. BRIDE	V.1	139
Petulant:	clash; snugs the Word, I shrug and am silent.	407	WAY WCRLD	I.1	447
Mrs Fain:	Immediately; I have a Word or two for Mr.	421	WAY WORLD	II.1	425
Foible:	Uncle; (he does not suspect a Word of your Ladyship;)	428	WAY WORLD	III.1	113
Lady Wish:	I will; I value your Judgment extreamly. On my Word	432	WAY WORLD	III.1	271
Sir Wilful:	Hold ye, hear me Friend; a Word with you in	437	WAY WORLD	III.1	468
Millamant:	now, and don't say a word.	452	WAY WORLD	IV.1	296
Millamant:	now, don't say a word.	452	WAY WORLD	IV.1 V	297
Sir Wilful:	Word, and I'll do't--Wilfull will do't, that's the Word--	455	WAY WORLD	IV.1	404
Lady Wish:	'tis with drinking your Health--O' my Word you are	455	WAY WORLD	IV.1	407
Sir Wilful:	Marry'd, say the Word, and send for the Piper, Wilfull	455	WAY WORLD	IV.1	411

World   (continued)
		PAGE	TITLE	ACT.SC	LINE
Maskwell:	Mercy on us, What will the Wickedness of this World	155	DOUEL DLR	III.1	196
Lady Ply:	privacy? I swear and declare in the face of the World I'm	159	DOUEL DLR	III.1	332
Lady Ply:	rather attempt it than any thing in the World, (Curtesies)	159	DOUEL DLR	III.1	341
Lady Ply:	for I'm sure there's nothing in the World that I would	159	DOUEL DLR	III.1	342
Lady Ply:	face cf the World that no body is more sensible of Favours	159	DOUEL DLR	III.1	351
Lady Ply:	you, Mr. Careless I don't know any thing in the World I	159	DOUEL DLR	III.1	353
Sir Paul:	man in the World; indeed that touches me near, very near.	161	DOUEL DLR	III.1	405
Sir Paul:	touch a Man for the World--at least not abcve once a	162	DOUEL DLR	III.1	433
Careless:	World.	162	DOUEL DLR	III.1	443
Lord Froth:	the World--you are never pleased but when we are all	162	DOUEL DLR	III.1	458
Cynthia:	think they are all in good nature with the World, and only	163	DOUEL DLR	III.1	482
Lord Froth:	had brought the Ape into the World her self.	165	DOUEL DLR	III.1	566
Lady Froth:	Three Quarters, but I swear she has a World of	167	DOUEL DLR	III.1	619
Cynthia:	Why shculd I call 'em Fools? The World thinks better of	167	DOUEL DLR	III.1	626
Cynthia:	Conversation are receiv'd and admir'd by the World--	167	DOUEL DLR	III.1	628
Lady Ply:	declare in the face of the World, never any body gain'd so	169	DOUEL DLR	IV.1	72
Lady Ply:	The last of any Man in the World, by my purity;	169	DOUEL DLR	IV.1	78
Lady Ply:	Conscience, or Hcnour, or any thing in the World.--	172	DOUEL DLR	IV.1	170
Sir Paul:	any of my Family that will bring Children into the World.	173	DOUEL DLR	IV.1	227
Sir Paul:	Estate would be left to the wide World, he? I hope you	174	DOUEL DLR	IV.1	254
Sir Paul:	know whether there be any thing at all in the World, or	179	DOUEL DLR	IV.1	450
Lord Touch:	World, and share my Fortunes.	182	DOUEL DLR	IV.1	564
Lady Touch:	immediate Lightning blast thee, me and the whole World	184	DOUEL DLR	IV.2	45
Maskwell:	World cf Love, cou'd be confin'd within the puny Province	199	DOUBL DLR	V.1	432
Maskwell:	gratifie your taste, and cheat the World, to prove a				
	faithful	199	DOUEL DLR	V.1	438
	As Nature gave the World to Man's first Age,	213	FOR LOVE	PRO.	13
	And tc our World, such Plenty ycu afford,	213	FOR LCVE	PRO.	16
Jeremy:	won't have a Friend left in the World, if you turn Poet	218	FOR LCVE	I.1	86
Scandal:	Rail? At whom? the whcle World? Impotent and	219	FOR LCVE	I.1	138
Valentine:	the Wcrld say of me, and of my forc'd Confinement?	220	FOR LCVE	I.1	158
Valentine:	the World say of me, and my forc'd Confinement?	220	FOR LCVE	I.1	V158
Scandal:	The Wcrld behaves it self, as it used to do on such	220	FOR LCVE	I.1	159
Scandal:	The Wcrld behaves it self, as it uses to do on such	220	FOR LCVE	I.1	V159
Valentine:	World: You have heard of a Booby-Brother of mine, that	225	FOR LCVE	I.1	332
Tattle:	him, that the World shall think the better of any Person	226	FOR LCVE	I.1	392
Tattle:	one and t'other, and every thing in the World; and, says I,	227	FCR LCVE	I.1	432
Mrs Frail:	You are the most mistaken in the World; there is	231	FCB LCVE	I.1	562
Angelica:	Siege? What a World of Fire and Candle, Matches and	237	FCR LCVE	II.1	81
Sr Sampson:	What brought you into the World? How came you here,	244	FOR LCVE	II.1	327
Sr Sampson:	Did you come a Voluntier into the World? Or did I	244	FCR LCVE	II.1	330
Sr Sampson:	go naked out of the World as you came into't.	244	FOR LCVE	II.1	338
Jeremy:	and I came up Stairs into the World; for I was born	245	FOR LCVE	II.1	381
Foresight:	World too, Friend.	245	FOR LCVE	II.1	384
Mrs Frail:	and speak openly one to another; I'm afraid the World	248	FOR LCVE	II.1	487
Tattle:	Oh Lord, I swear I wou'd not for the World--	250	FOR LCVE	II.1	553
Mrs Fore:	world to answer for, remember I wash my Bands of it,	251	FOR LCVE	II.1	578
Tattle:	most unfortunate Man in the World, and the most cruelly	255	FOR LCVE	III.1	82
Scandal:	little, yet says he has a World to say. Asks for his Father	266	FCR LCVE	III.1	498
Scandal:	upon the world.	272	FOR LCVE	III.1	701
Ben:	He, he, he; why that's true; just so for all the World it	273	FOR LCVE	III.1	721
Angelica:	trick--I'll try--I would disguise to all the World a	277	FOR LCVE	IV.1	54
Valentine:	It may be so--I did not know you--the World	280	FOR LCVE	IV.1	159
Valentine:	strange! But I am Truth, and come to give the World	280	FCB LCVE	IV.1	164
Valentine:	two greatest Monsters in the World are a Man and a	282	FOR LCVE	IV.1	263
Sr Sampson:	pox cn't, that I that know the World, and Men and	283	FOR LCVE	IV.1	286
Sr Sampson:	Fool in the Eye of the World, is a very hard Task. But,	299	FOR LCVE	V.1	67
Angelica:	Censure of the World: And she that marries a very Witty	299	FOR LCVE	V.1	72
Angelica:	O fie, Sir Sampscn, what would the World say?	300	FOR LOVE	V.1	117
Miss Prue:	thing, till I'm as tired as any thing in the World.	303	FOR LCVE	V.1	224
Tattle:	World we are.	309	FOR LCVE	V.1	443
Tattle:	The least in the World--That is for my Part, I	309	FCB LCVE	V.1	463
Angelica:	(to Valentine). Bad I the World to give you, it	312	FCB LCVE	V.1	560
Almeria:	Of that refulgent World, where I shall swim	340	M. BBIDE	II.2	27
Osmyn-Alph:	One, driv'n about the World like blasted Leaves	351	M. EBIDE	III.1	59
Osmyn-Alph:	And waking to the World and mortal Sense,	353	M. EBIDE	III.1	134
Almeria:	With Thee, the kneeling World should beg in vain	382	M. EBIDE	V.2	263
Witwoud:	Lady? Gad, I say any thing in the World to get this Fellow	402	WAY WCRLD	I.1	255
Witwoud:	World.	402	WAY WCRLD	I.1	260
Witwoud:	in the World,--he wou'd not be altogether contemptible.	403	WAY WORLD	I.1	293
Petulant:	--But there are Uncles and Nephews in the World	406	WAY WCRLD	I.1	429
Marwood:	the Wcrld the Injuries you have done me, both in my	415	WAY WCRLD	II.1	195
Fainall:	ways of Wedlock and this World. Will you yet be	415	WAY WCRLD	II.1	214
Fainall:	I would not hurt you for the World. Have I no	416	WAY WCRLD	II.1	227
Marwood:	self and the whole treacherous World.	416	WAY WCRLD	II.1	238
Fainall:	where to another World. I'll marry thee--Be pacify'd	416	WAY WCRLD	II.1	246
Millamant:	Complaisance for all the World beside. I swear, I never	433	WAY WCRLD	III.1	337
Fainall:	in the Way of the World. 'S death	442	WAY WORLD	III.1	631
Waitwell:	before I die--I wou'd gladly go out of the World with	458	WAY WORLD	IV.1	502
Lady Wish:	reconcile me to the bad World, or else I wou'd retire to	465	WAY WCRLD	V.1	132
Lady Wish:	and Purling Streams. Dear Marwood, let us leave the World,	465	WAY WCRLD	V.1	134
Lady Wish:	brought into the World.	465	WAY WCRLD	V.1	146
Mrs Fain:	so shall the World at a time Convenient.	466	WAY WCRLD	V.1	159
Fainall:	the way of the World. That shall not urge me to relinquish	474	WAY WCRLD	V.1	476
Mirabell:	Even sc Sir, 'tis the way of the World, Sir: of the	476	WAY WORLD	V.1	553
Mirabell:	Widdows of the World. I suppose this Deed may bear an	476	WAY WORLD	V.1	554

World's (3)
Mrs Frail:	The World's end! What, do you mean to banter	247	FOR LOVE	II.1	448
Mrs Fore:	You never were at the World's End?	247	FOR LOVE	II.1	456
Osmyn-Alph:	For this World's Bule, I wou'd nct wound thy	356	M. EBIDE	III.1	275

World's-End (2)
Mrs Fore:	World's-End.	247	FOR LOVE	II.1	447
Mrs Fore:	place call'd the World's-End? I'll swear you can keep your	247	FOR LCVE	II.1	451

Worldly (2)
Setter:	Why how now! prithee who art? lay by that Worldly	65	OLD BATCH	III.1	179

Worldly   (continued)
Scandal: Worldly Lucre carry you beyond your Judgment, nor   . . . 268 FOR LOVE   III.1 555
Worlds (1)
Fainall: and weep like Alexander, when he wanted other Worlds to   . 413 WAY WORLD II.1 116
Worms (1)
Leonora: Yet fresh and unconsum'd by Time, or Worms.   . . . . . 340 M. BRIDE   II.2   8
Worn (9)
Lucy: Strike Heartwell home, before the Bait's worn off the   . . 61 OLD BATCH III.1   10
Jeremy: Porter, worn out with pimping, and carrying Billet doux . 218 FOR LOVE   I.1   96
Valentine: and the Divine Part of me, my Mind, has worn this   . . 294 FOR LOVE   IV.1 702
Angelica: Coldness which I have always worn before you, should   . 313 FOR LOVE   V.1   606
Manuel: To see that Sable worn upon the Day   . . . . 333 M. BRIDE   I.1   295
Manuel: As they had wept in Blood, and worn the Night   . . . 367 M. BRIDE   IV.1 249
Mirabell: Care is taken for that--She is won and worn   . . . . 417 WAY WORLD II.1 288
Marwood: wou'd now and then find Days of Grace, and be worn for . 433 WAY WORLD III.1 302
Fainall: Encrease of fortune,--I cou'd have worn 'em tipt with   . 442 WAY WORLD III.1 646
Worn-out (1)
Jeremy: In the Form of a worn-out Punk, with Verses in her Hand, . 219 FOR LOVE   I.1   108
Wornout (1)
Scandal: and imperfect Lover; 'tis the last glimpse of Love to
wornout   . . . . 275 FOR LOVE   III.1 816
Worry'd (1)
Marwood: reputation worry'd at the Barr by a pack of Bawling   . 467 WAY WORLD V.1   210
Worse (18)
Lucy: Neither; but what was ten times worse, with damn'd,   . . 61 OLD BATCH III.1   18
Lady Touch: and can believe any thing worse, if it were laid to his
charge   . . . . 151 DOUBL DLR III.1   41
Nay, and what's worse, an Executioner.   . . . . . 204 DOUBL DLR EPI.   14
Scandal: Old Woman, any thing but Poet; a Modern Poet is worse, . 220 FOR LOVE   I.1   146
Angelica: --Nay, I know something worse, if I would   . . . . . 238 FOR LOVE   II.1 111
Mrs Fore: You have been at a worse place.   . . . . 247 FOR LOVE   II.1 444
Mrs Frail: I at a worse place, and with a man!   . . . . 247 FOR LOVE   II.1 445
Mrs Frail: (to her). Aye, aye, it's well it's no worse--Nay,   . 310 FOR LOVE   V.1   471
Still they proceed, and, at our Charge, write worse;   . 323 M. BRIDE   PRO.   23
Mirabell: Witwoud and Petulant; and what was worse, her   . . . 395 WAY WORLD I.1   22
Witwoud: from one Poet to another. And what's worse, 'tis as sure a . 401 WAY WORLD I.1   247
Witwoud: has been told; and you know she hates Mirabell, worse than . 408 WAY WORLD I.1   484
Mirabell: to the Occasion; a worse had not answer'd to the Purpose. . 417 WAY WORLD II.1 276
Mirabell: Your Health! Is there a worse Disease than the   . . . 421 WAY WORLD II.1 443
Marwood: worse than when you had her--I dare swear she had given . 442 WAY WORLD III.1 651
Waitwell: fare the worse for't--I shall have no appetite to   . 459 WAY WORLD IV.1 561
Lady Wish: Worse and Worse.   . . . . 468 WAY WORLD V.1   228
Worship (8)   see Mock-Worship
Sir Joseph: and a Man of Worship.   . . . . 101 OLD BATCH V.1   194
Boy: 'Tis directed to your Worship.   . . . . 161 DOUBL DLR III.1 397
Lady Touch: trusty Villain! I could worship thee.   . . . . . 199 DOUBL DLR V.1   455
Nurse: Pray Heav'n send your Worship good Luck, Marry   . . . 235 FOR LOVE   II.1   26
Nurse: Doings with my Masters Worship--Why, did you   . . . 238 FOR LOVE   II.1 100
Jeremy: begot me too:--Nay, and to tell your Worship   . . . . 245 FOR LOVE   II.1 361
Angelica: pretend to Worship, but have neither Zeal nor Faith: . 314 FOR LOVE   V.1   632
Foible: Ladyship's Feet and worship the Original.   . . . . . 423 WAY WORLD II.1 524
Worship's (2)
Setter: She was pumping me about how your Worship's Affairs   . . 99 OLD BATCH V.1   113
Nurse: What is your Worship's Pleasure?   . . . . 305 FOR LOVE   V.1   323
Worshipping (1)
Foible: Well, if worshipping of Pictures be a Sin   . . . . . 427 WAY WORLD III.1   77
Worst (11)
Sharper: 'Tis but trying, and being where I am at worst,   . . . 48 OLD BATCH II.1   16
Silvia: The worst of me, is, that I am your Wife--   . . . . 111 OLD BATCH V.2   133
For 'tis our way (you know) for fear o'th' worst,   . . 113 OLD BATCH EPI.   21
For if his Muse has play'd him false, the worst   . . . 125 DOUBL DLR PRO.   33
Valentine: Road is the worst way you can go--He that follows   . . 282 FOR LOVE   IV.1 253
Almeria: Am I, am I of all thy Woes the worst?   . . . . . 357 M. BRIDE   III.1 303
Sure scribbling Fools, call'd Poets, fare the worst.   . 393 WAY WORLD PRO.   2
Marwood: then know the worst; and be out of his Pain; but I wou'd . 411 WAY WORLD II.1   62
Foible: Nay, if that had been the worst I cou'd have born: But he . 427 WAY WORLD III.1   89
Fainall: If the worst come to the worst,--I'll turn my   . . . 444 WAY WORLD III.1 708
Worth (20)   see Penny-worth
Bellmour: worth your acquaintance--a little of thy Chymistry Tom, . 46 OLD BATCH I.1   345
Heartwell: worth for the purchase of thy Love--Say, is it mine then, . 72 OLD BATCH III.2   39
Bellmour: Nay, 'Faith, Madam, 'tis a pleasant one; and worth   . . 82 OLD BATCH IV.2   48
Setter: Person of Worth; be true to thy Trust, and be reputed   . 102 OLD BATCH V.1   227
Araminta: no need to forgive what is not worth my Anger.   . . . 106 OLD BATCH V.1   363
Lord Touch: shalt have due reward of all thy worth. Give me thy hand . 189 DOUBL DLR V.1   56
Lord Touch: Thou shalt enjoy it--if all I'm worth in   . . . . . 189 DOUBL DLR V.1   74
Lord Touch: worth your hearing.   . . . . 197 DOUBL DLR V.1   366
Cynthia: be worth your hearing.   . . . . 197 DOUBL DLR V.1   368
Valentine: A very rich Man.--Not worth a Groat.   . . . . . . 216 FOR LOVE   I.1   20
Sr Sampson: him; he is not worth your Consideration. The Rogue has . 259 FOR LOVE   III.1 240
Valentine: worth must pay for the Confession of my Senses; I'm   . 296 FOR LOVE   IV.1 773
Sr Sampson: ne're a young Fellow worth hanging--that's a very   . . 299 FOR LOVE   V.1   54
Sr Sampson: ne're a young Fellow worth hanging--that is a very   . . 299 FOR LOVE   V.1 V 54
Almeria: His Worth, his Truth, and Tenderness of Love.   . . . 328 M. BRIDE   I.1   103
Almeria: I doubt not of the Worth of Garcia's Deeds, ... 332 M. BRIDE   I.1   259
Osmyn-Alph: Will treasure here; more worth than Diadems,   . . . 353 M. BRIDE   III.1 137
Osmyn-Alph: I'll treasure as more worth than Diadems, ... 353 M. BRIDE   III.1 V137
Fainall: her of all she's worth, and we'll retire somewhere, any . 416 WAY WORLD V.1   245
Fainall: Not while you are worth a Groat, indeed my dear.   . . 475 WAY WORLD V.1   502
Worthless (2)
Scandal: worthless great Men, and dull rich Rogues, avoid a witty . 219 FOR LOVE   I.1   132
Gonsalez: O let me prostrate, pay my worthless Thanks   . . . . 334 M. BRIDE   I.1   338
Worths (0)   see Penny-worths
Worthy (11)
Lucy: may discover something in my Masque--Worthy Sir, a   . . 65 OLD BATCH III.1 155
Sir Joseph: let these worthy Gentlemen intercede for me.   . . . . 103 OLD BATCH V.1   245
Brisk: me perish, do I never say any thing worthy to be Laugh'd . 132 DOUBL DLR I.1   195

Worthy   (continued)

Maskwell:	and what is yet better, I have served a worthy Lord to	188	DOUEL DLR	V.1	25
Valentine:	more than Love, to make me worthy of you.	295	FOR LCVE	IV.1	727
Sr Sampson:	Madam, all my Affairs are scarce worthy to be laid at	299	FOR LCVE	V.1	94
Angelica:	cou'd not make me worthy of so generous and faithful a	312	FOR LCVE	V.1	561
Leonora:	By all the worthy and indulgent ways,	327	M. BBIDE	I.1	46
Manuel:	Worthy to be your Husband, and my Son.	334	M. BBIDE	I.1	334
Zara:	Worthy your private Ear, and this your Minister.	364	M. BBIDE	IV.1	130
Manuel:	In me, that can be worthy so great Services?	365	M. BBIDE	IV.1	158

Wou'd (161)

Belinda:	so bedeck'd, you wou'd have taken 'em for Friezland-Hens,	84	OLD BATCH	IV.3	29
Araminta:	Bless me, Cousin! Why wou'd you affront any	84	OLD BATCH	IV.3	35
Bellmour:	us.--I wou'd unrig.	96	OLD BATCH	V.1	7
Bellmour:	quickly, I'll follow you:--I wou'd not be known. (Exit	97	OLD BATCH	V.1	11
Sharper:	Now, were I ill-natur'd, wou'd I utterly disappoint	100	OLD BATCH	V.1	137
Setter:	Captain, I wou'd do any thing to serve you; but this	104	OLD BATCH	V.1	274
Heartwell:	And who wou'd you visit there, say you? (O'ons,	104	OLD BATCH	V.1	289
Araminta:	how insolent wou'd a real Pardon make you? But there's	106	OLD BATCH	V.1	362
Belinda:	Courtship, one wou'd think you meant a noble Entertainment:	106	OLD BATCH	V.1	373
Lord Touch:	Plyant has a large Eye, and wou'd centre every thing in	151	DOUEL DLR	III.1	6
Lady Touch:	His Defence! bless me, wou'd you have me	151	DOUEL DLR	III.1	31
Sir Paul:	you wou'd be private?	159	DOUBL DLB	III.1	322
Maskwell:	then were fine work indeed! her fury wou'd spare nothing,	190	DOUEL DLR	V.1	93
Jeremy:	suspicious Fellows like lawful Pads, that wou'd knock	221	FOR LCVE	I.1	203
Mrs Frail:	Unlucky Day, and wou'd not let me come abroad: But I	231	FOR LCVE	I.1	581
Scandal:	No, no; come to me if you wou'd see Pictures.	232	FOR LCVE	I.1	615
Foresight:	What, wou'd you be gadding too? Sure all Females	236	FOR LOVE	II.1	46
Sr Sampson:	By the Horns of the Moon, you wou'd say,	241	FOB LCVE	II.1	233
Sr Sampson:	wou'd my Son were an Egyptian Mummy for thy sake.	242	FOR LCVE	II.1	245
Sr Sampson:	How now, who sent for you? Ha! what wou'd you	242	FOR LCVE	II.1	261
Valentine:	Why, Sir, that you wou'd not go to the extremity	243	FCB LCVE	II.1	287
Sr Sampson:	and my Fatherly fondness wou'd fit like two Tallies.--	243	FOR LCVE	II.1	294
Sr Sampson:	What, wou'd you have your Mother a Whore!	244	FOR LCVE	II.1	318
Valentine:	provide for me, I desire you wou'd leave me as you found	244	FOR LCVE	II.1	335
Sr Sampson:	--If I had it again, I wou'd not give thee a Groat,	246	FOR LCVE	II.1	397
Jeremy:	I told you what your Visit wou'd come to.	246	FOB LCVE	II.1	406
Mrs Fore:	Besides, it wou'd not only reflect upon you, Sister, but me.	247	FOR LCVE	II.1	434
Mrs Fore:	Play the first day,--I warrant it wou'd break Mr. Tattle's	250	FOR LCVE	II.1	550
Tattle:	Oh Lord, I swear I wou'd not for the World--	250	FOR LCVE	II.1	553
Mrs Fore:	So he wou'd--but then leaving 'em	250	FOR LCVE	II.1	573
Angelica:	wou'd if you cou'd, no doubt on't.	255	FCB LOVE	III.1	95
Scandal:	wou'd have told me; I find, Madam, you don't know	256	FOR LOVE	III.1	110
Tattle:	find: For sure my intimate Friends wou'd have known--	256	FOR LCVE	III.1	113
Tattle:	He wou'd have brought me into the Spiritual Court, but	258	FCB LCVE	III.1	171
Mrs Frail:	That wou'd be pity, such a Handsome Young	261	FOR LCVE	III.1	304
Ben:	and may hap may'nt get 'em out again when he wou'd.	261	FOR LCVE	III.1	313
Ben:	you Mistress, wou'd you like going to Sea? Mess you're a	262	FCB LCVE	III.1	326
Scandal:	I prophesie it, and I wou'd not have the Fate of Cassandra,	268	FOR LCVE	III.1	546
Foresight:	I thank you, Mr. Scandal, indeed that wou'd be a	271	FOR LCVE	III.1	653
Scandal:	Domestick Thief; and he that wou'd secure his Pleasure,	271	FOR LGVE	III.1	676
Scandal:	Come, I know what you wou'd say,--you think	272	FOR LCVE	III.1	694
Mrs Frail:	wou'd not venture all in one Bottom.	273	FCB LCVE	III.1	724
Angelica:	tell me, for you know what I wou'd ask?	277	FOR LOVE	IV.1	60
Sr Sampson:	not foresee that the Moon wou'd predominate, and my	283	FOR LCVE	IV.1	281
Mrs Fore:	Last Night! and what wou'd your Impudence	284	FOR LCVE	IV.1	318
Ben:	Nay, nay, my mind run upon you,--but I wou'd not	285	FOR LCVE	IV.1	379
Ben:	and Kissing and Hugging, what wou'd you sheer off so?	286	FOR LCVE	IV.1	418
Ben:	wou'd you, and leave me aground?	286	FOR LCVE	IV.1	419
Ben:	Husband! Gad I wou'd not be your Husband, if you	287	FCR LCVE	IV.1	429
Ben:	wou'd have me; now I know your mind, tho'f you had	287	FOR LCVE	IV.1	430
Angelica:	Effects, I wou'd have striven; but that's too late.	294	FOR LCVE	IV.1	713
Angelica:	Wou'd any thing, but a Madman ccmplain of	296	FOR LCVE	IV.1	785
Sr Sampson:	wou'd she wou'd like me, then I shou'd hamper my ycung	298	FOR LCVE	V.1	49
Sr Sampson:	Rogues: Odd, wou'd she wou'd; faith and troth she's	298	FOR LCVE	V.1	50
Sr Sampson:	How, Madam! Wou'd I cou'd prove it.	299	FOR LCVE	V.1	89
Angelica:	thing that wou'd make me appear to be too much concern'd	299	FOR LOVE	V.1	91
Sr Sampson:	wou'd take my Advice in a Husband--	300	FOR LCVE	V.1	104
Tattle:	And sc you wou'd infer, that you and I are alike--	304	FOR LOVE	V.1	262
Tattle:	and I have a Secret in my Heart, which you wou'd be glad	305	FOR LCVE	V.1	289
Miss Prue:	Man; and if I can't have one, I wou'd go to sleep all my	305	FOR LCVE	V.1	309
Ben:	believe the Devil wou'd not venture aboard o' your	309	FOR LCVE	V.1	435
Tattle:	this Company wou'd speak of it.	310	FCB LCVE	V.1	477
Valentine:	I have heard as much, Sir; but I wou'd have it from	311	FOR LCVE	V.1	520
	He wou'd not lose thro' Prejudice his Cause;	324	M. BBIDE	PRO.	41
	Nor wou'd obtain precariously Applause.	324	M. EBIDE	PRO.	42
Almeria:	His fatal Refuge--Wou'd that I had fall'n	329	M. BBIDE	I.1	V117
Almeria:	They wou'd have marry'd me; but I had sworn	343	M. BBIDE	II.2	126
Almeria:	To Heav'n and thee; and sooner wou'd have dy'd--	343	M. EBIDE	II.2	127
Almeria:	Indeed I wou'd--Nay, I wou'd tell thee all	343	M. BBIDE	II.2	129
Osmyn-Alph:	With Grief, as wou'd draw Tears from Inhumanity.	352	M. BBIDE	III.1	115
Osmyn-Alph:	For this World's Rule, I wou'd not wound thy	356	M. BBIDE	III.1	275
Osmyn-Alph:	Grief wou'd not double thus, his Darts against me.	356	M. BBIDE	III.1	283
Fainall:	wou'd tempt the patience of a Stoick. What, some Coxcomb	395	WAY WORLD	I.1	19
Mirabell:	Woman wou'd be odious, serve but to make her more	399	WAY WORLD	I.1	162
Fainall:	Commendation wou'd go near to make me either Vain	402	WAY WORLD	I.1	262
Mirabell:	You had better step and ask his Wife; if you wou'd	402	WAY WORLD	I.1	266
Witwoud:	Come, come, you are malicious now, and wou'd	403	WAY WORLD	I.1	287
Witwoud:	in the World,--he wou'd not be altogether contemptible.	403	WAY WCRLD	I.1	293
Witwoud:	Mean, why he wou'd slip you out of this Chocolate-house,	405	WAY WORLD	I.1	369
Witwoud:	to the Door again in a trice; where he wou'd send in for	405	WAY WORLD	I.1	374
Witwoud:	wou'd come off--Ha, ha, ha; Gad I can't be angry	406	WAY WORLD	I.1	410
Mirabell:	Fame, wou'd shew as dim by these as a dead Whiting's	407	WAY WORLD	I.1	454
Mirabell:	Eye, by a Pearl of Orient; he wcu'd no more be seen by	407	WAY WORLD	I.1	455
Witwoud:	Mirabell wou'd be in some sort unfortunately fobb'd	408	WAY WORLD	I.1	489
Marwood:	O if he shou'd ever discover it, he wou'd	411	WAY WORLD	II.1	61
Marwood:	then know the worst; and be out of his Pain; but I wou'd	411	WAY WCRLD	II.1	62

Wou'd (continued)

Speaker	Quotation	PAGE	TITLE	ACT.SC	LINE
Mrs Fain:	Ingenious Mischief! Wou'd thou wert married	411	WAY WORLD	II.1	65
Marwood:	Wou'd I were.	411	WAY WORLD	II.1	67
Mrs Fain:	wou'd think it dissembl'd; for you have laid a Fault to	412	WAY WORLD	II.1	75
Mrs Fain:	pleasant Relation last Night: I wou'd fain hear it out.	412	WAY WORLD	II.1	99
Fainall:	You wou'd intimate then, as if there were a	413	WAY WORLD	II.1	126
Marwood:	she wou'd be thought.	413	WAY WORLD	II.1	129
Fainall:	Fortune; which then wou'd have descended to my Wife;--	415	WAY WORLD	II.1	205
Marwood:	and next to the Guilt with which you wou'd asperse me, I	415	WAY WORLD	II.1	220
Mrs Fain:	without Bounds, and wou'd you set Limits to that Aversion,	417	WAY WORLD	II.1	262
Mirabell:	Waitwell and Foible. I wou'd not tempt my Servant	417	WAY WORLD	II.1	291
Mirabell:	Yes, I think the good Lady wou'd marry any	418	WAY WORLD	II.1	311
Millamant:	. . . I fancy ones Hair wou'd not	419	WAY WORLD	II.1	V366
Mirabell:	You wou'd affect a Cruelty which is not in your	420	WAY WORLD	II.1	383
Mirabell:	I wou'd beg a little private Audience too--	421	WAY WORLD	II.1	427
Millamant:	Ha, ha, ha. What wou'd you give, that you cou'd help	422	WAY WORLD	II.1	458
Mirabell:	You are merry, Madam, but I wou'd perswade you	422	WAY WORLD	II.1	470
Foible:	I wou'd put her Ladyship's Picture in my Pocket to shew	423	WAY WORLD	II.1	521
Lady Wish:	O, he carries Poyson in his Tongue that wou'd	426	WAY WORLD	III.1	57
Foible:	Account, I'm sure you wou'd not suspect my Fidelity.	427	WAY WORLD	III.1	88
Lady Wish:	Audacious Villain! handle me, wou'd he durst	428	WAY WORLD	III.1	117
Foible:	of his success. I wou'd be seen as little as possible to speak	430	WAY WORLD	III.1	215
Marwood:	Woman! The Devil's an Ass: If I were a Painter, I wou'd	431	WAY WORLD	III.1	236
Marwood:	Methinks Mrs. Millamant and he wou'd make	432	WAY WORLD	III.1	266
Millamant:	Witwoud and he wou'd have quarrell'd.	432	WAY WORLD	III.1	294
Mincing:	I vow Mem, I thought once they wou'd have fit.	432	WAY WORLD	III.1	295
Marwood:	wou'd now and then find Days of Grace, and be worn for	433	WAY WORLD	III.1	302
Millamant:	I could consent to wear 'em, if they wou'd wear	433	WAY WORLD	III.1	304
Marwood:	you wou'd but appear bare fac'd now, and own Mirabell;	433	WAY WORLD	III.1	314
Millamant:	think he wou'd obey me; I wou'd command him to shew	433	WAY WORLD	III.1	339
Millamant:	sing the Song, I wou'd have learnt Yesterday. You shall	434	WAY WORLD	III.1	371
Witwoud:	this Fellow wou'd have bound me to a Maker of Felts.	440	WAY WORLD	III.1	562
Sir Wilful:	you wou'd have been in the fashion too, and have remember'd	441	WAY WORLD	III.1	603
Lady Wish:	Fie, fie, Nephew, you wou'd not pull off your	441	WAY WORLD	III.1	620
Fainall:	never lov'd her, or if I had, why that wou'd have been over	443	WAY WORLD	III.1	679
Sir Wilful:	troublesome, I wou'd have sought a walk with you.	448	WAY WORLD	IV.1	117
Mirabell:	Wou'd you have 'em both before Marriage? Or	449	WAY WORLD	IV.1	182
Mrs Fain:	wou'd fall into fits, and maybe not recover time enough to	452	WAY WORLD	IV.1	301
Sir Wilful:	but if you wou'd have me Marry my Cozen,--say the	455	WAY WORLD	IV.1	403
Waitwell:	and Poison me,--and I wou'd willingly starve him	458	WAY WORLD	IV.1	501
Waitwell:	before I die--I wou'd gladly go out of the World with	458	WAY WORLD	IV.1	502
Waitwell:	that Satisfaction.--That wou'd be some Comfort to	458	WAY WORLD	IV.1	503
Lady Wish:	Is he so Unnatural say you? truely I wou'd	458	WAY WORLD	IV.1	506
Lady Wish:	a Person who wou'd suffer racks in honour's cause, dear	459	WAY WORLD	IV.1	553
Lady Wish:	Letter--I wou'd open it in your presence, because I	460	WAY WORLD	IV.1	570
Lady Wish:	wou'd not make you Uneasie. If it shou'd make you	460	WAY WORLD	IV.1	571
Lady Wish:	Uneasie I wou'd burn it--speak if it do's--but	460	WAY WORLD	IV.1	572
Foible:	Chamber, but I wou'd not tell your Lady-ship to	461	WAY WORLD	IV.1	619
Foible:	Law in that case before I wou'd meddle or make.	463	WAY WORLD	V.1	45
Mincing:	My Lady wou'd speak with Mrs. Foible, Mem. Mr.	464	WAY WORLD	V.1	104
Mincing:	Foible; and wou'd you hide your self in my Lady's	465	WAY WORLD	V.1	106
Lady Wish:	reconcile me to the bad World, or else I wou'd retire to	465	WAY WORLD	V.1	132
Marwood:	More Temper wou'd look more like Innocence. But I have	466	WAY WORLD	V.1	161
Lady Wish:	wou'd ha' shriek'd, If she had but seen a Man, till she was	466	WAY WORLD	V.1	187
Lady Wish:	I warrant you, or she wou'd never have born	467	WAY WORLD	V.1	196
Lady Wish:	the Bases roar Blasphemy. O, she wou'd have swooned at	467	WAY WORLD	V.1	201
Marwood:	Nay this is nothing; if it wou'd end here,	468	WAY WORLD	V.1	229
Lady Wish:	this Barbarian, But she wou'd have him, tho' her Year was	469	WAY WORLD	V.1	303
Sir Wilful:	--S'heart! and I'm sorry for't. What wou'd you have?	470	WAY WORLD	V.1	315
Marwood:	This is precious Fooling, if it wou'd pass, but	471	WAY WORLD	V.1	354
Sir Wilful:	'Sheart an she shou'd her forehead wou'd wrinkle like the	471	WAY WORLD	V.1	363
Sir Wilful:	'Sheart and she shou'd her forehead wou'd wrinkle like the	471	WAY WORLD	V.1	V363
Sir Wilful:	An he do's not move me, wou'd I might never	472	WAY WORLD	V.1	392
Sir Wilful:	An he do's not move me, wou'd I may never	472	WAY WORLD	V.1	V392
Sir Wilful:	drink, to give her to him again,--I wou'd I might never	472	WAY WORLD	V.1	394
Mirabell:	But that you wou'd not accept of a Remedy from	473	WAY WORLD	V.1	450
Mincing:	Mercenary? No, if we wou'd have been Mercenary, we	474	WAY WORLD	V.1	489
Mincing:	shou'd have held our Tongues; You wou'd have brib'd	474	WAY WORLD	V.1	490
Sir Wilful:	on't, I must do't. And if these two Gentlemen wou'd	477	WAY WORLD	V.1	586
Millamant:	Why do's not the man take me? wou'd you have	477	WAY WORLD	V.1	594
Mirabell:	Ay, and over and over again; for I wou'd have you	477	WAY WORLD	V.1	596
Mirabell:	Ay, and over and over again; I wou'd have you	477	WAY WORLD	V.1	V596

Wou'dst (1)

Speaker	Quotation	PAGE	TITLE	ACT.SC	LINE
Lady Wish:	first. Here, here, under the Table--What wou'dst	426	WAY WORLD	III.1	34

Would (270)

Would'st (7)

Speaker	Quotation	PAGE	TITLE	ACT.SC	LINE
Bellmour:	Thou dost not know what thou would'st be at;	63	OLD BATCH	III.1	102
Sr Sampson:	--What, would'st thou have me turn Pelican, and	246	FOR LOVE	II.1	398
Osmyn-Alph:	What would'st thou? thou dost put me from thee.	342	M. BRIDE	II.2	101
Almeria:	Thou told'st me thou would'st think how we might meet	355	M. BRIDE	III.1	246
Osmyn-Alph:	O would'st thou be less killing, soft or kind,	356	M. BRIDE	III.1	V282
Manuel:	Rise, I command thee rise--and if thou would'st	368	M. BRIDE	IV.1	285
Gonsalez:	I think thou would'st not stop to do me Service.	371	M. BRIDE	IV.1	427

Wouldst (3)

Speaker	Quotation	PAGE	TITLE	ACT.SC	LINE
Bellmour:	whether thou wouldst have her angry or pleas'd. Couldst	63	OLD BATCH	III.1	103
Almeria:	If I should tell thee, wouldst thou pity me?	328	M. BRIDE	I.1	91
Almeria:	Tell me? I know thou wouldst, thou art compassionate.	328	M. BRIDE	I.1	92

Wound (7)

Speaker	Quotation	PAGE	TITLE	ACT.SC	LINE
Zara:	O thou dost wound me now, with this thy Goodness,	354	M. BRIDE	III.1	185
Osmyn-Alph:	For this World's Rule, I wou'd not wound thy	356	M. BRIDE	III.1	275
Almeria:	Why? why? to know it, cannot wound me more,	356	M. BRIDE	III.1	278
Almeria:	Thy second self should feel each other Wound,	356	M. BRIDE	III.1	287
Almeria:	Oh I am lost--there, Fate begins to wound.	368	M. BRIDE	IV.1	299
Alonzo:	Or who can wound the Dead?--I've from the Body,	379	M. BRIDE	V.2	114
Singer:	'Tis not to wound a wanton Boy	435	WAY WORLD	III.1	382

Write   (continued)

Cynthia:	Write, what?		138	DOUBL DLR	II.1	15
Lady Froth:	O Inconsistent! In Love, and not Write! if my		139	DOUBL DLR	II.1	20
Lady Froth:	a Woman of Letters, and not Write! Bless me! how can	.	139	DOUBL DLR	II.1	41
Brisk:	I'm wholly turn'd into Satyr. I confess I Write but seldom,	141	DOUBL DLR	II.1	116
Brisk:	I'm wholly turn'd into Satire. I confess I write but seldom,	141	DOUBL DLR	II.1	V116
Mellefont:	sight, and to lose so much time as to write to her.	. .	159	DOUBL DLR	III.1	318
Lady Froth:	I will; you'd oblige me extremely to write Notes	. . .	165	DOUBL DLR	III.1	554
Lord Touch:	to my Name; when next I see that Face, I'le write Villain	.	186	DOUBL DLR	IV.2	119
	But tho' he cannot Write, let him be freed	. . . .	204	DOUBL DLR	EPI.	35
Jeremy:	Was Epictetus a real Cook, or did he only write	. . . .	216	FOR LOVE	I.1	10
Jeremy:	Paper; you don't mean to write!		217	FOR LOVE	I.1	62
Valentine:	Yes, I do; I'll write a Play.		217	FOR LOVE	I.1	63
Scandal:	write the Name at the bottom.		230	FOR LOVE	I.1	539
Angelica:	to write poor innocent Servants Names in Blood, about a	.	238	FOR LOVE	II.1	109
Sr Sampson:	shake--I believe thou can'st write, Val: Ha, boy? Thou		281	FOR LOVE	IV.1	207
Sr Sampson:	can'st write thy Name, Val?--Jeremy, step and overtake		281	FOR LOVE	IV.1	208
	Still they proceed, and, at our Charge, write worse:	.	323	M. BRIDE	PRO.	23
	Each time they write, they venture all they've won:	.	393	WAY WORLD	PRO.	14
Millamant:	how to write Letters; and yet one has 'em, one does not	.	419	WAY WORLD	II.1	361
Millamant:	or Write.		436	WAY WORLD	III.1	427
Sir Wilful:	write my self; no offence to any Body, I hope; and Nephew	438	WAY WORLD	III.1	511
Sir Wilful:	Stile of your Letters, and write in a scrap of Paper gilt	439	WAY WORLD	III.1	541
Sir Wilful:	--You cou'd write News before you were out of your	.	439	WAY WORLD	III.1	548
Millamant:	to and from whom I please, to write and receive Letters,	.	450	WAY WORLD	IV.1	213
Witwoud:	Revenge--and hear me, if thou canst learn to write	. .	454	WAY WORLD	IV.1	372

Writer (0)   see Gazette-writer

Writers (1)

Marwood:	Short-hand Writers to the publick Press; and from thence	.	468	WAY WORLD	V.1	231

Writes (2)

Lady Ply:	swear he writes charmingly.		174	DOUBL DLR	IV.1	259
Waitwell:	hand? the Rascal writes a sort of a large hand; your	. .	460	WAY WORLD	IV.1	601

Writing (4)

Brisk:	Short, but there's Salt in't, my way of writing I'gad.	.	166	DOUBL DLR	III.1	602
Valentine:	draw the Writing--Mr. Trapland, you know this Man,	. .	224	FOR LOVE	I.1	320
Foible:	writing?		460	WAY WORLD	IV.1	605
Mirabell:	It is in Writing and with Papers of Concern; but	. . .	472	WAY WORLD	V.1	405

Writings (7)

Careless:	her Father Sir Paul Plyant, come to settle the Writings, this		129	DOUBL DLR	I.1	81
Lord Touch:	Writings are ready drawn, and wanted nothing but to be	.	189	DOUBL DLR	V.1	62
Maskwell:	That's right,--well, I'll secure the Writings;	. . .	193	DOUBL DLR	V.1	206
Valentine:	Therefore I would rail in my Writings, and be	. . . .	219	FOR LOVE	I.1	136
Sr Sampson:	draw up Writings of Settlement and Joynture--All shall	.	240	FOR LOVE	II.1	194
Waitwell:	Contains the Writings of my whole Estate, and deliver	. .	461	WAY WORLD	IV.1	634
	(Enter Waitwell with a Box of Writings.)	475	WAY WORLD	V.1	508

Written (7)

Sharper:	I am in disorder for what I have written. But something, I know		79	OLD BATCH	IV.1	159
Lady Touch:	they were written in thy heart, That I, with this, might lay	198	DOUBL DLR	V.1	396
Jeremy:	terrify'd Countenance, that looks as if he had written for	219	FOR LOVE	I.1	105
Foresight:	Prophesie written by Messehalah the Arabian, and thus	. .	236	FOR LOVE	II.1	49
Tattle:	No, Sir, 'tis written in my Heart. And safer there, Sir, than		292	FOR LOVE	IV.1	613
Mirabell:	You wrong him, his name is fairly written as shall	. . .	476	WAY WORLD	V.1	527
Mirabell:	written on the back may serve your occasions.	. . .	476	WAY WORLD	V.1	V549

Wrong (33)

Vainlove:	Hold hold, 'slife that's the wrong.		38	OLD BATCH	I.1	37
Bellmour:	No faith Frank you wrong her; she has been just	. . .	38	OLD BATCH	I.1	43
Belinda:	with their Feathers growing the wrong way.--O such	. .	84	OLD BATCH	IV.3	30
Araminta:	to a wrong Belief.--Unworthy, and ungrateful! Be	. . .	87	OLD BATCH	IV.3	173
Vainlove:	wrong her.--I begin to doubt.		99	OLD BATCH	V.1	98
Lady Ply:	--to wrong so good, so fair a Creature, and one that	. .	146	DOUBL DLR	II.1	290
Mellefont:	was I to wrong her? for yet I understand you not.	. . .	146	DOUBL DLR	II.1	296
Cynthia:	why have you look'd through the wrong end of the	. . .	168	DOUBL DLR	IV.1	24
Cynthia:	you have look'd through the wrong end of the	. . . . .	168	DOUBL DLR	IV.1	V 24
Lady Ply:	both Letters.--(Puts the wrong Letter hastily up, and gives him		174	DOUBL DLR	IV.1	263
Lord Touch:	I do him fresh wrong to question his forgiveness;	. . .	200	DOUBL DLR	V.1	481
Tattle:	she did me wrong--Well, well, that was	. . . . . .	227	FOR LOVE	I.1	422
Scandal:	No doubt on't. Well, but has she done you wrong, or	. .	228	FOR LOVE	I.1	476
Nurse:	Stocking with the wrong side outward.		235	FOR LOVE	II.1	28
Angelica:	I dare swear you wrong him, it is his own--And	. . . .	255	FOR LOVE	III.1	75
Valentine:	Nay, now you do me Wrong; for if any Interest	. . . .	295	FOR LOVE	IV.1	725
Jeremy:	Books backwards; may be you begin to read at the wrong	.	297	FOR LOVE	IV.1	806
Sr Sampson:	Not at all, Madam: Odsbud you wrong me; I	. . . . .	298	FOR LOVE	V.1	21
Tattle:	I fancy you have a wrong Notion of Faces.	. . . . .	304	FOR LOVE	V.1	265
Foresight:	How? What? A wrong Notion! How so?		304	FOR LOVE	V.1	266
Osmyn-Alph:	Wrong not my Love, to say too much.		343	M. BRIDE	II.2	119
Osmyn-Alph:	Wrong not my Love, to say too tenderly.		343	M. BRIDE	II.2	V119
Osmyn-Alph:	To guess at Right and Wrong; the twinkling Lamp	. . .	350	M. BRIDE	III.1	36
Osmyn-Alph:	You wrong me, beauteous Zara, to believe	. . . . .	354	M. BRIDE	III.1	169
Zara:	Thou hast the Wrong, 'till I redeem thee hence;	. . .	355	M. BRIDE	III.1	218
Almeria:	Thou dost me Wrong, and Grief too robs my	. . . . .	356	M. BRIDE	III.1	284
Fainall:	You do her wrong; for to give her her Due, she has	. .	399	WAY WORLD	I.1	151
Witwoud:	wrong him neither--And if he had but any Judgment	. .	403	WAY WORLD	I.1	292
Witwoud:	wrong him.--And if he had any Judgment	. . . . .	403	WAY WORLD	I.1	V292
Marwood:	You do me wrong.		413	WAY WORLD	II.1	142
Fainall:	--I believe you; I'm convinc'd I've done you wrong;	. .	416	WAY WORLD	II.1	242
Lady Wish:	Or else you wrong my Condescension--		459	WAY WORLD	IV.1	539
Mirabell:	You wrong him, his name is fairly written as shall	. .	476	WAY WORLD	V.1	527

Wrong'd (10)

Laetitia:	Who has wrong'd me to my Dearest? I hope my Jewel	. .	77	OLD BATCH	IV.1	80
Lady Touch:	Have you not wrong'd my Lord, who has		135	DOUBL DLR	I.1	309
Lady Touch:	have you not wrong'd him in the highest manner, in his	.	135	DOUBL DLR	I.1	311
Lady Ply:	much wrong'd.		171	DOUBL DLR	IV.1	160

Wrong'd (continued)
 Lady Ply: shall wrong'd Vertue fly for Reparation! I'll be Divorced . 179 DOUBL DLR IV.1 446
 Lord Touch: let me hasten to do Justice, in rewarding Virtue and wrong'd 203 DOUEL DLR V.1 582
 Gonsalez: How much Report has wrong'd your easie Faith. . . . . 377 M. BRIDE V.2 46
 Mrs Fain: I am wrong'd and abus'd, and so are you. 'Tis . . 466 WAY WCRLD V.1 153
 Lady Wish: be wrcng'd after all, ha? I don't know what to think,-- . 466 WAY WCBLD V.1 181
 Mirabell: be wrcng'd in this Savage manner. . . . . . 474 WAY WORLD V.1 461
Wrongfully (3)
 Almeria: And wrongfully have put to Death those Innocents: . . . 382 M. BRIDE V.2 248
 Almeria: And wrongfully have slain those Innocents: . . . . 382 M. BRIDE V.2 V248
 Mrs Fain: have aspers'd me wrongfully--I have prcv'd your . . . 475 WAY WCBLD V.1 499
Wrongs (5)
 Mellefont: known my wrongs--Nay, till I have made known ycurs, . . 186 DOUEL DLR IV.2 122
 Almeria: That thus couldst melt to see a Stranger's Wrongs. . . 327 M. EBIDE I.1 31
 Osmyn-Alph: The Spirit which was deaf to my own Wrcngs, . . . 351 M. EBIDE III.1 74
 Zara: Of these thy Wrongs; as she, whose barbarous Rage . . 353 M. EBIDE III.1 158
 Marwood: By all my Wrcngs I'll do't--I'll publish to . . . . 415 WAY WCRLD II.1 194
Wrote (1)
  And 'twas the prettiest Prologue, as he wrote it! . . . 35 OLD BATCH PRO. 21
Wrought (6)
 Bellmour: would have wrought thy Conversicn and been a Champion . . 42 OLD BATCH I.1 195
 Lord Touch: familiarly acquainted with it. This is a little Trick
  wrought . 151 DOUBL DLB III.1 14
 Maskwell: word,--how the Devil she wrought my Lord into . . 190 DOUEL DLR V.1 110
 Zara: Has also wrought this chilling Change of Temper. . . 379 M. BBIDE V.2 146
  He owns, with Toil, he wrought the following Scenes, . . 393 WAY WCBLD PRO. 22
 Lady Wish: wrought upon Foible to detect me, I'm ruin'd. Oh my dear . 426 WAY WCBLD III.1 53
Wrung (1)
 Lord Touch: but, by Encouragement, I wrung the secret from him; and . 191 DOUEL DLR V.1 137
Wry (1)
 Millamant: without Interrogatories or wry Faces on your part. To . . 450 WAY WCBLD IV.1 214
Y'are (3)
 Lady Touch: I'll hear no more.--Y' are False and . . . . . 135 DOUBL DLB I.1 299
 Heli: Y'are truly Noble. . . . . . . 338 M. EBIDE II.1 V 38
 Mirabell: One a Clock! (looking on his Watch) O y'are come-- . . 398 WAY WCBLD I.1 109
Yard (1)
 Lady Wish: Go hang out an old Prisoneer-gorget, with a yard of . . 462 WAY WOBLD V.1 14
Yawn (1)
 Almeria: Sure, 'tis the Friendly Yawn of Death for me; . . . 340 M. BRIDE II.2 14
Ye (22) see Hark-ye, Heark-ye
 Setter: Oh! I begin to smoak ye, thou art some fcrsaken Abigail, . 65 OLD EATCH III.1 183
 Sharper: Hearkee, Sir Joseph, a word with ye--In consideration . 69 OLD BATCH III.1 302
 Bellmour: Say you so?--Is that a Maxim among ye? . . . 106 OLD BATCH V.1 368
 Heartwell: How have I deserv'd this of you? Any of ye? Sir, have I . 109 OLD BATCH V.2 51
 Bellmour: you an Appetite to see us fall to before ye. Setter, Did . 112 OLD BATCH V.2 178
 Brisk: O ye Powers! O my Lady Froth, my Lady Froth! My Lady . 175 DOUBL DLR IV.1 309
 Sr Sampson: Body o' me, so do I.--Heark ye, Valentine, . . . 243 FOB LCVE II.1 279
  And a less Number New, would well content ye. . . . 323 M. EBIDE PRO. 2
 Osmyn-Alph: To Earth, and nail me, where I stand, ye Powers; . . . 341 M. EBIDE II.2 47
 Osmyn-Alph: Rivit and nail me, where I stand, ye Powers; . . . 341 M. EBIDE II.2 V 47
 Osmyn-Alph: To break these Chains. Off, off, ye Stains of Boyalty. . 352 M. EBIDE III.1 88
 Almeria: Ye Winds and Waves, I call ye all to witness. . . . 370 M. EBIDE IV.1 360
 Manuel: O, give me Patience, all ye Powers! no, rather, . . . 373 M. EBIDE V.1 35
 Manuel: This hour I throw ye off, and entertain . . . . 374 M. EBIDE V.1 64
 Zara: --Rain, rain ye Stars, spout from your burning Orbs . . 380 M. EBIDE V.2 V168
 Almeria: Giv'n me again frcm Death! O all ye Powers . . . . 383 M. EBIDE V.2 291
 Sir Wilful: Hold ye, hear me Friend; a Word with you in . . . 437 WAY WCBLD III.1 468
 Sir Wilful: Indeed! Hah! Look ye, look ye, you do? Nay, ... 448 WAY WCBLD IV.1 123
 Millamant: all ye douceurs, ye Someils du Matin, adieu--I can't
  do't, 'tis . 449 WAY WORLD IV.1 189
Yea (3)
 Sir Wilful: Hum! What sure 'tis not--Yea by'r Lady, ... 438 WAY WOBLD III.1 514
 Sir Wilful: Yea but 'tis, by the Bekin. Brother Anthony! What Tony . 438 WAY WOBLD III.1 515
 Sir Wilful: Yea but 'tis, by the Bekin. Brother Antony! What Tony . 438 WAY WOBLD III.1 V516
Year (20)
 Heartwell: courage, which you shew for the first year or two upon all . 43 OLD EATCH I.1 246
 Capt Bluff: not three words of Truth, the Year round, put into the . 52 OLD BATCH II.1 193
 Sharper: have their Year of Probation, before they are cloister'd in 104 OLD BATCH V.1 304
 Lady Ply: this three year past? Have I been white and unsulli'd
  even by . 145 DOUBL DLB II.1 255
 Sir Paul: year; I'm sure I have found it so; and alas, what's once a . 162 DOUBL DLR III.1 434
 Sir Paul: year to an Old Man, who would do good in his Generation? . 162 DOUBL DLR III.1 435
 Lady Ply: your next half year. . . . . . . 162 DOUBL DLR III.1 452
 Lady Ply: the next half year. . . . . 162 DOUBL DLR III.1 V452
 Sir Paul: pound a Year upon the Rogue as soon as ever he looks me . 173 DOUBL DLR IV.1 225
 Lord Touch: Circling Joys, tread round each happy Year of your long . 203 DOUBL DLR V.1 589
  To cultivate each Year a hungry Soil; . . . . 213 FCB LCVE PRO. 2
 Scandal: Widow in the Poultry--800 [Pounds] a Year Joynture, and . 223 FOR LCVE I.1 269
 Ben: our Landladies cnce a Year, get rid of a little Mony; and . 275 FOR LOVE III.1 802
  And One was thought sufficient for a Year: . . . . 323 M. EBIDE PRO. 4
  For in One Year, I think they're out of Date. . . . 323 M. EBIDE PRO. 6
 Almeria: Which are diffus'd thro' the revclving Year, . . . 330 M. EBIDE I.1 154
 Almeria: The Year, which I have vow'd to pay to Heav'n, . . . 333 M. EBIDE I.1 284
 Millamant: handsomer--And within a Year or two as young. . . . 434 WAY WOBLD III.1 359
 Lady Wish: pardons to ask than the Pope distributes in the Year of . 457 WAY WCBLD IV.1 486
 Lady Wish: this Barbarian, But she wou'd have him, tho' her Year was . 469 WAY WOBLD V.1 303
Years (21)
 Bellmour: may be as wicked as thou art at thy years. . . . . 43 OLD BATCH I.1 252
 Bellmour: of Lying and Swearing at the Years end. Besides, I have . 60 OLD BATCH II.2 222
 Heartwell: to? A Womans Toy; at these years! Death, a bearded . . 72 OLD EATCH III.2 46
 Fondlewife: of a Cuckold, and have been 3 Years Apprentice . . . 94 OLD BATCH IV.4 196
 Setter: time this Seven Years. . . . . . . 111 OLD BATCH V.2 143
 Lady Ply: these three Years past? Have I been white and unsulli'd
  even by . . . . 145 DOUEL DLB II.1 V255
 Careless: Sir Paul's nine years Courtship; how he has lain for . . 157 DOUBL DLB III.1 273
 Sir Paul: three Years past? Have I been swath'd in Blankets till I . 178 DOUBL DLR IV.1 424

Years (continued)

Speaker	Text	PAGE	TITLE	ACT.SC	LINE
Jeremy:	Name, has for the space cf Sev'n Years truly and faithfully	218	FOR LOVE	I.1	67
Valentine:	was sent to Sea three Years ago? This Brother, my Father	225	FCR LCVE	I.1	333
Nurse:	given Suck this Thirty Years.	238	FOR LCVE	II.1	V126
Mrs Frail:	Not by a Dozen Years wearing.--But I dc	247	FOR LCVE	II.1	461
Sr Sampson:	Years--I warrant he's grown--Call him in, bid	259	FCB LCVE	III.1	214
Sr Sampson:	Years; I writ you word, when you were at Legcrne.	261	FCR LCVE	III.1	293
Foresight:	Cheeks have been gather'd many Years;--ha! I do not	269	FOR LCVE	III.1	603
Ben:	at these years, there's more danger of your head's aking	286	FOR LOVE	IV.1	383
	When many Years were past, in Men again.	315	FCR LOVE	EPI.	18
Osmyn-Alph:	Give me more Weight, crush my declining Years	350	M. EBIDE	III.1	11
Marwood:	Marrying than Travelling at his Years. I hear he is turn'd	431	WAY WCRLD	III.1	260
Lady Wish:	Out upon't, out upon't, at years of Discretion,	455	WAY WCRLD	IV.1	384
Lady Wish:	to Impress upon her tender Years, a Young Odiua and	466	WAY WCRLD	V.1	185

Yellow (1)

Speaker	Text	PAGE	TITLE	ACT.SC	LINE
Lady Wish:	Yellow Colberteen again; do; an old gnaw'd Mask, two	462	WAY WCRLD	V.1	15

Yelp (1)

Speaker	Text	PAGE	TITLE	ACT.SC	LINE
Manuel:	Th' ignoble Currs, that yelp to fill the Cry,	362	M. EBIDE	IV.1	63

Yes (147)

Speaker	Text	PAGE	TITLE	ACT.SC	LINE
Vainlove:	Yes, Heartwell, that surly, cld, pretended Wcman-hater	40	OLD BATCH	I.1	118
Araminta:	Love a Man! yes, you would not love a Beast.	55	OLD EATCH	II.2	24
Araminta:	Yes, yes, I can see something near it when you and	55	OLD EATCH	II.2	36
Lucy:	Yes Yes, come, I warrant him, if you will go in and be	60	OLD EATCH	III.1	2
Lucy:	Yes, I know both Master and Man to be--	65	OLD EATCH	III.1	173
Fondlewife:	Yes--Why then!--Ay, but to say truth, She's fonder of	77	OLD EATCH	IV.1	59
Laetitia:	Yes it will break to oblige you.	77	OLD EATCH	IV.1	95
Vainlove:	Yes, when I feed my self--Eut I hate to be craw'd	80	OLD EATCH	IV.1	174
Vainlove:	No, she will be there this evening--Yes I will	80	OLD EATCH	IV.1	184
Setter:	Oh, Yes, Sir.	103	OLD EATCH	V.1	259
Belinda:	Yes: You flattering Men of the Mode have made	106	OLD BATCH	V.1	369
Belinda:	Yes: You fluttering Men of the Mode have made	106	OLD BATCH	V.1	V369
Lord Froth:	O yes, sometimes,--but I never Laugh.	133	DOUEL DLR	I.1	223
Cynthia:	Yes, yes, Madam, I'm not so Ignorant.--	139	DOUEL DLR	II.1	35
Mellefont:	O, yes, Madam.	140	DOUEL DLR	II.1	88
Lady Froth:	Did my Lord tell you? Yes I vow, and the Subject	141	DOUEL DLR	II.1	120
Lady Froth:	O yes, and Rapine, and Dacier upon Aristotle	142	DOUEL DLR	II.1	138
Lady Froth:	Yes, I believe I have.--Mr. Brisk, come will	142	DOUEL DLR	II.1	143
Maskwell:	a thing as Honesty? Yes, and whosoever has it about him,	150	DOUEL DLR	II.1	451
Lord Touch:	Yes, I believe I know some that have been	151	DOUEL DLR	III.1	13
Cynthia:	Yes, my Lord--(aside) I must humour this Fool.	162	DOUEL DLR	III.1	468
Footman:	Yes, Madam.	166	DOUEL DLR	III.1	607
Lady Touch:	Both indebted to him! yes, we are both	191	DOUEL DLR	V.1	142
Lord Touch:	Yes.	195	DOUEL DLR	V.1	314
Cynthia:	Yes.	196	DOUEL DLR	V.1	334
Lord Touch:	Yes, I will contain, tho' I cou'd burst.	199	DOUEL DLR	V.1	430
Mellefont:	your hand;--do you hold down your head? Yes, I am	202	DOUDL DLR	V.1	569
Valentine:	Yes.	216	FOR LCVE	I.1	23
Valentine:	Yes, I do; I'll write a Play.	217	FOR LCVE	I.1	63
Jeremy:	Yes, Sir.	222	FOR LCVE	I.1	215
Tattle:	No matter for that--Yes, yes, every body knows	227	FOR LCVE	I.1	427
Valentine:	Yes.	228	FOR LCVE	I.1	455
Scandal:	Yes, Mrs. Frail is a very fine Wcman, we all know	228	FCR LCVE	I.1	458
Scandal:	Yes Faith. Ask Valentine else.	228	FOR LCVE	I.1	472
Tattle:	I am strangely surpriz'd! Yes, yes, I can't deny't, if	229	FOR LCVE	I.1	481
Scandal:	Yes, all that have done him Favours, if you will	232	FOR LCVE	I.1	606
Scandal:	Yes Faith, I can shew you your own Picture, and	232	FOR LCVE	I.1	617
Scandal:	Yes, mine are most in black and white.--And yet	233	FOR LCVE	I.1	626
Scandal:	Yes, I have a Poet weighing Words, and selling	233	FOR LCVE	I.1	651
Servant:	Yes, Sir.	235	FOR LCVE	II.1	8
Foresight:	Yes, yes; while there's one Wcman left, the	237	FOR LCVE	II.1	64
Angelica:	Yes, I can make Oath of your unlawful Midnight	237	FOR LCVE	II.1	96
Angelica:	Yes, I saw you together, through the Key-hole of	238	FCR LOVE	II.1	106
Nurse:	Yes, Sir.	239	FCR LOVE	II.1	167
Valentine:	Yes, Sir, all that I presume to ask.--Eut what	243	FCR LOVE	II.1	290
Jeremy:	Yes, I have a reasonable good Ear, Sir, as to Jiggs and	245	FCR LCVE	II.1	373
Mrs Frail:	Yes marry will I--A great piece of business to	246	FCR LCVE	II.1	418
Miss Prue:	Yes; I may tell my Mother--And he says he'll	249	FOR LOVE	II.1	524
Tattle:	Yes, my Dear--I think I can guess--But	251	FOR LOVE	II.1	583
Miss Prue:	Yes, if you please.	251	FOR LOVE	II.1	590
Miss Prue:	Yes.	251	FOR LOVE	II.1	603
Tattle:	Pooh, Pox, you must not say yes already; I shan't care	251	FOR LCVE	II.1	604
Tattle:	Yes, if you would be well-bred. All well-bred Persons	251	FOR LCVE	II.1	610
Tattle:	Hum--Yes--But you must believe I speak	252	FOR LCVE	II.1	627
Scandal:	Yes, but I dare trust you; We were talking of	254	FOR LCVE	III.1	45
Tattle:	O Lord! yes indeed, Madam, several times.	255	FOR LCVE	III.1	79
Tattle:	Yes, I vow and swear I have: Lord, Madam, I'm the	255	FOR LCVE	III.1	81
Foresight:	my Pulses ha!--I have none--Mercy on me--hum--Yes,	269	FOR LCVE	III.1	606
Scandal:	Yes, yes, I hope this will be gone by Morning, taking	270	FOR LCVE	III.1	631
Nurse:	Yes, Sir.	270	FOR LOVE	III.1	642
Scandal:	Yes, Faith I do; I have a better Opinicn both of you	271	FOR LOVE	III.1	662
Scandal:	Yes, several, very honest;--they'll cheat a little at	271	FCR LCVE	III.1	666
Scandal:	Yes, Faith, I believe some Women are Vertuous too;	271	FCR LCVE	III.1	669
Scandal:	Yes Faith, I think so; I love tc speak my mind.	272	FCR LCVE	III.1	685
Jeremy:	Yes, Sir; you need make no great doubt of that; he	276	FOR LCVE	IV.1	3
Buckram:	O Lord, what must I say?--Yes, Sir.	280	FOR LCVE	IV.1	170
Mrs Fore:	O yes, now I remember, you were very	284	FOR LCVE	IV.1	327
Jeremy:	Yes, Sir; he says he'll favour it, and mistake her for	288	FOR LCVE	IV.1	482
Jeremy:	Yes, Madam; He has Intervals: But you see he begins	295	FOR LCVE	IV.1	747
Jenny:	(aside to Angelica). Yes, Madam, Sir Sampson will wait	296	FOR LCVE	IV.1	782
Miss Prue:	No? Yes but I would tho.	304	FOR LCVE	V.1	251
Valentine:	Yes, Sir.	311	FOR LCVE	V.1	536
Almeria:	Peace--No Cause! yes, there is Eternal Cause.	326	M. BRIDE	I.1	17
Almeria:	Yes.	342	M. EBIDE	II.2	102
Zara:	Yes, Traytor, Zara; lost, abandon'd Zara,	346	M. EBIDE	II.2	248
Osmyn-Alph:	To call thee mine? yes, thus, ev'n thus, to call	357	M. EBIDE	III.1	330
Zara:	Yes, thou shalt know, spite of thy past Distress,	361	M. EBIDE	III.1	455

Yes   (continued)
Manuel:	Yes, Guilt; they are the dumb Confessicns cf	368	M. BRIDE	IV.1	269
Almeria:	Yes, all my Father's wounding Wrath, tho' each	368	M. BRIDE	IV.1	307
Almeria:	Yes, I will strip off Life, and we will change:	370	M. BRIDE	IV.1	351
Selim:	Yes: But then, as if he thought	375	M. BRIDE	V.1	V 98
Zara:	Yes, Osmyn, yes; be Osmyn or Alphonso,	376	M. BRIDE	V.1	135
Almeria:	Yes, yes, I know to mourn; I'll sluce this Heart,	382	M. BRIDE	V.2	243
Almeria:	And living? yes, I will; I've been abus'd	383	M. BRIDE	V.2	295
Mirabell:	Yes, and Mrs. Marwood and three or four more,	396	WAY WORLD	I.1	28
Servant-M:	Yes, Sir.	398	WAY WCRLD	I.1	126
Betty:	Yes; what's your Business?	400	WAY WCRLD	I.1	182
Fainall:	Yes; he is half Brother to this Witwoud by a former	400	WAY WORLD	I.1	192
Witwoud:	as to that.--Yes, Faith, in a Controversie he'll	403	WAY WORLD	I.1	303
Betty:	Yes.	404	WAY WORLD	I.1	345
Mrs Fain:	Yes, for I have Lov'd with Indiscretion.	416	WAY WORLD	II.1	257
Mirabell:	Yes, upon Condition she consent to my Marriage	418	WAY WORLD	II.1	300
Mirabell:	Yes, upon Condition that she consent to my Marriage	418	WAY WORLD	II.1	V300
Mirabell:	Yes, I think the good Lady wou'd marry any	418	WAY WCRLD	II.1	311
Millamant:	Yes, the Vapours; Fools are Physicks for it, next	421	WAY WCRLD	II.1	445
Mirabell:	Yes.	424	WAY WCRLD	II.1	529
Lady Wish:	Taylor. Yes, he shall have my Niece with her Fortune, he	428	WAY WCRLD	III.1	135
Lady Wish:	Yes, but Tenderness becomes me best--A	429	WAY WORLD	III.1	167
Lady Wish:	a--Ha Foible? A swimminess in the Eyes--Yes, I'll	429	WAY WORLD	III.1	169
Lady Wish:	a--Ha Foible? A swimmingness in the Eyes--Yes, I'll	429	WAY WORLD	III.1	V169
Marwood:	Are you become a go-between of this Importance? Yes, I	431	WAY WORLD	III.1	226
Petulant:	Yes, it positively must, upon Prcof positive.	435	WAY WORLD	III.1	408
Witwoud:	Not I--Yes, I think it is he--I've almost	436	WAY WORLD	III.1	441
Sir Wilful:	My Aunt Sir, yes my Aunt Sir, and your Lady	437	WAY WORLD	III.1	452
Sir Wilful:	told you, Madam--Yes, I have settl'd my Concerns,	440	WAY WCRLD	III.1	573
Witwoud:	Yes, refin'd, like a Dutch Skipper from a	441	WAY WCRLD	III.1	590
Foible:	Yes, Madam. I have put Wax-Lights in the Sconces;	444	WAY WCRLD	IV.1	3
Foible:	Yes, Madam.	445	WAY WCRLD	IV.1	6
Lady Wish:	Yes, yes, I'll give the first Impression on a Couch--I wont	445	WAY WCRLD	IV.1	24
Lady Wish:	a little dangling off, Jogging in a thoughtful way--Yes--	445	WAY WCRLD	IV.1	26
Lady Wish:	and rise to meet him in a pretty disorder--Yes--O,	445	WAY WORLD	IV.1	28
Sir Wilful:	Yes; my Aunt would have it so,--I would gladly	446	WAY WCRLD	IV.1	73
Sir Wilful:	Yes; my Aunt will have it so,--I would gladly	446	WAY WCRLD	IV.1	V 73
Sir Wilful:	Yes,--your Servant. No offence I hope, Cozen.	447	WAY WCRLD	IV.1	102
Sir Wilful:	Not at present Cozen,--Yes, I made bold to	447	WAY WCRLD	IV.1	114
Millamant:	Ha, ha, ha. Yes, 'tis like I may.--You have nothing	448	WAY WCRLD	IV.1	132
Sir Wilful:	Enough, enough, Cozen, Yes, yes, all a case--	448	WAY WCRLD	IV.1	142
Sir Wilful:	All's one for that,--yes, yes, if your Concerns call you,	448	WAY WCRLD	IV.1	145
Witwoud:	out and piec'd in the sides like an unsiz'd Camlet,--Yes,	453	WAY WCRLD	IV.1	328
Witwoud:	yes the fray is compos'd; my Lady came in like a	453	WAY WCRLD	IV.1	329
Foible:	put upon his Clergy--Yes indeed, I enquir'd of the	463	WAY WCRLD	V.1	44
Lady Wish:	Abigails and Andrews! I'll couple you, Yes, I'll baste you	463	WAY WCRLD	V.1	52
Foible:	Yes, yes; I know it Madam; she was in my Lady's	464	WAY WCRLD	V.1	68
Foible:	Yes Madam; but my Lady did not see that part; We	464	WAY WORLD	V.1	78
Mincing:	Yes Mem, they have sent me to see if Sir Wilfull be	465	WAY WORLD	V.1	113
Foible:	Yes, yes Madam.	465	WAY WCRLD	V.1	120
Mincing:	O yes Mem, I'll vouch any thing for your Ladyship's	465	WAY WORLD	V.1	121
Marwood:	Lawyers? To be usherd in with an O Yes of Scandal; and	467	WAY WCRLD	V.1	V211
Fainall:	Yes, while the Instrument is drawing, to which you	469	WAY WCRLD	V.1	291
Foible:	Yes indeed Madam; I'll take my Bible-oath of it.	474	WAY WCRLD	V.1	478
Mirabell:	Yes Sir. I say that this Lady while a Widdow,	476	WAY WCRLD	V.1	540
Marwood:	Yes it shall have Vent--and to your	477	WAY WCRLD	V.1	565

Yester (1)
| Zara: | And shall the Wretch, whom yester Sun, beheld | 349 | M. BRIDE | II.2 | 364 |

Yesterday (5)
Bellmour:	yesterday.	40	OLD BATCH	I.1	134
Lucy:	Hook, Age will ccme; he nibbled fairly yesterday, and no	61	OLD BATCH	III.1	11
Jeremy:	that was so near turning Poet yesterday morning, can't be	276	FOR LCVE	IV.1	4
Tattle:	O Pox, that was Yesterday, Miss, that was a great	303	FOR LCVE	V.1	236
Millamant:	sing the Song, I wou'd have learnt Yesterday. You shall	434	WAY WORLD	III.1	371

Yet (228)

Yew (1)
| Brisk: | Spectacle; she's always chewing the Cud like an old Yew. | 165 | DOUBL DLR | III.1 | 568 |

Yez (1)
| Marwood: | Lawyers? To be usherd in with an O Yez of Scandal; and | 467 | WAY WORLD | V.1 | 211 |

Yield (16)
Bellmour:	she never yield?	63	OLD BATCH	III.1	111
Careless:	I'm almost at the end of my Cant, if she does not yield	170	DOUBL DLR	IV.1	95
Lady Ply:	can refrain to weep and yield to such sad Sayings.—	170	DOUBL DLR	IV.1	120
Lady Ply:	Oh, I yield my self all up to your uncontroulable	170	DOUBL DLR	IV.1	124
Maskwell:	his Case is desperate, and I believe he'll yield to any	199	DOUBL DLR	V.1	449
Valentine:	Scandal, have pity on him; he'll yield to any	230	FOR LCVE	I.1	523
Valentine:	Therefore I yield my Body as your Prisoner, and	313	FOR LCVE	V.1	615
Almeria:	If ever I do yield, or give consent,	330	M. BRIDE	I.1	185
Garcia:	But to devote, and yield my self for ever	334	M. BRIDE	I.1	336
Osmyn-Alph:	And thou perforce must yield, and aid his Transport,	358	M. BRIDE	III.1	360
Zara:	To yield him up--No, I will still conceal him,	363	M. BRIDE	IV.1	97
Almeria:	Thy Face, imploring thee that thou wilt yield;	368	M. BRIDE	IV.1	275
Gonsalez:	Wedded already--what if he should yield?	371	M. BRIDE	IV.1	405
Garcia:	And make 'em yield to Mercy of the Conquerour.	378	M. BRIDE	V.2	95
Selim:	And forc'd to yield your Letter with his Life:	380	M. BRIDE	V.2	181
Almeria:	And ccme prepar'd to yield my Throat--they shake	382	M. BRIDE	V.2	250

Yielding (2)
| Maskwell: | Opportunity, accomplish'd my Design; I prest the yielding | 136 | DOUBL DLR | I.1 | 369 |
| Lady Wish: | You must not attribute my yielding to any sinister appetite, | 458 | WAY WCRLD | IV.1 | 529 |

Yields (3)
Heartwell:	Debts, which by the time you have pay'd, yields no further	44	OLD BATCH	I.1	279
Heartwell:	And the first Stage a Down-hill Green-sword yields.	112	OLD BATCH	V.2	189
	Who to your Judgments yields all Resignation;	393	WAY WCRLD	PRO.	39

Yoke-fellow (1)
| Fondlewife: | have been a tender Husband, a tender Yoke-fellow; you | 95 | OLD BATCH | IV.4 | 249 |

Yon (1)
| Ben: | Why, Father came and found me squabling with yon | . . . | 285 | FOR LOVE | IV.1 | 363 |

Yond' (1)
| Sharper: | me: May be she mayn't be within. 'Tis but to yond' | . . | 104 | OLD BATCH | V.1 | 285 |

Yonder (13)
Sir Joseph:	did a little while ago.--Look yonder.--A-gad, if	. .	101	OLD BATCH	V.1	172
Sharper:	yonder. I have promised and vow'd some things in your	.	109	OLD BATCH	V.2	82
Brisk:	I shall burst else.--And yonder your Uncle my Lord	.	128	DOUBL DLR	I.1	53
Sir Paul:	exasperated,--but I will protect my Honour, and yonder	.	144	DOUBL DLR	II.1	232
Maskwell:	Thirst. Ha! yonder comes Mellefont thoughtful. Let me	.	155	DOUBL DLR	III.1	186
Lady Froth:	I will; you'd oblige me extremely to write Notes	.	165	DOUBL DLR	III.1	554
Maskwell:	O yonder he comes reading of it, for Heavens	. .	178	DOUBL DLR	IV.1	402
Maskwell:	an hour, yonder in my Lady's Dressing-Room; go by the	.	194	DOUBL DLR	V.1	239
Ben:	yonder.--	. .	285	FOR LOVE	IV.1	361
Perez:	Yonder, my Lord, behold the Noble Moor.	. . . . .	338	M. BRIDE	II.1	16
Almeria:	See, see, look yonder! where a grizled, pale	. . . .	371	M. BRIDE	IV.1	387
Mrs Fain:	Yonder Sir Wilfull's Drunk; and so noisy that	. . .	452	WAY WORLD	IV.1	310
Petulant:	and Baldwin yonder, thy half Brother is the rest--A gemini		454	WAY WORLD	IV.1	351
Petulant:	kiss'd your twin yonder in a humcur of reconciliation, till		454	WAY WORLD	IV.1	356

Yonder's (1)
| Careless: | 'Slife yonder's Sir Paul, but if he were not come, I'm | . | 171 | DOUBL DLR | IV.1 | 128 |

Yonders (1)
| Lady Touch: | yonders my Lord, I believe he's coming to find you, I'le | . | 188 | DOUBL DLR | V.1 | 7 |

You (3172)

You'd (14)
Sir Joseph:	know me, you'd nere say I were so ill natur'd.	. . . .	48	OLD BATCH	II.1	37
Belinda:	more. Ch Gad, I swear you'd make cne sick to hear you.	.	54	OLD BATCH	II.2	2
Setter:	And therefore you'd have him to set in your Ladies	. .	67	OLD BATCH	III.1	228
Silvia:	again, 'cause you'd have me be naught.	. . . .	74	OLD BATCH	III.2	112
Laetitia:	Nay, don't swear if you'd have me believe you; but	.	82	OLD BATCH	IV.2	69
Lady Froth:	I will; you'd oblige me extremely to write Notes	.	165	DOUBL DLR	III.1	554
Mrs Fore:	Countenance purely, you'd make an Admirable Player.	.	247	FOR LOVE	II.1	452
Mrs Frail:	O hang you; who'll believe you?--You'd be	. .	250	FOR LOVE	II.1	554
Mrs Frail:	hang'd before you'd confess--we knew you--	. .	250	FOR LOVE	II.1	555
Ben:	if you shou'd give such Language at Sea, you'd have a Cat	.	264	FOR LOVE	III.1	408
Mrs Fore:	Pish, you'd tell me so, tho' you did not think	. .	272	FOR LOVE	III.1	707
Scandal:	And you'd think sc, tho' I should not tell you so:	. .	272	FOR LOVE	III.1	709
Mrs Frail:	Well, but if you shou'd forsake me after all, you'd	.	273	FOR LOVE	III.1	728
Scandal:	You'd better let him go, Sir; and send for him if there	.	280	FOR LOVE	IV.1	189

You'l (7)
Belinda:	my Sol, I'm afraid you'l follow evil Courses.	. . . .	55	OLD BATCH	II.2	52
Araminta:	hearing. You'l bring my Cousin.	. . . .	60	OLD BATCH	II.2	209
Fondlewife:	Ifeck you'l break my Heart--Ifeck you will--See you have	.	78	OLD BATCH	IV.1	116
Lady Ply:	O fy, fy, Sir Paul, you'l put me out of Countenance	.	172	DOUBL DLR	IV.1	189
Sr Sampson:	Sirrah, you'l be hang'd; I shall live to see you	. .	243	FOR LOVE	II.1	303
Tattle:	you'l cry out, you must be sure to hold your Tcngue.	.	252	FOR LOVE	II.1	623
Scandal:	No don't; for then you'l tell us no more--Come, I'll	.	258	FOR LOVE	III.1	190

You'll (46)
Sir Joseph:	self--I'll give him the Lie if you'll stand to it.	. . .	69	OLD BATCH	III.1	307
Laetitia:	down upon our bed.--You'll disturb him; I can tread	.	91	OLD BATCH	IV.4	79
Laetitia:	Ah cruel Dear, how can you be so barbarous? You'll	.	95	OLD BATCH	IV.4	230
Heartwell:	I'll pay him well, if you'll break the Matter to him.	. .	97	OLD BATCH	V.1	20
Lucy:	Well, It is then: But you'll be secret?	. . . . .	98	OLD BATCH	V.1	52
Setter:	You'll remember the Conditions?--	. . . . . .	104	OLD BATCH	V.1	277
Setter:	mine. Here's Ccmpany coming, if you'll walk this way,	.	106	OLD BATCH	V.1	352
Sharper:	Hist,--Bellmour: If you'll bring the Ladies, make	.	107	OLD BATCH	V.1	390
Mellefont:	Yet, may be, you'll encourage a beginner;	. . . . .	113	OLD BATCH	EPI.	27
Sir Paul:	We'll come immediately, if you'll but go in, and	.	128	DOUBL DLR	I.1	46
Lord Froth:	With all my heart.--Mr. Brisk you'll come to	. . . .	133	DOUBL DLR	I.1	218
Brisk:	well, Mellefont, you'll be a happy Creature.	. . .	141	DOUBL DLR	II.1	110
Lady Touch:	in the World,--I hope you'll make me happy in	. . .	142	DOUBL DLR	II.1	132
Lady Ply:	O for Heaven's sake, my Lord, you'll ruine	. . . . .	153	DOUBL DLR	III.1	103
Sir Paul:	would refuse to a person sc meritorious--you'll	. .	159	DOUBL DLR	III.1	354
Sir Paul:	You'll scarcely believe me, when I shall tell you why	.	161	DOUBL DLR	III.1	430
Lord Froth:	You'll scarcely believe me, when I shall tell you--	. .	161	DOUBL DLR	III.1	V430
Mellefont:	I swear, my Dear, you'll spoil that Child, with	. .	166	DOUBL DLR	III.1	609
Lord Touch:	O I conceive you, you'll tell him so?	. . .	193	DOUBL DLR	V.1	226
Jeremy:	but too soon you'll know mine, and that Woman's shame.	.	202	DOUBL DLR	V.1	565
Valentine:	You'll grow Devilish fat upon this Paper-Diet.	. . .	216	FOR LOVE	I.1	5
Angelica:	You'll meet her.	. . . . . .	229	FOR LOVE	I.1	509
Mrs Fore:	come home--You'll have a Letter for Alimony to	. . .	239	FOR LOVE	II.1	134
Valentine:	Well, if you should, Mr. Tattle, you'll have a	. . .	250	FOR LOVE	II.1	577
	Estate, and I'll defer it as long as I can--Well,					
	you'll come	. . . . . .	259	FOR LOVE	III.1	227
Ben:	and then you'll carry your Keels above Water, he, he, he.	.	262	FOR LOVE	III.1	335
Scandal:	Well; You'll give me leave to wait upon you to	. . .	273	FOR LOVE	III.1	745
Jeremy:	(to Mrs. Frail). You'll meet, Madam;--I'll take	. . .	293	FOR LOVE	IV.1	671
Angelica:	Vigour before your time: You'll spend your Estate before	.	301	FOR LOVE	V.1	150
Jeremy:	you'll certainly be the Death of a Person that has a most		301	FOR LOVE	V.1	168
Angelica:	'Tis very true indeed, Uncle; I hope you'll be my	. .	308	FOR LOVE	V.1	393
Angelica:	O you'll agree very well in a little time; Custom	. .	310	FOR LOVE	V.1	481
Angelica:	be a good Father, or you'll never get a second Wife. I	.	312	FOR LOVE	V.1	572
Zara:	As you'll answer it, take heed	. . . .	360	M. BRIDE	III.1	447
Zara:	As you'll answer it, look, this Slave	. . . .	360	M. BRIDE	III.1	V447
Gonsalez:	Dear Madam, speak, or you'll incense the King.	. . .	367	M. BRIDE	IV.1	266
Mirabell:	vain how lost a Thing you'll be! Nay, 'tis true: Ycu are no		420	WAY WORLD	II.1	391
Millamant:	--You'll displease me--I think I must resolve	. .	422	WAY WORLD	II.1	449
Lady Wish:	may examine her with more freedcm--You'll pardon	. .	426	WAY WORLD	III.1	63
Marwood:	Indeed my Dear, you'll tear another Fan, if	. . . .	433	WAY WORLD	III.1	333
Lady Wish:	to chuse. When you have been abroad, Nephew, you'll	.	441	WAY WORLD	III.1	608
Lady Wish:	you'll pardon him, Madam--Gentlemen will you	. . .	441	WAY WORLD	III.1	623
Marwood:	now you'll be no more Jealous.	. . . . . .	444	WAY WORLD	III.1	713
Sir Wilful:	my leave--If so be you'll be so kind to make my Excuse,	.	446	WAY WORLD	IV.1	78
Sir Wilful:	S'heart you'll have time enough to toy after	. . .	477	WAY WORLD	V.1	V599
Sir Wilful:	S'heart you'll have him time enough to toy after	. . .	477	WAY WORLD	V.1	599

You're (68)
| Bellmour: | You're going to visit in return of Silvia's Letter-- | . . | 40 | OLD BATCH | I.1 | 115 |

You're   (continued)

Heartwell:	Good Mr. Young-fellow, you're mistaken; as	43	OLD BATCH	I.1	229
Lucy:	No, you're out; could we perswade him, that she doats . .	62	OLD BATCH	III.1	40
Lucy:	it you. Come Madam, you're like to have a happy time .	75	OLD BATCH	III.2	159
Araminta:	No, no; you're very well as can be.	83	OLD BATCH	IV.3	18
Belinda:	--Affront! Pshaw, how you're mistaken! The poor . . .	84	OLD BATCH	IV.3	39
Belinda:	you're a pure Man; Where did you get this excellent .	88	OLD BATCH	IV.3	196
Brisk:	trick; you're always spoiling Company by leaving it. .	128	DOUBL DLR	I.1	22
Brisk:	--and see what a condition you're like to be brought .	129	DOUBL DLR	I.1	58
Lord Froth:	Ridiculous! Sir Paul you're strangely mistaken, I . .	132	DOUBL DLR	I.1	190
Sir Paul:	us,--or call me when you're going to Joke, I'll be ready to	133	DOUBL DLR	I.1	219
Lady Froth:	you're a Judge; was ever any thing so well-bred as my .	140	DOUBL DLR	II.1	82
Mellefont:	You're thoughtful, Cynthia?	142	DOUBL DLR	II.1	149
Maskwell:	I'm glad you're come, for I could not contain my . .	156	DOUBL DLR	III.1	200
Lord Froth:	'tis such a sight to see some teeth--sure you're a great .	162	DOUBL DLR	III.1	460
Lady Ply:	you're too modest, Sir Paul.	172	DOUBL DLR	IV.1	186
Brisk:	Sir Paul, Gads-bud you're an uncivil Person, let me tell .	174	DOUBL DLR	IV.1	267
Brisk:	Daughter your self; you're always brooding over her like .	174	DOUBL DLR	IV.1	272
Mellefont:	done, left you to your self.--You're in a kind of Erasmus .	185	DOUBL DLR	IV.2	60
Mellefont:	out Cuckoldom with her Fingers, and you're running . .	187	DOUBL DLR	IV.2	132
Lady Touch:	that you're a Fool, Brother?	192	DOUBL DLR	V.1	166
Sir Paul:	A Fool; he, he, he, you're merry--no, no, not . . .	192	DOUBL DLR	V.1	167
Sir Paul:	You're a passionate Woman, gad'sbud,--but to say . .	192	DOUBL DLR	V.1	V195
Lady Froth:	Oh, no, I love it viclently,--my dear you're	201	DOUBL DLR	V.1	523
Jeremy:	Sir, you're a Gentleman, and probably understand . .	217	FOR LOVE	I.1	24
Jeremy:	upon you again. You're undone, Sir; you're ruin'd; you .	218	FOR LOVE	I.1	85
Trapland:	business.--You're a Wag.	223	FOR LOVE	I.1	282
Trapland:	Verily, give me a Glass,--you're a Wag,--	224	FOR LOVE	I.1	289
Angelica:	you keep her at Home, if you're Jealous when she's abroad?	237	FOR LOVE	II.1	70
Angelica:	you keep her at Home, if you're Jealous of her when she's				
	abroad?	237	FOR LOVE	II.1	V 70
Angelica:	Nay, now you're ungrateful.	255	FOR LOVE	III.1	84
Tattle:	Faith, Madam, you're in the right; no more I have, as .	256	FOR LOVE	III.1	100
Sr Sampson:	Faith and Troth you're a wise Woman, and I'm	260	FOR LOVE	III.1	257
Tattle:	Sir, you're welcome a-shore.	261	FOR LOVE	III.1	285
Ben:	you Mistress, wou'd you like going to Sea? Mess you're a .	262	FOR LOVE	III.1	326
Mrs Fore:	O, fie--I'll Swear you're Impudent.	272	FOR LOVE	III.1	705
Scandal:	I'll Swear you're Handsome.	272	FOR LOVE	III.1	706
Valentine:	You're a Woman,--One to whom Heav'n	292	FOR LOVE	IV.1	634
Angelica:	You're an absolute Courtier, Sir Sampson.	298	FOR LOVE	V.1	20
Sr Sampson:	Odd, you're cunning, a wary Baggage! Faith	300	FOR LOVE	V.1	124
Sr Sampson:	Odd, you're devilish Handsom; Faith and Troth, you're .	301	FOR LOVE	V.1	141
Angelica:	Hold, Sir Sampson--You're profuse of your	301	FOR LOVE	V.1	149
Tattle:	Ay faith, so she will, Jeremy: You're a good Friend to .	302	FOR LOVE	V.1	206
Tattle:	thing indeed--Fie, fie, you're a Woman now, and . .	303	FOR LOVE	V.1	243
Tattle:	you're a Woman, and don't know your own mind. . . .	304	FOR LOVE	V.1	253
Sr Sampson:	and I'm Lord of the Ascendant. Odd, you're an old Fellow, .	307	FOR LOVE	V.1	382
Sr Sampson:	Oons you're a Crocodile.	312	FOR LOVE	V.1	581
Sr Sampson:	You're an illiterate Fool, and I'm another, and . . .	313	FOR LOVE	V.1	583
Sr Sampson:	You're an illiterate Fool, and I'm another, ...	313	FOR LOVE	V.1	V583
	But we can't fear, since you're so good to save us, . .	315	FOR LOVE	EPI.	38
Zara:	You're grown a Favourite since last we parted; . . .	359	M. BRIDE	III.1	412
Zara:	I'm angry: you're deceiv'd. I came to set	360	M. BRIDE	III.1	417
Zara:	You're too secure: The Danger is more imminent . . .	364	M. BRIDE	IV.1	109
Manuel:	And lash against the Hook--by Heav'n you're all . . .	373	M. BRIDE	V.1	44
Witwoud:	speaks;--We have all our Failings; you're too hard . .	403	WAY WORLD	I.1	308
Mirabell:	the Women's Secrets--What you're a Cabalist, I . . .	407	WAY WORLD	I.1	449
Mincing:	You're such a Critick, Mr. Witwoud.	420	WAY WORLD	II.1	376
Millamant:	You're mistaken. Ridiculous!	433	WAY WORLD	III.1	332
Witwoud:	think you're in the Country, where great lubberly Brothers	439	WAY WORLD	III.1	534
Sir Wilful:	The Fashion's a Fool; and you're a Fop, dear	439	WAY WORLD	III.1	538
Sir Wilful:	When you're dispos'd, when you're dispos'd. Now's as .	448	WAY WORLD	IV.1	143
Sir Wilful:	When you're dispos'd. Now's as	448	WAY WORLD	IV.1	V143
Lady Wish:	will ever endure such a Borachio! you're an absolute .	455	WAY WORLD	IV.1	389
Mrs Fain:	I tell you Madam you're abus'd--stick to	466	WAY WORLD	V.1	173
Sir Wilful:	you're married; or if you will toy now; Let us have a .	477	WAY WORLD	V.1	600

You've (13)

Heartwell:	Ay there you've nick't it--there's the Devil upon . .	45	OLD BATCH	I.1	317
Belinda:	Man--you don't know what you've said, your Fever has .	54	OLD BATCH	II.2	V 6
Heartwell:	You've wrack'd my patience; begon, or By--	108	OLD BATCH	V.2	41
	You gain your End, and damn 'em when you've done. . .	113	OLD BATCH	EPI.	30
	You gain your Ends, and damn 'em when you've done. . .	113	OLD BATCH	EPI.	V 30
Mellefont:	So when you've swallow'd the Potion, you sweeten . .	156	DOUBL DLR	III.1	221
	The Freedom Man was born to, you've restor'd, . . .	213	FOR LOVE	PRO.	15
Sr Sampson:	You've had it already, Sir, I think I sent it you to . .	243	FOR LOVE	II.1	274
Ben:	spring a Leak. You have hit it indeed, Mess you've nick'd	273	FOR LOVE	III.1	726
Jeremy:	Ah, you've hit it, Sir; that's the matter with him, Sir; .	279	FOR LOVE	IV.1	137
Zara:	I am your Captive, and you've us'd me Nobly; . . .	364	M. BRIDE	IV.1	136
Manuel:	To cast beneath your Feet the Crown you've sav'd, . .	365	M. BRIDE	IV.1	159
Mirabell:	longer handsome when you've lost your Lover; your . .	420	WAY WORLD	II.1	392

Young (66)

	We've a young Author and his first born Play; . . .	35	OLD BATCH	PRO.	11
Heartwell:	young, termagant flashy sinners--you have all the guilt .	43	OLD BATCH	I.1	238
Bellmour:	Oyster-woman, to propagate young Fry for Bilingsgate-- .	45	OLD BATCH	I.1	299
Capt Bluff:	How how, my young Knight? Not for fear I hope; he . .	51	OLD BATCH	II.1	142
Capt Bluff:	How now, my young Knight? Not for fear I hope; he . .	51	OLD BATCH	II.1	V142
Heartwell:	S'death how the young Fellows will hoot me! I shall be .	63	OLD BATCH	III.1	78
Vainlove:	Or a young Wench, betwixt pleasure and	63	OLD BATCH	III.1	93
Vainlove:	Or a young Wench, between pleasure and	63	OLD BATCH	III.1	V 93
Bellmour:	I wonder why all our young Fellows should glory . . .	75	OLD BATCH	IV.1	6
Barnaby:	as ever he comes home--I could have brought young . .	76	OLD BATCH	IV.1	22
Fondlewife:	near my Doors. I say, he is a wanton young Levite and .	76	OLD BATCH	IV.1	26
Fondlewife:	of the Wife of thy Bosom?--Because she is young and .	76	OLD BATCH	IV.1	51
Araminta:	young, and your early baseness has prevented its growing .	87	OLD BATCH	IV.3	172
Sharper:	Why, I'll tell you: 'Tis a young Creature that Vainlove .	104	OLD BATCH	V.1	292
	I swear, young Bays within, is so dejected, . . .	113	OLD BATCH	EPI.	24

SYMBOLS AND NUMBERS

APPENDIXES

Appendix A
STAGE DIRECTIONS

PAGE	CHARACTER	DIRECTION	LINE
OLD BATCH III.1			
60		(The Street. Silvia and Lucy.)	
62		(Exeunt.)	58
62		(Enter Heartwell, Vainlove and Bellmour following.	59
63	Heartwell:	(Goes in.)	87
64		(Enter Setter.)	115
64	Vainlove:	(Exit.)	121
64		(Exit Bellmour.)	136
64		(Enter Lucy.)	144
65	Lucy:	(Puts on her Masque.)	157
66	Lucy:	(Unmasques.)	200
66	Lucy:	(Cries)	V211
67	Lucy:	(Exit.)	237
67	Setter:	(Exit after her.)	240
67		(Enter Sir Joseph Wittoll, Bluffe.)˙	241
68		(Enter Sharper, Bellmour.)	280
69	Sharper:	(Cuffs him.)	310
69	Sharper:	(Kicks him.)	318
69	Sharper:	(Kicks him.)	321
69	Sharper:	(Kicks him.)	326
70		(Exit Bellmour, Sharper.)	330
70	Capt Bluff:	(Draws.)	338
70	Capt Bluff:	(Putting up his Sword.)	350
70	Capt Bluff:	(Looks big.)	355
70		(Exeunt.)	365
OLD BATCH III.2			
71		(Scene Changes to Silvia's Lodgings.	
71		Enter Heartwell, Silvia.)	
71		(After the Song, a Dance of Antick.)	25
72	Heartwell:	(pulling out a Purse and chinking it)	35
74		(Enter Lucy.)	144
73	Heartwell:	(aside)	95
74	Silvia:	(Throws the Purse)	111
74	Silvia:	(Going.)	113
74	Heartwell:	(aside)	126
74	Silvia:	(Turns and Weeps.)	132
74	Heartwell:	(kisses her)	133
74	Heartwell:	(Exit.)	142
74		(Enter Lucy.)	144
75		(Exeunt.)	164
OLD BATCH IV.1			
75		(The Street Enter Bellmour in Fanatick habit, Setter.)	
75	Bellmour:	(Looking on his Watch.)	2
75		(Exeunt.)	12
75		(Enter Fondlewife and Barnaby.)	13
76		(Exit Barnaby.)	48
77		(Enter Laetitia)	64
77	Fondlewife:	(aside)	74
77	Laetitia:	(aside)	79
77	Laetitia:	(aside)	85
77	Laetitia:	(Crying)	89
77	Laetitia:	(Sighs.)	96
77	Fondlewife:	(aside)	97
78	Laetitia:	(aside)	102
78	Laetitia:	(aside)	V102
78	Laetitia:	(Sighs.)	113
78	Laetitia:	(aside)	119
78	Laetitia:	(She Kisses him.)	125
78	Laetitia:	(Sighs)	128
79	Laetitia:	(aside)	139
79		(Kiss.)	142
79	Laetitia:	(She goes in.)	149
79	Fondlewife:	(Exit.)	151
79		(Enter Vainlove, Sharper.)	152
79	Vainlove:	(Gives a letter.)	155
79	Sharper:	(reads)	156
80		(Exeunt.)	192
OLD BATCH IV.2			
80		(Scene changes to a chamber in Fondlewife's House.	
80		A Servant introducing Bellmour in Fanatick Habit, with a	
80		Patch upon one Eye, and a Book in his Hand.)	
80		(Exit Servant.)	3
81		(Enter Laetitia.)	9
81	Bellmour:	(Throwing off his Cloak, Patch, &c.)	13
81	Laetitia:	(discovering him, starts)	16
81	Laetitia:	(aside)	18
81	Bellmour:	(aside)	27
81	Bellmour:	(Pulls out the letter.)	33
81	Laetitia:	(aside)	34
81	Laetitia:	(Going.)	36
81	Laetitia:	(aside)	42
82	Laetitia:	(aside)	59
82	Bellmour:	(He kisses her.)	75
82	Laetitia:	(aside)	79

PAGE	CHARACTER	DIRECTION	LINE
V.1	[cont.]		
99	Setter:	(Whispers him.)	92
100	Vainlove:	(Exit.)	128
100		(Enter Bellmour.)	130
100	Bellmour:	(Exit.)	161
101		(Enter Sir Joseph and Bluffe.)	162
101	Sharper:	(Whispers.)	166
101	Capt Bluff:	(In a low Voice.)	182
101	Sir Joseph:	(Stealing away upon his Tip-toes.)	186
101	Capt Bluff:	(Almost whispering, and treading softly after him.)	190
102	Sharper:	(Aloud.)	197
102		(Bluffe frowns upon Sir Joseph.)	211
102	Sharper:	(To Setter.)	214
102	Sharper:	(Exit.)	220
103	Sir Joseph:	(Chinking a Purse.)	238
103	Sir Joseph:	(Gives him Gold.)	246
103	Capt Bluff:	(Shows Letters.)	266
103		(While Sir Joseph reads, Bluffe whispers Setter.)	273
104	Capt Bluff:	(Gives him Money)	279
104	Sir Joseph:	(Exit, with Bluffe.)	V282
104		(Enter Sharper, tugging in Heartwell.)	283
104	Heartwell:	(aside)	295
104	Heartwell:	(aside)	298
104	Sharper:	(Going.)	307
105	Heartwell:	(Exit.)	325
105		(Setter Entering.)	329
106		(Exeunt.)	354
106		(Enter Bellmour, Belinda, Araminta and Vainlove.)	355
106	Vainlove:	(to Araminta)	356
106	Belinda:	(to Bellmour)	364
106	Bellmour:	(aside)	371
107		(Enter Sharper.)	389
107	Sharper:	(Exit.)	394
107	Bellmour:	(To Belinda.)	397
107		(Exeunt.)	404

OLD BATCH
V.2

107		(Scene changes to Silvia's Lodgings.	
107		Enter Heartwell and Boy.)	
107		(Exit Boy.)	8
108		(Enter Bellmour, Belinda, Vainlove, Araminta.)	16
108		(Vainlove and Araminta talk a-part.)	21
109		(Enter Sharper.)	78
110	Sharper:	(Exit.)	92
110		(Re-enter Sharper, with Sir Joseph, Bluffe, Sylvia, Lucy,	95
110		Setter.)	96
110		(Lucy unmasks.)	111
110		(Araminta and Belinda unmask.)	117
111		(Sylvia unmasks.)	124
111		(Heartwell goes to Bellmour.)	130
112	Belinda:	(Giving her Hand.)	169
112	Vainlove:	(To Araminta.)	V172
112	Bellmour:	(Aside.)	176
112		(A Dance.)	181
112		(Exeunt Omnes.)	196

DOUBL DLR
I.1

127		(A Gallery in the Lord Touchwood's House,	
127		with Chambers adjoyning.)	
127		(Enter Careless, Crossing the Stage, with his Hat, Gloves,	
127		and Sword in his Hands; as just risen from Table:	
127		Mellefont following him.)	
128		(Enter Brisk.)	19
129	Brisk:	(Exit.)	63
131		(Enter Lord Touchwood, Lord Froth, Sir Paul Plyant,	170
131		and Brisk.)	171
133		(Exit Lord Touchwood and Sir Paul.)	221
134	Lord Froth:	(Takes out a Pocket-Glass, and looks in it.)	290
135	Brisk:	(Takes the Glass and looks.)	294
135		(Exeunt.)	297
135		(Enter Lady Touchwood, and Maskwell.)	298
136	Lady Touch:	(She Walks about Disorder'd.)	333
138		(Exeunt.)	423

DOUBL DLR
II.1

138		(Enter Lady Froth and Cynthia.)	
139	Cynthia:	(aside)	36
139		(Enter Lord Froth, Mellefont, Brisk.)	57
140	Cynthia:	(aside)	58
140	Lady Froth:	(Squeezes him by the hand, looks kindly on him, sighs, and	65
140		then laughs out.)	66
140	Lady Froth:	(Gives him a Pocket-glass.)	75
140	Lord Froth:	(He bows profoundly low, then kisses the Glass.)	79
141	Brisk:	(to Lady Froth)	115
142		(Exit Lady Froth and Brisk.)	146
142	Lord Froth:	(Exit.)	148
143		(Musicians crossing the Stage.)	174
143		(SONG.)	177
143		(To the Musick, they go out.)	193

PAGE	CHARACTER	DIRECTION	LINE

II.1 [cont.]

PAGE	CHARACTER	DIRECTION	LINE
143		(Enter Sir Paul Plyant and Lady Plyant.)	194
145		(Lady Plyant and Sir Paul come up to Mellefont.)	241
145	Mellefont:	(aside)	270
146		(Exit Sir Paul, and Cynthia.)	288
146	Mellefont:	(aside)	312
148	Lady Ply:	(Exit.)	373
148	Mellefont:	(after a pause)	374
148		(Enter Maskwell.)	380
149	Mellefont:	(Exit.)	438
150	Maskwell:	(Exit.)	V469

DOUBL DLR
III.1

PAGE	CHARACTER	DIRECTION	LINE
150		(Enter Lord Touchwood, and Lady Touchwood.)	
151	Lord Touch:	(half aside)	26
152	Lord Touch:	(aside)	44
154		(Exit Lord Touchwood.)	125
154		(Enter Maskwell.)	127
154	Maskwell:	(aside)	161
155		(Exit Lady Touchwood.)	173
155		(Maskwell pretending not to see him, walks by him, and	192
155		speaks as it were to himself.)	193
155		(Enter Mellefont musing.)	195
157	Maskwell:	(Exit.)	V261
157	Mellefont:	(Enter to him Careless.)	263
159	Mellefont:	(Exit.)	319
159		(Enter Sir Paul and Lady Plyant.)	320
159	Sir Paul:	(aside to her)	334
159	Lady Ply:	(Curtesies)	341
159	Lady Ply:	(Curtesies)	343
160		(Enter Boy with a Letter, . . .	392
160	Boy:	. . . carries it to Sir Paul.)	V392
161	Boy:	(Carries the Letter to my Lady and Exit.)	V401
161	Sir Paul:	(Cries.)	418
162	Lady Ply:	(Gives him the Letter.)	453
162		(Enter Lord Froth, Cynthia.)	454
162	Cynthia:	(aside)	468
163		(Enter Boy and whispers Sir Paul.)	488
163		(Exit Careless and Lady Plyant.)	496
163		(Exit Sir Paul.)	500
163		(Enter Lady Froth and Brisk.)	501
164	Lady Froth:	(pulls out a Paper.)	512
164	Lady Froth:	(Reads.)	514
164	Lady Froth:	(Reads.)	528
164	Lady Froth:	(reads)	534
165	Cynthia:	(aside)	577
166		(SONG.)	594
166	Lord Froth:	(sings)	595
166		(Enter Footman.)	603
167		(Exeunt.)	623
167	Cynthia:	(Exit.)	635

DOUBL DLR
IV.1

PAGE	CHARACTER	DIRECTION	LINE
167		(Enter Mellefont and Cynthia.)	
169		(Exeunt.)	67
169		(Enter Careless and Lady Plyant.)	68
169	Careless:	(Sighing)	77
169	Careless:	(in a Whining Tone)	85
170	Careless:	(Still Whining)	90
170	Careless:	(Aside.)	94
170	Careless:	(Aside.)	101
170	Lady Ply:	(Cries.)	121
170	Careless:	(Aside.)	123
171		(Enter Sir Paul and Cynthia.)	127
171	Careless:	(Gives her a Note)	130
171	Careless:	(Exit.)	131
171	Lady Ply:	(Aside.)	152
171	Cynthia:	(aside)	161
172	Cynthia:	(aside)	176
172	Cynthia:	(aside)	194
172	Sir Paul:	(He kisses her, and bows very low.)	196
173	Sir Paul:	(Bows and gives the Letter.)	219
173	Lady Ply:	(Aside.)	221
174	Lady Ply:	(Having read the Letter)	258
174	Lady Ply:	(Puts the wrong Letter hastily up, and gives him	263
174	Lady Ply:	her own)	264
174		(Enter Brisk.)	266
174		(Exit Cynthia.)	283
175	Lady Ply:	(Exit.)	285
175	Sir Paul:	(Exit.)	289
175	Brisk:	(Bows.)	297
175		(Enter Lady Froth.)	305
175	Brisk:	(sings)	306
175	Brisk:	(walking	306
175	Brisk:	about)	307
175	Brisk:	(Stands musing with his Arms a-cross.)	311
175	Brisk:	(Aside.)	317
177		(Embrace.)	360
177		(Enter Lord Froth.)	361
177	Brisk:	(Softly to her.)	364
177		(They pretend to practice part of a Country-Dance.)	371

	PAGE	CHARACTER	DIRECTION	LINE
IV.1	[cont.]			
	177	Lord Froth:	(aside)	372
	177	Brisk:	(aside)	379
	177	Brisk:	(To her)	384
	177		(Exeunt.)	388
	177		(Enter Lady Plyant, and Careless.)	389
	178		(Exeunt.)	404
	178		(Enter Sir Paul with the Letter.)	405
	178	Sir Paul:	(Reads)	408
	179		(Enter Lady Plyant.)	436
	179	Lady Ply:	(Snatches the Letter as in	441
	179	Lady Ply:	anger.)	442
	180	Lady Ply:	(Exit.)	489
	180		(Enter Careless.)	490
	180	Sir Paul:	(aside)	494
	181	Careless:	(aside)	V510
	181		(Exeunt.)	V511
	181		(Enter Mellefont and Maskwell severally.)	512
	161		(Mellefont, Maskwell, from different Doors.)	V512
	181	Mellefont:	(Exit.)	526
	181		(Enter Lord Touchwood.)	531
	183		(Exeunt, severally.)	592
DOUBL DLR				
IV.2	183		(Scene opening, shews Lady Touchwood's Chamber.)	
	183		(Mellefont, Solus.)	
	183	Mellefont:	(Goes behind the Hanging.)	6
	183	Mellefont:	(Goes behind the Hangings.)	V 6
	183		(Enter Lady Touchwood.)	7
	183		(Enter Maskwell.)	12
	184	Maskwell:	(Kisses her.)	25
	184	Lady Touch:	(Goes to the door.)	29
	184	Maskwell:	(aside)	30
	184	Mellefont:	(Leaps out.)	36
	184	Lady Touch:	(Shrieks.)	37
	184	Mellefont:	(Offers to Draw.)	38
	184	Maskwell:	(Runs out.)	40
	185	Lady Touch:	(aside)	64
	185	Lady Touch:	(She Weeps.)	67
	185		(Enter Lord Touchwood, Maskwell softly behind him.)	89
	185	Maskwell:	(Exit.)	92
	186	Lady Touch:	(kneeling)	94
	186	Lady Touch:	(Aside.)	95
	186	Lady Touch:	(aloud)	98
	186	Lord Touch:	(Draws, and runs at Mellefont, is held by Lady Touchwood.)	108
	187	**Lady Touch:**	(As she is going she turns back and smiles at him.)	134
	187		(Exeunt.)	140
	187	Mellefont:	(Exit.)	156
	187		(Scene shuts.)	157
DOUBL DLR				
V.1	187		(Enter Lady Touchwood and Maskwell.)	
	188	Lady Touch:	(Exit.)	9
	188		(Enter Lord Touchwood.)	15
	188	Lord Touch:	(aside)	21
	188	Lord Touch:	(aside)	27
	189	Maskwell:	(Seems to start, seeing my Lord.)	46
	189		(Maskwell pauses.)	68
	189	Lord Touch:	(Exit.)	84
	190		(Enter Mellefont.)	102
	190		(Exeunt.)	120
	190		(Enter Lord Touchwood, Lady Touchwood.)	121
	191	Lady Touch:	(aside)	134
	191	Lord Touch:	(Exit.)	141
	191		(Enter Sir Paul.)	158
	192	Lady Touch:	(Exit.)	194
	192	Sir Paul:	(Exit.)	198
	192		(Enter Mellefont, Maskwell, and Cynthia.)	199
	193	Maskwell:	(aside)	V230
	194	Mellefont:	(Exit.)	247
	194	Cynthia:	(Going.)	250
	194	Cynthia:	(Exit.)	261
	194	Maskwell:	(Goes to the Chamber Door and knocks.)	271
	194	Saygrace:	(looking out)	272
	195	Saygrace:	(enters)	280
	195	Saygrace:	(Exit.)	299
	195		(Enter Lord Touchwood.)	301
	195	Maskwell:	(Aside.)	308
	195	Maskwell:	(aside)	312
	196	Maskwell:	(aside)	322
	196		(Exeunt.)	331
	196		(Enter Careless and Cynthia.)	332
	196		(Enter Mellefont.)	340
	197		(Exeunt Mellefont and Careless.)	355
	197		(Enter Lord Touchwood.)	357
	197	Maskwell:	(within)	371
	197	Lady Touch:	(within)	372
	197		(They abscond.)	377
	197		(Enter Lady Touchwood with a Dagger, Maskwell.)	378
	198	Lady Touch:	(Goes to strike.)	393
	198	Lady Touch:	(weeps)	402

	PAGE	CHARACTER	DIRECTION	LINE
V.1	[cont.]			
	198	Lady Touch:	(Gives the Dagger.)	405
	198	Maskwell:	(aside)	412
	199	Maskwell:	(Gives the Dagger.)	452
	199	Lady Touch:	(Exit.)	460
	199	Maskwell:	(Exit.)	465
	199		(Cynthia, and Lord Touchwood, come forward.)	466
	200		(Exeunt.)	490
	200		(Enter Lord Froth, and Sir Paul.)	491
	201		(Enter Lady Froth, Brisk.)	516
	202		(Enter Lady Plyant, Careless, Cynthia.)	544
	202		(A great shriek from the corner of the Stage. Lady Touchwood	556
	202		runs out affrighted, my Lord after her, like a Parson.)	557
	202	Lady Touch:	(Runs out.)	562
	202		(Enter Mellefont lugging in Maskwell from the other side	566
	202		of the Stage, Mellefont like a Parson.)	567
	202		(Mellefont disguis'd in a Parson's Habit	V566
	202		and pulling in Maskwell.)	V567
	203		(They carry out Maskwell, who hangs down his head.)	577
	203		(Servants seize him.)	V577
	203		(Exeunt Omnes.)	597

FOR LOVE
I.1

	PAGE	CHARACTER	DIRECTION	LINE
	216		(Valentine in his Chamber Reading. Jeremy waiting.	
	216		Several Books upon the Table.)	
	216	Jeremy:	(Aside and taking away the Books.)	6
	219		(Enter Scandal.)	116
	220		(One Knocks.)	154
	220		(Exit Jeremy.)	156
	220		(Enter Jeremy.)	164
	221	Jeremy:	(Knocking)	182
	221		(Exit Jeremy.)	186
	221		(Re-enter Jeremy.)	201
	221	Valentine:	(Gives Money.)	209
	222	Scandal:	(Gives Money.)	217
	222		(Exit Jeremy.)	224
	222		(Enter Trapland and Jeremy.)	227
	222	Trapland:	(sits)	236
	222	Trapland:	(Drinks)	246
	222	Valentine:	(Drinks.)	253
	223		(They Drink.)	256
	223		(They Drink.)	277
	224	Trapland:	(Drinks.)	291
	224		(Enter Officer.)	294
	224		(Exit Officer.)	307
	224		(Enter Steward and Whispers Valentine.)	308
	224		(Steward who whispers.)	V308
	225		(Exeunt Steward, Trapland and Jeremy.)	327
	225		(Enter Jeremy.)	355
	225		(Exit Jeremy.)	361
	226		(Enter Tattle.)	381
	228	Tattle:	(Hums a Song.)	449
	229		(Enter Jeremy.)	504
	229		(Exit Jeremy.)	507
	230		(Enter Mrs. Frail.)	541
	234		(Enter Jeremy.)	660
	234		(Exeunt.)	682

FOR LOVE
II.1

	PAGE	CHARACTER	DIRECTION	LINE
	235		(A Room in Foresight's House. Foresight and Servant.)	
	235		(Enter Nurse.)	17
	236		(Enter Angelica.)	39
	236		(Exit Servant.)	43
	238	Nurse:	(crying)	125
	239		(Enter Servant.)	159
	239		(Exit Angelica and Servant.)	163
	239	Nurse:	(Exit.)	168
	240		(Enter Sir Sampson Legend with a Paper.)	171
	241	Foresight:	(Aside)	230
	242		(Enter Jeremy.)	260
	242		(Enter Valentine.)	271
	246		(Exeunt Sir Sampson and Foresight.)	405
	246		(Exeunt.)	413
	246		(Enter Mrs. Foresight and Mrs. Frail.)	414
	248	Mrs Fore:	(aside)	471
	249		(Enter Tattle, and Miss Prue.)	505
	251		(Exeunt Mrs. Foresight and Mrs. Frail.)	580
	251	Tattle:	(aside)	591
	252	Miss Prue:	(Runs and Kisses him.)	634
	252	Tattle:	(Kisses her.)	639
	252	Tattle:	(Kisses again.)	642
	253		(Exit Miss Prue.)	661
	253	Tattle:	(Exit after her.)	663

FOR LOVE
III.1

	PAGE	CHARACTER	DIRECTION	LINE
	253		(Enter Nurse.)	
	253	Nurse:	(peeps)	7
	253	Nurse:	(knocks)	11
	253	Nurse:	(Exit.)	13

	PAGE	CHARACTER	DIRECTION	LINE
M. BRIDE				
II.1				
	337		(Representing the Ile of a Temple.	
	337		Enter Garcia, Heli and Perez.)	
	338	Heli:	(Exit.)	39
	339		(Exeunt.)	50
	339		(Enter Almeria and Leonora.)	51
	339		(Exeunt.)	85
M. BRIDE				
II.2				
	340		(The Scene opening discovers a Place of Tombs. One	
	340		Monument fronting the View, greater than the rest. Enter Heli.)	
	340	Heli:	(Exit.)	4
	340		(Re-Enter, Almeria and Leonora.)	5
	340		(Osmyn ascending from the Tomb.)	34
	341	Osmyn-Alph:	(Coming forward.)	48
	341		(Enter Heli.)	57
	345		(Exit Almeria, Leonora, and Heli.)	213
	345		(Enter Zara attended by Selim.)	231
	348		(Enter the King, Perez, and Attendants.)	351
	348	Manuel:	(aside)	359
	349		(Guards carry off Osmyn.)	375
	349		(Exeunt Omnes.)	392
M. BRIDE				
III.1				
	349		(A Prison. Enter Osmyn alone, with a Paper.)	
	350	Osmyn-Alph:	(Reading.)	8
	350	Osmyn-Alph:	(Reading.)	15
	350		(Enter Heli.)	41
	352		(Exit Heli.)	124
	353		(Enter Zara veil'd.)	139
	353	Zara:	(Lifting her Veil.)	144
	355		(Exit Zara.)	221
	355		(Enter Almeria.)	234
	358		(Enter Zara, Perez, and Selim.)	375
	359		(Exit Perez.)	383
	359		(Exit Almeria.)	405
	359	Zara:	(aside)	406
	359	Zara:	(Aside.)	411
	360		(Enter Perez.)	446
	361		(Exeunt Omnes.)	459
M. BRIDE				
IV.1				
	361		(A Room of State. Enter Zara, and Selim.)	
	362		(Enter King, Gonsalez, Garcia, Perez.)	61
	363	Zara:	(aside to Selim)	90
	364		(Exeunt Garcia, Perez, and Attendants.)	135
	365		(Enter Perez.)	166
	365		(Exit Perez.)	173
	366		(Exeunt Zara and Selim.)	193
	367		(Enter Almeria and Leonora.)	242
	367		(Exit Leonora.)	246
	369		(Enter Leonora and Attendants.)	336
	369	Almeria:	(Faints.)	345
	370		(Exit King.)	367
	371	Almeria:	(Exit with attendants.)	395
	371		(Enter Alonzo.)	418
	372		(Exit Alonzo.)	443
	372	Gonsalez:	(Exit.)	448
M. BRIDE				
V.1				
	372		(A Room of State. Enter King, Perez, and Alonzo.)	
	373		(A Mute appears, and seeing the King retires.)	12
	373		(Exit Alonzo.)	14
	373		(Alonzo re-enters with a Paper.)	18
	373		(Alonzo follows him, and returns with a Paper.)	V 18
	373	Alonzo:	(Exit.)	31
	373	Manuel:	(Having read the Letter.)	34
	374	Manuel:	(reading)	52
	374	Manuel:	(reading)	59
	374	Manuel:	(Strikes him.)	70
	374		(Perez going.)	79
	374		(Exeunt.)	89
	374		(Enter Zara, and Selim.)	90
	376		(Exeunt.)	140
M. BRIDE				
V.2				
	376		(Scene changes to the Prison.	
	376		Enter Gonsalez, disguis'd like a Mute, with a Dagger.)	
	376		(Scene opening shews the Prison.	V
	376		Gonsalez alone, disguis'd like a Mute, with a Dagger.)	V
	376	Gonsalez:	(Looks in.)	5
	376	Gonsalez:	(Goes in.)	14
	376		(Enter Garcia and Alonzo.)	15

	PAGE	CHARACTER	DIRECTION	LINE
V.2	[cont.]			
	376		(Enter Gonsalez, bloody.)	23
	377		(Garcia goes in.)	47
	377	Garcia:	(returning)	51
	377		(They go in.)	62
	378		(Shout.)	89
	378	Alonzo:	(Goes in.)	99
	378		(Shout.)	101
	379	Garcia:	(Exit.)	108
	379		(Exeunt.)	129
	379		(Enter Zara, follow'd by Selim, and Two Mutes bearing	130
	379		the Bowls.)	131
	380		(Mutes go in.)	151
	380		(Exit Selim.)	154
	380		(The Mutes return and look affrighted.)	156
	380		(They go to the Scene which opens and shews the Body.)	161
	380		(Enter Selim.)	172
	380	Zara:	(Stabs him.)	176
	380	Selim:	(Dies.)	185
	381		(A Mute kneels and gives one of the Bowls.)	199
	381	Zara:	(Drinks.)	203
	381	Zara:	(Dies.)	212
	381		(The Mutes kneel and mourn over her.)	213
	381		(Enter Almeria and Leonora.)	214
	382		(They point at the Bowl on the Ground.)	252
	382		(They point to the other Cup.)	257
	382	Almeria:	(Coming nearer the Body, starts and lets fall the Cup.)	271
	382		(Enter Alphonso, Heli, Perez, with Garcia Prisoner,	273
	382		Guards and Attendants.)	274
	383	Almeria:	(She weeps.)	310
	384		(Exeunt Omnes.)	323

WAY WORLD
I.1

	PAGE	CHARACTER	DIRECTION	LINE
	395		(A Chocolate-house.	
	395		Mirabell and Fainall Rising from Cards. Betty waiting.)	
	398	Fainall:	(Exit.)	104
	398	Betty:	(Exit.)	107
	398	Mirabell:	(looking on his Watch)	109
	398		(Enter a Servant.)	110
	398		(Exit Servant.)	133
	398		(Re-Enter Fainall.)	134
	400		(Enter Messenger.)	180
	400		(Exit Messenger.)	186
	401		(Enter Witwoud.)	234
	404		(Enter Coachman.)	343
	404		(Exit Betty, and Coachman.)	352
	405		(Enter Petulant.)	381
	409		(Exeunt.)	543

WAY WORLD
II.1

	PAGE	CHARACTER	DIRECTION	LINE
	410		(St. James's Park. Enter Mrs. Fainall and Mrs. Marwood.)	
	412		(Enter Fainall and Mirabell.)	84
	412		(Exeunt Mrs. Fainall and Mirabell.)	108
	416		(Exeunt.)	250
	416		(Enter Mirabell and Mrs. Fainall.)	251
	418		(Enter Mrs. Millamant, Witwoud, and Mincing.)	322
	421	Mirabell:	(aside to Mrs. Fainall)	424
	421		(Exit Witwoud and Mrs. Fainall.)	428
	423	Millamant:	(Exit, with Mincing.)	V489
	423		(Enter Waitwell and Foible.)	504
	424	Mirabell:	(Gives Mony.)	535
	424	Foible:	(Looking out.)	544
	424		(Exit Foible.)	549
	424		(Exeunt.)	564

WAY WORLD
III.1

	PAGE	CHARACTER	DIRECTION	LINE
	425		(A Room in Lady Wishfort's House.	
	425		Lady Wishfort at her Toilet, Peg waiting.)	
	425	Lady Wish:	(Exit Peg)	21
	425		(Enter Peg with a Bottle and China-cup.)	26
	425		(One knocks.)	33
	426		(Enter Mrs. Marwood.)	42
	426	Lady Wish:	(To Peg.)	V 61
	426		(Exit Peg.)	62
	426		(Exit Marwood.)	68
	427		(Enter Foible.)	69
	427	Foible:	(aside)	84
	429	Lady Wish:	(Exit.)	182
	429		(Enter Mrs. Fainall.)	183
	430		(Enter Footman.)	218
	430		(Exeunt.)	223
	431		(Enter Mrs. Marwood.)	224
	431		(Enter Lady Wishfort.)	249
	431	Lady Wish:	(Calls)	256
	432		(Enter Foible.)	273
	432		(Exit Lady and Foible.)	282
	432		(Enter Mrs. Millamant and Mincing.)	283
	433	Millamant:	(Exit Mincing.)	327
	434		(Enter Mincing.)	367

Appendix B

INDEX OF COMMON WORDS

A (CONTINUED)
    FOR LOVE   (CONTINUED)
        228,241,243,249,251,253,254,255,257,262,264,265,287,295,302,304,311,314,315,316,317,319,319,
        319,320,322,322,324,325,326,330,339,342,342,356,361,361,362,369,370,372,377,383,385,390,392,
        397,397,404,406,408,413,413,414,414,415,421,423,425,429,437,437,452,457,461,462,464,464V,
        467,472,473,473,475,475,486,486V,493,498,503,505,507,508,508,509,514,514,514,516,534,534,535,
        545,576,595,596,601,602,638,641,646,650,653,662,664,666,671,671,675,677,677V,679,681,691,
        692,692,699,700,703,720,723,726,731,732,732,733,735,735,735,736,736,740,740,748,758,758,759,
        759,760,761,761,771,788,797,800,801,802,802,808,813,815,817; IV.1,8,16,20,21,21,21,23,23,24,27,
        30,35,35,43,45,48,53,54,64,69,70,79,88,89,102,107,111,131,133,133,133,134,149,171,175,184,193,
        196,212,240,244,249,254,256,258,262,263,263,266,266,268,271,272,274,279,287,289,290,291,335,
        342,349,360,365,365,367,368,375,381,385,399,401,408,409,410,410,425V,427,428,439,441,449,450,
        452,457,459,463,464,465,475,476,479,488,493,514,521,523,526,527,527,530,542,546,549,549,560,
        562,570,571,571,581,581,585,598,608,620,628,629,630,634,635,636,637,640,640,641,643,645,660,
        686,687,689,693,695,729,733,754,790,764,776,785,788,790,790V,795,795,801,808,810,811; V.1,D,5,
        6,14,14,18,19,19,22,22,24,25,26,28,28,30,31,33,33V,37,37V,39,47,51,54,54,54V,54V,57,59,62,62,
        62,64,65,66,66,67,68,69,70,70V,72,73V,74,74,77,79,80,81,81,82,83,90,95,95V,96,96,99,104,105,
        107,108,111,113,115,118,119,120,124,126,127,133,139,139,140,152,154,157,168,168,172,174,177,
        180,181,181,181,182,186,187,188,192,193,196,198,198,199,204,204,205,206,209,216,217,219,236,
        237,242,243,244,245,246,253,256,257,258,260,265,266,268,270,271,289,295,297,304,305,307,307,
        308,311,314,315,315,315,317,325,333,334,341,351,356,358,359,367,373,374,377,379,381,383,386,
        391,397,397,404,404,405,406,406,411,412,424,431,432,433,434,434,467,468,470,481,487,488,507,
        512,531,533,561,569,570,572,572,581,582,589,601,613,613V,620,621,637,637; EPI.,4,19,27,37,42,44
    M. BRIDE
        PRO.,2,4,20,20,31,34; I.1,1,2,30,31,48,73,110,120,124,127,141,164,165,179,230,253,290,292,293,
        315,315,322,348,348V,349,354,360,370,372,375,380,383,384,386,387,430,434,437,446,446V; II.1,D,
        8,8V,8V,21,52,53,66; II.2,D,75,99V,100,131,140,150,160,176,187,187V,195,195V,223,233,249,258,
        258V,272,272,289,302,309,309,315,330,336,341,371; III.1,D,D,6,50,53,53,108,112,141,170,180,183,
        206,222,241,251,277,316,325,353,412,458,458; IV.1,D,15,26,26,45,50,79,86,92,92V,102,122,129,
        151,189,190,200,232,233,236,237,279,281,281V,318,348,387,390,390,391,391V; V.1,D,12,18,18V,26,
        40,40,40V,40V,103,117,118,120,124,131; V.2,D,D,DV,DV,7,7,20,39,50,71,73,82,105,110,115,123,135,
        189,189V,193,193,199,200,221,222,229,229V,241,253,266,270,286,312,322,322; EPI.2,4,12,16,18,25
    WAY WORLD
        PRO.,3,5,18,21,30,32,35,38; I.1,D,1,6,8,9,11,19,25,31,33,38,39,44,47,51,62,70,71,71,72,74,75,
        77,86,90,91,94,95,96,109,110,114,119,130,136,138,140,142,145,145,146,156,156,158,159,170,173,
        179,183,192,208,212,213,224,225,230,232,240V,243,244,244,244,245,245,246,247,249,252,256,257,
        258,264,274,275,276,288,289,289,289V,289V,290,290,298,303,305,305,319,320,320,341,341,342,346V,
        350,353,359,361,372,373,374,376,379,383,384,384,390,394,395,395,408,408V,409,439,449,454,455,
        463,464,466,467,471,485,485,485,485,487,492,492,493,505,506,509,519,519,519V,522,527,537; II.1,
        29,48,57,75,78,80,98,100,103,110,114,120,126,157,163,165,185,206,210,210,211,211,212,212,
        213,248,248,269,269,270,271,271,272,275,276,296,298,303,308,312,313,313,315,318,318,319,324,
        324V,329,331,335,335V,339,339,343,348,352,353,353,353,357,357V,376,383,391,394,403,409,412,
        419,425,427,430,433,439,439,443,447,464,464,465,465,471V,474,477,491,491,492,492,493,493,494,
        495,495,511,514,520,538,545,559; III.1,D,6,7,20,26,27,28,28,29,31,31,35,36,45,54,75,77,90,93,
        95,104,110,113,118,130,131,131,132,134,144,151,152,156,162,164,164,166,167,168,168,169,169,
        169V,169V,175,176,178,180,184,201,212,217,226,227,227V,231,231,232,233,236,237,231,239,244V,
        247,247,254,254,267,267,286,288,296,296V,301,301,307,309,310,311,312,312,313,322,324,324,328,
        328,330,344,350,357,359,365,379,382,384,388,394,398,400,404,406,410,415,415,419,428,428V,432,
        443,443V,457,457V,461,462,468,473,487,489,505,523,523,524,524,528,532,535,538,538,540,541,542,
        545,545,546,546,547,547,547,556,556V,561,562,563,579,581,583,590,590,606,606,617,622,628,629,
        629,630,631V,632,633,633,635,637,637V,642,647,649,668,672,693,694,699,709,722; IV.1,4,18,23,24,
        26,26,28,29,29,32,63,65,74,76,94,101,116,117,118,121,140,142,163,175,176,177,179,190,191,192,
        203,206,206V,208,221,226,227,230,231,238,239,239,240,244,251,257,261,261,262,262,262V,262V,277,
        281,288,292,297,297V,298,302,315,316,329,333,338,346,347,348,350,351,356,357,359,363,366,368,
        371,373,375,381,381,387,389,392,394,400,402,406,410,410,414,414,422,422,424,425,426,426,436,
        438,440,444,445,447,447,450,456,457,462,471,472,474,474,479,481,489,492,495,495,496,509,
        521,524,524,525,528,535,536,549,553,556,558,558,559,563,565,573,573V,577,580,582,582,588,588,
        591,597,600,601,601,602,624,633,638,641; V.1,5,5,6,7,7,11,12,12,13,13,14,16,16,17,18,24,28,33,
        35,35,36,37,49,51,54,55V,59,59,62,63,65,84,93,96,97,98,99,99V,100,108,109,115,144,145,145,154,
        159,174,175,175V,176,178,178V,185,187,188,189,191,192,193,204,205,205V,209,210,212,213,214,215,
        215,216,220,225,242,272,273,285,306,314,317,318,322,325,328,331,336,345,364,366,367,367,367,
        369,373,380,382,385,393,397,401,410,417,427,427,432,440,443,443,450,459,470,481,495,502,508,
        524,537,540,550,570,579,583,591,591,591,600,607,608,616,618; EPI.,4,22,26,31

AM (362)
    OLD BATCH
        I.1,75,132,132V,135,137,142,253,347; II.1,16,62,64,72,122,122,134,200,211,227,236,241,244;
        II.2,10,58,81,107,109,173,186; III.1,63,63V,243,292,292,293; III.2,38,45,70,70,78,78V,80,80V,
        82,82,97,97,98; IV.1,28,52,74,109,159; IV.2,7,40,56,59,83,85; IV.3,1,2,5,5,78,90; IV.4,57,125,
        126,153,183,200,264; V.1,24,34,94,157,167,313,336,360; V.2,20,33,128,133; EPI.,17
    DOUBL DLR
        I.1,15,75,148,336,339,339,343,393; II.1,195,211,215,216,221,222,231,239,263,263V,309,310,323,
        323,323V,323V,335,375,393,402,433; III.1,24,29,34,38,47,50,121,132,228,383,389,414,414V,437,
        438; IV.1,57,98,103,141,178,192,209,293,339,411,433,533,537,552,552V,568,569; V.1,28,43,50,103,
        131,143,143V,177,196,257,305,316,401,410,415,470,569
    FOR LOVE
        I.1,40,49,56V,153,242,322,330,382,384,384,481,673; II.1,37,164,204,334,345,379,489; III.1,137,
        145,344,371,559,561,569,571,586,643,699; IV.1,59,70,83,83V,157,164,171,178,251,348,390,394,406,
        406,452,456,487,497,515,558,615,619,624,625,626,633,665,687,729,741,791; V.1,10,22,36,39,292,
        552,565,623
    M. BRIDE
        I.1,6,6,13,54,217; II.1,81,81V; II.2,70,76,77V,80,206,241,245,245,270,302,361; III.1,3,46,80,
        197,289,295,298,298V,303,303,349,367; IV.1,26,136,200,227,264,299,302,318,364,368,396,428; V.2,
        150,220,241,249,288,303; EPI,1
    WAY WORLD
        I.1,79,79V,86,121,137,141,144,150,184,394,447; II.1,45,50,80,95,101,124,125,135,209,209,338,
        344,359,561; III.1,4,142,148,159,188,254,263,357,357,509,510,574,579,614V,629,677,680,681,719;
        IV.1,48,57,67,75,161,180,224,292,308,316,326,410,484,492,492V,528,606,632; V.1,26,50,150,153,
        160,162,165,167,251,317,325,333,369,373,374,374V,416,460,608,609

AN (389)
    OLD BATCH
        I.1,60,64,77,78,90,157,211,214,250,278,288,298,312,332; II.1,8,32,57,88,198,199; II.2,25,26,
        28,129,171,171,213; III.1,91,91V,255,266; III.2,66,79,79V,143; IV.1,7,41,74,157,169; IV.2,38,

AN (CONTINUED)
   OLD BATCH   (CONTINUED)
       39; IV.3,51,78,153; IV.4,6,201,215,271; V.1,18,100,149,173,205,205,301,301,317,317,395; V.2,56,
       75,103,159,161,178; EPI.,15,16
   DOUBL DLR
       PRO.,13; I.1,120,130,201,362; II.1,90,118,119,157,163,171V,257,257V,435,450,452; III.1,9,32,
       37,117,144,171,174,216,268,270,270V,276,299,301,400,435,442,505,568,576,591,592; IV.1,81,202,
       267,273,290,399,407,473,528,552V,553,567,584; IV.2,41; V.1,23,239,273,273,274,292,317,426,492,
       529,537,542; EPI.,14
   FOR LOVE
       I.1,8,49,78,80,90,131,145,145,189,261,266,285,305,328,351,438,442,498,512,554,578,578,580,675;
       II.1,48,123,153,205,221,226,238,242,243,245,249,252,321,351,427,452,485,501,575; III.1,118,
       163,235,236,242,263,280,289,299,300,302,306,307,317,334,337,360,362,369,370,421,467,515,548,
       551,598,680,681,702,719,739,807; IV.1,46,63,85,92,124,175,238,289,307,382,392,425,425V,440,620,
       707,787,802; V.1,20,64,75,129,154,159,171,186,209,216,284,294,297,306,327,382,427,485,556,583,
       583V,592,607,620,622,627; EPI.,22,36
   M. BRIDE
       I.1,67,67V; II.1,30,63; III.1,326,419; IV.1,54,57,105,234; V.1,1; V.2,111,115V,122; EPI,4,31
   WAY WORLD
       I.1,35,72,76,93,190,204,218,230,232,248,258,290,323,338,407,434,443,471,481; II.1,9,18,48,97,
       105,113,153,156,270,286,307,317,320,352,410,417,420,421,469,508,531; III.1,6,29,36,51,58,60,
       138,148,233,236,237,255,416,422,426,502,505,505,525,554,557,574,586,628,631,640,667,669,681,
       701; IV.1,44,88,135,168,178,180,328,344,345,350,389,392,394,401,413,422,467,487,500,522,544,
       559,643,647; V.1,14,15,35,129,165,202,211,211V,212,227,318,351,360,363,382,384,385,392,392V,
       393,424,425,425,492,554

AND (3725)
   OLD BATCH
       PRO.,6,7,11,13,21; I.1,D,1,7,9,9V,11,11,20,21,22,24,24,25,25V,28,39,48,53,57,58,82,91,95,98,
       107,111,123,125,126,139,145,158,162,163,163,167,173,176,181,182,183,186,188,190,191,195,202,
       207,212,215,216,220,222,223,226,230,232,239,244,248,251,254,263,268,269,275,280,294,296,306,
       311,314,318,319,320,321,323,323V,326,327,340V,340,344,347,353,357,359,361,366,370,372,378,379,
       382; II.1,1,5,5V,9,16,19,31,36,36,55,58,65,67,68,73,77,89,89V,90,103,109,115,115,116,119,120,
       133,137,165,168,169,212,225; II.2,4,9,12,29,29,29,33,34,36,38,42,62,69,69,76,88,90,95,102,106,
       118,120,126,126,131,133,135,142,144,147,148,151,154,164,182,197,215,219,222,224,225; III.1,D,2,
       8,11,26,28,28,31,33,37,42,45,49,49,54,59,65,68,70,75,80,82,84,93,93V,100,122,123,128,147,149,
       151,151,152,161,163,173,175,180,181,184,188,191,198,205,207,210,226,228,234,236,238,242,243,
       243,249,250,250,251,255,259,274,276,284,290,297,300,301,320,324,328,328V,336,349,349; III.2,2,
       5,19V,19V,20V,24V,28,30,32,33,34,34,35,36,38,50,51,53,55,55V,56,63,66,67,68,71,72,76,80,80V,
       82,84,93,101,106,107,111,114,115,115,120,126,127,128,132,146,157,158,160,163,163V; IV.1,3,13,
       21,26,32,32,34,36,38,38V,43,46,49,51,52,52,53,54,54,55,56,60,62,68,70,90,109,118,130,137,144,
       156,161,164,165,166,167,169,172,178,179,185; IV.2,D,5,6,12,18,23,48,58,59,62,66,66,74; IV.3,D,
       2,13,19,24,31,42,43,45,45,47,51,52,53,57,63,64,68,78,79,88,91,99,99V,101,110,121,125,127,142,
       143,144,144,151,153,159,168,172,173,174,179,179,185,193,206; IV.4,D,6,14,22,24,39,50,53,66,70,
       78,83,91,103,112,115,135,139,148,157,170,172,177,179,182,183,188,190,196,203,209,210,219,225,
       228,239,240,241,241,244,245,250,252,265,266; V.1,D,5,9V,21,32,42,43,47,49,49V,53,60,61,70,
       71,81,83,84,88,96,96,97,105,115,116,117,120,126,141,146,160,162,164,167,174,176,190,194,203,
       208,215,218,218,222,224,227,231,233,239,240,244,253,253,255,256,256,257,284,289,291,293,295,
       295,298,300,306,308,310,337,344,355,375,377,402,403; V.2,D,14,20,21,53,55,55,57,69,69V,71,82,
       85,86,117,128,131,135,140,142,150,151,158,163,165,166,186,187,189,192,195; EPI.,2,5,22,29,30,
       30V
   DOUBL DLR
       PRO.,13,15,16; I.1,D,4,5,7,7V,9,9V,12,12V,15,17,23,26,27,34,38,46,47,53,54,55,58,60,65,69,75,
       80,84,93,95,104,105,106,108,112,114,116,127,129,129,130,133,134,136,137,156,161,161,162,162,
       165,171,173,181,182,183,187,217,217V,221,228,228V,238,239,241,255,255V,256,257,269,269,290,294,
       298,299,306,310,313,324,324V,327,331V,336,337,338,340,347,348,349,351,356,357,360,366,367,368,
       370,372,376,377,378,378V,394,398,400,402,402V,412,418; II.1,D,5,6,10,11,20,21,23,25,29,31,41,
       55,65,69,72,72,80,97,98,120,121,125,126,127,138,138,139,144,144V,146,147,150,150V,151,153,155,
       158,161,165,166,168,170,184,187,194,207,207V,210,217,217,220,223,225,231,232,234,236,241,242,
       243,247,252,255,255V,261,268,270,279,280,288,290,291,291V,294,301,301,304,310,312,314,316,317,
       318,322,323,323V,325,338,341,342,345,353,356,358,363,374,383,394,401,403,406,412,425,430,441,
       444,447,447,448,449,451,455,457,457,461,462,463,465,466,466,468; III.1,D,6,8,16,39,41,47,54,77,
       86,88,91,96,97,100,101,101,105,116,118,119,128,129,132,137,139,142,143,152,158,158,166,168,170,
       176,178,181,183,184,190,192,201,204,214,218,226,228,229,235,249,250,251,255,261,265,275,278,
       283,283V,289,289,290,290,291,291,300,306,308,308,312,313,315,315,318,320,326,328,332,344,352,
       368,372,379,381,381V,384,385,388,389,390,401V,409,410,412,416,424,434,459,461,462,463,469,475,
       476,482,483,488,496,501,503,508,508,524,535,539,539,541,542,543,545,547,547,552,556,556,560,
       571,574,575,586,587,600,606,610,612,620,627,627,628,629,629,630,631,634; IV.1,D,1,4,9,13,17,20,
       28,30,34,38,39,39V,48,49,51,55,62,63,65,68,70,70,71,77,82,91,94,97,98,99,100,101,116,117,120,
       126,127,132,143,148,152,164,174,175,176,182,185,190,191,196,208,209,216,218,219,223,247,251,
       253,259V,260,260,261,263,268,268,277,280,280,281,281,288,290,293,295,302,303,317,326,329,366,
       366,374,389,397,403,417,418,422,425V,427,429,431,454,458V,460,460,476,479,483V,487V,497,498,
       505,512,516,518,522,522V,523,529,535,537,538,555,564,568,571,571,572,578,582,590; IV.2,15,19,
       20,25,33,33,35,43,45,47,52,53,56,62,62,64,66,69,72,72V,77,82,85,86,93,108,113,130,132,134,
       141,142,144,144V,145,146,146,147,150; V.1,D,2,4,18,23,24,25,30,33,40,41,41,42,44,47,50,53,54,
       58,62,63,71,79,79,83,86,91,95,98,104,112,118,122,127,135,137,144,148,148V,153V,156,171,175,180,
       181,181,182,183,193V,199,204,207,208,218,223,224,237,238,240,242,255,255V,259,264,265,271,273,
       278,286,288,293,298,319,319V,329,332,337,345,345V,348,349,353,355,362,367,373,375,380,381,386,
       387,387V,394,400,403,409,410,412,418,422,438,445,447,449,457,462,463,466,471,474,484,486,487,
       489,491,494,519,531,536,543,552,560V,560V,563,565,567V,573,582,583,586,587,588,593; EPI.,11,13,
       14,15,18,19,20,23,24,24
   FOR LOVE
       PRO.,3,3,9,10,12,16,19,20,22,24,27,30,32,36,38,43,45; I.1,3,6,7,12,13,14,15,21,24,30,33,34,35,
       36,37,39,40,43,44,46,47,49,51,54,56,56V,67,68,79,96,97,100,106,107,125,132,134,134,136,138,147,
       149,158,158V,160,161,162,162,172,172,178,181,188,193,194,194V,197,198,204,205,210,211,214,218,
       219,227,229,231,240,242,248,250,257,265,269,285,286,287,287,290,297,297,298,299,308,311,315,
       319,327,338,339,340,341,344,353,363,364,364,365,366,371,373,374,374V,375,376,379,391,408,420,
       420,421,431,431,432,432,432,439,439,447,452,456,457,467V,483,496,501,516,528,559,564,567,
       572,577,578,581,582,583,583,585,592,593,597,601,602,603,609,610,617,618,625,626,626,627,629,
       632,632,633,637,643,644,644,645,647,651,652,655,656,674,675; II.1,D,13,15,15V,23,23,27,29,29,
       34,35,36,36,47,49,52,55,67,68,68,74,77,81,81,90,91,97,103,103,103,104,104,107,108,108,
       120,121,129,135,137,137,138,147,148,149,151,151,153,162,163,164,176,178,180,181,187,188,194,
       198,199,201,203,205,204,207,208,210,211,211,212,213,214,220,222,227,240,243,247,252,253,253,
       253,257,268,294,296,296,298,299,300,301,314,316,321,325,328,332V,334,337,341,345,347,348,361,

AND (CONTINUED)
  FOR LOVE   (CONTINUED)
        369,370,371,373,374,377,380,381,385,385,386,387,389,391,392,398,403,403,404,405,409,410,412,
        412,414,419,430,433,445,453,453V,476,478,481,482,485,487,489,490,491,492,497,498,501,503,503V,
        505,519,519,523,524,545,556,565,574,580,587,593,595,599,616,618,622,626,630,634,645,646,648,
        651,652,654,655,660; III.1,1,4,14V,15,24,25,26,41,57,67,69,75,81,82,90,104,109,132,135,139,143,
        144,145,153,154,156,158,160,162,170,174,176,176,192,200,205,208,209,222,223,227,233,235,237,
        242,247,249,254,257,257,261,265,267,272,273,274,278,283,290,291,294,295,310,313,317,322,324,
        327,327,330,332,335,342,359,371,374,376,376V,383,386,387,396,397,400,403,405,414,414,415,416,
        416,426,426V,427,432,435,442,444,447,448,452,455,458,474,476,477,483,484,486,489,497,499,499,
        510,514,515,515,516,516,522,524,530,532,534,537,544,546,548,552,552V,570,585,589,591,596,601,
        605,609,609,610,610,612,620,621,626,638,639,641,643,645,647,649,651,651,656,657,657,659,663,
        673,675,676,677,677V,682,684,687,689,700,709,710,712,717,723,736,738,743,746,758,759,766,767,
        771,778,785,787,788,796,797,800,801,802,808,811,813,816,817,818,820; IV.1,D,1,9,11,12,24,35,40,
        51,53,57,66,69,71,72,74,82,87,87,91,99,107,114,115,125,135,143,148,152,154,158,160,161,163,164,
        178,189,208,215,223,232,238,241,241,252,257,257,263,266,271,273,281,282,283,284,286,286,287,
        288,288,288,289,295,296,296V,298,308,311,312,318,321,323,328,328,330,336,336V,338,341,345,349,
        352,352,354,363,366,369,372,374,381,382,385,386,387,388,388,390,394,399,400,401,401,408,416,
        417,418,418,419,420,431,431,440,450,451,456,458,463,464,468,469,472,472,473,474,476,478,479,
        482,487,488,492,493,504,505,506,506,508,508,512,519,520,521,522,524,525,526,534,542,542,547,
        548,550,551,558,559,560,561,562,562,564,565,566,571,581,582,582,583,586,587,604,604,607,613,
        617,619,625,626,629,636,639,640,653,653,656,656,659,664,669,683,685,690,691,702,703,704,708,
        708,709,712,712V,716,717,719,724,724V,735,738,750,755,767,774,786,787,787,792,792,794,796,803,
        808,808,810,813; V.1,D,4,6,9,15,23V,25,32,36,37,37V,38,42,47,48,50,52,56,57,63,68,69,72,73,73V,
        82,84,95,95V,97,98,98,103,106,109,119,120,125,129,130,132,135,137,139,140,141,142,142,143,145,
        147,147,157,164,167,173,178,181,182,184,198,201,205,215,216,223,229,229,233,238,243,244,246,
        253,254,261,262,262,263,264,269,270,272,284,287,289,290,290,291,292,293,294,295,297,298,304,
        305,309,310,310,311,311V,315,317,318,319,320,324,326,327,329V,345,352,353,354,359,361,365,373,
        378,381,382,384,384,386,394,396,397,398,398,400,406,418,431,436,439,445,445,447,478,485,488,
        493,496,497,500,514,522,528,537,538,543,545,547,555,561,563,565,568,573,575,576,577,583,583,
        583V,584V,585V,585V,596,603,605,615,620,623,631,634; EPI.,9,10,14,17,25,25V,29,30,31,31,31,42
M. BRIDE
      PRO,2,4,10,16,19,23,35,37; I.1,4,5,9,11,18,21,24,25,27,28,29,30,40,40,43,44,44V,46,49,50,53,
        53V,63,64,81,83,85,85,86,97,100,100V,103,106,114,114,116,116V,120,121,124,125,127,130,131,135,
        136,141,141,144,145,146,148V,151,158,159,161,169,172,172V,173,180,180,181,184,190,195,197V,
        198V,199,203V,215,215,215V,215V,221,223,223V,225,230,232,232,235,236,236,239,240,241,241V,243,
        251,258,266,267,268,269,275,281,282V,285,286,286V,291,293,293,306,312,312,313,314,314,317,317,
        332,332,334,336,337,341,352,355,360,361,370,370,373,375,382,382,383,383,383,384,385,386,390,
        397,401,402,410,414,420,426,438,440,446V,451,452,457; II.1,D,6,11,14V,14V,20,21,24,26,27,31,32,
        35,46,46,46V,46V,48,51,58,61,62,64,65,66,67,67V,68,68V,71,74,74,79,82,83; II.2,5,8,13,15,18,18,
        19,39,21,23,26,26,28,36,39V,41,41V,45,46,46V,47,47V,53,55,61,63,67,67,68,70,72,84,88,90,90,
        97,103V,105,110,117,122,123,127,127,128V,130,132,138,141,146,150,151,153,155,155V,157,157V,159,
        162,163,173,173V,174,174V,177,181,183,189,193,197,203,206,208,211,212,213,214V,215,215V,226,
        232,236,237,239,240,242,253,256,260,263,265,269,269V,274,277,278,282,282V,284,285,287,290V,291,
        296,296,302,306,307V,308V,311,314,317,318,319,321,321,326,328,330,337,340,344,346,349V,351,354,
        355,358,362,364,366,367,369,373,374,378,378V,300,383,384,386,388,389,391; III.1,1,2,5,12,17,29,
        30,34,36,37,38,48,52,53,60,62,63,66,69,70,71,71V,71V,72V,75,77,82,84,85,8/,90,91,92,94,99,102,
        102V,104,110,121,125,131,134,134,141,150,152,153,155,155,159,160,163,165,165V,166,167,175,181,182,
        196,202,203,208,208,210,223,224,229,231,235,238,241,242,243,260,265,266,268,272,273,274,281,
        284,288,292,293,299,305,307,310,311,313,323,324,333,337,339,340,345,346,347,351,351V,351V,353,
        355,360,360,361,362,362,364,368,369,403,373,375,396,397,398,401,402,403V,407,409,410,413,424,
        429,439,440,441,450,453,456; IV.1,D,5,8,9,10,11,13V,16,17,21,24,25,26,33,34,41,44,52,57,60,64,
        65,78V,86,87V,98,106,108,118,124,126,130,134V,135,136,137,139,140,153,170,177,186,191,193,195,
        195,196,215,218,227,235,238,242,248,249,259,259,260,263,265,270,270V,274,277,280,280,283,283,
        284,285,290,293,295,297,303,305,309,312,313,314,317,318,323,326,326,328,331,333,334,336,343,
        348,350,351,353,359,359,360,365,366,376,379,381,382,388,389,389V,392,392V,401,407,409,422,
        432,437,442V,447; V.1,D,7,12,13V,15,16,18V,22,23,25,27,37,37V,39,40,43,44,48,48,59,63,64,65,66,
        72,78,82,84,86AV,86BV,86EV,86FV,88,88V,90,94,96,96V,100,103,106,107,109,110,112,120,121,125,
        128,133,134; V.2,2,9,12,13,15,18,21,27,29,31,34,37,38,39,45,49,51,55,67,68,72,79,83,85,92,95,
        103,103V,106,115,115V,118,123,128,130,132,133,137,138,138,139,139,140,141,144,145V,149,150,153,
        156,158,161,164V,165V,166V,167V,169V,171V,175,178,181,182,183,183V,186,193,196,197,199,201,205,
        208,211,213,214,222,223,229,229V,230,230V,239,241,242,244,245,248,248V,250,251,253,255,258,265,
        266,269,271,272,274,276,279,281,284,293,295,296,298,305,320,322; EPI,3,6,8,12,14,14V,20,24,26,
        26,28
WAY WORLD
      PRO.,4,20,29; I.1,D,6,11,15,17,20,22,22,26,28,28,31,37,40,51,54,54,57,59,61,62,62,70,71,75,78,
        87,90,94,96,102,115,118,121,125,128,129,130,131,139,142,142,154,158,161,165,165,169,170,173,
        176,179,205,210,214,214,216,218,220,222,224,225,227,230,231,231,247,249,257,257,266,287,288,
        289,289,289V,289V,290,292,292V,300,324,350,352,353,360,372,373,373,376,385,385,387,407,411,
        411V,413,420,429,430,435,438,439,439,443,447,460,463,466,480,482,482,483,484,488,492,494,518,
        520,526,542; II.1,D,2,4,5,7,8,8V,10,16,24,26,26,45,50,54,58,62,63,72,78,83,84,93,104,107,108,
        114,116,127,134,137,141,143,146,150,155,156,160,163,167,168,171,173,174,176,183,196,206,207,
        207,208,212,213,214,215,216,217,220,238,241,243,245,251,262,265,271,271,272,281,287,288,291,
        297,301,304,305,308,315,319,320,322,324,324,324V,324V,326,329,335,335V,341,350,361,370,372,374,
        374,378,386,387,388,390,395,397,404,405,405,411,411,417,428,452,455,466,468,482,482V,487,493,
        496,497,499,500,504,506,520,524,538,539,541,543,547,553,555,557,558,561,561V,563; III.1,19,21,
        26,28,46,61,61V,65,65,74,87,90,94,101,107,112,115,129,137,152,157,186,189,191,194,198,209,237,
        238,238,243V,245,247,264,266,269,276,279,282,283,294,301,302,302,311,312,314,315,316,316,341,
        342,345,350,355,359,368,374V,380,391,394,397,413,414,430,431,436,437,443,452,465,479,481,483,
        505,511,518,522,522,523,523,524,524,525,527,529,529,535,538,541,543,544,546,547,547,547,547,
        552,552,558,563,564,569,574,578,592,603,607,610,612,627,629,630,637,640,650,655,660,664,
        664,664,665,669,681,685,691,692,706,710,716,719,720,721; IV.1,D,2,4,5,7,11,11,15,15,17,21,25,
        27,27,28,30,31,42,46,49,51,56,57,65,71,88,105,115,122,125,129,137,144,155,158,160,164,167,168,
        171,172,173,181,183,194,198,199,201,203,203,205,207,209,212,213,213,215,223,233,237,241,242,
        243,246,249,250,253,261,265,266,267,268,270,273,274,275,277,281,291,293,297,300,301,304,310,
        312,314,328,330,330V,333,338,340,346,351,371,372,376,383,385,393,395,399,404,411,412,414,416,
        420,426,429,435,437,443,448,451,454,454,457,457,459,461,466,477,479,479,489,491,492,492V,494,
        501,501,507,514,514,515,515,515,516,523,524,545,546,549,552,554,559,562,567,588,592,592,614,
        616,623,625,629,634,638,642,643; V.1,D,5,6,16,17,21,30,43,52,53,63,66,69,70,72,84,87,89,95,98,
        99,106,109,112,114,123,124,128,128V,130,133,133,134,135,135,140,141,141,145,151,151,152,152,
        153,153,158,158,162,178,178V,182,184,185,192,194,197,198,198,199,199,200,202,204,208,209,211,
        211V,214,215,218,221,221,221V,221V,224,225,228,231,232,235,239,239,251,269,274,275,277,280,281,
        284,286,295,310,315,316,317,319,319,322,326,328,329,330,332,339,343,346,347,347,349,352,353V,
        359,363V,367,378,380,381,386,390,390,397,398,405,406,408,408V,413,422,423,423,424,433,435,436,

AND (CONTINUED)
    WAY WORLD   (CONTINUED)
        440,444,453,464,470,471,472,473,474,479,483,487,498,500,507,519,536,542,543,545,546,546,565,
        573,574,575,579,580,583,583,584,585,586,592,596,596,596V,596V,610; EPI.,7,10,15,19,22,27,28,33,
        36

ARE (606)
    OLD BATCH
        PRO.,3; I.1,6,30,150,218,240,243,260,272,273,331,358,386; II.1,32,79,88,100,113,136,158,162,
        176,179,192,248; II.2,14,46,58,72,74,76,78,85,97,118,120,135,136,144,151,152,216; III.1,57,98,
        190,264,290,322,323; III.2,34,56,77; IV.1,66,88,106,182; IV.2,20,22,24,24,29,46,62,62; IV.3,82,
        83,128,137; IV.4,8,42,127,129,130,161,172,173,191; V.1,33,37,44,64,175,231,269,271,304,358,372;
        V.2,26,27,61,66,70,83,100,107,131,132,139; EPI.,29
    DOUBL DLR
        PRO.,2,7,12,27; I.1,3,3V,11,11V,20,45,70,84,124,124V,163,233,257,284,299,337,359; II.1,97,98,
        154,166,215,247,299,341,359,384,447,466; III.1,36,42,111,167,223,228,293,307,313,338,358,380,
        445,458,458,482,577,628,634; IV.1,11,14,18,69,90,122,255,255V,269,290,300,301,362,377,387,431,
        504,518,532,540; IV.2,20,22,69,123; V.1,34,62,140,142,155,196,222,285,323,344,345,345V,400,521,
        530,530V,533,541,572,585,592; EPI.,5,19,21,22,23,29,29V
    FOR LOVE
        PRO.,37,38; I.1,39,47,76,151,161,185,191,195,272,301,313,318,364,397,430,503,505,527,528,536,
        547,562,603,609,625,626,627,654,676; II.1,1,35,47,66,72,74,76,78,138,201,203,215,299,314,324,
        326,339,347,347,377,388,411,477,477V,480,489,509,509V,513,519,534,548,611,615; III.1,35,42,134,
        149,151,151,181,223,249,251,380,409,412,449,456,514,524,528,533,542,553,556,559,560,568,607,
        658,660,669,670,673,684,692,702,790,804; IV.1,57,86,98,102,160,162,163,225,239,255,263,278,279,
        280,300,324,325,357,413,416,422,451,510,511,514,519,534,586,593,593V,594,617,623,635,637,638,
        638,770,784,786,792,809,815; V.1,41,57,65,87,88,94,106,144,167,188,222,256,262,268,337V,359,
        369,371,388,443,445,447,513,535,541,584V,590,613,613V,614,624,631; EPI.,7
    M. BRIDE
        PRO.,5; I.1,11,53,53V,55,56,60,154,195,197,197V,267,278,281,282V,386,387,452; II.1,28,49,80,
        80V; II.2,10,12,111,180,199V,315,321; III.1,64,70,266,293,328,362,363,367,386,404,404V; IV.1,
        74,80,111,133V,143,153,195,199,205,216,252,258,269,269V,310,331; V.1,55; V.2,28,39,113,132,157,
        205,228,238,240; EPI,29
    WAY WORLD
        PRO.,1,11,36; I.1,1,5,5,11,15,54,86,90,94,96,101,120,120,139,141,142,142,148,156,160,172,176,
        177,210,282,287,309,355,356,359,389,392,398,403,404,415,425,429,438,446,483,504,508,523,538;
        II.1,3,4,5,77,121,131,134,157,170,185,186,216,252,253,277,391,411,438,445,447,470,478,479,497,
        511; III.1,65,74,95,96,111,145,226,276,300,305,323,331,358,412,469,498,507,509,544,593,598,712,
        725; IV.1,2,11,39,47,55,70,124,128,170,199,211,217,230,293,345,367,407,424,440,442,465,527,545,
        549,587,604; V.1,89,129,131,153,235,265,275,322,341,343,343,346,347,356,382,415,432,432V,474,
        474V,492,493,502,514,521,588,601,606,614,623; EPI.,5,9,9,16,18,25

ART (105)
    OLD BATCH
        I.1,74,185,228,250,251,252; III.1,53,54,89,165,179,183,184,195,196; III.2,45,56,78,78V,79,79V;
        IV.1,50,50; IV.3,109; IV.4,15,143,198,251,251V; V.1,136,296,366; V.2,126,152
    DOUBL DLR
        I.1,23,33,362; II.1,131,463; III.1,205,265; IV.1,132,419,571; V.1,5,236V; EPI.,16
    FOR LOVE
        II.1,246,257; III.1,271,534; IV.1,168,400; V.1,180,259,267
    M. BRIDE
        PRO,36,37; I.1,52,52V,74,92,181,431; II.2,61,80,110,113,114,114V,121,132,151,152,333,336;
        III.1,318,318,332; IV.1,190,265,417,429; V.1,45,51; V.2,186
    WAY WORLD
        I.1,443,448,519,519V; III.1,23,151,152,155,518,519; IV.1,65,105,337,344,346,348,350,558; V.1,
        480

AT (446)
    OLD BATCH
        I.1,32,62V,84,92,98,129,169,204,252,281,286; II.1,16,106,112,183; II.2,80,81,133,198,208,219,
        222; III.1,8,47,98,102,134,193,225,285,348; III.2,18V,43,46,133,152,156,163,163V; IV.1,14,17,
        111,158; IV.2,23,49; IV.3,2,55,99,99V,108,120,128,144; IV.4,36,75,154,215,244; V.1,5,9V,10,83,
        88,103,116,150,156,237,272,276,328,331,336,351,365,377,382,393V,399; V.2,29,110,149,180; EPI.,
        12,29
    DOUBL DLR
        PRO.,18; I.1,11,11V,30,56,66,68,103,113,162,192,196,198,201,206,235,260,263,327,367,379; II.1,
        29,36,157,164,170,212,221,267,415,417,421,426,459; III.1,135,169,170,187,233,249,255,281,283,
        283V,284,285,305,350,433,466,477,480,483,491,535,559,576; IV.1,87,95,223,281,314,349,351,366,
        449,450; IV.2,19,108,134; V.1,48,243,253,270,564,581; EPI.,9,36
    FOR LOVE
        PRO.,28; I.1,14,18,25,35,80,92,93,101,138,140,168,180,182,225,287,328,349,373,387,389,445,453,
        539,572,599,618,674; II.1,6,37,38,41,58,63,70,70V,83,98,208,209,288,312,346,352,409,426,428,
        444,445,456,468,481,489,514,591,633; III.1,14V,112,155,155V,155V,156,157,170,206,290,293,308,
        321,344,379,383,399,408,430,443,472,472,483,488,488,592,666,765,787,800; IV.1,10,21,38,147,223,
        383,408,441,452,475,496,500,504,505,512,542,636,709,756,806; V.1,3,21,28,46,94,100,159,175,185,
        186,199,217,264,353,384,404,405,460,470,502,547,586V,609,609V; EPI.,1
    M. BRIDE
        PRO,19,23; I.1,9,13,24,52V,53,164,202,203V,254,278,310,321,367,367V,374,407,427,450; II.2,152,
        195V,229,229V,379V,385; III.1,6,37,38,41,58,63,70,70V,90,207,210,302,409,422,427; IV.1,3,53,92V,103,144,
        147,182,208,364,421,432,441; V.1,7,23,78; V.2,2,90,104,104V,127,163V,164V,232,233,252
    WAY WORLD
        PRO.,12; I.1,15,34,51,113,130,168,212,217,233,257,258,281,282,297,340,361,384,385,393,450,465,
        483; II.1,6,92,303,468,523,543; III.1,D,18,44,90,178,208,244V,260,423,425,463,576,664,700,711;
        IV.1,47,70,75,114,134,163,209,224,241,268,333,384,385,392,423,423,430,482,484,512,519,522,600,
        611; V.1,88,95,105,108,159,201,210,225,276,308,333,371,385,387,402,463,467,511,515,522,536,557

BE (1227)
    OLD BATCH
        PRO.,24,25; I.1,7,8,10,23,38,56,60,66,67,70,75,79,84,87,89,96,102,124,125,127,158,171,226,233,
        252,253,254,254,265,267V,268,270,270V,286,291,296,307,309,310,312,318,344,348,351,379; II.1,11,
        14,17,23,29,38,80,123,123V,129,136,143,159,181,182,198,215,229; II.2,8,10,12,13,64,65,83,
        86,87,107,114,124,127,139,141,145,153,169,173,175,220,226; III.1,2,12,68,70,78,79,82,102,104,
        105,134,149,154,158,161,173,174,195,207,210,217,220,224,231,236,253,256,266,286,292,292,292,
        293,297,300,308,323,324,336,340,343; III.2,73,75,83,89,96,112,124,126,128,138; IV.1,7,34,36,43,

BE (CONTINUED)
    OLD BATCH   (CONTINUED)
        60,92,108,110,119,135,136,140,174,182,184,186,191; IV.2,23,43,46,67,93; IV.3,18,36,58,81,87,93,
        102,104,104,105,110,131,135,152,153,173,188; IV.4,46,101,117,162,182,184,192,203,225,230,234,
        273; V.1,D,10,11,13,14,24,33,45,52,53,57,60,86,116,119,126,176,193,204,205,227,227,228,243,244,
        285,285,338,341,349,349,365; V.2,50,76,76,121,132,140,157,159,177; EPI.,2,2,16,22,27
    DOUBL DLR
        PRO.,11,14,20,25,34,35,35; I.1,26,58,66,69,70,84,125,133,138,153,156,157,158,158,159,180,195,
        203,203,219,219V,240,242,244,253,263,265,270,279,281,334,335,336,342,389,40C,410; II.1,18,36,
        58,105,107,110,128,134,139,169,171,171V,191,199,209,211,216,218,221,230,231,266,268,271,
        292,298,346,347,352,360,364,364,365,365V,367,370,377,414,423,434,436,442,456,463,465,465;
        III.1,16,17,35,39,43,44,46,48,55,55,65,68,72,75,76,87,104,106,107,138,141,159,214,219,219V,
        224,239,253,256,310,311,322,324,328,337,337,375,377,386,406,413,419,429,442,448,481; IV.1,7,39,
        39V,60,80,106,137,142,166,168,171,185,194,201,201V,212,212,216,223,247,254,280,338,341,418,420,
        420V,446,450,458,468,482V,499,502,527,527,533,538,553,576,585,590; IV.2,10,14,15,23,25,33,35,
        49,50,52,53,80,83,85,87,90,99,99,99V,115,155; V.1,3,8,13,18,22,38,48,59,62,90,91,92,94,113,
        114,125,125,138,145,149,150,163,165,182,190,208,210,211,230V,248,249,256,265,269,269V,273,279,
        287,288,290,293,300,302,319,319,319V,319V,320,321,324,327,328,352,368,369,373,397,426,432,440,
        444,463,474,476,482,506,547,568,586,591; EPI.,33,35
    FOR LCVE
        PRO.,32; I.1,22,25,29,41,50,53,57,73,75,83,100,112,136,142,143,145,149,175,182,183,187,196,
        225,257,298,301,322,324,362,363,376,378,387,397,405,409,442,465,473,483,491,508,514,516,517,
        518,520,521,538,556,570,572,578,591,646,659,659V,664,674,676; II.1,5,12,30,46,53,56,76,113,128,
        135,157,165,169,170,170V,172,178,184,193,195,197,214,216,230,280V,291,292,296,300,303,346,350,
        351,402,430,432,493,494,500V,551,554,570,576,594,610,620,621,623,652,655; III.1,101,105,124,
        130,154,175,208,218,251,289,296,301,301,304,306,311,334,343,351,352,357,366,391,398,428,428,
        461,462,475,487,487V,502,524,524,547,547,572,621,631,637,639,649,653,657,695,716,716,719,733,
        794,796; IV.1,4,16,43,48,61,71,73,74,99,107,107,115,116,135,142,143,159,190,221,222,238,243,
        248,254,280,282,288,308,317,369,381,397,413,414,426,429,474,496,500,502,507,522,528,532,535,
        548,550,552,554,563,619,629,638,646,657,657,662,670,672,686,697,699,708,737,750,755,762,771,
        774,801,806,809,813; V.1,2,10,22,52,58,76,82,90,91,94,100,115,115,161,161V,168,172,186,197,198,
        201,219,228,229,229,242,245,278,280,289,291,293,301,301V,305,311,311V,318,318,340,359,366,370,
        393,396,413,415,418,424,432,454,457,497,519,572,594,599,601,610,611; EPI.,2,22
    M. BRIDE
        I.1,57,59,72,97,139,172,172V,175,189,218,218V,220,248,286V,287,305,324,326V,334,362,398,403,
        408,408V,417,417V,431,443,443V,445,448,448V,449; II.1,30,34,36,77; II.2,49,67,108,108,142,142,
        149,165V,190,198,216V,217,252,314,321,324,330,341,350,356,363,379V,381,385; III.1,18,23,28,35,
        42,95,152,162,181,282,282V,288,296,302,333,334,343,406,425,426,439,443,450; IV.1,20,32,37,42,
        47,51,66,72,95,99,148,158,162V,171,205,220,229,239,239,245,252,279,328,352,353,371,371,379,408,
        411; V.1,1,29; V.2,55; V.1,85,86,86V,121,135,136; V.2,93,119,144,144V,174,186,301,309,315,315V
    WAY WORLD
        PRO.,15,21; I.1,15,33,39,43,55,56,76,77,82,82V,92,93,96,132,139,140,162,175,190,191,196,208,
        216,216,217,226,227,252,267,282,284,286,293,296,318,319,322,353,384,385,390,410,426,430,440,
        446,455,489,496,515,521,522,524,531,534; II.1,1,12,16,20,31,54,62,101,109,110,129,131,132,132V,
        145,160,176,187,188,100,212,214,241,246,249,259,270,274,315,328,391,396,438,451,452,453,
        454,455,471,471V,475,476,499,499,522,539,543,554,557,560,561,561V; III.1,77,119,119,122,156,
        156V,157,163,171,173,173,181,203,204,210,215,232,233,264,274,279,299,299V,302,309,322,338,340,
        346,361,362,362V,363,406,428,428V,435,496,508,525,531,550,563,631,631V,634,634,637V,642,653,
        654V,663,669,680,682,693,695,699,706,713,714,715; IV.1,12,22,27,40,53,78,78,81,84,116,116,125,
        130,135,158,160,164,174,183,185,194,195,200,204,204V,207,208,218,219,222,230,235,241,255,257,
        281,295,295,410,433,454,477,478,487,499,503,504,521,533,563,579,587,602,624,627,636,638,642;
        V.1,55,55V,59,63,111,113,122,135,140,180,181,195,203,211,211V,214,230,232,243,244,250,257,265,
        267,277,277,292,293,299,307,308,321,324,325,328,340,341,347,348,370,378,393,427,442,455,460,
        461,462,494,496,503,556,560,587,618,620; EPI.,2,4,6

BEEN (272)
    OLD BATCH
        I.1,43,99,99,180,183,184,188,192,195,197,368; II.1,8,19,30,117,124,152,205; III.1,23,275,275,
        276; III.2,145,148; IV.1,133,166; IV.3,2,41,49,116; IV.4,29,38,40,77,110,170,196,249,250,251;
        V.1,19,201,317,376,399; V.2,36,67,67V,68,69,69V,70,81,142
    DOUBL DLR
        PRO.,19,21; I.1,79,179,301,310,335,347,406; II.1,2,21,23,60,60V,61,69,255,255V,257,257V,421;
        III.1,13,19,20,130,150,177,214,317,393,424,466; IV.1,25,43,159,164,268,333,423,424,425,425V,
        432,439,457V,513,541,545,557; IV.2,17,68,75; V.1,12,146,425,437,509,519
    FOR LOVE
        I.1,90,119,122,152,163,180,254,264,393,572,573; II.1,143,268,299,367,391,423,423,440,444,644;
        III.1,61,103,114,140,201,205,208,246,287,289,289,292,442,521,528,541,603,617,620,624;
        IV.1,172,196,298,334,392,411,576,701,721,781; V.1,13,185,223,237,258,543
    M. BRIDE
        PRO.,1,35; I.1,4,24,52V,260,260,389,390; II.2,110; III.1,55,125,157,190,398,449,449V; IV.1,75,
        81,188,312,442,442V; V.1,105; V.2,3,83,254,295,317
    WAY WORLD
        PRO.,33; I.1,47,48,59,111,136,370,484,499,528; II.1,12,15,28,41,134,172,176,198,201,203,261,
        263,275,487,508,514; III.1,45,70,70,79,84,89,184,241,252,293,561,603,608,643,644,644,647,679;
        IV.1,74,208,311,327,359,361,482,509; V.1,28,33,40,43,46,47,48,85,143,144,148,149,182,197,314,
        348,387,481,489; EPI.,13

BUT (1167)
    OLD BATCH
        PRO.,5,10,14,15,26; I.1,6,19,19V,20,60,68,78,83,107,108,117,135,143,151,165,167,179,232,243,
        258,306,330,340V,348,353,361,366,379,380; II.1,9,16,23,30,36,45,79,83,87,93,94,97,105,108,110,
        111,128,132,145,146,147,152,154,158,168,179,181,196,198,218,241,244; II.2,31,33,41,54,86,109,
        117,121,129,173,181,199,204,210,216; III.1,18,27,52,57,110,112,142,146,171,192,193,209,260,261,
        273,290,322,323,331,348,360; III.2,15V,22V,49,57,65,69,74,86,94,100,104,109,116,117,127,128,
        137,153; IV.1,15,24,41,57,59,63,85,88,93,101,159,174,182,186; IV.2,26,27,32,41,54,69,80,83,85;
        IV.3,14,19,22,25,28,70,73,74,101,103,106,110,116,139,167,171,177; IV.4,2,52,85,91,92,127,128,
        144,162,165V,168,188,208,214,220,243,243V,250,268; V.1,4,6,34,40,52,65,76,94,105,110,126,141,
        145,148,151,154,185,201,244,244,248,262,269,274,282,285,298,303,305,336,346,362,374,375,380,
        384,385,393V,401; V.2,13,27,34,40,50,71,79,114,126,155,190,195; EPI.,17,19,26,28
    DOUBL DLR
        PRO.,23,25; I.1,7,7V,13,43,43V,46,51,52,60,71,83,94,98,105,111,119,142,155,158,168,181,192,
        198,222,223,235,237,240,250,262,263,265,321,327,331V,343,357,363,374,379,384,384V,388,390,400,
        414,418; II.1,9,9,11,31,38,40,45,84,85,98,105,115,116,116V,117,117,166,182,222,228,232,236,246,
        266,278,284,293,302,303,327,349,350,360,360,361,361,364,365,365V,366,371,376,377,394,408,409,

BUT (CONTINUED)
     DOUBL DLR   (CONTINUED)
          416,416V,420,433,448,450,454,456; III.1,17,38,50,65,72,73,74,75,85,90,95,116,122,135,151,166,
          176,176V,202,207,212,223,266,285,295,304,307,334,343,349,368,376,390,403,415,431,438,458,463,
          481,505,519,523,526,543,545,578,583,593,597,602,612,619; IV.1,2,4,17,21,26,41,44,44,59,61,128,
          133,134,138,147,150,157,167,179,183,207,211,244,299,325,328,328,329,331,334,365,368,372,407,
          419,431,432,460,476,485V,492,500,502,521,528,545,548,558,560,562; IV.2,2,5,14,39,51,53,73,86,
          90,142,149; V.1,6,22,43,48,62,73,88,111,124,127,137,138,139,152V,172,191,195,195V,200,203,208,
          220,233,236,236V,257,267,272,298,328,344,379,381,388,397,401,425,440,443,454,456,456V,495,497,
          525,532,565,581,596; EPI.,1,4,8,12,25,35
     FOR LOVE
          PRO.,18,19,44,46; I.1,25,35,41,47,69,73,82,94,97,110,141,141V,146,157,157V,191,259,286,300,
          314,314V,318,322,329,339,350,358,375,391,398,421,423,429,444,466,476,489,499,516,536,556,558,
          558V,561,563,566,570,581,597,601,605,610,612,641,643,659V; II.1,15,15V,33,37,61,66,102,113,115,
          118,124,125V,131,135,136,139,141,141,142,144,157,176,178,180,187,190,197,210,236,255,259,263,
          288,290,293,309,312,334,339,346,353,408,426,429,429,434,436,461,465,480,513,558,573,583,613,
          615,617,620,621,627,630,635,636,636V,648,651,658; III.1,22,29,45,61,89,94,119,121,124,135,149,
          150,171,173,187,206,225,247,308,327,330,338,344,359,380,385,395,407,421,460,462,486,486V,492,
          493,501,502,508,519,523,528,529,531,534,543,551,560,572,578,590,596,602,619,667,668,670,690V,
          692,702,715,718,728,735,780,815,819; IV.1,23,46,59,70,73,86,103,124,164,174,203,216,233,255,
          269,333,342,367,379,428,457,463,510,513,548,553,570,572,577,595,603,608,638,657,661,663,699,
          713,720,728,747,763,766,774,775,785,791,795,809; V.1,18,67,75,83,90,114,121,125,132,187,213,
          239,240,248,251,252,254,257,279,282,306,349,352,366,371,372,390,413,423,428,434,447,455,458,
          467,473,478,507,515,520,524,525,545,547,552,566,596,597,621,630,632; EPI.,5,17,28,35,38
     M. BRIDE
          PRO,22,25,29,34,36,40; I.1,12,34,71,74,82,98,107,118,118V,122,128,170,196,217,250,253,273,
          273V,277,301,316,336,342,366V,369,391,399,407,458,458,458,461; II.1,43,72,84; II.2,55,77,77V,
          126,135,135,158V,164,166,166V,176,188,202,207,210,220,223,228,237,243,256,316,334,337,346,370,
          382; III.1,1,2,13,19,22,24,24,32,45,52,108,109,164,175,216,216V,228,232,317,323,332,342,365,
          366,371,371V,373,395,418,423,440; IV.1,6,27,34,35,36,40,42,58,65,107,119,119V,161,163,163V,218,
          221,223,228,231,236,252,260,268,281,281V,282,289,358,380,399,412,425; V.1,87,87V,98,98V,103,
          119,121,139; V.2,20,33,64,66,106,111,113,124,124V,167V,178,179,189,190V,191,221,226,227,272,
          313; EPI.2,13
     WAY WORLD
          PRO.,13,17,23,30; I.1,37,55,79,79V,146,162,219,223,240,240V,241,252,258,259,264,273,276,292,
          330,358,429,452,466,467,471,487,500,500V,506,518,533,541; II.1,17,24,53,58,62,70,70,115,130,
          147,179,185,188,206,212,237,255,269,319,326,345,355,372,410,419,470,484,508,514,519; III.1,47,
          73,75,79,89,91,97,114,155,164,167,170,179V,196,202,204,206,217,230,231,240,251,255,292,305,313,
          314,319,341,360,361,368,373,377,384,394,398,407,409,415,420,447,515,516,516V,527,532,556,556V,
          556V,581,636,640,654V,706,715,717,721; IV.1,25,53,68,75,84,137,170,174,207,264,265,269,274,312,
          313,313V,382,403,406,410,414,439,455,487,492,492V,496,504,523,528,535,572,604,619,623,632,640;
          V.1,24,24,29,38,78,86,88,96,98,98,145,161,187,189,191,200,230,259,263,276,303,334,354,364,368,
          369,403,405,410,433,450,457,459,463,465,475,501,610; EPI.,3,13

BY (461)
     OLD BATCH
          PRO.,17; I.1,45,47,51,57,68,260,279,294,356,358,361; II.1,8,25,28,60,66,66,92,123,123V,128,
          167,175,204,207,232; I.2,35,135,141,179; III.1,19,56,57,132,141,162,179,206,207,252,268,277,
          304,343,352,357; III.2,59,77,105,131,133; IV.1,30,89,145,145,146,147,148,150,150,150,175,188;
          IV.2,11,52,67,72,73; IV.3,38,82,102,111,140; IV.4,24,29,54,61,170,206,208,235,273; V.1,109,
          141,185,268,326,330,402; V.2,41,87,109,125
     DOUBL DLR
          PRO.,23; I.1,22,23,26,27,29,94,117,242,322,364,367,393; II.1,65,98,152,155,173,207,207V,255,
          255V,300,398,435,456; III.1,3,15,59,62,68,146,174,177,187,192,232,238,257,302,315,315,579V,628;
          IV.1,1,78,164,173,204,211,238,239,240,281,281,298,341,345,399,408,413,430,476,497,503,537,585;
          IV.2,108,115,121,130; V.1,3,94,114,137,189,193,211,239,257,277,302,320,322,335,351,387,446,
          492,532,568
     FOR LOVE
          PRO.,37,43; I.1,66,80,90,135,143,143,181,187,295,424,466,483,483,520,537,546,546V,569,680;
          II.1,49,50,59,62,62,104,122,199,199,232,233,360,366,379,383,399,461,492,511,560,592,594,632;
          III.1,74,83,119,199,332,363,374,531,536,548,631,641,700,716,757; IV.1,82,149,192,198,242,258,
          289,399,400,438,540,577,639,651,659,670,718,724V,729,763,765,809,815; V.1,31,58,177,241,259,
          270,428,451,552; EPI.,33
     M. BRIDE
          PRO.,11,44; I.1,5,46,48,61,61V,122,136,186,236,265,275,297,314,319,382,383,409,409V,414,421,
          422,457; II.1,34,62; II.2,8,63,95,134V,193V,231,253,276,325,350,361; III.1,16,37,43,73,111,129,
          147,172,239; IV.1,38,57,86,114,177,189,207,232,294,388,407,434,434V,438; V.1,44,49,66; V.2,8,
          18,44,44V,71,119,130,180,224; EPI,6
     WAY WORLD
          PRO.,11,35; I.1,20,21,51,130,149,165,192,207,212,360,395,399,406,435,454,455,455,456,523,526,
          530,531,536; II.1,30,32,74,106,144,145,164,194,274,289,292,298,305,351,396,465,464,465,485,496,
          497,500,545; III.1,174,175,193,262,312,351,374,374V,463,503,516,516V,631V,637,637V,645,680,714;
          IV.1,9,226,313,313V,314,362,373,446,453,520,563,573,575,581,581V,582,593,613,630; V.1,13,28,
          87,133,135,178,193,197,210,212,215,230,251,281,282,284,360,372,376,417,425,487,537,544; EPI.,
          14,18

CAN (292)
     OLD BATCH
          I.1,58,69,88,161,352; II.1,38,45,109,187; II.2,36,47,118,123; III.1,62,198,226,295,360; III.2,
          51,74,109,129,129V,160; IV.1,36,108,115; IV.2,40,42,84; IV.3,18,73,97; IV.4,76,79,169,230,273;
          V.1,24,49,49V,103,105,133,198; V.2,24,79
     DOUBL DLR
          PRO.,34; I.1,166,180,200,306,329,345,352,386,413,414; II.1,41,105,213,236,271,293,344,352,356,
          358,358,364; III.1,1,25,41,46,166,188,208,208V,240,377,406,429,578,589,620; IV.1,84,106,120,
          157,169,200,221,231,278,338,380,552,574; IV.2,16,72,72V,81,124V,148,149; V.1,3,42,75,91,149,
          162,208,268,275,308,410,440,487; EPI.,34
     FOR LOVE
          PRO.,24; I.1,103,123,225,257,390,438,513,617,628,630; II.1,5,15,15V,61,96,119,122,212,278,301,
          370,432,451,493,498,501,540,583,602,614; III.1,24,29,153,154,227,365,366,501,547,683,791,808,
          814,819; IV.1,88,89,183,220,221,222,226,227,252,253,311,331,434,488,545,557,592,614,759,795;
          V.1,23,23V,61,90,226,339,425,494,548,577,578,590
     M. BRIDE
          PRO,11,38; I.1,109,274,386,411,418,432,432V; II.1,84; II.2,189,326,329; III.1,35,90,107,214,
          225,315,336; IV.1,59,101,115,158,179,297,320,431,444; V.1,139; V.2,114,147,173V,195,239,292,302

CAN (CONTINUED)
 WAY WORLD
  I.1,88,146,226,309,460; II.1,70,150,154,188,396,403,410,422,436,480,510; III.1,64,160,179V,
  205,320,320,356,358,426,617,650,656,687,703; IV.1,88,159,175,320,339,366,431,517,623; V.1,92,
  92,125,170,202,203,292,317,324,368,396,403,444,462,465,593,597,608; EPI.,19,26

COULD (109)
 OLD BATCH
  I.1,2,3,3V,306; II.1,125; II.2,31,220; III.1,19,30,32,32V,39,40,76,105,206,207; III.2,26,30;
  IV.1,22; IV.4,256; V.1,221; V.2,39; EPI.,4,20
 DOUBL DLR
  I.1,38,110; II.1,1,3,58,68,292,305,326,328,328V; III.1,115,200,245,449; IV.1,242,243,333,367,
  492,498,576; IV.2,46,141; V.1,282,376,425,426,455; EPI.,1,2
 FOR LOVE
  I.1,118,148,286,411; III.1,67,183,189,237,310,777; IV.1,130,461,652,653,712,712V; V.1,40,176,
  195,213,259,473,476,510,594
 M. BRIDE
  PRO.,24; I.1,29,47,393; II.1,7,14V; II.2,134V,184,196,196V,350; III.1,78,87,188,422; V.2,21,237
 WAY WORLD
  II.1,93,163,180,185,254,268,401,515; III.1,90,232,304

FOR (1181)
 OLD BATCH
  PRO.,8,10,23,25,26; I.1,56,62V,64,67,68,76,76,77,79,83,102,111,113,114,114,131,133,133V,142,
  148,148V,151,161,162,164,168,174,185,192,196,212,218,228,244,246,249,251,253,258,285,299,315,
  316,332,332,362,380,387,387; II.1,8,26,35,35V,54,54V,102,103,104,117,141,142,142V,147,153,158,
  161,164,196,202,207; II.2,15,124,127,129,132,134,137,140,168,177,216,219; III.1,15,54,83,
  127,132,153,163,169,196,245,248,249,251,254,255,265,274,320,325,346; III.2,23V,28,39,47,63,70,
  71,79,79V,86,88,106,119,148,149,157; IV.1,40,69,71,87,108,130,131,159,183; IV.2,74,80,86,87;
  IV.3,12,29,43,48,96,135,135,142,145,199,207; IV.4,15,28,36,128,167,177,192,206,209,213,220,
  224,228,236,264,268; V.1,15,43,58,59,69,75,122,147,157,167,207,228,231,233,236,245,280,341,351,
  376,379,396; V.2,27,28,33,86,121,131,148,151,154,155,158,175,182; EPI.,21,21
 DOUBL DLR
  PRO.,12,17,22,30,31,33; I.1,21,29,41,55,74,74,76,80,86,103,113,121,131,133,137,154,154,154V,
  179,197,226,226V,239,271,276,282,288,301,313,318,322,325,335,361,362,364,379,381,408,415; II.1,
  3,10,28,48,54,80,97,109,111,216,228,250,254,260,265,266,277,296,299,309,320,328,328V,339,343,
  350,367,368,370,392,401,404,412,413,432,439,452,455,457,458; III.1,8,17,42,79,96,97,103,113,
  123,129,141,194,200,247,254,269,273,276,281,298,310,311,316,333,342,344,352,370,391,404,413,
  433,451,472,477,481,486,511,515,519,519,520,520,529,542,569,569V,611,627,630,630; IV.1,14,23,
  25,32,59,62,63,81,116,138,148,161,163,175,176,179,179,180,228,233,235,245,288,300,336,345,348,
  352,352,402,418,420,420V,423,423,434,446,472,472,480,481V,499,513,521,521V,522,522V,561,566,
  571; IV.2,10,20,41,44,47,109,127,143; V.1,11,11,18,20,23,36,51,65,69,69,71,81,108,114,118,123,
  182,186,193V,230,235,236,236V,237,263,283,326,402,413,414,421,434,442,463,480,482,485,498,546,
  574; EPI.,10,13,26
 FOR LOVE
  PRO.,3,29,30,36; I.1,8,29,31,38,45,46,56,56V,67,69,75,91,94,97,97,105,120,123,129,129,140,142,
  225,241,258,279,340,347,351,366,369,370,384,388,390,391,393,404,427,429,438,515,563,565,582,
  593,614,614V,622,636,637,652,668; II.1,12,27,42,44,59,80,92,117,134,178,190,195,201,205,245,
  246,252,258,261,277,311,311,321,331V,335,360,362,381,387,454,460,464,489,500,502,522,553,578,
  605,618,621,658; III.1,18,21,29,31,34,35,36,36,39,46,48,54,55,59,66,77,102,108,109,109,113,131,
  135,145,146,154,161,172,174,177,188,188V,190,194,215,243,245,250,253,254,259,262,263,281,298,
  300,302,306,307,325,342,360,372,380,384,385,387,388,389,395,400,404,417,422,436,449,460,466,
  498,586,670,678,678,679,680,681,684,697,719,721,725,735,763,773,799,805,805V,808; IV.1,14,15,
  33,34,36,43,59,60,67,73,81,83,103,128,130,133,152,171,178,189,190,255,256,258,297,357,372,373,
  374,375,398,414,424,441,455,464,468,469,482,491,521,561,564,569,569V,585,614,628,639,641,645,
  659,663,665,688,689,697,701,711,724,724V,725,753,753V,773,789,792,811; V.1,45,63,68,74,76,105,
  108,111,112,121,153,154,169,175,179,186,187,190,203,219,220,223,270,277,288,294,295,306,310,
  311,311V,316,319,346,373,386,404,411,436,462,463,464,466,466,472,488,489,491,492,548,589,591,
  598,608,617,622,623; EPI.,3,7,9,23,35,40,44
 M. BRIDE
  PRO.,4,6,8,21,31,38; I.1,15,15V,28,29,37,38,68,75,95V,96,96V,102,109,128,134,144,144,165,166,
  171,175,179,253,276,285,298,325V,336,339V,454; II.1,52,75,81,81V; II.2,14,65,113,125,131,132,
  139,149,174,174V,184,198,236,236,236,238V,260,263,269V,274,275,280,298,315,336,342,343,368,371;
  III.1,5,13,19,33,44,64,70,98,102V,112,119,132V,156,168,196,233,248,263,275,325,326,327,366,
  389,436,436,437; IV.1,15,16,20,30,31,50,54,65,94,95,121,132V,192,240,241,244,263,283,310,322,
  325,333,353,374,385,393,393V,406,407; V.1,42,86DV,86EV,114,120,129; V.2,33,40,43,43V,44,44V,48,
  83,84,112,120,173V,178,184,187,189,189V,216,220,221,225,229,229V,233,256,256V,262,262V,321;
  EPI.,15,17
 WAY WORLD
  PRO.,3,6,9,23,25,32; I.1,11,25,34,62,63,79,79V,97,97V,137,142,145,146,151,156,158,159,159,183,
  197,199,201,201,228,239,275,282,282,318,330,330,353,366,368,374,375,377,379,421,431,442,
  458,460,466,469,473,478,508,512,517,537,542; II.1,16,74,75,85,86,86,112,143,217,218,227,257,
  258,288,307,309,324,324V,332,338,347,350,352,379,385,393,397,425,439,442,445,453,471,471V,498,
  506,506,514,560; III.1,27,29,96,105,106,114,115,126,138,139,153,157,207,211,212,220,233,241,
  243V,250,258,265,293,302,311,316,317,337,352,360,385,390,390,402,405,430,431,431,433,480,523,
  524,556,556V,565,576,586,602,605,622,639,671,677,680,683,684,702; IV.1,44,77,83,84,84,99,119,
  145,159,183,206,241,248,249,260,271,275,292,298,303,316,317V,333,353,369,374,400,402,411,419,
  440,448,457,473,479,483,496,498,558,585,592,618,623,633; V.1,10,36,40,42,48,48,62,66,72,90,121,
  130,145,145,150,176,183,193,214,216,236,240,267,269,285,294,301,307,319,320,329,332,364,373,
  373,374,374V,406,407,427,433,441,459,468,493,495,506,573,577,580,588,596,604,605,615,622; EPI.,
  12,13,15,28,31

FROM (275)
 OLD BATCH
  PRO.,4; I.1,45,125,236,256,346,369; II.1,48,131; II.2,40,136,200,225; III.1,23,29,41,96,148,
  166,256,258; IV.3,63,133; IV.4,54,72; V.1,208,264,267,268,269,271,337; V.2,76,77
 DOUBL DLR
  I.1,D,37,50,76,105,113,166,227,331V,344,396,414; II.1,39,272,276,317,464; III.1,37,51,98,163,
  203,252,270,270V,275,312,450,540; IV.1,117,215,410,512V,515,542,550,578; IV.2,118; V.1,41,137,
  156,210,294,376,533,556,566,591; EPI.,36
 FOR LOVE
  PRO.,10,14; I.1,70,84,124,206,341,373,661; II.1,62,250,288,297,481,649; III.1,39,70,76,150,
  310,310,459,549,772; IV.1,27,63,75,105,319,535,795; V.1,155,210,271,272,325,335,381,520; EPI.,
  4,20,20,33,40

PLAY
       ACT.SCENE,LINE REFERENCES

FROM (CONTINUED)
   M. BRIDE
        PRO,34,43; I.1,25,70,71,71V,161,194,286,286V,300,354,416,416V; II.1,5,36,40,46V; II.2,25,34,
        37,44,45,101,122,141,156,173,173V,250,252,258,258V,265,303,353,369,379,382; III.1,17,23,25,26,
        73,115,119,150,177,233,254,257,302,316,323,344,382; IV.1,29,151,152,214,253,317,324,377,386,
        392,393V,399; V.1,22,25,26; V.2,81,114,136,137,145,145V,168V,208,209,227,235,267,276,291,311,
        320; EPI,27
   WAY WORLD
        PRO.,17; I.1,D,183,237,245,247,294; II.1,8,8V,8V,22,93,96,141,434,499,558; III.1,105,192,231,
        231,232,428,428V,429,429V,507,590,687,693,701; IV.1,20,29,156,169,213,322,533,576,585,607; V.1,
        3,4,93,126,170,231,273,372,398,450,454,454,455,465,516,542,555,620; EPI.,32

HAD (309)
   OLD BATCH
        I.1,46V,50,51,99,184,208,227,233,359,364V; II.1,44,52,115,123,123V,125,126,144,196,199,205,
        237; II.2,29,43,44,177,223; III.1,145,275,276,277,319,328,328V,358,358; III.2,18V,145,146,148;
        IV.1,81; IV.2,43,64; IV.3,32,40,40V; IV.4,3,109,110; V.1,40,97,114,149,201,297; V.2,56,67,67V,
        69,69V,120,173
   DOUBL DLR
        PRO.,19; I.1,14,14V,79,108,111,118,118V,303,356,357,375,389; II.1,10,10,21,21,276,417; III.1,
        20,69,82,88,109,130,165,306,415,506,566; IV.1,43,142,165,177,215,268,468,477,498,516,521,521V,
        578; IV.2,24,71,77,149; V.1,51,73,192,193,252,326,359,417,425,431,431V
   FOR LOVE
        I.1,25,91,105,109,152,212,212,351,411,477,487; II.1,31,89,89V,110,143,143,274,349,395,397,
        423,423,438,619,629,644; III.1,17,32,88,101,104,109,114,150,164,170,172,201,205,294,294V,382,
        493,541,588,589,597,638,760,772,807,811; IV.1,260,334,335,336V,360,376,430,449,668,686,711,720,
        721,722,762; V.1,81,98,171,258,432,464,507,560,584V
   M. BRIDE
        I.1,38,39,117,117V,120,260,260,291,320,320V,361,389,390; II.2,126,377; III.1,54,54,143,177,
        190,300; IV.1,29,118,222,223,244,249,399; V.1,99; V.2,34,50,177,236
   WAY WORLD
        I.1,33,48,66,196,266,292,292V,370,383,409,411V,473,499; II.1,60,158,162,200,201,201,203,204,
        267,276,331,355,356,359,371,371V,429,433,520,531; III.1,86,89,90,206,241,274,299,299V,338,489,
        559,560,576,635,643,643,644,644,645,647,651,651,679,686; IV.1,167,208,242,318,326,361,362,425;
        V.1,42,63,87,93,187,221,221V,285,326,385,537,564,579

HAS (457)
   OLD BATCH
        PRO.,14; I.1,14,43,98,104,127,197,204,257,288,321,322,323,323V,340V,368,372,383; II.1,19,27,
        30,77,140,152; II.2,6,6V,128,131,163,218; III.1,29,32,32V,37,97,161,177,220,296; III.2,28,156;
        IV.1,60,62,74,79,80,166,169; IV.2,18,60; IV.3,65,92,118,129,154V,157,158,172,206; IV.4,29,38,
        40,78,133,165V,203; V.1,18,93,107,110,146,163,207,212,213,215,293,348,391,399; V.2,36; EPI.,8
   DOUBL DLR
        PRO.,33; I.1,43,43V,65,87,88,100,129,130,136,139,149,247,274,309; II.1,6,69,87,107,112,118,
        131,137,172,257,257V,285,382,393,402,428,451; III.1,4,6,7,97,137,152,164,181,272,273,277,282,
        283,283V,285,287,289,297,299,304,317,498,585,596,611,619; IV.1,25,150,151,159,163,166,174,180,
        201,201V,204,235,260,262,339,432,439,457V,493,521V,536,541,542,547,549,582; IV.2,23,24V,58,59,
        59,95,123,151; V.1,109,112,113,176,200,269V,309,310,315,358,437,470,538,543,543; EPI.,6,16
   FOR LOVE
        PRO.,40,43; I.1,21,55,55V,67,87,118,120,127,130,180,264,316,331,344,351,353,374,374V,393,419,
        450,476,479,505,558V,572,572,577,593,601,605,622,623; II.1,151,152,258,268,304,306,306V,309,
        352,386,391,392,455,464,492,515; III.1,3,3V,73,139,143,208,240,292,312,338,442,457,493,496,498,
        500,503,521,578,591,617,620,623,699,713,714,733; IV.1,8,10,30,35,82,123,130,181,298,302,404,
        455,457,459,533,679,702,716,747,770,811; V.1,5,42,84,111,168,204,260,336,508,576
   M. BRIDE
        PRO,1,35; I.1,1,79,192,192V,215V,256,257V,273,273V,318,434,440; III.1,58,67,79,118,157,159,
        173,196,222,228,321,457; IV.1,4,100,106,213,219,229,243,390; V.1,68; V.2,3,46,49,74,87,146,254,
        308V,316,317
   WAY WORLD
        PRO.,4,9,16,29,33; I.1,13,18,25,65,83,124,151,153,221,221V,227,244,289,289V,297,300,310,338,
        420,475,484,486; II.1,41,83,86,103,191,198,274,309,361,387,420,494,514,522,525,527,545; III.1,
        18,36,45,52,58,59,74,79,82,84,140,142,144,168,204,217,239,244,265,287,290,291,291,292,292,293,
        297,316,327,327,336,400,476,667,677,688; IV.1,34,46,179,311,402,422,428,428,474,482,509,511,
        512,513,513,523; V.1,26,27,76,77,79,85,105,108,182,259,280,348,401,408,408V,579

HAST (78)
   OLD BATCH
        I.1,45,180,183; II.1,147; III.1,89,91,91V,122,165,202; III.2,135,135V,153; IV.1,63,163,172;
        IV.4,234,250; V.2,153
   DOUBL DLR
        I.1,120; II.1,407,431; IV.1,236; V.1,398,398,403,454
   FOR LOVE
        I.1,437; III.1,287; IV.1,234,268
   M. BRIDE
        I.1,19,30,52V; II.2,78,79,86,87,87,110,117,132,153,272; III.1,218,279,279V,290,454,456; IV.1,
        1,232,287,329; V.1,83,101,107,110; V.2,109
   WAY WORLD
        I.1,441,444,533,534; III.1,28,30,70,70,73,80,80,455,455V; IV.1,64,65,342,557; V.1,481,568

HAVE (1331)
   OLD BATCH
        I.1,2,3,3V,23,25,25V,31,32,40,107,114,120,155,162,165,188,192,195,208,223,230,233,235,238,243,
        279,295,296,298,304,319,319,330,331,360,382; II.1,4,5,5,5V,11,26,27,29,48,72,85,88,109,111,
        112,117,125,126,128,131,132,135,144,169,185,212,220,224,224,233,234; II.2,3,4,9,26,28,29,59,
        102,104,122,176,181,186,207,207V,222,224; III.1,19,35,52,99,100,103,184,208,228,245,248,488,
        275,277,282,303,359; III.2,38,93,107,112,120,156,157,159; IV.1,18,22,23,40,67,69,77,82,83,84V,
        94,97,109,110,116,139,154,159,178,180,180; IV.2,4,29,31,35,38,40,41,45,69,87; IV.3,1,2,8,10V,
        11,29,49,68,74,91,95,115,116,117,142,145,154,164,169,170,183,195,199,207; IV.4,3,24,27,30,53,
        76,122,135,168,170,182,183,196,207,214,222,249,250,251; V.1,2,3,4,5,29,47,48,63,63V,68,125,142,
        156,168,215,230,243,248,251,264,304,317,341,357,369,369V,376,395; V.2,35,36,39,45,51,51,53,
        56,67,67V,70,71,81,82,102,114,115,120,142,158,176
   DOUBL DLR
        PRO.,1,6,15,24; I.1,9,9V,15,32,38,44,68,72,74,75,83,89,103,122,140,142,143,164,165,179,230,
        236,266,274,289,293,301,305,309,311,317,321,325,335,346,348,356,370,371,372,377,385,387,394,

                                        837

HAVE   (CONTINUED)
        DOUBL DLR   (CONTINUED)
        406,408; II.1,2,23,24,25,25V,39,44,60,60V,61,61,85,111,141,143,145,155,160,162,175,192,197,228,
        231,235,252,253,255,255V,259,279,280,281,303,318,320,335,345,358,383,399,399,418,421,432,460;
        III.1,13,19,31,46,51,57,70,81,90,97,97,100,114,115,131,132,139,144,160,160V,175,177,178,188,
        214,229,245,249,280,298,303,329,331,331V,348,368,393,396,402,407,411,411,424,424,434,438,446,
        466,483,484,489,543,558,570,627,631; IV.1,21,21,24,24V,31,66,74,104,110,118,119,134,135,136,
        136V,164,179,182,202,207,226,228,241,242,243,261,275,275,277,290,332,333,333,334,336,345,348,352,
        386,399,406,409,423,424,425,425V,426,437,463,478,483V,491,496,502,513,528,535,542,545,550,558,
        560,566,577,579; IV.2,8,16,26,42,51,54,55,65,68,72,72V,73,74,75,90,121,122,143,145,154; V.1,6,
        11,12,16,22,23,24,24,25,39,44,51,55,56,61,63,64,66,114,115,129,136,139,145,201,202,203,204,231,
        232,234,242,246,251,263,269,283,285,287,290,296,300,306,376,383,408,409,412,437,441,443,474,
        492,509,519,534,534V,540,542,548,583; EPI.,15
        FOR LOVE
            PRO.,9,12,12V; I.1,4,17,34,35,49,77,86,90,122,142,147,157,157V,163,166,169,171,189,212,240,
        247,249,254,296,305,314,314V,315,329,332,350,396,408,409,435,438,474,477,478,478,501,503,510,
        511,523,542,558,571,580,584,596,598,599,606,613,623,624,634,636,639,639V,642,642,644,649,651,
        652,657,666,668,671; II.1,12,27,30,31,66,82,115,119,124,127,131,134,148,173,190,193,207,207,
        210,220,222,226,241,244,249,251,251V,262,283,299,318,321,325,325,343,348,348,353,360,367,373,
        390,398,401,415,424,431,436,440,444,453,453V,473,486,488,488,489,490,493,501,508,512,517,541,
        548,577,596,619,636,636,636V,636V,636V; III.1,18,22,61,67,81,97,100,103,110,113,114,116,117,
        118,119,137,139,150,160,171,184,205,230,239,246,246,256,295,303,347,364,408,433,440,469,490,
        504,528,543,546,552,552V,598,603,606,624,640,662,678,678,682,690,690V,692,703,723,726,734,744,
        754,797,813; IV.1,6,48,57,69,70,86,131,131V,162,163,172,178,196,234,240,328,333,334,359,364,
        392,393,394,410,411,415,425,425V,430,450,463,464,465,470,479,489,489V,527,546,563,575,576,578,
        597,628,648,673V,681,701,709,709,712,712V,713,719,734,755,767,781,805; V.1,13,14,16,23,23V,30,
        44,45,59,60,64,75,80,82,126,127,157,171,178,184,185,203,212,222,223,226,237,250,258,265,267,
        287,288,289,291,304,307,309,314,315,334,385,408,426,427,466,473,491,502,518,520,520,531,533,
        543,546,554,555,570,574,575,586V,595,597,601,605,606,613,613V,619,623,629,630,632; EPI.,6,39,42
        M. BRIDE
            I.1,3,4,22,24,25,27,33,54,68,70,78,78V,80,82,102,102,106,143V,148,148V,190,203,203V,222,284,
        303,304,307,310,311,316,322,333,354,356,376,380,436,445,445V; II.1,41; II.2,89,92,93,95,98,116,
        116V,126,127,130,131,134V,143,144,150,194,228,229,229V,262,271,274,288,297,313,338,345; III.1,
        63,108,127,176,177,197,198,212,215,301,309,316,361,419,427; IV.1,18,40,51,56,58,75,80,81,83,96,
        129,138,143,150,162,169,176,178,185,188,244,245,254,279,294,305,306,309,311,312,313,338,370,
        380,423,426,435; V.1,4,54,105,117,123; V.2,70,91,111,155,189,189V,221,245,245V,247,248,248V,
        298,299,306
        WAY WORLD
            PRO.,24; I.1,2,11,36,47,51,59,66,83,91,92,111,117,122,136,146,179,179,183,190,191,202,232,232,
        271,275,278,280,308,339,366,390,419,422,434,435,439,518,527,528; II.1,4,12,15,20,28,41,45,46,
        63,71,75,100,120,134,137,139,139,140,157,172,174,176,195,198,199,200,202,205,210,212,227,229,
        235,248,255,257,258,261,261,263,268,272,275,280,283,307,309,329,331,333,333,346,347,347,425,
        450,456,487,488,490,507,509,528,542; III.1,3,3,50,72,75,89,102,102,103,104,135,178,184,193,198,
        211,229,234,238,242,246,252,255,269,286,288,294,295,311,365,371,384,393,398,404,406,421,437,
        442,505,551,561,562,564,572,573,581,583,603,603,604,608,639,640,646,656,679,704,709,710; IV.1,
        3,7,48,68,73,73V,74,91,113,117,132,134,140,182,210,216,221,229,232,284,285,291,291,292,293,295,
        299,306,313,313V,323,325,327,327,355,359,361,366,368,369,403,405,410,412,462,467,485,491,494,
        526,528,535,552,556,561,585,599,607,614,617; V.1,2,22,22,22,24,32,33,40,41,43,46,46,47,48,49,
        65,86,93,96,106,110,113,115,126,137,143,144,148,149,161,196,197,197,201,208,212,224,243,250,
        303,305,314,315,318,323,327,330,366,370,386,388,389,406,409,411,421,422,425,448,451,458,458,
        464,468,483,489,490,490,499,499,510,543,555,565,572,578,582,585,594,596,596V,599V,599,600,602,
        609,610; EPI.,7,13

HE (887)
        OLD BATCH
            PRO.,14,17,19,20,21; I.1,3V,17,21,21,84,109,121,124,126,126,127,158,176,179,197,201,204,211,
        212,219,220,224,283,283,288,322,323V,338,339V,340V,344,348,349,351,351,352,353,355,357,362,363,
        363,368,374,377,380,383,384,388; II.1,1,11,53,92,119,120,123,123,123V,123V,125,125,126,142,
        142V,148,152,167,178,181,181,215,215,219; II.2,95,128,131,141,163; III.1,1V,11,16,16,20,25,26,
        27,32,32V,47,91V,128,146,176,177,220,222,225,230,247,258,260,263,268,272,274,278,287,353,359;
        III.2,6,145,147; IV.1,11,11,22,26,27,28,79,134,134,134; IV.2,18,42,43,51,60,75; IV.3,58,120,
        130,131,132,147,154,154V; IV.4,10,52,90,90,95,102,154,165V,167,203; V.1,18,60,88,94,95,131,167,
        168,170,173,298,299,308,399; V.2,31,31V,46,54,176; EPI.,6,16
        DOUBL DLR
            PRO.,30,32; I.1,37,43,43V,133,139,149,156,157,181,184,184,184,189,189,189,208,208,212,212,212,
        230,230,230,231,231,231,274,280,323; II.1,30,43,46,51,53,54,76,79,101,107,126,248,248V,277,279;
        III.1,2,4,84,87,87,97,133,134,136,138,154,194,243,273,275,277,281,283,283V,284,286,288,288V,
        291,293,294,317,524,524,531,538,541,549,549V,562,589; IV.1,34,46,128,166,167,178,180,196,201,
        201V,223,224,225,229,254,255,255V,259,259V,260,273,275,275,275,284,402,403,421,439,444,461,
        470,479,520,548,568,582; IV.2,113,114,114,117,127,145,149; V.1,13,14,23,88,96,99,113,125,127,
        129,131,133,133V,145,167,167,167,174,188,200,232,234,269,269V,288,322,333,339,347,352,358,359,
        359,543; EPI.,6,7,16,35
        FOR LOVE
            PRO.,5,43,43,46; I.1,10,21,30,68,91,105,118,125,133,292,302,321,328,331,334,336,360,365,366,
        368,369,371,372,374,374V,375,378,379,388,450,513,558,558V,564,570,572,580,593,601,603,605,620,
        621,622,623,679; II.1,120,179,179,182,229,268,268,272,278,304,306V,309,368,370,386,521,524,526,
        543,544,573; III.1,109,109,122,125,143,171,172,206,207,211,218,220,224,234,240,243,306,306,306,
        313,316,320,335,335,335,398,416,417,420,421,437,457,459,461,466,497,498,500,501,502,503,507,
        520,521,522,538,549,550,550,551,611,611,620,623,626,627,646,676,698,699,714,717,721,721,721,
        733,770,772,777,784,785,787; IV.1,1,3,6,8,16,17,34,74,76,78,82,87,87,88,105,115,116,120,122,
        123,124,125,128,130,140,142,155,155,167,180,181,184,186,194,227,253,277,277,295,297,312,353,
        364,364,365,368,369,373,377,380,381,384,385,390,391,438,454,455,457,459,460,463,469,471,474,
        482,533,551,572,591,591,598,601,601,603,604,609,616,636,668,705,733,742,746,747,752,753,
        753V; V.1,1,5,6,82,111,122,192,254,317,317,319,321,334,339,395,396,543,576
        M. BRIDE
            PRO.37,41,43; I.1,11,45,67,114,136,169,363,366,366V,368,369,371,372,374,377,424,428V,429,438;
        II.1,22; II.2,60,63,63V,167,167V,208,208,223,244,295,301,301V,356,358,379V,380; III.1,3,133,
        133V,133V,286,396,450; IV.1,30,85,88,113,119V,210,298,331,333,342,342,353,356,374,405,408,409,
        414; V.1,8,8V,15,22,26,86,86V,92,97,97V,98,98V,99; V.2,6,19,20,61,100,152,187,190,190V,191,208,
        209,232,234,304; EPI.,13,30
        WAY WORLD
            PRO.,20,22,22,26,29,31,35; I.1,189,190,192,197,216,221,221V,224,226,227,228,228,229,244,250,
        252,276,292,292V,293,305,306,307,307,310,311,318,329,337,338,340,340,359,359V,363,365,365,369,
        371,374,379,379,400,404,411,411V,419,420,438,439,455,478,483,496,514; II.1,61,61,72,82,85,86,

HE   (CONTINUED)
    WAY WORLD   (CONTINUED)
        91,103,114,116,130,155,286,294,326,394,523; III.1,57,82,87,89,93,95,95,96,98,99,101,103,108,
        111,112,113,114,114,115,116,117,135,135,137,140,156,156,156V,156V,156V,157,160,172,176,211,240,
        244V,244,258,260,264,266,267,290,291,291,292,292,294,339,358,400,404,416,429,429,429V,429V,441,
        476,559,672,715,717; IV.1,12,27,33,57,176,294,312,314,357,382,400,414,422,432,436,474,482,506,
        509,511,512,513,513,521,522,523,587,603,603,613; V.1,26,29,30,38,40,41,42,43,71,85,89,105,109,
        110,221,221V,243,332,336,338,339,343,347,348,348,352,392,392V,401,408V,578,614; EPI.,7

HER (784)
    OLD BATCH
        I.1,40,43,46,46V,47,50,56,59,62V,64,98,116,119,119,120,120,122,161,162,168,172,172,174,183,
        185,263,263,265,269,316; II.2,94,210; III.1,31,41,103,109,110,113,113,132,132,157,190,240;
        III.2,22V,24V,40,55,55V,97,102,114,114,129,133,134V,157; IV.1,20,30,46,47,57,75,107,137,138,
        165,170,185,186,187,188,188; IV.2,11,64,75; IV.3,41,42,44,45,46,46,47,123,187,209; IV.4,33,97,
        97V,148,212,213,225,229,242,260,268; V.1,36,48,49,49V,58,59,73,98,103,104,104,105,105,115,
        115,117,126,127,127,152,153,155,198,212,216,216,219,224,254,255,256,257,257,258,268; V.2,1,5,6,
        53,138,140,169; EPI.,3,4
    DOUBL DLR
        PRO.,6; I.1,77,79,81,86,89,92,93,94,94,96,96,96V,97,101,104,105,106,106,108,115,115,116,118,
        118V,120,127,127,128,128,140,140,154,154V,156,159,275,411,414,415,416; II.1,59,179,181,182,265,
        296,300,310,378,383,398,402,409,409,417,419,425,425,426,427,428,430,433; III.1,7,10,175,176,
        176V,177,179,179,187,204,209,210,226,234,252,253,254,255,269,270,270V,271,271,274,275,296,
        296,298,301,303,305,315,315,317,317,317,318,334,376,381,381V,437,438,439,445,467,499,566,569,
        569V,570,570,575,575,581,584,586,588,599,599,611,613; IV.1,3,4,5,48,48,53,53,55,130,161,196,
        250,264,272,275,276,279,295,303,304,364,384,501,503,516,522,522V,523,523V,547,551; IV.2,1,2,5,
        25,124,132,137; V.1,2,3,11,93,94,109,118,131,138,147V,162,189,220,223,225,307,310,311,313,317,
        320,338,443,444,446,462,483,506,557
    FOR LOVE
        I.1,51,53,54,54,108,109,110,111,207,208,210,213,219,252,285,287,288,346,348,353,372,373,373,
        415,419,421,430,439,447,453,457,459,466,467,467V,475,477,493,506,509,513,538,613,674; II.1,6,
        21,70,70V,70V,72,152,153,162,258,259,472,501,535,535,539,539,563,567,639,663; III.1,3,3V,4,5,8,
        17,18,23,25,62,63,131,176,176,186,187,280,280V,411,413,440,441,442,443,457,458,458,578,579,731,
        731,741,752,754,765,770,771,773,774,775,777,787,810; IV.1,9,12,12,13,14,15,17,18,25,97,97,99,
        101,374,374,375,387,404,404,405,469,469,471,482,541,550,590,591,596,640,813,813; V.1,71,74,207,
        208,210,215,261,324,362,414,466,467,467,471,491,492,493,493,494,494,519,521
    M. BRIDE
        I.1,135,149,151,306,313,346,346V,351,353,354,354,367,367V,377,381,410,410,443,443V,456,457,
        458,458,459; II.1,31,46V; II.2,53,54,59,67,68,69,70,70,183,198,214,214V,216,216V,229,229V,352,
        353; III.1,46,107,144,229,231,388,394,396,401; IV.1,169,181,195,203,205,207,211,217,223,224,
        237,335,346,365,366,399,400; V.1,3,3,58,78,82,86CV,86CV,86EV,86FV,86FV; V.2,76,76,213,276,276,
        278,279,279,311
    WAY WORLD
        PRO.,6,7,9,10; I.1,10,20,22,24,35,37,38,40,42,43,45,45,60,64,65,70,70,71,72,73,75,78,82,82V,
        87,92,129,131,131,150,150,151,151,151,155,159,159,159,160,160,161,162,164,164,165,167,175,175,
        176,176,421,467,469,473,478; II.1,145,163,172,204,244,244,245,287,297,298,301,301,302,309,
        323,324,325,327,350,350,422,486,509,521,523,523,530,543,547,551,551; III.1,D,19,40,47,51,59,61,
        61,61V,61V,63,125,135,162,192,193,194,194,208,211,211,218,222,240,313,319,320,321,460,461,463,
        465,466,466,651,652,653V,654V,655,656,657,660,660,661,665,666,666,679,680,681,701,710,710;
        IV.1,37,37,38,80,237,312,428,428,429,429,576,618,618,629; V.1,76,105,119,182,184,185,188,190,
        191,193,194,205,205V,239,269,270,282,283,285,303,304,362,362,363,363V,390,394,417,458,465,536,
        537,538,542,546,583,592,592,597

HERE (220)
    OLD BATCH
        I.1,176,197,339V,371; II.1,19,22,22,139,146,159; II.2,96,98; III.1,66,153,251; III.2,34,34,
        110; IV.1,36,136,164,164; IV.3,55,67,67,176,178; IV.4,42,121,122,126,145,262,262; V.1,24,107,
        145,236,265,267,269,333; V.2,34; EPI.,18
    DOUBL DLR
        I.1,27,293,296V; II.1,54,74,171,171V,434; III.1,44,132,194,260,314,450,512; IV.1,35,91,249,
        303,403,441,475,505,529; IV.2,9,14,90; V.1,252,292,339,362,402,450,515; EPI.,13
    FOR LOVE
        PRO.,32; I.1,3,26,32,208,380,483,548; II.1,99,124,170V,173,180,187,272,300,327,328,328,334,
        410,465,484,503,503V,506,515,516,517; III.1,7,91,142,237,281,415,420,456,601,607,687,711,796;
        IV.1,18,90,96,101,125,126,150,193,221,237,249,274,353,415,475,537,581,589,721; V.1,2,222,297,
        324,374,438V,495,529,551; EPI.,42
    M. BRIDE
        I.1,278,413,449; II.2,76,76V,151,167,167V,169,206,228,261,349,349V; III.1,110,136V,137; IV.1,
        20,59,373; V.1,43,51,121; V.2,3,136,150,254
    WAY WORLD
        PRO.,36,36; I.1,123,181,344,364; II.1,228,252,323,501; III.1,34,34,76V,122,172,246,275,326V,
        438,447,455,470,470,508,536,586,621; IV.1,43,124,124,158,281,296,583,606; V.1,138,150,229,243,
        308,414,441,550

HIM (732)
    OLD BATCH
        I.1,58,62V,65,65,107,113,114,121,124,148,148V,158,207,219,256,264,349,351,353,357,361,361,364,
        364V,372; II.1,10,40,45,51,122,130,152,168,171,238; II.2,21,38,40,42,57,59,158,194,195; III.1,
        2,3,29,38,39,40,41,48,50,62,146,219,228,245,250,258,258,260,261,262,267,269,277,279,282,307,
        310,318,321,326; III.2,156; IV.1,25,125; IV.2,16,19,44,45,50,60; IV.3,63,78,132,146; IV.4,12,
        50,57,70,72,79,82,83,91,118,144,154,168,209,236,240,241; V.1,20,20,61,83,87,87,88,92,95,160,
        167,167,169,170,173,188,190,200,212,246,276,279,294,300,309,344; V.2,3,45,47,48,49,116,127;
        EPI.,10,25,25,26
    DOUBL DLR
        PRO.,33,34; I.1,D,32,43,43V,66,89,146,147,149,203,277,280,282,295,311,367,378,378V,387,400,
        400,401,403,413; II.1,31,42,54,55,65,75,142,197,200,202,202,205,245,246,247,273,274,451;
        III.1,92,98,100,101,132,144,145,148,152,152,158,162,163,165,167,192,192,263,284,290,293,300,
        453,506,508,525,541,548,565; IV.1,1,2,135,154,162,164,234,261,261,263,284,287,288,293,294,370,
        376,377,410,464,471,480,494,549,550,555,563,566,567,572,578; IV.2,9,89,117,134,136,137,149;
        V.1,24,58,77,85,98,115,136,137,140,142,143,143V,148,148V,150,226,227,242,242,259,259,287,346,
        348,353,354,418,446,447,457,479,480,481,482,483,574,577V; EPI.,35
    FOR LOVE
        I.1,17,70,100,124,161,275,292,304,310,319,359,362,378,390,392,414,450,450,523,559,582,601,606,
        607,623,624,662; II.1,40,165,166,174,178,182,244,312,358,408,494,495,521,543,552,563,568,634;

PLAY
ACT.SCENE,LINE REFERENCES

HIM (CONTINUED)
FOR LOVE   (CONTINUED)
    III.1,33,75,108,109,124,172,211,213,214,215,237,239,240,241,245,246,260,260,275,345,416,436,
    436,436,451,462,468,484,501,507,508,508,581,584,585,594,597,619,635,716; IV.1,10,11,30,36,40,
    49,51,53,71,73,78,80,81,81,83,117,129,131,131V,132,133,136,137,145,146,147,149,153,166,176,189,
    189,190,209,216,252,296,296V,305,306,306,311,335,343,345,350,350V,352,372,376,380,462,467,470,
    470,471,480,495,540,572,592,668,676,677,691,717,737,751,754,754V,755; V.1,6,8,83,84,110,196,
    201,202,232,244,263,264,264,300,301,301V,321,335,396,427,456,474,527,527,574,577,590
M. BRIDE
    I.1,37,167,171,211,263,298,368,369,381,425,429,441; II.1,11,18,18V,18V,19,24,28,46V,83; II.2,
    2,83,83,106,174V,175,294,325,326,342,360,368,370,374,390; III.1,10,13,19,24,27,119,129,452,
    452V; IV.1,8,12,18,50,56,58,76,86,94,97,97,182,204,209,211,231,241,280,294,373,401,413; V.1,13,
    13V,18V,25,41,47,47V,70,77,83,84; V.2,12,50,152,175,176,208,215,217,234,267,294,298
WAY WORLD
    PRO.,23,24; I.1,154,183,189,190,191,223,254,254,281,282,291,292,292V,297,309,309,312,322,327,
    330,347,349,360,364,366,370,411,411V,482,497,498,504,515,515,517; II.1,27,57,58,63,69,70,71,72,
    76,82,86,127,128,137,144,154,155,157,255,255,277,292,295,310,327,350,399,522,522; III.1,58,82,
    91,102,102,103,104,106,106,107,107,107,129,130,137,163,216,233,237,239,241,244V,246,338,339,
    342,351,354,354,440,442,442,477,481,488,488,488,491,605,611,623,643,671,672; IV.1,17,21,23,28,
    35,37,38,49,60,61,62,284,285,286,286,291,291,291,292,312,316,318,408,420,438,466,470,471,501,
    519,520,575,595,603,607; V.1,28,66,111,114,115,192,197,206,207,303,330,336,338,342,346,351,352,
    394,409,527,584,599

HIS (691)
OLD BATCH
    PRO.,11,12,17; I.1,3,3V,25,25V,57,88,107,123,141,147,159,205,224,262,289,321,321,323,323V,326,
    333,339V,352,357,365,374,376,382,385; II.1,45,52,131,149,149,153,220; II.2,30,32,128,132,137,
    137,148,148,149,149,193; III.1,8,20,22,23,26,31,42,42,128,129,139,143,145,147,148,161,188,261,
    311,339,350,359,361; III.2,117; IV.1,2,20,30,31,32,71,72; IV.2,D,13,18,49,51; IV.3,59,79,130,
    134,154,154,154V,154V,155; IV.4,D,12,12,14,31,75,90,97,97V,143,144,144,151,165V,203,209,237,237,
    241,273; V.1,88,132,174,186,187,234,297,379; V.2,30,55,122,123,188
DOUBL DLR
    PRO.,9,22,30,30,33; I.1,D,D,133,139,150,155,163,164,276,304,311,330V,330V,388; II.1,50,247,
    248,248V,272,273,276,283,283V,357,452,467; III.1,2,9,30,31,41,89,133,166,185,277,279,283,283V,
    288,288,288V,289,290,293,435,531,535,539,541,564,564,565,574; IV.1,2,47,182,201,201V,210,
    222,311,380,400,421,422,422,422,439,477,546,561,570,571; IV.2,26,143,144,144V,145,147,151; V.1,
    59,63,112,126,127,135,135,135,146,146,147V,153V,174,241,347,351,353,418,448,449,458,481,577
FOR LOVE
    PRO.,1,42,44; I.1,D,70,99,100,107,126,235,262,262,263,286,309,311,311,336,336,393,490,555,556,
    557,560,564,565,645,645,645,645,652; II.1,183,228,228V,264,268,269,309,353,386,392,393,393,
    393V,393V,493,500,500V,502,519,519,519; III.1,54,70,75,77,78,132,143,144,170,202,235,246,269,
    312,317,321,346,436,498,504,505,507,511,522,531,532,676,734,775,784; IV.1,7,8,21,33,34,35,36,
    57,62,64,75,76,85,88,104,105,106,113,116,117,138,143,146,168,180,186,190,216,227,232,251,254,
    266,297,298,300,302,312,344,352,381,466,471,474,508,509,519,519,520,520,528,529,533,549,551,
    582,688,690,695,718,753,753V; V.1,4,42,66,76,76,76,77,78,78,83,84,84,85,110,122,123,123,159,
    174,194,195,327,339,395,410,473,506,598
M. BRIDE
    PRO.,36,37,41; I.1,11,21,23,25,26,27,28,33,42,47,49,68,103,103,106,112,116,116,116V,117V,139,
    140,167V,213,213,215,216,227,236,237,242,257,257V,309,310,316,317,376,379,381,426,427,439,444,
    444V,445,445V,446,446V; II.1,20,27,28,31,33,41,46; II.2,39,21,22,23,39V,82,83,260,357,374,376,
    379,379,379V,381; III.1,14,14,23,27,66,113,129,135,136,136V,207,208,209,283,283V,320,322,360,
    376,397,401; IV.1,13V,15,17,19,21,24,27,28,51,54,100,112,139,177,182,186,231,321,334,349,372,
    404,407,438; V.1,10,10V,16,17,22,24,24,25,26,27,29,78,83,86AV,86AV,86EV,93,94,99,108; V.2,8,49,
    67,127,128,153,177,181,192,195,196,206,207,209,235,267; EPI,6,28
WAY WORLD
    PRO.,17,20,23,27,33; I.1,8,109,117,129,183,184,196,196,211,221,221V,223,224,232,266,277,279,
    284,291,310,318,323,326,326,327,330,331,372,380,406,407,482,514,517; II.1,25,62,76,76,77,103,
    106,114,156,158,159,160,270,274,341,352,464,465; III.1,57,59,91,94,94,94,104,134,134,193,193,
    198,204,209,215,238,241,242,244V,260,262,336,336,342,417,437,474,611,618,673,716,717; IV.1,13,
    18,20,34,173,176,437,517,524,595,604,614,617,621; V.1,26,39,44,193,194,197,221,221V,273,287,
    335,408,408V,410,410,525,527,581,614,622; EPI.,8

HOW (373)
OLD BATCH
    PRO.,1,20; I.1,17,17,35,38,126,180,282,290,293; II.1,42,51,142,142,142V,183,218; II.2,107,121,
    173,203; III.1,16,16,29,36,78,91,91V,110,116,168,171,179,201,222; III.2,35,36,55,55V,74,153;
    IV.1,3,25,25,67,68,68,119,137,139,153; IV.3,16,17,39,170,205; IV.4,4,64,122,195,202,222,230,
    234,239,259; V.1,56,110,113,154,253,253,260,290,308,312,316,340,362,376; V.2,9,31,31V,51,88,
    122; EPI.,14,23,23,28
DOUBL DLR
    PRO.,24; I.1,73,194,194,277,323,339,370,371,386,387,391,404,404,405; II.1,12,41,61,209,214,
    295,305,325,339,344,358,358,407,408,409,431; III.1,22,27,61,108,133,149,181,183,198,243,247,
    247,273,302,393,455,469,604,618; IV.1,109,126,139,169,329,362,368,562; IV.2,74,80,114; V.1,108,
    110,128,140,154,208,213,263,304,324,350,420,440,474,479,502,508,511,520,573; EPI.,1
FOR LOVE
    I.1,27,131,165,178,250,315,386,386V,391,391,400,413,444,485,490,552; II.1,25,29,88,93,95,146,
    146,202,202,261,285,312,327,377,432,507,518,540,544,559,595,597; III.1,53,142,290,290,295,325,
    375,531,558,561,571,613,803; IV.1,17,32,150,174,194,201,278,339,392,405,409,467,476,545,576,
    610,705,722,728,771; V.1,5,89,90,143,225,266,266,274,333,349,349,403,437,444,449,459,499,505,
    558,571,594,633,633V; EPI.,17,37
M. BRIDE
    PRO.,9; I.1,22,33,279,348,348V,404,404V; II.1,59; II.2,87,87,91,110,111,114,114V,130,158,158V,
    166,166,166V,166V,204,206,206,207,285,293,359; III.1,39,45,165,165V,166,237,238,239,246,345,
    347,349,399,433; IV.1,42,184,207,412; V.1,39,40,40V,41; V.2,46,63,96,317; EPI,14,14V
WAY WORLD
    I.1,108,254,362,409,432,470; II.1,28,52,361,390,391,415,436,484,557; III.1,6,87,356,455,455V,
    575,674,697; IV.1,15,17,115,320,379,388,432,591,591,609,615,615; V.1,28,30,110,125,376,462,520,
    575; EPI.,2,4,10

I (4109)
OLD BATCH
    PRO.,18,18,19,20,22,25,27; I.1,1,13,27,30,32,32,40,51,55,67,75,89,94,95,95,101,101,107,111,
    119,120,121,132,132,132V,132V,135,137,144,144,148,148V,157,159,167,169,172,173,174,185,188,188,
    192,210,222,227,230,231,233,235,253,272,284,284,291,295,295,296,296,302,304,304,309,309,312,

I (CONTINUED)
   FOR LOVE   (CONTINUED)
      606,614,614,619,623,625,631,633,637,640,640,643,645,647,649,650,650,651,651,653,656,658,662,
      662,668,669,670,683,685,685,690,690,690V,690V,694,697,699,709,710,713,714,716,723,731,734,739,
      742,754,794,806,808,809,809,813,814; IV.1,12,13,14,16,16,20,27,30,43,45,47,47,48,53,53,54,55,
      55,56,58,59,60,62,66,67,68,70,70,75,76,80,81,83,83,83V,86,87,88,89,89,97,97,103,108,128,
      131,131,131V,131V,132,145,157,159,164,166,170,171,171,172,178,178,183,185,190,196,202,204,207,
      212,214,218,218,220,226,226,249,251,260,261,272,286,309,311,315,320,327,333,333,340,341,348,
      356,356,359,367,369,370,371,373,375,376,379,382,384,385,390,391,392,393,394,405,406,406,
      411,414,415,425,425V,429,430,431,434,434,435,437,438,439,442,451,452,453,456,463,464,465,470,
      487,488,489,491,497,497,513,515,530,532,539,541,545,546,557,558,560,569,569V,572,575,576,
      578,591,594,595,597,597,607,608,609,610,615,619,619,623,624,625,626,628,633,639,639,640,641,
      648,648,652,652,654,655,656,657,659,665,670,674,675,685,686,687,687,695,697,698,699,709,711,
      711,712,712,712V,712V,713,719,719,721,722,726,726,729,741,749,750,753,753V,754,754V,755,755,
      759,762,765,766,791,791,799,805,812; V.1,5,8,10,13,15,19,21,23,23,23V,29,29,29,30,36,39,39,42,
      44,45,49,60,60,61,63,68,74,75,75,80,80,86,89,90,93,95,95V,96,97,103,105,106,119,119,120,125,
      125,126,127,135,143,144,153,161,161V,171,176,176,178,184,185,188,196,198,207,207,212,213,222,
      223,225,226,226,226,229,232,237,239,251,252,257,259,259,262,265,267,274,276,280,282,284,287,
      288,289,292,296,304,305,306,307,308,309,309,311,311V,313,318,326,328,332,334,334,336,344,346,
      348,351,361,366,367,369,370,372,373,383,393,410,412,413,423,424,426,431,433,434,445,445,446,
      447,447,455,455,457,457,460,463,464,465,466,467,467,472,475,475,476,483,483,490,491,494,504,
      507,507,511,515,520,522,523,524,524,525,533,543,544,546,548,552,555,555,560,565,566,568,
      570,572,574,574,577,577,584V,586V,590,592,595,598,605,606,608,611,615,621,622,623; EPI.,6,12,
      17,32,32,35,36,41,42
   M. BRIDE
      PRO.,6; I.1,6,6,13,20,26,29,38,54,54,55,57,59,65,66,66V,72,78,78V,80,80,87,91,92,94,94,94V,95,
      95V,98,98,100,100V,106,108,109,110,117,117V,137,137V,139,140,143V,148,144,145,148V,166,172,
      172V,173,173V,175,178,185,190,194,196,200,201,201V,202,202V,203,203V,204,207,213,217,251,251V,
      259,260,263,276,283,283V,284,307,322,326,326V,327,329,333,369,393,398,398,399,400,408,408V,409,
      409V,413,419,428V,435,436,441,453,456,458,458; II.1,10,11,18,18V,19,19,27,33,48,48,73,81,81V,
      82,84; II.2,1,9,16,27,32,47,47V,49,50,70,70,76,77,77V,77V,80,83,83,93,95,98,104,104,107,107,
      107V,107V,108,113,116V,117,125,125,126,129,129,130,130,131,139,142,143,144,149,150,157,157V,
      159,162,163,164,164,164,165,165V,169,169V,174,174V,177,178,178V,181,182,182V,183,184,184,191,
      194,195,195V,197,206,206,214,214V,228,229,229V,230V,241,245,245,254,254V,257,267,268,270,271,
      273,274,275,281,286,292,293,294,297,297,298,300,302,313,322,325,326,335,343,345,350,355,357,
      361,378,378V; III.1,1,3,6,33,33,33,45,46,46,51,51,80,83,87,89,90,105,107,108,108,109,111,120,
      136,152,170,177,184,188,190,197,197,201,212,214,215,218,219,230,233,237,242,242V,244,250,253,
      275,289,291,295,298,298V,303,303,349,350,350V,355V,361,367,369,379,392,399,406,411,415,417,421,
      422,423,430,435,436; IV.1,18,23,25,26,30,39,40,41,43,59,59,68,96,97,114,115,115,119,119V,122,129,
      136,138,142,149,150,163,163V,191,197,200,205,206,218,226,227,239,244,245,254,264,267,273,279,
      285,289,299,302,305,309,311,314,316,317,318,330,333,348,349,351,352,356,360,362,364,368,
      369,369,394,396,398,403,409,411,416,423,425,426,427,428,432,435,440,447; V.1,6,21,24,52,54,57,
      59,64,76,76V,86CV,101,114,117,118,120,122,123,126,129,137,139; V.2,11,70,87,105,128,150,165V,
      182,183V,186,188,189,189V,191,192,198,201,207,210,216,220,231,231V,234,240,241,243,246,249,254,
      258,262V,266,267,288,292,293,295,290,303,309,313; EPI.1,7
   WAY WORLD
      I.1,15,18,29,34,36,37,38,40,47,47,49,49,54,60,68,69,71,73,73,79,79V,85,85,99,121,131,136,137,
      138,141,144,150,159,164,165,166,168,173,179,179,179,183,184,190,191,196,199,204,237,255,
      256,256,258,258,259,259V,270,270,271,272,276,280,285,291,298,299,299V,302,302,309,311,312,316,
      330,340,366,375,378,378,379,383,386,387,390,392,394,397,405,405,409,410,423,428,428,428,433,
      434,442,446,446,447,448,449,450,458,460,467,468,473,477,487,492,499,500,500V,507,507,512,515,
      515,517,536,536,538; II.1,20,28,37,41,41,45,46,50,53,55,55,58,62,67,69,70,70,72,80,80,93,95,
      95,99,101,107,109,110,119,120,124,125,128,130,132,132V,134,135,136,140,143,145,153,154,162,172,
      176,179,183,188,188,189,196,198,201,206,209,209,210,212,217,219,220,225,227,227,229,230,235,
      239,240,240,242,254,254,254,257,261,269,278,280,291,295,307,308,309,311,325,326,331,333,333,
      338,339,344,344,344,346,346,347,347,353,354,355,356,359,359,360,364,364,365,366V,367,367,
      369,371,371V,378,379,379,380,382,385,388,419,425,427,430,432,441,449,449,453,456,456,457,460,
      460,464,470,473,475,479,487,490,509,509,514,515,515,518,519,521,527,527,530,530,540,541,544,
      554,559,560,561; III.1,3,3,3,4,12,17,21,27,32,47,47,51,61,61V,62,64,72,74,78,85,85,85,86,89,90,
      91,97,111,114,130,132,137,140,142,148,148,150,151,158,158,159,160,160,161,163,163,173,177,177,
      184,184,188,195,196,204,205,206,207,207,207,208,211,211,214,215,216,217,220,220,221,226,229,
      234,236,236,242,250,252,254,254,255,256,256,260,263,269,269,270,271,271,274,275,278,279,288,
      293,295,295,296V,304,335,337,337,338,339,341,343,344,348,348,349,351,352,354,355,357,357,358,
      360,371,387,388,389,398,400,401,404,406,412,415,422,425,425,439,441,441,442,447,461,462,467,
      470,473,476,477,478,484,487,493,497,508,510,510,511,515,517,526,532,539,542,557,558,560,560,
      564,567,567,570,571,573,574,576,578,578,578,579,580,580,580,580,580,581,581,583,601,602,602,
      605,614,614V,617,618,629,632,635,646,651,666,668,677,678,679,680,681,684,688,695,699,702,
      703,703,704,705,706,709,710,712,712,719,720,721,722,722; IV.1,3,15,17,18,19,19,24,35,38,39,43,
      46,48,57,58,61,62,65,67,68,73,73V,75,75,76,84,88,91,92,95,95,98,102,104,108,110,111,114,116,
      117,121,121,126,132,134,135,136,140,147,161,162,162,167,167,168,175,180,186,187,189,191,192,
      194,195,199,213,215,217,219,224,225,226,229,230,234,234,244,245,246,248,249,251,252,260,263,
      271,275,276,278,279,280,284,284,285,289,289,292,293,293,295,295,306,308,313,313V,314,316,
      316,316,325,325,326,326,327,327,355,366,366,368,368,405,409,410,423,423,425,431,432,433,437,
      446,461,467,470,484,485,487,491,491,499,501,502,502,504,506,508,528,531,534,534,535,538,540,
      540,542,556,557,561,569,570,570,572,575,578,581,581V,585,585,586,594,594,594,594V,594V,599,600,
      600,602,606,606,606,607,612,615,616,619,623,623,627,630,632,632,638,639; V.1,2,3,4,20,26,28,44,
      45,46,47,47,48,50,58,58,59,62,68,76,85,86,87,92,102,110,115,116,119,125,126,126,128V,132,141,
      144,147,150,151,153,158,158,160,161,162,164,165,167,173,177,177,181,182,183,183,196,202,206,
      241,241,244,245,248,249,250,254,258,266,273,277,288,293,294,299,306,308,312,314,314,316,316,
      316,316,318,322,323,325,326,327,328,330,333,334,335,335,336,337,337,341,342,347,349,351,366,
      369,370,370,371,372,373,374,374,374V,374V,379,384,388,388,389,392,392V,394,394,395,396,401,402,
      403,406,409,409,416,416,421,422,423,425,429,437,448,451,451,452,460,467,467,468,477,479,486,
      495,498,499,500,510,513,523,525,525,531,531,531,540,544,554,573,573,582,585,586,587,588,588,
      590,590,592,596,596V,597,598,608,608,608,609,610,615

IN (1521)
   OLD BATCH
      PRO.,1,26; I.1,3,3V,27,29,33,34,52,65,74,81,97,103,107,115,133,133V,137,138,167,199,201,202,
      206,207,211,218,220,223,231,240,247,266,268,271,295,297,305,306,313,332,341,365,388; II.1,24,
      47,49,59,65,66,66,71,73,78,81,94,94,101,102,113,160,169,180,182,189,195,201,205,215,230; II.2,
      4,DV,12,13,30,38,41,72,88,106,112,122,123,132,150,170,175,183,183V,206,207,211,221,226; III.1,
      2,9,17,17,19,27,34,34V,35,48,49,63,63V,68,79,80,80,82,87,106,107,108,130,134,146,155,175,193,
      196,202,204,213,221,222,225,228,231,248,249,272,302,316,323,323,333,340; III.2,3,16V,20V,42,57,
      58,96,103,117,121,135,135V,140,147,158; IV.1,D,7,23,28,31,45,49,60,81,83,101,111,144,144,145,

IN (CONTINUED)
    OLD BATCH (CONTINUED)
      149,159,178,185,186; IV.2,D,D,D,4,7,31,52,54,56,77; IV.3,10,10V,32,64,69,90,97,105,109,117,118,
      119,121,126,126,133,148,155,165,169,171,181,201; IV.4,D,6,12,16,17,18,19,20,28,30,30,35,42,62,
      68,74,77,89,92,95,110,117,127,132,142,143,153,158,161,172,188,195,201,202,205,209,238,240; V.1,
      D,6,12,38,44,46,48,57,69,82,97,102,108,109,118,132,139,175,182,187,187V,188,191,201,215,216,
      234,261,261V,278,283,304,328,331,338,349,357,364,372,375,382,383,384,393V,393V; V.2,11,23,28,
      82,145,151,155,170,177,180; EPI.,9,10,14
    DOUBL DLR
      PRO.,21,28; I.1,D,D,14,14V,46,47,94,97,99,104,106,109,116,117,139,148,155,156,159,160,165,210,
      214,238,238V,246,246,249,289,290,292,310,311,311,318,326,326,334,338,340,348,348,352,365,375,
      384,384V,388,396; II.1,2,20,52,61,69,72,96,97,98,115,132,132,147,158,171V,183,196,204,218,221,
      227,236,247,248,248V,254,261,268,278,302,313,318,329,345,375,387,389,397,397V,406,421,425,425,
      425,430,434,452; III.1,6,10,17,30,35,39,40,45,112,114,129,134,142,158,158,160,160V,166,167,170,
      171,177,180,208,208V,209,224,234,237,256,258,265,281,289,290,308,313,314,316,332,340,341,342,
      350,353,356,376,383,405,408,408,417,421,422,435,445,457,476,482,484,484,494,504,504,517,521,
      541,550V,563,571,574,578,579,606,624,625,633; IV.1,5,13,15,16,21,21,34,35,53,72,78,80,85,117,
      169,170,183,183,191,198,209,226,228,236,261,268,277,294,315,323,326,326,327,333,336,342,380,
      396,397,403,408,414,424,432,441,450,453,463,468,479,493,496,497,499,500,518,527,533,536,541,
      548,553,557,585; IV.2,22,60,64,71,73,77,83,87,93,125V,125V,142; V.1,54,55,59,65,74,86,94,97,
      103,105,106,114,115,117,126,138,139,147V,188,220,222,233,238,239,252,263,273,274,279,280,283,
      285,289,292,292,317,336,338,344,348,381,382,394,395,396,401,414,423,425,431,431V,441,442,446,
      448,451,451,483,485,506,566,566V,567,570,582,592,594; EPI.,12,16,19,25,32
    FOR LOVE
      PRO.,1,18,21,42; I.1,D,8,14,31,33,35,36,38,44,45,51,56,56V,78,86,91,108,108,114,136,139,173,
      190,208,213,219,223,249,257,259,262,269,270,287,297,304,309,331,352,365,369,370,374V,
      378,419,432,438,491,503,518,547,562,563,603,626,627,630,632,636,639,639V,645,656,678; II.1,D,6,
      30,30,37,55,65,66,69,71,80,99,109,110,115,121,129,173,193,210,226,235,253,257,259,263,275,
      296,297,309,353,356,380,380,382,392,402,419,430,433,437,441,441V,454,474,478,482,549,605,645,
      653,654; III.1,4,12,25,42,59,78,82,94,96,97,100,101,102,104,119,125,162,174,175,176,192,197,
      207,214,223,225,231,246,258,312,322,330,336,341,371,377,385,406,442,452,487,487V,502,503,507,
      522,531,532,536,539,541,569,587,600,612,632,637,651,657,661,693,695,697,720,724,731,734,736,
      766,809; IV.1,5,10,21,51,74,100,103,114,133,135,144,177,177,180,183,210,224,225,231,232,248,
      263,287,290,295,299,306,324,335,344,349,350,358,365,368,371,399,413,431,439,464,471,471,493,
      499,500,502,503,505,509,518,526,548,559,561,576,582,586,608,610,612,613,614,636,660,674,701,
      723,738,740,754,754V,776,784,810,813; V.1,D,3,26,31,35,66,67,75,83,87,92,95,95V,98,98,104,107,
      110,121,122,126,126,137,148,167,181,184,188,201,207,213,213,216,224,260,267,269,276,289,332,
      354,379,380,381,387,405,408,413,432,434,442,453,461,463,465,481,503,589,597,614,620,621,624,
      635; EPI.,2,3,17,18,23,24,37
    M. BRIDE
      PRO.6,13,14,21,37; I.1,8,23,28,42,74,105,110,113,117,127,141,167V,168,168,168V,189,197,197V,
      211,226,234,245,250,257,257V,264,266,267,280,281,281V,283V,285,291,296,308,317,318,375,384,392,
      392V,395,409,409V,431,437,453,454,455,459,460,461; II.1,5,9,30,32,34,80,76,77,80V; II.2,15,19,
      21,28,44,93,99,115,140,162,171,174,174V,187,187V,189,190,192,212,228,230V,233,253,269,269V,277,
      290,290V,323,325,328,328,378,378V,384,387; III.1,6,18,42,61,70,81,90,118,118,120,128,132,133V,
      154,155,224,260,265,267,272,288,301,332,340,403,397,397,407,441; IV.1,11,12,25,32,33,34,47,57,
      64,76,78,78V,89,103,125,133V,137,150,152,153,154,158,190,194,201,213,218,227,235,249,250; V.1,
      1,7,16,27,74,96,96V,111,112,117,119,129; V.2,5,14,36,42,47,60,62,79,99,103V,104V,115,115V,116,
      116V,120,151,159,169V,173,173V,190,190V,204,215,216,220,231,251,263,294,302,307,314,319; EPI,16
    WAY WORLD
      PRO.,7,11,20,37; I.1,20,24,24,37,41,47,67,70,75,76,100,114,119,136,157,161,164,170,173,173,
      185,187,197,213,220,245,255,259,259V,264,293,303,346,346V,374,374,385,394,415,418,429,448,453,
      461,488,489,500,500V,504,510,519,519V,522,538,539; II.1,2,3,13,17,19,19V,24,26,71,98,100,146,
      147,158,177,181,183,195,197,200,241,278,280,281,292,294,296,302,320,320,335,365,371,371V,383,
      384,397,436,447,448,451,452,469,474,480,491,493,495,499,508,511,514,521,526,533,545,555; III.1,
      D,4,31,35,36,37,40,40,43,48,51,57,62,82,86,104,126,133,137,145,169,169V,184,185,192,196,230,
      241,254,262,321,322,358,370,372,380,385,389,396,398,432,437,443,443V,446,446,448,449,449,457,
      457V,461,466,468,476,533,534,541,544,557,561,579,582,584,586,603,611,631,632,654V,666,673,685;
      IV.1,2,3,4,4,4,12,17,19,23,26,29,36,36,68,71,111,111,124,136,172,174,175,177,190,192,198,
      202,220,225,228,239,240,244,251,252,264,276,288,291,300,302,306,328,329,342,346,348,356,379,
      398,429,440,443,486,521,524,527,575,553,563,566,570,607,607,615,618,623,629,643,644; V.1,7,
      20,40,45,54,55,55V,56,68,72,74,75,94,106,108,136,138,143,165,171,176,184,188,189,191,194,209,
      211,211V,212,216,217,219,226,226V,227,244,263,273,276,278,280,282,294,296,314,326,328,331,346,
      348,351,352,372,383,388,405,408,408V,411,424,438,448,461,487,506,545,546,552,566,580,591,591,
      601,615,616,623; EPI.,11,11,33,35

INTO (126)
    OLD BATCH
      I.1,26,241,267V,292,307,359; II.1,60,193; II.2,207V; III.1,67,68,85,238,268,304; IV.2,38,40,
      90; IV.4,16,31,49,150; V.1,61,127,173,263; V.2,152
    DOUBL DLR
      PRO.,3; I.1,101,106,107; II.1,116,116V,144,144V,195,335,409,429; III.1,116,238,278,315,538,
      550,566; IV.1,227,286,296,315,343,421,515V,516; IV.2,78,144,144V; V.1,104,110,223,254,265,488,
      506
    FOR LOVE
      I.1,107,112,134,293,425,585; II.1,327,330,381; III.1,171,173,318,374,448,448,457,515,579;
      IV.1,106,254,367,549; V.1,178,451; EPI.,27
    M. BRIDE
      III.1,239,240,240V,268,368,399; IV.1,277; V.1,40,40V; V.2,84,91,206,279,283
    WAY WORLD
      I.1,31,71,184,230,373; II.1,253,553,559; III.1,49,59,62,138,287,621; IV.1,226,230,231,301,550,
      635; V.1,20,146,232

IS (1064)
    OLD BATCH
      PRO.,1,6; I.1,5,10,27,58,60,63,78,95,105,109,150,162,166,198,205,205,237,242,245,249,266,278,
      292,302,341,349,355,356,365,366,376,384; II.1,2,23,50,72,80,108,110,120,148,167,168; II.2,12,
      13,17,25,50,51,53,58,75,115,122,129,140,157,183,183V,202,212,213; III.1,51,60,64,66,146,148,
      150,152,153,192,197V,227,222,230,289,296,319,322,332; III.2,26,39,56,65,84,84,86,90,104,105,
      116,118,128,134V,151,155; IV.1,11,26,30,39,41,51,55,65,69,69,77,87,103,167,176; IV.2,2V,41,59,
      66,71; IV.3,15,41,67,67,73,73,118,120,126,134,176,178,201; IV.4,10,49,55,78,92,95,106,118,137,
      141,142,147,154,157,185,197,217,261,274; V.1,10,30,51,51V,52,60,74,84,108,123,170,192,228,229,
      229,232,241,244,275,300,301,363,368,372,384; V.2,63,127,133,134,145,155,195; EPI.,3,24

IS (CONTINUED)
  DOUBL DLR
      PRO.,3,25,30,31,34; I.1,21,77,79,122,124,124V,129,138,143,150,161,162,164,167,168,177,181,183,
      191,198,237,250,280,296V,316,324,324V,329V,350,386,408,412; II.1,1,28,51,68,115,121,126,163,
      164,168,217,233,234,236,248V,270,294,321,323,323V,329,340,342,348,356,357,377,381,430,448,449,
      450,453,455,463; III.1,12,14,18,38,54,66,99,136,156,177,178,184,191,218,219,219V,224,235,236,
      258,285,296,299,336,339,343,344,351,356,359,376,376,377,378,381,381V,386,410,410,412,422,431,
      441,465,469,473,475,478,503,509,541,542,565,605,606,610,618,629,633; IV.1,20,52,70,104,151,174,
      178,187,201,201V,203,218,239,240,274,284,395,412,444,448,475,477,503,505,515,515V,528,553,565,
      568,581,583; IV.2,4,10,19,72,108,113,134; V.1,2,13,25,28,43,49,57,75,77,78,85,101,124,126,144,
      144V,153V,234,253,267,297,318,333,345,345V,387,387V,423,449,451,451,475,494,494,578
  FOR LCVE
      PRO.,32; I.1,8,22,58,68,82,93,121,140,141,141V,146,187,214,214V,236,245,318,334,358,365,366,
      368,378,383,384,388,391,400,404,441,457,458,460,490,499,510V,548,562,564,567,568,570,603,614,
      633,641,649,679; II.1,2,6,6,11,44,47,55,58,59,65,71,127,128,146,150,160,180,182,182,183,198,
      223,242,256,257,272,280,298,298,300,311,429,431,477,477V,492,494,500,500,500V,500V,518,518,519,
      520,528,533,533,560,574,592,600,624,647; III.1,38,50,59,63,75,91,94,123,125,127,136,147,162,
      184,210,211,234,234,240,312,315,315,316,316,336,341,350,376,376V,386,395,466,505,513,516,520,
      520,536,547,548,560,572,581,586,605,635,675,681,689,689,697,698,720,722,815; IV.1,1,28,34,38,
      46,50,61,62,73,83,83V,95,100,114,120,122,125,128,136,140,144,147,154,155,158,160,185,191,230,
      237,249,253,265,270,294,295,298,344,366,404,447,458,516,529,530,541,554,558,589,598,606,637,
      646,750,752,790,776,787,790,790V,799,801,810; V.1,1,17,18,27,54V,66,67,73V,77,78,90,121,133,
      165,174,187,200,201,245,246,260,261,274,286,307,323,333,347,366,369,371,376,381,402,424,429,
      430,458,463,492,519,529,551,552,556,567,582,589,600,621,636; EPI.,24
  M. BRIDE
      PRO.,16,25,36; I.1,9,16,16V,17,17V,17,56V,57,58,60,73V,75,210V,213,226,244,250,279,288,288,289,
      306,321,330,330V,359,359V,362,363,368,428,428V,446V,458,458; II.1,52,58,59; II.2,37,56,56V,56V,
      60,66,75,76,76V,82,82,94,97,105,106,111,121,148,148,154,167,167V,180,188,199,199V,235,235,237,
      238,238V,249,261,273,302,308,308V,324,349,349V,389; III.1,7,14,25,30,31,31,45,48,48,81,85,86,
      142,153,251,325,328,329,337,346,381,441; IV.1,3,7,8,15,30,39,59,90,109,113,117,122,125,145,146,
      154,177,180,214,262,267,281,281V,302,303,342,356,358,374,377,400,406,411,445; V.1,6,32,54,116;
      V.2,4,17,19,28,32,41,42,48,88,135,173,184,187,211,219,232,232,275,297,313
  WAY WORLD
      PRO.,15; I.1,25,43,77,97,97V,97V,111,123,137,138,145,147,147V,181,187,189,192,199,204,214,218,
      224,226,227,228,250,273,283,323,342,344,357,365,378,379,418,418,453,456,465,466,478,481,482,
      494; II.1,14,43,46,72,91,96,114,124,130,155,232,233,233,233,235,236,239,286,288,288,296,316,
      317,363,374,383,384,386,393,394,403,435,437,439,442,443,474,495,495,498,499,502,543; III.1,17,
      33,76V,76V,76V,97,112,161,164,164,170,172,176,190,201,202,209,220,225,227,227V,231,251,260,289,
      310,312,317,325,326,326V,328,328,330,352,370,392,395,414,429,429V,432,441,453,462,466,475,487,
      502,520,527,528,575,586,587,615,626,641,690,691,700,701; IV.1,1,14,18,29,36,58,76,83,94,139,
      157,177,228,300,302,323,329,351,399,401,444,445,446,447,447,450,472,487,490,506,518,560,573,
      573V,588,603,604,610,621,641; V.1,54,66,82,101,105,107,108,114,138,138,139,142,216,229,268,271,
      279,291,298,306,306,307,332,336,348,354,362,387,405,414,414,419,438,445,457,457,463,470,493,
      504,527,535,548,571,575,578,584

IT (1163)
  OLD BATCH
      PRO.,10,14,16,21,22,24; I.1,48,49,55,60,66,67,78,78,90,90,98,102,103,124,128V,131,141,145,157,
      158,212,212,226,233,237,241,242,255,261,264,266,267V,284,291,294,317,324,341,383; II.1,8,28,32,
      34,53,65,72,77,81,85,85,93,109,112,115,121,159,161,180,201,212,230,232,233,234,235; II.2,10,36,
      48,49,58,61,86,121,132,134,169,206,208,208,219; III.1,20,20,23,25,26,27,28,46,51,51,91,91V,108,
      181,208,210,244,248,251,256,269,273,307,337,353; III.2,16,35,39,57,59,63,84,84,98,105,107,122,
      128,138,159; IV.1,4,39,57,69,69,70,77,83,84V,86,87,88,89,92,95,106,111,130,168,173,181,189;
      IV.2,41,46,57,63,84,90; IV.3,43,73,153,162,179,179,180,188,199; IV.4,97,97V,101,102,103,126,
      133,133,141,141,142,155,185,212,218,267; V.1,13,30,49,49V,51,51V,52,66,103,110,111,119,126,144,
      150,193,201,205,215,229,232,268,298,299,301,336,357; V.2,47,57,58,177; EPI.,5
  DOUBL DLR
      PRO.,11,17,18,18,19; I.1,22,29,39,67,91,91,101,107,121,124,124V,129,135,135V,147,157,165,177,
      180,236,238,238V,248,263,265,266,269,271,272,277,290,307,336,341,361,366,384,385,413,417,417,
      418; II.1,1,36,44,62,62,68,77,77V,80,122,126,151,163,168,173,176,217,220,236,254,276,289,292,
      294,298,298,304,310,319,322,323,323V,333,333,334,344,346,347,348,349,349,357,358,359,359,
      364,369,385,409,412,412,413,414,423,432,451,453; III.1,4,14,16,16,20,33,40,40,41,54,66,77,85,
      91,92,95,97,99,100,104,106,153,154,157,162,188,189,193,239,258,278,341,344,376,388,391,392V,
      395,396,403,410,410,412,417,426,426,428,428,434,436,449,451,519,519,551,551V,585,586,589,590,
      593,593,606,608,610; IV.1,7,11,13,21,21,58,60,73,92,94,97,102,104,109,145,146,151,152,153,153V,
      173,177,185,187,218,237,268,324,370,376,377,381,394,395,402,411,429,433,441,442,444,444,445,
      541,547,562,566; IV.2,19,27,47,61,72,99,99V,145; V.1,4,5,6,11,18,20,20,22,29,36,38,53,74,83,92,
      92,94,114,114,133,133V,136,139,139,144,144V,145,149,205,210,211,218,219,234,254,256,279,289,
      298,300,319,319V,321,321,328,383,387,387V,403,412,429,440,450,456V,476,521,523,549,564,595
  FOR LOVE
      PRO.,17,34; I.1,34,40,66,74,87,94,94,121,159,159,159V,159V,180,180,181,187,214,214V,234,258,
      262,275,276,314,314,314V,314V,316,339,359,377,390,393,403,423,431,480,482,490,561,565,659,659V;
      II.1,5,11,12,29,30,44,47,53,56,71,112,119,127,173,180,187,205,225,251,251V,274,274,278,282,
      293,297,300,301,302,355,366,371,397,408,423,427,434,435,458,462,468,502,518,528,533,533,535,
      549,550,578,584,592,594,600,616,619,624,630,636,636,636V,636V,637; III.1,36,38,46,46V,59,66,75,
      99,101,114,123,162,163,166,173,174,177,184,192,227,246,311,312,372,374,386,395,404,442,490,493,
      493,516,537,538,546,560,561,571,572,584,605,612,612,632,688,695,718,721,726,741,748,782,815;
      IV.1,11,16,17,20,26,78,87,88,105,137,144,145,159,206,216,217,217,218,219,219,220,222,226,228,
      229,230,230,231,231,232,234,269,366,373,377,442,454,460,461,465,482,484,484V,493,530,550,554,
      589,606,612,614,616,616,635,710,723,726,742,744,793,813; V.1,18,89,90,99,107,109,114,115,133,
      140,145,151,174,200,207,239,259,274,290,294,295,298,310,366,367,369,390,411,413,428,429,446,
      476,477,479,482,497,506,507,508,512,520,529,545,548,554,555,555,560,580,594,594,601,607,610,
      611,630; EPI.,41
  M. BRIDE
      I.1,56V,58,60,101,167,175,204,276,279,294,298,326,326V,326V,355,362,409,409V,430,448,449;
      II.1,28,36,46,46V,52,53,54,63,72; II.2,3,3,41,42,52,52,53,53,56,56V,56V,82,82,105,107,148,
      155V,186,187V,217,235,273,273,279,280,282,282V,289; III.1,7,14,26,62,111,116,119,142,149,153,
      162,167,177,179,181,183,184,189,278,279,279,279V,279V,340,366,410,424,447,447V; IV.1,20,31,37,
      39,67,72,93,95,99,113,142,160,178,190,197,203,206,218,220,293V,294,309,385,389,389,389V,391,
      391V,392,392V,393,393,393V,398,399,431,440; V.1,25,27,28,32,57,113; V.2,9,13,13,79,105,116,
      116V,121,144,144V,147,179,210,232
  WAY WORLD
      PRO.,34,37; I.1,25,54,63,117,123,170,227,233,279,334,339,390,461,466,467,488,491; II.1,17,18,
      37,39,43,60,61,75,77,93,99,113,124,131,132,132,132V,132V,165,175,182,183,187,189,191,199,201,

IT (CONTINUED)
  WAY WORLD   (CONTINUED)
    207,229,232,233,233,233,235,236,248,281,306,314,339,353,367V,369,372,373,396,397,403,422,437,
    438,445,451,456,461,484,486,516,554; III.1,18,58,76V,85,170,186,195,207,225,229,230,264,
    272,317,318,319,320,327,327,328,329,330,338,350,352,353,357,372,373,406,406,407,407,408,409,
    410,418,421,432,441,448,489,492,508,508,520,580,580,616,629,639,640,662,676,684,701,704,715,
    718; IV.1,30,73,73V,83,83,88,95,104,122,139,146,174,246,247,256,289,317,317V,337,340,368,373,
    398,412,447,481,533,538,550,570,571,572,572,573,575,576,583,583,596,597,598,604,610,625; V.1,
    47,68,92,98,98,99,99V,100,122,139,142,183,183,204,206,207,207,208,226,226V,229,230,238,238,248,
    249,267,273,305,318,331,341,354,355,370,384,384,385,387,393,405,406,406,423,427,441,448,460,
    460,463,475,475,478,501,512,535,541,564,565,618

MAY (354)
  OLD BATCH
    I.1,31,58,101,113,121,158,192,252,267V,270,270V,284,292,344,346,388; II.1,30,33,80,171; II.2,
    54,107,208,226; III.1,7,35,154,155,252,292,292,292,293; III.2,126,128,130,152; IV.1,7,27,70,
    109; IV.2,23,87; IV.3,58,58; IV.4,46,150,217,219; V.1,14,184,285,328,349,402; V.2,35,123,148,
    159,171,177,177; EPI.,27
  DOUBL DLR
    I.1,70,127,128,143,157; II.1,30,128,160,224,325,339,346,347,433,436,468; III.1,16,35,87,153,
    209,310,373,384,413,437,451,504,516,530,550,550V; IV.1,74,145,203,206,211,216,517,527,563,566;
    IV.2,24,24V,33,35,55,61,62,79; V.1,99,129,188,230V,233,240,288,294,324,328,367,373,375,443,
    446,447,450,476,506; EPI.,34
  FOR LOVE
    PRO.,11,26; I.1,66,72,79,140,187,220,378,474,490,560; II.1,30,30,152,243,300,353,502,524,613;
    III.1,91,124,208,225,313,334,343,374,376,376V,391,402,421,493,502,522,572,639,639,649,725,734,
    751,809; IV.1,48,59,63,67,81,105,159,184,191,343,386,386,440,442,484,484V,509,550,551,557,560,
    595,616,668,803,806; V.1,90,229,366,372,410,490,525,544,569,571,601; EPI.,22
  M. BRIDE
    PRO,36; I.1,85,151,187,443,443V,445; II.1,72,82; II.2,19,49,201,204,324; III.1,33,33,46,47,94,
    95,108,198,209,437,443; IV.1,47,51,58,70,99,162,162V,220,331,332,411,446; V.1,78; V.2,98,119,
    144,144V; EPI,22,23
  WAY WORLD
    I.1,59,90,131,252,281,322,354,430,439,461,496,517,539; II.1,16,22,131,132,132V,259,287,451,
    457,464,487; III.1,63,211,267,318,325,350,363,407,407,410,432,462,492,496,498,500,508,531,565,
    567,567,572,574,578,578,587,649,653,669; IV.1,8,12,39,124,128,130,132,135,148,174,219,226,230,
    257,276,313V,488,573,573V,638,639; V.1,100,141,183,257,295,338,392V,439,460,523,547,549,549V,
    554,558,587,601,618,622; EPI.,23

ME (1387)
  OLD BATCH
    PRO.,17,19,20,22; I.1,6,35,73,79,83,98,120,168,168,169,174,190,303,318; II.1,4,5,5V,14,22,23,
    37,39,43,58,74,77,91,101,118,119,119,121,124,143,185,203,218,224,225,237,242; II.2,3,9,27,41,
    42,44,57,91,101,102,124,124,160,164,173,177,183,183V; III.1,4,14,16,29,33,44,64,78,139,140,143,
    165,172,202,208,222,232,248,249,251,258,272,289,342; III.2,7,12V,13V,14V,28,29,42,42V,43,43,50,
    52,55,55V,58,61,71,92,93,94,100,100,105,112,119,121,122,140,141,145,145,146; IV.1,3,4,11,46,59,
    60,65,73,80,87,88,106,108,117,122,131,133,139,160; IV.2,15,19,24,40,44,50,52,69,72,80,86,88,92;
    IV.3,17,21,35,43,43,65,79,80,105,162,171,174,191,192,198,199; IV.4,27,47,47,47,53,54,73,82,88,
    91,106,107,128,166,166V,216,222,236,244,246; V.1,29,39,43,46,66,67,70,76,78,84,94,113,120,120,
    146,147,157,170,176,193,245,265,268,285,306,308,321,343,347,361; V.2,7V,23,45,50,57,60,61,90,
    93,126,133,153,166,179
  DOUBL DLR
    I.1,25,33,35,42,44,50,51,57,67,86,87,90,90V,91,99,103,115,116,124,124V,136,137,150,156,173,
    179,186,195,197,208,219,219V,237,241,249,251,253,254,258,262,263,267,282,291,291,292,306,317,
    321,336,341,349,351,355,360,364,380,380,385,395,396,397,399; II.1,22,41,84,85,94,104,118,121,
    125,130,132,136,197,199,204,207,207V,220,220,235,237,244,258,272,282,289,295,301,302,303,317,
    317,320,328,328V,330,332,333,334,337,344,369,369,393,395,402,406,408,425,426,439,442,457,460;
    III.1,31,31,42,46,48,52,53,56,56V,57,62,65,70,75,79,84,88,104,119,138,148,153,158,163,186,194,
    205,227,234,245,250,251,257,272,285,295,296,306,326,329,330,345,346,348,350,378,388,405,410,
    430,430V,457,505,512,527,554,557,583,587; IV.1,9,11,23,39,39V,46,47,58,71,73,77,79,86,91,92,99,
    99,104,110,116,117,151,187,189,192,204,207,215,225,234,256,260,267,271,296,307,319,319,323,325,
    337,338,343,344,344V,350,351,352,356,365,366,370,379,398,403,407,414,432,459,461,462,469,470,
    472,474,478,480,486V,493,508,536,542,542,547,549,562,566,574,574,582,584,588; IV.2,13,14,24,
    24V,28,45,47,65,70,75,83,84,95,102,104,130,149; V.1,30,40,54,56,64,71,78,86,88,89,105,112,133,
    133V,172,179,181,218,238,264,269,269V,277,282,292,303,313,318,324,330,338,348,369,371,374,380,
    385,386,400,406,409,413,416,454,471,534,534,534V,534V,538,542,545,545,550,558,558,560,578,582,
    586
  FOR LOVE
    PRO.,43; I.1,41,55,55V,64,71,95,157,157,157V,157V,158,158V,210,259,260,289,326,331,335,337,
    341,346,383,405,422,425,447,482,486,494,496,497,498,527,534,545,551,574V,580,581,584,588,590,
    594,608,615,662,664; II.1,45,67,87,135,138,147,158,167,178,184,186,190,202,222,229,241,249,
    279,283,288,306,306,306V,306V,320,329,334,335,335,336,340,340V,342,343,347,360,361,375,389,398,
    415,434,449,464,482,491,496,508,513,516,522,525,525,526,527,541,584,589,592,595,597,598,601,
    602,614,615,618,620,620,630,631,632,636,636,636V,636V,646,652; III.1,1,19,20,27,30,30V,55,66,
    70,110,112,161,171,185,212,220,225,229,243,271,273,274,292,301,329,343,349,353,356,376,376V,
    401,405,411,416,416,421,423,434,439,444,445,450,462,485,495,505,523,543,574,582,588,591,592,
    594,606,608,614,640,641,645,645,647,650,654,661,687,688,688,695,707,714,715,728,738,745,790;
    IV.1,26,28,42,44,48,58,59,60,69,73,80,116,123,127,128,135,145,154,155,157,166,169,173,180,184,
    198,201,202,206,217,220,226,228,240,241,243,247,290,321,325,329,363,364,368,373,391,398,419,
    427,430,442,456,458,461,463,468,476,486,491,494,560,561,568,575,587,588,618,622,627,631,648,
    676,680,693,702,705,709,716,717,722,725,727,728,731,767,784,792,812; V.1,1,2,6,9,15,21,23,23V,
    24,49,91,93,99,102,106,109,111,112,127,131,134,137,144,145,146,175,203,219,228,232,248,250,261,
    270,279,294,310,316,317,319,319,325,368,377,394,396,397,419,453,455,460,473,509,517V,524,532,
    533,549,561,577,596,623,635
  M. BRIDE
    I.1,20,35,35V,62,67,79,81,91,92,120,128,130,136,136,156,156,161,180,188,198,198V,273V,275,283,
    283V,289,324,335,338,341,404,434; II.1,4,21,25,26,36,45,67,67,67V,67V,68,68V,68V,69,69V,80,73,
    74,76,80V,81,81,81V; II.2,14,16,17,17V,21,21,30,31,31,36,42,43,43,43,46,47,47V,50,60,60,
    67,68,68,71,74,78,78,81,84,84,90,100,101,112,112V,118,118V,126,135,140,141,141,152,157,157V,
    234,252,255,264,266,273,289,290,290V,303,304,327,332,338,366,374,376,382; III.1,4,11,13,19,46,
    73,112,127,136,136V,140,156,160,164,165,165V,169,174,176,178,185,189,197,215,224,233,246,256,
    257,265,265,271,274,278,279,279V,280,283,283V,284,297,297,297,298,298,298V,306,307,313,316,333,
    355,368,370,376,389,393,395,416; IV.1,1,2,95,136,158,243,257,262,263,278,280,284,300,317,319,
    320,320,327,328,335,337,347,347,365,368,371,393V,403,410,427; V.1,30,35,36,36V,43,67,74,83,86V,

ME (CONTINUED)
    M. BRIDE   (CONTINUED)
        88V,97,97V,101,101,119,128,131; V.2,19,21,30,69,69,87,97,160,198,206,209,215,220,245,245V,247,
        275,280,291
    WAY WORLD
        I.1,29,79,79V,85,102,108,130,163,169,171,172,235,235,236,239,244,262,273,309,314,315,331,414,
        451,452,457,458; II.1,28,39,54,83,83,92,96,142,150,162,171,172,174,177,181,195,215,220,223,225,
        264,292,293,341,429,449,459,463,478,478,482,482V,486,488,514,519,546,561,561V; III.1,4,5,7,8,
        12,20,29,37,53,64,80,81,82,84,87,92,99,112,117,140,142,147,149,167,173,217,220,245,281,287,288,
        328,336,339,343,356,358,360,362,362V,390,418,454,468,517,545,560,562,596,617,665,671,676,678,
        687,687; IV.1,39,67,94,98,99,113,133,140,140,156,162,216,241,243,247,262,262V,302,307,339,353,
        365,372,373,394,395,397,403,467,468,469,473,501,504,509,532,533,551,580,591,591,613,625,633;
        V.1,24,26,30,30,32,33,34,34,35,38,40,49,69,74,113,132,141,163,164,171,171,177,268,290,307,312,
        330,336,350,372,372,378,392,392V,419,452,453,459,465,474,474V,476,481,499,512,517,546,561,578,
        594,595,611,616,617

MIGHT (81)
    OLD BATCH
        I.1,264; II.1,48,128,200,200V,215; II.2,176; III.1,158; IV.2,41; IV.3,36,170; IV.4,103,214,
        266; V.1,5,168; V.2,67,67V,70
    DOUBL DLR
        PRO.,24; II.1,39,418,423,424; III.1,337,419; IV.1,558; V.1,6,35,44,151,396
    FOR LOVE
        I.1,211; II.1,325,360,390,440; III.1,61,89,117,490,597,784; IV.1,681; V.1,82,96,212,258,413
    M. BRIDE
        I.1,137,139,377,398; II.1,28; III.1,199,227,246; IV.1,46,68,178,224,231,289; V.1,9,9V
    WAY WORLD
        PRO.,18; I.1,56,66; II.1,145,294,306,530; III.1,198,315,542,560,653V; IV.1,116,359; V.1,392,
        394

MUST (301)
    OLD BATCH
        I.1,7,9,9V,66,89,111,124,125,140,143,144,156,157,159,259,368; II.1,11,17,54,143,180,195,232;
        II.2,27,141,145,168,181; III.1,259; III.2,11V,41,61,72,100; IV.1,11,71,89; IV.3,121,136,152,
        154,154V,186; IV.4,24,161,187,224; V.1,41,54,61,119,180,204,336; V.2,104,106
    DOUBL DLR
        I.1,8,66,125,242,295,410; II.1,8,134,134,139,168,189,287,363,371,372,377,414,419; III.1,44,61,
        76,94,136,141,145,146,182,256,350,441,442,446,468,483; IV.1,71,73,98,99,101,136,136V,137,149,
        199,429,530; IV.2,90; V.1,36,90,92,94,95,114,125,127,174,176,265,267; EPI.,31,33
    FOR LOVE
        I.1,128,296,301,359,389,538,584,665; II.1,162,229,241,339,491,508,509,509V,511,523,531,532,
        534,585,588,596,597,598,598,599,599,604,606,607,609,611,612,614,615,616,617,620,620,621,623,
        626,627; III.1,22,224,229,339,346,350,382,449,507,579,677,677V,718; IV.1,43,55,116,170,275,297,
        513,539,619,709,719,773; V.1,86,114,122,198,217,227,241,244,304,305,491,517,517V,532,607,611,
        622; EPI.,14
    M. BRIDE
        I.1,57,62,102,172,172V,374,376; II.1,44; II.2,107V,194,198,223,363; III.1,33,162,244,360;
        IV.1,30,44,210,211,303,363; V.1,118; V.2,217,303,309
    WAY WORLD
        PRO.,20; I.1,99,194,284,298,350,396; II.1,2,14,16,22,76,113,114,222,314,364,401,421,449;
        III.1,99,149,152,153,192,275,343,406,407,408,409,506,724; IV.1,81,111,125,158,187,222,285,327,
        529,534,550,579,627,633; V.1,43,118,118,151,230,235,244,277,292,299,308,382,442,468,475,
        573,586,614; EPI.,7,34

MY (2064)
    OLD BATCH
        PRO.,15,26; I.1,9,9V,23,24,27,45,48,77,90,95,98,98,111,112,131,135,140,141,167,231,232,285,
        297,302,311,311,319,323,323V,331,335; II.1,5,5V,6V,30,34,36,53,55,55,58,76,83,94,104,111,112,
        119,131,139,140,140,140,142,142V,155,159,160,160,163,166,169,173,174,208,243; II.2,10,31,50,52,
        69,81,93,98,102,111,112,117,126,152,154,177,181,183,183V,209,218,219,223; III.1,6,15,16,30,35,
        45,52,68,70,75,75,76,100,106,107,140,142,142V,146,155,166,172,175,205,207,209,212,216,265,
        275,277,285,290,333,334,349,363; III.2,59,70,82,85,101,101,105,107,109,121,130,135,135V,138;
        IV.1,3,23,26,33,46,49,54,55,65,73,80,80,81,83,90,91,103,111,116,141,143,158,174,176,180; IV.2,
        2,2V,4,5,6,21,31,34,50,66,91; IV.3,1,10,10V,11,12,14,19,28,55,69,78,84,92,102,103,108,120,123,
        158,167,169,171,175,205; IV.4,3,4,13,13,15,16,24,30,43,47,58,65,66,67,71,74,74,76,110,132,139,
        147,149,151,157,169,169,170,195,202,202,206,211,213,220,231,243,243V,248,257,261,263,264,266,
        269,270; V.1,12,32,35,48,58,60,63,63V,72,74,100,102,125,140,151,160,181,191,206,223,225,233,
        240,240,247,278,290,295,306,309,310,319,322,332,333,334,337,363,364,364; V.2,39,41,49,66,67,
        67V,69,69V,76,77,109,118,125,136,138,140,145,148,158,167,175; EPI.,11,17,18
    DOUBL DLR
        PRO.,23; I.1,31,33,53,55,76,85,86,88,93,97,99,112,113,114,118,118V,126,126,133,135,135V,
        135V,136,138,138,150,150,152,165,183,192,194,194,210,218,227,231,233,235,237,250,274,276,283,
        284,289,291,291,292,295,309,317,318,320,322,325,326,326,338,338,339,340,342,344,346,347,349,
        352,365,366,368,369,381,392,398,399,406; II.1,8,20,23,25,25V,26,27,28,43,44,50,52,55,60,60,60V,
        62,63,64,68,73,74,74,76,76,80,82,96,101,101,102,111,111,112,117,120,121,124,126,127,127,129,
        134,139,142,172,192,196,202,204,206,212,214,217,221,231,232,233,234,236,238,252,254,259,264,
        267,268,270,276,278,280,297,312,317,326,335,341,342,349,350,353,355,360,374,375,376,382,397,
        397V,403,405,405V,406,410,420,422,423,424,429,440,441; III.1,1,1,5,11,11,15,16,24,27,35,35,36,
        42,42,50,51,59,59,64,65,67,69,89,91,96,101,103,105,109,112,114,115,115,118,120,128,134,143,144,
        146,150,151,152,155,157,157,160,160V,165,170,178,178,180,188,189,190,200,207,210,237,246,251,
        257,258,259,259,264,305,307,324,326,334,349,352,355,360,372,373,375,376,385,386,395,396,398,
        401V,402,404,415,416,417,419,431,436,440,441,455,461,466,468,472,475,480,489,498,548,556,558,
        559,561,567,589,590,593,602,609,614,615,616,620,621; IV.1,2,7,11,35,37,47,62,65,74,76,78,81,83,
        92,92,95,100,103,112,114,115,116,117,124,132,134,140,144,147,157,158,159,163,166,169,171,194,
        195,199,214,221,227,228,229,236,242,248,253,253,257,282,291,297,298,304,309,309,313,
        317,326,328,330,344,344V,351,357,359,363,367,369,376,377,381,383,384,384,412,413,413,415,428,
        430,442,445,453,457,470,492,496,498,499,509,509,509,515,515,515V,515V,523,523V,536,538,540,543,
        544,546,552,552V,560,561,563,564,565,573,576,583,585,588; IV.2,1,5,24,24V,46,52,53,62,64,72,
        72V,77,82,84,84,86,90,95,96,109,111,112,113,117,118,119,120,121,122,128,138,138,141,151; V.1,4,
        6,7,10,10,13,14,23,24,26,30,33,34,36,40,43,43,46,51,54,57,59,72,72,78,80,87,89,90,92,96,96,97,
        105,107,110,111,115,118,119,128,128,138,155,155,155,159,159,160,171,172,174,176,184,187,205,
        210,211,214,215,217,224,225,232,239,242,266,267,285,303,306,308,315,319,319V,322,333,336,337,
        338,343,344,356,359,365,373,374,376,391,397,398,399,401,402,404,412,416,420,424,427,428,436,
        461,463,467,468,472,472,474,478,482,486,487,493,493,496,499,502,504,512,517,519,523,525,526,

MY (CONTINUED)
    DOUBL DLR   (CONTINUED)
      527,527,538,546,551,551,554,557,574
    FOR LOVE
      I.1,53,75,91,122,136,158,158V,183,200,208,208,211,214,214V,216,218,222,228,243,246,259,260,
      318,322,326,333,335,336,338,338,340,340,384,394,394V,421,428,429,435,456,515,516,567,576,595,
      597,610,665,669,678; II.1,1,2,2,3,6,13,27,37,38,38,66,71,100,130,131,132,133,144,148,149,162,
      165,173,175,182,183,192,193,229,230,238,243,245,246,247,255,265,265,267,282,284,294,306,306V,
      324,337,339,345,363,379,379,390,395,395,399,410,421,454,458,463,467,472,480,484,497,499,509,
      509V,511,512,524,527,530,560,564,568,570,578,583,619,631,638,638,641,649,658,659; III.1,9,11,
      15,32,57,57,96,97,101,102,113,118,135,144,146,149,158,177,177,185,185,189,191,210,212,213,218,
      225,226,232,234,259,270,270,278,283,302,307,352,371,373,387,397,420,446,449,471,510,523,543,
      578,582,586,587,590,594,595,605,606,610,623,648,663,685,686,690,690V,713,718,729,736,741,742,
      743,746,747,797,808,808; IV.1,15,29,44,55,69,74,80,89,90,99,131,131V,178,193,199,223,225,230,
      231,237,239,243,265,272,281,302,316,324,351,353,357,362,370,372,375,379,380,384,387,391,393,
      417,447,452,464,535,560,569,569,569V,569V,579,595,606,612,613,617,625,626,654,655,656,685,
      690,698,702,715,716,718,767,773,777,796,796,814; V.1,7,37,37V,44,49,75,80,94,99,104,126,134,
      136,137,148,152,171,173,175,177,185,190,200,208,213,215,227,228,229,230,232,254,254,257,
      259,282,283,283,289,301,301V,307,309,316,318,318,347,347,384,388,393,403,457,461,463,464,465,
      472,473,478,480,489,498,500,517,519,533,534,540,543,545,545,547,562,562,566,577,579,585V,591,
      593,602,615; EPI.,35
    M. BRIDE
      I.1,8,28,35,35,35V,37,37,68,70,71,71V,74,76,76,76,79,89V,99,99V,102,109,111,119,131,134,136,
      148,148V,152,160,173,173V,183,184,192,192V,193,195,195,201,201,201V,201V,202V,206,214,217,224,
      246,246,248,250,253,255,263,271,272,274,281V,282,285,294,308,309,310,330,330V,334,336,337,338,
      340,340V,349,369,378,400,403,409,409V,411,414,450; II.1,6,7,16,19,25,64,66,69,69V,72,79,79,82,
      83; II.2,9,22,24,25,29,45,56,56V,76V,81,112,112V,115,119,119V,120,122,123,124,132,133,133,140,
      153,155,155,155V,155V,157V,159,162,170,170V,184,200,203,205,215V,216,239,239,243,253,269,
      269V,276,278,281,285,288,290,291,296,300,304,339,345,358,359,361,365,365,365V,365V,367,378,
      378V; III.1,2,6,9,10,11,13,17,18,19,39,44,73,74,75,77,79,80,81,85,90,93,99,104,105,111,123,126,
      142,147,148,153,160,170,179,187,193,196,202,213,220,224,233,235,236,236,236,236,252,253,254,
      277,281,284,292,304,304,305,305,317,318,318,329,341,345,346,348,350,351,351V,351V,352,352V,354,
      364,368,387,407,411,420,443,454; IV.1,25,29,29,39,41,93,117,141,146,150,156,184,192,228,233,
      234,271,274,282,291,307,309,315,316,333,337,338,342,350,352,356,358,372,379,386,392,392V,394,
      398,402,417,424,429,435,441; V.1,5,15,30,33,33,38,47,47V,65,68,71,72,76,86DV,86EV,88,88V,114,
      119,122,125,126,127,137,139; V.2,4,13,16,20,22,22,22,48,53,55,55,70,72,74,77,78,81,96,126,142,
      144V,145,147,166V,167V,183,183,183V,183V,190,190V,193,197,201,204,205,208,210,221,231,238,242,
      250,260,262,262V,268,269,276,278,282,293,293,297,297,297,299,300,302,304
    WAY WORLD
      I.1,18,23,24,26,46,60,78,168,169,172,176,193,193,235,237,245,250,250,256,270,273,279,288,294,
      311,314,315,399,411,411,411V,411V,436,444,445,451,466,468,483,492,507,514; II.1,16,16,17,19,
      19V,30,30,51,55,82,87,88,95,97,98,110,113,124,127,143,144,146,146,162,162,170,173,173,179,189,
      194,195,203,205,225,237,241,244,254,280,282,285,286,291,293,296,300,300V,305,308,332,333,340,
      366,371,371V,430,441,442,501,506,510,513,516,519,521,543,546,555,557,558,558,561,561V,563,563;
      III.1,4,49,49,53,62,88,102,112,135,141,150,170,171,180,186,191,193,195,206,207,207,209,219,
      219,228,251,255,257,263,271,274,288,289,293,320,323,325,329,333,358,366,373,401,422,445,450,
      452,452,453,458,499,500,511,557,558,568,571,572,573,606,617,618,622,630,635,636,637,637V,645,
      645,647,659,660,663,668,677,683,684,684,685,685,700,708,721; IV.1,23,34,37,45,49,66,68,73,73V,
      76,78,78,79,91,135,150,156,158,181,185,186,187,197,201,216,220,221,222,243,253,261,288,296,
      299,300,311,329,336,343,353,357,369,376,388,395,398,403,405,405,406,407,425,444,475,476,477,
      477,485,490,490,499,500,500,509,512,518,518,529,530,569,576,586,603,603,607,616,624,624,
      625,627,628,629,634,644,645; V.1,1,9,20,21,21,29,62,66,68,70,73,75,75,77,78,81,83,87,92,104,
      106,107,107,109,110,114,116,125,129,130,131,140,140,141,151,151,152,155,156,156,162,171,178,
      178V,183,203,205,224,239,239,239,250,258,266,268,270,278,286,295,302,304,305,309,321,327,329,
      335,348,349,388,390,390,396,398,402,402,404,406,412,416,418,421,422,423,425,434,435,435,436,
      441,445,447,448,451,453,457,459,464,464,472,477,478,480,502,525,534,575,578,582,584,588,595,
      598,603,609,611,614,615

NAY (197)
    OLD BATCH
      I.1,38,334; II.1,101,104,144,232,243,248; II.2,1,46,151; III.1,79,174,212,308,339; III.2,43,
      84,92,100,122,133; IV.1,58,98,100,100,105,115,117; IV.2,48,69,79; IV.3,61,97,111,131,195,201;
      IV.4,19,161,190,270; V.1,37,57,64,64,67,71,147,171,237,284,375; V.2,49,64,76
    DOUBL DLR
      I.1,41,187,240,253,355,383,385; I.1,38,76,155,257,257V,334,337,355,355,393; III.1,16,23,40,
      61,64,68,70,72,76,81,84,94,105,111,255,298,304,379; IV.1,156,214,244,469,485V,544; IV.2,39,97,
      122; V.1,19,92,129,182,276,424,428,453,512,568; EPI.,14
    FOR LOVE
      I.1,58,152,398,403,410,414,492,501; II.1,31,76,88,111,257,263,355,361,421,468,517,568; III.1,
      84,280,280V,283,299,306,338,385,519,519,714,739; IV.1,66,379,379,568,706,725,739; V.1,350,471,
      532
    M. BRIDE
      II.1,67,68V; II.2,129; III.1,76,318; IV.1,310; V.2,166V,309
    WAY WORLD
      I.1,71,159,291,375; II.1,210,222,239,391,478,559; III.1,74,89,188,188,291,292,695,705; IV.1,
      87,91,91,93,94,119,123,164,580; V.1,190,229,232,235,241,371,373,390,454

NEITHER (42)
    OLD BATCH
      I.1,172; III.1,18,271; III.2,109; IV.3,130; V.2,28
    DOUBL DLR
      I.1,314; II.1,25,25V,372; III.1,168,584,591; IV.1,15,136,136V,157,244,344
    FOR LOVE
      II.1,61; III.1,238,648,691,714; IV.1,73,97; V.1,22,64,66,352,467,632
    M. BRIDE
      II.2,77,329
    WAY WORLD
      I.1,292; II.1,560; III.1,163,292; IV.1,25,107,299,333

NEVER (221)
    OLD BATCH
      I.1,47,102,144,168,199,300,309,358; II.1,14,41,203; II.2,10,118,121,124,129,194,195; III.1,43,
      57,111,193,263; III.2,105,111,153; IV.1,41,171; IV.2,79; IV.3,72,174; IV.4,91,110,139,150,155,
      200; V.1,242,293,347,399

NEVER (CONTINUED)
    DOUBL DLR
        I.1,147,195,222,223,225,318,357; II.1,13,21,23,44,84,105,205,268,268,282,318,351,365,365V;
        III.1,114,265,286,293,316,458,526; IV.1,7,13,40,72,123,135,136,136V,147,149,165,167,199,278,
        453,573; IV.2,73,98,98,149,152; V.1,34,399
    FOR LOVE
        I.1,84,91,94,265,267,344,346,363,385,401,406,411,498,515,517,518,518,519,573; II.1,456,532,
        574,611; III.1,21,27,31,55,78,89,101,104,116,119,122,125,127,182,208,230,311,361,399,622,622,
        733; IV.1,67,96,291,333,432,497,572,657,662,789; V.1,55,213,280,464,465,504,544,572,593,610
    M. BRIDE
        I.1,108,175; II.2,125; III.1,54,118; IV.1,188,287,289,322,330; V.2,289
    WAY WORLD
        I.1,29,226,276,340,468,497; II.1,12,17,33,72,183,365,369; III.1,46,140,150,158,160,232,284,
        300,301,305,312,337,679; IV.1,52,72,87,175,180,200,204,204V,206,206V,222,289,416,481,481,627;
        V.1,189,191,196,253,255,342,375,392,392V,394,543

NO (767)
    OLD BATCH
        PRO.,5,16; I.1,2,43,114,151,162,198,279,309,332,335,351,366,374,379; II.1,4,21,25,33,40,40,81,
        94,125,128,190,196,200,200V,204,210,217; II.2,1,46,59,76,79,104,116; III.1,11,14,40,74,74V,181,
        187,198,234,236,236,256,271,271,328,328V,331,346,346,351,356,356,360,362; III.2,48,62,62,86,99,
        99,109,109,124,155; IV.1,83,83,106,106,115,124,127,131,131,184; IV.2,47,67,84,92; IV.3,18,18,
        77,106,169,177,187,209; IV.4,1,1,15,52,81,81,85,116,116,135,158,160,165V,218,224,228,228,248,
        248,259,268,273; V.1,4,123,132,142,156,242,242,261,261V,267,272,303,310,324,347,363,371,
        387; V.2,27,84,85,105,105,147,147; EPI.,12
    DOUBL DLR
        PRO.,2; I.1,7,7V,29,43,43,43,43V,43V,43V,74,111,120,122,192,224,225,226,226V,243,260,271,299,
        318,329V,345,346,393; II.1,27,141,141,159,164,211,230,271,325,328,329,338,338,344,348,350,356,
        366,370,370,391,391,454,456; III.1,29,46,61,64,81,93,93,93,146,147,189,202,210,212,228,228,239,
        267,306,351,399,400,427,427,428,428,429,439,440,459,519,574,577; IV.1,107,148,163,181,182,
        220,220,275,275,294,334,336,351,365,372,376,420,420V,451,457,468,552; IV.2,23,42,58; V.1,19,36,
        61,64,91,94,100,106,131,138,167,167,168,200,229,229,259,259,262,267,293,296,308,325,343,372,
        372,372V,372V,388,433,456,456V,505,505,523,525,532,536,596; EPI.,7
    FOR LOVE
        PRO.,42; I.1,34,71,74,144,171,181,207,210,249,257,274,281,281,281,283,317,324,331,358,363,377,
        404,427,428,468,469,476,477,495,531,533,555,563,574,574V,596,610,615,615,622,647,648,664; II.1,
        4,15,15V,60,136,170,170V,172,176,177,177,195,197,267,293,309,326,333,427,457,460,490,493,
        586,586,587,607,614,633,648,654; III.1,21,22,30,39,40,47,47,54,85,94,95,97,100,107,112,153,190,
        190,239,297,303,315,333,341,354,354,380,390,401,407,430,489,491,492,586,644,644,690,690V,764;
        IV.1,3,8,29,46,81,88,89,102,104,121,124,124,143,174,181,183,200,200,200V,200V,218,232,237,256,
        321,359,398,406,406,420,425,425V,434,445,473,518,552,554,554,591,591,601,613,614,615,623,625,
        665,676,679,695,750,752; V.1,16,27,34,44,44,76,87,152,152,180,194,219,219,245,245,250,250,251,
        280,287,326,351,369,427,466,469,471,484,492,497,506,517,517V,518,555; EPI.,14
    M. BRIDE
        PRO,26; I.1,16,16V,17,17V,19,17,34,53,53V,55,71,71V,72,73V,88,88V,152,175,201,201,201V,201V,
        206,292,320V,340,340V,443,452; II.1,58,73; II.2,116,116,116V,120,121,148,180,201,205,214,
        273; III.1,102,156,162,162,174,247,247,258,258,314,314,335,370,372,448,448V,451,451V,457; IV.1,
        35,35,59,97,170,279,281,281V,330,332,397,406,420; V.1,35,138; V.2,11,30,91,106,124V,173,173V,
        226,298; EPI.2,17
    WAY WORLD
        PRO.,9,17,24,30; I.1,4,7,63,115,201,207,239,241,242,251,264,273,280,297,297,297,298,315,318,
        318,318,319,323,323,334,336,339,339,363,412,413,428,455,468,474,514,514; II.1,20,58,227,235,
        240,312,325,349,360,372,379,391,407,409,472,483,495,542; III.1,1,2,3,4,11,38,39,124,160,161,
        252,290,320,328,393,394,418,418,419,420,420,420,484,486,487,493,511,515,526,542,588,650,682,
        682,682,682,713,714,720; IV.1,19,21,48,83,99,102,107,108,139,146,153,159,160,216,235,236,238,
        269,325,332,355,359,386,426,431,442,442,444,517,519,527,545,561,577,577,585,622,626,628; V.1,7,
        24,24,31,34,36,39,74,165,171,206,206,216,237,237,248,249,256,288,307,316,320,326,379,396,445,
        445,467,477,489,494,503,530,577,582,608; EPI.,12,19,34

NOR (122)
    OLD BATCH
        I.1,169,241; II.1,126,234; II.2,120; III.1,109; IV.2,85; IV.4,1; V.1,198; V.2,28
    DOUBL DLR
        I.1,56,77; II.1,25V,357,391; IV.1,15,137,158,449; V.1,35,72,105,162; EPI.,5
    FOR LOVE
        I.1,261,489,519,613; II.1,2,2,62,143,172,428; III.1,33,238,238,366,378,399,399,428,492,555,
        648,691; IV.1,74,96,97,97,250; V.1,64,66,447,459,459,593,632; EPI.,16
    M. BRIDE
        PRO,7,42; I.1,145,202V,218,248,453; II.1,18V; II.2,50,55,55,59,76,76V,77,77V,91,184,184,261,
        299,341; III.1,107,213,215,314,321,458; IV.1,39,255,302,330,396,399; V.1,3,3; V.2,1,1,76,106,
        134,134,188,192,270,270,290
    WAY WORLD
        PRO.,27; II.1,454; III.1,517,571; IV.1,53,108,201,202,206,206V,295,299,530; V.1,176,438,439

NOT (1193)
    OLD BATCH
        PRO.,14; I.1,6,27,60,63,75,84,133,133V,137,142,151,171,188,204,227,254,259,312,314,349,358;
        II.1,9,29,29,35,35V,65,115,142,142V,161,162,166,176,186,190,193,203,205,234,238; II.2,24,25,
        41,43,59,72,111,117,128,153,170,210; III.1,11,1V,4,25,44,52,60,64,73,74,74V,101,101V,102,106,
        106,125,147,149,160,161,209,218,236,237,238,271,290,292,297,303,313,332,339,343,348,353,357;
        III.2,8,11V,11V,12V,13V,42,42V,53,69,77,84,92,105,109,123,138; IV.1,11,25,56,58,65,81,85,
        88,98,101,126,160,163,175,180,186,188; IV.2,20,24,26,27,44,45,51,60,84; IV.3,5,32,58,83,91,92,
        115,121,129,131,139,162,168,169,171,206; IV.4,75,90,117,162,185,191,222,251,251V; V.1,D,10,11,
        32,33,44,54,61,74,94,120,140,144,147,166,167,213,254,255,279,299,303,323,360,363,376,379; V.2,
        5,6,23,39,42,67,67V,69,69V,105,115,122,134,175,179; EPI.,20
    DOUBL DLR
        PRO.,16,21,28; I.1,2,15,33,38,77,79,83,98,100,117,127,143,153,154,154V,203,203,244,246,249,
        257,258,269,271,280,288,308,309,311,317,321,322,334,335,342,346,348,348,355,371,373,386,387,
        388,394,419; II.1,3,3,6,8,18,20,35,41,53,62,97,103,107,126,131,139,159,170,184,211,216,220,245,
        246,263,263V,277,296,303,309,319,328V,339,349,357,357,363,371,379,386,417,432,450,462,463;
        III.1,7,38,43,46,47,66,67,69,75,76,78,87,94,97,106,128,145,146,172,200,239,239,242,
        258,270,270V,284,308,330,348,375,377,385,391,404,411,424,426,426,428,428,433,503,506,591,621,
        622,624,629,630; IV.1,27,43,44,66,95,98,109,128,135,149,177,179,214,243,262,268,269,273,292,
        303,325,352,420,420V,434,470,475,499,500,518,553,570,576,579; IV.2,9,16,22,26,47,71,80,83,90,

NOT (CONTINUED)
    DOUBL DLR   (CONTINUED)
      102,103,113,115,121,130; V.1,1,8,10,20,47,53,72,92,99,105,111,126,167,176,177,229,233,254,260,
      264,276,282,290,294,294,312,320,333,365,371,388,450,451,451,475,484,521,521,530,530V;548; EPI.,
      25
    FOR LOVE
      PRO.,36,40,45; I.1,20,45,68,97,113,127,153,180,198,219,220,245,255,261,266,313,376,387,399,
      401,402,421,442,448,460,487,489,494,510,510V,514,521,581,620,641; II.1,2,19,44,65,72,118,132,
      143,162,164,228,228V,241,246,287,300,304,316,317,324,324,325,358,358,389,397,407,434,446,461,
      471,474,481,508,509,509V,523,528,533,535,553,564,585,598,604,607,620,626,635,662; III.1,3,29,
      30V,47,59,85,94,96,105,108,140,145,170,181,183,235,237,240,241,243,281,297,321,329,339,341,
      344,346,351,364,370,382,383,389,395,429,430,449,459,461,492,502,507,513,519,520,524,525,540,
      546,547,549,550,554,556,559,560,564,568,600,603,614,621,635,688,689,707,709,724,734,790; IV.1,
      8,17,23,43,47,48,50,61,62,83,83V,120,121,125,144,155,156,157,159,161,166,206,239,243,246,247,
      249,281,309,312,323,325,330,331,342,372,379,391,406,409,429,486,491,549,606,623,626,627,629,
      646,697,734,741,753,753V,755,760,762,784,791,803,812,816; V.1,1,10,13,15,17,21,22,28,41,77,121,
      165,167,176,227,235,238,241,250,252,267,293,295,304,325,331,336,337V,355,370,371,371,379,388,
      390,404,405,414,426,430,435,459,484,505,541,561,575,588V,599,607,624,625,625,637; EPI.,17,35
    M. BRIDE
      PRO.,1,17,41; I.1,8,13,19,59,67,67V,87,88,88V,101,118,118V,218,218V,244,259,300,302,307,315,
      335,355,374,391,406,409,409V,435,436,439,443V; II.1,18,18V,23; II.2,50,59,69,74,76,76V,78,79,
      81,91,98,104,113,115,119,119V,120,134,149,164,183,207,210,216V,220,223,225,244,244,246,254,
      254V,261,271,288,298,298,299,331,332,333,336,341,347; III.1,13,19,24,78,97,100,100V,107,126,
      156,174,187,190,212,215,242,242V,255,256,264,266,275,283,283V,286,311,332,332,335,342,361,363,
      370,370,394,415,416,420,423,425,451,451V; IV.1,2,20,21,37,95,99,111,113,119,119V,146,170,178,
      197,199,204,212,218,230,237,264,301,304,319,338,358,364,366,368,372,373,421,423,427,442,442V;
      V.1,1,2,42,68,91,91V,97,108,116,118,120,123,128; V.2,21,76,97,111,124,184,187,191,229,229V,
      238,239,240,264,264V,300,314,320
    WAY WORLD
      PRO.,26,31,34; I.1,5,15,34,36,49,84,86,88,91,92,137,138,141,145,150,154,166,204,212,222,223,
      228,240,240V,293,307,311,334,338,376,392,394,422,428,435,438,478,487,500,500V,504,524,530,531,
      531,533,536; II.1,24,57,60,118,119,121,128,132V,143,148,163,184,200,209,210,222,225,227,
      232,233,233,233,235,237,240,275,276,291,346,350,361,366V,377,383,400,400,401,402,438,447,450,
      451,460,461,480,494,497,498,502,506,517,530,538,542; III.1,3,7,8,11,15,24,30,76V,80,80,88,
      90,113,155,156,156V,157,164,188,195,231,241,243,244,256,289,297,322,325,349,357,372,378,379,
      382,407,418,441,442,454,459,465,475,496,498,506,509,514,515,517,519,528,533,536,536,556,556,
      556V,556V,557,560,570,579,620,643,654V,657,666,684,688,695,696,703,706,722; IV.1,8,39,81,83,83,
      104,114,116,134,170,177,179,209,230,233,247,249,256,264,301,313,313V,315,317,317V,337,367,369,
      402,412,428,437,440,443,445,508,529,532,540,542,571,619,623,630; V.1,26,32,38,41,75,76,78,
      99,99V,144,148,148,149,149,165,217,248,249,257,267,269,286,304,305,312,313,344,356,357,361,372,
      372,373,383,392,392V,393,409,416,427,438,441,446,450,451,460,463,476,495,501,502,517,528,531,
      594,598,601,613

OF (2327)
    OLD BATCH
      I.1,10,12,20,23,29,33,49,56,57,61,64,69,75,80,80,80,81,82,83,91,95,102,105,106,115,116,117,
      120,121,127,128V,138,139,140,143,151,154,156,157,158,159,162,168,182,183,185,197,203,205,208,
      210,211,214,222,223,232,236,237,239,239,240,241,242,245,248,250,259,262,264,267V,275,276,
      280,281,288,289,292,295,296,300,302,303,305,306,307,310,310,311,311,318,322,322,328,328,341,
      345,355,357,360,365,366,370,371,372,377,378,379; II.1,3,34,45,52,53,55,56,58,59,60,63,68,71,
      73,73,77,82,88,98,105,111,118,118,132,139,145,148,162,163,163,168,188,193,197,198,199,205,214,
      219,219,220,228; II.2,5,15,17,25,31,32,37,39,57,89,106,108,111,123,127,138,144,146,152,154,165,
      222; III.1,9,15,21,29,34,34V,45,50,65,67,79,81,83,99,100,127,129,137,146,150,153,166,167,175,
      177,182,185,187,188,188,190,209,216,234,242,252,266,269,273,277,288,298,301,303,304,316,352,
      362,363,363; III.2,21V,25,37,39,49,50,56,58,77,80,80V,97,127,129,129V,130,149; IV.1,7,8,16,28,
      29,42,51,51,59,60,61,69,86,93,106,114,133,157,158,160,168,169,176,182; IV.2,7,10,25,51,54,58,
      64,85; IV.3,7,13,24,33,33,38,40,40V,43,44,46,48,54,54V,68,79,80,88,102,128,130,133,136,139,
      152,153,158,168,170,177,178,178V,189,197,200; IV.4,23,24,25,46,58,62,65,65,65,66,70,73,78,87,
      103,110,115,119,132,142,144,151,153,162,164,184,189,191,193,196,205,206,211,212,224,225,226,
      231,235,235,245,264,269,271; V.1,2,16,53,58,64,67,76,104,105,109,126,131,134,142,144,147,149,
      155,176,184,194,198,208,222,227,229,231,234,234,244,254,258,266,269,271,301,304,305,327,337,
      339,344,348,351,365,369,369V,379,381,381,383,386,392; V.2,9,10,18,51,51,52,64,66,71,81,103,119,
      122,123,133,135,139,152,165,168,173,173,191; EPI.,9,13,13,20
    DOUBL DLR
      PRO.,7,10,11,12,14,26; I.1,3,3V,8,11,11V,14,34,34,35,37,39,42,75,79,85,86,89,92,93,93,95,96,
      96V,97,97,104,107,112,116,149,199,199V,200,201,202,217,217V,229,239,256,286,292,330V,330V,344,
      348,349,349,349,365,376,378,378V,385,393,398,416; II.1,5,21,29,30,32,41,49,49V,50,50,86,87,107,
      131,156,156V,158,162,163,168,170,175,196,217,218,233,236,243,247,253,260,273,278,279,283,283V,
      289,291,291V,292,294,295,301,304,307,314,315,316,318,329,340,345,347,351,363,367,374,376,378,
      381,397,397V,398,401,414,417,426,441,444,448,450,456,468; III.1,3,8,9,15,19,24,37,66,92,101,
      104,117,124,136,137,142,147,148,154,157,160,168,196,198,204,215,224,225,226,229,229,230,
      235,245,254,256,258,260,272,276,277,277,277,282,287,287,292,296,302,307,312,317,317,332,
      337,339,351,351,352,355,357,370,372,373,375,377,381,381,381V,381V,384,385,393,402,427,437,451,
      451,457,461,465,466,469,471,472,473,481,486,494,516,530,540,556,564,565,570,574,581,584,
      591,602,619,624,625,626; IV.1,12,12V,18,24,24V,27,29,35,36,41,43,45,47,52,53,72,74,78,81,81,82,
      87,95,105,111,119,137,138,145,155,157,161,168,173,189,203,204,207,222,227,228,234,238,238,240,
      241,255,255V,292,293,295,302,304,316,326,332,366,371,378,398,400,402,410,411,413,415,417,425,
      425V,426V,426V,428,438,440,453,454,456,459,475,477,514,533,549,562,571,579,582,583,584,589;
      IV.2,3,9,11,22,24,24V,54,60,66,69,75,76,78,78,124,142,143,147,148,149,151; V.1,31,42,48,56,57,
      69,72,81,82,86,87,87,90,98,104,124,136,144,144V,152V,156,156,172,173,174,177,214,220,223,253,
      255,255V,263,269,269V,273,273,274,277,278,281,281V,310,311,313,341,354,375,380,395,426,431,
      431V,432,433,436,451,451,456,456V,462,469,472,472,477,503,526,526,527,531,531,539,542,551,556,
      567,570,571,576,581,589; EPI.,17,24,26,27,27,28,33
    FOR LOVE
      PRO.,7,17,25,27,36,39,47; I.1,15,17,27,29,33,36,56,56V,60,60,61,65,67,74,78,79,80,89,95,101,
      101,102,107,108,110,112,114,114,126,133,133,149,149,150,158,158,158V,181,188,188,188,190,190,
      191,196,199,205,218,229,236,236,254,332,332,335,335,340,341,343,345,348,351,353,367,368,369,
      370,372,376,378,383,392,394,394,394V,399,403,405,405,417,423,425,429,431,443,446,446,448,
      463,466,467,467V,475,486,515,521,526,528,537,560,568,569,573,576,578,579,597,598,605,618,623,
      624,632,639,657,675,676,677; II.1,5,19,29,32,45,47,48,58,59,70V,72,81,89,89V,96,102,105,106,
      107,112,121,127,128,130,130,154,183,194,198,200,212,212,219,219,221,222,223,223,227,228,228V,
      230,231,232,232,233,236,237,237,240,240,244,248,249,250,255,256,275,275,277,288,291,299,299,
      306,306V,310,331,338,340,340V,341,345,354,355,364,366,369,379,383,386,387,388,393,393V,395,395,
      399,400,418,424,425,433,441,441V,453,453V,464,478,482,485,490,493,497,500,500V,503,537,539,548,

OF (CONTINUED)
FOR LOVE (CONTINUED)
549,549,549,565,578,584,592,593,625,645; III.1,2,27,29,36,43,45,46,46V,52,56,57,67,68,70,71,74,
76,76,77,104,117,118,119,121,129,132,132,138,155,166,174,174,175,182,185,186,191,213,218,226,
226,241,262,316,329,372,373,374,375,404,411,411,413,413,426,461,462,464,477,484,486,486V,499,
500,501,511,516,530,534,535,536,539,539,545,546,548,551,554,587,589,589,597,598,602,612,617,
641,646,647,648,659,662,682,683,690,690V,698,733,740,744,750,753,754,790,802,809,815,816,817;
IV.1,3,7,15,25,26,33,34,42,46,56,58,63,64,68,68,69,90,98,100,106,106,122,132,142,173,197,
212,216,221,240,251,256,272,285,290,294,295,299,302,316,333,334,356,365,368,375,383,401,402,
410,427,450,452,456,458,471,479,507,516,523,524,548,559,564,578,579,581,597,598,605,607,614,
627,636,637,661,663,686,691,692,702,703,704,704,708,717,718,720,722,727,729,772,773,775,777,
785,786,788,788,789,796,802,808,813,814,815; V.1,13,22,34,35,36,37,37V,39,39,39,46,53,56,57,63,
67,71,72,73,73V,74,77,78,79,84,84,97,100,110,111,126,128,149,152,158,158V,166,168,174,176,177,
182,184,191,200,208,209,216,218,225,238,244,261,265,267,268,269,271,272,286,288,294,295,
297,308,315,327,344,354,362,376,381,382,385,391,399,406,420,427,430,451,464,468,472,476,477,
487,488,491,512,534,543,561,563,567,589,610,613,613V,629,629; EPI.,5,11,21,29
M. BRIDE
PRO.,5,6,10,10,12,12,15,18; I.1,7,35,35V,37,38,40,41,42,42,56V,58,58,61,61V,62,63,73,83,84,89V,
96,96V,103,104,113,114,126,139,148,147,148V,158,166,170,182,188,210,220,228,229,234,235,235,
241,242,242V,245,247,249,258,259,259,265,266,273,273V,282,282V,286,302,315,318,322,324,325,
325V,328,337,348V,364,396,422,427,428V,433,434,439,444,451; II.1,D,2,8,8V,10,13,15V,37,42,46,
53,55,59,65,80,70,75,76,78,80V; II.2,D,1,3,7,14,20,20V,27,28,30,36,51,64,64V,85,88,92,107,107V,
107V,109,120,128,128V,135,137,138,144,146,160,161,173,173V,174,185,187,187V,192,200,203,211,
217,217V,220,224,237,238,240,252,266,286,287,289,295,305,319,323,339,352,354,355,363,365,365V,
368,370,374,382; III.1,4,6,25,26,27,29,37,60,61,63,68,75,77,87,88,92,95,96,106,116,126,128,130,
132,132,132V,132V,133,133V,135,138,158,167,179,194,205,217,217V,223,224,226,227,231,235,238,
243,252,261,293,303,304,305,305,309,310,313,319,336,338,340,367,373,374,376,388,389,400,408,
426,427,429,441,442,455; IV.1,D,6,7,10,12,14,18,22,25,28,35,45,46,52,53,55,71,74,79,81,83,84,
98,105,106,123,126,134V,137,141,144,153,161,192,194,200,201,219,221,252,255,258,261,269,269V,
276,278,280,283,286,290,297,332,363,371,379,402,433,437,438; V.1,D,3,9V,10,10V,17,19,30,86CV,
104,111,124,132,132V; V.2,2,29,31,33,49,72,74,82,84,90,92,95,103,112,115,122,123,137,137,138,
141,143,144,144V,146,160,194,196,197,199,201,219,220,240,241,244,251,256,256V,269,281,282,284,
285,289,305,307,307V,317,319; EPI,10,12,24,26
WAY WORLD
PRO.,1,3,36,38; I.1,5,6,7,9,14,19,31,33,43,44,50,50,53,57,59,61,61,61,64,67,69,70,72,74,75,79,
79V,84,85,86,92,94,96,106,115,135,136,137,139,140,142,144,150,150,157,168,187,201,202,204,205,
205,210,211,218,221,221V,224,225,229,244,246,248,254,256,256,275,276,281,284,286,290,290,294,
310,314,320,321,326,330,341,350,351,364,369,392,413,419,445,451,455,471,478,481,482,487,493,
494,504,510,524,535,537,539,540; II.1,8,8V,9,14,20,21,48,55,55,62,63,76,77,95,97,104,110,113,
113,122,123,125,138,151,151,151V,159,160,166,168,175,180,180,197,199,203,204,206,212,213,214,
219,245,263,267,268,270,277,278,298,301,303,307,310,313,315,317,318,319,324,324V,330,332,338,
339,357,357V,384,389,399,407,408,408,414,416,417,421,433,436,440,444,447,453,455,469,480,485,
485V,486,488,488,490,491,492,493,495,496,500,501,501,520,523,542,562; III.1,1,29,32,44,46,54,
66,77,83,113,125,127,127V,140,141,152,162,168,168,178,202,212,215,226,231,234,239,243,245,246,
247,247,240,255,259,261,262,289,297,300,300,300,302,309,313,313,321,357,377,395,396,412,423,
437,499,499,500,503,512,531,535,541,541,546,548,550,553,553,555,560,562,563,570,582,583,
605,618,631,641,646,649,662,662,676,680,681,681,682,685,688,702,709,709,710,710,721; IV.1,8,55,
63,68,101,110,124,130,139,161,163,169,174,176,178,178,179,181,198,205,205,220,222,228,236,238,
249,251,254,262,262V,263,267,271,274,282,333,344,345,346,347,347,348,350,352,352,356,363,381,
384,387,388,424,467,485,486,488,490,491,493,494,496,498,500,502,507,508,516,527,530,531,532,
535,536,537,542,543,559,562,580,593,601,606,624,634,643,644; V.1,1,4,5,6,12,14,16,21,31,
43,44,49,51,74,80,82,92,98,127,127,128,128V,130,131,137,140,140,142,144,163,184,186,190,193,
202,205,205V,210,211,211V,216,218,224,233,251,260,263,263,269,272,275,278,279,281,309,329,331,
334,342,355,362,364,366,368,371,385,391,405,414,424,424,425,426,432,432V,437,444,448,450,458,
476,477,478,484,505,508,522,528,537,538,538,542,543,544,545,545,551,551,551,553,553,554,560,
590,614,618; EPI.,13,36

ON (283)
OLD BATCH
PRO.,12,15; I.1,123,221,333; II.1,21,248; II.2,94,126,220; III.1,41,66,157,181,358; III.2,40,
72; IV.1,2,4,91; IV.2,21,44; IV.3,54,54V,59,60,70,168; IV.4,86,86,102,127,192; V.1,66,79,163,
198; V.2,6,182,184; EPI.,19
DOUBL DLR
I.1,82,257,319; II.1,26,65,239; III.1,89,196,279,281,585; IV.1,198,230,251,288,384,461,559;
IV.2,51; V.1,73,218,234,289,365,367,433,435,493
FOR LOVE
I.1,50,159,159V,200,207,362,439,523,544,663; II.1,5,27,40,87,114,154,166,185,409; III.1,1,451,
464V,548,578,606,800; IV.1,426,457,470,485,571,635,678,700,705; V.1,55,109,115,302,344,566,609,
609V,625; EPI.,10
M. BRIDE
PRO.,16; I.1,111,112,120,125,130,149,160,179V,188,193,201,201V,231,277,277V,324,343,349,353,
367,367V,381,393,400,439,451; II.1,64,73,81V; II.2,13,28,72,73V,76V,100,159,181,230V,251,281,
294,301,303,304,304,305,306,306,310,317,367; III.1,29,50,80,83,94,131,166,171,257,259,298,298V,
337,338,339,343,352,352V,358; IV.1,45,48,160,167,186,231,250,253,319,327,333,366,375,401,447;
V.1,8,8V,27,42,73,126; V.2,17,69,69,170V,229,229V,245,245V,246,252,268,287,307,307V,321; EPI,
16,24,26
WAY WORLD
PRO.,10,18,25; I.1,3,12,29,109,213,214,360,372,386,406,515; II.1,140,207,269,435,538; III.1,
188,271,319,341,341,369,417,691; IV.1,24,176,214,257,269,340,470,476,492,492,492V,504,554;
V.1,9,169,221,221V,253,268,270,328,403,419,420,549,549V,589,602,613; EPI.,12,15

OR (457)
OLD BATCH
PRO.,9,20; I.1,8,10,16,42,96,99,116,144,212,246,247,263,352; II.1,28,66,66,66,160,160,190,230,
231; II.2,96,149,171; III.1,17,22,46,81,93,93V,95,103,171,172,259,265; III.2,60; IV.1,82,176;
IV.2,60,66; IV.3,17,32,175,176; IV.4,96,97,97V,218; V.1,3,127,271,306,309,322; V.2,30,35,39,
40,41,58,75,75,108,113,138
DOUBL DLR
PRO.,2,4; I.1,28,28V,36,97,110,115,192,202,219,219V,252,267,286,305; II.1,17,49,49V,50,53,300,
328,328V,387,407,442; III.1,49,87,189,246,271,271,313,372,447,473,532,533V,591; IV.1,29,36,60,
60,60,144,170,176,198,338,339,381,439,450,473,473,536; IV.2,129,153; V.1,14,75,129,176,192,
236,236V,245,268,274,306; EPI.,3,7,20
FOR LOVE
PRO.,34; I.1,10,26,27,29,32,73,80,101,106,111,113,145,292,310,347,354,384,420,447,466,476,519,

OR (CONTINUED)
    FOR LOVE   (CONTINUED)
        681; II.1,68,83,87,125V,215,215,216,217,224,326,330,375,402,421,438,438,439,490,504,549,593,
        607,607; III.1,4,30,30V,118,130,162,203,229,331,404,464,464V,467,486V,487,487V,505,509,511,563,
        671,735; IV.1,10,89,89,133,136,177,218,250,255,274,740,752,771,802,811; V.1,10,43,58,71,258,
        296,308,369,370,373,395,420,572,625; EPI.,23
    M. BRIDE
        PRO.,9,12,20,26,44; I.1,2,7,16V,66,66V,138,148,146,147,147,185,186,205,218V,249,394,427; II.1,
        7,8,8V,37,41,54,76; II.2,8,10,80,91,95,98,99,120,180,191,191,195,196V,223,251,326,357; III.1,
        31,62,79,138,172,176,184,207,226,240,240V,241,242V,248,254,282,282V,315,316,326,451V,452V;
        IV.1,38,42,42,43,157,168,185,211,266,267,361,384,386,416; V.1,73,75,75V,114,135; V.2,56,56,63,
        63,64,65,107,107,114,124,124V,135,147,207,216,236,236,320; EPI.,4
    WAY WORLD
        PRO.,35,40; I.1,23,28,80,160,167,246,261,263,277,305,310,316,341,358,396,423,433,451,485,486,
        530,537; II.1,3,26,26,169,281,411,425,438,465; III.1,9,96,131,133,149,156,156V,307,308,324,329,
        359,383,427,515,570,633,679,715,718,724,724; IV.1,60,72,74,157,182,201,214,218,236,270,340,426,
        439,439,451V,462,496,499,530,534,539,547,627,642,648; V.1,13,31,45,55,55V,111,112V,132,155,163,
        192,196,202,222,222V,226,226V,234,264,283,427,428,442,443,452,477,566,589,600

OUR (161)
    OLD BATCH
        PRO.,9; I.1,11,68,132,132,132V,132V,223; II.2,145,201; III.1,57,118,213; III.2,151,152,161;
        IV.1,6,29; IV.3,59,101,119,147; IV.4,79,245; V.1,342,342V,400; V.2,173,192; EPI.,5,21
    DOUBL DLR
        PRO.,9,19,27; I.1,37,173,217,217V; II.1,32,435; III.1,62,170,503,516,530,547; IV.1,22,26,161,
        239,239,374; V.1,58,196,215,231,244,279,475
    FOR LOVE
        PRO.,16,21,24; I.1,151,245,281,296,299; II.1,35,36,625; III.1,126,135,750,751,790,802; IV.1,
        104,659,708,790V; V.1,128,316,332,628; EPI.,6,7,25,25V,26,34,37
    M. BRIDE
        PRO.,22,23,35; I.1,123,126,133,278,279,279V,296,362,389; II.1,40; II.2,195,195V,221,221V,318;
        III.1,92,121,217,217V,259,261,321,328,328,336,340,372,390; IV.1,106,121,128V,132V,132V,134V,
        145; V.2,28,36,66,67,67,202,318,318V; EPI,27
    WAY WORLD
        PRO.,37; I.1,117,308; II.1,2,2,13,21,24,26,267,397,451,452; III.1,206,449; IV.1,257; V.1,82,
        94,135,261,490,580; EPI.,1

SHALL (400)
    OLD BATCH
        PRO.,18,19,25; I.1,84,144,173,309; II.1,14,51,60,67,134,198,230; II.2,15,88,178,186; III.1,78,
        82,135,137,171,263,313; III.2,96,121; IV.1,75,83,110,140,185; IV.2,87; IV.3,75,103,112,135,139,
        159,175; IV.4,45,193,194; V.1,168,242,309; V.2,29,34,109,138,145,176; EPI.,25
    DOUBL DLR
        PRO.,32; I.1,50,53,83,158,263,263,279,283,296,322,389,402,402V,419; II.1,44,77,77V,111,112,
        192,222,261,355,406,407,442; III.1,169,219,243,249,265,323,387,421,430,430V,527,598; IV.1,4,76,
        93,93V,123,195,247,369,374,386,446,448,482V,485V,529,573,585; IV.2,3,57,57,84,85,106,139,152;
        V.1,13,18,53,66,154,154,210,211,279,280,304,319V,324,391,479,536,551,554,568; EPI.,7
    FOR LOVE
        I.1,53,71,76,125,220,225,305,321,324,392,438,514,515,517,533,546,546V,571,592,658; II.1,118,
        132,148,149,165,194,200,214,216,239,291,303,512,587,652,662; III.1,16,19,39,159,175,212,217,
        218,229,260,297,361,437,446,473,474,475,476,477,510,511,651,791; IV.1,241,405,532,547,549,550,
        552,554,588,672,675; V.1,42,138,225,290,314,318,348,353,384,385,395,396,423,467,483,518,609,
        609V
    M. BRIDE
        PRO.,39; I.1,54,71,71V,175,326V,343,343V,354,448V,449; II.1,11; II.2,17,17V,27,107,142,143,149,
        190,209,210,216,216V,364,387,388; III.1,32,103,151,165,167,230,237,242,242V,248,358,399,418;
        IV.1,23,43,73,153,164,171,255,298,353,394,431,440; V.1,86CV,86DV; V.2,128,186,207,265,278,293,
        299,315,315V
    WAY WORLD
        PRO.,37; I.1,154,173,363,423,433,468,515,515; II.1,17,187,187,188,189,217,369,453,539; III.1,
        85,135,136,140,150,158,159,160,177,227,227V,242,250,279,351,371,467,505,580,622,681,699,701,
        711; IV.1,17,18,19,46,53,58,62,76,87,110,137,186,199,224,241,246,254,280,284,284,289,368,432,
        460,499,521,522,561,582,594,594,594,594V,624,643,646; V.1,54,59,62,137,159,244,252,261,
        265,268,293,307,337,342,352,375,376,395,426,427,429,434,460,464,476,495,496,527,532,560,560,
        565,603

SHE (449)
    OLD BATCH
        I.1,43,48,58,58,62V,65,98,103,121,162,165,166,168,171,184,205,208,264,265,269,327; III.1,39,
        40,97,111; III.2,15V,18V,19V,134,156; IV.1,51,53,60,62,74,98,114,125,149,166,167,169,184,185,
        189; IV.2,8; IV.3,42,43,137,179,187,188; IV.4,49,83,212,228,241,274; V.1,49,49V,93,94,95,97,
        113,150,198,200,212,213,215,254,255,258,265,268,285; V.2,5,125,127,159,175; EPI.,4
    DOUBL DLR
        I.1,87,95,98,109,111,114,116,118,119,129,161,333,408,410,412,413; II.1,181,183,184,238,257,
        257V,261,394,402,415,418,424,428,430,433; III.1,7,174,180,181,210,233,235,255,266,272,284,284,
        286,289,297,299,304,306,412,422,432,442,464,476,498,565,585,585,587,599,619; IV.1,2,95,150,151,
        152,162,198,252,273,292,295,296,303,500,516,517,521V,547,548; IV.2,4,4,67,123,124V,131,131,134,
        134; V.1,4,11,75,94,110,129,163,190,294,310,316,443
    FOR LOVE
        I.1,111,207,211,212,220,344,346,422,423,465,470,474,476,482,483,486,487,506,570,572,613,614;
        II.1,95,110,143,150,152,162,239,257,258,408,557,562,567,593,594; III.1,3,3V,17,61,127,440,441,
        441,578,585,585,752,752,764; IV.1,10,16,17,18,18,95,96,334,335,336V,337,541,541,645,646,679,
        800,801,810,812; V.1,49,50,70,70V,72,93,165,201,203,204,206,218,336,336,345,347,493
    M. BRIDE
        I.1,306,311,318,320,320V,346,346V,347,360,362,378,406,408,408V,441,444,444V,454,460; II.2,54,
        54,59,66,68,69,199,199V,202,250,359; III.1,45,54,54,57,157,158,161,161V,228,230,232; IV.1,184,
        204,206,209,213,219,220,222,223,224,231,236,293,293V,355,355V,363,366,397; V.1,3,9,9V,52,77,
        86DV,87,87V; V.2,275,310,315,315V
    WAY WORLD
        PRO.,4,8,9,10; I.1,25,40,41,43,48,74,75,75,83,85,88,131,151,153,163,465,475,476,477,484; II.1,
        128,129,288,300,300V,303,306,309,310,323,420,420,421,468,510,516,516,527,531,545,551; III.1,37,
        50,58,59,99,170,210,217,318,462,651,652,653V,654V,665,686,687,705; IV.1,155,236,300,428,428,
        472,560; V.1,68,70,76,79,118,169,180,180,186,187,187,188,191,194,195,196,201,206,259,280,302,
        303,306,322,360,361,361,363,363V,443,536,543,544,583

```
        PLAY
            ACT.SCENE,LINE REFERENCES

SHOULD (187)
      OLD BATCH
            I.1,226,235,265,268,286,303,352; II.2,20,139; III.1,5,21,101,101V,161,210,278; III.2,30,48,80,
            80V,92,95,139; IV.1,6,104,188,189,191; IV.2,42; IV.4,96,184; V.1,144; EPI.,13
      DOUBL DLR
            I.1,145,165,260,271,303,371,385; II.1,23,27,50,181,218,281,282,284,320,360; III.1,19,143,159,
            179,329,340,373,396,404,424,448,626; IV.1,27,46,55,80,111,152,194,249,251,298,409,452; IV.2,8,
            14; V.1,12,22,29,38,232,245,245,303,319,547
      FOR LOVE
            PRO.,4; I.1,175,363,398,450; II.1,12,128,189,351,435,473,577,635; III.1,396,396,459,461,709,
            717,783; IV.1,16,176,288,411,474,646,654,656,662,816; V.1,5,36,48,74,414,415,488,599,606
      M. BRIDE
            I.1,59,91,245,305,310,311,316,362,403,406,408,408V; II.2,125,203,379V; III.1,20,20V,22,93,213,
            250,287,314,450; IV.1,176,267,334,362,362,405,439; V.1,57,105,113,115; V.2,66,71,188,263,268
      WAY WORLD
            PRO.,19,34,35; I.1,82,82V,139,202,353,491; II.1,177,256,437; III.1,259,657,665,688,692; IV.1,
            167,300,499; V.1,143,168

SO (749)
      OLD BATCH
            PRO.,12; I.1,1,9,9V,52,97,109,124,133,133V,142,150,159,171,209,231,240,249,284,347; II.1,19,
            37,38,79,80,81,88,89,89V,100,102,108,113,126,152,187,203,222; II.2,25,26,64,65,97,101,114,122,
            124,139,163,176,203; III.1,154,238,242,256,263,267,286,301,313,320,342,342,351; III.2,30,43,57,
            71,88,93,114,121,122,123,141; IV.1,7,11,36,38,54,130,144,186; IV.2,10,37,46,53,71,79; IV.3,2,
            14,16,19,29,36,45,49,119,132,141,142,148,148,148,159; IV.4,40,119,170,185,187,188,230,234,238,
            248,264,274; V.1,38,74,90,97,99,108,119,140,171,179,232,256,275,291,349,366,368,372,382; V.2,
            108,113,121,134,171; EPI.,5,19,24,26
      DOUBL DLR
            PRO.,9; I.1,1,49,124,124V,142,159,183,188,197,212,228,228V,252,258,319,412,413; II.1,2,5,6,35,
            68,77,77V,82,106,107,263,263V,290,290,298,306,345,348,374,390,468; III.1,16,17,21,29,30,97,99,
            114,115,126,136,167,198,221,228,239,291,318,329,334,343,348,354,358,359,360,361,362,363,363,
            363,363,363V,363V,363V,363V,364,364,364,364,365,365,367,367,367,367,368,368,378,388,389,390,
            395,399,424,431,432,434,476,489,516,530,542,547,577,581,589,610,624; IV.1,10,12,14,18,43,63,70,
            70,72,82,90,90,97,106,108,108,129,145,155,157,167,168,177,185,194,221,232,243,247,261,290,292,
            319,368,437,442,444,459,460,460,460,465,481,508,510V,510V,510V,548,554; IV.2,32,33,41,100,139;
            V.1,3,10,13,24,55,81,81,81,123,125,210,221,222,222,224,226,227,228,240,254,300,318,319,319V,
            383,408,436,441,461,484,539,543,543; EPI.,6
      FOR LOVE
            PRO.,7,11,12,12V,14,33; I.1,16,21,53,122,171,180,219,220,271,349,457,514,521,536,583,638;
            II.1,29,164,184,279,347,387,403,514,525,547,557,571,573,594,614,662; III.1,67,91,147,151,164,
            182,185,258,276,276,278,283,300,324,331,333,342,364,380,389,390,393,395,398,400,429,434,510,
            532,568,570,570,586,614,620,621,626,630,633,650,682,684,685,707,708,709,709,716,721,734,807;
            IV.1,4,30,42,61,66,83,83V,84,159,217,222,246,268,299,301,317,340,364,366,368,370,378,380,380,
            381,385,391,413,418,432,435,441,536,573,607,617,640,664,691,775,808; V.1,22,143,160,201,201,
            205,206,207,212,227,231,233,233,238,239,262,266,287,319,321,351,381,402,408,415,415,425,426,
            432,444,460,480,561,600; EPI.,38
      M. BRIDE
            PRO.,1,11,15; I.1,61,61V,66,66V,68,118,118V,135,192V,288,327,362,375,415V,422,431,432,432V;
            II.1,30,47; II.2,52,80,80,86,97,103,103V,165V,194,216,216V,225,270,279,279V,280,330,331,337,
            337,347,361,362; III.1,26,105,114,126,151,164,164,170,179,197,217V,255,264,296,302,333,409,410,
            456; IV.1,72,102,145,147,158,174,182,190,207,290,416,444; V.1,6,29,85,123; V.2,150,232; EPI,25
      WAY WORLD
            PRO.,10,32,40; I.1,5,13,38,73,118,120,120,153,155,160,160,166,168,178,179,216,228,257,379,478,
            479,518,538; II.1,10,70,90,92,132,132V,164,258,285,296,345,356,373,374,374,375,408,415,419,454,
            455,478,502,513,522,527,531,550; III.1,17,32,75,75,84,96,170,203,209,220,229,232,255,284,300,
            301,308,338,340,341,342,345,346,346,355,365,433,467,492,510,518,525,525,544,545,547,677,
            681,684,686,692,693,697,697; IV.1,57,73,73V,77,78,78,83,84,87,116,177,179,199,269,291,294,296,
            310,317,317V,323,333,369,420,445,487,504,506,537,538,639; V.1,32,32,33,79,84,91,92,99,99V,153,
            158,159,160,167,195,257,319,321,367,411,462,479,483,553,609; EPI.,5,25,29,35

THAT (1384)
      OLD BATCH
            PRO.,16; I.1,21,21,39,42,49,65,78,87,109,118,120,150,151,152,158,184,190,191,216,219,224,240,
            242,242,248,251,257,270V,272,302,309,346,348,349,355,356,365,377,379,383; II.1,21,27,33,52,80,
            88,103,104,115,136,143,156,166,194,196,198,200,200V,235,239; II.2,5,9,28,30,37,89,95,118,123,
            125,129,135,166,167,171,176,179,221,223; III.1,21,32,32V,35,39,40,60,65,68,128,150,152,161,179,
            209,226,254,260,261,263,273,291,304,305,308,356,357; III.2,38,47,48,65,86,95,104,105,136,157,
            158,160,162; IV.1,19,27,31,32,36,54,56,62,81,88,104,110,119,139,181; IV.2,3,55,76,77; IV.3,12,55,
            73,96,104,108,118,120,149,164,183; IV.4,36,63,77,99,103,147,161,166,168,212,219,228,256,265;
            V.1,10,14,15,32,32,108,116,176,176,191,207,228,232,266,292,297,301,319,323,323,323,349,368,372,
            378,381,385,401; V.2,2,4,11,12,27,30,58,98,107,133,137,193; EPI.,13
      DOUBL DLR
            PRO.,30,34,35; I.1,11,31,72,78,88,88,110,122,124,126,138,157,164,239,291,303,314,318,319,350,
            350,362,362,375,403,410,412,413; II.1,23,43,47,50,67,71,71,71,105,109,112,150,231,234,280,283,
            283V,290,301,314,348,352,366,392,420,422,422,426,434,435,453,459; III.1,13,17,23,26,27,35,54,
            147,154,160,160V,184,185,199,207,229,244,268,270,270V,275,280,281,282,283,283V,285,285,295,299,
            300,311,323,323,328,329,336,339,342,344,351,357,377,378,379,381,381V,393,405,406,410,419,432,
            438,439,462,465,480,481,502,517,522,524,526,549,550,550V,580,581,586,609,630; IV.1,18,20,21,34,
            44,58,79,92,122,139,148,149,152,156,157,159,165,166,168,174,179,179,191,194,201,201V,203,210,
            227,229,234,249,250,268,292,317,327,339,401,417,420,420V,452,454,455,476,484V,486V,500,522,529,
            530,536,542,548,556,558,563,565,571,573,585; IV.2,2,30,55,76,77,119; V.1,5,24,35,39,42,52,54,
            55,77,99,109,115,116,128,151,151,166,177,205,210,211,218,232,236,254,268,288,294,315,319,319V,
            333,336,345,352,395,395,396,414,417,425,431,431V,437,437,441,443,475,483,535,565,575,595; EPI.,
            4,16,19,31
      FOR LOVE
            PRO.,26,32; I.1,8,18,35,35,45,46,53,55,66,68,87,89,92,92,105,129,172,175,181,191,203,219,225,
            266,332,350,369,377,379,383,384,385,388,391,392,400,402,404,405,410,411,416,417,420,420,422,
            424,424,427,431,460,474,513,528,537,544,564,580,590,606,623,624,641,677,677; II.1,11,30,33,54,
            57,75,119,121,125V,143,144,146,181,183,198,202,227,250,263,287,290,311,329,329,342,346,348,352,
            363,366,390,428,450,455,460,469,471,473,477,486,492,498,501,527,551,565,586,644; III.1,28,33,
            34,38,63,66,99,97,104,116,139,159,160,162,175,192,203,203,208,220,289,299,301,302,304,311,315,
            329,331,358,373,376,376V,380,385,389,396,415,416,419,419,422,449,452,494,507,508,509,509,543,
            548,556,560,572,586,591,597,604,623,650,653,660,676,678,698,699,699,703,714,715,716,735,739,
            772,783,789,790,791,794,819; IV.1,3,4,10,35,86,151,154,154,160,161,162,163,167,175,212,217,251,
```

THAT (CONTINUED)
    FOR LOVE   (CONTINUED)
        253,265,271,280,281,286,286,287,300,311,331,334,335,336V,341,366,367,367,373,381,385,395,395,
        408,409,413,435,438,439,451,453,457,469,508,510,526,550,551,557,560,595,597,609,610,636,640,
        642,648,680,687,759,776,810,815; V.1,17,19,30,35,40,54V,61,66,70,70V,72,81,87,90,91,96,121,165,
        168,170,190,193,232,236,236,239,240,242,260,262,268,274,292,366,371,379,386,395,406,425,432,
        451,463,479,491,494,517,517V,518,519,524,544,547,548,556,577,577,598,602,605,608,609,609,609V,
        609V,624,627,636,637; EPI.,4,16,20,21,39

    M. BRIDE
        PRO,31,32,39; I.1,3,29,31,38,42,43,59,80,95,104,117V,125,133,133,138,143,151,153,158,183,197,
        205,232,250,276,279,279V,290,295,296,300,301,302,316,324,326,326V,355,379,389,428,428V,430,435,
        437,439,443,443V,448,448V,458,458; II.1,11,42,44,72,78; II.2,11,15,27,35,35,37,49,51,81,89,151,
        152,165V,167,186,186V,201,228,230V,242,250,258,279,279V,289,310,318,330,338,343,356,358,363,
        370,370,372,385; III.1,2,4,22,37,55,89,96,109,120,143,145,149,154,154,161,163,173,180,182,190,
        207,219,249,250,253,257,258,271,292,293,294,296,299,300,311,314,325,335,337,337; IV.1,6,47,58,
        63,80,84,90,93,100,116,119,122,127,132V,137,142,149,158,160,161,162V,168,174,179,204,213,216,
        221,228,233,236,241,248,252,256,259,275,281,281,287,288,297,301,310,322,323,331,332,356,366,
        371,371,372,373,382,401,410,426,431,434; V.1,13,13V,46,54,55,55,69,73,77,92,113,114,130,130V;
        V.2,4,7,33,40,41,45,66,74,90,134,143,144,144V,150,187,188,189,189V,192,229,231,231V,236,239,
        259,259V,294,303,318; EPI,16,19,22

    WAY WORLD
        PRO,,18,21,36; I.1,8,18,47,55,56,73,74,78,79,84,87,95,113,131,138,147,160,163,164,166,168,185,
        187,199,201,202,229,256,283,285,298,299,299V,302,303,312,313,318,319,326,330,342,353,359,375,
        392,408,424,425,431,442,460,465,466,477,517,533,539,542; II.1,10,10,31,54,91,92,100,112,115,
        125,128,134,135,145,148,154,164,176,177,211,212,231,235,261,262,266,267,273,288,300V,305,306,
        312,317,351,363,381,385,388,397,403,419,420,421,430,435,458,460,464,467,472,482,488,493,495,
        516,516,518,519,520,523,530,545,545; III.1,14,33,50,52,57,62,76V,76V,81,86,89,114,115,125,139,
        142,168,185,188,189,196,200,208,209,211,234,241,245,284,287,293,296,296V,299V,321,328,329,354,
        361,361,370,372,383,390,405,405,415,420,425,426,433,455,455V,477,487,492,522,556,556V,559,560,
        575,575,578,586,612,614,614V,643,644,644,645,653,664,669,671,672,679,682,682,688,700,711,712,
        716; IV.1,8,12,21,39,43,46,67,76,84,84,99,101,115,116,122,125,127,145,158,170,171,172,175,198,
        200,217,229,234,235,245,247,264,269,310,320,323,354,399,400,420,421,445,446,447,468,473,499,
        503,503,504,508,511,512,513,513,535,547,578,585,585,586,592,610,611,635,636,643,647; V.1,2,3,4,
        26,45,58,58,69,70,78,79,94,110,112,112V,118,126,167,203,234V,258,277,278,300,302,305,319,326,
        328,330,334,342,349,364,388,389,396,403,419,450,457,476,481,494,529,535,536,540,576,577,601,
        605,609,611,613,615,623; EPI.,13,29

THE (3303)
    OLD BATCH
        PRO,,6,14,21,22,23; I.1,D,10,11,12,15,33,34,37,38,48,49,51,53,55,56,56,60,63,63,63,71,71,74,
        74,80,80,85,89,90,92,92,92,96,99,101,102,103,116,125,130,138,139,143,157,157,159,167,172,174,
        174,177,184,184,187,191,196,202,202,203,207,210,211,216,220,220,221,222,223,225,232,233,238,
        239,239,239,240,241,241,243,244,246,249,256,257,258,258,261,264,267V,270,270V,271,275,276,279,
        280,280,281,283,288,293,298,305,305,307,310,311,317,318,322,325,326,327,328,330V,340,341,
        356,359,359,365,366,370,371,373,376,377,380,387; II.1,2,2,3,13,13,17,23,25,34,47,51,52,56,58,
        59,60,62,65,67,71,72,73,77,78,78,81,89,89V,97,123,123V,165,167,168,169,175,182,188,188,193,193,
        195,199,204,205,205,207,208,219,229,232; II.2,8,9,12,13,13,13,14,15,18,28,31,34,34,39,51,56,56,
        61,69,81,88,91,97,100V,102,105,124,126,134,136,136,144,147,158,161,165,169,176,186,187,200,202,
        203,205,207,207V,215,218,222; III.1;D,9,10,10,12,15,29,32,32V,33,34,34V,47,49,63,63V,64,67,67,
        78,79,79,80,81,81,82,83,85,85,90,90,99,100,110,116,117,123,123,125,127,129,134,135,138,139,139,
        141,142,145,146,161,163,169,175,175,177,188,193,194,195,196,197V,202,202,204,205,216,217,218,
        231,239,249,249,250,252,252,254,256,259,264,266,283,284,286,287,288,288,295,296,307,316,352,
        357; III.2,3,10V,14V,16V,18V,21V,25,33,37,39,49,50,56,58,76,76,90,90,111,117,118,121,130,
        140,149,153; IV.1,D,1,8,10,16,17,23,28,29,34,38,38V,41,42,43,49,51,60,61,61,68,86,97,98,119,
        136,175,177,177V,178,179,183; IV.2,7,7,10,11,25,26,27,28,29V,34,40,50,52,53,53,55,55,56,56,
        63,73,85,89,92,92; IV.3,2,3,4,15,24,30,32,33,34,39,41,45,46,47,48,51,52,53,55,90,94,108,110,
        111,117,118,118,121,128,128,133,135,142,144,144,144,148,152,152,153,156,158,167,176,179,183,
        186,188,189,193,198,200,201,203,207; IV.4,D,11,21,23,23,24,30,49,51,51,57,61,64,65,66,68,68,73,
        78,81,82,83,83,87,92,94,99,103,105,106,107,110,115,127,132,132,133,135,136,136,142,150,158,162,
        164,167,171,172,183,189,190,191,194,195,199,205,211,215,220,226,226,234,235,239,244,244,245,
        251,251V,264,269,271; V.1,6,6,20,23,42,61,65,67,70,74,76,78,83,88,93,97,101,104,107,118,119,
        124,131,139,144,150,151,154,157,173,174,177,185,193,200,201,207,216,219,229,234,239,241,242,
        253,261,261V,263,277,278,288,297,298,305,306,327,335,337,338,344,348,349,350,351,369,369V,
        372,377,379,383,384,384,385,386,390,393V,398,401,402; V.2,10,15,17,18,29,35,42,44,52,57,59,66,
        87,93,100,109,110,122,123,125,133,145,148,152,166,173,177,180,187,189,191,194,195; EPI.,4,8,8,
        9,11,14,28

    DOUBL DLR
        PRO,,3,3,7,10,10,14,26,26,28,29,32,33; I.1,D,D,3,3V,4,8,9,9,9V,11,11V,11V,26,29,33,34,35,37,
        42,47,50,50,51,57,81,85,89,92,92,95,96,96V,97,104,109,110,113,119,124,124V,143,143,155,166,167,
        168,182,200,201,202,204,210,216,227,228,228,228V,228V,229,238,238V,245,246,246,249,256,260,268,
        273,273V,283,288,292,294,311,319,322,330V,331V,332V,344,348,350,366,369,376,376,378,378V,386,
        393,397,416; II.1,30,32,39,39,40,48,49,49V,55,65,79,81,96,97,111,115,120,122,131,131,132,133,
        144,144V,147,155,165,165,166,166,170,171,171V,172,173,174,175,175,176,189,189,193,196,214,226,
        233,234,247,252,253,258,273,289,293,294,294,295,302,304,305,306,306,307,308,308,308V,308V,312,
        314,314,315,316,317,327,329,332,335,340,341,350,352,361,361,367,377,378,382,383,384,387,397,
        397V,399,412,413,414,424,426,434,440,443,448,455,460,460,462,463; III.1,3,7,8,9,19,39,47,112,
        118,135,142,143,153,160,160V,161,177,182,196,204,215,221,224,225,230,235,236,242,244,249,251,
        258,268,272,274,275,277,280,281,282,287,287,296,301,302,308,313,332,332,341,342,350,350,351,
        352,353,380,381,381,381V,381V,401V,404,405,408,427,429,433,442,452V,453,458,459,469,482,493,
        495,502,504,504,508,509,511,513,515,518,519,519,523,523,524,526,529,532,536,538,550,550V,555,
        556,564,566,566,568,581,601,606,608,610,611,612,613,624,626,628,631,632,634; IV.1,1,4,12,12V,
        13,14,16,20,24,24,24V,24V,27,29,42,45,53,53,55,59,61,72,72,74,78,78,81,87,91,93,93V,95,101,105,
        105,122,137,137,144,146,153V,170,183,200,203,205,216,219,221,225,226,227,231,237,238,238,240,
        254,258,261,263,265,269,277,277,286,296,302,303,312,314,315,316,334,338,340,344,344V,351,362,
        366,366,378,392,393,396,405,408,408,410,412,421,426V,427,428,437,441,448,450,463,470,487V,506,
        517,522,522V,528,529,530,532,533,563,581; IV.2,3,6,6V,9,10,22,28,37,43,45,46,51,69,70,72,72V,
        73,75,76,76,81,98,111,123,125V,143,147,152; V.1,31,48,57,61,63,65,79,80,87,98,98,101,110,113,
        117,137,147V,152,179,180,185,188,196,201,206,207,208,214,219,220,223,233,233,237,239,241,
        246,249,252,252,253,255,255V,264,271,272,273,274,276,277,278,280,283,288,290,300,311,313,335,
        341,343,344,345,345V,348,381,384,398,405,415,416,422,424,431,431V,432,434,438,442,443,446,451,
        451,452,457,462,466,471,477,485,488,488,489,494,495,495,496,497,499,503,505,507,518,530,530V,
        531,533,539,555,556,556,566,567,570,594,596; EPI.,6,7,9,10,11,17,18,19,20,21,23,27,28,29,
        29V,32

THE (CONTINUED)
    FOR LOVE
        PRO.,1,4,4,7,7,8,13,15,20,25,27,30,39,41,41; I.1,D,6,15,28,36,36,52,55V,56,56V,59,61,66,67,74,
        77,78,79,80,82,86,88,89,89,90,91,92,92,93,94,97,100,101,101,106,107,108,110,111,114,114,118,
        118,126,126,127,135,138,140,141,141V,143,143,148,149,149,150,152,153,158,158V,159,159V,161,170,
        178,182,188,196,202,205,212,216,220,233,239,241,268,269,271,272,275,283,286,290,298,299,310,
        311,317,320,331,331,339,369,370,370,372,373,374,374V,375,376,392,392,394,394V,399,402,423,429,
        432,466,474,486,498,499,502,520,520,529,534,537,539,539,543,560,562,562,564,568,569,571,573,
        578,578,579,585,601,601,602,603,610,611,614,614V,618,623,661,664,669,671,676; II.1,1,5,6,12,20,
        23,25,28,48,49,51,55,57,57,58,59,59,59,59,64,72,78,79,84,89,89,89V,89V,97,101,103,104,106,107,
        107,108,110,121,123,127,128,128,129,130,136,137,137,137,138,139,141,146,154,165,173,180,
        186,188,190,195,197,199,199,200,201,207,208,208,210,211,211,219,219,220,221,222,223,227,228,
        228V,231,232,232,233,233,237,247,250,252,256,257,258,267,280,280V,287,288,296,297,298,306,
        306V,307,307,319,319,327,330,331,332,332V,338,341,346,355,360,366,374,375,376,379,381,383,387,
        392,394,400,424,425,429,446,448,451,454,456,487,492,494,497,502,548,549,550,553,560,584,600,
        618,645,649,651; III.1,2,6,6,8,11,12,14V,25,32,36,36,39,59,68,68,71,73,76,76,81,82,82,83,100,
        103,104,121,123,128,130,130,131,132,132,132,142,150,151,154,155,155V,155V,156,156,157,157,
        159,161,162,164,166,167,168,169,169,170,171,173,185,186,191,192,193,197,197,201,201,208,
        212,223,226,226,240,247,247,259,260,302,307,312,318,332,334,336,341,355,372,375,375,384,386,
        393,439,441,441,448,458,460,462,464,466,467,466,467,469,474,476,478,482,486,486,486V,486V,487,
        487,487V,487V,499,499,502,506,506,508,510,511,511,530,534,535,536,537,538,539,546,547,552,552V,
        554,579,584,585,587,591,597,600,602,612,637,641,647,647,647,648,648,651,677,682,696,697,697,
        699,701,719,721,727,730,750,751,763,766,769,774,776,781,803,804,814,815,816,817,820; IV.1,5,6,
        9,9,13,25,25,28,45,50,54,56,64,67,75,82,98,100,104,106,112,114,136,137,147,148,158,159,161,164,
        165,173,176,185,191,192,205,209,216,221,223,225,232,238,241,242,247,252,253,258,260,262,263,
        281,286,287,291,306,308,316,319,331,335,349,356,357,362,365,372,382,386,386,394,396,407,423,
        424,450,451,452,455,456,467,476,499,501,503,503,504,505,507,508,509,518,524,526,528,547,548,
        556,556,559,562,577,579,580,583,587,594,604,636,648,661,661,680,691,692,701,702,703,707,712,
        712V,717,734,749,754V,772,773,775,776,779,786,787,788,788,789,792,796,799,806,813; V.1,3,3,13,
        35,40,46,53,58,59,67,67,70,70V,71,72,73,73V,83,98,100,102,114,117,125,126,127,128,130,130,138,
        155,158,158V,158V,166,168,174,175,177,184,187,191,194,197,200,200,218,224,227,238,246,261,263,
        267,269,271,272,286,292,292,294,313,317,330,342,345,353,354,354,358,361,364,380,380,382,385,
        385,391,398,412,414,415,425,427,428,430,430,435,44C,441,442,442,451,455,458,460,463,463,464,
        478,489,495,497,508,511,512,525,528,529,549,551,552,557,560,566,567,568,574,584V,589,598,600,
        617,629,630,635,636; EPI.,2,4,40
    M. BRIDE
        PRO,1,8,9,9,15,16,25,28,30,33,34,38,39; I.1,10,10,26,38,40,40,41,41,41,46,49,50,51,58,63,73,
        73V,82,96,96V,104,108,111,112,115,115V,115V,120,125,126,130,130,131,134,137,137V,139,140,153,
        153,154,155,157,157,157,158,160,163,172,172V,178,197,197V,209,210,210V,221,226,228,231,232,
        233,235,237,238,245,247,249,258,259,261,265,267,268,269,269,270,284,286,295,301,303,322,325,
        325V,337,352,359,361,366,366V,429,433,438,451,455,457,459; II.1,D,2,4,9,15V,16,24,26,37,40,49,
        53,59,64,70,76,77; II.2,D,D,2,6,7,10,11,14,16,17,17V,19,26,34,36,37,44,85,85,88,88,92,161,
        161,173,173V,174,174V,181,185,191,192,200,203,224,225,226,226,235,238,238V,241,243,250,250,252,
        265,270,276,284,286,287,291,292,293,295,305,307,307,307,307V,307V,312,316,317,318,322,323,
        324,325,330,339,347,348,348,349,349V,351,352,353,356,363,364,365,365V,360,369,369,371,384,386,
        388; III.1,1,4,16,25,26,27,29,30,34,35,36,38,42,43,44,47,49,59,60,63,65,65,74,75,77,82,85,85,
        87,95,96,109,116,123,126,130,132,132V,133,13,3V,134,157,174,202,205,205,217,217V,218,227,228,
        230,230,235,238,243,251,261,267,291,298,298V,303,314,319,336,347,352,352V,355V,365,373,377,378,
        381,382,389,400,407,415,426,440,440,441,442,449,449V,451,451V,452,452V,454; IV.1,5,6,11,12,14,
        14,14V,18,20,22,24,28,37,46,53,55,56,59,60,62,63,73,81,82,84,87,87V,96,98,108,109,118,121,124,
        127,128V,131,131V,134V,144,147,151,152,153,154,156,159,160,163,163V,169,170,175,177,180,180,
        201,202,209,215,221,224,249,250,252,253,254,255,258,259,262,266,269,269V,277,280,283,308,310,
        311,324,327,329,337,381,385,393,393V,401,402,403,409,412,415,419,433,433,437,445,447; V.1,2,9,
        9V,10,10V,12,21,24,27,28,32,34,44,45,48,84,85,91,91V,91V,92,95,95,104,106,107,109,110,114,130,
        130V,133; V.2,D,DV,1,2,12,17,17,28,30,32,32,33,35,36,38,38,39,41,49,50,58,59,59,64,64,72,74,75,
        79,81,85,85V,86,86,86V,87,88,90,91,93,94,95,96,97,102,102V,103V,104,104V,112,114,114,115,115V,
        116,116,116V,117,117V,119,120,124,126,131,133,136,139,140,144,144V,149,152,153,156,161,161,
        167V,170V,170V,171V,173,173V,180,182,184,198,199,213,216,219,224,230,230V,234,240,244,244,249,
        252,252,257,259,259V,263,268,269,271,271,281,282,283,285,287,307,307V,311,317,319; EPI.,1,8,10,
        11,15,19,22,24,26,28,31
    WAY WORLD
        PRO.,2,7,8,11,15,22,24; I.1,6,7,7,9,19,31,34,37,44,52,53,54,55,57,59,61,64,67,69,72,73,76,79,
        79V,95,97,97V,100,100,106,108,111,115,116,122,124,125,128,142,144,144,145,145,157,166,185,187,
        191,199,201,205,205,205,210,211,212,215,216,220,220,220,221,229,233,238,240,245,248,255,257,
        259,259,259V,259V,277,283,285,293,294,297,299,299V,311,314,327,331,346,354,360,374,382,409,
        413,419,420,429,447,449,456,459,461,482,494,496,499,504,508,510,510,516,520,524,538,539; II.1,
        2,7,10,11,13,46,48,55,56,62,63,74,80,91,92,93,100,104,112,140,144,147,148,157,159,160,166,166,
        168,174,175,175,180,195,195,199,204,213,219,220,227,238,253,261,263,266,273,276,276,294,297,
        301,311,315,316,318,319,320,329,334,363,370,371,371V,373,384,389,393,393,395,395,395,399,402,
        414,416,417,429,433,435,443,445,453,468,469,480,485,485V,485V,486,494,496,499,500,501,524,
        533,539,539,550,556,560,562,562; III.1,5,5,9,9,11,12,18,19,20,22,24,33,34,35,36,37,48,50,65,65,
        66,72,79,82,84,89,92,121,121,125,126,129,132,133,133,145,147,152,162,169,169V,178,185,189,197,
        202,207,221,227,227V,236,238,246,248,286,289,297,299,309,310,311,316,317,317,325,327,329,337,
        338,341,352,355,368,370,371,377,377,383,384,387,395,395,396,398,423,428,430,430,431,431,431,
        434,437,442,446,457,457V,466,477,494,494,494,497,499,500,504,512,516,516V,534,536,538,540,542,
        549,551,552,555,555,559,568,569,571,572,575,583,603,611,621,631,631,641,658,658,662,662,678,
        685,695,696,700,702,702,703,703,706,708,708,709,715,716,720,721,725; IV.1,3,4,4,5,6,7,8,11,11,
        18,19,20,24,30,36,48,56,62,63,70,71,77,84,89,92,93,105,111,119,122,125,126,129,130,153,158,160,
        161,163,164,166,166,169,172,172,176,177,178,183,183,198,202,205,224,239,241,242,244,248,
        249,250,252,262,263,263,269,272,274,280,281,282,293,304,306,323,328,329,330V,331,332,340,351,
        358,362,364,369,381,397,403,404,411,411,417,417,422,427,429,430,439,439,440,440,446,451,451,
        451V,451V,456,463,463V,465,485,486,486,488,490,491,492,492V,492V,498,502,507,507,511,512,512,
        513,513,514,514,514,515,515,515,515,516,516,518,526,527,528,536,536,543,549,560,561,563,565,
        567,573,573V,593,600,601,608,611,615,615,622,634,637,644; V.1,16,19V,26,31,31,43,43,44,55,55V,
        56,61,70,72,72,74,75,79,82,101,125,127,127,128,128,128V,128V,130,130,132,134,136,138,142,144,
        146,159,184,186,190,191,192,193,200,201,202,205,205V,210,215,217,218,219,220,224,230,231,232,
        232,233,234V,242,251,256,260,266,268,271,276,279,281,284,291,294,294,322,326,329,339,339,341,
        345,353V,355,363,363V,366,368,370,393,404,411,415,436,444,448,476,476,477,484,487,487,493,504,
        506,510,514,520,522,522,529,538,544,545,547,548,549,549V,551,553,553,554,566,574,575,583,
        590,592,594,601,610,616,621; EPI.,10,11,20,24,28,28

THEE (243)
    OLD BATCH
        I.1,40,41,45,54,149,298,300; II.1,141,148; III.1,163,181,181,192,342; III.2,63,63,71,79V,80V,

THEE (CONTINUED)
    OLD BATCH   (CONTINUED)
        85,107,120,135,135V; IV.1,50,50,53,56,58,58,70,118,129,130,167; IV.4,193,199,207,251,256,259,
        262,270; V.1,34,54,59,71,138,141,143,147,281,365,365; V.2,126,150,152,154,184
    DOUBL DLR
        I.1,45,397; II.1,248,248V,278,279,407,437; III.1,204,257,262; IV.1,233,525; IV.2,44,45; V.1,
        59,83,245,388,397,455,563
    FOR LOVE
        I.1,438; II.1,236,248,397,399; III.1,74,270,273,288,357,425,465; IV.1,194,200V,202,229,487,
        489,489V,491,522,525,652,674; V.1,386,397
    M. BRIDE
        I.1,70,71,71V,73,91,94,94V,95,98,100V,109,143V,194,196,277,277V,307; II.2,32,32,32,89,93,95,
        96,100,101,112,112V,113,116,116V,122,123,124,127,129,131,134,134V,164,165,165V,166,183,200,204,
        205,212,241,242,243,268,269,269V,275,275,278,327,336,338,346; III.1,109,110,123,148,152,159,
        163,166,203,218,237,238,240,240V,244,250,254,257,316,329,330,331,334,348,442; IV.1,2,17,226,
        275,285,306,310,317,432,439; V.1,52,60,67,80,127,136,139; V.2,83,84,125,125V,125V,165V,166V,
        167V,175,259,259V,263,265
    WAY WORLD
        I.1,163,454,456,460,461; II.1,246; III.1,15,24,28,32,83,139,518; IV.1,186,374,438,439,476;
        V.1,312,495

THEIR (143)
    OLD BATCH
        PRO.,4; I.1,144,182; II.2,199; III.2,21V,33,37,77; IV.3,30,33,38,60,150; V.1,304,359; V.2,27,
        90
    DOUBL DLR
        PRO.,2; I.1,12,12,12V,12V,229; II.1,153,156,156V,383,444; III.1,168,309,309,484,484,579,579V;
        IV.1,302,497; V.1,48,477,509,593; EPI.,3,9,36
    FOR LOVE
        PRO.,8,8V,37,38; I.1,60,60,134,193,340,431,532,532V,533,534,535,574,574V,577,579,627,656,656;
        II.1,211,390; III.1,169,202,535; IV.1,479,511,513; V.1,634,634; EPI.,7,8,8,10,10
    M. BRIDE
        PRO.,14,19,25; I.1,158,159,240,391; II.1,22,47,60; II.2,12,193V,319; III.1,71,71V,84,210,428;
        IV.1,64,65,69,80,152,350,434,434V; V.1,48,94; V.2,104,104V,107,167V,251,306,308,308V
    WAY WORLD
        PRO.,28; I.1,29,50,387,529,531; II.1,4,202,434,436,498; III.1,326,326V,607,641,722; IV.1,4,
        172,199,330; V.1,89,177,515; EPI.,10,14,21

THEM (31)
    OLD BATCH
        I.1,306; III.2,88; V.2,28,87
    DOUBL DLR
        I.1,4,154,154V,163,232,234; II.1,11,348; III.1,312,481; IV.1,284; V.1,269V,287,304
    FOR LOVE
        I.1,57; II.1,571; IV.1,351,437,619; V.1,585V
    M. BRIDE
        I.1,129; II.1,75; IV.1,14V,52; V.1,55
    WAY WORLD
        III.1,420; V.1,114

THESE (88)
    OLD BATCH
        I.1,5,277; III.1,137,268; III.2,46; IV.3,75,80,82; V.1,245,265,269,317; V.2,90,165; EPI.,19
    DOUBL DLR
        II.1,255V; III.1,98,99,613,627; IV.2,81
    FOR LOVE
        I.1,27,37,184,598,633; II.1,223,350,388,441,547; III.1,213,276,292,523,541,602,622,780; IV.1,
        383,426,531,533,593,593V; V.1,53,302; EPI.,15,28,35
    M. BRIDE
        I.1,56,93,145,146,280,311,363,400; II.2,58V,62; III.1,5,88,158,243,248,328,344,350,350V; IV.1,
        152,268,373; V.2,31,82,159; EPI,27
    WAY WORLD
        I.1,359; II.1,399,423; III.1,469; IV.1,111,225,276; V.1,18,473,586,617; EPI.,21

THEY (293)
    OLD BATCH
        I.1,16,23,25,25V,251,253,357; II.1,4; II.2,78,79,198,217; III.1,286; III.2,36,65,86,103; IV.1,
        7; IV.2,22,24; IV.3,36,49,60,138; V.1,12,84,231,248,262,271,304,331,358,358; V.2,3,26,27
    DOUBL DLR
        PRO.,8; I.1,11,11V,49,89,118V,135,135V; II.1,151,193,281,282,346; III.1,42,300,311,313,314,
        477,482,483,484,578,629; IV.1,122,158,290,371; IV.2,69,148,155; V.1,264,265,285,377,396,509,
        515,547,577; EPI.,2,9,24,31
    FOR LOVE
        PRO.,11,37; I.1,28,38,48,175,185,256,277,287,318,348,349,349,350,528,603; II.1,21,90,225,347,
        375,410,503,503V,547,548,582,586,630; III.1,338,392,392,433,449,449,456,475,476,529,607,608,
        783,786,794,796; IV.1,475,594,617,805,808; V.1,36,38,55,56,57,95,95V,118,147,345,359,369,371,
        374,434,480,599,631; EPI.,3,8,10,11,12,13,15,30
    M. BRIDE
        PRO.,5,7,14,15,23,24; I.1,62,85,156,159,233,233,239,241,241V,274,425; II.2,89,126,223,362;
        III.1,103,301,363; IV.1,73,80,170,249,269,269V,270V; V.1,130; V.2,62,100,121,161,236,245V,246,
        246,250,252,253,256V,257; EPI,7,11,23
    WAY WORLD
        PRO.,13,14,14; I.1,29,33,49,50,52,101,113,118,120,142,160,169,172,392,395,396,398,403,411,
        411V,415,430,497,497,504,526,530,531; II.1,4,4,5,6,6,7,14,247,252,253,289,362,400,401,404,405,
        410,437,438,438,479,496,497; III.1,212,295,304,305,325,506,535,584,644,649,718; IV.1,8,39,138,
        146,171,217,218,313,313V,332,362; V.1,113,275,314,584,587; EPI.,6,13,14,19,26,32

THIS (746)
    OLD BATCH
        PRO.,1; I.1,33,53,70,79,82,95,147,260,270,335; II.1,2,2,7,11,15,17,17,22,50,133,168,183,202,
        202,214,217,228,229; II.2,12,17,53,101,106,121,165; III.1,19,64,130,151,268,289,311,319,322,
        328,328V,332,353; III.2,28,37,38,38,48,77,83,85; IV.1,10,87,93,104,154,158,160,167,171,184;
        IV.2,5,15,42,43,80; IV.3,10,10V,13,15,64,77,149,156,156V,157,196; IV.4,42,46,72,91,92,98,106,
        118,129,137,140,179,207,217; V.1,6,25,44,59,100,108,120,163,203,204,216,225,265,274,326,336,

THIS   (CONTINUED)
        OLD BATCH   (CONTINUED)
            352; V.2,51,63,93,102,120,125,143
        DOUBL DLR
            PRO.,1,9,25,31; I.1,16,17,21,67,68,73,81,97,98,121,126,256,364,384,384V,386,387; II.1,74,212,
            213,218,251,255,264,270,301,329,375,377,396,410,427,433,435; III.1,2,3,14,18,45,68,101,112,124,
            128,132,142,156,159,169,191,196,227,232,233,254,411,441,468,494,610,631; IV.1,25,28,39,39V,52,
            71,113,129,133,153,168,171,201,201V,212,234,234,235,235,277,367,373,412,423,433,442,447,448,
            455,461,469,482V,493,503,505,510V,523,523V,525,546,553,577; IV.2,2,34,43,44,47,62,66,75,79,85,
            107,142,151; V.1,29,38,41,45,65,71,85,111,124,134,144,144V,179,186,189,193,200,217,244,253,254,
            266,270,308,312,321,324,329,358,361,373,374,375,387,387V,391,396,402,407,413,437,440,450,461,
            470,475,488,573,578; EPI.,12
        FOR LOVE
            PRO.,9,14,24,40,41,46; I.1,5,25,52,55,55V,82,90,187,199,208,216,245,254,320,333,338,351,420,
            431,441,499,502,580,649,657; II.1,32,42,113,126V,128,185,189,230,298,298,311,352,357,366,385,
            387,411,424,466,469,512,522,528,592,624; III.1,56,74,147,152,152V,184,206,350,376,430,489,505,
            544,544,544,552,552V,570,590,592,596,631,660,687,789,805,805V; IV.1,11,14,46,61,92,115,158,183,
            214,221,294,309,333,349,388,427,574,583,702,703,719,719,722,729,756,774,784; V.1,46,134,167,
            225,286,297,344,376,376,402,413,426,458,477,515,546,553,563,567,579,582,589; EPI.,1,5,23,25,32,
            43
        M. BRIDE
            PRO,27; I.1,87,121,166,193,196,203,203V,220,223,223V,243,244,277,277V,280,283V,312,321,333,
            339V,342,353,398,440,450; II.1,1,2,7,55,59,70; II.2,1,75,88,111,116,116V,137,138,139,145,145V,
            145V,188,193,193V,235,238,238V,240,260,266,298,301,301V,323,334,335,353,354,382; III.1,7,7,14,
            25,67,101,127,128,133,133V,135,136,136V,141,151,166,167,176,185,190,190,192,194,197,210,212,
            222,225,237,275,301,325,326,327,327,328,329,354,362,364,403,399,403V,408,422,447,448; IV.1,11,
            38,60,71,79,83,87,87V,89,104,125,130,194,199,202,212,215,228,235,250,255,258,312,314,330,404,
            415,444; V.1,9V,22,33,43,64,66,81; V.2,24,29,29,37,42,57,63,73,75,78,84,92,123,142,144V,146,
            160,163V,168V,168V,168V,194,202,215,219,227,236,243,288,292,297,300,302; EPI.,3,30
        WAY WORLD
            PRO.,16,33; I.1,59,65,79V,138,192,210,255,365,366,369,378,384,393,395,406,418,418,441,486,494,
            536; II.1,106,201,214,239,248,248,264,289,289,309,448,498; III.1,6,36,44,142,190,199,226,227,
            227V,250,463,473,487,512,513,528,539,543,558,562,663,667,680,697,714; IV.1,44,68,80,94,95,116,
            147,148,157,228,313,313V,380,385,461,481,562,563,564,589,606,611,611,612,639,641; V.1,19,19V,
            22,50,66,71,82,91,101,171,203,229,230,235,251,271,276,295,298,299,303,306,308,323,324,329,333,
            354,389,437,438,441,444,455,461,465,493,493,495,504,505,517,540,545,546,554,560,580,617; EPI.,
            1,2,23

THOSE (70)
        OLD BATCH
            I.1,296,349,372; II.1,48,180,219; IV.2,21,72,72,73; IV.3,66; V.1,330; V.2,100
        DOUBL DLR
            II.1,33; III.1,50,338,340,349,511; IV.2,68; V.1,51,302
        FOR LOVE
            I.1,65,608,609; II.1,34,284,328,363,441V; IV.1,257,265; V.1,34,625
        M. BRIDE
            I.1,117,118V,125,394,403; III.1,119,300,456; IV.1,14,62,74,248,286,438; V.1,68,132; V.2,245,
            245V,248,248V
        WAY WORLD
            PRO.,1,27,36; I.1,86,161,210; II.1,21,43,365,413; III.1,192,245,334; IV.1,130,275; V.1,620

THOU (453)
        OLD BATCH
            I.1,38,74,155,180,183,185,194,228,250,252,282; II.1,147; III.1,77,89,89,91,91V,102,102,103,
            104,110,122,166,167,168,172,177,183,187,188,190,195,196,202,324; III.2,38,45,62,78,78V,79,79V,
            120,122,135,135V,154; IV.1,62,130,134,163,172,186; IV.3,46,109,167,168; IV.4,15,65,121,125,136,
            143,198,234,234,250,251,251V; V.1,34,99,136,157,296,366; V.2,42,127,151,153
        DOUBL DLR
            I.1,23,33,45,71,72,120,397,404,404; II.1,27,243,407,408,431; III.1,205,213,265; IV.1,125,132,
            133,223,236,419,571; IV.2,65,118; V.1,48,55,74,229,235,236V,388,398,398,399,403,453,454,571
        FOR LOVE
            I.1,401,437; II.1,235,236,246,251,251V,257,398; III.1,271,278,287,464,464V,473; IV.1,156,169,
            169,171,195,198,201,207,207,214,219,229,233,234,262,268,268,398,400,407,433,487,490,626,627,
            673,673,673V; V.1,180,386,397
        M. BRIDE
            I.1,19,19,30,32,34,52,52V,74,88,88,88V,90,91,92,92,99,99V,100,100V,101,102,181,181,184,197,
            198V,275,275,298,300,302,431; II.2,61,78,78,79,80,81,86,87,87,101,101,103,103,103V,103V,109,
            109,109,110,110,113,114,114V,117,121,122,132,132,151,152,156,157,157V,157V,158,158,158V,158V,
            166V,234,239,242,264,267,272,278,280,331,331,333,335,336,343,346,347; III.1,40,104,123,149,156,
            156,160,164,165,165V,167,178,178,185,186,215,218,246,246,256,257,264,266,272,279,279V,280,282,
            282V,284,290,302,306,308,308,308V,308V,310,311,317,318,318,332,341,343,349,360,385,423,434,436,
            453,454,455,456; IV.1,1,90,198,228,232,232V,247,263,265,270,270V,272,275,278,279,285,287,300,
            304,315,328,329,333,339,354,378,379,380,384,384,417,427,429,436; V.1,20,39,42,45,46,50,51,55,
            62,69,73,75,75V,83,87V,88,96,101,106,108,110,136,138; V.2,19,109,186,200,264,264V,289,303,317
        WAY WORLD
            I.1,368,441,443,444,445,448,452,456,519,519V,520,533,534,534; II.1,43,65; III.1,7,8,13,15,15,
            23,24,28,29,30,30,35,70,70,73,80,80,81,122,147,149,155,190,454,455,455V,459,460,464,464,517,
            518,519; IV.1,1,64,65,105,337,337,342,343,346,347,350,353,372,440,441,477,557,558,560; V.1,1,2,
            2,36,91,91,139,446,480,481,568

THY (272)
        OLD BATCH
            I.1,29,29,92,195,252,300,345; II.2,163; III.1,89,167,168,168,178,185,187,190,192,195,197,347;
            III.2,39,77,122; IV.1,51,58,71,71,163,164,166; IV.2,84,85; IV.3,168; IV.4,92; V.1,53,108,135,
            138,138,141,142,226,227; V.2,23,150,154
        DOUBL DLR
            I.1,5,36,39,121; II.1,245,245,245,275,278,279,284,381,441; III.1,455; IV.1,229,230,237,239,
            434,572; V.1,49,53,56,56,386,389,396,563
        FOR LOVE
            I.1,365; II.1,245,251,251V,256; III.1,298,464,464V,473; IV.1,157,158,201,206,208,220,234,264,
            488,521; V.1,180,396,396
        M. BRIDE
            I.1,33,72,73V,75,81,95,95V,180,299,340,340V,343V; II.1,3,54,67,67V,67V,68,69V; II.2,31,44,61,
            71,72,72,72,76V,76,76V,77,77V,79,84,96,97,104,116,116V,147,156,163,167,167V,201,202,212,218V,

THY (CONTINUED)
  M. BRIDE   (CONTINUED)
      219,268,278,282,282V,283,284,286,287,305,313,327,345,348; III.1,18,110,143,145,149,155,158,168,
      185,187,194,195,219,239,242,242V,243,248,252,265,266,268,272,273,273,274,274,275,281,287,
      289,296,297,299,299,300,303,306,307,309,309,313,358,359,367,455; IV.1,1,38,41,227,251,262,264,
      269V,270,270V,273,275,276,277,278,286,313,315,361,362,379,426,430,432,439,441; V.1,41,42,55,69,
      71,71,71,73,74,102,104,124; V.2,86,86V,178,201,280,281,283,284,286,304,313,314,316
  WAY WORLD
      I.1,452,453,534; III.1,14,30,31,35,455,455V,459; IV.1,351,371,478; V.1,446,447,496,569

TO (3352)
  OLD BATCH
      PRO.,3,9,10,18,24,25,27; I.1,6,19,19V,22,23,39,44,48,50,53,56,60,60,62V,63,75,76,80,83,88,90,
      96,98,108,108,112,115,123,124,126,127,131,132,132V,142,147,147,149,152,158,169,171,186,198,200,
      202,208,211,218,220,224,225,226,233,249,254,261,261,264,266,273,275,277,277,278,284,296,299,
      300,303,307,309,312,314,318,319,319,324,324,330,353,361,363,369,376,379,383; II.1,9,15,23,23,
      29,30,38,52,52,60,65,72,79,83,83,94,97,100,101,119,121,127,129,131,132,135,143,144,159,165,168,
      194,208,208,211,229,235,238,246; II.2,2,3,D,9,12,13,29,30,35,42,77,79,81,83,87,88,92,97,97,102,
      105,105,109,114,122,124,139,140,142,158,177,178,179,182,186,190,210,220,223,224; III.1,3,7,12,
      12,15,27,45,51,51,54,60,61,66,66,66,67,68,79,80,85,89,95,98,100,104,105,105,108,109,110,124,
      133,137,147,149,151,158,160,169,173,174,178,181,183,185,194,195,195,196,197V,202,212,213,216,
      217,218,218,220,220,224,228,232,235,250,253,256,258,262,266,273,282,285,294,297,304,307,316,
      323,323,324,327,329,336,343,353,356,357,360,363,364; III.2,D,20V,23V,30,32,33,36,37,46,47,48,
      50,54,59,64,68,82,83,87,87,87,87,92,93,94,98,102,108,116,117,139,141,151,151,152,159,161; IV.1,
      23,38,38V,40,43,43,46,59,60,65,77,80,85,86,87,88,89,90,95,104,107,108,111,130,136,137,137,139,
      140,140,141,154,165,167,174,178,181,187; IV.2,D,1,19,24,35,46,46,52,56,57,63,63,67,72,74,81,90;
      IV.3,D,5,21,24,32,33,41,59,61,62,70,71,72,78,78,79,85,91,93,102,105,110,115,116,119,122,123,
      127,136,137,138,139,154,154V,157,162,166,173,188,188,188,191,192,199,199,206; IV.4,D,6,33,49,
      63,72,77,78,83,97,97V,115,117,148,155,156,158,158,162,168,169,178,184,186,195,197,199,208,211,
      213,216,236,246,258,265,268; V.1,14,18,20,25,33,34,43,53,63V,65,66,70,71,75,78,84,91,98,104,
      115,116,120,124,129,148,150,152,154,164,170,175,181,188,193,196,201,207,212,213,214,215,216,
      216,219,222,225,227,228,230,234,244,257,264,274,285,299,306,336,338,341,343,344,349,356,357,
      359,363,364,365,365,374,377,381,383,384,387,388,391,395,397,401,401; V.2,D,10,12,23,30,30,39,
      45,48,49,54,55,72,76,81,83,84,86,90,93,98,100,102,122,127,129,130,132,136,167,171,172V,177,178,
      178,184; EPI.,2,6,7,9,15,18,19,22,25
  DOUBL DLR
      PRO.,1,4,5,8,10,11,20,22,26,27,34,35; I.1,4,12,12,12V,12V,14,14,14V,14V,14V,15,17,30,50,55,56,
      58,59,66,71,72,80,81,84,87,89,91,92,95,101,103,112,114,117,120,121,124,124V,125,125,127,127,
      128,128,131,136,138,140,149,149,156,156,157,158,160,163,173,195,199,199V,201,203,203,209,216,
      217,217V,218,219,219,219V,227,231,231,233,234,240,253,254,258,266,268,272,274,277,278,280,283,
      286,305,306,310,319,326,335,336,337,338,339,340,342,342,344,347,363,366,379,381,386,389,392,
      399,418,421,422; II.1,18,31,34,36,40,62,81,101,107,115,121,140,142,147,157,159,171,171V,173,
      175,182,191,193,197,199,209,211,216,220,223,227,227,235,241,250,257,257V,260,263,263V,266,266,
      272,290,294,296,298,298,306,306,308V,310,316,320,320,322,326,328,328V,330,348,350,352,369,382,
      387,389,399,400,400,401,402,402,403,410,410,412,421,424,425,428,432,433,440,442,446,446,
      447,458,463; III.1,9,24,29,34,35,37,39,40,40,41,43,46,48,48,51,53,55,56V,63,64,66,75,76,77,83,
      88,88,92,117,118,129,132,138,138,144,147,150,150,151,152,154,154,156,159,161,165,167,175,179,
      181,188,192,193,197,201,201,202,205,205,216,219,219V,224,229,242,245,246,248,249,252,253,258,
      263,266,267,285,288,288V,291,299,300,301,305,305,307,311,313,317,318,318,324,329,330,330,
      331,331V,333,334,337,337,338,339,350,354,375,388,392V,395,396,397,401V,410,411,414,414V,424,
      435,439,442,444,448,455,460,472,473,487,508,511,544,551,551V,554,555,563,571,573,574,592,610,
      611,621,624,625; IV.1,2,12,12V,31,34,37,38,40,45,48,57,60,70,91,92,94,103,109,116,120,120,
      124,133,134,135,136,136V,158,161,166,167,177,178,182,183,183,192,200,202,207,209,212,214,215,
      226,232,237,242,252,254,255,255V,257,264,265,265V,271,284,290,293,294,296,299,302,303,304,317,
      328,328,337,343,364,368,371,374,384,394,407,410,412,422,422,427,429,432,433,440,453,454,455,
      463,468,471,474,478,480,482V,483V,486V,488V,493,498,499,501,502,509,518,521,522,522V,523,523V,
      527,529,532,533,538,544,546,560,560,563,566,567,572,573,576,577,577,579,582,586,588; IV.2,5,5,
      10,15,15,16,17,23,26,29,38,42,46,47,60,63,66,68,71,71,73,75,84,84,98,99,99V,115,119,128,131,
      136,137,142,143,144,144V,145,145,148,155; V.1,3,5,7,12,17,25,40,43,46,59,62,79,89,90,96,96,98,
      100,101,111,113,115,115,124,133,133V,138,140,142,143,143V,146,147V,147V,148,148V,149,150,150,
      150,150,152V,165,173,176,176,177,179,183,192,195,195V,201,203,204,210,214,218,219,227,232,241,
      242,243,244,245,249,255,255V,264,266,266,266,268,269,269V,271,277,281,281V,287,295,302,305,309,
      317,318,319,319V,323,326,327,327,328,349,352,374,379,380,382,384,393,397,398,403,413,415,
      417,418,419,424,427,437,438,439,447,449,471,481,482,483,486,486,508,530,530V,548,574,582; EPI.,
      2,3,11,15,28,30,33,34
  FOR LOVE
      PRO.,2,6,13,15,16,31,38,40,44,45; I.1,7,13,22,27,31,32,35,41,43,49,53,54,55,55V,57,62,64,65,
      73,74,77,77,78,82,94,95,98,99,100,106,109,110,111,112,112,113,113,128,135,139,145,145,159,159V,
      173,177,178,181,183,187,191,194,194V,195,196,198,207,216,231,231,240,242,243,243,245,246,251,
      258,260,261,262,272,287,290,292,297,301,302,311,315,319,322,333,336,337,341,343,349,350,
      358,375,376,377,388,388,389,394,394V,396,397,401,402,405,409,410,411,414,420,424,424,431,439,
      442,462,463,473,474,478,479,487,489,490,497,505,511,523,527,538,547,555,557,557,564,565,578,
      582,583,591,591,596,596,609,613,614,614V,615,618,659,659V,662,664,666,669,672,674,674,678,680;
      II.1,47,48,52,66,68,78,83,84,84,99,109,116,119,134,140,143,152,160,164,166,169,170,170V,172,
      176,178,178,178,180,182,182,183,193,193,195,197,198,202,205,206,238,238,251,251V,269,269,274,
      283,283,284,286,287,290,291,303,306,306V,308,312,328,332,332V,334,346,349,349,361,366,373,391,
      394,401,402,402,406,407,408,415,415,418,419,430,438,438,438,446,448,458,462,463,469,479,486,
      487,492,494,494,497,500V,504,512,525,548,551,559,578,588,589,592,595,596,619,623,629,636,636V;
      III.1,4,4,5,8,22,32,33,44,46V,66,74,85,86,101,101,102,105,124,129,131,134,136,142,142,143,145,
      160,161,191,193,196V,200,202,211,215,218,220,221,226,228,229,232,232,239,239,251,255,258,261,
      262,263,263,264,272,273,296,300,303,309,310,310,311,317,317,326,330,334,348,352,356,360,362,
      365,367,369,377,378,378,379,385,385,386,387,387,392,397,398,402,406,411,412,413,413,416,422,
      424,435,440,452,469,473,473,475,475,475,483,493,496,497,498,500,500,503,503,504,505,508,535,
      538,547,550,552,552V,559,563,576,588,590,593,594,597,619,620,621,625,635,637,650,654,659,660,
      663,677,677V,683,685,686,687,695,696,713,714,715,716,741,742,742,743,745,745,761,765,774,
      786,790,799,805,805V,807,808,811,814,816,817; IV.1,5,5,8,21,24,35,36,43,44,47,48,54,55,58,59,
      70,71,71,71,73,73,85,90,99,99,107,109,115,135,148,150,164,166,166,197,199,210,228,234,238,
      248,250,250,260,260,280,304,306,307,308,309,312,314,317,328,329,335,344,348,350,350V,352,368,
      370,371,372,374,374,376,378,378,381,385,389,394,400,405,405,407,407,409,409,410,410,414,427,
      435,439,440,447,459,466,466,471,472,475,481,487,489,489V,490,491,494,502,509,525,527,528,528,
      532,542,546,562,563,568,569,569V,570,574,576,578,579,583,590,595,599,604,606,617,619,625,629,
      634,638,643,645,646,653,654,655,657,660,664,667,671,675,677,686,688,689,690,691,692,695,698,
      698,716,717,717,718,720,727,729,731,734,737,744,748,790,755,762,764,765,767,770,771,774,779,
      782,790,790V,801,806,809,812,816; V.1,10,16,18,22,35,46,58,58,61,65,65,71,73,73V,82,91,94,96,

TO (CONTINUED)
    FOR LOVE   (CONTINUED)
        100,107,108,110,114,123,127,131,143,151,161,161V,166,172,175,177,181,186,199,201,202,203,206,
        208,209,213,245,245,257,259,268,278,280,284,287,290,291,293,296,298,301V,305,305,309,327,331,
        335,350,350,351,359,359,368,370,384,388,398,404,405,408,411,417,417,418,426,428,428,429,433,
        454,455,457,458,467,469,471,482,483,486,493,500,509,509,510,512,519,522,530,532,534,541,545,
        546,548,552,556,560,560,563,571,574,574,577,590,591,607,608,610,611,614,614,622,628,630,632,
        633V,634,636; EPI.,2,4,8,9,15,16,22,26,26,33,34,38,39
    M. BRIDE
        PRO.,20,28,33,35,44; I.1,1,2,8,22,25,31,33,45,50,55,58,62,65,72,81,82,97,102,107,108,115,115V,
        121,122,129,132,136,152,156,167,167V,169,170,171,179,179V,180,183,186,209,214,215,218,218V,222,
        251,251V,254,264,270,273,273V,277,277V,278,281V,282,284,284,286V,287,288,289,292,295,299,302,
        304,306,307,307,309,311,312,313,314,319,321,321,323,328,334,335,335,336,342,343V,346,346V,350,
        352,355,361,373,373,374,394,397,417,417V,420,420,421,423,431,442,443V,448,449,450,456; II.1,1,
        3,4,5,6,7,9,10,10,23,24,25,26,28,29,30,34,36,41,43,45,61,66,67,68V,72,83,83; II.2,11,16,39,22,
        29,32,32,32,39V,41,42,42,47,61,84,85,86,88,90,90,90,93,93,96,96,98,104,105,106,113,116,116V,
        119,119V,123,124,124,127,131,131,133,133,137,139,140,147,149,150,165V,178,178V,179,179V,189,
        193V,204,205,210,218,218V,226,227,232,240,241,242,243,249,251,258,262,266,268,268,271,288,292,
        294,301,301V,303,311,314,314,316,317,321,322,338,341,342,344,353,356,357,366,366,366V,366V,368,
        371,372,373,376,383,385,386,390,390; III.1,18,23,30,32,34,36,42,44,46,48,49,52,53,54,56,62,65,
        66,70,71,71,74,76,75,81,83,83,84,88,94,97,99,117,125,132,132V,134,136,136V,141,169,171,173,
        176,179,187,189,198,203,205,216,216V,219,225,227,233,237,238,245,247,249,252,263,278,294,300,
        301,307,313,316,329,330,330,333,333,334,343,346,348,353,354,361,362,364,365,366,403,376,380,
        390,403V,417,419,420,426,427,428,441,448V,451,451V,452,452V,457; IV.1,2,3,5,6,21,22,24,27,28,
        36,36,37,37,39,40,42,51,52,54,56,56,58,62,63,66,77,85,87,87V,88,89,90,93,97,110,119,119V,140,
        142,144,147,148,159,162,163V,169,182,199,202,205,208,209,223,225,231,237,241,244,247,251,252,
        257,259,262,267,271,274,288,299,301,311,312,315,324,334,360,369,374,381,402,404,408,411,413,
        417,427; V.1,1,17,23,25,29,30,39,43,48,71,75,77,80,84,85,86CV,88,88V,109,115,116,120,121,122,
        123,127,128,129,139; V.2,D,8,12,13,30,32,35,37,50,56,56,65,65,75,76,78,79,86,86V,91,93,95,96,
        97,100,104V,107,113,117,121,124,124V,126,127,136,145,145V,153,161,165V,166V,167V,167V,173,175,
        177,181,191,192,193,202,217,230V,237,239,243,245,245V,248,249,250,255,255V,257,259V,276,279,
        280,286,290,300,301,303,314,314; EPI,5,7,10,11,15,18,23,25,28,29,31
    WAY WORLD
        PRO.,8,9,12,15,18,19,28,31,33,37,39; I.1,3,9,15,15,23,33,34,39,39,41,41,43,53,56,64,64,65,69,
        71,76,77,78,80,82,82V,85,86,87,91,92,93,96,97,97V,115,117,118,131,140,143,151,153,154,162,164,
        167,167,168,169,171,171,172,184,189,190,191,191,192,193,197,197,204,207,208,221,221V,227,232,
        233,247,255,262,271,271,276,280,281,282,286,296,302,303,323,327,331,338,359,360,363,364,365,
        365,370,372,374,385,390,409,418,419,420,426,435,444,446,452,466,467,481,481,488,491,512,514,
        520,522,524,532,533,534,538; II.1,5,6,12,12,12,13,15,15,18,19V,20,23,24,25,41,45,46,46,50,63,
        66,71,75,89,105,105,106,109,113,115,116,124,128,132,132V,136,143,145,146,153,158,159,162,163,
        169,169,172,173,173,174,175,179,181,186,191,194,202,205,206,213,215,220,226,228,236,237,240,
        246,255,259,262,266,270,273,274,275,276,276,278,280,280,281,283,287,292,293,293,300,300V,
        306,308,310,310,314,315,319,328,329,331,333,344,352,357,357V,361,362,372,382,389,390,409,410,
        413,416,417,424,429,430,430,433,438,439,441,446,450,454,455,463,471,471V,482,482V,483,484,
        487,491,496,498,499,499,500,509,521,522,523,552,556,557,559,563; III.1,29,37,43,51,53,60,61V,
        66,74,81,81,93,104,108,112,119,120,129,130,137,141,150,155,159,162,162,186,189,189,190,191,193,
        194,203,209,210,210,214,215,216,228,232,233,233,244V,245,254,256,258,265,276,279,304,306,313,
        329,336,338,338,339,340,342,347,356,357,365,368,370,373,382,384,398,400,404,406,416,418,419,
        420,423,423,426,432,444,446,461,471,481,488,488,500,511,512,522,528,533,540,544,550,551,559,
        559,559,559,560,561,562,563,563,566,567,572,574,581,582,584,604,608,614,614V,617,631,631V,634,
        634,636,640,642,642,645,649,655,656,659,660,661,661,665,666,668,671,683,684,688,689,
        688,689,700,701,702,708,709,716,718,719,722; IV.1,5,13,28,30,35,36,37,39,43,44,45,53,55,65,67,
        71,78,79,80,95,114,115,115,122,133,133,135,137,138,140,150,156,157,160,164,167,168,175,202,203,
        204,206,206V,210,212,213,213,214,216,216,218,219,221,221,223,226,229,236,237,238,239,242,
        244,245,247,247,262,262V,263,265,266,270,272,281,281,292,299,301,302,303,305,307,311,311,317,
        317V,337,361,366,368,372,373,376,381,408,409,410,421,426,437,439,440,450,451,451V,456,467,
        469,470,471,471,486,487,495,503,504,507,509,510,529,531,532,536,558,559,560,561,564,575,584,
        586,587,595,602,612,617,619,620,630,638,638; V.1,31,32,33,34,34,35,35,40,40,41,47,50,50,63,63,
        63,64,65,69,70,71,72,73,86,93,95,97,111,113,114,114,114,119,126,127,129,131,132,132,137,143,
        150,160,162,164,168,171,173,174,181,183,186,189,192,197,199,204,211,211V,213,214,214,217,
        224,231,232,244,250,253,255,259,261,262,266,266,288,290,291,299,308,317,320,320,321,325,325,
        326,328,329,331,335,336,337,340,343,347,348,350,353V,366,372,389,393,394,394,403,406,410,415,
        418,419,426,435,436,443,445,447,452,453,455,455,455,468,472,473,474,474V,476,484,484,488,
        496,507,517,524,546,547,552,557,563,565,570,575,575,576,581,582,585,595,599V,599,609,610,613,
        616,616,617,618,620,622; EPI.,2,4,6,18,20,22,24,26,27,29,30,34

UP (151)
    OLD BATCH
        I.1,34,78,103,144; II.2,83,147; III.1,48,83,188,272,275,341,341,342,342,343,346,350; IV.1,27,
        166; IV.2,74; IV.3,61,110,193; IV.4,10,14,103,105; V.1,49,49V,255,377,385
    DOUBL DLR
        I.1,47,134,168,253,254; II.1,161,198,200,241,248,248V,355,391; III.1,143,290; IV.1,124,153,
        153V,263,413; IV.2,146; V.1,244,468,522
    FOR LOVE
        I.1,15,28,32,91,119,299,311,359,366,369,506; II.1,36,77,103,131,133,194,304,331V,381,383;
        III.1,3,3V,35,42,465,466,581,778; IV.1,231,340,619; V.1,223,324,356,386,411; EPI.,39
    M. BRIDE
        II.2,39,39V,71,181; III.1,81,229,317,322,354; IV.1,97,348; V.2,78,226,278; EPI.8
    WAY WORLD
        I.1,23,115,129,208,324,385; II.1,362,363,366,367V,372; III.1,18,94,150,211,221,325,366,565,
        652,653V; IV.1,5,71,156,192,193,243,318,323,371,463,463V; V.1,10,96,238,238,239,244,360,389;
        EPI.,15

UPON (288)
    OLD BATCH
        I.1,94,141,141,171,189,190,198,246,317; II.1,56,59,112,149,153; II.2,77,104,147; III.1,82,126,
        163,168,245,297,300; III.2,26,29,31,71,128,152; IV.1,32,58,70,72,157; IV.2,D,53,55,76,77,92;
        IV.3,158; IV.4,44,53,79,163,164,165V,209,211,226,241,245,251; V.1,29,70,77,186,211,262,327,
        345,396; V.2,37,43,157
    DOUBL DLR
        PRO.,13; I.1,90,90V,120,122,132,137,150,151,164,229,378,378V,417; II.1,138,167,207,207V,260,
        314,340,353,406,444; III.1,2,63,88,151,180,210,212,274,292,328,329,339,459,467,588,617; IV.1,
        34,73,92,110,181,216,225,319,444,478,500,546,566; IV.2,19,26,87; V.1,36,218,251,443,462,469,553

PLAY
ACT.SCENE,LINE REFERENCES

UPON (CONTINUED)
FOR LOVE
PRO.,8,8V; I.1,D,5,13,18,61,85,93,99,126,152,153,358,374,421,456,465,516; II.1,54,153,160,221,
328,390,434,436,534,546; III.1,126,127,131,132,172,177,191,265,426,426V,466,545,598,639,646,
661,701,745,750; IV.1,23.48,56,58,148,162,360,379,393,415,461,468,480,526,547,580,618,675,766,
783; V.1,30,44,52,128,200,307,358,423,627
M. BRIDE
PRO,30; I.1,206,257,280,294,295; II.1,21,29,37; II.2,12,97,216,276; III.1,140,265,448; IV.1,
84,114,117,273,274; V.1,86EV; V.2,262,262V; EPI,19
WAY WORLD
I.1,45,53,57,100,251,309,441; II.1,6,39,63,83,177,294,300,300V,393,550; III.1,16,36,53,87,134,
248,408,409,409,497,567,662; IV.1,20,21,25,76,161,171,216,269,280,314,357,425,525; V.1,12,44,
98,185,193,222,222V,322,339,400,434,488,534,579,611

US (154)
OLD BATCH
I.1,11,91,123,131; II.1,123,123V,191; II.2,143,187,207,207V; III.2,152; IV.3,58,76,102,115;
IV.4,7,51,66,129; V.1,7,231; V.2,170,178
DOUBL DLR
PRO.,19; I.1,2,102,107,219,219V,418; II.1,95,162,168,171,173,175; III.1,196,487,559; IV.1,12,
12V,25,66,250,409,458V,519; V.1,118,243,278,422,428,486
FOR LOVE
I.1,296,349,495; II.1,5,477,477V,488,503,503V,545,569,570,571,593; III.1,190,221,316,481,484,
494,538,545,747,803; IV.1,99,278,350,350V,466,484V,485,547,557,580,662,700,706,708,789; V.1,
129,302,332,339,344,444,451,628; EPI.,5,6,10,11,27,38,39,39
M. BRIDE
PRO,16,21; I.1,125,129,137,137V; II.1,49,70; II.2,13; III.1,248,337,370; IV.1,106,145,317;
V.2,207,318,318V
WAY WORLD
I.1,520,524; II.1,6,7,8,8V,10,14,107,120,169,192,400,423; IV.1,200,206,206V,207,208,418,421;
V.1,98,134,136,488,491,600

WAS (414)
OLD BATCH
I.1,21,50,52,96,185,248,348,359,362,363; II.1,101,130,166,178,180,195,197,199,224,228; II.2,
11,131; III.1,18,27,56,176,271,273,274,284,339; III.2,101; IV.1,53,54,55,87,100,101,102,102V;
IV.2,25,27,52,77; IV.3,15,16,19,25,40,40V,42,147,162,171,198; IV.4,4,52,62,117,205,208,210,
216,243,243V,245; V.1,95,113,122,258,335; V.2,2,19; EPI.,18
DOUBL DLR
I.1,30,31,91,100,107,109,254,292,351,370,374,375,376; II.1,68,82,118,196,235,267,283V,296,304,
375,409,412,415,416,416V,423; III.1,21,23,54,87,114,128,178,188,201,275,288,288V,327,327V,379,
403,480,548,549,549,549V,552; IV.1,59,108,155,167,173,199,241,315,326,326,401,456,548,557;
IV.2,11,70,71,76,77; V.1,23,72,219,302,347,364,461,461,475
FOR LOVE
PRO.,15; I.1,10,18,41,172,258,266,333,338,407,422,423,446,502,580,610; II.1,12,13,88,93,130,
151,169,180,189,236,259,358,362,381,389,394,408,409,429,441,441V,443,567,630,644; III.1,51,66,
77,102,116,122,125,127,163,163,164,166,168,172,174,177,188V,202,203,203,205,258,259,373,373,
406,415,419,530,551,570,572,587,590,593,614,619,750,752,752,762,763; IV.1,4,15,34,83,83V,96,
202,291,309,319,340,365,375,384,390,572,641,726,726,765; V.1,15,81,107,236,236,239,257,344,379,
460,504,506,507,512,545,546,562,574,593,622; EPI.,21
M. BRIDE
PRO,4; I.1,65,66,66V,101,110,121,127,141,297,308,318,406; II.1,1,52,54; II.2,35,159,257,280,
301,301V,322,358,380; III.1,1,3,14,24,55,74,118; IV.1,31,102,117,123,208,251,281,281,281V,281V,
382,385,414; V.1,46,57; V.2,41,43,43V,50,63,135,139,180; EPI,31
WAY WORLD
I.1,20,22,26,38,47,50,54,70,74,75,85,115,166,166,193,271,279,371,371,451; II.1,72,165,211,240,
305,356,402,432,516,545; III.1,27,86,118,195,196,230,284,556,556V,557,558,558,602,632,652;
IV.1,52,167,331,332,358,359,543,602,611,613,615,617; V.1,19,19V,40,40,58,58,68,74,98,99,99V,
187,188,194,286,303,305,369,384,385,494,536; EPI.,22

WE (290)
OLD BATCH
PRO.,5,8; I.1,20,76,223; II.2,46,85,120,151,152,186; III.1,39,40,57,62,184,213; III.2,151,153;
IV.1,61; IV.2,37,46; IV.3,75,83,114,116,116,195; IV.4,122; V.1,200,328,374; V.2,9,10,70,173,
176,182,193
DOUBL DLR
I.1,45,175,180,283,284,359; II.1,21,27,160,160,426; III.1,141,169,214,321,348,388,446,458,525,
559,631; IV.1,11,12,12V,16,16,17,18,20,20,21,21,27,31,31,278,386,387,518; V.1,140,142,240,243,
246,252,477,551,585; EPI.,25
FOR LOVE
PRO.,14,21,23,26,27,29; I.1,295,296,298,424,426,450,458,548,571; II.1,83,199,424,425,477,477V,
481,488,501,543,555,568,569,585; III.1,22,22,45,124,134,179,223,308,311,346,361,369,376,376V,
433,446,492,531,623,684,710,718,791,799,799,800; IV.1,102,160,161,191,278,279,280,280,451,461,
562,563,598,664,668,790,790,790V,816; V.1,114,144,241,386,433,443,450,450,476,601,636; EPI.,14,
19,20,23,34,37,38,40
M. BRIDE
PRO,22,27,34; I.1,122,123,342; II.2,92,111,194,195,196,196V,196V,204,209,209V,210,210,317,324,
390,390,391,391; III.1,94,245,246,247,258,339,386,412; IV.1,70,128V,133V,199,303,351; V.2,66,
91,188,298
WAY WORLD
PRO.,7,29; I.1,2,116,118,202,308,480; II.1,1,1,6,8,8V,15,22,200,222,265,314,314,400,410,411,
450,453,507,540; III.1,299,299,299V,299V,300,311,393,394,396,401,438,448,505,551,697; IV.1,204,
204V,208,209,488,642; V.1,78,93,95,96,97,100,137,192,261,261,346,347,486,489,489,601,603; EPI.,
9

WERE (242)
OLD BATCH
PRO.,2; I.1,76,261,264,270,270V; II.1,31,37,121,181; II.2,79; III.1,158,213,256,316,328,328V,
348,351; III.2,22V,59,69,74; IV.3,21,46,114,119; IV.4,12,155,188; V.1,115,116,123,137,144,200,
221,262,265,299,319,378; V.2,18; EPI.,7,14
DOUBL DLR
PRO.,22; I.1,35,167,175,177,268,271,348; II.1,254,283,349,420; III.1,41,77,96,179,180,193,300,
391,404,559,561,587; IV.1,128,252,273,292,417,430,434,442,537,549; IV.2,2,17,41; V.1,93,151,
321,347,358,365,367,396,417,440,564

WERE (CONTINUED)
   FOR LOVE
      PRO.,19; I.1,106,111,511; II.1,83,90,188,245,263,285,377,385,400,456,558; III.1,45,188,237,
      250,255,258,293,308,312,327,329,369,372,387,429,488,529,530,780; IV.1,84,124,327,371,388,502,
      720; V.1,62,95V,108,114,118,155,427,450,458,488,504,532; EPI.,15,18,28
   M. BRIDE
      PRO,1,7,13,17; I.1,29,41,123,132,133,241,241V,360,372; II.2,184,195,195V,196,196V,299; III.1,
      129,311,331; IV.1,5,69,78,78V,160,236,369; V.2,40,102,102V,105,242,313
   WAY WORLD
      I.1,21,41,49,58,116,119,311,312,395,411,411V,477,487,512; II.1,8,8V,67,126,268,289,345,351,
      354,367V,400,438,492,505; III.1,236,540,548,554,682; IV.1,45,95,115,163,168,204,204V,209,314,
      364,603,610,620; V.1,18,48,95,95,97,145,190,327,342,393,416,605

WHAT (745)
   OLD BATCH
      PRO.,19,20,25; I.1,14,58,71,105,126,137,150,154,182,197,204,244,253,266,280,314,324,338,341,
      348,358,388; II.1,23,27,30,80,92,101,125,221,224,235,242; II.2,3,6,6V,49,51,179; III.1,18,25,
      45,50,102,116,153,165,209,217,234,264,293,315,344; III.2,45,100,119; IV.1,73,77,85,93,126,154,
      156,159,160,190; IV.2,24,39,42,83,88; IV.3,8,49,66,67,70,75,84,137,183,191; IV.4,33,45,76,98,
      130,144,162,173,177,192,194,214; V.1,23,24,31,33,46,69,187,187V,191,221,224,230,243,247,260,
      363,402; V.2,17,42,45,59,74,93,139,144,191,192,193; EPI.,11
   DOUBL DLR
      I.1,1,20,40,41,58,102,103,119,166,185,194,203,203,226,226V,246,260,286,305,329,354,383,384,
      384V,391,414,422; II.1,15,22,121,127,144V,157,204,213,215,216,236,244,263,263V,319,370,397,
      397V,418,443,461,462; III.1,60,74,79,86,148,156,167,174,178,196,198,209,213,219,219V,241,284,
      327,327V,331,331V,406,429,446,465,469,477,513,592,621; IV.1,8,31,57,119,132,158,299,349,357,
      395,406,419,438,448,459,467,473,501,504,507,568,579,581,582; IV.2,3,4,57,114,142,147,149; V.1,
      16,25,43,80,103,145,147,149,154,173,175,176,192,308,337,370,376,413,427,469,493,504,508,559;
      EPI.,2,12
   FOR LOVE
      PRO.,4,24; I.1,3,18,31,42,117,127,157,157,157V,157V,169,174,187,214,214V,240,264,268,275,330,
      350,357,407,417,421,435,439,448,461,463,463,479,492,497,554,558,558V,583,588,593; II.1,1,5,46,
      79,81,175,189,229,246,248,255,261,265,278,285,290,318,324,327,343,349,367,398,406,415,416,422,
      431,442,443,448,477V,509,509V,513,515,556,581,587,587,591,600,606,612; III.1,16,19,35,50,
      73,89,96,234,234,236,299,378,398,406,419,422,439,440,446,456,483,493,504,547,597,659,673,694,
      715,744; IV.1,28,47,58,60,79,95,120,122,135,140,166,168,170,193,225,230,230,237,249,250,255,
      260,270,277,277,283,295,302,305,315,318,365,367,369,392,416,418,422,426,434,454,490,496,539,
      594,611,618,625,627,641,662,673,673V,700,715,799; V.1,41,117,135,146,204,241,263,266,274,277,
      286,302,304,305,311,311V,323,326,369,372,403,502,509,523,532,567; EPI.,6,35
   M. BRIDE
      PRO,10,10,12,12; I.1,6,78,78V,98,272,302,313,318,330,330V,358V,385,385; II.1,84; II.2,9,77,
      77V,101,103,103V,111,149,169,169V,185,199,199V,223,237,258,258V,266,267,288,294,297,298,308,
      308V,315,329,334,336,354,362,380,381,390; III.1,7,20,20V,31,31,39,51,51,56,78,94,140,148,161,
      189,191,206,264,298V,308,317,346,362,365,385,425; IV.1,3,23,36,48,95,114,115,119,119V,122,141,
      157,157,184,198,213,219,222,223,239,248,267,268,302,315,339,341,354,384,405,406; V.1,2,20,105,
      117,129; V.2,6,10,21,22,29,53,53,53,64,73,98,109,113,147,152,155,191,218,225,233,253,254,256V,
      288; EPI,10,11,13
   WAY WORLD
      PRO.,13; I.1,3,19,22,26,41,45,82,82V,105,187,259,259V,261,271,278,301,316,318,337,354,365,368,
      398,404,430,444,449,460,476,494,505,515,529,529,530,531; II.1,8,8V,11,41,70,81,96,114,133,135,
      158,165,190,191,233,233,233,313,356,403,410,458,462,472,502; III.1,23,28,34,70,73,81,85,92,93,
      95,98,99,108,187,250,256,290,308,327,345,352,358,401,437,447,453,464,514,516,516V,517; IV.1,17,
      48,81,92,94,118,166,215,249,284,286,313,313V,331,358,368,437,460,470,518,556,558,610,640; V.1,
      29,34,46,49,122,157,158,181,204,208,315,317,388,403,453,453,492,510,521,529,548,555,603; EPI.,
      22

WHEN (314)
   OLD BATCH
      I.1,49,79,94,127,212,255,264,265,267V,327; II.1,122,242; II.2,36,42,128,136,224; III.1,95,278;
      III.2,70,78,78V,79,79V,80,80V,80V,127,137; IV.1,7,41,109,174,191; IV.3,80; IV.4,90,117,212,
      228,244; V.1,87,114,115,136,254,258,358,374; V.2,9,13,15,15,18,25,54,73,159; EPI.,30,30V
   DOUBL DLR
      I.1,28,28V,70,105,111,187,202,204,219,219V,229,247,260,355,361; II.1,63,73,98,117,153,179,189,
      189,221,222,236,285,298,439,461,462,467; III.1,22,57,106,110,169,221,286,306,311,376,417,430,
      430V,458,498,535,548,573; IV.1,14,14,125,142,187,241,262,322,377,498,502,518; IV.2,13,20,119,
      145; V.1,293,347,409,451,451,470,508; EPI.,30
   FOR LOVE
      PRO.,4,11,19; I.1,17,42,47,52,141,141V,176,250,314,314V,316,383,384,399,498,506; II.1,12,51,
      55,70,70V,189,224,224,417,474,614; III.1,224,293,313,476,588,764; IV.1,23,132,290,384,442,527,
      586,635,638,790,790,790V; V.1,36,120,122,203,308,310,328,490,492,511,600,611; EPI.,7,18
   M. BRIDE
      PRO,1; I.1,24,38,54,66,100,100V,111,121,124,134,168,168V,196,308,398,399,415,415V; II.1,19,31;
      II.2,144,160,182V,190,275,286,295,391; III.1,47,90,103,106,129,230,343,349; IV.1,30,42,411;
      V.1,41,77,83,86DV,101,126; V.2,136,202; EPI,14V,20
   WAY WORLD
      I.1,4,39,75,219,370,526,534; II.1,5,115,116,181,277,309,315,372,386,387,392,487; III.1,122,
      156,156V,264,351,378,388,389,398,400,535,543,549,580,608,612,651,700,717; IV.1,8,38,134,143,
      143,143V,170,193,219,220,230,240,254,317,392,613,617,620; V.1,20,71,95,119,175,175V,261,409,
      448,585; EPI.,14,31

WHERE (151)
   OLD BATCH
      PRO.,4; I.1,66,77,96,180,257; II.1,16,108; II.2,131; III.1,90,117,230; III.2,45,96,103; IV.1,
      84V; IV.2,86; IV.3,19,120,138,196; IV.4,8,117,261; V.1,83,115,117,131,170
   DOUBL DLR
      I.1,3,3V,20,91,143,181,246,350; II.1,271,323,323V; III.1,22; IV.1,16,125,284,445; V.1,66,162,
      164,406,508
   FOR LOVE
      I.1,21,140,272,527,645,653; II.1,208,425,465,469,646; III.1,48,51,179,211; IV.1,96,128,541;
      V.1,1,376,450,552
   M. BRIDE
      I.1,26,183,374,387; II.1,17,17,82; II.2,16,17,17V,27,47,47V,66,86,110,169,169V,178,178V,188,
      232,301,301V,302,357,383,387; III.1,3,68,85,86,86,86,100,100V,355V,372; IV.1,387,400,401,440;
      V.1,52,84,108; V.2,16,16,16,19,19,28,61,132,173,173V,228,275,288,304; EPI,7

WHERE (CONTINUED)
    WAY WORLD
        I.1,52,374,441,541; II.1,246,268; III.1,70,103,534,564; IV.1,224,304,465,487; V.1,200,216,374,
        374V,514

WHICH (231)
    OLD BATCH
        I.1,49,81,219,224,246,248,279,302,367; II.1,22,57,60,82; II.2,8,25,146,154; III.1,65,126,137,
        176,177,208,225; III.2,64; IV.1,56,92; IV.2,31,41; IV.3,94,127,160,183,188; IV.4,209; V.1,41,
        69,287,358,375; V.2,11,83,151,152
    DOUBL DLR
        I.1,111,351,356,389; II.1,54,295,318; III.1,38,48,50,55,135,159,189,202,252,276,295,328,338;
        IV.1,215,455,479,541,553,578; IV.2,123,151; V.1,12,29,35,51,65,77,218,310,327,539; EPI.,16,25,
        33
    FOR LOVE
        PRO.,12,12V,29; I.1,55,55V,109,191; II.1,110,152,284,618; III.1,536; IV.1,55,148,250,420,511,
        533,688,690,718,723,816; V.1,289,370,548,552,606,621; EPI.,5,25,25V
    M. BRIDE
        PRO.,14; I.1,85,113,144,154,228,244,260,284,290,296,356,363,395; II.1,22,42; II.2,95,123,133,
        139,218,218V,290,290V,292,317; III.1,16,66,74,76,109,120,136,136V,199,204,228,267,368,456;
        IV.1,9,77,79,203,251,341,364,408; V.1,26,110,114; V.2,119,161,294,307V; EPI,31
    WAY WORLD
        PRO.,3,8; I.1,34,57,73,83,93,97,97V,137,161,167,184,525; II.1,21,76,177,200,205,220,263,268,
        309,383,435,486,496,497,522; III.1,51,126,192,321,379,390,432,699,710; IV.1,198,222,242,247,
        257,271,633; V.1,85,165,242,279,280,285,291,293,385,386,411,542; EPI.,34

WHOM (55)
    OLD BATCH
        II.1,118; III.1,4,5; III.2,163,163V; V.2,114,115
    DOUBL DLR
        I.1,303,305; II.1,250; III.1,583; V.1,26
    FOR LOVE
        I.1,37,65,138,399,426; III.1,173,178,188,188V,207; IV.1,349,634; V.1,178; EPI.,12
    M. BRIDE
        I.1,171,333,428V,438; II.2,364; III.1,52,54,161V,172,233,436,437; IV.1,25,207,354; V.2,40,246;
        EPI,30
    WAY WORLD
        I.1,29,305,306,359V; II.1,93,122,283,395; III.1,190,385; IV.1,213

WHY (336)
    OLD BATCH
        I.1,5,55,119,137,156,170,277,291,342,383; II.1,19,38,136,187,192,192; II.2,57,93,160; III.1,4,
        20,63,63V,73,140,158,179,254,264; III.2,32,40,117; IV.1,6,50,50,52,59; IV.3,3,35,51,64; IV.4,
        47,68,150,187; V.1,112,120,288,292,296,300,341; EPI.,15
    DOUBL DLR
        I.1,2,11,11V,73,73,145,226,226V,248,248,252,385; II.1,43,105,214,275,278,297,392,460,465,466;
        III.1,82,226,236,248,268,407,419,430,585,626,629; IV.1,10,24,27,41,58,90,108,144,155,206,236,
        238,298,319,323,412,449,468,475,496,505; IV.2,130; V.1,33,85,125,125,169,185,186,214,217,222,
        227,262,385
    FOR LOVE
        I.1,34,83,120,122,126,133,255,387,398,398,401,437,463,473,494,512,636; II.1,25,69,86,100,169,
        199,287,300,314,323,333,333,351,352,365,370,371,389,435,441,441V,533,566,568,607,609; III.1,2,
        2,8,59,93,99,123,147,300,308,333,334,366,380,393,482,495,671,675,686,688,721,725,807,813; IV.1,
        33,96,99,142,167,219,220,224,261,265,279,363,390,391,396,433,535,612,643,746,749; V.1,16,114,
        228,232,233,235,300,337V,342,343,358,361,422,453,459,476,484,487
    M. BRIDE
        I.1,13,54,55,56,60,60,65,66,66V,67,67V,279V; II.2,74,91,103,103,103V,103V,122,199V,234,239,
        264,264,297,299,322,352; III.1,22,55,55,57,272,278,278,306,308,308V,308V; IV.1,221,247,250,265,
        384; V.1,75,75V; V.2,19,29,157,159
    WAY WORLD
        I.1,13,199,238,364,369,434,438,442,479; II.1,28,60,190,263,265,345,356,362,403,407,505,554;
        III.1,7,15,30,148,227,227V,257,330,355,428,428V,449,453,454,459,461,480,498,519,521,531,611,
        616,628,657,676,679,686,696,697; IV.1,337; V.1,148,180,346,382,475,594

WILL (582)
    OLD BATCH
        I.1,15,54,55,65,67,70,79,87,114,116,124,126,126,190,281,294,300,353,380; II.1,57,65,90,150,
        153,232,242,247; II.2,127,179,197,207,207V; III.1,1,1V,2,11,12,44,50,70,78,90,130,259,311,320;
        III.2,28,65,66,73,86,134,134V,138,139,158; IV.1,14,17,21,34,46,47,49,56,57,72,82,84V,94,94,94,
        95,110,111,116,119,134,136,139,175,182,184,184; IV.2,58,93; IV.3,9,81,104,143,177,182,188;
        IV.4,43,47,86,164,218,225,257,259,260,270; V.1,24,45,65,72,155,158,187,187V; V.2,30,129,157,
        170; EPI.,1,11,16
    DOUBL DLR
        PRO.,17,21; I.1,49,49,49,67,125,133,334,394,403,413,416,418,422; II.1,100,101,143,187,188,209,
        211,232,239,240,248,248V,369,437,439,454,456,459,465; III.1,17,17,57,59,61,72,75,104,107,116,
        120,121,138,147,157,159,166,172,189,196,233,237,254,294,327,327V,519,526,554; IV.1,7,116,129,
        146,147,226,227,286,288,288,295,317,329,421,459,467,502,523,570,572,584,587,590; IV.2,51,84,87,
        102,103,121,130; V.1,63,64,65,76,83,97,105,128,205,243,248,249,256,257,260,264,272,290,298,300,
        303,319,319V,327,343,371,381,383,406,430,441,457,463,484
    FOR LOVE
        PRO.,28; I.1,28,29,83,143,181,183,199,298,335,337,352,370,372,385,513,514,516,521,542,554,572,
        583,588,593,604,606,662,666,668,678; II.1,87,117,118,127,127,131,174,187,192,198,282,283,291,
        348,402,412,417,418,455,497,517,527,569,588,595,631,655; III.1,69,99,192,207,360,398,399,417,
        420,450,452,506,527,527,545,576,608,625,631,637,640,649,650,657,733,738; IV.1,129,143,228,246,
        254,305,377,421,439,442,469,471,490,491,492,493,496,497,500,501,503,504,505,507,510,590,597,
        608,670,674,676,680,733,750,771,774,782,812; V.1,130,132,197,206,240,274,300,307,334,356,386,
        411,434,479,480,482,514,538,538,548
    M. BRIDE
        I.1,18,72,144,145,167,175,195,207,248,362,453; II.1,71,73; II.2,20,20V,23,24,25,125,188,198,
        205,208,279,316; III.1,7,34,97,102,102V,105,121,137,152,184,202,232,247,273,339,345,345,347,
        347,350,350V,355V,404,404V,406,411,424; IV.1,20,32,53,55,97,108,128V,133V,149,191,260,330,348,
        351,351,352,415,425; V.1,52,59,76,76V,132,132V; V.2,93,201,230,266,295,298; EPI,30
    WAY WORLD
        I.1,139,213,216,217,230,319,339,341,458,463,476; II.1,1,11,25,101,104,107,118,183,190,214,243,

WILL (CONTINUED)
WAY WORLD (CONTINUED)
297,308,310,452,478,487,533,552,554,557; III.1,122,155,156,156,156V,156V,186,264,271,274,322,
369,499,588,599,623,661,663,666,672,699,705,720; IV.1,21,61,73V,104,140,146,181,183,193,389,
404,405,412,427,467,468,471,475,481,498,500,551,554,569,636,640,642; V.1,87,122,164,243,
258,266,277,280,281,290,293,294,340,341,350,380,401,402,406,423,441,467,477,479,495,500,600,
611,615; EPI.,8

WITH (969)
OLD BATCH
PRO.,7,7; I.1,3,3V,59,71,89,120,131,138,142,159,181,183,191,202,216,219,237,243,255,259,263,
270,270V,278,310,339V,370,381,383; II.1,36,76,104,122,124,135,148,189; II.2,31,32,44,90,95,
100V,153,160,164,169,171,187,207,207V; III.1,18,118,120,124,128,140,156,184,185,223,232,235,
302,305,308; III.2,6,42V,70,71,120; IV.1,20,20,27,33,47,49,75,92,109,130; IV.2,D,14,31,50,85;
IV.3,23,30,54,54V,79,80,105,132,153,162,198,209; IV.4,48,57,93,97,97V,110,136,178,201,224,264,
265; V.1,39,41,49,49V,54,66,72,82,89,91,96,138,140,145,152,160,230,233,251,280,282V,284,305,
361; V.2,1,14,57,85,95,137,186,192,194,195; EPI.,5
DOUBL DLR
I.1,D,D,30,62,69,80,85,87,88,98,114,122,134,203,203,203,203,218,242,284,295,313,320,327,327,
330V,336,362,367,373,388,406,415; II.1,26,36,55,59,61,69,200,223,224,225,225,252,261,273,278,
295,298,421,428; III.1,14,38,76,79,83,121,144,148,204,218,219,219V,222,225,262,271,279,280,286,
288,288,288V,288V,291,293,316,323,326,352,392,439,440,482,499,551,551V,556,559,564,574,585,587,
609; IV.1,2,31,38,73,86,275,276,294,304,306,308,311,370,376,377,383,405,410,422,427,443,491,
494,508,563; IV.2,1,3,62,120,132,152; V.1,31,51,78,83,90,112,127,144,144V,171,182,188,190,207,
217,224,241,273,286,298,333,337,351,378,385,396,416,424,445,448,507,522,538,541; EPI.,23
FOR LOVE
I.1,32,44,46,50,57,58,71,72,72,73,90,96,99,104,108,118,167,171,202,204,205,214V,216,238,276,
285,319,337,352,388,397,401,408,409,411,411,425,445,452,482,548,555,611,640,643,644,645,654,
655,677,681; II.1,27,28,69,100,136,144,153,171,221,229,239,247,251,251V,278,329,331,337,342,
352,358,362,368,420,427,430,439,445,463,480,484,486,535,552,571,638,651; III.1,8,62,63,70,105,
147,177,196V,231,245,251,253,254,259,259,307,343,345,353,370,379,423,438,444,450,462,467,471,
504,507,516,523,601,677,677V,695,714,715,748,773,775,776,796,801,803; IV.1,6,10,12,19,72,100,
104,105,107,111,113,136,137,147,209,229,236,238,244,276,285,305,306,331,335,336,336V,340,343,
347,351,363,387,400,408,451,465,511,512,523,532,577,582,598,616,620,621,626,630,661,676,693,
729; V.1,10,13,62,114,137,172,182,194,201,202,210,216,246,258,279,312,312V,337,341,375,424,
489,494,529,540,544,628; EPI.,28,31
M. BRIDE
PRO,40,40; I.1,4,39,149,155,156,161,171,198,198V,214,215,217,218,218V,223,223V,225,229,237,
239,248,251,251V,254,257,257V,274,313,323,360,370,379,388,389,396,399,400,411,424,426,461;
II.1,4,6,13,14V,20,21,33,69,69V,75,84; II.2,13,18,24,63,63V,69,71,124,153,182V,186,186V,197,
212,256,265,268,282,282V,312,318,343,346,372,374; III.1,D,12,12,57,58,69,82,99,105,115,117,125,
155,159,170,185,186,199,226,243,260,262,267,269,277,288,297,306,307,323,323,324,327,334,349,
350,350V,353,356V,369,374,387,389,428,452,452V; IV.1,1,8,13,14V,60,73,76,86,107,118,175,180,
215,217,235,247,253,263,264,271,282,289,293,293V,316,326,337,350,388,395,408,436; V.1,8V,18,
18V,23,45,47,47V,51,86AV,86PV,131,132,132V,139; V.2,D,DV,67,73,77,78,85,85V,86,94,102V,103,103,
103V,123,125,125V,126,140,157,164V,165V,181,238,263,273,282,285,296,306; EPI,11,13,21,30
WAY WORLD
PRO.,1,5,22,37; I.1,8,26,35,38,42,46,68,70,72,72,93,95,146,159,163,176,176,208,208,224,264,
278,347,354,356,411,411V,515,516,518,520,525; II.1,7,19,21,32,41,86,104,106,124,151,151,151,
151V,151V,151V,160,175,181,182,196,202,220,244,256,257,269,273,278,301,323,335,335V,337,349,
360,364,365,366,367V,373,386,387,387,442,466,467,472,489V,503,507,508,523,546,558; III.1,19,26,
31,35,48,49,50,63,64,66,82,84,94,125,130,134,135,138,141,159,186,221,225,230,235,237,245,247,
268,276,279,311,313,346,378,448,455,455V,468,499,544,549,618,632,636,642,646,650,660,678,686,
701,720; IV.1,5,12,25,31,40,45,66,74,113,117,129,149,163,183,215,217,218,246,248,252,253,257,
264,274,312,318,326,399,407,417,427,438,461,463,463V,463V,468,472,480,484,489,495,502,522,549,
565,569; V.1,5,11,14,16,17,26,42,81,85,100,104,105,129,165,168,176,189,211,211V,220,233,245,
278,284,293,306,349,367,390,404,405,407,432,432V,481,508,592,603; EPI.,5,17,21

WOULD (270)
OLD BATCH
PRO.,14; I.1,120,194,195,255,260,298,312,348,360; II.1,3,4,13,13,134,181,201,215; II.2,18,24,
28,33,40,125,142,142,173,175,192,193; III.1,15,20,27,66,112,249,275,277,303; III.2,51,92,93,
106,155; IV.1,32,107,114,177,177V,179,180; IV.2,45; IV.3,115,207; IV.4,12,53,213,222; V.1,151,
192; V.2,74,76; EPI.,4,7,26
DOUBL DLR
I.1,68,74,75,139,179,180,244,255,255V,269,334,341,342,343,377,395; II.1,23,25,25V,279,280,282,
282,319,432; III.1,77,106,114,124,139,239,239,342,354,432,435,444,444,498; IV.1,44,66,134,154,
216,228,241,250,253,254,296,332,417,420,420V,435,442,500,553,555; IV.2,26; V.1,11,29,36,39,67,
72,136,231,234,280,387,387V,418,434,454,546; EPI.,1
FOR LOVE
PRO.,23; I.1,42,90,136,139,157,157V,196,285,580,590,591; II.1,12,82,111,296,321,325,446,594,
610; III.1,114,235,297,502; IV.1,6,17,45,54,130,175,328,342,364,449,535,648,655,657,677,711;
V.1,2,64,75,76,99,109,117,118,194,242,250,251,252,426,484,515,555,580,595,629,633,633V
M. BRIDE
PRO,2; I.1,33,68,73,80,98,117,137,137V,194,204,242,242V,263,358V,369,436; II.1,33; II.2,178,
179V,223,258,258V,330; III.1,91,109,110,425; IV.1,305,309,311,369,389,389V,425; V.1,95; V.2,11,
40
WAY WORLD
I.1,36,117,346,346V,531; II.1,54,57,92,148,199,212,227,460; III.1,108,703; IV.1,48,49,66,67,
73,73,73V,352,436,614; V.1,245,305

YET (228)
OLD BATCH
I.1,123,135,140,199,237,284,344,356,358; II.1,207,216; II.2,60,120,166; III.1,14,76,272,276;
III.2,41,54,72,85,114; IV.1,43,71,104; V.1,95; EPI.,27
DOUBL DLR
I.1,88,353,354,354,399; II.1,49,49V,180,191,296,327,369,375,414; III.1,113,136,139,153,175,
190,438,524,547,565; IV.1,66,212,293,343,345,372,453,541; IV.2,61,143; V.1,13,25,28,33,53,359,
400,414,433,436,476,482
FOR LOVE
PRO.,28,42; I.1,40,94,374,374V,408,626,632; II.1,20,232; III.1,69,392,492,498,605,690; IV.1,8,
47,51,161,188,226,257,266,501,559,646,771,812; V.1,23,23V,38,194,290,293,295,384
M. BRIDE
I.1,128,181,190,194,286V,287,289,294,329,411,418,444,446V; II.1,23,77; II.2,2,8,59,79,100,144,

YET   (CONTINUED)
   M. BRIDE   (CONTINUED)
      214,214V,214V,263,312,336,338,384; III.1,14,33,51,78,180,188,203,251,318,320,322,371,371V,379,
      406,411,439; IV.1,96,98,99,115,146,194,213,305,314,318,328,363,368,410,425,426,446,447; V.1,4,
      82,91,91V; V.2,42,124,142,195,200,235,239,242,255,255V,266,303
   WAY WORLD
      I.1,93,137,226,423; II.1,50,100,185,200,214,232,233,234,235,244,252,271,341,361,396,413,452,
      499,500,503,563; III.1,1,38,355,450; IV.1,52; V.1,141,464,591,606,611; EPI.,20

YOU (3172)
   OLD BATCH
      PRO.,8,16,17,18,24; I.1,6,13,15,20,31,30,43,44,51,63,69,76,88,99,113,113,114,117,150,156,161,
      170,218,219,220,227,237,238,240,241,241,242,243,244,246,248,259,268,272,279,286,291,306,307,
      316,330,331,347,368,385; II.1,27,31,32,33,36,38,38,40,47,48,74,79,80,85,87,88,90,93,94,100,103,
      103,103,107,109,113,116,117,134,134,136,146,152,154,155,156,158,162,163,170,170,176,177,185,
      187,188,194,195,201,201,210,217,218,221,222,222,224,228,234,235,242,243,247,248,248; II.2,2,3,
      4,6,6,6V,7,8,14,20,21,24,27,30,31,33,33,36,37,37,40,41,42,43,43,43,47,49,51,54,56,56,57,58,59,
      60,72,79,81,86,88,88,89,93,97,97,101,105,107,109,112,114,123,123,125,142,144,146,147,153,160,
      167,168,172,173,176,177,179,183,183V,192,193,208; III.1,2,4,4,5,7,26,37,48,50,73,95,95,105,120,
      156,206,207,208,209,214,220,225,232,234,238,238,245,248,249,250,251,252,264,264,268,269,276,
      282,282,290,294,295,303,308,311,311,315,315,316,319,320,322,323,323,349,351,356,357,358,358,
      359,360; III.2,13V,28,30,31,33,43,51,53,54,57,61,61,61,68,71,74,79,80,88,92,92,93,94,99,99,100,
      100,106,106,111,111,119,125,145,155,159,161; IV.1,19,20,24,35,66,67,69,77,83,84V,87,88,88,90,
      90,93,94,94,95,98,106,106,108,109,109,110,112,116,116,121,122,124,131,132,132,133,144,144,
      145,181,182; IV.2,1,20,20,24,29,29,35,40,40,46,57,58,61,62,62,64,64,69,80,90,90; IV.3,1,13,14,
      15,16,20,21,22,22,29,35,49,66,67,82,88,95,96,103,105,112,115,115,142,143,143,146,150,157,158,
      159,164,171,181,196,208; IV.4,8,16,17,20,39,43,44,47,57,62,70,77,81,87,88,95,103,127,129,130,
      144,145,145,155,155,161,163,164,172,173,177,182,183,186,187,188,190,191,191,200,214,215,219,
      219,222,222,223,224,230,231,244,246,247,249,265,268,269,269; V.1,D,2,3,8,11,15,21,21,30,33,33,
      37,38,41,43,47,47,48,49,49V,60,63,63V,64,65,66,66,68,69,74,76,76,77,82,83,91,110,114,115,115,
      117,120,123,144,145,148,148,154,155,160,169,174,176,183,183,183V,183V,184,185,187,187V,188,191,
      195,210,218,236,237,251,252,262,263,274,278,280,289,289,292,293,321,334,342,342V,353,356,361,
      362,368,369,369V,372,373,380,395,402,403; V.2,1,22,29,34,36,45,47,51,54,55,57,57,61,61,66,73,
      74,80,81,83,85,87,88,105,107,113,115,120,129,131,131,134,138,139,142,158,170,178,179; EPI.,6,7,
      21,23,23,26,30,30V
   DOUBL DLR
      PRO.,12,35; I.1,2,14,14,14V,14V,18,20,20,25,28,28,28V,28V,29,30,31,41,42,49,51,54,55,60,62,66,
      67,83,84,122,124,124V,125,127,128,142,142,145,145,147,151,154,154V,154V,161,163,164,165,
      166,177,185,186,188,191,193,206,210,210,216,219V,233,244,244,248,249,251,252,253,254,255,255V,
      257,260,261,261,263,263,267,268,269,272,275,278,286,289,295,296,300,307,309,310,310,311,314,
      317,320,322,334,336,337,337,339,341,341,343,344,344,346,348,349,353,356,359,360,360,361,
      362,365,365,366,370,379,380,383,384V,385,386,387,388,390,391,394,395,402,402V,403,406,414;
      II.1,8,9,10,13,25,25V,32,33,34,39,40,42,61,64,73,74,77,77V,85,86,95,96,97,98,102,105,120,121,
      122,134,139,141,142,144,144,144V,144V,147,158,175,186,187,188,189,192,200,202,203,209,215,
      216,216,227,228,228,235,239,244,250,260,264,265,267,267,286,291,291V,296,297,298,299,306,320,
      320,330,334,334,338,339,342,345,346,347,355,358,359,363,366,367,368,371,383,386,387,392,
      392,400,400,401,402,404,412,413,417,417,419,428,432,434,440; III.1,1,11,27,27,30,31,33,36,40,
      43,46,53,56,56V,57,58,60,62,64,65,67,68,69,70,70,72,75,76,79,89,90,94,104,105,106,106,110,111,
      111,112,113,116,118,119,120,120,123,131,138,139,146,148,151,153,161,162,165,166,166,167,168,
      199,202,209,221,223,226,227,228,231,233,237,239,242,244,245,249,253,256,260,261,284,292,293,
      294,298,302,305,314,322,323,323,325,327,327V,328,329,331,331,331V,338,346,350,353,358,366,368,
      372,373,378,380,387,393,393,395,400,402,403,421,424,427,427,430,430V,444,444,446,448,448,451,
      457,458,466,477,483,493,497,497,502,503,506,508,508,511,512,513,518,520,525,527,542,544,545,
      550,550V,558,559,561,583,588,598,614,620,621,622; IV.1,6,9,24,24V,31,35,42,43,47,48,58,63,69,
      71,73,79,85,90,98,99,104,106,107,107,108,109,110,110,118,119,130,134,139,140,145,149,174,175,
      177,195,206,214,215,218,220,229,231,232,243,246,246,247,249,250,254,268,268,269,271,280,
      281,286,286,310,319,323,332,334,369,374,377,384,386,394,410,430,431,437,438,439,443,452,453,
      455,461,461,462,467,473,481,483V,485V,487V,487V,491,493,499,502,507,508,513,516,518,520,521,
      521V,527,532,535,540,542,545,549,550,552,552V,555,556,570,573,574,581,586; IV.2,11,13,13,16,17,
      41,41,42,43,51,51,55,59,60,61,61,68,72,72V,74,75,76,81,94,97,102,103,117,128,130; V.1,3,7,53,
      66,78,80,109,128,133,133V,139,143,143V,159,163,164,165,165,169,175,177,182,183,184,189,189,192,
      192,193,201,207,216,217,218,220,222,224,226,227,230V,231,233,241,248,254,257,273,274,278,280,
      281,281V,282,283,287,294,296,300,306,310,313,315,324,341,343,345,345V,347,349,349,367,371,374,
      375,376,379,383,385,386,391,400,409,411,413,413,417,417,419,423,425,435,439,444,446,447,450,
      476,485,487,487,502,521,527,528,530,530V,533,534,534V,536,540,541,542,545,548,550,554,561V,
      564,564,568,569,572,579,579,588; EPI.,34
   FOR LOVE
      PRO.,11,12,12V,16,28; I.1,7,25,27,29,31,31,34,37,39,42,43,45,47,47,62,64,71,72,73,76,76,77,79,
      85,85,86,103,123,127,128,131,140,141,141,141V,141V,142,143,147,151,157,157V,160,161,162,169,
      178,183,183,187,193,194,194V,195,231,231,233,235,235,240,242,243,246,250,254,255,258,259,265,
      267,271,272,301,305,313,314,314V,315,317,319,320,321,324,326,332,344,346,350,351,358,359,363,
      364,366,371,373,383,387,389,390,396,398,399,399,403,408,409,417,439,444,445,463,476,477,480,
      492,494,495,497,498,501,505,510,511,514,521,527,532,532V,536,538,542,544,547,547,548,551,554,
      562,566,566,568,576,583,584,585,587,588,590,591,592,594,596,597,598,604,606,615,616,617,628,
      630,649,657,659,659V,662,663,671,675,676,677,678; II.1,9,11,15,15V,23,27,46,61,62,67,68,70,70V,
      71,71,72,74,76,78,79,82,86,87,88,91,97,100,103,104,108,113,114,114,114,118,119,121,132,146,147,
      148,149,156,158,160,179,189,203,203,203,205,204,207,210,230,231,233,255,261,261,263,269,274,
      283,285,285,287,289,291,299,301,303,305,313,314,314,318,319,324,324,326,326,327,
      327,330,331V,332,332V,333,334,334,335,335,338,339,342,346,348,358,360,362,365,371,376,377,378,
      383,396,400,401,403,406,415,417,423,426,431,434,436,442,444,446,448,450,451,453,453V,
      456,458,463,465,466,469,469,477,477V,486,489,494,495,497,498,499,503,503V,506,507,508,508,509,
      509,509V,509V,511,513,515,516,517,523,531,532,534,534,536,538,538,541,554,554,555,559,562,566,
      566,566,577,582,587,588,588,589,590,595,596,597,598,598,599,599,602,604,605,607,607,607,
      610,611,611,612,614,614,614,615,615,615,616,616,617,618,619,619,620,620,621,621,622,623,626,
      627,631,633,635,643,644,646,649,650,652,652,654,655,657,658,660,662; III.1,6,10,11,23,24,27,28,
      28,29,30,30V,31,34,34,35,42,45,46,46V,50,57,59,59,65,69,75,88,88,90,91,94,95,99,99,103,110,112,
      114,114,131,131,145,166,178,178,181,187,191,194,212,217,222,231,232,237,249,250,256,258,258,
      259,266,269,272,272,280,280V,283,286,286,293,293,295,296,296,297,299,306,307,308,324,326,
      326,327,329,330,330,331,334,334,338,339,343,344,345,349,350,350,351,355,360,360,362,363,364,
      364,365,366,367,370,371,374,375,376,376,376V,378,379,380,385,389,391,396,398,399,399,400,
      401,402,402,403,405,405,407,407,408,410,410,411,412,416,417,417,419,425,429,430,430,440,
      447,450,483,500,502,514,515,519,523,524,525,527,528,529,533,540,541,555,556,556,559,560,
      560,563,564,566,568,568,576,579,584,586,588,590,596,598,613,616,630,637,638,639,640,644,653,
      659,660,660,662,664,665,678,678,682,684,687,687,692,692,694,694,696,700,702,703,707,709,719,

YOU (CONTINUED)
FOR LOVE (CONTINUED)

723,726,728,731,738,739,740,744,745,746,748,748,751,791,804,807,807,811; IV.1,3,20,38,42,50,55,
57,57,57,59,60,63,66,68,71,77,84,97,103,108,127,130,159,172,174,176,183,188,196,197,200,204,
217,221,222,228,241,246,247,253,255,256,280,284,297,301,305,311,315,315,321,323,325,325,327,
331,338,338,339,342,343,347,351,352,359,378,379,382,388,396,397,407,409,413,416,418,419,420,
420,422,424,426,429,430,431,435,436,437,437,438,439,441,442,442,449,449,455,457,463,464,471,
472,475,476,479,497,501,510,513,514,514,531,532,545,545,546,557,568,568,569,569V,575,577,578,
580,586,587,594,601,606,608,611,612,618,622,623,623,631,635,637,637,638,638,639,654,655,670,
675,677,678,680,688,689,690,693,697,699,700,709,709,710,711,712,712V,720,720,721,723,725,727,
728,741,742,743,745,747,749,749,759,762,766,767,770,771,772,781,783,784,791,791,792,792,795,
799,802,803,806; V.1,1,14,16,21,24,24,25,29,42,46,48,51,52,65,68,80,86,86,88,90,103,103,106,
108,109,111,118,119,120,125,125,130,130,132,132,135,136,138,138,143,151,152,153,158,158V,160,
167,177,179,188,216,217,220,222,223,223,226,228,228,228,229,229,230,231,232,233,233,235,235,
240,248,248,250,252,252,256,258,262,262,265,274,279,282,284,288,289,290,291,296,296,297,
298,300,300,314,315,326,328,331,337V,350,353,354,358,366,368,368,372,384,385,388,391,408,409,
414,415,417,420,420,422,422,424,424,436,453,453,462,475,480,482,484,485,490,490,491,494,502,
504,510,513,514,515,517,517V,518,518,522,531,532,532,535,538,538,541,554,560,568,570,571,571,
575,575,575,578,585V,590,591,592,593,595,595,597,606,607,611,613,613,613V,613V,614,617,619,622,
623,627,628,629,635; EPI.,39
M. BRIDE

PRO.,17,17; I.1,35,37,40,49,55,64,132,167,167V,207,243,273,273V,279,279V,281,281V,304,325V,326,
328,364,368,387,403,404,404V,413,414,429,436; II.1,25; II.2,171,178,178,178V,179V,181,181,198,
199V,216,216V,254,254V,255,256,258,258V,262,288,292,293,294,295,296,298,299,300,328,332,378,
378V,381,382; III.1,47,93,103,119,169,174,177,177,184,214,377,388,394,408,416,418,419,420,435,
437,443,452,452V; IV.1,12,40,44,50,60,110,111,113,116,116V,142,162,162V,179,185,186,188,244,
247,320,331,338,352,423; V.1,2,113; V.2,40,98,98,150,155,155,159,179,180,309; EPI,1
WAY WORLD

PRO.,31,38; I.1,1,3,3,4,5,5,11,13,15,17,18,20,26,33,41,50,54,66,83,83,90,90,91,93,94,95,96,97,
97V,99,100,111,120,122,127,127V,132,135,138,148,148,151,156,176,177,178,189,191,194,194,232,
232,240,240V,261,261,266,266,271,272,278,281,281,282,283,283,287,296,299,299V,309,322,339,350,
354,356,359,363,369,370,389,392,402,422,434,435,438,439,450,458,463,467,473,479,484,494,499,
502,502V,504,505,507,508,512,517,518,523,525,526,527,527,528,538,538,539; II.1,11,18,28,30,34,
41,42,57,60,68,71,74,75,77,78,78,81,82,85,86,89,96,98,107,118,121,124,126,131,134,135,136,137,
139,139,142,146,147,150,153,155,157,158,170,171,172,172,173,174,175,176,179,180,180,182,185,
185,185,186,187,188,190,195,196,196,200,201,207,214,216,217,218,220,221,227,228,230,230,241,
242,242,248,256,258,259,261,262,263,263,268,268,277,277,279,280,280,283,297,309,328,328,329,
330,345,347,348,350,354,363,377,377V,380,381,383,391,401,407,413,416,429,429,430,432,433,434,
436,437,438,447,448,450,456,457,458,458,460,462,470,470,472,477,478,479,480,482,482V,484,485,
485V,487,487,491,503,505,505,512,519,525,528,530,541,542,546,550,552; III.1,5,6,20,49,55,61,
61V,64,67,86,88,95,95,108,111,114,114,114,115,116,116,151,152,153,153,168,185,221,225,226,227,227V,
229,230,232,234,241,242,269,270,279,279,286,308,314,315,319,323,329,330,331,334,344,349,350,
351,358,360,360,364,369,371,419,439,445,448,468,476,479,480,481,483,489,498,498,499,500,503,
506,507,508,509,513,520,525,531,532,533,533,540,540,543,544,548,548,549,550,554,564,565,566,
570,573,576,588,593,598,599,600,601,602,603,600,617,620,622,623,625,639,640,643,650,650,651,
655,655,655,656,656,657,657,674,690,692,704,711,712; IV.1,7,45,45,46,55,60,61,67,67,70,81,87,
88,113,115,117,123,124,127,128,130,132,136,139,145,148,155,159,162,170,182,183,187,193,210,222,
224,225,226,230,232,234,235,237,239,240,240,240,242,245,247,254,261,264,269,286,290,292,293,
294,295,295,299,300,305,306,317,317V,318,318,318,320,323,339,339,345,352,364,367,379,387,388,
392,394,403,407,410,462,462,466,467,468,471,475,494,506,510,526,527,527,529,532,534,539,541,
543,545,551,552,554,567,571,571,573,573V,580,581,581,581V,582,583,584,584,586,587,597,598,600,
604,610,620,620,626,628,630,632,633,640,646; V.1,19,19,19V,19V,20,20,21,22,22,22,29,33,47,48,
49,49,52,52,53,53,54,69,84,86,95,106,118,126,128,128V,129,131,143,145,145,145,148,149,153,157,
158,160,164,167,168,170,173,174,175,175V,182,196,235,235,235,242,242,244,246,252,253,265,265,
267,285,290,291,295,300,315,320,326,327,338,340,341,344,356,360,361,375,376,381,382,382,
383,395,396,403,406,415,420,424,425,432,432V,433,434,439,440,448,450,451,458,460,460,462,464,
465,467,467,483,487,488,490,492,493,494,498,498,500,502,512,521,523,527,528,532,535,537,543,
547,547,555,558,560,560,563,564,572,593,594,595,596,596V,598,600,617,618; EPI.,3,4

YOUR (1340)
OLD BATCH

PRO.,9,10,13,27; I.1,69,87,112,192,221,230,236,243,245,245,245,248,281,314,315,320,345; II.1,
32,34,35,35V,41,49,54,54V,56,59,61,68,87,89,89V,101,102,104,107,137,146,147,157,158,162,171,
225; II.2,6,6V,11,15,22,25,38,41,42,50,68,77,86,95,105,106,108,117,123,146,155,167,177,182,192,
198,212,213; III.1,7,8,9,21,44,49,73,120,134,160,180,217,228,242,267,281,284,297,304,306,317,
319,323,341,348,358,360; III.2,68,124,147,160; IV.1,38,38V,78,94,103,131,161; IV.2,1,17,23,24,
25,32,38,49,81; IV.3,7,69,87,95,111,114,135,163,172,176,178,178V,207; IV.4,2,10,15,25,29,52,55,
73,86,86,151,153,158,163,163,164,178,189,191,193,201,206,208,210,211,216,225,237,238,264; V.1,
2,3,14,15,18,21,39,42,54,71,107,113,154,155,155,178,180,184,187,187V,192,203,218,237,261,261V,
322,357,372,396,396,401; V.2,33,34,36,50,52,52,54,64,67,67V,69,69V,71,72,82,133,134,144,168,
176,183; EPI.,20,25,30,30V
DOUBL DLR

I.1,7,7V,21,53,56,57,61,79,80,122,125,128,142,151,158,167,172,175,180,183,188,198,206,208,214,
222,233,255,255V,256,301,306,310,313,313,335,339,340,347,360,360,363,365,368,373,374,381,384,
384V,393,394,402,402V; II.1,1,6,7,8,21,26,36,38,72,72,73,80,84,93,98,99,109,112,115,118,130,
134,136,137,199,206,235,299,345,357,361,363,368,386,392,393,400,413,422,452,455; III.1,38,49,
51,63,66,82,82,88,91,105,111,116,117,139,164,167,202,215,222,223,224,230,246,250,255,321,325,
333,356,359,383,397,450,452,469,491,494,507,605,617; IV.1,23,36,43,55,62,63,65,73,75,86,87,87,
87,94,100,114,117,124,142,145,155,156,171,176,180,181,184,190,193,197,203,206,213,215,215,217,
241,248,251,257,264,265,265V,271,272,301,313,321,326,336,339,345,398,399,400,438,440,445,456,
465,469,476,479,482V,527,533,538,541,544,568,579,583,588,590,591; IV.2,15,33,42,52,56,60,83,84,
85,86,106,112,131,133; V.1,2,5,50,52,69,106,109,122,164,169,182,183,192,193V,222,238,277,278,
279,292,295,297,305,312,328,336,346,366,368,380,381,382,392,408,414,418,419,425,431,431V,436,
436,438,442,445,445,448,505,517,521,530,530V,538,543,553,569,570,570,583,585,587,589
FOR LOVE

PRO.,14,20,47; I.1,12,13,14,14,14,15,26,26,28,29,32,42,43,43,43,44,44,45,47,58,73,76,82,83,
127,128,142,151,160,163,178,184,196,197,198,199,200,205,205,251,258,295,302,303,304,313,
315,330,343,352,352,390,433,444,452,453,503,512,537,566,599,617,618,661,668,672,675,678,
678; II.1,18,26,45,67,69,77,87,96,102,102,103,104,105,108,115,115,116,116,120,157,206,235,237,
238,273,293,298,299,311,315,318,321,361,374,383,400,401,402,404,406,429,437,451,459,459,462,
464,482,526,531,537,540,612,612,613,613,617,623,645,646; III.1,5,38,52,54,55,56,63,65,67,70,91,
94,96,135,184,217,222,240,242,243,256,301,332,335,347,350,375,400,404,404,404,409,412,417,424,434,
435,435,450,496,555,556,563,563,564,565,572,577,582,582,588,614,616,616,626,635,639,657,661,
681,688,689,698,730,746; IV.1,1,30,38,64,103,108,109,118,134,136,184,193,279,282,282,283,283,

PLAY
ACT.SCENE,LINE REFERENCES

YOUR (CONTINUED)
FOR LOVE   (CONTINUED)
        283,284,284,285,293,294,318,322,326,337,348,360,383,389,413,415,417,426,429,430,431,436,479,
        516,570,576,585,610,624,692,692,704,722,723,735,735,759,760,766,770,777,803,803; V.1,34,35,39,
        40,41,45,45,60,86,92,95,95V,97,100,105,106,121,138,145,149,150,150,155,157,158,169,172,176,178,
        188,216,217,218,240,253,256,257,260,276,284,288,323,324,335,356,380,413,418,418,420,421,421V,
        423,423,429,432,433,435,437,485,501,502,509,537,537,541,563,573,573,597,609,609V,615,616,622,
        628,630; EPI.,29,43,44
    M. BRIDE
        PRO,29,30; I.1,16,16V,23,45,107,163,166,209,220,221,224,245,254,255,257,258,288,288,292,323,
        325,325V,326V,327,328,330,330V,332,334,350,359V,368,389,392,392V,406,406,448,448V; II.1,13,15V,
        35,71; II.2,176,177,178,179V,215,215V,329,358,362,385; III.1,68,93,95,98,103,106,117,380,381,
        409,416,422,429; IV.1,4,21,49,57,101,110,114,130,130,136,138,140,142,159,167,171,178,206,243,
        245,318,319,375,375,376,377,419,422,428,431,440; V.1,57,115,122; V.2,24,31,45,46,69,157,158,
        165V,168V,181,226,230,230V,247; EPI,5,29
    WAY WORLD
        PRO.,16,28,37,39,40; I.1,4,12,23,64,65,80,80,82,82V,98,105,132,135,140,157,177,182,213,214,
        235,249,254,261,265,286,296,356,371,395,395,399,422,423,433,512,523,524,525,539,540; II.1,31,
        36,39,74,95,125,136,138,138,140,141,154,156,157,177,181,184,184,184,189,191,198,198,199,239,
        247,247,258,259,277,281,283,287,292,304,307,321,337,349,351,357,357V,363,364,372,383,384,385,
        389,390,390,392,392,394,394,398,414,416,416,417,435,443,472,480,482,482V,506,507,510,511,520,
        533,536,541,547,552; III.1,9,17,43,74,87,90,99,108,113,115,127,127V,144,151,153,153,166,195,
        196,197,202,204,205,214,219,230,235,270,271,277,285,315,326,326V,348,363,392,412,439,451,452,
        453,469,475,497,502,502,507,507,520,521,521,522,523,524,528,529,529,529,529,541,548,551,564,
        565,571,582,583,594,595,596,597,598,599,602,604,604,607,614,614V,620,650,659,675; IV.1,43,68,
        71,72,86,100,102,110,145,147,149,149,156,211,214,217,219,228,232,234,236,237,245,264,265,279,
        280,296,298,303,356,369,370,375,381,385,393,394,407,409,423,423,424,431,442,443,444,445,445,
        446,457,473,479,491,507,508,550,569,570,581,581,581V,581V,586,595,601,619,630,635; V.1,10,11,
        18,19,23,27,30,39,41,42,42,46,53,54,80,85,105,106,112,112V,121,126,147,150,151,154,155,156,162,
        169,170,174,208,209,212,213,251,252,253,267,268,280,281,283,292,296,301,311,325,331,332,334,
        338,371,374,376,389,400,407,414,424,426,428,431,432,432V,432V,434,437,438,439,440,442,467,484,
        486,496,497,498,499,500,506,510,512,517,524,532,536,537,541,549,549V,555,558,563,565,572,574,
        577,578,613

YOURS (30)
    OLD BATCH
        II.1,198,214; III.2,110; IV.1,93
    DOUBL DLR
        III.1,137; IV.2,87,122; V.1,63,118,451,451,517
    FOR LOVE
        I.1,382,384; II.1,460,468; III.1,127; IV.1,726; V.1,534,562
    M. BRIDE
        I.1,195,281,282V,332,386; II.2,184; IV.1,39
    WAY WORLD
        III.1,288,521; V.1,209

865

Appendix C

WORDS IN ORDER OF FREQUENCY

4109 I	870 As	414 Was	293 They	236 Very
3725 And	784 Her	400 Shall	292 Can	234 Than
3352 To	767 No	398 Do	290 We	231 Which
3303 The	749 So	389 An	288 See Upon	228 Yet
3172 You	746 This	386 Ha	287 I'm	224 Enter Man
2772 A	745 What	373 How	283 Let On	221 Never
2327 Of	732 Him	371 Come	275 From	220 Here Out
2064 My	691 His	369 Well	274 Madam	209 Lady
1521 In	670 If	362 Am	272 Been Thy	202 Who
1387 Me	662 Sir	360 More	270 Would	198 Own
1384 That	621 All	359 Now	265 Don't	197 Nay
1340 Your	606 Are	354 May	264 There	189 Did
1331 Have	582 Will	345 Then	254 Mr Too	187 Should
1227 Be	489 I'll	336 Why	253 Make Say	183 Go
1193 Not	468 O	328 Love	251 Self	179 Give
1181 For	461 By	318 One	248 Tell	172 Some
1167 But	457 Has Or	314 When	243 Thee 'tis	171 Thing
1163 It	453 Thou	309 Had	242 Good Were	170 Take
1064 Is	449 She	302 Think	240 Any Lord	167 Dear
969 With	446 At	301 Must		162 Ay 'em Such Time
887 He	428 Know	296 Like		

161
Our
Wou'd
157
Much
155
Look
154
Us
153
Heart
That's
151
Up
Where
148
Oh
147
Yes
143
Their
141
Exit
135
Only
133
Wife
131
Again
130
Before
129
Little
128
Indeed
Made
126
Into
124
Face
123
Hear
122
Find
Nor
118
Body
117
Sure
Way
114
Hope
Mean
Speak
Woman
113
Can't
Day
Shou'd
112
Aside
111
Better
Friend
Leave
110
Done
109
Believe
Could

Thus
108
Great
Nothing
'Tis
World
107
Another
Eyes
Thought
106
Hand
105
Art
Ever
First
104
Does
There's
100
Life
99
Husband
Matter
Most
98
Heav'n
97
Old
96
Till
95
Enough
Marry
94
Hold
93
Faith
92
Mrs
Tho'
Won't
91
Father
Long
Poor
88
He's
These
86
Last
85
Still
83
Just
Night
Swear
82
Death
Gone
81
Might
Once
80
Since
Two
While
78
After
Call
Hast
77
Put

True
What's
76
Mirabell
Off
Without
75
Cannot
Cou'd
Down
Mind
Wit
74
Fool
Fortune
73
Pray
72
Devil
71
Both
Over
70
Get
Scandal
Those
69
Every
Exeunt
Together
Told
68
You're
67
About
Seen
Something
66
Away
Young
65
Ah
Honour
Part
Stay
64
Name
Person
Truth
63
Please
62
King
Paul
61
Alphonso
Being
Dost
Jeremy
Married
Ready
She's
60
Confess
Head
Help
Himself
Other
Passion
59
Ask
Mad
Nature
58
Fear
57
Aunt

Because
Foible
Men
Said
56
Alone
Comes
Set
Valentine
55
Keep
Meet
Sampson
Servant
Tattle
Things
Whom
54
Care
Fellow
Foresight
Here's
Letter
Word
53
Careless
Lost
52
Else
Ladyship
Osmyn
Soul
51
Always
Cause
Fine
Mellefont
Mine
Pox
Thank
50
Bring
Fainall
Found
Kiss
Morning
Pleasure
Reason
Says
49
Creature
It's
Lover
Mistress
Pardon
Secret
Son
48
Brother
Lie
On't
Pretty
Rowland
Warrant
47
Business
Coming
46
Already
Company
Cynthia
Shew
You'll
45
Gad
Haste
Honest
Joy
Play
Soon
Talk
Witwoud
44
Back

Die
Follow
Heard
Hour
None
O'
Same
43
Answer
Brisk
Far
I've
Live
Sight
Want
Wish
42
Between
Joseph
Neither
Power
Rather
Wilfull
41
Hopes
Read
Saw
40
Afraid
Bless
Hate
House
Maskwell
Means
Miss
Prithee
We'll
Words
39
Blood
Child
Fair
Fit
Half
Heaven
Lov'd
Next
Right
Stand
Uncle
38
Against
Bed
End
Hands
Place
Run
Women
37
Bellmour
Door
Doubt
False
Fools
Going
Jest
Marriage
Turn
Zara
36
Angelica
Born
Break
Came
Consent
Late
Laugh
Marwood
New
Whether
35
Arms
Best
Cousin
Light
Past
Revenge
Sharper

35 (CONT.)
T'other
Wait

34
Almeria
Bear
Damn'd
Daughter
Even
Home
Humour
Ill
Plain
Sister
Town
Under
Vainlove

33
Angry
Hard
Knew
Knows
Left
Petulant
Present
Reputation
Return
Rogue
Sense
Understand
Within
Wrong

32
Free
Full
Garcia
Gives
Glad
Its
Sake
Vow

31
Conscience
Dead
Each
Estate
I'le
Impossible
Least
Many
Master
Match
Them

30
Given
Kind
Liberty
Opportunity
Rest
Tongue
Villain
Yours

29
Comfort
Design
Drink
Excuse
Favour
Fie
Hell
Hither
Looks
Makes
Mother
Nephew
Odd
Remember
Setter
Sorry
Suppose
Therefore
Three
Vain

28
Alas
Beg
Chamber
Dare
Froth
Gave

Lady's
Less
Longer
Millamant
Often
Peace
Private
Rage
Seem
Seems
Service
Shalt
Though
Turn'd
Write

27
Besides
Expect
Gentleman
Goes
Happy
He'll
Hem
Hum
Jealous
Known
Methinks
Moment
Morrow
Opinion
Patience
Pity
Song
'twas

26
Abroad
Aye
Boy
Cruel
Fall
Loves
Mercy
Plot
Promise
Sirrah
Sun
Tears
Through
Voice
Whole

25
Behold
Fate
Grief
Quickly
Scene
Short
Temper

24
Agad
Alonzo
Beauty
Brought
Earth
Father's
Fire
Force
Frail
Friends
Glass
Grant
Handsome
Hang
I'd
Near
Occasion
Open
Order
Pay
Pound
Purpose
Room
Ruine
Save
Sea
Send
Sent
Touchwood

23
Araminta
Bid
Despair

Discover
Do's
Fly
Forgive
Heartwell
Lead
Letters
Quality
Serve
Strange
Who's
Whose
Wonder

22
Beyond
Concern'd
Gentlemen
Ladies
Loss
Lucy
Met
Ought
Paper
Plyant
Receive
Sex
Shan't
She'll
Slave
Sometimes
Thinking
Thro'
Try
Use
Walk
Where's
Ye

21
All's
Almost
Cold
Court
Cozen
Deceiv'd
Discover'd
Either
Family
Hence
Kisses
Mistaken
Need
Perez
Perhaps
Pleas'd
S'heart
Sin
Sit
Sleep
Thousand
Wretch
Years

20
Account
Appear
Captain
Carry
Condition
D'ye
Dream
Few
Fond
I'gad
Impudence
Innocence
Interest
Lay
Let's
Lose
Making
Mincing
Poets
Providence
Somewhat
Thanks
Trust
Wind
Worth
Year

19
Dance
Days
Deny
Faces

Fault
Feet
Forget
Forgot
Forth
Got
Having
Lies
Mouth
Nurse
Poet
Publick
Sign
Telling
Tender
Treachery
Trick
Troth
Went
Wise
Wishfort
Wits

18
Act
Bosom
Breast
Close
Coach
Compassion
Cuckold
D'ee
Deed
Deuce
Discovery
Eye
Fancy
Favours
Girl
Health
Laid
Law
Money
Pass
Prove
Pshaw
Question
Stars
Surpriz'd
Sweet
They're
Thoughts
Val
Weep
Welcome
Woman's
Worse

17
Acquaintance
Affair
Attend
Behind
Ben
Bound
Chance
Cocky
Command
Confusion
Country
Cry
Do'st
Do't
Enemy
Evening
Feel
Grace
Greater
Grow
High
Hours
Humble
Malice
Oblige
Parts
Perish
Resolv'd
Sad
Secure
Senses
Sort
Success
Taken
Undone
Warm
Witness

16
Age
Allow
Anger
Bad
Begin
Black
Breath
Call'd
Certain
Chains
Danger
Deal
Easie
Effect
Flesh
Friendship
Further
Grave
Hardly
Heh
Lips
Looking
May-hap
Memory
Merit
Mischief
Necessity
News
Noble
Possible
Presently
Proof
Quite
Receiv'd
Retire
Shame
Themselves
Vile
Visit
Weary
Yield

15
Air
Alive
Belinda
Canst
Chang'd
Common
Consider
Conversation
Dark
Entertain
Grown
Habit
Heaven's
Heli
Honesty
Hundred
I'me
Judge
Knight
Ladiship
Laughing
Lawyer
Living
Lordship
Low
Maid
Meant
Merry
Mistake
Monster
Musick
Mute
Mutes
Offence
One's
Others
Paid
Plays
Pooh
Pretended
Prevent
Rise
Round
Ruin'd
Selves
Speaks
Speed
Stage
Th'
'twere
Vertue
View
Watch

8 (CONT.)
Advice
Advise
Affection
Affront
Ago
Agree
Agreed
Amazement
Anselmo's
Appearance
Appears
Attendants
Bare
Begins
Blush
Bonds
Boys
Breeding
Captivity
Catch
Caught
Changes
Charity
Commands
Confidence
Consideration
Contain
Contract
Contrary
Contrive
Convenient
Cover
Cruelty
Cup
Dee
Degree
Deny'd
Dies
Discourse
Dispos'd
Due
Dull
Enquire
Equal
Expected
Fare
Fashion
Fetch
Fled
Follows
Foreign
Former
Forsooth
Fresh
Fruit
Future
Gallantry
Generous
Gold
Griefs
Hadst
Hates
Hearts
Heat
Hee
Heed
Heir
Husbands
Ignorance
Impatient
Inclinations
Indifference
Insolence
Instant
Instrument
Joys
Kill
Kindness
Know'st
Knowledge
Land
Lodgings
Loose
Loud
Man's
Marrying
Melt
Ne're
Nose
O'er
Oath
Object
Otherwise
Owe
Pains
Pair

Pit
Pleased
Prepare
Pretend
Prison
Quarter
Rain
Remains
Require
Reveng'd
Sacrifice
Sail
Serv'd
Sets
Share
Ship
Side
Sings
Sink
Slavery
Smell
Softly
Souls
Spirits
Spoke
Stands
Starve
Steward
Stink
Stop
Suffer'd
Suspected
Temptation
Tho
Trade
Transported
Treacherous
Turning
Twelve
'Twere
Twould
Understood
Unworthy
Utmost
Vulgar
Waiting
Ways
We're
Wealth
Wed
Wholly
Worship

7
Abandon'd
Absence
Absolute
Acquaint
Acquit
Adieu
Admit
Afternoon
Alderman
Also
Amour
Anchor
Ancient
Anon
Apprehension
Assist
Attempt
Attended
Awake
Bawd
Becomes
Behaviour
Belief
Betray
Bill
Bite
Books
Boots
Bottom
Box
Bride
Broken
Burst
Carried
Certainly
Charming
Cheeks
Clear
Colour
Comparison
Conjunction
Courage
Credit

Criticks
Damnation
Deceive
Deep
Deliver'd
Demonstration
Direct
Directed
Disappointed
Disguis'd
Distance
Distress
Draws
Dreadful
Dressing
Dy'd
E'en
Earnest
Empire
Employ'd
Employment
Empty
Endeavours
Ends
Entertainment
'ere
Escape
Example
Excellent
Experience
Expose
Fame
Fast
Five
Foh
Four
Frighted
Frippery
Gad'sbud
Gain'd
Giv'n
Giving
Growing
Handsom
Harry
Heark'ee
Hide
Holds
Honourable
Horse
However
I'th
Ifeck
Illiterate
Imagination
Inclination
Instructed
Invention
Jenny
Kindly
King's
Kiss'd
Knees
Lard
Lawful
Leaving
Likely
Lock
Lords
Master's
Matters
Mercenary
Miracle
Mistresses
Natural
Ned
Obey
Obliged
Observe
Odious
Offended
Office
Osmyn's
Pain
Papers
Passions
Patch
Perfidious
Pictures
Piety
Pish
Positively
Possession
Posture
Praise
Prevented
Project

Promis'd
Propose
Proud
Putting
Race
Rail
Rash
Relation
Relations
Remaining
Repent
Reputations
Requires
Return'd
Rogues
Root
Sacred
Satire
Satisfy'd
Sees
Seize
Seriously
Settle
Several
Severe
Shine
Shining
Sign'd
Silly
Silvia
Solitude
Sound
Spleen
Step
Stir
Storm
Surprizing
Suspicion
Taking
Tempt
Tenderness
Thence
Tho'f
Thoughtful
Throat
Throw
Tide
Title
Touch
Toy
Triumph
Try'd
'twill
Unfortunate
Unlucky
Unseen
Urg'd
Value
Victory
Virtue
Voyage
Waits
Wake
Walks
Week
Wherein
Wine
Woe
Womans
Would'st
Wound
Writings
Written
You'l
Youth

6
Abide
Absent
Actions
Admiration
Admittance
Adore
Afford
Aim
Akes
Alike
Amazed
Amongst
Apart
Arm
Arriv'd
Artifice
Authority
Baseness
Beast
Beauteous

Beget
Beheld
Bend
Birth
Bleed
Bore
Bows
Breaks
Bright
Brute
Carry'd
Causes
Censure
Charm'd
Cholick
Circle
Concerns
Conferr'd
Confess'd
Confesses
Confident
Confinement
Confound
Consenting
Consequently
Consult
Contemplation
Contemptible
Contriv'd
Convince
Cost
Could'st
Covent-Garden
Cure
Dares
Dash
Date
Deaf
Debts
Decay'd
Defer
Disorder
Dispose
Dissembling
Dress
Dress'd
Drinks
Drive
E'er
Early
Egyptian
Embraces
Engag'd
Entring
Envy
Errant
Errour
Escap'd
Ev'n
Exchange
Explain
Fact
Feast
Felt
Fidelity
Fill'd
Fish
Flame
Foes
Foible's
Foolish
Foul
Fox
Frailty
Frightful
Gain
Gallop
Garcia's
Garden
Gaze
Granted
Grows
Hall
Hanging
He'd
Heavy
Hist
Honours
Hook
Hot
Humph
Idle
Impatience
Impertinent
Impiety
Importance
Impression

4 (CONT.)

Approach	Distracted	Inclining	Play-house	Strangest
Approve	Disturb'd	Incomparable	Playing	Stretch'd
Arise	Divorced	Infinite	Poem	Strongest
Assur'd	Doom	Infirmities	Poems	Strumpet
Assurance	Dotage	Ingenious	Policy	Subject
Astrology	Dozen	Injustice	Port	Succeeded
Asunder	Drinking	Instead	Positive	Suck
Audience	Drudgery	Instinct	Prayer-Book	Suckling
Baggage	Dry'd	Instructions	Prerogative	Suddain
Balm	Eccho	Insupportable	Preserv'd	Suit
Banter	Education	Integrity	Prevailing	Sung
Beastly	Effects	Interr'd	Prey	Superfluity
Beau	Eloquent	Invasion	Prisoners	Superstitious
Bed-Chamber	Encouragement	Jack	Proceedings	Survive
Begets	Encrease	Jehu	Proper	Suspicions
Behave	Enemies	Jesu	Prosper	Swain
Below	Engaged	Join'd	Provide	Sweet-heart
Bestow	Enquiry	Joke	Province	Swim
Bodes	Entirely	Joyn	Provok'd	Swords
Boding	Erect	Key	Pull	Table
Bodkin	Err	Kneels	Punishment	Tea-Table
Borachio	Exceeding	Lady-ship	Purchas'd	Teat
Bowl	Excessive	Landed	Racks	Tedious
Bowls	Expects	Language	Railing	Temple
Brain	Expedition	Lasting	Rank	Tempted
Breaking	Expiring	Lastly	Rare	They'll
Breed	Express	Laughs	Raves	Think'st
Brib'd	Expression	Laying	Ravish	Thrown
Build	Failings	Leads	Reality	Thrust
Burns	Faints	Leasure	Reasons	Thyrsis
Busied	Fairly	Lets	Reduc'd	Tir'd
Butler	Fan	Likes	Refund	Titles
Buxom	Fat	Listen	Refus'd	Toilet
Candle	Fathers	Load	Reign	Traveller
Capable	Features	Lust	Rejoyce	Treasure
Cards	Fed	Lustre	Relate	Tribulation
Carries	Fever	Lye	Related	Troubled
Caus'd	Fiddle	Maker	Remov'd	Turks
Caution	Finely	March	Report	Twenty
Cell	Fits	Marries	Resemblance	Unmasks
Cellar	Flight	Meer	Resent	Unseasonable
Charmingly	Flourish	Merciful	Reserve	Used
Chaste	Fobb'd	Midwife	Restor'd	Uses
Choak	Foresee	Mighty	Reverse	Valentine's
Circumstance	Forgetting	Minds	Revolution	Valour
City	Foundation	Mock	Rights	Variety
Civility	Foy	Months	Risen	Veil
Cloak	French	Morals	Rises	Venus
Clouds	Friendly	Motion	Rising	Verses
Compose	Fruitful	Mummy	Roar	Vex'd
Compound	Futurity	Muse	Roof	Virgin
Conclude	'gad	Musing	Roses	Visits
Conducted	Gad's	Musty	Rules	Waking
Conference	Gay	Nails	S'bud	Wars
Confin'd	Gentlewoman	Naught	Sacrific'd	Wedded
Conquerour	Gentlewomen	Naughty	Sailor	Weeping
Considerable	Gild	Nearer	Satisfie	Wenches
Conspiracy	Gladly	Nice	Saygrace	Wherewithal
Constancy	Glory	Nine	Scoundrel	Whirlwind
Consulted	Gloves	Noon	Seeking	Whisper'd
Corrupt	God	Nun	Seeming	Widdow
Counsel	God's	O'th'	Seldom	Winning
Coy	Golden	Oak	Selling	Winter
Create	Grand	Oaths	Sensible	Wisdom
Crimes	Greatness	Obliging	Sermon	Wish'd
Critick	Green	Obstacle	Served	Writing
Crying	Groans	Obstinacy	Services	
Cue	Ha'	Obtain	Shift	3
Curious	Hackney-Coach	Ods	Shop	500
Curses	Happiest	Off'ring	Shout	[Pounds]
Curst	Harmless	Offences	Shrine	Accident
D'e	Harmony	Offensive	Sighing	Accomplice
Dancing	Hasty	Officer	Signifie	Accomplish'd
Darling	Hatred	Oft	Singing	Accomplishments
Dash'd	Hazard	Open'd	Single	Accounts
Daughter's	Hears	Opens	Skill	Action
Deare	Hinder	Original	Skin	Added
Decreed	Hint	Ours	Slain	Admirer
Deeds	Holding	Overtake	Smart	Admiring
Deeper	Hoods	Own'd	Sneer	Ador'd
Delicious	Horses	Pallace	Society	Adultery
Depend	Houses	Pardons	Softness	Advance
Deserves	Humane	Parent	Songs	Advances
Desperate	Humbly	Parish	Sons	Affections
Despise	Hurt	Partake	Sorrow	Afflicted
Destruction	Husband's	Partly	Sounds	Aid
Detected	Husht	Passage	Spent	Airs
Devotion	Hypocrisie	Pattern	Spoil'd	Airy
Difference	Ice	Paul's	Spoiling	Ake
Disappoint	Ile	Pen	Spoken	Alas-a-day
Disappointment	Ills	Penitent	Stab	Allow'd
Discovers	Immediate	Perdition	Stain	Allows
Disease	Imperfect	Perfection	Stare	Alter'd
Disinherit	Impertinence	Perplexity	Starting	Altogether
Displeasure	Imposture	Physiognomy	Stock	Amen
Distinguish	Incense	Pious	Stood	Amends
	Incest	Plagues	Stranger	Ample

Inhumanity
Injured
Ink
Inmost
Inn
Innocency
Innocents
Inprimis
Insignificant
Insipid
Inspir'd
Inspiration
Insult
Int'rest
Intent
Intention
Intercede
Interpreter
Interrogatories
Intervals
Intire
Into't
Introducing
Invented
Invincible
Inviolate
Iron
Irons
Island
Iteration
Jacket
Jade
James's
Jealousies
Jealousy
Jelly
Jesuite
Jew
Jezabel
Jilted
Joan
Joining
Joseph's
Joyn'd
Joynture
Jubilee
Judgments
Jugler
Juice
Juncture
Jury
Justifie
Keen
Keenest
Kettle
Kick
Kick'd
Kindle
Knave
Knew'st
Knight-hood
Knighthood
Lab'ring
Labour's
Labours
Lace
Lad
Lady-ship's
Lain
Lambs
Lamented
Lamp
Lampoon
Lampoons
Languishing
Lap-Dog
Lapland-Witch
Larger
Las
Lash
Latter
Lavender
Lawfully
Laws
Lawyers
Layn
Leaky
Lean
Leaps
Leer
Legacy
Legs
Lessen
Lessens
Let'n
Lethargy

Levell'd
Levite
Lew'd
Liable
Liberal
Libertine
License
Lifts
Lightning
Likeness
Lilly
Lines
Lingo
Lively
Loaden
Lodg'd
Lord-Harry
Lordship's
Lov'st
Lover's
Lower
Lowness
Lubberly
Lurk
Magnifie
Mahometan
Maiden-head
Maidens
Male-Contents
Mallice
Man-child
Manacled
Manag'd
Manly
Mann'd
Map
Marginal
Marri'd
Marwood's
Masque
Match'd
May'st
Meagre
Measures
Mechanick
Meditation
Melting
Melts
Members
Mend
Mender
Mens
Mentioning
Merchandize
Merciless
Mercy's
Mere
Meritorious
Message
Method
Methought
Mettle
Middle
Mien
Milk
Milky
Mingling
Ministers
Miracles
Miraculous
Mirrour
Mirrours
Mischance
Mislaid
Miss'd
Missing
Mix
Mode
Moment's
Monsters
Month's
Monument
Moral
Morality
Morsel
Mother-in-Law
Motions
Motto
Mould
Mourn'd
Mouth'd
Mouths
Movement
Muffled
Mumble
Mungril
Murderer

Murmurs
Musical
Musick-master
Mute's
Nail
Nam'd
Name's
Named
Napkin
Narrow
Nation
Nature's
Nearly
Neck
Necks
Needless
Needy
Nest
New-born
Nicety
Nick'd
Nigh
No-body
No-h
Nobility
Nod
Noisy
Noli prosequi
North
Notion
Notwithstanding
Novel
Novelty
Now-a-days
Now's
Number
Numbers
O're
Oafe
Obedient
Objects
Obscene
Obscure
Obscurity
Obstinate
Obtain'd
Obvious
Occupation
Occur
Ocean
Odly
Odzooks
Officious
Ogling
Omit
Opportunely
Oppress
Oracle
Orbs
Order'd
Orders
Orphan
Orthodox
Otherwhere
Out-live
Outragious
Outside
Outward
Over-reach'd
Overset
Overtaken
Overtaking
Owing
Painful
Painted
Painters
Paints
Palate
Palm
Panting
Par'd
Parents
Parlour
Parricide
Parrot
Particularly
Passes
Passive
Paternal
Paths
Patient
Pauh
Paultry
Pearl
Pedantick
Peeps
Penny

Perfect
Perforce
Permission
Permitted
Pernicious
Perplex
Perplex'd
Persian
Personal
Personally
Perswaded
Petulant's
Philistines
Philosophers
Pick
Pickle
Piece-meal
Piercing
Piercingly
Pimple
Pinch
Pinion'd
Pins
Piper
Pithy
Pitie
Pitiful
Plaid
Plate
Plausible
Players
Pleading
Pleads
Pleasantly
Plentiful
Plung'd
Plunge
Ply
Pocket-Glass
Poet's
Polishing
Pomp
Pond
Ponder
Pope
Porter
Possess
Possibly
Post
Postilion
Pour
Powder
Practices
Practis'd
Praises
Prating
Preach
Precise
Premunire
Pressing
Presumption
Pretensions
Prevention
Prig
Principal
Principally
Privilege
Probatum est
Proceeding
Procur'd
Prodigal
Produce
Professing
Profest
Prognosticates
Prohibit
Prone
Pronounc'd
Prophecy
Proportion
Propos'd
Prose
Protect
Proverbs
Provident
Proving
Provoked
Provokes
Prudence
Pry
Ptolomee
Publish
Pull'd
Pulse
Punish'd
Puny
Purgatory

Purging
Pursues
Pursuit
Puzzled
Quack
Quadrates
Qualifie
Quarrell'd
Queens
Quits
Quotha
Rack'd
Raffled
Raging
Raised
Rally
Ram
Ransome
Rarely
Rascally
Rave
Re-Enter
Readily
Reap
Rear
Reasoning
Recall'd
Receives
Recollect
Reconcile
Reconciliation
Recovers
Recreation
Redeem
Reduce
Refusal
Refuses
Regain
Regard
Regardless
Religiously
Remain
Remember'd
Remind
Remnants
Renew
Reparation
Repartee
Repeated
Repents
Reported
Represent
Representing
Reprieve
Reproaches
Reputed
Requir'd
Resemble
Resembles
Reserv'd
Resign'd
Resist
Resolute
Restless
Retard
Retinue
Retir'd
Retired
Retreat
Retrieve
Retrograde
Reveal'd
Reviv'd
Revive
Reviving
Revoking
Revolt
Revolted
Rewarding
Rewards
Rhetorick
Rhyming
Riches
Riddance
Ride
Riding
Rip
Rites
Rivals
Rive
Rivet
Rivets
Rob
Robe
Rock
Rod
Rogue's

1 (CONT.)

Flowing
Flown
Flung
Flush
Flutter
Fluttering
Fly-flap
Flyer
Flyes
Foaming
Foil'd
Folding
Folio
Folio's
Folk
Follower
Fonder
Fondest
Fondly
Fool'd
Fool's
Foot-men
Fopperies
Foppery
Foppish
For's
Forbearance
Forbidding
Forces
Fore-castle
Fore-see
Foregad
Foregod
Foreknow
Foremost
Foresaw
Foretel
Foretell
Forfeits
Forgiving
Forgivness
Forks
Forlorn
Form'd
Forma Pauperis
Forms
Fornicator
Forsee
Forswear
Forsworn
Fortifi'd
Fortitudes
Fortnight
Fortune's
Foster'd
Foul-mouth'd
Foundations
Foundress
Fountain
Fourty
Fram'd
France
Francis
Frankincense
Frankly
Frauds
Free-love's
Free-loves
Free'd
Freed
Freeholder
French-man
Frendship
Friar
Friers
Friezland-Hens
Frigat
Frightn'd
Frisoneer-gorget
Frivolous
Frollick
Front
Frontiers
Fronting
Frontless
Fronts
Frost-nip't
Frosty
Froth's
Frowning
Frozen
Fruitless
Fruz-Towr
Fry
Fryar
Fulfill'd

Full-blown
Fuller
Fully
Fulsamick
Fulsome
Fulsomely
Fumes
Furious
Furnace
Furnish'd
Furnishes
Furnival's
Furnivals
Fustian
Gadding
Gads-Daggers-
  Belts-Blades
Gadso
Gadzooks
Gaiety
'gainst
Gall
Gall'd-beast
Gallantries
Galley-slave
Galloper
Gang
Gaoler
Gap
Gape
Garb
Garments
Garret
Garter
Gash'd
Gashly
Gather'd
Gause
Gav'n
Gawdy
Gazette-writer
Gazettes
Gazetts
Gems
Gen'rous
Gender
Generals
Generously
Genuine
Gesture
Ghastly
Ghost
Ghosts
Gibbet-thief
Giddy-thing
Gilded
Gilds
Gilt
Gingling
Girl's
Girls
Giv'st
Give't
Giver
Glares
Glimmers
Glittering
Globe
Globes
Glooms
Gloomy
Glosses
Glossy
Glow
Glutton-like
Gnashing
Gnaw'd
Gnawing
Gnaws
Go-between
Goat
God-father
God-like
Godlike
Godliness
Godly
Godmother
Goe
Goods
Goose's
Gore
Gorg'd
Gorge
Gorgon
Gothick
Govern'd
Governante

Governs
Grac'd
Graceful
Gradually
Grain
Grandson
Grandsons
Granting
Grants
Grape
Grapple
Grasshopper
Gratefully
Grates
Gratifying
Gravely
Gray
Grazing
Greatly
Green-sword
Greenland
Gregory
Grey
Grey-pease
Grievance
Grievances
Grievous
Grimaces
Grinn
Grinning
Grins
Grizled
Groan
Grond
Grounded
Groundless
Groveling
Groves
Grudging
Grutch
Guardian
Guardians
Gudgeon
Guesse
Guided
Guilded
Guile
Guiltiness
Guinea
Gull'd
Gums
Gun
Guns
Gush
Gust
Gusto
Ha'n't
Habits
Habitual
Hack
Had'nt
Hadn't
Haggar'd
Hainous
Hairs
Hale
Half-way
Haling
Haly
Hammock
Hand-Gripings
Hand's
Handed
Handsomer
Handsomest
Handsomly
Hang-Dog
Hangings
Hangman
Hapned
Happens
Happyness
Hardest
Hare
Hare's-gall
Hares
Hark-ye
Harlot
Harlotry
Harness
Harrow
Harrows
Hartshorn
Hasten
Hatch
Hatch'd
Hatching

Haughty
Haule
Hawk
Hawkers
Hawks
Hazle
Head-Quarters
Headed
Headpiece
Healing
Healths
Heaps
Heark-ye
Heart-breaking
Heart-heavings
Heart-wounding
Hearted
Hearty
Heat's
Heathenish
Heavier
Heaving
Heavy-laden
Hebrew
Hector
Heeds
Heels
Heigh
Heiress
Hell-born
Helping
Helps
Hemp
Hens
Hen
Hen-peck'd
Henceforth
Henceforward
Her's
Hercules
Hereditary
Hermaphrodite
Hero
Heroically
Herself
Hey-day
Hides
Hieroglyphical
Hieroglyphick
High-fed
Higher
Highness
Hills
Hilt
Hinder'd
Hindered
Hindrance
Hinge
Hinges
Hinted
Hir'd
Hire
Hiss
Hiss'd-off
Hitherto
Hoard
Hoarse
Hoary
Hodgson
Hog's-bones
Hoh
Hoity
Holborn-hill
Holes
Holla
Hollows
Holy
Homage
Homely
Honestly
Honourably
Honoured
Hoofs
Hoot
Hopeful
Hopeless
Horn
Horn-Books
Horn-mad
Horrible
Horrors
Horrours
Horse-Race
Horse-nail
Hospitable
Hospitably
Hospital

Hot-headed
Housewifes
Hover
Hovering
Howe'er
Howe're
Howls
Huddle
Huffe
Hugely
Hulk
Hum'd
Humanum est errare
Humility
Humorist
Humours
Hums
Hunter
Hunting
Huntsmen
Hurry
Husbandman
Hussey
Hust
Hymenial
Hypocrisy
Hypocrite
Iambicks
Icicles
Ideot
Idiot-Race
Idleness
Idlers
Idolatry
Idols
If't
Ignoble
Ill-fated
Ill-humoured
Ill-manners
Ill-nature
Images
Imaginations
Imagined
Immerge
Immoderately
Immortal
Immortality
Immoveable
Impair'd
Impal'd
Impartial
Impatiently
Impediments
Imperceptible
Impertinently
Impetuous
Implement
Imploring
Import
Important
Imports
Importune
Importunes
Impos'd
Imposes
Impositions
Impossibility
Impostor
Impowr'd
Impregnable
Impress
Imprisonment
Improv'd
Improvement
Improving
Impudently
Imputation
Imputed
In statu quo
In vino veritas
Inanimate
Inauspicious
Incarnate
Incentive
Incessant
Incestuous
Inchanted
Inclines
Inconsiderable
Inconveniencies
Increase
Increases
Incredulous
Incumbent
Incumbrance
Incumbrances

Mumper
Mun
Mungrel
Murderers
Murther
Muscovite
Musicians
Musick-meetings
Musk-Doublet
Muslin
Mussulman
Mustard-seed
Muster
Mutter
Mutton
Mystically
Nadir
Nakedness
Narrowly
Nativities
Nativity
Natures
Nauseate
Ne
Nearest
Nearness
Necessaries
Necessities
Necklace
Needle
Negative
Neglected
Negligence
Negligently
Negotiate
Negotiation
Negro
Neighbourhood
Neighbours
Neighing
Neighs
Nemo omnibus horis
Nere
Nerves
Nettl'd
Never-slacking
Nevertheless
New-flushing
New-married
Newly
Nibbled
Nicely
Nick-Name
Nick't
Night-Gown
Night-Cap
Night-cap
Night's
Nightly
Nightwalkers
Nine-tails
Noblest
Nobly
Nodding
Noisie
Nol
Non Compos mentis
Non compos mentis
Nonsence
Nonsense
Noon-day
North-East
Northern
Nostrodamus
Nothing's
Notions
Notorious
Notoriously
Nourishment
Novels
Novice
Number's
Numberless
Nuptial
Nusance
Nutmeg
Nutmeg-Grater
Nutriment
O-law
O'Fortune
O'ds
O'er-cast
O'er-flow
O'er-joy'd
O'fashion
O'mind

O'nights
O'repaid
O'retake
O'seeing
O'sight
Oaf
Oafs
Oar
Obey'd
Objection
Objections
Obliges
Obliterated
Oblivion
Observers
Obstinately
Occasion'd
Occupy
Ocular
Odds
Odium
Odour
Oeconomy
Of's
Off-and-on
Off-spring
Off'rings
Offending
Offered
Offering
Officers
Officiously
Offspring
Oftentimes
Oftner
Oil
Oil'd
Older
Olio
Omen-hunter
Omission
Omissions
Omitted
One-and-twenty
One-ey'd
Onely
Opened
Opportune
Oppos'd
Oppose
Oppressed
Oppressing
Oppression
Orange-Brandy
Oratory
Orb
Ord'nary
Ordain'd
Ordered
Ordinary's
Ore
Orestes
Orient
Originals
Ornament
Oth'
Other-guess-toys
Otters
Ought'st
Out-Jilted
Out-Matrimony'd
Out-Witted
Out-blossom
Out-fac'd
Out-landish
Out-lie
Out-strip
Out-strip'd
Out-stripp'd
Outstays
Outwitted
Over-act
Over-hear
Over-joy'd
Over-rates
Over-run
Over-sea's
Overcharg'd
Overheard
Overlaid
Overnicely
Oversee
Overseen
Overspreads
Overstock'd
Ow'd
Ow'st

Owes
Owest
Owls
Ox
Oyl
Oyster
Oyster-woman
Oysters
Pace
Pack
Packthread
Pacquet
Pads
Pagan
Page
Pageantry
Paintings
Pairings
Paler
Pallaces
Pallat
Palpitation
Palpitations
Pam
Pampereth
Pancras
Pander
Panegyrick
Panegyricks
Pangs
Pant
Papa
Paper-Diet
Paper-Mill
Papist
Paradice
Paradise
Parallel
Pardonable
Parish-Priest
Parish-Searchers
Parliament
Parson's
Partial
Particle
Parties
Partlet
Partner
Partners
Partridge
Party-coloured
Pass par tout
Pass par toute
Passages
Passing-Bell
Passionately
Passively
Pasted
Pastimes
Pastor
Pastoral
Pat
Pater-noster
Path
Pathetick
Patriarchs
Pauses
Pavement
Paw
Paws
Paying
Payment
Peaceable
Peacefull
Peacefully
Peacock
Peals
Pecquet
Pedestals
Peel'd
Peep
Peeping
Peers
Pelican
Penal
Penance
Penetrating
Penitential
Penn'd
Pennance
Penny-worth
Penny-worths
Pens
Pension
Pent-house
Penthesilea
Peoples

Pepper
Perceiving
Peremptory
Perfected
Perfidiousness
Performance
Perfumes
Perilous
Permit
Permitting
Perquisite
Perruke
Perrukes
Persecuted
Perseveres
Persevering
Persist
Persisting
Personate
Perspective
Perspicuity
Persuade
Persuasive
Perswasion
Pertinently
Pertness
Peru
Peruke
Perusal
Perverseness
Perverting
Perverts
Pester'd
Pestilential
Petitions
Petrifie
Petticoat
Petticoats
Pheasant
Philander
Phillis
Philomaths
Philosophy
Phisician
Phoebus
Phosphorus
Phrases
Phuh
Physicks
Piaza
Piazza
Pick'd
Picking
Picque
Pidgeons
Piec'd
Pierc'd
Pierce
Pig
Pig-water
Pile
Pillag'd
Pillars
Pillory'd
Pilot
Pinch'd
Pincushions
Pineda
Pinn'd
Pinnace
Pinto
Piping
Pippins
Pistoll
Pitied
Pitying
Plague
Plain-Dealers
Plain-dealing
Plainly
Plaistred
Planets
Planted
Planting
Plato
Play-Book
Play-fellows
Play-House
Play'd
Play'll
Player
Player's
Pleaded
Pleasurable
Pliant
Plod
Plumb

Plumes
Plump
Plyant's
Plyants
Pocket-glass
Pocket-Tipstaves
Pockets
Point's
Pointed
'pointed
Pointing
Politick
Politicks
Polluted
Pompous
Pond'rous
Pontack's
Poorly
Poppy-Water
Poppy-water
Populace
Pore
Pores
Poring
Porpoise
Portbound
Portend
Portent
Portions
Portrait
Pos'd
Position
Possessing
Possessions
Postern
Posts
Pot-gun
Potent
Potion
Poultry
Pouting
Powder-Horn
Powder'd
Poysoning's
Practicable
Practise
Pragmatical
Praised
Pratled
Prattle
Praying
Pre-engag'd
Precariously
Precede
Precedes
Precipitated
Precipitation
Prediction
Predominate
Prefer
Preferment
Preferr'd
Preferring
Preheminence
Preliminary
Premeditated
Premeditation
Premises
Prentices
Preparation
Preparative
Prepared
Preposterous
Presage
Prescrib'd
Preserved
Preserving
Presidents
Press'd
Prest
Presum'd
Presumptive
Presumptuous
Pretender
Pretious
Prettily
Prevail'd
Prevails
Prevents
Pricking
Prickle
Priming
Primitive
Primly's
Principle
Principles
Pris'ners

Prisons
Privacies
Privateers
Probability
Probably
Probation
Probe
Proceeded
Proclaim
Proclaim'd
Proclamation
Proctor
Procured
Procuring
Prodigal's
Prodigality
Produc'd
Produces
Producing
Profane
Profession
Professor
Profit
Profited
Profligate
Profoundly
Profuse
Profusion
Progeny
Projection
Projector
Projects
Prologues
Promiscuous
Promoting
Promotion
Prompt
Prompts
Pronouncing
Prop
Propagate
Propagated
Prophane
Prophecies
Prophecy'd
Prophesies
Proportion'd
Proposal
Proposals
Proposed
Proposing
Proposition
Propria persona
Prosecute
Prospects
Prostituted
Prostitution
Protection
Protestant
Protesting
Proverb
Proverbially
Provides
Proxy
Prudent
Pryn
Psalm
Publishes
Puff
Pullvill'd
Pulp
Pulpit
Pulses
Pump
Pumping
Pumple
Punch
Punctually
Punishing
Punk
Punsters
Puppet
Purest
Purling
Purloyn'd
Purport
Pursuant
Pursued
Pushes
Put'n
Puzled
Puzzle
Py
Pylades
Pyramids
Pythagories

Quake
Quaker
Qualification
Qualify
Quality's
Qualm
Qualmsick
Quandary
Quarles
Quarrel'd
Quarrelling
Quarry
Quarters
Quench
Quench'd
Quenching
Question'd
Qui vult decipi
Quibble
Quiblers
Quicken
Quicksands
Quietness
Quill
Quilted
Quintessence
Quixote
Quoif
Quorum
Quoth
Rackets
Racking
Radish
Raffl'd
Rag
Ragged
Rags
Rail'd
Railer
Railings
Raillier
Rails
Rains
Rainy
Raising
Rakes
Rallery
Rally'd
Ramirez
Ran
Rancling
Range
Ranged
Rank-Husband
Rank-Wife
Rantipole
Rap
Rapine
Raptures
Rashly
Rat
Ratifie
Ratify'd
Rats-bane
Raved
Raving
Ravish'd
Ravished
Raymond
Rays
Re-composing
Re-enters
Re-inforce
Re-inspire
Reader
Readiness
Readmit
Rebate
Rebel-rate
Rebell
Rebellious
Rebuild
Recall
Recant
Recede
Receipt
Receipts
Received
Receiver
Receiving
Receptacle
Reception
Recesses
Reciprocal
Reckon
Reckoning
Reclaiming

Recollected
Recollection
Recompose
Reconcil'd
Reconciled
Reconcilement
Record
Recov'ring
Recover'd
Recovery
Red-hissing
Red'ning
Redeem'd
Redeliver
Redemption
Redfleck'd
Redned
Reeking
Refin'd
Refine
Refining
Reflected
Reflects
Reflux
Reform
Reform'd
Reformation
Refulgent
Refunding
Refusing
Regal
Regards
Register
Regularity
Reigns
Reimburse
Reinstate
Rejoicings
Relates
Relating
Releas'd
Releasing
Relent
Relenting
Relentless
Relies
Relieve
Relinquish
Rely
Remainder
Remarks
Remedied
Remedies
Remembers
Remembrances
Remorseless
Remorsless
Remote
Rend
Render'd
Renews
Renounc'd
Rent
Rent-roll
Repaid
Repay'd
Repeat
Repell
Repented
Repenting
Replies
Reply'd
Represented
Reprimanded
Reprobate
Reproof
Repulsed
Request's
Requested
Requests
Required
Requisite
Rescue
Rescued
Resembl'd
Resentments
Reserved
Resident
Resign
Resistance
Resists
Resolved
Resolves
Respected
Respectful
Respecting
Respiring

Respite
Restitution
Restoring
Restrain
Resume
Resumption
Retailer
Retaining
Retirement
Retires
Retrospection
Reunion
Rev'rend
Revealed
Reveals
Revelation
Revell'd
Revellers
Revelling
Revengful
Revenging
Revisit
Revoke
Revolves
Revolving
Reynard
Rhenish-wine
Rhime
Rhiming
Rhymes
Ribaldry
Ribbon
Richly
Ridicule
Ridiculing
Rigg'd
Rigging
Rightful
Rightly
Rigour
Rings
Ripe-horn-mad
Ripen'd
Riseings
Risk
Risque
Rival'd
Rival's
Rivers
Riveted
Roam
Roaring
Roasted
Roasting
Robb'd
Robs
Rode
Roderigo's
Roll'd
Roman
Romances
Rooted
Rope's
Ropes
Rosamond's
Rotation
Rots
Rough
Rout
Rowes
Rowl
Rowlands
Rows
Roxolana's
Royalty
Rubb'd
Rubbing
Ruby-Lips
Rudenes
Ruder
Rudiments
Rueful
Ruffian
Ruffians
Ruins
Rummer
Rumour
Rung
Russian
Rustick
Rustle
Rustling
Rusty
Saddest
Sagely
Sages
Sailing

Saist
Sake's
Salacious
Sallies
Sally-Port
Salop
Salopian
Sampler
Sampson's
Sampsons
Sancho
Sanctified
Sand
Sands
Sanguine
Sant
Sapiens dominabitur
Saracens
Sarazen
Sat
Sate
Satirical
Satisfactions
Satisfi'd
Saturn
Satyre
Satyrical
Sauce
Saul
Save-all
Say'd
Say'n
Say't
Sayn
Scabbard
Scabbards
Scaffolding
Scalding
Scales
Scandaliz'd
Scandalously
Scap'd
Scapes
'scaping
Scar
Scarlet
Scarron's
Scatter
Scatter'd
Sceptres
Schechemite
Scholar
Sciences
Scipio
Scoff
Sconces
Scornful
Scoundrels
Scourge
Scrap
Scrape
Scraps
Scratch
Scratch'd
Scratching
Scrawl
Scrawl'd
Screen
Scribbling
Scruple
Scrupulously
Scuffle
Sculler
Scut
Sea-Beast
Sea-Lover
Sea-wit
Seal'd
Seaman
Seamen
Search'd
Searcher
Searches
Season
Second-best
Secretaries
Secretary's
Sect
Secur'd
Secures
Sedate
Sedition
Seduc'd
Seducing
See'st
Seeds
Seeks

1 (CONT.)

Seizes
Self-Murder
Self-consuming
Self-content
Self-interest
Sence
Sends
Seneca
Sententious
Sentiments
Separate
Separate-
  maintenance
Separated
Separately
Separating
Serene
Serjeants
Serpent's
Serves
Servile
Setled
Settl'd
Sev'n
Sev'ral
Seven
Seventh
Severest
Sexes
Sextiles
Sha'n't
Sha'not
Sha'nt
Shackled
Shadow
Shaft
Shake-bag
Shaking
Sham-Settlement
Sham-sickness
Shar'd
Shared
Sharks
Sharp
Sharply
Shav'd
Sheafs
Shee'll
Sheer
Sheers
Shelves
Shepherd
Shepherdesses
Sheriff's
Shew'd
Shewing
Shewn
Shields
Shifted
Shill
Shilling
Shipping
Ships-Crew's
Shipwrack'd
Shoals
Shoar
Shocks
Shook
Short-liv'd
Shortest
Shortness
Shoud'st
Should'st
Shoulder
Show'r
Show'rs
Shrew'd
Shriek
Shriek'd
Shrinks
Shrivell'd
Shropshire
Shroud
Shrub
Shrug
Shuffled
Shuns
Shutting
Side-Box
Siege
Sifted
Sigillatum
Signal
Signatum
Significations
Signior

Silenc'd
Sillibub
Simpers
Simplicity
Singled
Singly
Sinister
Sinks
Sipping
Sister's
Sisterly
Skies
Skill'd
Skins
Skipper
Skull
Skull's
Skulls
Sky
Slabber
Slabber'd
Slander-mouth'd
Slander'd
Slanderous
Slap
Slap-dash
Slaughter
Sleek-face
Sleeve
Slides
'Slidikins
Slighting
Slily
Slipper
Slippers
Slovenly
Slumber
Slut
Small-beer
Small-pox
Smear'd
Smiling
Smock
Smooth
Smoothest
Smoothness
Smother'd
Snakes
Snarling
Sneering
Snipwel's
Snivel
Snow
Snow-House
Snowy
Snub
Snuff-Box
Snuff-box
Snugs
Soaker
Soar
Sober
Sobriety
Soforth
Softlier
Soh
Solacing
Soldier-like
Solemnly
Soles
Solicitations
Solicited
Soliciting
Soliloques
Soliloquies
Solitudes
Solus
Solve
Someils du Matin
Sonnet
Soothing
Soothsayer
Sop
Sophisticated
Sorceress
Sore
Sorrowful
Soul-racking
Sounding
South
Sow
Sowre
Space
Spain
Spanish
Spark
Sparkle

Sparks
Spectacle
Speechless
Speedy
Spelling
Spells
Sphere
Spice
Spider
Spiders
Spintext's
Spit
Spitfire
Splenatick
Spoon-meat
Spoons
Spot
Spotless
Spout
Spouting
Sprawling
Spring-Garden
Springs
Spumoso
Spur
Sputt'ring
Spys
Squabling
Squander
Square
Squeek
Squeezes
Squeezing
Squires
Squirrel
'st
Stables
Stabs
Staggers
Stain'd
Stains
Stale
Stalk
Stalking
Stalking-Horse
Stalks
Stallion
Stalls
Stamp
Stander
Star-Gazer
Star-gazing
Starch'd
Starling
Starry
Startles
Starv'd
Starves
State-Cook
Station
Statue
Statues
Stealing
Stedfast
Steeds
Steel
Steer'd
Steinkirk
Sternly
Stickle
Stiff'ning
Stifl'd
Stile
Still'd
Stilness
Stinkard
Stinking
Stirring
Stitch'd
Stock'd
Stoick
Stolen
Stomacher
Stomack
Stomacks
Stond
Stones
Stooping
Store
Storms
Straight
Straining
Strait-Laceing
Strammel
Stranger's
Strangers
Strangl'd

Strapping
Straw
Straying
Streaming
Streights
Strein
Stretch
Stretches
Stretching
Strew'd
Strictly
Striding
Strings
Strip'd
Stripling
Stripp'd
Stripping
Striven
Stroaking
Stroke
Strole
Stroling
Strove
Structure
Struggl'd
Struggle
Strumpets
Stuck
Students
Study
Study'd
Stumbl'd
Stumbled
Stun
Stunn'd
Stuns
Stupendous
Stupidity
Subborn'd
Subjected
Subjects
Sublimate
Submission
Submits
Subpoena
Substantially
Subtilty
Subtle
Subtlest
Succeeds
Sucking
Suckl'd
Suckle
Suddainly
Suddenness
Sue
Suff'ring
Suff'rings
Suffocating
Sugar-loaf
Sullenness
Sully'd
Summers-day
Summon
Summons
Sun's
Sunder
Superabundant
Superanuated
Superfluous
Superiority
Superiour
Supp'd
Supplemental
Suppliants
Supplies
Supporters
Supposed
Surfeit
Surgeons
Surges
Surlily
Surmount
Surprising
Surprizes
Surrender
Surveying
Suspicious
Suspiciously
Sussex
Sustenance
Swaddled
Swail'd
Swarming
Swathed
Sweeps
Sweet-Heart

Sweeten
Sweets
Swell
Swell'd
Swiftness
Swimminess
Swimming
Swimmingly
Swimmingness
Swing
Swinging
Swoll'n
Swollen
Swoon
Swooned
Sybills
Symphony
T'
T'amuze
T'impart
Tabby-Cat
Tabernacle
Tables
Taciturnity
Tack
Tack'd
Tag
Tainted
Taliacotius
Talk'st
Talked
Tall
Tallies
Tallow-Chandler
Tame
Tampering
Tantalized
Tapers
Tapestry-hanging
Tapster
Tarpaulin
Tarpawlin
Tartars
Tartary
Tast
Tasting
Tatter
Tatterdemallion
Tatters
Taunts
Taylor's
Tea-Cups
Tea-table
Teaches
Tearers
Teats
Teaze
Tedious-wasting
Teens
Tell'n
Temperately
Tempests
'tempted
Tempter
Tempting
Tempts
Tender-hearted
Tends
Tennis-Court
Tenor
Tenter
Termagant
Terminated
Terribly
Terrifies
Terrify'd
Testament
Teste a teste
Testify
Testimony
Tete a tete
Text
Thankless
That'n
Theatres
Theft
Ther's
Thereafter
Thereby
Thereunto
Thetis
They'd
Thick
Thick-Skull'd
Thigh
Thimble
Thinly

1 (CONT.)
Woman-bobb'd
Woman-hater
Womans-flesh
Womens
Wonderful
Wood-louse
Wooden
Wooing
Worded
Worlds
Worms
Worn-out
Wornout
Worry'd
Worshipping
Wou'dst
Wounding
Woundy
Wrack
Wrap'd
Wrapt
Wrecks
Wrench
Wrench'd
Wretchedly
Wrinckles
Wring
Writers
Wrote
Wrung
Wry
Yard
Yawn
Yellow
Yelp
Yester
Yew
Yez
Yoke-fellow
Yon
Yond'
Yonder's
Yonders
Young-fellow
Young-widow
Yourself
Zealot
Zealous
Zenith